THE DAILY WALK® BIBLE

The Daily Walk® BIBLE

BRUCE H. WILKINSON
Executive Editor

PAULA A. KIRK
General Editor

JOHN W. HOOVER
Editor

Walk Thru the Bible Ministries, Inc.
Atlanta, Georgia

Tyndale House Publishers, Inc.
Wheaton, Illinois

Library of Congress Cataloging-in-Publication Data

Bible. English. New Living Translation. 1996.
 The Daily Walk Bible / Bruce H. Wilkinson, executive editor; Paula A. Kirk, general editor; John W. Hoover, editor; Walk Thru the Bible Ministries, Inc.
  p. cm.
Daily devotionals accompanying Scriptures from the New Living Translation.
ISBN 0-8423-3259-6 (hc : alk. paper). ISBN 0-8423-3258-8 (sc : alk. paper)
1. Devotional calendars. I. Wilkinson, Bruce. II. Kirk, Paul. III. Hoover, John, date.
IV. Walk Thru the Bible (Educational ministry) V. Title.
BS195.N38 1995a
220.5'208—dc20   95-15687

08 07 06 05 04
12 11 10 9 8 7

Index
to the books of the Bible

Alphabetical Index
to the books of the Bible

Introduction

You are holding in your hands a book designed to help you in your spiritual walk with God. *The Daily Walk Bible* brings together the insightful devotionals from Walk Thru the Bible's *Daily Walk* reading guide and the popular New Living Translation.

As a result, you can spend a fruitful time each day in God's Word by gaining practical devotional insights related to the Scripture you've read. At the end of one year you will have read the Bible from cover to cover at an easy, manageable pace . . . and you will have enjoyed it! But more than that, you will find your relationship with the Lord deepening as you spend time reading and meditating on his Word.

Not only is *The Daily Walk Bible* appropriate for personal devotions, you can also use it with your children as a family devotional. And churches can use it in Bible study groups or simply to encourage congregational reading of God's Word.

As a result of using *The Daily Walk Bible,* you will see the Scriptures from Genesis to Revelation in a new light and be able to understand how they all fit together. You will experience firsthand how practical God's Word is as you find the answers to the perplexing problems you face each day. You will learn from great men and women of faith how to express your innermost thoughts to God . . . how to handle disappointments and heartaches . . . how to express joy and praise . . . how to draw on the unlimited power of God moment by moment . . . and so much more. And you will delight in sharing your newfound knowledge with others, helping them to cope in their chaotic world by turning to the life-changing Word of God.

The Daily Walk Bible will help transform your attitudes and energize you with confidence in your loving God by giving you new insight into his Scriptures. With the Bible as your foundation for living, you will never be the same again.

We at Walk Thru the Bible Ministries are thrilled to join together with Tyndale House Publishers to make this Bible-reading devotional tool available to you. The common purpose of our ministries is to help more Christians become rooted and grounded in the Scriptures.

And now, prepare yourself for the walk of your lifetime!

Bruce H. Wilkinson
President and Executive Editor
Walk Thru the Bible Ministries

How to Get the Most out of *The Daily Walk Bible*

The Daily Walk Bible is conveniently arranged for daily Bible reading 365 days of the year. Each section is dated with the month and the day; however, if you would like to start reading through the Bible at some time in the year other than January, simply use the optional reading track ("Day 231"), and put a check mark in the box to help you keep your place.

 Overview provides a foretaste for your Bible reading of the day. A convenient chart also summarizes the main ideas of the Scripture section.

 Your Daily Walk encourages you to think carefully about one scriptural insight from the day's reading and offers you specific ways to put the truths you will read into action in your own life. Principles from God's Word are explained practically to help you successfully cope with life today.

 Insight brings to light a fascinating scriptural or historical fact to build your total Bible knowledge.

Every seventh day, four times a month, you'll have the opportunity to pause and rest in your walk through the Bible with a special devotional reviewing the past several days' readings. After you *Look Back* at the broad sweep of your reading for the previous week, you can *Look Up* at God and consider what he wants to say to you through his Word and *Look Ahead* at what's to come. You can also use this seventh day to catch up on any reading from the past few days.

You will also find in *The Daily Walk Bible* a helpful introductory page for each of the sixty-six books of the Bible. A concise overview of the background and purpose of each book is followed by a useful chart summarizing its content and flow.

Every feature of *The Daily Walk Bible* is designed to help you get the most out of your devotional times with the Lord. It's the tool you have been looking for to bring the Bible alive for you!

Walk Thru the Bible Ministries

Walk Thru the Bible Ministries (WTB) unofficially began in the early 1970s in Portland, Oregon. A young teacher named Bruce Wilkinson developed an innovative way of teaching Old and New Testament surveys of the Bible.

From these small beginnings emerged the multifaceted Bible-teaching outreach that Dr. Wilkinson officially founded as a nonprofit ministry in 1976. WTB has grown into one of the leading Christian organizations in America with an international ministry extending to more than fifty countries representing some thirty-five languages. International branch offices are located in Australia, Great Britain, Singapore, New Zealand, South Africa, and Ukraine.

By focusing on the central themes of Scripture and their practical application, WTB has been able to develop and maintain wide acceptance in denominations and fellowships around the world. In addition, it has carefully initiated strategic ministry alliances with more than one hundred Christian organizations and missions of wide diversity and background.

WTB has four major outreach ministries: seminars, publishing, leadership training, and video.

Seminars. Since it began its seminar ministry more than two decades ago, WTB has instructed more than 2 million people worldwide through seminars taught by more than 1,600 certified teachers. People of all ages and religious persuasions have developed a deeper understanding of the Bible through these unique Old and New Testament surveys, and many have come to know Christ in a new and more personal way.

Publishing. WTB's publishing ministry began in 1978 with the launching of *The Daily Walk* magazine. Since then, WTB Publishing has continued to develop additional publications that enable individuals and families to maintain a meaningful habit of daily devotional time in the Word of God. The publications include *Closer Walk, Family Walk, LifeWalk, Quiet Walk, Youthwalk,* and *Tapestry.*

Leadership Training. WTB's Leadership Training ministry goes into the secular marketplace as well as churches and organizations to communicate biblical principles of leadership. There are several leadership modules available to fit the unique needs of each group. Each training module provides practical tools that make biblical truth relevant in both personal relationships and in the marketplace.

Video Training. The newest ministry of WTB is the video-training curriculum. In just a few short years, the WTB creative team has developed a number of leading video courses that have enjoyed widespread distribution. Video makes it possible to bring WTB's life-changing Bible teaching into churches and homes throughout the world.

WTB has had a consistent history of strategic ministry from the beginning. The organization strives to help fulfill the great commission in obedience to the Lord's call. With this mission in mind, WTB lives out its commitment to excellence with the highest standards of ethical conduct and integrity not only in ministry but also in its internal operational policies and procedures. No matter what the ministry, no matter where the ministry, WTB focuses on the Word of God and encourages people of all nations to grow in their knowledge of God and in unreserved obedience and service to him.

For more information about Walk Thru the Bible's publications, videos, or seminars in your area, write to *Walk Thru the Bible Ministries, P.O. Box 80587, Atlanta, GA 30366 or call (770) 458-9300.*

God's Word in Our Language

Do you speak Hebrew . . . or Aramaic . . . or Greek . . . or Latin . . . or German? Most Americans don't.

That is why the Bible you pick up and read today is such a remarkable accomplishment—and such a priceless treasure. You have many dedicated people to thank for the privilege of reading God's Word in your mother tongue.

The story of how we got the English Bible begins many centuries ago and many miles away. Written translations of the entire Hebrew (Old) Testament have existed since the third century B.C., when Jews living in Egypt discovered that their children could no longer understand the Hebrew Scriptures. The Greek translation that resulted has been given the name "Septuagint" (Latin for *seventy*), which reflects the tradition that it was translated by seventy elders in seventy sessions.

When Jesus lived in Israel, Aramaic was the language of the common people. But the four Gospel accounts, as well as Paul's letters and the rest of the New Testament, were written in Greek—the language of the Mediterranean world.

By the late fourth century, the spoken language of the Roman Empire was Latin. Few people could read or write Greek any longer, and a Latin translation was needed. About 382 the bishop of Rome asked a learned Bible scholar named Jerome to undertake the task, and the Vulgate or "common" Bible was produced. When Latin became the liturgical language of the church and the Bible became associated with the liturgy, it continued to be written and read in Latin.

After the conversion of the British Isles to Christianity, various monks attempted to translate the Vulgate into English. No complete English translation was available for many years, and Bible stories were commonly taught through pictures, carvings, and drama.

The first complete English Bible did not appear until the end of the fourteenth century. John Wycliffe, an English priest, began to preach in the *vernacular* language (English), rather than the *liturgical* language (Latin). Under his leadership the first translation of the entire Bible from Latin to English was completed in 1384.

As with all copies of the Bible up to this time, duplication was only possible by hand—a process that was slow, tedious, and expensive. With the invention of movable type in Mainz, Germany, production and distribution of the Bible entered a new era. The Latin Vulgate was the first Bible to appear in printed form. Produced by Johannes Gutenberg, it soon became known as the *Gutenberg Bible.*

The Reformation brought a renewed demand for the Bible in the language of the people. Martin Luther translated the Bible from Hebrew and Greek into German. When church authorities in England prohibited a similar English translation, Luther's counterpart, William Tyndale, went to Germany, where he translated the New Testament from the original Greek in 1526. Miles Coverdale, an English bishop, prepared the first complete English Bible from the original languages in 1535. His work was later revised, and portions can still be found today in the *Book of Common Prayer.*

English refugees living in France made the first Roman Catholic translation of the Bible from Latin into English, publishing the New Testament in Rheims, France, in 1582, and the Old Testament in Douay, France, in 1610. This translation is known today as the *Douay-Rheims* or *Douay Bible.*

In 1604, King James of England commissioned a group of fifty scholars to prepare a revision of earlier English translations of the Bible. The resulting King James (or Authorized) Version of 1611 was warmly and widely received. Acclaimed for its accuracy, readability, and poetic beauty, it soon became the most popular English Bible—a tribute held for more than 350 years.

God never changes (James 1:17), and God's Word never changes (Matthew 5:18). But human language—the vehicle for communicating God's changeless message—undergoes constant metamorphosis. In the twentieth century this has given impetus to numerous revisions and translations—the product of scholarly committees employing the most recent findings from archaeology and linguistics. Contemporary translations include:

American Standard Version (1901)
Revised Standard Version (1952)
Jerusalem Bible (1966)
New English Bible (1966)
New American Bible (1970)
New American Standard Bible (1971)
Good News Bible: Today's English Version (1976)
New International Version (1978)
New King James Version (1982)
New Jewish Publications Society Translation (1982)
Revised English Bible (1989)
New Revised Standard Version (1989)
Contemporary English Version (1995)
New Living Translation (1996)

In addition, popular paraphrases such as *The Living Bible* (1971), J. B. Phillips's *New Testament in Modern English* (1960), and Eugene Peterson's *The Message* (1993) have provided fresh, easy-to-read versions.

The English Bible—God's Word in our language. It is a priceless treasure in any generation, especially when millions of people today still do not have a single verse of Scripture in their mother tongue.

Take time to read a portion of your Bible each day, for God has something to say to you!

Seven Benefits from Reading Your Bible

Bible reading is more than a pleasant pastime. It can become a daily habit that will change your life.

God's Word holds out the promise of rich benefits for those who spend time reading it and taking its truths to heart. Here are just seven of the many ways your life can be better as you make the Bible your daily reading companion. All seven come from Psalm 119—a magnificent song of praise for God's Word.

1. **The Bible will help keep you from sin.** "I have hidden your word in my heart, that I might not sin against you" (verse 11).

2. **The Bible will lift your burdens.** "I weep with grief; encourage me by your word" (verse 28).

3. **The Bible will guide your steps.** "Your word is a lamp for my feet and a light for my path" (verse 105).

4. **The Bible will bring you joy.** "Your decrees are my treasure; they are truly my heart's delight" (verse 111).

5. **The Bible will lead you to wisdom.** "As your words are taught, they give light; even the simple can understand them" (verse 130).

6. **The Bible will give you peace.** "Those who love your law have great peace and do not stumble" (verse 165).

7. **The Bible will bring you back to God.** "I have wandered away like a lost sheep; come and find me, for I have not forgotten your commands" (verse 176).

A Note to Readers

With 40 million copies in print, *The Living Bible* has been meeting a great need in people's hearts for more than thirty years. But even good things can be improved, so ninety evangelical scholars from various theological backgrounds and denominations were commissioned in 1989 to begin revising *The Living Bible*. The end result of this seven-year process is the *Holy Bible*, New Living Translation—a general-purpose translation that is accurate, easy to read, and excellent for study.

The goal of any Bible translation is to convey the meaning of the ancient Hebrew and Greek texts as accurately as possible to the modern reader. The New Living Translation is based on the most recent scholarship in the theory of translation. The challenge for the translators was to create a text that would make the same impact in the life of modern readers that the original text had for the original readers. In the New Living Translation, this is accomplished by translating entire thoughts (rather than just words) into natural, everyday English. The end result is a translation that is easy to read and understand and that accurately communicates the meaning of the original text.

We believe that this new translation, which combines the latest in scholarship with the best in translation style, will speak to your heart. We present the New Living Translation with the prayer that God will use it to speak his timeless truth to the church and to the world in a fresh, new way.

The Publishers, July 1996

Introduction to the New Living Translation

TRANSLATION PHILOSOPHY AND METHODOLOGY

There are two general theories or methods of Bible translation. The first has been called "formal equivalence." According to this theory, the translator attempts to render each word of the original language into the receptor language and seeks to preserve the original word order and sentence structure as much as possible. The second has been called "dynamic equivalence" or "functional equivalence." The goal of this translation theory is to produce in the receptor language the closest natural equivalent of the message expressed by the original-language text—both in meaning and in style. Such a translation attempts to have the same impact on modern readers as the original had on its own audience.

A dynamic-equivalence translation can also be called a thought-for-thought translation, as contrasted with a formal-equivalence or word-for-word translation. Of course, to translate the thought of the original language requires that the text be interpreted accurately and then be rendered in understandable idiom. So the goal of any thought-for-thought translation is to be both reliable and eminently readable. Thus, as a thought-for-thought translation, the New Living Translation seeks to be both exegetically accurate and idiomatically powerful.

In making a thought-for-thought translation, the translators must do their best to enter into the thought patterns of the ancient authors and to present the same ideas, connotations, and effects in the receptor language. In order to guard against personal biases and to ensure the accuracy of the message, a thought-for-thought translation should be created by a group of scholars who employ the best exegetical tools and who also understand the receptor language very well. With these concerns in mind, the Bible Translation Committee assigned each book of the Bible to three different scholars. Each scholar made a thorough review of the assigned book and submitted suggested revisions to the appropriate general reviewer. The general reviewer reviewed and summarized these suggestions and then proposed a first-draft revision of the text. This draft served as the basis for several additional phases of exegetical and stylistic committee review. Then the Bible Translation Committee jointly reviewed and approved every verse in the final translation.

A thought-for-thought translation prepared by a group of capable scholars has the potential to represent the intended meaning of the original text even more accurately than a word-for-word translation. This is illustrated by the various renderings of the Hebrew word *hesed*. This term cannot be adequately translated by any single English word because it can connote love, mercy, grace, kindness, faithfulness, and loyalty. The context—not the lexicon—must determine which English term is selected for translation.

The value of a thought-for-thought translation can be illustrated by comparing 1 Kings 2:10 in the King James Version, the New International Version, and the New Living Translation. "So David slept with his fathers, and was buried in the city of David" (KJV). "Then David rested with his fathers and was buried in the City of David" (NIV). "Then David died and was buried in the City of David" (NLT). Only the New Living Translation clearly translates the real meaning of the Hebrew idiom "slept with his fathers" into contemporary English.

WRITTEN TO BE READ ALOUD

It is evident in Scripture that the biblical documents were written to be read aloud, often in public worship (see Nehemiah 8; Luke 4:16-20; 1 Timothy 4:13; Revelation 1:3). It is still the case today that more people will hear the Bible read aloud in church than are likely to read it for themselves. Therefore, a new translation must communicate with clarity and power when it is read aloud. For this reason, the New Living Translation is recommended as a Bible to be used for public reading. Its living language is not only easy to understand, but it also has an emotive quality that will make an impact on the listener.

THE TEXTS BEHIND THE NEW LIVING TRANSLATION

The translators of the Old Testament used the Masoretic Text of the Hebrew Bible as their standard text. They used the edition known as *Biblia Hebraica Stuttgartensia* (1977) with its up-to-date textual apparatus, a revision of Rudolf Kittel's *Biblia Hebraica* (Stuttgart, 1937). The translators also compared the Dead Sea Scrolls, the Septuagint and other Greek manuscripts, the Samaritan Pentateuch, the Syriac Peshitta, the Latin Vulgate, and any other versions or manuscripts that shed light on textual problems.

The translators of the New Testament used the two standard editions of the Greek New Testament: the *Greek New Testament*, published by the United Bible Societies (fourth revised edition, 1993), and *Novum Testamentum Graece*, edited by Nestle and Aland (twenty-seventh edition, 1993). These two editions, which have the same text but differ in punctuation and textual notes, represent the best in modern textual scholarship.

TRANSLATION ISSUES

The translators have made a conscious effort to provide a text that can be easily understood by the average reader of modern English. To this end, we have used the vocabulary and language structures commonly used by the average person. The result is a translation of the Scriptures written generally at the reading level of a junior high school student. We have avoided using language that is likely to become quickly dated or that reflects a narrow subdialect of English, with the goal of making the New Living Translation as broadly useful as possible.

But our concern for readability goes beyond the concerns of vocabulary and sentence structure. We are also concerned about historical and cultural barriers to understanding the Bible, and we have sought to translate terms shrouded in history or culture in ways that can be immediately understood by the contemporary reader. Thus, our goal of easy readability expresses itself in a number of other ways:

♦ Rather than translating ancient weights and measures literally, which communicates little to the modern reader, we have expressed them by means of recognizable contemporary equivalents. We have converted ancient weights and measures to modern English (American) equivalents, and we have rendered the literal Hebrew or Greek measures, along with metric equivalents, in textual footnotes.

♦ Instead of translating ancient currency values literally, we have generally expressed them in terms of weights in precious metals. In some cases we have used other common terms to communicate the message effectively. For example, "three shekels of silver" might become "three silver coins" or "three pieces of silver" to convey the intended message. Again, a rendering of the literal Hebrew or Greek is given in textual footnotes.

♦ Since the Hebrew lunar calendar fluctuates from year to year in relation to the solar calendar used today, we have translated Hebrew dates in a way that communicates with our modern readership. It was clear that we could not use the names of the Hebrew months, such as *Abib*, which are meaningless to the modern reader. Nor could we use a simple designation such as "first month," because the months of the

Hebrew lunar calendar do not correspond with the months of our calendar. Thus, we have often used seasonal references to communicate the time of year when something happened. For example, "the first month" (which occurs in March and April) might be translated "early spring." Where it is possible to define a specific ancient date in terms of our modern calendar, we use modern dates in the text. Textual footnotes then give the literal Hebrew date and state the rationale for our rendering. For example, Ezra 7:9 pinpoints the date when Ezra arrived in Jerusalem: "the first day of the fifth month." This was during the seventh year of King Artaxerxes' reign (Ezra 7:7). We translate that lunar date as August 4, with a footnote giving the Hebrew and identifying the year as 458 B.C.

◆ Since ancient references to the time of day differ from our modern methods of denoting time, we used renderings that are instantly understandable to the modern reader. Accordingly, we have rendered specific times of day by using approximate equivalents in terms of our common "o'clock" system. On occasion, translations such as "at dawn the next morning" or "as the sun began to set" have been used when the biblical reference is general.

◆ Many words in the original texts made sense to the original audience but communicate something quite different to the modern reader. In such cases, some liberty must be allowed in translation to communicate what was intended. Places identified by the term normally translated "city," for example, are often better identified as "towns" or "villages." Similarly, the term normally translated "mountain" is often better rendered "hill."

◆ Many words and phrases carry a great deal of cultural meaning that was obvious to the original readers but needs explanation in our own culture. For example, the phrase "they beat their breasts" (Luke 23:48) in ancient times meant that people were very upset. In our translation we chose to translate this phrase dynamically: "They went home *in deep sorrow.*" In some cases, however, we have simply illuminated the existing expression to make it immediately understandable. For example, we might have expanded the literal phrase to read "they beat their breasts *in sorrow.*"

◆ Metaphorical language is often difficult for contemporary readers to understand, so at times we have chosen to translate or illuminate the metaphor. For example, the ancient poet writes, "Your eyes are doves" (Song of Songs 1:15). To help the modern reader, who might be confused or distracted by a literal visualization of this image, we converted the metaphor to a simile to make the meaning immediately clear: "Your eyes are soft *like* doves." Here we also added the modifier "soft" to help the modern reader catch the significance of the metaphoric expression. A few chapters later, the poet writes, "Your neck is like the tower of David" (Song of Songs 4:4). We rendered it "Your neck is *as stately as* the tower of David" to clarify the intended positive meaning of the metaphor.

◆ We did not feel obligated to display all Hebrew poetry in English poetic form. Only the book of Psalms is set entirely in poetic lines. Other books, though poetic in nature, are set in prose for the sake of easier reading. Nonetheless, these prose renderings reflect the poetic language of the original Hebrew. Where a portion of text is explicitly said to be a poem or song, however, it has usually been set as such.

◆ One challenge we faced was in determining how to translate accurately the ancient biblical text that was originally written in a context where male-oriented terms were used to refer to humanity generally. We needed to respect the nature of the ancient context while also trying to make the translation clear to a modern audience that tends to read male-oriented language as applying only to males. Often the original text, though using masculine nouns and pronouns, clearly intends that the message be applied to both men and women. One example is found in the New Testament epistles, where the believers are called "brothers" *(adelphoi)*. Yet it is clear that these epistles were addressed to all the believers—male and female. Thus, we have usually translated this Greek word "brothers and sisters" in order to represent the historical situation more accurately.

We have also been sensitive to passages where the text applies generally to human beings or to the human condition. In many instances we have used plural pronouns (they, them) in place of the masculine singular (he, him). For example, a traditional rendering of Proverbs 22:6 is: "Train up a child in the way he should go, and when he is old he will not turn from it." We have rendered it: "Teach your children to choose the right path, and when they are older, they will remain upon it." At times, we have also replaced third person pronouns with the second person to ensure clarity. A traditional rendering of Proverbs 26:27 is: "He who digs a pit will fall into it, and he who rolls a stone, it will come back on him." We have rendered it: "If you set a trap for others, you will get caught in it yourself. If you roll a boulder down on others, it will roll back and crush you." All such decisions were driven by the concern to reflect accurately the intended meaning of the original texts of Scripture.

We should emphasize, however, that all masculine nouns and pronouns used to represent God (for example, "Father") have been maintained without exception. We believe that essential traits of God's revealed character can only be conveyed through the masculine language expressed in the original texts of Scripture.

LEXICAL CONSISTENCY IN TERMINOLOGY

For the sake of clarity, we have maintained lexical consistency in areas such as divine names, synoptic passages, rhetorical structures, and nontheological technical terms (i.e., liturgical, cultic, zoological, botanical, cultural, and legal terms). For theological terms, we have allowed a greater semantic range of acceptable English words or phrases for a single Hebrew or Greek word. We avoided weighty theological terms that do not readily communicate to many modern readers. For example, we avoided using words such as "justification," "sanctification," and "regeneration." In place of these words (which are carryovers from Latin), we provided renderings such as "we are made right with God," "we are made holy," and "we are born anew."

THE SPELLING OF PROPER NAMES

Many individuals in the Bible, especially the Old Testament, are known by more than one name or by a number of variant names (e.g., Uzziah/Azariah). For the sake of clarity, we have tried to use a single spelling for any one individual, footnoting the literal spelling whenever we differ from it. This is especially helpful in delineating the kings of Israel and Judah. King Joash/Jehoash of Israel has been consistently called Jehoash, while King Joash/Jehoash of Judah is called Joash. A similar distinction has been used to distinguish between Joram/Jehoram of Israel and Joram/Jehoram of Judah. All such decisions were made with the goal of clarifying the text for the reader. When the ancient biblical writers clearly had a theological purpose in their choice of a variant name (e.g., Eshbaal/Ish-bosheth), the different names have been maintained with an explanatory footnote.

THE RENDERING OF DIVINE NAMES

All appearances of *'el*, *'elohim*, or *'eloah* have been translated "God," except where the context demands the translation "god(s)." We have rendered the tetragrammaton (*YHWH*) consistently as "the LORD," utilizing a form with small capitals that is common among English translations. This will distinguish it from the name *'adonai*, which we render "Lord." When *'adonai* and *YHWH* appear in conjunction, we have rendered it "Sovereign LORD." This also distinguishes *'adonai YHWH* from cases where *YHWH* appears with *'elohim*, which is rendered "Lord God." When *YH* (the short form of *YHWH*) and *YHWH* appear together, we have rendered it "Lord God." The Hebrew word *'adon* is rendered "lord," or "master," or sometimes "sir."

In the New Testament, the Greek word *Christos* has been translated as "Messiah" when the context assumes a Jewish audience. When a Gentile audience can be assumed, *Christos* has been translated as "Christ." The Greek word *kurios* is consistently translated "Lord," except in four quotations of Psalm 110:1, where it is translated "Lord."

TEXTUAL FOOTNOTES

The New Living Translation provides several kinds of textual footnotes:

- ◆ All Old Testament passages that are clearly quoted in the New Testament are identified in a textual footnote in the New Testament.
- ◆ Some textual footnotes provide cultural and historical information on places, things, and people in the Bible that are probably obscure to modern readers. Such notes should aid the reader in understanding the message of the text. For example, in Acts 12:1, "King Herod" is named in this translation as "King Herod Agrippa" and is identified in a footnote as being "the nephew of Herod Antipas and a grandson of Herod the Great."
- ◆ When various ancient manuscripts contain different readings, these differences are often documented in footnotes. For instance, textual variants are footnoted when the variant reading is very familiar (usually through the King James Version). We have used footnotes when we have selected variant readings that differ from the Hebrew and Greek editions normally followed.
- ◆ When the meaning of a proper name (or a wordplay inherent in a proper name) is relevant to the meaning of the text, it is illuminated with a textual footnote. For example, the footnote at Genesis 3:20 reads: "*Eve* sounds like a Hebrew term that means 'to give life.' " This wordplay in the Hebrew illuminates the meaning of the text, which goes on to say that Eve "would be the mother of all people everywhere." If the meaning of the name is more certain, it is stated more simply. For example, the footnote at Genesis 16:11 reads: "*Ishmael* means 'God hears.' " In this case, Hagar named her son Ishmael after realizing that God had heard her cry for help.
- ◆ When we translate the meaning of a place-name that is often simply transliterated from the Hebrew or Greek, we provide a textual footnote showing the transliteration that appears in many English translations. For example, the name usually transliterated "Havvoth-jair" in Judges 10:4 has been translated "the Towns of Jair," with a footnote that gives the traditional transliteration: "Hebrew *Havvoth-jair*."
- ◆ Textual footnotes are also used to show alternative renderings. These are prefaced with the word "Or." On occasion, we also provide notes on words or phrases that represent a translation that departs from long-standing tradition. These notes are prefaced with the words "traditionally rendered." For example, a footnote to the translation "contagious skin disease" at Leviticus 13:2 says, "Traditionally rendered *leprosy*."

AS WE SUBMIT this translation of the Bible for publication, we recognize that any translation of the Scriptures is subject to limitations and imperfections. Anyone who has attempted to communicate the richness of God's Word into another language will realize it is impossible to make a perfect translation. Recognizing these limitations, we sought God's guidance and wisdom throughout this project. Now we pray that he will accept our efforts and use this translation for the benefit of the Church and of all people.

We pray that the New Living Translation will overcome some of the barriers of history, culture, and language that have kept people from reading and understanding God's

Word. We hope that readers unfamiliar with the Bible will find the words clear and easy to understand, and that readers well versed in the Scriptures will gain a fresh perspective. We pray that readers will gain insight and wisdom for living, but most of all that they will meet the God of the Bible and be forever changed by knowing him.

The Bible Translation Committee
JULY 1996

Holy Bible, New Living Translation
Bible Translation Team

PENTATEUCH
Daniel I. Block, General Reviewer
The Southern Baptist Theological Seminary

GENESIS
Allan Ross, *Trinity Episcopal Seminary*
Gordon Wenham, *The Cheltenham and Gloucester College of Higher Education*

EXODUS
Robert Bergen, *Hannibal-LaGrange College*
Daniel I. Block, *The Southern Baptist Theological Seminary*
Eugene Carpenter, *Bethel College, Mishawaka, Indiana*

LEVITICUS
David Baker, *Ashland Theological Seminary*
Victor Hamilton, *Asbury College*
Kenneth Mathews, *Beeson Divinity School, Samford University*

NUMBERS
Dale A. Brueggemann, *Assemblies of God Division of Foreign Missions*
Roland K. Harrison (deceased), *Wycliffe College*
Gerald L. Mattingly, *Johnson Bible College*

DEUTERONOMY
J. Gordon McConville, *The Cheltenham and Gloucester College of Higher Education*
Eugene H. Merrill, *Dallas Theological Seminary*
John A. Thompson, *University of Melbourne*

HISTORICAL BOOKS
Barry J. Beitzel, General Reviewer
Trinity Evangelical Divinity School

JOSHUA/JUDGES
Carl E. Armerding, *Schloss Mittersill Study Centre*
Barry J. Beitzel, *Trinity Evangelical Divinity School*
Lawson Stone, *Asbury Theological Seminary*

1 & 2 SAMUEL
Barry J. Beitzel, *Trinity Evangelical Divinity School*
V. Philips Long, *Covenant Theological Seminary*
J. Robert Vannoy, *Biblical Theological Seminary*

1 & 2 KINGS
Bill T. Arnold, *Asbury Theological Seminary*

William H. Barnes, *North Central University*
Frederic W. Bush, *Fuller Theological Seminary*

1 & 2 CHRONICLES
Raymond B. Dillard (deceased), *Westminster Theological Seminary*
David A. Dorsey, *Evangelical School of Theology*
Terry Eves, *Erskine College*

EZRA/NEHEMIAH/ESTHER/RUTH
William C. Williams, *Southern California College*
Hugh G. M. Williamson, *Oxford University*

POETRY
Tremper Longman III, General Reviewer
Westmont College

JOB
August Konkel, *Providence Theological Seminary*
Tremper Longman III, *Westmont College*
Al Wolters, *Redeemer College*

PSALMS 1–75
Mark D. Futato, *Westminster Theological Seminary in California*
Douglas Green, *Westminster Theological Seminary*
Richard Pratt, *Reformed Theological Seminary*

PSALMS 76–150
David M. Howard Jr., *Bethel Theological Seminary*
Raymond C. Ortlund Jr., *Trinity Evangelical Divinity School*
Willem VanGemeren, *Trinity Evangelical Divinity School*

PROVERBS
Ted Hildebrandt, *Grace College*
Richard Schultz, *Wheaton College*
Raymond C. Van Leeuwen, *Eastern College*

ECCLESIASTES/SONG OF SONGS
Daniel C. Fredericks, *Belhaven College*
David Hubbard (deceased), *Fuller Theological Seminary*
Tremper Longman III, *Westmont College*

PROPHETS
John N. Oswalt, General Reviewer
Wesley Biblical Seminary

ISAIAH
John N. Oswalt, *Wesley Biblical Seminary*
Gary Smith, *Bethel Theological Seminary*
John Walton, *Moody Bible Institute*

JEREMIAH/LAMENTATIONS
G. Herbert Livingston, *Asbury Theological Seminary*
Elmer A. Martens, *Mennonite Brethren Biblical Seminary*

EZEKIEL
Daniel I. Block, *The Southern Baptist Theological Seminary*
David H. Engelhard, *Calvin Theological Seminary*
David Thompson, *Asbury Theological Seminary*

DANIEL/HAGGAI/ZECHARIAH/MALACHI
Joyce Baldwin Caine (deceased), *Trinity College, Bristol*
Douglas Gropp, *Catholic University of America*
Roy Hayden, *Oral Roberts School of Theology*

HOSEA–ZEPHANIAH
Joseph Coleson, *Nazarene Theological Seminary*
Andrew Hill, *Wheaton College*
Richard Patterson, *Professor Emeritus, Liberty University*

GOSPELS AND ACTS
Grant R. Osborne, General Reviewer
Trinity Evangelical Divinity School

MATTHEW
Craig Blomberg, *Denver Conservative Baptist Seminary*
Donald A. Hagner, *Fuller Theological Seminary*
David Turner, *Grand Rapids Baptist Seminary*

MARK
Robert Guelich (deceased), *Fuller Theological Seminary*
Grant R. Osborne, *Trinity Evangelical Divinity School*

LUKE
Darrell Bock, *Dallas Theological Seminary*
Scot McKnight, *North Park College*
Robert Stein, *Bethel Theological Seminary*

JOHN
Gary M. Burge, *Wheaton College*
Philip W. Comfort, *Coastal Carolina University*
Marianne Meye Thompson, *Fuller Theological Seminary*

ACTS
D. A. Carson, *Trinity Evangelical Divinity School*
William J. Larkin, *Columbia Biblical Seminary*
Roger Mohrlang, *Whitworth College*

LETTERS AND REVELATION
Norman R. Ericson, General Reviewer
Wheaton College

ROMANS/GALATIANS
Gerald Borchert, *The Southern Baptist Theological Seminary*
Douglas J. Moo, *Trinity Evangelical Divinity School*
Thomas R. Schreiner, *Bethel Theological Seminary*

1 & 2 CORINTHIANS
Joseph Alexanian, *Trinity International University*
Linda Belleville, *North Park Theological Seminary*
Douglas A. Oss, *Central Bible College*
Robert Sloan, *Baylor University*

EPHESIANS–PHILEMON
Harold W. Hoehner, *Dallas Theological Seminary*
Moises Silva, *Gordon-Conwell Theological Seminary*
Klyne Snodgrass, *North Park Theological Seminary*

HEBREWS/JAMES/1 & 2 PETER/JUDE
Peter Davids, *Canadian Theological Seminary*
Norman R. Ericson, *Wheaton College*
William Lane (deceased), *Seattle Pacific University*
J. Ramsey Michaels, *S.W. Missouri State University*

1–3 JOHN/REVELATION
Greg Beale, *Gordon-Conwell Theological Seminary*
Robert Mounce, *Whitworth College*
M. Robert Mulholland Jr., *Asbury Theological Seminary*

SPECIAL REVIEWERS
F. F. Bruce (deceased), *University of Manchester*
Kenneth N. Taylor, *Tyndale House Publishers*

COORDINATING TEAM
Mark R. Norton, *Managing Editor and O.T. Coordinating Editor*
Philip W. Comfort, *N.T. Coordinating Editor*
Ronald A. Beers, *Executive Director and Stylist*
Mark D. Taylor, *Director and Chief Stylist*
Daniel W. Taylor, *Consultant*

Old Testament

The Old Testament traces the plan of God from the creation of the world to about 400 B.C. The Historical Books portray the birth, growth, development, and discipline of God's covenant people, Israel. Following their four hundred years of captivity in Egypt, God plants them in the land of Canaan, where they eventually establish a kingdom. The Poetical Books capture the emotions and heartbeat of men and women living during this historical period. And the Prophetical Books record God's repeated attempts to call his people back to the godly behavior they abandoned.

THE OLD TESTAMENT

HISTORICAL (17)		POETICAL (5)	PROPHETICAL (17)	
PENTATEUCH (5)	Genesis Exodus Leviticus Numbers Deuteronomy	Job Psalms Proverbs Ecclesiastes Song of Songs	Isaiah Jeremiah Lamentations Ezekiel Daniel	MAJOR (5)
HISTORICAL (12)	Joshua Judges Ruth 1 Samuel 2 Samuel 1 Kings 2 Kings 1 Chronicles 2 Chronicles Ezra Nehemiah Esther		Hosea Joel Amos Obadiah Jonah Micah Nahum Habakkuk Zephaniah Haggai Zechariah Malachi	MINOR (12)

New Testament

The New Testament continues to unfold the program of God from the birth of Jesus to about the end of the first century A.D. The record of Jesus' incomparable words and works is preserved in the four Gospels (Matthew—John). After his ascension, Jesus' followers spread the Good News of his message (Acts). One of these followers, Paul of Tarsus, penned many letters to churches and individuals, providing much-needed encouragement and instruction. The final nine books contain practical help for the followers of Jesus Christ.

THE NEW TESTAMENT

PAULINE EPISTLES: INDIVIDUALS				
1 Timothy	2 Timothy	Titus	Philemon	

PAULINE EPISTLES: CHURCHES				NON-PAULINE EPISTLES AND REVELATION
2 Thessalonians			Hebrews	
1 Thessalonians			James	
Colossians			1 Peter	
Philippians			2 Peter	
Ephesians			1 John	
Galatians			2 John	
2 Corinthians			3 John	
1 Corinthians			Jude	
Romans			Revelation	

Matthew	Mark	Luke	John	Acts
HISTORICAL BOOKS				

Genesis

GENESIS begins "in the beginning." Its fifty chapters sketch human history from Creation to Babel (Genesis 1–11) and from Abraham to Joseph (Genesis 12–50). The first eleven chapters introduce the Creator God and the beginnings of life, sin, judgment, family, worship, and salvation. The remainder of the book focuses on the lives of the four patriarchs of the faith—Abraham, Isaac, Jacob, and Joseph—from whom will come the nation Israel . . . and ultimately the Savior, Jesus Christ.

Focus	Four Great Events				Four Great People			
Divisions	Creation	Fall	Flood	Nations	Abraham	Isaac	Jacob	Joseph
	1	2 3	5 6	9 10 11	12	24 25	26 27	36 37	50
Topics	Primeval History				Patriarchal History			
	Beginning of the Human Race				Beginning of the Hebrew Race			
Place	East (Eden to Ur)				West (Canaan to Egypt)			
Time	Over 2,000 Years (20% of Genesis)				About 350 Years (80% of Genesis)			

JANUARY 1 □ DAY 1
GENESIS 1–2
"In the Beginning . . ."

OVERVIEW Genesis opens with two accounts of Creation. The first (1:1–2:4a) describes the events in chronological order; the second (2:4b-25) considers the events topically, in order to focus on one aspect of Creation. The first provides a wide-angle view of the creation of the universe; the second takes a zoom-lens look at man and woman, the climax of Creation—for they are the ones who will bear God's image and enjoy God's fellowship in the garden prepared especially for them.

Chapter 1	Chapter 2
Six Days of Creation Summarized	Sixth Day of Creation Scrutinized
Chronological	Topical

YOUR DAILY WALK
- What is the longest book you ever read?
- What is the greatest distance you ever walked?
- What is the biggest meal you ever ate?
- And what could these three curious questions possibly have in common?

That God created us from dust is no reason to treat another person like dirt.

In case you haven't guessed, they are all examples of big projects completed in small stages. You read that book one page at a time . . . covered that distance one step at a time . . . ate that meal one bite at a time. One page, one step, one bite might not seem like much when compared to the whole, but each brings you closer to your goal.

This year, with the help of *The Daily Walk Bible,* you'll be fulfilling what for many people has been a lifelong dream: to read through the Bible—all 1,189 chapters of it! And like thousands of other "daily walkers," you'll discover you *can* reach your goal—one day at a time! Are you ready to launch your exciting expedition through the Bible? It starts with the first words of Genesis: "In the beginning God created . . ."

INSIGHT The Days of Creation
If the days of Creation are arranged in two columns of three days each, you'll discover an interesting fact!

First God created the realm	Then God created the ruler
Day 1—Light	Day 4—Sun, Moon, & Stars
Day 2—Sky & Oceans	Day 5—Birds & Fish
Day 3—Dry Land	Day 6—Animals & People

C H A P T E R 1

In the beginning God created* the heavens and the earth. ²The earth was empty, a formless mass cloaked in darkness. And the Spirit of God was hovering over its surface. ³Then God said, "Let there be light," and there was light. ⁴And God saw that it was good. Then he separated the

1:1 Or *In the beginning when God created,* or *When God began to create.*

light from the darkness. ⁵God called the light "day" and the darkness "night." Together these made up one day.

⁶And God said, "Let there be space between the waters, to separate water from water." ⁷And so it was. God made this space to separate the waters above from the waters below. ⁸And God called the space "sky." This happened on the second day.

⁹And God said, "Let the waters beneath the sky be gathered into one place so dry ground may appear." And so it was. ¹⁰God named the dry ground "land" and the water "seas." And God saw that it was good. ¹¹Then God said, "Let the land burst forth with every sort of grass and seed-bearing plant. And let there be trees that grow seed-bearing fruit. The seeds will then produce the kinds of plants and trees from which they came." And so it was. ¹²The land was filled with seed-bearing plants and trees, and their seeds produced plants and trees of like kind. And God saw that it was good. ¹³This all happened on the third day.

¹⁴And God said, "Let bright lights appear in the sky to separate the day from the night. They will be signs to mark off the seasons, the days, and the years. ¹⁵Let their light shine down upon the earth." And so it was. ¹⁶For God made two great lights, the sun and the moon, to shine down upon the earth. The greater one, the sun, presides during the day; the lesser one, the moon, presides through the night. He also made the stars. ¹⁷God set these lights in the heavens to light the earth, ¹⁸to govern the day and the night, and to separate the light from the darkness. And God saw that it was good. ¹⁹This all happened on the fourth day.

²⁰And God said, "Let the waters swarm with fish and other life. Let the skies be filled with birds of every kind." ²¹So God created great sea creatures and every sort of fish and every kind of bird. And God saw that it was good. ²²Then God blessed them, saying, "Let the fish multiply and fill the oceans. Let the birds increase and fill the earth." ²³This all happened on the fifth day.

²⁴And God said, "Let the earth bring forth every kind of animal—livestock, small animals, and wildlife." And so it was. ²⁵God made all sorts of wild animals, livestock, and small animals, each able to re-

produce more of its own kind. And God saw that it was good.

²⁶Then God said, "Let us make people* in our image, to be like ourselves. They will be masters over all life—the fish in the sea, the birds in the sky, and all the livestock, wild animals,* and small animals."

²⁷ So God created people in his own image;
    God patterned them after himself;
    male and female he created them.

²⁸God blessed them and told them, "Multiply and fill the earth and subdue it. Be masters over the fish and birds and all the animals." ²⁹And God said, "Look! I have given you the seed-bearing plants throughout the earth and all the fruit trees for your food. ³⁰And I have given all the grasses and other green plants to the animals and birds for their food." And so it was. ³¹Then God looked over all he had made, and he saw that it was excellent in every way. This all happened on the sixth day.

CHAPTER 2

So the creation of the heavens and the earth and everything in them was completed. ²On the seventh day, having finished his task, God rested from all his work. ³And God blessed the seventh day and declared it holy, because it was the day when he rested from his work of creation.

⁴This is the account of the creation of the heavens and the earth.

When the LORD God made the heavens and the earth, ⁵there were no plants or grain growing on the earth, for the LORD God had not sent any rain. And no one was there to cultivate the soil. ⁶But water came up out of the ground and watered all the land. ⁷And the LORD God formed a man's body from the dust of the ground and breathed into it the breath of life. And the man became a living person.

⁸Then the LORD God planted a garden in Eden, in the east, and there he placed the man he had created. ⁹And the LORD God planted all sorts of trees in the garden— beautiful trees that produced delicious fruit. At the center of the garden he placed the tree of life and the tree of the knowledge of good and evil.

¹⁰A river flowed from the land of Eden,

1:26a Hebrew *man*; also in 1:27.   1:26b As in Syriac version; Hebrew reads *all the earth*.

watering the garden and then dividing into four branches. ¹¹One of these branches is the Pishon, which flows around the entire land of Havilah, where gold is found. ¹²The gold of that land is exceptionally pure; aromatic resin and onyx stone are also found there. ¹³The second branch is the Gihon, which flows around the entire land of Cush. ¹⁴The third branch is the Tigris, which flows to the east of Asshur. The fourth branch is the Euphrates.

¹⁵The LORD God placed the man in the Garden of Eden to tend and care for it. ¹⁶But the LORD God gave him this warning: "You may freely eat any fruit in the garden ¹⁷except fruit from the tree of the knowledge of good and evil. If you eat of its fruit, you will surely die."

¹⁸And the LORD God said, "It is not good for the man to be alone. I will make a companion who will help him." ¹⁹So the LORD God formed from the soil every kind of animal and bird. He brought them to Adam* to see what he would call them, and Adam chose a name for each one. ²⁰He gave names to all the livestock, birds, and wild animals. But still there was no companion suitable for him. ²¹So the LORD God caused Adam to fall into a deep sleep. He took one of Adam's ribs* and closed up the place from which he had taken it. ²²Then the LORD God made a woman from the rib and brought her to Adam.

²³"At last!" Adam exclaimed. "She is part of my own flesh and bone! She will be called 'woman,' because she was taken out of a man." ²⁴This explains why a man leaves his father and mother and is joined to his wife, and the two are united into one. ²⁵Now, although Adam and his wife were both naked, neither of them felt any shame.

2:19 Hebrew *the man,* and so throughout this chapter.   2:21 Or *took a part of Adam's side.*

JANUARY 2 □ DAY 2
GENESIS 3–5
From Paradise to Pain

 OVERVIEW What began as paradise is soon spoiled by sin. Satan, disguised as a serpent, tempts the woman by turning her gaze from God's bountiful provision (the many trees) to God's one prohibition (the single tree of the knowledge of good and evil). Adam and Eve's disobedience in eating from the forbidden tree results in their expulsion from the garden. The seeds of their sin quickly grow as their first son (Cain) commits the first murder. For generation after generation the spiral continues, setting the stage for God's judgment.

Chapter 3	Chapter 4	Chapter 5
The First Sin	The First Murder	The First Family Tree
Adam and Eve	Cain and Abel	Seth

 YOUR DAILY WALK Satan is a master at taking the blessings of God and turning them into something that brings a curse instead. If given the chance, he'll convince you to seek the pleasures of sex outside the bonds of marriage . . . to exchange the worship of the Creator for the worship of the creation . . . to substitute what is convenient for what is obedient. The temptation will be cunning, the promise inviting. But as Adam and Eve discovered, the painful consequences will far outweigh the temporary pleasures.

Satan, like a fisherman, baits his hook according to the appetite of the fish.

For many Christians, resisting temptation is difficult because they don't want to discourage it completely. God has promised to provide a way out (1 Corinthians 10:13), but that doesn't help if you keep leaving a forwarding address! Write the references of James 4:7 and 2 Timothy 2:22 in the margin next to Genesis 3. Look them up; read them twice; take them to heart!

 INSIGHT Cataloging a Curse

Genesis 3 introduces more than the beginning of sin. There you'll also find some of its consequences: crabgrass, labor pains, slithering snakes, and perspiration! After reading chapter 3, try to summarize each part of the curse as it relates to the following:

- the serpent (3:14)
- Satan (3:15)
- the woman (3:15-16)
- the man (3:17-19)

CHAPTER 3

Now the serpent was the shrewdest of all the creatures the LORD God had made. "Really?" he asked the woman. "Did God really say you must not eat any of the fruit in the garden?"

²"Of course we may eat it," the woman told him. ³"It's only the fruit from the tree at the center of the garden that we are not allowed to eat. God says we must not eat it or even touch it, or we will die."

⁴"You won't die!" the serpent hissed. ⁵"God knows that your eyes will be opened when you eat it. You will become just like God, knowing everything, both good and evil."

⁶The woman was convinced. The fruit looked so fresh and delicious, and it would make her so wise! So she ate some of the fruit. She also gave some to her husband, who was with her. Then he ate it, too. ⁷At that moment, their eyes were opened, and they suddenly felt shame at their nakedness. So they strung fig leaves together around their hips to cover themselves.

⁸Toward evening they heard the LORD God walking about in the garden, so they hid themselves among the trees. ⁹The LORD God called to Adam,* "Where are you?"

¹⁰He replied, "I heard you, so I hid. I was afraid because I was naked."

¹¹"Who told you that you were naked?" the LORD God asked. "Have you eaten the fruit I commanded you not to eat?"

¹²"Yes," Adam admitted, "but it was the woman you gave me who brought me the fruit, and I ate it."

¹³Then the LORD God asked the woman, "How could you do such a thing?"

"The serpent tricked me," she replied. "That's why I ate it."

¹⁴So the LORD God said to the serpent, "Because you have done this, you will be punished. You are singled out from all the domestic and wild animals of the whole earth to be cursed. You will grovel in the dust as long as you live, crawling along on your belly. ¹⁵From now on, you and the woman will be enemies, and your offspring and her offspring will be enemies. He will crush your head, and you will strike his heel."

¹⁶Then he said to the woman, "You will bear children with intense pain and suffering. And though your desire will be for your husband,* he will be your master."

¹⁷And to Adam he said, "Because you listened to your wife and ate the fruit I told you not to eat, I have placed a curse on the ground. All your life you will struggle to scratch a living from it. ¹⁸It will grow thorns and thistles for you, though you will eat of its grains. ¹⁹All your life you will sweat to produce food, until your dying day. Then you will return to the ground from which you came. For you were made from dust, and to the dust you will return."

²⁰Then Adam named his wife Eve,* because she would be the mother of all people everywhere. ²¹And the LORD God made clothing from animal skins for Adam and his wife.

²²Then the LORD God said, "The people have become as we are, knowing everything, both good and evil. What if they eat the fruit of the tree of life? Then they will live forever!" ²³So the LORD God banished Adam and his wife from the Garden of Eden, and he sent Adam out to cultivate the

---

3:9 Hebrew *the man*, and so throughout this chapter.   **3:16** Or *And though you may desire to control your husband.*   **3:20** *Eve* sounds like a Hebrew term that means "to give life."

ground from which he had been made.
²⁴After banishing them from the garden,
the LORD God stationed mighty angelic beings* to the east of Eden. And a flaming
sword flashed back and forth, guarding the
way to the tree of life.

CHAPTER 4

Now Adam* slept with his wife, Eve, and
she became pregnant. When the time came,
she gave birth to Cain,* and she said, "With
the LORD's help, I have brought forth* a
man!" ²Later she gave birth to a second son
and named him Abel.

When they grew up, Abel became a
shepherd, while Cain was a farmer. ³At
harvesttime Cain brought to the LORD a gift
of his farm produce, ⁴while Abel brought
several choice lambs from the best of his
flock. The LORD accepted Abel and his offering, ⁵but he did not accept Cain and his
offering. This made Cain very angry and
dejected.

⁶"Why are you so angry?" the LORD asked
him. "Why do you look so dejected? ⁷You
will be accepted if you respond in the right
way. But if you refuse to respond correctly,
then watch out! Sin is waiting to attack and
destroy you, and you must subdue it."

⁸Later Cain suggested to his brother,
Abel, "Let's go out into the fields."* And
while they were there, Cain attacked and
killed his brother.

⁹Afterward the LORD asked Cain,
"Where is your brother? Where is Abel?"

"I don't know!" Cain retorted. "Am I
supposed to keep track of him wherever he
goes?"

¹⁰But the LORD said, "What have you
done? Listen—your brother's blood cries
out to me from the ground! ¹¹You are hereby
banished from the ground you have defiled
with your brother's blood. ¹²No longer will
it yield abundant crops for you, no matter
how hard you work! From now on you will
be a homeless fugitive on the earth, constantly wandering from place to place."

¹³Cain replied to the LORD, "My punish-
ment* is too great for me to bear! ¹⁴You have
banished me from my land and from your
presence; you have made me a wandering
fugitive. All who see me will try to kill me!"

¹⁵The LORD replied, "They will not kill
you, for I will give seven times your punishment to anyone who does." Then the
LORD put a mark on Cain to warn anyone
who might try to kill him. ¹⁶So Cain left the
LORD's presence and settled in the land of
Nod,* east of Eden.

¹⁷Then Cain's wife became pregnant and
gave birth to a son, and they named him
Enoch. When Cain founded a city, he
named it Enoch after his son.

¹⁸ Enoch was the father of* Irad.

Irad was the father of Mehujael.

Mehujael was the father of Methushael.

Methushael was the father of Lamech.

¹⁹Lamech married two women—Adah
and Zillah. ²⁰Adah gave birth to a baby
named Jabal. He became the first of the
herdsmen who live in tents. ²¹His brother's name was Jubal, the first musician—
the inventor of the harp and flute. ²²To
Lamech's other wife, Zillah, was born
Tubal-cain. He was the first to work with
metal, forging instruments of bronze and
iron. Tubal-cain had a sister named Naamah.

²³One day Lamech said to Adah and Zil-
lah, "Listen to me, my wives. I have killed
a youth who attacked and wounded me.
²⁴If anyone who kills Cain is to be punished
seven times, anyone who takes revenge
against me will be punished seventy-seven
times!"

²⁵Adam slept with his wife again, and
she gave birth to another son. She named
him Seth,* for she said, "God has granted
me another son in place of Abel, the one
Cain killed." ²⁶When Seth grew up, he had
a son and named him Enosh. It was during
his lifetime that people first began to worship the LORD.

CHAPTER 5

This is the history of the descendants of
Adam. When God created people,* he
made them in the likeness of God. ²He created them male and female, and he blessed
them and called them "human."*

³When Adam was 130 years old, his son
Seth was born,* and Seth was the very
image of his father.* ⁴After the birth of

3:24 Hebrew *cherubim.*   **4:1a** Hebrew *the man.*   **4:1b** *Cain* sounds like a Hebrew term that can mean "bring forth" or "acquire."
4:1c Or *I have acquired.*   **4:8** As in Samaritan Pentateuch, Greek and Syriac versions, Latin Vulgate; Masoretic Text lacks "Let's go
out into the fields."   **4:13** Or *My sin.*   **4:16** *Nod* means "wandering."   **4:18** Or *the ancestor of,* and so throughout the verse.
4:25 *Seth* probably means "granted"; the name may also mean "appointed."   **5:1** Hebrew *man.*   **5:2** Hebrew *man.*   **5:3a** Or *his
son, the ancestor of Seth, was born;* similarly in 5:6, 9, 12, 15, 18, 21, 25.   **5:3b** Hebrew *was in his own likeness, after his image.*

Seth,* Adam lived another 800 years, and he had other sons and daughters. [5]He died at the age of 930.

[6]When Seth was 105 years old, his son Enosh was born. [7]After the birth of Enosh, Seth lived another 807 years, and he had other sons and daughters. [8]He died at the age of 912.

[9]When Enosh was 90 years old, his son Kenan was born. [10]After the birth of Kenan, Enosh lived another 815 years, and he had other sons and daughters. [11]He died at the age of 905.

[12]When Kenan was 70 years old, his son Mahalalel was born. [13]After the birth of Mahalalel, Kenan lived another 840 years, and he had other sons and daughters. [14]He died at the age of 910.

[15]When Mahalalel was 65 years old, his son Jared was born. [16]After the birth of Jared, Mahalalel lived 830 years, and he had other sons and daughters. [17]He died at the age of 895.

[18]When Jared was 162 years old, his son Enoch was born. [19]After the birth of Enoch, Jared lived another 800 years, and he had other sons and daughters. [20]He died at the age of 962.

[21]When Enoch was 65 years old, his son Methuselah was born. [22]After the birth of Methuselah, Enoch lived another 300 years in close fellowship with God, and he had other sons and daughters. [23]Enoch lived 365 years in all. [24]He enjoyed a close relationship with God throughout his life. Then suddenly, he disappeared because God took him.

[25]When Methuselah was 187 years old, his son Lamech was born. [26]After the birth of Lamech, Methuselah lived another 782 years, and he had other sons and daughters. [27]He died at the age of 969.

[28]When Lamech was 182 years old, his son Noah was born. [29]Lamech named his son Noah,* for he said, "He will bring us relief from the painful labor of farming this ground that the LORD has cursed." [30]After the birth of Noah, Lamech lived 595 years, and he had other sons and daughters. [31]He died at the age of 777.

[32]By the time Noah was 500 years old, he had three sons: Shem, Ham, and Japheth.

5:4 Or *After the birth of this ancestor of Seth;* similarly in 5:7, 10, 13, 16, 19, 22, 26.   **5:29** *Noah* sounds like a Hebrew term that can mean "relief" or "comfort."

JANUARY 3   ☐ DAY 3
GENESIS 6–9
Noah's Boat and God's Judgment

OVERVIEW As the generations begin to multiply on the face of the earth, the world's population greatly increases . . . and so does the world's wickedness (6:5). At last, God prepares to destroy humankind with a judgment of water. But one man and his family receive God's commendation, while the rest of humanity faces God's condemnation. Noah obediently undertakes a century-long shipbuilding project in preparation for saving his believing family. As the floodwaters rise, Noah's eight-member family rides high in God's loving protection.

Chapter 6	Chapter 7	Chapter 8	Chapter 9
Humankind's Corruption	God's Condemnation Executed	Ended	God's Covenant
Building the Boat	Riding in the Boat		Rainbow in the Sky

YOUR DAILY WALK When a man repeats a promise over and over, you can be pretty sure that he must have a problem keeping it. When God repeats a promise over and over, you can be absolutely sure that he doesn't!

God may not promise a comfortable journey, but he does guarantee a safe landing.

Is God trustworthy? Does he keep his word? When he makes a promise, is there an 80 . . . 90 . . . 100 percent chance it will come true? The ancient shipbuilder named Noah must have wrestled with such questions, for his very life and the lives of his family were totally bound up in the promises of God. Spend a few minutes evaluating God's "scorecard" on how well he kept his promises to Noah:

"I will begin forty days and forty nights of rain" (7:4). Yes or no?
"I will wipe from the earth all the living things I have created" (7:4). Yes or no?
"I will never again curse the earth" (8:21). Yes or no?
"I will remember my covenant" (9:15). Yes or no?

The rainbow in the sky (9:12-16) is God's eternal reminder that he will never repeat the watery horror of Noah's day. Keep an eye out for rainbows today in photographs and drawings—or even real ones! Let each one remind you (as it did Noah) that when you're resting on a promise from God, you needn't worry how deep the water gets!

INSIGHT Water, Water, Everywhere . . . and Very Little Else! In the account of the Flood, you will find phrases such as "the floods prevailed" (7:17), and "the waters rose higher and higher" (7:18). God wanted to make it clear that this was no ordinary flood and that his promise—to destroy "all living things that I have made"— was no idle threat.

CHAPTER 6

When the human population began to grow rapidly on the earth, [2]the sons of God saw the beautiful women of the human race and took any they wanted as their wives. [3]Then the LORD said, "My Spirit will not put up with humans for such a long time, for they are only mortal flesh. In the future, they will live no more than 120 years."

[4]In those days, and even afterward, giants* lived on the earth, for whenever the sons of God had intercourse with human women, they gave birth to children who became the heroes mentioned in legends of old.

[5]Now the LORD observed the extent of the people's wickedness, and he saw that all their thoughts were consistently and totally evil. [6]So the LORD was sorry he had ever made them. It broke his heart. [7]And the LORD said, "I will completely wipe out this human race that I have created. Yes, and I will destroy all the animals and birds, too. I am sorry I ever made them." [8]But Noah found favor with the LORD.

[9]This is the history of Noah and his family. Noah was a righteous man, the only blameless man living on earth at the time. He consistently followed God's will and enjoyed a close relationship with him. [10]Noah had three sons: Shem, Ham, and Japheth.

[11]Now the earth had become corrupt in God's sight, and it was filled with violence. [12]God observed all this corruption in the world, and he saw violence and depravity everywhere. [13]So God said to Noah, "I have decided to destroy all living creatures, for the earth is filled with violence because of them. Yes, I will wipe them all from the face of the earth!

[14]"Make a boat* from resinous wood and seal it with tar, inside and out. Then construct decks and stalls throughout its interior. [15]Make it 450 feet long, 75 feet wide, and 45 feet high.* [16]Construct an opening all the way around the boat, 18 inches* below the roof. Then put three decks inside the boat—bottom, middle, and upper— and put a door in the side.

[17]"Look! I am about to cover the earth with a flood that will destroy every living thing. Everything on earth will die! [18]But I solemnly swear to keep you safe in the boat, with your wife and your sons and

6:4 Hebrew *Nephilim.*   6:14 Traditionally rendered *an ark.*   6:15 Hebrew *300 cubits* [135 meters] *long, 50 cubits* [22.5 meters] *wide, and 30 cubits* [13.5 meters] *high.*   6:16 Hebrew *1 cubit* [45 centimeters].

their wives. ¹⁹Bring a pair of every kind of animal—a male and a female—into the boat with you to keep them alive during the flood. ²⁰Pairs of each kind of bird and each kind of animal, large and small alike, will come to you to be kept alive. ²¹And remember, take enough food for your family and for all the animals."

²²So Noah did everything exactly as God had commanded him.

CHAPTER 7
Finally, the day came when the LORD said to Noah, "Go into the boat with all your family, for among all the people of the earth, I consider you alone to be righteous. ²Take along seven pairs of each animal that I have approved for eating and for sacrifice, and take one pair of each of the others. ³Then select seven pairs of every kind of bird. There must be a male and a female in each pair to ensure that every kind of living creature will survive the flood. ⁴One week from today I will begin forty days and forty nights of rain. And I will wipe from the earth all the living things I have created."

⁵So Noah did exactly as the LORD had commanded him. ⁶He was 600 years old when the flood came, ⁷and he went aboard the boat to escape—he and his wife and his sons and their wives. ⁸With them were all the various kinds of animals—those approved for eating and sacrifice and those that were not—along with all the birds and other small animals. ⁹They came into the boat in pairs, male and female, just as God had commanded Noah. ¹⁰One week later, the flood came and covered the earth.

¹¹When Noah was 600 years old, on the seventeenth day of the second month, the underground waters burst forth on the earth, and the rain fell in mighty torrents from the sky. ¹²The rain continued to fall for forty days and forty nights. ¹³But Noah had gone into the boat that very day with his wife and his sons—Shem, Ham, and Japheth—and their wives. ¹⁴With them in the boat were pairs of every kind of breathing animal—domestic and wild, large and small—along with birds and flying insects of every kind. ¹⁵Two by two they came into the boat, ¹⁶male and female, just as God had commanded. Then the LORD shut them in.

¹⁷For forty days the floods prevailed, covering the ground and lifting the boat high above the earth. ¹⁸As the waters rose higher and higher above the ground, the boat floated safely on the surface. ¹⁹Finally, the water covered even the highest mountains on the earth, ²⁰standing more than twenty-two feet* above the highest peaks. ²¹All the living things on earth died—birds, domestic animals, wild animals, all kinds of small animals, and all the people. ²²Everything died that breathed and lived on dry land. ²³Every living thing on the earth was wiped out—people, animals both large and small, and birds. They were all destroyed, and only Noah was left alive, along with those who were with him in the boat. ²⁴And the water covered the earth for 150 days.

CHAPTER 8
But God remembered Noah and all the animals in the boat. He sent a wind to blow across the waters, and the floods began to disappear. ²The underground water sources ceased their gushing, and the torrential rains stopped. ³So the flood gradually began to recede. After 150 days, ⁴exactly five months from the time the flood began,* the boat came to rest on the mountains of Ararat. ⁵Two and a half months later,* as the waters continued to go down, other mountain peaks began to appear.

⁶After another forty days, Noah opened the window he had made in the boat ⁷and released a raven that flew back and forth until the earth was dry. ⁸Then he sent out a dove to see if it could find dry ground. ⁹But the dove found no place to land because the water was still too high. So it returned to the boat, and Noah held out his hand and drew the dove back inside. ¹⁰Seven days later, Noah released the dove again. ¹¹This time, toward evening, the bird returned to him with a fresh olive leaf in its beak. Noah now knew that the water was almost gone. ¹²A week later, he released the dove again, and this time it did not come back.

¹³Finally, when Noah was 601 years old, ten and a half months after the flood began,* Noah lifted back the cover to look. The water was drying up. ¹⁴Two more months went by,* and at last the earth was

7:20 Hebrew *15 cubits* [6.8 meters].   **8:4** Hebrew *on the seventeenth day of the seventh month;* see 7:11.   **8:5** Hebrew *On the first day of the tenth month;* see 7:11 and note on 8:4.   **8:13** Hebrew *on the first day of the first month;* see 7:11.   **8:14** Hebrew *The twenty-seventh day of the second month arrived;* see note on 8:13.

dry! [15]Then God said to Noah, [16]"Leave the boat, all of you. [17]Release all the animals and birds so they can breed and reproduce in great numbers." [18]So Noah, his wife, and his sons and their wives left the boat. [19]And all the various kinds of animals and birds came out, pair by pair.

[20]Then Noah built an altar to the LORD and sacrificed on it the animals and birds that had been approved for that purpose. [21]And the LORD was pleased with the sacrifice and said to himself, "I will never again curse the earth, destroying all living things, even though people's thoughts and actions are bent toward evil from childhood. [22]As long as the earth remains, there will be springtime and harvest, cold and heat, winter and summer, day and night."

CHAPTER 9

God blessed Noah and his sons and told them, "Multiply and fill the earth. [2]All the wild animals, large and small, and all the birds and fish will be afraid of you. I have placed them in your power. [3]I have given them to you for food, just as I have given you grain and vegetables. [4]But you must never eat animals that still have their life-blood in them. [5]And murder is forbidden. Animals that kill people must die, and any person who murders must be killed. [6]Yes, you must execute anyone who murders another person, for to kill a person is to kill a living being made in God's image. [7]Now you must have many children and repopulate the earth. Yes, multiply and fill the earth!"

[8]Then God told Noah and his sons, [9]"I am making a covenant with you and your descendants, [10]and with the animals you brought with you—all these birds and livestock and wild animals. [11]I solemnly promise never to send another flood to kill all living creatures and destroy the earth." [12]And God said, "I am giving you a sign as evidence of my eternal covenant with you and all living creatures. [13]I have placed my rainbow in the clouds. It is the sign of my permanent promise to you and to all the earth. [14]When I send clouds over the earth,

9:27 Hebrew *may he live in the tents of Shem.*

the rainbow will be seen in the clouds, [15]and I will remember my covenant with you and with everything that lives. Never again will there be a flood that will destroy all life. [16]When I see the rainbow in the clouds, I will remember the eternal covenant between God and every living creature on earth." [17]Then God said to Noah, "Yes, this is the sign of my covenant with all the creatures of the earth."

[18]Shem, Ham, and Japheth, the three sons of Noah, survived the Flood with their father. (Ham is the ancestor of the Canaanites.) [19]From these three sons of Noah came all the people now scattered across the earth.

[20]After the Flood, Noah became a farmer and planted a vineyard. [21]One day he became drunk on some wine he had made and lay naked in his tent. [22]Ham, the father of Canaan, saw that his father was naked and went outside and told his brothers. [23]Shem and Japheth took a robe, held it over their shoulders, walked backward into the tent, and covered their father's naked body. As they did this, they looked the other way so they wouldn't see him naked. [24]When Noah woke up from his drunken stupor, he learned what Ham, his youngest son, had done. [25]Then he cursed the descendants of Canaan, the son of Ham:

"A curse on the Canaanites!
May they be the lowest of servants
    to the descendants of Shem and
    Japheth."

[26]Then Noah said,

"May Shem be blessed by the LORD my
    God;
and may Canaan be his servant.
[27] May God enlarge the territory of
    Japheth,
    and may he share the prosperity of
    Shem;*
    and let Canaan be his servant."

[28]Noah lived another 350 years after the Flood. [29]He was 950 years old when he died.

JANUARY 4 ☐ DAY 4
GENESIS 10–11
Construction and Confusion

 OVERVIEW Starting with Noah and his three sons, God begins to repopulate the world. But since the root of sin has not been removed, the fruit of sin soon becomes apparent again in proud, disobedient actions. As Noah's descendants seek to build "a great city with a tower that reaches to the skies" (11:4), God brings the project to a halt by confusing their speech, causing them to disperse over the face of the earth—precisely as God had originally commanded (9:1).

Chapter 10			Chapter 11	
	Table of Nations			Tower of Babel	
Japheth	Ham	Shem	God's Judgment	Shem's Genealogy
1 5	6 20	21 32	1 9	10 32
Origin of the Nations			Dispersion of the Nations	

 YOUR DAILY WALK Even on television the sight is impressive. Delegates from around the world meet in the General Assembly of the United Nations to discuss world problems and seek solutions to international tensions. Most wear headsets—an eloquent reminder of the barriers that divide humanity—as they labor together to make the nations united in more than name alone.

The best way to put an idea across is to wrap it up in a person.

Centuries ago, humankind turned from God in rebellion. The result was confusion. Genesis 11 paints a pathetic picture of disoriented people separating from one another in distrust and bewilderment. And yet that scene is not so far removed from today's world. The Babel of the ancient world foreshadows the "babble" of the late twentieth century. Languages still divide; people are still perplexed. And God's solution for humanity's chaos is still the same: divine truth communicated through individuals who have experienced that truth. It's a message that is timeless: the good news of sins forgiven in Jesus Christ. No doubt you've shared this with someone in English; have you ever shared it with someone who speaks a different language? Your local Christian bookstore would be a good source of gospel tracts and Scripture portions in other languages. Today would be a great day to look for someone who needs to know that God speaks his or her language.

 INSIGHT Looking Down from Above
The Babel builders were proud of the mighty tower they thought would reach up to the skies (11:4). But from God's viewpoint (11:5), he had to come down to view their puny pinnacle far below!

CHAPTER 10
This is the history of the families of Shem, Ham, and Japheth, the three sons of Noah. Many children were born to them after the Flood.

² The descendants of Japheth were Gomer, Magog, Madai, Javan, Tubal, Meshech, and Tiras. ³ The descendants of Gomer were Ashkenaz, Riphath, and Togarmah.

⁴ The descendants of Javan were Elishah, Tarshish, Kittim, and Rodanim.* ⁵ Their descendants became the seafaring peoples in various lands, each tribe with its own language.

⁶ The descendants of Ham were Cush, Mizraim,* Put, and Canaan. ⁷ The descendants of Cush were Seba,

10:4 As in some Hebrew manuscripts and Greek version (see also 1 Chr 1:7); most Hebrew manuscripts read *Dodanim*.
10:6 Or *Egypt*; also in 10:13.

Havilah, Sabtah, Raamah, and Sabteca. The descendants of Raamah were Sheba and Dedan.

[8]One of Cush's descendants was Nimrod, who became a heroic warrior. [9]He was a mighty hunter in the LORD's sight.* His name became proverbial, and people would speak of someone as being "like Nimrod, a mighty hunter in the LORD's sight." [10]He built the foundation for his empire in the land of Babylonia,* with the cities of Babel, Erech, Akkad, and Calneh. [11]From there he extended his reign to Assyria, where he built Nineveh, Rehoboth-ir, Calah, [12]and Resen—the main city of the empire, located between Nineveh and Calah.

[13]Mizraim was the ancestor of the Ludites, Anamites, Lehabites, Naphtuhites, [14]Pathrusites, Casluhites, and the Caphtorites, from whom the Philistines came.*

[15]Canaan's oldest son was Sidon, the ancestor of the Sidonians. Canaan was also the ancestor of the Hittites, [16]Jebusites, Amorites, Girgashites, [17]Hivites, Arkites, Sinites, [18]Arvadites, Zemarites, and Hamathites. [19]Eventually the territory of Canaan spread from Sidon to Gerar, near Gaza, and to Sodom, Gomorrah, Admah, and Zeboiim, near Lasha.

[20]These were the descendants of Ham, identified according to their tribes, languages, territories, and nations.

[21]Sons were also born to Shem, the older brother of Japheth.* Shem was the ancestor of all the descendants of Eber. [22]The descendants of Shem were Elam, Asshur, Arphaxad, Lud, and Aram. [23]The descendants of Aram were Uz, Hul, Gether, and Mash.

[24]Arphaxad was the father of Shelah,* and Shelah was the father of Eber. [25]Eber had two sons. The first was named Peleg—"division"—for during his lifetime the people of the world were divided into different language groups and dispersed. His brother's name was Joktan.

[26]Joktan was the ancestor of Almodad, Sheleph, Hazarmaveth, Jerah, [27]Hadoram, Uzal, Diklah, [28]Obal, Abimael, Sheba, [29]Ophir, Havilah, and Jobab. [30]The descendants of Joktan lived in the area extending from Mesha toward the eastern hills of Sephar.

[31]These were the descendants of Shem, identified according to their tribes, languages, territories, and nations.

[32]These are the families that came from Noah's sons, listed nation by nation according to their lines of descent. The earth was populated with the people of these nations after the Flood.

CHAPTER 11

At one time the whole world spoke a single language and used the same words. [2]As the people migrated eastward, they found a plain in the land of Babylonia* and settled there. [3]They began to talk about construction projects. "Come," they said, "let's make great piles of burnt brick and collect natural asphalt to use as mortar. [4]Let's build a great city with a tower that reaches to the skies—a monument to our greatness! This will bring us together and keep us from scattering all over the world."

[5]But the LORD came down to see the city and the tower the people were building. [6]"Look!" he said. "If they can accomplish this when they have just begun to take advantage of their common language and political unity, just think of what they will do later. Nothing will be impossible for them! [7]Come, let's go down and give them different languages. Then they won't be able to understand each other."

[8]In that way, the LORD scattered them all over the earth; and that ended the building of the city. [9]That is why the city was called Babel,* because it was there that the LORD confused the people by giving them many languages, thus scattering them across the earth.

[10]This is the history of Shem's family.

When Shem was 100 years old, his son Arphaxad was born. This happened two years after the Flood. [11]After the birth of Arphaxad, Shem lived another

10:9 Hebrew a mighty hunter before the LORD; also in 10:9b.   10:10 Hebrew Shinar.   10:14 Hebrew Casluhites, from whom the Philistines came, Caphtorites. Compare Jer 47:4; Amos 9:7.   10:21 Or Shem, whose older brother was Japheth.   10:24 Greek version reads Arphaxad was the father of Cainan, Cainan was the father of Shelah.   11:2 Hebrew Shinar.   11:9 Babel sounds like a Hebrew term that means "confusion."

500 years and had other sons and daughters. ¹²When Arphaxad was 35 years old, his son Shelah was born.* ¹³After the birth of Shelah, Arphaxad lived another 403 years and had other sons and daughters.*

¹⁴When Shelah was 30 years old, his son Eber was born. ¹⁵After the birth of Eber, Shelah lived another 403 years and had other sons and daughters.

¹⁶When Eber was 34 years old, his son Peleg was born. ¹⁷After the birth of Peleg, Eber lived another 430 years and had other sons and daughters.

¹⁸When Peleg was 30 years old, his son Reu was born. ¹⁹After the birth of Reu, Peleg lived another 209 years and had other sons and daughters.

²⁰When Reu was 32 years old, his son Serug was born. ²¹After the birth of Serug, Reu lived another 207 years and had other sons and daughters. ²²When Serug was 30 years old, his son Nahor was born. ²³After the birth of

Nahor, Serug lived another 200 years and had other sons and daughters. ²⁴When Nahor was 29 years old, his son Terah was born. ²⁵After the birth of Terah, Nahor lived another 119 years and had other sons and daughters. ²⁶When Terah was 70 years old, he became the father of Abram, Nahor, and Haran.

²⁷This is the history of Terah's family. Terah was the father of Abram, Nahor, and Haran; and Haran had a son named Lot. ²⁸But while Haran was still young, he died in Ur of the Chaldeans, the place of his birth. He was survived by Terah, his father. ²⁹Meanwhile, Abram married Sarai, and his brother Nahor married Milcah, the daughter of their brother Haran. (Milcah had a sister named Iscah.) ³⁰Now Sarai was not able to have any children.

³¹Terah took his son Abram, his daughter-in-law Sarai, and his grandson Lot (his son Haran's child) and left Ur of the Chaldeans to go to the land of Canaan. But they stopped instead at the village of Haran and settled there. ³²Terah lived for 205 years* and died while still at Haran.

11:12 Or *his son, the ancestor of Shelah, was born;* similarly in 11:14, 16, 18, 20, 22, 24. **11:12-13** Greek version reads *¹²When Arphaxad was 135 years old, his son Cainan was born. ¹³After the birth of Cainan, Arphaxad lived another 430 years and had other sons and daughters, and then he died. When Cainan was 130 years old, his son Shelah was born. After the birth of Shelah, Cainan lived another 330 years and had other sons and daughters, and then he died.* **11:32** Some ancient versions read *145 years;* compare 11:26; 12:4.

JANUARY 5 ☐ DAY 5
GENESIS 12–14
Abram's Call and God's Promises

 OVERVIEW Having dealt with rebellious people for generations, God now begins to unfold his great plan of redemption—a plan beginning with one man, Abram. God calls Abram to leave his home in Ur of the Chaldeans and travel to a distant but unspecified new land. Responding in faith, Abram obeys with nothing to cling to but the promises of God—promises of a great name, a great nation, and a great blessing for all people. The journey is not without its moments of danger, as seen in the life of Lot. But through it all, Abram dares to believe God for what seems impossible, given his childless condition.

Chapter 12		Chapter 13	Chapter 14
Abram in Ur	Abram in Egypt	Abram in Canaan	Lot in Danger
1 9	10 20		
Calling	Compromising	Choosing	Conquering

YOUR DAILY WALK How long have you lived in your present home? If your answer is less than three years, you are typical! The average American family moves about once every three years.

The evidence of knowing God is obeying God.

Genesis 12:1-4 describes a similar "moving experience"—a God-fearing family obeys the voice of God, pulls up stakes in Ur, and heads for a new home more than a thousand miles away. But Hebrews 11:8 explains why this was no ordinary move! "Abraham obeyed. . . . He went without knowing where he was going." The command of God was clear, but the destination was not! That's faith—the kind that pleases God (Hebrews 11:6) and the kind God wants you to exercise today as you face similar situations in which his will may be clear . . . though the way he wants you to accomplish it is not. Abram found that you don't always need to know where you're going, provided you know whom you're following!

Call a family council this evening to discuss a decision you are facing involving career, home, or finances—and the way Abram's example can make your decision easier. Then memorize together this verse from tomorrow's reading about the basis for Abram's obedience, his faith in God: "And Abram believed the LORD, and the LORD declared him righteous because of his faith" (15:6).

 INSIGHT The True Test of Values
Lot's choice of the well-watered plains of Jordan was the beginning of his downfall, for it caused him to pitch his tent toward the wicked city of Sodom. By contrast, Abram was building his life on the promises of God. Lot chose for *himself* (13:11); Abram allowed *God* to choose for *him* (13:14-15). Which do you think was the better choice?

CHAPTER 12

Then the LORD told Abram, "Leave your country, your relatives, and your father's house, and go to the land that I will show you. ²I will cause you to become the father of a great nation. I will bless you and make you famous, and I will make you a blessing to others. ³I will bless those who bless you and curse those who curse you. All the families of the earth will be blessed through you."

⁴So Abram departed as the LORD had instructed him, and Lot went with him. Abram was seventy-five years old when he left Haran. ⁵He took his wife, Sarai, his nephew Lot, and all his wealth—his livestock and all the people who had joined his household at Haran—and finally arrived in Canaan. ⁶Traveling through Canaan, they came to a place near Shechem and set up camp beside the oak at Moreh. At that time, the area was inhabited by Canaanites.

⁷Then the LORD appeared to Abram and said, "I am going to give this land to your offspring.*" And Abram built an altar there to commemorate the LORD's visit. ⁸After that, Abram traveled southward and set up camp in the hill country between Bethel on the west and Ai on the east. There he built

an altar and worshiped the LORD. ⁹Then Abram traveled south by stages toward the Negev.

¹⁰At that time there was a severe famine in the land, so Abram went down to Egypt to wait it out. ¹¹As he was approaching the borders of Egypt, Abram said to Sarai, "You are a very beautiful woman. ¹²When the Egyptians see you, they will say, 'This is his wife. Let's kill him; then we can have her!' ¹³But if you say you are my sister, then the Egyptians will treat me well because of their interest in you, and they will spare my life."

¹⁴And sure enough, when they arrived in Egypt, everyone spoke of her beauty. ¹⁵When the palace officials saw her, they sang her praises to their king, the pharaoh, and she was taken into his harem. ¹⁶Then Pharaoh gave Abram many gifts because of her—sheep, cattle, donkeys, male and female servants, and camels.

¹⁷But the LORD sent a terrible plague upon Pharaoh's household because of Sarai, Abram's wife. ¹⁸So Pharaoh called for Abram and accused him sharply. "What is this you have done to me?" he demanded. "Why didn't you tell me she was your wife? ¹⁹Why were you willing to let me

12:7 Hebrew *seed.*

marry her, saying she was your sister? Here is your wife! Take her and be gone!" [20]Pharaoh then sent them out of the country under armed escort—Abram and his wife, with all their household and belongings.

CHAPTER 13

So they left Egypt and traveled north into the Negev—Abram with his wife and Lot and all that they owned, [2]for Abram was very rich in livestock, silver, and gold. [3]Then they continued traveling by stages toward Bethel, to the place between Bethel and Ai where they had camped before. [4]This was the place where Abram had built the altar, and there he again worshiped the LORD.

[5]Now Lot, who was traveling with Abram, was also very wealthy with sheep, cattle, and many tents. [6]But the land could not support both Abram and Lot with all their flocks and herds living so close together. There were too many animals for the available pastureland. [7]So an argument broke out between the herdsmen of Abram and Lot. At that time Canaanites and Perizzites were also living in the land.

[8]Then Abram talked it over with Lot. "This arguing between our herdsmen has got to stop," he said. "After all, we are close relatives! [9]I'll tell you what we'll do. Take your choice of any section of the land you want, and we will separate. If you want that area over there, then I'll stay here. If you want to stay in this area, then I'll move on to another place."

[10]Lot took a long look at the fertile plains of the Jordan Valley in the direction of Zoar. The whole area was well watered everywhere, like the garden of the LORD or the beautiful land of Egypt. (This was before the LORD had destroyed Sodom and Gomorrah.) [11]Lot chose that land for himself—the Jordan Valley to the east of them. He went there with his flocks and servants and parted company with his uncle Abram. [12]So while Abram stayed in the land of Canaan, Lot moved his tents to a place near Sodom, among the cities of the plain. [13]The people of this area were unusually wicked and sinned greatly against the LORD.

[14]After Lot was gone, the LORD said to Abram, "Look as far as you can see in every direction. [15]I am going to give all this land to you and your offspring* as a permanent possession. [16]And I am going to give you so

many descendants that, like dust, they cannot be counted! [17]Take a walk in every direction and explore the new possessions I am giving you." [18]Then Abram moved his camp to the oak grove owned by Mamre, which is at Hebron. There he built an altar to the LORD.

CHAPTER 14

About this time war broke out in the region. King Amraphel of Babylonia,* King Arioch of Ellasar, King Kedorlaomer of Elam, and King Tidal of Goiim [2]fought against King Bera of Sodom, King Birsha of Gomorrah, King Shinab of Admah, King Shemeber of Zeboiim, and the king of Bela (now called Zoar).

[3]The kings of Sodom, Gomorrah, Admah, Zeboiim, and Bela formed an alliance and mobilized their armies in Siddim Valley (that is, the valley of the Dead Sea*). [4]For twelve years they had all been subject to King Kedorlaomer, but now in the thirteenth year they rebelled.

[5]One year later, Kedorlaomer and his allies arrived. They conquered the Rephaites in Ashteroth-karnaim, the Zuzites in Ham, the Emites in the plain of Kiriathaim, [6]and the Horites in Mount Seir, as far as El-paran at the edge of the wilderness. [7]Then they swung around to En-mishpat (now called Kadesh) and destroyed the Amalekites, and also the Amorites living in Hazazon-tamar.

[8]But now the army of the kings of Sodom, Gomorrah, Admah, Zeboiim, and Bela (now called Zoar) prepared for battle in the valley of the Dead Sea* [9]against King Kedorlaomer of Elam and the kings of Goiim, Babylonia, and Ellasar—four kings against five. [10]As it happened, the valley was filled with tar pits. And as the army of the kings of Sodom and Gomorrah fled, some slipped into the tar pits, while the rest escaped into the mountains. [11]The victorious invaders then plundered Sodom and Gomorrah and began their long journey home, taking all the wealth and food with them. [12]They also captured Lot—Abram's nephew who lived in Sodom—and took everything he owned. [13]One of the men who escaped came and told Abram the Hebrew, who was camped at the oak grove belonging to Mamre the Amorite. Mamre and his relatives, Eshcol and Aner, were Abram's allies.

13:15 Hebrew *seed.*   14:1 Hebrew *Shinar;* also in 14:9.   14:3 Hebrew *Salt Sea.*   14:8 Hebrew *in Siddim Valley;* see 14:3.

[14]When Abram learned that Lot had been captured, he called together the men born into his household, 318 of them in all. He chased after Kedorlaomer's army until he caught up with them in Dan. [15]There he divided his men and attacked during the night from several directions. Kedorlaomer's army fled, but Abram chased them to Hobah, north of Damascus. [16]Abram and his allies recovered everything—the goods that had been taken, Abram's nephew Lot with his possessions, and all the women and other captives.

[17]As Abram returned from his victory over Kedorlaomer and his allies, the king of Sodom came out to meet him in the valley of Shaveh (that is, the King's Valley). [18]Then Melchizedek, the king of Salem and a priest of God Most High, brought him bread and wine. [19]Melchizedek blessed Abram with this blessing:

"Blessed be Abram by God Most High,
   Creator of heaven and earth.
[20] And blessed be God Most High,
   who has helped you conquer your
      enemies."

Then Abram gave Melchizedek a tenth of all the goods he had recovered.

[21]The king of Sodom told him, "Give back my people who were captured. But you may keep for yourself all the goods you have recovered."

[22]Abram replied, "I have solemnly promised the LORD, God Most High, Creator of heaven and earth, [23]that I will not take so much as a single thread or sandal thong from you. Otherwise you might say, 'I am the one who made Abram rich!' [24]All I'll accept is what these young men of mine have already eaten. But give a share of the goods to my allies—Aner, Eshcol, and Mamre."

JANUARY 6 □ DAY 6
GENESIS 15–17
God's Covenant with Abram

 OVERVIEW It is one thing to walk with God; it is something else to run ahead of God. God's promise to Abram of many descendants is amply repeated (12:2; 13:16; 15:4-5). But as the years pass with no evidence of fulfillment, Abram acts in foolish impatience. The result is a son, Ishmael, who becomes the heartbreak of his father and a constant reminder of the high price of unbelief. But God's promise stands sure! Though his promise is biologically impossible, Abram and Sarai will give birth to a son—a promise confirmed by new names for the parents-to-be: Abraham ("father of many") and Sarah ("princess").

Chapter 15	Chapter 16	Chapter 17
Abram's Covenant of Faith	Abram's Child of Impatience	Abram's Covenant Confirmed
Promise	Presumption	Prescribed Rite

 YOUR DAILY WALK Hindsight may be a harsh teacher, but its vision is always 20/20! The book of Genesis does not seek to cover up the frailties of Abraham and Sarah but includes them right along with the moments of shining faith and obedience. Why? So that we might learn from their example, good or bad!

Many people have turned and left the dock just before their ship came in.

In hindsight, what can you learn from Abraham's life about the danger of running ahead of God? Here are two lessons worth noting:
   (1) Abraham's God was too small. Abraham assumed that Sarah's

barrenness was a permanent obstacle to God's promise, forgetting that "nothing is impossible with God" (Luke 1:37).

(2) Abraham's patience was too short. He got in a hurry. He decided to fulfill a promise that God was responsible to fulfill.

Write out one of God's timeless promises to you (Philippians 4:19 would do nicely), and attach it to a clock you glance at regularly. This is a great way to remind yourself throughout the day that there's no better time of day to take God at his word!

 INSIGHT Who Gets the Estate?
In the ancient Near East, the heirs to a man's property on his death would be in this order: (1) the son of his first wife; (2) the son of another wife; (3) the son of a slave girl; (4) the ranking servant in his house. Using this "law of the land," who would have received the estate in 15:2-3? in 16:15?

CHAPTER 15

Afterward the LORD spoke to Abram in a vision and said to him, "Do not be afraid, Abram, for I will protect you, and your reward will be great."

²But Abram replied, "O Sovereign LORD, what good are all your blessings when I don't even have a son? Since I don't have a son, Eliezer of Damascus, a servant in my household, will inherit all my wealth. ³You have given me no children, so one of my servants will have to be my heir."

⁴Then the LORD said to him, "No, your servant will not be your heir, for you will have a son of your own to inherit everything I am giving you." ⁵Then the LORD brought Abram outside beneath the night sky and told him, "Look up into the heavens and count the stars if you can. Your descendants will be like that—too many to count!" ⁶And Abram believed the LORD, and the LORD declared him righteous because of his faith. ⁷Then the LORD told him, "I am the LORD who brought you out of Ur of the Chaldeans to give you this land."

⁸But Abram replied, "O Sovereign LORD, how can I be sure that you will give it to me?"

⁹Then the LORD told him, "Bring me a three-year-old heifer, a three-year-old female goat, a three-year-old ram, a turtledove, and a young pigeon." ¹⁰Abram took all these and killed them. He cut each one down the middle and laid the halves side by side. He did not, however, divide the birds in half. ¹¹Some vultures came down to eat the carcasses, but Abram chased them away. ¹²That evening, as the sun was going down, Abram fell into a deep sleep.

He saw a terrifying vision of darkness and horror.

¹³Then the LORD told Abram, "You can be sure that your descendants will be strangers in a foreign land, and they will be oppressed as slaves for four hundred years. ¹⁴But I will punish the nation that enslaves them, and in the end they will come away with great wealth. ¹⁵(But you will die in peace, at a ripe old age.) ¹⁶After four generations your descendants will return here to this land, when the sin of the Amorites has run its course."

¹⁷As the sun went down and it became dark, Abram saw a smoking firepot and a flaming torch pass between the halves of the carcasses. ¹⁸So the LORD made a covenant with Abram that day and said, "I have given this land to your descendants, all the way from the border of Egypt* to the great Euphrates River—¹⁹the land of the Kenites, Kenizzites, Kadmonites, ²⁰Hittites, Perizzites, Rephaites, ²¹Amorites, Canaanites, Girgashites, and Jebusites."

CHAPTER 16

But Sarai, Abram's wife, had no children. So Sarai took her servant, an Egyptian woman named Hagar, ²and gave her to Abram so she could bear his children. "The LORD has kept me from having any children," Sarai said to Abram. "Go and sleep with my servant. Perhaps I can have children through her." And Abram agreed. ³So Sarai, Abram's wife, took Hagar the Egyptian servant and gave her to Abram as a wife. (This happened ten years after Abram first arrived in the land of Canaan.)

⁴So Abram slept with Hagar, and she

15:18 Hebrew *the river of Egypt*, referring either to an eastern branch of the Nile River or to the brook of Egypt in the Sinai (see Num 34:5).

became pregnant. When Hagar knew she was pregnant, she began to treat her mistress Sarai with contempt. [5]Then Sarai said to Abram, "It's all your fault! Now this servant of mine is pregnant, and she despises me, though I myself gave her the privilege of sleeping with you. The LORD will make you pay for doing this to me!*"

[6]Abram replied, "Since she is your servant, you may deal with her as you see fit." So Sarai treated her harshly, and Hagar ran away.

[7]The angel of the LORD found Hagar beside a desert spring along the road to Shur. [8]The angel said to her, "Hagar, Sarai's servant, where have you come from, and where are you going?"

"I am running away from my mistress," she replied.

[9]Then the angel of the LORD said, "Return to your mistress and submit to her authority." [10]The angel added, "I will give you more descendants than you can count." [11]And the angel also said, "You are now pregnant and will give birth to a son. You are to name him Ishmael,* for the LORD has heard about your misery. [12]This son of yours will be a wild one—free and untamed as a wild donkey! He will be against everyone, and everyone will be against him. Yes, he will live at odds with the rest of his brothers."

[13]Thereafter, Hagar referred to the LORD, who had spoken to her, as "the God who sees me,"* for she said, "I have seen the One who sees me!" [14]Later that well was named Beer-lahairoi,* and it can still be found between Kadesh and Bered.

[15]So Hagar gave Abram a son, and Abram named him Ishmael. [16]Abram was eighty-six years old at that time.

CHAPTER 17
When Abram was ninety-nine years old, the LORD appeared to him and said, "I am God Almighty; serve me faithfully and live a blameless life. [2]I will make a covenant with you, by which I will guarantee to make you into a mighty nation." [3]At this, Abram fell face down in the dust. Then God said to him, [4]"This is my covenant with you: I will make you the father of not just one nation, but a multitude of nations! [5]What's more, I am changing your name. It will no longer be Abram; now you will be known as Abraham,* for you will be the father of many nations. [6]I will give you millions of descendants who will represent many nations. Kings will be among them!

[7]"I will continue this everlasting covenant between us, generation after generation. It will continue between me and your offspring* forever. And I will always be your God and the God of your descendants after you. [8]Yes, I will give all this land of Canaan to you and to your offspring forever. And I will be their God.

[9]"Your part of the agreement," God told Abraham, "is to obey the terms of the covenant. You and all your descendants have this continual responsibility. [10]This is the covenant that you and your descendants must keep: Each male among you must be circumcised; [11]the flesh of his foreskin must be cut off. This will be a sign that you and they have accepted this covenant. [12]Every male child must be circumcised on the eighth day after his birth. This applies not only to members of your family, but also to the servants born in your household and the foreign-born servants whom you have purchased. [13]All must be circumcised. Your bodies will thus bear the mark of my everlasting covenant. [14]Anyone who refuses to be circumcised will be cut off from the covenant family for violating the covenant."

[15]Then God added, "Regarding Sarai, your wife—her name will no longer be Sarai; from now on you will call her Sarah.* [16]And I will bless her and give you a son from her! Yes, I will bless her richly, and she will become the mother of many nations. Kings will be among her descendants!"

[17]Then Abraham bowed down to the ground, but he laughed to himself in disbelief. "How could I become a father at the age of one hundred?" he wondered. "Besides, Sarah is ninety; how could she have a baby?" [18]And Abraham said to God, "Yes, may Ishmael enjoy your special blessing!"

[19]But God replied, "Sarah, your wife, will bear you a son. You will name him Isaac,* and I will confirm my everlasting covenant with him and his descendants. [20]As for Ishmael, I will bless him also, just as you have asked. I will cause him to multiply and become a great nation. Twelve princes will be among his descendants.

[21]But my covenant is with Isaac, who will be born to you and Sarah about this time next year."

[22]That ended the conversation, and God left Abraham. [23]On that very day Abraham took his son Ishmael and every other male in his household and circumcised them, cutting off their foreskins, exactly as God had told him. [24]Abraham was ninety-nine years old at that time, [25]and Ishmael his son was thirteen. [26]Both were circumcised the same day, [27]along with all the other men and boys of the household, whether they were born there or bought as servants.

JANUARY 7 ☐ DAY 7
The God You Can Know

 LOOK BACK Congratulations! You've taken an exciting step in your spiritual walk through God's Word. Already you've read about God's masterful creation of the universe, the first sin and its spread throughout humanity, Noah and his boat, the Tower of Babel and the scattering of the nations, and God's promise to Abraham to make him a father of a nation special to God.

But now let's pause and refresh ourselves as we walk through the pages of Scripture. About every seventh day you'll have the opportunity to catch up on your reading from the week if you need to. But more than that, you'll have a chance to *look back* at what you've been reading, *look up* at God and consider what he wants to say to you through his Word, and *look ahead* at what's to come.

Don't hurry through these seventh-day devotionals. Instead, take the opportunity to rest in God's presence because you're not just reading through the Bible this year—you're beginning a walk with God himself . . . a walk that will last forever!

 LOOK UP Believe what you hear on the radio, and you might conclude that "God is watching us from a distance." Believe what you read in the book of Genesis, and you'll most certainly conclude that "God is close by, and he takes a personal interest in my life." And you'll be right!

The best way to face life's changes is to look to the unchanging God.

After all, look at the divine fingerprints clearly visible on the lives of Adam (who walked with God in the cool of the evening), Noah (who rode high above the floodwaters in a boat built with the aid of a blueprint from heaven—and notice in Genesis 7:16 who shut the door!), and Abram (selected by God to be the father of nations and the channel of blessing to the entire world). Not the picture of a distant, detached deity, but the portrait of a powerful yet personal God of Creation, who not only made you but wants to guide and provide for you each day of your life.

 LOOK AHEAD Even though you have only just begun to read through the Old Testament, pause for a moment to read an important verse from the New Testament. In it you will find one of the most compelling reasons to keep reading each and every day.

In Hebrews 11 you'll find enshrined the names of many of the heroes of faith you will be meeting "up close and personal" over the next few months. But notice the last half of verse 6: "Anyone who wants to come to him must believe that there is a God and that he rewards those who sincerely seek him."

The God of Creation is not an impersonal cosmic force but a personal, promise-keeping Friend and Guide. At times when God may seem far away and it feels as if he is watching you from a distance, you can be confident it was you, not he, that moved. The one who put the galaxies in space and is big enough to rule the universe is looking for men and women, boys and girls who earnestly desire to seek and find him.

The God who showed himself strong to Adam, Noah, and Abram thousands of years ago is still alive and well today, and he is the same God you will meet each day in the pages of his Word as you journey through *The Daily Walk Bible*. If you're not in the habit of doing so, why not begin keeping a journal to record your observations, insights, and action points? By the end of the year, you'll have a treasure chest of memories about your daily time with God—whether in the cool of the evening or the quiet of the morning, or sometime in between.

JANUARY 8 ☐ DAY 8
GENESIS 18–20
God's Judgment on Sodom

OVERVIEW Three heavenly messengers arrive with both good news and bad news for Abraham's family. The good news: Abraham and Sarah's long-awaited dream is about to come true! They will soon experience the joys of parenthood. The bad news: Sodom and Gomorrah will soon experience the full fury of God's judgment for their grievous sins. In response to Abraham's intercession, God spares Lot's family during Sodom's destruction, though their grudging departure reflects their lukewarm spiritual condition.

Chapter 18	Chapter 19	Chapter 20
Sodom's Doom Declared	Sodom and Gomorrah Destroyed	Abraham's Deceit
Saving Lot		Saving Sarah

YOUR DAILY WALK One day a man named Lot sat down at his desk, pulled out a sheet of paper, and wrote across the top: "Goals for My Life." Then he began to compile the goals that would shape the direction of his life:

Many people have the right aims in life; they just never get around to pulling the trigger.

1. To lose all sense of moral values.
2. To forfeit all spiritual authority in my home.
3. To exert no influence for good in my community.
4. To lose everyone and everything dear to me.

Ridiculous, you say? Then consider this: Lot set no such goals, yet he accomplished everything on that list! Those unwritten goals simply became the consequences of his worldly choices.

Lot had no spiritual goals in his life, but you should. Written goals help prevent the kind of purposeless drift that set Lot up for disaster. What do you want to accomplish specifically this year in the areas of Scripture memorization . . . time in God's Word . . . reading good Christian books . . . sharing your faith? Write them down; hang them up; pray them through; and with God's help watch them happen!

INSIGHT Where Are They Today?
From the offspring resulting from Lot's incest with his daughters came the forerunners of the Moabites and Ammonites (19:37-38), who—though related to them—were the Israelites' constant enemies. For their gross idolatry, both Moab and Ammon would later be destroyed (Amos 2:1-3; Ezekiel 25:1-7).

CHAPTER 18

The LORD appeared again to Abraham while he was camped near the oak grove belonging to Mamre. One day about noon, as Abraham was sitting at the entrance to his tent, ²he suddenly noticed three men standing nearby. He got up and ran to meet them, welcoming them by bowing low to the ground. ³"My lord," he said, "if it pleases you, stop here for a while. ⁴Rest in the shade of this tree while my servants get some water to wash your feet. ⁵Let me prepare some food to refresh you. Please stay awhile before continuing on your journey."

"All right," they said. "Do as you have said."

⁶So Abraham ran back to the tent and said to Sarah, "Quick! Get three measures* of your best flour, and bake some bread." ⁷Then Abraham ran out to the herd and chose a fat calf and told a servant to hurry and butcher it. ⁸When the food was ready, he took some cheese curds and milk and the roasted meat, and he served it to the men. As they ate, Abraham waited on them there beneath the trees.

⁹"Where is Sarah, your wife?" they asked him.

"In the tent," Abraham replied.

¹⁰Then one of them said, "About this time next year I will return, and your wife Sarah will have a son."

Now Sarah was listening to this conversation from the tent nearby. ¹¹And since Abraham and Sarah were both very old, and Sarah was long past the age of having children, ¹²she laughed silently to herself. "How could a worn-out woman like me have a baby?" she thought. "And when my master—my husband—is also so old?"

¹³Then the LORD said to Abraham, "Why did Sarah laugh? Why did she say, 'Can an old woman like me have a baby?' ¹⁴Is anything too hard for the LORD? About a year from now, just as I told you, I will return, and Sarah will have a son." ¹⁵Sarah was afraid, so she denied that she had laughed. But he said, "That is not true. You did laugh."

¹⁶Then the men got up from their meal and started on toward Sodom. Abraham went with them part of the way.

¹⁷"Should I hide my plan from Abraham?" the LORD asked. ¹⁸"For Abraham will become a great and mighty nation, and all the nations of the earth will be blessed through him. ¹⁹I have singled him out so that he will direct his sons and their families to keep the way of the LORD and do what is right and just. Then I will do for him all that I have promised." ²⁰So the LORD told Abraham, "I have heard that the people of Sodom and Gomorrah are extremely evil, and that everything they do is wicked. ²¹I am going down to see whether or not these reports are true. Then I will know."

²²The two other men went on toward Sodom, but the LORD remained with Abraham for a while. ²³Abraham approached him and said, "Will you destroy both innocent and guilty alike? ²⁴Suppose you find fifty innocent people there within the city—will you still destroy it, and not spare it for their sakes? ²⁵Surely you wouldn't do such a thing, destroying the innocent with the guilty. Why, you would be treating the innocent and the guilty exactly the same! Surely you wouldn't do that! Should not the Judge of all the earth do what is right?"

²⁶And the LORD replied, "If I find fifty innocent people in Sodom, I will spare the entire city for their sake."

²⁷Then Abraham spoke again. "Since I have begun, let me go on and speak further to my Lord, even though I am but dust and ashes. ²⁸Suppose there are only forty-five? Will you destroy the city for lack of five?"

And the LORD said, "I will not destroy it if I find forty-five."

²⁹Then Abraham pressed his request further. "Suppose there are only forty?"

And the LORD replied, "I will not destroy it if there are forty."

³⁰"Please don't be angry, my Lord," Abraham pleaded. "Let me speak—suppose only thirty are found?"

And the LORD replied, "I will not destroy it if there are thirty."

³¹Then Abraham said, "Since I have dared to speak to the Lord, let me continue—suppose there are only twenty?"

And the LORD said, "Then I will not destroy it for the sake of the twenty."

³²Finally, Abraham said, "Lord, please do not get angry; I will speak but once more! Suppose only ten are found there?"

And the LORD said, "Then, for the sake of the ten, I will not destroy it."

³³The LORD went on his way when he

18:6 Hebrew *3 seahs*, about 15 quarts or 18 liters.

had finished his conversation with Abraham, and Abraham returned to his tent.

CHAPTER 19

That evening the two angels came to the entrance of the city of Sodom, and Lot was sitting there as they arrived. When he saw them, he stood up to meet them. Then he welcomed them and bowed low to the ground. ²"My lords," he said, "come to my home to wash your feet, and be my guests for the night. You may then get up in the morning as early as you like and be on your way again."

"Oh no," they said, "we'll just spend the night out here in the city square."

³But Lot insisted, so at last they went home with him. He set a great feast before them, complete with fresh bread made without yeast. After the meal, ⁴as they were preparing to retire for the night, all the men of Sodom, young and old, came from all over the city and surrounded the house. ⁵They shouted to Lot, "Where are the men who came to spend the night with you? Bring them out so we can have sex with them."

⁶Lot stepped outside to talk to them, shutting the door behind him. ⁷"Please, my brothers," he begged, "don't do such a wicked thing. ⁸Look—I have two virgin daughters. Do with them as you wish, but leave these men alone, for they are under my protection."

⁹"Stand back!" they shouted. "Who do you think you are? We let you settle among us, and now you are trying to tell us what to do! We'll treat you far worse than those other men!" And they lunged at Lot and began breaking down the door. ¹⁰But the two angels reached out and pulled Lot in and bolted the door. ¹¹Then they blinded the men of Sodom so they couldn't find the doorway.

¹²"Do you have any other relatives here in the city?" the angels asked. "Get them out of this place—sons-in-law, sons, daughters, or anyone else. ¹³For we will destroy the city completely. The stench of the place has reached the LORD, and he has sent us to destroy it."

¹⁴So Lot rushed out to tell his daughters' fiancés, "Quick, get out of the city! The LORD is going to destroy it." But the young men thought he was only joking.

¹⁵At dawn the next morning the angels became insistent. "Hurry," they said to Lot. "Take your wife and your two daughters who are here. Get out of here right now, or you will be caught in the destruction of the city."

¹⁶When Lot still hesitated, the angels seized his hand and the hands of his wife and two daughters and rushed them to safety outside the city, for the LORD was merciful. ¹⁷"Run for your lives!" the angels warned. "Do not stop anywhere in the valley. And don't look back! Escape to the mountains, or you will die."

¹⁸"Oh no, my lords, please," Lot begged. ¹⁹"You have been so kind to me and saved my life, and you have granted me such mercy. But I cannot go to the mountains. Disaster would catch up to me there, and I would soon die. ²⁰See, there is a small village nearby. Please let me go there instead; don't you see how small it is? Then my life will be saved."

²¹"All right," the angel said, "I will grant your request. I will not destroy that little village. ²²But hurry! For I can do nothing until you are there." From that time on, that village was known as Zoar.*

²³The sun was rising as Lot reached the village. ²⁴Then the LORD rained down fire and burning sulfur from the heavens on Sodom and Gomorrah. ²⁵He utterly destroyed them, along with the other cities and villages of the plain, eliminating all life—people, plants, and animals alike. ²⁶But Lot's wife looked back as she was following along behind him, and she became a pillar of salt.

²⁷The next morning Abraham was up early and hurried out to the place where he had stood in the LORD's presence. ²⁸He looked out across the plain to Sodom and Gomorrah and saw columns of smoke and fumes, as from a furnace, rising from the cities there. ²⁹But God had listened to Abraham's request and kept Lot safe, removing him from the disaster that engulfed the cities on the plain.

³⁰Afterward Lot left Zoar because he was afraid of the people there, and he went to live in a cave in the mountains with his two daughters. ³¹One day the older daughter said to her sister, "There isn't a man anywhere in this entire area for us to marry. And our father will soon be too old to have

19:22 Zoar means "little."

children. ³²Come, let's get him drunk with wine, and then we will sleep with him. That way we will preserve our family line through our father." ³³So that night they got him drunk, and the older daughter went in and slept with her father. He was unaware of her lying down or getting up again.

³⁴The next morning the older daughter said to her younger sister, "I slept with our father last night. Let's get him drunk with wine again tonight, and you go in and sleep with him. That way our family line will be preserved." ³⁵So that night they got him drunk again, and the younger daughter went in and slept with him. As before, he was unaware of her lying down or getting up again. ³⁶So both of Lot's daughters became pregnant by their father.

³⁷When the older daughter gave birth to a son, she named him Moab.* He became the ancestor of the nation now known as the Moabites. ³⁸When the younger daughter gave birth to a son, she named him Ben-ammi.* He became the ancestor of the nation now known as the Ammonites.

CHAPTER 20
Now Abraham moved south to the Negev and settled for a while between Kadesh and Shur at a place called Gerar. ²Abraham told people there that his wife, Sarah, was his sister. So King Abimelech sent for her and had her brought to him at his palace.

³But one night God came to Abimelech in a dream and told him, "You are a dead man, for that woman you took is married."

⁴But Abimelech had not slept with her yet, so he said, "Lord, will you kill an innocent man? ⁵Abraham told me, 'She is my sister,' and she herself said, 'Yes, he is my brother.' I acted in complete innocence!"

⁶"Yes, I know you are innocent," God replied. "That is why I kept you from sinning against me; I did not let you touch her. ⁷Now return her to her husband, and he will pray for you, for he is a prophet. Then you will live. But if you don't return her to him, you can be sure that you and your entire household will die."

⁸Abimelech got up early the next morning and hastily called a meeting of all his servants. When he told them what had happened, great fear swept through the crowd. ⁹Then Abimelech called for Abraham. "What is this you have done to us?" he demanded. "What have I done to you that deserves treatment like this, making me and my kingdom guilty of this great sin? This kind of thing should not be done! ¹⁰Why have you done this to us?"

¹¹"Well," Abraham said, "I figured this to be a godless place. I thought, 'They will want my wife and will kill me to get her.' ¹²Besides, she is my sister—we both have the same father, though different mothers—and I married her. ¹³When God sent me to travel far from my father's home, I told her, 'Wherever we go, have the kindness to say that you are my sister.'"

¹⁴Then Abimelech took sheep and oxen and servants—both men and women—and gave them to Abraham, and he returned his wife, Sarah, to him. ¹⁵"Look over my kingdom, and choose a place where you would like to live," Abimelech told him. ¹⁶Then he turned to Sarah. "Look," he said, "I am giving your 'brother' a thousand pieces of silver* to compensate for any embarrassment I may have caused you. This will settle any claim against me in this matter."

¹⁷Then Abraham prayed to God, and God healed Abimelech, his wife, and the other women of the household, so they could have children. ¹⁸For the LORD had stricken all the women with infertility as a warning to Abimelech for having taken Abraham's wife.

19:37 *Moab* sounds like a Hebrew term that means "from father." *1,000 shekels of silver*, about 25 pounds or 11.4 kilograms in weight. 19:38 *Ben-ammi* means "son of my people." 20:16 Hebrew

JANUARY 9 □ DAY 9
GENESIS 21–24
Isaac—God's Promise in Flesh and Blood

OVERVIEW Today's reading describes the birth and early years of Isaac, the long-awaited son God had promised Abraham. After many years of learning to walk by faith, Abraham and Sarah experience the greatest joy of their lives: the miraculous birth of a son and heir and the one through whom God would form a great nation! The stage is set for Abraham's severest test—the command to sacrifice his treasured son as a burnt offering to God. Drawing upon a faith in God that has grown with the years, Abraham obeys, thereby learning another lesson in God's faithfulness. Sarah, who sees her son reach manhood, does not live to see him marry.

Chapter 21	Chapter 22	Chapter 23	Chapter 24
Birth of Isaac	Offering of Isaac	Death of Sarah	Marriage of Isaac
Isaac's Childhood		Isaac's Early Adulthood	

YOUR DAILY WALK "There is no such thing as an *accident,* only *incidents* in the perfect will of God." That's not just a glib maxim. It was spoken by a father whose teenage daughter had just undergone brain surgery after a car and bus collision. He meant that both the *type* and the *timing* of "accidents" are under God's wise control.

The best measure of a spiritual life is not its ecstasies but its obedience.

It is no coincidence that chapter 22, the offering of Isaac, begins with these words: "Later on God tested Abraham's faith and obedience." Why did God choose to test Abraham's faith and obedience at this point? Abraham had undergone many faith-stretching experiences, which are recorded in chapters 12–21. These experiences prepared Abraham for the big test—choosing to obey God even if obedience cost Abraham his son.

Are you learning the lessons today that will help you handle the tests God has for you tomorrow? Think of one faith-stretching situation you are facing today (a grumpy neighbor, a difficult boss, a houseful of kids). How might God use it to prepare you for tomorrow? Pause right now and ask him to make you teachable in today's tests so you'll be prepared for the bigger ones tomorrow.

INSIGHT Ephron's Generosity . . . or Was It?
As a burial place for Sarah, Abraham purchased the cave of Machpelah at Hebron from a Hittite named Ephron (23:3-16). In Hittite law, a property owner was subject to military duty. Abraham only wanted to buy the cave; Ephron urged him to take the whole field. In this way, Ephron freed himself from military obligation.

CHAPTER 21
Then the LORD did exactly what he had promised. ²Sarah became pregnant, and she gave a son to Abraham in his old age. It all happened at the time God had said it would. ³And Abraham named his son Isaac.* ⁴Eight days after Isaac was born, Abraham circumcised him as God had

commanded. ⁵Abraham was one hundred years old at the time.

⁶And Sarah declared, "God has brought me laughter! All who hear about this will laugh with me. ⁷For who would have dreamed that I would ever have a baby? Yet I have given Abraham a son in his old age!"

⁸As time went by and Isaac grew and

21:3 *Isaac* means "he laughs."

was weaned, Abraham gave a big party to celebrate the happy occasion. [9]But Sarah saw Ishmael—the son of Abraham and her Egyptian servant Hagar—making fun of Isaac. [10]So she turned to Abraham and demanded, "Get rid of that servant and her son. He is not going to share the family inheritance with my son, Isaac. I won't have it!"

[11]This upset Abraham very much because Ishmael was his son. [12]But God told Abraham, "Do not be upset over the boy and your servant wife. Do just as Sarah says, for Isaac is the son through whom your descendants will be counted. [13]But I will make a nation of the descendants of Hagar's son because he also is your son."

[14]So Abraham got up early the next morning, prepared food for the journey, and strapped a container of water to Hagar's shoulders. He sent her away with their son, and she walked out into the wilderness of Beersheba, wandering aimlessly. [15]When the water was gone, she left the boy in the shade of a bush. [16]Then she went and sat down by herself about a hundred yards* away. "I don't want to watch the boy die," she said, as she burst into tears.

[17]Then God heard the boy's cries, and the angel of God called to Hagar from the sky, "Hagar, what's wrong? Do not be afraid! God has heard the boy's cries from the place where you laid him. [18]Go to him and comfort him, for I will make a great nation from his descendants."

[19]Then God opened Hagar's eyes, and she saw a well. She immediately filled her water container and gave the boy a drink. [20]And God was with the boy as he grew up in the wilderness of Paran. He became an expert archer, [21]and his mother arranged a marriage for him with a young woman from Egypt.

[22]About this time, Abimelech came with Phicol, his army commander, to visit Abraham. "It is clear that God helps you in everything you do," Abimelech said. [23]"Swear to me in God's name that you won't deceive me, my children, or my grandchildren. I have been loyal to you, so now swear that you will be loyal to me and to this country in which you are living."

[24]Abraham replied, "All right, I swear to it!" [25]Then Abraham complained to Abim-

elech about a well that Abimelech's servants had taken violently from Abraham's servants.

[26]"This is the first I've heard of it," Abimelech said. "And I have no idea who is responsible. Why didn't you say something about this before?" [27]Then Abraham gave sheep and oxen to Abimelech, and they made a treaty. [28]But when Abraham took seven additional ewe lambs and set them off by themselves, [29]Abimelech asked, "Why are you doing that?"

[30]Abraham replied, "They are my gift to you as a public confirmation that I dug this well." [31]So ever since, that place has been known as Beersheba—"well of the oath"—because that was where they had sworn an oath. [32]After making their covenant, Abimelech left with Phicol, the commander of his army, and they returned home to the land of the Philistines. [33]Then Abraham planted a tamarisk tree at Beersheba, and he worshiped the LORD, the Eternal God, at that place. [34]And Abraham lived in Philistine country for a long time.

CHAPTER 22

Later on God tested Abraham's faith and obedience. "Abraham!" God called.

"Yes," he replied. "Here I am."

[2]"Take your son, your only son—yes, Isaac, whom you love so much—and go to the land of Moriah. Sacrifice him there as a burnt offering on one of the mountains, which I will point out to you."

[3]The next morning Abraham got up early. He saddled his donkey and took two of his servants with him, along with his son Isaac. Then he chopped wood to build a fire for a burnt offering and set out for the place where God had told him to go. [4]On the third day of the journey, Abraham saw the place in the distance. [5]"Stay here with the donkey," Abraham told the young men. "The boy and I will travel a little farther. We will worship there, and then we will come right back."

[6]Abraham placed the wood for the burnt offering on Isaac's shoulders, while he himself carried the knife and the fire. As the two of them went on together, [7]Isaac said, "Father?"

"Yes, my son," Abraham replied.

"We have the wood and the fire," said

21:16 Hebrew *a bowshot.*

the boy, "but where is the lamb for the sacrifice?"

8"God will provide a lamb, my son," Abraham answered. And they both went on together.

9When they arrived at the place where God had told Abraham to go, he built an altar and placed the wood on it. Then he tied Isaac up and laid him on the altar over the wood. 10And Abraham took the knife and lifted it up to kill his son as a sacrifice to the LORD. 11At that moment the angel of the LORD shouted to him from heaven, "Abraham! Abraham!"

"Yes," he answered. "I'm listening."

12"Lay down the knife," the angel said. "Do not hurt the boy in any way, for now I know that you truly fear God. You have not withheld even your beloved son from me."

13Then Abraham looked up and saw a ram caught by its horns in a bush. So he took the ram and sacrificed it as a burnt offering on the altar in place of his son. 14Abraham named the place "The LORD Will Provide."* This name has now become a proverb: "On the mountain of the LORD it will be provided."

15Then the angel of the LORD called again to Abraham from heaven, 16"This is what the LORD says: Because you have obeyed me and have not withheld even your beloved son, I swear by my own self that 17I will bless you richly. I will multiply your descendants into countless millions, like the stars of the sky and the sand on the seashore. They will conquer their enemies, 18and through your descendants,* all the nations of the earth will be blessed—all because you have obeyed me." 19Then they returned to Abraham's young men and traveled home again to Beersheba, where Abraham lived for quite some time.

20Soon after this, Abraham heard that Milcah, his brother Nahor's wife, had borne Nahor eight sons. 21The oldest was named Uz, the next oldest was Buz, followed by Kemuel (the father of Aram), 22Kesed, Hazo, Pildash, Jidlaph, and Bethuel. 23Bethuel became the father of Rebekah. 24In addition to his eight sons from Milcah, Nahor had four other children from his concubine Reumah. Their names were Tebah, Gaham, Tahash, and Maacah.

C H A P T E R   2 3

When Sarah was 127 years old, 2she died at Kiriath-arba (now called Hebron) in the land of Canaan. There Abraham mourned and wept for her. 3Then, leaving her body, he went to the Hittite elders and said, 4"Here I am, a stranger in a foreign land, with no place to bury my wife. Please let me have a piece of land for a burial plot."

5The Hittites replied to Abraham, 6"Certainly, for you are an honored prince among us. It will be a privilege to have you choose the finest of our tombs so you can bury her there."

7Then Abraham bowed low before them and said, 8"Since this is how you feel, be so kind as to ask Ephron son of Zohar 9to let me have the cave of Machpelah, down at the end of his field. I want to pay the full price, of course, whatever is publicly agreed upon, so I may have a permanent burial place for my family."

10Ephron was sitting there among the others, and he answered Abraham as the others listened, speaking publicly before all the elders of the town. 11"No, sir," he said to Abraham, "please listen to me. I will give you the cave and the field. Here in the presence of my people, I give it to you. Go and bury your dead."

12Abraham bowed again to the people of the land, 13and he replied to Ephron as everyone listened. "No, listen to me," he insisted. "I will buy it from you. Let me pay the full price for the field so I can bury my dead there."

14"Well," Ephron answered, 15"the land is worth four hundred pieces* of silver, but what is that between friends? Go ahead and bury your dead."

16So Abraham paid Ephron the amount he had suggested, four hundred pieces of silver, as was publicly agreed. 17He bought the plot of land belonging to Ephron at Machpelah, near Mamre. This included the field, the cave that was in it, and all the trees nearby. 18They became Abraham's permanent possession by the agreement made in the presence of the Hittite elders at the city gate. 19So Abraham buried Sarah there in Canaan, in the cave of Machpelah, near Mamre, which is at Hebron. 20The field and the cave were sold to Abraham by the Hittites as a permanent burial place.

22:14 Hebrew *Yahweh Yir'eh*.   22:18 Hebrew *seed*.   23:15 Hebrew *400 shekels*, about 10 pounds or 4.6 kilograms in weight; also in 23:16.

CHAPTER 24

Abraham was now a very old man, and the LORD had blessed him in every way. [2]One day Abraham said to the man in charge of his household, who was his oldest servant, [3]"Swear* by the LORD, the God of heaven and earth, that you will not let my son marry one of these local Canaanite women. [4]Go instead to my homeland, to my relatives, and find a wife there for my son Isaac."

[5]The servant asked, "But suppose I can't find a young woman who will travel so far from home? May I then take Isaac there to live among your relatives?"

[6]"No!" Abraham warned. "Be careful never to take my son there. [7]For the LORD, the God of heaven, who took me from my father's house and my native land, solemnly promised to give this land to my offspring.* He will send his angel ahead of you, and he will see to it that you find a young woman there to be my son's wife. [8]If she is unwilling to come back with you, then you are free from this oath. But under no circumstances are you to take my son there."

[9]So the servant took a solemn oath* that he would follow Abraham's instructions. [10]He loaded ten of Abraham's camels with gifts and set out, taking with him the best of everything his master owned. He traveled to Aram-naharaim* and went to the village where Abraham's brother Nahor had settled. [11]There the servant made the camels kneel down beside a well just outside the village. It was evening, and the women were coming out to draw water.

[12]"O LORD, God of my master," he prayed. "Give me success and show kindness to my master, Abraham. Help me to accomplish the purpose of my journey. [13]See, here I am, standing beside this spring, and the young women of the village are coming out to draw water. [14]This is my request. I will ask one of them for a drink. If she says, 'Yes, certainly, and I will water your camels, too!'—let her be the one you have appointed as Isaac's wife. By this I will know that you have shown kindness to my master."

[15]As he was still praying, a young woman named Rebekah arrived with a water jug on her shoulder. Her father was Bethuel, who was the son of Abraham's brother Nahor and his wife, Milcah. [16]Now Rebekah was very beautiful, and she was a virgin; no man had ever slept with her. She went down to the spring, filled her jug, and came up again. [17]Running over to her, the servant asked, "Please give me a drink."

[18]"Certainly, sir," she said, and she quickly lowered the jug for him to drink. [19]When he had finished, she said, "I'll draw water for your camels, too, until they have had enough!" [20]So she quickly emptied the jug into the watering trough and ran down to the well again. She kept carrying water to the camels until they had finished drinking. [21]The servant watched her in silence, wondering whether or not she was the one the LORD intended him to meet. [22]Then at last, when the camels had finished drinking, he gave her a gold ring for her nose and two large gold bracelets* for her wrists.

[23]"Whose daughter are you?" he asked. "Would your father have any room to put us up for the night?"

[24]"My father is Bethuel," she replied. "My grandparents are Nahor and Milcah. [25]Yes, we have plenty of straw and food for the camels, and we have a room for guests."

[26]The man fell down to the ground and worshiped the LORD. [27]"Praise be to the LORD, the God of my master, Abraham," he said. "The LORD has been so kind and faithful to Abraham, for he has led me straight to my master's relatives."

[28]The young woman ran home to tell her family about all that had happened. [29]Now Rebekah had a brother named Laban. [30]When he saw the nose-ring and the bracelets on his sister's wrists, and when he heard her story, he rushed out to the spring, where the man was still standing beside his camels. Laban said to him, [31]"Come and stay with us, you who are blessed by the LORD. Why do you stand here outside the village when we have a room all ready for you and a place prepared for the camels!"

[32]So the man went home with Laban, and Laban unloaded the camels, gave him straw to bed them down, fed them, and

24:3 Hebrew *Put your hand under my thigh, and I will make you swear.* 24:7 Hebrew *seed.* 24:9 Hebrew *put his hand under the thigh of Abraham his master and swore an oath.* 24:10 *Aram-naharaim* means "Aram of the two rivers," thought to have been located between the Euphrates and Balih Rivers in northwestern Mesopotamia. 24:22 Hebrew *a gold nose-ring weighing a half shekel* [0.2 ounces or 6 grams] *and two gold bracelets weighing 10 shekels* [4 ounces or 114 grams].

provided water for the camel drivers to wash their feet. ³³Then supper was served. But Abraham's servant said, "I don't want to eat until I have told you why I have come."

"All right," Laban said, "tell us your mission."

³⁴"I am Abraham's servant," he explained. ³⁵"And the LORD has blessed my master richly; he has become a great man. The LORD has given him flocks of sheep and herds of cattle, a fortune in silver and gold, and many servants and camels and donkeys. ³⁶When Sarah, my master's wife, was very old, she gave birth to my master's son, and my master has given him everything he owns. ³⁷And my master made me swear that I would not let Isaac marry one of the local Canaanite women. ³⁸Instead, I was to come to his relatives here in this far-off land, to his father's home. I was told to bring back a young woman from here to marry his son.

³⁹"'But suppose I can't find a young woman willing to come back with me?' I asked him. ⁴⁰'You will,' he told me, 'for the LORD, in whose presence I have walked, will send his angel with you and will make your mission successful. Yes, you must get a wife for my son from among my relatives, from my father's family. ⁴¹But if you go to my relatives and they refuse to let her come, you will be free from your oath.'

⁴²"So this afternoon when I came to the spring I prayed this prayer: 'O LORD, the God of my master, Abraham, if you are planning to make my mission a success, please guide me in a special way. ⁴³Here I am, standing beside this spring. I will say to some young woman who comes to draw water, "Please give me a drink of water!" ⁴⁴And she will reply, "Certainly! And I'll water your camels, too!" LORD, let her be the one you have selected to be the wife of my master's son.'

⁴⁵"Before I had finished praying these words, I saw Rebekah coming along with her water jug on her shoulder. She went down to the spring and drew water and filled the jug. So I said to her, 'Please give me a drink.' ⁴⁶She quickly lowered the jug from her shoulder so I could drink, and she said, 'Certainly, sir, and I will water your camels, too!' And she did. ⁴⁷When I asked her whose daughter she was, she told me, 'My father is Bethuel, the son of Nahor and

his wife, Milcah.' So I gave her the ring and the bracelets.

⁴⁸"Then I bowed my head and worshiped the LORD. I praised the LORD, the God of my master, Abraham, because he had led me along the right path to find a wife from the family of my master's relatives. ⁴⁹So tell me—will you or won't you show true kindness to my master? When you tell me, then I'll know what my next step should be, whether to move this way or that."

⁵⁰Then Laban and Bethuel replied, "The LORD has obviously brought you here, so what can we say? ⁵¹Here is Rebekah; take her and go. Yes, let her be the wife of your master's son, as the LORD has directed."

⁵²At this reply, Abraham's servant bowed to the ground and worshiped the LORD. ⁵³Then he brought out silver and gold jewelry and lovely clothing for Rebekah. He also gave valuable presents to her mother and brother. ⁵⁴Then they had supper, and the servant and the men with him stayed there overnight. But early the next morning, he said, "Send me back to my master."

⁵⁵"But we want Rebekah to stay at least ten days," her brother and mother said, "Then she can go."

⁵⁶But he said, "Don't hinder my return. The LORD has made my mission successful, and I want to report back to my master."

⁵⁷"Well," they said, "we'll call Rebekah and ask her what she thinks." ⁵⁸So they called Rebekah. "Are you willing to go with this man?" they asked her.

And she replied, "Yes, I will go."

⁵⁹So they said good-bye to Rebekah and sent her away with Abraham's servant and his men. The woman who had been Rebekah's childhood nurse went along with her. ⁶⁰They blessed her with this blessing as she parted:

"Our sister, may you become
    the mother of many millions!
May your descendants overcome
    all their enemies."

⁶¹Then Rebekah and her servants mounted the camels and left with Abraham's servant.

⁶²Meanwhile, Isaac, whose home was in the Negev, had returned from Beer-lahai-roi. ⁶³One evening as he was taking a walk out in the fields, meditating, he looked up and saw the camels coming. ⁶⁴When Rebekah looked up and saw Isaac, she quickly dismounted. ⁶⁵"Who is that man

walking through the fields to meet us?" she asked the servant.

And he replied, "It is my master." So Rebekah covered her face with her veil. [66]Then the servant told Isaac the whole story.

[67]And Isaac brought Rebekah into his mother's tent, and she became his wife. He loved her very much, and she was a special comfort to him after the death of his mother.

JANUARY 10 □ DAY 10
GENESIS 25–26
Isaac's Family and Fortune

 OVERVIEW Isaac's family, though presented only briefly in the book of Genesis, is immensely significant. Born to Isaac are twin sons who would later be the fathers of twin nations: Jacob (Israel) and Esau (Edom). Isaac repeats one of his father's most memorable mistakes (26:6-16), but in spite of all his failures, he hears the reassuring promise from God: "I will give all this land to you and your descendants, just as I solemnly promised Abraham, your father" (26:3).

Chapter 25		Chapter 26	
Birth of Twins	Battle for a Birthright	Deception in Gerar	Dispute in Gerar
1 26	27 34	1 11	12 35
Isaac's Family		Isaac's Faith and Failures	

 YOUR DAILY WALK Take a piece of paper and list everything you know about the life of Isaac. Then compare it with the following paragraph.

Faithfulness in little things is a big thing.

Isaac was Abraham's son, Rebekah's husband, and Jacob and Esau's father. He imitated his father and got tricked by his son. He dug a few wells and fathered a set of twins. In short, he generally did what God told him to do without much fanfare.

How would you like your epitaph to read: "He generally did what God told him to do"? There's not a lot of glamour in quiet faithfulness, but as far as God is concerned, it's more important than just about anything else. Maybe that's one reason Isaac gets equal billing with his father and son every time God identifies himself as "the God of Abraham, Isaac, and Jacob."

Has the Lord assigned you a supporting role that escapes the notice of the crowd? Not everyone can function without applause, but apparently God knows that you can by his grace. Thank God right now for the privilege of serving in the "Isaac Brigade," and ask him for that same steadfastness of spirit that produced God's commendation for Isaac!

 INSIGHT Abraham's Life—Filled to the Brim
The original Hebrew text of 25:8 reads, "Then Abraham . . . died in a good old age, an old man and *full.*" When Abraham breathed his last, he was full, not only of years, but also of trials and temptations . . . . victories and rewards . . . reminders and reassurances that God's promises to his posterity would surely come to pass.

CHAPTER 25

Now Abraham married again. Keturah was his new wife, ²and she bore him Zimran, Jokshan, Medan, Midian, Ishbak, and Shuah. ³Jokshan's two sons were Sheba and Dedan. Dedan's descendants were the Asshurites, Letushites, and Leummites. ⁴Midian's sons were Ephah, Epher, Hanoch, Abida, and Eldaah. These were all descendants of Abraham through Keturah.

⁵Abraham left everything he owned to his son Isaac. ⁶But before he died, he gave gifts to the sons of his concubines and sent them off to the east, away from Isaac.

⁷Abraham lived for 175 years, ⁸and he died at a ripe old age, joining his ancestors in death. ⁹His sons Isaac and Ishmael buried him in the cave of Machpelah, near Mamre, in the field of Ephron son of Zohar the Hittite. ¹⁰This was the field Abraham had purchased from the Hittites, where he had buried his wife Sarah. ¹¹After Abraham's death, God poured out rich blessings on Isaac, who settled near Beerlahairoi in the Negev.

¹²This is the history of the descendants of Ishmael, the son of Abraham through Hagar, Sarah's Egyptian servant. ¹³Here is a list, by their names and clans, of Ishmael's descendants: The oldest was Nebaioth, followed by Kedar, Adbeel, Mibsam, ¹⁴Mishma, Dumah, Massa, ¹⁵Hadad, Tema, Jetur, Naphish, and Kedemah. ¹⁶These twelve sons of Ishmael became the founders of twelve tribes that bore their names, listed according to the places they settled and camped. ¹⁷Ishmael finally died at the age of 137 and joined his ancestors in death. ¹⁸Ishmael's descendants were scattered across the country from Havilah to Shur, which is east of Egypt in the direction of Asshur. The clans descended from Ishmael camped close to one another.*

¹⁹This is the history of the family of Isaac, the son of Abraham. ²⁰When Isaac was forty years old, he married Rebekah, the daughter of Bethuel the Aramean from Paddan-aram and the sister of Laban. ²¹Isaac pleaded with the LORD to give Rebekah a child because she was childless. So the LORD answered Isaac's prayer, and his wife became pregnant with twins. ²²But the two children struggled with each other in her womb. So she went to ask the LORD about it. "Why is this happening to me?" she asked.

²³And the LORD told her, "The sons in your womb will become two rival nations. One nation will be stronger than the other; the descendants of your older son will serve the descendants of your younger son."

²⁴And when the time came, the twins were born. ²⁵The first was very red at birth. He was covered with so much hair that one would think he was wearing a piece of clothing. So they called him Esau.* ²⁶Then the other twin was born with his hand grasping Esau's heel. So they called him Jacob.* Isaac was sixty years old when the twins were born.

²⁷As the boys grew up, Esau became a skillful hunter, a man of the open fields, while Jacob was the kind of person who liked to stay at home. ²⁸Isaac loved Esau in particular because of the wild game he brought home, but Rebekah favored Jacob.

²⁹One day when Jacob was cooking some stew, Esau arrived home exhausted and hungry from a hunt. ³⁰Esau said to Jacob, "I'm starved! Give me some of that red stew you've made." (This was how Esau got his other name, Edom—"Red.")

³¹Jacob replied, "All right, but trade me your birthright for it."

³²"Look, I'm dying of starvation!" said Esau. "What good is my birthright to me now?"

³³So Jacob insisted, "Well then, swear to me right now that it is mine." So Esau swore an oath, thereby selling all his rights as the firstborn to his younger brother. ³⁴Then Jacob gave Esau some bread and lentil stew. Esau ate and drank and went on about his business, indifferent to the fact that he had given up his birthright.

CHAPTER 26

Now a severe famine struck the land, as had happened before in Abraham's time. So Isaac moved to Gerar, where Abimelech, king of the Philistines, lived.

²The LORD appeared to him there and said, "Do not go to Egypt. ³Do as I say, and stay here in this land. If you do, I will be with you and bless you. I will give all this land to you and your descendants, just as I solemnly promised Abraham, your father. ⁴I will cause your descendants to become

25:18 The meaning of the Hebrew is uncertain.   25:25 *Esau* sounds like a Hebrew term that means "hair."   25:26 *Jacob* means "he grasps the heel"; this can also figuratively mean "he deceives."

as numerous as the stars, and I will give them all these lands. And through your descendants* all the nations of the earth will be blessed. [5]I will do this because Abraham listened to me and obeyed all my requirements, commands, regulations, and laws."

[6]So Isaac stayed in Gerar. [7]And when the men there asked him about Rebekah, he said, "She is my sister." He was afraid to admit that she was his wife. He thought they would kill him to get her, because she was very beautiful. [8]But some time later, Abimelech, king of the Philistines, looked out a window and saw Isaac fondling Rebekah.

[9]Abimelech called for Isaac and exclaimed, "She is obviously your wife! Why did you say she was your sister?"

"Because I was afraid someone would kill me to get her from me," Isaac replied.

[10]"How could you treat us this way!" Abimelech exclaimed. "Someone might have taken your wife and slept with her, and you would have made us guilty of great sin." [11]Then Abimelech made a public proclamation: "Anyone who harms this man or his wife will die!"

[12]That year Isaac's crops were tremendous! He harvested a hundred times more grain than he planted, for the LORD blessed him. [13]He became a rich man, and his wealth only continued to grow. [14]He acquired large flocks of sheep and goats, great herds of cattle, and many servants. Soon the Philistines became jealous of him, [15]and they filled up all of Isaac's wells with earth. These were the wells that had been dug by the servants of his father, Abraham.

[16]And Abimelech asked Isaac to leave the country. "Go somewhere else," he said, "for you have become too rich and powerful for us."

[17]So Isaac moved to the Gerar Valley and lived there instead. [18]He reopened the wells his father had dug, which the Philistines had filled in after Abraham's death. Isaac renamed them, using the names Abraham had given them. [19]His shepherds also dug in the Gerar Valley and found a gushing spring.

[20]But then the local shepherds came and claimed the spring. "This is our water," they said, and they argued over it with Isaac's herdsmen. So Isaac named the well

"Argument,"* because they had argued about it with him. [21]Isaac's men then dug another well, but again there was a fight over it. So Isaac named it "Opposition."* [22]Abandoning that one, he dug another well, and the local people finally left him alone. So Isaac called it "Room Enough,"* for he said, "At last the LORD has made room for us, and we will be able to thrive."

[23]From there Isaac moved to Beersheba, [24]where the LORD appeared to him on the night of his arrival. "I am the God of your father, Abraham," he said. "Do not be afraid, for I am with you and will bless you. I will give you many descendants, and they will become a great nation. I will do this because of my promise to Abraham, my servant." [25]Then Isaac built an altar there and worshiped the LORD. He set up his camp at that place, and his servants dug a well.

[26]One day Isaac had visitors from Gerar. King Abimelech arrived with his adviser, Ahuzzath, and also Phicol, his army commander. [27]"Why have you come?" Isaac asked them. "This is obviously no friendly visit, since you sent me from your land in a most unfriendly way."

[28]They replied, "We can plainly see that the LORD is with you. So we decided we should have a treaty, a covenant between us. [29]Swear that you will not harm us, just as we did not harm you. We have always treated you well, and we sent you away from us in peace. And now look how the LORD has blessed you!"

[30]So Isaac prepared a great feast for them, and they ate and drank in preparation for the treaty ceremony. [31]Early the next morning, they each took a solemn oath of nonaggression. Then Isaac sent them home again in peace. [32]That very day Isaac's servants came and told him about a well they had dug. "We've found water!" they said. [33]So Isaac named the well "Oath,"* and from that time to this, the town that grew up there has been called Beersheba—"well of the oath."

[34]At the age of forty, Esau married a young woman named Judith, the daughter of Beeri the Hittite. He also married Basemath, the daughter of Elon the Hittite. [35]But Esau's wives made life miserable for Isaac and Rebekah.

26:4 Hebrew *seed.*   **26:20** Hebrew *Esek.*   **26:21** Hebrew *Sitnah.*   **26:22** Hebrew *Rehoboth.*   **26:33** Hebrew *Shibah*, which can mean "oath" or "seven."

JANUARY 11 ☐ DAY 11
GENESIS 27–31
Jacob's Dream and Flight from Esau

OVERVIEW The conflict that began in their mother's womb carries over into the adult lives of Esau and Jacob. After following Rebekah's plan to trick Isaac into giving him the patriarchal blessing, Jacob flees to Haran for safety. En route, he receives assurance from God in a dream that he is indeed the heir to the covenant promises. After twenty years in Haran learning painful lessons from his uncle Laban, Jacob returns to Canaan with his livestock, servants, and family—the nucleus from which God will fashion a new nation: Israel.

Chapter 27	Chapter 28	Chapters 29–30	Chapter 31
Jacob's Stolen Blessing	Jacob's Dream at Bethel	Jacob's Family	Jacob's Flight
Leaving Home		Longing for Home	

YOUR DAILY WALK The first important experience of a new Hebrew baby was receiving a name. Often the name given would describe the parents' hopes for the child or picture the child's personality. So an infant would tend to live up to his name!

Satan's primary tool is not an active sinner but an inactive saint.

You as a child of God bear the name *Christian*. And that raises a penetrating question: Are you living up to your name? Talk to your heavenly Father about it right now. If you are willing to be a Christian today in more than name alone, tell him so!

INSIGHT You Can't Tell the Patriarchs without a Program!

Order	Name	Meaning	Mother (Son)
1	Reuben	"Look, a son!"	Leah (1)
2	Simeon	"One who hears"	Leah (2)
3	Levi	"Being attached"	Leah (3)
4	Judah	"Praise"	Leah (4)
5	Dan	"To judge"	Bilhah (1)
6	Naphtali	"My struggle"	Bilhah (2)
7	Gad	"Good fortune"	Zilpah (1)
8	Asher	"Happy"	Zilpah (2)
9	Issachar	"Reward"	Leah (5)
10	Zebulun	"Honor"	Leah (6)
11	Joseph	"May he add"	Rachel (1)
12	Benjamin	"Son of my right hand"	Rachel (2)

CHAPTER 27

When Isaac was old and almost blind, he called for Esau, his older son, and said, "My son?"

"Yes, Father?" Esau replied.

²"I am an old man now," Isaac said, "and I expect every day to be my last. ³Take your bow and a quiver full of arrows out into the open country, and hunt some wild game for me. ⁴Prepare it just the way I like it so it's savory and good, and bring it here for me to eat. Then I will pronounce the blessing that belongs to you, my firstborn son, before I die."

⁵But Rebekah overheard the conversation. So when Esau left to hunt for the wild game, ⁶she said to her son Jacob, "I overheard your father asking Esau ⁷to prepare him a delicious meal of wild game. He wants to bless Esau in the LORD's presence before he dies. ⁸Now, my son, do exactly as I tell you. ⁹Go out to the flocks and bring me two fine young goats. I'll prepare your father's favorite dish from them. ¹⁰Take the food to your father; then he can eat it and bless you instead of Esau before he dies."

¹¹"But Mother!" Jacob replied. "He

won't be fooled that easily. Think how hairy Esau is and how smooth my skin is! [12]What if my father touches me? He'll see that I'm trying to trick him, and then he'll curse me instead of blessing me."

[13]"Let the curse fall on me, dear son," said Rebekah. "Just do what I tell you. Go out and get the goats."

[14]So Jacob followed his mother's instructions, bringing her the two goats. She took them and cooked a delicious meat dish, just the way Isaac liked it. [15]Then she took Esau's best clothes, which were there in the house, and dressed Jacob with them. [16]She made him a pair of gloves from the hairy skin of the young goats, and she fastened a strip of the goat's skin around his neck. [17]Then she gave him the meat dish, with its rich aroma, and some freshly baked bread. [18]Jacob carried the platter of food to his father and said, "My father?"

"Yes, my son," he answered. "Who is it—Esau or Jacob?"

[19]Jacob replied, "It's Esau, your older son. I've done as you told me. Here is the wild game, cooked the way you like it. Sit up and eat it so you can give me your blessing."

[20]Isaac asked, "How were you able to find it so quickly, my son?"

"Because the LORD your God put it in my path!" Jacob replied.

[21]Then Isaac said to Jacob, "Come over here. I want to touch you to make sure you really are Esau." [22]So Jacob went over to his father, and Isaac touched him. "The voice is Jacob's, but the hands are Esau's," Isaac said to himself. [23]But he did not recognize Jacob because Jacob's hands felt hairy just like Esau's. So Isaac pronounced his blessing on Jacob. [24]"Are you really my son Esau?" he asked.

"Yes, of course," Jacob replied.

[25]Then Isaac said, "Now, my son, bring me the meat. I will eat it, and then I will give you my blessing." So Jacob took the food over to his father, and Isaac ate it. He also drank the wine that Jacob served him. Then Isaac said, [26]"Come here and kiss me, my son."

[27]So Jacob went over and kissed him. And when Isaac caught the smell of his clothes, he was finally convinced, and he blessed his son. He said, "The smell of my son is the good smell of the open fields that the LORD has blessed. [28]May God always give you plenty of dew for healthy crops and good harvests of grain and wine. [29]May many nations become your servants. May you be the master of your brothers. May all your mother's sons bow low before you. All who curse you are cursed, and all who bless you are blessed."

[30]As soon as Isaac had blessed Jacob, and almost before Jacob had left his father, Esau returned from his hunting trip. [31]Esau prepared his father's favorite meat dish and brought it to him. Then he said, "I'm back, Father, and I have the wild game. Sit up and eat it so you can give me your blessing."

[32]But Isaac asked him, "Who are you?"

"Why, it's me, of course!" he replied. "It's Esau, your older son."

[33]Isaac began to tremble uncontrollably and said, "Then who was it that just served me wild game? I have already eaten it, and I blessed him with an irrevocable blessing before you came."

[34]When Esau understood, he let out a loud and bitter cry. "O my father, bless me, too!" he begged.

[35]But Isaac said, "Your brother was here, and he tricked me. He has carried away your blessing."

[36]Esau said bitterly, "No wonder his name is Jacob,* for he has deceived me twice, first taking my birthright and now stealing my blessing. Oh, haven't you saved even one blessing for me?"

[37]Isaac said to Esau, "I have made Jacob your master and have declared that all his brothers will be his servants. I have guaranteed him an abundance of grain and wine—what is there left to give?"

[38]Esau pleaded, "Not one blessing left for me? O my father, bless me, too!" Then Esau broke down and wept.

[39]His father, Isaac, said to him, "You will live off the land and what it yields, [40]and you will live by your sword. You will serve your brother for a time, but then you will shake loose from him and be free."

[41]Esau hated Jacob because he had stolen his blessing, and he said to himself, "My father will soon be dead and gone. Then I will kill Jacob."

[42]But someone got wind of what Esau was planning and reported it to Rebekah. She sent for Jacob and told him, "Esau is threatening to kill you. [43]This is what you

27:36 *Jacob* means "he grasps the heel"; this can also figuratively mean "he deceives."

should do. Flee to your uncle Laban in Haran. [44]Stay there with him until your brother's fury is spent. [45]When he forgets what you have done, I will send for you. Why should I lose both of you in one day?"

[46]Then Rebekah said to Isaac, "I'm sick and tired of these local Hittite women. I'd rather die than see Jacob marry one of them."

CHAPTER 28

So Isaac called for Jacob, blessed him, and said, "Do not marry any of these Canaanite women. [2]Instead, go at once to Paddan-aram, to the house of your grandfather Bethuel, and marry one of your uncle Laban's daughters. [3]May God Almighty bless you and give you many children. And may your descendants become a great assembly of nations! [4]May God pass on to you and your descendants the blessings he promised to Abraham. May you own this land where we now are foreigners, for God gave it to Abraham."

[5]So Isaac sent Jacob away, and he went to Paddan-aram to stay with his uncle Laban, his mother's brother, the son of Bethuel the Aramean.

[6]Esau heard that his father had blessed Jacob and sent him to Paddan-aram to find a wife, and that he had warned Jacob not to marry a Canaanite woman. [7]He also knew that Jacob had obeyed his parents and gone to Paddan-aram. [8]It was now very clear to Esau that his father despised the local Canaanite women. [9]So he visited his uncle Ishmael's family and married one of Ishmael's daughters, in addition to the wives he already had. His new wife's name was Mahalath. She was the sister of Nebaioth and the daughter of Ishmael, Abraham's son.

[10]Meanwhile, Jacob left Beersheba and traveled toward Haran. [11]At sundown he arrived at a good place to set up camp and stopped there for the night. Jacob found a stone for a pillow and lay down to sleep. [12]As he slept, he dreamed of a stairway that reached from earth to heaven. And he saw the angels of God going up and down on it. [13]At the top of the stairway stood the LORD, and he said, "I am the LORD, the God of your grandfather Abraham and the God of your father, Isaac. The ground you are lying on belongs to you. I will give it to you and your descendants. [14]Your descendants will be as numerous as the dust of the earth! They will cover the land from east to west and from north to south. All the families of the earth will be blessed through you and your descendants.* [15]What's more, I will be with you, and I will protect you wherever you go. I will someday bring you safely back to this land. I will be with you constantly until I have finished giving you everything I have promised."

[16]Then Jacob woke up and said, "Surely the LORD is in this place, and I wasn't even aware of it." [17]He was afraid and said, "What an awesome place this is! It is none other than the house of God—the gateway to heaven!" [18]The next morning he got up very early. He took the stone he had used as a pillow and set it upright as a memorial pillar. Then he poured olive oil over it. [19]He named the place Bethel—"house of God"—though the name of the nearby village was Luz.

[20]Then Jacob made this vow: "If God will be with me and protect me on this journey and give me food and clothing, [21]and if he will bring me back safely to my father, then I will make the LORD my God. [22]This memorial pillar will become a place for worshiping God, and I will give God a tenth of everything he gives me."

CHAPTER 29

Jacob hurried on, finally arriving in the land of the east. [2]He saw in the distance three flocks of sheep lying in an open field beside a well, waiting to be watered. But a heavy stone covered the mouth of the well. [3]It was the custom there to wait for all the flocks to arrive before removing the stone. After watering them, the stone would be rolled back over the mouth of the well. [4]Jacob went over to the shepherds and asked them, "Where do you live?"

"At Haran," they said.

[5]"Do you know a man there named Laban, the grandson of Nahor?"

"Yes, we do," they replied.

[6]"How is he?" Jacob asked.

"He's well and prosperous. Look, here comes his daughter Rachel with the sheep."

[7]"Why don't you water the flocks so they can get back to grazing?" Jacob asked.

28:14 Hebrew *seed*.

"They'll be hungry if you stop so early in the day."

⁸"We don't roll away the stone and begin the watering until all the flocks and shepherds are here," they replied.

⁹As this conversation was going on, Rachel arrived with her father's sheep, for she was a shepherd. ¹⁰And because she was his cousin, the daughter of his mother's brother, and because the sheep were his uncle's, Jacob went over to the well and rolled away the stone and watered his uncle's flock. ¹¹Then Jacob kissed Rachel, and tears came to his eyes. ¹²He explained that he was her cousin on her father's side, her aunt Rebekah's son. So Rachel quickly ran and told her father, Laban.

¹³As soon as Laban heard about Jacob's arrival, he rushed out to meet him and greeted him warmly. Laban then brought him home, and Jacob told him his story. ¹⁴"Just think, my very own flesh and blood!" Laban exclaimed.

After Jacob had been there about a month, ¹⁵Laban said to him, "You shouldn't work for me without pay just because we are relatives. How much do you want?"

¹⁶Now Laban had two daughters: Leah, who was the oldest, and her younger sister, Rachel. ¹⁷Leah had pretty eyes,* but Rachel was beautiful in every way, with a lovely face and shapely figure. ¹⁸Since Jacob was in love with Rachel, he told her father, "I'll work for you seven years if you'll give me Rachel, your younger daughter, as my wife."

¹⁹"Agreed!" Laban replied. "I'd rather give her to you than to someone outside the family."

²⁰So Jacob spent the next seven years working to pay for Rachel. But his love for her was so strong that it seemed to him but a few days. ²¹Finally, the time came for him to marry her. "I have fulfilled my contract," Jacob said to Laban. "Now give me my wife so we can be married."

²²So Laban invited everyone in the neighborhood to celebrate with Jacob at a wedding feast. ²³That night, when it was dark, Laban took Leah to Jacob, and he slept with her. ²⁴And Laban gave Leah a servant, Zilpah, to be her maid.

²⁵But when Jacob woke up in the morning—it was Leah! "What sort of trick is this?" Jacob raged at Laban. "I worked seven years for Rachel. What do you mean by this trickery?"

²⁶"It's not our custom to marry off a younger daughter ahead of the firstborn," Laban replied. ²⁷"Wait until the bridal week is over, and you can have Rachel, too—that is, if you promise to work another seven years for me."

²⁸So Jacob agreed to work seven more years. A week after Jacob had married Leah, Laban gave him Rachel, too. ²⁹And Laban gave Rachel a servant, Bilhah, to be her maid. ³⁰So Jacob slept with Rachel, too, and he loved her more than Leah. He then stayed and worked the additional seven years.

³¹But because Leah was unloved, the LORD let her have a child, while Rachel was childless. ³²So Leah became pregnant and had a son. She named him Reuben,* for she said, "The LORD has noticed my misery, and now my husband will love me." ³³She soon became pregnant again and had another son. She named him Simeon,* for she said, "The LORD heard that I was unloved and has given me another son." ³⁴Again she became pregnant and had a son. She named him Levi,* for she said, "Surely now my husband will feel affection for me, since I have given him three sons!" ³⁵Once again she became pregnant and had a son. She named him Judah,* for she said, "Now I will praise the LORD!" And then she stopped having children.

CHAPTER 30

When Rachel saw that she wasn't having any children, she became jealous of her sister. "Give me children, or I'll die!" she exclaimed to Jacob.

²Jacob flew into a rage. "Am I God?" he asked. "He is the only one able to give you children!"

³Then Rachel told him, "Sleep with my servant, Bilhah, and she will bear children for me." ⁴So Rachel gave him Bilhah to be his wife, and Jacob slept with her. ⁵Bilhah became pregnant and presented him with a son. ⁶Rachel named him Dan,* for she said, "God has vindicated me! He has heard my request and given me a son."

29:17 Or dull eyes. The meaning of the Hebrew is uncertain.　　29:32 Reuben means "Look, a son!" It also sounds like the Hebrew for "He has seen my misery."　　29:33 Simeon probably means "one who hears."　　29:34 Levi sounds like a Hebrew term that means "being attached" or "feeling affection for."　　29:35 Judah sounds like the Hebrew for "praise."　　30:6 Dan is a play on the Hebrew term meaning "to vindicate" or "to judge."

[7]Then Bilhah became pregnant again and gave Jacob a second son. [8]Rachel named him Naphtali,* for she said, "I have had an intense struggle with my sister, and I am winning!"

[9]Meanwhile, Leah realized that she wasn't getting pregnant anymore, so she gave her servant, Zilpah, to Jacob to be his wife. [10]Soon Zilpah presented him with another son. [11]Leah named him Gad,* for she said, "How fortunate I am!" [12]Then Zilpah produced a second son, [13]and Leah named him Asher,* for she said, "What joy is mine! The other women will consider me happy indeed!"

[14]One day during the wheat harvest, Reuben found some mandrakes growing in a field and brought the roots to his mother, Leah. Rachel begged Leah to give some of them to her. [15]But Leah angrily replied, "Wasn't it enough that you stole my husband? Now will you steal my son's mandrake roots, too?"

Rachel said, "I will let him sleep with you tonight in exchange for the mandrake roots."

[16]So that evening, as Jacob was coming home from the fields, Leah went out to meet him. "You must sleep with me tonight!" she said. "I have paid for you with some mandrake roots my son has found." So Jacob slept with her. [17]And God answered her prayers. She became pregnant again and gave birth to her fifth son. [18]She named him Issachar,* for she said, "God has rewarded me for giving my servant to my husband as a wife." [19]Then she became pregnant again and had a sixth son. [20]She named him Zebulun,* for she said, "God has given me good gifts for my husband. Now he will honor me, for I have given him six sons." [21]Later she gave birth to a daughter and named her Dinah.

[22]Then God remembered Rachel's plight and answered her prayers by giving her a child. [23]She became pregnant and gave birth to a son. "God has removed my shame," she said. [24]And she named him Joseph,* for she said, "May the LORD give me yet another son."

[25]Soon after Joseph was born to Rachel, Jacob said to Laban, "I want to go back home. [26]Let me take my wives and children, for I have earned them from you, and let me be on my way. You know I have fully paid for them with my service to you."

[27]"Please don't leave me," Laban replied, "for I have learned by divination that the LORD has blessed me because you are here. [28]How much do I owe you? Whatever it is, I'll pay it."

[29]Jacob replied, "You know how faithfully I've served you through these many years, and how your flocks and herds have grown. [30]You had little indeed before I came, and your wealth has increased enormously. The LORD has blessed you from everything I do! But now, what about me? When should I provide for my own family?"

[31]"What wages do you want?" Laban asked again.

Jacob replied, "Don't give me anything at all. Just do one thing, and I'll go back to work for you. [32]Let me go out among your flocks today and remove all the sheep and goats that are speckled or spotted, along with all the dark-colored sheep. Give them to me as my wages. [33]This will make it easy for you to see whether or not I have been honest. If you find in my flock any white sheep or goats that are not speckled, you will know that I have stolen them from you."

[34]"All right," Laban replied. "It will be as you have said." [35]But that very day Laban went out and removed all the male goats that were speckled and spotted, the females that were speckled and spotted with any white patches, and all the dark-colored sheep. He placed them in the care of his sons, [36]and they took them three days' distance from where Jacob was. Meanwhile, Jacob stayed and cared for Laban's flock.

[37]Now Jacob took fresh shoots from poplar, almond, and plane trees and peeled off strips of the bark to make white streaks on them. [38]Then he set up these peeled branches beside the watering troughs so Laban's flocks would see them as they came to drink, for that was when they mated. [39]So when the flocks mated in front of the white-streaked branches, all of their offspring were streaked, speckled, and spotted. [40]Jacob added them to his own flock, thus separating the lambs from Laban's flock. Then at mating time, he turned the flocks toward the streaked and dark-

---

30:8 *Naphtali* means "my struggle."   **30:11** *Gad* means "good fortune."   **30:13** *Asher* means "happy."   **30:18** *Issachar* sounds like a Hebrew term that means "reward."   **30:20** *Zebulun* probably means "honor."   **30:24** *Joseph* means "may he add."

colored rams in Laban's flock. This is how he built his flock from Laban's. [41]Whenever the stronger females were ready to mate, Jacob set up the peeled branches in front of them. [42]But he didn't do this with the weaker ones, so the weaker lambs belonged to Laban, and the stronger ones were Jacob's. [43]As a result, Jacob's flocks increased rapidly, and he became very wealthy, with many servants, camels, and donkeys.

CHAPTER 31

But Jacob soon learned that Laban's sons were beginning to grumble. "Jacob has robbed our father!" they said. "All his wealth has been gained at our father's expense." [2]And Jacob began to notice a considerable cooling in Laban's attitude toward him.

[3]Then the LORD said to Jacob, "Return to the land of your father and grandfather and to your relatives there, and I will be with you."

[4]Jacob called Rachel and Leah out to the field where he was watching the flocks, [5]so he could talk things over with them. "Your father has turned against me and is not treating me like he used to," he told them. "But the God of my father has been with me. [6]You know how hard I have worked for your father, [7]but he has tricked me, breaking his wage agreement with me again and again. But God has not allowed him to do me any harm. [8]For if he said the speckled animals were mine, the whole flock began to produce speckled lambs. And when he changed his mind and said I could have the streaked ones, then all the lambs were born streaked. [9]In this way, God has made me wealthy at your father's expense. [10]During the mating season, I had a dream and saw that the male goats mating with the flock were streaked, speckled, and spotted. [11]Then in my dream, the angel of God said to me, 'Jacob!' And I replied, 'Yes, I'm listening!' [12]The angel said, 'Look, and you will see that only the streaked, speckled, and spotted males are mating with the females of your flock. For I have seen all that Laban has done to you. [13]I am the God you met at Bethel, the place where you anointed the pillar of stone and made a vow to serve me. Now leave this country and return to the land you came from.'"

[14]Rachel and Leah said, "That's fine with us! There's nothing for us here—none of our father's wealth will come to us anyway. [15]He has reduced our rights to those of foreign women. He sold us, and what he received for us has disappeared. [16]The riches God has given you from our father are legally ours and our children's to begin with. So go ahead and do whatever God has told you."

[17]So Jacob put his wives and children on camels. [18]He drove the flocks in front of him—all the livestock he had acquired at Paddan-aram—and set out on his journey to the land of Canaan, where his father, Isaac, lived. [19]At the time they left, Laban was some distance away, shearing his sheep. Rachel stole her father's household gods and took them with her. [20]They set out secretly and never told Laban they were leaving. [21]Jacob took all his possessions with him and crossed the Euphrates River, heading for the territory of Gilead.

[22]Laban didn't learn of their flight for three days. [23]But when he did, he gathered a group of his relatives and set out in hot pursuit. He caught up with them seven days later in the hill country of Gilead. [24]But the previous night God had appeared to Laban in a dream. "Be careful about what you say to Jacob!" he was told.

[25]So when Laban caught up with Jacob as he was camped in the hill country of Gilead, he set up his camp not far from Jacob's. [26]"What do you mean by sneaking off like this?" Laban demanded. "Are my daughters prisoners, the plunder of war, that you have stolen them away like this? [27]Why did you slip away secretly? I would have given you a farewell party, with joyful singing accompanied by tambourines and harps. [28]Why didn't you let me kiss my daughters and grandchildren and tell them good-bye? You have acted very foolishly! [29]I could destroy you, but the God of your father appeared to me last night and told me, 'Be careful about what you say to Jacob!' [30]I know you feel you must go, and you long intensely for your childhood home, but why have you stolen my household gods?"

[31]"I rushed away because I was afraid," Jacob answered. "I said to myself, 'He'll take his daughters from me by force.' [32]But as for your household gods, let the person who has taken them die! If you find anything that belongs to you, I swear before all these relatives of ours, I will give it back

without question." But Jacob didn't know that Rachel had taken them.

[33]Laban went first into Jacob's tent to search there, then into Leah's, and then he searched the tents of the two concubines, but he didn't find the gods. Finally, he went into Rachel's tent. [34]Rachel had taken the household gods and had stuffed them into her camel saddle, and now she was sitting on them. So although Laban searched all the tents, he couldn't find them. [35]"Forgive my not getting up, Father," Rachel explained. "I'm having my monthly period." So despite his thorough search, Laban didn't find them.

[36]Then Jacob became very angry. "What did you find?" he demanded of Laban. "What is my crime? You have chased me as though I were a criminal. [37]You have searched through everything I own. Now show me what you have found that belongs to you! Set it out here in front of us, before our relatives, for all to see. Let them decide who is the real owner!

[38]"Twenty years I have been with you, and all that time I cared for your sheep and goats so they produced healthy offspring. In all those years I never touched a single ram of yours for food. [39]If any were attacked and killed by wild animals, did I show them to you and ask you to reduce the count of your flock? No, I took the loss! You made me pay for every animal stolen from the flocks, whether the loss was my fault or not. [40]I worked for you through the scorching heat of the day and through cold and sleepless nights. [41]Yes, twenty years— fourteen of them earning your two daughters, and six years to get the flock. And you have reduced my wages ten times! [42]In fact, except for the grace of God—the God of my grandfather Abraham, the awe-inspiring God of my father, Isaac—you would have sent me off without a penny to my name. But God has seen your cruelty and my hard

work. That is why he appeared to you last night and vindicated me."

[43]Then Laban replied to Jacob, "These women are my daughters, and these children are my grandchildren, and these flocks and all that you have—all are mine. But what can I do now to my own daughters and grandchildren? [44]Come now, and we will make a peace treaty, you and I, and we will live by its terms."

[45]So Jacob took a stone and set it up as a monument. [46]He also told his men to gather stones and pile them up in a heap. Jacob and Laban then sat down beside the pile of stones to share a meal. [47]They named it "Witness Pile," which is Jegarsahadutha in Laban's language and Galeed* in Jacob's.

[48]"This pile of stones will stand as a witness to remind us of our agreement," Laban said. [49]This place was also called Mizpah,* for Laban said, "May the LORD keep watch between us to make sure that we keep this treaty when we are out of each other's sight. [50]I won't know about it if you are harsh to my daughters or if you take other wives, but God will see it. [51]This heap of stones and this pillar [52]stand between us as a witness of our vows. I will not cross this line to harm you, and you will not cross it to harm me. [53]I call on the God of our ancestors—the God of your grandfather Abraham and the God of my grandfather Nahor—to punish either one of us who harms the other."

So Jacob took an oath before the awesome God of his father, Isaac, to respect the boundary line. [54]Then Jacob presented a sacrifice to God and invited everyone to a feast. Afterward they spent the night there in the hills. [55]Laban got up early the next morning, and he kissed his daughters and grandchildren and blessed them. Then he returned home.

31:47 *Jegar-sahadutha* means "witness pile" in Aramaic; *Galeed* means "witness pile" in Hebrew.   31:49 *Mizpah* means "watchtower."

JANUARY 12 □ DAY 12
GENESIS 32–36
Jacob's Encounter with Esau

 OVERVIEW Having survived the pursuit of his jealous uncle, Laban, Jacob now faces an even greater danger from his estranged brother, Esau. After sending his family across the Jabbok River, Jacob wrestles with the Angel of God until daybreak. God assures Jacob of his continued presence and leaves Jacob with both a new name—Israel ("one who struggles with God")—and a permanent limp as reminders of the encounter. Once reconciled to God, Jacob is ready to be reconciled to Esau and to return to Canaan as the vital link in God's continuing promises.

Chapter 32	Chapter 33	Chapter 34	Chapter 35	Chapter 36
Meeting God	Meeting Esau	Avenging Dinah	Returning to Bethel	Recounting Esau's Line
Jacob's Reconciliation		Jacob's Rededication		

 YOUR DAILY WALK David, Jabez, and Jacob. A more unlikely trio you will never meet! David, the mighty king of Israel . . . Jabez, an obscure figure from the pages of 1 Chronicles . . . Jacob, the schemer-turned-servant. Yet they shared a common experience. Do you know what it was?

All blessings carry responsibility, so don't pray for the first if you're not ready for the second.

David prayed, "May God be merciful and bless us" (Psalm 67:1). Jabez "prayed to the God of Israel, 'Oh, that you would bless me'" (1 Chronicles 4:10). Jacob wrestled with the Angel of God, not willing to let go "unless you bless me" (32:26). And in each case, God did precisely that! David's kingdom enjoyed unprecedented peace and prosperity; Jabez received from God what he had requested; and in response to Jacob's petition, the Angel of the Lord "blessed Jacob there" (32:29).

Is it possible God has a blessing in store for you—in the form of protection (like David), expanded responsibility (like Jabez), or renewed promises (like Jacob)—but that "the reason you don't have . . . is that you don't ask God for it" (James 4:2)? Use the prayer of David, Jabez, or Jacob to express the desire of your heart. And don't be surprised if God answers! He's in the business of blessing.

 INSIGHT Three Spiritual Milestones in Jacob's Life
Three times Jacob encountered the God of his forefathers. At Haran he was *redirected* by God (31:1-16); at Peniel he was *restored* by God (32:24-32); at Bethel he was *reassured* by God (35:1-15).

CHAPTER 32
As Jacob and his household started on their way again, angels of God came to meet him. ²When Jacob saw them, he exclaimed, "This is God's camp!" So he named the place Mahanaim.*

³Jacob now sent messengers to his brother, Esau, in Edom, the land of Seir. ⁴He told them, "Give this message to my mas-

ter Esau: 'Humble greetings from your servant Jacob! I have been living with Uncle Laban until recently, ⁵and now I own oxen, donkeys, sheep, goats, and many servants, both men and women. I have sent these messengers to inform you of my coming, hoping that you will be friendly to us.'"

⁶The messengers returned with the news that Esau was on his way to meet Jacob—

32:2 *Mahanaim* means "two camps."

with an army of four hundred men! [7]Jacob was terrified at the news. He divided his household, along with the flocks and herds and camels, into two camps. [8]He thought, "If Esau attacks one group, perhaps the other can escape."

[9]Then Jacob prayed, "O God of my grandfather Abraham and my father, Isaac—O LORD, you told me to return to my land and to my relatives, and you promised to treat me kindly. [10]I am not worthy of all the faithfulness and unfailing love you have shown to me, your servant. When I left home, I owned nothing except a walking stick, and now my household fills two camps! [11]O LORD, please rescue me from my brother, Esau. I am afraid that he is coming to kill me, along with my wives and children. [12]But you promised to treat me kindly and to multiply my descendants until they become as numerous as the sands along the seashore—too many to count."

[13]Jacob stayed where he was for the night and prepared a present for Esau: [14]two hundred female goats, twenty male goats, two hundred ewes, twenty rams, [15]thirty female camels with their young, forty cows, ten bulls, twenty female donkeys, and ten male donkeys. [16]He told his servants to lead them on ahead, each group of animals by itself, separated by a distance in between.

[17]He gave these instructions to the men leading the first group: "When you meet Esau, he will ask, 'Where are you going? Whose servants are you? Whose animals are these?' [18]You should reply, 'These belong to your servant Jacob. They are a present for his master Esau! He is coming right behind us.'" [19]Jacob gave the same instructions to each of the herdsmen and told them, "You are all to say the same thing to Esau when you see him. [20]And be sure to say, 'Your servant Jacob is right behind us.'" Jacob's plan was to appease Esau with the presents before meeting him face to face. "Perhaps," Jacob hoped, "he will be friendly to us." [21]So the presents were sent on ahead, and Jacob spent that night in the camp.

[22]But during the night Jacob got up and sent his two wives, two concubines, and eleven sons across the Jabbok River. [23]After they were on the other side, he sent over all his possessions. [24]This left Jacob all alone in the camp, and a man came and wrestled with him until dawn. [25]When the man saw that he couldn't win the match, he struck Jacob's hip and knocked it out of joint at the socket. [26]Then the man said, "Let me go, for it is dawn."

But Jacob panted, "I will not let you go unless you bless me."

[27]"What is your name?" the man asked.

He replied, "Jacob."

[28]"Your name will no longer be Jacob," the man told him. "It is now Israel,* because you have struggled with both God and men and have won."

[29]"What is your name?" Jacob asked him.

"Why do you ask?" the man replied. Then he blessed Jacob there.

[30]Jacob named the place Peniel—"face of God"—for he said, "I have seen God face to face, yet my life has been spared." [31]The sun rose as he left Peniel,* and he was limping because of his hip. [32]That is why even today the people of Israel don't eat meat from near the hip, in memory of what happened that night.

CHAPTER 33

Then, in the distance, Jacob saw Esau coming with his four hundred men. [2]Jacob now arranged his family into a column, with his two concubines and their children at the front, Leah and her children next, and Rachel and Joseph last. [3]Then Jacob went on ahead. As he approached his brother, he bowed low seven times before him. [4]Then Esau ran to meet him and embraced him affectionately and kissed him. Both of them were in tears.

[5]Then Esau looked at the women and children and asked, "Who are these people with you?"

"These are the children God has graciously given to me," Jacob replied. [6]Then the concubines came forward with their children and bowed low before him. [7]Next Leah came with her children, and they bowed down. Finally, Rachel and Joseph came and made their bows.

[8]"And what were all the flocks and herds I met as I came?" Esau asked.

Jacob replied, "They are gifts, my lord, to ensure your goodwill."

32:28 *Israel* means "God struggles" or "one who struggles with God."   **32:31** Hebrew *Penuel*, a variant name for Peniel.

⁹"Brother, I have plenty," Esau answered. "Keep what you have."

¹⁰"No, please accept them," Jacob said, "for what a relief it is to see your friendly smile. It is like seeing the smile of God! ¹¹Please take my gifts, for God has been very generous to me. I have more than enough." Jacob continued to insist, so Esau finally accepted them.

¹²"Well, let's be going," Esau said. "I will stay with you and lead the way."

¹³But Jacob replied, "You can see, my lord, that some of the children are very young, and the flocks and herds have their young, too. If they are driven too hard, they may die. ¹⁴So go on ahead of us. We will follow at our own pace and meet you at Seir."

¹⁵"Well," Esau said, "at least let me leave some of my men to guide and protect you."

"There is no reason for you to be so kind to me," Jacob insisted.

¹⁶So Esau started back to Seir that same day. ¹⁷Meanwhile, Jacob and his household traveled on to Succoth. There he built himself a house and made shelters for his flocks and herds. That is why the place was named Succoth.* ¹⁸Then they arrived safely at Shechem, in Canaan, and they set up camp just outside the town. ¹⁹Jacob bought the land he camped on from the family of Hamor, Shechem's father, for a hundred pieces of silver.* ²⁰And there he built an altar and called it El-Elohe-Israel.*

CHAPTER 34

One day Dinah, Leah's daughter, went to visit some of the young women who lived in the area. ²But when the local prince, Shechem son of Hamor the Hivite, saw her, he took her and raped her. ³But Shechem's love for Dinah was strong, and he tried to win her affection. ⁴He even spoke to his father about it. "Get this girl for me," he demanded. "I want to marry her."

⁵Word soon reached Jacob that his daughter had been defiled, but his sons were out in the fields herding cattle so he did nothing until they returned. ⁶Meanwhile, Hamor, Shechem's father, came out to discuss the matter with Jacob. ⁷He arrived just as Jacob's sons were coming in from the fields. They were shocked and furious that their sister had been raped. Shechem had done a disgraceful thing

against Jacob's family,* a thing that should never have been done.

⁸Hamor told Jacob and his sons, "My son Shechem is truly in love with your daughter, and he longs for her to be his wife. Please let him marry her. ⁹We invite you to let your daughters marry our sons, and we will give our daughters as wives for your young men. ¹⁰And you may live among us; the land is open to you! Settle here and trade with us. You are free to acquire property among us."

¹¹Then Shechem addressed Dinah's father and brothers. "Please be kind to me, and let me have her as my wife," he begged. "I will give whatever you require. ¹²No matter what dowry or gift you demand, I will pay it—only give me the girl as my wife."

¹³But Dinah's brothers deceived Shechem and Hamor because of what Shechem had done to their sister. ¹⁴They said to them, "We couldn't possibly allow this, because you aren't circumcised. It would be a disgrace for her to marry a man like you! ¹⁵But here is a solution. If every man among you will be circumcised like we are, ¹⁶we will intermarry with you and live here and unite with you to become one people. ¹⁷Otherwise we will take her and be on our way."

¹⁸Hamor and Shechem gladly agreed, ¹⁹and Shechem lost no time in acting on this request, for he wanted Dinah desperately. Shechem was a highly respected member of his family, ²⁰and he appeared with his father before the town leaders to present this proposal. ²¹"Those men are our friends," they said. "Let's invite them to live here among us and ply their trade. For the land is large enough to hold them, and we can intermarry with them. ²²But they will consider staying here only on one condition. Every one of us men must be circumcised, just as they are. ²³But if we do this, all their flocks and possessions will become ours. Come, let's agree to this so they will settle here among us."

²⁴So all the men agreed and were circumcised. ²⁵But three days later, when their wounds were still sore, two of Dinah's brothers, Simeon and Levi, took their swords, entered the town without opposition, and slaughtered every man there, ²⁶including Hamor and Shechem. They rescued Dinah from Shechem's house and returned to their camp. ²⁷Then all of Jacob's

33:17 *Succoth* means "shelters."   **33:19** Hebrew *100 kesitahs;* the value or weight of the kesitah is no longer known.
33:20 *El-Elohe-Israel* means "God, the God of Israel."   **34:7** Hebrew *in Israel.*

sons plundered the town because their sister had been defiled there. [28]They seized all the flocks and herds and donkeys—everything they could lay their hands on, both inside the town and outside in the fields. [29]They also took all the women and children and wealth of every kind.

[30]Afterward Jacob said to Levi and Simeon, "You have made me stink among all the people of this land—among all the Canaanites and Perizzites. We are so few that they will come and crush us. We will all be killed!"

[31]"Should he treat our sister like a prostitute?" they retorted angrily.

CHAPTER 35

God said to Jacob, "Now move on to Bethel and settle there. Build an altar there to worship me—the God who appeared to you when you fled from your brother, Esau."

[2]So Jacob told everyone in his household, "Destroy your idols, wash yourselves, and put on clean clothing. [3]We are now going to Bethel, where I will build an altar to the God who answered my prayers when I was in distress. He has stayed with me wherever I have gone."

[4]So they gave Jacob all their idols and their earrings, and he buried them beneath the tree near Shechem. [5]When they set out again, terror from God came over the people in all the towns of that area, and no one attacked them. [6]Finally, they arrived at Luz (now called Bethel) in Canaan. [7]Jacob built an altar there and named it El-bethel,* because God had appeared to him there at Bethel when he was fleeing from Esau.

[8]Soon after this, Rebekah's old nurse, Deborah, died. She was buried beneath the oak tree in the valley below Bethel. Ever since, the tree has been called the "Oak of Weeping."*

[9]God appeared to Jacob once again when he arrived at Bethel after traveling from Paddan-aram. God blessed him [10]and said, "Your name is no longer Jacob; you will now be called Israel."* [11]Then God said, "I am God Almighty. Multiply and fill the earth! Become a great nation, even many nations. Kings will be among your descendants! [12]And I will pass on to you the land I gave to Abraham and Isaac. Yes, I will give it to you and your descen-

dants." [13]Then God went up from the place where he had spoken to Jacob.

[14]Jacob set up a stone pillar to mark the place where God had spoken to him. He then poured wine over it as an offering to God and anointed the pillar with olive oil. [15]Jacob called the place Bethel—"house of God"—because God had spoken to him there.

[16]Leaving Bethel, they traveled on toward Ephrath (that is, Bethlehem). But Rachel's pains of childbirth began while they were still some distance away. [17]After a very hard delivery, the midwife finally exclaimed, "Don't be afraid—you have another son!" [18]Rachel was about to die, but with her last breath she named him Ben-oni; the baby's father, however, called him Benjamin.* [19]So Rachel died and was buried on the way to Ephrath (that is, Bethlehem). [20]Jacob set up a stone monument over her grave, and it can be seen there to this day.

[21]Jacob* then traveled on and camped beyond the tower of Eder. [22]While he was there, Reuben slept with Bilhah, his father's concubine, and someone told Jacob about it.

These are the names of the twelve sons of Jacob:

[23]The sons of Leah were Reuben (Jacob's oldest son), Simeon, Levi, Judah, Issachar, and Zebulun.
[24]The sons of Rachel were Joseph and Benjamin.
[25]The sons of Bilhah, Rachel's servant, were Dan and Naphtali.
[26]The sons of Zilpah, Leah's servant, were Gad and Asher.

These were the sons born to Jacob at Paddan-aram.

[27]So Jacob came home to his father Isaac in Mamre, which is near Kiriath-arba (now called Hebron), where Abraham had also lived. [28]Isaac lived for 180 years, [29]and he died at a ripe old age, joining his ancestors in death. Then his sons, Esau and Jacob, buried him.

CHAPTER 36

This is the history of the descendants of Esau (also known as Edom). [2]Esau married two young women from Canaan: Adah, the

---

35:7 El-bethel means "the God of Bethel."   35:8 Hebrew Allon-bacuth.   35:10 Jacob means "he grasps the heel"; this can also figuratively mean "he deceives"; Israel means "God struggles" or "one who struggles with God."   35:18 Ben-oni means "son of my sorrow"; Benjamin means "son of my right hand."   35:21 Hebrew Israel; also in 35:22a.

daughter of Elon the Hittite; and Oholibamah, the daughter of Anah and granddaughter of Zibeon the Hivite. [3]He also married his cousin Basemath, who was the daughter of Ishmael and the sister of Nebaioth. [4]Esau and Adah had a son named Eliphaz. Esau and Basemath had a son named Reuel. [5]Esau and Oholibamah had sons named Jeush, Jalam, and Korah. All these sons were born to Esau in the land of Canaan.

[6]Then Esau took his wives, children, household servants, cattle, and flocks—all the wealth he had gained in the land of Canaan—and moved away from his brother, Jacob. [7]There was not enough land to support them both because of all their cattle and livestock. [8]So Esau (also known as Edom) settled in the hill country of Seir.

[9]This is a list of Esau's descendants, the Edomites, who lived in the hill country of Seir.

[10]Among Esau's sons were Eliphaz, the son of Esau's wife Adah; and Reuel, the son of Esau's wife Basemath.
[11]The sons of Eliphaz were Teman, Omar, Zepho, Gatam, and Kenaz. [12]Eliphaz had another son named Amalek, born to Timna, his concubine. These were all grandchildren of Esau's wife Adah.
[13]The sons of Reuel were Nahath, Zerah, Shammah, and Mizzah. These were all grandchildren of Esau's wife Basemath.
[14]Esau also had sons through Oholibamah, the daughter of Anah and granddaughter of Zibeon. Their names were Jeush, Jalam, and Korah.

[15]Esau's children and grandchildren became the leaders of different clans.

The sons of Esau's oldest son, Eliphaz, became the leaders of the clans of Teman, Omar, Zepho, Kenaz, [16]Korah, Gatam, and Amalek. These clans in the land of Edom were descended from Eliphaz, the son of Esau and Adah.
[17]The sons of Esau's son Reuel became the leaders of the clans of Nahath, Zerah, Shammah, and Mizzah. These clans in the land of Edom were descended from Reuel, the son of Esau and Basemath.
[18]The sons of Esau and his wife Oholibamah became the leaders of the

clans of Jeush, Jalam, and Korah. These are the clans descended from Esau's wife Oholibamah, the daughter of Anah.

[19]These are all the clans descended from Esau (also known as Edom).

[20]These are the names of the tribes that descended from Seir the Horite, one of the families native to the land of Seir: Lotan, Shobal, Zibeon, Anah, [21]Dishon, Ezer, and Dishan. These were the Horite clans, the descendants of Seir, who lived in the land of Edom.

[22]The sons of Lotan were Hori and Heman. Lotan's sister was named Timna.
[23]The sons of Shobal were Alvan, Manahath, Ebal, Shepho, and Onam.
[24]The sons of Zibeon were Aiah and Anah. This is the Anah who discovered the hot springs in the wilderness while he was grazing his father's donkeys.
[25]The son of Anah was Dishon, and Oholibamah was his daughter.
[26]The sons of Dishon* were Hemdan, Eshban, Ithran, and Keran.
[27]The sons of Ezer were Bilhan, Zaavan, and Akan.
[28]The sons of Dishan were Uz and Aran.

[29]So the leaders of the Horite clans were Lotan, Shobal, Zibeon, Anah, [30]Dishon, Ezer, and Dishan. The Horite clans are named after their clan leaders, who lived in the land of Seir.

[31]These are the kings who ruled in Edom before there were kings in Israel*:
[32]Bela son of Beor, who ruled from his city of Dinhabah.
[33]When Bela died, Jobab son of Zerah from Bozrah became king.
[34]When Jobab died, Husham from the land of the Temanites became king.
[35]When Husham died, Hadad son of Bedad became king and ruled from the city of Avith. He was the one who destroyed the Midianite army in the land of Moab.
[36]When Hadad died, Samlah from the city of Masrekah became king.
[37]When Samlah died, Shaul from the city of Rehoboth on the Euphrates River* became king.

36:26 Hebrew *Dishan,* a variant name for Dishon; compare 36:21, 28.   **36:31** Or *before an Israelite king ruled over them.*
36:37 Hebrew *the river.*

³⁸When Shaul died, Baal-hanan son of Acbor became king.

³⁹When Baal-hanan died, Hadad* became king and ruled from the city of Pau. Hadad's wife was Mehetabel, the daughter of Matred and granddaughter of Me-zahab.

⁴⁰These are the leaders of the clans of Esau, who lived in the places named for them: Timna, Alvah, Jetheth, ⁴¹Oholibamah, Elah, Pinon, ⁴²Kenaz, Teman, Mibzar, ⁴³Magdiel, and Iram. These are the names of the clans of Esau, the ancestor of the Edomites, each clan giving its name to the area it occupied.

36:39 As in some Hebrew manuscripts, Samaritan Pentateuch, and Syriac version (see also 1 Chr 1:50); most Hebrew manuscripts read *Hadar*.

JANUARY 13 ☐ DAY 13
GENESIS 37–40
Joseph's Slavery in Egypt

 OVERVIEW Abraham . . . Isaac . . . Jacob . . . and now comes Joseph, the fourth major character in the Genesis account of the patriarchs (fathers of the faith). Favored by his father but alienated by his brothers, Joseph is sold into Egyptian slavery. Imprisoned for a crime he did not commit and ignored by the forgetful cup-bearer, Joseph finds his faith—and his integrity—sorely tested. Though Joseph doesn't realize it, through it all God is preparing him for an important role that will bring fruition to his childhood dreams.

Chapter 37	Chapter 38	Chapter 39	Chapter 40
Joseph's Slavery	Judah's Shame	Joseph's Integrity	Joseph's Imprisonment
Life in Jacob's Family		Life in Pharaoh's Prison	

 YOUR DAILY WALK "God, why did you let this happen to me?"

It is better to go straight than to move in the best of circles.

Have you ever felt the urge to ask that question? The average Christian does . . . about every twenty minutes or so! *Why* is a question Christians frequently ask—and God often leaves unanswered. Joseph must have been tempted often to ask for a heavenly explanation for his earthly troubles. Though God did not answer all of Joseph's questions, he did meet all of Joseph's needs (39:21)—and he has promised to do the same for you (Philippians 4:13, 19). That means giving you power over discouragement when you're down in the pits (37:24) . . . power over temptation from lustful thoughts (39:12) . . . purpose for living even when you're mistreated or ignored (39:20-21).

Joseph's faith in God fortified him to face the pit in Canaan, the prison in Egypt, and everything in between. You can develop a faith like that, too! Read about it in James 1:2-4. Then make a little sign that reads, Another Joseph under Construction, and put it by your telephone. That way every ring can provide a comforting reminder!

 INSIGHT Brothers in the Business

The members of the Ishmaelite caravan who bought Joseph from his brothers and sold him in Egypt were called Midianites (37:28, 36). Midian and Medan were two sons of Abraham and his second wife, Keturah (25:2). From them developed a nomadic people who, while blood brothers of the Jews, became their constant enemies (Judges 6:1).

CHAPTER 37

So Jacob settled again in the land of Canaan, where his father had lived.

2This is the history of Jacob's family. When Joseph was seventeen years old, he often tended his father's flocks with his half brothers, the sons of his father's wives Bilhah and Zilpah. But Joseph reported to his father some of the bad things his brothers were doing. 3Now Jacob* loved Joseph more than any of his other children because Joseph had been born to him in his old age. So one day he gave Joseph a special gift—a beautiful robe.* 4But his brothers hated Joseph because of their father's partiality. They couldn't say a kind word to him.

5One night Joseph had a dream and promptly reported the details to his brothers, causing them to hate him even more. 6"Listen to this dream," he announced. 7"We were out in the field tying up bundles of grain. My bundle stood up, and then your bundles all gathered around and bowed low before it!"

8"So you are going to be our king, are you?" his brothers taunted. And they hated him all the more for his dream and what he had said.

9Then Joseph had another dream and told his brothers about it. "Listen to this dream," he said. "The sun, moon, and eleven stars bowed low before me!"

10This time he told his father as well as his brothers, and his father rebuked him. "What do you mean?" his father asked. "Will your mother, your brothers, and I actually come and bow before you?" 11But while his brothers were jealous of Joseph, his father gave it some thought and wondered what it all meant.

12Soon after this, Joseph's brothers went to pasture their father's flocks at Shechem. 13When they had been gone for some time, Jacob said to Joseph, "Your brothers are over at Shechem with the flocks. I'm going to send you to them."

"I'm ready to go," Joseph replied.

14"Go and see how your brothers and the flocks are getting along," Jacob said. "Then come back and bring me word." So Jacob sent him on his way, and Joseph traveled to Shechem from his home in the valley of Hebron.

15When he arrived there, a man noticed him wandering around the countryside. "What are you looking for?" he asked.

16"For my brothers and their flocks," Joseph replied. "Have you seen them?"

17"Yes," the man told him, "but they are no longer here. I heard your brothers say they were going to Dothan." So Joseph followed his brothers to Dothan and found them there.

18When Joseph's brothers saw him coming, they recognized him in the distance and made plans to kill him. 19"Here comes that dreamer!" they exclaimed. 20"Come on, let's kill him and throw him into a deep pit. We can tell our father that a wild animal has eaten him. Then we'll see what becomes of all his dreams!"

21But Reuben came to Joseph's rescue. "Let's not kill him," he said. 22"Why should we shed his blood? Let's just throw him alive into this pit here. That way he will die without our having to touch him." Reuben was secretly planning to help Joseph escape, and then he would bring him back to his father.

23So when Joseph arrived, they pulled off his beautiful robe 24and threw him into the pit. This pit was normally used to store water, but it was empty at the time. 25Then, just as they were sitting down to eat, they noticed a caravan of camels in the distance coming toward them. It was a group of Ishmaelite traders taking spices, balm, and myrrh from Gilead to Egypt.

26Judah said to the others, "What can we gain by killing our brother? That would just give us a guilty conscience. 27Let's sell Joseph to those Ishmaelite traders. Let's not be responsible for his death; after all, he is our brother!" And his brothers agreed. 28So when the traders* came by, his brothers pulled Joseph out of the pit and sold him for twenty pieces* of silver, and the Ishmaelite traders took him along to Egypt.

29Some time later, Reuben returned to get Joseph out of the pit. When he discovered that Joseph was missing, he tore his clothes in anguish and frustration. 30Then he went back to his brothers and lamented, "The boy is gone! What can I do now?"

31Then Joseph's brothers killed a goat and dipped the robe in its blood. 32They took the beautiful robe to their father and asked him to identify it. "We found this in

37:3a Hebrew *Israel;* also in 37:13.   **37:3b** Traditionally rendered *a coat of many colors.* The exact meaning of the Hebrew is uncertain.   **37:28a** Hebrew *Midianites;* also in 37:36.   **37:28b** Hebrew *20 shekels,* about 8 ounces or 228 grams in weight.

the field," they told him. "It's Joseph's robe, isn't it?"

[33]Their father recognized it at once. "Yes," he said, "it is my son's robe. A wild animal has attacked and eaten him. Surely Joseph has been torn in pieces!" [34]Then Jacob tore his clothes and put on sackcloth. He mourned deeply for his son for many days. [35]His family all tried to comfort him, but it was no use. "I will die in mourning for my son," he would say, and then begin to weep.

[36]Meanwhile, in Egypt, the traders sold Joseph to Potiphar, an officer of Pharaoh, the king of Egypt. Potiphar was captain of the palace guard.

CHAPTER 38

About this time, Judah left home and moved to Adullam, where he visited a man named Hirah. [2]There he met a Canaanite woman, the daughter of Shua, and he married her. [3]She became pregnant and had a son, and Judah named the boy Er. [4]Then Judah's wife had another son, and she named him Onan. [5]And when she had a third son, she named him Shelah. At the time of Shelah's birth, they were living at Kezib.

[6]When his oldest son, Er, grew up, Judah arranged his marriage to a young woman named Tamar. [7]But Er was a wicked man in the LORD's sight, so the LORD took his life. [8]Then Judah said to Er's brother Onan, "You must marry Tamar, as our law requires of the brother of a man who has died. Her first son from you will be your brother's heir."

[9]But Onan was not willing to have a child who would not be his own heir. So whenever he had intercourse with Tamar, he spilled the semen on the ground to keep her from having a baby who would belong to his brother. [10]But the LORD considered it a wicked thing for Onan to deny a child to his dead brother. So the LORD took Onan's life, too.

[11]Then Judah told Tamar, his daughter-in-law, not to marry again at that time but to return to her parents' home. She was to remain a widow until his youngest son, Shelah, was old enough to marry her. (But Judah didn't really intend to do this because he was afraid Shelah would also die,

like his two brothers.) So Tamar went home to her parents.

[12]In the course of time Judah's wife died. After the time of mourning was over, Judah and his friend Hirah the Adullamite went to Timnah to supervise the shearing of his sheep. [13]Someone told Tamar that her father-in-law had left for the sheep-shearing at Timnah. [14]Tamar was aware that Shelah had grown up, but they had not called her to come and marry him. So she changed out of her widow's clothing and covered herself with a veil to disguise herself. Then she sat beside the road at the entrance to the village of Enaim, which is on the way to Timnah. [15]Judah noticed her as he went by and thought she was a prostitute, since her face was veiled. [16]So he stopped and propositioned her to sleep with him, not realizing that she was his own daughter-in-law.

"How much will you pay me?" Tamar asked.

[17]"I'll send you a young goat from my flock," Judah promised.

"What pledge will you give me so I can be sure you will send it?" she asked.

[18]"Well, what do you want?" he inquired.

She replied, "I want your identification seal, your cord, and the walking stick you are carrying." So Judah gave these items to her. She then let him sleep with her, and she became pregnant. [19]Afterward she went home, took off her veil, and put on her widow's clothing as usual.

[20]Judah asked his friend Hirah the Adullamite to take the young goat back to her and to pick up the pledges he had given her, but Hirah couldn't find her. [21]So he asked the men who lived there, "Where can I find the prostitute* who was sitting beside the road at the entrance to the village?"

"We've never had a prostitute here," they replied. [22]So Hirah returned to Judah and told him that he couldn't find her anywhere and that the men of the village had claimed they didn't have a prostitute there.

[23]"Then let her keep the pledges!" Judah exclaimed. "We tried our best to send her the goat. We'd be the laughingstock of the village if we went back again."

[24]About three months later, word reached Judah that Tamar, his daughter-in-

38:21 Hebrew *shrine prostitute;* also in 38:21b, 22.

law, was pregnant as a result of prostitution. "Bring her out and burn her!" Judah
shouted.

²⁵But as they were taking her out to kill
her, she sent this message to her father-in-
law: "The man who owns this identification seal and walking stick is the father of
my child. Do you recognize them?"

²⁶Judah admitted that they were his and
said, "She is more in the right than I am,
because I didn't keep my promise to let her
marry my son Shelah." But Judah never
slept with Tamar again.

²⁷In due season the time of Tamar's delivery arrived, and she had twin sons. ²⁸As
they were being born, one of them reached
out his hand, and the midwife tied a scarlet
thread around the wrist of the child who
appeared first, saying, "This one came out
first." ²⁹But then he drew back his hand,
and the other baby was actually the first to
be born. "What!" the midwife exclaimed.
"How did you break out first?" And ever
after, he was called Perez.* ³⁰Then the baby
with the scarlet thread on his wrist was
born, and he was named Zerah.*

CHAPTER 39
Now when Joseph arrived in Egypt with
the Ishmaelite traders, he was purchased
by Potiphar, a member of the personal staff
of Pharaoh, the king of Egypt. Potiphar
was the captain of the palace guard.

²The LORD was with Joseph and blessed
him greatly as he served in the home of his
Egyptian master. ³Potiphar noticed this
and realized that the LORD was with
Joseph, giving him success in everything
he did. ⁴So Joseph naturally became quite a
favorite with him. Potiphar soon put
Joseph in charge of his entire household
and entrusted him with all his business
dealings. ⁵From the day Joseph was put in
charge, the LORD began to bless Potiphar
for Joseph's sake. All his household affairs
began to run smoothly, and his crops and
livestock flourished. ⁶So Potiphar gave
Joseph complete administrative responsibility over everything he owned. With
Joseph there, he didn't have a worry in the
world, except to decide what he wanted to
eat!

Now Joseph was a very handsome and
well-built young man. ⁷And about this
time, Potiphar's wife began to desire him

and invited him to sleep with her. ⁸But
Joseph refused. "Look," he told her, "my
master trusts me with everything in his
entire household. ⁹No one here has more
authority than I do! He has held back nothing from me except you, because you are
his wife. How could I ever do such a
wicked thing? It would be a great sin
against God."

¹⁰She kept putting pressure on him day
after day, but he refused to sleep with her,
and he kept out of her way as much as
possible. ¹¹One day, however, no one else
was around when he was doing his work
inside the house. ¹²She came and grabbed
him by his shirt, demanding, "Sleep with
me!" Joseph tore himself away, but as he
did, his shirt came off. She was left holding
it as he ran from the house.

¹³When she saw that she had his shirt and
that he had fled, ¹⁴she began screaming.
Soon all the men around the place came
running. "My husband has brought this
Hebrew slave here to insult us!" she sobbed.
"He tried to rape me, but I screamed.
¹⁵When he heard my loud cries, he ran and
left his shirt behind with me."

¹⁶She kept the shirt with her, and when
her husband came home that night, ¹⁷she
told him her story. "That Hebrew slave
you've had around here tried to make a
fool of me," she said. ¹⁸"I was saved only
by my screams. He ran out, leaving his
shirt behind!"

¹⁹After hearing his wife's story, Potiphar
was furious! ²⁰He took Joseph and threw
him into the prison where the king's prisoners were held. ²¹But the LORD was with
Joseph there, too, and he granted Joseph
favor with the chief jailer. ²²Before long, the
jailer put Joseph in charge of all the other
prisoners and over everything that happened in the prison. ²³The chief jailer had
no more worries after that, because Joseph
took care of everything. The LORD was with
him, making everything run smoothly and
successfully.

CHAPTER 40
Some time later, Pharaoh's chief cup-bearer
and chief baker offended him. ²Pharaoh
became very angry with these officials,
³and he put them in the prison where
Joseph was, in the palace of Potiphar, the
captain of the guard. ⁴They remained in

38:29 *Perez* means "breaking out."   38:30 *Zerah* means "scarlet" or "brightness."

prison for quite some time, and Potiphar assigned Joseph to take care of them.

⁵One night the cup-bearer and the baker each had a dream, and each dream had its own meaning. ⁶The next morning Joseph noticed the dejected look on their faces. ⁷"Why do you look so worried today?" he asked.

⁸And they replied, "We both had dreams last night, but there is no one here to tell us what they mean."

"Interpreting dreams is God's business," Joseph replied. "Tell me what you saw."

⁹The cup-bearer told his dream first. "In my dream," he said, "I saw a vine in front of me. ¹⁰It had three branches that began to bud and blossom, and soon there were clusters of ripe grapes. ¹¹I was holding Pharaoh's wine cup in my hand, so I took the grapes and squeezed the juice into it. Then I placed the cup in Pharaoh's hand."

¹²"I know what the dream means," Joseph said. "The three branches mean three days. ¹³Within three days Pharaoh will take you out of prison and return you to your position as his chief cup-bearer. ¹⁴And please have some pity on me when you are back in his favor. Mention me to Pharaoh, and ask him to let me out of here. ¹⁵For I was kidnapped from my homeland, the land of the Hebrews, and now I'm here in jail, but I did nothing to deserve it."

¹⁶When the chief baker saw that the first dream had such a good meaning, he told his dream to Joseph, too. "In my dream," he said, "there were three baskets of pastries on my head. ¹⁷In the top basket were all kinds of bakery goods for Pharaoh, but the birds came and ate them."

¹⁸"I'll tell you what it means," Joseph told him. "The three baskets mean three days. ¹⁹Three days from now Pharaoh will cut off your head and impale your body on a pole. Then birds will come and peck away at your flesh."

²⁰Pharaoh's birthday came three days later, and he gave a banquet for all his officials and household staff. He sent for his chief cup-bearer and chief baker, and they were brought to him from the prison. ²¹He then restored the chief cup-bearer to his former position, ²²but he sentenced the chief baker to be impaled on a pole, just as Joseph had predicted. ²³Pharaoh's cup-bearer, however, promptly forgot all about Joseph, never giving him another thought.

JANUARY 14 ☐ DAY 14
A Faith That Stands the Test of Time

 LOOK BACK Buy a new appliance, and you'll be lucky to get a warranty with it that protects your purchase for ninety days. Buy a new car, and you might do a little better: five years or fifty thousand miles. But get ahold of the faith of Abraham, Isaac, Jacob, and Joseph, and you just might discover the genuine item that will endure for generations!

Over the past week you have read about the courageous faith of Abraham, who clung to the promises of God against all odds; the quiet faith of Isaac, who built altars, dug wells, and proclaimed the name of the Lord wherever he went; the struggling faith of Jacob, who wasn't content until he experienced God's blessing firsthand; and the patient faith of Joseph, whose confidence in God carried him literally from the pit to the palace. Four different men, four different sets of circumstances, but one thing in common: a faith in God that grew with the years.

 LOOK UP Definitions of faith are plentiful and at times helpful. Here are just a few. Faith is
- "Forsaking All, I Trust Him,"
- taking God at his Word,
- seeing the promises of God as present realities,
- living your life in such a way that it does not make sense unless God exists.

A faith that Genesis does more than define the faith of Abraham, Isaac, Jacob,
falters before and Joseph—it paints a portrait of faith in brush strokes of everyday
the finish living. Did you find yourself identifying with the struggles of Jacob?
was faulty yearning to know the God of Isaac? wishing your faith was as strong as
from the first. Abraham's? Then wait till you read the rest of Joseph's amazing story!
His faith in God will carry him through more than a decade in prison.

Faith is like a muscle that grows stronger through exercise. And the
exercise that builds a vibrant faith is the stress of facing daily circumstances with confidence in God.

Learning patience and persistence (like ninety-nine-year-old Abraham waiting for God to keep his promise); leaning on God to resolve a
bitter family feud (like Jacob seeking to be reunited with his estranged
brother, Esau); following God and doing what's right regardless of the
consequences (like Joseph, who ended up in the pit and in prison
through no fault of his own)—that's how to build a faith that stands
the test of time!

 LOOK AHEAD Perhaps you have been blessed with other models of
faith in your lifetime: a parent or family member who walked with God
for decades, a spiritual leader who practiced what he or she preached,
a friend or co-worker who talked to God in prayer as if God were in the
same room. Have you ever shared with that person what his or her
model of faith has meant to you? A note or phone call today would be
an excellent way to do so.

Models of faith are in short supply today, just as they were in
the days of the patriarchs. You can't get physically fit in a day, nor
can you develop the faith of a Jacob or a Joseph overnight. But
you can see your faith grow and deepen each day as you face life's
challenges in the strength of the Lord. Take one of those faith-
stretching circumstances or decisions you're facing right now, and
talk to your ever faithful God about it. Tell him that Abraham, Isaac,
Jacob, and Joseph sent you!

JANUARY 15 □ DAY 15
GENESIS 41–44
Joseph's Brothers in Egypt

 OVERVIEW During his imprisonment, Joseph gains a reputation as an
accurate interpreter of dreams. He is now called upon to use his God-
given ability to interpret the disturbing dreams of Pharaoh. Though
the interpretation is ominous, Pharaoh's response is overwhelming:
Joseph becomes prime minister of the land, with power second only to
Pharaoh himself! With a worldwide famine coming, Joseph becomes
Pharaoh's choice to administer a relief program to meet the challenge.
Joseph's new position allows him to confront his brothers with their
carefully concealed crime.

Chapter 41	Chapter 42	Chapter 43	Chapter 44
Joseph's Promotion	Jacob's Problem	Benjamin's Visit	Joseph's Vengeance
Faithfulness	Famine	Fear	Confession

YOUR DAILY WALK There are many skills you can learn in an after-noon: how to ride a bicycle, how to change the oil in your car, or how to bake a batch of cookies. Other skills take weeks to master: how to read a thousand words a minute, how to sing harmony, or how to drive a car. And then there are skills you will hone and develop for the rest of your life: how to work with people, how to study God's Word, or how to draw upon God's promises even when the circumstances aren't too promising.

It is possible to learn from an enemy things we can't learn from a friend.

Thirteen years of Joseph's life were spent in obscurity in Egypt. But they were not wasted years. God in his infinite wisdom knew that the man who emerged in chapter 41 would be different from the man who submerged in chapter 37.

It takes a world with trouble in it to train men and women for their high calling as children of God. Faced with trouble, some people (like Joseph) grow wings; others buy crutches. Which kind are you? Read Isaiah 40:31, and wherever you encounter the word *they*, substitute your own name. It's a promise aimed at you!

INSIGHT From Prison to Palace in One Day
At the tender age of seventeen, Joseph was sold into Egyptian slavery (37:2, 28). Thirteen years later he was in prison (41:46). But when the time was right, God promoted him from the prison to the palace . . . overnight! That's a much-needed reminder that God's "Graduate School of Growing" is seldom a one-year curriculum!

CHAPTER 41

Two years later, Pharaoh dreamed that he was standing on the bank of the Nile River. [2]In his dream, seven fat, healthy-looking cows suddenly came up out of the river and began grazing along its bank. [3]Then seven other cows came up from the river, but these were very ugly and gaunt. These cows went over and stood beside the fat cows. [4]Then the thin, ugly cows ate the fat ones! At this point in the dream, Pharaoh woke up.

[5]Soon he fell asleep again and had a second dream. This time he saw seven heads of grain on one stalk, with every kernel well formed and plump. [6]Then suddenly, seven more heads appeared on the stalk, but these were shriveled and withered by the east wind. [7]And these thin heads swallowed up the seven plump, well-formed heads! Then Pharaoh woke up again and realized it was a dream.

[8]The next morning, as he thought about it, Pharaoh became very concerned as to what the dreams might mean. So he called for all the magicians and wise men of Egypt and told them about his dreams, but not one of them could suggest what they meant. [9]Then the king's cup-bearer spoke up. "Today I have been reminded of my failure," he said. [10]"Some time ago, you were angry with the chief baker and me, and you imprisoned us in the palace of the captain of the guard. [11]One night the chief baker and I each had a dream, and each dream had a meaning. [12]We told the dreams to a young Hebrew man who was a servant of the captain of the guard. He told us what each of our dreams meant, [13]and everything happened just as he said it would. I was restored to my position as cup-bearer, and the chief baker was executed and impaled on a pole."

[14]Pharaoh sent for Joseph at once, and he was brought hastily from the dungeon. After a quick shave and change of clothes, he went in and stood in Pharaoh's presence. [15]"I had a dream last night," Pharaoh told him, "and none of these men can tell me what it means. But I have heard that you can interpret dreams, and that is why I have called for you."

[16]"It is beyond my power to do this," Joseph replied. "But God will tell you what it means and will set you at ease."

[17]So Pharaoh told him the dream. "I was standing on the bank of the Nile River," he said. [18]"Suddenly, seven fat, healthy-looking cows came up out of the river and began grazing along its bank. [19]But then seven other cows came up from the river. They were very thin and gaunt—in fact, I've never seen such ugly animals in all the land of Egypt. [20]These thin, ugly cows ate up the seven fat ones that had come out of the river first, [21]but afterward they were

still as ugly and gaunt as before! Then I woke up.

²²"A little later I had another dream. This time there were seven heads of grain on one stalk, and all seven heads were plump and full. ²³Then out of the same stalk came seven withered heads, shriveled by the east wind. ²⁴And the withered heads swallowed up the plump ones! I told these dreams to my magicians, but not one of them could tell me what they mean."

²⁵"Both dreams mean the same thing," Joseph told Pharaoh. "God was telling you what he is about to do. ²⁶The seven fat cows and the seven plump heads of grain both represent seven years of prosperity. ²⁷The seven thin, ugly cows and the seven withered heads of grain represent seven years of famine. ²⁸This will happen just as I have described it, for God has shown you what he is about to do. ²⁹The next seven years will be a period of great prosperity throughout the land of Egypt. ³⁰But afterward there will be seven years of famine so great that all the prosperity will be forgotten and wiped out. Famine will destroy the land. ³¹This famine will be so terrible that even the memory of the good years will be erased. ³²As for having the dream twice, it means that the matter has been decreed by God and that he will make these events happen soon.

³³"My suggestion is that you find the wisest man in Egypt and put him in charge of a nationwide program. ³⁴Let Pharaoh appoint officials over the land, and let them collect one-fifth of all the crops during the seven good years. ³⁵Have them gather all the food and grain of these good years into the royal storehouses, and store it away so there will be food in the cities. ³⁶That way there will be enough to eat when the seven years of famine come. Otherwise disaster will surely strike the land, and all the people will die."

³⁷Joseph's suggestions were well received by Pharaoh and his advisers. ³⁸As they discussed who should be appointed for the job, Pharaoh said, "Who could do it better than Joseph? For he is a man who is obviously filled with the spirit of God." ³⁹Turning to Joseph, Pharaoh said, "Since God has revealed the meaning of the dreams to you, you are the wisest man in the land! ⁴⁰I hereby appoint you to direct this project. You will manage my household and organize all my people. Only I will have a rank higher than yours."

⁴¹And Pharaoh said to Joseph, "I hereby put you in charge of the entire land of Egypt." ⁴²Then Pharaoh placed his own signet ring on Joseph's finger as a symbol of his authority. He dressed him in beautiful clothing and placed the royal gold chain about his neck. ⁴³Pharaoh also gave Joseph the chariot of his second-in-command, and wherever he went the command was shouted, "Kneel down!" So Joseph was put in charge of all Egypt. ⁴⁴And Pharaoh said to Joseph, "I am the king, but no one will move a hand or a foot in the entire land of Egypt without your approval."

⁴⁵Pharaoh renamed him Zaphenath-paneah* and gave him a wife—a young woman named Asenath, the daughter of Potiphera, priest of Heliopolis.* So Joseph took charge of the entire land of Egypt. ⁴⁶He was thirty years old when he entered the service of Pharaoh, the king of Egypt. And when Joseph left Pharaoh's presence, he made a tour of inspection throughout the land.

⁴⁷And sure enough, for the next seven years there were bumper crops everywhere. ⁴⁸During those years, Joseph took a portion of all the crops grown in Egypt and stored them for the government in nearby cities. ⁴⁹After seven years, the granaries were filled to overflowing. There was so much grain, like sand on the seashore, that the people could not keep track of the amount.

⁵⁰During this time, before the arrival of the first of the famine years, two sons were born to Joseph and his wife, Asenath, the daughter of Potiphera, priest of Heliopolis. ⁵¹Joseph named his older son Manasseh,* for he said, "God has made me forget all my troubles and the family of my father." ⁵²Joseph named his second son Ephraim,* for he said, "God has made me fruitful in this land of my suffering."

⁵³At last the seven years of plenty came to an end. ⁵⁴Then the seven years of famine began, just as Joseph had predicted. There were crop failures in all the surrounding countries, too, but in Egypt there was plenty of grain in the storehouses. ⁵⁵Throughout the land of Egypt the people

41:45a *Zaphenath-paneah* probably means "God speaks and lives." **41:45b** Hebrew *of On;* also in 41:50. **41:51** *Manasseh* sounds like a Hebrew term that means "causing to forget." **41:52** *Ephraim* sounds like a Hebrew term that means "fruitful."

began to starve. They pleaded with Pharaoh for food, and he told them, "Go to Joseph and do whatever he tells you." [56]So with severe famine everywhere in the land, Joseph opened up the storehouses and sold grain to the Egyptians. [57]And people from surrounding lands also came to Egypt to buy grain from Joseph because the famine was severe throughout the world.

CHAPTER 42
When Jacob heard that there was grain available in Egypt, he said to his sons, "Why are you standing around looking at one another? [2]I have heard there is grain in Egypt. Go down and buy some for us before we all starve to death." [3]So Joseph's ten older brothers went down to Egypt to buy grain. [4]Jacob wouldn't let Joseph's younger brother, Benjamin, go with them, however, for fear some harm might come to him. [5]So Jacob's* sons arrived in Egypt along with others to buy food, for the famine had reached Canaan as well.

[6]Since Joseph was governor of all Egypt and in charge of the sale of the grain, it was to him that his brothers came. They bowed low before him, with their faces to the ground. [7]Joseph recognized them instantly, but he pretended to be a stranger. "Where are you from?" he demanded roughly.

"From the land of Canaan," they replied. "We have come to buy grain."

[8]Joseph's brothers didn't recognize him, but Joseph recognized them. [9]And he remembered the dreams he had had many years before. He said to them, "You are spies! You have come to see how vulnerable our land has become."

[10]"No, my lord!" they exclaimed. "We have come to buy food. [11]We are all brothers and honest men, sir! We are not spies!"

[12]"Yes, you are!" he insisted. "You have come to discover how vulnerable the famine has made us."

[13]"Sir," they said, "there are twelve of us brothers, and our father is in the land of Canaan. Our youngest brother is there with our father, and one of our brothers is no longer with us."

[14]But Joseph insisted, "As I said, you are spies! [15]This is how I will test your story. I swear by the life of Pharaoh that you will not leave Egypt unless your youngest brother comes here. [16]One of you go and

get your brother! I'll keep the rest of you here, bound in prison. Then we'll find out whether or not your story is true. If it turns out that you don't have a younger brother, then I'll know you are spies."

[17]So he put them all in prison for three days. [18]On the third day Joseph said to them, "I am a God-fearing man. If you do as I say, you will live. [19]We'll see how honorable you really are. Only one of you will remain in the prison. The rest of you may go on home with grain for your families. [20]But bring your youngest brother back to me. In this way, I will know whether or not you are telling me the truth. If you are, I will spare you." To this they agreed.

[21]Speaking among themselves, they said, "This has all happened because of what we did to Joseph long ago. We saw his terror and anguish and heard his pleadings, but we wouldn't listen. That's why this trouble has come upon us."

[22]"Didn't I tell you not to do it?" Reuben asked. "But you wouldn't listen. And now we are going to die because we murdered him."

[23]Of course, they didn't know that Joseph understood them as he was standing there, for he had been speaking to them through an interpreter. [24]Now he left the room and found a place where he could weep. Returning, he talked some more with them. He then chose Simeon from among them and had him tied up right before their eyes.

[25]Joseph then ordered his servants to fill the men's sacks with grain, but he also gave secret instructions to return each brother's payment at the top of his sack. He also gave them provisions for their journey. [26]So they loaded up their donkeys with the grain and started for home.

[27]But when they stopped for the night and one of them opened his sack to get some grain to feed the donkeys, he found his money in the sack. [28]"Look!" he exclaimed to his brothers. "My money is here in my sack!" They were filled with terror and said to each other, "What has God done to us?" [29]So they came to their father, Jacob, in the land of Canaan and told him all that had happened.

[30]"The man who is ruler over the land spoke very roughly to us," they told him. "He took us for spies. [31]But we said, 'We

are honest men, not spies. [32]We are twelve brothers, sons of one father; one brother has disappeared, and the youngest is with our father in the land of Canaan.' [33]Then the man, the ruler of the land, told us, 'This is the way I will find out if you are honest men. Leave one of your brothers here with me, and take grain for your families and go on home. [34]But bring your youngest brother back to me. Then I will know that you are honest men and not spies. If you prove to be what you say, then I will give you back your brother, and you may come as often as you like to buy grain.'"

[35]As they emptied out the sacks, there at the top of each one was the bag of money paid for the grain. Terror gripped them, as it did their father. [36]Jacob exclaimed, "You have deprived me of my children! Joseph has disappeared, Simeon is gone, and now you want to take Benjamin, too. Everything is going against me!"

[37]Then Reuben said to his father, "You may kill my two sons if I don't bring Benjamin back to you. I'll be responsible for him."

[38]But Jacob replied, "My son will not go down with you, for his brother Joseph is dead, and he alone is left of his mother's children. If anything should happen to him, you would bring my gray head down to the grave in deep sorrow."

CHAPTER 43
But there was no relief from the terrible famine throughout the land. [2]When the grain they had brought from Egypt was almost gone, Jacob said to his sons, "Go again and buy us a little food."

[3]But Judah said, "The man wasn't joking when he warned that we couldn't see him again unless Benjamin came along. [4]If you let him come with us, we will go down and buy some food. [5]But if you don't let Benjamin go, we may as well stay at home. Remember that the man said, 'You won't be allowed to come and see me unless your brother is with you.'"

[6]"Why did you ever tell him you had another brother?" Jacob* moaned. "Why did you have to treat me with such cruelty?"

[7]"But the man specifically asked us about our family," they replied. "He wanted to know whether our father was still living, and he asked us if we had another brother so we told him. How could we have known he would say, 'Bring me your brother'?"

[8]Judah said to his father, "Send the boy with me, and we will be on our way. Otherwise we will all die of starvation—and not only we, but you and our little ones. [9]I personally guarantee his safety. If I don't bring him back to you, then let me bear the blame forever. [10]For we could have gone and returned twice by this time if you had let him come without delay."

[11]So their father, Jacob, finally said to them, "If it can't be avoided, then at least do this. Fill your bags with the best products of the land. Take them to the man as gifts—balm, honey, spices, myrrh, pistachio nuts, and almonds. [12]Take double the money that you found in your sacks, as it was probably someone's mistake. [13]Then take your brother and go back to the man. [14]May God Almighty give you mercy as you go before the man, that he might release Simeon and return Benjamin. And if I must bear the anguish of their deaths, then so be it."

[15]So they took Benjamin and the gifts and double the money and hurried to Egypt, where they presented themselves to Joseph. [16]When Joseph saw that Benjamin was with them, he said to the manager of his household, "These men will eat with me this noon. Take them inside and prepare a big feast." [17]So the man did as he was told and took them to Joseph's palace.

[18]They were badly frightened when they saw where they were being taken. "It's because of the money returned to us in our sacks," they said. "He plans to pretend that we stole it. Then he will seize us as slaves and take our donkeys."

[19]As the brothers arrived at the entrance to the palace, they went over to the man in charge of Joseph's household. [20]They said to him, "Sir, after our first trip to Egypt to buy food, [21]as we were returning home, we stopped for the night and opened our sacks. The money we had used to pay for the grain was there in our sacks. Here it is; we have brought it back again. [22]We also have additional money to buy more grain. We have no idea how the money got into our sacks."

[23]"Relax. Don't worry about it," the

43:6 Hebrew *Israel;* also in 43:11.

household manager told them. "Your God, the God of your ancestors, must have put it there. We collected your money all right." Then he released Simeon and brought him out to them.

²⁴The brothers were then led into the palace and given water to wash their feet and food for their donkeys. ²⁵They were told they would be eating there, so they prepared their gifts for Joseph's arrival at noon.

²⁶When Joseph came, they gave him their gifts and bowed low before him. ²⁷He asked them how they had been getting along, and then he said, "How is your father—the old man you spoke about? Is he still alive?"

²⁸"Yes," they replied. "He is alive and well." Then they bowed again before him.

²⁹Looking at his brother Benjamin, Joseph asked, "Is this your youngest brother, the one you told me about? May God be gracious to you, my son." ³⁰Then Joseph made a hasty exit because he was overcome with emotion for his brother and wanted to cry. Going into his private room, he wept there. ³¹Then he washed his face and came out, keeping himself under control. "Bring on the food!" he ordered.

³²Joseph ate by himself, and his brothers were served at a separate table. The Egyptians sat at their own table because Egyptians despise Hebrews and refuse to eat with them. ³³Joseph told each of his brothers where to sit, and to their amazement, he seated them in the order of their ages, from oldest to youngest. ³⁴Their food was served to them from Joseph's own table. He gave the largest serving to Benjamin—five times as much as to any of the others. So they all feasted and drank freely with him.

CHAPTER 44
When his brothers were ready to leave, Joseph gave these instructions to the man in charge of his household: "Fill each of their sacks with as much grain as they can carry, and put each man's money back into his sack. ²Then put my personal silver cup at the top of the youngest brother's sack, along with his grain money." So the household manager did as he was told.

³The brothers were up at dawn and set out on their journey with their loaded donkeys. ⁴But when they were barely out of the city, Joseph said to his household manager,

"Chase after them and stop them. Ask them, 'Why have you repaid an act of kindness with such evil? ⁵What do you mean by stealing my master's personal silver drinking cup, which he uses to predict the future? What a wicked thing you have done!'"

⁶So the man caught up with them and spoke to them in the way he had been instructed. ⁷"What are you talking about?" the brothers responded. "What kind of people do you think we are, that you accuse us of such a terrible thing? ⁸Didn't we bring back the money we found in our sacks? Why would we steal silver or gold from your master's house? ⁹If you find his cup with any one of us, let that one die. And all the rest of us will be your master's slaves forever."

¹⁰"Fair enough," the man replied, "except that only the one who stole it will be a slave. The rest of you may go free."

¹¹They quickly took their sacks from the backs of their donkeys and opened them. ¹²Joseph's servant began searching the oldest brother's sack, going on down the line to the youngest. The cup was found in Benjamin's sack! ¹³At this, they tore their clothing in despair, loaded the donkeys again, and returned to the city. ¹⁴Joseph was still at home when Judah and his brothers arrived, and they fell to the ground before him.

¹⁵"What were you trying to do?" Joseph demanded. "Didn't you know that a man such as I would know who stole it?"

¹⁶And Judah said, "Oh, my lord, what can we say to you? How can we plead? How can we prove our innocence? God is punishing us for our sins. My lord, we have all returned to be your slaves—we and our brother who had your cup in his sack."

¹⁷"No," Joseph said. "Only the man who stole the cup will be my slave. The rest of you may go home to your father."

¹⁸Then Judah stepped forward and said, "My lord, let me say just this one word to you. Be patient with me for a moment, for I know you could have me killed in an instant, as though you were Pharaoh himself.

¹⁹"You asked us, my lord, if we had a father or a brother. ²⁰We said, 'Yes, we have a father, an old man, and a child of his old age, his youngest son. His brother is dead, and he alone is left of his mother's children, and his father loves him very much.' ²¹And

you said to us, 'Bring him here so I can see him.' ²²But we said to you, 'My lord, the boy cannot leave his father, for his father would die.' ²³But you told us, 'You may not see me again unless your youngest brother is with you.' ²⁴So we returned to our father and told him what you had said. ²⁵And when he said, 'Go back again and buy us a little food,' ²⁶we replied, 'We can't unless you let our youngest brother go with us. We won't be allowed to see the man in charge of the grain unless our youngest brother is with us.' ²⁷Then my father said to us, 'You know that my wife had two sons, ²⁸and that one of them went away and never returned—doubtless torn to pieces by some wild animal. I have never seen him since. ²⁹If you take away his brother

from me, too, and any harm comes to him, you would bring my gray head down to the grave in deep sorrow.'

³⁰"And now, my lord, I cannot go back to my father without the boy. Our father's life is bound up in the boy's life. ³¹When he sees that the boy is not with us, our father will die. We will be responsible for bringing his gray head down to the grave in sorrow. ³²My lord, I made a pledge to my father that I would take care of the boy. I told him, 'If I don't bring him back to you, I will bear the blame forever.' ³³Please, my lord, let me stay here as a slave instead of the boy, and let the boy return with his brothers. ³⁴For how can I return to my father if the boy is not with me? I cannot bear to see what this would do to him."

JANUARY 16 ☐ DAY 16
GENESIS 45 – 47
Joseph's Family United in Egypt

OVERVIEW Today's reading contains the exciting conclusion to the story of Joseph and his unsuspecting brothers. After twice planting evidence on his brothers that would ensure their return to Egypt, Joseph cannot contain his secret any longer. In an emotion-packed scene, he reveals that he is the brother they sold into slavery and left for dead. But Joseph doesn't get revenge for their ill treatment of him. Instead he shows kindness to his brothers, acknowledging that God was behind it all to bring much good out of his difficult circumstances. As a result of Joseph's actions, his father, Jacob, moves to Egypt to spend his remaining years with his united family.

Chapter 45	Chapter 46	Chapter 47
Joseph's Surprise Announcement	Jacob's Move to Egypt	Jacob's Exaltation in Egypt
Joseph's Family Reunited	Joseph's Family Treated Kindly	

We should be thankful that God always turns out to be bigger than we thought.

YOUR DAILY WALK *Sovereignty* is a big word, but it is also a biblical concept that touches your life every day. God is sovereign. That means nothing takes him by surprise. Every experience in life, from the most pleasant to the most painful, has been allowed by God for a very special purpose. Joseph learned this important truth, although it took years of mistreatment to drive the point home. Addressing his brothers who sold him, he declared, "Yes, it was God who sent me here, not you" (45:8). God was at work even then.

Think back over your life and select one event that stands out as a time when it appeared that God had lost control of the situation. Perhaps it was a death in the family or the loss of a job or an unexpected accident. Now across that painful memory, mentally write the words,

"God was there." Write out a definition of sovereignty in your own words, and make it speak to your own situation. (For example: "Sovereignty means that God had a purpose in my recent job loss. He hasn't forgotten about me; he just has something better in store!")

 INSIGHT Why God Moved the Israelites to Egypt
It is not difficult to see the divine wisdom in moving Jacob's family to Egypt. In Egypt the Israelites would have to remain a separate, distinct people, for Jacob and his sons were shepherds, an abominable occupation to Egyptians and thus a natural barrier to intermarriage. For four hundred years the Israelites would multiply under these ideal conditions.

CHAPTER 45

Joseph could stand it no longer. "Out, all of you!" he cried out to his attendants. He wanted to be alone with his brothers when he told them who he was. ²Then he broke down and wept aloud. His sobs could be heard throughout the palace, and the news was quickly carried to Pharaoh's palace.

³"I am Joseph!" he said to his brothers. "Is my father still alive?" But his brothers were speechless! They were stunned to realize that Joseph was standing there in front of them. ⁴"Come over here," he said. So they came closer. And he said again, "I am Joseph, your brother whom you sold into Egypt. ⁵But don't be angry with yourselves that you did this to me, for God did it. He sent me here ahead of you to preserve your lives. ⁶These two years of famine will grow to seven, during which there will be neither plowing nor harvest. ⁷God has sent me here to keep you and your families alive so that you will become a great nation. ⁸Yes, it was God who sent me here, not you! And he has made me a counselor to Pharaoh—manager of his entire household and ruler over all Egypt.

⁹"Hurry, return to my father and tell him, 'This is what your son Joseph says: God has made me master over all the land of Egypt. Come down to me right away! ¹⁰You will live in the land of Goshen so you can be near me with all your children and grandchildren, your flocks and herds, and all that you have. ¹¹I will take care of you there, for there are still five years of famine ahead of us. Otherwise you and your household will come to utter poverty.'"

¹²Then Joseph said, "You can see for yourselves, and so can my brother Benjamin, that I really am Joseph! ¹³Tell my father how I am honored here in Egypt. Tell him about everything you have seen, and bring him to me quickly." ¹⁴Weeping with joy, he embraced Benjamin, and Benjamin also began to weep. ¹⁵Then Joseph kissed each of his brothers and wept over them, and then they began talking freely with him.

¹⁶The news soon reached Pharaoh: "Joseph's brothers have come!" Pharaoh was very happy to hear this and so were his officials.

¹⁷Pharaoh said to Joseph, "Tell your brothers to load their pack animals and return quickly to their homes in Canaan. ¹⁸Tell them to bring your father and all of their families, and to come here to Egypt to live. Tell them, 'Pharaoh will assign to you the very best territory in the land of Egypt. You will live off the fat of the land!' ¹⁹And tell your brothers to take wagons from Egypt to carry their wives and little ones and to bring your father here. ²⁰Don't worry about your belongings, for the best of all the land of Egypt is yours."

²¹So the sons of Jacob* did as they were told. Joseph gave them wagons, as Pharaoh had commanded, and he supplied them with provisions for the journey. ²²And he gave each of them new clothes—but to Benjamin he gave five changes of clothes and three hundred pieces* of silver! ²³He sent his father ten donkeys loaded with the good things of Egypt, and ten donkeys loaded with grain and all kinds of other food to be eaten on his journey. ²⁴So he sent his brothers off, and as they left, he called after them, "Don't quarrel along the way!" ²⁵And they left Egypt and returned to their father, Jacob, in the land of Canaan.

²⁶"Joseph is still alive!" they told him. "And he is ruler over all the land of Egypt!" Jacob was stunned at the news—he couldn't believe it. ²⁷But when they had given him Joseph's messages, and when he saw the wagons loaded with the food sent by Joseph, his spirit revived.

45:21 Hebrew *Israel;* also in 45:28.   45:22 Hebrew *300 shekels,* about 7.5 pounds or 3.4 kilograms in weight.

²⁸Then Jacob said, "It must be true! My son Joseph is alive! I will go and see him before I die."

CHAPTER 46

So Jacob* set out for Egypt with all his possessions. And when he came to Beersheba, he offered sacrifices to the God of his father, Isaac. ²During the night God spoke to him in a vision. "Jacob! Jacob!" he called.

"Here I am," Jacob replied.

³"I am God," the voice said, "the God of your father. Do not be afraid to go down to Egypt, for I will see to it that you become a great nation there. ⁴I will go with you down to Egypt, and I will bring your descendants back again. But you will die in Egypt with Joseph at your side."

⁵So Jacob left Beersheba, and his sons brought him to Egypt. They carried their little ones and wives in the wagons Pharaoh had provided for them. ⁶They brought their livestock, too, and all the belongings they had acquired in the land of Canaan. Jacob and his entire family arrived in Egypt— ⁷sons and daughters, grandsons and granddaughters—all his descendants.

⁸These are the names of the Israelites, the descendants of Jacob, who went with him to Egypt:

Reuben was Jacob's oldest son. ⁹The sons of Reuben were Hanoch, Pallu, Hezron, and Carmi.

¹⁰The sons of Simeon were Jemuel, Jamin, Ohad, Jakin, Zohar, and Shaul. (Shaul's mother was a Canaanite woman.)

¹¹The sons of Levi were Gershon, Kohath, and Merari.

¹²The sons of Judah were Er, Onan, Shelah, Perez, and Zerah. (But Er and Onan had died in the land of Canaan.) The sons of Perez were Hezron and Hamul.

¹³The sons of Issachar were Tola, Puah,* Jashub,* and Shimron.

¹⁴The sons of Zebulun were Sered, Elon, and Jahleel.

¹⁵These are the sons of Jacob who were born to Leah in Paddan-aram, along with their sister, Dinah. In all, Jacob's descendants through Leah numbered thirty-three.

¹⁶The sons of Gad were Zephon,* Haggi, Shuni, Ezbon, Eri, Arodi, and Areli.

¹⁷The sons of Asher were Imnah, Ishvah, Ishvi, and Beriah. Their sister was named Serah. Beriah's sons were Heber and Malkiel.

¹⁸These sixteen were descendants of Jacob through Zilpah, the servant given to Leah by her father, Laban.

¹⁹The sons of Jacob's wife Rachel were Joseph and Benjamin.

²⁰Joseph's sons, born in the land of Egypt, were Manasseh and Ephraim. Their mother was Asenath, daughter of Potiphera, priest of Heliopolis.*

²¹Benjamin's sons were Bela, Beker, Ashbel, Gera, Naaman, Ehi, Rosh, Muppim, Huppim, and Ard.

²²These fourteen were the descendants of Jacob and his wife Rachel.

²³The son of Dan was Hushim.

²⁴The sons of Naphtali were Jahzeel, Guni, Jezer, and Shillem.

²⁵These seven were the descendants of Jacob through Bilhah, the servant given to Rachel by her father, Laban.

²⁶So the total number of Jacob's direct descendants who went with him to Egypt, not counting his sons' wives, was sixty-six. ²⁷Joseph also had two sons* who had been born in Egypt. So altogether, there were seventy* members of Jacob's family in the land of Egypt.

²⁸Jacob sent Judah on ahead to meet Joseph and get directions to the land of Goshen. And when they all arrived there, ²⁹Joseph prepared his chariot and traveled to Goshen to meet his father. As soon as Joseph arrived, he embraced his father and wept on his shoulder for a long time. ³⁰Then Jacob said to Joseph, "Now let me die, for I have seen you with my own eyes and know you are still alive."

³¹And Joseph said to his brothers and to all their households, "I'll go and tell Pharaoh that you have all come from the land of Canaan to join me. ³²And I will tell him, 'These men are shepherds and livestock breeders. They have brought with them their flocks and herds and everything they

---

46:1 Hebrew *Israel*; also in 46:30.   46:13a As in Syriac version and Samaritan Pentateuch (see also 1 Chr 7:1); Hebrew reads *Puvah*.   46:13b As in some Greek manuscripts and Samaritan Pentateuch (see also Num 26:24; 1 Chr 7:1); Hebrew reads *Iob*.
46:16 As in Greek version and Samaritan Pentateuch (see also Num 26:15); Hebrew reads *Ziphion*.   46:20 Hebrew *of On*.
46:27a Greek version reads *nine sons*, probably including Joseph's grandsons through Ephraim and Manasseh (see 1 Chr 7:14-20).
46:27b Greek version reads *seventy-five*; see note on Exod 1:5.

own.' ³³So when Pharaoh calls for you and asks you about your occupation, ³⁴tell him, 'We have been livestock breeders from our youth, as our ancestors have been for many generations.' When you tell him this, he will let you live here in the land of Goshen, for shepherds are despised in the land of Egypt."

CHAPTER 47

So Joseph went to see Pharaoh and said, "My father and my brothers are here from Canaan. They came with all their flocks and herds and possessions, and they are now in the land of Goshen."

²Joseph took five of his brothers with him and presented them to Pharaoh. ³Pharaoh asked them, "What is your occupation?"

And they replied, "We are shepherds like our ancestors. ⁴We have come to live here in Egypt, for there is no pasture for our flocks in Canaan. The famine is very severe there. We request permission to live in the land of Goshen."

⁵And Pharaoh said to Joseph, "Now that your family has joined you here, ⁶choose any place you like for them to live. Give them the best land of Egypt—the land of Goshen will be fine. And if any of them have special skills, put them in charge of my livestock, too."

⁷Then Joseph brought his father, Jacob, and presented him to Pharaoh, and Jacob blessed Pharaoh. ⁸"How old are you?" Pharaoh asked him.

⁹Jacob replied, "I have lived for 130 hard years, but I am still not nearly as old as many of my ancestors." ¹⁰Then Jacob blessed Pharaoh again before he left.

¹¹So Joseph assigned the best land of Egypt—the land of Rameses—to his father and brothers, just as Pharaoh had commanded. ¹²And Joseph furnished food to his father and brothers in amounts appropriate to the number of their dependents.

¹³Meanwhile, the famine became worse and worse, and the crops continued to fail throughout Egypt and Canaan. ¹⁴Joseph collected all the money in Egypt and Canaan in exchange for grain, and he brought the money to Pharaoh's treasure-house. ¹⁵When the people of Egypt and Canaan ran out of money, they came to Joseph crying again for food. "Our money is gone," they said, "but give us bread. Why should we die?"

¹⁶"Well, then," Joseph replied, "since your money is gone, give me your livestock. I will give you food in exchange." ¹⁷So they gave their livestock to Joseph in exchange for food. Soon all the horses, flocks, herds, and donkeys of Egypt were in Pharaoh's possession. But at least they were able to purchase food for that year.

¹⁸The next year they came again and said, "Our money is gone, and our livestock are yours. We have nothing left but our bodies and land. ¹⁹Why should we die before your very eyes? Buy us and our land in exchange for food; we will then become servants to Pharaoh. Just give us grain so that our lives may be saved and so the land will not become empty and desolate."

²⁰So Joseph bought all the land of Egypt for Pharaoh. All the Egyptians sold him their fields because the famine was so severe, and their land then belonged to Pharaoh. ²¹Thus, all the people of Egypt became servants to Pharaoh.* ²²The only land he didn't buy was that belonging to the priests, for they were assigned food from Pharaoh and didn't need to sell their land.

²³Then Joseph said to the people, "See, I have bought you and your land for Pharaoh. I will provide you with seed, so you can plant the fields. ²⁴Then when you harvest it, a fifth of your crop will belong to Pharaoh. Keep four-fifths for yourselves, and use it to plant the next year's crop and to feed yourselves, your households, and your little ones."

²⁵"You have saved our lives!" they exclaimed. "May it please you, sir, to let us be Pharaoh's servants." ²⁶Joseph then made it a law throughout the land of Egypt—and it is still the law—that Pharaoh should receive one-fifth of all the crops grown on his land. But since Pharaoh had not taken over the priests' land, they were exempt from this payment.

²⁷So the people of Israel settled in the land of Goshen in Egypt. And before long, they began to prosper there, and their population grew rapidly. ²⁸Jacob lived for seventeen years after his arrival in Egypt, so he was 147 years old when he died. ²⁹As the time of his death drew near, he called for his son Joseph and said to him, "If you are pleased with me,

47:21 As in Greek version and Samaritan Pentateuch; Hebrew reads *He moved the people into the towns throughout the land of Egypt.*

swear most solemnly that you will honor this, my last request: Do not bury me in Egypt. ³⁰When I am dead, take me out of Egypt and bury me beside my ancestors." So

Joseph promised that he would. ³¹"Swear that you will do it," Jacob insisted. So Joseph gave his oath, and Jacob* bowed in worship as he leaned on his staff.*

47:31a Hebrew *Israel.*   47:31b As in Greek version; Hebrew reads *bowed in worship at the head of his bed.*

JANUARY 17 □ DAY 17
GENESIS 48 – 50
The Last Days of Jacob and Joseph

 OVERVIEW As Jacob's life in Egypt draws to a close, he summons Joseph's two sons and blesses them, exalting the younger, Ephraim, over the older, Manasseh. As his final act, Jacob prophetically outlines the future of his twelve sons. His desire for burial in Canaan testifies that the destiny of the nation still lies in the Promised Land. Joseph also dies after a faithful and prosperous life and adds his testimony that God will one day liberate his people.

Chapter 48	Chapter 49	Chapter 50	
Blessing the Sons of Joseph	Blessing the Sons of Jacob	Death and Burial of Jacob	Death and Burial of Joseph
1		21 22	26
Last Words		Last Resting Place	

 YOUR DAILY WALK On a scale of one to ten (with one being low and ten high), rate yourself on the following two statements:

For most of us, forgiveness comes easily. . . after we've gotten even.

- I am a forgiving person.
- I am quick to forget offenses against me.

You've probably heard the phrase "I'll forgive, but I won't forget." That's really just another way of saying, "I won't forgive." For true forgiveness involves totally putting out of our mind the wrong suffered. That's the way God forgives (Ephesians 4:32), and his brand of forgiveness is the model he expects us to follow as well.

Joseph exhibited the quality of full forgiveness with his brothers. After Jacob's death, the brothers feared revenge (50:15) even though Joseph had already forgiven them. Their pleas for mercy moved him to tears as he reassured his brothers that he had totally forgiven them.

If you have experienced God's forgiveness in Christ, you have the greatest motivation possible for forgiving others. In what relationships have you *forgiven* but not *forgotten* an offense against you? Talk to God about it right now. Thank him for the peace that only total forgiveness can bring. Then phone, write, or visit the offending party and share your newfound victory.

 INSIGHT "A Moving Epitaph" for Jacob and Joseph
Joseph's care in honoring his father Jacob's dying request to be buried in Canaan (49:29-30) was duplicated by Moses hundreds of years later. Moses carried out Joseph's last wish by transporting his remains back to Canaan (Exodus 13:19).

CHAPTER 48
One day not long after this, word came to Joseph that his father was failing rapidly. So Joseph went to visit him, and he took with him his two sons, Manasseh and Ephraim. [2]When Jacob heard that Joseph had arrived, he gathered his strength and sat up in bed to greet him.

[3]Jacob said to Joseph, "God Almighty appeared to me at Luz in the land of Canaan and blessed me. [4]He said to me, 'I will make you a multitude of nations, and I will give this land of Canaan to you and your descendants as an everlasting possession.' [5]Now I am adopting as my own sons these two boys of yours, Ephraim and Manasseh, who were born here in the land of Egypt before I arrived. They will inherit from me just as Reuben and Simeon will. [6]But the children born to you in the future will be your own. The land they inherit will be within the territories of Ephraim and Manasseh. [7]As I was returning from Paddan, Rachel died in the land of Canaan. We were still on the way, just a short distance from Ephrath (that is, Bethlehem). So with great sorrow I buried her there beside the road to Ephrath."

[8]Then Jacob* looked over at the two boys. "Are these your sons?" he asked.

[9]"Yes," Joseph told him, "these are the sons God has given me here in Egypt."

And Jacob said, "Bring them over to me, and I will bless them."

[10]Now Jacob was half blind because of his age and could hardly see. So Joseph brought the boys close to him, and Jacob kissed and embraced them. [11]Then Jacob said to Joseph, "I never thought I would see you again, but now God has let me see your children, too."

[12]Joseph took the boys from their grandfather's knees, and he bowed low to him. [13]Then he positioned the boys so Ephraim was at Jacob's left hand and Manasseh was at his right hand. [14]But Jacob crossed his arms as he reached out to lay his hands on the boys' heads. So his right hand was on the head of Ephraim, the younger boy, and his left hand was on the head of Manasseh, the older.

[15]Then he blessed Joseph and said, "May God, the God before whom my grandfather Abraham and my father, Isaac, walked, the God who has been my shepherd all my life, [16]and the angel who has kept me from all harm—may he bless these boys. May they preserve my name and the names of my grandfather Abraham and my father, Isaac. And may they become a mighty nation."

[17]But Joseph was upset when he saw that his father had laid his right hand on Ephraim's head. So he lifted it to place it on Manasseh's head instead. [18]"No, Father," he said, "this one over here is older. Put your right hand on his head."

[19]But his father refused. "I know what I'm doing, my son," he said. "Manasseh, too, will become a great people, but his younger brother will become even greater. His descendants will become a multitude of nations!" [20]So Jacob blessed the boys that day with this blessing: "The people of Israel will use your names to bless each other. They will say, 'May God make you as prosperous as Ephraim and Manasseh.'" In this way, Jacob put Ephraim ahead of Manasseh.

[21]Then Jacob said to Joseph, "I am about to die, but God will be with you and will bring you again to Canaan, the land of your ancestors. [22]And I give you an extra portion* beyond what I have given your brothers—the portion that I took from the Amorites with my sword and bow."

CHAPTER 49
Then Jacob called together all his sons and said, "Gather around me, and I will tell you what is going to happen to you in the days to come.

[2]   "Come and listen, O sons of Jacob;
        listen to Israel, your father.

[3]   "Reuben, you are my oldest son,
        the child of my vigorous youth.
     You are first on the list in rank and
        honor.
[4]   But you are as unruly as the waves of
        the sea,
     and you will be first no longer.
   For you slept with one of my wives;
        you dishonored me in my own bed.

[5]   "Simeon and Levi are two of a kind—
        men of violence.
[6]   O my soul, stay away from them.
     May I never be a party to their
        wicked plans.
   For in their anger they murdered men,
        and they crippled oxen just for sport.

48:8 Hebrew *Israel;* also in 48:10, 11, 13, 14, 21.   48:22 Or *give you the ridge of land.* The meaning of the Hebrew is uncertain.

7 Cursed be their anger, for it is fierce;
    cursed be their wrath, for it is cruel.
Therefore, I will scatter their
            descendants
    throughout the nation of Israel.

8 "Judah, your brothers will praise you.
    You will defeat your enemies.
    All your relatives will bow before
            you.
9 Judah is a young lion
    that has finished eating its prey.
Like a lion he crouches and lies down;
    like a lioness—who will dare to
            rouse him?
10 The scepter will not depart from Judah,
    nor the ruler's staff from his
            descendants,
until the coming of the one to whom it
            belongs,*
    the one whom all nations will obey.
11 He ties his foal to a grapevine,
    the colt of his donkey to a choice vine.
He washes his clothes in wine
    because his harvest is so plentiful.
12 His eyes are darker than wine,
    and his teeth are whiter than milk.

13 "Zebulun will settle on the shores of
            the sea
    and will be a harbor for ships;
    his borders will extend to Sidon.
14 "Issachar is a strong beast of burden,
    resting among the sheepfolds.*
15 When he sees how good the country-
            side is,
    how pleasant the land,
he will bend his shoulder to the task
    and submit to forced labor.

16 "Dan will govern his people
    like any other tribe in Israel.
17 He will be a snake beside the road,
    a poisonous viper along the path,
that bites the horse's heels
    so the rider is thrown off.
18 I trust in you for salvation, O LORD!

19 "Gad will be plundered by marauding
            bands,
    but he will turn and plunder them.

20 "Asher will produce rich foods,
    food fit for kings.

21 "Naphtali is a deer let loose,
    producing magnificent fawns.

22 "Joseph is a fruitful tree,
    a fruitful tree beside a fountain.
    His branches reach over the wall.
23 He has been attacked by archers,
    who shot at him and harassed him.
24 But his bow remained strong,
    and his arms were strengthened
by the Mighty One of Jacob,
    the Shepherd, the Rock of Israel.
25 May the God of your ancestors help
            you;
    may the Almighty bless you
with the blessings of the heavens above,
    blessings of the earth beneath,
    and blessings of the breasts and
            womb.
26 May the blessings of your ancestors
    be greater than the blessings of the
            eternal mountains,
    reaching to the utmost bounds of
            the everlasting hills.
These blessings will fall on the head
            of Joseph,
    who is a prince among his brothers.

27 "Benjamin is a wolf that prowls.
    He devours his enemies in the
            morning,
    and in the evening he divides the
            plunder."

28 These are the twelve tribes of Israel, and these are the blessings with which Jacob* blessed his twelve sons. Each received a blessing that was appropriate to him.

29 Then Jacob told them, "Soon I will die. Bury me with my father and grandfather in the cave in Ephron's field. 30 This is the cave in the field of Machpelah, near Mamre in Canaan, which Abraham bought from Ephron the Hittite for a permanent burial place. 31 There Abraham and his wife Sarah are buried. There Isaac and his wife, Rebekah, are buried. And there I buried Leah. 32 It is the cave that my grandfather Abraham bought from the Hittites." 33 Then when Jacob had finished this charge to his sons, he lay back in the bed, breathed his last, and died.

CHAPTER 50

Joseph threw himself on his father and wept over him and kissed him. 2 Then Joseph told his morticians to embalm the body. 3 The embalming process took forty days, and there was a period of national mourning for seventy days. [4]When the period of mourning was over, Joseph approached Pharaoh's advisers and asked them to speak to Pharaoh on his behalf. [5]He told them, "Tell Pharaoh that my father made me swear an oath. He said to me, 'I am about to die; take my body back to the land of Canaan, and bury me in our family's burial cave.' Now I need to go and bury my father. After his burial is complete, I will return without delay."

[6]Pharaoh agreed to Joseph's request. "Go and bury your father, as you promised," he said. [7]So Joseph went, with a great number of Pharaoh's counselors and advisers—all the senior officers of Egypt. [8]Joseph also took his brothers and the entire household of Jacob. But they left their little children and flocks and herds in the land of Goshen. [9]So a great number of chariots, cavalry, and people accompanied Joseph.

[10]When they arrived at the threshing floor of Atad, near the Jordan River, they held a very great and solemn funeral, with a seven-day period of mourning for Joseph's father. [11]The local residents, the Canaanites, renamed the place Abel-mizraim,* for they said, "This is a place of very deep mourning for these Egyptians." [12]So Jacob's sons did as he had commanded them. [13]They carried his body to the land of Canaan and buried it there in the cave of Machpelah. This is the cave that Abraham had bought for a permanent burial place in the field of Ephron the Hittite, near Mamre.

[14]Then Joseph returned to Egypt with his brothers and all who had accompanied him to his father's funeral. [15]But now that their father was dead, Joseph's brothers be-

came afraid. "Now Joseph will pay us back for all the evil we did to him," they said. [16]So they sent this message to Joseph: "Before your father died, he instructed us [17]to say to you: 'Forgive your brothers for the great evil they did to you.' So we, the servants of the God of your father, beg you to forgive us." When Joseph received the message, he broke down and wept. [18]Then his brothers came and bowed low before him. "We are your slaves," they said.

[19]But Joseph told them, "Don't be afraid of me. Am I God, to judge and punish you? [20]As far as I am concerned, God turned into good what you meant for evil. He brought me to the high position I have today so I could save the lives of many people. [21]No, don't be afraid. Indeed, I myself will take care of you and your families." And he spoke very kindly to them, reassuring them.

[22]So Joseph and his brothers and their families continued to live in Egypt. Joseph was 110 years old when he died. [23]He lived to see three generations of descendants of his son Ephraim and the children of Manasseh's son Makir, who were treated as if they were his own.

[24]"Soon I will die," Joseph told his brothers, "but God will surely come for you, to lead you out of this land of Egypt. He will bring you back to the land he vowed to give to the descendants of Abraham, Isaac, and Jacob."

[25]Then Joseph made the sons of Israel swear an oath, and he said, "When God comes to lead us back to Canaan, you must take my body back with you." [26]So Joseph died at the age of 110. They embalmed him, and his body was placed in a coffin in Egypt.

50:11 *Abel-mizraim* means "mourning of the Egyptians."

Exodus

DURING the nearly four hundred years since the close of Genesis, the descendants of the patriarchal family have experienced good news and bad news. The good news: They have grown into a nation numbering several million. The bad news: They have become oppressed slaves in the land of Egypt. Exodus is thus the story of redemption from slavery under Pharaoh through a covenant relationship with God. From Egypt to Sinai, Israel learns of the might and power of God, and of the importance of national worship.

Focus	Slavery		Salvation				Sanctification			
Divisions	Birth of Moses	Call of Moses	Conflict with Pharaoh	Exodus from Egypt	Red Sea Crossing	Journey to Sinai	Law and Ceremonies	Tabernacle Blueprint	Gold Calf	Tabernacle Dedication
	1	2 3	6 7	10 11	12 13	15 16	18 19	24 25	31 32	34 35 40
Topic	Deliverance from Oppression						Preparation for Worship			
	Getting Israel Out of Egypt						Getting Egypt Out of Israel			
Place	In Egypt		On the March				At Sinai			
Time	430 Years (15% of Exodus)		2 Months (30% of Exodus)				10 Months (55% of Exodus)			

JANUARY 18 ☐ DAY 18
EXODUS 1–2
Birth of Moses

OVERVIEW Exodus opens where Genesis leaves off: with Jacob's descendants multiplying in Egypt. A new ruler emerges who respects neither Joseph's memory nor the Israelites' human rights. Though Pharaoh attempts to kill all newborn Hebrew males, the infant Moses is providentially spared and raised in the very palace of the one who sought his death! At the age of forty Moses seeks to bring about the right thing (deliverance) in the wrong way (murder) and spends the next four decades of his life in exile, tending sheep in the Midian wilderness.

Chapter 1		Chapter 2		
Israel's Multiplication	Pharaoh's Mistreatment	Faith of Parents	Failure of Moses	Faithfulness of God
1 7	8 22	1 10	11 22	23 25
People Prepared for Deliverance		Deliverer Prepared for People		

YOUR DAILY WALK The man sitting by the well was lost in his thoughts. Dejection on every line of his face, he felt much older than his forty years. Moses was miserable—and with good reason.

Our God has a big eraser.

He had been the one man in all of Egypt who might have had a chance to bring relief to his people. He had position, training, natural ability, and the desire to help. But in one foolish act, he killed a man and forfeited all the advantages he had hoped to use.

Satan delights in convincing believers that they are of no use to God. And God delights in building cathedrals out of rubble. Moses' life needed reconstruction, to be sure! But when that rebuilding process was complete, he was a monument to God's grace.

Where in your life have you nearly given up hope that God could ever salvage the situation: your job? schooling? marriage? ministry? Before you throw in the towel, walk a mile in Moses' sandals. Study his failures. Learn about God's patience with him.

Then find your own "well" to sit by, and meditate on the encouraging words for discouraged disciples found in Exodus 4:11-12.

INSIGHT The Boat Revisited
The same Hebrew word for *boat* (as in Noah's) describes the vessel used by Moses' mother to hide him in the reeds. Once again we see God delivering his chosen from destruction by water after an obedient act of the faithful.

CHAPTER 1

These are the sons of Jacob* who went with their father to Egypt, each with his family: ²Reuben, Simeon, Levi, Judah, ³Issachar, Zebulun, Benjamin, ⁴Dan, Naphtali, Gad, and Asher. ⁵Joseph was already down in Egypt. In all, Jacob had seventy* direct descendants.

⁶In time, Joseph and each of his brothers died, ending that generation. ⁷But their descendants had many children and grandchildren. In fact, they multiplied so quickly

1:1 Hebrew *Israel.*   1:5 Dead Sea Scrolls and Greek version read *seventy-five;* see notes on Gen 46:27.

that they soon filled the land. [8]Then a new king came to the throne of Egypt who knew nothing about Joseph or what he had done. [9]He told his people, "These Israelites are becoming a threat to us because there are so many of them. [10]We must find a way to put an end to this. If we don't and if war breaks out, they will join our enemies and fight against us. Then they will escape from the country."

[11]So the Egyptians made the Israelites their slaves and put brutal slave drivers over them, hoping to wear them down under heavy burdens. They forced them to build the cities of Pithom and Rameses as supply centers for the king. [12]But the more the Egyptians oppressed them, the more quickly the Israelites multiplied! The Egyptians soon became alarmed [13]and decided to make their slavery more bitter still. [14]They were ruthless with the Israelites, forcing them to make bricks and mortar and to work long hours in the fields.

[15]Then Pharaoh, the king of Egypt, gave this order to the Hebrew midwives, Shiphrah and Puah: [16]"When you help the Hebrew women give birth, kill all the boys as soon as they are born. Allow only the baby girls to live." [17]But because the midwives feared God, they refused to obey the king and allowed the boys to live, too.

[18]Then the king called for the midwives. "Why have you done this?" he demanded. "Why have you allowed the boys to live?"

[19]"Sir," they told him, "the Hebrew women are very strong. They have their babies so quickly that we cannot get there in time! They are not slow in giving birth like Egyptian women."

[20]So God blessed the midwives, and the Israelites continued to multiply, growing more and more powerful. [21]And because the midwives feared God, he gave them families of their own.

[22]Then Pharaoh gave this order to all his people: "Throw all the newborn Israelite boys into the Nile River. But you may spare the baby girls."

CHAPTER 2
During this time, a man and woman from the tribe of Levi got married. [2]The woman became pregnant and gave birth to a son. She saw what a beautiful baby he was and kept him hidden for three months. [3]But when she could no longer hide him, she got a little basket made of papyrus reeds and waterproofed it with tar and pitch. She put the baby in the basket and laid it among the reeds along the edge of the Nile River. [4]The baby's sister then stood at a distance, watching to see what would happen to him.

[5]Soon after this, one of Pharaoh's daughters came down to bathe in the river, and her servant girls walked along the riverbank. When the princess saw the little basket among the reeds, she told one of her servant girls to get it for her. [6]As the princess opened it, she found the baby boy. His helpless cries touched her heart. "He must be one of the Hebrew children," she said.

[7]Then the baby's sister approached the princess. "Should I go and find one of the Hebrew women to nurse the baby for you?" she asked.

[8]"Yes, do!" the princess replied. So the girl rushed home and called the baby's mother.

[9]"Take this child home and nurse him for me," the princess told her. "I will pay you for your help." So the baby's mother took her baby home and nursed him.

[10]Later, when he was older, the child's mother brought him back to the princess, who adopted him as her son. The princess named him Moses,* for she said, "I drew him out of the water."

[11]Many years later, when Moses had grown up, he went out to visit his people, the Israelites, and he saw how hard they were forced to work. During his visit, he saw an Egyptian beating one of the Hebrew slaves. [12]After looking around to make sure no one was watching, Moses killed the Egyptian and buried him in the sand.

[13]The next day, as Moses was out visiting his people again, he saw two Hebrew men fighting. "What are you doing, hitting your neighbor like that?" Moses said to the one in the wrong.

[14]"Who do you think you are?" the man replied. "Who appointed you to be our prince and judge? Do you plan to kill me as you killed that Egyptian yesterday?"

Moses was badly frightened because he realized that everyone knew what he had done. [15]And sure enough, when Pharaoh heard about it, he gave orders to have Moses arrested and killed. But Moses fled

2:10 *Moses* sounds like a Hebrew term that means "to draw out."

from Pharaoh and escaped to the land of Midian.

When Moses arrived in Midian, he sat down beside a well. ¹⁶Now it happened that the priest of Midian had seven daughters who came regularly to this well to draw water and fill the water troughs for their father's flocks. ¹⁷But other shepherds would often come and chase the girls and their flocks away. This time, however, Moses came to their aid, rescuing the girls from the shepherds. Then he helped them draw water for their flocks.

¹⁸When the girls returned to Reuel, their father, he asked, "How did you get the flocks watered so quickly today?"

¹⁹"An Egyptian rescued us from the shepherds," they told him. "And then he drew water for us and watered our flocks."

²⁰"Well, where is he then?" their father asked. "Did you just leave him there? Go and invite him home for a meal!"

²¹Moses was happy to accept the invitation, and he settled down to live with them. In time, Reuel gave Moses one of his daughters, Zipporah, to be his wife. ²²Later they had a baby boy, and Moses named him Gershom,* for he said, "I have been a stranger in a foreign land."

²³Years passed, and the king of Egypt died. But the Israelites still groaned beneath their burden of slavery. They cried out for help, and their pleas for deliverance rose up to God. ²⁴God heard their cries and remembered his covenant promise to Abraham, Isaac, and Jacob. ²⁵He looked down on the Israelites and felt deep concern for their welfare.

2:22 *Gershom* sounds like a Hebrew term that means "a stranger there."

JANUARY 19 □ DAY 19
EXODUS 3–6
Confrontation with Pharaoh

 OVERVIEW After forty years of reflection, Moses concludes he is permanently disqualified from God's service. In a remarkable debate with the living God, Moses offers four excuses and begs God to send someone else as his spokesman. Finally, when God provides Aaron as a mouthpiece, Moses confronts Pharaoh with God's message. As predicted, Pharaoh not only denies God's demand but increases the miseries of the Hebrews. Moses' popularity with his people plummets, but God assures Moses that he will keep his promise of deliverance.

Chapters 3–4		Chapter 5	Chapter 6
Moses' Call by God	Moses' Excuses to God	Pharaoh's Response to Moses	God's Reassurance to Moses
3:1　　　　3:10	3:11　　　　4:31		
God Confronts Moses		Moses Confronts Pharaoh	

 YOUR DAILY WALK The church has been likened to a football game in which thousands of spectators desperately in need of exercise are watching a handful of players desperately in need of rest.

Are you a spectator or a player?

In God's strategy for successful living, character is more important than intelligence.

Before you can pull out your list of reasons excusing you from active duty in your local church, eavesdrop on an eighty-year-old shepherd as he argues with a burning bush. With good reason Moses anticipated resistance and rejection from his own people—to say nothing of Pharaoh. Besides, he had a speech impediment and an inferiority complex! Surely God was showing poor judgment (so Moses thought) in his choice of a deliverer for his people.

Patiently, thoroughly, God gave his rebuttal: I can use this bush, that staff in your hand, or even your stammering lips—whatever is available—to accomplish my plan and fulfill my promises. For all that you lack and everything you are not, I AM.

God probably isn't recruiting you to lead a nation out of bondage. But he definitely wants to show what he can accomplish through you. In response to his promise that "I AM all you need," will you answer, "I am available"?

 INSIGHT Speak Softly and Carry a Big Stick
Moses' staff was subsequently used by God to turn water into blood, bring hail and lightning, summon locusts, divide the Red Sea, bring water out of rocks, and signal victory in battle.

CHAPTER 3

One day Moses was tending the flock of his father-in-law, Jethro,* the priest of Midian, and he went deep into the wilderness near Sinai,* the mountain of God. ²Suddenly, the angel of the LORD appeared to him as a blazing fire in a bush. Moses was amazed because the bush was engulfed in flames, but it didn't burn up. ³"Amazing!" Moses said to himself. "Why isn't that bush burning up? I must go over to see this."

⁴When the LORD saw that he had caught Moses' attention, God called to him from the bush, "Moses! Moses!"

"Here I am!" Moses replied.

⁵"Do not come any closer," God told him. "Take off your sandals, for you are standing on holy ground." ⁶Then he said, "I am the God of your ancestors—the God of Abraham, the God of Isaac, and the God of Jacob." When Moses heard this, he hid his face in his hands because he was afraid to look at God.

⁷Then the LORD told him, "You can be sure I have seen the misery of my people in Egypt. I have heard their cries for deliverance from their harsh slave drivers. Yes, I am aware of their suffering. ⁸So I have come to rescue them from the Egyptians and lead them out of Egypt into their own good and spacious land. It is a land flowing with milk and honey—the land where the Canaanites, Hittites, Amorites, Perizzites, Hivites, and Jebusites live. ⁹The cries of the people of Israel have reached me, and I have seen how the Egyptians have oppressed them with heavy tasks. ¹⁰Now go, for I am sending you to Pharaoh. You will lead my people, the Israelites, out of Egypt."

¹¹"But who am I to appear before Pharaoh?" Moses asked God. "How can you expect me to lead the Israelites out of Egypt?"

¹²Then God told him, "I will be with you. And this will serve as proof that I have sent you: When you have brought the Israelites out of Egypt, you will return here to worship God at this very mountain."

¹³But Moses protested, "If I go to the people of Israel and tell them, 'The God of your ancestors has sent me to you,' they won't believe me. They will ask, 'Which god are you talking about? What is his name?' Then what should I tell them?"

¹⁴God replied, "I AM THE ONE WHO ALWAYS IS.* Just tell them, 'I AM has sent me to you.'" ¹⁵God also said, "Tell them, 'The LORD,* the God of your ancestors—the God of Abraham, the God of Isaac, and the God of Jacob—has sent me to you.' This will be my name forever; it has always been my name, and it will be used throughout all generations.

¹⁶"Now go and call together all the leaders of Israel. Tell them, 'The LORD, the God of your ancestors—the God of Abraham, Isaac, and Jacob—appeared to me in a burning bush. He said, "You can be sure that I am watching over you and have seen what is happening to you in Egypt. ¹⁷I promise to rescue you from the oppression of the Egyptians. I will lead you to the land now occupied by the Canaanites, Hittites, Amorites, Perizzites, Hivites, and Jebusites—a land flowing with milk and honey."'

¹⁸"The leaders of the people of Israel will accept your message. Then all of you must go straight to the king of Egypt and tell him, 'The LORD, the God of the Hebrews, has met with us. Let us go on a three-day

---

3:1a Moses' father-in-law went by two names, Jethro and Reuel.   **3:1b** Hebrew *Horeb*, another name for Sinai.   **3:14** Or *I AM WHO I AM*, or *I WILL BE WHAT I WILL BE*.   **3:15** Hebrew *Yahweh*; traditionally rendered *Jehovah*.

journey into the wilderness to offer sacrifices to the LORD our God.'

¹⁹"But I know that the king of Egypt will not let you go except under heavy pressure. ²⁰So I will reach out and strike at the heart of Egypt with all kinds of miracles. Then at last he will let you go. ²¹And I will see to it that the Egyptians treat you well. They will load you down with gifts so you will not leave empty-handed. ²²The Israelite women will ask for silver and gold jewelry and fine clothing from their Egyptian neighbors and their neighbors' guests. With this clothing, you will dress your sons and daughters. In this way, you will plunder the Egyptians!"

CHAPTER 4

But Moses protested again, "Look, they won't believe me! They won't do what I tell them. They'll just say, 'The LORD never appeared to you.'"

²Then the LORD asked him, "What do you have there in your hand?"

"A shepherd's staff," Moses replied.

³"Throw it down on the ground," the LORD told him. So Moses threw it down, and it became a snake! Moses was terrified, so he turned and ran away.

⁴Then the LORD told him, "Take hold of its tail." So Moses reached out and grabbed it, and it became a shepherd's staff again.

⁵"Perform this sign, and they will believe you," the LORD told him. "Then they will realize that the LORD, the God of their ancestors—the God of Abraham, the God of Isaac, and the God of Jacob—really has appeared to you."

⁶Then the LORD said to Moses, "Put your hand inside your robe." Moses did so, and when he took it out again, his hand was white as snow with leprosy.* ⁷"Now put your hand back into your robe again," the LORD said. Moses did, and when he took it out this time, it was as healthy as the rest of his body.

⁸"If they do not believe the first miraculous sign, they will believe the second," the LORD said. ⁹"And if they do not believe you even after these two signs, then take some water from the Nile River and pour it out on the dry ground. When you do, it will turn into blood."

¹⁰But Moses pleaded with the LORD,

"O Lord, I'm just not a good speaker. I never have been, and I'm not now, even after you have spoken to me. I'm clumsy with words."

¹¹"Who makes mouths?" the LORD asked him. "Who makes people so they can speak or not speak, hear or not hear, see or not see? Is it not I, the LORD? ¹²Now go, and do as I have told you. I will help you speak well, and I will tell you what to say."

¹³But Moses again pleaded, "Lord, please! Send someone else."

¹⁴Then the LORD became angry with Moses. "All right," he said. "What about your brother, Aaron the Levite? He is a good speaker. And look! He is on his way to meet you now. And when he sees you, he will be very glad. ¹⁵You will talk to him, giving him the words to say. I will help both of you to speak clearly, and I will tell you what to do. ¹⁶Aaron will be your spokesman to the people, and you will be as God to him, telling him what to say. ¹⁷And be sure to take your shepherd's staff along so you can perform the miraculous signs I have shown you."

¹⁸Then Moses went back home and talked it over with Jethro, his father-in-law. "With your permission," Moses said, "I would like to go back to Egypt to visit my family. I don't even know whether they are still alive."

"Go with my blessing," Jethro replied.

¹⁹Before Moses left Midian, the LORD said to him, "Do not be afraid to return to Egypt, for all those who wanted to kill you are dead."

²⁰So Moses took his wife and sons, put them on a donkey, and headed back to the land of Egypt. In his hand he carried the staff of God.

²¹Then the LORD reminded him, "When you arrive back in Egypt, go to Pharaoh and perform the miracles I have empowered you to do. But I will make him stubborn so he will not let the people go. ²²Then you will tell him, 'This is what the LORD says: Israel is my firstborn son. ²³I commanded you to let him go, so he could worship me. But since you have refused, be warned! I will kill your firstborn son!'"

²⁴On the journey, when Moses and his family had stopped for the night, the LORD confronted Moses* and was about to kill him. ²⁵But Zipporah, his wife, took a flint

---

4:6 Or *with a contagious skin disease.* The Hebrew word used here can describe various skin diseases.   **4:24** Or *confronted Moses' son;* Hebrew reads *confronted him.*

knife and circumcised her son. She threw the foreskin at Moses' feet and said, "What a blood-smeared bridegroom you are to me!" 26(When she called Moses a "blood-smeared bridegroom," she was referring to the circumcision.) After that, the LORD left him alone.

27Now the LORD had said to Aaron, "Go out into the wilderness to meet Moses." So Aaron traveled to the mountain of God, where he found Moses and greeted him warmly. 28Moses then told Aaron everything the LORD had commanded them to do and say. And he told him about the miraculous signs they were to perform.

29So Moses and Aaron returned to Egypt and called the leaders of Israel to a meeting. 30Aaron told them everything the LORD had told Moses, and Moses performed the miraculous signs as they watched. 31The leaders were soon convinced that the LORD had sent Moses and Aaron. And when they realized that the LORD had seen their misery and was deeply concerned for them, they all bowed their heads and worshiped.

CHAPTER 5

After this presentation to Israel's leaders, Moses and Aaron went to see Pharaoh. They told him, "This is what the LORD, the God of Israel, says: 'Let my people go, for they must go out into the wilderness to hold a religious festival in my honor.'"

2"Is that so?" retorted Pharaoh. "And who is the LORD that I should listen to him and let Israel go? I don't know the LORD, and I will not let Israel go."

3But Aaron and Moses persisted. "The God of the Hebrews has met with us," they declared. "Let us take a three-day trip into the wilderness so we can offer sacrifices to the LORD our God. If we don't, we will surely die by disease or the sword."

4"Who do you think you are," Pharaoh shouted, "distracting the people from their tasks? Get back to work! 5Look, there are many people here in Egypt, and you are stopping them from doing their work."

6That same day Pharaoh sent this order to the slave drivers and foremen he had set over the people of Israel: 7"Do not supply the people with any more straw for making bricks. Let them get it themselves! 8But don't reduce their production quotas by a single brick. They obviously don't have enough to

do. If they did, they wouldn't be talking about going into the wilderness to offer sacrifices to their God. 9Load them down with more work. Make them sweat! That will teach them to listen to these liars!"

10So the slave drivers and foremen informed the people: "Pharaoh has ordered us not to provide straw for you. 11Go and get it yourselves. Find it wherever you can. But you must produce just as many bricks as before!" 12So the people scattered throughout the land in search of straw.

13The slave drivers were brutal. "Meet your daily quota of bricks, just as you did before!" they demanded. 14Then they whipped the Israelite foremen in charge of the work crews. "Why haven't you met your quotas either yesterday or today?" they demanded.

15So the Israelite foremen went to Pharaoh and pleaded with him. "Please don't treat us like this," they begged. 16"We are given no straw, but we are still told to make as many bricks as before. We are beaten for something that isn't our fault! It is the fault of your slave drivers for making such unreasonable demands."

17But Pharaoh replied, "You're just lazy! You obviously don't have enough to do. If you did, you wouldn't be saying, 'Let us go, so we can offer sacrifices to the LORD.' 18Now, get back to work! No straw will be given to you, but you must still deliver the regular quota of bricks."

19Since Pharaoh would not let up on his demands, the Israelite foremen could see that they were in serious trouble. 20As they left Pharaoh's court, they met Moses and Aaron, who were waiting outside for them. 21The foremen said to them, "May the LORD judge you for getting us into this terrible situation with Pharaoh* and his officials. You have given them an excuse to kill us!"

22So Moses went back to the LORD and protested, "Why have you mistreated your own people like this, Lord? Why did you send me? 23Since I gave Pharaoh your message, he has been even more brutal to your people. You have not even begun to rescue them!"

CHAPTER 6

"Now you will see what I will do to Pharaoh," the LORD told Moses. "When he

5:21 Hebrew *for making us a stench in the nostrils of Pharaoh.*

feels my powerful hand upon him, he will let the people go. In fact, he will be so anxious to get rid of them that he will force them to leave his land!"

²And God continued, "I am the LORD. ³I appeared to Abraham, to Isaac, and to Jacob as God Almighty,* though I did not reveal my name, the LORD,* to them. ⁴And I entered into a solemn covenant with them. Under its terms, I swore to give them the land of Canaan, where they were living. ⁵You can be sure that I have heard the groans of the people of Israel, who are now slaves to the Egyptians. I have remembered my covenant with them.

⁶"Therefore, say to the Israelites: 'I am the LORD, and I will free you from your slavery in Egypt. I will redeem you with mighty power and great acts of judgment. ⁷I will make you my own special people, and I will be your God. And you will know that I am the LORD your God who has rescued you from your slavery in Egypt. ⁸I will bring you into the land I swore to give to Abraham, Isaac, and Jacob. It will be your very own property. I am the LORD!'"

⁹So Moses told the people what the LORD had said, but they wouldn't listen anymore. They had become too discouraged by the increasing burden of their slavery.

¹⁰Then the LORD said to Moses, ¹¹"Go back to Pharaoh, and tell him to let the people of Israel leave Egypt."

¹²"But LORD!" Moses objected. "My own people won't listen to me anymore. How can I expect Pharaoh to listen? I'm no orator!"

¹³But the LORD ordered Moses and Aaron to return to Pharaoh, king of Egypt, and to demand that he let the people of Israel leave Egypt.

¹⁴These are the ancestors of clans from some of Israel's tribes:

The descendants of Reuben, Israel's oldest son, included Hanoch, Pallu, Hezron, and Carmi. Their descendants became the clans of Reuben.
¹⁵The descendants of Simeon included Jemuel, Jamin, Ohad, Jakin, Zohar, and Shaul (whose mother was a Canaanite).

Their descendants became the clans of Simeon.
¹⁶These are the descendants of Levi, listed according to their family groups. In the first generation were Gershon, Kohath, and Merari. (Levi, their father, lived to be 137 years old.)
¹⁷ The descendants of Gershon included Libni and Shimei, each of whom is the ancestor of a clan.
¹⁸ The descendants of Kohath included Amram, Izhar, Hebron, and Uzziel. (Kohath lived to be 133 years old.)
¹⁹ The descendants of Merari included Mahli and Mushi.

These are the clans of the Levites, listed according to their genealogies.

²⁰Amram married his father's sister Jochebed, and she bore him Aaron and Moses. (Amram lived to be 137 years old.)
²¹The descendants of Izhar included Korah, Nepheg, and Zicri.
²²The descendants of Uzziel included Mishael, Elzaphan, and Sithri.
²³Aaron married Elisheba, the daughter of Amminadab and sister of Nahshon, and she bore him Nadab, Abihu, Eleazar, and Ithamar.
²⁴The descendants of Korah included Assir, Elkanah, and Abiasaph. Their descendants became the clans of Korah.
²⁵Eleazar son of Aaron married one of the daughters of Putiel, and she bore him Phinehas.

These are the ancestors of the Levite clans, listed according to their family groups.

²⁶The Aaron and Moses named in this list are the same Aaron and Moses to whom the LORD said, "Lead all the people of Israel out of the land of Egypt, division by division." ²⁷They are the ones who went to Pharaoh to ask permission to lead the people from the land of Egypt.

²⁸At that time, the LORD had said to them, ²⁹"I am the LORD! Give Pharaoh the message I have given you." ³⁰This is the same Moses who had argued with the LORD, saying, "I can't do it! I'm no orator. Why should Pharaoh listen to me?"

6:3a Hebrew *El Shaddai*.   6:3b Hebrew *Yahweh*; traditionally rendered *Jehovah*.

JANUARY 20 ☐ DAY 20
EXODUS 7–10
First Nine Plagues in Egypt

OVERVIEW Pharaoh's stubborn refusal to release the people prompts God to unleash nine devastating plagues against Egypt. Moved by this display of God's power, Pharaoh repeatedly promises to release the nation. But when the time arrives, his heart is hardened, and he breaks his word. To shatter Pharaoh's unyielding will, God prepares one last plague—the visit of the death angel to every unprepared home in the land.

Ch. 7	Chapter 8			Chapter 9			Chapter 10	
				First Nine Plagues upon Egypt				
Blood	Frogs	Gnats	Flies	Dead Livestock	Boils	Hail	Locusts	Darkness
1	15	16 19	20 32	1 7	8 12	13 35	1 20	21 29
				The gods of Egypt vs. the God of Israel				

One Almighty is more than all mighties.

YOUR DAILY WALK While on a trip, have you ever yielded to the temptation to take what you thought was a shortcut, only to find yourself hopelessly lost? Maybe you've experienced the same thing in your spiritual life as you looked for a shortcut to accomplish God's will.

"Alternate routes" may look very attractive, but they can often have unexpected consequences. Pharaoh offered Moses four shortcuts to releasing the people from bondage (8:25, 28; 10:11, 24). None of the four conformed to God's specific instructions. They were only attempts by Pharaoh to hide his refusal to obey God. Moses detected Pharaoh's motives, for he knew that *anything short of obedience is disobedience.*

That principle is still true today. There is no safe "alternate route" when the Bible clearly states, "This is what the LORD says." Nothing short of doing God's will in God's way will guarantee that you arrive at your intended destination! Look up the following verses to discover how God wants to guide you from the pages of his Word:
- The Bible is a _____ and a _____ (Psalm 119:105).
- The entrance of God's Word gives _____ (Psalm 119:130).
- The best place to hide God's Word is _____ (Psalm 119:11).

Now map out God's route to one of *your* destinations today!

INSIGHT Terror in the Sky
The locust, tool of divine judgment upon Egypt (Exodus 10) and numerous other nations in the pages of Scripture, is one of nature's most destructive creatures. A swarm of locusts may number more than one hundred thousand insects per square mile and can eat thousands of acres of vegetation in a single day.

CHAPTER 7
Then the LORD said to Moses, "Pay close attention to this. I will make you seem like God to Pharaoh. Your brother, Aaron, will be your prophet; he will speak for you. ²Tell Aaron everything I say to you and have him announce it to Pharaoh. He will demand that the people of Israel be allowed to leave Egypt. ³But I will cause Pharaoh to be stubborn so I can multiply my miraculous signs and wonders in the land of Egypt. ⁴Even then Pharaoh will refuse to listen to you. So I will crush Egypt with a series of disasters, after which I will lead the forces of Israel out with great acts of judgment. ⁵When I show the Egyptians my power and force them to let the Israelites go, they will realize that I am the LORD."

⁶So Moses and Aaron did just as the LORD had commanded them. ⁷Moses was eighty years old, and Aaron was eighty-three

at the time they made their demands to Pharaoh.

[8]Then the LORD said to Moses and Aaron, [9]"Pharaoh will demand that you show him a miracle to prove that God has sent you. When he makes this demand, say to Aaron, 'Throw down your shepherd's staff,' and it will become a snake."

[10]So Moses and Aaron went to see Pharaoh, and they performed the miracle just as the LORD had told them. Aaron threw down his staff before Pharaoh and his court, and it became a snake. [11]Then Pharaoh called in his wise men and magicians, and they did the same thing with their secret arts. [12]Their staffs became snakes, too! But then Aaron's snake swallowed up their snakes. [13]Pharaoh's heart, however, remained hard and stubborn. He still refused to listen, just as the LORD had predicted.

[14]Then the LORD said to Moses, "Pharaoh is very stubborn, and he continues to refuse to let the people go. [15]So go to Pharaoh in the morning as he goes down to the river. Stand on the riverbank and meet him there. Be sure to take along the shepherd's staff that turned into a snake. [16]Say to him, 'The LORD, the God of the Hebrews, has sent me to say, "Let my people go, so they can worship me in the wilderness." Until now, you have refused to listen to him. [17]Now the LORD says, "You are going to find out that I am the LORD." Look! I will hit the water of the Nile with this staff, and the river will turn to blood. [18]The fish in it will die, and the river will stink. The Egyptians will not be able to drink any water from the Nile.'"

[19]Then the LORD said to Moses: "Tell Aaron to point his staff toward the waters of Egypt—all its rivers, canals, marshes, and reservoirs. Everywhere in Egypt the water will turn into blood, even the water stored in wooden bowls and stone pots in the people's homes."

[20]So Moses and Aaron did just as the LORD had commanded them. As Pharaoh and all of his officials watched, Aaron raised his staff and hit the water of the Nile. Suddenly, the whole river turned to blood! [21]The fish in the river died, and the water became so foul that the Egyptians couldn't drink it. There was blood everywhere throughout the land of Egypt. [22]But again the magicians of Egypt used their secret arts, and they, too, turned water into blood. So Pharaoh's heart remained hard and stubborn. He refused to listen to Moses and Aaron, just as the LORD had predicted. [23]Pharaoh returned to his palace and put the whole thing out of his mind. [24]Then the Egyptians dug wells along the riverbank to get drinking water, for they couldn't drink from the river. [25]An entire week passed from the time the LORD turned the water of the Nile to blood.

CHAPTER 8

Then the LORD said to Moses, "Go to Pharaoh once again and tell him, 'This is what the LORD says: Let my people go, so they can worship me. [2]If you refuse, then listen carefully to this: I will send vast hordes of frogs across your entire land from one border to the other. [3]The Nile River will swarm with them. They will come up out of the river and into your houses, even into your bedrooms and onto your beds! Every home in Egypt will be filled with them. They will fill even your ovens and your kneading bowls. [4]You and your people will be overwhelmed by frogs!'"

[5]Then the LORD said to Moses, "Tell Aaron to point his shepherd's staff toward all the rivers, canals, and marshes of Egypt so there will be frogs in every corner of the land." [6]Aaron did so, and frogs covered the whole land of Egypt! [7]But the magicians were able to do the same thing with their secret arts. They, too, caused frogs to come up on the land.

[8]Then Pharaoh summoned Moses and Aaron and begged, "Plead with the LORD to take the frogs away from me and my people. I will let the people go, so they can offer sacrifices to the LORD."

[9]"You set the time!" Moses replied. "Tell me when you want me to pray for you, your officials, and your people. I will pray that you and your houses will be rid of the frogs. Then only the frogs in the Nile River will remain alive."

[10]"Do it tomorrow," Pharaoh said.

"All right," Moses replied, "it will be as you have said. Then you will know that no one is as powerful as the LORD our God. [11]All the frogs will be destroyed, except those in the river."

[12]So Moses and Aaron left Pharaoh, and Moses pleaded with the LORD about the frogs he had sent. [13]And the LORD did as Moses had promised. The frogs in the houses, the courtyards, and the fields all

died. ¹⁴They were piled into great heaps, and a terrible stench filled the land. ¹⁵But when Pharaoh saw that the frogs were gone, he hardened his heart. He refused to listen to Moses and Aaron, just as the LORD had predicted.

¹⁶So the LORD said to Moses, "Tell Aaron to strike the dust with his staff. The dust will turn into swarms of gnats throughout the land of Egypt." ¹⁷So Moses and Aaron did just as the LORD had commanded them. Suddenly, gnats infested the entire land, covering the Egyptians and their animals. All the dust in the land of Egypt turned into gnats. ¹⁸Pharaoh's magicians tried to do the same thing with their secret arts, but this time they failed. And the gnats covered all the people and animals.

¹⁹"This is the finger of God!" the magicians exclaimed to Pharaoh. But Pharaoh's heart remained hard and stubborn. He wouldn't listen to them, just as the LORD had predicted.

²⁰Next the LORD told Moses, "Get up early in the morning and meet Pharaoh as he goes down to the river. Say to him, 'This is what the LORD says: Let my people go, so they can worship me. ²¹If you refuse, I will send swarms of flies throughout Egypt. Your homes will be filled with them, and the ground will be covered with them. ²²But it will be very different in the land of Goshen, where the Israelites live. No flies will be found there. Then you will know that I am the LORD and that I have power even in the heart of your land. ²³I will make a clear distinction between your people and my people. This miraculous sign will happen tomorrow.'"

²⁴And the LORD did just as he had said. There were terrible swarms of flies in Pharaoh's palace and in every home in Egypt. The whole country was thrown into chaos by the flies.

²⁵Pharaoh hastily called for Moses and Aaron. "All right! Go ahead and offer sacrifices to your God," he said. "But do it here in this land. Don't go out into the wilderness."

²⁶But Moses replied, "That won't do! The Egyptians would detest the sacrifices that we offer to the LORD our God. If we offer them here where they can see us, they will be sure to stone us. ²⁷We must take a three-day trip into the wilderness to offer sacrifices to the LORD our God, just as he has commanded us."

²⁸"All right, go ahead," Pharaoh replied. "I will let you go to offer sacrifices to the LORD your God in the wilderness. But don't go too far away. Now hurry, and pray for me."

²⁹"As soon as I go," Moses said, "I will ask the LORD to cause the swarms of flies to disappear from you and all your people. But I am warning you, don't change your mind again and refuse to let the people go to sacrifice to the LORD."

³⁰So Moses left Pharaoh and asked the LORD to remove all the flies. ³¹And the LORD did as Moses asked and caused the swarms to disappear. Not a single fly remained in the land! ³²But Pharaoh hardened his heart again and refused to let the people go.

CHAPTER 9

"Go back to Pharaoh," the LORD commanded Moses. "Tell him, 'This is what the LORD, the God of the Hebrews, says: Let my people go, so they can worship me. ²If you continue to oppress them and refuse to let them go, ³the LORD will send a deadly plague to destroy your horses, donkeys, camels, cattle, and sheep. ⁴But the LORD will again make a distinction between the property of the Israelites and that of the Egyptians. Not a single one of Israel's livestock will die!'"

⁵The LORD announced that he would send the plague the very next day, ⁶and he did it, just as he had said. The next morning all the livestock of the Egyptians began to die, but the Israelites didn't lose a single animal from their flocks and herds. ⁷Pharaoh sent officials to see whether it was true that none of the Israelites' animals were dead. But even after he found it to be true, his heart remained stubborn. He still refused to let the people go.

⁸Then the LORD said to Moses and Aaron, "Take soot from a furnace, and have Moses toss it into the sky while Pharaoh watches. ⁹It will spread like fine dust over the whole land of Egypt, causing boils to break out on people and animals alike."

¹⁰So they gathered soot from a furnace and went to see Pharaoh. As Pharaoh watched, Moses tossed the soot into the air, and terrible boils broke out on the people and animals throughout Egypt. ¹¹Even the magicians were unable to stand before Moses, because the boils had broken out on

them, too. [12]But the LORD made Pharaoh even more stubborn, and he refused to listen, just as the LORD had predicted.

[13]Then the LORD said to Moses, "Get up early in the morning. Go to Pharaoh and tell him, 'The LORD, the God of the Hebrews, says: Let my people go, so they can worship me. [14]If you don't, I will send a plague that will really speak to you and your officials and all the Egyptian people. I will prove to you that there is no other God like me in all the earth. [15]I could have killed you all by now. I could have attacked you with a plague that would have wiped you from the face of the earth. [16]But I have let you live for this reason—that you might see my power and that my fame might spread throughout the earth. [17]But you are still lording it over my people, and you refuse to let them go. [18]So tomorrow at this time I will send a hailstorm worse than any in all of Egypt's history. [19]Quick! Order your livestock and servants to come in from the fields. Every person or animal left outside will die beneath the hail.'"

[20]Some of Pharaoh's officials believed what the LORD said. They immediately brought their livestock and servants in from the fields. [21]But those who had no respect for the word of the LORD left them out in the open.

[22]Then the LORD said to Moses, "Lift your hand toward the sky, and cause the hail to fall throughout Egypt, on the people, the animals, and the crops." [23]So Moses lifted his staff toward the sky, and the LORD sent thunder and hail, and lightning struck the earth. The LORD sent a tremendous hailstorm against all the land of Egypt. [24]Never in all the history of Egypt had there been a storm like that, with such severe hail and continuous lightning. [25]It left all of Egypt in ruins. Everything left in the fields was destroyed—people, animals, and crops alike. Even all the trees were destroyed. [26]The only spot in all Egypt without hail that day was the land of Goshen, where the people of Israel lived.

[27]Then Pharaoh urgently sent for Moses and Aaron. "I finally admit my fault," he confessed. "The LORD is right, and my people and I are wrong. [28]Please beg the LORD to end this terrifying thunder and hail. I will let you go at once."

[29]"All right," Moses replied. "As soon as I leave the city, I will lift my hands and pray to the LORD. Then the thunder and hail will stop. This will prove to you that the earth belongs to the LORD. [30]But as for you and your officials, I know that you still do not fear the LORD God as you should."

[31]All the flax and barley were destroyed because the barley was ripe and the flax was in bloom. [32]But the wheat and the spelt were not destroyed because they had not yet sprouted from the ground.

[33]So Moses left Pharaoh and went out of the city. As he lifted his hands to the LORD, all at once the thunder and hail stopped, and the downpour ceased. [34]When Pharaoh saw this, he and his officials sinned yet again by stubbornly refusing to do as they had promised. [35]Pharaoh refused to let the people leave, just as the LORD had predicted.

CHAPTER 10

Then the LORD said to Moses, "Return to Pharaoh and again make your demands. I have made him and his officials stubborn so I can continue to display my power by performing miraculous signs among them. [2]You will be able to tell wonderful stories to your children and grandchildren about the marvelous things I am doing among the Egyptians to prove that I am the LORD."

[3]So Moses and Aaron went to Pharaoh and said, "This is what the LORD, the God of the Hebrews, says: How long will you refuse to submit to me? Let my people go, so they can worship me. [4]If you refuse, watch out! For tomorrow I will cover the whole country with locusts. [5]There will be so many that you won't be able to see the ground. They will devour everything that escaped the hailstorm, including all the trees in the fields. [6]They will overrun your palaces and the homes of your officials and all the houses of Egypt. Never in the history of Egypt has there been a plague like this one!" And with that, Moses turned and walked out.

[7]The court officials now came to Pharaoh and appealed to him. "How long will you let these disasters go on? Please let the Israelites go to serve the LORD their God! Don't you realize that Egypt lies in ruins?"

[8]So Moses and Aaron were brought back to Pharaoh. "All right, go and serve the LORD your God," he said. "But tell me, just whom do you want to take along?"

[9]"Young and old, all of us will go," Moses replied. "We will take our sons and

daughters and our flocks and herds. We must all join together in a festival to the LORD."

¹⁰Pharaoh retorted, "The LORD will certainly need to be with you if you try to take your little ones along! I can see through your wicked intentions. ¹¹Never! Only the men may go and serve the LORD, for that is what you requested." And Pharaoh threw them out of the palace.

¹²Then the LORD said to Moses, "Raise your hand over the land of Egypt to bring on the locusts. Let them cover the land and eat all the crops still left after the hailstorm."

¹³So Moses raised his staff, and the LORD caused an east wind to blow all that day and through the night. When morning arrived, the east wind had brought the locusts. ¹⁴And the locusts swarmed over the land of Egypt from border to border. It was the worst locust plague in Egyptian history, and there has never again been one like it. ¹⁵For the locusts covered the surface of the whole country, making the ground look black. They ate all the plants and all the fruit on the trees that had survived the hailstorm. Not one green thing remained, neither tree nor plant, throughout the land of Egypt.

¹⁶Pharaoh quickly sent for Moses and Aaron. "I confess my sin against the LORD your God and against you," he said to them. ¹⁷"Forgive my sin only this once, and plead with the LORD your God to take away this terrible plague."

¹⁸So Moses left Pharaoh and pleaded with the LORD. ¹⁹The LORD responded by sending a strong west wind that blew the locusts out into the Red Sea.* Not a single locust remained in all the land of Egypt. ²⁰But the LORD made Pharaoh stubborn once again, and he did not let the people go.

²¹Then the LORD said to Moses, "Lift your hand toward heaven, and a deep and terrifying darkness will descend on the land of Egypt." ²²So Moses lifted his hand toward heaven, and there was deep darkness over the entire land for three days. ²³During all that time the people scarcely moved, for they could not see. But there was light as usual where the people of Israel lived.

²⁴Then Pharaoh called for Moses. "Go and worship the LORD," he said. "But let your flocks and herds stay here. You can even take your children with you."

²⁵"No," Moses said, "we must take our flocks and herds for sacrifices and burnt offerings to the LORD our God. ²⁶All our property must go with us; not a hoof can be left behind. We will have to choose our sacrifices for the LORD our God from among these animals. And we won't know which sacrifices he will require until we get there."

²⁷So the LORD hardened Pharaoh's heart once more, and he would not let them go. ²⁸"Get out of here!" Pharaoh shouted at Moses. "Don't ever let me see you again! The day you do, you will die!"

²⁹"Very well," Moses replied. "I will never see you again."

10:19 Hebrew *sea of reeds.*

JANUARY 21 □ DAY 21
Choices That Affect Your Destiny

 LOOK BACK Joseph and Moses, a study in contrasts. Joseph grew up in a typical Hebrew household; Moses was raised with an Egyptian silver spoon in his mouth. Joseph spent his early years in prison; Moses spent his early years in the palace. Joseph was nearly a murder victim; Moses fled as a fugitive because of a murder he had committed. Joseph was promoted to the position of prime minister in Egypt; Moses was demoted from a similar position!

And yet in many ways these two men were similar. Both encountered God under miraculous circumstances (Joseph in visions, Moses at the burning bush). Both were used by God in a remarkable way (Joseph to administer famine relief in Egypt, Moses to lead God's people out of Egyptian slavery). And both were faced with crucial decisions at pivotal moments in their lives—decisions that affected their destiny.

LOOK UP   Life is a series of choices and consequences. Decide today to step in front of a speeding car, and you will face the consequences of that choice for the rest of your life (as brief as that life may be!). Decide to harbor bitterness in your heart for something someone said or did to you, and you will experience the by-product of that bitterness. Decide to leave God out of your plans, and you will soon discover that life without God is foolish and unfulfilling (Psalm 14:1).

The person who provides for this life but takes no care for the next is wise for a moment but a fool forever.

Consider for a moment some of the "could haves" from the lives of Joseph and Moses. Joseph could have been bitter and unforgiving for what his brothers did to him—and with good reason. He could have shaken his fist at God for the injustice he experienced in the pit and in prison. He could have been angry with God for the years that were wasted because of other people's cruelty and lies. He could have taken the credit for being able to interpret Pharaoh's dreams. But in each case he chose to do something else.

Moses could have chosen to keep his true identity hidden. He could have ignored the plight of his countrymen. He could have settled down in Midian and nurtured a grudge against God for the rest of his life. He could have ignored the burning bush and the commission he received from God. He could have allowed his past mistakes and present feelings of inadequacy to keep him from obeying God. But in each case he chose to do something else.

In each case, Joseph and Moses were faced with a choice. And the path they chose determined the destination they reached.

LOOK AHEAD   Life is a matter of choices, not chances. And the choices you face today may be remarkably similar to those that confronted Joseph and Moses:
- Bitterness or forgiveness
- Anger or acceptance
- Self-promotion or seeking God's kingdom
- Self-pity over the past or putting the past behind you
- Comfortable compromise or painful obedience

Chances are good you won't find yourself standing before the world's most powerful leader. But then again, when you dare to choose wisely like a Joseph or a Moses, you never know.

JANUARY 22 ☐ DAY 22
EXODUS 11–12
Tenth Plague, Passover, and Exodus

OVERVIEW   In the end, it's no contest. Death touches every Egyptian family as the final plague brings destruction to every firstborn child and beast. But the Israelite homes escape death because their households are protected by the blood of a sacrificial animal killed as a substitute for the firstborn. Pharaoh, the stubborn monarch, commands the Hebrews to leave, and the long-awaited Exodus begins. The holiday called *Passover* thereafter becomes an annual memorial of the salvation of God's people from their Egyptian homes of slavery.

Chapter 11		Chapter 12	
Tenth Plague Announced	Passover Observed	Firstborn Destroyed	Exodus Begun
1	28	29 36	37 51
Packing Up		Moving Out	

YOUR DAILY WALK "Let each generation tell its children of your mighty acts" (Psalm 145:4).

If everyone turned gossip into prayer, there would be no more reason for gossip.

If someone were to write an article entitled "What to Do between God's Miracles," it might consist of a single word: *Remember.* The mighty supernatural acts of God on behalf of his people have been relatively few and far between. One of God's purposes for such spectacular demonstrations has been to reveal his power quietly at work behind the scenes. Because miracles like the ten plagues occurred infrequently, God's people were instructed to recall the past as a basis for faith in the present. And as an aid to feeble memories, God instituted memorials—such as the Passover—to be observed on a regular basis by his people throughout the generations.

What was a good idea then is a good idea now. Are there objects in your home that can serve to remind you of God's faithfulness in the past: a picture on the wall . . . a cancelled check . . . a scrapbook? Are there certain dates you could designate "Memorial Anniversaries" to recall special provisions of God? Select your own memorial today, and plan now to recall a mighty act of God in your life. Like Passover, let it become a yearly habit to recall God's goodness!

INSIGHT Israel's Severance Pay for Forced Labor
In their eagerness to remove the Israelites (and the plagues) from their land, the Egyptians turned over vast quantities of jewelry, gold, and clothing—fair payment for years of slave labor!

CHAPTER 11

Then the LORD said to Moses, "I will send just one more disaster on Pharaoh and the land of Egypt. After that, Pharaoh will let you go. In fact, he will be so anxious to get rid of you that he will practically force you to leave the country. ²Tell all the Israelite men and women to ask their Egyptian neighbors for articles of silver and gold."

³(Now the LORD had caused the Egyptians to look favorably on the people of Israel, and Moses was considered a very great man in the land of Egypt. He was respected by Pharaoh's officials and the Egyptian people alike.)

⁴So Moses announced to Pharaoh, "This is what the LORD says: About midnight I will pass through Egypt. ⁵All the firstborn sons will die in every family in Egypt, from the oldest son of Pharaoh, who sits on the throne, to the oldest son of his lowliest slave. Even the firstborn of the animals will die. ⁶Then a loud wail will be heard throughout the land of Egypt; there has never been such wailing before, and there never will be again. ⁷But among the Israelites it will be so peaceful that not even a dog will bark. Then you will know that the LORD makes a distinction between the Egyptians and the Israelites. ⁸All the officials of Egypt will come running to me, bowing low. 'Please leave!' they will beg. 'Hurry! And take all your followers with you.' Only then will I go!" Then, burning with anger, Moses left Pharaoh's presence.

⁹Now the LORD had told Moses, "Pharaoh will not listen to you. But this will give me the opportunity to do even more mighty miracles in the land of Egypt." ¹⁰Although Moses and Aaron did these miracles in Pharaoh's presence, the LORD hardened his heart so he wouldn't let the Israelites leave the country.

CHAPTER 12

Now the LORD gave the following instructions to Moses and Aaron while they were still in the land of Egypt: ²"From now on, this month will be the first month of the year for you. [3]Announce to the whole community that on the tenth day of this month each family must choose a lamb or a young goat for a sacrifice. [4]If a family is too small to eat an entire lamb, let them share the lamb with another family in the neighborhood. Whether or not they share in this way depends on the size of each family and how much they can eat. [5]This animal must be a one-year-old male, either a sheep or a goat, with no physical defects.

[6]"Take special care of these lambs until the evening of the fourteenth day of this first month. Then each family in the community must slaughter its lamb. [7]They are to take some of the lamb's blood and smear it on the top and sides of the doorframe of the house where the lamb will be eaten. [8]That evening everyone must eat roast lamb with bitter herbs and bread made without yeast. [9]The meat must never be eaten raw or boiled; roast it all, including the head, legs, and internal organs. [10]Do not leave any of it until the next day. Whatever is not eaten that night must be burned before morning.

[11]"Wear your traveling clothes as you eat this meal, as though prepared for a long journey. Wear your sandals, and carry your walking sticks in your hands. Eat the food quickly, for this is the LORD's Passover. [12]On that night I will pass through the land of Egypt and kill all the firstborn sons and firstborn male animals in the land of Egypt. I will execute judgment against all the gods of Egypt, for I am the LORD! [13]The blood you have smeared on your doorposts will serve as a sign. When I see the blood, I will pass over you. This plague of death will not touch you when I strike the land of Egypt.

[14]"You must remember this day forever. Each year you will celebrate it as a special festival to the LORD. [15]For seven days, you may eat only bread made without yeast. On the very first day you must remove every trace of yeast from your homes. Anyone who eats bread made with yeast at any time during the seven days of the festival will be cut off from the community of Israel. [16]On the first day of the festival, and again on the seventh day, all the people must gather for a time of special worship. No work of any kind may be done on these days except in the preparation of food.

[17]"Celebrate this Festival of Unleavened Bread, for it will remind you that I brought your forces out of the land of Egypt on this very day. This festival will be a permanent regulation for you, to be kept from generation to generation. [18]Only bread without yeast may be eaten from the evening of the fourteenth day of the month until the evening of the twenty-first day of the month. [19]During those seven days, there must be no trace of yeast in your homes. Anyone who eats anything made with yeast during this week will be cut off from the community of Israel. These same regulations apply to the foreigners living with you, as if they had been born among you. [20]I repeat, during those days you must not eat anything made with yeast. Wherever you live, eat only bread that has no yeast in it."

[21]Then Moses called for the leaders of Israel and said, "Tell each of your families to slaughter the lamb they have set apart for the Passover. [22]Drain each lamb's blood into a basin. Then take a cluster of hyssop branches and dip it into the lamb's blood. Strike the hyssop against the top and sides of the doorframe, staining it with the blood. And remember, no one is allowed to leave the house until morning. [23]For the LORD will pass through the land and strike down the Egyptians. But when he sees the blood on the top and sides of the doorframe, the LORD will pass over your home. He will not permit the Destroyer to enter and strike down your firstborn.

[24]"Remember, these instructions are permanent and must be observed by you and your descendants forever. [25]When you arrive in the land the LORD has promised to give you, you will continue to celebrate this festival. [26]Then your children will ask, 'What does all this mean? What is this ceremony about?' [27]And you will reply, 'It is the celebration of the LORD's Passover, for he passed over the homes of the Israelites in Egypt. And though he killed the Egyptians, he spared our families and did not destroy us.'" Then all the people bowed their heads and worshiped.

[28]So the people of Israel did just as the LORD had commanded through Moses and Aaron. [29]And at midnight the LORD killed all the firstborn sons in the land of Egypt, from the firstborn son of Pharaoh,

who sat on the throne, to the firstborn son of the captive in the dungeon. Even the firstborn of their livestock were killed. ³⁰Pharaoh and his officials and all the people of Egypt woke up during the night, and loud wailing was heard throughout the land of Egypt. There was not a single house where someone had not died.

³¹Pharaoh sent for Moses and Aaron during the night. "Leave us!" he cried. "Go away, all of you! Go and serve the LORD as you have requested. ³²Take your flocks and herds, and be gone. Go, but give me a blessing as you leave." ³³All the Egyptians urged the people of Israel to get out of the land as quickly as possible, for they thought, "We will all die!"

³⁴The Israelites took with them their bread dough made without yeast. They wrapped their kneading bowls in their spare clothing and carried them on their shoulders. ³⁵And the people of Israel did as Moses had instructed and asked the Egyptians for clothing and articles of silver and gold. ³⁶The LORD caused the Egyptians to look favorably on the Israelites, and they gave the Israelites whatever they asked for. So, like a victorious army, they plundered the Egyptians!

³⁷That night the people of Israel left Rameses and started for Succoth. There were about 600,000 men, plus all the women and children. And they were all traveling on foot. ³⁸Many people who were not Israelites went with them, along with the many flocks and herds. ³⁹Whenever they stopped to eat, they baked bread from the yeastless dough they had brought from Egypt. It was made without yeast because the people were rushed out of Egypt and had no time to wait for bread to rise.

⁴⁰The people of Israel had lived in Egypt for 430 years. ⁴¹In fact, it was on the last day of the 430th year that all the LORD's forces left the land. ⁴²This night had been reserved by the LORD to bring his people out from the land of Egypt, so this same night now belongs to him. It must be celebrated every year, from generation to generation, to remember the LORD's deliverance.

⁴³Then the LORD said to Moses and Aaron, "These are the regulations for the festival of Passover. No foreigners are allowed to eat the Passover lamb. ⁴⁴But any slave who has been purchased may eat it if he has been circumcised. ⁴⁵Hired servants and visiting foreigners may not eat it. ⁴⁶All who eat the lamb must eat it together in one house. You must not carry any of its meat outside, and you may not break any of its bones. ⁴⁷The whole community of Israel must celebrate this festival at the same time.

⁴⁸"If there are foreigners living among you who want to celebrate the LORD's Passover, let all the males be circumcised. Then they may come and celebrate the Passover with you. They will be treated just as if they had been born among you. But an uncircumcised male may never eat of the Passover lamb. ⁴⁹This law applies to everyone, whether a native-born Israelite or a foreigner who has settled among you."

⁵⁰So the people of Israel followed all the LORD's instructions to Moses and Aaron. ⁵¹And that very day the LORD began to lead the people of Israel out of Egypt, division by division.

JANUARY 23 □ DAY 23
EXODUS 13–15
Crossing the Red Sea

 OVERVIEW Things get worse for the Israelites before they get better. God leads his band of 3 million refugees to the intersection of Baalzephon and the Red Sea—a seemingly inescapable dead end. Pharaoh, experiencing yet another change of heart, dispatches a crack chariot division to bring the Israelite exodus to an end. Instead, the Egyptian army meets its end in the swirling waters of the Red Sea. Moses watches the people's panic turn to praise as they cross the sea bed dry-shod and sing a great song of jubilation to God their Savior.

Chapter 13	Chapter 14	Chapter 15
God's Guiding Cloud	Israel's Great Crossing	Moses' Grateful Chorus
Direction	Protection	Jubilation

The miraculous is absolutely basic to Christianity.

YOUR DAILY WALK You are seated in church when you hear the words, "Please bow your head and worship the Lord in the quietness of your own heart." You put aside your bulletin and close your eyes. Then you think to yourself, *What am I supposed to do now?*

Worshiping God is a skill seldom taught . . . and infrequently practiced. The root meaning of *worship* involves recognizing the "worth-ship" of another. It is a response to the greatness of God. People in the Bible worshiped God for who he was (his person) and what he did (his works), for his actions are always consistent with his character.

If you had been standing with the Israelites on the far banks of the Red Sea as the waters swallowed up the Egyptian army, you would have had no trouble responding in an attitude of worship! Even today you can join in their chorus of praise. Read through their song in chapter 15 again, making one list of God's *actions* (conduct), which prompted worship from his people, and a second list of what is proclaimed about God's *attributes* (character). Now you, too, should be ready to "sing the praises" of your God and Savior today!

INSIGHT Taking the Scenic Route
Israel's God and Guide (in the form of a cloudy pillar) steered the travelers away from the most direct route to Canaan for at least two reasons: (1) to avoid certain warfare, and (2) to take Israel to the mountain of God (3:12). The nation needed to learn to walk with God before learning to fight for God.

CHAPTER 13

Then the LORD said to Moses, [2] "Dedicate to me all the firstborn sons of Israel and every firstborn male animal. They are mine."

[3] So Moses said to the people, "This is a day to remember forever—the day you left Egypt, the place of your slavery. For the LORD has brought you out by his mighty power. (Remember, you are not to use any yeast.) [4] This day in early spring* will be the anniversary of your exodus. [5] You must celebrate this day when the LORD brings you into the land of the Canaanites, Hittites, Amorites, Hivites, and Jebusites. This is the land he swore to give your ancestors—a land flowing with milk and honey. [6] For seven days you will eat only bread without yeast. Then on the seventh day, you will celebrate a great feast to the LORD. [7] Eat only bread without yeast during those seven days. In fact, there must be no yeast in your homes or anywhere within the borders of your land during this time.

[8] "During these festival days each year, you must explain to your children why you are celebrating. Say to them, 'This is a celebration of what the LORD did for us when we left Egypt.' [9] This annual festival will be a visible reminder to you, like a mark branded on your hands or your forehead. Let it remind you always to keep the LORD's instructions in your minds and on your lips. After all, it was the LORD who rescued you from Egypt with great power.

[10] "So celebrate this festival at the appointed time each year. [11] And remember these instructions when the LORD brings you into the land he swore to give your ancestors long ago, the land where the Canaanites are now living. [12] All firstborn sons and firstborn male animals must be presented to the LORD. [13] A firstborn male donkey may be redeemed from the LORD by presenting a lamb in its place. But if you decide not to make the exchange, the donkey must be killed by breaking its neck. However, you must redeem every firstborn son.

13:4 Hebrew *in the month of Abib.* This month of the Hebrew lunar calendar usually occurs in March and April.

[14]"And in the future, your children will ask you, 'What does all this mean?' Then you will tell them, 'With mighty power the LORD brought us out of Egypt from our slavery. [15]Pharaoh refused to let us go, so the LORD killed all the firstborn males throughout the land of Egypt, both people and animals. That is why we now offer all the firstborn males to the LORD—except that the firstborn sons are always redeemed.' [16]Again I say, this ceremony will be like a mark branded on your hands or your forehead. It is a visible reminder that it was the LORD who brought you out of Egypt with great power."

[17]When Pharaoh finally let the people go, God did not lead them on the road that runs through Philistine territory, even though that was the shortest way from Egypt to the Promised Land. God said, "If the people are faced with a battle, they might change their minds and return to Egypt." [18]So God led them along a route through the wilderness toward the Red Sea,* and the Israelites left Egypt like a marching army.

[19]Moses took the bones of Joseph with him, for Joseph had made the sons of Israel swear that they would take his bones with them when God led them out of Egypt—as he was sure God would.

[20]Leaving Succoth, they camped at Etham on the edge of the wilderness. [21]The LORD guided them by a pillar of cloud during the day and a pillar of fire at night. That way they could travel whether it was day or night. [22]And the LORD did not remove the pillar of cloud or pillar of fire from their sight.

CHAPTER 14
Then the LORD gave these instructions to Moses: [2]"Tell the people to march toward Pi-hahiroth between Migdol and the sea. Camp there along the shore, opposite Baal-zephon. [3]Then Pharaoh will think, 'Those Israelites are confused. They are trapped between the wilderness and the sea!' [4]And once again I will harden Pharaoh's heart, and he will chase after you. I have planned this so I will receive great glory at the expense of Pharaoh and his armies. After this, the Egyptians will know that I am the LORD!" So the Israelites camped there as they were told.

[5]When word reached the king of Egypt that the Israelites were not planning to return to Egypt after three days, Pharaoh and his officials changed their minds. "What have we done, letting all these slaves get away?" they asked. [6]So Pharaoh called out his troops and led the chase in his chariot. [7]He took with him six hundred of Egypt's best chariots, along with the rest of the chariots of Egypt, each with a commander. [8]The LORD continued to strengthen Pharaoh's resolve, and he chased after the people of Israel who had escaped so defiantly. [9]All the forces in Pharaoh's army—all his horses, chariots, and charioteers—were used in the chase. The Egyptians caught up with the people of Israel as they were camped beside the shore near Pi-hahiroth, across from Baal-zephon.

[10]As Pharaoh and his army approached, the people of Israel could see them in the distance, marching toward them. The people began to panic, and they cried out to the LORD for help. [11]Then they turned against Moses and complained, "Why did you bring us out here to die in the wilderness? Weren't there enough graves for us in Egypt? Why did you make us leave? [12]Didn't we tell you to leave us alone while we were still in Egypt? Our Egyptian slavery was far better than dying out here in the wilderness!"

[13]But Moses told the people, "Don't be afraid. Just stand where you are and watch the LORD rescue you. The Egyptians that you see today will never be seen again. [14]The LORD himself will fight for you. You won't have to lift a finger in your defense!"

[15]Then the LORD said to Moses, "Why are you crying out to me? Tell the people to get moving! [16]Use your shepherd's staff—hold it out over the water, and a path will open up before you through the sea. Then all the people of Israel will walk through on dry ground. [17]Yet I will harden the hearts of the Egyptians, and they will follow the Israelites into the sea. Then I will receive great glory at the expense of Pharaoh and his armies, chariots, and charioteers. [18]When I am finished with Pharaoh and his army, all Egypt will know that I am the LORD!"

[19]Then the angel of God, who had been leading the people of Israel, moved to a

13:18 Hebrew *sea of reeds.*

position behind them, and the pillar of cloud also moved around behind them. ²⁰The cloud settled between the Israelite and Egyptian camps. As night came, the pillar of cloud turned into a pillar of fire, lighting the Israelite camp. But the cloud became darkness to the Egyptians, and they couldn't find the Israelites.

²¹Then Moses raised his hand over the sea, and the LORD opened up a path through the water with a strong east wind. The wind blew all that night, turning the seabed into dry land. ²²So the people of Israel walked through the sea on dry ground, with walls of water on each side! ²³Then the Egyptians—all of Pharaoh's horses, chariots, and charioteers—followed them across the bottom of the sea. ²⁴But early in the morning, the LORD looked down on the Egyptian army from the pillar of fire and cloud, and he threw them into confusion. ²⁵Their chariot wheels began to come off, making their chariots impossible to drive. "Let's get out of here!" the Egyptians shouted. "The LORD is fighting for Israel against us!"

²⁶When all the Israelites were on the other side, the LORD said to Moses, "Raise your hand over the sea again. Then the waters will rush back over the Egyptian chariots and charioteers." ²⁷So as the sun began to rise, Moses raised his hand over the sea. The water roared back into its usual place, and the LORD swept the terrified Egyptians into the surging currents. ²⁸The waters covered all the chariots and charioteers—the entire army of Pharaoh. Of all the Egyptians who had chased the Israelites into the sea, not a single one survived.

²⁹The people of Israel had walked through the middle of the sea on dry land, as the water stood up like a wall on both sides. ³⁰This was how the LORD rescued Israel from the Egyptians that day. And the Israelites could see the bodies of the Egyptians washed up on the shore. ³¹When the people of Israel saw the mighty power that the LORD had displayed against the Egyptians, they feared the LORD and put their faith in him and his servant Moses.

CHAPTER 15

Then Moses and the people of Israel sang this song to the LORD:

15:4 Hebrew *sea of reeds;* also in 15:22.

"I will sing to the LORD, for he has
    triumphed gloriously;
he has thrown both horse and rider
    into the sea.
² The LORD is my strength and my song;
    he has become my victory.
He is my God, and I will praise him;
    he is my father's God, and I will
    exalt him!
³ The LORD is a warrior;
    yes, the LORD is his name!
⁴ Pharaoh's chariots and armies,
    he has thrown into the sea.
The very best of Pharaoh's officers
    have been drowned in the Red Sea.*
⁵ The deep waters have covered them;
    they sank to the bottom like a stone.

⁶ "Your right hand, O LORD,
    is glorious in power.
Your right hand, O LORD,
    dashes the enemy to pieces.
⁷ In the greatness of your majesty,
    you overthrew those who rose
    against you.
Your anger flashed forth;
    it consumed them as fire burns straw.
⁸ At the blast of your breath, the waters
    piled up!
The surging waters stood straight
    like a wall;
in the middle of the sea the waters
    became hard.

⁹ "The enemy said, 'I will chase them,
    catch up with them, and destroy them.
I will divide the plunder,
    avenging myself against them.
I will unsheath my sword;
    my power will destroy them.'
¹⁰ But with a blast of your breath,
    the sea covered them.
They sank like lead
    in the mighty waters.

¹¹ "Who else among the gods is like you,
    O LORD?
    Who is glorious in holiness like you—
so awesome in splendor,
    performing such wonders?
¹² You raised up your hand,
    and the earth swallowed our
    enemies.

¹³ "With unfailing love you will lead
    this people whom you have
    ransomed.

You will guide them in your strength
   to the place where your holiness
   dwells.
¹⁴ The nations will hear and tremble;
   anguish will grip the people of
   Philistia.
¹⁵ The leaders of Edom will be terrified;
   the nobles of Moab will tremble.
All the people of Canaan will melt with
   fear;
¹⁶   terror and dread will overcome them.
Because of your great power,
   they will be silent like a stone,
until your people pass by, O LORD,
   until the people whom you
   purchased pass by.
¹⁷ You will bring them in and plant them
   on your own mountain—
   the place you have made as your
   home, O LORD,
   the sanctuary, O Lord, that your
   hands have made.
¹⁸ The LORD will reign forever and ever!"

¹⁹When Pharaoh's horses, chariots, and
charioteers rushed into the sea, the LORD
brought the water crashing down on them.
But the people of Israel had walked
through on dry land!

²⁰Then Miriam the prophet, Aaron's sister, took a tambourine and led all the
women in rhythm and dance. ²¹And Miriam sang this song:

"I will sing to the LORD, for he has
   triumphed gloriously;
   he has thrown both horse and rider
   into the sea."

²²Then Moses led the people of Israel
away from the Red Sea, and they moved out
into the Shur Desert. They traveled in this
desert for three days without water. ²³When
they came to Marah, they finally found water. But the people couldn't drink it because
it was bitter. (That is why the place was
called Marah, which means "bitter.")

²⁴Then the people turned against Moses.
"What are we going to drink?" they demanded.

²⁵So Moses cried out to the LORD for help,
and the LORD showed him a branch. Moses
took the branch and threw it into the water.
This made the water good to drink.

It was there at Marah that the LORD laid
before them the following conditions to test
their faithfulness to him: ²⁶"If you will
listen carefully to the voice of the LORD
your God and do what is right in his sight,
obeying his commands and laws, then I
will not make you suffer the diseases I sent
on the Egyptians; for I am the LORD who
heals you."

²⁷After leaving Marah, they came to
Elim, where there were twelve springs and
seventy palm trees. They camped there beside the springs.

JANUARY 24 ☐ DAY 24
EXODUS 16–18
Israel's Journey to Mount Sinai

 OVERVIEW Only days after the miracle of the Red Sea, grumbling
and discontent begin to surface among the people on the march. The
nation God delivered by faith must now learn to walk by faith, and they
have much to learn! Of prime concern is finding sufficient water and
food to sustain a caravan of 3 million people in the desolate wilderness.
A month into the journey, when food and water supplies are exhausted,
the people cry out anxiously to Moses. Miraculously, God provides
manna, quail, and water in abundance to remind them that he is the
source of their supply. Even Moses must learn this lesson. Exhausted
from attempting to administer the nation single-handedly, Moses
follows the advice of his father-in-law and selects seventy assistants to
help him with the work.

Chapter 16	Chapter 17	Chapter 18
Famine in the Wilderness	Thirst at Rephidim	Exhaustion in Moses' Office
Israel's Complaints		Moses' Co-workers

YOUR DAILY WALK Have you found that your *blessings* are also your biggest *problems?* The things you thought would bring you the greatest joy are in fact the things that cause you the most headaches; for instance, the new car (which spends more time in the shop than on the road), the long-awaited child (who now has the house in a state of siege), the unexpected promotion (which produced those equally unexpected ulcers).

God gives us the ingredients for our daily bread, but he expects us to do the baking.

Israel learned the hard way that *blessings bring responsibility*. Daily manna was a wonderful provision from God, but it had to be collected and eaten in a particular way. God's presence in the pillar of cloud and fire was comforting, but it meant unquestioned obedience. When the pillar moved, Israel moved.

Make a list of some of God's recent blessings to you, including the ones that seem to give you grief. Next to each, put an obligation that is yours if you enjoy the blessing as God intended.

INSIGHT A Subtle Prophecy
The water from the rock at Rephidim beautifully symbolizes Christ, our life-giver. The apostle Paul wrote that the Rock from which the Israelites drank was Christ (1 Corinthians 10:4). The life—and living water—that Jesus offers is available to you today! "If you are thirsty, come to me! If you believe in me, come and drink! For the Scriptures declare that rivers of living water will flow out from within" (John 7:37-38).

CHAPTER 16

Then they left Elim and journeyed into the Sin* Desert, between Elim and Mount Sinai. They arrived there a month after leaving Egypt.* ²There, too, the whole community of Israel spoke bitterly against Moses and Aaron.

³"Oh, that we were back in Egypt," they moaned. "It would have been better if the LORD had killed us there! At least there we had plenty to eat. But now you have brought us into this desert to starve us to death."

⁴Then the LORD said to Moses, "Look, I'm going to rain down food from heaven for you. The people can go out each day and pick up as much food as they need for that day. I will test them in this to see whether they will follow my instructions. ⁵Tell them to pick up twice as much as usual on the sixth day of each week."

⁶Then Moses and Aaron called a meeting of all the people of Israel and told them, "In the evening you will realize that it was the LORD who brought you out of the land of Egypt. ⁷In the morning you will see the glorious presence of the LORD. He has heard your complaints, which are against the LORD and not against us. ⁸The LORD will give you meat to eat in the evening and bread in the morning, for he has heard all your complaints against him. Yes, your complaints are against the LORD, not against us."

⁹Then Moses said to Aaron, "Say this to the entire community of Israel: 'Come into the LORD's presence, and hear his reply to your complaints.'" ¹⁰And as Aaron spoke to the people, they looked out toward the desert. Within the guiding cloud, they could see the awesome glory of the LORD.

¹¹And the LORD said to Moses, ¹²"I have heard the people's complaints. Now tell them, 'In the evening you will have meat to eat, and in the morning you will be filled with bread. Then you will know that I am the LORD your God.'"

¹³That evening vast numbers of quail arrived and covered the camp. The next morning the desert all around the camp

16:1a Not to be confused with the English word *sin.*   16:1b Hebrew *on the fifteenth day of the second month.* The Exodus had occurred on the fourteenth day of the first month (see 12:6).

was wet with dew. [14]When the dew disappeared later in the morning, thin flakes, white like frost, covered the ground. [15]The Israelites were puzzled when they saw it. "What is it?" they asked.

And Moses told them, "It is the food the LORD has given you. [16]The LORD says that each household should gather as much as it needs. Pick up two quarts* for each person."

[17]So the people of Israel went out and gathered this food—some getting more, and some getting less. [18]By gathering two quarts for each person, everyone had just enough. Those who gathered a lot had nothing left over, and those who gathered only a little had enough. Each family had just what it needed.

[19]Then Moses told them, "Do not keep any of it overnight." [20]But, of course, some of them didn't listen and kept some of it until morning. By then it was full of maggots and had a terrible smell. And Moses was very angry with them.

[21]The people gathered the food morning by morning, each family according to its need. And as the sun became hot, the food they had not picked up melted and disappeared. [22]On the sixth day, there was twice as much as usual on the ground—four quarts* for each person instead of two. The leaders of the people came and asked Moses why this had happened. [23]He replied, "The LORD has appointed tomorrow as a day of rest, a holy Sabbath to the LORD. On this day we will rest from our normal daily tasks. So bake or boil as much as you want today, and set aside what is left for tomorrow."

[24]The next morning the leftover food was wholesome and good, without maggots or odor. [25]Moses said, "This is your food for today, for today is a Sabbath to the LORD. There will be no food on the ground today. [26]Gather the food for six days, but the seventh day is a Sabbath. There will be no food on the ground for you on that day."

[27]Some of the people went out anyway to gather food, even though it was the Sabbath day. But there was none to be found. [28]"How long will these people refuse to obey my commands and instructions?" the LORD asked Moses. [29]"Do they not realize that I have given them the seventh day, the

Sabbath, as a day of rest? That is why I give you twice as much food on the sixth day, so there will be enough for two days. On the Sabbath day you must stay in your places. Do not pick up food from the ground on that day." [30]So the people rested on the seventh day.

[31]In time, the food became known as manna.* It was white like coriander seed, and it tasted like honey cakes.

[32]Then Moses gave them this command from the LORD: "Take two quarts of manna and keep it forever as a treasured memorial of the LORD's provision. By doing this, later generations will be able to see the bread that the LORD provided in the wilderness when he brought you out of Egypt."

[33]Moses said to Aaron, "Get a container and put two quarts of manna into it. Then store it in a sacred place* as a reminder for all future generations." [34]Aaron did this, just as the LORD had commanded Moses. He eventually placed it for safekeeping in the Ark of the Covenant.* [35]So the people of Israel ate manna for forty years until they arrived in the land of Canaan, where there were crops to eat.

[36](The container used to measure the manna was an omer, which held about two quarts.)*

CHAPTER 17
At the LORD's command, the people of Israel left the Sin* Desert and moved from place to place. Eventually they came to Rephidim, but there was no water to be found there. [2]So once more the people grumbled and complained to Moses. "Give us water to drink!" they demanded.

"Quiet!" Moses replied. "Why are you arguing with me? And why are you testing the LORD?"

[3]But tormented by thirst, they continued to complain, "Why did you ever take us out of Egypt? Why did you bring us here? We, our children, and our livestock will all die!"

[4]Then Moses pleaded with the LORD, "What should I do with these people? They are about to stone me!"

[5]The LORD said to Moses, "Take your shepherd's staff, the one you used when you struck the water of the Nile. Then call some of the leaders of Israel and walk on

---

16:16 Hebrew *1 omer* [2 liters]; also in 16:18, 32, 33.   **16:22** Hebrew *2 omers* [4 liters].   **16:31** *Manna* means "What is it?" See 16:15.
16:33 Hebrew *before the* LORD.   **16:34** Hebrew *in front of the Testimony.*   **16:36** Hebrew *An omer is one tenth of an ephah.*   **17:1** Not to be confused with the English word *sin.*

ahead of the people. [6]I will meet you by the rock at Mount Sinai.* Strike the rock, and water will come pouring out. Then the people will be able to drink." Moses did just as he was told; and as the leaders looked on, water gushed out.

[7]Moses named the place Massah—"the place of testing"—and Meribah—"the place of arguing"—because the people of Israel argued with Moses and tested the LORD by saying, "Is the LORD going to take care of us or not?"

[8]While the people of Israel were still at Rephidim, the warriors of Amalek came to fight against them. [9]Moses commanded Joshua, "Call the Israelites to arms, and fight the army of Amalek. Tomorrow, I will stand at the top of the hill with the staff of God in my hand."

[10]So Joshua did what Moses had commanded. He led his men out to fight the army of Amalek. Meanwhile Moses, Aaron, and Hur went to the top of a nearby hill. [11]As long as Moses held up the staff with his hands, the Israelites had the advantage. But whenever he lowered his hands, the Amalekites gained the upper hand. [12]Moses' arms finally became too tired to hold up the staff any longer. So Aaron and Hur found a stone for him to sit on. Then they stood on each side, holding up his hands until sunset. [13]As a result, Joshua and his troops were able to crush the army of Amalek.

[14]Then the LORD instructed Moses, "Write this down as a permanent record, and announce it to Joshua: I will blot out every trace of Amalek from under heaven." [15]Moses built an altar there and called it "The LORD Is My Banner."* [16]He said, "They have dared to raise their fist against the LORD's throne, so now* the LORD will be at war with Amalek generation after generation."

CHAPTER 18
Word soon reached Jethro, the priest of Midian and Moses' father-in-law, about all the wonderful things God had done for Moses and his people, the Israelites. He had heard about how the LORD had brought them safely out of Egypt.

[2]Some time before this, Moses had sent his wife, Zipporah, and his two sons to live with Jethro, his father-in-law. [3]The name of Moses' first son was Gershom,* for Moses had said when the boy was born, "I have been a stranger in a foreign land." [4]The name of his second son was Eliezer,* for Moses had said at his birth, "The God of my fathers was my helper; he delivered me from the sword of Pharaoh." [5]Jethro now came to visit Moses, and he brought Moses' wife and two sons with him. They arrived while Moses and the people were camped near the mountain of God. [6]Moses was told, "Jethro, your father-in-law, has come to visit you. Your wife and your two sons are with him."

[7]So Moses went out to meet his father-in-law. He bowed to him respectfully and greeted him warmly. They asked about each other's health and then went to Moses' tent to talk further. [8]Moses told his father-in-law about everything the LORD had done to rescue Israel from Pharaoh and the Egyptians. He also told him about the problems they had faced along the way and how the LORD had delivered his people from all their troubles. [9]Jethro was delighted when he heard about all that the LORD had done for Israel as he brought them out of Egypt.

[10]"Praise be to the LORD," Jethro said, "for he has saved you from the Egyptians and from Pharaoh. He has rescued Israel from the power of Egypt! [11]I know now that the LORD is greater than all other gods, because his people have escaped from the proud and cruel Egyptians."

[12]Then Jethro presented a burnt offering and gave sacrifices to God. As Jethro was doing this, Aaron and the leaders of Israel came out to meet him. They all joined him in a sacrificial meal in God's presence.

[13]The next day, Moses sat as usual to hear the people's complaints against each other. They were lined up in front of him from morning till evening.

[14]When Moses' father-in-law saw all that Moses was doing for the people, he said, "Why are you trying to do all this alone? The people have been standing here all day to get your help."

[15]Moses replied, "Well, the people come to me to seek God's guidance. [16]When an argument arises, I am the one who settles the case. I inform the people of God's decisions and teach them his laws and instructions."

17:6 Hebrew *Horeb*, another name for Sinai.   17:15 Hebrew *Yahweh Nissi*.   17:16 Or *Hands have been lifted up to the LORD's throne, and now.*   18:3 *Gershom* sounds like a Hebrew term that means "a stranger there."   18:4 *Eliezer* means "God is my helper."

[17]"This is not good!" his father-in-law exclaimed. [18]"You're going to wear yourself out—and the people, too. This job is too heavy a burden for you to handle all by yourself. [19]Now let me give you a word of advice, and may God be with you. You should continue to be the people's representative before God, bringing him their questions to be decided. [20]You should tell them God's decisions, teach them God's laws and instructions, and show them how to conduct their lives. [21]But find some capable, honest men who fear God and hate bribes. Appoint them as judges over groups of one thousand, one hundred, fifty, and ten. [22]These men can serve the people, resolving all the ordinary cases. Anything that is too important or too complicated can be brought to you. But they can take care of the smaller

matters themselves. They will help you carry the load, making the task easier for you. [23]If you follow this advice, and if God directs you to do so, then you will be able to endure the pressures, and all these people will go home in peace."

[24]Moses listened to his father-in-law's advice and followed his suggestions. [25]He chose capable men from all over Israel and made them judges over the people. They were put in charge of groups of one thousand, one hundred, fifty, and ten. [26]These men were constantly available to administer justice. They brought the hard cases to Moses, but they judged the smaller matters themselves.

[27]Soon after this, Moses said good-bye to his father-in-law, who returned to his own land.

JANUARY 25 ☐ DAY 25
EXODUS 19–20
The Ten Commandments

OVERVIEW Except for its size, Israel could scarcely be called a nation. Up to this point it was just a vast group of unorganized people. Self-government was impossible in Egypt, and as yet there are still no laws. But at Mount Sinai, in a setting designed to remove distractions and focus attention on God, the people receive their charter as God's chosen nation. After declaring their willingness to obey the commands they are about to receive, the Israelites spend two days preparing themselves to hear God. On the third day, beginning with an awe-inspiring display on Mount Sinai, God delivers the broad moral principles on which the nation's social and religious life will be based.

Chapter 19			Chapter 20	
A Promised Blessing 1 6	A Prepared People 7 15	A Powerful God 16 25	Four Commands Godward 1 11	Six Commands Humanward 12 26
The Setting			The Ten Commandments	

YOUR DAILY WALK "The Christian life is a bunch of do's and don'ts!" "The Christian life is liberty to do as I please!"

Stop! You're both wrong. To be sure, in Christ there is freedom from slavery to sin and release from the guilt of past failures. But *liberty* does not mean *license* to live as you please. Just because the Israelites were free from Egyptian slavery did not mean they were free to follow their every desire. God still wanted them to live as his chosen people, so he gave them rules for their daily conduct—not a list of do's and don'ts to spoil their fun, but a series of commands for their protection and profit.

The tablets at Sinai were given to show the need for the cross at Calvary.

Imagine what a football game would be like without rules: no boundaries, no clock, no referees, no time limit. Probably no fun! Rules are essential for the enjoyment of life.

As you read through the list of commandments today, try to think of at least one way in which each command would make your life happier or safer if you kept it unquestioningly. Is there one you need to work on today?

INSIGHT What Was the Hike up Sinai Like?
Mount Sinai is best identified with Jebel Musa, a 7,363-foot peak on the southern end of a granite mountain ridge two miles long and one mile wide. Before it stretches a plain adequate to hold Israel's camp.

CHAPTER 19

The Israelites arrived in the wilderness of Sinai exactly two months after they left Egypt.* ²After breaking camp at Rephidim, they came to the base of Mount Sinai and set up camp there.

³Then Moses climbed the mountain to appear before God. The LORD called out to him from the mountain and said, "Give these instructions to the descendants of Jacob, the people of Israel: ⁴'You have seen what I did to the Egyptians. You know how I brought you to myself and carried you on eagle's wings. ⁵Now if you will obey me and keep my covenant, you will be my own special treasure from among all the nations of the earth; for all the earth belongs to me. ⁶And you will be to me a kingdom of priests, my holy nation.' Give this message to the Israelites."

⁷Moses returned from the mountain and called together the leaders of the people and told them what the LORD had said. ⁸They all responded together, "We will certainly do everything the LORD asks of us." So Moses brought the people's answer back to the LORD.

⁹Then the LORD said to Moses, "I am going to come to you in a thick cloud so the people themselves can hear me as I speak to you. Then they will always have confidence in you."

Moses told the LORD what the people had said. ¹⁰Then the LORD told Moses, "Go down and prepare the people for my visit. Purify them today and tomorrow, and have them wash their clothing. ¹¹Be sure they are ready on the third day, for I will come down upon Mount Sinai as all the people watch. ¹²Set boundary lines that the people may not pass. Warn them, 'Be careful! Do not go up on the mountain or even touch its

boundaries. Those who do will certainly die! ¹³Any people or animals that cross the boundary must be stoned to death or shot with arrows. They must not be touched by human hands.' The people must stay away from the mountain until they hear one long blast from the ram's horn. Then they must gather at the foot of the mountain."

¹⁴So Moses went down to the people. He purified them for worship and had them wash their clothing. ¹⁵He told them, "Get ready for an important event two days from now. And until then, abstain from having sexual intercourse."

¹⁶On the morning of the third day, there was a powerful thunder and lightning storm, and a dense cloud came down upon the mountain. There was a long, loud blast from a ram's horn, and all the people trembled. ¹⁷Moses led them out from the camp to meet with God, and they stood at the foot of the mountain. ¹⁸All Mount Sinai was covered with smoke because the LORD had descended on it in the form of fire. The smoke billowed into the sky like smoke from a furnace, and the whole mountain shook with a violent earthquake. ¹⁹As the horn blast grew louder and louder, Moses spoke, and God thundered his reply for all to hear. ²⁰The LORD came down on the top of Mount Sinai and called Moses to the top of the mountain. So Moses climbed the mountain.

²¹Then the LORD told Moses, "Go back down and warn the people not to cross the boundaries. They must not come up here to see the LORD, for those who do will die. ²²Even the priests who regularly come near to the LORD must purify themselves, or I will destroy them."

²³"But, LORD, the people cannot come up on the mountain!" Moses protested. "You

---

19:1 Hebrew *in the third month . . . on the very day*, i.e., two lunar months to the day after leaving Egypt. This day of the Hebrew lunar calendar occurs in late May or early June; compare note on 13:4.

already told them not to. You told me to set boundaries around the mountain and to declare it off limits."

²⁴But the LORD said, "Go down anyway and bring Aaron back with you. In the meantime, do not let the priests or the people cross the boundaries to come up here. If they do, I will punish them."

²⁵So Moses went down to the people and told them what the LORD had said.

CHAPTER 20

Then God instructed the people as follows:

²"I am the LORD your God, who rescued you from slavery in Egypt.

³"Do not worship any other gods besides me.

⁴"Do not make idols of any kind, whether in the shape of birds or animals or fish. ⁵You must never worship or bow down to them, for I, the LORD your God, am a jealous God who will not share your affection with any other god! I do not leave unpunished the sins of those who hate me, but I punish the children for the sins of their parents to the third and fourth generations. ⁶But I lavish my love on those who love me and obey my commands, even for a thousand generations.

⁷"Do not misuse the name of the LORD your God. The LORD will not let you go unpunished if you misuse his name.

⁸"Remember to observe the Sabbath day by keeping it holy. ⁹Six days a week are set apart for your daily duties and regular work, ¹⁰but the seventh day is a day of rest dedicated to the LORD your God. On that day no one in your household may do any kind of work. This includes you, your sons and daughters, your male and female servants, your livestock, and any foreigners living among you. ¹¹For in six days the LORD made the heavens, the earth, the sea, and everything in them; then he rested on the seventh

day. That is why the LORD blessed the Sabbath day and set it apart as holy.

¹²"Honor your father and mother. Then you will live a long, full life in the land the LORD your God will give you.

¹³"Do not murder.

¹⁴"Do not commit adultery.

¹⁵"Do not steal.

¹⁶"Do not testify falsely against your neighbor.

¹⁷"Do not covet your neighbor's house. Do not covet your neighbor's wife, male or female servant, ox or donkey, or anything else your neighbor owns."

¹⁸When the people heard the thunder and the loud blast of the horn, and when they saw the lightning and the smoke billowing from the mountain, they stood at a distance, trembling with fear.

¹⁹And they said to Moses, "You tell us what God says, and we will listen. But don't let God speak directly to us. If he does, we will die!"

²⁰"Don't be afraid," Moses said, "for God has come in this way to show you his awesome power. From now on, let your fear of him keep you from sinning!"

²¹As the people stood in the distance, Moses entered into the deep darkness where God was.

²²And the LORD said to Moses, "Say this to the people of Israel: You are witnesses that I have spoken to you from heaven. ²³Remember, you must not make or worship idols of silver or gold.

²⁴"The altars you make for me must be simple altars of earth. Offer on such altars your sacrifices to me—your burnt offerings and peace offerings, your sheep and goats and your cattle. Build altars in the places where I remind you who I am, and I will come and bless you there. ²⁵If you build altars from stone, use only uncut stones. Do not chip or shape the stones with a tool, for that would make them unfit for holy use. ²⁶And you may not approach my altar by steps. If you do, someone might look up under the skirts of your clothing and see your nakedness.

JANUARY 26 □ DAY 26
EXODUS 21–24
Civil and Ceremonial Laws

OVERVIEW The law given by God to Israel at Sinai falls into three categories: moral laws (Exodus 20), civil and social laws (Exodus 21–23), and religious laws (Exodus 24—Leviticus). Today's reading contains the laws that comprise the Book of the Covenant (24:7) given along with the Ten Commandments. Following a formal ceremony ratifying the covenant, Moses is called again by God to Mount Sinai to receive further revelation.

Chapters 21–22	Chapter 23	Chapter 24
Relationships under the Law	Religious Observances under the Law	Ratification of the Law
Civil Laws	Ceremonial Laws	Compulsory Laws

YOUR DAILY WALK "If I've told you once, I've told you *a hundred times . . . !*"

Some things bear repeating, and even then they don't always sink in. God's word to Israel in the first two commandments could hardly have been clearer: No other gods . . . no idols. Yet he would later repeat those same warnings again and again. He wanted to impress upon his people the seriousness of his lordship and to make certain they understood the necessity for exclusive devotion to the God of Israel.

Where law ends, tyranny begins.

God knew full well the principle that you eventually worship what you serve. Therefore, whatever or whoever commands your attention becomes your god. Recognizing that fact can help you guard against idolatry. Here are two questions that may point to the real "lord" of your life:

1. What do you think about when your mind is in neutral?
2. What do you do during your idle moments?

Review your own loyalties, and then fill in the blank: "An objective observer of my life over the past week would conclude that _____ is my god." Is there something that needs to change so that you, like Israel, have "no other gods" besides the Lord?

INSIGHT A Forbidden Recipe

The prohibition against cooking a young goat in its mother's milk (23:19) made little sense to modern scholars until archaeological discoveries revealed that the practice was current in Canaan as a pagan magic spell connected with fertility rites.

CHAPTER 21

"Here are some other instructions you must present to Israel:

²"If you buy a Hebrew slave, he is to serve for only six years. Set him free in the seventh year, and he will owe you nothing for his freedom. ³If he was single when he became your slave and then married afterward, only he will go free in the seventh year. But if he was married before he became a slave, then his wife will be freed with him.

21:6 Or *before the judges.*

⁴"If his master gave him a wife while he was a slave, and they had sons or daughters, then the man will be free in the seventh year, but his wife and children will still belong to his master. ⁵But the slave may plainly declare, 'I love my master, my wife, and my children. I would rather not go free.' ⁶If he does this, his master must present him before God.* Then his master must take him to the door and publicly pierce his ear with an awl. After

that, the slave will belong to his master forever.

7"When a man sells his daughter as a slave, she will not be freed at the end of six years as the men are. 8If she does not please the man who bought her, he may allow her to be bought back again. But he is not allowed to sell her to foreigners, since he is the one who broke the contract with her. 9And if the slave girl's owner arranges for her to marry his son, he may no longer treat her as a slave girl, but he must treat her as his daughter. 10If he himself marries her and then takes another wife, he may not reduce her food or clothing or fail to sleep with her as his wife. 11If he fails in any of these three ways, she may leave as a free woman without making any payment.

12"Anyone who hits a person hard enough to cause death must be put to death. 13But if it is an accident and God allows it to happen, I will appoint a place where the slayer can run for safety. 14However, if someone deliberately attacks and kills another person, then the slayer must be dragged even from my altar and put to death.

15"Anyone who strikes father or mother must be put to death.

16"Kidnappers must be killed, whether they are caught in possession of their victims or have already sold them as slaves.

17"Anyone who curses father or mother must be put to death.

18"Now suppose two people quarrel, and one hits the other with a stone or fist, causing injury but not death. 19If the injured person is later able to walk again, even with a crutch, the assailant will be innocent. Nonetheless, the assailant must pay for time lost because of the injury and must pay for the medical expenses.

20"If a male or female slave is beaten and dies, the owner must be punished. 21If the slave recovers after a couple of days, however, then the owner should not be punished, since the slave is the owner's property.

22"Now suppose two people are fighting, and in the process, they hurt a pregnant woman so her child is born prematurely. If no further harm results, then the person responsible must pay damages in the amount the woman's husband demands and the judges approve. 23But if any harm

results, then the offender must be punished according to the injury. If the result is death, the offender must be executed. 24If an eye is injured, injure the eye of the person who did it. If a tooth gets knocked out, knock out the tooth of the person who did it. Similarly, the payment must be hand for hand, foot for foot, 25burn for burn, wound for wound, bruise for bruise.

26"If an owner hits a male or female slave in the eye and the eye is blinded, then the slave may go free because of the eye. 27And if an owner knocks out the tooth of a male or female slave, the slave should be released in payment for the tooth.

28"If a bull gores a man or woman to death, the bull must be stoned, and its flesh may not be eaten. In such a case, however, the owner will not be held liable. 29Suppose, on the other hand, that the owner knew the bull had gored people in the past, yet the bull was not kept under control. If this is true and if the bull kills someone, it must be stoned, and the owner must also be killed. 30However, the dead person's relatives may accept payment from the owner of the bull to compensate for the loss of life. The owner will have to pay whatever is demanded.

31"The same principle applies if the bull gores a boy or a girl. 32But if the bull gores a slave, either male or female, the slave's owner is to be given thirty silver coins* in payment, and the bull must be stoned.

33"Suppose someone digs or uncovers a well and fails to cover it, and then an ox or a donkey falls into it. 34The owner of the well must pay in full for the dead animal but then gets to keep it.

35"If someone's bull injures a neighbor's bull and the injured bull dies, then the two owners must sell the live bull and divide the money between them. Each will also own half of the dead bull. 36But if the bull was known from past experience to gore, yet its owner failed to keep it under control, the money will not be divided. The owner of the living bull must pay in full for the dead bull but then gets to keep it.

CHAPTER 22

"A fine must be paid by anyone who steals an ox or sheep and then kills or sells it. For oxen the fine is five oxen for each one

21:32 Hebrew *30 shekels of silver*, about 12 ounces or 342 grams in weight.

stolen. For sheep the fine is four sheep for each one stolen.

2"If a thief is caught in the act of breaking into a house and is killed in the process, the person who killed the thief is not guilty. 3But if it happens in daylight, the one who killed the thief is guilty of murder.

"A thief who is caught must pay in full for everything that was stolen. If payment is not made, the thief must be sold as a slave to pay the debt. 4If someone steals an ox or a donkey or a sheep and it is recovered alive, then the thief must pay double the value.

5"If an animal is grazing in a field or vineyard and the owner lets it stray into someone else's field to graze, then the animal's owner must pay damages in the form of high-quality grain or grapes.

6"If a fire gets out of control and goes into another person's field, destroying the sheaves or the standing grain, then the one who started the fire must pay for the lost crops.

7"Suppose someone entrusts money or goods to a neighbor, and they are stolen from the neighbor's house. If the thief is found, the fine is double the value of what was stolen. 8But if the thief is not found, God* will determine whether or not it was the neighbor who stole the property.

9"Suppose there is a dispute between two people as to who owns a particular ox, donkey, sheep, article of clothing, or anything else. Both parties must come before God* for a decision, and the person whom God declares* guilty must pay double to the other.

10"Now suppose someone asks a neighbor to care for a donkey, ox, sheep, or any other animal, but it dies or is injured or gets away, and there is no eyewitness to report just what happened. 11The neighbor must then take an oath of innocence in the presence of the LORD. The owner must accept the neighbor's word, and no payment will be required. 12But if the animal or property was stolen, payment must be made to the owner. 13If it was attacked by a wild animal, the carcass must be shown as evidence, and no payment will be required.

14"If someone borrows an animal from a neighbor and it is injured or killed, and if the owner was not there at the time, the person who borrowed it must pay for it.

15But if the owner is there, no payment is required. And no payment is required if the animal was rented because this loss was covered by the rental fee.

16"If a man seduces a virgin who is not engaged to anyone and sleeps with her, he must pay the customary dowry and accept her as his wife. 17But if her father refuses to let her marry him, the man must still pay the money for her dowry.

18"A sorceress must not be allowed to live.

19"Anyone who has sexual relations with an animal must be executed.

20"Anyone who sacrifices to any god other than the LORD must be destroyed.

21"Do not oppress foreigners in any way. Remember, you yourselves were once foreigners in the land of Egypt.

22"Do not exploit widows or orphans. 23If you do and they cry out to me, then I will surely help them. 24My anger will blaze forth against you, and I will kill you with the sword. Your wives will become widows, and your children will become fatherless.

25"If you lend money to a fellow Hebrew in need, do not be like a money lender, charging interest. 26If you take your neighbor's cloak as a pledge of repayment, you must return it by nightfall. 27Your neighbor will need it to stay warm during the night. If you do not return it and your neighbor cries out to me for help, then I will hear, for I am very merciful.

28"Do not blaspheme God* or curse anyone who rules over you.

29"Do not hold anything back when you give me the tithe of your crops and your wine.

"You must make the necessary payment for redemption of your firstborn sons.

30"You must also give me the firstborn of your cattle and sheep. Leave the newborn animal with its mother for seven days; then give it to me on the eighth day.

31"You are my own holy people. Therefore, do not eat any animal that has been attacked and killed by a wild animal. Throw its carcass out for the dogs to eat.

CHAPTER 23

"Do not pass along false reports. Do not cooperate with evil people by telling lies on the witness stand.

22:8 Or *the judges.*   22:9a Or *before the judges.*   22:9b Or *whom the judges declare.*   22:28 Or *Do not revile your judges.*

²"Do not join a crowd that intends to do evil. When you are on the witness stand, do not be swayed in your testimony by the opinion of the majority. ³And do not slant your testimony in favor of a person just because that person is poor.

⁴"If you come upon your enemy's ox or donkey that has strayed away, take it back to its owner. ⁵If you see the donkey of someone who hates you struggling beneath a heavy load, do not walk by. Instead, stop and offer to help.

⁶"Do not twist justice against people simply because they are poor.

⁷"Keep far away from falsely charging anyone with evil. Never put an innocent or honest person to death. I will not allow anyone guilty of this to go free.

⁸"Take no bribes, for a bribe makes you ignore something that you clearly see. A bribe always hurts the cause of the person who is in the right.

⁹"Do not oppress the foreigners living among you. You know what it is like to be a foreigner. Remember your own experience in the land of Egypt.

¹⁰"Plant and harvest your crops for six years, ¹¹but let the land rest and lie fallow during the seventh year. Then let the poor among you harvest any volunteer crop that may come up. Leave the rest for the animals to eat. The same applies to your vineyards and olive groves.

¹²"Work for six days, and rest on the seventh. This will give your ox and your donkey a chance to rest. It will also allow the people of your household, including your slaves and visitors, to be refreshed.

¹³"Be sure to obey all my instructions. And remember, never pray to or swear by any other gods. Do not even mention their names.

¹⁴"Each year you must celebrate three festivals in my honor. ¹⁵The first is the Festival of Unleavened Bread. For seven days you are to eat bread made without yeast, just as I commanded you before. This festival will be an annual event at the appointed time in early spring,* for that is the anniversary of your exodus from Egypt. Everyone must bring me a sacrifice at that time. ¹⁶You must also celebrate the Festival of Harvest,* when you bring me the first crops of your harvest. Finally, you are to celebrate the Festival of the Final Harvest* at the end of the harvest season. ¹⁷At these three times each year, every man in Israel must appear before the Sovereign LORD.

¹⁸"Sacrificial blood must never be offered together with bread that has yeast in it. And no sacrificial fat may be left unoffered until the next morning.

¹⁹"As you harvest each of your crops, bring me a choice sample of the first day's harvest. It must be offered to the LORD your God.

"You must not cook a young goat in its mother's milk.

²⁰"See, I am sending my angel before you to lead you safely to the land I have prepared for you. ²¹Pay attention to him, and obey all of his instructions. Do not rebel against him, for he will not forgive your sins. He is my representative—he bears my name. ²²But if you are careful to obey him, following all my instructions, then I will be an enemy to your enemies, and I will oppose those who oppose you. ²³For my angel will go before you and bring you into the land of the Amorites, Hittites, Perizzites, Canaanites, Hivites, and Jebusites, so you may live there. And I will destroy them. ²⁴Do not worship the gods of these other nations or serve them in any way, and never follow their evil example. Instead, you must utterly conquer them and break down their shameful idols.

²⁵"You must serve only the LORD your God. If you do, I will bless you with food and water, and I will keep you healthy. ²⁶There will be no miscarriages or infertility among your people, and I will give you long, full lives.

²⁷"I will send my terror upon all the people whose lands you invade, and they will panic before you. ²⁸I will send hornets ahead of you to drive out the Hivites, Canaanites, and Hittites. ²⁹But I will not do this all in one year because the land would become a wilderness, and the wild animals would become too many to control. ³⁰I will drive them out a little at a time until your population has increased enough to fill the land. ³¹And I will fix your boundaries from the Red Sea to the Mediterranean Sea,* and from the southern deserts to the Euphrates River.* I will help you defeat the people

23:15 Hebrew *in the month of Abib.* This month of the Hebrew lunar calendar usually occurs in March and April.   **23:16a** Or *Festival of Weeks.*   **23:16b** This was later called the Festival of Shelters; see Lev 23:33-36.   **23:31a** Hebrew *from the sea of reeds to the sea of the Philistines.*   **23:31b** Hebrew *the river.*

now living in the land, and you will drive them out ahead of you.

[32]"Make no treaties with them and have nothing to do with their gods. [33]Do not even let them live among you! If you do, they will infect you with their sin of idol worship, and that would be disastrous for you."

CHAPTER 24

Then the LORD instructed Moses: "Come up here to me, and bring along Aaron, Nadab, Abihu, and seventy of Israel's leaders. All of them must worship at a distance. [2]You alone, Moses, are allowed to come near to the LORD. The others must not come too close. And remember, none of the other people are allowed to climb on the mountain at all."

[3]When Moses had announced to the people all the teachings and regulations the LORD had given him, they answered in unison, "We will do everything the LORD has told us to do."

[4]Then Moses carefully wrote down all the LORD's instructions. Early the next morning he built an altar at the foot of the mountain. He also set up twelve pillars around the altar, one for each of the twelve tribes of Israel. [5]Then he sent some of the young men to sacrifice young bulls as burnt offerings and peace offerings to the LORD. [6]Moses took half the blood from these animals and drew it off into basins. The other half he splashed against the altar. [7]Then he took the Book of the Covenant and read it to the people. They all responded again, "We will do everything the LORD has commanded. We will obey."

[8]Then Moses sprinkled the blood from the basins over the people and said, "This blood confirms the covenant the LORD has made with you in giving you these laws."

[9]Then Moses, Aaron, Nadab, Abihu, and seventy of the leaders of Israel went up the mountain. [10]There they saw the God of Israel. Under his feet there seemed to be a pavement of brilliant sapphire, as clear as the heavens. [11]And though Israel's leaders saw God, he did not destroy them. In fact, they shared a meal together in God's presence!

[12]And the LORD said to Moses, "Come up to me on the mountain. Stay there while I give you the tablets of stone that I have inscribed with my instructions and commands. Then you will teach the people from them." [13]So Moses and his assistant Joshua climbed up the mountain of God.

[14]Moses told the other leaders, "Stay here and wait for us until we come back. If there are any problems while I am gone, consult with Aaron and Hur, who are here with you."

[15]Then Moses went up the mountain, and the cloud covered it. [16]And the glorious presence of the LORD rested upon Mount Sinai, and the cloud covered it for six days. On the seventh day the LORD called to Moses from the cloud. [17]The Israelites at the foot of the mountain saw an awesome sight. The awesome glory of the LORD on the mountaintop looked like a devouring fire. [18]Then Moses disappeared into the cloud as he climbed higher up the mountain. He stayed on the mountain forty days and forty nights.

JANUARY 27 ☐ DAY 27
EXODUS 25–27
Design of the Tabernacle

 OVERVIEW During Moses' stay on the mountain, God reveals his detailed plans for the Tabernacle in which he will dwell and receive his people's worship. No item is overlooked in God's design of this portable tent of worship. Everything is to be done "according to the design you were shown on the mountain" (26:30). The place of God's abode with Israel will be the central structure in the camp and the focus of the nation's attention and activities.

Chapter 25	Chapter 26	Chapter 27
Tabernacle Interior	Tabernacle Structure	Tabernacle Exterior
Items of Worship	Place of Worship	

YOUR DAILY WALK How big is *your* God?

God is neither shut up nor shut out of any place.

After you have studied the Tabernacle in detail, keep in mind this was a portable building, capable of being dismantled and carried about as Israel journeyed. Though God's presence uniquely inhabited the Tabernacle, the fact that it could be disassembled for travel served to remind the Israelites that their God could not be confined to four walls! He was with them in the fire and cloud; he could divide great seas and drown mighty armies; he could provide water from rocks and manna from the morning dew. Contrast this with the pagan gods of neighboring nations—powerless idols that had to be carried on their worshipers' shoulders (Isaiah 46:5-7). Israel's priests carried God's temporary *house* on their shoulders, but Israel's God carried *them!*

If at times you find yourself wishing your God were a little more flexible, yielding more to your own desires and expectations, consider this fact: If God were small enough for you to control, he would be too small to help you in time of need.

If you can, pay a visit to your church sometime today, and in the quiet, worshipful atmosphere of the silent sanctuary, spend a few minutes praising the God you serve—a God no building can contain!

INSIGHT How Would You Like to Hang These Drapes?

The Jewish historian Josephus explained that the veil that separated the Holy Place from the Most Holy Place was *four inches thick!* It was so strong that it could not be torn apart by horses tied to it, pulling in opposite directions.

CHAPTER 25

The LORD said to Moses, [2]"Tell the people of Israel that everyone who wants to may bring me an offering. [3]Here is a list of items you may accept on my behalf: gold, silver, and bronze; [4]blue, purple, and scarlet yarn; fine linen; goat hair for cloth; [5]tanned ram skins and fine goatskin leather; acacia wood; [6]olive oil for the lamps; spices for the anointing oil and the fragrant incense; [7]onyx stones, and other stones to be set in the ephod and the chestpiece.

[8]"I want the people of Israel to build me a sacred residence where I can live among them. [9]You must make this Tabernacle and its furnishings exactly according to the plans I will show you.

[10]"Make an Ark of acacia wood—a sacred chest 3¾ feet long, 2¼ feet wide, and 2¼ feet high.* [11]Overlay it inside and outside with pure gold, and put a molding of gold all around it. [12]Cast four rings of gold

for it, and attach them to its four feet, two rings on each side. [13]Make poles from acacia wood, and overlay them with gold. [14]Fit the poles into the rings at the sides of the Ark to carry it. [15]These carrying poles must never be taken from the rings; they are to be left there permanently. [16]When the Ark is finished, place inside it the stone tablets inscribed with the terms of the covenant,* which I will give to you.

[17]"Then make the Ark's cover—the place of atonement—out of pure gold. It must be 3¾ feet long and 2¼ feet wide. [18]Then use hammered gold to make two cherubim, and place them at the two ends of the atonement cover. [19]Attach the cherubim to each end of the atonement cover, making it all one piece. [20]The cherubim will face each other, looking down on the atonement cover with their wings spread out above it. [21]Place inside the Ark the stone tablets inscribed with the terms of the covenant,

25:10 Hebrew 2½ *cubits* [1.1 meters] *long,* 1½ *cubits* [0.7 meters] *wide, and* 1½ *cubits high.* In this chapter, the distance measures are calculated from the Hebrew cubit at a ratio of 18 inches or 45 centimeters per cubit.   **25:16** Hebrew *place inside it the Testimony;* also in 25:21.

which I will give to you. Then put the atonement cover on top of the Ark. [22]I will meet with you there and talk to you from above the atonement cover between the gold cherubim that hover over the Ark of the Covenant.* From there I will give you my commands for the people of Israel.

[23]"Then make a table of acacia wood, 3 feet long, 1½ feet wide, and 2¼ feet high. [24]Overlay it with pure gold and run a molding of gold around it. [25]Put a rim about three inches* wide around the top edge, and put a gold molding all around the rim. [26]Make four gold rings, and put the rings at the four corners by the four legs, [27]close to the rim around the top. These rings will support the poles used to carry the table. [28]Make these poles from acacia wood and overlay them with gold. [29]And make gold plates and dishes, as well as pitchers and bowls to be used in pouring out drink offerings. [30]You must always keep the special Bread of the Presence on the table before me.

[31]"Make a lampstand of pure, hammered gold. The entire lampstand and its decorations will be one piece—the base, center stem, lamp cups, buds, and blossoms. [32]It will have six branches, three branches going out from each side of the center stem. [33]Each of the six branches will hold a cup shaped like an almond blossom, complete with buds and petals. [34]The center stem of the lampstand will be decorated with four almond blossoms, complete with buds and petals. [35]One blossom will be set beneath each pair of branches where they extend from the center stem. [36]The decorations and branches must all be one piece with the stem, and they must be hammered from pure gold. [37]Then make the seven lamps for the lampstand, and set them so they reflect their light forward. [38]The lamp snuffers and trays must also be made of pure gold. [39]You will need seventy-five pounds* of pure gold for the lampstand and its accessories.

[40]"Be sure that you make everything according to the pattern I have shown you here on the mountain.

CHAPTER 26

"Make the Tabernacle from ten sheets of fine linen. These sheets are to be decorated with blue, purple, and scarlet yarn, with figures of cherubim skillfully embroidered into them. [2]Each sheet must be forty-two feet long and six feet wide.* All ten sheets must be exactly the same size. [3]Join five of these sheets together into one set; then join the other five sheets into a second set. [4]Put loops of blue yarn along the edge of the last sheet in each set. [5]The fifty loops along the edge of one set are to match the fifty loops along the edge of the other. [6]Then make fifty gold clasps to fasten the loops of the two sets of sheets together, making the Tabernacle a single unit.

[7]"Make heavy sheets of cloth from goat hair to cover the Tabernacle. There must be eleven of these sheets, [8]each forty-five feet long and six feet wide. All eleven of these sheets must be exactly the same size. [9]Join five of these together into one set, and join the other six into a second set. The sixth sheet of the second set is to be doubled over at the entrance of the sacred tent. [10]Put fifty loops along the edge of the last sheet in each set, [11]and fasten them together with fifty bronze clasps. In this way, the two sets will become a single unit. [12]An extra half sheet of this roof covering will be left to hang over the back of the Tabernacle, [13]and the covering will hang down an extra eighteen inches on each side. [14]On top of these coverings place a layer of tanned ram skins, and over them put a layer of fine goatskin leather. This will complete the roof covering.

[15]"The framework of the Tabernacle will consist of frames made of acacia wood. [16]Each frame must be 15 feet high and 2¼ feet wide. [17]There will be two pegs on each frame so they can be joined to the next frame. All the frames must be made this way. [18]Twenty of these frames will support the south side of the Tabernacle. [19]They will fit into forty silver bases—two bases under each frame. [20]On the north side there will also be twenty of these frames, [21]with their forty silver bases, two bases for each frame. [22]On the west side there will be six frames, [23]along with an extra frame at each corner. [24]These corner frames will be connected at the bottom and firmly attached at the top with a single ring, forming a single unit. Both of these corner frames will be made the same way. [25]So there will be eight frames on that end of the Tabernacle, supported by sixteen silver bases—two bases under each frame.

25:22 Or *Ark of the Testimony.*   **25:25** Hebrew *a handbreadth* [8 centimeters].   **25:39** Hebrew *1 talent* [34 kilograms].   **26:2** Hebrew *28 cubits* [12.6 meters] *long and 4 cubits* [1.8 meters] *wide.* In this chapter, the distance measures are calculated from the Hebrew cubit at a ratio of 18 inches or 45 centimeters per cubit.

26"Make crossbars of acacia wood to run across the frames, five crossbars for the north side of the Tabernacle 27and five for the south side. Also make five crossbars for the rear of the Tabernacle, which will face westward. 28The middle crossbar, halfway up the frames, will run all the way from one end of the Tabernacle to the other. 29Overlay the frames with gold and make gold rings to support the crossbars. Overlay the crossbars with gold as well.

30"Set up this Tabernacle according to the design you were shown on the mountain.

31"Across the inside of the Tabernacle hang a special curtain made of fine linen, with cherubim skillfully embroidered into the cloth using blue, purple, and scarlet yarn. 32Hang this inner curtain on gold hooks set into four posts made from acacia wood and overlaid with gold. The posts will fit into silver bases. 33When the inner curtain is in place, put the Ark of the Covenant* behind it. This curtain will separate the Holy Place from the Most Holy Place.

34"Then put the Ark's cover—the place of atonement—on top of the Ark of the Covenant inside the Most Holy Place. 35Place the table and lampstand across the room from each other outside the inner curtain. The lampstand must be placed on the south side, and the table must be set toward the north.

36"Make another curtain from fine linen for the entrance of the sacred tent, and embroider exquisite designs into it, using blue, purple, and scarlet yarn. 37Hang this curtain on gold hooks set into five posts made from acacia wood and overlaid with gold. The posts will fit into five bronze bases.

C H A P T E R   2 7
"Using acacia wood, make a square altar 7½ feet wide, 7½ feet long, and 4½ feet high.* 2Make a horn at each of the four corners of the altar so the horns and altar are all one piece. Overlay the altar and its horns with bronze. 3The ash buckets, shovels, basins, meat hooks, and firepans will all be made of bronze. 4Make a bronze grating, with a metal ring at each corner. 5Fit the grating halfway down into the firebox, resting it on the ledge built there. 6For moving the altar, make poles from acacia wood, and overlay them with bronze. 7To carry it,

put the poles into the rings at two sides of the altar. 8The altar must be hollow, made from planks. Be careful to build it just as you were shown on the mountain.

9"Then make a courtyard for the Tabernacle, enclosed with curtains made from fine linen. On the south side the curtains will stretch for 150 feet. 10They will be held up by twenty bronze posts that fit into twenty bronze bases. The curtains will be held up with silver hooks attached to the silver rods that are attached to the posts. 11It will be the same on the north side of the courtyard—150 feet of curtains held up by twenty posts fitted into bronze bases, with silver hooks and rods. 12The curtains on the west end of the courtyard will be 75 feet long, supported by ten posts set into ten bases. 13The east end will also be 75 feet long. 14The courtyard entrance will be on the east end, flanked by two curtains. The curtain on the right side will be 22½ feet long, supported by three posts set into three bases. 15The curtain on the left side will also be 22½ feet long, supported by three posts set into three bases.

16"For the entrance to the courtyard, make a curtain that is 30 feet long. Fashion it from fine linen, and decorate it with beautiful embroidery in blue, purple, and scarlet yarn. It will be attached to four posts that fit into four bases. 17All the posts around the courtyard must be connected by silver rods, using silver hooks. The posts are to be set in solid bronze bases. 18So the entire courtyard will be 150 feet long and 75 feet wide, with curtain walls 7½ feet high, made from fine linen. The bases supporting its walls will be made of bronze.

19"All the articles used in the work of the Tabernacle, including all the tent pegs used to support the Tabernacle and the courtyard curtains, must be made of bronze.

20"Tell the people of Israel to bring you pure olive oil for the lampstand, so it can be kept burning continually. 21The lampstand will be placed outside the inner curtain of the Most Holy Place in the Tabernacle.* Aaron and his sons will keep the lamps burning in the LORD's presence day and night. This is a permanent law for the people of Israel, and it must be kept by all future generations.

26:33 Or Ark of the Testimony; also in 26:34.   27:1 Hebrew 5 cubits [2.3 meters] wide, 5 cubits long, and 3 cubits [1.4 meters] high. In this chapter, the distance measures are calculated from the Hebrew cubit at a ratio of 18 inches or 45 centimeters per cubit. 27:21 Hebrew in the Tent of Meeting, outside of the inner curtain, in front of the Testimony.

JANUARY 28 ☐ DAY 28
Father Knows Best

LOOK BACK On center stage for the entire week of reading from the book of Exodus has been Moses, the humble servant-leader of the Hebrew people. Whether calling down plagues upon hard-hearted Pharaoh, leading God's people through the Red Sea and the wilderness, or receiving God's law at Mount Sinai, Moses demonstrates the attitudes of humility and authority. Entrusted with a high visibility role, Moses never flaunts his position or exploits his countrymen for personal gain. Rather, he leads them in the fear of the Lord. That's not to say Moses' patience isn't severely tried by God's stiff-necked people. (You have already read about six encounters between Moses and his rebellious countrymen, and four more confrontations lie just ahead.) But Moses' leadership is consistently marked by 20/20 vision—Exodus 20:20, that is: "Don't be afraid, . . . for God has come in this way to show you his awesome power. From now on, let your fear of him keep you from sinning!"

More than 35,000 laws have been written trying to improve upon what God said in the Ten Commandments.

LOOK UP Which is the longest word in the English language? The one that follows the announcement "And now a word from our sponsor."

Words communicate thoughts. If you want to know what someone is thinking, listen carefully to what he or she is saying. And if you want to know the most important thought on a person's heart, ask that person to express his or her thoughts in just ten words. Try it yourself! In the space provided, take ten words (or less) to capture the most important thought on your mind right now.

_____

_____

The Ten Commandments that Moses received on Mount Sinai contain more than ten words. But in them you will find ten thoughts that are near and dear to the heart of God. Think back over what you read this past week (or turn to Exodus 20 if you need a quick review), and summarize what God said about each of the following:

- Other gods (20:3)
- Idols (20:4-6)
- Cursing (20:7)
- Sabbath (20:8-11)
- Parents (20:12)
- Murder (20:13)
- Adultery (20:14)
- Stealing (20:15)
- Lying (20:16)
- Coveting (20:17)

And lest you conclude that the Ten Commandments are only found in the Old Testament, notice what Jesus said to the rich young ruler in Mark 10:19!

LOOK AHEAD It might be easy to conclude that God as described in the pages of the Old Testament is a God of do's and don'ts. After all, look at all the rules and regulations that the people of God were required to observe. But God often goes beyond telling his people *what* to do and tells them *why* they should do it. (Watch for the telltale words *for, because,* or *that,* which signal that God is about to include the *why* along with the *what.*) He wants his people to learn that "Father knows best."

As you continue your reading in the books of Exodus and Leviticus, don't get lost in the maze of statutes and ordinances. Remember to use Exodus 20:20 vision as you read. And if you're curious to know which of the hundreds of commandments is nearest and dearest to the heart of God, take a look at Matthew 22:34-40 and Mark 12:28-34!

JANUARY 29 □ DAY 29
EXODUS 28–31
Special Instructions for Priests

OVERVIEW No center of worship is complete without people to minister in it and utensils to use in the worship services. Exodus 28–31 describes the priests, Israel's representatives before God, who are chosen to lead the worship in the Tabernacle. Everything about them is special, from the clothing they wear to the elaborate sacrifices needed to prepare them for ministry, as well as the supplies and furnishings they use (such as incense, perfumes, oil, the altar, and the washbasin) in the Tabernacle worship. Even the designers and construction workers for the Tabernacle are handpicked by God.

Chapter 28	Chapter 29	Chapter 30	Chapter 31
Clothing for the Priests	Consecration of the Priests	Commands for the Priests	Craftsmen for the Tabernacle
Priestly Ministry			Priestly Carpenters

YOUR DAILY WALK Preparing the priest for service in the Tabernacle was no small chore (Exodus 29). The most curious part of the ceremony involved killing a ram and applying the blood to the tip of the priest's right ear, the thumb of his right hand, and the big toe of his right foot.

God deserves to be served with all the energy of which we are capable.

The blood was a picture of cleansing. Before the priest could minister before the Lord, he had to be clean from the sin that polluted him. Then he needed to be dedicated to the Lord from the top of his head to the bottom of his feet. Every part of him, from his ear (which hearkens to God's law) to his hand (which does God's will) to his foot (which follows in God's steps) had to be surrendered to the will of God.

Does God have that kind of control over your whole life? If not, starting with your head, give each part of your body to him in a prayer of dedication: "Lord, take my eyes; help me to look only at those things that please you. Take my ears; help me to listen only to those things that build up, not those that tear down . . ." Then you, like Israel's priest, will be ready to do his will—from head to toe!

INSIGHT Urim, You Win; and Thummim, You Lose
The Urim and Thummim were used to determine the will of God. Scholars have been unable to determine exactly what they were or how they were used. One theory is that the Urim and Thummim were two flat stones kept in the breastplate of the high priest. Each had one dark side and one light. They were tossed into the air and allowed to fall to the ground. Two dark sides showing meant yes, two light sides meant no, and one of each meant no reply.

CHAPTER 28

"Your brother, Aaron, and his sons, Nadab, Abihu, Eleazar, and Ithamar, will be set apart from the common people. They will be my priests and will minister to me. ²Make special clothing for Aaron to show his separation to God—beautiful garments that will lend dignity to his work. ³Instruct all those who have special skills as tailors to make the garments that will set Aaron apart from everyone else, so he may serve me as a priest. ⁴They are to make a chestpiece, an ephod, a robe, an embroidered tunic, a turban, and a sash. They will also make special garments for Aaron's sons to wear when they serve as priests before me. ⁵These items must be made of fine linen cloth and embroidered with gold thread and blue, purple, and scarlet yarn.

⁶"The ephod must be made of fine linen

cloth and skillfully embroidered with gold thread and blue, purple, and scarlet yarn. [7]It will consist of two pieces, front and back, joined at the shoulders with two shoulder-pieces. [8]And the sash will be made of the same materials: fine linen cloth embroidered with gold thread and blue, purple, and scarlet yarn. [9]Take two onyx stones and engrave on them the names of the tribes of Israel. [10]Six names will be on each stone, naming all the tribes in the order of their ancestors' births. [11]Engrave these names in the same way a gemcutter engraves a seal. Mount the stones in gold settings. [12]Fasten the two stones on the shoulder-pieces of the ephod as memorial stones for the people of Israel. Aaron will carry these names before the LORD as a constant reminder. [13]The settings are to be made of gold filigree, [14]and two cords made of pure gold will be attached to the settings on the shoulders of the ephod.

[15]"Then, with the most careful workmanship, make a chestpiece that will be used to determine God's will. Use the same materials as you did for the ephod: fine linen cloth embroidered with gold thread and blue, purple, and scarlet yarn. [16]This chestpiece will be made of two folds of cloth, forming a pouch nine inches* square. [17]Four rows of gemstones* will be attached to it. The first row will contain a red carnelian, a chrysolite, and an emerald. [18]The second row will contain a turquoise, a sapphire, and a white moonstone. [19]The third row will contain a jacinth, an agate, and an amethyst. [20]The fourth row will contain a beryl, an onyx, and a jasper. All these stones will be set in gold. [21]Each stone will represent one of the tribes of Israel, and the name of that tribe will be engraved on it as though it were a seal.

[22]"To attach the chestpiece to the ephod, make braided cords of pure gold. [23]Then make two gold rings and attach them to the top corners of the chestpiece. [24]The two gold cords will go through the rings on the chestpiece, [25]and the ends of the cords will be tied to the gold settings on the shoulder-pieces of the ephod. [26]Then make two more gold rings, and attach them to the two lower inside corners of the chestpiece next to the ephod. [27]And make two more gold rings and attach them to the ephod near the sash. [28]Then attach the bottom rings of the chestpiece to the rings on the ephod with blue cords. This will hold the chestpiece securely to the ephod above the beautiful sash. [29]In this way, Aaron will carry the names of the tribes of Israel on the chestpiece over his heart when he goes into the presence of the LORD in the Holy Place. Thus, the LORD will be reminded of his people continually. [30]Insert into the pocket of the chestpiece the Urim and Thummim, to be carried over Aaron's heart when he goes into the LORD's presence. Thus, Aaron will always carry the objects used to determine the LORD's will for his people whenever he goes in before the LORD.

[31]"Make the robe of the ephod entirely of blue cloth, [32]with an opening for Aaron's head in the middle of it. The opening will be reinforced by a woven collar* so it will not tear. [33]Make pomegranates out of blue, purple, and scarlet yarn, and attach them to the hem of the robe, with gold bells between them. [34]The gold bells and pomegranates are to alternate all the way around the hem. [35]Aaron will wear this robe whenever he enters the Holy Place to minister to the LORD, and the bells will tinkle as he goes in and out of the LORD's presence. If he wears it, he will not die.

[36]"Next make a medallion of pure gold. Using the techniques of an engraver, inscribe it with these words: SET APART AS HOLY TO THE LORD. [37]This medallion will be attached to the front of Aaron's turban by means of a blue cord. [38]Aaron will wear it on his forehead, thus bearing the guilt connected with any errors regarding the sacred offerings of the people of Israel. He must always wear it so the LORD will accept the people.

[39]"Weave Aaron's patterned tunic from fine linen cloth. Fashion the turban out of this linen as well. Also make him an embroidered sash.

[40]"Then for Aaron's sons, make tunics, sashes, and headdresses to give them dignity and respect. [41]Clothe Aaron and his sons with these garments, and then anoint and ordain them. Set them apart as holy so they can serve as my priests. [42]Also make linen underclothes for them, to be worn next to their bodies, reaching from waist to thigh. [43]These must be worn whenever Aaron and his sons enter the Tabernacle* or approach the altar in the Holy Place to per-

---

28:16 Hebrew *1 span* [23 centimeters].   28:17 The identification of some of these gemstones is uncertain.   28:32 The meaning of the Hebrew is uncertain.   28:43 Hebrew *Tent of Meeting.*

form their duties. Thus they will not incur guilt and die. This law is permanent for Aaron and his descendants.

CHAPTER 29

"This is the ceremony for the dedication of Aaron and his sons as priests: Take a young bull and two rams with no physical defects. [2]Then using fine wheat flour and no yeast, make loaves of bread, thin cakes mixed with olive oil, and wafers with oil poured over them. [3]Place these various kinds of bread in a single basket, and present them at the entrance of the Tabernacle, along with the young bull and the two rams.

[4]"Present Aaron and his sons at the entrance of the Tabernacle,* and wash them with water. [5]Then put Aaron's tunic on him, along with the embroidered robe of the ephod, the ephod itself, the chestpiece, and the sash. [6]And place on his head the turban with the gold medallion. [7]Then take the anointing oil and pour it over his head. [8]Next present his sons, and dress them in their tunics [9]with their woven sashes and their headdresses. They will then be priests forever. In this way, you will ordain Aaron and his sons.

[10]"Then bring the young bull to the entrance of the Tabernacle, and Aaron and his sons will lay their hands on its head. [11]You will then slaughter it in the LORD's presence at the entrance of the Tabernacle. [12]Smear some of its blood on the horns of the altar with your finger, and pour out the rest at the base of the altar. [13]Take all the fat that covers the internal organs, also the long lobe of the liver and the two kidneys with their fat, and burn them on the altar. [14]Then take the carcass (including the skin and the dung) outside the camp, and burn it as a sin offering.

[15]"Next Aaron and his sons must lay their hands on the head of one of the rams [16]as it is slaughtered. Its blood will be collected and sprinkled on the sides of the altar. [17]Cut up the ram and wash off the internal organs and the legs. Set them alongside the head and the other pieces of the body, [18]and burn them all on the altar. This is a burnt offering to the LORD, which is very pleasing to him.

[19]"Now take the other ram and have Aaron and his sons lay their hands on its head [20]as it is slaughtered. Collect the

blood and place some of it on the tip of the right earlobes of Aaron and his sons. Also put it on their right thumbs and the big toes of their right feet. Sprinkle the rest of the blood on the sides of the altar. [21]Then take some of the blood from the altar and mix it with some of the anointing oil. Sprinkle it on Aaron and his sons and on their clothes. In this way, they and their clothing will be set apart as holy to the LORD.

[22]"Since this is the ram for the ordination of Aaron and his sons, take the fat of the ram, including the fat tail and the fat that covers the internal organs. Also, take the long lobe of the liver, the two kidneys with their fat, and the right thigh. [23]Then take one loaf of bread, one cake mixed with olive oil, and one wafer from the basket of yeastless bread that was placed before the LORD. [24]Put all these in the hands of Aaron and his sons to be lifted up as a special gift to the LORD. [25]Afterward take the bread from their hands, and burn it on the altar as a burnt offering that will be pleasing to the LORD. [26]Then take the breast of Aaron's ordination ram, and lift it up in the LORD's presence as a special gift to him. Afterward keep it for yourself.

[27]"Set aside as holy the parts of the ordination ram that belong to Aaron and his sons. This includes the breast and the thigh that were lifted up before the LORD in the ordination ceremony. [28]In the future, whenever the people of Israel offer up peace offerings or thanksgiving offerings to the LORD, these parts will be the regular share of Aaron and his descendants.

[29]"Aaron's sacred garments must be preserved for his descendants who will succeed him, so they can be anointed and ordained in them. [30]Whoever is the next high priest after Aaron will wear these clothes for seven days before beginning to minister in the Tabernacle and the Holy Place.

[31]"Take the ram used in the ordination ceremony, and boil its meat in a sacred place. [32]Aaron and his sons are to eat this meat, along with the bread in the basket, at the Tabernacle entrance. [33]They alone may eat the meat and bread used for their atonement in the ordination ceremony. The ordinary people may not eat them, for these things are set apart and holy. [34]If any of the ordination meat or bread remains until the

29:4 Hebrew *Tent of Meeting;* also in 29:10, 11, 30, 32, 42, 44.

morning, it must be burned. It may not be eaten, for it is holy.

35"This is how you will ordain Aaron and his sons to their offices. The ordination ceremony will go on for seven days. 36Each day you must sacrifice a young bull as an offering for the atonement of sin. Afterward make an offering to cleanse the altar. Purify the altar by making atonement for it; make it holy by anointing it with oil. 37Make atonement for the altar every day for seven days. After that, the altar will be exceedingly holy, and whatever touches it will become holy.

38"This is what you are to offer on the altar. Offer two one-year-old lambs each day, 39one in the morning and the other in the evening. 40With one of them, offer two quarts of fine flour mixed with one quart of olive oil; also, offer one quart of wine* as a drink offering. 41Offer the other lamb in the evening, along with the same offerings of flour and wine as in the morning. It will be a fragrant offering to the LORD, an offering made by fire.

42"This is to be a daily burnt offering given from generation to generation. Offer it in the LORD's presence at the Tabernacle entrance, where I will meet you and speak with you. 43I will meet the people of Israel there, and the Tabernacle will be sanctified by my glorious presence. 44Yes, I will make the Tabernacle and the altar most holy, and I will set apart Aaron and his sons as holy, that they may be my priests. 45I will live among the people of Israel and be their God, 46and they will know that I am the LORD their God. I am the one who brought them out of Egypt so that I could live among them. I am the LORD their God.

CHAPTER 30

"Then make a small altar out of acacia wood for burning incense. 2It must be eighteen inches square and three feet high,* with horns at the corners carved from the same piece of wood as the altar. 3Overlay the top, sides, and horns of the altar with pure gold, and run a gold molding around the entire altar. 4Beneath the molding, on opposite sides of the altar, attach two gold rings to support the carrying poles. 5The poles are to be made of acacia wood and overlaid with gold. 6Place the incense altar just outside the inner curtain, opposite the Ark's cover—the place of atonement—that rests on the Ark of the Covenant.* I will meet with you there.

7"Every morning when Aaron trims the lamps, he must burn fragrant incense on the altar. 8And each evening when he tends to the lamps, he must again burn incense in the LORD's presence. This must be done from generation to generation. 9Do not offer any unholy incense on this altar, or any burnt offerings, grain offerings, or drink offerings.

10"Once a year Aaron must purify the altar by placing on its horns the blood from the offering made for the atonement of sin. This will be a regular, annual event from generation to generation, for this is the LORD's supremely holy altar."

11And the LORD said to Moses, 12"Whenever you take a census of the people of Israel, each man who is counted must pay a ransom for himself to the LORD. Then there will be no plagues among the people as you count them. 13His payment to the LORD will be one-fifth of an ounce* of silver. 14All who have reached their twentieth birthday must give this offering to the LORD. 15When this offering is given to the LORD to make atonement for yourselves, the rich must not give more, and the poor must not give less. 16Use this money for the care of the Tabernacle.* It will bring you, the Israelites, to the LORD's attention, and it will make atonement for your lives."

17And the LORD said to Moses, 18"Make a large bronze washbasin with a bronze pedestal. Put it between the Tabernacle and the altar, and fill it with water. 19Aaron and his sons will wash their hands and feet there 20before they go into the Tabernacle to appear before the LORD and before they approach the altar to burn offerings to the LORD. They must always wash before ministering in these ways, or they will die. 21This is a permanent law for Aaron and his descendants, to be kept from generation to generation."

22Then the LORD said to Moses, 23"Collect choice spices—12½ pounds of pure myrrh, 6¼ pounds* each of cinnamon and of sweet cane, 2412½ pounds of cassia, and

29:40 Hebrew 1/10 of an ephah [2 liters] of fine flour . . . 1/4 of a hin [1 liter] of olive oil . . . 1/4 of a hin of wine.   30:2 Hebrew 1 cubit [45 centimeters] square and 2 cubits [90 centimeters] high.   30:6 Or Ark of the Testimony; also in 30:26, 36.   30:13 Hebrew half a shekel [6 grams], according to the sanctuary shekel, 20 gerahs to each shekel.   30:16 Hebrew Tent of Meeting; also in 30:18, 20, 26, 36. 30:23 Hebrew 500 shekels [5.7 kilograms] of pure myrrh, 250 shekels [2.9 kilograms].

one gallon* of olive oil. 25Blend these ingredients into a holy anointing oil. 26Use this scented oil to anoint the Tabernacle, the Ark of the Covenant, 27the table and all its utensils, the lampstand and all its accessories, the incense altar, 28the altar of burnt offering with all its utensils, and the large washbasin with its pedestal. 29Sanctify them to make them entirely holy. After this, whatever touches them will become holy. 30Use this oil also to anoint Aaron and his sons, sanctifying them so they can minister before me as priests. 31And say to the people of Israel, 'This will always be my holy anointing oil. 32It must never be poured on the body of an ordinary person, and you must never make any of it for yourselves. It is holy, and you must treat it as holy. 33Anyone who blends scented oil like it or puts any of it on someone who is not a priest will be cut off from the community.'"

34These were the LORD's instructions to Moses concerning the incense: "Gather sweet spices—resin droplets, mollusk scent, galbanum, and pure frankincense—weighing out the same amounts of each. 35Using the usual techniques of the incense maker, refine it to produce a pure and holy incense. 36Beat some of it very fine and put some of it in front of the Ark of the Covenant, where I will meet with you in the Tabernacle. This incense is most holy. 37Never make this incense for yourselves. It is reserved for the LORD, and you must treat it as holy. 38Those who make it for their own enjoyment will be cut off from the community."

CHAPTER 31

The LORD also said to Moses, 2"Look, I have chosen Bezalel son of Uri, grandson of Hur, of the tribe of Judah. 3I have filled him with the Spirit of God, giving him great wisdom, intelligence, and skill in all kinds of crafts. 4He is able to create beautiful objects from gold, silver, and bronze. 5He is skilled in cutting and setting gemstones and in carving wood. Yes, he is a master at every craft!

6"And I have appointed Oholiab son of Ahisamach, of the tribe of Dan, to be his assistant. Moreover, I have given special skill to all the naturally talented craftsmen so they can make all the things I have instructed you to make: 7the Tabernacle itself; the Ark of the Covenant;* the Ark's cover—the place of atonement; all the furnishings of the Tabernacle; 8the table and all its utensils; the gold lampstand with all its accessories; the incense altar; 9the altar of burnt offering with all its utensils; the washbasin and its pedestal; 10the beautifully stitched, holy garments for Aaron the priest, and the garments for his sons to wear as they minister as priests; 11the anointing oil; and the special incense for the Holy Place. They must follow exactly all the instructions I have given you."

12The LORD then gave these further instructions to Moses: 13"Tell the people of Israel to keep my Sabbath day, for the Sabbath is a sign of the covenant between me and you forever. It helps you to remember that I am the LORD, who makes you holy. 14Yes, keep the Sabbath day, for it is holy. Anyone who desecrates it must die; anyone who works on that day will be cut off from the community. 15Work six days only, but the seventh day must be a day of total rest. I repeat: Because the LORD considers it a holy day, anyone who works on the Sabbath must be put to death. 16The people of Israel must keep the Sabbath day forever. 17It is a permanent sign of my covenant with them. For in six days the LORD made heaven and earth, but he rested on the seventh day and was refreshed."

18Then as the LORD finished speaking with Moses on Mount Sinai, he gave him the two stone tablets inscribed with the terms of the covenant,* written by the finger of God.

30:24 Hebrew *500 shekels* [5.7 kilograms] *of cassia, according to the sanctuary shekel, and 1 hin* [3.8 liters].   31:7 Hebrew *the Tent of Meeting; the Ark of the Testimony.*   31:18 Hebrew *the Testimony.*

JANUARY 30 ☐ DAY 30
EXODUS 32–34
Incident of the Gold Calf

OVERVIEW Six weeks have passed since the people made their solemn vow of fidelity to God. Concluding that Moses has died on the mountain, they insist on creating a replica of an Egyptian god and worshiping it. Coming upon this grotesque scene, Moses dashes the newly inscribed tablets to pieces, dramatically illustrating the broken covenant. He destroys the gold calf and orders the Levites to slay the guilty Israelites. Israel's repentance, Moses' selfless intercession, and God's faithfulness to his promises lead to a renewal of the covenant. New tablets are engraved, and Moses experiences yet another encounter with God on Mount Sinai.

Chapter 32		Chapter 33		Chapter 34
Covenant's Interruption	Moses' Intercession	Israel's Repentance	Moses' Request	Covenant's Renewal
1 6	7 35	1 17	18 23	
Israel's Rebellion		God's Restoration		

YOUR DAILY WALK "I just can't understand teenagers. One minute they want to be treated like adults; the next minute they act like children."

Never look back unless you want to go that way.

This oft-voiced exasperation of many a parent illustrates a fact about growth. The process of maturation does not proceed at a consistent pace. Everyone at one time or another reverts to former patterns of behavior.

The incident of the gold calf is but one of many cases of backsliding in Israel's history. One lesson is clear: Believers are not immune from reverting to old habits and patterns of living. It may occur in an unguarded moment, such as an outburst of temper. Or it may be the result of impatience, when God's timetable seems agonizingly slow.

Take a personal inventory of your spiritual life. Have you made a commitment to the Lord in recent weeks? If so, have you followed through on it or reverted to your previous behavior? If you see a "gold calf" in your life, deal with it now! You'll discover that "gold calves" make terrible "sacred cows"—but excellent hamburger!

INSIGHT The Gold Calf: A Lingering Legacy
Calf worship—or worshiping idols of any kind—was expressly forbidden in the law (20:4-6). Yet, at least once more in Israel's history, a gold calf spelled destruction for the people (see 1 Kings 12:28).

CHAPTER 32
When Moses failed to come back down the mountain right away, the people went to Aaron. "Look," they said, "make us some gods who can lead us. This man Moses, who brought us here from Egypt, has disappeared. We don't know what has happened to him."

²So Aaron said, "Tell your wives and sons and daughters to take off their gold earrings, and then bring them to me."

³All the people obeyed Aaron and brought him their gold earrings. ⁴Then Aaron took the gold, melted it down, and molded and tooled it into the shape of a calf. The people exclaimed, "O Israel, these are the gods who brought you out of Egypt!"

⁵When Aaron saw how excited the people were about it, he built an altar in front of the calf and announced, "Tomorrow there will be a festival to the LORD!"

⁶So the people got up early the next morning to sacrifice burnt offerings and

peace offerings. After this, they celebrated with feasting and drinking, and indulged themselves in pagan revelry.

⁷Then the LORD told Moses, "Quick! Go down the mountain! The people you brought from Egypt have defiled themselves. ⁸They have already turned from the way I commanded them to live. They have made an idol shaped like a calf, and they have worshiped and sacrificed to it. They are saying, 'These are your gods, O Israel, who brought you out of Egypt.'"

⁹Then the LORD said, "I have seen how stubborn and rebellious these people are. ¹⁰Now leave me alone so my anger can blaze against them and destroy them all. Then I will make you, Moses, into a great nation instead of them."

¹¹But Moses pleaded with the LORD his God not to do it. "O LORD!" he exclaimed. "Why are you so angry with your own people whom you brought from the land of Egypt with such great power and mighty acts? ¹²The Egyptians will say, 'God tricked them into coming to the mountains so he could kill them and wipe them from the face of the earth.' Turn away from your fierce anger. Change your mind about this terrible disaster you are planning against your people! ¹³Remember your covenant with your servants—Abraham, Isaac, and Jacob.* You swore by your own self, 'I will make your descendants as numerous as the stars of heaven. Yes, I will give them all of this land that I have promised to your descendants, and they will possess it forever.'"

¹⁴So the LORD withdrew his threat and didn't bring against his people the disaster he had threatened.

¹⁵Then Moses turned and went down the mountain. He held in his hands the two stone tablets inscribed with the terms of the covenant.* They were inscribed on both sides, front and back. ¹⁶These stone tablets were God's work; the words on them were written by God himself.

¹⁷When Joshua heard the noise of the people shouting below them, he exclaimed to Moses, "It sounds as if there is a war in the camp!"

¹⁸But Moses replied, "No, it's neither a cry of victory nor a cry of defeat. It is the sound of a celebration."

¹⁹When they came near the camp, Moses saw the calf and the dancing. In terrible anger, he threw the stone tablets to the ground, smashing them at the foot of the mountain. ²⁰He took the calf they had made and melted it in the fire. And when the metal had cooled, he ground it into powder and mixed it with water. Then he made the people drink it.

²¹After that, he turned to Aaron. "What did the people do to you?" he demanded. "How did they ever make you bring such terrible sin upon them?"

²²"Don't get upset, sir," Aaron replied. "You yourself know these people and what a wicked bunch they are. ²³They said to me, 'Make us some gods to lead us, for something has happened to this man Moses, who led us out of Egypt.' ²⁴So I told them, 'Bring me your gold earrings.' When they brought them to me, I threw them into the fire—and out came this calf!"

²⁵When Moses saw that Aaron had let the people get completely out of control—and much to the amusement of their enemies—²⁶he stood at the entrance to the camp and shouted, "All of you who are on the LORD's side, come over here and join me." And all the Levites came.

²⁷He told them, "This is what the LORD, the God of Israel, says: Strap on your swords! Go back and forth from one end of the camp to the other, killing even your brothers, friends, and neighbors." ²⁸The Levites obeyed Moses, and about three thousand people died that day.

²⁹Then Moses told the Levites, "Today you have been ordained for the service of the LORD, for you obeyed him even though it meant killing your own sons and brothers. Because of this, he will now give you a great blessing."

³⁰The next day Moses said to the people, "You have committed a terrible sin, but I will return to the LORD on the mountain. Perhaps I will be able to obtain forgiveness for you."

³¹So Moses returned to the LORD and said, "Alas, these people have committed a terrible sin. They have made gods of gold for themselves. ³²But now, please forgive their sin—and if not, then blot me out of the record you are keeping."

³³The LORD replied to Moses, "I will blot out whoever has sinned against me. ³⁴Now go, lead the people to the place I told you

32:13 Hebrew *Israel.*   **32:15** Hebrew *the Testimony.*

about. Look! My angel will lead the way before you! But when I call the people to account, I will certainly punish them for their sins."

³⁵And the LORD sent a great plague upon the people because they had worshiped the calf Aaron had made.

CHAPTER 33

The LORD said to Moses, "Now that you have brought these people out of Egypt, lead them to the land I solemnly promised Abraham, Isaac, and Jacob. I told them long ago that I would give this land to their descendants. ²And I will send an angel before you to drive out the Canaanites, Amorites, Hittites, Perizzites, Hivites, and Jebusites. ³Theirs is a land flowing with milk and honey. But I will not travel along with you, for you are a stubborn, unruly people. If I did, I would be tempted to destroy you along the way."

⁴When the people heard these stern words, they went into mourning and refused to wear their jewelry and ornaments. ⁵For the LORD had told Moses to tell them, "You are an unruly, stubborn people. If I were there among you for even a moment, I would destroy you. Remove your jewelry and ornaments until I decide what to do with you." ⁶So from the time they left Mount Sinai,* the Israelites wore no more jewelry.

⁷It was Moses' custom to set up the tent known as the Tent of Meeting far outside the camp. Everyone who wanted to consult with the LORD would go there.

⁸Whenever Moses went out to the Tent of Meeting, all the people would get up and stand in their tent entrances. They would all watch Moses until he disappeared inside. ⁹As he went into the tent, the pillar of cloud would come down and hover at the entrance while the LORD spoke with Moses. ¹⁰Then all the people would stand and bow low at their tent entrances. ¹¹Inside the Tent of Meeting, the LORD would speak to Moses face to face, as a man speaks to his friend. Afterward Moses would return to the camp, but the young man who assisted him, Joshua son of Nun, stayed behind in the Tent of Meeting.

¹²Moses said to the LORD, "You have been telling me, 'Take these people up to the Promised Land.' But you haven't told

me whom you will send with me. You call me by name and tell me I have found favor with you. ¹³Please, if this is really so, show me your intentions so I will understand you more fully and do exactly what you want me to do. Besides, don't forget that this nation is your very own people."

¹⁴And the LORD replied, "I will personally go with you, Moses. I will give you rest—everything will be fine for you."

¹⁵Then Moses said, "If you don't go with us personally, don't let us move a step from this place. ¹⁶If you don't go with us, how will anyone ever know that your people and I have found favor with you? How else will they know we are special and distinct from all other people on the earth?"

¹⁷And the LORD replied to Moses, "I will indeed do what you have asked, for you have found favor with me, and you are my friend."

¹⁸Then Moses had one more request. "Please let me see your glorious presence," he said.

¹⁹The LORD replied, "I will make all my goodness pass before you, and I will call out my name, 'the LORD,' to you. I will show kindness to anyone I choose, and I will show mercy to anyone I choose. ²⁰But you may not look directly at my face, for no one may see me and live." ²¹The LORD continued, "Stand here on this rock beside me. ²²As my glorious presence passes by, I will put you in the cleft of the rock and cover you with my hand until I have passed. ²³Then I will remove my hand, and you will see me from behind. But my face will not be seen."

CHAPTER 34

The LORD told Moses, "Prepare two stone tablets like the first ones. I will write on them the same words that were on the tablets you smashed. ²Be ready in the morning to come up Mount Sinai and present yourself to me there on the top of the mountain. ³No one else may come up with you. In fact, no one is allowed anywhere on the mountain. Do not even let the flocks or herds graze near the mountain."

⁴So Moses cut two tablets of stone like the first ones. Early in the morning he climbed Mount Sinai as the LORD had told him, carrying the two stone tablets in his hands.

33:6 Hebrew *Horeb,* another name for Sinai.

[5]Then the LORD came down in a pillar of cloud and called out his own name, "the LORD," as Moses stood there in his presence. [6]He passed in front of Moses and said, "I am the LORD, I am the LORD, the merciful and gracious God. I am slow to anger and rich in unfailing love and faithfulness. [7]I show this unfailing love to many thousands by forgiving every kind of sin and rebellion. Even so I do not leave sin unpunished, but I punish the children for the sins of their parents to the third and fourth generations."

[8]Moses immediately fell to the ground and worshiped. [9]And he said, "If it is true that I have found favor in your sight, O Lord, then please go with us. Yes, this is an unruly and stubborn people, but please pardon our iniquity and our sins. Accept us as your own special possession."

[10]The LORD replied, "All right. This is the covenant I am going to make with you. I will perform wonders that have never been done before anywhere in all the earth or in any nation. And all the people around you will see the power of the LORD—the awesome power I will display through you. [11]Your responsibility is to obey all the commands I am giving you today. Then I will surely drive out all those who stand in your way—the Amorites, Canaanites, Hittites, Perizzites, Hivites, and Jebusites.

[12]"Be very careful never to make treaties with the people in the land where you are going. If you do, you soon will be following their evil ways. [13]Instead, you must break down their pagan altars, smash the sacred pillars they worship, and cut down their carved images. [14]You must worship no other gods, but only the LORD, for he is a God who is passionate about his relationship with you.

[15]"Do not make treaties of any kind with the people living in the land. They are spiritual prostitutes, committing adultery against me by sacrificing to their gods. If you make peace with them, they will invite you to go with them to worship their gods, and you are likely to do it. [16]And you will accept their daughters, who worship other gods, as wives for your sons. Then they will cause your sons to commit adultery against me by worshiping other gods. [17]You must make no gods for yourselves at all.

[18]"Be sure to celebrate the Festival of Un-leavened Bread for seven days, just as I instructed you, at the appointed time each year in early spring,* for that was when you left Egypt.

[19]"Every firstborn male belongs to me—of both cattle and sheep. [20]A firstborn male donkey may be redeemed from the LORD by presenting a lamb in its place. But if you decide not to make the exchange, you must kill the donkey by breaking its neck. However, you must redeem every firstborn son. No one is allowed to appear before me without a gift.

[21]"Six days are set aside for work, but on the Sabbath day you must rest, even during the seasons of plowing and harvest. [22]And you must remember to celebrate the Festival of Harvest* with the first crop of the wheat harvest, and celebrate the Festival of the Final Harvest* at the end of the harvest season. [23]Three times each year all the men of Israel must appear before the Sovereign LORD, the God of Israel. [24]No one will attack and conquer your land when you go to appear before the LORD your God those three times each year. I will drive out the nations that stand in your way and will enlarge your boundaries.

[25]"You must not offer bread made with yeast as a sacrifice to me. And none of the meat of the Passover lamb may be kept over until the following morning. [26]You must bring the best of the first of each year's crop to the house of the LORD your God.

"You must not cook a young goat in its mother's milk."

[27]And the LORD said to Moses, "Write down all these instructions, for they represent the terms of my covenant with you and with Israel."

[28]Moses was up on the mountain with the LORD forty days and forty nights. In all that time he neither ate nor drank. At that time he wrote the terms of the covenant—the Ten Commandments—on the stone tablets.

[29]When Moses came down the mountain carrying the stone tablets inscribed with the terms of the covenant,* he wasn't aware that his face glowed because he had spoken to the LORD face to face. [30]And when Aaron and the people of Israel saw the radiance of Moses' face, they were afraid to come near him.

34:18 Hebrew *in the month of Abib.* This month of the Hebrew lunar calendar usually occurs in March and April.   **34:22a** Or *Festival of Weeks.*   **34:22b** This was later called the Festival of Shelters; see Lev 23:33-36.   **34:29** Hebrew *the Testimony.*

³¹But Moses called to them and asked Aaron and the community leaders to come over and talk with him. ³²Then all the people came, and Moses gave them the instructions the LORD had given him on Mount Sinai. ³³When Moses had finished speaking with them, he put a veil over his face. ³⁴But whenever he went into the Tent of Meeting to speak with the LORD, he removed the veil until he came out again. Then he would give the people whatever instructions the LORD had given him, ³⁵and the people would see his face aglow. Afterward he would put the veil on again until he returned to speak with the LORD.

JANUARY 31 ☐ DAY 31
EXODUS 35–40
Tabernacle Erected and Occupied

OVERVIEW The book of Exodus closes with a detailed account of the construction of the Tabernacle, the new place of residence for the God of Israel as he accompanies his people to Canaan. Notice the many steps involved in the project: Moses organizes the needed workers and materials; skilled artisans do the actual construction; Moses inspects the finished work; the Tabernacle is erected and the furniture set in place; and finally the glory of the Lord fills the Tabernacle, showing God's pleasure with the structure. From start to finish, the entire project is done "just as the LORD had commanded Moses."

Chapter 35	Chapters 36–39		Chapter 40	
Step 1: Preparation	Step 2: Construction	Step 3: Inspection	Step 4: Erection	Step 5: Occupation
	36:1 39:31	39:32 39:43	1 33	34 38
Tabernacle Completed	Tabernacle Occupied			

YOUR DAILY WALK God has always sought to dwell in the midst of his people. Think back to the opening chapters of Genesis, and what do you find? Adam and Eve in the garden. And in the cool of the evening God walks through the garden, seeking face-to-face fellowship with his creation.

How many friends would you have left if you started spending as much time with them as you do with God?

In today's reading, God's glory takes up residence in the Tabernacle in order to accompany the Israelites on their journey to Canaan. Later in Israel's history, God's presence will reside in Solomon's magnificent Temple. And today God's Holy Spirit indwells every child of God (1 Corinthians 6:19-20). The lesson is clear: God wants to identify himself with those who are truly his. More specifically, God wants to identify himself with *you*, fellowship with *you*, spend time with *you*, help *you* get to know him better.

How do you go about building a relationship like that? Jot down the first five things that come to mind. Now use your list to help you organize your day and assign priorities to your activities. Place "Time with God" at the top of the list. After all, that's *his* greatest desire: to walk and talk with you! If that's *your* greatest desire, tell him so right now.

INSIGHT "We've Come a Long Way, Baby"
Exodus begins with a mob of miserable slaves held captive in Egypt, yet ends with an emancipated nation in fellowship with God and on its way to Canaan. No wonder Exodus is called the "book of redemption"!

CHAPTER 35

Now Moses called a meeting of all the people and told them, "You must obey these instructions from the LORD. ²Each week, work for six days only. The seventh day is a day of total rest, a holy day that belongs to the LORD. Anyone who works on that day will die. ³Do not even light fires in your homes on that day."

⁴Then Moses said to all the people, "This is what the LORD has commanded. ⁵Everyone is invited to bring these offerings to the LORD: gold, silver, and bronze; ⁶blue, purple, and scarlet yarn; fine linen; goat hair for cloth; ⁷tanned ram skins and fine goatskin leather; acacia wood; ⁸olive oil for the lamps; spices for the anointing oil and the fragrant incense; ⁹onyx stones, and other stones to be set in the ephod and the chestpiece.

¹⁰"Come, all of you who are gifted craftsmen. Construct everything that the LORD has commanded: ¹¹the entire Tabernacle, including the sacred tent and its coverings, the clasps, frames, crossbars, posts, and bases; ¹²the Ark and its poles; the Ark's cover—the place of atonement; the inner curtain to enclose the Ark in the Most Holy Place; ¹³the table, its carrying poles, and all of its utensils; the Bread of the Presence; ¹⁴the lampstand and its accessories; the lamp cups and the oil for lighting; ¹⁵the incense altar and its carrying poles; the anointing oil and fragrant incense; the curtain for the entrance of the Tabernacle; ¹⁶the altar of burnt offering; the bronze grating of the altar and its carrying poles and utensils; the large washbasin with its pedestal; ¹⁷the curtains for the walls of the courtyard; the posts and their bases; the curtain for the entrance to the courtyard; ¹⁸the tent pegs of the Tabernacle and courtyard and their cords; ¹⁹the beautifully stitched clothing for the priests to wear while ministering in the Holy Place; the sacred garments for Aaron and his sons to wear while officiating as priests."

²⁰So all the people left Moses and went to their tents to prepare their gifts. ²¹If their hearts were stirred and they desired to do so, they brought to the LORD their offerings of materials for the Tabernacle* and its furnishings and for the holy garments. ²²Both men and women came, all whose hearts were willing. Some brought to the LORD

their offerings of gold—medallions, earrings, rings from their fingers, and necklaces. They presented gold objects of every kind to the LORD. ²³Others brought blue, purple, and scarlet yarn, fine linen, or goat hair for cloth. Some gave tanned ram skins or fine goatskin leather. ²⁴Others brought silver and bronze objects as their offering to the LORD. And those who had acacia wood brought it.

²⁵All the women who were skilled in sewing and spinning prepared blue, purple, and scarlet yarn, and fine linen cloth, and they brought them in. ²⁶All the women who were willing used their skills to spin and weave the goat hair into cloth. ²⁷The leaders brought onyx stones and the other gemstones to be used for the ephod and the chestpiece. ²⁸They also brought spices and olive oil for the light, the anointing oil, and the fragrant incense. ²⁹So the people of Israel—every man and woman who wanted to help in the work the LORD had given them through Moses—brought their offerings to the LORD.

³⁰And Moses told them, "The LORD has chosen Bezalel son of Uri, grandson of Hur, of the tribe of Judah. ³¹The LORD has filled Bezalel with the Spirit of God, giving him great wisdom, intelligence, and skill in all kinds of crafts. ³²He is able to create beautiful objects from gold, silver, and bronze. ³³He is skilled in cutting and setting gemstones and in carving wood. In fact, he has every necessary skill. ³⁴And the LORD has given both him and Oholiab son of Ahisamach, of the tribe of Dan, the ability to teach their skills to others. ³⁵The LORD has given them special skills as jewelers, designers, weavers, and embroiderers in blue, purple, and scarlet yarn on fine linen cloth. They excel in all the crafts needed for the work.

CHAPTER 36

"Bezalel, Oholiab, and the other craftsmen whom the LORD has gifted with wisdom, skill, and intelligence will construct and furnish the Tabernacle, just as the LORD has commanded."

²So Moses told Bezalel and Oholiab to begin the work, along with all those who were specially gifted by the LORD. ³Moses gave them the materials donated by the people for the completion of the sanctuary.

35:21 Hebrew *Tent of Meeting.*

Additional gifts were brought each morning. [4]But finally the craftsmen left their work to meet with Moses. [5]"We have more than enough materials on hand now to complete the job the LORD has given us to do!" they exclaimed.

[6]So Moses gave the command, and this message was sent throughout the camp: "Bring no more materials! You have already given more than enough." So the people stopped bringing their offerings. [7]Their contributions were more than enough to complete the whole project.

[8]The skilled weavers first made ten sheets from fine linen. One of the craftsmen then embroidered blue, purple, and scarlet cherubim into them. [9]Each sheet was exactly the same size—forty-two feet long and six feet wide.* [10]Five of these sheets were joined together to make one set, and a second set was made of the other five. [11]Fifty blue loops were placed along the edge of the last sheet in each set. [12]The fifty loops along the edge of the first set of sheets matched the loops along the edge of the second set. [13]Then fifty gold clasps were made to connect the loops on the edge of each set. Thus the Tabernacle was joined together in one piece.

[14]Above the Tabernacle, a roof covering was made from eleven sheets of cloth made from goat hair. [15]Each sheet was exactly the same size—forty-five feet long and six feet wide. [16]The craftsmen joined five of these sheets together to make one set, and the six remaining sheets were joined to make a second set. [17]Then they made fifty loops along the edge of the last sheet in each set. [18]They also made fifty small bronze clasps to couple the loops, so the two sets of sheets were firmly attached to each other. In this way, the roof covering was joined together in one piece. [19]Then they made two more layers for the roof covering. The first was made of tanned ram skins, and the second was made of fine goatskin leather.

[20]For the framework of the Tabernacle, they made frames of acacia wood standing on end. [21]Each frame was 15 feet high and 2¼ feet wide. [22]There were two pegs on each frame so they could be joined to the next frame. All the frames were made this way. [23]They made twenty frames to support the south side, [24]along with forty silver bases, two for each frame. [25]They also made twenty frames for the north side of the Tabernacle, [26]along with forty silver bases, two for each frame. [27]The west side of the Tabernacle, which was its rear, was made from six frames, [28]plus an extra frame at each corner. [29]These corner frames were connected at the bottom and firmly attached at the top with a single ring, forming a single unit from top to bottom. They made two of these, one for each rear corner. [30]So for the west side they made a total of eight frames, along with sixteen silver bases, two for each frame.

[31]Then they made five crossbars from acacia wood to tie the frames on the south side together. [32]They made another five for the north side and five for the west side. [33]The middle crossbar of the five was halfway up the frames, along each side, running from one end to the other. [34]The frames and crossbars were all overlaid with gold. The rings used to hold the crossbars were made of pure gold.

[35]The inner curtain was made of fine linen cloth, and cherubim were skillfully embroidered into it with blue, purple, and scarlet yarn. [36]This curtain was then attached to four gold hooks set into four posts of acacia wood. The posts were overlaid with gold and set into four silver bases.

[37]Then they made another curtain for the entrance to the sacred tent. It was made of fine linen cloth and embroidered with blue, purple, and scarlet yarn. [38]This curtain was connected by five hooks to five posts. The posts with their decorated tops and bands were overlaid with gold. The five bases were molded from bronze.

C H A P T E R   3 7

Next Bezalel made the Ark out of acacia wood. It was 3¾ feet long, 2¼ feet wide, and 2¼ feet high.* [2]It was overlaid with pure gold inside and out, and it had a molding of gold all the way around. [3]Four gold rings were fastened to its four feet, two rings at each side. [4]Then he made poles from acacia wood and overlaid them with gold. [5]He put the poles into the rings at the sides of the Ark to carry it.

[6]Then, from pure gold, he made the

36:9 Hebrew *28 cubits* [12.6 meters] *long and 4 cubits* [1.8 meters] *wide*. In this chapter, the distance measures are calculated from the Hebrew cubit at a ratio of 18 inches or 45 centimeters per cubit.   37:1 Hebrew *2½ cubits* [1.1 meters] *long*, *1½ cubits* [0.7 meters] *wide, and 1½ cubits high*. In this chapter, the distance measures are calculated from the Hebrew cubit at a ratio of 18 inches or 45 centimeters per cubit.

Ark's cover—the place of atonement. It was 3¾ feet long and 2¼ feet wide. ⁷He made two figures of cherubim out of hammered gold and placed them at the two ends of the atonement cover. ⁸They were made so they were actually a part of the atonement cover—it was all one piece. ⁹The cherubim faced each other as they looked down on the atonement cover, and their wings were stretched out above the atonement cover to protect it.

¹⁰Then he made a table out of acacia wood, 3 feet long, 1½ feet wide, and 2¼ feet high. ¹¹It was overlaid with pure gold, with a gold molding all around the edge. ¹²A rim about 3 inches* wide was attached along the edges of the table, and a gold molding ran around the rim. ¹³Then he cast four rings of gold and attached them to the four table legs ¹⁴next to the rim. These were made to hold the carrying poles in place. ¹⁵He made the carrying poles of acacia wood and overlaid them with gold. ¹⁶Next, using pure gold, he made the plates, dishes, bowls, and pitchers to be placed on the table. These utensils were to be used in pouring out drink offerings.

¹⁷Then he made the lampstand, again using pure, hammered gold. Its base, center stem, lamp cups, blossoms, and buds were all of one piece. ¹⁸The lampstand had six branches, three going out from each side of the center stem. ¹⁹Each of the six branches held a cup shaped like an almond blossom, complete with buds and petals. ²⁰The center stem of the lampstand was also decorated with four almond blossoms. ²¹One blossom was set beneath each pair of branches, where they extended from the center stem. ²²The decorations and branches were all one piece with the stem, and they were hammered from pure gold. ²³He also made the seven lamps, the lamp snuffers, and the trays, all of pure gold. ²⁴The entire lampstand, along with its accessories, was made from seventy-five pounds* of pure gold.

²⁵The incense altar was made of acacia wood. It was eighteen inches square and three feet high, with its corner horns made from the same piece of wood as the altar itself. ²⁶He overlaid the top, sides, and horns of the altar with pure gold and ran a gold molding around the edge. ²⁷Two gold rings were placed on opposite sides, beneath the molding, to hold the carrying poles. ²⁸The carrying poles were made of acacia wood and were overlaid with gold.

²⁹Then he made the sacred oil, for anointing the priests, and the fragrant incense, using the techniques of the most skilled incense maker.

CHAPTER 38

The altar for burning animal sacrifices also was constructed of acacia wood. It was 7½ feet square at the top and 4½ feet high.* ²There were four horns, one at each of the four corners, all of one piece with the rest. This altar was overlaid with bronze. ³Then he made all the bronze utensils to be used with the altar—the ash buckets, shovels, basins, meat hooks, and firepans. ⁴Next he made a bronze grating that rested on a ledge about halfway down into the firebox. ⁵Four rings were cast for each side of the grating to support the carrying poles. ⁶The carrying poles themselves were made of acacia wood and were overlaid with bronze. ⁷These poles were inserted into the rings at the side of the altar. The altar was hollow and was made from planks.

⁸The bronze washbasin and its bronze pedestal were cast from bronze mirrors donated by the women who served at the entrance of the Tabernacle.*

⁹Then he constructed the courtyard. The south wall was 150 feet long. It consisted of curtains made of fine linen. ¹⁰There were twenty posts, each with its own bronze base, and there were silver hooks and rods to hold up the curtains. ¹¹The north wall was also 150 feet long, with twenty bronze posts and bases and with silver hooks and rods. ¹²The west end was 75 feet wide. The walls were made from curtains supported by ten posts and bases and with silver hooks and rods. ¹³The east end was also 75 feet wide.

¹⁴The courtyard entrance was on the east side, flanked by two curtains. The curtain on the right side was 22½ feet long and was supported by three posts set into three bases. ¹⁵The curtain on the left side was also 22½ feet long and was supported by three posts set into three bases. ¹⁶All the curtains used in the courtyard walls were made of fine linen. ¹⁷Each post had a

37:12 Hebrew *a handbreadth* [8 centimeters].   **37:24** Hebrew *1 talent* [34 kilograms].   **38:1** Hebrew *5 cubits* [2.3 meters] *square at the top, and 3 cubits* [1.4 meters] *high.* In this chapter, the distance measures are calculated from the Hebrew cubit at a ratio of 18 inches or 45 centimeters per cubit.   **38:8** Hebrew *Tent of Meeting;* also in 38:30.

bronze base, and all the hooks and rods were silver. The tops of the posts were overlaid with silver, and the rods to hold up the curtains were solid silver.

[18] The curtain that covered the entrance to the courtyard was made of fine linen cloth and embroidered with blue, purple, and scarlet yarn. It was 30 feet long and 7½ feet high, just like the curtains of the courtyard walls. [19] It was supported by four posts set into four bronze bases. The tops of the posts were overlaid with silver, and the hooks and rods were also made of silver.

[20] All the tent pegs used in the Tabernacle and courtyard were made of bronze.

[21] Here is an inventory of the materials used in building the Tabernacle of the Covenant.* Moses directed the Levites to compile the figures, and Ithamar son of Aaron the priest served as recorder. [22] Bezalel son of Uri, grandson of Hur, of the tribe of Judah, was in charge of the whole project, just as the LORD had commanded Moses. [23] He was assisted by Oholiab son of Ahisamach, of the tribe of Dan, a craftsman expert at engraving, designing, and embroidering blue, purple, and scarlet yarn on fine linen cloth.

[24] The people brought gifts of gold totaling about 2,200 pounds,* all of which was used throughout the Tabernacle.

[25] The amount of silver that was given was about 7,545 pounds.* [26] It came from the tax of one-fifth of an ounce of silver* collected from each of those registered in the census. This included all the men who were twenty years old or older, 603,550 in all. [27] The 100 bases for the frames of the sanctuary walls and for the posts supporting the inner curtain required 7,500 pounds of silver, about 75 pounds for each base.* [28] The rest of the silver, about 45 pounds,* was used to make the rods and hooks and to overlay the tops of the posts.

[29] The people also brought 5,310 pounds* of bronze, [30] which was used for casting the bases for the posts at the entrance to the Tabernacle, and for the bronze altar with its bronze grating and altar utensils. [31] Bronze was also used to make the bases for the posts that supported the curtains around

the courtyard, the bases for the curtain at the entrance of the courtyard, and all the tent pegs used to hold the curtains of the courtyard in place.

CHAPTER 39

For the priests, the craftsmen made beautiful garments of blue, purple, and scarlet cloth—clothing to be worn while ministering in the Holy Place. This same cloth was used for Aaron's sacred garments, just as the LORD had commanded Moses.

[2] The ephod was made from fine linen cloth and embroidered with gold thread and blue, purple, and scarlet yarn. [3] A skilled craftsman made gold thread by beating gold into thin sheets and cutting it into fine strips. He then embroidered it into the linen with the blue, purple, and scarlet yarn.

[4] They made two shoulder-pieces for the ephod, which were attached to its corners so it could be tied down. [5] They also made an elaborate woven sash of the same materials: fine linen cloth; blue, purple, and scarlet yarn; and gold thread, just as the LORD had commanded Moses. [6] The two onyx stones, attached to the shoulder-pieces of the ephod, were set in gold filigree. The stones were engraved with the names of the tribes of Israel, just as initials are engraved on a seal. [7] These stones served as reminders to the LORD concerning the people of Israel. All this was done just as the LORD had commanded Moses.

[8] The chestpiece was made in the same style as the ephod, crafted from fine linen cloth and embroidered with gold thread and blue, purple, and scarlet yarn. [9] It was doubled over to form a pouch, nine inches* square. [10] Four rows of gemstones* were set across it. In the first row were a red carnelian, a chrysolite, and an emerald. [11] In the second row were a turquoise, a sapphire, and a white moonstone. [12] In the third row were a jacinth, an agate, and an amethyst. [13] In the fourth row were a beryl, an onyx, and a jasper. Each of these gemstones was set in gold. [14] The stones were engraved like a seal, each with the name of one of the twelve tribes of Israel.

38:21 Hebrew the Tabernacle, the Tabernacle of the Testimony.   38:24 Hebrew 29 talents [2,175 pounds or 986 kilograms] and 730 shekels [18.3 pounds or 8.3 kilograms], according to the sanctuary shekel.   38:25 Hebrew 100 talents [7,500 pounds or 3,400 kilograms] and 1,775 shekels [44.4 pounds or 20.2 kilograms], according to the sanctuary shekel.   38:26 Hebrew 1 beka [6 grams] per person, that is, half a shekel, according to the sanctuary shekel.   38:27 Hebrew 100 talents [3,400 kilograms] of silver, 1 talent [34 kilograms] for each base.   38:28 Hebrew 1,775 shekels [20.2 kilograms].   38:29 Hebrew 70 talents [5,250 pounds or 2,380 kilograms] and 2,400 shekels [60 pounds or 27.4 kilograms].   39:9 Hebrew 1 span [23 centimeters].   39:10 The identification of some of these gemstones is uncertain.

¹⁵To attach the chestpiece to the ephod, they made braided cords of pure gold. ¹⁶They also made two gold rings and attached them to the top corners of the chestpiece. ¹⁷The two gold cords were put through the gold rings on the chestpiece, ¹⁸and the ends of the cords were tied to the gold settings on the shoulder-pieces of the ephod. ¹⁹Two more gold rings were attached to the lower inside corners of the chestpiece next to the ephod. ²⁰Then two gold rings were attached to the ephod near the sash. ²¹Blue cords were used to attach the bottom rings of the chestpiece to the rings on the ephod. In this way, the chestpiece was held securely to the ephod above the beautiful sash. All this was done just as the LORD had commanded Moses.

²²The robe of the ephod was woven entirely of blue yarn, ²³with an opening for Aaron's head in the middle of it. The edge of this opening was reinforced with a woven collar,* so it would not tear. ²⁴Pomegranates were attached to the bottom edge of the robe. These were finely crafted of blue, purple, and scarlet yarn. ²⁵Bells of pure gold were placed between the pomegranates along the hem of the robe, ²⁶with bells and pomegranates alternating all around the hem. This robe was to be worn when Aaron ministered to the LORD, just as the LORD had commanded Moses.

²⁷Tunics were then made for Aaron and his sons from fine linen cloth. ²⁸The turban, the headdresses, and the underclothes were all made of this fine linen. ²⁹The sashes were made of fine linen cloth and embroidered with blue, purple, and scarlet yarn, just as the LORD had commanded Moses. ³⁰Finally, they made the sacred medallion of pure gold to be worn on the front of the turban. Using the techniques of an engraver, they inscribed it with these words: SET APART AS HOLY TO THE LORD. ³¹This medallion was tied to the turban with a blue cord, just as the LORD had commanded Moses.

³²And so at last the Tabernacle* was finished. The Israelites had done everything just as the LORD had commanded Moses. ³³And they brought the entire Tabernacle to Moses: the sacred tent with all its furnishings, the clasps, frames, crossbars,

posts, and bases; ³⁴the layers of tanned ram skins and fine goatskin leather; the inner curtain that enclosed the Most Holy Place; ³⁵the Ark of the Covenant* and its carrying poles; the Ark's cover—the place of atonement; ³⁶the table and all its utensils; the Bread of the Presence; ³⁷the gold lampstand and its accessories; the lamp cups and the oil for lighting; ³⁸the gold altar; the anointing oil; the fragrant incense; the curtain for the entrance of the sacred tent; ³⁹the bronze altar; the bronze grating; its poles and utensils; the large washbasin and its pedestal; ⁴⁰the curtains for the walls of the courtyard and the posts and bases holding them up; the curtain at the courtyard entrance; the cords and tent pegs; all the articles used in the operation of the Tabernacle; ⁴¹the beautifully crafted garments to be worn while ministering in the Holy Place—the holy garments for Aaron the priest and for his sons to wear while on duty.

⁴²So the people of Israel followed all of the LORD's instructions to Moses. ⁴³Moses inspected all their work and blessed them because it had been done as the LORD had commanded him.

CHAPTER 40

The LORD now said to Moses, ²"Set up the Tabernacle* on the first day of the new year.* ³Place the Ark of the Covenant* inside, and install the inner curtain to enclose the Ark within the Most Holy Place. ⁴Then bring in the table, and arrange the utensils on it. And bring in the lampstand, and set up the lamps.

⁵"Place the incense altar just outside the inner curtain, opposite the Ark of the Covenant. Set up the curtain made for the entrance of the Tabernacle. ⁶Place the altar of burnt offering in front of the Tabernacle entrance. ⁷Set the large washbasin between the Tabernacle* and the altar and fill it with water. ⁸Then set up the courtyard around the outside of the tent, and hang the curtain for the courtyard entrance.

⁹"Take the anointing oil and sprinkle it on the Tabernacle and on all its furnishings to make them holy. ¹⁰Sprinkle the anointing oil on the altar of burnt offering and its utensils, sanctifying them. Then the altar

---

39:23 The meaning of the Hebrew is uncertain.   39:32 Hebrew *the Tabernacle, the Tent of Meeting;* also in 39:40.   39:35 Or *Ark of the Testimony.*   40:2a Hebrew *the Tabernacle, the Tent of Meeting;* also in 40:6, 29.   40:2b Hebrew *the first day of the first month.* This day of the Hebrew lunar calendar occurs in March or early April.   40:3 Or *Ark of the Testimony;* also in 40:5, 21.   40:7 Hebrew *Tent of Meeting;* also in 40:12, 22, 24, 26, 30, 32, 34, 35.

will become most holy. [11]Next anoint the large washbasin and its pedestal to make them holy.

[12]"Bring Aaron and his sons to the entrance of the Tabernacle, and wash them with water. [13]Clothe Aaron with the holy garments and anoint him, setting him apart to serve me as a priest. [14]Then bring his sons and dress them in their tunics. [15]Anoint them as you did their father, so they may serve me as priests. With this anointing, Aaron's descendants are set apart for the priesthood forever, from generation to generation."

[16]Moses proceeded to do everything as the LORD had commanded him. [17]So the Tabernacle was set up on the first day of the new year.* [18]Moses put it together by setting its frames into their bases and attaching the crossbars and raising the posts. [19]Then he spread the coverings over the Tabernacle framework and put on the roof layers, just as the LORD had commanded him.

[20]He placed inside the Ark the stone tablets inscribed with the terms of the covenant,* and then he attached the Ark's carrying poles. He also set the Ark's cover—the place of atonement—on top of it. [21]Then he brought the Ark of the Covenant into the Tabernacle and set up the inner curtain to shield it from view, just as the LORD had commanded.

[22]Next he placed the table in the Tabernacle, along the north side of the Holy Place, just outside the inner curtain. [23]And he arranged the Bread of the Presence on the table that stands before the LORD, just as the LORD had commanded.

[24]He set the lampstand in the Tabernacle across from the table on the south side of the Holy Place. [25]Then he set up the lamps in the LORD's presence, just as the LORD had commanded. [26]He also placed the incense altar in the Tabernacle, in the Holy Place in front of the inner curtain. [27]On it he burned the fragrant incense made from sweet spices, just as the LORD had commanded.

[28]He attached the curtain at the entrance of the Tabernacle, [29]and he placed the altar of burnt offering near the Tabernacle entrance. On it he offered a burnt offering and a grain offering, just as the LORD had commanded.

[30]Next he placed the large washbasin between the Tabernacle and the altar. He filled it with water so the priests could use it to wash themselves. [31]Moses and Aaron and Aaron's sons washed their hands and feet in the basin. [32]Whenever they walked past the altar to enter the Tabernacle, they were to stop and wash, just as the LORD had commanded Moses.

[33]Then he hung the curtains forming the courtyard around the Tabernacle and the altar. And he set up the curtain at the entrance of the courtyard. So at last Moses finished the work.

[34]Then the cloud covered the Tabernacle, and the glorious presence of the LORD filled it. [35]Moses was no longer able to enter the Tabernacle because the cloud had settled down over it, and the Tabernacle was filled with the awesome glory of the LORD.

[36]Now whenever the cloud lifted from the Tabernacle and moved, the people of Israel would set out on their journey, following it. [37]But if the cloud stayed, they would stay until it moved again. [38]The cloud of the LORD rested on the Tabernacle during the day, and at night there was fire in the cloud so all the people of Israel could see it. This continued throughout all their journeys.

40:17 Hebrew *the first day of the first month, in the second year.* See note on 40:2b. **40:20** Hebrew *the Testimony.*

Leviticus

DELIVERED by God to Moses on Mount Sinai, the instructions of Leviticus pertain to Israel's personal and national life. Leviticus—the new nation's book of worship—derives its name from the tribe of Levi, which was entrusted with the ceremonial worship of God and the physical care of the Tabernacle. Leviticus solves the twin dilemmas of how a sinful people can achieve access to God (through animal sacrifices) and maintain fellowship with God (through obedience to his Word).

Focus	Sacrifice			Sanctification			
Divisions	Voluntary Offerings	Compulsory Offerings	Priestly Orders	Personal Purity	National Purity	Priestly Purity	Future Purity
	1 3	4 7	8 10	11 15	16 20	21 23	24 27
Topics	Access to God by Sacrifice			Fellowship with God by Obedience			
	Priests			Feasts			
Place	Mount Sinai						
Time	About One Month						

FEBRUARY 1 □ DAY 32
LEVITICUS 1–3
Three Voluntary Offerings

OVERVIEW Leviticus opens with a description of the five different sacrifices an Israelite could offer: three for those in fellowship with God (worship offerings) and two for those out of fellowship with God (compulsory offerings). The worship offerings were tailored to the person's ability to give, and each had a special significance. The burnt offering signified the devotion of the worshiper to God, the grain offering pointed to God's provision in life, and the peace offering pictured the thankful worshiper's fellowship with God.

Chapter 1	Chapter 2	Chapter 3
Burnt Offering	Grain Offering	Peace Offering
Worship Offerings		

YOUR DAILY WALK During a visit to Korea two American business-men were highly amused to see a young farmer hitched to a plow that was guided by his father. Later they learned that both father and son were Christians who sold their only ox to provide money for a new church building.

A drop of praise is unsuitable acknowledgment for an ocean of mercy.

"What a stupendous sacrifice!" exclaimed one of the businessmen.

"Not really," replied a missionary accompanying them. "They were only sorry they had but one ox to give to the Lord's work."

On one occasion Jesus was dining with a Pharisee named Simon when an immoral woman interrupted the dinner in a most startling way. She anointed Jesus' feet with expensive perfume, prompting the Lord to respond, "I tell you, her sins—and they are many—have been forgiven, so she has shown me much love. But a person who is forgiven little shows only little love" (Luke 7:47).

What is one tangible way in which you can show your gratitude today for God's great love and forgiveness? Select a twentieth-century sacrifice of praise you can offer him—perhaps in the form of a special offering or act of kindness—to say thank you to your heavenly Father who so richly deserves it!

INSIGHT Exodus and Leviticus: A Study in Contrasts

Exodus emphasizes:	*Leviticus emphasizes:*
Pardon	Purity
God's approach to people	People's approach to God
Salvation	Sanctification
"Let my people go"	"Be holy because I am holy"

CHAPTER 1

The LORD called to Moses from the Tabernacle* and said to him, ²"Give the following instructions to the Israelites: Whenever you present offerings to the LORD, you must bring animals from your flocks and herds.

³"If your sacrifice for a whole burnt offering is from the herd, bring a bull with no physical defects to the entrance of the

1:1 Hebrew *Tent of Meeting;* also in 1:3, 5.

Tabernacle so it will be accepted by the LORD. [4]Lay your hand on its head so the LORD will accept it as your substitute, thus making atonement for you. [5]Then slaughter the animal in the LORD's presence, and Aaron's sons, the priests, will present the blood by sprinkling it against the sides of the altar that stands in front of the Tabernacle. [6]When the animal has been skinned and cut into pieces, [7]the sons of Aaron the priest will build a wood fire on the altar. [8]Aaron's sons will then put the pieces of the animal, including its head and fat, on the wood fire. [9]But the internal organs and legs must first be washed with water. Then the priests will burn the entire sacrifice on the altar. It is a whole burnt offering made by fire, very pleasing to the LORD.

[10]"If your sacrifice for a whole burnt offering is from the flock, bring a male sheep or goat with no physical defects. [11]Slaughter the animal on the north side of the altar in the LORD's presence. Aaron's sons, the priests, will sprinkle its blood against the sides of the altar. [12]Then you must cut the animal in pieces, and the priests will lay the pieces of the sacrifice, including the head and fat, on top of the wood fire on the altar. [13]The internal organs and legs must first be washed with water. Then the priests will burn the entire sacrifice on the altar. It is a whole burnt offering made by fire, very pleasing to the LORD.

[14]"If you bring a bird as a burnt offering to the LORD, choose either a turtledove or a young pigeon. [15]The priest will take the bird to the altar, twist off its head, and burn the head on the altar. He must then let its blood drain out against the sides of the altar. [16]The priest must remove the crop and the feathers* and throw them to the east side of the altar among the ashes. [17]Then, grasping the bird by its wings, the priest will tear the bird apart, though not completely. Then he will burn it on top of the wood fire on the altar. It is a whole burnt offering made by fire, very pleasing to the LORD.

CHAPTER 2
"When you bring a grain offering to the LORD, the offering must consist of choice flour. You are to pour olive oil on it and sprinkle it with incense. [2]Bring this offering to one of Aaron's sons, and he will take a handful of the flour mixed with olive oil, together with all the incense, and burn this token portion on the altar fire. It is an offering made by fire, very pleasing to the LORD. [3]The rest of the flour will be given to Aaron and his sons. It will be considered a most holy part of the offerings given to the LORD by fire.

[4]"When you present some kind of baked bread as a grain offering, it must be made of choice flour mixed with olive oil but without any yeast. It may be presented in the form of cakes mixed with olive oil or wafers spread with olive oil. [5]If your grain offering is cooked on a griddle, it must be made of choice flour and olive oil, and it must contain no yeast. [6]Break it into pieces and pour oil on it; it is a kind of grain offering. [7]If your offering is prepared in a pan, it also must be made of choice flour and olive oil.

[8]"No matter how a grain offering has been prepared before being offered to the LORD, bring it to the priests who will present it at the altar. [9]The priests will take a token portion of the grain offering and burn it on the altar as an offering made by fire, and it will be very pleasing to the LORD. [10]The rest of the grain offering will be given to Aaron and his sons as their food. It will be considered a most holy part of the offerings given to the LORD by fire.

[11]"Do not use yeast in any of the grain offerings you present to the LORD, because no yeast or honey may be burned as an offering to the LORD by fire. [12]You may add yeast and honey to the offerings presented at harvesttime, but these must never be burned on the altar as an offering pleasing to the LORD. [13]Season all your grain offerings with salt, to remind you of God's covenant. Never forget to add salt to your grain offerings.

[14]"If you present a grain offering to the LORD from the first portion of your harvest, bring kernels of new grain that have been roasted on a fire. [15]Since it is a grain offering, put olive oil on it and sprinkle it with incense. [16]The priests will take a token portion of the roasted grain mixed with olive oil, together with all the incense, and burn it as an offering given to the LORD by fire.

1:16 Or *the crop and its contents.* The meaning of the Hebrew is uncertain.

CHAPTER 3
"If you want to present a peace offering from the herd, use either a bull or a cow. The animal you offer to the LORD must have no physical defects. ²Lay your hand on the animal's head, and slaughter it at the entrance of the Tabernacle.* Aaron's sons, the priests, will then sprinkle the animal's blood against the sides of the altar. ³Part of this peace offering must be presented to the LORD as an offering made by fire. This includes the fat around the internal organs, ⁴the two kidneys with the fat around them near the loins, and the lobe of the liver, which is to be removed with the kidneys. ⁵The sons of Aaron will burn these on the altar on top of the burnt offering on the wood fire. It is an offering made by fire, very pleasing to the LORD.

⁶"If you present a peace offering to the LORD from the flock, you may bring either a goat or a sheep. It may be either male or female, and it must have no physical defects. ⁷If you bring a sheep as your gift, present it to the LORD ⁸by laying your hand on its head and slaughtering it at the entrance of the Tabernacle. The sons of Aaron will then sprinkle the sheep's blood against the sides of the altar. ⁹Part of this peace offering must be presented to the LORD as an offering made by fire. This includes the fat of the entire tail cut off near the backbone, the fat around the internal organs, ¹⁰the two kidneys with the fat around them near the loins, and the lobe of the liver, which is to be removed with the kidneys. ¹¹The priest will burn them on the altar as food, an offering given to the LORD by fire.

¹²"If you bring a goat as your offering to the LORD, ¹³lay your hand on its head, and slaughter it at the entrance of the Tabernacle. Then the sons of Aaron will sprinkle the goat's blood against the sides of the altar. ¹⁴Part of this offering must be presented to the LORD as an offering made by fire. This part includes the fat around the internal organs, ¹⁵the two kidneys with the fat around them near the loins, and the lobe of the liver, which is to be removed with the kidneys. ¹⁶The priest will burn them on the altar as food, an offering made by fire; these will be very pleasing to the LORD. Remember, all the fat belongs to the LORD.

¹⁷"You must never eat any fat or blood. This is a permanent law for you and all your descendants, wherever they may live."

3:2 Hebrew *Tent of Meeting*; also in 3:8, 13.

FEBRUARY 2 ☐ DAY 33
LEVITICUS 4–7
Two Compulsory Offerings

OVERVIEW In addition to the three worship offerings, God gives instruction regarding two compulsory offerings—both required when sin had interrupted fellowship with him. The sin offering, which covered sins of uncleanness, neglect, or thoughtlessness, provided restoration for the sinner while reinforcing the seriousness of sin. The guilt offering, which covered sins of injury to God and others, provided compensation for the injured or offended party.

Chapter 4	Chapter 5	Chapters 6–7
Sin Offering	Guilt Offering	Law of the Offerings
Compulsory Offerings		Reviewing the Offerings

YOUR DAILY WALK What do a dented fender, a facial scar, and a stain on the carpet all have in common? (Hint: It has nothing to do with your teenage son!) Give up? They are all constant reminders of unpleasant experiences: the fire hydrant that ran into your car, the razor that "gotcha," the spill that ruined the rug.

Sin is so big   For the Israelites there was another collection of reminders: the
that it takes a bleating of a lamb, the smell of fresh blood, the sight of rising
Christ with smoke. All served to remind them that they were sinners. Every new
a cross to sin, even an unintentional one, demanded that another animal be
measure it. slain.

    Doesn't that make you appreciate all the more the death of Jesus
Christ for you? The fact that he died to set you free from the endless
requirement of additional sacrifices is indeed a great reason for rejoicing.
Remind yourself often today of Christ's once-for-all-time sacrifice for
you, and let that reminder bear the fruit of praise on your lips and in
your life.

INSIGHT   Sweet and Sour Offerings
Unlike the other three offerings, neither the sin nor the guilt offering
was a sweet fragrance to God because sin is never sweet to God. Those
two offerings foreshadowed many details of Christ's sacrificial death on
the cross:
- The sacrifice was without spot or blemish.
- Sin was transferred from the offerer to the sacrifice.
- The sacrifice died in the sinner's place.
- The sin sacrifice was offered outside the camp.

CHAPTER 4

Then the LORD said to Moses, 2"Give the Israelites the following instructions for dealing with those who sin unintentionally by doing anything forbidden by the LORD's commands.

3"If the high priest sins, bringing guilt upon the entire community, he must bring to the LORD a young bull with no physical defects. 4He must present the bull to the LORD at the entrance of the Tabernacle,* lay his hand on the bull's head, and slaughter it there in the LORD's presence. 5The priest on duty will then take some of the animal's blood into the Tabernacle, 6dip his finger into the blood, and sprinkle it seven times before the LORD in front of the inner curtain of the Most Holy Place. 7The priest will put some of the blood on the horns of the incense altar that stands in the LORD's presence in Tabernacle. The rest of the bull's blood must be poured out at the base of the altar of burnt offerings at the entrance of the Tabernacle. 8The priest must remove all the fat around the bull's internal organs, 9the two kidneys with the fat around them near the loins, and the lobe of the liver. 10Then he must burn them on the altar of burnt offerings, just as is done with the bull or cow sacrificed as a peace offering. 11But the rest of the bull—its hide, meat, head, legs, internal organs, and dung—12must be carried away to a ceremonially clean place outside the camp, the place where the ashes are thrown. He will burn it all on a wood fire in the ash heap.

13"If the entire Israelite community does something forbidden by the LORD and the matter escapes the community's notice, all the people will be guilty. 14When they discover their sin, the leaders of the community must bring a young bull for a sin offering and present it at the entrance of the Tabernacle. 15The leaders must then lay their hands on the bull's head and slaughter it there before the LORD. 16The priest will bring some of its blood into the Tabernacle, 17dip his finger into the blood, and sprinkle it seven times before the LORD in front of the inner curtain. 18He will then put some of the blood on the horns of the incense altar that stands in the LORD's presence in the Tabernacle. The rest of the blood must then be poured out at the base of the altar of burnt offerings at the entrance of the Tabernacle. 19The priest must remove all the animal's fat and burn it on the altar, 20following the same procedure as with the sin offering for the priest. In this way, the priest will make atonement for the people, and they will be forgiven. 21The priest must then take what is left of the bull outside the camp and burn it there, just as is done with the sin offering for the high priest. This is a sin offering for the entire community of Israel.

4:4 Hebrew *Tent of Meeting;* also in 4:5, 7, 14, 16, 18.

²²"If one of Israel's leaders does something forbidden by the LORD his God, he will be guilty even if he sinned unintentionally. ²³When he becomes aware of his sin, he must bring as his offering a male goat with no physical defects. ²⁴He is to lay his hand on the goat's head and slaughter it before the LORD at the place where burnt offerings are slaughtered. This will be his sin offering. ²⁵Then the priest will dip his finger into the blood of the sin offering, put it on the horns of the altar of burnt offerings, and pour out the rest of the blood at the base of the altar. ²⁶He must burn all the goat's fat on the altar, just as is done with the peace offering. In this way, the priest will make atonement for the leader's sin, and he will be forgiven.

²⁷"If any of the citizens of Israel* do something forbidden by the LORD, they will be guilty even if they sinned unintentionally. ²⁸When they become aware of their sin, they must bring as their offering a female goat with no physical defects. It will be offered for their sin. ²⁹They are to lay a hand on the head of the sin offering and slaughter it at the place where burnt offerings are slaughtered. ³⁰The priest will then dip his finger into the blood, put the blood on the horns of the altar of burnt offerings, and pour out the rest of the blood at the base of the altar. ³¹Those who are guilty must remove all the goat's fat, just as is done with the peace offering. Then the priest will burn the fat on the altar, and it will be very pleasing to the LORD. In this way, the priest will make atonement for them, and they will be forgiven.

³²"If any of the people bring a sheep as their sin offering, it must be a female with no physical defects. ³³They are to lay a hand on the head of the sin offering and slaughter it at the place where the burnt offerings are slaughtered. ³⁴The priest will then dip his finger into the blood, put it on the horns of the altar of burnt offerings, and pour out the rest of the blood at the base of the altar. ³⁵Those who are guilty must remove all the sheep's fat, just as is done with a sheep presented as a peace offering. Then the priest will burn the fat on the altar on top of the offerings given to the LORD by fire. In this way, the priest will make atonement for them, and they will be forgiven.

CHAPTER 5

"If any of the people are called to testify about something they have witnessed, but they refuse to testify, they will be held responsible and be subject to punishment.

²"Or if they touch something that is ceremonially unclean, such as the dead body of an animal that is ceremonially unclean—whether a wild animal, a domesticated animal, or an animal that scurries along the ground—they will be considered ceremonially unclean and guilty, even if they are unaware of their defilement.

³"Or if they come into contact with any source of human defilement, even if they don't realize they have been defiled, they will be considered guilty as soon as they become aware of it.

⁴"Or if they make a rash vow of any kind, whether its purpose is for good or bad, they will be considered guilty even if they were not fully aware of what they were doing at the time.

⁵"When any of the people become aware of their guilt in any of these ways, they must confess their sin ⁶and bring to the LORD as their penalty a female from the flock, either a sheep or a goat. This will be a sin offering to remove their sin, and the priest will make atonement for them.

⁷"If any of them cannot afford to bring a sheep, they must bring to the LORD two young turtledoves or two young pigeons as the penalty for their sin. One of the birds will be a sin offering, and the other will be a burnt offering. ⁸They must bring them to the priest, who will offer one of the birds as the sin offering. The priest will wring its neck but without severing its head from the body. ⁹Then he will sprinkle some of the blood of the sin offering against the sides of the altar, and the rest will be drained out at the base of the altar. ¹⁰The priest will offer the second bird as a whole burnt offering, following all the procedures that have been prescribed. In this way, the priest will make atonement for those who are guilty, and they will be forgiven.

¹¹"If any of the people cannot afford to bring young turtledoves or pigeons, they must bring two quarts* of choice flour for their sin offering. Since it is a sin offering, they must not mix it with olive oil or put any incense on it. ¹²They must take the

4:27 Hebrew *people of the land.*   5:11 Hebrew ¹/₁₀ *of an ephah* [2 liters].

flour to the priest, who will scoop out a handful as a token portion. He will burn this flour on the altar just like any other offering given to the LORD by fire. This will be their sin offering. [13]In this way, the priest will make atonement for those who are guilty, and they will be forgiven. The rest of the flour will belong to the priest, just as with the grain offering."

[14]Then the LORD said to Moses, [15]"If any of the people sin by unintentionally defiling the LORD's sacred property, they must bring to the LORD a ram from the flock as their guilt offering. The animal must have no physical defects, and it must be of the proper value in silver as measured by the standard sanctuary shekel.* [16]They must then make restitution for whatever holy things they have defiled by paying for the loss, plus an added penalty of 20 percent. When they give their payments to the priest, he will make atonement for them with the ram sacrificed as a guilt offering, and they will be forgiven.

[17]"If any of them sin by doing something forbidden by the LORD, even if it is done unintentionally, they will be held responsible. When they become aware of their guilt, [18]they must bring to the priest a ram from the flock as a guilt offering. The animal must have no physical defects, and it must be of the proper value. In this way, the priest will make atonement for those who are guilty, and they will be forgiven. [19]This is a guilt offering, for they have been guilty of an offense against the LORD."

CHAPTER 6

And the LORD said to Moses, [2]"Suppose some of the people sin against the LORD by falsely telling their neighbor that an item entrusted to their safekeeping has been lost or stolen. Or suppose they have been dishonest with regard to a security deposit, or they have taken something by theft or extortion. [3]Or suppose they find a lost item and lie about it, or they deny something while under oath, or they commit any other similar sin. [4]If they have sinned in any of these ways and are guilty, they must give back whatever they have taken by theft or extortion, whether a security deposit, or property entrusted to them, or a lost object that they claimed as their own, [5]or anything gained by swearing falsely. When

they realize their guilt, they must restore the principal amount plus a penalty of 20 percent to the person they have harmed. [6]They must then bring a guilt offering to the priest, who will present it before the LORD. This offering must be a ram with no physical defects or the animal's equivalent value in silver.* [7]The priest will then make atonement for them before the LORD, and they will be forgiven."

[8]Then the LORD said to Moses, [9]"Give Aaron and his sons the following instructions regarding the whole burnt offering. The burnt offering must be left on the altar until the next morning, and the altar fire must be kept burning all night. [10]The next morning, after dressing in his special linen clothing and undergarments, the priest on duty must clean out the ashes of the burnt offering and put them beside the altar. [11]Then he must change back into his normal clothing and carry the ashes outside the camp to a place that is ceremonially clean. [12]Meanwhile, the fire on the altar must be kept burning; it must never go out. Each morning the priest will add fresh wood to the fire and arrange the daily whole burnt offering on it. He must then burn the fat of the peace offerings on top of this daily whole burnt offering. [13]Remember, the fire must be kept burning on the altar at all times. It must never go out.

[14]"These are the instructions regarding the grain offering. Aaron's sons must present this offering to the LORD in front of the altar. [15]The priest on duty will take a handful of the choice flour that has been mixed with olive oil and sprinkled with incense. He will burn this token portion on the altar, and it will be very pleasing to the LORD. [16]After burning this handful, the rest of the flour will belong to Aaron and his sons for their food. It must, however, be baked without yeast and eaten in a sacred place within the courtyard of the Tabernacle.* [17]Remember, this flour may never be prepared with yeast. I have given it to the priests as their share of the offerings presented to me by fire. Like the sin offering and the guilt offering, it is most holy. [18]Any of Aaron's male descendants, from generation to generation, may eat of the grain offering, because it is their regular share of the offerings given to the LORD by fire.

5:15 Each sanctuary shekel was about 0.4 ounces or 11 grams in weight.　　**6:6** Or *and the animal must be of the proper value;* Hebrew lacks *in silver;* compare 5:15.　　**6:16** Hebrew *Tent of Meeting;* also in 6:26, 30.

Anyone or anything that touches this food will become holy."

¹⁹And the LORD said to Moses, ²⁰"On the day Aaron and his sons are anointed, they must bring to the LORD a grain offering of two quarts* of choice flour, half to be offered in the morning and half to be offered in the evening. ²¹It must be cooked on a griddle with olive oil, and it must be well mixed and broken* into pieces. You must present this grain offering, and it will be very pleasing to the LORD. ²²As the sons of the priests replace their fathers, they will be inducted into office by offering this same sacrifice on the day they are anointed. It is the LORD's regular share, and it must be completely burned up. ²³All such grain offerings of the priests must be entirely burned up. None of the flour may be eaten."

²⁴Then the LORD said to Moses, ²⁵"Give Aaron and his sons these further instructions regarding the sin offering. The animal given as a sin offering is most holy and must be slaughtered in the LORD's presence at the place where the burnt offerings are slaughtered. ²⁶The priest who offers the sacrifice may eat his portion in a sacred place within the courtyard of the Tabernacle. ²⁷Anything or anyone who touches the sacrificial meat will become holy, and if the sacrificial blood splatters anyone's clothing, it must be washed off in a sacred place. ²⁸If a clay pot is used to boil the sacrificial meat, it must be broken. If a bronze kettle is used, it must be scoured and rinsed thoroughly with water. ²⁹Only males from a priest's family may eat of this offering, for it is most holy. ³⁰If, however, the blood of a sin offering has been taken into the Tabernacle to make atonement in the Holy Place for the people's sins, none of that animal's meat may be eaten. It must be completely burned up.

CHAPTER 7

"These are the instructions for the guilt offering, which is most holy. ²The animal sacrificed as a guilt offering must be slaughtered where the burnt offerings are slaughtered, and its blood sprinkled against the sides of the altar. ³The priest will then offer all its fat on the altar, including the fat from the tail, the fat around the internal organs, ⁴the two kidneys with the

fat around them near the loins, and the lobe of the liver, which is to be removed with the kidneys. ⁵The priests will burn these parts on the altar as an offering to the LORD made by fire. It is a guilt offering. ⁶All males from a priest's family may eat the meat, and it must be eaten in a sacred place, for it is most holy.

⁷"For both the sin offering and the guilt offering, the meat of the sacrificed animal belongs to the priest in charge of the atonement ceremony. ⁸In the case of the whole burnt offering, the hide of the sacrificed animal also belongs to the priest. ⁹Any grain offering that has been baked in an oven, prepared in a pan, or cooked on a griddle belongs to the priest who presents it. ¹⁰All other grain offerings, whether flour mixed with olive oil or dry flour, are to be shared among all the priests and their sons.

¹¹"These are the instructions regarding the different kinds of peace offerings that may be presented to the LORD. ¹²If you present your peace offering as a thanksgiving offering, the usual animal sacrifice must be accompanied by various kinds of bread—loaves, wafers, and cakes—all made without yeast and soaked with olive oil. ¹³This peace offering of thanksgiving must also be accompanied by loaves of yeast bread. ¹⁴One of each kind of bread must be presented as a gift to the LORD. This bread will then belong to the priest who sprinkles the altar with blood from the sacrificed animal. ¹⁵The animal's meat must be eaten on the same day it is offered. None of it may be saved for the next morning.

¹⁶"However, if you bring an offering to fulfill a vow or as a freewill offering, the meat may be eaten on that same day, and whatever is left over may be eaten on the second day. ¹⁷But anything left over until the third day must be completely burned up. ¹⁸If any of the meat from this peace offering is eaten on the third day, it will not be accepted by the LORD. It will have no value as a sacrifice, and you will receive no credit for bringing it as an offering. By then, the meat will be contaminated; if you eat it, you will have to answer for your sin.

¹⁹"Meat that touches anything ceremonially unclean may not be eaten; it must be completely burned up. And as for meat that may be eaten, it may only be eaten by

6:20 Hebrew ¹/₁₀ of an ephah [2 liters].   6:21 The meaning of this Hebrew term is uncertain.

people who are ceremonially clean. [20]Anyone who is ceremonially unclean but eats meat from a peace offering that was presented to the LORD must be cut off from the community. [21]If anyone touches anything that is unclean, whether it is human defilement or an unclean animal, and then eats meat from the LORD's sacrifices, that person must be cut off from the community."

[22]Then the LORD said to Moses, [23]"Give the Israelites these instructions: You must never eat fat, whether from oxen or sheep or goats. [24]The fat of an animal found dead or killed by a wild animal may never be eaten, though it may be used for any other purpose. [25]Anyone who eats fat from an offering given to the LORD by fire must be cut off from the community. [26]Even in your homes, you must never eat the blood of any bird or animal. [27]Anyone who eats blood must be cut off from the community."

[28]Then the LORD said to Moses, [29]"Give these further instructions to the Israelites: When you present a peace offering to the LORD, bring part of it as a special gift to the LORD. [30]Present it to him with your own hands as an offering given to the LORD by fire. Bring the fat of the animal, together with the breast, and present it to the LORD by lifting it up before him. [31]Then the priest will burn the fat on the altar, but the breast will belong to Aaron and his sons. [32]You are to give the right thigh of your peace offering to the priest as a gift. [33]The right thigh must always be given to the priest who sprinkles the blood and offers the fat of the peace offering. [34]For I have designated the breast and the right thigh for the priests. It is their regular share of the peace offerings brought by the Israelites. [35]This is their share. It has been set apart for Aaron and his descendants from the offerings given to the LORD by fire from the time they were appointed to serve the LORD as priests. [36]The LORD commanded that the Israelites were to give these portions to the priests as their regular share from the time of the priests' anointing. This regulation applies throughout the generations to come."

[37]These are the instructions for the whole burnt offering, the grain offering, the sin offering, the guilt offering, the ordination offering, and the peace offering. [38]The LORD gave these instructions to Moses on Mount Sinai when he commanded the Israelites to bring their offerings to the LORD in the wilderness of Sinai.

FEBRUARY 3 □ DAY 34
LEVITICUS 8–10
Priestly Orders and Offense

 OVERVIEW After the sacrifices come the divine requirements for the priests who are to offer them. Moses consecrates Aaron and his four sons to minister in the Tabernacle. Sacrifices and ceremonies take place for seven consecutive days, after which Aaron begins his duties. The joyous inaugural week abruptly ends, however, with the disobedience and death of two of Aaron's sons, which leads to a divine announcement of restrictions concerning the priests' conduct.

Chapter 8	Chapter 9	Chapter 10
Consecration of the Priests	Ministry of the Priests	Restrictions on the Priests
Dedication	Duty	Disqualification

 YOUR DAILY WALK Has this ever happened to you? You are late for an appointment and pushing the speed limit—from the wrong direction. Suddenly you catch a glimpse of flashing lights in your rearview mirror. You watch in numb despair as a police car draws ever closer and

If you go against the grain of God's law, you get splinters!

finally pulls over . . . the car next to you! Would that experience change your driving habits (at least for the next few miles)?

One of the reasons God gave you the Old Testament was to provide flashing lights to warn you of dangerous situations. Others learned the hard way, but you don't have to—*if* you take their painful example to heart. Nadab and Abihu met an untimely death because they took God's holiness lightly. In a moment of proud disobedience they offered the wrong kind of fire in the wrong place and paid for that act with their lives.

At the dinner table this evening, read aloud 1 Corinthians 10:11. Then, beginning with the story of Nadab and Abihu, share "Lessons from the Lives of Old Testament People" from which you can benefit today. After all, you'll never live long enough to duplicate all the mistakes of others—nor do you have to!

 INSIGHT The High Priest's Wardrobe—Fit for One! There would be many priests, but only one high priest—only one who would represent the people before God by entering the Most Holy Place to make atonement. To signify this unique role, only the high priest wore the *ephod*—a sacred garment of gold, blue, purple, and scarlet thread, and fine-twined linen (8:6-13; see also Exodus 28:4-14).

CHAPTER 8

The LORD said to Moses, ²"Now bring Aaron and his sons, along with their special clothing, the anointing oil, the bull for the sin offering, the two rams, and the basket of unleavened bread ³to the entrance of the Tabernacle.* Then call the entire community of Israel to meet you there."

⁴So Moses followed the LORD's instructions, and all the people assembled at the Tabernacle entrance. ⁵Moses announced to them, "The LORD has commanded what I am now going to do!" ⁶Then he presented Aaron and his sons and washed them with water. ⁷He clothed Aaron with the embroidered tunic and tied the sash around his waist. He dressed him in the robe of the ephod, along with the ephod itself, and attached the ephod with its decorative sash. ⁸Then Moses placed the chestpiece on Aaron and put the Urim and the Thummim inside it. ⁹He placed on Aaron's head the turban with the gold medallion at its front, just as the LORD had commanded him.

¹⁰Then Moses took the anointing oil and anointed the Tabernacle and everything in it, thus making them holy. ¹¹He sprinkled the altar seven times, anointing it and all its utensils and the washbasin and its pedestal, making them holy. ¹²Then he poured some of the anointing oil on Aaron's head, thus anointing him and making him holy for his work. ¹³Next Moses presented Aar-

on's sons and clothed them in their embroidered tunics, their sashes, and their turbans, just as the LORD had commanded him.

¹⁴Then Moses brought in the bull for the sin offering, and Aaron and his sons laid their hands on its head ¹⁵as Moses slaughtered it. Moses took some of the blood, and with his finger he put it on the four horns of the altar to purify it. He poured out the rest of the blood at the base of the altar. In this way, he set the altar apart as holy and made atonement for it.* ¹⁶He took all the fat around the internal organs, the lobe of the liver, and the two kidneys and their fat, and he burned them all on the altar. ¹⁷The rest of the bull, including its hide, meat, and dung, was burned outside the camp, just as the LORD had commanded Moses.

¹⁸Then Moses presented the ram to the LORD for the whole burnt offering, and Aaron and his sons laid their hands on its head ¹⁹as Moses slaughtered it. Then Moses took the ram's blood and sprinkled it against the sides of the altar. ²⁰Next he cut the ram into pieces and burned the head, some of its pieces, and the fat on the altar. ²¹After washing the internal organs and the legs with water, Moses burned the entire ram on the altar as a whole burnt offering. It was an offering given to the LORD by fire, very pleasing to the LORD. All this was done just as the LORD had commanded Moses.

8:3 Hebrew *Tent of Meeting;* also in 8:4, 31, 33, 35.   **8:15** Or *that atonement may be made on it.*

²²Next Moses presented the second ram, which was the ram of ordination. Aaron and his sons laid their hands on its head ²³as Moses slaughtered it. Then Moses took some of its blood and put it on the lobe of Aaron's right ear, the thumb of his right hand, and the big toe of his right foot. ²⁴Next he presented Aaron's sons and put some of the blood on the lobe of their right ears, the thumb of their right hands, and the big toe of their right feet. He then sprinkled the rest of the blood against the sides of the altar.

²⁵Next he took the fat, including the fat from the tail, the fat around the internal organs, the lobe of the liver, and the two kidneys with their fat, along with the right thigh. ²⁶On top of these he placed a loaf of unleavened bread, a cake of unleavened bread soaked with olive oil, and a thin wafer spread with olive oil. All these were taken from the basket of bread made without yeast that was placed in the LORD's presence. ²⁷He gave all of these to Aaron and his sons, and he presented the portions by lifting them up before the LORD. ²⁸Moses then took all the offerings back and burned them on the altar on top of the burnt offering as an ordination offering. It was an offering given to the LORD by fire, very pleasing to the LORD. ²⁹Then Moses took the breast and lifted it up in the LORD's presence. This was Moses' share of the ram of ordination, just as the LORD had commanded him.

³⁰Next Moses took some of the anointing oil and some of the blood that was on the altar, and he sprinkled them on Aaron and his clothing and on his sons and their clothing. In this way, he made Aaron and his sons and their clothing holy.

³¹Then Moses said to Aaron and his sons, "Boil the rest of the meat at the Tabernacle entrance, and eat it along with the bread that is in the basket of ordination offerings, just as I commanded you. ³²Any meat or bread that is left over must then be burned up. ³³Do not leave the Tabernacle entrance for seven days, for that is the time it will take to complete the ordination ceremony. ³⁴What has been done today was commanded by the LORD in order to make atonement for you. ³⁵Remember, you must stay at the entrance of the Tabernacle day and night for seven days, doing everything the LORD requires. If you fail in this, you

will die. This is what the LORD has said." ³⁶So Aaron and his sons did everything the LORD had commanded through Moses.

CHAPTER 9

After the ordination ceremony, on the eighth day, Moses called together Aaron and his sons and the leaders of Israel. ²He said to Aaron, "Take a young bull for a sin offering and a ram for a whole burnt offering, both with no physical defects, and present them to the LORD. ³Then tell the Israelites to take a male goat for a sin offering for themselves and a year-old calf and a year-old lamb for a whole burnt offering, each with no physical defects. ⁴Also tell them to take a bull* and a ram for a peace offering and flour mixed with olive oil for a grain offering. Tell them to present all these offerings to the LORD because the LORD will appear to them today."

⁵So the people brought all of these things to the entrance of the Tabernacle,* just as Moses had commanded, and the whole community came and stood there in the LORD's presence. ⁶Then Moses told them, "When you have followed these instructions from the LORD, the glorious presence of the LORD will appear to you."

⁷Then Moses said to Aaron, "Approach the altar and present your sin offering and your whole burnt offering to make atonement for yourself. Then present the offerings to make atonement for the people, just as the LORD has commanded."

⁸So Aaron went to the altar and slaughtered the calf as a sin offering for himself. ⁹His sons brought him the blood, and he dipped his finger into it and put it on the horns of the altar. He poured out the rest of the blood at the base of the altar. ¹⁰Then he burned on the altar the fat, the kidneys, and the lobe of the liver from the sin offering, just as the LORD had commanded Moses. ¹¹The meat and the hide, however, he burned outside the camp.

¹²Next Aaron slaughtered the animal for the whole burnt offering. His sons brought him the blood, and he sprinkled it against the sides of the altar. ¹³They handed the animal to him piece by piece, including the head, and he burned each part on the altar. ¹⁴Then he washed the internal organs and the legs and also burned them on the altar as a whole burnt offering.

9:4 Or *cow*; also in 9:18, 19.   **9:5** Hebrew *Tent of Meeting*; also in 9:23.

¹⁵Next Aaron presented the sacrifices for the people. He slaughtered the people's goat and presented it as their sin offering, just as he had done previously for himself. ¹⁶Then he brought the whole burnt offering and presented it in the prescribed way. ¹⁷He also brought the grain offering, burning a handful of the flour on the altar, in addition to the regular morning burnt offering.

¹⁸Then Aaron slaughtered the bull and the ram for the people's peace offering. His sons brought him the blood, and he sprinkled it against the sides of the altar. ¹⁹Then he took the fat of the bull and the ram—the fat from the tail and from around the internal organs—along with the kidneys and the lobe of the liver. ²⁰He placed these fat parts on top of the breasts of these animals and then burned them on the altar. ²¹Aaron then lifted up the breasts and right thighs as an offering to the LORD, just as Moses had commanded.

²²After that, Aaron raised his hands toward the people and blessed them. Then, after presenting the sin offering, the whole burnt offering, and the peace offering, he stepped down from the altar. ²³Next Moses and Aaron went into the Tabernacle, and when they came back out, they blessed the people again, and the glorious presence of the LORD appeared to the whole community. ²⁴Fire blazed forth from the LORD's presence and consumed the burnt offering and the fat on the altar. When the people saw all this, they shouted with joy and fell face down on the ground.

CHAPTER 10

Aaron's sons Nadab and Abihu put coals of fire in their incense burners and sprinkled incense over it. In this way, they disobeyed the LORD by burning before him a different kind of fire than he had commanded. ²So fire blazed forth from the LORD's presence and burned them up, and they died there before the LORD.

³Then Moses said to Aaron, "This is what the LORD meant when he said,

'I will show myself holy
    among those who are near me.
I will be glorified
    before all the people.'"

And Aaron was silent.

⁴Then Moses called for Mishael and El-

zaphan, Aaron's cousins, the sons of Aaron's uncle Uzziel. He said to them, "Come and carry the bodies of your relatives away from the sanctuary to a place outside the camp." ⁵So they came forward and carried them out of the camp by their tunics as Moses had commanded.

⁶Then Moses said to Aaron and his sons Eleazar and Ithamar, "Do not mourn by letting your hair hang loose* or by tearing your clothes. If you do, you will die, and the LORD will be angry with the whole community of Israel. However, the rest of the Israelites, your relatives, may mourn for Nadab and Abihu, whom the LORD has destroyed by fire. ⁷But you are not to leave the entrance of the Tabernacle,* under penalty of death, for the anointing oil of the LORD is upon you." So they did as Moses commanded.

⁸Then the LORD said to Aaron, ⁹"You and your descendants must never drink wine or any other alcoholic drink before going into the Tabernacle. If you do, you will die. This is a permanent law for you, and it must be kept by all future generations. ¹⁰You are to distinguish between what is holy and what is ordinary, what is ceremonially unclean and what is clean. ¹¹And you must teach the Israelites all the laws that the LORD has given through Moses."

¹²Then Moses said to Aaron and his remaining sons, Eleazar and Ithamar, "Take what is left of the grain offering after the handful has been presented to the LORD by fire. Make sure there is no yeast in it, and eat it beside the altar, for it is most holy. ¹³It must be eaten in a sacred place, for it has been given to you and your descendants as your regular share of the offerings given to the LORD by fire. These are the commands I have been given. ¹⁴But the breast and thigh that were lifted up may be eaten in any place that is ceremonially clean. These parts have been given to you and to your sons and daughters as your regular share of the peace offerings presented by the people of Israel. ¹⁵The thigh and breast that are lifted up must be lifted up to the LORD along with the fat of the offerings given by fire. Then they will belong to you and your descendants forever, just as the LORD has commanded."

¹⁶When Moses demanded to know what had happened to the goat of the sin offer-

ing, he discovered that it had been burned up. As a result, he became very angry with Eleazar and Ithamar, Aaron's remaining sons. [17]"Why didn't you eat the sin offering in the sanctuary area?" he demanded. "It is a holy offering! It was given to you for removing the guilt of the community and for making atonement for the people before the LORD. [18]Since the animal's blood was not taken into the Holy Place, you

should have eaten the meat in the sanctuary area as I ordered you."

[19]Then Aaron answered Moses on behalf of his sons. "Today my sons presented both their sin offering and their burnt offering to the LORD," he said. "This kind of thing has also happened to me. Would the LORD have approved if I had eaten the sin offering today?" [20]And when Moses heard this, he approved.

FEBRUARY 4 ☐ DAY 35
LEVITICUS 11–15
Personal Purity in Daily Life

OVERVIEW Today's reading sets forth laws regarding clean and unclean food, childbirth, leprosy and other skin diseases, and discharges. Being a holy people demands a holy lifestyle. Ceremonial purity is an indispensable part of worshiping a holy God, though it imposes restrictions on one's conduct. For the Israelites this meant dietary laws, strict health requirements, and temporary quarantines after contact with potentially harmful substances. The word *unclean* occurs more than a hundred times in these chapters, showing that ceremonial uncleanness (which is, in fact, disobedience) is no small matter with God.

Chapter 11	Chapter 12	Chapters 13–14	Chapter 15
Rules Regarding Food	Rules Regarding Childbirth	Rules Regarding Leprosy	Rules Regarding Discharges
Home Matters		Health Matters	

YOUR DAILY WALK Rules and restrictions bring out the absolute worst in people! There is something about seeing a sign that says Wet Paint—Do Not Touch that makes us a little bit touchy. Signs such as Keep Off the Grass or Don't Feed the Chimps or Speed Limit 55 seem to whisper in our ears, "I dare you . . ."

What people uncover, God will cover; what people cover, God will uncover.

But did you ever stop to think why those rules are there? Someone is trying to look out for the best interests of you and others. They know that fresh paint looks better on park benches than on dresses; that grass stays prettier when a horde of people isn't trampling it to death; that chimps don't survive well on a diet of Chee-tos; and that gas—and people—last longer if you drive moderately. Such rules are for your own good.

The same was true for many of Israel's laws. God gave them for his people's protection. So no scavenger animals for dinner, no contact with leprous people, and plenty of baths! In today's passage look for ways God protected his people through the laws he gave.

INSIGHT A Holy People, a Horrible Disease
Leprosy in Old Testament times was regarded as hereditary and incurable. The leper was excluded from the camp, and only after quarantine and careful inspection would that person be declared "clean"

once again. Leprosy is often used in the New Testament as a picture of sin. Like leprosy, sin's treatment demands cleansing and constant alertness (1 Corinthians 11:31). The forgiveness of sin, like the healing of leprosy, can be effected by God alone.

CHAPTER 11

Then the LORD said to Moses and Aaron, [2]"Give the following instructions to the Israelites: The animals you may use for food [3]include those that have completely divided hooves and chew the cud. [4]You may not, however, eat the animals named here* because they either have split hooves or chew the cud, but not both. The camel may not be eaten, for though it chews the cud, it does not have split hooves. [5]The same is true of the rock badger* [6]and the hare, so they also may never be eaten. [7]And the pig may not be eaten, for though it has split hooves, it does not chew the cud. [8]You may not eat the meat of these animals or touch their dead bodies. They are ceremonially unclean for you.

[9]"As for marine animals, you may eat whatever has both fins and scales, whether taken from fresh water or salt water. [10]You may not, however, eat marine animals that do not have both fins and scales. You are to detest them, [11]and they will always be forbidden to you. You must never eat their meat or even touch their dead bodies. [12]I repeat, any marine animal that does not have both fins and scales is strictly forbidden to you.

[13]"These are the birds you must never eat because they are detestable for you: the eagle, the vulture, the osprey, [14]the buzzard, kites of all kinds, [15]ravens of all kinds, [16]the ostrich, the nighthawk, the seagull, hawks of all kinds, [17]the little owl, the cormorant, the great owl, [18]the white owl, the pelican, the carrion vulture, [19]the stork, herons of all kinds, the hoopoe, and the bat.

[20]"You are to consider detestable all swarming insects that walk along the ground. [21]However, there are some exceptions that you may eat. These include insects that jump with their hind legs: [22]locusts of all varieties, crickets, bald locusts, and grasshoppers. All these may be eaten. [23]But you are to consider detestable all other swarming insects that walk or crawl.

[24]"The following creatures make you ceremonially unclean. If you touch any of their dead bodies, you will be defiled until evening. [25]If you move the dead body of an unclean animal, you must immediately wash your clothes, and you will remain defiled until evening.

[26]"Any animal that has divided but unsplit hooves or that does not chew the cud is unclean for you. If you touch the dead body of such an animal, you will be defiled until evening. [27]Of the animals that walk on all fours, those that have paws are unclean for you. If you touch the dead body of such an animal, you will be defiled until evening. [28]If you pick up and move its carcass, you must immediately wash your clothes, and you will remain defiled until evening.

[29]"Of the small animals that scurry or creep on the ground, these are unclean for you: the mole, the mouse, the great lizard of all varieties, [30]the gecko, the monitor lizard, the common lizard, the sand lizard, and the chameleon. [31]All these small animals are unclean for you. If you touch the dead body of such an animal, you will be defiled until evening. [32]If such an animal dies and falls on something, that object, whatever its use, will be unclean. This is true whether the object is made of wood, cloth, leather, or sackcloth. It must be put into water, and it will remain defiled until evening. After that, it will be ceremonially clean and may be used again.

[33]"If such an animal dies and falls into a clay pot, everything in the pot will be defiled, and the pot must be smashed. [34]If the water used to cleanse an unclean object touches any food, all of that food will be defiled. And any beverage that is in such an unclean container will be defiled. [35]Any object on which the dead body of such an animal falls will be defiled. If it is a clay oven or cooking pot, it must be smashed to pieces. It has become defiled, and it will remain that way.

[36]"However, if the dead body of such an animal falls into a spring or a cistern, the water will still be clean. But anyone who removes the dead body will be defiled. [37]If the dead body falls on seed grain to be

11:4 The identification of some of the animals, birds, and insects in this chapter is uncertain.   11:5 Or *coney*, or *hyrax*.

planted in the field, the seed will still be considered clean. ³⁸But if the seed is wet when the dead body falls on it, the seed will be defiled.

³⁹"If an animal that is permitted for eating dies and you touch its carcass, you will be defiled until evening. ⁴⁰If you eat any of its meat or carry away its carcass, you must wash your clothes. Then you will remain defiled until evening.

⁴¹"Consider detestable any animal that scurries along the ground; such animals may never be eaten. ⁴²This includes all animals that slither along on their bellies, as well as those with four legs and those with many feet. All such animals are to be considered detestable. ⁴³Never defile yourselves by touching such animals. ⁴⁴After all, I, the LORD, am your God. You must be holy because I am holy. So do not defile yourselves by touching any of these animals that scurry along the ground. ⁴⁵I, the LORD, am the one who brought you up from the land of Egypt to be your God. You must therefore be holy because I am holy.

⁴⁶"These are the instructions regarding the land animals, the birds, and all the living things that move through the water or swarm over the earth, ⁴⁷so you can distinguish between what is unclean and may not be eaten and what is clean and may be eaten."

CHAPTER 12

The LORD said to Moses, "Give these instructions to the Israelites: ²When a woman becomes pregnant and gives birth to a son, she will be ceremonially unclean for seven days, just as she is defiled during her menstrual period. ³On the eighth day, the boy must be circumcised. ⁴Then the woman must wait for thirty-three days until the time of her purification from the blood of childbirth is completed. During this time of purification, she must not touch anything that is holy. And she must not go to the sanctuary until her time of purification is over. ⁵If a woman gives birth to a daughter, she will be ceremonially defiled for two weeks, just as she is defiled during her menstrual period. She must then wait another sixty-six days to be purified from the blood of childbirth.

⁶"When the time of purification is completed for either a son or a daughter, the woman must bring a year-old lamb for a whole burnt offering and a young pigeon or turtledove for a purification offering. She must take her offerings to the priest at the entrance of the Tabernacle.* ⁷The priest will then present them to the LORD and make atonement for her. Then she will be ceremonially clean again after her bleeding at childbirth. These are the instructions to be followed after the birth of a son or a daughter.

⁸"If a woman cannot afford to bring a sheep, she must bring two turtledoves or two young pigeons. One will be for the whole burnt offering and the other for the purification offering. The priest will sacrifice them, thus making atonement for her, and she will be ceremonially clean."

CHAPTER 13

The LORD said to Moses and Aaron, ²"If some of the people notice a swelling or a rash or a shiny patch on their skin that develops into a contagious skin disease,* they must be brought to Aaron the priest or to one of his sons. ³The priest will then examine the affected area of a person's skin. If the hair in the affected area has turned white and appears to be more than skin-deep, then it is a contagious skin disease, and the priest must pronounce the person ceremonially unclean.

⁴"But if the affected area of the skin is white but does not appear to be more than skin-deep, and if the hair in the spot has not turned white, the priest will put the infected person in quarantine for seven days. ⁵On the seventh day the priest will make another examination. If the affected area has not changed or spread on the skin, then the priest will put the person in quarantine for seven more days. ⁶The priest will examine the skin again on the seventh day. If the affected area has faded and not spread, the priest will pronounce the person ceremonially clean. It was only a temporary rash. So after washing the clothes, the person will be considered free of disease. ⁷But if the rash continues to spread after this examination and pronouncement by the priest, the infected person must return to be examined again. ⁸If the priest notices that the rash has spread, then he must pronounce this person ceremonially unclean, for it is a contagious skin disease.

12:6 Hebrew *Tent of Meeting.*   13:2 Traditionally rendered *leprosy.* The Hebrew word used throughout this passage is used to describe various skin diseases.

9"Anyone who develops a contagious skin disease must go to the priest for an examination. 10If the priest sees that some hair has turned white and an open sore appears in the affected area, 11it is clearly a contagious skin disease, and the priest must pronounce that person ceremonially unclean. In such cases, the person need not be quarantined for further observation because it is clear that the skin is defiled by the disease.

12"Now suppose the priest discovers after his examination that a rash has broken out all over someone's skin, covering the body from head to foot. 13In such cases, the priest must examine the infected person to see if the disease covers the entire body. If it does, he will pronounce the person ceremonially clean because the skin has turned completely white. 14But if any open sores appear, the infected person will be pronounced ceremonially unclean. 15The priest must make this pronouncement as soon as he sees an open sore because open sores indicate the presence of a contagious skin disease. 16However, if the open sores heal and turn white like the rest of the skin, the person must return to the priest. 17If, after another examination, the affected areas have indeed turned completely white, then the priest will pronounce the person ceremonially clean.

18"If anyone has had a boil on the skin that has started to heal, 19but a white swelling or a reddish white spot remains in its place, that person must go to the priest to be examined. 20If the priest finds the disease to be more than skin-deep, and if the hair in the affected area has turned white, then the priest must pronounce that person ceremonially unclean. It is a contagious skin disease that has broken out in the boil. 21But if the priest sees that there is no white hair in the affected area, and if it doesn't appear to be more than skin-deep and has faded, then the priest is to put the person in quarantine for seven days. 22If during that time the affected area spreads on the skin, the priest must pronounce the person ceremonially unclean, because it is a contagious skin disease. 23But if the area grows no larger and does not spread, it is merely the scar from the boil, and the priest will pronounce that person ceremonially clean.

24"If anyone has suffered a burn on the skin and the burned area changes color, becoming either a shiny reddish white or white, 25then the priest must examine it. If the hair in the affected area turns white and the problem appears to be more than skin-deep, a contagious skin disease has broken out in the burn. The priest must then pronounce that person ceremonially unclean, for it is clearly a contagious skin disease. 26But if the priest discovers that there is no white hair in the affected area and the problem appears to be no more than skin-deep and has faded, then the priest is to put the infected person in quarantine for seven days. 27If at the end of that time the affected area has spread on the skin, the priest must pronounce that person ceremonially unclean, for it is clearly a contagious skin disease. 28But if the affected area has not moved or spread on the skin and has faded, it is simply a scar from the burn. The priest must then pronounce the person ceremonially clean.

29"If anyone, whether a man or woman, has an open sore on the head or chin, 30the priest must examine the infection. If it appears to be more than skin-deep and fine yellow hair is found in the affected area, the priest must pronounce the infected person ceremonially unclean. The infection is a contagious skin disease of the head or chin. 31However, if the priest's examination reveals that the infection is only skin-deep and there is no black hair in the affected area, then he must put the person in quarantine for seven days. 32If at the end of that time the affected area has not spread and no yellow hair has appeared, and if the infection does not appear to be more than skin-deep, 33the infected person must shave off all hair except the hair on the affected area. Then the priest must put the person in quarantine for another seven days, 34and he will examine the infection again on the seventh day. If it has not spread and appears to be no more than skin-deep, the priest must pronounce that person ceremonially clean. After washing clothes, that person will be clean. 35But if the infection begins to spread after the person is pronounced clean, 36the priest must do another examination. If the infection has spread, he must pronounce the infected person ceremonially unclean, even without checking for yellow hair. 37But if it appears that the infection has stopped spreading and black hair has grown in the affected area, then the infection has healed. The priest will then pronounce the infected person ceremonially clean.

38"If anyone, whether a man or woman, has shiny white patches on the skin, 39the priest must examine the affected area. If the patch is only a pale white, this is a harmless skin rash, and the person is ceremonially clean.

40"If a man loses his hair and his head becomes bald, he is still ceremonially clean. 41And if he loses hair on his forehead, he simply has a bald forehead; he is still clean. 42However, if a reddish white infection appears on the front or the back of his head, this is a contagious skin disease. 43The priest must examine him, and if he finds swelling around the reddish white sore, 44the man is infected with a contagious skin disease and is unclean. The priest must pronounce him ceremonially unclean because of the infection.

45"Those who suffer from any contagious skin disease must tear their clothing and allow their hair to hang loose.* Then, as they go from place to place, they must cover their mouth and call out, 'Unclean! Unclean!' 46As long as the disease lasts, they will be ceremonially unclean and must live in isolation outside the camp.

47"Now suppose an infectious mildew* contaminates some woolen or linen clothing, 48some woolen or linen fabric, the hide of an animal, or anything made of leather. 49If the affected area in the clothing, the animal hide, the fabric, or the leather has turned bright green or a reddish color, it is contaminated with an infectious mildew and must be taken to the priest to be examined. 50After examining the affected spot, the priest will put it away for seven days. 51On the seventh day the priest must inspect it again. If the affected area has spread, the material is clearly contaminated by an infectious mildew and is unclean. 52The priest must burn the linen or wool clothing or the piece of leather because it has been contaminated by an infectious mildew. It must be completely destroyed by fire.

53"But if the priest examines it again and the affected spot has not spread in the clothing, the fabric, or the leather, 54the priest will order the contaminated object to be washed and then isolated for seven more days. 55Then the priest must inspect the object again. If he sees that the affected area has not changed appearance after being washed, even if it did not spread, the object is defiled. It must be completely burned up, whether it is contaminated on the inside or outside. 56But if the priest sees that the affected area has faded after being washed, he is to cut the spot from the clothing, the fabric, or the leather. 57If the spot reappears at a later time, however, the mildew is clearly spreading, and the contaminated object must be burned up. 58But if the spot disappears after the object is washed, it must be washed again; then it will be ceremonially clean.

59"These are the instructions for dealing with infectious mildew in woolen or linen clothing or fabric, or in anything made of leather. This is how the priest will determine whether these things are ceremonially clean or unclean."

CHAPTER 14
And the LORD said to Moses, 2"The following instructions must be followed by those seeking purification from a contagious skin disease.* Those who have been healed must be brought to the priest, 3who will examine them at a place outside the camp. If the priest finds that someone has been healed of the skin disease, 4he will perform a purification ceremony, using two wild birds of a kind permitted for food, along with some cedarwood, a scarlet cloth, and a hyssop branch. 5The priest will order one of the birds to be slaughtered over a clay pot that is filled with fresh springwater. 6He will then dip the living bird, along with the cedarwood, the scarlet cloth, and the hyssop branch, into the blood of the slaughtered bird. 7The priest will also sprinkle the dead bird's blood seven times over the person being purified, and the priest will pronounce that person to be ceremonially clean. At the end of the ceremony, the priest will set the living bird free so it can fly away into the open fields.

8"The people being purified must complete the cleansing ceremony by washing their clothes, shaving off all their hair, and bathing themselves in water. Then they will be ceremonially clean and may return to live inside the camp. However, they must still remain outside their tents for

---

13:45 Or *and uncover their heads.*   13:47 Traditionally rendered *leprosy.* The Hebrew term used throughout this passage is the same term used for the various skin diseases described in 13:1-46.   14:2 Traditionally rendered *leprosy.* See note at 13:2.

seven days. ⁹On the seventh day, they must again shave off all their hair, including the hair of the beard and eyebrows, and wash their clothes and bathe themselves in water. Then they will be pronounced ceremonially clean.

¹⁰"On the next day, the eighth day, each person cured of the skin disease must bring two male lambs and one female year-old lamb with no physical defects, along with five quarts* of choice flour mixed with olive oil and three-fifths of a pint* of olive oil. ¹¹Then the officiating priest will present that person for cleansing, along with the offerings, before the LORD at the entrance of the Tabernacle.* ¹²The priest will take one of the lambs and the olive oil and offer them as a guilt offering by lifting them up before the LORD. ¹³He will then slaughter the lamb there in the sacred area at the place where sin offerings and burnt offerings are slaughtered. As with the sin offering, the guilt offering will be given to the priest. It is a most holy offering. ¹⁴The priest will then take some of the blood from the guilt offering and put it on the tip of the healed person's right ear, on the thumb of the right hand, and on the big toe of the right foot.

¹⁵"Then the priest will pour some of the olive oil into the palm of his own left hand. ¹⁶He will dip his right finger into the oil and sprinkle it seven times before the LORD. ¹⁷The priest will then put some of the oil remaining in his left hand on the tip of the healed person's right ear, on the thumb of the right hand, and on the big toe of the right foot, in addition to the blood of the guilt offering. ¹⁸The oil remaining in the priest's hand will then be poured over the healed person's head. In this way, the priest will make atonement before the LORD for the person being cleansed.

¹⁹"Then the priest must offer the sin offering and again perform the atonement ceremony for the person cured of the skin disease. After that, the priest will slaughter the whole burnt offering ²⁰and offer it on the altar along with the grain offering. In this way, the priest will make atonement for the person being cleansed, and the healed person will be ceremonially clean.

²¹"But anyone who cannot afford two lambs must bring one male lamb for a guilt offering, along with two quarts* of choice flour mixed with olive oil as a grain offering and three-fifths of a pint of olive oil. The guilt offering will be presented by lifting it up, thus making atonement for the person being cleansed. ²²The person being cleansed must also bring two turtledoves or two young pigeons, whichever the person can afford. One of the pair must be used for a sin offering and the other for a whole burnt offering. ²³On the eighth day, the person being cleansed must bring the offerings to the priest for the cleansing ceremony to be performed in the LORD's presence at the Tabernacle entrance. ²⁴The priest will take the lamb for the guilt offering, along with the olive oil, and lift them up before the LORD as an offering to him. ²⁵Then the priest will slaughter the lamb for the guilt offering and put some of its blood on the tip of the person's right ear, on the thumb of the right hand, and on the big toe of the right foot.

²⁶"The priest will also pour some of the olive oil into the palm of his own left hand. ²⁷He will dip his right finger into the oil and sprinkle some of it seven times before the LORD. ²⁸The priest will then put some of the olive oil from his hand on the lobe of the person's right ear, on the thumb of the right hand, and on the big toe of the right foot, in addition to the blood of the guilt offering. ²⁹The oil that is still in the priest's hand will then be poured over the person's head. In this way, the priest will make atonement for the person being cleansed.

³⁰"Then the priest will offer the two turtledoves or the two young pigeons, whichever the person was able to afford. ³¹One of them is for a sin offering and the other for a whole burnt offering, to be presented along with the grain offering. In this way, the priest will make atonement before the LORD for the person being cleansed. ³²These are the instructions for cleansing those who have recovered from a contagious skin disease but who cannot afford to bring the sacrifices normally required for the ceremony of cleansing."

³³Then the LORD said to Moses and Aaron, ³⁴"When you arrive in Canaan, the land I am giving you as an inheritance, I may contaminate some of your houses with an infectious mildew.* ³⁵The owner of such a house must then go to the priest and

14:10a Hebrew *3/10 of an ephah* [5.4 liters].   14:10b Hebrew *1 log* [0.3 liters]; also in 14:21.   14:11 Hebrew *Tent of Meeting;* also in 14:23.   14:21 Hebrew *1/10 of an ephah* [2 liters].   14:34 Traditionally rendered *leprosy.* See note at 13:47.

say, 'It looks like my house has some kind of disease.' ³⁶Before the priest examines the house, he must have the house emptied so everything inside will not be pronounced unclean. Then the priest will go in and inspect the house. ³⁷If he finds bright green or reddish streaks on the walls of the house and the contamination appears to go deeper than the wall's surface, ³⁸he will leave the house and lock it up for seven days. ³⁹On the seventh day the priest must return for another inspection. If the mildew on the walls of the house has spread, ⁴⁰the priest must order that the stones from those areas be removed. The contaminated material will then be thrown into an area outside the town designated as ceremonially unclean. ⁴¹Next the inside walls of the entire house must be scraped thoroughly and the scrapings dumped in the unclean place outside the town. ⁴²Other stones will be brought in to replace the ones that were removed, and the walls will be replastered.

⁴³"But if the mildew reappears after all these things have been done, ⁴⁴the priest must return and inspect the house again. If he sees that the affected areas have spread, the walls are clearly contaminated with an infectious mildew, and the house is defiled. ⁴⁵It must be torn down, and all its stones, timbers, and plaster must be carried out of town to the place designated as ceremonially unclean. ⁴⁶Anyone who enters the house while it is closed will be considered ceremonially unclean until evening. ⁴⁷All who sleep or eat in the house must wash their clothing.

⁴⁸"But if the priest returns for his inspection and finds that the affected areas have not reappeared after the fresh plastering, then he will pronounce the house clean because the infectious mildew is clearly gone. ⁴⁹To purify the house the priest will need two birds, some cedarwood, a scarlet cloth, and a hyssop branch. ⁵⁰He will slaughter one of the birds over a clay pot that is filled with fresh springwater. ⁵¹Then he will dip the cedarwood, the hyssop branch, the scarlet cloth, and the living bird into the blood of the slaughtered bird, and he will sprinkle the house seven times. ⁵²After he has purified the house in this way, ⁵³he will release the living bird in the open fields outside the town. In this way, the priest will make atonement for the house, and it will be ceremonially clean.

⁵⁴"These are the instructions for dealing with the various kinds of contagious skin disease* and infectious mildew,* ⁵⁵whether in clothing, in a house, ⁵⁶in a swollen area of skin, in a skin rash, or in a shiny patch of skin. ⁵⁷These instructions must be followed when dealing with any contagious skin disease or infectious mildew, to determine when something is ceremonially clean or unclean."

CHAPTER 15

The LORD said to Moses and Aaron, ²"Give these further instructions to the Israelites: Any man who has a genital discharge* is ceremonially unclean because of it. ³This defilement applies whether the discharge continues or is stopped up. In either case the man is unclean. ⁴Any bedding on which he lies and anything on which he sits will be defiled.

⁵"So if you touch the man's bedding, you will be required to wash your clothes and bathe in water, and you will remain ceremonially defiled until evening. ⁶If you sit where the man with the discharge has sat, you will be required to wash your clothes and bathe in water. You will then remain defiled until evening. ⁷The same instructions apply if you touch the man who has the unclean discharge. ⁸And if he spits on you, you must undergo the same procedure. ⁹Any blanket on which the man rides will be defiled. ¹⁰If you touch or carry anything that was under him, you will be required to wash your clothes and bathe in water, and you will remain defiled until evening. ¹¹If the man touches you without first rinsing his hands, then you will be required to wash your clothes and bathe in water, and you will remain defiled until evening. ¹²Any clay pot touched by the man with the discharge must be broken, and every wooden utensil he touches must be rinsed with water.

¹³"When the man's discharge heals, he must count off a period of seven days. During that time, he must wash his clothes and bathe in fresh springwater. Then he will be ceremonially clean. ¹⁴On the eighth day he must bring two turtledoves or two young pigeons and present himself to the LORD at the entrance of the Tabernacle* and give his offerings to the priest. ¹⁵The priest will present the offerings there, one for a sin offering

14:54 Traditionally rendered *leprosy.* See notes at 13:2 and 13:47.   15:2 Hebrew *a discharge from his flesh;* also in 15:32.
15:14 Hebrew *Tent of Meeting;* also in 15:29.

and the other for a whole burnt offering. In this way, the priest will make atonement for the man before the LORD for his discharge.

[16] "Whenever a man has an emission of semen, he must wash his entire body, and he will remain ceremonially defiled until evening. [17] Any clothing or leather that comes in contact with the semen must be washed, and it will remain defiled until evening. [18] After having sexual intercourse, both the man and the woman must bathe, and they will remain defiled until evening.

[19] "Whenever a woman has her menstrual period, she will be ceremonially unclean for seven days. If you touch her during that time, you will be defiled until evening. [20] Anything on which she lies or sits during that time will be defiled. [21] If you touch her bed, you must wash your clothes and bathe in water, and you will remain defiled until evening. [22] The same applies if you touch an object on which she sits, [23] whether it is her bedding or any piece of furniture. [24] If a man has sexual intercourse with her during this time, her menstrual impurity will be transmitted to him. He will remain defiled for seven days, and any bed on which he lies will be defiled.

[25] "If the menstrual flow of blood continues for many days beyond the normal period, or if she discharges blood unrelated to her menstruation, the woman will be cere-monially unclean as long as the discharge continues. [26] Anything on which she lies or sits during that time will be defiled, just as it would be during her normal menstrual period. [27] If you touch her bed or anything on which she sits, you will be defiled. You will be required to wash your clothes and bathe in water, and you will remain defiled until evening.

[28] "When the woman's menstrual discharge stops, she must count off a period of seven days. After that, she will be ceremonially clean. [29] On the eighth day, she must bring two turtledoves or two young pigeons and present them to the priest at the entrance of the Tabernacle. [30] The priest will offer one for a sin offering and the other for a whole burnt offering. In this way, the priest will make atonement for her before the LORD for her menstrual discharge.

[31] "In this way, you will keep the people of Israel separate from things that will defile them, so they will not die as a result of defiling my Tabernacle that is right there among them. [32] These are the instructions for dealing with a man who has been defiled by a genital discharge or an emission of semen; [33] for dealing with a woman during her monthly menstrual period; for dealing with anyone, man or woman, who has had a bodily discharge of any kind; and for dealing with a man who has had intercourse with a woman during her period."

FEBRUARY 5 ☐ DAY 36
LEVITICUS 16–17
The Holiest Day of the Year

OVERVIEW The great Day of Atonement observed each year was Israel's most significant act of worship. On that day the nation gathered to watch expectantly as the high priest entered the Most Holy Place with the blood of atonement to cover the sins of the nation for another year. Because blood was the central ingredient in Israel's national and personal forgiveness, God prohibited its use for any purpose except sacrifice to him, for "it is the blood, representing life, that brings you atonement" (17:11).

Chapter 16	Chapter 17
Atonement by Blood	Abstaining from Blood
Life of the Nation	Life of the Flesh

YOUR DAILY WALK   Have you ever had to live with a gnawing uncertainty? a recurring illness? an overdue bill? a threat of legal action? The emotions of facing situations like those are intensely painful.

The wonder of the Cross is not the blood, but whose blood.

In Old Testament times the emotions that charged the air on every Day of Atonement were just as intense. As the high priest cautiously entered the Most Holy Place to make atonement for the sins of the nation, one question was uppermost in everyone's mind: Will God pass over our sins for another year?

The awful reality of the Day of Atonement was this: Sins were never fully *cleansed.* They were only temporarily *covered* and sent away on the head of the scapegoat. The debt of sin remained unpaid, like a promissory note deferred from year to year.

Aren't you glad Jesus Christ ended that uncertainty for all time? By his death the long-standing debt of sin was paid in full (Colossians 2:14). When you pay your bills this month, remind yourself—and one other person—of the price Jesus paid.

INSIGHT   Covered and Protected for Another Year
The words *atone, appease,* and *pacify* all come from the same Hebrew root meaning "to cover," which appears more than one hundred times in the Old Testament. The same root occurs in Genesis 6:14, where Noah is commanded to "make a boat from resinous wood and seal it with tar, inside and out." Just as the tar covered the boat and protected the boat's passengers, so the shed blood of the sacrifice stood between sinful humanity and the holy God whose law had been violated.

CHAPTER 16

The LORD spoke to Moses after the death of Aaron's two sons, who died when they burned a different kind of fire than the LORD had commanded.* ²The LORD said to Moses, "Warn your brother Aaron not to enter the Most Holy Place behind the inner curtain whenever he chooses; the penalty for intrusion is death. For the Ark's cover—the place of atonement—is there, and I myself am present in the cloud over the atonement cover.

³"When Aaron enters the sanctuary area, he must follow these instructions fully. He must first bring a young bull for a sin offering and a ram for a whole burnt offering. ⁴Then he must wash his entire body and put on his linen tunic and the undergarments worn next to his body. He must tie the linen sash around his waist and put the linen turban on his head. These are his sacred garments. ⁵The people of Israel must then bring him two male goats for a sin offering and a ram for a whole burnt offering.

⁶"Aaron will present the bull as a sin offering, to make atonement for himself and his family. ⁷Then he must bring the two male goats and present them to the LORD at the entrance of the Tabernacle.* ⁸He is to cast sacred lots to determine which goat will be sacrificed to the LORD and which one will be the scapegoat.* ⁹The goat chosen to be sacrificed to the LORD will be presented by Aaron as a sin offering. ¹⁰The goat chosen to be the scapegoat will be presented to the LORD alive. When it is sent away into the wilderness, it will make atonement for the people.

¹¹"Then Aaron will present the young bull as a sin offering for himself and his family. After he has slaughtered this bull for the sin offering, ¹²he will fill an incense burner with burning coals from the altar that stands before the LORD. Then, after filling both his hands with fragrant incense, he will carry the burner and incense behind the inner curtain. ¹³There in the LORD's presence, he will put the incense on the burning coals so that a cloud of incense will rise over the Ark's cover—the place of atonement—that rests on the Ark of the Covenant.* If he follows these instructions, he will not die. ¹⁴Then he must dip his finger into the blood of the bull and sprinkle it on the front of the atonement cover and then seven times against the front of the Ark.

16:1 Hebrew *when they approached the LORD's presence;* compare 10:1.   16:7 Hebrew *Tent of Meeting;* also in 16:16, 17, 20, 23, 33.
16:8 Hebrew *azazel,* which in this context means "the goat of removal"; also in 16:10, 26.   16:13 Hebrew *on the Testimony,* referring to the terms of God's covenant with Israel, which were kept in the Ark.

¹⁵"Then Aaron must slaughter the goat as a sin offering for the people and bring its blood behind the inner curtain. There he will sprinkle the blood on the atonement cover and against the front of the Ark, just as he did with the bull's blood. ¹⁶In this way, he will make atonement for the Most Holy Place, and he will do the same for the entire Tabernacle, because of the defiling sin and rebellion of the Israelites. ¹⁷No one else is allowed inside the Tabernacle while Aaron goes in to make atonement for the Most Holy Place. No one may enter until he comes out again after making atonement for himself, his family, and all the Israelites.

¹⁸"Then Aaron will go out to make atonement for the altar that stands before the LORD by smearing some of the blood from the bull and the goat on each of the altar's horns. ¹⁹Then he must dip his finger into the blood and sprinkle it seven times over the altar. In this way, he will cleanse it from Israel's defilement and return it to its former holiness.

²⁰"When Aaron has finished making atonement for the Most Holy Place, the Tabernacle, and the altar, he must bring the living goat forward. ²¹He is to lay both of his hands on the goat's head and confess over it all the sins and rebellion of the Israelites. In this way, he will lay the people's sins on the head of the goat; then he will send it out into the wilderness, led by a man chosen for this task. ²²After the man sets it free in the wilderness, the goat will carry all the people's sins upon itself into a desolate land.

²³"As Aaron enters the Tabernacle, he must take off the linen garments he wore when he entered the Most Holy Place, and he must leave the garments there. ²⁴Then he must bathe his entire body with water in a sacred place, put on his garments, and go out to sacrifice his own whole burnt offering and the whole burnt offering for the people. In this way, he will make atonement for himself and for the people. ²⁵He must also burn all the fat of the sin offering on the altar.

²⁶"The man chosen to send the goat out into the wilderness as a scapegoat must wash his clothes and bathe in water. Then he may return to the camp.

²⁷"The bull and goat given as sin offerings, whose blood Aaron brought into the Most Holy Place to make atonement for Israel, will be carried outside the camp to be burned. This includes the animals' hides, the internal organs, and the dung. ²⁸The man who does the burning must wash his clothes and bathe himself in water before returning to the camp.

²⁹"On the appointed day in early autumn,* you must spend the day fasting and not do any work. This is a permanent law for you, and it applies to those who are Israelites by birth, as well as to the foreigners living among you. ³⁰On this day, atonement will be made for you, and you will be cleansed from all your sins in the LORD's presence. ³¹It will be a Sabbath day of total rest, and you will spend the day in fasting. This is a permanent law for you. ³²In future generations, the atonement ceremony will be performed by the anointed high priest who serves in place of his ancestor Aaron. He will put on the holy linen garments ³³and make atonement for the Most Holy Place, the Tabernacle, the altar, the priests, and the entire community. ³⁴This is a permanent law for you, to make atonement for the Israelites once each year."

Moses followed all these instructions that the LORD had given to him.

CHAPTER 17

Then the LORD said to Moses, ²"Give Aaron and his sons and all the Israelites these commands from the LORD: ³If any Israelite sacrifices a bull* or a lamb or a goat anywhere inside or outside the camp ⁴and does not bring it to the entrance of the Tabernacle* to present it as an offering to the LORD, that person will be guilty of a capital offense.* Such a person has shed blood and must be cut off from the community. ⁵This rule will stop the Israelites from sacrificing animals in the open fields. It will cause them to bring their sacrifices to the priest at the entrance of the Tabernacle, so he can present them to the LORD as peace offerings. ⁶That way the priest will be able to sprinkle the blood and burn the fat on the LORD's altar at the entrance of the Tabernacle, and it will be very pleasing to the LORD. ⁷The people must no longer be unfaithful to the LORD by offering sacrifices to evil spirits* out in the fields. This is a permanent law for them, to be kept generation after generation.

16:29 Hebrew *On the tenth day of the seventh month.* This day of the Hebrew lunar calendar occurs in September or early October.   17:3 Or *cow.*   17:4a Hebrew *Tent of Meeting;* also in 17:5, 6, 9.   17:4b Hebrew *blood guilt.*   17:7 Or *goat idols.*

⁸"Give them this command as well, which applies both to Israelites and to the foreigners living among you. If you offer a whole burnt offering or a sacrifice ⁹and do not bring it to the entrance of the Tabernacle to offer it to the LORD, you will be cut off from the community.

¹⁰"And I will turn against anyone, whether an Israelite or a foreigner living among you, who eats or drinks blood in any form. I will cut off such a person from the community, ¹¹for the life of any creature is in its blood. I have given you the blood so you can make atonement for your sins. It is the blood, representing life, that brings you atonement. ¹²That is why I said to the Israelites: 'You and the foreigners who live among you must never eat or drink blood.'

¹³"And this command applies both to Is-raelites and to the foreigners living among you. If you go hunting and kill an animal or bird that is approved for eating, you must drain out the blood and cover it with earth. ¹⁴The life of every creature is in the blood. That is why I have told the people of Israel never to eat or drink it, for the life of any bird or animal is in the blood. So whoever eats or drinks blood must be cut off.

¹⁵"And this command also applies both to Israelites and the foreigners living among you. If you eat from the carcass of an animal that died a natural death or was killed by a wild animal, you must wash your clothes and bathe yourselves in water. Then you will remain ceremonially unclean until evening; after that, you will be considered clean. ¹⁶But if you do not wash your clothes and bathe, you will be held responsible."

FEBRUARY 6 □ DAY 37
LEVITICUS 18–20
A Holy People Uniquely His

 OVERVIEW In addition to the regulations governing national holiness, God provides Israel with laws governing personal conduct and purity in matters pertaining to the family, community, and society in general. Because of the central importance of obedience, God requires that violators be punished promptly and in a manner appropriate to the crime committed. God's strict guidelines for living reflect his desire that his people be holy and uniquely his.

Chapter 18	Chapter 19	Chapter 20
Abstaining from Sexual Sins	Abstaining from Social Sins	Avoiding the Penalty for Sins
Holy People		Holy God

 YOUR DAILY WALK The chapters you read today are not pleasant, for in them you will discover the depths to which fallen human nature is capable of sinking: incest, child sacrifice, prostitution, bestiality, homosexuality.

A Christian's spiritual health is exactly proportional to his or her devotion to God.

More than fourteen hundred years later, Paul would describe human nature in these dismaying words: "shameful envy, murder, fighting, deception, malicious . . . insolent, proud, and boastful . . . heartless and unforgiving" (Romans 1:18-31). Perhaps these lists look like today's headlines, for human nature has not changed over the generations.

With so many ways to go astray, is it any wonder that God must lay down so many rules for his children to follow before he can turn them loose in pagan Canaan? God desires that his people be transformed by their relationships with him—not conformed to their world.

How about you? Are you *transformed* by godliness or *conformed* to worldliness? (Or are you *deformed* by trying to be both?) Take a strip of paper and write down those areas of your life in which you may be too much of a conformist (dress, activities, personal life, speech). Use it as a bookmark in your Bible to remind you that "living what you read" is the transformation God desires.

 INSIGHT Ten Familiar Commands in an Unfamiliar Place
Last month you read Exodus 20:1-17, the passage containing the familiar Ten Commandments. But did you know most of the ten are also contained in Leviticus 19? Go prospecting through the chapter to see how many you can find. Happy hunting!

CHAPTER 18

Then the LORD said to Moses, [2]"Say this to your people, the Israelites: I, the LORD, am your God. [3]So do not act like the people in Egypt, where you used to live, or like the people of Canaan, where I am taking you. You must not imitate their way of life. [4]You must obey all my regulations and be careful to keep my laws, for I, the LORD, am your God. [5]If you obey my laws and regulations, you will find life through them. I am the LORD.

[6]"You must never have sexual intercourse with a close relative, for I am the LORD. [7]Do not violate your father by having sexual intercourse with your mother. She is your mother; you must never have intercourse with her. [8]Do not have sexual intercourse with any of your father's wives, for this would violate your father.

[9]"Do not have sexual intercourse with your sister or half sister, whether she is your father's daughter or your mother's daughter, whether she was brought up in the same family or somewhere else.

[10]"Do not have sexual intercourse with your granddaughter, whether your son's daughter or your daughter's daughter; that would violate you. [11]Do not have sexual intercourse with the daughter of any of your father's wives; she is your half sister. [12]Do not have intercourse with your aunt, your father's sister, because she is your father's close relative. [13]Do not have sexual intercourse with your aunt, your mother's sister, because she is your mother's close relative. [14]And do not violate your uncle, your father's brother, by having sexual intercourse with his wife; she also is your aunt. [15]Do not have sexual intercourse with your daughter-in-law; she is your son's wife. [16]Do not have intercourse with your brother's wife; this would violate your brother.

[17]"Do not have sexual intercourse with both a woman and her daughter or marry both a woman and her granddaughter, whether her son's daughter or her daughter's daughter. They are close relatives, and to do this would be a horrible wickedness.

[18]"Do not marry a woman and her sister because they will be rivals. But if your wife dies, then it is all right to marry her sister.

[19]"Do not violate a woman by having sexual intercourse with her during her period of menstrual impurity.

[20]"Do not defile yourself by having sexual intercourse with your neighbor's wife.

[21]"Do not give any of your children as a sacrifice to Molech, for you must not profane the name of your God. I am the LORD.

[22]"Do not practice homosexuality; it is a detestable sin.

[23]"A man must never defile himself by having sexual intercourse with an animal, and a woman must never present herself to a male animal in order to have intercourse with it; this is a terrible perversion.

[24]"Do not defile yourselves in any of these ways, because this is how the people I am expelling from the Promised Land have defiled themselves. [25]As a result, the entire land has become defiled. That is why I am punishing the people who live there, and the land will soon vomit them out. [26]You must strictly obey all of my laws and regulations, and you must not do any of these detestable things. This applies both to you who are Israelites by birth and to the foreigners living among you.

[27]"All these detestable activities are practiced by the people of the land where I am taking you, and the land has become defiled. [28]Do not give the land a reason to vomit you out for defiling it, as it will vomit out the people who live there now. [29]Whoever does any of these detestable things will be cut off from the community of Is-

rael. [30]So be careful to obey my laws, and do not practice any of these detestable activities. Do not defile yourselves by doing any of them, for I, the LORD, am your God."

CHAPTER 19

The LORD also said to Moses, [2]"Say this to the entire community of Israel: You must be holy because I, the LORD your God, am holy. [3]Each of you must show respect for your mother and father, and you must always observe my Sabbath days of rest, for I, the LORD, am your God. [4]Do not put your trust in idols or make gods of metal for yourselves. I, the LORD, am your God.

[5]"When you sacrifice a peace offering to the LORD, offer it properly so it will be accepted on your behalf. [6]You must eat it on the same day you offer it or on the next day at the latest. Any leftovers that remain until the third day must be burned. [7]If any of the offering is eaten on the third day, it will be contaminated, and I will not accept it. [8]If you eat it on the third day, you will answer for the sin of profaning what is holy to the LORD and must be cut off from the community.

[9]"When you harvest your crops, do not harvest the grain along the edges of your fields, and do not pick up what the harvesters drop. [10]It is the same with your grape crop—do not strip every last bunch of grapes from the vines, and do not pick up the grapes that fall to the ground. Leave them for the poor and the foreigners who live among you, for I, the LORD, am your God.

[11]"Do not steal.

"Do not cheat one another.

"Do not lie.

[12]"Do not use my name to swear a falsehood and so profane the name of your God. I am the LORD.

[13]"Do not cheat or rob anyone.

"Always pay your hired workers promptly.

[14]"Show your fear of God by treating the deaf with respect and by not taking advantage of the blind. I am the LORD.

[15]"Always judge your neighbors fairly, neither favoring the poor nor showing deference to the rich.

[16]"Do not spread slanderous gossip among your people.*

"Do not try to get ahead at the cost of your neighbor's life, for I am the LORD.

[17]"Do not nurse hatred in your heart for any of your relatives.

"Confront your neighbors directly so you will not be held guilty for their crimes.

[18]"Never seek revenge or bear a grudge against anyone, but love your neighbor as yourself. I am the LORD.

[19]"You must obey all my laws.

"Do not breed your cattle with other kinds of animals. Do not plant your field with two kinds of seed. Do not wear clothing woven from two different kinds of fabric.

[20]"If a man has sexual intercourse with a slave girl who is committed to become someone else's wife, compensation must be paid. But since she had not been freed at the time, the couple will not be put to death. [21]The man, however, must bring a ram as a guilt offering and present it to the LORD at the entrance of the Tabernacle.* [22]The priest will then make atonement for him before the LORD with the sacrificial ram of the guilt offering, and the man will be forgiven.

[23]"When you enter the land and plant fruit trees, leave the fruit unharvested for the first three years and consider it forbidden.* [24]In the fourth year the entire crop will be devoted to the LORD as an outburst of praise. [25]Finally, in the fifth year you may eat the fruit. In this way, its yield will be increased. I, the LORD, am your God.

[26]"Never eat meat that has not been drained of its blood.

"Do not practice fortune-telling or witchcraft.

[27]"Do not trim off the hair on your temples or clip the edges of your beards.

[28]"Never cut your bodies in mourning for the dead or mark your skin with tattoos, for I am the LORD.

[29]"Do not defile your daughter by making her a prostitute, or the land will be filled with promiscuity and detestable wickedness.

[30]"Keep my Sabbath days of rest and show reverence toward my sanctuary, for I am the LORD.

[31]"Do not rely on mediums and psychics, for you will be defiled by them. I, the LORD, am your God.

[32]"Show your fear of God by standing

19:16 Hebrew *Do not act as a merchant toward your own people.*   **19:21** Hebrew *Tent of Meeting.*   **19:23** Hebrew *consider it uncircumcised.*

up in the presence of elderly people and showing respect for the aged. I am the LORD.

33"Do not exploit the foreigners who live in your land. 34They should be treated like everyone else, and you must love them as you love yourself. Remember that you were once foreigners in the land of Egypt. I, the LORD, am your God.

35"Do not use dishonest standards when measuring length, weight, or volume. 36Your scales and weights must be accurate. Your containers for measuring dry goods or liquids must be accurate.* I, the LORD, am your God, who brought you out of the land of Egypt. 37You must be careful to obey all of my laws and regulations, for I am the LORD."

CHAPTER 20

The LORD said to Moses, 2"Give the Israelites these instructions, which apply to those who are Israelites by birth as well as to the foreigners living among you. If any among them devote their children as burnt offerings to Molech, they must be stoned to death by people of the community. 3I myself will turn against them and cut them off from the community, because they have defiled my sanctuary and profaned my holy name by giving their children to Molech. 4And if the people of the community ignore this offering of children to Molech and refuse to execute the guilty parents, 5then I myself will turn against them and cut them off from the community, along with all those who commit prostitution by worshiping Molech.

6"If any among the people are unfaithful by consulting and following mediums or psychics, I will turn against them and cut them off from the community. 7So set yourselves apart to be holy, for I, the LORD, am your God. 8Keep all my laws and obey them, for I am the LORD, who makes you holy.

9"All who curse their father or mother must be put to death. They are guilty of a capital offense.

10"If a man commits adultery with another man's wife, both the man and the woman must be put to death. 11If a man has intercourse with his father's wife, both the man and the woman must die, for they are guilty of a capital offense. 12If a man has

intercourse with his daughter-in-law, both must be put to death. They have acted contrary to nature and are guilty of a capital offense.

13"The penalty for homosexual acts is death to both parties. They have committed a detestable act and are guilty of a capital offense. 14If a man has intercourse with both a woman and her mother, such an act is terribly wicked. All three of them must be burned to death to wipe out such wickedness from among you.

15"If a man has sexual intercourse with an animal, he must be put to death, and the animal must be killed. 16If a woman approaches a male animal to have intercourse with it, she and the animal must both be put to death. Both must die, for they are guilty of a capital offense.

17"If a man has sexual intercourse with his sister, the daughter of either his father or his mother, it is a terrible disgrace. Both of them must be publicly cut off from the community. Since the man has had intercourse with his sister, he will suffer the consequences of his guilt. 18If a man has intercourse with a woman suffering from a hemorrhage,* both of them must be cut off from the community, because he exposed the source of her flow, and she allowed him to do it.

19"If a man has sexual intercourse with his aunt, whether his mother's sister or his father's sister, he has violated a close relative. Both parties are guilty of a capital offense. 20If a man has intercourse with his uncle's wife, he has violated his uncle. Both the man and woman involved are guilty of a capital offense and will die childless. 21If a man marries his brother's wife, it is an act of impurity. He has violated his brother, and the guilty couple will remain childless.

22"You must carefully obey all my laws and regulations; otherwise the land to which I am bringing you will vomit you out. 23Do not live by the customs of the people whom I will expel before you. It is because they do these terrible things that I detest them so much. 24But I have promised that you will inherit their land, a land flowing with milk and honey. I, the LORD, am your God, who has set you apart from all other people. 25"You must therefore make a distinction between ceremonially clean and unclean animals, and between clean and unclean birds. You must not defile yourselves by eating any animal or bird or creeping creature that I have forbidden. ²⁶You must be holy because I, the LORD, am holy. I have set you apart from all other people to be my very own.

²⁷"Men and women among you who act as mediums or psychics must be put to death by stoning. They are guilty of a capital offense."

FEBRUARY 7 □ DAY 38
A Blueprint for Worship

LOOK BACK If you have safely navigated through the Scripture readings for this past week, congratulations! Many who begin with great enthusiasm in January to read all the way through the Bible wonder if they are going to falter and fall by the wayside in February when they get to the book of Leviticus. It needn't be that way if you understand the intention of the Author!

In Exodus 25 through 30 you read about the divine blueprint for the Tabernacle, the ornate traveling tent that would be Israel's place of worship on the march to the Promised Land. In exquisite detail God set forth the plan, and Moses—assisted by skillful, Spirit-filled workmen—followed the plan to the last detail. Only when the job was done "just as the LORD had commanded Moses" did the glory of God fill the Tabernacle.

But who would assist those who came to the Tabernacle to worship? And how would they know how to offer acceptable sacrifices on behalf of the people? Leviticus provides a helpful handbook for the Levites and priests who carried the awesome responsibility of leading the nation in corporate and private worship.

LOOK UP What would you think of a restaurant chef who decided that the weights and measures in a recipe were "a needless bother" and ignored them in preparing your dinner?

You cannot walk with God and run with the devil.

What would you think of an auto mechanic who decided that a sledgehammer and machete were just as good as metric tools when it came to servicing your car?

What would you think of a surgeon who used hedge clippers because "I never was much good with a scalpel"?

Probably you would use someone else's services. Why? Because *how* you do something is as important as *what* you do. Well-meaning, inept chefs, mechanics, and surgeons just don't get the job done.

Think of worship the same way. It's not enough to *want* to worship God—you must consider carefully *how* you worship God. You cannot approach a holy God with soiled hands or an unclean heart. You cannot expect to please God by offering him what is unacceptable to him. You cannot call something insignificant when God has called it indispensable.

LOOK AHEAD Chuck Swindoll has commented that we in America are guilty of playing at our worship, worshiping our work, and working at our play. Worship, done properly, is hard work. It involves the entire person in an attitude of humility and dependence upon God, acknowledging the "worth-ship" of our Creator and Sustainer. Begin now to prepare for the next visit you will make to your local house of worship. Here are some verses to look up and meditate upon as you prepare to give God the honor and adoration he so richly deserves: 1 Chronicles 16:29; Psalm 95:6; John 4:24; Revelation 15:4.

And if you find that you just can't wait, feel free to worship him for a few minutes right now! You might want to read the words of Psalm 100 out loud as the expression of your heart.

FEBRUARY 8 ☐ DAY 39
LEVITICUS 21–23
Priestly Purity

 OVERVIEW Ministry to and for a holy people requires a holy priesthood. Because of their high calling, the priests accepted extra restrictions on their conduct and privileges. They had to be physically perfect and willing to avoid defilements that were permissible for others. The sacrifices they offered had to be without blemish. They were required to carry out their duties with meticulous attention to detail. Their busiest times of the year came during the holy convocations—joyous times of feasting and reflecting on God's goodness in dealing with Israel.

Chapter 21		Chapter 22	Chapter 23
Priestly Defilements	Priestly Defects	Priestly Duties	Important Days
1 15	16 24		
Holy Priests			Yearly Festivals

 YOUR DAILY WALK Here is a statement worth considering, especially if you are the hard-driving kind of person commonly labeled as a workaholic: Seven days without relaxation makes one weak.

Jesus knows we must come apart and rest awhile or else we may just plain come apart.

On the seventh day of each week the Israelites were commanded to rest from their labors. Seven times each year they enjoyed a "holy holiday" to commemorate important days in their nation's history. These were no mere business meetings but were times of feasting and festivity.

How long has it been since you set aside your work to spend time alone or with your family enjoying a leisurely activity? If your mind is constantly focused on your job, it will seldom be focused on God. In contrast, periodic times of refreshment and reflection will help to improve your attitude toward your work.

Look at your personal or family calendar, and prayerfully consider whether a vacation is long overdue. It needn't be long to be refreshing. But it does need to be a priority in your schedule if it is ever to become more than just a good idea.

INSIGHT How about This for a Vacation Schedule?
Life in the nation of Israel was not all work, work, work. There were nineteen days of national holiday: Passover, Unleavened Bread (seven days), Firstfruits, Pentecost, Trumpets, Day of Atonement, and Shelters (seven days). Counting the weekly Sabbath days of rest, that makes ten weeks of vacation a year!

CHAPTER 21

The LORD said to Moses, "Tell the priests to avoid making themselves ceremonially unclean by touching a dead relative [2]unless it is a close relative—mother or father, son or daughter, brother [3]or virgin sister who was dependent because she had no husband. [4]As a husband among his relatives,* he must not defile himself.

[5]"The priests must never shave their heads, trim the edges of their beards, or cut their bodies. [6]They must be set apart to God as holy and must never dishonor his name. After all, they are the ones who present the offerings to the LORD by fire, providing God with his food, and they must remain holy.

[7]"The priests must not marry women defiled by prostitution or women who have been divorced, for the priests must be set apart to God as holy. [8]You must treat them as holy because they offer up food to your God. You must consider them holy because I, the LORD, am holy, and I make you holy. [9]If a priest's daughter becomes a prostitute, defiling her father's holiness as well as herself, she must be burned to death.

[10]"The high priest, who has had the anointing oil poured on his head and has been ordained to wear the special priestly garments, must never let his hair hang loose* or tear his clothing. [11]He must never defile himself by going near a dead person, even if it is his father or mother. [12]He must not desecrate the sanctuary of his God by leaving it to attend his parents' funeral, because he has been made holy by the anointing oil of his God. I am the LORD.

[13]"The high priest must marry a virgin. [14]He must not marry a widow, a divorced woman, or a woman defiled by prostitution. She must be a virgin from his own clan, [15]that he may not dishonor his descendants among the members of his clan, because I, the LORD, have made him holy."

[16]Then the LORD said to Moses, [17]"Tell Aaron that in all future generations, his descendants who have physical defects will not qualify to offer food to their God. [18]No one who has a defect may come near to me, whether he is blind or lame, stunted or deformed, [19]or has a broken foot or hand, [20]or has a humped back or is a dwarf, or has a defective eye, or has oozing sores

or scabs on his skin, or has damaged testicles. [21]Even though he is a descendant of Aaron, his physical defects disqualify him from presenting offerings to the LORD by fire. Since he has a blemish, he may not offer food to his God. [22]However, he may eat from the food offered to God, including the holy offerings and the most holy offerings. [23]Yet because of his physical defect, he must never go behind the inner curtain or come near the altar, for this would desecrate my holy places. I am the LORD who makes them holy."

[24]So Moses gave these instructions to Aaron and his sons and to all the Israelites.

CHAPTER 22

The LORD said to Moses, [2]"Tell Aaron and his sons to treat the sacred gifts that the Israelites set apart for me with great care, so they do not profane my holy name. I am the LORD. [3]Remind them that if any of their descendants are ceremonially unclean when they approach the sacred food presented by the Israelites, they must be cut off from my presence. I am the LORD!

[4]"If any of the priests have a contagious skin disease* or any kind of discharge that makes them ceremonially unclean, they may not eat the sacred offerings until they have been pronounced clean. If any of the priests become unclean by touching a corpse, or are defiled by an emission of semen, [5]or by touching a creeping creature that is unclean, or by touching someone who is ceremonially unclean for any reason, [6]they will remain defiled until evening. They must not eat any of the sacred offerings until they have purified their bodies with water. [7]When the sun goes down, they will be clean again and may eat the sacred offerings. After all, this food has been set aside for them. [8]The priests may never eat an animal that has died a natural death or has been torn apart by wild animals, for this would defile them. I am the LORD. [9]Warn all the priests to follow these instructions carefully; otherwise they will be subject to punishment and die for violating them. I am the LORD who makes them holy.

[10]"No one outside a priest's family may ever eat the sacred offerings, even if the person lives in a priest's home or is one of his hired servants. [11]However, if the priest

---

21:4 The meaning of the Hebrew is uncertain.   21:10 Or *uncover his head.*   22:4 Traditionally rendered *leprosy.* See note at 13:2.

buys slaves with his own money, they may eat of his food. And if his slaves have children, they also may share his food. [12]If a priest's daughter marries someone outside the priestly family, she may no longer eat the sacred offerings. [13]But if she becomes a widow or is divorced and has no children to support her, and she returns to live in her father's home, she may eat her father's food again. But other than these exceptions, only members of the priests' families are allowed to eat the sacred offerings.

[14]"Anyone who eats the sacred offerings without realizing it must pay the priest for the amount eaten, plus an added penalty of 20 percent. [15]No one may defile the sacred offerings brought to the LORD by the Israelites [16]by allowing unauthorized people to eat them. The negligent priest would bring guilt upon the people and require them to pay compensation. I am the LORD, who makes them holy."

[17]And the LORD said to Moses, [18]"Give Aaron and his sons and all the Israelites these instructions, which apply to those who are Israelites by birth as well as to the foreigners living among you. If you offer a whole burnt offering to the LORD, whether to fulfill a vow or as a freewill offering, [19]it will be accepted only if it is a male animal with no physical defects. It may be either a bull, a ram, or a male goat. [20]Do not bring an animal with physical defects, because it won't be accepted on your behalf.

[21]"If you bring a peace offering to the LORD from the herd or flock, whether to fulfill a vow or as a freewill offering, you must offer an animal that has no physical defects of any kind. [22]An animal that is blind, injured, mutilated, or that has a growth, an open sore, or a scab must never be offered to the LORD by fire on the altar. [23]If the bull* or lamb is deformed or stunted, it may still be offered as a freewill offering, but it may not be offered to fulfill a vow. [24]If an animal has damaged testicles or is castrated, it may never be offered to the LORD. [25]You must never accept mutilated or defective animals from foreigners to be offered as a sacrifice to your God. Such animals will not be accepted on your behalf because they are defective."

[26]And the LORD said to Moses, [27]"When a bull or a ram or a male goat is born, it must be left with its mother for seven days.

From the eighth day on, it will be acceptable as an offering given to the LORD by fire. [28]But you must never slaughter a mother animal and her offspring on the same day, whether from the herd or the flock. [29]When you bring a thanksgiving offering to the LORD, it must be sacrificed properly so it will be accepted on your behalf. [30]Eat the entire sacrificial animal on the day it is presented. Don't leave any of it until the second day. I am the LORD.

[31]"You must faithfully keep all my commands by obeying them, for I am the LORD. [32]Do not treat my holy name as common and ordinary. I must be treated as holy by the people of Israel. It is I, the LORD, who makes you holy. [33]It was I who rescued you from Egypt, that I might be your very own God. I am the LORD."

CHAPTER 23

The LORD said to Moses, [2]"Give the Israelites instructions regarding the LORD's appointed festivals, the days when all of you will be summoned to worship me. [3]You may work for six days each week, but on the seventh day all work must come to a complete stop. It is the LORD's Sabbath day of complete rest, a holy day to assemble for worship. It must be observed wherever you live. [4]In addition to the Sabbath, the LORD has established festivals, the holy occasions to be observed at the proper time each year.

[5]"First comes the LORD's Passover, which begins at twilight on its appointed day in early spring.* [6]Then the day after the Passover celebration,* the Festival of Unleavened Bread begins. This festival to the LORD continues for seven days, and during that time all the bread you eat must be made without yeast. [7]On the first day of the festival, all the people must stop their regular work and gather for a sacred assembly. [8]On each of the next seven days, the people must present an offering to the LORD by fire. On the seventh day, the people must again stop all their regular work to hold a sacred assembly."

[9]Then the LORD told Moses [10]to give these instructions to the Israelites: "When you arrive in the land I am giving you and you harvest your first crops, bring the priest some grain from the first portion of your grain harvest. [11]On the day after the

22:23 Or *cow;* also in 22:27.   **23:5** Hebrew *on the fourteenth day of the first month.* This day of the Hebrew lunar calendar occurs in late March or early April.   **23:6** Hebrew *On the fifteenth day of the same month.*

Sabbath, the priest will lift it up before the LORD so it may be accepted on your behalf. [12] That same day you must sacrifice a year-old male lamb with no physical defects as a whole burnt offering to the LORD. [13] A grain offering must accompany it consisting of three quarts* of choice flour mixed with olive oil. It will be an offering given to the LORD by fire, and it will be very pleasing to him. Along with this sacrifice, you must also offer one quart* of wine as a drink offering. [14] Do not eat any bread or roasted grain or fresh kernels on that day until after you have brought this offering to your God. This is a permanent law for you, and it must be observed wherever you live.

[15] "From the day after the Sabbath, the day the bundle of grain was lifted up as an offering, count off seven weeks. [16] Keep counting until the day after the seventh Sabbath, fifty days later, and bring an offering of new grain to the LORD. [17] From wherever you live, bring two loaves of bread to be lifted up before the LORD as an offering. These loaves must be baked from three quarts of choice flour that contains yeast. They will be an offering to the LORD from the first of your crops. [18] Along with this bread, present seven one-year-old lambs with no physical defects, one bull, and two rams as burnt offerings to the LORD. These whole burnt offerings, together with the accompanying grain offerings and drink offerings, will be given to the LORD by fire and will be pleasing to him. [19] Then you must offer one male goat as a sin offering and two one-year-old male lambs as a peace offering.

[20] "The priest will lift up these offerings before the LORD, together with the loaves representing the first of your later crops. These offerings are holy to the LORD and will belong to the priests. [21] That same day, you must stop all your regular work and gather for a sacred assembly. This is a permanent law for you, and it must be observed wherever you live.

[22] "When you harvest the crops of your land, do not harvest the grain along the edges of your fields, and do not pick up what the harvesters drop. Leave it for the poor and the foreigners living among you. I, the LORD, am your God."

[23] The LORD told Moses [24] to give these instructions to the Israelites: "On the appointed day in early autumn,* you are to celebrate a day of complete rest. All your work must stop on that day. You will call the people to a sacred assembly—the Festival of Trumpets—with loud blasts from a trumpet. [25] You must do no regular work on that day. Instead, you are to present offerings to the LORD by fire."

[26] Then the LORD said to Moses, [27] "Remember that the Day of Atonement is to be celebrated on the ninth day after the Festival of Trumpets.* On that day you must humble yourselves, gather for a sacred assembly, and present offerings to the LORD by fire. [28] Do no work during that entire day because it is the Day of Atonement, when atonement will be made for you before the LORD your God, and payment will be made for your sins. [29] Anyone who does not spend that day in humility will be cut off from the community. [30] And I will destroy anyone among you who does any kind of work on that day. [31] You must do no work at all! This is a permanent law for you, and it must be observed wherever you live. [32] This will be a Sabbath day of total rest for you, and on that day you must humble yourselves. This time of rest and fasting will begin the evening before the Day of Atonement* and extend until evening of that day."

[33] And the LORD said to Moses, [34] "Tell the Israelites to begin the Festival of Shelters on the fifth day after the Day of Atonement.* This festival to the LORD will last for seven days. [35] It will begin with a sacred assembly on the first day, and all your regular work must stop. [36] On each of the seven festival days, you must present offerings to the LORD by fire. On the eighth day, you must gather again for a sacred assembly and present another offering to the LORD by fire. This will be a solemn closing assembly, and no regular work may be done that day.

[37] "These are the LORD's appointed annual festivals. Celebrate them by gathering in sacred assemblies to present all the various offerings to the LORD by fire—whole burnt offerings and grain offerings, sacrificial meals and drink offerings—each on its proper day. [38] These festivals must be

---

23:13a Hebrew *²⁄₁₀ of an ephah* [3.6 liters]; also in 23:17.   **23:13b** Hebrew *¼ of a hin* [1 liter].   **23:24** Hebrew *On the first day of the seventh month.* This day of the Hebrew lunar calendar occurs in September or early October.   **23:27** Hebrew *on the tenth day of the seventh month;* see 23:24 and the note there.   **23:32** Hebrew *the evening of the ninth day of the month;* see 23:24, 27 and the notes there.   **23:34** Hebrew *on the fifteenth day of the seventh month;* see 23:24, 27 and the notes there.

observed in addition to the LORD's regular Sabbath days. And these offerings must be given in addition to your personal gifts, the offerings you make to accompany your vows, and any freewill offerings that you present to the LORD.

39"Now, on the first day of the Festival of Shelters,* after you have harvested all the produce of the land, you will begin to celebrate this seven-day festival to the LORD. Remember that the first day and closing eighth day of the festival will be days of total rest. 40On the first day, gather fruit from citrus trees,* and collect palm fronds and other leafy branches and willows that grow by the streams. Then rejoice before the LORD your God for seven days. 41You must observe this seven-day festival to the LORD every year. This is a permanent law for you, and it must be kept by all future generations. 42During the seven festival days, all of you who are Israelites by birth must live in shelters. 43This will remind each new generation of Israelites that their ancestors had to live in shelters when I rescued them from the land of Egypt. I, the LORD, am your God."

44So Moses gave these instructions regarding the annual festivals of the LORD to the Israelites.

23:39 Hebrew *on the fifteenth day of the seventh month*; see 23:24 and the note there.   **23:40** Or *fruit from majestic trees.*

FEBRUARY 9 ☐ DAY 40
LEVITICUS 24–27
Future Purity in the Promised Land

OVERVIEW The book of Leviticus closes with instructions regarding conversation and conduct in the land. Blasphemy (which breaks the third commandment) is dealt with severely; vows and freewill offerings to the Lord must be carried out as promised. Sandwiched between these two discussions are rules regarding regular periods of rest for the land. Every seventh year the land must rest from sowing and reaping, and every fiftieth year marks a Jubilee, when debts are cancelled and possessions revert to their original owners. To provide for both the Sabbath year and the Year of Jubilee, God promises to bless in abundance the prior year (in much the same way he supplied double the daily manna the day before each Sabbath).

Chapter 24	Chapter 25	Chapter 26	Chapter 27
Blasphemy to the Lord	Rest for the Land	Blessing in the Land	Vows to the Lord
Unholy Lips	A Holy Land		Holy Lips

YOUR DAILY WALK Would you have the faith to do what God required of Israel? After every six years of farming the land, the Israelites were commanded to leave it unplanted for an entire year.

We live by faith, and faith lives by exercise.

In essence, God was asking them to place their source of livelihood completely in his hands. Leaning on his provision alone, they would experience the thrill of living by faith and watching God supply their daily needs. Imagine the excitement of watching farmland suddenly produce double and even triple its normal crop! God was saying to the people, "Just trust me."

God has staked his reputation on the fact that when you obey him, he will follow through on his promises. "Seek his will in all you do, and he will direct your paths" (Proverbs 3:6). "And he will give you all you need from day to day if you live for him and make the Kingdom of God your primary concern" (Matthew 6:33). Select one of these two verses and make it yours for today. Read your name into it, and claim it by faith.

 INSIGHT Don't Take Those Sabbatical Years Lightly!
God's command to let the land rest every seventh year (and again every fiftieth year) fell on deaf ears. Later, the people would go into captivity in Babylon and spend one year in exile for every sabbatical year they ignored (2 Chronicles 36:20-21).

CHAPTER 24

The LORD said to Moses, ²"Command the people of Israel to provide you with pure olive oil for the lampstand, so it can be kept burning continually. ³Aaron will set it up outside the inner curtain of the Most Holy Place in the Tabernacle* and must arrange to have the lamps tended continually, from evening until morning, before the LORD. This is a permanent law for you, and it must be kept by all future generations. ⁴The lamps on the pure gold lampstand must be tended continually in the LORD's presence.

⁵"You must bake twelve loaves of bread from choice flour, using three quarts* of flour for each loaf. ⁶Place the bread in the LORD's presence on the pure gold table, and arrange the loaves in two rows, with six in each row. ⁷Sprinkle some pure frankincense near each row. It will serve as a token offering, to be burned in place of the bread as an offering given to the LORD by fire. ⁸Every Sabbath day this bread must be laid out before the LORD on behalf of the Israelites as a continual part of the covenant. ⁹The loaves of bread belong to Aaron and his male descendants, who must eat them in a sacred place, for they represent a most holy portion of the offerings given to the LORD by fire."

¹⁰One day a man who had an Israelite mother and an Egyptian father got into a fight with one of the Israelite men. ¹¹During the fight, this son of an Israelite woman blasphemed the LORD's name. So the man was brought to Moses for judgment. His mother's name was Shelomith. She was the daughter of Dibri of the tribe of Dan. ¹²They put the man in custody until the LORD's will in the matter should become clear.

¹³Then the LORD said to Moses, ¹⁴"Take the blasphemer outside the camp, and tell all those who heard him to lay their hands on his head. Then let the entire community stone him to death. ¹⁵Say to the people of Israel: Those who blaspheme God will suffer the consequences of their guilt and be punished. ¹⁶Anyone who blasphemes the LORD's name must be stoned to death by the whole community of Israel. Any Israelite or foreigner among you who blasphemes the LORD's name will surely die.

¹⁷"Anyone who takes another person's life must be put to death.

¹⁸"Anyone who kills another person's animal must pay it back in full—a live animal for the animal that was killed.

¹⁹"Anyone who injures another person must be dealt with according to the injury inflicted—²⁰fracture for fracture, eye for eye, tooth for tooth. Whatever anyone does to hurt another person must be paid back in kind.

²¹"Whoever kills an animal must make full restitution, but whoever kills another person must be put to death.

²²"These same regulations apply to Israelites by birth and foreigners who live among you. I, the LORD, am your God."

²³After Moses gave all these instructions to the Israelites, they led the blasphemer outside the camp and stoned him to death, just as the LORD had commanded Moses.

CHAPTER 25

While Moses was on Mount Sinai, the LORD said to him, ²"Give these instructions to the Israelites: When you have entered the land I am giving you as an inheritance, the land itself must observe a Sabbath to the LORD every seventh year. ³For six years you may plant your fields and prune your vineyards and harvest your crops, ⁴but during the seventh year the land will enjoy a Sabbath year of rest to the LORD. Do not plant your crops or prune your vineyards during that entire year. ⁵And don't store away the

24:3 Hebrew *the curtain of the Testimony in the Tent of Meeting.*   24:5 Hebrew *²/₁₀ of an ephah* [3.6 liters].

crops that grow naturally or process the grapes that grow on your unpruned vines. The land is to have a year of total rest. [6]But you, your male and female slaves, your hired servants, and any foreigners who live with you may eat the produce that grows naturally during the Sabbath year. [7]And your livestock and the wild animals will also be allowed to eat of the land's bounty.

[8]"In addition, you must count off seven Sabbath years, seven years times seven, adding up to forty-nine years in all. [9]Then on the Day of Atonement of the fiftieth year,* blow the trumpets loud and long throughout the land. [10]This year will be set apart as holy, a time to proclaim release for all who live there. It will be a jubilee year for you, when each of you returns to the lands that belonged to your ancestors and rejoins your clan. [11]Yes, the fiftieth year will be a jubilee for you. During that year, do not plant any seeds or store away any of the crops that grow naturally, and do not process the grapes that grow on your unpruned vines. [12]It will be a jubilee year for you, and you must observe it as a special and holy time. You may, however, eat the produce that grows naturally in the fields that year. [13]In the Year of Jubilee each of you must return to the lands that belonged to your ancestors.

[14]"When you make an agreement with a neighbor to buy or sell property, you must never take advantage of each other. [15]When you buy land from your neighbor, the price of the land should be based on the number of years since the last jubilee. The seller will charge you only for the crop years left until the next Year of Jubilee. [16]The more the years, the higher the price; the fewer the years, the lower the price. After all, the person selling the land is actually selling you a certain number of harvests. [17]Show your fear of God by not taking advantage of each other. I, the LORD, am your God.

[18]"If you want to live securely in the land, keep my laws and obey my regulations. [19]Then the land will yield bumper crops, and you will eat your fill and live securely in it. [20]But you might ask, 'What will we eat during the seventh year, since we are not allowed to plant or harvest crops that year?' [21]The answer is, 'I will order my blessing for you in the sixth year,

so the land will produce a bumper crop, enough to support you for three years. [22]As you plant the seed in the eighth year, you will still be eating the produce of the previous year. In fact, you will eat from the old crop until the new harvest comes in the ninth year.' [23]And remember, the land must never be sold on a permanent basis because it really belongs to me. You are only foreigners and tenants living with me.

[24]"With every sale of land there must be a stipulation that the land can be redeemed at any time. [25]If any of your Israelite relatives go bankrupt and are forced to sell some inherited land, then a close relative, a kinsman redeemer, may buy it back for them. [26]If there is no one to redeem the land but the person who sold it manages to get enough money to buy it back, [27]then that person has the right to redeem it from the one who bought it. The price of the land will be based on the number of years until the next Year of Jubilee. After buying it back, the original owner may then return to the land. [28]But if the original owner cannot afford to redeem it, then it will belong to the new owner until the next Year of Jubilee. In the jubilee year, the land will be returned to the original owner.

[29]"Anyone who sells a house inside a walled city has the right to redeem it for a full year after its sale. During that time, the seller retains the right to buy it back. [30]But if it is not redeemed within a year, then the house within the walled city will become the permanent property of the buyer. It will not be returned to the original owner in the Year of Jubilee. [31]But a house in a village—a settlement without fortified walls—will be treated like property in the open fields. Such a house may be redeemed at any time and must be returned to the original owner in the Year of Jubilee.

[32]"The Levites always have the right to redeem any house they have sold within the cities belonging to them. [33]And any property that can be redeemed by the Levites—all houses within the Levitical cities—must be returned in the Year of Jubilee. After all, the cities reserved for the Levites are the only property they own in all Israel. [34]The strip of pastureland around each of the Levitical cities may never be sold. It is their permanent ancestral property.

25:9 Hebrew *on the tenth day of the seventh month, on the Day of Atonement;* see 23:27 and the note there.

35"If any of your Israelite relatives fall into poverty and cannot support themselves, support them as you would a resident foreigner and allow them to live with you. 36Do not demand an advance or charge interest on the money you lend them. Instead, show your fear of God by letting them live with you as your relatives. 37Remember, do not charge your relatives interest on anything you lend them, whether money or food. 38I, the LORD, am your God, who brought you out of Egypt to give you the land of Canaan and to be your God.

39"If any of your Israelite relatives go bankrupt and sell themselves to you, do not treat them as slaves. 40Treat them instead as hired servants or as resident foreigners who live with you, and they will serve you only until the Year of Jubilee. 41At that time they and their children will no longer be obligated to you, and they will return to their clan and ancestral property. 42The people of Israel are my servants, whom I brought out of the land of Egypt, so they must never be sold as slaves. 43Show your fear of God by treating them well; never exercise your power over them in a ruthless way.

44"However, you may purchase male or female slaves from among the foreigners who live among you. 45You may also purchase the children of such resident foreigners, including those who have been born in your land. You may treat them as your property, 46passing them on to your children as a permanent inheritance. You may treat your slaves like this, but the people of Israel, your relatives, must never be treated this way.

47"If a resident foreigner becomes rich, and if some of your Israelite relatives go bankrupt and sell themselves to such a foreigner, 48they still retain the right of redemption. They may be bought back by a close relative—49an uncle, a nephew, or anyone else who is closely related. They may also redeem themselves if they can get the money. 50The price of their freedom will be based on the number of years left until the next Year of Jubilee—whatever it would cost to hire a servant for that number of years. 51If many years still remain, they will repay most of what they received when they sold themselves. 52If only a few years remain until the Year of Jubilee, then they will repay a relatively small amount for their redemption. 53The foreigner must treat them as servants hired on a yearly basis. You must not allow a resident foreigner to treat any of your Israelite relatives ruthlessly. 54If any Israelites have not been redeemed by the time the Year of Jubilee arrives, then they and their children must be set free at that time. 55For the people of Israel are my servants, whom I brought out of the land of Egypt. I, the LORD, am your God.

CHAPTER 26

"Do not make idols or set up carved images, sacred pillars, or shaped stones to be worshiped in your land. I, the LORD, am your God. 2You must keep my Sabbath days of rest and show reverence for my sanctuary. I am the LORD.

3"If you keep my laws and are careful to obey my commands, 4I will send the seasonal rains. The land will then yield its crops, and the trees will produce their fruit. 5Your threshing season will extend until the grape harvest, and your grape harvest will extend until it is time to plant grain again. You will eat your fill and live securely in your land.

6"I will give you peace in the land, and you will be able to sleep without fear. I will remove the wild animals from your land and protect you from your enemies. 7In fact, you will chase down all your enemies and slaughter them with your swords. 8Five of you will chase a hundred, and a hundred of you will chase ten thousand! All your enemies will fall beneath the blows of your weapons.

9"I will look favorably upon you and multiply your people and fulfill my covenant with you. 10You will have such a surplus of crops that you will need to get rid of the leftovers from the previous year to make room for each new harvest. 11I will live among you, and I will not despise you. 12I will walk among you; I will be your God, and you will be my people. 13I, the LORD, am your God, who brought you from the land of Egypt so you would no longer be slaves. I have lifted the yoke of slavery from your neck so you can walk free with your heads held high.

14"However, if you do not listen to me or obey my commands, 15and if you break my covenant by rejecting my laws and treating my regulations with contempt, 16I will punish you. You will suffer from sudden terrors, with wasting diseases, and with burning fevers, causing your eyes to fail and your life to ebb away. You will plant your crops in vain because your enemies will eat them. [17]I will turn against you, and you will be defeated by all your enemies. They will rule over you, and you will run even when no one is chasing you!

[18]"And if, in spite of this, you still disobey me, I will punish you for your sins seven times over. [19]I will break down your arrogant spirit by making the skies above as unyielding as iron and the earth beneath as hard as bronze. [20]All your work will be for nothing, for your land will yield no crops, and your trees will bear no fruit.

[21]"If even then you remain hostile toward me and refuse to obey, I will inflict you with seven more disasters for your sins. [22]I will release wild animals that will kill your children and destroy your cattle, so your numbers will dwindle and your roads will be deserted.

[23]"And if you fail to learn a lesson from this and continue your hostility toward me, [24]then I myself will be hostile toward you, and I will personally strike you seven times over for your sins. [25]I will send armies against you to carry out these covenant threats. If you flee to your cities, I will send a plague to destroy you there, and you will be conquered by your enemies. [26]I will completely destroy your food supply, so the bread from one oven will have to be stretched to feed ten families. They will ration your food by weight, and even if you have food to eat, you will not be satisfied.

[27]"If after this you still refuse to listen and still remain hostile toward me, [28]then I will give full vent to my hostility. I will punish you seven times over for your sins. [29]You will eat the flesh of your own sons and daughters. [30]I will destroy your pagan shrines and cut down your incense altars. I will leave your corpses piled up beside your lifeless idols, and I will despise you. [31]I will make your cities desolate and destroy your places of worship, and I will take no pleasure in your offerings of incense. [32]Yes, I myself will devastate your land. Your enemies who come to occupy it will be utterly shocked at the destruction they see. [33]I will scatter you among the nations and attack you with my own weapons. Your land will become desolate, and your cities will lie in ruins. [34]Then at last the land will make up for its missed Sabbath years as it lies desolate during your years of exile in the land of your enemies. Then the land will finally rest and enjoy its Sabbaths. [35]As the land lies in ruins, it will take the rest you never allowed it to take every seventh year while you lived in it.

[36]"And for those of you who survive, I will demoralize you in the land of your enemies far away. You will live there in such constant fear that the sound of a leaf driven by the wind will send you fleeing. You will run as though chased by a warrior with a sword, and you will fall even when no one is pursuing you. [37]Yes, though no one is chasing you, you will stumble over each other in flight, as though fleeing in battle. You will have no power to stand before your enemies. [38]You will die among the foreign nations and be devoured in the land of your enemies. [39]Those still left alive will rot away in enemy lands because of their sins and the sins of their ancestors.

[40]"But at last my people will confess their sins and the sins of their ancestors for betraying me and being hostile toward me. [41]Finally, when I have given full expression to my hostility and have brought them to the land of their enemies, then at last their disobedient hearts will be humbled, and they will pay for their sins. [42]Then I will remember my covenant with Jacob, with Isaac, and with Abraham, and I will remember the land. [43]And the land will enjoy its years of Sabbath rest as it lies deserted. At last the people will receive the due punishment for their sins, for they rejected my regulations and despised my laws.

[44]"But despite all this, I will not utterly reject or despise them while they are in exile in the land of their enemies. I will not cancel my covenant with them by wiping them out. I, the LORD, am their God. [45]I will remember my ancient covenant with their ancestors, whom I brought out of Egypt while all the nations watched. I, the LORD, am their God."

[46]These are the laws, regulations, and instructions that the LORD gave to the Israelites through Moses on Mount Sinai.

CHAPTER 27

The LORD said to Moses, [2]"Give the following instructions to the Israelites: If you make a special vow to dedicate someone to the LORD by paying the value of that person,

³here is the scale of values to be used. A man between the ages of twenty and sixty is valued at fifty pieces of silver*; ⁴a woman of that age is valued at thirty pieces of silver. ⁵A boy between five and twenty is valued at twenty pieces of silver; a girl of that age is valued at ten pieces of silver. ⁶A boy between the ages of one month and five years is valued at five pieces of silver; a girl of that age is valued at three pieces of silver. ⁷A man older than sixty is valued at fifteen pieces of silver; a woman older than sixty is valued at ten pieces of silver. ⁸If you desire to make such a vow but cannot afford to pay the prescribed amount, go to the priest and he will evaluate your ability to pay. You will then pay the amount decided by the priest.

⁹"If your vow involves giving a clean animal—one that is acceptable as an offering to the LORD—then your gift to the LORD will be considered holy. ¹⁰The animal should never be exchanged or substituted for another—neither a good animal for a bad one nor a bad animal for a good one. But if such an exchange is in fact made, then both the original animal and the substitute will be considered holy. ¹¹But if your vow involves an unclean animal—one that is not acceptable as an offering to the LORD—then you must bring the animal to the priest. ¹²He will assess its value, and his assessment will be final. ¹³If you want to redeem the animal, you must pay the value set by the priest, plus 20 percent.

¹⁴"If you dedicate a house to the LORD, the priest must come to assess its value. The priest's assessment will be final. ¹⁵If you wish to redeem the house, you must pay the value set by the priest, plus 20 percent. Then the house will again belong to you.

¹⁶"If you dedicate to the LORD a piece of your ancestral property, its value will be assessed by the amount of seed required to plant it—fifty pieces of silver for an area that produces* five bushels* of barley seed. ¹⁷If the field is dedicated to the LORD in the Year of Jubilee, then the entire assessment will apply. ¹⁸But if the field is dedicated after the Year of Jubilee, the priest must assess the land's value in proportion to the years left until the next Year of Jubilee. ¹⁹If you decide to redeem the dedicated field, you must pay the land's value as assessed by the priest, plus 20 percent. Then the field will again belong to you. ²⁰But if you decide not to redeem the field, or if the field is sold to someone else by the priests, it can never be redeemed. ²¹When the field is released in the Year of Jubilee, it will be holy, a field specially set apart* for the LORD. It will become the property of the priests.

²²"If you dedicate to the LORD a field that you have purchased but which is not part of your ancestral property, ²³the priest must assess its value based on the years until the next Year of Jubilee. You must then give the assessed value of the land as a sacred donation to the LORD. ²⁴In the Year of Jubilee the field will be released to the original owner from whom you purchased it. ²⁵All the value assessments must be measured in terms of the standard sanctuary shekel.*

²⁶"You may not dedicate to the LORD the firstborn of your cattle or sheep because the firstborn of these animals already belong to him. ²⁷However, if it is the firstborn of a ceremonially unclean animal, you may redeem it by paying the priest's assessment of its worth, plus 20 percent. If you do not redeem it, the priest may sell it to someone else for its assessed value.

²⁸"However, anything specially set apart by the LORD—whether a person, an animal, or an inherited field—must never be sold or redeemed. Anything devoted in this way has been set apart for the LORD as holy. ²⁹A person specially set apart by the LORD for destruction cannot be redeemed. Such a person must be put to death.

³⁰"A tenth of the produce of the land, whether grain or fruit, belongs to the LORD and must be set apart to him as holy. ³¹If you want to redeem the LORD's tenth of the fruit or grain, you must pay its value, plus 20 percent. ³²The LORD also owns every tenth animal counted off from your herds and flocks. They are set apart to him as holy. ³³The tenth animal must not be selected on the basis of whether it is good or bad, and no substitutions will be allowed. If any exchange is in fact made, then both the original animal and the substituted one will be considered holy and cannot be redeemed."

³⁴These are the commands that the LORD gave to the Israelites through Moses on Mount Sinai.

27:3 Hebrew *50 shekels of silver, according to the standard sanctuary shekel,* each about 0.4 ounces or 11 grams in weight. The term *shekels* also appears in 27:4, 5, 6, 7, 16.   **27:16a** Or *requires.*   **27:16b** Hebrew *1 homer* [182 liters].   **27:21** The Hebrew term used here refers to the complete consecration of things or people to the LORD, either by destroying them or by giving them as an offering; also in 27:28, 29.   **27:25** Hebrew *measured according to the sanctuary shekel, 20 gerahs to each shekel.* Each sanctuary shekel was about 0.4 ounces or 11 grams in weight.

Numbers

BEGINNING with events about one year after the Exodus from Egypt, Numbers is the book of divine discipline, showing the painful consequences of wrong choices by God's chosen people. Because of the nation's unbelief, Israel's eleven-day journey becomes a forty-year ordeal. Numbers contains the records of two generations, two censuses, and two sets of instructions for enjoying the Promised Land. The lesson from history is clear: Obedience is the path to blessing in any generation.

Focus	Preparation			Punishment			Promise		
Divisions	The Nation Counted and Camped	The Nation Cleansed for Worship	The Nation Commences the Journey	Rebellion and Death in the Wilderness	The Staff, Red Heifer, and Rebellion	The Bronze Snake and Brash Seer	Recounting and Reviewing	The Last Days of a Great Leader	Laws of the Promised Land
	1 4	5 8	9 12	13 16	17 20	21 25	26 30	31 33	34 36
Topics	Old Generation			Degeneration			New Generation		
	A Bright Beginning			A Tragic Transition			The Grand Conclusion		
Place	On the Road to Kadesh			In the Wilderness			On the Road to Canaan		
Time	About 40 Years								

FEBRUARY 10 ☐ DAY 41
NUMBERS 1–4
The Nation Counted and Camped

 OVERVIEW With the nation of Israel now poised, ready to begin its march toward Canaan, God commands Moses to number the fighting men and arrange the tribes around the camp with the Tabernacle in the center. The census of the soldiers suggests a total population of 2 to 3 million people. The Levites are also counted and assigned specific tasks in connection with the care, erection, and transportation of the Tabernacle and its furnishings.

Chapter 1	Chapter 2	Chapter 3	Chapter 4
The Nation Counted	The Nation Camped	The Levites Arrayed	The Levites Assigned
God's People		God's Priests	

 YOUR DAILY WALK *Question:* Which part of your physical body is more important? Your eye or ear? Your arm or Adam's apple?

Question: Which part of the spiritual body of Christ is more important? The teacher or administrator? The pastor or exhorter? (Now check Ephesians 4:16 for the answer.)

Life is a lot like tennis—the goal is to learn to serve best.

Because God accomplishes his purposes through people, he has given each of his children specific gifts, talents, and skills to do his will. The sons of Merari, one family of the tribe of Levi, were told by God to carry parts of the Tabernacle—an assignment so specific that everything they carried was itemized piece by piece (4:29-32). Every man in that family knew exactly what his job was. And the importance of their work was clear to all, for their employer was none other than the Lord.

What act of service has God given you to do? The task may seem small compared to what others are doing, but God never asks you to compare yourself with others. He simply desires your faithfulness.

Use a few of the more insignificant parts of your physical body to complete this sentence: "I'm so glad my [little finger, kneecap, eyelash, etc.] is a *faithful* part of my body, and that's what I want to be known as in the body of Christ—a faithful member."

 INSIGHT Say, You Look Familiar!
God instructed Moses to arrange the twelve tribes in the camp of Israel by ancestry. The tribes were descended from four different mothers (the four wives of Jacob), and God placed those tribes that were the nearest of kin close to one another.

CHAPTER 1
One day in midspring,* during the second year after Israel's departure from Egypt, the LORD spoke to Moses in the Tabernacle* in the wilderness of Sinai. He said, [2] "Take a census of the whole community of Israel by their clans and families. List the names of all the men [3] twenty years old or older who are able to go to war. You and Aaron are to direct the project, [4] assisted by one family leader from each tribe."

1:1a Hebrew *On the first day of the second month.* This day of the Hebrew lunar calendar occurs in April or early May.   1:1b Hebrew *Tent of Meeting.*

⁵These are the tribes and the names of the leaders chosen for the task:

Tribe	Leader
Reuben	Elizur son of Shedeur
⁶ Simeon	Shelumiel son of Zurishaddai
⁷ Judah	Nahshon son of Amminadab
⁸ Issachar	Nethanel son of Zuar
⁹ Zebulun	Eliab son of Helon
¹⁰ Ephraim son of Joseph	Elishama son of Ammihud
Manasseh son of Joseph	Gamaliel son of Pedahzur
¹¹ Benjamin	Abidan son of Gideoni
¹² Dan	Ahiezer son of Ammishaddai
¹³ Asher	Pagiel son of Ocran
¹⁴ Gad	Eliasaph son of Deuel
¹⁵ Naphtali	Ahira son of Enan

¹⁶These tribal leaders, heads of their own families, were chosen from among all the people.

¹⁷Now Moses and Aaron and the chosen leaders ¹⁸called together the whole community of Israel on that very day.* All the people were registered according to their ancestry by their clans and families. The men of Israel twenty years old or older were registered, one by one, ¹⁹just as the LORD had commanded Moses. So Moses counted the people there in the wilderness of Sinai.

²⁰⁻²¹This is the number of men twenty years old or older who were able to go to war, each listed according to his own clan and family*:

Tribe	Number
Reuben (Jacob's* oldest son)	46,500
²²⁻²³ Simeon	59,300
²⁴⁻²⁵ Gad	45,650
²⁶⁻²⁷ Judah	74,600
²⁸⁻²⁹ Issachar	54,400
³⁰⁻³¹ Zebulun	57,400
³²⁻³³ Ephraim son of Joseph	40,500
³⁴⁻³⁵ Manasseh son of Joseph	32,200
³⁶⁻³⁷ Benjamin	35,400
³⁸⁻³⁹ Dan	62,700
⁴⁰⁻⁴¹ Asher	41,500
⁴²⁻⁴³ Naphtali	53,400

⁴⁴These were the men counted by Moses and Aaron and the twelve leaders of Israel, all listed according to their ancestral descent. ⁴⁵They were counted by families— all the men of Israel who were twenty years old or older and able to go to war. ⁴⁶The total number was 603,550.

⁴⁷But this total did not include the Levites. ⁴⁸For the LORD had said to Moses, ⁴⁹"Exempt the tribe of Levi from the census; do not include them when you count the rest of the Israelites. ⁵⁰You must put the Levites in charge of the Tabernacle of the Covenant,* along with its furnishings and equipment. They must carry the Tabernacle and its equipment as you travel, and they must care for it and camp around it. ⁵¹Whenever the Tabernacle is moved, the Levites will take it down and set it up again. Anyone else who goes too near the Tabernacle will be executed. ⁵²Each tribe of Israel will have a designated camping area with its own family banner. ⁵³But the Levites will camp around the Tabernacle of the Covenant to offer the people of Israel protection from the LORD's fierce anger. The Levites are responsible to stand guard around the Tabernacle."

⁵⁴So the Israelites did everything just as the LORD had commanded Moses.

CHAPTER 2

Then the LORD gave these instructions to Moses and Aaron: ²"Each tribe will be assigned its own area in the camp, and the various groups will camp beneath their family banners. The Tabernacle* will be located at the center of these tribal compounds.

³⁻⁴"The divisions of Judah, Issachar, and Zebulun are to camp toward the sunrise on the east side of the Tabernacle, beneath their family banners. These are the names of the tribes, their leaders, and the number of their available troops:

Tribe	Leader	Number
Judah	Nahshon son of Amminadab	74,600
⁵⁻⁶ Issachar	Nethanel son of Zuar	54,400
⁷⁻⁸ Zebulun	Eliab son of Helon	57,400

⁹So the total of all the troops on Judah's side of the camp is 186,400. These three tribes are to lead the way whenever the Israelites travel to a new campsite.

¹⁰⁻¹¹"The divisions of Reuben, Simeon, and Gad are to camp on the south side of the Tabernacle, beneath their family banners. These are the names of the tribes, their

1:18 Hebrew *on the first day of the second month;* see 1:1.   1:20-21a In the Hebrew text, *number of men . . . family* is repeated in 1:22, 24, 26, 28, 30, 32, 34, 36, 38, 40, 42.   1:20-21b Hebrew *Israel's.*   1:50 Or *Tabernacle of the Testimony;* also in 1:53.   2:2 Hebrew *Tent of Meeting;* also in 2:17.

leaders, and the number of their available troops:

Tribe	Leader	Number
Reuben . . .	Elizur son of Shedeur . .	46,500
12-13 Simeon. . . .	Shelumiel son of Zurishaddai.	59,300
14-15 Gad	Eliasaph son of Deuel* . .	45,650

16So the total of all the troops on Reuben's side of the camp is 151,450. These three tribes will be second in line whenever the Israelites travel.

17"Then the Levites will set out from the middle of the camp with the Tabernacle. All the tribes are to travel in the same order that they camp, each in position under the appropriate family banner.

18-19"The divisions of Ephraim, Manasseh, and Benjamin are to camp on the west side of the Tabernacle, beneath their family banners. These are the names of the tribes, their leaders, and the number of their available troops:

Tribe	Leader	Number
Ephraim . .	Elishama son of Ammihud	40,500
20-21 Manasseh . .	Gamaliel son of Pedahzur	32,200
22-23 Benjamin . .	Abidan son of Gideoni . .	35,400

24So the total of all the troops on Ephraim's side of the camp is 108,100, and they will follow the Levites in the line of march.

25-26"The divisions of Dan, Asher, and Naphtali are to camp on the north side of the Tabernacle, beneath their family banners. These are the names of the tribes, their leaders, and the number of their available troops:

Tribe	Leader	Number
Dan	Ahiezer son of Ammishaddai	62,700
27-28 Asher	Pagiel son of Ocran	41,500
29-30 Naphtali . .	Ahira son of Enan	53,400

31So the total of all the troops on Dan's side of the camp is 157,600. They are to bring up the rear whenever the Israelites move to a new campsite."

32In summary, the troops of Israel listed by their families totaled 603,550. 33The Levites were exempted from this census by the LORD's command to Moses. 34So the people of Israel did everything just as the LORD had commanded Moses. Each clan and family set up camp and marched un-

der their banners exactly as the LORD had instructed them.

CHAPTER 3

This is the family line of Aaron and Moses as it was recorded when the LORD spoke to Moses on Mount Sinai: 2Aaron's sons were Nadab (the firstborn), Abihu, Eleazar, and Ithamar. 3They were anointed and set apart to minister as priests. 4But Nadab and Abihu died in the LORD's presence in the wilderness of Sinai when they burned before the LORD a different kind of fire than he had commanded. Since they had no sons, this left only Eleazar and Ithamar to serve as priests with their father, Aaron.

5Then the LORD said to Moses, 6"Call forward the tribe of Levi and present them to Aaron the priest as his assistants. 7They will serve Aaron and the whole community, performing their sacred duties in and around the Tabernacle.* 8They will also maintain all the furnishings of the sacred tent,* serving in the Tabernacle on behalf of all the Israelites. 9Assign the Levites to Aaron and his sons as their assistants. 10Appoint Aaron and his sons to carry out the duties of the priesthood. Anyone else who comes too near the sanctuary must be executed!"

11And the LORD said to Moses, 12"I have chosen the Levites from among the Israelites as substitutes for all the firstborn sons of the people of Israel. The Levites are mine 13because all the firstborn sons are mine. From the day I killed all the firstborn sons of the Egyptians, I set apart for myself all the firstborn in Israel of both men and animals. They are mine; I am the LORD."

14The LORD spoke again to Moses, there in the wilderness of Sinai. He said, 15"Take a census of the tribe of Levi by its families and clans. Count every male who is one month old or older." 16So Moses counted them, just as the LORD had commanded.

17Levi had three sons, who were named Gershon, Kohath, and Merari.
18The clans descended from Gershon were named for two of his descendants, Libni and Shimei.
19The clans descended from Kohath were named for four of his descendants, Amram, Izhar, Hebron, and Uzziel.
20The clans descended from Merari were

named for two of his descendants, Mahli and Mushi.

These were the Levite clans, listed according to their family groups.

[21] The descendants of Gershon were composed of the clans descended from Libni and Shimei. [22] There were 7,500 males one month old or older among these Gershonite clans. [23] They were assigned the area to the west of the Tabernacle for their camp. [24] The leader of the Gershonite clans was Eliasaph son of Lael. [25] These two clans were responsible to care for the tent of the Tabernacle with its layers of coverings, its entry curtains, [26] the curtains of the courtyard that surrounded the Tabernacle and altar, the curtain at the courtyard entrance, the cords, and all the equipment related to their use.

[27] The descendants of Kohath were composed of the clans descended from Amram, Izhar, Hebron, and Uzziel. [28] There were 8,600* males one month old or older among these Kohathite clans. They were responsible for the care of the sanctuary. [29] They were assigned the area south of the Tabernacle for their camp. [30] The leader of the Kohathite clans was Elizaphan son of Uzziel. [31] These four clans were responsible for the care of the Ark, the table, the lampstand, the altars, the various utensils used in the sanctuary, the inner curtain, and all the equipment related to their use. [32] Eleazar the priest, Aaron's son, was the chief administrator over all the Levites, with special responsibility for the oversight of the sanctuary.

[33] The descendants of Merari were composed of the clans descended from Mahli and Mushi. [34] There were 6,200 males one month old or older among these Merarite clans. [35] They were assigned the area north of the Tabernacle for their camp. The leader of the Merarite clans was Zuriel son of Abihail. [36] These two clans were responsible for the care of the frames supporting the Tabernacle, the crossbars, the pillars, the bases, and all the equipment related to their use. [37] They were also responsible for the posts of the courtyard and all their bases, pegs, and cords.

[38] The area in front of the Tabernacle in the east toward the sunrise* was reserved for the tents of Moses and of Aaron and his sons, who had the final responsibility for the sanctuary on behalf of the people of Israel. Anyone other than a priest or Levite who came too near the sanctuary was to be executed.

[39] So among the Levite clans counted by Moses and Aaron at the LORD's command, there were 22,000 males one month old or older.

[40] Then the LORD said to Moses, "Now count all the firstborn sons in Israel who are one month old or older, and register each name. [41] The Levites will be reserved for me as substitutes for the firstborn sons of Israel; I am the LORD. And the Levites' livestock are mine as substitutes for the firstborn livestock of the whole nation of Israel."

[42] So Moses counted the firstborn sons of the people of Israel, just as the LORD had commanded. [43] The total number of firstborn sons who were one month old or older was 22,273.

[44] Now the LORD said to Moses, [45] "Take the Levites in place of the firstborn sons of the people of Israel. And take the livestock of the Levites as substitutes for the firstborn livestock of the people of Israel. The Levites will be mine; I am the LORD. [46] To redeem the 273 firstborn sons of Israel who are in excess of the number of Levites, [47] collect five pieces of silver for each person, each piece weighing the same as the standard sanctuary shekel.* [48] Give the silver to Aaron and his sons as the redemption price for the extra firstborn sons."

[49] So Moses collected redemption money for the firstborn sons of Israel who exceeded the number of Levites. [50] The silver collected on behalf of these firstborn sons of Israel came to about thirty-four pounds in weight.* [51] And Moses gave the redemption money to Aaron and his sons as the LORD had commanded.

CHAPTER 4
Then the LORD said to Moses and Aaron, [2] "Take a census of the clans and families of the Kohathite division of the Levite tribe. [3] Count all the men between the ages of thirty and fifty who qualify to work in the Tabernacle.*
[4] "The duties of the Kohathites at the Tab-

3:28 Some Greek manuscripts read *8,300;* see total in 3:39.   **3:38** Hebrew *toward the sunrise, in front of the Tent of Meeting.*
3:47 Hebrew *5 shekels* [2 ounces or 57 grams] *apiece, according to the sanctuary shekel, 20 gerahs to each shekel.*   **3:50** Hebrew
1,365 shekels [15.5 kilograms], *according to the sanctuary shekel.*   **4:3** Hebrew *Tent of Meeting;* also in 4:4, 15, 23, 25, 28, 30, 31,
33, 35, 37, 39, 41, 43, 47.

ernacle will relate to the most sacred objects. ⁵When the camp moves, Aaron and his sons must enter the Tabernacle first to take down the inner curtain and cover the Ark of the Covenant* with it. ⁶Then they must cover the inner curtain with fine goatskin leather, and the goatskin leather with a dark blue cloth. Finally, they must put the carrying poles of the Ark in place.

⁷"Next they must spread a blue cloth over the table, where the Bread of the Presence is displayed, and place the dishes, spoons, bowls, cups, and the special bread on the cloth. ⁸They must spread a scarlet cloth over that, and finally a covering of fine goatskin leather on top of the scarlet cloth. Then they must insert the carrying poles into the table.

⁹"Next they must cover the lampstand with a dark blue cloth, along with its lamps, lamp snuffers, trays, and special jars of olive oil. ¹⁰The lampstand with its utensils must then be covered with fine goatskin leather, and the bundle must be placed on a carrying frame.

¹¹"Aaron and his sons must also spread a dark blue cloth over the gold altar and cover this cloth with a covering of fine goatskin leather. Then they are to attach the carrying poles to the altar. ¹²All the remaining utensils of the sanctuary must be wrapped in a dark blue cloth, covered with fine goatskin leather, and placed on the carrying frame.

¹³"The ashes must be removed from the altar, and the altar must then be covered with a purple cloth. ¹⁴All the altar utensils—the firepans, hooks, shovels, basins, and all the containers—are to be placed on the cloth, and a covering of fine goatskin leather must be spread over them. Finally, the carrying poles must be put in place. ¹⁵When Aaron and his sons have finished covering the sanctuary and all the sacred utensils, the Kohathites will come and carry these things to the next destination. But they must not touch the sacred objects, or they will die. So these are the objects of the Tabernacle that the Kohathites must carry.

¹⁶"Eleazar son of Aaron the priest will be responsible for the oil of the lampstand, the fragrant incense, the daily grain offering, and the anointing oil. In fact, the supervi-

sion of the entire Tabernacle and everything in it will be Eleazar's responsibility."

¹⁷Then the LORD said to Moses and Aaron, ¹⁸"Don't let the Kohathite clans be destroyed from among the Levites! ¹⁹This is what you must do so they will live and not die when they approach the most sacred objects. Aaron and his sons must always go in with them and assign a specific duty or load to each person. ²⁰Otherwise they must not approach the sanctuary and look at the sacred objects for even a moment, or they will die."

²¹And the LORD said to Moses, ²²"Take a census of the clans and families of the Gershonite division of the tribe of Levi. ²³Count all the men between the ages of thirty and fifty who are eligible to serve in the Tabernacle.

²⁴"The duties of the Gershonites will be in the areas of general service and carrying loads. ²⁵They must carry the curtains of the Tabernacle, the Tabernacle itself with its coverings, the outer covering of fine goatskin leather, and the curtain for the Tabernacle entrance. ²⁶They are also to carry the curtains for the courtyard walls that surround the Tabernacle and altar, the curtain across the courtyard entrance, the necessary cords, and all the altar's accessories. The Gershonites are responsible for transporting all these items. ²⁷Aaron and his sons will direct the Gershonites regarding their duties, whether it involves moving or doing other work. They must assign the Gershonites the loads they are to carry. ²⁸So these are the duties assigned to the Gershonites at the Tabernacle. They will be directly responsible to Ithamar son of Aaron the priest.

²⁹"Now take a census of the clans and families of the Merarite division of the Levite tribe. ³⁰Count all the men between the ages of thirty and fifty who are eligible to serve in the Tabernacle.

³¹"Their duties at the Tabernacle will consist of carrying loads. They will be required to carry the frames of the Tabernacle, the crossbars, the pillars with their bases, ³²the posts for the courtyard walls with their bases, pegs, cords, accessories, and everything else related to their use. You must assign the various loads to each man by name. ³³So these are the duties of the Merarites at the Tabernacle. They are

4:5 Or *Ark of the Testimony.*

directly responsible to Ithamar son of Aaron the priest."

³⁴So Moses, Aaron, and the other leaders of the community counted the Kohathite division by its clans and families. ³⁵The count included all the men between thirty and fifty years of age who were eligible for service in the Tabernacle, ³⁶and the total number came to 2,750. ³⁷So this was the total of all those from the Kohathite clans who were eligible to serve at the Tabernacle. Moses and Aaron counted them, just as the LORD had commanded through Moses.

³⁸The Gershonite division was also counted by its clans and families. ³⁹The count included all the men between thirty and fifty years of age who were eligible for service in the Tabernacle, ⁴⁰and the total number came to 2,630. ⁴¹So this was the total of all those from the Gershonite clans who were eligible to serve at the Tabernacle. Moses and Aaron

counted them, just as the LORD had commanded.

⁴²The Merarite division was also counted by its clans and families. ⁴³The count included all the men between thirty and fifty years of age who were eligible for service in the Tabernacle, ⁴⁴and the total number came to 3,200. ⁴⁵So this was the total of all those from the Merarite clans who were eligible for service. Moses and Aaron counted them, just as the LORD had commanded through Moses.

⁴⁶So Moses, Aaron, and the leaders of Israel counted all the Levites by their clans and families. ⁴⁷All the men between thirty and fifty years of age who were eligible for service in the Tabernacle and for its transportation ⁴⁸numbered 8,580. ⁴⁹Each man was assigned his task and told what to carry, just as the LORD had commanded through Moses.

And so the census was completed, just as the LORD had commanded Moses.

FEBRUARY 11 ☐ DAY 42
NUMBERS 5–8
The Nation Cleansed for Worship

OVERVIEW God now further prepares the nation for the coming trip to Canaan by commanding Moses to deal with four specific problem areas: moral defilement, jealous suspicion, unmet needs in the Tabernacle, and uncleansed Levites in the service of the Lord. Israel's purity in moral conduct and interpersonal relationships is of utmost importance because the holy God of Israel lives in her camp (5:3).

Chapter 5	Chapter 6	Chapter 7	Chapter 8
Defilement in Morals	Dedication to Service	Offerings of the Leaders	Offerings of the Levites
Cleansing	Dedication		

YOUR DAILY WALK It is time for an easy, one-question quiz based on your reading of Leviticus and Numbers:

True or False: God demands holiness from his people.

A godly life is always the best advertisement for Christianity.

Absolutely true. But living a holy life is easier said than done because it involves maintaining personal purity while rubbing shoulders with a decidedly impure world.

As God prepared Israel to enter a land dominated by pagan influences, he knew his children would be exposed to all manner of idolatry and evil. So he required that they live a completely different way. His purpose was to *insulate* the Israelites from the influence of evil, but not to *isolate* them from the people to whom they could be a testimony. Israel was to witness about the true God in the midst of corruption, and the nation couldn't do that hidden away in the wilderness. Only as Israel's pagan neighbors saw the nation's godly lifestyle lived out before them would they be influenced toward righteousness.

Are the people around you influenced by your distinctive lifestyle, or do you blend inconspicuously into the world around you? Does your lifestyle *reflect* or *refute* your godly priorities and purity? Select one lifestyle goal for this coming week, and make it your "project in purity." Better yet, "team up" with another Daily Walker!

 INSIGHT Twelve Offerings in One Service
Even though the offerings of the twelve leaders of the tribes of Israel (given on the day the Tabernacle worship was inaugurated) were identical, each is recorded in great detail (7:10-83), showing God's pleasure with their individual (and generous) gifts.

CHAPTER 5

The LORD gave these instructions to Moses: [2]"Command the people of Israel to remove anyone from the camp who has a contagious skin disease* or a discharge, or who has been defiled by touching a dead person. [3]This applies to men and women alike. Remove them so they will not defile the camp, where I live among them." [4]So the Israelites did just as the LORD had commanded Moses and removed such people from the camp.

[5]Then the LORD said to Moses, [6]"Give these instructions to the people of Israel: If any of the people—men or women—betray the LORD by doing wrong to another person, they are guilty. [7]They must confess their sin and make full restitution for what they have done, adding a penalty of 20 percent and returning it to the person who was wronged. [8]But if the person who was wronged is dead, and there are no near relatives to whom restitution can be made, it belongs to the LORD and must be given to the priest, along with a ram for atonement. [9]All the sacred gifts that the Israelites bring to a priest will belong to him. [10]Each priest may keep the sacred donations that he receives."

[11]And the LORD said to Moses, [12]"Say to the people of Israel: 'Suppose a man's wife goes astray and is unfaithful to her husband. [13]Suppose she sleeps with another man, but there is no witness since she was not caught in the act. [14]If her husband becomes jealous and suspicious of his wife, even if she has not defiled herself, [15]the husband must bring his wife to the priest with an offering of two quarts* of barley

flour to be presented on her behalf. Do not mix it with olive oil or frankincense, for it is a jealousy offering—an offering of inquiry to find out if she is guilty.

[16]"'The priest must then present her before the LORD. [17]He must take some holy water in a clay jar and mix it with dust from the Tabernacle floor. [18]When he has presented her before the LORD, he must unbind her hair and place the offering of inquiry—the jealousy offering—in her hands to determine whether or not her husband's suspicions are justified. The priest will stand before her, holding the jar of bitter water that brings a curse to those who are guilty. [19]The priest will put the woman under oath and say to her, "If no other man has slept with you, and you have not defiled yourself by being unfaithful, may you be immune from the effects of this bitter water that causes the curse. [20]But if you have gone astray while under your husband's authority and defiled yourself by sleeping with another man"—[21]at this point the priest must put the woman under this oath—"then may the people see that the LORD's curse is upon you when he makes you infertile.* [22]Now may this water that brings the curse enter your body and make you infertile.*" And the woman will be required to say, "Yes, let it be so." [23]Then the priest will write these curses on a piece of leather and wash them off into the bitter water. [24]He will then make the woman drink the bitter water, so it may bring on the curse and cause bitter suffering in cases of guilt.

[25]"'Then the priest will take the jealousy offering from the woman's hand, lift it up

5:2 Traditionally rendered *leprosy*. The Hebrew word used here describes various skin diseases. 5:15 Hebrew *1/10 of an ephah* [2 liters]. 5:21 Hebrew *when he causes your thigh to waste away and your abdomen to swell*. 5:22 Hebrew *enter your body so that your abdomen swells and your thigh wastes away*.

before the LORD, and carry it to the altar. ²⁶He will take a handful as a token portion and burn it on the altar. Then he will require the woman to drink the water. ²⁷If she has defiled herself by being unfaithful to her husband, the water that brings the curse will cause bitter suffering. She will become infertile,* and her name will become a curse word among her people. ²⁸But if she has not defiled herself and is pure, she will be unharmed and will still be able to have children.

²⁹"'This is the ritual law for dealing with jealousy. If a woman defiles herself by being unfaithful to her husband, ³⁰or if a man is overcome with jealousy and suspicion that his wife has been unfaithful, the husband must present his wife before the LORD, and the priest will apply this entire ritual law to her. ³¹The husband will be innocent of any guilt in this matter, but his wife will be held accountable for her sin.'"

CHAPTER 6

Then the LORD said to Moses, "Speak to the people of Israel and give them these instructions: ²If some of the people, either men or women, take the special vow of a Nazirite, setting themselves apart to the LORD in a special way, ³they must give up wine and other alcoholic drinks. They must not use vinegar made from wine, they must not drink other fermented drinks or fresh grape juice, and they must not eat grapes or raisins. ⁴As long as they are bound by their Nazirite vow, they are not allowed to eat or drink anything that comes from a grapevine, not even the grape seeds or skins.

⁵"They must never cut their hair throughout the time of their vow, for they are holy and set apart to the LORD. That is why they must let their hair grow long. ⁶And they may not go near a dead body during the entire period of their vow to the LORD, ⁷even if their own father, mother, brother, or sister has died. They must not defile the hair on their head, because it is the symbol of their separation to God. ⁸This applies as long as they are set apart to the LORD.

⁹"If their hair is defiled because someone suddenly falls dead beside them, they must wait for seven days and then shave their heads. Then they will be cleansed from their defilement. ¹⁰On the eighth day they

must bring two turtledoves or two young pigeons to the priest at the entrance of the Tabernacle.* ¹¹The priest will offer one of the birds for a sin offering and the other for a burnt offering. In this way, he will make atonement for the guilt they incurred from the dead body. Then they must renew their vow that day and let their hair begin to grow again. ¹²The days of their vow that were completed before their defilement no longer count. They must rededicate themselves to the LORD for the full term of their vow, and each must bring a one-year-old male lamb for a guilt offering.

¹³"This is the ritual law of the Nazirites. At the conclusion of their time of separation as Nazirites, they must each go to the entrance of the Tabernacle ¹⁴and offer these sacrifices to the LORD: a one-year-old male lamb without defect for a burnt offering, a one-year-old female lamb without defect for a sin offering, a ram without defect for a peace offering, ¹⁵a basket of bread made without yeast—cakes of choice flour mixed with olive oil and wafers spread with olive oil—along with their prescribed grain offerings and drink offerings. ¹⁶The priest will present these offerings before the LORD: first the sin offering and the burnt offering; ¹⁷then the ram for a peace offering, along with the basket of bread made without yeast. The priest must also make the prescribed grain offering and drink offering.

¹⁸"Then the Nazirites will shave their hair at the entrance of the Tabernacle and put it on the fire beneath the peace-offering sacrifice. ¹⁹After each Nazirite's head has been shaved, the priest will take for each of them the boiled shoulder of the ram, one cake made without yeast, and one wafer made without yeast, and put them all into the Nazirite's hands. ²⁰The priest will then lift the gifts up before the LORD in a gesture of offering. These are holy portions for the priest, along with the breast and thigh pieces that were lifted up before the LORD. After this ceremony the Nazirites may again drink wine.

²¹"This is the ritual law of the Nazirites. If any Nazirites have vowed to give the LORD anything else beyond what is required by their normal Nazirite vow, they must fulfill their special vow exactly as they have promised."

5:27 Hebrew *Her body will swell and her thigh will waste away.*   **6:10** Hebrew *Tent of Meeting;* also in 6:13, 18.

²²Then the LORD said to Moses, ²³"Instruct Aaron and his sons to bless the people of Israel with this special blessing:

²⁴ 'May the LORD bless you
     and protect you.
²⁵ May the LORD smile on you
     and be gracious to you.
²⁶ May the LORD show you his favor
     and give you his peace.'

²⁷This is how Aaron and his sons will designate the Israelites as my people,* and I myself will bless them."

CHAPTER 7
On the day Moses set up the Tabernacle, he anointed it and set it apart as holy, along with all its furnishings and the altar with its utensils. ²Then the leaders of Israel—the tribal leaders who had organized the census—came and brought their offerings. ³Together they brought six carts and twelve oxen. There was a cart for every two leaders and an ox for each leader. They presented these to the LORD in front of the Tabernacle.

⁴Then the LORD said to Moses, ⁵"Receive their gifts and use these oxen and carts for the work of the Tabernacle.* Distribute them among the Levites according to the work they have to do." ⁶So Moses presented the carts and oxen to the Levites. ⁷He gave two carts and four oxen to the Gershonite division for their work, ⁸and four carts and eight oxen to the Merarite division for their work. All their work was done under the leadership of Ithamar son of Aaron the priest. ⁹But he gave none of the carts or oxen to the Kohathite division, since they were required to carry the sacred objects of the Tabernacle on their shoulders.

¹⁰The leaders also presented dedication gifts for the altar at the time it was anointed. They each placed their gifts before the altar. ¹¹The LORD said to Moses, "Let each leader bring his gift on a different day for the dedication of the altar."

¹²On the first day Nahshon son of Amminadab, leader of the tribe of Judah, presented his offering.
¹³The offering consisted of a silver platter weighing about 3¼ pounds and a silver basin of about 1¾ pounds.* These were both filled with grain offerings of choice flour mixed with olive oil. ¹⁴He also brought a gold container weighing about four ounces,* which was filled with incense. ¹⁵He brought a young bull, a ram, and a one-year-old male lamb as a burnt offering; ¹⁶a male goat for a sin offering; ¹⁷and two oxen, five rams, five male goats, and five one-year-old male lambs for a peace offering. This was the offering brought by Nahshon son of Amminadab.

¹⁸On the second day Nethanel son of Zuar, leader of the tribe of Issachar, presented his offering.
¹⁹The offering consisted of a silver platter weighing about 3¼ pounds and a silver basin of about 1¾ pounds. These were both filled with grain offerings of choice flour mixed with olive oil. ²⁰He also brought a gold container weighing about four ounces, which was filled with incense. ²¹He brought a young bull, a ram, and a one-year-old male lamb as a burnt offering; ²²a male goat for a sin offering; ²³and two oxen, five rams, five male goats, and five one-year-old male lambs for a peace offering. This was the offering brought by Nethanel son of Zuar.

²⁴On the third day Eliab son of Helon, leader of the tribe of Zebulun, presented his offering.
²⁵The offering consisted of a silver platter weighing about 3¼ pounds and a silver basin of about 1¾ pounds. These were both filled with grain offerings of choice flour mixed with olive oil. ²⁶He also brought a gold container weighing about four ounces, which was filled with incense. ²⁷He brought a young bull, a ram, and a one-year-old male lamb as a burnt offering; ²⁸a male goat for a sin offering; ²⁹and two oxen, five rams, five male goats, and five one-year-old male lambs for a peace offering. This was the offering brought by Eliab son of Helon.

³⁰On the fourth day Elizur son of Shedeur, leader of the tribe of Reuben, presented his offering.
³¹The offering consisted of a silver platter weighing about 3¼ pounds and a silver

---

6:27 Hebrew *will put my name on the people of Israel.*   **7:5** Hebrew *Tent of Meeting;* also in 7:89.   **7:13** Hebrew *silver platter weighing 130 shekels* [1.5 kilograms] *and a silver basin weighing 70 shekels* [0.8 kilograms], *according to the sanctuary shekel;* also in 7:19, 25, 31, 37, 43, 49, 55, 61, 67, 73, 79, 85.   **7:14** Hebrew *10 shekels* [114 grams]; also in 7:20, 26, 32, 38, 44, 50, 56, 62, 68, 74, 80, 86.

basin of about 1¾ pounds. These were both filled with grain offerings of choice flour mixed with olive oil. ³²He also brought a gold container weighing about four ounces, which was filled with incense. ³³He brought a young bull, a ram, and a one-year-old male lamb as a burnt offering; ³⁴a male goat for a sin offering; ³⁵and two oxen, five rams, five male goats, and five one-year-old male lambs for a peace offering. This was the offering brought by Elizur son of Shedeur.

³⁶On the fifth day Shelumiel son of Zurishaddai, leader of the tribe of Simeon, presented his offering.

³⁷The offering consisted of a silver platter weighing about 3¼ pounds and a silver basin of about 1¾ pounds. These were both filled with grain offerings of choice flour mixed with olive oil. ³⁸He also brought a gold container weighing about four ounces, which was filled with incense. ³⁹He brought a young bull, a ram, and a one-year-old male lamb as a burnt offering; ⁴⁰a male goat for a sin offering; ⁴¹and two oxen, five rams, five male goats, and five one-year-old male lambs for a peace offering. This was the offering brought by Shelumiel son of Zurishaddai.

⁴²On the sixth day Eliasaph son of Deuel, leader of the tribe of Gad, presented his offering.

⁴³The offering consisted of a silver platter weighing about 3¼ pounds and a silver basin of about 1¾ pounds. These were both filled with grain offerings of choice flour mixed with olive oil. ⁴⁴He also brought a gold container weighing about four ounces, which was filled with incense. ⁴⁵He brought a young bull, a ram, and a one-year-old male lamb as a burnt offering; ⁴⁶a male goat for a sin offering; ⁴⁷and two oxen, five rams, five male goats, and five one-year-old male lambs for a peace offering. This was the offering brought by Eliasaph son of Deuel.

⁴⁸On the seventh day Elishama son of Ammihud, leader of the tribe of Ephraim, presented his offering.

⁴⁹The offering consisted of a silver platter weighing about 3¼ pounds and a silver basin of about 1¾ pounds. These were both filled with grain offerings of choice flour mixed with olive oil. ⁵⁰He also brought a gold container weighing about four ounces, which was filled with incense. ⁵¹He brought a young bull, a ram, and a one-year-old male lamb as a burnt offering; ⁵²a male goat for a sin offering; ⁵³and two oxen, five rams, five male goats, and five one-year-old male lambs for a peace offering. This was the offering brought by Elishama son of Ammihud.

⁵⁴On the eighth day Gamaliel son of Pedahzur, leader of the tribe of Manasseh, presented his offering.

⁵⁵The offering consisted of a silver platter weighing about 3¼ pounds and a silver basin of about 1¾ pounds. These were both filled with grain offerings of choice flour mixed with olive oil. ⁵⁶He also brought a gold container weighing about four ounces, which was filled with incense. ⁵⁷He brought a young bull, a ram, and a one-year-old male lamb as a burnt offering; ⁵⁸a male goat for a sin offering; ⁵⁹and two oxen, five rams, five male goats, and five one-year-old male lambs for a peace offering. This was the offering brought by Gamaliel son of Pedahzur.

⁶⁰On the ninth day Abidan son of Gideoni, leader of the tribe of Benjamin, presented his offering.

⁶¹The offering consisted of a silver platter weighing about 3¼ pounds and a silver basin of about 1¾ pounds. These were both filled with grain offerings of choice flour mixed with olive oil. ⁶²He also brought a gold container weighing about four ounces, which was filled with incense. ⁶³He brought a young bull, a ram, and a one-year-old male lamb as a burnt offering; ⁶⁴a male goat for a sin offering; ⁶⁵and two oxen, five rams, five male goats, and five one-year-old male lambs for a peace offering. This was the offering brought by Abidan son of Gideoni.

⁶⁶On the tenth day Ahiezer son of Ammishaddai, leader of the tribe of Dan, presented his offering.

⁶⁷The offering consisted of a silver platter weighing about 3¼ pounds and a silver basin of about 1¾ pounds. These were both filled with grain offerings of choice flour mixed with olive oil. ⁶⁸He also

brought a gold container weighing about four ounces, which was filled with incense. [69]He brought a young bull, a ram, and a one-year-old male lamb as a burnt offering; [70]a male goat for a sin offering; [71]and two oxen, five rams, five male goats, and five one-year-old male lambs for a peace offering. This was the offering brought by Ahiezer son of Ammishaddai.

[72]On the eleventh day Pagiel son of Ocran, leader of the tribe of Asher, presented his offering.
[73]The offering consisted of a silver platter weighing about 3¼ pounds and a silver basin of about 1¾ pounds. These were both filled with grain offerings of choice flour mixed with olive oil. [74]He also brought a gold container weighing about four ounces, which was filled with incense. [75]He brought a young bull, a ram, and a one-year-old male lamb as a burnt offering; [76]a male goat for a sin offering; [77]and two oxen, five rams, five male goats, and five one-year-old male lambs for a peace offering. This was the offering brought by Pagiel son of Ocran.

[78]On the twelfth day Ahira son of Enan, leader of the tribe of Naphtali, presented his offering.
[79]The offering consisted of a silver platter weighing about 3¼ pounds and a silver basin of about 1¾ pounds. These were both filled with grain offerings of choice flour mixed with olive oil. [80]He also brought a gold container weighing about four ounces, which was filled with incense. [81]He brought a young bull, a ram, and a one-year-old male lamb as a burnt offering; [82]a male goat for a sin offering; [83]and two oxen, five rams, five male goats, and five one-year-old male lambs for a peace offering. This was the offering brought by Ahira son of Enan.

[84]So this was the dedication offering for the altar, brought by the leaders of Israel at the time it was anointed: twelve silver platters, twelve silver basins, and twelve gold incense containers. [85]In all, the silver objects weighed about 60 pounds,* about 3¼ pounds for each platter and 1¾ pounds for each basin. [86]The weight of the donated gold came to about three pounds,* about four ounces for each of the gold containers that were filled with incense. [87]Twelve bulls, twelve rams, and twelve one-year-old male lambs were donated for the burnt offerings, along with their prescribed grain offerings. Twelve male goats were brought for the sin offerings. [88]Twenty-four young bulls, sixty rams, sixty male goats, and sixty one-year-old male lambs were donated for the peace offerings. This was the dedication offering for the altar after it was anointed.

[89]Whenever Moses went into the Tabernacle to speak with the LORD, he heard the voice speaking to him from between the two cherubim above the Ark's cover—the place of atonement—that rests on the Ark of the Covenant.* The LORD spoke to him from there.

CHAPTER 8
The LORD said to Moses, [2]"Tell Aaron that when he sets up the seven lamps in the lampstand, he is to place them so their light shines forward." [3]So Aaron did this. He set up the seven lamps so they reflected their light forward, just as the LORD had commanded Moses. [4]The entire lampstand, from its base to its decorative blossoms, was made of beaten gold. It was built according to the exact design the LORD had shown Moses.

[5]Then the LORD said to Moses, [6]"Now set the Levites apart from the rest of the people of Israel and make them ceremonially clean. [7]Do this by sprinkling them with the water of purification. And have them shave their entire body and wash their clothing. Then they will be ceremonially clean. [8]Have them bring a young bull and a grain offering of choice flour mixed with olive oil, along with a second young bull for a sin offering. [9]Then assemble the whole community of Israel and present the Levites at the entrance of the Tabernacle.* [10]When you bring the Levites before the LORD, the people of Israel must lay their hands on them. [11]Aaron must present the Levites to the LORD as a special offering from the people of Israel, thus dedicating them to the LORD's service.
[12]"Next the Levites will lay their hands on the heads of the young bulls and present them to the LORD. One will be for a sin offering and the other for a burnt offering,

to make atonement for the Levites. ¹³Then have the Levites stand in front of Aaron and his sons, and present them as a special offering to the LORD. ¹⁴In this way, you will set the Levites apart from the rest of the people of Israel, and the Levites will belong to me. ¹⁵After this, they may go in and out of the Tabernacle to do their work, because you have purified them and presented them as a special offering.

¹⁶"Of all the people of Israel, the Levites are reserved for me. I have claimed them for myself in place of all the firstborn sons of the Israelites; I have taken the Levites as their substitutes. ¹⁷For all the firstborn males among the people of Israel are mine, both people and animals. I set them apart for myself on the night I killed all the first-born sons of the Egyptians. ¹⁸Yes, I claim the Levites in place of all the firstborn sons of Israel. ¹⁹And of all the Israelites, I have assigned the Levites to Aaron and his sons. They will serve in the Tabernacle on behalf of the Israelites and make atonement for

them so no plague will strike them when they approach the sanctuary."

²⁰So Moses, Aaron, and the whole community of Israel dedicated the Levites, carefully following all the LORD's instructions to Moses. ²¹The Levites purified themselves and washed their clothes, and Aaron presented them to the LORD as a special offering. He then performed the rite of atonement over them to purify them. ²²From then on the Levites went into the Tabernacle to perform their duties, helping Aaron and his sons. So they carried out all the commands that the LORD gave Moses concerning the Levites.

²³The LORD also instructed Moses, ²⁴"This is the rule the Levites must follow: They must begin serving in the Tabernacle at the age of twenty-five, ²⁵and they must retire at the age of fifty. ²⁶After retirement they may assist their fellow Levites by performing guard duty at the Tabernacle, but they may not officiate in the service. This is how you will assign duties to the Levites."

FEBRUARY 12 ☐ DAY 43
NUMBERS 9–12
The Nation Commences the Journey

 OVERVIEW After a special celebration of the Passover at Mount Sinai, the people watch as the cloud of his presence begins to move. Trumpets blare forth the exciting news: It is time to march! No sooner has Sinai faded from view than the congregation begins to grumble and complain. The manna is monotonous . . . water is scarce . . . the journey is hard. Egypt would have been far better than this! For every *problem* there is a corresponding *provision* from God until at last the people arrive at an oasis in the wilderness called Kadesh—the last scheduled stop before they enter the Promised Land. It is time for a crucial test of the people's commitment to walk by faith.

Chapter 9	Chapter 10	Chapter 11	Chapter 12
A Cloud to Guide	A Call to March	Complaining about Manna	Complaining about Moses
Getting Ready to March		Grumbling on the March	

 YOUR DAILY WALK Have you ever spent the night in a wilderness? If so, you will have little trouble identifying with the complaints of the Israelites as they begin their march from Mount Sinai to the Promised Land.

The wilderness is a hostile place. By day the sun beats down mercilessly, and the temperature soars. (God knew this and provided a

The reason so traveling umbrella—the cloud.) Food is scarce and water is virtually
many people nonexistent in a wilderness—unless, of course, you are eating manna
know the from the dew and drinking water from rocks!
solution is   Do you see God's hand of provision in the life of his nation? More
that they important, do you see God's hand of provision in your life? Repeatedly,
created the the Israelites expressed *grumbling* instead of *gratitude*. Why not enjoy
problem. the blessing they missed by spending the next few minutes praising
God for his daily provision!

INSIGHT   Guided by a Cloud . . . and by Hobab
Though God provided divine guidance for the people in the form of
the cloud of his presence, this did not preclude human agents. Moses
persuaded his brother-in-law, Hobab, to act as a guide (10:31). God
not only gives direction through his Word and through his Holy Spirit,
he also uses people to guide our steps along life's journey.

CHAPTER 9

The LORD gave these instructions to Moses in early spring,* during the second year after Israel's departure from Egypt, while he and the rest of the Israelites were in the wilderness of Sinai: ²"Tell the Israelites to celebrate the Passover at the proper time, ³at twilight on the appointed day in early spring.* Be sure to follow all my laws and regulations concerning this celebration."

⁴So Moses told the people to celebrate the Passover ⁵in the wilderness of Sinai as twilight fell on the appointed day.* And they celebrated the festival there, just as the LORD had commanded Moses. ⁶But some of the men had been ceremonially defiled by touching a dead person, so they could not offer their Passover lambs that day. So they came to Moses and Aaron that day ⁷and said, "We have become ceremonially unclean by touching a dead person. But why should we be excluded from presenting the LORD's offering at the proper time with the rest of the Israelites?"

⁸Moses answered, "Wait here until I have received instructions for you from the LORD."

⁹This was the LORD's reply: ¹⁰"Say to the Israelites: 'If any of the people now or in future generations are ceremonially unclean at Passover time because of touching a dead body, or if they are on a journey and cannot be present at the ceremony, they may still celebrate the LORD's Passover. ¹¹They must offer the Passover sacrifice one month later,* at twilight on the appointed day. They must eat the lamb at that time with bitter herbs and bread made

without yeast. ¹²They must not leave any of the lamb until the next morning, and they must not break any of its bones. They must follow all the normal regulations concerning the Passover.

¹³"'But those who are ceremonially clean and not away on a trip, yet still refuse to celebrate the Passover at the regular time, will be cut off from the community of Israel for failing to present the LORD's offering at the proper time. They will suffer the consequences of their guilt. ¹⁴And if foreigners living among you want to celebrate the Passover to the LORD, they must follow these same laws and regulations. The same laws apply both to you and to the foreigners living among you.'"

¹⁵The Tabernacle was set up, and on that day the cloud covered it.* Then from evening until morning the cloud over the Tabernacle appeared to be a pillar of fire. ¹⁶This was the regular pattern—at night the cloud changed to the appearance of fire. ¹⁷When the cloud lifted from over the sacred tent, the people of Israel followed it. And wherever the cloud settled, the people of Israel camped. ¹⁸In this way, they traveled at the LORD's command and stopped wherever he told them to. Then they remained where they were as long as the cloud stayed over the Tabernacle. ¹⁹If the cloud remained over the Tabernacle for a long time, the Israelites stayed for a long time, just as the LORD commanded. ²⁰Sometimes the cloud would stay over the Tabernacle for only a few days, so the people would stay for only a few days. Then at the LORD's command they would break camp. ²¹Sometimes the

9:1 Hebrew *in the first month*. This month of the Hebrew lunar calendar usually occurs in March and April.   **9:3** Hebrew *on the fourteenth day of the first month*. This day of the Hebrew lunar calendar occurs in late March or early April.   **9:5** Hebrew *on the fourteenth day of the first month*; see note on 9:3.   **9:11** Hebrew *on the fourteenth day of the second month*. This day of the Hebrew lunar calendar occurs in late April or early May.   **9:15** Hebrew *covered the Tabernacle, the Tent of the Testimony.*

cloud stayed only overnight and moved on the next morning. But day or night, when the cloud lifted, the people broke camp and followed. [22]Whether the cloud stayed above the Tabernacle for two days, a month, or a year, the people of Israel stayed in camp and did not move on. But as soon as it lifted, they broke camp and moved on. [23]So they camped or traveled at the LORD's command, and they did whatever the LORD told them through Moses.

CHAPTER 10

Now the LORD said to Moses, [2]"Make two trumpets of beaten silver to be used for summoning the people to assemble and for signaling the breaking of camp. [3]When both trumpets are blown, the people will know that they are to gather before you at the entrance of the Tabernacle.* [4]But if only one is blown, then only the leaders of the tribes of Israel will come to you.

[5]"When you sound the signal to move on, the tribes on the east side of the Tabernacle will break camp and move forward. [6]When you sound the signal a second time, the tribes on the south will follow. You must sound short blasts to signal moving on. [7]But when you call the people to an assembly, blow the trumpets using a different signal. [8]Only the priests, Aaron's descendants, are allowed to blow the trumpets. This is a permanent law to be followed from generation to generation.

[9]"When you arrive in your own land and go to war against your enemies, you must sound the alarm with these trumpets so the LORD your God will remember you and rescue you from your enemies. [10]Blow the trumpets in times of gladness, too, sounding them at your annual festivals and at the beginning of each month to rejoice over your burnt offerings and peace offerings. The trumpets will remind the LORD your God of his covenant with you. I am the LORD your God."

[11]One day in midspring,* during the second year after Israel's departure from Egypt, the cloud lifted from the Tabernacle of the Covenant.* [12]So the Israelites set out from the wilderness of Sinai and traveled on in stages until the cloud stopped in the wilderness of Paran. [13]When the time to move arrived, the LORD gave the order through Moses. [14]The

tribes that camped with Judah headed the march with their banner, under the leadership of Nahshon son of Amminadab. [15]The tribe of Issachar was led by Nethanel son of Zuar. [16]The tribe of Zebulun was led by Eliab son of Helon.

[17]Then the Tabernacle was taken down, and the Gershonite and Merarite divisions of the Levites were next in the line of march, carrying the Tabernacle with them. [18]Then the tribes that camped with Reuben set out with their banner, under the leadership of Elizur son of Shedeur. [19]The tribe of Simeon was led by Shelumiel son of Zurishaddai. [20]The tribe of Gad was led by Eliasaph son of Deuel.

[21]Next came the Kohathite division of the Levites, carrying the sacred objects from the Tabernacle. When they arrived at the next camp, the Tabernacle would already be set up at its new location. [22]Then the tribes that camped with Ephraim set out with their banner, under the leadership of Elishama son of Ammihud. [23]The tribe of Manasseh was led by Gamaliel son of Pedahzur. [24]The tribe of Benjamin was led by Abidan son of Gideoni.

[25]Last of all, the tribes that camped with Dan set out under their banner. They served as the rear guard for all the tribal camps. The tribe of Dan headed this group, under the leadership of Ahiezer son of Ammishaddai. [26]The tribe of Asher was led by Pagiel son of Ocran. [27]The tribe of Naphtali was led by Ahira son of Enan.

[28]This was the order in which the tribes marched, division by division.

[29]One day Moses said to his brother-in-law, Hobab son of Reuel the Midianite, "We are on our way to the Promised Land. Come with us and we will treat you well, for the LORD has given wonderful promises to Israel!"

[30]But Hobab replied, "No, I will not go. I must return to my own land and family."

[31]"Please don't leave us," Moses pleaded. "You know the places in the wilderness where we should camp. [32]Come, be our guide and we will share with you all the good things that the LORD does for us."

[33]They marched for three days after leaving the mountain of the LORD, with the Ark of the LORD's covenant moving ahead of them to show them where to stop and rest. [34]As they moved on each day, the cloud of

10:3 Hebrew *Tent of Meeting.*   10:11a Hebrew *On the twentieth day of the second month.* This day of the Hebrew lunar calendar occurs in late April or early May.   10:11b Or *Tabernacle of the Testimony.*

the LORD hovered over them. ³⁵And whenever the Ark set out, Moses would cry, "Arise, O LORD, and let your enemies be scattered! Let them flee before you!" ³⁶And when the Ark was set down, he would say, "Return, O LORD, to the countless thousands of Israel!"

CHAPTER 11

The people soon began to complain to the LORD about their hardships; and when the LORD heard them, his anger blazed against them. Fire from the LORD raged among them and destroyed the outskirts of the camp. ²The people screamed to Moses for help; and when he prayed to the LORD, the fire stopped. ³After that, the area was known as Taberah—"the place of burning"—because fire from the LORD had burned among them there.

⁴Then the foreign rabble who were traveling with the Israelites began to crave the good things of Egypt, and the people of Israel also began to complain. "Oh, for some meat!" they exclaimed. ⁵"We remember all the fish we used to eat for free in Egypt. And we had all the cucumbers, melons, leeks, onions, and garlic that we wanted. ⁶But now our appetites are gone, and day after day we have nothing to eat but this manna!"

⁷The manna looked like small coriander seeds, pale yellow in color.* ⁸The people gathered it from the ground and made flour by grinding it with hand mills or pounding it in mortars. Then they boiled it in a pot and made it into flat cakes. These cakes tasted like they had been cooked in olive oil. ⁹The manna came down on the camp with the dew during the night.

¹⁰Moses heard all the families standing in front of their tents weeping, and the LORD became extremely angry. Moses was also very aggravated. ¹¹And Moses said to the LORD, "Why are you treating me, your servant, so miserably? What did I do to deserve the burden of a people like this? ¹²Are they my children? Am I their father? Is that why you have told me to carry them in my arms—like a nurse carries a baby—to the land you swore to give their ancestors? ¹³Where am I supposed to get meat for all these people? They keep complaining and saying, 'Give us meat!' ¹⁴I can't carry all these people by myself! The load

is far too heavy! ¹⁵I'd rather you killed me than treat me like this. Please spare me this misery!"

¹⁶Then the LORD said to Moses, "Summon before me seventy of the leaders of Israel. Bring them to the Tabernacle* to stand there with you. ¹⁷I will come down and talk to you there. I will take some of the Spirit that is upon you, and I will put the Spirit upon them also. They will bear the burden of the people along with you, so you will not have to carry it alone.

¹⁸"And tell the people to purify themselves, for tomorrow they will have meat to eat. Tell them, 'The LORD has heard your whining and complaints: "If only we had meat to eat! Surely we were better off in Egypt!" Now the LORD will give you meat, and you will have to eat it. ¹⁹And it won't be for just a day or two, or for five or ten or even twenty. ²⁰You will eat it for a whole month until you gag and are sick of it. For you have rejected the LORD, who is here among you, and you have complained to him, "Why did we ever leave Egypt?"'"

²¹But Moses said, "There are 600,000 foot soldiers here with me, and yet you promise them meat for a whole month! ²²Even if we butchered all our flocks and herds, would that satisfy them? Even if we caught all the fish in the sea, would that be enough?"

²³Then the LORD said to Moses, "Is there any limit to my power? Now you will see whether or not my word comes true!"

²⁴So Moses went out and reported the LORD's words to the people. Then he gathered the seventy leaders and stationed them around the Tabernacle.* ²⁵And the LORD came down in the cloud and spoke to Moses. He took some of the Spirit that was upon Moses and put it upon the seventy leaders. They prophesied as the Spirit rested upon them, but that was the only time this happened.

²⁶Two men, Eldad and Medad, were still in the camp when the Spirit rested upon them. They were listed among the leaders but had not gone out to the Tabernacle, so they prophesied there in the camp. ²⁷A young man ran and reported to Moses, "Eldad and Medad are prophesying in the camp!" ²⁸Joshua son of Nun, who had been Moses' personal assistant since his youth, protested, "Moses, my master, make them stop!"

11:7 Hebrew *the color of gum resin.*   11:16 Hebrew *Tent of Meeting.*   11:24 Hebrew *the tent;* also in 11:26.

²⁹But Moses replied, "Are you jealous for my sake? I wish that all the LORD's people were prophets, and that the LORD would put his Spirit upon them all!" ³⁰Then Moses returned to the camp with the leaders of Israel.

³¹Now the LORD sent a wind that brought quail from the sea and let them fall into the camp and all around it! For many miles in every direction from the camp there were quail flying about three feet above the ground.* ³²So the people went out and caught quail all that day and throughout the night and all the next day, too. No one gathered less than fifty bushels*! They spread the quail out all over the camp. ³³But while they were still eating the meat, the anger of the LORD blazed against the people, and he caused a severe plague to break out among them. ³⁴So that place was called Kibroth-hattaavah—"the graves of craving"—because they buried the people there who had craved meat from Egypt. ³⁵From there the Israelites traveled to Hazeroth, where they stayed for some time.

CHAPTER 12
While they were at Hazeroth, Miriam and Aaron criticized Moses because he had married a Cushite woman. ²They said, "Has the LORD spoken only through Moses? Hasn't he spoken through us, too?" But the LORD heard them.

³Now Moses was more humble than any other person on earth. ⁴So immediately the LORD called to Moses, Aaron, and Miriam and said, "Go out to the Tab-

ernacle,* all three of you!" And the three of them went out. ⁵Then the LORD descended in the pillar of cloud and stood at the entrance of the Tabernacle.* "Aaron and Miriam!" he called, and they stepped forward. ⁶And the LORD said to them, "Now listen to me! Even with prophets, I the LORD communicate by visions and dreams. ⁷But that is not how I communicate with my servant Moses. He is entrusted with my entire house. ⁸I speak to him face to face, directly and not in riddles! He sees the LORD as he is. Should you not be afraid to criticize him?"

⁹The LORD was furious with them, and he departed. ¹⁰As the cloud moved from above the Tabernacle, Miriam suddenly became white as snow with leprosy.* When Aaron saw what had happened, ¹¹he cried out to Moses, "Oh, my lord! Please don't punish us for this sin we have so foolishly committed. ¹²Don't let her be like a stillborn baby, already decayed at birth."

¹³So Moses cried out to the LORD, "Heal her, O God, I beg you!"

¹⁴And the LORD said to Moses, "If her father had spit in her face, wouldn't she have been defiled for seven days? Banish her from the camp for seven days, and after that she may return."

¹⁵So Miriam was excluded from the camp for seven days, and the people waited until she was brought back before they traveled again. ¹⁶Then they left Hazeroth and camped in the wilderness of Paran.

11:31 Or *there were quail 3 feet* [2 cubits or 90 centimeters] *deep on the ground.*   11:32 Hebrew *10 homers* [1.8 kiloliters].
12:4 Hebrew *Tent of Meeting.*   12:5 Hebrew *the tent;* also in 12:10.   12:10 Or *with a contagious skin disease.* The Hebrew word used here can describe various skin diseases.

FEBRUARY 13 ☐ DAY 44
NUMBERS 13–16
Rebellion and Death in the Wilderness

 OVERVIEW As Israel camps at the edge of Canaan, the Lord commands Moses to select one man from each tribe to form a scouting party to report on conditions in the land. The scouts travel into Canaan and return with a report that stuns the people. The land is full of giants and fortified cities. By a vote of ten to two, the scouts officially discourage the nation from claiming the land, and Caleb and Joshua's voices of faith are drowned out as the people cry, "Back to Egypt!" God punishes his children for their lack of faith by sentencing them to forty years of wandering in the wilderness—one year for each day the scouts surveyed the land.

Chapter 13	Chapter 14	Chapter 15	Chapter 16
A Discouraging Word	A Disheartened People	A Divine Law	A Disobedient Korah
Rebellion against God		Judgment from God	

YOUR DAILY WALK Action and reaction have more in common than their spelling. They are inseparable halves of everything you do.

Because "no man is an island," your actions touch the lives of those close to you—family, friends, and associates. Therefore, the decisions you make today spill over into the lives of others tomorrow—whether for good or evil.

Courage is the knowledge of how to fear what ought to be feared and how not to fear what ought not to be feared.

The Israelites who rejected God at Kadesh quickly realized the painful consequences of their willful disobedience. If they had remained faithful to God, not only they but their children as well would have enjoyed the blessings of the land immediately. Instead, parents and children alike suffered through forty years of wilderness wanderings until the unbelieving generation had all died.

Are you facing a seemingly insurmountable problem today—your own private "Canaan," full of giants and walled cities? Remember, in times like this it's the size of your God—not the size of your giants—that counts. Take a few minutes today to share your "Canaan" with a prayer partner or family member. Then together ask God to help you make decisions that impact others for *good* and for *God.*

INSIGHT Warning! Warning! Warning!
Israel's revolt at Kadesh provides such a significant lesson on the price of unbelief that it is mentioned three times in the New Testament: 1 Corinthians 10:1-12; Hebrews 3:7-11; 4:1-11.

CHAPTER 13
The LORD now said to Moses, [2]"Send men to explore the land of Canaan, the land I am giving to Israel. Send one leader from each of the twelve ancestral tribes." [3]So Moses did as the LORD commanded him. He sent out twelve men, all tribal leaders of Israel, from their camp in the wilderness of Paran. [4]These were the tribes and the names of the leaders:

Tribe	Leader
Reuben	Shammua son of Zaccur
[5] Simeon	Shaphat son of Hori
[6] Judah	Caleb son of Jephunneh
[7] Issachar	Igal son of Joseph
[8] Ephraim	Hoshea son of Nun
[9] Benjamin	Palti son of Raphu
[10] Zebulun	Gaddiel son of Sodi
[11] Manasseh son of Joseph	Gaddi son of Susi
[12] Dan	Ammiel son of Gemalli
[13] Asher	Sethur son of Michael
[14] Naphtali	Nahbi son of Vophsi
[15] Gad	Geuel son of Maki

[16]These are the names of the men Moses sent to explore the land. By this time Moses had changed Hoshea's name to Joshua.*

[17]Moses gave the men these instructions as he sent them out to explore the land: "Go northward through the Negev into the hill country. [18]See what the land is like and find out whether the people living there are strong or weak, few or many. [19]What kind of land do they live in? Is it good or bad? Do their towns have walls or are they unprotected? [20]How is the soil? Is it fertile or poor? Are there many trees? Enter the land boldly, and bring back samples of the crops you see." (It happened to be the season for harvesting the first ripe grapes.)

[21]So they went up and explored the land from the wilderness of Zin as far as Rehob,

13:16 *Hoshea* (see 13:8) means "salvation"; *Joshua* means "The LORD is salvation."

near Lebo-hamath. ²²Going northward, they passed first through the Negev and arrived at Hebron, where Ahiman, Sheshai, and Talmai—all descendants of Anak—lived. (The ancient town of Hebron was founded seven years before the Egyptian city of Zoan.) ²³When they came to what is now known as the valley of Eshcol, they cut down a cluster of grapes so large that it took two of them to carry it on a pole between them! They also took samples of the pomegranates and figs. ²⁴At that time the Israelites renamed the valley Eshcol—"cluster"—because of the cluster of grapes they had cut there.

²⁵After exploring the land for forty days, the men returned ²⁶to Moses, Aaron, and the people of Israel at Kadesh in the wilderness of Paran. They reported to the whole community what they had seen and showed them the fruit they had taken from the land. ²⁷This was their report to Moses: "We arrived in the land you sent us to see, and it is indeed a magnificent country—a land flowing with milk and honey. Here is some of its fruit as proof. ²⁸But the people living there are powerful, and their cities and towns are fortified and very large. We also saw the descendants of Anak who are living there! ²⁹The Amalekites live in the Negev, and the Hittites, Jebusites, and Amorites live in the hill country. The Canaanites live along the coast of the Mediterranean Sea* and along the Jordan Valley."

³⁰But Caleb tried to encourage the people as they stood before Moses. "Let's go at once to take the land," he said. "We can certainly conquer it!"

³¹But the other men who had explored the land with him answered, "We can't go up against them! They are stronger than we are!" ³²So they spread discouraging reports about the land among the Israelites: "The land we explored will swallow up any who go to live there. All the people we saw were huge. ³³We even saw giants* there, the descendants of Anak. We felt like grasshoppers next to them, and that's what we looked like to them!"

CHAPTER 14
Then all the people began weeping aloud, and they cried all night. ²Their voices rose in a great chorus of complaint against Moses and Aaron. "We wish we had died

in Egypt, or even here in the wilderness!" they wailed. ³"Why is the LORD taking us to this country only to have us die in battle? Our wives and little ones will be carried off as slaves! Let's get out of here and return to Egypt!" ⁴Then they plotted among themselves, "Let's choose a leader and go back to Egypt!"

⁵Then Moses and Aaron fell face down on the ground before the people of Israel. ⁶Two of the men who had explored the land, Joshua son of Nun and Caleb son of Jephunneh, tore their clothing. ⁷They said to the community of Israel, "The land we explored is a wonderful land! ⁸And if the LORD is pleased with us, he will bring us safely into that land and give it to us. It is a rich land flowing with milk and honey, and he will give it to us! ⁹Do not rebel against the LORD, and don't be afraid of the people of the land. They are only helpless prey to us! They have no protection, but the LORD is with us! Don't be afraid of them!"

¹⁰But the whole community began to talk about stoning Joshua and Caleb. Then the glorious presence of the LORD appeared to all the Israelites from above the Tabernacle.* ¹¹And the LORD said to Moses, "How long will these people reject me? Will they never believe me, even after all the miraculous signs I have done among them? ¹²I will disown them and destroy them with a plague. Then I will make you into a nation far greater and mightier than they are!"

¹³"But what will the Egyptians think when they hear about it?" Moses pleaded with the LORD. "They know full well the power you displayed in rescuing these people from Egypt. ¹⁴They will tell this to the inhabitants of this land, who are well aware that you are with this people. They know, LORD, that you have appeared in full view of your people in the pillar of cloud that hovers over them. They know that you go before them in the pillar of cloud by day and the pillar of fire by night. ¹⁵Now if you slaughter all these people, the nations that have heard of your fame will say, ¹⁶'The LORD was not able to bring them into the land he swore to give them, so he killed them in the wilderness.'

¹⁷"Please, Lord, prove that your power is as great as you have claimed it to be. For you said, ¹⁸'The LORD is slow to anger and rich in unfailing love, forgiving every kind

13:29 Hebrew *the sea.*   13:33 Hebrew *nephilim.*   14:10 Hebrew *Tent of Meeting.*

of sin and rebellion. Even so he does not leave sin unpunished, but he punishes the children for the sins of their parents to the third and fourth generations.' [19]Please pardon the sins of this people because of your magnificent, unfailing love, just as you have forgiven them ever since they left Egypt."

[20]Then the LORD said, "I will pardon them as you have requested. [21]But as surely as I live, and as surely as the earth is filled with the LORD's glory, [22]not one of these people will ever enter that land. They have seen my glorious presence and the miraculous signs I performed both in Egypt and in the wilderness, but again and again they tested me by refusing to listen. [23]They will never even see the land I swore to give their ancestors. None of those who have treated me with contempt will enter it. [24]But my servant Caleb is different from the others. He has remained loyal to me, and I will bring him into the land he explored. His descendants will receive their full share of that land. [25]Now turn around and don't go on toward the land where the Amalekites and Canaanites live. Tomorrow you must set out for the wilderness in the direction of the Red Sea.*"

[26]Then the LORD said to Moses and Aaron, [27]"How long will this wicked nation complain about me? I have heard everything the Israelites have been saying. [28]Now tell them this: 'As surely as I live, I will do to you the very things I heard you say. I, the LORD, have spoken! [29]You will all die here in this wilderness! Because you complained against me, none of you who are twenty years old or older and were counted in the census [30]will enter the land I swore to give you. The only exceptions will be Caleb son of Jephunneh and Joshua son of Nun. [31]'You said your children would be taken captive. Well, I will bring them safely into the land, and they will enjoy what you have despised. [32]But as for you, your dead bodies will fall in this wilderness. [33]And your children will be like shepherds, wandering in the wilderness forty years. In this way, they will pay for your faithlessness, until the last of you lies dead in the wilderness.

[34]'Because the men who explored the land were there for forty days, you must wander in the wilderness for forty years— a year for each day, suffering the consequences of your sins. You will discover what it is like to have me for an enemy.' [35]I, the LORD, have spoken! I will do these things to every member of the community who has conspired against me. They will all die here in this wilderness!"

[36]Then the ten scouts who had incited the rebellion against the LORD by spreading discouraging reports about the land [37]were struck dead with a plague before the LORD. [38]Of the twelve who had explored the land, only Joshua and Caleb remained alive.

[39]When Moses reported the LORD's words to the Israelites, there was much sorrow among the people. [40]So they got up early the next morning and set out for the hill country of Canaan. "Let's go," they said. "We realize that we have sinned, but now we are ready to enter the land the LORD has promised us."

[41]But Moses said, "Why are you now disobeying the LORD's orders to return to the wilderness? It won't work. [42]Do not go into the land now. You will only be crushed by your enemies because the LORD is not with you. [43]When you face the Amalekites and Canaanites in battle, you will be slaughtered. The LORD will abandon you because you have abandoned the LORD."

[44]But the people pushed ahead toward the hill country of Canaan, despite the fact that neither Moses nor the Ark of the LORD's covenant left the camp. [45]Then the Amalekites and the Canaanites who lived in those hills came down and attacked them and chased them as far as Hormah.

CHAPTER 15

The LORD told Moses to give these instructions to the people of Israel: [2]"When you finally settle in the land I am going to give you, [3]and you want to please the LORD with a burnt offering or any other offering given by fire, the sacrifice must be an animal from your flocks of sheep and goats or from your herds of cattle. When it is an ordinary burnt offering, a sacrifice to fulfill a vow, a freewill offering, or a special sacrifice at any of the annual festivals, [4]whoever brings it must also give to the LORD a grain offering of two quarts* of choice flour mixed with one quart* of olive oil. [5]For each lamb offered as a whole burnt offering, you must

14:25 Hebrew *sea of reeds*.   **15:4a** Hebrew ¹/₁₀ *of an ephah* [2 liters].   **15:4b** Hebrew ¹/₄ *of a hin* [1 liter]; also in 15:5.

also present one quart of wine for a drink offering.

⁶"If the sacrifice is a ram, give three quarts* of choice flour mixed with two and a half pints* of olive oil, ⁷and give two and a half pints of wine for a drink offering. This sacrifice will be very pleasing to the LORD.

⁸"When you present a young bull as a burnt offering or a sacrifice in fulfillment of a special vow or as a peace offering to the LORD, ⁹then the grain offering accompanying it must include five quarts* of choice flour mixed with two quarts* of olive oil, ¹⁰plus two quarts of wine for the drink offering. This will be an offering made by fire, very pleasing to the LORD.

¹¹"These are the instructions for what is to accompany each sacrificial bull, ram, lamb, or young goat. ¹²Each of you must do this with each offering you present. ¹³If you native Israelites want to present an offering by fire that is pleasing to the LORD, you must follow all these instructions. ¹⁴And if any foreigners living among you want to present an offering by fire, pleasing to the LORD, they must follow the same procedures. ¹⁵Native Israelites and foreigners are the same before the LORD and are subject to the same laws. This is a permanent law for you. ¹⁶The same instructions and regulations will apply both to you and to the foreigners living among you."

¹⁷The LORD also said to Moses at this time, ¹⁸"Give the people of Israel the following instructions: When you arrive in the land where I am taking you, ¹⁹you will eat from the crops that grow there. But you must set some aside as a gift to the LORD. ²⁰Present a cake from the first of the flour you grind and set it aside as a gift, as you do with the first grain from the threshing floor. ²¹Throughout the generations to come, you are to present this offering to the LORD each year from the first of your ground flour.

²²"But suppose some of you unintentionally fail to carry out all these commands that the LORD has given you through Moses. ²³And suppose some of your descendants in the future fail to do everything the LORD has commanded through Moses. ²⁴If the mistake was done unintentionally, and the community was unaware of it, the whole community must present a

young bull for a burnt offering. It will be pleasing to the LORD, and it must be offered along with the prescribed grain offering and drink offering and with one male goat for a sin offering. ²⁵With it the priest will make atonement for the whole community of Israel, and they will be forgiven. For it was an unintentional sin, and they have corrected it with their offering given to the LORD by fire and by their sin offering. ²⁶The whole community of Israel will be forgiven, including the foreigners living among you, for the entire population was involved in the sin.

²⁷"If the unintentional sin is committed by an individual, the guilty person must bring a one-year-old female goat for a sin offering. ²⁸The priest will make atonement for the guilty person before the LORD, and that person will be forgiven. ²⁹This same law applies both to native Israelites and the foreigners living among you.

³⁰"But those who brazenly violate the LORD's will, whether native Israelites or foreigners, blaspheme the LORD, and they must be cut off from the community. ³¹Since they have treated the LORD's word with contempt and deliberately disobeyed his commands, they must be completely cut off and suffer the consequences of their guilt."

³²One day while the people of Israel were in the wilderness, they caught a man gathering wood on the Sabbath day. ³³He was apprehended and taken before Moses, Aaron, and the rest of the community. ³⁴They held him in custody because they did not know what to do with him. ³⁵Then the LORD said to Moses, "The man must be put to death! The whole community must stone him outside the camp." ³⁶So the whole community took the man outside the camp and stoned him to death, just as the LORD had commanded Moses.

³⁷And the LORD said to Moses, ³⁸"Say to the people of Israel: 'Throughout the generations to come you must make tassels for the hems of your clothing and attach the tassels at each corner with a blue cord. ³⁹The tassels will remind you of the commands of the LORD, and that you are to obey his commands instead of following your own desires and going your own ways, as you are prone to do. ⁴⁰The tassels will help you remember that you must obey all my com-

15:6a Hebrew ²/₁₀ of an ephah [3.6 liters].   15:6b Hebrew ¹/₃ of a hin [1.3 liters]; also in 15:7.   15:9a Hebrew ³/₁₀ of an ephah [5.4 liters].   15:9b Hebrew ¹/₂ of a hin [2 liters]; also in 15:10.

mands and be holy to your God. ⁴¹I am the LORD your God who brought you out of the land of Egypt that I might be your God. I am the LORD your God!'"

CHAPTER 16
One day Korah son of Izhar, a descendant of Kohath son of Levi, conspired with Dathan and Abiram, the sons of Eliab, and On son of Peleth, from the tribe of Reuben. ²They incited a rebellion against Moses, involving 250 other prominent leaders, all members of the assembly. ³They went to Moses and Aaron and said, "You have gone too far! Everyone in Israel has been set apart by the LORD, and he is with all of us. What right do you have to act as though you are greater than anyone else among all these people of the LORD?"

⁴When Moses heard what they were saying, he threw himself down with his face to the ground. ⁵Then he said to Korah and his followers, "Tomorrow morning the LORD will show us who belongs to him and who is holy. The LORD will allow those who are chosen to enter his holy presence. ⁶You, Korah, and all your followers must do this: Take incense burners, ⁷and burn incense in them tomorrow before the LORD. Then we will see whom the LORD chooses as his holy one. You Levites are the ones who have gone too far!"

⁸Then Moses spoke again to Korah: "Now listen, you Levites! ⁹Does it seem a small thing to you that the God of Israel has chosen you from among all the people of Israel to be near him as you serve in the LORD's Tabernacle and to stand before the people to minister to them? ¹⁰He has given this special ministry only to you and your fellow Levites, but now you are demanding the priesthood as well! ¹¹The one you are really revolting against is the LORD! And who is Aaron that you are complaining about him?"

¹²Then Moses summoned Dathan and Abiram, the sons of Eliab, but they replied, "We refuse to come! ¹³Isn't it enough that you brought us out of Egypt, a land flowing with milk and honey, to kill us here in this wilderness, and that you now treat us like your subjects? ¹⁴What's more, you haven't brought us into the land flowing with milk and honey or given us an inheritance of fields and vineyards. Are you trying to fool us? We will not come."

¹⁵Then Moses became very angry and said to the LORD, "Do not accept their offerings! I have not taken so much as a donkey from them, and I have never hurt a single one of them." ¹⁶And Moses said to Korah, "Come here tomorrow and present yourself before the LORD with all your followers. Aaron will also be here. ¹⁷Be sure that each of your 250 followers brings an incense burner with incense on it, so you can present them before the LORD. Aaron will also bring his incense burner."

¹⁸So these men came with their incense burners, placed burning coals and incense on them, and stood at the entrance of the Tabernacle* with Moses and Aaron. ¹⁹Meanwhile, Korah had stirred up the entire community against Moses and Aaron, and they all assembled at the Tabernacle entrance. Then the glorious presence of the LORD appeared to the whole community, ²⁰and the LORD said to Moses and Aaron, ²¹"Get away from these people so that I may instantly destroy them!"

²²But Moses and Aaron fell face down on the ground. "O God, the God and source of all life," they pleaded. "Must you be angry with all the people when only one man sins?"

²³And the LORD said to Moses, ²⁴"Then tell all the people to get away from the tents of Korah, Dathan, and Abiram."

²⁵So Moses got up and rushed over to the tents of Dathan and Abiram, followed closely by the Israelite leaders. ²⁶"Quick!" he told the people. "Get away from the tents of these wicked men, and don't touch anything that belongs to them. If you do, you will be destroyed for their sins." ²⁷So all the people stood back from the tents of Korah, Dathan, and Abiram. Then Dathan and Abiram came out and stood at the entrances of their tents with their wives and children and little ones.

²⁸And Moses said, "By this you will know that the LORD has sent me to do all these things that I have done—for I have not done them on my own. ²⁹If these men die a natural death, then the LORD has not sent me. ³⁰But if the LORD performs a miracle and the ground opens up and swallows them and all their belongings, and they go down alive into the grave, then you will know that these men have despised the LORD."

16:18 Hebrew *Tent of Meeting;* also in 16:19, 42, 43, 50.

[31]He had hardly finished speaking the words when the ground suddenly split open beneath them. [32]The earth opened up and swallowed the men, along with their households and the followers who were standing with them, and everything they owned. [33]So they went down alive into the grave, along with their belongings. The earth closed over them, and they all vanished. [34]All of the people of Israel fled as they heard their screams, fearing that the earth would swallow them, too. [35]Then fire blazed forth from the LORD and burned up the 250 men who were offering incense.

[36]And the LORD said to Moses, [37]"Tell Eleazar son of Aaron the priest to pull all the incense burners from the fire, for they are holy. Also tell him to scatter the burning incense [38]from the burners of these men who have sinned at the cost of their lives. He must then hammer the metal of the incense burners into a sheet as a covering for the altar, for these burners have become holy because they were used in the LORD's presence. The altar covering will then serve as a warning to the people of Israel."

[39]So Eleazar the priest collected the 250 bronze incense burners that had been used by the men who died in the fire, and they were hammered out into a sheet of metal to cover the altar. [40]This would warn the Israelites that no unauthorized man—no one who was not a descendant of Aaron—should ever enter the LORD's presence to burn incense. If anyone did,

the same thing would happen to him as happened to Korah and his followers. Thus, the LORD's instructions to Moses were carried out.

[41]But the very next morning the whole community began muttering again against Moses and Aaron, saying, "You two have killed the LORD's people!" [42]As the people gathered to protest to Moses and Aaron, they turned toward the Tabernacle and saw that the cloud had covered it, and the glorious presence of the LORD appeared.

[43]Moses and Aaron came and stood at the entrance of the Tabernacle, [44]and the LORD said to Moses, [45]"Get away from these people so that I can instantly destroy them!" But Moses and Aaron fell face down on the ground.

[46]And Moses said to Aaron, "Quick, take an incense burner and place burning coals on it from the altar. Lay incense on it and carry it quickly among the people to make atonement for them. The LORD's anger is blazing among them—the plague has already begun."

[47]Aaron did as Moses told him and ran out among the people. The plague indeed had already begun, but Aaron burned the incense and made atonement for them. [48]He stood between the living and the dead until the plague was stopped. [49]But 14,700 people died in that plague, in addition to those who had died in the incident involving Korah. [50]Then because the plague had stopped, Aaron returned to Moses at the entrance of the Tabernacle.

FEBRUARY 14 ☐ DAY 45
Holy Habits for a Holy People

 LOOK BACK Repetition is the key to retention. (Let me say that again.) Repetition is the key to retention. If you feel comfortable making notations in your Bible, the portions of Leviticus and Numbers you have read this past week have given you plenty of opportunity to mark words and phrases that are frequently repeated: "clean . . . unclean . . . atonement . . . I, the LORD, am your God . . . holy." They serve as a reminder that a holy God demanded nothing less than holy people in a holy camp. And when that holiness was interrupted by defilement or disobedience, God had already provided a way for the priest to make atonement (covering) for the sin. The sounds of animals being slaughtered, the smell of spilled blood and roasting flesh, the sight of smoke rising constantly from the altar—these were all too familiar to the nation. Without the shedding of blood there could be no forgiveness of sin or fellowship with God.

LOOK UP Take a handful of mud and coat your hands thoroughly. Now answer a series of questions.

Whitewashing the pump will not purify the water.

1. What would it take to get your hands clean enough to do work in the garage? (No problem. Just wipe them on your overalls, and that should do the trick.)

2. What would it take to get your hands clean enough to be allowed at the dinner table? (Soap and water might be needed there!)

3. What would it take to get your hands clean enough to put on your best white shirt or blouse without soiling it? (Lots of soap and hot water!)

4. What would it take to get your hands clean enough to do abdominal surgery? (Soap, water, a strong disinfectant, and lots of scrubbing time.)

As one exasperated parent put it: "Cleanliness may be next to godliness, but around our house it's next to impossible."

But here's one more question to ponder:

5. What would it take to get your hands clean enough for God to allow you into heaven? (As one little boy was heard to exclaim: "You mean only people with clean hands get into heaven? Then I'm a goner!") Turn to Psalm 24:3-4, and see what God's Word says about clean hands!

LOOK AHEAD Heaven is a prepared place for a prepared people. Jesus prayed, "Father, may your name be honored" (Luke 11:2). He knew that God, who is holy, cannot tolerate the presence of that which is unholy or defiled. So how is it possible for imperfect people to get to heaven? If no soap on earth can rid the stain of sin, what hope is there for any of us?

Answer: None at all . . . apart from the cleansing work of Jesus Christ, God's Son. "And what God wants is for us to be made holy by the sacrifice of the body of Jesus Christ once for all time" (Hebrews 10:10). What no soap, disinfectant, or miracle detergent could do for our sinful condition, Jesus accomplished by his death, burial, and resurrection. "The blood of Jesus, his Son, cleanses us from every sin" (1 John 1:7).

"Have you washed your hands?" Mothers tend to ask questions like that a lot.

"Do you have clean hands and a pure heart?" The Father in heaven will one day ask you that question. If you're not sure what answer you would give, make Hebrews 10 your meditation today!

FEBRUARY 15 ☐ DAY 46
NUMBERS 17–20
The Staff, Red Heifer, and Rebellion

OVERVIEW Two sounds accompany the people as they wander in the wilderness: the *rumbling* of a nation on the march and the *grumbling* of the people as they complain about the food, water, and leadership. Mutiny against Moses and Aaron is avoided when God provides the miracle of Aaron's budding staff. In addition, the Levites are reaffirmed in their service in the Tabernacle, and the sacrifice of the red heifer

provides a constant source of cleansing from the ever present defilement of death. Yet, the grumbling continues. In a moment of anger,
Moses does the right thing (bringing forth water) in the wrong way
(striking the rock instead of speaking to it), thereby forfeiting his
privilege to set foot in the Promised Land.

Chapter 17	Chapter 18	Chapter 19	Chapter 20
Staff of Aaron	Responsibilities of the Levites	Sacrifice of the Red Heifer	Sin of the People and Moses
Priesthood Established		Purity Enforced	

People always remember a kind deed—particularly if it was their own.

YOUR DAILY WALK Imagine for a moment that God has appeared
to you to announce you will no longer be permitted to hold down a
paying job or own property. Instead, you are to spend your full time in
his service, and your compensation will be whatever your countrymen
give to the Lord! Would that *comfort* you or *concern* you?

According to 18:20-21, those were basically God's instructions to
Aaron and his descendants! Your local church today is in many ways a
faith ministry like the priesthood of Aaron. You, like the Israelites, have
been commanded to support the work of the Lord so God can be
magnified in your community. Which word best describes your giving
habits to your church: a *comfort* . . . or a *concern* to those ministering
to you? Now read Acts 20:35, and enjoy a blessing this week!

INSIGHT A Family That Never Set Foot in Canaan
Moses, his sister Miriam, and his brother Aaron, never enjoyed the bless-
ings of the Promised Land. Numbers 20 details the fate of each of these
three family members. Check out the details about
• Miriam (20:1)
• Moses (20:7-13)
• Aaron (20:22-29)

CHAPTER 17
Then the LORD said to Moses, ²"Take
twelve wooden staffs, one from each of Israel's ancestral tribes, and inscribe each
tribal leader's name on his staff. ³Inscribe
Aaron's name on the staff of the tribe of
Levi, for there must be one staff for the
leader of each ancestral tribe. ⁴Put these
staffs in the Tabernacle in front of the Ark
of the Covenant,* where I meet with you.
⁵Buds will sprout on the staff belonging to
the man I choose. Then I will finally put an
end to this murmuring and complaining
against you."

⁶So Moses gave the instructions to the
people of Israel, and each of the twelve
tribal leaders, including Aaron, brought
Moses a staff. ⁷Moses put the staffs in the
LORD's presence in the Tabernacle of the
Covenant.* ⁸When he went into the Tabernacle of the Covenant the next day, he
found that Aaron's staff, representing the

tribe of Levi, had sprouted, blossomed, and
produced almonds!

⁹When Moses brought all the staffs out
from the LORD's presence, he showed them
to the people. Each man claimed his own
staff. ¹⁰And the LORD said to Moses: "Place
Aaron's staff permanently before the Ark
of the Covenant* as a warning to rebels.
This should put an end to their complaints
against me and prevent any further
deaths." ¹¹So Moses did as the LORD commanded him.

¹²Then the people of Israel said to Moses,
"We are as good as dead! We are ruined!
¹³Everyone who even comes close to the
Tabernacle of the LORD dies. We are all
doomed!"

CHAPTER 18
The LORD now said to Aaron: "You, your
sons, and your relatives from the tribe of
Levi will be held responsible for any of-

17:4 Hebrew *in the Tent of Meeting before the Testimony.*   17:7 Or *Tabernacle of the Testimony;* also in 17:8.   17:10 Hebrew *before the Testimony.*

fenses related to the sanctuary. But you and your sons alone will be held liable for violations connected with the priesthood. ²"Bring your relatives of the tribe of Levi to assist you and your sons as you perform the sacred duties in front of the Tabernacle of the Covenant.* ³But as the Levites go about their duties under your supervision, they must be careful not to touch any of the sacred objects or the altar. If they do, both you and they will die. ⁴The Levites must join with you to fulfill their responsibilities for the care and maintenance of the Tabernacle,* but no one who is not a Levite may officiate with you.

⁵"You yourselves must perform the sacred duties within the sanctuary and at the altar. If you follow these instructions, the LORD's anger will never again blaze against the people of Israel. ⁶I myself have chosen your fellow Levites from among the Israelites to be your special assistants. They are dedicated to the LORD for service in the Tabernacle. ⁷But you and your sons, the priests, must personally handle all the sacred service associated with the altar and everything within the inner curtain. I am giving you the priesthood as your special gift of service. Any other person who comes too near the sanctuary will be put to death."

⁸The LORD gave these further instructions to Aaron: "I have put the priests in charge of all the holy gifts that are brought to me by the people of Israel. I have given these offerings to you and your sons as your regular share. ⁹You are allotted the portion of the most holy offerings that is kept from the fire. From all the most holy offerings—including the grain offerings, sin offerings, and guilt offerings—that portion belongs to you and your sons. ¹⁰You must eat it as a most holy offering. All the males may eat of it, and you must treat it as most holy.

¹¹"All the other offerings presented to me by the Israelites by lifting them up before the altar also belong to you as your regular share. Any member of your family who is ceremonially clean, male and female alike, may eat of these offerings.

¹²"I also give you the harvest gifts brought by the people as offerings to the LORD—the best of the olive oil, wine, and grain. ¹³All the firstfruits of the land that the people present to the LORD belong to you. Any member of your family who is ceremonially clean may eat this food.

¹⁴"Whatever is specially set apart for the LORD* also belongs to you.

¹⁵"The firstborn of every mother, whether human or animal, that is offered to the LORD will be yours. But you must always redeem your firstborn sons and the firstborn males of ritually unclean animals. ¹⁶Redeem them when they are one month old. The redemption price is five pieces of silver, each piece weighing the same as the standard sanctuary shekel.*

¹⁷"However, you may not redeem the firstborn of cattle, sheep, or goats. They are holy and have been set apart for the LORD. Sprinkle their blood on the altar, and burn their fat as an offering given by fire, very pleasing to the LORD. ¹⁸The meat of these animals will be yours, just like the breast and right thigh that are presented by lifting them up before the altar. ¹⁹Yes, I am giving you all these holy offerings that the people of Israel bring to the LORD. They are for you and your sons and daughters, to be eaten as your regular share. This is an unbreakable covenant* between the LORD and you and your descendants."

²⁰And the LORD said to Aaron, "You priests will receive no inheritance of land or share of property among the people of Israel. I am your inheritance and your share. ²¹As for the tribe of Levi, your relatives, I will pay them for their service in the Tabernacle with the tithes from the entire land of Israel.

²²"From now on, Israelites other than the priests and Levites are to stay away from the Tabernacle. If they come too near, they will be judged guilty and die. ²³The Levites must serve at the Tabernacle, and they will be held responsible for any offenses against it. This is a permanent law among you. But the Levites will receive no inheritance of land among the Israelites, ²⁴because I have given them the Israelites' tithes, which have been set apart as offerings to the LORD. This will be the Levites' share. That is why I said they would receive no inheritance of land among the Israelites."

18:2 Or *Tabernacle of the Testimony.*   18:4 Hebrew *Tent of Meeting*; also in 18:6, 21, 22, 23, 31.   18:14 The Hebrew term used here refers to the complete consecration of things or people to the LORD, either by destroying them or by giving them as an offering. 18:16 Hebrew *5 shekels* [about 2 ounces or 57 grams] *of silver, according to the sanctuary shekel, 20 gerahs to each shekel.*   18:19 Hebrew *a covenant of salt.*

25The LORD also told Moses, 26"Say this to the Levites: 'When you receive the tithes from the Israelites, give a tenth of the tithes you receive—a tithe of the tithe—to the LORD as a gift. 27The LORD will consider this to be your harvest offering, as though it were the first grain from your own threshing floor or wine from your own winepress. 28You must present one-tenth of the tithe received from the Israelites as a gift to the LORD. From this you must present the LORD's portion to Aaron the priest. 29Be sure to set aside the best portions of the gifts given to you as your gifts to the LORD.'

30"Also say to the Levites: 'When you present the best part, it will be considered as though it came from your own threshing floor or winepress. 31You Levites and your families may eat this food anywhere you wish, for it is your compensation for serving in the Tabernacle. 32You will not be considered guilty for accepting the LORD's tithes if you give the best portion to the priests. But be careful not to treat the holy gifts of the people of Israel as though they were common. If you do, you will die.'"

CHAPTER 19

The LORD said to Moses and Aaron, 2"Here is another ritual law required by the LORD: Tell the people of Israel to bring you a red heifer that has no physical defects and has never been yoked to a plow. 3Give it to Eleazar the priest, and it will be taken outside the camp and slaughtered in his presence. 4Eleazar will take some of its blood on his finger and sprinkle it seven times toward the front of the Tabernacle.* 5As Eleazar watches, the heifer must be burned—its hide, meat, blood, and dung. 6Eleazar the priest must then take cedarwood, a hyssop branch, and scarlet thread and throw them into the fire where the heifer is burning.

7"Then the priest must wash his clothes and bathe himself in water. Afterward he may return to the camp, though he will remain ceremonially unclean until evening. 8The man who burns the animal must also wash his clothes and bathe in water, and he, too, will remain unclean until evening. 9Then someone who is ceremonially clean will gather up the ashes of the heifer and place them in a purified place outside the camp. They will be kept there for the people of Israel to use in the water for the

purification ceremony. This ceremony is performed for the removal of sin. 10The man who gathers up the ashes of the heifer must also wash his clothes, and he will remain ceremonially unclean until evening. This is a permanent law for the people of Israel and any foreigners who live among them.

11"All those who touch a dead human body will be ceremonially unclean for seven days. 12They must purify themselves on the third and seventh days with the water of purification; then they will be purified. But if they do not do this on the third and seventh days, they will continue to be unclean even after the seventh day. 13All those who touch a dead body and do not purify themselves in the proper way defile the LORD's Tabernacle and will be cut off from the community of Israel. Since the water of purification was not sprinkled on them, their defilement continues.

14"This is the ritual law that applies when someone dies in a tent: Those who enter that tent, and those who were inside when the death occurred, will be ceremonially unclean for seven days. 15Any container in the tent that was not covered with a lid is also defiled. 16And if someone outdoors touches the corpse of someone who was killed with a sword or who died a natural death, or if someone touches a human bone or a grave, that person will be unclean for seven days.

17"To remove the defilement, put some of the ashes from the burnt purification offering in a jar and pour fresh water over them. 18Then someone who is ceremonially clean must take a hyssop branch and dip it into the water. That person must sprinkle the water on the tent, on all the furnishings in the tent, and on anyone who was in the tent, or anyone who has touched a human bone, or has touched a person who was killed or who died naturally, or has touched a grave. 19On the third and seventh days the ceremonially clean person must sprinkle the water on those who are unclean. Then on the seventh day the people being cleansed must wash their clothes and bathe themselves, and that evening they will be cleansed of their defilement.

20"But those who become defiled and do not purify themselves will be cut off from

19:4 Hebrew *Tent of Meeting.*

the community, for they have defiled the sanctuary of the LORD. Since the water of purification has not been sprinkled on them, they remain defiled. ²¹This is a permanent law. Those who sprinkle the water of purification must afterward wash their clothes, and anyone who touches the water of purification will remain defiled until evening. ²²Anything and anyone that a defiled person touches will be ceremonially defiled until evening."

CHAPTER 20
In early spring* the people of Israel arrived in the wilderness of Zin and camped at Kadesh. While they were there, Miriam died and was buried.

²There was no water for the people to drink at that place, so they rebelled against Moses and Aaron. ³The people blamed Moses and said, "We wish we had died in the LORD's presence with our brothers! ⁴Did you bring the LORD's people into this wilderness to die, along with all our livestock? ⁵Why did you make us leave Egypt and bring us here to this terrible place? This land has no grain, figs, grapes, or pomegranates. And there is no water to drink!"

⁶Moses and Aaron turned away from the people and went to the entrance of the Tabernacle,* where they fell face down on the ground. Then the glorious presence of the LORD appeared to them, ⁷and the LORD said to Moses, ⁸"You and Aaron must take the staff and assemble the entire community. As the people watch, command the rock over there to pour out its water. You will get enough water from the rock to satisfy all the people and their livestock."

⁹So Moses did as he was told. He took the staff from the place where it was kept before the LORD. ¹⁰Then he and Aaron summoned the people to come and gather at the rock. "Listen, you rebels!" he shouted. "Must we bring you water from this rock?" ¹¹Then Moses raised his hand and struck the rock twice with the staff, and water gushed out. So all the people and their livestock drank their fill.

¹²But the LORD said to Moses and Aaron, "Because you did not trust me enough to demonstrate my holiness to the people of Israel, you will not lead them into the land I am giving them!" ¹³This place was known as the waters of Meribah,* because it was

where the people of Israel argued with the LORD, and where he demonstrated his holiness among them.

¹⁴While Moses was at Kadesh, he sent ambassadors to the king of Edom with this message:

"This message is from your relatives, the people of Israel: You know all the hardships we have been through, ¹⁵and that our ancestors went down to Egypt. We lived there a long time and suffered as slaves to the Egyptians. ¹⁶But when we cried out to the LORD, he heard us and sent an angel who brought us out of Egypt. Now we are camped at Kadesh, a town on the border of your land. ¹⁷Please let us pass through your country. We will be careful not to go through your fields and vineyards. We won't even drink water from your wells. We will stay on the king's road and never leave it until we have crossed the opposite border."

¹⁸But the king of Edom said, "Stay out of my land or I will meet you with an army!"

¹⁹The Israelites answered, "We will stay on the main road. If any of our livestock drinks your water, we will pay for it. We only want to pass through your country and nothing else."

²⁰But the king of Edom replied, "Stay out! You may not pass through our land." With that he mobilized his army and marched out to meet them with an imposing force. ²¹Because Edom refused to allow Israel to pass through their country, Israel was forced to turn around.

²²The whole community of Israel left Kadesh as a group and arrived at Mount Hor. ²³Then the LORD said to Moses and Aaron at Mount Hor on the border of the land of Edom, ²⁴"The time has come for Aaron to join his ancestors in death. He will not enter the land I am giving the people of Israel, because the two of you rebelled against my instructions concerning the waters of Meribah. ²⁵Now take Aaron and his son Eleazar up Mount Hor. ²⁶There you will remove Aaron's priestly garments and put them on Eleazar, his son. Aaron will die there and join his ancestors."

²⁷So Moses did as the LORD commanded. The three of them went up Mount Hor together as the whole community watched.

20:1 Hebrew *In the first month.* This month of the Hebrew lunar calendar usually occurs in March and April.   **20:6** Hebrew *Tent of Meeting.*   **20:13** *Meribah* means "arguing."

²⁸At the summit, Moses removed the priestly garments from Aaron and put them on Eleazar, Aaron's son. Then Aaron died there on top of the mountain, and Moses and Eleazar went back down. ²⁹When the people realized that Aaron had died, all Israel mourned for him thirty days.

FEBRUARY 16 ☐ DAY 47
NUMBERS 21–25
The Bronze Snake and Brash Seer

 OVERVIEW There is warfare on the march to the Promised Land as the Israelites defeat the opposing Canaanites, Amorites, and Bashanites—but the victories are soured by Israel's persistent complaining. Once again God's hand of discipline falls, this time in the form of poisonous snakes. The reputation of Israel's God precedes the nation on its relentless march, causing the king of Moab to hire Balaam for the purpose of cursing Israel. The plot backfires when Balaam blesses Israel and predicts her future prosperity. But while Balaam could not bring misfortune upon Israel through a curse, the people of God bring it upon themselves through idolatry and mixed marriages.

Chapter 21	Chapters 22–24	Chapter 25
Conquest in the Midst of Complaining	Blessing in Spite of Balak	Defeat in the Midst of Disobedience
Bronze Snake	Balaam	Baal of Peor

 YOUR DAILY WALK Look up the words *sovereignty* and *reign* in the dictionary, and read what it says about each. Chances are, the definitions will sound somewhat similar.

If God lights the candle, none can blow it out.

Balak, king of Moab, knew his days were numbered. In a desperate attempt to preserve his life and the life of his nation, he hired Balaam to bring down a curse upon Israel. Yet God so controlled the circumstances that Balaam uttered blessings instead of cursings. Rather than bring harm to Israel, Balaam became an agent of God's blessing upon Israel. And all of this happened while the nation remained completely unaware of the threat to its safety! That is sovereignty: God reigning in the affairs of his people.

Sometimes it's difficult to see God's sovereignty in the present, but you can clearly observe it in the past. Looking back over the first few weeks of this year, how many times can you see God's sovereignty at work, protecting, guarding, and keeping you from physical harm?

 INSIGHT Immortalizing Balaam's Words
When Samuel Morse was looking for a suitable phrase to test out his new invention, the telegraph, his thoughts turned to the great statement of God's sovereignty in Numbers 23:23 (KJV): "What hath God wrought!"—an appropriate first "word by wire."

CHAPTER 21
The Canaanite king of Arad, who lived in the Negev, heard that the Israelites were approaching on the road to Atharim. So he attacked the Israelites and took some of them as prisoners. ²Then the people of Israel made this vow to the LORD: "If you will help us conquer these people, we will com-

pletely destroy* all their towns." ³The LORD heard their request and gave them victory over the Canaanites. The Israelites completely destroyed them and their towns, and the place has been called Hormah* ever since.

⁴Then the people of Israel set out from Mount Hor, taking the road to the Red Sea* to go around the land of Edom. But the people grew impatient along the way, ⁵and they began to murmur against God and Moses. "Why have you brought us out of Egypt to die here in the wilderness?" they complained. "There is nothing to eat here and nothing to drink. And we hate this wretched manna!"

⁶So the LORD sent poisonous snakes among them, and many of them were bitten and died. ⁷Then the people came to Moses and cried out, "We have sinned by speaking against the LORD and against you. Pray that the LORD will take away the snakes." So Moses prayed for the people.

⁸Then the LORD told him, "Make a replica of a poisonous snake and attach it to the top of a pole. Those who are bitten will live if they simply look at it!" ⁹So Moses made a snake out of bronze and attached it to the top of a pole. Whenever those who were bitten looked at the bronze snake, they recovered!

¹⁰The Israelites traveled next to Oboth and camped there. ¹¹Then they went on to Iye-abarim, in the wilderness on the eastern border of Moab. ¹²From there they traveled to the valley of Zered Brook and set up camp. ¹³Then they moved to the far side of the Arnon River, in the wilderness adjacent to the territory of the Amorites. The Arnon is the boundary line between the Moabites and the Amorites. ¹⁴For this reason *The Book of the Wars of the LORD* speaks of "the town of Waheb in the area of Suphah, and the ravines; and the Arnon River ¹⁵and its ravines, which extend as far as the settlement of Ar on the border of Moab."

¹⁶From there the Israelites traveled to Beer,* which is the well where the LORD said to Moses, "Assemble the people, and I will give them water." ¹⁷There the Israelites sang this song:

"Spring up, O well!
    Yes, sing about it!
¹⁸ Sing of this well,
    which princes dug,
which great leaders hollowed out
    with their scepters and staffs."

Then the Israelites left the wilderness and proceeded on through Mattanah, ¹⁹Nahaliel, and Bamoth. ²⁰Then they went to the valley in Moab where Pisgah Peak overlooks the wasteland.*

²¹The Israelites now sent ambassadors to King Sihon of the Amorites with this message:

²²"Let us travel through your land. We will stay on the king's road until we have crossed your territory. We will not trample your fields or touch your vineyards or drink your well water."

²³But King Sihon refused to let them cross his land. Instead, he mobilized his entire army and attacked Israel in the wilderness, engaging them in battle at Jahaz. ²⁴But the Israelites slaughtered them and occupied their land from the Arnon River to the Jabbok River. They went only as far as the Ammonite border because the boundary of the Ammonites was fortified.*

²⁵So Israel captured all the towns of the Amorites and settled in them, including the city of Heshbon and its surrounding villages. ²⁶Heshbon had been the capital of King Sihon of the Amorites. He had conquered a former Moabite king and seized all his land as far as the Arnon River. ²⁷For this reason the ancient poets wrote this about him:

"Come to Heshbon, city of Sihon!
    May it be restored and rebuilt.
²⁸ A fire flamed forth from Heshbon,
    a blaze from the city of Sihon.
It burned the city of Ar in Moab;
    it destroyed the rulers of the Arnon heights.
²⁹ Your destruction is certain, O people of Moab!
    You are finished, O worshipers of Chemosh!
Chemosh has left his sons as refugees,
    and his daughters as captives of Sihon, the Amorite king.
³⁰ We have utterly destroyed them,
    all the way from Heshbon to Dibon.

21:2 The Hebrew term used here refers to the complete consecration of things or people to the LORD, either by destroying them or by giving them as an offering; also in 21:3.   21:3 *Hormah* means "destruction."   21:4 Hebrew *sea of reeds*.   21:16 *Beer* means "well."   21:20 Or *overlooks Jeshimon*.   21:24 Or *because the terrain of the Ammonite frontier was rugged;* Hebrew *because the boundary of the Ammonites was strong*.

We have completely wiped them out
as far away as Nophah and
Medeba.*"

³¹So the people of Israel occupied the
territory of the Amorites. ³²After Moses
sent men to explore the Jazer area, they
captured all the towns in the region and
drove out the Amorites who lived there.
³³Then they turned and marched toward
Bashan, but King Og of Bashan and all his
people attacked them at Edrei. ³⁴The LORD
said to Moses, "Do not be afraid of him, for
I have given you victory over Og and his
entire army, giving you all his land. You
will do the same to him as you did to King
Sihon of the Amorites, who ruled in Heshbon." ³⁵And Israel was victorious and
killed King Og, his sons, and his subjects;
not a single survivor remained. Then Israel
occupied their land.

CHAPTER 22

Then the people of Israel traveled to the
plains of Moab and camped east of the
Jordan River, across from Jericho. ²Balak
son of Zippor, the Moabite king, knew
what the Israelites had done to the Amorites. ³And when they saw how many Israelites there were, he and his people were
terrified. ⁴The king of Moab said to the
leaders of Midian, "This mob will devour
everything in sight, like an ox devours
grass!"

So Balak, king of Moab, ⁵sent messengers
to Balaam son of Beor, who was living in
his native land of Pethor* near the Euphrates River.* He sent this message to request
that Balaam come to help him:

"A vast horde of people has arrived
from Egypt. They cover the face of the
earth and are threatening me. ⁶Please
come and curse them for me because
they are so numerous. Then perhaps
I will be able to conquer them and
drive them from the land. I know that
blessings fall on the people you bless.
I also know that the people you curse
are doomed."

⁷Balak's messengers, officials of both
Moab and Midian, set out and took money
with them to pay Balaam to curse Israel.
They went to Balaam and urgently explained to him what Balak wanted. ⁸"Stay

here overnight," Balaam said. "In the
morning I will tell you whatever the LORD
directs me to say." So the officials from
Moab stayed there with Balaam.

⁹That night God came to Balaam and
asked him, "Who are these men with you?"

¹⁰So Balaam said to God, "Balak son of
Zippor, king of Moab, has sent me this message: ¹¹'A vast horde of people has come
from Egypt and has spread out over the
whole land. Come at once to curse them.
Perhaps then I will be able to conquer them
and drive them from the land.'"

¹²"Do not go with them," God told Balaam. "You are not to curse these people,
for I have blessed them!"

¹³The next morning Balaam got up and
told Balak's officials, "Go on home! The
LORD will not let me go with you."

¹⁴So the Moabite officials returned to
King Balak and reported, "Balaam refused
to come with us." ¹⁵Then Balak tried again.
This time he sent a larger number of even
more distinguished officials than those he
had sent the first time. ¹⁶They went to Balaam and gave him this message:

"This is what Balak son of Zippor says:
Please don't let anything stop you from
coming. ¹⁷I will pay you well and do
anything you ask of me. Just come and
curse these people for me!"

¹⁸But Balaam answered them, "Even if
Balak were to give me a palace filled with
silver and gold, I would be powerless to do
anything against the will of the LORD my
God. ¹⁹But stay here one more night to see
if the LORD has anything else to say to me."

²⁰That night God came to Balaam and
told him, "Since these men have come for
you, get up and go with them. But be sure
to do only what I tell you to do."

²¹So the next morning Balaam saddled
his donkey and started off with the Moabite officials. ²²But God was furious that Balaam was going, so he sent the angel of the
LORD to stand in the road to block his way.
As Balaam and two servants were riding
along, ²³Balaam's donkey suddenly saw
the angel of the LORD standing in the road
with a drawn sword in his hand. The donkey bolted off the road into a field, but
Balaam beat it and turned it back onto the
road. ²⁴Then the angel of the LORD stood at
a place where the road narrowed between

21:30 Or *until fire spread to Medeba.* The meaning of the Hebrew is uncertain.   22:5a Or *who was at Pethor in the land of the Amavites.*
22:5b Hebrew *the river.*

two vineyard walls. ²⁵When the donkey saw the angel of the LORD standing there, it tried to squeeze by and crushed Balaam's foot against the wall. So Balaam beat the donkey again. ²⁶Then the angel of the LORD moved farther down the road and stood in a place so narrow that the donkey could not get by at all. ²⁷This time when the donkey saw the angel, it lay down under Balaam. In a fit of rage Balaam beat it again with his staff.

²⁸Then the LORD caused the donkey to speak. "What have I done to you that deserves your beating me these three times?" it asked Balaam.

²⁹"Because you have made me look like a fool!" Balaam shouted. "If I had a sword with me, I would kill you!"

³⁰"But I am the same donkey you always ride on," the donkey answered. "Have I ever done anything like this before?"

"No," he admitted.

³¹Then the LORD opened Balaam's eyes, and he saw the angel of the LORD standing in the roadway with a drawn sword in his hand. Balaam fell face down on the ground before him.

³²"Why did you beat your donkey those three times?" the angel of the LORD demanded. "I have come to block your way because you are stubbornly resisting me. ³³Three times the donkey saw me and shied away; otherwise, I would certainly have killed you by now and spared the donkey."

³⁴Then Balaam confessed to the angel of the LORD, "I have sinned. I did not realize you were standing in the road to block my way. I will go back home if you are against my going."

³⁵But the angel of the LORD told him, "Go with these men, but you may say only what I tell you to say." So Balaam went on with Balak's officials. ³⁶When King Balak heard that Balaam was on the way, he went out to meet him at a Moabite town on the Arnon River at the border of his land.

³⁷"Did I not send you an urgent invitation? Why didn't you come right away?" Balak asked Balaam. "Didn't you believe me when I said I would reward you richly?"

³⁸Balaam replied, "I have come, but I have no power to say just anything. I will speak only the messages that God gives me." ³⁹Then Balaam accompanied Balak to Kiriath-huzoth, ⁴⁰where the king sacrificed

cattle and sheep. He sent portions of the meat to Balaam and the officials who were with him. ⁴¹The next morning Balak took Balaam up to Bamoth-baal. From there he could see the people of Israel spread out below him.

CHAPTER 23

Balaam said to King Balak, "Build me seven altars here, and prepare seven young bulls and seven rams for a sacrifice." ²Balak followed his instructions, and the two of them sacrificed a young bull and a ram on each altar.

³Then Balaam said to Balak, "Stand here by your burnt offerings, and I will go to see if the LORD will respond to me. Then I will tell you whatever he reveals to me." So Balaam went alone to the top of a hill, ⁴and God met him there. Balaam said to him, "I have prepared seven altars and have sacrificed a young bull and a ram on each altar."

⁵Then the LORD gave Balaam a message for King Balak and said, "Go back to Balak and tell him what I told you."

⁶When Balaam returned, the king was standing beside his burnt offerings with all the officials of Moab. ⁷This was the prophecy Balaam delivered:

"Balak summoned me to come from Aram;
    the king of Moab brought me from the eastern hills.
'Come,' he said, 'curse Jacob for me!
    Come and announce Israel's doom.'
⁸ But how can I curse
    those whom God has not cursed?
How can I condemn
    those whom the LORD has not condemned?
⁹ I see them from the cliff tops;
    I watch them from the hills.
I see a people who live by themselves,
    set apart from other nations.
¹⁰ Who can count Jacob's descendants, as numerous as dust?
    Who can count even a fourth of Israel's people?
Let me die like the righteous;
    let my life end like theirs."

¹¹Then King Balak demanded of Balaam, "What have you done to me? I brought you to curse my enemies. Instead, you have blessed them!"

¹²But Balaam replied, "Can I say anything except what the LORD tells me?"

¹³Then King Balak told him, "Come with me to another place. There you will see only a portion of the nation of Israel. Curse at least that many!" ¹⁴So Balak took Balaam to the plateau of Zophim on Pisgah Peak. He built seven altars there and offered a young bull and a ram on each altar.

¹⁵Then Balaam said to the king, "Stand here by your burnt offering while I go to meet the LORD."

¹⁶So the LORD met Balaam and gave him a message. Then he said, "Go back to Balak and give him this message."

¹⁷So Balaam returned to the place where the king and the officials of Moab were standing beside Balak's burnt offerings. "What did the LORD say?" Balak asked eagerly.

¹⁸This was the prophecy Balaam delivered:

"Rise up, Balak, and listen!
     Hear me, son of Zippor.
¹⁹ God is not a man, that he should lie.
     He is not a human, that he should
          change his mind.
Has he ever spoken and failed to act?
     Has he ever promised and not
          carried it through?
²⁰ I received a command to bless;
     he has blessed, and I cannot
          reverse it!
²¹ No misfortune is in sight for Jacob;
     no trouble is in store for Israel.
For the LORD their God is with them;
     he has been proclaimed their king.
²² God has brought them out of Egypt;
     he is like a strong ox for them.
²³ No curse can touch Jacob;
     no sorcery has any power against
          Israel.
For now it will be said of Jacob,
     'What wonders God has done for
          Israel!'
²⁴ These people rise up like a lioness;
     like a majestic lion they stand.
They refuse to rest
     until they have feasted on prey,
     drinking the blood of the
          slaughtered!"

²⁵Then Balak said to Balaam, "If you aren't going to curse them, at least don't bless them!"

²⁶But Balaam replied, "Didn't I tell you that I must do whatever the LORD tells me?"

²⁷Then King Balak said to Balaam, "Come, I will take you to yet another place. Perhaps it will please God to let you curse them from there."

²⁸So Balak took Balaam to the top of Mount Peor, overlooking the wasteland.* ²⁹Balaam again told Balak, "Build me seven altars and prepare me seven young bulls and seven rams for a sacrifice." ³⁰So Balak did as Balaam ordered and offered a young bull and a ram on each altar.

CHAPTER 24

By now Balaam realized that the LORD intended to bless Israel, so he did not resort to divination as he often did. Instead, he turned and looked out toward the wilderness, ²where he saw the people of Israel camped, tribe by tribe. Then the Spirit of God came upon him, ³and this is the prophecy he delivered:

"This is the prophecy of Balaam son of
     Beor,
     the prophecy of the man whose eyes
          see clearly,
⁴ who hears the words of God,
     who sees a vision from the Almighty,
     who falls down with eyes wide open:
⁵ How beautiful are your tents, O Jacob;
     how lovely are your homes, O Israel!
⁶ They spread before me like groves of
     palms,
     like fruitful gardens by the riverside.
They are like aloes planted by the LORD,
     like cedars beside the waters.
⁷ Water will gush out in buckets;
     their offspring are supplied with all
          they need.
Their king will be greater than Agag;
     their kingdom will be exalted.
⁸ God brought them up from Egypt,
     drawing them along like a wild ox.
He devours all the nations that oppose
     him,
     breaking their bones in pieces,
     shooting them with arrows.
⁹ Like a lion, Israel crouches and lies
     down;
     like a lioness, who dares to arouse her?
Blessed is everyone who blesses you,
     O Israel,
     and cursed is everyone who curses
          you."

23:28 Or overlooking Jeshimon.

[10]King Balak flew into a rage against Balaam. He angrily clapped his hands and shouted, "I called you to curse my enemies! Instead, you have blessed them three times. [11]Now get out of here! Go back home! I had planned to reward you richly, but the LORD has kept you from your reward."

[12]Balaam told Balak, "Don't you remember what I told your messengers? I said, [13]'Even if Balak were to give me a palace filled with silver and gold, I am powerless to do anything against the will of the LORD.' I told you that I could say only what the LORD says! [14]Now I am returning to my own people. But first let me tell you what the Israelites will do to your people in the future."

[15]This is the prophecy Balaam delivered:

"This is the message of Balaam son of Beor,
  the prophecy of the man whose eyes see clearly,
[16] who hears the words of God,
  who has knowledge from the Most High,
  who sees a vision from the Almighty,
  who falls down with eyes wide open:
[17] I see him, but not in the present time.
  I perceive him, but far in the distant future.
A star will rise from Jacob;
  a scepter will emerge from Israel.
It will crush the foreheads of Moab's people,
  cracking the skulls of the people of Sheth.
[18] Edom will be taken over,
  and Seir, its enemy, will be conquered,
  while Israel continues on in triumph.
[19] A ruler will rise in Jacob
  who will destroy the survivors of Ir."

[20]Then Balaam looked over at the people of Amalek and delivered this prophecy:

"Amalek was the greatest of nations,
  but its destiny is destruction!"

[21]Then he looked over at the Kenites and prophesied:

"You are strongly situated;
  your nest is set in the rocks.
[22] But the Kenites will be destroyed
  when Assyria* takes you captive."

[23]Balaam concluded his prophecies by saying:

"Alas, who can survive when God does this?
[24]   Ships will come from the coasts of Cyprus*;
  they will oppress both Assyria and Eber,
  but they, too, will be utterly destroyed."

[25]Then Balaam and Balak returned to their homes.

CHAPTER 25

While the Israelites were camped at Acacia,* some of the men defiled themselves by sleeping with the local Moabite women. [2]These women invited them to attend sacrifices to their gods, and soon the Israelites were feasting with them and worshiping the gods of Moab. [3]Before long Israel was joining in the worship of Baal of Peor, causing the LORD's anger to blaze against his people.

[4]The LORD issued the following command to Moses: "Seize all the ringleaders and execute them before the LORD in broad daylight, so his fierce anger will turn away from the people of Israel." [5]So Moses ordered Israel's judges to execute everyone who had joined in worshiping Baal of Peor.

[6]Just then one of the Israelite men brought a Midianite woman into the camp, right before the eyes of Moses and all the people, as they were weeping at the entrance of the Tabernacle.* [7]When Phinehas son of Eleazar and grandson of Aaron the priest saw this, he jumped up and left the assembly. Then he took a spear [8]and rushed after the man into his tent. Phinehas thrust the spear all the way through the man's body and into the woman's stomach. So the plague against the Israelites was stopped, [9]but not before 24,000 people had died.

[10]Then the LORD said to Moses, [11]"Phinehas son of Eleazar and grandson of Aaron the priest has turned my anger away from the Israelites by displaying passionate zeal among them on my behalf. So I have stopped destroying all Israel as I had intended to do in my anger. [12]So tell him that I am making my special covenant of peace with him. [13]In this covenant, he and his descendants will be priests for all time,

because he was zealous for his God and made atonement for the people of Israel."

14The Israelite man killed with the Midianite woman was named Zimri son of Salu, the leader of a family from the tribe of Simeon. 15The woman's name was Cozbi; she was the daughter of Zur, the leader of a Midianite clan.

16Then the LORD said to Moses, 17"Attack the Midianites and destroy them, 18because they assaulted you with deceit by tricking you into worshiping Baal of Peor, and because of Cozbi, the daughter of a Midianite leader, who was killed on the day of the plague at Peor."

FEBRUARY 17 ☐ DAY 48
NUMBERS 26–30
Recounting and Reviewing

 OVERVIEW Nearly forty years have passed; the unbelieving generation has vanished from the scene, and a new generation has grown to take its place. Once again it is time to number the people and assess Israel's military might. In spite of divine judgments that take the lives of more than thirty-eight thousand people (16:49; 25:9), the nation's fighting force still totals more than six hundred thousand. Moses, who has led the people from the beginning, will never live to see the conquest of Canaan. It remains for his successor, Joshua, to lead the people to victory.

Chapter 26	Chapter 27	Chapters 28–30
Repeating the Census	Replacing the Commander in Chief	Recounting the Code of Worship
A New Generation	A New General	A General Review

 YOUR DAILY WALK If you were suddenly incapacitated, who would be qualified to pick up your responsibilities and duties as they relate to . . . your job? . . . your family? . . . your church? As Moses approached

The object of teaching is to enable those taught to get along without a teacher.

his final days as Israel's leader, God instructed him not to leave "the people of the LORD . . . like sheep without a shepherd" (27:17). Moses was commanded to take Joshua, lay his hands on him, deliver a charge to him before all the people, and "transfer your authority to him" (27:20). In this way the transition of leadership would be smooth so that when the man of God died, the work of God would not falter.

That's good advice for any generation. Are you letting others remain dependent upon you at home and church, or are you busy discipling them to one day take your place and carry on the work you've begun? Complete this sentence: "Knowing that no individual is indispensable in the program of God, today I will help prepare [whom?] to continue the work I am currently doing [where?] by [how?]."

INSIGHT Picking Your Lot by Lots (26:52-56)
There were two aspects to the partitioning of the land of Canaan. The size of each tribe's parcel was determined by the second census, each tribe receiving territory in proportion to the size of its population. The location of each tribe's parcel was determined by lot so that no tribe could grumble about the quality of its land.

CHAPTER 26

After the plague had ended, the LORD said to Moses and to Eleazar son of Aaron, the priest, ²"Take a census of all the men of Israel who are twenty years old or older, to find out how many of each family are of military age." ³At that time the entire nation of Israel was camped on the plains of Moab beside the Jordan River, across from Jericho.

So Moses and Eleazar the priest issued these census instructions to the leaders of Israel: ⁴"Count all the men of Israel twenty years old and older, just as the LORD commanded Moses." This is the census record of all the descendants of Israel who came out of Egypt.

⁵These were the clans descended from Reuben, Jacob's* oldest son:
The Hanochite clan, named after its ancestor Hanoch.
The Palluite clan, named after its ancestor Pallu.
⁶ The Hezronite clan, named after its ancestor Hezron.
The Carmite clan, named after its ancestor Carmi.

⁷The men from all the clans of Reuben numbered 43,730.

⁸Pallu was the ancestor of Eliab, ⁹and Eliab was the father of Nemuel, Dathan, and Abiram. This Dathan and Abiram are the same community leaders who conspired with Korah against Moses and Aaron, defying the LORD. ¹⁰But the earth opened up and swallowed them with Korah, and 250 of their followers were destroyed that day by fire from the LORD. This served as a warning to the entire nation of Israel. ¹¹However, the sons of Korah did not die that day.

¹²These were the clans descended from the sons of Simeon:
The Nemuelite clan, named after its ancestor Nemuel.
The Jaminite clan, named after its ancestor Jamin.
The Jakinite clan, named after its ancestor Jakin.
¹³ The Zerahite clan, named after its ancestor Zerah.
The Shaulite clan, named after its ancestor Shaul.

¹⁴The men from all the clans of Simeon numbered 22,200.

¹⁵These were the clans descended from the sons of Gad:
The Zephonite clan, named after its ancestor Zephon.
The Haggite clan, named after its ancestor Haggi.
The Shunite clan, named after its ancestor Shuni.
¹⁶ The Oznite clan, named after its ancestor Ozni.
The Erite clan, named after its ancestor Eri.
¹⁷ The Arodite clan, named after its ancestor Arodi.*
The Arelite clan, named after its ancestor Areli.

¹⁸The men from all the clans of Gad numbered 40,500.

¹⁹Judah had two sons, Er and Onan, who had died in the land of Canaan. ²⁰But the following clans descended from Judah's surviving sons:
The Shelanite clan, named after its ancestor Shelah.
The Perezite clan, named after its ancestor Perez.
The Zerahite clan, named after its ancestor Zerah.

²¹These were the subclans descended from the Perezites:
The Hezronites, named after their ancestor Hezron.
The Hamulites, named after their ancestor Hamul.

²²The men from all the clans of Judah numbered 76,500.

²³These were the clans descended from the sons of Issachar:
The Tolaite clan, named after its ancestor Tola.
The Puite clan, named after its ancestor Puah.*
²⁴ The Jashubite clan, named after its ancestor Jashub.
The Shimronite clan, named after its ancestor Shimron.

²⁵The men from all the clans of Issachar numbered 64,300.

26 These were the clans descended from the sons of Zebulun:

The Seredite clan, named after its ancestor Sered.

The Elonite clan, named after its ancestor Elon.

The Jahleelite clan, named after its ancestor Jahleel.

27 The men from all the clans of Zebulun numbered 60,500.

28 Two clans were descended from Joseph through Manasseh and Ephraim.

29 These were the clans descended from Manasseh:

The Makirite clan, named after its ancestor Makir.

The Gileadite clan, named after its ancestor Gilead, Makir's son.

30 These were the subclans descended from the Gileadites:

The Iezerites, named after their ancestor Iezer.

The Helekites, named after their ancestor Helek.

31 The Asrielites, named after their ancestor Asriel.

The Shechemites, named after their ancestor Shechem.

32 The Shemidaites, named after their ancestor Shemida.

The Hepherites, named after their ancestor Hepher.

33 Hepher's son, Zelophehad, had no sons, but his daughters' names were Mahlah, Noah, Hoglah, Milcah, and Tirzah.

34 The men from all the clans of Manasseh numbered 52,700.

35 These were the clans descended from the sons of Ephraim:

The Shuthelahite clan, named after its ancestor Shuthelah.

The Bekerite clan, named after its ancestor Beker.

The Tahanite clan, named after its ancestor Tahan.

36 This was the subclan descended from the Shuthelahites:

The Eranites, named after their ancestor Eran.

37 The men from all the clans of Ephraim numbered 32,500.

These clans of Manasseh and Ephraim were all descendants of Joseph.

38 These were the clans descended from the sons of Benjamin:

The Belaite clan, named after its ancestor Bela.

The Ashbelite clan, named after its ancestor Ashbel.

The Ahiramite clan, named after its ancestor Ahiram.

39 The Shuphamite clan, named after its ancestor Shupham.*

The Huphamite clan, named after its ancestor Hupham.

40 These were the subclans descended from the Belaites:

The Ardites, named after their ancestor Ard.*

The Naamites, named after their ancestor Naaman.

41 The men from all the clans of Benjamin numbered 45,600.

42 These were the clans descended from the sons of Dan:

The Shuhamite clan, named after its ancestor Shuham.

43 All the clans of Dan were Shuhamite clans, and the men from these clans numbered 64,400.

44 These were the clans descended from the sons of Asher:

The Imnite clan, named after its ancestor Imnah.

The Ishvite clan, named after its ancestor Ishvi.

The Beriite clan, named after its ancestor Beriah.

45 These were the subclans descended from the Beriites:

The Heberites, named after their ancestor Heber.

The Malkielites, named after their ancestor Malkiel.

46 Asher also had a daughter named Serah.

47 The men from all the clans of Asher numbered 53,400.

26:39 As in some Hebrew manuscripts, Samaritan Pentateuch, Greek and Syriac versions, and Latin Vulgate; most Hebrew manuscripts read *Shephupham.*   **26:40** As in Samaritan Pentateuch, some Greek manuscripts, and Latin Vulgate; Hebrew lacks *named after their ancestor Ard.*

[48] These were the clans descended from the sons of Naphtali:

The Jahzeelite clan, named after its ancestor Jahzeel.

The Gunite clan, named after its ancestor Guni.

[49] The Jezerite clan, named after its ancestor Jezer.

The Shillemite clan, named after its ancestor Shillem.

[50] The men from all the clans of Naphtali numbered 45,400.

[51] So the total number of Israelite men counted in the census numbered 601,730.

[52] Then the LORD said to Moses, [53] "Divide the land among the tribes in proportion to their populations, as indicated by the census. [54] Give the larger tribes more land and the smaller tribes less land, each group's inheritance reflecting the size of its population. [55] Make sure you assign the land by lot, and define the inheritance of each ancestral tribe by means of the census listings. [56] Each inheritance must be assigned by lot among the larger and smaller tribal groups."

[57] This is the census record for the Levites who were counted according to their clans:

The Gershonite clan, named after its ancestor Gershon.

The Kohathite clan, named after its ancestor Kohath.

The Merarite clan, named after its ancestor Merari.

[58] The Libnites, the Hebronites, the Mahlites, the Mushites, and the Korahites were all subclans of the Levites.

Now Kohath was the ancestor of Amram, [59] and Amram's wife was named Jochebed. She also was a descendant of Levi, born among the Levites in the land of Egypt. Amram and Jochebed became the parents of Aaron, Moses, and their sister, Miriam. [60] To Aaron were born Nadab, Abihu, Eleazar, and Ithamar. [61] But Nadab and Abihu died when they burned before the LORD a different kind of fire than he had commanded.

[62] The men from the Levite clans who were one month old or older numbered 23,000. But the Levites were not included in the total census figure of the people of Israel because they were not given an inheritance of land when it was divided among the Israelites.

[63] So these are the census figures of the people of Israel as prepared by Moses and Eleazar the priest on the plains of Moab beside the Jordan River, across from Jericho. [64] Not one person that was counted in this census had been among those counted in the previous census taken by Moses and Aaron in the wilderness of Sinai. [65] For the LORD had said of them, "They will all die in the wilderness." The only exceptions were Caleb son of Jephunneh and Joshua son of Nun.

CHAPTER 27

One day a petition was presented by the daughters of Zelophehad—Mahlah, Noah, Hoglah, Milcah, and Tirzah. Their father, Zelophehad, was the son of Hepher, son of Gilead, son of Makir, son of Manasseh, son of Joseph. [2] These women went and stood before Moses, Eleazar the priest, the tribal leaders, and the entire community at the entrance of the Tabernacle.* [3] "Our father died in the wilderness without leaving any sons," they said. "But he was not among Korah's followers, who rebelled against the LORD. He died because of his own sin. [4] Why should the name of our father disappear just because he had no sons? Give us property along with the rest of our relatives."

[5] So Moses brought their case before the LORD. [6] And the LORD replied to Moses, [7] "The daughters of Zelophehad are right. You must give them an inheritance of land along with their father's relatives. Assign them the property that would have been given to their father. [8] Moreover announce this to the people of Israel: 'If a man dies and has no sons, then give his inheritance to his daughters. [9] And if he has no daughters, turn his inheritance over to his brothers. [10] If he has no brothers, give his inheritance to his father's brothers. [11] But if his father has no brothers, pass on his inheritance to the nearest relative in his clan. The Israelites must observe this as a general legal requirement, just as the LORD commanded Moses.'"

[12] One day the LORD said to Moses, "Climb to the top of the mountains east of the river,* and look out over the land I have given the people of Israel. [13] After you have

27:2 Hebrew *Tent of Meeting.*　　27:12 Hebrew *the mountains of Abarim.*

seen it, you will die as Aaron your brother did, [14]for you both rebelled against my instructions in the wilderness of Zin. When the people of Israel rebelled, you failed to demonstrate my holiness to them at the waters." (These are the waters of Meribah at Kadesh* in the wilderness of Zin.)

[15]Then Moses said to the LORD, [16]"O LORD, the God of the spirits of all living things, please appoint a new leader for the community. [17]Give them someone who will lead them into battle, so the people of the LORD will not be like sheep without a shepherd."

[18]The LORD replied, "Take Joshua son of Nun, who has the Spirit in him, and lay your hands on him. [19]Present him to Eleazar the priest before the whole community, and publicly commission him with the responsibility of leading the people. [20]Transfer your authority to him so the whole community of Israel will obey him. [21]When direction from the LORD is needed, Joshua will stand before Eleazar the priest, who will determine the LORD's will by means of sacred lots.* This is how Joshua and the rest of the community of Israel will discover what they should do."

[22]So Moses did as the LORD commanded and presented Joshua to Eleazar the priest and the whole community. [23]Moses laid his hands on him and commissioned him to his responsibilities, just as the LORD had commanded through Moses.

CHAPTER 28

The LORD said to Moses, [2]"Give these instructions to the people of Israel: The offerings you present to me by fire on the altar are my food, and they are very pleasing to me. See to it that they are brought at the appointed times and offered according to my instructions.

[3]"Say to them: When you present your daily whole burnt offerings to the LORD, you must offer two one-year-old male lambs with no physical defects. [4]One lamb will be sacrificed in the morning and the other in the evening. [5]With each lamb you must offer a grain offering of two quarts* of choice flour mixed with one quart* of olive oil. [6]This is the regular burnt offering ordained at Mount Sinai, an offering made by fire, very pleasing to the LORD. [7]Along with it you must present the proper drink offering, consisting of one quart of fermented drink with each lamb, poured out in the Holy Place as an offering to the LORD. [8]Offer the second lamb in the evening with the same grain offering and drink offering. It, too, is an offering made by fire, very pleasing to the LORD.

[9]"On the Sabbath day, sacrifice two one-year-old male lambs with no physical defects. They must be accompanied by a grain offering of three quarts* of choice flour mixed with olive oil, and a drink offering. [10]This is the whole burnt offering to be presented each Sabbath day, in addition to the regular daily burnt offering and its accompanying drink offering.

[11]"On the first day of each month, present an extra burnt offering to the LORD of two young bulls, one ram, and seven one-year-old male lambs, all with no physical defects. [12]These will be accompanied by grain offerings of choice flour mixed with olive oil—five quarts* with each bull, three quarts with the ram, [13]and two quarts with each lamb. This burnt offering must be presented by fire, and it will be very pleasing to the LORD. [14]You must also give a drink offering with each sacrifice: two quarts* of wine with each bull, two and a half pints* for the ram, and one quart* for each lamb. Present this monthly burnt offering on the first day of each month throughout the year.

[15]"Also, on the first day of each month you must offer one male goat for a sin offering to the LORD. This is in addition to the regular daily burnt offering and its accompanying drink offering.

[16]"On the appointed day in early spring,* you must celebrate the LORD's Passover. [17]On the following day a joyous, seven-day festival will begin, but no bread made with yeast may be eaten. [18]On the first day of the festival you must call a sacred assembly of the people. None of your regular work may be done on that day. [19]You must present as a burnt offering to the LORD two young bulls, one ram, and seven one-year-old male lambs, all with no physical defects. [20]These will be accompa-

27:14 Hebrew *waters of Meribath-kadesh.*   **27:21** Hebrew *of the Urim.*   **28:5a** Hebrew *1/10 of an ephah* [2 liters]; also in 28:13, 21, 29.
28:5b Hebrew *1/4 of a hin* [1 liter]; also in 28:7.   **28:9** Hebrew *2/10 of an ephah* [3.6 liters]; also in 28:12, 20, 28.   **28:12** Hebrew *3/10 of
an ephah* [5.4 liters]; also in 28:20, 28.   **28:14a** Hebrew *1/2 of a hin* [2 liters].   **28:14b** Hebrew *1/3 of a hin* [1.3 liters].   **28:14c** Hebrew
1/4 of a hin [1 liter].   **28:16** Hebrew *On the fourteenth day of the first month.* This day of the Hebrew lunar calendar occurs in late
March or early April.

nied by grain offerings of choice flour mixed with olive oil—five quarts with each bull, three quarts with the ram, [21]and two quarts with each of the seven lambs. [22]You must also offer a male goat as a sin offering, to make atonement for yourselves. [23]You will present these offerings in addition to your regular morning sacrifices. [24]On each of the seven days of the festival, this is how you will prepare the food offerings to be presented by fire, very pleasing to the LORD. These will be offered in addition to the regular whole burnt offerings and drink offerings. [25]On the seventh day of the festival you must call another holy assembly of the people. None of your regular work may be done on that day.

[26]"On the first day of the Festival of Harvest,* when you present the first of your new grain to the LORD, you must call a holy assembly of the people. None of your regular work may be done on that day. [27]A special whole burnt offering will be offered that day, very pleasing to the LORD. It will consist of two young bulls, one ram, and seven one-year-old male lambs. [28]These will be accompanied by grain offerings of choice flour mixed with olive oil—five quarts with each bull, three quarts with the ram, [29]and two quarts with each of the seven lambs. [30]Also, offer one male goat to make atonement for yourselves. [31]These special burnt offerings, along with their drink offerings, are in addition to the regular daily burnt offering and its accompanying grain offering. Be sure that all the animals you sacrifice have no physical defects.

CHAPTER 29

"The Festival of Trumpets will be celebrated on the appointed day in early autumn* each year. You must call a solemn assembly of all the people on that day, and no regular work may be done. [2]On that day you must present a burnt offering, very pleasing to the LORD. It will consist of one young bull, one ram, and seven one-year-old male lambs, all with no physical defects. [3]These must be accompanied by grain offerings of choice flour mixed with olive oil—five quarts* with the bull, three quarts* with the ram, [4]and two quarts*

with each of the seven lambs. [5]In addition, you must sacrifice a male goat as a sin offering, to make atonement for yourselves. [6]These special sacrifices are in addition to your regular monthly and daily burnt offerings, and they must be given with their prescribed grain offerings and drink offerings. These offerings are given to the LORD by fire and are very pleasing to him.

[7]"Ten days later,* you must call another holy assembly of all the people. On that day, the Day of Atonement, the people must go without food, and no regular work may be done. [8]You must present a burnt offering, very pleasing to the LORD. It will consist of one young bull, one ram, and seven one-year-old male lambs, all with no physical defects. [9]These offerings must be accompanied by the prescribed grain offerings of choice flour mixed with olive oil—five quarts of choice flour with the bull, three quarts of choice flour with the ram, [10]and two quarts of choice flour with each of the seven lambs. [11]You must also sacrifice one male goat for a sin offering. This is in addition to the sin offering of atonement and the regular daily burnt offering with its grain offering, and their accompanying drink offerings.

[12]"Five days later,* you must call yet another holy assembly of all the people, and on that day no regular work may be done. It is the beginning of the Festival of Shelters, a seven-day festival to the LORD. [13]That day you must present a special whole burnt offering by fire, very pleasing to the LORD. It will consist of thirteen young bulls, two rams, and fourteen one-year-old male lambs, all with no physical defects. [14]Each of these offerings must be accompanied by a grain offering of choice flour mixed with olive oil—five quarts for each of the thirteen bulls, three quarts for each of the two rams, [15]and two quarts for each of the fourteen lambs. [16]You must also sacrifice a male goat as a sin offering, in addition to the regular daily burnt offering with its accompanying grain offering and drink offering.

[17]"On the second day of this seven-day festival, sacrifice twelve young bulls, two rams, and fourteen one-year-old male lambs, all with no physical defects. [18]Each

---

of these offerings of bulls, rams, and lambs must be accompanied by the prescribed grain offering and drink offering. [19] You must also sacrifice a male goat as a sin offering, in addition to the regular daily burnt offering with its accompanying grain offering and drink offering.

[20] "On the third day of the festival, sacrifice eleven young bulls, two rams, and fourteen one-year-old male lambs, all with no physical defects. [21] Each of these offerings of bulls, rams, and lambs must be accompanied by the prescribed grain offering and drink offering. [22] You must also sacrifice a male goat as a sin offering, in addition to the regular daily burnt offering with its accompanying grain offering and drink offering.

[23] "On the fourth day of the festival, sacrifice ten young bulls, two rams, and fourteen one-year-old male lambs, all with no physical defects. [24] Each of these offerings of bulls, rams, and lambs must be accompanied by the prescribed grain offering and drink offering. [25] You must also sacrifice a male goat as a sin offering, in addition to the regular daily burnt offering with its accompanying grain offering and drink offering.

[26] "On the fifth day of the festival, sacrifice nine young bulls, two rams, and fourteen one-year-old male lambs, all with no physical defects. [27] Each of these offerings of bulls, rams, and lambs must be accompanied by the prescribed grain offering and drink offering. [28] You must also sacrifice a male goat as a sin offering, in addition to the regular daily burnt offering with its accompanying grain offering and drink offering.

[29] "On the sixth day of the festival, sacrifice eight young bulls, two rams, and fourteen one-year-old male lambs, all with no physical defects. [30] Each of these offerings of bulls, rams, and lambs must be accompanied by the prescribed grain offering and drink offering. [31] You must also sacrifice a male goat as a sin offering, in addition to the regular daily burnt offering with its accompanying grain offering and drink offering.

[32] "On the seventh day of the festival, sacrifice seven young bulls, two rams, and fourteen one-year-old male lambs, all with no physical defects. [33] Each of these offerings of bulls, rams, and lambs must be accompanied by the prescribed grain offering

and drink offering. [34] You must also sacrifice one male goat as a sin offering, in addition to the regular daily burnt offering with its accompanying grain offering and drink offering.

[35] "On the eighth day of the festival, call all the people to another holy assembly. You must do no regular work on that day. [36] You must present a burnt offering, very pleasing to the LORD. It will consist of one young bull, one ram, and seven one-year-old male lambs, all with no physical defects. [37] Each of these offerings must be accompanied by the prescribed grain offering and drink offering. [38] You must also sacrifice one male goat as a sin offering, in addition to the regular daily burnt offering with its accompanying grain offering and drink offering.

[39] "You must present these offerings to the LORD at your annual festivals. These are in addition to the sacrifices and offerings you present in connection with vows, or as freewill offerings, burnt offerings, grain offerings, drink offerings, or peace offerings."

[40] So Moses gave all of these instructions to the people of Israel, just as the LORD had commanded him.

CHAPTER 30

Now Moses summoned the leaders of the tribes of Israel and told them, "This is what the LORD has commanded: [2] A man who makes a vow to the LORD or makes a pledge under oath must never break it. He must do exactly what he said he would do.

[3] "If a young woman makes a vow to the LORD or a pledge under oath while she is still living at her father's home, [4] and her father hears of the vow or pledge but says nothing, then all her vows and pledges will stand. [5] But if her father refuses to let her fulfill the vow or pledge on the day he hears of it, then all her vows and pledges will become invalid. The LORD will forgive her because her father would not let her fulfill them.

[6] "Now suppose a young woman takes a vow or makes an impulsive pledge and later marries. [7] If her husband learns of her vow or pledge and raises no objections on the day he hears of it, her vows and pledges will stand. [8] But if her husband refuses to accept her vow or impulsive pledge on the day he hears of it, he nullifies her commit-

ments, and the LORD will forgive her. ⁹If, however, a woman is a widow or is divorced, she must fulfill all her vows and pledges no matter what.

¹⁰"Suppose a woman is married and living in her husband's home when she makes a vow or pledge. ¹¹If her husband hears of it and does nothing to stop her, her vow or pledge will stand. ¹²But if her husband refuses to accept it on the day he hears of it, her vow or pledge will be nullified, and the LORD will forgive her. ¹³So her

husband may either confirm or nullify any vows or pledges she makes to deny herself. ¹⁴But if he says nothing on the day he hears of it, then he is agreeing to it. ¹⁵If he waits more than a day and then tries to nullify a vow or pledge, he will suffer the consequences of her guilt."

¹⁶These are the regulations the LORD gave Moses concerning relationships between a man and his wife, and between a father and a young daughter who still lives at home.

FEBRUARY 18 □ DAY 49
NUMBERS 31–33
The Last Days of a Great Leader

OVERVIEW The final days of Moses' administration are just as productive as the first! As Israel's commander in chief, he leads a highly successful campaign against Midian; as administrator, he handles wisely the request of the tribes of Reuben and Gad that they be allowed to settle east of the Jordan River. He grants permission, provided the two tribes assist the other ten in conquering the Promised Land first. The remainder of the book of Numbers is a review of the Israelites' travels from Egypt to Moab.

Chapter 31	Chapter 32	Chapter 33
The Midianites Removed	A Problem Resolved	A Journey Recounted
Moses' Leadership	Moses' Wisdom	Moses' Travels

A little sin will add to your trouble, subtract from your energy, and multiply your difficulties.

YOUR DAILY WALK It could easily happen to you. You're doing some work around the house when suddenly your hand slips, and you come up with a finger full of splinters. After a half hour of "surgery," you figure you've pulled them all out, only to discover later that you (ouch) missed a few! At that point, the fact that you removed *most* of the splinters doesn't help much. It is the few remaining ones that really matter.

God clearly directed Israel to completely rid the land of its pagan inhabitants when the time came for conquest. He warned that any Canaanites left behind would become like painful splinters and thorns to the Israelites (33:55-56). Disobeying God, Israel failed to rid the land of its pagan populace and was eventually corrupted by immorality and idolatry. The nation was *victimized* by forces it should have *controlled*.

Are there any "splinters" in your spiritual life—secret sins . . . nagging habits . . . little things you know displease God? Carry a pair of tweezers with you today as a reminder that what you fail to remove now will only fester and cause more pain in the future.

INSIGHT Do Easy Paths Lead to Easy Living?
Moses handled the requests of the tribes of Reuben and Gad and the half-tribe of Manasseh in a prudent manner. However, their choice to remain outside the Promised Land in the rich grazing lands of Trans-jordan was comparable to Lot's selfish decision. And their choice manifested similar results of unbelief and conformity to the worldly standards of those about them (see 1 Chronicles 5:25-26).

CHAPTER 31

Then the LORD said to Moses, [2]"Take vengeance on the Midianites for leading the Israelites into idolatry. After that, you will die and join your ancestors."

[3]So Moses said to the people, "Choose some men to fight the LORD's war of vengeance against Midian. [4]From each tribe of Israel, send one thousand men into battle." [5]So they chose one thousand men from each tribe of Israel, a total of twelve thousand men armed for battle. [6]Then Moses sent them out, a thousand men from each tribe, and Phinehas son of Eleazar the priest led them into battle. They carried along the holy objects of the sanctuary and the trumpets for sounding the charge. [7]They attacked Midian just as the LORD had commanded Moses, and they killed all the men. [8]All five of the Midianite kings—Evi, Rekem, Zur, Hur, and Reba—died in the battle. They also killed Balaam son of Beor with the sword.

[9]Then the Israelite army captured the Midianite women and children and seized their cattle and flocks and all their wealth as plunder. [10]They burned all the towns and villages where the Midianites had lived. [11]After they had gathered the plunder and captives, both people and animals, [12]they brought them all to Moses and Eleazar the priest, and to the whole community of Israel, which was camped on the plains of Moab beside the Jordan River, across from Jericho. [13]Moses, Eleazar the priest, and all the leaders of the people went to meet them outside the camp. [14]But Moses was furious with all the military commanders* who had returned from battle.

[15]"Why have you let all the women live?" he demanded. [16]"These are the very ones who followed Balaam's advice and caused the people of Israel to rebel against the LORD at Mount Peor. They are the ones who caused the plague to strike the LORD's people. [17]Now kill all the boys and all the women who have slept with a man. [18]Only

the young girls who are virgins may live; you may keep them for yourselves. [19]And all of you who have killed anyone or touched a dead body must stay outside the camp for seven days. You must purify yourselves and your captives on the third and seventh days. [20]Also, purify all your clothing and everything made of leather, goat hair, or wood."

[21]Then Eleazar the priest said to the men who were in the battle, "The LORD has given Moses this requirement of the law: [22]Anything made of gold, silver, bronze, iron, tin, or lead—[23]that is, metals that do not burn—must be passed through fire in order to be made ceremonially pure. These metal objects must then be further purified with the water of purification. But everything that burns must be purified by the water alone. [24]On the seventh day you must wash your clothes and be purified. Then you may return to the camp."

[25]And the LORD said to Moses, [26]"You and Eleazar the priest and the family leaders of each tribe are to make a list of all the plunder taken in the battle, including the people and animals. [27]Then divide the plunder into two parts, and give half to the men who fought the battle and half to the rest of the people. [28]But first give the LORD his share of the captives, cattle, donkeys, sheep, and goats that belong to the army. Set apart one out of every five hundred as the LORD's share. [29]Give this share of their half to Eleazar the priest as an offering to the LORD. [30]Also take one of every fifty of the captives, cattle, donkeys, sheep, and goats in the half that belongs to the people of Israel. Give this share to the Levites in charge of maintaining the LORD's Tabernacle." [31]So Moses and Eleazar the priest did as the LORD commanded Moses.

[32]The plunder remaining from the spoils that the fighting men had taken totaled 675,000 sheep, [33]72,000 cattle, [34]61,000 donkeys, [35]and 32,000 young girls.

[36]So the half of the plunder given to the fighting men totaled 337,500 sheep, [37]of

31:14 Hebrew *the commanders of thousands, and the commanders of hundreds;* also in 31:48, 52, 54.

which 675 were the LORD's share; [38]36,000 cattle, of which 72 were the LORD's share; [39]30,500 donkeys, of which 61 were the LORD's share; [40]16,000 young girls, of whom 32 were the LORD's share. [41]Moses gave all the LORD's share to Eleazar the priest, just as the LORD had directed him.

[42]The half of the plunder belonging to the people of Israel, which Moses had separated from the half belonging to the fighting men, [43]amounted to 337,500 sheep, [44]36,000 cattle, [45]30,500 donkeys, [46]and 16,000 young girls. [47]From the half-share given to the people, Moses took one of every fifty prisoners and animals and gave them to the Levites who maintained the LORD's Tabernacle. All this was done just as the LORD had commanded Moses.

[48]Then all the military commanders came to Moses [49]and said, "Sir, we have accounted for all the men who went out to battle under our command; not one of us is missing! [50]So we are presenting the items of gold we captured as an offering to the LORD from our share of the plunder—armbands, bracelets, rings, earrings, and necklaces. This will make atonement for our lives before the LORD."

[51]So Moses and Eleazar the priest received the gold from all the military commanders, all kinds of jewelry and crafted objects. [52]In all, the gold that the commanders presented as a gift to the LORD weighed about 420 pounds.* [53]All the fighting men had taken some of the plunder for themselves. [54]So Moses and Eleazar the priest accepted the gifts from the military commanders and brought the gold to the Tabernacle* as a reminder to the LORD that the people of Israel belong to him.

CHAPTER 32

Now the tribes of Reuben and Gad owned vast numbers of livestock. So when they saw that the lands of Jazer and Gilead were ideally suited for their flocks and herds, [2]they came to Moses, Eleazar the priest, and the other leaders of the people. They said, [3]"Ataroth, Dibon, Jazer, Nimrah, Heshbon, Elealeh, Sebam, Nebo, and Beon—[4]the LORD has conquered this whole area for the people of Israel. It is ideally suited for all our flocks and herds. [5]If we have found favor with you, please let us

have this land as our property instead of giving us land across the Jordan River."

[6]"Do you mean you want to stay back here while your brothers go across and do all the fighting?" Moses asked the Reubenites and Gadites. [7]"Are you trying to discourage the rest of the people of Israel from going across to the land the LORD has given them? [8]This is what your ancestors did when I sent them from Kadesh-barnea to explore the land. [9]After they went up to the valley of Eshcol and scouted the land, they discouraged the people of Israel from entering the land the LORD was giving them. [10]Then the LORD was furious with them, and he vowed, [11]'Of all those I rescued from Egypt, no one who is twenty years old or older will ever see the land I solemnly promised to Abraham, Isaac, and Jacob, for they have not obeyed me completely. [12]The only exceptions are Caleb son of Jephunneh the Kenizzite and Joshua son of Nun, for they have wholeheartedly followed the LORD.'

[13]"The LORD was furious with Israel and made them wander in the wilderness for forty years until the whole generation that sinned against him had died. [14]But here you are, a brood of sinners, doing exactly the same thing! You are making the LORD even angrier with Israel. [15]If you turn away from him like this and he abandons them again in the wilderness, you will be responsible for destroying this entire nation!"

[16]But they responded to Moses, "We simply want to build sheepfolds for our flocks and fortified cities for our wives and children. [17]Then we will arm ourselves and lead our fellow Israelites into battle until we have brought them safely to their inheritance. Meanwhile, our families will stay in the fortified cities we build here, so they will be safe from any attacks by the local people. [18]We will not return to our homes until all the people of Israel have received their inheritance of land. [19]But we do not want any of the land on the other side of the Jordan. We would rather live here on the east side where we have received our inheritance."

[20]Then Moses said, "If you keep your word and arm yourselves for the LORD's battles, [21]and if your troops cross the Jordan until the LORD has driven out his enemies, [22]then you may return when the land

31:52 Hebrew *16,750 shekels* [191 kilograms].   **31:54** Hebrew *Tent of Meeting*.

is finally subdued before the LORD. You will have discharged your duty to the LORD and to the rest of the people of Israel. And the land on the east side of the Jordan will be your inheritance from the LORD. ²³But if you fail to keep your word, then you will have sinned against the LORD, and you may be sure that your sin will find you out. ²⁴Go ahead and build towns for your families and sheepfolds for your flocks, but do everything you have said."

²⁵Then the people of Gad and Reuben replied, "We are your servants and will follow your instructions exactly. ²⁶Our children, wives, flocks, and cattle will stay here in the towns of Gilead. ²⁷But, sir, all who are able to bear arms will cross over to fight for the LORD, just as you have said."

²⁸So Moses gave orders to Eleazar, Joshua, and the tribal leaders of Israel. ²⁹He said, "If all the men of Gad and Reuben who are able to fight the LORD's battles cross the Jordan with you, then when the land is conquered, you must give them the land of Gilead as their property. ³⁰But if they refuse to cross over and march ahead of you, then they must accept land with the rest of you in the land of Canaan."

³¹The tribes of Gad and Reuben said again, "Sir, we will do as the LORD has commanded! ³²We will cross the Jordan into Canaan fully armed to fight for the LORD, but our inheritance of land will be here on this side of the Jordan."

³³So Moses assigned to the tribes of Gad, Reuben, and half the tribe of Manasseh son of Joseph the territory of King Sihon of the Amorites and the land of King Og of Bashan—the whole land with its towns and surrounding lands.

³⁴The people of Gad built the towns of Dibon, Ataroth, Aroer, ³⁵Atroth-shophan, Jazer, Jogbehah, ³⁶Beth-nimrah, and Beth-haran. These were all fortified cities with sheepfolds for their flocks.

³⁷The people of Reuben built the towns of Heshbon, Elealeh, Kiriathaim, ³⁸Nebo, Baal-meon, and Sibmah. They changed the names of some of the towns they conquered and rebuilt.

³⁹Then the descendants of Makir of the tribe of Manasseh went to Gilead and conquered it, and they drove out the Amorites, who were living there. ⁴⁰So Moses gave Gilead to the Makirites, descendants of Manasseh, and they lived there. ⁴¹The people of Jair, another clan of the tribe of Manasseh, captured many of the towns in Gilead and changed the name of that region to the Towns of Jair.* ⁴²Meanwhile, a man named Nobah captured the town of Kenath and its surrounding villages, and he renamed that area Nobah after himself.

CHAPTER 33

This is the itinerary the Israelites followed as they marched out of Egypt under the leadership of Moses and Aaron. ²At the LORD's direction, Moses kept a written record of their progress. These are the stages of their march, identified by the different places they stopped along the way.

³They set out from the city of Rameses on the morning after the first Passover celebration in early spring.* The people of Israel left defiantly, in full view of all the Egyptians. ⁴Meanwhile, the Egyptians were burying all their firstborn sons, whom the LORD had killed the night before. The LORD had defeated the gods of Egypt that night with great acts of judgment!

⁵After leaving Rameses, the Israelites set up camp at Succoth.

⁶Then they left Succoth and camped at Etham on the edge of the wilderness.

⁷They left Etham and turned back toward Pi-hahiroth, opposite Baal-zephon, and camped near Migdol.

⁸They left Pi-hahiroth and crossed the Red Sea* into the wilderness beyond. Then they traveled for three days into the Etham wilderness and camped at Marah.

⁹They left Marah and camped at Elim, where there are twelve springs of water and seventy palm trees.

¹⁰They left Elim and camped beside the Red Sea.*

¹¹They left the Red Sea and camped in the Sin* Desert.

¹²They left the Sin Desert and camped at Dophkah.

¹³They left Dophkah and camped at Alush.

32:41 Hebrew *Havvoth-jair.*   33:3 Hebrew *on the fifteenth day of the first month.* This day of the Hebrew lunar calendar occurs in late March or early April.   33:8 Hebrew *the sea.*   33:10 Hebrew *sea of reeds;* also in 33:11.   33:11 Not to be confused with the English word *sin.*

¹⁴They left Alush and camped at Rephidim, where there was no water for the people to drink.

¹⁵They left Rephidim and camped in the wilderness of Sinai.

¹⁶They left the wilderness of Sinai and camped at Kibroth-hattaavah.

¹⁷They left Kibroth-hattaavah and camped at Hazeroth.

¹⁸They left Hazeroth and camped at Rithmah.

¹⁹They left Rithmah and camped at Rimmon-perez.

²⁰They left Rimmon-perez and camped at Libnah.

²¹They left Libnah and camped at Rissah.

²²They left Rissah and camped at Kehelathah.

²³They left Kehelathah and camped at Mount Shepher.

²⁴They left Mount Shepher and camped at Haradah.

²⁵They left Haradah and camped at Makheloth.

²⁶They left Makheloth and camped at Tahath.

²⁷They left Tahath and camped at Terah.

²⁸They left Terah and camped at Mithcah.

²⁹They left Mithcah and camped at Hashmonah.

³⁰They left Hashmonah and camped at Moseroth.

³¹They left Moseroth and camped at Bene-jaakan.

³²They left Bene-jaakan and camped at Hor-haggidgad.

³³They left Hor-haggidgad and camped at Jotbathah.

³⁴They left Jotbathah and camped at Abronah.

³⁵They left Abronah and camped at Ezion-geber.

³⁶They left Ezion-geber and camped at Kadesh in the wilderness of Zin.

³⁷They left Kadesh and camped at Mount Hor, at the border of Edom.

³⁸While they were at the foot of Mount Hor, Aaron the priest was directed by the LORD to go up the mountain, and there he died. This happened on a day in midsummer,* during the fortieth year after Israel's departure from Egypt. ³⁹Aaron was 123 years old when he died there on Mount Hor.

⁴⁰It was then that the Canaanite king of Arad, who lived in the Negev in the land of Canaan, heard that the people of Israel were approaching his land.

⁴¹Meanwhile, the Israelites left Mount Hor and camped at Zalmonah.

⁴²Then they left Zalmonah and camped at Punon.

⁴³They left Punon and camped at Oboth.

⁴⁴They left Oboth and camped at Iye-abarim on the border of Moab.

⁴⁵They left Iye-abarim* and camped at Dibon-gad.

⁴⁶They left Dibon-gad and camped at Almon-diblathaim.

⁴⁷They left Almon-diblathaim and camped in the mountains east of the river,* near Mount Nebo.

⁴⁸They left the mountains east of the river and camped on the plains of Moab beside the Jordan River, across from Jericho. ⁴⁹Along the Jordan River they camped from Beth-jeshimoth as far as Abel-shittim on the plains of Moab.

⁵⁰While they were camped near the Jordan River on the plains of Moab opposite Jericho, the LORD said to Moses, ⁵¹"Speak to the Israelites and tell them: 'When you cross the Jordan River into the land of Canaan, ⁵²you must drive out all the people living there. You must destroy all their carved and molten images and demolish all their pagan shrines. ⁵³Take possession of the land and settle in it, because I have given it to you to occupy. ⁵⁴You must distribute the land among the clans by sacred lot and in proportion to their size. A larger inheritance of land will be allotted to each of the larger clans, and a smaller inheritance will be allotted to each of the smaller clans. The decision of the sacred lot is final. In this way, the land will be divided among your ancestral tribes. ⁵⁵But if you fail to drive out the people who live in the land, those who remain will be like splinters in your eyes and thorns in your sides. They will harass you in the land where you live. ⁵⁶And I will do to you what I had planned to do to them.'"

33:38 Hebrew *on the first day of the fifth month.* This day of the Hebrew lunar calendar occurs in July or early August.   **33:45** As in 33:44; Hebrew reads *Iyim,* another name for Iye-abarim.   **33:47** Hebrew *the mountains of Abarim;* also in 33:48.

FEBRUARY 19 ☐ DAY 50
NUMBERS 34–36
Laws of the Promised Land

OVERVIEW Perhaps no greater promises can be found in the pages of Scripture than those contained in Numbers 34–36, little-read chapters introduced with the phrase, "When you come into the land of Canaan . . . " (34:2). What follows is a detailed description of inheritances in the land of Canaan—the promise of thousands of square miles of real estate—when as yet the nation of Israel does not possess so much as a spadeful! Representatives from each of the twelve tribes cast lots for land they as yet do not own; the Levites are *given* forty-eight cities, not one of which has as yet been conquered. Fortified by faith, the people prepare to fight battles that have already been won!

Chapter 34	Chapter 35	Chapter 36
Borders around the Land	Refuge within the Land	Inheritance of the Land
Military Protection	Legal Protection	

YOUR DAILY WALK With eyes riveted to the television screen, a group of hometown hockey fans howls its approval as the match progresses. When the home team falls behind 1–0 in the first period, the fans are delighted; when the score goes to 2–0 in the second period, the excitement grows; when in the third period the home team still trails 2–1, they go crazy with joy. Why? Because they're watching a videotape of the game, and they already know that the final score will be 3–2, in favor of the home team! The fans are confident their team will emerge victorious in the end.

Television has turned the family circle into a semicircle.

In the same way, the Israelites could face the walled cities and giant warriors of Canaan confident that their victory had already been won—in God's strength.

Tape the words of Luke 1:37 to the corner of your television screen to remind you that when the battle is the Lord's, the outcome is already certain.

INSIGHT Cities of Refuge, Savior of Refuge (35:32)
For the murderer of innocent blood, there was no refuge from death. But for the accidental slayer, six cities would later be designated as places of protection (Joshua 20). Notice the parallels between these cities of refuge in the Old Testament and the Savior of refuge in the New Testament: Both were
- of divine origin,
- necessary to save from death,
- accessible to all, and
- all-sufficient for salvation.

CHAPTER 34
Then the LORD said to Moses, ²"Give these instructions to the Israelites: When you come into the land of Canaan, which I am giving you as your special possession, these will be the boundaries. ³The southern portion of your country will extend from the wilderness of Zin, along the edge of

Edom. The southern boundary will begin on the east at the Dead Sea.* ⁴It will then run south past Scorpion Pass* in the direction of Zin. Its southernmost point will be Kadesh-barnea, from which it will go to Hazar-addar, and on to Azmon. ⁵From Azmon the boundary will turn toward the brook of Egypt and end at the Mediterranean Sea.*

⁶"Your western boundary will be the coastline of the Mediterranean Sea.

⁷"Your northern boundary will begin at the Mediterranean Sea and run eastward to Mount Hor, ⁸then to Lebo-hamath, and on through Zedad ⁹and Ziphron to Hazar-enan. This will be your northern boundary.

¹⁰"The eastern boundary will start at Hazar-enan and run south to Shepham, ¹¹then down to Riblah on the east side of Ain. From there the boundary will run down along the eastern edge of the Sea of Galilee,* ¹²and then along the Jordan River to the Dead Sea. These are the boundaries of your land."

¹³Then Moses told the Israelites, "This is the territory you are to divide among yourselves by sacred lot. The LORD commands that the land be divided up among the nine and a half remaining tribes. ¹⁴The families of the tribes of Reuben, Gad, and half the tribe of Manasseh have already received their inheritance of land ¹⁵on the east side of the Jordan River, across from Jericho."

¹⁶And the LORD said to Moses, ¹⁷"These are the men who are to divide the land among the people: Eleazar the priest and Joshua son of Nun. ¹⁸Also enlist one leader from each tribe to help them with the task. ¹⁹These are the tribes and the names of the leaders:

Tribe	Leader
Judah.............	Caleb son of Jephunneh
²⁰ Simeon	Shemuel son of Ammihud
²¹ Benjamin.............	Elidad son of Kislon
²² Dan	Bukki son of Jogli
²³ Manasseh son of Joseph........	Hanniel son of Ephod
²⁴ Ephraim son of Joseph.........	Kemuel son of Shiphtan
²⁵ Zebulun	Elizaphan son of Parnach
²⁶ Issachar...............	Paltiel son of Azzan
²⁷ Asher..............	Ahihud son of Shelomi
²⁸ Naphtali	Pedahel son of Ammihud

²⁹These are the men the LORD has appointed to oversee the dividing of the land of Canaan among the Israelites."

CHAPTER 35

While Israel was camped beside the Jordan on the plains of Moab, across from Jericho, the LORD said to Moses, ²"Instruct the people of Israel to give to the Levites from their property certain towns to live in, along with the surrounding pasturelands. ³These towns will be their homes, and the surrounding lands will provide pasture for their cattle, flocks, and other livestock. ⁴The pastureland assigned to the Levites around these towns will extend 1,500 feet* from the town walls in every direction. ⁵Measure off 3,000 feet* outside the town walls in every direction—east, south, west, north—with the town at the center. This area will serve as the larger pastureland for the towns.

⁶"You must give the Levites six cities of refuge, where a person who has accidentally killed someone can flee for safety. In addition, give them forty-two other towns. ⁷In all, forty-eight towns with the surrounding pastureland will be given to the Levites. ⁸These towns will come from the property of the people of Israel. The larger tribes will give more towns to the Levites, while the smaller tribes will give fewer. Each tribe will give in proportion to its inheritance."

⁹And the LORD said to Moses, ¹⁰"Say this to the people of Israel: 'When you cross the Jordan into the land of Canaan, ¹¹designate cities of refuge for people to flee to if they have killed someone accidentally. ¹²These cities will be places of protection from a dead person's relatives who want to avenge the death. The slayer must not be killed before being tried by the community. ¹³Designate six cities of refuge for yourselves, ¹⁴three on the east side of the Jordan River and three on the west in the land of Canaan. ¹⁵These cities are for the protection of Israelites, resident foreigners, and traveling merchants. Anyone who accidentally kills someone may flee there for safety.

¹⁶"'But if someone strikes and kills another person with a piece of iron, it must be presumed to be murder, and the murderer must be executed. ¹⁷Or if someone strikes and kills another person with a large stone,

it is murder, and the murderer must be executed. ¹⁸The same is true if someone strikes and kills another person with a wooden weapon. It must be presumed to be murder, and the murderer must be executed. ¹⁹The victim's nearest relative is responsible for putting the murderer to death. When they meet, the avenger must execute the murderer. ²⁰So if in premeditated hostility someone pushes another person or throws a dangerous object and the person dies, it is murder. ²¹Or if someone angrily hits another person with a fist and the person dies, it is murder. In such cases, the victim's nearest relative must execute the murderer when they meet.

²²"'But suppose someone pushes another person without premeditated hostility, or throws something that unintentionally hits another person, ²³or accidentally drops a stone on someone, though they were not enemies, and the person dies. ²⁴If this should happen, the assembly must follow these regulations in making a judgment between the slayer and the avenger, the victim's nearest relative. ²⁵They must protect the slayer from the avenger, and they must send the slayer back to live in a city of refuge until the death of the high priest.

²⁶"'But if the slayer leaves the city of refuge, ²⁷and the victim's nearest relative finds him outside the city limits and kills him, it will not be considered murder. ²⁸The slayer should have stayed inside the city of refuge until the death of the high priest. But after the death of the high priest, the slayer may return to his own property. ²⁹These are permanent laws for you to observe from generation to generation, wherever you may live.

³⁰"'All murderers must be executed, but only if there is more than one witness. No one may be put to death on the testimony of only one witness. ³¹Also, you must never accept a ransom payment for the life of someone judged guilty of murder and subject to execution; murderers must always be put to death. ³²And never accept a ransom payment from someone who has fled to a city of refuge, allowing the slayer to return to his property before the death of the high priest. ³³This will ensure that the land where you live will not be polluted, for murder pollutes the land. And no atonement can be made for murder except by the execution of the murderer. ³⁴You must not defile the land where you are going to live, for I live there myself. I am the LORD, who lives among the people of Israel.'"

CHAPTER 36

Then the heads of the clan of Gilead—descendants of Makir, son of Manasseh, son of Joseph—came to Moses and the family leaders of Israel with a petition. ²They said, "Sir, the LORD instructed you to divide the land by sacred lot among the people of Israel. You were told by the LORD to give the inheritance of our brother Zelophehad to his daughters. ³But if any of them marries a man from another tribe, their inheritance of land will go with them to the tribe into which they marry. In this way, the total area of our tribal land will be reduced. ⁴Then when the Year of Jubilee comes, their inheritance of land will be added to that of the new tribe, causing it to be lost forever to our ancestral tribe."

⁵So Moses gave the Israelites this command from the LORD: "The men of the tribe of Joseph are right. ⁶This is what the LORD commands concerning the daughters of Zelophehad: Let them marry anyone they like, as long as it is within their own ancestral tribe. ⁷None of the inherited land may pass from tribe to tribe, for the inheritance of every tribe must remain fixed as it was first allotted. ⁸The daughters throughout the tribes of Israel who are in line to inherit property must marry within their tribe, so that all the Israelites will keep their ancestral property. ⁹No inheritance may pass from one tribe to another; each tribe of Israel must hold on to its allotted inheritance of land."

¹⁰The daughters of Zelophehad did as the LORD commanded Moses. ¹¹Mahlah, Tirzah, Hoglah, Milcah, and Noah all married cousins on their father's side. ¹²They married into the clans of Manasseh son of Joseph. Thus, their inheritance of land remained within their ancestral tribe.

¹³These are the commands and regulations that the LORD gave to the people of Israel through Moses while they were camped on the plains of Moab beside the Jordan River, across from Jericho.

Deuteronomy

THE LAST of the five books of Moses, Deuteronomy reviews the forty-year period of the nation's walk with God and previews the new relationship soon to begin in Canaan. Taking the form of a series of sermons, the book addresses the new generation emerging from the wilderness march. Moses reminds them of the central importance of obedience and stresses holiness as a way of life. Everything—possession of the land, victory over enemies, prosperity, and enjoyment of life—depends on these valuable lessons.

Focus	Backward			Inward			Upward	
Divisions	Reviewing the Wanderings	Renewing God's Demands for Obedience	Remembering Lessons in Obedience	Religious Laws for Canaan	Civil Laws for Canaan	Societal Laws for Canaan	Commitment to the Covenant	Farewell and Death of Moses
	1 4	5 7	8 11	12 16	17 20	21 26	27 30	31 34
Topics	Lessons from the Past			Lessons for the Future			Lessons of a Leader	
	The Obedient Life			The Orderly Life			One Man's Life	
Place	Moab (North of the Dead Sea)							
Time	About 2 Months							

FEBRUARY 20 □ DAY 51
DEUTERONOMY 1–4
Reviewing the Wanderings

OVERVIEW The first of Moses' three sermons in the book of Deuteronomy looks back over the history of the nation and traces God's dealings with his people. Because of unbelief the Israelites failed to possess the land God had promised them. But even their disobedience could not annul the promise of God. Israel would one day dwell in the land, though an entire generation had died in the wilderness for failing to believe God. True to his word, God overthrew nation after nation during Israel's relentless march to the Jordan River. The lesson from the past is painfully transparent: Blessing and victory follow obedience, but disobedience brings only defeat and heartache.

Chapter 1	Chapter 2	Chapter 3	Chapter 4
Postponement of the Land	Promise of the Land	Possession of the Land	Principle from the Land: Obey!
Looking to the Past			Learning from the Past

YOUR DAILY WALK What have you learned during the months or years you've been walking with the Lord?

To overlook one's own faults is to miss a valuable free education.

The story is told of a high school teacher who spoke with excessive pride of her thirty-eight years of mediocre teaching experience. Her principal responded with a chuckle, "Well, that's not quite correct. Actually she's a first-year teacher—thirty-eight times over!" Do you see the difference? Each year that teacher was making the same mistakes she made during her first year—mistakes that should have been corrected long ago! She never profited from her past errors and so was destined to repeat them again and again.

Moses tried to shake the nation of Israel from its complacency by pointing out the deadly consequences of past disobedience. As you read today's section, you can almost hear him plead with the people to open their eyes and learn from their sordid history.

How about you? Are you wiser in the ways of God today for having seen him work in the past? Sometime this week, share with someone a "history lesson" from your life that is making a difference in your walk with God today!

INSIGHT Words Worth Repeating

How much practical application do Moses' sermons to his people in the book of Deuteronomy carry? Just ask Jesus, who *three times* quoted this book to fend off Satan in the wilderness, one for each offer Satan made (Matthew 4:1-10). (By the way, it worked!)

CHAPTER 1

This book records the words that Moses spoke to all the people of Israel while they were in the wilderness east of the Jordan River. They were camped in the Jordan Val-

ley* near Suph, between Paran on one side and Tophel, Laban, Hazeroth, and Dizahab on the other. ²Normally it takes only eleven days to travel from Mount Sinai* to Kadesh-barnea, going by way of Mount

1:1 Hebrew *the Arabah;* also in 1:7.   1:2 Hebrew *Horeb,* another name for Sinai; also in 1:6, 19.

Seir. [3]But forty years after the Israelites left Mount Sinai, on a day in midwinter,* Moses gave these speeches to the Israelites, telling them everything the LORD had commanded him to say. [4]This was after he had defeated King Sihon of the Amorites, who had ruled in Heshbon, and King Og of Bashan, who had ruled in Ashtaroth and Edrei.

[5]So Moses addressed the people of Israel while they were in the land of Moab east of the Jordan River. He began to explain the law as follows: [6]"When we were at Mount Sinai, the LORD our God said to us, 'You have stayed at this mountain long enough. [7]It is time to break camp and move on. Go to the hill country of the Amorites and to all the neighboring regions—the Jordan Valley, the hill country, the western foothills,* the Negev, and the coastal plain. Go to the land of the Canaanites and to Lebanon, and all the way to the great Euphrates River. [8]I am giving all this land to you! Go in and occupy it, for it is the land the LORD swore to give to your ancestors Abraham, Isaac, and Jacob, and to all their descendants.'

[9]"At that time I told you, 'You are too great a burden for me to carry all by myself. [10]The LORD your God has made you as numerous as the stars! [11]And may the LORD, the God of your ancestors, multiply you a thousand times more and bless you as he promised! [12]But how can I settle all your quarrels and problems by myself? [13]Choose some men from each tribe who have wisdom, understanding, and a good reputation, and I will appoint them as your leaders.'

[14]"You agreed that my plan was a good one. [15]So I took the wise and respected men you had selected from your tribes and appointed them to serve as judges and officials over you. Some were responsible for a thousand people, some for a hundred, some for fifty, and some for ten. [16]I instructed the judges, 'You must be perfectly fair at all times, not only to fellow Israelites, but also to the foreigners living among you. [17]When you make decisions, never favor those who are rich; be fair to lowly and great alike. Don't be afraid of how they will react, for you are judging in the place of God. Bring me any cases that are too difficult for you, and I will handle them.' [18]And at that time I gave you instructions about everything you were to do.

[19]"Then, just as the LORD our God directed us, we left Mount Sinai and traveled through the great and terrifying wilderness, which you yourselves saw, and headed toward the hill country of the Amorites. When we arrived at Kadesh-barnea, [20]I said to you, 'You have now reached the land that the LORD our God is giving us. [21]Look! He has placed it in front of you. Go and occupy it as the LORD, the God of your ancestors, has promised you. Don't be afraid! Don't be discouraged!'

[22]"But you responded, 'First, let's send out scouts to explore the land for us. They will advise us on the best route to take and decide which towns we should capture.' [23]This seemed like a good idea to me, so I chose twelve scouts, one from each of your tribes. [24]They crossed into the hills and came to the valley of Eshcol and explored it. [25]They picked some of its fruit and brought it back to us. And they reported that the land the LORD our God had given us was indeed a good land.

[26]"But you rebelled against the command of the LORD your God and refused to go in. [27]You murmured and complained in your tents and said, 'The LORD must hate us, bringing us here from Egypt to be slaughtered by these Amorites. [28]How can we go on? Our scouts have demoralized us with their report. They say that the people of the land are taller and more powerful than we are, and that the walls of their towns rise high into the sky! They have even seen giants there—the descendants of Anak!'

[29]"But I said to you, 'Don't be afraid! [30]The LORD your God is going before you. He will fight for you, just as you saw him do in Egypt. [31]And you saw how the LORD your God cared for you again and again here in the wilderness, just as a father cares for his child. Now he has brought you to this place.' [32]But even after all he did, you refused to trust the LORD your God, [33]who goes before you looking for the best places to camp, guiding you by a pillar of fire at night and a pillar of cloud by day.

[34]"When the LORD heard your complaining, he became very angry. So he solemnly swore, [35]'Not one of you from this entire wicked generation will live to see the good

1:3 Hebrew *on the first day of the eleventh month.* This day of the Hebrew lunar calendar occurs in January or early February.
1:7 Hebrew *the Shephelah.*

land I swore to give your ancestors, ³⁶except Caleb son of Jephunneh. He will see this land because he has followed the LORD completely. I will give to him and his descendants some of the land he walked over during his scouting mission.'

³⁷"And the LORD was also angry with me because of you. He said to me, 'You will never enter the Promised Land! ³⁸Instead, your assistant, Joshua son of Nun, will lead the people into the land. Encourage him as he prepares to enter it. ³⁹I will give the land to your innocent children. You were afraid they would be captured, but they will be the ones who occupy it. ⁴⁰As for you, turn around now and go on back through the wilderness toward the Red Sea.*'

⁴¹"Then you confessed, 'We have sinned against the LORD! We will go into the land and fight for it, as the LORD our God has told us.' So your men strapped on their weapons, thinking it would be easy to conquer the hill country.

⁴²"But the LORD said to me, 'Tell them not to attack, for I will not go with them. If they do, they will be crushed by their enemies.' ⁴³This is what I told you, but you would not listen. Instead, you again rebelled against the LORD's command and arrogantly went into the hill country to fight. ⁴⁴But the Amorites who lived there came out against you like a swarm of bees. They chased and battered you all the way from Seir to Hormah. ⁴⁵Then you returned and wept before the LORD, but he refused to listen. ⁴⁶So you stayed there at Kadesh for a long time.

CHAPTER 2

"Then we turned around and set out across the wilderness toward the Red Sea,* just as the LORD had instructed me, and we wandered around Mount Seir for a long time. ²Then at last the LORD said to me, ³'You have been wandering around in this hill country long enough; turn northward. ⁴Give these orders to the people: "You will be passing through the country belonging to your relatives the Edomites, the descendants of Esau, who live in Seir. The Edomites will feel threatened, so be careful. ⁵Don't bother them, for I have given them all the hill country around Mount Seir as their property, and I will not give you any of their land. ⁶Pay them for whatever food

or water you use. ⁷The LORD your God has blessed everything you have done and has watched your every step through this great wilderness. During these forty years, the LORD your God has been with you and provided for your every need so that you lacked nothing."' ⁸So we went past our relatives, the descendants of Esau, who live in Seir, and avoided the road through the Arabah Valley that comes up from Elath and Ezion-geber.

"Then as we traveled northward along the desert route through Moab, ⁹the LORD warned us, 'Do not bother the Moabites, the descendants of Lot, or start a war with them. I have given them Ar as their property, and I will not give you any of their land.'"

¹⁰(A numerous and powerful race of giants called the Emites had once lived in the area of Ar. They were as tall as the Anakites, another race of giants. ¹¹Both the Emites and the Anakites are often referred to as the Rephaites, but the Moabites called them Emites. ¹²In earlier times the Horites had lived at Mount Seir, but they were driven out and displaced by the descendants of Esau. In a similar way the peoples in Canaan were driven from the land that the LORD had assigned to Israel.)

¹³Moses continued, "Then the LORD told us to cross Zered Brook, and we did. ¹⁴So thirty-eight years passed from the time we first arrived at Kadesh-barnea until we finally crossed Zered Brook! For the LORD had vowed that this could not happen until all the men old enough to fight in battle had died in the wilderness. ¹⁵The LORD had lifted his hand against them until all of them had finally died.

¹⁶"When all the men of fighting age had died, ¹⁷the LORD said to me, ¹⁸'Today you will cross the border of Moab at Ar ¹⁹and enter the land of Ammon. But do not bother the Ammonites, the descendants of Lot, or start a war with them. I have given the land of Ammon to them as their property, and I will not give you any of their land.'"

²⁰(That area, too, was once considered the land of the Rephaites, though the Ammonites referred to them as Zamzummites. ²¹They were a numerous and powerful race, as tall as the Anakites. But the LORD destroyed them so the Ammonites could

1:40 Hebrew *sea of reeds.*   2:1 Hebrew *sea of reeds.*

occupy their land. [22]He had similarly helped the descendants of Esau at Mount Seir, for he destroyed the Horites so they could settle there in their place. The descendants of Esau live there to this day. [23]A similar thing happened when the Caphtorites from Crete* invaded and destroyed the Avvites, who had lived in villages in the area of Gaza.)

[24]Moses continued, "Then the LORD said, 'Now cross the Arnon Gorge! Look, I will help you defeat Sihon the Amorite, king of Heshbon, and I will give you his land. Attack him and begin to occupy the land. [25]Beginning today I will make all people throughout the earth terrified of you. When they hear reports about you, they will tremble with dread and fear.'

[26]"Then from the wilderness of Kedemoth I sent ambassadors to King Sihon of Heshbon with this proposal of peace: [27]'Let us pass through your land. We will stay on the main road and won't turn off into the fields on either side. [28]We will pay for every bite of food we eat and all the water we drink. All we want is permission to pass through your land. [29]The descendants of Esau at Mount Seir allowed us to go through their country, and so did the Moabites, who live in Ar. Let us pass through until we cross the Jordan into the land the LORD our God has given us.' [30]But King Sihon refused to allow you to pass through, because the LORD your God made Sihon stubborn and defiant so he could help you defeat them, as he has now done.

[31]"Then the LORD said to me, 'Look, I have begun to hand King Sihon and his land over to you. Begin now to conquer and occupy his land.' [32]Then King Sihon declared war on us and mobilized his forces at Jahaz. [33]But the LORD our God handed him over to us, and we crushed him, his sons, and all his people. [34]We conquered all his towns and completely destroyed* everyone—men, women, and children. Not a single person was spared. [35]We took all the livestock as plunder for ourselves, along with anything of value from the towns we ransacked.

[36]"The LORD our God helped us conquer Aroer on the edge of the Arnon Gorge, the town in the gorge, and the whole area as far as Gilead. No town had walls too strong for us. [37]However, we stayed away from the Ammonites along the Jabbok River and the towns in the hill country—all the places the LORD our God had commanded us to leave alone.

CHAPTER 3

"Next we headed for the land of Bashan, where King Og and his army attacked us at Edrei. [2]But the LORD told me, 'Do not be afraid of him, for I have given you victory over Og and his army, giving you his entire land. Treat him just as you treated King Sihon of the Amorites, who ruled in Heshbon.' [3]So the LORD our God handed King Og and all his people over to us, and we killed them all. [4]We conquered all sixty of his towns, the entire Argob region in his kingdom of Bashan. [5]These were all fortified cities with high walls and barred gates. We also took many unwalled villages at the same time. [6]We completely destroyed* the kingdom of Bashan, just as we had destroyed King Sihon of Heshbon. We destroyed* all the people in every town we conquered—men, women, and children alike. [7]But we kept all the livestock for ourselves and took plunder from all the towns.

[8]"We now possessed all the land of the two Amorite kings east of the Jordan River—from the Arnon Gorge to Mount Hermon. [9](Mount Hermon is called Sirion by the Sidonians; the Amorites call it Senir.) [10]We had now conquered all the cities on the plateau, and all Gilead and Bashan as far as the towns of Salecah and Edrei, which were part of Og's kingdom in Bashan. [11](Incidentally, King Og of Bashan was the last of the giant Rephaites. His iron bed was more than thirteen feet long and six feet wide.* It can still be seen in the Ammonite city of Rabbah.)

[12]"When we took possession of this land, I gave the territory beyond Aroer along the Arnon Gorge, plus half of the hill country of Gilead with its towns, to the tribes of Reuben and Gad. [13]Then I gave the rest of Gilead and all of Bashan—Og's former kingdom—to the half-tribe of Manasseh. (The Argob region of Bashan used to be known as the land of the Rephaites. [14]Jair, a leader from the tribe of Manasseh, acquired the whole Argob region in Bashan

2:23 Hebrew *from Caphtor.*   2:34 The Hebrew term used here refers to the complete consecration of things or people to the LORD, either by destroying them or by giving them as an offering.   3:6 The Hebrew term used here refers to the complete consecration of things or people to the LORD, either by destroying them or by giving them as an offering.   3:11 Hebrew *9 cubits* [4.1 meters] *long and 4 cubits* [1.8 meters] *wide.*

all the way to the borders of the Geshurites and Maacathites. Jair renamed this region after himself, calling it the Towns of Jair,* as it is still known today.) [15]I gave Gilead to the clan of Makir. [16]And to the tribes of Reuben and Gad I gave the area extending from Gilead to the middle of the Arnon Gorge, all the way to the Jabbok River on the Ammonite frontier. [17]They also received the Jordan Valley, including the Jordan River and its eastern banks, all the way from the Sea of Galilee down to the Dead Sea,* with the slopes of Pisgah on the east.

[18]"At that time I gave this command to the tribes that will live east of the Jordan: 'Although the LORD your God has given you this land as your property, all your fighting men must cross the Jordan, armed and ready to protect your Israelite relatives. [19]Your wives, children, and numerous livestock, however, may stay behind in the towns I have given you. [20]When the LORD has given security to the rest of the Israelites, as he has to you, and when they occupy the land the LORD your God is giving them across the Jordan River, then you may return here to the land I have given you.'

[21]"At that time I said to Joshua, 'You have seen all that the LORD your God has done to these two kings. He will do the same to all the kingdoms on the west side of the Jordan. [22]Do not be afraid of the nations there, for the LORD your God will fight for you.'

[23]"At that time I pleaded with the LORD and said, [24]'O Sovereign LORD, I am your servant. You have only begun to show me your greatness and power. Is there any god in heaven or on earth who can perform such great deeds as yours? [25]Please let me cross the Jordan to see the wonderful land on the other side, the beautiful hill country and the Lebanon mountains.'

[26]"But the LORD was angry with me because of you, and he would not listen to me. 'That's enough!' he ordered. 'Speak of it no more. [27]You can go to Pisgah Peak and view the land in every direction, but you may not cross the Jordan River. [28]But commission Joshua and encourage him, for he will lead the people across the Jordan. He will give them the land you now see before you.' [29]So we stayed in the valley near Beth-peor.

CHAPTER 4

"And now, Israel, listen carefully to these laws and regulations that I am about to teach you. Obey them so that you may live, so you may enter and occupy the land the LORD, the God of your ancestors, is giving you. [2]Do not add to or subtract from these commands I am giving you from the LORD your God. Just obey them. [3]You saw what the LORD did to you at Baal-peor, where the LORD your God destroyed everyone who had worshiped the god Baal of Peor. [4]But all of you who were faithful to the LORD your God are still alive today.

[5]"You must obey these laws and regulations when you arrive in the land you are about to enter and occupy. The LORD my God gave them to me and commanded me to pass them on to you. [6]If you obey them carefully, you will display your wisdom and intelligence to the surrounding nations. When they hear about these laws, they will exclaim, 'What other nation is as wise and prudent as this!' [7]For what great nation has a god as near to them as the LORD our God is near to us whenever we call on him? [8]And what great nation has laws and regulations as fair as this body of laws that I am giving you today?

[9]"But watch out! Be very careful never to forget what you have seen the LORD do for you. Do not let these things escape from your mind as long as you live! And be sure to pass them on to your children and grandchildren. [10]Tell them especially about the day when you stood before the LORD your God at Mount Sinai,* where he told me, 'Summon the people before me, and I will instruct them. That way, they will learn to fear me as long as they live, and they will be able to teach my laws to their children.' [11]You came near and stood at the foot of the mountain, while the mountain was burning with fire. Flames shot into the sky, shrouded in black clouds and deep darkness. [12]And the LORD spoke to you from the fire. You heard his words but didn't see his form; there was only a voice. [13]He proclaimed his covenant, which he commanded you to keep—the Ten Commandments—and wrote them on two stone tablets. [14]It was at that time that the LORD commanded me to issue the laws and regulations you must obey in the land you are about to enter and occupy.

3:14 Hebrew *Havvoth-jair.*   **3:17** Hebrew *from Kinnereth to the sea of the Arabah, the Salt Sea.*   **4:10** Hebrew *Horeb,* another name for Sinai; also in 4:15.

¹⁵"But be careful! You did not see the LORD's form on the day he spoke to you from the fire at Mount Sinai. ¹⁶So do not corrupt yourselves by making a physical image in any form—whether of a man or a woman, ¹⁷an animal or a bird, ¹⁸a creeping creature or a fish. ¹⁹And when you look up into the sky and see the sun, moon, and stars—all the forces of heaven—don't be seduced by them and worship them. The LORD your God designated these heavenly bodies for all the peoples of the earth. ²⁰Remember that the LORD rescued you from the burning furnace of Egypt to become his own people and special possession; that is what you are today.

²¹"But the LORD was very angry with me because of you. He vowed that I would never cross the Jordan River into the good land the LORD your God is giving you as your special possession. ²²Though you will cross the Jordan to occupy the land, I will die here on this side of the river. ²³So be careful not to break the covenant the LORD your God has made with you. You will break it if you make idols of any shape or form, for the LORD your God has absolutely forbidden this. ²⁴The LORD your God is a devouring fire, a jealous God.

²⁵"In the future, when you have children and grandchildren and have lived in the land a long time, do not corrupt yourselves by making idols of any kind. This is evil in the sight of the LORD your God and will arouse his anger.

²⁶"Today I call heaven and earth as witnesses against you. If you disobey me, you will quickly disappear from the land you are crossing the Jordan to occupy. You will live there only a short time; then you will be utterly destroyed. ²⁷For the LORD will scatter you among the nations, where only a few of you will survive. ²⁸There, in a foreign land, you will worship idols made from wood and stone, gods that neither see nor hear nor eat nor smell. ²⁹From there you will search again for the LORD your God. And if you search for him with all your heart and soul, you will find him.

³⁰"When those bitter days have come upon you far in the future, you will finally return to the LORD your God and listen to what he tells you. ³¹For the LORD your God is merciful—he will not abandon you or destroy you or forget the solemn covenant he made with your ancestors.

³²"Search all of history, from the time God created people on the earth until now. Then search from one end of the heavens to the other. See if anything as great as this has ever happened before. ³³Has any nation ever heard the voice of God* speaking from fire—as you did—and survived? ³⁴Has any other god taken one nation for himself by rescuing it from another by means of trials, miraculous signs, wonders, war, awesome power, and terrifying acts? Yet that is what the LORD your God did for you in Egypt, right before your very eyes.

³⁵"He showed you these things so you would realize that the LORD is God and that there is no other god. ³⁶He let you hear his voice from heaven so he could instruct you. He let you see his great fire here on earth so he could speak to you from it. ³⁷Because he loved your ancestors, he chose to bless their descendants and personally brought you out of Egypt with a great display of power. ³⁸He drove out nations far greater than you, so he could bring you in and give you their land as a special possession, as it is today. ³⁹So remember this and keep it firmly in mind: The LORD is God both in heaven and on earth, and there is no other god! ⁴⁰If you obey all the laws and commands that I will give you today, all will be well with you and your children. Then you will enjoy a long life in the land the LORD your God is giving you for all time."

⁴¹Then Moses set apart three cities of refuge east of the Jordan River, ⁴²where anyone who had accidentally killed someone without having any previous hostility could flee for safety. ⁴³These were the cities: Bezer on the wilderness plateau for the tribe of Reuben; Ramoth in Gilead for the tribe of Gad; Golan in Bashan for the tribe of Manasseh.

⁴⁴This is the law that Moses handed down to the Israelites. ⁴⁵These are the stipulations, laws, and regulations that Moses gave to the people of Israel when they left Egypt, ⁴⁶and as they camped in the valley near Beth-peor east of the Jordan River. (This land was formerly occupied by the Amorites under King Sihon of Heshbon. He and his people had been destroyed by Moses and the Israelites as they came up from Egypt. ⁴⁷Israel conquered his land

4:33 Or *voice of a god.*

and that of King Og of Bashan—the two Amorite kings east of the Jordan. [48]So Israel conquered all the area from Aroer at the edge of the Arnon Gorge to Mount Sirion,* also called Mount Hermon. [49]And they took the eastern bank of the Jordan Valley as far south as the Dead Sea,* below the slopes of Pisgah.)

4:48 As in Syriac version (see also 3:9); Hebrew reads *Mount Sion. the sea of the Arabah.*

4:49 Hebrew *took the Arabah on the east side of the Jordan as far as the sea of the Arabah.*

FEBRUARY 21 ☐ DAY 52
Lessons in the Wilderness

LOOK BACK In a book entitled *Numbers* you'd expect to find statistics and figures prominent, and this past week's reading has not disappointed! After an initial census to determine the strength of the fighting force, God instructed Moses to cleanse and consecrate the nation for worship and warfare. After a special celebration of the Passover at Mount Sinai, the people began the journey with great expectations. But rejoicing soon turned to rebellion, leading to a fateful decision at the desert of Paran and forty years of fruitless wandering in the wilderness. Even in the midst of death and discouragement, God's grace was evident in the form of daily provisions of manna and water. The bronze snake was God's lifesaving antidote for poisonous snakes, and a talking donkey showed Balaam the folly of trying to curse God's people. A second census (nearly forty years after the first) showed that the loss of a generation through unbelief had not decimated the nation. It would now remain for the new generation to learn from the errors of its elders.

LOOK UP You cannot get from Mount Sinai to the Promised Land without passing through the wilderness. The issue was not whether the children of Israel would pass through the wilderness (they would), but rather how long they would camp there. What should have been an eleven-day experience became a forty-year nightmare. What should have been a brief, uncomfortable inconvenience became instead a "terminal illness" for an entire generation. What should have produced a few blisters and first-degree burns ended up costing 1.2 million people their lives.

Most people don't mind obstacles, as long as they don't get in their way.

A wilderness is never pleasant (unless it is on a picture postcard). It tends to be dry, barren, lifeless, and uncomfortable. You tend to get thirsty there and find yourself yearning to be in a place of rest and refreshment.

But as you continue your Daily Walk through the Bible, you will discover something intriguing: Many of God's choicest servants spent time in this kind of an environment. Moses did (forty years, to be exact). David did. John the Baptist did. The apostle Paul did. And even our Lord was tempted for forty days in a barren wilderness region near the Dead Sea.

LOOK AHEAD A season in the wilderness does something interesting for a tree: It causes the roots to go down deeper in search of life-giving moisture. And the result is a stronger tree that is better able to weather the storms of life.

The same is true of the man or woman of God who faces the hot blast of desertlike conditions. What may at first glance appear to be barren, fruitless days on the "backside of God's blessing" may, in fact, be preparing you for days of great fruit bearing just ahead. Wilderness times will come—expect them! But don't allow the heat to make you bitter or disobedient toward God. "So let [endurance] grow, for when your endurance is fully developed, you will be strong in character and ready for anything" (James 1:4).

The tragedy of the book of Numbers is not that the nation went through the wilderness, but that through disobedience they camped there so long.

By the way, where are you camped these days?

FEBRUARY 22 ☐ DAY 53
DEUTERONOMY 5–7
Reviewing God's Demands

 OVERVIEW The second (and longest) of Moses' three sermons begins in chapter 5 and ends in chapter 26. Moses begins by reviewing the Ten Commandments, the foundational expression of God's moral requirements for humanity. He then stresses the importance of loving God and passing on his law to succeeding generations. Moses realizes the need for the people of Israel to keep the law and teach future generations God's commands if they are to be what God desires of his children: an obedient people who conquer their foes in the strength God provides.

Chapter 5	Chapter 6	Chapter 7
Restating the Ten Commandments	Revealing a New Command	Repeating a Future Hope
Laws from Sinai	Law of Love	Certainty of Victory

 YOUR DAILY WALK If a *god* is defined as anything that has the potential to replace God as the focus of your life, what will be the most dangerous god you encounter today at work? . . . at home? . . . on your campus? . . . in your leisure-time activities?

Idolatry is anything that cools your desire for Christ.

As Moses repeated God's law to the people, he emphasized one command: "'Do not worship any other gods besides [the LORD]'" (5:7). Why that command? Because he had indelible memories of the gold calf incident at Mount Sinai. He knew the ever present danger of substituting *something* for the all-important *someone.* In addition, Moses had keen foresight. He knew the religious "climate" into which the people were about to move: a land filled with idolatry and unabashed immorality, which, if permitted, would turn the Israelites away from God.

Go back over your list of potential gods. Have you allowed one or more to take a controlling interest in your life? If so, make a note for yourself of the ones that need to be rooted out. Then invite the one true God to return to his desired (and proper) place in your life.

 INSIGHT Hear Ye, Hear Ye!
Deuteronomy 6:4 begins the celebrated Hebrew Shema ("listen"), which consists of 6:4-9, 11:13-21, and Numbers 15:37-41, and is recited twice daily by pious Jews. The command "Listen, Israel" in some variation is repeated a total of seven times in this book (4:1; 5:1; 6:3-4; 9:1; 20:3; 27:9) to emphasize Moses' appeal for obedience on the part of the nation.

CHAPTER 5

Moses called all the people of Israel together and said, "Listen carefully to all the laws and regulations I am giving you today. Learn them and be sure to obey them! ²"While we were at Mount Sinai,* the LORD our God made a covenant with us. ³The LORD did not make this covenant long ago with our ancestors, but with all of us who are alive today. ⁴The LORD spoke to you face to face from the heart of the fire on the mountain. ⁵I stood as an intermediary between you and the LORD, for you were afraid of the fire and did not climb the mountain. He spoke to me, and I passed his words on to you. This is what he said:

⁶"'I am the LORD your God, who rescued you from slavery in Egypt.
⁷"'Do not worship any other gods besides me.
⁸"'Do not make idols of any kind, whether in the shape of birds or animals or fish. ⁹You must never worship or bow down to them, for I, the LORD your God, am a jealous God who will not share your affection with any other god! I do not leave unpunished the sins of those who hate me, but I punish the children for the sins of their parents to the third and fourth generations. ¹⁰But I lavish my love on those who love me and obey my commands, even for a thousand generations.
¹¹"'Do not misuse the name of the LORD your God. The LORD will not let you go unpunished if you misuse his name.
¹²"'Observe the Sabbath day by keeping it holy, as the LORD your God has commanded you. ¹³Six days a week are set apart for your daily duties and regular work, ¹⁴but the seventh day is a day of rest dedicated to the LORD your God. On that day no one in your household may do any kind of work. This includes you, your sons and daughters, your male and female servants, your oxen and donkeys and other livestock, and any foreigners living among you. All your male and female servants must rest as you do. ¹⁵Remember that you were once slaves in Egypt and that the LORD your God brought you out with amazing power and mighty deeds. That is why the LORD your God has commanded you to observe the Sabbath day.

¹⁶"'Honor your father and mother, as the LORD your God commanded you. Then you will live a long, full life in the land the LORD your God will give you.
¹⁷"'Do not murder.
¹⁸"'Do not commit adultery.
¹⁹"'Do not steal.
²⁰"'Do not testify falsely against your neighbor.
²¹"'Do not covet your neighbor's wife. Do not covet your neighbor's house or land, male or female servant, ox or donkey, or anything else your neighbor owns.'

²²"The LORD spoke these words with a loud voice to all of you from the heart of the fire, surrounded by clouds and deep darkness. This was all he said at that time, and he wrote his words on two stone tablets and gave them to me. ²³But when you heard the voice from the darkness, while the mountain was blazing with fire, all your tribal leaders came to me. ²⁴They said, 'The LORD our God has shown us his glory and greatness, and we have heard his voice from the heart of the fire. Today we have seen God speaking to humans, and yet we live! ²⁵But now, why should we die? If the LORD our God speaks to us again, we will certainly die and be consumed by this awesome fire. ²⁶Can any living thing hear the voice of the living God from the heart of the fire and yet survive? ²⁷You go and listen to what the LORD our God says. Then come and tell us everything he tells you, and we will listen and obey.'

²⁸"The LORD heard your request and said to me, 'I have heard what the people have said to you, and they are right. ²⁹Oh, that they would always have hearts like this, that they might fear me and obey all my commands! If they did, they and their descendants would prosper forever. ³⁰Go and tell them to return to their tents. ³¹But you stay here with me so I can give you all my commands, laws, and regulations. You will teach them to the people so they can obey them in the land I am giving to them as their inheritance.'"

³²So Moses told the people, "You must obey all the commands of the LORD your God, following his instructions in every detail. ³³Stay on the path that the LORD your God has commanded you to follow. Then you will live long and prosperous

5:2 Hebrew *Horeb,* another name for Sinai.

lives in the land you are about to enter and occupy.

CHAPTER 6

"These are all the commands, laws, and regulations that the LORD your God told me to teach you so you may obey them in the land you are about to enter and occupy, [2]and so you and your children and grandchildren might fear the LORD your God as long as you live. If you obey all his laws and commands, you will enjoy a long life. [3]Listen closely, Israel, to everything I say. Be careful to obey. Then all will go well with you, and you will have many children in the land flowing with milk and honey, just as the LORD, the God of your ancestors, promised you.

[4]"Hear, O Israel! The LORD is our God, the LORD alone.* [5]And you must love the LORD your God with all your heart, all your soul, and all your strength. [6]And you must commit yourselves wholeheartedly to these commands I am giving you today. [7]Repeat them again and again to your children. Talk about them when you are at home and when you are away on a journey, when you are lying down and when you are getting up again. [8]Tie them to your hands as a reminder, and wear them on your forehead. [9]Write them on the doorposts of your house and on your gates.

[10]"The LORD your God will soon bring you into the land he swore to give your ancestors Abraham, Isaac, and Jacob. It is a land filled with large, prosperous cities that you did not build. [11]The houses will be richly stocked with goods you did not produce. You will draw water from cisterns you did not dig, and you will eat from vineyards and olive trees you did not plant. When you have eaten your fill in this land, [12]be careful not to forget the LORD, who rescued you from slavery in the land of Egypt. [13]You must fear the LORD your God and serve him. When you take an oath, you must use only his name.

[14]"You must not worship any of the gods of neighboring nations, [15]for the LORD your God, who lives among you, is a jealous God. His anger will flare up against you and wipe you from the face of the earth. [16]Do not test the LORD your God as you did when you complained at Massah. [17]You

must diligently obey the commands of the LORD your God—all the stipulations and laws he has given you. [18]Do what is right and good in the LORD's sight, so all will go well with you. Then you will enter and occupy the good land that the LORD solemnly promised to give your ancestors. [19]You will drive out all the enemies living in your land, just as the LORD said you would.

[20]"In the future your children will ask you, 'What is the meaning of these stipulations, laws, and regulations that the LORD our God has given us?' [21]Then you must tell them, 'We were Pharaoh's slaves in Egypt, but the LORD brought us out of Egypt with amazing power. [22]Before our eyes the LORD did miraculous signs and wonders, dealing terrifying blows against Egypt and Pharaoh and all his people. [23]He brought us out of Egypt so he could give us this land he had solemnly promised to give our ancestors. [24]And the LORD our God commanded us to obey all these laws and to fear him for our own prosperity and well-being, as is now the case. [25]For we are righteous when we obey all the commands the LORD our God has given us.'

CHAPTER 7

"When the LORD your God brings you into the land you are about to enter and occupy, he will clear away many nations ahead of you: the Hittites, Girgashites, Amorites, Canaanites, Perizzites, Hivites, and Jebusites. These seven nations are all more powerful than you. [2]When the LORD your God hands these nations over to you and you conquer them, you must completely destroy* them. Make no treaties with them and show them no mercy. [3]Do not intermarry with them, and don't let your daughters and sons marry their sons and daughters. [4]They will lead your young people away from me to worship other gods. Then the anger of the LORD will burn against you, and he will destroy you. [5]Instead, you must break down their pagan altars and shatter their sacred pillars. Cut down their Asherah poles and burn their idols. [6]For you are a holy people, who belong to the LORD your God. Of all the people on earth, the LORD your God has chosen you to be his own special treasure.

6:4 Or *The LORD our God is one LORD,* or *The LORD our God, the LORD is one,* or *The LORD is our God, the LORD is one.*   7:2 The Hebrew term used here refers to the complete consecration of things or people to the LORD, either by destroying them or by giving them as an offering; also in 7:26.

[7]"The LORD did not choose you and lavish his love on you because you were larger or greater than other nations, for you were the smallest of all nations! [8]It was simply because the LORD loves you, and because he was keeping the oath he had sworn to your ancestors. That is why the LORD rescued you with such amazing power from your slavery under Pharaoh in Egypt. [9]Understand, therefore, that the LORD your God is indeed God. He is the faithful God who keeps his covenant for a thousand generations and constantly loves those who love him and obey his commands. [10]But he does not hesitate to punish and destroy those who hate him. [11]Therefore, obey all these commands, laws, and regulations I am giving you today.

[12]"If you listen to these regulations and obey them faithfully, the LORD your God will keep his covenant of unfailing love with you, as he solemnly promised your ancestors. [13]He will love you and bless you and make you into a great nation. He will give you many children and give fertility to your land and your animals. When you arrive in the land he swore to give your ancestors, you will have large crops of grain, grapes, and olives, and great herds of cattle, sheep, and goats. [14]You will be blessed above all the nations of the earth. None of your men or women will be childless, and all your livestock will bear young. [15]And the LORD will protect you from all sickness. He will not let you suffer from the terrible diseases you knew in Egypt, but he will bring them all on your enemies!

[16]"You must destroy all the nations the LORD your God hands over to you. Show them no mercy and do not worship their gods. If you do, they will trap you. [17]Per-

haps you will think to yourselves, 'How can we ever conquer these nations that are so much more powerful than we are?' [18]But don't be afraid of them! Just remember what the LORD your God did to Pharaoh and to all the land of Egypt. [19]Remember the great terrors the LORD your God sent against them. You saw it all with your own eyes! And remember the miraculous signs and wonders, and the amazing power he used when he brought you out of Egypt. The LORD your God will use this same power against the people you fear. [20]And then the LORD your God will send hornets* to drive out the few survivors still hiding from you!

[21]"No, do not be afraid of those nations, for the LORD your God is among you, and he is a great and awesome God. [22]The LORD your God will drive those nations out ahead of you little by little. You will not clear them away all at once, for if you did, the wild animals would multiply too quickly for you. [23]But the LORD your God will hand them over to you. He will throw them into complete confusion until they are destroyed. [24]He will put their kings in your power, and you will erase their names from the face of the earth. No one will be able to stand against you, and you will destroy them all.

[25]"You must burn their idols in fire, and do not desire the silver or gold with which they are made. Do not take it or it will become a snare to you, for it is detestable to the LORD your God. [26]Do not bring any detestable objects into your home, for then you will be set apart for destruction just like them. You must utterly detest such things, for they are set apart for destruction.

7:20 Or *will spread panic,* or *will send a plague.* The meaning of the Hebrew is uncertain.

FEBRUARY 23 ☐ DAY 54
DEUTERONOMY 8–11
Remembering Lessons in Obedience

OVERVIEW Moses continues his second sermon by calling upon Israel to remember God's miraculous care throughout the wilderness experience. As he provided abundantly in the past, so he will provide in the future. But Israel must not forget its sinful past—especially the gold calf incident and its tragic consequences. The choice is Israel's to make. If she will love and obey, God will shower her with blessings; if she rebels, God's judgment must surely follow.

Chapter 8	Chapter 9	Chapters 10–11
Remember the Lord's Provision	Remember Israel's Provocation	Respond with Obedience
God's Part	Moses' Part	The Nation's Part

When your heart is filled with faith, there is no room left for fear.

YOUR DAILY WALK The sons of Anak were a race of giants greatly feared by the Israelites. When the spies made their report about the Promised Land (Numbers 13:26-33), it included two specific references to the Anakites: first, an observation that was true ("We also saw the descendants of Anak who are living there!" Numbers 13:28); second, an interpretation that was false ("We can't go up against them! They are stronger than we are!" Numbers 13:31). For forty years these towering giants had stood as a taunting symbol of the nation's unbelief. So tall and formidable were they that the nation had coined a saying, "'Who can stand up to the Anakites?'" (Deuteronomy 9:2). But Moses assured the Israelites that God specializes in dealing with Anakites! God would go before his people to destroy the giants and give them the land as he had promised.

Where are you facing "Anakites" in your life? What impossible situation seems to stand squarely in the way of your spiritual progress? God's word to Israel is also aimed at you: "But the LORD your God will cross over ahead of you like a devouring fire to destroy them" (9:3). Stop by a grocery store today, and buy a giant-sized box of something you need, as a token of your faith in God to handle your "giant-sized" situation.

INSIGHT Phylacteries—A "Binding" Practice
The Pharisees of Jesus' day (and orthodox Jews of today) practiced Deuteronomy 11:18 by tying phylacteries, small receptacles containing verses of Scripture, to their foreheads and left arms during morning prayers.

CHAPTER 8
"Be careful to obey all the commands I am giving you today. Then you will live and multiply, and you will enter and occupy the land the LORD swore to give your ancestors. ²Remember how the LORD your God led you through the wilderness for forty years, humbling you and testing you to prove your character, and to find out whether or not you would really obey his commands. ³Yes, he humbled you by letting you go hungry and then feeding you with manna, a food previously unknown to you and your ancestors. He did it to teach you that people need more than bread for their life; real life comes by feeding on every word of the LORD. ⁴For all these forty years your clothes didn't wear out, and your feet didn't blister or swell. ⁵So you should realize that just as a parent

disciplines a child, the LORD your God disciplines you to help you.

⁶"So obey the commands of the LORD your God by walking in his ways and fearing him. ⁷For the LORD your God is bringing you into a good land of flowing streams and pools of water, with springs that gush forth in the valleys and hills. ⁸It is a land of wheat and barley, of grapevines, fig trees, pomegranates, olives, and honey. ⁹It is a land where food is plentiful and nothing is lacking. It is a land where iron is as common as stone, and copper is abundant in the hills. ¹⁰When you have eaten your fill, praise the LORD your God for the good land he has given you.

¹¹"But that is the time to be careful! Beware that in your plenty you do not forget the LORD your God and disobey his commands, regulations, and laws. ¹²For when you have

become full and prosperous and have built fine homes to live in, [13] and when your flocks and herds have become very large and your silver and gold have multiplied along with everything else, [14] that is the time to be careful. Do not become proud at that time and forget the LORD your God, who rescued you from slavery in the land of Egypt. [15] Do not forget that he led you through the great and terrifying wilderness with poisonous snakes and scorpions, where it was so hot and dry. He gave you water from the rock! [16] He fed you with manna in the wilderness, a food unknown to your ancestors. He did this to humble you and test you for your own good. [17] He did it so you would never think that it was your own strength and energy that made you wealthy. [18] Always remember that it is the LORD your God who gives you power to become rich, and he does it to fulfill the covenant he made with your ancestors.

[19] "But I assure you of this: If you ever forget the LORD your God and follow other gods, worshiping and bowing down to them, you will certainly be destroyed. [20] Just as the LORD has destroyed other nations in your path, you also will be destroyed for not obeying the LORD your God.

CHAPTER 9

"Hear, O Israel! Today you are about to cross the Jordan River to occupy the land belonging to nations much greater and more powerful than you. They live in cities with walls that reach to the sky! [2] They are strong and tall—descendants of the famous Anakite giants. You've heard the saying, 'Who can stand up to the Anakites?' [3] But the LORD your God will cross over ahead of you like a devouring fire to destroy them. He will subdue them so that you will quickly conquer them and drive them out, just as the LORD has promised.

[4] "After the LORD your God has done this for you, don't say to yourselves, 'The LORD has given us this land because we are so righteous!' No, it is because of the wickedness of the other nations that he is doing it. [5] It is not at all because you are such righteous, upright people that you are about to occupy their land. The LORD your God will drive these nations out ahead of you only because of their wickedness, and to fulfill the oath he had sworn to your ancestors Abraham, Isaac, and Jacob. [6] I will say it again: The

LORD your God is not giving you this good land because you are righteous, for you are not—you are a stubborn people.

[7] "Remember how angry you made the LORD your God out in the wilderness. From the day you left Egypt until now, you have constantly rebelled against him. [8] Remember how angry you made the LORD at Mount Sinai,* where he was ready to destroy you. [9] That was when I was on the mountain receiving the tablets of stone inscribed with the covenant that the LORD had made with you. I was there for forty days and forty nights, and all that time I ate nothing and drank no water. [10] The LORD gave me the covenant, the tablets on which God himself had written all the words he had spoken to you from the fire on the mountain.

[11] "At the end of the forty days and nights, the LORD handed me the two stone tablets with the covenant inscribed on them. [12] Then the LORD said to me, 'Go down immediately because the people you led out of Egypt have become corrupt. They have already turned from the way I commanded them to live and have cast an idol for themselves from gold.'

[13] "The LORD said to me, 'I have been watching this people, and they are extremely stubborn. [14] Leave me alone so I may destroy them and erase their name from under heaven. Then I will make a mighty nation of your descendants, a nation larger and more powerful than they are.'

[15] "So I came down from the fiery mountain, holding in my hands the two stone tablets of the covenant. [16] There below me I could see the gold calf you had made in your terrible sin against the LORD your God. How quickly you had turned from the path the LORD had commanded you to follow! [17] So I raised the stone tablets and dashed them to the ground. I smashed them before your very eyes. [18] Then for forty days and nights I lay prostrate before the LORD, neither eating bread nor drinking water. I did this because you had sinned by doing what the LORD hated, thus making him very angry. [19] How I feared for you, for the LORD was ready to destroy you. But again he listened to me. [20] The LORD was so angry with Aaron that he wanted to destroy him. But I prayed for Aaron, and the LORD spared him. [21] I took your sin—the calf you had made—and I melted it in the fire and ground it into fine

9:8 Hebrew *Horeb*, another name for Sinai.

dust. I threw the dust into the stream that cascades down the mountain.

22"You also made the LORD angry at Taberah,* Massah,* and Kibroth-hattaavah.* 23And at Kadesh-barnea the LORD sent you out with this command: 'Go up and take the land I have given you.' But you rebelled against the command of the LORD your God and refused to trust him or obey him. 24Yes, you have been rebelling against the LORD as long as I have known you.

25"That is why I fell down and lay before the LORD for forty days and nights when he was ready to destroy you. 26I prayed to the LORD and said, 'O Sovereign LORD, do not destroy your own people. They are your special possession, redeemed from Egypt by your mighty power and glorious strength. 27Overlook the stubbornness and sin of these people, but remember instead your servants Abraham, Isaac, and Jacob. 28If you destroy these people, the Egyptians will say, "The LORD destroyed them because he wasn't able to bring them to the land he had sworn to give them." Or they might say, "He destroyed them because he hated them; he brought them into the wilderness to slaughter them." 29But they are your people and your special possession, whom you brought from Egypt by your mighty power and glorious strength.'

CHAPTER 10

"At that time the LORD said to me, 'Prepare two stone tablets like the first ones, and make a sacred chest of wood to keep them in. Return to me on the mountain, 2and I will write on the tablets the same words that were on the ones you smashed. Then place the tablets in the sacred chest—the Ark of the Covenant.'

3"So I made a chest of acacia wood and cut two stone tablets like the first two, and I took the tablets up the mountain. 4The LORD again wrote the terms of the covenant—the Ten Commandments—on them and gave them to me. They were the same words the LORD had spoken to you from the heart of the fire on the mountain as you were assembled below. 5Then I came down and placed the tablets in the Ark of the Covenant, which I had made, just as the LORD commanded me. And the tablets are still there in the Ark.

6"The people of Israel set out from the wells of the people of Jaakan* and traveled to Moserah, where Aaron died and was buried. His son Eleazar became the high priest in his place. 7Then they journeyed to Gudgodah, and from there to Jotbathah, a land with brooks of water. 8At that time the LORD set apart the tribe of Levi to carry the Ark of the LORD's covenant, to minister before the LORD, and to pronounce blessings in his name. These are still their duties. 9That is why the Levites have no share or inheritance reserved for them among the other Israelite tribes. The LORD himself is their inheritance, as the LORD your God told them.

10"As I said before, I stayed on the mountain in the LORD's presence for forty days and nights, as I had done the first time. And once again the LORD yielded to my pleas and didn't destroy you. 11But the LORD said to me, 'Get up and lead the people into the land I swore to give their ancestors, so they may take possession of it.'

12"And now, Israel, what does the LORD your God require of you? He requires you to fear him, to live according to his will, to love and worship him with all your heart and soul, 13and to obey the LORD's commands and laws that I am giving you today for your own good. 14The highest heavens and the earth and everything in it all belong to the LORD your God. 15Yet the LORD chose your ancestors as the objects of his love. And he chose you, their descendants, above every other nation, as is evident today. 16Therefore, cleanse your sinful hearts and stop being stubborn.

17"The LORD your God is the God of gods and Lord of lords. He is the great God, mighty and awesome, who shows no partiality and takes no bribes. 18He gives justice to orphans and widows. He shows love to the foreigners living among you and gives them food and clothing. 19You, too, must show love to foreigners, for you yourselves were once foreigners in the land of Egypt. 20You must fear the LORD your God and worship him and cling to him. Your oaths must be in his name alone. 21He is your God, the one who is worthy of your praise, the one who has done mighty miracles that you yourselves have seen. 22When your ancestors went down into Egypt, there were only seventy of them. But now the LORD your God has made you as numerous as the stars in the sky!

9:22a *Taberah* means "place of burning." See Num 11:1-3.   9:22b *Massah* means "place of testing." See Exod 17:1-7.   9:22c *Kibroth-hattaavah* means "graves of craving." See Num 11:31-34.   10:6 Or *set out from Beeroth of Bene-jaakan.*

CHAPTER 11

"You must love the LORD your God and obey all his requirements, laws, regulations, and commands. ²Listen! I am not talking now to your children, who have never experienced the discipline of the LORD your God or seen his greatness and awesome power. ³They weren't there to see the miraculous signs and wonders he performed in Egypt against Pharaoh and all his land. ⁴They didn't see what the LORD did to the armies of Egypt and to their horses and chariots—how he drowned them in the Red Sea* as they were chasing you, and how he has kept them devastated to this very day! ⁵They didn't see how the LORD cared for you in the wilderness until you arrived here. ⁶They weren't there to see what he did to Dathan and Abiram (the sons of Eliab, a descendant of Reuben) when the earth opened up and swallowed them, along with their households and tents and every living thing that belonged to them. ⁷But you have seen all the LORD's mighty deeds with your own eyes!

⁸"Therefore, be careful to obey every command I am giving you today, so you may have strength to go in and occupy the land you are about to enter. ⁹If you obey, you will enjoy a long life in the land the LORD swore to give to your ancestors and to you, their descendants—a land flowing with milk and honey! ¹⁰For the land you are about to enter and occupy is not like the land of Egypt from which you came, where you planted your seed and dug out irrigation ditches with your foot as in a vegetable garden. ¹¹It is a land of hills and valleys with plenty of rain—¹²a land that the LORD your God cares for. He watches over it day after day throughout the year!

¹³"If you carefully obey all the commands I am giving you today, and if you love the LORD your God with all your heart and soul, and if you worship him, ¹⁴then he will send the rains in their proper seasons so you can harvest crops of grain, grapes for wine, and olives for oil. ¹⁵He will give you lush pastureland for your cattle to graze in, and you yourselves will have plenty to eat.

¹⁶"But do not let your heart turn away from the LORD to worship other gods. ¹⁷If you do, the LORD's anger will burn against you. He will shut up the sky and hold back the rain, and your harvests will fail. Then you will quickly die in that good land the LORD is now giving you. ¹⁸So commit yourselves completely to these words of mine. Tie them to your hands as a reminder, and wear them on your forehead. ¹⁹Teach them to your children. Talk about them when you are at home and when you are away on a journey, when you are lying down and when you are getting up again. ²⁰Write them on the doorposts of your house and on your gates, ²¹so that as long as the sky remains above the earth, you and your children may flourish in the land the LORD swore to give your ancestors.

²²"Be careful to obey all the commands I give you; show love to the LORD your God by walking in his ways and clinging to him. ²³Then the LORD will drive out all the nations in your land, though they are much greater and stronger than you. ²⁴Wherever you set your feet, the land will be yours. Your frontiers will stretch from the wilderness in the south to Lebanon in the north, and from the Euphrates River in the east to the Mediterranean Sea in the west.* ²⁵No one will be able to stand against you, for the LORD your God will send fear and dread ahead of you, as he promised you, wherever you go in the whole land.

²⁶"Today I am giving you the choice between a blessing and a curse! ²⁷You will be blessed if you obey the commands of the LORD your God that I am giving you today. ²⁸You will receive a curse if you reject the commands of the LORD your God and turn from his way by worshiping foreign gods.

²⁹"When the LORD your God brings you into the land to possess it, you must pronounce a blessing from Mount Gerizim and a curse from Mount Ebal. ³⁰(These two mountains are west of the Jordan River in the land of the Canaanites who live in the Jordan Valley,* near the town of Gilgal. They are located toward the west, not far from the oaks of Moreh.) ³¹For you are about to cross the Jordan to occupy the land the LORD your God is giving you. When you are living in that land, ³²you must be careful to obey all the laws and regulations I am giving you today.

11:4 Hebrew *sea of reeds.*   11:24 Hebrew *to the western sea.*   11:30 Hebrew *the Arabah.*

FEBRUARY 24 □ DAY 55
DEUTERONOMY 12–16
Religious Laws for Canaan

 OVERVIEW From the general principles of the law and exhortations to obedience, Moses now moves to more specific regulations governing life in the Promised Land. God himself would specify the place and manner of worship, and Israel must reject all idolatrous practices. Purity, tithing, release from debt, and servanthood are all ways in which Israel can demonstrate her unique relationship with God. And the nation must be careful to observe all the feast days that mark important events in her miraculous history.

Chapter 12	Chapter 13	Chapter 14	Chapter 15	Chapter 16
Regulations for a Holy Land Involving				
Offerings	False Gods	Food	Finances	Festivals
"Obey . . . all my commands . . . that all will go well with you" (12:28)				

 YOUR DAILY WALK Today pierced ears are considered by some to be highly fashionable. But in Israel ears were pierced for a vastly different reason!

Service is the overflow of superabounding devotion.

In today's reading Moses gives instructions concerning the release of servants after a six-year period. Once in a while there arose a situation in which a servant so loved his master that he did not wish to be set free. He would prefer to remain under his master's protection, devoted to his work, rather than to set out on his own. As a perpetual sign of this new relationship, the master would pierce the servant's ear, thereby proclaiming to the world: "This is my beloved servant; I am perpetually his beloved master."

What about your ears? Have they been pierced yet for the Lord? Are you the property of the Father, ready to do his will as a loving servant? If not, give God your ears—and life—right now!

 INSIGHT "What We Do This Day . . . Don't" (12:8)
The disruption of life caused by the conquest of the land east of the Jordan may have made orderly worship impossible. This verse may have been intended to prohibit the use of private altars for worship or sacrifice. Once in the land, only one place of worship would be sanctioned: the Tabernacle in Jerusalem.

CHAPTER 12
"These are the laws and regulations you must obey as long as you live in the land the LORD, the God of your ancestors, is giving you.

2"When you drive out the nations that live there, you must destroy all the places where they worship their gods—high on the mountains, up on the hills, and under every green tree. 3Break down their altars and smash their sacred pillars. Burn their Asherah poles and cut down their carved idols. Erase the names of their gods from those places!

4"Do not worship the LORD your God in the way these pagan peoples worship their gods. 5Rather, you must seek the LORD your God at the place he himself will choose from among all the tribes for his name to be honored. 6There you will bring to the LORD your burnt offerings, your sacrifices, your tithes, your special gifts, your offerings to fulfill a vow, your freewill offerings, and your offerings of the firstborn animals of your flocks and herds. 7There you and your families will feast in the presence of the LORD your God, and you will rejoice in all you have accomplished because the LORD your God has blessed you.

8"Today you are doing whatever you

please, but that is not how it will be [9]when you arrive in the place of rest the LORD your God is giving you. [10]You will soon cross the Jordan River and live in the land the LORD your God is giving you as a special possession. When he gives you rest and security from all your enemies, [11]you must bring everything I command you—your burnt offerings, your sacrifices, your tithes, your special gifts, and your offerings to fulfill a vow—to the place the LORD your God will choose for his name to be honored. [12]You must celebrate there with your sons and daughters and all your servants in the presence of the LORD your God. And remember the Levites who live in your towns, for they will have no inheritance of land as their own. [13]Be careful not to sacrifice your burnt offerings just anywhere. [14]You may do so only at the place the LORD will choose within one of your tribal territories. There you must offer your burnt offerings and do everything I command you.

[15]"But you may butcher animals for meat in any town, wherever you want, just as you do now with gazelle and deer. You may eat as many animals as the LORD your God gives you. All of you, whether ceremonially clean or unclean, may eat that meat. [16]The only restriction is that you are not to eat the blood. You must pour it out on the ground like water.

[17]"But your offerings must not be eaten at home—neither the tithe of your grain and new wine and olive oil, nor the firstborn of your flocks and herds, nor an offering to fulfill a vow, nor your freewill offerings, nor your special gifts. [18]You must eat these in the presence of the LORD your God at the place he will choose. Eat them there with your children, your servants, and the Levites who live in your towns, celebrating in the presence of the LORD your God in all you do. [19]Be very careful never to forget the Levites as long as you live in your land.

[20]"When the LORD your God enlarges your territory as he has promised, you may eat meat whenever you want. [21]It might happen that the place the LORD your God chooses for his name to be honored is a long way from your home. If so, you may butcher any of the cattle or sheep the LORD has given you, and you may eat the meat at your home as I have commanded you. [22]Anyone, whether ceremonially clean or unclean, may eat that meat,

just as you do now with gazelle and deer. [23]The only restriction is never to eat the blood, for the blood is the life, and you must not eat the life with the meat. [24]Instead, pour out the blood on the ground like water. [25]Do not eat the blood; then all will go well with you and your children, because you will be doing what pleases the LORD. [26]Take your sacred gifts and your offerings given to fulfill a vow to the place the LORD chooses to dwell. [27]You must offer the meat and blood of your burnt offerings on the altar of the LORD your God. The blood of your other sacrifices must be poured out beside the altar of the LORD your God, but you may eat the meat. [28]Be careful to obey all my commands so that all will go well with you and your children, because you will be doing what pleases the LORD your God.

[29]"When the LORD your God destroys the nations and you drive them out and occupy their land, [30]do not be trapped into following their example in worshiping their gods. Do not say, 'How do these nations worship their gods? I want to follow their example.' [31]You must not do this to the LORD your God. These nations have committed many detestable acts that the LORD hates, all in the name of their gods. They have even burned their sons and daughters as sacrifices to their gods. [32]Carefully obey all the commands I give you. Do not add to them or subtract from them.

CHAPTER 13

"Suppose there are prophets among you, or those who have dreams about the future, and they promise you signs or miracles, [2]and the predicted signs or miracles take place. If the prophets then say, 'Come, let us worship the gods of foreign nations,' [3]do not listen to them. The LORD your God is testing you to see if you love him with all your heart and soul. [4]Serve only the LORD your God and fear him alone. Obey his commands, listen to his voice, and cling to him. [5]The false prophets or dreamers who try to lead you astray must be put to death, for they encourage rebellion against the LORD your God, who brought you out of slavery in the land of Egypt. Since they try to keep you from following the LORD your God, you must execute them to remove the evil from among you.

⁶"Suppose your brother, son, daughter, beloved wife, or closest friend comes to you secretly and says, 'Let us go worship other gods'—gods that neither you nor your ancestors have known. ⁷They might suggest that you worship the gods of peoples who live nearby or who come from the ends of the earth. ⁸If they do this, do not give in or listen, and have no pity. Do not spare or protect them. ⁹You must put them to death! You must be the one to initiate the execution; then all the people must join in. ¹⁰Stone the guilty ones to death because they have tried to draw you away from the LORD your God, who rescued you from the land of Egypt, the place of slavery. ¹¹Then all Israel will hear about it and be afraid, and such wickedness will never again be done among you.

¹²"Suppose you hear in one of the towns the LORD your God is giving you ¹³that some worthless rabble among you have led their fellow citizens astray by encouraging them to worship foreign gods. ¹⁴In such cases, you must examine the facts carefully. If you find it is true and can prove that such a detestable act has occurred among you, ¹⁵you must attack that town and completely destroy* all its inhabitants, as well as all the livestock. ¹⁶Then you must pile all the plunder in the middle of the street and burn it. Put the entire town to the torch as a burnt offering to the LORD your God. That town must remain a ruin forever; it may never be rebuilt. ¹⁷Keep none of the plunder that has been set apart for destruction. Then the LORD will turn from his fierce anger and be merciful to you. He will have compassion on you and make you a great nation, just as he solemnly promised your ancestors.

¹⁸"The LORD your God will be merciful only if you obey him and keep all the commands I am giving you today, doing what is pleasing to him.

CHAPTER 14

"Since you are the people of the LORD your God, never cut yourselves or shave the hair above your foreheads for the sake of the dead. ²You have been set apart as holy to the LORD your God, and he has chosen you to be his own special treasure from all the nations of the earth.

³"You must not eat animals that are ceremonially unclean. ⁴These are the animals* you may eat: the ox, the sheep, the goat, ⁵the deer, the gazelle, the roebuck, the wild goat, the ibex, the antelope, and the mountain sheep.

⁶"Any animal that has split hooves and chews the cud may be eaten, ⁷but if the animal doesn't have both, it may not be eaten. So you may not eat the camel, the hare, or the rock badger.* They chew the cud but do not have split hooves. ⁸And the pig may not be eaten, for though it has split hooves, it does not chew the cud. All these animals are ceremonially unclean for you. You may not eat or even touch the dead bodies of such animals.

⁹"As for marine animals, you may eat whatever has both fins and scales. ¹⁰You may not, however, eat marine animals that do not have both fins and scales. They are ceremonially unclean for you.

¹¹"You may eat any bird that is ceremonially clean. ¹²These are the birds you may not eat: the eagle, the vulture, the osprey, ¹³the buzzard, kites of all kinds, ¹⁴ravens of all kinds, ¹⁵the ostrich, the nighthawk, the seagull, hawks of all kinds, ¹⁶the little owl, the great owl, the white owl, ¹⁷the pelican, the carrion vulture, the cormorant, ¹⁸the stork, herons of all kinds, the hoopoe, and the bat.

¹⁹"All flying insects are ceremonially unclean for you and may not be eaten. ²⁰But you may eat any winged creature that is ceremonially clean.

²¹"Do not eat anything that has died a natural death. You may give it to a foreigner living among you, or you may sell it to a foreigner. But do not eat it yourselves, for you are set apart as holy to the LORD your God.

"Do not boil a young goat in its mother's milk.

²²"You must set aside a tithe of your crops—one-tenth of all the crops you harvest each year. ²³Bring this tithe to the place the LORD your God chooses for his name to be honored, and eat it there in his presence. This applies to your tithes of grain, new wine, olive oil, and the firstborn males of your flocks and herds. The purpose of tithing is to teach you always to fear the LORD your God. ²⁴Now the place the LORD your

13:15 The Hebrew term used here refers to the complete consecration of things or people to the LORD, either by destroying them or by giving them as an offering; also in 13:17.   14:4 The identification of some of the animals and birds listed in this chapter is uncertain.   14:7 Or *coney,* or *hyrax.*

God chooses for his name to be honored might be a long way from your home. ²⁵If so, you may sell the tithe portion of your crops and herds and take the money to the place the LORD your God chooses. ²⁶When you arrive, use the money to buy anything you want—an ox, a sheep, some wine, or beer. Then feast there in the presence of the LORD your God and celebrate with your household. ²⁷And do not forget the Levites in your community, for they have no inheritance as you do.

²⁸"At the end of every third year bring the tithe of all your crops and store it in the nearest town. ²⁹Give it to the Levites, who have no inheritance among you, as well as to the foreigners living among you, the orphans, and the widows in your towns, so they can eat and be satisfied. Then the LORD your God will bless you in all your work.

CHAPTER 15

"At the end of every seventh year you must cancel your debts. ²This is how it must be done. Creditors must cancel the loans they have made to their fellow Israelites. They must not demand payment from their neighbors or relatives, for the LORD's time of release has arrived. ³This release from debt, however, applies only to your fellow Israelites—not to the foreigners living among you. ⁴There should be no poor among you, for the LORD your God will greatly bless you in the land he is giving you as a special possession. ⁵You will receive this blessing if you carefully obey the commands of the LORD your God that I am giving you today. ⁶The LORD your God will bless you as he has promised. You will lend money to many nations but will never need to borrow! You will rule many nations, but they will not rule over you!

⁷"But if there are any poor people in your towns when you arrive in the land the LORD your God is giving you, do not be hard-hearted or tightfisted toward them. ⁸Instead, be generous and lend them whatever they need. ⁹Do not be mean-spirited and refuse someone a loan because the year of release is close at hand. If you refuse to make the loan and the needy person cries out to the LORD, you will be considered guilty of sin. ¹⁰Give freely without begrudging it, and the LORD your God will

bless you in everything you do. ¹¹There will always be some among you who are poor. That is why I am commanding you to share your resources freely with the poor and with other Israelites in need.

¹²"If an Israelite man or woman voluntarily becomes your servant and serves you for six years, in the seventh year you must set that servant free.

¹³"When you release a male servant, do not send him away empty-handed. ¹⁴Give him a generous farewell gift from your flock, your threshing floor, and your winepress. Share with him some of the bounty with which the LORD your God has blessed you. ¹⁵Remember that you were slaves in the land of Egypt and the LORD your God redeemed you! That is why I am giving you this command. ¹⁶But suppose your servant says, 'I will not leave you,' because he loves you and your family, and he is well off with you. ¹⁷In that case, take an awl and push it through his earlobe into the door. After that, he will be your servant for life.

"You must do the same for your female servants.

¹⁸"Do not consider it a hardship when you release your servants. Remember that for six years they have given you the services worth double the wages of hired workers, and the LORD your God will bless you in all you do.

¹⁹"You must set aside for the LORD your God all the firstborn males from your flocks and herds. Do not use the firstborn of your herds to work your fields, and do not shear the firstborn of your flocks. ²⁰Instead, you and your family must eat these animals in the presence of the LORD your God each year at the place he chooses. ²¹But if this firstborn animal has any defect, such as being lame or blind, or if anything else is wrong with it, you must not sacrifice it to the LORD your God. ²²Instead, use it for food for your family at home. Anyone may eat it, whether ceremonially clean or unclean, just as anyone may eat a gazelle or deer. ²³But do not eat the blood. You must pour it out on the ground like water.

CHAPTER 16

"In honor of the LORD your God, always celebrate the Passover at the proper time in early spring,* for that was when the LORD your God brought you out of Egypt by

16:1 Hebrew *in the month of Abib.* This month of the Hebrew lunar calendar usually occurs in March and April.

night. ²Your Passover sacrifice may be from either the flock or the herd, and it must be sacrificed to the LORD your God at the place he chooses for his name to be honored. ³Eat it with bread made without yeast. For seven days eat only bread made without yeast, as you did when you escaped from Egypt in such a hurry. Eat this bread—the bread of suffering—so that you will remember the day you departed from Egypt as long as you live. ⁴Let no yeast be found in any house throughout your land for seven days. And do not let any of the meat of the Passover lamb remain until the next morning.

⁵"The Passover must not be eaten in the towns that the LORD your God is giving you. ⁶It must be offered at the place the LORD your God will choose for his name to be honored. Sacrifice it there as the sun goes down on the anniversary of your exodus from Egypt. ⁷Roast the lamb and eat it in the place the LORD your God chooses. Then go back to your tents the next morning. ⁸For the next six days you may not eat bread made with yeast. On the seventh day the people must assemble before the LORD your God, and no work may be done on that day.

⁹"Count off seven weeks from the beginning of your grain harvest. ¹⁰Then you must celebrate the Festival of Harvest* to honor the LORD your God. Bring him a freewill offering in proportion to the blessings you have received from him. ¹¹It is a time to celebrate before the LORD your God at the place he chooses for his name to be honored. Celebrate with your whole family, all your servants, the Levites from your towns, and the foreigners, orphans, and widows who live among you. ¹²Remember

16:10 Or *Festival of Weeks;* also in 16:16.

that you were slaves in Egypt, so be careful to obey all these laws.

¹³"Another celebration, the Festival of Shelters, must be observed for seven days at the end of the harvest season, after the grain has been threshed and the grapes have been pressed. ¹⁴This festival will be a happy time of rejoicing with your family, your servants, and with the Levites, foreigners, orphans, and widows from your towns. ¹⁵For seven days celebrate this festival to honor the LORD your God at the place he chooses, for it is the LORD your God who gives you bountiful harvests and blesses all your work. This festival will be a time of great joy for all.

¹⁶"Each year every man in Israel must celebrate these three festivals: the Festival of Unleavened Bread, the Festival of Harvest, and the Festival of Shelters. They must appear before the LORD your God at the place he chooses on each of these occasions, and they must bring a gift to the LORD. ¹⁷All must give as they are able, according to the blessings given to them by the LORD your God.

¹⁸"Appoint judges and officials for each of your tribes in all the towns the LORD your God is giving you. They will judge the people fairly throughout the land. ¹⁹You must never twist justice or show partiality. Never accept a bribe, for bribes blind the eyes of the wise and corrupt the decisions of the godly. ²⁰Let true justice prevail, so you may live and occupy the land that the LORD your God is giving you.

²¹"You must never set up an Asherah pole beside the altar of the LORD your God. ²²And never set up sacred pillars for worship, for the LORD your God hates them.

FEBRUARY 25 □ DAY 56
DEUTERONOMY 17–20
Civil Laws for Canaan

 OVERVIEW Because Israel was a civil society as well as a religious community, laws governing national affairs were as vital as religious statutes. In today's reading Moses delivers a set of regulations providing for justice and impartiality in the settling of a wide variety of situations that might arise in the life of the nation. Included are laws governing kings, priests, and prophets; peacetime and war; national and international affairs; the guilty and the innocent.

Chapter 17	Chapter 18	Chapter 19	Chapter 20
Choosing a King	Testing a Prophet	Providing a Refuge	Waging a War
National Affairs			International Affairs

YOUR DAILY WALK　"Now, I don't know if this is true or not, but did you hear about so-and-so . . . ?"

Envy is usually the mother of gossip.

If you've ever been the subject of such talk, you know the pain and destructiveness of hearsay. God hates rumor, hearsay, and gossip. That's why he designated a system of justice in Israel whereby no action could be taken against an accused person until two or three witnesses had testified to the truthfulness of the accusation (17:6-7). This law required a thorough investigation and gave the accused the right to be confronted by his accusers. The system was so effective that it became standard practice in the New Testament for handling church discipline (2 Corinthians 13:1). Jesus reaffirmed the Old Testament law when he said, "If another believer sins against you, go privately and point out the fault. . . . But if you are unsuccessful, take one or two others with you and go back again, so that everything you say may be confirmed by two or three witnesses" (Matthew 18:15-16).

God's principle is clear: You are responsible to investigate a charge of wrongdoing against a fellow Christian before acting on it or telling someone else about it. Find an electrical fuse and carry it with you today as a reminder to "short-circuit" rumors and hearsay before they cause a "power failure" in your spiritual life!

INSIGHT　The Motive behind the Monarch (17:14)
Although Israel's request for a king would seem harmless enough, 1 Samuel 8:4-9 reveals that this desire for a human monarch was indicative of Israel's refusal to retain God as her true King.

CHAPTER 17

"Never sacrifice a sick or defective ox or sheep to the LORD your God, for he detests such gifts.

²"Suppose a man or woman among you, in one of your towns that the LORD your God is giving you, has done evil in the sight of the LORD your God and has violated the covenant ³by serving other gods or by worshiping the sun, the moon, or any of the forces of heaven, which I have strictly forbidden. ⁴When you hear about it, investigate the matter thoroughly. If it is true that this detestable thing has been done in Israel, ⁵then that man or woman must be taken to the gates of the town and stoned to death. ⁶But never put a person to death on the testimony of only one witness. There must always be at least two or three witnesses. ⁷The witnesses must throw the first stones, and then all the people will join

in. In this way, you will purge all evil from among you.

⁸"Suppose a case arises in a local court that is too hard for you to decide—for instance, whether someone is guilty of murder or only of manslaughter, or a difficult lawsuit, or a case involving different kinds of assault. Take such cases to the place the LORD your God will choose, ⁹where the Levitical priests and the judge on duty will hear the case and decide what to do. ¹⁰The decision they make at the place the LORD chooses will always stand. You must do exactly what they say. ¹¹After they have interpreted the law and reached a verdict, the sentence they impose must be fully executed; do not modify it in any way. ¹²Anyone arrogant enough to reject the verdict of the judge or of the priest who represents the LORD your God must be put to death. Such evil must be purged from Israel.

¹³Then everyone will hear about it and be afraid to act so arrogantly.

¹⁴"You will soon arrive in the land the LORD your God is giving you, and you will conquer it and settle there. Then you may begin to think, 'We ought to have a king like the other nations around us.' ¹⁵If this happens, be sure that you select as king the man the LORD your God chooses. You must appoint a fellow Israelite, not a foreigner. ¹⁶The king must not build up a large stable of horses for himself, and he must never send his people to Egypt to buy horses there, for the LORD has told you, 'You must never return to Egypt.' ¹⁷The king must not take many wives for himself, because they will lead him away from the LORD. And he must not accumulate vast amounts of wealth in silver and gold for himself.

¹⁸"When he sits on the throne as king, he must copy these laws on a scroll for himself in the presence of the Levitical priests. ¹⁹He must always keep this copy of the law with him and read it daily as long as he lives. That way he will learn to fear the LORD his God by obeying all the terms of this law. ²⁰This regular reading will prevent him from becoming proud and acting as if he is above his fellow citizens. It will also prevent him from turning away from these commands in the smallest way. This will ensure that he and his descendants will reign for many generations in Israel.

CHAPTER 18

"Remember that the Levitical priests and the rest of the tribe of Levi will not be given an inheritance of land like the other tribes in Israel. Instead, the priests and Levites will eat from the offerings given to the LORD by fire, for that is their inheritance. ²They will have no inheritance of their own among the Israelites. The LORD himself is their inheritance, just as he promised them.

³"These are the parts the priests may claim as their share from the oxen and sheep that the people bring as offerings: the shoulder, the cheeks, and the stomach. ⁴You must also give to the priests the first share of the grain, the new wine, the olive oil, and the wool at shearing time. ⁵For the LORD your God chose the tribe of Levi out of all your tribes to minister in the LORD's name forever.

⁶"Any Levite who so desires may come from any town in Israel, from wherever he is living, to the place the LORD chooses. ⁷He may minister there in the name of the LORD his God, just like his fellow Levites who are serving the LORD there. ⁸He may eat his share of the sacrifices and offerings, even if he has a private source of income.

⁹"When you arrive in the land the LORD your God is giving you, be very careful not to imitate the detestable customs of the nations living there. ¹⁰For example, never sacrifice your son or daughter as a burnt offering.* And do not let your people practice fortune-telling or sorcery, or allow them to interpret omens, or engage in witchcraft, ¹¹or cast spells, or function as mediums or psychics, or call forth the spirits of the dead. ¹²Anyone who does these things is an object of horror and disgust to the LORD. It is because the other nations have done these things that the LORD your God will drive them out ahead of you. ¹³You must be blameless before the LORD your God. ¹⁴The people you are about to displace consult with sorcerers and fortune-tellers, but the LORD your God forbids you to do such things.

¹⁵"The LORD your God will raise up for you a prophet like me from among your fellow Israelites, and you must listen to that prophet. ¹⁶For this is what you yourselves requested of the LORD your God when you were assembled at Mount Sinai.* You begged that you might never again have to listen to the voice of the LORD your God or see this blazing fire for fear you would die.

¹⁷"Then the LORD said to me, 'Fine, I will do as they have requested. ¹⁸I will raise up a prophet like you from among their fellow Israelites. I will tell that prophet what to say, and he will tell the people everything I command him. ¹⁹I will personally deal with anyone who will not listen to the messages the prophet proclaims on my behalf. ²⁰But any prophet who claims to give a message from another god or who falsely claims to speak for me must die.' ²¹You may wonder, 'How will we know whether the prophecy is from the LORD or not?' ²²If the prophet predicts something in the LORD's name and it does not happen, the LORD did not give the message. That prophet has spoken on his own and need not be feared.

18:10 Or *never make your son or daughter pass through the fire.*   **18:16** Hebrew *Horeb,* another name for Sinai.

CHAPTER 19

"The LORD your God will soon destroy the nations whose land he is giving you, and you will displace them and settle in their towns and homes. ²Then you must set apart three cities of refuge in the land the LORD your God is giving you to occupy. ³Divide the land the LORD your God is giving you into three districts, with one of these cities in each district. Keep the roads to these cities in good repair so that anyone who has killed someone can flee there for safety.

⁴"If someone accidentally kills a neighbor without harboring any previous hatred, the slayer may flee to any of these cities and be safe. ⁵For example, suppose someone goes into the forest with a neighbor to cut wood. And suppose one of them swings an ax and the ax head flies off the handle, killing the other person. In such cases, the slayer could flee to one of the cities of refuge and be safe. ⁶If the distance to the nearest city of refuge was too far, an enraged avenger might be able to chase down and kill the person who caused the death. The slayer would die, even though there was no death sentence and the first death had been an accident. ⁷That is why I am commanding you to set aside three cities of refuge.

⁸"If the LORD your God enlarges your territory, as he solemnly promised your ancestors, and gives you all the land he promised them, ⁹you must designate three additional cities of refuge. (He will give you this land if you obey all the commands I have given you—if you always love the LORD your God and walk in his ways.) ¹⁰That way you will prevent the death of innocent people in the land the LORD your God is giving you as a special possession, and you will not be held responsible for murder.

¹¹"But suppose someone hates a neighbor and deliberately ambushes and murders that neighbor and then escapes to one of the cities of refuge. ¹²In that case, the leaders of the murderer's hometown must have the murderer brought back from the city of refuge and handed over to the dead person's avenger to be killed. ¹³Do not feel sorry for that murderer! Purge the guilt of murder from Israel so all may go well with you.

¹⁴"When you arrive in the land the LORD your God is giving you as a special possession, never steal someone's land by moving the boundary markers your ancestors set up to mark their property.

¹⁵"Never convict anyone of a crime on the testimony of just one witness. The facts of the case must be established by the testimony of two or three witnesses. ¹⁶If a malicious witness comes forward and accuses someone of a crime, ¹⁷then both the accuser and accused must appear before the priests and judges who are on duty before the LORD. ¹⁸They must be closely questioned, and if the accuser is found to be lying, ¹⁹the accuser will receive the punishment intended for the accused. In this way, you will cleanse such evil from among you. ²⁰Those who hear about it will be afraid to do such an evil thing again. ²¹You must never show pity! Your rule should be life for life, eye for eye, tooth for tooth, hand for hand, foot for foot.

CHAPTER 20

"When you go out to fight your enemies and you face horses and chariots and an army greater than your own, do not be afraid. The LORD your God, who brought you safely out of Egypt, is with you! ²Before you go into battle, the priest will come forward to speak with the troops. ³He will say, 'Listen to me, all you men of Israel! Do not be afraid as you go out to fight today! Do not lose heart or panic. ⁴For the LORD your God is going with you! He will fight for you against your enemies, and he will give you victory!'

⁵"Then the officers of the army will address the troops and say, 'Has anyone just built a new house but not yet dedicated it? If so, go home! You might be killed in the battle, and someone else would dedicate your house! ⁶Has anyone just planted a vineyard but not yet eaten any of its fruit? If so, go home! You might die in battle, and someone else would eat from it! ⁷Has anyone just become engaged? Well, go home and get married! You might die in the battle, and someone else would marry your fiancée.' ⁸Then the officers will also say, 'Is anyone terrified? If you are, go home before you frighten anyone else.' ⁹When the officers have finished saying this to their troops, they will announce the names of the unit commanders.

¹⁰"As you approach a town to attack it, first offer its people terms for peace. ¹¹If they accept your terms and open the gates to you, then all the people inside will serve you in forced labor. ¹²But if they refuse to make

peace and prepare to fight, you must attack the town. [13]When the LORD your God hands it over to you, kill every man in the town. [14]But you may keep for yourselves all the women, children, livestock, and other plunder. You may enjoy the spoils of your enemies that the LORD your God has given you. [15]But these instructions apply only to distant towns, not to the towns of nations nearby.

[16]"As for the towns of the nations the LORD your God is giving you as a special possession, destroy every living thing in them. [17]You must completely destroy* the Hittites, Amorites, Canaanites, Perizzites,

Hivites, and Jebusites, just as the LORD your God has commanded you. [18]This will keep the people of the land from teaching you their detestable customs in the worship of their gods, which would cause you to sin deeply against the LORD your God.

[19]"When you are besieging a town and the war drags on, do not destroy the trees. Eat the fruit, but do not cut down the trees. They are not enemies that need to be attacked! [20]But you may cut down trees that you know are not valuable for food. Use them to make the equipment you need to besiege the town until it falls.

20:17 The Hebrew term used here refers to the complete consecration of things or people to the LORD, either by destroying them or by giving them as an offering.

FEBRUARY 26 ☐ DAY 57
DEUTERONOMY 21–26
Societal Laws for Canaan

 OVERVIEW The concluding portion of Moses' second sermon contains a variety of wise guidelines for life in the Promised Land. Moses anticipates (and resolves) situations that could arise to disrupt the smooth functioning of Israel's society. In areas as diverse as marriage, capital punishment, purity, and tithing, Moses provides God's view of what should and should not be done.

Chapters 21–22	Chapters 23–25	Chapter 26
Domestic Relationships	Defending the Weak	Donations to God
Family Matters	National Matters	Tabernacle Matters

 YOUR DAILY WALK A man whose life was notoriously cluttered and confused asked that this epitaph be etched on his tombstone: "Organized at last!"

Many errors in life result from an inability to sit still long enough to read what God has written.

If you sometimes have trouble planning ahead for challenging situations, you may find Moses' example in today's reading very helpful. He greatly served Israel by giving the people clear directions in anticipation of a number of difficult situations. What can you learn from him?

Take the matter of potentially sinful situations. You have a child with disciplinary problems. You have a boss or fellow employee who irritates you. Why not plan right now the biblical, God-honoring response you will make the next time that situation arises? Make three columns on a sheet of paper, and write down (1) the anticipated situation; (2) your natural response; and (3) your prayerful, planned response. Keep that sheet handy and, with God's help, plan ahead to glorify him in the midst of a difficult situation!

INSIGHT High-Rise Living, Old Testament Style
God directed that all homes be built with restraining walls or fences around the roof (22:8). In a society where rooftops were used as recreation areas or extra bedrooms, this was wise to avoid accidental deaths!

CHAPTER 21

"Suppose someone is found murdered in a field in the land the LORD your God is giving you, and you don't know who committed the murder. ²In such cases, your leaders and judges must determine which town is nearest the body. ³Then the leaders of that town must select a young cow that has never been trained or yoked to a plow. ⁴They must lead it to a valley that is neither plowed nor planted with a stream running through it. There they must break the cow's neck. ⁵The Levitical priests must go there also, for the LORD your God has chosen them to minister before him and to pronounce blessings in the LORD's name. And they are to decide all lawsuits and punishments.

⁶"The leaders of the town nearest the body must wash their hands over the young cow whose neck was broken. ⁷Then they must say, 'Our hands did not shed this blood, nor did we see it happen. ⁸O LORD, forgive your people Israel whom you have redeemed. Do not charge your people Israel with the guilt of murdering an innocent person.' Then they will be absolved of the guilt of this person's blood. ⁹By following these instructions and doing what is right in the LORD's sight, you will cleanse the guilt of murder from your community.

¹⁰"Suppose you go to war against your enemies and the LORD your God hands them over to you and you take captives. ¹¹And suppose you see among the captives a beautiful woman, and you are attracted to her and want to marry her. ¹²If this happens, you may take her to your home, where she must shave her head, cut her fingernails, ¹³and change all her clothes. Then she must remain in your home for a full month, mourning for her father and mother. After that you may marry her. ¹⁴But if you marry her and then decide you do not like her, you must let her go free. You may not sell her or treat her as a slave, for you have humiliated her.

¹⁵"Suppose a man has two wives, but he loves one and not the other, and both have given him sons. And suppose the firstborn son is the son of the wife he does not love.

¹⁶When the man divides the inheritance, he may not give the larger inheritance to his younger son, the son of the wife he loves. ¹⁷He must give the customary double portion to his oldest son, who represents the strength of his father's manhood and who owns the rights of the firstborn son, even though he is the son of the wife his father does not love.

¹⁸"Suppose a man has a stubborn, rebellious son who will not obey his father or mother, even though they discipline him. ¹⁹In such cases, the father and mother must take the son before the leaders of the town. ²⁰They must declare: 'This son of ours is stubborn and rebellious and refuses to obey. He is a worthless drunkard.' ²¹Then all the men of the town must stone him to death. In this way, you will cleanse this evil from among you, and all Israel will hear about it and be afraid.

²²"If someone has committed a crime worthy of death and is executed and then hanged on a tree, ²³the body must never remain on the tree overnight. You must bury the body that same day, for anyone hanging on a tree is cursed of God. Do not defile the land the LORD your God is giving you as a special possession.

CHAPTER 22

"If you see your neighbor's ox or sheep wandering away, don't pretend not to see it. Take it back to its owner. ²If it does not belong to someone nearby or you don't know who the owner is, keep it until the owner comes looking for it; then return it. ³Do the same if you find your neighbor's donkey, clothing, or anything else your neighbor loses. Don't pretend you did not see it.

⁴"If you see your neighbor's ox or donkey lying on the road, do not look the other way. Go and help your neighbor get it to its feet!

⁵"A woman must not wear men's clothing, and a man must not wear women's clothing. The LORD your God detests people who do this.

⁶"If you find a bird's nest on the ground

or in a tree and there are young ones or eggs in it with the mother sitting in the nest, do not take the mother with the young. ⁷You may take the young, but let the mother go, so you may prosper and enjoy a long life.

⁸"Every new house you build must have a barrier around the edge of its flat rooftop. That way you will not bring the guilt of bloodshed on your household if someone falls from the roof.

⁹"Do not plant any other crop between the rows of your vineyard. If you do, you are forbidden to use either the grapes from the vineyard or the produce of the other crop.

¹⁰"Do not plow with an ox and a donkey harnessed together.

¹¹"Do not wear clothing made of wool and linen woven together.

¹²"You must put tassels on the four corners of your cloaks.

¹³"Suppose a man marries a woman and, after sleeping with her, changes his mind about her ¹⁴and falsely accuses her of having slept with another man. He might say, 'I discovered she was not a virgin when I married her.' ¹⁵If the man does this, the woman's father and mother must bring the proof of her virginity to the leaders of the town. ¹⁶Her father must tell them, 'I gave my daughter to this man to be his wife, and now he has turned against her. ¹⁷He has accused her of shameful things, claiming that she was not a virgin when he married her. But here is the proof of my daughter's virginity.' Then they must spread the cloth before the judges. ¹⁸The judges must then punish the man. ¹⁹They will fine him one hundred pieces of silver,* for he falsely accused a virgin of Israel. The payment will be made to the woman's father. The woman will then remain the man's wife, and he may never divorce her.

²⁰"But suppose the man's accusations are true, and her virginity could not be proved. ²¹In such cases, the judges must take the girl to the door of her father's home, and the men of the town will stone her to death. She has committed a disgraceful crime in Israel by being promiscuous while living in her parents' home. Such evil must be cleansed from among you.

²²"If a man is discovered committing adultery, both he and the other man's wife must be killed. In this way, the evil will be cleansed from Israel.

²³"Suppose a man meets a young woman, a virgin who is engaged to be married, and he has sexual intercourse with her. If this happens within a town, ²⁴you must take both of them to the gates of the town and stone them to death. The woman is guilty because she did not scream for help. The man must die because he violated another man's wife. In this way, you will cleanse the land of evil.

²⁵"But if the man meets the engaged woman out in the country, and he rapes her, then only the man should die. ²⁶Do nothing to the young woman; she has committed no crime worthy of death. This case is similar to that of someone who attacks and murders a neighbor. ²⁷Since the man raped her out in the country, it must be assumed that she screamed, but there was no one to rescue her.

²⁸"If a man is caught in the act of raping a young woman who is not engaged, ²⁹he must pay fifty pieces of silver* to her father. Then he must marry the young woman because he violated her, and he will never be allowed to divorce her.

³⁰"A man must not have intercourse with his father's wife, for this would violate his father.

CHAPTER 23

"If a man's testicles are crushed or his penis is cut off, he may not be included in the assembly of the LORD.

²"Those of illegitimate birth and their descendants for ten generations may not be included in the assembly of the LORD.

³"No Ammonites or Moabites, or any of their descendants for ten generations, may be included in the assembly of the LORD. ⁴These nations did not welcome you with food and water when you came out of Egypt. Instead, they tried to hire Balaam son of Beor from Pethor in Aramnaharaim* to curse you. ⁵(But the LORD your God would not listen to Balaam. He turned the intended curse into a blessing because the LORD your God loves you.) ⁶You must never, as long as you live, try to help the Ammonites or the Moabites in any way.

22:19 Hebrew *100 shekels of silver,* about 2.5 pounds or 1.1 kilograms in weight.   22:29 Hebrew *50 shekels of silver,* about 1.25 pounds or 570 grams in weight.   23:4 *Aram-naharaim* means "Aram of the two rivers," thought to have been located between the Euphrates and Balih Rivers in northwestern Mesopotamia.

[7]"Do not detest the Edomites or the Egyptians, because the Edomites are your relatives, and you lived as foreigners among the Egyptians. [8]The third generation of Egyptians who came with you from Egypt may enter the assembly of the LORD.

[9]"When you go to war against your enemies, stay away from everything impure. [10]"Any man who becomes ceremonially defiled because of a nocturnal emission must leave the camp and stay away all day. [11]Toward evening he must bathe himself, and at sunset he may return to the camp.

[12]"Mark off an area outside the camp for a latrine. [13]Each of you must have a spade as part of your equipment. Whenever you relieve yourself, you must dig a hole with the spade and cover the excrement. [14]The camp must be holy, for the LORD your God moves around in your camp to protect you and to defeat your enemies. He must not see any shameful thing among you, or he might turn away from you.

[15]"If slaves should escape from their masters and take refuge with you, do not force them to return. [16]Let them live among you in whatever town they choose, and do not oppress them.

[17]"No Israelite man or woman may ever become a temple prostitute. [18]Do not bring to the house of the LORD your God any offering from the earnings of a prostitute, whether a man or a woman, for both are detestable to the LORD your God.

[19]"Do not charge interest on the loans you make to a fellow Israelite, whether it is money, food, or anything else that may be loaned with interest. [20]You may charge interest to foreigners, but not to Israelites, so the LORD your God may bless you in everything you do in the land you are about to enter and occupy.

[21]"When you make a vow to the LORD your God, be prompt in doing whatever you promised him. For the LORD your God demands that you promptly fulfill all your vows. If you don't, you will be guilty of sin. [22]However, it is not a sin to refrain from making a vow. [23]But once you have voluntarily made a vow, be careful to do as you have said, for you have made a vow to the LORD your God.

[24]"You may eat your fill of grapes from your neighbor's vineyard, but do not take any away in a basket. [25]And you may pluck a few heads of your neighbor's grain by hand, but you may not harvest it with a sickle.

CHAPTER 24

"Suppose a man marries a woman but later discovers something about her that is shameful. So he writes her a letter of divorce, gives it to her, and sends her away. [2]If she then leaves and marries another man [3]and the second husband also divorces her or dies, [4]the former husband may not marry her again, for she has been defiled. That would be detestable to the LORD. You must not bring guilt upon the land the LORD your God is giving you as a special possession.

[5]"A newly married man must not be drafted into the army or given any other special responsibilities. He must be free to be at home for one year, bringing happiness to the wife he has married.

[6]"It is wrong to take a pair of millstones, or even just the upper millstone, as a pledge, for the owner uses it to make a living.

[7]"If anyone kidnaps a fellow Israelite and treats him as a slave or sells him, the kidnapper must die. You must cleanse the evil from among you.

[8]"Watch all contagious skin diseases* carefully and follow the instructions of the Levitical priests; obey the commands I have given them. [9]Remember what the LORD your God did to Miriam as you were coming from Egypt.

[10]"If you lend anything to your neighbor, do not enter your neighbor's house to claim the security. [11]Stand outside and the owner will bring it out to you. [12]If your neighbor is poor and has only a cloak to give as security, do not keep the cloak overnight. [13]Return the cloak to its owner by sunset so your neighbor can sleep in it and bless you. And the LORD your God will count it as a righteous act.

[14]"Never take advantage of poor laborers, whether fellow Israelites or foreigners living in your towns. [15]Pay them their wages each day before sunset because they are poor and are counting on it. Otherwise they might cry out to the LORD against you, and it would be counted against you as sin.

[16]"Parents must not be put to death for the sins of their children, nor the children

---

24:8 Traditonally rendered *leprosy*. The Hebrew word used here can describe various skin diseases.

for the sins of their parents. Those worthy of death must be executed for their own crimes.

[17]"True justice must be given to foreigners living among you and to orphans, and you must never accept a widow's garment in pledge of her debt. [18]Always remember that you were slaves in Egypt and that the LORD your God redeemed you. That is why I have given you this command.

[19]"When you are harvesting your crops and forget to bring in a bundle of grain from your field, don't go back to get it. Leave it for the foreigners, orphans, and widows. Then the LORD your God will bless you in all you do. [20]When you beat the olives from your olive trees, don't go over the boughs twice. Leave some of the olives for the foreigners, orphans, and widows. [21]This also applies to the grapes in your vineyard. Do not glean the vines after they are picked, but leave any remaining grapes for the foreigners, orphans, and widows. [22]Remember that you were slaves in the land of Egypt. That is why I am giving you this command.

CHAPTER 25

"Suppose two people take a dispute to court, and the judges declare that one is right and the other is wrong. [2]If the person in the wrong is sentenced to be flogged, the judge will command him to lie down and be beaten in his presence with the number of lashes appropriate to the crime. [3]No more than forty lashes may ever be given; more than forty lashes would publicly humiliate your neighbor.

[4]"Do not keep an ox from eating as it treads out the grain.

[5]"If two brothers are living together on the same property and one of them dies without a son, his widow must not marry outside the family. Instead, her husband's brother must marry her and fulfill the duties of a brother-in-law. [6]The first son she bears to him will be counted as the son of the dead brother, so that his name will not be forgotten in Israel. [7]But if the dead man's brother refuses to marry the widow, she must go to the town gate and say to the leaders there, 'My husband's brother refuses to preserve his brother's name in Israel—he refuses to marry me.' [8]The leaders of the town will then summon him and try to reason with him. If he still insists that he

doesn't want to marry her, [9]the widow must walk over to him in the presence of the leaders, pull his sandal from his foot, and spit in his face. She will then say, 'This is what happens to a man who refuses to raise up a son for his brother.' [10]Ever afterward his family will be referred to as 'the family of the man whose sandal was pulled off'!

[11]"If two Israelite men are fighting and the wife of one tries to rescue her husband by grabbing the testicles of the other man, [12]her hand must be cut off without pity.

[13]"You must use accurate scales when you weigh out merchandise, [14]and you must use full and honest measures. [15]Yes, use honest weights and measures, so that you will enjoy a long life in the land the LORD your God is giving you. [16]Those who cheat with dishonest weights and measures are detestable to the LORD your God.

[17]"Never forget what the Amalekites did to you as you came from Egypt. [18]They attacked you when you were exhausted and weary, and they struck down those who were lagging behind. They had no fear of God. [19]Therefore, when the LORD your God has given you rest from all your enemies in the land he is giving you as a special possession, you are to destroy the Amalekites and erase their memory from under heaven. Never forget this!

CHAPTER 26

"When you arrive in the land the LORD your God is giving you as a special possession and you have conquered it and settled there, [2]put some of the first produce from each harvest into a basket and bring it to the place the LORD your God chooses for his name to be honored. [3]Go to the priest in charge at that time and say to him, 'With this gift I acknowledge that the LORD your God has brought me into the land he swore to give our ancestors.' [4]The priest will then take the basket from your hand and set it before the altar of the LORD your God. [5]You must then say in the presence of the LORD your God, 'My ancestor Jacob was a wandering Aramean who went to live in Egypt. His family was few in number, but in Egypt they became a mighty and numerous nation. [6]When the Egyptians mistreated and humiliated us by making us their slaves, [7]we cried out to the LORD, the God of our ancestors.

He heard us and saw our hardship, toil, and oppression. [8]So the LORD brought us out of Egypt with amazing power, overwhelming terror, and miraculous signs and wonders. [9]He brought us to this place and gave us this land flowing with milk and honey! [10]And now, O LORD, I have brought you a token of the first crops you have given me from the ground.' Then place the produce before the LORD your God and worship him. [11]Afterward go and celebrate because of all the good things the LORD your God has given to you and your household. Remember to include the Levites and the foreigners living among you in the celebration.

[12]"Every third year you must offer a special tithe of your crops. You must give these tithes to the Levites, foreigners, orphans, and widows so that they will have enough to eat in your towns. [13]Then you must declare in the presence of the LORD your God, 'I have taken the sacred gift from my house and have given it to the Levites, foreigners, orphans, and widows, just as you commanded me. I have not violated or forgotten any of your commands. [14]I have not eaten any of it while in mourning; I have not touched it while I was ceremonially unclean; and I have not offered any of it to the dead. I have obeyed the LORD my God and have done everything you commanded me. [15]Look down from your holy dwelling place in heaven and bless your people Israel and the land you have given us—a land flowing with milk and honey—just as you solemnly promised our ancestors.'

[16]"Today the LORD your God has commanded you to obey all these laws and regulations. You must commit yourself to them without reservation. [17]You have declared today that the LORD is your God. You have promised to obey his laws, commands, and regulations by walking in his ways and doing everything he tells you. [18]The LORD has declared today that you are his people, his own special treasure, just as he promised, and that you must obey all his commands. [19]And if you do, he will make you greater than any other nation. Then you will receive praise, honor, and renown. You will be a nation that is holy to the LORD your God, just as he promised."

FEBRUARY 27 ☐ DAY 58
DEUTERONOMY 27–30
Commitment to the Covenant

 OVERVIEW In today's reading Moses concludes his presentation of the new law for the new generation. First, he sets forth the consequences of obeying and of violating the covenant. Complete surrender to God's will as revealed in the laws will bring blessing upon the nation, the family, and the individual. Crops will flourish, cattle will multiply, and daily needs will be met. On the other hand, disobedience will result in disaster: pestilence, plagues, and ultimately removal from the land. The responsibility is left squarely on the shoulders of the people. They are free to choose the path they will take, but they are not free to escape the consequences of their fateful choice.

Chapter 27	Chapter 28	Chapter 29	Chapter 30
Curses for Disobedience	Blessings for Obedience	The Covenant's Demands	A Life-or-Death Decision
The Covenant Concluded		The Covenant Ratified	

 YOUR DAILY WALK Do you ever find the will of God elusive or unclear? You have an important decision to make, and you want to do the right thing. You want to honor God. But which direction should

Perfect you turn? First, turn to the word of God. God has something to say to
conformity to you, and it's written in the Bible. All that remains is for you to read and
the will of God obey it!
is the sole   God is not in the business of hiding his will or making it difficult to
sovereign and understand. To the Israelites Moses wrote, "This command I am giving
perfect liberty. you today is not too difficult for you to understand or perform. It is not
up in heaven, so distant that you must ask, 'Who will go to heaven and
bring it down so we can hear and obey it?'" (30:11-12). God's will for
you is not a heavenly fog; it is a down-to-earth reality you can understand.

Read Deuteronomy 30:11-20 twice. Then list three things that
characterize God's will for you today. Don't worry about the things in
the Bible you don't understand; worry about the things you do! And
"do whatever he tells you" (John 2:5).

 INSIGHT The Day the Slave Markets Were Glutted
The horrible curse of 28:68 literally came true! After the fall of Jerusalem
in A.D. 70, the slave markets of Egypt became so glutted with captive
Israelites that there were not enough buyers for them all. God always
keeps his promises—good and bad.

CHAPTER 27

Then Moses and the leaders of Israel charged the people as follows: "Keep all these commands that I am giving you to-day. ²When you cross the Jordan River and enter the land the LORD your God is giving you, set up some large stones and coat them with plaster. ³Then write all the terms of this law on them. I repeat, you will soon cross the river to enter the land the LORD your God is giving you, a land flowing with milk and honey, just as the LORD, the God of your ancestors, prom-ised you. ⁴When you cross the Jordan, set up these stones at Mount Ebal and coat them with plaster, as I am commanding you today. ⁵Then build an altar there to the LORD your God, using natural stones. ⁶Do not shape the stones with an iron tool. On the altar you must offer burnt offer-ings to the LORD your God. ⁷Sacrifice peace offerings on it also, and feast there with great joy before the LORD your God. ⁸On the stones coated with plaster, you must clearly write all the terms of this law."

⁹Then Moses and the Levitical priests addressed all Israel as follows: "O Israel, be quiet and listen! Today you have become the people of the LORD your God. ¹⁰So obey the LORD your God by keeping all these commands and laws that I am giving you today."

¹¹That same day Moses gave this charge to the people: ¹²"When you cross the Jor-dan River, the tribes of Simeon, Levi,

Judah, Issachar, Joseph, and Benjamin must stand on Mount Gerizim to proclaim a blessing over the people. ¹³And the tribes of Reuben, Gad, Asher, Zebulun, Dan, and Naphtali must stand on Mount Ebal to pro-claim a curse. ¹⁴Then the Levites must shout to all the people of Israel:

¹⁵'Cursed is anyone who carves or
casts idols and secretly sets them up.
These idols, the work of craftsmen,
are detestable to the LORD.'
And all the people will reply, 'Amen.'

¹⁶'Cursed is anyone who despises
father or mother.'
And all the people will reply, 'Amen.'

¹⁷'Cursed is anyone who steals property
from a neighbor by moving a boundary
marker.'
And all the people will reply, 'Amen.'

¹⁸'Cursed is anyone who leads a blind
person astray on the road.'
And all the people will reply, 'Amen.'

¹⁹'Cursed is anyone who is unjust to
foreigners, orphans, and widows.'
And all the people will reply, 'Amen.'

²⁰'Cursed is anyone who has sexual
intercourse with his father's wife, for
he has violated his father.'
And all the people will reply, 'Amen.'

²¹'Cursed is anyone who has sexual
intercourse with an animal.'
And all the people will reply, 'Amen.'

²²'Cursed is anyone who has sexual intercourse with his sister, whether she is the daughter of his father or his mother.'

And all the people will reply, 'Amen.'

²³'Cursed is anyone who has sexual intercourse with his mother-in-law.'

And all the people will reply, 'Amen.'

²⁴'Cursed is anyone who kills another person in secret.'

And all the people will reply, 'Amen.'

²⁵'Cursed is anyone who accepts payment to kill an innocent person.'

And all the people will reply, 'Amen.'

²⁶'Cursed is anyone who does not affirm the terms of this law by obeying them.'

And all the people will reply, 'Amen.'

CHAPTER 28

"If you fully obey the LORD your God by keeping all the commands I am giving you today, the LORD your God will exalt you above all the nations of the world. ²You will experience all these blessings if you obey the LORD your God:

³ You will be blessed in your towns and in the country.
⁴ You will be blessed with many children and productive fields.
You will be blessed with fertile herds and flocks.
⁵ You will be blessed with baskets overflowing with fruit, and with kneading bowls filled with bread.
⁶ You will be blessed wherever you go, both in coming and in going.

⁷"The LORD will conquer your enemies when they attack you. They will attack you from one direction, but they will scatter from you in seven!

⁸"The LORD will bless everything you do and will fill your storehouses with grain. The LORD your God will bless you in the land he is giving you.

⁹"If you obey the commands of the LORD your God and walk in his ways, the LORD will establish you as his holy people as he solemnly promised to do. ¹⁰Then all the nations of the world will see that you are a people claimed by the LORD, and they will stand in awe of you.

¹¹"The LORD will give you an abundance of good things in the land he swore to give your ancestors—many children, numerous livestock, and abundant crops. ¹²The LORD will send rain at the proper time from his rich treasury in the heavens to bless all the work you do. You will lend to many nations, but you will never need to borrow from them. ¹³If you listen to these commands of the LORD your God and carefully obey them, the LORD will make you the head and not the tail, and you will always have the upper hand. ¹⁴You must not turn away from any of the commands I am giving you today to follow after other gods and worship them.

¹⁵"But if you refuse to listen to the LORD your God and do not obey all the commands and laws I am giving you today, all these curses will come and overwhelm you:

¹⁶ You will be cursed in your towns and in the country.
¹⁷ You will be cursed with baskets empty of fruit, and with kneading bowls empty of bread.
¹⁸ You will be cursed with few children and barren fields.
You will be cursed with infertile herds and flocks.
¹⁹ You will be cursed wherever you go, both in coming and in going.

²⁰"The LORD himself will send against you curses, confusion, and disillusionment in everything you do, until at last you are completely destroyed for doing evil and forsaking me. ²¹The LORD will send diseases among you until none of you are left in the land you are about to enter and occupy. ²²The LORD will strike you with wasting disease, fever, and inflammation, with scorching heat and drought, and with blight and mildew. These devastations will pursue you until you die. ²³The skies above will be as unyielding as bronze, and the earth beneath will be as hard as iron. ²⁴The LORD will turn your rain into sand and dust, and it will pour down from the sky until you are destroyed.

²⁵"The LORD will cause you to be defeated by your enemies. You will attack your enemies from one direction, but you will scatter from them in seven! You will be an object of horror to all the kingdoms of the earth. ²⁶Your dead bodies will be food for the birds and wild animals, and no one will be there to chase them away.

27"The LORD will afflict you with the boils of Egypt and with tumors, scurvy, and the itch, from which you cannot be cured. 28The LORD will strike you with madness, blindness, and panic. 29You will grope around in broad daylight, just like a blind person groping in the darkness, and you will not succeed at anything you do. You will be oppressed and robbed continually, and no one will come to save you.

30"You will be engaged to a woman, but another man will ravish her. You will build a house, but someone else will live in it. You will plant a vineyard, but you will never enjoy its fruit. 31Your ox will be butchered before your eyes, but you won't get a single bite of the meat. Your donkey will be driven away, never to be returned. Your sheep will be given to your enemies, and no one will be there to help you. 32You will watch as your sons and daughters are taken away as slaves. Your heart will break as you long for them, but nothing you do will help. 33A foreign nation you have never heard about will eat the crops you worked so hard to grow. You will suffer under constant oppression and harsh treatment. 34You will go mad because of all the tragedy around you. 35The LORD will cover you from head to foot with incurable boils.

36"The LORD will exile you and the king you crowned to a nation unknown to you and your ancestors. Then in exile you will worship gods of wood and stone! 37You will become an object of horror, a proverb and a mockery among all the nations to which the LORD sends you.

38"You will plant much but harvest little, for locusts will eat your crops. 39You will plant vineyards and care for them, but you will not drink the wine or eat the grapes, for worms will destroy the vines. 40You will grow olive trees throughout your land, but you will never use the olive oil, for the trees will drop the fruit before it is ripe. 41You will have sons and daughters, but you will not keep them, for they will be led away into captivity. 42Swarms of insects will destroy your trees and crops. 43The foreigners living among you will become stronger and stronger, while you become weaker and weaker. 44They will lend money to you, not you to them. They will be the head, and you will be the tail!

45"If you refuse to listen to the LORD your God and to obey the commands and laws he has given you, all these curses will pursue and overtake you until you are destroyed. 46These horrors will serve as a sign and warning among you and your descendants forever. 47Because you have not served the LORD your God with joy and enthusiasm for the abundant benefits you have received, 48you will serve your enemies whom the LORD will send against you. You will be left hungry, thirsty, naked, and lacking in everything. They will oppress you harshly until you are destroyed.

49"The LORD will bring a distant nation against you from the end of the earth, and it will swoop down on you like an eagle. It is a nation whose language you do not understand, 50a fierce and heartless nation that shows no respect for the old and no pity for the young. 51Its armies will devour your livestock and crops, and you will starve to death. They will leave you no grain, new wine, olive oil, calves, or lambs, bringing about your destruction. 52They will lay siege to your cities until all the fortified walls in your land—the walls you trusted to protect you—are knocked down. They will attack all the towns in the land the LORD your God has given you. 53The siege will be so severe that you will eat the flesh of your own sons and daughters, whom the LORD your God has given you. 54The most tenderhearted man among you will have no compassion for his own brother, his beloved wife, and his surviving children. 55He will refuse to give them a share of the flesh he is devouring—the flesh of one of his own children—because he has nothing else to eat during the siege that your enemy will inflict on all your towns. 56The most tender and delicate woman among you—so delicate she would not so much as touch her feet to the ground—will be cruel to the husband she loves and to her own son or daughter. 57She will hide from them the afterbirth and the new baby she has borne, so that she herself can secretly eat them. She will have nothing else to eat during the siege and terrible distress that your enemy will inflict on all your towns.

58"If you refuse to obey all the terms of this law that are written in this book, and if you do not fear the glorious and awesome name of the LORD your God, 59then the LORD will overwhelm both you and your children with indescribable plagues. These plagues will be intense and without relief, making you miserable and unbearably sick. [60]He will bring against you all the diseases of Egypt that you feared so much, and they will claim you. [61]The LORD will bring against you every sickness and plague there is, even those not mentioned in this Book of the Law, until you are destroyed. [62]Though you are as numerous as the stars in the sky, few of you will be left because you would not listen to the LORD your God.

[63]"Just as the LORD has found great pleasure in helping you to prosper and multiply, the LORD will find pleasure in destroying you, until you disappear from the land you are about to enter and occupy. [64]For the LORD will scatter you among all the nations from one end of the earth to the other. There you will worship foreign gods that neither you nor your ancestors have known, gods made of wood and stone! [65]There among those nations you will find no place of security and rest. And the LORD will cause your heart to tremble, your eyesight to fail, and your soul to despair. [66]Your lives will hang in doubt. You will live night and day in fear, with no reason to believe that you will see the morning light. [67]In the morning you will say, 'If only it were night!' And in the evening you will say, 'If only it were morning!' You will say this because of your terror at the awesome horrors you see around you. [68]Then the LORD will send you back to Egypt in ships, a journey I promised you would never again make. There you will offer to sell yourselves to your enemies as slaves, but no one will want to buy you."

CHAPTER 29
These are the terms of the covenant the LORD commanded Moses to make with the Israelites while they were in the land of Moab, in addition to the covenant he had made with them at Mount Sinai.*

[2]Moses summoned all the Israelites and said to them, "You have seen with your own eyes everything the LORD did in Egypt to Pharaoh and all his servants and his whole country—[3]all the great tests of strength, the miraculous signs, and the amazing wonders. [4]But to this day the LORD has not given you minds that understand, nor eyes that see, nor ears that hear! [5]For forty years I led you through the wilderness, yet your clothes and sandals did

not wear out. [6]You had no bread or wine or other strong drink, but he gave you food so you would know that he is the LORD your God. [7]When we came here, King Sihon of Heshbon and King Og of Bashan came out to fight against us, but we defeated them. [8]We took their land and gave it to the tribes of Reuben and Gad and to the half-tribe of Manasseh as their inheritance.

[9]"Therefore, obey the terms of this covenant so that you will prosper in everything you do. [10]All of you—your tribal leaders, your judges, your officers, all the men of Israel—are standing today before the LORD your God. [11]With you are your little ones, your wives, and the foreigners living among you who chop your wood and carry your water. [12]You are standing here today to enter into a covenant with the LORD your God. The LORD is making this covenant with you today, and he has sealed it with an oath. [13]He wants to confirm you today as his people and to confirm that he is your God, just as he promised you, and as he swore to your ancestors Abraham, Isaac, and Jacob. [14]But you are not the only ones with whom the LORD is making this covenant with its obligations. [15]The LORD your God is making this covenant with you who stand in his presence today and also with all future generations of Israel.

[16]"Surely you remember how we lived in the land of Egypt and how we traveled through the lands of enemy nations as we left. [17]You have seen their detestable idols made of wood, stone, silver, and gold. [18]The LORD made this covenant with you so that no man, woman, family, or tribe among you would turn away from the LORD our God to worship these gods of other nations, and so that no root among you would bear bitter and poisonous fruit. [19]Let none of those who hear the warnings of this curse consider themselves immune, thinking, 'I am safe, even though I am walking in my own stubborn way.' This would lead to utter ruin! [20]The LORD will not pardon such people. His anger and jealousy will burn against them. All the curses written in this book will come down on them, and the LORD will erase their names from under heaven. [21]The LORD will separate them from all the tribes of Israel, to pour out on them all the covenant curses recorded in this Book of the Law.

29:1 Hebrew *Horeb*, another name for Sinai.

22"Then the generations to come, both your own descendants and the foreigners who come from distant lands, will see the devastation of the land and the diseases the LORD will send against it. 23They will find its soil turned into sulfur and salt, with nothing planted and nothing growing, not even a blade of grass. It will be just like Sodom and Gomorrah, Admah and Zeboiim, which the LORD destroyed in his anger. 24The surrounding nations will ask, 'Why has the LORD done this to his land? Why was he so angry?'

25"And they will be told, 'This happened because the people of the land broke the covenant they made with the LORD, the God of their ancestors, when he brought them out of the land of Egypt. 26They turned to serve and worship other gods that were foreign to them, gods that the LORD had not designated for them. 27That is why the LORD's anger burned against this land, bringing down on it all the curses recorded in this book. 28In great anger and fury the LORD uprooted his people from their land and exiled them to another land, where they still live today!'

29"There are secret things that belong to the LORD our God, but the revealed things belong to us and our descendants forever, so that we may obey these words of the law.

CHAPTER 30

"Suppose all these things happen to you—the blessings and the curses I have listed—and you meditate on them as you are living among the nations to which the LORD your God has exiled you. 2If at that time you return to the LORD your God, and you and your children begin wholeheartedly to obey all the commands I have given you today, 3then the LORD your God will restore your fortunes. He will have mercy on you and gather you back from all the nations where he has scattered you. 4Though you are at the ends of the earth, the LORD your God will go and find you and bring you back again. 5He will return you to the land that belonged to your ancestors, and you will possess that land again. He will make you even more prosperous and numerous than your ancestors!

6"The LORD your God will cleanse your heart and the hearts of all your descendants so that you will love him with all your heart and soul, and so you may live! 7The LORD your God will inflict all these curses on your enemies and persecutors. 8Then you will again obey the LORD and keep all the commands I am giving you today. 9The LORD your God will make you successful in everything you do. He will give you many children and numerous livestock, and your fields will produce abundant harvests, for the LORD will delight in being good to you as he was to your ancestors. 10The LORD your God will delight in you if you obey his voice and keep the commands and laws written in this Book of the Law, and if you turn to the LORD your God with all your heart and soul.

11"This command I am giving you today is not too difficult for you to understand or perform. 12It is not up in heaven, so distant that you must ask, 'Who will go to heaven and bring it down so we can hear and obey it?' 13It is not beyond the sea, so far away that you must ask, 'Who will cross the sea to bring it to us so we can hear and obey it?' 14The message is very close at hand; it is on your lips and in your heart so that you can obey it.

15"Now listen! Today I am giving you a choice between prosperity and disaster, between life and death. 16I have commanded you today to love the LORD your God and to keep his commands, laws, and regulations by walking in his ways. If you do this, you will live and become a great nation, and the LORD your God will bless you and the land you are about to enter and occupy. 17But if your heart turns away and you refuse to listen, and if you are drawn away to serve and worship other gods, 18then I warn you now that you will certainly be destroyed. You will not live a long, good life in the land you are crossing the Jordan to occupy.

19"Today I have given you the choice between life and death, between blessings and curses. I call on heaven and earth to witness the choice you make. Oh, that you would choose life, that you and your descendants might live! 20Choose to love the LORD your God and to obey him and commit yourself to him, for he is your life. Then you will live long in the land the LORD swore to give your ancestors Abraham, Isaac, and Jacob."

FEBRUARY 28 ☐ DAY 59
DEUTERONOMY 31–34
Farewell and Death of Moses

OVERVIEW Moses' long and illustrious life is drawing to a close. During his final days as Israel's leader, he delivers some significant words of counsel to the priests, Levites, his successor, Joshua, and the entire nation. He has learned much during his 120-year walk with God, and his final words of warning and encouragement deserve careful attention. To make his last utterances easily remembered, Moses writes them down in the form of a song, which he teaches to the people. After blessing each of the twelve tribes, Moses climbs Mount Nebo for a final look at the Promised Land, and there he dies—still in the prime of life!

Chapter 31	Chapter 32	Chapter 33	Chapter 34
Moses' Successor	Moses' Song	Moses' Farewell	Moses' Funeral
The Final Days of Moses			

No one is so old as the one who has outlived enthusiasm.

YOUR DAILY WALK Do you have trouble identifying with a great Old Testament saint such as Moses? After all, in many ways Moses was unique in history. He stood in the very presence of God, performed miracles before Pharaoh, parted the Red Sea, turned rocks into drinking fountains, and died at the age of 120, still full of youthful vigor.

And yet the Bible paints Moses in very human tones. He spent the first two-thirds of his life wrestling with his calling before he finally yielded to God's will. Being a man of action, he found it frustrating to administer the affairs of a large, rebellious nation. Finally, in a moment of impatience and anger, he disobeyed God's direct instructions, thus denying himself the opportunity to set foot in the Promised Land. And yet, God's commentary on Moses is this: "There has never been another prophet like Moses, whom the LORD knew face to face" (34:10).

Let the words of Deuteronomy 29:29 provide a fresh motivation for you to *know* and *do* God's will next month as you follow in the footsteps of Moses!

INSIGHT The Promised Land at Last
Sadly, Moses, deliverer of his people, never set foot in the Promised Land. Or did he? Though he climbs Mount Nebo for one last faraway look at Canaan before his death, he is seen *inside* the Promised Land years later on the mountain where Jesus was transfigured (Matthew 17:3; Luke 9:30-31).

CHAPTER 31
When Moses had finished saying* these things to all the people of Israel, ²he said, "I am now 120 years old and am no longer able to lead you. The LORD has told me that I will not cross the Jordan River. ³But the LORD your God himself will cross over ahead of you. He will destroy the nations living there, and you will take possession of their land. Joshua is your new leader, and he will go with you, just as the LORD

promised. ⁴The LORD will destroy the nations living in the land, just as he destroyed Sihon and Og, the kings of the Amorites. ⁵The LORD will hand over to you the people who live there, and you will deal with them as I have commanded you. ⁶Be strong and courageous! Do not be afraid of them! The LORD your God will go ahead of you. He will neither fail you nor forsake you."

⁷Then Moses called for Joshua, and as all Israel watched he said to him, "Be strong

31:1 As in Dead Sea Scrolls and Greek version; Masoretic Text reads *Moses went and spoke.*

and courageous! For you will lead these people into the land that the LORD swore to give their ancestors. You are the one who will deliver it to them as their inheritance. [8]Do not be afraid or discouraged, for the LORD is the one who goes before you. He will be with you; he will neither fail you nor forsake you."

[9]So Moses wrote down this law and gave it to the priests, who carried the Ark of the LORD's covenant, and to the leaders of Israel. [10]Then Moses gave them this command: "At the end of every seventh year, the Year of Release, during the Festival of Shelters, [11]you must read this law to all the people of Israel when they assemble before the LORD your God at the place he chooses. [12]Call them all together—men, women, children, and the foreigners living in your towns—so they may listen and learn to fear the LORD your God and carefully obey all the terms of this law. [13]Do this so that your children who have not known these laws will hear them and will learn to fear the LORD your God. Do this as long as you live in the land you are crossing the Jordan to occupy."

[14]Then the LORD said to Moses, "The time has come for you to die. Call Joshua and take him with you to the Tabernacle,* and I will commission him there." So Moses and Joshua went and presented themselves at the Tabernacle. [15]And the LORD appeared to them in a pillar of cloud at the entrance to the sacred tent.

[16]The LORD said to Moses, "You are about to die and join your ancestors. After you are gone, these people will begin worshiping foreign gods, the gods of the land where they are going. They will abandon me and break the covenant I have made with them. [17]Then my anger will blaze forth against them. I will abandon them, hiding my face from them, and they will be destroyed. Terrible trouble will come down on them, so that they will say, 'These disasters have come because God is no longer among us!' [18]At that time I will hide my face from them on account of all the sins they have committed by worshiping other gods.

[19]"Now write down the words of this song, and teach it to the people of Israel. Teach them to sing it, so it may serve as a witness against them. [20]For I will bring them into the land I swore to give their ancestors—a land flowing with milk and honey. There they will become prosperous; they will eat all the food they want and become well nourished. Then they will begin to worship other gods; they will despise me and break my covenant. [21]Then great disasters will come down on them, and this song will stand as evidence against them, for it will never be forgotten by their descendants. I know what these people are like, even before they have entered the land I swore to give them." [22]So that very day Moses wrote down the words of the song and taught it to the Israelites.

[23]Then the LORD commissioned Joshua son of Nun with these words: "Be strong and courageous! You must bring the people of Israel into the land I swore to give them. I will be with you."

[24]When Moses had finished writing down this entire body of law in a book, [25]he gave these instructions to the Levites who carried the Ark of the LORD's covenant: [26]"Take this Book of the Law and place it beside the Ark of the Covenant of the LORD your God, so it may serve as a witness against the people of Israel. [27]For I know how rebellious and stubborn you are. Even now, while I am still with you, you have rebelled against the LORD. How much more rebellious will you be after my death! [28]Now summon all the leaders and officials of your tribes so that I can speak to them and call heaven and earth to witness against them. [29]I know that after my death you will become utterly corrupt and will turn from the path I have commanded you to follow. In the days to come, disaster will come down on you, for you will make the LORD very angry by doing what is evil in his sight."

[30]So Moses recited this entire song to the assembly of Israel:

CHAPTER 32

1　"Listen, O heavens, and I will speak!
　　Hear, O earth, the words that I say!
2　My teaching will fall on you like rain;
　　my speech will settle like dew.
　My words will fall like rain on tender grass,
　　like gentle showers on young plants.
3　I will proclaim the name of the LORD;
　　how glorious is our God!

31:14 Hebrew *Tent of Meeting*; also in 31:14b.

4 He is the Rock; his work is perfect.
   Everything he does is just and fair.
He is a faithful God who does no
      wrong;
   how just and upright he is!

5 "But they have acted corruptly toward
      him;
   when they act like that, are they
      really his children?*
They are a deceitful and twisted
   generation.
6 Is this the way you repay the LORD,
   you foolish and senseless people?
Isn't he your Father who created you?
   Has he not made you and
      established you?
7 Remember the days of long ago;
   think about the generations past.
Ask your father and he will inform you.
   Inquire of your elders, and they will
      tell you.
8 When the Most High assigned lands
      to the nations,
   when he divided up the human race,
he established the boundaries of the
   peoples
   according to the number of angelic
      beings.*
9 For the people of Israel belong to the
   LORD;
   Jacob is his special possession.

10 "He found them in a desert land,
   in an empty, howling wasteland.
He surrounded them and watched
   over them;
   he guarded them as his most
      precious possession.*
11 Like an eagle that rouses her chicks
   and hovers over her young,
so he spread his wings to take them in
   and carried them aloft on his pinions.
12 The LORD alone guided them;
   they lived without any foreign gods.
13 He made them ride over the highlands;
   he let them feast on the crops of the
      fields.
He nourished them with honey from
   the cliffs,
   with olive oil from the hard rock.
14 He fed them curds from the herd and
      milk from the flock,
   together with the fat of lambs and
      goats.

He gave them choice rams and goats
      from Bashan,
   together with the choicest wheat.
You drank the finest wine,
   made from the juice of grapes.
15 But Israel* soon became fat and unruly;
   the people grew heavy, plump, and
      stuffed!
Then they abandoned the God who
   had made them;
   they made light of the Rock of their
      salvation.
16 They stirred up his jealousy by
      worshiping foreign gods;
   they provoked his fury with
      detestable acts.
17 They offered sacrifices to demons,
      non-gods,
   to gods they had not known before,
   to gods only recently arrived,
   to gods their ancestors had never
      feared.
18 You neglected the Rock who had
      fathered you;
   you forgot the God who had given
      you birth.

19 "The LORD saw this and was filled with
      loathing.
   He was provoked to anger by his
      own sons and daughters.
20 He said, 'I will abandon them;
   I will see to their end!
For they are a twisted generation,
   children without integrity.
21 They have roused my jealousy by
      worshiping non-gods;
   they have provoked my fury with
      useless idols.
Now I will rouse their jealousy by
   blessing other nations;
   I will provoke their fury by blessing
      the foolish Gentiles.
22 For my anger blazes forth like fire
   and burns to the depths of the grave.*
It devours the earth and all its crops
   and ignites the foundations of the
      mountains.
23 I will heap disasters upon them
   and shoot them down with my
      arrows.
24 I will send against them wasting
      famine,
   burning fever, and deadly disease.

32:5 The meaning of the Hebrew is uncertain.   32:8 As in Dead Sea Scrolls, which read of the sons of God, and Greek version, which
reads of the angels of god; Masoretic Text reads of the sons of Israel.   32:10 Hebrew as the apple of his eye.   32:15 Hebrew Jeshurun, a
term of endearment for Israel.   32:22 Hebrew of Sheol.

They will be troubled by the fangs of
	wild beasts,
	by poisonous snakes that glide in
		the dust.
25 Outside, the sword will bring death,
	and inside, terror will strike
both young men and young women,
	both infants and the aged.
26 I decided to scatter them,*
	so even the memory of them would
		disappear.
27 But I feared the taunt of the enemy,
	that their adversaries might
		misunderstand and say,
	"Our power has triumphed!
	It was not the LORD who did this!"'

28 "Israel is a nation that lacks sense;
	the people are foolish, without
		understanding.
29 Oh, that they were wise and could
		understand this!
	Oh, that they might know their fate!
30 How could one person chase a
		thousand of them,
	and two people put ten thousand
		to flight,
unless their Rock had sold them,
	unless the LORD had given them up?
31 But the rock of our enemies is not like
		our Rock,
	as even they recognize.*
32 Their vine grows from the vine of Sodom,
	from the vineyards of Gomorrah.
Their grapes are poison,
	and their clusters are bitter.
33 Their wine is the venom of snakes,
	the deadly poison of vipers.

34 "'I am storing up these things,
	sealing them away within my
		treasury.
35 I will take vengeance; I will repay those
		who deserve it.
	In due time their feet will slip.
Their day of disaster will arrive,
	and their destiny will overtake them.'

36 "Indeed, the LORD will judge his
		people,
	and he will change his mind about*
		his servants,
when he sees their strength is gone
	and no one is left, slave or free.
37 Then he will ask, 'Where are their gods,
	the rocks they fled to for refuge?

38 Where now are those gods,
	who ate the fat of their sacrifices
	and drank the wine of their offerings?
Let those gods arise and help you!
	Let them provide you with shelter!
39 Look now; I myself am he!
	There is no god other than me!
I am the one who kills and gives life;
	I am the one who wounds and heals;
	no one delivers from my power!
40 Now I raise my hand to heaven
	and declare, "As surely as I live,
41 when I sharpen my flashing sword
	and begin to carry out justice,
I will bring vengeance on my enemies
	and repay those who hate me.
42 I will make my arrows drunk with
		blood,
	and my sword will devour flesh—
the blood of the slaughtered and the
		captives,
	and the heads of the enemy leaders."'

43 "Rejoice with him, O heavens,
	and let all the angels of God worship
		him,*
	for he will avenge the blood of his
		servants.
He will take vengeance on his enemies
	and cleanse his land and his people."

44So Moses came with Joshua* son of
Nun and recited all the words of this song
to the people. 45When Moses had finished
reciting these words to Israel, 46he added:
"Take to heart all the words I have given
you today. Pass them on as a command to
your children so they will obey every word
of this law. 47These instructions are not
mere words—they are your life! By obeying them you will enjoy a long life in the
land you are crossing the Jordan River to
occupy."

48That same day the LORD said to
Moses, 49"Go to Moab, to the mountains
east of the river,* and climb Mount Nebo,
which is across from Jericho. Look out
across the land of Canaan, the land I am
giving to the people of Israel as their own
possession. 50Then you must die there on
the mountain and join your ancestors,
just as Aaron, your brother, died on
Mount Hor and joined his ancestors. 51For
both of you broke faith with me among
the Israelites at the waters of Meribah at

32:26 As in Greek version; the meaning of the Hebrew is uncertain.	32:31 The meaning of the Hebrew is uncertain. Greek version
reads *our enemies are fools.*	32:36 Or *will take revenge for.*	32:43 As in Dead Sea Scrolls and Greek version; Masoretic Text reads
Rejoice with his people, O nations.	32:44 Hebrew *Hoshea,* a variant name for Joshua.	32:49 Hebrew *the mountains of Abarim.*

Kadesh* in the wilderness of Zin. You failed to demonstrate my holiness to the people of Israel there. ⁵²So you will see the land from a distance, but you may not enter the land I am giving to the people of Israel."

CHAPTER 33
This is the blessing that Moses, the man of God, gave to the people of Israel before his death:

² "The LORD came from Mount Sinai
  and dawned upon us* from Mount
    Seir;
he shone forth from Mount Paran
  and came from Meribah-kadesh
  with flaming fire at his right hand.*
³ Indeed, you love the people;
  all your holy ones are in your hands.
They follow in your steps
  and accept your instruction.
⁴ Moses charged us with the law,
  the special possession of the
    assembly of Israel.*
⁵ The LORD became king in Israel*—
  when the leaders of the people
    assembled,
  when the tribes of Israel gathered."

⁶Moses said this about the tribe of Reuben:*

  "Let the tribe of Reuben live and not
    die out,
  even though their tribe is small."

⁷Moses said this about the tribe of Judah:

  "O LORD, hear the cry of Judah
    and bring them again to their people.
  Give them strength to defend their
    cause;
    help them against their enemies!"

⁸Moses said this about the tribe of Levi:

  "O LORD, you have given the sacred
    lots*
  to your faithful servants the Levites.
  You put them to the test at Massah
    and contended with them at the
      waters of Meribah.
⁹ The Levites obeyed your word
  and guarded your covenant.
They were more loyal to you
  than to their parents, relatives, and
    children.

¹⁰ Now let them teach your regulations
    to Jacob;
  let them give your instructions to
    Israel.
They will present incense before you
  and offer whole burnt offerings on
    the altar.
¹¹ Bless the Levites, O LORD,
  and accept all their work.
Crush the loins of their enemies;
  strike down their foes so they never
    rise again."

¹²Moses said this about the tribe of Benjamin:

  "The people of Benjamin are loved
    by the LORD
  and live in safety beside him.
He surrounds them continuously
  and preserves them from every
    harm."

¹³Moses said this about the tribes of Joseph:

  "May their land be blessed by the LORD
    with the choice gift of rain from the
      heavens,
    and water from beneath the earth;
¹⁴ with the riches that grow in the sun,
  and the bounty produced each
    month;
¹⁵ with the finest crops of the ancient
    mountains,
  and the abundance from the
    everlasting hills;
¹⁶ with the best gifts of the earth and its
    fullness,
  and the favor of the one who
    appeared in the burning bush.
May these blessings rest on Joseph's
  head,
  crowning the brow of the prince
    among his brothers.
¹⁷ Joseph has the strength and majesty
    of a young bull;
  his power is like the horns of a wild
    ox.
He will gore distant nations,
  driving them to the ends of the earth.
This is my blessing for the multitudes
    of Ephraim
  and the thousands of Manasseh."

¹⁸Moses said this about the tribes of Zebulun and Issachar*:

32:51 Hebrew waters of Meribath-kadesh.   33:2a As in Greek and Syriac versions; Hebrew reads upon them.   33:2b Or came from myriads of holy ones, from the south, from his mountain slopes. The meaning of the Hebrew is uncertain.   33:4 Hebrew of Jacob.   33:5 Hebrew in Jeshurun, a term of endearment for Israel.   33:6 Hebrew lacks Moses said this about the tribe of Reuben. 33:8 Hebrew given your Thummim and Urim. See Exod 28:30.   33:18 Hebrew lacks and Issachar.

"May the people of Zebulun prosper
   in their expeditions abroad.
May the people of Issachar prosper
   at home in their tents.
[19] They summon the people to the
      mountain
   to offer proper sacrifices there.
They benefit from the riches of the sea
   and the hidden treasures of the sand."

[20]Moses said this about the tribe of Gad:

"Blessed is the one who enlarges Gad's
      territory!
Gad is poised there like a lion
   to tear off an arm or a head.
[21] The people of Gad took the best land
      for themselves;
   a leader's share was assigned to them.
When the leaders of the people were
      assembled,
   they carried out the LORD's justice
   and obeyed his regulations for
      Israel."

[22]Moses said this about the tribe of Dan:

"Dan is a lion's cub,
   leaping out from Bashan."

[23]Moses said this about the tribe of Naphtali:

"O Naphtali, you are rich in favor
   and full of the LORD's blessings;
may you possess the west and the
   south."

[24]Moses said this about the tribe of Asher:

"May Asher be blessed above other
      sons;
   may he be esteemed by his brothers;
   may he bathe his feet in olive oil.
[25] May the bolts of your gates be of iron
      and bronze;
   may your strength match the length
      of your days!"

[26] "There is no one like the God of Israel.*
   He rides across the heavens to help
      you,
   across the skies in majestic splendor.
[27] The eternal God is your refuge,
   and his everlasting arms are under
      you.
He thrusts out the enemy before you;
   it is he who cries, 'Destroy them!'

[28] So Israel will live in safety,
   prosperous Jacob in security,
in a land of grain and wine,
   while the heavens drop down dew.
[29] How blessed you are, O Israel!
   Who else is like you, a people saved
      by the LORD?
He is your protecting shield
   and your triumphant sword!
Your enemies will bow low before you,
   and you will trample on their backs!"

CHAPTER 34

Then Moses went to Mount Nebo from the plains of Moab and climbed Pisgah Peak, which is across from Jericho. And the LORD showed him the whole land, from Gilead as far as Dan; [2]all the land of Naphtali; the land of Ephraim and Manasseh; all the land of Judah, extending to the Mediterranean Sea*; [3]the Negev; the Jordan Valley with Jericho—the city of palms—as far as Zoar. [4]Then the LORD said to Moses, "This is the land I promised on oath to Abraham, Isaac, and Jacob, and I told them I would give it to their descendants. I have now allowed you to see it, but you will not enter the land."

[5]So Moses, the servant of the LORD, died there in the land of Moab, just as the LORD had said. [6]He was buried* in a valley near Beth-peor in Moab, but to this day no one knows the exact place. [7]Moses was 120 years old when he died, yet his eyesight was clear, and he was as strong as ever. [8]The people of Israel mourned thirty days for Moses on the plains of Moab, until the customary period of mourning was over.

[9]Now Joshua son of Nun was full of the spirit of wisdom, for Moses had laid his hands on him. So the people of Israel obeyed him and did everything just as the LORD had commanded Moses.

[10]There has never been another prophet like Moses, whom the LORD knew face to face. [11]The LORD sent Moses to perform all the miraculous signs and wonders in the land of Egypt against Pharaoh, all his servants, and his entire land. [12]And it was through Moses that the LORD demonstrated his mighty power and terrifying acts in the sight of all Israel.

33:26 Hebrew *of Jeshurun*, a term of endearment for Israel.   **34:2** Hebrew *the western sea*.   **34:6** Hebrew *He buried him*, that is, "The LORD buried him." Samaritan Pentateuch and some Greek manuscripts read *They buried him*.

FEBRUARY 29 ☐ DAY 60
All God Requires

LOOK BACK "Take two," says your doctor, instructing you to take two tablets of medication every day until you feel better.

"Take two," says the director, instructing the actors to repeat a part of the drama that didn't come off right the first time.

Both would be accurate summaries of the chapters you have read this past week. "Take two tablets of the law," says Moses, and make them, not your daily *medication,* but your daily *meditation.* In so doing, the new generation would avoid the folly and heartache of their parents, who died in the desert rather than in the land of milk and honey. The nation is given a second chance to discover that the law is designed, not to restrict and shackle, but to align the nation with God's holy purposes, resulting in provision, protection, and prolonged life (5:32-33).

It's a lesson God wants parents to teach their children, and Israel to teach the nations around them: "And now, Israel, what does the LORD your God require of you? He requires you to fear him, to live according to his will, to love and worship him with all your heart and soul, and to obey the LORD's commands and laws that I am giving you today *for your own good*" (10:12-13, emphasis added).

A person who "knows everything" has a lot to learn.

LOOK UP What does the highway patrol in your state require of motorists if they are going to use the highways? (Stay within the speed limit; don't endanger others; keep your car under control; don't drive without a license—simple things designed for the well-being of all.) Would you say that the highway patrol is heavy-handed and unfair to make such demands of motorists who want to drive on the highways, or that it is their intent to ensure that everyone is able to use and enjoy the highways to the fullest? The latter, of course.

In the same way, the Author of Life, who ought to know how life was meant to be lived, desires you to discover how to live life to the fullest. After all, it was Jesus who said, "My purpose is to give life in all its fullness" (John 10:10). God is no cosmic killjoy, out to make you miserable with needless rules and regulations. His commands and warnings are for our ultimate good, and those who ignore them are an accident waiting to happen.

You can be sure if God says something more than once (such as the Ten Commandments in Exodus 20 and Deuteronomy 5), it's no accident!

LOOK AHEAD Perhaps the prophet Micah said it best. Read his words out loud twice, looking for the answer to the question, What is God expecting me to do?

"No, O people, the LORD has already told you what is good, and this is what he requires: to do what is right, to love mercy, and to walk humbly with your God" (Micah 6:8).

Now close your eyes, tell God what you read, and what you intend to do about it.

Joshua

THE BOOK of Joshua is a tale of war and peace. In the first twelve chapters, the people of Israel conquer the land of Canaan. Through three military campaigns involving more than thirty enemy armies, they learn a valuable lesson under Joshua's capable leadership: Victory comes through faith in God and obedience to his Word rather than by military might or numerical superiority. In the final twelve chapters, peace reigns as the people of God divide up their new homeland.

Focus	Divide and Conquer				Divide and Settle			
Divisions	Preparation	Central Campaign	Moving South & North		Portions for 5 Tribes	Portions for 7 Tribes	Joshua's Last Words	
	1 5	6 8	9 12	13	17 18	21 22		24
Topics	Possessing Canaan				Partitioning Canaan			
	Subduing the Land				Settling the Land			
Place	9½ Tribes West of the Jordan (Canaan) 2½ Tribes East of the Jordan (Transjordan)							
Time	About 7 Years				About 18 Years			

MARCH 1 ☐ DAY 61
JOSHUA 1–5
Preparation of the People for War

 OVERVIEW Moses, "the LORD's servant," is dead. In his place stands General Joshua, one of only two adults surviving the forty years of wilderness wandering. Joshua must guide the nation across the flood-swollen Jordan River and into battle against the fortified cities of Canaan—certainly not an assignment for the fainthearted! Spying out the city of Jericho . . . crossing the Jordan . . . circumcising the new generation—each step brings comforting reminders of God's promise to fight on behalf of his people.

Chapter 1	Chapter 2	Chapters 3–4	Chapter 5
Commands for Joshua	Close Call at Jericho	Crossing the Jordan	Commemorating the Passover
"Be strong"	"Spy out"	"Go into"	"Circumcise"

 YOUR DAILY WALK The coach is giving his pregame pep talk to the local football team. To the players, the opposing team looks enormous, obviously outweighing (and no doubt outplaying) them at every position. Somehow the coach's encouragement rings hollow: "OK, men, now I want you to go out there and be strong . . . be courageous . . . don't let their size terrify you." But then an amazing thing happens. The coach, a man of unequaled strength and skill, lays aside his whistle and playbook, dons a jersey, and announces to the team: "I will be your quarterback, and in my strength we cannot fail. So be strong!"

Confidence is the feeling you have just before you fully understand the situation.

The opening chapter of Joshua was no mere divine pep talk. Rather, God was providing Joshua with the bedrock assurance he needed to face the towering giants and fortified strongholds of Canaan. Humanly speaking, the battle seemed already lost; but from God's perspective, the battle was already won—because it would be fought in his strength! What is one situation in your life today in which you too can draw courage from the promise of Joshua 1:5?

 INSIGHT Joshua, the Renamed General
Joshua's original name was *Hoshea* (Numbers 13:8), which means "salvation." But during the wilderness wanderings Moses changed his name to *Jehoshua*, "the LORD is salvation" (Numbers 13:16). *Joshua* is a contracted form of *Jehoshua* and the Hebrew form of the New Testament Greek name *Jesus*.

CHAPTER 1
After the death of Moses the LORD's servant, the LORD spoke to Joshua son of Nun, Moses' assistant. He said, ²"Now that my servant Moses is dead, you must lead my people across the Jordan River into the land I am giving them. ³I promise you what I

promised Moses: 'Everywhere you go, you will be on land I have given you—⁴from the Negev Desert in the south to the Lebanon mountains in the north, from the Euphrates River on the east to the Mediterranean Sea* on the west, and all the land of the Hittites.' ⁵No one will be able to stand their ground

1:4 Hebrew *the Great Sea.*

against you as long as you live. For I will be with you as I was with Moses. I will not fail you or abandon you.

⁶"Be strong and courageous, for you will lead my people to possess all the land I swore to give their ancestors. ⁷Be strong and very courageous. Obey all the laws Moses gave you. Do not turn away from them, and you will be successful in everything you do. ⁸Study this Book of the Law continually. Meditate on it day and night so you may be sure to obey all that is written in it. Only then will you succeed. ⁹I command you—be strong and courageous! Do not be afraid or discouraged. For the LORD your God is with you wherever you go."

¹⁰Joshua then commanded the leaders of Israel, ¹¹"Go through the camp and tell the people to get their provisions ready. In three days you will cross the Jordan River and take possession of the land the LORD your God has given you."

¹²Then Joshua called together the tribes of Reuben, Gad, and the half-tribe of Manasseh. He told them, ¹³"Remember what Moses, the servant of the LORD, commanded you: 'The LORD your God is giving you rest and has given you this land.' ¹⁴Your wives, children, and cattle may remain here on the east side of the Jordan River, but your warriors, fully armed, must lead the other tribes across the Jordan to help them conquer their territory. Stay with them ¹⁵until the LORD gives rest to them as he has given rest to you, and until they, too, possess the land the LORD your God is giving them. Only then may you settle here on the east side of the Jordan River in the land that Moses, the servant of the LORD, gave you."

¹⁶They answered Joshua, "We will do whatever you command us, and we will go wherever you send us. ¹⁷We will obey you just as we obeyed Moses. And may the LORD your God be with you as he was with Moses. ¹⁸Anyone who rebels against your word and does not obey your every command will be put to death. So be strong and courageous!"

CHAPTER 2

Then Joshua secretly sent out two spies from the Israelite camp at Acacia.* He instructed them, "Spy out the land on the other side of the Jordan River, especially around Jericho." So the two men set out

and came to the house of a prostitute named Rahab and stayed there that night.

²But someone told the king of Jericho, "Some Israelites have come here tonight to spy out the land." ³So the king of Jericho sent orders to Rahab: "Bring out the men who have come into your house. They are spies sent here to discover the best way to attack us."

⁴Rahab, who had hidden the two men, replied, "The men were here earlier, but I didn't know where they were from. ⁵They left the city at dusk, as the city gates were about to close, and I don't know where they went. If you hurry, you can probably catch up with them." ⁶(But she had taken them up to the roof and hidden them beneath piles of flax.) ⁷So the king's men went looking for the spies along the road leading to the shallow crossing places of the Jordan River. And as soon as the king's men had left, the city gate was shut.

⁸Before the spies went to sleep that night, Rahab went up on the roof to talk with them. ⁹"I know the LORD has given you this land," she told them. "We are all afraid of you. Everyone is living in terror. ¹⁰For we have heard how the LORD made a dry path for you through the Red Sea* when you left Egypt. And we know what you did to Sihon and Og, the two Amorite kings east of the Jordan River, whose people you completely destroyed.* ¹¹No wonder our hearts have melted in fear! No one has the courage to fight after hearing such things. For the LORD your God is the supreme God of the heavens above and the earth below. ¹²Now swear to me by the LORD that you will be kind to me and my family since I have helped you. Give me some guarantee that ¹³when Jericho is conquered, you will let me live, along with my father and mother, my brothers and sisters, and all their families."

¹⁴"We offer our own lives as a guarantee for your safety," the men agreed. "If you don't betray us, we will keep our promise when the LORD gives us the land."

¹⁵Then, since Rahab's house was built into the city wall, she let them down by a rope through the window. ¹⁶"Escape to the hill country," she told them. "Hide there for three days until the men who are searching for you have returned; then go on your way."

¹⁷Before they left, the men told her, "We

2:1 Hebrew *Shittim*.   2:10a Hebrew *sea of reeds*.   2:10b The Hebrew term used here refers to the complete consecration of things or people to the LORD, either by destroying them or by giving them as an offering.

can guarantee your safety [18]only if you leave this scarlet rope hanging from the window. And all your family members—your father, mother, brothers, and all your relatives—must be here inside the house. [19]If they go out into the street, they will be killed, and we cannot be held to our oath. But we swear that no one inside this house will be killed—not a hand will be laid on any of them. [20]If you betray us, however, we are not bound by this oath in any way."

[21]"I accept your terms," she replied. And she sent them on their way, leaving the scarlet rope hanging from the window.

[22]The spies went up into the hill country and stayed there three days. The men who were chasing them had searched everywhere along the road, but they finally returned to the city without success. [23]Then the two spies came down from the hill country, crossed the Jordan River, and reported to Joshua all that had happened to them. [24]"The LORD will certainly give us the whole land," they said, "for all the people in the land are terrified of us."

CHAPTER 3

Early the next morning Joshua and all the Israelites left Acacia* and arrived at the banks of the Jordan River, where they camped before crossing. [2]Three days later, the Israelite leaders went through the camp [3]giving these instructions to the people: "When you see the Levitical priests carrying the Ark of the Covenant of the LORD your God, follow them. [4]Since you have never traveled this way before, they will guide you. Stay about a half mile* behind them, keeping a clear distance between you and the Ark. Make sure you don't come any closer."

[5]Then Joshua told the people, "Purify yourselves, for tomorrow the LORD will do great wonders among you."

[6]In the morning Joshua said to the priests, "Lift up the Ark of the Covenant and lead the people across the river." And so they started out.

[7]The LORD told Joshua, "Today I will begin to make you great in the eyes of all the Israelites. Now they will know that I am with you, just as I was with Moses. [8]Give these instructions to the priests who are carrying the Ark of the Covenant: 'When you reach the banks of the Jordan River, take a few steps into the river and stop.'"

[9]So Joshua told the Israelites, "Come and listen to what the LORD your God says. [10]Today you will know that the living God is among you. He will surely drive out the Canaanites, Hittites, Hivites, Perizzites, Girgashites, Amorites, and Jebusites. [11]Think of it! The Ark of the Covenant, which belongs to the Lord of the whole earth, will lead you across the Jordan River! [12]Now choose twelve men, one from each tribe. [13]The priests will be carrying the Ark of the LORD, the Lord of all the earth. When their feet touch the water, the flow of water will be cut off upstream, and the river will pile up there in one heap."

[14]When the people set out to cross the Jordan, the priests who were carrying the Ark of the Covenant went ahead of them. [15]Now it was the harvest season, and the Jordan was overflowing its banks. But as soon as the feet of the priests who were carrying the Ark touched the water at the river's edge, [16]the water began piling up at a town upstream called Adam, which is near Zarethan. And the water below that point flowed on to the Dead Sea* until the riverbed was dry. Then all the people crossed over near the city of Jericho. [17]Meanwhile, the priests who were carrying the Ark of the LORD's covenant stood on dry ground in the middle of the riverbed as the people passed by them. They waited there until everyone had crossed the Jordan on dry ground.

CHAPTER 4

When all the people were safely across the river, the LORD said to Joshua, [2]"Now choose twelve men, one from each tribe. [3]Tell the men to take twelve stones from where the priests are standing in the middle of the Jordan and pile them up at the place where you camp tonight."

[4]So Joshua called together the twelve men [5]and told them, "Go into the middle of the Jordan, in front of the Ark of the LORD your God. Each of you must pick up one stone and carry it out on your shoulder—twelve stones in all, one for each of the twelve tribes. [6]We will use these stones to build a memorial. In the future, your children will ask, 'What do these stones mean to you?' [7]Then you can tell them, 'They remind us that the Jordan River stopped flowing when the Ark of the LORD's cove-

nant went across.' These stones will stand as a permanent memorial among the people of Israel."

[8]So the men did as Joshua told them. They took twelve stones from the middle of the Jordan River, one for each tribe, just as the LORD had commanded Joshua. They carried them to the place where they camped for the night and constructed the memorial there.

[9]Joshua also built another memorial of twelve stones in the middle of the Jordan, at the place where the priests who carried the Ark of the Covenant were standing. The memorial remains there to this day.

[10]The priests who were carrying the Ark stood in the middle of the river until all of the LORD's instructions, which Moses had given to Joshua, were carried out. Meanwhile, the people hurried across the riverbed. [11]And when everyone was on the other side, the priests crossed over with the Ark of the LORD. [12]The armed warriors from the tribes of Reuben, Gad, and the half-tribe of Manasseh led the Israelites across the Jordan, just as Moses had directed. [13]These warriors—about forty thousand strong—were ready for battle, and they crossed over to the plains of Jericho in the LORD's presence.

[14]That day the LORD made Joshua great in the eyes of all the Israelites, and for the rest of his life they revered him as much as they had revered Moses.

[15]The LORD had said to Joshua, [16]"Command the priests carrying the Ark of the Covenant* to come up out of the riverbed." [17]So Joshua gave the command. [18]And as soon as the priests carrying the Ark of the LORD's covenant came up out of the riverbed, the Jordan River flooded its banks as before.

[19]The people crossed the Jordan on the tenth day of the first month—the month that marked their exodus from Egypt.* They camped at Gilgal, east of Jericho. [20]It was there at Gilgal that Joshua piled up the twelve stones taken from the Jordan River. [21]Then Joshua said to the Israelites, "In the future, your children will ask, 'What do these stones mean?' [22]Then you can tell them, 'This is where the Israelites crossed the Jordan on dry ground.' [23]For the LORD your God dried up the river right before your eyes, and he kept it dry until you were all across, just as he did at the Red Sea* when he dried it up until we had all crossed over. [24]He did this so that all the nations of the earth might know the power of the LORD, and that you might fear the LORD your God forever."

CHAPTER 5

When all the Amorite kings west of the Jordan and all the Canaanite kings who lived along the Mediterranean coast* heard how the LORD had dried up the Jordan River so the people of Israel could cross, they lost heart and were paralyzed with fear.

[2]At that time the LORD told Joshua, "Use knives of flint to make the Israelites a circumcised people again." [3]So Joshua made flint knives and circumcised the entire male population of Israel at Gibeath-haaraloth.*

[4]Joshua had to circumcise them because all the men who were old enough to bear arms when they left Egypt had died in the wilderness. [5]Those who left Egypt had all been circumcised, but none of those born after the Exodus, during the years in the wilderness, had been circumcised. [6]The Israelites wandered in the wilderness for forty years until all the men who were old enough to bear arms when they left Egypt had died. For they had disobeyed the LORD, and the LORD vowed he would not let them enter the land he had sworn to give us—a land flowing with milk and honey. [7]So Joshua circumcised their sons who had not been circumcised on the way to the Promised Land—those who had grown up to take their fathers' places. [8]After all the males had been circumcised, they rested in the camp until they were healed.

[9]Then the LORD said to Joshua, "Today I have rolled away the shame of your slavery in Egypt." So that place has been called Gilgal* to this day.

[10]While the Israelites were camped at Gilgal on the plains of Jericho, they celebrated Passover on the evening of the fourteenth day of the first month—the month that marked their exodus from Egypt.* [11]The very next day they began to eat unleavened bread and roasted grain

4:16 Hebrew *Ark of the Testimony.* **4:19** Hebrew *the tenth day of the first month.* This day of the Hebrew lunar calendar occurs in late March or early April. **4:23** Hebrew *sea of reeds.* **5:1** Hebrew *along the sea.* **5:3** *Gibeath-haaraloth* means "hill of foreskins." **5:9** *Gilgal* sounds like the Hebrew word *galal,* meaning "to roll." **5:10** Hebrew *the fourteenth day of the first month.* This day of the Hebrew lunar calendar occurs in late March or early April.

harvested from the land. ¹²No manna appeared that day, and it was never seen again. So from that time on the Israelites ate from the crops of Canaan.

¹³As Joshua approached the city of Jericho, he looked up and saw a man facing him with sword in hand. Joshua went up to him and asked, "Are you friend or foe?"

¹⁴"Neither one," he replied. "I am commander of the LORD's army."

At this, Joshua fell with his face to the ground in reverence. "I am at your command," Joshua said. "What do you want your servant to do?"

¹⁵The commander of the LORD's army replied, "Take off your sandals, for this is holy ground." And Joshua did as he was told.

MARCH 2 ☐ DAY 62
JOSHUA 6–8
Central Campaign

 OVERVIEW Standing like a taunting giant in the path of the approaching Israelites is the walled fortress of Jericho. There can be no skirting the issue: Jericho must be conquered. But how? The strategy God delivers to Joshua is truly unique and is designed to ensure that if the walls fall down, there can be only one explanation—God did it! Joshua leads the people on a daily lap around the city walls, culminating in a seven-lap marathon on the seventh day. At last comes the moment to shout . . . and Jericho's walls turn to rubble. But even in victory the people of God disobey. Achan steals some of the forbidden booty, resulting in death and defeat for the Israelite army.

Chapter 6	Chapter 7	Chapter 8
Obedient Victory at Jericho	Disobedient Defeat at Ai	Obedient Rematch at Ai
The Thrill of Victory	The Agony of Defeat	

 YOUR DAILY WALK *Hate* is a strong word. And to say that God hates is even stronger!

Yet the Bible lists many things that God hates: idolatry (Deuteronomy 16:22), wickedness (Psalm 45:7), pride, lying, murder, discord, mischief-making (Proverbs 6:16-19)—in a word, SIN!

There is no biblical authority for believing there is any such thing as a little sin.

Today's reading explains one reason why God finds sin so abhorrent: It leaves scars on the innocent as well as the guilty. Achan's sin—seemingly so private and harmless—resulted in thirty-six lives needlessly lost in battle and an entire nation left in disarray.

Are you tempted to disobey God today, concluding, "It's my life and I can do with it as I please"? Then stop and consider. What will disobedience cost you personally? How will it affect others around you? God has strength for you to be an overcomer instead (Romans 8:37). Will you turn to him right now and use that strength?

 INSIGHT Long Odds at Ai
Overconfident from their smashing victory at Jericho, the people urge Joshua to send only a token force against Ai (7:3). Joshua agrees, sending only three thousand soldiers (7:4). In their own strength—and facing an enemy that outnumbers them four-to-one (8:25)—the Israelite troops suffer a staggering defeat. The lesson is clear: With God on your side, you cannot lose; without him, you cannot win!

CHAPTER 6

Now the gates of Jericho were tightly shut because the people were afraid of the Israelites. No one was allowed to go in or out. ²But the LORD said to Joshua, "I have given you Jericho, its king, and all its mighty warriors. ³Your entire army is to march around the city once a day for six days. ⁴Seven priests will walk ahead of the Ark, each carrying a ram's horn. On the seventh day you are to march around the city seven times, with the priests blowing the horns. ⁵When you hear the priests give one long blast on the horns, have all the people give a mighty shout. Then the walls of the city will collapse, and the people can charge straight into the city."

⁶So Joshua called together the priests and said, "Take up the Ark of the Covenant, and assign seven priests to walk in front of it, each carrying a ram's horn." ⁷Then he gave orders to the people: "March around the city, and the armed men will lead the way in front of the Ark of the LORD."

⁸After Joshua spoke to the people, the seven priests with the rams' horns started marching in the presence of the LORD, blowing the horns as they marched. And the priests carrying the Ark of the LORD's covenant followed behind them. ⁹Armed guards marched both in front of the priests and behind the Ark, with the priests continually blowing the horns. ¹⁰"Do not shout; do not even talk," Joshua commanded. "Not a single word from any of you until I tell you to shout. Then shout!" ¹¹So the Ark of the LORD was carried around the city once that day, and then everyone returned to spend the night in the camp.

¹²Joshua got up early the next morning, and the priests again carried the Ark of the LORD. ¹³The seven priests with the rams' horns marched in front of the Ark of the LORD, blowing their horns. Armed guards marched both in front of the priests with the horns and behind the Ark of the LORD. All this time the priests were sounding their horns. ¹⁴On the second day they marched around the city once and returned to the camp. They followed this pattern for six days.

¹⁵On the seventh day the Israelites got up at dawn and marched around the city as they had done before. But this time they went around the city seven times.

¹⁶The seventh time around, as the priests sounded the long blast on their horns, Joshua commanded the people, "Shout! For the LORD has given you the city! ¹⁷The city and everything in it must be completely destroyed* as an offering to the LORD. Only Rahab the prostitute and the others in her house will be spared, for she protected our spies. ¹⁸Do not take any of the things set apart for destruction, or you yourselves will be completely destroyed, and you will bring trouble on all Israel. ¹⁹Everything made from silver, gold, bronze, or iron is sacred to the LORD and must be brought into his treasury."

²⁰When the people heard the sound of the horns, they shouted as loud as they could. Suddenly, the walls of Jericho collapsed, and the Israelites charged straight into the city from every side and captured it. ²¹They completely destroyed everything in it—men and women, young and old, cattle, sheep, donkeys—everything.

²²Then Joshua said to the two spies, "Keep your promise. Go to the prostitute's house and bring her out, along with all her family."

²³The young men went in and brought out Rahab, her father, mother, brothers, and all the other relatives who were with her. They moved her whole family to a safe place near the camp of Israel.

²⁴Then the Israelites burned the city and everything in it. Only the things made from silver, gold, bronze, or iron were kept for the treasury of the LORD's house. ²⁵So Joshua spared Rahab the prostitute and her relatives who were with her in the house, because she had hidden the spies Joshua sent to Jericho. And she lives among the Israelites to this day.

²⁶At that time Joshua invoked this curse:

"May the curse of the LORD fall on anyone
    who tries to rebuild the city of
    Jericho.
At the cost of his firstborn son,
    he will lay its foundation.
At the cost of his youngest son,
    he will set up its gates."

²⁷So the LORD was with Joshua, and his name became famous throughout the land.

6:17 The Hebrew term used here refers to the complete consecration of things or people to the LORD, either by destroying them or by giving them as an offering; also in 6:18, 21.

CHAPTER 7

But Israel was unfaithful concerning the things set apart for the LORD.* A man named Achan had stolen some of these things, so the LORD was very angry with the Israelites. Achan was the son of Carmi, of the family of Zimri,* of the clan of Zerah, and of the tribe of Judah.

²Joshua sent some of his men from Jericho to spy out the city of Ai, east of Bethel, near Beth-aven. ³When they returned, they told Joshua, "It's a small town, and it won't take more than two or three thousand of us to destroy it. There's no need for all of us to go there."

⁴So approximately three thousand warriors were sent, but they were soundly defeated. The men of Ai ⁵chased the Israelites from the city gate as far as the quarries,* and they killed about thirty-six who were retreating down the slope. The Israelites were paralyzed with fear at this turn of events, and their courage melted away.

⁶Joshua and the leaders of Israel tore their clothing in dismay, threw dust on their heads, and bowed down facing the Ark of the LORD until evening. ⁷Then Joshua cried out, "Sovereign LORD, why did you bring us across the Jordan River if you are going to let the Amorites kill us? If only we had been content to stay on the other side! ⁸Lord, what am I to say, now that Israel has fled from its enemies? ⁹For when the Canaanites and all the other people living in the land hear about it, they will surround us and wipe us off the face of the earth. And then what will happen to the honor of your great name?"

¹⁰But the LORD said to Joshua, "Get up! Why are you lying on your face like this? ¹¹Israel has sinned and broken my covenant! They have stolen the things that I commanded to be set apart for me. And they have not only stolen them; they have also lied about it and hidden the things among their belongings. ¹²That is why the Israelites are running from their enemies in defeat. For now Israel has been set apart for destruction. I will not remain with you any longer unless you destroy the things among you that were set apart for destruction.

¹³"Get up! Command the people to pu-

rify themselves in preparation for tomorrow. For this is what the LORD, the God of Israel, says: Hidden among you, O Israel, are things set apart for the LORD. You will never defeat your enemies until you remove these things. ¹⁴In the morning you must present yourselves by tribes, and the LORD will point out the tribe to which the guilty man belongs. That tribe must come forward with its clans, and the LORD will point out the guilty clan. That clan will then come forward, and the LORD will point out the guilty family. Finally, each member of the guilty family must come one by one. ¹⁵The one who has stolen what was set apart for destruction will himself be burned with fire, along with everything he has, for he has broken the covenant of the LORD and has done a horrible thing in Israel."

¹⁶Early the next morning Joshua brought the tribes of Israel before the LORD, and the tribe of Judah was singled out. ¹⁷Then the clans of Judah came forward, and the clan of Zerah was singled out. Then the families of Zerah came before the LORD, and the family of Zimri was singled out. ¹⁸Every member of Zimri's family was brought forward person by person, and Achan was singled out.

¹⁹Then Joshua said to Achan, "My son, give glory to the LORD, the God of Israel, by telling the truth. Make your confession and tell me what you have done. Don't hide it from me."

²⁰Achan replied, "I have sinned against the LORD, the God of Israel. ²¹For I saw a beautiful robe imported from Babylon,* two hundred silver coins,* and a bar of gold weighing more than a pound.* I wanted them so much that I took them. They are hidden in the ground beneath my tent, with the silver buried deeper than the rest."

²²So Joshua sent some men to make a search. They ran to the tent and found the stolen goods hidden there, just as Achan had said, with the silver buried beneath the rest. ²³They took the things from the tent and brought them to Joshua and all the Israelites. Then they laid them on the ground in the presence of the LORD.

²⁴Then Joshua and all the Israelites took

Achan, the silver, the robe, the bar of gold, his sons, daughters, cattle, donkeys, sheep, tent, and everything he had, and they brought them to the valley of Achor. ²⁵Then Joshua said to Achan, "Why have you brought trouble on us? The LORD will now bring trouble on you." And all the Israelites stoned Achan and his family and burned their bodies. ²⁶They piled a great heap of stones over Achan, which remains to this day. That is why the place has been called the Valley of Trouble* ever since. So the LORD was no longer angry.

CHAPTER 8

Then the LORD said to Joshua, "Do not be afraid or discouraged. Take the entire army and attack Ai, for I have given to you the king of Ai, his people, his city, and his land. ²You will destroy them as you destroyed Jericho and its king. But this time you may keep the captured goods and the cattle for yourselves. Set an ambush behind the city."

³So Joshua and the army of Israel set out to attack Ai. Joshua chose thirty thousand fighting men and sent them out at night ⁴with these orders: "Hide in ambush close behind the city and be ready for action. ⁵When our main army attacks, the men of Ai will come out to fight as they did before, and we will run away from them. ⁶We will let them chase us until they have all left the city. For they will say, 'The Israelites are running away from us as they did before.' ⁷Then you will jump up from your ambush and take possession of the city, for the LORD your God will give it to you. ⁸Set the city on fire, as the LORD has commanded. You have your orders."

⁹So they left that night and lay in ambush between Bethel and the west side of Ai. But Joshua remained among the people in the camp that night. ¹⁰Early the next morning Joshua roused his men and started toward Ai, accompanied by the leaders of Israel. ¹¹They camped on the north side of Ai, with a valley between them and the city. ¹²That night Joshua sent five thousand men to lie in ambush between Bethel and Ai, on the west side of the city. ¹³So they stationed the main army north of the city and the ambush west of the city. Joshua himself spent that night in the valley.

¹⁴When the king of Ai saw the Israelites

across the valley, he and all his army hurriedly went out early the next morning and attacked the Israelites at a place overlooking the Jordan Valley.* But he didn't realize there was an ambush behind the city. ¹⁵Joshua and the Israelite army fled toward the wilderness as though they were badly beaten, ¹⁶and all the men in the city were called out to chase after them. In this way, they were lured away from the city. ¹⁷There was not a man left in Ai or Bethel* who did not chase after the Israelites, and the city was left wide open.

¹⁸Then the LORD said to Joshua, "Point your spear toward Ai, for I will give you the city." Joshua did as he was commanded. ¹⁹As soon as Joshua gave the signal, the men in ambush jumped up and poured into the city. They quickly captured it and set it on fire.

²⁰When the men of Ai looked behind them, smoke from the city was filling the sky, and they had nowhere to go. For the Israelites who had fled in the direction of the wilderness now turned on their pursuers. ²¹When Joshua and the other Israelites saw that the ambush had succeeded and that smoke was rising from the city, they turned and attacked the men of Ai. ²²Then the Israelites who were inside the city came out and started killing the enemy from the rear. So the men of Ai were caught in a trap, and all of them died. Not a single person survived or escaped. ²³Only the king of Ai was taken alive and brought to Joshua.

²⁴When the Israelite army finished killing all the men outside the city, they went back and finished off everyone inside. ²⁵So the entire population of Ai was wiped out that day—twelve thousand in all. ²⁶For Joshua kept holding out his spear until everyone who had lived in Ai was completely destroyed.* ²⁷Only the cattle and the treasures of the city were not destroyed, for the Israelites kept these for themselves, as the LORD had commanded Joshua. ²⁸So Ai* became a permanent mound of ruins, desolate to this very day.

²⁹Joshua hung the king of Ai on a tree and left him there until evening. At sunset the Israelites took down the body and threw it in front of the city gate. They piled a great heap of stones over him that can still be seen today.

7:26 Hebrew *valley of Achor.*   **8:14** Hebrew *the Arabah.*   **8:17** Some manuscripts lack *or Bethel.*   **8:26** The Hebrew term used here refers to the complete consecration of things or people to the LORD, either by destroying them or by giving them as an offering. **8:28** *Ai* means "ruin."

³⁰Then Joshua built an altar to the LORD, the God of Israel, on Mount Ebal. ³¹He followed the instructions that Moses the LORD's servant had written in the Book of the Law: "Make me an altar from stones that are uncut and have not been shaped with iron tools." Then on the altar they presented burnt offerings and peace offerings to the LORD. ³²And as the Israelites watched, Joshua copied the law of Moses onto the stones of the altar.*

³³Then all the Israelites—foreigners and citizens alike—along with the leaders, officers, and judges, were divided into two groups. One group stood at the foot of

8:32 Or *onto stones.*

Mount Gerizim, the other at the foot of Mount Ebal. Each group faced the other, and between them stood the Levitical priests carrying the Ark of the LORD's covenant. This was all done according to the instructions Moses, the servant of the LORD, had given for blessing the people of Israel.

³⁴Joshua then read to them all the blessings and curses Moses had written in the Book of the Law. ³⁵Every command Moses had ever given was read to the entire assembly, including the women and children and the foreigners who lived among the Israelites.

MARCH 3 □ DAY 63
JOSHUA 9–12
Moving South and North

OVERVIEW "Divide and conquer" is a classic strategy for military conquest, and Joshua uses it to perfection. With Jericho and Ai secured, he has accomplished phase one—dividing the land in half, thereby isolating the northern and southern confederacies. Next he begins a "mopping up" operation in the south and north. But the thrill of victory is tempered by the knowledge of what should have been. The Gibeonites, hearing the sad fate of Jericho and Ai, trick Joshua into signing a pact of protection, causing the Israelites to defend rather than defeat one of their enemies.

Chapter 9	Chapter 10	Chapter 11	Chapter 12
Craftiness of Gibeon	Conquest of Five Kings	Conquest of the North	Counting Up the Score
Southern Campaign		Northern Campaign	

Understanding can wait; obedience can't.

YOUR DAILY WALK "Dr. Livingstone, I presume?" Fortunately for Sir Henry Stanley on that fateful day in 1871 deep in the heart of central Africa, he "presumed" correctly. But more often than not, presumption can get you into trouble—particularly if it is presumption about God's Word.

Yesterday you read about Achan, a man who presumed that God wouldn't mind if he stole a few trinkets from the crumbling ruins of Jericho—and paid for it with his life. Today you read about godly Joshua falling into a presumptuous sin by failing to consult the Lord. The Scriptures make it very clear that presumption can bring pretty serious consequences!

What important decision are you facing today? Don't presume you can make a wise choice without God's help. With his Spirit indwelling you and his Word available to you, he can guide you into a wise course of action—if you'll let him.

INSIGHT A Hungry Homeland
Earlier the scouts described Canaan as a land that "will swallow up any who go to live there" (Numbers 13:32). During the seven-year conquest, Joshua's army destroyed thirty-one kings and most of the Canaanites, making the scouts' statement ironically prophetic!

CHAPTER 9

Now all the kings west of the Jordan heard about what had happened. (These were the kings of the Hittites, Amorites, Canaanites, Perizzites, Hivites, and Jebusites, who lived in the hill country, in the western foothills,* and along the coast of the Mediterranean Sea* as far north as the Lebanon mountains.) ²These kings quickly combined their armies to fight against Joshua and the Israelites.

³But when the people of Gibeon heard what had happened to Jericho and Ai, ⁴they resorted to deception to save themselves. They sent ambassadors to Joshua, loading their donkeys with weathered saddlebags and old patched wineskins. ⁵They put on ragged clothes and worn-out, patched sandals. And they took along dry, moldy bread for provisions. ⁶When they arrived at the camp of Israel at Gilgal, they told Joshua and the men of Israel, "We have come from a distant land to ask you to make a peace treaty with us."

⁷The Israelites replied to these Hivites, "How do we know you don't live nearby? For if you do, we cannot make a treaty with you."

⁸They replied, "We will be your servants."

"But who are you?" Joshua demanded. "Where do you come from?"

⁹They answered, "We are from a very distant country. We have heard of the might of the LORD your God and of all he did in Egypt. ¹⁰We have also heard what he did to the two Amorite kings east of the Jordan River—King Sihon of Heshbon and King Og of Bashan (who lived in Ashtaroth). ¹¹So our leaders and our people instructed us, 'Prepare for a long journey. Go meet with the people of Israel and declare our people to be their servants, and ask for peace.'

¹²"This bread was hot from the ovens when we left. But now, as you can see, it is dry and moldy. ¹³These wineskins were new when we filled them, but now they are

old and cracked. And our clothing and sandals are worn out from our long, hard trip."

¹⁴So the Israelite leaders examined their bread, but they did not consult the LORD. ¹⁵Then Joshua went ahead and signed a peace treaty with them, and the leaders of Israel ratified their agreement with a binding oath.

¹⁶Three days later, the facts came out—these people of Gibeon lived nearby! ¹⁷The Israelites set out at once to investigate and reached their towns in three days. The names of these towns were Gibeon, Kephirah, Beeroth, and Kiriath-jearim. ¹⁸But the Israelites did not attack the towns, for their leaders had made a vow to the LORD, the God of Israel.

The people of Israel grumbled against their leaders because of the treaty. ¹⁹But the leaders replied, "We have sworn an oath in the presence of the LORD, the God of Israel. We cannot touch them. ²⁰We must let them live, for God would be angry with us if we broke our oath. ²¹Let them live. But we will make them chop the wood and carry the water for the entire community."

So the Israelites kept their promise to the Gibeonites. ²²But Joshua called together the Gibeonite leaders and said, "Why did you lie to us? Why did you say that you live in a distant land when you live right here among us? ²³May you be cursed! From now on you will chop wood and carry water for the house of my God."

²⁴They replied, "We did it because we were told that the LORD your God instructed his servant Moses to conquer this entire land and destroy all the people living in it. So we feared for our lives because of you. That is why we have done it. ²⁵Now we are at your mercy—do whatever you think is right."

²⁶Joshua did not allow the people of Israel to kill them. ²⁷But that day he made the Gibeonites the woodchoppers and water carriers for the people of Israel and for the altar of the LORD—wherever the LORD would choose to build it. That arrangement continues to this day.

9:1a Hebrew *the Shephelah.*   9:1b Hebrew *the Great Sea.*

CHAPTER 10

Now Adoni-zedek, king of Jerusalem, heard that Joshua had captured and completely destroyed* Ai and killed its king, just as he had destroyed the city of Jericho and killed its king. He also learned that the Gibeonites had made peace with Israel and were now their allies. ²He and his people became very afraid when they heard all this because Gibeon was a large city—as large as the royal cities and larger than Ai. And the Gibeonite men were mighty warriors. ³So King Adoni-zedek of Jerusalem sent messengers to several other kings: Hoham of Hebron, Piram of Jarmuth, Japhia of Lachish, and Debir of Eglon. ⁴"Come and help me destroy Gibeon," he urged them, "for they have made peace with Joshua and the people of Israel." ⁵So these five Amorite kings combined their armies for a united attack. They moved all their troops into place and attacked Gibeon.

⁶The men of Gibeon quickly sent messengers to Joshua at Gilgal, "Don't abandon your servants now!" they pleaded. "Come quickly and save us! For all the Amorite kings who live in the hill country have come out against us with their armies."

⁷So Joshua and the entire Israelite army left Gilgal and set out to rescue Gibeon. ⁸"Do not be afraid of them," the LORD said to Joshua, "for I will give you victory over them. Not a single one of them will be able to stand up to you."

⁹Joshua traveled all night from Gilgal and took the Amorite armies by surprise. ¹⁰The LORD threw them into a panic, and the Israelites slaughtered them in great numbers at Gibeon. Then the Israelites chased the enemy along the road to Beth-horon and attacked them at Azekah and Makkedah, killing them along the way. ¹¹As the Amorites retreated down the road from Beth-horon, the LORD destroyed them with a terrible hailstorm that continued until they reached Azekah. The hail killed more of the enemy than the Israelites killed with the sword.

¹²On the day the LORD gave the Israelites victory over the Amorites, Joshua prayed to the LORD in front of all the people of Israel. He said,

"Let the sun stand still over Gibeon,
    and the moon over the valley of
    Aijalon."

¹³So the sun and moon stood still until the Israelites had defeated their enemies.

Is this event not recorded in *The Book of Jashar**? The sun stopped in the middle of the sky, and it did not set as on a normal day. ¹⁴The LORD fought for Israel that day. Never before or since has there been a day like that one, when the LORD answered such a request from a human being.

¹⁵Then Joshua and the Israelite army returned to their camp at Gilgal.

¹⁶During the battle, the five kings escaped and hid in a cave at Makkedah. ¹⁷When Joshua heard that they had been found, ¹⁸he issued this command: "Cover the opening of the cave with large rocks and place guards at the entrance to keep the kings inside. ¹⁹The rest of you continue chasing the enemy and cut them down from the rear. Don't let them get back to their cities, for the LORD your God has given you victory over them."

²⁰So Joshua and the Israelite army continued the slaughter and wiped out the five armies except for a tiny remnant that managed to reach their fortified cities. ²¹Then the Israelites returned safely to their camp at Makkedah. After that, no one dared to speak a word against Israel.

²²Then Joshua said, "Remove the rocks covering the opening of the cave and bring the five kings to me." ²³So they brought the five kings out of the cave—the kings of Jerusalem, Hebron, Jarmuth, Lachish, and Eglon. ²⁴Joshua told the captains of his army, "Come and put your feet on the kings' necks." And they did as they were told.

²⁵"Don't ever be afraid or discouraged," Joshua told his men. "Be strong and courageous, for the LORD is going to do this to all of your enemies." ²⁶Then Joshua killed each of the five kings and hung them on five trees until evening.

²⁷As the sun was going down, Joshua gave instructions for the bodies of the kings to be taken down from the trees and thrown into the cave where they had been hiding. Then they covered the opening of the cave with a large pile of stones, which remains to this very day.

²⁸That same day Joshua completely destroyed the city of Makkedah, killing everyone in it, including the king. Not one person in the city was left alive. He killed the king of Makkedah as he had killed the

10:1 The Hebrew term used here refers to the complete consecration of things or people to the LORD, either by destroying them or by giving them as an offering; also in 10:28, 35, 37, 39, 40.   10:13 Or *The Book of the Upright*.

king of Jericho. ²⁹Then Joshua and the Israelites went to Libnah and attacked it. ³⁰There, too, the LORD gave them the city and its king. They slaughtered everyone in the city and left no survivors. Then Joshua killed the king of Libnah just as he had killed the king of Jericho.

³¹From Libnah, Joshua and the Israelites went to Lachish and attacked it. ³²And the LORD gave it to them on the second day. Here, too, the entire population was slaughtered, just as at Libnah. ³³During the attack on Lachish, King Horam of Gezer had arrived with his army to help defend the city. But Joshua's men killed him and destroyed his entire army.

³⁴Then Joshua and the Israelite army went to Eglon and attacked it. ³⁵They captured it in one day, and as at Lachish, they completely destroyed everyone in the city. ³⁶After leaving Eglon, they attacked Hebron, ³⁷capturing it and all of its surrounding towns. And just as they had done at Eglon, they completely destroyed the entire population. Not one person was left alive. ³⁸Then they turned back and attacked Debir. ³⁹They captured the city, its king, and all of its surrounding villages. And they killed everyone in it, leaving no survivors. They completely destroyed Debir just as they had destroyed Libnah and Hebron.

⁴⁰So Joshua conquered the whole region—the kings and people of the hill country, the Negev, the western foothills,* and the mountain slopes. He completely destroyed everyone in the land, leaving no survivors, just as the LORD, the God of Israel, had commanded. ⁴¹Joshua slaughtered them from Kadesh-barnea to Gaza and from Goshen to Gibeon. ⁴²In a single campaign Joshua conquered all these kings and their land, for the LORD, the God of Israel, was fighting for his people. ⁴³Then Joshua and the Israelite army returned to their camp at Gilgal.

CHAPTER 11

When King Jabin of Hazor heard what had happened, he sent urgent messages to the following kings: King Jobab of Madon; the king of Shimron; the king of Acshaph; ²all the kings of the northern hill country; the kings in the Jordan Valley* south of Galilee*; the kings in the western foothills*; the kings of Naphothdor on the west; ³the kings of Canaan, both east and west; the kings of the Amorites; the kings of the Hittites; the kings of the Perizzites; the kings in the Jebusite hill country; and the Hivites in the towns on the slopes of Mount Hermon, in the land of Mizpah.

⁴All these kings responded by mobilizing their warriors and uniting to fight against Israel. Their combined armies, along with a vast array of horses and chariots, covered the landscape like the sand on the seashore. ⁵They established their camp around the water near Merom to fight against Israel.

⁶Then the LORD said to Joshua, "Do not be afraid of them. By this time tomorrow they will all be dead. Cripple their horses and burn their chariots."

⁷So Joshua and his warriors traveled to the water near Merom and attacked suddenly. ⁸And the LORD gave them victory over their enemies. The Israelites chased them as far as Great Sidon and Misrephoth-maim, and eastward into the valley of Mizpah, until not one enemy warrior was left alive. ⁹Then Joshua crippled the horses and burned all the chariots, as the LORD had instructed.

¹⁰Joshua then turned back and captured Hazor and killed its king. (Hazor had at one time been the capital of the federation of all these kingdoms.) ¹¹The Israelites completely destroyed* every living thing in the city. Not a single person was spared. And then Joshua burned the city.

¹²Joshua slaughtered all the other kings and their people, completely destroying them, just as Moses, the servant of the LORD, had commanded. ¹³However, Joshua did not burn any of the cities built on mounds except Hazor. ¹⁴And the Israelites took all the captured goods and cattle of the ravaged cities for themselves, but they killed all the people. ¹⁵As the LORD had commanded his servant Moses, so Moses commanded Joshua. And Joshua did as he was told, carefully obeying all of the LORD's instructions to Moses.

¹⁶So Joshua conquered the entire region—the hill country, the Negev, the land of Goshen, the western foothills, the Jordan Valley, and the mountains and lowlands of Israel. ¹⁷The Israelite territory now extended all the

---

10:40 Hebrew *the Shephelah.*   **11:2a** Hebrew *the Arabah;* also in 11:16.   **11:2b** Hebrew *of Kinnereth.*   **11:2c** Hebrew *the Shephelah;* also in 11:16.   **11:11** The Hebrew term used here refers to the complete consecration of things or people to the LORD, either by destroying them or by giving them as an offering; also in 11:12, 20, 21.

way from Mount Halak, which leads up to Seir, to Baal-gad at the foot of Mount Hermon in the valley of Lebanon. Joshua killed all the kings of those territories, [18]waging war for a long time to accomplish this. [19]No one in this region made peace with the Israelites except the Hivites of Gibeon. All the others were defeated. [20]For the LORD hardened their hearts and caused them to fight the Israelites instead of asking for peace. So they were completely and mercilessly destroyed, as the LORD had commanded Moses.

[21]During this period, Joshua destroyed all the descendants of Anak, who lived in the hill country of Hebron, Debir, Anab, and the entire hill country of Judah and Israel. He killed them all and completely destroyed their towns. [22]Not one was left in all the land of Israel, though some still remained in Gaza, Gath, and Ashdod.

[23]So Joshua took control of the entire land, just as the LORD had instructed Moses. He gave it to the people of Israel as their special possession, dividing the land among the tribes. So the land finally had rest from war.

CHAPTER 12

These are the kings east of the Jordan River who had been killed and whose land was taken. Their territory extended from the Arnon Gorge to Mount Hermon and included all the land east of the Jordan Valley.*

[2]King Sihon of the Amorites, who lived in Heshbon, was defeated. His kingdom included Aroer, on the edge of the Arnon Gorge, and extended from the middle of the Arnon Gorge to the Jabbok River, which serves as a boundary for the Ammonites. This territory included half of the present area of Gilead, which lies north of the Jabbok River. [3]Sihon also controlled the Jordan Valley as far north as the western shores of the Sea of Galilee* and as far south as the Dead Sea,* from Beth-jeshimoth to the slopes of Pisgah.

[4]King Og of Bashan, the last of the Rephaites, lived at Ashtaroth and Edrei. [5]He ruled a territory stretching from Mount Hermon to Salecah in the north and to all of Bashan in the east, and westward to the boundaries of the kingdoms of Geshur and Maacah. His kingdom included the northern half of Gilead, the other portion of which was in the

territory of King Sihon of Heshbon. [6]Moses, the servant of the LORD, and the Israelites had destroyed the people of King Sihon and King Og. And Moses gave their land to the tribes of Reuben, Gad, and the half-tribe of Manasseh.

[7]The following is a list of the kings Joshua and the Israelite armies defeated on the west side of the Jordan, from Baal-gad in the valley of Lebanon to Mount Halak, which leads up to Seir. (Joshua allotted this land to the tribes of Israel as their inheritance, [8]including the hill country, the western foothills,* the Jordan Valley, the mountain slopes, the Judean wilderness, and the Negev. The people who lived in this region were the Hittites, the Amorites, the Canaanites, the Perizzites, the Hivites, and the Jebusites.) These are the kings Israel defeated:

[9] The king of Jericho
  The king of Ai, near Bethel
[10] The king of Jerusalem
  The king of Hebron
[11] The king of Jarmuth
  The king of Lachish
[12] The king of Eglon
  The king of Gezer
[13] The king of Debir
  The king of Geder
[14] The king of Hormah
  The king of Arad
[15] The king of Libnah
  The king of Adullam
[16] The king of Makkedah
  The king of Bethel
[17] The king of Tappuah
  The king of Hepher
[18] The king of Aphek
  The king of Lasharon
[19] The king of Madon
  The king of Hazor
[20] The king of Shimron-meron
  The king of Acshaph
[21] The king of Taanach
  The king of Megiddo
[22] The king of Kedesh
  The king of Jokneam in Carmel
[23] The king of Dor in the city of
    Naphoth-dor*
  The king of Goyim in Gilgal*
[24] The king of Tirzah.

In all, thirty-one kings and their cities were destroyed.

12:1 Hebrew *the Arabah;* also in 12:3, 8. **12:3a** Hebrew *sea of Kinnereth.* **12:3b** Hebrew *the sea of the Arabah, the Salt Sea.* **12:8** Hebrew *the Shephelah.* **12:23a** Hebrew *Naphath-dor,* a variant name for Naphoth-dor. **12:23b** Greek version reads *Goyim in Galilee.*

MARCH 4 ☐ DAY 64
JOSHUA 13–17
Portions for Five Tribes

OVERVIEW The conquest is complete, and now it is time to assign portions of the land to the tribes that have fought so valiantly in the strength of the Lord. Reuben, Gad, and half the tribe of Manasseh have previously requested land east of the Jordan, and now receive their new homesteads. Caleb, still full of vigor at the age of eighty-five, requests and receives Hebron in Judah's area as his inheritance—even though it contains giants and walled cities!

Chapter 13	Chapter 14	Chapter 15	Chapters 16–17
Portions for			
2½ Tribes	Caleb	Judah	Joseph's Sons
East of Jordan	West of Jordan		

YOUR DAILY WALK Joshua 14 features Caleb, and at first glance he may appear to be a proud, self-reliant soldier. After all, how often do you hear an eighty-five-year-old claim to have the energy of someone half his age? But Caleb wasn't blowing his own horn. Rather, he was boasting in the Lord: "I followed the LORD my God completely. . . . Now, as you can see, the LORD has kept me alive" (14:8, 10). He was merely giving credit where credit was due!

When we are truly witnessing, we are not talking about ourselves but about Christ.

Stop right now and brag a little about the Lord. Think of one way God has shown himself strong on your behalf over the past week, and tell a friend or loved one about it sometime today. Then you'll be doing what Caleb, the soldier, (and David, the psalmist) loved to do so much: "I will boast only in the LORD" (Psalm 34:2).

INSIGHT Locating the Allocator of the Land
Who, in fact, made the final decision regarding *which* tribe received *which* parcel of land? According to 13:1-6, it was Joshua; 14:1 suggests Eleazar and the heads of the families; 14:5 implies the people as a whole. One commentator has suggested that Eleazar cast the lots, assisted by the heads of families; the people accepted the allocations; and Joshua took the ultimate responsibility.

CHAPTER 13
When Joshua was an old man, the LORD said to him, "You are growing old, and much land remains to be conquered. ²The people still need to occupy the land of the Philistines and the Geshurites—³territory that belongs to the Canaanites. This land extends from the stream of Shihor, which is on the boundary of Egypt, northward to the boundary of Ekron, ⁴and includes the five Philistine cities of Gaza, Ashdod, Ashkelon, Gath, and Ekron. The land of the Avvites in the south also remains to be conquered. In the north, this area has not yet been conquered: all the land of the Canaanites, including Mearah (which belongs to the Sidonians), stretching northward to Aphek on the border of the Amo-

rites; ⁵the land of the Gebalites and all of the Lebanon mountain area to the east, from Baal-gad beneath Mount Hermon to Lebo-hamath; ⁶and all the hill country from Lebanon to Misrephoth-maim, including all the land of the Sidonians.

"I will drive these people out of the land for the Israelites. So be sure to give this land to Israel as a special possession, just as I have commanded you. ⁷Include all this territory as Israel's inheritance when you divide the land among the nine tribes and the half-tribe of Manasseh."

⁸Half the tribe of Manasseh and the tribes of Reuben and Gad had already received their inheritance on the east side of

the Jordan, for Moses, the servant of the LORD, had previously assigned this land to them.

⁹Their territory extended from Aroer on the edge of the Arnon Gorge (including the town in the middle of the gorge) to the plain beyond Medeba, as far as Dibon. ¹⁰It also included all the towns of King Sihon of the Amorites, who reigned in Heshbon, and extended as far as the borders of Ammon. ¹¹It included Gilead, the territory of the kingdoms of Geshur and Maacah, all of Mount Hermon, all of Bashan as far as Salecah, ¹²and all the territory of King Og of Bashan, who had reigned in Ashtaroth and Edrei. King Og was the last of the Rephaites, for Moses had attacked them and driven them out. ¹³But the Israelites failed to drive out the people of Geshur and Maacah, so they continue to live among the Israelites to this day.

¹⁴Moses did not assign any land to the tribe of Levi. Instead, as the LORD had promised them, their inheritance came from the offerings burned on the altar to the LORD, the God of Israel.

¹⁵Moses had assigned the following area to the families of the tribe of Reuben.

¹⁶Their territory extended from Aroer on the edge of the Arnon Gorge (including the town in the middle of the gorge) to the plain beyond Medeba. ¹⁷It included Heshbon and the other towns on the plain—Dibon, Bamoth-baal, Beth-baal-meon, ¹⁸Jahaz, Kedemoth, Mephaath, ¹⁹Kiriathaim, Sibmah, Zereth-shahar on the hill above the valley, ²⁰Beth-peor, the slopes of Pisgah, and Beth-jeshimoth. ²¹The land of Reuben also included all the towns of the plain and the entire kingdom of Sihon. Sihon was the Amorite king who had reigned in Heshbon and was killed by Moses along with the chiefs of Midian—Evi, Rekem, Zur, Hur, and Reba—princes living in the region who were allied with Sihon. ²²The Israelites also killed Balaam the magician, the son of Beor. ²³The Jordan River marked the western boundary for the tribe of Reuben. The towns and villages in this area were given as an inheritance to the families of the tribe of Reuben.

²⁴Moses had assigned the following area to the families of the tribe of Gad.

²⁵Their territory included Jazer, all the towns of Gilead, and half of the land of Ammon, as far as the town of Aroer just west of Rabbah. ²⁶It extended from Heshbon to Ramath-mizpeh and Betonim, and from Mahanaim to Lo-debar.* ²⁷In the valley were Beth-haram, Beth-nimrah, Succoth, Zaphon, and the rest of the kingdom of King Sihon of Heshbon. The Jordan River was the western border, extending as far north as the Sea of Galilee.* ²⁸The towns and villages in this area were given as an inheritance to the families of the tribe of Gad.

²⁹Moses had assigned the following area to the families of the half-tribe of Manasseh.

³⁰Their territory extended from Mahanaim, including all of Bashan, all the former kingdom of King Og, and the sixty towns of Jair in Bashan. ³¹It also included half of Gilead and King Og's royal cities of Ashtaroth and Edrei. All this was given to the descendants of Makir, who was Manasseh's son.

³²These are the allotments Moses had made while he was on the plains of Moab, across the Jordan River, east of Jericho. ³³But Moses gave no land to the tribe of Levi, for the LORD, the God of Israel, had promised to be their inheritance.

CHAPTER 14
The remaining tribes of Israel inherited land in Canaan as allotted by Eleazar the priest, Joshua son of Nun, and the tribal leaders. ²These nine and a half tribes received their inheritance by means of sacred lots, in accordance with the LORD's command through Moses. ³Moses had already given an inheritance of land to the two and a half tribes on the east side of the Jordan River. ⁴The tribe of Joseph had become two separate tribes—Manasseh and Ephraim. And the Levites were given no land at all, only towns to live in and the surrounding pasturelands for their flocks and herds. ⁵So the distribution of the land was in strict

13:26 Or to the territory of Debir.   13:27 Hebrew sea of Kinnereth.

accordance with the LORD's instructions to Moses.

⁶A delegation from the tribe of Judah, led by Caleb son of Jephunneh the Kenizzite, came to Joshua at Gilgal. Caleb said to Joshua, "Remember what the LORD said to Moses, the man of God, about you and me when we were at Kadesh-barnea. ⁷I was forty years old when Moses, the servant of the LORD, sent me from Kadesh-barnea to explore the land of Canaan. I returned and gave from my heart a good report, ⁸but my brothers who went with me frightened the people and discouraged them from entering the Promised Land. For my part, I followed the LORD my God completely. ⁹So that day Moses promised me, 'The land of Canaan on which you were just walking will be your special possession and that of your descendants forever, because you wholeheartedly followed the LORD my God.'

¹⁰"Now, as you can see, the LORD has kept me alive and well as he promised for all these forty-five years since Moses made this promise—even while Israel wandered in the wilderness. Today I am eighty-five years old. ¹¹I am as strong now as I was when Moses sent me on that journey, and I can still travel and fight as well as I could then. ¹²So I'm asking you to give me the hill country that the LORD promised me. You will remember that as scouts we found the Anakites living there in great, walled cities. But if the LORD is with me, I will drive them out of the land, just as the LORD said."

¹³So Joshua blessed Caleb son of Jephunneh and gave Hebron to him as an inheritance. ¹⁴Hebron still belongs to the descendants of Caleb son of Jephunneh the Kenizzite because he wholeheartedly followed the LORD, the God of Israel. ¹⁵(Previously Hebron had been called Kiriath-arba. It had been named after Arba, a great hero of the Anakites.)

And the land had rest from war.

CHAPTER 15

The land assigned to the families of the tribe of Judah reached southward to the border of Edom, with the wilderness of Zin being its southernmost point.

²The southern boundary began at the south bay of the Dead Sea,* ³ran south of Scorpion Pass* into the wilderness of Zin and went south of Kadesh-barnea to Hezron. Then it went up to Addar, where it turned toward Karka. ⁴From there it passed to Azmon, until it finally reached the brook of Egypt, which it followed to the Mediterranean Sea.* This was their* southern boundary.

⁵The eastern boundary extended along the Dead Sea to the mouth of the Jordan River.

The northern boundary began at the bay where the Jordan River empties into the Dead Sea, ⁶crossed to Beth-hoglah, then proceeded north of Beth-arabah to the stone of Bohan. (Bohan was Reuben's son.) ⁷From that point it went through the valley of Achor to Debir, turning north toward Gilgal, which is across from the slopes of Adummim on the south side of the valley. From there the border extended to the springs at En-shemesh and on to En-rogel. ⁸The boundary then passed through the valley of the son of Hinnom, along the southern slopes of the Jebusites, where the city of Jerusalem is located. Then it went west to the top of the mountain above the valley of Hinnom, and on up to the northern end of the valley of Rephaim. ⁹From there the border extended from the top of the mountain to the spring at the waters of Nephtoah,* and from there to the towns on Mount Ephron. Then it turned toward Baalah (that is, Kiriath-jearim). ¹⁰The border circled west of Baalah to Mount Seir, passed along to the town of Kesalon on the northern slope of Mount Jearim, and went down to Beth-shemesh and on to Timnah. ¹¹The boundary line then proceeded to the slope of the hill north of Ekron, where it turned toward Shikkeron and Mount Baalah. It passed Jabneel and ended at the Mediterranean Sea.

¹²The western boundary was the shoreline of the Mediterranean Sea.*

These are the boundaries for the families of the tribe of Judah.

¹³The LORD instructed Joshua to assign some of Judah's territory to Caleb son of Jephunneh. So Caleb was given the city of Arba (that is, Hebron), which had been named after Anak's ancestor. ¹⁴Caleb drove

---

15:2 Hebrew *the Salt Sea;* also in 15:5.　　**15:3** Hebrew *Akrabbim.*　　**15:4a** Hebrew *the sea;* also in 15:11.　　**15:4b** Hebrew *your.*
15:9 Or *the spring at Me-nephtoah.*　　**15:12** Hebrew *the Great Sea;* also in 15:47.

out the three Anakites—Sheshai, Ahiman, and Talmai—descendants of Anak. [15]Then he fought against the people living in the town of Debir (formerly called Kiriath-sepher). [16]Caleb said, "I will give my daughter Acsah in marriage to the one who attacks and captures Kiriath-sepher." [17]Othniel, the son of Caleb's brother Kenaz, was the one who conquered it, so Acsah became Othniel's wife.

[18]When Acsah married Othniel, she urged him* to ask her father for an additional field. As she got down off her donkey, Caleb asked her, "What is it? What can I do for you?"

[19]She said, "Give me a further blessing. You have been kind enough to give me land in the Negev; please give me springs as well." So Caleb gave her the upper and lower springs.

[20]This was the inheritance given to the families of the tribe of Judah.

[21]The towns of Judah situated along the borders of Edom in the extreme south are Kabzeel, Eder, Jagur, [22]Kinah, Dimonah, Adadah, [23]Kedesh, Hazor, Ithnan, [24]Ziph, Telem, Bealoth, [25]Hazor-hadattah, Kerioth-hezron (that is, Hazor), [26]Amam, Shema, Moladah, [27]Hazar-gaddah, Heshmon, Beth-pelet, [28]Hazar-shual, Beersheba, Biziothiah, [29]Baalah, Iim, Ezem, [30]Eltolad, Kesil, Hormah, [31]Ziklag, Madmannah, Sansannah, [32]Lebaoth, Shilhim, Ain, and Rimmon. In all, there were twenty-nine of these towns with their surrounding villages.

[33]The following towns situated in the western foothills* were also given to Judah: Eshtaol, Zorah, Ashnah, [34]Zanoah, En-gannim, Tappuah, Enam, [35]Jarmuth, Adullam, Socoh, Azekah, [36]Shaaraim, Adithaim, Gederah, and Gederothaim. In all, there were fourteen towns with their surrounding villages.

[37]Also included were Zenan, Hadashah, Migdal-gad, [38]Dilean, Mizpeh, Joktheel, [39]Lachish, Bozkath, Eglon, [40]Cabbon, Lahmam, Kitlish, [41]Gederoth, Beth-dagon, Naamah, and Makkedah—sixteen towns with their surrounding villages. [42]Besides these, there were Libnah, Ether, Ashan, [43]Iphtah, Ashnah, Nezib, [44]Keilah, Aczib, and Mareshah—

nine towns with their surrounding villages.

[45]The territory of the tribe of Judah also included all the towns and villages of Ekron. [46]From Ekron the boundary extended west and included the towns near Ashdod with their surrounding villages. [47]It also included Ashdod with its towns and villages and Gaza with its towns and villages, as far as the brook of Egypt and along the coast of the Mediterranean Sea.

[48]Judah also received the following towns in the hill country: Shamir, Jattir, Socoh, [49]Dannah, Kiriath-sannah (that is, Debir), [50]Anab, Eshtemoh, Anim, [51]Goshen, Holon, and Giloh—eleven towns with their surrounding villages. [52]Also included were the towns of Arab, Dumah, Eshan, [53]Janim, Beth-tappuah, Aphekah, [54]Humtah, Kiriath-arba (that is, Hebron), and Zior—nine towns with their surrounding villages.

[55]Besides these, there were Maon, Carmel, Ziph, Juttah, [56]Jezreel, Jokdeam, Zanoah, [57]Kain, Gibeah, and Timnah—ten towns with their surrounding villages.

[58]In addition, there were Halhul, Beth-zur, Gedor, [59]Maarath, Beth-anoth, and Eltekon—six towns with their surrounding villages. [60]There were also Kiriath-baal (that is, Kiriath-jearim) and Rabbah—two towns with their surrounding villages.

[61]In the wilderness there were the towns of Beth-arabah, Middin, Secacah, [62]Nibshan, the City of Salt, and En-gedi—six towns with their surrounding villages.

[63]But the tribe of Judah could not drive out the Jebusites, who lived in the city of Jerusalem, so the Jebusites live there among the people of Judah to this day.

CHAPTER 16

The allotment to the descendants of Joseph extended from the Jordan River near Jericho, east of the waters of Jericho, through the wilderness and into the hill country of Bethel. [2]From Bethel (that is, Luz)* it ran over to Ataroth in the territory of the Arkites. [3]Then it descended westward to the

15:18 Some Greek manuscripts read *Othniel urged her.*   15:33 Hebrew *the Shephelah.*   16:2 As in Greek version (also see 18:13); Hebrew reads *From Bethel to Luz.*

territory of the Japhletites as far as Lower Beth-horon, then to Gezer and on over to the Mediterranean Sea.*

⁴The families of Joseph's sons, Manasseh and Ephraim, received their inheritance.

⁵The following territory was given to the families of the tribe of Ephraim as their inheritance.

The eastern boundary of their inheritance began at Ataroth-addar. From there it ran to Upper Beth-horon, ⁶then on to the Mediterranean Sea. The northern boundary began at the Mediterranean, ran east past Micmethath, then curved eastward past Taanath-shiloh to the east of Janoah. ⁷From Janoah it turned southward to Ataroth and Naarah, touched Jericho, and ended at the Jordan River. ⁸From Tappuah the border extended westward, following the Kanah Ravine to the Mediterranean Sea. This is the inheritance given to the families of the tribe of Ephraim.

⁹Ephraim was also given some towns with surrounding villages in the territory of the half-tribe of Manasseh. ¹⁰They did not drive the Canaanites out of Gezer, however, so the people of Gezer live as slaves among the people of Ephraim to this day.

CHAPTER 17

The next allotment of land was given to the half-tribe of Manasseh, the descendants of Joseph's older son. Gilead and Bashan on the east side of the Jordan had already been given to the family of Makir because he was a great warrior. (Makir was Manasseh's oldest son and was the father of Gilead.) ²Land on the west side of the Jordan was allotted to the remaining families within the tribe of Manasseh: Abiezer, Helek, Asriel, Shechem, Hepher, and Shemida.

³However, Zelophehad son of Hepher, who was a descendant of Manasseh, Makir, and Gilead, had no sons. Instead, he had five daughters. Their names were Mahlah, Noah, Hoglah, Milcah, and Tirzah. ⁴These women came to Eleazar the priest, Joshua son of Nun, and the Israelite leaders and said, "The LORD commanded Moses to give us an inheritance along with the men of our tribe."

So Joshua gave them an inheritance

along with their uncles, as the LORD had commanded. ⁵As a result, Manasseh's inheritance came to ten parcels of land, in addition to the land of Gilead and Bashan across the Jordan River, ⁶because the female descendants of Manasseh received an inheritance along with the male descendants. (The land of Gilead was given to the rest of the male descendants of Manasseh.)

⁷The boundary of the tribe of Manasseh extended from the border of Asher to Micmethath, which is east of Shechem. Then the boundary went south from Micmethath to the people living near the spring of Tappuah. ⁸(The land surrounding Tappuah belonged to Manasseh, but the town of Tappuah, on the border of Manasseh's territory, belonged to the tribe of Ephraim.) ⁹From the spring of Tappuah, the border of Manasseh followed the northern side of the Kanah Ravine to the Mediterranean Sea.* (Several towns in Manasseh's territory belonged to the tribe of Ephraim.) ¹⁰The land south of the ravine belonged to Ephraim, and the land north of the ravine belonged to Manasseh, with the Mediterranean Sea forming Manasseh's western border. North of Manasseh was the territory of Asher, and to the east was the territory of Issachar.

¹¹The following towns within the territory of Issachar and Asher were given to Manasseh: Beth-shan,* Ibleam, Dor (that is, Naphoth-dor),* Endor, Taanach, and Megiddo, with their respective villages. ¹²But the descendants of Manasseh were unable to occupy these towns. They could not drive out the Canaanites who continued to live there. ¹³Later on, however, when the Israelites became strong enough, they forced the Canaanites to work as slaves. But they did not drive them out of the land.

¹⁴The descendants of Joseph came to Joshua and asked, "Why have you given us only one portion of land when the LORD has given us so many people?"

¹⁵Joshua replied, "If the hill country of Ephraim is not large enough for you, clear out land for yourselves in the forest where the Perizzites and Rephaites live."

¹⁶They said, "The hill country is not

16:3 Hebrew *the sea*; also in 16:6, 8.   17:9 Hebrew *the sea*; also in 17:10.   17:11a Hebrew *Beth-shean*, a variant name for Beth-shan; also in 17:16.   17:11b The meaning of the Hebrew here is uncertain.

enough for us, and the Canaanites in the lowlands around Beth-shan and the valley of Jezreel have iron chariots—they are too strong for us."

¹⁷Then Joshua said to the tribes of Ephraim and Manasseh, the descendants of Joseph, "Since you are so large and strong, you will be given more than one portion. ¹⁸The forests of the hill country will be yours as well. Clear as much of the land as you wish and live there. And I am sure you can drive out the Canaanites from the valleys, too, even though they are strong and have iron chariots."

MARCH 5 ☐ DAY 65
JOSHUA 18–21
Portions for Seven Tribes

 OVERVIEW Seven tribes remain to receive their hard-earned "property inheritance." After ordering a survey of the land, Joshua divides it into seven parcels and distributes it by lot. In addition, six cities of refuge are designated to protect innocent slayers. The Levites, whose inheritance is the priesthood rather than property, are given forty-eight cities in which to live. With the Tabernacle in place in Shiloh, the task of dividing up the land is complete.

Chapter 18		Chapter 19	Chapter 20	Chapter 21
Portions for			Protection for	Provision for
Benjamin		6 Tribes	Slayers	Levites
A Hard-Earned Reward			A Gracious Refuge	

 YOUR DAILY WALK Today's passage will either excite you or embalm you!

On the surface it appears to be little more than a long list of unknown towns, obscure families, and meaningless details. You'll be tempted to skim the material—and skip the blessing God has for you.

God will keep all his promises whether you believe them or not!

Put yourself in Joshua's sandals for a moment. Imagine that your home state is the Promised Land. For seven long years you have been taking stronghold after stronghold in the quest to rid the land of its pagan occupants. Then one morning trumpets blare forth the news: The war is over! The land is yours. Victory is complete. It is time to celebrate and to learn which part of the new territory will be your home.

You listen breathlessly as Joshua describes its borders: "Norman and Norma Christian, your family now owns all of Jefferson County, from Route 16 to the state line." You pinch yourself. After all the years of waiting, it's finally happened. God has kept his word!

Does that do anything for your faith in God and your confidence in his promises to care for you? If so, write the words of Philippians 4:19 on a card, sign it, and date it. Let it be a reminder today—and every day—that you are taking God at his word!

 INSIGHT Growing Room for the Tribe of Dan

Dan's allotment was a small territory compressed between the northwestern hills of Judah and the Mediterranean Sea—a portion that proved too small for Dan's 64,400 families (Numbers 26:42-43). The majority of the tribe migrated farther north and settled in Laish—with disastrous consequences (Judges 18).

CHAPTER 18

Now that the land was under Israelite control, the entire Israelite assembly gathered at Shiloh and set up the Tabernacle.* [2]But there remained seven tribes who had not yet been allotted their inheritance.

[3]Then Joshua asked them, "How long are you going to wait before taking possession of the remaining land the LORD, the God of your ancestors, has given to you? [4]Select three men from each tribe, and I will send them out to survey the unconquered territory. They will return to me with a written report of their proposed divisions of the inheritance. [5]The scouts will map the land into seven sections, excluding Judah's territory in the south and Joseph's territory in the north. [6]Then I will cast sacred lots in the presence of the LORD our God to decide which section will be assigned to each tribe. [7]However, the Levites will not receive any land. Their role as priests of the LORD is their inheritance. And the tribes of Gad, Reuben, and the half-tribe of Manasseh won't receive any more land, for they have already received their inheritance, which Moses, the servant of the LORD, gave them on the east side of the Jordan River."

[8]As the men who were mapping out the land started on their way, Joshua commanded them, "Go and survey the land. Then return to me with your written report, and I will assign the land to the tribes by casting sacred lots in the presence of the LORD here at Shiloh." [9]The men did as they were told and mapped the entire territory into seven sections, listing the towns in each section. Then they returned to Joshua in the camp at Shiloh. [10]There at Shiloh, Joshua cast sacred lots in the presence of the LORD to determine which tribe should have each section.

[11]The first allotment of land went to the families of the tribe of Benjamin. It lay between the territory previously assigned to the tribes of Judah and Joseph.

[12]The northern boundary began at the Jordan River, went north of the slope of Jericho, then west through the hill country and the wilderness of Beth-aven. [13]From there the boundary went south to Luz (that is, Bethel)

and proceeded down to Ataroth-addar to the top of the hill south of Lower Beth-horon.

[14]The boundary then ran south along the western edge of the hill facing Beth-horon, ending at the village of Kiriath-baal (that is, Kiriath-jearim), one of the towns belonging to the tribe of Judah. This was the western boundary.

[15]The southern boundary began at the outskirts of Kiriath-jearim. From there it ran westward* to the spring at the waters of Nephtoah,* [16]and down to the base of the mountain beside the valley of the son of Hinnom, at the northern end of the valley of Rephaim. From there it went down the valley of Hinnom, crossing south of the slope where the Jebusites lived, and continued down to En-rogel. [17]From En-rogel the boundary proceeded northeast to En-shemesh and on to Geliloth (which is across from the slopes of Adummim). Then it went down to the stone of Bohan. (Bohan was Reuben's son.) [18]From there it passed along the north side of the slope overlooking the Jordan Valley.* The border then went down into the valley, [19]ran past the north slope of Beth-hoglah, and ended at the north bay of the Dead Sea,* which is the southern end of the Jordan River.

[20]The eastern boundary was the Jordan River.

This was the inheritance for the families of the tribe of Benjamin.

[21]These were the towns given to the families of the tribe of Benjamin.

Jericho, Beth-hoglah, Emek-keziz, [22]Beth-arabah, Zemaraim, Bethel, [23]Avvim, Parah, Ophrah, [24]Kephar-ammoni, Ophni, and Geba—twelve towns with their villages. [25]Also Gibeon, Ramah, Beeroth, [26]Mizpeh, Kephirah, Mozah, [27]Rekem, Irpeel, Taralah, [28]Zela, Haeleph, Jebus (that is, Jerusalem), Gibeah, and Kiriath-jearim*—fourteen towns with their villages.

This was the inheritance given to the families of the tribe of Benjamin.

18:1 Hebrew *Tent of Meeting.*   18:15a Or *it went to Ephron, and.* The meaning of the Hebrew is uncertain.   18:15b Or *the spring at Me-nephtoah.*   18:18 Hebrew *the Arabah.*   18:19 Hebrew *Salt Sea.*   18:28 As in Greek version; Hebrew reads *Kiriath.*

CHAPTER 19

The second allotment of land went to the families of the tribe of Simeon. Their inheritance was surrounded by Judah's territory.

²Simeon's inheritance included Beer-sheba, Sheba, Moladah, ³Hazar-shual, Balah, Ezem, ⁴Eltolad, Bethul, Hormah, ⁵Ziklag, Beth-marcaboth, Hazar-susah, ⁶Beth-lebaoth, and Sharuhen—thirteen towns with their villages. ⁷It also included Ain, Rimmon, Ether, and Ashan—four towns with their villages, ⁸including all the villages as far south as Baalath-beer (also known as Ramah of the Negev).

This was the inheritance of the families of the tribe of Simeon. ⁹Their inheritance came from part of what had been given to Judah because Judah's territory was too large for them. So the tribe of Simeon received an inheritance within the territory of Judah.

¹⁰The third allotment of land went to the families of the tribe of Zebulun.

The boundary of Zebulun's inheritance started at Sarid. ¹¹From there it went west, going past Maralah, touching Dabbesheth, and proceeding to the brook east of Jokneam. ¹²In the other direction, the boundary line went east from Sarid to the border of Kisloth-tabor, and from there to Daberath and up to Japhia. ¹³Then it continued east to Gath-hepher, Eth-kazin, and Rimmon and turned toward Neah. ¹⁴The northern boundary of Zebulun passed Hannathon and ended at the valley of Iphtah-el. ¹⁵The towns in these areas included Kattath, Nahalal, Shimron, Idalah, and Bethlehem—twelve towns with their surrounding villages.

¹⁶This was the inheritance of the families of the tribe of Zebulun.

¹⁷The fourth allotment of land went to the families of the tribe of Issachar.

¹⁸Its boundaries included the following towns: Jezreel, Kesulloth, Shunem, ¹⁹Hapharaim, Shion, Anaharath, ²⁰Rabbith, Kishion, Ebez, ²¹Remeth, En-gannim, En-haddah, and Beth-pazzez. ²²The boundary also touched Tabor, Shahazumah, and Beth-shemesh, ending at the Jordan River—sixteen towns with their surrounding villages.

²³This was the inheritance of the families of the tribe of Issachar.

²⁴The fifth allotment of land went to the families of the tribe of Asher.

²⁵Its boundaries included these towns: Helkath, Hali, Beten, Acshaph, ²⁶Allammelech, Amad, and Mishal. The boundary on the west went from Carmel to Shihor-libnath, ²⁷turned east toward Beth-dagon, and ran as far as Zebulun in the valley of Iphtah-el, running north to Beth-emek and Neiel. It then continued north to Cabul, ²⁸Abdon,* Rehob, Hammon, Kanah, and as far as Greater Sidon. ²⁹Then the boundary turned toward Ramah and the fortified city of Tyre and came to the Mediterranean Sea* at Hosah. The territory also included Mehebel, Aczib, ³⁰Ummah, Aphek, and Rehob—twenty-two towns with their surrounding villages.

³¹This was the inheritance of the families of the tribe of Asher.

³²The sixth allotment of land went to the families of the tribe of Naphtali.

³³Its boundary ran from Heleph, from the oak at Zaanannim, and extended across to Adami-nekeb, Jabneel, and as far as Lakkum, ending at the Jordan River. ³⁴The western boundary ran past Aznoth-tabor, then to Hukkok, and touched the boundary of Zebulun in the south, the boundary of Asher on the west, and the Jordan River* on the east. ³⁵The fortified cities included in this territory were Ziddim, Zer, Hammath, Rakkath, Kinnereth, ³⁶Adamah, Ramah, Hazor, ³⁷Kedesh, Edrei, En-hazor, ³⁸Yiron, Migdal-el, Horem, Beth-anath, and Beth-shemesh—nineteen cities with their surrounding villages.

³⁹This was the inheritance of the families of the tribe of Naphtali.

⁴⁰The seventh and last allotment of land went to the families of the tribe of Dan.

⁴¹The towns within Dan's inheritance included Zorah, Eshtaol, Ir-shemesh, ⁴²Shaalabbin, Aijalon, Ithlah, ⁴³Elon, Timnah, Ekron, ⁴⁴Eltekeh, Gibbethon,

---

19:28 As in some Hebrew manuscripts (see also 21:30); most Hebrew manuscripts read *Ebron.*   **19:29** Hebrew *the sea.*
19:34 Hebrew *and Judah at the Jordan River.*

Baalath, [45]Jehud, Bene-berak, Gath-rimmon, [46]and Me-jarkon, also Rakkon along with the territory across from Joppa.

[47]But the tribe of Dan had trouble taking possession of their land, so they fought against the town of Laish.* They captured it, slaughtered its people, and settled there. They renamed the city Dan after their ancestor.

[48]This was the inheritance of the families of the tribe of Dan—these towns with their villages.

[49]After all the land was divided among the tribes, the Israelites gave a special piece of land to Joshua as his inheritance. [50]For the LORD had said he could have any town he wanted. He chose Timnath-serah in the hill country of Ephraim. He rebuilt the town and lived there.

[51]These are the territories that Eleazar the priest, Joshua son of Nun, and the tribal leaders gave as an inheritance to the tribes of Israel by casting sacred lots in the presence of the LORD at the entrance of the Tabernacle* at Shiloh. So the division of the land was completed.

CHAPTER 20

The LORD said to Joshua, [2]"Now tell the Israelites to designate the cities of refuge, as I instructed Moses. [3]Anyone who kills another person unintentionally can run to one of these cities and be protected from the relatives of the one who was killed, for the relatives may seek to avenge the killing.

[4]"Upon reaching one of these cities, the one who caused the accidental death will appear before the leaders at the city gate and explain what happened. They must allow the accused to enter the city and live there among them. [5]If the relatives of the victim come to avenge the killing, the leaders must not release the accused to them, for the death was accidental. [6]But the person who caused the death must stay in that city and be tried by the community and found innocent. Then the one declared innocent because the death was accidental must continue to live in that city until the death of the high priest who was in office at the time of the accident. After that, the one found innocent is free to return home."

[7]The following cities were designated as cities of refuge: Kedesh of Galilee, in the hill country of Naphtali; Shechem, in the hill country of Ephraim; and Kiriath-arba (that is, Hebron), in the hill country of Judah. [8]On the east side of the Jordan River, across from Jericho, the following cities were designated as cities of refuge: Bezer, in the wilderness plain of the tribe of Reuben; Ramoth in Gilead, in the territory of the tribe of Gad; and Golan in Bashan, in the land of the tribe of Manasseh. [9]These cities were set apart for Israelites as well as the foreigners living among them. Anyone who accidentally killed another person could take refuge in one of these cities. In this way, they could escape being killed in revenge prior to standing trial before the community.

CHAPTER 21

Then the leaders of the tribe of Levi came to consult with Eleazar the priest, Joshua son of Nun, and the leaders of the other tribes of Israel. [2]They spoke to them at Shiloh in the land of Canaan, saying, "The LORD instructed Moses to give us towns to live in and pasturelands for our cattle." [3]So by the command of the LORD the Levites were given as their inheritance the following towns with their pasturelands.

[4]The descendants of Aaron, who were members of the Kohathite clan within the tribe of Levi, were given thirteen towns that were originally assigned to the tribes of Judah, Simeon, and Benjamin. [5]The other families of the Kohathite clan were allotted ten towns from the territories of Ephraim, Dan, and the half-tribe of Manasseh.

[6]The clan of Gershon received thirteen towns from the tribes of Issachar, Asher, Naphtali, and the half-tribe of Manasseh in Bashan.

[7]The clan of Merari received twelve cities from the tribes of Reuben, Gad, and Zebulun.

[8]So the Israelites obeyed the LORD's command to Moses and assigned these towns and pasturelands to the Levites by casting sacred lots.

[9]The Israelites gave the following towns from the tribes of Judah and Simeon [10]to the descendants of Aaron, who were members of the Kohathite clan within the tribe of Levi, since the sacred lot fell to them first: [11]Kiriath-arba (that is, Hebron), in the hill

---

19:47 Hebrew *Leshem*, another name for Laish.   **19:51** Hebrew *Tent of Meeting*.

country of Judah, along with its surrounding pasturelands. (Arba was an ancestor of Anak.) [12]But the fields beyond the city and the surrounding villages were given to Caleb son of Jephunneh.

[13]The following towns with their pasturelands were given to the descendants of Aaron the priest: Hebron (a city of refuge for those who accidentally killed someone), Libnah, [14]Jattir, Eshtemoa, [15]Holon, Debir, [16]Ain, Juttah, and Beth-shemesh—nine towns from these two tribes.

[17]From the tribe of Benjamin the priests were given the following towns with their surrounding pasturelands: Gibeon, Geba, [18]Anathoth, and Almon—four towns. [19]So thirteen towns were given to the priests, the descendants of Aaron.

[20]The rest of the Kohathite clan from the tribe of Levi was allotted these towns and pasturelands from the tribe of Ephraim: [21]Shechem (a city of refuge for those who accidentally killed someone), Gezer, [22]Kibzaim, and Beth-horon—four towns.

[23]The following towns and pasturelands were allotted to the priests from the tribe of Dan: Eltekeh, Gibbethon, [24]Aijalon, and Gath-rimmon—four towns.

[25]The half-tribe of Manasseh allotted the following towns with their pasturelands to the priests: Taanach and Gath-rimmon—two towns. [26]So ten towns with their pasturelands were given to the rest of the Kohathite clan.

[27]The descendants of Gershon, another clan within the tribe of Levi, received two towns with their pasturelands from the half-tribe of Manasseh: Golan in Bashan (a city of refuge) and Be-eshterah.

[28]From the tribe of Issachar they received

21:36 Hebrew *Jahzah*, a variant name for Jahaz.

Kishion, Daberath, [29]Jarmuth, and Engannim—four towns with their pasturelands.

[30]From the tribe of Asher they received Mishal, Abdon, [31]Helkath, and Rehob—four towns and their pasturelands.

[32]From the tribe of Naphtali they received Kedesh in Galilee (a city of refuge), Hammoth-dor, and Kartan—three towns with their pasturelands.

[33]So thirteen towns and their pasturelands were allotted to the clan of Gershon.

[34]The rest of the Levites—the Merari clan—were given the following towns from the tribe of Zebulun: Jokneam, Kartah, [35]Dimnah, and Nahalal—four towns with their pasturelands.

[36]From the tribe of Reuben they received Bezer, Jahaz,* [37]Kedemoth, and Mephaath—four towns with their pasturelands.

[38]From the tribe of Gad they received Ramoth in Gilead (a city of refuge), Mahanaim, [39]Heshbon, and Jazer—four towns with their pasturelands. [40]So twelve towns were allotted to the clan of Merari.

[41]The total number of towns and pasturelands within Israelite territory given to the Levites came to forty-eight. [42]Every one of these towns had pasturelands surrounding it.

[43]So the LORD gave to Israel all the land he had sworn to give their ancestors, and they conquered it and settled there. [44]And the LORD gave them rest on every side, just as he had solemnly promised their ancestors. None of their enemies could stand against them, for the LORD helped them conquer all their enemies. [45]All of the good promises that the LORD had given Israel came true.

MARCH 6 ☐ DAY 66
JOSHUA 22–24
Joshua's Last Words

OVERVIEW In his one-hundred-plus years, Joshua has seldom seen an uneventful day—and the closing chapters of his life are no exception! Scarcely have the tribes unpacked in their new homeland when civil war threatens to break out. A memorial built by the eastern tribes is misinterpreted as an idol by their western neighbors, and only quick action by Joshua prevents bloodshed. Years later, in the final hours of Joshua's life, he gathers the nation together and delivers an emotional charge, pleading with them to remain true to the Lord—yet knowing full well they would depart from him. He concludes with a ringing challenge: "Choose today whom you will serve. . . . But as for me and my family, we will serve the LORD" (24:15).

Chapter 22	Chapter 23	Chapter 24
An Altar Misinterpreted	A Charge Given: "Be Faithful to the Lord"	A Covenant Renewed "We Will Serve the Lord"
National Conflict	National Challenge	National Commitment

 YOUR DAILY WALK   When a person lies on his or her deathbed facing the final hours of earthly life, you can be sure he or she won't fritter away those precious moments in small talk. Every word will be fraught with importance. Listen carefully, for that person is sharing his or her innermost thoughts.

A person can't go anywhere while he or she is straddling a fence.

Joshua gathered his dwindling strength and made one last appeal to Israel for a fresh resolve to put away idolatry and serve God alone. After all, it was God who brought their fathers out of Egypt. It was God who parted the Red Sea and decimated the Egyptian army. It was God who stopped the Jordan, flattened Jericho, and put the Canaanite armies to flight. It was God who gave them a land they did not deserve, cities they had not built, and vineyards they did not plant. Is it any wonder Joshua drew an imaginary line in the dust and declared, "Choose today whom you will serve"?

What is keeping you from making a clear-cut commitment to serve God? Has something or someone replaced God as the object of your affection? Choose this day whom you will serve.

 INSIGHT   Joshua's One Glaring Failure
When Moses died, his right-hand man, Joshua, stepped in to fill the void. When Joshua died, he did not have a right-hand man to take over. The resulting lack of trained leadership set the stage for the chaotic period of the judges when "the people did whatever seemed right in their own eyes."

CHAPTER 22
Then Joshua called together the tribes of Reuben, Gad, and the half-tribe of Manasseh. ²He told them, "You have done as Moses, the servant of the LORD, commanded you, and you have obeyed every order I have given you. ³You have not deserted the other tribes, even though the campaign has lasted for such a long time. You have been careful to obey the commands of the LORD your God up to the present day. ⁴And now the LORD your God has given the other tribes rest, as he promised them. So go home now to the land Moses, the servant of the LORD, gave you on the east side of the Jordan River. ⁵But be very careful to obey all the commands and the law that Moses gave to you. Love the LORD your God, walk in all his ways, obey his commands, be faithful to him, and

serve him with all your heart and all your soul."

⁶So Joshua blessed them and sent them home. ⁷Now Moses had given the land of Bashan to the half-tribe of Manasseh east of the Jordan. The other half of the tribe was given land west of the Jordan. As Joshua sent them away, he blessed them ⁸and said, "Share with your relatives back home the great wealth you have taken from your enemies. Share with them your large herds of cattle, your silver and gold, your bronze and iron, and your clothing."

⁹So the men of Reuben, Gad, and the half-tribe of Manasseh left the rest of Israel at Shiloh in the land of Canaan. They started the journey back to their own land of Gilead, the territory that belonged to them according to the LORD's command through Moses.

[10]But while they were still in Canaan, before they crossed the Jordan River, Reuben, Gad, and the half-tribe of Manasseh built a very large altar near the Jordan River at a place called Geliloth.

[11]When the rest of Israel heard they had built the altar at Geliloth west of the Jordan River, in the land of Canaan, [12]the whole assembly gathered at Shiloh and prepared to go to war against their brother tribes. [13]First, however, they sent a delegation led by Phinehas son of Eleazar, the priest. They crossed the river to talk with the tribes of Reuben, Gad, and the half-tribe of Manasseh. [14]In this delegation were ten high officials of Israel, one from each of the ten tribes, and each a leader within the family divisions of Israel.

[15]When they arrived in the land of Gilead, they said to the tribes of Reuben, Gad, and the half-tribe of Manasseh, [16]"The whole community of the LORD demands to know why you are betraying the God of Israel. How could you turn away from the LORD and build an altar in rebellion against him? [17]Was our sin at Peor not enough? We are not yet fully cleansed of it, even after the plague that struck the entire assembly of the LORD. [18]And yet today you are turning away from following the LORD. If you rebel against the LORD today, he will be angry with all of us tomorrow. [19]If you need the altar because your land is defiled, then join us on our side of the river, where the LORD lives among us in his Tabernacle, and we will share our land with you. But do not rebel against the LORD or draw us into your rebellion by building another altar for yourselves. There is only one true altar of the LORD our God. [20]Didn't God punish all the people of Israel when Achan, a member of the clan of Zerah, sinned by stealing the things set apart for the LORD*? He was not the only one who died because of that sin."

[21]Then the people of Reuben, Gad, and the half-tribe of Manasseh answered these high officials: [22]"The LORD alone is God! The LORD alone is God! We have not built the altar in rebellion against the LORD. If we have done so, do not spare our lives this day. But the LORD knows, and let all Israel know, too, [23]that we have not built an altar for ourselves to turn away from the LORD. Nor will we use it for our burnt offerings or grain offerings or peace offerings. If we

have built it for this purpose, may the LORD himself punish us.

[24]"We have built this altar because we fear that in the future your descendants will say to ours, 'What right do you have to worship the LORD, the God of Israel? [25]The LORD has placed the Jordan River as a barrier between our people and your people. You have no claim to the LORD.' And your descendants may make our descendants stop worshiping the LORD. [26]So we decided to build the altar, not for burnt sacrifices, [27]but as a memorial. It will remind our descendants and your descendants that we, too, have the right to worship the LORD at his sanctuary with our burnt offerings, sacrifices, and peace offerings. Then your descendants will not be able to say to ours, 'You have no claim to the LORD.' [28]If they say this, our descendants can reply, 'Look at this copy of the LORD's altar that our ancestors made. It is not for burnt offerings or sacrifices; it is a reminder of the relationship both of us have with the LORD.' [29]Far be it from us to rebel against the LORD or turn away from him by building our own altar for burnt offerings, grain offerings, or sacrifices. Only the altar of the LORD our God that stands in front of the Tabernacle may be used for that purpose."

[30]When Phinehas the priest and the high officials heard this from the tribes of Reuben, Gad, and the half-tribe of Manasseh, they were satisfied. [31]Phinehas son of Eleazar, the priest, replied to them, "Today we know the LORD is among us because you have not sinned against the LORD as we thought. Instead, you have rescued Israel from being destroyed by the LORD."

[32]Then Phinehas son of Eleazar, the priest, and the ten high officials left the tribes of Reuben and Gad in Gilead and returned to the land of Canaan to tell the Israelites what had happened. [33]And all the Israelites were satisfied and praised God and spoke no more of war against Reuben and Gad. [34]The people of Reuben and Gad named the altar "Witness,"* for they said, "It is a witness between us and them that the LORD is our God, too."

CHAPTER 23

The years passed, and the LORD had given the people of Israel rest from all their enemies. Joshua, who was now very old, [2]called

22:20 The Hebrew term used here refers to the complete consecration of things or people to the LORD, either by destroying them or by giving them as an offering.   22:34 Hebrew *edh*. Some manuscripts lack this word.

together all the elders, leaders, judges, and officers of Israel. He said to them, "I am an old man now. ³You have seen everything the LORD your God has done for you during my lifetime. The LORD your God has fought for you against your enemies. ⁴I have allotted to you as an inheritance all the land of the nations yet unconquered, as well as the land of those we have already conquered—from the Jordan River to the Mediterranean Sea* in the west. ⁵This land will be yours, for the LORD your God will drive out all the people living there now. You will live there instead of them, just as the LORD your God promised you.

⁶"So be strong! Be very careful to follow all the instructions written in the Book of the Law of Moses. Do not deviate from them in any way. ⁷Make sure you do not associate with the other people still remaining in the land. Do not even mention the names of their gods, much less swear by them or worship them. ⁸But be faithful to the LORD your God as you have done until now.

⁹"For the LORD has driven out great and powerful nations for you, and no one has yet been able to defeat you. ¹⁰Each one of you will put to flight a thousand of the enemy, for the LORD your God fights for you, just as he has promised. ¹¹So be very careful to love the LORD your God.

¹²"But if you turn away from him and intermarry with the survivors of these nations remaining among you, ¹³then know for certain that the LORD your God will no longer drive them out from your land. Instead, they will be a snare and a trap to you, a pain in your side and a thorn in your eyes, and you will be wiped out from this good land the LORD your God has given you.

¹⁴"Soon I will die, going the way of all the earth. Deep in your hearts you know that every promise of the LORD your God has come true. Not a single one has failed! ¹⁵But as surely as the LORD your God has given you the good things he promised, he will also bring disaster on you if you disobey him. He will completely wipe you out from this good land he has given you. ¹⁶If you break the covenant of the LORD your God by worshiping and serving other gods, his anger will burn against you, and you will quickly be wiped out from the good land he has given you."

CHAPTER 24

Then Joshua summoned all the people of Israel to Shechem, along with their elders, leaders, judges, and officers. So they came and presented themselves to God.

²Joshua said to the people, "This is what the LORD, the God of Israel, says: Your ancestors, including Terah, the father of Abraham and Nahor, lived beyond the Euphrates River,* and they worshiped other gods. ³But I took your ancestor Abraham from the land beyond the Euphrates and led him into the land of Canaan. I gave him many descendants through his son Isaac. ⁴To Isaac I gave Jacob and Esau. To Esau I gave the hill country of Seir, while Jacob and his children went down into Egypt.

⁵"Then I sent Moses and Aaron, and I brought terrible plagues on Egypt; and afterward I brought you out as a free people. ⁶But when your ancestors arrived at the Red Sea,* the Egyptians chased after you with chariots and horses. ⁷When you cried out to the LORD, I put darkness between you and the Egyptians. I brought the sea crashing down on the Egyptians, drowning them. With your very own eyes you saw what I did. Then you lived in the wilderness for many years.

⁸"Finally, I brought you into the land of the Amorites on the east side of the Jordan. They fought against you, but I gave you victory over them, and you took possession of their land. ⁹Then Balak son of Zippor, king of Moab, started a war against Israel. He asked Balaam son of Beor to curse you, ¹⁰but I would not listen to him. Instead, I made Balaam bless you, and so I rescued you from Balak.

¹¹"When you crossed the Jordan River and came to Jericho, the men of Jericho fought against you. There were also many others who fought you, including the Amorites, the Perizzites, the Canaanites, the Hittites, the Girgashites, the Hivites, and the Jebusites. But I gave you victory over them. ¹²And I sent hornets ahead of you to drive out the two kings of the Amorites. It was not your swords or bows that brought you victory. ¹³I gave you land you had not worked for, and I gave you cities you did not build— the cities in which you are now living. I gave you vineyards and olive groves for food, though you did not plant them.

¹⁴"So honor the LORD and serve him

23:4 Hebrew *the Great Sea.*   24:2 Hebrew *the river;* also in 24:3, 14, 15.   24:6 Hebrew *sea of reeds.*

wholeheartedly. Put away forever the idols your ancestors worshiped when they lived beyond the Euphrates River and in Egypt. Serve the LORD alone. [15]But if you are unwilling to serve the LORD, then choose today whom you will serve. Would you prefer the gods your ancestors served beyond the Euphrates? Or will it be the gods of the Amorites in whose land you now live? But as for me and my family, we will serve the LORD."

[16]The people replied, "We would never forsake the LORD and worship other gods. [17]For the LORD our God is the one who rescued us and our ancestors from slavery in the land of Egypt. He performed mighty miracles before our very eyes. As we traveled through the wilderness among our enemies, he preserved us. [18]It was the LORD who drove out the Amorites and the other nations living here in the land. So we, too, will serve the LORD, for he alone is our God."

[19]Then Joshua said to the people, "You are not able to serve the LORD, for he is a holy and jealous God. He will not forgive your rebellion and sins. [20]If you forsake the LORD and serve other gods, he will turn against you and destroy you, even though he has been so good to you."

[21]But the people answered Joshua, saying, "No, we are determined to serve the LORD!"

[22]"You are accountable for this decision," Joshua said. "You have chosen to serve the LORD."

"Yes," they replied, "we are accountable."

[23]"All right then," Joshua said, "destroy the idols among you, and turn your hearts to the LORD, the God of Israel."

[24]The people said to Joshua, "We will serve the LORD our God. We will obey him alone."

[25]So Joshua made a covenant with the people that day at Shechem, committing them to a permanent and binding contract between themselves and the LORD. [26]Joshua recorded these things in the Book of the Law of God. As a reminder of their agreement, he took a huge stone and rolled it beneath the oak tree beside the Tabernacle of the LORD.

[27]Joshua said to all the people, "This stone has heard everything the LORD said to us. It will be a witness to testify against you if you go back on your word to God."

[28]Then Joshua sent the people away, each to his own inheritance.

[29]Soon after this, Joshua son of Nun, the servant of the LORD, died at the age of 110. [30]They buried him in the land he had inherited, at Timnath-serah in the hill country of Ephraim, north of Mount Gaash.

[31]Israel served the LORD throughout the lifetime of Joshua and of the leaders who outlived him—those who had personally experienced all that the LORD had done for Israel.

[32]The bones of Joseph, which the Israelites had brought along with them when they left Egypt, were buried at Shechem, in the parcel of ground Jacob had bought from the sons of Hamor for one hundred pieces of silver.* This land was located in the territory allotted to the tribes of Ephraim and Manasseh, the descendants of Joseph.

[33]Eleazar son of Aaron also died. He was buried in the hill country of Ephraim, in the town of Gibeah, which had been given to his son Phinehas.

24:32 Hebrew *100 kesitahs;* the value or weight of the kesitah is no longer known.

MARCH 7 ☐ DAY 67
Leading the Way

 LOOK BACK Last month we read about Moses' leadership of God's people. Now we've just finished the book of Joshua, in which the general by that name filled Moses' sandals. Leadership transitions are never easy. Any time a leader of the stature and longevity of a Moses passes from the scene, there is good reason for the followers to be nervous: How will our new leader compare with his predecessor? Will he be kind or cruel? Will he walk in the footsteps of his predecessor? Will he have his own agenda or follow God faithfully?

What allowed the transition to move smoothly from Moses to Joshua, in the final analysis, was the realization that the nation's true leader had never changed—only the human instrument through whom that leader worked. Joshua the servant of Moses became Joshua the servant of LORD and continued the pattern of servant leadership the nation had known for forty years. After a fitting farewell for Moses, Joshua led the nation on a memorable crossing of the flood-swollen Jordan River and began a seven-year campaign to conquer and cleanse the Promised Land. Out of a total of thirty-one battles, Joshua would lose only one (can you name it?)—a temporary setback quickly corrected.

LOOK UP With small children, leadership is seldom a problem. When playing "Follow the Leader," everyone takes a turn.

But what about leadership in the household of faith? Are leaders made or born? And how do you know when you have the qualifications for leadership?

Be careful if you think you are leading people—they may be chasing you.

Regardless of your present role of leadership or "followership" in the family of God, it is a worthy ambition to aspire to become a leader (1 Timothy 3:1). But leadership is not for everyone. In fact, the qualifications set forth in 1 Timothy 3 and Titus 1 may surprise you. They have nothing to do with your net worth, your degrees, or the number of civic clubs you belong to. Leadership isn't something to be earned. It is a recognition of spiritual maturity, proven character, and the reputation you have developed both inside and outside the church.

If you aspire to help "manage the ministry" within the family of God, then ask yourself, How well have I managed the other responsibilities I have been entrusted with? Have I managed well my physical body? . . . my mind? . . . my money? . . . my family? . . . my tongue? . . . my reputation? Am I worthy of respect? Am I self-controlled? . . . hospitable? . . . teachable? . . . above reproach? . . . mature? . . . honest in all my dealings? If the answer to these questions is yes, then an expanded leadership role may be appropriate for you.

LOOK AHEAD Regardless of whether an enlarged leadership responsibility may be in your future, the attitude of a servant-leader ought to be your ambition. Listen to this exhortation from the apostle Peter: "Care for the flock of God entrusted to you. Watch over it *willingly,* not grudgingly—not for what you will get out of it, but because you are *eager* to serve God. Don't lord it over the people assigned to your care, but lead them by your *good example.* . . . And all of you, *serve* each other in *humility*" (1 Peter 5:2-5, emphasis added).

Leaders like that are always in short supply—perhaps because they are too humble to admit they have what it takes.

Judges

FOLLOWING the conquest of Canaan, Israel plunges into a 350-year period of national deterioration. A monotonous and deadly pattern develops: The people fall into sin, God disciplines them with foreign oppression, the people cry out in repentance, God raises up a deliverer, peace is restored. The cycle of sin repeats itself a total of seven times in the book. But God, ever faithful to his covenant people, extends his grace again and again by sending such leaders as Deborah, Gideon, and Samson.

Focus	Deterioration	Deliverance					Depravity
Divisions	Introduction to the Judges	First 5 Judges	Gideon, the Hesitant Hero	Gideon's Son and 6 Judges	Samson, the Carnal Champion		2 Examples of National Degradation
	1 2	3 5	6 8	9 12	13 16		17 21
Topics	Situation	Sin, Servitude, and Salvation					Shocking Decline
	Religious Laxity	Political Uncertainty					Moral Anarchy
Place	Canaan and Transjordan						
Time	About 350 Years						

MARCH 8 ☐ DAY 68
JUDGES 1–5
First Five Judges

OVERVIEW Efforts by Judah, Simeon, and the other tribes to purge the land of its pagan inhabitants are not completely successful. Pockets of godless influence remain, always a source of spiritual stumbling to Israel. Over and over the cycle repeats itself. Israel falls into national immorality and idolatry, causing God to allow powerful neighboring countries to oppress and enslave her. When the people cry out in repentance, God responds to their renewed commitment by raising up yet another judge to deliver them. But the cycle soon begins again as the nation's spiritual temperature grows steadily colder.

Chapters 1–2	Chapter 3			Chapters 4–5
Background of the Judges	Three Early Judges			Deborah and Barak
	Othniel	Ehud	Shamgar	
1	11 / 12	30 / 31		
God's Message	God's Messengers			God's Miracles

When a sin is fashionable, Christians should be out of fashion.

YOUR DAILY WALK Look up Romans 12:1-2, and read it several times. Now write down some ways in which you could easily "copy the behavior and customs of this world."

You will spend nearly every day of your earthly life surrounded by unbelievers. And when you stop to think about it, you really have no choice in the matter. To eliminate all contact with non-Christians, as Paul writes, would require leaving the world (1 Corinthians 5:9-10). Besides, how can you witness to unbelievers and lead them to the Savior if you spend no time with them?

But while you must have contact with the world, you are commanded not to "copy the behavior and customs of this world." That was Israel's problem. Her people not only had contact with sinners (as a result of their failure to obey God and clear them out), but they also embraced the sinner's sin. They became indistinguishable from the heathen.

Here is a sentence to ponder and complete: One way in which my lifestyle differs from the world around me because of my commitment to Christ is _____. If you have trouble supplying an answer, consult 1 Peter 2:9-17 for suggestions!

INSIGHT Reconstructing the Colorful Period of the Judges
An excellent way to trace the cyclical period of the judges is by color-coding your Bible. Select five colored pens, and use one color to high-light each part of the "sin cycle": *sin, servitude, supplication, salvation, silence* (you'll use each pen seven times).

CHAPTER 1
After Joshua died, the Israelites asked the LORD, "Which tribe should attack the Canaanites first?"

²The LORD answered, "Judah, for I have given them victory over the land."

³The leaders of Judah said to their rela-tives from the tribe of Simeon, "Join with us to fight against the Canaanites living in the territory allotted to us. Then we will help you conquer your territory." So the men of Simeon went with Judah.

⁴When the men of Judah attacked, the LORD gave them victory over the Canaanites

and Perizzites, and they killed ten thousand enemy warriors at the town of Bezek. [5]While at Bezek they encountered King Adoni-bezek and fought against him, and the Canaanites and Perizzites were defeated. [6]Adoni-bezek escaped, but the Israelites soon captured him and cut off his thumbs and big toes. [7]Adoni-bezek said, "I once had seventy kings with thumbs and big toes cut off, eating scraps from under my table. Now God has paid me back for what I did to them." They took him to Jerusalem, and he died there.

[8]The men of Judah attacked Jerusalem and captured it, killing all its people and setting the city on fire. [9]Then they turned south to fight the Canaanites living in the hill country, the Negev, and the western foothills.* [10]Judah marched against the Canaanites in Hebron (formerly called Kiriath-arba), defeating the forces of Sheshai, Ahiman, and Talmai. [11]From there they marched against the people living in the town of Debir (formerly called Kiriath-sepher).

[12]Then Caleb said, "I will give my daughter Acsah in marriage to the one who attacks and captures Kiriath-sepher." [13]Othniel, the son of Caleb's younger brother Kenaz, was the one who conquered it, so Acsah became Othniel's wife.

[14]When Acsah married Othniel, she urged him* to ask her father for an additional field. As she got down off her donkey, Caleb asked her, "What is it? What can I do for you?"

[15]She said, "Give me a further blessing. You have been kind enough to give me land in the Negev; please give me springs as well." So Caleb gave her the upper and lower springs.

[16]When the tribe of Judah left Jericho,* the Kenites, who were descendants of Moses' father-in-law, traveled with them into the wilderness of Judah. They settled among the people there, near the town of Arad in the Negev.

[17]Then Judah joined with Simeon to fight against the Canaanites living in Zephath, and they completely destroyed* the town. So the town was named Hormah.* [18]In addition, Judah captured the cities of Gaza, Ashkelon, and Ekron, along with their surrounding territories.

[19]The LORD was with the people of Judah, and they took possession of the hill country. But they failed to drive out the people living in the plains because the people there had iron chariots. [20]The city of Hebron was given to Caleb as Moses had promised. And Caleb drove out the people living there, who were descendants of the three sons of Anak. [21]The tribe of Benjamin, however, failed to drive out the Jebusites, who were living in Jerusalem. So to this day the Jebusites live in Jerusalem among the people of Benjamin.

[22]The descendants of Joseph attacked the town of Bethel, and the LORD was with them. [23]They sent spies to Bethel (formerly known as Luz), [24]who confronted a man coming out of the city. They said to him, "Show us a way into the city, and we will have mercy on you." [25]So he showed them a way in, and they killed everyone in the city except for this man and his family. [26]Later the man moved to the land of the Hittites, where he built a city. He named the city Luz, and it is known by that name to this day.

[27]The tribe of Manasseh failed to drive out the people living in Beth-shan,* Taanach, Dor, Ibleam, Megiddo, and their surrounding villages, because the Canaanites were determined to stay in that region. [28]When the Israelites grew stronger, they forced the Canaanites to work as slaves, but they never did drive them out of the land.

[29]The tribe of Ephraim also failed to drive out the Canaanites living in Gezer, and so the Canaanites continued to live there among them.

[30]The tribe of Zebulun also failed to drive out the Canaanites living in Kitron and Nahalol, who continued to live among them. But they forced them to work as slaves.

[31]The tribe of Asher also failed to drive out the residents of Acco, Sidon, Ahlab, Aczib, Helbah, Aphik, and Rehob. [32]In fact, because they did not drive them out, the Canaanites dominated the land where the people of Asher lived.

[33]The tribe of Naphtali also failed to drive out the residents of Beth-shemesh and Beth-anath. Instead, the Canaanites dominated the land where they lived. Nev-

1:9 Hebrew *the Shephelah.*   1:14 Greek version and Latin Vulgate read *he urged her.*   1:16 Hebrew *the city of palms.*   1:17a The Hebrew term used here refers to the complete consecration of things or people to the LORD, either by destroying them or by giving them as an offering.   1:17b *Hormah* means "destruction."   1:27 Hebrew *Beth-shean,* a variant name for Beth-shan.

ertheless, the people of Beth-shemesh and Beth-anath were sometimes forced to work as slaves for the people of Naphtali.

[34]As for the tribe of Dan, the Amorites forced them into the hill country and would not let them come down into the plains. [35]The Amorites were determined to stay in Mount Heres, Aijalon, and Shaalbim, but when the descendants of Joseph became stronger, they forced the Amorites to work as slaves. [36]The boundary of the Amorites ran from Scorpion Pass* to Sela and continued upward from there.

CHAPTER 2

The angel of the LORD went up from Gilgal to Bokim with a message for the Israelites. He told them, "I brought you out of Egypt into this land that I swore to give your ancestors, and I said I would never break my covenant with you. [2]For your part, you were not to make any covenants with the people living in this land; instead, you were to destroy their altars. Why, then, have you disobeyed my command? [3]Since you have done this, I will no longer drive out the people living in your land. They will be thorns in your sides, and their gods will be a constant temptation to you." [4]When the angel of the LORD finished speaking, the Israelites wept loudly. [5]So they called the place "Weeping,"* and they offered sacrifices to the LORD.

[6]After Joshua sent the people away, each of the tribes left to take possession of the land allotted to them. [7]And the Israelites served the LORD throughout the lifetime of Joshua and the leaders who outlived him—those who had seen all the great things the LORD had done for Israel.

[8]Then Joshua son of Nun, the servant of the LORD, died at the age of 110. [9]They buried him in the land he had inherited, at Timnath-serah* in the hill country of Ephraim, north of Mount Gaash.

[10]After that generation died, another generation grew up who did not acknowledge the LORD or remember the mighty things he had done for Israel. [11]Then the Israelites did what was evil in the LORD's sight and worshiped the images of Baal. [12]They abandoned the LORD, the God of their ancestors, who had brought them out of Egypt. They chased after other gods, worshiping the gods of the people around

them. And they angered the LORD. [13]They abandoned the LORD to serve Baal and the images of Ashtoreth. [14]This made the LORD burn with anger against Israel, so he handed them over to marauders who stole their possessions. He sold them to their enemies all around, and they were no longer able to resist them. [15]Every time Israel went out to battle, the LORD fought against them, bringing them defeat, just as he promised. And the people were very distressed.

[16]Then the LORD raised up judges to rescue the Israelites from their enemies. [17]Yet Israel did not listen to the judges but prostituted themselves to other gods, bowing down to them. How quickly they turned away from the path of their ancestors, who had walked in obedience to the LORD's commands. [18]Whenever the LORD placed a judge over Israel, he was with that judge and rescued the people from their enemies throughout the judge's lifetime. For the LORD took pity on his people, who were burdened by oppression and suffering. [19]But when the judge died, the people returned to their corrupt ways, behaving worse than those who had lived before them. They followed other gods, worshiping and bowing down to them. And they refused to give up their evil practices and stubborn ways.

[20]So the LORD burned with anger against Israel. He said, "Because these people have violated the covenant I made with their ancestors and have ignored my commands, [21]I will no longer drive out the nations that Joshua left unconquered when he died. [22]I did this to test Israel—to see whether or not they would obey the LORD as their ancestors did." [23]That is why the LORD did not quickly drive the nations out or allow Joshua to conquer them all.

CHAPTER 3

The LORD left certain nations in the land to test those Israelites who had not participated in the wars of Canaan. [2]He did this to teach warfare to generations of Israelites who had no experience in battle. [3]These were the nations: the Philistines (those living under the five Philistine rulers), all the Canaanites, the Sidonians, and the Hivites living in the hill country of Lebanon from Mount Baal-hermon to Lebo-hamath.

1:36 Hebrew *Akrabbim*.   2:5 Hebrew *Bokim*.   2:9 Hebrew *Timnath-heres*, a variant name for Timnath-serah.

⁴These people were left to test the Israelites—to see whether they would obey the commands the LORD had given to their ancestors through Moses.

⁵So Israel lived among the Canaanites, Hittites, Amorites, Perizzites, Hivites, and Jebusites, ⁶and they intermarried with them. Israelite sons married their daughters, and Israelite daughters were given in marriage to their sons. And the Israelites worshiped their gods.

⁷The Israelites did what was evil in the LORD's sight. They forgot about the LORD their God, and they worshiped the images of Baal and the Asherah poles. ⁸Then the LORD burned with anger against Israel, and he handed them over to King Cushan-rishathaim of Aram-naharaim.* And the Israelites were subject to Cushan-rishathaim for eight years.

⁹But when Israel cried out to the LORD for help, the LORD raised up a man to rescue them. His name was Othniel, the son of Caleb's younger brother, Kenaz. ¹⁰The Spirit of the LORD came upon him, and he became Israel's judge. He went to war against King Cushan-rishathaim of Aram, and the LORD gave Othniel victory over him. ¹¹So there was peace in the land for forty years. Then Othniel son of Kenaz died.

¹²Once again the Israelites did what was evil in the LORD's sight, so the LORD gave King Eglon of Moab control over Israel. ¹³Together with the Ammonites and Amalekites, Eglon attacked Israel and took possession of Jericho.* ¹⁴And the Israelites were subject to Eglon of Moab for eighteen years.

¹⁵But when Israel cried out to the LORD for help, the LORD raised up a man to rescue them. His name was Ehud son of Gera, of the tribe of Benjamin, who was left-handed. The Israelites sent Ehud to deliver their tax money to King Eglon of Moab. ¹⁶So Ehud made himself a double-edged dagger that was eighteen inches* long, and he strapped it to his right thigh, keeping it hidden under his clothing. ¹⁷He brought the tax money to Eglon, who was very fat. ¹⁸After delivering the payment, Ehud sent home those who had carried the tax money.

¹⁹But when Ehud reached the stone carvings near Gilgal, he turned back. He came to Eglon and said, "I have a secret message for you." So the king commanded his servants to be silent and sent them all out of the room. ²⁰Ehud walked over to Eglon as he was sitting alone in a cool upstairs room and said, "I have a message for you from God!" As King Eglon rose from his seat, ²¹Ehud reached with his left hand, pulled out the dagger strapped to his right thigh, and plunged it into the king's belly. ²²The dagger went so deep that the handle disappeared beneath the king's fat. So Ehud left the dagger in, and the king's bowels emptied. ²³Then Ehud closed and locked the doors and climbed down the latrine and escaped through the sewage access.

²⁴After Ehud was gone, the king's servants returned and found the doors to the upstairs room locked. They thought he might be using the latrine, ²⁵so they waited. But when the king didn't come out after a long delay, they became concerned and got a key. And when they opened the door, they found their master dead on the floor.

²⁶While the servants were waiting, Ehud escaped, passing the idols on his way to Seirah. ²⁷When he arrived in the hill country of Ephraim, Ehud sounded a call to arms. Then he led a band of Israelites down from the hills. ²⁸"Follow me," he said, "for the LORD has given you victory over Moab your enemy." So they followed him. And the Israelites took control of the shallows of the Jordan River across from Moab, preventing anyone from crossing. ²⁹They attacked the Moabites and killed about ten thousand of their strongest and bravest warriors. Not one of them escaped. ³⁰So Moab was conquered by Israel that day, and the land was at peace for eighty years.

³¹After Ehud, Shamgar son of Anath rescued Israel. He killed six hundred Philistines with an ox goad.

CHAPTER 4

After Ehud's death, the Israelites again did what was evil in the LORD's sight. ²So the LORD handed them over to King Jabin of Hazor, a Canaanite king. The commander of his army was Sisera, who lived in Harosheth-haggoyim. ³Sisera, who had nine hundred iron chariots, ruthlessly oppressed the Israelites for twenty years. Then the Israelites cried out to the LORD for help.

⁴Deborah, the wife of Lappidoth, was a

3:8 *Aram-naharaim* means "Aram of the two rivers," thought to have been located between the Euphrates and Balih Rivers in northwestern Mesopotamia. **3:13** Hebrew *the city of palms.* **3:16** Hebrew *1 cubit* [45 centimeters].

prophet who had become a judge in Israel. [5]She would hold court under the Palm of Deborah, which stood between Ramah and Bethel in the hill country of Ephraim, and the Israelites came to her to settle their disputes. [6]One day she sent for Barak son of Abinoam, who lived in Kedesh in the land of Naphtali. She said to him, "This is what the LORD, the God of Israel, commands you: Assemble ten thousand warriors from the tribes of Naphtali and Zebulun at Mount Tabor. [7]I will lure Sisera, commander of Jabin's army, along with his chariots and warriors, to the Kishon River. There I will give you victory over him."

[8]Barak told her, "I will go, but only if you go with me!"

[9]"Very well," she replied, "I will go with you. But since you have made this choice, you will receive no honor. For the LORD's victory over Sisera will be at the hands of a woman." So Deborah went with Barak to Kedesh. [10]At Kedesh, Barak called together the tribes of Zebulun and Naphtali, and ten thousand warriors marched up with him. Deborah also marched with them.

[11]Now Heber the Kenite, a descendant of Moses' brother-in-law* Hobab, had moved away from the other members of his tribe and pitched his tent by the Oak of Zaanannim, near Kedesh.

[12]When Sisera was told that Barak son of Abinoam had gone up to Mount Tabor, [13]he called for all nine hundred of his iron chariots and all of his warriors, and they marched from Harosheth-haggoyim to the Kishon River.

[14]Then Deborah said to Barak, "Get ready! Today the LORD will give you victory over Sisera, for the LORD is marching ahead of you." So Barak led his ten thousand warriors down the slopes of Mount Tabor into battle. [15]When Barak attacked, the LORD threw Sisera and all his charioteers and warriors into a panic. Then Sisera leaped down from his chariot and escaped on foot. [16]Barak chased the enemy and their chariots all the way to Harosheth-haggoyim, killing all of Sisera's warriors. Not a single one was left alive.

[17]Meanwhile, Sisera ran to the tent of Jael, the wife of Heber the Kenite, because Heber's family was on friendly terms with King Jabin of Hazor. [18]Jael went out to meet Sisera and said to him, "Come into my tent,

sir. Come in. Don't be afraid." So he went into her tent, and she covered him with a blanket.

[19]"Please give me some water," he said. "I'm thirsty." So she gave him some milk to drink and covered him again.

[20]"Stand at the door of the tent," he told her. "If anybody comes and asks you if there is anyone here, say no."

[21]But when Sisera fell asleep from exhaustion, Jael quietly crept up to him with a hammer and tent peg. Then she drove the tent peg through his temple and into the ground, and so he died.

[22]When Barak came looking for Sisera, Jael went out to meet him. She said, "Come, and I will show you the man you are looking for." So he followed her into the tent and found Sisera lying there dead, with the tent peg through his temple.

[23]So on that day Israel saw God subdue Jabin, the Canaanite king. [24]And from that time on Israel became stronger and stronger against King Jabin, until they finally destroyed him.

CHAPTER 5

On that day Deborah and Barak son of Abinoam sang this song:

[2] "When Israel's leaders take charge,
      and the people gladly follow—
    bless the LORD!

[3] "Listen, you kings!
      Pay attention, you mighty rulers!
    For I will sing to the LORD.
      I will lift up my song to the LORD, the
        God of Israel.

[4] "LORD, when you set out from Seir
      and marched across the fields of
        Edom,
    the earth trembled
      and the cloudy skies poured down
        rain.
[5] The mountains quaked at the coming
        of the LORD.
      Even Mount Sinai shook in the
        presence of the LORD, the God of
        Israel.

[6] "In the days of Shamgar son of Anath,
      and in the days of Jael,
    people avoided the main roads,
      and travelers stayed on crooked side
        paths.

7 There were few people left in the
    villages of Israel—
    until Deborah arose as a mother for
      Israel.
8 When Israel chose new gods,
    war erupted at the city gates.
    Yet not a shield or spear could be seen
      among forty thousand warriors in
      Israel!
9 My heart goes out to Israel's leaders,
    and to those who gladly followed.
    Bless the LORD!

10 "You who ride on fine donkeys
    and sit on fancy saddle blankets,
      listen!
    And you who must walk along the
      road, listen!
11 Listen to the village musicians*
    gathered at the watering holes.
    They recount the righteous victories
      of the LORD,
    and the victories of his villagers in
      Israel.
    Then the people of the LORD
      marched down to the city gates.

12 "Wake up, Deborah, wake up!
    Wake up, wake up, and sing a song!
    Arise, Barak!
      Lead your captives away, son of
      Abinoam!
13 "Down from Tabor marched the
      remnant against the mighty.
    The people of the LORD marched
      down against mighty warriors.
14 They came down from Ephraim—a
      land that once belonged to the
      Amalekites,
    and Benjamin also followed you.
    From Makir the commanders marched
      down;
    from Zebulun came those who carry
      the rod of authority.
15 The princes of Issachar were with
      Deborah and Barak.
    They followed Barak, rushing into
      the valley.
    But in the tribe of Reuben
      there was great indecision.
16 Why did you sit at home among the
      sheepfolds—
    to hear the shepherds whistle for
      their flocks?
    In the tribe of Reuben
      there was great indecision.

17 Gilead remained east of the Jordan.
    And Dan, why did he stay home?
    Asher sat unmoved at the seashore,
      remaining in his harbors.
18 But Zebulun risked his life,
    as did Naphtali, on the battlefield.

19 "The kings of Canaan fought at
      Taanach near Megiddo's springs,
    but they carried off no treasures of
      battle.
20 The stars fought from heaven.
    The stars in their orbits fought
      against Sisera.
21 The Kishon River swept them away—
    that ancient river, the Kishon.
    March on, my soul, with courage!
22 Then the horses' hooves hammered the
      ground,
    the galloping, galloping of Sisera's
      mighty steeds.
23 'Let the people of Meroz be cursed,'
      said the angel of the LORD.
    'Let them be utterly cursed
    because they did not come to help the
      LORD,
    to help the LORD against the mighty
      warriors.'

24 "Most blessed is Jael,
    the wife of Heber the Kenite.
    May she be blessed above all women
      who live in tents.
25 Sisera asked for water,
    and Jael gave him milk.
    In a bowl fit for kings,
      she brought him yogurt.
26 Then with her left hand she reached for
      a tent peg,
    and with her right hand she reached
      for the workman's hammer.
    She hit Sisera, crushing his head.
    She pounded the tent peg through
      his head, piercing his temples.
27 He sank, he fell,
    he lay dead at her feet.

28 "From the window Sisera's mother
      looked out.
    Through the window she watched
      for his return, saying,
    'Why is his chariot so long in coming?
    Why don't we hear the sound of
      chariot wheels?'
29 A reply comes from her wise women,
    and she repeats these words to
      herself:

5:11 The meaning of the Hebrew is uncertain.

³⁰ 'They are dividing the captured goods
        they found—
    a woman or two for every man.
  There are gorgeous robes for Sisera,
    and colorful, beautifully
      embroidered robes for me.'

³¹ "LORD, may all your enemies die as
        Sisera did!
    But may those who love you rise like
        the sun at full strength!"

Then there was peace in the land for forty
years.

MARCH 9 □ DAY 69
JUDGES 6–8
Gideon, the Hesitant Hero

OVERVIEW Israel's oppression under Midian is brief but severe, as
Midian forcibly takes Israel's harvest. Gideon, called by a divine messenger to deliver God's people, is a reluctant savior and doubtful candidate
for greatness. It takes a pair of confirming signs (first a soggy fleece,
then a dry one) to convince Gideon that God can use him. But once
his faith is sparked, Gideon watches as God removes all the props upon
which he might have trusted: his army (reduced 99 percent); his weapons (reduced to pitchers, torches, and trumpets); and his military strategy (reduced to a single command: "Stand still!"). When a miracle of
deliverance occurs, there can be only one explanation—God did it!

Chapter 6	Chapter 7	Chapter 8
Call of Gideon	Defeat of Midian	Rest for Israel
God's Man	God's Plan	God's Glory

YOUR DAILY WALK Are you a skeptic—the kind of person who never
takes anything at face value, asks a lot of questions, and always requires
confirmation of the facts? Then you will appreciate the life of Gideon!

If seeing is believing, the true skeptic will refuse to look.

In 1 Corinthians 1:22, Paul comments that the "Jews . . . want a
sign," and such was the case with Gideon. Faced with an overwhelming assignment and equipped with rather dubious human qualifications
for the task, Gideon needed a bolstered faith before he was ready to
answer God's call. Nowhere in the passage did God chide Gideon for
his request for a confirming sign. Rather, he gladly and patiently provided what Gideon needed to overcome his inferiority complex.

When the will of God is clear, to demand a sign is evidence of unwillingness to obey. When God's will is uncertain, but you are earnestly
seeking to find it (like Gideon), God will make it clear to you. Take a
decision you are wrestling with today, and ask God to confirm his will
through the Bible, Christian counsel, circumstances, or inner assurance.
But, remember, once you know what he wants you to do, delayed
obedience is really disobedience.

INSIGHT God Plus One: An Unbeatable Team (7:14)
In Leviticus 26:8, God had promised Israel that "Five of you will chase a
hundred [a ratio of one to twenty], and a hundred of you will chase ten
thousand [one to one hundred]!" With Gideon's band of 300 men, God
fulfilled that promise and proved he doesn't worry about the odds!

CHAPTER 6

Again the Israelites did what was evil in the LORD's sight. So the LORD handed them over to the Midianites for seven years. ²The Midianites were so cruel that the Israelites fled to the mountains, where they made hiding places for themselves in caves and dens. ³Whenever the Israelites planted their crops, marauders from Midian, Amalek, and the people of the east would attack Israel, ⁴camping in the land and destroying crops as far away as Gaza. They left the Israelites with nothing to eat, taking all the sheep, oxen, and donkeys. ⁵These enemy hordes, coming with their cattle and tents as thick as locusts, arrived on droves of camels too numerous to count. And they stayed until the land was stripped bare. ⁶So Israel was reduced to starvation by the Midianites. Then the Israelites cried out to the LORD for help.

⁷When they cried out to the LORD because of Midian, ⁸the LORD sent a prophet to the Israelites. He said, "This is what the LORD, the God of Israel, says: I brought you up out of slavery in Egypt ⁹and rescued you from the Egyptians and from all who oppressed you. I drove out your enemies and gave you their land. ¹⁰I told you, 'I am the LORD your God. You must not worship the gods of the Amorites, in whose land you now live.' But you have not listened to me."

¹¹Then the angel of the LORD came and sat beneath the oak tree at Ophrah, which belonged to Joash of the clan of Abiezer. Gideon son of Joash had been threshing wheat at the bottom of a winepress to hide the grain from the Midianites. ¹²The angel of the LORD appeared to him and said, "Mighty hero, the LORD is with you!"

¹³"Sir," Gideon replied, "if the LORD is with us, why has all this happened to us? And where are all the miracles our ancestors told us about? Didn't they say, 'The LORD brought us up out of Egypt'? But now the LORD has abandoned us and handed us over to the Midianites."

¹⁴Then the LORD turned to him and said, "Go with the strength you have and rescue Israel from the Midianites. I am sending you!"

¹⁵"But Lord," Gideon replied, "how can I rescue Israel? My clan is the weakest in the whole tribe of Manasseh, and I am the least in my entire family!"

¹⁶The LORD said to him, "I will be with you. And you will destroy the Midianites as if you were fighting against one man."

¹⁷Gideon replied, "If you are truly going to help me, show me a sign to prove that it is really the LORD speaking to me. ¹⁸Don't go away until I come back and bring my offering to you."

The LORD answered, "I will stay here until you return."

¹⁹Gideon hurried home. He cooked a young goat, and with half a bushel* of flour he baked some bread without yeast. Then, carrying the meat in a basket and the broth in a pot, he brought them out and presented them to the angel, who was under the oak tree.

²⁰The angel of God said to him, "Place the meat and the unleavened bread on this rock, and pour the broth over it." And Gideon did as he was told. ²¹Then the angel of the LORD touched the meat and bread with the staff in his hand, and fire flamed up from the rock and consumed all he had brought. And the angel of the LORD disappeared.

²²When Gideon realized that it was the angel of the LORD, he cried out, "Sovereign LORD, I have seen the angel of the LORD face to face!"

²³"It is all right," the LORD replied. "Do not be afraid. You will not die." ²⁴And Gideon built an altar to the LORD there and named it "The LORD Is Peace."* The altar remains in Ophrah in the land of the clan of Abiezer to this day.

²⁵That night the LORD said to Gideon, "Take the second best bull from your father's herd, the one that is seven years old. Pull down your father's altar to Baal, and cut down the Asherah pole standing beside it. ²⁶Then build an altar to the LORD your God here on this hill, laying the stones carefully. Sacrifice the bull as a burnt offering on the altar, using as fuel the wood of the Asherah pole you cut down." ²⁷So Gideon took ten of his servants and did as the LORD had commanded. But he did it at night because he was afraid of the other members of his father's household and the people of the town. He knew what would happen if they found out who had done it.

²⁸Early the next morning, as the people of the town began to stir, someone discovered that the altar of Baal had been knocked

6:19 Hebrew *1 ephah* [18 liters].   **6:24** Hebrew *Yahweh Shalom*.

down and that the Asherah pole beside it was gone. In their place a new altar had been built, and it had the remains of a sacrifice on it. ²⁹The people said to each other, "Who did this?" And after asking around and making a careful search, they learned that it was Gideon, the son of Joash.

³⁰"Bring out your son," they shouted to Joash. "He must die for destroying the altar of Baal and for cutting down the Asherah pole."

³¹But Joash shouted to the mob, "Why are you defending Baal? Will you argue his case? Whoever pleads his case will be put to death by morning! If Baal truly is a god, let him defend himself and destroy the one who knocked down his altar!" ³²From then on Gideon was called Jerubbaal, which means "Let Baal defend himself," because he knocked down Baal's altar.

³³Soon afterward the armies of Midian, Amalek, and the people of the east formed an alliance against Israel and crossed the Jordan, camping in the valley of Jezreel. ³⁴Then the Spirit of the LORD took possession of Gideon. He blew a ram's horn as a call to arms, and the men of the clan of Abiezer came to him. ³⁵He also sent messengers throughout Manasseh, Asher, Zebulun, and Naphtali, summoning their warriors, and all of them responded.

³⁶Then Gideon said to God, "If you are truly going to use me to rescue Israel as you promised, ³⁷prove it to me in this way. I will put some wool on the threshing floor tonight. If the fleece is wet with dew in the morning but the ground is dry, then I will know that you are going to help me rescue Israel as you promised." ³⁸And it happened just that way. When Gideon got up the next morning, he squeezed the fleece and wrung out a whole bowlful of water.

³⁹Then Gideon said to God, "Please don't be angry with me, but let me make one more request. This time let the fleece remain dry while the ground around it is wet with dew." ⁴⁰So that night God did as Gideon asked. The fleece was dry in the morning, but the ground was covered with dew.

CHAPTER 7
So Jerubbaal (that is, Gideon) and his army got up early and went as far as the spring of Harod. The armies of Midian

were camped north of them in the valley near the hill of Moreh. ²The LORD said to Gideon, "You have too many warriors with you. If I let all of you fight the Midianites, the Israelites will boast to me that they saved themselves by their own strength. ³Therefore, tell the people, 'Whoever is timid or afraid may leave* and go home.'" Twenty-two thousand of them went home, leaving only ten thousand who were willing to fight.

⁴But the LORD told Gideon, "There are still too many! Bring them down to the spring, and I will sort out who will go with you and who will not." ⁵When Gideon took his warriors down to the water, the LORD told him, "Divide the men into two groups. In one group put all those who cup water in their hands and lap it up with their tongues like dogs. In the other group put all those who kneel down and drink with their mouths in the stream." ⁶Only three hundred of the men drank from their hands. All the others got down on their knees and drank with their mouths in the stream. ⁷The LORD told Gideon, "With these three hundred men I will rescue you and give you victory over the Midianites. Send all the others home." ⁸So Gideon collected the provisions and rams' horns of the other warriors and sent them home. But he kept the three hundred men with him.

Now the Midianite camp was in the valley just below Gideon. ⁹During the night, the LORD said, "Get up! Go down into the Midianite camp, for I have given you victory over them! ¹⁰But if you are afraid to attack, go down to the camp with your servant Purah. ¹¹Listen to what the Midianites are saying, and you will be greatly encouraged. Then you will be eager to attack."

So Gideon took Purah and went down to the outposts of the enemy camp. ¹²The armies of Midian, Amalek, and the people of the east had settled in the valley like a swarm of locusts. Their camels were like grains of sand on the seashore—too many to count! ¹³Gideon crept up just as a man was telling his friend about a dream. The man said, "I had this dream, and in my dream a loaf of barley bread came tumbling down into the Midianite camp. It hit a tent, turned it over, and knocked it flat!"

¹⁴His friend said, "Your dream can mean only one thing—God has given Gideon son

7:3 Hebrew *leave Mount Gilead*. The identity of Mount Gilead is uncertain in this context. It is perhaps used here as another name for Mount Gilboa.

of Joash, the Israelite, victory over all the armies united with Midian!"

¹⁵When Gideon heard the dream and its interpretation, he thanked God. Then he returned to the Israelite camp and shouted, "Get up! For the LORD has given you victory over the Midianites!" ¹⁶He divided the three hundred men into three groups and gave each man a ram's horn and a clay jar with a torch in it. ¹⁷Then he said to them, "Keep your eyes on me. When I come to the edge of the camp, do just as I do. ¹⁸As soon as my group blows the rams' horns, those of you on the other sides of the camp blow your horns and shout, 'For the LORD and for Gideon!'"

¹⁹It was just after midnight, after the changing of the guard, when Gideon and the one hundred men with him reached the outer edge of the Midianite camp. Suddenly, they blew the horns and broke their clay jars. ²⁰Then all three groups blew their horns and broke their jars. They held the blazing torches in their left hands and the horns in their right hands and shouted, "A sword for the LORD and for Gideon!" ²¹Each man stood at his position around the camp and watched as all the Midianites rushed around in a panic, shouting as they ran. ²²When the three hundred Israelites blew their horns, the LORD caused the warriors in the camp to fight against each other with their swords. Those who were not killed fled to places as far away as Beth-shittah near Zererah and to the border of Abel-meholah near Tabbath.

²³Then Gideon sent for the warriors of Naphtali, Asher, and Manasseh, who joined in the chase after the fleeing army of Midian. ²⁴Gideon also sent messengers throughout the hill country of Ephraim, saying, "Come down to attack the Midianites. Cut them off at the shallows of the Jordan River at Beth-barah." And the men of Ephraim did as they were told. ²⁵They captured Oreb and Zeeb, the two Midianite generals, killing Oreb at the rock of Oreb, and Zeeb at the winepress of Zeeb. And they continued to chase the Midianites. Afterward the Israelites brought the heads of Oreb and Zeeb to Gideon, who was by the Jordan.

CHAPTER 8
Then the people of Ephraim asked Gideon, "Why have you treated us this way? Why

didn't you send for us when you first went out to fight the Midianites?" And they argued heatedly with Gideon.

²But Gideon replied, "What have I done compared to you? Aren't the last grapes of Ephraim's harvest better than the entire crop of my little clan of Abiezer? ³God gave you victory over Oreb and Zeeb, the generals of the Midianite army. What have I done compared to that?" When the men of Ephraim heard Gideon's answer, they were no longer angry.

⁴Gideon then crossed the Jordan River with his three hundred men, and though they were exhausted, they continued to chase the enemy. ⁵When they reached Succoth, Gideon asked the leaders of the town, "Will you please give my warriors some food? They are very tired. I am chasing Zebah and Zalmunna, the kings of Midian."

⁶But the leaders of Succoth replied, "You haven't caught Zebah and Zalmunna yet. Catch them first, and then we will feed your warriors."

⁷So Gideon said, "After the LORD gives me victory over Zebah and Zalmunna, I will return and tear your flesh with the thorns and briers of the wilderness."

⁸From there Gideon went up to Peniel* and asked for food, but he got the same answer. ⁹So he said to the people of Peniel, "After I return in victory, I will tear down this tower."

¹⁰By this time Zebah and Zalmunna were in Karkor with a remnant of 15,000 warriors—all that remained of the allied armies of the east—for 120,000 had already been killed. ¹¹Gideon circled around by the caravan route east of Nobah and Jogbehah, taking the Midianite army by surprise. ¹²Zebah and Zalmunna, the two Midianite kings, fled, but Gideon chased them down and captured all their warriors.

¹³After this, Gideon returned by way of Heres Pass. ¹⁴There he captured a young man from Succoth and demanded that he write down the names of all the seventy-seven rulers and leaders in the town. ¹⁵Gideon then returned to Succoth and said to the leaders, "Here are Zebah and Zalmunna. When we were here before, you taunted me, saying, 'You haven't caught Zebah and Zalmunna yet. Catch them first, and then we will feed your exhausted war-

8:8 Hebrew *Penuel*, a variant name for Peniel; also in 8:9, 17.

riors.'" ¹⁶Then Gideon took the leaders of the town and taught them a lesson, punishing them with thorns and briers from the wilderness. ¹⁷He also knocked down the tower of Peniel and killed all the men in the town.

¹⁸Then Gideon asked Zebah and Zalmunna, "The men you killed at Tabor— what were they like?"

"Like you," they replied. "They all had the look of a king's son."

¹⁹"They were my brothers!" Gideon exclaimed. "As surely as the LORD lives, I wouldn't kill you if you hadn't killed them."

²⁰Turning to Jether, his oldest son, he said, "Kill them!" But Jether did not draw his sword, for he was only a boy and was afraid.

²¹Then Zebah and Zalmunna said to Gideon, "Don't ask a boy to do a man's job! Do it yourself!" So Gideon killed them both and took the royal ornaments from the necks of their camels.

²²Then the Israelites said to Gideon, "Be our ruler! You and your son and your grandson will be our rulers, for you have rescued us from Midian."

²³But Gideon replied, "I will not rule over you, nor will my son. The LORD will rule over you! ²⁴However, I have one request. Each of you can give me an earring out of the treasures you collected from your fallen enemies." (The enemies, being Ishmaelites, all wore gold earrings.)

²⁵"Gladly!" they replied. They spread out a cloak, and each one threw in a gold earring he had gathered. ²⁶The weight of the gold earrings was forty-three pounds,* not including the crescents and pendants, the royal clothing of the kings, or the chains around the necks of their camels. ²⁷Gideon made a sacred ephod from the gold and put it in Ophrah, his hometown. But soon all the Israelites prostituted themselves by worshiping it, and it became a trap for Gideon and his family.

²⁸That is the story of how Israel subdued Midian, which never recovered. Throughout the rest of Gideon's lifetime—about forty years—the land was at peace.

²⁹Then Gideon* son of Joash returned home. ³⁰He had seventy sons, for he had many wives. ³¹He also had a concubine in Shechem, who bore him a son named Abimelech. ³²Gideon died when he was very old, and he was buried in the grave of his father, Joash, at Ophrah in the land of the clan of Abiezer.

³³As soon as Gideon was dead, the Israelites prostituted themselves by worshiping the images of Baal, making Baal-berith their god. ³⁴They forgot the LORD their God, who had rescued them from all their enemies surrounding them. ³⁵Nor did they show any loyalty to the family of Jerubbaal (that is, Gideon), despite all the good he had done for Israel.

8:26 Hebrew *1,700 shekels* [19.4 kilograms].   8:29 Hebrew *Jerubbaal*; see 6:32.

MARCH 10 ☐ DAY 70
JUDGES 9–12
Gideon's Son and Six Judges

 OVERVIEW Abimelech, Gideon's son by a concubine, is never called a judge in Israel, though he sets himself up as king and murders his seventy brothers. As Jotham (the only surviving brother) predicts, Abimelech dies as violently as he lived. The brief records of two minor judges, Tola and Jair, are followed by a lengthy treatment of Jephthah in the days of oppression by the Philistines and Ammonites. In contrast to Gideon, who sought to appease the tribe of Ephraim, Jephthah ends up going to war against Ephraim. His action-filled reign as judge is best remembered for his presumptuous vow, which seals forever the fate of his virgin daughter. The section closes with a brief look at three other minor judges who are most noteworthy for their enormous families!

Chapter 9	Chapter 10	Chapter 11	Chapter 12
God's Retribution	God's Rebuke	Jephthah's Vow	Jephthah's Vengeance
Abimelech	Tola/Jair	Jephthah and 3 Other Judges	

YOUR DAILY WALK   Should Christians take oaths or make vows today? Those who respond no will find ample support for their view in the tragic consequences of Jephthah's presumptuous vow (11:30-31, 34-40).

No one can be called mature who does not learn from his own mistakes.

Vows are not to be taken lightly. But the real tragedy of Jephthah was his unwillingness to admit he had acted foolishly and had made a mistake. A willingness to admit errors and seek help is an evidence of maturity and strength, not a weakness.

Is there a family member or friend you have wronged through a mistake? Going to that person, admitting you were wrong, asking for forgiveness, and making restitution for any damage can open new opportunities for fellowship and service with him or her. God wants you to be an open, honest person with a realistic view of yourself—one who (unlike Jephthah) is quick to admit mistakes and knows when to seek wise counsel.

INSIGHT   A Deadly Slip of the Tongue
The forty-two thousand Ephraimites Jephthah slew were identified by the fact that they said, *Sibboleth* instead of *Shibboleth* (12:6). But they aren't the only ones in Scripture who were betrayed by an accent. When Peter was in the high priest's courtyard the night Jesus was arrested, he was accused of being a follower of Jesus because of his Galilean speech (Matthew 26:73)!

CHAPTER 9

One day Gideon's* son Abimelech went to Shechem to visit his mother's brothers. He said to them and to the rest of his mother's family, ²"Ask the people of Shechem whether they want to be ruled by all seventy of Gideon's sons or by one man. And remember, I am your own flesh and blood!"

³So Abimelech's uncles spoke to all the people of Shechem on his behalf. And after listening to their proposal, they decided in favor of Abimelech because he was their relative. ⁴They gave him seventy silver coins from the temple of Baal-berith, which he used to hire some soldiers who agreed to follow him. ⁵He took the soldiers to his father's home at Ophrah, and there, on one stone, they killed all seventy of his half brothers. But the youngest brother, Jotham, escaped and hid. ⁶Then the people of Shechem and Beth-millo called a meeting under the oak beside the pillar* at Shechem and made Abimelech their king.

⁷When Jotham heard about this, he climbed to the top of Mount Gerizim and shouted, "Listen to me, people of Shechem! Listen to me if you want God to listen to you! ⁸Once upon a time the trees decided to elect a king. First they said to the olive tree, 'Be our king!' ⁹But it refused, saying, 'Should I quit producing the olive oil that blesses both God and people, just to wave back and forth over the trees?'

¹⁰"Then they said to the fig tree, 'You be our king!' ¹¹But the fig tree also refused, saying, 'Should I quit producing my sweet fruit just to wave back and forth over the trees?'

¹²"Then they said to the grapevine, 'You be our king!' ¹³But the grapevine replied, 'Should I quit producing the wine that cheers both God and people, just to wave back and forth over the trees?'

¹⁴"Then all the trees finally turned to the thornbush and said, 'Come, you be our king!' ¹⁵And the thornbush replied, 'If you truly want to make me your king, come

9:1 Hebrew *Jerubbaal's* (see 6:32); also in 9:2, 24.   **9:6** The meaning of the Hebrew is uncertain.

and take shelter in my shade. If not, let fire come out from me and devour the cedars of Lebanon.'

[16]"Now make sure you have acted honorably and in good faith by making Abimelech your king, and that you have done right by Gideon* and all of his descendants. Have you treated my father with the honor he deserves? [17]For he fought for you and risked his life when he rescued you from the Midianites. [18]But now you have revolted against my father and his descendants, killing his seventy sons on one stone. And you have chosen his slave woman's son, Abimelech, to be your king just because he is your relative. [19]If you have acted honorably and in good faith toward Gideon and his descendants, then may you find joy in Abimelech, and may he find joy in you. [20]But if you have not acted in good faith, then may fire come out from Abimelech and devour the people of Shechem and Beth-millo; and may fire come out from the people of Shechem and Beth-millo and devour Abimelech!" [21]Then Jotham escaped and lived in Beer because he was afraid of his brother Abimelech.

[22]After Abimelech had ruled over Israel for three years, [23]God stirred up trouble* between Abimelech and the people of Shechem, and they revolted. [24]In the events that followed, God punished Abimelech and the men of Shechem for murdering Gideon's seventy sons. [25]The people of Shechem set an ambush for Abimelech on the hilltops and robbed everyone who passed that way. But someone warned Abimelech about their plot.

[26]At that time Gaal son of Ebed moved to Shechem with his brothers and gained the confidence of the people of Shechem. [27]During the annual harvest festival at Shechem, held in the temple of the local god, the wine flowed freely, and everyone began cursing Abimelech. [28]"Who is Abimelech?" Gaal shouted. "He's not a true descendant of Shechem!* Why should we be Abimelech's servants? He's merely the son of Gideon, and Zebul is his administrator. Serve the men of Hamor, who are Shechem's true descendants. Why should we serve Abimelech? [29]If I were in charge, I would get rid of Abimelech. I would say* to him, 'Get

some more soldiers, and come out and fight!'"

[30]But when Zebul, the leader of the city, heard what Gaal was saying, he was furious. [31]He sent messengers to Abimelech in Arumah,* telling him, "Gaal son of Ebed and his brothers have come to live in Shechem, and now they are inciting the city to rebel against you. [32]Come by night with an army and hide out in the fields. [33]In the morning, as soon as it is daylight, storm the city. When Gaal and those who are with him come out against you, you can do with them as you wish."

[34]So Abimelech and his men went by night and split into four groups, stationing themselves around Shechem. [35]Gaal was standing at the city gates when Abimelech and his army came out of hiding. [36]When Gaal saw them, he said to Zebul, "Look, there are people coming down from the hilltops!"

Zebul replied, "It's just the shadows of the hills that look like men."

[37]But again Gaal said, "No, people are coming down from the hills.* And another group is coming down the road past the Diviners' Oak.*"

[38]Then Zebul turned on him triumphantly. "Now where is that big mouth of yours?" he demanded. "Wasn't it you that said, 'Who is Abimelech, and why should we be his servants?' The men you mocked are right outside the city! Go out and fight them!"

[39]Gaal then led the men of Shechem into battle against Abimelech, [40]but he was defeated and ran away. Many of Shechem's warriors were killed, and the ground was covered with dead bodies all the way to the city gate. [41]Abimelech stayed in Arumah, and Zebul drove Gaal and his brothers out of Shechem.

[42]The next day the people of Shechem went out into the fields to battle. When Abimelech heard about it, [43]he divided his men into three groups and set an ambush in the fields. When Abimelech saw the people coming out of the city, he and his men jumped up from their hiding places and attacked them. [44]Abimelech and his group stormed the city gate to keep the men of Shechem from getting back in, while Abimelech's other two groups cut

9:16 Hebrew *Jerubbaal* (see 6:32); also in 9:19, 28, 57.   9:23 Hebrew *sent a disturbing spirit.*   9:28 Hebrew *Who is Shechem?*
9:29 As in Greek version; Hebrew reads *And he said.*   9:31 Hebrew *Tormah;* see 9:41.   9:37a Or *the center of the land.*
9:37b Hebrew *Elon-meonenim.*

them down in the fields. ⁴⁵The battle went on all day before Abimelech finally captured the city. He killed the people, leveled the city, and scattered salt all over the ground.

⁴⁶When the people who lived in the tower of Shechem heard what had happened, they took refuge within the walls of the temple of Baal-berith.* ⁴⁷Someone reported to Abimelech that the people were gathered together in the temple, ⁴⁸so he led his forces to Mount Zalmon. He took an ax and chopped some branches from a tree, and he put them on his shoulder. "Quick, do as I have done!" he told his men. ⁴⁹So each of them cut down some branches, following Abimelech's example. They piled the branches against the walls of the temple and set them on fire. So all the people who had lived in the tower of Shechem died, about a thousand men and women.

⁵⁰Then Abimelech attacked the city of Thebez and captured it. ⁵¹But there was a strong tower inside the city, and the entire population fled to it. They barricaded themselves in and climbed up to the roof of the tower. ⁵²Abimelech followed them to attack the tower. But as he prepared to set fire to the entrance, ⁵³a woman on the roof threw down a millstone that landed on Abimelech's head and crushed his skull. ⁵⁴He said to his young armor bearer, "Draw your sword and kill me! Don't let it be said that a woman killed Abimelech!" So the young man stabbed him with his sword, and he died. ⁵⁵When Abimelech's men saw that he was dead, they disbanded and returned to their homes.

⁵⁶Thus, God punished Abimelech for the evil he had done against his father by murdering his seventy brothers. ⁵⁷God also punished the men of Shechem for all their evil. So the curse of Jotham son of Gideon came true.

CHAPTER 10

After Abimelech's death, Tola, the son of Puah and descendant of Dodo, came to rescue Israel. He was from the tribe of Issachar but lived in the town of Shamir in the hill country of Ephraim. ²He was Israel's judge for twenty-three years. When he died, he was buried in Shamir.

³After Tola died, a man from Gilead named Jair judged Israel for twenty-two years. ⁴His thirty sons rode around on thirty donkeys, and they owned thirty towns in the land of Gilead, which are still called the Towns of Jair.* ⁵When Jair died, he was buried in Kamon.

⁶Again the Israelites did evil in the LORD's sight. They worshiped images of Baal and Ashtoreth, and the gods of Aram, Sidon, Moab, Ammon, and Philistia. Not only this, but they abandoned the LORD and no longer served him at all. ⁷So the LORD burned with anger against Israel, and he handed them over to the Philistines and the Ammonites, ⁸who began to oppress them that year. For eighteen years they oppressed all the Israelites east of the Jordan River in the land of the Amorites (that is, in Gilead). ⁹The Ammonites also crossed to the west side of the Jordan and attacked Judah, Benjamin, and Ephraim. The Israelites were in great distress. ¹⁰Finally, they cried out to the LORD, saying, "We have sinned against you because we have abandoned you as our God and have served the images of Baal."

¹¹The LORD replied, "Did I not rescue you from the Egyptians, the Amorites, the Ammonites, the Philistines, ¹²the Sidonians, the Amalekites, and the Maonites? When they oppressed you, you cried out to me, and I rescued you. ¹³Yet you have abandoned me and served other gods. So I will not rescue you anymore. ¹⁴Go and cry out to the gods you have chosen! Let them rescue you in your hour of distress!"

¹⁵But the Israelites pleaded with the LORD and said, "We have sinned. Punish us as you see fit, only rescue us today from our enemies." ¹⁶Then the Israelites put aside their foreign gods and served the LORD. And he was grieved by their misery.

¹⁷At that time the armies of Ammon had gathered for war and were camped in Gilead, preparing to attack Israel's army at Mizpah. ¹⁸The leaders of Gilead said to each other, "Whoever attacks the Ammonites first will become ruler over all the people of Gilead."

CHAPTER 11

Now Jephthah of Gilead was a great warrior. He was the son of Gilead, but his mother was a prostitute. ²Gilead's wife also had several sons, and when these half brothers grew up, they chased Jephthah off

9:46 Hebrew *El-berith*, another name for Baal-berith; compare 9:4.   10:4 Hebrew *Havvoth-jair*.

the land. "You will not get any of our father's inheritance," they said, "for you are the son of a prostitute." ³So Jephthah fled from his brothers and lived in the land of Tob. Soon he had a large band of rebels following him.

⁴At about this time, the Ammonites began their war against Israel. ⁵When the Ammonites attacked, the leaders of Gilead sent for Jephthah in the land of Tob. They said, ⁶"Come and be our commander! Help us fight the Ammonites!"

⁷But Jephthah said to them, "Aren't you the ones who hated me and drove me from my father's house? Why do you come to me now when you're in trouble?"

⁸"Because we need you," they replied. "If you will lead us in battle against the Ammonites, we will make you ruler over all the people of Gilead."

⁹Jephthah said, "If I come with you and if the LORD gives me victory over the Ammonites, will you really make me ruler over all the people?"

¹⁰"The LORD is our witness," the leaders replied. "We promise to do whatever you say."

¹¹So Jephthah went with the leaders of Gilead, and he became their ruler and commander of the army. At Mizpah, in the presence of the LORD, Jephthah repeated what he had said to the leaders.

¹²Then Jephthah sent messengers to the king of Ammon, demanding to know why Israel was being attacked. ¹³The king of Ammon answered Jephthah's messengers, "When the Israelites came out of Egypt, they stole my land from the Arnon River to the Jabbok River and all the way to the Jordan. Now then, give back the land peaceably."

¹⁴Jephthah sent this message back to the Ammonite king:

¹⁵"This is what Jephthah says: Israel did not steal any land from Moab or Ammon. ¹⁶When the people of Israel arrived at Kadesh on their journey from Egypt after crossing the Red Sea,* ¹⁷they sent messengers to the king of Edom asking for permission to pass through his land. But their request was denied. Then they asked the king of Moab for similar permission, but he wouldn't let them pass through either.

So the people of Israel stayed in Kadesh.

¹⁸"Finally, they went around Edom and Moab through the wilderness. They traveled along Moab's eastern border and camped on the other side of the Arnon River. But they never once crossed the Arnon River into Moab.

¹⁹"Then Israel sent messengers to King Sihon of the Amorites, who ruled from Heshbon, asking for permission to cross through his land to get to their destination. ²⁰But King Sihon didn't trust Israel to pass through his land. Instead, he mobilized his army at Jahaz and attacked them. ²¹But the LORD, the God of Israel, gave his people victory over King Sihon. So Israel took control of all the land of the Amorites, who lived in that region, ²²from the Arnon River to the Jabbok River, and from the wilderness to the Jordan.

²³"So you see, it was the LORD, the God of Israel, who took away the land from the Amorites and gave it to Israel. Why, then, should we give it to you? ²⁴You keep whatever your god Chemosh gives you, and we will keep whatever the LORD our God gives us. ²⁵Are you any better than Balak son of Zippor, king of Moab? Did he try to make a case against Israel for disputed land? Did he go to war? No, of course not. ²⁶But now after three hundred years you make an issue of this! Israel has been living here all this time, spread across the land from Heshbon to Aroer and in all the towns along the Arnon River. Why have you made no effort to recover it before now? ²⁷I have not sinned against you. Rather, you have wronged me by attacking me. Let the LORD, who is judge, decide today which of us is right—Israel or Ammon."

²⁸But the king of Ammon paid no attention to Jephthah's message.

²⁹At that time the Spirit of the LORD came upon Jephthah, and he went throughout the land of Gilead and Manasseh, including Mizpah in Gilead, and led an army against the Ammonites. ³⁰And Jephthah made a vow to the LORD. He said, "If you give me victory over the Ammonites, ³¹I will give to the LORD the first thing coming out of my house to greet me when I return

11:16 Hebrew *sea of reeds.*

in triumph. I will sacrifice it as a burnt offering."

[32]So Jephthah led his army against the Ammonites, and the LORD gave him victory. [33]He thoroughly defeated the Ammonites from Aroer to an area near Minnith—twenty towns—and as far away as Abel-keramim. Thus Israel subdued the Ammonites.

[34]When Jephthah returned home to Mizpah, his daughter—his only child—ran out to meet him, playing on a tambourine and dancing for joy. [35]When he saw her, he tore his clothes in anguish. "My daughter!" he cried out. "My heart is breaking! What a tragedy that you came out to greet me. For I have made a vow to the LORD and cannot take it back."

[36]And she said, "Father, you have made a promise to the LORD. You must do to me what you have promised, for the LORD has given you a great victory over your enemies, the Ammonites. [37]But first let me go up and roam in the hills and weep with my friends for two months, because I will die a virgin."

[38]"You may go," Jephthah said. And he let her go away for two months. She and her friends went into the hills and wept because she would never have children. [39]When she returned home, her father kept his vow, and she died a virgin. So it has become a custom in Israel [40]for young Israelite women to go away for four days each year to lament the fate of Jephthah's daughter.

CHAPTER 12

Then the tribe of Ephraim mobilized its army and crossed over to Zaphon. They sent this message to Jephthah: "Why didn't you call for us to help you fight against Ammon? We are going to burn down your house with you in it!"

[2]"I summoned you at the beginning of the dispute, but you refused to come!"

Jephthah said. "You failed to help us in our struggle against Ammon. [3]So I risked my life and went to battle without you, and the LORD gave me victory over the Ammonites. So why have you come to fight me?"

[4]The leaders of Ephraim responded, "The men of Gilead are nothing more than rejects from Ephraim and Manasseh." So Jephthah called out his army and attacked the men of Ephraim and defeated them.

[5]Jephthah captured the shallows of the Jordan, and whenever a fugitive from Ephraim tried to go back across, the men of Gilead would challenge him. "Are you a member of the tribe of Ephraim?" they would ask. If the man said, "No, I'm not," [6]they would tell him to say "Shibboleth." If he was from Ephraim, he would say "Sibboleth," because people from Ephraim cannot pronounce the word correctly. Then they would take him and kill him at the shallows of the Jordan River. So forty-two thousand Ephraimites were killed at that time.

[7]Jephthah was Israel's judge for six years. When he died, he was buried in one of the towns of Gilead.

[8]After Jephthah, Ibzan became Israel's judge. He lived in Bethlehem, [9]and he had thirty sons and thirty daughters. He married his daughters to men outside his clan and brought in thirty young women from outside his clan to marry his sons. Ibzan judged Israel for seven years. [10]When he died, he was buried at Bethlehem.

[11]After him, Elon from Zebulun became Israel's judge. He judged Israel for ten years. [12]When he died, he was buried at Aijalon in Zebulun.

[13]After Elon died, Abdon son of Hillel, from Pirathon, became Israel's judge. [14]He had forty sons and thirty grandsons, who rode on seventy donkeys. He was Israel's judge for eight years. [15]Then he died and was buried at Pirathon in Ephraim, in the hill country of the Amalekites.

MARCH 11 ☐ DAY 71
JUDGES 13–16
Samson, the Carnal Champion

OVERVIEW The life of Samson is a study in unfulfilled potential. The only child of an elderly couple, designated by God a Nazirite from birth, blessed with superhuman strength, and commissioned to "rescue Israel from the Philistines" (13:5), Samson instead spends most of his life fulfilling his own passions and desires. His lack of self-control eventually results in blindness and bondage. But God gives him one last portion of power, and in his death Samson destroys more Philistines than during his entire life of compromise.

Chapter 13	Chapter 14	Chapter 15	Chapter 16
Manoah's Prayer	Samson's Power	Samson's Passion	Samson's Passing
Calling		Compromise	

Forgiveness warms the heart and cools the sting.

YOUR DAILY WALK Here are some of the wisest words ever penned by Benjamin Franklin: "Doing an injury puts you below your enemy; revenging one makes you but even with him; forgiving one sets you above him." You may want to create a plaque or stitchery featuring them!

Revenge is one of the most natural—and destructive—of all human responses. Rather than reacting to a wrong with forgiveness, the most common reaction is to commit another wrong—namely, lashing out at the other person. Such was the problem with Samson. He spent much of his time burning with anger (14:19) and doing harm to those who had wronged him (15:3). But his temper only complicated the problem, never corrected it.

What is your response when someone has wronged you? Do you count to ten before blasting off, or do you go into orbit immediately? To help you cultivate a proper response to others, put this verse to work today: "A gentle answer turns away wrath, but harsh words stir up anger" (Proverbs 15:1). Be the one to break anger's destructive cycle in your interactions with others today.

INSIGHT Nazirite or Nazarene: What's the Difference?
Many confuse the two terms *Nazirite* and *Nazarene*. Jesus, a Nazarene, was so called because he lived in Nazareth. Samson, a Nazirite, was so called because he did not drink wine or touch dead bodies or cut his hair—all prohibitions of a Nazirite vow. (For added details concerning this vow, see Numbers 6:1-21.)

CHAPTER 13

Again the Israelites did what was evil in the LORD's sight, so the LORD handed them over to the Philistines, who kept them in subjection for forty years.

²In those days, a man named Manoah from the tribe of Dan lived in the town of Zorah. His wife was unable to become pregnant, and they had no children. ³The angel of the LORD appeared to Manoah's wife and said, "Even though you have been unable to have children, you will soon become pregnant and give birth to a son. ⁴You must not drink wine or any other alcoholic drink or eat any forbidden food. ⁵You will become pregnant and give birth to a son, and his hair must never be cut. For he will be dedicated to God as a Nazirite from birth. He will rescue Israel from the Philistines."

⁶The woman ran and told her husband, "A man of God appeared to me! He was

like one of God's angels, terrifying to look at. I didn't ask where he was from, and he didn't tell me his name. [7]But he told me, 'You will become pregnant and give birth to a son. You must not drink wine or any other alcoholic drink or eat any forbidden food. For your son will be dedicated to God as a Nazirite from the moment of his birth until the day of his death.'"

[8]Then Manoah prayed to the LORD. He said, "Lord, please let the man of God come back to us again and give us more instructions about this son who is to be born."

[9]God answered his prayer, and the angel of God appeared once again to his wife as she was sitting in the field. But her husband, Manoah, was not with her. [10]So she quickly ran and told her husband, "The man who appeared to me the other day is here again!"

[11]Manoah ran back with his wife and asked, "Are you the man who talked to my wife the other day?"

"Yes," he replied, "I am."

[12]So Manoah asked him, "When your words come true, what kind of rules should govern the boy's life and work?"

[13]The angel of the LORD replied, "Be sure your wife follows the instructions I gave her. [14]She must not eat grapes or raisins, drink wine or any other alcoholic drink, or eat any forbidden food."

[15]Then Manoah said to the angel of the LORD, "Please stay here until we can prepare a young goat for you to eat."

[16]"I will stay," the angel of the LORD replied, "but I will not eat anything. However, you may prepare a burnt offering as a sacrifice to the LORD." (Manoah didn't realize it was the angel of the LORD.)

[17]Then Manoah asked the angel of the LORD, "What is your name? For when all this comes true, we want to honor you."

[18]"Why do you ask my name?" the angel of the LORD replied. "You wouldn't understand if I told you."

[19]Then Manoah took a young goat and a grain offering and offered it on a rock as a sacrifice to the LORD. And as Manoah and his wife watched, the LORD did an amazing thing. [20]As the flames from the altar shot up toward the sky, the angel of the LORD ascended in the fire. When Manoah and his wife saw this, they fell with their faces to the ground.

[21]The angel did not appear again to Manoah and his wife. Manoah finally realized it was the angel of the LORD, [22]and he said to his wife, "We will die, for we have seen God!"

[23]But his wife said, "If the LORD were going to kill us, he wouldn't have accepted our burnt offering and grain offering. He wouldn't have appeared to us and told us this wonderful thing and done these miracles."

[24]When her son was born, they named him Samson. And the LORD blessed him as he grew up. [25]And in Mahaneh-dan, which is located between the towns of Zorah and Eshtaol, the Spirit of the LORD began to take hold of him.

CHAPTER 14

One day when Samson was in Timnah, he noticed a certain Philistine woman. [2]When he returned home, he told his father and mother, "I want to marry a young Philistine woman I saw in Timnah."

[3]His father and mother objected strenuously, "Isn't there one woman in our tribe or among all the Israelites you could marry? Why must you go to the pagan Philistines to find a wife?"

But Samson told his father, "Get her for me. She is the one I want." [4]His father and mother didn't realize the LORD was at work in this, creating an opportunity to disrupt the Philistines, who ruled over Israel at that time.

[5]As Samson and his parents were going down to Timnah, a young lion attacked Samson near the vineyards of Timnah. [6]At that moment the Spirit of the LORD powerfully took control of him, and he ripped the lion's jaws apart with his bare hands. He did it as easily as if it were a young goat. But he didn't tell his father or mother about it. [7]When Samson arrived in Timnah, he talked with the woman and was very pleased with her.

[8]Later, when he returned to Timnah for the wedding, he turned off the path to look at the carcass of the lion. And he found that a swarm of bees had made some honey in the carcass. [9]He scooped some of the honey into his hands and ate it along the way. He also gave some to his father and mother, and they ate it. But he didn't tell them he had taken the honey from the carcass of the lion.

[10]As his father was making final arrangements for the marriage, Samson threw a

party at Timnah, as was the custom of the day. [11]Thirty young men from the town were invited to be his companions. [12]Samson said to them, "Let me tell you a riddle. If you solve my riddle during these seven days of the celebration, I will give you thirty plain linen robes and thirty fancy robes. [13]But if you can't solve it, then you must give me thirty linen robes and thirty fancy robes."

"All right," they agreed, "let's hear your riddle."

[14]So he said:

"From the one who eats came
        something to eat;
    out of the strong came something
        sweet."

Three days later they were still trying to figure it out. [15]On the fourth* day they said to Samson's wife, "Get the answer to the riddle from your husband, or we will burn down your father's house with you in it. Did you invite us to this party just to make us poor?"

[16]So Samson's wife came to him in tears and said, "You don't love me; you hate me! You have given my people a riddle, but you haven't told me the answer."

"I haven't even given the answer to my father or mother," he replied. "Why should I tell you?" [17]So she cried whenever she was with him and kept it up for the rest of the celebration. At last, on the seventh day, he told her the answer because of her persistent nagging. Then she gave the answer to the young men.

[18]So before sunset of the seventh day, the men of the town came to Samson with their answer:

"What is sweeter than honey?
    What is stronger than a lion?"

Samson replied, "If you hadn't plowed with my heifer, you wouldn't have found the answer to my riddle!" [19]Then the Spirit of the LORD powerfully took control of him. He went down to the town of Ashkelon, killed thirty men, took their belongings, and gave their clothing to the men who had answered his riddle. But Samson was furious about what had happened, and he went back home to live with his father and mother. [20]So his wife was given in marriage

to the man who had been Samson's best man at the wedding.

CHAPTER 15

Later on, during the wheat harvest, Samson took a young goat as a present to his wife. He intended to sleep with her, but her father wouldn't let him in. [2]"I really thought you hated her," her father explained, "so I gave her in marriage to your best man. But look, her sister is more beautiful than she is. Marry her instead."

[3]Samson said, "This time I cannot be blamed for everything I am going to do to you Philistines." [4]Then he went out and caught three hundred foxes. He tied their tails together in pairs, and he fastened a torch to each pair of tails. [5]Then he lit the torches and let the foxes run through the fields of the Philistines. He burned all their grain to the ground, including the grain still in piles and all that had been bundled. He also destroyed their grapevines and olive trees.

[6]"Who did this?" the Philistines demanded.

"Samson," was the reply, "because his father-in-law from Timnah gave Samson's wife to be married to his best man." So the Philistines went and got the woman and her father and burned them to death.

[7]"Because you did this," Samson vowed, "I will take my revenge on you, and I won't stop until I'm satisfied!" [8]So he attacked the Philistines with great fury and killed many of them. Then he went to live in a cave in the rock of Etam.

[9]The Philistines retaliated by setting up camp in Judah and raiding the town of Lehi. [10]The men of Judah asked the Philistines, "Why have you attacked us?"

The Philistines replied, "We've come to capture Samson. We have come to pay him back for what he did to us."

[11]So three thousand men of Judah went down to get Samson at the cave in the rock of Etam. They said to Samson, "Don't you realize the Philistines rule over us? What are you doing to us?"

But Samson replied, "I only paid them back for what they did to me."

[12]But the men of Judah told him, "We have come to tie you up and hand you over to the Philistines."

14:15 As in Greek version; Hebrew reads *seventh*.

MARCH 11 / JUDGES 16   292

"All right," Samson said. "But promise that you won't kill me yourselves."

13"We will tie you up and hand you over to the Philistines," they replied. "We won't kill you." So they tied him up with two new ropes and led him away from the rock.

14As Samson arrived at Lehi, the Philistines came shouting in triumph. But the Spirit of the LORD powerfully took control of Samson, and he snapped the ropes on his arms as if they were burnt strands of flax, and they fell from his wrists. 15Then he picked up a donkey's jawbone that was lying on the ground and killed a thousand Philistines with it. 16And Samson said,

"With the jawbone of a donkey,
    I've made heaps on heaps!
With the jawbone of a donkey,
    I've killed a thousand men!"

17When he finished speaking, he threw away the jawbone; and the place was named Jawbone Hill.*

18Now Samson was very thirsty, and he cried out to the LORD, "You have accomplished this great victory by the strength of your servant. Must I now die of thirst and fall into the hands of these pagan people?" 19So God caused water to gush out of a hollow in the ground at Lehi, and Samson was revived as he drank. Then he named that place "The Spring of the One Who Cried Out,"* and it is still in Lehi to this day. 20Samson was Israel's judge for twenty years, while the Philistines ruled the land.

CHAPTER 16

One day Samson went to the Philistine city of Gaza and spent the night with a prostitute. 2Word soon spread that Samson was there, so the men of Gaza gathered together and waited all night at the city gates. They kept quiet during the night, saying to themselves, "When the light of morning comes, we will kill him."

3But Samson stayed in bed only until midnight. Then he got up, took hold of the city gates with its two posts, and lifted them, bar and all, right out of the ground. He put them on his shoulders and carried them all the way to the top of the hill across from Hebron.

4Later Samson fell in love with a woman named Delilah, who lived in the valley of Sorek. 5The leaders of the Philistines went to her and said, "Find out from Samson what makes him so strong and how he can be overpowered and tied up securely. Then each of us will give you eleven hundred pieces* of silver."

6So Delilah said to Samson, "Please tell me what makes you so strong and what it would take to tie you up securely."

7Samson replied, "If I am tied up with seven new bowstrings that have not yet been dried, I will be as weak as anyone else."

8So the Philistine leaders brought Delilah seven new bowstrings, and she tied Samson up with them. 9She had hidden some men in one of the rooms of her house, and she cried out, "Samson! The Philistines have come to capture you!" But Samson snapped the bowstrings as if they were string that had been burned in a fire. So the secret of his strength was not discovered.

10Afterward Delilah said to him, "You made fun of me and told me a lie! Now please tell me how you can be tied up securely."

11Samson replied, "If I am tied up with brand-new ropes that have never been used, I will be as weak as anyone else."

12So Delilah took new ropes and tied him up with them. The men were hiding in the room as before, and again Delilah cried out, "Samson! The Philistines have come to capture you!" But Samson snapped the ropes from his arms as if they were thread.

13Then Delilah said, "You have been making fun of me and telling me lies! Won't you please tell me how you can be tied up securely?"

Samson replied, "If you weave the seven braids of my hair into the fabric on your loom and tighten it with the loom shuttle,* I will be as weak as anyone else."

So while he slept, Delilah wove the seven braids of his hair into the fabric 14and tightened it with the loom shuttle. Again she cried out, "Samson! The Philistines have come to capture you!" But Samson woke up, pulled back the loom shuttle, and yanked his hair away from the loom and the fabric.

15Then Delilah pouted, "How can you say you love me when you don't confide in me? You've made fun of me three times now, and you still haven't told me what

15:17 Hebrew *Ramath-lehi.*   15:19 Hebrew *En-hakkore.*   16:5 Hebrew *1,100 shekels,* about 28 pounds or 12.5 kilograms in weight.   16:13 As in Greek version; Hebrew lacks *on your loom and tighten it with the loom shuttle.*

makes you so strong!" [16]So day after day she nagged him until he couldn't stand it any longer.

[17]Finally, Samson told her his secret. "My hair has never been cut," he confessed, "for I was dedicated to God as a Nazirite from birth. If my head were shaved, my strength would leave me, and I would become as weak as anyone else."

[18]Delilah realized he had finally told her the truth, so she sent for the Philistine leaders. "Come back one more time," she said, "for he has told me everything." So the Philistine leaders returned and brought the money with them. [19]Delilah lulled Samson to sleep with his head in her lap, and she called in a man to shave off his hair, making his capture certain. And his strength left him. [20]Then she cried out, "Samson! The Philistines have come to capture you!"

When he woke up, he thought, "I will do as before and shake myself free." But he didn't realize the LORD had left him.

[21]So the Philistines captured him and gouged out his eyes. They took him to Gaza, where he was bound with bronze chains and made to grind grain in the prison. [22]But before long his hair began to grow back.

[23]The Philistine leaders held a great festival, offering sacrifices and praising their god, Dagon. They said, "Our god has given us victory over our enemy Samson!"

[24]When the people saw him, they praised their god, saying, "Our god has delivered our enemy to us! The one who killed so many of us is now in our power!"

[25]Half drunk by now, the people demanded, "Bring out Samson so he can perform for us!" So he was brought from the prison and made to stand at the center of the temple, between the two pillars supporting the roof.

[26]Samson said to the servant who was leading him by the hand, "Place my hands against the two pillars. I want to rest against them." [27]The temple was completely filled with people. All the Philistine leaders were there, and there were about three thousand on the roof who were watching Samson and making fun of him.

[28]Then Samson prayed to the LORD, "Sovereign LORD, remember me again. O God, please strengthen me one more time so that I may pay back the Philistines for the loss of my eyes." [29]Then Samson put his hands on the center pillars of the temple and pushed against them with all his might. [30]"Let me die with the Philistines," he prayed. And the temple crashed down on the Philistine leaders and all the people. So he killed more people when he died than he had during his entire lifetime.

[31]Later his brothers and other relatives went down to get his body. They took him back home and buried him between Zorah and Eshtaol, where his father, Manoah, was buried. Samson had been Israel's judge for twenty years.

MARCH 12 ☐ DAY 72
JUDGES 17–21
Two Examples of National Degradation

 OVERVIEW The closing chapters of Judges provide graphic snapshots of the spiritual and moral degeneration of a nation in which "the people did whatever seemed right in their own eyes" (17:6; 21:25). Chronologically, these events belong with chapter 3, but thematically they form a fitting conclusion to the book. The spiritual decline is illustrated by Micah, who carves his own idol, consecrates his own son as priest, and hires a traveling Levite to minister on his behalf! The tribe of Dan confiscates both the idol and the priest to serve their own interests instead. The story of the Levite and his concubine is a grisly flashback to the days of Sodom and Gomorrah. In the ensuing civil war, the tribe of Benjamin is decimated, and efforts to repopulate it result in little more than anarchy.

Chapter 17	Chapter 18	Chapter 19	Chapters 20–21
Man-Made Religion	Idolatrous Religion	Violent Immorality	Violent Vengeance
Religious Confusion		Moral and Civil Confusion	

YOUR DAILY WALK Is it possible that one of the reasons the forces of evil and wickedness are so successful is that the children of God are simply naive?

Those who believe that people aren't so bad must never have been parents.

When you read chapters in the Bible like Judges 17–21, your immediate reaction may be, "It can't happen here." No one wants to believe the veneer of civilization is really that thin and fragile. But until you recognize the problem, there is little hope of finding a solution.

Check up on your own IQ (Information Quotient). Do you know what the crime rate is in your area? What percent of your community is unchurched? How many babies were aborted last year? How many incidents of divorce, child abuse, homosexuality, and substance abuse were recorded? If you don't know, a local social service agency can tell you. Knowing some of those statistics can help you pray more intelligently (and perhaps enable you to make a difference for Christ by helping some of the hurting people who are responsible for those statistics).

INSIGHT My, How Times Have Changed!
The book of Joshua records the history of the nation of Israel in days of victory with faith in God, spiritual vision, strength, and unity. But as you read in Judges of Israel's defeats, unbelief, apostasy, worldliness, weakness, and anarchy, you may have thought you were reading about an entirely different nation!

CHAPTER 17

A man named Micah lived in the hill country of Ephraim. ²One day he said to his mother, "I heard you curse the thief who stole eleven hundred pieces* of silver from you. Well, here they are. I was the one who took them."

"The LORD bless you for admitting it," his mother replied. ³He returned the money to her, and she said, "I now dedicate these silver coins to the LORD. In honor of my son, I will have an image carved and an idol cast." ⁴So his mother took two hundred of the silver coins to a silversmith, who made them into an image and an idol. And these were placed in Micah's house.

⁵Micah set up a shrine, and he made a sacred ephod and some household idols. Then he installed one of his sons as the priest. ⁶In those days Israel had no king, so the people did whatever seemed right in their own eyes.

⁷One day a young Levite from Bethlehem in Judah ⁸arrived in that area of

Ephraim, looking for a good place to live. He happened to stop at Micah's house as he was traveling through. ⁹"Where are you from?" Micah asked him.

And he replied, "I am a Levite from Bethlehem in Judah, and I am looking for a place to live."

¹⁰"Stay here with me," Micah said, "and you can be a father and priest to me. I will give you ten pieces* of silver a year, plus a change of clothes and your food." ¹¹The Levite agreed to this and became like one of Micah's sons. ¹²So Micah ordained the Levite as his personal priest, and he lived in Micah's house. ¹³"I know the LORD will bless me now," Micah said, "because I have a Levite serving as my priest."

CHAPTER 18

Now in those days Israel had no king. And the tribe of Dan was trying to find a place to settle, for they had not yet driven out the people who lived in the land assigned to them. ²So the men of Dan chose five war-

17:2 Hebrew *1,100 shekels*, about 28 pounds or 12.5 kilograms in weight.   17:10 Hebrew *10 shekels*, about 4 ounces or 114 grams in weight.

riors from among their clans, who lived in the towns of Zorah and Eshtaol, to scout out a land for them to settle in.

When these warriors arrived in the hill country of Ephraim, they came to Micah's home and spent the night there. ³Noticing the young Levite's accent, they took him aside and asked him, "Who brought you here, and what are you doing? Why are you here?" ⁴He told them about his agreement with Micah and that he was Micah's personal priest.

⁵Then they said, "Ask God whether or not our journey will be successful."

⁶"Go in peace," the priest replied. "For the LORD will go ahead of you on your journey."

⁷So the five men went on to the town of Laish, where they noticed the people living carefree lives, like the Sidonians; they were peaceful and secure. The people were also wealthy because their land was very fertile. And they lived a great distance from Sidon and had no allies nearby.

⁸When the men returned to Zorah and Eshtaol, their relatives asked them, "What did you find?"

⁹The men replied, "Let's attack! We have seen the land, and it is very good. You should not hesitate to go and take possession of it. ¹⁰When you get there, you will find the people living carefree lives. God has given us a spacious and fertile land, lacking in nothing!"

¹¹So six hundred warriors from the tribe of Dan set out from Zorah and Eshtaol. ¹²They camped at a place west of Kiriath-jearim in Judah, which is called Mahaneh-dan* to this day. ¹³Then they went up into the hill country of Ephraim and came to the house of Micah.

¹⁴The five men who had scouted out the land around Laish said to the others, "There is a shrine here with a sacred ephod, some household idols, a carved image, and a cast idol. It's obvious what we ought to do." ¹⁵So the five men went over to Micah's house, where the young Levite lived, and greeted him kindly. ¹⁶As the six hundred warriors from the tribe of Dan stood just outside the gate, ¹⁷the five spies entered the shrine and took the carved image, the sacred ephod, the household idols, and the cast idol.

¹⁸When the priest saw the men carrying all the sacred objects out of Micah's shrine, he said, "What are you doing?"

¹⁹"Be quiet and come with us," they said. "Be a father and priest to all of us. Isn't it better to be a priest for an entire tribe of Israel than just for the household of one man?" ²⁰The young priest was quite happy to go with them, so he took along the sacred ephod, the household idols, and the carved image. ²¹They started on their way again, placing their children, livestock, and possessions in front of them.

²²When the people from the tribe of Dan were quite a distance from Micah's home, Micah and some of his neighbors came chasing after them. ²³They were shouting as they caught up with them. The men of Dan turned around and said, "What do you want? Why have you called these men together and chased after us like this?"

²⁴"What do you mean, What do I want?" Micah replied. "You've taken away all my gods and my priest, and I have nothing left!"

²⁵The men of Dan said, "Watch what you say! Some of us are short-tempered, and they might get angry and kill you and your family." ²⁶So the men of Dan went on their way. When Micah saw that there were too many of them for him to attack, he turned around and went home.

²⁷Then, with Micah's idols and his priest, the men of Dan came to the town of Laish, whose people were peaceful and secure. They attacked and killed all the people and burned the town to the ground. ²⁸There was no one to rescue the residents of the town, for they lived a great distance from Sidon and had no allies nearby. This happened in the valley near Beth-rehob.

Then the people of the tribe of Dan rebuilt the town and lived there. ²⁹They renamed the town Dan after their ancestor, Israel's son, but it had originally been called Laish.

³⁰Then they set up the carved image, and they appointed Jonathan son of Gershom, a descendant of Moses,* as their priest. This family continued as priests for the tribe of Dan until the Exile. ³¹So Micah's carved image was worshiped by the tribe of Dan as long as the Tabernacle of God remained at Shiloh.

18:12 *Mahaneh-dan* means "the camp of Dan." 18:30 As in an ancient Hebrew tradition, some Greek manuscripts, and Latin Vulgate; Masoretic Text reads *of Manasseh.*

CHAPTER 19

Now in those days Israel had no king. There was a man from the tribe of Levi living in a remote area of the hill country of Ephraim. One day he brought home a woman from Bethlehem in Judah to be his concubine. [2]But she was unfaithful to him and returned to her father's home in Bethlehem. After about four months, [3]her husband took a servant and an extra donkey to Bethlehem to persuade her to come back. When he arrived at her father's house, she took him inside, and her father welcomed him. [4]Her father urged him to stay awhile, so he stayed three days, eating, drinking, and sleeping there.

[5]On the fourth day the man was up early, ready to leave, but the woman's father said, "Have something to eat before you go." [6]So the two of them sat down together and had something to eat and drink. Then the woman's father said, "Please stay the night and enjoy yourself." [7]The man got up to leave, but his father-in-law kept urging him to stay, so he finally gave in and stayed the night. [8]On the morning of the fifth day he was up early again, ready to leave, and again the woman's father said, "Have something to eat; then you can leave some time this afternoon." So they had another day of feasting.

[9]That afternoon, as he and his concubine and servant were preparing to leave, his father-in-law said, "Look, it's getting late. Stay the night and enjoy yourself. Tomorrow you can get up early and be on your way."

[10]But this time the man was determined to leave. So he took his two saddled donkeys and his concubine and headed in the direction of Jebus (that is, Jerusalem). [11]It was late in the day when they reached Jebus, and the man's servant said to him, "It's getting too late to travel; let's stay in this Jebusite city tonight."

[12]"No," his master said, "we can't stay in this foreign city where there are no Israelites. We will go on to Gibeah. [13]We will find a place to spend the night in either Gibeah or Ramah." [14]So they went on. The sun was setting as they came to Gibeah, a town in the land of Benjamin, [15]so they stopped there to spend the night. They rested in the town square, but no one took them in for the night.

[16]That evening an old man came home from his work in the fields. He was from the hill country of Ephraim, but he was living in Gibeah in the territory of Benjamin. [17]When he saw the travelers sitting in the town square, he asked them where they were from and where they were going.

[18]"We have been in Bethlehem in Judah," the man replied. "We are on our way home to a remote area in the hill country of Ephraim, and we're going to the Tabernacle of the LORD. But no one has taken us in for the night, [19]even though we have everything we need. We have straw and fodder for our donkeys and plenty of bread and wine for ourselves."

[20]"You are welcome to stay with me," the old man said. "I will give you anything you might need. But whatever you do, don't spend the night in the square." [21]So he took them home with him and fed their donkeys. After they washed their feet, they had supper together.

[22]While they were enjoying themselves, some of the wicked men in the town surrounded the house. They began beating at the door and shouting to the old man, "Bring out the man who is staying with you so we can have sex with him."

[23]The old man stepped outside to talk to them. "No, my brothers, don't do such an evil thing. For this man is my guest, and such a thing would be shameful. [24]Here, take my virgin daughter and this man's concubine. I will bring them out to you, and you can do whatever you like to them. But don't do such a shameful thing to this man."

[25]But they wouldn't listen to him. Then the Levite took his concubine and pushed her out the door. The men of the town abused her all night, taking turns raping her until morning. Finally, at dawn, they let her go. [26]At daybreak the woman returned to the house where her husband was staying. She collapsed at the door of the house and lay there until it was light.

[27]When her husband opened the door to leave, he found her there. She was lying face down, with her hands on the threshold. [28]He said, "Get up! Let's go!" But there was no answer.* So he put her body on his donkey and took her home.

[29]When he got home, he took a knife and cut his concubine's body into twelve

19:28 Greek version adds *for she was dead.*

pieces. Then he sent one piece to each tribe of Israel. [30]Everyone who saw it said, "Such a horrible crime has not been committed since Israel left Egypt. Shouldn't we speak up and do something about this?"

CHAPTER 20

Then all the Israelites, from Dan to Beer-sheba and from the land of Gilead, came together in one large assembly and stood in the presence of the LORD at Mizpah. [2]The leaders of all the people and all the tribes of Israel—400,000 warriors armed with swords—took their positions in the assembly of the people of God. [3](Word soon reached the land of Benjamin that the other tribes had gone up to Mizpah.) The Israelites then asked how this terrible crime had happened.

[4]The Levite, the husband of the woman who had been murdered, said, "My concubine and I came to Gibeah, a town in the land of Benjamin, to spend the night. [5]That night some of the leaders of Gibeah surrounded the house, planning to kill me, and they raped my concubine until she was dead. [6]So I cut her body into twelve pieces and sent the pieces throughout the land of Israel, for these men have committed this terrible and shameful crime. [7]Now then, the entire community of Israel must decide what should be done about this!"

[8]And all the people stood up together and replied, "Not one of us will return home. [9]Instead, we will draw lots to decide who will attack Gibeah. [10]One tenth of the men from each tribe will be chosen to supply the warriors with food, and the rest of us will take revenge on Gibeah* for this shameful thing they have done in Israel." [11]So all the Israelites were united, and they gathered together to attack the town.

[12]The Israelites sent messengers to the tribe of Benjamin, saying, "What a terrible thing has been done among you! [13]Give up these evil men from Gibeah so we can execute them and purge Israel of this evil."

But the people of Benjamin would not listen. [14]Instead, they came from their towns and gathered at Gibeah to fight the Israelites. [15]Twenty-six thousand of their warriors armed with swords arrived in Gibeah to join the seven hundred warriors who lived there. [16]Seven hundred of Benjamin's warriors were left-handed, each of whom could sling a rock and hit a target within a hairsbreadth, without missing. [17]Israel had 400,000 warriors armed with swords, not counting Benjamin's warriors.

[18]Before the battle the Israelites went to Bethel and asked God, "Which tribe should lead the attack against the people of Benjamin?"

The LORD answered, "Judah is to go first."

[19]So the Israelites left early the next morning and camped near Gibeah. [20]Then they advanced toward Gibeah to attack the men of Benjamin. [21]But Benjamin's warriors, who were defending the town, came out and killed twenty-two thousand Israelites in the field that day.

[22]But the Israelites took courage and assembled at the same place they had fought the previous day. [23](For they had gone up to Bethel and wept in the presence of the LORD until evening. Then they asked the LORD, "Should we fight against our relatives from Benjamin again?" And the LORD said, "Go out and fight against them.")

[24]So they went out to fight against the warriors of Benjamin, [25]but the men of Benjamin killed another eighteen thousand Israelites, all of whom were experienced with a sword.

[26]Then all the Israelites went up to Bethel and wept in the presence of the LORD and fasted until evening. They also brought burnt offerings and peace offerings to the LORD. [27]And the Israelites went up seeking direction from the LORD. (In those days the Ark of the Covenant of God was in Bethel, [28]and Phinehas son of Eleazar and grandson of Aaron was the priest.) The Israelites asked the LORD, "Should we fight against our relatives from Benjamin again or should we stop?"

The LORD said, "Go! Tomorrow I will give you victory over them."

[29]So the Israelites set an ambush all around Gibeah. [30]They went out on the third day and assembled at the same place as before. [31]When the warriors of Benjamin came out to attack, they were drawn away from the town. And as they had done before, they began to kill the Israelites. About thirty Israelites died in the open fields and along the roads leading to Bethel and Gibeah. [32]Then the warriors of Benjamin

20:10 Hebrew *Geba*, in this case, a variant for Gibeah; also in 20:33.

shouted, "We're defeating them as we did in the first battle!" But the Israelites had agreed in advance to run away so that the men of Benjamin would chase them along the roads and be drawn away from the town. ³³When the main group of Israelite warriors reached Baal-tamar, they turned and prepared to attack. Then the Israelites hiding in ambush west of Gibeah jumped up from where they were ³⁴and advanced against Benjamin from behind. The fighting was so heavy that Benjamin didn't realize the impending disaster. ³⁵So the LORD helped Israel defeat Benjamin, and that day the Israelites killed 25,100 of Benjamin's warriors, all of whom were experienced with a sword. ³⁶Then the men of Benjamin saw that they were beaten.

The Israelites had retreated from Benjamin's warriors in order to give those hiding in ambush more room to maneuver. ³⁷Then those who were in hiding rushed in from all sides and killed everyone in the town. ³⁸They sent up a large cloud of smoke from the town, ³⁹which was the signal for the Israelites to turn and attack Benjamin's warriors.

By that time Benjamin's warriors had killed about thirty Israelites, and they shouted, "We're defeating them as we did in the first battle!" ⁴⁰But when the warriors of Benjamin looked behind them and saw the smoke rising into the sky from every part of the town, ⁴¹the Israelites turned and attacked. At this point Benjamin's warriors realized disaster was near and became terrified. ⁴²So they ran toward the wilderness, but the Israelites chased after them and killed them. ⁴³The Israelites surrounded the men of Benjamin and were relentless in chasing them down, finally overtaking them east of Gibeah. ⁴⁴Eighteen thousand of Benjamin's greatest warriors died in that day's battle. ⁴⁵The survivors fled into the wilderness toward the rock of Rimmon, but Israel killed five thousand of them along the road. They continued the chase until they had killed another two thousand near Gidom.

⁴⁶So the tribe of Benjamin lost twenty-five thousand brave warriors that day, ⁴⁷leaving only six hundred men who escaped to the rock of Rimmon, where they lived for four months. ⁴⁸Then the Israelites

returned and slaughtered every living thing in all the towns—the people, the cattle—everything. They also burned down every town they came to.

CHAPTER 21

The Israelites had vowed at Mizpah never to give their daughters in marriage to a man from the tribe of Benjamin. ²And the people went to Bethel and sat in the presence of God until evening, raising their voices and weeping bitterly. ³"O LORD, God of Israel," they cried out, "why has this happened? Now one of our tribes is missing!"

⁴Early the next morning the people built an altar and presented their burnt offerings and peace offerings on it. ⁵Then they said, "Was any tribe of Israel not represented when we held our council in the presence of the LORD at Mizpah?" At that time they had taken a solemn oath in the LORD's presence, vowing that anyone who refused to come must die.

⁶The Israelites felt deep sadness for Benjamin and said, "Today we have lost one of the tribes from our family; it is nearly wiped out. ⁷How can we find wives for the few who remain, since we have sworn by the LORD not to give them our daughters in marriage?"

⁸So they asked, "Was anyone absent when we presented ourselves to the LORD at Mizpah?" And they discovered that no one from Jabesh-gilead had attended. ⁹For after they counted all the people, no one from Jabesh-gilead was present. ¹⁰So they sent twelve thousand warriors to Jabesh-gilead with orders to kill everyone there, including women and children. ¹¹"This is what you are to do," they said. "Completely destroy* all the males and every woman who is not a virgin." ¹²Among the residents of Jabesh-gilead they found four hundred young virgins who had never slept with a man, and they brought them to the camp at Shiloh in the land of Canaan.

¹³The Israelite assembly sent a peace delegation to the little remnant of Benjamin who were living at the rock of Rimmon. ¹⁴Then the men of Benjamin returned to their homes, and the four hundred women of Jabesh-gilead who were spared were

21:11 The Hebrew term used here refers to the complete consecration of things or people to the LORD, either by destroying them or by giving them as an offering.

given to them as wives. But there were not enough women for all of them.

¹⁵The people felt sorry for Benjamin because the LORD had left this gap in the tribes of Israel. ¹⁶So the Israelite leaders asked, "How can we find wives for the few who remain, since all the women of the tribe of Benjamin are dead? ¹⁷There must be heirs for the survivors so that an entire tribe of Israel will not be lost forever. ¹⁸But we cannot give them our own daughters in marriage because we have sworn with a solemn oath that anyone who does this will fall under God's curse."

¹⁹Then they thought of the annual festival of the LORD held in Shiloh, between Lebonah and Bethel, along the east side of the road that goes from Bethel to Shechem. ²⁰They told the men of Benjamin who still needed wives, "Go and hide in the vineyards. ²¹When the women of Shiloh come out for their dances, rush out from the vineyards, and each of you can take one of them home to be your wife! ²²And when their fathers and brothers come to us in protest, we will tell them, 'Please be understanding. Let them have your daughters, for we didn't find enough wives for them when we destroyed Jabesh-gilead. And you are not guilty of breaking the vow since you did not give your daughters in marriage to them.'"

²³So the men of Benjamin did as they were told. They kidnapped the women who took part in the celebration and carried them off to the land of their own inheritance. Then they rebuilt their towns and lived in them. ²⁴So the assembly of Israel departed by tribes and families, and they returned to their own homes.

²⁵In those days Israel had no king, so the people did whatever seemed right in their own eyes.

Ruth

AGAINST the dark backdrop of the time of the judges in Israel—filled with apostasy and judgment—the story of Ruth is a cameo of love and redemption. Ruth, a young widow, leaves her native Moab to help her mother-in-law and gathers grain in the fields belonging to a relative, Boaz, who grows to love this faithful woman. The two marry and become the great-grandparents of King David, ancestor of Jesus Christ. By marrying the widow and redeeming the family's property, Boaz is a picture of Christ as the "family redeemer."

Focus	Ruth's Faithfulness Revealed		Ruth's Faithfulness Rewarded	
Divisions	Ruth's Decision	Ruth's Devotion	Ruth's Deliverer	Ruth's Delight
	1:1 1:22	2:1 2:23	3:1 3:18	4:1 4:22
Topics	Ruth and Naomi		Ruth and Boaz	
	Going with Naomi	Gathering Grain for Naomi	Loved by Boaz	Married to Boaz
Place	Moab	Fields in Bethlehem	Threshing Floor in Bethlehem	Home in Bethlehem
Time	About 30 Years			

MARCH 13 ☐ DAY 73
RUTH 1–4
Ruth: An Old Testament Love Story

 OVERVIEW Yesterday you read five of the darkest chapters in all of Scripture; today you're reading four of the brightest. The remarkable thing to keep in mind is this: The events described in both portions take place at approximately the same time! The book of Ruth is a cameo story of love, devotion, and redemption set in the black context of the era of the judges. It is the story of a Moabite woman who was willing to forsake her pagan heritage in order to cling to the people of Israel and the God of Israel. Because of her *faithfulness* in a time of national *faithlessness,* God rewards her by giving her a new husband (Boaz), a baby son (Obed), and a privileged position in the lineage of Christ (she is the great-grandmother of King David).

Chapter 1	Chapter 2	Chapter 3	Chapter 4
Ruth's Decision	Ruth's Devotion	Ruth's Deliverer	Ruth's Delight
Love Revealed		Love Rewarded	

 YOUR DAILY WALK After reading Ruth's four-chapter love story, turn to Hebrews 11:6. The words will have a familiar ring, but don't slide over them casually. Then ask yourself this question: Do I truly believe that God rewards those who diligently seek him?

The world crowns success, but God crowns faithfulness.

Think back over the difficult decisions that confronted Ruth: staying in her homeland of Moab, where she was known and loved, or moving to Israel, where she was largely unknown and unloved; starting a new home of her own, or living with her bereaved mother-in-law; worshiping the familiar gods of Moab, or worshiping the true God of Israel. As she diligently sought to walk with God in the midst of a godless nation, Ruth learned firsthand that God rewards God-seekers!

Are you struggling with misfortune, bereavement, or strange new surroundings today? Take heart from Ruth's example. Why not share with your in-laws (if you have some) a difficult decision you are facing today, and ask them to join you in prayer!

 INSIGHT Typecasting in the Book of Ruth
Notice how the characters' names foreshadow the action in the book of Ruth: *Naomi,* "pleasant"; *Elimelech,* "my God is King"; *Mahlon,* "sick"; *Kilion,* "pining"; *Orpah,* "stubbornness"; *Ruth,* "friendship"; *Boaz,* "in him is strength."

CHAPTER 1
In the days when the judges ruled in Israel, a man from Bethlehem in Judah left the country because of a severe famine. He took his wife and two sons and went to live in the country of Moab. ²The man's name was Elimelech, and his wife was Naomi. Their two sons were Mahlon and Kilion. They were Ephrathites from Bethlehem in the land of Judah. During their stay in Moab, ³Elimelech died and Naomi was left with her two sons. ⁴The two sons married Moabite women. One married a woman named Orpah, and the other a woman named Ruth. But about ten years later, ⁵both Mahlon and Kilion died. This

left Naomi alone, without her husband or sons.

⁶Then Naomi heard in Moab that the LORD had blessed his people in Judah by giving them good crops again. So Naomi and her daughters-in-law got ready to leave Moab to return to her homeland. ⁷With her two daughters-in-law she set out from the place where she had been living, and they took the road that would lead them back to Judah.

⁸But on the way, Naomi said to her two daughters-in-law, "Go back to your mothers' homes instead of coming with me. And may the LORD reward you for your kindness to your husbands and to me. ⁹May the LORD bless you with the security of another marriage." Then she kissed them good-bye, and they all broke down and wept.

¹⁰"No," they said. "We want to go with you to your people."

¹¹But Naomi replied, "Why should you go on with me? Can I still give birth to other sons who could grow up to be your husbands? ¹²No, my daughters, return to your parents' homes, for I am too old to marry again. And even if it were possible, and I were to get married tonight and bear sons, then what? ¹³Would you wait for them to grow up and refuse to marry someone else? No, of course not, my daughters! Things are far more bitter for me than for you, because the LORD himself has caused me to suffer."

¹⁴And again they wept together, and Orpah kissed her mother-in-law good-bye. But Ruth insisted on staying with Naomi. ¹⁵"See," Naomi said to her, "your sister-in-law has gone back to her people and to her gods. You should do the same."

¹⁶But Ruth replied, "Don't ask me to leave you and turn back. I will go wherever you go and live wherever you live. Your people will be my people, and your God will be my God. ¹⁷I will die where you die and will be buried there. May the LORD punish me severely if I allow anything but death to separate us!" ¹⁸So when Naomi saw that Ruth had made up her mind to go with her, she stopped urging her.

¹⁹So the two of them continued on their journey. When they came to Bethlehem, the entire town was stirred by their arrival. "Is it really Naomi?" the women asked.

²⁰"Don't call me Naomi," she told them. "Instead, call me Mara,* for the Almighty has made life very bitter for me. ²¹I went away full, but the LORD has brought me home empty. Why should you call me Naomi when the LORD has caused me to suffer* and the Almighty has sent such tragedy?"

²²So Naomi returned from Moab, accompanied by her daughter-in-law Ruth, the young Moabite woman. They arrived in Bethlehem at the beginning of the barley harvest.

CHAPTER 2

Now there was a wealthy and influential man in Bethlehem named Boaz, who was a relative of Naomi's husband, Elimelech.

²One day Ruth said to Naomi, "Let me go out into the fields to gather leftover grain behind anyone who will let me do it."

And Naomi said, "All right, my daughter, go ahead." ³So Ruth went out to gather grain behind the harvesters. And as it happened, she found herself working in a field that belonged to Boaz, the relative of her father-in-law, Elimelech.

⁴While she was there, Boaz arrived from Bethlehem and greeted the harvesters. "The LORD be with you!" he said.

"The LORD bless you!" the harvesters replied.

⁵Then Boaz asked his foreman, "Who is that girl over there?"

⁶And the foreman replied, "She is the young woman from Moab who came back with Naomi. ⁷She asked me this morning if she could gather grain behind the harvesters. She has been hard at work ever since, except for a few minutes' rest over there in the shelter."

⁸Boaz went over and said to Ruth, "Listen, my daughter. Stay right here with us when you gather grain; don't go to any other fields. Stay right behind the women working in my field. ⁹See which part of the field they are harvesting, and then follow them. I have warned the young men not to bother you. And when you are thirsty, help yourself to the water they have drawn from the well."

¹⁰Ruth fell at his feet and thanked him warmly. "Why are you being so kind to me?" she asked. "I am only a foreigner."

¹¹"Yes, I know," Boaz replied. "But I also

1:20 *Naomi* means "pleasant"; *Mara* means "bitter."   1:21 Or *has testified against me.*

know about the love and kindness you have shown your mother-in-law since the death of your husband. I have heard how you left your father and mother and your own land to live here among complete strangers. ¹²May the LORD, the God of Israel, under whose wings you have come to take refuge, reward you fully."

¹³"I hope I continue to please you, sir," she replied. "You have comforted me by speaking so kindly to me, even though I am not as worthy as your workers."

¹⁴At lunchtime Boaz called to her, "Come over here and help yourself to some of our food. You can dip your bread in the wine if you like." So she sat with his harvesters, and Boaz gave her food—more than she could eat.

¹⁵When Ruth went back to work again, Boaz ordered his young men, "Let her gather grain right among the sheaves without stopping her. ¹⁶And pull out some heads of barley from the bundles and drop them on purpose for her. Let her pick them up, and don't give her a hard time!"

¹⁷So Ruth gathered barley there all day, and when she beat out the grain that evening, it came to about half a bushel.* ¹⁸She carried it back into town and showed it to her mother-in-law. Ruth also gave her the food that was left over from her lunch.

¹⁹"So much!" Naomi exclaimed. "Where did you gather all this grain today? Where did you work? May the LORD bless the one who helped you!"

So Ruth told her mother-in-law about the man in whose field she had worked. And she said, "The man I worked with today is named Boaz."

²⁰"May the LORD bless him!" Naomi told her daughter-in-law. "He is showing his kindness to us as well as to your dead husband.* That man is one of our closest relatives, one of our family redeemers."

²¹Then Ruth said, "What's more, Boaz even told me to come back and stay with his harvesters until the entire harvest is completed."

²²"This is wonderful!" Naomi exclaimed. "Do as he said. Stay with his workers right through the whole harvest. You will be safe there, unlike in other fields."

²³So Ruth worked alongside the women in Boaz's fields and gathered grain with

them until the end of the barley harvest. Then she worked with them through the wheat harvest, too. But all the while she lived with her mother-in-law.

CHAPTER 3

One day Naomi said to Ruth, "My daughter, it's time that I found a permanent home for you, so that you will be provided for. ²Boaz is a close relative of ours, and he's been very kind by letting you gather grain with his workers. Tonight he will be winnowing barley at the threshing floor. ³Now do as I tell you—take a bath and put on perfume and dress in your nicest clothes. Then go to the threshing floor, but don't let Boaz see you until he has finished his meal. ⁴Be sure to notice where he lies down; then go and uncover his feet and lie down there. He will tell you what to do."

⁵"I will do everything you say," Ruth replied. ⁶So she went down to the threshing floor that night and followed the instructions of her mother-in-law.

⁷After Boaz had finished his meal and was in good spirits, he lay down beside the heap of grain and went to sleep. Then Ruth came quietly, uncovered his feet, and lay down. ⁸Around midnight, Boaz suddenly woke up and turned over. He was surprised to find a woman lying at his feet! ⁹"Who are you?" he demanded.

"I am your servant Ruth," she replied. "Spread the corner of your covering over me, for you are my family redeemer."

¹⁰"The LORD bless you, my daughter!" Boaz exclaimed. "You are showing more family loyalty now than ever by not running after a younger man, whether rich or poor. ¹¹Now don't worry about a thing, my daughter. I will do what is necessary, for everyone in town knows you are an honorable woman. ¹²But there is one problem. While it is true that I am one of your family redeemers, there is another man who is more closely related to you than I am. ¹³Stay here tonight, and in the morning I will talk to him. If he is willing to redeem you, then let him marry you. But if he is not willing, then as surely as the LORD lives, I will marry you! Now lie down here until morning."

¹⁴So Ruth lay at Boaz's feet until the morning, but she got up before it was light enough for people to recognize each other. For Boaz said, "No one must know that a

2:17 Hebrew *about an ephah* [18 liters].   2:20 Hebrew *to the living and to the dead.*

woman was here at the threshing floor." [15]Boaz also said to her, "Bring your cloak and spread it out." He measured out six scoops* of barley into the cloak and helped her put it on her back. Then Boaz* returned to the town.

[16]When Ruth went back to her mother-in-law, Naomi asked, "What happened, my daughter?"

Ruth told Naomi everything Boaz had done for her, [17]and she added, "He gave me these six scoops of barley and said, 'Don't go back to your mother-in-law empty-handed.'"

[18]Then Naomi said to her, "Just be patient, my daughter, until we hear what happens. The man won't rest until he has followed through on this. He will settle it today."

CHAPTER 4

So Boaz went to the town gate and took a seat there. When the family redeemer he had mentioned came by, Boaz called out to him, "Come over here, friend. I want to talk to you." So they sat down together. [2]Then Boaz called ten leaders from the town and asked them to sit as witnesses. [3]And Boaz said to the family redeemer, "You know Naomi, who came back from Moab. She is selling the land that belonged to our relative Elimelech. [4]I felt that I should speak to you about it so that you can redeem it if you wish. If you want the land, then buy it here in the presence of these witnesses. But if you don't want it, let me know right away, because I am next in line to redeem it after you."

The man replied, "All right, I'll redeem it."

[5]Then Boaz told him, "Of course, your purchase of the land from Naomi also requires that you marry Ruth, the Moabite widow. That way, she can have children who will carry on her husband's name and keep the land in the family."

[6]"Then I can't redeem it," the family redeemer replied, "because this might endanger my own estate. You redeem the land; I cannot do it."

[7]In those days it was the custom in Israel for anyone transferring a right of purchase to remove his sandal and hand it to the other party. This publicly validated the transaction. [8]So the other family redeemer drew off his sandal as he said to Boaz, "You buy the land."

[9]Then Boaz said to the leaders and to the crowd standing around, "You are witnesses that today I have bought from Naomi all the property of Elimelech, Kilion, and Mahlon. [10]And with the land I have acquired Ruth, the Moabite widow of Mahlon, to be my wife. This way she can have a son to carry on the family name of her dead husband and to inherit the family property here in his hometown. You are all witnesses today."

[11]Then the leaders and all the people standing there replied, "We are witnesses! May the LORD make the woman who is now coming into your home like Rachel and Leah, from whom all the nation of Israel descended! May you be great in Ephrathah and famous in Bethlehem. [12]And may the LORD give you descendants by this young woman who will be like those of our ancestor Perez, the son of Tamar and Judah."

[13]So Boaz married Ruth and took her home to live with him. When he slept with her, the LORD enabled her to become pregnant, and she gave birth to a son. [14]And the women of the town said to Naomi, "Praise the LORD who has given you a family redeemer today! May he be famous in Israel. [15]May this child restore your youth and care for you in your old age. For he is the son of your daughter-in-law who loves you so much and who has been better to you than seven sons!"

[16]Naomi took care of the baby and cared for him as if he were her own. [17]The neighbor women said, "Now at last Naomi has a son again!" And they named him Obed. He became the father of Jesse and the grandfather of David.

[18]This is their family line beginning with their ancestor Perez:

Perez was the father of Hezron.
[19] Hezron was the father of Ram.
  Ram was the father of Amminadab.
[20] Amminadab was the father of Nahshon.
  Nahshon was the father of Salmon.
[21] Salmon was the father of Boaz.
  Boaz was the father of Obed.
[22] Obed was the father of Jesse.
  Jesse was the father of David.

3:15a Hebrew *six measures*, an unknown quantity.   3:15b Most Hebrew manuscripts read *he;* many Hebrew manuscripts, Syriac version, and Latin Vulgate read *she*.

MARCH 14 □ DAY 74
Against the Odds

LOOK BACK This week you have read about the judges of Israel, military leaders who fought to deliver the nation from the effects of its persistent sin. More than a dozen are described in the book of Judges, but Deborah and Gideon are two of the best. Deborah, a prophetess and songwriter, is instrumental in delivering the nation from Canaanite oppression. Gideon, a timid man with dubious credentials, leads the world's most unusual military band in the destruction of Midian's army—without a shot being fired!

Casting a shadow bigger than life across the last half of the book of Judges is Samson, a man with incredible physical strength and equally remarkable moral weakness. Set apart by his parents from birth for special service to God, Samson ends his life in failure and dishonor. His great potential and equally great moral collapse mirror the condition of the nation, which becomes so corrupt and degraded by the end of the book that even shocking brutality and immorality no longer cause the people to blush. Against this dark backdrop, the story of Ruth shines as a bright exception. Ruth the Moabitess forfeits the security of her homeland for the privilege of knowing the one true God.

When we put our cares in God's hands, he puts his peace in our hearts.

LOOK UP The plans may be man's, but the odds are God's. And chances are good you wouldn't want to face the odds Gideon faced as God whittled down his fighting force to something that would bring great glory to the Lord of hosts. Get your pen or pencil, and let's do a little arithmetic:

(1) How large was the Midianite army before the battle began? (According to Judges 8:10, there were only 15,000 soldiers left after 120,000 had fallen in battle. That would make a total of ____,000 enemy soldiers to begin with.)

(2) According to Judges 7:3, Gideon had 10,000 soldiers left after 22,000 had gone home fearful. Add those two numbers together, and he had started with ____,000 men.

(3) That means initially Gideon faced "odds" of 135,000:32,000 or roughly 4:1. What did God say about those odds (Judges 7:2)?

_____

(4) After the fearful ones left, Gideon's army was reduced to just ____,000. The Midianite army was still the same size: ____,000. Now Gideon faced odds of 135,000:10,000 or roughly 13:1. What did God say about those odds (Judges 7:4)?

_____

(5) After the water-drinking experience, Gideon's army was further reduced to just _____ men (Judges 7:7). Meanwhile the Midianite army was still the same size: ____,000. That means Gideon now faced odds of 135,000:300 or roughly 450:1. And what did God say about those odds (Judges 7:7)? _____

LOOK AHEAD God delights to bring great victory out of certain defeat. At times he seems to go out of his way to ensure that the odds are overwhelmingly against his people so that when victory is achieved, there can be only one explanation: God did it!

Would you have had the courage to do what Gideon did? Before you conclude that Gideon was some sort of Old Testament "super saint," recall that when the story began he was cowering in a winepress trying to escape the all-seeing eye of the Midianites (Judges 6:11-12). This was just a humble servant willing to obey God in spite of the odds.

Perhaps the odds look no better from where you are standing as you look at your own prospects for victory over a physical disability, an uncertain future, a family situation that defies solution. Give God a chance to show himself strong, and you may see the odds swing decidedly in your favor!

1 Samuel

AS Israel's last judge, Samuel is raised up by God to bring to a close this chaotic period in the nation's history. To restore order, God instructs Samuel to anoint an impressive soldier named Saul. Though qualified outwardly, Saul is soon disqualified inwardly. Once again Samuel takes his anointing flask in search of a king—one with a heart like God's. Thus, 1 Samuel recounts the rise and decline of Saul and sets the stage for Israel's greatest monarch, David.

Focus	Final Judge		First King		King-Elect			
Divisions	The Dedicated Servant	The Faithful Servant	The Chosen King	The Rejected King	The Secret King-Elect	The Pursued King-Elect	The Recognized King-Elect	The Exiled King-Elect
	1 3	4 8	9 12	13 15	16 19	20 23	24 26	27 31
Topics	Samuel		Saul		David			
	Rebuilding		Rebelling		Running			
Place	Israel in Canaan							
Time	About 94 Years							

MARCH 15 ☐ DAY 75
1 SAMUEL 1–3
Samuel, the Dedicated Servant

OVERVIEW As the period of the judges draws to a close, God blesses a man named Elkanah and his barren wife, Hannah, with a son. The child Samuel, destined to be the last judge and first great prophet in Israel, is dedicated to the Lord's service and grows up in the household of Eli the priest. Through Samuel God delivers an ear-tingling message of judgment upon Eli's house for his failure to discipline his wayward sons. Samuel's obedience from earliest childhood demonstrates to "All the people of Israel from one end of the land to the other . . . that Samuel was confirmed as a prophet of the LORD" (3:20).

Chapter 1		Chapter 2		Chapter 3
Hannah's Request	God's Reward	Hannah's Rejoicing	Eli's Rejection	Samuel's Response
1 18	19 28	1 11	12 36	
Birth of Samuel		Boyhood of Samuel		

Keep your heart right, even when it is sorely wounded.

YOUR DAILY WALK Your best friend comes to you and says, "I've been praying about something for weeks, and God still hasn't answered my prayer. Can you tell me why?" What would you tell that person? How many reasons can you think of why God might not answer a certain prayer?

According to the Bible, unanswered prayer may result from
• sin in the life of the person praying (Psalm 66:18)
• lack of faith (James 1:6-7)
• not praying according to God's will (1 John 5:14)
• praying from impure motives (James 4:3)

But what if you pray, meet all the requirements, and still don't receive an answer (like Hannah)? The answer is simple, yet complex: God is sovereign. He answers prayer in his time and for his purposes. Hannah prayed and wept and longed for a child. At the right time God gave her a son who would be a blessing to the entire nation.

Today, compile an "unanswered prayer list" of those requests you've been praying about for some time. Across the top, write "Remember Hannah" as a reminder that God never leaves a prayer unanswered too long.

INSIGHT A Prayer God Loves to Answer
Hannah is one of several Bible women who, in answer to specific prayer, was blessed with a son. How many others can you name? (Hint: Genesis 17:15-16; 25:21; 30:22; Luke 1:13).

CHAPTER 1
There was a man named Elkanah who lived in Ramah* in the hill country of Ephraim. He was the son of Jeroham and grandson of Elihu, from the family of Tohu and the clan of Zuph. ²Elkanah had two wives, Hannah and Peninnah. Peninnah had children, while Hannah did not.

³Each year Elkanah and his family would travel to Shiloh to worship and sacrifice to the LORD Almighty at the Tabernacle. The priests of the LORD at that time

1:1 Hebrew *Ramathaim-zophim;* compare 1:19.

were the two sons of Eli—Hophni and Phinehas. [4]On the day Elkanah presented his sacrifice, he would give portions of the sacrifice to Peninnah and each of her children. [5]But he gave Hannah a special portion* because he loved her very much, even though the LORD had given her no children. [6]But Peninnah made fun of Hannah because the LORD had closed her womb. [7]Year after year it was the same—Peninnah would taunt Hannah as they went to the Tabernacle.* Hannah would finally be reduced to tears and would not even eat.

[8]"What's the matter, Hannah?" Elkanah would ask. "Why aren't you eating? Why be so sad just because you have no children? You have me—isn't that better than having ten sons?"

[9]Once when they were at Shiloh, Hannah went over to the Tabernacle* after supper to pray to the LORD. Eli the priest was sitting at his customary place beside the entrance. [10]Hannah was in deep anguish, crying bitterly as she prayed to the LORD. [11]And she made this vow: "O LORD Almighty, if you will look down upon my sorrow and answer my prayer and give me a son, then I will give him back to you. He will be yours for his entire lifetime, and as a sign that he has been dedicated to the LORD, his hair will never be cut."*

[12]As she was praying to the LORD, Eli watched her. [13]Seeing her lips moving but hearing no sound, he thought she had been drinking. [14]"Must you come here drunk?" he demanded. "Throw away your wine!"

[15]"Oh no, sir!" she replied, "I'm not drunk! But I am very sad, and I was pouring out my heart to the LORD. [16]Please don't think I am a wicked woman! For I have been praying out of great anguish and sorrow."

[17]"In that case," Eli said, "cheer up! May the God of Israel grant the request you have asked of him."

[18]"Oh, thank you, sir!" she exclaimed. Then she went back and began to eat again, and she was no longer sad.

[19]The entire family got up early the next morning and went to worship the LORD once more. Then they returned home to Ramah. When Elkanah slept with Hannah, the LORD remembered her request, [20]and in due time she gave birth to a son. She named him Samuel,* for she said, "I asked the LORD for him."

[21]The next year Elkanah, Peninnah, and their children went on their annual trip to offer a sacrifice to the LORD. [22]But Hannah did not go. She told her husband, "Wait until the baby is weaned. Then I will take him to the Tabernacle and leave him there with the LORD permanently."*

[23]"Whatever you think is best," Elkanah agreed. "Stay here for now, and may the LORD help you keep your promise." So she stayed home and nursed the baby.

[24]When the child was weaned, Hannah took him to the Tabernacle in Shiloh. They brought along a three-year-old bull* for the sacrifice and half a bushel* of flour and some wine. [25]After sacrificing the bull, they took the child to Eli. [26]"Sir, do you remember me?" Hannah asked. "I am the woman who stood here several years ago praying to the LORD. [27]I asked the LORD to give me this child, and he has given me my request. [28]Now I am giving him to the LORD, and he will belong to the LORD his whole life." And they* worshiped the LORD there.

CHAPTER 2

Then Hannah prayed:

"My heart rejoices in the LORD!
    Oh, how the LORD has blessed me!
Now I have an answer for my enemies,
    as I delight in your deliverance.
[2] No one is holy like the LORD!
    There is no one besides you;
    there is no Rock like our God.

[3] "Stop acting so proud and haughty!
    Don't speak with such arrogance!
The LORD is a God who knows your
        deeds;
    and he will judge you for what you
        have done.
[4] Those who were mighty are mighty
        no more;
    and those who were weak are now
        strong.
[5] Those who were well fed are now
        starving;
    and those who were starving are
        now full.

1:5 Or *a double portion.* The meaning of the Hebrew is uncertain.   **1:7** Hebrew *the house of the LORD;* also in 1:24.   **1:9** Hebrew *the Temple of the LORD.*   **1:11** Some manuscripts add *He will drink neither wine nor intoxicants.*   **1:20** *Samuel* sounds like the Hebrew term for "asked of God" or "heard by God."   **1:22** Some manuscripts add *I will offer him as a Nazirite for all time.*   **1:24a** As in Dead Sea Scrolls, Greek and Syriac versions; Masoretic Text reads *3 bulls.*   **1:24b** Hebrew *and an ephah* [18 liters].   **1:28** Or *he.*

The barren woman now has seven
children;
but the woman with many children
will have no more.
6 The LORD brings both death and life;
he brings some down to the grave
but raises others up.
7 The LORD makes one poor and another
rich;
he brings one down and lifts
another up.
8 He lifts the poor from the dust—
yes, from a pile of ashes!
He treats them like princes,
placing them in seats of honor.

"For all the earth is the LORD's,
and he has set the world in order.
9 He will protect his godly ones,
but the wicked will perish in
darkness.
No one will succeed by strength alone.
10   Those who fight against the LORD
will be broken.
He thunders against them from heaven;
the LORD judges throughout the
earth.
He gives mighty strength to his king;
he increases the might of his
anointed one."

11 Then Elkanah and Hannah returned
home to Ramah without Samuel. And the
boy became the LORD's helper, for he assisted Eli the priest.

12 Now the sons of Eli were scoundrels
who had no respect for the LORD 13 or for
their duties as priests. Whenever anyone
offered a sacrifice, Eli's sons would send
over a servant with a three-pronged fork.
While the meat of the sacrificed animal was
still boiling, 14 the servant would stick the
fork into the pot and demand that whatever it brought up be given to Eli's sons. All
the Israelites who came to worship at Shiloh were treated this way. 15 Sometimes the
servant would come even before the animal's fat had been burned on the altar. He
would demand raw meat before it had
been boiled so that it could be used for
roasting. 16 The man offering the sacrifice might
reply, "Take as much as you want, but the
fat must first be burned." Then the servant
would demand, "No, give it to me now, or

I'll take it by force." 17 So the sin of these
young men was very serious in the LORD's
sight, for they treated the LORD's offerings
with contempt.

18 Now Samuel, though only a boy, was
the LORD's helper. He wore a linen tunic
just like that of a priest.* 19 Each year his
mother made a small coat for him and
brought it to him when she came with her
husband for the sacrifice. 20 Before they returned home, Eli would bless Elkanah and
his wife and say, "May the LORD give you
other children to take the place of this one
she gave to the LORD.*" 21 And the LORD
gave Hannah three sons and two daughters. Meanwhile, Samuel grew up in the
presence of the LORD.

22 Now Eli was very old, but he was
aware of what his sons were doing to the
people of Israel. He knew, for instance, that
his sons were seducing the young women
who assisted at the entrance of the Tabernacle.* 23 Eli said to them, "I have been hearing reports from the people about the
wicked things you are doing. Why do you
keep sinning? 24 You must stop, my sons!
The reports I hear among the LORD's
people are not good. 25 If someone sins
against another person, God* can mediate
for the guilty party. But if someone sins
against the LORD, who can intercede?" But
Eli's sons wouldn't listen to their father, for
the LORD was already planning to put them
to death.

26 Meanwhile, as young Samuel grew
taller, he also continued to gain favor with
the LORD and with the people.

27 One day a prophet came to Eli and
gave him this message from the LORD:
"Didn't I reveal myself to your ancestors
when the people of Israel were slaves in
Egypt? 28 I chose your ancestor Aaron* from
among all his relatives to be my priest, to
offer sacrifices on my altar, to burn incense,
and to wear the priestly garments* as he
served me. And I assigned the sacrificial
offerings to you priests. 29 So why do you
scorn my sacrifices and offerings? Why do
you honor your sons more than me—for
you and they have become fat from the best
offerings of my people!

30 "Therefore, the LORD, the God of Israel,
says: The terrible things you are doing cannot continue! I had promised that your

branch of the tribe of Levi* would always be my priests. But I will honor only those who honor me, and I will despise those who despise me. ³¹I will put an end to your family, so it will no longer serve as my priests. All the members of your family will die before their time. None will live to a ripe old age. ³²You will watch with envy as I pour out prosperity on the people of Israel. But no members of your family will ever live out their days. ³³Those who are left alive will live in sadness and grief, and their children will die a violent death.* ³⁴And to prove that what I have said will come true, I will cause your two sons, Hophni and Phinehas, to die on the same day!

³⁵"Then I will raise up a faithful priest who will serve me and do what I tell him to do. I will bless his descendants, and his family will be priests to my anointed kings forever. ³⁶Then all of your descendants will bow before his descendants, begging for money and food. 'Please,' they will say, 'give us jobs among the priests so we will have enough to eat.'"

CHAPTER 3

Meanwhile, the boy Samuel was serving the LORD by assisting Eli. Now in those days messages from the LORD were very rare, and visions were quite uncommon.

²One night Eli, who was almost blind by now, had just gone to bed. ³The lamp of God had not yet gone out, and Samuel was sleeping in the Tabernacle* near the Ark of God. ⁴Suddenly, the LORD called out, "Samuel! Samuel!"

"Yes?" Samuel replied. "What is it?" ⁵He jumped up and ran to Eli. "Here I am. What do you need?"

"I didn't call you," Eli replied. "Go on back to bed." So he did.

⁶Then the LORD called out again, "Samuel!"

Again Samuel jumped up and ran to Eli. "Here I am," he said. "What do you need?"

"I didn't call you, my son," Eli said. "Go on back to bed."

⁷Samuel did not yet know the LORD because he had never had a message from the LORD before. ⁸So now the LORD called a third time, and once more Samuel jumped up and ran to Eli. "Here I am," he said. "What do you need?"

Then Eli realized it was the LORD who was calling the boy. ⁹So he said to Samuel, "Go and lie down again, and if someone calls again, say, 'Yes, LORD, your servant is listening.'" So Samuel went back to bed.

¹⁰And the LORD came and called as before, "Samuel! Samuel!"

And Samuel replied, "Yes, your servant is listening."

¹¹Then the LORD said to Samuel, "I am about to do a shocking thing in Israel. ¹²I am going to carry out all my threats against Eli and his family. ¹³I have warned him continually that judgment is coming for his family, because his sons are blaspheming God* and he hasn't disciplined them. ¹⁴So I have vowed that the sins of Eli and his sons will never be forgiven by sacrifices or offerings."

¹⁵Samuel stayed in bed until morning, then got up and opened the doors of the Tabernacle* as usual. He was afraid to tell Eli what the LORD had said to him. ¹⁶But Eli called out to him, "Samuel, my son."

"Here I am," Samuel replied.

¹⁷"What did the LORD say to you? Tell me everything. And may God punish you if you hide anything from me!" ¹⁸So Samuel told Eli everything; he didn't hold anything back. "It is the LORD's will," Eli replied. "Let him do what he thinks best."

¹⁹As Samuel grew up, the LORD was with him, and everything Samuel said was wise and helpful. ²⁰All the people of Israel from one end of the land to the other knew that Samuel was confirmed as a prophet of the LORD. ²¹The LORD continued to appear at Shiloh and gave messages to Samuel there at the Tabernacle. ⁴:¹And Samuel's words went out to all the people of Israel.

2:30 Hebrew *that your house and your father's house.*   **2:33** As in Dead Sea Scrolls, which read *die by the sword;* Masoretic Text reads *die like mortals.*   **3:3** Hebrew *the Temple of the LORD.*   **3:13** As in Greek version; Hebrew reads *his sons have made themselves contemptible.*   **3:15** Hebrew *the house of the LORD.*

MARCH 16 ☐ DAY 76
1 SAMUEL 4–8
Samuel, the Faithful Servant

OVERVIEW The Philistines, enemies and oppressors of Israel since the days of Samson, are God's instrument of judgment upon Eli and his wicked sons. Using the Ark of God as a good-luck charm, Israel carries it into battle and is soundly defeated. The Ark is captured, and Hophni and Phinehas (who carried it into battle) are slain—events that serve as a deathblow for Eli. Truly *Ichabod* ("Where is the glory?") can be written over Israel. But though the symbol of God's presence is gone, God himself is still very much alive! He afflicts the Philistines with grievous plagues, even causing the Philistine objects of worship to fall down before the Ark. When at last the Ark is returned, Samuel leads the nation in repentance before God and victory over the enemy. But the days of the judges are numbered, for the people demand a king "like the nations around us" (8:20)—a request with painful repercussions.

Chapter 4	Chapters 5–6	Chapter 7	Chapter 8
The Ark Removed	The Ark Returned	The Nation Repentant	A King Requested
Defeat in the Nation		Revival in the Nation	

YOUR DAILY WALK There are really only two things you can do with someone else's mistakes: (1) You can learn from them, or (2) you can duplicate them.

What a father says to his children is not heard by the world, but it will be heard by posterity.

Samuel should have learned the necessity of proper parental discipline from his observance of Eli's failure with his sons. But apparently he did not because his own sons were equally undisciplined. They were covetous, took bribes, and perverted justice—just like Hophni and Phinehas! How could such a tragic turn of events repeat itself? How could Samuel duplicate Eli's folly? How could any generation not learn from its predecessors?

Answer: Neglect. Samuel's circuit-riding schedule (7:15-17) left scant time to spend with his children during their formative years. How about you? Does your schedule reflect that your children are a priority in your life? Make an appointment to take each one to breakfast sometime next week. It will be time well spent—for both of you!

INSIGHT The Heartbreak of Having a King
In the space of eight verses, Samuel warns the people of at least ten painful consequences of having a king (8:11-18). How many can you find? (Hint: Watch for the telltale words *the king will.*)

CHAPTER 4
At that time Israel was at war with the Philistines. The Israelite army was camped near Ebenezer, and the Philistines were at Aphek. ²The Philistines attacked and defeated the army of Israel, killing four thousand men. ³After the battle was over, the army of Israel retreated to their camp, and their leaders asked, "Why did the LORD allow us to be defeated by the Philistines?"

4:3 Or *he*.

Then they said, "Let's bring the Ark of the Covenant of the LORD from Shiloh. If we carry it into battle with us, it* will save us from our enemies."

⁴So they sent men to Shiloh to bring back the Ark of the Covenant of the LORD Almighty, who is enthroned between the cherubim. Hophni and Phinehas, the sons of Eli, helped carry the Ark of God to where the battle was being fought. ⁵When the

Israelites saw the Ark of the Covenant of the LORD coming into the camp, their shout of joy was so loud that it made the ground shake!

⁶"What's going on?" the Philistines asked. "What's all the shouting about in the Hebrew camp?" When they were told it was because the Ark of the LORD had arrived, ⁷they panicked. "The gods have* come into their camp!" they cried. "This is a disaster! We have never had to face anything like this before! ⁸Who can save us from these mighty gods of Israel? They are the same gods who destroyed the Egyptians with plagues when Israel was in the wilderness. ⁹Fight as you never have before, Philistines! If you don't, we will become the Hebrews' slaves just as they have been ours!"

¹⁰So the Philistines fought desperately, and Israel was defeated again. The slaughter was great; thirty thousand Israelite men died that day. The survivors turned and fled to their tents. ¹¹The Ark of God was captured, and Hophni and Phinehas, the two sons of Eli, were killed.

¹²A man from the tribe of Benjamin ran from the battlefront and arrived at Shiloh later that same day. He had torn his clothes and put dust on his head to show his grief. ¹³Eli was waiting beside the road to hear the news of the battle, for his heart trembled for the safety of the Ark of God. When the messenger arrived and told what had happened, an outcry resounded throughout the town. ¹⁴"What is all the noise about?" Eli asked.

The messenger rushed over to Eli, ¹⁵who was ninety-eight years old and blind. ¹⁶He said to Eli, "I have just come from the battlefront—I was there this very day."

"What happened?" Eli demanded.

¹⁷"Israel has been defeated," the messenger replied. "Thousands of Israelite troops are dead on the battlefield. Your two sons, Hophni and Phinehas, were killed, too. And the Ark of God has been captured."

¹⁸When the messenger mentioned what had happened to the Ark, Eli fell backward from his seat beside the gate. He broke his neck and died, for he was old and very fat. He had led Israel for forty years.

¹⁹Eli's daughter-in-law, the wife of Phinehas, was pregnant and near her time of delivery. When she heard that the Ark of God had been captured and that her husband and father-in-law were dead, her labor pains suddenly began. ²⁰She died in childbirth, but before she passed away the midwives tried to encourage her. "Don't be afraid," they said. "You have a baby boy!" But she did not answer or respond in any way.

²¹She named the child Ichabod—"Where is the glory?"—murmuring, "Israel's glory is gone." She named him this because the Ark of God had been captured and because her husband and her father-in-law were dead. ²²Then she said, "The glory has departed from Israel, for the Ark of God has been captured."

C H A P T E R 5

After the Philistines captured the Ark of God, they took it from the battleground at Ebenezer to the city of Ashdod. ²They carried the Ark of God into the temple of Dagon and placed it beside the idol of Dagon. ³But when the citizens of Ashdod went to see it the next morning, Dagon had fallen with his face to the ground in front of the Ark of the LORD! So they set the idol up again. ⁴But the next morning the same thing happened—the idol had fallen face down before the Ark of the LORD again. This time his head and hands had broken off and were lying in the doorway. Only the trunk of his body was left intact. ⁵That is why to this day neither the priests of Dagon nor anyone who enters the temple of Dagon will step on its threshold.

⁶Then the LORD began to afflict the people of Ashdod and the nearby villages with a plague of tumors.* ⁷When the people realized what was happening, they cried out, "We can't keep the Ark of the God of Israel here any longer! He is against us! We will all be destroyed along with our god Dagon." ⁸So they called together the rulers of the five Philistine cities and asked, "What should we do with the Ark of the God of Israel?"

The rulers discussed it and replied, "Move it to the city of Gath." So they moved the Ark of the God of Israel to Gath. ⁹But when the Ark arrived at Gath, the LORD began afflicting its people, young and old, with a plague of tumors, and there was a great panic. ¹⁰So they sent the Ark of God to the city

---

4:7 Or *A god has.*   **5:6** Greek version and Latin Vulgate read *tumors. And rats appeared in their land, and death and destruction were throughout the city.*

of Ekron, but when the people of Ekron saw it coming they cried out, "They are bringing the Ark of the God of Israel here to kill us, too!" [11] So the people summoned the rulers again and begged them, "Please send the Ark of the God of Israel back to its own country, or it* will kill us all." For the plague from God had already begun, and great fear was sweeping across the city. [12] Those who didn't die were afflicted with tumors; and there was weeping everywhere.

CHAPTER 6

The Ark of the LORD remained in Philistine territory seven months in all. [2] Then the Philistines called in their priests and diviners and asked them, "What should we do about the Ark of the LORD? Tell us how to return it to its own land."

[3] "Send the Ark of the God of Israel back, along with a gift," they were told. "Send a guilt offering so the plague will stop. Then, if the plague doesn't stop, you will know that God didn't send the plague after all."

[4] "What sort of guilt offering should we send?" they asked.

And they were told, "Since the plague has struck both you and your five rulers, make five gold tumors and five gold rats, just like those that have ravaged your land. [5] Make these things to show honor to the God of Israel. Perhaps then he will stop afflicting you, your gods, and your land. [6] Don't be stubborn and rebellious as Pharaoh and the Egyptians were. They wouldn't let Israel go until God had ravaged them with dreadful plagues. [7] Now build a new cart, and find two cows that have just had calves. Make sure the cows have never been yoked to a cart. Hitch the cows to the cart, but shut their calves away from them in a pen. [8] Put the Ark of the LORD on the cart, and beside it place a chest containing the gold rats and gold tumors. Then let the cows go wherever they want. [9] If they cross the border of our land and go to Beth-shemesh, we will know it was the LORD who brought this great disaster upon us. If they don't, we will know that the plague was simply a coincidence and was not sent by the LORD at all."

[10] So these instructions were carried out. Two cows with newborn calves were hitched to the cart, and their calves were shut up in a pen. [11] Then the Ark of the LORD and the chest containing the gold rats and gold tumors were placed on the cart. [12] And sure enough, the cows went straight along the road toward Bethshemesh, lowing as they went. The Philistine rulers followed them as far as the border of Beth-shemesh.

[13] The people of Beth-shemesh were harvesting wheat in the valley, and when they saw the Ark, they were overjoyed! [14] The cart came into the field of a man named Joshua and stopped beside a large rock. So the people broke up the wood of the cart for a fire and killed the cows and sacrificed them to the LORD as a burnt offering. [15] Several men of the tribe of Levi lifted the Ark of the LORD and the chest containing the gold rats and gold tumors from the cart and placed them on the large rock. Many burnt offerings and sacrifices were offered to the LORD that day by the people of Bethshemesh. [16] The five Philistine rulers watched all this and then returned to Ekron that same day.

[17] The five gold tumors that were sent by the Philistines as a guilt offering to the LORD were gifts from the rulers of Ashdod, Gaza, Ashkelon, Gath, and Ekron. [18] The five gold rats represented the five Philistine cities and their surrounding villages, which were controlled by the five rulers. The large rock at Beth-shemesh, where they set the Ark of the LORD, still stands in the field of Joshua as a reminder of what happened there.

[19] But the LORD killed seventy men* from Beth-shemesh because they looked into the Ark of the LORD. And the people mourned greatly because of what the LORD had done. [20] "Who is able to stand in the presence of the LORD, this holy God?" they cried out. "Where can we send the Ark from here?" [21] So they sent messengers to the people at Kiriath-jearim and told them, "The Philistines have returned the Ark of the LORD. Please come here and get it!"

CHAPTER 7

So the men of Kiriath-jearim came to get the Ark of the LORD. They took it to the hillside home of Abinadab and ordained Eleazar, his son, to be in charge of it. [2] The Ark remained in Kiriath-jearim for a long time—twenty years in all. During that

---

5:11 Or *he.*   6:19 As in a few Hebrew manuscripts; most Hebrew manuscripts and Greek version read *50,070 men.* Perhaps the text should be understood to read *the LORD killed 70 men and 50 oxen.*

time, all Israel mourned because it seemed that the LORD had abandoned them.

³Then Samuel said to all the people of Israel, "If you are really serious about wanting to return to the LORD, get rid of your foreign gods and your images of Ashtoreth. Determine to obey only the LORD; then he will rescue you from the Philistines." ⁴So the Israelites destroyed their images of Baal and Ashtoreth and worshiped only the LORD.

⁵Then Samuel told them, "Come to Mizpah, all of you. I will pray to the LORD for you." ⁶So they gathered there and, in a great ceremony, drew water from a well and poured it out before the LORD. They also went without food all day and confessed that they had sinned against the LORD. So it was at Mizpah that Samuel became Israel's judge.

⁷When the Philistine rulers heard that all Israel had gathered at Mizpah, they mobilized their army and advanced. The Israelites were badly frightened when they learned that the Philistines were approaching. ⁸"Plead with the LORD our God to save us from the Philistines!" they begged Samuel. ⁹So Samuel took a young lamb and offered it to the LORD as a whole burnt offering. He pleaded with the LORD to help Israel, and the LORD answered.

¹⁰Just as Samuel was sacrificing the burnt offering, the Philistines arrived for battle. But the LORD spoke with a mighty voice of thunder from heaven, and the Philistines were thrown into such confusion that the Israelites defeated them. ¹¹The men of Israel chased them from Mizpah to Beth-car, slaughtering them all along the way.

¹²Samuel then took a large stone and placed it between the towns of Mizpah and Jeshanah.* He named it Ebenezer—"the stone of help"—for he said, "Up to this point the LORD has helped us!" ¹³So the Philistines were subdued and didn't invade Israel again for a long time. And throughout Samuel's lifetime, the LORD's powerful hand was raised against the Philistines. ¹⁴The Israelite towns near Ekron and Gath that the Philistines had captured were restored to Israel, along with the rest of the territory that the Philistines had taken. And there was also peace between Israel and the Amorites in those days.

¹⁵Samuel continued as Israel's judge for the rest of his life. ¹⁶Each year he traveled around, setting up his court first at Bethel, then at Gilgal, and then at Mizpah. He judged the people of Israel at each of these places. ¹⁷Then he would return to his home at Ramah, and he would hear cases there, too. And Samuel built an altar to the LORD at Ramah.

CHAPTER 8

As Samuel grew old, he appointed his sons to be judges over Israel. ²Joel and Abijah, his oldest sons, held court in Beersheba. ³But they were not like their father, for they were greedy for money. They accepted bribes and perverted justice.

⁴Finally, the leaders of Israel met at Ramah to discuss the matter with Samuel. ⁵"Look," they told him, "you are now old, and your sons are not like you. Give us a king like all the other nations have."

⁶Samuel was very upset with their request and went to the LORD for advice. ⁷"Do as they say," the LORD replied, "for it is me they are rejecting, not you. They don't want me to be their king any longer. ⁸Ever since I brought them from Egypt they have continually forsaken me and followed other gods. And now they are giving you the same treatment. ⁹Do as they ask, but solemnly warn them about how a king will treat them."

¹⁰So Samuel passed on the LORD's warning to the people. ¹¹"This is how a king will treat you," Samuel said. "The king will draft your sons into his army and make them run before his chariots. ¹²Some will be commanders of his troops, while others will be slave laborers. Some will be forced to plow in his fields and harvest his crops, while others will make his weapons and chariot equipment. ¹³The king will take your daughters from you and force them to cook and bake and make perfumes for him. ¹⁴He will take away the best of your fields and vineyards and olive groves and give them to his own servants. ¹⁵He will take a tenth of your harvest and distribute it among his officers and attendants. ¹⁶He will want your male and female slaves and demand the finest of your cattle* and donkeys for his own use. ¹⁷He will demand a tenth of your flocks, and you will be his slaves.

7:12 As in Greek version; Hebrew reads *Shen.*   8:16 As in Greek version; Hebrew reads *young men.*

18When that day comes, you will beg for relief from this king you are demanding, but the LORD will not help you."

19But the people refused to listen to Samuel's warning. "Even so, we still want a king," they said. 20"We want to be like the nations around us. Our king will govern us and lead us into battle."

21So Samuel told the LORD what the people had said, 22and the LORD replied, "Do as they say, and give them a king." Then Samuel agreed and sent the people home.

MARCH 17 ☐ DAY 77
1 SAMUEL 9–12
Saul, the Chosen King

OVERVIEW Part of Samuel's "rebuilding program" for the nation involves anointing the first king, a giant of a man named Saul. Installed as king at Mizpah, proven in battle against the Ammonites, and confirmed as king at Gilgal, Saul shows promising potential as the leader of God's people. But as Samuel points out in his farewell address, the very presence of a human king shows the rebellious attitude of the nation toward their divine king (12:19-20) and foreshadows disaster to come.

Chapter 9	Chapter 10	Chapter 11	Chapter 12
Selecting a King	Crowning a King	Confirming a King	Counseling a King
Saul's Coronation			Samuel's Caution

YOUR DAILY WALK Try as you may, you will not find listed among the spiritual gifts in the New Testament the gift of criticism. But criticizing the actions and motives of others continues to be a popular Christian sport. After all, it's a game everyone can play, with no age limit or experience required. And it's especially gratifying when the criticism is justified—when the other person is truly out of line.

No one so thoroughly appreciates the value of constructive criticism as the one who is giving it.

Samuel had every right to judge the people for demanding a king. Their motives were wrong, and Samuel knew it; their end would be destruction, and Samuel knew it. But after delivering his blistering rebuke to the people, Samuel tempered it with love. Like a tender father disciplining an erring son, Samuel allowed his true affections to show through. "You have certainly done wrong . . . [but] I will certainly not sin against the LORD by ending my prayers for you" (12:20, 23). Though the failure of others gave him reason to criticize, it instead drove him to his knees.

How do you react when others stumble and fall? Are you quick to criticize or quick to intercede? Samuel turned his criticisms into a cause for prayer; think of one person for whom you'll practice doing the same today.

INSIGHT Lend Me Your Ear
The phrase "the LORD had told Samuel" (9:15) literally means "the LORD had uncovered Samuel's ear," an expression derived from the Middle East practice of pushing aside another man's hair or the corner of his turban in order to whisper a secret into his ear.

CHAPTER 9

Kish was a rich, influential man from the tribe of Benjamin. He was the son of Abiel and grandson of Zeror, from the family of Becorath and the clan of Aphiah. [2]His son Saul was the most handsome man in Israel—head and shoulders taller than anyone else in the land.

[3]One day Kish's donkeys strayed away, and he told Saul, "Take a servant with you, and go look for them." [4]So Saul took one of his servants and traveled all through the hill country of Ephraim, the land of Shalishah, the Shaalim area, and the entire land of Benjamin, but they couldn't find the donkeys anywhere. [5]Finally, they entered the region of Zuph, and Saul said to his servant, "Let's go home. By now my father will be more worried about us than about the donkeys!"

[6]But the servant said, "I've just thought of something! There is a man of God who lives here in this town. He is held in high honor by all the people because everything he says comes true. Let's go find him. Perhaps he can tell us which way to go."

[7]"But we don't have anything to offer him," Saul replied. "Even our food is gone, and we don't have a thing to give him."

[8]"Well," the servant said, "I have one small silver piece.* We can at least offer it to him and see what happens!" [9](In those days if people wanted a message from God, they would say, "Let's go and ask the seer," for prophets used to be called seers.)

[10]"All right," Saul agreed, "let's try it!" So they started into the town where the man of God was.

[11]As they were climbing a hill toward the town, they met some young women coming out to draw water. So Saul and his servant asked, "Is the seer here today?"

[12]"Yes," they replied. "Stay right on this road. He is at the town gates. He has just arrived to take part in a public sacrifice up on the hill. [13]Hurry and catch him before he goes up the hill to eat. The guests won't start until he arrives to bless the food."

[14]So they entered the town, and as they passed through the gates, Samuel was coming out toward them to climb the hill. [15]Now the LORD had told Samuel the previous day, [16]"About this time tomorrow I will send you a man from the land of Benjamin. Anoint him to be the leader of my people, Israel. He will rescue them from the Philistines, for I have looked down on my people in mercy and have heard their cry."

[17]When Samuel noticed Saul, the LORD said, "That's the man I told you about! He will rule my people."

[18]Just then Saul approached Samuel at the gateway and asked, "Can you please tell me where the seer's house is?"

[19]"I am the seer!" Samuel replied. "Go on up the hill ahead of me to the place of sacrifice, and we'll eat there together. In the morning I will tell you what you want to know and send you on your way. [20]And don't worry about those donkeys that were lost three days ago, for they have been found. And I am here to tell you that you and your family are the focus of all Israel's hopes."

[21]Saul replied, "But I'm only from Benjamin, the smallest tribe in Israel, and my family is the least important of all the families of that tribe! Why are you talking like this to me?"

[22]Then Samuel brought Saul and his servant into the great hall and placed them at the head of the table, honoring them above the thirty special guests. [23]Samuel then instructed the cook to bring Saul the finest cut of meat, the piece that had been set aside for the guest of honor. [24]So the cook brought it in and placed it before Saul. "Go ahead and eat it," Samuel said. "I was saving it for you even before I invited these others!" So Saul ate with Samuel.

[25]After the feast, when they had returned to the town, Samuel took Saul up to the roof of the house and prepared a bed for him there.* [26]At daybreak the next morning, Samuel called up to Saul, "Get up! It's time you were on your way." So Saul got ready, and he and Samuel left the house together. [27]When they reached the edge of town, Samuel told Saul to send his servant on ahead. After the servant was gone, Samuel said, "Stay here, for I have received a special message for you from God."

CHAPTER 10

Then Samuel took a flask of olive oil and poured it over Saul's head. He kissed Saul on the cheek and said, "I am doing this because the LORD has appointed you to be

9:8 Hebrew *¼ shekel of silver*, about 0.1 ounces or 3 grams in weight. **9:25** As in Greek version; Hebrew reads *and talked with him there.*

the leader of his people Israel.* [2]When you leave me today, you will see two men beside Rachel's tomb at Zelzah, on the border of Benjamin. They will tell you that the donkeys have been found and that your father is worried about you and is asking, 'Have you seen my son?'

[3]"When you get to the oak of Tabor, you will see three men coming toward you who are on their way to worship God at Bethel. One will be bringing three young goats, another will have three loaves of bread, and the third will be carrying a skin of wine. [4]They will greet you and offer you two of the loaves, which you are to accept.

[5]"When you arrive at Gibeah of God,* where the garrison of the Philistines is located, you will meet a band of prophets coming down from the altar on the hill. They will be playing a harp, a tambourine, a flute, and a lyre, and they will be prophesying. [6]At that time the Spirit of the LORD will come upon you with power, and you will prophesy with them. You will be changed into a different person. [7]After these signs take place, do whatever you think is best, for God will be with you. [8]Then go down to Gilgal ahead of me and wait for me there seven days. I will join you there to sacrifice burnt offerings and peace offerings. When I arrive, I will give you further instructions."

[9]As Saul turned and started to leave, God changed his heart, and all Samuel's signs were fulfilled that day. [10]When Saul and his servant arrived at Gibeah, they saw the prophets coming toward them. Then the Spirit of God came upon Saul, and he, too, began to prophesy. [11]When his friends heard about it, they exclaimed, "What? Is Saul a prophet? How did the son of Kish become a prophet?" [12]But one of the neighbors responded, "It doesn't matter who his father is; anyone can become a prophet."* So that is the origin of the saying "Is Saul a prophet?"

[13]When Saul had finished prophesying, he climbed the hill to the altar. [14]"Where in the world have you been?" Saul's uncle asked him.

"We went to look for the donkeys," Saul replied, "but we couldn't find them. So we went to the prophet Samuel to ask him where they were."

[15]"Oh? And what did he say?" his uncle asked.

[16]"He said the donkeys had been found," Saul replied. But Saul didn't tell his uncle that Samuel had anointed him to be king.

[17]Later Samuel called all the people of Israel to meet before the LORD at Mizpah. [18]And he gave them this message from the LORD, the God of Israel: "I brought you from Egypt and rescued you from the Egyptians and from all of the nations that were oppressing you. [19]But though I have done so much for you, you have rejected me and said, 'We want a king instead!' Now, therefore, present yourselves before the LORD by tribes and clans."

[20]So Samuel called the tribal leaders together before the LORD, and the tribe of Benjamin was chosen.* [21]Then he brought each family of the tribe of Benjamin before the LORD, and the family of the Matrites was chosen. And finally Saul son of Kish was chosen from among them. But when they looked for him, he had disappeared! [22]So they asked the LORD, "Where is he?"

And the LORD replied, "He is hiding among the baggage." [23]So they found him and brought him out, and he stood head and shoulders above anyone else.

[24]Then Samuel said to all the people, "This is the man the LORD has chosen as your king. No one in all Israel is his equal!"

And all the people shouted, "Long live the king!"

[25]Then Samuel told the people what the rights and duties of a king were. He wrote them down on a scroll and placed it before the LORD. Then Samuel sent the people home again.

[26]When Saul returned to his home at Gibeah, a band of men whose hearts God had touched became his constant companions. [27]But there were some wicked men who complained, "How can this man save us?" And they despised him and refused to bring him gifts. But Saul ignored them.*

10:1 Greek version reads *Israel. And you will rule over the LORD's people and save them from their enemies around them. This will be the sign to you that the LORD has appointed you to be leader over his inheritance.*   **10:5** Hebrew *Gibeath-elohim.*   **10:12** Hebrew responded, *"Who is their father?"*   **10:20** Hebrew *chosen by lot;* also in 10:21.   **10:27** Dead Sea Scroll 4QSamᵃ continues: *Nahash, king of the Ammonites, had been grievously oppressing the Gadites and Reubenites who lived east of the Jordan River. He gouged out the right eye of each of the Israelites living there, and he didn't allow anyone to come and rescue them. In fact, of all the Israelites east of the Jordan, there wasn't a single one whose right eye Nahash had not gouged out. But there were seven thousand men who had escaped from the Ammonites, and they had settled in Jabesh-gilead.*

CHAPTER 11

About a month later,* King Nahash of Ammon led his army against the Israelite city of Jabesh-gilead. But the citizens of Jabesh asked for peace. "Make a treaty with us, and we will be your servants," they pleaded.

²"All right," Nahash said, "but only on one condition. I will gouge out the right eye of every one of you as a disgrace to all Israel!"

³"Give us seven days to send messengers throughout Israel!" replied the leaders of Jabesh. "If none of our relatives will come to save us, we will agree to your terms."

⁴When the messengers came to Gibeah, Saul's hometown, and told the people about their plight, everyone broke into tears. ⁵Saul was plowing in the field, and when he returned to town, he asked, "What's the matter? Why is everyone crying?" So they told him about the message from Jabesh.

⁶Then the Spirit of God came mightily upon Saul, and he became very angry. ⁷He took two oxen and cut them into pieces and sent the messengers to carry them throughout Israel with this message: "This is what will happen to the oxen of anyone who refuses to follow Saul and Samuel into battle!" And the LORD made the people afraid of Saul's anger, and all of them came out together as one. ⁸When Saul mobilized them at Bezek, he found that there were 300,000 men of Israel, in addition to 30,000* from Judah.

⁹So Saul sent the messengers back to Jabesh-gilead to say, "We will rescue you by noontime tomorrow!" What joy there was throughout the city when that message arrived!

¹⁰The men of Jabesh then told their enemies, "Tomorrow we will come out to you, and you can do to us as you wish." ¹¹But before dawn the next morning, Saul arrived, having divided his army into three detachments. He launched a surprise attack against the Ammonites and slaughtered them the whole morning. The remnant of their army was so badly scattered that no two of them were left together.

¹²Then the people exclaimed to Samuel, "Now where are those men who said Saul

shouldn't rule over us? Bring them here, and we will kill them!"

¹³But Saul replied, "No one will be executed today, for today the LORD has rescued Israel!"

¹⁴Then Samuel said to the people, "Come, let us all go to Gilgal to reaffirm Saul's kingship." ¹⁵So they went to Gilgal, and in a solemn ceremony before the LORD they crowned him king. Then they offered peace offerings to the LORD, and Saul and all the Israelites were very happy.

CHAPTER 12

Then Samuel addressed the people again: "I have done as you asked and given you a king. ²I have selected him ahead of my own sons, and I stand here, an old, gray-haired man. I have served as your leader since I was a boy. ³Now tell me as I stand before the LORD and before his anointed one—whose ox or donkey have I stolen? Have I ever cheated any of you? Have I ever oppressed you? Have I ever taken a bribe? Tell me and I will make right whatever I have done wrong."

⁴"No," they replied, "you have never cheated or oppressed us in any way, and you have never taken even a single bribe."

⁵"The LORD and his anointed one are my witnesses," Samuel declared, "that you can never accuse me of robbing you."

"Yes, it is true," they replied.

⁶"It was the LORD who appointed Moses and Aaron," Samuel continued. "He brought your ancestors out of the land of Egypt. ⁷Now stand here quietly before the LORD as I remind you of all the great things the LORD has done for you and your ancestors.

⁸"When the Israelites were* in Egypt and cried out to the LORD, he sent Moses and Aaron to rescue them from Egypt and to bring them into this land. ⁹But the people soon forgot about the LORD their God, so he let them be conquered by Sisera, the general of Hazor's army, and by the Philistines and the king of Moab.

¹⁰"Then they cried to the LORD again and confessed, 'We have sinned by turning away from the LORD and worshiping the images of Baal and Ashtoreth. But we will worship you and you alone if you will rescue us from our enemies.' ¹¹Then

11:1 As in Greek version; Hebrew lacks *About a month later.*   **11:8** Dead Sea Scrolls and Greek version read *70,000.*   **12:8** Hebrew *When Jacob was.*

the LORD sent Gideon,* Barak,* Jephthah, and Samuel* to save you, and you lived in safety.

¹²"But when you were afraid of Nahash, the king of Ammon, you came to me and said that you wanted a king to reign over you, even though the LORD your God was already your king. ¹³All right, here is the king you have chosen. Look him over. You asked for him, and the LORD has granted your request.

¹⁴"Now if you will fear and worship the LORD and listen to his voice, and if you do not rebel against the LORD's commands, and if you and your king follow the LORD your God, then all will be well. ¹⁵But if you rebel against the LORD's commands and refuse to listen to him, then his hand will be as heavy upon you as it was upon your ancestors.

¹⁶"Now stand here and see the great thing the LORD is about to do. ¹⁷You know that it does not rain at this time of the year during the wheat harvest. I will ask the LORD to send thunder and rain today. Then you will realize how wicked you have been in asking the LORD for a king!"

¹⁸So Samuel called to the LORD, and the LORD sent thunder and rain. And all the people were terrified of the LORD and of Samuel. ¹⁹"Pray to the LORD your God for us, or we will die!" they cried out to Samuel. "For now we have added to our sins by asking for a king."

²⁰"Don't be afraid," Samuel reassured them. "You have certainly done wrong, but make sure now that you worship the LORD with all your heart and that you don't turn your back on him in any way. ²¹Don't go back to worshiping worthless idols that cannot help or rescue you—they really are useless! ²²The LORD will not abandon his chosen people, for that would dishonor his great name. He made you a special nation for himself.

²³"As for me, I will certainly not sin against the LORD by ending my prayers for you. And I will continue to teach you what is good and right. ²⁴But be sure to fear the LORD and sincerely worship him. Think of all the wonderful things he has done for you. ²⁵But if you continue to sin, you and your king will be destroyed."

12:11a Hebrew *Jerubbaal*, another name for Gideon; see Judg 7:1. **12:11c** Greek and Syriac versions read *Samson*.

12:11b As in Greek and Syriac versions; Hebrew reads *Bedan*.

MARCH 18 ☐ DAY 78
1 SAMUEL 13–15
Saul, the Rejected King

OVERVIEW After his promising beginning, Saul soon begins to show his true colors. When a Philistine invasion threatens, Saul takes over the role of the priest and offers sacrifices himself in defiance of God's clear command. Later, an impulsive oath nearly costs Saul the life of his devoted son Jonathan. Finally, Saul is given a make-or-break assignment: Destroy the Amalekites and all they possess. However, Saul chooses to spare the choicest livestock and the king of the land. Confronted with his disobedience, Saul passes the blame to the people, prompting the prophet to declare, "[The LORD] has rejected you" (15:26).

Chapter 13	Chapter 14	Chapter 15
Saul's Impatience	Saul's Impulsiveness	Saul's Incomplete Obedience
Tested and Rebuked		Tested and Rejected

YOUR DAILY WALK Have you discovered that God's heavenly time-table doesn't always make good earthly sense?

You know God has the perfect marriage partner for you, but as the years slip by you grow more and more impatient. . . .

Patience is accepting a difficult situation without giving God a deadline for removing it.

You know God wants you to succeed in your work, but year after year you labor at the same task with no promotion in sight. . . .

You know God wants you to help win the world for him, but after twelve years of teaching fifth-grade Sunday school . . .

When Saul offered the sacrifices that only priests were permitted to offer, it cost him more than God's approval; it also cost him the king-dom. Because God's timetable didn't coincide with Saul's, Israel's first king responded impatiently. In the process he discovered there is something worse than having to wait for God—and that is wishing you had!

Are you becoming impatient with God's timetable for your life? Then do some "wait" watching today. Look up these verses and meditate upon their truth: Isaiah 25:9; 30:18; 40:31.

INSIGHT A Sword in the Hand, But None in the Land

The Philistines had the military advantage over Israel because they held the monopoly on iron and strictly controlled its use among subject peoples (13:19-22). Swords and spears were very rare. The monopoly was broken when Saul and David overthrew the Philistines and armed the Israelites.

CHAPTER 13

Saul was thirty* years old when he became king, and he reigned for forty-two years.*

²Saul selected three thousand special troops from the army of Israel and sent the rest of the men home. He took two thousand of the chosen men with him to Micmash and the hill country of Bethel. The other thousand went with Saul's son Jonathan to Gibeah in the land of Benjamin.

³Soon after this, Jonathan attacked and defeated the garrison of Philistines at Geba. The news spread quickly among the Philistines that Israel was in revolt, so Saul sounded the call to arms throughout Israel. ⁴He announced that the Philistine garrison at Geba had been destroyed, and he warned the people that the Philistines now hated the Israelites more than ever. So the entire Israelite army mobilized again and met Saul at Gilgal.

⁵The Philistines mustered a mighty army of three thousand* chariots, six thousand horsemen, and as many warriors as the grains of sand along the seashore! They camped at Micmash east of Beth-aven. ⁶When the men of Israel saw the vast number of enemy troops, they lost their nerve entirely and tried to hide in caves, holes, rocks, tombs, and cisterns. ⁷Some of them

crossed the Jordan River and escaped into the land of Gad and Gilead.

Meanwhile, Saul stayed at Gilgal, and his men were trembling with fear. ⁸Saul waited there seven days for Samuel, as Samuel had instructed him earlier, but Samuel still didn't come. Saul realized that his troops were rapidly slipping away. ⁹So he demanded, "Bring me the burnt offering and the peace offerings!" And Saul sacrificed the burnt offering himself. ¹⁰Just as Saul was finishing with the burnt offering, Samuel arrived. Saul went out to meet and welcome him, ¹¹but Samuel said, "What is this you have done?"

Saul replied, "I saw my men scattering from me, and you didn't arrive when you said you would, and the Philistines are at Micmash ready for battle. ¹²So I said, 'The Philistines are ready to march against us, and I haven't even asked for the LORD's help!' So I felt obliged to offer the burnt offering myself before you came."

¹³"How foolish!" Samuel exclaimed. "You have disobeyed the command of the LORD your God. Had you obeyed, the LORD would have established your kingdom over Israel forever. ¹⁴But now your dynasty must end, for the LORD has sought out a man after his own heart. The LORD has already chosen him to be king over his

13:1a As in a few Greek manuscripts; the number is missing in the Hebrew.   13:1b Hebrew *reigned . . . and two*; the number is incomplete in the Hebrew. Compare Acts 13:21.   13:5 As in Greek and Syriac versions; Hebrew reads *30,000*.

people, for you have not obeyed the LORD's command."

¹⁵Samuel then left Gilgal and went on his way, but the rest of the troops went with Saul to meet the army. They went up from Gilgal to Gibeah in the land of Benjamin.* When Saul counted the men who were still with him, he found only six hundred left! ¹⁶Saul and Jonathan and the troops with them were staying at Geba, near Gibeah, in the land of Benjamin. The Philistines set up their camp at Micmash. ¹⁷Three raiding parties soon left the camp of the Philistines. One went north toward Ophrah in the land of Shual, ¹⁸another went west to Beth-horon, and the third moved toward the border above the valley of Zeboim near the wilderness.

¹⁹There were no blacksmiths in the land of Israel in those days. The Philistines wouldn't allow them for fear they would make swords and spears for the Hebrews. ²⁰So whenever the Israelites needed to sharpen their plowshares, picks, axes, or sickles,* they had to take them to a Philistine blacksmith. ²¹(The schedule of charges was as follows: a quarter of an ounce of silver* for sharpening a plowshare or a pick, and an eighth of an ounce* for sharpening an ax, a sickle, or an ox goad.) ²²So none of the people of Israel had a sword or spear, except for Saul and Jonathan.

²³The pass at Micmash had meanwhile been secured by a contingent of the Philistine army.

CHAPTER 14

One day Jonathan said to the young man who carried his armor, "Come on, let's go over to where the Philistines have their outpost." But Jonathan did not tell his father what he was doing. ²Meanwhile, Saul and his six hundred men were camped on the outskirts of Gibeah, around the pomegranate tree at Migron. ³(Among Saul's men was Ahijah the priest, who was wearing the linen ephod. Ahijah was the son of Ahitub, Ichabod's brother. Ahitub was the son of Phinehas and the grandson of Eli, the priest of the LORD who had served at Shiloh.)

No one realized that Jonathan had left the Israelite camp. ⁴To reach the Philistine outpost, Jonathan had to go down between two rocky cliffs that were called Bozez and Seneh. ⁵The cliff on the north was in front of Micmash, and the one on the south was in front of Geba. ⁶"Let's go across to see those pagans," Jonathan said to his armor bearer. "Perhaps the LORD will help us, for nothing can hinder the LORD. He can win a battle whether he has many warriors or only a few!"

⁷"Do what you think is best," the youth replied. "I'm with you completely, whatever you decide."

⁸"All right then," Jonathan told him. "We will cross over and let them see us. ⁹If they say to us, 'Stay where you are or we'll kill you,' then we will stop and not go up to them. ¹⁰But if they say, 'Come on up and fight,' then we will go up. That will be the LORD's sign that he will help us defeat them."

¹¹When the Philistines saw them coming, they shouted, "Look! The Hebrews are crawling out of their holes!" ¹²Then they shouted to Jonathan, "Come on up here, and we'll teach you a lesson!"

"Come on, climb right behind me," Jonathan said to his armor bearer, "for the LORD will help us defeat them!" ¹³So they climbed up using both hands and feet, and the Philistines fell back as Jonathan and his armor bearer killed them right and left. ¹⁴They killed about twenty men in all, and their bodies were scattered over about half an acre.* ¹⁵Suddenly, panic broke out in the Philistine army, both in the camp and in the field, including even the outposts and raiding parties. And just then an earthquake struck, and everyone was terrified.

¹⁶Saul's lookouts in Gibeah saw a strange sight—the vast army of Philistines began to melt away in every direction. ¹⁷"Find out who isn't here," Saul ordered. And when they checked, they found that Jonathan and his armor bearer were gone. ¹⁸Then Saul shouted to Ahijah, "Bring the ephod here!" For at that time Ahijah was wearing the ephod in front of the Israelites.* ¹⁹But while Saul was talking to the priest, the shouting and confusion in the Philistine camp grew louder and louder. So Saul said to Ahijah, "Never mind; let's get going!"* ²⁰Then Saul and his six hundred men

---

13:15 As in Greek version; Hebrew reads *Samuel left Gilgal and went to Gibeah in the land of Benjamin.*   13:20 As in Greek version; Hebrew reads *or plowshares.*   13:21a Hebrew *1 pim* [8 grams].   13:21b Hebrew *1/3 of a shekel* [4 grams].   14:14 Hebrew *half a yoke;* a "yoke" was the amount of land plowed by a pair of yoked oxen in one day.   14:18 As in some Greek manuscripts; Hebrew reads *"Bring the Ark of God." For at that time the Ark of God was with the Israelites.*   14:19 Hebrew *Withdraw your hand.*

rushed out to the battle and found the Philistines killing each other. There was terrible confusion everywhere. ²¹Even the Hebrews who had gone over to the Philistine army revolted and joined in with Saul, Jonathan, and the rest of the Israelites. ²²Likewise, the men who were hiding in the hills joined the chase when they saw the Philistines running away. ²³So the LORD saved Israel that day, and the battle continued to rage even out beyond Beth-aven.

²⁴Now the men of Israel were worn out that day, because Saul had made them take an oath, saying, "Let a curse fall on anyone who eats before evening—before I have full revenge on my enemies." So no one ate a thing all day, ²⁵even though they found honeycomb on the ground in the forest. ²⁶They didn't even touch the honey because they all feared the oath they had taken.

²⁷But Jonathan had not heard his father's command, and he dipped a stick into a piece of honeycomb and ate the honey. After he had eaten it, he felt much better. ²⁸But one of the men saw him and said, "Your father made the army take a strict oath that anyone who eats food today will be cursed. That is why everyone is weary and faint."

²⁹"My father has made trouble for us all!" Jonathan exclaimed. "A command like that only hurts us. See how much better I feel now that I have eaten this little bit of honey. ³⁰If the men had been allowed to eat freely from the food they found among our enemies, think how many more we could have killed!"

³¹But hungry as they were, they chased and killed the Philistines all day from Micmash to Aijalon, growing more and more faint. ³²That evening they flew upon the battle plunder and butchered the sheep, cattle, and calves, but they ate them without draining the blood. ³³Someone reported to Saul, "Look, the men are sinning against the LORD by eating meat that still has blood in it."

"That is very wrong," Saul said. "Find a large stone and roll it over here. ³⁴Then go out among the troops and tell them, 'Bring the cattle and sheep here to kill them and drain the blood. Do not sin against the LORD by eating meat with the blood still in it.'" So that night all the troops brought their animals and slaughtered them there.

³⁵And Saul built an altar to the LORD, the first one he had ever built.

³⁶Then Saul said, "Let's chase the Philistines all night and destroy every last one of them."

His men replied, "We'll do whatever you think is best."

But the priest said, "Let's ask God first." ³⁷So Saul asked God, "Should we go after the Philistines? Will you help us defeat them?" But God made no reply that day.

³⁸Then Saul said to the leaders, "Something's wrong! I want all my army commanders to come here. We must find out what sin was committed today. ³⁹I vow by the name of the LORD who rescued Israel that the sinner will surely die, even if it is my own son Jonathan!" But no one would tell him what the trouble was. ⁴⁰Then Saul said, "Jonathan and I will stand over here, and all of you stand over there." And the people agreed.

⁴¹Then Saul prayed, "O LORD, God of Israel, please show us who is guilty and who is innocent. Are Jonathan and I guilty, or is the sin among the others?"* And Jonathan and Saul were chosen* as the guilty ones, and the people were declared innocent.

⁴²Then Saul said, "Now choose* between me and Jonathan." And Jonathan was shown to be the guilty one.

⁴³"Tell me what you have done," Saul demanded of Jonathan.

"I tasted a little honey," Jonathan admitted. "It was only a little bit on the end of a stick. Does that deserve death?"

⁴⁴"Yes, Jonathan," Saul said, "you must die! May God strike me dead if you are not executed for this."

⁴⁵But the people broke in and said to Saul, "Should Jonathan, who saved Israel today, die? Far from it! As surely as the LORD lives, not one hair on his head will be touched, for he has been used of God to do a mighty miracle today." So the people rescued Jonathan, and he was not put to death. ⁴⁶Then Saul called back the army from chasing the Philistines, and the Philistines returned home.

⁴⁷Now when Saul had secured his grasp on Israel's throne, he fought against his enemies in every direction—against Moab, Ammon, Edom, the kings of Zobah, and the Philistines. And wherever he turned, he

---

14:41a Greek version adds *If the fault is with me or my son Jonathan, respond with Urim; but if the men of Israel are at fault, respond with Thummim.*   **14:41b** Hebrew *chosen by lot.*   **14:42** Hebrew *draw lots.*

was victorious. ⁴⁸He did great deeds and conquered the Amalekites, saving Israel from all those who had plundered them.

⁴⁹Saul's sons included Jonathan, Ishbosheth,* and Malkishua. He also had two daughters: Merab, who was older, and Michal. ⁵⁰Saul's wife was Ahinoam, the daughter of Ahimaaz. The commander of Saul's army was his cousin Abner, his uncle Ner's son. ⁵¹Abner's father, Ner, and Saul's father, Kish, were brothers; both were sons of Abiel.

⁵²The Israelites fought constantly with the Philistines throughout Saul's lifetime. So whenever Saul saw a young man who was brave and strong, he drafted him into his army.

CHAPTER 15

One day Samuel said to Saul, "I anointed you king of Israel because the LORD told me to. Now listen to this message from the LORD! ²This is what the LORD Almighty says: 'I have decided to settle accounts with the nation of Amalek for opposing Israel when they came from Egypt. ³Now go and completely destroy* the entire Amalekite nation—men, women, children, babies, cattle, sheep, camels, and donkeys.'"

⁴So Saul mobilized his army at Telaim. There were 200,000 troops in addition to 10,000 men from Judah. ⁵Then Saul went to the city of Amalek and lay in wait in the valley. ⁶Saul sent this message to the Kenites: "Move away from where the Amalekites live or else you will die with them. For you were kind to the people of Israel when they came up from Egypt." So the Kenites packed up and left.

⁷Then Saul slaughtered the Amalekites from Havilah all the way to Shur, east of Egypt. ⁸He captured Agag, the Amalekite king, but completely destroyed everyone else. ⁹Saul and his men spared Agag's life and kept the best of the sheep and cattle, the fat calves and lambs—everything, in fact, that appealed to them. They destroyed only what was worthless or of poor quality.

¹⁰Then the LORD said to Samuel, ¹¹"I am sorry that I ever made Saul king, for he has not been loyal to me and has again refused to obey me." Samuel was so deeply moved when he heard this that he cried out to the LORD all night.

¹²Early the next morning Samuel went to find Saul. Someone told him, "Saul went to Carmel to set up a monument to himself; then he went on to Gilgal."

¹³When Samuel finally found him, Saul greeted him cheerfully. "May the LORD bless you," he said. "I have carried out the LORD's command!"

¹⁴"Then what is all the bleating of sheep and lowing of cattle I hear?" Samuel demanded.

¹⁵"It's true that the army spared the best of the sheep and cattle," Saul admitted. "But they are going to sacrifice them to the LORD your God. We have destroyed everything else."

¹⁶Then Samuel said to Saul, "Stop! Listen to what the LORD told me last night!"

"What was it?" Saul asked.

¹⁷And Samuel told him, "Although you may think little of yourself, are you not the leader of the tribes of Israel? The LORD has anointed you king of Israel. ¹⁸And the LORD sent you on a mission and told you, 'Go and completely destroy the sinners, the Amalekites, until they are all dead.' ¹⁹Why haven't you obeyed the LORD? Why did you rush for the plunder and do exactly what the LORD said not to do?"

²⁰"But I did obey the LORD," Saul insisted. "I carried out the mission he gave me. I brought back King Agag, but I destroyed everyone else. ²¹Then my troops brought in the best of the sheep and cattle and plunder to sacrifice to the LORD your God in Gilgal."

²²But Samuel replied, "What is more pleasing to the LORD: your burnt offerings and sacrifices or your obedience to his voice? Obedience is far better than sacrifice. Listening to him is much better than offering the fat of rams. ²³Rebellion is as bad as the sin of witchcraft, and stubbornness is as bad as worshiping idols. So because you have rejected the word of the LORD, he has rejected you from being king."

²⁴Then Saul finally admitted, "Yes, I have sinned. I have disobeyed your instructions and the LORD's command, for I was afraid of the people and did what they demanded. ²⁵Oh, please, forgive my sin now and go with me to worship the LORD."

²⁶But Samuel replied, "I will not return

14:49 Hebrew *Ishvi*, a variant name for Ishbosheth; also known as Eshbaal.   15:3 The Hebrew term used here refers to the complete consecration of things or people to the LORD, either by destroying them or by giving them as an offering; also in 15:8, 9, 15, 18, 20, 21.

with you! Since you have rejected the LORD's command, he has rejected you from being the king of Israel."

²⁷As Samuel turned to go, Saul grabbed at him to try to hold him back and tore his robe. ²⁸And Samuel said to him, "See? The LORD has torn the kingdom of Israel from you today and has given it to someone else—one who is better than you. ²⁹And he who is the Glory of Israel will not lie, nor will he change his mind, for he is not human that he should change his mind!"

³⁰Then Saul pleaded again, "I know I have sinned. But please, at least honor me before the leaders and before my people by going with me to worship the LORD your God." ³¹So Samuel finally agreed and went with him, and Saul worshiped the LORD.

³²Then Samuel said, "Bring King Agag to me." Agag arrived full of smiles, for he thought, "Surely the worst is over, and I have been spared!"* ³³But Samuel said, "As your sword has killed the sons of many mothers, now your mother will be childless." And Samuel cut Agag to pieces before the LORD at Gilgal. ³⁴Then Samuel went home to Ramah, and Saul returned to his house at Gibeah. ³⁵Samuel never went to meet with Saul again, but he mourned constantly for him. And the LORD was sorry he had ever made Saul king of Israel.

15:32 Dead Sea Scrolls and Greek version read *Agag arrived hesitantly, for he thought, "Surely this is the bitterness of death."*

MARCH 19 ☐ DAY 79
1 SAMUEL 16–19
David, the Secret King-Elect

 OVERVIEW While Saul is losing favor with God, the shepherd boy David is being secretly anointed by Samuel as Saul's replacement. From that moment on, the lives of Saul and David will be intricately intertwined. Because of his skill as a musician, David is selected to play for King Saul and soothe his troubled mind. Next, David becomes a national hero by challenging and killing Goliath, the Philistine giant whom Saul himself actually should have fought. Clearly, God is with David—an observation that drives Saul into a jealous frenzy and puts David's life in jeopardy.

Chapter 16		Chapter 17	Chapters 18–19
David the King-Elect	David the Musician	David the Fighter	David the Fugitive
1 13	14 23		
In the Field	In the Court	In the Valley	On the Run

 YOUR DAILY WALK It is one thing to keep a level head when things are running smoothly. It is quite another to behave wisely when you are on the run, pressure is on, the future seems uncertain, and every breath you take may be your last!

Most of us don't put our best foot forward until we get the other one in hot water.

David faced a peculiar set of pressures. God was with him, causing his every endeavor to prosper. And because of his constant success and growing acclaim, David's life became more and more uncertain! Because "the LORD was with [David]" (18:14), Saul sought to snuff out David's life. Yet, in spite of the temptation to retaliate and grow bitter, David did what was right and "continued to succeed in everything he did" (18:14).

Are you in a similar situation at your job? . . . in your home? . . . or on your campus? Because of God's blessing upon your life or ministry, are you faced with jealous opposition and undeserved suffering? God wants you, like David, to maintain an honorable attitude and blameless behavior in the face of persecution. Turn to Matthew 10:16, and notice what it says: *Wary* and *harmless* should be your watchwords!

 INSIGHT David, First-Rate Candidate for King
David's qualifications, as stated by one of Saul's own servants (16:18), were impeccable: He was good-looking, a fine musician, a skilled warrior, and a quick learner, and the Lord was with him. Everything that a king needed for success, David had. Little wonder that Saul was jealous.

CHAPTER 16
Finally, the LORD said to Samuel, "You have mourned long enough for Saul. I have rejected him as king of Israel. Now fill your horn with olive oil and go to Bethlehem. Find a man named Jesse who lives there, for I have selected one of his sons to be my new king."

²But Samuel asked, "How can I do that? If Saul hears about it, he will kill me."

"Take a heifer with you," the LORD replied, "and say that you have come to make a sacrifice to the LORD. ³Invite Jesse to the sacrifice, and I will show you which of his sons to anoint for me."

⁴So Samuel did as the LORD instructed him. When he arrived at Bethlehem, the leaders of the town became afraid. "What's wrong?" they asked. "Do you come in peace?"

⁵"Yes," Samuel replied. "I have come to sacrifice to the LORD. Purify yourselves and come with me to the sacrifice." Then Samuel performed the purification rite for Jesse and his sons and invited them, too.

⁶When they arrived, Samuel took one look at Eliab and thought, "Surely this is the LORD's anointed!" ⁷But the LORD said to Samuel, "Don't judge by his appearance or height, for I have rejected him. The LORD doesn't make decisions the way you do! People judge by outward appearance, but the LORD looks at a person's thoughts and intentions."

⁸Then Jesse told his son Abinadab to step forward and walk in front of Samuel. But Samuel said, "This is not the one the LORD has chosen." ⁹Next Jesse summoned Shammah, but Samuel said, "Neither is this the one the LORD has chosen." ¹⁰In the same way all seven of Jesse's sons were presented to Samuel. But Samuel said to Jesse, "The LORD has not chosen any of these." ¹¹Then Samuel asked, "Are these all the sons you have?"

"There is still the youngest," Jesse replied. "But he's out in the fields watching the sheep."

"Send for him at once," Samuel said. "We will not sit down to eat until he arrives."

¹²So Jesse sent for him. He was ruddy and handsome, with pleasant eyes. And the LORD said, "This is the one; anoint him."

¹³So as David stood there among his brothers, Samuel took the olive oil he had brought and poured it on David's head. And the Spirit of the LORD came mightily upon him from that day on. Then Samuel returned to Ramah.

¹⁴Now the Spirit of the LORD had left Saul, and the LORD sent a tormenting spirit that filled him with depression and fear. ¹⁵Some of Saul's servants suggested a remedy. "It is clear that a spirit from God is tormenting you," they said. ¹⁶"Let us find a good musician to play the harp for you whenever the tormenting spirit is bothering you. The harp music will quiet you, and you will soon be well again."

¹⁷"All right," Saul said. "Find me someone who plays well and bring him here."

¹⁸One of the servants said to Saul, "The son of Jesse is a talented harp player. Not only that; he is brave and strong and has good judgment. He is also a fine-looking young man, and the LORD is with him."

¹⁹So Saul sent messengers to Jesse to say, "Send me your son David, the shepherd." ²⁰Jesse responded by sending David to Saul, along with a young goat and a donkey loaded down with food and wine. ²¹So David went to Saul and served him. Saul liked David very much, and David became one of Saul's armor bearers.

²²Then Saul sent word to Jesse asking, "Please let David join my staff, for I am very pleased with him." ²³And whenever the tormenting spirit from God troubled Saul, David would play the harp. Then Saul would feel better, and the tormenting spirit would go away.

CHAPTER 17

The Philistines now mustered their army for battle and camped between Socoh in Judah and Azekah at Ephes-dammim. ²Saul countered by gathering his troops near the valley of Elah. ³So the Philistines and Israelites faced each other on opposite hills, with the valley between them.

⁴Then Goliath, a Philistine champion from Gath, came out of the Philistine ranks to face the forces of Israel. He was a giant of a man, measuring over nine feet* tall! ⁵He wore a bronze helmet and a coat of mail that weighed 125 pounds.* ⁶He also wore bronze leggings, and he slung a bronze javelin over his back. ⁷The shaft of his spear was as heavy and thick as a weaver's beam, tipped with an iron spearhead that weighed fifteen pounds.* An armor bearer walked ahead of him carrying a huge shield.

⁸Goliath stood and shouted across to the Israelites, "Do you need a whole army to settle this? Choose someone to fight for you, and I will represent the Philistines. We will settle this dispute in single combat! ⁹If your man is able to kill me, then we will be your slaves. But if I kill him, you will be our slaves! ¹⁰I defy the armies of Israel! Send me a man who will fight with me!" ¹¹When Saul and the Israelites heard this, they were terrified and deeply shaken.

¹²Now David was the son of a man named Jesse, an Ephrathite from Bethlehem in the land of Judah. Jesse was an old man at that time, and he had eight sons in all. ¹³Jesse's three oldest sons—Eliab, Abinadab, and Shammah—had already joined Saul's army to fight the Philistines. ¹⁴David was the youngest of Jesse's sons. Since David's three oldest brothers were in the army, they stayed with Saul's forces all the time. ¹⁵But David went back and forth between working for Saul and helping his father with the sheep in Bethlehem.

¹⁶For forty days, twice a day, morning and evening, the Philistine giant strutted in front of the Israelite army.

¹⁷One day Jesse said to David, "Take this half-bushel* of roasted grain and these ten loaves of bread to your brothers. ¹⁸And give these ten cuts of cheese to their captain. See how your brothers are getting along, and bring me back a letter from them.*"

¹⁹David's brothers were with Saul and the Israelite army at the valley of Elah, fighting against the Philistines. ²⁰So David left the sheep with another shepherd and set out early the next morning with the gifts. He arrived at the outskirts of the camp just as the Israelite army was leaving for the battlefield with shouts and battle cries. ²¹Soon the Israelite and Philistine forces stood facing each other, army against army. ²²David left his things with the keeper of supplies and hurried out to the ranks to greet his brothers. ²³As he was talking with them, he saw Goliath, the champion from Gath, come out from the Philistine ranks, shouting his challenge to the army of Israel.

²⁴As soon as the Israelite army saw him, they began to run away in fright. ²⁵"Have you seen the giant?" the men were asking. "He comes out each day to challenge Israel. And have you heard about the huge reward the king has offered to anyone who kills him? The king will give him one of his daughters for a wife, and his whole family will be exempted from paying taxes!"

²⁶David talked to some others standing there to verify the report. "What will a man get for killing this Philistine and putting an end to his abuse of Israel?" he asked them. "Who is this pagan Philistine anyway, that he is allowed to defy the armies of the living God?" ²⁷And David received the same reply as before: "What you have been hearing is true. That is the reward for killing the giant."

²⁸But when David's oldest brother, Eliab, heard David talking to the men, he was angry. "What are you doing around here anyway?" he demanded. "What about those few sheep you're supposed to be taking care of? I know about your pride and dishonesty. You just want to see the battle!"

²⁹"What have I done now?" David replied. "I was only asking a question!" ³⁰He walked over to some others and asked them the same thing and received the same answer. ³¹Then David's question was reported to King Saul, and the king sent for him.

³²"Don't worry about a thing," David told Saul. "I'll go fight this Philistine!"

³³"Don't be ridiculous!" Saul replied. "There is no way you can go against this

---

17:4 Hebrew *6 cubits and 1 span* [which totals about 9.75 feet or 3 meters]; Greek version and Dead Sea Scrolls read *4 cubits and 1 span* [which totals about 6.75 feet or 2 meters].   17:5 Hebrew *5,000 shekels* [57 kilograms].   17:7 Hebrew *600 shekels* [6.8 kilograms].   17:17 Hebrew *ephah* [18 liters].   17:18 Hebrew *and take their pledge.*

Philistine. You are only a boy, and he has been in the army since he was a boy!"

[34]But David persisted. "I have been taking care of my father's sheep," he said. "When a lion or a bear comes to steal a lamb from the flock, [35]I go after it with a club and take the lamb from its mouth. If the animal turns on me, I catch it by the jaw and club it to death. [36]I have done this to both lions and bears, and I'll do it to this pagan Philistine, too, for he has defied the armies of the living God! [37]The LORD who saved me from the claws of the lion and the bear will save me from this Philistine!"

Saul finally consented. "All right, go ahead," he said. "And may the LORD be with you!"

[38]Then Saul gave David his own armor—a bronze helmet and a coat of mail. [39]David put it on, strapped the sword over it, and took a step or two to see what it was like, for he had never worn such things before. "I can't go in these," he protested. "I'm not used to them." So he took them off again. [40]He picked up five smooth stones from a stream and put them in his shepherd's bag. Then, armed only with his shepherd's staff and sling, he started across to fight Goliath.

[41]Goliath walked out toward David with his shield bearer ahead of him, [42]sneering in contempt at this ruddy-faced boy. [43]"Am I a dog," he roared at David, "that you come at me with a stick?" And he cursed David by the names of his gods. [44]"Come over here, and I'll give your flesh to the birds and wild animals!" Goliath yelled.

[45]David shouted in reply, "You come to me with sword, spear, and javelin, but I come to you in the name of the LORD Almighty—the God of the armies of Israel, whom you have defied. [46]Today the LORD will conquer you, and I will kill you and cut off your head. And then I will give the dead bodies of your men to the birds and wild animals, and the whole world will know that there is a God in Israel! [47]And everyone will know that the LORD does not need weapons to rescue his people. It is his battle, not ours. The LORD will give you to us!"

[48]As Goliath moved closer to attack, David quickly ran out to meet him. [49]Reaching into his shepherd's bag and taking out a stone, he hurled it from his sling and hit the Philistine in the forehead. The

stone sank in, and Goliath stumbled and fell face downward to the ground. [50]So David triumphed over the Philistine giant with only a stone and sling. And since he had no sword, [51]he ran over and pulled Goliath's sword from its sheath. David used it to kill the giant and cut off his head.

When the Philistines saw that their champion was dead, they turned and ran. [52]Then the Israelites gave a great shout of triumph and rushed after the Philistines, chasing them as far as Gath* and the gates of Ekron. The bodies of the dead and wounded Philistines were strewn all along the road from Shaaraim, as far as Gath and Ekron. [53]Then the Israelite army returned and plundered the deserted Philistine camp. [54](David took Goliath's head to Jerusalem, but he stored the Philistine's armor in his own tent.)

[55]As Saul watched David go out to fight Goliath, he asked Abner, the general of his army, "Abner, whose son is he?"

"I really don't know," Abner said.

[56]"Well, find out!" the king told him.

[57]After David had killed Goliath, Abner brought him to Saul with the Philistine's head still in his hand. [58]"Tell me about your father, my boy," Saul said.

And David replied, "His name is Jesse, and we live in Bethlehem."

CHAPTER 18
After David had finished talking with Saul, he met Jonathan, the king's son. There was an immediate bond of love between them, and they became the best of friends. [2]From that day on Saul kept David with him at the palace and wouldn't let him return home. [3]And Jonathan made a special vow to be David's friend, [4]and he sealed the pact by giving him his robe, tunic, sword, bow, and belt.

[5]Whatever Saul asked David to do, David did it successfully. So Saul made him a commander in his army, an appointment that was applauded by the fighting men and officers alike. [6]But something happened when the victorious Israelite army was returning home after David had killed Goliath. Women came out from all the towns along the way to celebrate and to cheer for King Saul, and they sang and danced for joy with tambourines and cymbals.* [7]This was their song:

17:52 As in some Greek manuscripts; Hebrew reads *a valley.*   18:6 The type of instrument represented by the final word is uncertain.

"Saul has killed his thousands,
   and David his ten thousands!"

⁸This made Saul very angry. "What's this?" he said. "They credit David with ten thousands and me with only thousands. Next they'll be making him their king!" ⁹So from that time on Saul kept a jealous eye on David.

¹⁰The very next day, in fact, a tormenting spirit from God overwhelmed Saul, and he began to rave like a madman. David began to play the harp, as he did whenever this happened. But Saul, who had a spear in his hand, ¹¹suddenly hurled it at David, intending to pin him to the wall. But David jumped aside and escaped. This happened another time, too, ¹²for Saul was afraid of him, and he was jealous because the LORD had left him and was now with David. ¹³Finally, Saul banned him from his presence and appointed him commander over only a thousand men, but David faithfully led his troops into battle.

¹⁴David continued to succeed in everything he did, for the LORD was with him. ¹⁵When Saul recognized this, he became even more afraid of him. ¹⁶But all Israel and Judah loved David because he was so successful at leading his troops into battle.

¹⁷One day Saul said to David, "I am ready to give you my older daughter, Merab, as your wife. But first you must prove yourself to be a real warrior by fighting the LORD's battles." For Saul thought to himself, "I'll send him out against the Philistines and let them kill him rather than doing it myself."

¹⁸"Who am I, and what is my family in Israel that I should be the king's son-in-law?" David exclaimed. "My father's family is nothing!" ¹⁹So* when the time came for the wedding, Saul gave Merab in marriage to Adriel, a man from Meholah.

²⁰In the meantime, Saul's daughter Michal had fallen in love with David, and Saul was delighted when he heard about it. ²¹"Here's another chance to see him killed by the Philistines!" Saul said to himself. But to David he said, "I have a way for you to become my son-in-law after all!"

²²Then Saul told his men to say confidentially to David, "The king really likes you, and so do we. Why don't you accept the king's offer and become his son-in-law?"

²³When Saul's men said these things to David, he replied, "How can a poor man from a humble family afford the bride price for the daughter of a king?"

²⁴When Saul's men reported this back to the king, ²⁵he told them, "Tell David that all I want for the bride price is one hundred Philistine foreskins! Vengeance on my enemies is all I really want." But what Saul had in mind was that David would be killed in the fight.

²⁶David was delighted to accept the offer. So before the time limit expired, ²⁷he and his men went out and killed two hundred Philistines and presented all their foreskins to the king. So Saul gave Michal to David to be his wife.

²⁸When the king realized how much the LORD was with David and how much Michal loved him, ²⁹he became even more afraid of him, and he remained David's enemy for the rest of his life. ³⁰Whenever the Philistine army attacked, David was more successful against them than all the rest of Saul's officers. So David's name became very famous throughout the land.

CHAPTER 19

Saul now urged his servants and his son Jonathan to assassinate David. But Jonathan, because of his close friendship with David, ²told him what his father was planning. "Tomorrow morning," he warned him, "you must find a hiding place out in the fields. ³I'll ask my father to go out there with me, and I'll talk to him about you. Then I'll tell you everything I can find out."

⁴The next morning Jonathan spoke with his father about David, saying many good things about him. "Please don't sin against David," Jonathan pleaded. "He's never done anything to harm you. He has always helped you in any way he could. ⁵Have you forgotten about the time he risked his life to kill the Philistine giant and how the LORD brought a great victory to Israel as a result? You were certainly happy about it then. Why should you murder an innocent man like David? There is no reason for it at all!"

⁶So Saul listened to Jonathan and vowed, "As surely as the LORD lives, David will not be killed." ⁷Afterward Jonathan called David and told him what had happened. Then he took David to see Saul, and everything was as it had been before.

18:19 Or *But.*

⁸War broke out shortly after that, and David led his troops against the Philistines. He attacked them with such fury that they all ran away.

⁹But one day as Saul was sitting at home, the tormenting spirit from the LORD suddenly came upon him again. As David played his harp for the king, ¹⁰Saul hurled his spear at David in an attempt to kill him. But David dodged out of the way and escaped into the night, leaving the spear stuck in the wall.

¹¹Then Saul sent troops to watch David's house. They were told to kill David when he came out the next morning. But Michal, David's wife, warned him, "If you don't get away tonight, you will be dead by morning." ¹²So she helped him climb out through a window, and he escaped. ¹³Then she took an idol* and put it in his bed, covered it with blankets, and put a cushion of goat's hair at its head. ¹⁴When the troops came to arrest David, she told them he was sick and couldn't get out of bed.

¹⁵"Then bring him to me in his bed," Saul ordered, "so I can kill him as he lies there!" And he sent them back to David's house. ¹⁶But when they came to carry David out, they discovered that it was only an idol in

19:13 Hebrew *teraphim;* also in 19:16.

the bed with a cushion of goat's hair at its head.

¹⁷"Why have you tricked me and let my enemy escape?" Saul demanded of Michal.

"I had to," Michal replied. "He threatened to kill me if I didn't help him."

¹⁸So David got away and went to Ramah to see Samuel, and he told him all that Saul had done to him. Then Samuel took David with him to live at Naioth. ¹⁹When the report reached Saul that David was at Naioth in Ramah, ²⁰he sent troops to capture him. But when they arrived and saw Samuel and the other prophets prophesying, the Spirit of God came upon Saul's men, and they also began to prophesy. ²¹When Saul heard what had happened, he sent other troops, but they, too, prophesied! The same thing happened a third time! ²²Finally, Saul himself went to Ramah and arrived at the great well in Secu. "Where are Samuel and David?" he demanded.

"They are at Naioth in Ramah," someone told him. ²³But on the way to Naioth the Spirit of God came upon Saul, and he, too, began to prophesy! ²⁴He tore off his clothes and lay on the ground all day and all night, prophesying in the presence of Samuel. The people who were watching exclaimed, "What? Is Saul a prophet, too?"

MARCH 20 □ DAY 80
1 SAMUEL 20–23
David, the Pursued King-Elect

 OVERVIEW Ironically, as the rift grows between David and Saul, the relationship deepens between David and Saul's son Jonathan. Knowing he himself will never sit upon the throne of Israel, Jonathan seeks to assist and protect the pursued king-elect. He alerts David to his father's murderous intent and sends David on the first leg of a journey that will cover hundreds of miles and span nearly a decade. From Nob . . . to Gath . . . to Adullam . . . to the wilderness of Ziph, the king-elect is hunted by the king-rejected in a desperate and deadly game of hide-and-seek, from which only one will emerge victorious.

Chapter 20	Chapter 21	Chapter 22	Chapter 23
David's Faithful Friend Jonathan	Nob	David's Frantic Flight to Adullam	Ziph
A Friend Indeed	A Fugitive in Need		

YOUR DAILY WALK Have you found a Jonathan in your Christian life:
- someone who knows you fully and accepts you completely?
- someone with whom you can share your deepest hurts?
- someone who will listen without lecturing . . . comfort without condemning . . . encourage without criticizing?
- someone who will defend you when you're not around?
- someone whose greatest joy comes from your happiness?
- someone who watches out for your well-being, even at the potential risk of his own?
- someone who grieves when you are grieved, rejoices when you are promoted, bleeds when you are wounded?

The more hot arguments you win, the fewer warm friends you'll have.

Jonathans are rare, perhaps because the key to finding a Jonathan is becoming a David. Friendship is costly, demanding sacrifice and sensitivity; but that's what makes it so precious. Have you discovered the priceless treasure of finding—or becoming—a Jonathan?

INSIGHT The Nob of a Hill Called Nob
Nob, also known as "the city of the priests" (22:19), was located about one mile north of Jerusalem on a ridge overlooking what later became the site of Solomon's Temple. During the time of David, the Tabernacle was located in Nob, and national worship was conducted from there.

CHAPTER 20

David now fled from Naioth in Ramah and found Jonathan. "What have I done?" he exclaimed. "What is my crime? How have I offended your father that he is so determined to kill me?"

²"That's not true!" Jonathan protested. "I'm sure he's not planning any such thing, for he always tells me everything he's going to do, even the little things. I know he wouldn't hide something like this from me. It just isn't so!"

³Then David took an oath before Jonathan and said, "Your father knows perfectly well about our friendship, so he has said to himself, 'I won't tell Jonathan—why should I hurt him?' But I swear to you that I am only a step away from death! I swear it by the LORD and by your own soul!"

⁴"Tell me what I can do!" Jonathan exclaimed.

⁵David replied, "Tomorrow we celebrate the new moon festival. I've always eaten with your father on this occasion, but tomorrow I'll hide in the field and stay there until the evening of the third day. ⁶If your father asks where I am, tell him I asked permission to go home to Bethlehem for an annual family sacrifice. ⁷If he says, 'Fine!' then you will know all is well. But if he is angry and loses his temper, then you will know he was planning to kill me. ⁸Show me this kindness as my sworn friend—for we made a covenant together before the

LORD—or kill me yourself if I have sinned against your father. But please don't betray me to him!"

⁹"Never!" Jonathan exclaimed. "You know that if I had the slightest notion my father was planning to kill you, I would tell you at once."

¹⁰Then David asked, "How will I know whether or not your father is angry?"

¹¹"Come out to the field with me," Jonathan replied. And they went out there together. ¹²Then Jonathan told David, "I promise by the LORD, the God of Israel, that by this time tomorrow, or the next day at the latest, I will talk to my father and let you know at once how he feels about you. If he speaks favorably about you, I will let you know. ¹³But if he is angry and wants you killed, may the LORD kill me if I don't warn you so you can escape and live. May the LORD be with you as he used to be with my father. ¹⁴And may you treat me with the faithful love of the LORD as long as I live. But if I die, ¹⁵treat my family with this faithful love, even when the LORD destroys all your enemies."

¹⁶So Jonathan made a covenant with David,* saying, "May the LORD destroy all your enemies!" ¹⁷And Jonathan made David reaffirm his vow of friendship again, for Jonathan loved David as much as he loved himself.

¹⁸Then Jonathan said, "Tomorrow we celebrate the new moon festival. You will

20:16 Hebrew *with the house of David.*

be missed when your place at the table is empty. ¹⁹The day after tomorrow, toward evening, go to the place where you hid before, and wait there by the stone pile.* ²⁰I will come out and shoot three arrows to the side of the stone pile as though I were shooting at a target. ²¹Then I will send a boy to bring the arrows back. If you hear me tell him, 'They're on this side,' then you will know, as surely as the LORD lives, that all is well, and there is no trouble. ²²But if I tell him, 'Go farther—the arrows are still ahead of you,' then it will mean that you must leave immediately, for the LORD is sending you away. ²³And may the LORD make us keep our promises to each other, for he has witnessed them."

²⁴So David hid himself in the field, and when the new moon festival began, the king sat down to eat. ²⁵He sat at his usual place against the wall, with Jonathan sitting opposite him* and Abner beside him. But David's place was empty. ²⁶Saul didn't say anything about it that day, for he said to himself, "Something must have made David ceremonially unclean. Yes, that must be why he's not here." ²⁷But when David's place was empty again the next day, Saul asked Jonathan, "Why hasn't the son of Jesse been here for dinner either yesterday or today?"

²⁸Jonathan replied, "David earnestly asked me if he could go to Bethlehem. ²⁹He wanted to take part in a family sacrifice. His brother demanded that he be there, so I told him he could go. That's why he isn't here."

³⁰Saul boiled with rage at Jonathan. "You stupid son of a whore!"* he swore at him. "Do you think I don't know that you want David to be king in your place, shaming yourself and your mother? ³¹As long as that son of Jesse is alive, you'll never be king. Now go and get him so I can kill him!"

³²"But what has he done?" Jonathan demanded. "Why should he be put to death?" ³³Then Saul hurled his spear at Jonathan, intending to kill him. So at last Jonathan realized that his father was really determined to kill David. ³⁴Jonathan left the table in fierce anger and refused to eat all that day, for he was crushed by his father's shameful behavior toward David.

³⁵The next morning, as agreed, Jonathan went out into the field and took a young boy with him to gather his arrows. ³⁶"Start running," he told the boy, "so you can find the arrows as I shoot them." So the boy ran, and Jonathan shot an arrow beyond him. ³⁷When the boy had almost reached the arrow, Jonathan shouted, "The arrow is still ahead of you. ³⁸Hurry, hurry, don't wait." So the boy quickly gathered up the arrows and ran back to his master. ³⁹He, of course, didn't understand what Jonathan meant; only Jonathan and David knew. ⁴⁰Then Jonathan gave his bow and arrows to the boy and told him to take them back to the city.

⁴¹As soon as the boy was gone, David came out from where he had been hiding near the stone pile.* Then David bowed to Jonathan with his face to the ground. Both of them were in tears as they embraced each other and said good-bye, especially David. ⁴²At last Jonathan said to David, "Go in peace, for we have made a pact in the LORD's name. We have entrusted each other and each other's children into the LORD's hands forever." Then David left, and Jonathan returned to the city.

CHAPTER 21

David went to the city of Nob to see Ahimelech the priest. Ahimelech trembled when he saw him. "Why are you alone?" he asked. "Why is no one with you?"

²"The king has sent me on a private matter," David said. "He told me not to tell anyone why I am here. I have told my men where to meet me later. ³Now, what is there to eat? Give me five loaves of bread or anything else you have."

⁴"We don't have any regular bread," the priest replied. "But there is the holy bread, which I guess you can have if your young men have not slept with any women recently."

⁵"Don't worry," David replied. "I never allow my men to be with women when they are on a campaign. And since they stay clean even on ordinary trips, how much more on this one!"

⁶So, since there was no other food available, the priest gave him the holy bread—the Bread of the Presence that was placed before the LORD in the Tabernacle. It had just been replaced that day with fresh bread.

20:19 Hebrew *the stone Ezel.* The meaning of the Hebrew is uncertain. *standing.* 20:30 Hebrew *You son of a perverse and rebellious woman.* 20:25 As in Greek version; Hebrew reads *with Jonathan* 20:41 As in Greek version; Hebrew reads *near the south edge.*

[7]Now Doeg the Edomite, Saul's chief herdsman, was there that day for ceremonial purification.*

[8]David asked Ahimelech, "Do you have a spear or sword? The king's business was so urgent that I didn't even have time to grab a weapon!"

[9]"I only have the sword of Goliath the Philistine, whom you killed in the valley of Elah," the priest replied. "It is wrapped in a cloth behind the ephod. Take that if you want it, for there is nothing else here."

"There is nothing like it!" David replied. "Give it to me!"

[10]So David escaped from Saul and went to King Achish of Gath. [11]But Achish's officers weren't happy about his being there. "Isn't this David, the king of the land?" they asked. "Isn't he the one the people honor with dances, singing, 'Saul has killed his thousands, and David his ten thousands'?"

[12]David heard these comments and was afraid of what King Achish might do to him. [13]So he pretended to be insane, scratching on doors and drooling down his beard. [14]Finally, King Achish said to his men, "Must you bring me a madman? [15]We already have enough of them around here! Why should I let someone like this be my guest?"

CHAPTER 22
So David left Gath and escaped to the cave of Adullam. Soon his brothers and other relatives joined him there. [2]Then others began coming—men who were in trouble or in debt or who were just discontented—until David was the leader of about four hundred men.

[3]Later David went to Mizpeh in Moab, where he asked the king, "Would you let my father and mother live here under royal protection until I know what God is going to do for me?" [4]The king agreed, and David's parents stayed in Moab while David was living in his stronghold.

[5]One day the prophet Gad told David, "Leave the stronghold and return to the land of Judah." So David went to the forest of Hereth. [6]The news of his arrival in Judah soon reached Saul. At the time, the king was sitting beneath a tamarisk tree on the hill at Gibeah, holding his spear and surrounded by his officers.

[7]"Listen here, you men of Benjamin!" Saul shouted when he heard the news.

"Has David promised you fields and vineyards? Has he promised to make you commanders in his army? [8]Is that why you have conspired against me? For not one of you has ever told me that my own son is on David's side. You're not even sorry for me. Think of it! My own son—encouraging David to try and kill me!"

[9]Then Doeg the Edomite, who was standing there with Saul's men, spoke up. "When I was at Nob," he said, "I saw David talking to Ahimelech the priest. [10]Ahimelech consulted the LORD to find out what David should do. Then he gave David food and the sword of Goliath the Philistine."

[11]King Saul immediately sent for Ahimelech and all his family, who served as priests at Nob. [12]When they arrived, Saul shouted at him, "Listen to me, you son of Ahitub!"

"What is it, my king?" Ahimelech asked.

[13]"Why have you and David conspired against me?" Saul demanded. "Why did you give him food and a sword? Why have you inquired of God for him? Why did you encourage him to revolt against me and to come here and attack me?"

[14]"But sir," Ahimelech replied, "is there anyone among all your servants who is as faithful as David, your son-in-law? Why, he is the captain of your bodyguard and a highly honored member of your household! [15]This was certainly not the first time I had consulted God for him! Please don't accuse me and my family in this matter, for I knew nothing of any plot against you."

[16]"You will surely die, Ahimelech, along with your entire family!" the king shouted. [17]And he ordered his bodyguards, "Kill these priests of the LORD, for they are allies and conspirators with David! They knew he was running away from me, but they didn't tell me!" But Saul's men refused to kill the LORD's priests.

[18]Then the king said to Doeg, "You do it." So Doeg turned on them and killed them, eighty-five priests in all, all still wearing their priestly tunics. [19]Then he went to Nob, the city of the priests, and killed the priests' families—men and women, children and babies, and all the cattle, donkeys, and sheep.

[20]Only Abiathar, one of the sons of Ahimelech, escaped and fled to David. [21]When he told David that Saul had killed the

21:7 Hebrew *was detained before the* LORD.

priests of the LORD, ²²David exclaimed, "I knew it! When I saw Doeg there that day, I knew he would tell Saul. Now I have caused the death of all your father's family. ²³Stay here with me, and I will protect you with my own life, for the same person wants to kill us both."

CHAPTER 23

One day news came to David that the Philistines were at Keilah stealing grain from the threshing floors. ²David asked the LORD, "Should I go and attack them?"

"Yes, go and save Keilah," the LORD told him.

³But David's men said, "We're afraid even here in Judah. We certainly don't want to go to Keilah to fight the whole Philistine army!"

⁴So David asked the LORD again, and again the LORD replied, "Go down to Keilah, for I will help you conquer the Philistines."

⁵So David and his men went to Keilah. They slaughtered the Philistines and took all their livestock and rescued the people of Keilah. ⁶Abiathar the priest went to Keilah with David, taking the ephod with him to get answers for David from the LORD.

⁷Saul soon learned that David was at Keilah. "Good!" he exclaimed. "We've got him now! God has handed him over to me, for he has trapped himself in a walled city!"

⁸So Saul mobilized his entire army to march to Keilah and attack David and his men. ⁹But David learned of Saul's plan and told Abiathar the priest to bring the ephod and ask the LORD what he should do. ¹⁰And David prayed, "O LORD, God of Israel, I have heard that Saul is planning to come and destroy Keilah because I am here. ¹¹Will the men of Keilah surrender me to him?* And will Saul actually come as I have heard? O LORD, God of Israel, please tell me."

And the LORD said, "He will come."

¹²Again David asked, "Will these men of Keilah really betray me and my men to Saul?"

And the LORD replied, "Yes, they will betray you."

¹³So David and his men—about six hundred of them now—left Keilah and began roaming the countryside. Word soon reached Saul that David had escaped, so he

didn't go to Keilah after all. ¹⁴David now stayed in the strongholds of the wilderness and in the hill country of Ziph. Saul hunted him day after day, but God didn't let him be found.

¹⁵One day near Horesh, David received the news that Saul was on the way to Ziph to search for him and kill him. ¹⁶Jonathan went to find David and encouraged him to stay strong in his faith in God. ¹⁷"Don't be afraid," Jonathan reassured him. "My father will never find you! You are going to be the king of Israel, and I will be next to you, as my father is well aware." ¹⁸So the two of them renewed their covenant of friendship before the LORD. Then Jonathan returned home, while David stayed at Horesh.

¹⁹But now the men of Ziph went to Saul in Gibeah and betrayed David to him. "We know where David is hiding," they said. "He is in the strongholds of Horesh on the hill of Hakilah, which is in the southern part of Jeshimon. ²⁰Come down whenever you're ready, O king, and we will catch him and hand him over to you!"

²¹"The LORD bless you," Saul said. "At last someone is concerned about me! ²²Go and check again to be sure of where he is staying and who has seen him there, for I know that he is very crafty. ²³Discover his hiding places, and come back with a more definite report. Then I'll go with you. And if he is in the area at all, I'll track him down, even if I have to search every hiding place in Judah!"

²⁴So the men of Ziph returned home ahead of Saul. Meanwhile, David and his men had moved into the wilderness of Maon in the Arabah Valley south of Jeshimon. ²⁵When David heard that Saul and his men were searching for him, he went even farther into the wilderness to the great rock, and he remained there in the wilderness of Maon. But Saul kept after him. ²⁶He and David were now on opposite sides of a mountain. Just as Saul and his men began to close in on David and his men, ²⁷an urgent message reached Saul that the Philistines were raiding Israel again. ²⁸So Saul quit the chase and returned to fight the Philistines. Ever since that time, the place where David was camped has been called the Rock of Escape.* ²⁹David then went to live in the strongholds of En-gedi.

23:11 Some manuscripts lack the first sentence of 23:11.   23:28 Hebrew *Sela-hammahlekoth.*

MARCH 21 □ DAY 81
True Strength

LOOK BACK The young boy Samuel shows that you don't have to be old—just attentive—to hear and obey the voice of God.

Though "tuned in" to God in many ways, Samuel neglects the proper discipline of his sons, resulting in a national call for a king. In spite of dire predictions of what a king would do, God instructs Samuel to anoint Saul, a man of great physical stature but scant spiritual character. Saul's early *successes* soon give way to disobedient *excesses*, resulting in God's verdict of "rejected" and the anointing of Saul's successor. David, the young shepherd boy plucked from the pasture, would soon sing and "sling" his way into the hearts of his countrymen. But the path to the palace would be fraught with danger, discouragement, and deadly intrigue as David runs for his life from a crazed King Saul.

LOOK UP Q: Who had more strength—Samuel or Samson?
A: It all depends upon your definition of *strength*.

If by *strength* you mean "the physical ability to bring down the house," then it's no contest. He-man Samson beats little boy Samuel every time.

Good character is like good soup—it is usually homemade.

But if by *strength* you mean inner moral character, the ability to do what is right even when no one is watching, godliness, self-control, and ethical integrity, then little boy Samuel beats Samson hands down.

Samson spent his entire life seeing how close to the edge of moral collapse he could get without falling over. In the end he lost his sight, his influence, and eventually his life. To be sure, God won a great victory over the Philistines at Samson's death, but imagine how many other victories were never achieved because of Samson's compromising stance toward right and wrong.

By contrast, even in his early years Samuel was intent on hearing and obeying God's voice. "The LORD was with him, and everything Samuel said was wise and helpful" (3:19). Samuel never seemed to tire of "tuning in" to what God was trying to say. He wanted to get as close to God as possible, lest he miss a single word. It's true that Samuel's later years were marked by the failure of overcommitment as he reaped the tearful harvest of having neglected the discipline of his sons. But over his life could be written the epitaph "He yearned to hear God's voice."

LOOK AHEAD What a strange, upside-down world we live in when those receiving the greatest public applause and financial reward are those who can dunk a basketball, act in front of a camera, or sell a million albums—with no regard to their moral character or ethical conduct.

By contrast, those in line for God's recognition and reward are those who "realize their need for him . . . are gentle . . . are merciful . . . work for peace . . . and are persecuted because they live for God" (Matthew 5:3-10). No, you're not likely to see them in the spotlight this side of heaven. But when God hands out his "Well done, . . . good and faithful servant" awards (Matthew 25:21, 23), you can be sure there will be some surprises!

Incidentally, which type of recognition are you striving to receive?

MARCH 22 □ DAY 82
1 SAMUEL 24–26
David, the Recognized King-Elect

OVERVIEW In today's reading you will encounter four different people and will view each from God's perspective. The focus is not on their external appearance but on their internal motivation, for "people judge by outward appearance, but the LORD looks at a person's thoughts and intentions" (16:7). David demonstrates a heart of true compassion and righteousness when he twice refuses to kill the helpless king. Saul portrays a heart of repentance when he humbly acknowledges his sin of pursuing David. Nabal reveals his foolish heart by refusing to assist the king-elect. Nabal's wife, Abigail, shows her discerning heart by offering to David and his weary men the hospitality that her reckless husband withheld.

Chapter 24	Chapter 25	Chapter 26
A Demonstration of Righteousness	A Demonstration of Foolishness	A Demonstration of Faithfulness
David Spares Saul	Abigail Spares Nabal	David Spares Saul Again

YOUR DAILY WALK "If I ran the show, I would . . ."

Have you ever been convinced you could do a better job than the leader in charge? If so, how did you handle the situation? Were you openly supportive . . . or openly critical?

The best thing to do behind a person's back is pat it.

David showed unique strength of character when faced with an inept, jealous leader. Though David fled for his life, he never fought for his rights, even when twice given the opportunity to rid himself of his pursuer. David's conduct demonstrates that a righteous person recognizes God's chosen leader even when the leader fails.

How do you respond to the leaders God has placed over you? Do you honor them with the respect due their position? Do you permit them the luxury of an occasional mistake? (After all, what if you hadn't been given a second, third, or even fourth chance?) Take the time today to write an encouraging note to one of your civic, national, or spiritual leaders, pledging your continued support as that individual exercises God-given authority.

INSIGHT A Fragile Peace with a Fickle King

Although chapter 26 ends on a note of reconciliation (vv. 21-25), David is wise enough not to return with King Saul. As the opening verse of tomorrow's reading will show, from that time on, no trust remained between the two rivals.

CHAPTER 24

After Saul returned from fighting the Philistines, he was told that David had gone into the wilderness of En-gedi. ²So Saul chose three thousand special troops from throughout Israel and went to search for David and his men near the rocks of the wild goats. ³At the place where the road passes some sheepfolds, Saul went into a cave to relieve himself. But as it happened, David and his men were hiding in that very cave!

⁴"Now's your opportunity!" David's men whispered to him. "Today is the day the LORD was talking about when he said, 'I will certainly put Saul into your power, to do with as you wish.'" Then David crept forward and cut off a piece of Saul's robe.

⁵But then David's conscience began bothering him because he had cut Saul's robe. ⁶"The LORD knows I shouldn't have done it," he said to his men. "It is a serious thing to attack the LORD's anointed one, for

the LORD himself has chosen him." ⁷So David sharply rebuked his men and did not let them kill Saul.

After Saul had left the cave and gone on his way, ⁸David came out and shouted after him, "My lord the king!" And when Saul looked around, David bowed low before him. ⁹Then he shouted to Saul, "Why do you listen to the people who say I am trying to harm you? ¹⁰This very day you can see with your own eyes it isn't true. For the LORD placed you at my mercy back there in the cave, and some of my men told me to kill you, but I spared you. For I said, 'I will never harm him—he is the LORD's anointed one.' ¹¹Look, my father, at what I have in my hand. It is a piece of your robe! I cut it off, but I didn't kill you. This proves that I am not trying to harm you and that I have not sinned against you, even though you have been hunting for me to kill me. ¹²The LORD will decide between us. Perhaps the LORD will punish you for what you are trying to do to me, but I will never harm you. ¹³As that old proverb says, 'From evil people come evil deeds.' So you can be sure I will never harm you. ¹⁴Who is the king of Israel trying to catch anyway? Should he spend his time chasing one who is as worthless as a dead dog or a flea? ¹⁵May the LORD judge which of us is right and punish the guilty one. He is my advocate, and he will rescue me from your power!"

¹⁶Saul called back, "Is that really you, my son David?" Then he began to cry. ¹⁷And he said to David, "You are a better man than I am, for you have repaid me good for evil. ¹⁸Yes, you have been wonderfully kind to me today, for when the LORD put me in a place where you could have killed me, you didn't do it. ¹⁹Who else would let his enemy get away when he had him in his power? May the LORD reward you well for the kindness you have shown me today. ²⁰And now I realize that you are surely going to be king, and Israel will flourish under your rule. ²¹Now, swear to me by the LORD that when that happens you will not kill my family and destroy my line of descendants!"

²²So David promised, and Saul went home. But David and his men went back to their stronghold.

CHAPTER 25

Now Samuel died, and all Israel gathered for his funeral. They buried him near his home at Ramah.

Then David moved down to the wilderness of Maon.* ²There was a wealthy man from Maon who owned property near the village of Carmel. He had three thousand sheep and a thousand goats, and it was sheep-shearing time. ³This man's name was Nabal, and his wife, Abigail, was a sensible and beautiful woman. But Nabal, a descendant of Caleb, was mean and dishonest in all his dealings.

⁴When David heard that Nabal was shearing his sheep, ⁵he sent ten of his young men to Carmel. He told them to deliver this message: ⁶"Peace and prosperity to you, your family, and everything you own! ⁷I am told that you are shearing your sheep and goats. While your shepherds stayed among us near Carmel, we never harmed them, and nothing was ever stolen from them. ⁸Ask your own servants, and they will tell you this is true. So would you please be kind to us, since we have come at a time of celebration? Please give us any provisions you might have on hand." ⁹David's young men gave this message to Nabal and waited for his reply.

¹⁰"Who is this fellow David?" Nabal sneered. "Who does this son of Jesse think he is? There are lots of servants these days who run away from their masters. ¹¹Should I take my bread and water and the meat I've slaughtered for my shearers and give it to a band of outlaws who come from who knows where?" ¹²So David's messengers returned and told him what Nabal had said.

¹³"Get your swords!" was David's reply as he strapped on his own. Four hundred men started off with David, and two hundred remained behind to guard their equipment.

¹⁴Meanwhile, one of Nabal's servants went to Abigail and told her, "David sent men from the wilderness to talk to our master, and he insulted them. ¹⁵But David's men were very good to us, and we never suffered any harm from them. Nothing was stolen from us the whole time they were with us. ¹⁶In fact, day and night they were like a wall of protection to us and the sheep. ¹⁷You'd better think fast, for there is going to be trouble for our master and his whole family.

25:1 As in Greek version; Hebrew reads *Paran.*

He's so ill-tempered that no one can even talk to him!"

¹⁸Abigail lost no time. She quickly gathered two hundred loaves of bread, two skins of wine, five dressed sheep, nearly a bushel* of roasted grain, one hundred raisin cakes, and two hundred fig cakes. She packed them on donkeys and said to her servants, ¹⁹"Go on ahead. I will follow you shortly." But she didn't tell her husband what she was doing.

²⁰As she was riding her donkey into a mountain ravine, she saw David and his men coming toward her. ²¹David had just been saying, "A lot of good it did to help this fellow. We protected his flocks in the wilderness, and nothing he owned was lost or stolen. But he has repaid me evil for good. ²²May God deal with me severely if even one man of his household is still alive tomorrow morning!"

²³When Abigail saw David, she quickly got off her donkey and bowed low before him. ²⁴She fell at his feet and said, "I accept all blame in this matter, my lord. Please listen to what I have to say. ²⁵I know Nabal is a wicked and ill-tempered man; please don't pay any attention to him. He is a fool, just as his name suggests.* But I never even saw the messengers you sent.

²⁶"Now, my lord, as surely as the LORD lives and you yourself live, since the LORD has kept you from murdering and taking vengeance into your own hands, let all your enemies be as cursed as Nabal is. ²⁷And here is a present I have brought to you and your young men. ²⁸Please forgive me if I have offended in any way. The LORD will surely reward you with a lasting dynasty, for you are fighting the LORD's battles. And you have not done wrong throughout your entire life.

²⁹"Even when you are chased by those who seek your life, you are safe in the care of the LORD your God, secure in his treasure pouch! But the lives of your enemies will disappear like stones shot from a sling! ³⁰When the LORD has done all he promised and has made you leader of Israel, ³¹don't let this be a blemish on your record. Then you won't have to carry on your conscience the staggering burden of needless bloodshed and vengeance. And when the LORD has done these great things for you, please remember me!"

³²David replied to Abigail, "Praise the LORD, the God of Israel, who has sent you to meet me today! ³³Thank God for your good sense! Bless you for keeping me from murdering the man and carrying out vengeance with my own hands. ³⁴For I swear by the LORD, the God of Israel, who has kept me from hurting you, that if you had not hurried out to meet me, not one of Nabal's men would be alive tomorrow morning." ³⁵Then David accepted her gifts and told her, "Return home in peace. We will not kill your husband."

³⁶When Abigail arrived home, she found that Nabal had thrown a big party and was celebrating like a king. He was very drunk, so she didn't tell him anything about her meeting with David until the next morning. ³⁷The next morning when he was sober, she told him what had happened. As a result he had a stroke,* and he lay on his bed paralyzed. ³⁸About ten days later, the LORD struck him and he died.

³⁹When David heard that Nabal was dead, he said, "Praise the LORD, who has paid back Nabal and kept me from doing it myself. Nabal has received the punishment for his sin." Then David wasted no time in sending messengers to Abigail to ask her to become his wife.

⁴⁰When the messengers arrived at Carmel, they told Abigail, "David has sent us to ask if you will marry him."

⁴¹She bowed low to the ground and responded, "Yes, I am even willing to become a slave to David's servants!" ⁴²Quickly getting ready, she took along five of her servant girls as attendants, mounted her donkey, and went with David's messengers. And so she became his wife. ⁴³David also married Ahinoam from Jezreel, making both of them his wives. ⁴⁴Saul, meanwhile, had given his daughter Michal, David's wife, to a man from Gallim named Palti son of Laish.

CHAPTER 26
Now some messengers from Ziph came back to Saul at Gibeah to tell him, "David is hiding on the hill of Hakilah, which overlooks Jeshimon." ²So Saul took three thousand of his best troops and went to hunt him down in the wilderness of Ziph. ³Saul camped along the road beside the hill of Hakilah, near Jeshimon, where David was

---

25:18 Hebrew *5 seahs* [30 liters].   **25:25** The name *Nabal* means "fool."   **25:37** Hebrew *his heart failed him.*

hiding. But David knew of Saul's arrival, [4]so he sent out spies to watch his movements.

[5]David slipped over to Saul's camp one night to look around. Saul and his general, Abner son of Ner, were sleeping inside a ring formed by the slumbering warriors. [6]"Will anyone volunteer to go in there with me?" David asked Ahimelech the Hittite and Abishai son of Zeruiah, Joab's brother.

"I'll go with you," Abishai replied. [7]So David and Abishai went right into Saul's camp and found him asleep, with his spear stuck in the ground beside his head. Abner and the warriors were lying asleep around him. [8]"God has surely handed your enemy over to you this time!" Abishai whispered to David. "Let me thrust that spear through him. I'll pin him to the ground, and I won't need to strike twice!"

[9]"No!" David said. "Don't kill him. For who can remain innocent after attacking the LORD's anointed one? [10]Surely the LORD will strike Saul down someday, or he will die in battle or of old age. [11]But the LORD forbid that I should kill the one he has anointed! But I'll tell you what—we'll take his spear and his jug of water and then get out of here!"

[12]So David took the spear and jug of water that were near Saul's head. Then he and Abishai got away without anyone seeing them or even waking up, because the LORD had put Saul's men into a deep sleep. [13]David climbed the hill opposite the camp until he was at a safe distance. [14]Then he shouted down to Abner and Saul, "Wake up, Abner!"

"Who is it?" Abner demanded.

[15]"Well, Abner, you're a great man, aren't you?" David taunted. "Where in all Israel is there anyone as mighty? So why haven't you guarded your master the king when some-

one came to kill him? [16]This isn't good at all! I swear by the LORD that you and your men deserve to die, because you failed to protect your master, the LORD's anointed! Look around! Where are the king's spear and the jug of water that were beside his head?"

[17]Saul recognized David's voice and called out, "Is that you, my son David?"

And David replied, "Yes, my lord the king. [18]Why are you chasing me? What have I done? What is my crime? [19]But now let my lord the king listen to his servant. If the LORD has stirred you up against me, then let him accept my offering. But if this is simply a human scheme, then may those involved be cursed by the LORD. For you have driven me from my home, so I can no longer live among the LORD's people and worship as I should. [20]Must I die on foreign soil, far from the presence of the LORD? Why has the king of Israel come out to search for a single flea? Why does he hunt me down like a partridge on the mountains?"

[21]Then Saul confessed, "I have sinned. Come back home, my son, and I will no longer try to harm you, for you valued my life today. I have been a fool and very, very wrong."

[22]"Here is your spear, O king," David replied. "Let one of your young men come over and get it. [23]The LORD gives his own reward for doing good and for being loyal, and I refused to kill you even when the LORD placed you in my power, for you are the LORD's anointed one. [24]Now may the LORD value my life, even as I have valued yours today. May he rescue me from all my troubles."

[25]And Saul said to David, "Blessings on you, my son David. You will do heroic deeds and be a great conqueror." Then David went away, and Saul returned home.

MARCH 23 □ DAY 83
1 SAMUEL 27–31
David, the Exiled King-Elect

 OVERVIEW After Saul's second brush with death in the wilderness of Ziph, he discontinues the hunt for David. But the reprieve is only temporary, as David expects from past experience. Fleeing again to Gath of Philistia (the hometown of Goliath!), David pretends that he has defected to the enemy. In fact, he is busy destroying Philistine strongholds without leaving a single survivor to disclose his ingenious plan. When the Philistine kings mount a united war against Israel, David narrowly escapes fighting against his own nation. He returns instead to Ziklag to find it destroyed by the Amalekites, whom he pursues and defeats. Meanwhile, Saul is confronted with a Philistine invasion. Since the Spirit of God has left him, he seeks direction by divination—and receives instead a prediction of death and defeat.

Chapter 27	Chapter 28	Chapter 29	Chapter 30	Chapter 31
David's Defection	Saul's Distress	David's Dismissal	Amalekites' Defeat	Saul's Death
End of a Deadly Chase			End of a Dynasty	

YOUR DAILY WALK In contemporary English, the word *tragedy* is used to describe any severe adversity, regardless of its cause. But more specifically, a tragedy is a calamity that results from a wrong decision arising from a flawed character. Using this definition, Saul's life was a true tragedy. It held much promise of success for himself and the nation, yet it ended in defeat and disgrace—all because pride and self-will led him to rebel against God's commands.

The number of times the average person says no to temptation is once weakly.

Becoming a Christian doesn't mark the end of your battle with sin and temptation; in many ways it marks the beginning! As a Christian you still have a fallen nature that seeks to express itself in your daily actions. You also have a personal will that desires to direct your life. Both need to come under the lordship of Jesus Christ. Take the four major areas of your life (spiritual, social, physical, emotional) and give each back to God right now, asking for his help to make your attitudes, decisions, and actions pleasing to him.

INSIGHT A King's Life Comes Full Circle
First Samuel ends on a fitting note. Saul's first official act had been to rescue Jabesh Gilead (1 Samuel 11). Now its citizens have an opportunity to repay his kindness . . . posthumously (31:8-13).

CHAPTER 27

But David kept thinking to himself, "Someday Saul is going to get me. The best thing for me to do is escape to the Philistines. Then Saul will stop hunting for me, and I will finally be safe."

²So David took his six hundred men and their families and went to live at Gath under the protection of King Achish. ³David brought his two wives along with him—Ahinoam of Jezreel and Abigail of Carmel, Nabal's widow. ⁴Word soon reached Saul that David had fled to Gath, so he stopped hunting for him.

⁵One day David said to Achish, "If it is all right with you, we would rather live in one of the country towns instead of here in the royal city." ⁶So Achish gave him the town of Ziklag (which still belongs to the kings of Judah to this day), ⁷and they lived there among the Philistines for a year and four months.

⁸David and his men spent their time raiding the Geshurites, the Girzites, and the Amalekites—people who had lived near Shur, along the road to Egypt, since ancient times. ⁹David didn't leave one person alive in the villages he attacked. He took the sheep, cattle, donkeys, camels, and clothing before returning home to see King Achish.

¹⁰"Where did you make your raid today?" Achish would ask.

And David would reply, "Against the south of Judah, the Jerahmeelites, and the Kenites."

¹¹No one was left alive to come to Gath and tell where he had really been. This happened again and again while he was living among the Philistines. ¹²Achish believed David and thought to himself, "By now the people of Israel must hate him bitterly. Now he will have to stay here and serve me forever!"

CHAPTER 28

About that time the Philistines mustered their armies for another war with Israel. King Achish told David, "You and your men will be expected to join me in battle."

²"Very well!" David agreed. "Now you will see for yourself what we can do."

Then Achish told David, "I will make you my personal bodyguard for life."

³Meanwhile, Samuel had died, and all Israel had mourned for him. He was buried in Ramah, his hometown. And Saul had banned all mediums and psychics from the land of Israel.

⁴The Philistines set up their camp at Shunem, and Saul and the armies of Israel camped at Gilboa. ⁵When Saul saw the vast Philistine army, he became frantic with fear. ⁶He asked the LORD what he should do, but the LORD refused to answer him, either by dreams or by sacred lots* or by the prophets. ⁷Saul then said to his advisers, "Find a woman who is a medium, so I can go and ask her what to do."

His advisers replied, "There is a medium at Endor."

⁸So Saul disguised himself by wearing ordinary clothing instead of his royal robes. Then he went to the woman's home at night, accompanied by two of his men. "I have to talk to a man who has died," he said. "Will you call up his spirit for me?"

⁹"Are you trying to get me killed?" the woman demanded. "You know that Saul has expelled all the mediums and psychics from the land. Why are you setting a trap for me?"

¹⁰But Saul took an oath in the name of the LORD and promised, "As surely as the LORD lives, nothing bad will happen to you for doing this."

¹¹Finally, the woman said, "Well, whose spirit do you want me to call up?"

"Call up Samuel," Saul replied.

¹²When the woman saw Samuel, she screamed, "You've deceived me! You are Saul!"

¹³"Don't be afraid!" the king told her. "What do you see?"

"I see a god* coming up out of the earth," she said.

¹⁴"What does he look like?" Saul asked.

"He is an old man wrapped in a robe," she replied. Saul realized that it was Samuel, and he fell to the ground before him.

¹⁵"Why have you disturbed me by calling me back?" Samuel asked.

"Because I am in deep trouble," Saul replied. "The Philistines are at war with us, and God has left me and won't reply by prophets or dreams. So I have called for you to tell me what to do."

¹⁶But Samuel replied, "Why ask me if the LORD has left you and has become your enemy? ¹⁷The LORD has done just as he said he would. He has taken the kingdom from you and given it to your rival, David. ¹⁸The LORD has done this because you did not obey his instructions concerning the Amalekites. ¹⁹What's more, the LORD will hand you and the army of Israel over to the Philistines tomorrow, and you and your sons will be here with me. The LORD will bring the entire army of Israel down in defeat."

²⁰Saul fell full length on the ground, paralyzed with fright because of Samuel's words. He was also faint with hunger, for he had eaten nothing all day and all night. ²¹When the woman saw how distraught he was, she said, "Sir, I obeyed your command at the risk of my life. ²²Now do what I say, and let me give you something to eat so you can regain your strength for the trip back."

²³But Saul refused. The men who were with him also urged him to eat, so he finally yielded and got up from the ground and sat on the couch. ²⁴The woman had been fattening a calf, so she hurried out and killed it. She kneaded dough and baked unleavened bread. ²⁵She brought the meal to Saul and his men, and they ate it. Then they went out into the night.

CHAPTER 29

The entire Philistine army now mobilized at Aphek, and the Israelites camped at the spring in Jezreel. ²As the Philistine rulers were leading out their troops in groups of one hundred and one thousand, David and his men marched at the rear with King Achish. ³But the Philistine commanders demanded, "What are these Hebrews doing here?"

And Achish told them, "This is David, the man who ran away from King Saul of Israel. He's been with me for years, and I've never found a single fault in him since he defected to me."

28:6 Hebrew *by Urim.*   28:13 Or *gods.*

[4]But the Philistine commanders were angry. "Send him back!" they demanded. "He can't go into the battle with us. What if he turns against us? Is there any better way for him to reconcile himself with his master than by turning on us in battle? [5]Isn't this the same David about whom the women of Israel sing in their dances, 'Saul has killed his thousands, and David his ten thousands'?"

[6]So Achish finally summoned David and his men. "I swear by the LORD," he told them, "you are some of the finest men I've ever met. I think you should go with us, but the other Philistine rulers won't hear of it. [7]Please don't upset them, but go back quietly."

[8]"What have I done to deserve this treatment?" David demanded. "Why can't I fight the enemies of my lord, the king?"

[9]But Achish insisted, "As far as I'm concerned, you're as perfect as an angel of God. But my commanders are afraid to have you with them in the battle. [10]Now get up early in the morning, and leave with your men as soon as it gets light." [11]So David headed back into the land of the Philistines, while the Philistine army went on to Jezreel.

CHAPTER 30

Three days later, when David and his men arrived home at their town of Ziklag, they found that the Amalekites had made a raid into the Negev and had burned Ziklag to the ground. [2]They had carried off the women and children and everyone else but without killing anyone. [3]When David and his men saw the ruins and realized what had happened to their families, [4]they wept until they could weep no more. [5]David's two wives, Ahinoam of Jezreel and Abigail, the widow of Nabal of Carmel, were among those captured. [6]David was now in serious trouble because his men were very bitter about losing their wives and children, and they began to talk of stoning him. But David found strength in the LORD his God.

[7]Then he said to Abiathar the priest, "Bring me the ephod!" So Abiathar brought it. [8]Then David asked the LORD, "Should I chase them? Will I catch them?"

And the LORD told him, "Yes, go after them. You will surely recover everything that was taken from you!" [9]So David and

his six hundred men set out, and they soon came to Besor Brook. [10]But two hundred of the men were too exhausted to cross the brook, so David continued the pursuit with his four hundred remaining troops.

[11]Some of David's troops found an Egyptian man in a field and brought him to David. They gave him some bread to eat and some water to drink. [12]They also gave him part of a fig cake and two clusters of raisins because he hadn't had anything to eat or drink for three days and nights. It wasn't long before his strength returned.

[13]"To whom do you belong, and where do you come from?" David asked him.

"I am an Egyptian—the slave of an Amalekite," he replied. "My master left me behind three days ago because I was sick. [14]We were on our way back from raiding the Kerethites in the Negev, the territory of Judah, and the land of Caleb, and we had just burned Ziklag."

[15]"Will you lead me to them?" David asked.

The young man replied, "If you swear by God's name that you will not kill me or give me back to my master, then I will guide you to them."

[16]So the Egyptian led them to the Amalekite encampment. When David and his men arrived, the Amalekites were spread out across the fields, eating and drinking and dancing with joy because of the vast amount of plunder they had taken from the Philistines and the land of Judah. [17]David and his men rushed in among them and slaughtered them throughout that night and the entire next day until evening. None of the Amalekites escaped except four hundred young men who fled on camels. [18]David got back everything the Amalekites had taken, and he rescued his two wives. [19]Nothing was missing: small or great, son or daughter, nor anything else that had been taken. David brought everything back. [20]His troops rounded up all the flocks and herds and drove them on ahead. "These all belong to David as his reward!" they said.

[21]When they reached Besor Brook and met the two hundred men who had been too tired to go with them, David greeted them joyfully. [22]But some troublemakers among David's men said, "They didn't go with us, so they can't have any of the plunder. Give them their wives and children, and tell them to be gone."

²³But David said, "No, my brothers! Don't be selfish with what the LORD has given us. He has kept us safe and helped us defeat the enemy. ²⁴Do you think anyone will listen to you when you talk like this? We share and share alike—those who go to battle and those who guard the equipment." ²⁵From then on David made this a law for all of Israel, and it is still followed.

²⁶When he arrived at Ziklag, David sent part of the plunder to the leaders of Judah, who were his friends. "Here is a present for you, taken from the LORD's enemies," he said. ²⁷The gifts were sent to the leaders of the following towns where David and his men had been: Bethel, Ramoth-negev, Jattir, ²⁸Aroer, Siphmoth, Eshtemoa, ²⁹Racal,* the towns of the Jerahmeelites, the towns of the Kenites, ³⁰Hormah, Bor-ashan, Athach, ³¹Hebron, and all the other places they had visited.

CHAPTER 31

Now the Philistines attacked Israel, forcing the Israelites to flee. Many were slaughtered on the slopes of Mount Gilboa. ²The Philistines closed in on Saul and his sons, and they killed three of his sons—Jonathan, Abinadab, and Malkishua. ³The fighting grew very fierce around Saul, and the Philistine archers caught up with him and wounded him severely. ⁴Saul groaned to his armor bearer, "Take your sword and kill me before these pagan Philistines run

30:29 Greek version reads *Carmel.*

me through and humiliate me." But his armor bearer was afraid and would not do it. So Saul took his own sword and fell on it. ⁵When his armor bearer realized that Saul was dead, he fell on his own sword and died beside the king. ⁶So Saul, three of his sons, his armor bearer, and his troops all died together that same day.

⁷When the Israelites on the other side of the Jezreel Valley and beyond the Jordan saw that their army had been routed and that Saul and his sons were dead, they abandoned their towns and fled. So the Philistines moved in and occupied their towns.

⁸The next day, when the Philistines went out to strip the dead, they found the bodies of Saul and his three sons on Mount Gilboa. ⁹So they cut off Saul's head and stripped off his armor. Then they proclaimed the news of Saul's death in their pagan temple and to the people throughout the land of Philistia. ¹⁰They placed his armor in the temple of the Ashtoreths, and they fastened his body to the wall of the city of Beth-shan.

¹¹But when the people of Jabesh-gilead heard what the Philistines had done to Saul, ¹²their warriors traveled all night to Beth-shan and took the bodies of Saul and his sons down from the wall. They brought them to Jabesh, where they burned the bodies. ¹³Then they took their remains and buried them beneath the tamarisk tree at Jabesh, and they fasted for seven days.

2 Samuel

THE BOOK of 2 Samuel chronicles the remarkable forty-year reign of King David, a man who lives at the halfway point between Moses and Christ (about 1000 B.C.). David's triumphs and successes bring Israel to the very zenith of her power. But his all-too-human weaknesses become a national scandal, leading to rebellion within his own family and temporary exile for himself and his court. Through it all, David seeks God zealously and confesses his sins promptly.

Focus	Success			Sin			Suffering
Divisions	David, King of Judah	David, King of Israel	David's Growing Kingdom	David's Tragic Downfall	Absalom's Quest to Rule	David's Return to the Throne	David's Final Days
	1　　　4	5　　　7	8　　10	11　　　　14	15　　8	19　20	21　24
Topics	David's Rise			David's Demise			
	Victory and Expansion			Violence and Struggle			
Place	Hebron			Jerusalem			
Time	7½ Years			33 Years			

MARCH 24 ☐ DAY 84
2 SAMUEL 1–4
David, King of Judah

OVERVIEW Second Samuel continues the narrative of 1 Samuel and chronicles David's rise to prominence as Israel's leader. After mourning the deaths of Saul and Jonathan, David assumes the throne as king over Judah. But Saul's dynasty is not to be replaced without a fight! Ishbosheth, Saul's son, claims the throne of Israel, initiating seven years of bloody civil war, intrigue, defections, assassinations, suspense, rival factions, and rebellions. But when at last the opposition has been quelled, David rules as king over a united kingdom.

Chapter 1	Chapters 2–3	Chapter 4
David Weeps	David Wars	David Wins
Mourning Saul's Death	Fighting Saul's House	

YOUR DAILY WALK Look up Matthew 12:25, and thoughtfully read it twice. Now ask yourself these two questions:
1. How was this verse proved true in David's kingdom?
2. What does this verse mean in my home?

The family altar would alter many a family.

In David's day many individuals were striving for positions of leadership and power. Some would even scheme, kill, or change sides to gain their personal ends. The result was chaos, frustration, and death until the nation was united under one head.

Many activities compete for your attention. Television, clubs, school activities, civic functions, church meetings—all demand your time and energy. In many homes the result is confusion, frustration, and lack of family unity.

Families, like nations, function best when they operate under one head. Hold a family council to talk about leadership in your home. Spend some time looking at Bible passages dealing with headship in the home (Ephesians 5:22–6:4; Colossians 3:18-21). Then select a family goal for the coming week—something that will honor the Lord and benefit each family member!

INSIGHT Did You Ever Read the One by . . .
Lost in the ancient world, the book of Jasher was apparently a collection of verse describing great events in Israel's history. It contained an account of Joshua's triumph at the battle of Gibeon (Joshua 10:12-13) as well as David's lament over Saul and Jonathan. Second Chronicles 9:29 mentions other writings that have been lost.

CHAPTER 1
After the death of Saul, David returned from his victory over the Amalekites and spent two days in Ziklag. ²On the third day after David's return, a man arrived from the Israelite battlefront. He had torn his clothes and put dirt on his head to show that he was in mourning. He fell to the ground before David in deep respect.

³"Where have you come from?" David asked.

"I escaped from the Israelite camp," the man replied.

[4]"What happened?" David demanded. "Tell me how the battle went."

The man replied, "Our entire army fled. Many men are dead and wounded on the battlefield, and Saul and his son Jonathan have been killed."

[5]"How do you know that Saul and Jonathan are dead?" David demanded.

[6]The young man answered, "I happened to be on Mount Gilboa. I saw Saul there leaning on his spear with the enemy chariots closing in on him. [7]When he turned and saw me, he cried out for me to come to him. 'How can I help?' I asked him. [8]And he said to me, 'Who are you?' I replied, 'I am an Amalekite.' [9]Then he begged me, 'Come over here and put me out of my misery, for I am in terrible pain and want to die.'

[10]"So I killed him," the Amalekite told David, "for I knew he couldn't live. Then I took his crown and one of his bracelets so I could bring them to you, my lord."

[11]David and his men tore their clothes in sorrow when they heard the news. [12]They mourned and wept and fasted all day for Saul and his son Jonathan, and for the LORD's army and the nation of Israel, because so many had died that day. [13]Then David said to the young man who had brought the news, "Where are you from?"

And he replied, "I am a foreigner, an Amalekite, who lives in your land."

[14]"Were you not afraid to kill the LORD's anointed one?" David asked. [15]Then David said to one of his men, "Kill him!" So the man thrust his sword into the Amalekite and killed him. [16]"You die self-condemned," David said, "for you yourself confessed that you killed the LORD's anointed one."

[17]Then David composed a funeral song for Saul and Jonathan. [18]Later he commanded that it be taught to all the people of Judah. It is known as the Song of the Bow, and it is recorded in *The Book of Jashar*.*

[19] Your pride and joy, O Israel, lies dead
on the hills!
How the mighty heroes have fallen!
[20] Don't announce the news in Gath,
or the Philistines will rejoice.
Don't proclaim it in the streets of
Ashkelon,
or the pagans will laugh in triumph.

[21] O mountains of Gilboa,
let there be no dew or rain upon you
or your slopes.
For there the shield of the mighty was
defiled;
the shield of Saul will no longer be
anointed with oil.
[22] Both Saul and Jonathan killed their
strongest foes;
they did not return from battle
empty-handed.

[23] How beloved and gracious were Saul
and Jonathan!
They were together in life and in
death.
They were swifter than eagles;
they were stronger than lions.

[24] O women of Israel, weep for Saul,
for he dressed you in fine clothing
and gold ornaments.

[25] How the mighty heroes have fallen
in battle!
Jonathan lies dead upon the hills.
[26] How I weep for you, my brother
Jonathan!
Oh, how much I loved you!
And your love for me was deep,
deeper than the love of women!

[27] How the mighty heroes have fallen!
Stripped of their weapons, they lie
dead.

CHAPTER 2

After this, David asked the LORD, "Should I move back to Judah?"

And the LORD replied, "Yes."

Then David asked, "Which town should I go to?"

And the LORD replied, "Hebron."

[2]David's wives were Ahinoam from Jezreel and Abigail, the widow of Nabal from Carmel. So David and his wives [3]and his men and their families all moved to Judah, and they settled near the town of Hebron. [4]Then Judah's leaders came to David and crowned him king over the tribe of Judah.

When David heard that the men of Jabesh-gilead had buried Saul, [5]he sent them this message: "May the LORD bless you for being so loyal to your king and giving him a decent burial. [6]May the LORD be loyal to you in return and reward you with his unfailing love! And I, too, will

1:18 Or *The Book of the Upright.*

reward you for what you have done. [7]And now that Saul is dead, I ask you to be my strong and loyal subjects like the people of Judah, who have anointed me as their new king."

[8]But Abner son of Ner, the commander of Saul's army, had already gone to Mahanaim with Saul's son Ishbosheth.* [9]There he proclaimed Ishbosheth king over Gilead, Jezreel, Ephraim, Benjamin, the land of the Ashurites, and all the rest of Israel. [10]Ishbosheth was forty years old when he became king, and he ruled from Mahanaim for two years. Meanwhile, the tribe of Judah remained loyal to David. [11]David made Hebron his capital, and he ruled as king of Judah for seven and a half years.

[12]One day Abner led some of Ishbosheth's troops from Mahanaim to Gibeon. [13]About the same time, Joab son of Zeruiah led David's troops from Hebron, and they met Abner at the pool of Gibeon. The two groups sat down there, facing each other from opposite sides of the pool. [14]Then Abner suggested to Joab, "Let's have a few of our warriors put on an exhibition of hand-to-hand combat."

"All right," Joab agreed. [15]So twelve men were chosen from each side to fight against each other. [16]Each one grabbed his opponent by the hair and thrust his sword into the other's side so that all of them died. The place has been known ever since as the Field of Swords.* [17]The two armies then began to fight each other, and by the end of the day Abner and the men of Israel had been defeated by the forces of David.

[18]Joab, Abishai, and Asahel, the three sons of Zeruiah, were among David's forces that day. Asahel could run like a deer, [19]and he began chasing Abner. He was relentless and single-minded in his pursuit. [20]When Abner looked back and saw him coming, he called out, "Is that you, Asahel?"

"Yes, it is," he replied.

[21]"Go fight someone else!" Abner warned. "Take on one of the younger men and strip him of his weapons." But Asahel refused and kept right on chasing Abner.

[22]Again Abner shouted to him, "Get away from here! I will never be able to face your brother Joab if I have to kill you!" [23]But Asahel would not give up, so Abner thrust the butt end of his spear through Asahel's stomach, and the spear came out through his back. He stumbled to the ground and died there. And everyone who came by that spot stopped and stood still when they saw Asahel lying there.

[24]When Joab and Abishai found out what had happened, they set out after Abner. The sun was just going down as they arrived at the hill of Ammah near Giah, along the road to the wilderness of Gibeon. [25]Abner's troops from the tribe of Benjamin regrouped there at the top of the hill to take a stand. [26]Abner shouted down to Joab, "Must we always solve our differences with swords? Don't you realize the only thing we will gain is bitterness toward each other? When will you call off your men from chasing their Israelite brothers?"

[27]Then Joab said, "God only knows what would have happened if you hadn't spoken, for we would have chased you all night if necessary." [28]So Joab blew his trumpet, and his men stopped chasing the troops of Israel.

[29]All that night Abner and his men retreated through the Jordan Valley.* They crossed the Jordan River, traveling all through the morning,* and they did not stop until they arrived at Mahanaim.

[30]Meanwhile, Joab and his men also returned home. When Joab counted his casualties, he discovered that only nineteen men were missing, in addition to Asahel. [31]But three hundred and sixty of Abner's men, all from the tribe of Benjamin, had been killed. [32]Joab and his men took Asahel's body to Bethlehem and buried him there beside his father. Then they traveled all night and reached Hebron at daybreak.

CHAPTER 3

That was the beginning of a long war between those who had been loyal to Saul and those who were loyal to David. As time passed David became stronger and stronger, while Saul's dynasty became weaker and weaker.

[2]These were the sons who were born to David in Hebron:

The oldest was Amnon, whose mother was Ahinoam of Jezreel.

[3] The second was Kileab, whose mother was Abigail, the widow of Nabal from Carmel.

2:8 Also known as *Eshbaal.*   **2:16** Hebrew *Helkath-hazzurim.*   **2:29a** Hebrew *the Arabah.*   **2:29b** Or *continued on through the Bithron.* The meaning of the Hebrew is uncertain.

The third was Absalom, whose mother was Maacah, the daughter of Talmai, king of Geshur.

⁴ The fourth was Adonijah, whose mother was Haggith.

The fifth was Shephatiah, whose mother was Abital.

⁵ The sixth was Ithream, whose mother was David's wife Eglah.

These sons were all born to David in Hebron.

⁶As the war went on, Abner became a powerful leader among those who were loyal to Saul's dynasty. ⁷One day Ishbosheth,* Saul's son, accused Abner of sleeping with one of his father's concubines, a woman named Rizpah. ⁸Abner became furious. "Am I a Judean dog to be kicked around like this?" he shouted. "After all I have done for you and your father by not betraying you to David, is this my reward—that you find fault with me about this woman? ⁹May God deal harshly with me if I don't help David get all that the LORD has promised him! ¹⁰I should just go ahead and give David the rest of Saul's kingdom. I should set him up as king over Israel as well as Judah, from Dan to Beersheba." ¹¹Ishbosheth didn't dare say another word because he was afraid of what Abner might do.

¹²Then Abner sent messengers to David, saying, "Let's make an agreement, and I will help turn the entire nation of Israel over to you."

¹³"All right," David replied, "but I will not negotiate with you unless you bring back my wife Michal, Saul's daughter, when you come."

¹⁴David then sent this message to Ishbosheth, Saul's son: "Give me back my wife Michal, for I bought her with the lives of one hundred Philistines." ¹⁵So Ishbosheth took Michal away from her husband Palti* son of Laish. ¹⁶Palti followed along behind her as far as Bahurim, weeping as he went. Then Abner told him, "Go back home!" So Palti returned.

¹⁷Meanwhile, Abner had consulted with the leaders of Israel. "For some time now," he told them, "you have wanted to make David your king. ¹⁸Now is the time! For the LORD has said, 'I have chosen David to save my people from the Philistines and from all

their other enemies.'" ¹⁹Abner also spoke with the leaders of the tribe of Benjamin. Then he went to Hebron to tell David that all the people of Israel and Benjamin supported him.

²⁰When Abner came to Hebron with his twenty men, David entertained them with a great feast. ²¹Then Abner said to David, "Let me go and call all the people of Israel to your side. They will make a covenant with you to make you their king. Then you will be able to rule over everything your heart desires." So David sent Abner safely on his way.

²²But just after Abner left, Joab and some of David's troops returned from a raid, bringing much plunder with them. ²³When Joab was told that Abner had just been there visiting the king and had been sent away in safety, ²⁴he rushed to see the king. "What have you done?" he demanded. "What do you mean by letting Abner get away? ²⁵You know perfectly well that he came to spy on you and to discover everything you are doing!"

²⁶Joab then left David and sent messengers to catch up with Abner. They found him at the pool of Sirah and brought him back with them. But David knew nothing about it. ²⁷When Abner arrived at Hebron, Joab took him aside at the gateway as if to speak with him privately. But then he drew his dagger and killed Abner in revenge for killing his brother Asahel.

²⁸When David heard about it, he declared, "I vow by the LORD that I and my people are innocent of this crime against Abner. ²⁹Joab and his family are the guilty ones. May his family in every generation be cursed with a man who has open sores or leprosy* or who walks on crutches* or who dies by the sword or who begs for food!"

³⁰So Joab and his brother Abishai killed Abner because Abner had killed their brother Asahel at the battle of Gibeon.

³¹Then David said to Joab and all those who were with him, "Tear your clothes and put on sackcloth. Go into deep mourning for Abner." And King David himself walked behind the procession to the grave. ³²They buried Abner in Hebron, and the king and all the people wept at his graveside. ³³Then the king sang this funeral song for Abner:

3:7 Also known as *Eshbaal*.   3:15 As in 1 Sam 25:44; Hebrew reads *Paltiel*, a variant name for Palti.   3:29a Or *or a contagious skin disease*. The Hebrew word used here can describe various skin diseases.   3:29b Or *who is effeminate*; Hebrew reads *who handles a spindle*.

"Should Abner have died as fools die?
³⁴ Your hands were not bound;
    your feet were not chained.
No, you were murdered—
    the victim of a wicked plot."

All the people wept again for Abner. ³⁵David had refused to eat anything the day of the funeral, and now everyone begged him to eat. But David had made a vow, saying, "May God kill me if I eat anything before sundown." ³⁶This pleased the people very much. In fact, everything the king did pleased them! ³⁷So everyone in Judah and Israel knew that David was not responsible for Abner's death.

³⁸Then King David said to the people, "Do you not realize that a great leader and a great man has fallen today in Israel? ³⁹And even though I am the anointed king, these two sons of Zeruiah—Joab and Abishai—are too strong for me to control. So may the LORD repay these wicked men for their wicked deeds."

CHAPTER 4

When Ishbosheth* heard about Abner's death at Hebron, he lost all courage, and his people were paralyzed with fear. ²Now there were two brothers, Baanah and Recab, who were captains of Ishbosheth's raiding parties. They were sons of Rimmon, a member of the tribe of Benjamin who lived in Beeroth. The town of Beeroth is now part of Benjamin's territory ³because the original people of Beeroth fled to Gittaim, where they still live as foreigners.

⁴(Saul's son Jonathan had a son named Mephibosheth,* who was crippled as a child. He was five years old when Saul and Jonathan were killed at the battle of Jezreel. When news of the battle reached the capital, the child's nurse grabbed him and fled. But she fell and dropped him as she was running, and he became crippled as a result.)

⁵One day Recab and Baanah, the sons of Rimmon from Beeroth, went to Ishbosheth's home around noon as he was taking a nap. ⁶The doorkeeper, who had been sifting wheat, became drowsy and fell asleep. So Recab and Baanah slipped past the doorkeeper, went into Ishbosheth's bedroom, and stabbed him in the stomach. Then they escaped. ⁷But before leaving, they cut off his head as he lay there on his bed. Taking his head with them, they fled across the Jordan Valley* through the night. ⁸They arrived at Hebron and presented Ishbosheth's head to David. "Look!" they exclaimed. "Here is the head of Ishbosheth, the son of your enemy Saul who tried to kill you. Today the LORD has given you revenge on Saul and his entire family!"

⁹But David said to Recab and Baanah, "As surely as the LORD lives, the one who saves me from my enemies, I will tell you the truth. ¹⁰Once before, someone told me, 'Saul is dead,' thinking he was bringing me good news. But I seized him and killed him at Ziklag. That's the reward I gave him for his news! ¹¹Now what reward should I give the wicked men who have killed an innocent man in his own house and on his own bed? Should I not also demand your very lives?" ¹²So David ordered his young men to kill them, and they did. They cut off their hands and feet and hung their bodies beside the pool in Hebron. Then they took Ishbosheth's head and buried it in Abner's tomb in Hebron.

4:1 Also known as *Eshbaal*. 4:4 Also known as *Meribbaal*. 4:7 Hebrew *the Arabah*.

MARCH 25   □ DAY 85
2 SAMUEL 5–7
David's Reign over a United Nation

OVERVIEW Initially, David's rule extends only over the tribe of Judah. But with the death of Ishbosheth, all Israel transfers her allegiance to David as the rightful ruler. After making Jerusalem his new capital, David wastes no time in bringing the Ark of God back from Kiriath-jearim where it had sat for years. Intent on building a beautiful house for God, David learns that God will build an eternal house for him instead: His throne, family, and kingdom will be established forever, and he will take his place among the great men of history.

Chapter 5	Chapter 6	Chapter 7	
Reuniting the Nation	Returning the Ark	A House for God Planned	A House for David Promised
David's Power	David's Passion	David's Plan	David's Praise

YOUR DAILY WALK The motto "Attempt great things for God, expect great things from God" would provide an apt summary of David's early years in office as king over the twelve tribes of Israel. He moved speedily to implement his godly convictions both politically and religiously, reversing the godless influences of his predecessor, Saul. And though God would not permit him to fulfill certain dreams (such as building the Temple), he never rebuked David for his motives or discouraged him from attempting other great enterprises for him.

One person with a dream is equal to ninety-nine who only have interests.

Building projects for God are costly. They demand vision . . . time . . . sacrifice . . . perseverance. The great Christian schools we enjoy today, the majestic churches whose pulpits are aflame with righteousness, the missionary organizations that touch millions of lives spiritually and physically—each began with a dream in the heart of a committed child of God.

Do you have a dream of how God might want to use you? . . . your family? . . . your church? . . . your skills? . . . your resources to impact your world for him? If not, allow God to implant a dream for his glory; then dream it, plan it, pursue it—and as God enables—achieve it!

INSIGHT Chronicling a Coronation
The account of David's coronation in 2 Samuel covers just three verses (5:1-3). For a fuller treatment of this very impressive ceremony, read 1 Chronicles 12:23-40, which describes the massive assembly of more than 340,000 troops for the gala event.

CHAPTER 5

Then all the tribes of Israel went to David at Hebron and told him, "We are all members of your family. ²For a long time, even while Saul was our king, you were the one who really led Israel. And the LORD has told you, 'You will be the shepherd of my people Israel. You will be their leader.'" ³So there at Hebron, David made a covenant with the leaders of Israel before the LORD. And they anointed him king of Israel.

⁴David was thirty years old when he began to reign, and he reigned forty years in all. ⁵He had reigned over Judah from Hebron for seven years and six months, and from Jerusalem he reigned over all Israel and Judah for thirty-three years.

⁶David then led his troops to Jerusalem to fight against the Jebusites. "You'll never get in here," the Jebusites taunted. "Even the blind and lame could keep you out!"

For the Jebusites thought they were safe. ⁷But David captured the fortress of Zion, now called the City of David.

⁸When the insulting message from the defenders of the city reached David, he told his own troops, "Go up through the water tunnel into the city and destroy those 'lame' and 'blind' Jebusites. How I hate them." That is the origin of the saying, "The blind and the lame may not enter the house."* ⁹So David made the fortress his home, and he called it the City of David. He built additional fortifications around the city, starting at the Millo* and working inward. ¹⁰And David became more and more powerful, because the LORD God Almighty was with him.

¹¹Then King Hiram of Tyre sent messengers to David, along with carpenters and stonemasons to build him a palace. Hiram also sent many cedar logs for lumber.

5:8 The meaning of this saying is uncertain.   5:9 Or *the supporting terraces.* The meaning of the Hebrew is uncertain.

¹²And David realized that the LORD had made him king over Israel and had made his kingdom great for the sake of his people Israel.

¹³After moving from Hebron to Jerusalem, David married more wives and concubines, and he had many sons and daughters. ¹⁴These are the names of David's sons who were born in Jerusalem: Shimea,* Shobab, Nathan, Solomon, ¹⁵Ibhar, Elishua, Nepheg, Japhia, ¹⁶Elishama, Eliada, and Eliphelet.

¹⁷When the Philistines heard that David had been anointed king of Israel, they mobilized all their forces to capture him. But David was told they were coming and went into the stronghold. ¹⁸The Philistines arrived and spread out across the valley of Rephaim. ¹⁹So David asked the LORD, "Should I go out to fight the Philistines? Will you hand them over to me?"

The LORD replied, "Yes, go ahead. I will certainly give you the victory."

²⁰So David went to Baal-perazim and defeated the Philistines there. "The LORD has done it!" David exclaimed. "He burst through my enemies like a raging flood!" So David named that place Baal-perazim (which means "the Lord who bursts through"). ²¹The Philistines had abandoned their idols there, so David and his troops confiscated them.

²²But after a while the Philistines returned and again spread out across the valley of Rephaim. ²³And once again David asked the LORD what to do. "Do not attack them straight on," the LORD replied. "Instead, circle around behind them and attack them near the balsam trees. ²⁴When you hear a sound like marching feet in the tops of the balsam trees, attack! That will be the signal that the LORD is moving ahead of you to strike down the Philistines." ²⁵So David did what the LORD commanded, and he struck down the Philistines all the way from Gibeon* to Gezer.

CHAPTER 6

Then David mobilized thirty thousand special troops. ²He led them to Baalah of Judah* to bring home the Ark of God, which bears the name of the LORD Almighty, who is enthroned between the cherubim. ³They placed the Ark of God on a new cart and brought it from the hillside home of Abinadab. Uzzah and Ahio, Abinadab's sons, were guiding the cart ⁴with the Ark of God on it, with Ahio walking in front. ⁵David and all the people of Israel were celebrating before the LORD with all their might, singing songs* and playing all kinds of musical instruments—lyres, harps, tambourines, castanets, and cymbals.

⁶But when they arrived at the threshing floor of Nacon, the oxen stumbled, and Uzzah put out his hand to steady the Ark of God. ⁷Then the LORD's anger blazed out against Uzzah for doing this, and God struck him dead beside the Ark of God. ⁸David was angry because the LORD's anger had blazed out against Uzzah. He named that place Perez-uzzah (which means "outbreak against Uzzah"). It is still called that today.

⁹David was now afraid of the LORD and asked, "How can I ever bring the Ark of the LORD back into my care?" ¹⁰So David decided not to move the Ark of the LORD into the City of David. He took it instead to the home of Obed-edom of Gath. ¹¹The Ark of the LORD remained there with the family of Obed-edom for three months, and the LORD blessed him and his entire household.

¹²Then King David was told, "The LORD has blessed Obed-edom's home and everything he has because of the Ark of God." So David went there and brought the Ark to the City of David with a great celebration. ¹³After the men who were carrying it had gone six steps, they stopped and waited so David could sacrifice an ox and a fattened calf. ¹⁴And David danced before the LORD with all his might, wearing a priestly tunic.* ¹⁵So David and all Israel brought up the Ark of the LORD with much shouting and blowing of trumpets.

¹⁶But as the Ark of the LORD entered the City of David, Michal, the daughter of Saul, looked down from her window. When she saw King David leaping and dancing before the LORD, she was filled with contempt for him.

¹⁷The Ark of the LORD was placed inside the special tent that David had prepared for it. And David sacrificed burnt offerings and peace offerings to the LORD. ¹⁸When he had finished, David blessed the people in

---

5:14 As in parallel text at 1 Chr 3:5; Hebrew reads *Shammua*, a variant name for Shimea.   **5:25** As in Greek version (see also 1 Chr 14:16); Hebrew reads *Geba*.   **6:2** *Baalah of Judah* is another name for Kiriath-jearim; compare 1 Chr 13:6.   **6:5** As in Greek version (see also 1 Chr 13:8); Hebrew reads *cypress trees*.   **6:14** Hebrew *a linen ephod*.

the name of the LORD Almighty. [19]Then he gave a gift of food to every man and woman in Israel: a loaf of bread, a cake of dates,* and a cake of raisins. Then everyone went home.

[20]When David returned home to bless his family, Michal came out to meet him and said in disgust, "How glorious the king of Israel looked today! He exposed himself to the servant girls like any indecent person might do!"

[21]David retorted to Michal, "I was dancing before the LORD, who chose me above your father and his family! He appointed me as the leader of Israel, the people of the LORD. So I am willing to act like a fool in order to show my joy in the LORD. [22]Yes, and I am willing to look even more foolish than this, but I will be held in honor by the girls of whom you have spoken!" [23]So Michal, the daughter of Saul, remained childless throughout her life.

CHAPTER 7

When the LORD had brought peace to the land and King David was settled in his palace, [2]David summoned Nathan the prophet. "Look!" David said. "Here I am living in this beautiful cedar palace, but the Ark of God is out in a tent!"

[3]Nathan replied, "Go ahead and do what you have in mind, for the LORD is with you."

[4]But that same night the LORD said to Nathan,

[5]"Go and tell my servant David, 'This is what the LORD says: Are you the one to build me a temple to live in? [6]I have never lived in a temple, from the day I brought the Israelites out of Egypt until now. My home has always been a tent, moving from one place to another. [7]And I have never once complained to Israel's leaders, the shepherds of my people Israel. I have never asked them, "Why haven't you built me a beautiful cedar temple?"'

[8]"Now go and say to my servant David, 'This is what the LORD Almighty says: I chose you to lead my people Israel when you were just a shepherd boy, tending your sheep out in the pasture. [9]I have been with you wherever you have gone, and I have destroyed all your enemies. Now I will make your name famous throughout the earth!

[10]And I have provided a permanent homeland for my people Israel, a secure place where they will never be disturbed. It will be their own land where wicked nations won't oppress them as they did in the past, [11]from the time I appointed judges to rule my people. And I will keep you safe from all your enemies.

"'And now the LORD declares that he will build a house for you—a dynasty of kings! [12]For when you die, I will raise up one of your descendants, and I will make his kingdom strong. [13]He is the one who will build a house—a temple—for my name. And I will establish the throne of his kingdom forever. [14]I will be his father, and he will be my son. If he sins, I will use other nations to punish him. [15]But my unfailing love will not be taken from him as I took it from Saul, whom I removed before you. [16]Your dynasty and your kingdom will continue for all time before me, and your throne will be secure forever.'"

[17]So Nathan went back to David and told him everything the LORD had said.

[18]Then King David went in and sat before the LORD and prayed, "Who am I, O Sovereign LORD, and what is my family, that you have brought me this far? [19]And now, Sovereign LORD, in addition to everything else, you speak of giving me a lasting dynasty! Do you deal with everyone this way,* O Sovereign LORD? [20]What more can I say? You know what I am really like, Sovereign LORD. [21]For the sake of your promise and according to your will, you have done all these great things and have shown them to me.

[22]"How great you are, O Sovereign LORD! There is no one like you—there is no other God. We have never even heard of another god like you! [23]What other nation on earth is like Israel? What other nation, O God, have you redeemed from slavery to be your own people? You made a great name for yourself when you rescued your people from Egypt. You performed awesome miracles and drove out the nations and gods that stood in their way. [24]You made Israel your people forever, and you, O LORD, became their God.

[25]"And now, O LORD God, do as you have promised concerning me and my family. Confirm it as a promise that will last

---

6:19 Or *a portion of meat.* The meaning of the Hebrew is uncertain. 7:19 The meaning of the Hebrew is uncertain.

forever. ²⁶And may your name be honored forever so that all the world will say, 'The LORD Almighty is God over Israel!' And may the dynasty of your servant David be established in your presence.

²⁷"O LORD Almighty, God of Israel, I have been bold enough to pray this prayer because you have revealed that you will build a house for me—an eternal dynasty! ²⁸For you are God, O Sovereign LORD. Your words are truth, and you have promised these good things to me, your servant. ²⁹And now, may it please you to bless me and my family so that our dynasty may continue forever before you. For when you grant a blessing to your servant, O Sovereign LORD, it is an eternal blessing!"

MARCH 26 ☐ DAY 86
2 SAMUEL 8–10
David's Growing Kingdom

OVERVIEW Once the internal security of the nation has been restored, David begins the task of securing and enlarging its borders. The Philistines, Moabites, and Arameans fall in quick succession before Israel's mighty army. But in spite of David's many military conquests, his tenderness and compassion are evident in his invitation to Mephibosheth, crippled son of Jonathan, to live in the king's palace. When the Ammonites question another of David's acts of kindness, he teaches them a stern lesson in respect.

Chapter 8	Chapter 9	Chapter 10
David Expands the Kingdom	David Expresses His Kindness	David Extends His Justice
Moab	Mephibosheth	Ammon

YOUR DAILY WALK When was the last time you
- visited a shut-in?
- cooked a meal for someone outside your family?
- offered to take an elderly person shopping?
- did something for someone who couldn't repay you?

To feel sorry for the needy is not the mark of a Christian—to help them is.

King David demonstrated great depth of character when he showed mercy to Jonathan's crippled son. Kings seldom concerned themselves with the welfare of the disadvantaged, and the heirs of former monarchs were usually killed, not comforted. But out of a heart of compassion and because he had made a covenant with Jonathan, David took the unprecedented step of making Mephibosheth an adopted member of his family. With no thought of repayment or publicity, David acted in faithfulness to his friend by caring for Mephibosheth.

Where has God brought a Mephibosheth across your path? You may not find it very convenient . . . or glamorous . . . or financially rewarding to help that person. But remember, "I assure you, when you did it to one of the least of these my brothers and sisters," Jesus said, "you were doing it to me" (Matthew 25:40).

INSIGHT Flaunting the Kindness of the King
Compare the response of Mephibosheth (9:8) with that of the Ammonites (10:1-4) when each was extended King David's kindness. Mephibosheth was humbly grateful and dwelt in the palace, but the Ammonites remained proudly arrogant and died on the battlefield.

CHAPTER 8
After this, David subdued and humbled the Philistines by conquering Gath, their largest city.* ²David also conquered the land of Moab. He made the people lie down on the ground in a row, and he measured them off in groups with a length of rope. He measured off two groups to be executed for every one group to be spared. The Moabites who were spared became David's servants and brought him tribute money.

³David also destroyed the forces of Hadadezer son of Rehob, king of Zobah, when Hadadezer marched out to strengthen his control along the Euphrates River. ⁴David captured seventeen hundred charioteers* and twenty thousand foot soldiers. Then he crippled all but one hundred of the chariot horses.

⁵When Arameans from Damascus arrived to help Hadadezer, David killed twenty-two thousand of them. ⁶Then he placed several army garrisons in Damascus, the Aramean capital, and the Arameans became David's subjects and brought him tribute money. So the LORD gave David victory wherever he went. ⁷David brought the gold shields of Hadadezer's officers to Jerusalem, ⁸along with a large amount of bronze from Hadadezer's cities of Tebah* and Berothai.

⁹When King Toi of Hamath heard that David had destroyed the army of Hadadezer, ¹⁰he sent his son Joram to congratulate David on his success. Hadadezer and Toi had long been enemies, and there had been many wars between them. Joram presented David with many gifts of silver, gold, and bronze. ¹¹King David dedicated all these gifts to the LORD, along with the silver and gold he had set apart from the other nations he had subdued—¹²Edom,* Moab, Ammon, Philistia, and Amalek—and from Hadadezer son of Rehob, king of Zobah.

¹³So David became very famous. After his return he destroyed eighteen thousand Edomites* in the Valley of Salt. ¹⁴He placed army garrisons throughout Edom, and all the Edomites became David's subjects.

This was another example of how the LORD made David victorious wherever he went.

¹⁵David reigned over all Israel and was fair to everyone. ¹⁶Joab son of Zeruiah was commander of the army. Jehoshaphat son of Ahilud was the royal historian. ¹⁷Zadok son of Ahitub and Ahimelech son of Abiathar were the priests. Seraiah was the court secretary. ¹⁸Benaiah son of Jehoiada was captain of the king's bodyguard.* David's sons served as priestly leaders.*

CHAPTER 9
One day David began wondering if anyone in Saul's family was still alive, for he had promised Jonathan that he would show kindness to them. ²He summoned a man named Ziba, who had been one of Saul's servants. "Are you Ziba?" the king asked.

"Yes sir, I am," Ziba replied.

³The king then asked him, "Is anyone still alive from Saul's family? If so, I want to show God's kindness to them in any way I can."

Ziba replied, "Yes, one of Jonathan's sons is still alive, but he is crippled."

⁴"Where is he?" the king asked.

"In Lo-debar," Ziba told him, "at the home of Makir son of Ammiel." ⁵So David sent for him and brought him from Makir's home. ⁶His name was Mephibosheth*; he was Jonathan's son and Saul's grandson. When he came to David, he bowed low in great fear and said, "I am your servant."

⁷But David said, "Don't be afraid! I've asked you to come so that I can be kind to you because of my vow to your father, Jonathan. I will give you all the land that once belonged to your grandfather Saul, and you may live here with me at the palace!"

⁸Mephibosheth fell to the ground before the king. "Should the king show such kindness to a dead dog like me?" he exclaimed.

⁹Then the king summoned Saul's servant Ziba and said, "I have given your master's grandson everything that belonged to Saul and his family. ¹⁰You and your sons and servants are to farm the land for him to produce food for his family. But Mephibosheth will live here at the palace with me."

Ziba, who had fifteen sons and twenty

8:1 Hebrew *by conquering Metheg-ammah*, a name which means "the bridle," possibly referring to the size of the city or the tribute money taken from it. Compare 1 Chr 18:1.   8:4 Greek version reads *1,000 chariots and 7,000 charioteers*; compare 1 Chr 18:4.   8:8 As in some Greek manuscripts (see also 1 Chr 18:8); Hebrew reads *Betah*.   8:12 As in a few Hebrew manuscripts and Greek and Syriac versions (see also 8:14; 1 Chr 18:11); most Hebrew manuscripts read *Aram*.   8:13 As in a few Hebrew manuscripts and Greek and Syriac versions (see also 8:14; 1 Chr 18:12); most Hebrew manuscripts read *Arameans*.   8:18a Hebrew *of the Kerethites and Pelethites*.   8:18b Hebrew *David's sons were priests*; compare parallel text at 1 Chr 18:17.   9:6 Also known as *Meribbaal*.

servants, replied, [11]"Yes, my lord; I will do all that you have commanded." And from that time on, Mephibosheth ate regularly with David, as though he were one of his own sons. [12]Mephibosheth had a young son named Mica. And from then on, all the members of Ziba's household were Mephibosheth's servants. [13]And Mephibosheth, who was crippled in both feet, moved to Jerusalem to live at the palace.

CHAPTER 10

Some time after this, King Nahash of the Ammonites died, and his son Hanun became king. [2]David said, "I am going to show complete loyalty to Hanun because his father, Nahash, was always completely loyal to me." So David sent ambassadors to express sympathy to Hanun about his father's death.

But when David's ambassadors arrived in the land of Ammon, [3]Hanun's advisers said to their master, "Do you really think these men are coming here to honor your father? No! David has sent them to spy out the city so that they can come in and conquer it!" [4]So Hanun seized David's ambassadors and shaved off half of each man's beard, cut off their robes at the buttocks, and sent them back to David in shame. [5]When David heard what had happened, he sent messengers to tell the men to stay at Jericho until their beards grew out, for they were very embarrassed by their appearance.

[6]Now the people of Ammon realized how seriously they had angered David, so they hired twenty thousand Aramean mercenaries from the lands of Beth-rehob and Zobah, one thousand from the king of Maacah, and twelve thousand from the land of Tob. [7]When David heard about this, he sent Joab and the entire Israelite army to fight them. [8]The Ammonite troops drew up their battle lines at the entrance of the city gates, while the Arameans from Zobah and Rehob and the men from Tob and Maacah positioned themselves to fight in the open fields.

[9]When Joab saw that he would have to fight on two fronts, he chose the best troops in his army. He placed them under his personal command and led them out to fight the Arameans in the fields. [10]He left the rest of the army under the command of his brother Abishai, who was to attack the Ammonites. [11]"If the Arameans are too strong for me, then come over and help me," Joab told his brother. "And if the Ammonites are too strong for you, I will come and help you. [12]Be courageous! Let us fight bravely to save our people and the cities of our God. May the LORD's will be done."

[13]When Joab and his troops attacked, the Arameans began to run away. [14]And when the Ammonites saw the Arameans running, they ran from Abishai and retreated into the city. After the battle was over, Joab returned to Jerusalem.

[15]The Arameans now realized that they were no match for Israel. So when they regrouped, [16]they were joined by additional Aramean troops summoned by Hadadezer from the other side of the Euphrates River.* These troops arrived at Helam under the command of Shobach, the commander of all Hadadezer's forces. [17]When David heard what was happening, he mobilized all Israel, crossed the Jordan River, and led the army to Helam. The Arameans positioned themselves there in battle formation and then attacked David. [18]But again the Arameans fled from the Israelites. This time David's forces killed seven hundred charioteers and forty thousand horsemen,* including Shobach, the commander of their army. [19]When Hadadezer and his Aramean allies realized they had been defeated by Israel, they surrendered to them and became their subjects. After that, the Arameans were afraid to help the Ammonites.

10:16 Hebrew *the river.*   10:18 Some Greek manuscripts read *foot soldiers;* compare parallel text at 1 Chr 19:18.

MARCH 27 ☐ DAY 87
2 SAMUEL 11–14
David's Tragic Downfall

OVERVIEW Today's section marks a tragic turning point in David's life. While idling in the palace instead of fighting on the battlefield, David yields to temptation and commits adultery with Bathsheba—an act the king then attempts to hide with lies, deceit, and eventually murder. Though David's sin is grave, his response to the uncovering of that sin is exemplary: "I have sinned against the LORD" (12:13). Forgiveness and restoration follow, but there can be no reversing the ugly consequences of David's act: death for the unnamed infant and open revolt in David's household and nation.

Chapter 11	Chapter 12	Chapters 13–14
David's Wrongdoing	Nathan's Rebuke	David's Regret
A Palace Corrupted		A Family Divided

One test of a person's strength is that person's knowledge of his or her weakness.

YOUR DAILY WALK Take a sheet of paper and write on it: "Things That Could Never Happen to Me." Then make a list of at least five moral, spiritual, and financial disasters that you feel certain could never happen to you: bankruptcy, divorce, prodigal children, nervous break-down, etc.

David's reign was marked by material wealth, military success, social prestige, and the promise of future prosperity. From all outward appearances, things couldn't have been better for the king and his magnificent kingdom.

But in David's heart, a steady erosion was taking place in his ability to withstand temptation—a spiritual slide away from God prompted by an undisciplined life of passion, polygamy, and idle pleasure. When the moment of temptation came, David had no power to resist, and the rest is history.

Where is erosion taking place in your spiritual life? Where are you setting yourself up for future heartache by ignoring danger signs in the present? Look again at your list of "impossible disasters," and scratch out the word *never* in the title. Tragedy could happen to you, just as it did to David, if you take your eyes off the Lord.

INSIGHT Heavy, Heavy Hangs over Your Head
A "hand on the head" (13:19; compare Jeremiah 2:37) was the sign that terrible calamity had befallen the victim and that the hand of God was against him or her—a heavy burden indeed!

CHAPTER 11
The following spring, the time of year when kings go to war, David sent Joab and the Israelite army to destroy the Ammonites. In the process they laid siege to the city of Rabbah. But David stayed behind in Jerusalem.

²Late one afternoon David got out of bed after taking a nap and went for a stroll on the roof of the palace. As he looked out over the city, he noticed a woman of un-usual beauty taking a bath. ³He sent someone to find out who she was, and he was told, "She is Bathsheba, the daughter of Eliam and the wife of Uriah the Hittite." ⁴Then David sent for her; and when she came to the palace, he slept with her. (She had just completed the purification rites after having her menstrual period.) Then she returned home. ⁵Later, when Bathsheba discovered that she was pregnant, she sent a message to inform David.

⁶So David sent word to Joab: "Send me Uriah the Hittite." ⁷When Uriah arrived, David asked him how Joab and the army were getting along and how the war was progressing. ⁸Then he told Uriah, "Go on home and relax." David even sent a gift to Uriah after he had left the palace. ⁹But Uriah wouldn't go home. He stayed that night at the palace entrance with some of the king's other servants.

¹⁰When David heard what Uriah had done, he summoned him and asked, "What's the matter with you? Why didn't you go home last night after being away for so long?"

¹¹Uriah replied, "The Ark and the armies of Israel and Judah are living in tents,* and Joab and his officers are camping in the open fields. How could I go home to wine and dine and sleep with my wife? I swear that I will never be guilty of acting like that."

¹²"Well, stay here tonight," David told him, "and tomorrow you may return to the army." So Uriah stayed in Jerusalem that day and the next. ¹³Then David invited him to dinner and got him drunk. But even then he couldn't get Uriah to go home to his wife. Again he slept at the palace entrance.

¹⁴So the next morning David wrote a letter to Joab and gave it to Uriah to deliver. ¹⁵The letter instructed Joab, "Station Uriah on the front lines where the battle is fiercest. Then pull back so that he will be killed." ¹⁶So Joab assigned Uriah to a spot close to the city wall where he knew the enemy's strongest men were fighting. ¹⁷And Uriah was killed along with several other Israelite soldiers.

¹⁸Then Joab sent a battle report to David. ¹⁹He told his messenger, "Report all the news of the battle to the king. ²⁰But he might get angry and ask, 'Why did the troops go so close to the city? Didn't they know there would be shooting from the walls? ²¹Wasn't Gideon's son Abimelech killed* at Thebez by a woman who threw a millstone down on him?' Then tell him, 'Uriah the Hittite was killed, too.'"

²²So the messenger went to Jerusalem and gave a complete report to David. ²³"The enemy came out against us," he said. "And as we chased them back to the city gates, ²⁴the archers on the wall shot arrows at us. Some of our men were killed, including Uriah the Hittite."

²⁵"Well, tell Joab not to be discouraged," David said. "The sword kills one as well as another! Fight harder next time, and conquer the city!"

²⁶When Bathsheba heard that her husband was dead, she mourned for him. ²⁷When the period of mourning was over, David sent for her and brought her to the palace, and she became one of his wives. Then she gave birth to a son. But the LORD was very displeased with what David had done.

CHAPTER 12

So the LORD sent Nathan the prophet to tell David this story: "There were two men in a certain town. One was rich, and one was poor. ²The rich man owned many sheep and cattle. ³The poor man owned nothing but a little lamb he had worked hard to buy. He raised that little lamb, and it grew up with his children. It ate from the man's own plate and drank from his cup. He cuddled it in his arms like a baby daughter. ⁴One day a guest arrived at the home of the rich man. But instead of killing a lamb from his own flocks for food, he took the poor man's lamb and killed it and served it to his guest."

⁵David was furious. "As surely as the LORD lives," he vowed, "any man who would do such a thing deserves to die! ⁶He must repay four lambs to the poor man for the one he stole and for having no pity."

⁷Then Nathan said to David, "You are that man! The LORD, the God of Israel, says, 'I anointed you king of Israel and saved you from the power of Saul. ⁸I gave you his house and his wives and the kingdoms of Israel and Judah. And if that had not been enough, I would have given you much, much more. ⁹Why, then, have you despised the word of the LORD and done this horrible deed? For you have murdered Uriah and stolen his wife. ¹⁰From this time on, the sword will be a constant threat to your family, because you have despised me by taking Uriah's wife to be your own.

¹¹"Because of what you have done, I, the LORD, will cause your own household to rebel against you. I will give your wives to another man, and he will go to bed with them in public view. ¹²You did it secretly,

but I will do this to you openly in the sight of all Israel.'"

[13]Then David confessed to Nathan, "I have sinned against the LORD."

Nathan replied, "Yes, but the LORD has forgiven you, and you won't die for this sin. [14]But you have given the enemies of the LORD great opportunity to despise and blaspheme him, so your child will die."

[15]After Nathan returned to his home, the LORD made Bathsheba's baby deathly ill. [16]David begged God to spare the child. He went without food and lay all night on the bare ground. [17]The leaders of the nation pleaded with him to get up and eat with them, but he refused. [18]Then on the seventh day the baby died. David's advisers were afraid to tell him. "He was so broken up about the baby being sick," they said. "What will he do to himself when we tell him the child is dead?"

[19]But when David saw them whispering, he realized what had happened. "Is the baby dead?" he asked.

"Yes," they replied. [20]Then David got up from the ground, washed himself, put on lotions, and changed his clothes. Then he went to the Tabernacle and worshiped the LORD. After that, he returned to the palace and ate. [21]His advisers were amazed. "We don't understand you," they told him. "While the baby was still living, you wept and refused to eat. But now that the baby is dead, you have stopped your mourning and are eating again."

[22]David replied, "I fasted and wept while the child was alive, for I said, 'Perhaps the LORD will be gracious to me and let the child live.' [23]But why should I fast when he is dead? Can I bring him back again? I will go to him one day, but he cannot return to me."

[24]Then David comforted Bathsheba, his wife, and slept with her. She became pregnant and gave birth to a son, and they named him Solomon. The LORD loved the child [25]and sent word through Nathan the prophet that his name should be Jedidiah—"beloved of the LORD"—because the LORD loved him.

[26]Meanwhile, Joab and the Israelite army were successfully ending their siege of Rabbah, the capital of Ammon. [27]Joab sent messengers to tell David, "I have fought against Rabbah and captured its water supply.* [28]Now bring the rest of the army and finish the job, so you will get credit for the victory instead of me."

[29]So David led the rest of his army to Rabbah and captured it. [30]David removed the crown from the king's head,* and it was placed on David's own head. The crown was made of gold and set with gems, and it weighed about seventy-five pounds.* David took a vast amount of plunder from the city. [31]He also made slaves of the people of Rabbah and forced them to labor with saws, picks, and axes, and to work in the brick kilns. That is how he dealt with the people of all the Ammonite cities. Then David and his army returned to Jerusalem.

C H A P T E R 1 3

David's son Absalom had a beautiful sister named Tamar. And Amnon, her half brother, fell desperately in love with her. [2]Amnon became so obsessed with Tamar that he became ill. She was a virgin, and it seemed impossible that he could ever fulfill his love for her.

[3]Now Amnon had a very crafty friend— his cousin Jonadab. He was the son of David's brother Shimea.* [4]One day Jonadab said to Amnon, "What's the trouble? Why should the son of a king look so dejected morning after morning?"

So Amnon told him, "I am in love with Tamar, Absalom's sister."

[5]"Well," Jonadab said, "I'll tell you what to do. Go back to bed and pretend you are sick. When your father comes to see you, ask him to let Tamar come and prepare some food for you. Tell him you'll feel better if she feeds you."

[6]So Amnon pretended to be sick. And when the king came to see him, Amnon asked him, "Please let Tamar come to take care of me and cook something for me to eat." [7]So David agreed and sent Tamar to Amnon's house to prepare some food for him.

[8]When Tamar arrived at Amnon's house, she went to the room where he was lying down so he could watch her mix some dough. Then she baked some special bread for him. [9]But when she set the serving tray before him, he refused to eat. "Everyone get out of here," Amnon told his servants.

12:27 Or *captured the city of water.* **12:30a** Greek version reads *removed the crown of Milcom;* compare 1 Kgs 11:5. Milcom, also called Molech, was the god of the Ammonites. **12:30b** Hebrew *1 talent* [34 kilograms]. **13:3** Hebrew *Shimeah* (also in 13:32), a variant name for Shimea; compare 1 Chr 2:13.

So they all left. ¹⁰Then he said to Tamar, "Now bring the food into my bedroom and feed it to me here." So Tamar took it to him. ¹¹But as she was feeding him, he grabbed her and demanded, "Come to bed with me, my darling sister."

¹²"No, my brother!" she cried. "Don't be foolish! Don't do this to me! You know what a serious crime it is to do such a thing in Israel. ¹³Where could I go in my shame? And you would be called one of the greatest fools in Israel. Please, just speak to the king about it, and he will let you marry me."

¹⁴But Amnon wouldn't listen to her, and since he was stronger than she was, he raped her. ¹⁵Then suddenly Amnon's love turned to hate, and he hated her even more than he had loved her. "Get out of here!" he snarled at her.

¹⁶"No, no!" Tamar cried. "To reject me now is a greater wrong than what you have already done to me."

But Amnon wouldn't listen to her. ¹⁷He shouted for his servant and demanded, "Throw this woman out, and lock the door behind her!"

¹⁸So the servant put her out. She was wearing a long, beautiful robe,* as was the custom in those days for the king's virgin daughters. ¹⁹But now Tamar tore her robe and put ashes on her head. And then, with her face in her hands, she went away crying.

²⁰Her brother Absalom saw her and asked, "Is it true that Amnon has been with you? Well, don't be so upset. Since he's your brother anyway, don't worry about it." So Tamar lived as a desolate woman in Absalom's house. ²¹When King David heard what had happened, he was very angry. ²²And though Absalom never spoke to Amnon about it, he hated Amnon deeply because of what he had done to his sister.

²³Two years later, when Absalom's sheep were being sheared at Baal-hazor near Ephraim, Absalom invited all the king's sons to come to a feast. ²⁴He went to the king and said, "My sheep-shearers are now at work. Would the king and his servants please come to celebrate the occasion with me?"

²⁵The king replied, "No, my son. If we all came, we would be too much of a burden on you." Absalom pressed him, but the king wouldn't come, though he sent his thanks.

²⁶"Well, then," Absalom said, "if you can't come, how about sending my brother Amnon instead?"

"Why Amnon?" the king asked. ²⁷But Absalom kept on pressing the king until he finally agreed to let all his sons attend, including Amnon.

²⁸Absalom told his men, "Wait until Amnon gets drunk; then at my signal, kill him! Don't be afraid. I'm the one who has given the command. Take courage and do it!" ²⁹So at Absalom's signal they murdered Amnon. Then the other sons of the king jumped on their mules and fled.

³⁰As they were on the way back to Jerusalem, this report reached David: "Absalom has killed all your sons; not one is left alive!" ³¹The king jumped up, tore his robe, and fell prostrate on the ground. His advisers also tore their clothes in horror and sorrow.

³²But just then Jonadab, the son of David's brother Shimea, arrived and said, "No, not all your sons have been killed! It was only Amnon! Absalom has been plotting this ever since Amnon raped his sister Tamar. ³³No, your sons aren't all dead! It was only Amnon." ³⁴Meanwhile Absalom escaped.

Then the watchman on the Jerusalem wall saw a great crowd coming toward the city from the west. He ran to tell the king, "I see a crowd of people coming from the Horonaim road* along the side of the hill."

³⁵"Look!" Jonadab told the king. "There they are now! Your sons are coming, just as I said." ³⁶They soon arrived, weeping and sobbing, and the king and his officials wept bitterly with them. ³⁷And David mourned many days for his son Amnon.

Absalom fled to his grandfather, Talmai son of Ammihud, the king of Geshur. ³⁸He stayed there in Geshur for three years. ³⁹And David, now reconciled to Amnon's death, longed to be reunited with his son Absalom.*

CHAPTER 14

Joab realized how much the king longed to see Absalom. ²So he sent for a woman from Tekoa who had a reputation for great wisdom. He said to her, "Pretend you are in mourning; wear mourning clothes and don't bathe or wear any perfume. Act like a woman who has been in deep sorrow for

---

13:18 Or *a robe with sleeves,* or *an ornamented robe.* The meaning of the Hebrew is uncertain.   **13:34** As in Greek version; Hebrew reads *from the road behind him.*   **13:39** Or *no longer felt a need to go out after Absalom.*

a long time. ³Then go to the king and tell him the story I am about to tell you." Then Joab told her what to say.

⁴When the woman approached the king, she fell with her face down to the floor in front of him and cried out, "O king! Help me!"

⁵"What's the trouble?" the king asked.

"I am a widow," she replied. ⁶"My two sons had a fight out in the field. And since no one was there to stop it, one of them was killed. ⁷Now the rest of the family is demanding, 'Let us have your son. We will execute him for murdering his brother. He doesn't deserve to inherit his family's property.' But if I do that, I will have no one left, and my husband's name and family will disappear from the face of the earth."

⁸"Leave it to me," the king told her. "Go home, and I'll see to it that no one touches him."

⁹"Oh, thank you, my lord," she replied. "And I'll take the responsibility if you are criticized for helping me like this."

¹⁰"Don't worry about that!" the king said. "If anyone objects, bring them to me. I can assure you they will never complain again!"

¹¹Then she said, "Please swear to me by the LORD your God that you won't let anyone take vengeance against my son. I want no more bloodshed."

"As surely as the LORD lives," he replied, "not a hair on your son's head will be disturbed!"

¹²"Please let me ask one more thing of you!" she said.

"Go ahead," he urged. "Speak!"

¹³She replied, "Why don't you do as much for all the people of God as you have promised to do for me? You have convicted yourself in making this decision, because you have refused to bring home your own banished son. ¹⁴All of us must die eventually. Our lives are like water spilled out on the ground, which cannot be gathered up again. That is why God tries to bring us back when we have been separated from him. He does not sweep away the lives of those he cares about—and neither should you!

¹⁵"But I have come to plead with you for my son because my life and my son's life have been threatened. I said to myself, 'Perhaps the king will listen to me ¹⁶and rescue us from those who would cut us off from

God's people. ¹⁷Yes, the king will give us peace of mind again.' I know that you are like an angel of God and can discern good from evil. May the LORD your God be with you."

¹⁸"I want to know one thing," the king replied.

"Yes, my lord?" she asked.

¹⁹"Did Joab send you here?"

And the woman replied, "My lord the king, how can I deny it? Nobody can hide anything from you. Yes, Joab sent me and told me what to say. ²⁰He did it to place the matter before you in a different light. But you are as wise as an angel of God, and you understand everything that happens among us!"

²¹So the king sent for Joab and told him, "All right, go and bring back the young man Absalom."

²²Joab fell to the ground before the king and blessed him and said, "At last I know that I have gained your approval, for you have granted me this request!"

²³Then Joab went to Geshur and brought Absalom back to Jerusalem. ²⁴But the king gave this order: "Absalom may go to his own house, but he must never come into my presence." So Absalom did not see the king.

²⁵Now no one in Israel was as handsome as Absalom. From head to foot, he was the perfect specimen of a man. ²⁶He cut his hair only once a year, and then only because it was too heavy to carry around. When he weighed it out, it came to five pounds!* ²⁷He had three sons and one daughter. His daughter's name was Tamar, and she was very beautiful.

²⁸Absalom lived in Jerusalem for two years without getting to see the king. ²⁹Then Absalom sent for Joab to ask him to intercede for him, but Joab refused to come. Absalom sent for him a second time, but again Joab refused to come. ³⁰So Absalom said to his servants, "Go and set fire to Joab's barley field, the field next to mine." So they set his field on fire, as Absalom had commanded.

³¹Then Joab came to Absalom and demanded, "Why did your servants set my field on fire?"

³²And Absalom replied, "Because I wanted you to ask the king why he brought me back from Geshur if he didn't intend to

14:26 Hebrew *200 shekels* [2.3 kilograms] *by the royal standard.*

see me. I might as well have stayed there. Let me see the king; if he finds me guilty of anything, then let him execute me." ³³So Joab told the king what Absalom had said. Then at last David summoned his estranged son, and Absalom came and bowed low before the king, and David kissed him.

MARCH 28 ☐ DAY 88
Learning to WOTL

LOOK BACK Here is a hint to help you keep track of 1 and 2 Samuel and 1 and 2 Kings:
- 1 Samuel describes the life of Samuel and the first king he anointed (Saul).
- 2 Samuel describes the life of the second king Samuel anointed (David).
- 1 Kings describes the life of the last king to rule over one kingdom (Solomon).
- 2 Kings describes the demise of two kingdoms (Israel and Judah).

LOOK UP Have you learned how to WOTL yet?

No, we're not talking about how to waddle like a duck but rather how to **W**ait **O**n **T**he **L**ord, like the young shepherd boy David did. The youngest of eight brothers, entrusted with the unenviable "chore" of tending the family's flocks, David could have viewed his job as monotonous and his future as bleak. Instead, he looked for and found constructive ways to pass the time while tending the sheep.

There are times when God asks nothing of his children except silence, patience, and tears.

Notice the way this young shepherd is described in 1 Samuel 16:18. He had earned a remarkable reputation in the obscurity of the sheepfold:
- "a talented harp player"; he was an accomplished musician who practiced long hours, though his only audience consisted of sheep and stars.
- "[a] brave and strong [young man]"; he taught bears and lions not to fool with his flock.
- "a fine-looking young man"; he lived in the bush but didn't look like one.
- "the LORD is with him"; God's blessing upon his life was evident to all.

LOOK AHEAD It's not much fun tending sheep. The hours are long, the task demanding, the pay disappointing—and the sheep almost never say *thaaaaaaanks*.

But it's remarkable how many people take on the challenge nonetheless: teachers, their students; parents, their infant children; ministers, their congregations. They understand the importance of a long-term perspective, the need for patience and determination if a harvest is ever to be realized in the next generation.

David saw each day as an opportunity to develop his walk with God. He composed songs, practiced his lyre and sling, defended his flock against all predators, and sought to develop himself in body, soul, and spirit. Twice presented with a tempting opportunity to cut short the wait, David chose to WOTL rather than lift his hand against King Saul. Write *WOTL* on a three-by-five-inch card, and place it where you're likely to see it often today (such as next to the telephone or refrigerator). Let it remind you that you're never *late* when you *wait* on the Lord!

MARCH 29 ☐ DAY 89
2 SAMUEL 15–18
Absalom's Quest to Rule

OVERVIEW Absalom, David's handsome but undisciplined son, initiates a plot to take away the reins of leadership from his father. True to Nathan's prophecy (12:11-12), Absalom first sows seeds of discontent in Israel, then leads an invasion against Jerusalem that forces David to flee for his life. The nation temporarily sides with Absalom until his humiliating death, while hanging from an oak tree, cuts short his brief revolt. Though David wins the battle, he loses a son, leaving him a broken parent who has paid a staggering price for lax discipline.

Chapter 15	Chapter 16	Chapter 17	Chapter 18
Absalom's Conspiracy	Shimei's Curse	Ahithophel's Counsel	Joab's Cruelty
Starting a Rebellion		Stopping a Rebellion	

The alternative to discipline is disaster.

YOUR DAILY WALK "This is going to hurt me more than it hurts you" is probably one of the most "unbelievable" things a parent can say to a child—at least from the child's perspective! Though the parent's words are sincere, the child finds them hard to believe since it isn't Mom or Dad who feels the sting of the paddle.

Discipline, regardless of the form it takes, is never pleasant for the moment (Hebrews 12:11). But it is necessary in order to ensure that both parent and child aren't hurt even more in the future when they begin to reap the consequences of a lack of discipline.

King David, preoccupied with his royal duties, allowed his wayward son to continue in disobedience. Had David attempted to curb Absalom's rebellion, it would have been painful to be sure—but not nearly as painful as the grief David experienced when his son died a rebel. Do you see discipline as a pain to be avoided or as a means of avoiding pain? In the margin, write down three reasons why children need to be disciplined in love. If you're a parent, learn from David's sad example. If you're not a parent, pass along your insights to someone who can use them!

INSIGHT The High Cost of High-Mindedness
Absalom was noted for being a fine physical specimen who gloried in his phenomenal head of hair, from which seven pounds were trimmed annually. Ironically, it was his ego that led him astray (14:25-26) and his hair that trapped him and led to his death.

CHAPTER 15
After this, Absalom bought a chariot and horses, and he hired fifty footmen to run ahead of him. ²He got up early every morning and went out to the gate of the city. When people brought a case to the king for judgment, Absalom would ask where they were from, and they would tell him their tribe. ³Then Absalom would say, "You've really got a strong case here! It's too bad the king doesn't have anyone to hear it. ⁴I wish

I were the judge. Then people could bring their problems to me, and I would give them justice!" ⁵And when people tried to bow before him, Absalom wouldn't let them. Instead, he took them by the hand and embraced them. ⁶So in this way, Absalom stole the hearts of all the people of Israel.

⁷After four years,* Absalom said to the king, "Let me go to Hebron to offer a sacrifice to the LORD in fulfillment of a vow I

15:7 As in Greek and Syriac versions; Hebrew reads *40 years.*

made to him. [8]For while I was at Geshur, I promised to sacrifice to him in Hebron if he would bring me back to Jerusalem."

[9]"All right," the king told him. "Go and fulfill your vow."

So Absalom went to Hebron. [10]But while he was there, he sent secret messengers to every part of Israel to stir up a rebellion against the king. "As soon as you hear the trumpets," his message read, "you will know that Absalom has been crowned king in Hebron." [11]He took two hundred men from Jerusalem with him as guests, but they knew nothing of his intentions. [12]While he was offering the sacrifices, he sent for Ahithophel, one of David's counselors who lived in Giloh. Soon many others also joined Absalom, and the conspiracy gained momentum.

[13]A messenger soon arrived in Jerusalem to tell King David, "All Israel has joined Absalom in a conspiracy against you!"

[14]"Then we must flee at once, or it will be too late!" David urged his men. "Hurry! If we get out of the city before he arrives, both we and the city of Jerusalem will be spared from disaster."

[15]"We are with you," his advisers replied. "Do what you think is best." [16]So the king and his household set out at once. He left no one behind except ten of his concubines to keep the palace in order. [17]The king and his people set out on foot, and they paused at the edge of the city [18]to let David's troops move past to lead the way. There were six hundred Gittites who had come with David from Gath, along with the king's bodyguard.*

[19]Then the king turned to Ittai, the captain of the Gittites, and asked, "Why are you coming with us? Go on back with your men to King Absalom, for you are a guest in Israel, a foreigner in exile. [20]You arrived only yesterday, and now should I force you to wander with us? I don't even know where we will go. Go on back and take your troops with you, and may the LORD show you his unfailing love and faithfulness.*"

[21]But Ittai said to the king, "I vow by the LORD and by your own life that I will go wherever you go, no matter what happens—whether it means life or death."

[22]David replied, "All right, come with us." So Ittai and his six hundred men and their families went along.

[23]There was deep sadness throughout the land as the king and his followers passed by. They crossed the Kidron Valley and then went out toward the wilderness.

[24]Abiathar and Zadok and the Levites took the Ark of the Covenant of God and set it down beside the road. Then they offered sacrifices there until everyone had passed by. [25]David instructed Zadok to take the Ark of God back into the city. "If the LORD sees fit," David said, "he will bring me back to see the Ark and the Tabernacle again. [26]But if he is through with me, then let him do what seems best to him."

[27]Then the king told Zadok the priest, "Look,* here is my plan. You and Abiathar* should return quietly to the city with your son Ahimaaz and Abiathar's son Jonathan. [28]I will stop at the shallows of the Jordan River* and wait there for a message from you. Let me know what happens in Jerusalem before I disappear into the wilderness." [29]So Zadok and Abiathar took the Ark of God back to the city and stayed there.

[30]David walked up the road that led to the Mount of Olives, weeping as he went. His head was covered and his feet were bare as a sign of mourning. And the people who were with him covered their heads and wept as they climbed the mountain. [31]When someone told David that his adviser Ahithophel was now backing Absalom, David prayed, "O LORD, let Ahithophel give Absalom foolish advice!"

[32]As they reached the spot at the top of the Mount of Olives where people worshiped God, David found Hushai the Arkite waiting for him. Hushai had torn his clothing and put dirt on his head as a sign of mourning. [33]But David told him, "If you go with me, you will only be a burden. [34]Return to Jerusalem and tell Absalom, 'I will now be your adviser, just as I was your father's adviser in the past.' Then you can frustrate and counter Ahithophel's advice. [35]Zadok and Abiathar, the priests, are there. Tell them the plans that are being made to capture me, [36]and they will send their sons Ahimaaz and Jonathan to find me and tell me what is going on." [37]So David's friend

15:18 Hebrew *the Kerethites and Pelethites.*   **15:20** As in Greek version; Hebrew reads *and may unfailing love and faithfulness go with you.*   **15:27a** As in Greek version; Hebrew reads *Are you a seer?* or *Do you see?*   **15:27b** Hebrew lacks *and Abiathar;* compare 15:29. **15:28** Hebrew *at the crossing points of the wilderness.*

Hushai returned to Jerusalem, getting there just as Absalom arrived.

CHAPTER 16

David was just past the top of the hill when Ziba, the servant of Mephibosheth,* caught up with him. He was leading two donkeys loaded with two hundred loaves of bread, one hundred clusters of raisins, one hundred bunches of summer fruit, and a skin of wine. ²"What are these for?" the king asked Ziba.

And Ziba replied, "The donkeys are for your people to ride on, and the bread and summer fruit are for the young men to eat. The wine is to be taken with you into the wilderness for those who become faint."

³"And where is Mephibosheth?" the king asked him.

"He stayed in Jerusalem," Ziba replied. "He said, 'Today I will get back the kingdom of my grandfather Saul.'"

⁴"In that case," the king told Ziba, "I give you everything Mephibosheth owns."

"Thank you, sir," Ziba replied. "I will always do whatever you want me to do."

⁵As David and his party passed Bahurim, a man came out of the village cursing them. It was Shimei son of Gera, a member of Saul's family. ⁶He threw stones at the king and the king's officers and all the mighty warriors who surrounded them. ⁷"Get out of here, you murderer, you scoundrel!" he shouted at David. ⁸"The LORD is paying you back for murdering Saul and his family. You stole his throne, and now the LORD has given it to your son Absalom. At last you will taste some of your own medicine, you murderer!"

⁹"Why should this dead dog curse my lord the king?" Abishai son of Zeruiah demanded. "Let me go over and cut off his head!"

¹⁰"No!" the king said. "What am I going to do with you sons of Zeruiah! If the LORD has told him to curse me, who am I to stop him?" ¹¹Then David said to Abishai and the other officers, "My own son is trying to kill me. Shouldn't this relative of Saul* have even more reason to do so? Leave him alone and let him curse, for the LORD has told him to do it. ¹²And perhaps the LORD will see that I am being wronged and will bless me because of these

curses." ¹³So David and his men continued on, and Shimei kept pace with them on a nearby hillside, cursing as he went and throwing stones at David and tossing dust into the air.

¹⁴The king and all who were with him grew weary along the way, so they rested when they reached the Jordan River.*

¹⁵Meanwhile, Absalom and his men arrived at Jerusalem, accompanied by Ahithophel. ¹⁶When David's friend Hushai the Arkite arrived, he went immediately to see Absalom. "Long live the king!" he exclaimed. "Long live the king!"

¹⁷"Is this the way you treat your friend David?" Absalom asked him. "Why aren't you with him?"

¹⁸"I'm here because I work for the man who is chosen by the LORD and by Israel," Hushai replied. ¹⁹"And anyway, why shouldn't I serve you? I helped your father, and now I will help you!"

²⁰Then Absalom turned to Ahithophel and asked him, "What should I do next?"

²¹Ahithophel told him, "Go and sleep with your father's concubines, for he has left them here to keep the house. Then all Israel will know that you have insulted him beyond hope of reconciliation, and they will give you their support." ²²So they set up a tent on the palace roof where everyone could see it, and Absalom went into the tent to sleep with his father's concubines.

²³Absalom followed Ahithophel's advice, just as David had done. For every word Ahithophel spoke seemed as wise as though it had come directly from the mouth of God.

CHAPTER 17

Now Ahithophel urged Absalom, "Let me choose twelve thousand men to start out after David tonight. ²I will catch up to him while he is weary and discouraged. He and his troops will panic, and everyone will run away. Then I will kill only the king, ³and I will bring all the people back to you as a bride returns to her husband. After all, it is only this man's life that you seek.* Then all the people will remain unharmed and peaceful." ⁴This plan seemed good to Absalom and to all the other leaders of Israel.

⁵But then Absalom said, "Bring in Hu-

16:1 Also known as *Meribbaal.*　　**16:11** Hebrew *this Benjaminite.*　　**16:14** As in Greek version (see also 17:16); Hebrew reads *when they reached their destination.*　　**17:3** As in Greek version; Hebrew reads *like the return of all is the man whom you seek.*

shai the Arkite. Let's see what he thinks about this." ⁶When Hushai arrived, Absalom told him what Ahithophel had said. Then he asked, "What is your opinion? Should we follow Ahithophel's advice? If not, speak up."

⁷"Well," Hushai replied, "this time I think Ahithophel has made a mistake. ⁸You know your father and his men; they are mighty warriors. Right now they are probably as enraged as a mother bear who has been robbed of her cubs. And remember that your father is an experienced soldier. He won't be spending the night among the troops. ⁹He has probably already hidden in some pit or cave. And when he comes out and attacks and a few of your men fall, there will be panic among your troops, and everyone will start shouting that your men are being slaughtered. ¹⁰Then even the bravest of them, though they have the heart of a lion, will be paralyzed with fear. For all Israel knows what a mighty man your father is and how courageous his warriors are.

¹¹"I suggest that you mobilize the entire army of Israel, bringing them from as far away as Dan and Beersheba. That way you will have an army as numerous as the sand on the seashore. And I think that you should personally lead the troops. ¹²When we find David, we can descend on him like the dew that falls to the ground, so that not one of his men is left alive. ¹³And if David has escaped into some city, you will have the entire army of Israel there at your command. Then we can take ropes and drag the walls of the city into the nearest valley until every stone is torn down."

¹⁴Then Absalom and all the leaders of Israel said, "Hushai's advice is better than Ahithophel's." For the LORD had arranged to defeat the counsel of Ahithophel, which really was the better plan, so that he could bring disaster upon Absalom!

¹⁵Then Hushai reported to Zadok and Abiathar, the priests, what Ahithophel had said and what he himself had suggested instead. ¹⁶"Quick!" he told them. "Find David and urge him not to stay at the shallows of the Jordan River* tonight. He must go across at once into the wilderness beyond. Otherwise he will die and his entire army with him."

¹⁷Jonathan and Ahimaaz had been stay-ing at En-rogel so as not to be seen entering and leaving the city. Arrangements had been made for a servant girl to bring them the message they were to take to King David. ¹⁸But a boy saw them leaving En-rogel to go to David, and he told Absalom about it. Meanwhile, they escaped to Bahurim, where a man hid them inside a well in his courtyard. ¹⁹The man's wife put a cloth over the top of the well with grain on it to dry in the sun; so no one suspected they were there.

²⁰When Absalom's men arrived, they asked her, "Have you seen Ahimaaz and Jonathan?"

She replied, "They were here, but they crossed the brook." Absalom's men looked for them without success and returned to Jerusalem.

²¹Then the two men crawled out of the well and hurried on to King David. "Quick!" they told him, "cross the Jordan tonight!" And they told him how Ahithophel had advised that he be captured and killed. ²²So David and all the people with him went across the Jordan River during the night, and they were all on the other bank before dawn.

²³Meanwhile, Ahithophel was publicly disgraced when Absalom refused his advice. So he saddled his donkey, went to his hometown, set his affairs in order, and hanged himself. He died there and was buried beside his father.

²⁴David soon arrived at Mahanaim. By now, Absalom had mobilized the entire army of Israel and was leading his troops across the Jordan River. ²⁵Absalom had appointed Amasa as commander of his army, replacing Joab, who had been commander under David. (Amasa was Joab's cousin. His father was Jether,* an Ishmaelite.* His mother, Abigail daughter of Nahash, was the sister of Joab's mother, Zeruiah.) ²⁶Absalom and the Israelite army set up camp in the land of Gilead.

²⁷When David arrived at Mahanaim, he was warmly greeted by Shobi son of Nahash of Rabbah, an Ammonite, and by Makir son of Ammiel of Lo-debar, and by Barzillai of Gilead from Rogelim. ²⁸They brought sleeping mats, cooking pots, serving bowls, wheat and barley flour, roasted grain, beans, lentils, ²⁹honey, butter, sheep, and cheese for David and those

17:16 Hebrew *at the crossing points of the wilderness.* 17:25a Hebrew *Ithra*, a variant name for Jether. 17:25b As in some Greek manuscripts (see also 1 Chr 2:17); Hebrew reads *an Israelite.*

who were with him. For they said, "You must all be very tired and hungry and thirsty after your long march through the wilderness."

CHAPTER 18

David now appointed generals and captains to lead his troops. ²One-third were placed under Joab, one-third under Joab's brother Abishai son of Zeruiah, and one-third under Ittai the Gittite. The king told his troops, "I am going out with you."

³But his men objected strongly. "You must not go," they urged. "If we have to turn and run—and even if half of us die—it will make no difference to Absalom's troops; they will be looking only for you. You are worth ten thousand of us, and it is better that you stay here in the city and send us help if we need it."

⁴"If you think that's the best plan, I'll do it," the king finally agreed. So he stood at the gate of the city as all the divisions of troops passed by. ⁵And the king gave this command to Joab, Abishai, and Ittai: "For my sake, deal gently with young Absalom." And all the troops heard the king give this order to his commanders.

⁶So the battle began in the forest of Ephraim, ⁷and the Israelite troops were beaten back by David's men. There was a great slaughter, and twenty thousand men laid down their lives that day. ⁸The battle raged all across the countryside, and more men died because of the forest than were killed by the sword.

⁹During the battle, Absalom came unexpectedly upon some of David's men. He tried to escape on his mule, but as he rode beneath the thick branches of a great oak, his head got caught. His mule kept going and left him dangling in the air. ¹⁰One of David's men saw what had happened and told Joab, "I saw Absalom dangling in a tree."

¹¹"What?" Joab demanded. "You saw him there and didn't kill him? I would have rewarded you with ten pieces of silver* and a hero's belt!"

¹²"I wouldn't do it for a thousand pieces of silver,*" the man replied. "We all heard the king say to you and Abishai and Ittai, 'For my sake, please don't harm young Absalom.' ¹³And if I had betrayed the king by

killing his son—and the king would certainly find out who did it—you yourself would be the first to abandon me."

¹⁴"Enough of this nonsense," Joab said. Then he took three daggers and plunged them into Absalom's heart as he dangled from the oak still alive. ¹⁵Ten of Joab's young armor bearers then surrounded Absalom and killed him. ¹⁶Then Joab blew the trumpet, and his men returned from chasing the army of Israel. ¹⁷They threw Absalom's body into a deep pit in the forest and piled a great heap of stones over it. And the army of Israel fled to their homes.

¹⁸During his lifetime, Absalom had built a monument to himself in the King's Valley, for he had said, "I have no son to carry on my name." He named the monument after himself, and it is known as Absalom's Monument to this day.

¹⁹Then Zadok's son Ahimaaz said, "Let me run to the king with the good news that the LORD has saved him from his enemy Absalom."

²⁰"No," Joab told him, "it wouldn't be good news to the king that his son is dead. You can be my messenger some other time, but not today."

²¹Then Joab said to a man from Cush, "Go tell the king what you have seen." The man bowed and ran off.

²²But Ahimaaz continued to plead with Joab, "Whatever happens, please let me go, too."

"Why should you go, my son?" Joab replied. "There will be no reward for you."

²³"Yes, but let me go anyway," he begged.

Joab finally said, "All right, go ahead." Then Ahimaaz took a shortcut across the plain of the Jordan and got to Mahanaim ahead of the man from Cush.

²⁴While David was sitting at the city gate, the watchman climbed to the roof of the gateway by the wall. As he looked, he saw a lone man running toward them. ²⁵He shouted the news down to David, and the king replied, "If he is alone, he has news."

As the messenger came closer, ²⁶the watchman saw another man running toward them. He shouted down, "Here comes another one!"

The king replied, "He also will have news."

18:11 Hebrew *10 shekels of silver*, about 4 ounces or 114 grams in weight.   18:12 Hebrew *1,000 shekels*, about 25 pounds or 11.4 kilograms in weight.

²⁷"The first man runs like Ahimaaz son of Zadok," the watchman said.

"He is a good man and comes with good news," the king replied.

²⁸Then Ahimaaz cried out to the king, "All is well!" He bowed low with his face to the ground and said, "Blessed be the LORD your God, who has handed over the rebels who dared to stand against you."

²⁹"What about young Absalom?" the king demanded. "Is he all right?"

Ahimaaz replied, "When Joab told me to come, there was a lot of commotion. But I didn't know what was happening."

³⁰"Wait here," the king told him. So Ahimaaz stepped aside.

³¹Then the man from Cush arrived and said, "I have good news for my lord the king. Today the LORD has rescued you from all those who rebelled against you."

³²"What about young Absalom?" the king demanded. "Is he all right?"

And the Cushite replied, "May all of your enemies, both now and in the future, be as that young man is!"

³³The king was overcome with emotion. He went up to his room over the gateway and burst into tears. And as he went, he cried, "O my son Absalom! My son, my son Absalom! If only I could have died instead of you! O Absalom, my son, my son."

MARCH 30 ☐ DAY 90
2 SAMUEL 19–20
David's Return to the Throne

OVERVIEW David's grief over the death of Absalom causes him to overlook the people who risked their lives to help restore his rule over Israel. Alerted to the danger of this situation by General Joab, David responds by accompanying his faithful followers in a triumphal return to Jerusalem. But though David has been successful in putting down one rebellion, he must soon confront another in the person of Sheba. Only when it has been crushed can David reign over a reunited kingdom.

Chapter 19		Chapter 20
Joab's Rebuke	David's Return	Sheba's Revolt
1 14	15 43	
David's Throne Restored		David's Throne Threatened

YOUR DAILY WALK In a humorous television commercial, a man nervously rehearses the words he will use to tell his boss he has bad breath (which, of course, can only be eliminated by using a particular brand of mouthwash). Fortunately for the employee, the boss discovers the "cure" on his own, thus avoiding the confrontation.

There is a vast difference between putting your nose in other people's business and putting your heart in other people's problems.

Two men in David's life faced situations far more serious than that of telling the king he needed to freshen his breath. Both were used by God to "freshen up" David's spiritual life and jar him back to reality. When David was seeking to cover up his sin with Bathsheba, Nathan boldly announced to the king, "You are that man!" (12:7)—words that helped David come to grips with his sin. Later, as David mourned the death of Absalom, Joab prevented mutiny in the army by exhorting his commander in chief, "Now go out there and congratulate the troops" (19:7)—strong words that could have cost Joab his job or his life. Yet he had the courage to exhort his king and friend.

Do you have the holy boldness of a Nathan or a Joab? When those you love need to hear the truth about themselves, can you speak the truth in love? To help you recognize the importance of sensitive confrontation, meditate on Proverbs 27:6: "Wounds from a friend are better than many kisses from an enemy."

 INSIGHT Politics in David's Day
Compare the list of David's "cabinet members" in 20:23-26 with an earlier list in 8:15-18 and watch for the differences. Can you spot who has been replaced and who is still "in office"?

CHAPTER 19

Word soon reached Joab that the king was weeping and mourning for Absalom. ²As the troops heard of the king's deep grief for his son, the joy of that day's victory was turned into deep sadness. ³They crept back into the city as though they were ashamed and had been beaten in battle. ⁴The king covered his face with his hands and kept on weeping, "O my son Absalom! O Absalom, my son, my son!"

⁵Then Joab went to the king's room and said to him, "We saved your life today and the lives of your sons, your daughters, and your wives and concubines. Yet you act like this, making us feel ashamed, as though we had done something wrong. ⁶You seem to love those who hate you and hate those who love you. You have made it clear today that we mean nothing to you. If Absalom had lived and all of us had died, you would be pleased. ⁷Now go out there and congratulate the troops, for I swear by the LORD that if you don't, not a single one of them will remain here tonight. Then you will be worse off than you have ever been." ⁸So the king went out and sat at the city gate, and as the news spread throughout the city that he was there, everyone went to him.

Meanwhile, the Israelites who supported Absalom had fled to their homes. ⁹And throughout the tribes of Israel there was much discussion and argument going on. The people were saying, "The king saved us from our enemies, the Philistines, but Absalom chased him out of the country. ¹⁰Now Absalom, whom we anointed to rule over us, is dead. Let's ask David to come back and be our king again."

¹¹Then King David sent Zadok and Abiathar, the priests, to say to the leaders of Judah, "Why are you the last ones to reinstate the king? For I have heard that all Israel is ready, and only you are holding out. ¹²Yet you are my relatives, my own tribe, my own flesh and blood! Why are you the last ones to welcome me back?"

¹³And David told them to tell Amasa, "Since you are my nephew, may God strike me dead if I do not appoint you as commander of my army in place of Joab." ¹⁴Then Amasa convinced all the leaders of Judah, and they responded unanimously. They sent word to the king, "Return to us, and bring back all those who are with you."

¹⁵So the king started back to Jerusalem. And when he arrived at the Jordan River, the people of Judah came to Gilgal to meet him and escort him across the river. ¹⁶Then Shimei son of Gera, the man from Bahurim in Benjamin, hurried across with the men of Judah to welcome King David. ¹⁷A thousand men from the tribe of Benjamin were with him, including Ziba, the servant of Saul, and Ziba's fifteen sons and twenty servants. They rushed down to the Jordan to arrive ahead of the king. ¹⁸They all crossed the ford and worked hard ferrying the king's household across the river, helping them in every way they could.

As the king was about to cross the river, Shimei fell down before him. ¹⁹"My lord the king, please forgive me," he pleaded. "Forget the terrible thing I did when you left Jerusalem. ²⁰I know how much I sinned. That is why I have come here today, the very first person in all Israel* to greet you."

²¹Then Abishai son of Zeruiah said, "Shimei should die, for he cursed the LORD's anointed king!"

²²"What am I going to do with you sons of Zeruiah!" David exclaimed. "This is not a day for execution but for celebration! I am once again the king of Israel!" ²³Then, turning to Shimei, David vowed, "Your life will be spared."

²⁴Now Mephibosheth,* Saul's grandson, arrived from Jerusalem to meet the king. He had not washed his feet or clothes nor trimmed his beard since the day the king left Jerusalem. ²⁵"Why didn't you come with me, Mephibosheth?" the king asked him.

19:20 Hebrew *the house of Joseph.*   **19:24** Also known as *Meribbaal.*

[26]Mephibosheth replied, "My lord the king, my servant Ziba deceived me. I told him, 'Saddle my donkey so that I can go with the king.' For as you know I am crippled. [27]Ziba has slandered me by saying that I refused to come. But I know that you are like an angel of God, so do what you think is best. [28]All my relatives and I could expect only death from you, my lord, but instead you have honored me among those who eat at your own table! So how can I complain?"

[29]"All right," David replied. "My decision is that you and Ziba will divide your land equally between you."

[30]"Give him all of it," Mephibosheth said. "I am content just to have you back again, my lord!"

[31]Barzillai of Gilead now arrived from Rogelim to conduct the king across the Jordan. [32]He was very old, about eighty, and very wealthy. He was the one who had provided food for the king during his stay in Mahanaim. [33]"Come across with me and live in Jerusalem," the king said to Barzillai. "I will take care of you there."

[34]"No," he replied, "I am far too old for that. [35]I am eighty years old today, and I can no longer enjoy anything. Food and wine are no longer tasty, and I cannot hear the musicians as they play. I would only be a burden to my lord the king. [36]Just to go across the river with you is all the honor I need! [37]Then let me return again to die in my own town, where my father and mother are buried. But here is my son Kimham. Let him go with you and receive whatever good things you want to give him."

[38]"Good," the king agreed. "Kimham will go with me, and I will do for him whatever I would have done for you." [39]So all the people crossed the Jordan with the king. After David had blessed and embraced him, Barzillai returned to his own home. [40]The king then went on to Gilgal, taking Kimham with him. All the army of Judah and half the army of Israel escorted him across the river.

[41]But the men of Israel complained to the king that the men of Judah had gotten to do most of the work in helping him cross the Jordan. [42]"Why not?" the men of Judah replied. "The king is one of our own tribe. Why should this make you angry? We have

charged him nothing. And he hasn't fed us or even given us gifts!"

[43]"But there are ten tribes in Israel," the others replied. "So we have ten times as much right to the king as you do. Why did you treat us with such contempt? Remember, we were the first to speak of bringing him back to be our king again." The argument continued back and forth, and the men of Judah were very harsh in their replies.

CHAPTER 20

Then a troublemaker named Sheba son of Bicri, a man from the tribe of Benjamin, blew a trumpet and shouted, "We have nothing to do with David. We want no part of this son of Jesse. Come on, you men of Israel, let's all go home!" [2]So the men of Israel deserted David and followed Sheba. But the men of Judah stayed with their king and escorted him from the Jordan River to Jerusalem.

[3]When the king arrived at his palace in Jerusalem, he instructed that the ten concubines he had left to keep house should be placed in seclusion. Their needs were to be cared for, he said, but he would no longer sleep with them. So each of them lived like a widow until she died.

[4]Then the king instructed Amasa to mobilize the army of Judah within three days and to report back at that time. [5]So Amasa went out to notify the troops, but it took him longer than the three days he had been given. [6]Then David said to Abishai, "That troublemaker Sheba is going to hurt us more than Absalom did. Quick, take my troops and chase after him before he gets into a fortified city where we can't reach him."

[7]So Abishai and Joab set out after Sheba with an elite guard from Joab's army and the king's own bodyguard.* [8]As they arrived at the great stone in Gibeon, Amasa met them, coming from the opposite direction. Joab was wearing his uniform with a dagger strapped to his belt. As he stepped forward to greet Amasa, he secretly slipped the dagger from its sheath. [9]"How are you, my cousin?" Joab said and took him by the beard with his right hand as though to kiss him. [10]Amasa didn't notice the dagger in his left hand, and Joab stabbed him in the stomach with it so that his insides gushed out onto the ground. Joab did not need to

20:7 Hebrew *the Kerethites and Pelethites*; also in 20:23.

strike again, and Amasa soon died. Joab and his brother Abishai left him lying there and continued after Sheba.

[11]One of Joab's young officers shouted to Amasa's troops, "If you are for Joab and David, come and follow Joab." [12]But Amasa lay in his blood in the middle of the road, and Joab's officer saw that a crowd was gathering around to stare at him. So he pulled him off the road into a field and threw a cloak over him. [13]With Amasa's body out of the way, everyone went on with Joab to capture Sheba.

[14]Meanwhile, Sheba had traveled across Israel to mobilize his own clan of Bicri at the city of Abel-beth-maacah. [15]When Joab's forces arrived, they attacked Abel-beth-maacah and built a ramp against the city wall and began battering it down. [16]But a wise woman in the city called out to Joab, "Listen to me, Joab. Come over here so I can talk to you." [17]As he approached, the woman asked, "Are you Joab?"

"I am," he replied.

So she said, "Listen carefully to your servant."

"I'm listening," he said.

[18]Then she continued, "There used to be a saying, 'If you want to settle an argument,

ask advice at the city of Abel.' [19]I am one who is peace loving and faithful in Israel. But you are destroying a loyal city. Why do you want to destroy what belongs to the LORD?"

[20]And Joab replied, "Believe me, I don't want to destroy your city! [21]All I want is a man named Sheba son of Bicri from the hill country of Ephraim, who has revolted against King David. If you hand him over to me, we will leave the city in peace."

"All right," the woman replied, "we will throw his head over the wall to you." [22]Then the woman went to the people with her wise advice, and they cut off Sheba's head and threw it out to Joab. So he blew the trumpet and called his troops back from the attack, and they all returned to their homes. Joab returned to the king at Jerusalem.

[23]Joab once again became the commander of David's army. Benaiah son of Jehoiada was commander of the king's bodyguard. [24]Adoniram* was in charge of the labor force. Jehoshaphat son of Ahilud was the royal historian. [25]Sheva was the court secretary. Zadok and Abiathar were the priests. [26]Ira the Jairite was David's personal priest.

20:24 As in Greek version (see also 1 Kgs 4:6; 5:14); Hebrew reads *Adoram*.

MARCH 31 ☐ DAY 91
2 SAMUEL 21–24
David's Final Words and Acts

OVERVIEW Today's section covers six topics that, although out of strict chronological order, form an appendix supplementing the main body of 2 Samuel and, as such, provide a fitting conclusion to the book. The topics include a severe famine sent in judgment for Saul's treatment of the Gibeonites (whom he was committed by oath to protect—21:1); a series of wars with Philistia (apparently toward the very end of David's life—21:15-22); a beautiful psalm of deliverance and praise (including David's last words—23:1-7); a list of David's mighty men of valor (with one startling addition—Uriah!); a sinful census (apparently motivated by pride); and the severe punishment by pestilence that followed it. The closing paragraph of the book portrays David in his most natural pose: worshiping the Lord in humility.

Chapter 21	Chapters 22-23	Chapter 24
Famine and Philistines	Music and Mighty Men	A Proud Census and Painful Punishment
	David's Final Words and Acts	

YOUR DAILY WALK Are you on God's list of "mighty men and women"? Don't answer too quickly. God's choices may surprise you!

A man can be no bigger than the number of people for whom he genuinely cares.

David composed a list of thirty-seven soldiers from his vast armies, thirty-seven men who, in his estimation, deserved the title "mighty." Most of his selections make good sense. After all, who could possibly forget Adino the Eznite, who killed eight hundred men single-handedly? Or Eleazar, the son of Dodai, who one day fought Philistines until his hand "was too tired to lift his sword"! But there are some curious additions as well. Three men broke through the Philistine lines to bring thirsty King David a cup of cold water from the well of Bethlehem—and for that they received the same praise as a warrior who slew hundreds.

Stop and think of one specific act you can do today that would be mighty in God's eyes. (Remember, even a cup of cold water given in his name will not go unrewarded.) Now include it in your schedule, and do it! You'll be "mighty" glad you did.

INSIGHT Real Estate Rich with Significance
The book closes with David purchasing the threshing floor on Mount Moriah—the place where Abraham offered Isaac centuries before and where Solomon's Temple would soon stand.

CHAPTER 21
There was a famine during David's reign that lasted for three years, so David asked the LORD about it. And the LORD said, "The famine has come because Saul and his family are guilty of murdering the Gibeonites."

²So King David summoned the Gibeonites. They were not part of Israel but were all that was left of the nation of the Amorites. Israel had sworn not to kill them, but Saul, in his zeal, had tried to wipe them out. ³David asked them, "What can I do for you to make amends? Tell me so that the LORD will bless his people again."

⁴"Well, money won't do it," the Gibeonites replied. "And we don't want to see the Israelites executed in revenge."

"What can I do then?" David asked. "Just tell me and I will do it for you."

⁵Then they replied, "It was Saul who planned to destroy us, to keep us from having any place at all in Israel. ⁶So let seven of Saul's sons or grandsons be handed over to us, and we will execute them before the LORD at Gibeon, on the mountain of the LORD.*"

"All right," the king said, "I will do it."

⁷David spared Jonathan's son Mephibosheth,* who was Saul's grandson, because of the oath David and Jonathan had sworn before the LORD. ⁸But he gave them Saul's two sons Armoni and Mephibosheth, whose mother was Rizpah daughter of Aiah. He also gave them the five sons of Saul's daughter Merab,* the wife of Adriel son of Barzillai from Meholah. ⁹The men of Gibeon executed them on the mountain before the LORD. So all seven of them died together at the beginning of the barley harvest.

¹⁰Then Rizpah, the mother of two of the men, spread sackcloth on a rock and stayed there the entire harvest season. She prevented vultures from tearing at their bodies during the day and stopped wild animals from eating them at night. ¹¹When David learned what Rizpah, Saul's concubine, had done, ¹²he went to the people of Jabesh-gilead and asked for the bones of Saul and his son Jonathan. (When Saul and Jonathan had died in a battle with the Philistines, it was the people of Jabesh-gilead who had retrieved their bodies from the public square of the Philistine city of

21:6 As in Greek version (see also 21:9); Hebrew reads *at Gibeah of Saul, the chosen of the* LORD.   21:7 Also known as *Meribbaal.*
21:8 As in a few Hebrew and Greek manuscripts and Syriac version (see also 1 Sam 18:19); most Hebrew manuscripts read *Michal.*

Beth-shan.) ¹³So David brought the bones of Saul and Jonathan, as well as the bones of the men the Gibeonites had executed. ¹⁴He buried them all in the tomb of Kish, Saul's father, at the town of Zela in the land of Benjamin. After that, God ended the famine in the land of Israel.

¹⁵Once again the Philistines were at war with Israel. And when David and his men were in the thick of battle, David became weak and exhausted. ¹⁶Ishbi-benob was a descendant of the giants*; his bronze spearhead weighed more than seven pounds,* and he was armed with a new sword. He had cornered David and was about to kill him. ¹⁷But Abishai son of Zeruiah came to his rescue and killed the Philistine. After that, David's men declared, "You are not going out to battle again! Why should we risk snuffing out the light of Israel?"

¹⁸After this, there was another battle against the Philistines at Gob. As they fought, Sibbecai from Hushah killed Saph, another descendant of the giants. ¹⁹In still another battle at Gob, Elhanan son of Jair* from Bethlehem killed the brother of Goliath of Gath.* The handle of his spear was as thick as a weaver's beam! ²⁰In another battle with the Philistines at Gath, a huge man with six fingers on each hand and six toes on each foot—a descendant of the giants—²¹defied and taunted Israel. But he was killed by Jonathan, the son of David's brother Shimea.* ²²These four Philistines were descended from the giants of Gath, but they were killed by David and his warriors.

CHAPTER 22

David sang this song to the LORD after the LORD had rescued him from all his enemies and from Saul. ²These are the words he sang:

"The LORD is my rock, my fortress, and
my savior;
³   my God is my rock, in whom I find
protection.
He is my shield, the strength of my
salvation, and my stronghold,
my high tower, my savior, the one
who saves me from violence.

⁴ I will call on the LORD, who is worthy
of praise,
for he saves me from my enemies.

⁵ "The waves of death surrounded me;
the floods of destruction swept over
me.
⁶ The grave* wrapped its ropes around
me;
death itself stared me in the face.
⁷ But in my distress I cried out to the
LORD;
yes, I called to my God for help.
He heard me from his sanctuary;
my cry reached his ears.

⁸ "Then the earth quaked and trembled;
the foundations of the heavens shook;
they quaked because of his anger.
⁹ Smoke poured from his nostrils;
fierce flames leaped from his mouth;
glowing coals flamed forth from him.
¹⁰ He opened the heavens and came down;
dark storm clouds were beneath his
feet.
¹¹ Mounted on a mighty angel,* he flew,
soaring* on the wings of the wind.
¹² He shrouded himself in darkness,
veiling his approach with dense rain
clouds.
¹³ A great brightness shone before him,
and bolts of lightning blazed forth.
¹⁴ The LORD thundered from heaven;
the Most High gave a mighty shout.
¹⁵ He shot his arrows and scattered his
enemies;
his lightning flashed, and they were
confused.
¹⁶ Then at the command of the LORD,
at the blast of his breath,
the bottom of the sea could be seen,
and the foundations of the earth
were laid bare.

¹⁷ "He reached down from heaven and
rescued me;
he drew me out of deep waters.
¹⁸ He delivered me from my powerful
enemies,
from those who hated me and were
too strong for me.
¹⁹ They attacked me at a moment when
I was weakest,
but the LORD upheld me.

21:16a As in Greek version; Hebrew reads *a descendant of the Rephaites*; also in 21:18, 20, 22.   21:16b Hebrew *300 shekels* [3.4 kilograms].   21:19a As in parallel text at 1 Chr 20:5; Hebrew reads *son of Jaare-oregim*.   21:19b As in parallel text at 1 Chr 20:5; Hebrew reads *killed Goliath of Gath*.   21:21 As in parallel text at 1 Chr 20:7; Hebrew reads *Shimei*, a variant name for Shimea.   22:6 Hebrew *Sheol*.   22:11a Hebrew *cherub*.   22:11b As in some Hebrew manuscripts (see also Ps 18:10); other Hebrew manuscripts read *appearing*.

²⁰ He led me to a place of safety;
  he rescued me because he delights
    in me.
²¹ The LORD rewarded me for doing right;
  he compensated me because of my
    innocence.
²² For I have kept the ways of the LORD;
  I have not turned from my God to
    follow evil.
²³ For all his laws are constantly before
    me;
  I have never abandoned his
    principles.
²⁴ I am blameless before God;
  I have kept myself from sin.
²⁵ The LORD rewarded me for doing right,
  because of my innocence in his sight.

²⁶ "To the faithful you show yourself
    faithful;
  to those with integrity you show
    integrity.
²⁷ To the pure you show yourself pure,
  but to the wicked you show yourself
    hostile.
²⁸ You rescue those who are humble,
  but your eyes are on the proud to
    humiliate them.
²⁹ O LORD, you are my light;
  yes, LORD, you light up my darkness.
³⁰ In your strength I can crush an army;
  with my God I can scale any wall.

³¹ "As for God, his way is perfect.
  All the LORD's promises prove true.
  He is a shield for all who look to him
    for protection.
³² For who is God except the LORD?
  Who but our God is a solid rock?
³³ God is my strong fortress;
  he has made my way safe.
³⁴ He makes me as surefooted as a deer,
  leading me safely along the
    mountain heights.
³⁵ He prepares me for battle;
  he strengthens me to draw a bow
    of bronze.
³⁶ You have given me the shield of your
    salvation;
  your help* has made me great.
³⁷ You have made a wide path for my feet
  to keep them from slipping.

³⁸ "I chased my enemies and destroyed
    them;
  I did not stop until they were
    conquered.

³⁹ I consumed them; I struck them down
    so they could not get up;
  they fell beneath my feet.
⁴⁰ You have armed me with strength
    for the battle;
  you have subdued my enemies
    under my feet.
⁴¹ You made them turn and run;
  I have destroyed all who hated me.
⁴² They called for help, but no one came
    to rescue them.
  They cried to the LORD, but he
    refused to answer them.
⁴³ I ground them as fine as the dust of the
    earth;
  I swept them into the gutter like dirt.

⁴⁴ "You gave me victory over my accusers.
  You preserved me as the ruler over
    nations;
  people I don't even know now serve
    me.
⁴⁵ Foreigners cringe before me;
  as soon as they hear of me, they
    submit.
⁴⁶ They all lose their courage
  and come trembling from their
    strongholds.

⁴⁷ "The LORD lives! Blessed be my rock!
  May God, the rock of my salvation,
    be exalted!
⁴⁸ He is the God who pays back those
    who harm me;
  he subdues the nations under me
⁴⁹   and rescues me from my enemies.
  You hold me safe beyond the reach
    of my enemies;
  you save me from violent opponents.
⁵⁰ For this, O LORD, I will praise you
    among the nations;
  I will sing joyfully to your name.
⁵¹ You give great victories to your king;
  you show unfailing love to your
    anointed,
  to David and all his descendants
    forever."

CHAPTER 23
These are the last words of David:

  "David, the son of Jesse, speaks—
  David, the man to whom God gave
    such wonderful success,
  David, the man anointed by the God
    of Jacob,
  David, the sweet psalmist of Israel.

22:36 As in Dead Sea Scrolls; most Hebrew manuscripts read *your answering.*

2 "The Spirit of the LORD speaks through
    me;
    his words are upon my tongue.
3 The God of Israel spoke.
    The Rock of Israel said to me:
    'The person who rules righteously,
    who rules in the fear of God,
4 he is like the light of the morning,
    like the sunrise bursting forth in a
      cloudless sky,
    like the refreshing rains that bring
      tender grass from the earth.'

5 "It is my family God has chosen!
    Yes, he has made an everlasting
      covenant with me.
    His agreement is eternal, final, sealed.
    He will constantly look after my
      safety and success.
6 But the godless are like thorns to be
      thrown away,
    for they tear the hand that touches
      them.
7 One must be armed to chop them
      down;
    they will be utterly consumed with
      fire."

8 These are the names of David's mightiest men. The first was Jashobeam the Hacmonite,* who was commander of the Three—the three greatest warriors among David's men. He once used his spear to kill eight hundred enemy warriors in a single battle.*

9 Next in rank among the Three was Eleazar son of Dodai, a descendant of Ahoah. Once Eleazar and David stood together against the Philistines when the entire Israelite army had fled. 10 He killed Philistines until his hand was too tired to lift his sword, and the LORD gave him a great victory that day. The rest of the army did not return until it was time to collect the plunder!

11 Next in rank was Shammah son of Agee from Harar. One time the Philistines gathered at Lehi and attacked the Israelites in a field full of lentils. The Israelite army fled, 12 but Shammah held his ground in the middle of the field and beat back the Philistines. So the LORD brought about a great victory.

13 Once during harvesttime, when David was at the cave of Adullam, the Philistine army was camped in the valley of Rephaim. The Three (who were among the Thirty—an elite group among David's fighting men) went down to meet him there. 14 David was staying in the stronghold at the time, and a Philistine detachment had occupied the town of Bethlehem. 15 David remarked longingly to his men, "Oh, how I would love some of that good water from the well in Bethlehem, the one by the gate." 16 So the Three broke through the Philistine lines, drew some water from the well, and brought it back to David. But he refused to drink it. Instead, he poured it out before the LORD. 17 "The LORD forbid that I should drink this!" he exclaimed. "This water is as precious as the blood of these men who risked their lives to bring it to me." So David did not drink it. This is an example of the exploits of the Three.

18 Abishai son of Zeruiah, the brother of Joab, was the leader of the Thirty.* He once used his spear to kill three hundred enemy warriors in a single battle. It was by such feats that he became as famous as the Three. 19 Abishai was the most famous of the Thirty* and was their commander, though he was not one of the Three.

20 There was also Benaiah son of Jehoiada, a valiant warrior from Kabzeel. He did many heroic deeds, which included killing two of Moab's mightiest warriors. Another time he chased a lion down into a pit. Then, despite the snow and slippery ground, he caught the lion and killed it. 21 Another time, armed only with a club, he killed a great Egyptian warrior who was armed with a spear. Benaiah wrenched the spear from the Egyptian's hand and killed him with it. 22 These are some of the deeds that made Benaiah almost as famous as the Three. 23 He was more honored than the other members of the Thirty, though he was not one of the Three. And David made him commander of his bodyguard.

24 Other members of the Thirty included:

    Asahel, Joab's brother;
    Elhanan son of Dodo from Bethlehem;
25 Shammah from Harod;
    Elika from Harod;
26 Helez from Pelon*;
    Ira son of Ikkesh from Tekoa;

23:8a As in parallel text at 1 Chr 11:11; Hebrew reads *Josheb-basshebeth the Tahkemonite.*   **23:8b** As in some Greek manuscripts (see also 1 Chr 11:11); the Hebrew is uncertain, though it might be rendered *the Three. It was Adino the Eznite who killed eight hundred men at one time.*   **23:18** As in a few Hebrew manuscripts and Syriac version; most Hebrew manuscripts read *the Three.*   **23:19** As in Syriac version; Hebrew reads *the Three.*   **23:26** As in parallel text at 1 Chr 11:27 (see also 1 Chr 27:10); Hebrew reads *from Palti.*

27 Abiezer from Anathoth;
   Sibbecai* from Hushah;
28 Zalmon from Ahoah;
   Maharai from Netophah;
29 Heled* son of Baanah from Netophah;
   Ithai* son of Ribai from Gibeah (from
      the tribe of Benjamin);
30 Benaiah from Pirathon;
   Hurai* from Nahale-gaash*;
31 Abi-albon the Arbathite;
   Azmaveth from Bahurim;
32 Eliahba from Shaalbon;
   the sons of Jashen;
33 Jonathan son of Shagee* from Harar;
   Ahiam son of Sharar from Harar;
34 Eliphelet son of Ahasbai from Maacah;
   Eliam son of Ahithophel from Giloh;
35 Hezro from Carmel;
   Paarai from Arba;
36 Igal son of Nathan from Zobah;
   Bani from Gad;
37 Zelek from Ammon;
   Naharai from Beeroth (Joab's armor
      bearer);
38 Ira from Jattir;
   Gareb from Jattir;
39 Uriah the Hittite.

There were thirty-seven in all.

CHAPTER 24
Once again the anger of the LORD burned against Israel, and he caused David to harm them by taking a census. "Go and count the people of Israel and Judah," the LORD told him.

2So the king said to Joab, the commander of his army, "Take a census of all the people in the land—from Dan in the north to Beersheba in the south—so that I may know how many people there are."

3But Joab replied to the king, "May the LORD your God let you live until there are a hundred times as many people in your kingdom as there are now! But why do you want to do this?"

4But the king insisted that they take the census, so Joab and his officers went out to count the people of Israel. 5First they crossed the Jordan and camped at Aroer, south of the town in the valley, in the direction of Gad. Then they went on to Jazer, 6then to Gilead in the land of Tahtim-

hodshi* and to Dan-jaan and around to Sidon. 7Then they came to the stronghold of Tyre, and all the cities of the Hivites and Canaanites. Finally, they went south to Judah as far as Beersheba. 8Having gone through the entire land, they completed their task in nine months and twenty days and then returned to Jerusalem. 9Joab reported the number of people to the king. There were 800,000 men of military age in Israel and 500,000 in Judah.

10But after he had taken the census, David's conscience began to bother him. And he said to the LORD, "I have sinned greatly and shouldn't have taken the census. Please forgive me, LORD, for doing this foolish thing."

11The next morning the word of the LORD came to the prophet Gad, who was David's seer. This was the message: 12"Go and say to David, 'This is what the LORD says: I will give you three choices. Choose one of these punishments, and I will do it.'"

13So Gad came to David and asked him, "Will you choose three* years of famine throughout the land, three months of fleeing from your enemies, or three days of severe plague throughout your land? Think this over and let me know what answer to give the LORD."

14"This is a desperate situation!" David replied to Gad. "But let us fall into the hands of the LORD, for his mercy is great. Do not let me fall into human hands."

15So the LORD sent a plague upon Israel that morning, and it lasted for three days. Seventy thousand people died throughout the nation. 16But as the death angel was preparing to destroy Jerusalem, the LORD relented and said to the angel, "Stop! That is enough!" At that moment the angel of the LORD was by the threshing floor of Araunah the Jebusite.

17When David saw the angel, he said to the LORD, "I am the one who has sinned and done wrong! But these people are innocent—what have they done? Let your anger fall against me and my family."

18That day Gad came to David and said to him, "Go and build an altar to the LORD on the threshing floor of Araunah the Jebusite."

19So David went to do what the LORD

23:27 As in some Greek manuscripts (see also 1 Chr 11:29); Hebrew reads *Mebunnai*.   23:29a As in some Hebrew manuscripts (see also 1 Chr 11:30); most Hebrew manuscripts read *Heleb*.   23:29b As in parallel text at 1 Chr 11:31; Hebrew reads *Ittai*.   23:30a As in some Greek manuscripts (see also 1 Chr 11:32); Hebrew reads *Hiddai*.   23:30b Or *from the ravines of Gaash*.   23:33 As in parallel text at 1 Chr 11:34; Hebrew reads *Jonathan, Shammah*; some Greek manuscripts read *Jonathan son of Shammah*.   24:6 Greek version reads *to Gilead and to Kadesh in the land of the Hittites*.   24:13 As in Greek version (see also 1 Chr 21:12); Hebrew reads *seven*.

had commanded him. [20]When Araunah saw the king and his men coming toward him, he came forward and bowed before the king with his face to the ground. [21]"Why have you come, my lord?" Araunah asked.

And David replied, "I have come to buy your threshing floor and to build an altar to the LORD there, so that the LORD will stop the plague."

[22]"Take it, my lord, and use it as you wish," Araunah said to David. "Here are oxen for the burnt offering, and you can use the threshing tools and ox yokes for wood to build a fire on the altar. [23]I will give it all to you, and may the LORD your God accept your sacrifice."

[24]But the king replied to Araunah, "No, I insist on buying it, for I cannot present burnt offerings to the LORD my God that have cost me nothing." So David paid him fifty pieces of silver* for the threshing floor and the oxen. [25]David built an altar there to the LORD and offered burnt offerings and peace offerings. And the LORD answered his prayer, and the plague was stopped.

24:24 Hebrew *50 shekels of silver,* about 20 ounces or 570 grams in weight.

1 Kings

AS 1 Kings opens, the golden era of David's reign is drawing to a close, and David's son Solomon prepares to take the throne. While Solomon is able to fulfill his father's dream by building the Temple in Jerusalem, he fails to center his life on the faith it signified (1 Kings 1–11). Solomon's death marks the end of a unified nation of twelve tribes and introduces the chaotic period of the divided kingdom, with Israel in the north and Judah in the south (1 Kings 12–22).

Focus	A King's Divided Heart			A Divided Kingdom		
Divisions	Solomon's Commission: A Throne from God	Solomon's Construction: A Temple for God	Solomon's Compromise: Turning from God	Israel's Civil War	Ahab's Battle with Elijah	Ahab's Battle with Syria
	1 4	5 8	9 11	12 16	17 19	20 22
Topics	The Glory Years			The Declining Years		
		One King (Solomon)		Many Kings	One Prophet (Elijah)	
Place	Jerusalem			Northern Kingdom: Israel Southern Kingdom: Judah		
Time	About 40 Years			About 90 Years		

APRIL 1 ☐ DAY 92
1 KINGS 1–4
Solomon's Commission: A Throne from God

OVERVIEW The final days of David's forty-year reign provide bitter-sweet reminders of his conduct as king: bitter memories of past family failures as seen in Adonijah's attempt to usurp the throne and sweet recollections of a promised dynasty as personified in Solomon, the king-elect. After David's death, Solomon steps into the enormous responsibilities as God's anointed. When confronted by God with the invitation "Ask, and I will give it to you!" (3:5), Solomon responds, "Give me an understanding mind so that I can govern your people well" (3:9)—a request God is only too willing to grant. In addition, God provides the things Solomon could have asked for but didn't: wealth, victory, fame, and long life.

	Chapter 1		Chapter 2	Chapters 3–4
1	A False "King" Overthrown 27	28 A New King Anointed 53	Justice in the Palace	Wisdom in the Palace
	Solomon's Rise		Solomon's Rule	

YOUR DAILY WALK Think back over the great personalities of the past century. Would you like to have been
- the son or daughter of Albert Einstein?
- the center fielder who succeeded Mickey Mantle?
- the conductor who picked up the baton of Arthur Fiedler?

Wise men talk because they have something to say; fools, because they have to say something.

Following in the footsteps of greatness is never easy. Imagine the burden that Solomon carried as he assumed the reins of power formerly held by his father David. And yet, in God's strength and wisdom, he did it, taking the nation of Israel to even greater heights spiritually and economically. Instead of falling over his father's reputation, Solomon followed in his father's footsteps . . . and then some.

Write the words of 1 Kings 3:9 on a piece of paper, and place it by the shoes you will wear tomorrow. Let this verse remind you that God has new paths of service for you to blaze, regardless of who has preceded you.

INSIGHT I'd Like the Chef to Prepare . . .
Solomon's court, which included his enormous harem, his ministers, officials, family members, and servants, required two or three meals a day, just like everyone else. Solomon appointed twelve governors over various regions of Israel to supply the necessary provisions—a job worthy of a military quartermaster corps.

CHAPTER 1
Now King David was very old, and no matter how many blankets covered him, he could not keep warm. ²So his advisers told him, "We will find a young virgin who will wait on you and be your nurse. She will lie in your arms and keep you warm." ³So they searched throughout the country for a beautiful girl, and they found Abishag from Shunem and brought her to the king. ⁴The girl was very beautiful, and she waited on the king and took care of him. But the king had no sexual relations with her.

⁵About that time David's son Adonijah, whose mother was Haggith, decided to make himself king in place of his aged father. So he provided himself with chariots and horses* and recruited fifty men to run in front of him. ⁶Now his father, King David, had never disciplined him at any time, even by asking, "What are you doing?" Adonijah was a very handsome man and had been born next after Absalom. ⁷Adonijah took Joab son of Zeruiah and Abiathar the priest into his confidence, and they agreed to help him become king. ⁸But among those who remained loyal to David and refused to support Adonijah were Zadok the priest, Benaiah son of Jehoiada, Nathan the prophet, Shimei, Rei, and David's personal bodyguard.

⁹Adonijah went to the stone of Zoheleth* near the spring of En-rogel, where he sacrificed sheep, oxen, and fattened calves. He invited all his brothers—the other sons of King David—and all the royal officials of Judah. ¹⁰But he did not invite Nathan the prophet, or Benaiah, or the king's bodyguard, or his brother Solomon.

¹¹Then Nathan the prophet went to Bathsheba, Solomon's mother, and asked her, "Did you realize that Haggith's son, Adonijah, has made himself king and that our lord David doesn't even know about it? ¹²If you want to save your own life and the life of your son Solomon, follow my counsel. ¹³Go at once to King David and say to him, 'My lord, didn't you promise me that my son Solomon would be the next king and would sit upon your throne? Then why has Adonijah become king?' ¹⁴And while you are still talking with him, I will come and confirm everything you have said."

¹⁵So Bathsheba went into the king's bedroom. He was very old now, and Abishag was taking care of him. ¹⁶Bathsheba bowed low before him.

"What can I do for you?" he asked her.

¹⁷She replied, "My lord, you vowed to me by the LORD your God that my son Solomon would be the next king and would sit on your throne. ¹⁸But instead, Adonijah has become the new king, and you do not even know about it. ¹⁹He has sacrificed many oxen, fattened calves, and sheep, and he has invited all your sons and Abiathar the priest and Joab, the commander of the army. But he did not invite

your servant Solomon. ²⁰And now, my lord the king, all Israel is waiting for your decision as to who will become king after you. ²¹If you do not act, my son Solomon and I will be treated as criminals as soon as you are dead."

²²While she was still speaking with the king, Nathan the prophet arrived. ²³The king's advisers told him, "Nathan the prophet is here to see you."

Nathan went in and bowed low before the king. ²⁴He asked, "My lord, have you decided that Adonijah will be the next king and that he will sit on your throne? ²⁵Today he has sacrificed many oxen, fattened calves, and sheep, and he has invited your sons to attend the celebration. He also invited Joab, the commander of the army,* and Abiathar the priest. They are feasting and drinking with him and shouting, 'Long live King Adonijah!' ²⁶But I myself, your servant, was not invited; neither were Zadok the priest, Benaiah son of Jehoiada, nor Solomon. ²⁷Has my lord really done this without letting any of his servants know who should be the next king?"

²⁸"Call Bathsheba," David said. So she came back in and stood before the king. ²⁹And the king vowed, "As surely as the LORD lives, who has rescued me from every danger, ³⁰today I decree that your son Solomon will be the next king and will sit on my throne, just as I swore to you before the LORD, the God of Israel."

³¹Then Bathsheba bowed low before him again and exclaimed, "May my lord King David live forever!"

³²Then King David ordered, "Call Zadok the priest, Nathan the prophet, and Benaiah son of Jehoiada." When they came into the king's presence, ³³the king said to them, "Take Solomon and my officers down to Gihon Spring. Solomon is to ride on my personal mule. ³⁴There Zadok the priest and Nathan the prophet are to anoint him king over Israel. Then blow the trumpets and shout, 'Long live King Solomon!' ³⁵When you bring him back here, he will sit on my throne. He will succeed me as king, for I have appointed him to be ruler over Israel and Judah."

³⁶"Amen!" Benaiah son of Jehoiada replied. "May the LORD, the God of my lord the king, decree it to be so. ³⁷And may the LORD be with Solomon as he has been with

1:5 Or and charioteers.   1:9 Or to the Serpent's Stone; Greek version supports reading Zoheleth as a proper name.   1:25 As in Greek version; Hebrew reads invited the commanders of the army.

you, and may he make Solomon's reign even greater than yours!"

³⁸So Zadok the priest, Nathan the prophet, Benaiah son of Jehoiada, and the king's bodyguard* took Solomon down to Gihon Spring, and Solomon rode on King David's personal mule. ³⁹There Zadok the priest took a flask of olive oil from the sacred tent and poured it on Solomon's head. Then the trumpets were blown, and all the people shouted, "Long live King Solomon!" ⁴⁰And all the people returned with Solomon to Jerusalem, playing flutes and shouting for joy. The celebration was so joyous and noisy that the earth shook with the sound.

⁴¹Adonijah and his guests heard the celebrating and shouting just as they were finishing their banquet. When Joab heard the sound of trumpets, he asked, "What's going on? Why is the city in such an uproar?"

⁴²And while he was still speaking, Jonathan son of Abiathar the priest arrived. "Come in," Adonijah said to him, "for you are a good man. You must have good news."

⁴³"Not at all!" Jonathan replied. "Our lord King David has just declared Solomon king! ⁴⁴The king sent him down to Gihon Spring with Zadok the priest, Nathan the prophet, and Benaiah son of Jehoiada, protected by the king's bodyguard. They had him ride on the king's own mule, ⁴⁵and Zadok and Nathan have anointed him as the new king. They have just returned, and the whole city is celebrating and rejoicing. That's what all the noise is about. ⁴⁶Moreover, Solomon is now sitting on the royal throne as king. ⁴⁷All the royal officials went to King David and congratulated him, saying, 'May your God make Solomon's fame even greater than your own, and may Solomon's kingdom be even greater than yours!' Then the king bowed his head in worship as he lay in his bed, ⁴⁸and he spoke these words: 'Blessed be the LORD, the God of Israel, who today has chosen someone to sit on my throne while I am still alive to see it.'"

⁴⁹Then all of Adonijah's guests jumped up in panic from the banquet table and quickly went their separate ways. ⁵⁰Adonijah himself was afraid of Solomon, so he rushed to the sacred tent and caught hold of the horns of the altar. ⁵¹Word soon reached Solomon that Adonijah had seized the horns of the altar and that he was pleading, "Let Solomon swear today that he will not kill me!"

⁵²Solomon replied, "If he proves himself to be loyal, he will not be harmed.* But if he does not, he will die." ⁵³So King Solomon summoned Adonijah, and they brought him down from the altar. He came and bowed low before the king, and Solomon dismissed him, saying, "Go on home."

CHAPTER 2
As the time of King David's death approached, he gave this charge to his son Solomon: ²"I am going where everyone on earth must someday go. Take courage and be a man. ³Observe the requirements of the LORD your God and follow all his ways. Keep each of the laws, commands, regulations, and stipulations written in the law of Moses so that you will be successful in all you do and wherever you go. ⁴If you do this, then the LORD will keep the promise he made to me: 'If your descendants live as they should and follow me faithfully with all their heart and soul, one of them will always sit on the throne of Israel.'

⁵"And there is something else. You know that Joab son of Zeruiah murdered my two army commanders, Abner son of Ner and Amasa son of Jether. He pretended that it was an act of war, but it was done in a time of peace,* staining his belt and sandals with the blood of war. ⁶Do with him what you think best, but don't let him die in peace.

⁷"Be kind to the sons of Barzillai of Gilead. Make them permanent guests of the king, for they took care of me when I fled from your brother Absalom.

⁸"And remember Shimei son of Gera, the man from Bahurim in Benjamin. He cursed me with a terrible curse as I was fleeing to Mahanaim. When he came down to meet me at the Jordan River, I swore by the LORD that I would not kill him. ⁹But that oath does not make him innocent. You are a wise man, and you will know how to arrange a bloody death for him."

¹⁰Then David died and was buried in the City of David. ¹¹He had reigned over Israel for forty years, seven of them in Hebron

1:38 Hebrew *the Kerethites and Pelethites;* also in 1:44.   **1:52** Hebrew *not a hair on his head will be touched.*   **2:5** Or *He murdered them during a time of peace as revenge for deaths they had caused in time of war.*

and thirty-three in Jerusalem. [12]Solomon succeeded him as king, replacing his father, David, and he was firmly established on the throne.

[13]One day Adonijah, whose mother was Haggith, came to see Bathsheba, Solomon's mother. "Have you come to make trouble?" she asked him.

"No," he said, "I come in peace. [14]In fact, I have a favor to ask of you."

"What is it?" she asked.

[15]He replied, "As you know, the kingdom was mine; everyone expected me to be the next king. But the tables were turned, and everything went to my brother instead; for that is the way the LORD wanted it. [16]So now I have just one favor to ask of you. Please don't turn me down."

"What is it?" she asked.

[17]He replied, "Speak to King Solomon on my behalf, for I know he will do anything you request. Ask him to give me Abishag, the girl from Shunem, as my wife."

[18]"All right," Bathsheba replied. "I will speak to the king for you."

[19]So Bathsheba went to King Solomon to speak on Adonijah's behalf. The king rose from his throne to meet her, and he bowed down before her. When he sat down on his throne again, he ordered that a throne be brought for his mother, and she sat at his right hand.

[20]"I have one small request to make of you," she said. "I hope you won't turn me down."

"What is it, my mother?" he asked. "You know I won't refuse you."

[21]"Then let your brother Adonijah marry Abishag, the girl from Shunem," she replied.

[22]"How can you possibly ask me to give Abishag to Adonijah?" Solomon demanded. "You might as well be asking me to give him the kingdom! You know that he is my older brother, and that he has Abiathar the priest and Joab son of Zeruiah on his side." [23]Then King Solomon swore solemnly by the LORD: "May God strike me dead if Adonijah has not sealed his fate with this request. [24]The LORD has confirmed me and placed me on the throne of my father, David; he has established my dynasty as he promised. So as surely as the LORD lives, Adonijah will die this very day!" [25]So King Solomon ordered Benaiah son of Jehoiada to execute him, and Adonijah was put to death.

[26]Then the king said to Abiathar the priest, "Go back to your home in Anathoth. You deserve to die, but I will not kill you now, because you carried the Ark of the Sovereign LORD for my father, and you suffered right along with him through all his troubles." [27]So Solomon deposed Abiathar from his position as priest of the LORD, thereby fulfilling the decree the LORD had made at Shiloh concerning the descendants of Eli.

[28]Although he had not followed Absalom earlier, Joab had also joined Adonijah's revolt. When Joab heard about Adonijah's death, he ran to the sacred tent of the LORD and caught hold of the horns of the altar. [29]When news of this reached King Solomon, he sent Benaiah son of Jehoiada to execute him.

[30]Benaiah went into the sacred tent of the LORD and said to Joab, "The king orders you to come out!"

But Joab answered, "No, I will die here." So Benaiah returned to the king and told him what Joab had said.

[31]"Do as he said," the king replied. "Kill him there beside the altar and bury him. This will remove the guilt of his senseless murders from me and from my father's family. [32]Then the LORD will repay him for the murders of two men who were more righteous and better than he. For my father was no party to the deaths of Abner son of Ner, commander of the army of Israel, and Amasa son of Jether, commander of the army of Judah. [33]May Joab and his descendants be forever guilty of these murders, and may the LORD grant peace to David and his descendants and to his throne forever."

[34]So Benaiah son of Jehoiada returned to the sacred tent and killed Joab, and Joab was buried at his home in the wilderness. [35]Then the king appointed Benaiah to command the army in place of Joab, and he installed Zadok the priest to take the place of Abiathar.

[36]The king then sent for Shimei and told him, "Build a house here in Jerusalem and live there. But don't step outside the city to go anywhere else. [37]On the day you cross the Kidron Valley, you will surely die; your blood will be on your own head."

[38]Shimei replied, "Your sentence is fair; I will do whatever my lord the king commands." So Shimei lived in Jerusalem for a long time.

[39] But three years later, two of Shimei's slaves escaped to King Achish of Gath. When Shimei learned where they were, [40] he saddled his donkey and went to Gath to search for them. When he had found them, he took them back to Jerusalem.

[41] Solomon heard that Shimei had left Jerusalem and had gone to Gath and returned. [42] So he sent for Shimei and demanded, "Didn't I make you swear by the LORD and warn you not to go anywhere else, or you would surely die? And you replied, 'The sentence is fair; I will do as you say.' [43] Then why haven't you kept your oath to the LORD and obeyed my command?"

[44] The king also said to Shimei, "You surely remember all the wicked things you did to my father, King David. May the LORD punish you for them. [45] But may I receive the LORD's rich blessings, and may one of David's descendants always sit on this throne." [46] Then, at the king's command, Benaiah son of Jehoiada took Shimei outside and killed him.

So the kingdom was now firmly in Solomon's grip.

CHAPTER 3

Solomon made an alliance with Pharaoh, the king of Egypt, and married one of his daughters. He brought her to live in the City of David until he could finish building his palace and the Temple of the LORD and the wall around the city. [2] At that time the people of Israel sacrificed their offerings at local altars, for a temple honoring the name of the LORD had not yet been built.

[3] Solomon loved the LORD and followed all the instructions of his father, David, except that Solomon, too, offered sacrifices and burned incense at the local altars. [4] The most important of these altars was at Gibeon, so the king went there and sacrificed one thousand burnt offerings. [5] That night the LORD appeared to Solomon in a dream, and God said, "What do you want? Ask, and I will give it to you!"

[6] Solomon replied, "You were wonderfully kind to my father, David, because he was honest and true and faithful to you. And you have continued this great kindness to him today by giving him a son to succeed him. [7] O LORD my God, now you have made me king instead of my father, David, but I am like a little child who doesn't know his way around. [8] And here I am among your own chosen people, a nation so great they are too numerous to count! [9] Give me an understanding mind so that I can govern your people well and know the difference between right and wrong. For who by himself is able to govern this great nation of yours?"

[10] The Lord was pleased with Solomon's reply and was glad that he had asked for wisdom. [11] So God replied, "Because you have asked for wisdom in governing my people and have not asked for a long life or riches for yourself or the death of your enemies—[12] I will give you what you asked for! I will give you a wise and understanding mind such as no one else has ever had or ever will have! [13] And I will also give you what you did not ask for—riches and honor! No other king in all the world will be compared to you for the rest of your life! [14] And if you follow me and obey my commands as your father, David, did, I will give you a long life."

[15] Then Solomon woke up and realized it had been a dream. He returned to Jerusalem and stood before the Ark of the Lord's covenant, where he sacrificed burnt offerings and peace offerings. Then he invited all his officials to a great banquet.

[16] Some time later, two prostitutes came to the king to have an argument settled. [17] "Please, my lord," one of them began, "this woman and I live in the same house. I gave birth to a baby while she was with me in the house. [18] Three days later, she also had a baby. We were alone; there were only two of us in the house. [19] But her baby died during the night when she rolled over on it. [20] Then she got up in the night and took my son from beside me while I was asleep. She laid her dead child in my arms and took mine to sleep beside her. [21] And in the morning when I tried to nurse my son, he was dead! But when I looked more closely in the morning light, I saw that it wasn't my son at all."

[22] Then the other woman interrupted, "It certainly was your son, and the living child is mine."

"No," the first woman said, "the dead one is yours, and the living one is mine." And so they argued back and forth before the king.

[23] Then the king said, "Let's get the facts straight. Both of you claim the living child is yours, and each says that the dead child

belongs to the other. 24All right, bring me a sword." So a sword was brought to the king. 25Then he said, "Cut the living child in two and give half to each of these women!"

26Then the woman who really was the mother of the living child, and who loved him very much, cried out, "Oh no, my lord! Give her the child—please do not kill him!"

But the other woman said, "All right, he will be neither yours nor mine; divide him between us!"

27Then the king said, "Do not kill him, but give the baby to the woman who wants him to live, for she is his mother!"

28Word of the king's decision spread quickly throughout all Israel, and the people were awed as they realized the great wisdom God had given him to render decisions with justice.

CHAPTER 4

So Solomon was king over all Israel, 2and these were his high officials:

Azariah son of Zadok was the priest.
3 Elihoreph and Ahijah, the sons of Shisha, were court secretaries.
Jehoshaphat son of Ahilud was the royal historian.
4 Benaiah son of Jehoiada was commander of the army.
Zadok and Abiathar were the priests.
5 Azariah son of Nathan presided over the district governors.
Zabud son of Nathan, a priest, was a trusted adviser to the king.
6 Ahishar was manager of palace affairs.
Adoniram son of Abda was in charge of the labor force.

7Solomon also had twelve district governors who were over all Israel. They were responsible for providing food from the people for the king's household. Each of them arranged provisions for one month of the year.

8These are the names of the twelve governors:

Ben-hur, in the hill country of Ephraim.
9 Ben-deker, in Makaz, Shaalbim, Beth-shemesh, and Elon-bethhanan.
10 Ben-hesed, in Arubboth, including Socoh and all the land of Hepher.
11 Ben-abinadab, in Naphoth-dor.* (He was married to Taphath, one of Solomon's daughters.)
12 Baana son of Ahilud, in Taanach and Megiddo, all of Beth-shan* near Zarethan below Jezreel, and all the territory from Beth-shan to Abel-meholah and over to Jokmeam.
13 Ben-geber, in Ramoth-gilead, including the Towns of Jair (named for Jair son of Manasseh) in Gilead, and in the Argob region of Bashan, including sixty great fortified cities with gates barred with bronze.
14 Ahinadab son of Iddo, in Mahanaim.
15 Ahimaaz, in Naphtali. (He was married to Basemath, another of Solomon's daughters.)
16 Baana son of Hushai, in Asher and in Aloth.
17 Jehoshaphat son of Paruah, in Issachar.
18 Shimei son of Ela, in Benjamin.
19 Geber son of Uri, in the land of Gilead,* including the territories of King Sihon of the Amorites and King Og of Bashan.

And there was one governor over the land of Judah.*

20The people of Judah and Israel were as numerous as the sand on the seashore. They were very contented, with plenty to eat and drink. 21King Solomon ruled all the kingdoms from the Euphrates River* to the land of the Philistines, as far south as the border of Egypt. The conquered peoples of those lands sent tribute money to Solomon and continued to serve him throughout his lifetime.

22The daily food requirements for Solomon's palace were 150 bushels of choice flour and 300 bushels of meal,* 23ten oxen from the fattening pens, twenty pasture-fed cattle, one hundred sheep or goats, as well as deer, gazelles, roebucks, and choice fowl.

24Solomon's dominion extended over all the kingdoms west of the Euphrates River, from Tiphsah to Gaza. And there was peace throughout the entire land. 25Throughout the lifetime of Solomon, all of Judah and Israel lived in peace and safety. And from Dan to Beersheba, each family had its own home and garden.

4:11 Hebrew Naphath-dor, a variant name for Naphoth-dor.   4:12 Hebrew Beth-shean, a variant name for Beth-shan; also in 4:12b.   4:19a Greek version reads of Gad; compare 4:13.   4:19b As in some Greek manuscripts; Hebrew lacks of Judah. The meaning of the Hebrew is uncertain.   4:21 Hebrew the river; also in 4:24.   4:22 Hebrew 30 cors [5.5 kiloliters] of choice flour and 60 cors [11 kiloliters] of meal.

²⁶Solomon had four thousand* stalls for his chariot horses and twelve thousand horses.* ²⁷The district governors faithfully provided food for King Solomon and his court, each during his assigned month. ²⁸They also brought the necessary barley and straw for the royal horses in the stables.

²⁹God gave Solomon great wisdom and understanding, and knowledge too vast to be measured. ³⁰In fact, his wisdom exceeded that of all the wise men of the East and the wise men of Egypt. ³¹He was wiser than anyone else, including Ethan the Ezrahite and Heman, Calcol, and Darda—the sons of Mahol. His fame spread throughout all the surrounding nations. ³²He composed some 3,000 proverbs and wrote 1,005 songs. ³³He could speak with authority about all kinds of plants, from the great cedar of Lebanon to the tiny hyssop that grows from cracks in a wall. He could also speak about animals, birds, reptiles, and fish. ³⁴And kings from every nation sent their ambassadors to listen to the wisdom of Solomon.

4:26a As in some Greek manuscripts (see also 2 Chr 9:25); Hebrew reads 40,000.   4:26b Or 12,000 charioteers.

APRIL 2 ☐ DAY 93
1 KINGS 5–8
Solomon's Construction: A Temple for God

OVERVIEW David's lifelong dream to build a house for God now becomes Solomon's consuming passion. Building upon the ample preparations of his father, Solomon secures the remaining supplies and manpower to accomplish the task: cedar from Lebanon, huge stones from mountain quarries, conscripted laborers from all over the country. Seven long years pass before the work is finished and worship can begin. Elders, Levites, priests, and the people congregate to exalt the God whom no earthly house can contain. When at last the glory of the Lord fills the Temple, Solomon lifts his hands toward heaven and leads the nation in a stirring prayer of praise and petition.

Chapter 5	Chapter 6	Chapter 7	Chapter 8
Temple Builders	Temple Blueprint	Temple Construction	Temple Consecration

"So I am planning to build a Temple to honor . . . the Lord my God." (5:5)

YOUR DAILY WALK If your prayer life has been a little anemic lately, spend some extra moments savoring chapter 8.

Prayer at its best employs four statements: Thank you; I'm sorry; teach me; go with me.

In the space of thirty-one verses (8:23-53), Solomon pours out his heart to God in a prayer of unparalleled worship and adoration. With hands held high to heaven (v. 22) and kneeling in humility before the Lord (v. 54), Solomon recalls God's covenant promises to his people. Knowing full well that God cannot be contained by the Temple he has built (v. 27), Solomon is equally confident that God answers prayers in keeping with his covenant (v. 23). Then Solomon makes seven specific petitions covering different cases in which future prayers would be offered to God in the Temple. (Can you find all seven, each containing the phrase "hear from heaven"?)

How confident are you that God hears and answers your prayers when they are consistent with his promises? Make 1 John 5:14 your meditation for the day: "And we can be confident that he will listen to us whenever we ask him for anything in line with his will." Then pray with the same confidence that Solomon prayed!

INSIGHT Unholey Walls for a Holy Temple (7:9)
Walls in Solomon's time were commonly made of sun-dried mud or
sandstone blocks, often with gaps between. The wealthy would avoid
this problem by substituting expensive, close-fitting hewn stones. This
was the building method used for the Temple.

CHAPTER 5

King Hiram of Tyre had always been a loyal friend of David, so when he learned that David's son Solomon was the new king of Israel, Hiram sent ambassadors to congratulate him. ²Then Solomon sent this message back to Hiram:

³"You know that my father, David, was not able to build a Temple to honor the name of the LORD his God because of the many wars he waged with surrounding nations. He could not build until the LORD gave him victory over all his enemies. ⁴But now the LORD my God has given me peace on every side, and I have no enemies and all is well. ⁵So I am planning to build a Temple to honor the name of the LORD my God, just as he instructed my father that I should do. For the LORD told him, 'Your son, whom I will place on your throne, will build the Temple to honor my name.' ⁶Now please command that cedars from Lebanon be cut for me. Let my men work alongside yours, and I will pay your men whatever wages you ask. As you know, there is no one among us who can cut timber like you Sidonians!"

⁷When Hiram received Solomon's message, he was very pleased and said, "Praise the LORD for giving David a wise son to be king of the great nation of Israel." ⁸Then he sent this reply to Solomon:

"I have received your message, and I will do as you have asked concerning the timber. I can supply you with both cedar and cypress. ⁹My servants will bring the logs from the Lebanon mountains to the Mediterranean Sea and build them into rafts. We will float them along the coast to whatever place you choose. Then we will break the rafts apart and deliver the timber to you. You can pay me with food for my household."

¹⁰So Hiram produced for Solomon as much cedar and cypress timber as he desired. ¹¹In return Solomon sent him an annual payment of 100,000 bushels* of wheat for his household and 110,000 gallons* of olive oil. ¹²So the LORD gave great wisdom to Solomon just as he had promised. And Hiram and Solomon made a formal alliance of peace.

¹³Then King Solomon enlisted 30,000 laborers from all Israel. ¹⁴He sent them to Lebanon in shifts, 10,000 every month, so that each man would be one month in Lebanon and two months at home. Adoniram was in charge of this labor force. ¹⁵Solomon also enlisted 70,000 common laborers, 80,000 stonecutters in the hill country, ¹⁶and 3,600* foremen to supervise the work. ¹⁷At the king's command, the stonecutters quarried and shaped costly blocks of stone for the foundation of the Temple. ¹⁸Men from the city of Gebal helped Solomon's and Hiram's builders prepare the timber and stone for the Temple.

CHAPTER 6

It was in midspring,* during the fourth year of Solomon's reign, that he began the construction of the Temple of the LORD. This was 480 years after the people of Israel were delivered from their slavery in the land of Egypt.

²The Temple that King Solomon built for the LORD was 90 feet long, 30 feet wide, and 45 feet high.* ³The foyer at the front of the Temple was 30 feet wide, running across the entire width of the Temple. It projected outward 15 feet from the front of the Temple. ⁴Solomon also made narrow, recessed windows throughout the Temple.

⁵A complex of rooms was built against the outer walls of the Temple, all the way around the sides and rear of the building. ⁶The complex was three stories high, the

5:11a Hebrew *20,000 cors* [3,640 kiloliters]. 5:11b As in Greek version, which reads *20,000 baths* [420 kiloliters] (see also 2 Chr 2:10); Hebrew reads *20 cors*, about 800 gallons or 3.6 kiloliters in volume. 5:16 As in some Greek manuscripts (see also 2 Chr 2:2, 18); Hebrew reads *3,300.* 6:1 Hebrew *in the month of Ziv, which is the second month.* This month of the Hebrew lunar calendar usually occurs in April and May. 6:2 Hebrew *60 cubits* [27 meters] *long, 20 cubits* [9 meters] *wide, and 30 cubits* [13.5 meters] *high.* In this chapter, the distance measures are calculated from the Hebrew cubit at a ratio of 18 inches or 45 centimeters per cubit.

bottom floor being 7½ feet wide, the second floor 9 feet wide, and the top floor 10½ feet wide. The rooms were connected to the walls of the Temple by beams resting on ledges built out from the wall. So the beams were not inserted into the walls themselves.

7The stones used in the construction of the Temple were prefinished at the quarry, so the entire structure was built without the sound of hammer, ax, or any other iron tool at the building site.

8The entrance to the bottom floor* was on the south side of the Temple. There were winding stairs going up to the second floor, and another flight of stairs between the second and third floors. 9After completing the Temple structure, Solomon put in a ceiling made of beams and planks of cedar. 10As already stated, there was a complex of rooms on three sides of the building, attached to the Temple walls by cedar timbers. Each story of the complex was 7½ feet high.

11Then the LORD gave this message to Solomon: 12"Concerning this Temple you are building, if you keep all my laws and regulations and obey all my commands, I will fulfill through you the promise I made to your father, David. 13I will live among the people of Israel and never forsake my people."

14So Solomon finished building the Temple. 15The entire inside, from floor to ceiling, was paneled with wood. He paneled the walls and ceilings with cedar, and he used cypress for the floors. 16He partitioned off an inner sanctuary—the Most Holy Place—at the far end of the Temple. It was 30 feet deep and was paneled with cedar from floor to ceiling. 17The main room of the Temple, outside the Most Holy Place, was 60 feet long. 18Cedar paneling completely covered the stone walls throughout the Temple, and the paneling was decorated with carvings of gourds and open flowers.

19Solomon prepared the inner sanctuary in the rear of the Temple, where the Ark of the LORD's covenant would be placed. 20This inner sanctuary was 30 feet long, 30 feet wide, and 30 feet high. Solomon overlaid its walls and ceiling with pure gold. He also overlaid the altar made of cedar.* 21Then he overlaid the rest of the Temple's interior with pure gold, and he made gold chains to protect the entrance to the Most Holy Place. 22So he finished overlaying the entire Temple with gold, including the altar that belonged to the Most Holy Place.

23Within the inner sanctuary Solomon placed two cherubim made of olive wood, each 15 feet tall. 24The wingspan of each of the cherubim was 15 feet, each wing being 7½ feet long. 25The two cherubim were identical in shape and size; 26each was 15 feet tall. 27Solomon placed them side by side in the inner sanctuary of the Temple. Their outspread wings reached from wall to wall, while their inner wings touched at the center of the room. 28He overlaid the two cherubim with gold.

29All the walls of the inner sanctuary and the main room were decorated with carvings of cherubim, palm trees, and open flowers. 30The floor in both rooms was overlaid with gold.

31For the entrance to the inner sanctuary, Solomon made double doors of olive wood with five-sided doorposts. 32These doors were decorated with carvings of cherubim, palm trees, and open flowers, and the doors were overlaid with gold.

33Then he made four-sided doorposts of olive wood for the entrance to the Temple. 34There were two folding doors of cypress wood, and each door was hinged to fold back upon itself. 35These doors were decorated with carvings of cherubim, palm trees, and open flowers, and the doors were overlaid with gold.

36The walls of the inner courtyard were built so that there was one layer of cedar beams after every three layers of hewn stone.

37The foundation of the LORD's Temple was laid in midspring* of the fourth year of Solomon's reign. 38The entire building was completed in every detail by midautumn* of the eleventh year of his reign. So it took seven years to build the Temple.

CHAPTER 7
Solomon also built a palace for himself, and it took him thirteen years to complete the construction.

2One of Solomon's buildings was called

the Palace of the Forest of Lebanon. It was 150 feet long, 75 feet wide, and 45 feet high.* The great cedar ceiling beams rested on four rows of cedar pillars. ³It had a cedar roof supported by forty-five rafters that rested on three rows of pillars, fifteen in each row. ⁴On each of the side walls there were three rows of windows facing each other. ⁵All the doorways were rectangular in frame; they were in sets of three, facing each other.

⁶He also built the Hall of Pillars, which was 75 feet long and 45 feet wide. There was a porch at its front, covered by a canopy that was supported by pillars.

⁷There was also the Hall of the Throne, also known as the Hall of Judgment, where Solomon sat to hear legal matters. It was paneled with cedar from floor to ceiling.* ⁸Solomon's living quarters surrounded a courtyard behind this hall; they were built the same way. He also built similar living quarters for Pharaoh's daughter, one of his wives. ⁹All these buildings were built entirely from huge, costly blocks of stone, cut and trimmed to exact measure on all sides. ¹⁰Some of the huge foundation stones were 15 feet long, and some were 12 feet long. ¹¹The costly blocks of stone used in the walls were also cut to measure, and cedar beams were also used. ¹²The walls of the great courtyard were built so that there was one layer of cedar beams after every three layers of hewn stone, just like the walls of the inner courtyard of the LORD's Temple with its entrance foyer.

¹³King Solomon then asked for a man named Huram* to come from Tyre, ¹⁴for he was a craftsman skilled in bronze work. He was half Israelite, since his mother was a widow from the tribe of Naphtali, and his father had been a foundry worker from Tyre. So he came to work for King Solomon.

¹⁵Huram cast two bronze pillars, each 27 feet tall and 18 feet in circumference. ¹⁶For the tops of the pillars he made capitals of molded bronze, each 7½ feet tall. ¹⁷Each capital was decorated with seven sets of latticework and interwoven chains. ¹⁸He also made two rows of pomegranates that encircled the latticework to decorate the capitals over the pillars. ¹⁹The capitals on the columns inside the foyer were shaped like lilies, and they were 6 feet tall. ²⁰Each capital on the two pillars had two hundred pomegranates in two rows around them, beside the rounded surface next to the latticework. ²¹Huram set the pillars at the entrance of the Temple, one toward the south and one toward the north. He named the one on the south Jakin, and the one on the north Boaz.* ²²The capitals on the pillars were shaped like lilies. And so the work on the pillars was finished.

²³Then Huram cast a large round tank, 15 feet across from rim to rim; it was called the Sea. It was 7½ feet deep and about 45 feet in circumference. ²⁴The Sea was encircled just below its rim by two rows of decorative gourds. There were about six gourds per foot* all the way around, and they had been cast as part of the tank. ²⁵The Sea rested on a base of twelve bronze oxen, all facing outward. Three faced north, three faced west, three faced south, and three faced east. ²⁶The walls of the Sea were about three inches* thick, and its rim flared out like a cup and resembled a lily blossom. It could hold about 11,000 gallons* of water.

²⁷Huram also made ten bronze water carts, each 6 feet long, 6 feet wide, and 4½ feet tall. ²⁸They were constructed with side panels braced with crossbars. ²⁹Both the panels and the crossbars were decorated with carved lions, oxen, and cherubim. Above and below the lions and oxen were wreath decorations. ³⁰Each of these carts had four bronze wheels and bronze axles. At each corner of the carts were supporting posts for the bronze basins; these supports were decorated with carvings of wreaths on each side. ³¹The top of each cart had a circular frame for the basin. It projected 1½ feet above the cart's top like a round pedestal, and its opening was 2¼ feet across; it was decorated on the outside with carvings of wreaths. The panels of the carts were square, not round. ³²Under the panels were four wheels that were connected to axles that had been cast as one unit with the cart. The wheels were 2¼ feet in diameter

7:2 Hebrew *100 cubits* [45 meters] *long, 50 cubits* [22.5 meters] *wide, and 30 cubits* [13.5 meters] *high*. In this chapter, the distance measures are calculated from the Hebrew cubit at a ratio of 18 inches or 45 centimeters per cubit.   7:7 As in Syriac version and Latin Vulgate; Hebrew reads *from floor to floor*.   7:13 Hebrew *Hiram* (also in 7:40, 45); compare 2 Chr 2:13. This is not the same person mentioned in 5:1.   7:21 Jakin probably means "he establishes"; Boaz probably means "in him is strength."   7:24 Or *20 gourds per meter;* Hebrew reads *10 per cubit*.   7:26a Hebrew *a handbreadth* [8 centimeters].   7:26b Hebrew *2,000 baths* [42 kiloliters].

33and were similar to chariot wheels. The axles, spokes, rims, and hubs were all cast from molten bronze.

34There were supports at each of the four corners of the carts, and these, too, were cast as one unit with the cart. 35Around the top of each cart there was a rim 9 inches wide.* The supports and side panels were cast as one unit with the cart. 36Carvings of cherubim, lions, and palm trees decorated the panels and supports wherever there was room, and there were wreaths all around. 37All ten water carts were the same size and were made alike, for each was cast from the same mold.

38Huram also made ten bronze basins, one for each cart. Each basin was 6 feet across and could hold 220 gallons* of water. 39He arranged five water carts on the south side of the Temple and five on the north side. The Sea was placed at the southeast corner of the Temple. 40He also made the necessary pots, shovels, and basins.

So at last Huram completed everything King Solomon had assigned him to make for the Temple of the LORD:

41 two pillars,
   two bowl-shaped capitals on top of the
      pillars,
   two networks of chains that decorated
      the capitals,
42 four hundred pomegranates that
      hung from the chains on the capitals
      (two rows of pomegranates for each
      of the chain networks that were hung
      around the capitals on top of the
      pillars),
43 the ten water carts holding the ten
      basins,
44 the Sea and the twelve oxen under it,
45 the pots, the shovels, and the basins.

All these utensils for the Temple of the LORD that Huram made for Solomon were made of burnished bronze. 46The king had them cast in clay molds in the Jordan Valley between Succoth and Zarethan. 47Solomon did not weigh all the utensils because there were so many; the weight of the bronze could not be measured.

48So Solomon made all the furnishings of the Temple of the LORD:

the gold altar,
the gold table for the Bread of the
   Presence,
49 the gold lampstands, five on the south
   and five on the north, in front of the
   Most Holy Place,
the flower decorations, lamps, and
   tongs, all of gold,
50 the cups, lamp snuffers, basins, dishes,
   and firepans, all of pure gold,
the doors for the entrances to the Most
   Holy Place and the main room of the
   Temple, with their fronts overlaid
   with gold.

51So King Solomon finished all his work on the Temple of the LORD. Then Solomon brought all the gifts his father, David, had dedicated—the silver, the gold, and the other utensils—and he stored them in the treasuries of the LORD's Temple.

CHAPTER 8

Solomon then summoned the leaders of all the tribes and families of Israel to assemble in Jerusalem. They were to bring the Ark of the LORD's covenant from its location in the City of David, also known as Zion, to its new place in the Temple. 2They all assembled before the king at the annual Festival of Shelters in early autumn.* 3When all the leaders of Israel arrived, the priests picked up the Ark. 4Then the priests and Levites took the Ark of the LORD, along with the Tabernacle* and all its sacred utensils, and carried them up to the Temple. 5King Solomon and the entire community of Israel sacrificed sheep and oxen before the Ark in such numbers that no one could keep count!

6Then the priests carried the Ark of the LORD's covenant into the inner sanctuary of the Temple—the Most Holy Place—and placed it beneath the wings of the cherubim. 7The cherubim spread their wings over the Ark, forming a canopy over the Ark and its carrying poles. 8These poles were so long that their ends could be seen from the front entrance of the Temple's main room—the Holy Place—but not from outside it. They are still there to this day. 9Nothing was in the Ark except the two stone tablets that Moses had placed there at Mount Sinai,* where the LORD made a cov-

7:35 Hebrew *half a cubit wide* [22.5 centimeters].   7:38 Hebrew *40 baths* [840 liters].   8:2 Hebrew *at the festival in the month Ethanim, which is the seventh month.* The Festival of Shelters began on the fifteenth day of the seventh month on the Hebrew lunar calendar. This occurs on our calendar in late September or early October.   8:4 Hebrew *Tent of Meeting.*   8:9 Hebrew *at Horeb,* another name for Sinai.

enant with the people of Israel as they were leaving the land of Egypt.

¹⁰As the priests came out of the inner sanctuary, a cloud filled the Temple of the LORD. ¹¹The priests could not continue their work because the glorious presence of the LORD filled the Temple.

¹²Then Solomon prayed, "O LORD, you have said that you would live in thick darkness. ¹³But I have built a glorious Temple for you, where you can live forever!"

¹⁴Then the king turned around to the entire community of Israel standing before him and gave this blessing: ¹⁵"Blessed be the LORD, the God of Israel, who has kept the promise he made to my father, David. ¹⁶For he told my father, 'From the day I brought my people Israel out of Egypt, I have never chosen a city among the tribes of Israel as the place where a temple should be built to honor my name. But now I have chosen David to be king over my people.'"

¹⁷Then Solomon said, "My father, David, wanted to build this Temple to honor the name of the LORD, the God of Israel. ¹⁸But the LORD told him, 'It is right for you to want to build the Temple to honor my name, ¹⁹but you are not the one to do it. One of your sons will build it instead.'

²⁰"And now the LORD has done what he promised, for I have become king in my father's place. I have built this Temple to honor the name of the LORD, the God of Israel. ²¹And I have prepared a place there for the Ark, which contains the covenant that the LORD made with our ancestors when he brought them out of Egypt."

²²Then Solomon stood with his hands lifted toward heaven before the altar of the LORD in front of the entire community of Israel. ²³He prayed, "O LORD, God of Israel, there is no God like you in all of heaven or earth. You keep your promises and show unfailing love to all who obey you and are eager to do your will. ²⁴You have kept your promise to your servant David, my father. You made that promise with your own mouth, and today you have fulfilled it with your own hands. ²⁵And now, O LORD, God of Israel, carry out your further promise to your servant David, my father. For you said to him, 'If your descendants guard their behavior as you have done, they will always reign over Israel.' ²⁶Now, O God of Israel, fulfill this promise to your servant David, my father.

²⁷"But will God really live on earth? Why, even the highest heavens cannot contain you. How much less this Temple I have built! ²⁸Listen to my prayer and my request, O LORD my God. Hear the cry and the prayer that your servant is making to you today. ²⁹May you watch over this Temple both day and night, this place where you have said you would put your name. May you always hear the prayers I make toward this place. ³⁰May you hear the humble and earnest requests from me and your people Israel when we pray toward this place. Yes, hear us from heaven where you live, and when you hear, forgive.

³¹"If someone wrongs another person and is required to take an oath of innocence in front of the altar at this Temple, ³²then hear from heaven and judge between your servants—the accuser and the accused. Punish the guilty party and acquit the one who is innocent.

³³"If your people Israel are defeated by their enemies because they have sinned against you, and if they turn to you and call on your name and pray to you here in this Temple, ³⁴then hear from heaven and forgive their sins and return them to this land you gave their ancestors.

³⁵"If the skies are shut up and there is no rain because your people have sinned against you, and then they pray toward this Temple and confess your name and turn from their sins because you have punished them, ³⁶then hear from heaven and forgive the sins of your servants, your people Israel. Teach them to do what is right, and send rain on your land that you have given to your people as their special possession.

³⁷"If there is a famine in the land, or plagues, or crop disease, or attacks of locusts or caterpillars, or if your people's enemies are in the land besieging their towns—whatever the trouble is—³⁸and if your people offer a prayer concerning their troubles or sorrow, raising their hands toward this Temple, ³⁹then hear from heaven where you live, and forgive. Give your people whatever they deserve, for you alone know the human heart. ⁴⁰Then they will fear you and walk in your ways as long as they live in the land you gave to our ancestors.

⁴¹"And when foreigners hear of you and come from distant lands to worship your great name—⁴²for they will hear of you and of your mighty miracles and your power—

and when they pray toward this Temple, [43]then hear from heaven where you live, and grant what they ask of you. Then all the people of the earth will come to know and fear you, just as your own people Israel do. They, too, will know that this Temple I have built bears your name.

[44]"If your people go out at your command to fight their enemies, and if they pray to the LORD toward this city that you have chosen and toward this Temple that I have built for your name, [45]then hear their prayers from heaven and uphold their cause.

[46]"If they sin against you—and who has never sinned?—you may become angry with them and let their enemies conquer them and take them captive to a foreign land far or near. [47]But in that land of exile, they may turn to you again in repentance and pray, 'We have sinned, done evil, and acted wickedly.' [48]Then if they turn to you with their whole heart and soul and pray toward the land you gave to their ancestors, toward this city you have chosen, and toward this Temple I have built to honor your name, [49]then hear their prayers from heaven where you live. Uphold their cause [50]and forgive your people who have sinned against you. Make their captors merciful to them, [51]for they are your people—your special possession—whom you brought out of the iron-smelting furnace of Egypt.

[52]"May your eyes be open to my requests and to the requests of your people Israel. Hear and answer them whenever they cry out to you. [53]For when you brought our ancestors out of Egypt, O Sovereign LORD, you told your servant Moses that you had separated Israel from among all the nations of the earth to be your own special possession."

[54]When Solomon finished making these prayers and requests to the LORD, he stood up in front of the altar of the LORD, where he had been kneeling with his hands raised toward heaven. [55]He stood there and shouted this blessing over the entire community of Israel: [56]"Praise the LORD who has given rest to his people Israel, just as he promised. Not one word has failed of all the wonderful promises he gave through his servant Moses. [57]May the LORD our God be with us as he was with our ancestors; may he never forsake us. [58]May he give us the desire to do his will in everything and to obey all the commands, laws, and regulations that he gave our ancestors. [59]And may these words that I have prayed in the presence of the LORD be before him constantly, day and night, so that the LORD our God may uphold my cause and the cause of his people Israel, fulfilling our daily needs. [60]May people all over the earth know that the LORD is God and that there is no other god. [61]And may you, his people, always be faithful to the LORD our God. May you always obey his laws and commands, just as you are doing today."

[62]Then the king and all Israel with him offered sacrifices to the LORD. [63]Solomon sacrificed peace offerings to the LORD numbering 22,000 oxen and 120,000 sheep. And so the king and all Israel dedicated the Temple of the LORD. [64]That same day the king dedicated the central area of the courtyard in front of the LORD's Temple. He offered burnt offerings, grain offerings, and the fat of peace offerings there, because the bronze altar in the LORD's presence was too small to handle so many offerings.

[65]Then Solomon and all Israel celebrated the Festival of Shelters* in the presence of the LORD their God. A large crowd had gathered from as far away as Lebo-hamath in the north to the brook of Egypt in the south. The celebration went on for fourteen days in all—seven days for the dedication of the altar and seven days for the Festival of Shelters.* [66]After the festival was over,* Solomon sent the people home. They blessed the king as they went, and they were all joyful and happy because the LORD had been good to his servant David and to his people Israel.

8:65a Hebrew *the festival;* see note on 8:2.   **8:65b** Hebrew *seven days and seven days, fourteen days;* compare parallel text at 2 Chr 7:8-10.   **8:66** Hebrew *On the eighth day,* probably referring to the day following the seven-day Festival of Shelters; compare parallel text at 2 Chr 7:9-10.

APRIL 3 ☐ DAY 94
1 KINGS 9–11
Solomon's Compromise: Turning from God

 OVERVIEW With the completion of the Temple in Jerusalem, Solomon reaches the zenith of his reign. At this crucial moment, God brings both a promise and a warning to his kingly representative. If Solomon will continue to walk in the footsteps of his father, David, God promises to bless and prosper him. But if Solomon strays into paths of idolatry and immorality, God warns that he will severely discipline both the king and his people. Hardly has the ring of God's words left Solomon's ears when he begins to amass wealth and wives—the very things that will lead to his undoing. Earthly pursuits and pagan women soon turn his heart away from God, leading to yet another declaration from God: "I will surely tear the kingdom away from you and give it to one of your servants" (11:11).

Chapter 9	Chapter 10	Chapter 11
Warning to Solomon	Wealth of Solomon	Wives of Solomon
Solomon's Fame		Solomon's Failure

 YOUR DAILY WALK In the margin make a list of three or more issues about which you are currently straddling the fence (that is, you are considering the different sides of the issue but as yet haven't come to a firm conviction regarding which side you want to take).

The highest reward for a person's toil is not what he or she gets for it but rather what he or she becomes by it.

Straddling the proverbial fence may be desirable when an issue is still in question. But once the proper course of action is clear, fence-straddling can be dangerous—even deadly. Solomon straddled the fence in his relationship with God. He worshiped God one day and pagan gods the next; he built his life upon God's promises one day, then disregarded them the next; he sought God's wisdom one day but ignored God's warnings the next. And in the end his divided heart resulted in a divided kingdom.

Take an issue on which you are straddling the fence, and search the Scriptures until God's mind on the matter is clear to you. Then decide what—with God's help—you can do in the next week to declare which side you're on!

 INSIGHT Three Strikes and You're Out
Deuteronomy 17:14-20 sets forth God's three commands specifically aimed at Israel's kings in the Promised Land (vv. 16-17, 19). What was Solomon's "batting average" on these three important prohibitions (10:28; 11:3, 6-8)?

CHAPTER 9

So Solomon finished building the Temple of the LORD, as well as the royal palace. He completed everything he had planned to do. ²Then the LORD appeared to Solomon a second time, as he had done before at Gibeon. ³The LORD said to him, "I have heard your prayer and your request. I have set apart this Temple you have built so that my name will be honored there forever. I will always watch over it and care for it. ⁴As for you, if you will follow me with integrity and godliness, as David your father did, always obeying my commands and keeping my laws and regulations, ⁵then I will establish the throne of your dynasty over Israel forever. For I made this promise to your father, David: 'You will never fail to have a successor on the throne of Israel.'

[6]"But if you or your descendants abandon me and disobey my commands and laws, and if you go and worship other gods, [7]then I will uproot the people of Israel from this land I have given them. I will reject this Temple that I have set apart to honor my name. I will make Israel an object of mockery and ridicule among the nations. [8]And though this Temple is impressive now, it will become an appalling sight for all who pass by. They will scoff and ask, 'Why did the LORD do such terrible things to his land and to his Temple?' [9]And the answer will be, 'Because his people forgot the LORD their God, who brought their ancestors out of Egypt, and they worshiped other gods instead. That is why the LORD has brought all these disasters upon them.'"

[10]Now at the end of the twenty years during which Solomon built the Temple of the LORD and the royal palace, [11]Solomon gave twenty towns in the land of Galilee to King Hiram of Tyre as payment for all the cedar and cypress lumber and gold he had furnished for the construction of the buildings. [12]Hiram came from Tyre to see the towns Solomon had given him, but he was not at all pleased with them. [13]"What kind of towns are these, my brother?" he asked. "These towns are worthless!" So Hiram called that area Cabul—"worthless"—as it is still known today. [14]Hiram had sent Solomon nine thousand pounds* of gold.

[15]This is the account of the forced labor that Solomon conscripted to build the LORD's Temple, the royal palace, the Millo,* the wall of Jerusalem, and the cities of Hazor, Megiddo, and Gezer. [16](The king of Egypt had attacked and captured Gezer, killing the Canaanite population and burning it down. He gave the city to his daughter as a wedding gift when she married Solomon. [17]So Solomon rebuilt the city of Gezer.) He also built up the towns of Lower Beth-horon, [18]Baalath, and Tamar* in the desert, within his land. [19]He built towns as supply centers and constructed cities where his chariots and horses* could be kept. He built to his heart's content in Jerusalem and Lebanon and throughout the entire realm.

[20]There were still some people living in the land who were not Israelites, including Amorites, Hittites, Perizzites, Hivites, and Jebusites. [21]These were descendants of the nations that Israel had not completely destroyed.* So Solomon conscripted them for his labor force, and they serve in the labor force to this day. [22]But Solomon did not conscript any of the Israelites for forced labor. Instead, he assigned them to serve as fighting men, government officials, officers in his army, commanders of his chariots, and charioteers. [23]He also appointed 550 of them to supervise the various projects.

[24]After Solomon moved his wife, Pharaoh's daughter, from the City of David to the new palace he had built for her, he constructed the Millo.

[25]Three times each year Solomon offered burnt offerings and peace offerings to the LORD on the altar he had built. He also burned incense to the LORD. And so he finished the work of building the Temple.

[26]Later King Solomon built a fleet of ships at Ezion-geber, a port near Elath* in the land of Edom, along the shore of the Red Sea.* [27]Hiram sent experienced crews of sailors to sail the ships with Solomon's men. [28]They sailed to Ophir and brought back to Solomon some sixteen tons* of gold.

CHAPTER 10

When the queen of Sheba heard of Solomon's reputation, which brought honor to the name of the LORD, she came to test him with hard questions. [2]She arrived in Jerusalem with a large group of attendants and a great caravan of camels loaded with spices, huge quantities of gold, and precious jewels. When she met with Solomon, they talked about everything she had on her mind. [3]Solomon answered all her questions; nothing was too hard for the king to explain to her. [4]When the queen of Sheba realized how wise Solomon was, and when she saw the palace he had built, [5]she was breathless. She was also amazed at the food on his tables, the organization of his officials and their splendid clothing, the cupbearers and their robes, and the burnt offerings Solomon made at the Temple of the LORD.

[6]She exclaimed to the king, "Everything I heard in my country about your achieve-

9:14 Hebrew *120 talents* [4 metric tons].   **9:15** Or *the supporting terraces;* also in 9:24.   **9:18** The marginal *Qere* reading of the Masoretic Text reads *Tadmor.*   **9:19** Or *and charioteers.*   **9:21** The Hebrew term used here refers to the complete consecration of things or people to the LORD, either by destroying them or by giving them as an offering.   **9:26a** As in Greek version (see also 2 Kgs 14:22; 16:6); Hebrew reads *Eloth.*   **9:26b** Hebrew *sea of reeds.*   **9:28** Hebrew *420 talents* [14 metric tons].

ments and wisdom is true! [7] I didn't believe it until I arrived here and saw it with my own eyes. Truly I had not heard the half of it! Your wisdom and prosperity are far greater than what I was told. [8] How happy these people must be! What a privilege for your officials to stand here day after day, listening to your wisdom! [9] The LORD your God is great indeed! He delights in you and has placed you on the throne of Israel. Because the LORD loves Israel with an eternal love, he has made you king so you can rule with justice and righteousness."

[10] Then she gave the king a gift of nine thousand pounds* of gold, and great quantities of spices and precious jewels. Never again were so many spices brought in as those the queen of Sheba gave to Solomon.

[11] (When Hiram's ships brought gold from Ophir, they also brought rich cargoes of almug wood and precious jewels. [12] The king used the almug wood to make railings for the Temple of the LORD and the royal palace, and to construct harps and lyres for the musicians. Never before or since has there been such a supply of beautiful almug wood.)

[13] King Solomon gave the queen of Sheba whatever she asked for, besides all the other customary gifts he had so generously given. Then she and all her attendants left and returned to their own land.

[14] Each year Solomon received about twenty-five tons* of gold. [15] This did not include the additional revenue he received from merchants and traders, all the kings of Arabia, and the governors of the land.

[16] King Solomon made two hundred large shields of hammered gold, each containing over fifteen pounds* of gold. [17] He also made three hundred smaller shields of hammered gold, each containing nearly four pounds* of gold. The king placed these shields in the Palace of the Forest of Lebanon.

[18] Then the king made a huge ivory throne and overlaid it with pure gold. [19] The throne had six steps and a rounded back. On both sides of the seat were armrests, with the figure of a lion standing on each side of the throne. [20] Solomon made twelve other lion figures, one standing on each end of each of the six steps. No other throne in all the world could be compared with it!

[21] All of King Solomon's drinking cups were solid gold, as were all the utensils in the Palace of the Forest of Lebanon. They were not made of silver because silver was considered of little value in Solomon's day!

[22] The king had a fleet of trading ships* that sailed with Hiram's fleet. Once every three years the ships returned, loaded down with gold, silver, ivory, apes, and peacocks.*

[23] So King Solomon became richer and wiser than any other king in all the earth. [24] People from every nation came to visit him and to hear the wisdom God had given him. [25] Year after year, everyone who came to visit brought him gifts of silver and gold, clothing, weapons, spices, horses, and mules.

[26] Solomon built up a huge force of chariots and horses. He had fourteen hundred chariots and twelve thousand horses.* He stationed many of them in the chariot cities, and some near him in Jerusalem. [27] The king made silver as plentiful in Jerusalem as stones. And valuable cedarwood was as common as the sycamore wood that grows in the foothills of Judah.* [28] Solomon's horses were imported from Egypt* and from Cilicia*; the king's traders acquired them from Cilicia at the standard price. [29] At that time, Egyptian chariots delivered to Jerusalem could be purchased for 600 pieces of silver,* and horses could be bought for 150 pieces of silver.* Many of these were then resold to the kings of the Hittites and the kings of Aram.

CHAPTER 11

Now King Solomon loved many foreign women. Besides Pharaoh's daughter, he married women from Moab, Ammon, Edom, Sidon, and from among the Hittites. [2] The LORD had clearly instructed his people not to intermarry with those nations, because the women they married would lead them to worship their gods. Yet Solomon insisted on loving them anyway. [3] He had seven hundred wives and three hundred concubines. And sure enough, they led his heart away from the LORD. [4] In

---

10:10 Hebrew 120 talents [4 metric tons].　10:14 Hebrew 666 talents [23 metric tons].　10:16 Hebrew 600 shekels [6.8 kilograms].　10:17 Hebrew 3 minas [1.8 kilograms].　10:22a Hebrew fleet of ships of Tarshish.　10:22b Or and baboons.　10:26 Or 12,000 charioteers.　10:27 Hebrew the Shephelah.　10:28a Possibly Muzur, a district near Cilicia; also in 10:29.　10:28b Hebrew Kue, probably another name for Cilicia.　10:29a Hebrew 600 shekels of silver, about 15 pounds or 6.8 kilograms in weight.　10:29b Hebrew 150 [shekels], about 3.8 pounds or 1.7 kilograms in weight.

Solomon's old age, they turned his heart to worship their gods instead of trusting only in the LORD his God, as his father, David, had done. [5]Solomon worshiped Ashtoreth, the goddess of the Sidonians, and Molech,* the detestable god of the Ammonites. [6]Thus, Solomon did what was evil in the LORD's sight; he refused to follow the LORD completely, as his father, David, had done. [7]On the Mount of Olives, east of Jerusalem, he even built a shrine for Chemosh, the detestable god of Moab, and another for Molech, the detestable god of the Ammonites. [8]Solomon built such shrines for all his foreign wives to use for burning incense and sacrificing to their gods.

[9]The LORD was very angry with Solomon, for his heart had turned away from the LORD, the God of Israel, who had appeared to him twice. [10]He had warned Solomon specifically about worshiping other gods, but Solomon did not listen to the LORD's command. [11]So now the LORD said to him, "Since you have not kept my covenant and have disobeyed my laws, I will surely tear the kingdom away from you and give it to one of your servants. [12]But for the sake of your father, David, I will not do this while you are still alive. I will take the kingdom away from your son. [13]And even so, I will let him be king of one tribe, for the sake of my servant David and for the sake of Jerusalem, my chosen city."

[14]Then the LORD raised up Hadad the Edomite, a member of Edom's royal family, to be an enemy against Solomon. [15]Years before, David had gone to Edom with Joab, his army commander, to bury some Israelites who had died in battle. While there, the Israelite army had killed nearly every male in Edom. [16]Joab and the army had stayed there for six months, killing them. [17]But Hadad and a few of his father's royal officials had fled. (Hadad was a very small child at the time.) [18]They escaped from Midian and went to Paran, where others joined them. Then they traveled to Egypt and went to Pharaoh, who gave them a home, food, and some land. [19]Pharaoh grew very fond of Hadad, and he gave him a wife—the sister of Queen Tahpenes. [20]She bore him a son, Genubath, who was brought up in Pharaoh's palace among Pharaoh's own sons.

[21]When the news reached Hadad in Egypt that David and his commander Joab were both dead, he said to Pharaoh, "Let me return to my own country."

[22]"Why?" Pharaoh asked him. "What do you lack here? How have we disappointed you that you want to go home?"

"Nothing is wrong," he replied. "But even so, I must return home."

[23]God also raised up Rezon son of Eliada to be an enemy against Solomon. Rezon had fled from his master, King Hadadezer of Zobah, [24]and had become the leader of a gang of rebels. After David conquered Hadadezer, Rezon and his men fled to Damascus, where he became king. [25]Rezon was Israel's bitter enemy for the rest of Solomon's reign, and he made trouble, just as Hadad did. Rezon hated Israel intensely and continued to reign in Aram.

[26]Another rebel leader was Jeroboam son of Nebat, one of Solomon's own officials. He came from the city of Zeredah in Ephraim, and his mother was Zeruah, a widow. [27]This is the story behind his rebellion. Solomon was rebuilding the Millo* and repairing the walls of the city of his father, David. [28]Jeroboam was a very capable young man, and when Solomon saw how industrious he was, he put him in charge of the labor force from the tribes of Ephraim and Manasseh.*

[29]One day as Jeroboam was leaving Jerusalem, the prophet Ahijah from Shiloh met him on the road, wearing a new cloak. The two of them were alone in a field, [30]and Ahijah took the new cloak he was wearing and tore it into twelve pieces. [31]Then he said to Jeroboam, "Take ten of these pieces, for this is what the LORD, the God of Israel, says: 'I am about to tear the kingdom from the hand of Solomon, and I will give ten of the tribes to you! [32]But I will leave him one tribe for the sake of my servant David and for the sake of Jerusalem, which I have chosen out of all the tribes of Israel. [33]For Solomon has abandoned me and worshiped Ashtoreth, the goddess of the Sidonians; Chemosh, the god of Moab; and Molech, the god of the Ammonites. He has not followed my ways and done what is pleasing in my sight. He has not obeyed my laws and regulations as his father, David, did.

[34]"'But I will not take the entire kingdom from Solomon at this time. For the sake of

my servant David, the one whom I chose and who obeyed my commands and laws, I will let Solomon reign for the rest of his life. ³⁵But I will take the kingdom away from his son and give ten of the tribes to you. ³⁶His son will have one tribe so that the descendants of David my servant will continue to reign* in Jerusalem, the city I have chosen to be the place for my name. ³⁷And I will place you on the throne of Israel, and you will rule over all that your heart desires. ³⁸If you listen to what I tell you and follow my ways and do whatever I consider to be right, and if you obey my laws and commands, as my servant David did, then I will always be with you. I will

11:36 Hebrew *will continue to have a lamp.*

establish an enduring dynasty for you as I did for David, and I will give Israel to you. ³⁹But I will punish the descendants of David because of Solomon's sin—though not forever.'"

⁴⁰Solomon tried to kill Jeroboam, but he fled to King Shishak of Egypt and stayed there until Solomon died.

⁴¹The rest of the events in Solomon's reign, including his wisdom, are recorded in *The Book of the Acts of Solomon.* ⁴²Solomon ruled in Jerusalem over all Israel for forty years. ⁴³When Solomon died, he was buried in the city of his father, David. Then his son Rehoboam became the next king.

APRIL 4 ☐ DAY 95
1 KINGS 12–16
Israel's Civil War

 OVERVIEW What was sown by Solomon is now reaped by Rehoboam. Solomon's great wealth was accumulated partially through excessive taxation of the people. Rehoboam, his son, faced with the choice of decreasing or increasing taxes, foolishly follows the leading of his young advisors. He increases the tax burden of the people, prompting open revolt and the fracturing of the kingdom. One nation becomes two, with Jeroboam ruling the ten tribes in the north (Israel) and Rehoboam ruling only two tribes in the south (Judah). Jeroboam charts a godless course of idol worship in Israel that every one of his successors will imitate. In Judah the picture is somewhat brighter as godly kings (such as Asa) introduce periodic revivals that, although short-lived, profoundly influence their nation for God.

Chapters 12–13	Chapter 14	Chapters 15–16
Reign by Jeroboam	Reign by Rehoboam	Reigns of Eight Kings
Israel	Judah	Israel and Judah

 YOUR DAILY WALK Rate the following six influences in the order that you feel they have affected the lives of your children (or your own life if you are not a parent). Use 1 for "most influential," 2 for "next most influential," etc.

Others will follow your footsteps more easily than they will follow your advice.

____ Television	____ Church
____ Parents	____ Friends
____ School	____ Brothers/Sisters

The epitaph "He walked in the ways of his father" could be penned over almost every king you will read about in today's section. With surprising regularity the son became a carbon copy of his father, patterning his spiritual and moral actions after those of his parent.

Parent, if your children walk in your ways, will you be happy or horrified? Tonight before putting them to bed, give them the above quiz. Then discuss ways that as a family you can walk in the way of the Lord.

INSIGHT Six Decades of Kingly Calamity
Of the six kings of Israel in today's reading, only two died of natural causes. Two others were murdered, one was stricken by God, and one committed suicide—all in the space of fifty-seven years!

CHAPTER 12

Rehoboam went to Shechem, where all Israel had gathered to make him king. ²When Jeroboam son of Nebat heard of Solomon's death, he returned from Egypt,* for he had fled to Egypt to escape from King Solomon. ³The leaders of Israel sent for Jeroboam, and the whole assembly of Israel went to speak with Rehoboam. ⁴"Your father was a hard master," they said. "Lighten the harsh labor demands and heavy taxes that your father imposed on us. Then we will be your loyal subjects."

⁵Rehoboam replied, "Give me three days to think this over. Then come back for my answer." So the people went away.

⁶Then King Rehoboam went to discuss the matter with the older men who had counseled his father, Solomon. "What is your advice?" he asked. "How should I answer these people?"

⁷The older counselors replied, "If you are willing to serve the people today and give them a favorable answer, they will always be your loyal subjects."

⁸But Rehoboam rejected the advice of the elders and instead asked the opinion of the young men who had grown up with him and who were now his advisers. ⁹"What is your advice?" he asked them. "How should I answer these people who want me to lighten the burdens imposed by my father?"

¹⁰The young men replied, "This is what you should tell those complainers: 'My little finger is thicker than my father's waist—if you think he was hard on you, just wait and see what I'll be like! ¹¹Yes, my father was harsh on you, but I'll be even harsher! My father used whips on you, but I'll use scorpions!'"

¹²Three days later, Jeroboam and all the people returned to hear Rehoboam's decision, just as the king had requested. ¹³But Rehoboam spoke harshly to them, for he rejected the advice of the older counselors ¹⁴and followed the counsel of his younger advisers. He told the people, "My father was harsh on you, but I'll be even harsher! My father used whips on you, but I'll use scorpions!" ¹⁵So the king paid no attention to the people's demands. This turn of events was the will of the LORD, for it fulfilled the LORD's message to Jeroboam son of Nebat through the prophet Ahijah from Shiloh.

¹⁶When all Israel realized that the king had rejected their request, they shouted, "Down with David and his dynasty! We have no share in Jesse's son! Let's go home, Israel! Look out for your own house, O David!" So the people of Israel returned home. ¹⁷But Rehoboam continued to rule over the Israelites who lived in the towns of Judah.

¹⁸King Rehoboam sent Adoniram,* who was in charge of the labor force, to restore order, but all Israel stoned him to death. When this news reached King Rehoboam, he quickly jumped into his chariot and fled to Jerusalem. ¹⁹The northern tribes of Israel have refused to be ruled by a descendant of David to this day.

²⁰When the people of Israel learned of Jeroboam's return from Egypt, they called an assembly and made him king over all Israel. So only the tribe of Judah remained loyal to the family of David.

²¹When Rehoboam arrived at Jerusalem, he mobilized the armies of Judah and Benjamin—180,000 select troops—to fight against the army of Israel and to restore the kingdom to himself. ²²But God said to Shemaiah, the man of God, ²³"Say to Rehoboam son of Solomon, king of Judah, and to all the people of Judah and Benjamin, ²⁴'This is what the LORD says: Do not fight against your relatives, the Israelites. Go back home, for what has happened is my doing!'" So they obeyed the message of the

12:2 As in Greek version and Latin Vulgate (see also 2 Chr 10:2); Hebrew reads *he lived in Egypt.*   **12:18** As in some Greek manuscripts and Syriac version (see also 4:6; 5:14); Hebrew reads *Adoram.*

LORD and went home, as the LORD had commanded.

²⁵Jeroboam then built up the city of Shechem in the hill country of Ephraim, and it became his capital. Later he went and built up the town of Peniel.* ²⁶Jeroboam thought to himself, "Unless I am careful, the kingdom will return to the dynasty of David. ²⁷When they go to Jerusalem to offer sacrifices at the Temple of the LORD, they will again give their allegiance to King Rehoboam of Judah. They will kill me and make him their king instead."

²⁸So on the advice of his counselors, the king made two gold calves. He said to the people, "It is too much trouble for you to worship in Jerusalem. O Israel, these are the gods who brought you out of Egypt!"

²⁹He placed these calf idols at the southern and northern ends of Israel—in Bethel and in Dan. ³⁰This became a great sin, for the people worshiped them, traveling even as far as Dan.

³¹Jeroboam built shrines at the pagan high places and ordained priests from the rank and file of the people—those who were not from the priestly tribe of Levi. ³²Jeroboam also instituted a religious festival in Bethel, held on a day in midautumn,* similar to the annual Festival of Shelters in Judah. There at Bethel he himself offered sacrifices to the calves he had made. And it was at Bethel that he appointed priests for the pagan shrines he had made. ³³So on the appointed day in midautumn, a day that he himself had designated, Jeroboam offered sacrifices on the altar at Bethel. He instituted a religious festival for Israel, and he went up to the altar to burn incense.

CHAPTER 13

At the LORD's command, a man of God from Judah went to Bethel, and he arrived there just as Jeroboam was approaching the altar to offer a sacrifice. ²Then at the LORD's command, he shouted, "O altar, altar! This is what the LORD says: A child named Josiah will be born into the dynasty of David. On you he will sacrifice the priests from the pagan shrines who come here to burn incense, and human bones will be burned on you." ³That same day the man of God gave a sign to prove his message, and he said, "The LORD has promised to give this sign:

This altar will split apart, and its ashes will be poured out on the ground."

⁴King Jeroboam was very angry with the man of God for speaking against the altar. So he pointed at the man and shouted, "Seize that man!" But instantly the king's hand became paralyzed in that position, and he couldn't pull it back. ⁵At the same time a wide crack appeared in the altar, and the ashes poured out, just as the man of God had predicted in his message from the LORD.

⁶The king cried out to the man of God, "Please ask the LORD your God to restore my hand again!" So the man of God prayed to the LORD, and the king's hand became normal again.

⁷Then the king said to the man of God, "Come to the palace with me and have something to eat, and I will give you a gift."

⁸But the man of God said to the king, "Even if you gave me half of everything you own, I would not go with you. I would not eat any food or drink any water in this place. ⁹For the LORD gave me this command: 'You must not eat any food or drink any water while you are there, and do not return to Judah by the same way you came.'" ¹⁰So he left Bethel and went home another way.

¹¹As it happened, there was an old prophet living in Bethel, and his sons came home and told him what the man of God had done in Bethel that day. They also told him what he had said to the king. ¹²The old prophet asked them, "Which way did he go?" So they told their father which road the man of God had taken. ¹³"Quick, saddle the donkey," the old man said. And when they had saddled the donkey for him, ¹⁴he rode after the man of God and found him sitting under an oak tree.

The old prophet asked him, "Are you the man of God who came from Judah?"

"Yes," he replied, "I am."

¹⁵Then he said to the man of God, "Come home with me and eat some food."

¹⁶"No, I cannot," he replied. "I am not allowed to eat any food or drink any water here in this place. ¹⁷For the LORD gave me this command: 'You must not eat any food or drink any water while you are there, and do not return to Judah by the same way you came.'"

12:25 Hebrew *Penuel*, a variant name for Peniel.   12:32 Hebrew *on the fifteenth day of the eighth month* (also in 12:33). This day of the Hebrew lunar calendar occurs in late October or early November, exactly one month after the annual Festival of Shelters in Judah (see Lev 23:34).

[18]But the old prophet answered, "I am a prophet, too, just as you are. And an angel gave me this message from the LORD: 'Bring him home with you, and give him food to eat and water to drink.'" But the old man was lying to him. [19]So they went back together, and the man of God ate some food and drank some water at the prophet's home.

[20]Then while they were sitting at the table, a message from the LORD came to the old prophet. [21]He cried out to the man of God from Judah, "This is what the LORD says: You have defied the LORD's message and have disobeyed the command the LORD your God gave you. [22]You came back to this place and ate food and drank water where he told you not to eat or drink. Because of this, your body will not be buried in the grave of your ancestors."

[23]Now after the man of God had finished eating and drinking, the prophet saddled his own donkey for him, [24]and the man of God started off again. But as he was traveling along, a lion came out and killed him. His body lay there on the road, with the donkey and the lion standing beside it. [25]People came by and saw the body lying in the road and the lion standing beside it, and they went and reported it in Bethel, where the old prophet lived.

[26]When the old prophet heard the report, he said, "It is the man of God who disobeyed the LORD's command. The LORD has fulfilled his word by causing the lion to attack and kill him."

[27]Then the prophet said to his sons, "Saddle a donkey for me." So they saddled a donkey, [28]and he went out and found the body lying in the road. The donkey and lion were still standing there beside it, for the lion had not eaten the body nor attacked the donkey. [29]So the prophet laid the body of the man of God on the donkey and took it back to the city to mourn over him and bury him. [30]He laid the body in his own grave, crying out in grief, "Oh, my brother!"

[31]Afterward the prophet said to his sons, "When I die, bury me in the grave where the man of God is buried. Lay my bones beside his bones. [32]For the message the LORD told him to proclaim against the altar in Bethel and against the pagan shrines in the towns of Samaria will surely come true."

[33]But even after this, Jeroboam did not turn from his evil ways. He continued to choose priests from the rank and file of the people. Anyone who wanted to could become a priest for the pagan shrines. [34]This became a great sin and resulted in the destruction of Jeroboam's kingdom and the death of all his family.

CHAPTER 14

At that time Jeroboam's son Abijah became very sick. [2]So Jeroboam told his wife, "Disguise yourself so that no one will recognize you as the queen. Then go to the prophet Ahijah at Shiloh—the man who told me I would become king. [3]Take him a gift of ten loaves of bread, some cakes, and a jar of honey, and ask him what will happen to the boy."

[4]So Jeroboam's wife went to Ahijah's home at Shiloh. He was an old man now and could no longer see. [5]But the LORD had told Ahijah, "Jeroboam's wife will come here, pretending to be someone else. She will ask you about her son, for he is very sick. You must give her the answer that I give you."

[6]So when Ahijah heard her footsteps at the door, he called out, "Come in, wife of Jeroboam! Why are you pretending to be someone else?" Then he told her, "I have bad news for you. [7]Give your husband, Jeroboam, this message from the LORD, the God of Israel: 'I promoted you from the ranks of the common people and made you ruler over my people Israel. [8]I ripped the kingdom away from the family of David and gave it to you. But you have not been like my servant David, who obeyed my commands and followed me with all his heart and always did whatever I wanted him to do. [9]You have done more evil than all who lived before you. You have made other gods and have made me furious with your gold calves. And since you have turned your back on me, [10]I will bring disaster on your dynasty and kill all your sons, slave or free alike. I will burn up your royal dynasty as one burns up trash until it is all gone. [11]I, the LORD, vow that the members of your family who die in the city will be eaten by dogs, and those who die in the field will be eaten by vultures.'"

[12]Then Ahijah said to Jeroboam's wife, "Go on home, and when you enter the city, the child will die. [13]All Israel will mourn for him and bury him. He is the only mem-

ber of your family who will have a proper burial, for this child is the only good thing that the LORD, the God of Israel, sees in the entire family of Jeroboam. ¹⁴And the LORD will raise up a king over Israel who will destroy the family of Jeroboam. This will happen today, even now! ¹⁵Then the LORD will shake Israel like a reed whipped about in a stream. He will uproot the people of Israel from this good land that he gave their ancestors and will scatter them beyond the Euphrates River,* for they have angered the LORD by worshiping Asherah poles. ¹⁶He will abandon Israel because Jeroboam sinned and made all of Israel sin along with him."

¹⁷So Jeroboam's wife returned to Tirzah, and the child died just as she walked through the door of her home. ¹⁸When the people of Israel buried him, they mourned for him, as the LORD had promised through the prophet Ahijah.

¹⁹The rest of the events of Jeroboam's reign, all his wars and how he ruled, are recorded in *The Book of the History of the Kings of Israel.* ²⁰Jeroboam reigned in Israel twenty-two years. When Jeroboam died, his son Nadab became the next king.

²¹Meanwhile, Rehoboam son of Solomon was king in Judah. He was forty-one years old when he became king, and he reigned seventeen years in Jerusalem, the city the LORD had chosen from among all the tribes of Israel as the place to honor his name. Rehoboam's mother was Naamah, an Ammonite woman. ²²During Rehoboam's reign, the people of Judah did what was evil in the LORD's sight, arousing his anger with their sin, for it was even worse than that of their ancestors. ²³They built pagan shrines and set up sacred pillars and Asherah poles on every high hill and under every green tree. ²⁴There were even shrine prostitutes throughout the land. The people imitated the detestable practices of the pagan nations the LORD had driven from the land ahead of the Israelites.

²⁵In the fifth year of King Rehoboam's reign, King Shishak of Egypt came up and attacked Jerusalem. ²⁶He ransacked the Temple of the LORD and the royal palace and stole everything, including all the gold shields Solomon had made. ²⁷Afterward Rehoboam made bronze shields as substi-

tutes, and he entrusted them to the care of the palace guard officers. ²⁸Whenever the king went to the Temple of the LORD, the guards would carry them along and then return them to the guardroom.

²⁹The rest of the events in Rehoboam's reign and all his deeds are recorded in *The Book of the History of the Kings of Judah.* ³⁰There was constant war between Rehoboam and Jeroboam. ³¹When Rehoboam died, he was buried among his ancestors in the City of David. His mother was Naamah, an Ammonite woman. Then his son Abijam* became the next king.

CHAPTER 15
Abijam* began to rule over Judah in the eighteenth year of Jeroboam's reign in Israel. ²He reigned in Jerusalem three years. His mother was Maacah, the daughter of Absalom.* ³He committed the same sins as his father before him, and his heart was not right with the LORD his God, as the heart of his ancestor David had been. ⁴But for David's sake, the LORD his God allowed his dynasty to continue,* and he gave Abijam a son to rule after him in Jerusalem. ⁵For David had done what was pleasing in the LORD's sight and had obeyed the LORD's commands throughout his life, except in the affair concerning Uriah the Hittite.

⁶There was war between Abijam and Jeroboam* throughout Abijam's reign. ⁷The rest of the events in Abijam's reign and all his deeds are recorded in *The Book of the History of the Kings of Judah.* There was constant war between Abijam and Jeroboam. ⁸When Abijam died, he was buried in the City of David. Then his son Asa became the next king.

⁹Asa began to rule over Judah in the twentieth year of Jeroboam's reign in Israel. ¹⁰He reigned in Jerusalem forty-one years. His grandmother* was Maacah, the daughter of Absalom. ¹¹Asa did what was pleasing in the LORD's sight, as his ancestor David had done. ¹²He banished the shrine prostitutes from the land and removed all the idols his ancestors had made. ¹³He even deposed his grandmother Maacah from her position as queen mother because she had made an obscene Asherah pole. He cut down the pole and burned it in the Kidron Valley. ¹⁴Although the pagan shrines were

not completely removed, Asa remained faithful to the LORD throughout his life. [15]He brought into the Temple of the LORD the silver and gold and the utensils that he and his father had dedicated.

[16]There was constant war between King Asa of Judah and King Baasha of Israel. [17]King Baasha of Israel invaded Judah and fortified Ramah in order to prevent anyone from entering or leaving King Asa's territory in Judah. [18]Asa responded by taking all the silver and gold that was left in the treasuries of the LORD's Temple and the royal palace. He sent it with some of his officials to Ben-hadad son of Tabrimmon and grandson of Hezion, the king of Aram, who was ruling in Damascus, along with this message:

> [19]"Let us renew the treaty that existed between your father and my father. See, I am sending you a gift of silver and gold. Break your treaty with King Baasha of Israel so that he will leave me alone."

[20]Ben-hadad agreed to King Asa's request and sent his armies to attack Israel. They conquered the towns of Ijon, Dan, Abel-beth-maacah, and all Kinnereth, with all the land of Naphtali. [21]As soon as Baasha of Israel heard what was happening, he abandoned his project of fortifying Ramah and withdrew to Tirzah. [22]Then King Asa sent an order throughout Judah, requiring that everyone, without exception, help to carry away the building stones and timbers that Baasha had been using to fortify Ramah. Asa used these materials to fortify the town of Geba in Benjamin and the town of Mizpah.

[23]The rest of the events in Asa's reign, the extent of his power, and the names of the cities he built are recorded in *The Book of the History of the Kings of Judah*. In his old age his feet became diseased. [24]When Asa died, he was buried with his ancestors in the City of David. Then his son Jehoshaphat became the next king.

[25]Nadab son of Jeroboam began to rule over Israel in the second year of King Asa's reign in Judah. He reigned in Israel two years. [26]But he did what was evil in the LORD's sight and followed the example of his father, continuing the sins of idolatry that Jeroboam had led Israel to commit.

[27]Then Baasha son of Ahijah, from the tribe of Issachar, plotted against Nadab and assassinated him while he and the Israelite army were laying siege to the Philistine town of Gibbethon. [28]Baasha killed Nadab in the third year of King Asa's reign in Judah, and he became the next king of Israel. [29]He immediately killed all the descendants of King Jeroboam, so that not one of the royal family was left, just as the LORD had promised concerning Jeroboam by the prophet Ahijah from Shiloh. [30]This was done because Jeroboam had aroused the anger of the LORD, the God of Israel, by the sins he had committed and the sins he had led Israel to commit. [31]The rest of the events in Nadab's reign and all his deeds are recorded in *The Book of the History of the Kings of Israel*.

[32]There was constant war between Asa and King Baasha of Israel. [33]Baasha began to rule over Israel in the third year of King Asa's reign in Judah. Baasha reigned in Tirzah twenty-four years. [34]But he did what was evil in the LORD's sight and followed the example of Jeroboam, continuing the sins of idolatry that Jeroboam had led Israel to commit.

CHAPTER 16

This message from the LORD was delivered to King Baasha by the prophet Jehu son of Hanani: [2]"I lifted you out of the dust to make you ruler of my people Israel, but you have followed the evil example of Jeroboam. You have aroused my anger by causing my people to sin. [3]So now I will destroy you and your family, just as I destroyed the descendants of Jeroboam son of Nebat. [4]Those of your family who die in the city will be eaten by dogs, and those who die in the field will be eaten by the vultures."

[5]The rest of the events in Baasha's reign and the extent of his power are recorded in *The Book of the History of the Kings of Israel*. [6]When Baasha died, he was buried in Tirzah. Then his son Elah became the next king.

[7]This message from the LORD had been spoken against Baasha and his family through the prophet Jehu son of Hanani. It was delivered because Baasha had done what was evil in the LORD's sight, arousing him to anger by his sins, just like the family of Jeroboam, and also because Baasha had destroyed the family of Jeroboam.

[8]Elah son of Baasha began to rule over

Israel from Tirzah in the twenty-sixth year of King Asa's reign in Judah. He reigned in Israel two years. [9]Then Zimri, who commanded half of the royal chariots, made plans to kill him. One day in Tirzah, Elah was getting drunk at the home of Arza, the supervisor of the palace. [10]Zimri walked in and struck him down and killed him. This happened in the twenty-seventh year of King Asa's reign in Judah. Then Zimri became the next king.

[11]Zimri immediately killed the entire royal family of Baasha, and he did not leave a single male child. He even destroyed distant relatives and friends. [12]So Zimri destroyed the dynasty of Baasha as the LORD had promised through the prophet Jehu. [13]This happened because of the sins of Baasha and his son Elah and because of all the sins they led Israel to commit, arousing the anger of the LORD, the God of Israel, with their idols. [14]The rest of the events in Elah's reign and all his deeds are recorded in *The Book of the History of the Kings of Israel.*

[15]Zimri began to rule over Israel from Tirzah in the twenty-seventh year of King Asa's reign in Judah, but he reigned only seven days. When the army of Israel, which was then engaged in attacking the Philistine town of Gibbethon, [16]heard that Zimri had assassinated the king, they chose Omri, commander of the army, as their new king. [17]So Omri led the army of Israel away from Gibbethon to attack Tirzah, Israel's capital. [18]When Zimri saw that the city had been taken, he went into the citadel of the king's house and burned it down over himself and died in the flames. [19]For he, too, had done what was evil in the LORD's sight and followed the example of Jeroboam, continuing the sins of idolatry that Jeroboam had led Israel to commit. [20]The rest of the events of Zimri's reign and his conspiracy are recorded in *The Book of the History of the Kings of Israel.*

[21]But now the people of Israel were divided into two groups. Half the people tried to make Tibni son of Ginath their king, while the other half supported Omri. [22]But Omri's supporters defeated the supporters of Tibni son of Ginath. So Tibni was killed, and Omri became the next king.

[23]Omri began to rule over Israel in the thirty-first year of King Asa's reign in Judah. He reigned twelve years in all, six of them in Tirzah. [24]Then Omri bought the hill now known as Samaria from its owner, Shemer, for 150 pounds of silver.* He built a city on it and called the city Samaria in honor of Shemer. [25]But Omri did what was evil in the LORD's sight, even more than any of the kings before him. [26]He followed the example of Jeroboam, continuing the sins of idolatry that Jeroboam had led Israel to commit. Thus, he aroused the anger of the LORD, the God of Israel. [27]The rest of the events in Omri's reign, the extent of his power, and all his deeds are recorded in *The Book of the History of the Kings of Israel.* [28]When Omri died, he was buried in Samaria. Then his son Ahab became the next king.

[29]Ahab son of Omri began to rule over Israel in the thirty-eighth year of King Asa's reign in Judah. He reigned in Samaria twenty-two years. [30]But Ahab did what was evil in the LORD's sight, even more than any of the kings before him. [31]And as though it were not enough to live like Jeroboam, he married Jezebel, the daughter of King Ethbaal of the Sidonians, and he began to worship Baal. [32]First he built a temple and an altar for Baal in Samaria. [33]Then he set up an Asherah pole. He did more to arouse the anger of the LORD, the God of Israel, than any of the other kings of Israel before him.

[34]It was during his reign that Hiel, a man from Bethel, rebuilt Jericho. When he laid the foundations, his oldest son, Abiram, died. And when he finally completed it by setting up the gates, his youngest son, Segub, died. This all happened according to the message from the LORD concerning Jericho spoken by Joshua son of Nun.

16:24 Hebrew *for 2 talents* [68 kilograms] *of silver.*

APRIL 5 ☐ DAY 96
1 KINGS 17–19
Ahab's Battle with Elijah

OVERVIEW Without fanfare or announcement, the prophet Elijah bursts upon the scene of Israel's history to predict a severe drought during the reign of King Ahab. At the peak of the drought, the prophet returns to challenge Ahab and the prophets of Baal to a "battle of the gods" on Mount Carmel. In a fiery display of power and majesty, God consumes the offering, wood, stones, dirt, and water of Elijah's sacrifice, proving to the onlooking nation that he alone is the Lord God. When the news of Elijah's victory reaches Queen Jezebel, she vows to end his life. Once again the prophet returns to seclusion where God ministers to his exhausted and discouraged servant.

Chapter 17	Chapter 18	Chapter 19
Elijah and the Widow of Zarephath	Elijah and the Prophets of Baal	Elijah and the Fear of Jezebel
God's Provision	God's Power	God's Persistence

YOUR DAILY WALK When was the last time you suffered a bout of depression or self-pity? Do you remember what caused it? How long did it last? What finally helped you to overcome it?

To hatch despair, just brood over your troubles.

In 1 Kings 19 you will see Elijah in one of those blue moods of depression, his thoughts filled with self-pity: "I have zealously served the LORD God Almighty. . . . I alone am left, and now they are trying to kill me" (19:10). Did you notice when the prophet of God fell into the doldrums of depression? It was immediately after one of the greatest spiritual victories of his life! He had just confronted wicked Ahab and 450 of his pagan prophets and won by a score of 450 to nothing! Then . . . depression set in.

Think back to the last low time in your walk with God. What happened immediately before it? Were you perhaps physically or emotionally drained from ministering to the needs of others? Elijah found strength to continue by hearing the gentle whisper of God (19:12). Spend some extra moments in prayer and meditation today. It's one sure cure for a run-down spiritual battery!

INSIGHT Before All Else Fails, Read the Directions!
Sometimes the greatest challenge is sitting long enough to learn God's will, rather than acting first and praying later. Read 17:2, 5, 8, 10, and 18:1-2 to discover Elijah's pattern for godly service.

CHAPTER 17

Now Elijah, who was from Tishbe in Gilead, told King Ahab, "As surely as the LORD, the God of Israel, lives—the God whom I worship and serve—there will be no dew or rain during the next few years unless I give the word!"

²Then the LORD said to Elijah, ³"Go to the east and hide by Kerith Brook at a place east of where it enters the Jordan River. ⁴Drink from the brook and eat what the ravens bring you, for I have commanded them to bring you food."

⁵So Elijah did as the LORD had told him and camped beside Kerith Brook. ⁶The ravens brought him bread and meat each morning and evening, and he drank from the brook. ⁷But after a while the brook dried up, for there was no rainfall anywhere in the land.

⁸Then the LORD said to Elijah, ⁹"Go and live in the village of Zarephath, near the

city of Sidon. There is a widow there who will feed you. I have given her my instructions."

¹⁰So he went to Zarephath. As he arrived at the gates of the village, he saw a widow gathering sticks, and he asked her, "Would you please bring me a cup of water?" ¹¹As she was going to get it, he called to her, "Bring me a bite of bread, too."

¹²But she said, "I swear by the LORD your God that I don't have a single piece of bread in the house. And I have only a handful of flour left in the jar and a little cooking oil in the bottom of the jug. I was just gathering a few sticks to cook this last meal, and then my son and I will die."

¹³But Elijah said to her, "Don't be afraid! Go ahead and cook that 'last meal,' but bake me a little loaf of bread first. Afterward there will still be enough food for you and your son. ¹⁴For this is what the LORD, the God of Israel, says: There will always be plenty of flour and oil left in your containers until the time when the LORD sends rain and the crops grow again!"

¹⁵So she did as Elijah said, and she and Elijah and her son continued to eat from her supply of flour and oil for many days. ¹⁶For no matter how much they used, there was always enough left in the containers, just as the LORD had promised through Elijah.

¹⁷Some time later, the woman's son became sick. He grew worse and worse, and finally he died. ¹⁸She then said to Elijah, "O man of God, what have you done to me? Have you come here to punish my sins by killing my son?"

¹⁹But Elijah replied, "Give me your son." And he took the boy's body from her, carried him up to the upper room, where he lived, and laid the body on his bed. ²⁰Then Elijah cried out to the LORD, "O LORD my God, why have you brought tragedy on this widow who has opened her home to me, causing her son to die?"

²¹And he stretched himself out over the child three times and cried out to the LORD, "O LORD my God, please let this child's life return to him." ²²The LORD heard Elijah's prayer, and the life of the child returned, and he came back to life! ²³Then Elijah brought him down from the upper room and gave him to his mother. "Look, your son is alive!" he said.

²⁴Then the woman told Elijah, "Now I know for sure that you are a man of God, and that the LORD truly speaks through you."

CHAPTER 18

After many months passed, in the third year of the drought, the LORD said to Elijah, "Go and present yourself to King Ahab. Tell him that I will soon send rain!" ²So Elijah went to appear before Ahab.

Meanwhile, the famine had become very severe in Samaria. ³So Ahab summoned Obadiah, who was in charge of the palace. (Now Obadiah was a devoted follower of the LORD. ⁴Once when Jezebel had tried to kill all the LORD's prophets, Obadiah had hidden one hundred of them in two caves. He had put fifty prophets in each cave and had supplied them with food and water.) ⁵Ahab said to Obadiah, "We must check every spring and valley to see if we can find enough grass to save at least some of my horses and mules." ⁶So they divided the land between them. Ahab went one way by himself, and Obadiah went another way by himself.

⁷As Obadiah was walking along, he saw Elijah coming toward him. Obadiah recognized him at once and fell to the ground before him. "Is it really you, my lord Elijah?" he asked.

⁸"Yes, it is," Elijah replied. "Now go and tell your master I am here."

⁹"Oh, sir," Obadiah protested, "what harm have I done to you that you are sending me to my death at the hands of Ahab? ¹⁰For I swear by the LORD your God that the king has searched every nation and kingdom on earth from end to end to find you. And each time when he was told, 'Elijah isn't here,' King Ahab forced the king of that nation to swear to the truth of his claim. ¹¹And now you say, 'Go and tell your master that Elijah is here'! ¹²But as soon as I leave you, the Spirit of the LORD will carry you away to who knows where. When Ahab comes and cannot find you, he will kill me. Yet I have been a true servant of the LORD all my life. ¹³Has no one told you, my lord, about the time when Jezebel was trying to kill the LORD's prophets? I hid a hundred of them in two caves and supplied them with food and water. ¹⁴And now you say, 'Go and tell your master that Elijah is here'! Sir, if I do that, I'm as good as dead!"

¹⁵But Elijah said, "I swear by the LORD Almighty, in whose presence I stand, that I will present myself to Ahab today."

¹⁶So Obadiah went to tell Ahab that Elijah had come, and Ahab went out to meet him. ¹⁷"So it's you, is it—Israel's troublemaker?" Ahab asked when he saw him.

¹⁸"I have made no trouble for Israel," Elijah replied. "You and your family are the troublemakers, for you have refused to obey the commands of the LORD and have worshiped the images of Baal instead. ¹⁹Now bring all the people of Israel to Mount Carmel, with all 450 prophets of Baal and the 400 prophets of Asherah, who are supported by Jezebel."

²⁰So Ahab summoned all the people and the prophets to Mount Carmel. ²¹Then Elijah stood in front of them and said, "How long are you going to waver between two opinions? If the LORD is God, follow him! But if Baal is God, then follow him!" But the people were completely silent.

²²Then Elijah said to them, "I am the only prophet of the LORD who is left, but Baal has 450 prophets. ²³Now bring two bulls. The prophets of Baal may choose whichever one they wish and cut it into pieces and lay it on the wood of their altar, but without setting fire to it. I will prepare the other bull and lay it on the wood on the altar, but not set fire to it. ²⁴Then call on the name of your god, and I will call on the name of the LORD. The god who answers by setting fire to the wood is the true God!" And all the people agreed.

²⁵Then Elijah said to the prophets of Baal, "You go first, for there are many of you. Choose one of the bulls and prepare it and call on the name of your god. But do not set fire to the wood."

²⁶So they prepared one of the bulls and placed it on the altar. Then they called on the name of Baal all morning, shouting, "O Baal, answer us!" But there was no reply of any kind. Then they danced wildly around the altar they had made.

²⁷About noontime Elijah began mocking them. "You'll have to shout louder," he scoffed, "for surely he is a god! Perhaps he is deep in thought, or he is relieving himself. Or maybe he is away on a trip, or he is asleep and needs to be wakened!"

²⁸So they shouted louder, and following their normal custom, they cut themselves with knives and swords until the blood gushed out. ²⁹They raved all afternoon until the time of the evening sacrifice, but still there was no reply, no voice, no answer.

³⁰Then Elijah called to the people, "Come over here!" They all crowded around him as he repaired the altar of the LORD that had been torn down. ³¹He took twelve stones, one to represent each of the tribes of Israel,* ³²and he used the stones to rebuild the LORD's altar. Then he dug a trench around the altar large enough to hold about three gallons.* ³³He piled wood on the altar, cut the bull into pieces, and laid the pieces on the wood. Then he said, "Fill four large jars with water, and pour the water over the offering and the wood." After they had done this, ³⁴he said, "Do the same thing again!" And when they were finished, he said, "Now do it a third time!" So they did as he said, ³⁵and the water ran around the altar and even overflowed the trench.

³⁶At the customary time for offering the evening sacrifice, Elijah the prophet walked up to the altar and prayed, "O LORD, God of Abraham, Isaac, and Jacob,* prove today that you are God in Israel and that I am your servant. Prove that I have done all this at your command. ³⁷O LORD, answer me! Answer me so these people will know that you, O LORD, are God and that you have brought them back to yourself."

³⁸Immediately the fire of the LORD flashed down from heaven and burned up the young bull, the wood, the stones, and the dust. It even licked up all the water in the ditch! ³⁹And when the people saw it, they fell on their faces and cried out, "The LORD is God! The LORD is God!"

⁴⁰Then Elijah commanded, "Seize all the prophets of Baal. Don't let a single one escape!" So the people seized them all, and Elijah took them down to the Kishon Valley and killed them there.

⁴¹Then Elijah said to Ahab, "Go and enjoy a good meal! For I hear a mighty rainstorm coming!"

⁴²So Ahab prepared a feast. But Elijah climbed to the top of Mount Carmel and fell to the ground and prayed. ⁴³Then he said to his servant, "Go and look out toward the sea."

The servant went and looked, but he re-

18:31 Hebrew *each of the tribes of the sons of Jacob to whom the* LORD *had said, "Your name will be Israel."*   18:32 Hebrew *2 seahs* [12 liters] *of seed.*   18:36 Hebrew *and Israel.*

turned to Elijah and said, "I didn't see anything." Seven times Elijah told him to go and look, and seven times he went. ⁴⁴Finally the seventh time, his servant told him, "I saw a little cloud about the size of a hand rising from the sea."

Then Elijah shouted, "Hurry to Ahab and tell him, 'Climb into your chariot and go back home. If you don't hurry, the rain will stop you!'"

⁴⁵And sure enough, the sky was soon black with clouds. A heavy wind brought a terrific rainstorm, and Ahab left quickly for Jezreel. ⁴⁶Now the LORD gave special strength to Elijah. He tucked his cloak into his belt and ran ahead of Ahab's chariot all the way to the entrance of Jezreel.

CHAPTER 19

When Ahab got home, he told Jezebel what Elijah had done and that he had slaughtered the prophets of Baal. ²So Jezebel sent this message to Elijah: "May the gods also kill me if by this time tomorrow I have failed to take your life like those whom you killed."

³Elijah was afraid and fled for his life. He went to Beersheba, a town in Judah, and he left his servant there. ⁴Then he went on alone into the desert, traveling all day. He sat down under a solitary broom tree and prayed that he might die. "I have had enough, LORD," he said. "Take my life, for I am no better than my ancestors."

⁵Then he lay down and slept under the broom tree. But as he was sleeping, an angel touched him and told him, "Get up and eat!" ⁶He looked around and saw some bread baked on hot stones and a jar of water! So he ate and drank and lay down again.

⁷Then the angel of the LORD came again and touched him and said, "Get up and eat some more, for there is a long journey ahead of you."

⁸So he got up and ate and drank, and the food gave him enough strength to travel forty days and forty nights to Mount Sinai,* the mountain of God. ⁹There he came to a cave, where he spent the night.

But the LORD said to him, "What are you doing here, Elijah?"

¹⁰Elijah replied, "I have zealously served the LORD God Almighty. But the people of Israel have broken their covenant with you, torn down your altars, and killed every one

of your prophets. I alone am left, and now they are trying to kill me, too."

¹¹"Go out and stand before me on the mountain," the LORD told him. And as Elijah stood there, the LORD passed by, and a mighty windstorm hit the mountain. It was such a terrible blast that the rocks were torn loose, but the LORD was not in the wind. After the wind there was an earthquake, but the LORD was not in the earthquake. ¹²And after the earthquake there was a fire, but the LORD was not in the fire. And after the fire there was the sound of a gentle whisper. ¹³When Elijah heard it, he wrapped his face in his cloak and went out and stood at the entrance of the cave.

And a voice said, "What are you doing here, Elijah?"

¹⁴He replied again, "I have zealously served the LORD God Almighty. But the people of Israel have broken their covenant with you, torn down your altars, and killed every one of your prophets. I alone am left, and now they are trying to kill me, too."

¹⁵Then the LORD told him, "Go back the way you came, and travel to the wilderness of Damascus. When you arrive there, anoint Hazael to be king of Aram. ¹⁶Then anoint Jehu son of Nimshi to be king of Israel, and anoint Elisha son of Shaphat from Abel-meholah to replace you as my prophet. ¹⁷Anyone who escapes from Hazael will be killed by Jehu, and those who escape Jehu will be killed by Elisha! ¹⁸Yet I will preserve seven thousand others in Israel who have never bowed to Baal or kissed him!"

¹⁹So Elijah went and found Elisha son of Shaphat plowing a field with a team of oxen. There were eleven teams of oxen ahead of him, and he was plowing with the twelfth team. Elijah went over to him and threw his cloak across his shoulders and walked away again. ²⁰Elisha left the oxen standing there, ran after Elijah, and said to him, "First let me go and kiss my father and mother good-bye, and then I will go with you!"

Elijah replied, "Go on back! But consider what I have done to you."

²¹Elisha then returned to his oxen, killed them, and used the wood from the plow to build a fire to roast their flesh. He passed around the meat to the other plowmen, and they all ate. Then he went with Elijah as his assistant.

19:8 Hebrew *Horeb*, another name for Sinai.

APRIL 6 ☐ DAY 97
1 KINGS 20–22
Ahab's Battle with Aram

OVERVIEW Ahab's life illustrates the disastrous consequences of persistent disobedience. Even after seeing God's power exhibited on Mount Carmel, Ahab refuses to seek his assistance against the Aramean army. Twice God gives Ahab victory over the Arameans, yet the king responds by sparing Ben-Hadad rather than killing him as the Lord had commanded. For Ahab's refusal to obey, a prophet declares that the king of Israel will forfeit his life for the life of the king of Aram. True to the prophet's word, Ahab suffers a mortal (and divinely guided) wound in the third campaign that was waged against Aram.

Chapter 20	Chapter 21	Chapter 22
Samaria under Siege	Vying for Naboth's Vineyard	Dying on the Field of Battle
Ahab's Life		Ahab's Death

YOUR DAILY WALK There are many ways you can discover that it is dangerous to jump off a ten-story building: You can read about the law of gravity in a book. You can learn from the sad experience of someone who tried it. You can listen to the wise counsel of a fireman or physician who claims it would be "hazardous to your health." Or you can jump. Each provides the information you are seeking; the only difference is the amount of pain involved in gaining that information.

A person becomes wise by observing what happens when he or she isn't.

God wanted Ahab to learn that he alone is Lord of the nations. Fire at Mount Carmel . . . victory over vast armies . . . drought and rain—each was for Ahab's benefit: "Then you will know that I am the LORD" (20:13, 28). Only after being mortally wounded did Ahab learn the lesson, but then it was too late.

What about you? Jot down in the margin a few of the signs of God's sovereignty that you have observed in recent days. How should you respond? How will you respond . . . today?

INSIGHT 1 Kings in Capsule Form
The book of 1 Kings ("one kings") traces the rise and fall of "one king-dom." Solomon, the king who built the Temple for God, was not care-ful to guard the temple of his own heart. After his death the kingdom splits, as does the spiritual loyalty of the people. The book of 2 Kings ("two kings") traces the decline of these "two kingdoms" at the hands of Assyria and Babylonia.

CHAPTER 20
Now King Ben-hadad of Aram mobilized his army, supported by the chariots and horses of thirty-two allied kings. They went to besiege Samaria, the Israelite capi-tal, and launched attacks against it. ²Ben-hadad sent messengers into the city to relay this message to King Ahab of Israel: "This is what Ben-hadad says: ³'Your silver and gold are mine, and so are the best of your wives and children!'"

⁴"All right, my lord," Ahab replied. "All that I have is yours!"

⁵Soon Ben-hadad's messengers returned again and said, "This is what Ben-hadad says: 'I have already demanded that you give me your silver, gold, wives, and chil-dren. ⁶But about this time tomorrow I will send my officials to search your palace and the homes of your people. They will take away everything you consider valuable!'"

⁷Then Ahab summoned all the leaders of

the land and said to them, "Look how this man is stirring up trouble! I already agreed when he sent the message demanding that I give him my wives and children and silver and gold."

⁸"Don't give in to any more demands," the leaders and people advised.

⁹So Ahab told the messengers from Ben-hadad, "Say this to my lord the king: 'I will give you everything you asked for the first time, but this last demand of yours I simply cannot meet.'" So the messengers returned to Ben-hadad with the response.

¹⁰Then Ben-hadad sent this message to Ahab: "May the gods bring tragedy on me, and even worse than that, if there remains enough dust from Samaria to provide more than a handful for each of my soldiers."

¹¹The king of Israel sent back this answer: "A warrior still dressing for battle should not boast like a warrior who has already won."

¹²This reply of Ahab's reached Ben-hadad and the other kings as they were drinking in their tents.* "Prepare to attack!" Ben-hadad commanded his officers. So they prepared to attack the city.

¹³Then a prophet came to see King Ahab and told him, "This is what the LORD says: Do you see all these enemy forces? Today I will hand them all over to you. Then you will know that I am the LORD."

¹⁴Ahab asked, "How will he do it?"

And the prophet replied, "This is what the LORD says: The troops of the provincial commanders will do it."

"Should we attack first?" Ahab asked.

"Yes," the prophet answered.

¹⁵So Ahab mustered the troops of the 232 provincial commanders. Then he called out the rest of his army of seven thousand men. ¹⁶About noontime, as Ben-hadad and the thirty-two allied kings were still in their tents getting drunk, ¹⁷the troops of the provincial commanders marched out of the city. As they approached, Ben-hadad's scouts reported to him, "Some troops are coming from Samaria."

¹⁸"Take them alive," Ben-hadad commanded, "whether they have come for peace or for war."

¹⁹But by now Ahab's provincial commanders had led the army out to fight. ²⁰Each Israelite soldier killed his Aramean opponent, and suddenly the entire Aramean army panicked and fled. The Israel-

ites chased them, but King Ben-hadad and a few others escaped on horses. ²¹However, the other horses and chariots were destroyed, and the Arameans were killed in a great slaughter.

²²Afterward the prophet said to King Ahab, "Get ready for another attack by the king of Aram next spring."

²³After their defeat, Ben-hadad's officers said to him, "The Israelite gods are gods of the hills; that is why they won. But we can beat them easily on the plains. ²⁴Only this time replace the kings with field commanders! ²⁵Recruit another army like the one you lost. Give us the same number of horses, chariots, and men, and we will fight against them in the plains. There's not a shadow of a doubt that we will beat them." So King Ben-hadad did as they suggested.

²⁶The following spring he called up the Aramean army and marched out against Israel, this time at Aphek. ²⁷Israel then mustered its army, set up supply lines, and moved into the battle. But the Israelite army looked like two little flocks of goats in comparison to the vast Aramean forces that filled the countryside!

²⁸Then the man of God went to the king of Israel and said, "This is what the LORD says: The Arameans have said that the LORD is a god of the hills and not of the plains. So I will help you defeat this vast army. Then you will know that I am the LORD."

²⁹The two armies camped opposite each other for seven days, and on the seventh day the battle began. The Israelites killed 100,000 Aramean foot soldiers in one day. ³⁰The rest fled behind the walls of Aphek, but the wall fell on them and killed another 27,000. Ben-hadad fled into the city and hid in a secret room. ³¹Ben-hadad's officers said to him, "Sir, we have heard that the kings of Israel are very merciful. So let's humble ourselves by wearing sackcloth and putting ropes on our heads. Then perhaps King Ahab will let you live."

³²So they put on sackcloth and ropes and went to the king of Israel and begged, "Your servant Ben-hadad says, 'Please let me live!'"

The king of Israel responded, "Is he still alive? He is my brother!"

³³The men were quick to grasp at this straw of hope, and they replied, "Yes, your brother Ben-hadad!"

20:12 Or *in Succoth;* also in 20:16.

"Go and get him," the king of Israel told them. And when Ben-hadad arrived, Ahab invited him up into his chariot!

³⁴Ben-hadad told him, "I will give back the towns my father took from your father, and you may establish places of trade in Damascus, as my father did in Samaria."

Then Ahab said, "I will let you go under these conditions." So they made a treaty, and Ben-hadad was set free.

³⁵Meanwhile, the LORD instructed one of the group of prophets to say to another man, "Strike me!" But the man refused to strike the prophet. ³⁶Then the prophet told him, "Because you have not obeyed the voice of the LORD, a lion will kill you as soon as you leave me." And sure enough, when he had gone, a lion attacked and killed him.

³⁷Then the prophet turned to another man and said, "Strike me!" So he struck the prophet and wounded him.

³⁸The prophet waited for the king beside the road, having placed a bandage over his eyes to disguise himself. ³⁹As the king passed by, the prophet called out to him, "Sir, I was in the battle, and a man brought me a prisoner. He said, 'Guard this man; if for any reason he gets away, you will either die or pay a fine of seventy-five pounds* of silver!' ⁴⁰But while I was busy doing something else, the prisoner disappeared!"

"Well, it's your own fault," the king replied. "You have determined your own judgment."

⁴¹Then the prophet pulled the bandage from his eyes, and the king of Israel recognized him as one of the prophets. ⁴²And the prophet told him, "This is what the LORD says: Because you have spared the man I said must be destroyed,* now you must die in his place, and your people will die instead of his people." ⁴³So the king of Israel went home to Samaria angry and sullen.

CHAPTER 21
King Ahab had a palace in Jezreel, and near the palace was a vineyard owned by a man named Naboth. ²One day Ahab said to Naboth, "Since your vineyard is so convenient to the palace, I would like to buy it to use as a vegetable garden. I will give you a better vineyard in exchange, or if you prefer, I will pay you for it."

³But Naboth replied, "The LORD forbid that I should give you the inheritance that was passed down by my ancestors." ⁴So Ahab went home angry and sullen because of Naboth's answer. The king went to bed with his face to the wall and refused to eat!

⁵"What in the world is the matter?" his wife, Jezebel, asked him. "What has made you so upset that you are not eating?"

⁶"I asked Naboth to sell me his vineyard or to trade it, and he refused!" Ahab told her.

⁷"Are you the king of Israel or not?" Jezebel asked. "Get up and eat and don't worry about it. I'll get you Naboth's vineyard!"

⁸So she wrote letters in Ahab's name, sealed them with his seal, and sent them to the elders and other leaders of the city where Naboth lived. ⁹In her letters she commanded: "Call the citizens together for fasting and prayer and give Naboth a place of honor. ¹⁰Find two scoundrels* who will accuse him of cursing God and the king. Then take him out and stone him to death."

¹¹So the elders and other leaders followed the instructions Jezebel had written in the letters. ¹²They called for a fast and put Naboth at a prominent place before the people. ¹³Then two scoundrels accused him before all the people of cursing God and the king. So he was dragged outside the city and stoned to death. ¹⁴The city officials then sent word to Jezebel, "Naboth has been stoned to death."

¹⁵When Jezebel heard the news, she said to Ahab, "You know the vineyard Naboth wouldn't sell you? Well, you can have it now! He's dead!" ¹⁶So Ahab immediately went down to the vineyard to claim it.

¹⁷But the LORD said to Elijah, who was from Tishbe, ¹⁸"Go down to meet King Ahab, who rules in Samaria. He will be at Naboth's vineyard in Jezreel, taking possession of it. ¹⁹Give him this message: 'This is what the LORD says: Isn't killing Naboth bad enough? Must you rob him, too? Because you have done this, dogs will lick your blood outside the city just as they licked the blood of Naboth!'"

²⁰"So my enemy has found me!" Ahab exclaimed to Elijah.

"Yes," Elijah answered, "I have come because you have sold yourself to what is evil in the LORD's sight. ²¹The LORD is going to bring disaster to you and sweep you away. He will not let a single one of your male descendants, slave or free alike, survive in Israel! ²²He is going to destroy your family as

20:39 Hebrew *1 talent* [34 kilograms].   20:42 The Hebrew term used here refers to the complete consecration of things or people to the LORD, either by destroying them or by giving them as an offering.   21:10 Hebrew *two sons of Belial;* also in 21:13.

he did the family of Jeroboam son of Nebat and the family of Baasha son of Ahijah, for you have made him very angry and have led all of Israel into sin. ²³The LORD has also told me that the dogs of Jezreel will eat the body of your wife, Jezebel, at the city wall. ²⁴The members of your family who die in the city will be eaten by dogs, and those who die in the field will be eaten by vultures."

²⁵No one else so completely sold himself to what was evil in the LORD's sight as did Ahab, for his wife, Jezebel, influenced him. ²⁶He was especially guilty because he worshiped idols just as the Amorites had done—the people whom the LORD had driven from the land ahead of the Israelites.

²⁷When Ahab heard this message, he tore his clothing, dressed in sackcloth, and fasted. He even slept in sackcloth and went about in deep mourning.

²⁸Then another message from the LORD came to Elijah, who was from Tishbe: ²⁹"Do you see how Ahab has humbled himself before me? Because he has done this, I will not do what I promised during his lifetime. It will happen to his sons; I will destroy all his descendants."

CHAPTER 22

For three years there was no war between Aram and Israel. ²Then during the third year, King Jehoshaphat of Judah went to visit King Ahab of Israel. ³During the visit, Ahab said to his officials, "Do you realize that the Arameans are still occupying our city of Ramoth-gilead? And we haven't done a thing about it!" ⁴Then he turned to Jehoshaphat and asked, "Will you join me in fighting against Ramoth-gilead?"

And Jehoshaphat replied to King Ahab, "Why, of course! You and I are brothers, and my troops are yours to command. Even my horses are at your service." ⁵Then Jehoshaphat added, "But first let's find out what the LORD says."

⁶So King Ahab summoned his prophets, about four hundred of them, and asked them, "Should I go to war against Ramoth-gilead or not?"

They all replied, "Go right ahead! The Lord will give you a glorious victory!"

⁷But Jehoshaphat asked, "Isn't there a prophet of the LORD around, too? I would like to ask him the same question."

⁸King Ahab replied, "There is still one prophet of the LORD, but I hate him. He never prophesies anything but bad news for me! His name is Micaiah son of Imlah."

"You shouldn't talk like that," Jehoshaphat said. "Let's hear what he has to say."

⁹So the king of Israel called one of his officials and said, "Quick! Go and get Micaiah son of Imlah."

¹⁰King Ahab of Israel and King Jehoshaphat of Judah, dressed in their royal robes, were sitting on thrones at the threshing floor near the gate of Samaria. All of Ahab's prophets were prophesying there in front of them. ¹¹One of them, Zedekiah son of Kenaanah, made some iron horns and proclaimed, "This is what the LORD says: With these horns you will gore the Arameans to death!"

¹²All the other prophets agreed. "Yes," they said, "go up to Ramoth-gilead and be victorious, for the LORD will give you victory!"

¹³Meanwhile, the messenger who went to get Micaiah said to him, "Look, all the prophets are promising victory for the king. Be sure that you agree with them and promise success."

¹⁴But Micaiah replied, "As surely as the LORD lives, I will say only what the LORD tells me to say."

¹⁵When Micaiah arrived before the king, Ahab asked him, "Micaiah, should we go to war against Ramoth-gilead or not?"

And Micaiah replied, "Go right ahead! The LORD will give the king a glorious victory!"

¹⁶But the king replied sharply, "How many times must I demand that you speak only the truth when you speak for the LORD?"

¹⁷So Micaiah told him, "In a vision I saw all Israel scattered on the mountains, like sheep without a shepherd. And the LORD said, 'Their master has been killed. Send them home in peace.'"

¹⁸"Didn't I tell you?" the king of Israel said to Jehoshaphat. "He does it every time. He never prophesies anything but bad news for me."

¹⁹Then Micaiah continued, "Listen to what the LORD says! I saw the LORD sitting on his throne with all the armies of heaven around him, on his right and on his left. ²⁰And the LORD said, 'Who can entice Ahab to go into battle against Ramoth-gilead so that he can be killed there?' There were many suggestions, ²¹until finally a spirit approached the LORD and said, 'I can do it!'

²²"'How will you do this?' the LORD asked.

"And the spirit replied, 'I will go out and inspire all Ahab's prophets to speak lies.'

"'You will succeed,' said the LORD. 'Go ahead and do it.'

23"So you see, the LORD has put a lying spirit in the mouths of your prophets. For the LORD has determined disaster for you."

24Then Zedekiah son of Kenaanah walked up to Micaiah and slapped him across the face. "When did the Spirit of the LORD leave me to speak to you?" he demanded.

25And Micaiah replied, "You will find out soon enough when you find yourself hiding in some secret room!"

26King Ahab of Israel then ordered, "Arrest Micaiah and take him back to Amon, the governor of the city, and to my son Joash. 27Give them this order from the king: 'Put this man in prison, and feed him nothing but bread and water until I return safely from the battle!'"

28But Micaiah replied, "If you return safely, the LORD has not spoken through me!" Then he added to those standing around, "Take note of what I have said."

29So the king of Israel and King Jehoshaphat of Judah led their armies against Ramoth-gilead. 30Now King Ahab said to Jehoshaphat, "As we go into battle, I will disguise myself so no one will recognize me, but you wear your royal robes." So Ahab disguised himself, and they went into battle.

31Now the king of Aram had issued these orders to his thirty-two charioteers: "Attack only the king of Israel!" 32So when the Aramean charioteers saw Jehoshaphat in his royal robes, they went after him. "There is the king of Israel!" they shouted. But when Jehoshaphat cried out, 33the charioteers realized he was not the king of Israel, and they stopped chasing him.

34An Aramean soldier, however, randomly shot an arrow at the Israelite troops, and the arrow hit the king of Israel between the joints of his armor. "Get me out of here!" Ahab groaned to the driver of his chariot. "I have been badly wounded!" 35The battle raged all that day, and Ahab was propped up in his chariot facing the Arameans. The blood from his wound ran down to the floor of his chariot, and as evening arrived he died. 36Just as the sun was setting, the cry ran through his troops: "It's all over—return

home!" 37So the king died, and his body was taken to Samaria and buried there. 38Then his chariot was washed beside the pool of Samaria, where the prostitutes bathed, and dogs came and licked the king's blood, just as the LORD had promised.

39The rest of the events in Ahab's reign and the story of the ivory palace and the cities he built are recorded in *The Book of the History of the Kings of Israel*. 40When Ahab died, he was buried among his ancestors. Then his son Ahaziah became the next king.

41Jehoshaphat son of Asa began to rule over Judah in the fourth year of King Ahab's reign in Israel. 42He was thirty-five years old when he became king, and he reigned in Jerusalem twenty-five years. His mother was Azubah, the daughter of Shilhi. 43Jehoshaphat was a good king, following the example of his father, Asa. He did what was pleasing in the LORD's sight. During his reign, however, he failed to remove all the pagan shrines, and the people still offered sacrifices and burned incense there. 44Jehoshaphat also made peace with the king of Israel.

45The rest of the events in Jehoshaphat's reign, the extent of his power, and the wars he waged are recorded in *The Book of the History of the Kings of Judah*. 46He banished from the land the rest of the shrine prostitutes, who still continued their practices from the days of his father, Asa. 47There was no king in Edom at that time, only a deputy.

48Jehoshaphat also built a fleet of trading ships* to sail to Ophir for gold. But the ships never set sail, for they were wrecked at Ezion-geber. 49At that time Ahaziah son of Ahab proposed to Jehoshaphat, "Let my men sail an expedition with your men." But Jehoshaphat refused the offer.

50When Jehoshaphat died, he was buried with his ancestors in the City of David. Then his son Jehoram became the next king.

51Ahaziah son of Ahab began to rule over Israel in the seventeenth year of King Jehoshaphat's reign in Judah. He reigned in Samaria two years. 52But he did what was evil in the LORD's sight, following the example of his father and mother and the example of Jeroboam son of Nebat, who had led Israel into the sin of idolatry. 53He served Baal and worshiped him, arousing the anger of the LORD, the God of Israel, just as his father had done.

22:48 Hebrew *fleet of ships of Tarshish.*

APRIL 7 □ DAY 98
The Danger of a Divided Heart

LOOK BACK Solomon's request for wisdom from God, combined with his commitment to walk in the footsteps of his father (3:3), ensure that Solomon's reign will mark the Golden Age of Israel's kings. People come from as far away as Africa to see for themselves the splendor and wisdom of Solomon's administration—and they are not disappointed.

Blessed with an international reputation and indescribable wealth, Solomon sets out to fulfill the dream of his father, David: a suitable Temple in which to worship the God of heaven. Curiously, God's house takes only half as long to build as Solomon's own house.

Soon there are other warning signs that all is not well in Solomon's palace. Wealth, women, weapons of war, and worship of idols soon crowd God out of Solomon's heart. Under the selfish leadership of his son Rehoboam, Solomon's kingdom fractures. Under the godless leadership of such kings as Jeroboam and Ahab, the twin kingdoms disintegrate. The call goes out for a striking figure with a penetrating message: Elijah from Tishbe.

LOOK UP What would you think of an athlete who ran as fast as the wind . . . for the first half of the race, then walked the rest of the way and came in dead last?

The inconsistent Christian is one of the devil's best workers.

What would you think of a builder whose high-rise buildings were strong and safe . . . for the first ten stories but were marked by shoddy workmanship and half-finished rooms on the rest of the floors?

What would you think of a baker whose bread and pastries had a marvelous aroma . . . but upon taking a bite you discovered they were half-baked?

Chances are you would look for someone who gave as much attention to the *finish* as to the *start*. In every pursuit of life—whether running, building, baking, or serving God—a job half done is little better than a job that was never begun.

Solomon's reign started with great promise and potential. The king who "became richer and wiser than any other in all the earth" (10:23) seemed to have everything going for him. But in his final years, the wisest man who ever lived began to play the fool. Once his heart had focused on God alone, but now Solomon's heart was turned to other loves: foreign women, fast chariots, glittering wealth. And when the last (and saddest) chapter of his life was written, the king with a divided heart had left behind a divided kingdom.

LOOK AHEAD The Bible has many sobering things to say about the danger of halfheartedness. The church at Laodicea was neither hot nor cold. It was merely lukewarm in its zeal for God. And notice God's surprising reaction to a church like that (Revelation 3:15-16).

Neglect and preoccupation can be lethal, as Solomon observed when he wrote about the field of a slothful man in Proverbs 24:30-34. Without knowing it, Solomon was writing a parable about his own life. Don't let his words become a parable about your life. If you have made a halfhearted commitment to God or a family member, what better time than today to put your whole heart into it.

2 Kings

IN 1 Kings one nation becomes two; in 2 Kings two nations become one. Nineteen consecutive evil kings consistently lead Israel downhill. Even the miracle-working ministry of Elisha cannot stop the nation's slide. Meanwhile, to the south, the occasional good king in Judah is powerless to reform the evils of his many bad predecessors. The "tale of two nations" ends disastrously: Israel is dispersed by Assyria (2 Kings 1–17); Judah is marched off to exile by Babylon (2 Kings 18–25).

Focus	Two Nations Become One					
Divisions	Reign of Joram	Record of Elisha	Jehu's Revenge / Joash's Reforms	Ruin of Israel	Reforms of Hezekiah	Ruin of Judah
	1 3	4 8	9 12	13 17	18 21	22 25
Topics	Elisha	Kings and Queens of Israel and Judah				
	Downfall of Israel				Downfall of Judah	
Place	Israel and Judah				Judah	
Time	About 130 Years				About 155 Years	

APRIL 8 ☐ DAY 99
2 KINGS 1–3
Reign of Joram

OVERVIEW While 1 Kings centers around the ministry of Elijah, 2 Kings focuses on the ministry of Elisha. After Elijah makes his last prophetic utterance—the prediction of Ahaziah's death for turning to lifeless idols rather than to the living God—he is taken up to heaven in a whirlwind, leaving his understudy, Elisha, to continue the prophetic work of calling the nation back to God. With the cloak of Elijah on his shoulders and a double portion of Elijah's spirit to fortify him, Elisha wastes no time in beginning his prophetic and miraculous ministry. He predicts that God will fill the valleys of Edom with water, enabling King Joram to defeat the forces of Moab and turn back the enemy threat.

Chapter 1	Chapter 2	Chapter 3
Fire from Heaven	Whirlwind from Heaven	Water from Heaven
Elijah's Ministry Ends and Elisha's Ministry Begins		

YOUR DAILY WALK If a miracle is defined as "something so difficult that only God can do it," what area of your life is most in need of a miracle? And how does it compare with these "miracle stories"?

Though you may ask God to do something for you, he generally wants to do something in you.

The Lord said to Abraham, "Is anything too hard for the LORD?" (Genesis 18:14). And Abraham fathered Isaac at age one hundred.

When Elisha instructed Joram to dig trenches in the valley because God was going to fill them with water in spite of a drought, Elisha assured the king, "But this is only a simple thing for the LORD" (2 Kings 3:18). The next morning the waters came.

Jeremiah affirmed, "Nothing is too hard for you"(Jeremiah 32:17). And God delivered his people from exile.

The angel told Mary, "For nothing is impossible with God" (Luke 1:37). And a virgin gave birth to the Savior.

What challenge in your life seems too big for anyone but God? Write your name by one of the stories above as your testimony of confidence in God's ability to do the impossible in your life as well.

INSIGHT Going to School with the Prophets
The "group of prophets" (1 Kings 20:35; 2 Kings 2:3, 5, 7, 15; 4:1, 38; 5:22; 6:1) were probably young men studying the law and the history of Israel in order to teach the people. Samuel may have set up these schools as part of his circuit-riding ministry (1 Samuel 7:15-17).

CHAPTER 1
After King Ahab's death, the nation of Moab declared its independence from Israel.

²One day Israel's new king, Ahaziah, fell through the latticework of an upper room at his palace in Samaria, and he was seriously injured. So he sent messengers to the

temple of Baal-zebub, the god of Ekron, to ask whether he would recover.

³But the angel of the LORD told Elijah, who was from Tishbe, "Go and meet the messengers of the king of Samaria and ask them, 'Why are you going to Baal-zebub, the god of Ekron, to ask whether the king will get well? Is there no God in Israel?

[4]Now, therefore, this is what the LORD says: You will never leave the bed on which you are lying, but you will surely die.'" So Elijah went to deliver the message.

[5]When the messengers returned to the king, he asked them, "Why have you returned so soon?"

[6]They replied, "A man came up to us and said, 'Go back to the king and give him this message from the LORD: Why are you sending men to Baal-zebub, the god of Ekron, to ask whether you will get well? Is there no God in Israel? Now, since you have done this, you will never leave the bed on which you are lying, but you will surely die.'"

[7]"Who was this man?" the king demanded. "What did he look like?"

[8]They replied, "He was a hairy man,* and he wore a leather belt around his waist."

"It was Elijah from Tishbe!" the king exclaimed. [9]Then he sent an army captain with fifty soldiers to arrest him. They found him sitting on top of a hill. The captain said to him, "Man of God, the king has commanded you to come along with us."

[10]But Elijah replied to the captain, "If I am a man of God, let fire come down from heaven and destroy you and your fifty men!" Then fire fell from heaven and killed them all.

[11]So the king sent another captain with fifty men. The captain said to him, "Man of God, the king says that you must come down right away."

[12]Elijah replied, "If I am a man of God, let fire come down from heaven and destroy you and your fifty men!" And again the fire of God fell from heaven and killed them all.

[13]Once more the king sent a captain with fifty men. But this time the captain fell to his knees before Elijah. He pleaded with him, "O man of God, please spare my life and the lives of these, your fifty servants. [14]See how the fire from heaven has destroyed the first two groups. But now please spare my life!"

[15]Then the angel of the LORD said to Elijah, "Don't be afraid. Go with him." So Elijah got up and went to the king.

[16]And Elijah said to the king, "This is what the LORD says: Why did you send messengers to Baal-zebub, the god of Ekron, to ask whether you will get well? Is there no God in Israel? Now, since you have done this, you will never leave the bed on which you are lying, but you will surely die."

[17]So Ahaziah died, just as the LORD had promised through Elijah. Since Ahaziah did not have a son to succeed him, his brother Joram* became the next king. This took place in the second year of the reign of Jehoram son of Jehoshaphat, king of Judah. [18]The rest of the events in Ahaziah's reign are recorded in *The Book of the History of the Kings of Israel.*

CHAPTER 2

When the LORD was about to take Elijah up to heaven in a whirlwind, Elijah and Elisha were traveling from Gilgal. [2]And Elijah said to Elisha, "Stay here, for the LORD has told me to go to Bethel."

But Elisha replied, "As surely as the LORD lives and you yourself live, I will never leave you!" So they went on together to Bethel.

[3]The group of prophets from Bethel came to Elisha and asked him, "Did you know that the LORD is going to take your master away from you today?"

"Quiet!" Elisha answered. "Of course I know it."

[4]Then Elijah said to Elisha, "Stay here, for the LORD has told me to go to Jericho."

But Elisha replied again, "As surely as the LORD lives and you yourself live, I will never leave you." So they went on together to Jericho.

[5]Then the group of prophets from Jericho came to Elisha and asked him, "Did you know that the LORD is going to take your master away from you today?"

"Quiet!" he answered again. "Of course I know it."

[6]Then Elijah said to Elisha, "Stay here, for the LORD has told me to go to the Jordan River."

But again Elisha replied, "As surely as the LORD lives and you yourself live, I will never leave you." So they went on together.

[7]Fifty men from the group of prophets also went and watched from a distance as Elijah and Elisha stopped beside the Jordan River. [8]Then Elijah folded his cloak together and struck the water with it. The river divided, and the two of them went across on dry ground!

1:8 Or *He was wearing clothing made of hair.*   1:17 Hebrew *Jehoram,* a variant name for Joram.

⁹When they came to the other side, Elijah said to Elisha, "What can I do for you before I am taken away?"

And Elisha replied, "Please let me become your rightful successor."*

¹⁰"You have asked a difficult thing," Elijah replied. "If you see me when I am taken from you, then you will get your request. But if not, then you won't."

¹¹As they were walking along and talking, suddenly a chariot of fire appeared, drawn by horses of fire. It drove between them, separating them, and Elijah was carried by a whirlwind into heaven. ¹²Elisha saw it and cried out, "My father! My father! The chariots and charioteers of Israel!" And as they disappeared from sight, Elisha tore his robe in two.

¹³Then Elisha picked up Elijah's cloak and returned to the bank of the Jordan River. ¹⁴He struck the water with the cloak and cried out, "Where is the LORD, the God of Elijah?" Then the river divided, and Elisha went across.

¹⁵When the group of prophets from Jericho saw what happened, they exclaimed, "Elisha has become Elijah's successor!"* And they went to meet him and bowed down before him. ¹⁶"Sir," they said, "just say the word and fifty of our strongest men will search the wilderness for your master. Perhaps the Spirit of the LORD has left him on some mountain or in some valley."

"No," Elisha said, "don't send them." ¹⁷But they kept urging him until he was embarrassed, and he finally said, "All right, send them." So fifty men searched for three days but did not find Elijah. ¹⁸Elisha was still at Jericho when they returned. "Didn't I tell you not to go?" he asked.

¹⁹Now the leaders of the town of Jericho visited Elisha. "We have a problem, my lord," they told him. "This town is located in beautiful natural surroundings, as you can see. But the water is bad, and the land is unproductive."

²⁰Elisha said, "Bring me a new bowl with salt in it." So they brought it to him. ²¹Then he went out to the spring that supplied the town with water and threw the salt into it. And he said, "This is what the LORD says: I have made this water wholesome. It will no longer cause death or infertility.*" ²²And sure enough! The water has remained wholesome ever since, just as Elisha said.

²³Elisha left Jericho and went up to Bethel. As he was walking along the road, a group of boys from the town began mocking and making fun of him. "Go away, you baldhead!" they chanted. "Go away, you baldhead!" ²⁴Elisha turned around and looked at them, and he cursed them in the name of the LORD. Then two bears came out of the woods and mauled forty-two of them. ²⁵From there Elisha went to Mount Carmel and finally returned to Samaria.

CHAPTER 3

Ahab's son Joram* began to rule over Israel in the eighteenth year of King Jehoshaphat's reign in Judah. He reigned in Samaria twelve years. ²He did what was evil in the LORD's sight, but he was not as wicked as his father and mother. He at least tore down the sacred pillar of Baal that his father had set up. ³Nevertheless he continued in the sins of idolatry that Jeroboam son of Nebat had led the people of Israel to commit.

⁴King Mesha of Moab and his people were sheep breeders. They used to pay the king of Israel an annual tribute of 100,000 lambs and the wool of 100,000 rams. ⁵But after Ahab's death, the king of Moab rebelled against the king of Israel. ⁶So King Joram mustered the army of Israel and marched from Samaria. ⁷On the way, he sent this message to King Jehoshaphat of Judah: "The king of Moab has rebelled against me. Will you help me fight him?"

And Jehoshaphat replied, "Why, of course! You and I are brothers, and my troops are yours to command. Even my horses are at your service." ⁸Then Jehoshaphat asked, "What route will we take?"

"We will attack from the wilderness of Edom," Joram replied. ⁹The king of Edom and his troops joined them, and all three armies traveled along a roundabout route through the wilderness for seven days. But there was no water for the men or their pack animals.

¹⁰"What should we do?" the king of Israel cried out. "The LORD has brought the three of us here to let the king of Moab defeat us."

¹¹But King Jehoshaphat of Judah asked, "Is there no prophet of the LORD with us? If there is, we can ask the LORD what to do."

One of King Joram's officers replied,

2:9 Hebrew *Let me inherit a double share of your spirit.*   2:15 Hebrew *The spirit of Elijah rests upon Elisha.*   2:21 Or *or make the land unproductive.*   3:1 Hebrew *Jehoram,* a variant name for Joram; also in 3:6.

"Elisha son of Shaphat is here. He used to be Elijah's personal assistant.*"

¹²Jehoshaphat said, "Then the LORD will speak through him." So the kings of Israel, Judah, and Edom went to consult with Elisha.

¹³"I want no part of you," Elisha said to the king of Israel. "Go to the pagan prophets of your father and mother!"

But King Joram said, "No! For it was the LORD who called us three kings here to be destroyed by the king of Moab!"

¹⁴Elisha replied, "As surely as the LORD Almighty lives, whom I serve, I would not bother with you except for my respect for King Jehoshaphat of Judah. ¹⁵Now bring me someone who can play the harp."

While the harp was being played, the power of the LORD came upon Elisha, ¹⁶and he said, "This is what the LORD says: This dry valley will be filled with pools of water! ¹⁷You will see neither wind nor rain, says the LORD, but this valley will be filled with water. You will have plenty for yourselves and for your cattle and your other animals. ¹⁸But this is only a simple thing for the LORD, for he will make you victorious over the army of Moab! ¹⁹You will conquer the best of their cities, even the fortified ones. You will cut down all their trees, stop up all their springs, and ruin all their good land with stones."

²⁰And sure enough, the next day at about the time when the morning sacrifice was offered, water suddenly appeared! It was flowing from the direction of Edom, and soon there was water everywhere.

²¹Meanwhile, when the people of Moab heard about the three armies marching against them, they mobilized every man who could fight, young and old, and stationed themselves along their border. ²²But when they got up the next morning, the sun was shining across the water, making it look as red as blood. ²³"It's blood!" the Moabites exclaimed. "The three armies have attacked and killed each other! Let's go and collect the plunder!"

²⁴When they arrived at the Israelite camp, the army of Israel rushed out and attacked the Moabites, who turned and ran. The army of Israel chased them into the land of Moab, destroying everything as they went. ²⁵They destroyed the cities, covered their good land with stones, stopped up the springs, and cut down the good trees. Finally, only Kir-hareseth was left, but even that came under attack.*

²⁶When the king of Moab saw that he was losing the battle, he led seven hundred of his warriors in a desperate attempt to break through the enemy lines near the king of Edom, but they failed to escape. ²⁷So he took his oldest son, who would have been the next king, and sacrificed him as a burnt offering on the wall. As a result, the anger against Israel was great, so they withdrew and returned to their own land.

3:11 Hebrew *He used to pour water on the hands of Elijah.*   3:25 Hebrew *until only Kir-hareseth was left, with its stones, but the slingers surrounded and attacked it.*

APRIL 9 ☐ DAY 100
2 KINGS 4–8
Record of Elisha

 OVERVIEW Elisha, the great miracle worker of God, performs no fewer than nine miracles in the space of today's section: providing an "oil well" for a destitute widow, giving new life to a dead boy, making poisoned stew harmless, multiplying bread for a hungry crowd, curing a leprous army captain, making an ax head defy the law of gravity, reading the mind of an enemy king, opening the eyes of a servant to see the angels of God, and closing the eyes of the enemy to the same spectacle. In each case, God's power at work in the *individual* shows his readiness to do the same in the *nation* he has called his own.

Chapter 4	Chapter 5	Chapters 6–8
Elisha and the Woman from Shunem	Elisha and the Aramean Captain	Elisha and the Aramean King
Provision	Purification	Protection

YOUR DAILY WALK   If you wear glasses, then you're probably familiar with the term *myopia*. Myopia, simply defined, is improper focus. Images appear fuzzy or blurred because the eye is incapable of bringing the light to a sharp focus. Physical myopia can be detected and compensated for quite easily.

It is not the darkness that blocks your vision so much as what is between you and God.

But there is a similar visual problem in the spiritual realm. Let's call it "spiritual myopia." The symptoms: clear focus when it comes to identifying problems, obstacles, and difficulties in everyday life, but great difficulty in focusing on the reservoir of power and protection God has provided to meet those problems head-on. Spiritual myopia is the condition from which Elisha's servant suffered when he focused on the *problem* (6:15) but not the *provision* (6:17). He saw only a horde of Arameans, while Elisha saw the host of angels.

On a three-by-five-inch card, draw a small eye chart (similar to what you would find in an optometrist's office) using the words of 2 Kings 6:16 and place it on your mirror or mantel. Let it remind you often of the importance of proper spiritual focus in your walk with God.

INSIGHT   How to Fly off the Handle
In biblical times the iron head of an ax was attached to the handle by thongs. Thus, it was common for the head to fly off the handle whenever the thongs broke or slipped. Accidents with axes were so common that a special provision was included in the law of Moses to handle such cases (Deuteronomy 19:1-6).

CHAPTER 4

One day the widow of one of Elisha's fellow prophets came to Elisha and cried out to him, "My husband who served you is dead, and you know how he feared the LORD. But now a creditor has come, threatening to take my two sons as slaves."

²"What can I do to help you?" Elisha asked. "Tell me, what do you have in the house?"

"Nothing at all, except a flask of olive oil," she replied.

³And Elisha said, "Borrow as many empty jars as you can from your friends and neighbors. ⁴Then go into your house with your sons and shut the door behind you. Pour olive oil from your flask into the jars, setting the jars aside as they are filled."

⁵So she did as she was told. Her sons brought many jars to her, and she filled one after another. ⁶Soon every container was full to the brim!

"Bring me another jar," she said to one of her sons.

"There aren't any more!" he told her. And then the olive oil stopped flowing.

⁷When she told the man of God what had happened, he said to her, "Now sell the olive oil and pay your debts, and there will be enough money left over to support you and your sons."

⁸One day Elisha went to the town of Shunem. A wealthy woman lived there, and she invited him to eat some food. From then on, whenever he passed that way, he would stop there to eat.

⁹She said to her husband, "I am sure this man who stops in from time to time is a holy man of God. ¹⁰Let's make a little room for him on the roof and furnish it with a bed, a table, a chair, and a lamp. Then he will have a place to stay whenever he comes by."

¹¹One day Elisha returned to Shunem, and he went up to his room to rest. ¹²He said to his servant Gehazi, "Tell the woman I want to speak to her." When she arrived, ¹³Elisha said to Gehazi, "Tell her that we

appreciate the kind concern she has shown us. Now ask her what we can do for her. Does she want me to put in a good word for her to the king or to the commander of the army?"

"No," she replied, "my family takes good care of me."

14Later Elisha asked Gehazi, "What do you think we can do for her?"

He suggested, "She doesn't have a son, and her husband is an old man."

15"Call her back again," Elisha told him. When the woman returned, Elisha said to her as she stood in the doorway, 16"Next year at about this time you will be holding a son in your arms!"

"No, my lord!" she protested. "Please don't lie to me like that, O man of God."

17But sure enough, the woman soon became pregnant. And at that time the following year she had a son, just as Elisha had said.

18One day when her child was older, he went out to visit his father, who was working with the harvesters. 19Suddenly he complained, "My head hurts! My head hurts!"

His father said to one of the servants, "Carry him home to his mother."

20So the servant took him home, and his mother held him on her lap. But around noontime he died. 21She carried him up to the bed of the man of God, then shut the door and left him there. 22She sent a message to her husband: "Send one of the servants and a donkey so that I can hurry to the man of God and come right back."

23"Why today?" he asked. "It is neither a new moon festival nor a Sabbath."

But she said, "It's all right." 24So she saddled the donkey and said to the servant, "Hurry! Don't slow down on my account unless I tell you to."

25As she approached the man of God at Mount Carmel, Elisha saw her in the distance. He said to Gehazi, "Look, the woman from Shunem is coming. 26Run out to meet her and ask her, 'Is everything all right with you, with your husband, and with your child?'"

"Yes," the woman told Gehazi, "everything is fine."

27But when she came to the man of God at the mountain, she fell to the ground before him and caught hold of his feet. Gehazi began to push her away, but the man of God said, "Leave her alone. Something is troubling her deeply, and the LORD has not told me what it is."

28Then she said, "It was you, my lord, who said I would have a son. And didn't I tell you not to raise my hopes?"

29Then Elisha said to Gehazi, "Get ready to travel; take my staff and go! Don't talk to anyone along the way. Go quickly and lay the staff on the child's face."

30But the boy's mother said, "As surely as the LORD lives and you yourself live, I won't go home unless you go with me." So Elisha returned with her.

31Gehazi hurried on ahead and laid the staff on the child's face, but nothing happened. There was no sign of life. He returned to meet Elisha and told him, "The child is still dead."

32When Elisha arrived, the child was indeed dead, lying there on the prophet's bed. 33He went in alone and shut the door behind him and prayed to the LORD. 34Then he lay down on the child's body, placing his mouth on the child's mouth, his eyes on the child's eyes, and his hands on the child's hands. And the child's body began to grow warm again! 35Elisha got up and walked back and forth in the room a few times. Then he stretched himself out again on the child. This time the boy sneezed seven times and opened his eyes!

36Then Elisha summoned Gehazi. "Call the child's mother!" he said. And when she came in, Elisha said, "Here, take your son!" 37She fell at his feet, overwhelmed with gratitude. Then she picked up her son and carried him downstairs.

38Elisha now returned to Gilgal, but there was a famine in the land. One day as the group of prophets was seated before him, he said to his servant, "Put on a large kettle and make some stew for these men."

39One of the young men went out into the field to gather vegetables and came back with a pocketful of wild gourds. He shredded them and put them into the kettle without realizing they were poisonous. 40But after the men had eaten a bite or two they cried out, "Man of God, there's poison in this stew!" So they would not eat it.

41Elisha said, "Bring me some flour." Then he threw it into the kettle and said, "Now it's all right; go ahead and eat." And then it did not harm them!

42One day a man from Baal-shalishah brought the man of God a sack of fresh grain and twenty loaves of barley bread made from the first grain of his harvest. Elisha said, "Give it to the group of prophets* so they can eat."

⁴³"What?" his servant exclaimed. "Feed one hundred people with only this?"

But Elisha repeated, "Give it to the group of prophets so they can eat, for the LORD says there will be plenty for all. There will even be some left over!" ⁴⁴And sure enough, there was plenty for all and some left over, just as the LORD had promised.

CHAPTER 5

The king of Aram had high admiration for Naaman, the commander of his army, because through him the LORD had given Aram great victories. But though Naaman was a mighty warrior, he suffered from leprosy.*

²Now groups of Aramean raiders had invaded the land of Israel, and among their captives was a young girl who had been given to Naaman's wife as a maid. ³One day the girl said to her mistress, "I wish my master would go to see the prophet in Samaria. He would heal him of his leprosy."

⁴So Naaman told the king what the young girl from Israel had said. ⁵"Go and visit the prophet," the king told him. "I will send a letter of introduction for you to carry to the king of Israel." So Naaman started out, taking as gifts 750 pounds of silver, 150 pounds of gold,* and ten sets of clothing. ⁶The letter to the king of Israel said: "With this letter I present my servant Naaman. I want you to heal him of his leprosy."

⁷When the king of Israel read it, he tore his clothes in dismay and said, "This man sends me a leper to heal! Am I God, that I can kill and give life? He is only trying to find an excuse to invade us again."

⁸But when Elisha, the man of God, heard about the king's reaction, he sent this message to him: "Why are you so upset? Send Naaman to me, and he will learn that there is a true prophet here in Israel."

⁹So Naaman went with his horses and chariots and waited at the door of Elisha's house. ¹⁰But Elisha sent a messenger out to him with this message: "Go and wash yourself seven times in the Jordan River. Then your skin will be restored, and you will be healed of leprosy."

¹¹But Naaman became angry and stalked away. "I thought he would surely come out to meet me!" he said. "I expected him to wave his hand over the leprosy and call on the name of the LORD his God and heal me! ¹²Aren't the Abana River and Pharpar River of Damascus better than all the rivers of Israel put together? Why shouldn't I wash in them and be healed?" So Naaman turned and went away in a rage.

¹³But his officers tried to reason with him and said, "Sir, if the prophet had told you to do some great thing, wouldn't you have done it? So you should certainly obey him when he says simply to go and wash and be cured!" ¹⁴So Naaman went down to the Jordan River and dipped himself seven times, as the man of God had instructed him. And his flesh became as healthy as a young child's, and he was healed!

¹⁵Then Naaman and his entire party went back to find the man of God. They stood before him, and Naaman said, "I know at last that there is no God in all the world except in Israel. Now please accept my gifts."

¹⁶But Elisha replied, "As surely as the LORD lives, whom I serve, I will not accept any gifts." And though Naaman urged him to take the gifts, Elisha refused.

¹⁷Then Naaman said, "All right, but please allow me to load two of my mules with earth from this place, and I will take it back home with me. From now on I will never again offer any burnt offerings or sacrifices to any other god except the LORD. ¹⁸However, may the LORD pardon me in this one thing. When my master the king goes into the temple of the god Rimmon to worship there and leans on my arm, may the LORD pardon me when I bow, too."

¹⁹"Go in peace," Elisha said. So Naaman started home again.

²⁰But Gehazi, Elisha's servant, said to himself, "My master should not have let this Aramean get away without accepting his gifts. As surely as the LORD lives, I will chase after him and get something from him." ²¹So Gehazi set off after him.

When Naaman saw him running after him, he climbed down from his chariot and went to meet him. "Is everything all right?" Naaman asked.

²²"Yes," Gehazi said, "but my master has sent me to tell you that two young prophets from the hill country of Ephraim have just

4:42 Hebrew *to the people;* also in 4:43.　　**5:1** Or *from a contagious skin disease.* The Hebrew word used here and throughout this passage can describe various skin diseases.　　**5:5** Hebrew *10 talents* [340 kilograms] *of silver, 6,000 shekels* [68 kilograms] *of gold.*

arrived. He would like 75 pounds* of silver and two sets of clothing to give to them."

23"By all means, take 150 pounds* of silver," Naaman insisted. He gave him two sets of clothing, tied up the money in two bags, and sent two of his servants to carry the gifts for Gehazi. 24But when they arrived at the hill, Gehazi took the gifts from the servants and sent the men back. Then he hid the gifts inside the house.

25When he went in to his master, Elisha asked him, "Where have you been, Gehazi?"

"I haven't been anywhere," he replied.

26But Elisha asked him, "Don't you realize that I was there in spirit when Naaman stepped down from his chariot to meet you? Is this the time to receive money and clothing and olive groves and vineyards and sheep and oxen and servants? 27Because you have done this, you and your children and your children's children will suffer from Naaman's leprosy forever." When Gehazi left the room, he was leprous; his skin was as white as snow.

CHAPTER 6

One day the group of prophets came to Elisha and told him, "As you can see, this place where we meet with you is too small. 2Let's go down to the Jordan River, where there are plenty of logs. There we can build a new place for us to meet."

"All right," he told them, "go ahead."

3"Please come with us," someone suggested.

"I will," he said.

4When they arrived at the Jordan, they began cutting down trees. 5But as one of them was chopping, his ax head fell into the river. "Ah, my lord!" he cried. "It was a borrowed ax!"

6"Where did it fall?" the man of God asked. When he showed him the place, Elisha cut a stick and threw it into the water. Then the ax head rose to the surface and floated. 7"Grab it," Elisha said to him. And the man reached out and grabbed it.

8When the king of Aram was at war with Israel, he would confer with his officers and say, "We will mobilize our forces at such and such a place."

9But immediately Elisha, the man of God, would warn the king of Israel, "Do not go near that place, for the Arameans are planning to mobilize their troops there." 10So the king of Israel would send word to the place indicated by the man of God, warning the people there to be on their guard. This happened several times.

11The king of Aram became very upset over this. He called in his officers and demanded, "Which of you is the traitor? Who has been informing the king of Israel of my plans?"

12"It's not us, my lord," one of the officers replied. "Elisha, the prophet in Israel, tells the king of Israel even the words you speak in the privacy of your bedroom!"

13The king commanded, "Go and find out where Elisha is, and we will send troops to seize him."

And the report came back: "Elisha is at Dothan." 14So one night the king of Aram sent a great army with many chariots and horses to surround the city. 15When the servant of the man of God got up early the next morning and went outside, there were troops, horses, and chariots everywhere.

"Ah, my lord, what will we do now?" he cried out to Elisha.

16"Don't be afraid!" Elisha told him. "For there are more on our side than on theirs!" 17Then Elisha prayed, "O LORD, open his eyes and let him see!" The LORD opened his servant's eyes, and when he looked up, he saw that the hillside around Elisha was filled with horses and chariots of fire.

18As the Aramean army advanced toward them, Elisha prayed, "O LORD, please make them blind." And the LORD did as Elisha asked. 19Then Elisha went out and told them, "You have come the wrong way! This isn't the right city! Follow me, and I will take you to the man you are looking for." And he led them to Samaria. 20As soon as they had entered Samaria, Elisha prayed, "O LORD, now open their eyes and let them see." And the LORD did, and they discovered that they were in Samaria.

21When the king of Israel saw them, he shouted to Elisha, "My father, should I kill them?"

22"Of course not!" Elisha told him. "Do we kill prisoners of war? Give them food and drink and send them home again to their master."

23So the king made a great feast for them and then sent them home to their king.

5:22 Hebrew 1 talent [34 kilograms].   5:23 Hebrew 2 talents [68 kilograms].

After that, the Aramean raiders stayed away from the land of Israel.

²⁴Some time later, however, King Benhadad of Aram mobilized his entire army and besieged Samaria. ²⁵As a result there was a great famine in the city. After a while even a donkey's head sold for two pounds of silver, and a cup of dove's dung cost about two ounces* of silver.

²⁶One day as the king of Israel was walking along the wall of the city, a woman called to him, "Please help me, my lord the king!"

²⁷"If the LORD doesn't help you, what can I do?" he retorted. "I have neither food nor wine to give you." ²⁸But then the king asked, "What is the matter?"

She replied, "This woman proposed that we eat my son one day and her son the next. ²⁹So we cooked my son and ate him. Then the next day I said, 'Kill your son so we can eat him,' but she had hidden him."

³⁰When the king heard this, he tore his clothes in despair. And as the king walked along the wall, the people could see that he was wearing sackcloth underneath next to his skin. ³¹"May God kill me if I don't execute Elisha son of Shaphat this very day," the king vowed.

³²Elisha was sitting in his house at a meeting with the leaders of Israel when the king sent a messenger to summon him. But before the messenger arrived, Elisha said to the leaders, "A murderer has sent a man to kill me. When he arrives, shut the door and keep him out. His master will soon follow him."

³³While Elisha was still saying this, the messenger arrived. And the king* said, "It is the LORD who has brought this trouble on us! Why should I wait any longer for the LORD?"

CHAPTER 7

Elisha replied, "Hear this message from the LORD! This is what the LORD says: By this time tomorrow in the markets of Samaria, five quarts of fine flour will cost only half an ounce of silver,* and ten quarts of barley grain will cost only half an ounce of silver.*"

²The officer assisting the king said to the man of God, "That couldn't happen even if the LORD opened the windows of heaven!"

But Elisha replied, "You will see it happen, but you won't be able to eat any of it!"

³Now there were four men with leprosy* sitting at the entrance of the city gates. "Why should we sit here waiting to die?" they asked each other. ⁴"We will starve if we stay here, and we will starve if we go back into the city. So we might as well go out and surrender to the Aramean army. If they let us live, so much the better. But if they kill us, we would have died anyway."

⁵So that evening they went out to the camp of the Arameans, but no one was there! ⁶For the Lord had caused the whole army of Aram to hear the clatter of speeding chariots and the galloping of horses and the sounds of a great army approaching. "The king of Israel has hired the Hittites and Egyptians* to attack us!" they cried out. ⁷So they panicked and fled into the night, abandoning their tents, horses, donkeys, and everything else, and they fled for their lives.

⁸When the lepers arrived at the edge of the camp, they went into one tent after another, eating, drinking wine, and carrying out silver and gold and clothing and hiding it. ⁹Finally, they said to each other, "This is not right. This is wonderful news, and we aren't sharing it with anyone! If we wait until morning, some terrible calamity will certainly fall upon us. Come on, let's go back and tell the people at the palace."

¹⁰So they went back to the city and told the gatekeepers what had happened—that they had gone out to the Aramean camp and no one was there! The horses and donkeys were tethered and the tents were all in order, but there was not a single person around. ¹¹Then the gatekeepers shouted the news to the people in the palace.

¹²The king got out of bed in the middle of the night and told his officers, "I know what has happened. The Arameans know we are starving, so they have left their camp and have hidden in the fields. They are expecting us to leave the city, and then they will take us alive and capture the city."

¹³One of his officers replied, "We had better send out scouts to check into this. Let them take five of the remaining horses. If

6:25 Hebrew *sold for 80 shekels* [0.9 kilograms] *of silver, and* ¼ *of a cab* [0.3 liters] *of dove's dung cost 5 shekels* [57 grams]. *Dove's dung may be a variety of wild vegetable.*   **6:33** Hebrew *he.*   **7:1a** Hebrew *1 seah* [6 liters] *of fine flour will cost 1 shekel* [11 grams]; also in 7:16, 18.   **7:1b** Hebrew *2 seahs* [12 liters] *of barley grain will cost 1 shekel* [11 grams]; also in 7:16, 18.   **7:3** Or *with a contagious skin disease.* The Hebrew word used here and throughout this passage can describe various skin diseases.   **7:6** Possibly *and the people of Muzur,* a district near Cilicia.

something happens to them, it won't be a greater loss than if they stay here and die with the rest of us."

¹⁴So two chariots with horses were prepared, and the king sent scouts to see what had happened to the Aramean army. ¹⁵They went all the way to the Jordan River, following a trail of clothing and equipment that the Arameans had thrown away in their mad rush to escape. The scouts returned and told the king about it. ¹⁶Then the people of Samaria rushed out and plundered the Aramean camp. So it was true that five quarts of fine flour were sold that day for half an ounce of silver, and ten quarts of barley grain were sold for half an ounce of silver, just as the LORD had promised. ¹⁷The king appointed his officer to control the traffic at the gate, but he was knocked down and trampled to death as the people rushed out.

So everything happened exactly as the man of God had predicted when the king came to his house. ¹⁸The man of God had said to the king, "By this time tomorrow in the markets of Samaria, five quarts of fine flour will cost half an ounce of silver, and ten quarts of barley grain will cost half an ounce of silver." ¹⁹The king's officer had replied, "That couldn't happen even if the LORD opened the windows of heaven!" And the man of God had said, "You will see it happen, but you won't be able to eat any of it!" ²⁰And so it was, for the people trampled him to death at the gate!

CHAPTER 8

Elisha had told the woman whose son he had brought back to life, "Take your family and move to some other place, for the LORD has called for a famine on Israel that will last for seven years." ²So the woman did as the man of God instructed. She took her family and lived in the land of the Philistines for seven years.

³After the famine ended she returned to the land of Israel, and she went to see the king about getting back her house and land. ⁴As she came in, the king was talking with Gehazi, the servant of the man of God. The king had just said, "Tell me some stories about the great things Elisha has done." ⁵And Gehazi was telling the king about the time Elisha had brought a boy back to life. At that very moment, the

mother of the boy walked in to make her appeal to the king.

"Look, my lord!" Gehazi exclaimed. "Here is the woman now, and this is her son—the very one Elisha brought back to life!"

⁶"Is this true?" the king asked her. And she told him that it was. So he directed one of his officials to see to it that everything she had lost was restored to her, including the value of any crops that had been harvested during her absence.

⁷Now Elisha went to Damascus, the capital of Aram, where King Ben-hadad lay sick. Someone told the king that the man of God had come. ⁸When the king heard the news, he said to Hazael, "Take a gift to the man of God. Then tell him to ask the LORD if I will get well again."

⁹So Hazael loaded down forty camels with the finest products of Damascus as a gift for Elisha. He went in to him and said, "Your servant Ben-hadad, the king of Aram, has sent me to ask you if he will recover."

¹⁰And Elisha replied, "Go and tell him, 'You will recover.' But the LORD has shown me that he will actually die!" ¹¹Elisha stared at Hazael* with a fixed gaze until Hazael became uneasy. Then the man of God started weeping.

¹²"What's the matter, my lord?" Hazael asked him.

Elisha replied, "I know the terrible things you will do to the people of Israel. You will burn their fortified cities, kill their young men, dash their children to the ground, and rip open their pregnant women!"

¹³Then Hazael replied, "How could a nobody like me* ever accomplish such a great feat?"

But Elisha answered, "The LORD has shown me that you are going to be the king of Aram."

¹⁴When Hazael went back, the king asked him, "What did Elisha tell you?"

And Hazael replied, "He told me that you will surely recover."

¹⁵But the next day Hazael took a blanket, soaked it in water, and held it over the king's face until he died. Then Hazael became the next king of Aram.

¹⁶Jehoram son of King Jehoshaphat of Judah began to rule over Judah in the fifth

8:11 Hebrew *He stared at him.*   **8:13** Hebrew *a dog.*

year of King Joram's reign in Israel. Joram was the son of Ahab. [17]Jehoram was thirty-two years old when he became king, and he reigned in Jerusalem eight years. [18]But Jehoram followed the example of the kings of Israel and was as wicked as King Ahab, for he had married one of Ahab's daughters. So Jehoram did what was evil in the LORD's sight. [19]But the LORD was not willing to destroy Judah, for he had made a covenant with David and promised that his descendants would continue to rule forever.*

[20]During Jehoram's reign, the Edomites revolted against Judah and crowned their own king. [21]So Jehoram* went with all his chariots to attack the town of Zair.* The Edomites surrounded him and his charioteers, but he escaped at night under cover of darkness. Jehoram's army, however, deserted him and fled. [22]Edom has been independent from Judah to this day. The town of Libnah revolted about that same time.

[23]The rest of the events in Jehoram's reign and all his deeds are recorded in The *Book of the History of the Kings of Judah.* [24]When Jehoram died, he was buried with his ancestors in the City of David. Then his son Ahaziah became the next king.

[25]Ahaziah son of Jehoram began to rule over Judah in the twelfth year of King Joram's reign in Israel. King Joram was the son of Ahab. [26]Ahaziah was twenty-two years old when he became king, and he reigned in Jerusalem one year. His mother was Athaliah, a granddaughter of King Omri of Israel. [27]Ahaziah followed the evil example of King Ahab's family, doing what was evil in the LORD's sight, because he was related by marriage to the family of Ahab.

[28]Ahaziah joined King Joram of Israel in his war against King Hazael of Aram at Ramoth-gilead. When King Joram was wounded in the battle, [29]he returned to Jezreel to recover from his wounds. While Joram was there, King Ahaziah of Judah went to visit him.

8:19 Hebrew *promised to give a lamp to David and his descendants forever.*   8:21a Hebrew *Joram,* a variant name for Jehoram; also in 8:23, 24.   8:21b Greek version reads *Seir.*

APRIL 10 ☐ DAY 101
2 KINGS 9–12
Jehu's Revenge, Joash's Reforms

 OVERVIEW Anointed king over Israel at Elisha's direction, Jehu wastes no time in carrying out his mission. He heads straight for the city of Jezreel, where Joram is recuperating from his battle wounds. There he slays the ruling heir of Ahab's house in the vineyard of Naboth for which Ahab had committed murder a generation before! But Jehu is far from finished. In addition, he kills Ahaziah, king of Judah (who was making an untimely visit to Joram), Jezebel (Joram's wicked mother-in-law), and finally the entire surviving family of Ahab, thus fulfilling God's sentence of death. But while Jehu is executing judgment in Israel, a different and potentially more dangerous execution is taking place in Judah. Athaliah, Ahab's daughter and the mother of Ahaziah, seizes the throne and seeks to liquidate the rest of the royal line. The sole surviving heir, Joash, grows up to be Judah's youngest monarch and one of its greatest reformers.

Chapter 9	Chapter 10	Chapter 11	Chapter 12
Jehu Kills Two Kings	Jehu Kills Ahab's Family	Athaliah Kills Her Own Family	Joash Repairs the Temple
Jehu's Ministry of Judgment		Joash's Ministry of Reform	

YOUR DAILY WALK Whatever else you can say about Jehu (and you can say plenty!), his single-minded attention to the task God had given him is exemplary. Jehu was a man with a divine calling, a man with a mission, who lost no time in carrying it out. He brought to fulfillment the prophecy of Elijah against the house of Ahab (1 Kings 21:19-24) and completely rid Israel of the heathen worship of Baal for a time. God approved of Jehu's ministry and rewarded him for it.

Get on fire for God, and people will watch you burn.

How do you tackle the assignment God has set before you? carelessly? halfheartedly? or with the zeal of a Jehu? Whether you are a student or a parent, a minister or an office worker, you can put your heart into your work—if the God of Jehu is in your heart.

INSIGHT Judgment Can Be Murder

Jehu was anointed as God's instrument for the task of exterminating the house of Ahab and, along with it, the worship of Baal. Baalism was so viciously cruel that only a person of Jehu's relentlessness could have done the job. By the end, Jehu had indeed wiped out the entire house of Ahab and had thoroughly purged the nation of Baal worshipers.

CHAPTER 9

Meanwhile, Elisha the prophet had summoned a member of the group of prophets. "Get ready to go to Ramoth-gilead," he told him. "Take this vial of olive oil with you, ²and find Jehu son of Jehoshaphat and grandson of Nimshi. Call him into a back room away from his friends, ³and pour the oil over his head. Say to him, 'This is what the LORD says: I anoint you to be the king over Israel.' Then open the door and run for your life!"

⁴So the young prophet did as he was told and went to Ramoth-gilead. ⁵When he arrived there, he found Jehu sitting in a meeting with the other army officers. "I have a message for you, Commander," he said.

"For which one of us?" Jehu asked.

"For you, Commander," he replied.

⁶So Jehu left the others and went into the house. Then the young prophet poured the oil on Jehu's head and said, "This is what the LORD, the God of Israel, says: I anoint you king over the LORD's people, Israel. ⁷You are to destroy the family of Ahab, your master. In this way, I will avenge the murder of my prophets and all the LORD's servants who were killed by Jezebel. ⁸The entire family of Ahab must be wiped out—every male, slave and free alike, in Israel. ⁹I will destroy the family of Ahab as I destroyed the families of Jeroboam son of Nebat and of Baasha son of Ahijah. ¹⁰Dogs will eat Ahab's wife, Jezebel, at the plot of land in Jezreel, and no one will bury her." Then the young prophet opened the door and ran.

¹¹Jehu went back to his fellow officers, and one of them asked him, "What did that crazy fellow want? Is everything all right?"

"You know the way such a man babbles on," Jehu replied.

¹²"You're lying," they said. "Tell us." So Jehu told them what the man had said and that at the LORD's command he had been anointed king over Israel.

¹³They quickly spread out their cloaks on the bare steps and blew a trumpet, shouting, "Jehu is king!"

¹⁴So Jehu son of Jehoshaphat and grandson of Nimshi formed a conspiracy against King Joram. (Now Joram had been with the army at Ramoth-gilead, defending Israel against the forces of King Hazael of Aram. ¹⁵But Joram* had been wounded in the fighting and had returned to Jezreel to recover from his wounds.) So Jehu told the men with him, "Since you want me to be king, don't let anyone escape to Jezreel to report what we have done."

¹⁶Then Jehu got into a chariot and rode to Jezreel to find King Joram, who was lying there wounded. King Ahaziah of Judah was there, too, for he had gone to visit him. ¹⁷The watchman on the tower of Jezreel saw Jehu and his company approaching, so he shouted to Joram, "I see a company of troops coming!"

"Send out a rider to find out if they are coming in peace," King Joram shouted back.

¹⁸So a rider went out to meet Jehu and said, "The king wants to know whether you are coming in peace."

Jehu replied, "What do you know about peace? Get behind me!"

9:15 Hebrew *Jehoram*, a variant name for Joram; also in 9:17, 21, 22, 23, 24.

The watchman called out to the king, "The rider has met them, but he is not returning."

[19]So the king sent out a second rider. He rode up to them and demanded, "The king wants to know whether you come in peace."

Again Jehu answered, "What do you know about peace? Get behind me!"

[20]The watchman exclaimed, "The rider has met them, but he isn't returning either! It must be Jehu son of Nimshi, for he is driving so recklessly."

[21]"Quick! Get my chariot ready!" King Joram commanded.

Then King Joram of Israel and King Ahaziah of Judah rode out in their chariots to meet Jehu. They met him at the field that had belonged to Naboth of Jezreel. [22]King Joram demanded, "Do you come in peace, Jehu?"

Jehu replied, "How can there be peace as long as the idolatry and witchcraft of your mother, Jezebel, are all around us?"

[23]Then King Joram reined the chariot horses around and fled, shouting to King Ahaziah, "Treason, Ahaziah!" [24]Then Jehu drew his bow and shot Joram between the shoulders. The arrow pierced his heart, and he sank down dead in his chariot.

[25]Jehu said to Bidkar, his officer, "Throw him into the field of Naboth of Jezreel. Do you remember when you and I were riding along behind his father, Ahab? The LORD pronounced this message against him: [26]'I solemnly swear that I will repay him here on Naboth's property, says the LORD, for the murder of Naboth and his sons that I saw yesterday.' So throw him out on Naboth's field, just as the LORD said."

[27]When King Ahaziah of Judah saw what was happening, he fled along the road to Beth-haggan. Jehu rode after him, shouting, "Shoot him, too!" So they shot Ahaziah in his chariot at the Ascent of Gur, near Ibleam. He was able to go on as far as Megiddo, but he died there. [28]His officials took him by chariot to Jerusalem, where they buried him with his ancestors in the City of David. [29]Ahaziah's reign over Judah had begun in the eleventh year of King Joram's reign in Israel.

[30]When Jezebel, the queen mother, heard that Jehu had come to Jezreel, she painted her eyelids and fixed her hair and sat at a window. [31]When Jehu entered the gate of the palace, she shouted at him, "Have you come in peace, you murderer? You are just like Zimri, who murdered his master!"

[32]Jehu looked up and saw her at the window and shouted, "Who is on my side?" And two or three eunuchs looked out at him. [33]"Throw her down!" Jehu yelled. So they threw her out the window, and some of her blood spattered against the wall and on the horses. And Jehu trampled her body under his horses' hooves.

[34]Then Jehu went into the palace and ate and drank. Afterward he said, "Someone go and bury this cursed woman, for she is the daughter of a king." [35]But when they went out to bury her, they found only her skull, her feet, and her hands.

[36]When they returned and told Jehu, he stated, "This fulfills the message from the LORD, which he spoke through his servant Elijah from Tishbe: 'At the plot of land in Jezreel, dogs will eat Jezebel's flesh. [37]Her body will be scattered like dung on the field of Jezreel, so that no one will be able to recognize her.'"

CHAPTER 10
Now Ahab had seventy sons living in the city of Samaria. So Jehu wrote a letter and sent copies to Samaria, to the officials of the city,* to the leaders of the people, and to the guardians of King Ahab's sons. The letter said, [2]"The king's sons are with you, and you have at your disposal chariots, horses, a fortified city, and weapons. As soon as you receive this letter, [3]select the best qualified of King Ahab's sons to be your king, and prepare to fight for Ahab's dynasty."

[4]But they were paralyzed with fear and said, "Two kings couldn't stand against this man! What can we do?" [5]So the palace and city administrators, together with the other leaders and the guardians of the king's sons, sent this message to Jehu: "We are your servants and will do anything you tell us. We will not make anyone king; do whatever you think is best."

[6]Jehu responded with a second letter: "If you are on my side and are going to obey me, bring the heads of the king's sons to me at Jezreel at about this time tomorrow."

Now the seventy sons of the king were being cared for by the leaders of Samaria, where they had been raised since childhood. [7]When the letter arrived, the leaders

10:1 As in some Greek manuscripts and Latin Vulgate (see also 10:6); Hebrew reads *of Jezreel.*

killed all seventy of the king's sons. They placed their heads in baskets and presented them to Jehu at Jezreel. [8]A messenger went to Jehu and said, "They have brought the heads of the king's sons."

So Jehu ordered, "Pile them in two heaps at the entrance of the city gate, and leave them there until morning."

[9]In the morning he went out and spoke to the crowd that had gathered around them. "You aren't to blame," he told them. "I am the one who conspired against my master and killed him. But who killed all these? [10]You can be sure that the message of the LORD that was spoken concerning Ahab's family will not fail. The LORD declared through his servant Elijah that this would happen." [11]Then Jehu killed all of Ahab's relatives living in Jezreel and all his important officials, personal friends, and priests. So Ahab was left without a single survivor.

[12]Then Jehu set out for Samaria. Along the way, while he was at Beth-eked of the Shepherds, [13]he met some relatives of King Ahaziah of Judah. "Who are you?" he asked them.

And they replied, "We are relatives of King Ahaziah. We are going to visit the sons of King Ahab and the queen mother."

[14]"Take them alive!" Jehu shouted to his men. And they captured all forty-two of them and killed them at the well of Beth-eked. None of them escaped.

[15]When Jehu left there, he met Jehonadab son of Recab, who was coming to meet him. After they had greeted each other, Jehu said to him, "Are you as loyal to me as I am to you?"

"Yes, I am," Jehonadab replied.

"If you are," Jehu said, "then give me your hand." So Jehonadab put out his hand, and Jehu helped him into the chariot. [16]Then Jehu said, "Now come with me, and see how devoted I am to the LORD." So Jehonadab rode along with him. [17]When Jehu arrived in Samaria, he killed everyone who was left there from Ahab's family, just as the LORD had promised through Elijah.

[18]Then Jehu called a meeting of all the people of the city and said to them, "Ahab hardly worshiped Baal at all compared to the way I will worship him! [19]Summon all the prophets and worshipers of Baal, and call together all his priests. See to it that every one of them comes, for I am going to offer a great sacrifice to Baal. Any of Baal's worshipers who fail to come will be put to death." But Jehu's plan was to destroy all the worshipers of Baal.

[20]Then Jehu ordered, "Prepare a solemn assembly to worship Baal!" So they did. [21]He sent messengers throughout all Israel summoning those who worshiped Baal. They all came and filled the temple of Baal from one end to the other. [22]And Jehu instructed the keeper of the wardrobe, "Be sure that every worshiper of Baal wears one of these robes." So robes were given to them.

[23]Then Jehu went into the temple of Baal with Jehonadab son of Recab. Jehu said to the worshipers of Baal, "Make sure that only those who worship Baal are here. Don't let anyone in who worships the LORD!" [24]So they were all inside the temple to offer sacrifices and burnt offerings. Now Jehu had surrounded the building with eighty of his men and had warned them, "If you let anyone escape, you will pay for it with your own life."

[25]As soon as Jehu had finished sacrificing the burnt offering, he commanded his guards and officers, "Go in and kill all of them. Don't let a single one escape!" So they killed them all with their swords, and the guards and officers dragged their bodies outside. Then Jehu's men went into the fortress* of the temple of Baal. [26]They dragged out the sacred pillar used in the worship of Baal and destroyed it. [27]They broke down the sacred pillar of Baal and wrecked the temple of Baal, converting it into a public toilet. That is what it is used for to this day. [28]Thus, Jehu destroyed every trace of Baal worship from Israel. [29]He did not, however, destroy the gold calves at Bethel and Dan, the great sin that Jeroboam son of Nebat had led Israel to commit.

[30]Nonetheless the LORD said to Jehu, "You have done well in following my instructions to destroy the family of Ahab. Because of this I will cause your descendants to be the kings of Israel down to the fourth generation." [31]But Jehu did not obey the law of the LORD, the God of Israel, with all his heart. He refused to turn from the sins of idolatry that Jeroboam had led Israel to commit.

10:25 Hebrew *city*.

³²At about that time the LORD began to reduce the size of Israel's territory. King Hazael conquered several sections of the country ³³east of the Jordan River, including all of Gilead, Gad, Reuben, and Manasseh. He conquered the area from the town of Aroer by the Arnon Gorge to as far north as Gilead and Bashan.

³⁴The rest of the events in Jehu's reign and all his deeds and achievements are recorded in *The Book of the History of the Kings of Israel.* ³⁵When Jehu died, he was buried with his ancestors in Samaria. Then his son Jehoahaz became the next king. ³⁶In all, Jehu reigned over Israel from Samaria for twenty-eight years.

CHAPTER 11

When Athaliah, the mother of King Ahaziah of Judah, learned that her son was dead, she set out to destroy the rest of the royal family. ²But Ahaziah's sister Jehosheba, the daughter of King Jehoram,* took Ahaziah's infant son, Joash, and stole him away from among the rest of the king's children, who were about to be killed. Jehosheba put Joash and his nurse in a bedroom to hide him from Athaliah, so the child was not murdered. ³Joash and his nurse remained hidden in the Temple of the LORD for six years while Athaliah ruled over the land.

⁴In the seventh year of Athaliah's reign, Jehoiada the priest summoned the commanders, the Carite mercenaries, and the guards to come to the Temple of the LORD. He made a pact with them and made them swear an oath of loyalty there in the LORD's Temple; then he showed them the king's son.

⁵Jehoiada told them, "This is what you must do. A third of you who are on duty on the Sabbath are to guard the royal palace itself. ⁶Another third of you are to stand guard at the Sur Gate. And the final third must stand guard behind the palace guard. These three groups will all guard the palace. ⁷The other two units who are off duty on the Sabbath must stand guard for the king at the LORD's Temple. ⁸Form a bodyguard for the king and keep your weapons in hand. Any unauthorized person who approaches you must be killed. Stay right beside the king at all times."

⁹So the commanders did everything just as Jehoiada the priest ordered. The commanders took charge of the men reporting for duty that Sabbath, as well as those who were going off duty. They brought them all to Jehoiada the priest, ¹⁰and he supplied them with the spears and shields that had once belonged to King David and were stored in the Temple of the LORD. ¹¹The guards stationed themselves around the king, with their weapons ready. They formed a line from the south side of the Temple around to the north side and all around the altar.

¹²Then Jehoiada brought out Joash, the king's son, and placed the crown on his head. He presented Joash with a copy of God's covenant and proclaimed him king. They anointed him, and all the people clapped their hands and shouted, "Long live the king!"

¹³When Athaliah heard all the noise made by the guards and the people, she hurried to the LORD's Temple to see what was happening. ¹⁴And she saw the newly crowned king standing in his place of authority by the pillar, as was the custom at times of coronation. The officers and trumpeters were surrounding him, and people from all over the land were rejoicing and blowing trumpets. When Athaliah saw all this, she tore her clothes in despair and shouted, "Treason! Treason!"

¹⁵Then Jehoiada the priest ordered the commanders who were in charge of the troops, "Take her out of the Temple, and kill anyone who tries to rescue her. Do not kill her here in the Temple of the LORD." ¹⁶So they seized her and led her out to the gate where horses enter the palace grounds, and she was killed there.

¹⁷Then Jehoiada made a covenant between the LORD and the king and the people that they would be the LORD's people. He also made a covenant between the king and the people. ¹⁸And all the people of the land went over to the temple of Baal and tore it down. They demolished the altars and smashed the idols to pieces, and they killed Mattan the priest of Baal in front of the altars.

Jehoiada the priest stationed guards at the Temple of the LORD. ¹⁹Then the commanders, the Carite mercenaries, the guards, and all the people of the land escorted the king from the Temple of the

11:2 Hebrew *Joram*, a variant name for Jehoram.

LORD. They went through the gate of the guards and into the palace, and the king took his seat on the royal throne. ²⁰So all the people of the land rejoiced, and the city was peaceful because Athaliah had been killed at the king's palace.

²¹Joash* was seven years old when he became king.

CHAPTER 12

Joash* began to rule over Judah in the seventh year of King Jehu's reign in Israel. He reigned in Jerusalem forty years. His mother was Zibiah, from Beersheba. ²All his life Joash did what was pleasing in the LORD's sight because Jehoiada the priest instructed him. ³Yet even so, he did not destroy the pagan shrines, and the people still offered sacrifices and burned incense there.

⁴One day King Joash said to the priests, "Collect all the money brought as a sacred offering to the LORD's Temple, whether it is a regular assessment, a payment of vows, or a voluntary gift. ⁵Let the priests take some of that money to pay for whatever repairs are needed at the Temple."

⁶But by the twenty-third year of Joash's reign, the priests still had not repaired the Temple. ⁷So King Joash called for Jehoiada and the other priests and asked them, "Why haven't you repaired the Temple? Don't use any more gifts for your own needs. From now on, it must all be spent on getting the Temple into good condition." ⁸So the priests agreed not to collect any more money from the people, and they also agreed not to undertake the repairs of the Temple themselves.

⁹Then Jehoiada the priest bored a hole in the lid of a large chest and set it on the right-hand side of the altar at the entrance of the Temple of the LORD. The priests guarding the entrance put all of the people's contributions into the chest. ¹⁰Whenever the chest became full, the court

secretary and the high priest counted the money that had been brought to the LORD's Temple and put it into bags. ¹¹Then they gave the money to the construction supervisors, who used it to pay the people working on the LORD's Temple—the carpenters, the builders, ¹²the masons, and the stonecutters. They also used the money to buy timber and cut stone for repairing the LORD's Temple, and they paid any other expenses related to the Temple's restoration.

¹³The money brought to the Temple was not used for making silver cups, lamp snuffers, basins, trumpets, or other articles of gold or silver for the Temple of the LORD. ¹⁴It was paid out to the workmen, who used it for the Temple repairs. ¹⁵No accounting was required from the construction supervisors, because they were honest and faithful workers. ¹⁶However, the money that was contributed for guilt offerings and sin offerings was not brought into the LORD's Temple. It was given to the priests for their own use.

¹⁷About this time King Hazael of Aram went to war against Gath and captured it. Then he turned to attack Jerusalem. ¹⁸King Joash collected all the sacred objects that Jehoshaphat, Jehoram, and Ahaziah, the previous kings of Judah, had dedicated, along with what he himself had dedicated. He sent them all to Hazael, along with all the gold in the treasuries of the LORD's Temple and the royal palace. So Hazael called off his attack on Jerusalem.

¹⁹The rest of the events in Joash's reign and all his deeds are recorded in *The Book of the History of the Kings of Judah.* ²⁰But his officers plotted against him and assassinated him at Beth-millo on the road to Silla. ²¹The assassins were Jozabad son of Shimeath and Jehozabad son of Shomer—both trusted advisers. Joash was buried with his ancestors in the City of David. Then his son Amaziah became the next king.

11:21 Hebrew *Jehoash,* a variant name for Joash.   12:1 Hebrew *Jehoash,* a variant name for Joash; also in 12:2, 4, 6, 7, 18.

APRIL 11 ☐ DAY 102
2 KINGS 13–17
Ruin of Israel

OVERVIEW On his deathbed, Elisha offers King Joash of Israel the opportunity to utterly rout his Aramean enemy. But the king's lack of faith results in something far short of complete victory and presents a picture of the problem that has plagued Israel's kings for centuries. The alliance between Israel and Judah, secured under Jehoshaphat, now gives way to constant warfare. Anarchy and apostasy rip the land of Israel as first one king and then another is assassinated. When Israel and Aram form an alliance against Judah, Ahaz (king of Judah) buys the help of Assyria. But the downward spiral continues, and soon the ten tribes in the north are deported to the remotest corners of the Assyrian Empire, while other conquered peoples are imported to fill the vacuum.

Chapter 13	Chapter 14	Chapter 15	Chapters 16–17
Elisha Dies	Jeroboam II Reigns	Seven Kings Reign	Assyria Prevails
Decline in Israel		Dispersion of Israel	

The power of man can never reverse the sentence of God.

YOUR DAILY WALK Historians and political scientists have developed elaborate explanations for the conquest of Israel and later of Judah. "These were small countries," they say, "in the buffer zone between large, powerful neighbors to the south [Egypt] and north [Assyria and Babylonia]." But the Bible states that the conquest and exile were God's judgment because of the sin of his people. Israel abandoned the Lord, turned to idols, and ignored the repeated message of God's prophets to "shape up or ship out." They had no one to blame but themselves.

That biblical principle remains in force today for nations as well as individuals, Christians as well as unbelievers. God will deal with an individual, with a family, or with a nation according to the unchanging principle that "you will always reap what you sow" (Galatians 6:7). By the way, when was the last time you "sowed" a word for God by means of a brief phone call or letter to one of your elected officials? If an issue is crucial and God has spoken in his Word concerning it, can you afford to remain silent?

INSIGHT It's a Long Way to Captivity
In the Assyrian dispersion many Israelites were resettled in northern Mesopotamia (more than four hundred miles away) and others in the area of the Medes (a full thousand miles from Samaria).

CHAPTER 13
Jehoahaz son of Jehu began to rule over Israel in the twenty-third year of King Joash's reign in Judah. He reigned in Samaria seventeen years. ²But he did what was evil in the LORD's sight. He followed the example of Jeroboam son of Nebat, continuing the sins of idolatry that Jeroboam son of Nebat had led Israel to commit. ³So the LORD was very angry with Israel, and he allowed King Hazael of Aram and his son Ben-hadad to defeat them time after time.

⁴Then Jehoahaz prayed for the LORD's help, and the LORD heard his prayer. The LORD could see how terribly the king of Aram was oppressing Israel. ⁵So the LORD raised up a deliverer to rescue the Israelites from the tyranny of the Arameans. Then Israel lived in safety again as they had in former days. ⁶But they continued to sin, following the evil example of Jeroboam. They even set up an Asherah pole in Samaria. ⁷Finally, Jehoahaz's army was reduced to fifty mounted troops, ten chariots,

and ten thousand foot soldiers. The king of Aram had killed the others like they were dust under his feet.

[8]The rest of the events in Jehoahaz's reign and all his deeds, including the extent of his power, are recorded in *The Book of the History of the Kings of Israel.* [9]When Jehoahaz died, he was buried in Samaria with his ancestors. Then his son Jehoash* became the next king.

[10]Jehoash son of Jehoahaz began to rule over Israel in the thirty-seventh year of King Joash's reign in Judah. He reigned in Samaria sixteen years. [11]But he did what was evil in the LORD's sight. He refused to turn from the sins of idolatry that Jeroboam son of Nebat had led Israel to commit. [12]The rest of the events in Jehoash's reign and all his deeds, including the extent of his power and his war with King Amaziah of Judah, are recorded in *The Book of the History of the Kings of Israel.* [13]When Jehoash died, he was buried with his ancestors in Samaria. Then his son Jeroboam II became the next king.

[14]When Elisha was in his last illness, King Jehoash of Israel visited him and wept over him. "My father! My father! The chariots and charioteers of Israel!" he cried.

[15]Elisha told him, "Get a bow and some arrows." And the king did as he was told. [16]Then Elisha told the king of Israel to put his hand on the bow, and Elisha laid his own hands on the king's hands. [17]Then he commanded, "Open that eastern window," and he opened it. Then he said, "Shoot!" So he did.

Then Elisha proclaimed, "This is the LORD's arrow, full of victory over Aram, for you will completely conquer the Arameans at Aphek. [18]Now pick up the other arrows and strike them against the ground." So the king picked them up and struck the ground three times. [19]But the man of God was angry with him. "You should have struck the ground five or six times!" he exclaimed. "Then you would have beaten Aram until they were entirely destroyed. Now you will be victorious only three times."

[20]Then Elisha died and was buried. Groups of Moabite raiders used to invade the land each spring. [21]Once when some Israelites were burying a man, they spied a band of these raiders. So they hastily threw the body they were burying into the tomb of Elisha. But as soon as the body touched Elisha's bones, the dead man revived and jumped to his feet!

[22]King Hazael of Aram had oppressed Israel during the entire reign of King Jehoahaz. [23]But the LORD was gracious to the people of Israel, and they were not totally destroyed. He pitied them because of his covenant with Abraham, Isaac, and Jacob. And to this day he still has not completely destroyed them or banished them from his presence.

[24]King Hazael of Aram died, and his son Ben-hadad became the next king. [25]Then Jehoash son of Jehoahaz recaptured from Ben-hadad son of Hazael the towns that Hazael had taken from Jehoash's father, Jehoahaz. Jehoash defeated Ben-hadad on three occasions, and so recovered the Israelite towns.

CHAPTER 14

Amaziah son of Joash began to rule over Judah in the second year of the reign of King Jehoash* of Israel. [2]Amaziah was twenty-five years old when he became king, and he reigned in Jerusalem twenty-nine years. His mother was Jehoaddin, from Jerusalem. [3]Amaziah did what was pleasing in the LORD's sight, but not like his ancestor David. Instead, he followed the example of his father, Joash. [4]Amaziah did not destroy the pagan shrines, where the people offered sacrifices and burned incense.

[5]When Amaziah was well established as king, he executed the men who had assassinated his father. [6]However, he did not kill the children of the assassins, for he obeyed the command of the LORD written in the Book of the Law of Moses: "Parents must not be put to death for the sins of their children, nor the children for the sins of their parents. Those worthy of death must be executed for their own crimes."*

[7]It was Amaziah who killed ten thousand Edomites in the Valley of Salt. He also conquered Sela and changed its name to Joktheel, as it is called to this day.

[8]One day Amaziah sent this challenge to Israel's king Jehoash, the son of Jehoahaz and grandson of Jehu: "Come and meet me in battle!"

[9]But King Jehoash of Israel replied to King Amaziah of Judah with this story:

13:9 Hebrew *Joash*, a variant name for Jehoash; also in 13:10, 12, 13, 14, 25.   14:1 Hebrew *Joash*, a variant name for Jehoash; also in 14:13, 23, 27.   14:6 Deut 24:16.

"Out in the Lebanon mountains a thistle sent a message to a mighty cedar tree: 'Give your daughter in marriage to my son.' But just then a wild animal came by and stepped on the thistle, crushing it! ¹⁰You have indeed destroyed Edom and are very proud about it. Be content with your victory and stay at home! Why stir up trouble that will bring disaster on you and the people of Judah?"

¹¹But Amaziah refused to listen, so King Jehoash of Israel mobilized his army against King Amaziah of Judah. The two armies drew up their battle lines at Beth-shemesh in Judah. ¹²Judah was routed by the army of Israel, and its army scattered and fled for home. ¹³King Jehoash of Israel captured King Amaziah of Judah at Beth-shemesh and marched on to Jerusalem. Then Jehoash ordered his army to demolish six hundred feet* of Jerusalem's wall, from the Ephraim Gate to the Corner Gate. ¹⁴He carried off all the gold and silver and all the utensils from the Temple of the LORD, as well as from the palace treasury. He also took hostages and returned to Samaria.

¹⁵The rest of the events in Jehoash's reign, including the extent of his power and his war with King Amaziah of Judah, are recorded in The Book of the History of the Kings of Israel. ¹⁶When Jehoash died, he was buried with his ancestors in Samaria. Then his son Jeroboam II became the next king.

¹⁷King Amaziah of Judah lived on for fifteen years after the death of King Jehoash of Israel. ¹⁸The rest of the events in Amaziah's reign are recorded in The Book of the History of the Kings of Judah. ¹⁹There was a conspiracy against Amaziah's life in Jerusalem, and he fled to Lachish. But his enemies sent assassins after him, and they killed him there. ²⁰They brought him back to Jerusalem on a horse, and he was buried with his ancestors in the City of David.

²¹The people of Judah then crowned Amaziah's sixteen-year-old son, Uzziah,* as their next king. ²²After his father's death, Uzziah rebuilt the town of Elath and restored it to Judah.

²³Jeroboam II, the son of Jehoash, began to rule over Israel in the fifteenth year of King Amaziah's reign in Judah. Jeroboam reigned in Samaria forty-one years. ²⁴He

did what was evil in the LORD's sight. He refused to turn from the sins of idolatry that Jeroboam son of Nebat had led Israel to commit. ²⁵Jeroboam II recovered the territories of Israel between Lebo-hamath and the Dead Sea,* just as the LORD, the God of Israel, had promised through Jonah son of Amittai, the prophet from Gath-hepher. ²⁶For the LORD saw the bitter suffering of everyone in Israel, and how they had absolutely no one to help them. ²⁷And because the LORD had not said he would blot out the name of Israel completely, he used Jeroboam II, the son of Jehoash, to save them.

²⁸The rest of the events in the reign of Jeroboam II and all his deeds, including the extent of his power, his wars, and how he recovered for Israel both Damascus and Hamath, which had belonged to Judah,* are recorded in The Book of the History of the Kings of Israel. ²⁹When Jeroboam II died, he was buried with his ancestors, the kings of Israel. Then his son Zechariah became the next king.

CHAPTER 15

Uzziah* son of Amaziah began to rule over Judah in the twenty-seventh year of the reign of King Jeroboam II of Israel. ²He was sixteen years old when he became king, and he reigned in Jerusalem fifty-two years. His mother was Jecoliah, from Jerusalem. ³He did what was pleasing in the LORD's sight, just as his father, Amaziah, had done. ⁴But he did not destroy the pagan shrines, where the people offered sacrifices and burned incense. ⁵The LORD struck the king with leprosy,* which lasted until the day of his death; he lived in a house by himself. The king's son Jotham was put in charge of the royal palace, and he governed the people of the land.

⁶The rest of the events in Uzziah's reign and all his deeds are recorded in The Book of the History of the Kings of Judah. ⁷When Uzziah died, he was buried near his ancestors in the City of David. Then his son Jotham became the next king.

⁸Zechariah son of Jeroboam II began to rule over Israel in the thirty-eighth year of King Uzziah's reign in Judah. He reigned in Samaria six months. ⁹Zechariah did what was evil in the LORD's sight, as his ancestors had done. He refused to turn

14:13 Hebrew *400 cubits* [180 meters].   14:21 Hebrew *Azariah*, a variant name for Uzziah.   14:25 Hebrew *the sea of the Arabah.*
14:28 Or *to Yaudi.*   15:1 Hebrew *Azariah*, a variant name for Uzziah; also in 15:6, 7, 8, 17, 23, 27.   15:5 Or *with a contagious skin disease.* The Hebrew word used here and throughout this passage can describe various skin diseases.

from the sins of idolatry that Jeroboam son of Nebat had led Israel to commit. ¹⁰Then Shallum son of Jabesh conspired against Zechariah, assassinated him in public,* and became the next king. ¹¹The rest of the events in Zechariah's reign are recorded in *The Book of the History of the Kings of Israel.* ¹²So the LORD's message to Jehu came true: "Your descendants will be kings of Israel down to the fourth generation."

¹³Shallum son of Jabesh began to rule over Israel in the thirty-ninth year of King Uzziah's reign in Judah. Shallum reigned in Samaria only one month. ¹⁴Then Menahem son of Gadi went to Samaria from Tirzah and assassinated him, and he became the next king. ¹⁵The rest of the events in Shallum's reign, including his conspiracy, are recorded in *The Book of the History of the Kings of Israel.*

¹⁶At that time Menahem destroyed the town of Tappuah* and all the surrounding countryside as far as Tirzah, because its citizens refused to surrender the town. He killed the entire population and ripped open the pregnant women.

¹⁷Menahem son of Gadi began to rule over Israel in the thirty-ninth year of King Uzziah's reign in Judah. He reigned in Samaria ten years. ¹⁸But Menahem did what was evil in the LORD's sight. During his entire reign, he refused to turn from the sins of idolatry that Jeroboam son of Nebat had led Israel to commit. ¹⁹Then King Tiglath-pileser* of Assyria invaded the land. But Menahem paid him thirty-seven tons* of silver to gain his support in tightening his grip on royal power. ²⁰Menahem extorted the money from the rich of Israel, demanding that each of them pay twenty ounces* of silver in the form of a special tax. So the king of Assyria turned from attacking Israel and did not stay in the land. ²¹The rest of the events in Menahem's reign and all his deeds are recorded in *The Book of the History of the Kings of Israel.* ²²When Menahem died, his son Pekahiah became the next king.

²³Pekahiah son of Menahem began to rule over Israel in the fiftieth year of King Uzziah's reign in Judah. He reigned in Samaria two years. ²⁴But Pekahiah did what was evil in the LORD's sight. He refused to turn from the sins of idolatry that Jeroboam son of Nebat had led Israel to commit.

²⁵Then Pekah son of Remaliah, the commander of Pekahiah's army, conspired against him. With fifty men from Gilead, Pekah assassinated the king, along with Argob and Arieh, in the citadel of the palace at Samaria. Pekah then became the next king of Israel. ²⁶The rest of the events in Pekahiah's reign and all his deeds are recorded in *The Book of the History of the Kings of Israel.*

²⁷Pekah son of Remaliah began to rule over Israel in the fifty-second year of King Uzziah's reign in Judah. He reigned in Samaria twenty years. ²⁸But Pekah did what was evil in the LORD's sight. He refused to turn from the sins of idolatry that Jeroboam son of Nebat had led Israel to commit. ²⁹During his reign, King Tiglath-pileser of Assyria attacked Israel again, and he captured the towns of Ijon, Abel-beth-maacah, Janoah, Kedesh, and Hazor. He also conquered the regions of Gilead, Galilee, and Naphtali, and he took the people to Assyria as captives. ³⁰Then Hoshea son of Elah conspired against Pekah and assassinated him. He began to rule over Israel in the twentieth year of Jotham son of Uzziah. ³¹The rest of the events in Pekah's reign and all his deeds are recorded in *The Book of the History of the Kings of Israel.*

³²Jotham son of Uzziah began to rule over Judah in the second year of King Pekah's reign in Israel. ³³He was twenty-five years old when he became king, and he reigned in Jerusalem sixteen years. His mother was Jerusha, the daughter of Zadok.

³⁴Jotham did what was pleasing in the LORD's sight, just as his father Uzziah had done. ³⁵But he did not destroy the pagan shrines, where the people offered sacrifices and burned incense. He was the one who rebuilt the upper gate of the Temple of the LORD.

³⁶The rest of the events in Jotham's reign and all his deeds are recorded in *The Book of the History of the Kings of Judah.* ³⁷In those days the LORD began to send King Rezin of Aram and King Pekah of Israel to attack Judah. ³⁸When Jotham died, he was buried with his ancestors in the City of David. Then his son Ahaz became the next king.

15:10 Or *at Ibleam.*   **15:16** As in some Greek manuscripts; Hebrew reads *Tiphsah.*   **15:19a** Hebrew *Pul,* another name for Tiglath-pileser.   **15:19b** Hebrew *1,000 talents* [34 metric tons].   **15:20** Hebrew *50 shekels* [570 grams].

CHAPTER 16

Ahaz son of Jotham began to rule over Judah in the seventeenth year of King Pekah's reign in Israel. [2]Ahaz was twenty years old when he became king, and he reigned in Jerusalem sixteen years. He did not do what was pleasing in the sight of the LORD his God, as his ancestor David had done. [3]Instead, he followed the example of the kings of Israel, even sacrificing his own son in the fire.* He imitated the detestable practices of the pagan nations the LORD had driven from the land ahead of the Israelites. [4]He offered sacrifices and burned incense at the pagan shrines and on the hills and under every green tree.

[5]Then King Rezin of Aram and King Pekah of Israel declared war on Ahaz. They besieged Jerusalem but did not conquer it. [6]At that time the king of Edom* recovered the town of Elath for Edom.* He drove out the people of Judah and sent Edomites* to live there, as they do to this day.

[7]King Ahaz sent messengers to King Tiglath-pileser of Assyria with this message: "I am your servant and your vassal.* Come up and rescue me from the attacking armies of Aram and Israel." [8]Then Ahaz took the silver and gold from the Temple of the LORD and the palace treasury and sent it as a gift to the Assyrian king. [9]So the Assyrians attacked the Aramean capital of Damascus and led its population away as captives, resettling them in Kir. They also killed King Rezin.

[10]King Ahaz then went to Damascus to meet with King Tiglath-pileser of Assyria. While he was there, he noticed an unusual altar. So he sent a model of the altar to Uriah the priest, along with its design in full detail. [11]Uriah built an altar just like it by following the king's instructions, and it was ready for the king when he returned from Damascus. [12]When the king returned, he inspected the altar and made offerings on it. [13]The king presented a burnt offering and a grain offering, poured a drink offering over it, and sprinkled the blood of peace offerings on it.

[14]Then King Ahaz removed the old bronze altar from the front of the LORD's Temple, which had stood between the entrance and the new altar, and placed it on the north side of the new altar. [15]He said to Uriah the priest, "Use the new altar for the morning sacrifices of burnt offering, the evening grain offering, the king's burnt offering and grain offering, and the offerings of the people, including their drink offerings. The blood from the burnt offerings and sacrifices should be sprinkled over the new altar. The old bronze altar will be only for my personal use." [16]Uriah the priest did just as King Ahaz instructed him.

[17]Then the king removed the side panels and basins from the portable water carts. He also removed the Sea from the backs of the bronze oxen and placed it on the stone pavement. [18]In deference to the king of Assyria, he also removed the canopy that had been constructed inside the palace for use on the Sabbath day,* as well as the king's outer entrance to the Temple of the LORD.

[19]The rest of the events in Ahaz's reign and his deeds are recorded in *The Book of the History of the Kings of Judah*. [20]When Ahaz died, he was buried with his ancestors in the City of David. Then his son Hezekiah became the next king.

CHAPTER 17

Hoshea son of Elah began to rule over Israel in the twelfth year of King Ahaz's reign in Judah. He reigned in Samaria nine years. [2]He did what was evil in the LORD's sight, but not as much as the kings of Israel who ruled before him.

[3]King Shalmaneser of Assyria attacked and defeated King Hoshea, so Israel was forced to pay heavy annual tribute to Assyria. [4]Then Hoshea conspired against the king of Assyria by asking King So of Egypt* to help him shake free of Assyria's power and by refusing to pay the annual tribute to Assyria. When the king of Assyria discovered this treachery, he arrested him and put him in prison for his rebellion.

[5]Then the king of Assyria invaded the entire land, and for three years he besieged Samaria. [6]Finally, in the ninth year of King Hoshea's reign, Samaria fell, and the people of Israel were exiled to Assyria. They were settled in colonies in Halah, along the banks of the Habor River in Gozan, and among the cities of the Medes.

[7]This disaster came upon the nation of Israel because the people worshiped other

---

16:3 Or *even making his son pass through the fire.*   **16:6a** As in Latin Vulgate; Hebrew reads *Rezin king of Aram.*   **16:6b** As in Latin Vulgate; Hebrew reads *Aram.*   **16:6c** As in marginal *Qere* reading of the Masoretic Text, Greek version, and Latin Vulgate; Hebrew reads *Arameans.*   **16:7** Hebrew *your son.*   **16:18** The meaning of the Hebrew is uncertain.   **17:4** Or *by asking the king of Egypt at Sais.*

gods, sinning against the LORD their God, who had brought them safely out of their slavery in Egypt. ⁸They had imitated the practices of the pagan nations the LORD had driven from the land before them, as well as the practices the kings of Israel had introduced. ⁹The people of Israel had also secretly done many things that were not pleasing to the LORD their God. They built pagan shrines for themselves in all their towns, from the smallest outpost to the largest walled city. ¹⁰They set up sacred pillars and Asherah poles at the top of every hill and under every green tree. ¹¹They burned incense at the shrines, just like the nations the LORD had driven from the land ahead of them. So the people of Israel had done many evil things, arousing the LORD's anger. ¹²Yes, they worshiped idols, despite the LORD's specific and repeated warnings. ¹³Again and again the LORD had sent his prophets and seers to warn both Israel and Judah: "Turn from all your evil ways. Obey my commands and laws, which are contained in the whole law that I commanded your ancestors and which I gave you through my servants the prophets."

¹⁴But the Israelites would not listen. They were as stubborn as their ancestors and refused to believe in the LORD their God. ¹⁵They rejected his laws and the covenant he had made with their ancestors, and they despised all his warnings. They worshiped worthless idols and became worthless themselves. They followed the example of the nations around them, disobeying the LORD's command not to imitate them. ¹⁶They defied all the commands of the LORD their God and made two calves from metal. They set up an Asherah pole and worshiped Baal and all the forces of heaven. ¹⁷They even sacrificed their own sons and daughters in the fire.* They consulted fortune-tellers and used sorcery and sold themselves to evil, arousing the LORD's anger.

¹⁸And because the LORD was angry, he swept them from his presence. Only the tribe of Judah remained in the land. ¹⁹But even the people of Judah refused to obey the commands of the LORD their God. They walked down the same evil paths that Israel had established. ²⁰So the LORD rejected all the descendants of Israel. He punished them by handing them over to their attackers until they were destroyed. ²¹For when

the LORD tore Israel away from the kingdom of David, they chose Jeroboam son of Nebat as their king. Then Jeroboam drew Israel away from following the LORD and made them commit a great sin. ²²And the people of Israel persisted in all the evil ways of Jeroboam. They did not turn from these sins of idolatry ²³until the LORD finally swept them away, just as all his prophets had warned would happen. So Israel was carried off to the land of Assyria, where they remain to this day.

²⁴And the king of Assyria transported groups of people from Babylon, Cuthah, Avva, Hamath, and Sepharvaim and resettled them in the towns of Samaria, replacing the people of Israel. So the Assyrians took over Samaria and the other towns of Israel. ²⁵But since these foreign settlers did not worship the LORD when they first arrived, the LORD sent lions among them to kill some of them.

²⁶So a message was sent to the king of Assyria: "The people whom you have resettled in the towns of Israel* do not know how to worship the God of the land. He has sent lions among them to destroy them because they have not worshiped him correctly."

²⁷The king of Assyria then commanded, "Send one of the exiled priests from Samaria back to Israel. Let him teach the new residents the religious customs of the God of the land." ²⁸So one of the priests who had been exiled from Samaria returned to Bethel and taught the new residents how to worship the LORD.

²⁹But these various groups of foreigners also continued to worship their own gods. In town after town where they lived, they placed their idols at the pagan shrines that the people of Israel had built. ³⁰Those from Babylon worshiped idols of their god Succoth-benoth. Those from Cuthah worshiped their god Nergal. And those from Hamath worshiped Ashima. ³¹The Avvites worshiped their gods Nibhaz and Tartak. And the people from Sepharvaim even burned their own children as sacrifices to Adrammelech and Anammelech.

³²These new residents worshiped the LORD, but they appointed from among themselves priests to offer sacrifices at the pagan shrines. ³³And though they worshiped the LORD, they continued to follow the religious customs of the nations from

17:17 Or *They even made their sons and daughters pass through the fire.*   17:26 Hebrew *of Samaria;* also in 17:29.

which they came. ³⁴And this is still going on among them today. They follow their former practices instead of truly worshiping the LORD and obeying the laws, regulations, instructions, and commands he gave the descendants of Jacob, whose name he changed to Israel. ³⁵For the LORD had made a covenant with the descendants of Jacob and commanded them: "Do not worship any other gods or bow before them or serve them or offer sacrifices to them. ³⁶Worship only the LORD, who brought you out of Egypt with such mighty miracles and power. You must worship him and bow before him; offer sacrifices to him alone. ³⁷Be careful to obey all the laws, regulations, instructions, and commands that he wrote for you. You must not worship any other gods. ³⁸Do not forget the covenant I made with you, and do not worship other gods. ³⁹You must worship only the LORD your God. He is the one who will rescue you from all your enemies."

⁴⁰But the people would not listen and continued to follow their old ways. ⁴¹So while these new residents worshiped the LORD, they also worshiped their idols. And to this day their descendants do the same.

APRIL 12 □ DAY 103
2 KINGS 18–21
Reforms of Hezekiah

 OVERVIEW With the captivity and deportation of Israel, the curtain drops on the northern ten tribes. But what of their countrymen in the south? Will they learn from Israel's calamity and turn back to God? At this crucial juncture, God raises up Hezekiah, who does "what [is] pleasing in the LORD's sight, just as his ancestor David had done" (18:3). Spiritually, Hezekiah institutes sweeping reforms to bring the nation back to a wholehearted worship of God. Politically, he refuses to pay tribute any longer to Assyria, choosing instead to trust God for protection from reprisal. In answer to his prayer, God decimates the Assyrian army, breaking the back of that once mighty nation. However, by the time of his death, Hezekiah's pride and family negligence ensure that Judah's days are numbered.

Chapter 18	Chapter 19	Chapter 20	Chapter 21
Assyria at the Door	Assyria on the Run	Hezekiah on His Deathbed	Manasseh on the Rampage
Hezekiah's National Problems		Hezekiah's Personal Problems	

 YOUR DAILY WALK If you're looking for some help in your prayer life, why not spend some time studying an Old Testament character whose every recorded prayer was answered!

People may spurn your appeals, reject your messages, and oppose your arguments, but they are helpless against your prayers.

Hezekiah was a man of faith (18:5) and a man of prayer. His first reaction when confronted with a problem was to bring it before the Lord. Whether the problem was 185,000 uninvited Assyrians (19:35) or a painful illness (20:1, 7), Hezekiah took it to the Lord in prayer. And when he prayed, things happened!

Prayer is not a magic formula, but verbal communication with the sovereign God of creation. Examine your own prayer habits. Are they built on a personal relationship with God? Are you strengthening your prayer life with daily exercise? Are you more comfortable talking to God today than you were a year ago? Try this: Every time you get into or out of your car today, spend a few seconds in prayer. You'll find it habit-forming!

INSIGHT Smashing a Pagan Python
Hezekiah's zealous reforms included even the destruction of the bronze
snake Moses had made in the wilderness (Numbers 21:8-9), to which
the people were burning incense.

CHAPTER 18

Hezekiah son of Ahaz began to rule over Judah in the third year of King Hoshea's reign in Israel. ²He was twenty-five years old when he became king, and he reigned in Jerusalem twenty-nine years. His mother was Abijah,* the daughter of Zechariah. ³He did what was pleasing in the LORD's sight, just as his ancestor David had done. ⁴He removed the pagan shrines, smashed the sacred pillars, and knocked down the Asherah poles. He broke up the bronze serpent that Moses had made, because the people of Israel had begun to worship it by burning incense to it. The bronze serpent was called Nehushtan.*

⁵Hezekiah trusted in the LORD, the God of Israel. There was never another king like him in the land of Judah, either before or after his time. ⁶He remained faithful to the LORD in everything, and he carefully obeyed all the commands the LORD had given Moses. ⁷So the LORD was with him, and Hezekiah was successful in everything he did. He revolted against the king of Assyria and refused to pay him tribute. ⁸He also conquered the Philistines as far distant as Gaza and its territory, from their smallest outpost to their largest walled city.

⁹During the fourth year of Hezekiah's reign, which was the seventh year of King Hoshea's reign in Israel, King Shalmaneser of Assyria attacked Israel and began a siege on the city of Samaria. ¹⁰Three years later, during the sixth year of King Hezekiah's reign and the ninth year of King Hoshea's reign in Israel, Samaria fell. ¹¹At that time the king of Assyria deported the Israelites to Assyria and put them in colonies in Halah, along the banks of the Habor River in Gozan, and among the cities of the Medes. ¹²For they had refused to listen to the LORD their God. Instead, they had violated his covenant—all the laws the LORD had given through his servant Moses.

¹³In the fourteenth year of King Hezekiah's reign, King Sennacherib of Assyria came to attack the fortified cities of Judah and conquered them. ¹⁴King Hezekiah sent this message to the king of Assyria at Lachish: "I have done wrong. I will pay whatever tribute money you demand if you will only go away." The king of Assyria then demanded a settlement of more than eleven tons of silver and about one ton of gold.* ¹⁵To gather this amount, King Hezekiah used all the silver stored in the Temple of the LORD and in the palace treasury. ¹⁶Hezekiah even stripped the gold from the doors of the LORD's Temple and from the doorposts he had overlaid with gold, and he gave it all to the Assyrian king.

¹⁷Nevertheless the king of Assyria sent his commander in chief, his field commander, and his personal representative from Lachish with a huge army to confront King Hezekiah in Jerusalem. The Assyrians stopped beside the aqueduct that feeds water into the upper pool, near the road leading to the field where cloth is bleached. ¹⁸They summoned King Hezekiah, but the king sent these officials to meet with them: Eliakim son of Hilkiah, the palace administrator, Shebna the court secretary, and Joah son of Asaph, the royal historian.

¹⁹Then the Assyrian king's personal representative sent this message to King Hezekiah:

"This is what the great king of Assyria says: What are you trusting in that makes you so confident? ²⁰Do you think that mere words can substitute for military skill and strength? Which of your allies will give you any military backing against Assyria? ²¹Will Egypt? If you lean on Egypt, you will find it to be a stick that breaks beneath your weight and pierces your hand. The pharaoh of Egypt is completely unreliable!

²²"But perhaps you will say, 'We are trusting in the LORD our God!' But isn't he the one who was insulted by King Hezekiah? Didn't Hezekiah tear down his shrines and altars and make everyone in Judah worship only at the altar here in Jerusalem?

²³"I'll tell you what! My master, the

18:2 As in parallel text at 2 Chr 29:1; Hebrew reads *Abi*, a variant name for Abijah.   18:4 *Nehushtan* sounds like the Hebrew terms that mean "snake," "bronze," and "unclean thing."   18:14 Hebrew *300 talents* [10 metric tons] *of silver and 30 talents* [1 metric ton] *of gold.*

king of Assyria, will strike a bargain with you. If you can find two thousand horsemen in your entire army, he will give you two thousand horses for them to ride on! 24With your tiny army, how can you think of challenging even the weakest contingent of my master's troops, even with the help of Egypt's chariots and horsemen*? 25What's more, do you think we have invaded your land without the LORD's direction? The LORD himself told us, 'Go and destroy it!'"

26Then Eliakim son of Hilkiah, Shebna, and Joah said to the king's representative, "Please speak to us in Aramaic, for we understand it well. Don't speak in Hebrew, for the people on the wall will hear."

27But Sennacherib's representative replied, "My master wants everyone in Jerusalem to hear this, not just you. He wants them to know that if you do not surrender, this city will be put under siege. The people will become so hungry and thirsty that they will eat their own dung and drink their own urine."

28Then he stood and shouted in Hebrew to the people on the wall, "Listen to this message from the great king of Assyria! 29This is what the king says: Don't let King Hezekiah deceive you. He will never be able to rescue you from my power. 30Don't let him fool you into trusting in the LORD by saying, 'The LORD will rescue us! This city will never be handed over to the Assyrian king.'

31"Don't listen to Hezekiah! These are the terms the king of Assyria is offering: Make peace with me—open the gates and come out. Then I will allow each of you to continue eating from your own garden and drinking from your own well. 32Then I will arrange to take you to another land like this one—a country with bountiful harvests of grain and wine, bread and vineyards, olive trees and honey—a land of plenty. Choose life instead of death!

"Don't listen to Hezekiah when he tries to mislead you by saying, 'The LORD will rescue us!' 33Have the gods of any other nations ever saved their people from the king of Assyria? 34What happened to the gods of Hamath and Arpad? And what about the gods of Sepharvaim, Hena, and Ivvah? Did they rescue Samaria from my

power? 35What god of any nation has ever been able to save its people from my power? Name just one! So what makes you think that the LORD can rescue Jerusalem?"

36But the people were silent and did not answer because Hezekiah had told them not to speak. 37Then Eliakim son of Hilkiah, the palace administrator, Shebna the court secretary, and Joah son of Asaph, the royal historian, went back to Hezekiah. They tore their clothes in despair, and they went in to see the king and told him what the Assyrian representative had said.

CHAPTER 19

When King Hezekiah heard their report, he tore his clothes and put on sackcloth and went into the Temple of the LORD to pray. 2And he sent Eliakim the palace administrator, Shebna the court secretary, and the leading priests, all dressed in sackcloth, to the prophet Isaiah son of Amoz. 3They told him, "This is what King Hezekiah says: This is a day of trouble, insult, and disgrace. It is like when a child is ready to be born, but the mother has no strength to deliver it. 4But perhaps the LORD your God has heard the Assyrian representative defying the living God and will punish him for his words. Oh, pray for those of us who are left!"

5After King Hezekiah's officials delivered the king's message to Isaiah, 6the prophet replied, "Say to your master, 'This is what the LORD says: Do not be disturbed by this blasphemous speech against me from the Assyrian king's messengers. 7Listen! I myself will move against him, and the king will receive a report from Assyria telling him that he is needed at home. Then I will make him want to return to his land, where I will have him killed with a sword.'"

8Meanwhile, the Assyrian representative left Jerusalem and went to consult his king, who had left Lachish and was attacking Libnah. 9Soon afterward King Sennacherib received word that King Tirhakah of Ethiopia* was leading an army to fight against him. Before leaving to meet the attack, he sent this message back to Hezekiah in Jerusalem:

10"This message is for King Hezekiah of Judah. Don't let this God you trust deceive you with promises that

18:24 Or *and charioteers.*   19:9 Hebrew *of Cush.*

Jerusalem will not be captured by the king of Assyria. [11] You know perfectly well what the kings of Assyria have done wherever they have gone. They have crushed everyone who stood in their way! Why should you be any different? [12] Have the gods of other nations rescued them—such nations as Gozan, Haran, Rezeph, and the people of Eden who were in Tel-assar? The former kings of Assyria destroyed them all! [13] What happened to the king of Hamath and the king of Arpad? What happened to the kings of Sephar-vaim, Hena, and Ivvah?"

[14] After Hezekiah received the letter and read it, he went up to the LORD's Temple and spread it out before the LORD. [15] And Hezekiah prayed this prayer before the LORD: "O LORD, God of Israel, you are enthroned between the mighty cherubim! You alone are God of all the kingdoms of the earth. You alone created the heavens and the earth. [16] Listen to me, O LORD, and hear! Open your eyes, O LORD, and see! Listen to Sennacherib's words of defiance against the living God.

[17] "It is true, LORD, that the kings of Assyria have destroyed all these nations, just as the message says. [18] And they have thrown the gods of these nations into the fire and burned them. But of course the Assyrians could destroy them! They were not gods at all—only idols of wood and stone shaped by human hands. [19] Now, O LORD our God, rescue us from his power; then all the kingdoms of the earth will know that you alone, O LORD, are God."

[20] Then Isaiah son of Amoz sent this message to Hezekiah: "This is what the LORD, the God of Israel, says: I have heard your prayer about King Sennacherib of Assyria. [21] This is the message that the LORD has spoken against him:

'The virgin daughter of Zion
    despises you and laughs at you.
The daughter of Jerusalem
    scoffs and shakes her head as you flee.

[22] 'Whom do you think you have been
        insulting and ridiculing?
    Against whom did you raise your
        voice?
At whom did you look in such proud
        condescension?
    It was the Holy One of Israel!

[23] By your messengers you have mocked
        the Lord.
    You have said, "With my many
        chariots
I have conquered the highest
        mountains—
    yes, the remotest peaks of Lebanon.
I have cut down its tallest cedars
    and its choicest cypress trees.
I have reached its farthest corners
    and explored its deepest forests.
[24] I have dug wells in many a foreign land
    and refreshed myself with their
        water.
I even stopped up the rivers of Egypt
    so that my armies could go across!"

[25] 'But have you not heard?
    It was I, the LORD, who decided this
        long ago.
Long ago I planned what I am now
        causing to happen,
    that you should crush fortified cities
        into heaps of rubble.
[26] That is why their people have so little
        power
    and are such easy prey for you.
They are as helpless as the grass,
    as easily trampled as tender green
        shoots.
They are like grass sprouting on a
        housetop,
    easily scorched by the sun.

[27] 'But I know you well—
    your comings and goings and all
        you do.
    I know the way you have raged
        against me.
[28] And because of your arrogance against
        me,
    which I have heard for myself,
I will put my hook in your nose
    and my bridle in your mouth.
I will make you return
    by the road on which you came.'"

[29] Then Isaiah said to Hezekiah, "Here is the proof that the LORD will protect this city from Assyria's king. This year you will eat only what grows up by itself, and next year you will eat what springs up from that. But in the third year you will plant crops and harvest them; you will tend vineyards and eat their fruit. [30] And you who are left in Judah, who have escaped the ravages of the siege, will take root again in your own soil, and you will flourish and multiply.

³¹For a remnant of my people will spread out from Jerusalem, a group of survivors from Mount Zion. The passion of the LORD Almighty will make this happen!

³²"And this is what the LORD says about the king of Assyria: His armies will not enter Jerusalem to shoot their arrows. They will not march outside its gates with their shields and build banks of earth against its walls. ³³The king will return to his own country by the road on which he came. He will not enter this city, says the LORD. ³⁴For my own honor and for the sake of my servant David, I will defend it."

³⁵That night the angel of the LORD went out to the Assyrian camp and killed 185,000 Assyrian troops. When the surviving Assyrians* woke up the next morning, they found corpses everywhere. ³⁶Then King Sennacherib of Assyria broke camp and returned to his own land. He went home to his capital of Nineveh and stayed there. ³⁷One day while he was worshiping in the temple of his god Nisroch, his sons Adrammelech and Sharezer killed him with their swords. They then escaped to the land of Ararat, and another son, Esarhaddon, became the next king of Assyria.

CHAPTER 20
About that time Hezekiah became deathly ill, and the prophet Isaiah son of Amoz went to visit him. He gave the king this message: "This is what the LORD says: Set your affairs in order, for you are going to die. You will not recover from this illness."

²When Hezekiah heard this, he turned his face to the wall and prayed to the LORD, ³"Remember, O LORD, how I have always tried to be faithful to you and do what is pleasing in your sight." Then he broke down and wept bitterly.

⁴But before Isaiah had left the middle courtyard, this message came to him from the LORD: ⁵"Go back to Hezekiah, the leader of my people. Tell him, 'This is what the LORD, the God of your ancestor David, says: I have heard your prayer and seen your tears. I will heal you, and three days from now you will get out of bed and go to the Temple of the LORD. ⁶I will add fifteen years to your life, and I will rescue you and this city from the king of Assyria. I will do this to defend my honor and for the sake of my servant David.'"

⁷Then Isaiah said to Hezekiah's servants, "Make an ointment from figs and spread it over the boil." They did this, and Hezekiah recovered!

⁸Meanwhile, Hezekiah had said to Isaiah, "What sign will the LORD give to prove that he will heal me and that I will go to the Temple of the LORD three days from now?"

⁹Isaiah replied, "This is the sign that the LORD will give you to prove he will do as he promised. Would you like the shadow on the sundial to go forward ten steps or backward ten steps?"

¹⁰"The shadow always moves forward," Hezekiah replied. "Make it go backward instead." ¹¹So Isaiah asked the LORD to do this, and he caused the shadow to move ten steps backward on the sundial of Ahaz!

¹²Soon after this, Merodach-baladan son of Baladan, king of Babylon, sent Hezekiah his best wishes and a gift, for he had heard that Hezekiah had been very sick. ¹³Hezekiah welcomed the Babylonian envoys and showed them everything in his treasure-houses—the silver, the gold, the spices, and the aromatic oils. He also took them to see his armory and showed them all his other treasures—everything! There was nothing in his palace or kingdom that Hezekiah did not show them.

¹⁴Then Isaiah the prophet went to King Hezekiah and asked him, "What did those men want? Where were they from?"

Hezekiah replied, "They came from the distant land of Babylon."

¹⁵"What did they see in your palace?" Isaiah asked.

"They saw everything," Hezekiah replied. "I showed them everything I own—all my treasures."

¹⁶Then Isaiah said to Hezekiah, "Listen to this message from the LORD: ¹⁷The time is coming when everything you have—all the treasures stored up by your ancestors—will be carried off to Babylon. Nothing will be left, says the LORD. ¹⁸Some of your own descendants will be taken away into exile. They will become eunuchs who will serve in the palace of Babylon's king."

¹⁹Then Hezekiah said to Isaiah, "This message you have given me from the LORD is good." But the king was thinking, "At least there will be peace and security during my lifetime."

19:35 Hebrew When they.

[20]The rest of the events in Hezekiah's reign, including the extent of his power and how he built a pool and dug a tunnel to bring water into the city, are recorded in *The Book of the History of the Kings of Judah.* [21]When Hezekiah died, his son Manasseh became the next king.

CHAPTER 21

Manasseh was twelve years old when he became king, and he reigned in Jerusalem fifty-five years. His mother was Hephzibah. [2]He did what was evil in the LORD's sight, imitating the detestable practices of the pagan nations whom the LORD had driven from the land ahead of the Israelites. [3]He rebuilt the pagan shrines his father, Hezekiah, had destroyed. He constructed altars for Baal and set up an Asherah pole, just as King Ahab of Israel had done. He also bowed before all the forces of heaven and worshiped them. [4]He even built pagan altars in the Temple of the LORD, the place where the LORD had said his name should be honored. [5]He built these altars for all the forces of heaven in both courtyards of the LORD's Temple. [6]Manasseh even sacrificed his own son in the fire.* He practiced sorcery and divination, and he consulted with mediums and psychics. He did much that was evil in the LORD's sight, arousing his anger.

[7]Manasseh even took an Asherah pole he had made and set it up in the Temple, the very place where the LORD had told David and his son Solomon: "My name will be honored here forever in this Temple and in Jerusalem—the city I have chosen from among all the other tribes of Israel. [8]If the Israelites will obey my commands—the whole law that was given through my servant Moses—I will not send them into exile from this land that I gave their ancestors." [9]But the people refused to listen, and Manasseh led them to do even more evil than the pagan nations whom the LORD had destroyed when the Israelites entered the land.

[10]Then the LORD said through his servants the prophets: [11]"King Manasseh of Judah has done many detestable things. He is even more wicked than the Amorites, who lived in this land before Israel. He has led the people of Judah into idolatry. [12]So this is what the LORD, the God of Israel, says: I will bring such disaster on Jerusalem and Judah that the ears of those who hear about it will tingle with horror. [13]I will judge Jerusalem by the same standard I used for Samaria and by the same measure I used for the family of Ahab. I will wipe away the people of Jerusalem as one wipes a dish and turns it upside down. [14]Then I will reject even those few of my people who are left, and I will hand them over as plunder for their enemies. [15]For they have done great evil in my sight and have angered me ever since their ancestors came out of Egypt."

[16]Manasseh also murdered many innocent people until Jerusalem was filled from one end to the other with innocent blood. This was in addition to the sin that he caused the people of Judah to commit, leading them to do evil in the LORD's sight.

[17]The rest of the events in Manasseh's reign and all his deeds, including the sins he committed, are recorded in *The Book of the History of the Kings of Judah.* [18]When Manasseh died, he was buried in the palace garden, the garden of Uzza. Then his son Amon became the next king.

[19]Amon was twenty-two years old when he became king, and he reigned in Jerusalem two years. His mother was Meshullemeth, the daughter of Haruz from Jotbah. [20]He did what was evil in the LORD's sight, just as his father, Manasseh, had done. [21]He followed the example of his father, worshiping the same idols that his father had worshiped. [22]He abandoned the LORD, the God of his ancestors, and he refused to follow the LORD's ways.

[23]Then Amon's own servants plotted against him and assassinated him in his palace. [24]But the people of the land killed all those who had conspired against King Amon, and they made his son Josiah the next king.

[25]The rest of the events in Amon's reign and all his deeds are recorded in *The Book of the History of the Kings of Judah.* [26]He was buried in his tomb in the garden of Uzza. Then his son Josiah became the next king.

21:6 Or *even made his son pass through the fire.*

APRIL 13 ☐ DAY 104
2 KINGS 22–25
Ruin of Judah

OVERVIEW Those who do not learn from history are destined to repeat it, and Judah is no exception. Though Israel has been swept away in judgment, the southern kingdom continues its pagan "business as usual." Good King Josiah makes a last desperate attempt to turn the nation back to God. He locates the long-lost Book of the Law and institutes sweeping reforms. But though he can impose a change of *actions* on the people, only wholehearted repentance can change the *attitudes* of godlessness and self-indulgence that are the root of the problem. When Josiah dies, his successors revert to their pagan patterns and practices. At last, God brings down the curtain on the southern kingdom as Babylonian soldiers topple the walls, homes, and Temple of once-mighty Jerusalem.

Chapter 22	Chapter 23	Chapter 24	Chapter 25
Recovery of the Law	Reform of the Nation	Siege of Jerusalem	Fall of Jerusalem
Reform by Josiah		Removal by Nebuchadnezzar	

YOUR DAILY WALK What is the most important book in the world to you? Assuming your answer is "the Bible" . . .

How many days this month have you spent time in the Bible? Assuming your answer is at least one . . .

The degree of our spiritual vigor is in direct proportion to the time we spend in God's Word.

How did you respond to the truth you encountered there? Assuming your answer is an honest one . . .

Are you satisfied with how you responded to that truth? Assuming your answer is anything less than a resounding yes . . .

Reread 2 Kings 23:2-3. The power of God's Word to change lives is perhaps nowhere more evident than in those two verses. The Word pierced where no man-made sword could reach: to the very heart of the king, priests, prophets, and people, turning their hearts collectively back to God. The result: a national spiritual awakening.

God's Word convicts, but only you can commit yourself to doing God's will. Is there an area of your life where a response is overdue? THINK.

INSIGHT The Short and Long and Short and Long of It
The length of time each of the last four kings in Judah reigned is easy to remember once you see the pattern. The sequence is 3 months—11 years—3 months—11 years.

CHAPTER 22
Josiah was eight years old when he became king, and he reigned in Jerusalem thirty-one years. His mother was Jedidah, the daughter of Adaiah from Bozkath. ²He did what was pleasing in the LORD's sight and followed the example of his ancestor David. He did not turn aside from doing what was right.

³In the eighteenth year of his reign, King Josiah sent Shaphan son of Azaliah and

grandson of Meshullam, the court secretary, to the Temple of the LORD. He told him, ⁴"Go up to Hilkiah the high priest and have him count the money the gatekeepers have collected from the people at the LORD's Temple. ⁵Entrust this money to the men assigned to supervise the Temple's restoration. Then they can use it to pay workers to repair the Temple of the LORD. ⁶They will need to hire carpenters, builders, and masons. Also have them buy the timber and the cut stone needed to repair the Temple. [7]But there will be no need for the construction supervisors to keep account of the money they receive, for they are honest people."

[8]Hilkiah the high priest said to Shaphan the court secretary, "I have found the Book of the Law in the LORD's Temple!" Then Hilkiah gave the scroll to Shaphan, and he read it.

[9]Shaphan returned to the king and reported, "Your officials have given the money collected at the Temple of the LORD to the workers and supervisors at the Temple." [10]Shaphan also said to the king, "Hilkiah the priest has given me a scroll." So Shaphan read it to the king.

[11]When the king heard what was written in the Book of the Law, he tore his clothes in despair. [12]Then he gave these orders to Hilkiah the priest, Ahikam son of Shaphan, Acbor son of Micaiah, Shaphan the court secretary, and Asaiah the king's personal adviser: [13]"Go to the Temple and speak to the LORD for me and for the people and for all Judah. Ask him about the words written in this scroll that has been found. The LORD's anger is burning against us because our ancestors have not obeyed the words in this scroll. We have not been doing what this scroll says we must do."

[14]So Hilkiah the priest, Ahikam, Acbor, Shaphan, and Asaiah went to the newer Mishneh section* of Jerusalem to consult with the prophet Huldah. She was the wife of Shallum son of Tikvah and grandson of Harhas, the keeper of the Temple wardrobe. [15]She said to them, "The LORD, the God of Israel, has spoken! Go and tell the man who sent you, [16]'This is what the LORD says: I will destroy this city and its people, just as I stated in the scroll you read. [17]For my people have abandoned me and worshiped pagan gods, and I am very angry with them for everything they have done. My anger is burning against this place, and it will not be quenched.'

[18]"But go to the king of Judah who sent you to seek the LORD and tell him: 'This is what the LORD, the God of Israel, says concerning the message you have just heard: [19]You were sorry and humbled yourself before the LORD when you heard what I said against this city and its people, that this land would be cursed and become deso-

late. You tore your clothing in despair and wept before me in repentance. So I have indeed heard you, says the LORD. [20]I will not send the promised disaster against this city until after you have died and been buried in peace. You will not see the disaster I am going to bring on this place.'" So they took her message back to the king.

CHAPTER 23

Then the king summoned all the leaders of Judah and Jerusalem. [2]And the king went up to the Temple of the LORD with all the people of Judah and Jerusalem, and the priests, and the prophets—all the people from the least to the greatest. There the king read to them the entire Book of the Covenant that had been found in the LORD's Temple. [3]The king took his place of authority beside the pillar and renewed the covenant in the LORD's presence. He pledged to obey the LORD by keeping all his commands, regulations, and laws with all his heart and soul. In this way, he confirmed all the terms of the covenant that were written in the scroll, and all the people pledged themselves to the covenant.

[4]Then the king instructed Hilkiah the high priest and the leading priests and the Temple gatekeepers to remove from the LORD's Temple all the utensils that were used to worship Baal, Asherah, and all the forces of heaven. The king had all these things burned outside Jerusalem on the terraces of the Kidron Valley, and he carried the ashes away to Bethel. [5]He did away with the pagan priests, who had been appointed by the previous kings of Judah, for they had burned incense at the pagan shrines throughout Judah and even in the vicinity of Jerusalem. They had also offered incense to Baal, and to the sun, the moon, the constellations, and to all the forces of heaven. [6]The king removed the Asherah pole from the LORD's Temple and took it outside Jerusalem to the Kidron Valley, where he burned it. Then he ground the pole to dust and threw the dust in the public cemetery. [7]He also tore down the houses of the shrine prostitutes that were inside the Temple of the LORD, where the women wove coverings for the Asherah pole.

[8]Josiah brought back to Jerusalem all the priests of the LORD, who were living in other towns of Judah. He also defiled all

22:14 Or *the Second Quarter,* a newer section of Jerusalem.

the pagan shrines, where they had burned incense, from Geba to Beersheba. He destroyed the shrines at the entrance to the gate of Joshua, the governor of Jerusalem. This gate was located to the left of the city gate as one enters the city. ⁹The priests who had served at the pagan shrines were not allowed to serve at the LORD's altar in Jerusalem, but they were allowed to eat unleavened bread with the other priests.

¹⁰Then the king defiled the altar of Topheth in the valley of Ben-hinnom, so no one could ever again use it to sacrifice a son or daughter in the fire* as an offering to Molech. ¹¹He removed from the entrance of the LORD's Temple the horse statues that the former kings of Judah had dedicated to the sun. They were near the quarters of Nathan-melech the eunuch, an officer of the court. The king also burned the chariots dedicated to the sun.

¹²Josiah tore down the altars that the kings of Judah had built on the palace roof above the upper room of Ahaz. The king destroyed the altars that Manasseh had built in the two courtyards of the LORD's Temple. He smashed them to bits and scattered the pieces in the Kidron Valley. ¹³The king also desecrated the pagan shrines east of Jerusalem and south of the Mount of Corruption, where King Solomon of Israel had built shrines for Ashtoreth, the detestable goddess of the Sidonians; and for Chemosh, the detestable god of the Moabites; and for Molech,* the detestable god of the Ammonites. ¹⁴He smashed the sacred pillars and cut down the Asherah poles. Then he desecrated these places by scattering human bones over them.

¹⁵The king also tore down the altar at Bethel, the pagan shrine that Jeroboam son of Nebat had made when he led Israel into sin. Josiah crushed the stones to dust and burned the Asherah pole. ¹⁶Then as Josiah was looking around, he noticed several tombs in the side of the hill. He ordered that the bones be brought out, and he burned them on the altar at Bethel to desecrate it. This happened just as the LORD had promised through the man of God as Jeroboam stood beside the altar at the festival. Then Josiah turned and looked up at the tomb of the man of God* who had predicted these things. ¹⁷"What is that monument over there?" Josiah asked.

And the people of the town told him, "It is the tomb of the man of God who came from Judah and predicted the very things that you have just done to the altar at Bethel!"

¹⁸Josiah replied, "Leave it alone. Don't disturb his bones." So they did not burn his bones or those of the old prophet from Samaria.

¹⁹Then Josiah demolished all the buildings at the pagan shrines in the towns of Samaria, just as he had done at Bethel. They had been built by the various kings of Israel and had made the LORD very angry. ²⁰He executed the priests of the pagan shrines on their own altars, and he burned human bones on the altars to desecrate them. Finally, he returned to Jerusalem.

²¹King Josiah then issued this order to all the people: "You must celebrate the Passover to the LORD your God, as it is written in the Book of the Covenant." ²²There had not been a Passover celebration like that since the time when the judges ruled in Israel, throughout all the years of the kings of Israel and Judah. ²³This Passover was celebrated to the LORD in Jerusalem during the eighteenth year of King Josiah's reign.

²⁴Josiah also exterminated the mediums and psychics, the household gods, and every other kind of idol worship, both in Jerusalem and throughout the land of Judah. He did this in obedience to all the laws written in the scroll that Hilkiah the priest had found in the LORD's Temple. ²⁵Never before had there been a king like Josiah, who turned to the LORD with all his heart and soul and strength, obeying all the laws of Moses. And there has never been a king like him since.

²⁶Even so, the LORD's anger burned against Judah because of all the great evils of King Manasseh, and he did not hold back his fierce anger from them. ²⁷For the LORD had said, "I will destroy Judah just as I have destroyed Israel. I will banish the people from my presence and reject my chosen city of Jerusalem and the Temple where my name was to be honored."

²⁸The rest of the events in Josiah's reign and all his deeds are recorded in *The Book of the History of the Kings of Judah.*

²⁹While Josiah was king, Pharaoh Neco, king of Egypt, went to the Euphrates River to help the king of Assyria. King Josiah

23:10 Or *to make a son or daughter pass through the fire.*   23:13 Hebrew *Milcom,* a variant name for Molech.   23:16 As in Greek version; Hebrew lacks *as Jeroboam stood beside the altar at the festival. Then Josiah turned and looked up at the tomb of the man of God.*

marched out with his army to fight him, but King Neco killed him when they met at Megiddo. [30]Josiah's officers took his body back in a chariot from Megiddo to Jerusalem and buried him in his own tomb. Then the people anointed his son Jehoahaz and made him the next king.

[31]Jehoahaz was twenty-three years old when he became king, and he reigned in Jerusalem three months. His mother was Hamutal, the daughter of Jeremiah from Libnah. [32]He did what was evil in the LORD's sight, just as his ancestors had done.

[33]Pharaoh Neco put Jehoahaz in prison at Riblah in the land of Hamath to prevent him from ruling from Jerusalem. He also demanded that Judah pay 7,500 pounds of silver and 75 pounds of gold* as tribute. [34]Pharaoh Neco then installed Eliakim, another of Josiah's sons, to reign in place of his father, and he changed Eliakim's name to Jehoiakim. Jehoahaz was taken to Egypt as a prisoner, where he died.

[35]In order to get the silver and gold demanded as tribute by Pharaoh Neco, Jehoiakim collected a tax from the people of Judah, requiring them to pay in proportion to their wealth.

[36]Jehoiakim was twenty-five years old when he became king, and he reigned in Jerusalem eleven years. His mother was Zebidah, the daughter of Pedaiah from Rumah. [37]He did what was evil in the LORD's sight, just as his ancestors had done.

CHAPTER 24

During Jehoiakim's reign, King Nebuchadnezzar of Babylon invaded the land of Judah. Jehoiakim surrendered and paid him tribute for three years but then rebelled. [2]Then the LORD sent bands of Babylonian,* Aramean, Moabite, and Ammonite raiders against Judah to destroy it, just as the LORD had promised through his prophets. [3]These disasters happened to Judah according to the LORD's command. He had decided to remove Judah from his presence because of the many sins of Manasseh. [4]He had filled Jerusalem with innocent blood, and the LORD would not forgive this.

[5]The rest of the events in Jehoiakim's reign and all his deeds are recorded in *The Book of the History of the Kings of Judah.* [6]When Jehoiakim died, his son Jehoiachin became the next king. [7]The king of Egypt never returned after that, for the king of Babylon occupied the entire area formerly claimed by Egypt—from the brook of Egypt to the Euphrates River.

[8]Jehoiachin was eighteen years old when he became king, and he reigned in Jerusalem three months. His mother was Nehushta, the daughter of Elnathan from Jerusalem. [9]Jehoiachin did what was evil in the LORD's sight, just as his father had done.

[10]During Jehoiachin's reign, the officers of King Nebuchadnezzar of Babylon came up against Jerusalem and besieged it. [11]Nebuchadnezzar himself arrived at the city during the siege. [12]Then King Jehoiachin, along with his advisers, nobles, and officials, and the queen mother, surrendered to the Babylonians.

In the eighth year of Nebuchadnezzar's reign, he took Jehoiachin prisoner. [13]As the LORD had said beforehand, Nebuchadnezzar carried away all the treasures from the LORD's Temple and the royal palace. They cut apart all the gold vessels that King Solomon of Israel had placed in the Temple. [14]King Nebuchadnezzar took ten thousand captives from Jerusalem, including all the princes and the best of the soldiers, craftsmen, and smiths. So only the poorest people were left in the land.

[15]Nebuchadnezzar led King Jehoiachin away as a captive to Babylon, along with his wives and officials, the queen mother, and all Jerusalem's elite. [16]He also took seven thousand of the best troops and one thousand craftsmen and smiths, all of whom were strong and fit for war. [17]Then the king of Babylon installed Mattaniah, Jehoiachin's uncle, as the next king, and he changed Mattaniah's name to Zedekiah.

[18]Zedekiah was twenty-one years old when he became king, and he reigned in Jerusalem eleven years. His mother was Hamutal, the daughter of Jeremiah from Libnah. [19]But Zedekiah did what was evil in the LORD's sight, just as Jehoiakim had done. [20]So the LORD, in his anger, finally banished the people of Jerusalem and Judah from his presence and sent them into exile.

Then Zedekiah rebelled against the king of Babylon.

23:33 Hebrew *100 talents* [3.4 metric tons] *of silver and 1 talent* [34 kilograms] *of gold.*   24:2 Or *Chaldean.*

CHAPTER 25

So on January 15,* during the ninth year of Zedekiah's reign, King Nebuchadnezzar of Babylon led his entire army against Jerusalem. They surrounded the city and built siege ramps against its walls. ²Jerusalem was kept under siege until the eleventh year of King Zedekiah's reign.

³By July 18 of Zedekiah's eleventh year,* the famine in the city had become very severe, with the last of the food entirely gone. ⁴Then a section of the city wall was broken down, and all the soldiers made plans to escape from the city. But since the city was surrounded by the Babylonians,* they waited for nightfall and fled through the gate between the two walls behind the king's gardens. They made a dash across the fields, in the direction of the Jordan Valley.*

⁵But the Babylonians chased after them and caught the king on the plains of Jericho, for by then his men had all abandoned him. ⁶They brought him to the king of Babylon at Riblah, where sentence was passed against him. ⁷The king of Babylon made Zedekiah watch as all his sons were killed. Then they gouged out Zedekiah's eyes, bound him in bronze chains, and led him away to Babylon.

⁸On August 14 of that year,* which was the nineteenth year of Nebuchadnezzar's reign, Nebuzaradan, captain of the guard, an official of the Babylonian king, arrived in Jerusalem. ⁹He burned down the Temple of the LORD, the royal palace, and all the houses of Jerusalem. He destroyed all the important buildings in the city. ¹⁰Then the captain of the guard supervised the entire Babylonian* army as they tore down the walls of Jerusalem. ¹¹Nebuzaradan, captain of the guard, then took as exiles those who remained in the city, along with the rest of the people and the troops who had declared their allegiance to the king of Babylon. ¹²But the captain of the guard allowed some of the poorest people to stay behind in Judah to care for the vineyards and fields.

¹³The Babylonians broke up the bronze pillars, the bronze water carts, and the bronze Sea that were at the LORD's Temple, and they carried all the bronze away to Babylon. ¹⁴They also took all the pots, shovels, lamp snuffers, dishes, and all the other bronze utensils used for making sacrifices at the Temple. ¹⁵Nebuzaradan, captain of the guard, also took the firepans and basins, and all the other utensils made of pure gold or silver.

¹⁶The bronze from the two pillars, the water carts, and the Sea was too great to be weighed. These things had been made for the LORD's Temple in the days of King Solomon. ¹⁷Each of the pillars was 27 feet* tall. The bronze capital on top of each pillar was 7½ feet* high and was decorated with a network of bronze pomegranates all the way around.

¹⁸The captain of the guard took with him as prisoners Seraiah the chief priest, his assistant Zephaniah, and the three chief gatekeepers. ¹⁹And of the people still hiding in the city, he took an officer of the Judean army, five of the king's personal advisers, the army commander's chief secretary, who was in charge of recruitment, and sixty other citizens. ²⁰Nebuzaradan the commander took them all to the king of Babylon at Riblah. ²¹And there at Riblah, in the land of Hamath, the king of Babylon had them all put to death. So the people of Judah were sent into exile from their land.

²²Then King Nebuchadnezzar appointed Gedaliah son of Ahikam and grandson of Shaphan as governor over the people left in Judah. ²³When all the army commanders and their men learned that the king of Babylon had appointed Gedaliah as governor, they joined him at Mizpah. These included Ishmael son of Nethaniah, Johanan son of Kareah, Seraiah son of Tanhumeth the Netophathite, and Jaazaniah son of the Maacathite, and all their men.

²⁴Gedaliah vowed to them that the Babylonian officials meant them no harm. "Live in the land and serve the king of Babylon, and all will go well for you," he promised. ²⁵But in midautumn of that year,* Ishmael son of Nethaniah and grandson of Elishama, who was of the

25:1 Hebrew *on the tenth day of the tenth month,* of the Hebrew calendar. A number of events in 2 Kings can be cross-checked with dates in surviving Babylonian records and related accurately to our modern calendar. This event occurred on January 15, 588 B.C. 25:3 Hebrew *By the ninth day,* that is, "of the fourth month of Zedekiah's eleventh year" (compare Jer 52:6 and the note there). This event of the Hebrew lunar calendar occurred on July 18, 586 B.C.; also see note on 25:1.   25:4a Or *the Chaldeans;* also in 25:5, 13, 25, 26. 25:4b Hebrew *the Arabah.*   25:8 Hebrew *On the seventh day of the fifth month,* of the Hebrew calendar. This day was August 14, 586 B.C.; also see note on 25:1.   25:10 Or *Chaldean;* also in 25:24.   25:17a Hebrew *18 cubits* [8.1 meters].   25:17b As in parallel texts at 1 Kgs 7:16, 2 Chr 3:15, and Jer 52:22, all of which read *5 cubits* [2.3 meters]; Hebrew reads *3 cubits,* which is 4.5 feet or 1.4 meters.   25:25 Hebrew *in the seventh month,* of the Hebrew calendar. This month occurred in October and November 586 B.C.

royal family, went to Mizpah with ten men and assassinated Gedaliah and everyone with him, both Judeans and Babylonians.

²⁶Then all the people of Judah, from the least to the greatest, as well as the army commanders, fled in panic to Egypt, for they were afraid of what the Babylonians would do to them.

²⁷In the thirty-seventh year of King Jehoiachin's exile in Babylon, Evil-merodach ascended to the Babylonian throne. He was kind to Jehoiachin and released him from prison on April 2 of that year.* ²⁸He spoke pleasantly to Jehoiachin and gave him preferential treatment over all the other exiled kings in Babylon. ²⁹He supplied Jehoiachin with new clothes to replace his prison garb and allowed him to dine at the king's table for the rest of his life. ³⁰The Babylonian king also gave him a regular allowance to cover his living expenses until the day of his death.

25:27 Hebrew *on the twenty-seventh day of the twelfth month*, of the Hebrew calendar. This day was April 2, 561 B.C.; also see note on 25:1.

APRIL 14 □ DAY 105
Prayers God Delights to Answer

 LOOK BACK One nation under Solomon (Israel) becomes two nations fractured by civil war (Israel and Judah). Beginning with 1 Kings 12, you have been reading the parallel histories of these two kingdoms.

Elijah's prophetic ministry (1 Kings) is mostly public and national in scope. His encounter with the prophets of Baal on Mount Carmel is a classic "battle of the gods," and his prayer life an example to all believers (James 5:17-18). By contrast, his successor, Elisha (2 Kings), ministers with equal power and a double portion of Elijah's spirit, but mostly in private, one-on-one encounters.

The northern kingdom of Israel, clearly on a collision course with disaster since the days of Ahab, finally meets its fate at the hands of the cruel Assyrians. The surviving kingdom of Judah narrowly averts a similar end and is revived during the reign of good king Hezekiah. His zealous reforms and heartfelt prayers temporarily turn the tide of national apostasy and halfhearted religion.

 LOOK UP When you pray, does God *(a)* always answer your prayers? *(b)* sometimes answer your prayers? *(c)* seldom answer your prayers?

If the frequency of God's answers makes you suspect you still have

True prayer is a way of life, not just an emergency detour. much to learn about prayer, you are in good company. Even Jesus' closest traveling companions came to him one day and said, "Lord, teach us to pray" (Luke 11:1). It was a request Jesus was only too happy to grant!

In your reading of 1 and 2 Kings you have encountered two remarkable examples of people who prayed the kinds of prayers God delights to answer.

Elijah prayed a prayer of *self-sacrifice*. In order to bring his countrymen to a spiritual crossroads, Elijah prayed that it wouldn't rain—knowing that if God answered his prayer, Elijah's own brook would dry up, and his life would be in jeopardy.

Hezekiah prayed a prayer of *total dependence*. Spreading before the Lord the threatening letter he had received from the Assyrian general, Hezekiah affirmed that God and God alone had the power to deliver his people. Hezekiah's confidence was not in his wealth, his wisdom, the size of his army, or the eloquence of his words—but in God's omnipotent greatness.

LOOK AHEAD Close your time in the Word today by following the exhortation of Peter (one of the disciples who asked Jesus to teach him to pray) in 1 Peter 5:5-7: "And all of you, serve each other in humility, for 'God sets himself against the proud, but he shows favor to the humble.' So humble yourselves under the mighty power of God, and in his good time he will honor you. Give all your worries and cares to God, for he cares about what happens to you."

Think of a problem or decision you are facing right now, and pray it through like Elijah or Hezekiah. Lay your request before the Lord; be honest and transparent before him. Are you willing to obey God totally, even if it means personal inconvenience or risk? Are you willing to lean on God alone, even if others criticize or ostracize you? Tell him so right now!

It's a humbling thing to acknowledge that you cannot solve your own problems—but when you let God be your problem solver, don't be surprised if you see enemies flee and fireworks begin!

1 Chronicles

THE TWO books of Chronicles are priestly recollections and interpretations of the historical facts surrounding God's people from the reign of David to the Babylonian exile. First Chronicles recounts the righteous reign of David. Chapters 1–9 date David's ancestry back to Adam, and chapters 10–29 focus on the details of David's administration. The book's emphasis is on proper worship of the one true God—a worship David's life consistently exemplifies.

Focus	David's Line	David's Reign			
Divisions	David's Ancestors	David's Early Years as King	David's Kingdom and Covenant	David's Preparations for Temple Worship	David's Final Words and Deeds
	1 9	10 16	17 21	22 27	28 29
Topics	Genealogy	Biography			
	Ancestry	Anointing	Administration		Advice
Place	United Kingdom of Israel				
Time	Many Years	About 40 Years			

APRIL 15 ☐ DAY 106
1 CHRONICLES 1–9
David's Ancestors

OVERVIEW Chronicles gives a priestly perspective on the history of God's people. The anonymous chronicler (possibly Ezra) carefully weds the nation's history with the sovereign hand of God to show God's purposes at work in the affairs of his people. For generations God has been preparing a people (the Jews), a king (David), and a kingdom (Judah) through whom he would bless the world. In spite of the nation's unbelief, disobedience, and even displacement from the land, God's plan for them is still at work—a warming comfort for those about to return to rubble-strewn Jerusalem after a seventy-year absence.

Chapters 1–3	Chapters 4–8	Chapter 9
Genealogy from Adam to Exile	Genealogy of the Twelve Tribes	Genealogy after the Exile
Family Tree of David and Israel		

YOUR DAILY WALK One wag has commented, "Always treat your mother and father with respect, for without them you might be somebody else!"

Never try to make your son or daughter another you; one is enough.

The chronicler spends nine chapters showing how important it was for God's people to trace their roots and cling to their ancestral ties. Why? Because many of God's promises were made to an individual and his descendants, such as Abraham (Genesis 15) and David (2 Samuel 7). Take away the roots, and you take away the promises. For a people languishing in exile and wondering if God had forgotten them, their heritage became their hope.

Do a little New Testament research to discover what your rich heritage is because of your position in the family of God. Start with Galatians 3:29; 4:7; Titus 3:7; James 2:5; 1 Peter 1:3-4.

INSIGHT Shame on a Name
Baal is not a proper name but a title: "master." It is used to describe the owner of a house, land, or cattle. During the period of the judges, it was applied by many to the Lord and appeared in many individuals' names. (For example, see Judges 7:1.) But *Baal* was also the name of the chief male god of Canaan. Later, scribes found the custom of using *Baal* in personal names so abhorrent that they put the word *bosheth* (which means "shame") in place of *Baal*. Hence the name *Ishbosheth* in place of *Eshbaal* (8:33; see 2 Samuel 2:8) and *Mephibosheth* in place of *Meribbaal* (8:34; see 2 Samuel 9:6).

CHAPTER 1
The descendants of Adam were Seth, Enosh, ²Kenan, Mahalalel, Jared, ³Enoch, Methuselah, Lamech, ⁴and Noah.
The sons of Noah were* Shem, Ham, and Japheth.

⁵The descendants of Japheth were Gomer, Magog, Madai, Javan, Tubal, Meshech, and Tiras.
⁶The descendants of Gomer were Ashkenaz, Riphath,* and Togarmah.

1:4 As in Greek version (see also Gen 5:3-32); Hebrew lacks *The sons of Noah were.*   **1:6** As in some Hebrew manuscripts and Greek version (see also Gen 10:3); most Hebrew manuscripts read *Diphath.*

⁷The descendants of Javan were Elishah, Tarshish, Kittim, and Rodanim.

⁸The descendants of Ham were Cush, Mizraim,* Put, and Canaan.

⁹The descendants of Cush were Seba, Havilah, Sabtah, Raamah, and Sabteca. The descendants of Raamah were Sheba and Dedan. ¹⁰Cush was also the ancestor of Nimrod, who was known across the earth as a heroic warrior.

¹¹Mizraim was the ancestor of the Ludites, Anamites, Lehabites, Naphtuhites, ¹²Pathrusites, Casluhites, and the Caphtorites, from whom the Philistines came.*

¹³Canaan's oldest son was Sidon, the ancestor of the Sidonians. Canaan was also the ancestor of the Hittites, ¹⁴Jebusites, Amorites, Girgashites, ¹⁵Hivites, Arkites, Sinites, ¹⁶Arvadites, Zemarites, and Hamathites.

¹⁷The descendants of Shem were Elam, Asshur, Arphaxad, Lud, and Aram.

The descendants of Aram were* Uz, Hul, Gether, and Mash.*

¹⁸Arphaxad was the father of Shelah. Shelah was the father of Eber. ¹⁹Eber had two sons. The first was named Peleg—"division"—for during his lifetime the people of the world were divided into different language groups and dispersed. His brother's name was Joktan.

²⁰Joktan was the ancestor of Almodad, Sheleph, Hazarmaveth, Jerah, ²¹Hadoram, Uzal, Diklah, ²²Obal,* Abimael, Sheba, ²³Ophir, Havilah, and Jobab. All these were descendants of Joktan.

²⁴So this is the family line descended from Shem: Arphaxad, Shelah,* ²⁵Eber, Peleg, Reu, ²⁶Serug, Nahor, Terah, ²⁷and Abram, later known as Abraham.

²⁸The sons of Abraham were Isaac and Ishmael.

²⁹The sons of Ishmael were Nebaioth (the oldest), Kedar, Adbeel, Mibsam, ³⁰Mishma, Dumah, Massa, Hadad, Tema, ³¹Jetur, Naphish, and Kedemah. These were the sons of Ishmael.

³²The sons of Keturah, Abraham's concubine, were Zimran, Jokshan, Medan, Midian, Ishbak, and Shuah. The sons of Jokshan were Sheba and Dedan.

³³ The sons of Midian were Ephah, Epher, Hanoch, Abida, and Eldaah.

All these were sons of Abraham by his concubine Keturah.

³⁴Abraham was the father of Isaac. The sons of Isaac were Esau and Israel.*

³⁵The sons of Esau were Eliphaz, Reuel, Jeush, Jalam, and Korah.

³⁶The sons of Eliphaz were Teman, Omar, Zepho,* Gatam, Kenaz, and Amalek, who was born to Timna.*

³⁷The sons of Reuel were Nahath, Zerah, Shammah, and Mizzah.

³⁸The sons of Seir were Lotan, Shobal, Zibeon, Anah, Dishon, Ezer, and Dishan.

³⁹The sons of Lotan were Hori and Heman.* Lotan's sister was named Timna.

⁴⁰The sons of Shobal were Alvan,* Manahath, Ebal, Shepho,* and Onam. The sons of Zibeon were Aiah and Anah.

⁴¹The son of Anah was Dishon. The sons of Dishon were Hemdan,* Eshban, Ithran, and Keran.

⁴²The sons of Ezer were Bilhan, Zaavan, and Akan.*

The sons of Dishan* were Uz and Aran.

⁴³These are the kings who ruled in Edom before there were kings in Israel*:

Bela son of Beor, who ruled from his city of Dinhabah.

⁴⁴When Bela died, Jobab son of Zerah from Bozrah became king.

⁴⁵When Jobab died, Husham from the land of the Temanites became king.

⁴⁶When Husham died, Hadad son of Bedad became king and ruled from the city of Avith. He was the one who

---

1:8 Or *Egypt;* also in 1:11.   **1:12** Hebrew *Casluhites, from whom the Philistines came, Caphtorites.* See Jer 47:4; Amos 9:7.   **1:17a** As in one Hebrew manuscript and some Greek manuscripts (see also Gen 10:23); most Hebrew manuscripts lack *The descendants of Aram were.*   **1:17b** As in parallel text at Gen 10:23; Hebrew reads *and Meshech.*   **1:22** As in some Hebrew manuscripts and Syriac version (see also Gen 10:28); most Hebrew manuscripts read *Ebal.*   **1:24** Some Greek manuscripts read *Arphaxad, Cainan, Shelah.* See notes on Gen 10:24; 11:12-13.   **1:34** *Israel* is the name that God gave to Jacob.   **1:36a** As in many Hebrew manuscripts and a few Greek manuscripts (see also Gen 36:11); most Hebrew manuscripts read *Zephi.*   **1:36b** As in some Greek manuscripts (see also Gen 36:12); Hebrew reads *Kenaz, Timna, and Amalek.*   **1:39** As in parallel text at Gen 36:22; Hebrew reads *and Homam.*   **1:40a** As in many Hebrew manuscripts and a few Greek manuscripts (see also Gen 36:23); most Hebrew manuscripts read *Alian.*   **1:40b** As in some Hebrew manuscripts (see also Gen 36:23); most Hebrew manuscripts read *Shephi.*   **1:41** As in many Hebrew manuscripts and some Greek manuscripts (see also Gen 36:26); most Hebrew manuscripts read *Hamran.*   **1:42a** As in many Hebrew and Greek manuscripts (see also Gen 36:27); most Hebrew manuscripts read *Jaakan.*   **1:42b** Hebrew *Dishon;* compare 1:38 and parallel text at Gen 36:28.   **1:43** Or *before an Israelite king ruled over them.*

destroyed the Midianite army in the land of Moab.

⁴⁷When Hadad died, Samlah from the city of Masrekah became king.

⁴⁸When Samlah died, Shaul from the city of Rehoboth on the Euphrates River* became king.

⁴⁹When Shaul died, Baal-hanan son of Acbor became king.

⁵⁰When Baal-hanan died, Hadad became king and ruled from the city of Pau.* His wife was Mehetabel, the daughter of Matred and granddaughter of Me-zahab. ⁵¹Then Hadad died.

The clan leaders of Edom were Timna, Alvah,* Jetheth, ⁵²Oholibamah, Elah, Pinon, ⁵³Kenaz, Teman, Mibzar, ⁵⁴Magdiel, and Iram. These were the clan leaders of Edom.

CHAPTER 2

The sons of Israel* were Reuben, Simeon, Levi, Judah, Issachar, Zebulun, ²Dan, Joseph, Benjamin, Naphtali, Gad, and Asher.

³Judah had three sons through Bathshua, a Canaanite woman. Their names were Er, Onan, and Shelah. But the oldest son, Er, was a wicked man, so the LORD killed him. ⁴Later Judah had twin sons through Tamar, his widowed daughter-in-law. Their names were Perez and Zerah. So Judah had five sons in all.

⁵The sons of Perez were Hezron and Hamul.

⁶The sons of Zerah were Zimri, Ethan, Heman, Calcol, and Darda*—five in all.

⁷Achan* son of Carmi, one of Zerah's descendants, brought disaster on Israel by taking plunder that had been set apart for the LORD.*

⁸The son of Ethan was Azariah.

⁹The sons of Hezron were Jerahmeel, Ram, and Caleb.*

¹⁰ Ram was the father of Amminadab. Amminadab was the father of Nahshon, a leader of Judah.

¹¹ Nahshon was the father of Salmon.* Salmon was the father of Boaz.

¹² Boaz was the father of Obed. Obed was the father of Jesse.

¹³Jesse's first son was Eliab, his second was Abinadab, his third was Shimea, ¹⁴his fourth was Nethanel, his fifth was Raddai, ¹⁵his sixth was Ozem, and his seventh was David.

¹⁶Their sisters were named Zeruiah and Abigail. Zeruiah had three sons named Abishai, Joab, and Asahel.

¹⁷Abigail married a man named Jether, an Ishmaelite, and they had a son named Amasa.

¹⁸Hezron's son Caleb had two wives named Azubah and Jerioth. Azubah's sons were named Jesher, Shobab, and Ardon. ¹⁹After Azubah died, Caleb married Ephrathah,* and they had a son named Hur. ²⁰Hur was the father of Uri. Uri was the father of Bezalel.

²¹When Hezron was sixty years old, he married Gilead's sister, the daughter of Makir. They had a son named Segub. ²²Segub was the father of Jair, who ruled twenty-three towns in the land of Gilead. ²³(Later Geshur and Aram captured the Towns of Jair* and also took Kenath and its sixty surrounding villages.) All these were descendants of Makir, the father of Gilead.

²⁴Soon after Hezron died in the town of Caleb-ephrathah, his wife Abijah gave birth to a son named Ashhur (the father of* Tekoa).

²⁵The sons of Jerahmeel, the oldest son of Hezron, were Ram (the oldest), Bunah, Oren, Ozem, and Ahijah. ²⁶Jerahmeel had a second wife named Atarah. She was the mother of Onam.

²⁷The sons of Ram, the oldest son of Jerahmeel, were Maaz, Jamin, and Eker.

²⁸The sons of Onam were Shammai and Jada. The sons of Shammai were Nadab and Abishur.

²⁹ The sons of Abishur and his wife Abihail were Ahban and Molid.

³⁰ The sons of Nadab were Seled and Appaim. Seled died without children, ³¹but Appaim had a son named Ishi.

1:48 Hebrew *the river.*   1:50 As in many Hebrew manuscripts, some Greek manuscripts, Syriac version, and Latin Vulgate (see also Gen 36:39); most Hebrew manuscripts read *Pai.*   1:51 As in parallel text at Gen 36:40; Hebrew reads *Aliah.*   2:1 *Israel* is the name that God gave to Jacob.   2:6 As in many Hebrew manuscripts, some Greek manuscripts, and Syriac version (see also 1 Kgs 4:31); Hebrew reads *Dara.*   2:7a Hebrew *Achar;* compare Josh 7:1. *Achar* means "disaster."   2:7b The Hebrew term used here refers to the complete consecration of things or people to the LORD, either by destroying them or by giving them as an offering. 2:9 Hebrew *Kelubai,* a variant name for Caleb; compare 2:18.   2:11 As in Greek version (see also Ruth 4:21); Hebrew reads *Salma.* 2:19 Hebrew *Ephrath,* a variant name for Ephrathah; compare 2:50 and 4:4.   2:23 Or *captured Havvoth-jair.*   2:24 Or *the founder of;* also in 2:42, 45, 49-52 and perhaps other instances where the text reads *the father of.*

The son of Ishi was Sheshan. Sheshan had a descendant named Ahlai.

[32]Shammai's brother, Jada, had two sons named Jether and Jonathan. Jether died without children, [33]but Jonathan had two sons named Peleth and Zaza. These were all descendants of Jerahmeel.

[34]Sheshan had no sons, though he did have daughters. He also had an Egyptian servant named Jarha. [35]Sheshan gave one of his daughters to be the wife of Jarha, and they had a son named Attai.

[36] Attai was the father of Nathan. Nathan was the father of Zabad.

[37] Zabad was the father of Ephlal. Ephlal was the father of Obed.

[38] Obed was the father of Jehu. Jehu was the father of Azariah.

[39] Azariah was the father of Helez. Helez was the father of Eleasah.

[40] Eleasah was the father of Sismai. Sismai was the father of Shallum.

[41] Shallum was the father of Jekamiah. Jekamiah was the father of Elishama.

[42]The oldest son of Caleb, the brother of Jerahmeel, was Mesha, the father of Ziph. Caleb's second son was Mareshah, the father of Hebron.*

[43]The sons of Hebron were Korah, Tappuah, Rekem, and Shema. [44]Shema was the father of Raham. Raham was the father of Jorkeam. Rekem was the father of Shammai. [45]The son of Shammai was Maon. Maon was the father of Beth-zur.

[46]Caleb's concubine Ephah gave birth to Haran, Moza, and Gazez. Haran was the father of Gazez.

[47]The sons of Jahdai were Regem, Jotham, Geshan, Pelet, Ephah, and Shaaph.

[48]Another of Caleb's concubines, Maacah, gave birth to Sheber and Tirhanah. [49]She also gave birth to Shaaph (the father of Madmannah) and Sheva (the father of Macbenah and Gibea). Caleb also had a daughter named Acsah.

[50]These were all descendants of Caleb. The sons of Hur, the oldest son of Caleb's wife Ephrathah, were Shobal (the father of Kiriath-jearim), [51]Salma (the father of Bethlehem), and Hareph (the father of Beth-gader).

[52]The descendants of Shobal (the father of Kiriath-jearim) were Haroeh, half the Manahathites, [53]and the families of Kiriath-jearim—the Ithrites, Puthites, Shumathites, and Mishraites, from whom came the people of Zorah and Eshtaol.

[54]The descendants of Salma were Bethlehem, the Netophathites, Atroth-beth-joab, the other half of the Manahathites, the Zorites, [55]and the families of scribes living at Jabez—the Tirathites, Shimeathites, and Sucathites. All these were Kenites who descended from Hammath, the father of the family of Recab.*

CHAPTER 3

These were the sons who were born to David in Hebron:

The oldest was Amnon, whose mother was Ahinoam of Jezreel.

The second was Kileab,* whose mother was Abigail from Carmel.

[2] The third was Absalom, whose mother was Maacah, the daughter of Talmai, king of Geshur.

The fourth was Adonijah, whose mother was Haggith.

[3] The fifth was Shephatiah, whose mother was Abital.

The sixth was Ithream, whose mother was Eglah.

[4]These six sons were born to David in Hebron, where he reigned seven and a half years.

Then David moved the capital to Jerusalem, where he reigned another thirty-three years. [5]The sons born to David in Jerusalem included Shimea, Shobab, Nathan, and Solomon. Bathsheba,* the daughter of Ammiel, was the mother of these sons. [6]David also had nine other sons: Ibhar, Elishua,* Elpelet,* [7]Nogah, Nepheg, Japhia, [8]Elishama, Eliada, and Eliphelet.

[9]These were the sons of David, not including the sons of his concubines. David also had a daughter named Tamar.

[10]The descendants of Solomon were Rehoboam, Abijah, Asa, Jehoshaphat, [11]Jehoram,* Ahaziah, Joash, [12]Amaziah,

Uzziah,* Jotham, [13]Ahaz, Hezekiah, Manasseh, [14]Amon, and Josiah.

[15]The sons of Josiah were Johanan (the oldest), Jehoiakim (the second), Zedekiah (the third), and Jehoahaz* (the fourth).

[16]Jehoiakim was succeeded by his son Jehoiachin; he, in turn, was succeeded by his uncle Zedekiah.*

[17]The sons of Jehoiachin,* who was taken prisoner by the Babylonians, were Shealtiel, [18]Malkiram, Pedaiah, Shenazzar, Jekamiah, Hoshama, and Nedabiah.

[19]The sons of Pedaiah were Zerubbabel and Shimei.

The sons of Zerubbabel were Meshullam and Hananiah. He also had a daughter named Shelomith. [20]His five other sons were Hashubah, Ohel, Berekiah, Hasadiah, and Jushab-hesed.

[21]The sons of Hananiah were Pelatiah and Jeshaiah. Jeshaiah's son was Rephaiah. Rephaiah's son was Arnan. Arnan's son was Obadiah. Obadiah's son was Shecaniah.

[22]Shecaniah's descendants were Shemaiah and his sons, Hattush, Igal, Bariah, Neariah, and Shaphat—six in all.

[23]The sons of Neariah were Elioenai, Hizkiah, and Azrikam—three in all.

[24]The sons of Elioenai were Hodaviah, Eliashib, Pelaiah, Akkub, Johanan, Delaiah, and Anani—seven in all.

CHAPTER 4

Some of the descendants of Judah were Perez, Hezron, Carmi, Hur, and Shobal. [2]Shobal's son Reaiah was the father of Jahath. Jahath was the father of Ahumai and Lahad. These were the families of the Zorathites.

[3]The descendants of * Etam were Jezreel, Ishma, Idbash, Hazzelelponi (his daughter), [4]Penuel (the father of * Gedor), and Ezer (the father of Hushah). These were the descendants of Hur (the firstborn of Ephrathah), the ancestor of Bethlehem.

[5]Ashhur (the father of Tekoa) had two wives, named Helah and Naarah. [6]Naarah gave birth to Ahuzzam, Hepher, Temeni, and Haahashtari. [7]Helah gave birth to

Zereth, Izhar, Ethnan, [8]and Koz, who became the ancestor of Anub, Zobebah, and all the families of Aharhel son of Harum.

[9]There was a man named Jabez who was more distinguished than any of his brothers. His mother named him Jabez* because his birth had been so painful. [10]He was the one who prayed to the God of Israel, "Oh, that you would bless me and extend my lands! Please be with me in all that I do, and keep me from all trouble and pain!" And God granted him his request.

[11]Kelub (the brother of Shuhah) was the father of Mehir. Mehir was the father of Eshton. [12]Eshton was the father of Beth-rapha, Paseah, and Tehinnah. Tehinnah was the father of Ir-nahash. These were the descendants of Recah.

[13]The sons of Kenaz were Othniel and Seraiah. Othniel's sons were Hathath and Meonothai.* [14]Meonothai was the father of Ophrah. Seraiah was the father of Joab, the founder of the Valley of Craftsmen,* so called because many craftsmen lived there.

[15]The sons of Caleb son of Jephunneh were Iru, Elah, and Naam. The son of Elah was Kenaz.

[16]The sons of Jehallelel were Ziph, Ziphah, Tiria, and Asarel.

[17]The sons of Ezrah were Jether, Mered, Epher, and Jalon. Mered married an Egyptian woman, who became the mother of Miriam, Shammai, and Ishbah (the father of Eshtemoa). [18]Mered also married a woman of Judah, who became the mother of Jered (the father of Gedor), Heber (the father of Soco), and Jekuthiel (the father of Zanoah). Mered's Egyptian wife was named Bithiah, and she was an Egyptian princess.

[19]Hodiah's wife was the sister of Naham. One of her sons was the father of Keilah the Garmite, and another was the father of Eshtemoa the Maacathite.

[20]The sons of Shimon were Amnon, Rinnah, Ben-hanan, and Tilon.

The descendants of Ishi were Zoheth and Ben-zoheth.

3:12 Hebrew *Azariah,* a variant name for Uzziah.   3:15 Hebrew *Shallum,* another name for Jehoahaz.   3:16 Hebrew *The descendants of Jehoiakim were his son Jeconiah* [a variant name for Jehoiachin] *and his son Zedekiah.*   3:17 Hebrew *Jeconiah,* a variant name for Jehoiachin.   4:3 As in Greek version; Hebrew reads *father of.* The meaning of the Hebrew is uncertain.   4:4 Or *the founder of;* also in 4:12, 14, 17-18, and perhaps other instances where the text reads *the father of.*   4:9 *Jabez* sounds like a Hebrew term meaning "distress" or "pain."   4:13 As in some Greek manuscripts and Latin Vulgate; Hebrew lacks *and Meonothai.*   4:14 Or *Joab, the father of Ge-harashim.*

²¹Shelah was one of Judah's sons. The descendants of Shelah were Er (the father of Lecah), Laadah (the father of Mareshah), the families of linen workers at Beth-ashbea, ²²Jokim, the people of Cozeba, Joash, and Saraph, who ruled over Moab and Jashubi-lehem. These names all come from ancient records. ²³They were the potters who lived in Netaim and Gederah. They all worked for the king.

²⁴The sons of Simeon were Nemuel, Jamin, Jarib, Zerah, and Shaul.

²⁵The descendants of Shaul were Shallum, Mibsam, and Mishma.

²⁶The descendants of Mishma were Hammuel, Zaccur, and Shimei.

²⁷Shimei had sixteen sons and six daughters, but none of his brothers had large families. So Simeon's tribe never became as large as the tribe of Judah.

²⁸They lived in Beersheba, Moladah, Hazar-shual, ²⁹Bilhah, Ezem, Tolad, ³⁰Bethuel, Hormah, Ziklag, ³¹Bethmarcaboth, Hazar-susim, Beth-biri, and Shaaraim. These towns were under their control until the time of King David.

³²Their descendants also lived in Etam, Ain, Rimmon, Token, and Ashan—five towns ³³and their surrounding villages as far away as Baalath.* This was their territory, and these names are recorded in their family genealogy.

³⁴Other descendants of Simeon included Meshobab, Jamlech, Joshah son of Amaziah, ³⁵Joel, Jehu son of Joshibiah, son of Seraiah, son of Asiel, ³⁶Elioenai, Jaakobah, Jeshohaiah, Asaiah, Adiel, Jesimiel, Benaiah, ³⁷and Ziza son of Shiphi, son of Allon, son of Jedaiah, son of Shimri, son of Shemaiah.

³⁸These were the names of some of the leaders of Simeon's wealthy clans, ³⁹who traveled to the region of Gedor, in the east part of the valley, seeking pastureland for their flocks. ⁴⁰They found lush pastures there, and the land was quiet and peaceful. Some of Ham's descendants had been living in the region of Gedor. ⁴¹But during the reign of King Hezekiah of Judah, the leaders of Simeon invaded it and completely destroyed* the homes of the descendants of Ham and of the Meunites. They killed everyone who lived there and took the land for themselves, because they wanted its good pastureland for their flocks. ⁴²Five hundred of these invaders from the tribe of Simeon went to Mount Seir, led by Pelatiah, Neariah, Rephaiah, and Uzziel—all sons of Ishi. ⁴³They destroyed the few Amalekites who had survived, and they have lived there ever since.

CHAPTER 5

The oldest son of Israel* was Reuben. But since he dishonored his father by sleeping with one of his father's concubines, his birthright was given to the sons of his brother Joseph. For this reason, Reuben is not listed in the genealogy as the firstborn son. ²It was the descendants of Judah that became the most powerful tribe and provided a ruler for the nation,* but the birthright belonged to Joseph.

³The sons of Reuben, the oldest son of Israel, were Hanoch, Pallu, Hezron, and Carmi.

⁴The descendants of Joel were Shemaiah, Gog, Shimei, ⁵Micah, Reaiah, Baal, ⁶and Beerah.

Beerah was the leader of the Reubenites when they were taken into captivity by King Tiglath-pileser* of Assyria.

⁷Beerah's relatives are listed in their genealogy by their clans: Jeiel (the leader), Zechariah, ⁸and Bela son of Azaz, son of Shema, son of Joel.

These Reubenites lived in the area that stretches from Aroer to Nebo and Baal-meon. ⁹And since they had so many cattle in the land of Gilead, they spread eastward toward the edge of the desert that stretches to the Euphrates River.

¹⁰During the reign of Saul, the Reubenites defeated the Hagrites in battle. Then they moved into the Hagrite settlements all along the eastern edge of Gilead.

¹¹Across from the Reubenites in the land of Bashan lived the descendants of

---

4:33 As in some Greek manuscripts (see also Josh 19:8); Hebrew reads *Baal*.   4:41 The Hebrew term used here refers to the complete consecration of things or people to the LORD, either by destroying them or by giving them as an offering.   5:1 *Israel* is the name that God gave to Jacob.   5:2 Or *and from Judah came a prince*.   5:6 Hebrew *Tilgath-pilneser*, a variant name for Tiglath-pileser; also in 5:26.

Gad, who were spread as far east as Salecah. ¹²Joel was the leader in the land of Bashan, and Shapham was second-in-command, along with Janai and Shaphat. ¹³Their relatives, the leaders of seven other clans, were Michael, Meshullam, Sheba, Jorai, Jacan, Zia, and Eber. ¹⁴These were all descendants of Abihail son of Huri, son of Jaroah, son of Gilead, son of Michael, son of Jeshishai, son of Jahdo, son of Buz. ¹⁵Ahi son of Abdiel, son of Guni, was the leader of their clans.

¹⁶The Gadites lived in the land of Gilead, in Bashan and its villages, and throughout the Sharon Plain. ¹⁷All of these were listed in the genealogical records during the days of King Jotham of Judah and King Jeroboam of Israel.

¹⁸There were 44,760 skilled warriors in the armies of Reuben, Gad, and the half-tribe of Manasseh. They were all skilled in combat and armed with shields, swords, and bows. ¹⁹They waged war against the Hagrites, the Jeturites, the Naphishites, and the Nodabites. ²⁰They cried out to God during the battle, and he answered their prayer because they trusted in him. So the Hagrites and all their allies were defeated. ²¹The plunder taken from the Hagrites included 50,000 camels, 250,000 sheep, 2,000 donkeys, and 100,000 captives. ²²Many of the Hagrites were killed in the battle because God was fighting against them. So they lived in their land until they were taken away into exile.

²³The half-tribe of Manasseh spread through the land from Bashan to Baal-hermon, Senir, and Mount Hermon. They were very numerous. ²⁴These were the leaders of their clans: Epher, Ishi, Eliel, Azriel, Jeremiah, Hodaviah, and Jahdiel. Each of these men had a great reputation as a warrior and leader. ²⁵But they were unfaithful and violated their covenant with the God of their ancestors. They worshiped the gods of the nations that God had destroyed. ²⁶So the God of Israel caused King Pul of Assyria (also known as Tiglath-pileser) to invade the land and lead away the people of Reuben, Gad, and the half-tribe of Manasseh as captives. The Assyrians exiled them to Halah, Habor, Hara, and the Gozan River, where they remain to this day.

CHAPTER 6

The sons of Levi were Gershon, Kohath, and Merari. ²The descendants of Kohath included Amram, Izhar, Hebron, and Uzziel. ³The children of Amram were Aaron, Moses, and Miriam.

The sons of Aaron were Nadab, Abihu, Eleazar, and Ithamar.

⁴ Eleazar was the father of Phinehas. Phinehas was the father of Abishua.
⁵ Abishua was the father of Bukki. Bukki was the father of Uzzi.
⁶ Uzzi was the father of Zerahiah. Zerahiah was the father of Meraioth.
⁷ Meraioth was the father of Amariah. Amariah was the father of Ahitub.
⁸ Ahitub was the father of Zadok. Zadok was the father of Ahimaaz.
⁹ Ahimaaz was the father of Azariah. Azariah was the father of Johanan.
¹⁰ Johanan was the father of Azariah, the high priest at the Temple built by Solomon in Jerusalem.
¹¹ Azariah was the father of Amariah. Amariah was the father of Ahitub.
¹² Ahitub was the father of Zadok. Zadok was the father of Shallum.
¹³ Shallum was the father of Hilkiah. Hilkiah was the father of Azariah.
¹⁴ Azariah was the father of Seraiah. Seraiah was the father of Jehozadak, ¹⁵who went into exile when the LORD sent the people of Judah and Jerusalem into captivity under Nebuchadnezzar.

¹⁶The sons of Levi were Gershon,* Kohath, and Merari. ¹⁷The descendants of Gershon included Libni and Shimei. ¹⁸The descendants of Kohath included Amram, Izhar, Hebron, and Uzziel. ¹⁹The descendants of Merari included Mahli and Mushi.

The following were the Levite clans, listed according to their ancestral descent:

²⁰The descendants of Gershon included Libni, Jahath, Zimmah, ²¹Joah, Iddo, Zerah, and Jeatherai. ²²The descendants of Kohath included Amminadab, Korah, Assir, ²³Elkanah, Abiasaph,* Assir, ²⁴Tahath, Uriel, Uzziah, and Shaul.

6:16 Hebrew *Gershom,* a variant name for Gershon (see 6:1); also in 6:17, 20, 43, 62, 71.   6:23 Hebrew *Ebiasaph,* a variant name for Abiasaph (also in 6:37); compare parallel text at Exod 6:24.

²⁵The descendants of Elkanah included Amasai, Ahimoth, ²⁶Elkanah, Zophai, Nahath, ²⁷Eliab, Jeroham, Elkanah, and Samuel.*

²⁸The sons of Samuel were Joel* (the older) and Abijah (the second).

²⁹The descendants of Merari included Mahli, Libni, Shimei, Uzzah, ³⁰Shimea, Hag- giah, and Asaiah.

³¹David assigned the following men to lead the music at the house of the LORD after he put the Ark there. ³²They ministered with music there at the Tabernacle* until Solomon built the Temple of the LORD in Jerusalem. Then they carried on their work there, following all the regulations handed down to them. ³³These are the men who served, along with their sons:

Heman the musician was from the clan of Kohath. His genealogy was traced back through Joel, Samuel, ³⁴Elkanah, Jeroham, Eliel, Toah, ³⁵Zuph, Elkanah, Mahath, Amasai, ³⁶Elkanah, Joel, Azariah, Zephaniah, ³⁷Tahath, Assir, Abiasaph, Korah, ³⁸Izhar, Kohath, Levi, and Israel.*

³⁹Heman's first assistant was Asaph from the clan of Gershon.* Asaph's genealogy was traced back through Berekiah, Shimea, ⁴⁰Michael, Baaseiah, Malkijah, ⁴¹Ethni, Zerah, Adaiah, ⁴²Ethan, Zimmah, Shimei, ⁴³Jahath, Gershon, and Levi.

⁴⁴Heman's second assistant was Ethan from the clan of Merari. Ethan's genealogy was traced back through Kishi, Abdi, Malluch, ⁴⁵Hashabiah, Amaziah, Hilkiah, ⁴⁶Amzi, Bani, Shemer, ⁴⁷Mahli, Mushi, Merari, and Levi.

⁴⁸Their relatives, also Levites, were appointed to various other tasks in the Tabernacle, the house of God.

⁴⁹Only Aaron and his descendants served as priests. They presented the offerings on the altar of burnt offering and the altar of incense, and they performed all the other duties related to the Most Holy Place. They made atonement for Israel by following all the commands that Moses, the servant of God, had given them.

⁵⁰The descendants of Aaron were Eleazar, Phinehas, Abishua, ⁵¹Bukki, Uzzi, Zerahiah, ⁵²Meraioth, Amariah, Ahitub, ⁵³Zadok, and Ahimaaz.

⁵⁴This is a record of the towns and territory assigned by means of sacred lots to the descendants of Aaron who were from the clan of Kohath. ⁵⁵This included Hebron and its surrounding pasturelands in Judah, ⁵⁶but the fields and outlying areas were given to Caleb son of Jephunneh. ⁵⁷So the descendants of Aaron were given the following towns, each with its surrounding pasturelands: Hebron (a city of refuge), Libnah, Jattir, Eshtemoa, ⁵⁸Holon,* Debir, ⁵⁹Ain,* Juttah,* and Beth-shemesh. ⁶⁰And from the territory of Benjamin they were given Gibeon,* Geba, Alemeth, and Anathoth, each with its pasturelands. So a total of thirteen towns was given to the descendants of Aaron. ⁶¹The remaining descendants of Kohath received ten towns from the territory of the half-tribe of Manasseh by means of sacred lots.

⁶²The descendants of Gershon received by sacred lots thirteen towns from the territories of Issachar, Asher, Naphtali, and from the Bashan area of Manasseh, east of the Jordan.

⁶³The descendants of Merari received by sacred lots twelve towns from the territories of Reuben, Gad, and Zebulun.

⁶⁴So the people of Israel assigned all these towns and pasturelands to the Levites. ⁶⁵The towns in the territories of Judah, Simeon, and Benjamin, mentioned above, were also assigned by means of sacred lots.

⁶⁶The descendants of Kohath received from the territory of Ephraim these towns, each with its surrounding pasturelands: ⁶⁷Shechem (a city of refuge in the hill country of Ephraim), Gezer, ⁶⁸Jokmeam, Beth-horon, ⁶⁹Aijalon, and Gathrimmon. ⁷⁰The remaining descendants of Kohath were assigned these towns from the territory of the half-tribe of Manasseh: Aner and Bileam, each with its pasturelands.

⁷¹The descendants of Gershon received from the territory of the half-tribe of Manasseh the town of Golan in Bashan with its

6:27 As in some Greek manuscripts (see also 6:33-34); Hebrew lacks *and Samuel*.   **6:28** As in some Greek manuscripts and the Syriac version (see also 6:33 and 1 Sam 8:2); Hebrew lacks *Joel*.   **6:32** Hebrew *the Tabernacle, the Tent of Meeting*.   **6:38** *Israel* is the name that God gave to Jacob.   **6:39** Hebrew lacks *from the clan of Gershon; see 6:43*.   **6:58** As in parallel text at Josh 21:15; Hebrew reads *Hilen*.   **6:59a** As in parallel text at Josh 21:16; Hebrew reads *Ashan*.   **6:59b** As in Syriac version (see also Josh 21:16); Hebrew lacks *Juttah*.   **6:60** As in parallel text at Josh 21:17; Hebrew lacks *Gibeon*.

pasturelands and Ashtaroth with its pasturelands. [72] From the territory of Issachar, they were given Kedesh, Daberath, [73] Ramoth, and Anem, with their pasturelands. [74] From the territory of Asher, they received Mashal, Abdon, [75] Hukok, and Rehob, each with its pasturelands. [76] From the territory of Naphtali, they were given Kedesh in Galilee, Hammon, and Kiriathaim, each with its pasturelands.

[77] The remaining descendants of Merari received from the territory of Zebulun the towns of Jokneam, Kartah,* Rimmono, and Tabor, each with its pasturelands. [78] From the territory of Reuben, east of the Jordan River opposite Jericho, they received Bezer (a desert town), Jahaz,* [79] Kedemoth, and Mephaath, each with its pasturelands. [80] And from the territory of Gad, they received Ramoth in Gilead, Mahanaim, [81] Heshbon, and Jazer, each with its pasturelands.

CHAPTER 7

The four sons of Issachar were Tola, Puah, Jashub, and Shimron. [2] The sons of Tola were Uzzi, Rephaiah, Jeriel, Jahmai, Ibsam, and Shemuel. Each of them was the leader of an ancestral clan. At the time of King David, the total number of men available for military service from these families was 22,600. [3] The son of Uzzi was Izrahiah. The sons of Izrahiah were Michael, Obadiah, Joel, and Isshiah. These five became the leaders of clans. [4] The total number of men available for military service among their descendants was 36,000, for all five of them had many wives and many sons.

[5] The total number of men available for military service from all the clans of the tribe of Issachar was 87,000. All of them were listed in their tribal genealogy. [6] Three of Benjamin's sons were Bela, Beker, and Jediael. [7] The sons of Bela were Ezbon, Uzzi, Uzziel, Jerimoth, and Iri. These five warriors were the leaders of clans. The total number of men available for military service among their descendants was 22,034. All of them were listed in their family genealogy.

[8] The sons of Beker were Zemirah, Joash, Eliezer, Elioenai, Omri, Jeremoth, Abijah, Anathoth, and Alemeth. [9] According to their family genealogy, there were 20,200 men available for military service among their descendants, in addition to their clan leaders.

[10] The son of Jediael was Bilhan. The sons of Bilhan were Jeush, Benjamin, Ehud, Kenaanah, Zethan, Tarshish, and Ahishahar. [11] They were the leaders of the clans of Jediael, and their descendants included 17,200 men available for military service.

[12] The sons of Ir were Shuppim and Huppim. Hushim was the son of Aher.

[13] The sons of Naphtali were Jahzeel,* Guni, Jezer, and Shillem.* They were all descendants of Jacob's wife Bilhah.

[14] The sons of Manasseh, born to his Aramean concubine, were Asriel and Makir. Makir was the father of Gilead. [15] Makir found wives for Huppim and Shuppim. Makir's sister was named Maacah. One of his descendants was Zelophehad, who had only daughters. [16] Makir's wife, Maacah, gave birth to a son whom she named Peresh. His brother's name was Sheresh. The sons of Peresh were Ulam and Rakem. [17] The son of Ulam was Bedan. All these were considered Gileadites, descendants of Makir son of Manasseh. [18] Makir's sister Hammoleketh gave birth to Ishhod, Abiezer, and Mahlah. [19] The sons of Shemida were Ahian, Shechem, Likhi, and Aniam.

[20] The descendants of Ephraim were Shuthelah, Bered, Tahath, Eleadah, Tahath, [21] Zabad, and Shuthelah.

Ephraim's sons Ezer and Elead were killed trying to steal livestock from the local farmers near Gath. [22] Their father, Ephraim, mourned for them a long time, and his relatives came to comfort him. [23] Afterward Ephraim slept with his wife, and she became pregnant and gave birth to a son. Ephraim named him Beriah* because of the tragedy his family had suffered.

[24] Ephraim had a daughter named Sheerah. She built the towns of Lower

---

6:77 As in Greek version (see also Josh 21:34); Hebrew lacks *Jokneam, Kartah.*   **6:78** Hebrew *Jahzah,* a variant name for Jahaz.
7:13a As in parallel text at Gen 46:24; Hebrew reads *Jahziel,* a variant name for Jahzeel.   **7:13b** As in some Hebrew and Greek manuscripts (see also Gen 46:24; Num 26:49); most Hebrew manuscripts read *Shallum.*   **7:23** *Beriah* sounds like a Hebrew term meaning "tragedy" or "misfortune."

and Upper Beth-horon and Uzzen-sheerah. ²⁵Ephraim's line of descent was Rephah, Resheph, Telah, Tahan, ²⁶Ladan, Ammihud, Elishama, ²⁷Nun, and Joshua.

²⁸The descendants of Ephraim lived in the territory that included Bethel and its surrounding towns to the south, Naaran to the east, Gezer and its villages to the west, and Shechem and its surrounding villages to the north as far as Ayyah and its towns. ²⁹Along the border of Manasseh were the towns of Beth-shan,* Taanach, Megiddo, Dor, and their surrounding villages. The descendants of Joseph son of Israel* lived in these towns.

³⁰The sons of Asher were Imnah, Ishvah, Ishvi, and Beriah. They had a sister named Serah.

³¹The sons of Beriah were Heber and Malkiel (the father of Birzaith).

³²The sons of Heber were Japhlet, Shomer, and Hotham. They had a sister named Shua.

³³The sons of Japhlet were Pasach, Bimhal, and Ashvath.

³⁴The sons of Shomer were Ahi, Rohgah, Hubbah, and Aram.

³⁵The sons of his brother Helem* were Zophah, Imna, Shelesh, and Amal.

³⁶The sons of Zophah were Suah, Harnepher, Shual, Beri, Imrah, ³⁷Bezer, Hod, Shamma, Shilshah, Ithran,* and Beera.

³⁸The sons of Jether were Jephunneh, Pispah, and Ara.

³⁹The sons of Ulla were Arah, Hanniel, and Rizia.

⁴⁰Each of these descendants of Asher was the head of an ancestral clan. They were all skilled warriors and prominent leaders. There were 26,000 men available for military service among the descendants listed in their tribal genealogy.

CHAPTER 8

The sons of Benjamin, in order of age, included Bela (the oldest), Ashbel, Aharah, ²Nohah, and Rapha. ³The sons of Bela were Addar, Gera, Abihud,* ⁴Abishua, Naaman, Ahoah, ⁵Gera, Shephuphan, and Huram.

⁶The sons of Ehud, leaders of the clans living at Geba, were driven out and moved to Manahath. ⁷Ehud's sons were Naaman, Ahijah, and Gera. Gera, the father of Uzza and Ahihud, led them when they moved.

⁸After Shaharaim divorced his wives Hushim and Baara, he had children in the land of Moab. ⁹Hodesh, his new wife, gave birth to Jobab, Zibia, Mesha, Malcam, ¹⁰Jeuz, Sakia, and Mirmah. These sons all became the leaders of clans. ¹¹Shaharaim's wife Hushim had already given birth to Abitub and Elpaal. ¹²The sons of Elpaal were Eber, Misham, Shemed (who built Ono and Lod and their villages), ¹³Beriah, and Shema. They were the leaders of the clans living in Aijalon, and they drove out the inhabitants of Gath.

¹⁴Ahio, Shashak, Jeremoth, ¹⁵Zebadiah, Arad, Eder, ¹⁶Michael, Ishpah, and Joha were the sons of Beriah.

¹⁷Zebadiah, Meshullam, Hizki, Heber, ¹⁸Ishmerai, Izliah, and Jobab were the sons of Elpaal.

¹⁹Jakim, Zicri, Zabdi, ²⁰Elienai, Zillethai, Eliel, ²¹Adaiah, Beraiah, and Shimrath were the sons of Shimei.

²²Ishpan, Eber, Eliel, ²³Abdon, Zicri, Hanan, ²⁴Hananiah, Elam, Anthothijah, ²⁵Iphdeiah, and Penuel were the sons of Shashak.

²⁶Shamsherai, Shehariah, Athaliah, ²⁷Jaareshiah, Elijah, and Zicri were the sons of Jeroham.

²⁸These were the leaders of the ancestral clans, and they were listed in their tribal genealogy. They all lived in Jerusalem.

²⁹Jeiel* (the father of* Gibeon) lived in Gibeon. His wife's name was Maacah, ³⁰and his oldest son was named Abdon. Jeiel's other sons were Zur, Kish, Baal, Ner,* Nadab, ³¹Gedor, Ahio, Zechariah,* ³²and Mikloth, who was the father of Shimeam.* All these families lived near each other in Jerusalem.

³³Ner was the father of Kish. Kish was the father of Saul. Saul was the father

---

7:29a Hebrew *Beth-shean*, a variant name for Beth-shan.   7:29b *Israel* is the name that God gave to Jacob.   7:35 Possibly another name for *Hotham*; compare 7:32.   7:37 Possibly another name for *Jether*; compare 7:38.   8:3 Possibly *Gera the father of Ehud*; compare 8:6.   8:29a As in some Greek manuscripts (see also 9:35); Hebrew lacks *Jeiel*.   8:29b Or *the founder of*.   8:30 As in some Greek manuscripts (see also 9:36); Hebrew lacks *Ner*.   8:31 As in parallel text at 9:37; Hebrew reads *Zeker*, a variant name for Zechariah.   8:32 As in parallel text at 9:38; Hebrew reads *Shimeah*, a variant name for Shimeam.

of Jonathan, Malkishua, Abinadab, and Eshbaal. [34]Jonathan was the father of Meribbaal. Meribbaal was the father of Micah. [35]Micah was the father of Pithon, Melech, Tahrea,* and Ahaz.

[36] Ahaz was the father of Jadah.* Jadah was the father of Alemeth, Azmaveth, and Zimri. Zimri was the father of Moza.

[37] Moza was the father of Binea. Binea was the father of Rephaiah.* Rephaiah was the father of Eleasah. Eleasah was the father of Azel.

[38]Azel had six sons: Azrikam, Bokeru, Ishmael, Sheariah, Obadiah, and Hanan. These were the sons of Azel. [39]Azel's brother Eshek had three sons: Ulam (the oldest), Jeush (the second), and Eliphelet (the third). [40]The sons of Ulam were all skilled warriors and expert archers. They had many sons and grandsons—150 in all.

All these were descendants of Benjamin.

CHAPTER 9

All Israel was listed in the genealogical record in *The Book of the Kings of Israel.*

The people of Judah were exiled to Babylon because they were unfaithful to the LORD. [2]The first to return to their property in their former towns were common people. With them came some of the priests, Levites, and Temple assistants. [3]People from the tribes of Judah, Benjamin, Ephraim, and Manasseh came and settled in Jerusalem.

[4]One family that returned was that of Uthai son of Ammihud, son of Omri, son of Imri, son of Bani, a descendant of Perez son of Judah.

[5]Others returned from the Shilonite clan, including Asaiah (the oldest) and his sons.

[6]From the Zerahite clan, Jeuel returned with his relatives.

In all, 690 families from the tribe of Judah returned.

[7]From the tribe of Benjamin came Sallu son of Meshullam, son of Hodaviah, son of Hassenuah; [8]Ibneiah son of

Jeroham; Elah son of Uzzi, son of Micri; Meshullam son of Shephatiah, son of Reuel, son of Ibnijah.

[9]These men were all leaders of clans, and they were listed in their tribal genealogy. In all, 956 families from the tribe of Benjamin returned.

[10]Among the priests who returned were Jedaiah, Jehoiarib, Jakin, [11]Azariah son of Hilkiah, son of Meshullam, son of Zadok, son of Meraioth, son of Ahitub. Azariah was the chief officer of the house of God.

[12]Other returning priests were Adaiah son of Jeroham, son of Pashhur, son of Malkijah, and Maasai son of Adiel, son of Jahzerah, son of Meshullam, son of Meshillemith, son of Immer.

[13]In all, 1,760 priests returned. They were heads of clans and very able men. They were responsible for ministering at the house of God.

[14]The Levites who returned were Shemaiah son of Hasshub, son of Azrikam, son of Hashabiah, a descendant of Merari; [15]Bakbakkar; Heresh; Galal; Mattaniah son of Mica, son of Zicri, son of Asaph; [16]Obadiah son of Shemaiah, son of Galal, son of Jeduthun; and Berekiah son of Asa, son of Elkanah, who lived in the area of Netophah.

[17]The gatekeepers who returned were Shallum, Akkub, Talmon, Ahiman, and their relatives. Shallum was the chief gatekeeper. [18]Prior to this time, they were responsible for the King's Gate on the east side. These men served as gatekeepers for the camps of the Levites. [19]Shallum was the son of Kore, a descendant of Abiasaph,* from the clan of Korah. He and his relatives, the Korahites, were responsible for guarding the entrance to the sanctuary, just as their ancestors had guarded the Tabernacle in the camp of the LORD.

[20]Phinehas son of Eleazar had been in charge of the gatekeepers in earlier times, and the LORD had been with him. [21]And later Zechariah son of Meshelemiah had been responsible for guarding the entrance to the Tabernacle.*

[22]In all, there were 212 gatekeepers in those days, and they were listed by

8:35 As in parallel text at 9:41; Hebrew reads *Tarea,* a variant name for Tahrea.   8:36 As in parallel text at 9:42; Hebrew reads *Jehoaddah,* a variant name for Jadah.   8:37 As in parallel text at 9:43; Hebrew reads *Raphah,* a variant name for Rephaiah. 9:19 Hebrew *Ebiasaph,* a variant name for Abiasaph; compare Exod 6:24.   9:21 Hebrew *Tent of Meeting.*

genealogies in their villages. David and Samuel the seer had appointed their ancestors because they were reliable men. [23]These gatekeepers and their descendants, by their divisions, were responsible for guarding the entrance to the house of the LORD, the house that was formerly a tent. [24]The gatekeepers were stationed on all four sides—east, west, north, and south. [25]From time to time, their relatives in the villages came to share their duties for seven-day periods.

[26]The four chief gatekeepers, all Levites, were in an office of great trust, for they were responsible for the rooms and treasuries at the house of God. [27]They would spend the night around the house of God, since it was their duty to guard it. It was also their job to open the gates every morning.

[28]Some of the gatekeepers were assigned to care for the various utensils used in worship. They checked them in and out to avoid any loss. [29]Others were responsible for the furnishings, the items in the sanctuary, and the supplies such as choice flour, wine, olive oil, incense, and spices. [30]But it was the priests who prepared the spices and incense. [31]Mattithiah, a Levite and the oldest son of Shallum the Korahite, was entrusted with baking the bread used in the offerings. [32]And some members of the clan of Kohath were in charge of preparing the bread to be set on the table each Sabbath day.

[33]The musicians, all prominent Levites, lived at the Temple. They were exempt from other responsibilities there since they were on duty at all hours. [34]All these men lived in Jerusalem. They were the heads of Levite families and were listed as prominent leaders in their tribal genealogy.

[35]Jeiel (the father of* Gibeon) lived in Gibeon. His wife's name was Maacah, [36]and his oldest son was named Abdon. Jeiel's other sons were Zur, Kish, Baal, Ner, Nadab, [37]Gedor, Ahio, Zechariah, and Mikloth. [38]Mikloth was the father of Shimeam. All these families lived near each other in Jerusalem.

[39]Ner was the father of Kish. Kish was the father of Saul. Saul was the father of Jonathan, Malkishua, Abinadab, and Eshbaal.

[40]Jonathan was the father of Meribbaal. Meribbaal was the father of Micah. [41]The sons of Micah were Pithon, Melech, Tahrea, and Ahaz.*

[42] Ahaz was the father of Jadah.*
Jadah was the father of Alemeth,
    Azmaveth, and Zimri.
Zimri was the father of Moza.

[43] Moza was the father of Binea.
Binea's son was Rephaiah.
Rephaiah's son was Eleasah.
Eleasah's son was Azel.

[44]Azel had six sons, and their names were Azrikam, Bokeru, Ishmael, Sheariah, Obadiah, and Hanan. These were the sons of Azel.

9:35 Or *the founder of.*   **9:41** As in Syriac version and Latin Vulgate (see also 8:35); Hebrew lacks *and Ahaz.*   **9:42** As in some Hebrew manuscripts and Greek version (see also 8:36); Hebrew reads *Jarah.*

APRIL 16 ☐ DAY 107
1 CHRONICLES 10–16
David's Early Years as King

 OVERVIEW Because Chronicles is written from the perspective of a priest, not a palace dweller, the Temple and Temple worship are central themes in the chronicler's work. Thus, David's efforts to return the Ark of the Covenant to its rightful place—an event that is scarcely mentioned in 2 Samuel—consumes three entire chapters in today's reading! With right motives but wrong methods, David learns that God's will done in something other than God's way is not God's will.

When at last the Ark is installed in Jerusalem, there is cause for national rejoicing, for God's presence is in the midst of his people.

Chapter 10	Chapters 11–12	Chapters 13–15	Chapter 16
David's Accession	David's Army	David's Ark Adventures	David's Anthem of Praise
David on the Throne		David on His Knees	

YOUR DAILY WALK "It must be OK. After all, I'm doing it for God." That statement reflects a common misconception about what it means to serve God. But does the end justify the means in serving God?

Motivation is what gets you started; habit is what keeps you going.

David had a godly ambition. He wanted to return the Ark to its rightful place in Jerusalem. But in his zeal, he paid no attention to God's law regarding how the Ark should be carried (Numbers 4:15). Instead, he substituted a *convenient* way for the *obedient* way, and the result was that Uzzah lost his life.

Sincerity in serving God is important, but it is possible to be sincerely wrong. Select an area of service that you participate in weekly. Then answer this question: What does the Bible say about *how* I should do this? Motives and methods—both are important in God's service.

INSIGHT Valiant Warriors, Loyal Friends
David's mighty men were an elite group of warriors, famous for their courage in battle, their personal valor, and their leadership. For instance, Benaiah earned his reputation by two acts: killing a lion in a pit and killing an Egyptian giant with the giant's own weapon. Above all, the mighty men showed loyalty to David—a character quality of great worth in the turbulent political intrigues of the day.

CHAPTER 10

Now the Philistines attacked Israel, forcing the Israelites to flee. Many were slaughtered on the slopes of Mount Gilboa. ²The Philistines closed in on Saul and his sons, and they killed three of his sons—Jonathan, Abinadab, and Malkishua. ³The fighting grew very fierce around Saul, and the Philistine archers caught up with him and wounded him severely. ⁴Saul groaned to his armor bearer, "Take your sword and run me through before these pagan Philistines come and humiliate me." But his armor bearer was afraid and would not do it. So Saul took his own sword and fell on it. ⁵When his armor bearer realized that Saul was dead, he fell on his own sword and died. ⁶So Saul and his three sons died there together, bringing his dynasty to an end.

⁷When the Israelites in the Jezreel Valley saw that their army had been routed and that Saul and his sons were dead, they abandoned their towns and fled. So the Philistines moved in and occupied their towns.

⁸The next day when the Philistines went out to strip the dead, they found the bodies of Saul and his sons on Mount Gilboa. ⁹So they stripped off Saul's armor and cut off his head. Then they proclaimed the news of Saul's death before their idols and to the people throughout the land of Philistia. ¹⁰They placed his armor in the temple of their gods, and they fastened his head to the wall in the temple of Dagon.

¹¹But when the people of Jabesh-gilead heard what the Philistines had done to Saul, ¹²their warriors went out and brought the bodies of Saul and his three sons back to Jabesh. Then they buried their remains beneath the oak tree at Jabesh, and they fasted for seven days.

¹³So Saul died because he was unfaithful to the LORD. He failed to obey the LORD's command, and he even consulted a medium ¹⁴instead of asking the LORD for guidance. So the LORD killed him and turned his kingdom over to David son of Jesse.

CHAPTER 11

Then all Israel went to David at Hebron and told him, "We are all members of your family. ²For a long time, even while Saul was our king, you were the one who really led Israel. And the LORD your God has told you, 'You will be the shepherd of my people Israel. You will be their leader.'" ³So there at Hebron David made a covenant with the leaders of Israel before the LORD. They anointed him king of Israel, just as the LORD had promised through Samuel.

⁴Then David and all Israel went to Jerusalem (or Jebus, as it used to be called), where the Jebusites, original inhabitants of the land, lived. ⁵The people of Jebus said to David, "You will never get in here!" But David captured the fortress of Zion, now called the City of David.

⁶David had said to his troops, "Whoever leads the attack against the Jebusites will become the commander of my armies!" And Joab, the son of David's sister Zeruiah, led the attack, so he became the commander of David's armies.

⁷David made the fortress his home, and that is why it is called the City of David. ⁸He extended the city from the Millo* to the surrounding area, while Joab rebuilt the rest of Jerusalem. ⁹And David became more and more powerful, because the LORD Almighty was with him.

¹⁰These are the leaders of David's mighty men. Together with all Israel, they determined to make David their king, just as the LORD had promised concerning Israel. ¹¹Here is the record of David's mightiest men:

The first was Jashobeam the Hacmonite, who was commander of the Three—the three greatest warriors among David's men.* He once used his spear to kill three hundred enemy warriors in a single battle.

¹²Next in rank among the Three was Eleazar son of Dodai,* a descendant of Ahoah. ¹³He was with David in the battle against the Philistines at Pas-dammim. The battle took place in a field full of barley, and the Israelite army fled. ¹⁴But Eleazar and David held their ground in the middle of the field and beat back the Philistines. So the LORD saved them by giving them a great victory.

¹⁵Once when David was at the rock near the cave of Adullam, the Philistine army was camped in the valley of Rephaim. The Three (who were among the Thirty—an elite group among David's fighting men) went down to meet him there. ¹⁶David was staying in the stronghold at the time, and a Philistine detachment had occupied the town of Bethlehem. ¹⁷David remarked longingly to his men, "Oh, how I would love some of that good water from the well in Bethlehem, the one by the gate." ¹⁸So the Three broke through the Philistine lines, drew some water from the well, and brought it back to David. But David refused to drink it. Instead, he poured it out before the LORD. ¹⁹"God forbid that I should drink this!" he exclaimed. "This water is as precious as the blood of these men who risked their lives to bring it to me." So David did not drink it. This is an example of the exploits of the Three.

²⁰Abishai, the brother of Joab, was the leader of the Thirty.* He once used his spear to kill three hundred enemy warriors in a single battle. It was by such feats that he became as famous as the Three. ²¹Abishai was the most famous of the Thirty and was their commander, though he was not one of the Three.

²²There was also Benaiah son of Jehoiada, a valiant warrior from Kabzeel. He did many heroic deeds, which included killing two of Moab's mightiest warriors. Another time he chased a lion down into a pit. Then, despite the snow and slippery ground, he caught the lion and killed it. ²³Another time, armed with only a club, he killed an Egyptian warrior who was seven and a half feet* tall and whose spear was as thick as a weaver's beam. Benaiah wrenched the spear from the Egyptian's hand and killed him with it. ²⁴These are some of the deeds that made Benaiah as famous as the Three. ²⁵He was more honored than the other members of the Thirty, though he was not one of the Three. And David made him commander of his bodyguard.

²⁶These were also included among David's mighty men:

Asahel, Joab's brother;
Elhanan son of Dodo from Bethlehem;

11:8 Or *the supporting terraces.* The meaning of the Hebrew is uncertain.   **11:11** As in some Greek manuscripts (see also 2 Sam 23:8); Hebrew *commander of the Thirty,* or *commander of the captains.*   **11:12** As in parallel text at 2 Sam 23:9 (see also 1 Chr 27:4); Hebrew reads *Dodo,* a variant name for Dodai.   **11:20** As in Syriac version; Hebrew reads *the Three;* also in 11:21.   **11:23** Hebrew *5 cubits* [2.3 meters].

27 Shammah from Harod;*
   Helez from Pelon;
28 Ira son of Ikkesh from Tekoa;
   Abiezer from Anathoth;
29 Sibbecai from Hushah;
   Zalmon* from Ahoah;
30 Maharai from Netophah;
   Heled son of Baanah from Netophah;
31 Ithai son of Ribai from Gibeah (from
   the tribe of Benjamin);
   Benaiah from Pirathon;
32 Hurai from near Nahale-gaash*;
   Abi-albon* the Arbathite;
33 Azmaveth from Bahurim*;
   Eliahba from Shaalbon;
34 the sons of Jashen* from Gizon;
   Jonathan son of Shagee from Harar;
35 Ahiam son of Sharar* from Harar;
   Eliphal son of Ur;
36 Hepher from Mekerah;
   Ahijah from Pelon;
37 Hezro from Carmel;
   Paarai* son of Ezbai;
38 Joel, the brother of Nathan;
   Mibhar son of Hagri;
39 Zelek from Ammon;
   Naharai from Beeroth (Joab's armor
   bearer);
40 Ira from Jattir;
   Gareb from Jattir;
41 Uriah the Hittite;
   Zabad son of Ahlai;
42 Adina son of Shiza, the Reubenite
   leader who had thirty men with him;
43 Hanan son of Maacah;
   Joshaphat from Mithna;
44 Uzzia from Ashtaroth;
   Shama and Jeiel, the sons of Hotham,
   from Aroer;
45 Jediael son of Shimri;
   Joha, his brother, from Tiz;
46 Eliel from Mahavah;
   Jeribai and Joshaviah, the sons
   of Elnaam;
   Ithmah from Moab;
47 Eliel and Obed;
   Jaasiel from Zobah.

CHAPTER 12

The following men joined David at Ziklag while he was hiding from Saul son of Kish. They were among the warriors who fought beside David in battle. 2All of them were expert archers, and they could shoot arrows or sling stones with their left hand as well as their right. They were all relatives of Saul from the tribe of Benjamin. 3Their leader was Ahiezer son of Shemaah from Gibeah; his brother Joash was second-in-command. These were the other warriors:

   Jeziel and Pelet, sons of Azmaveth;
   Beracah and Jehu from Anathoth;
4 Ishmaiah from Gibeon, a famous
      warrior and leader among the Thirty;
   Jeremiah, Jahaziel, Johanan, and Jozabad
      from Gederah;
5 Eluzai, Jerimoth, Bealiah, Shemariah,
      and Shephatiah from Haruph;
6 Elkanah, Isshiah, Azarel, Joezer, and
      Jashobeam, who were Korahites;
7 Joelah and Zebadiah, sons of Jeroham
      from Gedor.

8Some brave and experienced warriors from the tribe of Gad also defected to David while he was at the stronghold in the wilderness. They were expert with both shield and spear, as fierce as lions and as swift as deer on the mountains.

9 Ezer was their leader.
   Obadiah was second.
   Eliab was third.
10 Mishmannah was fourth.
   Jeremiah was fifth.
11 Attai was sixth.
   Eliel was seventh.
12 Johanan was eighth.
   Elzabad was ninth.
13 Jeremiah was tenth.
   Macbannai was eleventh.

14These warriors from Gad were army commanders. The weakest among them could take on a hundred regular troops, and the strongest could take on a thousand! 15They crossed the Jordan River during its seasonal flooding at the beginning of the year and drove out all the people living in the lowlands on both the east and west banks.

16Others from Benjamin and Judah came to David at the stronghold. 17David went out to meet them and said, "If you have come in peace to help me, we are friends. But if you have come to betray me to my

---

11:27 As in parallel text at 2 Sam 23:25; Hebrew reads *Shammoth from Haror.*   11:29 As in parallel text at 2 Sam 23:28; Hebrew reads *Ilai.*   11:32a Or *from the ravines of Gaash.*   11:32b As in parallel text at 2 Sam 23:31; Hebrew reads *Abiel.*   11:33 As in parallel text at 2 Sam 23:31; Hebrew reads *Baharum.*   11:34 As in parallel text at 2 Sam 23:32; Hebrew reads *sons of Hashem.*   11:35 As in parallel text at 2 Sam 23:33; Hebrew reads *son of Sacar.*   11:37 As in parallel text at 2 Sam 23:35; Hebrew reads *Naarai.*

enemies when I am innocent, then may the God of our ancestors see and judge you."

[18]Then the Spirit came upon Amasai, who later became a leader among the Thirty, and he said,

"We are yours, David!
We are on your side, son of Jesse.
Peace and prosperity be with you,
and success to all who help you,
for your God is the one who helps
you."

So David let them join him, and he made them officers over his troops.

[19]Some men from Manasseh defected from the Israelite army and joined David when he went with the Philistines to fight against Saul. But as it turned out, the Philistine leaders refused to let David and his men go with them. After much discussion, they sent them back, for they said, "It will cost us our lives if David switches loyalties to Saul and turns against us."

[20]Here is a list of the men from Manasseh who defected to David as he was returning to Ziklag: Adnah, Jozabad, Jediael, Michael, Jozabad, Elihu, and Zillethai. Each commanded a thousand troops from the tribe of Manasseh. [21]They helped David chase down bands of raiders, for they were all brave and able warriors who became commanders in his army. [22]Day after day more men joined David until he had a great army, like the army of God.

[23]These are the numbers of armed warriors who joined David at Hebron. They were all eager to see David become king instead of Saul, just as the LORD had promised.

[24]From the tribe of Judah, there were 6,800 warriors armed with shields and spears.

[25]From the tribe of Simeon, there were 7,100 warriors.

[26]From the tribe of Levi, there were 4,600 troops. [27]This included Jehoiada, leader of the family of Aaron, who had 3,700 under his command. [28]This also included Zadok, a young warrior, with twenty-two members of his family who were all officers.

[29]From the tribe of Benjamin, Saul's relatives, there were 3,000 warriors. Most of the men from Benjamin had remained loyal to Saul until this time.

[30]From the tribe of Ephraim, there were 20,800 warriors, each famous in his own clan.

[31]From the half-tribe of Manasseh west of the Jordan, 18,000 men were sent for the express purpose of helping David become king.

[32]From the tribe of Issachar, there were 200 leaders of the tribe with their relatives. All these men understood the temper of the times and knew the best course for Israel to take.

[33]From the tribe of Zebulun, there were 50,000 skilled warriors. They were fully armed and prepared for battle and completely loyal to David.

[34]From the tribe of Naphtali, there were 1,000 officers and 37,000 warriors armed with shields and spears.

[35]From the tribe of Dan, there were 28,600 warriors, all prepared for battle.

[36]From the tribe of Asher, there were 40,000 trained warriors, all prepared for battle.

[37]From the east side of the Jordan River— where the tribes of Reuben and Gad and the half-tribe of Manasseh lived— there were 120,000 troops armed with every kind of weapon.

[38]All these men came in battle array to Hebron with the single purpose of making David the king of Israel. In fact, all Israel agreed that David should be their king. [39]They feasted and drank with David for three days, for preparations had been made by their relatives for their arrival. [40]And people from as far away as Issachar, Zebulun, and Naphtali brought food on donkeys, camels, mules, and oxen. Vast supplies of flour, fig cakes, raisins, wine, olive oil, cattle, and sheep were brought to the celebration. There was great joy throughout the land of Israel.

CHAPTER 13
David consulted with all his officials, including the generals and captains of his army. [2]Then he addressed the entire assembly of Israel as follows: "If you approve and if it is the will of the LORD our God, let us send messages to all the Israelites throughout the land, including the priests and Levites in their towns and pasturelands. Let us invite them to come and join us. [3]It is time to bring back the Ark of our God, for we neglected it during the reign of Saul."

[4]The whole assembly agreed to this, for

the people could see it was the right thing to do. ⁵So David summoned all the people of Israel, from one end of the country to the other,* to join in bringing the Ark of God from Kiriath-jearim. ⁶Then David and all Israel went to Baalah of Judah (also called Kiriath-jearim) to bring back the Ark of God, which bears the name of the LORD who is enthroned between the cherubim. ⁷They transported the Ark of God from the house of Abinadab on a new cart, with Uzzah and Ahio guiding it. ⁸David and all Israel were celebrating before God with all their might, singing and playing all kinds of musical instruments—lyres, harps, tambourines, cymbals, and trumpets.

⁹But when they arrived at the threshing floor of Nacon,* the oxen stumbled, and Uzzah put out his hand to steady the Ark. ¹⁰Then the LORD's anger blazed out against Uzzah, and he struck him dead because he had laid his hand on the Ark. So Uzzah died there in the presence of God. ¹¹David was angry because the LORD's anger had blazed out against Uzzah. He named that place Perez-uzzah (which means "outbreak against Uzzah"). It is still called that today.

¹²David was now afraid of God and asked, "How can I ever bring the Ark of God back into my care?" ¹³So David decided not to move the Ark into the City of David. He took it instead to the home of Obed-edom of Gath. ¹⁴The Ark of God remained there with the family of Obed-edom for three months, and the LORD blessed him and his entire household.

CHAPTER 14

Now King Hiram of Tyre sent messengers to David, along with stonemasons and carpenters to build him a palace. Hiram also sent many cedar logs for lumber. ²And David realized that the LORD had made him king over Israel and had made his kingdom very great for the sake of his people Israel.

³Then David married more wives in Jerusalem, and they had many sons and daughters. ⁴These are the names of David's sons who were born in Jerusalem: Shimea,* Shobab, Nathan, Solomon, ⁵Ibhar, Elishua, Elpelet, ⁶Nogah, Nepheg, Japhia, ⁷Elishama, Eliada,* and Eliphelet.

⁸When the Philistines heard that David had been anointed king over all Israel, they mobilized all their forces to capture him. But David was told they were coming, so he and his men marched out to meet them. ⁹The Philistines had arrived in the valley of Rephaim and raided it. ¹⁰So David asked God, "Should I go out to fight the Philistines? Will you hand them over to me?"

The LORD replied, "Yes, go ahead. I will give you the victory."

¹¹So David and his troops went to Baal-perazim and defeated the Philistines there. "God has done it!" David exclaimed. "He used me to burst through my enemies like a raging flood!" So that place was named Baal-perazim (which means "the Lord who bursts through"). ¹²The Philistines had abandoned their idols* there, so David gave orders to burn them up.

¹³But after a while, the Philistines returned and raided the valley again. ¹⁴And once again David asked God what to do. "Do not attack them straight on," God replied. "Instead, circle around behind them and attack them near the balsam trees. ¹⁵When you hear a sound like marching feet in the tops of the balsam trees, attack! That will be the signal that God is moving ahead of you to strike down the Philistines." ¹⁶So David did what God commanded, and he struck down the Philistine army all the way from Gibeon to Gezer.

¹⁷So David's fame spread everywhere, and the LORD caused all the nations to fear David.

CHAPTER 15

David now built several buildings for himself in the City of David. He also prepared a place for the Ark of God and set up a special tent there to shelter it. ²Then he issued these instructions: "When we transport the Ark of God this time, no one except the Levites may carry it. The LORD has chosen them to carry the Ark of the LORD and to minister before him forever."

³Then David summoned all the Israelites to Jerusalem to bring the Ark of the LORD to the place he had prepared for it. ⁴These are the priests* and Levites who were called together:

13:5 Hebrew *from the Shihor of Egypt to Lebo-hamath.*   13:9 As in parallel text at 2 Sam 6:6; Hebrew reads *Kidon.*   14:4 Hebrew *Shammua,* a variant name for Shimea; compare 3:5.   14:7 Hebrew *Beeliada,* a variant name for Eliada; compare 3:8 and parallel text at 2 Sam 5:16.   14:12 Hebrew *their gods;* compare parallel text at 2 Sam 5:21.   15:4 Hebrew *descendants of Aaron.*

⁵There were 120 from the clan of Kohath, with Uriel as their leader. ⁶There were 220 from the clan of Merari, with Asaiah as their leader. ⁷There were 130 from the clan of Gershon,* with Joel as their leader. ⁸There were 200 descendants of Elizaphan, with Shemaiah as their leader. ⁹There were 80 descendants of Hebron, with Eliel as their leader. ¹⁰There were 112 descendants of Uzziel, with Amminadab as their leader.

¹¹Then David summoned the priests, Zadok and Abiathar, and these Levite leaders: Uriel, Asaiah, Joel, Shemaiah, Eliel, and Amminadab. ¹²He said to them, "You are the leaders of the Levite families. You must purify yourselves and all your fellow Levites, so you can bring the Ark of the LORD, the God of Israel, to the place I have prepared for it. ¹³Because you Levites did not carry the Ark the first time, the anger of the LORD our God burst out against us. We failed to ask God how to move it in the proper way." ¹⁴So the priests and the Levites purified themselves in order to bring the Ark of the LORD, the God of Israel, to Jerusalem. ¹⁵Then the Levites carried the Ark of God on their shoulders with its carrying poles, just as the LORD had instructed Moses.

¹⁶David also ordered the Levite leaders to appoint a choir of Levites who were singers and musicians to sing joyful songs to the accompaniment of lyres, harps, and cymbals. ¹⁷So the Levites appointed Heman son of Joel, Asaph son of Berekiah, and Ethan son of Kushaiah from the clan of Merari to direct the musicians. ¹⁸The following men were chosen as their assistants: Zechariah, Jaaziel, Shemiramoth, Jehiel, Unni, Eliab, Benaiah, Maaseiah, Mattithiah, Eliphelehu, Mikneiah, and the gatekeepers, Obed-edom and Jeiel. ¹⁹Heman, Asaph, and Ethan were chosen to sound the bronze cymbals. ²⁰Zechariah, Aziel, Shemiramoth, Jehiel, Unni, Eliab, Maaseiah, and Benaiah were chosen to play the lyres.* ²¹Mattithiah, Eliphelehu, Mikneiah, Obed-edom, Jeiel, and Azaziah were chosen to play the harps.* ²²Kenaniah, the head Levite, was chosen as the choir leader because of his skill.

²³Berekiah and Elkanah were chosen to guard the Ark. ²⁴Shebaniah, Joshaphat, Nethanel, Amasai, Zechariah, Benaiah, and Eliezer—all of whom were priests—were chosen to blow the trumpets as they marched in front of the Ark of God. Obed-edom and Jehiah were chosen to guard the Ark.

²⁵Then David and the leaders of Israel and the generals of the army went to the home of Obed-edom to bring the Ark of the LORD's covenant up to Jerusalem with a great celebration. ²⁶And because God was clearly helping the Levites as they carried the Ark of the LORD's covenant, they sacrificed seven bulls and seven lambs. ²⁷David was dressed in a robe of fine linen, as were the Levites who carried the Ark, the singers, and Kenaniah the song leader. David was also wearing a priestly tunic.* ²⁸So all Israel brought up the Ark of the LORD's covenant to Jerusalem with shouts of joy, the blowing of horns and trumpets, the crashing of cymbals, and loud playing on harps and lyres.

²⁹But as the Ark of the LORD's covenant entered the City of David, Michal, the daughter of Saul, looked down from her window. When she saw King David dancing and leaping for joy, she was filled with contempt for him.

CHAPTER 16
So they brought the Ark of God into the special tent David had prepared for it, and they sacrificed burnt offerings and peace offerings before God. ²When he had finished, David blessed the people in the name of the LORD. ³Then he gave a gift of food to every man and woman in Israel: a loaf of bread, a cake of dates,* and a cake of raisins.

⁴David appointed the following Levites to lead the people in worship before the Ark of the LORD by asking for his blessings and giving thanks and praise to the LORD, the God of Israel. ⁵Asaph, the leader of this group, sounded the cymbals. His assistants were Zechariah (the second), then Jeiel, Shemiramoth, Jehiel, Mattithiah, Eliab, Benaiah, Obed-edom, and Jeiel. They played the harps and lyres. ⁶The priests, Benaiah

15:7 Hebrew *Gershom*, a variant name for Gershon.   15:20 Hebrew adds *according to Alamoth*, which is probably a musical term. The meaning of the Hebrew is uncertain.   15:21 Hebrew adds *according to the Sheminith*, which is probably a musical term. The meaning of the Hebrew is uncertain.   15:27 Hebrew *a linen ephod.*   16:3 Or *a portion of meat.* The meaning of the Hebrew is uncertain.

and Jahaziel, played the trumpets regularly before the Ark of God's covenant.

⁷That day David gave to Asaph and his fellow Levites this song of thanksgiving to the LORD:

⁸ Give thanks to the LORD and proclaim
    his greatness.
    Let the whole world know what he
      has done.
⁹ Sing to him; yes, sing his praises.
    Tell everyone about his miracles.
¹⁰ Exult in his holy name;
    O worshipers of the LORD, rejoice!
¹¹ Search for the LORD and for his
     strength,
    and keep on searching.
¹² Think of the wonderful works he has
     done,
    the miracles, and the judgments he
     handed down,
¹³ O children of Israel, God's servant,
    O descendants of Jacob, God's
     chosen one.

¹⁴ He is the LORD our God.
    His rule is seen throughout the land.
¹⁵ He always stands by his covenant*—
    the commitment he made to a
     thousand generations.
¹⁶ This is the covenant he made with
     Abraham
    and the oath he swore to Isaac.
¹⁷ He confirmed it to Jacob as a decree,
    to the people of Israel as a never-
     ending treaty:
¹⁸ "I will give you the land of Canaan
    as your special possession."

¹⁹ He said this when they were few in
     number,
    a tiny group of strangers in Canaan.
²⁰ They wandered back and forth
     between nations,
    from one kingdom to another.
²¹ Yet he did not let anyone oppress them.
    He warned kings on their behalf:
²² "Do not touch these people I have
     chosen,
    and do not hurt my prophets."

²³ Let the whole earth sing to the LORD!
    Each day proclaim the good news
     that he saves.
²⁴ Publish his glorious deeds among the
     nations.

    Tell everyone about the amazing
     things he does.
²⁵ Great is the LORD! He is most worthy
    of praise!
    He is to be revered above all gods.
²⁶ The gods of other nations are merely
     idols,
    but the LORD made the heavens!
²⁷ Honor and majesty surround him;
    strength and beauty are in his
     dwelling.

²⁸ O nations of the world, recognize the
     LORD,
    recognize that the LORD is glorious
     and strong.
²⁹ Give to the LORD the glory he deserves!
    Bring your offering and come to
     worship him.
    Worship the LORD in all his holy
     splendor.
³⁰ Let all the earth tremble before him.
    The world is firmly established and
     cannot be shaken.
³¹ Let the heavens be glad, and let the
     earth rejoice!
    Tell all the nations that the LORD is
     king.
³² Let the sea and everything in it shout
     his praise!
    Let the fields and their crops burst
     forth with joy!
³³ Let the trees of the forest rustle with
     praise before the LORD!
    For he is coming to judge the earth.

³⁴ Give thanks to the LORD, for he is good!
    His faithful love endures forever.
³⁵ Cry out, "Save us, O God of our
     salvation!
    Gather and rescue us from among
     the nations,
    so we can thank your holy name
     and rejoice and praise you."
³⁶ Blessed be the LORD, the God of Israel,
    from everlasting to everlasting!

And all the people shouted "Amen!" and praised the LORD.

³⁷David arranged for Asaph and his fellow Levites to minister regularly before the Ark of the LORD's covenant, doing whatever needed to be done each day. ³⁸This group included Obed-edom (son of Jeduthun), Hosah, and sixty-eight other Levites as gatekeepers.

16:15 As in some Greek manuscripts (see also Ps 105:8); Hebrew reads *Remember his covenant forever.*

³⁹Meanwhile, David stationed Zadok the priest and his fellow priests at the Tabernacle of the LORD on the hill of Gibeon, where they continued to minister before the LORD. ⁴⁰They sacrificed the regular burnt offerings to the LORD each morning and evening on the altar set aside for that purpose, obeying everything written in the law of the LORD, which he had given to Israel. ⁴¹David also appointed Heman, Jeduthun, and the others chosen by name to give thanks to the LORD, "for his faithful love endures forever." ⁴²They used their trumpets, cymbals, and other instruments to accompany the songs of praise to God. And the sons of Jeduthun were appointed as gatekeepers.

⁴³Then all the people returned to their homes, and David returned home to bless his family.

APRIL 17 ☐ DAY 108
1 CHRONICLES 17–21
David's Kingdom and Covenant

 OVERVIEW David's dream of building a fitting place for God to dwell and be worshiped meets with the prophet's approval . . . and God's disapproval. Solomon, not David, is God's choice to erect the Temple. But while David's house for God must be postponed, God has a house for David that begins immediately and never ends: an eternal kingdom and perpetual dynasty. In peacetime and war, through times of faithfulness and faltering, God keeps his promise by preserving David's line.

Chapter 17	Chapter 18	Chapters 19–20	Chapter 21
An Eternal House	An Extended Kingdom	An Exterminated Enemy	An Evil Idea
Covenant	Conquest		Census

 YOUR DAILY WALK If a chronicler were to write the priestly view of your life, what would he include? And what would he exclude from his account?

There are some Christians who can't be called pilgrims because they never make any progress.

There are some notable omissions in the book of 1 Chronicles. Try as you might, you will find nothing about Saul's reign or David's sin with Bathsheba, Absalom's rebellion or Adonijah's attempted coup. Why are these bleak events in Israel's history deleted? Not to whitewash the story of the nation, but to put the emphasis on God's positive purpose for the nation's existence. In spite of repeated human failings, God's program for his people will be accomplished!

If you were to diagram your own spiritual pilgrimage, chances are it wouldn't have any more ups and downs than Israel's. And God is just as committed to *your* spiritual maturity and the fulfilling of his purpose for your life. "And I am sure that God, who began the good work within you, will continue his work until it is finally finished on that day when Christ Jesus comes back again" (Philippians 1:6). Pretend that you are the chronicler writing the autobiography of your own walk with God. What spiritual milestones would you highlight? Jot them down in your journal or inside the cover of this Bible. But leave room—God isn't finished yet!

INSIGHT How's That Name Again?
David's secretary, Seraiah, of 18:16 is also called Shisha (1 Kings 4:3) and Sheva (2 Samuel 20:25). The variations in spelling are perhaps due to a non-Hebrew origin for his name, giving rise to different transliterations.

CHAPTER 17

Now when David was settled in his palace, he said to Nathan the prophet, "Here I am living in this beautiful cedar palace, but the Ark of the LORD's covenant is out in a tent!" ²Nathan replied, "Go ahead with what you have in mind, for God is with you." ³But that same night God said to Nathan,

⁴"Go and tell my servant David, 'This is what the LORD says: You are not the one to build me a temple to live in. ⁵I have never lived in a temple, from the day I brought the Israelites out of Egypt until now. My home has always been a tent, moving from one place to another. ⁶And I never once complained to Israel's leaders,* the shepherds of my people. I have never asked them, "Why haven't you built me a beautiful cedar temple?"'

⁷"Now go and say to my servant David, 'This is what the LORD Almighty says: I chose you to lead my people Israel when you were just a shepherd boy, tending your sheep out in the pasture. ⁸I have been with you wherever you have gone, and I have destroyed all your enemies. Now I will make your name famous throughout the earth! ⁹And I have provided a permanent homeland for my people Israel, a secure place where they will never be disturbed. It will be their own land where wicked nations won't oppress them as they did in the past, ¹⁰from the time I appointed judges to rule my people. And I will subdue all your enemies.

" 'And now I declare that the LORD will build a house for you—a dynasty of kings! ¹¹For when you die, I will raise up one of your sons, and I will make his kingdom strong. ¹²He is the one who will build a house—a temple—for me. And I will establish his throne forever. ¹³I will be his father, and he will be my son. I will not take my unfailing love from him as I took it from Saul, who ruled before you. ¹⁴I will establish him over my dynasty and my kingdom for all time, and his throne will be secure forever.'"

¹⁵So Nathan went back to David and told him everything the LORD had said.

¹⁶Then King David went in and sat before the LORD and prayed, "Who am I, O LORD God, and what is my family, that you have brought me this far? ¹⁷And now, O God, in addition to everything else, you speak of giving me a lasting dynasty! You speak as though I were someone very great,* O LORD God! ¹⁸What more can I say about the way you have honored me? You know what I am really like. ¹⁹For my sake, O LORD, and according to your will, you have done all these great things and have made them known.

²⁰"O LORD, there is no one like you—there is no other God. We have never even heard of another god like you! ²¹What other nation on earth is like Israel? What other nation, O God, have you redeemed from slavery to be your own people? You made a great name for yourself when you rescued your people from Egypt. You performed awesome miracles and drove out the nations that stood in their way. ²²You chose Israel to be your people forever, and you, O LORD, have become their God.

²³"And now, O LORD, do as you have promised concerning me and my family. May it be a promise that will last forever. ²⁴And may your name be established and honored forever so that all the world will say, 'The LORD Almighty is God over Israel!' And may the dynasty of your servant David be established in your presence.

²⁵"O my God, I have been bold enough to pray this prayer because you have revealed that you will build a house for me—an eternal dynasty! ²⁶For you are God, O LORD. And you have promised these good things to me, your servant. ²⁷And now, it has pleased you to bless me and my family so that our dynasty will continue forever before you. For when you grant a blessing, O LORD, it is an eternal blessing!"

17:6 As in Greek version (see also 2 Sam 7:7); Hebrew reads *judges*.　　17:17 The meaning of the Hebrew is uncertain.

CHAPTER 18

After this, David subdued and humbled the Philistines by conquering Gath and its surrounding towns. [2]David also conquered the land of Moab, and the Moabites became David's subjects and brought him tribute money.

[3]Then David destroyed the forces of King Hadadezer of Zobah, as far as Hamath,* when Hadadezer marched out to strengthen his control along the Euphrates River. [4]David captured one thousand chariots, seven thousand charioteers, and twenty thousand foot soldiers. Then he crippled all but one hundred of the chariot horses.

[5]When Arameans from Damascus arrived to help Hadadezer, David killed twenty-two thousand of them. [6]Then he placed several army garrisons in Damascus, the Aramean capital, and the Arameans became David's subjects and brought him tribute money. So the LORD gave David victory wherever he went. [7]David brought the gold shields of Hadadezer's officers to Jerusalem, [8]along with a large amount of bronze from Hadadezer's cities of Tebah* and Cun. Later Solomon melted the bronze and used it for the Temple. He molded it into the bronze Sea, the pillars, and the various bronze utensils used at the Temple.

[9]When King Toi* of Hamath heard that David had destroyed the army of King Hadadezer of Zobah, [10]he sent his son Joram* to congratulate David on his success. Hadadezer and Toi had long been enemies, and there had been many wars between them. Joram presented David with many gifts of gold, silver, and bronze. [11]King David dedicated all these gifts to the LORD, along with the silver and gold he had taken from the other nations he had subdued—Edom, Moab, Ammon, Philistia, and Amalek.

[12]Abishai son of Zeruiah destroyed eighteen thousand Edomites in the Valley of Salt. [13]He placed army garrisons throughout Edom, and all the Edomites became David's subjects. This was another example of how the LORD made David victorious wherever he went.

[14]David reigned over all Israel and was fair to everyone. [15]Joab son of Zeruiah was commander of the army. Jehoshaphat son of Ahilud was the royal historian. [16]Zadok son of Ahitub and Ahimelech* son of Abiathar were the priests. Seraiah* was the court secretary. [17]Benaiah son of Jehoiada was captain of the king's bodyguard.* David's sons served as the king's chief assistants.

CHAPTER 19

Some time after this, King Nahash of the Ammonites died, and his son Hanun* became king. [2]David said, "I am going to show complete loyalty to Hanun because his father, Nahash, was always completely loyal to me." So David sent ambassadors to express sympathy to Hanun about his father's death.

But when David's ambassadors arrived in the land of Ammon, [3]Hanun's advisers said to him, "Do you really think these men are coming here to honor your father? No! David has sent them to spy out the land so that they can come in and conquer it!" [4]So Hanun seized David's ambassadors and shaved their beards, cut off their robes at the buttocks, and sent them back to David in shame. [5]When David heard what had happened, he sent messengers to tell the men to stay at Jericho until their beards grew out, for they were very embarrassed by their appearance.

[6]Now the people of Ammon realized how seriously they had angered David, so Hanun and the Ammonites sent thirty-eight tons* of silver to hire chariots and troops from Aram-naharaim, Aram-maacah, and Zobah. [7]They also hired thirty-two thousand chariots and secured the support of the king of Maacah and his army. These forces camped at Medeba, where they were joined by the Ammonite troops that Hanun had recruited from his own towns. [8]When David heard about this, he sent Joab and all his warriors to fight them. [9]The Ammonite troops drew up their battle lines at the gate of the city, while other kings positioned themselves to fight in the open fields.

[10]When Joab saw that he would have to

18:3 The meaning of the Hebrew is uncertain.   18:8 Hebrew reads *Tibhath,* a variant name for Tebah; compare parallel text at 2 Sam 8:8.   18:9 As in parallel text at 2 Sam 8:9; Hebrew reads *Tou;* also in 18:10.   18:10 As in parallel text at 2 Sam 8:10; Hebrew reads *Hadoram,* a variant name for Joram.   18:16a As in some Hebrew manuscripts, Syriac version, and Latin Vulgate (see also 2 Sam 8:17); most Hebrew manuscripts read *Abimelech.*   18:16b As in parallel text at 2 Sam 8:17; Hebrew reads *Shavsha.* 18:17 Hebrew *of the Kerethites and Pelethites.*   19:1 Hebrew lacks *Hanun;* compare parallel text at 2 Sam 10:1.   19:6 Hebrew *1,000 talents* [34 metric tons].

fight on two fronts, he chose the best troops in his army. He placed them under his personal command and led them out to fight the Arameans in the fields. [11]He left the rest of the army under the command of his brother Abishai, who was to attack the Ammonites. [12]"If the Arameans are too strong for me, then come over and help me," Joab told his brother. "And if the Ammonites are too strong for you, I will help you. [13]Be courageous! Let us fight bravely to save our people and the cities of our God. May the LORD's will be done."

[14]When Joab and his troops attacked, the Arameans began to run away. [15]And when the Ammonites saw the Arameans running, they ran from Abishai and retreated into the city. Then Joab returned to Jerusalem.

[16]The Arameans now realized that they were no match for Israel, so they summoned additional Aramean troops from the other side of the Euphrates River.* These troops arrived under the command of Shobach,* the commander of all Hadadezer's forces. [17]When David heard what was happening, he mobilized all Israel, crossed the Jordan River, and positioned his troops in battle formation. Then he engaged the enemy troops in battle, and they fought against him. [18]But again the Arameans fled from the Israelites. This time David's forces killed seven thousand charioteers and forty thousand foot soldiers, including Shobach, the commander of their army. [19]When the servants of Hadadezer realized they had been defeated by Israel, they surrendered to David and became his subjects. After that, the Arameans were no longer willing to help the Ammonites.

CHAPTER 20

The following spring, the time of year when kings go to war, Joab led the Israelite army in successful attacks against the towns and villages of the Ammonites. In the process they laid siege to the city of Rabbah and destroyed it. But David had stayed behind in Jerusalem.

[2]When David arrived at Rabbah, he removed the crown from the king's head,* and it was placed on David's own head. The crown was made of gold and set with gems, and it weighed about seventy-five pounds.* David took a vast amount of plunder from the city. [3]He also made slaves of the people of Rabbah and forced them to labor with saws, picks, and axes.* That is how he dealt with the people of all the Ammonite cities. Then David and his army returned to Jerusalem.

[4]After this, war broke out with the Philistines at Gezer. As they fought, Sibbecai from Hushah killed Saph,* a descendant of the giants,* and so the Philistines were subdued. [5]During another battle with the Philistines, Elhanan son of Jair killed Lahmi, the brother of Goliath of Gath. The handle of Lahmi's spear was as thick as a weaver's beam! [6]In another battle with the Philistines at Gath, a huge man with six fingers on each hand and six toes on each foot—a descendant of the giants—[7]defied and taunted Israel. But he was killed by Jonathan, the son of David's brother Shimea. [8]These Philistines were descendants of the giants of Gath, but they were killed by David and his warriors.

CHAPTER 21

Satan rose up against Israel and caused David to take a census of the Israelites. [2]David gave these orders to Joab and his commanders: "Take a census of all the people in the land—from Beersheba in the south to Dan in the north—and bring me the totals so I may know how many there are."

[3]But Joab replied, "May the LORD increase the number of his people a hundred times over! But why, my lord, do you want to do this? Are they not all your servants? Why must you cause Israel to sin?"

[4]But the king insisted that Joab take the census, so Joab traveled throughout Israel to count the people. Then he returned to Jerusalem [5]and reported the number of people to David. There were 1,100,000 men of military age in Israel, and 470,000 in Judah. [6]But Joab did not include the tribes of Levi and Benjamin in the census because he was so distressed at what the king had made him do.

[7]God was very displeased with the

19:16a Hebrew the river.   19:16b As in parallel text at 2 Sam 10:16; Hebrew reads Shophach; also in 19:18.   20:2a Greek version and Latin Vulgate read removed the crown of Milcom; compare 1 Kgs 11:5. Milcom, also called Molech, was the god of the Ammonites.   20:2b Hebrew 1 talent [34 kilograms].   20:3 As in parallel text at 2 Sam 12:31; Hebrew reads and saws.   20:4a As in parallel text at 2 Sam 21:18; Hebrew reads Sippai.   20:4b Hebrew descendant of the Rephaites; also in 20:6, 8.

census, and he punished Israel for it. [8]Then David said to God, "I have sinned greatly and shouldn't have taken the census. Please forgive me for doing this foolish thing."

[9]Then the LORD spoke to Gad, David's seer. This was the message: [10]"Go and say to David, 'This is what the LORD says: I will give you three choices. Choose one of these punishments, and I will do it.'"

[11]So Gad came to David and said, "These are the choices the LORD has given you. [12]You may choose three years of famine, three months of destruction by your enemies, or three days of severe plague as the angel of the LORD brings devastation throughout the land of Israel. Think this over and let me know what answer to give the LORD."

[13]"This is a desperate situation!" David replied to Gad. "But let me fall into the hands of the LORD, for his mercy is very great. Do not let me fall into human hands."

[14]So the LORD sent a plague upon Israel, and seventy thousand people died as a result. [15]And God sent an angel to destroy Jerusalem. But just as the angel was preparing to destroy it, the LORD relented and said to the death angel, "Stop! That is enough!" At that moment the angel of the LORD was standing by the threshing floor of Araunah* the Jebusite.

[16]David looked up and saw the angel of the LORD standing between heaven and earth with his sword drawn, stretched out over Jerusalem. So David and the leaders of Israel put on sackcloth to show their distress and fell down with their faces to the ground. [17]And David said to God, "I am the one who called for the census! I am the one who has sinned and done wrong! But these people are innocent—what have they done? O LORD my God, let your anger fall against me and my family, but do not destroy your people."

[18]Then the angel of the LORD told Gad to instruct David to build an altar to the LORD at the threshing floor of Araunah the Jebusite. [19]So David obeyed the instructions the LORD had given him through Gad. [20]Araunah, who was busy threshing wheat at the time, turned and saw the angel there. His four sons, who were with him, ran away and hid. [21]When Araunah saw the king approaching, he left his threshing floor and bowed to the ground before David.

[22]David said to Araunah, "Let me buy this threshing floor from you at its full price. Then I will build an altar to the LORD there, so that he will stop the plague."

[23]"Take it, my lord, and use it as you wish," Araunah said to David. "Here are oxen for the burnt offerings, and you can use the threshing tools for wood to build a fire on the altar. And take the wheat for the grain offering. I will give it all to you."

[24]But the king replied to Araunah, "No, I insist on paying what it is worth. I cannot take what is yours and give it to the LORD. I will not offer a burnt offering that has cost me nothing!" [25]So David gave Araunah six hundred pieces of gold* in payment for the threshing floor. [26]David built an altar there to the LORD and sacrificed burnt offerings and peace offerings. And when David prayed, the LORD answered him by sending fire from heaven to burn up the offering on the altar. [27]Then the LORD spoke to the angel, who put the sword back into its sheath.

[28]When David saw that the LORD had answered his prayer, he offered sacrifices there at Araunah's threshing floor. [29]At that time, the Tabernacle of the LORD and the altar that Moses made in the wilderness were located at the hill of Gibeon. [30]But David was not able to go there to inquire of God, because he was terrified by the drawn sword of the angel of the LORD.

21:15 As in parallel text at 2 Sam 24:16; Hebrew reads *Ornan*, another name for Araunah; also in 21:18-28.   21:25 Hebrew *600 shekels of gold*, about 15 pounds or 6.8 kilograms in weight.

APRIL 18 ☐ DAY 109
1 CHRONICLES 22–27
David's Preparations for the Temple

 OVERVIEW Though David is denied the privilege of building the Temple in Jerusalem, he nevertheless can begin preparations for that mammoth project. Every detail—from selecting a site to securing materials—must be carefully planned and coordinated. Most important, David spends his time training the foreman who will oversee the entire project: Solomon, his son. David informs Solomon of God's decision to have his Temple built by a man of peace and tells his son of the detailed preparations that have already been made. Finally, David sends Solomon off to the task with a command and a promise: "Now begin the work, and may the LORD be with you" (22:16).

Chapter 22	Chapters 23–24	Chapter 25	Chapters 26–27
David's Charge to Solomon	David's Commissioning of the		
	Levites	Musicians	Officers
Father to Son	Leader to Followers		

 YOUR DAILY WALK How successful are you at making other people successful?

Length of service for God is not nearly as important as breadth and depth of service.

Divide a sheet of paper in half, and label the left side "Things I am doing to make myself successful." Fill in that column with all the activities you do to make yourself successful spiritually (e.g., praying), physically (jogging), vocationally (reading), etc.

Now title the right column "Things I am doing to make _____ successful." Add the name of a spouse, child, employee, or someone else in whose life you have an influence. Then complete as before.

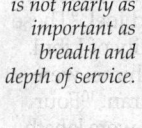

Which was easier to fill out: the right side or the left? Now stop and think: Even though God would not allow David to be successful in his desire to build the Temple (left column), he did allow David to make preparations for his son Solomon to successfully complete the task (right column). What specific action can you begin today to help the person you named become successful in his or her God-given roles?

 INSIGHT Priestly Lots for Lots of Priests
With the growing population came a growing number of priests, seemingly far more than were needed in the Temple of Jerusalem. So they were divided into twenty-four "lots," with each group serving for a two-week period each year and being on call during the feast days (24:1-19).

CHAPTER 22
Then David said, "This will be the location for the Temple of the LORD God and the place of the altar for Israel's burnt offerings!"

²So David gave orders to call together the foreigners living in Israel, and he assigned them the task of preparing blocks of stone for building the Temple of God. ³David provided large amounts of iron for the nails that would be needed for the doors in the gates and for the clamps, and

more bronze than they could ever weigh. ⁴He also provided innumerable cedar logs, for the men of Tyre and Sidon had brought vast amounts of cedar to David. ⁵David said, "My son Solomon is still young and inexperienced, and the Temple of the LORD must be a magnificent structure, famous and glorious throughout the world. So I will begin making preparations for it now." So David collected vast amounts of building materials before his death.

⁶Then David sent for his son Solomon and instructed him to build a Temple for the LORD, the God of Israel. ⁷"I wanted to build a Temple to honor the name of the LORD my God," David told him. ⁸"But the LORD said to me, 'You have killed many men in the great battles you have fought. And since you have shed so much blood before me, you will not be the one to build a Temple to honor my name. ⁹But you will have a son who will experience peace and rest. I will give him peace with his enemies in all the surrounding lands. His name will be Solomon,* and I will give peace and quiet to Israel during his reign. ¹⁰He is the one who will build a Temple to honor my name. He will be my son, and I will be his father. And I will establish the throne of his kingdom over Israel forever.'

¹¹"Now, my son, may the LORD be with you and give you success as you follow his instructions in building the Temple of the LORD your God. ¹²And may the LORD give you wisdom and understanding, that you may obey the law of the LORD your God as you rule over Israel. ¹³For if you carefully obey the laws and regulations that the LORD gave to Israel through Moses, you will be successful. Be strong and courageous; do not be afraid or lose heart!

¹⁴"I have worked hard to provide materials for building the Temple of the LORD—nearly four thousand tons of gold, nearly forty thousand tons of silver,* and so much iron and bronze that it cannot be weighed. I have also gathered lumber and stone for the walls, though you may need to add more. ¹⁵You have many skilled stonemasons and carpenters and craftsmen of every kind available to you. ¹⁶They are expert goldsmiths and silversmiths and workers of bronze and iron. Now begin the work, and may the LORD be with you!"

¹⁷Then David ordered all the leaders of Israel to assist Solomon in this project. ¹⁸"The LORD your God is with you," he declared. "He has given you peace with the surrounding nations. He has handed them over to me, and they are now subject to the LORD and his people. ¹⁹Now seek the LORD your God with all your heart. Build the sanctuary of the LORD God so that you can bring the Ark of the LORD's covenant and the holy vessels of God into the Temple built to honor the LORD's name."

CHAPTER 23

When David was an old man, he appointed his son Solomon to be king over Israel. ²David summoned all the political leaders of Israel, together with the priests and Levites, for the coronation ceremony. ³All the Levites who were thirty years old or older were counted, and the total came to thirty-eight thousand. ⁴Then David said, "Twenty-four thousand of them will supervise the work at the Temple of the LORD. Six thousand are to serve as officials and judges. ⁵Four thousand will work as gatekeepers, and another four thousand will praise the LORD with the musical instruments I have made." ⁶Then David divided the Levites into divisions named after the clans descended from the three sons of Levi—Gershon, Kohath, and Merari.

⁷The Gershonite family units were defined by their lines of descent from Libni* and Shimei, the sons of Gershon. ⁸Three of the descendants of Libni were Jehiel (the family leader), Zetham, and Joel. ⁹These were the leaders of the family of Libni.

Three of the descendants of Shimei were Shelomoth, Haziel, and Haran. ¹⁰Four other descendants of Shimei were Jahath, Ziza,* Jeush, and Beriah. ¹¹Jahath was the family leader, and Ziza was next. Jeush and Beriah were counted as a single family because neither had many sons.

¹²The descendants of Kohath included Amram, Izhar, Hebron, and Uzziel.

¹³The sons of Amram were Aaron and Moses. Aaron and his descendants were set apart to dedicate the most holy things, to offer sacrifices in the LORD's presence, to serve the LORD, and to pronounce blessings in his name forever.

¹⁴As for Moses, the man of God, his sons were included with the tribe of Levi. ¹⁵The sons of Moses were Gershom and Eliezer.

¹⁶ The descendants of Gershom included Shebuel, the family leader.

¹⁷ Eliezer had only one son, Rehabiah, the family leader. Rehabiah had numerous descendants.

22:9 *Solomon* sounds like and is probably derived from the Hebrew word for "peace." **22:14** Hebrew *100,000 talents* [3,400 metric tons] *of gold, 1,000,000 talents* [34,000 metric tons] *of silver.* **23:7** Hebrew *Ladan* (also in 23:8-9), another name for Libni; compare 6:17. **23:10** As in Greek version and Latin Vulgate (see also 23:11); Hebrew reads *Zina.*

18 The descendants of Izhar included Shelomith, the family leader.

19 The descendants of Hebron included Jeriah (the family leader), Amariah (the second), Jahaziel (the third), and Jekameam (the fourth).

20 The descendants of Uzziel included Micah (the family leader) and Isshiah (the second).

21 The descendants of Merari included Mahli and Mushi.

The sons of Mahli were Eleazar and Kish. 22 Eleazar died with no sons, only daughters. His daughters married their cousins, the sons of Kish.

23 The three sons of Mushi were Mahli, Eder, and Jerimoth.

24 These were the descendants of Levi by clans, the leaders of their family groups, registered carefully by name. Each had to be twenty years old or older to qualify for service in the house of the LORD. 25 For David said, "The LORD, the God of Israel, has given us peace, and he will always live in Jerusalem. 26 Now the Levites will no longer need to carry the Tabernacle and its utensils from place to place." 27 It was according to David's final instructions that all the Levites twenty years old or older were registered for service.

28 The work of the Levites was to assist the priests, the descendants of Aaron, as they served at the house of the LORD. They also took care of the courtyards and side rooms, helped perform the ceremonies of purification, and served in many other ways in the house of God. 29 They were in charge of the sacred bread that was set out on the table, the choice flour for the grain offerings, the wafers made without yeast, the cakes cooked in olive oil, and the other mixed breads. They were also responsible to check all the weights and measures. 30 And each morning and evening they stood before the LORD to sing songs of thanks and praise to him. 31 They assisted with the burnt offerings that were presented to the LORD on Sabbath days, at new moon celebrations, and at all the appointed festivals. The proper number of Levites served in the LORD's presence at all times, following all the procedures they had been given.

32 And so, under the supervision of the priests, the Levites watched over the Tabernacle and the Temple* and faithfully carried out their duties of service at the house of the LORD.

CHAPTER 24

This is how Aaron's descendants, the priests, were divided into groups for service. The sons of Aaron were Nadab, Abihu, Eleazar, and Ithamar. 2 But Nadab and Abihu died before their father did, and they had no sons. So only Eleazar and Ithamar were left to carry on as priests.

3 With the help of Zadok, who was a descendant of Eleazar, and of Ahimelech, who was a descendant of Ithamar, David divided Aaron's descendants into groups according to their various duties. 4 Eleazar's descendants were divided into sixteen groups and Ithamar's into eight, for there were more family leaders among the descendants of Eleazar.

5 All tasks were assigned to the various groups by means of sacred lots so that no preference would be shown, for there were many qualified officials serving God in the sanctuary from among the descendants of both Eleazar and Ithamar. 6 Shemaiah son of Nethanel, a Levite, acted as secretary and wrote down the names and assignments in the presence of the king, Zadok the priest, Ahimelech son of Abiathar, and the family leaders of the priests and Levites. The descendants of Eleazar and Ithamar took turns casting lots.

7 The first lot fell to Jehoiarib.
The second lot fell to Jedaiah.

8 The third lot fell to Harim.
The fourth lot fell to Seorim.

9 The fifth lot fell to Malkijah.
The sixth lot fell to Mijamin.

10 The seventh lot fell to Hakkoz.
The eighth lot fell to Abijah.

11 The ninth lot fell to Jeshua.
The tenth lot fell to Shecaniah.

12 The eleventh lot fell to Eliashib.
The twelfth lot fell to Jakim.

13 The thirteenth lot fell to Huppah.
The fourteenth lot fell to Jeshebeab.

14 The fifteenth lot fell to Bilgah.
The sixteenth lot fell to Immer.

15 The seventeenth lot fell to Hezir.
The eighteenth lot fell to Happizzez.

16 The nineteenth lot fell to Pethahiah.
The twentieth lot fell to Jehezkel.

23:32 Hebrew *the Tent of Meeting and the sanctuary.*

17 The twenty-first lot fell to Jakin.
  The twenty-second lot fell to Gamul.
18 The twenty-third lot fell to Delaiah.
  The twenty-fourth lot fell to Maaziah.

19Each group carried out its duties in the house of the LORD according to the procedures established by their ancestor Aaron in obedience to the commands of the LORD, the God of Israel.

20These were the other family leaders descended from Levi:

From the descendants of Amram,
  the leader was Shebuel.*
From the descendants of Shebuel,
  the leader was Jehdeiah.
21 From the descendants of Rehabiah,
  the leader was Isshiah.
22 From the descendants of Izhar,
  the leader was Shelomith.*
From the descendants of Shelomith,
  the leader was Jahath.
23 From the descendants of Hebron, Jeriah was the leader,* Amariah was second-in-command, Jahaziel was third, and Jekameam was fourth.
24 From the descendants of Uzziel,
  the leader was Micah.
From the descendants of Micah, the leader was Shamir, 25along with Isshiah, the brother of Micah.
From the descendants of Isshiah,
  the leader was Zechariah.
26 From the descendants of Merari,
  the leaders were Mahli and Mushi.
From the descendants of Jaaziah,
  the leader was Beno.
27 From the descendants of Merari through Jaaziah, the leaders were Beno, Shoham, Zaccur, and Ibri.
28 From the descendants of Mahli, the leader was Eleazar, though he had no sons.
29 From the descendants of Kish, the leader was Jerahmeel.
30 From the descendants of Mushi, the leaders were Mahli, Eder, and Jerimoth.

These were the descendants of Levi in their various families. 31Like the descendants of Aaron, they were assigned to their duties by means of sacred lots, without regard to age or rank. It was done in the presence of King David, Zadok, Ahimelech, and the family leaders of the priests and the Levites.

CHAPTER 25

David and the army commanders then appointed men from the families of Asaph, Heman, and Jeduthun to proclaim God's messages to the accompaniment of harps, lyres, and cymbals. Here is a list of their names and their work:

2From the sons of Asaph, there were Zaccur, Joseph, Nethaniah, and Asarelah. They worked under the direction of their father, Asaph, who proclaimed God's messages by the king's orders. 3Jeduthun had six sons: Gedaliah, Zeri, Jeshaiah, Shimei,* Hashabiah, and Mattithiah. They worked under the direction of their father, Jeduthun, who proclaimed God's messages to the accompaniment of the harp, offering thanks and praise to the LORD. 4Heman's sons were Bukkiah, Mattaniah, Uzziel, Shubael,* Jerimoth, Hananiah, Hanani, Eliathah, Geddalti, Romamti-ezer, Joshbekashah, Mallothi, Hothir, and Mahazioth. 5All these were the sons of Heman, the king's seer, for God had honored him with fourteen sons and three daughters.

6All these men were under the direction of their fathers as they made music at the house of the LORD. Their responsibilities included the playing of cymbals, lyres, and harps at the house of God. Asaph, Jeduthun, and Heman reported directly to the king. 7They and their families were all trained in making music before the LORD, and each of them—288 in all—was an accomplished musician. 8The musicians were appointed to their particular term of service by means of sacred lots, without regard to whether they were young or old, teacher or student.

9   The first lot fell to Joseph of the Asaph clan and twelve of his sons and relatives.*
  The second lot fell to Gedaliah and twelve of his sons and relatives.

24:20 Hebrew Shubael (also in 24:20b), a variant name for Shebuel; compare 23:16 and 26:24.   24:22 Hebrew Shelomoth (also in 24:22b), a variant name for Shelomith; compare 23:18.   24:23 Hebrew From the descendants of Jeriah; compare 23:19.   25:3 As in one Hebrew manuscript and some Greek manuscripts (see also 25:17); most Hebrew manuscripts lack Shimei.   25:4 Hebrew Shebuel, a variant name for Shubael; compare 25:20.   25:9 As in Greek version; Hebrew lacks and twelve of his sons and relatives.

¹⁰ The third lot fell to Zaccur and twelve of his sons and relatives.

¹¹ The fourth lot fell to Zeri* and twelve of his sons and relatives.

¹² The fifth lot fell to Nethaniah and twelve of his sons and relatives.

¹³ The sixth lot fell to Bukkiah and twelve of his sons and relatives.

¹⁴ The seventh lot fell to Asarelah* and twelve of his sons and relatives.

¹⁵ The eighth lot fell to Jeshaiah and twelve of his sons and relatives.

¹⁶ The ninth lot fell to Mattaniah and twelve of his sons and relatives.

¹⁷ The tenth lot fell to Shimei and twelve of his sons and relatives.

¹⁸ The eleventh lot fell to Uzziel* and twelve of his sons and relatives.

¹⁹ The twelfth lot fell to Hashabiah and twelve of his sons and relatives.

²⁰ The thirteenth lot fell to Shubael and twelve of his sons and relatives.

²¹ The fourteenth lot fell to Mattithiah and twelve of his sons and relatives.

²² The fifteenth lot fell to Jerimoth* and twelve of his sons and relatives.

²³ The sixteenth lot fell to Hananiah and twelve of his sons and relatives.

²⁴ The seventeenth lot fell to Joshbeka-shah* and twelve of his sons and relatives.

²⁵ The eighteenth lot fell to Hanani and twelve of his sons and relatives.

²⁶ The nineteenth lot fell to Mallothi and twelve of his sons and relatives.

²⁷ The twentieth lot fell to Eliathah and twelve of his sons and relatives.

²⁸ The twenty-first lot fell to Hothir and twelve of his sons and relatives.

²⁹ The twenty-second lot fell to Geddalti* and twelve of his sons and relatives.

³⁰ The twenty-third lot fell to Mahazioth and twelve of his sons and relatives.

³¹ The twenty-fourth lot fell to Romamti-ezer and twelve of his sons and relatives.

CHAPTER 26

These are the divisions of the gatekeepers:

From the Korahites, there was Meshel-emiah son of Kore, of the family of Asaph. ²The sons of Meshelemiah were Zechariah (the oldest), Jediael (the second), Zebadiah (the third), Jathniel (the fourth), ³Elam (the fifth), Jeho-hanan (the sixth), and Eliehoenai (the seventh).

⁴The sons of Obed-edom, also gatekeepers, were Shemaiah (the oldest), Jehozabad (the second), Joah (the third), Sacar (the fourth), Nethanel (the fifth), ⁵Ammiel (the sixth), Issachar (the seventh), and Peullethai (the eighth). God had richly blessed Obed-edom.

⁶Obed-edom's son Shemaiah had sons with great ability who earned positions of great authority in the clan. ⁷Their names were Othni, Rephael, Obed, and Elzabad. Their relatives, Elihu and Semakiah, were also very capable men.

⁸All of these descendants of Obed-edom, including their sons and grand-sons—sixty-two of them in all—were very capable men, well qualified for their work.

⁹Meshelemiah's eighteen sons and relatives were also very capable men.

¹⁰Hosah, of the Merari clan, appointed Shimri as the leader among his sons, though he was not the oldest. ¹¹His other sons included Hilkiah (the second), Tebaliah (the third), and Zechariah (the fourth). Hosah's sons and relatives, who served as gate-keepers, numbered thirteen in all.

¹²These divisions of the gatekeepers were named for their family leaders, and like the other Levites, they served at the house of the LORD. ¹³They were assigned by families for guard duty at the various gates, with-out regard to age or training, for it was all decided by means of sacred lots.

¹⁴The responsibility for the east gate went to Meshelemiah* and his group. The north gate was assigned to his son Zecha-riah, a man of unusual wisdom. ¹⁵The south gate went to Obed-edom, and his sons were put in charge of the storehouses. ¹⁶Shuppim and Hosah were assigned the west gate and the gateway leading up to the Temple.* Guard duties were divided evenly. ¹⁷Six Levites were assigned each day to the east gate, four to the north gate,

25:11 Hebrew Izri, a variant name for Zeri; compare 25:3.   25:14 Hebrew Jesharelah, a variant name for Asarelah; compare 25:2.
25:18 Hebrew Azarel, a variant name for Uzziel; compare 25:4.   25:22 Hebrew Jeremoth, a variant name for Jerimoth; compare 25:4.
25:24 Hebrew Joshbekasha, a variant name for Joshbekashah; compare 25:4.   25:29 Hebrew Giddalti, a variant name for Geddalti;
compare 25:4.   26:14 Hebrew Shelemiah, a variant name for Meshelemiah; compare 26:2.   26:16 Or the gate of Shalleketh on the
upper road (also in 26:18). The meaning of the Hebrew is uncertain.

four to the south gate, and two to each of the storehouses. [18]Six were assigned each day to the west gate, four to the gateway leading up to the Temple, and two to the courtyard.*

[19]These were the divisions of the gatekeepers from the clans of Korah and Merari.

[20]Other Levites, led by Ahijah, were in charge of the treasuries of the house of God and the storerooms. [21]From the family of Libni* in the clan of Gershon, Jehiel* was the leader. [22]The sons of Jehiel, Zetham and his brother Joel, were in charge of the treasuries of the house of the LORD.

[23]These are the leaders that descended from Amram, Izhar, Hebron, and Uzziel:

[24]From the clan of Amram, Shebuel was a descendant of Gershom son of Moses. He was the chief officer of the treasuries. [25]His relatives through Eliezer were Rehabiah, Jeshaiah, Joram, Zicri, and Shelomoth.

[26]Shelomoth and his relatives were in charge of the treasuries that held all the things dedicated to the LORD by King David, the family leaders, and the generals and captains and other officers of the army. [27]These men had dedicated some of the plunder they had gained in battle to maintain the house of the LORD. [28]Shelomoth and his relatives also cared for the items dedicated to the LORD by Samuel the seer, Saul son of Kish, Abner son of Ner, and Joab son of Zeruiah. All the other dedicated items were in their care, too.

[29]From the clan of Izhar came Kenaniah. He and his sons were appointed to serve as public administrators and judges throughout Israel.

[30]From the clan of Hebron came Hashabiah. He and his relatives—seventeen hundred capable men—were put in charge of the Israelite lands west of the Jordan River. They were responsible for all matters related to the things of the LORD and the service of the king in that area.

[31]Also from the clan of Hebron came Jeriah,* who was the leader of the Hebronites according to the genealogical records. (In the fortieth year of David's reign, a search was made in the records, and capable men from the clan of Hebron were found at Jazer in the land of Gilead.) [32]There were twenty-seven hundred capable men among the relatives of Jeriah. King David sent them to the east side of the Jordan River and put them in charge of the tribes of Reuben and Gad and the half-tribe of Manasseh. They were responsible for all matters related to the things of God and the service of the king.

CHAPTER 27

This is the list of Israelite generals and captains, and their officers, who served the king by supervising the army divisions that were on duty each month of the year. Each division served for one month and had twenty-four thousand troops.

[2]Jashobeam son of Zabdiel was commander of the first division, which was on duty during the first month. There were twenty-four thousand troops in his division. [3]He was a descendant of Perez and was in charge of all the army officers for the first month.

[4]Dodai, a descendant of Ahoah, was commander of the second division, which was on duty during the second month. There were twenty-four thousand troops in his division, and Mikloth was his chief officer.

[5]Benaiah son of Jehoiada the priest was commander of the third division, which was on duty during the third month. There were twenty-four thousand troops in his division. [6]This was the Benaiah who commanded David's elite military group known as the Thirty. His son Ammizabad was his chief officer.

[7]Asahel, the brother of Joab, was commander of the fourth division, which was on duty during the fourth month. There were twenty-four thousand troops in his division. Asahel was succeeded by his son Zebadiah.

[8]Shammah* the Izrahite was commander of the fifth division, which was on duty during the fifth month. There were twenty-four thousand troops in his division.

[9]Ira son of Ikkesh from Tekoa was

26:18 Or *the colonnade.* The meaning of the Hebrew is uncertain.   26:21a Hebrew *Ladan,* another name for Libni; compare 6:17.
26:21b Hebrew *Jehieli* (also in 26:22), a variant name for Jehiel; compare 23:8.   26:31 Hebrew *Jerijah,* a variant name for Jeriah; compare 23:19.   27:8 Hebrew *Shamhuth,* another name for Shammah; compare 11:27 and 2 Sam 23:25.

commander of the sixth division, which was on duty during the sixth month. There were twenty-four thousand troops in his division.

¹⁰Helez, a descendant of Ephraim from Pelon, was commander of the seventh division, which was on duty during the seventh month. There were twenty-four thousand troops in his division.

¹¹Sibbecai, a descendant of Zerah from Hushah, was commander of the eighth division, which was on duty during the eighth month. There were twenty-four thousand troops in his division.

¹²Abiezer from Anathoth in the territory of Benjamin was commander of the ninth division, which was on duty during the ninth month. There were twenty-four thousand troops in his division.

¹³Maharai, a descendant of Zerah from Netophah, was commander of the tenth division, which was on duty during the tenth month. There were twenty-four thousand troops in his division.

¹⁴Benaiah from Pirathon in Ephraim was commander of the eleventh division, which was on duty during the eleventh month. There were twenty-four thousand troops in his division.

¹⁵Heled,* a descendant of Othniel from Netophah, was commander of the twelfth division, which was on duty during the twelfth month. There were twenty-four thousand troops in his division.

¹⁶The following were the tribes of Israel and their leaders:

Tribe	Leader
Reuben	Eliezer son of Zicri
Simeon	Shephatiah son of Maacah
¹⁷ Levi	Hashabiah son of Kemuel
Aaron (the priests)	Zadok
¹⁸ Judah	Elihu (a brother of David)
Issachar	Omri son of Michael
¹⁹ Zebulun	Ishmaiah son of Obadiah
Naphtali	Jeremoth son of Azriel
²⁰ Ephraim	Hoshea son of Azaziah
Manasseh (west)	Joel son of Pedaiah
²¹ Manasseh (east*)	Iddo son of Zechariah
Benjamin	Jaasiel son of Abner
²² Dan	Azarel son of Jeroham

These were the leaders of the tribes of Israel.

²³When David took his census, he did not count those who were younger than twenty years of age, because the LORD had promised to make the Israelites as numerous as the stars in heaven. ²⁴Joab began the census but never finished it because the anger of God broke out against Israel. The final total was never recorded in King David's official records.

²⁵Azmaveth son of Adiel was in charge of the palace treasuries.

Jonathan son of Uzziah was in charge of the regional treasuries throughout the towns, villages, and fortresses of Israel.

²⁶Ezri son of Kelub was in charge of the field workers who farmed the king's lands.

²⁷Shimei from Ramah was in charge of the king's vineyards.

Zabdi from Shepham was responsible for the grapes and the supplies of wine.

²⁸Baal-hanan from Geder was in charge of the king's olive groves and sycamore-fig trees in the foothills of Judah.*

Joash was responsible for the supplies of olive oil.

²⁹Shitrai from Sharon was in charge of the cattle on the Sharon Plain.

Shaphat son of Adlai was responsible for the cattle in the valleys.

³⁰Obil the Ishmaelite was in charge of the camels.

Jehdeiah from Meronoth was in charge of the donkeys.

³¹Jaziz the Hagrite was in charge of the king's sheep.

All these officials were overseers of King David's property.

³²Jonathan, David's uncle, was a wise counselor to the king, a man of great insight, and a scribe. Jehiel the Hacmonite was responsible to teach the king's sons. ³³Ahithophel was the royal adviser. Hushai the Arkite was the king's friend. ³⁴Ahithophel was succeeded by Jehoiada son of Benaiah and by Abiathar. Joab was commander of the Israelite army.

27:15 Hebrew *Heldai,* a variant name for Heled; compare 11:30 and 2 Sam 23:29.　　27:21 Hebrew *in Gilead.*　　27:28 Hebrew *the Shephelah.*

APRIL 19 ☐ DAY 110
1 CHRONICLES 28–29
David's Final Words and Deeds

 OVERVIEW Compare the opening chapters of David's life with the closing ones, and you will come to a startling conclusion: David ended his life the same way he began it—with humble confidence in God. In spite of his great and numerous accomplishments, he never let greatness go to his head. David's final words to Solomon and the nation reflect the same wholehearted devotion to God that he first expressed as a youthful shepherd in the pasturelands of Judea. With the dream of his heart (building a temple) entrusted to his son and the tokens of God's blessing all around him, David died "at a ripe old age, having enjoyed long life, wealth, and honor. Then his son Solomon ruled in his place" (29:28).

Chapter 28		Chapter 29	
David's Final Words to Israel	to Solomon	David's Final Act of Worship	David's Fitting Epitaph
1 8	9 21	1 21	22 30
Advice		Adoration	Acclaim

 YOUR DAILY WALK Close your study of David's life in 1 Chronicles by reading his prayer slowly and prayerfully. Is his expression of thanksgiving to God the prayer of your heart?

The person who forgets the language of gratitude can never be on speaking terms with happiness.

"Yours, O LORD, is the greatness, the power, the glory, the victory, and the majesty. Everything in the heavens and on earth is yours, O LORD, and this is your kingdom. We adore you as the one who is over all things. Riches and honor come from you alone, for you rule over everything. Power and might are in your hand, and it is at your discretion that people are made great and given strength. O our God, we thank you and praise your glorious name" (29:11-13).

David offered this prayer in gratitude for the generous, voluntary contributions of the congregation for the service of God's house. Why not prepare a special offering for your church this weekend?

 INSIGHT All That Glitters Is Not Gold (It May Be Silver!)
Don't miss the incredible statistics (29:4-7) that describe the materials David set aside for building the Temple: 300 tons of gold, 675 tons of silver, and nearly 4,000 tons of iron! Find the current price of gold and silver, and calculate what those tons of precious metals would be worth today!

CHAPTER 28

David summoned all his officials to Jerusalem—the leaders of the tribes, the commanders of the twelve army divisions, the other generals and captains, the overseers of the royal property and livestock, the palace officials, the mighty men, and all the other warriors in the kingdom. ²David rose and stood before them and addressed them as follows: "My brothers and my people! It was my desire to build a temple where the Ark of the LORD's covenant, God's footstool, could rest permanently. I made the necessary preparations for building it, ³but God said to me, 'You must not build a temple to honor my name, for you are a warrior and have shed much blood.'

⁴"Yet the LORD, the God of Israel, has chosen me from among all my father's family to be king over Israel forever. For he has chosen the tribe of Judah to rule, and from among the families of Judah, he chose my father's family. And from among my father's sons, the LORD was pleased to make me king over all Israel. ⁵And from among my sons—for the LORD has given

me many children—he chose Solomon to succeed me on the throne of his kingdom of Israel. [6]He said to me, 'Your son Solomon will build my Temple and its courtyards, for I have chosen him as my son, and I will be his father. [7]And if he continues to obey my commands and regulations as he does now, I will make his kingdom last forever.' [8]So now, with God as our witness, I give you this charge for all Israel, the LORD's assembly: Be careful to obey all the commands of the LORD your God, so that you may possess this good land and leave it to your children as a permanent inheritance.

[9]"And Solomon, my son, get to know the God of your ancestors. Worship and serve him with your whole heart and with a willing mind. For the LORD sees every heart and understands and knows every plan and thought. If you seek him, you will find him. But if you forsake him, he will reject you forever. [10]So take this seriously. The LORD has chosen you to build a Temple as his sanctuary. Be strong, and do the work."

[11]Then David gave Solomon the plans for the Temple and its surroundings, including the treasuries, the upstairs rooms, the inner rooms, and the inner sanctuary where the Ark's cover—the place of atonement—would be kept. [12]David also gave Solomon all the plans he had in mind* for the courtyards of the LORD's Temple, the outside rooms, the treasuries of God's Temple, and the rooms for the dedicated gifts. [13]The king also gave Solomon the instructions concerning the work of the various divisions of priests and Levites in the Temple of the LORD. And he gave specifications for the items in the LORD's Temple which were to be used for worship and sacrifice.

[14]David gave instructions regarding how much gold and silver should be used to make the necessary items. [15]He told Solomon the amount of gold needed for the gold lampstands and lamps, and the amount of silver for the silver lampstands and lamps, depending on how each would be used. [16]He designated the amount of gold for the table on which the Bread of the Presence would be placed and the amount of silver for other tables.

[17]David also designated the amount of gold for the solid gold meat hooks used to handle the sacrificial meat and for the ba-

sins, pitchers, and dishes, as well as the amount of silver for every dish. [18]Finally, he designated the amount of refined gold for the altar of incense and for the gold cherubim, whose wings were stretched out over the Ark of the LORD's covenant. [19]"Every part of this plan," David told Solomon, "was given to me in writing from the hand of the LORD.*"

[20]Then David continued, "Be strong and courageous, and do the work. Don't be afraid or discouraged by the size of the task, for the LORD God, my God, is with you. He will not fail you or forsake you. He will see to it that all the work related to the Temple of the LORD is finished correctly. [21]The various divisions of priests and Levites will serve in the Temple of God. Others with skills of every kind will volunteer, and the leaders and the entire nation are at your command."

CHAPTER 29

Then King David turned to the entire assembly and said, "My son Solomon, whom God has chosen to be the next king of Israel, is still young and inexperienced. The work ahead of him is enormous, for the Temple he will build is not just another building—it is for the LORD God himself! [2]Using every resource at my command, I have gathered as much as I could for building the Temple of my God. Now there is enough gold, silver, bronze, iron, and wood, as well as great quantities of onyx, other precious stones, costly jewels, and all kinds of fine stone and marble. [3]And now because of my devotion to the Temple of my God, I am giving all of my own private treasures of gold and silver to help in the construction. This is in addition to the building materials I have already collected for his holy Temple. [4]I am donating more than 112 tons of gold* from Ophir and over 262 tons of refined silver* to be used for overlaying the walls of the buildings [5]and for the other gold and silver work to be done by the craftsmen. Now then, who will follow my example? Who is willing to give offerings to the LORD today?"

[6]Then the family leaders, the leaders of the tribes of Israel, the generals and captains of the army, and the king's administrative officers all gave willingly. [7]For

28:12 Or *the plans of the spirit that was with him.*   **28:19** Or *was written under the direction of the LORD.*   **29:4a** Hebrew *3,000 talents* [102 metric tons] *of gold.*   **29:4b** Hebrew *7,000 talents* [238 metric tons] *of silver.*

the construction of the Temple of God, they gave almost 188 tons of gold,* 10,000 gold coins,* about 375 tons of silver,* about 675 tons of bronze,* and about 3,750 tons of iron.* ⁸They also contributed numerous precious stones, which were deposited in the treasury of the house of the LORD under the care of Jehiel, a descendant of Gershon. ⁹The people rejoiced over the offerings, for they had given freely and wholeheartedly to the LORD, and King David was filled with joy.

¹⁰Then David praised the LORD in the presence of the whole assembly: "O LORD, the God of our ancestor Israel,* may you be praised forever and ever! ¹¹Yours, O LORD, is the greatness, the power, the glory, the victory, and the majesty. Everything in the heavens and on earth is yours, O LORD, and this is your kingdom. We adore you as the one who is over all things. ¹²Riches and honor come from you alone, for you rule over everything. Power and might are in your hand, and it is at your discretion that people are made great and given strength.

¹³"O our God, we thank you and praise your glorious name! ¹⁴But who am I, and who are my people, that we could give anything to you? Everything we have has come from you, and we give you only what you have already given us! ¹⁵We are here for only a moment, visitors and strangers in the land as our ancestors were before us. Our days on earth are like a shadow, gone so soon without a trace.

¹⁶"O LORD our God, even these materials that we have gathered to build a Temple to honor your holy name come from you! It all belongs to you! ¹⁷I know, my God, that you examine our hearts and rejoice when you find integrity there. You know I have done all this with good motives, and I have watched your people offer their gifts willingly and joyously.

¹⁸"O LORD, the God of our ancestors Abraham, Isaac, and Israel, make your people always want to obey you. See to it that their love for you never changes. ¹⁹Give my son Solomon the wholehearted desire to obey all your commands, decrees, and principles, and to build this Temple, for which I have made all these preparations."

²⁰Then David said to the whole assembly, "Give praise to the LORD your God!" And the entire assembly praised the LORD, the God of their ancestors, and they bowed low and knelt before the LORD and the king.

²¹The next day they brought a thousand bulls, a thousand rams, and a thousand male lambs as burnt offerings to the LORD. They also brought drink offerings and many other sacrifices on behalf of Israel. ²²They feasted and drank in the LORD's presence with great joy that day.

And again they crowned David's son Solomon as their new king. They anointed him before the LORD as their leader, and they anointed Zadok as their priest. ²³So Solomon took the throne of the LORD in place of his father, David, and he prospered greatly, and all Israel obeyed him. ²⁴All the royal officials, the army commanders, and the sons of King David pledged their loyalty to King Solomon. ²⁵And the LORD exalted Solomon so the entire nation of Israel stood in awe of him, and he gave Solomon even greater wealth and honor than his father.

²⁶So David son of Jesse reigned over all Israel. ²⁷He ruled Israel for forty years in all, seven years from Hebron and thirty-three years from Jerusalem. ²⁸He died at a ripe old age, having enjoyed long life, wealth, and honor. Then his son Solomon ruled in his place. ²⁹All the events of King David's reign, from beginning to end, are written in *The Record of Samuel the Seer, The Record of Nathan the Prophet,* and *The Record of Gad the Seer.* ³⁰These accounts include the mighty deeds of his reign and everything that happened to him and to Israel and to all the surrounding kingdoms.

29:7a Hebrew *5,000 talents* [170 metric tons] *of gold.* **29:7b** Hebrew *10,000 darics* [a Persian coin] *of gold,* about 185 pounds or 84 kilograms in weight. **29:7c** Hebrew *10,000 talents* [340 metric tons] *of silver.* **29:7d** Hebrew *18,000 talents* [612 metric tons] *of bronze.* **29:7e** Hebrew *100,000 talents* [3,400 metric tons] *of iron.* **29:10** *Israel* is the name that God gave to Jacob.

2 Chronicles

THE BOOK of 2 Chronicles begins with the construction of Solomon's Temple and concludes with Cyrus's edict to rebuild the Temple more than four hundred years later! In between, 2 Chronicles is the story of fading glory—the downward spiral of the kingdom of Judah in spite of the energetic efforts of a handful of reformers. The Temple and Temple worship remain central throughout the book, although the people stray far from it and ultimately pay the price for their waywardness.

Focus	Descendants of King David								
Divisions	Solomon's Magnificent Temple	Solomon's Worship and Works	Rebellion against Rehoboam	Reigns of Abijah and Asa	Reform under Jehoshaphat	Reigns of Jehoram to Amaziah	Reigns of Uzziah to Ahaz	Reform under Hezekiah	Reigns of Judah's Last Kings
	1 5	6 9	10 12	13 16	17 20	21 25	26 28	29 32	33 36
Topics	Solomon's Glory				Judah's Decline				
	Construction of the Temple				Desecration of the Temple				
Place	Southern Kingdom of Judah								
Time	About 40 Years				About 400 Years				

APRIL 20 ☐ DAY 111
2 CHRONICLES 1–5
Solomon's Magnificent Temple

OVERVIEW Solomon's wealth and wisdom are legendary. But they pale by comparison to the one project with which history would later connect his name: Solomon's Temple. In only seven years, Solomon uses the efforts of 153,000 workers to fashion tons of gold and silver, brass and cedar, into a breathtaking abode for the God who is "greater than any other" (2:5). When at last the task is complete, the glory of God fills the Temple with such radiance that even the people who work there must temporarily evacuate—a token of God's pleasure with the finished project.

Chapter 1	Chapters 2–3	Chapter 4	Chapter 5
Solomon's Wealth and Wisdom	Solomon's Wondrous Temple Fashioned	Furnished	Filled
Promise from God	Place to Worship God		

YOUR DAILY WALK What is your reaction when you encounter a wealthy businessman? . . . a wealthy politician? . . . a wealthy Christian? . . . a wealthy minister? Do the terms *rich* and *Christian* seem contradictory?

Don't knock the rich. When was the last time you were hired by somebody poor?

The real issue for a Christian living in an age of plenty is not how much money he or she has. Christians can be rich or poor, in or out of the will of God. The rich man in James 5 is not so much a man who possesses much as he is a man who is preoccupied with what he possesses. King Solomon had much, but he recognized it all as a gift from God (1:11-12), which, if used wisely, would become a constant source of blessing to himself and others.

How can you use a part of your material blessings from God to become in turn a blessing in someone else's life today? To be truly rich, reach out!

INSIGHT Temples Old and New
When you come across the word *temple* in your Bible, be sure to check the context. Is the author speaking of
- Solomon's Temple?
- Zerubbabel's Temple? (Ezra 3:8—the one built to replace Solomon's Temple after Nebuchadnezzar destroyed it in 586 B.C.)
- Herod's Temple? (Matthew 24:1; John 2:20—Zerubbabel's Temple expanded and elaborated that stood in Jesus' day)
- Ezekiel's Temple? (Ezekiel 40–48—a temple as yet unbuilt whose details were given to Ezekiel in a vision)
- Diana's temple? (Acts 19:27—a pagan shrine in Ephesus and one of the seven wonders of the ancient world)

CHAPTER 1

Solomon, the son of King David, now took firm control of the kingdom, for the LORD his God was with him and made him very powerful. ²He called together all Israel—the generals and captains of the army, the judges, and all the political and clan leaders. ³Then Solomon led the entire assembly to the hill at Gibeon where God's Tabernacle* was located. This was the Tabernacle that Moses, the LORD's servant, had constructed in the wilderness. ⁴David had already moved the Ark of God from Kiriath-jearim to the special tent he had prepared for it in Jerusalem. ⁵But the bronze altar made by Bezalel son of Uri and grandson of Hur was still at Gibeon in front of the Tabernacle of the LORD. So Solomon and the people gathered in front of it to consult the LORD. ⁶There in front of the Tabernacle, Solomon went up to the bronze altar in the LORD's presence and sacrificed a thousand burnt offerings on it.

⁷That night God appeared to Solomon in a dream and said, "What do you want? Ask, and I will give it to you!"

⁸Solomon replied to God, "You have been so faithful and kind to my father, David, and now you have made me king in his place. ⁹Now, LORD God, please keep your promise to David my father, for you have made me king over a people as numerous as the dust of the earth! ¹⁰Give me wisdom and knowledge to rule them properly, for who is able to govern this great nation of yours?"

¹¹God said to Solomon, "Because your greatest desire is to help your people, and you did not ask for personal wealth and honor or the death of your enemies or even a long life, but rather you asked for wisdom and knowledge to properly govern my people, ¹²I will certainly give you the wisdom and knowledge you requested. And I will also give you riches, wealth, and honor such as no other king has ever had before you or will ever have again!" ¹³Then Solomon returned to Jerusalem from the Tabernacle at the hill of Gibeon, and he reigned over Israel.

¹⁴Solomon built up a huge military force, which included fourteen hundred chariots and twelve thousand horses.* He stationed many of them in the chariot cities, and some near him in Jerusalem. ¹⁵During Solomon's reign, silver and gold were as plentiful in Jerusalem as stones. And valuable cedarwood was as common as the sycamore wood that grows in the foothills of Judah.* ¹⁶Solomon's horses were imported

from Egypt* and from Cilicia*; the king's traders acquired them from Cilicia at the standard price. ¹⁷At that time, Egyptian chariots delivered to Jerusalem could be purchased for 600 pieces of silver,* and horses could be bought for 150 pieces of silver.* Many of these were then resold to the kings of the Hittites and the kings of Aram.

CHAPTER 2

Solomon now decided that the time had come to build a Temple for the LORD and a royal palace for himself. ²He enlisted a force of 70,000 common laborers, 80,000 stonecutters in the hill country, and 3,600 foremen. ³Solomon also sent this message to King Hiram* at Tyre:

"Send me cedar logs like the ones that were supplied to my father, David, when he was building his palace. ⁴I am about to build a Temple to honor the name of the LORD my God. It will be a place set apart to burn incense and sweet spices before him, to display the special sacrificial bread, and to sacrifice burnt offerings each morning and evening, on the Sabbaths, at new moon celebrations, and at the other appointed festivals of the LORD our God. He has commanded Israel to do these things forever.

⁵"This will be a magnificent Temple because our God is an awesome God, greater than any other. ⁶But who can really build him a worthy home? Not even the highest heavens can contain him! So who am I to consider building a Temple for him, except as a place to burn sacrifices to him?

⁷"So send me a master craftsman who can work with gold, silver, bronze, and iron; someone who is expert at dyeing purple, scarlet, and blue cloth; and a skilled engraver who can work with the craftsmen of Judah and Jerusalem who were selected by my father, David. ⁸Also send me cedar, cypress, and almug* logs from Lebanon, for I know that your men are without equal at cutting timber. I will send my men to help them. ⁹An immense amount of timber will be

1:3 Hebrew *Tent of Meeting*; also in 1:6, 13.   **1:14** Or *12,000 charioteers*.   **1:15** Hebrew *the Shephelah*.   **1:16a** Possibly *Muzur*, a district near Cilicia; also in 1:17.   **1:16b** Hebrew *Kue*, probably another name for Cilicia.   **1:17a** Hebrew *600 shekels of silver*, about 15 pounds or 6.8 kilograms in weight.   **1:17b** Hebrew *150 shekels*, about 3.8 pounds or 1.7 kilograms in weight.   **2:3** Hebrew *Huram*, a variant name for Hiram; also in 2:11, 12.   **2:8** Hebrew *algum*, a variant name for almug; compare 9:10-11 and parallel text at 1 Kgs 10:11-12.

needed, for the Temple I am going to build will be very large and magnificent. ¹⁰I will pay your men 100,000 bushels of crushed wheat, 100,000 bushels of barley,* 110,000 gallons of wine, and 110,000 gallons of olive oil.*"

¹¹King Hiram sent this letter of reply to Solomon:

"It is because the LORD loves his people that he has made you their king! ¹²Blessed be the LORD, the God of Israel, who made the heavens and the earth! He has given David a wise son, gifted with skill and understanding, who will build a Temple for the LORD and a royal palace for himself.

¹³"I am sending you a master craftsman named Huram-abi. He is a brilliant man, ¹⁴the son of a woman from Dan in Israel; his father is from Tyre. He is skillful at making things from gold, silver, bronze, and iron. He also knows all about stonework, carpentry, and weaving. He is an expert in dyeing purple, blue, and scarlet cloth and in working with linen. He is also an engraver and can follow any design given to him. He will work with your craftsmen and those appointed by my lord David, your father.

¹⁵"Send along the wheat, barley, olive oil, and wine that you mentioned. ¹⁶We will cut whatever timber you need from the Lebanon mountains and will float the logs in rafts down the coast of the Mediterranean Sea to Joppa. From there you can transport the logs up to Jerusalem."

¹⁷Solomon took a census of all foreigners in the land of Israel, like the census his father had taken, and he counted 153,600. ¹⁸He enlisted 70,000 of them as common laborers, 80,000 as stonecutters in the hill country, and 3,600 as foremen.

CHAPTER 3

So Solomon began to build the Temple of the LORD in Jerusalem on Mount Moriah, where the LORD had appeared to Solomon's father, King David. The Temple was built on the threshing floor of Araunah* the Jebusite, the site that David had selected. ²The construction began in midspring,* during the fourth year of Solomon's reign.

³The foundation for the Temple of God was ninety feet long and thirty feet wide.* ⁴The foyer at the front of the Temple was thirty feet wide, running across the entire width of the Temple. The inner walls of the foyer and the ceiling were overlaid with pure gold. The roof of the foyer was thirty feet* high.

⁵The main room of the Temple was paneled with cypress wood, overlaid with pure gold, and decorated with carvings of palm trees and chains. ⁶The walls of the Temple were decorated with beautiful jewels and with pure gold from the land of Parvaim. ⁷All the walls, beams, doors, and thresholds throughout the Temple were overlaid with gold, and figures of cherubim were carved on the walls.

⁸The Most Holy Place was thirty feet wide, corresponding to the width of the Temple, and it was also thirty feet deep. Its interior was overlaid with about twenty-three tons* of pure gold. ⁹They used gold nails that weighed about twenty ounces* each. The walls of the upper rooms were also overlaid with pure gold.

¹⁰Solomon made two figures shaped like cherubim and overlaid them with gold. These were placed in the Most Holy Place. ¹¹The total wingspan of the two cherubim standing side by side was 30 feet. One wing of the first figure was 7½ feet long, and it touched the Temple wall. The other wing, also 7½ feet long, touched one of the wings of the second figure. ¹²In the same way, the second figure had one wing 7½ feet long that touched the opposite wall. The other wing, also 7½ feet long, touched the wing of the first figure. ¹³So the wingspan of both cherubim together was 30 feet. They both stood and faced out toward the main room of the Temple. ¹⁴Across the entrance of the Most Holy Place, Solomon hung a curtain made of fine linen and blue, purple, and scarlet yarn, with figures of cherubim embroidered on it.

¹⁵For the front of the Temple, Solomon

2:10a Hebrew *20,000 cors* [3,640 kiloliters] *of crushed wheat, 20,000 cors of barley.*   2:10b Hebrew *20,000 baths* [420 kiloliters] *of wine, and 20,000 baths of olive oil.*   3:1 Hebrew reads *Ornan,* another name for Araunah; compare 2 Sam 24:16.   3:2 Hebrew *on the second day of the second month.* This day of the Hebrew lunar calendar occurs in April or early May.   3:3 Hebrew *60 cubits* [27 meters] *long and 20 cubits* [9 meters] *wide.* In this chapter, the distance measures are calculated from the Hebrew cubit at a ratio of 18 inches or 45 centimeters per cubit.   3:4 As in some Greek and Syriac manuscripts, which read *20 cubits* [9 meters]; Hebrew reads *120 cubits,* which is 180 feet or 54 meters.   3:8 Hebrew *600 talents* [20.4 metric tons].   3:9 Hebrew *50 shekels* [570 grams].

made two pillars that were 27 feet* tall, each topped by a capital extending upward another 7½ feet. ¹⁶He made a network of interwoven chains and used them to decorate the tops of the pillars. He also made one hundred decorative pomegranates and attached them to the chains. ¹⁷Then he set up the two pillars at the entrance of the Temple, one to the south of the entrance and the other to the north. He named the one on the south Jakin, and the one on the north Boaz.*

CHAPTER 4

Solomon also made a bronze altar 30 feet long, 30 feet wide, and 15 feet high.* ²Then he cast a large round tank, 15 feet across from rim to rim; it was called the Sea. It was 7½ feet deep and about 45 feet in circumference. ³The Sea was encircled just below its rim by two rows of figures that resembled oxen. There were about six oxen per foot* all the way around, and they had been cast as part of the tank.

⁴The Sea rested on a base of twelve bronze oxen, all facing outward. Three faced north, three faced west, three faced south, and three faced east. ⁵The walls of the Sea were about three inches* thick, and its rim flared out like a cup and resembled a lily blossom. It could hold about 16,500 gallons* of water.

⁶He also made ten basins for water to wash the offerings, five to the south of the Sea and five to the north. The priests used the Sea itself, and not the basins, for their own washing.

⁷Solomon then cast ten gold lampstands according to the specifications that had been given and put them in the Temple. Five were placed against the south wall, and five were placed against the north wall. ⁸He also built ten tables and placed them in the Temple, five along the south wall and five along the north wall. Then he molded one hundred gold basins.

⁹Solomon also built a courtyard for the priests and the large outer courtyard. He made doors for the courtyard entrances and overlaid them with bronze. ¹⁰The Sea was placed near the southeast corner of the Temple.

¹¹Huram-abi also made the necessary pots, shovels, and basins.

So at last Huram-abi completed everything King Solomon had assigned him to make for the Temple of God:

¹² two pillars,
two bowl-shaped capitals on top of the pillars,
two networks of chains that decorated the capitals,
¹³ four hundred pomegranates that hung from the chains on the capitals (two rows of pomegranates for each of the chain networks that were hung around the capitals on top of the pillars),
¹⁴ the water carts holding the basins,
¹⁵ the Sea and the twelve oxen under it,
¹⁶ the pots, the shovels, the meat hooks, and all the related utensils.

Huram-abi made all these things out of burnished bronze for the Temple of the LORD, just as King Solomon had requested. ¹⁷The king had them cast in clay molds in the Jordan Valley between Succoth and Zarethan.* ¹⁸Such great quantities of bronze were used that its weight could not be determined.

¹⁹So Solomon made all the furnishings for the Temple of God:

the gold altar;
the tables for the Bread of the Presence;
²⁰ the lampstands and their lamps of pure gold to burn in front of the Most Holy Place as prescribed;
²¹ the flower decorations, lamps, and tongs, all of pure gold;
²² the lamp snuffers, basins, dishes, and firepans, all of pure gold;
the doors for the entrances to the Most Holy Place and the main room of the Temple, overlaid with gold.

CHAPTER 5

When Solomon had finished all the work related to building the Temple of the LORD, he brought in the gifts dedicated by his father, King David, including all the silver and gold and all the utensils. These were stored in the treasuries of the Temple of God.

3:15 As in Syriac version (see also 1 Kgs 7:15; 2 Kgs 25:17; Jer 52:21), which reads *18 cubits* [8.1 meters]; Hebrew reads *35 cubits,* which is 52.5 feet or 15.8 meters.   **3:17** Jakin probably means "he establishes"; Boaz probably means "in him is strength."   **4:1** Hebrew *20 cubits* [9 meters] *long, 20 cubits wide, and 10 cubits* [4.5 meters] *high.* In this chapter, the distance measures are calculated from the Hebrew cubit at a ratio of 18 inches or 45 centimeters per cubit.   **4:3** Or *20 oxen per meter;* Hebrew reads *10 per cubit.*   **4:5a** Hebrew *a handbreadth* [8 centimeters].   **4:5b** Hebrew *3,000 baths* [63 kiloliters].   **4:17** As in parallel text at 1 Kgs 7:46; Hebrew reads *Zeredah.*

²Solomon then summoned the leaders of all the tribes and families of Israel to assemble in Jerusalem. They were to bring the Ark of the LORD's covenant from its location in the City of David, also known as Zion, to its new place in the Temple. ³They all assembled before the king at the annual Festival of Shelters in early autumn.* ⁴When all the leaders of Israel arrived, the Levites moved the Ark, ⁵along with the special tent* and all its sacred utensils. The Levitical priests carried them all up to the Temple. ⁶King Solomon and the entire community of Israel sacrificed sheep and oxen before the Ark in such numbers that no one could keep count!

⁷Then the priests carried the Ark of the LORD's covenant into the inner sanctuary of the Temple—the Most Holy Place—and placed it beneath the wings of the cherubim. ⁸The cherubim spread their wings out over the Ark, forming a canopy over the Ark and its carrying poles. ⁹These poles were so long that their ends could be seen from the front entrance of the Temple's main room—the Holy Place—but not from outside it. They are still there to this day. ¹⁰Nothing was in the Ark except the two stone tablets that Moses had placed there at Mount Sinai,* when the LORD made a covenant with the people of Israel after they left Egypt.

¹¹Then the priests left the Holy Place. All the priests who were present had purified themselves, whether or not they were on duty that day. ¹²And the Levites who were musicians—Asaph, Heman, Jeduthun, and all their sons and brothers—were dressed in fine linen robes and stood at the east side of the altar playing cymbals, harps, and lyres. They were joined by 120 priests who were playing trumpets. ¹³The trumpeters and singers performed together in unison to praise and give thanks to the LORD. Accompanied by trumpets, cymbals, and other instruments, they raised their voices and praised the LORD with these words:

"He is so good!
His faithful love endures forever!"

At that moment a cloud filled the Temple of the LORD. ¹⁴The priests could not continue their work because the glorious presence of the LORD filled the Temple of God.

5:3 Hebrew *at the festival that is in the seventh month.* The Festival of Shelters began on the fifteenth day of the seventh month of the Hebrew lunar calendar. This occurs on our calendar in late September or early October.   5:5 Hebrew *Tent of Meeting.*
5:10 Hebrew *Horeb,* another name for Sinai.

APRIL 21 ☐ DAY 112
Sounds of Celebration

 LOOK BACK The end of 2 Kings marks the end of two kingdoms. Assyria ransacks Israel, dispersing its population in the process (2 Kings 17). Babylonia descends upon defenseless Jerusalem, destroying its walls, burning its Temple, and dislocating many of its inhabitants (2 Kings 25).

Beginning with 1 Chronicles, the story takes a leap back in time, returning again to the days of King David. Don't worry, there's nothing wrong with your Bible. The books of 1 and 2 Chronicles retrace the same portion of the story you have already read in 2 Samuel through 2 Kings. Only this time you will see it through the eyes of a priest (perhaps Ezra, though we don't know for sure).

Parts of the story that were covered briefly in 2 Samuel through 2 Kings now unfold with exciting new detail in 1 and 2 Chronicles. Other accounts you've read in the books of Kings are omitted completely in the books of Chronicles in order to focus on the events that have the most profound spiritual impact upon David and his descendants. You'll enjoy this "second look" at the man after God's own heart (David), the son who followed in his footsteps (Solomon), and the descendants who perpetuated his dynasty (Judah).

LOOK UP In a few short weeks we'll reach the book of Psalms—the longest book in the Bible and the halfway point in your journey through the Bible. But you needn't wait till then to begin to read and enjoy these majestic anthems of praise and adoration penned by King David, for in 1 Chronicles 16 you'll discover portions of three psalms blended into one:

Since we fight for the liberty to worship, should we not make more use of that liberty?

Verses 8-22 are drawn from Psalm 105:1-15.
Verses 23-33 come from Psalm 96:1-13.
Verses 34-36 echo Psalm 106:1, 47-48.

As David and his appointed assistants ministered before the Lord, they found their hearts tugging in three directions: *upward* (in spontaneous praise to God), *outward* (in public testimony and thanksgiving for God's greatness), and *inward* (in humble dependence upon God). As you read the words of 1 Chronicles 16, you can almost hear the music ascending to heaven as the king and his people sing for joy before the Lord.

LOOK AHEAD Whether you are vocally gifted, instrumentally talented, or "musically challenged," you will find ample motivation this week to sing to the Lord . . . praise the Lord . . . and give thanks to the Lord in musical worship. Set aside a few minutes to lift your voice or play your instrument to the glory of God. (No audience necessary but the Lord!) Here are the titles of several hymns and gospel songs you may want to use to focus your thoughts (along with the Scripture from which they are drawn):

- "How Great Thou Art" (Psalm 86:10)
- "Great Is the Lord" (Psalm 145:3)
- "Be Exalted, O God" (Psalm 57:10-11)
- "O Worship the King" (Psalm 104:1)
- "A Mighty Fortress Is Our God" (Psalm 46:1-7)
- "Holy, Holy, Holy" (Revelation 4:8)

Have you ever thought of composing your own poem of praise or song of celebration? Remember, God delights to hear our "joyful noise" made in adoration of him.

APRIL 22 ☐ DAY 113
2 CHRONICLES 6–9
Solomon's Worship and Works

OVERVIEW Humbly on his knees with hands outstretched to heaven, Solomon inaugurates the Temple worship with a moving prayer of consecration. This is more than the dedication of a building, however. It is also the dedication of a nation to make the Temple of God and the God of the Temple the center of everyday life. God appears to Solomon by night to make this promise: If Solomon will walk in the steps of his father, David, God will establish his dynasty forever. True to his word, God blesses Solomon's early years with immense wealth, national allegiance, and international fame.

Chapter 6	Chapter 7	Chapter 8	Chapter 9	
Solomon's Prayer	God's Promise	Solomon's Fame	Solomon's Fortune	Solomon's Funeral
			1 28	29 31
Solomon's Worship		Solomon's Wealth		

YOUR DAILY WALK If your prayer life is normal, you have probably prayed often for God to bless you. But when was the last time you blessed God?

Bless the Lord today; he blesses you every day.

There is something God desires from you, something he is incapable of providing for himself. Naturally it's not money or power or possessions. God owns the cattle on a thousand hills (Psalm 50:10). He is high above all people (Psalm 99:2). So what could he possibly want that he does not already possess?

He wants your *praise.* Praise is a response of gratitude and worship to the goodness and blessing of God, a heartfelt thank-you from one of God's creatures for the benefits provided by the loving Creator. At the dedication of the Temple, Solomon "turned around to the entire community of Israel . . . and gave this blessing" (6:3). And then he did what his father, David, had urged in Psalm 103:2. "Praise the LORD, I tell myself, and never forget the good things he does for me." Count how many blessings Solomon mentions in 6:4-11. (Can you find a dozen?) Then turn each benefit into an occasion to bless the Lord in a prayer of praise.

INSIGHT The Offering That Lasted a Fortnight

At the inauguration of the Temple, Solomon offered 22,000 bulls and 120,000 sheep in a peace offering to God (1 Kings 8:63). According to Leviticus, the peace offering was to be eaten by the offerer, which helps explain the fifteen days of feasting and the fact that the people returned home "joyful and happy" (7:5-10).

CHAPTER 6

Then Solomon prayed, "O LORD, you have said that you would live in thick darkness. ²But I have built a glorious Temple for you, where you can live forever!"

³Then the king turned around to the entire community of Israel standing before him and gave this blessing: ⁴"Blessed be the LORD, the God of Israel, who has kept the promise he made to my father, David. For he told my father, ⁵'From the day I brought my people out of Egypt, I have never chosen a city among the tribes of Israel as the place where a temple should be built to honor my name. Nor have I chosen a king to lead my people Israel. ⁶But now I have chosen Jerusalem as that city, and David as that king.'"

⁷Then Solomon said, "My father, David, wanted to build this Temple to honor the name of the LORD, the God of Israel. ⁸But the LORD told him, 'It is right for you to want to build the Temple to honor my name, ⁹but you will not be the one to do it. One of your sons will build it instead.'

¹⁰"And now the LORD has done what he promised, for I have become king in my father's place. I have built this Temple to honor the name of the LORD, the God of Israel. ¹¹There I have placed the Ark, and in the Ark is the covenant that the LORD made with the people of Israel."

¹²Then Solomon stood with his hands spread out before the altar of the LORD in front of the entire community of Israel. ¹³He had made a bronze platform 7½ feet long, 7½ feet wide, and 4½ feet high* and had placed it at the center of the Temple's outer courtyard. He stood on the platform before the entire assembly, and then he knelt down and lifted his hands toward heaven. ¹⁴He prayed, "O LORD, God of Israel, there is no God like you in all of heaven and earth. You keep your promises

6:13 Hebrew *5 cubits* [2.3 meters] *long, 5 cubits wide, and 3 cubits* [1.4 meters] *high.*

and show unfailing love to all who obey you and are eager to do your will. [15]You have kept your promise to your servant David, my father. You made that promise with your own mouth, and today you have fulfilled it with your own hands. [16]And now, O LORD, God of Israel, carry out your further promise to your servant David, my father. For you said to him, 'If your descendants guard their behavior and obey my law as you have done, they will always reign over Israel.' [17]Now, O LORD, God of Israel, fulfill this promise to your servant David.

[18]"But will God really live on earth among people? Why, even the highest heavens cannot contain you. How much less this Temple I have built! [19]Listen to my prayer and my request, O LORD my God. Hear the cry and the prayer that your servant is making to you. [20]May you watch over this Temple both day and night, this place where you have said you would put your name. May you always hear the prayers I make toward this place. [21]May you hear the humble and earnest requests from me and your people Israel when we pray toward this place. Yes, hear us from heaven where you live, and when you hear, forgive.

[22]"If someone wrongs another person and is required to take an oath of innocence in front of the altar at this Temple, [23]then hear from heaven and judge between your servants—the accuser and the accused. Punish the guilty party, and acquit the one who is innocent.

[24]"If your people Israel are defeated by their enemies because they have sinned against you, and if they turn to you and call on your name and pray to you here in this Temple, [25]then hear from heaven and forgive their sins and return them to this land you gave their ancestors.

[26]"If the skies are shut up and there is no rain because your people have sinned against you, and then they pray toward this Temple and confess your name and turn from their sins because you have punished them, [27]then hear from heaven and forgive the sins of your servants, your people Israel. Teach them to do what is right, and send rain on your land that you have given to your people as their special possession.

[28]"If there is a famine in the land, or plagues, or crop disease, or attacks of locusts or caterpillars, or if your people's enemies are in the land besieging their towns—whatever the trouble is—[29]and if your people offer a prayer concerning their troubles or sorrow, raising their hands toward this Temple, [30]then hear from heaven where you live, and forgive. Give your people whatever they deserve, for you alone know the human heart. [31]Then they will fear you and walk in your ways as long as they live in the land you gave to our ancestors.

[32]"And when foreigners hear of you and your mighty miracles, and they come from distant lands to worship your great name and to pray toward this Temple, [33]then hear from heaven where you live, and grant what they ask of you. Then all the people of the earth will come to know and fear you, just as your own people Israel do. They, too, will know that this Temple I have built bears your name.

[34]"If your people go out at your command to fight their enemies, and if they pray to you toward this city that you have chosen and toward this Temple that I have built for your name, [35]then hear their prayers from heaven and uphold their cause.

[36]"If they sin against you—and who has never sinned?—you may become angry with them and let their enemies conquer them and take them captive to a foreign land far or near. [37]But in that land of exile, they may turn to you again in repentance and pray, 'We have sinned, done evil, and acted wickedly.' [38]Then if they turn to you with their whole heart and soul and pray toward the land you gave to their ancestors, toward this city you have chosen, and toward this Temple I have built to honor your name, [39]then hear their prayers from heaven where you live. Uphold their cause and forgive your people who have sinned against you.

[40]"O my God, be attentive to all the prayers made to you in this place. [41]And now, O LORD God, arise and enter this resting place of yours, where your magnificent Ark has been placed. May your priests, O LORD God, be clothed with salvation, and may your saints rejoice in your goodness. [42]O LORD God, do not reject your anointed one. Remember your unfailing love for your servant David.*"

6:42 Or *Remember the faithfulness of your servant David.*

CHAPTER 7

When Solomon finished praying, fire flashed down from heaven and burned up the burnt offerings and sacrifices, and the glorious presence of the LORD filled the Temple. ²The priests could not even enter the Temple of the LORD because the glorious presence of the LORD filled it. ³When all the people of Israel saw the fire coming down and the glorious presence of the LORD filling the Temple, they fell face down on the ground and worshiped and praised the LORD, saying,

"He is so good!
His faithful love endures forever!"

⁴Then the king and all the people offered sacrifices to the LORD. ⁵King Solomon offered a sacrifice of 22,000 oxen and 120,000 sheep. And so the king and all the people dedicated the Temple of God. ⁶The priests took their assigned positions, and so did the Levites who were singing, "His faithful love endures forever!" They accompanied the singing with music from the instruments King David had made for praising the LORD. On the other side of the Levites, the priests blew the trumpets, while all Israel stood.

⁷Solomon then dedicated the central area of the courtyard in front of the LORD's Temple so they could present burnt offerings and the fat from peace offerings there. He did this because the bronze altar he had built could not handle all the burnt offerings, grain offerings, and sacrificial fat.

⁸For the next seven days they celebrated the Festival of Shelters* with huge crowds gathered from all the tribes of Israel. They came from as far away as Lebo-hamath in the north, to the brook of Egypt in the south. ⁹On the eighth day they had a closing ceremony, for they had celebrated the dedication of the altar for seven days and the Festival of Shelters for seven days. ¹⁰Then at the end of the celebration,* Solomon sent the people home. They were all joyful and happy because the LORD had been so good to David and Solomon and to his people Israel.

¹¹So Solomon finished building the Temple of the LORD, as well as the royal palace. He completed everything he had planned to do. ¹²Then one night the LORD appeared to Solomon and said, "I have heard your prayer and have chosen this Temple as the place for making sacrifices. ¹³At times I might shut up the heavens so that no rain falls, or I might command locusts to devour your crops, or I might send plagues among you. ¹⁴Then if my people who are called by my name will humble themselves and pray and seek my face and turn from their wicked ways, I will hear from heaven and will forgive their sins and heal their land. ¹⁵I will listen to every prayer made in this place, ¹⁶for I have chosen this Temple and set it apart to be my home forever. My eyes and my heart will always be here.

¹⁷"As for you, if you follow me as your father, David, did and obey all my commands, laws, and regulations, ¹⁸then I will not let anyone take away your throne. This is the same promise I gave your father, David, when I said, 'You will never fail to have a successor who rules over Israel.'

¹⁹"But if you abandon me and disobey the laws and commands I have given you, and if you go and worship other gods, ²⁰then I will uproot the people of Israel from this land of mine that I have given them. I will reject this Temple that I have set apart to honor my name. I will make it a spectacle of contempt among the nations. ²¹And though this Temple is impressive now, it will become an appalling sight to all who pass by. They will ask, 'Why has the LORD done such terrible things to his land and to his Temple?' ²²And the answer will be, 'Because his people abandoned the LORD, the God of their ancestors, who brought them out of Egypt, and they worshiped other gods instead. That is why he brought all these disasters upon them.'"

CHAPTER 8

It was now twenty years since Solomon had become king, and the great building projects of the LORD's Temple and his own royal palace were completed. ²Solomon now turned his attention to rebuilding the towns that King Hiram* had given him, and he settled Israelites in them. ³It was at this time, too, that Solomon fought against the city of Hamath-zobah and conquered it. ⁴He rebuilt Tadmor in the desert and built towns in the region of Hamath as supply centers. ⁵He fortified the cities of

7:8 Hebrew *the festival* (also in 7:9); see note on 5:3.   7:10 Hebrew *Then on the twenty-seventh day of the seventh month.* This day of the Hebrew lunar calendar occurs in late September or early October.   8:2 Hebrew *Huram,* a variant name for Hiram; also in 8:18.

Upper Beth-horon and Lower Beth-horon, rebuilding their walls and installing barred gates. ⁶He also rebuilt Baalath and other supply centers at this time and constructed cities where his chariots and horses* could be kept. He built to his heart's content in Jerusalem and Lebanon and throughout the entire realm.

⁷There were still some people living in the land who were not Israelites, including Hittites, Amorites, Perizzites, Hivites, and Jebusites. ⁸These were descendants of the nations that Israel had not completely destroyed. So Solomon conscripted them for his labor force, and they serve in the labor force to this day. ⁹But Solomon did not conscript any of the Israelites for forced labor. Instead, he assigned them to serve as fighting men, officers in his army, commanders of his chariots, and charioteers. ¹⁰King Solomon also appointed 250 of them to supervise the various projects.

¹¹Solomon moved his wife, Pharaoh's daughter, from the City of David to the new palace he had built for her. He said, "My wife must not live in King David's palace, for the Ark of the LORD has been there, and it is holy ground."

¹²Then Solomon sacrificed burnt offerings to the LORD on the altar he had built in front of the foyer of the Temple. ¹³The number of sacrifices varied from day to day according to the commands Moses had given. Extra sacrifices were offered on the Sabbaths, on new moon festivals, and at the three annual festivals—the Passover celebration, the Festival of Harvest,* and the Festival of Shelters. ¹⁴In assigning the priests to their duties, Solomon followed the regulations of his father, David. He also assigned the Levites to lead the people in praise and to assist the priests in their daily duties. And he assigned the gatekeepers to their gates by their divisions, following the commands of David, the man of God. ¹⁵Solomon did not deviate in any way from David's commands concerning the priests and Levites and the treasuries.

¹⁶So Solomon made sure that all the work related to building the Temple of the LORD was carried out, from the day its foundation was laid to the day of its completion.

¹⁷Later Solomon went to Ezion-geber and Elath,* ports in the land of Edom, along the shore of the Red Sea.* ¹⁸Hiram sent him ships commanded by his own officers and manned by experienced crews of sailors. These ships sailed to the land of Ophir with Solomon's men and brought back to Solomon almost seventeen tons* of gold.

CHAPTER 9

When the queen of Sheba heard of Solomon's reputation, she came to Jerusalem to test him with hard questions. She arrived with a large group of attendants and a great caravan of camels loaded with spices, huge quantities of gold, and precious jewels. ²When she met with Solomon, they talked about everything she had on her mind. Solomon answered all her questions; nothing was too hard for him to explain to her. ³When the queen of Sheba realized how wise Solomon was, and when she saw the palace he had built, ⁴she was breathless. She was also amazed at the food on his tables, the organization of his officials and their splendid clothing, the cup-bearers and their robes, and the burnt offerings Solomon made at the Temple of the LORD.

⁵She exclaimed to the king, "Everything I heard in my country about your achievements and wisdom is true! ⁶I didn't believe it until I arrived here and saw it with my own eyes. Truly I had not heard the half of it! Your wisdom is far greater than what I was told. ⁷How happy these people must be! What a privilege for your officials to stand here day after day, listening to your wisdom! ⁸The LORD your God is great indeed! He delights in you and has placed you on the throne to rule for him. Because God loves Israel so much and desires this kingdom to last forever, he has made you king so you can rule with justice and righteousness."

⁹Then she gave the king a gift of nine thousand pounds* of gold, and great quantities of spices and precious jewels. Never before had there been spices as fine as those the queen of Sheba gave to Solomon.

¹⁰(When the crews of Hiram and Solomon brought gold from Ophir, they also brought rich cargoes of almug wood* and precious jewels. ¹¹The king used the almug wood to make steps* for the Temple of the

---

8:6 Or *and charioteers.* 8:13 Or *Festival of Weeks.* 8:17a As in Greek version (see also 2 Kgs 14:22; 16:6); Hebrew reads *Eloth.* 8:17b Hebrew *the sea.* 8:18 Hebrew *450 talents* [15.3 metric tons]. 9:9 Hebrew *120 talents* [4 metric tons]. 9:10 Hebrew *algum wood* (also in 9:11); compare parallel text at 1 Kgs 10:11-12. 9:11 Or *gateways.* The meaning of the Hebrew is uncertain.

LORD and the royal palace, and to construct harps and lyres for the musicians. Never before had there been such beautiful instruments in Judah.)

[12]King Solomon gave the queen of Sheba whatever she asked for—gifts of greater value than the gifts she had given him. Then she and all her attendants left and returned to their own land.

[13]Each year Solomon received about 25 tons* of gold. [14]This did not include the additional revenue he received from merchants and traders. All the kings of Arabia and the governors of the land also brought gold and silver to Solomon.

[15]King Solomon made two hundred large shields of hammered gold, each containing over 15 pounds* of gold. [16]He also made three hundred smaller shields of hammered gold, each containing about 7½ pounds* of gold. The king placed these shields in the Palace of the Forest of Lebanon.

[17]Then the king made a huge ivory throne and overlaid it with pure gold. [18]The throne had six steps, and there was a footstool of gold attached to it. On both sides of the seat were armrests, with the figure of a lion standing on each side of the throne. [19]Solomon made twelve other lion figures, one standing on each end of each of the six steps. No other throne in all the world could be compared with it!

[20]All of King Solomon's drinking cups were solid gold, as were all the utensils in the Palace of the Forest of Lebanon. They were not made of silver because silver was considered of little value in Solomon's day!

[21]The king had a fleet of trading ships* manned by the sailors sent by Hiram.* Once every three years the ships returned, loaded down with gold, silver, ivory, apes, and peacocks.*

[22]So King Solomon became richer and wiser than any other king in all the earth. [23]Kings from every nation came to visit him and to hear the wisdom God had given him. [24]Year after year, everyone who came to visit brought him gifts of silver and gold, clothing, weapons, spices, horses, and mules.

[25]Solomon had four thousand stalls for his chariot horses and twelve thousand horses.* He stationed many of them in the chariot cities, and some near him in Jerusalem. [26]He ruled over all the kings from the Euphrates River* to the land of the Philistines and the border of Egypt. [27]The king made silver as plentiful in Jerusalem as stones. And valuable cedarwood was as common as the sycamore wood that grows in the foothills of Judah.* [28]Solomon's horses were imported from Egypt* and many other countries.

[29]The rest of the events of Solomon's reign, from beginning to end, are recorded in *The Record of Nathan the Prophet* and in *The Prophecy of Ahijah from Shiloh,* and also in *The Visions of Iddo the Seer,* concerning Jeroboam son of Nebat. [30]Solomon ruled in Jerusalem over all Israel for forty years. [31]When he died, he was buried in the city of his father, David. Then his son Rehoboam became the next king.

9:13 Hebrew *666 talents* [23 metric tons].   9:15 Hebrew *600 shekels* [6.8 kilograms].   9:16 Hebrew *300 shekels* [3.4 kilograms]. 9:21a Hebrew *fleet of ships that could sail to Tarshish.*   9:21b Hebrew *Huram,* a variant name for Hiram.   9:21c Or *and baboons.* 9:25 Or *12,000 charioteers.*   9:26 Hebrew *the river.*   9:27 Hebrew *the Shephelah.*   9:28 Possibly *Muzur,* a district near Cilicia.

APRIL 23 ☐ DAY 114
2 CHRONICLES 10–12
Rebellion against Rehoboam

 OVERVIEW Everything about Rehoboam is divided: from his counselors to his kingdom to his heart attitude toward God. While 1 Kings recounted the predicament in which Rehoboam found himself, Chronicles centers around the divine purpose behind it all: "So the king paid no attention to the people's demand. This turn of events was the will of God, for it fulfilled the prophecy of the LORD" (10:15). The result is open hostility between the north and south and the formation of two distinct national entities: Israel and Judah. After three years of outward compliance with God's law, Rehoboam once again shows his true colors by forsaking God and drawing away most of the people. At his death these words provide the divine commentary on his life: "But he was an evil king, for he did not seek the LORD with all his heart" (12:14).

Chapter 10		Chapter 11	Chapter 12
A Divided Opinion	A Divided Nation	A Divided Heart	A Defaced Temple
1　　　　15	16　　　　19		
Rehoboam's Political Life		Rehoboam's Spiritual Life	

YOUR DAILY WALK Here are some symptoms of a halfhearted love for God taken from the life of Rehoboam:

The more a person takes the needs of others to heart, the more he or she will take his or her own heart to God.

- Your words and actions promote division, not peace.
- You rely on your own strength, rather than God's.
- You worship God only when it is expedient for you.
- You distort God's plan and purpose for the family.
- You acknowledge God only when you feel helpless.

Rehoboam's self-serving indifference came to a sudden halt when God brought him face-to-face with death in the person of Shishak, king of Egypt. In humble helplessness, Rehoboam acknowledged his own wickedness and God's righteousness.

Are you halfhearted in your love for God? Then clear the channels of communication with him. Admit your waywardness, acknowledge his righteousness, and get back in step with him. Don't wait until you're staring death in the face to set things right.

INSIGHT Double Coverage for Good News
The chronicler does not recognize the kings of the northern kingdom, Israel. From his viewpoint, only the descendants of David are legitimate rulers of the nation, even though it is sadly divided. Furthermore, the reigns of the eight good kings of Judah are given twice as much coverage as the twelve evil rulers.

CHAPTER 10

Rehoboam went to Shechem, where all Israel had gathered to make him king. ²When Jeroboam son of Nebat heard of Solomon's death, he returned from Egypt, for he had fled to Egypt to escape from King Solomon. ³The leaders of Israel sent for Jeroboam, and he and all Israel went together to speak with Rehoboam. ⁴"Your father was a hard master," they said. "Lighten the harsh labor demands and heavy taxes that your father imposed on us. Then we will be your loyal subjects."

⁵Rehoboam replied, "Come back in three days for my answer." So the people went away.

⁶Then King Rehoboam went to discuss the matter with the older men who had counseled his father, Solomon. "What is your advice?" he asked. "How should I answer these people?"

⁷The older counselors replied, "If you are good to the people and show them kindness and do your best to please them, they will always be your loyal subjects."

⁸But Rehoboam rejected the advice of the elders and instead asked the opinion of the young men who had grown up with him and who were now his advisers. ⁹"What is your advice?" he asked them. "How should I answer these people who want me to lighten the burdens imposed by my father?"

¹⁰The young men replied, "This is what you should tell those complainers: 'My little finger is thicker than my father's waist—if you think he was hard on you, just wait and see what I'll be like! ¹¹Yes, my father was harsh on you, but I'll be even harsher! My father used whips on you, but I'll use scorpions!'"

¹²Three days later, Jeroboam and all the people returned to hear Rehoboam's decision, just as the king had requested. ¹³But

Rehoboam spoke harshly to them, for he rejected the advice of the older counselors [14]and followed the counsel of his younger advisers. He told the people, "My father was harsh on you, but I'll be even harsher! My father used whips on you, but I'll use scorpions!" [15]So the king paid no attention to the people's demands. This turn of events was the will of God, for it fulfilled the prophecy of the LORD spoken to Jeroboam son of Nebat by the prophet Ahijah from Shiloh.

[16]When all Israel realized that the king had rejected their request, they shouted, "Down with David and his dynasty! We have no share in Jesse's son! Let's go home, Israel! Look out for your own house, O David!" So all Israel returned home. [17]But Rehoboam continued to rule over the Israelites who lived in the towns of Judah.

[18]King Rehoboam sent Adoniram,* who was in charge of the labor force, to restore order, but the Israelites stoned him to death. When this news reached King Rehoboam, he quickly jumped into his chariot and fled to Jerusalem. [19]The northern tribes of Israel have refused to be ruled by a descendant of David to this day.

CHAPTER 11

When Rehoboam arrived at Jerusalem, he mobilized the armies of Judah and Benjamin—180,000 select troops—to fight against the army of Israel and to restore the kingdom to himself. [2]But the LORD said to Shemaiah, the man of God, [3]"Say to Rehoboam son of Solomon, king of Judah, and to all the Israelites in Judah and Benjamin: [4]'This is what the LORD says: Do not fight against your relatives. Go back home, for what has happened is my doing!'" So they obeyed the message of the LORD and did not fight against Jeroboam.

[5]Rehoboam remained in Jerusalem and fortified various cities for the defense of Judah. [6]He built up Bethlehem, Etam, Tekoa, [7]Beth-zur, Soco, Adullam, [8]Gath, Mareshah, Ziph, [9]Adoraim, Lachish, Azekah, [10]Zorah, Aijalon, and Hebron. These became the fortified cities of Judah and Benjamin. [11]Rehoboam strengthened their defenses and stationed commanders in them. In each of them, he stored supplies of food, olive oil, and wine. [12]He also put shields and spears in these towns as a fur-

ther safety measure. So only Judah and Benjamin remained under his control.

[13]But all the priests and Levites living among the northern tribes of Israel sided with Rehoboam. [14]The Levites even abandoned their homes and property and moved to Judah and Jerusalem, because Jeroboam and his sons would not allow them to serve the LORD as priests. [15]Jeroboam appointed his own priests to serve at the pagan shrines, where they worshiped the goat and calf idols he had made. [16]From all over Israel, those who sincerely wanted to worship the LORD, the God of Israel, followed the Levites to Jerusalem, where they could offer sacrifices to the LORD, the God of their ancestors. [17]This strengthened the kingdom of Judah, and for three years they supported Rehoboam son of Solomon and earnestly sought to obey the LORD as they had done during the reigns of David and Solomon.

[18]Rehoboam married his cousin Mahalath, the daughter of David's son Jerimoth and of Abihail, the daughter of Eliab. (Eliab was one of David's brothers, a son of Jesse.) [19]Mahalath had three sons—Jeush, Shemariah, and Zaham.

[20]Later Rehoboam married another cousin, Maacah, the daughter of Absalom. Maacah gave birth to Abijah, Attai, Ziza, and Shelomith. [21]Rehoboam loved Maacah more than any of his other wives and concubines. In all, he had eighteen wives and sixty concubines, and they gave birth to twenty-eight sons and sixty daughters. [22]Rehoboam made Maacah's son Abijah chief among the princes, making it clear that he would be the next king. [23]Rehoboam also wisely gave responsibilities to his other sons and stationed them in the fortified cities throughout the land of Judah and Benjamin. He provided them with generous provisions and arranged for each of them to have several wives.

CHAPTER 12

But when Rehoboam was firmly established and strong, he abandoned the law of the LORD, and all Israel followed him in this sin. [2]Because they were unfaithful to the LORD, King Shishak of Egypt attacked Jerusalem in the fifth year of King Rehoboam's reign. [3]He came with twelve hundred chariots, sixty thousand horsemen,

10:18 Hebrew *Hadoram*, a variant name for Adoniram; compare 1 Kgs 4:6; 5:14; 12:18.

and a countless army of foot soldiers, including Libyans, Sukkites, and Ethiopians.* [4]Shishak conquered Judah's fortified cities and then advanced to attack Jerusalem.

[5]The prophet Shemaiah then met with Rehoboam and Judah's leaders, who had all fled to Jerusalem because of Shishak. Shemaiah told them, "This is what the LORD says: You have abandoned me, so I am abandoning you to Shishak."

[6]The king and the leaders of Israel humbled themselves and said, "The LORD is right in doing this to us!"

[7]When the LORD saw their change of heart, he gave this message to Shemaiah: "Since the people have humbled themselves, I will not completely destroy them and will soon give them some relief. I will not use Shishak to pour out my anger on Jerusalem. [8]But they will become his subjects, so that they can learn how much better it is to serve me than to serve earthly rulers."

[9]So King Shishak of Egypt came to Jerusalem and took away all the treasures of the Temple of the LORD and of the royal palace, including all of Solomon's gold shields. [10]King Rehoboam later replaced them with

12:3 Hebrew *and Cushites.*

bronze shields and entrusted them to the care of the captain of his bodyguard. [11]Whenever the king went to the Temple of the LORD, the guards would carry them along and then return them to the guardroom. [12]Because Rehoboam humbled himself, the LORD's anger was turned aside, and he did not destroy him completely. And there was still goodness in the land of Judah.

[13]King Rehoboam firmly established himself in Jerusalem and continued to rule. He was forty-one years old when he became king, and he reigned seventeen years in Jerusalem, the city the LORD had chosen from among all the tribes of Israel as the place to honor his name. Rehoboam's mother was Naamah, a woman from Ammon. [14]But he was an evil king, for he did not seek the LORD with all his heart.

[15]The rest of the events of Rehoboam's reign, from beginning to end, are recorded in *The Record of Shemaiah the Prophet* and in *The Record of Iddo the Seer,* which are part of the genealogical record. Rehoboam and Jeroboam were continually at war with each other. [16]When Rehoboam died, he was buried in the City of David. Then his son Abijah became the next king.

APRIL 24 ☐ DAY 115
2 CHRONICLES 13–16
Reigns of Abijah and Asa

 OVERVIEW Abijah, who "committed the same sins as his father before him" (1 Kings 15:3), nevertheless is used by God to judge an even more corrupt king, Jeroboam in the North. Through Abijah God vindicates the Temple in Jerusalem as the true place of worship. By contrast, Abijah's son Asa demonstrates a faith in God unparalleled since the days of Solomon and David! He removes idols, restores pure worship, and reminds God often of his promise to fight on behalf of his people: "O LORD, no one but you can help the powerless against the mighty! Help us, O LORD our God, for we trust in you alone. It is in your name that we have come against this vast horde" (14:11).

Chapter 13	Chapters 14–15	Chapter 16
Abijah's Civil Struggle	Asa's Reliance on God	Asa's Treaty with Aram
Divine Deliverance		Divine Discipline

YOUR DAILY WALK Today's section contains a divine "classified ad." God is looking for a certain kind of person—someone to do an important job for him. Do you have the qualifications for the position?

The capital of heaven is the heart in which God is enthroned as king.

"Wanted: People with a heart loyal to God. No age limit. Experience not necessary. Educational background immaterial. Physical limitations no problem. Open to anyone, regardless of race, color, sex, or national origin. Equal opportunity employer. No mandatory retirement age."

That's the gist of 16:9. God is searching diligently for men and women, boys and girls, whose heart attitude is right toward him. No matter if you're weak; God has strength in abundance! He's looking for those who are willing to make their lives a showcase for his power. Are you interested in the position? Then give heaven a call right now. (It's toll-free.) God is standing by to talk to you personally.

Just tell him Asa sent you!

INSIGHT Calling Out the Troops, One and All

In the war between Abijah and Jeroboam, 1.2 million troops were committed to the battle—800,000 for Israel and 400,000 for Judah (13:3). Compare these numbers with the census figures recorded in 2 Samuel 24:9 and 1 Chronicles 21:5. This was all-out war!

CHAPTER 13

Abijah began to rule over Judah in the eighteenth year of Jeroboam's reign in Israel. ²He reigned in Jerusalem three years. His mother was Maacah,* a daughter of Uriel from Gibeah.

Then war broke out between Abijah and Jeroboam. ³Judah, led by King Abijah, fielded 400,000 seasoned warriors, while Jeroboam mustered 800,000 courageous men from Israel. ⁴When the army of Judah arrived in the hill country of Ephraim, Abijah stood on Mount Zemaraim and shouted to Jeroboam and the Israelite army: "Listen to me! ⁵Don't you realize that the LORD, the God of Israel, made an unbreakable covenant* with David, giving him and his descendants the throne of Israel forever? ⁶Yet Jeroboam son of Nebat, who was a mere servant of David's son Solomon, became a traitor to his master. ⁷Then a whole gang of scoundrels joined him, defying Solomon's son Rehoboam when he was young and inexperienced and could not stand up to them. ⁸Do you really think you can stand against the kingdom of the LORD that is led by the descendants of David? Your army is vast indeed, but with you are those gold calves that Jeroboam made as your gods! ⁹And you have chased away the priests of the LORD and the Levites and have appointed your own priests, just like the pagan nations. You let anyone become a priest these days! Whoever comes to be dedicated with a

young bull and seven rams can become a priest of these so-called gods of yours!

¹⁰"But as for us, the LORD is our God, and we have not abandoned him. Only the descendants of Aaron serve the LORD as priests, and the Levites alone may help them in their work. ¹¹They present burnt offerings and fragrant incense to the LORD every morning and evening. They place the Bread of the Presence on the holy table, and they light the gold lampstand every evening. We are following the instructions of the LORD our God, but you have abandoned him. ¹²So you see, God is with us. He is our leader. His priests blow their trumpets and lead us into battle against you. O people of Israel, do not fight against the LORD, the God of your ancestors, for you will not succeed!"

¹³Meanwhile, Jeroboam had secretly sent part of his army around behind the men of Judah to ambush them. ¹⁴When Judah realized that they were being attacked from the front and the rear, they cried out to the LORD for help. Then the priests blew the trumpets, ¹⁵and the men of Judah began to shout. At the sound of their battle cry, God defeated Jeroboam and the Israelite army and routed them before Abijah and the army of Judah. ¹⁶The Israelite army fled from Judah, and God handed them over to Judah in defeat. ¹⁷Abijah and his army inflicted heavy losses on them; there were 500,000 casualties among Israel's finest troops that day. ¹⁸So Judah defeated Israel

13:2 As in most Greek manuscripts and Syriac version (see also 2 Chr 11:20-21; 1 Kgs 15:2); Hebrew reads *Micaiah.*   **13:5** Hebrew *a covenant of salt.*

because they trusted in the LORD, the God of their ancestors. [19]Abijah and his army pursued Jeroboam's troops and captured some of his towns, including Bethel, Jeshanah, and Ephron, along with their surrounding villages.

[20]So Jeroboam of Israel never regained his power during Abijah's lifetime, and finally the LORD struck him down and he died. [21]By contrast, Abijah of Judah grew more and more powerful. He married fourteen wives and had twenty-two sons and sixteen daughters. [22]The rest of the events of Abijah's reign, including his words and deeds, are recorded in *The Commentary of Iddo the Prophet.*

CHAPTER 14

When Abijah died, he was buried in the City of David. Then his son Asa became the next king. There was peace in the land for ten years, [2]for Asa did what was pleasing and good in the sight of the LORD his God. [3]He removed the pagan altars and the shrines. He smashed the sacred pillars and cut down the Asherah poles. [4]He commanded the people of Judah to seek the LORD, the God of their ancestors, and to obey his law and his commands. [5]Asa also removed the pagan shrines, as well as the incense altars from every one of Judah's towns. So Asa's kingdom enjoyed a period of peace. [6]During those peaceful years, he was able to build up the fortified cities throughout Judah. No one tried to make war against him at this time, for the LORD was giving him rest from his enemies. [7]Asa told the people of Judah, "Let us build towns and fortify them with walls, towers, gates, and bars. The land is ours because we sought the LORD our God, and he has given us rest from our enemies." So they went ahead with these projects and brought them to completion.

[8]King Asa had an army of 300,000 warriors from the tribe of Judah, armed with large shields and spears. He also had an army of 280,000 warriors from the tribe of Benjamin, armed with small shields and bows. Both armies were composed of courageous fighting men.

[9]Once an Ethiopian* named Zerah attacked Judah with an army of a million men* and three hundred chariots. They ad-

vanced to the city of Mareshah, [10]so Asa deployed his armies for battle in the valley north of Mareshah.* [11]Then Asa cried out to the LORD his God, "O LORD, no one but you can help the powerless against the mighty! Help us, O LORD our God, for we trust in you alone. It is in your name that we have come against this vast horde. O LORD, you are our God; do not let mere men prevail against you!"

[12]So the LORD defeated the Ethiopians* in the presence of Asa and the army of Judah, and the enemy fled. [13]Asa and his army pursued them as far as Gerar, and so many Ethiopians fell that they were unable to rally. They were destroyed by the LORD and his army, and the army of Judah carried off vast quantities of plunder. [14]While they were at Gerar, they attacked all the towns in that area, and terror from the LORD came upon the people there. As a result, vast quantities of plunder were taken from these towns, too. [15]They also attacked the camps of herdsmen and captured many sheep and camels before finally returning to Jerusalem.

CHAPTER 15

Then the Spirit of God came upon Azariah son of Oded, [2]and he went out to meet King Asa as he was returning from the battle. "Listen to me, Asa!" he shouted. "Listen, all you people of Judah and Benjamin! The LORD will stay with you as long as you stay with him! Whenever you seek him, you will find him. But if you abandon him, he will abandon you. [3]For a long time, Israel was without the true God, without a priest to teach them, and without God's law. [4]But whenever you were in distress and turned to the LORD, the God of Israel, and sought him out, you found him. [5]During those dark times, it was not safe to travel. Problems troubled the nation on every hand. [6]Nation fought against nation, and city against city, for God was troubling you with every kind of problem. [7]And now, you men of Judah, be strong and courageous, for your work will be rewarded."

[8]When Asa heard this message from Azariah the prophet,* he took courage and removed all the idols in the land of Judah and Benjamin and in the towns he had

captured in the hill country of Ephraim. And he repaired the altar of the LORD, which stood in front of the foyer of the LORD's Temple.

⁹Then Asa called together all the people of Judah and Benjamin, along with the people of Ephraim, Manasseh, and Simeon who had settled among them. Many had moved to Judah during Asa's reign when they saw that the LORD his God was with him. ¹⁰The people gathered at Jerusalem in late spring,* during the fifteenth year of Asa's reign. ¹¹On that day they sacrificed to the LORD some of the animals they had taken as plunder in the battle— seven hundred oxen and seven thousand sheep and goats. ¹²Then they entered into a covenant to seek the LORD, the God of their ancestors, with all their heart and soul. ¹³They agreed that anyone who refused to seek the LORD, the God of Israel, would be put to death—whether young or old, man or woman. ¹⁴They shouted out their oath of loyalty to the LORD with trumpets blaring and horns sounding. ¹⁵All were happy about this covenant, for they had entered into it with all their hearts. Eagerly they sought after God, and they found him. And the LORD gave them rest from their enemies on every side.

¹⁶King Asa even deposed his grandmother Maacah from her position as queen mother because she had made an obscene Asherah pole. He cut down the pole, broke it up, and burned it in the Kidron Valley. ¹⁷Although the pagan shrines were not completely removed from Israel, Asa remained fully committed to the LORD throughout his life. ¹⁸He brought into the Temple of God the silver and gold and the utensils that he and his father had dedicated. ¹⁹So there was no more war until the thirty-fifth year of Asa's reign.

CHAPTER 16

In the thirty-sixth year of Asa's reign, King Baasha of Israel invaded Judah and fortified Ramah in order to prevent anyone from entering or leaving King Asa's territory in Judah. ²Asa responded by taking the silver and gold from the treasuries of the LORD's Temple and from the royal palace. He sent it to King Ben-hadad of Aram, who was ruling in Damascus, along with this message:

³"Let us renew the treaty that existed between your father and my father. See, I am sending you a gift of silver and gold. Break your treaty with King Baasha of Israel so that he will leave me alone."

⁴Ben-hadad agreed to King Asa's request and sent his armies to attack Israel. They conquered the towns of Ijon, Dan, Abel-beth-maacah,* and all the store cities in Naphtali. ⁵As soon as Baasha of Israel heard what was happening, he abandoned his project of fortifying Ramah. ⁶Then King Asa called out all the men of Judah to carry away the building stones and timbers that Baasha had been using to fortify Ramah. Asa used these materials to fortify the towns of Geba and Mizpah.

⁷At that time Hanani the seer came to King Asa and told him, "Because you have put your trust in the king of Aram instead of in the LORD your God, you missed your chance to destroy the army of the king of Aram. ⁸Don't you remember what happened to the Ethiopians* and Libyans and their vast army, with all of their chariots and horsemen*? At that time you relied on the LORD, and he handed them all over to you. ⁹The eyes of the LORD search the whole earth in order to strengthen those whose hearts are fully committed to him. What a fool you have been! From now on, you will be at war." ¹⁰Asa became so angry with Hanani for saying this that he threw him into prison. At that time, Asa also began to oppress some of his people.

¹¹The rest of the events of Asa's reign, from beginning to end, are recorded in *The Book of the Kings of Judah and Israel.* ¹²In the thirty-ninth year of his reign, Asa developed a serious foot disease. Even when the disease became life threatening, he did not seek the LORD's help but sought help only from his physicians. ¹³So he died in the forty-first year of his reign. ¹⁴He was buried in the tomb he had carved out for himself in the City of David. He was laid on a bed perfumed with sweet spices and ointments, and at his funeral the people built a huge fire in his honor.

15:10 Hebrew *in the third month.* This month of the Hebrew lunar calendar usually occurs in May and June.   16:4 As in parallel text at 1 Kgs 15:20; Hebrew reads *Abel-maim,* another name for Abel-beth-maacah.   16:8a Hebrew *Cushites.*   16:8b Or *and chariroteers.*

APRIL 25 ☐ DAY 116
2 CHRONICLES 17–20
Reform under Jehoshaphat

OVERVIEW Building upon the foundation of his reformer father, Asa, Jehoshaphat appoints Levites to travel around the country carrying the law of the Lord and teaching the people the ways of the Lord. A quarter-century of godly leadership is nearly cut short by a foolish alliance between Jehoshaphat and Ahab, king of Israel. After being rebuked for his momentary lapse of faith, Jehoshaphat continues his reforming ways by destroying idols in the land and appointing judges to render righteous and impartial decisions in the courts.

Chapter 17	Chapter 18	Chapter 19	Chapter 20
Jehoshaphat's Teachers	Ahab's Death	Jehoshaphat's Judges	Moab's Defeat
Revival in the Cities		Reform in the Courts	

Pessimism is pulling tomorrow's cloud over today's sunshine.

YOUR DAILY WALK When times of crisis come to your family, how do you respond? Does the pressure pull you apart or weld you closer together? Do you find yourself praying less as a family or more?

Jehoshaphat faced a crisis. The Moabites and Ammonites were massing their troops in preparation for an all-out assault on Judah. Jehoshaphat had every right to be afraid . . . withdrawn . . . worried . . . and indecisive. But instead, his response was exemplary. He gathered all Judah together to seek help from the Lord. In an unprecedented national call to prayer, "all the men of Judah stood before the LORD with their little ones, wives, and children," (20:13)—a prayer meeting involving every member of the family!

Is that what happens in your home? If not, gather your family together to discuss a crisis you are facing as a family or as a nation. Allow each person to pray for God's strength and wisdom in the midst of the crisis. You'll find your love deepening for the God to whom you pray, as well as for the people you pray with and those you pray for.

INSIGHT Beating Yourself at Your Own Game
As part of God's divine strategy for giving Jehoshaphat the victory over Moab and Ammon, "they turned on each other" (20:23, i.e., the enemy forces fought and killed each other). Can you think of another Old Testament battle where the same thing happened? (Hint: See Judges 7:22.)

CHAPTER 17
Then Jehoshaphat, Asa's son, became the next king. He strengthened Judah to stand against any attack from Israel. ²He stationed troops in all the fortified cities of Judah, and he assigned additional garrisons to the land of Judah and to the towns of Ephraim that his father, Asa, had conquered.

³The LORD was with Jehoshaphat because he followed the example of his father's early years* and did not worship

the images of Baal. ⁴He sought his father's God and obeyed his commands instead of following the practices of the kingdom of Israel. ⁵So the LORD established Jehoshaphat's control over the kingdom of Judah. All the people of Judah brought gifts to Jehoshaphat, so he became very wealthy and highly esteemed. ⁶He was committed to the ways of the LORD. He knocked down the pagan shrines and destroyed the Asherah poles.

⁷In the third year of his reign, Jehoshaphat

17:3 Some Hebrew manuscripts read *the example of his father, David.*

sent out his officials to teach in all the towns of Judah. These officials included Ben-hail, Obadiah, Zechariah, Nethanel, and Micaiah. [8]He sent Levites along with them, including Shemaiah, Nethaniah, Zebadiah, Asahel, Shemiramoth, Jehonathan, Adonijah, Tobijah, and Tob-adonijah. He also sent out the priests, Elishama and Jehoram. [9]They took copies of the Book of the Law of the LORD and traveled around through all the towns of Judah, teaching the people.

[10]Then the fear of the LORD fell over all the surrounding kingdoms so that none of them declared war on Jehoshaphat. [11]Some of the Philistines brought him gifts and silver as tribute, and the Arabs brought seventy-seven hundred rams and seventy-seven hundred male goats.

[12]So Jehoshaphat became more and more powerful and built fortresses and store cities throughout Judah. [13]He stored numerous supplies in Judah's towns and stationed an army of seasoned troops at Jerusalem. [14]His army was enrolled according to ancestral clans.

From Judah, there were 300,000 troops organized in units of one thousand, under the command of Adnah. [15]Next in command was Jehohanan, who commanded 280,000 troops. [16]Next was Amasiah son of Zicri, who volunteered for the LORD's service, with 200,000 troops under his command.

[17]From Benjamin, there were 200,000 troops equipped with bows and shields. They were under the command of Eliada, a veteran soldier. [18]Next in command was Jehozabad, who commanded 180,000 armed men.

[19]These were the troops stationed in Jerusalem to serve the king, besides those Jehoshaphat stationed in the fortified cities throughout Judah.

CHAPTER 18

Now Jehoshaphat enjoyed great riches and high esteem, and he arranged for his son to marry the daughter of King Ahab of Israel. [2]A few years later, he went to Samaria to visit Ahab, who prepared a great banquet for him and his officials. They butchered great numbers of sheep and oxen for the feast. Then Ahab enticed Jehoshaphat to join forces with him to attack Ramoth-gilead. [3]"Will you join me in fighting against Ramoth-gilead?" Ahab asked.

And Jehoshaphat replied, "Why, of course! You and I are brothers, and my troops are yours to command. We will certainly join you in battle." [4]Then Jehoshaphat added, "But first let's find out what the LORD says."

[5]So King Ahab summoned his prophets, four hundred of them, and asked them, "Should we go to war against Ramoth-gilead or not?"

They all replied, "Go ahead, for God will give you a great victory!"

[6]But Jehoshaphat asked, "Isn't there a prophet of the LORD around, too? I would like to ask him the same question."

[7]King Ahab replied, "There is still one prophet of the LORD, but I hate him. He never prophesies anything but bad news for me! His name is Micaiah son of Imlah."

"You shouldn't talk like that," Jehoshaphat said. "Let's hear what he has to say."

[8]So the king of Israel called one of his officials and said, "Quick! Go and get Micaiah son of Imlah."

[9]King Ahab of Israel and King Jehoshaphat of Judah, dressed in their royal robes, were sitting on thrones at the threshing floor near the gate of Samaria. All of Ahab's prophets were prophesying there in front of them. [10]One of them, Zedekiah son of Kenaanah, made some iron horns and proclaimed, "This is what the LORD says: With these horns you will gore the Arameans to death!"

[11]All the other prophets agreed. "Yes," they said, "go up to Ramoth-gilead and be victorious. The LORD will give you a glorious victory!"

[12]Meanwhile, the messenger who went to get Micaiah said to him, "Look, all the prophets are promising victory for the king. Be sure that you agree with them and promise success."

[13]But Micaiah replied, "As surely as the LORD lives, I will say only what my God tells me to say."

[14]When Micaiah arrived before the king, Ahab asked him, "Micaiah, should we go to war against Ramoth-gilead or not?"

And Micaiah replied, "Go right ahead! It will be a glorious victory!"

[15]But the king replied sharply, "How many times must I demand that you speak only the truth when you speak for the LORD?"

¹⁶So Micaiah told him, "In a vision I saw all Israel scattered on the mountains, like sheep without a shepherd. And the LORD said, 'Their master has been killed. Send them home in peace.'"

¹⁷"Didn't I tell you?" the king of Israel said to Jehoshaphat. "He does it every time. He never prophesies anything but bad news for me."

¹⁸Then Micaiah continued, "Listen to what the LORD says! I saw the LORD sitting on his throne with all the armies of heaven on his right and on his left. ¹⁹And the LORD said, 'Who can entice King Ahab of Israel to go into battle against Ramoth-gilead so that he can be killed there?' There were many suggestions, ²⁰until finally a spirit approached the LORD and said, 'I can do it!'

"'How will you do this?' the LORD asked.

²¹"And the spirit replied, 'I will go out and inspire all Ahab's prophets to speak lies.'

"'You will succeed,' said the LORD. 'Go ahead and do it.'

²²"So you see, the LORD has put a lying spirit in the mouths of your prophets. For the LORD has determined disaster for you."

²³Then Zedekiah son of Kenaanah walked up to Micaiah and slapped him across the face. "When did the Spirit of the LORD leave me to speak to you?" he demanded.

²⁴And Micaiah replied, "You will find out soon enough, when you find yourself hiding in some secret room!"

²⁵King Ahab of Israel then ordered, "Arrest Micaiah and take him back to Amon, the governor of the city, and to my son Joash. ²⁶Give them this order from the king: 'Put this man in prison, and feed him nothing but bread and water until I return safely from the battle!'"

²⁷But Micaiah replied, "If you return safely, the LORD has not spoken through me!" Then he added to those standing around, "Take note of what I have said."

²⁸So the king of Israel and King Jehoshaphat of Judah led their armies against Ramoth-gilead. ²⁹Now King Ahab said to Jehoshaphat, "As we go into battle, I will disguise myself so no one will recognize me, but you wear your royal robes." So Ahab disguised himself, and they went into battle.

³⁰Now the king of Aram had issued these orders to his charioteers: "Attack only the king of Israel!" ³¹So when the Aramean charioteers saw Jehoshaphat in his royal robes, they went after him. "There is the king of Israel!" they shouted. But Jehoshaphat cried out to the LORD to save him, and God helped him by turning the attack away from him. ³²As soon as the charioteers realized he was not the king of Israel, they stopped chasing him.

³³An Aramean soldier, however, randomly shot an arrow at the Israelite troops, and the arrow hit the king of Israel between the joints of his armor. "Get me out of here!" Ahab groaned to the driver of his chariot. "I have been badly wounded!" ³⁴The battle raged all that day, and Ahab propped himself up in his chariot facing the Arameans until evening. Then, just as the sun was setting, he died.

CHAPTER 19

When King Jehoshaphat of Judah arrived safely home to Jerusalem, ²Jehu son of Hanani the seer went out to meet him. "Why should you help the wicked and love those who hate the LORD?" he asked the king. "What you have done has brought the LORD's anger against you. ³There is some good in you, however, for you have removed the Asherah poles throughout the land, and you have committed yourself to seeking God."

⁴So Jehoshaphat lived in Jerusalem, but he went out among the people, traveling from Beersheba to the hill country of Ephraim, encouraging the people to return to the LORD, the God of their ancestors. ⁵He appointed judges throughout the nation in all the fortified cities, ⁶and he gave them these instructions: "Always think carefully before pronouncing judgment. Remember that you do not judge to please people but to please the LORD. He will be with you when you render the verdict in each case that comes before you. ⁷Fear the LORD and judge with care, for the LORD our God does not tolerate perverted justice, partiality, or the taking of bribes."

⁸Jehoshaphat appointed some of the Levites and priests and clan leaders in Israel to serve as judges in Jerusalem for cases concerning both the law of the LORD and civil disputes. ⁹These were his instructions to them: "You must always act in the fear of the LORD, with integrity and with undivided hearts. ¹⁰Whenever a case comes to you from fellow citizens in an outlying

town, whether a murder case or some other violation of God's instructions, commands, laws, or regulations, you must warn them not to sin against the LORD, so that his anger will not come against you and them. Do this and you will not be guilty.

¹¹"Amariah the high priest will have final say in all cases concerning the LORD. Zebadiah son of Ishmael, a leader from the tribe of Judah, will have final say in all civil cases. The Levites will assist you in making sure that justice is served. Take courage as you fulfill your duties, and may the LORD be with those who do what is right."

CHAPTER 20

After this, the armies of the Moabites, Ammonites, and some of the Meunites* declared war on Jehoshaphat. ²Messengers came and told Jehoshaphat, "A vast army from Edom* is marching against you from beyond the Dead Sea.* They are already at Hazazon-tamar." (This was another name for En-gedi.) ³Jehoshaphat was alarmed by this news and sought the LORD for guidance. He also gave orders that everyone throughout Judah should observe a fast. ⁴So people from all the towns of Judah came to Jerusalem to seek the LORD.

⁵Jehoshaphat stood before the people of Judah and Jerusalem in front of the new courtyard at the Temple of the LORD. ⁶He prayed, "O LORD, God of our ancestors, you alone are the God who is in heaven. You are ruler of all the kingdoms of the earth. You are powerful and mighty; no one can stand against you! ⁷O our God, did you not drive out those who lived in this land when your people arrived? And did you not give this land forever to the descendants of your friend Abraham? ⁸Your people settled here and built this Temple for you. ⁹They said, 'Whenever we are faced with any calamity such as war, disease, or famine, we can come to stand in your presence before this Temple where your name is honored. We can cry out to you to save us, and you will hear us and rescue us.'

¹⁰"And now see what the armies of Ammon, Moab, and Mount Seir are doing. You would not let our ancestors invade those nations when Israel left Egypt, so they went around them and did not destroy them. ¹¹Now see how they reward us! For they have come to throw us out of your

land, which you gave us as an inheritance. ¹²O our God, won't you stop them? We are powerless against this mighty army that is about to attack us. We do not know what to do, but we are looking to you for help."

¹³As all the men of Judah stood before the LORD with their little ones, wives, and children, ¹⁴the Spirit of the LORD came upon one of the men standing there. His name was Jahaziel son of Zechariah, son of Benaiah, son of Jeiel, son of Mattaniah, a Levite who was a descendant of Asaph. ¹⁵He said, "Listen, King Jehoshaphat! Listen, all you people of Judah and Jerusalem! This is what the LORD says: Do not be afraid! Don't be discouraged by this mighty army, for the battle is not yours, but God's. ¹⁶Tomorrow, march out against them. You will find them coming up through the ascent of Ziz at the end of the valley that opens into the wilderness of Jeruel. ¹⁷But you will not even need to fight. Take your positions; then stand still and watch the LORD's victory. He is with you, O people of Judah and Jerusalem. Do not be afraid or discouraged. Go out there tomorrow, for the LORD is with you!"

¹⁸Then King Jehoshaphat bowed down with his face to the ground. And all the people of Judah and Jerusalem did the same, worshiping the LORD. ¹⁹Then the Levites from the clans of Kohath and Korah stood to praise the LORD, the God of Israel, with a very loud shout.

²⁰Early the next morning the army of Judah went out into the wilderness of Tekoa. On the way Jehoshaphat stopped and said, "Listen to me, all you people of Judah and Jerusalem! Believe in the LORD your God, and you will be able to stand firm. Believe in his prophets, and you will succeed." ²¹After consulting the leaders of the people, the king appointed singers to walk ahead of the army, singing to the LORD and praising him for his holy splendor. This is what they sang:

"Give thanks to the LORD;
    his faithful love endures forever!"

²²At the moment they began to sing and give praise, the LORD caused the armies of Ammon, Moab, and Mount Seir to start fighting among themselves. ²³The armies of Moab and Ammon turned against their allies from Mount Seir and killed every one

20:1 As in some Greek manuscripts (see also 26:7); Hebrew reads *Ammonites.*   20:2a As in one Hebrew manuscript; most Hebrew manuscripts and ancient versions read *Aram.*   20:2b Hebrew *the sea.*

of them. After they had finished off the army of Seir, they turned on each other.

²⁴So when the army of Judah arrived at the lookout point in the wilderness, there were dead bodies lying on the ground for as far as they could see. Not a single one of the enemy had escaped. ²⁵King Jehoshaphat and his men went out to gather the plunder. They found vast amounts of equipment, cloth-ing,* and other valuables—more than they could carry. There was so much plunder that it took them three days just to collect it all! ²⁶On the fourth day they gathered in the Valley of Blessing,* which got its name that day because the people praised and thanked the LORD there. It is still called the Valley of Blessing today.

²⁷Then they returned to Jerusalem, with Jehoshaphat leading them, full of joy that the LORD had given them victory over their enemies. ²⁸They marched into Jerusalem to the music of harps, lyres, and trumpets and proceeded to the Temple of the LORD. ²⁹When the surrounding kingdoms heard that the LORD himself had fought against the enemies of Israel, the fear of God came over them. ³⁰So Jehoshaphat's kingdom was at peace, for his God had given him rest on every side.

³¹So Jehoshaphat ruled over the land of Judah. He was thirty-five years old when he became king, and he reigned in Jerusalem twenty-five years. His mother was Azubah, the daughter of Shilhi. ³²Jehoshaphat was a good king, following the ways of his father, Asa. He did what was pleasing in the LORD's sight. ³³During his reign, however, he failed to remove all the pagan shrines, and the people never fully committed themselves to following the God of their ancestors. ³⁴The rest of the events of Jehoshaphat's reign, from beginning to end, are recorded in *The Record of Jehu Son of Hanani*, which is in-cluded in *The Book of the Kings of Israel*.

³⁵But near the end of his life, King Je-hoshaphat of Judah made an alliance with King Ahaziah of Israel, who was a very wicked man.* ³⁶Together they built a fleet of trading ships* at the port of Ezion-geber. ³⁷Then Eliezer son of Dodavahu from Ma-reshah prophesied against Jehoshaphat. He said, "Because you have allied yourself with King Ahaziah, the LORD will destroy your work." So the ships met with disaster and never put out to sea.*

20:25 As in some Hebrew manuscripts and Latin Vulgate; most Hebrew manuscripts read *corpses*.   20:26 Hebrew *valley of Beracah*.   20:35 Or *who made him do what was wrong*.   20:36 Hebrew *fleet of ships that could go to Tarshish*.   20:37 Hebrew *never set sail for Tarshish*.

APRIL 26 ☐ DAY 117
2 CHRONICLES 21–25
Reigns of Jehoram to Amaziah

OVERVIEW Jehoshaphat's spiritual gains in the nation are all too soon wiped out by the wicked reigns of Jehoram, Ahaziah, and Athaliah. Before reading the tale of intrigue and bloodshed, be sure you under-stand the family relationships between the main characters and the significance of little Joash's survival as the sole remaining heir of David's dynasty.

```
        North (Israel)                                      South (Judah)
  Ahab ───────── Jezebel                                   Jehoshaphat
  (husband)    │    (wife)                                      │
        Athaliah ───────── (wife/husband) ───────── Jehoram (son)
        (daughter)                                             │
                                                     Ahaziah (son)
                                                             │
                                                        Joash (son)
```

Chapter 21	Chapter 22		Chapters 23–24	Chapter 25
Idolatry in the Palace			Inconsistency in the Palace	
Jehoram	Ahaziah	Athaliah	Joash	Amaziah
	1 9	10 12		
"Evil in the LORD's sight"			"What was pleasing in the LORD's sight"	

YOUR DAILY WALK There are two parts to any military conquest: (1) the initial assault, and (2) the "mopping up" operation that deals with any lingering resistance. Keeping that in mind, consider this principle that holds true both in military and spiritual realms: Pockets of resistance, if left unchallenged, can lead to rebellion. Dealing with those pockets is not optional; it is essential if complete victory is to be achieved.

When evil thoughts come into your heart, dash them at once on the rock of Christ.

Study the life of good king Joash, and you will quickly detect some pockets of resistance in his spiritual life: idolatry (24:18), insensitivity to the message of God's prophet (24:19-21), and cruelty in the face of kindness (24:22). How about you? Are there any areas of your life that have become pockets of resistance, such as

- Finances?
- Time with God?
- Thought life?
- Pride?
- Gossip?
- Time with family?

Pick an area of resistance and deal with it today!

INSIGHT The Reign of Joash—Judah's History in Miniature
The life of Joash reads like a condensed history of Judah. He began his reign by living righteously, yet in later years abandoned the Lord, killed the prophet who rebuked him, was defeated by a foreign power, and died a humiliating death for his many crimes.

CHAPTER 21

When Jehoshaphat died, he was buried with his ancestors in the City of David. Then his son Jehoram became the next king. ²Jehoram's brothers—the other sons of Jehoshaphat—were Azariah, Jehiel, Zechariah, Azariahu, Michael, and Shephatiah. ³Their father had given each of them valuable gifts of silver, gold, and costly items, and also the ownership of some of Judah's fortified cities. However, Jehoram became king because he was the oldest. ⁴But when Jehoram had become solidly established as king, he killed all his brothers and some of the other leaders of Israel.

⁵Jehoram was thirty-two years old when he became king, and he reigned in Jerusalem eight years. ⁶But Jehoram followed the example of the kings of Israel and was as wicked as King Ahab, for he had married one of Ahab's daughters. So Jehoram did what was evil in the LORD's sight. ⁷But the LORD was not willing to destroy David's dynasty, for he had made a covenant with David and promised that his descendants would continue to rule forever.*

⁸During Jehoram's reign, the Edomites revolted against Judah and crowned their own king. ⁹So Jehoram went to attack Edom with his full army and all his chariots. The Edomites surrounded him and his charioteers, but he escaped at night under cover of darkness. ¹⁰Edom has been independent from Judah to this day. The town of Libnah revolted about that same time, because Jehoram had abandoned the LORD, the God of his ancestors. ¹¹He had built pagan shrines in the hill country of Judah and had led the people of Jerusalem and Judah to give themselves to pagan gods.

¹²Then Elijah the prophet wrote Jehoram this letter:

"This is what the LORD, the God of your ancestor David, says: You have not followed the good example of your father, Jehoshaphat, or your grandfather King Asa of Judah. ¹³Instead, you have been as evil as the kings of Israel. You have led the people of Jerusalem and Judah to worship idols, just as King Ahab did in Israel. And you have even killed

21:7 Hebrew *promised to give a lamp to David and his descendants forever.*

your own brothers, men who were better than you. ¹⁴So now the LORD is about to strike you, your people, your children, your wives, and all that is yours with a heavy blow. ¹⁵You yourself will be stricken with a severe intestinal disease until it causes your bowels to come out."

¹⁶Then the LORD stirred up the Philistines and the Arabs, who lived near the Ethiopians,* to attack Jehoram. ¹⁷They marched against Judah, broke down its defenses, and carried away everything of value in the royal palace, including his sons and his wives. Only his youngest son, Ahaziah,* was spared.

¹⁸It was after this that the LORD struck Jehoram with the severe intestinal disease. ¹⁹In the course of time, at the end of two years, the disease caused his bowels to come out, and he died in agony. His people did not build a great fire to honor him at his funeral as they had done for his ancestors. ²⁰Jehoram was thirty-two years old when he became king, and he reigned in Jerusalem eight years. No one was sorry when he died. He was buried in the City of David, but not in the royal cemetery.

CHAPTER 22

Then the people of Jerusalem made Ahaziah, Jehoram's youngest son, their next king. The marauding bands of Arabs had killed all the older sons. So Ahaziah son of Jehoram reigned as king of Judah. ²Ahaziah was twenty-two* years old when he became king, and he reigned in Jerusalem one year. His mother was Athaliah, a granddaughter of King Omri of Israel. ³Ahaziah also followed the evil example of King Ahab's family, for his mother encouraged him in doing wrong. ⁴He did what was evil in the LORD's sight, just as Ahab had done. After the death of his father, members of Ahab's family became his advisers, and they led him to ruin.

⁵Following their evil advice, Ahaziah made an alliance with King Joram,* the son of King Ahab of Israel. They went out to fight King Hazael of Aram at Ramoth-gilead, and the Arameans wounded Joram in the battle. ⁶Joram returned to Jezreel to recover from his wounds, and King Aha-

ziah* of Judah went to Jezreel to visit him. ⁷But this turned out to be a fatal mistake, for God had decided to punish Ahaziah. It was during this visit that Ahaziah went out with Joram to meet Jehu son of Nimshi, whom the LORD had appointed to end the dynasty of Ahab.

⁸While Jehu was executing judgment against the family of Ahab, he happened to meet some of Judah's officials and Ahaziah's relatives* who were attending Ahaziah. So Jehu killed them all. ⁹Then Jehu's men searched for Ahaziah, and they found him hiding in the city of Samaria. They brought him to Jehu, who killed him. Ahaziah was given a decent burial because the people said, "He was the grandson of Jehoshaphat—a man who sought the LORD with all his heart." None of the surviving members of Ahaziah's family was capable of ruling the kingdom.

¹⁰When Athaliah, the mother of King Ahaziah of Judah, learned that her son was dead, she set out to destroy the rest of Judah's royal family. ¹¹But Ahaziah's sister Jehosheba,* the daughter of King Jehoram, took Ahaziah's infant son, Joash, and stole him away from among the rest of the king's children, who were about to be killed. She put Joash and his nurse in a bedroom. In this way, Jehosheba, the wife of Jehoiada the priest, hid the child so that Athaliah could not murder him. ¹²Joash remained hidden in the Temple of God for six years while Athaliah ruled over the land.

CHAPTER 23

In the seventh year of Athaliah's reign, Jehoiada the priest decided to act. He got up his courage and made a pact with five army commanders: Azariah son of Jeroham, Ishmael son of Jehohanan, Azariah son of Obed, Maaseiah son of Adaiah, and Elishaphat son of Zicri. ²These men traveled secretly throughout Judah and summoned the Levites and clan leaders in Judah's towns to come to Jerusalem. ³They all gathered at the Temple of God, where they made a covenant with Joash, the young king.

Jehoiada said to them, "The time has come for the king's son to reign! The LORD has promised that a descendant of David

---

21:16 Hebrew *the Cushites.*   21:17 Hebrew *Jehoahaz,* a variant name for Ahaziah; compare 22:1.   22:2 As in some Greek manuscripts and Syriac version (see also 2 Kgs 8:26); Hebrew reads *forty-two.*   22:5 Hebrew *Jehoram,* a variant name for Joram; also in 22:6, 7.   22:6 Some Hebrew manuscripts, Greek and Syriac versions, and Latin Vulgate (see also 2 Kgs 8:29); most Hebrew manuscripts read *Azariah.*   22:8 As in Greek version (see also 2 Kgs 10:13); Hebrew reads *and sons of the brothers of Ahaziah.*   22:11 As in parallel text at 2 Kgs 11:2; Hebrew reads *Jehoshabeath,* a variant name for Jehosheba.

will be our king. ⁴This is what you must do. When the priests and Levites come on duty on the Sabbath, a third of them will serve as gatekeepers. ⁵Another third will go over to the royal palace, and the final third will be at the Foundation Gate. Everyone else should stay in the courtyards of the LORD's Temple. ⁶Remember, only the priests and Levites on duty may enter the Temple of the LORD, for they are set apart as holy. The rest of the people must obey the LORD's instructions and stay outside. ⁷You Levites, form a bodyguard for the king and keep your weapons in hand. Any unauthorized person who enters the Temple must be killed. Stay right beside the king at all times."

⁸So the Levites and the people did everything just as Jehoiada the priest ordered. The commanders took charge of the men reporting for duty that Sabbath, as well as those who were going off duty. Jehoiada the priest did not let anyone go home after their shift ended. ⁹Then Jehoiada supplied the commanders with the spears and shields that had once belonged to King David and were stored in the Temple of God. ¹⁰He stationed the guards around the king, with their weapons ready. They formed a line from the south side of the Temple around to the north side and all around the altar.

¹¹Then Jehoiada and his sons brought out Joash, the king's son, and placed the crown on his head. They presented Joash with a copy of God's laws and proclaimed him king. Then they anointed him, and everyone shouted, "Long live the king!"

¹²When Athaliah heard the noise of the people running and the shouts of praise to the king, she hurried to the LORD's Temple to see what was happening. ¹³And she saw the newly crowned king standing in his place of authority by the pillar at the Temple entrance. The officers and trumpeters were surrounding him, and people from all over the land were rejoicing and blowing trumpets. Singers with musical instruments were leading the people in a great celebration. When Athaliah saw all this, she tore her clothes in despair and shouted, "Treason! Treason!"

¹⁴Then Jehoiada the priest ordered the commanders who were in charge of the troops, "Take her out of the Temple, and kill anyone who tries to rescue her. Do not kill her here in the Temple of the LORD." ¹⁵So

they seized her and led her out to the gate where horses enter the palace grounds, and they killed her there.

¹⁶Then Jehoiada made a covenant between himself and the king and the people that they would be the LORD's people. ¹⁷And all the people went over to the temple of Baal and tore it down. They demolished the altars and smashed the idols, and they killed Mattan the priest of Baal in front of the altars.

¹⁸Jehoiada now put the Levitical priests in charge of the Temple of the LORD, following all the instructions given by David. He also commanded them to present burnt offerings to the LORD, as prescribed by the law of Moses, and to sing and rejoice as David had instructed. ¹⁹He stationed gatekeepers at the gates of the LORD's Temple to keep those who were ceremonially unclean from entering.

²⁰Then the commanders, nobles, rulers, and all the people escorted the king from the Temple of the LORD. They went through the Upper Gate and into the palace, and they seated the king on the royal throne. ²¹So all the people of the land rejoiced, and the city was peaceful because Athaliah had been killed.

CHAPTER 24

Joash was seven years old when he became king, and he reigned in Jerusalem forty years. His mother was Zibiah, from Beersheba. ²Joash did what was pleasing in the LORD's sight throughout the lifetime of Jehoiada the priest. ³Jehoiada chose two wives for Joash, and he had sons and daughters.

⁴Some time later, Joash decided to repair and restore the Temple of the LORD. ⁵He summoned the priests and Levites and gave them these instructions: "Go at once to all the towns of Judah and collect the required annual offerings, so that we can repair the Temple of your God. Do not delay!" But the Levites did not act right away.

⁶So the king called for Jehoiada the high priest and asked him, "Why haven't you demanded that the Levites go out and collect the Temple taxes from the towns of Judah and from Jerusalem? Moses, the servant of the LORD, levied this tax on the community of Israel in order to maintain the Tabernacle of the Covenant.*"

⁷Over the years, the followers of wicked

24:6 Hebrew *Tent of the Testimony.*

Athaliah had broken into the Temple of God, and they had used all the dedicated things from the Temple of the LORD to worship the images of Baal. [8]So now Joash gave instructions for a chest to be made and set outside the gate leading to the Temple of the LORD. [9]Then a proclamation was sent throughout Judah and Jerusalem, telling the people to bring to the LORD the tax that Moses, the servant of God, had required of the Israelites in the wilderness. [10]This pleased all the leaders and the people, and they gladly brought their money and filled the chest with it.

[11]Whenever the chest became full, the Levites carried it to the king's officials. Then the court secretary and an officer of the high priest counted the money and took the chest back to the Temple again. This went on day after day, and a large amount of money was collected. [12]The king and Jehoiada gave the money to the construction supervisors, who hired masons and carpenters to restore the Temple of the LORD. They also hired metalworkers, who made articles of iron and bronze for the LORD's Temple.

[13]So the men in charge of the renovation worked hard, and they made steady progress. They restored the Temple of God according to its original design and strengthened it. [14]When all the repairs were finished, they brought the remaining money to the king and Jehoiada. It was used to make utensils for the Temple of the LORD—utensils for worship services and for burnt offerings, including ladles and other vessels made of gold and silver. And the burnt offerings were sacrificed continually in the Temple of the LORD during the lifetime of Jehoiada the priest.

[15]Jehoiada lived to a very old age, finally dying at 130. [16]He was buried among the kings in the City of David, because he had done so much good in Israel for God and his Temple.

[17]But after Jehoiada's death, the leaders of Judah came and bowed before King Joash and persuaded the king to listen to their advice. [18]They decided to abandon the Temple of the LORD, the God of their ancestors, and they worshiped Asherah poles and idols instead! Then the anger of God burned against Judah and Jerusalem because of their sin. [19]The LORD sent prophets to bring them back to him, but the people would not listen.

[20]Then the Spirit of God came upon Zechariah son of Jehoiada the priest. He stood before the people and said, "This is what God says: Why do you disobey the LORD's commands so that you cannot prosper? You have abandoned the LORD, and now he has abandoned you!"

[21]Then the leaders plotted to kill Zechariah, and by order of King Joash himself, they stoned him to death in the courtyard of the LORD's Temple. [22]That was how King Joash repaid Jehoiada for his love and loyalty—by killing his son. Zechariah's last words as he died were, "May the LORD see what they are doing and hold them accountable!"

[23]At the beginning of the year, the Aramean army marched against Joash. They invaded Judah and Jerusalem and killed all the leaders of the nation. Then they sent all the plunder back to their king in Damascus. [24]Although the Arameans attacked with only a small army, the LORD helped them conquer the much larger army of Judah. The people of Judah had abandoned the LORD, the God of their ancestors, so judgment was executed against Joash.

[25]The Arameans withdrew, leaving Joash severely wounded. But his own officials decided to kill him for murdering the son of Jehoiada the priest. They assassinated him as he lay in bed. Then he was buried in the City of David, but not in the royal cemetery. [26]The assassins were Jozabad,* the son of an Ammonite woman named Shimeath, and Jehozabad, the son of a Moabite woman named Shomer.*

[27]The complete story about the sons of Joash, the prophecies about him, and the record of his restoration of the Temple of God are written in *The Commentary on the Book of the Kings*. When Joash died, his son Amaziah became the next king.

CHAPTER 25

Amaziah was twenty-five years old when he became king, and he reigned in Jerusalem twenty-nine years. His mother was Jehoaddin,* from Jerusalem. [2]Amaziah did what was pleasing in the LORD's sight, but not wholeheartedly.

[3]When Amaziah was well established as king, he executed the men who had assassinated his father. [4]However, he did not kill the children of the assassins, for he obeyed

24:26a As in parallel text at 2 Kgs 12:21; Hebrew reads *Zabad*.   24:26b As in parallel text at 2 Kgs 12:21; Hebrew reads *Shimrith*.
25:1 As in parallel text at 2 Kgs 14:2; Hebrew reads *Jehoaddan*, a variant name for Jehoaddin.

the command of the LORD written in the Book of the Law of Moses: "Parents must not be put to death for the sins of their children, nor the children for the sins of their parents. Those worthy of death must be executed for their own crimes."*

5Another thing Amaziah did was to organize the army, assigning leaders to each clan from Judah and Benjamin. Then he took a census and found that he had an army of 300,000 men twenty years old and older, all trained in the use of spear and shield. 6He also paid about 7,500 pounds* of silver to hire 100,000 experienced fighting men from Israel.

7But a man of God came to the king and said, "O king, do not hire troops from Israel, for the LORD is not with Israel. He will not help those people of Ephraim! 8If you let them go with your troops into battle, you will be defeated no matter how well you fight. God will overthrow you, for he has the power to help or to frustrate."

9Amaziah asked the man of God, "But what should I do about the silver I paid to hire the army of Israel?"

The man of God replied, "The LORD is able to give you much more than this!" 10So Amaziah discharged the hired troops and sent them back to Ephraim. This made them angry with Judah, and they returned home in a great rage.

11Then Amaziah summoned his courage and led his army to the Valley of Salt, where they killed ten thousand Edomite troops from Seir. 12They captured another ten thousand and took them to the top of a cliff and threw them off, dashing them to pieces on the rocks below.

13Meanwhile, the hired troops that Amaziah had sent home raided several of the towns of Judah between Samaria and Bethhoron, killing three thousand people and carrying off great quantities of plunder.

14When King Amaziah returned from defeating the Edomites, he brought with him idols taken from the people of Seir. He set them up as his own gods, bowed down in front of them, and presented sacrifices to them! 15This made the LORD very angry, and he sent a prophet to ask, "Why have you worshiped gods who could not even save their own people from you?"

16But the king interrupted him and said,

"Since when have I asked your advice? Be quiet now before I have you killed!"

So the prophet left with this warning: "I know that God has determined to destroy you because you have done this and have not accepted my counsel."

17After consulting with his advisers, King Amaziah of Judah sent this challenge to Israel's king Jehoash,* the son of Jehoahaz and grandson of Jehu: "Come and meet me in battle!"

18But King Jehoash of Israel replied to King Amaziah of Judah with this story: "Out in the Lebanon mountains, a thistle sent a message to a mighty cedar tree: 'Give your daughter in marriage to my son.' But just then a wild animal came by and stepped on the thistle, crushing it! 19You may be very proud of your conquest of Edom, but my advice is to stay home. Why stir up trouble that will bring disaster on you and the people of Judah?"

20But Amaziah would not listen, for God was arranging to destroy him for worshiping the gods of Edom. 21So King Jehoash of Israel mobilized his army against King Amaziah of Judah. The two armies drew up their battle lines at Bethshemesh in Judah. 22Judah was routed by the army of Israel, and its army scattered and fled for home. 23King Jehoash of Israel captured King Amaziah of Judah at Beth-shemesh and brought him back to Jerusalem. Then Jehoash ordered his army to demolish six hundred feet* of Jerusalem's wall, from the Ephraim Gate to the Corner Gate. 24He carried off all the gold and silver and all the utensils from the Temple of God that had been in the care of Obed-edom. He also seized the treasures of the royal palace, along with hostages, and then returned to Samaria.

25King Amaziah of Judah lived on for fifteen years after the death of King Jehoash of Israel. 26The rest of the events of Amaziah's reign, from beginning to end, are recorded in *The Book of the Kings of Judah and Israel.* 27After Amaziah turned away from the LORD, there was a conspiracy against his life in Jerusalem, and he fled to Lachish. But his enemies sent assassins after him, and they killed him there. 28They brought him back to Jerusalem on a horse, and he was buried with his ancestors in the City of David.*

25:4 Deut 24:16.   25:6 Hebrew *100 talents* [3.4 metric tons].   25:17 Hebrew *Joash,* a variant name for Jehoash; also in 25:18, 21, 23, 25.   25:23 Hebrew *400 cubits* [180 meters].   25:28 As in some Hebrew manuscripts and other ancient versions (see also 2 Kgs 14:20); most Hebrew manuscripts read *the city of Judah.*

APRIL 27 ☐ DAY 118
2 CHRONICLES 26–28
Reigns of Uzziah to Ahaz

OVERVIEW Uzziah's fifty-two-year reign can be summarized in a dozen words: "As long as the king sought the LORD, God gave him success" (26:5). His administration sparkles with military, architectural, and agricultural achievements. But the luster is dimmed in his final years when he intrudes into the priests' functions and dies of leprosy. His son Jotham picks up where his father left off by becoming "powerful because he was careful to live in obedience to the LORD his God" (27:6). But after nearly seven decades of godly national leadership, Ahaz emerges to undo much of what his father and grandfather had accomplished. Forbidden alliances, infant sacrifices, and rank idolatry bring the nation of Judah to its knees "because of King Ahaz . . . for he had encouraged his people to sin and had been utterly unfaithful to the LORD" (28:19).

Chapter 26	Chapter 27	Chapter 28
Uzziah, Usurper in the Temple	Jotham, Giant on the Battlefield	Ahaz, Heathen in the Palace
Pride	Prosperity	Pollution

YOUR DAILY WALK Take a few minutes to complete the following statements:

When you see a worthy person, emulate him or her; when you see an unworthy person, examine yourself.

"You will stay stronger and healthier *physically* if you . . ."
"You will stay stronger and healthier *financially* if you . . ."
"You will stay stronger and healthier *emotionally* if you . . ."
Now that you have the hang of it, try the really hard one!
"You will stay stronger and healthier *spiritually* if you . . ."

Just as there are God-given principles for physical, financial, and emotional health, so, too, there are God-given principles for spiritual health. Keep them and you will enjoy the benefits; violate them and you will pay the penalty. Uzziah and Jotham learned that painful lesson. Have you? Take your own counsel (as revealed in the way you completed the last sentence), compare it with Scripture, and look for a way to put it to work today.

INSIGHT A Century of Unemployed Prophets
As long as Judah's kings were obeying God's commands, there was no need for the prophet's ultimatum: Shape up or judgment will fall! That message was reserved for wicked kings and wicked times in the nation. Thus, during the century of godly leadership under Joash, Amaziah, Uzziah, and Jotham (835–732 B.C.), prophets were largely out of work!

CHAPTER 26

The people of Judah then crowned Amaziah's sixteen-year-old son, Uzziah, as their next king. ²After his father's death, Uzziah rebuilt the town of Elath* and restored it to Judah. ³Uzziah was sixteen when he became king, and he reigned in Jerusalem fifty-two years. His mother was Jecoliah, from Jerusalem. ⁴He did what was pleasing

in the LORD's sight, just as his father, Amaziah, had done. ⁵Uzziah sought God during the days of Zechariah, who instructed him in the fear of God. And as long as the king sought the LORD, God gave him success.

⁶He declared war on the Philistines and broke down the walls of Gath, Jabneh, and Ashdod. Then he built new towns in the

26:2 As in Greek version (see also 2 Kgs 14:22; 16:6); Hebrew reads *Eloth*.

Ashdod area and in other parts of Philistia. [7]God helped him not only with his wars against the Philistines, but also in his battles with the Arabs of Gur* and in his wars with the Meunites. [8]The Meunites* paid annual tribute to him, and his fame spread even to Egypt, for he had become very powerful.

[9]Uzziah built fortified towers in Jerusalem at the Corner Gate, at the Valley Gate, and at the angle in the wall. [10]He also constructed forts in the wilderness and dug many water cisterns, because he kept great herds of livestock in the foothills of Judah* and on the plains. He was also a man who loved the soil. He had many workers who cared for his farms and vineyards, both on the hillsides and in the fertile valleys.

[11]Uzziah had an army of well-trained warriors, ready to march into battle, unit by unit. This great army of fighting men had been mustered and organized by Jeiel, the secretary of the army, and his assistant, Maaseiah. They were under the direction of Hananiah, one of the king's officials. [12]Twenty-six hundred clan leaders commanded these regiments of seasoned warriors. [13]The army consisted of 307,500 men, all elite troops. They were prepared to assist the king against any enemy. [14]Uzziah provided the entire army with shields, spears, helmets, coats of mail, bows, and sling stones. [15]And he produced machines mounted on the walls of Jerusalem, designed by brilliant men to shoot arrows and hurl stones* from the towers and the corners of the wall. His fame spread far and wide, for the LORD helped him wonderfully until he became very powerful.

[16]But when he had become powerful, he also became proud, which led to his downfall. He sinned against the LORD his God by entering the sanctuary of the LORD's Temple and personally burning incense on the altar. [17]Azariah the high priest went in after him with eighty other priests of the LORD, all brave men. [18]They confronted King Uzziah and said, "It is not for you, Uzziah, to burn incense to the LORD. That is the work of the priests alone, the sons of Aaron who are set apart for this work. Get out of the sanctuary, for

you have sinned. The LORD God will not honor you for this!"

[19]Uzziah was furious and refused to set down the incense burner he was holding. But as he was standing there with the priests before the incense altar in the LORD's Temple, leprosy* suddenly broke out on his forehead. [20]When Azariah and the other priests saw the leprosy, they rushed him out. And the king himself was eager to get out because the LORD had struck him. [21]So King Uzziah had leprosy until the day he died. He lived in isolation, excluded from the Temple of the LORD. His son Jotham was put in charge of the royal palace, and he governed the people of the land.

[22]The rest of the events of Uzziah's reign, from beginning to end, are recorded by the prophet Isaiah son of Amoz. [23]So Uzziah died, and since he had leprosy, he was buried nearby in a burial field belonging to the kings. Then his son Jotham became the next king.

CHAPTER 27

Jotham was twenty-five years old when he became king, and he reigned in Jerusalem sixteen years. His mother was Jerusha, the daughter of Zadok. [2]He did what was pleasing in the LORD's sight, just as his father, Uzziah, had done. But unlike him, Jotham did not enter the Temple of the LORD. Nevertheless, the people continued in their corrupt ways.

[3]Jotham rebuilt the Upper Gate to the LORD's Temple and also did extensive rebuilding on the wall at the hill of Ophel. [4]He built towns in the hill country of Judah and constructed fortresses and towers in the wooded areas. [5]Jotham waged war against the Ammonites and conquered them. For the next three years, he received from them an annual tribute of 7,500 pounds* of silver, 50,000 bushels of wheat, and 50,000 bushels of barley.*

[6]King Jotham became powerful because he was careful to live in obedience to the LORD his God.

[7]The rest of the events of Jotham's reign, including his wars and other activities, are recorded in The Book of the Kings of Israel and Judah. [8]He was twenty-five years old when

26:7 As in Greek version; Hebrew reads Gur-baal.   26:8 As in Greek version; Hebrew reads Ammonites. Compare 26:7.   26:10 Hebrew the Shephelah.   26:15 Or designed by brilliant men to protect those who shot arrows and stones.   26:19 Or a contagious skin disease. The Hebrew word used here and throughout this passage can describe various skin diseases.   27:5a Hebrew 100 talents [3.4 metric tons].   27:5b Hebrew 10,000 cors [1,820 kiloliters] of wheat, and 10,000 cors of barley.

he became king, and he reigned in Jerusalem sixteen years. ⁹When he died, he was buried in the City of David, and his son Ahaz became the next king.

CHAPTER 28

Ahaz was twenty years old when he became king, and he reigned in Jerusalem sixteen years. He did not do what was pleasing in the sight of the LORD, as his ancestor David had done. ²Instead, he followed the example of the kings of Israel and cast images for the worship of Baal. ³He offered sacrifices in the valley of the son of Hinnom, even sacrificing his own sons in the fire.* He imitated the detestable practices of the pagan nations whom the LORD had driven from the land ahead of the Israelites. ⁴He offered sacrifices and burned incense at the pagan shrines and on the hills and under every green tree.

⁵That is why the LORD his God allowed the king of Aram to defeat Ahaz and to exile large numbers of his people to Damascus. The armies of Israel also defeated Ahaz and inflicted many casualties on his army. ⁶In a single day Pekah son of Remaliah, Israel's king, killed 120,000 of Judah's troops because they had abandoned the LORD, the God of their ancestors. ⁷Then Zicri, a warrior from Ephraim, killed Maaseiah, the king's son; Azrikam, the king's palace commander; and Elkanah, the king's second-in-command. ⁸The armies of Israel captured 200,000 women and children from Judah and took tremendous amounts of plunder, which they took back to Samaria.

⁹But a prophet of the LORD named Oded was there in Samaria when the army of Israel returned home. He went out to meet them and said, "The LORD, the God of your ancestors, was angry with Judah and let you defeat them. But you have gone too far, killing them without mercy, and all heaven is disturbed. ¹⁰And now you are planning to make slaves of these people from Judah and Jerusalem. What about your own sins against the LORD your God? ¹¹Listen to me and return these captives you have taken, for they are your own relatives. Watch out, because now the LORD's fierce anger has been turned against you!"

¹²Then some of the leaders of Israel*—

Azariah son of Jehohanan, Berekiah son of Meshillemoth, Jehizkiah son of Shallum, and Amasa son of Hadlai—agreed with this and confronted the men returning from battle. ¹³"You must not bring the prisoners here!" they declared. "We cannot afford to add to our sins and guilt. Our guilt is already great, and the LORD's fierce anger is already turned against Israel."

¹⁴So the warriors released the prisoners and handed over the plunder in the sight of all the leaders and people. ¹⁵Then the four men mentioned by name came forward and distributed clothes from the plunder to the prisoners who were naked. They provided clothing and sandals to wear, gave them enough food and drink, and dressed their wounds with olive oil. They put those who were weak on donkeys and took all the prisoners back to their own land—to Jericho, the city of palms. Then they returned to Samaria.

¹⁶About that time King Ahaz of Judah asked the king of Assyria for help against his enemies. ¹⁷The armies of Edom had again invaded Judah and taken captives. ¹⁸And the Philistines had raided towns located in the foothills of Judah* and in the Negev. They had already captured Beth-shemesh, Aijalon, Gederoth, Soco with its villages, Timnah with its villages, and Gimzo with its villages, and the Philistines had occupied these towns. ¹⁹The LORD was humbling Judah because of King Ahaz of Judah,* for he had encouraged his people to sin and had been utterly unfaithful to the LORD. ²⁰So when King Tiglath-pileser* of Assyria arrived, he oppressed King Ahaz instead of helping him. ²¹Ahaz took valuable items from the LORD's Temple, the royal palace, and from the homes of his officials and gave them to the king of Assyria as tribute. But even this did not help him.

²²And when trouble came to King Ahaz, he became even more unfaithful to the LORD. ²³He offered sacrifices to the gods of Damascus who had defeated him, for he said, "These gods helped the kings of Aram, so they will help me, too, if I sacrifice to them." But instead, they led to his ruin and the ruin of all Israel. ²⁴The king took the utensils from the Temple of God and broke them into pieces. He shut the doors of the LORD's Temple so that no one could worship there and then set up altars to

---

28:3 Or *even making his sons pass through the fire.*   28:12 Hebrew *Ephraim,* referring to the northern kingdom of Israel.
28:18 Hebrew *the Shephelah.*   28:19 Hebrew *of Israel.*   28:20 Hebrew *Tilgath-pilneser,* a variant name for Tiglath-pileser.

pagan gods in every corner of Jerusalem. [25] He made pagan shrines in all the towns of Judah for offering sacrifices to other gods. In this way, he aroused the anger of the LORD, the God of his ancestors.

[26] The rest of the events of Ahaz's reign and all his dealings, from beginning to end, are recorded in *The Book of the Kings of Judah and Israel.* [27] When King Ahaz died, he was buried in Jerusalem but not in the royal cemetery. Then his son Hezekiah became the next king.

APRIL 28 ☐ DAY 119
Ageless Obedience

 LOOK BACK First Chronicles provides a priestly view of David's reign. Second Chronicles continues this "divine editorial" by focusing on David's descendants, the kings who ruled over the southern kingdom of Judah. Kings whose names were barely mentioned in 2 Kings receive extensive space in 2 Chronicles, and for good reason. Asa, Jehoshaphat, Joash, Uzziah, and Jotham led reforms that helped to restore righteousness and postpone judgment for decades. They made a difference in their generation because they walked with God and used their God-given influence for good.

Notice how the chronicler highlights both the *what* of their reign and the *why* behind their success (emphasis added):

"The LORD was with Jehoshaphat *because* he followed the example of his father's early years" (2 Chronicles 17:3).

"*As long as* [Uzziah] sought the LORD, God gave him success" (2 Chronicles 26:5).

"King Jotham became powerful *because* he was careful to live in obedience to the LORD his God" (2 Chronicles 27:6).

Sadly, the influence of these godly kings is largely blunted by the cumulative effect of many more ungodly kings. The spiral is clearly downward, and time is running out for Judah.

 LOOK UP There were no headlines in Uzziah's day, but if there had been, they might have read: "Teenager Takes Over Reins of Government."

Obedience sheds light on the hidden things of God.

At the tender age of sixteen, the boy-king Uzziah began a reign that would eventually stretch more than half a century. Barely old enough to drive a chariot, Uzziah suddenly found himself steering an entire nation! Armed with a healthy fear of God, a robust commitment to do what was right, and a circle of godly advisers, Uzziah wasted no time "going to school" on his nation. Here's how his report card might have looked, according to 2 Chronicles 26:

Achievements: "He declared war . . . and broke down the walls of Gath, Jabneh, and Ashdod."

Architecture: "He built new towns . . . fortified towers . . . and dug many water cisterns . . ."

Agriculture: "He kept great herds of livestock . . . He had many workers who cared for his farms and vineyards . . ."

Armed forces: He had "an army . . . of 307,500 men, all elite troops."

Accolades: "His fame spread far and wide, for . . . he became very powerful."

Straight A's in his kingly curriculum, to be sure. And yet, when the final report card was in, Uzziah had failed in the role of king because "when he had become powerful, he also became proud, which led to his downfall" (26:16). Arrogance and presumption later in life resulted in his being stricken with leprosy and dying a tragic death.

LOOK AHEAD Believe it or not, an even younger king than Uzziah once sat upon the throne of Judah—a seven-year-old named Joash (2 Chronicles 24:1)! Faithfulness to God knows no age limit. Whether young or old, you are the right age to seek God and obey him with a whole heart.

The apostle Paul underscored this point when he told his youthful understudy Timothy, "Don't let anyone think less of you because you are young. Be an example to all believers in what you teach, in the way you live, in your love, your faith, and your purity" (1 Timothy 4:12).

Now there's a homework assignment you can spend a lifetime completing!

APRIL 29 ☐ DAY 120
2 CHRONICLES 29–32
Reform under Hezekiah

OVERVIEW Ahaz's son Hezekiah inherits a nation that is spiritually cold, militarily weak, and politically disorganized. And brutal Assyrian forces threaten Judah's very existence. What should Hezekiah do first: reorganize the palace or rearm his troops? Wisely he chooses to reestablish the worship of God as the nation's top priority. In the first month of his administration, Hezekiah reopens and repairs the house of the Lord, restores observance of the Passover, and declares war on idol worship and pagan practices. When the Assyrians come, Hezekiah handles the danger as he has handled so many decisions before: on his knees. God answers Hezekiah's prayer and honors his faith by bringing Assyria to defeat without a single Israelite soldier being lost in battle!

Chapter 29	Chapters 30–31	Chapter 32
Hezekiah's Rapid Reforms	Hezekiah's Passover Preparations	Hezekiah's Divine Deliverance
Correction	Celebration	Confrontation

YOUR DAILY WALK Some of the kings in 2 Chronicles are described in as few as nine verses (e.g., Jotham, 27:1-9); others command as much as four chapters (e.g., Jehoshaphat and Hezekiah). Can you suggest a reason for this uneven treatment and selective emphasis on Judah's kings?

Faith is the tendril by which the soul clings to God.

God's Word is not blind to the failures of his children, but neither is it stingy in its praise of those who lived out their faith day by day. Do you need a godly model to encourage you in your walk with God? Then look no further than such heroes of the faith as Solomon, Asa, Jehoshaphat, Joash, or Hezekiah.

Walking by faith is not an impossible assignment. In God's strength it can be done. They did it . . . and so can you! Complete this sentence: "The hero of the faith from 2 Chronicles I most admire is _____ because _____."

INSIGHT The Day the People Led the Priests in Worship
In the days of Ahaz, the priests had done nothing to oppose the godless activities of the king (2 Kings 16:10-16). Now the zeal of the people in returning to the worship of the Lord and observance of the Passover shamed the priests into action. They, too, sanctified themselves and brought burnt offerings to the Temple (30:15).

CHAPTER 29

Hezekiah was twenty-five years old when he became the king of Judah, and he reigned in Jerusalem twenty-nine years. His mother was Abijah, the daughter of Zechariah. ²He did what was pleasing in the LORD's sight, just as his ancestor David had done.

³In the very first month of the first year of his reign, Hezekiah reopened the doors of the Temple of the LORD and repaired them. ⁴He summoned the priests and Levites to meet him at the courtyard east of the Temple. ⁵He said to them, "Listen to me, you Levites! Purify yourselves, and purify the Temple of the LORD, the God of your ancestors. Remove all the defiled things from the sanctuary. ⁶Our ancestors were unfaithful and did what was evil in the sight of the LORD our God. They abandoned the LORD and his Temple; they turned their backs on him. ⁷They also shut the doors to the Temple's foyer, and they snuffed out the lamps. They stopped burning incense and presenting burnt offerings at the sanctuary of the God of Israel. ⁸That is why the LORD's anger has fallen upon Judah and Jerusalem. He has made us an object of dread, horror, and ridicule, as you can so plainly see. ⁹Our fathers have been killed in battle, and our sons and daughters and wives are in captivity. ¹⁰But now I will make a covenant with the LORD, the God of Israel, so that his fierce anger will turn away from us. ¹¹My dear Levites, do not neglect your duties any longer! The LORD has chosen you to stand in his presence, to minister to him, and to lead the people in worship and make offerings to him."

¹²Then these Levites got right to work:

From the clan of Kohath: Mahath son of Amasai and Joel son of Azariah.
From the clan of Merari: Kish son of Abdi and Azariah son of Jehallelel.
From the clan of Gershon: Joah son of Zimmah and Eden son of Joah.
¹³ From the family of Elizaphan: Shimri and Jeiel.
From the family of Asaph: Zechariah and Mattaniah.
¹⁴ From the family of Heman: Jehiel and Shimei.
From the family of Jeduthun: Shemaiah and Uzziel.

¹⁵These men called together their fellow Levites, and they purified themselves. Then they began to purify the Temple of the LORD, just as the king had commanded. They were careful to follow all the LORD's instructions in their work. ¹⁶The priests went into the sanctuary of the Temple of the LORD to cleanse it, and they took out to the Temple courtyard all the defiled things they found. From there the Levites carted it all out to the Kidron Valley.

¹⁷The work began on a day in early spring,* and in eight days they had reached the foyer of the LORD's Temple. Then they purified the Temple of the LORD itself, which took another eight days. So the entire task was completed in sixteen days.

¹⁸Then the Levites went to King Hezekiah and gave him this report: "We have purified the Temple of the LORD, the altar of burnt offering with all its utensils, and the table of the Bread of the Presence with all its utensils. ¹⁹We have also recovered all the utensils taken by King Ahaz when he was unfaithful and closed the Temple. They are now in front of the altar of the LORD, purified and ready for use."

²⁰Early the next morning King Hezekiah gathered the city officials and went to the Temple of the LORD. ²¹They brought seven bulls, seven rams, seven lambs, and seven male goats as a sin offering for the kingdom, for the Temple, and for Judah. The king commanded the priests, who were descendants of Aaron, to sacrifice the animals on the altar of the LORD. ²²So they killed the bulls, and the priests took the blood and sprinkled it on the altar. Next they killed the rams and sprinkled their blood on the altar. And finally, they did the same with the lambs. ²³The male goats for the sin offering were then brought before the king and the assembly of people, who laid their hands on them. ²⁴The priests then killed the goats as a sin offering and sprinkled their blood on the altar to make atonement for the sins of all Israel. The king had specifically commanded that this burnt offering and sin offering should be made for all Israel.

²⁵King Hezekiah then stationed the Levites at the Temple of the LORD with cymbals, harps, and lyres. He obeyed all the commands that the LORD had given to King David through Gad, the king's seer, and the

prophet Nathan. ²⁶The Levites then took their positions around the Temple with the instruments of David, and the priests took their positions with the trumpets. ²⁷Then Hezekiah ordered that the burnt offering be placed on the altar. As the burnt offering was presented, songs of praise to the LORD were begun, accompanied by the trumpets and other instruments of David, king of Israel. ²⁸The entire assembly worshiped the LORD as the singers sang and the trumpets blew, until all the burnt offerings were finished. ²⁹Then the king and everyone with him bowed down in worship. ³⁰King Hezekiah and the officials ordered the Levites to praise the LORD with the psalms of David and Asaph the seer. So they offered joyous praise and bowed down in worship.

³¹Then Hezekiah declared, "The dedication ceremony has come to an end. Now bring your sacrifices and thanksgiving offerings to the Temple of the LORD." So the people brought their sacrifices and thanksgiving offerings, and those whose hearts were willing brought burnt offerings, too. ³²The people brought to the LORD seventy bulls, one hundred rams, and two hundred lambs for burnt offerings. ³³They also brought six hundred bulls and three thousand sheep as sacrifices. ³⁴But there were too few priests to prepare all the burnt offerings, so their relatives the Levites helped them until the work was finished and until more priests had been purified. For the Levites had been more conscientious about purifying themselves than the priests. ³⁵There was an abundance of burnt offerings, along with the usual drink offerings, and a great deal of fat from the many peace offerings. So the Temple of the LORD was restored to service. ³⁶And Hezekiah and all the people rejoiced greatly because of what God had done for the people, for everything had been accomplished so quickly.

CHAPTER 30

King Hezekiah now sent word to all Israel and Judah, and he wrote letters of invitation to Ephraim and Manasseh. He asked everyone to come to the Temple of the LORD at Jerusalem to celebrate the Passover of the LORD, the God of Israel. ²The king, his officials, and all the community of Jerusalem decided to celebrate Passover a month later than usual.* ³They were unable to celebrate it at the regular time because not enough priests could be purified by then, and the people had not yet assembled at Jerusalem. ⁴This plan for keeping the Passover seemed right to the king and all the people. ⁵So they sent a proclamation throughout all Israel, from Beersheba in the south to Dan in the north, inviting everyone to come to Jerusalem to celebrate the Passover of the LORD, the God of Israel. The people had not been celebrating it in great numbers as prescribed in the law.

⁶At the king's command, messengers were sent throughout Israel and Judah. They carried letters which said:

"O people of Israel, return to the LORD, the God of Abraham, Isaac, and Israel,* so that he will return to the few of us who have survived the conquest of the Assyrian kings. ⁷Do not be like your ancestors and relatives who abandoned the LORD, the God of their ancestors, and became an object of derision, as you yourselves can see. ⁸Do not be stubborn, as they were, but submit yourselves to the LORD. Come to his Temple which he has set apart as holy forever. Worship the LORD your God so that his fierce anger will turn away from you. ⁹For if you return to the LORD, your relatives and your children will be treated mercifully by their captors, and they will be able to return to this land. For the LORD your God is gracious and merciful. If you return to him, he will not continue to turn his face from you."

¹⁰The messengers went from town to town throughout Ephraim and Manasseh and as far as the territory of Zebulun. But most of the people just laughed at the messengers and made fun of them. ¹¹However, some from Asher, Manasseh, and Zebulun humbled themselves and went to Jerusalem. ¹²At the same time, God's hand was on the people in the land of Judah, giving them a strong desire to unite in obeying the orders of the king and his officials, who were following the word of the LORD. ¹³And so a huge crowd assembled at Jerusalem in midspring* to celebrate Passover and the Festival of Unleavened Bread. ¹⁴They set to work and removed the pagan

30:2 Hebrew *in the second month.* This month of the Hebrew lunar calendar usually occurs in April and May. **30:6** *Israel* is the name that God gave to Jacob. **30:13** Hebrew *in the second month.* This month of the Hebrew lunar calendar usually occurs in April and May.

altars from Jerusalem. They took away all the incense altars and threw them into the Kidron Valley.

[15]On the appointed day in midspring, one month later than usual,* the people slaughtered their Passover lambs. Then the priests and Levites became ashamed, so they purified themselves and brought burnt offerings to the Temple of the LORD. [16]They took their places at the Temple according to the regulations found in the law of Moses, the man of God. The Levites brought the sacrificial blood to the priests, who then sprinkled it on the altar.

[17]Since many of the people there had not purified themselves, the Levites had to slaughter their Passover lambs for them, to set them apart for the LORD. [18]Most of those who came from Ephraim, Manasseh, Issachar, and Zebulun had not purified themselves. But King Hezekiah prayed for them, and they were allowed to eat the Passover meal anyway, even though this was contrary to God's laws. For Hezekiah said, "May the LORD, who is good, pardon those [19]who decide to follow the LORD, the God of their ancestors, even though they are not properly cleansed for the ceremony." [20]And the LORD listened to Hezekiah's prayer and healed the people.

[21]So the people of Israel who were present in Jerusalem celebrated the Festival of Unleavened Bread for seven days with great joy. Each day the Levites and priests sang to the LORD, accompanied by loud instruments.* [22]Hezekiah encouraged the Levites for the skill they displayed as they served the LORD. So for seven days the celebration continued. Peace offerings were sacrificed, and the people confessed their sins to the LORD, the God of their ancestors.

[23]The entire assembly then decided to continue the festival another seven days, so they celebrated joyfully for another week. [24]King Hezekiah gave the people one thousand bulls and seven thousand sheep for offerings, and the officials donated one thousand bulls and ten thousand sheep. Meanwhile, many more priests purified themselves.

[25]The entire assembly of Judah rejoiced, including the priests, the Levites, all who came from the land of Israel, the foreigners who came to the festival, and all those who lived in Judah. [26]There was great joy in the city, for Jerusalem had not seen a celebration like this one since the days of Solomon, King David's son. [27]Then the Levitical priests stood and blessed the people, and God heard them from his holy dwelling in heaven.

CHAPTER 31

Now when the festival ended, the Israelites who attended went to all the towns of Judah, Benjamin, Ephraim, and Manasseh, and they smashed the sacred pillars, cut down the Asherah poles, and removed the pagan shrines and altars. After this, the Israelites returned to their own towns and homes.

[2]Hezekiah then organized the priests and Levites into divisions to offer the burnt offerings and peace offerings, and to worship and give thanks and praise to the LORD at the gates of the Temple. [3]The king also made a personal contribution of animals for the daily morning and evening burnt offerings, as well as for the weekly Sabbath festivals and monthly new moon festivals, and for the other annual festivals as required in the law of the LORD. [4]In addition, he required the people in Jerusalem to bring the prescribed portion of their income to the priests and Levites, so they could devote themselves fully to the law of the LORD.

[5]The people responded immediately and generously with the first of their crops and grain, new wine, olive oil, honey, and all the produce of their fields. They brought a tithe of all they owned. [6]The people who had moved to Judah from Israel, and the people of Judah themselves, brought in the tithes of their cattle and sheep and a tithe of the things that had been dedicated to the LORD their God, and they piled them up in great heaps. [7]The first of these tithes was brought in late spring,* and the heaps continued to grow until early autumn.* [8]When Hezekiah and his officials came and saw these huge piles, they thanked the LORD and his people Israel!

[9]"Where did all this come from?" Hezekiah asked the priests and Levites.

[10]And Azariah the high priest, from the

30:15 Hebrew *On the fourteenth day of the second month.* This day of the Hebrew lunar calendar occurs in late April or early May. **30:21** Or *sang to the LORD with all their strength.*   **31:7a** Hebrew *in the third month.* This month of the Hebrew lunar calendar usually occurs in May and June.   **31:7b** Hebrew *in the seventh month.* This month of the Hebrew lunar calendar usually occurs in September and October.

family of Zadok, replied, "Since the people began bringing their gifts to the LORD's Temple, we have had enough to eat and plenty to spare, for the LORD has blessed his people."

[11]Hezekiah decided to have storerooms prepared in the Temple of the LORD, and this was done. [12]Then all the gifts and tithes were faithfully brought to the Temple. Conaniah the Levite was put in charge, assisted by his brother Shimei. [13]The supervisors under them were Jehiel, Azaziah, Nahath, Asahel, Jerimoth, Jozabad, Eliel, Ismakiah, Mahath, and Benaiah. These appointments were made by King Hezekiah and Azariah, the chief official in the Temple of God.

[14]Kore son of Imnah the Levite, who was the gatekeeper at the East Gate, was put in charge of distributing the freewill offerings of God, the gifts, and the things that had been dedicated to the LORD. [15]His faithful assistants were Eden, Miniamin, Jeshua, Shemaiah, Amariah, and Shecaniah. They distributed the gifts among the families of priests in their towns, by their divisions, dividing the gifts fairly among young and old alike. [16]They also distributed the gifts to all males three years old or older, regardless of their place in the genealogical records, who came daily to the LORD's Temple to perform their official duties, by their divisions. [17]And they distributed gifts to the priests who were listed in the genealogical records by families, and to the Levites twenty years old or older who were listed according to their jobs and their divisions. [18]Food allotments were also given to all the families listed in the genealogical records, including the little babies, the wives, and the sons and daughters. For they had all been faithful in purifying themselves. [19]As for the priests, the descendants of Aaron, who were living in the open villages around the towns, men were appointed to distribute portions to every male among the priests and to all the Levites listed in the genealogical records.

[20]In this way, King Hezekiah handled the distribution throughout all Judah, doing what was pleasing and good in the sight of the LORD his God. [21]In all that he did in the service of the Temple of God and in his efforts to follow the law and the commands,

Hezekiah sought his God wholeheartedly. As a result, he was very successful.

CHAPTER 32

After Hezekiah had faithfully carried out this work, King Sennacherib of Assyria invaded Judah. He laid siege to the fortified cities, giving orders for his army to break through their walls. [2]When Hezekiah realized that Sennacherib also intended to attack Jerusalem, [3]he consulted with his officials and military advisers, and they decided to stop the flow of the springs outside the city. [4]They organized a huge work crew to stop the flow of the springs, cutting off the brook that ran through the fields. For they said, "Why should the kings of Assyria come here and find plenty of water?"

[5]Then Hezekiah further strengthened his defenses by repairing the wall wherever it was broken down and by adding to the fortifications and constructing a second wall outside the first. He also reinforced the Millo* in the City of David and manufactured large numbers of weapons and shields. [6]He appointed military officers over the people and asked them to assemble before him in the square at the city gate. Then Hezekiah encouraged them with this address: [7]"Be strong and courageous! Don't be afraid of the king of Assyria or his mighty army, for there is a power far greater on our side! [8]He may have a great army, but they are just men. We have the LORD our God to help us and to fight our battles for us!" These words greatly encouraged the people.

[9]Then King Sennacherib of Assyria, while still besieging the town of Lachish, sent officials to Jerusalem with this message for Hezekiah and all the people in the city:

[10]"This is what King Sennacherib of Assyria says: What are you trusting in that makes you think you can survive my siege of Jerusalem? [11]Hezekiah has said, 'The LORD our God will rescue us from the king of Assyria.' Surely Hezekiah is misleading you, sentencing you to death by famine and thirst! [12]Surely you must realize that Hezekiah is the very person who destroyed all the LORD's shrines and altars. He commanded Judah and Jerusalem to worship at only

32:5 Or *the supporting terraces.*

the one altar at the Temple and to make sacrifices on it alone.

¹³"Surely you must realize what I and the other kings of Assyria before me have done to all the people of the earth! Were any of the gods of those nations able to rescue their people from my power? ¹⁴Name just one time when any god, anywhere, was able to rescue his people from me! What makes you think your God can do any better? ¹⁵Don't let Hezekiah fool you! Don't let him deceive you like this! I say it again— no god of any nation has ever yet been able to rescue his people from me or my ancestors. How much less will your God rescue you from my power!"

¹⁶And Sennacherib's officials further mocked the LORD God and his servant Hezekiah, heaping insult upon insult. ¹⁷The king also sent letters scorning the LORD, the God of Israel. He wrote, "Just as the gods of all the other nations failed to rescue their people from my power, so the God of Hezekiah will also fail." ¹⁸The Assyrian officials who brought the letters shouted this in the Hebrew language to the people gathered on the walls of the city, trying to terrify them so it would be easier to capture the city. ¹⁹These officials talked about the God of Jerusalem as though he were one of the pagan gods, made by human hands.

²⁰Then King Hezekiah and the prophet Isaiah son of Amoz cried out in prayer to God in heaven. ²¹And the LORD sent an angel who destroyed the Assyrian army with all its commanders and officers. So Sennacherib returned home in disgrace to his own land. And when he entered the temple of his god, some of his own sons killed him there with a sword. ²²That is how the LORD rescued Hezekiah and the people of Jerusalem from King Sennacherib of Assyria and from all the others who threatened them. So there was peace at last throughout the land. ²³From then on King Hezekiah became highly respected among the surrounding nations, and many gifts for the LORD arrived at Jerusalem, with valuable presents for King Hezekiah, too.

²⁴About that time, Hezekiah became deathly ill. He prayed to the LORD, who healed him and gave him a miraculous sign. ²⁵But Hezekiah did not respond appropriately to the kindness shown him, and he became proud. So the LORD's anger came against him and against Judah and Jerusalem. ²⁶Then Hezekiah repented of his pride, and the people of Jerusalem humbled themselves. So the LORD's anger did not come against them during Hezekiah's lifetime.

²⁷Hezekiah was very wealthy and held in high esteem. He had to build special treasury buildings for his silver, gold, precious stones, and spices, and for his shields and other valuable items. ²⁸He also constructed many storehouses for his grain, new wine, and olive oil; and he made many stalls for his cattle and folds for his flocks of sheep and goats. ²⁹He built many towns and acquired vast flocks and herds, for God had given him great wealth. ³⁰He blocked up the upper spring of Gihon and brought the water down through a tunnel to the west side of the City of David. And so he succeeded in everything he did.

³¹However, when ambassadors arrived from Babylon to ask about the remarkable events that had taken place in the land, God withdrew from Hezekiah in order to test him and to see what was really in his heart.

³²The rest of the events of Hezekiah's reign and his acts of devotion are recorded in *The Vision of the Prophet Isaiah Son of Amoz*, which is included in *The Book of the Kings of Judah and Israel*. ³³When Hezekiah died, he was buried in the upper area of the royal cemetery, and all Judah and Jerusalem honored him at his death. Then his son Manasseh became the next king.

APRIL 30 ☐ DAY 121
2 CHRONICLES 33–36
Reigns of Judah's Last Kings

OVERVIEW The book of 2 Chronicles closes with bad news and good news. The bad news begins with the fifty-five-year reign of Manasseh, the longest ruling and most corrupt king in Judah. His reign of horror creates such a sinful situation in the nation that even the reforms of his successor, Josiah, cannot divert the coming judgment. Ultimately, the Babylonians sweep down upon Jerusalem, destroying the Temple, breaking down the walls, and carrying the inhabitants into exile in Babylon, where they will remain for seventy long years. But the book ends on a note of hope and good news! God has not forgotten his exiled nation. Seventy years later he raises up the Persian king Cyrus to give a proclamation: The people of Jerusalem are free to return home and rebuild the Temple of their God in Jerusalem.

Chapter 33	Chapters 34–35	Chapter 36
Manasseh's Evil	Josiah's Excellence	Judah's Exile
Law Ignored	Law Restored	People Removed

Better to master one mountain than a thousand foothills.

YOUR DAILY WALK Congratulations, you made it! You have finished another month of reading through the Bible. Your mind is probably buzzing with names and places you have encountered this month. But before you tackle next month's reading, spend a few minutes reviewing the books of Kings and Chronicles. Flip back through the pages, and then answer these questions:
• Who was your favorite character?
• Who was your least favorite character?
• Which day's reading did you enjoy the most?
• Which "Insight" did you enjoy the most?
• Which "Daily Walk" was most meaningful?
• How have you grown in your spiritual life this month?

INSIGHT Don't Throw Away God's Gifts to the Family
The ritual murder of children in the name of religion was common in heathen nations. Archaeologists have uncovered piles of ashes and infant skeletons around heathen altars. For God's people to engage in such demonic practices was against God's law; for their king to be the foremost practitioner of the occult—as was Manasseh—was complete apostasy, deserving of God's judgment.

CHAPTER 33
Manasseh was twelve years old when he became king, and he reigned in Jerusalem fifty-five years. ²He did what was evil in the LORD's sight, imitating the detestable practices of the pagan nations whom the LORD had driven from the land ahead of the Israelites. ³He rebuilt the pagan shrines his father Hezekiah had destroyed. He constructed altars for the images of Baal and

set up Asherah poles. He also bowed before all the stars of heaven and worshiped them. ⁴He even built pagan altars in the Temple of the LORD, the place where the LORD had said his name should be honored forever. ⁵He put these altars for the stars of heaven in both courtyards of the LORD's Temple. ⁶Manasseh even sacrificed his own sons in the fire* in the valley of the son of Hinnom. He practiced sorcery, divination,

33:6 Or *even made his sons pass through the fire.*

and witchcraft, and he consulted with mediums and psychics. He did much that was evil in the LORD's sight, arousing his anger. [7]Manasseh even took a carved idol he had made and set it up in God's Temple, the very place where God had told David and his son Solomon: "My name will be honored here forever in this Temple and in Jerusalem—the city I have chosen from among all the other tribes of Israel. [8]If the Israelites will obey my commands—all the instructions, laws, and regulations given through Moses—I will not send them into exile from this land that I gave their ancestors." [9]But Manasseh led the people of Judah and Jerusalem to do even more evil than the pagan nations whom the LORD had destroyed when the Israelites entered the land.

[10]The LORD spoke to Manasseh and his people, but they ignored all his warnings. [11]So the LORD sent the Assyrian armies, and they took Manasseh prisoner. They put a ring through his nose, bound him in bronze chains, and led him away to Babylon. [12]But while in deep distress, Manasseh sought the LORD his God and cried out humbly to the God of his ancestors. [13]And when he prayed, the LORD listened to him and was moved by his request for help. So the LORD let Manasseh return to Jerusalem and to his kingdom. Manasseh had finally realized that the LORD alone is God!

[14]It was after this that Manasseh rebuilt the outer wall of the City of David, from west of the Gihon Spring in the Kidron Valley to the Fish Gate, and continuing around the hill of Ophel, where it was built very high. And he stationed his military officers in all of the fortified cities of Judah. [15]Manasseh also removed the foreign gods from the hills and the idol from the LORD's Temple. He tore down all the altars he had built on the hill where the Temple stood and all the altars that were in Jerusalem, and he dumped them outside the city. [16]Then he restored the altar of the LORD and sacrificed peace offerings and thanksgiving offerings on it. He also encouraged the people of Judah to worship the LORD, the God of Israel. [17]However, the people still sacrificed at the pagan shrines, but only to the LORD their God.

[18]The rest of the events of Manasseh's reign, his prayer to God, and the words the seers spoke to him in the name of the LORD, the God of Israel, are recorded in *The Book of the Kings of Israel.* [19]Manasseh's prayer, the account of the way God answered him, and an account of all his sins and unfaithfulness are recorded in *The Record of the Seers.** It includes a list of the locations where he built pagan shrines and set up Asherah poles and idols before he repented. [20]When Manasseh died, he was buried at his palace. Then his son Amon became the next king.

[21]Amon was twenty-two years old when he became king, and he reigned in Jerusalem two years. [22]He did what was evil in the LORD's sight, just as his father Manasseh had done. He worshiped and sacrificed to all the idols his father had made. [23]But unlike his father, he did not humble himself before the LORD. Instead, Amon sinned even more.

[24]At last Amon's own officials plotted against him and assassinated him in his palace. [25]But the people of the land killed all those who had conspired against King Amon, and they made his son Josiah the next king.

CHAPTER 34

Josiah was eight years old when he became king, and he reigned in Jerusalem thirty-one years. [2]He did what was pleasing in the LORD's sight and followed the example of his ancestor David. He did not turn aside from doing what was right.

[3]During the eighth year of his reign, while he was still young, Josiah began to seek the God of his ancestor David. Then in the twelfth year, he began to purify Judah and Jerusalem, destroying all the pagan shrines, the Asherah poles, and the carved idols and cast images. [4]He saw to it that the altars for the images of Baal and their incense altars were torn down. He also made sure that the Asherah poles, the carved idols, and the cast images were smashed and scattered over the graves of those who had sacrificed to them. [5]Then he burned the bones of the pagan priests on their own altars, and so he purified Judah and Jerusalem.

[6]He did the same thing in the towns of Manasseh, Ephraim, and Simeon, even as far as Naphtali. [7]He destroyed the pagan altars and the Asherah poles, and he

crushed the idols into dust. He cut down the incense altars throughout the land of Israel and then returned to Jerusalem.

[8]In the eighteenth year of his reign, after he had purified the land and the Temple, Josiah appointed Shaphan son of Azaliah, Maaseiah the governor of Jerusalem, and Joah son of Joahaz, the royal historian, to repair the Temple of the LORD his God. [9]They gave Hilkiah the high priest the money that had been collected by the Levites who served as gatekeepers at the Temple of God. The gifts were brought by people from Manasseh, Ephraim, and from all the remnant of Israel, as well as from all Judah, Benjamin, and the people of Jerusalem. [10]He entrusted the money to the men assigned to supervise the restoration of the LORD's Temple. Then they paid the workers who did the repairs and renovation. [11]Thus, they hired carpenters and masons and purchased cut stone for the walls and timber for the rafters and beams. They restored what earlier kings of Judah had allowed to fall into ruin.

[12]The workers served faithfully under the leadership of Jahath and Obadiah, Levites of the Merarite clan, and Zechariah and Meshullam, Levites of the Kohathite clan. Other Levites, all of whom were skilled musicians, [13]were put in charge of the laborers of the various trades. Still others assisted as secretaries, officials, and gatekeepers.

[14]As Hilkiah the high priest was recording the money collected at the LORD's Temple, he found the Book of the Law of the LORD as it had been given through Moses. [15]Hilkiah said to Shaphan the court secretary, "I have found the Book of the Law in the LORD's Temple!" Then Hilkiah gave the scroll to Shaphan.

[16]Shaphan took the scroll to the king and reported, "Your officials are doing everything they were assigned to do. [17]The money that was collected at the Temple of the LORD has been given to the supervisors and workmen." [18]Shaphan also said to the king, "Hilkiah the priest has given me a scroll." So Shaphan read it to the king.

[19]When the king heard what was written in the law, he tore his clothes in despair. [20]Then he gave these orders to Hilkiah, Ahikam son of Shaphan, Acbor son of Micaiah,* Shaphan the court secretary, and Asaiah the king's personal adviser: [21]"Go to the Temple and speak to the LORD for me and for all the remnant of Israel and Judah. Ask him about the words written in this scroll that has been found. The LORD's anger has been poured out against us because our ancestors have not obeyed the word of the LORD. We have not been doing what this scroll says we must do."

[22]So Hilkiah and the other men went to the newer Mishneh section* of Jerusalem to consult with the prophet Huldah. She was the wife of Shallum son of Tikvah and grandson of Harhas,* the keeper of the Temple wardrobe. [23]She said to them, "The LORD, the God of Israel, has spoken! Go and tell the man who sent you, [24]'This is what the LORD says: I will certainly destroy this city and its people. All the curses written in the scroll you have read will come true. [25]For the people of Judah have abandoned me and worshiped pagan gods, and I am very angry with them for everything they have done. My anger will be poured out against this place, and nothing will be able to stop it.'

[26]"But go to the king of Judah who sent you to seek the LORD and tell him: 'This is what the LORD, the God of Israel, says concerning the message you have just heard: [27]You were sorry and humbled yourself before God when you heard what I said against this city and its people. You humbled yourself and tore your clothing in despair and wept before me in repentance. So I have indeed heard you, says the LORD. [28]I will not send the promised disaster against this city and its people until after you have died and been buried in peace. You will not see the disaster I am going to bring on this place.'" So they took her message back to the king.

[29]Then the king summoned all the leaders of Judah and Jerusalem. [30]And the king went up to the Temple of the LORD with all the people of Judah and Jerusalem and the priests and the Levites—all the people from the greatest to the least. There the king read to them the entire Book of the Covenant that had been found in the LORD's Temple. [31]The king took his place of authority beside the pillar and renewed the covenant in the LORD's presence. He pledged to obey the LORD by keeping all his commands, regulations, and laws with all

34:20 As in parallel text at 2 Kgs 22:12; Hebrew reads *Abdon son of Micah.* **34:22a** Or *the Second Quarter,* a newer section of Jerusalem. **34:22b** As in parallel text at 2 Kgs 22:14; Hebrew reads *son of Tokhath, son of Hasrah.*

his heart and soul. He promised to obey all the terms of the covenant that were written in the scroll. [32]And he required everyone in Jerusalem and the people of Benjamin to make a similar pledge. As the people of Jerusalem did this, they renewed their covenant with God, the God of their ancestors.

[33]So Josiah removed all detestable idols from the entire land of Israel and required everyone to worship the LORD their God. And throughout the rest of his lifetime, they did not turn away from the LORD, the God of their ancestors.

CHAPTER 35

Then Josiah announced that the Passover of the LORD would be celebrated in Jerusalem on the appointed day in early spring.* The Passover lambs were slaughtered at twilight of that day. [2]Josiah also assigned the priests to their duties and encouraged them in their work at the Temple of the LORD. [3]He issued this order to the Levites, who had been set apart to serve the LORD and were teachers in Israel: "Since the Ark is now in Solomon's Temple and you do not need to carry it back and forth on your shoulders, spend your time serving the LORD your God and his people Israel. [4]Report for duty according to the family divisions of your ancestors, following the written instructions of King David of Israel and the instructions of his son Solomon. [5]Then stand in your appointed holy places and help the families assigned to you as they bring their offerings to the Temple. [6]Slaughter the Passover lambs, purify yourselves, and prepare to help those who come. Follow all the instructions that the LORD gave through Moses."

[7]Then Josiah contributed from his personal property thirty thousand lambs and young goats for the people's Passover offerings, and three thousand bulls. [8]The king's officials also made willing contributions to the people, priests, and Levites. Hilkiah, Zechariah, and Jehiel, the administrators of God's Temple, gave the priests twenty-six hundred lambs and young goats and three hundred bulls as Passover offerings. [9]The Levite leaders—Conaniah and his brothers Shemaiah and Nethanel, and Hashabiah, Jeiel, and Jozabad—gave five thousand lambs and young goats and

five hundred bulls to the Levites for their Passover offerings.

[10]When everything was ready for the Passover celebration, the priests and the Levites took their places, organized by their divisions, according to the king's orders. [11]The Levites then slaughtered the Passover lambs and presented the blood to the priests, who sprinkled the blood on the altar while the Levites prepared the animals. [12]They divided the burnt offerings among the people by their family groups, so they could offer them to the LORD according to the instructions recorded in the Book of Moses. They did the same with the bulls. [13]Then they roasted the Passover lambs as prescribed; and they boiled the holy offerings in pots, kettles, and pans, and brought them out quickly so the people could eat them.

[14]Afterward the Levites prepared a meal for themselves and for the priests, because the priests had been busy from morning till night offering the burnt offerings and the fat portions. The Levites took responsibility for all these preparations. [15]The musicians, descendants of Asaph, were in their assigned places, following the orders given by David, Asaph, Heman, and Jeduthun, the king's seer. The gatekeepers guarded the gates and did not need to leave their posts of duty, for their meals were brought to them by their fellow Levites.

[16]The entire ceremony for the LORD's Passover was completed that day. All the burnt offerings were sacrificed on the altar of the LORD, as King Josiah had ordered. [17]All the Israelites present in Jerusalem celebrated Passover and the Festival of Unleavened Bread for seven days. [18]Never since the time of the prophet Samuel had there been such a Passover. None of the kings of Israel had ever kept a Passover as Josiah did, involving all the priests and Levites, all the people of Jerusalem, and people from all over Judah and Israel. [19]This Passover celebration took place in the eighteenth year of Josiah's reign.

[20]After Josiah had finished restoring the Temple, King Neco of Egypt led his army up from Egypt to do battle at Carchemish on the Euphrates River, and Josiah and his army marched out to fight him. [21]But King Neco sent ambassadors to Josiah with this message:

35:1 Hebrew *on the fourteenth day of the first month.* This day of the Hebrew lunar calendar occurs in late March or early April.

"What do you want with me, king of Judah? I have no quarrel with you today! I only want to fight the nation with which I am at war. And God has told me to hurry! Do not interfere with God, who is with me, or he will destroy you."

22But Josiah refused to listen to Neco, to whom God had indeed spoken, and he would not turn back. Instead, he led his army into battle on the plain of Megiddo. He laid aside his royal robes so the enemy would not recognize him. 23But the enemy archers hit King Josiah with their arrows and wounded him. He cried out to his men, "Take me from the battle, for I am badly wounded!"

24So they lifted Josiah out of his chariot and placed him in another chariot. Then they brought him back to Jerusalem, where he died. He was buried there in the royal cemetery. And all Judah and Jerusalem mourned for him. 25The prophet Jeremiah composed funeral songs for Josiah, and to this day choirs still sing these sad songs about his death. These songs of sorrow have become a tradition and are recorded in *The Book of Laments.* 26The rest of the events of Josiah's reign and his acts of devotion done according to the written law of the LORD, 27from beginning to end, are recorded in *The Book of the Kings of Israel and Judah.*

CHAPTER 36

Then the people of the land took Josiah's son Jehoahaz and made him the next king in Jerusalem. 2Jehoahaz* was twenty-three years old when he became king, but he reigned only three months. 3Then he was deposed by Neco, the king of Egypt, who demanded a tribute from Judah of 7,500 pounds of silver and 75 pounds of gold.* 4The king of Egypt appointed Eliakim, the brother of Jehoahaz, as the next king of Judah and Jerusalem, and he changed Eliakim's name to Jehoiakim. Then Neco took Jehoahaz to Egypt as a prisoner.

5Jehoiakim was twenty-five years old when he became king, and he reigned in Jerusalem eleven years. But he did what was evil in the sight of the LORD his God. 6Then King Nebuchadnezzar of Babylon came to Jerusalem and captured it, and he bound Jehoiakim in chains and led him away to Babylon. 7Nebuchadnezzar also took some of the treasures from the Temple of the LORD, and he placed them in his palace* in Babylon. 8The rest of the events of Jehoiakim's reign, including all the evil things he did and everything found against him, are recorded in *The Book of the Kings of Israel and Judah.* Then his son Jehoiachin became the next king.

9Jehoiachin was eighteen* years old when he became king, but he reigned in Jerusalem only three months and ten days. Jehoiachin did what was evil in the LORD's sight. 10In the spring of the following year, Jehoiachin was summoned to Babylon by King Nebuchadnezzar. Many treasures from the Temple of the LORD were taken to Babylon at that time. And Nebuchadnezzar appointed Jehoiachin's uncle,* Zedekiah, to be the next king in Judah and Jerusalem.

11Zedekiah was twenty-one years old when he became king, and he reigned in Jerusalem eleven years. 12He did what was evil in the sight of the LORD his God, and he refused to humble himself in the presence of the prophet Jeremiah, who spoke for the LORD. 13He also rebelled against King Nebuchadnezzar, even though he had taken an oath of loyalty in God's name. Zedekiah was a hard and stubborn man, refusing to turn to the LORD, the God of Israel.

14All the leaders of the priests and the people became more and more unfaithful. They followed the pagan practices of the surrounding nations, desecrating the Temple of the LORD in Jerusalem.

15The LORD, the God of their ancestors, repeatedly sent his prophets to warn them, for he had compassion on his people and his Temple. 16But the people mocked these messengers of God and despised their words. They scoffed at the prophets until the LORD's anger could no longer be restrained and there was no remedy.

17So the LORD brought the king of Babylon against them. The Babylonians* killed Judah's young men, even chasing after them into the Temple. They had no pity on the people, killing both young and old, men and women, healthy and sick. God

36:2 Hebrew *Joahaz,* a variant name for Jehoahaz; also in 36:4.   36:3 Hebrew *100 talents* [3.4 metric tons] *of silver and 1 talent* [34 kilograms] *of gold.*   36:7 Or *temple.*   36:9 As in one Hebrew manuscript, some Greek manuscripts, and Syriac version (see also 2 Kgs 24:8); most Hebrew manuscripts read *eight.*   36:10 As in parallel text at 2 Kgs 24:17; Hebrew reads *brother,* or *relative.*   36:17 Or *Chaldeans.*

handed them all over to Nebuchadnezzar. [18]The king also took home to Babylon all the utensils, large and small, used in the Temple of God, and the treasures from both the LORD's Temple and the royal palace. He also took with him all the royal princes. [19]Then his army set fire to the Temple of God, broke down the walls of Jerusalem, burned all the palaces, and completely destroyed everything of value.* [20]The few who survived were taken away to Babylon, and they became servants to the king and his sons until the kingdom of Persia came to power. [21]So the message of the LORD spoken through Jeremiah was fulfilled. The land finally enjoyed its Sabbath rest, lying desolate for seventy years, just as the prophet had said.

[22]In the first year of King Cyrus of Persia,* the LORD fulfilled Jeremiah's prophecy by stirring the heart of Cyrus to put this proclamation into writing and to send it throughout his kingdom:

[23]"This is what King Cyrus of Persia says: The LORD, the God of heaven, has given me all the kingdoms of the earth. He has appointed me to build him a Temple at Jerusalem in the land of Judah. All of you who are the LORD's people may return to Israel for this task. May the LORD your God be with you!"

36:19 Or *destroyed all the valuable Temple utensils.*   **36:22** The first year of Cyrus's reign was 538 B.C.

Ezra

THE JEWS held captive in Babylonia for seventy years are allowed at last to return to their homeland. The book of Ezra begins with the proclamation of King Cyrus of Persia and the homeward journey of the first returnees under Zerubbabel (Ezra 1–6). With the Temple rebuilt, a second group returns under Ezra the priest, this time to rebuild the spiritual vitality of the nation (Ezra 7–10). Between those two homecomings you'll find a fifty-eight-year interlude during which the book of Esther takes place.

Focus	Restoration of the Temple				Reformation of the People	
Divisions	Commission of the Temple Builders	Completion of the Temple Project	The Book of Esther		Commission of the Spiritual Leaders	Completion of the Spiritual Reforms
	1	3 4	6	7	8 9	10
Topics	Return under Zerubbabel		58-Year Gap		Return under Ezra	
	Building Construction				Rebuilding Commitment	
Place	Persia to Jerusalem				Persia to Jerusalem	
Time	23 Years (538–515 B.C.)				1 Year (457 B.C.)	

MAY 1 □ DAY 122
EZRA 1–3
Commission of the Temple Builders

OVERVIEW At last the wearisome Babylonian captivity is at an end. With the proclamation of King Cyrus, permitting the people to leave Persia and return to their homeland, the hard work of rebuilding the nation can begin. Nearly fifty thousand pilgrims journey with Zerubbabel back to Jerusalem to rebuild the Temple. But laying the Temple foundation brings tears of remembrance as the builders recall the splendor that was once Solomon's Temple—a splendor never to be regained.

Chapter 1	Chapter 2	Chapter 3
A Call for Temple Builders	A Catalog of Temple Builders	Commencing to Build the Temple
Proclamation	Presentation	Progress

Little people with little minds jog through life in little ruts, smugly resisting all changes that would jar their little worlds.

YOUR DAILY WALK How long have you lived at your present location? Based on the national average, one family in three will move this year. And that means if you have lived in the place you call home for five years or longer, you are a vanishing breed!

Pulling up stakes is never easy. Anticipation and anxiety can make the ordeal as difficult emotionally as it is physically. Consider the caravan of pioneers listed in Ezra 2. The trail ahead of them was long—a hike of nearly a thousand miles. There was the constant danger of ambush from robbers, especially since the people were transporting a wealth of Temple treasures (1:9-11). Notwithstanding, God had stirred up the hearts of the people to respond to the invitation of a pagan king. With such internal compulsion and external confirmation, how could they help but move out for God!

Is God calling you to pull up stakes—to move to a new home, a new school, a new church, a new job, a new level of commitment to him? Then here is a motto you may want to copy and display in your home or office: "Even a long, dangerous journey can be faced confidently when God is leading the expedition."

INSIGHT Cyrus, God's Pagan Messiah
About 150 years before the dramatic proclamation of Ezra 1:1-4, Isaiah delivered a detailed prophecy concerning King Cyrus (Isaiah 44:28–45:7). Because the Lord would prompt Cyrus to do all these things for the Jews, he is called "my shepherd" (Isaiah 44:28) and "his anointed one" (literally, *messiah*; Isaiah 45:1).

CHAPTER 1

In the first year of King Cyrus of Persia,* the LORD fulfilled Jeremiah's prophecy by stirring the heart of Cyrus to put this proclamation into writing and to send it throughout his kingdom:

1:1 The first year of Cyrus's reign was 538 B.C.

2"This is what King Cyrus of Persia says: The LORD, the God of heaven, has given me all the kingdoms of the earth. He has appointed me to build him a Temple at Jerusalem in the land of Judah. 3All of you who are his people may return to

Jerusalem in Judah to rebuild this Temple of the LORD, the God of Israel, who lives in Jerusalem. And may your God be with you! ⁴Those who live in any place where Jewish survivors are found should contribute toward their expenses by supplying them with silver and gold, supplies for the journey, and livestock, as well as a freewill offering for the Temple of God in Jerusalem."

⁵Then God stirred the hearts of the priests and Levites and the leaders of the tribes of Judah and Benjamin to return to Jerusalem to rebuild the Temple of the LORD. ⁶And all their neighbors assisted by giving them vessels of silver and gold, supplies for the journey, and livestock. They gave them many choice gifts in addition to all the freewill offerings.

⁷King Cyrus himself brought out the valuable items which King Nebuchadnezzar had taken from the LORD's Temple in Jerusalem and had placed in the temple of his own gods. ⁸Cyrus directed Mithredath, the treasurer of Persia, to count these items and present them to Sheshbazzar, the leader of the exiles returning to Judah.*

⁹These were the items Cyrus donated:

gold trays	30
silver trays	1,000
silver censers*	29
¹⁰ gold bowls	30
silver bowls	410
other items	1,000

¹¹In all, 5,400 gold and silver items were turned over to Sheshbazzar to take back to Jerusalem when the exiles returned there from Babylon.

CHAPTER 2
Here is the list of the Jewish exiles of the provinces who returned from their captivity to Jerusalem and to the other towns of Judah. They had been deported to Babylon by King Nebuchadnezzar. ²Their leaders were Zerubbabel, Jeshua, Nehemiah, Seraiah, Reelaiah, Mordecai, Bilshan, Mispar, Bigvai, Rehum, and Baanah. This is the number of the men of Israel who returned from exile:

³ The family of Parosh 2,172
⁴ The family of Shephatiah 372

⁵ The family of Arah 775
⁶ The family of Pahath-moab
     (descendants of Jeshua and Joab) 2,812
⁷ The family of Elam 1,254
⁸ The family of Zattu 945
⁹ The family of Zaccai 760
¹⁰ The family of Bani 642
¹¹ The family of Bebai 623
¹² The family of Azgad 1,222
¹³ The family of Adonikam 666
¹⁴ The family of Bigvai 2,056
¹⁵ The family of Adin 454
¹⁶ The family of Ater
     (descendants of Hezekiah) 98
¹⁷ The family of Bezai 323
¹⁸ The family of Jorah 112
¹⁹ The family of Hashum 223
²⁰ The family of Gibbar 95
²¹ The people of Bethlehem 123
²² The people of Netophah 56
²³ The people of Anathoth 128
²⁴ The people of Beth-azmaveth* 42
²⁵ The peoples of Kiriath-jearim,*
     Kephirah, and Beeroth 743
²⁶ The peoples of Ramah and Geba 621
²⁷ The people of Micmash 122
²⁸ The peoples of Bethel and Ai 223
²⁹ The citizens of Nebo 52
³⁰ The citizens of Magbish 156
³¹ The citizens of Elam 1,254
³² The citizens of Harim 320
³³ The citizens of Lod, Hadid, and Ono 725
³⁴ The citizens of Jericho 345
³⁵ The citizens of Senaah 3,630

³⁶These are the priests who returned from exile:
     The family of Jedaiah
     (through the line of Jeshua) 973
³⁷ The family of Immer 1,052
³⁸ The family of Pashhur 1,247
³⁹ The family of Harim 1,017

⁴⁰These are the Levites who returned from exile:
     The families of Jeshua and Kadmiel
     (descendants of Hodaviah) 74
⁴¹ The singers of the family of
     Asaph 128
⁴² The gatekeepers of the families
     of Shallum, Ater, Talmon, Akkub,
     Hatita, and Shobai 139

⁴³The descendants of the following
     Temple servants returned from exile:
     Ziha, Hasupha, Tabbaoth,

1:8 Hebrew *Sheshbazzar, the prince of Judah.*   1:9 The meaning of this Hebrew word is uncertain.   2:24 As in parallel text at Neh 7:28; Hebrew reads *Azmaveth.*   2:25 As in some Hebrew manuscripts and Greek version (see also Neh 7:29); Hebrew reads *Kiriath-arim.*

44 Keros, Siaha, Padon,
45 Lebanah, Hagabah, Akkub,
46 Hagab, Shalmai,* Hanan,
47 Giddel, Gahar, Reaiah,
48 Rezin, Nekoda, Gazzam,
49 Uzza, Paseah, Besai,
50 Asnah, Meunim, Nephusim,
51 Bakbuk, Hakupha, Harhur,
52 Bazluth, Mehida, Harsha,
53 Barkos, Sisera, Temah,
54 Neziah, and Hatipha.

55 The descendants of these servants of
   King Solomon returned from exile:
   Sotai, Sophereth,* Peruda,
56 Jaalah, Darkon, Giddel,
57 Shephatiah, Hattil,
   Pokereth-hazzebaim, and Ami.

58 In all, the Temple servants and the descendants of Solomon's servants numbered 392.

59 Another group returned to Jerusalem
at this time from the towns of Tel-melah,
Tel-harsha, Kerub, Addan, and Immer.
However, they could not prove that they or
their families were descendants of Israel.
60 This group consisted of the families of
Delaiah, Tobiah, and Nekoda—a total of
652 people.
61 Three families of priests—Hobaiah,
Hakkoz, and Barzillai—also returned to Jerusalem. (This Barzillai had married a
woman who was a descendant of Barzillai
of Gilead, and he had taken her family
name.) 62 But they had lost their genealogical records, so they were not allowed to
serve as priests. 63 The governor would not
even let them eat the priests' share of food
from the sacrifices until there was a priest
who could consult the LORD about the matter by means of sacred lots.*

64 So a total of 42,360 people returned to
Judah, 65 in addition to 7,337 servants and
200 singers, both men and women. 66 They
took with them 736 horses, 245 mules, 67 435
camels, and 6,720 donkeys.

68 When they arrived at the Temple of the
LORD in Jerusalem, some of the family leaders gave generously toward the rebuilding
of God's Temple on its original site, 69 and

each leader gave as much as he could. The
total of their gifts came to 61,000 gold
coins,* 6,250 pounds* of silver, and 100
robes for the priests.

70 So the priests, the Levites, the singers,
the gatekeepers, the Temple servants, and
some of the common people settled in villages near Jerusalem. The rest of the people
returned to the other towns of Judah from
which they had come.

CHAPTER 3
Now in early autumn,* when the Israelites
had settled in their towns, all the people
assembled together as one person in Jerusalem. 2 Then Jeshua son of Jehozadak*
with his fellow priests and Zerubbabel son
of Shealtiel with his family began to rebuild
the altar of the God of Israel so they could
sacrifice burnt offerings on it, as instructed
in the law of Moses, the man of God. 3 Even
though the people were afraid of the local
residents, they rebuilt the altar at its old
site. Then they immediately began to sacrifice burnt offerings on the altar to the LORD.
They did this each morning and evening.

4 They celebrated the Festival of Shelters
as prescribed in the law of Moses, sacrificing the burnt offerings specified for each
day of the festival. 5 They also offered the
regular burnt offerings and the offerings
required for the new moon celebrations
and the other annual festivals to the LORD.
Freewill offerings were also sacrificed to
the LORD by the people. 6 Fifteen days before the Festival of Shelters began,* the
priests had begun to sacrifice burnt offerings to the LORD. This was also before they
had started to lay the foundation of the
LORD's Temple.

7 Then they hired masons and carpenters
and bought cedar logs from the people of
Tyre and Sidon, paying them with food,
wine, and olive oil. The logs were brought
down from the Lebanon mountains and
floated along the coast of the Mediterranean Sea to Joppa, for King Cyrus had
given permission for this.

8 The construction of the Temple of God
began in midspring,* during the second

2:46 As in the marginal Qere reading of the Masoretic Text (see also Neh 7:48); Hebrew text reads Shamlai.   2:55 As in parallel
text at Neh 7:57; Hebrew reads Hassophereth.   2:63 Hebrew consult the Urim and Thummim about the matter.   2:69a Hebrew 61,000
darics of gold, about 1,100 pounds or 500 kilograms in weight.   2:69b Hebrew 5,000 minas [3 metric tons].   3:1 Hebrew in the
seventh month. The year is not specific, so it may have been during Cyrus's first year (538 B.C.) or second year (537 B.C.). The seventh
month of the Hebrew lunar calendar occurred in September/October 538 B.C. and October/November 537 B.C.   3:2 Hebrew
Jozadak, a variant name for Jehozadak; also in 3:8.   3:6 Hebrew On the first day of the seventh month. This day of the Hebrew lunar
calendar occurs in September or October. The Festival of Shelters began on the fifteenth day of the seventh month.   3:8 Hebrew
in the second month. This month of the Hebrew lunar calendar occurred in April and May 536 B.C.

year after they arrived in Jerusalem. The work force was made up of everyone who had returned from exile, including Zerubbabel son of Shealtiel, Jeshua son of Jehozadak and his fellow priests, and all the Levites. The Levites who were twenty years old or older were put in charge of rebuilding the LORD's Temple. ⁹The workers at the Temple of God were supervised by Jeshua with his sons and relatives, and Kadmiel and his sons, all descendants of Hodaviah.* They were helped in this task by the Levites of the family of Henadad.

¹⁰When the builders completed the foundation of the LORD's Temple, the priests put on their robes and took their places to blow their trumpets. And the Levites, descendants of Asaph, clashed their cymbals to praise the LORD, just as King David had prescribed. ¹¹With praise and thanks, they sang this song to the LORD:

"He is so good!
     His faithful love for Israel endures forever!"

Then all the people gave a great shout, praising the LORD because the foundation of the LORD's Temple had been laid.

¹²Many of the older priests, Levites, and other leaders remembered the first Temple, and they wept aloud when they saw the new Temple's foundation. The others, however, were shouting for joy. ¹³The joyful shouting and weeping mingled together in a loud commotion that could be heard far in the distance.

3:9 Hebrew *sons of Judah* (i.e., *bene Yehudah*). *Bene* might also be read here as the proper name Binnui; *Yehudah* is probably another name for Hodaviah. Compare 2:40; Neh 7:43; 1 Esdras 5:58.

MAY 2 ☐ DAY 123
EZRA 4–6
Completion of the Temple Project

OVERVIEW The task of rebuilding the Temple involves more than simply organizing men and materials. Antagonism from local citizens soon arises to threaten the project. Deceitful offers of help, open attack, false accusations—each must be handled by Zerubbabel with conviction and courage. Although the builders are temporarily stopped, the prophets Haggai and Zechariah emerge to exhort the people not to throw in the trowel, so to speak. Darius, a sympathetic new Persian king, at last ends the fifteen-year construction delay by reconfirming the proclamation of Cyrus: God's Temple must be completed!

Chapter 4	Chapter 5	Chapter 6
Restraining the Builders	Reinstating the Builders	Reaching the Goal
Opposition	Resolution	Completion

YOUR DAILY WALK In the margin see if you can list at least ten instant products that are popular today: instant coffee, instant cameras, etc.

Ours is an "instant" society in which immediate results have become our expectation. And yet there are many endeavors for God that will only be accomplished if the long-range perspective is maintained. Parenting a child . . . developing a spiritual gift . . . discipling a new Christian . . . gaining an education—all these take time, the investment of years of practice and patience and perseverance, if the goal is to be achieved.

If Zerubbabel had allowed the short-term discouragements to deter him from his long-range determination to rebuild the Temple, he never would have finished the task. But with his goal clearly in view and his

When you cannot remove an obstacle, plow around it. But in God's strength, keep plowing.

faith firmly fixed in God, Zerubbabel was able to stay on target . . . for more than twenty years!

Use one of your long-range roles or goals to complete this sentence: "Though I may not experience instant success in my goal of _____ _____, with God's help I will commit myself to be faithful a day at a time, beginning today."

 INSIGHT Ezra the Priest—Which Way Did He Go? In a book entitled *Ezra,* you would expect the title character to play a prominent role. With the help of a Bible concordance (or just by retracing your steps), see how many times Ezra's name appears in the first six chapters. The answer may surprise you!

CHAPTER 4

The enemies of Judah and Benjamin heard that the exiles were rebuilding a Temple to the LORD, the God of Israel. ²So they approached Zerubbabel and the other leaders and said, "Let us build with you, for we worship your God just as you do. We have sacrificed to him ever since King Esarhaddon of Assyria brought us here."

³But Zerubbabel, Jeshua, and the other leaders of Israel replied, "You may have no part in this work, for we have nothing in common. We alone will build the Temple for the LORD, the God of Israel, just as King Cyrus of Persia commanded us."

⁴Then the local residents tried to discourage and frighten the people of Judah to keep them from their work. ⁵They bribed agents to work against them and to frustrate their aims. This went on during the entire reign of King Cyrus of Persia and lasted until King Darius of Persia took the throne.

⁶Years later when Xerxes* began his reign, the enemies of Judah wrote him a letter of accusation against the people of Judah and Jerusalem. ⁷And even later, during the reign of King Artaxerxes of Persia,* the enemies of Judah, led by Bishlam, Mithredath, and Tabeel, sent a letter to Artaxerxes in the Aramaic language, and it was translated for the king. ⁸Rehum* the governor and Shimshai the court secretary wrote the letter, telling King Artaxerxes about the situation in Jerusalem. ⁹They greeted the king for all their colleagues—the judges and local leaders, the people of Tarpel, the Persians, the Babylonians, and the people of Erech and Susa (that is, Elam). ¹⁰They also sent greetings from the rest of the people whom the great and noble Ashurbanipal* had deported and relocated in Samaria and throughout the neighboring lands of the province west of the Euphrates River. ¹¹This is a copy of the letter they sent him:

"To Artaxerxes, from your loyal subjects in the province west of the Euphrates River.

¹²"Please be informed that the Jews who came here to Jerusalem from Babylon are rebuilding this rebellious and evil city. They have already laid the foundation for its walls and will soon complete them. ¹³But we wish you to know that if this city is rebuilt and its walls are completed, it will be much to your disadvantage, for the Jews will then refuse to pay their tribute, customs, and tolls to you.

¹⁴"Since we are loyal to you as your subjects and we do not want to see you dishonored in this way, we have sent you this information. ¹⁵We suggest that you search your ancestors' records, where you will discover what a rebellious city this has been in the past. In fact, it was destroyed because of its long history of sedition against the kings and countries who attempted to control it. ¹⁶We declare that if this city is rebuilt and its walls are completed, the province west of the Euphrates River will be lost to you."

¹⁷Then Artaxerxes made this reply:

"To Rehum the governor, Shimshai the court secretary, and their colleagues living in Samaria and throughout the province west of the Euphrates River.

¹⁸"Greetings. The letter you sent has been translated and read to me. ¹⁹I have ordered a search to be made of the

4:6 Hebrew *Ahasuerus,* another name for Xerxes. He reigned 486–465 B.C.   **4:7** Artaxerxes reigned 465–424 B.C.   **4:8** The original text of 4:8–6:18 is in Aramaic.   **4:10** Aramaic *Osnappar,* another name for Ashurbanipal.

records and have indeed found that Jerusalem has in times past been a hotbed of insurrection against many kings. In fact, rebellion and sedition are normal there! 20Powerful kings have ruled over Jerusalem and the entire province west of the Euphrates River and have received vast tribute, customs, and tolls. 21Therefore, issue orders to have these people stop their work. That city must not be rebuilt except at my express command. 22Do not delay, for we must not permit the situation to get out of control."

23When this letter from King Artaxerxes was read to Rehum, Shimshai, and their colleagues, they hurried to Jerusalem and forced the Jews to stop building.

24The work on the Temple of God in Jerusalem had stopped, and it remained at a standstill until the second year of the reign of King Darius of Persia.*

CHAPTER 5

At that time the prophets Haggai and Zechariah son of Iddo prophesied in the name of the God of Israel to the Jews in Judah and Jerusalem. 2Zerubbabel son of Shealtiel and Jeshua son of Jehozadak* responded by beginning the task of rebuilding the Temple of God in Jerusalem. And the prophets of God were with them and helped them.

3But Tattenai, governor of the province west of the Euphrates, and Shethar-bozenai and their colleagues soon arrived in Jerusalem and asked, "Who gave you permission to rebuild this Temple and restore this structure?" 4They also asked for a list of the names of all the people who were working on the Temple. 5But because their God was watching over them, the leaders of the Jews were not prevented from building until a report was sent to Darius and he returned his decision.

6This is the letter that Tattenai the governor, Shethar-bozenai, and the other officials of the province west of the Euphrates River sent to King Darius:

7"Greetings to King Darius. 8We wish to inform you that we went to the construction site of the Temple of the great God in the province of Judah. It is being rebuilt with specially prepared stones, and timber is being laid in its walls. The work is going forward with great energy and success. 9We asked the leaders, 'Who gave you permission to rebuild this Temple and restore this structure?' 10And we demanded their names so that we could tell you who the leaders were.

11"This was their answer: 'We are the servants of the God of heaven and earth, and we are rebuilding the Temple that was built here many years ago by a great king of Israel. 12But because our ancestors angered the God of heaven, he abandoned them to King Nebuchadnezzar of Babylon,* who destroyed this Temple and exiled the people to Babylonia. 13However, King Cyrus of Babylon,* during the first year of his reign, issued a decree that the Temple of God should be rebuilt. 14King Cyrus returned the gold and silver utensils that Nebuchadnezzar had taken from the Temple of God in Jerusalem and had placed in the temple of Babylon. These items were taken from that temple and delivered into the safekeeping of a man named Sheshbazzar, whom King Cyrus appointed as governor of Judah. 15The king instructed him to return the utensils to their place in Jerusalem and to rebuild the Temple of God there as it had been before. 16So this Sheshbazzar came and laid the foundations of the Temple of God in Jerusalem. The people have been working on it ever since, though it is not yet completed.'

17"So now, if it pleases the king, we request that you search in the royal archives of Babylon to discover whether King Cyrus ever issued a decree to rebuild God's Temple in Jerusalem. And then let the king send us his decision in this matter."

CHAPTER 6

So King Darius issued orders that a search be made in the Babylonian archives, where treasures were stored. 2But it was at the fortress at Ecbatana in the province of Media that a scroll was found. This is what it said:

4:24 The second year of Darius's reign was 520 B.C.   5:2 Aramaic *Jozadak*, a variant name for Jehozadak.   5:12 Aramaic *Nebuchadnezzar the Chaldean.*   5:13 King Cyrus of Persia is here identified as the king of Babylon because Persia had conquered the Babylonian Empire.

³"Memorandum:

"In the first year of King Cyrus's reign, a decree was sent out concerning the Temple of God at Jerusalem. It must be rebuilt on the site where Jews used to offer their sacrifices, retaining the original foundations. Its height will be ninety feet, and its width will be ninety feet.* ⁴Every three layers of specially prepared stones will be topped by a layer of timber. All expenses will be paid by the royal treasury. ⁵And the gold and silver utensils, which were taken to Babylon by Nebuchadnezzar from the Temple of God in Jerusalem, will be taken back to Jerusalem and put into God's Temple as they were before."

⁶So King Darius sent this message:

"To Tattenai, governor of the province west of the Euphrates River, to Shethar-bozenai, and to your colleagues and other officials west of the Euphrates:

"Stay away from there! ⁷Do not disturb the construction of the Temple of God. Let it be rebuilt on its former site, and do not hinder the governor of Judah and the leaders of the Jews in their work. ⁸Moreover I hereby decree that you are to help these leaders of the Jews as they rebuild this Temple of God. You must pay the full construction costs without delay from my taxes collected in your province so that the work will not be discontinued. ⁹Give the priests in Jerusalem whatever is needed in the way of young bulls, rams, and lambs for the burnt offerings presented to the God of heaven. And without fail, provide them with the wheat, salt, wine, and olive oil that they need each day. ¹⁰Then they will be able to offer acceptable sacrifices to the God of heaven and pray for me and my sons. ¹¹"Those who violate this decree in any way will have a beam pulled from their house. Then they will be tied to it and flogged, and their house will be reduced to a pile of rubble.* ¹²May the God who has chosen the city of Jerusalem as the place to honor his name

destroy any king or nation that violates this command and destroys this Temple. I, Darius, have issued this decree. Let it be obeyed with all diligence."

¹³Tattenai, governor of the province west of the Euphrates River, and Shethar-bozenai and their colleagues complied at once with the command of King Darius. ¹⁴So the Jewish leaders continued their work, and they were greatly encouraged by the preaching of the prophets Haggai and Zechariah son of Iddo. The Temple was finally finished, as had been commanded by the God of Israel and decreed by Cyrus, Darius, and Artaxerxes, the kings of Persia. ¹⁵The Temple was completed on March 12,* during the sixth year of King Darius's reign.

¹⁶The Temple of God was then dedicated with great joy by the people of Israel, the priests, the Levites, and the rest of the people who had returned from exile. ¹⁷During the dedication ceremony for the Temple of God, one hundred young bulls, two hundred rams, and four hundred lambs were sacrificed. And twelve male goats were presented as a sin offering for the twelve tribes of Israel. ¹⁸Then the priests and Levites were divided into their various divisions to serve at the Temple of God in Jerusalem, following all the instructions recorded in the Book of Moses.

¹⁹On April 21* the returned exiles celebrated Passover. ²⁰The priests and Levites had purified themselves and were ceremonially clean. So they slaughtered the Passover lamb for all the returned exiles, for the other priests, and for themselves. ²¹The Passover meal was eaten by the people of Israel who had returned from exile and by the others in the land who had turned from their immoral customs to worship the LORD, the God of Israel. ²²They ate the Passover meal and celebrated the Festival of Unleavened Bread for seven days. There was great joy throughout the land because the LORD had changed the attitude of the king of Assyria* toward them, so that he helped them to rebuild the Temple of God, the God of Israel.

6:3 Aramaic *Its height will be 60 cubits* [27 meters], *and its width will be 60 cubits.* It is commonly held that this verse should be emended to read: "Its height will be 45 feet, its length will be 90 feet, and its width will be 30 feet"; compare 1 Kgs 6:2. The emendation regarding the width is supported by the Syriac version.   **6:11** Aramaic *a dunghill.*   **6:15** Aramaic *on the third day of the month Adar,* of the Hebrew calendar. This event occurred on March 12, 515 B.C.; also see note on 3:1.   **6:19** Hebrew *On the fourteenth day of the first month,* of the Hebrew calendar. This event occurred on April 21, 515 B.C.; also see note on 3:1.   **6:22** King Darius of Persia is here identified as the king of Assyria because Persia had conquered the Babylonian Empire, which included the earlier Assyrian Empire.

MAY 3 ☐ DAY 124
EZRA 7–8
Commission of the Spiritual Leaders

OVERVIEW Chapter 7 breaks a fifty-eight-year silence with the introduction of a priest and teacher named Ezra. Another kingly proclamation,
this time by Artaxerxes, sets the stage for Ezra to return to Jerusalem,
accompanied by 1,753 priests, Levites, and laymen. After praying and
fasting, Ezra and his caravan begin the four-month journey, weighted down
with treasures for the Temple and buoyed up by their confidence in God.

Chapter 7	Chapter 8
Preparations for the Return	Protection during the Return
Ezra's Commission	Ezra's Companions

YOUR DAILY WALK Have you ever tried to help God out by doing for
him what he has already promised to do for himself?

We would worry less about what others think of us if we realized how seldom they do.

Abraham tried it (Genesis 16) by fathering Ishmael, even though
God had promised to give him a son by Sarah. Saul tried it (1 Samuel
17:38-39) by covering David with the king's bulky armor, but the young
shepherd boy knew God wanted him to use a proven, less cumbersome
method to defeat the giant Goliath.

Ezra was tempted to try it, too. When presented with the chance
to enlist pagan soldiers and horsemen as a protection against enemies
along the way, Ezra went to his knees and received the assurance of
something he had previously told pagan king Artaxerxes: "Our God
protects all those who worship him, but his fierce anger rages against
those who abandon him" (8:22). Armed with that confidence, Ezra
and the people set out on a four-month adventure in trusting God.
And God proved his faithfulness once more!

How are you tempted to substitute human crutches for wholehearted
trust in the Lord? Where do you turn when things get tough? To your
checkbook? . . . investments? . . . friends? . . . job security? . . . spouse?
. . . or to the Lord? Turn to him right now in confident prayer, and
watch him guide your pilgrimage!

INSIGHT Three Leaders, Three Backgrounds
God chose three very different men to lead the three Jerusalem "home-
comings." Zerubbabel was a prince of Judah; Ezra was a priest and
Levite; and Nehemiah was a politician from an unspecified tribe.

CHAPTER 7

Many years later, during the reign of King
Artaxerxes of Persia,* there was a man named
Ezra. He was the son* of Seraiah, son of Azariah, son of Hilkiah, ²son of Shallum, son of
Zadok, son of Ahitub, ³son of Amariah, son
of Azariah, son* of Meraioth, ⁴son of Zerahiah, son of Uzzi, son of Bukki, ⁵son of
Abishua, son of Phinehas, son of Eleazar, son
of Aaron the high priest. ⁶This Ezra was a
scribe, well versed in the law of Moses, which

the LORD, the God of Israel, had given to the
people of Israel. He came up to Jerusalem from
Babylon, and the king gave him everything
he asked for, because the gracious hand of
the LORD his God was on him. ⁷Some of the
people of Israel, as well as some of the priests,
Levites, singers, gatekeepers, and Temple
servants, traveled up to Jerusalem with him
in the seventh year of King Artaxerxes' reign.

⁸Ezra arrived in Jerusalem in August* of
that year. ⁹He had left Babylon on April 8*

7:1a Artaxerxes reigned 465–424 B.C.   **7:1b** Or *descendant;* see 1 Chr 6:14.   **7:3** Or *descendant;* see 1 Chr 6:6-10.   **7:8** Hebrew *in
the fifth month.* This month of the Hebrew lunar calendar occurred in August and September 458 B.C.   **7:9a** Hebrew *on the first day
of the first month,* of the Hebrew calendar. This event occurred on April 8, 458 B.C.; also see note on 3:1.

and came to Jerusalem on August 4,* for the gracious hand of his God was on him. [10]This was because Ezra had determined to study and obey the law of the LORD and to teach those laws and regulations to the people of Israel.

[11]King Artaxerxes had given a copy of the following letter to Ezra, the priest and scribe who studied and taught the commands and laws of the LORD to Israel:

[12]"Greetings* from Artaxerxes, the king of kings, to Ezra the priest, the teacher of the law of the God of heaven.

[13]"I decree that any of the people of Israel in my kingdom, including the priests and Levites, may volunteer to return to Jerusalem with you. [14]I and my Council of Seven hereby instruct you to conduct an inquiry into the situation in Judah and Jerusalem, based on your God's law, which is in your hand. [15]We also commission you to take with you some silver and gold, which we are freely presenting as an offering to the God of Israel who lives in Jerusalem.

[16]"Moreover you are to take any silver and gold which you may obtain from the province of Babylon, as well as the freewill offerings of the people and the priests that are presented for the Temple of their God in Jerusalem. [17]These donations are to be used specifically for the purchase of bulls, rams, lambs, and the appropriate grain offerings and drink offerings, all of which will be offered on the altar of the Temple of your God in Jerusalem. [18]Any money that is left over may be used in whatever way you and your colleagues feel is the will of your God. [19]But as for the utensils we are entrusting to you for the service of the Temple of your God, deliver them in full to the God of Jerusalem. [20]If you run short of money for anything necessary for your God's Temple or for any similar needs, you may requisition funds from the royal treasury.

[21]"I, Artaxerxes the king, hereby send this decree to all the treasurers in the province west of the Euphrates River: 'You are to give Ezra whatever he requests of you, for he is a priest and teacher of the law of the God of heaven. [22]You are to give him up to 7,500 pounds* of silver, 500 bushels* of wheat, 550 gallons of wine, 550 gallons of olive oil,* and an unlimited supply of salt. [23]Be careful to provide whatever the God of heaven demands for his Temple, for why should we risk bringing God's anger against the realm of the king and his sons? [24]I also decree that no priest, Levite, singer, gatekeeper, Temple servant, or other worker in this Temple of God will be required to pay taxes of any kind.'

[25]"And you, Ezra, are to use the wisdom God has given you to appoint magistrates and judges who know your God's laws to govern all the people in the province west of the Euphrates River. If the people are not familiar with those laws, you must teach them. [26]Anyone who refuses to obey the law of your God and the law of the king will be punished immediately by death, banishment, confiscation of goods, or imprisonment."

[27]Praise the LORD, the God of our ancestors, who made the king want to beautify the Temple of the LORD in Jerusalem! [28]And praise him for demonstrating such unfailing love to me by honoring me before the king, his council, and all his mighty princes! I felt encouraged because the gracious hand of the LORD my God was on me. And I gathered some of the leaders of Israel to return with me to Jerusalem.

CHAPTER 8

Here is a list of the family leaders and the genealogies of those who came with me from Babylon during the reign of King Artaxerxes:

[2] From the family of Phinehas: Gershom.
From the family of Ithamar: Daniel.
[3] From the family of David: Hattush son of Shecaniah.
From the family of Parosh: Zechariah and 150 other men.
[4] From the family of Pahath-moab: Eliehoenai son of Zerahiah and 200 other men.
[5] From the family of Zattu*: Shecaniah son of Jahaziel and 300 other men.
[6] From the family of Adin: Ebed son of Jonathan and 50 other men.

7:9b Hebrew *on the first day of the fifth month,* of the Hebrew calendar. This event occurred on August 4, 458 B.C.; also see note on 3:1. 7:12 The original text of 7:12-26 is in Aramaic. 7:22a Aramaic *100 talents* [3.4 metric tons]. 7:22b Aramaic *100 cors* [18.2 kiloliters]. 7:22c Aramaic *100 baths* [2.1 kiloliters] *of wine, 100 baths of olive oil.* 8:5 As in some Greek manuscripts (see also 1 Esdras 8:32); Hebrew lacks *Zattu.*

⁷ From the family of Elam: Jeshaiah son of Athaliah and 70 other men.

⁸ From the family of Shephatiah: Zebadiah son of Michael and 80 other men.

⁹ From the family of Joab: Obadiah son of Jehiel and 218 other men.

¹⁰ From the family of Bani*: Shelomith son of Josiphiah and 160 other men.

¹¹ From the family of Bebai: Zechariah son of Bebai and 28 other men.

¹² From the family of Azgad: Johanan son of Hakkatan and 110 other men.

¹³ From the family of Adonikam, who came later*: Eliphelet, Jeuel, Shemaiah, and 60 other men.

¹⁴ From the family of Bigvai: Uthai, Zaccur, and 70 other men.

¹⁵I assembled the exiles at the Ahava Canal, and we camped there for three days while I went over the lists of the people and the priests who had arrived. I found that not one Levite had volunteered to come along. ¹⁶So I sent for Eliezer, Ariel, Shemaiah, Elnathan, Jarib, Elnathan, Nathan, Zechariah, and Meshullam, who were leaders of the people. I also sent for Joiarib and Elnathan, who were very wise men. ¹⁷I sent them to Iddo, the leader of the Levites at Casiphia, to ask him and his relatives and the Temple servants to send us ministers for the Temple of God at Jerusalem. ¹⁸Since the gracious hand of our God was on us, they sent us a man named Sherebiah, along with eighteen of his sons and brothers. He was a very astute man and a descendant of Mahli, who was a descendant of Levi son of Israel.* ¹⁹They also sent Hashabiah, together with Jeshaiah from the descendants of Merari, and twenty of his sons and brothers, ²⁰and 220 Temple servants. The Temple servants were assistants to the Levites—a group of Temple workers first instituted by King David. They were all listed by name.

²¹And there by the Ahava Canal, I gave orders for all of us to fast and humble ourselves before our God. We prayed that he would give us a safe journey and protect us, our children, and our goods as we traveled. ²²For I was ashamed to ask the king for soldiers and horsemen to accompany us and protect us from enemies along the way. After all, we had told the king, "Our God protects all those who worship him, but his fierce anger rages against those who abandon him." ²³So we fasted and earnestly prayed that our God would take care of us, and he heard our prayer.

²⁴I appointed twelve leaders of the priests—Sherebiah, Hashabiah, and ten other priests—²⁵to be in charge of transporting the silver, the gold, the gold bowls, and the other items that the king, his council, his leaders, and the people of Israel had presented for the Temple of God. ²⁶I weighed the treasure as I gave it to them and found the totals to be as follows:

24 tons* of silver,
7,500 pounds* of silver utensils,
7,500 pounds* of gold,
²⁷ 20 gold bowls, equal in value to 1,000 gold coins,*
2 fine articles of polished bronze, as precious as gold.

²⁸And I said to these priests, "You and these treasures have been set apart as holy to the LORD. This silver and gold is a freewill offering to the LORD, the God of our ancestors. ²⁹Guard these treasures well until you present them, without an ounce lost, to the leading priests, the Levites, and the leaders of Israel at the storerooms of the LORD's Temple in Jerusalem." ³⁰So the priests and the Levites accepted the task of transporting these treasures to the Temple of our God in Jerusalem.

³¹We broke camp at the Ahava Canal on April 19* and started off to Jerusalem. And the gracious hand of our God protected us and saved us from enemies and bandits along the way. ³²So at last we arrived safely in Jerusalem, where we rested for three days.

³³On the fourth day after our arrival, the silver, gold, and other valuables were weighed at the Temple of our God and entrusted to Meremoth son of Uriah the priest and to Eleazar son of Phinehas, along with Jozabad son of Jeshua and Noadiah son of Binnui—both of whom were Levites. ³⁴Everything was accounted for by number and weight, and the total weight was officially recorded.

³⁵Then the exiles who had returned from captivity sacrificed burnt offerings to the God of Israel. They presented twelve oxen for the people of Israel, as well as ninety-six

8:10 As in some Greek manuscripts (see also 1 Esdras 8:36); Hebrew lacks *Bani*.   **8:13** The meaning of the Hebrew for this phrase is uncertain.   **8:18** *Israel* is the name that God gave to Jacob.   **8:26a** Hebrew *650 talents* [22 metric tons].   **8:26b** Hebrew *100 talents* [3.4 metric tons].   **8:26c** Hebrew *100 talents* [3.4 metric tons].   **8:27** Hebrew *1,000 darics*, about 19 pounds or 8.6 kilograms in weight.   **8:31** Hebrew *on the twelfth day of the first month*, of the Hebrew calendar. This event occurred on April 19, 458 B.C.; see note on 7:9a.

rams and seventy-seven lambs. They also offered twelve goats as a sin offering. All this was given as a burnt offering to the LORD. ³⁶ The king's decrees were delivered to his lieutenants and the governors of the province west of the Euphrates River, who then cooperated by supporting the people and the Temple of God.

MAY 4 ☐ DAY 125
EZRA 9–10
Completion of the Spiritual Reforms

 OVERVIEW Upon his arrival in Jerusalem, Ezra is greeted by reports of pollution in the city. Spiritually mixed marriages—expressly forbidden in the law of God—are taking place among people and priesthood alike. The news brings instant anguish to the "well versed in the law of Moses" (7:6). Identifying himself with his disobedient countrymen, Ezra intercedes with an emotional prayer of confession. The guilty parties, moved by Ezra's example, assemble to bring forth fruits befitting repentance. In spite of poor weather, the difficult and time-consuming job of restoring purity in Israel's family life begins.

Chapter 9		Chapter 10
Ezra's Anguish	Ezra's Acknowledgment	Ezra's Action
1	4 5	15
Pollution Discovered		Purging Demanded

 YOUR DAILY WALK The statement "Confession is good for the soul" is not a biblical quote, but it is a biblical concept. Look up the following verses to see what each says about the importance of confession:

Confession without change is just a game.

• Acts 19:18-20
• James 5:16
• 1 John 1:9

Real confession involves two elements: (1) an acknowledgment of wrong committed and (2) a forsaking of wrong conduct. Ezra 9–10 describes a grievous condition in Jerusalem, a situation that demanded both acknowledging ("we have been unfaithful," 10:2) and forsaking ("separate yourselves," 10:11). Though the cure was perhaps as painful as the disease, God was pleased with the nation's prompt and wholehearted confession.

Is confession overdue in your life today? There's no better time to complete this prayer: "God, I acknowledge that I have sinned against you, and beginning today with your help I will forsake _____ _____."

 INSIGHT Putting Yourself into Your Prayers
More than thirty occurrences of the plural pronouns *us, we,* and *our* in Ezra's prayer of intercession (9:5-15) show that Ezra—though innocent of the charges—identified himself with the condition of his countrymen. Do you pray that way for your family, church, and nation?

CHAPTER 9
But then the Jewish leaders came to me and said, "Many of the people of Israel, and even some of the priests and Levites, have not kept themselves separate from the other peoples living in the land. They have taken up the detestable practices of the Canaanites, Hittites, Perizzites, Jebusites, Ammonites,

Moabites, Egyptians, and Amorites. [2]For the men of Israel have married women from these people and have taken them as wives for their sons. So the holy race has become polluted by these mixed marriages. To make matters worse, the officials and leaders are some of the worst offenders."

[3]When I heard this, I tore my clothing, pulled hair from my head and beard, and sat down utterly shocked. [4]Then all who trembled at the words of the God of Israel came and sat with me because of this unfaithfulness of his people. And I sat there utterly appalled until the time of the evening sacrifice.

[5]At the time of the sacrifice, I stood up from where I had sat in mourning with my clothes torn. I fell to my knees, lifted my hands to the LORD my God. [6]I prayed, "O my God, I am utterly ashamed; I blush to lift up my face to you. For our sins are piled higher than our heads, and our guilt has reached to the heavens. [7]Our whole history has been one of great sin. That is why we and our kings and our priests have been at the mercy of the pagan kings of the land. We have been killed, captured, robbed, and disgraced, just as we are today.

[8]"But now we have been given a brief moment of grace, for the LORD our God has allowed a few of us to survive as a remnant. He has given us security in this holy place. Our God has brightened our eyes and granted us some relief from our slavery. [9]For we were slaves, but in his unfailing love our God did not abandon us in our slavery. Instead, he caused the kings of Persia to treat us favorably. He revived us so that we were able to rebuild the Temple of our God and repair its ruins. He has given us a protective wall in Judah and Jerusalem.

[10]"And now, O our God, what can we say after all of this? For once again we have ignored your commands! [11]Your servants the prophets warned us that the land we would possess was totally defiled by the detestable practices of the people living there. From one end to the other, the land is filled with corruption. [12]You told us not to let our daughters marry their sons, and not to let our sons marry their daughters, and not to help those nations in any way. You promised that if we avoided these things, we would become a prosperous nation. You promised that we would enjoy the good pro-

duce of the land and leave this prosperity to our children as an inheritance forever.

[13]"Now we are being punished because of our wickedness and our great guilt. But we have actually been punished far less than we deserve, for you, our God, have allowed some of us to survive as a remnant. [14]But now we are again breaking your commands and intermarrying with people who do these detestable things. Surely your anger will destroy us until even this little remnant no longer survives. [15]O LORD, God of Israel, you are just. We stand before you in our guilt as nothing but an escaped remnant, though in such a condition none of us can stand in your presence."

CHAPTER 10

While Ezra prayed and made this confession, weeping and throwing himself to the ground in front of the Temple of God, a large crowd of people from Israel—men, women, and children—gathered and wept bitterly with him. [2]Then Shecaniah son of Jehiel, a descendant of Elam, said to Ezra, "We confess that we have been unfaithful to our God, for we have married these pagan women of the land. But there is hope for Israel in spite of this. [3]Let us now make a covenant with our God to divorce our pagan wives and to send them away with their children. We will follow the advice given by you and by the others who respect the commands of our God. We will obey the law of God. [4]Take courage, for it is your duty to tell us how to proceed in setting things straight, and we will cooperate fully."

[5]So Ezra stood up and demanded that the leaders of the priests and the Levites and all the people of Israel swear that they would do as Shecaniah had said. And they all swore a solemn oath. [6]Then Ezra left the front of the Temple of God and went to the room of Jehohanan son of Eliashib. He spent the night* there, but he did not eat any food or drink. He was still in mourning because of the unfaithfulness of the returned exiles. [7]Then a proclamation was made throughout Judah and Jerusalem that all the returned exiles should come to Jerusalem. [8]Those who failed to come within three days would, if the leaders and elders so decided, forfeit all their property and be expelled from the assembly of the exiles.

[9]Within three days, all the people of Judah

10:6 As in parallel text at 1 Esdras 9:2; Hebrew reads *He went.*

and Benjamin had gathered in Jerusalem. This took place on December 19,* and all the people were sitting in the square before the Temple of God. They were trembling both because of the seriousness of the matter and because it was raining. [10]Then Ezra the priest stood and said to them: "You have sinned, for you have married pagan women. Now we are even more deeply under condemnation than we were before. [11]Confess your sin to the LORD, the God of your ancestors, and do what he demands. Separate yourselves from the people of the land and from these pagan women."

[12]Then the whole assembly raised their voices and answered, "Yes, you are right; we must do as you say!" [13]Then they added, "This isn't something that can be done in a day or two, for many of us are involved in this extremely sinful affair. This is the rainy season, so we cannot stay out here much longer. [14]Let our leaders act on behalf of us all. Everyone who has a pagan wife will come at the scheduled time with the leaders and judges of his city, so that the fierce anger of our God may be turned away from us concerning this affair." [15]Only Jonathan son of Asahel and Jahzeiah son of Tikvah opposed this course of action, and Meshullam and Shabbethai the Levite supported them.

[16]So this was the plan that they followed. Ezra selected leaders to represent their families, designating each of the representatives by name. On December 29,* the leaders sat down to investigate the matter. [17]By March 27 of the next year* they had finished dealing with all the men who had married pagan wives.

[18]These are the priests who had married pagan wives:

From the family of Jeshua son of Jehozadak* and his brothers: Maaseiah, Eliezer, Jarib, and Gedaliah. [19]They vowed to divorce their wives, and they each acknowledged their guilt by offering a ram as a guilt offering. [20]From the family of Immer: Hanani and Zebadiah. [21]From the family of Harim: Maaseiah, Elijah, Shemaiah, Jehiel, and Uzziah. [22]From the family of Pashhur: Elioenai, Maaseiah, Ishmael, Nethanel, Jozabad, and Elasah.

[23]These are the Levites who were guilty: Jozabad, Shimei, Kelaiah (also called Kelita), Pethahiah, Judah, and Eliezer.

[24]This is the singer who was guilty: Eliashib.

These are the gatekeepers who were guilty: Shallum, Telem, and Uri.

[25]These are the other people of Israel who were guilty:

From the family of Parosh: Ramiah, Izziah, Malkijah, Mijamin, Eleazar, Hashabiah,* and Benaiah. [26]From the family of Elam: Mattaniah, Zechariah, Jehiel, Abdi, Jeremoth, and Elijah. [27]From the family of Zattu: Elioenai, Eliashib, Mattaniah, Jeremoth, Zabad, and Aziza. [28]From the family of Bebai: Jehohanan, Hananiah, Zabbai, and Athlai. [29]From the family of Bani: Meshullam, Malluch, Adaiah, Jashub, Sheal, and Jeremoth. [30]From the family of Pahath-moab: Adna, Kelal, Benaiah, Maaseiah, Mattaniah, Bezalel, Binnui, and Manasseh. [31]From the family of Harim: Eliezer, Ishijah, Malkijah, Shemaiah, Shimeon, [32]Benjamin, Malluch, and Shemariah. [33]From the family of Hashum: Mattenai, Mattattah, Zabad, Eliphelet, Jeremai, Manasseh, and Shimei. [34]From the family of Bani: Maadai, Amram, Uel, [35]Benaiah, Bedeiah, Keluhi, [36]Vaniah, Meremoth, Eliashib, [37]Mattaniah, Mattenai, and Jaasu. [38]From the family of Binnui*: Shimei, [39]Shelemiah, Nathan, Adaiah, [40]Macnadebai, Shashai, Sharai, [41]Azarel, Shelemiah, Shemariah, [42]Shallum, Amariah, and Joseph. [43]From the family of Nebo: Jeiel, Mattithiah, Zabad, Zebina, Jaddai, Joel, and Benaiah.

[44]Each of these men had a pagan wife, and some even had children by these wives.*

10:9 Hebrew *on the twentieth day of the ninth month,* of the Hebrew calendar. This event occurred on December 19, 458 B.C.; also see note on 7:9a.   **10:16** Hebrew *On the first day of the tenth month,* of the Hebrew calendar. This event occurred on December 29, 458 B.C.; also see note on 7:9a.   **10:17** Hebrew *By the first day of the first month,* of the Hebrew calendar. This event occurred on March 27, 457 B.C.; also see note on 7:9a.   **10:18** Hebrew *Jozadak,* a variant name for Jehozadak.   **10:25** As in parallel text at 1 Esdras 9:26; Hebrew reads *Malkijah.*   **10:37-38** As in Greek version; Hebrew reads *Jaasu,* [38]*Bani, Binnui.*   **10:44** Or *and they sent them away with their children.* The meaning of the Hebrew is uncertain.

Nehemiah

A CONTEMPORARY of Ezra and cupbearer to the king of Persia, Nehemiah leads the third and final return of the Jews to Jerusalem after the Babylonian exile. Under his leadership the people undertake the enormous task of rebuilding the holy city's battered walls, destroyed almost a century earlier. Despite opposition from without and abuse from within, the task is completed in only fifty-two days—a feat that even Israel's enemies must attribute to God's power.

Focus	New Walls			New Worship	Renewed Nation
Divisions	Wall Plans Conceived	Wall Plans Commenced	Wall Plans Concluded	Renewed Worship Commenced	Renewed Nation Cleansed
	1	2 3	4 5	7 8	10 11	13
Topics	Reconstructing the City			Reforming the Citizens	
	Security			Purity	
Place	Jerusalem				
Time	About 25 Years (445–420 B.C.)				

MAY 5 ☐ DAY 126
NEHEMIAH 1–2
Wall Plans Conceived

OVERVIEW   Nearly a century has passed since Zerubbabel led the first group of Jewish hostages from Babylon back to their homeland. But though the Temple stands complete, inviting worshipers from near and far, the walls lie in rubble, inviting enemy attacks. Nehemiah, cupbearer to King Artaxerxes of Persia, hears this heartbreaking news. With a carefully and prayerfully conceived plan, he is ready when the king inquires, "How can I help you?" (2:4). Accompanied by army and cavalry units, Nehemiah returns to Jerusalem to inspect the damage and infuse his countrymen with the will to raise the walls.

	Chapter 1		Chapter 2
	Jerusalem's Broken Walls	Nehemiah's Broken Heart	Nehemiah's Building Plans
1	3	4	11
	Problem	Prayer	Preparation

YOUR DAILY WALK   Find a small electric appliance (an iron will do nicely), plug it in, and turn it on. Does it work? Were you surprised that it worked? If not, why not?

Prayer can do anything God can do.

What would you think of a person who, upon plugging in an iron and finding that it didn't work, responded, "Well, I guess it just wasn't God's will for it to get hot"? Irons are supposed to get hot! And when they don't, you need to check the connections because something is obviously wrong. You expect a hot iron . . . and rightly so!

Now consider your prayer life. Does it "get hot"? That is, does God answer your prayers in regular, discernible ways? Or are you surprised when an answer to prayer comes? Your expectation should be answered prayer, for God has staked his reputation on it. Nehemiah learned that exciting truth, and you can, too! Spend a few extra minutes basking in these biblical prayer promises: Jeremiah 33:3; Matthew 7:7-11; John 16:24; 1 John 5:14-15. Pick one and "plug it in" to your prayer life today. Watch for God's answer . . . and be thankful when it comes! That's what prayer is all about.

INSIGHT   Persian Cup-bearer: Servant or Something Else?
Nehemiah was more than a royal waiter. His duties included confidant, adviser, administrator, bodyguard, and food taster (to protect the king from poisoning)—a position of high trust and authority. Today we would call him a prime minister.

CHAPTER 1

These are the memoirs of Nehemiah son of Hacaliah.

In late autumn of the twentieth year of King Artaxerxes' reign,* I was at the fortress of Susa. ²Hanani, one of my brothers, came to visit me with some other men who had just arrived from Judah. I asked them about the Jews who had survived the captivity and about how things were going in

1:1 Hebrew *In the month of Kislev of the twentieth year.* A number of dates in the book of Nehemiah can be cross-checked with dates in surviving Persian records and related accurately to our modern calendar. This month of the Hebrew lunar calendar occurred in November and December 446 B.C. The *twentieth year* probably refers to the reign of King Artaxerxes I; compare 2:1; 5:14.

Jerusalem. ³They said to me, "Things are not going well for those who returned to the province of Judah. They are in great trouble and disgrace. The wall of Jerusalem has been torn down, and the gates have been burned."

⁴When I heard this, I sat down and wept. In fact, for days I mourned, fasted, and prayed to the God of heaven. ⁵Then I said, "O LORD, God of heaven, the great and awesome God who keeps his covenant of unfailing love with those who love him and obey his commands, ⁶listen to my prayer! Look down and see me praying night and day for your people Israel. I confess that we have sinned against you. Yes, even my own family and I have sinned! ⁷We have sinned terribly by not obeying the commands, laws, and regulations that you gave us through your servant Moses.

⁸"Please remember what you told your servant Moses: 'If you sin, I will scatter you among the nations. ⁹But if you return to me and obey my commands, even if you are exiled to the ends of the earth, I will bring you back to the place I have chosen for my name to be honored.'

¹⁰"We are your servants, the people you rescued by your great power and might. ¹¹O Lord, please hear my prayer! Listen to the prayers of those of us who delight in honoring you. Please grant me success now as I go to ask the king* for a great favor. Put it into his heart to be kind to me."

In those days I was the king's cup-bearer.

CHAPTER 2

Early the following spring,* during the twentieth year of King Artaxerxes' reign, I was serving the king his wine. I had never appeared sad in his presence before this time. ²So the king asked me, "Why are you so sad? You aren't sick, are you? You look like a man with deep troubles."

Then I was badly frightened, ³but I replied, "Long live the king! Why shouldn't I be sad? For the city where my ancestors are buried is in ruins, and the gates have been burned down."

⁴The king asked, "Well, how can I help you?"

With a prayer to the God of heaven, ⁵I replied, "If it please Your Majesty and if you are pleased with me, your servant, send me to Judah to rebuild the city where my ancestors are buried."

⁶The king, with the queen sitting beside him, asked, "How long will you be gone? When will you return?" So the king agreed, and I set a date for my departure.

⁷I also said to the king, "If it please Your Majesty, give me letters to the governors of the province west of the Euphrates River, instructing them to let me travel safely through their territories on my way to Judah. ⁸And please send a letter to Asaph, the manager of the king's forest, instructing him to give me timber. I will need it to make beams for the gates of the Temple fortress, for the city walls, and for a house for myself." And the king granted these requests, because the gracious hand of God was on me.

⁹When I came to the governors of the province west of the Euphrates River, I delivered the king's letters to them. The king, I should add, had sent along army officers and horsemen to protect me. ¹⁰But when Sanballat the Horonite and Tobiah the Ammonite official heard of my arrival, they were very angry that someone had come who was interested in helping Israel.

¹¹Three days after my arrival at Jerusalem, ¹²I slipped out during the night, taking only a few others with me. I had not told anyone about the plans God had put in my heart for Jerusalem. We took no pack animals with us, except the donkey that I myself was riding. ¹³I went out through the Valley Gate, past the Jackal's Well,* and over to the Dung Gate to inspect the broken walls and burned gates. ¹⁴Then I went to the Fountain Gate and to the King's Pool, but my donkey couldn't get through the rubble. ¹⁵So I went up the Kidron Valley* instead, inspecting the wall before I turned back and entered again at the Valley Gate.

¹⁶The city officials did not know I had been out there or what I was doing, for I had not yet said anything to anyone about my plans. I had not yet spoken to the religious and political leaders, the officials, or anyone else in the administration. ¹⁷But now I said to them, "You know full well the tragedy of our city. It lies in ruins, and its gates are burned. Let us rebuild the wall of Jerusalem and rid ourselves of this disgrace!" ¹⁸Then I told them about how the

---

1:11 Hebrew *stand before this man.*   2:1 Hebrew *In the month of Nisan.* This month of the Hebrew lunar calendar occurred in April and May 445 B.C.   2:13 Or *Serpent's Well.*   2:15 Hebrew *the valley.*

gracious hand of God had been on me, and about my conversation with the king.

They replied at once, "Good! Let's rebuild the wall!" So they began the good work.

[19] But when Sanballat, Tobiah, and Geshem the Arab heard of our plan, they scoffed contemptuously. "What are you doing, rebelling against the king like this?" they asked.

[20] But I replied, "The God of heaven will help us succeed. We his servants will start rebuilding this wall. But you have no stake or claim in Jerusalem."

MAY 6 ☐ DAY 127
NEHEMIAH 3–4
Wall Plans Commenced

OVERVIEW Nehemiah's dream of rebuilding the walls now becomes contagious! The people rise up in unison, trowels in hand, to begin repairing the eight gates and more than two miles of wall surrounding the city. Nehemiah's strategy is simple: Give each person a vested interest in the work. To ensure both speed and quality of workmanship, he assigns each worker the portion of the wall nearest the worker's own house! There's a lot of incentive to do a good job when you know that if enemies break through a defective portion of the wall, the first people jeopardized will be your own family. But soon the entire project is threatened by outside opposition. Harmless ridicule gives way to threats of violence, and Nehemiah responds with a combination of prayer and preparation.

Chapter 3	Chapter 4		
Repairing the Walls	Ridiculing the Workers	Rallying the Workers Prayerfully	Militarily
1	3 | 4	12 | 13	23
The Work Initiated	The Work Interrupted		

Too many people pray like little children who knock on doors, then run away.

YOUR DAILY WALK "Pray like it's up to God; then act like it's up to you." Those words are found nowhere in Scripture, but they contain more than a little truth. Over and over, God has told you to take your problems and anxieties to him. "Don't worry about anything; instead, pray about everything. Tell God what you need, and thank him for all he has done" (Philippians 4:6). Take a lesson from Nehemiah. When troubles come, turn your problems into prayers . . . pronto!

But once you have prayed through your problems, don't expect angels to finish building your walls! Pick up your trowel and finish the job God has given you. "Work . . . For God is working in you" (Philippians 2:12-13) is a great balance to achieve.

Pick a situation in your life that needs *prayer* coupled with *preparation*. Pray it through, work it out, and share it with a friend or family member!

INSIGHT The Special Gate for God
Among the list of gates is the East Gate (3:29), through which the shekinah glory (a visible manifestation of the presence of God) left and by which it will return. Ezekiel sees the return of God's glory through the East Gate (Ezekiel 43:1-17) to reside in the Temple's Most Holy Place during the kingdom age, as he had seen its departure during the fall of Jerusalem.

CHAPTER 3

Then Eliashib the high priest and the other priests started to rebuild at the Sheep Gate. They dedicated it and set up its doors, building the wall as far as the Tower of the Hundred, which they dedicated, and the Tower of Hananel. ²People from the city of Jericho worked next to them, and beyond them was Zaccur son of Imri.

³The Fish Gate was built by the sons of Hassenaah. They did the whole thing— laid the beams, hung the doors, and put the bolts and bars in place. ⁴Meremoth son of Uriah and grandson of Hakkoz repaired the next section of wall. Beside him were Meshullam son of Berekiah and grandson of Meshezabel, and then Zadok son of Baana. ⁵Next were the people from Tekoa, though their leaders refused to help.

⁶The Old City Gate* was repaired by Joiada son of Paseah and Meshullam son of Besodeiah. They laid the beams, set up the doors, and installed the bolts and bars. ⁷Next to them were Melatiah from Gibeon, Jadon from Meronoth, and people from Gibeon and Mizpah, the headquarters of the governor of the province west of the Euphrates River. ⁸Next was Uzziel son of Harhaiah, a goldsmith by trade, who also worked on the wall. Beyond him was Hananiah, a manufacturer of perfumes. They left out* a section of Jerusalem as far as the Broad Wall.

⁹Rephaiah son of Hur, the leader of half the district of Jerusalem, was next to them on the wall. ¹⁰Next Jedaiah son of Harumaph repaired the wall beside his own house, and next to him was Hattush son of Hashabneiah. ¹¹Then came Malkijah son of Harim and Hasshub son of Pahathmoab, who repaired the Tower of the Ovens, in addition to another section of the wall. ¹²Shallum son of Hallohesh and his daughters repaired the next section. He was the leader of the other half of the district of Jerusalem.

¹³The people from Zanoah, led by Hanun, rebuilt the Valley Gate, hung its doors, and installed the bolts and bars. They also repaired the fifteen hundred feet* of wall to the Dung Gate.

¹⁴The Dung Gate was repaired by Malkijah son of Recab, the leader of the Beth-hakkerem district. After rebuilding it,

he hung the doors and installed the bolts and bars.

¹⁵Shallum son of Col-hozeh, the leader of the Mizpah district, repaired the Fountain Gate. He rebuilt it, roofed it, hung its doors, and installed its bolts and bars. Then he repaired the wall of the pool of Siloam* near the king's garden, and he rebuilt the wall as far as the stairs that descend from the City of David. ¹⁶Next to him was Nehemiah son of Azbuk, the leader of half the district of Bethzur. He rebuilt the wall to a place opposite the royal cemetery as far as the water reservoir and the House of the Warriors.

¹⁷Next was a group of Levites working under the supervision of Rehum son of Bani. Then came Hashabiah, the leader of half the district of Keilah, who supervised the building of the wall on behalf of his own district. ¹⁸Next down the line were his countrymen led by Binnui* son of Henadad, the leader of the other half of the district of Keilah.

¹⁹Next to them, Ezer son of Jeshua, the leader of Mizpah, repaired another section of wall opposite the armory by the buttress. ²⁰Next to him was Baruch son of Zabbai, who repaired an additional section from the buttress to the door of the home of Eliashib the high priest. ²¹Meremoth son of Uriah and grandson of Hakkoz rebuilt another section of the wall extending from a point opposite the door of Eliashib's house to the side of the house.

²²Then came the priests from the surrounding region. ²³After them, Benjamin, Hasshub, and Azariah son of Maaseiah and grandson of Ananiah repaired the sections next to their own houses. ²⁴Next was Binnui son of Henadad, who rebuilt another section of the wall from Azariah's house to the buttress and the corner. ²⁵Palal son of Uzai carried on the work from a point opposite the buttress and the corner to the upper tower that projects from the king's house beside the court of the guard. Next to him were Pedaiah son of Parosh ²⁶and the Temple servants living on the hill of Ophel, who repaired the wall as far as the Water Gate toward the east and the projecting tower. ²⁷Then came the people of Tekoa, who repaired another section opposite the great projecting tower and over to the wall of Ophel.

3:6 Or *The Mishneh Gate*, or *The Jeshanah Gate*.   **3:8** Or *They restored.*   **3:13** Hebrew *1,000 cubits* [450 meters].   **3:15** Hebrew *pool of Shelah*, another name for the pool of Siloam.   **3:18** As in a few Hebrew manuscripts, some Greek manuscripts, and Syriac version (see also 3:24; 10:9); most Hebrew manuscripts read *Bavvai.*

[28] The priests repaired the wall up the hill from the Horse Gate, each one doing the section immediately opposite his own house. [29] Next Zadok son of Immer also rebuilt the wall next to his own house, and beyond him was Shemaiah son of Shecaniah, the gatekeeper of the East Gate. [30] Next Hananiah son of Shelemiah and Hanun, the sixth son of Zalaph, repaired another section, while Meshullam son of Berekiah rebuilt the wall next to his own house. [31] Malkijah, one of the goldsmiths, repaired the wall as far as the housing for the Temple servants and merchants, opposite the Inspection Gate. Then he continued as far as the upper room at the corner. [32] The other goldsmiths and merchants repaired the wall from that corner to the Sheep Gate.

CHAPTER 4

Sanballat was very angry when he learned that we were rebuilding the wall. He flew into a rage and mocked the Jews, [2] saying in front of his friends and the Samarian army officers, "What does this bunch of poor, feeble Jews think they are doing? Do they think they can build the wall in a day if they offer enough sacrifices? Look at those charred stones they are pulling out of the rubbish and using again!"

[3] Tobiah the Ammonite, who was standing beside him, remarked, "That stone wall would collapse if even a fox walked along the top of it!"

[4] Then I prayed, "Hear us, O our God, for we are being mocked. May their scoffing fall back on their own heads, and may they themselves become captives in a foreign land! [5] Do not ignore their guilt. Do not blot out their sins, for they have provoked you to anger here in the presence of* the builders."

[6] At last the wall was completed to half its original height around the entire city, for the people had worked very hard. [7] But when Sanballat and Tobiah and the Arabs, Ammonites, and Ashdodites heard that the work was going ahead and that the gaps in the wall were being repaired, they became furious. [8] They all made plans to come and fight against Jerusalem and to bring about confusion there. [9] But we prayed to our God and guarded the city day and night to protect ourselves.

[10] Then the people of Judah began to complain that the workers were becoming tired. There was so much rubble to be moved that we could never get it done by ourselves. [11] Meanwhile, our enemies were saying, "Before they know what's happening, we will swoop down on them and kill them and end their work."

[12] The Jews who lived near the enemy came and told us again and again, "They will come from all directions and attack us!"* [13] So I placed armed guards behind the lowest parts of the wall in the exposed areas. I stationed the people to stand guard by families, armed with swords, spears, and bows.

[14] Then as I looked over the situation, I called together the leaders and the people and said to them, "Don't be afraid of the enemy! Remember the Lord, who is great and glorious, and fight for your friends, your families, and your homes!"

[15] When our enemies heard that we knew of their plans and that God had frustrated them, we all returned to our work on the wall. [16] But from then on, only half my men worked while the other half stood guard with spears, shields, bows, and coats of mail. The officers stationed themselves behind the people of Judah [17] who were building the wall. The common laborers carried on their work with one hand supporting their load and one hand holding a weapon. [18] All the builders had a sword belted to their side. The trumpeter stayed with me to sound the alarm.

[19] Then I explained to the nobles and officials and all the people, "The work is very spread out, and we are widely separated from each other along the wall. [20] When you hear the blast of the trumpet, rush to wherever it is sounding. Then our God will fight for us!"

[21] We worked early and late, from sunrise to sunset. And half the men were always on guard. [22] I also told everyone living outside the walls to move into Jerusalem. That way they and their servants could go on guard duty at night as well as work during the day. [23] During this time, none of us—not I, nor my relatives, nor my servants, nor the guards who were with me—ever took off our clothes. We carried our weapons with us at all times, even when we went for water.*

4:5 Or *for they have thrown insults in the face of.*   4:12 The meaning of the Hebrew is uncertain.   4:23 Hebrew *Each his weapon the water.* The meaning of the Hebrew is uncertain.

MAY 7 ☐ DAY 128
Strength of the Lord

 LOOK BACK Hezekiah and Ezra. Their names sound alike and have similar meanings. *Ezra* means "help"; *Hezekiah* means "God strengthens." But there the similarity ends. Hezekiah was a king; Ezra was a priest. They never met since they lived hundreds of years apart in different parts of the world: Hezekiah in Jerusalem; Ezra in Persia. Hezekiah was trying to protect his nation from enemy attack; Ezra was intent on rebuilding his nation after seventy years of exile.

And yet these two heroes of the Old Testament accomplished great things for God because they shared a common passion to read, study, and obey the law of God. They were able to provide help and strength in the lives of others because their own lives were anchored to the unchanging foundation of God's Word.

Hezekiah and Ezra, Ruth and Esther—what a rich heritage of heroes and heroines you'll find in the pages of the Old Testament. Men and women who walked with God in uncertain days, made tough decisions, faced giant-sized enemies, prayed powerful prayers, and accomplished mighty feats in the strength of the Lord.

 LOOK UP Ezra learned firsthand about the hand of the Lord his God (Ezra 7:6, 9; 8:18, 22). When an attribute of God is described in human terms, it's called an anthropomorphism. Here are just a few of the many ways in which God is described in human terms. Can you explain the significance of each analogy?

The finger that points the way is part of the hand that provides the need.

The "hand" of the Lord (Joshua 4:24, NIV) helps us come to grips with his _____:

The "voice" of the Lord (1 Samuel 15:22, NIV) speaks of his _____ _____.

The "eyes" of the Lord (2 Chronicles 16:9) causes us to view his ____ _____.

The "arm" of the Lord (Isaiah 51:9, NIV) refers to his _____.

When a boxer throws a jab, his intent is to cause his opponent to feel the power of his hand. All the strength of the boxer is channeled and directed through his hand. In the same way, God desires to channel his power through the life of the believer. Ezra's life was full of God's power because Ezra's heart and mind were full of God's Word.

 LOOK AHEAD If you're experiencing a season of weakness or fruit-lessness in your spiritual life, perhaps you need to check your "power supply." A branch that is wilted and fruitless has obviously become severed from the vine, its source of strength and life (John 15:1-8).

Happiness, fruitfulness, prosperity—each is the heritage of anyone who makes the law of the Lord his or her daily meditation (Psalm 1:1-3). It's a truth Ezra learned, and so can you.

To meditate is to chew the cud, drawing nourishment from the life-giving truths of the Bible just like a cow draws nourishment from the life-giving grass. And typically one "chew" isn't enough! There is ample reason to meditate upon the same passage over and over again, for God delights to give fresh insight from previously digested passages!

Thumb back through the readings you've covered so far this year, and find a favorite passage or devotional. Read it again thoughtfully, reflecting on how the intervening months have helped to sharpen your insight into its meaning and application.

MAY 8 □ DAY 129
NEHEMIAH 5–8:1
Wall Plans Concluded

OVERVIEW Internal strife in the Israelite camp causes as much unrest as the attacks from outside the camp. The people are suffering under financial stress imposed by their Persian masters. Worse yet, the Hebrews are exacting interest from their own brothers who have borrowed to pay their debts. After correcting this abuse, Nehemiah again turns his attention toward the threats from without. He refuses to be lured into an assassination plot on his life, nor will he be intimidated by the threats of a slanderous letter. After fifty-two days of building and battling, the walls stand completed. At last the order can go forth to repopulate the holy city of Jerusalem!

Chapter 5	Chapter 6				Chapters 7–8
Interest Abolished	Murder Averted	Deceit Avoided	Mission Accomplished	Population Assigned	
1 4	5 14	15 19	7:1 8:1
Opposition			Outcome		

Injustice anywhere is a threat to justice everywhere.

YOUR DAILY WALK How do you react when you see the poor exploited? Does your heart beat a little faster . . . your temperature go up a degree or two? Now imagine it is a member of your family being exploited. How would you respond to that?

Lack of grain and oppressive Persian rule had forced some of the Hebrews in Jerusalem to mortgage their homes and sell themselves into slavery in order to pay their debts. When Nehemiah heard that the rich were extorting money from their own countrymen, his reaction was immediate . . . and unmistakable!

You may never have exacted interest from someone suffering hardships, but have you been guilty of taking advantage of another Christian by ignoring his or her difficult circumstances? Carry your money somewhere other than in your wallet or purse today, and let the empty wallet (or purse) remind you of the usury tactics of Nehemiah's day. Then look for a way to assist, rather than simply avoid, a Christian brother or sister who is in difficult financial straits.

INSIGHT Doing Wrong to Do Right Is Wrong, Right?
Shemaiah's offer of safety in the Temple for Nehemiah (6:10-14) was a direct violation of God's law that forbade laymen from entering the sanctuary. Even if Shemaiah had been telling the truth (which he wasn't), to enter the Temple would have been a fatal mistake.

CHAPTER 5

About this time some of the men and their wives raised a cry of protest against their fellow Jews. ²They were saying, "We have such large families. We need more money just so we can buy the food we need to survive." ³Others said, "We have mortgaged our fields, vineyards, and homes to get food during the famine." ⁴And others said, "We have already borrowed to the limit on our fields and vineyards to pay our taxes. ⁵We belong to the same family,

and our children are just like theirs. Yet we must sell our children into slavery just to get enough money to live. We have already sold some of our daughters, and we are helpless to do anything about it, for our fields and vineyards are already mortgaged to others."

⁶When I heard their complaints, I was very angry. ⁷After thinking about the situation, I spoke out against these nobles and officials. I told them, "You are oppressing your own relatives by charging them inter-

est when they borrow money!" Then I called a public meeting to deal with the problem.

[8] At the meeting I said to them, "The rest of us are doing all we can to redeem our Jewish relatives who have had to sell themselves to pagan foreigners, but you are selling them back into slavery again. How often must we redeem them?" And they had nothing to say in their defense.

[9] Then I pressed further, "What you are doing is not right! Should you not walk in the fear of our God in order to avoid being mocked by enemy nations? [10] I myself, as well as my brothers and my workers, have been lending the people money and grain, but now let us stop this business of loans. [11] You must restore their fields, vineyards, olive groves, and homes to them this very day. Repay the interest you charged on their money, grain, wine, and olive oil."

[12] Then they replied, "We will give back everything and demand nothing more from the people. We will do as you say." Then I called the priests and made the nobles and officials formally vow to do what they had promised.

[13] I shook out the fold of my robe and said, "If you fail to keep your promise, may God shake you from your homes and from your property!"

The whole assembly responded, "Amen," and they praised the LORD. And the people did as they had promised.

[14] I would like to mention that for the entire twelve years that I was governor of Judah—from the twentieth until the thirty-second year of the reign of King Artaxerxes*—neither I nor my officials drew on our official food allowance. [15] This was quite a contrast to the former governors who had laid heavy burdens on the people, demanding a daily ration of food and wine, besides a pound* of silver. Even their assistants took advantage of the people. But because of my fear of God, I did not act that way. [16] I devoted myself to working on the wall and refused to acquire any land. And I required all my officials to spend time working on the wall. [17] I asked for nothing, even though I regularly fed 150 Jewish officials at my table, besides all the visitors from other lands! [18] The provisions required at my expense for each day were one ox, six fat sheep, and a large number of domestic fowl. And every ten days we needed a large supply of all kinds of wine. Yet I refused to claim the governor's food allowance because the people were already having a difficult time.

[19] Remember, O my God, all that I have done for these people, and bless me for it.

CHAPTER 6
When Sanballat, Tobiah, Geshem the Arab, and the rest of our enemies found out that I had finished rebuilding the wall and that no gaps remained—though we had not yet hung the doors in the gates—[2] Sanballat and Geshem sent me a message asking me to meet them at one of the villages* in the plain of Ono. But I realized they were plotting to harm me, [3] so I replied by sending this message to them: "I am doing a great work! I cannot stop to come and meet with you."

[4] Four times they sent the same message, and each time I gave the same reply. [5] The fifth time, Sanballat's servant came with an open letter in his hand, [6] and this is what it said:

"Geshem* tells me that everywhere he goes he hears that you and the Jews are planning to rebel and that is why you are building the wall. According to his reports, you plan to be their king. [7] He also reports that you have appointed prophets to prophesy about you in Jerusalem, saying, 'Look! There is a king in Judah!'

"You can be very sure that this report will get back to the king, so I suggest that you come and talk it over with me."

[8] My reply was, "You know you are lying. There is no truth in any part of your story." [9] They were just trying to intimidate us, imagining that they could break our resolve and stop the work. So I prayed for strength to continue the work.

[10] Later I went to visit Shemaiah son of Delaiah and grandson of Mehetabel, who was confined to his home. He said, "Let us meet together inside the Temple of God and bolt the doors shut. Your enemies are coming to kill you tonight."

[11] But I replied, "Should someone in my position run away from danger? Should someone in my position enter the Temple

---

5:14 That is, from 445 to 433 B.C.   **5:15** Hebrew *40 shekels* [456 grams].   **6:2** As in Greek version; Hebrew reads *at Kephirim*. **6:6** Hebrew *Gashmu,* another name for Geshem.

to save his life? No, I won't do it!" [12]I realized that God had not spoken to him, but that he had uttered this prophecy against me because Tobiah and Sanballat had hired him. [13]They were hoping to intimidate me and make me sin by following his suggestion. Then they would be able to accuse and discredit me.

[14]Remember, O my God, all the evil things that Tobiah and Sanballat have done. And remember Noadiah the prophet and all the prophets like her who have tried to intimidate me.

[15]So on October 2* the wall was finally finished—just fifty-two days after we had begun. [16]When our enemies and the surrounding nations heard about it, they were frightened and humiliated. They realized that this work had been done with the help of our God.

[17]During those fifty-two days, many letters went back and forth between Tobiah and the officials of Judah. [18]For many in Judah had sworn allegiance to him because his father-in-law was Shecaniah son of Arah and because his son Jehohanan was married to the daughter of Meshullam son of Berekiah. [19]They kept telling me what a wonderful man Tobiah was, and then they told him everything I said. And Tobiah sent many threatening letters to intimidate me.

CHAPTER 7

After the wall was finished and I had hung the doors in the gates, the gatekeepers, singers, and Levites were appointed. [2]I gave the responsibility of governing Jerusalem to my brother Hanani, along with Hananiah, the commander of the fortress, for he was a faithful man who feared God more than most. [3]I said to them, "Do not leave the gates open during the hottest part of the day.* And while the gatekeepers are still on duty, have them shut and bar the doors. Appoint the residents of Jerusalem to act as guards, everyone on a regular watch. Some will serve at their regular posts and some in front of their own homes."

[4]At that time the city was large and spacious, but the population was small. And only a few houses were scattered throughout the city. [5]So my God gave me the idea to call together all the leaders of the city, along with the ordinary citizens, for registration. I had found the genealogical record of those who had first returned to Judah. This is what was written there:

[6]"Here is the list of the Jewish exiles of the provinces who returned from their captivity to Jerusalem and to the other towns of Judah. They had been deported to Babylon by King Nebuchadnezzar. [7]Their leaders were Zerubbabel, Jeshua, Nehemiah, Seraiah,* Reelaiah,* Nahamani, Mordecai, Bilshan, Mispar,* Bigvai, Rehum,* and Baanah. This is the number of men of Israel who returned from exile:

[8] The family of Parosh		2,172
[9] The family of Shephatiah		372
[10] The family of Arah		652
[11] The family of Pahath-moab		
(descendants of Jeshua and Joab)		2,818
[12] The family of Elam		1,254
[13] The family of Zattu		845
[14] The family of Zaccai		760
[15] The family of Bani*		648
[16] The family of Bebai		628
[17] The family of Azgad		2,322
[18] The family of Adonikam		667
[19] The family of Bigvai		2,067
[20] The family of Adin		655
[21] The family of Ater		
(descendants of Hezekiah)		98
[22] The family of Hashum		328
[23] The family of Bezai		324
[24] The family of Jorah*		112
[25] The family of Gibbar*		95
[26] The peoples of Bethlehem		
and Netophah		188
[27] The people of Anathoth		128
[28] The people of Beth-azmaveth		42
[29] The peoples of Kiriath-jearim,		
Kephirah, and Beeroth		743
[30] The peoples of Ramah and Geba		621
[31] The people of Micmash		122
[32] The peoples of Bethel and Ai		123
[33] The people of Nebo		52
[34] The citizens of Elam		1,254
[35] The citizens of Harim		320
[36] The citizens of Jericho		345
[37] The citizens of Lod, Hadid, and Ono		721
[38] The citizens of Senaah		3,930

6:15 Hebrew *on the twenty-fifth day of the month Elul,* of the Hebrew calendar. This event occurred on October 2, 445 B.C.; also see note on 1:1.   **7:3** Or *Keep the gates of Jerusalem closed until the sun is hot.*   **7:7a** As in parallel text at Ezra 2:2; Hebrew reads *Azariah.*   **7:7b** As in parallel text at Ezra 2:2; Hebrew reads *Raamiah.*   **7:7c** As in parallel text at Ezra 2:2; Hebrew reads *Mispereth.*   **7:7d** As in parallel text at Ezra 2:2; Hebrew reads *Nehum.*   **7:15** As in parallel text at Ezra 2:10; Hebrew reads *Binnui.*   **7:24** As in parallel text at Ezra 2:18; Hebrew reads *Hariph.*   **7:25** As in parallel text at Ezra 2:20; Hebrew reads *Gibeon.*

39 "These are the priests who returned from exile:

The family of Jedaiah
(through the line of Jeshua). 973
40 The family of Immer 1,052
41 The family of Pashhur 1,247
42 The family of Harim 1,017

43 "These are the Levites who returned from exile:

The families of Jeshua and Kadmiel
(descendants of Hodaviah*) 74
44 The singers of the family of Asaph 148
45 The gatekeepers of the families of
Shallum, Ater, Talmon, Akkub,
Hatita, and Shobai 138

46 "The descendants of the following
Temple servants returned from exile:
Ziha, Hasupha, Tabbaoth,
47 Keros, Siaha,* Padon,
48 Lebanah, Hagabah, Shalmai,
49 Hanan, Giddel, Gahar,
50 Reaiah, Rezin, Nekoda,
51 Gazzam, Uzza, Paseah,
52 Besai, Meunim, Nephusim,*
53 Bakbuk, Hakupha, Harhur,
54 Bazluth,* Mehida, Harsha,
55 Barkos, Sisera, Temah,
56 Neziah, and Hatipha.

57 "The descendants of these servants of
King Solomon returned from exile:
Sotai, Sophereth, Peruda,*
58 Jaalah,* Darkon, Giddel,
59 Shephatiah, Hattil,
Pokereth-hazzebaim, and Ami.*

60 "In all, the Temple servants and the descendants of Solomon's servants numbered 392.

61 "Another group returned to Jerusalem at this time from the towns of Tel-melah, Tel-harsha, Kerub, Addan,* and Immer. However, they could not prove that they or their families were descendants of Israel. 62 This group included the families of Delaiah, Tobiah, and Nekoda—a total of 642 people.

63 "Three families of priests—Hobaiah, Hakkoz, and Barzillai—also returned to Jerusalem. (This Barzillai had married a woman who was a descendant of Barzillai of Gilead, and he had taken her family name.) 64 But they had lost their genealogical records, so they were not allowed to serve as priests. 65 The governor would not even let them eat the priests' share of food from the sacrifices until there was a priest who could consult the LORD about the matter by means of sacred lots.*

66 "So a total of 42,360 people returned to Judah, 67 in addition to 7,337 servants and 245 singers, both men and women. 68 They took with them 736 horses, 245 mules,* 69 435 camels, and 6,720 donkeys.

70 "Some of the family leaders gave gifts for the work. The governor gave to the treasury 1,000 gold coins,* 50 gold basins, and 530 robes for the priests. 71 The other leaders gave to the treasury a total of 20,000 gold coins* and some 2,750 pounds* of silver for the work. 72 The rest of the people gave 20,000 gold coins, about 2,500 pounds* of silver, and 67 robes for the priests.

73 "So the priests, the Levites, the gatekeepers, the singers, the Temple servants, along with some of the people—that is to say, all Israel—settled in their own towns."

Now in midautumn,* when the Israelites had settled in their towns, 8:1 all the people assembled together as one person at the square just inside the Water Gate. They asked Ezra the scribe to bring out the Book of the Law of Moses, which the LORD had given for Israel to obey.

7:43 As in parallel text at Ezra 2:40; Hebrew reads Hodevah.   7:47 As in parallel text at Ezra 2:44; Hebrew reads Sia.
7:52 As in parallel text at Ezra 2:50; Hebrew reads Nephushesim.   7:54 As in parallel text at Ezra 2:52; Hebrew reads Bazlith.
7:57 As in parallel text at Ezra 2:55; Hebrew reads Perida.   7:58 As in parallel text at Ezra 2:56; Hebrew reads Jaala.   7:59 As in parallel text at Ezra 2:57; Hebrew reads Amon.   7:61 As in parallel text at Ezra 2:59; Hebrew reads Addon.   7:65 Hebrew consult the Urim and Thummim about the matter.   7:68 As in some Hebrew manuscripts (see also Ezra 2:66); most Hebrew manuscripts lack this verse.   7:70 Hebrew 1,000 darics of gold, about 19 pounds or 8.6 kilograms in weight.   7:71a Hebrew 20,000 darics of gold, about 375 pounds or 170 kilograms in weight; also in 7:72.   7:71b Hebrew 2,200 minas [1.3 metric tons].   7:72 Hebrew 2,000 minas [1.2 metric tons].   7:73 Hebrew in the seventh month. This month of the Hebrew lunar calendar occurred in October and November 445 B.C.

MAY 9 □ DAY 130
NEHEMIAH 8:2–10
Renewed Worship Commenced

OVERVIEW The first half of Nehemiah's account describes the construction of the city walls; the second half contains instruction for the city worshipers. Beginning with chapter 8 the account becomes biographical rather than autobiographical as Nehemiah deals with the spiritual rather than the physical well-being of the inhabitants of Jerusalem. Revival breaks out when the Word of God is translated, "broadcast," and explained for the common people. The preaching of Ezra the priest produces heartfelt confession, wholehearted worship, and refreshing resolve to bring the nation's wayward conduct in line with the nation's covenant relationship with God.

Chapter 8		Chapter 9	Chapter 10
Reading the Law	Restoring the Law	Responding to the Law	Resolving to Keep the Law
2 12	13 18		
Conviction	Commemoration	Confession	Commitment

Freedom decays as material society expands.

YOUR DAILY WALK This evening go through your house and gather up every trace of Scripture you can find: every copy of the Bible . . . every Bible motto or poster hanging on your walls . . . every hymnbook or gospel recording . . . every gospel tract or Christian biography. Pile them all together on a table in the living room. Then find a book of matches and strike one as you ponder this sobering thought: Someday you may lose the priceless freedom you enjoy today of surrounding yourself with God's Word.

If that ever happened, how much of God's Word would you have hidden away in your heart, where no tyrant can invade (Psalm 119:11)? Ezra's reading of the long-neglected Book of the Law produced tears of gladness and grief—gladness over the return of God's Word to a place of primacy in the nation, and grief that the nation had drifted so far from God's will and way. It could never happen in our country . . . or could it? And isn't it worth five minutes of prayer daily to help see that it won't?

INSIGHT Ezra, the Elusive Priest
Ezra did not appear until chapter 7 of the book that bears his own name, and he does not appear until chapter 8 of the book of Nehemiah—a natural dividing point for the book. Chapters 1–7 center around the *work* of God in building the wall; chapters 8–13 focus on the *worship* of God in obedience to the law.

CHAPTER 8

²So on October 8* Ezra the priest brought the scroll of the law before the assembly, which included the men and women and all the children old enough to understand. ³He faced the square just inside the Water Gate from early morning until noon and read aloud to everyone who could understand. All the people paid close attention to the Book of the Law. ⁴Ezra the scribe stood on a high wooden platform that had been made for the occasion. To his right stood Mattithiah, Shema, Anaiah, Uriah, Hilkiah, and Maaseiah. To his left stood Pedaiah, Mishael, Malkijah, Hashum, Hashbaddanah, Zechariah, and Meshullam. ⁵Ezra stood on the platform in full view of all the people. When they saw him open the book, they all rose to their feet.

⁶Then Ezra praised the LORD, the great

8:2 Hebrew *on the first day of the seventh month,* of the Hebrew calendar. This event occurred on October 8, 445 B.C.; also see note on 1:1.

God, and all the people chanted, "Amen! Amen!" as they lifted their hands toward heaven. Then they bowed down and worshiped the LORD with their faces to the ground.

[7]Now the Levites—Jeshua, Bani, Sherebiah, Jamin, Akkub, Shabbethai, Hodiah, Maaseiah, Kelita, Azariah, Jozabad, Hanan, and Pelaiah—instructed the people who were standing there. [8]They read from the Book of the Law of God and clearly explained the meaning of what was being read, helping the people understand each passage. [9]Then Nehemiah the governor, Ezra the priest and scribe, and the Levites who were interpreting for the people said to them, "Don't weep on such a day as this! For today is a sacred day before the LORD your God." All the people had been weeping as they listened to the words of the law.

[10]And Nehemiah* continued, "Go and celebrate with a feast of choice foods and sweet drinks, and share gifts of food with people who have nothing prepared. This is a sacred day before our Lord. Don't be dejected and sad, for the joy of the LORD is your strength!"

[11]And the Levites, too, quieted the people, telling them, "Hush! Don't weep! For this is a sacred day." [12]So the people went away to eat and drink at a festive meal, to share gifts of food, and to celebrate with great joy because they had heard God's words and understood them.

[13]On October 9* the family leaders and the priests and Levites met with Ezra to go over the law in greater detail. [14]As they studied the law, they discovered that the LORD had commanded through Moses that the Israelites should live in shelters during the festival to be held that month.* [15]He had said that a proclamation should be made throughout their towns and especially in Jerusalem, telling the people to go to the hills to get branches from olive, wild olive, myrtle, palm, and fig trees. They were to use these branches to make shelters in which they would live during the festival, as it was prescribed in the law.

[16]So the people went out and cut branches and used them to build shelters on the roofs of their houses, in their courtyards, in the courtyards of God's Temple, or in the squares just inside the Water Gate and the Ephraim Gate. [17]So everyone who had returned from captivity lived in these shelters for the seven days of the festival, and everyone was filled with great joy! The Israelites had not celebrated this way since the days of Joshua son of Nun. [18]Ezra read from the Book of the Law of God on each of the seven days of the festival. Then on the eighth day they held a solemn assembly, as was required by law.

CHAPTER 9

On October 31* the people returned for another observance. This time they fasted and dressed in sackcloth and sprinkled dust on their heads. [2]Those of Israelite descent separated themselves from all foreigners as they confessed their own sins and the sins of their ancestors. [3]The Book of the Law of the LORD their God was read aloud to them for about three hours.* Then for three more hours they took turns confessing their sins and worshiping the LORD their God. [4]Some of the Levites were standing on the stairs, crying out to the LORD their God. Their names were Jeshua, Bani, Kadmiel, Shebaniah, Bunni, Sherebiah, Bani, and Kenani.

[5]Then the leaders of the Levites—Jeshua, Kadmiel, Bani, Hashabneiah, Sherebiah, Hodiah, Shebaniah, and Pethahiah—called out to the people: "Stand up and praise the LORD your God, for he lives from everlasting to everlasting!"

Then they continued, "Praise his glorious name! It is far greater than we can think or say. [6]You alone are the LORD. You made the skies and the heavens and all the stars. You made the earth and the seas and everything in them. You preserve and give life to everything, and all the angels of heaven worship you.

[7]"You are the LORD God, who chose Abram and brought him from Ur of the Chaldeans and renamed him Abraham. [8]When he had proved himself faithful, you made a covenant with him to give him and his descendants the land of the Canaanites, Hittites, Amorites, Perizzites, Jebusites, and Girgashites. And you have done what

8:10 Hebrew *he.*   8:13 Hebrew *On the second day,* of the seventh month of the Hebrew calendar. This event occurred on October 9, 445 B.C.; also see notes on 1:1 and 8:2.   8:14 Hebrew *in the seventh month.* This month of the Hebrew lunar calendar usually occurs in September and October. See Lev 23:39-43.   9:1 Hebrew *On the twenty-fourth day of that same month,* the seventh month of the Hebrew calendar. This event occurred on October 31, 445 B.C.; also see note on 1:1.   9:3 Hebrew *for a quarter of a day.*

you promised, for you are always true to your word.

9"You saw the sufferings and sorrows of our ancestors in Egypt, and you heard their cries from beside the Red Sea.* 10You displayed miraculous signs and wonders against Pharaoh, his servants, and all his people, for you knew how arrogantly the Egyptians were treating them. You have a glorious reputation that has never been forgotten. 11You divided the sea for your people so they could walk through on dry land! And then you hurled their enemies into the depths of the sea. They sank like stones beneath the mighty waters. 12You led our ancestors by a pillar of cloud during the day and a pillar of fire at night so that they could find their way.

13"You came down on Mount Sinai and spoke to them from heaven. You gave them regulations and instructions that were just, and laws and commands that were true. 14You instructed them concerning the laws of your holy Sabbath. And you commanded them, through Moses your servant, to obey all your commands, laws, and instructions.

15"You gave them bread from heaven when they were hungry and water from the rock when they were thirsty. You commanded them to go and take possession of the land you had sworn to give them. 16But our ancestors were a proud and stubborn lot, and they refused to obey your commands.

17"They refused to listen and did not remember the miracles you had done for them. Instead, they rebelled and appointed a leader to take them back to their slavery in Egypt! But you are a God of forgiveness, gracious and merciful, slow to become angry, and full of unfailing love and mercy. You did not abandon them, 18even though they made an idol shaped like a calf and said, 'This is your god who brought you out of Egypt!' They sinned and committed terrible blasphemies. 19But in your great mercy you did not abandon them to die in the wilderness. The pillar of cloud still led them forward by day, and the pillar of fire showed them the way through the night. 20You sent your good Spirit to instruct them, and you did not stop giving them bread from heaven or water for their thirst. 21For forty years you sustained them in the

wilderness. They lacked nothing in all that time. Their clothes did not wear out, and their feet did not swell!

22"Then you helped our ancestors conquer great kingdoms and many nations, and you placed your people in every corner of the land. They completely took over the land of King Sihon of Heshbon and the land of King Og of Bashan. 23You made their descendants as numerous as the stars in the sky and brought them into the land you had promised to their ancestors. 24They went in and took possession of the land. You subdued whole nations before them. Even the kings and the Canaanites, who inhabited the land, were powerless! Your people could deal with them as they pleased. 25Our ancestors captured fortified cities and fertile land. They took over houses full of good things, with cisterns already dug and vineyards and olive groves and orchards in abundance. So they ate until they were full and grew fat and enjoyed themselves in all your blessings.

26"But despite all this, they were disobedient and rebelled against you. They threw away your law, they killed the prophets who encouraged them to return to you, and they committed terrible blasphemies. 27So you handed them over to their enemies. But in their time of trouble they cried to you, and you heard them from heaven. In great mercy, you sent them deliverers who rescued them from their enemies.

28"But when all was going well, your people turned to sin again, and once more you let their enemies conquer them. Yet whenever your people cried to you again for help, you listened once more from heaven. In your wonderful mercy, you rescued them repeatedly! 29You warned them to return to your law, but they became proud and obstinate and disobeyed your commands. They did not follow your regulations, by which people will find life if only they obey. They stubbornly turned their backs on you and refused to listen. 30In your love, you were patient with them for many years. You sent your Spirit, who, through the prophets, warned them about their sins. But still they wouldn't listen! So once again you allowed the pagan inhabitants of the land to conquer them. 31But in your great mercy, you did not destroy them

9:9 Hebrew *sea of reeds.*

completely or abandon them forever. What a gracious and merciful God you are!

[32]"And now, our God, the great and mighty and awesome God, who keeps his covenant of unfailing love, do not let all the hardships we have suffered be as nothing to you. Great trouble has come upon us and upon our kings and princes and priests and prophets and ancestors from the days when the kings of Assyria first triumphed over us until now. [33]Every time you punished us you were being just. We have sinned greatly, and you gave us only what we deserved. [34]Our kings, princes, priests, and ancestors did not obey your law or listen to your commands and solemn warnings. [35]Even while they had their own kingdom, they did not serve you even though you showered your goodness on them. You gave them a large, fertile land, but they refused to turn from their wickedness.

[36]"So now today we are slaves here in the land of plenty that you gave to our ancestors! We are slaves among all this abundance! [37]The lush produce of this land piles up in the hands of the kings whom you have set over us because of our sins. They have power over us and our cattle. We serve them at their pleasure, and we are in great misery.

[38]"Yet in spite of all this,* we are making a solemn promise and putting it in writing. On this sealed document are the names of our princes and Levites and priests."

CHAPTER 10

The document was ratified and sealed with the following names:

Nehemiah the governor, the son of Hacaliah.

The priests who signed were Zedekiah, [2]Seraiah, Azariah, Jeremiah, [3]Pashhur, Amariah, Malkijah, [4]Hattush, Shebaniah, Malluch, [5]Harim, Meremoth, Obadiah, [6]Daniel, Ginnethon, Baruch, [7]Meshullam, Abijah, Mijamin, [8]Maaziah, Bilgai, and Shemaiah. These were the priests.

[9]The Levites who signed were Jeshua son of Azaniah, Binnui from the family of Henadad, Kadmiel, [10]and their fellow Levites: Shebaniah, Hodiah, Kelita, Pelaiah, Hanan, [11]Mica, Rehob, Hashabiah, [12]Zaccur, Sherebiah, Shebaniah, [13]Hodiah, Bani, and Beninu.

[14]The leaders who signed were Parosh, Pahath-moab, Elam, Zattu, Bani, [15]Bunni, Azgad, Bebai, [16]Adonijah, Bigvai, Adin, [17]Ater, Hezekiah, Azzur, [18]Hodiah, Hashum, Bezai, [19]Hariph, Anathoth, Nebai, [20]Magpiash, Meshullam, Hezir, [21]Meshezabel, Zadok, Jaddua, [22]Pelatiah, Hanan, Anaiah, [23]Hoshea, Hananiah, Hasshub, [24]Hallohesh, Pilha, Shobek, [25]Rehum, Hashabnah, Maaseiah, [26]Ahiah, Hanan, Anan, [27]Malluch, Harim, and Baanah.

[28]The rest of the people—the priests, Levites, gatekeepers, singers, Temple servants, and all who had separated themselves from the pagan people of the land in order to serve God, and who were old enough to understand—[29]now all heartily bound themselves with an oath. They vowed to accept the curse of God if they failed to obey the law of God as issued by his servant Moses. They solemnly promised to carefully follow all the commands, laws, and regulations of the LORD their Lord.

[30]"We promise not to let our daughters marry the pagan people of the land, nor to let our sons marry their daughters. [31]We further promise that if the people of the land should bring any merchandise or grain to be sold on the Sabbath or on any other holy day, we will refuse to buy it. And we promise not to do any work every seventh year and to cancel the debts owed to us by other Jews.

[32]"In addition, we promise to obey the command to pay the annual Temple tax of an eighth of an ounce of silver,* so that there will be enough money to care for the Temple of our God. [33]This will provide for the Bread of the Presence; for the regular grain offerings and burnt offerings; for the offerings on the Sabbaths, the new moon celebrations, and the annual festivals; for the holy offerings; and for the sin offerings to make atonement for Israel. It will also provide for the other items necessary for the work of the Temple of our God.

[34]"We have cast sacred lots to determine when—at regular times each year—the families of the priests, Levites, and the common people should bring wood to God's Temple to be burned on the altar of the LORD our God, as required in the law.

[35]"We promise always to bring the first

9:38 Or *Because of all this.*   10:32 Hebrew *tax of 1/3 of a shekel* [4 grams].

part of every harvest to the LORD's Temple—whether it be a crop from the soil or from our fruit trees. [36] We agree to give to God our oldest sons and the firstborn of all our herds and flocks, just as the law requires. We will present them to the priests who minister in the Temple of our God. [37] We will store the produce in the storerooms of the Temple of our God. We will bring the best of our flour and other grain offerings, the best of our fruit, and the best of our new wine and olive oil. And we promise to bring to the Levites a tenth of everything our land produces, for it is the Levites who collect the tithes in all our rural towns. [38] A priest—a descendant of Aaron—will be with the Levites as they receive these tithes. And a tenth of all that is collected as tithes will be delivered by the Levites to the Temple of our God and placed in the storerooms. [39] The people and the Levites must bring these offerings of grain, new wine, and olive oil to the Temple and place them in the sacred containers near the ministering priests, the gatekeepers, and the singers.

"So we promise together not to neglect the Temple of our God."

MAY 10 ☐ DAY 131
NEHEMIAH 11–13
Renewed Nation Cleansed

OVERVIEW With his time in Jerusalem nearly at an end, Nehemiah busies himself with the final duties of his mission. He oversees the redistribution of the people in the cities—one tenth of the population in Jerusalem and the rest in surrounding suburbs. A massive ceremony is held in which two processions of praising people march along the walls to dedicate them to God. Nine years after returning to Persia, Nehemiah again hears disturbing news from his homeland. He returns to correct abuses in the Temple and deal again with the stubborn problem of mixed marriages.

Chapter 11	Chapter 12	Chapter 13
Resettling the People	Recognizing the People	Reforming the People
New Homes	Old Names	Old Problems

YOUR DAILY WALK It is sad but true that those who do not learn from history are destined to repeat it. The closing chapters of Nehemiah provide a sobering warning . . . and an opportunity to learn from the past.

Prayer becomes a flat and arduous business when we refuse to follow the lights and leads God has given us.

The people under Nehemiah had made several vows in chapter 10: They agreed to obey God's Word, abstain from intermarriage with pagans, keep the Sabbath, and support Temple worship. Less than a decade later, they had broken every promise!

Today would be a great time to renew old promises and vows before the Lord. If you are married, spend some quiet moments with your spouse, reminding one another of the vows you made on your wedding day. Confess your areas of failure, and praise your partner for the vow he or she has faithfully kept. If you are single, reflect on your extra privilege (and responsibility) to serve God with undivided attention (1 Corinthians 7:32-33).

If you have made a promise to serve God faithfully, take some time to renew that promise today. If you've never done so, this would be a great time to start!

INSIGHT Nehemiah's Prophetic Partner
Malachi, who lived and ministered during the same time as Nehemiah,
spoke to the moral condition of the Jews who returned to Jerusalem.
You might want to read his short, four-chapter book in connection with
Nehemiah. Malachi paints a bleak picture of coldhearted indifference
toward God—a condition that persisted for four hundred years until the
appearance of the Messiah (John 1:29).

CHAPTER 11

Now the leaders of the people were living in Jerusalem, the holy city, at this time. A tenth of the people from the other towns of Judah and Benjamin were chosen by sacred lots to live there, too, while the rest stayed where they were. ²And the people commended everyone who volunteered to resettle in Jerusalem.

³Here is a list of the names of the provincial officials who came to Jerusalem. Most of the people, priests, Levites, Temple servants, and descendants of Solomon's servants continued to live in their own homes in the various towns of Judah, ⁴but some of the people from Judah and Benjamin resettled in Jerusalem.

From the tribe of Judah: Athaiah son of Uzziah, son of Zechariah, son of Amariah, son of Shephatiah, son of Mahalalel, of the family of Perez; ⁵and Maaseiah son of Baruch, son of Colhozeh, son of Hazaiah, son of Adaiah, son of Joiarib, son of Zechariah, of the family of Shelah.* ⁶There were also 468 descendants of Perez who lived in Jerusalem—all outstanding men.

⁷From the tribe of Benjamin: Sallu son of Meshullam, son of Joed, son of Pedaiah, son of Kolaiah, son of Maaseiah, son of Ithiel, son of Jeshaiah; ⁸and after him there were Gabbai and Sallai, and a total of 928 relatives. ⁹Their chief officer was Joel son of Zicri, who was assisted by Judah son of Hassenuah, second-in-command over the city.

¹⁰From the priests: Jedaiah son of Joiarib; Jakin; ¹¹and Seraiah son of Hilkiah, son of Meshullam, son of Zadok, son of Meraioth, son of Ahitub, the supervisor of the Temple of God; ¹²together with 822 of their associates, who worked at the Temple. Also, there was Adaiah son of Jeroham, son of Pelaliah, son of Amzi, son of Zechariah, son of Pashhur, son of Malkijah; ¹³and 242 of his associates, who were heads of their families. There were also Amashsai son of Azarel, son of Ahzai, son of Meshillemoth, son of Immer; ¹⁴and 128 of his outstanding associates. Their chief officer was Zabdiel son of Haggedolim.

¹⁵From the Levites: Shemaiah son of Hasshub, son of Azrikam, son of Hashabiah, son of Bunni; ¹⁶Shabbethai and Jozabad, who were in charge of the work outside the Temple of God; ¹⁷Mattaniah son of Mica, son of Zabdi, a descendant of Asaph, who opened the thanksgiving services with prayer; Bakbukiah, who was Mattaniah's assistant; and Abda son of Shammua, son of Galal, son of Jeduthun. ¹⁸In all, there were 284 Levites in the holy city.

¹⁹From the gatekeepers: Akkub, Talmon, and 172 of their associates, who guarded the gates.

²⁰The other priests, Levites, and the rest of the Israelites lived wherever their family inheritance was located in any of the towns of Judah. ²¹However, the Temple servants, whose leaders were Ziha and Gishpa, all lived on the hill of Ophel.

²²The chief officer of the Levites in Jerusalem was Uzzi son of Bani, son of Hashabiah, son of Mattaniah, son of Mica, a descendant of Asaph, whose family served as singers at God's Temple. ²³They were under royal orders, which determined their daily activities.

²⁴Pethahiah son of Meshezabel, a descendant of Zerah son of Judah, was the king's agent in all matters of public administration.

²⁵Some of the people of Judah lived in Kiriath-arba with its villages, Dibon with its villages, and Jekabzeel with its villages. ²⁶They also lived in Jeshua, Moladah, Bethpelet, ²⁷Hazar-shual, Beersheba with its villages, ²⁸Ziklag, and Meconah with its villages. ²⁹They were also in En-rimmon, Zorah, Jarmuth, ³⁰Zanoah, and Adullam with their villages. They were also in Lachish and its nearby fields and Azekah

11:5 Hebrew *son of the Shilonite.*

with its surrounding villages. So the people of Judah were living all the way from Beer-sheba to the valley of Hinnom.

³¹Some of the people of Benjamin lived at Geba, Micmash, Aija, and Bethel with its surrounding villages. ³²They were also in Anathoth, Nob, Ananiah, ³³Hazor, Ramah, Gittaim, ³⁴Hadid, Zeboim, Neballat, ³⁵Lod, Ono, and the Valley of Craftsmen.* ³⁶Some of the Levites who lived in Judah were sent to live with the tribe of Benjamin.

CHAPTER 12
Here is the list of the priests and Levites who had returned with Zerubbabel son of Shealtiel and Jeshua the high priest:

    Seraiah, Jeremiah, Ezra,
² Amariah, Malluch, Hattush,
³ Shecaniah, Harim,* Meremoth,
⁴ Iddo, Ginnethon,* Abijah,
⁵ Miniamin, Moadiah,* Bilgah,
⁶ Shemaiah, Joiarib, Jedaiah,
⁷ Sallu, Amok, Hilkiah, and Jedaiah.

These were the leaders of the priests and their associates in the days of Jeshua.

⁸The Levites who had returned with them were Jeshua, Binnui, Kadmiel, Sherebiah, Judah, and Mattaniah, who with his associates was in charge of the songs of thanksgiving. ⁹Their associates, Bakbukiah and Unni, stood opposite them during the service.

¹⁰ Jeshua the high priest was the father of Joiakim.
    Joiakim was the father of Eliashib.
    Eliashib was the father of Joiada.
¹¹ Joiada was the father of Johanan.*
    Johanan was the father of Jaddua.

¹²Now when Joiakim was high priest, the family leaders of the priests were as follows:

    Meraiah was leader of the family of Seraiah.
    Hananiah was leader of the family of Jeremiah.
¹³ Meshullam was leader of the family of Ezra.
    Jehohanan was leader of the family of Amariah.

¹⁴ Jonathan was leader of the family of Malluch.*
    Joseph was leader of the family of Shecaniah.*
¹⁵ Adna was leader of the family of Harim.
    Helkai was leader of the family of Meremoth.*
¹⁶ Zechariah was leader of the family of Iddo.
    Meshullam was leader of the family of Ginnethon.
¹⁷ Zicri was leader of the family of Abijah.
    There was also a* leader of the family of Miniamin.
    Piltai was leader of the family of Moadiah.
¹⁸ Shammua was leader of the family of Bilgah.
    Jehonathan was leader of the family of Shemaiah.
¹⁹ Mattenai was leader of the family of Joiarib.
    Uzzi was leader of the family of Jedaiah.
²⁰ Kallai was leader of the family of Sallu.*
    Eber was leader of the family of Amok.
²¹ Hashabiah was leader of the family of Hilkiah.
    Nethanel was leader of the family of Jedaiah.

²²During the reign of Darius II of Persia,* a list was compiled of the family leaders of the Levites and the priests in the days of the following high priests: Eliashib, Joiada, Johanan, and Jaddua. ²³The heads of the Levite families were recorded in *The Book of History* down to the days of Johanan, the grandson* of Eliashib.

²⁴These were the family leaders of the Levites: Hashabiah, Sherebiah, Jeshua, Binnui,* Kadmiel, and other associates, who stood opposite them during the ceremonies of praise and thanksgiving, one section responding to the other, just as commanded by David, the man of God. ²⁵This included Mattaniah, Bakbukiah, and Obadiah.

Meshullam, Talmon, and Akkub were the gatekeepers in charge of the storerooms at the gates. ²⁶These all served in the days of Joiakim son of Jeshua, son of Jehoza-

11:35 Or *and Ge-harashim.*   **12:3** Hebrew *Rehum;* compare 7:42; 12:15; Ezra 2:39.   **12:4** As in some Hebrew manuscripts and Latin Vulgate (see also 12:16); most Hebrew manuscripts read *Ginnethoi.*   **12:5** Hebrew *Mijamin, Maadiah;* compare 12:17. **12:11** Hebrew *Jonathan;* compare 12:22.   **12:14a** As in Greek version (see also 10:4; 12:2); Hebrew reads *Malluchi.*   **12:14b** As in many Hebrew manuscripts, some Greek manuscripts, and Syriac version (see also 12:3); most Hebrew manuscripts read *Shebaniah.* **12:15** As in some Greek manuscripts (see also 12:3); Hebrew reads *Meraioth.*   **12:17** Hebrew lacks the name of this family leader. **12:20** Hebrew *Sallai;* compare 12:7.   **12:22** Hebrew *Darius the Persian.*   **12:23** Hebrew *son;* compare 12:10-11.   **12:24** Hebrew *son of* (i.e., *ben*), which should probably be read here as the proper name Binnui; compare Ezra 3:9 and the note there.

dak,* and in the days of Nehemiah the governor and of Ezra the priest and scribe.

²⁷During the dedication of the new wall of Jerusalem, the Levites throughout the land were asked to come to Jerusalem to assist in the ceremonies. They were to take part in the joyous occasion with their songs of thanksgiving and with the music of cymbals, lyres, and harps. ²⁸The singers were brought together from Jerusalem and its surrounding villages and from the villages of the Netophathites. ²⁹They also came from Beth-gilgal and the area of Geba and Azmaveth, for the singers had built their own villages around Jerusalem. ³⁰The priests and Levites first dedicated themselves, then the people, the gates, and the wall.

³¹I led the leaders of Judah to the top of the wall and organized two large choirs to give thanks. One of the choirs proceeded southward* along the top of the wall to the Dung Gate. ³²Hoshaiah and half the leaders of Judah followed them, ³³along with Azariah, Ezra, Meshullam, ³⁴Judah, Benjamin, Shemaiah, Jeremiah, ³⁵and some priests who played trumpets. Then came Zechariah son of Jonathan, son of Shemaiah, son of Mattaniah, son of Micaiah, son of Zaccur, a descendant of Asaph. ³⁶And finally came Zechariah's colleagues Shemaiah, Azarel, Milalai, Gilalai, Maai, Nethanel, Judah, and Hanani. They used the musical instruments prescribed by David, the man of God. Ezra the scribe led this procession. ³⁷At the Fountain Gate they went straight up the steps on the ascent of the city wall toward the City of David. They passed the house of David and then proceeded to the Water Gate on the east.

³⁸The second choir went northward* around the other way to meet them. I followed them, with the other half of the people, along the top of the wall past the Tower of the Ovens to the Broad Wall, ³⁹then past the Ephraim Gate to the Old City Gate,* past the Fish Gate and the Tower of Hananel, and went on to the Tower of the Hundred. Then we continued on to the Sheep Gate and stopped at the Guard Gate.

⁴⁰The two choirs that were giving thanks then proceeded to the Temple of God, where they took their places. So did I, together with the group of leaders who were with me. ⁴¹We went together with the trumpet-playing priests—Eliakim, Maaseiah, Miniamin, Micaiah, Elioenai, Zechariah, and Hananiah—⁴²and the singers—Maaseiah, Shemaiah, Eleazar, Uzzi, Jehohanan, Malkijah, Elam, and Ezer. They played and sang loudly and clearly under the direction of Jezrahiah the choir director.

⁴³Many sacrifices were offered on that joyous day, for God had given the people cause for great joy. The women and children also participated in the celebration, and the joy of the people of Jerusalem could be heard far away.

⁴⁴On that day men were appointed to be in charge of the storerooms for the gifts, the first part of the harvest, and the tithes. They were responsible to collect these from the fields as required by the law for the priests and Levites, for all the people of Judah valued the priests and Levites and their work. ⁴⁵They performed the service of their God and the service of purification, as required by the laws of David and his son Solomon, and so did the singers and the gatekeepers. ⁴⁶The custom of having choir directors to lead the choirs in hymns of praise and thanks to God began long ago in the days of David and Asaph. ⁴⁷So now, in the days of Zerubbabel and of Nehemiah, the people brought a daily supply of food for the singers, the gatekeepers, and the Levites. The Levites, in turn, gave a portion of what they received to the priests, the descendants of Aaron.

CHAPTER 13
On that same day, as the Book of Moses was being read, the people found a statement which said that no Ammonite or Moabite should ever be permitted to enter the assembly of God. ²For they had not been friendly to the Israelites when they left Egypt. Instead, they hired Balaam to curse them, though our God turned the curse into a blessing. ³When this law was read, all those of mixed ancestry were immediately expelled from the assembly.

⁴Before this had happened, Eliashib the priest, who had been appointed as supervisor of the storerooms of the Temple of our God and who was also a relative of Tobiah,

⁵had converted a large storage room and placed it at Tobiah's disposal. The room had previously been used for storing the grain offerings, frankincense, Temple utensils, and tithes of grain, new wine, olive oil, and the special portion set aside for the priests. Moses had decreed that these offerings belonged to the Levites, the singers, and the gatekeepers.

⁶I was not in Jerusalem at that time, for I had returned to the king in the thirty-second year of the reign of King Artaxerxes of Babylon,* though I later received his permission to return. ⁷When I arrived back in Jerusalem and learned the extent of this evil deed of Eliashib—that he had provided Tobiah with a room in the courtyards of the Temple of God—⁸I became very upset and threw all of Tobiah's belongings from the room. ⁹Then I demanded that the rooms be purified, and I brought back the utensils for God's Temple, the grain offerings, and the frankincense.

¹⁰I also discovered that the Levites had not been given what was due them, so they and the singers who were to conduct the worship services had all returned to work their fields. ¹¹I immediately confronted the leaders and demanded, "Why has the Temple of God been neglected?" Then I called all the Levites back again and restored them to their proper duties. ¹²And once more all the people of Judah began bringing their tithes of grain, new wine, and olive oil to the Temple storerooms.

¹³I put Shelemiah the priest, Zadok the scribe, and Pedaiah, one of the Levites, in charge of the storerooms. And I appointed Hanan son of Zaccur and grandson of Mattaniah as their assistant. These men had an excellent reputation, and it was their job to make honest distributions to their fellow Levites.

¹⁴Remember this good deed, O my God, and do not forget all that I have faithfully done for the Temple of my God.

¹⁵One Sabbath day I saw some men of Judah treading their winepresses. They were also bringing in bundles of grain and loading them on their donkeys. And on that day they were bringing their wine, grapes, figs, and all sorts of produce to Jerusalem to sell. So I rebuked them for selling their produce on the Sabbath. ¹⁶There were also some men

from Tyre bringing in fish and all kinds of merchandise. They were selling it on the Sabbath to the people of Judah—and in Jerusalem at that!

¹⁷So I confronted the leaders of Judah, "Why are you profaning the Sabbath in this evil way? ¹⁸Wasn't it enough that your ancestors did this sort of thing, so that our God brought the present troubles upon us and our city? Now you are bringing even more wrath upon the people of Israel by permitting the Sabbath to be desecrated in this way!" ¹⁹So I commanded that from then on the gates of the city should be shut as darkness fell every Friday evening,* not to be opened until the Sabbath ended. I also sent some of my own servants to guard the gates so that no merchandise could be brought in on the Sabbath day. ²⁰The merchants and tradesmen with a variety of wares camped outside Jerusalem once or twice. ²¹But I spoke sharply to them and said, "What are you doing out here, camping around the wall? If you do this again, I will arrest you!" And that was the last time they came on the Sabbath. ²²Then I commanded the Levites to purify themselves and to guard the gates in order to preserve the holiness of the Sabbath.

Remember this good deed also, O my God! Have compassion on me according to your great and unfailing love.

²³About the same time I realized that some of the men of Judah had married women from Ashdod, Ammon, and Moab. ²⁴Even worse, half their children spoke in the language of Ashdod or some other people and could not speak the language of Judah at all. ²⁵So I confronted them and called down curses on them. I beat some of them and pulled out their hair. I made them swear before God that they would not let their children intermarry with the pagan people of the land.

²⁶"Wasn't this exactly what led King Solomon of Israel into sin?" I demanded. "There was no king from any nation who could compare to him, and God loved him and made him king over all Israel. But even he was led into sin by his foreign wives. ²⁷How could you even think of committing this sinful deed and acting unfaithfully toward God by marrying foreign women?"

13:6 The thirty-second year of Artaxerxes was 433 B.C.   13:19 Hebrew *on the day before the Sabbath.*

^28One of the sons of Joiada* son of Eliashib the high priest had married a daughter of Sanballat the Horonite, so I banished him from my presence.

^29Remember them, O my God, for they have defiled the priesthood and the promises and vows of the priests and Levites.

13:28 Hebrew *Jehoiada,* a variant name for Joiada.

^30So I purged out everything foreign and assigned tasks to the priests and Levites, making certain that each knew his work. ^31I also made sure that the supply of wood for the altar was brought at the proper times and that the first part of the harvest was collected for the priests.

Remember this in my favor, O my God.

Esther

WHILE Zerubbabel, Ezra, and Nehemiah led some fifty thousand people to their homeland, many more were reluctant to leave their adopted home in Persia. Esther's story takes place against this Persian background. Chosen to replace the banished queen, Esther soon finds herself—and her countrymen—threatened by a bizarre plot. Her faithful and courageous action saves God's people from destruction and provides the occasion for an annual celebration still observed by Jews today: the Festival of Purim.

Focus	Grave Danger		Great Deliverance	
Divisions	Esther's Exaltation	Haman's Cunning Plot	Haman's Humiliation	Mordecai's Exaltation
	1 2	3 4	5 7	8 10
Topics	Feast of Xerxes	Fast of Mordecai	Feasts of Esther	Feast of Purim
	Exaltation	Persecution	Preservation	Commemoration
Place	Persia			
Time	About 10 Years (483–473 B.C.)			

MAY 11 ☐ DAY 132
ESTHER 1–2
Esther's Exaltation

OVERVIEW The book of Esther is the story of a beautiful Jewish girl who rises from obscurity to prominence when she becomes the new queen of Persia. Although God's name is not mentioned anywhere in the account, his hand is visible everywhere as he places Esther in the Persian palace and her cousin Mordecai's name in the Persian chronicles "for just such a time as this" (4:14).

Chapter 1		Chapter 2	
Xerxes' Dinner	Vashti's Divorce	Esther's Coronation	Mordecai's Loyalty
1 9	10 22	1 18	19 23
Banishment		Bravery	

Man proposes, God disposes.

YOUR DAILY WALK "Of all the bad luck! Why did that have to happen to me?"

It's truly amazing how quickly we credit our setbacks in life to "bad luck" and our successes to "hard work"!

As you read the book of Esther, you'll find a remarkable assortment of setbacks and successes. (Divide a sheet of paper in half, and see how many of each you can record over the next four days!) But one common thread runs through them all: God was at work behind the scenes. Esther's unexpected promotion, Mordecai's forgotten act of heroism—neither was an accident! Rather, God was weaving a beautiful lesson on sovereignty from the threads in their lives, showing that in their day—as in yours—God is in control.

It's a truth found not only in the book of Esther. Read about it as well in Exodus 4:11; Psalm 115:3; Daniel 4:17, 25, 32; Romans 8:28.

INSIGHT A Fatal Plot at a Fateful Moment

At a strategic moment, Mordecai became aware of a plot devised by two eunuchs of the royal bodyguard to put King Xerxes to death (2:21-23). On this occasion, Mordecai secretly passed the news to Esther, Esther reported it in Mordecai's name, the conspirators were hanged, and the incident was written up in *The Book of the History of King Xerxes' Reign*. Ironically, about fifteen years later Xerxes would finally lose his life as a result of a similar plot.

CHAPTER 1

This happened in the days of King Xerxes,* who reigned over 127 provinces stretching from India to Ethiopia.* ²At that time he ruled his empire from his throne at the fortress of Susa. ³In the third year of his reign, he gave a banquet for all his princes and officials. He invited all the military officers of Media and Persia, as well as the noblemen and provincial officials. ⁴The celebration lasted six months*—a tremendous display of the opulent wealth and glory of his empire.

⁵When it was all over, the king gave a special banquet for all the palace servants and officials—from the greatest to the least. It lasted for seven days and was held at Susa in the courtyard of the palace garden.

1:1a Hebrew *Ahasuerus*, another name for Xerxes; also throughout the book of Esther.   **1:1b** Hebrew *to Cush*.   **1:4** Hebrew *180 days*.

⁶The courtyard was decorated with beautifully woven white and blue linen hangings, fastened by purple ribbons to silver rings embedded in marble pillars. Gold and silver couches stood on a mosaic pavement of porphyry, marble, mother-of-pearl, and other costly stones. ⁷Drinks were served in gold goblets of many designs, and there was an abundance of royal wine, just as the king had commanded. ⁸The only restriction on the drinking was that no one should be compelled to take more than he wanted. But those who wished could have as much as they pleased, for the king had instructed his staff to let everyone decide this matter for himself.

⁹Queen Vashti gave a banquet for the women of the palace at the same time.

¹⁰On the seventh day of the feast, when King Xerxes was half drunk with wine, he told Mehuman, Biztha, Harbona, Bigtha, Abagtha, Zethar, and Carcas, the seven eunuchs who attended him, ¹¹to bring Queen Vashti to him with the royal crown on her head. He wanted all the men to gaze on her beauty, for she was a very beautiful woman. ¹²But when they conveyed the king's order to Queen Vashti, she refused to come. This made the king furious, and he burned with anger.

¹³He immediately consulted with his advisers, who knew all the Persian laws and customs, for he always asked their advice. ¹⁴The names of these men were Carshena, Shethar, Admatha, Tarshish, Meres, Marsena, and Memucan—seven high officials of Persia and Media. They were his closest associates and held the highest positions in the empire. ¹⁵"What must be done to Queen Vashti?" the king demanded. "What penalty does the law provide for a queen who refuses to obey the king's orders, properly sent through his eunuchs?"

¹⁶Memucan answered the king and his princes, "Queen Vashti has wronged not only the king but also every official and citizen throughout your empire. ¹⁷Women everywhere will begin to despise their husbands when they learn that Queen Vashti has refused to appear before the king. ¹⁸Before this day is out, the wife of every one of us, your officials throughout the empire, will hear what the queen did and will start talking to their husbands the same way. There will be no end to the contempt and

anger throughout your realm. ¹⁹So if it please the king, we suggest that you issue a written decree, a law of the Persians and Medes that cannot be revoked. It should order that Queen Vashti be forever banished from your presence and that you choose another queen more worthy than she. ²⁰When this decree is published throughout your vast empire, husbands everywhere, whatever their rank, will receive proper respect from their wives!"

²¹The king and his princes thought this made good sense, so he followed Memucan's counsel. ²²He sent letters to all parts of the empire, to each province in its own script and language, proclaiming that every man should be the ruler of his home.

CHAPTER 2
But after Xerxes' anger had cooled, he began thinking about Vashti and what she had done and the decree he had made. ²So his attendants suggested, "Let us search the empire to find beautiful young virgins for the king. ³Let the king appoint agents in each province to bring these beautiful young women into the royal harem at Susa. Hegai, the eunuch in charge, will see that they are all given beauty treatments. ⁴After that, the young woman who pleases you most will be made queen instead of Vashti." This advice was very appealing to the king, so he put the plan into effect immediately.

⁵Now at the fortress of Susa there was a certain Jew named Mordecai son of Jair. He was from the tribe of Benjamin and was a descendant of Kish and Shimei. ⁶His family* had been exiled from Jerusalem to Babylon by King Nebuchadnezzar, along with King Jehoiachin* of Judah and many others. ⁷This man had a beautiful and lovely young cousin, Hadassah, who was also called Esther. When her father and mother had died, Mordecai adopted her into his family and raised her as his own daughter. ⁸As a result of the king's decree, Esther, along with many other young women, was brought to the king's harem at the fortress of Susa and placed in Hegai's care. ⁹Hegai was very impressed with Esther and treated her kindly. He quickly ordered a special menu for her and provided her with beauty treatments. He also assigned her seven maids specially chosen

2:6a Hebrew *He.*   **2:6b** Hebrew *Jeconiah,* a variant name for Jehoiachin.

from the king's palace, and he moved her and her maids into the best place in the harem.

[10]Esther had not told anyone of her nationality and family background, for Mordecai had told her not to. [11]Every day Mordecai would take a walk near the courtyard of the harem to ask about Esther and to find out what was happening to her. [12]Before each young woman was taken to the king's bed, she was given the prescribed twelve months of beauty treatments—six months with oil of myrrh, followed by six months with special perfumes and ointments. [13]When the time came for her to go in to the king, she was given her choice of whatever clothing or jewelry she wanted to enhance her beauty. [14]That evening she was taken to the king's private rooms, and the next morning she was brought to the second harem,* where the king's wives lived. There she would be under the care of Shaashgaz, another of the king's eunuchs. She would live there for the rest of her life, never going to the king again unless he had especially enjoyed her and requested her by name.

[15]When it was Esther's turn* to go to the king, she accepted the advice of Hegai, the eunuch in charge of the harem. She asked for nothing except what he suggested, and she was admired by everyone who saw her.

[16]When Esther was taken to King Xerxes at the royal palace in early winter* of the seventh year of his reign, [17]the king loved her more than any of the other young women. He was so delighted with her that he set the royal crown on her head and declared her queen instead of Vashti. [18]To celebrate the occasion, he gave a banquet in Esther's honor for all his princes and servants, giving generous gifts to everyone and declaring a public festival for the provinces.

[19]Even after all the young women had been transferred to the second harem* and Mordecai had become a palace official, [20]Esther continued to keep her nationality and family background a secret. She was still following Mordecai's orders, just as she did when she was living in his home.

[21]One day as Mordecai was on duty at the palace, two of the king's eunuchs, Bigthana* and Teresh—who were guards at the door of the king's private quarters—became angry at King Xerxes and plotted to assassinate him. [22]But Mordecai heard about the plot and passed the information on to Queen Esther. She then told the king about it and gave Mordecai credit for the report. [23]When an investigation was made and Mordecai's story was found to be true, the two men were hanged on a gallows.* This was all duly recorded in *The Book of the History of King Xerxes' Reign.*

2:14 Or *to another part of the harem.*   **2:15** Hebrew *the turn of Esther, the daughter of Abihail, who was Mordecai's uncle, who had adopted her.*   **2:16** Hebrew *in the tenth month, the month of Tebeth.* A number of dates in the book of Esther can be cross-checked with dates in surviving Persian records and related accurately to our modern calendar. This month of the Hebrew lunar calendar occurred in December 479 B.C. and January 478 B.C.   **2:19** The meaning of the Hebrew is uncertain.   **2:21** Hebrew *Bigthan;* compare 6:2.   **2:23** Or *on a pole.*

MAY 12 ☐ DAY 133
ESTHER 3–4
Haman's Cunning Plot

 OVERVIEW Esther has been made queen without her nationality being known. But now a new danger arises in the person of Haman, another recipient of a kingly promotion. Mordecai, who has already proven his loyalty to the king, refuses to "worship" Haman as the king has decreed, prompting Haman to respond with insane anger. Both Mordecai and his countrymen must die. False charges and a sizable bribe secure what Haman desires: the king's permission to liquidate the Jewish population. Now Queen Esther is faced with a life-and-death decision. Should she risk revealing her nationality in order to dissuade the king? Or should she protect her life and watch her countrymen be exterminated?

Chapter 3				Chapter 4			
Haman's Promotion		Haman's Plot		Mordecai's Fast		Esther's Faith	
1	5	6	15	1	12	13	17
A Deadly Plan				A Desperate Decision			

YOUR DAILY WALK "If I must die, I am willing to die." Is this the fatalistic cry of a queen resigned to her death, or the faith-inspired statement of a woman who serves a sovereign God?

Only when we place ourselves in God's hands can we bring glory to him and growth to ourselves.

Don't miss the context: Mordecai has just warned Esther that she will not escape Haman's plot just because she is the queen. And he challenges her with this thought: "What's more, who can say but that you have been elevated to the palace for just such a time as this?" Paraphrased, he was saying: "Esther, God has placed you in a strategic place at a critical moment to be the instrument of deliverance for his people. Your presence in the palace is not by accident, but by divine appointment."

Do you find yourself in a situation similar to Esther's where you wish you could hide in the palace, so to speak? Then get ready! God has put you where you are for a purpose.

INSIGHT The High Price of Cold Blood
One commentator has valued the Hebrew talent of silver at $12,000. That means Haman was willing to pay $120 million to exterminate the Jews—a fabulous sum for a Persian hit man!

CHAPTER 3

Some time later, King Xerxes promoted Haman son of Hammedatha the Agagite to prime minister, making him the most powerful official in the empire next to the king himself. [2] All the king's officials would bow down before Haman to show him respect whenever he passed by, for so the king had commanded. But Mordecai refused to bow down or show him respect.

[3] Then the palace officials at the king's gate asked Mordecai, "Why are you disobeying the king's command?" [4] They spoke to him day after day, but still he refused to comply with the order. So they spoke to Haman about this to see if he would tolerate Mordecai's conduct, since Mordecai had told them he was a Jew.

[5] When Haman saw that Mordecai would not bow down or show him respect, he was filled with rage. [6] So he decided it was not enough to lay hands on Mordecai alone. Since he had learned that Mordecai was a Jew, he decided to destroy all the Jews throughout the entire empire of Xerxes.

[7] So in the month of April,* during the twelfth year of King Xerxes' reign, lots were cast (the lots were called *purim*) to determine the best day and month to take action. And the day selected was March 7, nearly a year later.*

[8] Then Haman approached King Xerxes and said, "There is a certain race of people scattered through all the provinces of your empire. Their laws are different from those of any other nation, and they refuse to obey even the laws of the king. So it is not in the king's interest to let them live. [9] If it please Your Majesty, issue a decree that they be destroyed, and I will give 375 tons* of silver to the government administrators so they can put it into the royal treasury."

[10] The king agreed, confirming his decision by removing his signet ring from his finger and giving it to Haman son of Hammedatha the Agagite—the enemy of the Jews. [11] "Keep the money," the king told Haman, "but go ahead and do as you like with these people."

[12] On April 17* Haman called in the king's secretaries and dictated letters to the princes,

3:7a Hebrew *in the first month, the month of Nisan.* This month of the Hebrew lunar calendar occurred in April and May 474 B.C.; also see note on 2:16. 3:7b As in Greek version, which reads *the thirteenth day of the twelfth month, the month of Adar* (see also 3:13). Hebrew reads *in the twelfth month,* of the Hebrew calendar. The date selected was March 7, 473 B.C.; also see note on 2:16. 3:9 Hebrew *10,000 talents* [340 metric tons]. 3:12 Hebrew *On the thirteenth day of the first month,* of the Hebrew calendar. This event occurred on April 17, 474 B.C.; also see note on 2:16.

the governors of the respective provinces, and the local officials of each province in their own scripts and languages. These letters were signed in the name of King Xerxes, sealed with his ring, [13]and sent by messengers into all the provinces of the empire. The letters decreed that all Jews—young and old, including women and children—must be killed, slaughtered, and annihilated on a single day. This was scheduled to happen nearly a year later on March 7.* The property of the Jews would be given to those who killed them. [14]A copy of this decree was to be issued in every province and made known to all the people, so that they would be ready to do their duty on the appointed day. [15]At the king's command, the decree went out by the swiftest messengers, and it was proclaimed in the fortress of Susa. Then the king and Haman sat down to drink, but the city of Susa fell into confusion.

CHAPTER 4

When Mordecai learned what had been done, he tore his clothes, put on sackcloth and ashes, and went out into the city, crying with a loud and bitter wail. [2]He stood outside the gate of the palace, for no one was allowed to enter while wearing clothes of mourning. [3]And as news of the king's decree reached all the provinces, there was great mourning among the Jews. They fasted, wept, and wailed, and many people lay in sackcloth and ashes.

[4]When Queen Esther's maids and eunuchs came and told her about Mordecai, she was deeply distressed. She sent clothing to him to replace the sackcloth, but he refused it. [5]Then Esther sent for Hathach, one of the king's eunuchs who had been appointed as her attendant. She ordered him to go to Mordecai and find out what

was troubling him and why he was in mourning. [6]So Hathach went out to Mordecai in the square in front of the palace gate.

[7]Mordecai told him the whole story and told him how much money Haman had promised to pay into the royal treasury for the destruction of the Jews. [8]Mordecai gave Hathach a copy of the decree issued in Susa that called for the death of all Jews, and he asked Hathach to show it to Esther. He also asked Hathach to explain it to her and to urge her to go to the king to beg for mercy and plead for her people. [9]So Hathach returned to Esther with Mordecai's message.

[10]Then Esther told Hathach to go back and relay this message to Mordecai: [11]"The whole world knows that anyone who appears before the king in his inner court without being invited is doomed to die unless the king holds out his gold scepter. And the king has not called for me to come to him in more than a month." [12]So Hathach gave Esther's message to Mordecai.

[13]Mordecai sent back this reply to Esther: "Don't think for a moment that you will escape there in the palace when all other Jews are killed. [14]If you keep quiet at a time like this, deliverance for the Jews will arise from some other place, but you and your relatives will die. What's more, who can say but that you have been elevated to the palace for just such a time as this?"

[15]Then Esther sent this reply to Mordecai: [16]"Go and gather together all the Jews of Susa and fast for me. Do not eat or drink for three days, night or day. My maids and I will do the same. And then, though it is against the law, I will go in to see the king. If I must die, I am willing to die." [17]So Mordecai went away and did as Esther told him.

3:13 Hebrew *on the thirteenth day of the twelfth month, the month of Adar,* of the Hebrew calendar. The date selected was March 7, 473 B.C.; also see note on 2:16.

MAY 13 ☐ DAY 134
ESTHER 5–7
Haman's Humiliation

OVERVIEW Esther knows full well that entering the king's throne room uninvited could prove hazardous to her health. But Esther courageously discovers that God has once again prepared the way. She invites Xerxes and Haman to a special banquet in their honor and there repeats the invitation for the next day as well. But before that fateful second banquet,

Haman builds a gallows seventy-five feet high on which to hang Mordecai; Xerxes discovers Mordecai's unrewarded heroism; and Haman watches the honor he had craved go to Mordecai. At the second banquet Haman is unmasked and dies the very death he had planned for Mordecai.

Chapter 5	Chapter 6	Chapter 7
Haman's Haughtiness	Haman's Humiliation	Haman's Hanging
First Banquet	Forgotten Bravery	Fateful Banquet

Believing supplications are forecasts of the future.

YOUR DAILY WALK Do you believe in prayer? Do you really? Esther believed in prayer enough to go before the king at an unappointed time with an unlikely request, though it could have meant swift death (4:11, 16; 5:2). Would you have done that?

The story is told of a midwestern town suffering under a searing drought. All the townspeople finally decided it was time to gather the clergy and assemble for prayer. The whole town turned out to pray for rain, but only one person, a small girl, brought her umbrella.

When you pray, are you like the townspeople or the little girl? Do you, like Esther, pray first and then live in the confidence of God's answer? Are your prayers specific enough that, when God answers, you notice a difference? In the margin write down a specific request for provision, protection, or guidance. For the next week focus your prayers on that item. You might even want to put your umbrella in an unusual place to remind you throughout the week to watch for God's answer!

INSIGHT The Hanging All Susa Would See
The excessive height of Haman's gallows (seventy-five feet, or at least as high as the city walls) was designed to ensure that Mordecai's downfall would be a citywide spectacle, visible both inside and outside the walls. Instead, Haman himself received the notoriety!

CHAPTER 5

Three days later, Esther put on her royal robes and entered the inner court of the palace, just across from the king's hall. The king was sitting on his royal throne, facing the entrance. [2]When he saw Queen Esther standing there in the inner court, he welcomed her, holding out the gold scepter to her. So Esther approached and touched its tip.

[3]Then the king asked her, "What do you want, Queen Esther? What is your request? I will give it to you, even if it is half the kingdom!"

[4]And Esther replied, "If it please Your Majesty, let the king and Haman come today to a banquet I have prepared for the king."

[5]The king turned to his attendants and said, "Tell Haman to come quickly to a banquet, as Esther has requested." So the king and Haman went to Esther's banquet.

[6]And while they were drinking wine, the king said to Esther, "Now tell me what you really want. What is your request? I will give it to you, even if it is half the kingdom!"

[7]Esther replied, "This is my request and deepest wish. [8]If Your Majesty is pleased with me and wants to grant my request, please come with Haman tomorrow to the banquet I will prepare for you. Then tomorrow I will explain what this is all about."

[9]What a happy man Haman was as he left the banquet! But when he saw Mordecai sitting at the gate, not standing up or trembling nervously before him, he was furious. [10]However, he restrained himself and went on home. Then he gathered together his friends and Zeresh, his wife, [11]and boasted to them about his great wealth and his many children. He bragged about the honors the king had given him

and how he had been promoted over all the other officials and leaders.

¹²Then Haman added, "And that's not all! Queen Esther invited only me and the king himself to the banquet she prepared for us. And she has invited me to dine with her and the king again tomorrow!" ¹³Then he added, "But all this is meaningless as long as I see Mordecai the Jew just sitting there at the palace gate."

¹⁴So Haman's wife, Zeresh, and all his friends suggested, "Set up a gallows* that stands seventy-five feet* tall, and in the morning ask the king to hang Mordecai on it. When this is done, you can go on your merry way to the banquet with the king." This pleased Haman immensely, and he ordered the gallows set up.

CHAPTER 6

That night the king had trouble sleeping, so he ordered an attendant to bring the historical records of his kingdom so they could be read to him. ²In those records he discovered an account of how Mordecai had exposed the plot of Bigthana and Teresh, two of the eunuchs who guarded the door to the king's private quarters. They had plotted to assassinate the king. ³"What reward or recognition did we ever give Mordecai for this?" the king asked.

His attendants replied, "Nothing has been done."

⁴"Who is that in the outer court?" the king inquired. Now, as it happened, Haman had just arrived in the outer court of the palace to ask the king to hang Mordecai from the gallows* he had prepared.

⁵So the attendants replied to the king, "Haman is out there."

"Bring him in," the king ordered. ⁶So Haman came in, and the king said, "What should I do to honor a man who truly pleases me?"

Haman thought to himself, "Whom would the king wish to honor more than me?" ⁷So he replied, "If the king wishes to honor someone, ⁸he should bring out one of the king's own royal robes, as well as the king's own horse with a royal emblem on its head. ⁹Instruct one of the king's most noble princes to dress the man in the king's robe and to lead him through the city square on the king's own horse. Have the prince shout as they go, 'This is what happens to those the king wishes to honor!'"

¹⁰"Excellent!" the king said to Haman. "Hurry and get the robe and my horse, and do just as you have said for Mordecai the Jew, who sits at the gate of the palace. Do not fail to carry out everything you have suggested."

¹¹So Haman took the robe and put it on Mordecai, placed him on the king's own horse, and led him through the city square, shouting, "This is what happens to those the king wishes to honor!" ¹²Afterward Mordecai returned to the palace gate, but Haman hurried home dejected and completely humiliated.

¹³When Haman told his wife, Zeresh, and all his friends what had happened, they said, "Since Mordecai—this man who has humiliated you—is a Jew, you will never succeed in your plans against him. It will be fatal to continue to oppose him." ¹⁴While they were still talking, the king's eunuchs arrived to take Haman to the banquet Esther had prepared.

CHAPTER 7

So the king and Haman went to Queen Esther's banquet. ²And while they were drinking wine that day, the king again asked her, "Tell me what you want, Queen Esther. What is your request? I will give it to you, even if it is half the kingdom!"

³And so Queen Esther replied, "If Your Majesty is pleased with me and wants to grant my request, my petition is that my life and the lives of my people will be spared. ⁴For my people and I have been sold to those who would kill, slaughter, and annihilate us. If we had only been sold as slaves, I could remain quiet, for that would have been a matter too trivial to warrant disturbing the king."

⁵"Who would do such a thing?" King Xerxes demanded. "Who would dare touch you?"

⁶Esther replied, "This wicked Haman is our enemy." Haman grew pale with fright before the king and queen. ⁷Then the king jumped to his feet in a rage and went out into the palace garden.

But Haman stayed behind to plead for his life with Queen Esther, for he knew that he was doomed. ⁸In despair he fell on the couch where Queen Esther was reclining,

5:14a Or *a pole.*   5:14b Hebrew *50 cubits* [22.5 meters].   6:4 Or *from the pole.*

just as the king returned from the palace garden. "Will he even assault the queen right here in the palace, before my very eyes?" the king roared. And as soon as the king spoke, his attendants covered Haman's face, signaling his doom.

⁹Then Harbona, one of the king's eunuchs, said, "Haman has set up a gallows*

that stands seventy-five feet* tall in his own courtyard. He intended to use it to hang Mordecai, the man who saved the king from assassination."

"Then hang Haman on it!" the king ordered. ¹⁰So they hanged Haman on the gallows he had set up for Mordecai, and the king's anger was pacified.

7:9a Or *a pole*; also in 7:10.   7:9b Hebrew *50 cubits* [22.5 meters].

MAY 14 □ DAY 135
Going and Coming with God

 LOOK BACK "Go home!" (That's what Artaxerxes told Nehemiah to do.) "Stay put!" (That, in essence, is what Mordecai told Esther to do.)

Sounds a bit confusing until you realize that both commands were God's will for his choice servants. When Nehemiah saw there was a rebuilding job to do hundreds of miles away in his beloved Jerusalem, he prayerfully began to form a plan to tackle the job. When the king inquired, Nehemiah was ready.

By contrast, Esther saw a need right where she lived in Persia. Her Jewish countrymen were threatened with annihilation at the hands of wicked Haman. With the help of her cousin Mordecai, Esther fasted, prayed, and formed a plan. And when the king inquired, Esther was ready.

Each faced withering opposition and seemingly insurmountable odds. They both had plenty of reason never to attempt what they did! And each saw God work a miracle through his available servant. What exciting walks of faith to study and model your life after as you seek to obey God in the daily decisions of life.

 LOOK UP Rome wasn't built in a day. Neither are most other things that have the potential to touch many lives or accomplish great good. But careful planning, combined with fervent prayer and plenty of hard work, can accomplish things for God that would never be possible on the spur of the moment.

We must ask ourselves, How much of eternity is in what we are doing?

Here is a partial list of long-range projects you might want to consider. If one person can't accomplish them alone, why not share your vision and burden with a circle of close praying friends, and see if God might want you to tackle something together:

• Get completely out of debt (including any mortgages on your own house).
• Start a backyard Bible class or weekly evangelistic Bible study in your neighborhood.
• Begin a recreation program with inner-city youth.
• Write a book.
• Take a short-term mission trip to another country.
• Call your former classmates from high school or college, and tell them the difference Jesus has made in your life.
• Build a low-cost house for a family who is dependent on government aid.
• Run for public office.
• Go back to school and finish that bachelor's, master's, or doctoral degree.

LOOK AHEAD No one believed Nehemiah could rebuild the walls of Jerusalem that lay in rubble and ruin. Fortified by long hours of prayer and tears, and joined by fifty thousand of his motivated countrymen, they completed the task miraculously in fifty-two days despite intense opposition!

No one believed Esther could stay the death sentence hanging over her countrymen. But with her heart prepared through prayer and fasting, and counseled by her godly cousin, Mordecai, Esther ventured into the very presence of the king to make her bold request. As a result, thousands of Jews were spared.

No one may believe that you can accomplish what God has laid upon your heart either . . . until you attempt it in the strength of the Lord.

MAY 15 ☐ DAY 136
ESTHER 8–10
Mordecai's Exaltation

OVERVIEW A Persian law sealed with the king's ring could never be revoked. And although Haman is dead, the king's decree calling for the extermination of the Jewish race lives on. Mordecai, who now occupies Haman's former position of power, issues a counter-decree allowing the Jews to defend themselves on the same day as Haman's edict. When the day of destruction arrives, the enemies of the Jews—not the Jews themselves—are annihilated. Future generations will henceforth celebrate the Festival of Purim (so named for the lots Haman cast and God directed), recalling the days of earnest appeal to God and the stunning deliverance he provided.

Chapter 8	Chapter 9	Chapter 10
Mordecai's Vindication	The Jews' Vengeance	Mordecai's Veneration
Promotion	Protection	Praise

To know God's will is life's greatest treasure; to do God's will is life's greatest pleasure.

YOUR DAILY WALK Think back over the troubles of the Jews as recorded in the historical books of the Bible. During the years of the judges and kings they experienced wars, famines, political upheavals, shattered families, and premature death. Later came captivity, dispersion, and exile at the hands of the Assyrians and Babylonians. During the four hundred years between the close of the Old Testament and the opening of the New, they would be characterized by coldhearted indifference, culminating in the outright rejection of the Messiah. They would be dispersed worldwide once again; attempts would be made to liquidate them once and for all. And yet, as you look at your map of the Middle East today, there boldly stands the tiny nation of Israel—still very much a part of God's continuing plan.

If God can bring his chosen people through centuries of chaotic history and preserve them from extinction in spite of unbelief, disobedience, and indifference, what do you suppose he is capable of doing in your life . . . especially if he has your cooperation? God wants to make Esther's story your story; will you let him?

INSIGHT The Verse That Says It All—or Nearly So!
There is something striking about Esther 8:9. Can you discover what it is? (Hint: John 11:35 is just the opposite!) Give up? The fifty-six words contained in that verse make it the longest in the Bible.

CHAPTER 8

On that same day King Xerxes gave the estate of Haman, the enemy of the Jews, to Queen Esther. Then Mordecai was brought before the king, for Esther had told the king how they were related. ²The king took off his signet ring—which he had taken back from Haman—and gave it to Mordecai. And Esther appointed Mordecai to be in charge of Haman's property.

³Now once more Esther came before the king, falling down at his feet and begging him with tears to stop Haman's evil plot against the Jews. ⁴Again the king held out the gold scepter to Esther. So she rose and stood before him ⁵and said, "If Your Majesty is pleased with me and if he thinks it is right, send out a decree reversing Haman's orders to destroy the Jews throughout all the provinces of the king. ⁶For how can I endure to see my people and my family slaughtered and destroyed?"

⁷Then King Xerxes said to Queen Esther and Mordecai the Jew, "I have given Esther the estate of Haman, and he has been hanged on the gallows* because he tried to destroy the Jews. ⁸Now go ahead and send a message to the Jews in the king's name, telling them whatever you want, and seal it with the king's signet ring. But remember that whatever is written in the king's name and sealed with his ring can never be revoked."

⁹So on June 25* the king's secretaries were summoned. As Mordecai dictated, they wrote a decree to the Jews and to the princes, governors, and local officials of all the 127 provinces stretching from India to Ethiopia.* The decree was written in the scripts and languages of all the peoples of the empire, including the Jews. ¹⁰Mordecai wrote in the name of King Xerxes and sealed the message with the king's signet ring. He sent the letters by swift messengers, who rode horses especially bred for the king's service.

¹¹The king's decree gave the Jews in every city authority to unite to defend their lives. They were allowed to kill, slaughter, and annihilate anyone of any nationality or province who might attack them or their children and wives, and to take the property of their enemies. ¹²The day chosen for this event throughout all the provinces of King Xerxes was March 7 of the next year.* ¹³A copy of this decree was to be recognized as law in every province and proclaimed to all the people. That way the Jews would be ready on that day to take revenge on their enemies. ¹⁴So urged on by the king's command, the messengers rode out swiftly on horses bred for the king's service. The same decree was also issued at the fortress of Susa.

¹⁵Then Mordecai put on the royal robe of blue and white and the great crown of gold, and he wore an outer cloak of fine linen and purple. And the people of Susa celebrated the new decree. ¹⁶The Jews were filled with joy and gladness and were honored everywhere. ¹⁷In every city and province, wherever the king's decree arrived, the Jews rejoiced and had a great celebration and declared a public festival and holiday. And many of the people of the land became Jews themselves, for they feared what the Jews might do to them.

CHAPTER 9

So on March 7* the two decrees of the king were put into effect. On that day, the enemies of the Jews had hoped to destroy them, but quite the opposite happened. ²The Jews gathered in their cities throughout all the king's provinces to defend themselves against anyone who might try to harm them. But no one could make a stand against them, for everyone was afraid of them. ³And all the commanders of the provinces, the princes, the governors, and the royal officials helped the Jews for fear of Mordecai. ⁴For Mordecai had been promoted in the king's palace, and his fame spread throughout all the provinces as he became more and more powerful.

⁵But the Jews went ahead on the ap-

8:7 Or *on the pole.*   **8:9a** Hebrew *on the twenty-third day of the third month, the month of Sivan,* of the Hebrew calendar. This event occurred on June 25, 474 B.C.; also see note on 2:16.   **8:9b** Hebrew *to Cush.*   **8:12** Hebrew *the thirteenth day of the twelfth month, the month of Adar,* of the Hebrew calendar. The date selected was March 7, 473 B.C.; also see note on 2:16.   **9:1** Hebrew *on the thirteenth day of the twelfth month, the month of Adar,* of the Hebrew calendar. This event occurred on March 7, 473 B.C.; also see note on 2:16.

pointed day and struck down their enemies with the sword. They killed and annihilated their enemies and did as they
pleased with those who hated them. [6]They
killed five hundred people in the fortress of
Susa. [7]They also killed Parshandatha, Dal-
phon, Aspatha, [8]Poratha, Adalia, Aridatha,
[9]Parmashta, Arisai, Aridai, and Vaizatha—
[10]the ten sons of Haman son of Hammedatha, the enemy of the Jews. But they did not
take any plunder.

[11]That evening, when the king was informed of the number of people killed in
the fortress of Susa, [12]he called for Queen
Esther and said, "The Jews have killed five
hundred people in the fortress of Susa
alone and also Haman's ten sons. If they
have done that here, what has happened in
the rest of the provinces? But now, what
more do you want? It will be granted to
you; tell me and I will do it."

[13]And Esther said, "If it please Your Majesty, give the Jews in Susa permission to do
again tomorrow as they have done today,
and have the bodies of Haman's ten sons
hung from the gallows.*"

[14]So the king agreed, and the decree was
announced in Susa. They also hung the
bodies of Haman's ten sons from the gallows. [15]Then the Jews at Susa gathered together on March 8* and killed three
hundred more people, though again they
took no plunder.

[16]Meanwhile, the other Jews throughout
the king's provinces had gathered together
to defend their lives. They gained relief
from all their enemies, killing seventy-five
thousand of those who hated them. But
they did not take any plunder. [17]Through-
out the provinces this was done on
March 7.* Then on the following day* they
rested, celebrating their victory with a day
of feasting and gladness. [18]But the Jews at
Susa continued killing their enemies on the
second day also, and then rested on the
third day,* making that their day of feasting and gladness. [19]So to this day, rural
Jews living in unwalled villages celebrate
an annual festival and holiday in late winter,* when they rejoice and send gifts to
each other.

[20]Mordecai recorded these events and
sent letters to the Jews near and far,
throughout all the king's provinces, [21]en-
couraging them to celebrate an annual festival on these two days. [22]He told them to
celebrate these days with feasting and
gladness and by giving gifts to each other
and to the poor. This would commemorate
a time when the Jews gained relief from
their enemies, when their sorrow was
turned into gladness and their mourning
into joy.

[23]So the Jews adopted Mordecai's suggestion and began this annual custom.
[24]Haman son of Hammedatha the Agagite,
the enemy of the Jews, had plotted to crush
and destroy them on the day and month
determined by casting lots (the lots were
called *purim*). [25]But when Esther came before the king, he issued a decree causing
Haman's evil plot to backfire, and Haman
and his sons were hanged on the gallows.
[26](That is why this celebration is called Purim, because it is the ancient word for casting lots.) So because of Mordecai's letter
and because of what they had experienced,
[27]the Jews throughout the realm agreed to
inaugurate this tradition and to pass it on
to their descendants and to all who became
Jews. They declared they would never fail
to celebrate these two prescribed days at
the appointed time each year. [28]These days
would be remembered and kept from generation to generation and celebrated by
every family throughout the provinces and
cities of the empire. These days would
never cease to be celebrated among the
Jews, nor would the memory of what happened ever die out among their descendants.

[29]Then Queen Esther, the daughter of
Abihail, along with Mordecai the Jew,
wrote another letter putting the queen's
full authority behind Mordecai's letter to
establish the Festival of Purim. [30]In addition, letters wishing peace and security
were sent to the Jews throughout the 127
provinces of the empire of Xerxes. [31]These
letters established the Festival of Purim—
an annual celebration of these days at the
appointed time, decreed by both Mordecai
the Jew and Queen Esther. (The people decided to observe this festival, just as they
had decided for themselves and their descendants to establish the times of fasting

9:13 Or *the pole;* also in 9:14, 25.   **9:15** Hebrew *the fourteenth day of the month of Adar,* of the Hebrew calendar. This event occurred
on March 8, 473 B.C.; also see note on 2:16.   **9:17a** Hebrew *on the thirteenth day of the month of Adar,* of the Hebrew calendar. This
event occurred on March 7, 473 B.C.; also see note on 2:16.   **9:17b** Hebrew *on the fourteenth day,* of the Hebrew month of Adar.
9:18 Hebrew *killing their enemies on the thirteenth day and the fourteenth day, and then rested on the fifteenth day,* of the Hebrew month
of Adar.   **9:19** Hebrew *on the fourteenth day of the month of Adar.* This day of the Hebrew lunar calendar usually occurs in March.

and mourning.) ³²So the command of Esther confirmed the practices of Purim, and it was all written down in the records.

CHAPTER 10
King Xerxes imposed tribute throughout his empire, even to the distant coastlands. ²His great achievements and the full account of the greatness of Mordecai, whom the king had promoted, are recorded in *The Book of the History of the Kings of Media and Persia*. ³Mordecai the Jew became the prime minister, with authority next to that of King Xerxes himself. He was very great among the Jews, who held him in high esteem, because he worked for the good of his people and was a friend at the royal court for all of them.

Job

THE BOOK of Job examines one of life's most perplexing questions. It introduces a pious man of God named Job, who lived perhaps four thousand years ago. In a sudden series of catastrophes, Job loses his family, fame, fortune, and fitness. For more than thirty chapters he searches his soul and debates his best friends to find a reason for his misfortune. After exhausting the conventional wisdom of his counselors, Job is confronted by God himself, and his demanding *why* melts into humble worship.

Focus	Situation	Search			Solution
Divisions	Controversy between the Lord and Satan	Controversy with Job's Four Friends:	Cycle 1 { Eliphaz and Job (4–7) / Bildad and Job (8–10) / Zophar and Job (11–14) } Cycle 2 { Eliphaz and Job (15–17) / Bildad and Job (18–19) / Zophar and Job (20–21) } Cycle 3 { Eliphaz and Job (22–24) / Bildad and Job (25–31) / Elihu (32–37) }		Controversy between the Lord and Job
	1 3	4		37	38 42
Topics	Dialogue in Heaven	Dialogue on Earth			Dialogue between Heaven & Earth
	The Onset of Suffering	The Failure of Human Wisdom			The Final Word from God
Place	Land of Uz (North Arabia)				
Time	Patriarchal Period (about 2000 B.C.)				

MAY 16 ☐ DAY 137
JOB 1–3
Controversy between the Lord and Satan

OVERVIEW Southeast of the Dead Sea lies the land of Uz, a sheep and cattle ranching region and home of the wealthy herdsman Job. Job's exemplary life of service for God is placed in the furnace of testing. In a heavenly drama (unknown to Job but revealed to the reader), Satan accuses Job of serving God for material reward. By divine permission, Satan tests Job by removing all that he holds dear: his family, wealth, health, and prestige. Yet through it all Job maintains his steadfast worship of God, though nagging questions remain.

Chapter 1		Chapter 2		Chapter 3
Satan's First Attack		Satan's Second Attack		Job's Agony
Planned	Performed	Planned	Performed	
1 11	12 22	1 6	7 13	
Disaster				Doubt

YOUR DAILY WALK What is your first response when someone points a finger at you? Do you find it a painful or a pleasant experience?

There is someone who takes great delight in pointing an accusing finger at your life. One of his names is *devil* (1 Peter 5:8), which literally means "slanderer." (Some of his other names are equally revealing—see Matthew 12:24; 13:19; Luke 10:18; John 8:44; Ephesians 6:12; Revelation 9:11; 12:10; 20:2).

Of all the devil's tools for making us miserable, discouragement is his finest and most frequently used.

Now that you know something about your enemy, you'll want to know how you—like Job—can stand firm against his fiery attacks. Job, who experienced the worst Satan could hurl against him, maintained an attitude of confident trust in his sovereign God.

Did that mean . . .
• Job deserved the treatment he received? (2:3)
• all of Job's questions were answered? (3:11-12, 23)

The answer in both cases is no! But even though Job's misery came unexplained and undeserved, Job demonstrated in the midst of it an unshakable confidence in the one who held his life in his very hands. It wasn't *what* he knew but *whom* he knew that gave him strength to stand against any trial.

INSIGHT A Name from Ancient Times
The name of both the book and its hero, Job (Hebrew, *iyyob*), appears in extrabiblical texts as early as 2000 B.C., indicating that Job is perhaps the oldest book of the Bible.

CHAPTER 1

There was a man named Job who lived in the land of Uz. He was blameless, a man of complete integrity. He feared God and stayed away from evil. ²He had seven sons and three daughters. ³He owned seven thousand sheep, three thousand camels, five hundred teams of oxen, and five hun-dred female donkeys, and he employed many servants. He was, in fact, the richest person in that entire area.

⁴Every year when Job's sons had birth-days, they invited their brothers and sisters to join them for a celebration. On these occasions they would get together to eat and drink. ⁵When these celebrations ended—

and sometimes they lasted several days—Job would purify his children. He would get up early in the morning and offer a burnt offering for each of them. For Job said to himself, "Perhaps my children have sinned and have cursed God in their hearts." This was Job's regular practice.

⁶One day the angels* came to present themselves before the LORD, and Satan the Accuser came with them. ⁷"Where have you come from?" the LORD asked Satan.

And Satan answered the LORD, "I have been going back and forth across the earth, watching everything that's going on."

⁸Then the LORD asked Satan, "Have you noticed my servant Job? He is the finest man in all the earth—a man of complete integrity. He fears God and will have nothing to do with evil."

⁹Satan replied to the LORD, "Yes, Job fears God, but not without good reason! ¹⁰You have always protected him and his home and his property from harm. You have made him prosperous in everything he does. Look how rich he is! ¹¹But take away everything he has, and he will surely curse you to your face!"

¹²"All right, you may test him," the LORD said to Satan. "Do whatever you want with everything he possesses, but don't harm him physically." So Satan left the LORD's presence.

¹³One day when Job's sons and daughters were dining at the oldest brother's house, ¹⁴a messenger arrived at Job's home with this news: "Your oxen were plowing, with the donkeys feeding beside them, ¹⁵when the Sabeans raided us. They stole all the animals and killed all the farmhands. I am the only one who escaped to tell you."

¹⁶While he was still speaking, another messenger arrived with this news: "The fire of God has fallen from heaven and burned up your sheep and all the shepherds. I am the only one who escaped to tell you."

¹⁷While he was still speaking, a third messenger arrived with this news: "Three bands of Chaldean raiders have stolen your camels and killed your servants. I am the only one who escaped to tell you."

¹⁸While he was still speaking, another messenger arrived with this news: "Your sons and daughters were feasting in their oldest brother's home. ¹⁹Suddenly, a powerful wind swept in from the desert and hit the house on all sides. The house collapsed, and all your children are dead. I am the only one who escaped to tell you."

²⁰Job stood up and tore his robe in grief. Then he shaved his head and fell to the ground before God. ²¹He said,

"I came naked from my mother's
    womb,
    and I will be stripped of everything
        when I die.
The LORD gave me everything I had,
    and the LORD has taken it away.
Praise the name of the LORD!"

²²In all of this, Job did not sin by blaming God.

CHAPTER 2

One day the angels* came again to present themselves before the LORD, and Satan the Accuser came with them. ²"Where have you come from?" the LORD asked Satan.

And Satan answered the LORD, "I have been going back and forth across the earth, watching everything that's going on."

³Then the LORD asked Satan, "Have you noticed my servant Job? He is the finest man in all the earth—a man of complete integrity. He fears God and will have nothing to do with evil. And he has maintained his integrity, even though you persuaded me to harm him without cause."

⁴Satan replied to the LORD, "Skin for skin—he blesses you only because you bless him. A man will give up everything he has to save his life. ⁵But take away his health, and he will surely curse you to your face!"

⁶"All right, do with him as you please," the LORD said to Satan. "But spare his life." ⁷So Satan left the LORD's presence, and he struck Job with a terrible case of boils from head to foot.

⁸Then Job scraped his skin with a piece of broken pottery as he sat among the ashes. ⁹His wife said to him, "Are you still trying to maintain your integrity? Curse God and die."

¹⁰But Job replied, "You talk like a godless woman. Should we accept only good things from the hand of God and never anything bad?" So in all this, Job said nothing wrong.

1:6 Hebrew *the sons of God.*   2:1 Hebrew *the sons of God.*

¹¹Three of Job's friends were Eliphaz the Temanite, Bildad the Shuhite, and Zophar the Naamathite. When they heard of the tragedy he had suffered, they got together and traveled from their homes to comfort and console him. ¹²When they saw Job from a distance, they scarcely recognized him. Wailing loudly, they tore their robes and threw dust into the air over their heads to demonstrate their grief. ¹³Then they sat on the ground with him for seven days and nights. And no one said a word, for they saw that his suffering was too great for words.

CHAPTER 3

At last Job spoke, and he cursed the day of his birth. ²He said:

³"Cursed be the day of my birth, and cursed be the night when I was conceived. ⁴Let that day be turned to darkness. Let it be lost even to God on high, and let it be shrouded in darkness. ⁵Yes, let the darkness and utter gloom claim it for its own. Let a black cloud overshadow it, and let the darkness terrify it. ⁶Let that night be blotted off the calendar, never again to be counted among the days of the year, never again to appear among the months. ⁷Let that night be barren. Let it have no joy. ⁸Let those who are experts at cursing—those who are ready to rouse the sea monster*— curse that day. ⁹Let its morning stars re-

3:8 Hebrew *rouse Leviathan.*

main dark. Let it hope for light, but in vain; may it never see the morning light. ¹⁰Curse it for its failure to shut my mother's womb, for letting me be born to all this trouble.

¹¹"Why didn't I die at birth as I came from the womb? ¹²Why did my mother let me live? Why did she nurse me at her breasts? ¹³For if I had died at birth, I would be at peace now, asleep and at rest. ¹⁴I would rest with the world's kings and prime ministers, famous for their great construction projects. ¹⁵I would rest with wealthy princes whose palaces were filled with gold and silver. ¹⁶Why was I not buried like a stillborn child, like a baby who never lives to see the light? ¹⁷For in death the wicked cease from troubling, and the weary are at rest. ¹⁸Even prisoners are at ease in death, with no guards to curse them. ¹⁹Rich and poor are there alike, and the slave is free from his master.

²⁰"Oh, why should light be given to the weary, and life to those in misery? ²¹They long for death, and it won't come. They search for death more eagerly than for hidden treasure. ²²It is a blessed relief when they finally die, when they find the grave. ²³Why is life given to those with no future, those destined by God to live in distress? ²⁴I cannot eat for sighing; my groans pour out like water. ²⁵What I always feared has happened to me. What I dreaded has come to be. ²⁶I have no peace, no quietness. I have no rest; instead, only trouble comes."

MAY 17 ☐ DAY 138
JOB 4–7
Eliphaz and Job (First Debate)

OVERVIEW Onto the stage now step three counselors to begin a series of poetic debates with Job, which will stretch from chapter 4 through chapter 31. These three personal friends, previously introduced in 2:11, represent three differing points of view as they analyze Job's sorry plight. Eliphaz, the senior spokesman, bases much of his insight on personal experience. Courteously, Eliphaz reasons from the general assumption that all people stand guilty before a perfect God. All suffering results from sin—a diagnosis that proves inadequate in Job's case. Job expresses disappointment with Eliphaz's counsel and challenges him to identify anything standing between Job and his God.

Chapter 4	Chapter 5	Chapter 6	Chapter 7
Sin's Suffering	Sin's Solution	The Sufferer's Sorrow	The Sufferer's Self-Analysis
Counsel by Eliphaz		Evaluation by Job	

YOUR DAILY WALK Put yourself in this fatherly role for a moment.
You have just come home from work to find a baseball and bat lying in front of the scattered remains of what used to be your patio window. Without investigating further (an open-and-shut case, you conclude), you storm into the house, corral the guilty party, and administer a sound spanking. Satisfied that justice has been served, you sit down with the evening paper . . . just as your wife returns with the boy next door who has confessed to the whole thing!

No one gives advice with more enthusiasm than an ignorant person.

Jumping to conclusions is not nearly as good an exercise as digging for the facts. The Bible tells us to be "quick to listen, slow to speak, and slow to get angry" (James 1:19). Take a counseling lesson from the book of Job. What situation today requires you to act as referee? Spend adequate time looking at all the issues first. Give your counsel only after thoughtful, prayerful consideration of all the facts.

INSIGHT What's Ailing You?
Job's disease included all of these symptoms: boils (2:7), itching (2:8), disfigurement (2:12), loss of appetite (3:24), severe depression (3:24-25), broken skin (7:5), red eyes (16:16), bad breath (19:17), constant pain (30:17), discoloration and fever (30:30), and an emaciated appearance (33:21).

CHAPTER 4

Then Eliphaz the Temanite replied to Job:

2"Will you be patient and let me say a word? For who could keep from speaking out?

3"In the past you have encouraged many a troubled soul to trust in God; you have supported those who were weak. 4Your words have strengthened the fallen; you steadied those who wavered. 5But now when trouble strikes, you faint and are broken. 6Does your reverence for God give you no confidence? Shouldn't you believe that God will care for those who are upright?

7"Stop and think! Does the innocent person perish? When has the upright person been destroyed? 8My experience shows that those who plant trouble and cultivate evil will harvest the same. 9They perish by a breath from God. They vanish in a blast of his anger. 10Though they are fierce young lions, they will all be broken and destroyed. 11The fierce lion will starve, and the cubs of the lioness will be scattered.

12"This truth was given me in secret, as though whispered in my ear. 13It came in a vision at night as others slept. 14Fear

gripped me; I trembled and shook with terror. 15A spirit* swept past my face. Its wind sent shivers up my spine. 16It stopped, but I couldn't see its shape. There was a form before my eyes, and a hushed voice said, 17"Can a mortal be just and upright before God? Can a person be pure before the Creator?'

18"If God cannot trust his own angels and has charged some of them with folly, 19how much less will he trust those made of clay! Their foundation is dust, and they are crushed as easily as moths. 20They are alive in the morning, but by evening they are dead, gone forever without a trace. 21Their tent collapses; they die in ignorance.

CHAPTER 5

"You may cry for help, but no one listens. You may turn to the angels,* but they give you no help. 2Surely resentment destroys the fool, and jealousy kills the simple. 3From my experience, I know that fools who turn from God may be successful for the moment, but then comes sudden disaster. 4Their children are abandoned far from help, with no one to defend them. 5Their

4:15 Or *wind.*   5:1 Hebrew *the holy ones.*

harvests are stolen, and their wealth satisfies the thirst of many others, not themselves! [6]But evil does not spring from the soil, and trouble does not sprout from the earth. [7]People are born for trouble as predictably as sparks fly upward from a fire.

[8]"My advice to you is this: Go to God and present your case to him. [9]For he does great works too marvelous to understand. He performs miracles without number. [10]He gives rain for the earth. He sends water for the fields. [11]He gives prosperity to the poor and humble, and he takes sufferers to safety. [12]He frustrates the plans of the crafty, so their efforts will not succeed. [13]He catches those who think they are wise in their own cleverness, so that their cunning schemes are thwarted. [14]They grope in the daylight as though they were blind; they see no better in the daytime than at night. [15]He rescues the poor from the cutting words of the strong. He saves them from the clutches of the powerful. [16]And so at last the poor have hope, and the fangs of the wicked are broken.

[17]"But consider the joy of those corrected by God! Do not despise the chastening of the Almighty when you sin. [18]For though he wounds, he also bandages. He strikes, but his hands also heal. [19]He will rescue you again and again so that no evil can touch you. [20]He will save you from death in time of famine, from the power of the sword in time of war. [21]You will be safe from slander and will have no fear of destruction when it comes. [22]You will laugh at destruction and famine; wild animals will not terrify you. [23]You will be at peace with the stones of the field, and its wild animals will be at peace with you. [24]You will know that your home is kept safe. When you visit your pastures, nothing will be missing. [25]Your children will be many; your descendants will be as plentiful as grass! [26]You will live to a good old age. You will not be harvested until the proper time!

[27]"We have found from experience that all this is true. Listen to my counsel, and apply it to yourself."

CHAPTER 6

Then Job spoke again:

[2]"If my sadness could be weighed and my troubles be put on the scales, [3]they would be heavier than all the sands of the sea. That is why I spoke so rashly. [4]For the Almighty has struck me down with his arrows. He has sent his poisoned arrows deep within my spirit. All God's terrors are arrayed against me. [5]Don't I have a right to complain? Wild donkeys bray when they find no green grass, and oxen low when they have no food. [6]People complain when there is no salt in their food. And how tasteless is the uncooked white of an egg! [7]My appetite disappears when I look at it; I gag at the thought of eating it!

[8]"Oh, that I might have my request, that God would grant my hope. [9]I wish he would crush me. I wish he would reach out his hand and kill me. [10]At least I can take comfort in this: Despite the pain, I have not denied the words of the Holy One. [11]But I do not have the strength to endure. I do not have a goal that encourages me to carry on. [12]Do I have strength as hard as stone? Is my body made of bronze? [13]No, I am utterly helpless, without any chance of success.

[14]"One should be kind to a fainting friend, but you have accused me without the slightest fear of the Almighty. [15]My brother, you have proved as unreliable as a seasonal brook that overflows its banks in the spring [16]when it is swollen with ice and melting snow. [17]But when the hot weather arrives, the water disappears. The brook vanishes in the heat. [18]The caravans turn aside to be refreshed, but there is nothing there to drink, and so they perish in the desert. [19]With high hopes, the caravans from Tema and from Sheba stop for water, [20]but finding none, their hopes are dashed. [21]You, too, have proved to be of no help. You have seen my calamity, and you are afraid. [22]But why? Have I ever asked you for a gift? Have I begged you to use any of your wealth on my behalf? [23]Have I ever asked you to rescue me from my enemies? Have I asked you to save me from ruthless people?

[24]"All I want is a reasonable answer—then I will keep quiet. Tell me, what have I done wrong? [25]Honest words are painful, but what do your criticisms amount to? [26]Do you think your words are convincing when you disregard my cry of desperation? [27]You would even send an orphan into slavery* or sell a friend. [28]Look at me! Would I lie to your face? [29]Stop assuming my guilt, for I am righteous. Don't be so

6:27 Hebrew *even gamble over an orphan.*

unjust. ³⁰Do you think I am lying? Don't I know the difference between right and wrong?

CHAPTER 7

"Is this not the struggle of all humanity? A person's life is long and hard, like that of a hired hand, ²like a worker who longs for the day to end, like a servant waiting to be paid. ³I, too, have been assigned months of futility, long and weary nights of misery. ⁴When I go to bed, I think, 'When will it be morning?' But the night drags on, and I toss till dawn. ⁵My skin is filled with worms and scabs. My flesh breaks open, full of pus.

⁶"My days are swifter than a weaver's shuttle flying back and forth. They end without hope. ⁷O God, remember that my life is but a breath, and I will never again experience pleasure. ⁸You see me now, but not for long. Your eyes will be on me, but I will be dead. ⁹Just as a cloud dissipates and vanishes, those who die will not come back. ¹⁰They are gone forever from their home—never to be seen again.

¹¹"I cannot keep from speaking. I must express my anguish. I must complain in my bitterness. ¹²Am I a sea monster that you place a guard on me? ¹³If I think, 'My bed will comfort me, and I will try to forget my misery with sleep,' ¹⁴you shatter me with dreams. You terrify me with visions. ¹⁵I would rather die of strangulation than go on and on like this. ¹⁶I hate my life. I do not want to go on living. Oh, leave me alone for these few remaining days.

¹⁷"What are mere mortals, that you should make so much of us? ¹⁸For you examine us every morning and test us every moment. ¹⁹Why won't you leave me alone—even for a moment*? ²⁰Have I sinned? What have I done to you, O watcher of all humanity? Why have you made me your target? Am I a burden to you? ²¹Why not just pardon my sin and take away my guilt? For soon I will lie down in the dust and die. When you look for me, I will be gone."

7:19 Hebrew *long enough to swallow my spittle.*

MAY 18 □ DAY 139
JOB 8–10
Bildad and Job (First Debate)

 OVERVIEW Eliphaz has based his arguments on a cause-and-effect view of sin and suffering. Now Bildad the Shuhite arises to argue the same case, but from the perspective of tradition rather than experience. He calls on Job to meditate upon the attribute of God's justice as seen repeatedly in history. God shows his salvation and mercy to the upright, but brings down the wicked. Therefore, there can be only one conclusion regarding Job's plight: He is guilty of some secret sin. Again the suffering patriarch concedes that God is perfect and just, but he also maintains his own innocence—and expresses his bewilderment as he struggles to understand his suffering.

Chapter 8	Chapter 9	Chapter 10
"God Is Just"	"I Know God Is Just!"	"Why Then Do I Suffer?"
Bildad's Comments	Job's Concession	Job's Confusion

 YOUR DAILY WALK The need for someone who can reconcile a holy God and sinful humanity is as old as the early chapters of Genesis. The sin of Adam and Eve in the Garden of Eden (Genesis 3:6) interrupted their fellowship with God, brought forth God's anger and judgment, and placed a barrier between God and humanity. Later, prophets would

The best of represent God to the people, and priests would establish God's order
saints have on earth for humanity. Yet throughout the Old Testament there was
borne the worst never one who could fully heal the breach. To do that would require
of sufferings. a man to be God and God to become a man.

Job lived during a period of history when a perfect and sinless mediator was unknown. The one who alone can bring God and humanity together and restore that lost fellowship is Jesus Christ (1 Timothy 2:5). Do you know Jesus as your personal Savior and Mediator before God? He is waiting to bring you to God, to settle the sin problem that has estranged you from him, to lay his loving hand upon you right now (Psalm 139:5-6). Will you let him?

 INSIGHT Here Comes the Judge
The word translated *mediator* in 9:33 does not merely mean a judge who decides what is right. He is one who mediates between or reconciles two parties by bringing them together and then lays his hands on them both as a mutual friend.

CHAPTER 8
Then Bildad the Shuhite replied to Job:
²"How long will you go on like this? Your words are a blustering wind. ³Does God twist justice? Does the Almighty twist what is right? ⁴Your children obviously sinned against him, so their punishment was well deserved. ⁵But if you pray to God and seek the favor of the Almighty, ⁶if you are pure and live with complete integrity, he will rise up and restore your happy home. ⁷And though you started with little, you will end with much.

⁸"Just ask the former generation. Pay attention to the experience of our ancestors. ⁹For we were born but yesterday and know so little. Our days on earth are as transient as a shadow. ¹⁰But those who came before us will teach you. They will teach you from the wisdom of former generations.

¹¹"Can papyrus reeds grow where there is no marsh? Can bulrushes flourish where there is no water? ¹²While they are still flowering, not ready to be cut, they begin to wither. ¹³Such is the fate of all who forget God. The hope of the godless comes to nothing. ¹⁴Everything they count on will collapse. They are leaning on a spiderweb. ¹⁵They cling to their home for security, but it won't last. They try to hold it fast, but it will not endure. ¹⁶The godless seem so strong, like a lush plant growing in the sunshine, its branches spreading across the garden. ¹⁷Its roots grow down through a pile of rocks to hold it firm. ¹⁸But when it is uprooted, it isn't even missed! ¹⁹That is the end of its life, and others spring up from the earth to replace it.

²⁰"But look! God will not reject a person of integrity, nor will he make evildoers prosper. ²¹He will yet fill your mouth with laughter and your lips with shouts of joy. ²²Those who hate you will be clothed with shame, and the tent of the wicked will be destroyed."

CHAPTER 9
Then Job spoke again:
²"Yes, I know this is all true in principle. But how can a person be declared innocent in the eyes of God? ³If someone wanted to take God to court,* would it be possible to answer him even once in a thousand times? ⁴For God is so wise and so mighty. Who has ever challenged him successfully?

⁵"Without warning, he moves the mountains, overturning them in his anger. ⁶He shakes the earth from its place, and its foundations tremble. ⁷If he commands it, the sun won't rise and the stars won't shine. ⁸He alone has spread out the heavens and marches on the waves of the sea. ⁹He made all the stars—the Bear, Orion, the Pleiades, and the constellations of the southern sky. ¹⁰His great works are too marvelous to understand. He performs miracles without number.

¹¹"Yet when he comes near, I cannot see him. When he moves on, I do not see him go. ¹²If he sends death to snatch someone away, who can stop him? Who dares to ask him, 'What are you doing?' ¹³And God does not restrain his anger. The mightiest forces against him* are crushed beneath his feet.

9:3 Or *If God wanted to take a person to court.*   9:13 Hebrew *The helpers of Rahab,* the name of a mythical sea monster that represents chaos in ancient literature.

¹⁴"And who am I, that I should try to answer God or even reason with him? ¹⁵Even if I were innocent, I would have no defense. I could only plead for mercy. ¹⁶And even if I summoned him and he responded, he would never listen to me. ¹⁷For he attacks me without reason,* and he multiplies my wounds without cause. ¹⁸He will not let me catch my breath, but fills me instead with bitter sorrows. ¹⁹As for strength, he has it. As for justice, who can challenge him? ²⁰Though I am innocent, my own mouth would pronounce me guilty. Though I am blameless, it* would prove me wicked.

²¹"I am innocent, but it makes no difference to me—I despise my life. ²²Innocent or wicked, it is all the same to him. That is why I say, 'He destroys both the blameless and the wicked.' ²³He laughs when a plague suddenly kills the innocent. ²⁴The whole earth is in the hands of the wicked, and God blinds the eyes of the judges and lets them be unfair. If not he, then who?

²⁵"My life passes more swiftly than a runner. It flees away, filled with tragedy. ²⁶It disappears like a swift boat, like an eagle that swoops down on its prey. ²⁷If I decided to forget my complaints, if I decided to end my sadness and be cheerful, ²⁸I would dread all the pain he would send. For I know you will not hold me innocent, O God. ²⁹Whatever happens, I will be found guilty. So what's the use of trying? ³⁰Even if I were to wash myself with soap and cleanse my hands with lye to make them absolutely clean, ³¹you would plunge me into a muddy ditch, and I would be so filthy my own clothing would hate me.

³²"God is not a mortal like me, so I cannot argue with him or take him to trial. ³³If only there were a mediator who could bring us together, but there is none. ³⁴The mediator could make God stop beating me, and I would no longer live in terror of his punishment. ³⁵Then I could speak to him without fear, but I cannot do that in my own strength.

CHAPTER 10

"I am disgusted with my life. Let me complain freely. I will speak in the bitterness of my soul. ²I will say to God, 'Don't simply condemn me—tell me the charge you are bringing against me. ³What do you gain by oppressing me? Why do you reject me, the work of your own hands, while sending joy and prosperity to the wicked? ⁴Are your eyes only those of a human? Do you see things as people see them? ⁵Is your lifetime merely human? Is your life so short ⁶that you are in a hurry to probe for my guilt, to search for my sin? ⁷Although you know I am not guilty, no one can rescue me from your power.

⁸"'You formed me with your hands; you made me, and yet you completely destroy me. ⁹Remember that I am made of dust—will you turn me back to dust so soon? ¹⁰You guided my conception and formed me in the womb.* ¹¹You clothed me with skin and flesh, and you knit my bones and sinews together. ¹²You gave me life and showed me your unfailing love. My life was preserved by your care.

¹³"'Yet your real motive—I know this was your intent—¹⁴was to watch me, and if I sinned, you would not forgive my iniquity. ¹⁵If I am guilty, too bad for me. And even if I'm innocent, I am filled with shame and misery so that I can't hold my head high. ¹⁶And if I hold my head high, you hunt me like a lion and display your awesome power against me. ¹⁷Again and again you witness against me. You pour out an ever-increasing volume of anger upon me and bring fresh armies against me.

¹⁸"'Why, then, did you bring me out of my mother's womb? Why didn't you let me die at birth? ¹⁹Then I would have been spared this miserable existence. I would have gone directly from the womb to the grave. ²⁰I have only a little time left, so leave me alone—that I may have a little moment of comfort ²¹before I leave for the land of darkness and utter gloom, never to return. ²²It is a land as dark as midnight, a land of utter gloom where confusion reigns and the light is as dark as midnight.'"

9:17 As in Syriac version; Hebrew reads *with a storm.*   **9:20** Or *he.*   **10:10** Hebrew *You poured me out like milk and curdled me like cheese.*

MAY 19 ☐ DAY 140
JOB 11–14
Zophar and Job (First Debate)

OVERVIEW Zophar wastes little time boring straight to the heart of the matter (as he interprets it). By comparison with Eliphaz and Bildad, he is almost brutal in his bluntness. "Should I remain silent while you babble on? . . . If only God would speak; if only he would tell you what he thinks! . . . God is doubtless punishing you far less than you deserve" (11:3, 5-6). He appeals to God's great wisdom and control, which dwarf those of vain and ignorant men, and urges Job to return to God, where he will find both security and hope. Job responds with a lengthy defense in which he acknowledges God's power, defends his own integrity, and reaffirms his steadfast confidence in God.

Chapter 11		Chapter 12	Chapter 13	Chapter 14
"God Is in Control"	"Turn Back to Him"	"I Never Left Him"	"You're No Help"	"Help Me, God"
1 12	13 20			
Zophar's Plea for Piety		Job's Persistent Denial		

YOUR DAILY WALK Few passages in Scripture paint as dark a picture of depression as that found in Job 14. What makes it more remarkable is that the author is describing a believer. Believers are not immune to the despair and despondency that accompany painful circumstances.

If we could avoid that portion of suffering we bring upon ourselves, we might be surprised at how little would be left.

But believers do have a reservoir for coping with depression that the world knows nothing about!
• They know God is on their side (Romans 8:31).
• They know God is in control of both the oppressed and the oppressor (Job 12:16).
• They know justice will ultimately triumph (Job 13:18).
Are you given to times of depression about a particular circumstance in your life? The answer is not to dwell on your circumstance but on the greatness of your Creator. He is your salvation (13:16); he numbers your every step (14:16); and he cares about you. Spend some quiet moments pondering his greatness until you can respond as Job did: "Praise the name of the LORD" (1:21).

INSIGHT Zophar, the Friend Job Could Do Without
Zophar (whose name means "hairy" or "rough") appears as a mean, self-made authority who thought he understood Job's problem (and didn't), making life all the more miserable for Job, who wanted to understand his problem (and couldn't)!

CHAPTER 11

Then Zophar the Naamathite replied to Job:

²"Shouldn't someone answer this torrent of words? Is a person proved innocent just by talking a lot? ³Should I remain silent while you babble on? When you mock God, shouldn't someone make you ashamed? ⁴You claim, 'My teaching is pure,' and 'I am clean in the sight of God.' ⁵If only God would speak; if only he would

tell you what he thinks! ⁶If only he would tell you the secrets of wisdom, for true wisdom is not a simple matter. Listen! God is doubtless punishing you far less than you deserve!

⁷"Can you solve the mysteries of God? Can you discover everything there is to know about the Almighty? ⁸Such knowledge is higher than the heavens—but who are you? It is deeper than the underworld*—what can you know in comparison to him? ⁹It

11:8 Hebrew *Sheol.*

is broader than the earth and wider than the sea. ¹⁰If God comes along and puts a person in prison, or if he calls the court to order, who is going to stop him? ¹¹For he knows those who are false, and he takes note of all their sins. ¹²An empty-headed person won't become wise any more than a wild donkey can bear human offspring*!

¹³"If only you would prepare your heart and lift up your hands to him in prayer! ¹⁴Get rid of your sins and leave all iniquity behind you. ¹⁵Then your face will brighten in innocence. You will be strong and free of fear. ¹⁶You will forget your misery. It will all be gone like water under the bridge. ¹⁷Your life will be brighter than the noonday. Any darkness will be as bright as morning. ¹⁸You will have courage because you will have hope. You will be protected and will rest in safety. ¹⁹You will lie down unafraid, and many will look to you for help. ²⁰But the wicked will lose hope. They have no escape. Their hope becomes despair."

CHAPTER 12

Then Job spoke again:

²"You really know everything, don't you? And when you die, wisdom will die with you! ³Well, I know a few things myself—and you're no better than I am. Who doesn't know these things you've been saying? ⁴Yet my friends laugh at me. I am a man who calls on God and receives an answer. I am a just and blameless man, yet they laugh at me. ⁵People who are at ease mock those in trouble. They give a push to people who are stumbling. ⁶But even robbers are left in peace, and those who provoke God—and God has them in his power—live in safety!

⁷"Ask the animals, and they will teach you. Ask the birds of the sky, and they will tell you. ⁸Speak to the earth, and it will instruct you. Let the fish of the sea speak to you. ⁹They all know that the LORD has done this. ¹⁰For the life of every living thing is in his hand, and the breath of all humanity. ¹¹Just as the mouth tastes good food, so the ear tests the words it hears. ¹²Wisdom belongs to the aged, and understanding to those who have lived many years.

¹³"But true wisdom and power are with God; counsel and understanding are his. ¹⁴What he destroys cannot be rebuilt. When he closes in on someone, there is no escape. ¹⁵If he holds back the rain, the earth becomes a desert. If he releases the waters, they flood the earth.

¹⁶"Yes, strength and wisdom are with him; deceivers and deceived are both in his power. ¹⁷He leads counselors away stripped of good judgment; he drives judges to madness. ¹⁸He removes the royal robe of kings. With ropes around their waist, they are led away. ¹⁹He leads priests away stripped of status; he overthrows the mighty. ²⁰He silences the trusted adviser, and he removes the insight of the elders. ²¹He pours disgrace upon princes and confiscates weapons from the strong.

²²"He floods the darkness with light; he brings light to the deepest gloom. ²³He raises up nations, and he destroys them. He makes nations expand, and he abandons them. ²⁴He takes away the understanding of kings, and he leaves them wandering in a wasteland without a path. ²⁵They grope in the darkness without a light. He makes them stagger like drunkards.

CHAPTER 13

"Look, I have seen many instances such as you describe. I understand what you are saying. ²I know as much as you do. You are no better than I am. ³Oh, how I long to speak directly to the Almighty. I want to argue my case with God himself. ⁴For you are smearing me with lies. As doctors, you are worthless quacks. ⁵Please be quiet! That's the smartest thing you could do. ⁶Listen to my charge; pay attention to my arguments.

⁷"Are you defending God by means of lies and dishonest arguments? ⁸You should be impartial witnesses, but will you slant your testimony in his favor? Will you argue God's case for him? ⁹Be careful that he doesn't find out what you are doing! Or do you think you can fool him as easily as you fool people? ¹⁰No, you will be in serious trouble with him if even in your hearts you slant your testimony in his favor. ¹¹Doesn't his majesty strike terror into your heart? Does not your fear of him seize you? ¹²Your statements have about as much value as ashes. Your defense is as fragile as a clay pot.

¹³"Be silent now and leave me alone. Let me speak—and I will face the consequences. ¹⁴Yes, I will take my life in my

11:12 Or *bear a tame colt.*

hands and say what I really think. ¹⁵God might kill me, but I cannot wait. I am going to argue my case with him. ¹⁶But this is what will save me: that I am not godless. If I were, I would be thrown from his presence.

¹⁷"Listen closely to what I am about to say. Hear me out. ¹⁸I have prepared my case; I will be proved innocent. ¹⁹Who can argue with me over this? If you could prove me wrong, I would remain silent until I die.

²⁰"O God, there are two things I beg of you, and I will be able to face you. ²¹Remove your hand from me, and don't terrify me with your awesome presence. ²²Now summon me, and I will answer! Or let me speak to you, and you reply. ²³Tell me, what have I done wrong? Show me my rebellion and my sin. ²⁴Why do you turn away from me? Why do you consider me your enemy? ²⁵Would you terrify a leaf that is blown by the wind? Would you chase a dry stalk of grass?

²⁶"You write bitter accusations against me and bring up all the sins of my youth. ²⁷You put my feet in stocks. You watch all my paths. You trace all my footprints. ²⁸I waste away like rotting wood, like a moth-eaten coat.

CHAPTER 14

"How frail is humanity! How short is life, and how full of trouble! ²Like a flower, we blossom for a moment and then wither. Like the shadow of a passing cloud, we quickly disappear. ³Must you keep an eye on such a frail creature and demand an accounting from me? ⁴Who can create purity in one born impure? No one! ⁵You have decided the length of our lives. You know how many months we will live, and

we are not given a minute longer. ⁶So give us a little rest, won't you? Turn away your angry stare. We are like hired hands, so let us finish the task you have given us.

⁷"If a tree is cut down, there is hope that it will sprout again and grow new branches. ⁸Though its roots have grown old in the earth and its stump decays, ⁹at the scent of water it may bud and sprout again like a new seedling.

¹⁰"But when people die, they lose all strength. They breathe their last, and then where are they? ¹¹As water evaporates from a lake and as a river disappears in drought, ¹²people lie down and do not rise again. Until the heavens are no more, they will not wake up nor be roused from their sleep.

¹³"I wish you would hide me with the dead and forget me there until your anger has passed. But mark your calendar to think of me again! ¹⁴If mortals die, can they live again? This thought would give me hope, and through my struggle I would eagerly wait for release. ¹⁵You would call and I would answer, and you would yearn for me, your handiwork. ¹⁶For then you would count my steps, instead of watching for my sins. ¹⁷My sins would be sealed in a pouch, and you would cover over my iniquity.

¹⁸"But as mountains fall and crumble and as rocks fall from a cliff, ¹⁹as water wears away the stones and floods wash away the soil, so you destroy people's hope. ²⁰You always overpower them, and then they pass from the scene. You disfigure them in death and send them away. ²¹They never know if their sons grow up in honor or sink to insignificance. ²²They are absorbed in their own pain and grief."

MAY 20 ☐ DAY 141
JOB 15–17
Eliphaz and Job (Second Debate)

OVERVIEW Like a second wave of attacking soldiers, the three counselors launch their second cycle of debates without giving Job so much as a moment's rest! Eliphaz again leads the assault, this time increasing the intensity of his verbal attack. He describes Job's words as worthless talk; he denies that Job understands anything new or

true about God; and he broadly condemns all wickedness in man—
a thinly disguised slander of Job's character. Job rejects these bitter
accusations. Then, speaking to himself, he agonizes over God's
apparent plot to destroy him. Depression once again overwhelms him.

Chapter 15	Chapter 16	Chapter 17
Eliphaz's Broken Record	Job's Broken Heart	Job's Broken Hope
Wicked People Die	God Shatters Me	God, Deliver Me

YOUR DAILY WALK "Anything true is not new; anything new is not true."

Your ability to learn depends in part on your ability to relinquish what you have held.

This closed-minded attitude that excludes any possibility of learning is a perfect description of the elder counselor, Eliphaz (15:9-10, 17-19). Such is the fate of all who claim to know it all by reason of their years of experience. Age alone, whether chronological or spiritual, is no sure measure of a person's wisdom.

Maintain a teachable spirit today. Take an index card with you everywhere you go, and write down at least four new thoughts that other people express today. Be a ready learner. Don't attempt to convince the other person of your point of view until first you are sure you understand his or hers. Then at the end of the day, evaluate the things you have written down. Are they biblical? Are they practical? Are they appropriate? See if you can learn something new and useful today.

And remember this little slogan: If you think you're green, you'll grow; if you think you're ripe, you'll rot.

INSIGHT The Agony of Defeat
When a wounded bull has spent his last energy, he will often scrape at the ground with his horns. Job sensed that he was doomed. In 16:15 he likens himself to a defeated animal who has laid his head in the dust— a pathetic picture of a discouraged saint.

CHAPTER 15
Then Eliphaz the Temanite replied:

2"You are supposed to be a wise man, and yet you give us all this foolish talk. You are nothing but a windbag. 3It isn't right to speak so foolishly. What good do such words do? 4Have you no fear of God, no reverence for him? 5Your sins are telling your mouth what to say. Your words are based on clever deception. 6But why should I condemn you? Your own mouth does!

7"Were you the first person ever born? Were you born before the hills were made? 8Were you listening at God's secret council? Do you have a monopoly on wisdom? 9What do you know that we don't? What do you understand that we don't? 10On our side are aged, gray-haired men much older than your father!

11"Is God's comfort too little for you? Is his gentle word not enough? 12What has captured your reason? What has weakened

your vision, 13that you turn against God and say all these evil things? 14Can a mortal be pure? Can a human be just? 15Why, God doesn't even trust the angels*! Even the heavens cannot be absolutely pure in his sight. 16How much less pure is a corrupt and sinful person with a thirst for wickedness!

17"If you will listen, I will answer you from my own experience. 18And it is confirmed by the experience of wise men who have heard the same thing from their fathers, 19those to whom the land was given long before any foreigners arrived.

20"Wicked people are in pain throughout their lives. 21They are surrounded by terrors, and even on good days they fear the attack of the destroyer. 22They dare not go out into the darkness for fear they will be murdered. 23They wander abroad for bread, saying, 'Where is it?'* They know their ruin is certain. 24That dark day

15:15 Hebrew *the holy ones.*   15:23 Greek version reads *He is appointed to be food for a vulture.*

terrifies them. They live in distress and anguish, like a king preparing for an attack. ²⁵For they have clenched their fists against God, defying the Almighty. ²⁶Holding their strong shields, they defiantly charge against him.

²⁷"These wicked people are fat and rich, ²⁸but their cities will be ruined. They will live in abandoned houses that are ready to tumble down. ²⁹They will not continue to be rich. Their wealth will not endure, and their possessions will no longer spread across the horizon.

³⁰"They will not escape the darkness. The flame will burn them up, and the breath of God will destroy everything they have. ³¹Let them no longer trust in empty riches. They are only fooling themselves, for emptiness will be their only reward. ³²They will be cut down in the prime of life, and all they counted on will disappear. ³³They will be like a vine whose grapes are harvested before they are ripe, like an olive tree that sheds its blossoms so the fruit cannot form. ³⁴For the godless are barren. Their homes, enriched through bribery, will be consumed by fire. ³⁵They conceive trouble and evil, and their hearts give birth only to deceit."

CHAPTER 16

Then Job spoke again:

²"I have heard all this before. What miserable comforters you are! ³Won't you ever stop your flow of foolish words? What have I said that makes you speak so endlessly? ⁴I could say the same things if you were in my place. I could spout off my criticisms against you and shake my head at you. ⁵But that's not what I would do. I would speak in a way that helps you. I would try to take away your grief. ⁶But as it is, my grief remains no matter how I defend myself. And it does not help if I refuse to speak.

⁷"O God, you have ground me down and devastated my family. ⁸You have reduced me to skin and bones—as proof, they say, of my sins. ⁹God hates me and tears angrily at my flesh. He gnashes his teeth at me and pierces me with his eyes. ¹⁰People jeer and laugh at me. They slap my cheek in contempt. A mob gathers against me. ¹¹God has handed me over to sinners. He has tossed me into the hands of the wicked.

¹²"I was living quietly until he broke me apart. He took me by the neck and dashed me to pieces. Then he set me up as his target. ¹³His archers surrounded me, and his arrows pierced me without mercy. The ground is wet with my blood.* ¹⁴Again and again he smashed me, charging at me like a warrior. ¹⁵Here I sit in sackcloth. I have surrendered, and I sit in the dust. ¹⁶My eyes are red with weeping; darkness covers my eyes. ¹⁷Yet I am innocent, and my prayer is pure.

¹⁸"O earth, do not conceal my blood. Let it cry out on my behalf. ¹⁹Even now my witness is in heaven. My advocate is there on high. ²⁰My friends scorn me, but I pour out my tears to God. ²¹Oh, that someone would mediate between God and me, as a person mediates between friends. ²²For soon I must go down that road from which I will never return.

CHAPTER 17

"My spirit is crushed, and I am near death. The grave is ready to receive me. ²I am surrounded by mockers. I watch how bitterly they taunt me.

³"You must defend my innocence, O God, since no one else will stand up for me. ⁴You have closed their minds to understanding, but do not let them triumph. ⁵They denounce their companions for their own advantage, so let their children faint with hunger.

⁶"God has made a mockery of me among the people; they spit in my face. ⁷My eyes are dim with weeping, and I am but a shadow of my former self. ⁸The upright are astonished when they see me. The innocent are aroused against the ungodly. ⁹The righteous will move onward and forward, and those with pure hearts will become stronger and stronger.

¹⁰"As for all of you, come back and try again! But I will not find a wise man among you. ¹¹My days are over. My hopes have disappeared. My heart's desires are broken. ¹²They say that night is day and day is night; how they pervert the truth! ¹³I might go to the grave and make my bed in darkness. ¹⁴And I might call the grave my father, and the worm my mother and my sister. ¹⁵But where then is my hope? Can anyone find it? ¹⁶No, my hope will go down with me to the grave. We will rest together in the dust!"

16:13 Hebrew *my gall.*

MAY 21 ☐ DAY 142
Our God Reigns

LOOK BACK Your reading this week has carried you from the palace of Queen Esther to the pit of Job's suffering. You've seen God deliver his people from certain death and allow his servant Job to experience suffering to the point of death. You've seen God's mighty arm at work in the days of Esther, and you've seen God strangely quiet and inactive in the midst of Job's sufferings. You've read about Mordecai's promotion for looking out for the welfare of his people and Job's agonizing calamities even though he was "the finest man in all the earth—a man of complete integrity" (2:3).

Perhaps you've wondered, *What's going on here, anyway? Is this really the same God at work? How can he be so benevolent to one of his children and seemingly so cruel and passive toward another?*

If so, you are not alone! Job asked himself many of those same questions. He struggled with the why of his predicament: God, where are you when it hurts? Why have you allowed such sadness and pain to come into my life? What have I done to deserve all this? The answers Job found—and which you will find, too, as you continue to read—changed forever the way he looked at the God of creation.

LOOK UP Reputation is what others think you are; character is what God knows you are. And when your reputation and character are both blameless, you have integrity—the ring of authenticity in the life of the child of God.

The longer you dwell on your misfortunes, the greater is their power to harm you.

Integrity is behaving in the dark just as you would in the light. It is being what you say you are and doing what you said you would even when no one is watching. It is consistency of character, with no hidden agenda or twisted motive.

Integrity is what causes you to tell the truth, regardless of how tempting it might be to shade the truth. It's what prompts you to tell the cashier you've received too much change, to give back the wallet someone lost without first counting its contents, to drive one mile under (rather than over) the speed limit, to be one minute early (rather than late) for an appointment, to stand up for what is right even if you stand alone.

When Job's world came crashing down around him, he no doubt faced an avalanche of emotional responses: fear, frustration, anger, bitterness, confusion, bewilderment. Unknown to Job, a celestial drama was unfolding between God and Satan—with Job as the center of attention! God was inviting Satan to observe one of his choicest servants and to discover what a blameless and upright man looks like—one who holds fast to his integrity. Job's character in the crucible of adversity was so remarkable, even his wife found it unbelievable (2:9)!

LOOK AHEAD Do you hold to your integrity in the midst of trying circumstances? Here's a little quiz to help you measure your "Integrity Quotient": *If you knew no one was watching or would ever know . . .*

- How much would someone have to pay you to get you to lie or shade the truth?
- How long would you watch a sexually suggestive TV program before you changed the channel?
- How much "too much" would a cashier have to pay you before you went to the trouble of pointing out the error and returning the money?
- How bad would things have to get before you were tempted to curse God?

MAY 22 ☐ DAY 143
JOB 18–19
Bildad and Job (Second Debate)

 OVERVIEW Bildad continues the seemingly endless debate by painting a horrifying picture of the terror and destruction awaiting the wicked. Job is pained, but he refuses to collapse under the pressure of his counselors-turned-accusers. Once again placing the responsibility for his plight on the Lord, Job dwells on the history of his disaster. He has been abandoned by family and friends, servants and spouse. Yet in spite of his despair, there is reason to hope. For Job knows that the future holds the promise both of resurrection and his ultimate vindication from wrong.

Chapter 18		Chapter 19		
Bildad's Hostility	Bildad's Harassment	Job's Hurt	Job's History	Job's Hope
1 4	5 21	1 12	13 22	23 29
Bildad's Taunts		Job's Thoughts		

 YOUR DAILY WALK "There is no medicine like hope, no incentive so great, no tonic so powerful as expectation of something better tomorrow."

There is no medicine like hope.

It is one thing to speak of hope when things look doubtful . . . when the future is uncertain . . . when circumstances are crowding in. It is something else to speak of hope when there is no doubt about the present (it is a disaster), when the future is certain (and definitely uninviting), when circumstances have crushed you to the floor. Hope in the midst of utter turmoil cannot simply be starry-eyed optimism; it must be built upon bedrock reality.

Job's testimony in 19:25-26 was no mere poetic sentiment. (Remember his plight; it was hopeless!) Rather, Job was drawing strength from the person to whom he had entrusted his life and from the promises that person had made on his behalf.

Imagine that you have been deprived of possessions, health, and loved ones. Could you proclaim with Job that your hope was still in the Lord? Pick one of God's many promises (1 Corinthians 10:13 would do nicely), and make it your "Project Hope" today!

 INSIGHT Count to Ten . . . Slowly
Ten is a prominent number in the Bible indicating patient endurance. Jacob endured ten changes in his wages (Genesis 31:7); the Israelites tempted God ten times with their rebellion (Numbers 14:22); and Job put up with ten insults from his companions (Job 19:3).

CHAPTER 18

Then Bildad the Shuhite replied:

2"How long before you stop talking? Speak sense if you want us to answer! 3Do you think we are cattle? Do you think we have no intelligence? 4You may tear your hair out in anger, but will that cause the earth to be abandoned? Will it make rocks fall from a cliff?

5"The truth remains that the light of the wicked will be snuffed out. The sparks of their fire will not glow. 6The light in their tent will grow dark. The lamp hanging above them will be quenched. 7The confident stride of the wicked will be shortened. Their own schemes will be their downfall.

8"The wicked walk into a net. They fall into a pit that's been dug in the path. 9A trap grabs them by the heel. A noose tightens around them. 10A snare lies hidden in the ground. A rope lies coiled on their path. 11"Terrors surround the wicked and trouble them at every step. ¹²Their vigor is depleted by hunger, and calamity waits for them to stumble. ¹³Disease eats their skin; death devours their limbs. ¹⁴They are torn from the security of their tent, and they are brought down to the king of terrors. ¹⁵The home of the wicked will disappear beneath a fiery barrage of burning sulfur. ¹⁶Their roots will dry up, and their branches will wither. ¹⁷All memory of their existence will perish from the earth. No one will remember them. ¹⁸They will be thrust from light into darkness, driven from the world. ¹⁹They will have neither children nor grandchildren, nor any survivor in their home country. ²⁰People in the west are appalled at their fate; people in the east are horrified. ²¹They will say, 'This was the home of a wicked person, the place of one who rejected God.'"

CHAPTER 19
Then Job spoke again:

²"How long will you torture me? How long will you try to break me with your words? ³Ten times now you have meant to insult me. You should be ashamed of dealing with me so harshly. ⁴And even if I have sinned, that is my concern, not yours. ⁵You are trying to overcome me, using my humiliation as evidence of my sin, ⁶but it is God who has wronged me. I cannot defend myself, for I am like a city under siege.

⁷"I cry out for help, but no one hears me. I protest, but there is no justice. ⁸God has blocked my way and plunged my path into darkness. ⁹He has stripped me of my honor and removed the crown from my head. ¹⁰He has demolished me on every side, and I am finished. He has destroyed my hope. ¹¹His fury burns against me; he counts me

19:26 Or *without my body I will see God.*

as an enemy. ¹²His troops advance. They build up roads to attack me. They camp all around my tent.

¹³"My relatives stay far away, and my friends have turned against me. ¹⁴My neighbors and my close friends are all gone. ¹⁵The members of my household have forgotten me. The servant girls consider me a stranger. I am like a foreigner to them. ¹⁶I call my servant, but he doesn't come; I even plead with him! ¹⁷My breath is repulsive to my wife. I am loathsome to my own family. ¹⁸Even young children despise me. When I stand to speak, they turn their backs on me. ¹⁹My close friends abhor me. Those I loved have turned against me. ²⁰I have been reduced to skin and bones and have escaped death by the skin of my teeth.

²¹"Have mercy on me, my friends, have mercy, for the hand of God has struck me. ²²Why must you persecute me as God does? Why aren't you satisfied with my anguish?

²³"Oh, that my words could be written. Oh, that they could be inscribed on a monument, ²⁴carved with an iron chisel and filled with lead, engraved forever in the rock.

²⁵"But as for me, I know that my Redeemer lives, and that he will stand upon the earth at last. ²⁶And after my body has decayed, yet in my body I will see God*! ²⁷I will see him for myself. Yes, I will see him with my own eyes. I am overwhelmed at the thought!

²⁸"How dare you go on persecuting me, saying, 'It's his own fault'? ²⁹I warn you, you yourselves are in danger of punishment for your attitude. Then you will know that there is judgment."

MAY 23   ☐ DAY 144
JOB 20–21
Zophar and Job (Second Debate)

OVERVIEW Zophar—who specializes in easy answers to difficult questions—now makes his last public appearance. His comments are addressed to "the wicked" (20:5) but are aimed straight at Job. The wicked will be cut off; sin and riches will devour him; those he oppressed shall see his defeat; and the fury of God's wrath shall strike him down. Then Job interrupts. The wicked do sometimes prosper and enjoy the luxury of their wealth, but they ultimately die just like every-one else. The wicked are mighty in power while they live, but then comes their destruction by God. Job concludes, "How can you comfort me? All your explanations are wrong" (21:34).

Chapter 20		Chapter 21	
Righteous Indignation	Repeated Insight	Understandable Impatience	Undeniable Injustice
1 3	4 29	1 6	7 34
Zophar's Insistence		Job's Innocence	

YOUR DAILY WALK How can you explain the seeming inequities in the world today? The wicked generally go unpunished, the rich get richer, the poor get poorer, the swindler prospers, while the honest man goes bankrupt. Isn't God concerned about such things?

Do not pray that the poor be fed unless you are willing to provide the bread.

If you have pondered thoughts like those, you're not alone. Centuries ago, Job asked the same penetrating questions about the prosperity of the wicked. He looked around him and saw distorted business ethics, perverted justice, unpunished criminals, and unjust suffering. Everywhere he looked there was cause for pessimism—until he looked up!

And suddenly everything snapped into sharp focus. The God of eternity works out his plan from the perspective of eternity. In the end, all accounts will be settled justly. But for now, God calls upon the righteous to trust him, leave vengeance in his hands, and walk by faith.

Pick an unfair situation from daily life, and look at it from God's perspective. What do you see? How will you respond?

INSIGHT Words with a Hollow (and Familiar) Ring
In his rebuttal, Job skillfully employs the words of his opponents. For example, in the space of a single verse (21:28), Job paraphrases (and parodies) the words of all three counselors: Bildad (8:22), Eliphaz (15:34), and Zophar (20:26).

CHAPTER 20
Then Zophar the Naamathite replied:

2"I must reply because I am greatly disturbed. 3I have had to endure your insults, but now my spirit prompts me to reply.

4"Don't you realize that ever since people were first placed on the earth, 5the triumph of the wicked has been short-lived and the joy of the godless has been only temporary? 6Though the godless man's pride reaches to the heavens and though his head touches the clouds, 7yet he will perish forever, thrown away like his own dung. Those who knew him will ask, 'Where is he?' 8He will fade like a dream and not be found. He will vanish like a vision in the night. 9Neither his friends nor his family will ever see him again. 10His children will beg from the poor, for he must give back his ill-gotten wealth. 11He was just a young man, but his bones will lie in the dust.

12"He enjoyed the taste of his wickedness, letting it melt under his tongue. 13He savored it, holding it long in his mouth. 14But suddenly, the food he has eaten turns sour within him, a poisonous venom in his stomach. 15He will vomit the wealth he swallowed. God won't let him keep it down. 16He will suck the poison of snakes. The viper will kill him. 17He will never again enjoy abundant streams of olive oil or rivers of milk and honey. 18His labors will not be rewarded. His wealth will bring him no joy. 19For he oppressed the poor and left them destitute. He foreclosed on their homes. 20He was always greedy but never satisfied. Of all the things he dreamed about, nothing remains. 21Nothing is left after he finishes gorging himself; therefore, his prosperity will not endure.

22"In the midst of plenty, he will run into trouble, and disasters will destroy him. 23May God give him a bellyful of trouble. May God rain down his anger upon him. 24He will try to escape, but God's arrow will pierce him. 25The arrow is pulled from his body, and the arrow-head glistens with blood.* The terrors of death are upon him.

26"His treasures will be lost in deepest darkness. A wildfire will devour his goods, consuming all he has left. 27The heavens will reveal his guilt, and the earth will give testimony against him. 28A flood will sweep away his house. God's anger will descend on him in torrents. 29This is the fate that awaits the wicked. It is the inheritance decreed by God."

CHAPTER 21
Then Job spoke again:

2"Listen closely to what I am saying. You can console me by listening to me. 3Bear with me, and let me speak. After I have spoken, you may mock me.

4"My complaint is with God, not with people. No wonder I'm so impatient. 5Look at me and be stunned. Put your hand over your mouth in shock. 6When I think about what I am saying, I shudder. My body trembles.

7"The truth is that the wicked live to a good old age. They grow old and wealthy. 8They live to see their children grow to maturity, and they enjoy their grandchildren. 9Their homes are safe from every fear, and God does not punish them. 10Their bulls never fail to breed. Their cows bear calves without miscarriage. 11Their children skip about like lambs in a flock of sheep. 12They sing with tambourine and harp. They make merry to the sound of the flute. 13They spend their days in prosperity; then they go down to the grave in peace. 14All this, even though they say to God, 'Go away. We want no part of you and your ways.15Who is the Almighty, and why should we obey him? What good will it do

20:25 Hebrew *with gall.*

us if we pray?' 16But their prosperity is not of their own doing, so I will have nothing to do with that kind of thinking.

17"Yet the wicked get away with it time and time again. They rarely have trouble, and God skips them when he distributes sorrows in his anger. 18Are they driven before the wind like straw? Are they carried away by the storm? Not at all!

19"'Well,' you say, 'at least God will punish their children!' But I say that God should punish the ones who sin, not their children! Let them feel their own penalty. 20Let their own eyes see their destruction. Let them drink deeply of the anger of the Almighty. 21For when they are dead, they will not care what happens to their family.

22"But who can teach a lesson to God, the supreme Judge? 23One person dies in prosperity and security, 24the very picture of good health. 25Another person dies in bitter poverty, never having tasted the good life. 26Both alike are buried in the same dust, both eaten by the same worms.

27"Look, I know your thoughts. I know the schemes you plot against me. 28You will tell me of rich and wicked people who came to disaster because of their sins. 29But I tell you to ask those who have been around, and they can tell you the truth. 30Evil people are spared in times of calamity and are allowed to escape. 31No one rebukes them openly. No one repays them for what they have done. 32When they are carried to the grave, an honor guard keeps watch at their tomb. 33A great funeral procession goes to the cemetery. Many pay their respects as the body is laid to rest and the earth gives sweet repose.

34"How can you comfort me? All your explanations are wrong!"

MAY 24 ☐ DAY 145
JOB 22–24
Eliphaz Silenced (Third Debate)

OVERVIEW Job's self-appointed counselors have run out of arguments—but not out of words. In the final round of debates, Eliphaz and Bildad take turns accusing Job of being the "wicked man" they have been describing all along. Eliphaz, following his cause-and-effect view of sin and suffering, continues to search for a secret sin in Job's life. In a desperate plea for acquittal, Job turns his glance heavenward. He laments that God is hard to find (23:8-9), and yet acknowledges that God's purposes are single-minded, unchanging, and beneficial for those who patiently wait upon him.

Chapter 22		Chapter 23	Chapter 24
"Don't Sin"	"Do Repent"	"Don't Hide from Me"	"Do Vindicate Me"
1 20	21 30		
Eliphaz to Job		Job to God	

YOUR DAILY WALK There is at least one thing Eliphaz and Job agreed upon—they both were appalled at the treatment received by the orphans.

We must learn to regard people less in the light of what they do or fail to do and more in the light of what they suffer.

Eliphaz stated in 22:9 that the wicked crushed the strength (literally, "arms") of orphans. The rightful privileges and means of support for orphans were taken away. Their boundary markers were moved; their flocks were driven off; they were left cold, hungry, and at the mercy of the elements. But the God of all mercy had not forgotten them.

God has a special place in his heart for the fatherless and orphaned. Psalm 82:3 exhorts us to "give fair judgment to the poor and the orphan." Do you know of a single-parent home in your neighborhood or a family that is destitute because of unemployment or illness? You can (and should) pray for them, but don't stop there. Carve out some time to spend with a fatherless youngster. Call up a needy neighbor and invite him or her over for dinner. Get involved in the lives of another family. If you have Christ, you have something to share!

INSIGHT Old Testament Cattle Rustling

Job 24:3 states that the wicked "take donkeys from the poor and father-less." Such an act would be damaging beyond repair. Orphan children would be unable to round up or recover the stolen livestock—a picture of utter helplessness and desperation. But such coldhearted acts are not hidden from the Lord.

CHAPTER 22

Then Eliphaz the Temanite replied:

2"Can a person's actions be of benefit to God? Can even a wise person be helpful to him? 3Is it any pleasure to the Almighty if you are righteous? Would it be any gain to him if you were perfect? 4Is it because of your reverence for him that he accuses and judges you? 5Not at all! It is because of your wickedness! Your guilt has no limit!

6"For example, you must have lent money to your friend and then kept the clothing he gave you as a pledge. Yes, you stripped him to the bone. 7You must have refused water for the thirsty and food for the hungry. 8After all, you think the land belongs to the powerful and that those who are privileged have a right to it! 9You must have sent widows away without helping them and crushed the strength of orphans. 10That is why you are surrounded by traps and sudden fears. 11That is why you cannot

see in the darkness, and waves of water cover you.

12"God is so great—higher than the heavens, higher than the farthest stars. 13But you reply, 'That's why God can't see what I am doing! How can he judge through the thick darkness? 14For thick clouds swirl about him, and he cannot see us. He is way up there, walking on the vault of heaven.'

15"Will you continue on the old paths where evil people have walked? 16They were snatched away in the prime of life, and the foundations of their lives were washed away forever. 17For they said to God, 'Leave us alone! What can the Almighty do for us?' 18But they forgot that he had filled their homes with good things, so I will have nothing to do with that kind of thinking.

19"Now the righteous will be happy to see the wicked destroyed, and the innocent will laugh them to scorn. 20They will say,

'Surely our enemies have been destroyed. The last of them have been consumed in the fire.'

²¹"Stop quarreling with God! If you agree with him, you will have peace at last, and things will go well for you. ²²Listen to his instructions, and store them in your heart. ²³If you return to the Almighty and clean up your life, you will be restored. ²⁴Give up your lust for money, and throw your precious gold into the river. ²⁵Then the Almighty himself will be your treasure. He will be your precious silver!

²⁶"Then you will delight yourself in the Almighty and look up to God. ²⁷You will pray to him, and he will hear you, and you will fulfill your vows to him. ²⁸Whatever you decide to do will be accomplished, and light will shine on the road ahead of you. ²⁹If someone is brought low and you say, 'Help him up,' God will save the downcast. ³⁰Then even sinners will be rescued by your pure hands."

CHAPTER 23

Then Job spoke again:

²"My complaint today is still a bitter one, and I try hard not to groan aloud. ³If only I knew where to find God, I would go to his throne and talk with him there. ⁴I would lay out my case and present my arguments. ⁵Then I would listen to his reply and understand what he says to me. ⁶Would he merely argue with me in his greatness? No, he would give me a fair hearing. ⁷Fair and honest people can reason with him, so I would be acquitted by my Judge.

⁸"I go east, but he is not there. I go west, but I cannot find him. ⁹I do not see him in the north, for he is hidden. I turn to the south, but I cannot find him. ¹⁰But he knows where I am going. And when he has tested me like gold in a fire, he will pronounce me innocent.

¹¹"For I have stayed in God's paths; I have followed his ways and not turned aside. ¹²I have not departed from his commands but have treasured his word in my heart. ¹³Nevertheless, his mind concerning me remains unchanged, and who can turn him from his purposes? Whatever he wants to do, he does. ¹⁴So he will do for me all he has planned. He controls my destiny. ¹⁵No wonder I am so terrified in his presence. When I think of it, terror grips me. ¹⁶God has made my heart faint; the Al-

mighty has terrified me. ¹⁷Darkness is all around me; thick, impenetrable darkness is everywhere.

CHAPTER 24

"Why doesn't the Almighty open the court and bring judgment? Why must the godly wait for him in vain? ²Evil people steal land by moving the boundary markers. They steal flocks of sheep, ³and they even take donkeys from the poor and fatherless. A poor widow must surrender her valuable ox as collateral for a loan. ⁴The poor are kicked aside; the needy must hide together for safety. ⁵Like the wild donkeys in the desert, the poor must spend all their time just getting enough to keep body and soul together. They go into the desert to search for food for their children. ⁶They harvest a field they do not own, and they glean in the vineyards of the wicked. ⁷All night they lie naked in the cold, without clothing or covering. ⁸They are soaked by mountain showers, and they huddle against the rocks for want of a home.

⁹"The wicked snatch a widow's child from her breast; they take the baby as a pledge for a loan. ¹⁰The poor must go about naked, without any clothing. They are forced to carry food while they themselves are starving. ¹¹They press out olive oil without being allowed to taste it, and they tread in the winepress as they suffer from thirst. ¹²The groans of the dying rise from the city, and the wounded cry for help, yet God does not respond to their moaning.

¹³"Wicked people rebel against the light. They refuse to acknowledge its ways. They will not stay in its paths. ¹⁴The murderer rises in the early dawn to kill the poor and needy; at night he is a thief. ¹⁵The adulterer waits for the twilight, for he says, 'No one will see me then.' He masks his face so no one will know him. ¹⁶They break into houses at night and sleep in the daytime. They are not acquainted with the light. ¹⁷The black night is their morning. They ally themselves with the terrors of the darkness.

¹⁸"But they disappear from the earth as quickly as foam is swept down a river. Everything they own is cursed, so that no one enters their vineyard. ¹⁹Death consumes sinners just as drought and heat consume snow. ²⁰Even the sinner's own

mother will forget him. Worms will find him sweet to eat. No one will remember him. Wicked people are broken like a tree in the storm. ²¹For they have taken advantage of the childless who have no protecting sons. They refuse to help the needy widows.

²²"God, in his power, drags away the rich. They may rise high, but they have no assurance in life. ²³They may be allowed to live in security, but God is always watching them. ²⁴And though they are great now, in a moment they will be gone like all others, withered like heads of grain.

²⁵"Can anyone claim otherwise? Who can prove me wrong?"

MAY 25 □ DAY 146
JOB 25–28
Bildad and Zophar Silenced (Third Debate)

OVERVIEW The prosecution rests its case at last. All arguments have been expended. In one final, angry, impatient outburst, Bildad repeats his well-worn case. A person cannot be justified before a high and holy God. Job, who agrees with Bildad's concept of a great God, contends that God is far bigger than even Bildad has yet shown. Insisting upon his own innocence, Job describes God as the one who wisely and justly rewards the righteous. Although humans have plumbed the depths of the earth to find rich minerals, they have yet to find anything as valuable or precious as the wisdom of God.

Chapter 25	Chapter 26	Chapter 27	Chapter 28
"God Is Distant"	"God Is Powerful"	"God Is Just"	"God Is Wise"
Pessimism		Optimism	

YOUR DAILY WALK Here is a good thought from the book of Ecclesiastes to add to your Bible reading today: "Don't be quick-tempered, for anger is the friend of fools" (Ecclesiastes 7:9).

He who can suppress a moment's anger may prevent a day of sorrow.

When words have all been used up, tempers usually flare and fists fly! Such was the case with Bildad. All his arguments had been refuted. There was nothing left to say. So he struck out in anger and showed the shallowness of his own counsel.

Work on your "anger factor" today. If possible, carry a thermometer with you in your coat pocket or purse. Or draw one on a note card with the words of Ecclesiastes 7:9 on the back, and tuck it in your pocket. Whenever you begin to boil about a problem today—a disagreement with your spouse, a traffic jam, a missed appointment, a tedious assignment, an unexpected disappointment—pull out your thermometer. Count the degree markings slowly ("96 . . . 97 . . . 98 . . ."). Then ask yourself these two questions: Is it worth making a fool of myself? And, Is the God I serve big enough to handle it? Then deal with your problem in God's way.

INSIGHT How Much Is Wisdom Really Worth?
Job stated that wisdom is more priceless than the earth's gold (28:12-17). Just how valuable is that? One gold field in South Africa alone has produced 49.4 million ounces. At an average price of $395 per ounce, that represents a "gold mine" of over $19 billion!

CHAPTER 25

Then Bildad the Shuhite replied:

²"God is powerful and dreadful. He enforces peace in the heavens. ³Who is able to count his heavenly army? Does his light not shine on all the earth? ⁴How can a mere mortal stand before God and claim to be righteous? Who in all the earth is pure? ⁵God is so glorious that even the moon and stars scarcely shine compared to him. ⁶How much less are mere people, who are but worms in his sight?"

CHAPTER 26

Then Job spoke again:

²"How you have helped the powerless! How you have saved a person who has no strength! ³How you have enlightened my stupidity! What wise things you have said! ⁴Where have you gotten all these wise sayings? Whose spirit speaks through you?

⁵"The dead tremble in their place beneath the waters. ⁶The underworld* is naked in God's presence. There is no cover for the place of destruction. ⁷God stretches the northern sky over empty space and hangs the earth on nothing. ⁸He wraps the rain in his thick clouds, and the clouds do not burst with the weight. ⁹He shrouds his throne with his clouds. ¹⁰He created the horizon when he separated the waters; he set the boundaries for day and night. ¹¹The foundations of heaven tremble at his rebuke. ¹²By his power the sea grew calm. By his skill he crushed the great sea monster.* ¹³His Spirit made the heavens beautiful, and his power pierced the gliding serpent.

¹⁴"These are some of the minor things he does, merely a whisper of his power. Who can understand the thunder of his power?"

CHAPTER 27

Job continued speaking:

²"I make this vow by the living God, who has taken away my rights, by the Almighty who has embittered my soul. ³As long as I live, while I have breath from God, ⁴my lips will speak no evil, and my tongue will speak no lies. ⁵I will never concede that you are right; until I die, I will defend my innocence. ⁶I will maintain my innocence without wavering. My conscience is clear for as long as I live.

⁷"May my enemy be punished like the wicked, my adversary like evil men. ⁸For what hope do the godless have when God cuts them off and takes away their life? ⁹Will God listen to their cry when trouble comes upon them? ¹⁰Can they take delight in the Almighty? Can they call to God at any time?

¹¹"I will teach you about God's power. I will not conceal anything that concerns the Almighty. ¹²But I don't need to, for you yourselves have seen all this; yet you are saying all these useless things to me.

¹³"This is what the wicked will receive from God; this is their inheritance from the Almighty. ¹⁴If they have a multitude of children, their children will die in war or starve to death. ¹⁵Those who survive will be brought down to the grave by a plague, with no one to mourn them, not even their wives.

¹⁶"Evil people may have all the money in the world, and they may store away mounds of clothing. ¹⁷But the righteous will wear that clothing, and the innocent will divide all that money. ¹⁸The houses built by the wicked are as fragile as a spiderweb, as flimsy as a shelter made of branches.

¹⁹"The wicked go to bed rich but wake up to find that all their wealth is gone. ²⁰Terror overwhelms them, and they are blown away in the storms of the night. ²¹The east wind carries them away, and they are gone. It sweeps them away. ²²It whirls down on them without mercy. They struggle to flee from its power. ²³But everyone jeers at them and mocks them.

CHAPTER 28

"People know how to mine silver and refine gold. ²They know how to dig iron from the earth and smelt copper from stone. ³They know how to put light into darkness and explore the farthest, darkest regions of the earth as they search for ore. ⁴They sink a mine shaft into the earth far from where anyone lives. They descend on ropes, swinging back and forth. ⁵Bread comes from the earth, but below the surface the earth is melted as by fire.

⁶"People know how to find sapphires and gold dust—⁷treasures that no bird of prey can see, no falcon's eye observe—⁸for they are deep within the mines. No wild animal has ever walked upon those

---

26:6 Hebrew *Sheol.*   26:12 Hebrew *Rahab*, the name of a mythical sea monster that represents chaos in ancient literature.

treasures; no lion has set his paw there. ⁹People know how to tear apart flinty rocks and overturn the roots of mountains. ¹⁰They cut tunnels in the rocks and uncover precious stones. ¹¹They dam up the trickling streams and bring to light the hidden treasures.

¹²"But do people know where to find wisdom? Where can they find understanding? ¹³No one knows where to find it, for it is not found among the living. ¹⁴'It is not here,' says the ocean. 'Nor is it here,' says the sea.

¹⁵"It cannot be bought for gold or silver. ¹⁶Its value is greater than all the gold of Ophir, greater than precious onyx stone or sapphires. ¹⁷Wisdom is far more valuable than gold and crystal. It cannot be purchased with jewels mounted in fine gold. ¹⁸Coral and valuable rock crystal are worthless in trying to get it. The price of wisdom is far above pearls. ¹⁹Topaz from

28:19 Hebrew *from Cush.*

Ethiopia* cannot be exchanged for it. Its value is greater than the purest gold.

²⁰"But do people know where to find wisdom? Where can they find understanding? ²¹For it is hidden from the eyes of all humanity. Even the sharp-eyed birds in the sky cannot discover it. ²²But Destruction and Death say, 'We have heard a rumor of where wisdom can be found.'

²³"God surely knows where it can be found, ²⁴for he looks throughout the whole earth, under all the heavens. ²⁵He made the winds blow and determined how much rain should fall. ²⁶He made the laws of the rain and prepared a path for the lightning. ²⁷Then, when he had done all this, he saw wisdom and measured it. He established it and examined it thoroughly. ²⁸And this is what he says to all humanity: 'The fear of the Lord is true wisdom; to forsake evil is real understanding.'"

MAY 26 ☐ DAY 147
JOB 29–31
Job's Final Plea (Third Debate)

 OVERVIEW Job's advisers have at last grown silent, but the problem of his suffering persists. Nearly overcome by depression, he longs for the good old days when he enjoyed his wealth and the presence of his children. In contrast to his former position of status and prestige, Job now experiences mockery from the young men of the city. And ever present is the excruciating pain of his loathsome disease. Job pauses. He thinks back over his life. Is there some area of sin he has overlooked? No. Has he manifested any bitter or negligent attitude toward his neighbors? No. Has he demonstrated an attitude of insensitivity toward God or others? No. And so with his personal and public life an open book before God, Job rests his case.

Chapter 29	Chapter 30	Chapter 31
The Good Old Days	The Bad New Days	A Personal Inventory
Job Remembers		Job Reexamines

 YOUR DAILY WALK All good store managers periodically take stock of their inventory. They carefully examine their goods to see what they have on hand and what they don't, what they need to buy for their shelves and what they need to throw away. And they do this at regular intervals.

Suffering can produce great depths of character, mature understanding, warm compassion, and rich spirituality.

That's precisely what Job did in chapter 31. He took stock of his life to see where his character, conduct, and spiritual life were deficient. Although there was no grave area of sin, Job's attitude of confession prepared him for God's instruction later.

When was the last time you took personal inventory in your life? Right now, check up on your personal thought life, your behavior toward others, and your walk with God. Confess your areas of sinful neglect, thank God for your areas of strength, and map out a project today to begin "restocking the shelves" in places where you are weak.

INSIGHT Job's Moral Inventory
Notice the three areas of Job's self-examination: (1) *personal life* (31:1-12)—he checked for the sins of lust, lying, and adultery; (2) *public life* (31:13-23)—he checked his treatment of servants, widows, orphans, and the needy; and (3) *spiritual life* (31:24-40)—he checked his use of money, worship of God, attitude toward revenge, use of hospitality, and purity of motives.

CHAPTER 29

Job continued speaking:

2"I long for the years gone by when God took care of me, 3when he lighted the way before me and I walked safely through the darkness. 4In my early years, the friendship of God was felt in my home. 5The Almighty was still with me, and my children were around me. 6In those days my cows produced milk in abundance, and my olive groves poured out streams of olive oil.

7"Those were the days when I went to the city gate and took my place among the honored leaders. 8The young stepped aside when they saw me, and even the aged rose in respect at my coming. 9The princes stood in silence and put their hands over their mouths. 10The highest officials of the city stood quietly, holding their tongues in respect.

11"All who heard of me praised me. All who saw me spoke well of me. 12For I helped the poor in their need and the orphans who had no one to help them. 13I helped those who had lost hope, and they blessed me. And I caused the widows' hearts to sing for joy. 14All I did was just and honest. Righteousness covered me like a robe, and I wore justice like a turban. 15I served as eyes for the blind and feet for the lame. 16I was a father to the poor and made sure that even strangers received a fair trial. 17I broke the jaws of godless oppressors and made them release their victims.

18"I thought, 'Surely I will die surrounded by my family after a long, good life. 19For I am like a tree whose roots reach the water, whose branches are refreshed with the dew. 20New honors are constantly bestowed on me, and my strength is continually renewed.'

21"Everyone listened to me and valued my advice. They were silent as they waited for me to speak. 22And after I spoke, they had nothing to add, for my counsel satisfied them. 23They longed for me to speak as they longed for rain. They waited eagerly, for my words were as refreshing as the spring rain. 24When they were discouraged, I smiled at them. My look of approval was precious to them. 25I told them what they should do and presided over them as their chief. I lived as a king among his troops and as one who comforts those who mourn.

CHAPTER 30

"But now I am mocked by those who are younger than I, by young men whose fathers are not worthy to run with my sheepdogs. 2A lot of good they are to me—those worn-out wretches! 3They are gaunt with hunger and flee to the deserts and the wastelands, desolate and gloomy. 4They eat coarse leaves, and they burn the roots of shrubs for heat. 5They are driven from civilization, and people shout after them as if they were thieves. 6So now they live in frightening ravines and in caves and among the rocks. 7They sound like animals as they howl among the bushes; they huddle together for shelter beneath the nettles. 8They are nameless fools, outcasts of civilization.

9"And now their sons mock me with their vulgar song! They taunt me! 10They despise me and won't come near me, except to spit in my face. 11For God has cut the cords of my tent. He has humbled me, so they have thrown off all restraint. ¹²These outcasts oppose me to my face. They send me sprawling; they lay traps in my path. ¹³They block my road and do everything they can to hasten my calamity, knowing full well that I have no one to help me. ¹⁴They come at me from all directions. They rush upon me when I am down. ¹⁵I live in terror now. They hold me in contempt, and my prosperity has vanished as a cloud before a strong wind.

¹⁶"And now my heart is broken. Depression haunts my days. ¹⁷My weary nights are filled with pain as though something were relentlessly gnawing at my bones. ¹⁸With a strong hand, God grabs my garment. He grips me by the collar of my tunic. ¹⁹He has thrown me into the mud. I have become as dust and ashes.

²⁰"I cry to you, O God, but you don't answer me. I stand before you, and you don't bother to look. ²¹You have become cruel toward me. You persecute me with your great power. ²²You throw me into the whirlwind and destroy me in the storm. ²³And I know that you are sending me to my death—the destination of all who live.

²⁴"Surely no one would turn against the needy when they cry for help. ²⁵Did I not weep for those in trouble? Was I not deeply grieved for the needy? ²⁶So I looked for good, but evil came instead. I waited for the light, but darkness fell. ²⁷My heart is troubled and restless. Days of affliction have come upon me. ²⁸I walk in gloom, without sunlight. I stand in the public square and cry for help. ²⁹But instead, I am considered a brother to jackals and a companion to ostriches. ³⁰My skin has turned dark, and my bones burn with fever. ³¹My harp plays sad music, and my flute accompanies those who weep.

CHAPTER 31

"I made a covenant with my eyes not to look with lust upon a young woman. ²What has God above chosen for us? What is our inheritance from the Almighty on high? ³It is calamity for the wicked, misfortune for those who do evil. ⁴He sees everything I do and every step I take.

⁵"Have I lied to anyone or deceived anyone? ⁶Let God judge me on the scales of justice, for he knows my integrity. ⁷If I have

strayed from his pathway, or if my heart has lusted for what my eyes have seen, or if I am guilty of any other sin, ⁸then let someone else harvest the crops I have planted, and let all that I have planted be uprooted.

⁹"If my heart has been seduced by a woman, or if I have lusted for my neighbor's wife, ¹⁰then may my wife belong to another man; may other men sleep with her. ¹¹For lust is a shameful sin, a crime that should be punished. ¹²It is a devastating fire that destroys to hell. It would wipe out everything I own.

¹³"If I have been unfair to my male or female servants, if I have refused to hear their complaints, ¹⁴how could I face God? What could I say when he questioned me about it? ¹⁵For God created both me and my servants. He created us both.

¹⁶"Have I refused to help the poor, or crushed the hopes of widows who looked to me for help? ¹⁷Have I been stingy with my food and refused to share it with hungry orphans? ¹⁸No, from childhood I have cared for orphans, and all my life I have cared for widows. ¹⁹Whenever I saw someone who was homeless and without clothes, ²⁰did they not praise me for providing wool clothing to keep them warm? ²¹If my arm has abused an orphan because I thought I could get away with it, ²²then let my shoulder be wrenched out of place! Let my arm be torn from its socket! ²³That would be better than facing the judgment sent by God. For if the majesty of God opposes me, what hope is there?

²⁴"Have I put my trust in money or felt secure because of my gold? ²⁵Does my happiness depend on my wealth and all that I own? ²⁶Have I looked at the sun shining in the skies, or the moon walking down its silver pathway, ²⁷and been secretly enticed in my heart to worship them? ²⁸If so, I should be punished by the judges, for it would mean I had denied the God of heaven.

²⁹"Have I ever rejoiced when my enemies came to ruin or become excited when harm came their way? ³⁰No, I have never cursed anyone or asked for revenge. ³¹My servants have never let others go hungry. ³²I have never turned away a stranger but have opened my doors to everyone. ³³Have I tried to hide my sins as people normally do, hiding my guilt in a closet? ³⁴Have I feared the crowd and its contempt, so that

I refused to acknowledge my sin and would not go outside? ³⁵"If only I had someone who would listen to me and try to see my side! Look, I will sign my name to my defense. Let the Almighty show me that I am wrong. Let my accuser write out the charges against me. ³⁶I would face the accusation proudly. I would treasure it like a crown. ³⁷For I

would tell him exactly what I have done. I would come before him like a prince. ³⁸"If my land accuses me and all its furrows weep together, ³⁹or if I have stolen its crops or murdered its owners, ⁴⁰then let thistles grow on that land instead of wheat and weeds instead of barley."

Job's words are ended.

MAY 27 □ DAY 148
JOB 32–34
Elihu and Job (Part One)

OVERVIEW Job's three "comfortless counselors" fall silent at last, their arguments exhausted, with Job no nearer a solution to his suffering. Enter Elihu, a younger contemporary of Eliphaz, Bildad, and Zophar, to offer his counsel. He begins by analyzing Job's response to his suffering and his insistence that God provide answers to his questions. Elihu points out that the Sovereign's actions are often educational, not merely disciplinary, in the life of his subjects. Using many quotes from Job's previous responses, Elihu gives a lengthy defense of God's dealings with humans. His conclusion: "God will not do wrong. The Almighty cannot twist justice" (34:12).

Chapter 32	Chapter 33	Chapter 34
"Both Sides, Listen to Me"	"God Is Greater than Any Person"	"God Will Not Do Wrong"
Elihu's Request	Elihu's Response	

Most of our suspicions of others are aroused by our knowledge of ourselves.

YOUR DAILY WALK Can you think of three occupations from the world of government, business, medicine, or sports that demand absolute impartiality if the job is to be done correctly? Write them in the space provided:

_____

_____

_____

Did you think of things like: Supreme Court judge, personnel manager, surgeon, or umpire? These are all examples of jobs requiring impartiality in the workaday world. But what about in the Christian life? How impartial does God want *you* to be?

Have you ever given preferential treatment to a prominent guest at church? Have you ever made a special effort to avoid someone who obviously came from a different ethnic, financial, or spiritual background than you? If so, you were exercising partiality. According to James 2:9, God looks on such favoritism as sin.

Elihu realized that God is absolutely impartial (34:16-20) and expects his children to be the same! Check up on your own personal contacts in your neighborhood, office, or church. What needs to change about your treatment of others so that James 2:1 is not true of you?

INSIGHT Words to Be Sampled and Savored
Elihu quoted a proverb, "Just as the mouth tastes good food, the ear
tests the words it hears" (34:3), in order to urge his listeners to test his
words as carefully as a gourmet cook would taste his delicacies.

CHAPTER 32

Job's three friends refused to reply further to him because he kept insisting on his innocence.

²Then Elihu son of Barakel the Buzite, of the clan of Ram, became angry. He was angry because Job refused to admit that he had sinned and that God was right in punishing him. ³He was also angry with Job's three friends because they had condemned God* by their inability to answer Job's arguments. ⁴Elihu had waited for the others to speak because they were older than he. ⁵But when he saw that they had no further reply, he spoke out angrily.

⁶Elihu son of Barakel the Buzite said, "I am young and you are old, so I held back and did not dare to tell you what I think. ⁷I thought, 'Those who are older should speak, for wisdom comes with age.' ⁸Surely it is God's Spirit within people, the breath of the Almighty within them, that makes them intelligent. ⁹But sometimes the elders are not wise. Sometimes the aged do not understand justice. ¹⁰So listen to me and let me express my opinion.

¹¹"I have waited all this time, listening very carefully to your arguments, listening to you grope for words. ¹²I have listened, but not one of you has refuted Job or answered his arguments. ¹³And don't tell me, 'He is too wise for us. Only God can convince him.' ¹⁴If Job had been arguing with me, I would not answer with that kind of logic! ¹⁵You sit there baffled, with no further response. ¹⁶Should I continue to wait, now that you are silent? Must I also remain silent? ¹⁷No, I will say my piece. I will speak my mind. I surely will. ¹⁸For I am pent up and full of words, and the spirit within me urges me on. ¹⁹I am like a wine cask without a vent. My words are ready to burst out! ²⁰I must speak to find relief, so let me give my answers. ²¹I won't play favorites or try to flatter anyone. ²²And if I tried, my Creator would soon do away with me.

CHAPTER 33

"Listen, Job, to what I have to say. ²Now that I have begun to speak, let me continue. ³I speak with all sincerity; I speak the truth. ⁴For the Spirit of God has made me, and the breath of the Almighty gives me life. ⁵Answer me, if you can; make your case and take your stand.

⁶"Look, you and I are the same before God. I, too, was formed from clay. ⁷So you don't need to be afraid of me. I am not some great person to make you nervous and afraid.

⁸"You have said it in my hearing. I have heard your very words. ⁹You said, 'I am pure; I am innocent; I have not sinned. ¹⁰God is picking a quarrel with me, and he considers me to be his enemy. ¹¹He puts my feet in the stocks and watches every move I make.'

¹²"In this you are not right, and I will show you why. As you yourself have said, 'God is greater than any person.' ¹³So why are you bringing a charge against him? You say, 'He does not respond to people's complaints.' ¹⁴But God speaks again and again, though people do not recognize it. ¹⁵He speaks in dreams, in visions of the night when deep sleep falls on people as they lie in bed. ¹⁶He whispers in their ear and terrifies them with his warning. ¹⁷He causes them to change their minds; he keeps them from pride. ¹⁸He keeps them from the grave, from crossing over the river of death. ¹⁹Or God disciplines people with sickness and pain, with ceaseless aching in their bones. ²⁰They lose their appetite and do not care for even the most delicious food. ²¹They waste away to skin and bones. ²²They are at death's door; the angels of death wait for them.

²³"But if a special messenger from heaven is there to intercede for a person, to declare that he is upright, ²⁴God will be gracious and say, 'Set him free. Do not make him die, for I have found a ransom for his life.' ²⁵Then his body will become as healthy as a child's, firm and youthful again. ²⁶When he prays to God, he will be accepted. And God will receive him with

32:3 As in ancient Hebrew scribal tradition; the Masoretic Text makes no reference to God.

joy and restore him to good standing. ²⁷He will declare to his friends, 'I sinned, but it was not worth it. ²⁸God rescued me from the grave, and now my life is filled with light.'

²⁹"Yes, God often does these things for people. ³⁰He rescues them from the grave so they may live in the light of the living. ³¹Mark this well, Job. Listen to me, and let me say more. ³²But if you have anything to say, go ahead. I want to hear it, for I am anxious to see you justified. ³³But if not, then listen to me. Keep silent and I will teach you wisdom!"

CHAPTER 34
Then Elihu said:

²"Listen to me, you wise men. Pay attention, you who have knowledge. ³'Just as the mouth tastes good food, the ear tests the words it hears.' ⁴So let us discern for ourselves what is right; let us learn together what is good. ⁵For Job has said, 'I am innocent, but God has taken away my rights. ⁶I am innocent, but they call me a liar. My suffering is incurable, even though I have not sinned.'

⁷"Has there ever been a man as arrogant as Job, with his thirst for irreverent talk? ⁸He seeks the companionship of evil people. He spends his time with wicked men. ⁹He has even said, 'Why waste time trying to please God?'

¹⁰"Listen to me, you who have understanding. Everyone knows that God doesn't sin! The Almighty can do no wrong. ¹¹He repays people according to their deeds. He treats people according to their ways. ¹²There is no truer statement than this: God will not do wrong. The Almighty cannot twist justice. ¹³Who put the world in his care? Who has set the whole world in place? ¹⁴If God were to take back his spirit* and withdraw his breath, ¹⁵all life would cease, and humanity would turn again to dust.

34:14 Or *his Spirit.*

¹⁶"Listen now and try to understand. ¹⁷Could God govern if he hated justice? Are you going to condemn the almighty Judge? ¹⁸For he says to kings and nobles, 'You are wicked and unjust.' ¹⁹He doesn't care how great a person may be, and he doesn't pay any more attention to the rich than to the poor. He made them all. ²⁰In a moment they die. At midnight they all pass away; the mighty are removed without human hand.

²¹"For God carefully watches the way people live; he sees everything they do. ²²No darkness is thick enough to hide the wicked from his eyes. ²³For it is not up to mortals to decide when to come before God in judgment. ²⁴He brings the mighty to ruin without asking anyone, and he sets up others in their places. ²⁵He watches what they do, and in the night he overturns them, destroying them. ²⁶He openly strikes them down for their wickedness. ²⁷For they turned aside from following him. They have no respect for any of his ways. ²⁸So they cause the poor to cry out, catching God's attention. Yes, he hears the cries of the needy. ²⁹When he is quiet, who can make trouble? But when he hides his face, who can find him? ³⁰He prevents the godless from ruling so they cannot be a snare to the people.

³¹"Why don't people say to God, 'I have sinned, but I will sin no more'? ³²Or 'I don't know what evil I have done; tell me, and I will stop at once'?

³³"Must God tailor his justice to your demands? But you have rejected him! The choice is yours, not mine. Go ahead, share your wisdom with us. ³⁴After all, bright people will tell me, and wise people will hear me say, ³⁵'Job speaks without knowledge; his words lack insight.' ³⁶Job, you deserve the maximum penalty for the wicked way you have talked. ³⁷For now you have added rebellion and blasphemy against God to your other sins."

MAY 28 □ DAY 149
Searching for Answers
(in All the Wrong Places)

LOOK BACK Debates have a tendency of going round and round, back and forth. And Job's debate with his three persistent friends is no different, as the verbal Ping-Pong match continues chapter after chapter.

Eliphaz, Bildad, and Zophar have taken turns attacking Job's credibility and affirming God's justice. From their vantage point, Job deserves what he is getting. With each round of debate, the arguments become more pointed and the atmosphere more charged. Diplomacy and tact give way to allegations and attack. The interaction produces plenty of heat but not much light, as Job struggles to defend himself before God and man and find a satisfying answer to the confusing circumstances that have befallen him.

When argument and accusation fail to produce a solution, anger takes over. The third and final round of "debate" demonstrates that there has been a noticeable "hardening of the attitudes" on the part of Job and his three self-appointed counselors. Job continues to maintain his integrity; his friends continue to insist God's ways and wisdom are unimpeachable. And the stalemate continues.

LOOK UP What do you know for sure—not hope, or wish, or think, or accept as conventional wisdom—but *know* with absolute certainty? Notice the strength of Job's assertions in chapter 27:
"By the living God . . ." (v. 2)
"While I have breath from God . . ." (v. 3)
"As long as I live . . ." (v. 6)

*The fire of God
in your heart
will melt
the lead in
your feet.*

These are not the hopeful musings of an incurable optimist, but the gut-wrenching convictions of an embattled saint. Job knows for sure that wickedness and deceit have no place in his response to unexplained suffering. And he knows with equal confidence that integrity and righteousness are always the God-honoring alternative. Regardless of how dark the night or bewildering the circumstances, it's always safe to trust the Lord.

LOOK AHEAD No one yearns to be crushed; no one welcomes the pain and pressure of adversity. Crushing is a painful, agonizing process—and the scars it leaves behind are real. But only through crushing can God release the full fragrance of his mercy in the life of the man or woman of God. If you are feeling the heat and pressure of painful circumstances today, then you are in good company! Place a copy of these triumphant words of Job in a prominent place and make them yours:

"But as for me, I know that my Redeemer lives, and that he will stand upon the earth at last. And after my body has decayed, yet in my body I will see God! I will see him for myself. Yes, I will see him with my own eyes. I am overwhelmed at the thought!" (19:25-27)

MAY 29 ☐ DAY 150
JOB 35-37
Elihu and Job (Part Two)

OVERVIEW Elihu deals with two of Job's most persistent complaints: What profit is there for acting righteously when you end up suffering anyway (35:1-8), and why doesn't God listen to the cries of a broken heart (35:9-16)? In the first case, Elihu concludes that God's perfect justice is not determined or altered by human behavior. Concerning unanswered prayer, Elihu argues that the only prayers God ignores are those that are proud and empty (35:12-13). God is sovereign over history and nature. His character is awesome and his ways unsearchable. "We cannot imagine the power of the Almighty" (37:23).

Chapter 35		Chapter 37
"We Are Not like God"		"God Is Not like Us"
Our Conduct	Our Pride	His Power
Elihu's Exhortation		Elihu's Explanation

YOUR DAILY WALK Here are three of the most difficult words any Christian will ever have to utter: *I don't know.*

Somehow the notion has developed that being unable to explain God's actions and attributes is a sign of spiritual weakness or immaturity. Job repeatedly took God to task because of the seemingly unreasonable things God was doing in his life. Knowing that God was absolutely just and impartial, Job concluded that God owed him an explanation. But it took young Elihu to remind Job of another important truth about God: His ways are different from human ways. In the words of the prophet Isaiah, "'My thoughts are completely different from yours,' says the LORD. 'And my ways are far beyond anything you could imagine'" (Isaiah 55:8).

A Christian with absolutely no doubts or questions is overlooking something.

Just as you must trust the surgeon to do his skillful work even though you do not understand all his techniques, so God is asking you to trust him to accomplish his purposes in your life—even though it may involve "surgery" you will not understand this side of heaven.

INSIGHT What's in a Name?

Many times Bible names characterize their bearers. In the case of Elihu, his name captures the major theme of his message on the sovereignty of God. *Elihu* means "He is my God!" Do you know the meaning of your name and those of your family members?

CHAPTER 35

Then Elihu said:

²"Do you think it is right for you to claim, 'I am righteous before God'? ³Yet you also ask, 'What's the use of living a righteous life? How will it benefit me?'

⁴"I will answer you and all your friends, too. ⁵Look up into the sky and see the clouds high above you. ⁶If you sin, what do you accomplish against him? Even if you sin again and again, what effect will it have on him? ⁷If you are good, is this some great gift to him? What could you possibly give

him? ⁸No, your sins affect only people like yourself, and your good deeds affect only other people.

⁹"The oppressed cry out beneath the wrongs that are done to them. They groan beneath the power of the mighty. ¹⁰Yet they don't ask, 'Where is God my Creator, the one who gives songs in the night? ¹¹Where is the one who makes us wiser than the animals and birds?'

¹²"And if they do cry out and God does not answer, it is because of their pride. ¹³But it is wrong to say God doesn't listen,

to say the Almighty isn't concerned. [14]And it is even more false to say he doesn't see what is going on. He will bring about justice if you will only wait. [15]But do you cry out against him because he does not respond in anger? [16]Job, you have protested in vain. You have spoken like a fool."

CHAPTER 36

Elihu continued speaking:

[2]"Let me go on, and I will show you the truth of what I am saying. For I have not finished defending God! [3]I will give you many illustrations of the righteousness of my Creator. [4]I am telling you the honest truth, for I am a man of well-rounded knowledge.

[5]"God is mighty, yet he does not despise anyone! He is mighty in both power and understanding. [6]He does not let the wicked live but gives justice to the afflicted. [7]His eyes never leave the innocent, but he establishes and exalts them with kings forever. [8]If troubles come upon them and they are enslaved and afflicted, [9]he takes the trouble to show them the reason. He shows them their sins, for they have behaved proudly. [10]He gets their attention and says they must turn away from evil.

[11]"If they listen and obey God, then they will be blessed with prosperity throughout their lives. All their years will be pleasant. [12]But if they refuse to listen to him, they will perish in battle and die from lack of understanding. [13]For the godless are full of resentment. Even when he punishes them, they refuse to cry out to him for help. [14]They die young after wasting their lives in immoral living. [15]But by means of their suffering, he rescues those who suffer. For he gets their attention through adversity.

[16]"God has led you away from danger, giving you freedom. You have prospered in a wide and pleasant valley. [17]But you are too obsessed with judgment on the godless. Don't worry, justice will be upheld. [18]But watch out, or you may be seduced with wealth. Don't let yourself be bribed into sin. [19]Could all your wealth and mighty efforts keep you from distress? [20]Do not long for the cover of night, for that is when people will be destroyed.

[21]Be on guard! Turn back from evil, for it was to prevent you from getting into a life of evil that God sent this suffering.

[22]"Look, God is all-powerful. Who is a teacher like him? [23]No one can tell him what to do. No one can say to him, 'You have done wrong.' [24]Instead, glorify his mighty works, singing songs of praise. [25]Everyone has seen these things, but only from a distance.

[26]"Look, God is exalted beyond what we can understand. His years are without number. [27]He draws up the water vapor and then distills it into rain. [28]The rain pours down from the clouds, and everyone benefits from it. [29]Can anyone really understand the spreading of the clouds and the thunder that rolls forth from heaven? [30]See how he spreads the lightning around him and how it lights up the depths of the sea. [31]By his mighty acts he governs the people, giving them food in abundance. [32]He fills his hands with lightning bolts. He hurls each at its target. [33]The thunder announces his presence; the storm announces his indignant anger.*

CHAPTER 37

"My heart pounds as I think of this. It leaps within me. [2]Listen carefully to the thunder of God's voice as it rolls from his mouth. [3]It rolls across the heavens, and his lightning flashes out in every direction. [4]Then comes the roaring of the thunder—the tremendous voice of his majesty. He does not restrain the thunder when he speaks. [5]God's voice is glorious in the thunder. We cannot comprehend the greatness of his power.

[6]"He directs the snow to fall on the earth and tells the rain to pour down. [7]Everyone stops working at such a time so they can recognize his power. [8]The wild animals hide in the rocks or in their dens. [9]The stormy wind comes from its chamber, and the driving winds bring the cold. [10]God's breath sends the ice, freezing wide expanses of water. [11]He loads the clouds with moisture, and they flash with his lightning. [12]The clouds turn around and around under his direction. They do whatever he commands throughout the earth. [13]He causes things to happen on earth, either as a punishment or as a sign of his unfailing love.

36:33 Or *even the cattle know when a storm is coming.* The meaning of the Hebrew is uncertain.

[14]"Listen, Job; stop and consider the wonderful miracles of God! [15]Do you know how God controls the storm and causes the lightning to flash forth from his clouds? [16]Do you understand how he balances the clouds with wonderful perfection and skill? [17]When you are sweltering in your clothes and the south wind dies down and everything is still, [18]he makes the skies reflect the heat like a giant mirror. Can you do that?

[19]"You think you know so much, so teach the rest of us what to say to God. We are too ignorant to make our own arguments. [20]Should God be told that I want to speak? Can we speak when we are confused? [21]We cannot look at the sun, for it shines brightly in the sky when the wind clears away the clouds. [22]Golden splendor comes from the mountain of God. He is clothed in dazzling splendor. [23]We cannot imagine the power of the Almighty, yet he is so just and merciful that he does not oppress us. [24]No wonder people everywhere fear him. People who are truly wise show him reverence."

MAY 30 □ DAY 151
JOB 38–39
Controversy between the Lord and Job

 OVERVIEW Job does not answer Elihu. The sufferer awaits the words of the one he has sought for thirty-seven chapters! At last God speaks to Job out of a whirlwind. But rather than answer Job's persistent questions, God ministers to the needs of Job's heart. He guides Job on a panoramic sweep of nature, showing Job the vastness of the mind and works of God and the insignificance of puny humans. Using a series of pointed questions, the infinite God challenges Job to answer: "Where were you when I laid the foundations of the earth?" (38:4). "Do you realize the extent of the earth?" (38:18). "Have you given the horse its strength?" (39:19). "Are you the one who makes the hawk soar and spread its wings to the south?" (39:26). Clearly, the answer to all of those is no. The God of creation rules the world. Though a God of justice and mercy, he is intimately acquainted with all his creatures.

Chapter 38	Chapter 39
The Vastness of God's Creativity in the Physical World	The Variety of God's Creativity in the Animal World
A Bigger Picture of Job's God	

 YOUR DAILY WALK Nature is not God (as pantheism claims), but God is revealed by nature (Romans 1:18-21). You have read today how God's works in the world of nature demonstrate his power and glory.

The greatness of the Promiser enhances the greatness of the promises.

With this thought in mind, do an outdoor "daily walk" today. See how many characteristics or attributes of God you can find by observing the natural world around you. Then look for an application of each characteristic of God to your life today.

For example, observe the sun. It rises every day—same time, same place. This shows God is unchangeable. And if God is unchanging, then his promises aren't fickle. They can be relied on today and tomorrow and forever! Now see what else you can learn from nature about God's infinity (not limited by space), eternity (not limited by time), omnipresence (everywhere present), and omnipotence (unlimited power). Better yet, do this while you take a walk with a friend!

INSIGHT A Challenge That Can Get You into Deep Trouble
Drop a heavy anchor into the Pacific Ocean over the Marianas Trench,
and an hour later it still will not have touched bottom—nearly seven
miles below! This sheds new light on God's challenge to Job in 38:16.

CHAPTER 38

Then the LORD answered Job from the whirlwind:

²"Who is this that questions my wisdom with such ignorant words? ³Brace yourself, because I have some questions for you, and you must answer them.

⁴"Where were you when I laid the foundations of the earth? Tell me, if you know so much. ⁵Do you know how its dimensions were determined and who did the surveying? ⁶What supports its foundations, and who laid its cornerstone ⁷as the morning stars sang together and all the angels* shouted for joy?

⁸"Who defined the boundaries of the sea as it burst from the womb, ⁹and as I clothed it with clouds and thick darkness? ¹⁰For I locked it behind barred gates, limiting its shores. ¹¹I said, 'Thus far and no farther will you come. Here your proud waves must stop!'

¹²"Have you ever commanded the morning to appear and caused the dawn to rise in the east? ¹³Have you ever told the daylight to spread to the ends of the earth, to bring an end to the night's wickedness? ¹⁴For the features of the earth take shape as the light approaches, and the dawn is robed in red. ¹⁵The light disturbs the haunts of the wicked, and it stops the arm that is raised in violence.

¹⁶"Have you explored the springs from which the seas come? Have you walked about and explored their depths? ¹⁷Do you know where the gates of death are located? Have you seen the gates of utter gloom? ¹⁸Do you realize the extent of the earth? Tell me about it if you know!

¹⁹"Where does the light come from, and where does the darkness go? ²⁰Can you take it to its home? Do you know how to get there? ²¹But of course you know all this! For you were born before it was all created, and you are so very experienced!

²²"Have you visited the treasuries of the snow? Have you seen where the hail is made and stored? ²³I have reserved it for the time of trouble, for the day of battle and war. ²⁴Where is the path to the origin of light? Where is the home of the east wind?

²⁵"Who created a channel for the torrents of rain? Who laid out the path for the lightning? ²⁶Who makes the rain fall on barren land, in a desert where no one lives? ²⁷Who sends the rain that satisfies the parched ground and makes the tender grass spring up?

²⁸"Does the rain have a father? Where does dew come from? ²⁹Who is the mother of the ice? Who gives birth to the frost from the heavens? ³⁰For the water turns to ice as hard as rock, and the surface of the water freezes.

³¹"Can you hold back the movements of the stars? Are you able to restrain the Pleiades or Orion? ³²Can you ensure the proper sequence of the seasons or guide the constellation of the Bear with her cubs across the heavens? ³³Do you know the laws of the universe and how God rules the earth?

³⁴"Can you shout to the clouds and make it rain? ³⁵Can you make lightning appear and cause it to strike as you direct it? ³⁶Who gives intuition and instinct? ³⁷Who is wise enough to count all the clouds? Who can tilt the water jars of heaven, ³⁸turning the dry dust to clumps of mud?

³⁹"Can you stalk prey for a lioness and satisfy the young lions' appetites ⁴⁰as they lie in their dens or crouch in the thicket? ⁴¹Who provides food for the ravens when their young cry out to God as they wander about in hunger?

CHAPTER 39

"Do you know when the mountain goats give birth? Have you watched as the wild deer are born? ²Do you know how many months they carry their young? Are you aware of the time of their delivery? ³They crouch down to give birth to their young and deliver their offspring. ⁴Their young grow up in the open fields, then leave their parents and never return.

⁵"Who makes the wild donkey wild? ⁶I have placed it in the wilderness; its home is the wasteland. ⁷It hates the noise of the city, and it has no driver to shout at it. ⁸The

38:7 Hebrew *sons of God.*

mountains are its pastureland, where it searches for every blade of grass.

⁹"Will the wild ox consent to being tamed? Will it stay in your stall? ¹⁰Can you hitch a wild ox to a plow? Will it plow a field for you? ¹¹Since it is so strong, can you trust it? Can you go away and trust the ox to do your work? ¹²Can you rely on it to return, bringing your grain to the threshing floor?

¹³"The ostrich flaps her wings grandly, but they are no match for the feathers of the stork. ¹⁴She lays her eggs on top of the earth, letting them be warmed in the dust. ¹⁵She doesn't worry that a foot might crush them or that wild animals might destroy them. ¹⁶She is harsh toward her young, as if they were not her own. She is unconcerned though they die, ¹⁷for God has deprived her of wisdom. He has given her no understanding. ¹⁸But whenever she jumps up to run, she passes the swiftest horse with its rider.

¹⁹"Have you given the horse its strength or clothed its neck with a flowing mane? ²⁰Did you give it the ability to leap forward like a locust? Its majestic snorting is something to hear! ²¹It paws the earth and rejoices in its strength. When it charges to war, ²²it is unafraid. It does not run from the sword. ²³The arrows rattle against it, and the spear and javelin flash. ²⁴Fiercely it paws the ground and rushes forward into battle when the trumpet blows. ²⁵It snorts at the sound of the bugle. It senses the battle even at a distance. It quivers at the noise of battle and the shout of the captain's commands.

²⁶"Are you the one who makes the hawk soar and spread its wings to the south? ²⁷Is it at your command that the eagle rises to the heights to make its nest? ²⁸It lives on the cliffs, making its home on a distant, rocky crag. ²⁹From there it hunts its prey, keeping watch with piercing eyes. ³⁰Its nestlings gulp down blood, for it feeds on the carcass of the slaughtered."

MAY 31 ☐ DAY 152
JOB 40 – 42
Job's Response and Reward

 OVERVIEW Though Job is willing to acknowledge God's power and wisdom, there yet remains the question of God's judgment (40:8). Once again God challenges Job to a face-to-face confrontation, this time over the issue of God's justice. Through interrogation, invitation, and illustration, God brings Job to the point of repentance for his presumptuous attitude. Now Job is willing to trust God completely, even though he doesn't completely understand his ways!

Chapters 40–41	Chapter 42	
God's Challenge to Job: "Can You Rule in My Place?"	Job's Response to God: Repentance	Job's Reward from God: Riches
1	6 7	17
The Sinfulness of Criticizing God		

 YOUR DAILY WALK Nowhere in the book of Job does God answer any of the burning questions that caused so much debate between Job and his friends. He simply answers the needs of Job's heart. God does not explain each phase of the battle, but he makes Job more than a conqueror in it. Job's knowledge of God before his trials was primarily secondhand, "I had heard about you before" (42:5), perhaps from his parents, friends, and acquaintances. But now, after passing through the fire of adversity, he sees God more clearly and knows that he can trust God personally.

Pray for a faith that will not shrink when washed in the waters of affliction.

God doesn't put just any of his children through a Job-like experience. Remember chapter 1 ' It was because of Job's God-fearing lifestyle that God permitted him to be tested by Satan in order that his devotion might run even deeper. Are you facing a severe test of your faith today? View it not as a sign that God has left you but as a token of his desire to deepen and strengthen your commitment to him. Complete this sentence: "Though I do not understand why, God is asking me to show my trust in him by _____, and I will!"

INSIGHT Double for Your Trouble
As his reward for faithfulness under fire, Job received back from God twice as many sheep, camels, oxen, and donkeys as he had had before, but not twice as many children (since he would one day see again the ones he had lost).

CHAPTER 40

Then the LORD said to Job, ²"Do you still want to argue with the Almighty? You are God's critic, but do you have the answers?"

³Then Job replied to the LORD, ⁴"I am nothing—how could I ever find the answers? I will put my hand over my mouth in silence. ⁵I have said too much already. I have nothing more to say."

⁶Then the LORD answered Job from the whirlwind:

⁷"Brace yourself, because I have some questions for you, and you must answer them. ⁸Are you going to discredit my justice and condemn me so you can say you are right? ⁹Are you as strong as God, and can you thunder with a voice like his? ¹⁰All right then, put on your robes of state, your majesty and splendor. ¹¹Give vent to your anger. Let it overflow against the proud. ¹²Humiliate the proud with a glance; walk on the wicked where they stand. ¹³Bury them in the dust. Imprison them in the world of the dead. ¹⁴Then even I would praise you, for your own strength would save you.

¹⁵"Take a look at the mighty hippopotamus.* I made it, just as I made you. It eats grass like an ox. ¹⁶See its powerful loins and the muscles of its belly. ¹⁷Its tail is as straight as a cedar. The sinews of its thighs are tightly knit together. ¹⁸Its bones are tubes of bronze. Its limbs are bars of iron. ¹⁹It is a prime example of God's amazing handiwork. Only its Creator can threaten it. ²⁰The mountains offer it their best food, where all the wild animals play. ²¹It lies down under the lotus plants, hidden by the reeds. ²²The lotus plants give it shade among the willows beside the stream. ²³It is not disturbed by raging rivers, not even when the swelling Jordan rushes down upon it. ²⁴No one can catch it off guard or put a ring in its nose and lead it away.

CHAPTER 41

"Can you catch a crocodile* with a hook or put a noose around its jaw? ²Can you tie it with a rope through the nose or pierce its jaw with a spike? ³Will it beg you for mercy or implore you for pity? ⁴Will it agree to work for you? Can you make it be your slave for life? ⁵Can you make it a pet like a bird, or give it to your little girls to play with? ⁶Will merchants try to buy it? Will they sell it in their shops? ⁷Will its hide be hurt by darts, or its head by a harpoon? ⁸If you lay a hand on it, you will never forget the battle that follows, and you will never try it again!

⁹"No, it is useless to try to capture it. The hunter who attempts it will be thrown down. ¹⁰And since no one dares to disturb the crocodile, who would dare to stand up to me? ¹¹Who will confront me and remain safe*? Everything under heaven is mine.

¹²"I want to emphasize the tremendous strength in the crocodile's limbs and throughout its enormous frame. ¹³Who can strip off its hide, and who can penetrate its double layer of armor*? ¹⁴Who could pry open its jaws? For its teeth are terrible! ¹⁵The overlapping scales on its back make a shield. ¹⁶They are close together so no air can get between them. ¹⁷They lock together so nothing can penetrate them.

¹⁸"When it sneezes, it flashes light! Its eyes are like the red of dawn. ¹⁹Fire and sparks leap from its mouth. ²⁰Smoke streams from its nostrils like steam from a boiling pot

---

40:15 Hebrew *at behemoth.*   **41:1** Hebrew *Leviathan;* also throughout the following passage.   **41:11** As in Greek version; Hebrew reads *confront me that I must pay.*   **41:13** As in Greek version; Hebrew reads *its bridle.*

on a fire of dry rushes. ²¹Yes, its breath would kindle coals, for flames shoot from its mouth.

²²"The tremendous strength in its neck strikes terror wherever it goes. ²³Its flesh is hard and firm, not soft and fat. ²⁴Its heart is as hard as rock, as hard as a millstone. ²⁵When it rises, the mighty are afraid, gripped by terror. ²⁶No sword can stop it, nor spear nor dart nor pointed shaft. ²⁷To the crocodile, iron is nothing but straw, and bronze is rotten wood. ²⁸Arrows cannot make it flee. Stones shot from a sling are as ineffective as straw. ²⁹Clubs do no good, and it laughs at the swish of the javelins. ³⁰Its belly is covered with scales as sharp as glass. They tear up the ground as it drags through the mud.

³¹"The crocodile makes the water boil with its commotion. It churns the depths. ³²The water glistens in its wake. One would think the sea had turned white. ³³There is nothing else so fearless anywhere on earth. ³⁴Of all the creatures, it is the proudest. It is the king of beasts."

CHAPTER 42
Then Job replied to the LORD:

²"I know that you can do anything, and no one can stop you. ³You ask, 'Who is this that questions my wisdom with such ignorance?' It is I. And I was talking about things I did not understand, things far too wonderful for me.

⁴"You said, 'Listen and I will speak! I have some questions for you, and you must answer them.'

⁵"I had heard about you before, but now I have seen you with my own eyes. ⁶I take back everything I said, and I sit in dust and ashes to show my repentance."

⁷After the LORD had finished speaking to Job, he said to Eliphaz the Temanite: "I am angry with you and with your two friends, for you have not been right in what you said about me, as my servant Job was. ⁸Now take seven young bulls and seven rams and go to my servant Job and offer a burnt offering for yourselves. My servant Job will pray for you, and I will accept his prayer on your behalf. I will not treat you as you deserve, for you have not been right in what you said about me, as my servant Job was."

⁹So Eliphaz the Temanite, Bildad the Shuhite, and Zophar the Naamathite did as the LORD commanded them, and the LORD accepted Job's prayer.

¹⁰When Job prayed for his friends, the LORD restored his fortunes. In fact, the LORD gave him twice as much as before! ¹¹Then all his brothers, sisters, and former friends came and feasted with him in his home. And they consoled him and comforted him because of all the trials the LORD had brought against him. And each of them brought him a gift of money* and a gold ring.

¹²So the LORD blessed Job in the second half of his life even more than in the beginning. For now he had fourteen thousand sheep, six thousand camels, one thousand teams of oxen, and one thousand female donkeys. ¹³He also gave Job seven more sons and three more daughters. ¹⁴He named his first daughter Jemimah, the second Keziah, and the third Keren-happuch. ¹⁵In all the land there were no other women as lovely as the daughters of Job. And their father put them into his will along with their brothers.

¹⁶Job lived 140 years after that, living to see four generations of his children and grandchildren. ¹⁷Then he died, an old man who had lived a long, good life.

42:11 Hebrew a *kesitah*; the value or weight of the kesitah is no longer known.

Psalms

WRITTEN by at least seven authors (of which David is the most notable), the book of Psalms spans one thousand years of Israel's rich history—from the time of Moses to the return from exile in Babylonia. The word *psalm* comes from a Greek word meaning "a song sung to the accompaniment of a plucked instrument." Used as the Temple hymnbook, the Psalms express the diversity of human emotion—praise to God in good times, fear of enemies in bad times, and an overriding confidence in God's goodness, majesty, and power.

Section	Book 1 (1–41)	Book 2 (42–72)	Book 3 (73–89)	Book 4 (90–106)	Book 5 (107–150)
Chief Author	David	David/ Asaph	Asaph	Anony-mous	David
No. of Psalms	41	31	17	17	44
Summary of Content	Songs of Worship	Hymns of National Interest		Anthems of Praise	
Possible Compiler	David	Hezekiah/Josiah		Ezra/Nehemiah	
Dates of Compilation	c. 1020–970 B.C.	c. 970–610 B.C.		Until c. 430 B.C.	
Topical Similarity to Pentateuch	Genesis: Mankind and Creation	Exodus: Delivered and Redeemed	Leviticus: Worship and Sanctuary	Numbers: Wilderness and Wandering	Deut: Scripture and Praise
Closing Doxology	41:13	72:18-19	89:52	106:48	150:1-6
Span of Authorship	About 1,000 Years (c. 1410–430 B.C.)				

JUNE 1 □ DAY 153
PSALMS 1–6
The Last Laugh

OVERVIEW The gateway to the book of Psalms is guarded by two major declarations concerning God's revelation of himself: He can be known through his Word, which brings blessing (Psalm 1), and he can be known in the person of his Son, who rules over creation (2). The servant of God can cling to him with confidence, knowing that God's help and consolation are assured in both good times and bad. No foe (3) nor failure (4), no frustration (5) nor cause for fainting (6) can change the fact that God is in control.

Psalm 1	Psalm 2	Psalm 3	Psalm 4	Psalm 5	Psalm 6
God's Word Prospers	God's Son Prevails	God's Servant Is Protected from			
		Foes	Failure	Frustration	Fainting
Proclamation		Petition			

YOUR DAILY WALK Laughter has been called the sensation of feeling good all over and showing it principally in one place. Everyone enjoys a good laugh . . . unless the laugh is at his or her expense. Then laughter can become a painful, rather than a pleasurable, experience.

The singing of a hymn should be a conversation between friends.

Psalm 2 describes the world's rulers gathered together. With great fury and indignation, they shake their fists in the face of God and threaten to overthrow his rule (2:3). And what is God's response to their impressive show of power and independence?

A cosmic guffaw, loud enough to shake the heavens (2:4), at the absurdity of the nations' rejecting the sovereign Creator who fashioned them! From God's perspective, it is a fool indeed who will not fall down and acknowledge his greatness. And those who put their trust in him are truly blessed.

Find a copy of today's newspaper, and spend a few minutes scanning it for news of the nations. Over each frightening or discouraging headline, write the words *God is in control!* That's a truth no one—king or commoner—can avoid.

INSIGHT Something Old, Something New

These words summarize the relationship between the Old and New Testaments: *The New is in the Old contained; the Old is in the New explained.* This statement can be proved by noting how the New Testament writers quote and explain portions of Psalm 2 in Acts 4:25-26 (quoting Psalm 2:1-2) and in Acts 13:33 and Hebrews 5:5 (both quoting Psalm 2:7).

BOOK ONE (Psalms 1–41)

PSALM 1

¹ Oh, the joys of those
who do not follow the advice of the
wicked,
or stand around with sinners,
or join in with scoffers.

² But they delight in doing everything
the LORD wants;
day and night they think about his
law.
³ They are like trees planted along the
riverbank,
bearing fruit each season without fail.

Their leaves never wither,
and in all they do, they prosper.

4 But this is not true of the wicked.
They are like worthless chaff,
scattered by the wind.
5 They will be condemned at the time
of judgment.
Sinners will have no place among
the godly.

6 For the LORD watches over the path
of the godly,
but the path of the wicked leads to
destruction.

PSALM 2

1 Why do the nations rage?
Why do the people waste their time
with futile plans?
2 The kings of the earth prepare for battle;
the rulers plot together
against the LORD
and against his anointed one.
3 "Let us break their chains," they cry,
"and free ourselves from this slavery."

4 But the one who rules in heaven laughs.
The Lord scoffs at them.
5 Then in anger he rebukes them,
terrifying them with his fierce fury.
6 For the LORD declares, "I have placed
my chosen king on the throne
in Jerusalem, my holy city.*"

7 The king proclaims the LORD's decree:
"The LORD said to me, 'You are my son.*
Today I have become your Father.*
8 Only ask, and I will give you the
nations as your inheritance,
the ends of the earth as your
possession.
9 You will break them with an iron rod
and smash them like clay pots.'"

10 Now then, you kings, act wisely!
Be warned, you rulers of the earth!
11 Serve the LORD with reverent fear,
and rejoice with trembling.
12 Submit to God's royal son, or he will
become angry,
and you will be destroyed in the
midst of your pursuits—
for his anger can flare up in an
instant.

But what joy for all who find protection
in him!

PSALM 3

*A psalm of David, regarding the time David fled
from his son Absalom.*

1 O LORD, I have so many enemies;
so many are against me.
2 So many are saying,
"God will never rescue him!"
                              *Interlude**

3 But you, O LORD, are a shield around me,
my glory, and the one who lifts my
head high.
4 I cried out to the LORD,
and he answered me from his holy
mountain.   *Interlude*

5 I lay down and slept.
I woke up in safety,
for the LORD was watching over me.
6 I am not afraid of ten thousand enemies
who surround me on every side.

7 Arise, O LORD!
Rescue me, my God!
Slap all my enemies in the face!
Shatter the teeth of the wicked!

8 Victory comes from you, O LORD.
May your blessings rest on your
people.   *Interlude*

PSALM 4

*For the choir director: A psalm of David, to be
accompanied by stringed instruments.*

1 Answer me when I call,
O God who declares me innocent.
Take away my distress.
Have mercy on me and hear my
prayer.

2 How long will you people ruin my
reputation?
How long will you make these
groundless accusations?
How long will you pursue lies?
                              Interlude

3 You can be sure of this:
The LORD has set apart the godly for
himself.
The LORD will answer when I call to
him.

4 Don't sin by letting anger gain control
over you.
Think about it overnight and remain
silent.   *Interlude*

2:6 Hebrew *on Zion, my holy mountain.*   2:7a Or *Son;* also in 2:12.   2:7b Or *Today I reveal you as my son.*   3:2 Hebrew *Selah.* The
meaning of this word is uncertain, though it is probably a musical or literary term. It is rendered *Interlude* throughout the Psalms.

5 Offer proper sacrifices,
   and trust in the LORD.

6 Many people say, "Who will show us
   better times?"
   Let the smile of your face shine on
   us, LORD.
7 You have given me greater joy
   than those who have abundant
   harvests of grain and wine.

8 I will lie down in peace and sleep,
   for you alone, O LORD, will keep me
   safe.

PSALM 5

*For the choir director: A psalm of David, to be
accompanied by the flute.*

1 O LORD, hear me as I pray;
   pay attention to my groaning.
2 Listen to my cry for help, my King and
   my God,
   for I will never pray to anyone but you.
3 Listen to my voice in the morning, LORD.
   Each morning I bring my requests to
   you and wait expectantly.

4 O God, you take no pleasure in
   wickedness;
   you cannot tolerate the slightest sin.
5 Therefore, the proud will not be
   allowed to stand in your presence,
   for you hate all who do evil.
6 You will destroy those who tell lies.
   The LORD detests murderers and
   deceivers.

7 Because of your unfailing love, I can
   enter your house;
   with deepest awe I will worship at
   your Temple.
8 Lead me in the right path, O LORD,
   or my enemies will conquer me.
   Tell me clearly what to do,
   and show me which way to turn.

9 My enemies cannot speak one truthful
   word.
   Their deepest desire is to destroy
   others.
   Their talk is foul, like the stench from
   an open grave.
   Their speech is filled with flattery.

6: TITLE Hebrew *with stringed instruments; according to the sheminith.*

10 O God, declare them guilty.
   Let them be caught in their own
   traps.
   Drive them away because of their
   many sins,
   for they rebel against you.

11 But let all who take refuge in you
   rejoice;
   let them sing joyful praises forever.
   Protect them,
   so all who love your name may be
   filled with joy.
12 For you bless the godly, O LORD,
   surrounding them with your shield
   of love.

PSALM 6

*For the choir director: A psalm of David, to be
accompanied by an eight-stringed instrument.**

1 O LORD, do not rebuke me in your
   anger
   or discipline me in your rage.
2 Have compassion on me, LORD, for I
   am weak.
   Heal me, LORD, for my body is in
   agony.
3 I am sick at heart.
   How long, O LORD, until you restore
   me?

4 Return, O LORD, and rescue me.
   Save me because of your unfailing
   love.
5 For in death, who remembers you?
   Who can praise you from the grave?

6 I am worn out from sobbing.
   Every night tears drench my bed;
   my pillow is wet from weeping.
7 My vision is blurred by grief;
   my eyes are worn out because of all
   my enemies.

8 Go away, all you who do evil,
   for the LORD has heard my crying.
9 The LORD has heard my plea;
   the LORD will answer my prayer.
10 May all my enemies be disgraced and
   terrified.
   May they suddenly turn back in
   shame.

JUNE 2 ☐ DAY 154
PSALMS 7–12
Let's Just Praise the Lord

 OVERVIEW The enemies of God's people are also the enemies of God. Responding to these enemies is David's burden in each of the psalms in today's reading. In the face of dangerous opposition, David seeks God's justice (Psalm 7), protection (9–10), and deliverance (11–12). The God who created people to rule over his creation is the God who will one day silence and subdue his enemies (8).

Psalm 7	Psalm 8	Psalms 9–10	Psalms 11–12
Desire for Vindication	Delight in Creation	Defense against Enemies	Deliverance from the Wicked
The Righteous Look to God		God Looks after the Righteous	

One who is sincere is sincere in all places and at all times.

YOUR DAILY WALK A famous author once commented that "one of the difficulties in language is that all our words have lost their edge from loose usage." Sadly, the church is not immune to this phenomenon. Christian clichés develop so quickly . . . so subtly. Almost before you realize what's happening, words that once prompted heartfelt response have turned into empty shells, phrases spoken more from habit than from the heart.

The exercise of praising God never became a well-worn routine for David. Rather, it involved a deliberate, reasoned response to God. The first two verses of Psalm 9 summarize David's pattern of praise. First, he rejoices in God's person; then he publicly proclaims God's wondrous ways. Put them together, and you have meditation turned into communication, inward delight turned into outward demonstration. In a word, *praise*.

Try David's plan for praising the Lord. Take an aspect of God's character that you discover while reading today's passage, and translate it into the language of praise to God by singing a hymn, composing a short poem of praise, or reading aloud the words of Psalm 9. Make this a habit, and you—like David—will become a person after God's own heart!

 INSIGHT The Psalm with the Split Personality
The absence of a title in Psalm 10 and the sequence of initial letters in the Hebrew text (every other verse of Psalms 9–10 begins with a successive letter of the Hebrew alphabet, forming a handy and memorable acrostic) have led many commentators to conclude that Psalms 9–10 were originally one long song composed by David.

PSALM 7
A psalm of David, which he sang to the LORD concerning Cush of the tribe of Benjamin.

¹ I come to you for protection, O LORD
my God.
Save me from my persecutors—
rescue me!
² If you don't, they will maul me like a lion,
tearing me to pieces with no one to
rescue me.

³ O LORD my God, if I have done wrong
or am guilty of injustice,
⁴ if I have betrayed a friend
or plundered my enemy without
cause,
⁵ then let my enemies capture me.
Let them trample me into the
ground.
Let my honor be left in the dust.
Interlude

⁶ Arise, O LORD, in anger!
   Stand up against the fury of my
      enemies!
   Wake up, my God, and bring justice!
⁷ Gather the nations before you.
   Sit on your throne high above them.
⁸ The LORD passes judgment on the
      nations.
   Declare me righteous, O LORD,
      for I am innocent, O Most High!
⁹ End the wickedness of the ungodly,
      but help all those who obey you.
   For you look deep within the mind
      and heart,
         O righteous God.

¹⁰ God is my shield,
      saving those whose hearts are true
         and right.
¹¹ God is a judge who is perfectly fair.
   He is angry with the wicked every
      day.

¹² If a person does not repent,
      God* will sharpen his sword;
   he will bend and string his bow.
¹³ He will prepare his deadly weapons
      and ignite his flaming arrows.

¹⁴ The wicked conceive evil;
      they are pregnant with trouble
         and give birth to lies.
¹⁵ They dig a pit to trap others
      and then fall into it themselves.
¹⁶ They make trouble,
      but it backfires on them.
   They plan violence for others,
      but it falls on their own heads.

¹⁷ I will thank the LORD because he is
      just;
   I will sing praise to the name of the
      LORD Most High.

PSALM 8

*For the choir director: A psalm of David, to be
accompanied by a stringed instrument.**

¹ O LORD, our Lord, the majesty of your
      name fills the earth!
   Your glory is higher than the heavens.

² You have taught children and nursing
      infants
   to give you praise.*
   They silence your enemies
      who were seeking revenge.

³ When I look at the night sky and see
      the work of your fingers—
   the moon and the stars you have set
      in place—
⁴ what are mortals that you should think
      of us,
   mere humans that you should care
      for us?*
⁵ For you made us only a little lower
      than God,*
   and you crowned us with glory and
      honor.
⁶ You put us in charge of everything you
      made,
   giving us authority over all things—
⁷ the sheep and the cattle
      and all the wild animals,
⁸ the birds in the sky, the fish in the sea,
   and everything that swims the ocean
      currents.

⁹ O LORD, our Lord, the majesty of your
      name fills the earth!

PSALM 9

*For the choir director: A psalm of David, to be sung
to the tune "Death of the Son."*

¹ I will thank you, LORD, with all my
      heart;
   I will tell of all the marvelous things
      you have done.
² I will be filled with joy because of you.
   I will sing praises to your name,
      O Most High.

³ My enemies turn away in retreat;
      they are overthrown and destroyed
         before you.
⁴ For you have judged in my favor;
      from your throne, you have judged
         with fairness.

⁵ You have rebuked the nations and
      destroyed the wicked;
   you have wiped out their names
      forever.
⁶ My enemies have met their doom;
      their cities are perpetual ruins.
   Even the memory of their uprooted
      cities is lost.

⁷ But the LORD reigns forever,
      executing judgment from his throne.
⁸ He will judge the world with justice
      and rule the nations with fairness.

7:12 Hebrew *he.*   **8:** TITLE Hebrew *according to the gittith.*   **8:2** As in Greek version; Hebrew reads *to show strength.*   **8:4** Hebrew
what is man that you should think of him, the son of man that you should care for him?   **8:5** Or *a little lower than the angels;* Hebrew
reads *Elohim.*

⁹ The LORD is a shelter for the oppressed,
  a refuge in times of trouble.
¹⁰ Those who know your name trust in
   you,
   for you, O LORD, have never
     abandoned anyone who searches
     for you.

¹¹ Sing praises to the LORD who reigns in
   Jerusalem.*
   Tell the world about his
     unforgettable deeds.
¹² For he who avenges murder cares for
   the helpless.
   He does not ignore those who cry
     to him for help.

¹³ LORD, have mercy on me.
   See how I suffer at the hands of those
     who hate me.
   Snatch me back from the jaws of
     death.
¹⁴ Save me, so I can praise you publicly at
   Jerusalem's gates,
   so I can rejoice that you have rescued
     me.

¹⁵ The nations have fallen into the pit
   they dug for others.
   They have been caught in their own
     trap.
¹⁶ The LORD is known for his justice.
   The wicked have trapped themselves
     in their own snares.
                         *Quiet Interlude**

¹⁷ The wicked will go down to the grave.*
   This is the fate of all the nations who
     ignore God.
¹⁸ For the needy will not be forgotten
   forever;
   the hopes of the poor will not always
     be crushed.

¹⁹ Arise, O LORD!
   Do not let mere mortals defy you!
   Let the nations be judged in your
     presence!
²⁰ Make them tremble in fear, O LORD.
   Let them know they are merely
     human.   *Interlude*

PSALM 10

¹ O LORD, why do you stand so far away?
  Why do you hide when I need you
    the most?
² Proud and wicked people viciously
  oppress the poor.

Let them be caught in the evil they
  plan for others.
³ For they brag about their evil desires;
  they praise the greedy and curse the
    LORD.
⁴ These wicked people are too proud to
  seek God.
  They seem to think that God is
    dead.
⁵ Yet they succeed in everything they
  do.
  They do not see your punishment
    awaiting them.
  They pour scorn on all their enemies.
⁶ They say to themselves, "Nothing bad
  will ever happen to us!
  We will be free of trouble forever!"

⁷ Their mouths are full of cursing, lies,
  and threats.
  Trouble and evil are on the tips of
    their tongues.
⁸ They lurk in dark alleys,
  murdering the innocent who pass by.

They are always searching
  for some helpless victim.
⁹ Like lions they crouch silently,
  waiting to pounce on the helpless.
  Like hunters they capture their victims
    and drag them away in nets.
¹⁰ The helpless are overwhelmed and
   collapse;
   they fall beneath the strength of the
     wicked.
¹¹ The wicked say to themselves, "God
   isn't watching!
   He will never notice!"

¹² Arise, O LORD!
   Punish the wicked, O God!
   Do not forget the helpless!
¹³ Why do the wicked get away with
   cursing God?
   How can they think, "God will never
     call us to account"?

¹⁴ But you do see the trouble and grief
   they cause.
   You take note of it and punish
     them.
   The helpless put their trust in you.
   You are the defender of orphans.

¹⁵ Break the arms of these wicked, evil
   people!
   Go after them until the last one is
     destroyed!

9:11 Hebrew *Zion*; also in 9:14.   **9:16** Hebrew *Higgaion Selah*. The meaning of this phrase is uncertain.   **9:17** Hebrew *to Sheol*.

16 The LORD is king forever and ever!
　　Let those who worship other gods
　　　be swept from the land.
17 LORD, you know the hopes of the
　　　helpless.
　　Surely you will listen to their cries
　　　and comfort them.
18 You will bring justice to the orphans
　　　and the oppressed,
　　so people can no longer terrify
　　　them.

PSALM 11

For the choir director: A psalm of David.

1 I trust in the LORD for protection.
　　So why do you say to me,
　"Fly to the mountains for safety!
2 　The wicked are stringing their bows
　　and setting their arrows in the
　　　bowstrings.
　　They shoot from the shadows at
　　　those who do right.
3 The foundations of law and order have
　　　collapsed.
　　What can the righteous do?"

4 But the LORD is in his holy Temple;
　　the LORD still rules from heaven.
　He watches everything closely,
　　examining everyone on earth.
5 The LORD examines both the righteous
　　and the wicked.
　He hates everyone who loves
　　violence.
6 He rains down blazing coals on the
　　wicked,
　　punishing them with burning sulfur
　　and scorching winds.

12: TITLE Hebrew *according to the sheminith.*

7 For the LORD is righteous, and he loves
　　justice.
　　Those who do what is right will see
　　　his face.

PSALM 12

*For the choir director: A psalm of David, to be
accompanied by an eight-stringed instrument.**

1 Help, O LORD, for the godly are fast
　　disappearing!
　　The faithful have vanished from the
　　　earth!
2 Neighbors lie to each other,
　　speaking with flattering lips and
　　　insincere hearts.
3 May the LORD bring their flattery to
　　an end
　　and silence their proud tongues.
4 They say, "We will lie to our hearts'
　　content.
　　Our lips are our own—who can
　　stop us?"
5 The LORD replies, "I have seen violence
　　done to the helpless,
　　and I have heard the groans of the
　　poor.
　Now I will rise up to rescue them,
　　as they have longed for me to do."
6 The LORD's promises are pure,
　　like silver refined in a furnace,
　　purified seven times over.
7 Therefore, LORD, we know you will
　　protect the oppressed,
　　preserving them forever from this
　　lying generation,
8 even though the wicked strut about,
　　and evil is praised throughout the
　　land.

JUNE 3　□ DAY 155
PSALMS 13–18
No Fooling

OVERVIEW Today, as in David's day, believers in God face many
challenges to their faith, both from their own fearful hearts (Psalm 13)
and from those who foolishly deny God's existence (14). The answer?
Walking in fellowship with God (15), being sustained by the promises
of God (16), and drawing upon God's ever-available resources (17–18).

Psalm 13	Psalm 14	Psalms 15–16	Psalm 17	Psalm 18
Anxious Believers	Atheistic Fools	Promise of Life	Prayer for Protection	Praise for Preservation
Challenged Faith		Confident Faith		

If God gives himself to us in promises, we must give ourselves to him in duties.

YOUR DAILY WALK Webster defines an *atheist* as "one who denies the existence of God." But Webster stops short of answering the question "Why do atheists refuse to believe in God?" How would you answer that question? Is it because

- they cannot accept God rationally or intellectually?
- they are untaught and ignorant of the things of God?
- they are unwilling to repent of sin in their lives?

While each of those answers may, in fact, be true, Psalm 14 highlights the root problem. Atheism is the by-product of a proud unwillingness to acknowledge sin before a holy God. David's use of such descriptions as "corrupt . . . evil . . . wicked" shows that the basic issue is moral, not intellectual.

Understanding that will help you the next time you share your faith. Rather than trying to prove God's existence (a common approach), focus instead on forgiveness in Jesus Christ. Intellectual objections can—and should—be answered. But only the grace of God can remove the guilt and stain of sin. Though you may not have the answers to all of the questions, you can be confident you have the answer to the need of every human heart because you have Christ in *your* heart! And that truth will prompt you to join David in praising God: "But I trust in your unfailing love. I will rejoice because you have rescued me. I will sing to the LORD because he has been so good to me" (13:5-6).

INSIGHT Haven't I Sung That Somewhere Before?
If the words of Psalm 18 seem familiar, it's probably because you read them before in 2 Samuel 22. Do you recall the occasion that prompted David to compose these verses?

PSALM 13
For the choir director: A psalm of David.

¹ O LORD, how long will you forget me?
   Forever?
   How long will you look the other way?
² How long must I struggle with anguish
      in my soul,
   with sorrow in my heart every day?
   How long will my enemy have the
      upper hand?

³ Turn and answer me, O LORD my God!
   Restore the light to my eyes, or I will
      die.
⁴ Don't let my enemies gloat, saying,
   "We have defeated him!"
   Don't let them rejoice at my downfall.

⁵ But I trust in your unfailing love.
   I will rejoice because you have
      rescued me.
⁶ I will sing to the LORD
   because he has been so good to me.

PSALM 14
For the choir director: A psalm of David.

¹ Only fools say in their hearts,
   "There is no God."
   They are corrupt, and their actions are
      evil;
   no one does good!

² The LORD looks down from heaven
      on the entire human race;
   he looks to see if there is even one with
      real understanding,
   one who seeks for God.
³ But no, all have turned away from
      God;
   all have become corrupt.
   No one does good,
      not even one!

⁴ Will those who do evil never learn?
   They eat up my people like bread;
   they wouldn't think of praying to the
      LORD.

5 Terror will grip them,
  for God is with those who obey him.
6 The wicked frustrate the plans of the
    oppressed,
  but the LORD will protect his people.

7 Oh, that salvation would come from
    Mount Zion to rescue Israel!
  For when the LORD restores his
    people,
  Jacob will shout with joy, and Israel
    will rejoice.

PSALM 15
A psalm of David.

1 Who may worship in your sanctuary,
    LORD?
  Who may enter your presence on
    your holy hill?

2 Those who lead blameless lives
    and do what is right,
  speaking the truth from sincere hearts.
3 Those who refuse to slander others
    or harm their neighbors
    or speak evil of their friends.
4 Those who despise persistent sinners,
    and honor the faithful followers of
      the LORD
    and keep their promises even when
      it hurts.
5 Those who do not charge interest on
    the money they lend,
    and who refuse to accept bribes to
      testify against the innocent.

  Such people will stand firm forever.

PSALM 16
A psalm of David.

1 Keep me safe, O God,
    for I have come to you for refuge.

2 I said to the LORD, "You are my Master!
    All the good things I have are from
      you."
3 The godly people in the land
    are my true heroes!
    I take pleasure in them!
4 Those who chase after other gods will
    be filled with sorrow.
    I will not take part in their sacrifices
    or even speak the names of their gods.

5 LORD, you alone are my inheritance,
    my cup of blessing.
    You guard all that is mine.

6 The land you have given me is a
    pleasant land.
    What a wonderful inheritance!

7 I will bless the LORD who guides me;
    even at night my heart instructs
      me.
8 I know the LORD is always with me.
    I will not be shaken, for he is right
      beside me.

9 No wonder my heart is filled with
    joy,
    and my mouth* shouts his praises!
    My body rests in safety.
10 For you will not leave my soul among
    the dead*
    or allow your godly one* to rot in the
      grave.
11 You will show me the way of life,
    granting me the joy of your presence
    and the pleasures of living with you
      forever.

PSALM 17
A prayer of David.

1 O LORD, hear my plea for justice.
    Listen to my cry for help.
    Pay attention to my prayer,
    for it comes from an honest heart.
2 Declare me innocent,
    for you know those who do right.

3 You have tested my thoughts and
    examined my heart in the night.
    You have scrutinized me and found
      nothing amiss,
    for I am determined not to sin in
      what I say.
4 I have followed your commands,
    which have kept me from going
      along with cruel and evil people.
5 My steps have stayed on your path;
    I have not wavered from following
      you.

6 I am praying to you because I know
    you will answer, O God.
    Bend down and listen as I pray.
7 Show me your unfailing love in
    wonderful ways.
    You save with your strength
    those who seek refuge from their
      enemies.
8 Guard me as the apple of your eye.
    Hide me in the shadow of your
      wings.

16:9 As in Greek version; Hebrew reads *glory.*   **16:10a** Hebrew *in Sheol.*   **16:10b** Or *your Holy One.*

⁹ Protect me from wicked people who
attack me,
from murderous enemies who
surround me.

¹⁰ They are without pity.
Listen to their boasting.
¹¹ They track me down, surround me,
and throw me to the ground.
¹² They are like hungry lions, eager to
tear me apart—
like young lions in hiding, waiting
for their chance.

¹³ Arise, O LORD!
Stand against them and bring them
to their knees!
Rescue me from the wicked with
your sword!
¹⁴ Save me by your mighty hand, O LORD,
from those whose only concern is
earthly gain.
May they have their punishment in full.
May their children inherit more of
the same,
and may the judgment continue to
their children's children.

¹⁵ But because I have done what is right,
I will see you.
When I awake, I will be fully
satisfied,
for I will see you face to face.

PSALM 18

*For the choir director: A psalm of David, the
servant of the LORD. He sang this song to the
LORD on the day the LORD rescued him from
all his enemies and from Saul.*

¹ I love you, LORD; you are my strength.
² The LORD is my rock, my fortress, and
my savior;
my God is my rock, in whom I find
protection.
He is my shield, the strength of my
salvation, and my stronghold.
³ I will call on the LORD, who is worthy
of praise,
for he saves me from my enemies.

⁴ The ropes of death surrounded me;
the floods of destruction swept over
me.
⁵ The grave* wrapped its ropes around
me;
death itself stared me in the face.

⁶ But in my distress I cried out to the
LORD;
yes, I prayed to my God for help.
He heard me from his sanctuary;
my cry reached his ears.

⁷ Then the earth quaked and trembled;
the foundations of the mountains
shook;
they quaked because of his anger.
⁸ Smoke poured from his nostrils;
fierce flames leaped from his mouth;
glowing coals flamed forth from him.
⁹ He opened the heavens and came
down;
dark storm clouds were beneath his
feet.
¹⁰ Mounted on a mighty angel,* he flew,
soaring on the wings of the wind.
¹¹ He shrouded himself in darkness,
veiling his approach with dense rain
clouds.
¹² The brilliance of his presence broke
through the clouds,
raining down hail and burning coals.
¹³ The LORD thundered from heaven;
the Most High gave a mighty shout.*
¹⁴ He shot his arrows and scattered his
enemies;
his lightning flashed, and they were
greatly confused.
¹⁵ Then at your command, O LORD,
at the blast of your breath,
the bottom of the sea could be seen,
and the foundations of the earth
were laid bare.

¹⁶ He reached down from heaven and
rescued me;
he drew me out of deep waters.
¹⁷ He delivered me from my powerful
enemies,
from those who hated me and were
too strong for me.
¹⁸ They attacked me at a moment when
I was weakest,
but the LORD upheld me.
¹⁹ He led me to a place of safety;
he rescued me because he delights
in me.
²⁰ The LORD rewarded me for doing right;
he compensated me because of my
innocence.
²¹ For I have kept the ways of the LORD;
I have not turned from my God to
follow evil.

18:5 Hebrew *Sheol*. 18:10 Hebrew *a cherub*. 18:13 As in Greek version (see also 2 Sam 22:14); Hebrew adds *raining down hail and burning coals.*

²² For all his laws are constantly before
     me;
     I have never abandoned his
        principles.
²³ I am blameless before God;
     I have kept myself from sin.
²⁴ The LORD rewarded me for doing right,
     because of the innocence of my
        hands in his sight.

²⁵ To the faithful you show yourself
        faithful;
     to those with integrity you show
        integrity.
²⁶ To the pure you show yourself pure,
     but to the wicked you show yourself
        hostile.
²⁷ You rescue those who are humble,
     but you humiliate the proud.
²⁸ LORD, you have brought light to my life;
     my God, you light up my darkness.
²⁹ In your strength I can crush an army;
     with my God I can scale any wall.

³⁰ As for God, his way is perfect.
     All the LORD's promises prove true.
     He is a shield for all who look to him
        for protection.
³¹ For who is God except the LORD?
     Who but our God is a solid rock?
³² God arms me with strength;
     he has made my way safe.
³³ He makes me as surefooted as a deer,
     leading me safely along the
        mountain heights.
³⁴ He prepares me for battle;
     he strengthens me to draw a bow
        of bronze.
³⁵ You have given me the shield of your
        salvation.
     Your right hand supports me;
     your gentleness has made me great.
³⁶ You have made a wide path for my feet
     to keep them from slipping.

³⁷ I chased my enemies and caught them;
     I did not stop until they were
        conquered.

³⁸ I struck them down so they could not
        get up;
     they fell beneath my feet.
³⁹ You have armed me with strength for
        the battle;
     you have subdued my enemies
        under my feet.
⁴⁰ You made them turn and run;
     I have destroyed all who hated me.
⁴¹ They called for help, but no one came
        to rescue them.
     They cried to the LORD, but he
        refused to answer them.
⁴² I ground them as fine as dust carried
        by the wind.
     I swept them into the gutter like dirt.

⁴³ You gave me victory over my accusers.
     You appointed me as the ruler over
        nations;
     people I don't even know now serve
        me.
⁴⁴ As soon as they hear of me, they
        submit;
     foreigners cringe before me.
⁴⁵ They all lose their courage
     and come trembling from their
        strongholds.

⁴⁶ The LORD lives! Blessed be my rock!
     May the God of my salvation be
        exalted!
⁴⁷ He is the God who pays back those
        who harm me;
     he subdues the nations under me
⁴⁸   and rescues me from my enemies.
     You hold me safe beyond the reach
        of my enemies;
     you save me from violent opponents.
⁴⁹ For this, O LORD, I will praise you
        among the nations;
     I will sing joyfully to your name.
⁵⁰ You give great victories to your king;
     you show unfailing love to your
        anointed,
     to David and all his descendants
        forever.

JUNE 4 ☐ DAY 156
PSALMS 19–24
In God We Trust

OVERVIEW God's involvement in the lives of his people is the dominant theme of the psalms in today's reading. God reveals himself in the world and in the Word (Psalm 19); he gives enablement and victory to those who do battle for him (20–21); he sends his Messiah to suffer on the cross (22), shepherd his people (23), and establish his rule over the earth (24). Indeed, he is worthy to be trusted!

Psalm 19	Psalm 20	Psalm 21	Psalms 22–24
Works and Words	Prayer before Victory	Praise after Victory	Portraits of Messiah
Revelation	Reliance		Redeemer

They are well kept whom God keeps.

YOUR DAILY WALK Question: What do retirement funds, college degrees, and nuclear submarines have in common?

Answer: They are all designed to give you a sense of security. Security for your future, security for your vocation, security for your protection. But do they?

Security in an increasingly insecure world is one of today's most sought after—and elusive—commodities.

Nearly three thousand years ago, the ultimate military weapons were the chariot and the horse. Armies that could field a cavalry or chariot brigade were considered virtually invincible.

But Israel was to be different. God's law forbade her king to multiply horses (Deuteronomy 17:16). Rather than put her confidence in strategic arms, Israel was to trust in the everlasting arms, for God had promised to fight for his people. That is why David's affirmation of trust in a delivering God (Psalm 20:7) is so appropriate. It's the answer to the national security problem—both in his day and yours.

On scratch paper, list in pencil five things the world says will make you secure. Then across the list, write in ink the words of Psalm 20:7: "We boast in the LORD our God." America's coins are stamped "In God We Trust." What sentiment is stamped on your heart?

INSIGHT And Speaking of Chariots . . .

Israel's security was often threatened by chariot-equipped armies. What was the outcome of the skirmishes described in Exodus 14? in Judges 4? in 2 Kings 6?

PSALM 19
For the choir director: A psalm of David.

¹ The heavens tell of the glory of God.
  The skies display his marvelous
    craftsmanship.
² Day after day they continue to speak;
  night after night they make him
    known.
³ They speak without a sound or a word;
  their voice is silent in the skies;*

⁴ yet their message has gone out to all
    the earth,
  and their words to all the world.

The sun lives in the heavens
  where God placed it.
⁵ It bursts forth like a radiant bride-
    groom
  after his wedding.
It rejoices like a great athlete
  eager to run the race.

19:3 Or *There is no speech or language where their voice is not heard.*

⁶ The sun rises at one end of the heavens
  and follows its course to the other
  end.
  Nothing can hide from its heat.

⁷ The law of the LORD is perfect,
  reviving the soul.
The decrees of the LORD are
  trustworthy,
  making wise the simple.
⁸ The commandments of the LORD are
  right,
  bringing joy to the heart.
The commands of the LORD are clear,
  giving insight to life.
⁹ Reverence for the LORD is pure,
  lasting forever.
The laws of the LORD are true;
  each one is fair.
¹⁰ They are more desirable than gold,
  even the finest gold.
They are sweeter than honey,
  even honey dripping from the comb.
¹¹ They are a warning to those who hear
  them;
  there is great reward for those who
  obey them.

¹² How can I know all the sins lurking
  in my heart?
  Cleanse me from these hidden
  faults.
¹³ Keep me from deliberate sins!
  Don't let them control me.
Then I will be free of guilt
  and innocent of great sin.

¹⁴ May the words of my mouth and the
  thoughts of my heart
  be pleasing to you,
  O LORD, my rock and my redeemer.

PSALM 20
For the choir director: A psalm of David.

¹ In times of trouble, may the LORD
  respond to your cry.
  May the God of Israel* keep you safe
  from all harm.
² May he send you help from his
  sanctuary
  and strengthen you from Jerusalem.*
³ May he remember all your gifts
  and look favorably on your burnt
  offerings.   *Interlude*

⁴ May he grant your heart's desire
  and fulfill all your plans.

⁵ May we shout for joy when we hear
  of your victory,
  flying banners to honor our God.
May the LORD answer all your prayers.

⁶ Now I know that the LORD saves his
  anointed king.
He will answer him from his holy
  heaven
  and rescue him by his great power.
⁷ Some nations boast of their armies and
  weapons,*
  but we boast in the LORD our God.
⁸ Those nations will fall down and
  collapse,
  but we will rise up and stand firm.

⁹ Give victory to our king, O LORD!
  Respond to our cry for help.

PSALM 21
For the choir director: A psalm of David.

¹ How the king rejoices in your strength,
  O LORD!
He shouts with joy because of your
  victory.
² For you have given him his heart's desire;
  you have held back nothing that he
  requested.   *Interlude*

³ You welcomed him back with success
  and prosperity.
You placed a crown of finest gold
  on his head.
⁴ He asked you to preserve his life,
  and you have granted his request.
The days of his life stretch on forever.
⁵ Your victory brings him great honor,
  and you have clothed him with
  splendor and majesty.
⁶ You have endowed him with eternal
  blessings.
You have given him the joy of being
  in your presence.
⁷ For the king trusts in the LORD.
The unfailing love of the Most High
  will keep him from stumbling.

⁸ You will capture all your enemies.
Your strong right hand will seize all
  those who hate you.
⁹ You will destroy them as in a flaming
  furnace
  when you appear.
The LORD will consume them in his
  anger;
  fire will devour them.

20:1 Hebrew *of Jacob*.   20:2 Hebrew *Zion*.   20:7 Hebrew *chariots and horses*.

¹⁰ You will wipe their children from the
         face of the earth;
      they will never have descendants.
¹¹ Although they plot against you,
      their evil schemes will never succeed.
¹² For they will turn and run
      when they see your arrows aimed
         at them.

¹³ We praise you, LORD, for all your
         glorious power.
      With music and singing we celebrate
         your mighty acts.

PSALM 22

*For the choir director: A psalm of David, to be sung
to the tune "Doe of the Dawn."*

¹ My God, my God! Why have you
      forsaken me?
   Why do you remain so distant?
   Why do you ignore my cries for help?
² Every day I call to you, my God, but
      you do not answer.
   Every night you hear my voice, but
      I find no relief.

³ Yet you are holy.
      The praises of Israel surround your
         throne.
⁴ Our ancestors trusted in you,
      and you rescued them.
⁵ You heard their cries for help and
         saved them.
      They put their trust in you and were
         never disappointed.

⁶ But I am a worm and not a man.
      I am scorned and despised by all!
⁷ Everyone who sees me mocks me.
      They sneer and shake their heads,
         saying,
⁸ "Is this the one who relies on the LORD?
      Then let the LORD save him!
   If the LORD loves him so much,
      let the LORD rescue him!"

⁹ Yet you brought me safely from my
      mother's womb
   and led me to trust you when I was
      a nursing infant.
¹⁰ I was thrust upon you at my birth.
      You have been my God from the
         moment I was born.

¹¹ Do not stay so far from me,
      for trouble is near,
      and no one else can help me.

¹² My enemies surround me like a herd
         of bulls;
      fierce bulls of Bashan have hemmed
         me in!
¹³ Like roaring lions attacking their prey,
      they come at me with open mouths.
¹⁴ My life is poured out like water,
      and all my bones are out of joint.
   My heart is like wax,
      melting within me.
¹⁵ My strength has dried up like
         sunbaked clay.
      My tongue sticks to the roof of my
         mouth.
      You have laid me in the dust and left
         me for dead.

¹⁶ My enemies surround me like a pack
         of dogs;
      an evil gang closes in on me.
      They have pierced my hands and
         feet.
¹⁷ I can count every bone in my body.
      My enemies stare at me and gloat.
¹⁸ They divide my clothes among
         themselves
      and throw dice* for my garments.

¹⁹ O LORD, do not stay away!
      You are my strength; come quickly
         to my aid!
²⁰ Rescue me from a violent death;
      spare my precious life from these
         dogs.
²¹ Snatch me from the lions' jaws,
      and from the horns of these wild
         oxen.

²² Then I will declare the wonder of your
         name to my brothers and sisters.
      I will praise you among all your
         people.
²³ Praise the LORD, all you who fear him!
      Honor him, all you descendants of
         Jacob!
      Show him reverence, all you
         descendants of Israel!
²⁴ For he has not ignored the suffering
         of the needy.
      He has not turned and walked
         away.
      He has listened to their cries for
         help.
²⁵ I will praise you among all the people;
      I will fulfill my vows in the presence
         of those who worship you.

22:18 Hebrew *cast lots.*

²⁶ The poor will eat and be satisfied.
  All who seek the LORD will praise
    him.
  Their hearts will rejoice with
    everlasting joy.
²⁷ The whole earth will acknowledge the
    LORD and return to him.
  People from every nation will bow
    down before him.
²⁸ For the LORD is king!
  He rules all the nations.

²⁹ Let the rich of the earth feast and
    worship.
  Let all mortals—those born to
    die—bow down in his presence.
³⁰ Future generations will also serve him.
  Our children will hear about the
    wonders of the Lord.
³¹ His righteous acts will be told to those
    yet unborn.
  They will hear about everything he
    has done.

PSALM 23
A psalm of David.

¹ The LORD is my shepherd;
  I have everything I need.
² He lets me rest in green meadows;
  he leads me beside peaceful streams.
³   He renews my strength.
  He guides me along right paths,
    bringing honor to his name.

⁴ Even when I walk
    through the dark valley of death,*
  I will not be afraid,
    for you are close beside me.
  Your rod and your staff
    protect and comfort me.

⁵ You prepare a feast for me
    in the presence of my enemies.
  You welcome me as a guest,

23:4 Or *the darkest valley.*   24:6 Hebrew *of Jacob.*

anointing my head with oil.
  My cup overflows with blessings.
⁶ Surely your goodness and unfailing
    love will pursue me
  all the days of my life,
  and I will live in the house of the LORD
    forever.

PSALM 24
A psalm of David.

¹ The earth is the LORD's, and everything
    in it.
  The world and all its people belong
    to him.
² For he laid the earth's foundation on
    the seas
  and built it on the ocean depths.

³ Who may climb the mountain of the
    LORD?
  Who may stand in his holy place?
⁴ Only those whose hands and hearts are
    pure,
  who do not worship idols
    and never tell lies.
⁵ They will receive the LORD's blessing
    and have right standing with God
      their savior.
⁶ They alone may enter God's presence
    and worship the God of Israel.*
                                    Interlude

⁷ Open up, ancient gates!
    Open up, ancient doors,
    and let the King of glory enter.
⁸ Who is the King of glory?
    The LORD, strong and mighty,
    the LORD, invincible in battle.
⁹ Open up, ancient gates!
    Open up, ancient doors,
    and let the King of glory enter.
¹⁰ Who is the King of glory?
    The LORD Almighty—
    he is the King of glory.   *Interlude*

JUNE 5 ☐ DAY 157
PSALMS 25–30
Praise and Thanks

OVERVIEW A growing relationship with God includes a growing
understanding of what he can accomplish in your life as you trust
in him. He will guide you in his way (Psalm 25), vindicate you when

you're wronged (26), and protect you when you're in danger (27–28). David's response—and the response God desires from every true believer—is an outpouring of heartfelt praise (29) and thanksgiving (30).

Psalm 25	Psalm 26	Psalm 27	Psalm 28	Psalm 29	Psalm 30
Watching for God's		Waiting for God's		Worshiping God in	
Direction	Defense	Salvation	Strength	Person	Power
Petition					Praise

YOUR DAILY WALK *Praise* and *thanks*. Are those terms synonymous, or is there a difference between them?

God is still on the throne, we're still on his footstool, and there's only a knee's distance between.

Psalms 29 and 30 provide a helpful illustration of the difference. Psalm 29, a paean of praise, focuses on God's glory as revealed in an earthshaking thunderstorm. Psalm 30, a testimony of thanksgiving, centers on David's experience of divine deliverance and his resulting gratitude to God. Psalm 29 illustrates praise, which is God-centered, focusing on God's glory as revealed in his mighty attributes and works. Psalm 30 illustrates thanksgiving, which is more human-centered, highlighting David's gratitude for God's involvement in his life.

Understanding the difference between the two can add a new dimension to your prayer life! It's easy to develop the habit of me-centered prayers in which your problems are central. And though petition is an important part of prayer (Matthew 7:7-8), it is not the only part. As you take time to pray today, begin instead with praise for God's glory and character (you-centered prayer). Make it a pattern in your praying that before you get caught up in your own concerns, you get caught up in God's greatness. Then you, like the psalmist, will be both praising and thanking the Lord!

INSIGHT The Praise-Packed Psalms
Praise and thanksgiving permeate the Psalms—a fact seen in the repetition of the terms *praise* (175 times), *thanks* (32 times), and *thanksgiving* (8 times). It's difficult to miss the psalmist's intent that you learn to "praise the LORD" and "give thanks to the Lord"!

PSALM 25
A psalm of David.

¹ To you, O LORD, I lift up my soul.
² I trust in you, my God!
Do not let me be disgraced,
or let my enemies rejoice in my
defeat.
³ No one who trusts in you will ever be
disgraced,
but disgrace comes to those who try
to deceive others.
⁴ Show me the path where I should
walk, O LORD;
point out the right road for me to
follow.
⁵ Lead me by your truth and teach me,
for you are the God who saves me.
All day long I put my hope in you.
⁶ Remember, O LORD, your unfailing
love and compassion,

which you have shown from long
ages past.
⁷ Forgive the rebellious sins of my youth;
look instead through the eyes of your
unfailing love,
for you are merciful, O LORD.
⁸ The LORD is good and does what is right;
he shows the proper path to those
who go astray.
⁹ He leads the humble in what is right,
teaching them his way.
¹⁰ The LORD leads with unfailing love and
faithfulness
all those who keep his covenant and
obey his decrees.
¹¹ For the honor of your name, O LORD,
forgive my many, many sins.
¹² Who are those who fear the LORD?
He will show them the path they
should choose.

¹³ They will live in prosperity,
   and their children will inherit the
      Promised Land.
¹⁴ Friendship with the LORD is reserved
   for those who fear him.
   With them he shares the secrets of his
      covenant.
¹⁵ My eyes are always looking to the
   LORD for help,
   for he alone can rescue me from the
      traps of my enemies.

¹⁶ Turn to me and have mercy on me,
   for I am alone and in deep distress.
¹⁷ My problems go from bad to worse.
   Oh, save me from them all!
¹⁸ Feel my pain and see my trouble.
   Forgive all my sins.
¹⁹ See how many enemies I have,
   and how viciously they hate me!
²⁰ Protect me! Rescue my life from them!
   Do not let me be disgraced, for I trust
      in you.
²¹ May integrity and honesty protect me,
   for I put my hope in you.

²² O God, ransom Israel
   from all its troubles.

PSALM 26
A psalm of David.

¹ Declare me innocent, O LORD,
   for I have acted with integrity;
   I have trusted in the LORD without
      wavering.
² Put me on trial, LORD, and
   cross-examine me.
   Test my motives and affections.
³ For I am constantly aware of your
      unfailing love,
   and I have lived according to your
      truth.

⁴ I do not spend time with liars
   or go along with hypocrites.
⁵ I hate the gatherings of those who do
      evil,
   and I refuse to join in with the
      wicked.

⁶ I wash my hands to declare my
      innocence.
   I come to your altar, O LORD,
⁷ singing a song of thanksgiving
   and telling of all your miracles.
⁸ I love your sanctuary, LORD,
   the place where your glory shines.

⁹ Don't let me suffer the fate of sinners.
   Don't condemn me along with
      murderers.
¹⁰ Their hands are dirty with wicked
      schemes,
   and they constantly take bribes.

¹¹ But I am not like that; I do what is right.
   So in your mercy, save me.
¹² I have taken a stand,
   and I will publicly praise the LORD.

PSALM 27
A psalm of David.

¹ The LORD is my light and my
      salvation—
   so why should I be afraid?
   The LORD protects me from danger—
   so why should I tremble?

² When evil people come to destroy me,
   when my enemies and foes attack
      me,
   they will stumble and fall.
³ Though a mighty army surrounds me,
   my heart will know no fear.
   Even if they attack me,
   I remain confident.

⁴ The one thing I ask of the LORD—
   the thing I seek most—
   is to live in the house of the LORD all
      the days of my life,
   delighting in the LORD's perfections
   and meditating in his Temple.
⁵ For he will conceal me there when
      troubles come;
   he will hide me in his sanctuary.
   He will place me out of reach on a
      high rock.
⁶ Then I will hold my head high,
   above my enemies who surround me.
   At his Tabernacle I will offer sacrifices
      with shouts of joy,
   singing and praising the LORD with
      music.

⁷ Listen to my pleading, O LORD.
   Be merciful and answer me!
⁸ My heart has heard you say, "Come
      and talk with me."
   And my heart responds, "LORD, I am
      coming."
⁹ Do not hide yourself from me.
   Do not reject your servant in anger.
   You have always been my helper.
   Don't leave me now; don't abandon me,
   O God of my salvation!

¹⁰ Even if my father and mother abandon
       me,
    the LORD will hold me close.

¹¹ Teach me how to live, O LORD.
    Lead me along the path of honesty,
    for my enemies are waiting for me
       to fall.
¹² Do not let me fall into their hands.
    For they accuse me of things I've
       never done
    and breathe out violence against me.
¹³ Yet I am confident that I will see the
       LORD's goodness
    while I am here in the land of the
       living.

¹⁴ Wait patiently for the LORD.
    Be brave and courageous.
    Yes, wait patiently for the LORD.

PSALM 28
A psalm of David.

¹ O LORD, you are my rock of safety.
    Please help me; don't refuse to
       answer me.
  For if you are silent,
    I might as well give up and die.
² Listen to my prayer for mercy
    as I cry out to you for help,
    as I lift my hands toward your holy
       sanctuary.

³ Don't drag me away with the wicked—
    with those who do evil—
  those who speak friendly words to
       their neighbors
    while planning evil in their hearts.
⁴ Give them the punishment they so
       richly deserve!
    Measure it out in proportion to their
       wickedness.
  Pay them back for all their evil deeds!
    Give them a taste of what they have
       done to others.
⁵ They care nothing for what the LORD
       has done
    or for what his hands have made.
  So he will tear them down like old
       buildings,
    and they will never be rebuilt!

⁶ Praise the LORD!
    For he has heard my cry for mercy.
⁷ The LORD is my strength, my shield
       from every danger.
    I trust in him with all my heart.

He helps me, and my heart is filled
       with joy.
    I burst out in songs of thanksgiving.

⁸ The LORD protects his people
    and gives victory to his anointed
       king.
⁹ Save your people!
    Bless Israel, your special possession!
  Lead them like a shepherd,
    and carry them forever in your
       arms.

PSALM 29
A psalm of David.

¹ Give honor to the LORD, you angels;
    give honor to the LORD for his glory
       and strength.
² Give honor to the LORD for the glory
       of his name.
    Worship the LORD in the splendor
       of his holiness.

³ The voice of the LORD echoes above
       the sea.
    The God of glory thunders.
    The LORD thunders over the mighty
       sea.
⁴ The voice of the LORD is powerful;
    the voice of the LORD is full of
       majesty.
⁵ The voice of the LORD splits the mighty
       cedars;
    the LORD shatters the cedars of
       Lebanon.
⁶ He makes Lebanon's mountains skip
       like a calf
    and Mount Hermon* to leap like
       a young bull.
⁷ The voice of the LORD strikes with
       lightning bolts.
⁸ The voice of the LORD makes the desert
       quake;
    the LORD shakes the desert of
       Kadesh.
⁹ The voice of the LORD twists mighty
       oaks*
    and strips the forests bare.
  In his Temple everyone shouts,
       "Glory!"

¹⁰ The LORD rules over the floodwaters.
    The LORD reigns as king forever.
¹¹ The LORD gives his people strength.
    The LORD blesses them with peace.

29:6 Hebrew *Sirion,* another name for Mount Hermon.   29:9 Or *causes the deer to writhe in labor.*

PSALM 30

A psalm of David, sung at the dedication of the Temple.

¹ I will praise you, LORD, for you have
    rescued me.
  You refused to let my enemies
    triumph over me.
² O LORD my God, I cried out to you
    for help,
  and you restored my health.
³ You brought me up from the grave,
    O LORD.
  You kept me from falling into the pit
    of death.

⁴ Sing to the LORD, all you godly ones!
    Praise his holy name.
⁵ His anger lasts for a moment,
    but his favor lasts a lifetime!
  Weeping may go on all night,
    but joy comes with the morning.

⁶ When I was prosperous I said,
    "Nothing can stop me now!"

⁷ Your favor, O LORD, made me as secure
    as a mountain.
  Then you turned away from me, and
    I was shattered.

⁸ I cried out to you, O LORD.
    I begged the Lord for mercy, saying,
⁹ "What will you gain if I die,
    if I sink down into the grave?
  Can my dust praise you from the
    grave?
  Can it tell the world of your
    faithfulness?
¹⁰ Hear me, LORD, and have mercy on me.
    Help me, O LORD."

¹¹ You have turned my mourning into
    joyful dancing.
  You have taken away my clothes of
    mourning and clothed me with joy,
¹² that I might sing praises to you and not
    be silent.
  O LORD my God, I will give you
    thanks forever!

JUNE 6 □ DAY 158
PSALMS 31–35
A Musical Manifesto

OVERVIEW Think of today's reading as forming a pyramid. The outer two psalms (31 and 35) form the foundation and deal with believers' struggles against their enemies. In each case David finds his refuge from external foes in God alone. In the next level of the pyramid (32 and 34), David faces internal woes: unconfessed sin and secret fear. In each situation the psalmist learns from his failures in the past so that he (and all who read his words) might respond rightly to similar perils in the future. The peak of the pyramid is formed by a beautiful psalm of praise to God whose "plans stand firm forever" (33:11).

Psalm 31	Psalm 32	Psalm 33	Psalms 34–35
Refuge for the Ravaged	Restoration for the Repentant	Rejoicing for the Righteous	Rescue for the Rejected
God's Care over His Children			

YOUR DAILY WALK A little boy who loved to listen to music was bitterly disappointed because he could neither play nor sing. But a kindly gentleman encouraged him with these words: "There are many ways of making music. What matters is the song in your heart." That little boy—Antonio Stradivari—took the man at his word and became the world's greatest violin maker.

  Perhaps you have an equally low estimation of your own singing

Music strikes in ability. If so, Psalm 33:1-3 will challenge you with the privilege and
me a profound responsibility of singing joyfully to the Lord. As if anticipating excuses,
contemplation the psalmist opens with the command to sing. This is not just a sugges-
of the First tion! The character of God makes musical expression an appropriate
Composer. part of worship, including instrumental arrangements (v. 2), songs
of your own creation, and rousing expressions of praise (v. 3). Your
sovereign Creator is worthy of them all.

It's time to sing! Find a hymnbook—and, if possible, a willing friend
or two—for a time of musical rejoicing in the Lord.

INSIGHT Scripture Memory Old Testament Style
Psalm 34 is one of seven acrostics in the book of Psalms. Each verse
begins with a different letter of the Hebrew alphabet, a definite memory
aid. In this way the reader could trace and remember David's sequence
of thought.

PSALM 31
For the choir director: A psalm of David.

¹ O LORD, I have come to you for
protection;
don't let me be put to shame.
Rescue me, for you always do what
is right.
² Bend down and listen to me;
rescue me quickly.
Be for me a great rock of safety,
a fortress where my enemies cannot
reach me.

³ You are my rock and my fortress.
For the honor of your name, lead me
out of this peril.
⁴ Pull me from the trap my enemies set
for me,
for I find protection in you alone.
⁵ I entrust my spirit into your hand.
Rescue me, LORD, for you are a
faithful God.

⁶ I hate those who worship worthless
idols.
I trust in the LORD.
⁷ I am overcome with joy because of
your unfailing love,
for you have seen my troubles,
and you care about the anguish of
my soul.
⁸ You have not handed me over to my
enemy
but have set me in a safe place.

⁹ Have mercy on me, LORD, for I am in
distress.
My sight is blurred because of my
tears.
My body and soul are withering
away.

¹⁰ I am dying from grief;
my years are shortened by sadness.
Misery* has drained my strength;
I am wasting away from within.
¹¹ I am scorned by all my enemies
and despised by my neighbors—
even my friends are afraid to come
near me.
When they see me on the street,
they turn the other way.
¹² I have been ignored as if I were dead,
as if I were a broken pot.
¹³ I have heard the many rumors about
me,
and I am surrounded by terror.
My enemies conspire against me,
plotting to take my life.

¹⁴ But I am trusting you, O LORD,
saying, "You are my God!"
¹⁵ My future is in your hands.
Rescue me from those who hunt me
down relentlessly.
¹⁶ Let your favor shine on your servant.
In your unfailing love, save me.
¹⁷ Don't let me be disgraced, O LORD,
for I call out to you for help.
Let the wicked be disgraced;
let them lie silent in the grave.
¹⁸ May their lying lips be silenced—
those proud and arrogant lips that
accuse the godly.

¹⁹ Your goodness is so great!
You have stored up great blessings
for those who honor you.
You have done so much for those who
come to you for protection,
blessing them before the watching
world.

31:10 Or *Sin.*

20 You hide them in the shelter of your
      presence,
   safe from those who conspire against
      them.
   You shelter them in your presence,
      far from accusing tongues.
21 Praise the LORD,
   for he has shown me his unfailing
      love.
   He kept me safe when my city was
      under attack.
22 In sudden fear I had cried out,
   "I have been cut off from the LORD!"
   But you heard my cry for mercy
      and answered my call for help.
23 Love the LORD, all you faithful ones!
   For the LORD protects those who are
      loyal to him,
   but he harshly punishes all who are
      arrogant.
24 So be strong and take courage,
   all you who put your hope in the
      LORD!

PSALM 32
A psalm of David.

1 Oh, what joy for those
   whose rebellion is forgiven,
   whose sin is put out of sight!
2 Yes, what joy for those
   whose record the LORD has cleared of
      sin,
   whose lives are lived in complete
      honesty!
3 When I refused to confess my sin,
   I was weak and miserable,
   and I groaned all day long.
4 Day and night your hand of discipline
      was heavy on me.
   My strength evaporated like water in
      the summer heat.   *Interlude*
5 Finally, I confessed all my sins to you
   and stopped trying to hide them.
   I said to myself, "I will confess my
      rebellion to the LORD."
   And you forgave me! All my guilt is
      gone.   *Interlude*
6 Therefore, let all the godly confess their
      rebellion to you while there is time,
   that they may not drown in the
      floodwaters of judgment.
7 For you are my hiding place;
   you protect me from trouble.

   You surround me with songs of
      victory.   *Interlude*
8 The LORD says, "I will guide you along
      the best pathway for your life.
   I will advise you and watch over you.
9 Do not be like a senseless horse or mule
      that needs a bit and bridle to keep it
      under control."
10 Many sorrows come to the wicked,
   but unfailing love surrounds those
      who trust the LORD.
11 So rejoice in the LORD and be glad, all
      you who obey him!
   Shout for joy, all you whose hearts
      are pure!

PSALM 33
1 Let the godly sing with joy to the LORD,
   for it is fitting to praise him.
2 Praise the LORD with melodies on the
      lyre;
   make music for him on the
      ten-stringed harp.
3 Sing new songs of praise to him;
   play skillfully on the harp and sing
      with joy.
4 For the word of the LORD holds true,
   and everything he does is worthy of
      our trust.
5 He loves whatever is just and good,
   and his unfailing love fills the earth.
6 The LORD merely spoke,
   and the heavens were created.
   He breathed the word,
   and all the stars were born.
7 He gave the sea its boundaries
   and locked the oceans in vast
      reservoirs.
8 Let everyone in the world fear the
      LORD,
   and let everyone stand in awe of him.
9 For when he spoke, the world began!
   It appeared at his command.
10 The LORD shatters the plans of the
      nations
   and thwarts all their schemes.
11 But the LORD's plans stand firm forever;
   his intentions can never be shaken.
12 What joy for the nation whose God is
      the LORD,
   whose people he has chosen for his
      own.

¹³ The LORD looks down from heaven
  and sees the whole human race.
¹⁴ From his throne he observes
  all who live on the earth.
¹⁵ He made their hearts,
  so he understands everything they
  do.
¹⁶ The best-equipped army cannot save
  a king,
  nor is great strength enough to save
  a warrior.
¹⁷ Don't count on your warhorse to give
  you victory—
  for all its strength, it cannot save you.

¹⁸ But the LORD watches over those who
  fear him,
  those who rely on his unfailing love.
¹⁹ He rescues them from death
  and keeps them alive in times of
  famine.

²⁰ We depend on the LORD alone to save
  us.
  Only he can help us, protecting us
  like a shield.
²¹ In him our hearts rejoice,
  for we are trusting in his holy name.
²² Let your unfailing love surround us,
  LORD,
  for our hope is in you alone.

PSALM 34

A psalm of David, regarding the time he pretended to be insane in front of Abimelech, who sent him away.

¹ I will praise the LORD at all times.
  I will constantly speak his praises.
² I will boast only in the LORD;
  let all who are discouraged take
  heart.
³ Come, let us tell of the LORD's greatness;
  let us exalt his name together.

⁴ I prayed to the LORD, and he answered
  me,
  freeing me from all my fears.
⁵ Those who look to him for help will be
  radiant with joy;
  no shadow of shame will darken
  their faces.
⁶ I cried out to the LORD in my suffering,
  and he heard me.
  He set me free from all my fears.
⁷ For the angel of the LORD guards all
  who fear him,
  and he rescues them.

⁸ Taste and see that the LORD is good.
  Oh, the joys of those who trust in him!
⁹ Let the LORD's people show him
  reverence,
  for those who honor him will have
  all they need.
¹⁰ Even strong young lions sometimes go
  hungry,
  but those who trust in the LORD will
  never lack any good thing.

¹¹ Come, my children, and listen to me,
  and I will teach you to fear the LORD.
¹² Do any of you want to live
  a life that is long and good?
¹³ Then watch your tongue!
  Keep your lips from telling lies!
¹⁴ Turn away from evil and do good.
  Work hard at living in peace with
  others.

¹⁵ The eyes of the LORD watch over those
  who do right;
  his ears are open to their cries for help.
¹⁶ But the LORD turns his face against
  those who do evil;
  he will erase their memory from the
  earth.

¹⁷ The LORD hears his people when they
  call to him for help.
  He rescues them from all their
  troubles.
¹⁸ The LORD is close to the brokenhearted;
  he rescues those who are crushed in
  spirit.

¹⁹ The righteous face many troubles,
  but the LORD rescues them from each
  and every one.
²⁰ For the LORD protects them from
  harm—
  not one of their bones will be broken!

²¹ Calamity will surely overtake the
  wicked,
  and those who hate the righteous
  will be punished.
²² But the LORD will redeem those who
  serve him.
  Everyone who trusts in him will be
  freely pardoned.

PSALM 35

A psalm of David.

¹ O LORD, oppose those who oppose me.
  Declare war on those who are attacking me.

² Put on your armor, and take up your
   shield.
    Prepare for battle, and come to my
     aid.
³ Lift up your spear and javelin
   and block the way of my enemies.
   Let me hear you say,
    "I am your salvation!"

⁴ Humiliate and disgrace those trying
    to kill me;
   turn them back in confusion.
⁵ Blow them away like chaff in the
    wind—
   a wind sent by the angel of the LORD.
⁶ Make their path dark and slippery,
   with the angel of the LORD pursuing
   them.
⁷ Although I did them no wrong,
   they laid a trap for me.
   Although I did them no wrong,
   they dug a pit for me.
⁸ So let sudden ruin overtake them!
   Let them be caught in the snare they
    set for me!
   Let them fall to destruction in the pit
   they dug for me.
⁹ Then I will rejoice in the LORD.
   I will be glad because he rescues me.
¹⁰ I will praise him from the bottom of my
   heart:
   "LORD, who can compare with you?
   Who else rescues the weak and helpless
    from the strong?
   Who else protects the poor and
    needy from those who want to rob
    them?"
¹¹ Malicious witnesses testify against me.
   They accuse me of things I don't
    even know about.
¹² They repay me with evil for the good
    I do.
   I am sick with despair.
¹³ Yet when they were ill,
   I grieved for them.
   I even fasted and prayed for them,
   but my prayers returned
    unanswered.
¹⁴ I was sad, as though they were my
    friends or family,
   as if I were grieving for my own
    mother.

¹⁵ But they are glad now that I am in
   trouble;
   they gleefully join together against
    me.
   I am attacked by people I don't even
    know;
   they hurl slander at me continually.
¹⁶ They mock me with the worst kind of
   profanity,
   and they snarl at me.

¹⁷ How long, O Lord, will you look on
   and do nothing?
   Rescue me from their fierce attacks.
   Protect my life from these lions!
¹⁸ Then I will thank you in front of the
   entire congregation.
   I will praise you before all the people.

¹⁹ Don't let my treacherous enemies
   rejoice over my defeat.
   Don't let those who hate me without
    cause
   gloat over my sorrow.
²⁰ They don't talk of peace;
   they plot against innocent people
   who are minding their own business.
²¹ They shout that they have seen me
    doing wrong.
   "Aha," they say. "Aha!
   With our own eyes we saw him
    do it!"

²² O LORD, you know all about this.
   Do not stay silent.
   Don't abandon me now, O Lord.
²³ Wake up! Rise to my defense!
   Take up my case, my God and my
    Lord.
²⁴ Declare me "not guilty," O LORD my
    God, for you give justice.
   Don't let my enemies laugh about
    me in my troubles.
²⁵ Don't let them say, "Look! We have
    what we wanted!
   Now we will eat him alive!"

²⁶ May those who rejoice at my troubles
   be humiliated and disgraced.
   May those who triumph over me
   be covered with shame and dishonor.
²⁷ But give great joy to those
   who have stood with me in my
    defense.
   Let them continually say, "Great is the
    LORD,
   who enjoys helping his servant."
²⁸ Then I will tell everyone of your justice
   and goodness,
   and I will praise you all day long.

JUNE 7 □ DAY 159
Hitting the Prophetic Bull's-Eye

LOOK BACK The book of Job introduced you to the *sovereignty* of God. The book of Psalms will help you learn to *worship* God.

Psalms is the longest book in the Bible, and you'll need an entire month to read your way through it. But don't let the size of the book overwhelm you. Think of it as 150 "songs of the heart"—poems set to music by David, Asaph, Moses, Solomon, and others as they walked with God and reflected on the many facets of his character.

You'll find a psalm for every mood: excitement and depression, gladness and gloom, expectation and exasperation. The human experiences behind the psalms bring the authors' words to life (don't miss the superscriptions at the beginning of many of the psalms—they give important historical information about the occasion on which the psalm was written). You may want to review what you have already read in 2 Samuel and 1 Chronicles as a backdrop for the psalms David wrote.

Psalms is more than a big book of meter and verse. Think of it as God's love letter to you. He wants you to get to know him better, for to know him is to love him as Shepherd, Guide, Provider, Protector, and King.

LOOK UP The Psalms are more than a treasure chest of poetry and praise. They are also the source of many of the messianic prophecies in the Old Testament.

The humble Carpenter of Nazareth was also the mighty Architect of the Universe.

Hundreds of years before the birth of Christ, God used the pen of the psalmist to predict with remarkable precision the details concerning the birth, life, ministry, death, and resurrection of Jesus of Nazareth. As you continue to read through the Old Testament, find a spiral notebook and begin a "Portfolio of Prophecies" about the Messiah. Here is a partial list from the Psalms to get you started:

A Messianic Prediction in the Psalms . . .	. . . Fulfilled in the New Testament
All things would be put under his feet (8:6).	Hebrews 2:8
He would be resurrected from the dead (16:10).	Mark 16:6-7
He would be forsaken by God (22:1).	Matthew 27:46
He would be scorned and mocked (22:7-8).	Luke 23:35
His hands and feet would be pierced (22:16).	John 20:25, 27
Soldiers would gamble for his clothes (22:18).	Matthew 27:35-36
Not one of his bones would be broken (34:20).	John 19:32-36
He would be hated without a cause (35:19).	John 15:25
Zeal for God's house would consume him (69:9).	John 2:17
He would be given wine mixed with poison to drink (69:21).	Matthew 27:34

LOOK AHEAD Imagine that you have been given the task of predicting the birth of a child eight hundred years from today. You must correctly predict his name, place of birth, time of birth, circumstances surrounding his birth, how he will live, how he will minister, how he will die, and what his final words will be before he dies.

"Why, that's impossible!" you say. And you'd be quite right . . . unless, of course, you were declaring God's message with a prophet's unerring accuracy. Aren't you glad you serve a God like that? Don't you wish everyone did? Share what you have learned about the messianic prophecies of Jesus with one other person this week, and invite him or her to meet the Messiah in a personal, life-changing way.

JUNE 8 ☐ DAY 160
PSALMS 36–41
Looking Up from Down Under

OVERVIEW Every honest believer admits to having ups and downs, and David is no exception. In the face of great wickedness, he takes comfort in God's loving care (Psalms 36–37). Despite inner conflict with guilt and discouragement, he finds strength in God's help (38–39). Out of the darkness of his circumstances, David proclaims a shining testimony of God's deliverance and mercy (40–41). No matter what life may bring, David knows that in God he has found a source of strength to rise above his circumstances rather than sink beneath them.

Psalms 36–37	Psalms 38–39	Psalms 40–41
Opposition from Without	Oppression from Within	Overcoming by God's Mercy
Trials	Turmoil	Testimony

YOUR DAILY WALK Think about it: "Ninety-five percent of all adults surveyed readily admit to having occasional times of depression; the other 5 percent were too depressed to respond to the survey." Does that humorous thought depress you or encourage you?

A head hung in despair cannot scan the horizon of God's provision.

Discouragement, depression, personal loss, a sense of hopelessness— they're the universal experience of people. Psalm 40 describes one such moment in the life of King David—a time he likened to being in "the pit of despair." There he learned that the question is not, Will I find myself from time to time in the pits?—you will! Rather, the question is, What will I do once I find myself there?

David discovered a way to move from the mire (v. 2) to the choir (v. 3). Resisting the temptation to complain, get bitter, give up, or grow angry, David cried out to God, waited for God to answer, and carefully gave God the credit when it came!

Take time today to call up a friend you sense may be "in the pits," and share David's testimony from Psalm 40. As you reach out to someone in need, you'll be amazed how God will encourage you both!

INSIGHT Lend Me Your Ears for Life
Israel's law made provision for a servant who, having fulfilled his obligations of service, loved his master and wanted to devote the rest of his life to his lord's service. This commitment was signified and sealed by piercing the servant's ear. You can read about this picturesque symbol of total devotion in Deuteronomy 15:12-17.

PSALM 36
For the choir director: A psalm of David, the servant of the LORD.

¹ Sin whispers to the wicked, deep within their hearts.
They have no fear of God to restrain them.
² In their blind conceit,
they cannot see how wicked they really are.
³ Everything they say is crooked and deceitful.
They refuse to act wisely or do what is good.

⁴ They lie awake at night, hatching sinful plots.
Their course of action is never good.
They make no attempt to turn from evil.

⁵ Your unfailing love, O LORD, is as vast as the heavens;
your faithfulness reaches beyond the clouds.
⁶ Your righteousness is like the mighty mountains,
your justice like the ocean depths.

You care for people and animals alike,
O Lord.

7 How precious is your unfailing love,
O God!
All humanity finds shelter
in the shadow of your wings.

8 You feed them from the abundance of
your own house,
letting them drink from your rivers
of delight.

9 For you are the fountain of life,
the light by which we see.

10 Pour out your unfailing love on those
who love you;
give justice to those with honest
hearts.

11 Don't let the proud trample me;
don't let the wicked push me around.

12 Look! They have fallen!
They have been thrown down, never
to rise again.

PSALM 37

A psalm of David.

1 Don't worry about the wicked.
Don't envy those who do wrong.

2 For like grass, they soon fade away.
Like springtime flowers, they soon
wither.

3 Trust in the Lord and do good.
Then you will live safely in the land
and prosper.

4 Take delight in the Lord,
and he will give you your heart's
desires.

5 Commit everything you do to the Lord.
Trust him, and he will help you.

6 He will make your innocence as clear
as the dawn,
and the justice of your cause will
shine like the noonday sun.

7 Be still in the presence of the Lord,
and wait patiently for him to act.
Don't worry about evil people who
prosper
or fret about their wicked schemes.

8 Stop your anger!
Turn from your rage!
Do not envy others—
it only leads to harm.

9 For the wicked will be destroyed,
but those who trust in the Lord will
possess the land.

10 In a little while, the wicked will
disappear.
Though you look for them, they will
be gone.

11 Those who are gentle and lowly will
possess the land;
they will live in prosperous security.

12 The wicked plot against the godly;
they snarl at them in defiance.

13 But the Lord just laughs,
for he sees their day of judgment
coming.

14 The wicked draw their swords
and string their bows
to kill the poor and the oppressed,
to slaughter those who do right.

15 But they will be stabbed through the
heart with their own swords,
and their bows will be broken.

16 It is better to be godly and have little
than to be evil and possess much.

17 For the strength of the wicked will be
shattered,
but the Lord takes care of the godly.

18 Day by day the Lord takes care of the
innocent,
and they will receive a reward that
lasts forever.

19 They will survive through hard times;
even in famine they will have more
than enough.

20 But the wicked will perish.
The Lord's enemies are like flowers
in a field—
they will disappear like smoke.

21 The wicked borrow and never repay,
but the godly are generous givers.

22 Those blessed by the Lord will inherit
the land,
but those cursed by him will die.

23 The steps of the godly are directed by
the Lord.
He delights in every detail of their lives.

24 Though they stumble, they will not fall,
for the Lord holds them by the hand.

25 Once I was young, and now I am old.
Yet I have never seen the godly
forsaken,
nor seen their children begging for
bread.

26 The godly always give generous loans
to others,
and their children are a blessing.

²⁷ Turn from evil and do good,
and you will live in the land forever.
²⁸ For the LORD loves justice,
and he will never abandon the godly.

He will keep them safe forever,
but the children of the wicked will
perish.
²⁹ The godly will inherit the land
and will live there forever.

³⁰ The godly offer good counsel;
they know what is right from wrong.
³¹ They fill their hearts with God's law,
so they will never slip from his
path.

³² Those who are evil spy on the godly,
waiting for an excuse to kill them.
³³ But the LORD will not let the wicked
succeed
or let the godly be condemned when
they are brought before the judge.

³⁴ Don't be impatient for the LORD to act!
Travel steadily along his path.
He will honor you, giving you the land.
You will see the wicked destroyed.

³⁵ I myself have seen it happen—
proud and evil people thriving like
mighty trees.
³⁶ But when I looked again, they were
gone!
Though I searched for them, I could
not find them!

³⁷ Look at those who are honest and
good,
for a wonderful future lies before
those who love peace.
³⁸ But the wicked will be destroyed;
they have no future.

³⁹ The LORD saves the godly;
he is their fortress in times of trouble.
⁴⁰ The LORD helps them,
rescuing them from the wicked.
He saves them,
and they find shelter in him.

PSALM 38

*A psalm of David, to bring us to the LORD's
remembrance.*

¹ O LORD, don't rebuke me in your
anger!
Don't discipline me in your rage!
² Your arrows have struck deep,
and your blows are crushing me.

³ Because of your anger, my whole body
is sick;
my health is broken because of my
sins.
⁴ My guilt overwhelms me—
it is a burden too heavy to bear.
⁵ My wounds fester and stink
because of my foolish sins.
⁶ I am bent over and racked with pain.
My days are filled with grief.
⁷ A raging fever burns within me,
and my health is broken.
⁸ I am exhausted and completely
crushed.
My groans come from an anguished
heart.

⁹ You know what I long for, Lord;
you hear my every sigh.
¹⁰ My heart beats wildly, my strength fails,
and I am going blind.
¹¹ My loved ones and friends stay away,
fearing my disease.
Even my own family stands at a
distance.
¹² Meanwhile, my enemies lay traps for
me;
they make plans to ruin me.
They think up treacherous deeds all
day long.
¹³ But I am deaf to all their threats.
I am silent before them as one who
cannot speak.
¹⁴ I choose to hear nothing,
and I make no reply.

¹⁵ For I am waiting for you, O LORD.
You must answer for me, O Lord my
God.
¹⁶ I prayed, "Don't let my enemies gloat
over me
or rejoice at my downfall."
¹⁷ I am on the verge of collapse,
facing constant pain.
¹⁸ But I confess my sins;
I am deeply sorry for what I have
done.
¹⁹ My enemies are many;
they hate me though I have done
nothing against them.
²⁰ They repay me evil for good
and oppose me because I stand for
the right.

²¹ Do not abandon me, LORD.
Do not stand at a distance, my God.
²² Come quickly to help me, O Lord my
savior.

PSALM 39
For Jeduthun, the choir director: A psalm of David.

¹ I said to myself, "I will watch what I do
and not sin in what I say.
  I will curb my tongue
    when the ungodly are around me."
² But as I stood there in silence—
    not even speaking of good things—
    the turmoil within me grew to the
      bursting point.
³ My thoughts grew hot within me
    and began to burn,
    igniting a fire of words:
⁴ "LORD, remind me how brief my time
    on earth will be.
  Remind me that my days are
    numbered,
    and that my life is fleeing away.
⁵ My life is no longer than the width of
    my hand.
  An entire lifetime is just a moment to
    you;
    human existence is but a breath."
							Interlude
⁶ We are merely moving shadows,
    and all our busy rushing ends in
      nothing.
  We heap up wealth for someone else
    to spend.
⁷ And so, Lord, where do I put my hope?
    My only hope is in you.
⁸ Rescue me from my rebellion,
    for even fools mock me when I rebel.
⁹ I am silent before you; I won't say a
    word.
  For my punishment is from you.
¹⁰ Please, don't punish me anymore!
  I am exhausted by the blows from
    your hand.
¹¹ When you discipline people for their
    sins,
    their lives can be crushed like the life
      of a moth.
  Human existence is as frail as breath.
							Interlude
¹² Hear my prayer, O LORD!
  Listen to my cries for help!
  Don't ignore my tears.
  For I am your guest—
    a traveler passing through,
    as my ancestors were before me.
¹³ Spare me so I can smile again
    before I am gone and exist no more.

PSALM 40
For the choir director: A psalm of David.

¹ I waited patiently for the LORD to help
    me,
    and he turned to me and heard my
      cry.
² He lifted me out of the pit of despair,
    out of the mud and the mire.
  He set my feet on solid ground
    and steadied me as I walked along.
³ He has given me a new song to sing,
    a hymn of praise to our God.
  Many will see what he has done and be
    astounded.
  They will put their trust in the LORD.

⁴ Oh, the joys of those who trust the
    LORD,
    who have no confidence in the proud,
    or in those who worship idols.
⁵ O LORD my God, you have done many
    miracles for us.
  Your plans for us are too numerous
    to list.
  If I tried to recite all your wonderful
    deeds,
    I would never come to the end of
      them.
⁶ You take no delight in sacrifices or
    offerings.
  Now that you have made me listen,
    I finally understand—
  you don't require burnt offerings or
    sin offerings.
⁷ Then I said, "Look, I have come.
  And this has been written about me
    in your scroll:
⁸ I take joy in doing your will, my God,
    for your law is written on my heart."
⁹ I have told all your people about your
    justice.
  I have not been afraid to speak out,
    as you, O LORD, well know.
¹⁰ I have not kept this good news hidden
    in my heart;
  I have talked about your faithfulness
    and saving power.
  I have told everyone in the great
    assembly
    of your unfailing love and
      faithfulness.
¹¹ LORD, don't hold back your tender
    mercies from me.
  My only hope is in your unfailing
    love and faithfulness.

¹² For troubles surround me—
  too many to count!
They pile up so high
  I can't see my way out.
They are more numerous than the hairs
  on my head.
  I have lost all my courage.

¹³ Please, LORD, rescue me!
  Come quickly, LORD, and help me.
¹⁴ May those who try to destroy me
  be humiliated and put to shame.
May those who take delight in my
  trouble
  be turned back in disgrace.
¹⁵ Let them be horrified by their shame,
  for they said, "Aha! We've got him
  now!"

¹⁶ But may all who search for you
  be filled with joy and gladness.
May those who love your salvation
  repeatedly shout, "The LORD is
  great!"

¹⁷ As for me, I am poor and needy,
  but the Lord is thinking about me
  right now.
You are my helper and my savior.
  Do not delay, O my God.

PSALM 41

For the choir director: A psalm of David.

¹ Oh, the joys of those who are kind to
  the poor.
  The LORD rescues them in times of
  trouble.
² The LORD protects them
  and keeps them alive.
He gives them prosperity
  and rescues them from their enemies.

³ The LORD nurses them when they are
  sick
  and eases their pain and discomfort.

⁴ "O LORD," I prayed, "have mercy on
  me.
  Heal me, for I have sinned against
  you."

⁵ But my enemies say nothing but evil
  about me.
  "How soon will he die and be
  forgotten?" they ask.
⁶ They visit me as if they are my friends,
  but all the while they gather gossip,
  and when they leave, they spread it
  everywhere.
⁷ All who hate me whisper about me,
  imagining the worst for me.
⁸ "Whatever he has, it is fatal," they say.
  "He will never get out of that bed!"
⁹ Even my best friend, the one I trusted
  completely,
  the one who shared my food,
  has turned against me.

¹⁰ LORD, have mercy on me.
  Make me well again, so I can pay
  them back!
¹¹ I know that you are pleased with me,
  for you have not let my enemy
  triumph over me.
¹² You have preserved my life because
  I am innocent;
  you have brought me into your
  presence forever.

¹³ Bless the LORD, the God of Israel,
  who lives forever from eternal ages
  past.
  Amen and amen!

JUNE 9 ☐ DAY 161
PSALMS 42–49
A Mighty Fortress

 OVERVIEW Book Two of Psalms begins with a collection of psalms
attributed to the descendants of Korah. The first two express the longing of the troubled soul for God (Psalms 42–43), followed by a prayer
for victory in the midst of trouble (44). By contrast, Psalms 45–48 extol
God's majesty (45), protection (46), and power (47–48). The section
concludes with wise instruction concerning true riches (49).

Psalms 42–44	Psalms 45–48	Psalm 49
Appealing for God's Help	Acclaiming God's Greatness	Acknowledging God's Sufficiency
Yearning	Yielding	

YOUR DAILY WALK Every tomorrow has two handles: the handle of anxiety and the handle of faith. Which will you use to get a "handle" on your day?

Anxiety never strengthens you for tomorrow; it only weakens you for today.

Second only to the fear of standing before a large audience is the widespread phobia known as "fear of the unknown." In a day when pressing problems greatly outnumber available solutions in matters of national and international concern, where do you turn for stability?

You turn to the same refuge the psalmist found.

In Psalm 46 the descendants of Korah portray the worst calamities imaginable upon earth: earthquakes, landslides, and a raging sea (vv. 2-3). And when everything seems to be breaking loose, they proclaim that there remains an immovable Refuge: the God of Israel.

Before you close your Bible today, follow the instructions of verse 10. Remove as many distractions as possible, and take a few minutes to be silent before the Lord. Turn over to him any fears you may be harboring; then write down the words of Psalm 46:10 on a three-by-five-inch card and carry it with you throughout the day. When fear, like acid, begins to eat away at your peace of mind, pull out your reminder from the descendants of Korah and refresh your memory. Your Refuge is "the same yesterday, today, and forever" (Hebrews 13:8).

INSIGHT And Now a Word about the Authors
The descendants of Korah were Levites, descendants of the man who died for his rebellion against Moses (Numbers 16). One part of the family became temple gatekeepers (1 Chronicles 9:19) and another the singers and musicians in the temple choir (1 Chronicles 6:31-47).

BOOK TWO (Psalms 42–72)

PSALM 42

For the choir director: A psalm of the descendants of Korah.

¹ As the deer pants for streams of water,
   so I long for you, O God.
² I thirst for God, the living God.
   When can I come and stand before him?
³ Day and night, I have only tears for food,
   while my enemies continually taunt me, saying,
   "Where is this God of yours?"

⁴ My heart is breaking
   as I remember how it used to be:
I walked among the crowds of worshipers,
   leading a great procession to the house of God,
singing for joy and giving thanks—
   it was the sound of a great celebration!

⁵ Why am I discouraged?
   Why so sad?
I will put my hope in God!
   I will praise him again—
   my Savior and ⁶my God!

Now I am deeply discouraged,
   but I will remember your kindness—
from Mount Hermon, the source of the Jordan,
   from the land of Mount Mizar.
⁷ I hear the tumult of the raging seas
   as your waves and surging tides sweep over me.

⁸ Through each day the LORD pours his unfailing love upon me,
   and through each night I sing his songs,
   praying to God who gives me life.

⁹ "O God my rock," I cry,
   "Why have you forsaken me?
Why must I wander in darkness,
   oppressed by my enemies?"

¹⁰ Their taunts pierce me like a fatal
       wound.
     They scoff, "Where is this God of
       yours?"

¹¹ Why am I discouraged?
     Why so sad?
   I will put my hope in God!
   I will praise him again—
     my Savior and my God!

PSALM 43

¹ O God, take up my cause!
     Defend me against these ungodly
       people.
   Rescue me from these unjust liars.
² For you are God, my only safe haven.
     Why have you tossed me aside?
   Why must I wander around in darkness,
     oppressed by my enemies?

³ Send out your light and your truth;
     let them guide me.
   Let them lead me to your holy mountain,
     to the place where you live.
⁴ There I will go to the altar of God,
     to God—the source of all my joy.
   I will praise you with my harp,
     O God, my God!

⁵ Why am I discouraged?
     Why so sad?
   I will put my hope in God!
   I will praise him again—
     my Savior and my God!

PSALM 44

*For the choir director: A psalm of the descendants
of Korah.*

¹ O God, we have heard it with our own
       ears—
     our ancestors have told us
   of all you did in other days,
     in days long ago:
² You drove out the pagan nations
     and gave all the land to our ancestors;
   you crushed their enemies,
     setting our ancestors free.
³ They did not conquer the land with
       their swords;
     it was not their own strength that
       gave them victory.
   It was by your mighty power that they
       succeeded;
     it was because you favored them and
       smiled on them.

44:4 Hebrew *for Jacob.*

⁴ You are my King and my God.
     You command victories for your
       people.*
⁵ Only by your power can we push back
       our enemies;
     only in your name can we trample
       our foes.
⁶ I do not trust my bow;
     I do not count on my sword to save
       me.
⁷ It is you who gives us victory over our
       enemies;
     it is you who humbles those who
       hate us.
⁸ O God, we give glory to you all day
       long
     and constantly praise your name.
                                              Interlude

⁹ But now you have tossed us aside in
       dishonor.
     You no longer lead our armies to
       battle.
¹⁰ You make us retreat from our enemies
     and allow them to plunder our land.
¹¹ You have treated us like sheep waiting
       to be slaughtered;
     you have scattered us among the
       nations.
¹² You sold us—your precious
       people—for a pittance.
     You valued us at nothing at all.
¹³ You have caused all our neighbors to
       mock us.
     We are an object of scorn and
       derision to the nations around us.
¹⁴ You have made us the butt of their
       jokes;
     we are scorned by the whole world.
¹⁵ We can't escape the constant
       humiliation;
     shame is written across our faces.
¹⁶ All we hear are the taunts of our
       mockers.
     All we see are our vengeful enemies.

¹⁷ All this has happened despite our
       loyalty to you.
     We have not violated your covenant.
¹⁸ Our hearts have not deserted you.
     We have not strayed from your
       path.
¹⁹ Yet you have crushed us in the desert.
     You have covered us with darkness
       and death.

20 If we had turned away from worshiping
   our God
      or spread our hands in prayer to
      foreign gods,
21 God would surely have known it,
      for he knows the secrets of every
      heart.
22 For your sake we are killed every
   day;
      we are being slaughtered like sheep.

23 Wake up, O Lord! Why do you sleep?
      Get up! Do not reject us forever.
24 Why do you look the other way?
      Why do you ignore our suffering
      and oppression?
25 We collapse in the dust,
      lying face down in the dirt.
26 Rise up! Come and help us!
      Save us because of your unfailing
      love.

PSALM 45

*For the choir director: A psalm of the descendants of
Korah, to be sung to the tune "Lilies." A love song.*

1 My heart overflows with a beautiful
      thought!
      I will recite a lovely poem to the king,
      for my tongue is like the pen of a
      skillful poet.

2 You are the most handsome of all.
      Gracious words stream from your
      lips.
      God himself has blessed you forever.
3 Put on your sword, O mighty warrior!
      You are so glorious, so majestic!
4 In your majesty, ride out to victory,
      defending truth, humility, and justice.
      Go forth to perform awe-inspiring
      deeds!
5 Your arrows are sharp,
      piercing your enemies' hearts.
      The nations fall before you,
      lying down beneath your feet.

6 Your throne, O God,* endures forever
   and ever.
      Your royal power is expressed in
      justice.
7 You love what is right and hate what is
   wrong.
      Therefore God, your God, has
      anointed you,
      pouring out the oil of joy on you
      more than on anyone else.

8 Your robes are perfumed with myrrh,
      aloes, and cassia.
      In palaces decorated with ivory,
      you are entertained by the music of
      harps.
9 Kings' daughters are among your
   concubines.
      At your right side stands the queen,
      wearing jewelry of finest gold from
      Ophir!

10 Listen to me, O royal daughter; take to
   heart what I say.
      Forget your people and your home-
      land far away.
11 For your royal husband delights in
      your beauty;
      honor him, for he is your lord.
12 The princes of Tyre* will shower you
      with gifts.
      People of great wealth will entreat
      your favor.
13 The bride, a princess, waits within her
   chamber,
      dressed in a gown woven with gold.
14 In her beautiful robes, she is led to the
   king,
      accompanied by her bridesmaids.
15 What a joyful, enthusiastic procession
      as they enter the king's palace!

16 Your sons will become kings like their
   father.
      You will make them rulers over many
      lands.

17 I will bring honor to your name in every
   generation.
      Therefore, the nations will praise you
      forever and ever.

PSALM 46

*For the choir director: A psalm of the descendants
of Korah, to be sung by soprano voices.* A song.*

1 God is our refuge and strength,
      always ready to help in times of trouble.
2 So we will not fear, even if earthquakes
   come
      and the mountains crumble into the
      sea.
3 Let the oceans roar and foam.
      Let the mountains tremble as the
      waters surge!   *Interlude*

4 A river brings joy to the city of our God,
      the sacred home of the Most High.

45:6 Or *Your divine throne.*   45:12 Hebrew *The daughter of Tyre.*   46: TITLE Hebrew *according to alamoth.*

⁵ God himself lives in that city; it cannot
    be destroyed.
  God will protect it at the break of day.
⁶ The nations are in an uproar,
    and kingdoms crumble!
  God thunders,
    and the earth melts!

⁷ The LORD Almighty is here among us;
    the God of Israel* is our fortress.
                                                Interlude

⁸ Come, see the glorious works of the
    LORD:
  See how he brings destruction upon
    the world
⁹ and causes wars to end throughout the
    earth.
  He breaks the bow and snaps the
    spear in two;
  he burns the shields with fire.

¹⁰ "Be silent, and know that I am God!
    I will be honored by every nation.
    I will be honored throughout the
      world."
¹¹ The LORD Almighty is here among us;
    the God of Israel is our fortress.
                                                Interlude

PSALM 47

*For the choir director: A psalm of the descendants
of Korah.*

¹ Come, everyone, and clap your hands
    for joy!
  Shout to God with joyful praise!
² For the LORD Most High is awesome.
    He is the great King of all the earth.
³ He subdues the nations before us,
    putting our enemies beneath our feet.
⁴ He chose the Promised Land as our
    inheritance,
  the proud possession of Jacob's
    descendants, whom he loves.
                                                Interlude

⁵ God has ascended with a mighty shout.
    The LORD has ascended with
      trumpets blaring.
⁶ Sing praise to God, sing praises;
    sing praise to our King, sing praises!
⁷ For God is the King over all the earth.
    Praise him with a psalm!
⁸ God reigns above the nations,
    sitting on his holy throne.

⁹ The rulers of the world have gathered
    together.
  They join us in praising the God of
    Abraham.
  For all the kings of the earth belong
    to God.
  He is highly honored everywhere.

PSALM 48

A psalm of the descendants of Korah. A song.

¹ How great is the LORD,
    and how much we should praise
      him
  in the city of our God,
    which is on his holy mountain!
² It is magnificent in elevation—
    the whole earth rejoices to see it!
  Mount Zion, the holy mountain,*
    is the city of the great King!
³ God himself is in Jerusalem's towers.
    He reveals himself as her defender.

⁴ The kings of the earth joined forces
    and advanced against the city.
⁵ But when they saw it, they were
    stunned;
  they were terrified and ran away.
⁶ They were gripped with terror,
    like a woman writhing in the pain
      of childbirth
⁷ or like the mighty ships of Tarshish
    being shattered by a powerful east
      wind.

⁸ We had heard of the city's glory,
    but now we have seen it ourselves—
    the city of the LORD Almighty.
  It is the city of our God;
    he will make it safe forever.
                                                Interlude

⁹ O God, we meditate on your unfailing
    love
  as we worship in your Temple.
¹⁰ As your name deserves, O God,
    you will be praised to the ends of the
      earth.
  Your strong right hand is filled with
    victory.
¹¹ Let the people on Mount Zion rejoice.
    Let the towns of Judah be glad,
    for your judgments are just.
¹² Go, inspect the city of Jerusalem.*
    Walk around and count the many
      towers.

46:7 Hebrew *of Jacob;* also in 46:11.   **48:2** Or *Mount Zion, in the far north;* Hebrew reads *Mount Zion, the heights of Zaphon.*
48:12 Hebrew *Zion.*

¹³ Take note of the fortified walls,
   and tour all the citadels,
that you may describe them
   to future generations.
¹⁴ For that is what God is like.
   He is our God forever and ever,
   and he will be our guide until we die.

PSALM 49

*For the choir director: A psalm of the descendants
of Korah.*

¹ Listen to this, all you people!
   Pay attention, everyone in the world!
² High and low,
   rich and poor—listen!
³ For my words are wise,
   and my thoughts are filled with
      insight.
⁴ I listen carefully to many proverbs
   and solve riddles with inspiration
      from a harp.

⁵ There is no need to fear when times of
      trouble come,
   when enemies are surrounding me.
⁶ They trust in their wealth
   and boast of great riches.
⁷ Yet they cannot redeem themselves
      from death*
   by paying a ransom to God.
⁸ Redemption does not come so easily,
   for no one can ever pay enough
⁹ to live forever
   and never see the grave.

¹⁰ Those who are wise must finally die,
   just like the foolish and senseless,
   leaving all their wealth behind.
¹¹ The grave is their eternal home,

49:7 Or *no one can redeem the life of another.*

where they will stay forever.
They may name their estates after
      themselves,
   but they leave their wealth to others.
¹² They will not last long despite their
      riches—
   they will die like the animals.
¹³ This is the fate of fools,
   though they will be remembered as
      being so wise.   *Interlude*

¹⁴ Like sheep, they are led to the grave,
   where death will be their shepherd.
In the morning the godly will rule over
      them.
   Their bodies will rot in the grave,
   far from their grand estates.
¹⁵ But as for me, God will redeem my life.
   He will snatch me from the power of
      death.   *Interlude*

¹⁶ So don't be dismayed when the wicked
      grow rich,
   and their homes become ever more
      splendid.
¹⁷ For when they die, they carry nothing
      with them.
   Their wealth will not follow them
      into the grave.
¹⁸ In this life they consider themselves
      fortunate,
   and the world loudly applauds their
      success.
¹⁹ But they will die like all others before
      them
   and never again see the light of day.
²⁰ People who boast of their wealth don't
      understand
   that they will die like the animals.

JUNE 10 ☐ DAY 162
PSALMS 50–54
Betrayed but Triumphant

OVERVIEW God in his righteousness deals with sin in the lives of
believers and unbelievers alike. For those who claim a false righteousness characterized by outward devotion but inward wickedness, there is
warning and rebuke (Psalm 50). For those who acknowledge and turn
from sin, there is forgiveness and restoration (51). The evil liar (52) and
the foolish atheist (53) face destruction, but the righteous one who
suffers at the hands of evil men can trust in God's ultimate victory (54).

Psalm 50	Psalm 51	Psalms 52–53	Psalm 54
Conviction of the Hypocrite	Confession of the Penitent	Condemnation of the Treacherous	Comfort for the Afflicted
God, the Righteous Judge			

YOUR DAILY WALK Take it from David: There is something worse than being wounded by an enemy—and that is being wounded by a friend. And when a trusted associate or fellow worker has stabbed you in the back, how should you handle the natural feelings of resentment that come?

You never so touch the ocean of God's love as when you forgive and love your enemies.

Answer: Handle them with prayer. When Doeg the Edomite reported David's whereabouts to King Saul, it must have come as no surprise to either Saul or David, for Doeg was a known ally of the king. But when the Ziphites—whose border town of Keilah David had personally rescued from a Philistine onslaught (1 Samuel 23:1-5)—betrayed their deliverer, the sting must have been intense.

Anger . . . bitterness . . . revenge . . . a desire to run. All are natural responses to betrayal. But none resolves the issue or helps the one betrayed. For that you must turn to God, who alone can heal the wound with a spirit of forgiveness and love. (See David's example in 52:8-9; 54:6-7; 55:22.)

Have you been wounded by a friend in recent days? Then finish this prayer: "Lord, you know I have every right to treat _____ as my enemy. Though I could respond naturally, help me in your strength to respond supernaturally."

INSIGHT The Carbon Copy Psalm

If upon reading Psalm 53 you get the distinct impression you have read that material before, you're right! Psalms 14 and 53 are almost identical. The titles differ slightly, one verse is omitted (which one?), and the name *God* is substituted for LORD in three places in Psalm 53. Upon reflection, can you suggest a reason why the message of Psalm 14 might be important enough to repeat in Psalm 53?

PSALM 50
A psalm of Asaph.

¹ The mighty God, the LORD, has spoken;
    he has summoned all humanity from
      east to west!
² From Mount Zion, the perfection of
    beauty,
    God shines in glorious radiance.
³ Our God approaches with the noise of
    thunder.
    Fire devours everything in his way,
    and a great storm rages around him.
⁴ Heaven and earth will be his witnesses
    as he judges his people:
⁵ "Bring my faithful people to me—
    those who made a covenant with me
      by giving sacrifices."
⁶ Then let the heavens proclaim his
    justice,
    for God himself will be the judge.
          Interlude

⁷ "O my people, listen as I speak.
    Here are my charges against you,
      O Israel:
    I am God, your God!
⁸ I have no complaint about your
    sacrifices
    or the burnt offerings you constantly
      bring to my altar.
⁹ But I want no more bulls from your
    barns;
    I want no more goats from your pens.
¹⁰ For all the animals of the forest are mine,
    and I own the cattle on a thousand
      hills.
¹¹ Every bird of the mountains
    and all the animals of the field
      belong to me.
¹² If I were hungry, I would not mention
    it to you,
    for all the world is mine and
      everything in it.

13 I don't need the bulls you sacrifice;
  I don't need the blood of goats.
14 What I want instead is your true thanks
    to God;
  I want you to fulfill your vows to the
    Most High.
15 Trust me in your times of trouble,
  and I will rescue you,
  and you will give me glory."

16 But God says to the wicked:
  "Recite my laws no longer,
  and don't pretend that you obey me.
17 For you refuse my discipline
  and treat my laws like trash.
18 When you see a thief, you help him,
  and you spend your time with
    adulterers.
19 Your mouths are filled with wicked-
    ness,
  and your tongues are full of lies.
20 You sit around and slander a brother—
  your own mother's son.
21 While you did all this, I remained
    silent,
  and you thought I didn't care.
  But now I will rebuke you,
  listing all my charges against you.
22 Repent, all of you who ignore me,
  or I will tear you apart,
  and no one will help you.
23 But giving thanks is a sacrifice that
    truly honors me.
  If you keep to my path,
  I will reveal to you the salvation of
    God."

PSALM 51

*For the choir director: A psalm of David, regarding
the time Nathan the prophet came to him after
David had committed adultery with Bathsheba.*

1 Have mercy on me, O God,
  because of your unfailing love.
  Because of your great compassion,
  blot out the stain of my sins.
2 Wash me clean from my guilt.
  Purify me from my sin.

3 For I recognize my shameful deeds—
  they haunt me day and night.
4 Against you, and you alone, have I
    sinned;
  I have done what is evil in your sight.
  You will be proved right in what you
    say,
  and your judgment against me is just.

5 For I was born a sinner—
  yes, from the moment my mother
    conceived me.
6 But you desire honesty from the heart,
  so you can teach me to be wise in my
    inmost being.

7 Purify me from my sins,* and I will be
    clean;
  wash me, and I will be whiter than
    snow.
8 Oh, give me back my joy again;
  you have broken me—
  now let me rejoice.
9 Don't keep looking at my sins.
  Remove the stain of my guilt.
10 Create in me a clean heart, O God.
  Renew a right spirit within me.
11 Do not banish me from your presence,
  and don't take your Holy Spirit from
    me.
12 Restore to me again the joy of your
    salvation,
  and make me willing to obey you.
13 Then I will teach your ways to sinners,
  and they will return to you.
14 Forgive me for shedding blood, O God
    who saves;
  then I will joyfully sing of your forgive-
    ness.
15 Unseal my lips, O Lord,
  that I may praise you.
16 You would not be pleased with sacrifices,
  or I would bring them.
  If I brought you a burnt offering,
  you would not accept it.
17 The sacrifice you want is a broken spirit.
  A broken and repentant heart, O God,
  you will not despise.

18 Look with favor on Zion and help her;
  rebuild the walls of Jerusalem.
19 Then you will be pleased with worthy
    sacrifices
  and with our whole burnt offerings;
  and bulls will again be sacrificed on
    your altar.

PSALM 52

*For the choir director: A psalm of David, regarding
the time Doeg the Edomite told Saul that Ahimelech
had given refuge to David.*

1 You call yourself a hero, do you?
  Why boast about this crime of yours,
  you who have disgraced God's
    people?

51:7 Hebrew *Purify me with the hyssop branch.*

² All day long you plot destruction.
   Your tongue cuts like a sharp razor;
   you're an expert at telling lies.
³ You love evil more than good
   and lies more than truth.   *Interlude*

⁴ You love to say things that harm others,
   you liar!
⁵ But God will strike you down once and
      for all.
   He will pull you from your home
   and drag you from the land of the
      living.   *Interlude*

⁶ The righteous will see it and be amazed.
   They will laugh and say,
⁷ "Look what happens to mighty
      warriors
   who do not trust in God.
   They trust their wealth instead
   and grow more and more bold in
      their wickedness."

⁸ But I am like an olive tree,
   thriving in the house of God.
   I trust in God's unfailing love
   forever and ever.
⁹ I will praise you forever, O God,
   for what you have done.
   I will wait for your mercies
   in the presence of your people.

PSALM 53
For the choir director: A meditation of David.

¹ Only fools say in their hearts,
   "There is no God."
   They are corrupt, and their actions are
      evil;
   no one does good!

² God looks down from heaven
   on the entire human race;
   he looks to see if there is even one with
      real understanding,
   one who seeks for God.
³ But no, all have turned away from God;
   all have become corrupt.
   No one does good,
      not even one!

⁴ Will those who do evil never learn?
   They eat up my people like bread;
   they wouldn't think of praying to
      God.
⁵ But then terror will grip them,
   terror like they have never known
      before.
   God will scatter the bones of your
      enemies.
   You will put them to shame, for God
      has rejected them.

⁶ Oh, that salvation would come from
      Mount Zion to rescue Israel!
   For when God restores his people,
   Jacob will shout with joy, and Israel
      will rejoice.

PSALM 54
For the choir director: A meditation of David,
regarding the time the Ziphites came and said to
Saul, "We know where David is hiding." To be
accompanied by stringed instruments.

¹ Come with great power, O God, and
      rescue me!
   Defend me with your might.
² O God, listen to my prayer.
   Pay attention to my plea.

³ For strangers are attacking me;
   violent men are trying to kill me.
   They care nothing for God.   *Interlude*

⁴ But God is my helper.
   The Lord is the one who keeps me
      alive!
⁵ May my enemies' plans for evil be
      turned against them.
   Do as you promised and put an end
      to them.

⁶ I will sacrifice a voluntary offering to
      you;
   I will praise your name, O LORD,
      for it is good.
⁷ For you will rescue me from my
      troubles
   and help me to triumph over my
      enemies.

JUNE 11 ☐ DAY 163
PSALMS 55–59
The Link of Faith

OVERVIEW Great peril can cause great discouragement; it can also disclose great faith in God. Although David cries out in anguish to God when faced with the betrayal of a friend (Psalm 55), the vicious pursuit of an enemy (56–57), and the hatred of violent judges (58), at the same time he demonstrates great confidence in God's ability to vindicate him at the proper time and in the proper way (59).

Psalm 55	Psalms 56–57	Psalm 58	Psalm 59
Deceitful Betrayers	Dangerous Enemies	Distorted Judge	Defiant Attacker
God, the Faithful Deliverer			

YOUR DAILY WALK When the forecast calls for storms, ships need a strong anchor; buildings, a sure foundation; trees, a deep root system. In each case, their very survival through the storm depends upon a strong link to that which cannot be moved.

The beginning of anxiety is the end of faith; the beginning of true faith is the end of anxiety.

David's anchor in stormy circumstances was an unshakable faith in an unchanging God. Each psalm in today's reading describes an unsettling, disrupting influence that swept into his life. David pictures these onslaughts as a wild storm (55:8), as fierce lions (57:4), as deadly snakes (58:4-5), and as vicious dogs (59:6). But rather than focus on the forces swirling around him, David concentrates on his link of faith to God (55:22; 56:10-11; 57:11; 58:11; 59:9). And since his anchor is fixed to an immovable Rock, David finds that he, too, is immovable.

Is there a storm on the horizon in your life? Are you facing fierce opposition because of your faith? Using David's expressions of trust as your model, compose in your own words a two- or three-sentence statement of your confidence in the God who never changes. Post your statement on a bulletin board or bathroom mirror, where it can remind you in coming days that you needn't fear the storms of life if you have a sure foundation—an anchor in the Lord.

INSIGHT Self-Portrait of a Traitor
Though the identity of the traitor described in Psalm 55:12-14 remains unknown to us, ironically David was painting a graphic picture of his own treachery toward Uriah the Hittite, one of David's staunchest allies and the victim of his murderous plot (2 Samuel 11).

PSALM 55
For the choir director: A psalm of David, to be accompanied by stringed instruments.

1 Listen to my prayer, O God.
  Do not ignore my cry for help!
2 Please listen and answer me,
    for I am overwhelmed by my
      troubles.
3 My enemies shout at me,
    making loud and wicked threats.
  They bring trouble on me,
    hunting me down in their anger.

4 My heart is in anguish.
    The terror of death overpowers me.
5 Fear and trembling overwhelm me.
    I can't stop shaking.
6 Oh, how I wish I had wings like a dove;
    then I would fly away and rest!
7 I would fly far away
    to the quiet of the wilderness.
                                                    Interlude
8 How quickly I would escape—
    far away from this wild storm of
      hatred.

⁹ Destroy them, Lord, and confuse their
      speech,
      for I see violence and strife in the
         city.
¹⁰ Its walls are patrolled day and night
      against invaders,
      but the real danger is wickedness
         within the city.
¹¹ Murder and robbery are everywhere
         there;
      threats and cheating are rampant
         in the streets.

¹² It is not an enemy who taunts me—
      I could bear that.
   It is not my foes who so arrogantly
         insult me—
      I could have hidden from them.
¹³ Instead, it is you—my equal,
      my companion and close friend.
¹⁴ What good fellowship we enjoyed
      as we walked together to the house
         of God.

¹⁵ Let death seize my enemies by
         surprise;
      let the grave* swallow them alive,
      for evil makes its home within
         them.

¹⁶ But I will call on God,
      and the LORD will rescue me.
¹⁷ Morning, noon, and night
      I plead aloud in my distress,
      and the LORD hears my voice.
¹⁸ He rescues me and keeps me safe
      from the battle waged against me,
      even though many still oppose me.
¹⁹ God, who is king forever,
      will hear me and will humble them.
                              Interlude
   For my enemies refuse to change their
         ways;
      they do not fear God.

²⁰ As for this friend of mine, he betrayed
         me;
      he broke his promises.
²¹ His words are as smooth as cream,
      but in his heart is war.
   His words are as soothing as lotion,
      but underneath are daggers!

²² Give your burdens to the LORD,
      and he will take care of you.
   He will not permit the godly to slip
      and fall.

²³ But you, O God, will send the wicked
      down to the pit of destruction.
   Murderers and liars will die young,
      but I am trusting you to save me.

PSALM 56

For the choir director: A psalm of David, regarding the time the Philistines seized him in Gath. To be sung to the tune "Dove on Distant Oaks."

¹ O God, have mercy on me.
      The enemy troops press in on me.
      My foes attack me all day long.
² My slanderers hound me constantly,
      and many are boldly attacking me.
³ But when I am afraid,
      I put my trust in you.
⁴ O God, I praise your word.
      I trust in God, so why should I be
         afraid?
      What can mere mortals do to me?

⁵ They are always twisting what I say;
      they spend their days plotting ways
         to harm me.
⁶ They come together to spy on me—
      watching my every step, eager to
         kill me.
⁷ Don't let them get away with their
         wickedness;
      in your anger, O God, throw them
         to the ground.

⁸ You keep track of all my sorrows.
      You have collected all my tears in
         your bottle.
      You have recorded each one in your
         book.

⁹ On the very day I call to you for help,
      my enemies will retreat.
      This I know: God is on my side.*
¹⁰ O God, I praise your word.
      Yes, LORD, I praise your word.
¹¹ I trust in God, so why should I be
         afraid?
      What can mere mortals do to me?

¹² I will fulfill my vows to you, O God,
      and offer a sacrifice of thanks for
         your help.
¹³ For you have rescued me from death;
      you have kept my feet from
         slipping.
   So now I can walk in your presence,
         O God,
      in your life-giving light.

55:15 Hebrew *let Sheol.*   56:9 Or *By this I will know that God is on my side.*

PSALM 57

For the choir director: A psalm of David, regarding the time he fled from Saul and went into the cave. To be sung to the tune "Do Not Destroy!"

¹ Have mercy on me, O God, have
    mercy!
  I look to you for protection.
I will hide beneath the shadow of your
    wings
  until this violent storm is past.

² I cry out to God Most High,
  to God who will fulfill his purpose
    for me.
³ He will send help from heaven to save
    me,
  rescuing me from those who are out
    to get me.   *Interlude*
My God will send forth his unfailing
    love and faithfulness.

⁴ I am surrounded by fierce lions
  who greedily devour human
    prey—
whose teeth pierce like spears and
    arrows,
  and whose tongues cut like swords.

⁵ Be exalted, O God, above the highest
    heavens!
  May your glory shine over all the
    earth.

⁶ My enemies have set a trap for me.
  I am weary from distress.
They have dug a deep pit in my path,
  but they themselves have fallen
    into it.   *Interlude*

⁷ My heart is confident in you, O God;
  no wonder I can sing your praises!
⁸ Wake up, my soul!
  Wake up, O harp and lyre!
  I will waken the dawn with my
    song.
⁹ I will thank you, Lord, in front of all
    the people.
  I will sing your praises among the
    nations.
¹⁰ For your unfailing love is as high as the
    heavens.
  Your faithfulness reaches to the
    clouds.

¹¹ Be exalted, O God, above the highest
    heavens.
  May your glory shine over all the
    earth.

PSALM 58

For the choir director: A psalm of David, to be sung to the tune "Do Not Destroy!"

¹ Justice—do you rulers know the meaning
    of the word?
  Do you judge the people fairly?
² No, all your dealings are crooked;
  you hand out violence instead of
    justice.
³ These wicked people are born sinners;
  even from birth they have lied and
    gone their own way.
⁴ They spit poison like deadly snakes;
  they are like cobras that refuse to
    listen,
⁵ ignoring the tunes of the snake
    charmers,
  no matter how skillfully they play.

⁶ Break off their fangs, O God!
  Smash the jaws of these lions,
    O Lord!
⁷ May they disappear like water into
    thirsty ground.
  Make their weapons useless in their
    hands.*
⁸ May they be like snails that dissolve
    into slime,
  like a stillborn child who will never
    see the sun.
⁹ God will sweep them away, both
    young and old,
  faster than a pot heats on an open
    flame.

¹⁰ The godly will rejoice when they see
    injustice avenged.
  They will wash their feet in the blood
    of the wicked.
¹¹ Then at last everyone will say,
  "There truly is a reward for those
    who live for God;
  surely there is a God who judges
    justly here on earth."

PSALM 59

For the choir director: A psalm of David, regarding the time Saul sent soldiers to watch David's house in order to kill him. To be sung to the tune "Do Not Destroy!"

¹ Rescue me from my enemies, O God.
  Protect me from those who have
    come to destroy me.
² Rescue me from these criminals;
  save me from these murderers.

58:7 Or *Let them be trodden down and wither like grass.* The meaning of the Hebrew is uncertain.

³ They have set an ambush for me.
　Fierce enemies are out there waiting,
　though I have done them no wrong,
　　O Lord.
⁴ Despite my innocence, they prepare to
　　kill me.
　Rise up and help me! Look on my
　　plight!
⁵ O Lord God Almighty, the God of
　　Israel,
　rise up to punish hostile nations.
　Show no mercy to wicked traitors.
　　　　　　　　　　　　　Interlude

⁶ They come at night,
　snarling like vicious dogs
　as they prowl the streets.
⁷ Listen to the filth that comes from their
　　mouths,
　the piercing swords that fly from
　　their lips.
　"Who can hurt us?" they sneer.

⁸ But Lord, you laugh at them.
　You scoff at all the hostile nations.
⁹ You are my strength; I wait for you to
　　rescue me,
　for you, O God, are my place of safety.
¹⁰ In his unfailing love, my God will come
　　and help me.
　He will let me look down in triumph
　　on all my enemies.

59:13 Hebrew *in Jacob.*　　**59:15** Or *and growl if they don't get enough.*

¹¹ Don't kill them, for my people soon
　　forget such lessons;
　stagger them with your power, and
　　bring them to their knees,
　　O Lord our shield.
¹² Because of the sinful things they say,
　because of the evil that is on their
　　lips,
　let them be captured by their pride,
　　their curses, and their lies.
¹³ Destroy them in your anger!
　Wipe them out completely!
　Then the whole world will know
　that God reigns in Israel.*　*Interlude*

¹⁴ My enemies come out at night,
　snarling like vicious dogs
　as they prowl the streets.
¹⁵ They scavenge for food
　but go to sleep unsatisfied.*

¹⁶ But as for me, I will sing about your
　　power.
　I will shout with joy each morning
　　because of your unfailing love.
　For you have been my refuge,
　　a place of safety in the day of distress.

¹⁷ O my Strength, to you I sing praises,
　for you, O God, are my refuge,
　the God who shows me unfailing
　　love.

JUNE 12 ☐ DAY 164
PSALMS 60–66
Through the Night Watches

 OVERVIEW The freedom to be transparent before God, to express to him exactly how you feel, is an important part of prayer. David's prayer life reveals the deepest emotions of his heart. The welfare of his nation (Psalm 60) and the duties of his office (61) weigh heavily upon him. He yearns for a growing relationship with God (62–64)—a relationship his enemies do not experience. He stands in awe of God's powerful creation (65) and revels in God's matchless salvation (66), inviting all who read his words to "come and see what our God has done" (66:5).

Psalms 60–61	Psalms 62–64	Psalms 65–66
Prosperity for the Nation and King	Protection for the Seeking Soul	Praise for the God Who Provides
Supplication		Acclamation

YOUR DAILY WALK Psalm 63 was penned by David "when [he] was in the wilderness of Judah," a desolate region where water is scarce, vegetation is almost nonexistent, and the heat of the day makes every activity a burden.

No daily meal is complete without the bread of life.

These barren surroundings prompted David to write, "My soul thirsts for you; my whole body longs for you in this parched and weary land" (v. 1). Soul and body, David longs to be in the presence of God.

David knows that the thirst and hunger he feels for God will be satisfied as he follows hard after him. "You satisfy me more than the richest of foods" (v. 5). In seeking God early, David finds elements of God's character to reflect upon late into the night (v. 6). Because God has helped him, David rejoices "in the shadow of [His] protecting wings" (v. 7). In cleaving to God, David finds God upholding him (v. 8).

Jesus told his followers, "God blesses those who are hungry and thirsty for justice, for they will receive it in full" (Matthew 5:6). How is your spiritual appetite? Carve out some time to be alone with God today for fifteen minutes or so of "thirst quenching." Enjoy his presence; feast on his Word; let him satisfy the yearning of your heart.

INSIGHT A Sleepless Night for a Thirsty Soul
In Bible times, the night was divided into three periods or "watches" for soldiers and shepherds: sunset to approximately 10:00 P.M., 10:00 P.M. to 2:00 A.M., and 2:00 A.M. to dawn. Now read Psalm 63:6 to discover a telltale sign of David's devotion to God!

PSALM 60

For the choir director: A psalm of David useful for teaching, regarding the time David fought Aram-naharaim and Aram-zobah, and Joab returned and killed twelve thousand Edomites in the Valley of Salt. To be sung to the tune "Lily of the Testimony."

¹ You have rejected us, O God, and
    broken our defenses.
  You have been angry with us; now
    restore us to your favor.
² You have shaken our land and split it
    open.
  Seal the cracks before it completely
    collapses.
³ You have been very hard on us,
    making us drink wine that sent us
    reeling.
⁴ But you have raised a banner for those
    who honor you—
  a rallying point in the face of attack.
                                    Interlude

⁵ Use your strong right arm to save us,
    and rescue your beloved people.
⁶ God has promised this by his holiness*:
  "I will divide up Shechem with joy.
  I will measure out the valley of
    Succoth.
⁷ Gilead is mine,
    and Manasseh is mine.
  Ephraim will produce my warriors,
    and Judah will produce my kings.

⁸ Moab will become my lowly servant,
    and Edom will be my slave.
  I will shout in triumph over the
    Philistines."

⁹ But who will bring me into the fortified
    city?
  Who will bring me victory over
    Edom?
¹⁰ Have you rejected us, O God?
  Will you no longer march with our
    armies?
¹¹ Oh, please help us against our
    enemies,
    for all human help is useless.
¹² With God's help we will do mighty
    things,
    for he will trample down our foes.

PSALM 61

For the choir director: A psalm of David, to be accompanied by stringed instruments.

¹ O God, listen to my cry!
    Hear my prayer!
² From the ends of the earth,
    I will cry to you for help,
    for my heart is overwhelmed.
  Lead me to the towering rock of safety,
³   for you are my safe refuge,
    a fortress where my enemies cannot
    reach me.

60:6 Or *in his sanctuary.*

⁴ Let me live forever in your sanctuary,
  safe beneath the shelter of your
      wings!   *Interlude*
⁵ For you have heard my vows, O God.
  You have given me an inheritance
      reserved for those who fear your
      name.

⁶ Add many years to the life of the king!
  May his years span the generations!
⁷ May he reign under God's protection
      forever.
  Appoint your unfailing love and
      faithfulness to watch over him.

⁸ Then I will always sing praises to your
      name
  as I fulfill my vows day after day.

PSALM 62
For Jeduthun, the choir director: A psalm of David.

¹ I wait quietly before God,
  for my salvation comes from him.
² He alone is my rock and my salvation,
  my fortress where I will never be
      shaken.

³ So many enemies against one man—
  all of them trying to kill me.
  To them I'm just a broken-down wall
  or a tottering fence.
⁴ They plan to topple me from my high
      position.
  They delight in telling lies about me.
  They are friendly to my face,
  but they curse me in their hearts.
                                   Interlude

⁵ I wait quietly before God,
  for my hope is in him.
⁶ He alone is my rock and my salvation,
  my fortress where I will not be shaken.
⁷ My salvation and my honor come from
      God alone.
  He is my refuge, a rock where no
      enemy can reach me.

⁸ O my people, trust in him at all times.
  Pour out your heart to him,
  for God is our refuge.   *Interlude*

⁹ From the greatest to the lowliest—
  all are nothing in his sight.
  If you weigh them on the scales,
  they are lighter than a puff of air.
¹⁰ Don't try to get rich
  by extortion or robbery.
  And if your wealth increases,
  don't make it the center of your life.

¹¹ God has spoken plainly,
  and I have heard it many times:
  Power, O God, belongs to you;
¹²   unfailing love, O Lord, is yours.
  Surely you judge all people
  according to what they have done.

PSALM 63
A psalm of David, regarding a time when David
was in the wilderness of Judah.

¹ O God, you are my God;
  I earnestly search for you.
  My soul thirsts for you;
  my whole body longs for you
  in this parched and weary land
  where there is no water.

² I have seen you in your sanctuary
  and gazed upon your power and
      glory.
³ Your unfailing love is better to me than
      life itself;
  how I praise you!
⁴ I will honor you as long as I live,
  lifting up my hands to you in prayer.
⁵ You satisfy me more than the richest of
      foods.
  I will praise you with songs of joy.

⁶ I lie awake thinking of you,
  meditating on you through the night.
⁷ I think how much you have helped me;
  I sing for joy in the shadow of your
      protecting wings.
⁸ I follow close behind you;
  your strong right hand holds me
      securely.

⁹ But those plotting to destroy me will
      come to ruin.
  They will go down into the depths
      of the earth.
¹⁰ They will die by the sword
  and become the food of jackals.

¹¹ But the king will rejoice in God.
  All who trust in him will praise him,
  while liars will be silenced.

PSALM 64
For the choir director: A psalm of David.

¹ O God, listen to my complaint.
  Do not let my enemies' threats
      overwhelm me.
² Protect me from the plots of the wicked,
  from the scheming of those who do
      evil.

3 Sharp tongues are the swords they
    wield;
    bitter words are the arrows they aim.
4 They shoot from ambush at the
    innocent,
    attacking suddenly and fearlessly.
5 They encourage each other to do evil
    and plan how to set their traps.
    "Who will ever notice?" they ask.
6 As they plot their crimes, they say,
    "We have devised the perfect plan!"
    Yes, the human heart and mind are
    cunning.

7 But God himself will shoot them down.
    Suddenly, his arrows will pierce
    them.
8 Their own words will be turned against
    them, destroying them.
    All who see it happening will shake
    their heads in scorn.
9 Then everyone will stand in awe,
    proclaiming the mighty acts of God,
    realizing all the amazing things he
    does.

10 The godly will rejoice in the LORD
    and find shelter in him.
    And those who do what is right
    will praise him.

PSALM 65
For the choir director: A psalm of David. A song.

1 What mighty praise, O God,
    belongs to you in Zion.
    We will fulfill our vows to you,
2   for you answer our prayers,
    and to you all people will come.
3 Though our hearts are filled with
    sins,
    you forgive them all.
4 What joy for those you choose to bring
    near,
    those who live in your holy courts.
    What joys await us
    inside your holy Temple.

5 You faithfully answer our prayers with
    awesome deeds,
    O God our savior.
    You are the hope of everyone on earth,
    even those who sail on distant seas.
6 You formed the mountains by your
    power
    and armed yourself with mighty
    strength.

7 You quieted the raging oceans
    with their pounding waves
    and silenced the shouting of the
    nations.
8 Those who live at the ends of the earth
    stand in awe of your wonders.
    From where the sun rises to where it
    sets,
    you inspire shouts of joy.

9 You take care of the earth and water it,
    making it rich and fertile.
    The rivers of God will not run dry;
    they provide a bountiful harvest of
    grain,
    for you have ordered it so.
10 You drench the plowed ground with
    rain,
    melting the clods and leveling the
    ridges.
    You soften the earth with showers
    and bless its abundant crops.
11 You crown the year with a bountiful
    harvest;
    even the hard pathways overflow
    with abundance.
12 The wilderness becomes a lush pasture,
    and the hillsides blossom with joy.
13 The meadows are clothed with flocks
    of sheep,
    and the valleys are carpeted with
    grain.
    They all shout and sing for joy!

PSALM 66
For the choir director: A psalm. A song.

1 Shout joyful praises to God, all the
    earth!
2   Sing about the glory of his name!
    Tell the world how glorious he is.
3 Say to God, "How awesome are your
    deeds!
    Your enemies cringe before your
    mighty power.
4 Everything on earth will worship you;
    they will sing your praises,
    shouting your name in glorious
    songs."   *Interlude*

5 Come and see what our God has done,
    what awesome miracles he does for
    his people!
6 He made a dry path through the Red
    Sea,*
    and his people went across on foot.
    Come, let us rejoice in who he is.

66:6 Hebrew *the sea.*

⁷ For by his great power he rules forever.
   He watches every movement of the
      nations;
   let no rebel rise in defiance.

Interlude

⁸ Let the whole world bless our God
   and sing aloud his praises.
⁹ Our lives are in his hands,
   and he keeps our feet from
      stumbling.
¹⁰ You have tested us, O God;
   you have purified us like silver
      melted in a crucible.
¹¹ You captured us in your net
   and laid the burden of slavery on our
      backs.
¹² You sent troops to ride across our
      broken bodies.
   We went through fire and flood.
   But you brought us to a place of
      great abundance.

¹³ Now I come to your Temple with burnt
      offerings

to fulfill the vows I made to you—
¹⁴ yes, the sacred vows you heard me
      make
   when I was in deep trouble.
¹⁵ That is why I am sacrificing burnt
      offerings to you—
   the best of my rams as a pleasing
      aroma.
   And I will sacrifice bulls and goats.

Interlude

¹⁶ Come and listen, all you who fear God,
   and I will tell you what he did for me.
¹⁷ For I cried out to him for help,
   praising him as I spoke.
¹⁸ If I had not confessed the sin in my
      heart,
   my Lord would not have listened.
¹⁹ But God did listen!
   He paid attention to my prayer.

²⁰ Praise God, who did not ignore my
      prayer
   and did not withdraw his unfailing
      love from me.

JUNE 13 ☐ DAY 165
PSALMS 67–72
Your Burden Bearer

OVERVIEW Book Two of Psalms concludes with six proclamations showing that God is worthy of praise and trust. The nations acknowledge God's righteous rule (Psalm 67), exulting in his care of the fatherless and homeless (68). He hears the cry of the distressed (69), speedily delivers the oppressed (70), strengthens the feeble (71), and exercises dominion over kings and kingdoms (72). Truly "all kings will bow before him, and all nations will serve him" (72:11).

Psalm 67	Psalm 68	Psalms 69–70	Psalm 71	Psalm 72
"Extol the Lord"	"Exalt the Lord"	"Don't Delay, Lord"	"Don't Desert Me, Lord"	"Bless the Lord"
Praise		Pleading		Prayer

YOUR DAILY WALK It has been well said, "Our days are identical suitcases—all the same size—but some people can pack more into them than others."

   In the midst of your busy schedule, never lose sight of the fact that God is busy, too—on your behalf! After you read Psalm 68 today, see if you can discover and jot down at least five things God has promised to do for you today—and every day.

   In our computerized world where people are often reduced to face-less records, it's encouraging to know there is someone to whom you'll

We have no power from God unless we live in the persuasion that we have none of our own.

never be just a number. Someone who carries you in his arms. Someone who enters into your joys and sorrows, exchanging your heavy burdens for his light ones (Matthew 11:28-30).

Five times, in Psalm 68, strength is mentioned—strength God longs to demonstrate on behalf of his people. Have you drawn upon that strength today, enabling you to do in his strength what you would be powerless to do in your own? After all, "the God of Israel gives power and strength to his people" (68:35).

 INSIGHT The Final Stop on a Four-Hundred-Year Journey
The exact occasion for which David composed Psalm 68 is not known, but quite possibly it marked the bringing of the Ark of the Covenant into Jerusalem (2 Samuel 6:12). This joyous event is the climax of a journey begun centuries before at Mount Sinai. There the Ark had been fashioned; from there it went before Israel into the Promised Land. Now the Ark reaches the summit of Mount Zion, where it will reside as the symbol of God's abiding presence.

PSALM 67

For the choir director: A psalm, to be accompanied by stringed instruments. A song.

¹ May God be merciful and bless us.
  May his face shine with favor upon
    us.   *Interlude*
² May your ways be known throughout
    the earth,
  your saving power among people
    everywhere.
³ May the nations praise you, O God.
  Yes, may all the nations praise you.

⁴ How glad the nations will be, singing
    for joy,
  because you govern them with
    justice
  and direct the actions of the whole
    world.   *Interlude*
⁵ May the nations praise you, O God.
  Yes, may all the nations praise you.

⁶ Then the earth will yield its harvests,
  and God, our God, will richly bless
    us.
⁷ Yes, God will bless us,
  and people all over the world will
    fear him.

PSALM 68

For the choir director: A psalm of David. A song.

¹ Arise, O God, and scatter your enemies.
  Let those who hate God run for their
    lives.
² Drive them off like smoke blown by the
    wind.
  Melt them like wax in fire.
  Let the wicked perish in the presence
    of God.

³ But let the godly rejoice.
  Let them be glad in God's presence.
  Let them be filled with joy.

⁴ Sing praises to God and to his name!
  Sing loud praises to him who rides
    the clouds.
  His name is the LORD—
    rejoice in his presence!

⁵ Father to the fatherless, defender of
    widows—
  this is God, whose dwelling is holy.
⁶ God places the lonely in families;
  he sets the prisoners free and gives
    them joy.
  But for rebels, there is only famine
    and distress.

⁷ O God, when you led your people from
    Egypt,
  when you marched through the
    wilderness,   *Interlude*
⁸ the earth trembled, and the heavens
    poured rain
  before you, the God of Sinai,
  before God, the God of Israel.
⁹ You sent abundant rain, O God,
  to refresh the weary Promised
    Land.
¹⁰ There your people finally settled,
  and with a bountiful harvest, O God,
  you provided for your needy people.

¹¹ The Lord announces victory,
  and throngs of women shout the
    happy news.
¹² Enemy kings and their armies flee,
  while the women of Israel divide the
    plunder.

¹³ Though they lived among the sheep-
folds,
now they are covered with silver and
gold,
as a dove is covered by its wings.
¹⁴ The Almighty scattered the enemy kings
like a blowing snowstorm on Mount
Zalmon.
¹⁵ The majestic mountains of Bashan
stretch high into the sky.
¹⁶ Why do you look with envy, O rugged
mountains,
at Mount Zion, where God has chosen
to live,
where the LORD himself will live
forever?
¹⁷ Surrounded by unnumbered thousands
of chariots,
the Lord came from Mount Sinai into
his sanctuary.
¹⁸ When you ascended to the heights,
you led a crowd of captives.
You received gifts from the people,
even from those who rebelled against
you.
Now the LORD God will live among
us here.
¹⁹ Praise the Lord; praise God our savior!
For each day he carries us in his
arms.   *Interlude*
²⁰ Our God is a God who saves!
The Sovereign LORD rescues us from
death.
²¹ But God will smash the heads of his
enemies,
crushing the skulls of those who love
their guilty ways.
²² The Lord says, "I will bring my
enemies down from Bashan;
I will bring them up from the depths
of the sea.
²³ You, my people, will wash your feet in
their blood,
and even your dogs will get their
share!"
²⁴ Your procession has come into view,
O God—
the procession of my God and King
as he goes into the sanctuary.
²⁵ Singers are in front, musicians are
behind;
with them are young women playing
tambourines.

²⁶ Praise God, all you people of Israel;
praise the LORD, the source of Israel's
life.
²⁷ Look, the little tribe of Benjamin leads
the way.
Then comes a great throng of rulers
from Judah
and all the rulers of Zebulun and
Naphtali.
²⁸ Summon your might, O God.
Display your power, O God, as you
have in the past.
²⁹ The kings of the earth are bringing
tribute
to your Temple in Jerusalem.
³⁰ Rebuke these enemy nations—
these wild animals lurking in the
reeds,
this herd of bulls among the weaker
calves.
Humble those who demand tribute
from us.*
Scatter the nations that delight in
war.
³¹ Let Egypt come with gifts of precious
metals;
let Ethiopia* bow in submission to
God.
³² Sing to God, you kingdoms of the earth.
Sing praises to the Lord.   *Interlude*
³³ Sing to the one who rides across the
ancient heavens,
his mighty voice thundering from
the sky.
³⁴ Tell everyone about God's power.
His majesty shines down on Israel;
his strength is mighty in the heavens.
³⁵ God is awesome in his sanctuary.
The God of Israel gives power and
strength to his people.

Praise be to God!

PSALM 69

*For the choir director: A psalm of David, to be sung
to the tune "Lilies."*

¹ Save me, O God,
for the floodwaters are up to my
neck.
² Deeper and deeper I sink into the
mire;
I can't find a foothold to stand on.
I am in deep water,
and the floods overwhelm me.

68:30 Or *Humble them until they submit, bringing pieces of silver as tribute.*   68:31 Hebrew *Cush.*

³ I am exhausted from crying for help;
  my throat is parched and dry.
My eyes are swollen with weeping,
  waiting for my God to help me.

⁴ Those who hate me without cause
  are more numerous than the hairs
    on my head.
These enemies who seek to destroy me
  are doing so without cause.
They attack me with lies,
  demanding that I give back what
    I didn't steal.

⁵ O God, you know how foolish I am;
  my sins cannot be hidden from you.
⁶ Don't let those who trust in you
    stumble because of me,
  O Sovereign LORD Almighty.
Don't let me cause them to be
    humiliated,
  O God of Israel.
⁷ For I am mocked and shamed for your
    sake;
  humiliation is written all over my face.
⁸ Even my own brothers pretend they
    don't know me;
  they treat me like a stranger.
⁹ Passion for your house burns within me,
  so those who insult you are also
    insulting me.
¹⁰ When I weep and fast before the LORD,
  they scoff at me.
¹¹ When I dress in sackcloth to show
    sorrow,
  they make fun of me.
¹² I am the favorite topic of town gossip,
  and all the drunkards sing about me.

¹³ But I keep right on praying to you,
    LORD,
  hoping this is the time you will show
    me favor.
In your unfailing love, O God,
  answer my prayer with your sure
    salvation.
¹⁴ Pull me out of the mud;
  don't let me sink any deeper!
Rescue me from those who hate me,
  and pull me from these deep waters.
¹⁵ Don't let the floods overwhelm me,
  or the deep waters swallow me,
  or the pit of death devour me.

¹⁶ Answer my prayers, O LORD,
  for your unfailing love is wonderful.
Turn and take care of me,
  for your mercy is so plentiful.

¹⁷ Don't hide from your servant;
  answer me quickly, for I am in deep
    trouble!
¹⁸ Come and rescue me;
  free me from all my enemies.

¹⁹ You know the insults I endure—
  the humiliation and disgrace.
You have seen all my enemies
  and know what they have said.
²⁰ Their insults have broken my heart,
  and I am in despair.
If only one person would show some
    pity;
  if only one would turn and comfort
    me.
²¹ But instead, they give me poison for
    food;
  they offer me sour wine to satisfy my
    thirst.

²² Let the bountiful table set before them
    become a snare,
  and let their security become a trap.
²³ Let their eyes go blind so they cannot
    see,
  and let their bodies grow weaker and
    weaker.
²⁴ Pour out your fury on them;
  consume them with your burning
    anger.
²⁵ May their homes become desolate
  and their tents be deserted.
²⁶ To those you have punished, they add
    insult to injury;
  they scoff at the pain of those you
    have hurt.
²⁷ Pile their sins up high,
  and don't let them go free.
²⁸ Erase their names from the Book of Life;
  don't let them be counted among the
    righteous.

²⁹ I am suffering and in pain.
  Rescue me, O God, by your saving
    power.
³⁰ Then I will praise God's name with
    singing,
  and I will honor him with thanks-
    giving.
³¹ For this will please the LORD more than
    sacrificing an ox
  or presenting a bull with its horns
    and hooves.
³² The humble will see their God at work
    and be glad.
  Let all who seek God's help live in
    joy.

³³ For the LORD hears the cries of his
        needy ones;
    he does not despise his people who
        are oppressed.

³⁴ Praise him, O heaven and earth,
        the seas and all that move in them.
³⁵ For God will save Jerusalem*
        and rebuild the towns of Judah.
    His people will live there
        and take possession of the land.
³⁶ The descendants of those who obey
        him will inherit the land,
    and those who love him will live
        there in safety.

PSALM 70

*For the choir director: A psalm of David, to bring
us to the LORD's remembrance.*

¹ Please, God, rescue me!
        Come quickly, LORD, and help me.
² May those who try to destroy me
        be humiliated and put to shame.
    May those who take delight in my
        trouble
        be turned back in disgrace.
³ Let them be horrified by their shame,
        for they said, "Aha! We've got him
        now!"
⁴ But may all who search for you
        be filled with joy and gladness.
    May those who love your salvation
        repeatedly shout, "God is great!"
⁵ But I am poor and needy;
        please hurry to my aid, O God.
    You are my helper and my savior;
        O LORD, do not delay!

PSALM 71

¹ O LORD, you are my refuge;
        never let me be disgraced.
² Rescue me! Save me from my enemies,
        for you are just.
    Turn your ear to listen and set me
        free.
³ Be to me a protecting rock of safety,
        where I am always welcome.
    Give the order to save me,
        for you are my rock and my fortress.

⁴ My God, rescue me from the power of
        the wicked,
    from the clutches of cruel oppressors.
⁵ O Lord, you alone are my hope.
    I've trusted you, O LORD, from
        childhood.

69:35 Hebrew *Zion.*

⁶ Yes, you have been with me from birth;
        from my mother's womb you have
        cared for me.
    No wonder I am always praising you!

⁷ My life is an example to many,
        because you have been my strength
        and protection.
⁸ That is why I can never stop praising
        you;
    I declare your glory all day long.

⁹ And now, in my old age, don't set me
        aside.
    Don't abandon me when my
        strength is failing.
¹⁰ For my enemies are whispering against
        me.
    They are plotting together to kill me.
¹¹ They say, "God has abandoned him.
        Let's go and get him,
        for there is no one to help him now."

¹² O God, don't stay away.
        My God, please hurry to help me.
¹³ Bring disgrace and destruction on
        those who accuse me.
    May humiliation and shame cover
        those who want to harm me.

¹⁴ But I will keep on hoping for you to
        help me;
    I will praise you more and more.
¹⁵ I will tell everyone about your
        righteousness.
    All day long I will proclaim your
        saving power,
        for I am overwhelmed by how much
        you have done for me.
¹⁶ I will praise your mighty deeds,
        O Sovereign LORD.
    I will tell everyone that you alone are
        just and good.

¹⁷ O God, you have taught me from my
        earliest childhood,
    and I have constantly told others
        about the wonderful things you do.
¹⁸ Now that I am old and gray,
        do not abandon me, O God.
    Let me proclaim your power to this
        new generation,
        your mighty miracles to all who
        come after me.

¹⁹ Your righteousness, O God, reaches to
        the highest heavens.

You have done such wonderful
  things.
Who can compare with you, O God?
²⁰ You have allowed me to suffer much
  hardship,
    but you will restore me to life again
    and lift me up from the depths of the
      earth.
²¹ You will restore me to even greater
  honor
    and comfort me once again.

²² Then I will praise you with music on
  the harp,
    because you are faithful to your
      promises, O God.
  I will sing for you with a lyre,
    O Holy One of Israel.
²³ I will shout for joy and sing your
  praises,
    for you have redeemed me.
²⁴ I will tell about your righteous deeds
  all day long,
    for everyone who tried to hurt me
    has been shamed and humiliated.

PSALM 72
A psalm of Solomon.

¹ Give justice to the king, O God,
    and righteousness to the king's son.
² Help him judge your people in the
    right way;
    let the poor always be treated fairly.
³ May the mountains yield prosperity
    for all,
    and may the hills be fruitful,
    because the king does what is right.
⁴ Help him to defend the poor,
    to rescue the children of the needy,
    and to crush their oppressors.
⁵ May he live* as long as the sun shines,
    as long as the moon continues in the
      skies.
    Yes, forever!
⁶ May his reign be as refreshing as the
    springtime rains—
    like the showers that water the earth.
⁷ May all the godly flourish during his
    reign.
    May there be abundant prosperity
    until the end of time.

⁸ May he reign from sea to sea,
    and from the Euphrates River* to the
      ends of the earth.
⁹ Desert nomads will bow before him;
    his enemies will fall before him in
      the dust.
¹⁰ The western kings of Tarshish and the
      islands
    will bring him tribute.
  The eastern kings of Sheba and Seba
    will bring him gifts.
¹¹ All kings will bow before him,
    and all nations will serve him.

¹² He will rescue the poor when they cry
      to him;
    he will help the oppressed, who have
      no one to defend them.
¹³ He feels pity for the weak and the
      needy,
    and he will rescue them.
¹⁴ He will save them from oppression and
      from violence,
    for their lives are precious to him.

¹⁵ Long live the king!
    May the gold of Sheba be given to
      him.
  May the people always pray for him
    and bless him all day long.
¹⁶ May there be abundant crops
      throughout the land,
    flourishing even on the mountain-
      tops.
  May the fruit trees flourish as they do
      in Lebanon,
    sprouting up like grass in a field.
¹⁷ May the king's name endure forever;
    may it continue as long as the sun
      shines.
  May all nations be blessed through him
    and bring him praise.

¹⁸ Bless the LORD God, the God of Israel,
    who alone does such wonderful
      things.
¹⁹ Bless his glorious name forever!
    Let the whole earth be filled with his
      glory.
  Amen and amen!

²⁰ (This ends the prayers of David son of
    Jesse.)

72:5 As in Greek version; Hebrew reads *May they fear you.*   72:8 Hebrew *the river.*

JUNE 14 □ DAY 166
It's All in the Call

 LOOK BACK As the psalmist spotlights the character of God, he finds himself adjusting his conduct accordingly. God's love reaches to the heavens; therefore, there is no need to fret. God is an ever-present help in trouble; therefore, there is no reason to be downcast. God's greatness is astounding; therefore, let his praises be known to all.

By contrast, humans are frail and finite, sinful and guilty. The psalmist's cry for mercy and forgiveness is met by God's promise of cleansing and comfort. Seeing God's greatness and grandeur puts the psalmist in line to draw upon God's strength and supply. It's a lesson each new generation must learn—and one of the best places to learn it is at the knee of silver-haired saints who have walked with God for a lifetime (71:18).

 LOOK UP Even a five-year-old child knows the significance of the telephone number 9-1-1. It's the magic number that unlocks incredible lifesaving resources in a matter of seconds. Those confronted with a life-threatening situation have only to call 9-1-1 to find help in time of

The melody of praise is best played with the notes of praise, adoration, confession, and thanksgiving.

need, comfort in the face of danger, and protection from the forces that would seek to harm and destroy.

But stop for a moment and ask yourself this question: Why do people in trouble reach for the phone and dial 9-1-1? Is it because

• they *think* someone might be on the other end of the line to hear their plea?
• they *hope* there is help to be found somewhere?
• they *wish* there were a solution to their dilemma? or
• they *know* that someone who is trained, ready, willing, and able to help is poised to respond the instant their call arrives?

Think of Psalm 70 as the psalmist's 9-1-1 prayer: "Please, God, rescue me! Come quickly, LORD, and help me. . . . please hurry to my aid, O God. You are my helper and my savior; O LORD, do not delay" (70:1, 5).

And why does the psalmist call upon the Lord? Not because he hopes or thinks or wishes or wonders if God will come to his rescue, but because "[God] *will* rescue the poor when they cry to him. . . . He *feels* pity for the weak and the needy. . . . He *will* save them from oppression and from violence" (Psalm 72:12-14, emphasis added). It's the same idea expressed by Jeremiah the prophet when he said, "The LORD . . . says this: Ask me and I will tell you some remarkable secrets about what is going to happen here" (Jeremiah 33:2-3).

 LOOK AHEAD When life seems to be out of control and circumstances are as bewildering as a three-alarm fire, you have several options as to how you will respond. You can lean on your own strength and understanding, even though you've been warned not to (Proverbs 3:5). You can surround yourself with busyness or indulge yourself in pleasure, but that won't remove the feelings of fear and inadequacy. You can ignore your problems and hope they will go away, but chances are they won't.

Or you can call upon the Lord, the only one who has promised never to leave you or forsake you (Matthew 28:20; Hebrews 13:5). It may sound like a simple solution—and in some ways it is. But with a Tower of Strength and Mercy like that awaiting your call twenty-four hours a day, why would anyone look elsewhere for help?

JUNE 15 ☐ DAY 167
PSALMS 73–77
People's Questions, God's Answers

OVERVIEW Book Three of Psalms begins with several selections by Asaph, a gifted musician appointed by David to direct the Levitical choirs. Asaph first probes the hard question, Why do the wicked flourish (Psalm 73) while Israel flounders (74)? By focusing on God's justice (75–76) and God's faithfulness to his people (77), Asaph discovers a solid foundation of hope, even as the wicked seem to get away with murder.

Psalm 73	Psalm 74	Psalms 75–76	Psalm 77
Prosperity of the Evil	Plight of the Righteous	Praise for God's Justice	Promise of God's Favor
Questions		Answers	

YOUR DAILY WALK A sheriff was asked by a local resident, "Do you think you will ever eliminate crime?"

If you don't want the fruits of sin in your life, stay out of sin's orchard.

The sheriff wisely replied, "I'm not naive enough to think that crime can ever be eliminated. There were prostitutes and pickpockets in the days of Christ. There was gambling and debauchery in the days of the prophets. There will always be some who submit to the soft, glittery pleasures of the world, and it will always be for the spiritually strong to lead them back."

His words ring true in a day when, according to FBI statistics, one serious crime is committed in this country every 2 seconds . . . one robbery every 10 seconds . . . one murder every 5.8 minutes.

Asaph, in observing the criminal element in his day, was honest enough to ask God some searching questions: Is godliness really worth the struggle? Have I made the wrong choice? (73:13-14). Implied in those words is another protest: God, do you really care?

If you've asked the same questions, you need what Asaph found: perspective. As he drew close to the Lord (73:17), the psalmist saw that the wicked would be repaid for their sinfulness and the faithful would receive a great reward. All this will happen in God's perfect timing.

In the meantime, you need strength for today—strength to forgo the expedient and concentrate on the obedient.

INSIGHT Asaph—No Second Fiddle When It Comes to Music
Asaph was one of the singers appointed by David to direct the choir of Levites (1 Chronicles 15:16, 19). Later, he was ranked with David as one of Israel's finest musicians (Nehemiah 12:46).

BOOK THREE (Psalms 73–89)
PSALM 73
A psalm of Asaph.

¹ Truly God is good to Israel,
to those whose hearts are pure.

² But as for me, I came so close to the edge of the cliff!
My feet were slipping, and I was almost gone.

³ For I envied the proud

when I saw them prosper despite their wickedness.

⁴ They seem to live such a painless life;
their bodies are so healthy and strong.

⁵ They aren't troubled like other people
or plagued with problems like everyone else.

⁶ They wear pride like a jeweled necklace,
and their clothing is woven of cruelty.

⁷ These fat cats have everything
   their hearts could ever wish for!
⁸ They scoff and speak only evil;
   in their pride they seek to crush
      others.
⁹ They boast against the very heavens,
   and their words strut throughout the
      earth.
¹⁰ And so the people are dismayed and
      confused,
   drinking in all their words.
¹¹ "Does God realize what is going on?"
      they ask.
   "Is the Most High even aware of
      what is happening?"
¹² Look at these arrogant people—
   enjoying a life of ease while their
      riches multiply.

¹³ Was it for nothing that I kept my heart
      pure
   and kept myself from doing wrong?
¹⁴ All I get is trouble all day long;
   every morning brings me pain.

¹⁵ If I had really spoken this way,
   I would have been a traitor to your
      people.
¹⁶ So I tried to understand why the
      wicked prosper.
   But what a difficult task it is!
¹⁷ Then one day I went into your
      sanctuary, O God,
   and I thought about the destiny of
      the wicked.
¹⁸ Truly, you put them on a slippery path
   and send them sliding over the cliff
      to destruction.
¹⁹ In an instant they are destroyed,
   swept away by terrors.
²⁰ Their present life is only a dream
   that is gone when they awake.
   When you arise, O Lord,
   you will make them vanish from this
      life.

²¹ Then I realized how bitter I had become,
   how pained I had been by all I had
      seen.
²² I was so foolish and ignorant—
   I must have seemed like a senseless
      animal to you.
²³ Yet I still belong to you;
   you are holding my right hand.
²⁴ You will keep on guiding me with your
      counsel,
   leading me to a glorious destiny.

²⁵ Whom have I in heaven but you?
   I desire you more than anything on
      earth.
²⁶ My health may fail, and my spirit may
      grow weak,
   but God remains the strength of my
      heart;
   he is mine forever.

²⁷ But those who desert him will perish,
   for you destroy those who abandon
      you.
²⁸ But as for me, how good it is to be near
      God!
   I have made the Sovereign LORD my
      shelter,
   and I will tell everyone about the
      wonderful things you do.

PSALM 74
A psalm of Asaph.

¹ O God, why have you rejected us
      forever?
   Why is your anger so intense against
      the sheep of your own pasture?
² Remember that we are the people you
      chose in ancient times,
   the tribe you redeemed as your own
      special possession!
   And remember Jerusalem,* your
      home here on earth.
³ Walk through the awful ruins of the
      city;
   see how the enemy has destroyed
      your sanctuary.
⁴ There your enemies shouted their
      victorious battle cries;
   there they set up their battle
      standards.
⁵ They chopped down the entrance
   like woodcutters in a forest.
⁶ With axes and picks,
   they smashed the carved paneling.
⁷ They set the sanctuary on fire, burning
      it to the ground.
   They utterly defiled the place that
      bears your holy name.
⁸ Then they thought, "Let's destroy
      everything!"
   So they burned down all the places
      where God was worshiped.
⁹ We see no miraculous signs
   as evidence that you will save us.
   All the prophets are gone;
   no one can tell us when it will end.

74:2 Hebrew *Mount Zion.*

¹⁰ How long, O God, will you allow our
 enemies to mock you?
  Will you let them dishonor your
   name forever?
¹¹ Why do you hold back your strong
 right hand?
  Unleash your powerful fist and
   deliver a deathblow.

¹² You, O God, are my king from ages past,
 bringing salvation to the earth.
¹³ You split the sea by your strength
 and smashed the sea monster's
  heads.
¹⁴ You crushed the heads of Leviathan
 and let the desert animals eat him.
¹⁵ You caused the springs and streams to
 gush forth,
  and you dried up rivers that never
   run dry.
¹⁶ Both day and night belong to you;
 you made the starlight* and the sun.
¹⁷ You set the boundaries of the earth,
 and you make both summer and
  winter.

¹⁸ See how these enemies scoff at you,
 LORD.
  A foolish nation has dishonored your
   name.
¹⁹ Don't let these wild beasts destroy your
 doves.
  Don't forget your afflicted people
   forever.
²⁰ Remember your covenant promises,
 for the land is full of darkness and
  violence!
²¹ Don't let the downtrodden be
 constantly disgraced!
  Instead, let these poor and needy
   ones give praise to your name.

²² Arise, O God, and defend your cause.
 Remember how these fools insult
  you all day long.
²³ Don't overlook these things your
 enemies have said.
  Their uproar of rebellion grows ever
   louder.

PSALM 75

*For the choir director: A psalm of Asaph, to be sung
to the tune "Do Not Destroy!" A song.*

¹ We thank you, O God!
 We give thanks because you are near.

People everywhere tell of your
 mighty miracles.

² God says, "At the time I have planned,
 I will bring justice against the wicked.
³ When the earth quakes and its people
 live in turmoil,
  I am the one who keeps its
   foundations firm.   *Interlude*

⁴ "I warned the proud, 'Stop your
 boasting!'
  I told the wicked, 'Don't raise your
   fists!
⁵ Don't lift your fists in defiance at the
 heavens
  or speak with rebellious arrogance.'"

⁶ For no one on earth—from east or west,
 or even from the wilderness—
  can raise another person up.
⁷ It is God alone who judges;
 he decides who will rise and who
  will fall.
⁸ For the LORD holds a cup in his hand;
 it is full of foaming wine mixed with
  spices.
  He pours the wine out in judgment,
   and all the wicked must drink it,
    draining it to the dregs.

⁹ But as for me, I will always proclaim
 what God has done;
  I will sing praises to the God of
   Israel.*

¹⁰ For God says, "I will cut off the
 strength of the wicked,
  but I will increase the power of the
   godly."

PSALM 76

*For the choir director: A psalm of Asaph, to be
accompanied by stringed instruments. A song.*

¹ God is well known in Judah;
 his name is great in Israel.
² Jerusalem* is where he lives;
 Mount Zion is his home.
³ There he breaks the arrows of the
 enemy,
  the shields and swords and weapons
   of his foes.   *Interlude*

⁴ You are glorious and more majestic
 than the everlasting mountains.*
⁵ The mightiest of our enemies have
 been plundered.

74:16 Or *moon;* Hebrew reads *light.*   75:9 Hebrew *of Jacob.*   76:2 Hebrew *Salem,* another name for Jerusalem.   76:4 As in Greek
version; Hebrew reads *than mountains filled with beasts of prey.*

They lie before us in the sleep of
    death.
No warrior could lift a hand against
    us.
6 When you rebuked them, O God of
    Jacob,
their horses and chariots stood still.

7 No wonder you are greatly feared!
    Who can stand before you when
        your anger explodes?
8 From heaven you sentenced your
    enemies;
the earth trembled and stood silent
    before you.
9 You stand up to judge those who do
    evil, O God,
and to rescue the oppressed of the
    earth.   *Interlude*

10 Human opposition only enhances your
    glory,
for you use it as a sword of judgment.*

11 Make vows to the LORD your God, and
    fulfill them.
Let everyone bring tribute to the
    Awesome One.
12 For he breaks the spirit of princes
    and is feared by the kings of the
        earth.

PSALM 77
For Jeduthun, the choir director: A psalm of Asaph.

1 I cry out to God without holding back.
    Oh, that God would listen to me!
2 When I was in deep trouble,
    I searched for the Lord.
All night long I pray, with hands lifted
    toward heaven, pleading.
There can be no joy for me until he
    acts.
3 I think of God, and I moan,
    overwhelmed with longing for his
        help.   *Interlude*

4 You don't let me sleep.
    I am too distressed even to pray!
5 I think of the good old days, long since
    ended,
6   when my nights were filled with
    joyful songs.

I search my soul and think about the
    difference now.
7 Has the Lord rejected me forever?
    Will he never again show me favor?
8 Is his unfailing love gone forever?
    Have his promises permanently
        failed?
9 Has God forgotten to be kind?
    Has he slammed the door on his
        compassion?   *Interlude*

10 And I said, "This is my fate,
    that the blessings of the Most High
        have changed to hatred."
11 I recall all you have done, O LORD;
    I remember your wonderful deeds
        of long ago.
12 They are constantly in my thoughts.
    I cannot stop thinking about them.

13 O God, your ways are holy.
    Is there any god as mighty as you?
14 You are the God of miracles and
    wonders.
You demonstrate your awesome
    power among the nations.
15 You have redeemed your people by
    your strength,
the descendants of Jacob and of
    Joseph by your might.   *Interlude*

16 When the Red Sea* saw you, O God,
    its waters looked and trembled!
The sea quaked to its very depths.
17 The clouds poured down their rain;
    the thunder rolled and crackled in
        the sky.
Your arrows of lightning flashed.
18 Your thunder roared from the
    whirlwind;
the lightning lit up the world!
The earth trembled and shook.
19 Your road led through the sea,
    your pathway through the mighty
        waters—
a pathway no one knew was there!
20 You led your people along that road
    like a flock of sheep,
with Moses and Aaron as their
    shepherds.

76:10 The meaning of the Hebrew is uncertain.   **77:16** Hebrew *the waters.*

JUNE 16 ☐ DAY 168
PSALMS 78–83
Warmth for Cold Hearts

OVERVIEW Asaph's final contribution to the Psalter is found in today's reading. There he recounts Israel's history of disobedience (Psalm 78) and cries out to God to restore his people to the place of blessing (79–80). A lament over the nation's failure to obey God (81) is followed by an appeal for God's justice to prevail over Israel's oppressors (82–83).

Psalm 78	Psalms 79–80	Psalm 81	Psalms 82–83
Israel's Rebellion	Israel's Restoration	Israel's Stubbornness	Israel's Savior
Admission	Appeal	Admonition	Petition

The more we count the blessings we have, the less we crave the luxuries we haven't.

YOUR DAILY WALK A woman asked her physician, "Doctor, why am I seized with these restless longings for the glamorous and faraway?"

"My dear lady," he replied, "those are the usual symptoms of abundant comfort in the home and ingratitude in the heart."

Three times in Psalm 78 Asaph points out how the nation Israel put God to the test by placing demands on God (v. 18), forgetting his past deliverance (v. 42), and disobeying his commands (v. 56). In each case, the problem was ingratitude—the subtle temptation first to grow accustomed to . . . then to expect . . . and finally to demand . . . the blessings of God.

Ingratitude in the face of God's gracious provision chipped away at the nation's relationship with God. Is ingratitude doing the same in your life? How do you relate to the blessings of God? Has abundance produced apathy or appreciation? Has your heart grown cold from the consistency of God's provision?

This gospel hymn is still a timely reminder:
"Count your blessings, name them one by one;
Count your many blessings, see what God hath done!"
Try it! In the next two minutes can you list twenty-five ways God has enriched your life—twenty-five blessings for which you want to tell him thanks? Remember, it is with gratitude that life becomes rich!

INSIGHT A Millennium of God's Mercy
Psalm 78, the second longest psalm, might well be subtitled "From Zoan to Zion." In the space of just fifty-seven verses (vv. 12-68) Asaph traces Israel's history from slavery in Egypt to David's rule in Zion—a thousand-year record of God's faithfulness!

PSALM 78
A psalm of Asaph.

¹ O my people, listen to my teaching.
  Open your ears to what I am saying,
² for I will speak to you in a parable.
I will teach you hidden lessons from
  our past—
³ stories we have heard and know,
  stories our ancestors handed down
  to us.
⁴ We will not hide these truths from our
  children

but will tell the next generation
  about the glorious deeds of the
  LORD.
We will tell of his power and the
  mighty miracles he did.
⁵ For he issued his decree to Jacob;
  he gave his law to Israel.
He commanded our ancestors
  to teach them to their children,
⁶ so the next generation might know
  them—
  even the children not yet born—

that they in turn might teach their children.

7 So each generation can set its hope anew on God,
remembering his glorious miracles and obeying his commands.

8 Then they will not be like their ancestors—
stubborn, rebellious, and unfaithful,
refusing to give their hearts to God.

9 The warriors of Ephraim, though fully armed,
turned their backs and fled when the day of battle came.

10 They did not keep God's covenant,
and they refused to live by his law.

11 They forgot what he had done—
the wonderful miracles he had shown them,

12 the miracles he did for their ancestors in Egypt, on the plain of Zoan.

13 For he divided the sea before them and led them through!
The water stood up like walls beside them!

14 In the daytime he led them by a cloud,
and at night by a pillar of fire.

15 He split open the rocks in the wilderness to give them plenty of water, as from a gushing spring.

16 He made streams pour from the rock,
making the waters flow down like a river!

17 Yet they kept on with their sin,
rebelling against the Most High in the desert.

18 They willfully tested God in their hearts,
demanding the foods they craved.

19 They even spoke against God himself, saying,
"God can't give us food in the desert.

20 Yes, he can strike a rock so water gushes out,
but he can't give his people bread and meat."

21 When the LORD heard them, he was angry.
The fire of his wrath burned against Jacob.
Yes, his anger rose against Israel,

22 for they did not believe God or trust him to care for them.

23 But he commanded the skies to open—
he opened the doors of heaven—

24 and rained down manna for them to eat.
He gave them bread from heaven.

25 They ate the food of angels!
God gave them all they could hold.

26 He released the east wind in the heavens
and guided the south wind by his mighty power.

27 He rained down meat as thick as dust—
birds as plentiful as the sands along the seashore!

28 He caused the birds to fall within their camp
and all around their tents.

29 The people ate their fill.
He gave them what they wanted.

30 But before they finished eating this food they had craved,
while the meat was yet in their mouths,

31 the anger of God rose against them,
and he killed their strongest men;
he struck down the finest of Israel's young men.

32 But in spite of this, the people kept on sinning.
They refused to believe in his miracles.

33 So he ended their lives in failure and gave them years of terror.

34 When God killed some of them, the rest finally sought him.
They repented and turned to God.

35 Then they remembered that God was their rock,
that their redeemer was the Most High.

36 But they followed him only with their words;
they lied to him with their tongues.

37 Their hearts were not loyal to him.
They did not keep his covenant.

38 Yet he was merciful and forgave their sins
and didn't destroy them all.
Many a time he held back his anger and did not unleash his fury!

39 For he remembered that they were merely mortal,
gone in a moment like a breath of wind, never to return.

40 Oh, how often they rebelled against him in the desert
and grieved his heart in the wilderness.

41 Again and again they tested God's patience
and frustrated the Holy One of Israel.
42 They forgot about his power
and how he rescued them from their enemies.
43 They forgot his miraculous signs in Egypt,
his wonders on the plain of Zoan.
44 For he turned their rivers into blood,
so no one could drink from the streams.
45 He sent vast swarms of flies to consume them
and hordes of frogs to ruin them.
46 He gave their crops to caterpillars;
their harvest was consumed by locusts.
47 He destroyed their grapevines with hail
and shattered their sycamores with sleet.
48 He abandoned their cattle to the hail,
their livestock to bolts of lightning.
49 He loosed on them his fierce anger—
all his fury, rage, and hostility.
He dispatched against them
a band of destroying angels.
50 He turned his anger against them;
he did not spare the Egyptians' lives
but handed them over to the plague.
51 He killed the oldest son in each Egyptian family,
the flower of youth throughout the land of Egypt.*
52 But he led his own people like a flock of sheep,
guiding them safely through the wilderness.
53 He kept them safe so they were not afraid;
but the sea closed in upon their enemies.
54 He brought them to the border of his holy land,
to this land of hills he had won for them.
55 He drove out the nations before them;
he gave them their inheritance by lot.
He settled the tribes of Israel into their homes.
56 Yet though he did all this for them,
they continued to test his patience.

They rebelled against the Most High
and refused to follow his decrees.
57 They turned back and were as faithless as their parents had been.
They were as useless as a crooked bow.
58 They made God angry by building altars to other gods;
they made him jealous with their idols.
59 When God heard them, he was very angry,
and he rejected Israel completely.
60 Then he abandoned his dwelling at Shiloh,
the Tabernacle where he had lived among the people.
61 He allowed the Ark of his might to be captured;
he surrendered his glory into enemy hands.
62 He gave his people over to be butchered by the sword,
because he was so angry with his own people—his special possession.
63 Their young men were killed by fire;
their young women died before singing their wedding songs.
64 Their priests were slaughtered,
and their widows could not mourn their deaths.
65 Then the Lord rose up as though waking from sleep,
like a mighty man aroused from a drunken stupor.
66 He routed his enemies
and sent them to eternal shame.
67 But he rejected Joseph's descendants;
he did not choose the tribe of Ephraim.
68 He chose instead the tribe of Judah,
Mount Zion, which he loved.
69 There he built his towering sanctuary,
as solid and enduring as the earth itself.
70 He chose his servant David,
calling him from the sheep pens.
71 He took David from tending the ewes and lambs
and made him the shepherd of Jacob's descendants—
God's own people, Israel.
72 He cared for them with a true heart
and led them with skillful hands.

78:51 Hebrew *in the tents of Ham.*

PSALM 79

A psalm of Asaph.

1 O God, pagan nations have conquered
    your land, your special possession.
  They have defiled your holy Temple
    and made Jerusalem a heap of ruins.
2 They have left the bodies of your
    servants
    as food for the birds of heaven.
  The flesh of your godly ones
    has become food for the wild
    animals.
3 Blood has flowed like water all around
    Jerusalem;
  no one is left to bury the dead.
4 We are mocked by our neighbors,
  an object of scorn and derision to
    those around us.

5 O Lord, how long will you be angry
    with us? Forever?
  How long will your jealousy burn
    like fire?
6 Pour out your wrath on the nations
    that refuse to recognize you—
  on kingdoms that do not call upon
    your name.
7 For they have devoured your people
    Israel,*
  making the land a desolate
    wilderness.
8 Oh, do not hold us guilty for our
    former sins!
  Let your tenderhearted mercies
    quickly meet our needs,
  for we are brought low to the dust.
9 Help us, O God of our salvation!
  Help us for the honor of your name.
  Oh, save us and forgive our sins
    for the sake of your name.
10 Why should pagan nations be allowed
    to scoff,
  asking, "Where is their God?"
  Show us your vengeance against the
    nations,
  for they have spilled the blood of
    your servants.
11 Listen to the moaning of the prisoners.
  Demonstrate your great power by
    saving those condemned to die.

12 O Lord, take sevenfold vengeance on
    our neighbors
  for the scorn they have hurled at you.
13 Then we your people, the sheep of
    your pasture,
will thank you forever and ever,
  praising your greatness from
    generation to generation.

PSALM 80

*For the choir director: A psalm of Asaph, to be sung
to the tune "Lilies of the Covenant."*

1 Please listen, O Shepherd of Israel,
  you who lead Israel* like a flock.
  O God, enthroned above the cherubim,
    display your radiant glory
2 to Ephraim, Benjamin, and Manasseh.
  Show us your mighty power.
  Come to rescue us!

3 Turn us again to yourself, O God.
  Make your face shine down upon us.
  Only then will we be saved.

4 O Lord God Almighty,
  how long will you be angry and
    reject our prayers?
5 You have fed us with sorrow
  and made us drink tears by the
    bucketful.
6 You have made us the scorn of
    neighboring nations.
  Our enemies treat us as a joke.

7 Turn us again to yourself, O God
    Almighty.
  Make your face shine down upon us.
  Only then will we be saved.

8 You brought us from Egypt as though
    we were a tender vine;
  you drove away the pagan nations
    and transplanted us into your
    land.
9 You cleared the ground for us,
  and we took root and filled the land.
10 The mountains were covered with our
    shade;
  the mighty cedars were covered with
    our branches.
11 We spread our branches west to the
    Mediterranean Sea,
  our limbs east to the Euphrates
    River.*
12 But now, why have you broken down
    our walls
  so that all who pass may steal our
    fruit?
13 The boar from the forest devours us,
  and the wild animals feed on us.

14 Come back, we beg you, O God
    Almighty.

79:7 Hebrew *Jacob.*   80:1 Hebrew *Joseph.*   80:11 Hebrew *west to the sea, . . . east to the river.*

Look down from heaven and see our
plight.
Watch over and care for this vine
15 that you yourself have planted,
    this son you have raised for your-
    self.
16 For we are chopped up and burned by
    our enemies.
    May they perish at the sight of your
    frown.
17 Strengthen the man you love,
    the son of your choice.
18 Then we will never forsake you again.
    Revive us so we can call on your
    name once more.

19 Turn us again to yourself, O LORD God
    Almighty.
    Make your face shine down upon us.
    Only then will we be saved.

PSALM 81

*For the choir director: A psalm of Asaph, to be
accompanied by a stringed instrument.**

1 Sing praises to God, our strength.
   Sing to the God of Israel.*
2 Sing! Beat the tambourine.
   Play the sweet lyre and the harp.
3 Sound the trumpet for a sacred feast
   when the moon is new,
   when the moon is full.
4 For this is required by the laws of
   Israel;
   it is a law of the God of Jacob.
5 He made it a decree for Israel*
   when he attacked Egypt to set us
   free.

   I heard an unknown voice that said,
6 "Now I will relieve your shoulder of
   its burden;
   I will free your hands from their
   heavy tasks.
7 You cried to me in trouble, and I saved
   you;
   I answered out of the thundercloud.
   I tested your faith at Meribah,
   when you complained that there
   was no water.   *Interlude*

8 "Listen to me, O my people, while
   I give you stern warnings.
   O Israel, if you would only listen!
9 You must never have a foreign god;
   you must not bow down before a
   false god.

10 For it was I, the LORD your God,
    who rescued you from the land of
    Egypt.
    Open your mouth wide, and I will
    fill it with good things.
11 "But no, my people wouldn't listen.
    Israel did not want me around.
12 So I let them follow their blind and
    stubborn way,
    living according to their own desires.
13 But oh, that my people would listen
    to me!
    Oh, that Israel would follow me,
    walking in my paths!
14 How quickly I would then subdue their
    enemies!
    How soon my hands would be upon
    their foes!
15 Those who hate the LORD would cringe
    before him;
    their desolation would last forever.
16 But I would feed you with the best of
    foods.
    I would satisfy you with wild honey
    from the rock."

PSALM 82

A psalm of Asaph.

1 God presides over heaven's court;
   he pronounces judgment on the
   judges:
2 "How long will you judges hand down
   unjust decisions?
   How long will you shower special
   favors on the wicked?   *Interlude*

3 "Give fair judgment to the poor and
   the orphan;
   uphold the rights of the oppressed
   and the destitute.
4 Rescue the poor and helpless;
   deliver them from the grasp of evil
   people.
5 But these oppressors know nothing;
   they are so ignorant!
   And because they are in darkness,
   the whole world is shaken to the core.
6 I say, 'You are gods
   and children of the Most High.
7 But in death you are mere men.
   You will fall as any prince,
   for all must die.'"

8 Rise up, O God, and judge the earth,
   for all the nations belong to you.

81: TITLE Hebrew *according to the gittith.*   **81:1** Hebrew *of Jacob.*   **81:5** Hebrew *for Joseph.*

PSALM 83
A psalm of Asaph. A song.

¹ O God, don't sit idly by,
   silent and inactive!
² Don't you hear the tumult of your
      enemies?
   Don't you see what your arrogant
      enemies are doing?
³ They devise crafty schemes against
      your people,
   laying plans against your precious ones.
⁴ "Come," they say, "let us wipe out
      Israel as a nation.
   We will destroy the very memory of
      its existence."
⁵   This was their unanimous decision.
   They signed a treaty as allies against
      you—
⁶   these Edomites and Ishmaelites,
      Moabites and Hagrites,
⁷   Gebalites, Ammonites, and
         Amalekites,
   and people from Philistia and Tyre.
⁸ Assyria has joined them, too,
   and is allied with the descendants of
      Lot.   *Interlude*

⁹ Do to them as you did to the Midianites
   or as you did to Sisera and Jabin at
      the Kishon River.

¹⁰ They were destroyed at Endor,
   and their decaying corpses fertilized
      the soil.
¹¹ Let their mighty nobles die as Oreb and
      Zeeb did.
   Let all their princes die like Zebah
      and Zalmunna,
¹² for they said, "Let us seize for our own
      use
   these pasturelands of God!"

¹³ O my God, blow them away like whirl-
      ing dust,
   like chaff before the wind!
¹⁴ As a fire roars through a forest
   and as a flame sets mountains
      ablaze,
¹⁵ chase them with your fierce storms;
   terrify them with your tempests.
¹⁶ Utterly disgrace them
   until they submit to your name,
      O LORD.
¹⁷ Let them be ashamed and terrified
      forever.
   Make them failures in everything
      they do,
¹⁸ until they learn that you alone are
      called the LORD,
   that you alone are the Most High,
      supreme over all the earth.

JUNE 17 ☐ DAY 169
PSALMS 84–89
A Promise-Keeping God

OVERVIEW Several different authors are represented in the six psalms in today's reading. The descendants of Korah yearn to be in God's presence (Psalm 84) and to see the nation restored to fellowship with God (85). David seeks the great and merciful God amid opposition (86), while the descendants of Korah proclaim the greatness of the city of God (87). The final two laments record the mournful cry of Heman when he was afflicted (88) and the pleading of Ethan, who remembers God's words to Israel (89).

Psalms 84–85	Psalms 86–87	Psalms 88–89
Longing for God	Looking to God	Leaning on God
Desire	Dependence	Doxology

YOUR DAILY WALK If someone has made a promise to you and then circumstances change, making it seemingly impossible for that person to keep his or her word, you are faced with a choice: You can either let your problems cast a shadow on the promise or allow the promise to shed light on your problems. It all depends on the trustworthiness—and power—of the promise maker.

You cannot starve a person who is feeding on God's promises.

God made a promise to David (89:3-4). You'll find it recorded in 2 Samuel 7:13-16. God promised David an everlasting family line, throne, and kingdom. On at least two occasions the "royal family" was reduced to only a single member (2 Chronicles 21:4; 22:8-12). Did that mean God's promise was in danger? Not at all! It only highlighted the importance of daily faith in the Promise Maker, for when the darkness is most severe, God's promises only shine more brightly.

To spark your faith in the God who keeps his word, find a sheet of paper and label one side "Promises God Made to People in the Bible but Never Kept"; the other, "Promises God Made—and Kept—to People in the Bible." Then do your own survey of Noah . . . Abraham . . . Jonah . . . and others. You'll find only one side of the paper filling up! What did these people discover about the promises of God? And does that cast a shadow or shed light on God's promises to you?

INSIGHT Unmasking a Maschil
Psalm 89 is a contemplation (Hebrew, *maschil*), a song of wisdom or insight designed to help you, the reader, reach your goal in life. Thirteen psalms are contemplations.

PSALM 84

For the choir director: A psalm of the descendants of Korah, to be accompanied by a stringed instrument.*

¹ How lovely is your dwelling place,
   O LORD Almighty.
² I long, yes, I faint with longing
   to enter the courts of the LORD.
With my whole being, body and soul,
   I will shout joyfully to the living God.
³ Even the sparrow finds a home there,
   and the swallow builds her nest
   and raises her young—
   at a place near your altar,
   O LORD Almighty, my King and my
      God!
⁴ How happy are those who can live in
      your house,
   always singing your praises.
                              Interlude
⁵ Happy are those who are strong in the
      LORD,
   who set their minds on a pilgrimage
      to Jerusalem.
⁶ When they walk through the Valley of
      Weeping,*
   it will become a place of refreshing
      springs,

where pools of blessing collect after
   the rains!
⁷ They will continue to grow stronger,
   and each of them will appear before
      God in Jerusalem.*

⁸ O LORD God Almighty, hear my
      prayer.
   Listen, O God of Israel.*   *Interlude*

⁹ O God, look with favor upon the king,
      our protector!
   Have mercy on the one you have
      anointed.

¹⁰ A single day in your courts
   is better than a thousand anywhere
      else!
I would rather be a gatekeeper in the
   house of my God
than live the good life in the homes
   of the wicked.
¹¹ For the LORD God is our light and
      protector.
   He gives us grace and glory.
No good thing will the LORD withhold
   from those who do what is right.
¹² O LORD Almighty,
   happy are those who trust in you.

84: TITLE Hebrew *according to the gittith.*   **84:6** Hebrew *valley of Baca.*   **84:7** Hebrew *Zion.*   **84:8** Hebrew *of Jacob.*

PSALM 85

For the choir director: A psalm of the descendants of Korah.

¹ LORD, you have poured out amazing
     blessings on your land!
     You have restored the fortunes of
     Israel.*
² You have forgiven the guilt of your
     people—
     yes, you have covered all their sins.
                           Interlude

³ You have withdrawn your fury.
     You have ended your blazing anger.
⁴ Now turn to us again, O God of our
     salvation.
     Put aside your anger against us.
⁵ Will you be angry with us always?
     Will you prolong your wrath to
     distant generations?
⁶ Won't you revive us again,
     so your people can rejoice in you?
⁷ Show us your unfailing love, O LORD,
     and grant us your salvation.

⁸ I listen carefully to what God the LORD
     is saying,
     for he speaks peace to his people, his
     faithful ones.
     But let them not return to their foolish
     ways.
⁹ Surely his salvation is near to those
     who honor him;
     our land will be filled with his glory.

¹⁰ Unfailing love and truth have met
     together.
     Righteousness and peace have kissed!
¹¹ Truth springs up from the earth,
     and righteousness smiles down from
     heaven.
¹² Yes, the LORD pours down his blessings.
     Our land will yield its bountiful crops.
¹³ Righteousness goes as a herald before
     him,
     preparing the way for his steps.

PSALM 86

A prayer of David.

¹ Bend down, O LORD, and hear my
     prayer;
     answer me, for I need your help.
² Protect me, for I am devoted to you.
     Save me, for I serve you and trust
     you.
     You are my God.

³ Be merciful, O Lord,
     for I am calling on you constantly.
⁴ Give me happiness, O Lord,
     for my life depends on you.
⁵ O Lord, you are so good, so ready to
     forgive,
     so full of unfailing love for all who
     ask your aid.
⁶ Listen closely to my prayer, O LORD;
     hear my urgent cry.
⁷ I will call to you whenever trouble
     strikes,
     and you will answer me.

⁸ Nowhere among the pagan gods is
     there a god like you, O Lord.
     There are no other miracles like
     yours.
⁹ All the nations—and you made each
     one—
     will come and bow before you, Lord;
     they will praise your great and holy
     name.
¹⁰ For you are great and perform great
     miracles.
     You alone are God.

¹¹ Teach me your ways, O LORD,
     that I may live according to your
     truth!
     Grant me purity of heart,
     that I may honor you.
¹² With all my heart I will praise you,
     O Lord my God.
     I will give glory to your name forever,
¹³ for your love for me is very great.
     You have rescued me from the
     depths of death*!

¹⁴ O God, insolent people rise up against
     me;
     violent people are trying to kill me.
     And you mean nothing to them.
¹⁵ But you, O Lord, are a merciful and
     gracious God,
     slow to get angry,
     full of unfailing love and truth.
¹⁶ Look down and have mercy on me.
     Give strength to your servant;
     yes, save me, for I am your servant.
¹⁷ Send me a sign of your favor.
     Then those who hate me will be put
     to shame,
     for you, O LORD, help and comfort
     me.

85:1 Hebrew *of Jacob.*   **86:13** Hebrew *of Sheol.*

PSALM 87

A psalm of the descendants of Korah. A song.

¹ On the holy mountain stands the city
    founded by the LORD.
² He loves the city of Jerusalem
    more than any other city in Israel.*
³ O city of God,
    what glorious things are said of you!
                                            Interlude

⁴ I will record Egypt* and Babylon
    among those who know me—
    also Philistia and Tyre, and even
        distant Ethiopia.*
    They have all become citizens of
        Jerusalem!
⁵ And it will be said of Jerusalem,*
    "Everyone has become a citizen here."
    And the Most High will personally
        bless this city.
⁶ When the LORD registers the nations,
    he will say, "This one has become a
        citizen of Jerusalem."   *Interlude*

⁷ At all the festivals, the people will sing,
    "The source of my life is in
        Jerusalem!"

PSALM 88

*For the choir director: A psalm of the descendants
of Korah, to be sung to the tune "The Suffering of
Affliction." A psalm of Heman the Ezrahite. A song.*

¹ O LORD, God of my salvation,
    I have cried out to you day and night.
² Now hear my prayer;
    listen to my cry.
³ For my life is full of troubles,
    and death draws near.
⁴ I have been dismissed as one who is
        dead,
    like a strong man with no strength left.
⁵ They have abandoned me to death,
    and I am as good as dead.
  I am forgotten,
    cut off from your care.
⁶ You have thrust me down to the lowest
        pit,
    into the darkest depths.
⁷ Your anger lies heavy on me;
    wave after wave engulfs me.
                                            Interlude

⁸ You have caused my friends to loathe me;
    you have sent them all away.
  I am in a trap with no way of escape.

⁹ My eyes are blinded by my tears.
  Each day I beg for your help, O LORD;
    I lift my pleading hands to you for
        mercy.
¹⁰ Of what use to the dead are your
        miracles?
  Do the dead get up and praise you?
                                            Interlude

¹¹ Can those in the grave declare your
        unfailing love?
  In the place of destruction, can they
        proclaim your faithfulness?
¹² Can the darkness speak of your
        miracles?
  Can anyone in the land of forgetful-
        ness talk about your righteousness?

¹³ O LORD, I cry out to you.
  I will keep on pleading day by day.
¹⁴ O LORD, why do you reject me?
  Why do you turn your face away
        from me?
¹⁵ I have been sickly and close to death
        since my youth.
  I stand helpless and desperate before
        your terrors.
¹⁶ Your fierce anger has overwhelmed me.
  Your terrors have cut me off.
¹⁷ They swirl around me like floodwaters
        all day long.
  They have encircled me completely.
¹⁸ You have taken away my companions
        and loved ones;
    only darkness remains.

PSALM 89

A psalm of Ethan the Ezrahite.

¹ I will sing of the tender mercies of the
        LORD forever!
  Young and old will hear of your
        faithfulness.
² Your unfailing love will last forever.
  Your faithfulness is as enduring as
        the heavens.

³ The LORD said, "I have made a solemn
        agreement with David, my chosen
        servant.
  I have sworn this oath to him:
⁴ 'I will establish your descendants as
        kings forever;
    they will sit on your throne from
        now until eternity.'"   *Interlude*

87:2 Hebrew *He loves the gates of Zion more than all the dwellings of Jacob.*   87:4a Hebrew *Rahab,* the name of a mythical sea
monster that represents chaos in ancient literature. The name is used here as a poetic name for Egypt.   87:4b Hebrew *Cush.*
87:5 Hebrew *Zion.*

5 All heaven will praise your miracles,
    LORD;
    myriads of angels will praise you for
    your faithfulness.
6 For who in all of heaven can compare
    with the LORD?
    What mightiest angel is anything like
    the LORD?
7 The highest angelic powers stand in
    awe of God.
    He is far more awesome than those
    who surround his throne.
8 O LORD God Almighty!
    Where is there anyone as mighty as
    you, LORD?
    Faithfulness is your very character.

9 You are the one who rules the oceans.
    When their waves rise in fearful
    storms, you subdue them.
10 You are the one who crushed the great
    sea monster.*
    You scattered your enemies with
    your mighty arm.
11 The heavens are yours, and the earth
    is yours;
    everything in the world is yours—
    you created it all.
12 You created north and south.
    Mount Tabor and Mount Hermon
    praise your name.
13 Powerful is your arm!
    Strong is your hand!
    Your right hand is lifted high in
    glorious strength.
14 Your throne is founded on two strong
    pillars—righteousness and justice.
    Unfailing love and truth walk before
    you as attendants.
15 Happy are those who hear the joyful
    call to worship,
    for they will walk in the light of your
    presence, LORD.
16 They rejoice all day long in your
    wonderful reputation.
    They exult in your righteousness.
17 You are their glorious strength.
    Our power is based on your favor.
18 Yes, our protection comes from the LORD,
    and he, the Holy One of Israel, has
    given us our king.

19 You once spoke in a vision to your
    prophet and said,
    "I have given help to a warrior.

I have selected him from the common
    people to be king.
20 I have found my servant David.
    I have anointed him with my holy oil.
21 I will steady him,
    and I will make him strong.
22 His enemies will not get the best of
    him,
    nor will the wicked overpower him.
23 I will beat down his adversaries before
    him
    and destroy those who hate him.
24 My faithfulness and unfailing love will
    be with him,
    and he will rise to power because
    of me.
25 I will extend his rule from the
    Mediterranean Sea in the west
    to the Tigris and Euphrates rivers
    in the east.*
26 And he will say to me, 'You are my
    Father,
    my God, and the Rock of my
    salvation.'
27 I will make him my firstborn son,
    the mightiest king on earth.
28 I will love him and be kind to him
    forever;
    my covenant with him will never
    end.
29 I will preserve an heir for him;
    his throne will be as endless as the
    days of heaven.
30 But if his sons forsake my law
    and fail to walk in my ways,
31 if they do not obey my decrees
    and fail to keep my commands,
32 then I will punish their sin with the rod,
    and their disobedience with beating.
33 But I will never stop loving him,
    nor let my promise to him fail.
34 No, I will not break my covenant;
    I will not take back a single word I
    said.
35 I have sworn an oath to David,
    and in my holiness I cannot lie:
36 His dynasty will go on forever;
    his throne is as secure as the sun,
37 as eternal as the moon,
    my faithful witness in the sky!"
                                    Interlude

38 But now you have rejected him.
    Why are you so angry with the one
    you chose as king?

89:10 Hebrew *Rahab,* the name of a mythical sea monster that represents chaos in ancient literature.   89:25 Hebrew *I will set his hand on the sea, his right hand on the rivers.*

39 You have renounced your covenant
      with him,
   for you have thrown his crown in the
      dust.
40 You have broken down the walls
      protecting him
   and laid in ruins every fort
      defending him.
41 Everyone who comes along has robbed
      him
   while his neighbors mock.
42 You have strengthened his enemies
      against him
   and made them all rejoice.
43 You have made his sword useless
   and have refused to help him in
      battle.
44 You have ended his splendor
   and overturned his throne.
45 You have made him old before his time
   and publicly disgraced him.

                                    Interlude

46 O LORD, how long will this go on?

Will you hide yourself forever?
   How long will your anger burn like
      fire?
47 Remember how short my life is,
   how empty and futile this human
      existence!
48 No one can live forever; all will die.
   No one can escape the power of the
      grave.   *Interlude*

49 Lord, where is your unfailing love?
   You promised it to David with a
      faithful pledge.
50 Consider, Lord, how your servants are
      disgraced!
   I carry in my heart the insults of so
      many people.
51 Your enemies have mocked me,
      O LORD;
   they mock the one you anointed as
      king.
52 Blessed be the LORD forever!
   Amen and amen!

JUNE 18 □ DAY 170
PSALMS 90–97
God's Seal of Approval

OVERVIEW Book Four opens with the oldest of the psalms, Moses' testimony of faith in an eternal God (Psalm 90). God's people find their refuge (91) and their joy (92) in the God who reigns over all (93) and avenges the wrongs done to his own (94). The invitation is extended for all to worship (95), sing praises (96), and gladly acknowledge the incomparable greatness of the God of Israel (97).

Psalms 90–92	Psalms 93–94	Psalms 95–97
God's People	God's Person	God's Praise
Mortal	Mighty	Majestic

YOUR DAILY WALK Because of its smallness, you seldom notice it unless you are looking for it. Yet thousands of items sold today display it proudly.

The person who does good for God's glory seeks neither praise nor reward but is sure of both in the end.

What is it? A seal of approval granted by a testing agency such as the Good Housekeeping Institute. For many shoppers, the presence—or absence—of such a recommendation has a significant impact on their decision to buy the product.

In Psalm 90 Moses speaks of another "seal of approval"—this one found, not on a product, but on a life; one issued, not by a testing agency, but by God himself. In contrast to the briefness of human life, God reserves his stamp of approval for endeavors of eternal significance. Earthly products soon rust or wear out, but God's seal of approval is the mark of eternity on a life. Whatever is done apart from God ends in death; whatever is accomplished for his glory lasts for eternity (Matthew 6:19-21).

Look for a seal of approval on a product or appliance you have around the house. Carefully remove the seal, and put it in a prominent place in your home or office to remind you throughout the day to live for God's approval—with eternity's values in view.

 INSIGHT The Dark Background of Psalm 90
Verses 7-12 seem to indicate that Moses wrote Psalm 90 during the time of wilderness wandering—the forty-year period when six hundred thousand Israelite men (and their wives) died for unbelief (Numbers 14:21-23). What clearer reminder of Israel's mortality could there be (Psalm 90:9-10) than an average of *one funeral every twenty minutes, twenty-four hours a day, for forty years!*

BOOK FOUR (Psalms 90–106)
PSALM 90
A prayer of Moses, the man of God.

¹ Lord, through all the generations
    you have been our home!
² Before the mountains were created,
    before you made the earth and the
        world,
    you are God, without beginning or
        end.

³ You turn people back to dust, saying,
    "Return to dust!"
⁴ For you, a thousand years are as
        yesterday!
    They are like a few hours!
⁵ You sweep people away like dreams
        that disappear
    or like grass that springs up in the
        morning.
⁶ In the morning it blooms and flourishes,
    but by evening it is dry and withered.
⁷ We wither beneath your anger;
    we are overwhelmed by your fury.
⁸ You spread out our sins before you—
    our secret sins—and you see them all.
⁹ We live our lives beneath your wrath.
    We end our lives with a groan.

¹⁰ Seventy years are given to us!
    Some may even reach eighty.
    But even the best of these years are
        filled with pain and trouble;
    soon they disappear, and we are
        gone.
¹¹ Who can comprehend the power of
        your anger?
    Your wrath is as awesome as the fear
        you deserve.

¹² Teach us to make the most of our time,
    so that we may grow in wisdom.
¹³ O LORD, come back to us!
    How long will you delay?
    Take pity on your servants!
¹⁴ Satisfy us in the morning with your
        unfailing love,
    so we may sing for joy to the end of
        our lives.
¹⁵ Give us gladness in proportion to our
        former misery!
    Replace the evil years with good.
¹⁶ Let us see your miracles again;
    let our children see your glory at
        work.
¹⁷ And may the Lord our God show us
        his approval
    and make our efforts successful.
    Yes, make our efforts successful!

PSALM 91
¹ Those who live in the shelter of the
        Most High
    will find rest in the shadow of the
        Almighty.
² This I declare of the LORD:
    He alone is my refuge, my place of
        safety;
    he is my God, and I am trusting him.
³ For he will rescue you from every trap
    and protect you from the fatal plague.
⁴ He will shield you with his wings.
    He will shelter you with his feathers.
    His faithful promises are your armor
        and protection.
⁵ Do not be afraid of the terrors of the
        night,
    nor fear the dangers of the day,

⁶ nor dread the plague that stalks in
darkness,
nor the disaster that strikes at
midday.
⁷ Though a thousand fall at your side,
though ten thousand are dying
around you,
these evils will not touch you.
⁸ But you will see it with your eyes;
you will see how the wicked are
punished.

⁹ If you make the LORD your refuge,
if you make the Most High your
shelter,
¹⁰ no evil will conquer you;
no plague will come near your
dwelling.
¹¹ For he orders his angels
to protect you wherever you go.
¹² They will hold you with their hands
to keep you from striking your foot
on a stone.
¹³ You will trample down lions and
poisonous snakes;
you will crush fierce lions and
serpents under your feet!

¹⁴ The LORD says, "I will rescue those
who love me.
I will protect those who trust in my
name.
¹⁵ When they call on me, I will answer;
I will be with them in trouble.
I will rescue them and honor them.
¹⁶ I will satisfy them with a long life
and give them my salvation."

PSALM 92

A psalm to be sung on the LORD's Day. A song.

¹ It is good to give thanks to the LORD,
to sing praises to the Most High.
² It is good to proclaim your unfailing
love in the morning,
your faithfulness in the evening,
³ accompanied by the harp and lute
and the harmony of the lyre.
⁴ You thrill me, LORD, with all you have
done for me!
I sing for joy because of what you
have done.
⁵ O LORD, what great miracles you do!
And how deep are your thoughts.
⁶ Only an ignorant person would not
know this!
Only a fool would not understand it.

⁷ Although the wicked flourish like weeds,
and evildoers blossom with success,
there is only eternal destruction
ahead of them.
⁸ But you are exalted in the heavens.
You, O LORD, continue forever.
⁹ Your enemies, LORD, will surely perish;
all evildoers will be scattered.
¹⁰ But you have made me as strong as
a wild bull.
How refreshed I am by your power!
¹¹ With my own eyes I have seen the
downfall of my enemies;
with my own ears I have heard the
defeat of my wicked opponents.
¹² But the godly will flourish like palm
trees
and grow strong like the cedars of
Lebanon.
¹³ For they are transplanted into the
LORD's own house.
They flourish in the courts of our
God.
¹⁴ Even in old age they will still produce
fruit;
they will remain vital and green.
¹⁵ They will declare, "The LORD is just!
He is my rock!
There is nothing but goodness in
him!"

PSALM 93

¹ The LORD is king! He is robed in majesty.
Indeed, the LORD is robed in majesty
and armed with strength.
The world is firmly established;
it cannot be shaken.

² Your throne, O LORD, has been
established from time immemorial.
You yourself are from the everlasting
past.
³ The mighty oceans have roared,
O LORD.
The mighty oceans roar like thunder;
the mighty oceans roar as they
pound the shore.
⁴ But mightier than the violent raging of
the seas,
mightier than the breakers on the
shore—
the LORD above is mightier than
these!
⁵ Your royal decrees cannot be changed.
The nature of your reign, O LORD, is
holiness forever.

PSALM 94

1 O Lord, the God to whom vengeance
    belongs,
  O God of vengeance, let your
    glorious justice be seen!
2 Arise, O judge of the earth.
  Sentence the proud to the penalties
    they deserve.
3 How long, O Lord?
  How long will the wicked be allowed
    to gloat?
4 Hear their arrogance!
  How these evildoers boast!
5 They oppress your people, Lord,
  hurting those you love.
6 They kill widows and foreigners
  and murder orphans.
7 "The Lord isn't looking," they say,
  "and besides, the God of Israel*
    doesn't care."

8 Think again, you fools!
  When will you finally catch on?
9 Is the one who made your ears deaf?
  Is the one who formed your eyes
    blind?
10 He punishes the nations—won't he
    also punish you?
  He knows everything—doesn't
    he also know what you are
    doing?
11 The Lord knows people's thoughts,
  that they are worthless!

12 Happy are those whom you discipline,
    Lord,
  and those whom you teach from
    your law.
13 You give them relief from troubled
    times
  until a pit is dug for the wicked.
14 The Lord will not reject his people;
  he will not abandon his own special
    possession.
15 Judgment will come again for the
    righteous,
  and those who are upright will have
    a reward.

16 Who will protect me from the wicked?
  Who will stand up for me against
    evildoers?
17 Unless the Lord had helped me,
  I would soon have died.
18 I cried out, "I'm slipping!"
  and your unfailing love, O Lord,
    supported me.

19 When doubts filled my mind,
  your comfort gave me renewed hope
    and cheer.
20 Can unjust leaders claim that God is on
    their side—
  leaders who permit injustice by their
    laws?
21 They attack the righteous
  and condemn the innocent to death.
22 But the Lord is my fortress;
  my God is a mighty rock where I can
    hide.
23 God will make the sins of evil people
    fall back upon them.
  He will destroy them for their sins.
  The Lord our God will destroy them.

PSALM 95

1 Come, let us sing to the Lord!
  Let us give a joyous shout to the rock
    of our salvation!
2 Let us come before him with thanksgiving.
  Let us sing him psalms of praise.
3 For the Lord is a great God,
  the great King above all gods.
4 He owns the depths of the earth,
  and even the mightiest mountains
    are his.
5 The sea belongs to him, for he made it.
  His hands formed the dry land, too.

6 Come, let us worship and bow down.
  Let us kneel before the Lord our
    maker,
7   for he is our God.
  We are the people he watches over,
    the sheep under his care.

  Oh, that you would listen to his voice
    today!
8 The Lord says, "Don't harden your
    hearts as Israel did at Meribah,
  as they did at Massah in the
    wilderness.
9 For there your ancestors tried my
    patience;
  they courted my wrath though they
    had seen my many miracles.
10 For forty years I was angry with them,
    and I said,
  'They are a people whose hearts turn
    away from me.
  They refuse to do what I tell them.'
11 So in my anger I made a vow:
  'They will never enter my place of
    rest.'"

94:7 Hebrew *of Jacob.*

PSALM 96

1 Sing a new song to the LORD!
  Let the whole earth sing to the LORD!
2 Sing to the LORD; bless his name.
  Each day proclaim the good news
    that he saves.
3 Publish his glorious deeds among the
    nations.
  Tell everyone about the amazing
    things he does.
4 Great is the LORD! He is most worthy
    of praise!
  He is to be revered above all the
    gods.
5 The gods of other nations are merely
    idols,
  but the LORD made the heavens!
6 Honor and majesty surround him;
  strength and beauty are in his
    sanctuary.
7 O nations of the world, recognize the
    LORD;
  recognize that the LORD is glorious
    and strong.
8 Give to the LORD the glory he
    deserves!
  Bring your offering and come to
    worship him.
9 Worship the LORD in all his holy
    splendor.
  Let all the earth tremble before him.
10 Tell all the nations that the LORD is
    king.
  The world is firmly established and
    cannot be shaken.
  He will judge all peoples fairly.

11 Let the heavens be glad, and let the
    earth rejoice!
  Let the sea and everything in it shout
    his praise!
12   Let the fields and their crops burst
    forth with joy!
  Let the trees of the forest rustle with
    praise 13before the LORD!

97:8 Hebrew *Zion.*

For the LORD is coming!
  He is coming to judge the earth.
He will judge the world with
    righteousness
  and all the nations with his truth.

PSALM 97

1 The LORD is king! Let the earth rejoice!
  Let the farthest islands be glad.
2 Clouds and darkness surround him.
  Righteousness and justice are the
    foundation of his throne.
3 Fire goes forth before him
  and burns up all his foes.
4 His lightning flashes out across the
    world.
  The earth sees and trembles.
5 The mountains melt like wax before
    the LORD,
  before the Lord of all the earth.
6 The heavens declare his righteousness;
  every nation sees his glory.
7 Those who worship idols are
    disgraced—
  all who brag about their worthless
    gods—
  for every god must bow to him.
8 Jerusalem* has heard and rejoiced,
  and all the cities of Judah are glad
  because of your justice, LORD!
9 For you, O LORD, are most high over
    all the earth;
  you are exalted far above all gods.

10 You who love the LORD, hate evil!
  He protects the lives of his godly
    people
  and rescues them from the power
    of the wicked.
11 Light shines on the godly,
  and joy on those who do right.
12 May all who are godly be happy in the
    LORD
  and praise his holy name!

JUNE 19 ☐ DAY 171
PSALMS 98–103
A Joyful Noise

OVERVIEW Perhaps no other six psalms picture God's praiseworthy character as graphically as the ones in today's reading. God in his righteousness (Psalm 98), in his exalted place of authority (99), and in his everlasting mercy (100) demands and deserves admiration and adoration by his people. In view of God's character, the psalmist pledges his obedience (101), expresses his dependence (102), and acknowledges his gratitude for God's rich blessings (103).

Psalm 98	Psalm 99	Psalm 100	Psalms 101–103
Singing God's Justice	Speaking God's Forgiveness	Shouting God's Faithfulness	Living Life Gratefully
	Reverence		Response

YOUR DAILY WALK You'll notice in Psalm 98:4 (and again in 100:1) that you are not required to make beautiful music but only a joyful shout to the Lord. Even monotones can vocalize their praise to the Lord!

Where the benefits received are infinite, the praises cannot be too extravagant.

The writer of Psalm 98 knew what rejoicing in the Lord meant. Have you learned his secret? When God has done something wonderful in your life, when you are bubbling over with appreciation for his mighty deeds, how can you express your joy? How can you say thank you to God in a way that befits his majesty and splendor?

Answer: You can sing! "Sing a new song to the LORD, . . . Shout to the LORD . . . Sing your praise to the LORD with the harp, with the harp and melodious song" (vv. 1, 4-5). One thing you can take with you throughout the day is a song. Spend the next few minutes singing some of your favorite hymns or choruses. Think about the words as you sing them. You'll have a song in your heart all day!

INSIGHT Praise Expressed Full Circle
In Psalm 103, David constructs a "circle of praise" in which the entire universe breaks forth in a doxology to God:
- Himself: "I tell myself" (vv. 1-5)
- The people of Israel (vv. 6-18)
- The armies of angels (vv. 19-22)

Finally, David ends where he began: "As for me—I, too, will praise the LORD."

PSALM 98
A psalm.

1 Sing a new song to the LORD,
    for he has done wonderful deeds.
He has won a mighty victory
    by his power and holiness.
2 The LORD has announced his victory
    and has revealed his righteousness
        to every nation!
3 He has remembered his promise to love
    and be faithful to Israel.
The whole earth has seen the
        salvation of our God.

4 Shout to the LORD, all the earth;
    break out in praise and sing for joy!
5 Sing your praise to the LORD with the
        harp,
    with the harp and melodious song,
6   with trumpets and the sound of the
        ram's horn.
Make a joyful symphony before the
    LORD, the King!

7 Let the sea and everything in it shout
        his praise!
    Let the earth and all living things
        join in.

8 Let the rivers clap their hands in
glee!
Let the hills sing out their songs of
joy 9before the LORD.
For the LORD is coming to judge the
earth.
He will judge the world with justice,
and the nations with fairness.

PSALM 99

1 The LORD is king!
Let the nations tremble!
He sits on his throne between the
cherubim.
Let the whole earth quake!
2 The LORD sits in majesty in Jerusalem,*
supreme above all the nations.
3 Let them praise your great and
awesome name.
Your name is holy!
4 Mighty king, lover of justice,
you have established fairness.
You have acted with justice
and righteousness throughout Israel.*
5 Exalt the LORD our God!
Bow low before his feet, for he is
holy!

6 Moses and Aaron were among his
priests;
Samuel also called on his name.
They cried to the LORD for help,
and he answered them.
7 He spoke to them from the pillar of
cloud,
and they followed the decrees and
principles he gave them.
8 O LORD our God, you answered them.
You were a forgiving God,
but you punished them when they
went wrong.

9 Exalt the LORD our God
and worship at his holy mountain in
Jerusalem,
for the LORD our God is holy!

PSALM 100

A psalm of thanksgiving.

1 Shout with joy to the LORD, O earth!
2 Worship the LORD with gladness.
Come before him, singing with joy.
3 Acknowledge that the LORD is God!
He made us, and we are his.
We are his people, the sheep of his
pasture.

4 Enter his gates with thanksgiving;
go into his courts with praise.
Give thanks to him and bless his
name.
5 For the LORD is good.
His unfailing love continues forever,
and his faithfulness continues to
each generation.

PSALM 101

A psalm of David.

1 I will sing of your love and justice.
I will praise you, LORD, with songs.
2 I will be careful to live a blameless life—
when will you come to my aid?
I will lead a life of integrity
in my own home.
3 I will refuse to look at
anything vile and vulgar.
I hate all crooked dealings;
I will have nothing to do with them.
4 I will reject perverse ideas
and stay away from every evil.
5 I will not tolerate people who slander
their neighbors.
I will not endure conceit and pride.

6 I will keep a protective eye on the godly,
so they may dwell with me in safety.
Only those who are above reproach
will be allowed to serve me.
7 I will not allow deceivers to serve me,
and liars will not be allowed to enter
my presence.
8 My daily task will be to ferret out
criminals
and free the city of the LORD from
their grip.

PSALM 102

*A prayer of one overwhelmed with trouble, pouring
out problems before the LORD.*

1 LORD, hear my prayer!
Listen to my plea!
2 Don't turn away from me
in my time of distress.
Bend down your ear
and answer me quickly when I call
to you,
3 for my days disappear like smoke,
and my bones burn like red-hot coals.
4 My heart is sick, withered like grass,
and I have lost my appetite.
5 Because of my groaning,
I am reduced to skin and bones.

99:2 Hebrew *Zion.*   **99:4** Hebrew *Jacob.*

⁶ I am like an owl in the desert,
  like a lonely owl in a far-off
    wilderness.
⁷ I lie awake,
  lonely as a solitary bird on the roof.
⁸ My enemies taunt me day after day.
  They mock and curse me.
⁹ I eat ashes instead of my food.
  My tears run down into my drink
¹⁰ because of your anger and wrath.
  For you have picked me up and
    thrown me out.
¹¹ My life passes as swiftly as the evening
    shadows.
  I am withering like grass.

¹² But you, O LORD, will rule forever.
  Your fame will endure to every
    generation.
¹³ You will arise and have mercy on
    Jerusalem*—
  and now is the time to pity her,
  now is the time you promised to help.
¹⁴ For your people love every stone in her
    walls
  and show favor even to the dust in
    her streets.
¹⁵ And the nations will tremble before the
    LORD.
  The kings of the earth will tremble
    before his glory.
¹⁶ For the LORD will rebuild Jerusalem.
  He will appear in his glory.
¹⁷ He will listen to the prayers of the
    destitute.
  He will not reject their pleas.

¹⁸ Let this be recorded for future
    generations,
  so that a nation yet to be created will
    praise the LORD.
¹⁹ Tell them the LORD looked down
  from his heavenly sanctuary.
  He looked to the earth from heaven
²⁰ to hear the groans of the prisoners,
  to release those condemned to die.
²¹ And so the LORD's fame will be
    celebrated in Zion,
  his praises in Jerusalem,
²² when multitudes gather together
  and kingdoms come to worship the
    LORD.

²³ He has cut me down in midlife,
  shortening my days.
²⁴ But I cried to him, "My God, who lives
    forever,

don't take my life while I am still so
    young!
²⁵ In ages past you laid the foundation
    of the earth,
  and the heavens are the work of your
    hands.
²⁶ Even they will perish, but you remain
    forever;
  they will wear out like old clothing.
  You will change them like a garment,
    and they will fade away.
²⁷ But you are always the same;
  your years never end.
²⁸ The children of your people
  will live in security.
  Their children's children
  will thrive in your presence."

PSALM 103
A psalm of David.

¹ Praise the LORD, I tell myself;
  with my whole heart, I will praise
    his holy name.
² Praise the LORD, I tell myself,
  and never forget the good things he
    does for me.
³ He forgives all my sins
  and heals all my diseases.
⁴ He ransoms me from death
  and surrounds me with love and
    tender mercies.
⁵ He fills my life with good things.
  My youth is renewed like the
    eagle's!
⁶ The LORD gives righteousness
  and justice to all who are treated
    unfairly.
⁷ He revealed his character to Moses
  and his deeds to the people of Israel.
⁸ The LORD is merciful and gracious;
  he is slow to get angry and full of
    unfailing love.
⁹ He will not constantly accuse us,
  nor remain angry forever.
¹⁰ He has not punished us for all our
    sins,
  nor does he deal with us as we
    deserve.
¹¹ For his unfailing love toward those
    who fear him
  is as great as the height of the
    heavens above the earth.
¹² He has removed our rebellious acts
  as far away from us as the east is
    from the west.

102:13 Hebrew *Zion*; also in 102:16.

13 The LORD is like a father to his
    children,
  tender and compassionate to those
    who fear him.
14 For he understands how weak we
    are;
  he knows we are only dust.
15 Our days on earth are like grass;
  like wildflowers, we bloom and
    die.
16 The wind blows, and we are gone—
  as though we had never been
    here.
17 But the love of the LORD remains forever
  with those who fear him.
  His salvation extends to the children's
    children

18 of those who are faithful to his
    covenant,
  of those who obey his commandments!
19 The LORD has made the heavens his
    throne;
  from there he rules over everything.
20 Praise the LORD, you angels of his,
  you mighty creatures who carry out
    his plans,
  listening for each of his commands.
21 Yes, praise the LORD, you armies of angels
  who serve him and do his will!
22 Praise the LORD, everything he has
    created,
  everywhere in his kingdom.
  As for me—I, too, will praise the LORD.

JUNE 20 ☐ DAY 172
PSALMS 104–106
Growing or Groaning? (Psalm 106)

OVERVIEW Book Four of Psalms closes with three majestic portraits
of God. He is the powerful God of creation (Psalm 104, a psalm that
closely parallels the creation account of Genesis 1); he is the faithful
God of the covenant, who formed a mighty nation out of people in
slavery (105); he is the long-suffering God, who patiently disciplines
but never deserts the objects of his love—a stiff-necked people (106).

Psalm 104	Psalm 105	Psalm 106
The Fullness of God's Creation	The Faithfulness of God to His People in Their Foundation	in Their Failures
God of Power	God of Patience	

YOUR DAILY WALK Memories, like fire, can both bless with warmth
and burn with searing heat. As you look back over the first half of this
year, do your memories give you more pleasure or pain?

Use the past as a springboard, not a sofa.

Probably you experienced a bit of both sensations. As the psalmist
reviewed Israel's history, he delighted in the faithfulness of God, who
never failed his people, and despaired over the faithlessness of Israel,
who repeatedly disobeyed God. The nation's history speaks eloquently
of the pain of waywardness and the persistence of God in guiding his
people down the path of righteousness and blessing.

If you were asked to write *The History of My Life: Part I*, would it read
like Psalm 106? Would it include pleasant memories of God's provision
and painful memories of your rebellious moments? Have you thanked
God for the former? Have you experienced God's forgiveness for the
latter (1 John 1:9)? And have you learned a lesson in the process? Or
are you—like the Israelites in Psalm 106—repeating your errors and
forfeiting God's blessings?

Find a few minutes to take a quiet walk alone today, with just God and your thoughts for companions. Reminisce over the first six months of this year: the good times (thank him for them) and the bad (confess your rebellious moments to him). Ask God to help you grow wiser—not just older—for the rest of the year.

 INSIGHT A Psalmist's Paraphrase of Genesis 1:1–2:3
Psalm 104 closely parallels the seven days of creation found in Genesis 1–2. Read through both passages side by side and notice how each section of the psalm acts as a free translation of the corresponding passage in Genesis. Can you match up all seven days of creation?

PSALM 104

¹ Praise the LORD, I tell myself;
  O LORD my God, how great you are!
You are robed with honor and with
    majesty;
²   you are dressed in a robe of light.
You stretch out the starry curtain of the
    heavens;
³   you lay out the rafters of your home
    in the rain clouds.
You make the clouds your chariots;
  you ride upon the wings of the wind.
⁴ The winds are your messengers;
  flames of fire are your servants.

⁵ You placed the world on its foundation
  so it would never be moved.
⁶ You clothed the earth with floods of
    water,
    water that covered even the
    mountains.
⁷ At the sound of your rebuke, the water
    fled;
    at the sound of your thunder, it fled
    away.
⁸ Mountains rose and valleys sank
  to the levels you decreed.
⁹ Then you set a firm boundary for the
    seas,
    so they would never again cover the
    earth.
¹⁰ You make the springs pour water into
    ravines,
    so streams gush down from the
    mountains.
¹¹ They provide water for all the animals,
  and the wild donkeys quench their
    thirst.
¹² The birds nest beside the streams
  and sing among the branches of the
    trees.
¹³ You send rain on the mountains from
    your heavenly home,
    and you fill the earth with the fruit of
    your labor.

¹⁴ You cause grass to grow for the cattle.
  You cause plants to grow for people
    to use.
  You allow them to produce food from
    the earth—
¹⁵   wine to make them glad,
    olive oil as lotion for their skin,
    and bread to give them strength.
¹⁶ The trees of the LORD are well cared
    for—
    the cedars of Lebanon that he
    planted.
¹⁷ There the birds make their nests,
  and the storks make their homes in
    the firs.
¹⁸ High in the mountains are pastures for
    the wild goats,
    and the rocks form a refuge for rock
    badgers.*
¹⁹ You made the moon to mark the
    seasons
    and the sun that knows when to set.
²⁰ You send the darkness, and it becomes
    night,
    when all the forest animals prowl
    about.
²¹ Then the young lions roar for their
    food,
    but they are dependent on God.
²² At dawn they slink back
  into their dens to rest.
²³ Then people go off to their work;
  they labor until the evening shadows
    fall again.
²⁴ O LORD, what a variety of things you
    have made!
  In wisdom you have made them all.
  The earth is full of your creatures.
²⁵ Here is the ocean, vast and wide,
  teeming with life of every kind,
  both great and small.
²⁶ See the ships sailing along,
  and Leviathan, which you made to
    play in the sea.

104:18 Or *coneys,* or *hyraxes.*

²⁷ Every one of these depends on you
   to give them their food as they need
   it.
²⁸ When you supply it, they gather it.
   You open your hand to feed them,
   and they are satisfied.
²⁹ But if you turn away from them, they
   panic.
   When you take away their breath,
   they die
   and turn again to dust.
³⁰ When you send your Spirit, new life is
   born
   to replenish all the living of the earth.

³¹ May the glory of the LORD last forever!
   The LORD rejoices in all he has made!
³² The earth trembles at his glance;
   the mountains burst into flame at his
   touch.
³³ I will sing to the LORD as long as I live.
   I will praise my God to my last
   breath!
³⁴ May he be pleased by all these
   thoughts about him,
   for I rejoice in the LORD.
³⁵ Let all sinners vanish from the face of
   the earth;
   let the wicked disappear forever.
   As for me—I will praise the LORD!

   Praise the LORD!

PSALM 105
¹ Give thanks to the LORD and proclaim
   his greatness.
   Let the whole world know what he
   has done.
² Sing to him; yes, sing his praises.
   Tell everyone about his miracles.
³ Exult in his holy name;
   O worshipers of the LORD, rejoice!
⁴ Search for the LORD and for his
   strength,
   and keep on searching.
⁵ Think of the wonderful works he has
   done,
   the miracles and the judgments he
   handed down,
⁶ O children of Abraham, God's servant,
   O descendants of Jacob, God's
   chosen one.
⁷ He is the LORD our God.
   His rule is seen throughout the land.
⁸ He always stands by his covenant—
   the commitment he made to a
   thousand generations.

⁹ This is the covenant he made with
   Abraham
   and the oath he swore to Isaac.
¹⁰ He confirmed it to Jacob as a decree,
   to the people of Israel as a
   never-ending treaty:
¹¹ "I will give you the land of Canaan
   as your special possession."
¹² He said this when they were few in
   number,
   a tiny group of strangers in Canaan.
¹³ They wandered back and forth
   between nations,
   from one kingdom to another.
¹⁴ Yet he did not let anyone oppress them.
   He warned kings on their behalf:
¹⁵ "Do not touch these people I have
   chosen,
   and do not hurt my prophets."
¹⁶ He called for a famine on the land of
   Canaan,
   cutting off its food supply.
¹⁷ Then he sent someone to Egypt ahead
   of them—
   Joseph, who was sold as a slave.
¹⁸ There in prison, they bruised his feet
   with fetters
   and placed his neck in an iron collar.
¹⁹ Until the time came to fulfill his word,
   the LORD tested Joseph's character.
²⁰ Then Pharaoh sent for him and set him
   free;
   the ruler of the nation opened his
   prison door.
²¹ Joseph was put in charge of all the
   king's household;
   he became ruler over all the king's
   possessions.
²² He could instruct the king's aides as he
   pleased
   and teach the king's advisers.

²³ Then Israel arrived in Egypt;
   Jacob lived as a foreigner in the land
   of Ham.
²⁴ And the LORD multiplied the people of
   Israel
   until they became too mighty for
   their enemies.
²⁵ Then he turned the Egyptians against
   the Israelites,
   and they plotted against the LORD's
   servants.

²⁶ But the LORD sent Moses his servant,
   along with Aaron, whom he had
   chosen.

27 They performed miraculous signs
        among the Egyptians,
    and miracles in the land of Ham.
28 The LORD blanketed Egypt in darkness,
    for they had defied his commands to
        let his people go.
29 He turned the nation's water into blood,
    poisoning all the fish.
30 Then frogs overran the land;
    they were found even in the king's
        private rooms.
31 When he spoke, flies descended on the
        Egyptians,
    and gnats swarmed across Egypt.
32 Instead of rain, he sent murderous hail,
    and flashes of lightning
        overwhelmed the land.
33 He ruined their grapevines and fig trees
    and shattered all the trees.
34 He spoke, and hordes of locusts came—
    locusts beyond number.
35 They ate up everything green in the
        land,
    destroying all the crops.
36 Then he killed the oldest child in each
        Egyptian home,
    the pride and joy of each family.

37 But he brought his people safely out
        of Egypt, loaded with silver and
        gold;
    there were no sick or feeble people
        among them.
38 Egypt was glad when they were gone,
    for the dread of them was great.
39 The LORD spread out a cloud above
        them as a covering
    and gave them a great fire to light
        the darkness.
40 They asked for meat, and he sent them
        quail;
    he gave them manna—bread from
        heaven.
41 He opened up a rock, and water
        gushed out
    to form a river through the dry and
        barren land.
42 For he remembered his sacred promise
    to Abraham his servant.
43 So he brought his people out of Egypt
        with joy,
    his chosen ones with rejoicing.
44 He gave his people the lands of pagan
        nations,
    and they harvested crops that others
        had planted.

45 All this happened so they would follow
        his principles
    and obey his laws.

Praise the LORD!

PSALM 106

1 Praise the LORD!

  Give thanks to the LORD, for he is good!
    His faithful love endures forever.
2 Who can list the glorious miracles of
        the LORD?
    Who can ever praise him half
        enough?
3 Happy are those who deal justly with
        others
    and always do what is right.

4 Remember me, too, LORD, when you
        show favor to your people;
    come to me with your salvation.
5 Let me share in the prosperity of your
        chosen ones.
    Let me rejoice in the joy of your
        people;
    let me praise you with those who are
        your heritage.

6 Both we and our ancestors have sinned.
    We have done wrong! We have acted
        wickedly!
7 Our ancestors in Egypt
    were not impressed by the LORD's
        miracles.
  They soon forgot his many acts of
        kindness to them.
    Instead, they rebelled against him at
        the Red Sea.*
8 Even so, he saved them—
    to defend the honor of his name
    and to demonstrate his mighty power.
9 He commanded the Red Sea* to divide,
    and a dry path appeared.
  He led Israel across the sea bottom
    that was as dry as a desert.
10 So he rescued them from their enemies
    and redeemed them from their foes.
11 Then the water returned and covered
        their enemies;
    not one of them survived.
12 Then at last his people believed his
        promises.
    Then they finally sang his praise.

13 Yet how quickly they forgot what he
        had done!
    They wouldn't wait for his counsel!

106:7 Hebrew *at the sea, the sea of reeds.*   106:9 Hebrew *sea of reeds;* also in 106:22.

¹⁴ In the wilderness, their desires ran wild,
  testing God's patience in that dry
  land.
¹⁵ So he gave them what they asked for,
  but he sent a plague along with it.
¹⁶ The people in the camp were jealous of
  Moses
  and envious of Aaron, the LORD's
  holy priest.
¹⁷ Because of this, the earth opened up;
  it swallowed Dathan
  and buried Abiram and the other
  rebels.
¹⁸ Fire fell upon their followers;
  a flame consumed the wicked.

¹⁹ The people made a calf at Mount Sinai*;
  they bowed before an image made of
  gold.
²⁰ They traded their glorious God
  for a statue of a grass-eating ox!
²¹ They forgot God, their savior,
  who had done such great things in
  Egypt—
²² such wonderful things in that land,
  such awesome deeds at the Red Sea.
²³ So he declared he would destroy them.
  But Moses, his chosen one, stepped
  between the LORD and the people.
  He begged him to turn from his
  anger and not destroy them.

²⁴ The people refused to enter the
  pleasant land,
  for they wouldn't believe his
  promise to care for them.
²⁵ Instead, they grumbled in their tents
  and refused to obey the LORD.
²⁶ Therefore, he swore
  that he would kill them in the
  wilderness,
²⁷ that he would scatter their descendants
  among the nations,
  exiling them to distant lands.

²⁸ Then our ancestors joined in the
  worship of Baal at Peor;
  they even ate sacrifices offered to the
  dead!
²⁹ They angered the LORD with all these
  things,
  so a plague broke out among them.
³⁰ But Phinehas had the courage to step in,
  and the plague was stopped.
³¹ So he has been regarded as a righteous
  man
  ever since that time.

³² At Meribah, too, they angered the LORD,
  causing Moses serious trouble.
³³ They made Moses angry,*
  and he spoke foolishly.

³⁴ Israel failed to destroy the nations in
  the land,
  as the LORD had told them to.
³⁵ Instead, they mingled among the pagans
  and adopted their evil customs.
³⁶ They worshiped their idols,
  and this led to their downfall.
³⁷ They even sacrificed their sons
  and their daughters to the demons.
³⁸ They shed innocent blood,
  the blood of their sons and daughters.
  By sacrificing them to the idols of
  Canaan,
  they polluted the land with murder.
³⁹ They defiled themselves by their evil
  deeds,
  and their love of idols was adultery
  in the LORD's sight.

⁴⁰ That is why the LORD's anger burned
  against his people,
  and he abhorred his own special
  possession.
⁴¹ He handed them over to pagan nations,
  and those who hated them ruled
  over them.
⁴² Their enemies crushed them
  and brought them under their cruel
  power.
⁴³ Again and again he delivered them,
  but they continued to rebel against
  him,
  and they were finally destroyed by
  their sin.
⁴⁴ Even so, he pitied them in their distress
  and listened to their cries.
⁴⁵ He remembered his covenant with them
  and relented because of his unfailing
  love.
⁴⁶ He even caused their captors
  to treat them with kindness.

⁴⁷ O LORD our God, save us!
  Gather us back from among the
  nations,
  so we can thank your holy name
  and rejoice and praise you.

⁴⁸ Blessed be the LORD, the God of Israel,
  from everlasting to everlasting!
  Let all the people say, "Amen!"

  Praise the LORD!

106:19 Hebrew *at Horeb,* another name for Sinai.   106:33 Hebrew *They embittered his spirit.*

JUNE 21 □ DAY 173
Don't Forget to Remember!

LOOK BACK The psalms you have read this past week ask and answer some of the intriguing *why* questions everyone is tempted to ask from time to time: Why do the wicked seem to get away with murder (Psalm 73)? Why has God seemingly rejected us (74, 77)? Why is God so patient with his people (78)? Why do the pagans question God's very existence (79)? Why does God judge his people (80)? Why does God sometimes seem to hide his face (88)?

The answers are as clear as the character of God. He is eternal (90), omnipotent (91), majestic (93), righteous (97), compassionate, gracious (103), creative (104), and promise-keeping (106). In short, "the LORD is God" (100:3), and to love him and fear him is to unlock many of the secrets of this life and the next (103).

LOOK UP Try this pop quiz on important bits of trivia:
1. When is your spouse's (or mother's) birthday?
2. What is your social security number?
3. If you have a will, who is the executor?
4. If you have a safe-deposit box, what is its number?
5. When were the batteries last changed in your smoke detectors?

When it comes to important information, the best advice is also the simplest: Don't forget! Perhaps you are in the habit of writing down important birthdays or anniversaries on a master calendar . . . keeping important documents in a special place . . . changing the batteries in your smoke detectors whenever you change your clocks to (or from) daylight saving time.

The person who will not command his or her thoughts will soon lose command of his or her actions.

The psalmist David has a similar reminder for you in Psalm 103. He wants you to remember who God is (his attributes) . . . what he has done (his activities) . . . how well he knows you (his omniscience) . . . how much he is in control (his sovereignty) . . . and how worthy he is to be praised. But none of that information will do you any good if you don't remember it!

LOOK AHEAD Think of Psalm 103 as a mother lode of golden truths about the God you serve. It takes only a few minutes of meditation and reflection to discover shimmering bits of insight about the greatness of your God. Try it! Take the next five minutes and see how many of these statements you can complete, using the words you have read in Psalm 103.

Don't forget . . . what God has done:

_____

Don't forget . . . what God is like:

_____

Don't forget . . . what God is *not* like:

_____

Don't forget . . . how much God loves you:

_____

Don't forget . . . how well God knows you:

_____

Don't forget . . . how much God is in control:

_____

Don't forget . . . how worthy God is to be praised:

_____

And lest you forget what you have just remembered, tie a string around your finger (or place a ribbon on the antenna of your car). Then when someone asks you what the string or ribbon is for (and they will), be ready to give an answer for the hope that is in you (1 Peter 3:15).

JUNE 22 ☐ DAY 174
PSALMS 107–110
Handling Slander (Psalm 109)

OVERVIEW Book Five begins with a vibrant note of thanksgiving for God's deliverance from danger (Psalm 107). David voices praise for God's help against his enemies (108), then cries out for vindication against those who have slandered him (109). But whether his enemies prosper or suffer swift punishment, David knows the future lies securely in the hands of God's righteous Ruler who will triumph over all (110).

Psalm 107	Psalm 108	Psalm 109	Psalm 110
God's Redeemed	God's Remnant	God's Reproached	God's Ruler
Testifying	Trusting		Triumphant

No greater injury can be inflicted upon someone than to wound his or her reputation.

YOUR DAILY WALK Character assassination. It's a malady you won't find in any medical text. And if it happens to you, chances are you won't end up in a hospital emergency room. But the pain is still acute, the damage severe, the recovery slow, the scars difficult to remove.

How do you react when you've been unjustly accused and maliciously slandered? David responded with some of the strongest words to be found in Scripture (109:6-20). In fact, these denunciations sound so uncharacteristic of the "sweet singer of Israel" that some commentators have suggested David's accuser (rather than David) is the one being quoted.

But David was zealous to defend the righteousness of God wherever it was attacked. His harsh cries were his way of expressing hatred for sin.

But the question remains: How do you handle a slanderous attack? David's advice would be this: Seek God's help and let him vindicate you (Psalm 109:26-27); let your enemies bring shame upon their own heads, rather than trying to do it yourself (v. 29); continue to praise the Lord throughout the ordeal (v. 30).

INSIGHT Psalms of Vengeance
Psalm 109 is just one of a number of "imprecatory" psalms in which the author asks God to judge his enemies (others include 7, 35, 55, 58, 59, 69, 79, 137, 139). In his indignation over sin, the psalmist cries out for God's swift and just punishment of evil.

BOOK FIVE (Psalms 107–150)
P S A L M   1 0 7
¹ Give thanks to the LORD, for he is good!
   His faithful love endures forever.
² Has the LORD redeemed you? Then speak out!

Tell others he has saved you from your enemies.
³ For he has gathered the exiles from many lands,
   from east and west, from north and south.

⁴ Some wandered in the desert,
   lost and homeless.
⁵ Hungry and thirsty,
   they nearly died.
⁶ "LORD, help!" they cried in their
      trouble,
   and he rescued them from their
      distress.
⁷ He led them straight to safety,
   to a city where they could live.
⁸ Let them praise the LORD for his great
      love
   and for all his wonderful deeds to
      them.
⁹ For he satisfies the thirsty
   and fills the hungry with good
      things.

¹⁰ Some sat in darkness and deepest
      gloom,
   miserable prisoners in chains.
¹¹ They rebelled against the words of
      God,
   scorning the counsel of the Most
      High.
¹² That is why he broke them with hard
      labor;
   they fell, and no one helped them
      rise again.
¹³ "LORD, help!" they cried in their
      trouble,
   and he saved them from their
      distress.
¹⁴ He led them from the darkness and
      deepest gloom;
   he snapped their chains.
¹⁵ Let them praise the LORD for his great
      love
   and for all his wonderful deeds to
      them.
¹⁶ For he broke down their prison gates
      of bronze;
   he cut apart their bars of iron.

¹⁷ Some were fools in their rebellion;
   they suffered for their sins.
¹⁸ Their appetites were gone,
   and death was near.
¹⁹ "LORD, help!" they cried in their
      trouble,
   and he saved them from their
      distress.
²⁰ He spoke, and they were healed—
   snatched from the door of death.
²¹ Let them praise the LORD for his great
      love
   and for all his wonderful deeds to
      them.

²² Let them offer sacrifices of thanksgiving
   and sing joyfully about his glorious
      acts.

²³ Some went off in ships,
   plying the trade routes of the world.
²⁴ They, too, observed the LORD's power
      in action,
   his impressive works on the deepest
      seas.
²⁵ He spoke, and the winds rose,
   stirring up the waves.
²⁶ Their ships were tossed to the heavens
   and sank again to the depths;
   the sailors cringed in terror.
²⁷ They reeled and staggered like drunk-
      ards
   and were at their wits' end.
²⁸ "LORD, help!" they cried in their trouble,
   and he saved them from their distress.
²⁹ He calmed the storm to a whisper
   and stilled the waves.
³⁰ What a blessing was that stillness
   as he brought them safely into harbor!
³¹ Let them praise the LORD for his great
      love
   and for all his wonderful deeds to
      them.
³² Let them exalt him publicly before the
      congregation
   and before the leaders of the nation.

³³ He changes rivers into deserts,
   and springs of water into dry land.
³⁴ He turns the fruitful land into salty
      wastelands,
   because of the wickedness of those
      who live there.
³⁵ But he also turns deserts into pools of
      water,
   the dry land into flowing springs.
³⁶ He brings the hungry to settle there
   and build their cities.
³⁷ They sow their fields, plant their
      vineyards,
   and harvest their bumper crops.
³⁸ How he blesses them!
   They raise large families there,
   and their herds of cattle increase.

³⁹ When they decrease in number and
      become impoverished
   through oppression, trouble, and
      sorrow,
⁴⁰ the LORD pours contempt on their
      princes,
   causing them to wander in trackless
      wastelands.

41 But he rescues the poor from their
distress
and increases their families like vast
flocks of sheep.
42 The godly will see these things and be
glad,
while the wicked are stricken silent.
43 Those who are wise will take all this
to heart;
they will see in our history the
faithful love of the LORD.

PSALM 108

A psalm of David. A song.

1 My heart is confident in you, O God;
no wonder I can sing your praises!
Wake up, my soul!
2   Wake up, O harp and lyre!
I will waken the dawn with my song.
3 I will thank you, LORD, in front of all
the people.
I will sing your praises among the
nations.
4 For your unfailing love is higher than
the heavens.
Your faithfulness reaches to the
clouds.
5 Be exalted, O God, above the highest
heavens.
May your glory shine over all the
earth.

6 Use your strong right arm to save me,
and rescue your beloved people.
7 God has promised this by his holiness*:
"I will divide up Shechem with joy.
I will measure out the valley of
Succoth.
8 Gilead is mine,
and Manasseh is mine.
Ephraim will produce my warriors,
and Judah will produce my kings.
9 Moab will become my lowly servant,
and Edom will be my slave.
I will shout in triumph over the
Philistines."
10 But who will bring me into the fortified
city?
Who will bring me victory over
Edom?
11 Have you rejected us, O God?
Will you no longer march with our
armies?
12 Oh, please help us against our enemies,
for all human help is useless.

108:7 Or *in his sanctuary.*

13 With God's help we will do mighty
things,
for he will trample down our foes.

PSALM 109

For the choir director: A psalm of David.

1 O God, whom I praise,
don't stand silent and aloof
2 while the wicked slander me
and tell lies about me.
3 They are all around me with their
hateful words,
and they fight against me for no
reason.
4 I love them, but they try to destroy
me—
even as I am praying for them!
5 They return evil for good,
and hatred for my love.

6 Arrange for an evil person to turn on
him.
Send an accuser to bring him to
trial.
7 When his case is called for judgment,
let him be pronounced guilty.
Count his prayers as sins.
8 Let his years be few;
let his position be given to someone
else.
9 May his children become fatherless,
and may his wife become a widow.
10 May his children wander as beggars;
may they be evicted from their
ruined homes.
11 May creditors seize his entire estate,
and strangers take all he has earned.
12 Let no one be kind to him;
let no one pity his fatherless
children.
13 May all his offspring die.
May his family name be blotted
out in a single generation.
14 May the LORD never forget the sins
of his ancestors;
may his mother's sins never be
erased from the record.
15 May these sins always remain before
the LORD,
but may his name be cut off from
human memory.
16 For he refused all kindness to others;
he persecuted the poor and needy,
and he hounded the brokenhearted
to death.

¹⁷ He loved to curse others;
  now you curse him.
He never blessed others;
  now don't you bless him.
¹⁸ Cursing is as much a part of him as his
    clothing,
  or as the water he drinks,
  or the rich food he eats.
¹⁹ Now may his curses return and cling
    to him like clothing;
  may they be tied around him like a
    belt.

²⁰ May those curses become the LORD's
    punishment for my accusers
  who are plotting against my life.
²¹ But deal well with me, O Sovereign
    LORD,
  for the sake of your own reputation!
Rescue me because you are so faithful
    and good.
²² For I am poor and needy,
  and my heart is full of pain.
²³ I am fading like a shadow at dusk;
  I am falling like a grasshopper that is
    brushed aside.
²⁴ My knees are weak from fasting,
  and I am skin and bones.
²⁵ I am an object of mockery to people
    everywhere;
  when they see me, they shake their
    heads.

²⁶ Help me, O LORD my God!
  Save me because of your unfailing
    love.
²⁷ Let them see that this is your doing,
  that you yourself have done it, LORD.
²⁸ Then let them curse me if they like,
  but you will bless me!
When they attack me, they will be
    disgraced!

110:2 Hebrew *Zion*.

But I, your servant, will go right on
  rejoicing!
²⁹ Make their humiliation obvious to all;
  clothe my accusers with disgrace.
³⁰ But I will give repeated thanks to the
    LORD,
  praising him to everyone.
³¹ For he stands beside the needy,
  ready to save them from those who
    condemn them.

PSALM 110
A psalm of David.

¹ The LORD said to my Lord,
  "Sit in honor at my right hand
until I humble your enemies,
  making them a footstool under your
    feet."

² The LORD will extend your powerful
    dominion from Jerusalem*;
  you will rule over your enemies.
³ In that day of battle,
  your people will serve you willingly.
Arrayed in holy garments,
  your vigor will be renewed each day
    like the morning dew.
⁴ The LORD has taken an oath and will
    not break his vow:
  "You are a priest forever in the line
    of Melchizedek."
⁵ The Lord stands at your right hand
    to protect you.
He will strike down many kings in
    the day of his anger.
⁶ He will punish the nations
  and fill them with their dead;
he will shatter heads
  over the whole earth.
⁷ But he himself will be refreshed from
    brooks along the way.
He will be victorious.

JUNE 23 ☐ DAY 175
PSALMS 111–118
God Understands

OVERVIEW The reasons for praising God are innumerable, but today's psalms will give you a few to start with! You can praise him for his tender care (Psalm 111), his blessings for the upright (112), his remembrance of the poor (113), his watchfulness over Israel (114, 115), his restoration of the sorrowing (116), and his enduring love (117–118).

Psalm 111	Psalm 112	Psalms 113–115	Psalms 116–118
Faithful Care	Fearing Child	Life, Love, and Liberty	Death, Devotion, and Destruction
God's Delight		God's Deeds	God's Deliverance

YOUR DAILY WALK "Judge a tree by its fruit; not by its leaves" (Euripides).

If people speak ill of you, live so that no one will believe them.

"Examine the contents, not the bottle" (Jewish Talmud).

"You can't judge a book by its cover" (Anonymous).

Three ways of saying the same thing: The only thing worse than making a surface judgment is being the victim of one!

What do you do when you suffer from superficial evaluations by your friends, superiors, or co-workers? Where can you turn when your actions or motives are misunderstood?

Turn to the one who experienced being misunderstood himself— "the stone rejected by the builders" who has today "become the cornerstone" (118:22). Christ knew what it meant to be rejected unjustly . . . condemned wrongfully . . . crucified unmercifully. He knows what you are going through. That's why you can come to him confidently to experience his presence (118:6), help (118:7), and protection (118:8-14) in times of misunderstanding.

Three times in the New Testament, Psalm 118:22 is quoted to show that human misunderstanding cannot thwart the good purposes of God (Matthew 21:42; Acts 4:11; 1 Peter 2:7). Put your initials next to one of those passages as your silent testimony of confidence in God's ability to do the same in your life today!

INSIGHT Psalm 118, the Palm Sunday Psalm

Just before Jesus quoted from Psalm 118 in Matthew 21, he had entered Jerusalem on the back of a colt to the acclamations of the multitude shouting the words of Psalm 118:26. (What are they? See Matthew 21:9.)

PSALM 111

1 Praise the LORD!

I will thank the LORD with all my heart
as I meet with his godly people.
2 How amazing are the deeds of the
LORD!
All who delight in him should
ponder them.
3 Everything he does reveals his glory
and majesty.
His righteousness never fails.

4 Who can forget the wonders he
performs?
How gracious and merciful is our
LORD!
5 He gives food to those who trust
him;
he always remembers his covenant.
6 He has shown his great power to his
people
by giving them the lands of other
nations.

7 All he does is just and good,
  and all his commandments are
    trustworthy.
8 They are forever true,
  to be obeyed faithfully and with
    integrity.
9 He has paid a full ransom for his
    people.
  He has guaranteed his covenant with
    them forever.
  What a holy, awe-inspiring name he
    has!
10 Reverence for the LORD is the
    foundation of true wisdom.
  The rewards of wisdom come to all
    who obey him.

  Praise his name forever!

PSALM 112

1 Praise the LORD!

  Happy are those who fear the LORD.
    Yes, happy are those who delight in
      doing what he commands.
2 Their children will be successful
    everywhere;
  an entire generation of godly people
    will be blessed.
3 They themselves will be wealthy,
    and their good deeds will never be
      forgotten.
4 When darkness overtakes the godly,
    light will come bursting in.
  They are* generous, compassionate,
    and righteous.
5 All goes well for those who are
    generous,
  who lend freely and conduct their
    business fairly.
6 Such people will not be overcome by
    evil circumstances.
  Those who are righteous will be long
    remembered.
7 They do not fear bad news;
    they confidently trust the LORD to
      care for them.
8 They are confident and fearless
    and can face their foes triumphantly.
9 They give generously to those in need.
    Their good deeds will never be
      forgotten.
  They will have influence and honor.
10 The wicked will be infuriated when
    they see this.
  They will grind their teeth in anger;

they will slink away, their hopes
  thwarted.

PSALM 113

1 Praise the LORD!

  Yes, give praise, O servants of the LORD.
    Praise the name of the LORD!
2 Blessed be the name of the LORD
    forever and ever.
3 Everywhere—from east to west—
    praise the name of the LORD.
4 For the LORD is high above the nations;
    his glory is far greater than the
      heavens.
5 Who can be compared with the LORD
    our God,
  who is enthroned on high?
6 Far below him are the heavens and the
    earth.
  He stoops to look,
7 and he lifts the poor from the dirt
    and the needy from the garbage
      dump.
8 He sets them among princes,
    even the princes of his own people!
9 He gives the barren woman a home,
    so that she becomes a happy mother.

  Praise the LORD!

PSALM 114

1 When the Israelites escaped from
    Egypt—
  when the family of Jacob left that
    foreign land—
2 the land of Judah became God's
    sanctuary,
  and Israel became his kingdom.

3 The Red Sea* saw them coming and
    hurried out of their way!
  The water of the Jordan River turned
    away.
4 The mountains skipped like rams,
    the little hills like lambs!
5 What's wrong, Red Sea, that made you
    hurry out of their way?
  What happened, Jordan River, that
    you turned away?
6 Why, mountains, did you skip like
    rams?
  Why, little hills, like lambs?

7 Tremble, O earth, at the presence of the
    Lord,
  at the presence of the God of Israel.*

112:4 Greek version reads *The LORD is.*   114:3 Hebrew *the sea;* also in 114:5.   114:7 Hebrew *of Jacob.*

⁸ He turned the rock into pools of water;
   yes, springs of water came from solid
      rock.

PSALM 115

¹ Not to us, O LORD, but to you goes all
      the glory
   for your unfailing love and faithful-
      ness.
² Why let the nations say,
   "Where is their God?"
³ For our God is in the heavens,
   and he does as he wishes.
⁴ Their idols are merely things of silver
      and gold,
   shaped by human hands.
⁵ They cannot talk, though they have
      mouths,
   or see, though they have eyes!
⁶ They cannot hear with their ears,
   or smell with their noses,
⁷   or feel with their hands,
   or walk with their feet,
   or utter sounds with their throats!
⁸ And those who make them are just like
      them,
   as are all who trust in them.

⁹ O Israel, trust the LORD!
   He is your helper; he is your shield.
¹⁰ O priests of Aaron, trust the LORD!
   He is your helper; he is your shield.
¹¹ All you who fear the LORD, trust the
      LORD!
   He is your helper; he is your shield.

¹² The LORD remembers us,
   and he will surely bless us.
   He will bless the people of Israel
   and the family of Aaron, the priests.
¹³ He will bless those who fear the LORD,
   both great and small.

¹⁴ May the LORD richly bless
   both you and your children.
¹⁵ May you be blessed by the LORD,
   who made heaven and earth.
¹⁶ The heavens belong to the LORD,
   but he has given the earth to all
      humanity.

¹⁷ The dead cannot sing praises to the LORD,
   for they have gone into the silence
      of the grave.
¹⁸ But we can praise the LORD
   both now and forever!

Praise the LORD!

PSALM 116

¹ I love the LORD because he hears
   and answers my prayers.
² Because he bends down and listens,
   I will pray as long as I have breath!
³ Death had its hands around my
      throat;
   the terrors of the grave* overtook
      me.
   I saw only trouble and sorrow.
⁴ Then I called on the name of the LORD:
   "Please, LORD, save me!"
⁵ How kind the LORD is! How good
      he is!
   So merciful, this God of ours!
⁶ The LORD protects those of childlike
      faith;
   I was facing death, and then he
      saved me.
⁷ Now I can rest again,
   for the LORD has been so good to me.
⁸ He has saved me from death,
   my eyes from tears,
   my feet from stumbling.
⁹ And so I walk in the LORD's presence
   as I live here on earth!
¹⁰ I believed in you, so I prayed,
   "I am deeply troubled, LORD."
¹¹ In my anxiety I cried out to you,
   "These people are all liars!"
¹² What can I offer the LORD
   for all he has done for me?
¹³ I will lift up a cup symbolizing his
      salvation;
   I will praise the LORD's name for
      saving me.
¹⁴ I will keep my promises to the LORD
   in the presence of all his people.

¹⁵ The LORD's loved ones are precious
      to him;
   it grieves him when they die.
¹⁶ O LORD, I am your servant;
   yes, I am your servant, the son of
      your handmaid,
   and you have freed me from my
      bonds!
¹⁷ I will offer you a sacrifice of
      thanksgiving
   and call on the name of the LORD.
¹⁸ I will keep my promises to the LORD
   in the presence of all his people,
¹⁹ in the house of the LORD,
   in the heart of Jerusalem.

Praise the LORD!

116:3 Hebrew *of Sheol.*

PSALM 117

¹ Praise the LORD, all you nations.
　　Praise him, all you people of the
　　earth.
² For he loves us with unfailing love;
　　the faithfulness of the LORD endures
　　forever.

　　Praise the LORD!

PSALM 118

¹ Give thanks to the LORD, for he is
　　good!
　　His faithful love endures forever.

² Let the congregation of Israel repeat:
　　"His faithful love endures forever."
³ Let Aaron's descendants, the priests,
　　repeat:
　　"His faithful love endures forever."
⁴ Let all who fear the LORD repeat:
　　"His faithful love endures forever."

⁵ In my distress I prayed to the LORD,
　　and the LORD answered me and
　　rescued me.
⁶ The LORD is for me, so I will not be
　　afraid.
　　What can mere mortals do to me?
⁷ Yes, the LORD is for me; he will help me.
　　I will look in triumph at those who
　　hate me.
⁸ It is better to trust the LORD
　　than to put confidence in people.
⁹ It is better to trust the LORD
　　than to put confidence in princes.

¹⁰ Though hostile nations surrounded me,
　　I destroyed them all in the name of
　　the LORD.
¹¹ Yes, they surrounded and attacked me,
　　but I destroyed them all in the name
　　of the LORD.
¹² They swarmed around me like bees;
　　they blazed against me like a roaring
　　flame.
　　But I destroyed them all in the name
　　of the LORD.

¹³ You did your best to kill me, O my
　　enemy,
　　but the LORD helped me.
¹⁴ The LORD is my strength and my song;
　　he has become my victory.
¹⁵ Songs of joy and victory are sung in the
　　camp of the godly.
　　The strong right arm of the LORD has
　　done glorious things!
¹⁶ The strong right arm of the LORD is
　　raised in triumph.
　　The strong right arm of the LORD has
　　done glorious things!
¹⁷ I will not die, but I will live
　　to tell what the LORD has done.
¹⁸ The LORD has punished me severely,
　　but he has not handed me over to
　　death.

¹⁹ Open for me the gates where the
　　righteous enter,
　　and I will go in and thank the LORD.
²⁰ Those gates lead to the presence of the
　　LORD,
　　and the godly enter there.
²¹ I thank you for answering my prayer
　　and saving me!

²² The stone rejected by the builders
　　has now become the cornerstone.
²³ This is the LORD's doing,
　　and it is marvelous to see.
²⁴ This is the day the LORD has made.
　　We will rejoice and be glad in it.
²⁵ Please, LORD, please save us.
　　Please, LORD, please give us success.
²⁶ Bless the one who comes in the name
　　of the LORD.
　　We bless you from the house of the
　　LORD.
²⁷ The LORD is God, shining upon us.
　　Bring forward the sacrifice and put it
　　on the altar.
²⁸ You are my God, and I will praise you!
　　You are my God, and I will exalt you!

²⁹ Give thanks to the LORD, for he is good!
　　His faithful love endures forever.

JUNE 24 ☐ DAY 176
PSALM 119
The Riches of God's Revelation

OVERVIEW The wonders of God's Word fill the 176 verses of Psalm 119—the longest song and the longest chapter in the Bible. Like a prism breaking a beam of light into colors, the psalmist holds aloft the Word of God to examine it from different angles. Six synonyms for Scripture dominate the psalm—each with a lesson:

- *Law*—God's Word reveals his will.
- *Decrees*—God's Word is faithful and true.
- *Commandments*—God's Word gives particular instructions.
- *Principles*—God's Word has binding force and permanence.
- *Commands*—God's Word possesses authority.
- *Word*—God's Word contains truth in all its forms.

Psalm 119
The Riches of God's Revelation in 22 Stanzas
"Oh, how I love your law! I think about it all day long" (v. 97).

YOUR DAILY WALK Why do you study God's Word? Could you list a dozen reasons for making God's inspired Word the focus of your daily meditation?

You could if you were the author of Psalm 119! The motivation for studying the Bible should never be solely a what's-in-it-for-me? mentality. An understanding of the benefits you will enjoy from a daily time in God's Word can only encourage you to spend more time mastering— and being mastered by—the book of books.

Martin Luther said, "I have done nothing; the Word has done and accomplished everything."

Psalm 119 resembles a treasure chest of benefits. For every eight verses, see if you can discover one benefit. For example, in verses 1-8, following God's Word spares the believer from disgrace; in verses 9-16, obedience to God's Word purifies the believer.

INSIGHT From *A* to *Z*
When the psalmist wrote 119, he began each eight verse section with a different letter from the Hebrew alphabet, which has twenty-two letters. From memory, can you think of Bible verses that begin with each of the twenty-six letters of the English alphabet? For example, *A:* "All of us have strayed away like sheep" (Isaiah 53:6). Ten or fewer means your memory work needs dusting off!

PSALM 119

¹ Happy are people of integrity,
   who follow the law of the LORD.
² Happy are those who obey his decrees
   and search for him with all their
      hearts.
³ They do not compromise with evil,
   and they walk only in his paths.
⁴ You have charged us
   to keep your commandments carefully.

⁵ Oh, that my actions would consistently
   reflect your principles!
⁶ Then I will not be disgraced
   when I compare my life with your
      commands.
⁷ When I learn your righteous laws,
   I will thank you by living as I
      should!
⁸ I will obey your principles.
   Please don't give up on me!

119 This psalm is a Hebrew acrostic poem; there are 22 stanzas, one for each letter of the Hebrew alphabet. The 8 verses within each stanza begin with the Hebrew letter of its section.

⁹ How can a young person stay pure?
    By obeying your word and following
        its rules.
¹⁰ I have tried my best to find you—
    don't let me wander from your
        commands.
¹¹ I have hidden your word in my heart,
    that I might not sin against you.
¹² Blessed are you, O LORD;
    teach me your principles.
¹³ I have recited aloud
    all the laws you have given us.
¹⁴ I have rejoiced in your decrees
    as much as in riches.
¹⁵ I will study your commandments
    and reflect on your ways.
¹⁶ I will delight in your principles
    and not forget your word.

¹⁷ Be good to your servant,
    that I may live and obey your word.
¹⁸ Open my eyes to see
    the wonderful truths in your law.
¹⁹ I am but a foreigner here on earth;
    I need the guidance of your
        commands.
    Don't hide them from me!
²⁰ I am overwhelmed continually
    with a desire for your laws.
²¹ You rebuke those cursed proud ones
    who wander from your commands.
²² Don't let them scorn and insult me,
    for I have obeyed your decrees.
²³ Even princes sit and speak against me,
    but I will meditate on your
        principles.
²⁴ Your decrees please me;
    they give me wise advice.

²⁵ I lie in the dust, completely
        discouraged;
    revive me by your word.
²⁶ I told you my plans, and you answered.
    Now teach me your principles.
²⁷ Help me understand the meaning of
        your commandments,
    and I will meditate on your
        wonderful miracles.
²⁸ I weep with grief;
    encourage me by your word.
²⁹ Keep me from lying to myself;
    give me the privilege of knowing
        your law.
³⁰ I have chosen to be faithful;
    I have determined to live by your
        laws.

³¹ I cling to your decrees.
    LORD, don't let me be put to shame!
³² If you will help me,
    I will run to follow your commands.

³³ Teach me, O LORD,
    to follow every one of your
        principles.
³⁴ Give me understanding and I will obey
        your law;
    I will put it into practice with all my
        heart.
³⁵ Make me walk along the path of your
        commands,
    for that is where my happiness is
        found.
³⁶ Give me an eagerness for your decrees;
    do not inflict me with love for money!
³⁷ Turn my eyes from worthless things,
    and give me life through your word.*
³⁸ Reassure me of your promise,
    which is for those who honor you.
³⁹ Help me abandon my shameful ways;
    your laws are all I want in life.
⁴⁰ I long to obey your commandments!
    Renew my life with your goodness.

⁴¹ LORD, give to me your unfailing love,
    the salvation that you promised me.
⁴² Then I will have an answer for those
        who taunt me,
    for I trust in your word.
⁴³ Do not snatch your word of truth from
        me,
    for my only hope is in your laws.
⁴⁴ I will keep on obeying your law
    forever and forever.
⁴⁵ I will walk in freedom,
    for I have devoted myself to your
        commandments.
⁴⁶ I will speak to kings about your decrees,
    and I will not be ashamed.
⁴⁷ How I delight in your commands!
    How I love them!
⁴⁸ I honor and love your commands.
    I meditate on your principles.

⁴⁹ Remember your promise to me,
    for it is my only hope.
⁵⁰ Your promise revives me;
    it comforts me in all my troubles.
⁵¹ The proud hold me in utter contempt,
    but I do not turn away from your law.
⁵² I meditate on your age-old laws;
    O LORD, they comfort me.
⁵³ I am furious with the wicked,
    those who reject your law.

119:37 Some manuscripts read *in your ways.*

⁵⁴ Your principles have been the music
    of my life
        throughout the years of my
        pilgrimage.
⁵⁵ I reflect at night on who you are, O LORD,
    and I obey your law because of this.
⁵⁶ This is my happy way of life:
    obeying your commandments.

⁵⁷ LORD, you are mine!
    I promise to obey your words!
⁵⁸ With all my heart I want your blessings.
    Be merciful just as you promised.
⁵⁹ I pondered the direction of my life,
    and I turned to follow your statutes.
⁶⁰ I will hurry, without lingering,
    to obey your commands.
⁶¹ Evil people try to drag me into sin,
    but I am firmly anchored to your law.
⁶² At midnight I rise to thank you
    for your just laws.
⁶³ Anyone who fears you is my friend—
    anyone who obeys your
        commandments.
⁶⁴ O LORD, the earth is full of your unfail-
    ing love;
        teach me your principles.

⁶⁵ You have done many good things for
    me, LORD,
        just as you promised.
⁶⁶ I believe in your commands;
    now teach me good judgment and
        knowledge.
⁶⁷ I used to wander off until you
    disciplined me;
        but now I closely follow your word.
⁶⁸ You are good and do only good;
    teach me your principles.
⁶⁹ Arrogant people have made up lies
    about me,
        but in truth I obey your
        commandments with all my heart.
⁷⁰ Their hearts are dull and stupid,
    but I delight in your law.
⁷¹ The suffering you sent was good for
    me,
        for it taught me to pay attention to
        your principles.
⁷² Your law is more valuable to me
    than millions in gold and silver!

⁷³ You made me; you created me.
    Now give me the sense to follow
        your commands.
⁷⁴ May all who fear you find in me a
    cause for joy,
        for I have put my hope in your word.

⁷⁵ I know, O LORD, that your decisions are
    fair;
        you disciplined me because I
        needed it.
⁷⁶ Now let your unfailing love comfort
    me,
        just as you promised me, your
        servant.
⁷⁷ Surround me with your tender mercies
    so I may live,
        for your law is my delight.
⁷⁸ Bring disgrace upon the arrogant
    people who lied about me;
        meanwhile, I will concentrate on
        your commandments.
⁷⁹ Let me be reconciled
    with all who fear you and know
        your decrees.
⁸⁰ May I be blameless in keeping your
    principles;
        then I will never have to be ashamed.

⁸¹ I faint with longing for your salvation;
    but I have put my hope in your
        word.
⁸² My eyes are straining to see your
    promises come true.
        When will you comfort me?
⁸³ I am shriveled like a wineskin in the
    smoke, exhausted with waiting.
        But I cling to your principles and
        obey them.
⁸⁴ How long must I wait?
    When will you punish those who
        persecute me?
⁸⁵ These arrogant people who hate your
    law
        have dug deep pits for me to fall into.
⁸⁶ All your commands are trustworthy.
    Protect me from those who hunt me
        down without cause.
⁸⁷ They almost finished me off,
    but I refused to abandon your
        commandments.
⁸⁸ In your unfailing love, spare my life;
    then I can continue to obey your
        decrees.

⁸⁹ Forever, O LORD,
    your word stands firm in heaven.
⁹⁰ Your faithfulness extends to every
    generation,
        as enduring as the earth you created.
⁹¹ Your laws remain true today,
    for everything serves your plans.
⁹² If your law hadn't sustained me with
    joy,
        I would have died in my misery.

[93] I will never forget your
   commandments,
      for you have used them to restore
      my joy and health.
[94] I am yours; save me!
      For I have applied myself to obey
      your commandments.
[95] Though the wicked hide along the way
   to kill me,
      I will quietly keep my mind on your
      decrees.
[96] Even perfection has its limits,
      but your commands have no limit.

[97] Oh, how I love your law!
      I think about it all day long.
[98] Your commands make me wiser than
   my enemies,
      for your commands are my constant
      guide.
[99] Yes, I have more insight than my
   teachers,
      for I am always thinking of your
      decrees.
[100] I am even wiser than my elders,
      for I have kept your commandments.
[101] I have refused to walk on any path of
   evil,
      that I may remain obedient to your
      word.
[102] I haven't turned away from your laws,
      for you have taught me well.
[103] How sweet are your words to my
   taste;
      they are sweeter than honey.
[104] Your commandments give me
   understanding;
      no wonder I hate every false way
      of life.

[105] Your word is a lamp for my feet
      and a light for my path.
[106] I've promised it once, and I'll promise
   again:
      I will obey your wonderful laws.
[107] I have suffered much, O LORD;
      restore my life again, just as you
      promised.
[108] LORD, accept my grateful thanks
      and teach me your laws.
[109] My life constantly hangs in the balance,
      but I will not stop obeying your law.
[110] The wicked have set their traps for me
   along your path,
      but I will not turn from your
      commandments.
[111] Your decrees are my treasure;
      they are truly my heart's delight.

[112] I am determined to keep your principles,
      even forever, to the very end.

[113] I hate those who are undecided about
   you,
      but my choice is clear—I love your
      law.
[114] You are my refuge and my shield;
      your word is my only source of hope.
[115] Get out of my life, you evil-minded
   people,
      for I intend to obey the commands of
      my God.
[116] LORD, sustain me as you promised, that
   I may live!
      Do not let my hope be crushed.
[117] Sustain me, and I will be saved;
      then I will meditate on your
      principles continually.
[118] But you have rejected all who stray
      from your principles.
      They are only fooling themselves.
[119] All the wicked of the earth are the scum
   you skim off;
      no wonder I love to obey your
      decrees!
[120] I tremble in fear of you;
      I fear your judgments.

[121] Don't leave me to the mercy of my
   enemies,
      for I have done what is just and right.
[122] Please guarantee a blessing for me.
      Don't let those who are arrogant
      oppress me!
[123] My eyes strain to see your deliverance,
      to see the truth of your promise
      fulfilled.
[124] I am your servant;
      deal with me in unfailing love,
      and teach me your principles.
[125] Give discernment to me, your servant;
      then I will understand your decrees.
[126] LORD, it is time for you to act,
      for these evil people have broken
      your law.
[127] Truly, I love your commands
      more than gold, even the finest gold.
[128] Truly, each of your commandments is
   right.
      That is why I hate every false way.

[129] Your decrees are wonderful.
      No wonder I obey them!
[130] As your words are taught, they give
   light;
      even the simple can understand
      them.

131 I open my mouth, panting expectantly,
    longing for your commands.
132 Come and show me your mercy,
    as you do for all who love your
      name.
133 Guide my steps by your word,
    so I will not be overcome by any evil.
134 Rescue me from the oppression of evil
    people;
    then I can obey your commandments.
135 Look down on me with love;
    teach me all your principles.
136 Rivers of tears gush from my eyes
    because people disobey your law.

137 O LORD, you are righteous,
    and your decisions are fair.
138 Your decrees are perfect;
    they are entirely worthy of our trust.
139 I am overwhelmed with rage,
    for my enemies have disregarded
      your words.
140 Your promises have been thoroughly
    tested;
    that is why I love them so much.
141 I am insignificant and despised,
    but I don't forget your
      commandments.
142 Your justice is eternal,
    and your law is perfectly true.
143 As pressure and stress bear down on
    me,
    I find joy in your commands.
144 Your decrees are always fair;
    help me to understand them, that I
      may live.

145 I pray with all my heart; answer me,
    LORD!
    I will obey your principles.
146 I cry out to you; save me,
    that I may obey your decrees.
147 I rise early, before the sun is up;
    I cry out for help and put my hope in
      your words.
148 I stay awake through the night,
    thinking about your promise.
149 In your faithful love, O LORD, hear my
    cry;
    in your justice, save my life.
150 Those lawless people are coming near
    to attack me;
    they live far from your law.
151 But you are near, O LORD,
    and all your commands are true.
152 I have known from my earliest days
    that your decrees never change.

153 Look down upon my sorrows and
    rescue me,
    for I have not forgotten your law.
154 Argue my case; take my side!
    Protect my life as you promised.
155 The wicked are far from salvation,
    for they do not bother with your
      principles.
156 LORD, how great is your mercy;
    in your justice, give me back my
      life.
157 Many persecute and trouble me,
    yet I have not swerved from your
      decrees.
158 I hate these traitors
    because they care nothing for your
      word.
159 See how I love your commandments,
    LORD.
    Give back my life because of your
      unfailing love.
160 All your words are true;
    all your just laws will stand forever.

161 Powerful people harass me without
    cause,
    but my heart trembles only at your
      word.
162 I rejoice in your word
    like one who finds a great treasure.
163 I hate and abhor all falsehood,
    but I love your law.
164 I will praise you seven times a day
    because all your laws are just.
165 Those who love your law have great
    peace
    and do not stumble.
166 I long for your salvation, LORD,
    so I have obeyed your commands.
167 I have obeyed your decrees,
    and I love them very much.
168 Yes, I obey your commandments and
    decrees,
    because you know everything I do.

169 O LORD, listen to my cry;
    give me the discerning mind you
      promised.
170 Listen to my prayer;
    rescue me as you promised.
171 Let my lips burst forth with praise,
    for you have taught me your
      principles.
172 Let my tongue sing about your word,
    for all your commands are right.
173 Stand ready to help me,
    for I have chosen to follow your
      commandments.

174 O LORD, I have longed for your
      salvation,
      and your law is my delight.
175 Let me live so I can praise you,
      and may your laws sustain me.

176 I have wandered away like a lost
      sheep;
      come and find me,
      for I have not forgotten your
      commands.

JUNE 25 ☐ DAY 177

PSALMS 120–127
Hymn of the Highway

OVERVIEW Psalms 120–134, which each bear the title "A song for the ascent to Jerusalem," were orginally sung by Jewish worshipers on their thrice-yearly pilgrimages to Jerusalem for the festival of Passover, the Festival of Harvest, and the Festival of Shelters. These travel tunes reflect the thoughts of a pilgrim away from home, longing for peace, protection, and provision.

Psalm 120	Psalm 121	Psalms 122–123	Psalms 124–125	Psalms 126–127
Life among Liars	Trust of the Traveler	Joy in Jerusalem	Praise for Protection	Hope in God's Heritage
Pilgrimage			Provision	

When you pray, do you give God instructions, or do you report for duty?

YOUR DAILY WALK The world of the psalmist—of about 1000 B.C.—has given way to the global village of A.D. 2000. Advances in communication and transportation have radically altered the way people live. Distances that would have taken David days to traverse can now be covered by car in hours . . . by jet plane in minutes. Where once message delivery took weeks, you can now pick up the phone and speak with someone half a world away.

Thanks to technology, much has changed. But two things remain the same: the speed with which you can reach God in prayer (Psalm 120) and the need for safety as you travel (Psalm 121). Every time you buckle up your seat belt today, remind yourself that "the LORD keeps watch over you as you come and go" (121:8). And every time you dial a phone number today, let the first ring remind you that "I took my troubles to the LORD; I cried out to him, and he answered my prayer" (120:1).

INSIGHT Smitten by the Moon . . . or Something More?
A common Hebrew figure of speech is the *merism,* which uses two extremes to speak of the totality of something. A few examples will illustrate the point (emphasis added):

"In the beginning God created *the heavens and the earth*" (and everything in between, a merism for *all of creation; Genesis* 1:1).

"O LORD, . . . You know when *I sit down or stand up*" (a merism for *my every movement throughout the day; Psalm* 139:1-2).

Now read Psalm 121:6. Using the principle of interpreting merisms as suggested by the examples above, how would you translate the psalmist's thought?

PSALM 120
A song for the ascent to Jerusalem.

1 I took my troubles to the LORD;
    I cried out to him, and he answered
    my prayer.
2 Rescue me, O LORD, from liars
    and from all deceitful people.
3 O deceptive tongue, what will God do
    to you?
    How will he increase your
    punishment?
4 You will be pierced with sharp arrows
    and burned with glowing coals.

5 How I suffer among these scoundrels
    of Meshech!
    It pains me to live with these people
    from Kedar!
6 I am tired of living here
    among people who hate peace.
7 As for me, I am for peace;
    but when I speak, they are for war!

PSALM 121
A song for the ascent to Jerusalem.

1 I look up to the mountains—
    does my help come from there?
2 My help comes from the LORD,
    who made the heavens and the
    earth!

3 He will not let you stumble and fall;
    the one who watches over you will
    not sleep.
4 Indeed, he who watches over Israel
    never tires and never sleeps.

5 The LORD himself watches over you!
    The LORD stands beside you as your
    protective shade.
6 The sun will not hurt you by day,
    nor the moon at night.
7 The LORD keeps you from all evil
    and preserves your life.
8 The LORD keeps watch over you as you
    come and go,
    both now and forever.

PSALM 122
*A song for the ascent to Jerusalem. A psalm
of David.*

1 I was glad when they said to me,
    "Let us go to the house of the LORD."
2 And now we are standing here
    inside your gates, O Jerusalem.
3 Jerusalem is a well-built city,
    knit together as a single unit.

4 All the people of Israel—the LORD's
    people—
    make their pilgrimage here.
    They come to give thanks to the name
    of the LORD
    as the law requires.
5 Here stand the thrones where judgment
    is given,
    the thrones of the dynasty of David.

6 Pray for the peace of Jerusalem.
    May all who love this city prosper.
7 O Jerusalem, may there be peace within
    your walls
    and prosperity in your palaces.
8 For the sake of my family and friends,
    I will say,
    "Peace be with you."
9 For the sake of the house of the LORD
    our God,
    I will seek what is best for you,
    O Jerusalem.

PSALM 123
A song for the ascent to Jerusalem.

1 I lift my eyes to you,
    O God, enthroned in heaven.
2 We look to the LORD our God for his
    mercy,
    just as servants keep their eyes on
    their master,
    as a slave girl watches her mistress
    for the slightest signal.

3 Have mercy on us, LORD, have mercy,
    for we have had our fill of contempt.
4 We have had our fill of the scoffing of
    the proud
    and the contempt of the arrogant.

PSALM 124
*A song for the ascent to Jerusalem. A psalm
of David.*

1 If the LORD had not been on our side—
    let Israel now say—
2 if the LORD had not been on our side
    when people rose up against us,
3 they would have swallowed us alive
    because of their burning anger
    against us.
4 The waters would have engulfed us;
    a torrent would have overwhelmed
    us.
5 Yes, the raging waters of their fury
    would have overwhelmed our very
    lives.

⁶ Blessed be the LORD,
    who did not let their teeth tear us
        apart!
⁷ We escaped like a bird from a hunter's
        trap.
    The trap is broken, and we are free!
⁸ Our help is from the LORD,
    who made the heavens and the earth.

PSALM 125
A song for the ascent to Jerusalem.

¹ Those who trust in the LORD are as
        secure as Mount Zion;
    they will not be defeated but will
        endure forever.
² Just as the mountains surround and
        protect Jerusalem,
    so the LORD surrounds and protects
        his people, both now and forever.
³ The wicked will not rule the godly,
    for then the godly might be forced
        to do wrong.
⁴ O LORD, do good to those who are
        good,
    whose hearts are in tune with you.
⁵ But banish those who turn to crooked
        ways, O LORD.
    Take them away with those who do
        evil.
    And let Israel have quietness and
        peace.

PSALM 126
A song for the ascent to Jerusalem.

¹ When the LORD restored his exiles to
        Jerusalem,*
    it was like a dream!
² We were filled with laughter,
    and we sang for joy.

126:1 Hebrew *Zion.*

And the other nations said,
    "What amazing things the LORD has
        done for them."
³ Yes, the LORD has done amazing things
        for us!
    What joy!

⁴ Restore our fortunes, LORD,
    as streams renew the desert.
⁵ Those who plant in tears
    will harvest with shouts of joy.
⁶ They weep as they go to plant their
        seed,
    but they sing as they return with the
        harvest.

PSALM 127
*A song for the ascent to Jerusalem. A psalm
of Solomon.*

¹ Unless the LORD builds a house,
    the work of the builders is useless.
    Unless the LORD protects a city,
        guarding it with sentries will do no
            good.
² It is useless for you to work so hard
        from early morning until late at night,
    anxiously working for food to eat;
        for God gives rest to his loved ones.

³ Children are a gift from the LORD;
    they are a reward from him.
⁴ Children born to a young man
    are like sharp arrows in a warrior's
        hands.
⁵ How happy is the man whose quiver
        is full of them!
    He will not be put to shame when he
        confronts his accusers at the city
            gates.

JUNE 26 ☐ DAY 178
PSALMS 128–134
Portraits of Harmony

OVERVIEW The pilgrim, continuing his journey to Jerusalem, contemplates the blessings of God upon his family (Psalm 128), the deliverance by God from danger (129) and depression (130), the sufficiency of God (131), the joy of serving God (132), and the unity of the household of God (133). An outburst of praise concludes the pilgrim's journey (134).

Psalm 128	Psalms 129–130	Psalm 131	Psalm 132	Psalms 133–134
Children from God	Crying Out to God	Contentment in God	Covenant of God	Communion with God's People
Satisfaction			Strength	

YOUR DAILY WALK Psalm 133 uses two Old Testament illustrations to describe the beautiful harmony of God's people dwelling together in unity (133:1). The first picture is of Aaron's anointing. When the high priest was anointed (Exodus 29:7; 30:22-25, 30), the ceremony involved the messy procedure of pouring special oil upon the priest's head. But the costly fragrant lotion pictured the beauty of the priest's spiritual role in bringing the nation to God. In the same way, unity in the brotherhood of believers is a pleasing fragrance to God and an attractive aroma to those in the world who find peace so elusive.

Too often Christian unity can be illustrated by two cold porcupines huddling together— they need each other, but they needle each other.

The second picture is of the dew on Mount Hermon. In an arid land where rainfall is scarce, the dew brings life-sustaining moisture to parched ground. Through the long, dry summers in Palestine, plants survive and blossom because of the dew. Unity in the brotherhood of believers is like that dew: a gift from God to bring blessing and fruitfulness in an otherwise barren world.

Have Christians today achieved this biblical ideal of unity? For the answer, first look at your own life. Read John 17:11, 21; then ask: Do my relationships in the body of Christ provide the fragrance of ointment and the refreshment of dew? What needs to change?

INSIGHT Ascent to the Holy City
Jerusalem, also known as Mount Zion, is located on a hill rising 2,600 feet above sea level. Because of its elevation, pilgrims arriving from any direction must go "up to Jerusalem." The Temple and walls rising above the surrounding terrain must have provided a breathtaking first glimpse for those marching to the holy city.

PSALM 128
A song for the ascent to Jerusalem.

¹ How happy are those who fear the
 LORD—
 all who follow his ways!
² You will enjoy the fruit of your labor.
 How happy you will be! How rich
 your life!
³ Your wife will be like a fruitful vine,
 flourishing within your home.
 And look at all those children!
 There they sit around your table
 as vigorous and healthy as young
 olive trees.
⁴ That is the LORD's reward
 for those who fear him.
⁵ May the LORD continually bless you
 from Zion.
 May you see Jerusalem prosper as
 long as you live.

⁶ May you live to enjoy your
 grandchildren.
 And may Israel have quietness and
 peace.

PSALM 129
A song for the ascent to Jerusalem.

¹ From my earliest youth my enemies
 have persecuted me—
 let Israel now say—
² from my earliest youth my enemies
 have persecuted me,
 but they have never been able to
 finish me off.
³ My back is covered with cuts,
 as if a farmer had plowed long
 furrows.
⁴ But the LORD is good;
 he has cut the cords used by the
 ungodly to bind me.

5 May all who hate Jerusalem*
  be turned back in shameful defeat.
6 May they be as useless as grass on a
    rooftop,
  turning yellow when only half grown,
7   ignored by the harvester,
  despised by the binder.
8 And may those who pass by refuse to
    give them this blessing:
  "The LORD's blessings be upon you;
  we bless you in the LORD's name."

PSALM 130
A song for the ascent to Jerusalem.

1 From the depths of despair, O LORD,
  I call for your help.
2 Hear my cry, O Lord.
  Pay attention to my prayer.

3 LORD, if you kept a record of our sins,
  who, O Lord, could ever survive?
4 But you offer forgiveness,
  that we might learn to fear you.

5 I am counting on the LORD;
  yes, I am counting on him.
  I have put my hope in his word.
6 I long for the Lord
  more than sentries long for the dawn,
  yes, more than sentries long for the
    dawn.

7 O Israel, hope in the LORD;
  for with the LORD there is unfailing
    love
  and an overflowing supply of
    salvation.
8 He himself will free Israel
  from every kind of sin.

PSALM 131
*A song for the ascent to Jerusalem. A psalm
of David.*

1 LORD, my heart is not proud;
  my eyes are not haughty.
  I don't concern myself with matters too
    great
  or awesome for me.
2 But I have stilled and quieted myself,
  just as a small child is quiet with its
    mother.
  Yes, like a small child is my soul
    within me.

3 O Israel, put your hope in the LORD—
  now and always.

PSALM 132
A song for the ascent to Jerusalem.

1 LORD, remember David
  and all that he suffered.
2 He took an oath before the LORD.
  He vowed to the Mighty One of
    Israel,*
3 "I will not go home;
  I will not let myself rest.
4 I will not let my eyes sleep
  nor close my eyelids in slumber
5   until I find a place to build a house
    for the LORD,
  a sanctuary for the Mighty One of
    Israel."
6 We heard that the Ark was in Ephrathah;
  then we found it in the distant
    countryside of Jaar.
7 Let us go to the dwelling place of the
    LORD;
  let us bow low before him.
8 Arise, O LORD, and enter your sanctuary,
  along with the Ark, the symbol of
    your power.
9 Your priests will be agents of salvation;
  may your loyal servants sing for joy.
10 For the sake of your servant David,
   do not reject the king you chose for
     your people.
11 The LORD swore to David
   a promise he will never take back:
   "I will place one of your descendants
     on your throne.
12 If your descendants obey the terms
     of my covenant
   and follow the decrees that I teach
     them,
   then your royal line will never end."

13 For the LORD has chosen Jerusalem*;
   he has desired it as his home.
14 "This is my home where I will live
     forever," he said.
   "I will live here, for this is the place
     I desired.
15 I will make this city prosperous
   and satisfy its poor with food.
16 I will make its priests the agents of
     salvation;
   its godly people will sing for joy.
17 Here I will increase the power of David;
   my anointed one will be a light for
     my people.
18 I will clothe his enemies with shame,
   but he will be a glorious king."

129:5 Hebrew *Zion.*   **132:2** Hebrew *of Jacob;* also in 132:5.   **132:13** Hebrew *Zion.*

PSALM 133

A song for the ascent to Jerusalem. A psalm of David.

¹ How wonderful it is, how pleasant,
   when brothers live together in
      harmony!
² For harmony is as precious as the
      fragrant anointing oil
   that was poured over Aaron's
      head,
   that ran down his beard
   and onto the border of his robe.
³ Harmony is as refreshing as the dew
      from Mount Hermon
   that falls on the mountains of
      Zion.

134:3 Hebrew *Zion.*

And the LORD has pronounced his
   blessing,
   even life forevermore.

PSALM 134

A song for the ascent to Jerusalem.

¹ Oh, bless the LORD, all you servants
      of the LORD,
   you who serve as night watchmen
      in the house of the LORD.
² Lift your hands in holiness,
   and bless the LORD.

³ May the LORD, who made heaven
      and earth,
   bless you from Jerusalem.*

JUNE 27 ☐ DAY 179
PSALMS 135–139
The God Who Is There

OVERVIEW From the heights of joy to the depths of sorrow, today's reading spans a wide range of emotions. In recalling past dealings with God—both in creation and in the redemption of God's people—the psalmist breaks forth in glad songs of praise (Psalms 135–136). Reliving the desperate days of exile, the psalmist expresses deep sorrow (137). But even times of trouble can be met with acclamation (138) by remembering God's infinite knowledge and unceasing presence (139).

Psalms 135–136	Psalm 137	Psalms 138–139
Adoration for God's Mighty Acts	Agony of the Exile	Awe at God's Greatness
Worship	Weeping	Wonder

Prayer is a shield to the soul, a sacrifice to God, and a scourge for Satan.

YOUR DAILY WALK Three of God's attributes are beautifully depicted in Psalm 139: his omniscience (he knows everything about you), his omnipresence (he goes everywhere with you), and his omnipotence (he is infinitely powerful, enough to meet your every need).

The question arises, If all that is true, then why should I pray? There are many good reasons to pray, but here are just three:
• Pray because God has commanded it (Jeremiah 33:3).
• Pray because God delights in giving good gifts to those who ask (Matthew 7:7-11).
• Pray because prayer changes things . . . but mostly, prayer changes people, and that means prayer changes *you!*

Notice in Psalm 139 how David's attitude changes. In the opening verses David is cautious, almost fearful, at the thought that his life is an open book before God. But by the end, he is humble and eager to please God—even in the secret compartments of his life. Do you need to pray David's prayer today (vv. 23-24)?

INSIGHT Mercy, Mercy, Mercy
Before you read Psalm 136, reflect on a few of the many ways in which
translators have captured the refrain "His faithful love endures forever"
(repeated twenty-six times in the psalm):
- "His kindness never fails" (Moffatt).
- "His steadfast love endures for ever" (Revised Standard Version).
- "His mercy endures forever" (New King James Version).

PSALM 135

¹ Praise the LORD!

Praise the name of the LORD!
Praise him, you who serve the LORD,
²   you who serve in the house of the
      LORD,
   in the courts of the house of our God.
³ Praise the LORD, for the LORD is good;
   celebrate his wonderful name with
      music.
⁴ For the LORD has chosen Jacob for
      himself,
   Israel for his own special treasure.

⁵ I know the greatness of the LORD—
   that our Lord is greater than any
      other god.
⁶ The LORD does whatever pleases him
      throughout all heaven and earth,
   and on the seas and in their depths.
⁷ He causes the clouds to rise over the
      earth.
   He sends the lightning with the rain
   and releases the wind from his
      storehouses.
⁸ He destroyed the firstborn in each
      Egyptian home,
   both people and animals.
⁹ He performed miraculous signs and
      wonders in Egypt;
   Pharaoh and all his people watched.
¹⁰ He struck down great nations
   and slaughtered mighty kings—
¹¹   Sihon king of the Amorites,
   Og king of Bashan,
   and all the kings of Canaan.
¹² He gave their land as an inheritance,
   a special possession to his people
      Israel.
¹³ Your name, O LORD, endures forever;
   your fame, O LORD, is known to
      every generation.
¹⁴ For the LORD will vindicate his people
   and have compassion on his servants.

¹⁵ Their idols are merely things of silver
      and gold,
   shaped by human hands.

¹⁶ They cannot talk, though they have
      mouths,
   or see, though they have eyes!
¹⁷ They cannot hear with their ears
   or smell with their noses.
¹⁸ And those who make them are just like
      them,
   as are all who trust in them.

¹⁹ O Israel, praise the LORD!
   O priests of Aaron, praise the LORD!
²⁰ O Levites, praise the LORD!
   All you who fear the LORD, praise the
      LORD!
²¹ The LORD be praised from Zion,
   for he lives here in Jerusalem.

Praise the LORD!

PSALM 136

¹ Give thanks to the LORD, for he is good!
      His faithful love endures forever.
² Give thanks to the God of gods.
      His faithful love endures forever.
³ Give thanks to the Lord of lords.
      His faithful love endures forever.

⁴ Give thanks to him who alone does
      mighty miracles.
      His faithful love endures forever.
⁵ Give thanks to him who made the
      heavens so skillfully.
      His faithful love endures forever.
⁶ Give thanks to him who placed the
      earth on the water.
      His faithful love endures forever.
⁷ Give thanks to him who made the
      heavenly lights—
      His faithful love endures forever.
⁸   the sun to rule the day,
      His faithful love endures forever.
⁹   and the moon and stars to rule the
      night.
      His faithful love endures forever.

¹⁰ Give thanks to him who killed the
      firstborn of Egypt.
      His faithful love endures forever.
¹¹ He brought Israel out of Egypt.
      His faithful love endures forever.

¹² He acted with a strong hand and
    powerful arm.
       His faithful love endures forever.
¹³ Give thanks to him who parted the Red
    Sea.*
       His faithful love endures forever.
¹⁴ He led Israel safely through,
       His faithful love endures forever.
¹⁵   but he hurled Pharaoh and his army
    into the sea.
       His faithful love endures forever.
¹⁶ Give thanks to him who led his people
    through the wilderness.
       His faithful love endures forever.
¹⁷ Give thanks to him who struck down
    mighty kings.
       His faithful love endures forever.
¹⁸ He killed powerful kings—
       His faithful love endures forever.
¹⁹   Sihon king of the Amorites,
       His faithful love endures forever.
²⁰   and Og king of Bashan.
       His faithful love endures forever.
²¹ God gave the land of these kings as an
    inheritance—
       His faithful love endures forever.
²²   a special possession to his servant
    Israel.
       His faithful love endures forever.

²³ He remembered our utter weakness.
       His faithful love endures forever.
²⁴ He saved us from our enemies.
       His faithful love endures forever.
²⁵ He gives food to every living thing.
       His faithful love endures forever.

²⁶ Give thanks to the God of heaven.
       His faithful love endures forever.

PSALM 137

¹ Beside the rivers of Babylon, we sat
    and wept
    as we thought of Jerusalem.*
² We put away our lyres,
    hanging them on the branches of the
    willow trees.
³ For there our captors demanded a song
    of us.
    Our tormentors requested a joyful
    hymn:
    "Sing us one of those songs of
    Jerusalem!"
⁴ But how can we sing the songs of the
    LORD
    while in a foreign land?

⁵ If I forget you, O Jerusalem,
    let my right hand forget its skill upon
    the harp.
⁶ May my tongue stick to the roof of my
    mouth
    if I fail to remember you,
    if I don't make Jerusalem my highest
    joy.

⁷ O LORD, remember what the Edomites
    did
    on the day the armies of Babylon
    captured Jerusalem.
    "Destroy it!" they yelled.
    "Level it to the ground!"
⁸ O Babylon, you will be destroyed.
    Happy is the one who pays you back
    for what you have done to us.
⁹ Happy is the one who takes your babies
    and smashes them against the rocks!

PSALM 138

A psalm of David.

¹ I give you thanks, O LORD, with all my
    heart;
    I will sing your praises before the
    gods.
² I bow before your holy Temple as I
    worship.
    I will give thanks to your name
    for your unfailing love and
    faithfulness,
    because your promises are backed
    by all the honor of your name.
³ When I pray, you answer me;
    you encourage me by giving me the
    strength I need.

⁴ Every king in all the earth will give you
    thanks, O LORD,
    for all of them will hear your words.
⁵ Yes, they will sing about the LORD's
    ways,
    for the glory of the LORD is very
    great.
⁶ Though the LORD is great, he cares for
    the humble,
    but he keeps his distance from the
    proud.

⁷ Though I am surrounded by troubles,
    you will preserve me against the
    anger of my enemies.
    You will clench your fist against my
    angry enemies!
    Your power will save me.

136:13 Hebrew *sea of reeds;* also in 136:15.   **137:1** Hebrew *Zion;* also in 137:3.

8 The LORD will work out his plans for
   my life—
     for your faithful love, O LORD,
     endures forever.
     Don't abandon me, for you made me.

PSALM 139
For the choir director: A psalm of David.

1 O LORD, you have examined my heart
   and know everything about me.
2 You know when I sit down or stand up.
   You know my every thought when
     far away.
3 You chart the path ahead of me
   and tell me where to stop and rest.
   Every moment you know where I am.
4 You know what I am going to say
   even before I say it, LORD.
5 You both precede and follow me.
   You place your hand of blessing on
     my head.
6 Such knowledge is too wonderful for
   me,
     too great for me to know!

7 I can never escape from your spirit!
   I can never get away from your
     presence!
8 If I go up to heaven, you are there;
   if I go down to the place of the
     dead,* you are there.
9 If I ride the wings of the morning,
   if I dwell by the farthest oceans,
10 even there your hand will guide me,
    and your strength will support me.
11 I could ask the darkness to hide me
    and the light around me to become
      night—
12   but even in darkness I cannot hide
      from you.
   To you the night shines as bright as day.
   Darkness and light are both alike to
     you.

13 You made all the delicate, inner parts of
    my body
     and knit me together in my mother's
     womb.
14 Thank you for making me so
    wonderfully complex!
     Your workmanship is marvelous—
     and how well I know it.
15 You watched me as I was being formed
    in utter seclusion,
     as I was woven together in the dark
     of the womb.
16 You saw me before I was born.
    Every day of my life was recorded
     in your book.
   Every moment was laid out
     before a single day had passed.
17 How precious are your thoughts about
    me,* O God!
     They are innumerable!
18 I can't even count them;
     they outnumber the grains of sand!
   And when I wake up in the morning,
     you are still with me!

19 O God, if only you would destroy the
    wicked!
     Get out of my life, you murderers!
20 They blaspheme you;
     your enemies take your name in vain.
21 O LORD, shouldn't I hate those who
    hate you?
     Shouldn't I despise those who resist
     you?
22 Yes, I hate them with complete hatred,
     for your enemies are my enemies.
23 Search me, O God, and know my heart;
    test me and know my thoughts.
24 Point out anything in me that offends
    you,
     and lead me along the path of ever-
     lasting life.

139:8 Hebrew *to Sheol*.   **139:17** Or *How precious to me are your thoughts.*

JUNE 28 □ DAY 180
Thanks, and Thanks Again

 LOOK BACK Metaphors abound in the Psalms. Already you have discovered that God is your shepherd, light, salvation, rock, fortress, refuge,
strength, defense, glory, and judge. The list will continue to grow as
you read further in this magnificent "diary of devotion." When you
learn a new truth *about* God, don't forget to respond in worship *to*

God. Psalms was not written for your information but for your transformation.

For a change of pace, try reading a portion of the Psalms just before
you go to bed at night. Or leave your Bible open to the Psalms, and
make it your meditation the first thing in the morning. Stick a small
copy of the Psalms in your pocket or purse, and "chew" on a psalm as
you enjoy lunch. If you have access to the Bible on cassette tape, try
listening to a portion of the book of Psalms as you drive back and forth
to work. In the process you'll be taking to heart the first psalm: "Oh,
the joys of those . . . [who] delight in doing everything the LORD wants;
day and night they think about his law. They are like trees planted along
the riverbank, bearing fruit each season without fail. Their leaves never
wither, and in all they do, they prosper" (Psalm 1:1-3).

LOOK UP Find a dictionary and look up the word *refrain*. What definition
does the author suggest?

*God's work
of creation is
done; our work
of praising is
just begun.*

Now compare that definition with this one: "A refrain is the reverber-
ation of the heart when touched by the greatness of God." It is a heartfelt exclamation that deserves to be repeated—and so it is! Refrains are
what you have discovered in several of the psalms you read this past
week. Think of them as divine "ditto marks" that highlight a particular
facet of God's character or program. Repetition needn't be redundant
if the motive behind it is to underscore something of great importance.

Can you find the *refrain* in each of the following psalms? (Hint: Look
for the portion of the verse that is repeated virtually verbatim.)

- Psalm 107:6, 13, 19, 28
- Psalm 107:8, 15, 21, 31
- Psalm 136 (every verse!)

LOOK AHEAD Thanksgiving ought to be more than a holiday on the
calendar. God intends it to be the attitude of your heart. How can you
know for sure? He said so . . . twenty-six times!

In Psalm 136 the psalmist rehearses dozens of memorable moments
from the history of God's people to stimulate an "attitude of gratitude."
As you read the psalm, you begin to anticipate the refrain that concludes
each and every verse: "His faithful love endures forever." Can you find
a reference in the historical books of the Old Testament (the first seventeen books, Genesis through Esther) to which the psalmist is referring
in each verse? For example, verses 7-9 are a reminder of what God did
in Genesis 1:14-19. How many others can you find? And if you feel like
joining the psalmist in his heartfelt refrain, well, don't refrain!

JUNE 29 □ DAY 181
PSALMS 140–145
A Heart like God's

OVERVIEW The six psalms you will read today contain David's
prayer for protection from those who would harm him (Psalms
140–141), as well as his testimony of trust in the one who is his
refuge and portion (142–143). Because David has seen God's care
over his life in the past (144), his faith is fortified to look for God's
provision in the future (145).

Psalms 140–141	Psalms 142–143	Psalm 144	Psalm 145
Protection from Evil People	Preservation from Enemies	Provision for Needs	Praise for God's Grace
Receiving from God			Responding to God

YOUR DAILY WALK Wanted: A Man after God's Own Heart. The "position available"? The throne of Israel. The one involved in the "job search"? The God of Abraham, Isaac, and Jacob.

David, the man after God's own heart, didn't do his devotions; he lived them.

When God wanted a man to do his will (1 Samuel 13:14), he found what he was looking for in an obscure lad from the pasturelands of Judea. Notice some of the qualities of David's character that many of his later writings reveal:
- Confidence in God in time of danger (Psalm 140:1, 4, 7)
- Hunger for righteousness (141:3-4)
- Transparent honesty before God (142:1-2)
- A good memory for God's past dealings (143:5)
- A desire to see God's justice prevail (144:5-8)
- Overflowing praise to God (145:1-21)

God is looking for similar individuals today—people with a heart like David's; that is, people with a heart like God's (2 Chronicles 16:9). After studying David's heart as revealed in Psalms 140–145, are you interested in applying for the position? Tell God so!

INSIGHT The Case of the Missing Letter

David's last psalm (Psalm 145) is also the last of eight acrostic psalms based on the Hebrew alphabet. One letter of the alphabet, nun, was omitted from the Hebrew text, causing the Hebrew reader to "stumble" at verse 14 (much the same way you might if you were reading the sequence "J, K, L, M, O, P"). But wouldn't you agree that verse 14 is a good one to "catch" yourself on?

PSALM 140
For the choir director: A psalm of David.

1 O LORD, rescue me from evil people.
　Preserve me from those who are
　　violent,
2 those who plot evil in their hearts
　and stir up trouble all day long.
3 Their tongues sting like a snake;
　the poison of a viper drips from their
　　lips.   *Interlude*

4 O LORD, keep me out of the hands of
　the wicked.
　Preserve me from those who are
　　violent,
　for they are plotting against me.
5 The proud have set a trap to catch me;
　they have stretched out a net;
　they have placed traps all along the
　　way.   *Interlude*

6 I said to the LORD, "You are my God!"
　Listen, O LORD, to my cries for mercy!
7 O Sovereign LORD, my strong savior,
　you protected me on the day of battle.

8 LORD, do not give in to their evil
　　desires.
　Do not let their evil schemes succeed,
　O God.   *Interlude*

9 Let my enemies be destroyed
　by the very evil they have planned
　　for me.
10 Let burning coals fall down on their
　　heads,
　or throw them into the fire,
　or into deep pits from which they
　　can't escape.
11 Don't let liars prosper here in our
　　land.
　Cause disaster to fall with great force
　　on the violent.

12 But I know the LORD will surely help
　　those they persecute;
　he will maintain the rights of the
　　poor.
13 Surely the godly are praising your
　　name,
　for they will live in your presence.

PSALM 141

A psalm of David.

¹ O LORD, I am calling to you. Please
    hurry!
  Listen when I cry to you for help!
² Accept my prayer as incense offered
    to you,
  and my upraised hands as an
    evening offering.

³ Take control of what I say, O LORD,
  and keep my lips sealed.
⁴ Don't let me lust for evil things;
  don't let me participate in acts of
    wickedness.
  Don't let me share in the delicacies
    of those who do evil.

⁵ Let the godly strike me!
  It will be a kindness!
  If they reprove me, it is soothing
    medicine.
  Don't let me refuse it.

  But I am in constant prayer
    against the wicked and their deeds.
⁶ When their leaders are thrown down
    from a cliff,
  they will listen to my words and find
    them pleasing.
⁷ Even as a farmer breaks up the soil and
    brings up rocks,
  so the bones of the wicked will be
    scattered without a decent burial.

⁸ I look to you for help, O Sovereign
    LORD.
  You are my refuge; don't let them kill
    me.
⁹ Keep me out of the traps they have set
    for me,
  out of the snares of those who do evil.
¹⁰ Let the wicked fall into their own
    snares,
  but let me escape.

PSALM 142

*A psalm of David, regarding his experience in the
cave. A prayer.*

¹ I cry out to the LORD;
  I plead for the LORD's mercy.
² I pour out my complaints before him
  and tell him all my troubles.
³ For I am overwhelmed,
  and you alone know the way I
    should turn.
  Wherever I go,
  my enemies have set traps for me.

⁴ I look for someone to come and help
    me,
  but no one gives me a passing
    thought!
  No one will help me;
  no one cares a bit what happens
    to me.
⁵ Then I pray to you, O LORD.
  I say, "You are my place of refuge.
  You are all I really want in life.
⁶ Hear my cry,
  for I am very low.
  Rescue me from my persecutors,
  for they are too strong for me.
⁷ Bring me out of prison
  so I can thank you.
  The godly will crowd around me,
  for you treat me kindly."

PSALM 143

A psalm of David.

¹ Hear my prayer, O LORD;
  listen to my plea!
  Answer me because you are faithful
    and righteous.
² Don't bring your servant to trial!
  Compared to you, no one is perfect.
³ My enemy has chased me.
  He has knocked me to the ground.
  He forces me to live in darkness like
    those in the grave.
⁴ I am losing all hope;
  I am paralyzed with fear.
⁵ I remember the days of old.
  I ponder all your great works.
  I think about what you have done.
⁶ I reach out for you.
  I thirst for you as parched land
    thirsts for rain.   *Interlude*

⁷ Come quickly, LORD, and answer me,
  for my depression deepens.
  Don't turn away from me,
  or I will die.
⁸ Let me hear of your unfailing love to
    me in the morning,
  for I am trusting you.
  Show me where to walk,
  for I have come to you in prayer.
⁹ Save me from my enemies, LORD;
  I run to you to hide me.
¹⁰ Teach me to do your will,
  for you are my God.
  May your gracious Spirit lead me
    forward
  on a firm footing.

[11] For the glory of your name, O LORD,
　　save me.
　　　In your righteousness, bring me out
　　　　of this distress.
[12] In your unfailing love, cut off all my
　　enemies
　　　and destroy all my foes,
　　　for I am your servant.

PSALM 144
A psalm of David.

[1] Bless the LORD, who is my rock.
　　He gives me strength for war
　　and skill for battle.
[2] He is my loving ally and my fortress,
　　my tower of safety, my deliverer.
　　He stands before me as a shield, and
　　　I take refuge in him.
　　He subdues the nations* under me.

[3] O LORD, what are mortals that you
　　should notice us,
　　　mere humans that you should care
　　　　for us?
[4] For we are like a breath of air;
　　our days are like a passing shadow.

[5] Bend down the heavens, LORD, and
　　come down.
　　Touch the mountains so they billow
　　　smoke.
[6] Release your lightning bolts and scatter
　　your enemies!
　　Release your arrows and confuse them!
[7] Reach down from heaven and rescue
　　me;
　　　deliver me from deep waters,
　　　from the power of my enemies.
[8] Their mouths are full of lies;
　　they swear to tell the truth, but they
　　　lie.

[9] I will sing a new song to you, O God!
　　I will sing your praises with a
　　　ten-stringed harp.
[10] For you grant victory to kings!
　　You are the one who rescued your
　　　servant David.
[11] Save me from the fatal sword!
　　Rescue me from the power of my
　　　enemies.
　　Their mouths are full of lies;
　　　they swear to tell the truth, but they
　　　　lie.

[12] May our sons flourish in their youth
　　like well-nurtured plants.

May our daughters be like graceful
　　pillars,
　　carved to beautify a palace.
[13] May our farms be filled
　　with crops of every kind.
May the flocks in our fields multiply
　　by the thousands,
　　even tens of thousands,
[14]　and may our oxen be loaded down
　　with produce.
May there be no breached walls, no
　　forced exile,
　　no cries of distress in our squares.
[15] Yes, happy are those who have it like
　　this!
　　Happy indeed are those whose God
　　is the LORD.

PSALM 145
A psalm of praise of David.

[1] I will praise you, my God and King,
　　and bless your name forever and
　　　ever.
[2] I will bless you every day,
　　and I will praise you forever.
[3] Great is the LORD! He is most worthy
　　of praise!
　　His greatness is beyond discovery!

[4] Let each generation tell its children
　　of your mighty acts.
[5] I will meditate* on your majestic,
　　glorious splendor
　　and your wonderful miracles.
[6] Your awe-inspiring deeds will be on
　　every tongue;
　　I will proclaim your greatness.
[7] Everyone will share the story of your
　　wonderful goodness;
　　they will sing with joy of your
　　　righteousness.

[8] The LORD is kind and merciful,
　　slow to get angry, full of unfailing
　　　love.
[9] The LORD is good to everyone.
　　He showers compassion on all his
　　　creation.
[10] All of your works will thank you,
　　LORD,
　　and your faithful followers will bless
　　　you.
[11] They will talk together about the glory
　　of your kingdom;
　　they will celebrate examples of your
　　　power.

144:2 Some manuscripts read *my people.*　　**145:5** Some manuscripts read *They will speak.*

12 They will tell about your mighty deeds
and about the majesty and glory of
your reign.
13 For your kingdom is an everlasting
kingdom.
You rule generation after generation.

The LORD is faithful in all he says;
he is gracious in all he does.*
14 The LORD helps the fallen
and lifts up those bent beneath their
loads.
15 All eyes look to you for help;
you give them their food as they
need it.
16 When you open your hand,
you satisfy the hunger and thirst of
every living thing.

17 The LORD is righteous in everything he
does;
he is filled with kindness.
18 The LORD is close to all who call on
him,
yes, to all who call on him sincerely.
19 He fulfills the desires of those who fear
him;
he hears their cries for help and
rescues them.
20 The LORD protects all those who love
him,
but he destroys the wicked.
21 I will praise the LORD,
and everyone on earth will bless his
holy name
forever and forever.

145:13 The last two lines of 145:13 are not found in many of the ancient manuscripts.

JUNE 30 ☐ DAY 182
PSALMS 146–150
A Lifestyle of Praise

 OVERVIEW It is appropriate in a book with the Hebrew title *tehillim*—which means "praises"—that the final five selections should be filled with precisely that. First, the individual believer voices praise for God's trustworthiness (Psalm 146); next, the nation of Israel praises God for his tender care (147); then all creation praises God for his power (148); God's choice servants join the chorus by extolling God for his love (149); finally, accompanied by a grand orchestra of instruments, all living things praise our matchless, mighty God (150).

Psalm 146	Psalm 147	Psalm 148	Psalm 149	Psalm 150
"Praise the LORD!"				
My Soul	My Nation	Creation	His Saints	Everyone
"How good it is to sing praises to our God!" (147:1).				

 YOUR DAILY WALK Congratulations! Today you will finish reading the longest book of the Bible—the believer's handbook of worship.

Praising and adoring God is the noblest part of the saint's work on earth, as it will be his chief employ in heaven.

While you are catching your breath and preparing to begin the book of Proverbs tomorrow, pause long enough to ask yourself one question: Is there anything different about my walk with God today for having spent the past month in the book of Psalms?

Psalm 147:1 gives three reasons for God's people to praise him: (1) It is good in God's eyes; (2) it is pleasant (delightful) to the one doing the praising; and (3) it is beautiful for all who share the praise experience.

Praise is like a bride's wedding ring. The bride's husband rejoices to see her wear it; she herself delights in it; and it testifies to others of the beauty of the couple's relationship. Tie a small piece of colored yarn around a ring you are wearing to remind you throughout the day that it's always in style to adorn your life with praise to God.

INSIGHT Inspired Psalms, Inspiring Psalms
The Psalter has become the hymnbook of the ages. It is read, recited, or sung virtually every day. And in the majestic strains of more recent hymns based on its verses (such as Martin Luther's "A Mighty Fortress Is Our God" and Isaac Watts's "O God, Our Help in Ages Past"), the message of the Psalter still rings around the world.

PSALM 146

¹ Praise the LORD!

Praise the LORD, I tell myself.
² I will praise the LORD as long as I live.
  I will sing praises to my God even
    with my dying breath.

³ Don't put your confidence in powerful
    people;
  there is no help for you there.
⁴ When their breathing stops, they return
    to the earth,
  and in a moment all their plans come
    to an end.
⁵ But happy are those who have the God
    of Israel* as their helper,
  whose hope is in the LORD their God.
⁶ He is the one who made heaven and
    earth,
  the sea, and everything in them.
  He is the one who keeps every promise
    forever,
⁷ who gives justice to the oppressed
    and food to the hungry.
  The LORD frees the prisoners.
⁸ The LORD opens the eyes of the blind.
  The LORD lifts the burdens of those
    bent beneath their loads.
  The LORD loves the righteous.
⁹ The LORD protects the foreigners
    among us.
  He cares for the orphans and
    widows,
  but he frustrates the plans of the
    wicked.

¹⁰ The LORD will reign forever.
  O Jerusalem,* your God is King in
    every generation!

  Praise the LORD!

PSALM 147

¹ Praise the LORD!

  How good it is to sing praises to our
    God!
  How delightful and how right!
² The LORD is rebuilding Jerusalem
  and bringing the exiles back to Israel.

³ He heals the brokenhearted,
  binding up their wounds.
⁴ He counts the stars
  and calls them all by name.
⁵ How great is our Lord! His power is
    absolute!
  His understanding is beyond compre-
    hension!
⁶ The LORD supports the humble,
  but he brings the wicked down into
    the dust.

⁷ Sing out your thanks to the LORD;
  sing praises to our God,
    accompanied by harps.
⁸ He covers the heavens with clouds,
  provides rain for the earth,
  and makes the green grass grow in
    mountain pastures.
⁹ He feeds the wild animals,
  and the young ravens cry to him for
    food.
¹⁰ The strength of a horse does not
    impress him;
  how puny in his sight is the strength
    of a man.
¹¹ Rather, the LORD's delight is in those
    who honor him,
  those who put their hope in his
    unfailing love.

¹² Praise the LORD, O Jerusalem!
  Praise your God, O Zion!
¹³ For he has fortified the bars of your
    gates
  and blessed your children within you.
¹⁴ He sends peace across your nation
  and satisfies you with plenty of the
    finest wheat.
¹⁵ He sends his orders to the world—
  how swiftly his word flies!
¹⁶ He sends the snow like white wool;
  he scatters frost upon the ground like
    ashes.
¹⁷ He hurls the hail like stones.
  Who can stand against his freezing
    cold?
¹⁸ Then, at his command, it all melts.
  He sends his winds, and the ice thaws.

146:5 Hebrew *of Jacob.*   **146:10** Hebrew *Zion.*

¹⁹ He has revealed his words to Jacob,
  his principles and laws to Israel.
²⁰ He has not done this with any other
    nation;
  they do not know his laws.

Praise the LORD!

PSALM 148

¹ Praise the LORD!

  Praise the LORD from the heavens!
  Praise him from the skies!
² Praise him, all his angels!
  Praise him, all the armies of heaven!
³ Praise him, sun and moon!
  Praise him, all you twinkling stars!
⁴ Praise him, skies above!
  Praise him, vapors high above the
    clouds!
⁵ Let every created thing give praise to
    the LORD,
  for he issued his command, and they
    came into being.
⁶ He established them forever and
    forever.
  His orders will never be revoked.

⁷ Praise the LORD from the earth,
  you creatures of the ocean depths,
⁸ fire and hail, snow and storm,
  wind and weather that obey him,
⁹ mountains and all hills,
  fruit trees and all cedars,
¹⁰ wild animals and all livestock,
  reptiles and birds,
¹¹ kings of the earth and all people,
  rulers and judges of the earth,
¹² young men and maidens,
  old men and children.
¹³ Let them all praise the name of the ·
    LORD.
  For his name is very great;
  his glory towers over the earth and
    heaven!
¹⁴ He has made his people strong,
  honoring his godly ones—
  the people of Israel who are close to
    him.

Praise the LORD!

149:2 Hebrew *Zion.*

PSALM 149

¹ Praise the LORD!

  Sing to the LORD a new song.
  Sing his praises in the assembly of
    the faithful.
² O Israel, rejoice in your Maker.
  O people of Jerusalem,* exult in your
    King.
³ Praise his name with dancing,
  accompanied by tambourine and
    harp.
⁴ For the LORD delights in his people;
  he crowns the humble with salvation.
⁵ Let the faithful rejoice in this honor.
  Let them sing for joy as they lie on
    their beds.
⁶ Let the praises of God be in their
    mouths,
  and a sharp sword in their hands—
⁷ to execute vengeance on the nations
  and punishment on the peoples,
⁸ to bind their kings with shackles
  and their leaders with iron chains,
⁹ to execute the judgment written against
    them.
  This is the glory of his faithful ones.

Praise the LORD!

PSALM 150

¹ Praise the LORD!

  Praise God in his heavenly dwelling;
  praise him in his mighty heaven!
² Praise him for his mighty works;
  praise his unequaled greatness!
³ Praise him with a blast of the trumpet;
  praise him with the lyre and harp!
⁴ Praise him with the tambourine and
    dancing;
  praise him with stringed instruments
    and flutes!
⁵ Praise him with a clash of cymbals;
  praise him with loud clanging
    cymbals.
⁶ Let everything that lives sing praises
    to the LORD!

Praise the LORD!

Proverbs

ONE of the most practical books in the Old Testament is Proverbs—timeless teaching for everyday living. A collection of approximately nine hundred inspired precepts, Proverbs provides godly counsel for virtually every facet of human relationships. These maxims deal with folly and wisdom, pride and humility, vengeance and justice, laziness and initiative, poverty and wealth, enemies and friends, lust and love, anger and anxiety, masters and servants, life and death.

Focus	Skillful Living in the Fear of the Lord					
Divisions	A Father's Words of Wisdom	Proverbs of Solomon (First Collection)	Words of Wisdom and Folly	Proverbs of Solomon (Second Collection)	Wisdom of Twos, Threes, and Fours	Alphabet of a Virtuous Wife
	1 9	10 21	22 24	25 29	30	31
Topics	Solomon				Agur	Lemuel
	Commendation	Counsel			Comparison	
Place	Judah				Unknown	
Time	Written and Compiled about 950–700 B.C.					

JULY 1 ☐ DAY 183
PROVERBS 1–4
A Father's Words of Wisdom

OVERVIEW Proverbs is the book of heavenly wisdom for your earthly walk. Solomon states his purpose in the opening verses: "to teach people wisdom and discipline" (1:2). Wisdom in life begins with the fear of the Lord (1:7)—reverential respect for God and careful attention to the moral and ethical principles of his Word.

Chapter 1	Chapter 2	Chapter 3	Chapter 4
Beginning of Wisdom	Benefits of Wisdom	Searching for Wisdom	Supremacy of Wisdom
Fear God	Know God	Trust God	Hear God

YOUR DAILY WALK The young bank clerk was being promoted to vice president—a position of great responsibility and one for which he felt ill-equipped. Approaching the wise and aged bank president, he asked, "But, sir, what is the secret of success in my new position?"

A good learner is one whose ears get as much use as his or her mouth.

The president replied, "Right decisions."

"And what, sir, is the secret of making right decisions?"

Again the president was quick to respond: "Experience."

"And what, sir, is the secret of gaining experience?"

The president smiled as he replied, "Wrong decisions."

In life, as in banking, the goal is to make right decisions—decisions that honor God, promote growth, bring blessing to others. Proverbs was written to help you make those kinds of decisions both in your personal and professional life.

But it is also a realistic book. Others have made foolish and naive decisions in the past—and you can learn from their mistakes. "To err is human . . . ," or so the saying goes. But to repeat those errors is both tragic and unnecessary.

As you begin to read Proverbs, do so with a notebook and pen in hand. Jot down your insights on "wise choices" and "foolish choices." Solomon's God-given wisdom and experience will steer you into right decisions . . . if you'll leave the driving to God!

INSIGHT A Structural Summary of Proverbs
Fatherly Proverbs—"my child" (1–9)
Antithetic Proverbs—"but" (10–15)
Synthetic Proverbs—"and" (16–22)
Extended Proverbs—more than one verse (23–31)

CHAPTER 1

These are the proverbs of Solomon, David's son, king of Israel.

²The purpose of these proverbs is to teach people wisdom and discipline, and to help them understand wise sayings. ³Through these proverbs, people will receive instruction in discipline, good con-duct, and doing what is right, just, and fair. ⁴These proverbs will make the simple-minded clever. They will give knowledge and purpose to young people.

⁵Let those who are wise listen to these proverbs and become even wiser. And let those who understand receive guidance ⁶by exploring the depth of meaning in

these proverbs, parables, wise sayings, and riddles.

[7]Fear of the LORD is the beginning of knowledge. Only fools despise wisdom and discipline.

[8]Listen, my child,* to what your father teaches you. Don't neglect your mother's teaching. [9]What you learn from them will crown you with grace and clothe you with honor.

[10]My child, if sinners entice you, turn your back on them! [11]They may say, "Come and join us. Let's hide and kill someone! Let's ambush the innocent! [12]Let's swallow them alive as the grave swallows its victims. Though they are in the prime of life, they will go down into the pit of death. [13]And the loot we'll get! We'll fill our houses with all kinds of things! [14]Come on, throw in your lot with us; we'll split our loot with you."

[15]Don't go along with them, my child! Stay far away from their paths. [16]They rush to commit crimes. They hurry to commit murder. [17]When a bird sees a trap being set, it stays away. [18]But not these people! They set an ambush for themselves; they booby-trap their own lives! [19]Such is the fate of all who are greedy for gain. It ends up robbing them of life.

[20]Wisdom shouts in the streets. She cries out in the public square. [21]She calls out to the crowds along the main street, and to those in front of city hall. [22]"You simpletons!" she cries. "How long will you go on being simpleminded? How long will you mockers relish your mocking? How long will you fools fight the facts? [23]Come here and listen to me! I'll pour out the spirit of wisdom upon you and make you wise.

[24]"I called you so often, but you didn't come. I reached out to you, but you paid no attention. [25]You ignored my advice and rejected the correction I offered. [26]So I will laugh when you are in trouble! I will mock you when disaster overtakes you—[27]when calamity overcomes you like a storm, when you are engulfed by trouble, and when anguish and distress overwhelm you.

[28]"I will not answer when they cry for help. Even though they anxiously search for me, they will not find me. [29]For they hated knowledge and chose not to fear the LORD. [30]They rejected my advice and paid no attention when I corrected them. [31]That is why they must eat the bitter fruit of living their own way. They must experience the full terror of the path they have chosen. [32]For they are simpletons who turn away from me—to death. They are fools, and their own complacency will destroy them. [33]But all who listen to me will live in peace and safety, unafraid of harm."

CHAPTER 2

My child,* listen to me and treasure my instructions. [2]Tune your ears to wisdom, and concentrate on understanding. [3]Cry out for insight and understanding. [4]Search for them as you would for lost money or hidden treasure. [5]Then you will understand what it means to fear the LORD, and you will gain knowledge of God. [6]For the LORD grants wisdom! From his mouth come knowledge and understanding. [7]He grants a treasure of good sense to the godly. He is their shield, protecting those who walk with integrity. [8]He guards the paths of justice and protects those who are faithful to him.

[9]Then you will understand what is right, just, and fair, and you will know how to find the right course of action every time. [10]For wisdom will enter your heart, and knowledge will fill you with joy. [11]Wise planning will watch over you. Understanding will keep you safe.

[12]Wisdom will save you from evil people, from those whose speech is corrupt. [13]These people turn from right ways to walk down dark and evil paths. [14]They rejoice in doing wrong, and they enjoy evil as it turns things upside down. [15]What they do is crooked, and their ways are wrong.

[16]Wisdom will save you from the immoral woman, from the flattery of the adulterous woman. [17]She has abandoned her husband and ignores the covenant she made before God. [18]Entering her house leads to death; it is the road to hell.* [19]The man who visits her is doomed. He will never reach the paths of life.

[20]Follow the steps of good men instead, and stay on the paths of the righteous. [21]For only the upright will live in the land, and those who have integrity will remain in it. [22]But the wicked will be removed from the land, and the treacherous will be destroyed.

1:8 Hebrew *my son;* also in 1:10, 15.   **2:1** Hebrew *My son.*   **2:18** Hebrew *to the spirits of the dead.*

CHAPTER 3

My child,* never forget the things I have taught you. Store my commands in your heart, [2]for they will give you a long and satisfying life. [3]Never let loyalty and kindness get away from you! Wear them like a necklace; write them deep within your heart. [4]Then you will find favor with both God and people, and you will gain a good reputation.

[5]Trust in the LORD with all your heart; do not depend on your own understanding. [6]Seek his will in all you do, and he will direct your paths.

[7]Don't be impressed with your own wisdom. Instead, fear the LORD and turn your back on evil. [8]Then you will gain renewed health and vitality.

[9]Honor the LORD with your wealth and with the best part of everything your land produces. [10]Then he will fill your barns with grain, and your vats will overflow with the finest wine.

[11]My child, don't ignore it when the LORD disciplines you, and don't be discouraged when he corrects you. [12]For the LORD corrects those he loves, just as a father corrects a child* in whom he delights.

[13]Happy is the person who finds wisdom and gains understanding. [14]For the profit of wisdom is better than silver, and her wages are better than gold. [15]Wisdom is more precious than rubies; nothing you desire can compare with her. [16]She offers you life in her right hand, and riches and honor in her left. [17]She will guide you down delightful paths; all her ways are satisfying. [18]Wisdom is a tree of life to those who embrace her; happy are those who hold her tightly.

[19]By wisdom the LORD founded the earth; by understanding he established the heavens. [20]By his knowledge the deep fountains of the earth burst forth, and the clouds poured down rain.

[21]My child, don't lose sight of good planning and insight. Hang on to them, [22]for they fill you with life and bring you honor and respect. [23]They keep you safe on your way and keep your feet from stumbling. [24]You can lie down without fear and enjoy pleasant dreams. [25]You need not be afraid of disaster or the destruction that comes upon the wicked, [26]for the LORD is your security. He will keep your foot from being caught in a trap.

[27]Do not withhold good from those who deserve it when it's in your power to help them. [28]If you can help your neighbor now, don't say, "Come back tomorrow, and then I'll help you."

[29]Do not plot against your neighbors, for they trust you. [30]Don't make accusations against someone who hasn't wronged you.

[31]Do not envy violent people; don't copy their ways. [32]Such wicked people are an abomination to the LORD, but he offers his friendship to the godly.

[33]The curse of the LORD is on the house of the wicked, but his blessing is on the home of the upright.

[34]The LORD mocks at mockers, but he shows favor to the humble.

[35]The wise inherit honor, but fools are put to shame!

CHAPTER 4

My children,* listen to me. Listen to your father's instruction. Pay attention and grow wise, [2]for I am giving you good guidance. Don't turn away from my teaching. [3]For I, too, was once my father's son, tenderly loved by my mother as an only child.

[4]My father told me, "Take my words to heart. Follow my instructions and you will live. [5]Learn to be wise, and develop good judgment. Don't forget or turn away from my words. [6]Don't turn your back on wisdom, for she will protect you. Love her, and she will guard you. [7]Getting wisdom is the most important thing you can do! And whatever else you do, get good judgment. [8]If you prize wisdom, she will exalt you. Embrace her and she will honor you. [9]She will place a lovely wreath on your head; she will present you with a beautiful crown."

[10]My child,* listen to me and do as I say, and you will have a long, good life. [11]I will teach you wisdom's ways and lead you in straight paths. [12]If you live a life guided by wisdom, you won't limp or stumble as you run. [13]Carry out my instructions; don't forsake them. Guard them, for they will lead you to a fulfilled life.

[14]Do not do as the wicked do or follow the path of evildoers. [15]Avoid their haunts. Turn away and go somewhere else, [16]for evil people cannot sleep until they have done their evil deed for the day. They can-

3:1 Hebrew *My son;* also in 3:11, 21.   3:12 Hebrew *a son.*   4:1 Hebrew *My sons.*   4:10 Hebrew *My son;* also in 4:20.

not rest unless they have caused someone to stumble. [17]They eat wickedness and drink violence!

[18]The way of the righteous is like the first gleam of dawn, which shines ever brighter until the full light of day. [19]But the way of the wicked is like complete darkness. Those who follow it have no idea what they are stumbling over.

[20]Pay attention, my child, to what I say. Listen carefully. [21]Don't lose sight of my words. Let them penetrate deep within

your heart, [22]for they bring life and radiant health to anyone who discovers their meaning.

[23]Above all else, guard your heart, for it affects everything you do.*

[24]Avoid all perverse talk; stay far from corrupt speech.

[25]Look straight ahead, and fix your eyes on what lies before you. [26]Mark out a straight path for your feet; then stick to the path and stay safe. [27]Don't get sidetracked; keep your feet from following evil.

4:23 Hebrew *for from it flow the springs of life.*

JULY 2 ☐ DAY 184
PROVERBS 5–9
A Father's Exhortation on Wisdom

 OVERVIEW The word *wisdom* in Hebrew is a feminine noun. Thus, it is natural for Solomon to personify it as a woman—a virtuous woman—in contrast to the foolish and immoral ways of a harlot. Both wisdom and folly beckon with similar invitations. "Come home with me" (9:4, 16). But the invitation you choose to accept will determine whether you find virtue or vice. Solomon warns his son, and all those reading his words, to watch out for sin's clever disguise and wise up to the importance of following God's instructions.

Chapters 5–6	Chapter 7	Chapter 8	Chapter 9
Warning against		Appeal for	
Adultery	Adulteresses	Wisdom	Watchfulness
Watch Out!		Wise Up!	

 YOUR DAILY WALK Few people plan to ruin their lives. Yet many a life ends in ruin. Why? Because someone else planned to ruin it for them.

Satan is alive and well . . . and craftily cunning in his attempts to destroy the moral fiber of God's children. His alternate route to God's ordained pattern for love, sex, marriage, and family is both attractive and inviting (7:10-23). The naive will play with fire—and get burned (6:28-29). The foolish will take the bait—and find that every kick offered by Satan also contains a kickback.

Wisdom opens the eyes to both the glories of heaven and the hollowness of earth.

The path leading to adultery is broad and inviting. Tragically, it is a path many find irresistible. But though the trail is well worn, no one need follow its deadly course. Whether young or old, married or single, Solomon's message is aimed at the heart: Don't play with matches—especially if the match belongs to someone else! Carry a book of matches with you today to keep that warning fresh in your mind and heart.

 INSIGHT Christ in the Proverbs
Notice the description of wisdom in chapter 8: It is divine (8:22-31); it is the source of life (8:35-36); it is righteous and moral (8:8-9); it is

available to all (8:1-6, 32-35). This wisdom became incarnate in Christ—"in him lie hidden all the treasures of wisdom and knowledge" (Colossians 2:3) and "God made Christ to be wisdom itself (1 Corinthians 1:30). Do you know that wisdom firsthand?

CHAPTER 5

My son, pay attention to my wisdom; listen carefully to my wise counsel. ²Then you will learn to be discreet and will store up knowledge.

³The lips of an immoral woman are as sweet as honey, and her mouth is smoother than oil. ⁴But the result is as bitter as poison, sharp as a double-edged sword. ⁵Her feet go down to death; her steps lead straight to the grave.* ⁶For she does not care about the path to life. She staggers down a crooked trail and doesn't even realize where it leads.

⁷So now, my sons, listen to me. Never stray from what I am about to say: ⁸Run from her! Don't go near the door of her house! ⁹If you do, you will lose your honor and hand over to merciless people everything you have achieved in life. ¹⁰Strangers will obtain your wealth, and someone else will enjoy the fruit of your labor. ¹¹Afterward you will groan in anguish when disease consumes your body, ¹²and you will say, "How I hated discipline! If only I had not demanded my own way! ¹³Oh, why didn't I listen to my teachers? Why didn't I pay attention to those who gave me instruction? ¹⁴I have come to the brink of utter ruin, and now I must face public disgrace."

¹⁵Drink water from your own well—share your love only with your wife.* ¹⁶Why spill the water of your springs in public, having sex with just anyone?* ¹⁷You should reserve it for yourselves. Don't share it with strangers.

¹⁸Let your wife be a fountain of blessing for you. Rejoice in the wife of your youth. ¹⁹She is a loving doe, a graceful deer. Let her breasts satisfy you always. May you always be captivated by her love. ²⁰Why be captivated, my son, with an immoral woman, or embrace the breasts of an adulterous woman?

²¹For the LORD sees clearly what a man does, examining every path he takes. ²²An evil man is held captive by his own sins; they are ropes that catch and hold him.

²³He will die for lack of self-control; he will be lost because of his incredible folly.

CHAPTER 6

My child,* if you co-sign a loan for a friend or guarantee the debt of someone you hardly know—²if you have trapped yourself by your agreement and are caught by what you said—³quick, get out of it if you possibly can! You have placed yourself at your friend's mercy. Now swallow your pride; go and beg to have your name erased. ⁴Don't put it off. Do it now! Don't rest until you do. ⁵Save yourself like a deer escaping from a hunter, like a bird fleeing from a net.

⁶Take a lesson from the ants, you lazybones. Learn from their ways and be wise! ⁷Even though they have no prince, governor, or ruler to make them work, ⁸they labor hard all summer, gathering food for the winter. ⁹But you, lazybones, how long will you sleep? When will you wake up? I want you to learn this lesson: ¹⁰A little extra sleep, a little more slumber, a little folding of the hands to rest—¹¹and poverty will pounce on you like a bandit; scarcity will attack you like an armed robber.

¹²Here is a description of worthless and wicked people: They are constant liars, ¹³signaling their true intentions to their friends by making signs with their eyes and feet and fingers. ¹⁴Their perverted hearts plot evil. They stir up trouble constantly. ¹⁵But they will be destroyed suddenly, broken beyond all hope of healing.

¹⁶There are six things the LORD hates—no, seven things he detests:
¹⁷ haughty eyes,
a lying tongue,
hands that kill the innocent,
¹⁸ a heart that plots evil,
feet that race to do wrong,
¹⁹ a false witness who pours out lies,
a person who sows discord among brothers.

²⁰My son, obey your father's commands, and don't neglect your mother's teaching. ²¹Keep their words always in your heart.

5:5 Hebrew *to Sheol.*   5:15 Hebrew *Drink water from your own cistern, flowing water from your own well.*   5:16 Hebrew *Why spill your springs in public, your streams in the streets?*   6:1 Hebrew *My son.*

Tie them around your neck. [22]Wherever you walk, their counsel can lead you. When you sleep, they will protect you. When you wake up in the morning, they will advise you. [23]For these commands and this teaching are a lamp to light the way ahead of you. The correction of discipline is the way to life.

[24]These commands and this teaching will keep you from the immoral woman, from the smooth tongue of an adulterous woman. [25]Don't lust for her beauty. Don't let her coyness seduce you. [26]For a prostitute will bring you to poverty, and sleeping with another man's wife may cost you your very life. [27]Can a man scoop fire into his lap and not be burned? [28]Can he walk on hot coals and not blister his feet? [29]So it is with the man who sleeps with another man's wife. He who embraces her will not go unpunished.

[30]Excuses might be found for a thief who steals because he is starving. [31]But if he is caught, he will be fined seven times as much as he stole, even if it means selling everything in his house to pay it back. [32]But the man who commits adultery is an utter fool, for he destroys his own soul. [33]Wounds and constant disgrace are his lot. His shame will never be erased. [34]For the woman's husband will be furious in his jealousy, and he will have no mercy in his day of vengeance. [35]There is no compensation or bribe that will satisfy him.

CHAPTER 7

Follow my advice, my son; always treasure my commands. [2]Obey them and live! Guard my teachings as your most precious possession.* [3]Tie them on your fingers as a reminder. Write them deep within your heart.

[4]Love wisdom like a sister; make insight a beloved member of your family. [5]Let them hold you back from an affair with an immoral woman, from listening to the flattery of an adulterous woman.

[6]I was looking out the window of my house one day [7]and saw a simpleminded young man who lacked common sense. [8]He was crossing the street near the house of an immoral woman. He was strolling down the path by her house [9]at twilight, as the day was fading, as the dark of night set in. [10]The woman approached him, dressed

seductively and sly of heart. [11]She was the brash, rebellious type who never stays at home. [12]She is often seen in the streets and markets, soliciting at every corner.

[13]She threw her arms around him and kissed him, and with a brazen look she said, [14]"I've offered my sacrifices and just finished my vows. [15]It's you I was looking for! I came out to find you, and here you are! [16]My bed is spread with colored sheets of finest linen imported from Egypt. [17]I've perfumed my bed with myrrh, aloes, and cinnamon. [18]Come, let's drink our fill of love until morning. Let's enjoy each other's caresses, [19]for my husband is not home. He's away on a long trip. [20]He has taken a wallet full of money with him, and he won't return until later in the month."

[21]So she seduced him with her pretty speech. With her flattery she enticed him. [22]He followed her at once, like an ox going to the slaughter or like a trapped stag, [23]awaiting the arrow that would pierce its heart. He was like a bird flying into a snare, little knowing it would cost him his life.

[24]Listen to me, my sons, and pay attention to my words. [25]Don't let your hearts stray away toward her. Don't wander down her wayward path. [26]For she has been the ruin of many; numerous men have been her victims. [27]Her house is the road to the grave.* Her bedroom is the den of death.

CHAPTER 8

Listen as wisdom calls out! Hear as understanding raises her voice! [2]She stands on the hilltop and at the crossroads. [3]At the entrance to the city, at the city gates, she cries aloud, [4]"I call to you, to all of you! I am raising my voice to all people. [5]How naive you are! Let me give you common sense. O foolish ones, let me give you understanding. [6]Listen to me! For I have excellent things to tell you. Everything I say is right, [7]for I speak the truth and hate every kind of deception. [8]My advice is wholesome and good. There is nothing crooked or twisted in it. [9]My words are plain to anyone with understanding, clear to those who want to learn.

[10]"Choose my instruction rather than silver, and knowledge over pure gold. [11]For wisdom is far more valuable than

7:2 Hebrew *as the apple of your eye.*   7:27 Hebrew *to Sheol.*

rubies. Nothing you desire can be compared with it. [12]"I, Wisdom, live together with good judgment. I know where to discover knowledge and discernment. [13]All who fear the LORD will hate evil. That is why I hate pride, arrogance, corruption, and perverted speech. [14]Good advice and success belong to me. Insight and strength are mine. [15]Because of me, kings reign, and rulers make just laws. [16]Rulers lead with my help, and nobles make righteous judgments.

[17]"I love all who love me. Those who search for me will surely find me. [18]Unending riches, honor, wealth, and justice are mine to distribute. [19]My gifts are better than the purest gold, my wages better than sterling silver! [20]I walk in righteousness, in paths of justice. [21]Those who love me inherit wealth, for I fill their treasuries.

[22]"The LORD formed me from the beginning, before he created anything else. [23]I was appointed in ages past, at the very first, before the earth began. [24]I was born before the oceans were created, before the springs bubbled forth their waters. [25]Before the mountains and the hills were formed, I was born—[26]before he had made the earth and fields and the first handfuls of soil.

[27]"I was there when he established the heavens, when he drew the horizon on the oceans. [28]I was there when he set the clouds above, when he established the deep fountains of the earth. [29]I was there when he set the limits of the seas, so they would not spread beyond their boundaries. And when he marked off the earth's foundations, [30]I was the architect at his side. I was his constant delight, rejoicing always in his presence. [31]And how happy I was with what he created—his wide world and all the human family!

[32]"And so, my children,* listen to me, for happy are all who follow my ways. [33]Listen to my counsel and be wise. Don't ignore it.

8:32 Hebrew *my sons.*   **9:18** Hebrew *in Sheol.*

[34]"Happy are those who listen to me, watching for me daily at my gates, waiting for me outside my home! [35]For whoever finds me finds life and wins approval from the LORD. [36]But those who miss me have injured themselves. All who hate me love death."

CHAPTER 9

Wisdom has built her spacious house with seven pillars. [2]She has prepared a great banquet, mixed the wines, and set the table. [3]She has sent her servants to invite everyone to come. She calls out from the heights overlooking the city. [4]"Come home with me," she urges the simple. To those without good judgment, she says, [5]"Come, eat my food, and drink the wine I have mixed. [6]Leave your foolish ways behind, and begin to live; learn how to be wise."

[7]Anyone who rebukes a mocker will get a smart retort. Anyone who rebukes the wicked will get hurt. [8]So don't bother rebuking mockers; they will only hate you. But the wise, when rebuked, will love you all the more. [9]Teach the wise, and they will be wiser. Teach the righteous, and they will learn more.

[10]Fear of the LORD is the beginning of wisdom. Knowledge of the Holy One results in understanding.

[11]Wisdom will multiply your days and add years to your life. [12]If you become wise, you will be the one to benefit. If you scorn wisdom, you will be the one to suffer.

[13]The woman named Folly is loud and brash. She is ignorant and doesn't even know it. [14]She sits in her doorway on the heights overlooking the city. [15]She calls out to men going by who are minding their own business. [16]"Come home with me," she urges the simple. To those without good judgment, she says, [17]"Stolen water is refreshing; food eaten in secret tastes the best!" [18]But the men don't realize that her former guests are now in the grave.*

JULY 3 ☐ DAY 185
PROVERBS 10–13
Wisdom vs. Folly

 OVERVIEW Proverbs is more than a book on how to be wise. If you choose, it can also be a book on how to be foolish. Every wise course of action to pursue is contrasted with a foolish course of action to avoid. These four chapters, and the verses extending through chapter 22, are mainly comprised of authentic proverbs—proverbs in which a contrast is introduced by the word *but*.

Chapter 10	Chapter 11	Chapter 12	Chapter 13
Lips and Labor	Riches and Reward	Snares and Sluggards	Prudence and Poverty
Faithfulness Contrasted with Folly			

 YOUR DAILY WALK A young child awakens and, for the next hour, resists all his parent's attempts to get him dressed, fed, and on his way to school. If you were his parent, how would you feel?

The opposite of ignorance in the spiritual realm is not knowledge but obedience.

The same child awakens, goes to his closet, selects his clothes, and dresses himself without being asked. The net result is the same: He is dressed. But how do you as his parent feel?

A wise son obeys his father willingly; a foolish son only does so grudgingly or under compulsion. Which characterizes your obedience to your heavenly Father? Read 10:1 thoughtfully. Then complete this sentence: Today I want to bring gladness (rather than heaviness) to the heart of God by gladly (rather than grudgingly) obeying him in the matter of _____. Now that's putting wisdom to work!

 INSIGHT The Fool's Self-Destruction
When people rebel against God, they end up destroying themselves. They fall beneath their own load of sin (11:5) and are trapped by their own sin (29:6). Ponder the timelessness of God's wisdom as you consider the results of abortion, drug abuse, broken homes, and homosexuality in our day.

C H A P T E R 1 0
The proverbs of Solomon:

A wise child* brings joy to a father; a foolish child brings grief to a mother.

²Ill-gotten gain has no lasting value, but right living can save your life.

³The LORD will not let the godly starve to death, but he refuses to satisfy the craving of the wicked.

⁴Lazy people are soon poor; hard workers get rich.

⁵A wise youth works hard all summer; a youth who sleeps away the hour of opportunity brings shame.

⁶The godly are showered with blessings; evil people cover up their harmful intentions.

⁷We all have happy memories of the godly, but the name of a wicked person rots away.

⁸The wise are glad to be instructed, but babbling fools fall flat on their faces.

⁹People with integrity have firm footing, but those who follow crooked paths will slip and fall.

¹⁰People who wink at wrong cause trouble, but a bold reproof promotes peace.*

¹¹The words of the godly lead to life; evil people cover up their harmful intentions.

¹²Hatred stirs up quarrels, but love covers all offenses.

¹³Wise words come from the lips of people with understanding, but fools will be punished with a rod.

¹⁴Wise people treasure knowledge, but the babbling of a fool invites trouble.

10:1 Hebrew *son*; also in 10:1b.   10:10 As in Greek version; Hebrew reads *but babbling fools fall flat on their faces.*

[15]The wealth of the rich is their fortress; the poverty of the poor is their calamity.

[16]The earnings of the godly enhance their lives, but evil people squander their money on sin.

[17]People who accept correction are on the pathway to life, but those who ignore it will lead others astray.

[18]To hide hatred is to be a liar; to slander is to be a fool.

[19]Don't talk too much, for it fosters sin. Be sensible and turn off the flow!

[20]The words of the godly are like sterling silver; the heart of a fool is worthless.

[21]The godly give good advice, but fools are destroyed by their lack of common sense.

[22]The blessing of the LORD makes a person rich, and he adds no sorrow with it.

[23]Doing wrong is fun for a fool, while wise conduct is a pleasure to the wise.

[24]The fears of the wicked will all come true; so will the hopes of the godly.

[25]Disaster strikes like a cyclone, whirling the wicked away, but the godly have a lasting foundation.

[26]Lazy people are a pain to their employer. They are like smoke in the eyes or vinegar that sets the teeth on edge.

[27]Fear of the LORD lengthens one's life, but the years of the wicked are cut short.

[28]The hopes of the godly result in happiness, but the expectations of the wicked are all in vain.

[29]The LORD protects the upright but destroys the wicked.

[30]The godly will never be disturbed, but the wicked will be removed from the land.

[31]The godly person gives wise advice, but the tongue that deceives will be cut off.

[32]The godly speak words that are helpful, but the wicked speak only what is corrupt.

CHAPTER 11

The LORD hates cheating, but he delights in honesty.

[2]Pride leads to disgrace, but with humility comes wisdom.

[3]Good people are guided by their honesty; treacherous people are destroyed by their dishonesty.

[4]Riches won't help on the day of judgment, but right living is a safeguard against death.

[5]The godly are directed by their honesty; the wicked fall beneath their load of sin.

[6]The godliness of good people rescues them; the ambition of treacherous people traps them.

[7]When the wicked die, their hopes all perish, for they rely on their own feeble strength.

[8]God rescues the godly from danger, but he lets the wicked fall into trouble.

[9]Evil words destroy one's friends; wise discernment rescues the godly.

[10]The whole city celebrates when the godly succeed; they shout for joy when the godless die.

[11]Upright citizens bless a city and make it prosper, but the talk of the wicked tears it apart.

[12]It is foolish to belittle a neighbor; a person with good sense remains silent.

[13]A gossip goes around revealing secrets, but those who are trustworthy can keep a confidence.

[14]Without wise leadership, a nation falls; with many counselors, there is safety.

[15]Guaranteeing a loan for a stranger is dangerous; it is better to refuse than to suffer later.

[16]Beautiful women obtain wealth, and violent men get rich.

[17]Your own soul is nourished when you are kind, but you destroy yourself when you are cruel.

[18]Evil people get rich for the moment, but the reward of the godly will last.

[19]Godly people find life; evil people find death.

[20]The LORD hates people with twisted hearts, but he delights in those who have integrity.

[21]You can be sure that evil people will be punished, but the children of the godly will go free.

[22]A woman who is beautiful but lacks discretion is like a gold ring in a pig's snout.

[23]The godly can look forward to happiness, while the wicked can expect only wrath.

[24]It is possible to give freely and become more wealthy, but those who are stingy will lose everything.

[25]The generous prosper and are satisfied; those who refresh others will themselves be refreshed.

[26]People curse those who hold their

grain for higher prices, but they bless the one who sells to them in their time of need.

²⁷If you search for good, you will find favor; but if you search for evil, it will find you!

²⁸Trust in your money and down you go! But the godly flourish like leaves in spring.

²⁹Those who bring trouble on their families inherit only the wind. The fool will be a servant to the wise.

³⁰The godly are like trees that bear life-giving fruit, and those who save lives are wise.

³¹If the righteous are rewarded here on earth, how much more true that the wicked and the sinner will get what they deserve!

CHAPTER 12
To learn, you must love discipline; it is stupid to hate correction.

²The LORD approves of those who are good, but he condemns those who plan wickedness.

³Wickedness never brings stability; only the godly have deep roots.

⁴A worthy wife is her husband's joy and crown; a shameful wife saps his strength.

⁵The plans of the godly are just; the advice of the wicked is treacherous.

⁶The words of the wicked are like a murderous ambush, but the words of the godly save lives.

⁷The wicked perish and are gone, but the children of the godly stand firm.

⁸Everyone admires a person with good sense, but a warped mind is despised.

⁹It is better to be a nobody with a servant than to be self-important but have no food.

¹⁰The godly are concerned for the welfare of their animals, but even the kindness of the wicked is cruel.

¹¹Hard work means prosperity; only fools idle away their time.

¹²Thieves are jealous of each other's loot, while the godly bear their own fruit.

¹³The wicked are trapped by their own words, but the godly escape such trouble.

¹⁴People can get many good things by the words they say; the work of their hands also gives them many benefits.

¹⁵Fools think they need no advice, but the wise listen to others.

¹⁶A fool is quick-tempered, but a wise person stays calm when insulted.

¹⁷An honest witness tells the truth; a false witness tells lies.

¹⁸Some people make cutting remarks, but the words of the wise bring healing.

¹⁹Truth stands the test of time; lies are soon exposed.

²⁰Deceit fills hearts that are plotting evil; joy fills hearts that are planning peace!

²¹No real harm befalls the godly, but the wicked have their fill of trouble.

²²The LORD hates those who don't keep their word, but he delights in those who do.

²³Wise people don't make a show of their knowledge, but fools broadcast their folly.

²⁴Work hard and become a leader; be lazy and become a slave.

²⁵Worry weighs a person down; an encouraging word cheers a person up.

²⁶The godly give good advice to their friends;* the wicked lead them astray.

²⁷Lazy people don't even cook the game they catch, but the diligent make use of everything they find.

²⁸The way of the godly leads to life; their path does not lead to death.

CHAPTER 13
A wise child* accepts a parent's discipline; a young mocker refuses to listen.

²Good people enjoy the positive results of their words, but those who are treacherous crave violence.

³Those who control their tongue will have a long life; a quick retort can ruin everything.

⁴Lazy people want much but get little, but those who work hard will prosper and be satisfied.

⁵Those who are godly hate lies; the wicked come to shame and disgrace.

⁶Godliness helps people all through life, while the evil are destroyed by their wickedness.

⁷Some who are poor pretend to be rich; others who are rich pretend to be poor.

⁸The rich can pay a ransom, but the poor won't even get threatened.

⁹The life of the godly is full of light and joy, but the sinner's light is snuffed out.

¹⁰Pride leads to arguments; those who take advice are wise.

¹¹Wealth from get-rich-quick schemes quickly disappears; wealth from hard work grows.

¹²Hope deferred makes the heart sick,

12:26 Or *The godly are cautious in friendship,* or *the godly are freed from evil.* The meaning of the Hebrew is uncertain.
13:1 Hebrew *son.*

but when dreams come true, there is life and joy.

¹³People who despise advice will find themselves in trouble; those who respect it will succeed.

¹⁴The advice of the wise is like a life-giving fountain; those who accept it avoid the snares of death.

¹⁵A person with good sense is respected; a treacherous person walks a rocky road.

¹⁶Wise people think before they act; fools don't and even brag about it!

¹⁷An unreliable messenger stumbles into trouble, but a reliable messenger brings healing.

¹⁸If you ignore criticism, you will end in poverty and disgrace; if you accept criticism, you will be honored.

¹⁹It is pleasant to see dreams come true,

but fools will not turn from evil to attain them.

²⁰Whoever walks with the wise will become wise; whoever walks with fools will suffer harm.

²¹Trouble chases sinners, while blessings chase the righteous!

²²Good people leave an inheritance to their grandchildren, but the sinner's wealth passes to the godly.

²³A poor person's farm may produce much food, but injustice sweeps it all away.

²⁴If you refuse to discipline your children, it proves you don't love them; if you love your children, you will be prompt to discipline them.

²⁵The godly eat to their hearts' content, but the belly of the wicked goes hungry.

JULY 4 ☐ DAY 186
PROVERBS 14–17
Wisdom in Daily Conduct

 OVERVIEW For a quick overview of today's reading, notice the first verse of each chapter. Solomon offers God's perspective on the home (14:1; 17:1), the tongue (15:1), and the heart (16:1). If you are skillful in those three areas of life, you are well on your way to establishing harmony in your interpersonal relationships.

Chapter 14	Chapter 15	Chapter 16	Chapter 17
Cribs and Crowns	Herbs and Ears	Kings and Conduct	Peacemakers and Troublemakers
Fear the Lord		Follow the Lord	

 YOUR DAILY WALK As you read through today's passage, look for the word *Lord,* and circle it every time it appears.

God writes with a pen that never blots, speaks with a tongue that never slips, and acts with a hand that never fails.

The frequent repetition of *Lord* acts as a constant reminder that Proverbs is not just a collection of secular maxims or a Farmer's Almanac of wit and wisdom. The counsel it contains is not recorded primarily for society as a whole but rather to instruct the people of God on how to live godly lives in an ungodly world.

The name *Lord* appears eighty-nine times in the book, and twenty-five times in today's reading alone. (How many times can you find it in chapter 16?) As one commentator has remarked, "It is good to be reminded over and over again that the Lord is the key to all righteous living, as its author, standard, inspirer, empowerer, judge, and rewarder."

Write the word *Lord* on an index card, and place it in a conspicuous place where you will see it often during the day (your refrigerator, car dashboard, bathroom mirror). Let it be a constant reminder to you today that the Lord is the answer, regardless of what the question might be! Then try to think of one way in which God has shown himself to be your author, standard, inspirer, empowerer, judge, and rewarder.

 INSIGHT The Lord Is Here, but God Is Strangely Absent
The word translated "God" appears only eight times in Proverbs, compared to eighty-nine times for LORD. LORD is the title God uses most frequently when dealing with his chosen people; God is a less intimate term, used mostly in his dealings with humankind as a whole. Thus, Proverbs was written primarily for the family of God—which explains why its precepts don't always make sense to the world.

CHAPTER 14

A wise woman builds her house; a foolish woman tears hers down with her own hands.

²Those who follow the right path fear the LORD; those who take the wrong path despise him.

³The talk of fools is a rod for their backs,* but the words of the wise keep them out of trouble.

⁴An empty stable stays clean, but no income comes from an empty stable.

⁵A truthful witness does not lie; a false witness breathes lies.

⁶A mocker seeks wisdom and never finds it, but knowledge comes easily to those with understanding.

⁷Stay away from fools, for you won't find knowledge there.

⁸The wise look ahead to see what is coming, but fools deceive themselves.

⁹Fools make fun of guilt, but the godly acknowledge it and seek reconciliation.

¹⁰Each heart knows its own bitterness, and no one else can fully share its joy.

¹¹The house of the wicked will perish, but the tent of the godly will flourish.

¹²There is a path before each person that seems right, but it ends in death.

¹³Laughter can conceal a heavy heart; when the laughter ends, the grief remains.

¹⁴Backsliders get what they deserve; good people receive their reward.

¹⁵Only simpletons believe everything they are told! The prudent carefully consider their steps.

¹⁶The wise are cautious* and avoid danger; fools plunge ahead with great confidence.

¹⁷Those who are short-tempered do foolish things, and schemers are hated.

¹⁸The simpleton is clothed with folly, but the wise person is crowned with knowledge.

¹⁹Evil people will bow before good people; the wicked will bow at the gates of the godly.

²⁰The poor are despised even by their neighbors, while the rich have many "friends."

²¹It is sin to despise one's neighbors; blessed are those who help the poor.

²²If you plot evil, you will be lost; but if you plan good, you will be granted unfailing love and faithfulness.

²³Work brings profit, but mere talk leads to poverty!

²⁴Wealth is a crown for the wise; the effort of fools yields only folly.

²⁵A truthful witness saves lives, but a false witness is a traitor.

²⁶Those who fear the LORD are secure; he will be a place of refuge for their children.

²⁷Fear of the LORD is a life-giving fountain; it offers escape from the snares of death.

²⁸A growing population is a king's glory; a dwindling nation is his doom.

²⁹Those who control their anger have great understanding; those with a hasty temper will make mistakes.

³⁰A relaxed attitude lengthens life; jealousy rots it away.

³¹Those who oppress the poor insult their Maker, but those who help the poor honor him.

³²The wicked are crushed by their sins, but the godly have a refuge when they die.

³³Wisdom is enshrined in an understanding heart; wisdom is not* found among fools.

³⁴Godliness exalts a nation, but sin is a disgrace to any people.

³⁵A king rejoices in servants who know what they are doing; he is angry with those who cause trouble.

14:3 Hebrew *a rod of pride.*   **14:16** Hebrew *The wise fear.*   **14:33** As in Greek version; Hebrew lacks *not.*

CHAPTER 15

A gentle answer turns away wrath, but harsh words stir up anger.

²The wise person makes learning a joy; fools spout only foolishness.

³The LORD is watching everywhere, keeping his eye on both the evil and the good.

⁴Gentle words bring life and health; a deceitful tongue crushes the spirit.

⁵Only a fool despises a parent's discipline; whoever learns from correction is wise.

⁶There is treasure in the house of the godly, but the earnings of the wicked bring trouble.

⁷Only the wise can give good advice; fools cannot do so.

⁸The LORD hates the sacrifice of the wicked, but he delights in the prayers of the upright.

⁹The LORD despises the way of the wicked, but he loves those who pursue godliness.

¹⁰Whoever abandons the right path will be severely punished; whoever hates correction will die.

¹¹Even the depths of Death and Destruction* are known by the LORD. How much more does he know the human heart!

¹²Mockers don't love those who rebuke them, so they stay away from the wise.

¹³A glad heart makes a happy face; a broken heart crushes the spirit.

¹⁴A wise person is hungry for truth, while the fool feeds on trash.

¹⁵For the poor, every day brings trouble; for the happy heart, life is a continual feast.

¹⁶It is better to have little with fear for the LORD than to have great treasure with turmoil.

¹⁷A bowl of soup with someone you love is better than steak with someone you hate.

¹⁸A hothead starts fights; a cool-tempered person tries to stop them.

¹⁹A lazy person has trouble all through life; the path of the upright is easy!

²⁰Sensible children bring joy to their father; foolish children despise their mother.

²¹Foolishness brings joy to those who have no sense; a sensible person stays on the right path.

²²Plans go wrong for lack of advice; many counselors bring success.

²³Everyone enjoys a fitting reply; it is wonderful to say the right thing at the right time!

²⁴The path of the wise leads to life above; they leave the grave* behind.

²⁵The LORD destroys the house of the proud, but he protects the property of widows.

²⁶The LORD despises the thoughts of the wicked, but he delights in pure words.

²⁷Dishonest money brings grief to the whole family, but those who hate bribes will live.

²⁸The godly think before speaking; the wicked spout evil words.

²⁹The LORD is far from the wicked, but he hears the prayers of the righteous.

³⁰A cheerful look brings joy to the heart; good news makes for good health.

³¹If you listen to constructive criticism, you will be at home among the wise.

³²If you reject criticism, you only harm yourself; but if you listen to correction, you grow in understanding.

³³Fear of the LORD teaches a person to be wise; humility precedes honor.

CHAPTER 16

We can gather our thoughts, but the LORD gives the right answer.

²People may be pure in their own eyes, but the LORD examines their motives.

³Commit your work to the LORD, and then your plans will succeed.

⁴The LORD has made everything for his own purposes, even the wicked for punishment.

⁵The LORD despises pride; be assured that the proud will be punished.

⁶Unfailing love and faithfulness cover sin; evil is avoided by fear of the LORD.

⁷When the ways of people please the LORD, he makes even their enemies live at peace with them.

⁸It is better to be poor and godly than rich and dishonest.

⁹We can make our plans, but the LORD determines our steps.

¹⁰The king speaks with divine wisdom; he must never judge unfairly.

¹¹The LORD demands fairness in every business deal; he sets the standard.

¹²A king despises wrongdoing, for his rule depends on his justice.

15:11 Hebrew *Sheol and Abaddon.*   **15:24** Hebrew *Sheol.*

¹³The king is pleased with righteous lips; he loves those who speak honestly.

¹⁴The anger of the king is a deadly threat; the wise do what they can to appease it.

¹⁵When the king smiles, there is life; his favor refreshes like a gentle rain.

¹⁶How much better to get wisdom than gold, and understanding than silver!

¹⁷The path of the upright leads away from evil; whoever follows that path is safe.

¹⁸Pride goes before destruction, and haughtiness before a fall.

¹⁹It is better to live humbly with the poor than to share plunder with the proud.

²⁰Those who listen to instruction will prosper; those who trust the LORD will be happy.

²¹The wise are known for their understanding, and instruction is appreciated if it's well presented.

²²Discretion is a life-giving fountain to those who possess it, but discipline is wasted on fools.

²³From a wise mind comes wise speech; the words of the wise are persuasive.

²⁴Kind words are like honey—sweet to the soul and healthy for the body.

²⁵There is a path before each person that seems right, but it ends in death.

²⁶It is good for workers to have an appetite; an empty stomach drives them on.

²⁷Scoundrels hunt for scandal; their words are a destructive blaze.

²⁸A troublemaker plants seeds of strife; gossip separates the best of friends.

²⁹Violent people deceive their companions, leading them down a harmful path.

³⁰With narrowed eyes, they plot evil; without a word, they plan their mischief.

³¹Gray hair is a crown of glory; it is gained by living a godly life.

³²It is better to be patient than powerful; it is better to have self-control than to conquer a city.

³³We may throw the dice, but the LORD determines how they fall.

CHAPTER 17

A dry crust eaten in peace is better than a great feast with strife.

²A wise slave will rule over the master's shameful sons and will share their inheritance.

³Fire tests the purity of silver and gold, but the LORD tests the heart.

⁴Wrongdoers listen to wicked talk; liars pay attention to destructive words.

⁵Those who mock the poor insult their Maker; those who rejoice at the misfortune of others will be punished.

⁶Grandchildren are the crowning glory of the aged; parents are the pride of their children.

⁷Eloquent speech is not fitting for a fool; even less are lies fitting for a ruler.

⁸A bribe seems to work like magic for those who give it; they succeed in all they do.

⁹Disregarding another person's faults preserves love; telling about them separates close friends.

¹⁰A single rebuke does more for a person of understanding than a hundred lashes on the back of a fool.

¹¹Evil people seek rebellion, but they will be severely punished.

¹²It is safer to meet a bear robbed of her cubs than to confront a fool caught in folly.

¹³If you repay evil for good, evil will never leave your house.

¹⁴Beginning a quarrel is like opening a floodgate, so drop the matter before a dispute breaks out.

¹⁵The LORD despises those who acquit the guilty and condemn the innocent.

¹⁶It is senseless to pay tuition to educate a fool who has no heart for wisdom.

¹⁷A friend is always loyal, and a brother is born to help in time of need.

¹⁸It is poor judgment to co-sign a friend's note, to become responsible for a neighbor's debts.

¹⁹Anyone who loves to quarrel loves sin; anyone who speaks boastfully* invites disaster.

²⁰The crooked heart will not prosper; the twisted tongue tumbles into trouble.

²¹It is painful to be the parent of a fool; there is no joy for the father of a rebel.

²²A cheerful heart is good medicine, but a broken spirit saps a person's strength.

²³The wicked accept secret bribes to pervert justice.

²⁴Sensible people keep their eyes glued on wisdom, but a fool's eyes wander to the ends of the earth.

17:19 Or *who builds up defenses;* Hebrew reads *who makes a high gate.*

²⁵A foolish child* brings grief to a father and bitterness to a mother.

²⁶It is wrong to fine the godly for being good or to punish nobles for being honest!

²⁷A truly wise person uses few words;

17:25 Hebrew *son.*

a person with understanding is even-tempered.

²⁸Even fools are thought to be wise when they keep silent; when they keep their mouths shut, they seem intelligent.

JULY 5 ☐ DAY 187
PROVERBS 18–21
Wisdom in Daily Choices

OVERVIEW Had all the proverbs composed by Solomon during his lifetime been a part of the inspired book of Proverbs, it would have stretched to more than three thousand verses (1 Kings 4:32)—making it by far the longest book in the Bible! But the nine hundred or so inspired maxims actually contained in Proverbs will provide a lifetime of challenge on the daily issues of life: speech, conduct, money, avoiding evil, maintaining proper motives, and walking in integrity.

Chapter 18	Chapter 19	Chapter 20	Chapter 21
Noble Neighbors	Princes and Paupers	Mockers and Meddlers	Haughtiness and Heartache
Responding to People			Responding to God

Child training is chiefly a matter of knowing which end of the child to pat— and when.

YOUR DAILY WALK A teacher sent home this note pinned to the coat of an unruly student: "Dear Mrs. Jones: I regret to inform you that your son Robert is disruptive. He needs a good spanking, and I strongly urge you to give him one." The next day this reply came back pinned to Bobby's jacket: "Dear Mrs. Smith: Spank him yourself; he hasn't disobeyed me!"

The right discipline tailored to the right person in the right situation—that's the challenge of anyone entrusted with leadership authority. But beware! There is something potentially as dangerous as exercising *no* discipline—that is, exercising the same discipline in every situation.

According to 19:25, there are three kinds of temperament and three kinds of discipline, one appropriate to each temperament. How would Solomon tell you to discipline the following?

The mocker: _____

The simple-minded: _____

The wise: _____

Now ask the Lord, "In whose life do you desire me to be a discerning disciplinarian?"

INSIGHT How's Your Heart?

Open-heart surgery is not a twentieth-century invention as you might have thought. It's as old as the book of Proverbs. As you read through the book, you'll discover the word *heart* used more than fifty times, showing it is through the heart—and a proper heart attitude—that you find and apply God's wisdom for your Christian walk.

CHAPTER 18
A recluse is self-indulgent, snarling at every sound principle of conduct.

²Fools have no interest in understand-

ing; they only want to air their own opinions.

³When the wicked arrive, contempt, shame, and disgrace are sure to follow.

⁴A person's words can be life-giving water; words of true wisdom are as refreshing as a bubbling brook.

⁵It is wrong for a judge to favor the guilty or condemn the innocent.

⁶Fools get into constant quarrels; they are asking for a beating.

⁷The mouths of fools are their ruin; their lips get them into trouble.

⁸What dainty morsels rumors are—but they sink deep into one's heart.

⁹A lazy person is as bad as someone who destroys things.

¹⁰The name of the LORD is a strong fortress; the godly run to him and are safe.

¹¹The rich think of their wealth as an impregnable defense; they imagine it is a high wall of safety.

¹²Haughtiness goes before destruction; humility precedes honor.

¹³What a shame, what folly, to give advice before listening to the facts!

¹⁴The human spirit can endure a sick body, but who can bear it if the spirit is crushed?

¹⁵Intelligent people are always open to new ideas. In fact, they look for them.

¹⁶Giving a gift works wonders; it may bring you before important people!

¹⁷Any story sounds true until someone sets the record straight.

¹⁸Casting lots can end arguments and settle disputes between powerful opponents.

¹⁹It's harder to make amends with an offended friend than to capture a fortified city. Arguments separate friends like a gate locked with iron bars.

²⁰Words satisfy the soul as food satisfies the stomach; the right words on a person's lips bring satisfaction.

²¹Those who love to talk will experience the consequences, for the tongue can kill or nourish life.

²²The man who finds a wife finds a treasure and receives favor from the LORD.

²³The poor plead for mercy; the rich answer with insults.

²⁴There are "friends" who destroy each other, but a real friend sticks closer than a brother.

CHAPTER 19
It is better to be poor and honest than to be a fool and dishonest.

²Zeal without knowledge is not good; a person who moves too quickly may go the wrong way.

³People ruin their lives by their own foolishness and then are angry at the LORD.

⁴Wealth makes many "friends"; poverty drives them away.

⁵A false witness will not go unpunished, nor will a liar escape.

⁶Many beg favors from a prince; everyone is the friend of a person who gives gifts!

⁷If the relatives of the poor despise them, how much more will their friends avoid them. The poor call after them, but they are gone.

⁸To acquire wisdom is to love oneself; people who cherish understanding will prosper.

⁹A false witness will not go unpunished, and a liar will be destroyed.

¹⁰It isn't right for a fool to live in luxury or for a slave to rule over princes!

¹¹People with good sense restrain their anger; they earn esteem by overlooking wrongs.

¹²The king's anger is like a lion's roar, but his favor is like dew on the grass.

¹³A foolish child* is a calamity to a father; a nagging wife annoys like a constant dripping.

¹⁴Parents can provide their sons with an inheritance of houses and wealth, but only the LORD can give an understanding wife.

¹⁵A lazy person sleeps soundly—and goes hungry.

¹⁶Keep the commandments and keep your life; despising them leads to death.

¹⁷If you help the poor, you are lending to the LORD—and he will repay you!

¹⁸Discipline your children while there is hope. If you don't, you will ruin their lives.

¹⁹Short-tempered people must pay their own penalty. If you rescue them once, you will have to do it again.

²⁰Get all the advice and instruction you can, and be wise the rest of your life.

²¹You can make many plans, but the LORD's purpose will prevail.

²²Loyalty makes a person attractive. And it is better to be poor than dishonest.

²³Fear of the LORD gives life, security, and protection from harm.

²⁴Some people are so lazy that they won't even lift a finger to feed themselves.

19:13 Hebrew *son;* also in 19:27.

²⁵If you punish a mocker, the simple-minded will learn a lesson; if you reprove the wise, they will be all the wiser.

²⁶Children who mistreat their father or chase away their mother are a public disgrace and an embarrassment.

²⁷If you stop listening to instruction, my child, you have turned your back on knowledge.

²⁸A corrupt witness makes a mockery of justice; the mouth of the wicked gulps down evil.

²⁹Mockers will be punished, and the backs of fools will be beaten.

CHAPTER 20

Wine produces mockers; liquor leads to brawls. Whoever is led astray by drink cannot be wise.

²The king's fury is like a lion's roar; to rouse his anger is to risk your life.

³Avoiding a fight is a mark of honor; only fools insist on quarreling.

⁴If you are too lazy to plow in the right season, you will have no food at the harvest.

⁵Though good advice lies deep within a person's heart, the wise will draw it out.

⁶Many will say they are loyal friends, but who can find one who is really faithful?

⁷The godly walk with integrity; blessed are their children after them.

⁸When a king judges, he carefully weighs all the evidence, distinguishing the bad from the good.

⁹Who can say, "I have cleansed my heart; I am pure and free from sin"?

¹⁰The LORD despises double standards of every kind.

¹¹Even children are known by the way they act, whether their conduct is pure and right.

¹²Ears to hear and eyes to see—both are gifts from the LORD.

¹³If you love sleep, you will end in poverty. Keep your eyes open, and there will be plenty to eat!

¹⁴The buyer haggles over the price, saying, "It's worthless," then brags about getting a bargain!

¹⁵Wise speech is rarer and more valuable than gold and rubies.

¹⁶Be sure to get collateral from anyone who guarantees the debt of a stranger. Get a deposit if someone guarantees the debt of a foreigner.*

¹⁷Stolen bread tastes sweet, but it turns to gravel in the mouth.

¹⁸Plans succeed through good counsel; don't go to war without the advice of others.

¹⁹A gossip tells secrets, so don't hang around with someone who talks too much.

²⁰If you curse your father or mother, the lamp of your life will be snuffed out.

²¹An inheritance obtained early in life is not a blessing in the end.

²²Don't say, "I will get even for this wrong." Wait for the LORD to handle the matter.

²³The LORD despises double standards; he is not pleased by dishonest scales.

²⁴How can we understand the road we travel? It is the LORD who directs our steps.

²⁵It is dangerous to make a rash promise to God before counting the cost.

²⁶A wise king finds the wicked, lays them out like wheat, then runs the crushing wheel over them.

²⁷The LORD's searchlight penetrates the human spirit,* exposing every hidden motive.

²⁸Unfailing love and faithfulness protect the king; his throne is made secure through love.

²⁹The glory of the young is their strength; the gray hair of experience is the splendor of the old.

³⁰Physical punishment cleanses away evil;* such discipline purifies the heart.

CHAPTER 21

The king's heart is like a stream of water directed by the LORD; he turns it wherever he pleases.

²People may think they are doing what is right, but the LORD examines the heart.

³The LORD is more pleased when we do what is just and right than when we give him sacrifices.

⁴Haughty eyes, a proud heart, and evil actions are all sin.

⁵Good planning and hard work lead to prosperity, but hasty shortcuts lead to poverty.

⁶Wealth created by lying is a vanishing mist and a deadly trap.*

⁷Because the wicked refuse to do what is

20:16 An alternate reading in the Hebrew text is *the debt of an adulterous woman;* compare 27:13.   20:27 Or *The human spirit is the* LORD's *searchlight.*   20:30 The meaning of the Hebrew is uncertain.   21:6 As in Greek version; Hebrew reads *mist for those who seek death.*

just, their violence boomerangs and destroys them.

⁸The guilty walk a crooked path; the innocent travel a straight road.

⁹It is better to live alone in the corner of an attic than with a contentious wife in a lovely home.

¹⁰Evil people love to harm others; their neighbors get no mercy from them.

¹¹A simpleton can learn only by seeing mockers punished; a wise person learns from instruction.

¹²The Righteous One* knows what is going on in the homes of the wicked; he will bring the wicked to disaster.

¹³Those who shut their ears to the cries of the poor will be ignored in their own time of need.

¹⁴A secret gift calms anger; a secret bribe pacifies fury.

¹⁵Justice is a joy to the godly, but it causes dismay among evildoers.

¹⁶The person who strays from common sense will end up in the company of the dead.

¹⁷Those who love pleasure become poor; wine and luxury are not the way to riches.

¹⁸Sometimes the wicked are punished to save the godly, and the treacherous for the upright.

21:12 Or *The righteous man.*

¹⁹It is better to live alone in the desert than with a crabby, complaining wife.

²⁰The wise have wealth and luxury, but fools spend whatever they get.

²¹Whoever pursues godliness and unfailing love will find life, godliness, and honor.

²²The wise conquer the city of the strong and level the fortress in which they trust.

²³If you keep your mouth shut, you will stay out of trouble.

²⁴Mockers are proud and haughty; they act with boundless arrogance.

²⁵The desires of lazy people will be their ruin, for their hands refuse to work. ²⁶They are always greedy for more, while the godly love to give!

²⁷God loathes the sacrifice of an evil person, especially when it is brought with ulterior motives.

²⁸A false witness will be cut off, but an attentive witness will be allowed to speak.

²⁹The wicked put up a bold front, but the upright proceed with care.

³⁰Human plans, no matter how wise or well advised, cannot stand against the LORD.

³¹The horses are prepared for battle, but the victory belongs to the LORD.

JULY 6 ☐ DAY 188
PROVERBS 22–24
Words of Wise Men

 OVERVIEW No one needs wisdom more than those in positions of authority and responsibility. Parents, teachers, civic leaders, pastors—the need is the same: skill in making moral, ethical, and spiritual decisions consistent with God's Word and will. Why? Because their choices impact not only their lives but also the lives of those they are attempting to lead into righteous paths of conduct and character.

Chapter 22	Chapter 23	Chapter 24
The King's Humility	The King's Habits	The King's House
Character	Conduct	Consistency

 YOUR DAILY WALK Motto on a procrastinator's desk: Never put off till tomorrow what you can put off till the day after tomorrow! Laziness is nothing new. The apostle Paul wrestled with the problem in the church at Thessalonica (2 Thessalonians 3:10-11). And the book

Those who expect to repent tomorrow usually die today. of Proverbs paints a graphic picture of the danger of laziness (24:30-34). The lazy person can expect his endeavors and possessions to crumble and fall apart—not from doing *wrong,* but from doing *nothing.* The end result: an impoverished person whose destruction has come suddenly . . . a day at a time.

What has been left undone in your life? Have you been putting off reading a good Christian book, beginning an exercise program, writing some overdue letters, visiting a shut-in or relative?

Go outside right now, and pull a weed or two from the nearest patch of grass. Then bring your "object lesson" indoors, take out a sheet of paper, and write down five neglected tasks you need to complete by the end of the month. Arrange them in order of priority, and put a date by each, showing when you intend to complete them. Then tackle "Project #1" today. You'll be amazed how fast your list—and the weeds it represents—will start to disappear!

 INSIGHT Good . . . and Good for You!
Complete these three verses from today's section to discover some "good" news!
"Choose a good _____ over great riches" (22:1).
"Eat _____, for it is good" (24:13).
"_____ are showered on those who convict the guilty" (24:25).

CHAPTER 22

Choose a good reputation over great riches, for being held in high esteem is better than having silver or gold.

²The rich and the poor have this in common: The LORD made them both.

³A prudent person foresees the danger ahead and takes precautions; the simpleton goes blindly on and suffers the consequences.

⁴True humility and fear of the LORD lead to riches, honor, and long life.

⁵The deceitful walk a thorny, treacherous road; whoever values life will stay away.

⁶Teach your children to choose the right path, and when they are older, they will remain upon it.

⁷Just as the rich rule the poor, so the borrower is servant to the lender.

⁸Those who plant seeds of injustice will harvest disaster, and their reign of terror will end.

⁹Blessed are those who are generous, because they feed the poor.

¹⁰Throw out the mocker, and fighting, quarrels, and insults will disappear.

¹¹Anyone who loves a pure heart and gracious speech is the king's friend.

¹²The LORD preserves knowledge, but he ruins the plans of the deceitful.

¹³The lazy person is full of excuses, saying, "If I go outside, I might meet a lion in the street and be killed!"

¹⁴The mouth of an immoral woman is a deep pit; those living under the LORD's displeasure will fall into it.

¹⁵A youngster's heart is filled with foolishness, but discipline will drive it away.

¹⁶A person who gets ahead by oppressing the poor or by showering gifts on the rich will end in poverty.

¹⁷Listen to the words of the wise; apply your heart to my instruction. ¹⁸For it is good to keep these sayings deep within yourself, always ready on your lips. ¹⁹I am teaching you today—yes, you—so you will trust in the LORD. ²⁰I have written thirty sayings for you, filled with advice and knowledge. ²¹In this way, you may know the truth and bring an accurate report to those who sent you.

²²Do not rob the poor because they are poor or exploit the needy in court. ²³For the LORD is their defender. He will injure anyone who injures them.

²⁴Keep away from angry, short-tempered people, ²⁵or you will learn to be like them and endanger your soul.

²⁶Do not co-sign another person's note or put up a guarantee for someone else's loan. ²⁷If you can't pay it, even your bed will be snatched from under you.

²⁸Do not steal your neighbor's property by moving the ancient boundary markers set up by your ancestors.

²⁹Do you see any truly competent workers? They will serve kings rather than ordinary people.

CHAPTER 23

When dining with a ruler, pay attention to what is put before you. ²If you are a big eater, put a knife to your throat, ³and don't desire all the delicacies—deception may be involved.

⁴Don't weary yourself trying to get rich. Why waste your time? ⁵For riches can disappear as though they had the wings of a bird!

⁶Don't eat with people who are stingy; don't desire their delicacies. ⁷"Eat and drink," they say, but they don't mean it. They are always thinking about how much it costs. ⁸You will vomit up the delicious food they serve, and you will have to take back your words of appreciation for their "kindness."

⁹Don't waste your breath on fools, for they will despise the wisest advice.

¹⁰Don't steal the land of defenseless orphans by moving the ancient boundary markers, ¹¹for their Redeemer is strong. He himself will bring their charges against you.

¹²Commit yourself to instruction; attune your ears to hear words of knowledge.

¹³Don't fail to correct your children. They won't die if you spank them. ¹⁴Physical discipline may well save them from death.*

¹⁵My child,* how I will rejoice if you become wise. ¹⁶Yes, my heart will thrill when you speak what is right and just.

¹⁷Don't envy sinners, but always continue to fear the LORD. ¹⁸For surely you have a future ahead of you; your hope will not be disappointed.

¹⁹My child, listen and be wise. Keep your heart on the right course. ²⁰Do not carouse with drunkards and gluttons, ²¹for they are on their way to poverty. Too much sleep clothes a person with rags.

²²Listen to your father, who gave you life, and don't despise your mother's experience when she is old. ²³Get the truth and don't ever sell it; also get wisdom, discipline, and discernment. ²⁴The father of godly children has cause for joy. What a pleasure it is to have wise children.* ²⁵So give your parents joy! May she who gave you birth be happy.

²⁶O my son, give me your heart. May your eyes delight in my ways of wisdom. ²⁷A prostitute is a deep pit; an adulterous woman is treacherous.* ²⁸She hides and waits like a robber, looking for another victim who will be unfaithful to his wife.

²⁹Who has anguish? Who has sorrow? Who is always fighting? Who is always complaining? Who has unnecessary bruises? Who has bloodshot eyes? ³⁰It is the one who spends long hours in the taverns, trying out new drinks. ³¹Don't let the sparkle and smooth taste of wine deceive you. ³²For in the end it bites like a poisonous serpent; it stings like a viper. ³³You will see hallucinations, and you will say crazy things. ³⁴You will stagger like a sailor tossed at sea, clinging to a swaying mast. ³⁵And you will say, "They hit me, but I didn't feel it. I didn't even know it when they beat me up. When will I wake up so I can have another drink?"

CHAPTER 24

Don't envy evil people; don't desire their company. ²For they spend their days plotting violence, and their words are always stirring up trouble.

³A house is built by wisdom and becomes strong through good sense. ⁴Through knowledge its rooms are filled with all sorts of precious riches and valuables.

⁵A wise man is mightier than a strong man,* and a man of knowledge is more powerful than a strong man. ⁶So don't go to war without wise guidance; victory depends on having many counselors.

⁷Wisdom is too much for a fool. When the leaders gather, the fool has nothing to say.

⁸A person who plans evil will get a reputation as a troublemaker. ⁹The schemes of a fool are sinful; everyone despises a mocker.

¹⁰If you fail under pressure, your strength is not very great.

¹¹Rescue those who are unjustly sentenced to death; don't stand back and let them die. ¹²Don't try to avoid responsibility by saying you didn't know about it. For God knows all hearts, and he sees you. He keeps watch over your soul, and he knows you knew! And he will judge all people according to what they have done.

¹³My child,* eat honey, for it is good, and the honeycomb is sweet to the taste. ¹⁴In the same way, wisdom is sweet to your soul. If you find it, you will have a bright future, and your hopes will not be cut short.

¹⁵Do not lie in wait like an outlaw at the home of the godly. And don't raid the house where the godly live. ¹⁶They may trip seven times, but each time they will

23:14 Hebrew from Sheol.   23:15 Hebrew My son; also in 23:19.   23:24 Hebrew a wise son.   23:27 Hebrew is a narrow well.
24:5 As in Greek version; Hebrew reads A wise man is strength.   24:13 Hebrew My son; also in 24:21.

rise again. But one calamity is enough to lay the wicked low.

¹⁷Do not rejoice when your enemies fall into trouble. Don't be happy when they stumble. ¹⁸For the LORD will be displeased with you and will turn his anger away from them.

¹⁹Do not fret because of evildoers; don't envy the wicked. ²⁰For the evil have no future; their light will be snuffed out.

²¹My child, fear the LORD and the king, and don't associate with rebels. ²²For you will go down with them to sudden disaster. Who knows where the punishment from the LORD and the king will end?

²³Here are some further sayings of the wise:

It is wrong to show favoritism when passing judgment. ²⁴A judge who says to the wicked, "You are innocent," will be cursed by many people and denounced by the na-

tions. ²⁵But blessings are showered on those who convict the guilty.

²⁶It is an honor to receive an honest reply. ²⁷Develop your business first before building your house.

²⁸Do not testify spitefully against innocent neighbors; don't lie about them. ²⁹And don't say, "Now I can pay them back for all their meanness to me! I'll get even!"

³⁰I walked by the field of a lazy person, the vineyard of one lacking sense. ³¹I saw that it was overgrown with thorns. It was covered with weeds, and its walls were broken down. ³²Then, as I looked and thought about it, I learned this lesson: ³³A little extra sleep, a little more slumber, a little folding of the hands to rest—³⁴and poverty will pounce on you like a bandit; scarcity will attack you like an armed robber.

JULY 7 ☐ DAY 189
Learning the Skill of Living

 LOOK BACK The closer you find yourself to the end of the book of Psalms, the greater becomes the crescendo of praise. Psalms 144–146 encourage you to praise God personally; Psalms 147–150 exhort you to praise God corporately. But whether you are alone or in a crowd, the result is the same: God, who is worthy of our highest adoration, receives from his creation the glory he so richly deserves.

Worshiping the Lord includes a healthy reverence for the Lord, for "fear of the LORD is the beginning of wisdom" (Proverbs 9:10). In more than nine hundred nuggets of common (and uncommon) sense, Solomon challenges the reader of Proverbs to hunt for, embrace, and employ heavenly wisdom for each earthly decision.

Making something beautiful out of the raw materials of life is God's plan and purpose for each of his children. But whether you choose the life of wisdom or the life of a fool, the choice is up to you!

 LOOK UP Proverbs is such a treasure chest of insight that you'll want to read it more than once. In fact, you may want to begin the habit of reading one chapter from Proverbs each day of the month (e.g., on the twenty-fourth day of the month, read Proverbs 24). As you read, notice the different kinds of proverbs and the lessons to be learned from each:

A wise person will desire no more than he or she may get justly, use soberly, distribute cheerfully, and leave contentedly.

Contrasting proverbs use the word *but* to set up a comparison. "The wise inherit honor, but fools are put to shame" (3:35).

Cause/effect proverbs use the words *then* or *for* to show the cause-and-effect relationship of actions and reactions. "Honor the LORD with your wealth . . . Then he will fill your barns with grain" (3:9-10).

Numerical proverbs make a statement, then itemize a list. "There are six things the LORD hates—no, seven things he detests: haughty eyes, a lying tongue, . . ." (6:16-19).

Comparative proverbs use the word *better* to suggest something . . . better! "It is better to have little with fear for the LORD than to have great treasure with turmoil" (15:16).

LOOK AHEAD If a carpenter can take a block of wood and turn it into a beautiful piece of furniture, we say that that person is a gifted craftsman.

If a conductor can shape the myriad skills of an entire orchestra to produce the sounds of a symphony, we say that that person is a musical genius.

And if a man or woman, boy or girl, can take the raw materials of life and shape them skillfully according to the blueprint God has provided in his Word, we say that that person is wise. It has nothing to do with IQ and everything to do with obedience! You can be wise with an IQ of 70; you can be a fool with an IQ of 170. The choice is up to you.

Whether you are a parent struggling to discipline a child . . . a teenager wrestling with peer pressure . . . or a rising executive tempted to follow the crowd in an unethical choice, you'll find Proverbs brimming with insight for living. Pick a topic you are eager to study from God's perspective, and retrace your steps through the book of Proverbs. Don't be surprised if God provides some heavenly (un)common sense!

JULY 8 ☐ DAY 190
PROVERBS 25–29
Wise Words from the King

OVERVIEW Today's section contains proverbs written by Solomon but compiled and arranged by King Hezekiah perhaps 250 years later. They represent a timeless treasure from a sovereign to his subjects: warnings against spiritual erosion and instructions regarding godly lifestyles. Solomon touches on many personalities and walks of life: the rich and the poor, false witnesses and friends, the lazy and the diligent, the deceitful and the dependable. In each case there is a right response and a proper perspective for the upright of heart.

Chapter 25	Chapter 26	Chapter 27	Chapter 28	Chapter 29
Gold and Good News	Whips and Lips	Kisses and Curses	Laws and Lions	Flattery and Fools
Wise Words for All Walks of Life				

YOUR DAILY WALK
Many verses in Proverbs could be called homilies in similes, sermons in the form of a comparison using the words *like* or *as*. In fact, the Hebrew word for *proverb* comes from a root meaning "to be like." Can you match up each statement with the thing it is "like," according to Proverbs?

Truth is always narrow, but error goes off in all directions.

___1. "Singing cheerful songs to a person whose heart is heavy is as bad . . ."

___2. "A quarrelsome person starts fights . . ."

___3. "As iron sharpens iron . . ."

___4. "A wicked ruler is as dangerous to the poor . . ."

a. "as easily as hot embers light charcoal or fire lights wood" (26:21).

b. "as a lion or bear attacking them" (28:15).

c. "as stealing someone's jacket in cold weather" (25:20).

d. "a friend sharpens a friend" (27:17).

Can you explain each comparison? More important, can you think of a way to exemplify the truth of one of these proverbs today?

INSIGHT Counsel by Comparison in Chapter 25

As you read chapter 25, see if you can locate at least one helpful piece of counsel regarding these everyday situations:
• Receiving honor
• Answering a quarrelsome person
• Ministering to a depressed friend
• Eating sweets
• Staying with a friend

CHAPTER 25

These are more proverbs of Solomon, collected by the advisers of King Hezekiah of Judah.

²It is God's privilege to conceal things and the king's privilege to discover them.

³No one can discover the height of heaven, the depth of the earth, or all that goes on in the king's mind!

⁴Remove the dross from silver, and the sterling will be ready for the silversmith. ⁵Remove the wicked from the king's court, and his reign will be made secure by justice.

⁶Don't demand an audience with the king or push for a place among the great. ⁷It is better to wait for an invitation than to be sent to the end of the line, publicly disgraced!

Just because you see something, ⁸don't be in a hurry to go to court. You might go down before your neighbors in shameful defeat. ⁹So discuss the matter with them privately. Don't tell anyone else, ¹⁰or others may accuse you of gossip. Then you will never regain your good reputation.

¹¹Timely advice is as lovely as golden apples in a silver basket.

¹²Valid criticism is as treasured by the one who heeds it as jewelry made from finest gold.

¹³Faithful messengers are as refreshing as snow in the heat of summer. They revive the spirit of their employer.

¹⁴A person who doesn't give a promised gift is like clouds and wind that don't bring rain.

¹⁵Patience can persuade a prince, and soft speech can crush strong opposition.

¹⁶Do you like honey? Don't eat too much of it, or it will make you sick!

¹⁷Don't visit your neighbors too often, or you will wear out your welcome.

¹⁸Telling lies about others is as harmful as hitting them with an ax, wounding them with a sword, or shooting them with a sharp arrow.

¹⁹Putting confidence in an unreliable person is like chewing with a toothache or walking on a broken foot.

²⁰Singing cheerful songs to a person whose heart is heavy is as bad as stealing someone's jacket in cold weather or rubbing salt in a wound.

²¹If your enemies are hungry, give them food to eat. If they are thirsty, give them water to drink. ²²You will heap burning coals on their heads, and the LORD will reward you.

²³As surely as a wind from the north brings rain, so a gossiping tongue causes anger!

²⁴It is better to live alone in the corner of an attic than with a contentious wife in a lovely home.

²⁵Good news from far away is like cold water to the thirsty.

²⁶If the godly compromise with the wicked, it is like polluting a fountain or muddying a spring.

²⁷Just as it is not good to eat too much honey, it is not good for people to think about all the honors they deserve.

²⁸A person without self-control is as defenseless as a city with broken-down walls.

CHAPTER 26

Honor doesn't go with fools any more than snow with summer or rain with harvest.

²Like a fluttering sparrow or a darting swallow, an unfair curse will not land on its intended victim.

³Guide a horse with a whip, a donkey with a bridle, and a fool with a rod to his back!

⁴When arguing with fools, don't answer their foolish arguments, or you will become as foolish as they are.

⁵When arguing with fools, be sure to answer their foolish arguments, or they will become wise in their own estimation.

⁶Trusting a fool to convey a message is as foolish as cutting off one's feet or drinking poison!

⁷In the mouth of a fool, a proverb becomes as limp as a paralyzed leg.

⁸Honoring a fool is as foolish as tying a stone to a slingshot.

⁹A proverb in a fool's mouth is as dangerous as a thornbush brandished by a drunkard.

¹⁰An employer who hires a fool or a bystander is like an archer who shoots recklessly.

¹¹As a dog returns to its vomit, so a fool repeats his folly.

¹²There is more hope for fools than for people who think they are wise.

¹³The lazy person is full of excuses, saying, "I can't go outside because there might be a lion on the road! Yes, I'm sure there's a lion out there!"

¹⁴As a door turns back and forth on its hinges, so the lazy person turns over in bed.

¹⁵Some people are so lazy that they won't lift a finger to feed themselves.

¹⁶Lazy people consider themselves smarter than seven wise counselors.

¹⁷Yanking a dog's ears is as foolish as interfering in someone else's argument.

¹⁸Just as damaging as a mad man shooting a lethal weapon ¹⁹is someone who lies to a friend and then says, "I was only joking."

²⁰Fire goes out for lack of fuel, and quarrels disappear when gossip stops.

²¹A quarrelsome person starts fights as easily as hot embers light charcoal or fire lights wood.

²²What dainty morsels rumors are—but they sink deep into one's heart.

²³Smooth* words may hide a wicked heart, just as a pretty glaze covers a common clay pot.

²⁴People with hate in their hearts may sound pleasant enough, but don't believe them. ²⁵Though they pretend to be kind, their hearts are full of all kinds of evil. ²⁶While their hatred may be concealed by trickery, it will finally come to light for all to see.

²⁷If you set a trap for others, you will get caught in it yourself. If you roll a boulder down on others, it will roll back and crush you.

²⁸A lying tongue hates its victims, and flattery causes ruin.

CHAPTER 27
Don't brag about tomorrow, since you don't know what the day will bring.

²Don't praise yourself; let others do it!

³A stone is heavy and sand is weighty, but the resentment caused by a fool is heavier than both.

⁴Anger is cruel, and wrath is like a flood, but who can survive the destructiveness of jealousy?

⁵An open rebuke is better than hidden love!

⁶Wounds from a friend are better than many kisses from an enemy.

⁷Honey seems tasteless to a person who is full, but even bitter food tastes sweet to the hungry.

⁸A person who strays from home is like a bird that strays from its nest.

⁹The heartfelt counsel of a friend is as sweet as perfume and incense.

¹⁰Never abandon a friend—either yours or your father's. Then in your time of need, you won't have to ask your relatives for assistance. It is better to go to a neighbor than to a relative who lives far away.

¹¹My child,* how happy I will be if you turn out to be wise! Then I will be able to answer my critics.

¹²A prudent person foresees the danger ahead and takes precautions. The simpleton goes blindly on and suffers the consequences.

¹³Be sure to get collateral from anyone who guarantees the debt of a stranger. Get a deposit if someone guarantees the debt of an adulterous woman.

¹⁴If you shout a pleasant greeting to your neighbor too early in the morning, it will be counted as a curse!

¹⁵A nagging wife is as annoying as the constant dripping on a rainy day. ¹⁶Trying to stop her complaints is like trying to stop the wind or hold something with greased hands.

¹⁷As iron sharpens iron, a friend sharpens a friend.

¹⁸Workers who tend a fig tree are allowed to eat its fruit. In the same way, workers who protect their employer's interests will be rewarded.

¹⁹As a face is reflected in water, so the heart reflects the person.

²⁰Just as Death and Destruction* are

26:23 As in Greek version; Hebrew reads *Burning.*   27:11 Hebrew *My son.*   27:20 Hebrew *Sheol and Abaddon.*

never satisfied, so human desire is never satisfied.

²¹Fire tests the purity of silver and gold, but a person is tested by being praised.

²²You cannot separate fools from their foolishness, even though you grind them like grain with mortar and pestle.

²³Know the state of your flocks, and put your heart into caring for your herds, ²⁴for riches don't last forever, and the crown might not be secure for the next generation. ²⁵After the hay is harvested, the new crop appears, and the mountain grasses are gathered in, ²⁶your sheep will provide wool for clothing, and your goats will be sold for the price of a field. ²⁷And you will have enough goats' milk for you, your family, and your servants.

CHAPTER 28

The wicked run away when no one is chasing them, but the godly are as bold as lions.

²When there is moral rot within a nation, its government topples easily. But with wise and knowledgeable leaders, there is stability.

³A poor person who oppresses the poor is like a pounding rain that destroys the crops.

⁴To reject the law is to praise the wicked; to obey the law is to fight them.

⁵Evil people don't understand justice, but those who follow the LORD understand completely.

⁶It is better to be poor and honest than rich and crooked.

⁷Young people who obey the law are wise; those who seek out worthless companions bring shame to their parents.

⁸A person who makes money by charging interest will lose it. It will end up in the hands of someone who is kind to the poor.

⁹The prayers of a person who ignores the law are despised.

¹⁰Those who lead the upright into sin will fall into their own trap, but the honest will inherit good things.

¹¹Rich people picture themselves as wise, but their real poverty is evident to the poor.

¹²When the godly succeed, everyone is glad. When the wicked take charge, people go into hiding.

¹³People who cover over their sins will not prosper. But if they confess and forsake them, they will receive mercy.

¹⁴Blessed are those who have a tender conscience,* but the stubborn are headed for serious trouble.

¹⁵A wicked ruler is as dangerous to the poor as a lion or bear attacking them.

¹⁶Only a stupid prince will oppress his people, but a king will have a long reign if he hates dishonesty and bribes.

¹⁷A murderer's tormented conscience will drive him into the grave. Don't protect him!

¹⁸The honest will be rescued from harm, but those who are crooked will be destroyed.

¹⁹Hard workers have plenty of food; playing around brings poverty.

²⁰The trustworthy will get a rich reward. But the person who wants to get rich quick will only get into trouble.

²¹Showing partiality is never good, yet some will do wrong for something as small as a piece of bread.

²²A greedy person tries to get rich quick, but it only leads to poverty.

²³In the end, people appreciate frankness more than flattery.

²⁴Robbing your parents and then saying, "What's wrong with that?" is as serious as committing murder.

²⁵Greed causes fighting; trusting the LORD leads to prosperity.

²⁶Trusting oneself is foolish, but those who walk in wisdom are safe.

²⁷Whoever gives to the poor will lack nothing. But a curse will come upon those who close their eyes to poverty.

²⁸When the wicked take charge, people hide. When the wicked meet disaster, the godly multiply.

CHAPTER 29

Whoever stubbornly refuses to accept criticism will suddenly be broken beyond repair.

²When the godly are in authority, the people rejoice. But when the wicked are in power, they groan.

³The man who loves wisdom brings joy to his father, but if he hangs around with prostitutes, his wealth is wasted.

⁴A just king gives stability to his nation, but one who demands bribes destroys it.

⁵To flatter people is to lay a trap for their feet.

28:14 Hebrew *those who fear.*

⁶Evil people are trapped by sin, but the righteous escape, shouting for joy.

⁷The godly know the rights of the poor; the wicked don't care to know.

⁸Mockers can get a whole town agitated, but those who are wise will calm anger.

⁹If a wise person takes a fool to court, there will be ranting and ridicule but no satisfaction.

¹⁰The bloodthirsty hate the honest, but the upright seek out the honest.

¹¹A fool gives full vent to anger, but a wise person quietly holds it back.

¹²If a ruler honors liars, all his advisers will be wicked.

¹³The poor and the oppressor have this in common—the LORD gives light to the eyes of both.

¹⁴A king who is fair to the poor will have a long reign.

¹⁵To discipline and reprimand a child produces wisdom, but a mother is disgraced by an undisciplined child.

¹⁶When the wicked are in authority, sin increases. But the godly will live to see the tyrant's downfall.

¹⁷Discipline your children, and they will give you happiness and peace of mind.

¹⁸When people do not accept divine guidance, they run wild. But whoever obeys the law is happy.

¹⁹For a servant, mere words are not enough—discipline is needed. For the words may be understood, but they are not heeded.

²⁰There is more hope for a fool than for someone who speaks without thinking.

²¹A servant who is pampered from childhood will later become a rebel.

²²A hot-tempered person starts fights and gets into all kinds of sin.

²³Pride ends in humiliation, while humility brings honor.

²⁴If you assist a thief, you are only hurting yourself. You will be punished if you report the crime, but you will be cursed if you don't.

²⁵Fearing people is a dangerous trap, but to trust the LORD means safety.

²⁶Many seek the ruler's favor, but justice comes from the LORD.

²⁷The godly despise the wicked; the wicked despise the godly.

JULY 9 ☐ DAY 191
PROVERBS 30–31
Alphabet of a Virtuous Wife

 OVERVIEW Proverbs closes with the wise counsel of two godly men: Agur and Lemuel. Using numerical proverbs and pictures from the natural world, Agur summarizes many of the themes that have been woven throughout the book: wisdom and folly, greed and gluttony, adultery and hypocrisy. Then in a beautiful acrostic poem—one in which each verse begins with a succeeding letter of the Hebrew alphabet—Lemuel extols the virtuous wife and mother.

Chapter 30	Chapter 31	
Wisdom in Twos, Threes, and Fours	Wisdom from a Godly Mother	Wisdom for a Godly Wife
1	9 10	31
Advice from Agur	Lectures from Lemuel	

 YOUR DAILY WALK Nothing is as contemporary as the question of women's rights and roles—both inside and outside the home. And nothing generates more heat and less light than debating the issue

Virtue has more admirers than followers.

without first consulting God's Word on the subject.

In Proverbs 31:10-31 Lemuel profiles a woman who is godly, industrious, creative, sensitive, multitalented . . . and a wife and mother! She wears many different hats: seamstress (v. 13), merchant (v. 14), cook (v. 15), real estate agent (v. 16), gardener (v. 16), physical fitness enthusiast (v. 17), community volunteer (v. 20). But her energies are directed primarily toward the home. "She carefully watches all that goes on in her household" (v. 27) and is a blessing to her family.

Wives, God has placed you in the home, not to stifle your creativity, but to stimulate it! Think of your home as a laboratory and Proverbs 31 as your lab manual. Pick one verse and make it your "Experiment in Fulfilled Womanhood" today.

And if you're not a wife, consider how your life has been enriched by a "Mrs. Far-above-Rubies"—and let her know today how much you appreciate her!

 INSIGHT Where Has All the Time Gone?
Home weaving looms of Bible times were often inefficient and time consuming. No wonder this virtuous woman's candle didn't go out at night. She spent much of her time making beautiful clothing from scratch for the family and the family business.

CHAPTER 30
The message of Agur son of Jakeh. An oracle.*

I am weary, O God; I am weary and worn out, O God.* ²I am too ignorant to be human, and I lack common sense. ³I have not mastered human wisdom, nor do I know the Holy One.

⁴Who but God goes up to heaven and comes back down? Who holds the wind in his fists? Who wraps up the oceans in his cloak? Who has created the whole wide world? What is his name—and his son's name? Tell me if you know!

⁵Every word of God proves true. He defends all who come to him for protection. ⁶Do not add to his words, or he may rebuke you, and you will be found a liar. ⁷O God, I beg two favors from you before I die. ⁸First, help me never to tell a lie. Second, give me neither poverty nor riches! Give me just enough to satisfy my needs. ⁹For if I grow rich, I may deny you and say, "Who is the LORD?" And if I am too poor, I may steal and thus insult God's holy name.

¹⁰Never slander a person to his employer. If you do, the person will curse you, and you will pay for it.

¹¹Some people curse their father and do not thank their mother. ¹²They feel pure, but they are filthy and unwashed. ¹³They are proud beyond description and disdainful. ¹⁴They devour the poor with teeth as sharp as swords or knives. They destroy the needy from the face of the earth.

¹⁵The leech has two suckers that cry out, "More, more!"* There are three other things—no, four!—that are never satisfied: ¹⁶ the grave,
the barren womb,
the thirsty desert,
the blazing fire.

¹⁷The eye that mocks a father and despises a mother will be plucked out by ravens of the valley and eaten by vultures.

¹⁸There are three things that amaze me—no, four things I do not understand: ¹⁹ how an eagle glides through the sky,
how a snake slithers on a rock,
how a ship navigates the ocean,
how a man loves a woman.
²⁰Equally amazing is how an adulterous woman can satisfy her sexual appetite, shrug her shoulders, and then say, "What's wrong with that?"

²¹There are three things that make the earth tremble—no, four it cannot endure: ²² a slave who becomes a king,
an overbearing fool who prospers,
²³ a bitter woman who finally gets a
husband,
a servant girl who supplants her
mistress.

²⁴There are four things on earth that are small but unusually wise:
²⁵ Ants—they aren't strong,
but they store up food for the winter.
²⁶ Rock badgers*—they aren't powerful,
but they make their homes among
the rocky cliffs.

30:1a Or *son of Jakeh from Massa.*   **30:1b** The Hebrew can also be translated *The man declares this to Ithiel, to Ithiel and to Ucal.*
30:15 Hebrew *two daughters who cry out, "Give, give!"*   **30:26** Or *coneys,* or *hyraxes.*

²⁷ Locusts—they have no king,
   but they march like an army in ranks.
²⁸ Lizards—they are easy to catch,
   but they are found even in kings'
      palaces.

²⁹There are three stately monarchs on the earth—no, four:
³⁰ the lion, king of animals, who won't
   turn aside for anything,
³¹ the strutting rooster,
   the male goat,
   a king as he leads his army.

³²If you have been a fool by being proud or plotting evil, don't brag about it—cover your mouth with your hand in shame.

³³As the beating of cream yields butter, and a blow to the nose causes bleeding, so anger causes quarrels.

CHAPTER 31

These are the sayings of King Lemuel, an oracle* that his mother taught him.

²O my son, O son of my womb, O son of my promises, ³do not spend your strength on women, on those who ruin kings.

⁴And it is not for kings, O Lemuel, to guzzle wine. Rulers should not crave liquor. ⁵For if they drink, they may forget their duties and be unable to give justice to those who are oppressed. ⁶Liquor is for the dying, and wine for those in deep depression. ⁷Let them drink to forget their poverty and remember their troubles no more.

⁸Speak up for those who cannot speak for themselves; ensure justice for those who are perishing. ⁹Yes, speak up for the poor and helpless, and see that they get justice.

¹⁰Who can find a virtuous and capable wife? She is worth more than precious rubies. ¹¹Her husband can trust her, and she will greatly enrich his life. ¹²She will not hinder him but help him all her life.

¹³She finds wool and flax and busily spins it. ¹⁴She is like a merchant's ship; she brings her food from afar. ¹⁵She gets up before dawn to prepare breakfast for her household and plan the day's work for her servant girls. ¹⁶She goes out to inspect a field and buys it; with her earnings she plants a vineyard.

¹⁷She is energetic and strong, a hard worker. ¹⁸She watches for bargains; her lights burn late into the night. ¹⁹Her hands are busy spinning thread, her fingers twisting fiber.

²⁰She extends a helping hand to the poor and opens her arms to the needy.

²¹She has no fear of winter for her household because all of them have warm* clothes. ²²She quilts her own bedspreads. She dresses like royalty in gowns of finest cloth.

²³Her husband is well known, for he sits in the council meeting with the other civic leaders.

²⁴She makes belted linen garments and sashes to sell to the merchants.

²⁵She is clothed with strength and dignity, and she laughs with no fear of the future. ²⁶When she speaks, her words are wise, and kindness is the rule when she gives instructions. ²⁷She carefully watches all that goes on in her household and does not have to bear the consequences of laziness.

²⁸Her children stand and bless her. Her husband praises her: ²⁹"There are many virtuous and capable women in the world, but you surpass them all!"

³⁰Charm is deceptive, and beauty does not last; but a woman who fears the LORD will be greatly praised. ³¹Reward her for all she has done. Let her deeds publicly declare her praise.

31:1 Or *of Lemuel, king of Massa.*   **31:21** As in Greek version; Hebrew *scarlet.*

Ecclesiastes

THE AUTHOR of Ecclesiastes (traditionally thought to be Solomon) enjoyed power, wealth, and access to all of life's pursuits and pleasures. After experiencing a full measure of life "under the sun," he declares it all to be futile and unsatisfying. Only as he lives "above the sun"—with an eye toward God—does life become meaningful and fulfilling. Ultimate satisfaction comes not from the good things of life but from the Giver of life, the one we are to fear, honor, and obey.

Focus	Exploration			Exhortation		
Divisions	All Is Meaningless	Meaninglessness of Doing	Meaninglessness of Having	Meaninglessness of Being	Using Life Well	Source of True Living
	1	2 4	5 6	7 9	10 11	12
Topics	Exploring Life's Inconsistencies			Explaining Life's Inconsistencies		
	Fickleness of Life vs. Fear of the Lord					
Place	Under the Sun					
Time	Decades of Searching (in the Days of King Solomon)					

JULY 10 ☐ DAY 192
ECCLESIASTES 1–6
Exploring Life's Inconsistencies

 OVERVIEW Truly life is an enigma . . . a riddle . . . a puzzle. From the perspective of those who do not know God, there can only be one word for it: *meaningless.* That's the word the Teacher uses in 1:2—and twenty-four other times in the book—to describe the futility of life apart from God. And he ought to know! Every earthly prescription for happiness has been tried . . . and found wanting. Only when life is viewed as a precious gift "from the hand of God" (2:24) does it begin to come into sharp focus—a focus only possible *above* the sun, so to speak.

Chapter 1	Chapters 2–4	Chapters 5–6
The Meaninglessness of Everything	The Futility of Work	The Futility of Wealth
Premise	Proof	

 YOUR DAILY WALK What would you think if your life began at the age of eighty and gradually approached eighteen? Would you live it differently?

Life asks no questions that faith cannot answer.

The Teacher has no illusions about life. He has learned from firsthand experience that nothing under the sun will bring lasting satisfaction. But even in the midst of his voyage into meaninglessness, the Teacher grows wiser, for he discovers the hand of God at work (2:24; 9:1). God is the Giver of "wisdom, knowledge, and joy" (2:26). He enables people to "eat and drink and enjoy the fruits of their labor" (3:13).

Why not plan a "praise party" for this evening? With family or friends, fix a special meal specifically for the purpose of thanking God publicly for his good gifts. You'll find that it is habit-forming!

 INSIGHT The Teacher: Solomon or Someone Else?
Compare the description of the Teacher in Ecclesiastes with the corresponding description of Solomon in 1 Kings.

Who Is the Teacher? (Ecclesiastes)	*Who Is Solomon?* (1 Kings)
• King David's son (1:1)	_____ (2:1)
• a ruler in Jerusalem (1:1)	_____ (8:1)
• searcher of understanding (1:13)	_____ (3:12)
• builder and gardener (2:4-6)	_____ (7:1-12)
• collector of treasure (2:7-10)	_____ (10:14-29)

Decide for yourself: Is "the Teacher" Solomon . . . or someone else?

CHAPTER 1

These are the words of the Teacher,* King David's son, who ruled in Jerusalem.

²"Everything is meaningless," says the Teacher, "utterly meaningless!"

³What do people get for all their hard work? ⁴Generations come and go, but nothing really changes. ⁵The sun rises and sets and hurries around to rise again. ⁶The wind blows south and north, here and there, twisting back and forth, getting nowhere. ⁷The rivers run into the sea, but the

1:1 Hebrew *Koheleth;* this term is rendered "the Teacher" throughout this book.

sea is never full. Then the water returns again to the rivers and flows again to the sea. [8]Everything is so weary and tiresome! No matter how much we see, we are never satisfied. No matter how much we hear, we are not content.

[9]History merely repeats itself. It has all been done before. Nothing under the sun is truly new. [10]What can you point to that is new? How do you know it didn't already exist long ago? [11]We don't remember what happened in those former times. And in future generations, no one will remember what we are doing now.

[12]I, the Teacher, was king of Israel, and I lived in Jerusalem. [13]I devoted myself to search for understanding and to explore by wisdom everything being done in the world. I soon discovered that God has dealt a tragic existence to the human race. [14]Everything under the sun is meaningless, like chasing the wind. [15]What is wrong cannot be righted. What is missing cannot be recovered.

[16]I said to myself, "Look, I am wiser than any of the kings who ruled in Jerusalem before me. I have greater wisdom and knowledge than any of them." [17]So I worked hard to distinguish wisdom from foolishness. But now I realize that even this was like chasing the wind. [18]For the greater my wisdom, the greater my grief. To increase knowledge only increases sorrow.

CHAPTER 2
I said to myself, "Come now, let's give pleasure a try. Let's look for the 'good things' in life." But I found that this, too, was meaningless. [2]"It is silly to be laughing all the time," I said. "What good does it do to seek only pleasure?" [3]After much thought, I decided to cheer myself with wine. While still seeking wisdom, I clutched at foolishness. In this way, I hoped to experience the only happiness most people find during their brief life in this world.

[4]I also tried to find meaning by building huge homes for myself and by planting beautiful vineyards. [5]I made gardens and parks, filling them with all kinds of fruit trees. [6]I built reservoirs to collect the water to irrigate my many flourishing groves. [7]I bought slaves, both men and women, and others were born into my household. I also owned great herds and flocks, more than any of the kings who lived in Jerusalem

before me. [8]I collected great sums of silver and gold, the treasure of many kings and provinces. I hired wonderful singers, both men and women, and had many beautiful concubines. I had everything a man could desire!

[9]So I became greater than any of the kings who ruled in Jerusalem before me. And with it all, I remained clear-eyed so that I could evaluate all these things. [10]Anything I wanted, I took. I did not restrain myself from any joy. I even found great pleasure in hard work, an additional reward for all my labors. [11]But as I looked at everything I had worked so hard to accomplish, it was all so meaningless. It was like chasing the wind. There was nothing really worthwhile anywhere.

[12]So I decided to compare wisdom and folly, and anyone else would come to the same conclusions I did. [13]Wisdom is of more value than foolishness, just as light is better than darkness. [14]For the wise person sees, while the fool is blind. Yet I saw that wise and foolish people share the same fate. [15]Both of them die. Just as the fool will die, so will I. So of what value is all my wisdom? Then I said to myself, "This is all so meaningless!" [16]For the wise person and the fool both die, and in the days to come, both will be forgotten.

[17]So now I hate life because everything done here under the sun is so irrational. Everything is meaningless, like chasing the wind. [18]I am disgusted that I must leave the fruits of my hard work to others. [19]And who can tell whether my successors will be wise or foolish? And yet they will control everything I have gained by my skill and hard work. How meaningless!

[20]So I turned in despair from hard work. It was not the answer to my search for satisfaction in this life. [21]For though I do my work with wisdom, knowledge, and skill, I must leave everything I gain to people who haven't worked to earn it. This is not only foolish but highly unfair. [22]So what do people get for all their hard work? [23]Their days of labor are filled with pain and grief; even at night they cannot rest. It is all utterly meaningless.

[24]So I decided there is nothing better than to enjoy food and drink and to find satisfaction in work. Then I realized that this pleasure is from the hand of God. [25]For who can eat or enjoy anything apart from him? [26]God gives wisdom, knowledge, and

joy to those who please him. But if a sinner becomes wealthy, God takes the wealth away and gives it to those who please him. Even this, however, is meaningless, like chasing the wind.

CHAPTER 3
¹ There is a time for everything,
   a season for every activity under
      heaven.
² A time to be born and a time to die.
   A time to plant and a time to harvest.
³ A time to kill and a time to heal.
   A time to tear down and a time
      to rebuild.
⁴ A time to cry and a time to laugh.
   A time to grieve and a time to dance.
⁵ A time to scatter stones and a time
      to gather stones.
   A time to embrace and a time to turn
      away.
⁶ A time to search and a time to lose.
   A time to keep and a time to throw
      away.
⁷ A time to tear and a time to mend.
   A time to be quiet and a time to
      speak up.
⁸ A time to love and a time to hate.
   A time for war and a time for peace.

⁹What do people really get for all their hard work? ¹⁰I have thought about this in connection with the various kinds of work God has given people to do. ¹¹God has made everything beautiful for its own time. He has planted eternity in the human heart, but even so, people cannot see the whole scope of God's work from beginning to end. ¹²So I concluded that there is nothing better for people than to be happy and to enjoy themselves as long as they can. ¹³And people should eat and drink and enjoy the fruits of their labor, for these are gifts from God.

¹⁴And I know that whatever God does is final. Nothing can be added to it or taken from it. God's purpose in this is that people should fear him. ¹⁵Whatever exists today and whatever will exist in the future has already existed in the past. For God calls each event back in its turn.*

¹⁶I also noticed that throughout the world there is evil in the courtroom. Yes, even the courts of law are corrupt! ¹⁷I said to myself, "In due season God will judge everyone, both good and bad, for all their deeds."

¹⁸Then I realized that God allows people to continue in their sinful ways so he can test them. That way, they can see for themselves that they are no better than animals. ¹⁹For humans and animals both breathe the same air,* and both die. So people have no real advantage over the animals. How meaningless! ²⁰Both go to the same place— the dust from which they came and to which they must return. ²¹For who can prove that the human spirit goes upward and the spirit of animals goes downward into the earth? ²²So I saw that there is nothing better for people than to be happy in their work. That is why they are here! No one will bring them back from death to enjoy life in the future.

CHAPTER 4
Again I observed all the oppression that takes place in our world. I saw the tears of the oppressed, with no one to comfort them. The oppressors have great power, and the victims are helpless. ²So I concluded that the dead are better off than the living. ³And most fortunate of all are those who were never born. For they have never seen all the evil that is done in our world.

⁴Then I observed that most people are motivated to success by their envy of their neighbors. But this, too, is meaningless, like chasing the wind.

⁵Foolish people refuse to work and almost starve. ⁶They feel it is better to be lazy and barely survive than to work hard, especially when in the long run everything is so futile.

⁷I observed yet another example of meaninglessness in our world. ⁸This is the case of a man who is all alone, without a child or a brother, yet who works hard to gain as much wealth as he can. But then he asks himself, "Who am I working for? Why am I giving up so much pleasure now?" It is all so meaningless and depressing.

⁹Two people can accomplish more than twice as much as one; they get a better return for their labor. ¹⁰If one person falls, the other can reach out and help. But people who are alone when they fall are in real trouble. ¹¹And on a cold night, two under the same blanket can gain warmth from each other. But how can one be warm

alone? [12]A person standing alone can be attacked and defeated, but two can stand back-to-back and conquer. Three are even better, for a triple-braided cord is not easily broken.

[13]It is better to be a poor but wise youth than to be an old and foolish king who refuses all advice. [14]Such a youth could come from prison and succeed. He might even become king, though he was born in poverty. [15]Everyone is eager to help such a youth, even to help him take the throne. [16]He might become the leader of millions and be very popular. But then the next generation grows up and rejects him! So again, it is all meaningless, like chasing the wind.

CHAPTER 5

As you enter the house of God, keep your ears open and your mouth shut! Don't be a fool who doesn't realize that mindless offerings to God are evil. [2]And don't make rash promises to God, for he is in heaven, and you are only here on earth. So let your words be few.

[3]Just as being too busy gives you nightmares, being a fool makes you a blabbermouth.

[4]So when you make a promise to God, don't delay in following through, for God takes no pleasure in fools. Keep all the promises you make to him. [5]It is better to say nothing than to promise something that you don't follow through on. [6]In such cases, your mouth is making you sin. And don't defend yourself by telling the Temple messenger that the promise you made was a mistake. That would make God angry, and he might wipe out everything you have achieved.

[7]Dreaming all the time instead of working is foolishness. And there is ruin in a flood of empty words. Fear God instead.

[8]If you see a poor person being oppressed by the powerful and justice being miscarried throughout the land, don't be surprised! For every official is under orders from higher up, and matters of justice only get lost in red tape and bureaucracy. [9]Even the king milks the land for his own profit!*

[10]Those who love money will never have enough. How absurd to think that wealth brings true happiness! [11]The more you have, the more people come to help you spend it. So what is the advantage of wealth—except perhaps to watch it run through your fingers!

[12]People who work hard sleep well, whether they eat little or much. But the rich are always worrying and seldom get a good night's sleep.

[13]There is another serious problem I have seen in the world. Riches are sometimes hoarded to the harm of the saver, [14]or they are put into risky investments that turn sour, and everything is lost. In the end, there is nothing left to pass on to one's children. [15]People who live only for wealth come to the end of their lives as naked and empty-handed as on the day they were born.

[16]And this, too, is a very serious problem. As people come into this world, so they depart. All their hard work is for nothing. They have been working for the wind, and everything will be swept away. [17]Throughout their lives, they live under a cloud—frustrated, discouraged, and angry.

[18]Even so, I have noticed one thing, at least, that is good. It is good for people to eat well, drink a good glass of wine, and enjoy their work—whatever they do under the sun—for however long God lets them live. [19]And it is a good thing to receive wealth from God and the good health to enjoy it. To enjoy your work and accept your lot in life—that is indeed a gift from God. [20]People who do this rarely look with sorrow on the past, for God has given them reasons for joy.

CHAPTER 6

There is another serious tragedy I have seen in our world. [2]God gives great wealth and honor to some people and gives them everything they could ever want, but then he doesn't give them the health to enjoy it. They die, and others get it all! This is meaningless—a sickening tragedy.

[3]A man might have a hundred children and live to be very old. But if he finds no satisfaction in life and in the end does not even get a decent burial, I say he would have been better off born dead. [4]I realize that his birth would have been meaningless and ended in darkness. He wouldn't even have had a name, [5]and he would never have seen the sun or known of its existence. Yet he would have had more peace than he has in growing up to be an

unhappy man. ⁶He might live a thousand years twice over but not find contentment. And since he must die like everyone else—well, what's the use?

⁷All people spend their lives scratching for food, but they never seem to have enough. ⁸Considering this, do wise people really have any advantage over fools? Do poor people gain anything by being wise and knowing how to act in front of others?

⁹Enjoy what you have rather than desiring what you don't have. Just dreaming about nice things is meaningless; it is like chasing the wind.

¹⁰Everything has already been decided. It was known long ago what each person would be. So there's no use arguing with God about your destiny.

¹¹The more words you speak, the less they mean. So why overdo it?

¹²In the few days of our empty lives, who knows how our days can best be spent? And who can tell what will happen in the future after we are gone?

JULY 11 ☐ DAY 193
ECCLESIASTES 7–12
Explaining Life's Inconsistencies

OVERVIEW Not only is there futility in what you do and in what you have, but apart from God there is futility in what you are. Good people are treated as if they were wicked (8:14). One sinner can destroy the work of many good men (9:18). Even moral, upright character seems to profit nothing. But once again, God's perspective turns futility into purpose. "But even though a person sins a hundred times and still lives a long time, I know that those who fear God will be better off" (8:12). "Young man, it's wonderful to be young! Enjoy every minute of it. Do everything you want to do; take it all in. But remember that you must give an account to God for everything you do" (11:9).

Chapters 7–10	Chapters 11–12
The Meaninglessness of Being (Wise, Good, Mortal)	The Solution to Life's Meaninglessness: "Fear God and Obey Him"
Life under the Sun	Life above the Sun

A useless life is only an early death.

YOUR DAILY WALK Every blessing from God carries with it a corresponding responsibility.

Are you young (11:9-10)? Then God holds you accountable for the way you use your strength and vitality.

Are you a member of the Geritol generation (12:1-7)? Don't use that as an alibi! God holds you equally accountable for the years of experience you have accumulated.

In the final two verses of Ecclesiastes, the Teacher summarizes his thoughts. Life at any age apart from God is meaningless and futile, regardless of how wise, wealthy, or industrious you are. Things can never fill the void that God desires to fill in your life. Therefore, "fear God and obey his commands" (12:13).

Analyze your life according to what you do, what you have, and what you are. Is God the focus of your activities? Is God more important than your possessions? Is God the center of your being? If not, what changes do you need to make today?

INSIGHT Reflections on Old Age
The Teacher paints a pessimistic picture of old age in Ecclesiastes 12:3. For example, he writes of limbs that "tremble with age," strong legs that "grow weak," teeth that "will be too few to do their work," and eyes that "will be blind." Despite his negative view, old age does have some benefits—like life experience and wisdom.

CHAPTER 7

A good reputation is more valuable than the most expensive perfume. In the same way, the day you die is better than the day you are born.

²It is better to spend your time at funerals than at festivals. For you are going to die, and you should think about it while there is still time.

³Sorrow is better than laughter, for sadness has a refining influence on us.

⁴A wise person thinks much about death, while the fool thinks only about having a good time now.

⁵It is better to be criticized by a wise person than to be praised by a fool! ⁶Indeed, a fool's laughter is quickly gone, like thorns crackling in a fire. This also is meaningless.

⁷Extortion turns wise people into fools, and bribes corrupt the heart.

⁸Finishing is better than starting. Patience is better than pride.

⁹Don't be quick-tempered, for anger is the friend of fools.

¹⁰Don't long for "the good old days," for you don't know whether they were any better than today.

¹¹Being wise is as good as being rich; in fact, it is better. ¹²Wisdom or money can get you almost anything, but it's important to know that only wisdom can save your life.

¹³Notice the way God does things; then fall into line. Don't fight the ways of God, for who can straighten out what he has made crooked?

¹⁴Enjoy prosperity while you can. But when hard times strike, realize that both come from God. That way you will realize that nothing is certain in this life.

¹⁵In this meaningless life, I have seen everything, including the fact that some good people die young and some wicked people live on and on. ¹⁶So don't be too good or too wise! Why destroy yourself? ¹⁷On the other hand, don't be too wicked either—don't be a fool! Why should you die before your time? ¹⁸So try to walk a middle course—but those who fear God will succeed either way.

¹⁹A wise person is stronger than the ten leading citizens of a town!

²⁰There is not a single person in all the earth who is always good and never sins.

²¹Don't eavesdrop on others—you may hear your servant laughing at you. ²²For you know how often you yourself have laughed at others.

²³All along I have tried my best to let wisdom guide my thoughts and actions. I said to myself, "I am determined to be wise." But it didn't really work. ²⁴Wisdom is always distant and very difficult to find. ²⁵I searched everywhere, determined to find wisdom and to understand the reason for things. I was determined to prove to myself that wickedness is stupid and that foolishness is madness.

²⁶I discovered that a seductive woman is more bitter than death. Her passion is a trap, and her soft hands will bind you. Those who please God will escape from her, but sinners will be caught in her snare.

²⁷"This is my conclusion," says the Teacher. "I came to this result after looking into the matter from every possible angle. ²⁸Just one out of every thousand men I interviewed can be said to be upright, but not one woman! ²⁹I discovered that God created people to be upright, but they have each turned to follow their own downward path."

CHAPTER 8

How wonderful to be wise, to be able to analyze and interpret things. Wisdom lights up a person's face, softening its hardness.

²Obey the king because you have vowed before God to do this. ³Don't try to avoid doing your duty, and don't take a stand with those who plot evil. For the king will punish those who disobey him. ⁴The king's command is backed by great power. No one can resist or question it. ⁵Those who obey him will not be punished. Those who are wise will find a time and a way to do what is right. ⁶Yes, there is a time and a way

for everything, even as people's troubles lie heavily upon them.

⁷Indeed, how can people avoid what they don't know is going to happen? ⁸None of us can hold back our spirit from departing. None of us has the power to prevent the day of our death. There is no escaping that obligation, that dark battle. And in the face of death, wickedness will certainly not rescue those who practice it.

⁹I have thought deeply about all that goes on here in the world, where people have the power to hurt each other. ¹⁰I have seen wicked people buried with honor. How strange that they were the very ones who frequented the Temple and are praised* in the very city where they committed their crimes! ¹¹When a crime is not punished, people feel it is safe to do wrong. ¹²But even though a person sins a hundred times and still lives a long time, I know that those who fear God will be better off. ¹³The wicked will never live long, good lives, for they do not fear God. Their days will never grow long like the evening shadows.

¹⁴And this is not all that is meaningless in our world. In this life, good people are often treated as though they were wicked, and wicked people are often treated as though they were good. This is so meaningless!

¹⁵So I recommend having fun, because there is nothing better for people to do in this world than to eat, drink, and enjoy life. That way they will experience some happiness along with all the hard work God gives them.

¹⁶In my search for wisdom, I tried to observe everything that goes on all across the earth. I discovered that there is ceaseless activity, day and night. ¹⁷This reminded me that no one can discover everything God has created in our world, no matter how hard they work at it. Not even the wisest people know everything, even if they say they do.

CHAPTER 9

This, too, I carefully explored: Even though the actions of godly and wise people are in God's hands, no one knows whether or not God will show them favor in this life. ²The same destiny ultimately awaits everyone, whether they are righteous or wicked, good or bad,* ceremonially clean or unclean, religious or irreligious. Good people receive the same treatment as sinners, and people who take oaths are treated like people who don't.

³It seems so tragic that one fate comes to all. That is why people are not more careful to be good. Instead, they choose their own mad course, for they have no hope. There is nothing ahead but death anyway. ⁴There is hope only for the living. For as they say, "It is better to be a live dog than a dead lion!"

⁵The living at least know they will die, but the dead know nothing. They have no further reward, nor are they remembered. ⁶Whatever they did in their lifetime—loving, hating, envying—is all long gone. They no longer have a part in anything here on earth. ⁷So go ahead. Eat your food and drink your wine with a happy heart, for God approves of this! ⁸Wear fine clothes, with a dash of cologne!

⁹Live happily with the woman you love through all the meaningless days of life that God has given you in this world. The wife God gives you is your reward for all your earthly toil. ¹⁰Whatever you do, do well. For when you go to the grave, there will be no work or planning or knowledge or wisdom.

¹¹I have observed something else in this world of ours. The fastest runner doesn't always win the race, and the strongest warrior doesn't always win the battle. The wise are often poor, and the skillful are not necessarily wealthy. And those who are educated don't always lead successful lives. It is all decided by chance, by being at the right place at the right time.

¹²People can never predict when hard times might come. Like fish in a net or birds in a snare, people are often caught by sudden tragedy.

¹³Here is another bit of wisdom that has impressed me as I have watched the way our world works. ¹⁴There was a small town with only a few people living in it, and a great king came with his army and besieged it. ¹⁵There was a poor, wise man living there who knew how to save the town, and so it was rescued. But afterward no one thought any more about him. ¹⁶Then I realized that though wisdom is better than strength, those who are wise will be despised if they are poor. What they

8:10 As in some Hebrew manuscripts and Greek version; many Hebrew manuscripts read *and are forgotten.*   9:2 As in Greek and Syriac versions, and Latin Vulgate; Hebrew lacks *or bad.*

say will not be appreciated for long. ¹⁷But even so, the quiet words of a wise person are better than the shouts of a foolish king. ¹⁸A wise person can overcome weapons of war, but one sinner can destroy much that is good.

CHAPTER 10

Dead flies will cause even a bottle of perfume to stink! Yes, an ounce of foolishness can outweigh a pound of wisdom and honor.

²The hearts of the wise lead them to do right, and the hearts of the foolish lead them to do evil. ³You can identify fools just by the way they walk down the street!

⁴If your boss is angry with you, don't quit! A quiet spirit can overcome even great mistakes.

⁵There is another evil I have seen as I have watched the world go by. Kings and rulers make a grave mistake ⁶if they give foolish people great authority, and if they fail to give people of proven worth their rightful place of dignity. ⁷I have even seen servants riding like princes—and princes walking like servants.

⁸When you dig a well, you may fall in. When you demolish an old wall, you could be bitten by a snake. ⁹When you work in a quarry, stones might fall and crush you! When you chop wood, there is danger with each stroke of your ax! Such are the risks of life.

¹⁰Since a dull ax requires great strength, sharpen the blade. That's the value of wisdom; it helps you succeed.

¹¹It does no good to charm a snake after it has bitten you.

¹²It is pleasant to listen to wise words, but the speech of fools brings them to ruin.

¹³Since fools base their thoughts on foolish premises, their conclusions will be wicked madness.

¹⁴Foolish people claim to know all about the future and tell everyone the details! But who can really know what is going to happen?

¹⁵Fools are so exhausted by a little work that they have no strength for even the simplest tasks.

¹⁶Destruction is certain for the land whose king is a child* and whose leaders feast in the morning. ¹⁷Happy is the land whose king is a nobleman and whose lead-

ers feast only to gain strength for their work, not to get drunk.

¹⁸Laziness lets the roof leak, and soon the rafters begin to rot.

¹⁹A party gives laughter, and wine gives happiness, and money gives everything!

²⁰Never make light of the king, even in your thoughts. And don't make fun of a rich man, either. A little bird may tell them what you have said.

CHAPTER 11

Give generously, for your gifts will return to you later.* ²Divide your gifts among many, for you do not know what risks might lie ahead.

³When the clouds are heavy, the rains come down.

When a tree falls, whether south or north, there it lies.

⁴If you wait for perfect conditions, you will never get anything done.

⁵God's ways are as hard to discern as the pathways of the wind, and as mysterious as a tiny baby being formed in a mother's womb.

⁶Be sure to stay busy and plant a variety of crops, for you never know which will grow—perhaps they all will.

⁷Light is sweet; it's wonderful to see the sun! ⁸When people live to be very old, let them rejoice in every day of life. But let them also remember that the dark days will be many. Everything still to come is meaningless.

⁹Young man, it's wonderful to be young! Enjoy every minute of it. Do everything you want to do; take it all in. But remember that you must give an account to God for everything you do. ¹⁰So banish grief and pain, but remember that youth, with a whole life before it, still faces the threat of meaninglessness.

CHAPTER 12

Don't let the excitement of youth cause you to forget your Creator. Honor him in your youth before you grow old and no longer enjoy living. ²It will be too late then to remember him, when the light of the sun and moon and stars is dim to your old eyes, and there is no silver lining left among the clouds. ³Your limbs will tremble with age, and your strong legs will grow weak. Your teeth will be too few to

---

10:16 Or *whose king is a servant.*   **11:1** Hebrew *Throw your bread on the waters, for after many days you will find it again.*

do their work, and you will be blind, too.
⁴And when your teeth are gone, keep
your lips tightly closed when you eat!
Even the chirping of birds will wake you
up. But you yourself will be deaf and
tuneless, with a quavering voice. ⁵You
will be afraid of heights and of falling,
white-haired and withered, dragging
along without any sexual desire. You will
be standing at death's door. And as you
near your everlasting home, the mourners
will walk along the streets.

⁶Yes, remember your Creator now while
you are young, before the silver cord of
life snaps and the golden bowl is broken.
Don't wait until the water jar is smashed
at the spring and the pulley is broken at
the well. ⁷For then the dust will return to
the earth, and the spirit will return to God
who gave it.

12:12 Hebrew *my son.*

⁸"All is meaningless," says the Teacher,
"utterly meaningless."

⁹Because the Teacher was wise, he taught
the people everything he knew. He collected proverbs and classified them. ¹⁰In-
deed, the Teacher taught the plain truth,
and he did so in an interesting way.

¹¹A wise teacher's words spur students
to action and emphasize important truths.
The collected sayings of the wise are like
guidance from a shepherd.

¹²But, my child,* be warned: There is no
end of opinions ready to be expressed.
Studying them can go on forever and become very exhausting!

¹³Here is my final conclusion: Fear God
and obey his commands, for this is the duty
of every person. ¹⁴God will judge us for
everything we do, including every secret
thing, whether good or bad.

Song of Songs

KING SOLOMON, who wrote over a thousand songs, calls this his "song of songs." Full of oriental imagery, the Song of Songs recounts his marrying a country maiden. While it extols the bliss of married love and the burning devotion of spouses to one another, it also speaks of the heartaches of marriage. Though some interpreters consider it a fictional drama and others view it as a literal event of Solomon's life, all have caught an intimate glimpse of God's fervent love for his people within these lyrics.

Focus	Fostering of Love		Faithfulness of Love	
Divisions	Adoration of Lover	Joined to Lover	Separated from Lover	Devoted to Lover
	1:1　　　　3:5	3:6　　　　5:1	5:2　　　　7:9	7:10　　　　8:14
Topics	Courtship	Consummation	Conflict	Cultivation
	Love Growing	Love Fulfilled	Love Tried	Love Enduring
Place	Israel, in the Country and the Palace			
Time	Perhaps 1 Year			

JULY 12 ☐ DAY 194
SONG OF SONGS 1–8
Extolling Marital Love

OVERVIEW Song of Songs is a love song written by Solomon that abounds in metaphor and oriental imagery. Historically, it depicts the wooing and wedding of a shepherdess by King Solomon and the joys and heartaches of their love for each other. Many have seen in the book a majestic picture of God's love for his people, Israel, and of Christ's love for his bride, the church. As human love finds its highest fulfillment in the love of husband and wife, so spiritual love finds its highest fulfillment in the love of the Creator for his creation.

Chapters 1–3	Chapter 4	Chapters 5–6	Chapters 7–8
Falling in Love	United in Love	Divided in Love	Devoted in Love
Fostering of Love		Faithfulness of Love	

YOUR DAILY WALK True or False: Love means never having to say you're sorry.

Nothing in this lost world bears the imprint of the Son of God so surely as forgiveness.

Modern-day balladeers seem to imply by that statement that apologizing is out of vogue when true love exists. Nothing could be further from the truth. If the young woman had followed that ill-guided advice instead of seeking her lover's forgiveness, she might still be in the locked bedroom!

But on the other side of the coin, Solomon's response to his lover's request for forgiveness is equally noteworthy. It would have been easy for him to take advantage of the apologizing partner and make her suffer through a series of *I told you so*'s. But look at Solomon's response in 6:4-10. He compliments her beauty and dignity, praises her hair and bright smile, and sets her apart as the one and only woman for him. In short, he reassures her of his forgiveness and continuing love.

What a pattern for forgiving and being forgiven in family disputes! Have you wronged your mate . . . or parent . . . or child through something you have said or done? Then take the initiative in asking for forgiveness. Remember, "Love means *wanting* to say you're sorry . . . and in God's strength *doing* it!"

INSIGHT Potent Lessons from a Moving Love Story
Apart from its historical significance, the Song of Songs pictures for the reader the strength of Christ's love (8:7), his delight in hearing and answering prayer (8:13), and the danger of failing to respond immediately to his knocking (5:2-6).

CHAPTER 1
This is Solomon's song of songs, more wonderful than any other.

Young Woman:* ²"Kiss me again and again, for your love is sweeter than wine. ³How fragrant your cologne, and how pleasing your name! No wonder all the young women love you! ⁴Take me with

you. Come, let's run! Bring me into your bedroom, O my king.*"
Young Women of Jerusalem: "How happy we are for him! We praise his love even more than wine."
Young Woman: "How right that the young women love you!
⁵"I am dark and beautiful, O women of Jerusalem, tanned as the dark tents

1:1 The headings identifying the speakers are not in the original text, though the Hebrew usually gives clues by means of the gender of the person speaking.   1:4 Or *The king has brought me into his bedroom.*

of Kedar. Yes, even as the tents of Solomon!

6"Don't look down on me, you fair city girls, just because my complexion is so dark. The sun has burned my skin. My brothers were angry with me and sent me out to tend the vineyards in the hot sun. Now see what it has done to me!*

7"Tell me, O my love, where are you leading your flock today? Where will you rest your sheep at noon? For why should I wander like a prostitute* among the flocks of your companions?"

Young Man: 8"If you don't know, O most beautiful woman, follow the trail of my flock to the shepherds' tents, and there feed your young goats. 9What a lovely filly you are, my beloved one!* 10How lovely are your cheeks, with your earrings setting them afire! How stately is your neck, accented with a long string of jewels. 11We will make earrings of gold for you and beads of silver."

Young Woman: 12"The king is lying on his couch, enchanted by the fragrance of my perfume. 13My lover is like a sachet of myrrh lying between my breasts. 14He is like a bouquet of flowers in the gardens of En-gedi."

Young Man: 15"How beautiful you are, my beloved, how beautiful! Your eyes are soft like doves."

Young Woman: 16"What a lovely, pleasant sight you are, my love, as we lie here on the grass, 17shaded by cedar trees and spreading firs."

CHAPTER 2

Young Woman: "I am the rose of Sharon, the lily of the valley."

Young Man: 2"Yes, compared to other women, my beloved is like a lily among thorns."

Young Woman: 3"And compared to other youths, my lover is like the finest apple tree in the orchard. I am seated in his delightful shade, and his fruit is delicious to eat. 4He brings me to the banquet hall, so everyone can see how much he loves me. 5Oh, feed me with your love—your 'raisins' and your 'apples'—for I am utterly lovesick!

6His left hand is under my head, and his right hand embraces me.

7"Promise me, O women of Jerusalem, by the swift gazelles and the deer of the wild, not to awaken love until the time is right.*

8"Ah, I hear him—my lover! Here he comes, leaping on the mountains and bounding over the hills. 9My lover is like a swift gazelle or a young deer. Look, there he is behind the wall! Now he is looking in through the window, gazing into the room.

10"My lover said to me, 'Rise up, my beloved, my fair one, and come away. 11For the winter is past, and the rain is over and gone. 12The flowers are springing up, and the time of singing birds has come, even the cooing of turtledoves. 13The fig trees are budding, and the grapevines are in blossom. How delicious they smell! Yes, spring is here! Arise, my beloved, my fair one, and come away.'"

Young Man: 14"My dove is hiding behind some rocks, behind an outcrop on the cliff. Let me see you; let me hear your voice. For your voice is pleasant, and you are lovely."

Young Women of Jerusalem: 15"Quick! Catch all the little foxes before they ruin the vineyard of your love, for the grapevines are all in blossom."

Young Woman: 16"My lover is mine, and I am his. He feeds among the lilies! 17Before the dawn comes and the shadows flee away, come back to me, my love. Run like a gazelle or a young stag on the rugged mountains.*"

CHAPTER 3

Young Woman: "One night as I lay in bed, I yearned deeply for my lover, but he did not come. 2So I said to myself, 'I will get up now and roam the city, searching for him in all its streets and squares.' But my search was in vain. 3The watchmen stopped me as they made their rounds, and I said to them, 'Have you seen him anywhere, this one I love so much?' 4A little while later I found him and held him. I didn't let him go until I had brought him to my childhood

1:6 Hebrew *My own vineyard I have neglected.*   1:7 Hebrew *like a veiled woman.*   1:9 Hebrew *I compare you, my beloved, to a mare among Pharaoh's chariots.*   2:7 Or *not to awaken love until it is ready.*   2:17 Or *on the hills of Bether.*

home, into my mother's bedroom, where I had been conceived.

5"Promise me, O women of Jerusalem, by the swift gazelles and the deer of the wild, not to awaken love until the time is right.*"

Young Women of Jerusalem: 6"Who is this sweeping in from the deserts like a cloud of smoke along the ground? Who is it that smells of myrrh and frankincense and every other spice? 7Look, it is Solomon's carriage, with sixty of Israel's mightiest men surrounding it. 8They are all skilled swordsmen and experienced warriors. Each one wears a sword on his thigh, ready to defend the king against an attack during the night.

9"King Solomon has built a carriage for himself from wood imported from Lebanon's forests. 10Its posts are of silver, its canopy is gold, and its seat is upholstered in purple cloth. Its interior was a gift of love from the young women of Jerusalem."

Young Woman: 11"Go out to look upon King Solomon, O young women of Jerusalem.* See the crown with which his mother crowned him on his wedding day, the day of his gladness."

CHAPTER 4

Young Man: "How beautiful you are, my beloved, how beautiful! Your eyes behind your veil are like doves. Your hair falls in waves, like a flock of goats frisking down the slopes of Gilead. 2Your teeth are as white as sheep, newly shorn and washed. They are perfectly matched; not one is missing. 3Your lips are like a ribbon of scarlet. Oh, how beautiful your mouth! Your cheeks behind your veil are like pomegranate halves—lovely and delicious. 4Your neck is as stately as the tower of David, jeweled with the shields of a thousand heroes. 5Your breasts are like twin fawns of a gazelle, feeding among the lilies. 6Before the dawn comes and the shadows flee away, I will go to the mountain of myrrh and to the hill of frankincense. 7You are so beautiful, my beloved, so perfect in every part.

8"Come with me from Lebanon, my bride. Come down* from the top of Mount Amana, from Mount Senir and Mount Hermon, where lions have their dens and panthers prowl. 9You have ravished my heart, my treasure, my bride. I am overcome by one glance of your eyes, by a single bead of your necklace. 10How sweet is your love, my treasure, my bride! How much better it is than wine! Your perfume is more fragrant than the richest of spices. 11Your lips, my bride, are as sweet as honey. Yes, honey and cream are under your tongue. The scent of your clothing is like that of the mountains and the cedars of Lebanon.

12"You are like a private garden, my treasure, my bride! You are like a spring that no one else can drink from, a fountain of my own. 13You are like a lovely orchard bearing precious fruit, with the rarest of perfumes: 14nard and saffron, calamus and cinnamon, myrrh and aloes, perfume from every incense tree, and every other lovely spice. 15You are a garden fountain, a well of living water, as refreshing as the streams from the Lebanon mountains."

Young Woman: 16"Awake, north wind! Come, south wind! Blow on my garden and waft its lovely perfume to my lover. Let him come into his garden and eat its choicest fruits."

CHAPTER 5

Young Man: "I am here in my garden, my treasure, my bride! I gather my myrrh with my spices and eat my honeycomb with my honey. I drink my wine with my milk."

Young Women of Jerusalem: "Oh, lover and beloved, eat and drink! Yes, drink deeply of this love!"

Young Woman: 2"One night as I was sleeping, my heart awakened in a dream. I heard the voice of my lover. He was knocking at my bedroom door. 'Open to me, my darling, my treasure, my lovely dove,' he said, 'for I have been out in the night. My head is soaked with dew, my hair with the wetness of the night.'

3"But I said, 'I have taken off my robe. Should I get dressed again? I have washed my feet. Should I get them soiled?'

3:5 Or *not to awaken love until it is ready.*   3:11 Hebrew *Zion.*   4:8 Or *Look down.*

⁴"My lover tried to unlatch the door, and my heart thrilled within me. ⁵I jumped up to open it. My hands dripped with perfume, my fingers with lovely myrrh, as I pulled back the bolt. ⁶I opened to my lover, but he was gone. I yearned for even his voice! I searched for him, but I couldn't find him anywhere. I called to him, but there was no reply. ⁷The watchmen found me as they were making their rounds; they struck and wounded me. The watchman on the wall tore off my veil.

⁸"Make this promise to me, O women of Jerusalem! If you find my beloved one, tell him that I am sick with love."

Young Women of Jerusalem: ⁹"O woman of rare beauty, what is it about your loved one that brings you to tell us this?"

Young Woman: ¹⁰"My lover is dark and dazzling, better than ten thousand others! ¹¹His head is the finest gold, and his hair is wavy and black. ¹²His eyes are like doves beside brooks of water; they are set like jewels. ¹³His cheeks are like sweetly scented beds of spices. His lips are like perfumed lilies. His breath is like myrrh. ¹⁴His arms are like round bars of gold, set with chrysolite. His body is like bright ivory, aglow with sapphires. ¹⁵His legs are like pillars of marble set in sockets of the finest gold, strong as the cedars of Lebanon. None can rival him. ¹⁶His mouth is altogether sweet; he is lovely in every way. Such, O women of Jerusalem, is my lover, my friend."

CHAPTER 6

Young Women of Jerusalem: "O rarest of beautiful women, where has your lover gone? We will help you find him."

Young Woman: ²"He has gone down to his garden, to his spice beds, to graze and to gather the lilies. ³I am my lover's, and my lover is mine. He grazes among the lilies!"

Young Man: ⁴"O my beloved, you are as beautiful as the lovely town of Tirzah. Yes, as beautiful as Jerusalem! You are as majestic as an army with banners! ⁵Look away, for your eyes overcome me! Your hair falls in waves, like a flock of goats frisking down the slopes of Gilead. ⁶Your teeth are as white as newly washed sheep. They are perfectly matched; not one is missing. ⁷Your cheeks behind your veil are like pomegranate halves—lovely and delicious. ⁸There may be sixty wives, all queens, and eighty concubines and unnumbered virgins available to me. ⁹But I would still choose my dove, my perfect one, the only beloved daughter of her mother! The young women are delighted when they see her; even queens and concubines sing her praises! ¹⁰'Who is this,' they ask, 'arising like the dawn, as fair as the moon, as bright as the sun, as majestic as an army with banners?'

¹¹"I went down into the grove of nut trees and out to the valley to see the new growth brought on by spring. I wanted to see whether the grapevines were budding yet, or whether the pomegranates were blossoming. ¹²Before I realized it, I found myself in my princely bed with my beloved one.*"

Young Women of Jerusalem: ¹³"Return, return to us, O maid of Shulam. Come back, come back, that we may see you once again."

Young Man: "Why do you gaze so intently at this young woman of Shulam, as she moves so gracefully between two lines of dancers?*"

CHAPTER 7

Young Man: "How beautiful are your sandaled feet, O queenly maiden. Your rounded thighs are like jewels, the work of a skilled craftsman. ²Your navel is as delicious as a goblet filled with wine. Your belly is lovely, like a heap of wheat set about with lilies. ³Your breasts are like twin fawns of a gazelle. ⁴Your neck is as stately as an ivory tower. Your eyes are like the sparkling pools in Heshbon by the gate of Bath-rabbim. Your nose is as fine as the tower of Lebanon overlooking Damascus. ⁵Your head is as majestic as Mount Carmel, and the sheen of your hair radiates royalty. A king is held captive in your queenly tresses.

⁶"Oh, how delightful you are, my

6:12 Or *among the royal chariots of my people,* or *among the chariots of Amminadab.* The meaning of the Hebrew is uncertain.   **6:13** Or *as you would at the movements of two armies?* or *as you would at the dance of Mahanaim?* The meaning of the Hebrew is uncertain.

beloved; how pleasant for utter delight! [7]You are tall and slim like a palm tree, and your breasts are like its clusters of dates. [8]I said, 'I will climb up into the palm tree and take hold of its branches.' Now may your breasts be like grape clusters, and the scent of your breath like apples. [9]May your kisses be as exciting as the best wine, smooth and sweet, flowing gently over lips and teeth.*"

Young Woman: [10]"I am my lover's, the one he desires. [11]Come, my love, let us go out into the fields and spend the night among the wildflowers.* [12]Let us get up early and go out to the vineyards. Let us see whether the vines have budded, whether the blossoms have opened, and whether the pomegranates are in flower. And there I will give you my love. [13]There the mandrakes give forth their fragrance, and the rarest fruits are at our doors, the new as well as old, for I have stored them up for you, my lover."

CHAPTER 8

Young Woman: "Oh, if only you were my brother, who nursed at my mother's breast. Then I could kiss you no matter who was watching, and no one would criticize me. [2]I would bring you to my childhood home, and there you would teach me. I would give you spiced wine to drink, my sweet pomegranate wine. [3]Your left hand would be under my head and your right hand would embrace me.

[4]"I want you to promise, O women of Jerusalem, not to awaken love until the time is right.*"

Young Women of Jerusalem: [5]"Who is this coming up from the desert, leaning on her lover?"

Young Woman: "I aroused you under the apple tree, where your mother gave you birth, where in great pain she delivered you. [6]Place me like a seal over your heart, or like a seal on your arm. For love is as strong as death, and its jealousy is as enduring as the grave. Love flashes like fire, the brightest kind of flame. [7]Many waters cannot quench love; neither can rivers drown it. If a man tried to buy love with everything he owned, his offer would be utterly despised."

The Young Woman's Brothers: [8]"We have a little sister too young for breasts. What will we do if someone asks to marry her? [9]If she is chaste, we will strengthen and encourage her. But if she is promiscuous, we will shut her off from men.*"

Young Woman: [10]"I am chaste, and I am now full breasted. And my lover is content with me.

[11]"Solomon has a vineyard at Baal-hamon, which he rents to some farmers there. Each of them pays one thousand pieces of silver* for its use. [12]But as for my own vineyard, O Solomon, you can take my thousand pieces of silver. And I will give two hundred pieces of silver* to those who care for its vines."

Young Man: [13]"O my beloved, lingering in the gardens, how wonderful that your companions can listen to your voice. Let me hear it, too!"

Young Woman: [14]"Come quickly, my love! Move like a swift gazelle or a young deer on the mountains of spices."

7:9 As in Greek and Syriac versions and Latin Vulgate; Hebrew reads *over lips of sleepers.*   **7:11** Or *in the villages.*   **8:4** Or *not to awaken love until it is ready.*   **8:9** Hebrew *If she is a wall, we will build battlements of silver on her; but if she is a door, we will surround her with panels of cedar.*   **8:11** Hebrew *1,000 shekels of silver,* about 25 pounds or 11.4 kilograms in weight; also in 8:12.   **8:12** Hebrew *200 [shekels],* about 5 pounds or 2.3 kilograms in weight.

Isaiah

THE BOOK of Isaiah, the mother lode of Hebrew prophecy, sets forth a lifetime of preaching by the statesman and prophet for whom it is named. In the first thirty-nine chapters, the prophet stresses righteousness, holiness, and the justice of God, announcing God's terrible judgment upon a world stained crimson with sin (1:18). But the last twenty-seven chapters portray God's glory and compassion and the undeserved favor he bestows. The Messiah will come as a Savior to bear a cross and as a Sovereign to wear a crown.

Focus	Condemnation			Interlude	Consolation		
Divisions	Judgment Is Coming upon . . . Judah (1–12)	the Nations (13–27)	the World (28–35)	Judah's Day of Judgment	God's Sovereignty	God's Salvation	God's Restoration
	1		35	36 39	40 48	49 57	58 66
Topics	Horror			History	Hope		
	Groaning under God's Judgment (1:4)				Glorying in God's Salvation (40:1-2)		
Place	Judah and Her Neighbors				Israel and the World		
Time	About 40 Years (722–681 B.C.)				Thousands of Years		

JULY 13 ☐ DAY 195
ISAIAH 1–4
Judah's Shallow Religion

 OVERVIEW *The date:* About 740 B.C. *The setting:* Judah, the southern kingdom. Judah faces extinction at the hands of the cruel Assyrians. In this crucial hour of national emergency, God sends Isaiah—a unique man with an unpleasant message. The nation of Judah is rotten to the core and ripe for judgment. Her habitual sins of idolatry, hypocrisy, injustice, and corruption have not escaped the notice of her holy God. His righteous wrath will soon fall upon king and commoner alike, that all might learn that the Lord Almighty cannot and will not be mocked.

Chapter 1	Chapter 2	Chapter 3	Chapter 4
A Nation Denounced	A House Cleansed	A People Humbled	A Prince Announced
Iniquity		Indignation	"In That Day"

 YOUR DAILY WALK The truth hurts.

No one minds looking into a mirror, provided the image reflected back is flattering to the viewer. But allow that mirror to reflect a painful truth about a person's appearance, and you just might end up with a broken mirror—and some hurt feelings!

People used to argue as to whether the world was square or round— but the Bible says it is crooked!

Isaiah held up the mirror of God's Word before the people of Judah to show how stained with sin the nation had become. And when he did, neither the prophet nor the people liked what they saw! Yet in spite of the bleak reflection, there was hope if only the people would respond to God's invitation.

Find a piece of white cotton material (a cotton ball will do nicely), and stain it with a few drops of red food coloring. Now try to wash it as clean and white as it was originally.

Give up? Isaiah 1:18 will show you how to enjoy cleansing from even the most stubborn stain of sin. Have you been washed as "clean as freshly fallen snow" by the blood of Christ?

 INSIGHT Pattern of a Prophet's Pronouncements

When broadly outlined, many of Isaiah's messages are strikingly similar: (1) accusation, (2) threat of judgment, (3) exhortation to repentance, and (4) promise of blessing. See if you can apply this general outline to Isaiah's first message in chapter 1. (Hint: Divide the chapter at verses 10, 16, and 21.)

CHAPTER 1

These visions concerning Judah and Jerusalem came to Isaiah son of Amoz during the reigns of Uzziah, Jotham, Ahaz, and Hezekiah—all kings of Judah.

²Hear, O heavens! Listen, O earth! This is what the LORD says: "The children I raised and cared for have turned against me.

³Even the animals—the donkey and the ox—know their owner and appreciate his care, but not my people Israel. No matter what I do for them, they still do not understand."

⁴Oh, what a sinful nation they are! They are loaded down with a burden of guilt. They are evil and corrupt children who

have turned away from the LORD. They have despised the Holy One of Israel, cutting themselves off from his help.

⁵Why do you continue to invite punishment? Must you rebel forever? Your head is injured, and your heart is sick. ⁶You are sick from head to foot—covered with bruises, welts, and infected wounds—without any ointments or bandages. ⁷Your country lies in ruins, and your cities are burned. As you watch, foreigners plunder your fields and destroy everything they see. ⁸Jerusalem* stands abandoned like a watchman's shelter in a vineyard or field after the harvest is over. It is as helpless as a city under siege. ⁹If the LORD Almighty had not spared a few of us, we would have been wiped out as completely as Sodom and Gomorrah.

¹⁰Listen to the LORD, you leaders of Israel! Listen to the law of our God, people of Israel. You act just like the rulers and people of Sodom and Gomorrah. ¹¹"I am sick of your sacrifices," says the LORD. "Don't bring me any more burnt offerings! I don't want the fat from your rams or other animals. I don't want to see the blood from your offerings of bulls and rams and goats. ¹²Why do you keep parading through my courts with your worthless sacrifices? ¹³The incense you bring me is a stench in my nostrils! Your celebrations of the new moon and the Sabbath day, and your special days for fasting—even your most pious meetings—are all sinful and false. I want nothing more to do with them. ¹⁴I hate all your festivals and sacrifices. I cannot stand the sight of them! ¹⁵From now on, when you lift up your hands in prayer, I will refuse to look. Even though you offer many prayers, I will not listen. For your hands are covered with the blood of your innocent victims. ¹⁶Wash yourselves and be clean! Let me no longer see your evil deeds. Give up your wicked ways. ¹⁷Learn to do good. Seek justice. Help the oppressed. Defend the orphan. Fight for the rights of widows.

¹⁸"Come now, let us argue this out," says the LORD. "No matter how deep the stain of your sins, I can remove it. I can make you as clean as freshly fallen snow. Even if you are stained as red as crimson, I can make you as white as wool. ¹⁹If you will only obey me and let me help you, then you will have plenty to eat. ²⁰But if you keep turning away and refusing to listen, you will be destroyed by your enemies. I, the LORD, have spoken!"

²¹See how Jerusalem, once so faithful, has become a prostitute. Once the home of justice and righteousness, she is now filled with murderers. ²²Once like pure silver, you have become like worthless slag. Once so pure, you are now like watered-down wine. ²³Your leaders are rebels, the companions of thieves. All of them take bribes and refuse to defend the orphans and the widows.

²⁴Therefore, the Lord, the LORD Almighty, the Mighty One of Israel, says, "I will pour out my fury on you, my enemies! ²⁵I will turn against you. I will melt you down and skim off your slag. I will remove all your impurities. ²⁶Afterward I will give you good judges and wise counselors like the ones you used to have. Then Jerusalem will again be called the Home of Justice and the Faithful City."

²⁷Because the LORD is just and righteous, the repentant people of Jerusalem* will be redeemed. ²⁸But all sinners will be completely destroyed, for they refuse to come to the LORD.

²⁹Shame will cover you when you think of the times you offered sacrifices to idols in your groves of sacred oaks. You will blush when you think of all the sins you committed in your sacred gardens. ³⁰You will wither away like an oak or garden without water. ³¹The strongest among you will disappear like burning straw. Your evil deeds are the spark that will set the straw on fire, and no one will be able to put it out.

CHAPTER 2

This is another vision that Isaiah son of Amoz saw concerning Judah and Jerusalem:

²In the last days, the Temple of the LORD in Jerusalem will become the most important place on earth. People from all over the world will go there to worship. ³Many nations will come and say, "Come, let us go up to the mountain of the LORD, to the Temple of the God of Israel.* There he will teach us his ways, so that we may obey him." For in those days the LORD's teaching and his word will go out from Jerusalem.

⁴The LORD will settle international disputes. All the nations will beat their swords

1:8 Hebrew *The daughter of Zion.*   1:27 Hebrew *Zion.*   2:3 Hebrew *of Jacob;* also in 2:5, 6.

into plowshares and their spears into pruning hooks. All wars will stop, and military training will come to an end. ⁵Come, people of Israel, let us walk in the light of the LORD!

⁶The LORD has rejected the people of Israel because they have made alliances with foreigners from the East who practice magic and divination, just like the Philistines. ⁷Israel has vast treasures of silver and gold and many horses and chariots. ⁸The land is filled with idols. The people bow down and worship these things they have made. ⁹So now everyone will be humbled and brought low. The LORD cannot simply ignore their sins!

¹⁰Crawl into caves in the rocks. Hide from the terror of the LORD and the glory of his majesty. ¹¹The day is coming when your pride will be brought low and the LORD alone will be exalted. ¹²In that day the LORD Almighty will punish the proud, bringing them down to the dust. ¹³He will cut down the tall cedars of Lebanon and the mighty oaks of Bashan. ¹⁴He will level the high mountains and hills. ¹⁵He will break down every high tower and wall. ¹⁶He will destroy the great trading ships* and all the small boats in the harbor. ¹⁷The arrogance of all people will be brought low. Their pride will lie in the dust. The LORD alone will be exalted! ¹⁸Idols will be utterly abolished and destroyed.

¹⁹When the LORD rises to shake the earth, his enemies will crawl with fear into holes in the ground. They will hide in caves in the rocks from the terror of the LORD and the glory of his majesty. ²⁰They will abandon their gold and silver idols to the moles and bats. ²¹They will crawl into caverns and hide among the jagged rocks at the tops of cliffs. In this way, they will try to escape the terror of the LORD and the glory of his majesty as he rises to shake the earth.

²²Stop putting your trust in mere humans. They are as frail as breath. How can they be of help to anyone?

CHAPTER 3
The Lord, the LORD Almighty, will cut off the supplies of food and water from Jerusalem and Judah. ²He will destroy all the nation's leaders—the heroes, soldiers, judges, prophets, diviners, elders, ³army officers, honorable citizens, advisers, skilled magicians,

and expert enchanters. ⁴Then he will appoint children to rule over them, and anarchy will prevail. ⁵People will take advantage of each other—man against man, neighbor fighting neighbor. Young people will revolt against authority, and nobodies will sneer at honorable people.

⁶In those days a man will say to his brother, "Since you have a cloak, you be our leader! Take charge of this heap of ruins!"

⁷"No!" he will reply. "I can't help. I don't have any extra food or clothes. Don't ask me to get involved!"

⁸Judah and Jerusalem will lie in ruins because they speak out against the LORD and refuse to obey him. They have offended his glorious presence among them. ⁹The very look on their faces gives them away and displays their guilt. They sin openly like the people of Sodom. They are not one bit ashamed. How terrible it will be for them! They have brought about their own destruction.

¹⁰But all will be well for those who are godly. Tell them, "You will receive a wonderful reward!" ¹¹But say to the wicked, "Your destruction is sure. You, too, will get what you deserve. Your well-earned punishment is on the way."

¹²Children oppress my people, and women rule over them. O my people, can't you see what fools your rulers are? They are leading you down a pretty garden path to destruction.

¹³The LORD takes his place in court. He is the great prosecuting attorney, presenting his case against his people! ¹⁴The leaders and the princes will be the first to feel the LORD's judgment. "You have ruined Israel, which is my vineyard. You have taken advantage of the poor, filling your barns with grain extorted from helpless people. ¹⁵How dare you grind my people into the dust like that!" demands the Lord, the LORD Almighty.

¹⁶Next the LORD will judge the women of Jerusalem,* who walk around with their noses in the air, with tinkling ornaments on their ankles. Their eyes rove among the crowds, flirting with the men. ¹⁷The Lord will send a plague of scabs to ornament their heads. Yes, the LORD will make them bald for all to see!

¹⁸The Lord will strip away their artful beauty—their ornaments, headbands, and crescent necklaces; ¹⁹their earrings,

2:16 Hebrew *every ship of Tarshish*.   3:16 Hebrew *the daughters of Zion.*

bracelets, and veils of shimmering gauze. [20]Gone will be their scarves, ankle chains, sashes, perfumes, and charms; [21]their rings, jewels, [22]party clothes, gowns, capes, and purses; [23]their mirrors, linen garments, head ornaments, and shawls. [24]Instead of smelling of sweet perfume, they will stink. They will wear ropes for sashes, and their well-set hair will fall out. They will wear rough sackcloth instead of rich robes. Their beauty will be gone. Only shame will be left to them.

[25]The men of the city will die in battle. [26]The gates of Jerusalem* will weep and mourn. The city will be like a ravaged woman, huddled on the ground.

CHAPTER 4

In that day few men will be left alive. Seven women will fight over each of them and say, "Let us all marry you! We will provide our own food and clothing. Only let us be called by your name so we won't be mocked as old maids."

[2]But in the future, Israel—the branch of the LORD—will be lush and beautiful, and the fruit of the land will be the pride of its people. [3]All those whose names are written down, who have survived the destruction of Jerusalem, will be a holy people. [4]The Lord will wash the moral filth from the women of Jerusalem.* He will cleanse Jerusalem of its bloodstains by a spirit of judgment that burns like fire. [5]Then the LORD will provide shade for Jerusalem* and all who assemble there. There will be a canopy of smoke and cloud throughout the day and clouds of fire at night, covering the glorious land. [6]It will be a shelter from daytime heat and a hiding place from storms and rain.

3:26 Hebrew *Zion.*   **4:4** Hebrew *from the daughters of Zion.*   **4:5** Hebrew *Mount Zion.*

JULY 14 ☐ DAY 196
Search for Significance

LOOK BACK Proverbs, Ecclesiastes, Song of Songs—three books historically attributed to King Solomon, the wisest man who ever lived. But notice how these books parallel the downward spiral of his life: Song of Songs (when Solomon early in life was full of youthful passion and fervor); Proverbs (when Solomon in his midlife had learned much about the importance of choices, good and bad); and finally, Ecclesiastes (when Solomon in later life had discovered the bitterness of empty pursuits, and the high price of chasing the wind and reaping the whirlwind).

By contrast, Isaiah sets his compass on the commission he receives from the Lord and follows it with the determination of a laser beam. For more than fifty years, spanning the administrations of four kings of Judah, Isaiah stays true to his calling—delivering a ringing indictment upon God's disobedient people.

LOOK UP One of Satan's most effective tools to distract, disable, and ultimately destroy God's people is the phrase "If only . . ."

"If only I could get a high school or college degree, then I'd be on my way."

Most people don't know what they want, but it is something different from what they have.

"If only I could find a good job, then I'd have status and worth."

"If only I could get married and have a family, then I'd be truly happy."

"If only I could win the lottery, then I'd be set for life."

"If only I could write a best-selling book, then I'd be someone important."

"If only [you complete the sentence now!]."

Take it from Solomon, the wisest . . . richest . . . most accomplished . . . most published . . . most married . . . most you-name-it individual in the Bible. If you are looking for significance and satisfaction in the pursuits of life, you are in for a rude disappointment. Purpose and meaning can never be found there; they are found only in the Giver of life himself. That's why at the end of his twelve-chapter odyssey, Solomon concludes with these words: "Fear God and obey his commands, for this is the duty of every person" (Ecclesiastes 12:13). The hymn writer put it this way:

"Trust and obey, for there's no other way,
To be happy in Jesus, but to trust and obey."

LOOK AHEAD
Take a few moments to thoughtfully complete this "Significance Survey." It just might change the way you look at your "net worth" and accomplishments.

1. I have $_____ in the bank right now, but my real riches are what I have because I am in Christ (Ephesians 1:3).

2. I have earned a _____ degree, but I realize that all I can boast about is my relationship with God (Jeremiah 9:23-24).

3. I am respected in my community because of _____, but whatever has been to my profit I consider loss for the sake of Christ (Philippians 3:7).

4. I have written _____ books and articles, but in the final analysis, all that matters is what I have done with the Book, God's Word.

Society today is marked by an obsession with significance. It's a pursuit as old as the days of Solomon—and just as fruitless unless God is the center and circumference of the search. Let your search end with him, and you will never be disappointed.

JULY 15 □ DAY 197
ISAIAH 5–8
Judah's Untamed Wickedness

OVERVIEW No sooner does Isaiah complete his scathing indictment upon Judah than he turns to share a comforting word of encouragement. God's displeasure with the unrighteous harvest of the vineyard he has planted (Israel and Judah) causes him to commission his prophet (Isaiah) to deliver a declaration of doom. But after the prophet's message of heartache comes a balm of hope. The Messiah will be born of a virgin, hostilities will cease, and Judah's enemies will be brought low. Isaiah's response in the face of such unusual announcements? "I will wait for the LORD. . . . My only hope is in him" (8:17).

Chapter 5	Chapter 6	Chapter 7	Chapter 8
Wild Grapes	Woeful Prophet	Prediction of an Infant	Prediction of an Invasion
Israel	Isaiah	Immanuel	Assyria

YOUR DAILY WALK You cannot impart what you do not possess. In Isaiah's case, before he could be used by God to call the people back to holy living, he himself had to be cleansed and prepared for holy service.

It was important for Isaiah to have an indelible vision of the Lord in all his holiness, for Isaiah's mission would be to preach to a people of

Seeing God for who he is will open your eyes to who you are. unclean lips and hardened hearts. Before he could confront kings and princes, he needed a firsthand glimpse of the King of the universe sitting on his "lofty throne" (6:1, 5). Only then was Isaiah ready to exchange his sinful inadequacy ("Woe is me", NKJV) for God's holy adequacy ("Go, and tell", NKJV).

Cleansing . . . calling . . . commitment. That pattern is still valid today. God is looking for men and women who will respond to his holiness by volunteering for holy service.

"Woe . . . Go . . ." Put those two words in your pocket—and on your heart—for they are the key to fulfilling your God-given calling today and every day.

INSIGHT The Six-Decade Servant of God
According to 6:1, Isaiah's long ministry began in the year of King Uzziah's death (about 740 B.C.). It would, according to 1:1, continue through the reigns of Jotham (739–731), Ahaz (731–715), and Hezekiah (715–685)—a period of nearly sixty years!

CHAPTER 5

Now I will sing a song for the one I love about his vineyard:

My beloved has a vineyard
  on a rich and fertile hill.
2 He plowed the land, cleared its stones,
  and planted it with choice vines.
In the middle he built a watchtower
  and carved a winepress in the nearby
    rocks.
Then he waited for a harvest of sweet
    grapes,
  but the grapes that grew were wild
    and sour.
3 "Now, you people of Jerusalem and
    Judah,
  you have heard the case; you be the
    judges.
4 What more could I have done
  to cultivate a rich harvest?
Why did my vineyard give me wild
    grapes
  when I expected sweet ones?
5 Now this is what I am going to do to
    my vineyard:
I will tear down its fences
  and let it be destroyed.
I will break down its walls
  and let the animals trample it.
6 I will make it a wild place.
  I will not prune the vines or hoe the
    ground.
  I will let it be overgrown with briers
    and thorns.
  I will command the clouds
    to drop no more rain on it."

7 This is the story of the LORD's people.
  They are the vineyard of the LORD
    Almighty.
  Israel and Judah are his pleasant
    garden.
  He expected them to yield a crop of
    justice,
    but instead he found bloodshed.
  He expected to find righteousness,
    but instead he heard cries of
      oppression.

8 Destruction is certain for you who buy up property so others have no place to live. Your homes are built on great estates so you can be alone in the land. 9 But the LORD Almighty has sealed your awful fate. With my own ears I heard him say, "Many beautiful homes will stand deserted, the owners dead or gone. 10 Ten acres* of vineyard will not produce even six gallons* of wine. Ten measures of seed will yield only one measure* of grain."

11 Destruction is certain for you who get up early to begin long drinking bouts that last late into the night. 12 You furnish lovely music and wine at your grand parties; the harps, lyres, tambourines, and flutes are superb! But you never think about the LORD or notice what he is doing. 13 So I will send my people into exile far away because they do not know me. The great and honored among them will starve, and the common people will die of thirst.

14 The grave* is licking its chops in anticipation of Jerusalem, this delicious morsel. Her great and lowly will be swallowed up, with all her drunken crowds. 15 In that day

5:10a Hebrew *A ten yoke,* that is, the area of land plowed by ten teams of oxen in one day.   5:10b Hebrew *a bath* [21 liters].
5:10c Hebrew *A homer* [5 bushels or 182 liters] *of seed will yield only an ephah* [0.5 bushels or 18.2 liters].   5:14 Hebrew *Sheol.*

the arrogant will be brought down to the dust; the proud will be humbled. [16]But the LORD Almighty is exalted by his justice. The holiness of God is displayed by his righteousness. [17]In those days flocks will feed among the ruins; lambs and kids* will pasture there.

[18]Destruction is certain for those who drag their sins behind them, tied with cords of falsehood. [19]They even mock the Holy One of Israel and say, "Hurry up and do something! Quick, show us what you can do. We want to see what you have planned."

[20]Destruction is certain for those who say that evil is good and good is evil; that dark is light and light is dark; that bitter is sweet and sweet is bitter.

[21]Destruction is certain for those who think they are wise and consider themselves to be clever.

[22]Destruction is certain for those who are heroes when it comes to drinking, who boast about all the liquor they can hold. [23]They take bribes to pervert justice. They let the wicked go free while punishing the innocent.

[24]Therefore, they will all disappear like burning straw. Their roots will rot and their flowers wither, for they have rejected the law of the LORD Almighty. They have despised the word of the Holy One of Israel. [25]That is why the anger of the LORD burns against his people. That is why he has raised his fist to crush them. The hills tremble, and the rotting bodies of his people are thrown as garbage into the streets. But even then the LORD's anger will not be satisfied. His fist is still poised to strike!

[26]He will send a signal to the nations far away. He will whistle to those at the ends of the earth, and they will come racing toward Jerusalem. [27]They will not get tired or stumble. They will run without stopping for rest or sleep. Not a belt will be loose, not a sandal thong broken. [28]Their arrows will be sharp and their bows ready for battle. Sparks will fly from their horses' hooves as the wheels of their chariots spin like the wind. [29]Roaring like lions, they will pounce on their prey. They will seize my people and carry them off into captivity, and no one will be there to rescue them. [30]The enemy nations will growl over their victims like the roaring

of the sea. A cloud of darkness and sorrow will hover over Israel. The clouds will blot out the light.

CHAPTER 6

In the year King Uzziah died, I saw the Lord. He was sitting on a lofty throne, and the train of his robe filled the Temple. [2]Hovering around him were mighty seraphim, each with six wings. With two wings they covered their faces, with two they covered their feet, and with the remaining two they flew. [3]In a great chorus they sang, "Holy, holy, holy is the LORD Almighty! The whole earth is filled with his glory!" [4]The glorious singing shook the Temple to its foundations, and the entire sanctuary was filled with smoke.

[5]Then I said, "My destruction is sealed, for I am a sinful man and a member of a sinful race. Yet I have seen the King, the LORD Almighty!"

[6]Then one of the seraphim flew over to the altar, and he picked up a burning coal with a pair of tongs. [7]He touched my lips with it and said, "See, this coal has touched your lips. Now your guilt is removed, and your sins are forgiven."

[8]Then I heard the Lord asking, "Whom should I send as a messenger to my people? Who will go for us?"

And I said, "Lord, I'll go! Send me."

[9]And he said, "Yes, go. But tell my people this: 'You will hear my words, but you will not understand. You will see what I do, but you will not perceive its meaning.' [10]Harden the hearts of these people. Close their ears, and shut their eyes. That way, they will not see with their eyes, hear with their ears, understand with their hearts, and turn to me for healing."

[11]Then I said, "Lord, how long must I do this?"

And he replied, "Until their cities are destroyed, with no one left in them. Until their houses are deserted and the whole country is an utter wasteland. [12]Do not stop until the LORD has sent everyone away to distant lands and the entire land of Israel lies deserted. [13]Even if only a tenth—a remnant—survive, it will be invaded again and burned. Israel will remain a stump, like a tree that is cut down, but the stump will be a holy seed that will grow again."

5:17 As in Greek version; Hebrew reads *strangers*.

CHAPTER 7

During the reign of Ahaz son of Jotham and grandson of Uzziah, Jerusalem was attacked by King Rezin of Aram and King Pekah of Israel, the son of Remaliah. The city withstood the attack, however, and was not taken.

2The news had come to the royal court: "Aram is allied with Israel* against us!" So the hearts of the king and his people trembled with fear, just as trees shake in a storm.

3Then the LORD said to Isaiah, "Go out to meet King Ahaz, you and your son Shear-jashub.* You will find the king at the end of the aqueduct that feeds water into the upper pool, near the road leading to the field where cloth is bleached. 4Tell him to stop worrying. Tell him he doesn't need to fear the fierce anger of those two burned-out embers, King Rezin of Aram and Pekah son of Remaliah.

5"Yes, the kings of Aram and Israel are coming against you. They are saying, 6'We will invade Judah and throw its people into panic. Then we will fight our way into Jerusalem and install the son of Tabeel as Judah's king.'

7"But this is what the Sovereign LORD says: This invasion will never happen, 8because Aram is no stronger than its capital, Damascus. And Damascus is no stronger than its king, Rezin. As for Israel, within sixty-five years it will be crushed and completely destroyed. 9Israel is no stronger than its capital, Samaria. And Samaria is no stronger than its king, Pekah son of Remaliah. You do not believe me? If you want me to protect you, learn to believe what I say."

10Not long after this, the LORD sent this message to King Ahaz: 11"Ask me for a sign, Ahaz, to prove that I will crush your enemies as I have promised. Ask for anything you like, and make it as difficult as you want."

12But the king refused. "No," he said, "I wouldn't test the LORD like that."

13Then Isaiah said, "Listen well, you royal family of David! You aren't satisfied to exhaust my patience. You exhaust the patience of God as well! 14All right then, the Lord himself will choose the sign. Look! The virgin* will conceive a child! She will give birth to a son and will call him Immanuel—'God is with us.' 15By the time this child is old enough to eat curds and honey, he will know enough to choose what is

right and reject what is wrong. 16But before he knows right from wrong, the two kings you fear so much—the kings of Israel and Aram—will both be dead.

17"The LORD will bring a terrible curse on you, your nation, and your family. You will soon experience greater terror than has been known in all the years since Solomon's empire was divided into Israel and Judah. The mighty king of Assyria will come with his great army!"

18In that day the LORD will whistle for the army of Upper Egypt and for the army of Assyria. They will swarm around you like flies. Like bees, they will sting and kill. 19They will come in vast hordes, spreading across the whole land. They will settle in the fertile areas and also in the desolate valleys, caves, and thorny places. 20In that day the Lord will take this "razor"—these Assyrians you have hired to protect you—and use it to shave off everything: your land, your crops, and your people.*

21When they finally stop plundering, a farmer will be fortunate to have a cow and two sheep left. 22The few people still left in the land will live on curds and wild honey because that is all the land will produce. 23In that day the lush vineyards, now worth as much as a thousand pieces of silver,* will become patches of briers and thorns. 24The entire land will be one vast brier patch, a hunting ground overrun by wildlife. 25No one will go to the fertile hillsides where the gardens once grew, for briers and thorns will cover them. Cattle, sheep, and goats will graze there.

CHAPTER 8

Again the LORD said to me, "Make a large signboard and clearly write this name on it: Maher-shalal-hash-baz.*" 2I asked Uriah the priest and Zechariah son of Jeberekiah, both known as honest men, to testify that I had written it before the child was conceived.

3Then I slept with my wife, and she became pregnant and had a son. And the LORD said, "Call him Maher-shalal-hash-baz. 4This name prophesies that within a couple of years, before this child is old enough to say 'Papa' or 'Mama,' the king of Assyria will invade both Damascus and Samaria and carry away their riches."

5Then the LORD spoke to me again and

7:2 Hebrew *Ephraim*, referring to the northern kingdom of Israel; also in 7:5, 8, 9, 17.   7:3 *Shear-jashub* means "A remnant will return."   7:14 Or *young woman*.   7:20 Hebrew *shave off the head, the hair of the legs, and the beard*.   7:23 Hebrew *1,000 shekels of silver*, about 25 pounds or 11.4 kilograms in weight.   8:1 *Maher-shalal-hash-baz* means "Swift to plunder and quick to spoil."

said, [6]"The people of Judah have rejected my gentle care* and are rejoicing over what will happen to King Rezin and King Pekah. [7]Therefore, the Lord will overwhelm them with a mighty flood from the Euphrates River*—the king of Assyria and all his mighty armies. [8]This flood will overflow all its channels and sweep into Judah. It will submerge Immanuel's land from one end to the other.

[9]"The Assyrians will cry, 'Do your best to defend yourselves, but you will be shattered! Listen all you nations. Prepare for battle—and die! Yes, die! [10]Call your councils of war, develop your strategies, prepare your plans of attack—and then die! For God is with us!*'"

[11]The LORD has said to me in the strongest terms: "Do not think like everyone else does. [12]Do not be afraid that some plan conceived behind closed doors will be the end of you. [13]Do not fear anything except the LORD Almighty. He alone is the Holy One. If you fear him, you need fear nothing else. [14]He will keep you safe. But to Israel and Judah he will be a stone that causes people to stumble and a rock that makes them fall. And for the people of Jerusalem he will be a trap that entangles them. [15]Many of them will stumble and fall, never to rise again. Many will be captured."

[16]I will write down all these things as a testimony of what the LORD will do. I will entrust it to my disciples, who will pass it down to future generations. [17]I will wait for the LORD to help us, though he has turned away from the people of Israel.* My only hope is in him. [18]I and the children the LORD has given me have names* that reveal the plans the LORD Almighty has for his people. [19]So why are you trying to find out the future by consulting mediums and psychics? Do not listen to their whisperings and mutterings. Can the living find out the future from the dead? Why not ask your God?

[20]"Check their predictions against my testimony," says the LORD. "If their predictions are different from mine, it is because there is no light or truth in them. [21]My people will be led away as captives, weary and hungry. And because they are hungry, they will rage and shake their fists at heaven and curse their king and their God. [22]Wherever they look, there will be trouble and anguish and dark despair. They will be thrown out into the darkness."

8:6 Hebrew *rejected the gently flowing waters of Shiloah.*   **8:7** Hebrew *the river.*   **8:10** Hebrew *Immanuel!*   **8:17** Hebrew *the house of Jacob.*   **8:18** Isaiah means "The LORD will save"; *Shear-jashub* means "A remnant will return"; and *Maher-shalal-hash-baz* means "Swift to plunder and quick to spoil."

JULY 16 ☐ DAY 198
ISAIAH 9–12
Judah's Darkness and Dawn

OVERVIEW Chapters 9–12 (along with 7 and 8, which you read yesterday) have been called "The Book of Immanuel" because of the many prophecies and allusions regarding the Messiah:

He would be born of a virgin (7:14).
He would be given the name *Immanuel,* "God is with us" (7:14).
He would be a stumbling block to Israel (8:14).
He would be a great light to the nations (9:2).
He would be a ruler, counselor, and prince (9:6).
He would come from the line of David (11:1).

Is it any wonder the redeemed gather together for a grand chorus of praise and worship at the thought of their Immanuel?

Chapter 9	Chapter 10	Chapter 11	Chapter 12
Prince of Peace	Promise of Punishment	Promise of Peace	Postlude of Praise
Exhortation	Explanation		Exaltation

YOUR DAILY WALK Titles can be deceiving.

The more you think about Christ, the more you think of him.

A young executive was describing with evident pride his recent promotion to the position of vice president. "Aw, that's nothing," responded a friend. "Vice presidents are a dime a dozen. Why, I'll bet there's even a vice president of peanuts at the supermarket."

"You're on!" exclaimed the executive, as he dialed the store on the phone. "May I speak to the vice president of peanuts, please?"

The reply came back, "Packaged or bulk?"

By contrast, the titles you will find attributed to Christ are highly significant! His name will be called "Wonderful, Counselor"—and God alone is "a wonderful teacher" (28:29). He is the "Mighty God"—the same term used to describe "the LORD, the Holy One of Israel" (10:20-21). Thus, his titles underscore his deity.

Share with a person today the significance of one of the names of Jesus. Ask God to open a door of witness through it!

INSIGHT First to Feel the Groan, First to See the Glory

The land of Zebulun and Naphtali—the first region to succumb to the Assyrian onslaught within months of Isaiah's meeting with Ahaz (7:1-9)—would also be the first to see the glory of the Lord (9:1-2) . . . a striking prophecy that went unheeded when the Messiah came (John 1:46; 7:52).

CHAPTER 9

Nevertheless, that time of darkness and despair will not go on forever. The land of Zebulun and Naphtali will soon be humbled, but there will be a time in the future when Galilee of the Gentiles, which lies along the road that runs between the Jordan and the sea, will be filled with glory. ²The people who walk in darkness will see a great light—a light that will shine on all who live in the land where death casts its shadow. ³Israel will again be great, and its people will rejoice as people rejoice at harvesttime. They will shout with joy like warriors dividing the plunder. ⁴For God will break the chains that bind his people and the whip that scourges them, just as he did when he destroyed the army of Midian with Gideon's little band. ⁵In that day of peace, battle gear will no longer be issued. Never again will uniforms be bloodstained by war. All such equipment will be burned.

⁶For a child is born to us, a son is given to us. And the government will rest on his shoulders. These will be his royal titles: Wonderful Counselor,* Mighty God, Everlasting Father, Prince of Peace. ⁷His ever expanding, peaceful government will never end. He will rule forever with fairness and justice from the throne of his ancestor David. The passionate commitment of the LORD Almighty will guarantee this!

⁸The Lord has spoken out against that braggart Israel, ⁹and the people of Israel* and Samaria will soon discover it. In their pride and arrogance they say, ¹⁰"Our land lies in ruins now, but we will rebuild it better than before. We will replace the broken bricks with cut stone, the fallen sycamore trees with cedars." ¹¹The LORD will reply to their bragging by bringing Rezin's enemies, the Assyrians, against them— ¹²along with Arameans from the east and Philistines from the west. With bared fangs, they will devour Israel. But even then the LORD's anger will not be satisfied. His fist is still poised to strike. ¹³For after all this punishment, the people will still not repent and turn to the LORD Almighty.

¹⁴Therefore, in a single day, the LORD will destroy both the head and the tail, the palm branch and the reed. ¹⁵The leaders of Israel are the head, and the lying prophets are the tail. ¹⁶For the leaders of the people have led them down the path of destruction. ¹⁷That is why the Lord has no joy in the young men and no mercy on even the widows and orphans. For they are all hypocrites, speaking wickedness with lies. But even then the LORD's anger will not be satisfied. His fist is still poised to strike.

¹⁸This wickedness is like a brushfire. It burns not only briers and thorns but the forests, too. Its burning sends up vast clouds of smoke. ¹⁹The land is blackened by the fury of the LORD Almighty. The

9:6 Or *Wonderful, Counselor.*   **9:9** Hebrew *of Ephraim,* referring to the northern kingdom of Israel.

people are fuel for the fire, and no one spares anyone else. ²⁰They fight against their own neighbors to steal food, but they will still be hungry. In the end they will even eat their own children.* ²¹Manasseh will feed on Ephraim, Ephraim will feed on Manasseh, and both will devour Judah. But even then the LORD's anger will not be satisfied. His fist is still poised to strike.

CHAPTER 10

Destruction is certain for the unjust judges, for those who issue unfair laws. ²They deprive the poor, the widows, and the orphans of justice. Yes, they rob widows and fatherless children! ³What will you do when I send desolation upon you from a distant land? To whom will you turn for help? Where will your treasures be safe? ⁴I will not help you. You will stumble along as prisoners or lie among the dead. But even then the LORD's anger will not be satisfied. His fist is still poised to strike.

⁵"Destruction is certain for Assyria, the whip of my anger. Its military power is a club in my hand. ⁶Assyria will enslave my people, who are a godless nation. It will plunder them, trampling them like dirt beneath its feet. ⁷But the king of Assyria will not know that it is I who sent him. He will merely think he is attacking my people as part of his plan to conquer the world. ⁸He will say, 'Each of my princes will soon be a king, ruling a conquered land. ⁹We will destroy Calno just as we did Carchemish. Hamath will fall before us as Arpad did. And we will destroy Samaria just as we did Damascus. ¹⁰Yes, we have finished off many a kingdom whose gods were far greater than those in Jerusalem and Samaria. ¹¹So when we have defeated Samaria and her gods, we will destroy Jerusalem with hers.'"

¹²After the Lord has used the king of Assyria to accomplish his purposes in Jerusalem, he will turn against the king of Assyria and punish him—for he is proud and arrogant. ¹³He boasts, "By my own power and wisdom I have won these wars. By my own strength I have captured many lands, destroyed their kings, and carried off their treasures. ¹⁴By my greatness I have robbed their nests of riches and gathered up kingdoms as a farmer gathers eggs. No one can

even flap a wing against me or utter a peep of protest."

¹⁵Can the ax boast greater power than the person who uses it? Is the saw greater than the person who saws? Can a whip strike unless a hand is moving it? Can a cane walk by itself?

¹⁶Listen now, king of Assyria! Because of all your evil boasting, the Lord, the LORD Almighty, will send a plague among your proud troops, and a flaming fire will ignite your glory. ¹⁷The LORD, the Light of Israel and the Holy One, will be a flaming fire that will destroy them. In a single night he will burn those thorns and briers, the Assyrians. ¹⁸Assyria's vast army is like a glorious forest, yet it will be destroyed. The LORD will completely destroy Assyria's warriors, and they will waste away like sick people in a plague. ¹⁹Only a few from all that mighty army will survive—so few that a child could count them!

²⁰Then at last those left in Israel and Judah* will trust the LORD, the Holy One of Israel. They will no longer depend on the Assyrians, who would destroy them. ²¹A remnant of them will return* to the Mighty God. ²²But though the people of Israel are as numerous as the sand on the seashore, only a few of them will return at that time. The LORD has rightly decided to destroy his people. ²³Yes, the Lord, the LORD Almighty, has already decided to consume them.

²⁴So this is what the Lord, the LORD Almighty, says: "My people in Jerusalem,* do not be afraid of the Assyrians when they oppress you just as the Egyptians did long ago. ²⁵It will not last very long. In a little while my anger against you will end, and then my anger will rise up to destroy them."

²⁶The LORD Almighty will beat them with his whip, as he did when Gideon triumphed over the Midianites at the rock of Oreb, or when the LORD's staff was raised to drown the Egyptian army in the sea. ²⁷In that day the LORD will end the bondage of his people. He will break the yoke of slavery and lift it from their shoulders.*

²⁸Look, the mighty armies of Assyria are coming! They are now at Aiath, now at Migron. They are storing some of their equipment at Micmash. ²⁹They are crossing the pass and are staying overnight at Geba. Fear strikes the city of Ramah. All the

---

9:20 Or *eat their own arms.*   10:20 Hebrew *and the house of Jacob.*   10:21 Hebrew *Shear-jashub;* see 7:3; 8:18.   10:24 Hebrew *Zion.*
10:27 As in Greek version; Hebrew reads *The yoke will be broken, for you have grown so fat.*

people of Gibeah—the city of Saul—are running for their lives. ³⁰Well may you scream in terror, you people of Gallim! Shout out a warning to Laishah, for the mighty army comes. Poor Anathoth, what a fate is yours! ³¹There go the people of Madmenah, all fleeing. And the citizens of Gebim are preparing to run. ³²But the enemy stops at Nob for the rest of that day. He shakes his fist at Mount Zion in Jerusalem.

³³But look! The Lord, the LORD Almighty, will chop down the mighty tree! He will destroy all that vast army of Assyria—officers and high officials alike. ³⁴The Mighty One will cut down the enemy as an ax cuts down the forest trees in Lebanon.

CHAPTER 11

Out of the stump of David's family* will grow a shoot—yes, a new Branch bearing fruit from the old root. ²And the Spirit of the LORD will rest on him—the Spirit of wisdom and understanding, the Spirit of counsel and might, the Spirit of knowledge and the fear of the LORD. ³He will delight in obeying the LORD. He will never judge by appearance, false evidence, or hearsay. ⁴He will defend the poor and the exploited. He will rule against the wicked and destroy them with the breath of his mouth. ⁵He will be clothed with fairness and truth.

⁶In that day the wolf and the lamb will live together; the leopard and the goat will be at peace. Calves and yearlings will be safe among lions, and a little child will lead them all. ⁷The cattle will graze among bears. Cubs and calves will lie down together. And lions will eat grass as the livestock do. ⁸Babies will crawl safely among poisonous snakes. Yes, a little child will put its hand in a nest of deadly snakes and pull it out unharmed. ⁹Nothing will hurt or destroy in all my holy mountain. And as the waters fill the sea, so the earth will be filled with people who know the LORD.

¹⁰In that day the heir to David's throne* will be a banner of salvation to all the world. The nations will rally to him, for the land where he lives will be a glorious place. ¹¹In that day the Lord will bring back a remnant of his people for the second time,

returning them to the land of Israel from Assyria, Lower Egypt, Upper Egypt, Ethiopia,* Elam, Babylonia,* Hamath, and all the distant coastlands.

¹²He will raise a flag among the nations for Israel to rally around. He will gather the scattered people of Judah from the ends of the earth. ¹³Then at last the jealousy between Israel* and Judah will end. They will not fight against each other anymore. ¹⁴They will join forces to swoop down on Philistia to the west. Together they will attack and plunder the nations to the east. They will occupy all the lands of Edom, Moab, and Ammon.

¹⁵The LORD will make a dry path through the Red Sea.* He will wave his hand over the Euphrates River,* sending a mighty wind to divide it into seven streams that can easily be crossed. ¹⁶He will make a highway from Assyria for the remnant there, just as he did for Israel long ago when they returned from Egypt.

CHAPTER 12

In that day you will sing:

"Praise the LORD!
He was angry with me,
   but now he comforts me.
² See, God has come to save me.
   I will trust in him and not be afraid.
The LORD GOD is my strength and my
      song;
   he has become my salvation."

³With joy you will drink deeply from the fountain of salvation! ⁴In that wonderful day you will sing:

"Thank the LORD!
   Praise his name!
Tell the world what he has done.
   Oh, how mighty he is!
⁵ Sing to the LORD,
   for he has done wonderful things.
   Make known his praise around the
      world.
⁶ Let all the people of Jerusalem* shout
      his praise with joy!
   For great is the Holy One of Israel
      who lives among you."

11:1 Hebrew *the line of Jesse.* Jesse was King David's father.   11:10 Hebrew *the root of Jesse.*   11:11a Hebrew *Pathros, Cush.*
11:11b Hebrew *Shinar.*   11:13 Hebrew *Ephraim,* referring to the northern kingdom of Israel.   11:15a Hebrew *sea of Egypt.*
11:15b Hebrew *the river.*   12:6 Hebrew *Zion.*

JULY 17 ☐ DAY 199
ISAIAH 13–16
Woes on Babylon and Moab

OVERVIEW God is sovereign over his nation; he is also sovereign over all nations. No empire or tribe on earth is exempt from the judgment of God when wickedness replaces righteousness. Isaiah now turns his verbal missiles upon the Gentile nations, which will melt away before the furnace of God's wrath for their opposition to his people and plan. Babylon is faced with the gloomy prospect of being dominated by the Medes (it happened in 539 B.C.). The cities of Moab can look forward to being sacked (it happened in 701 B.C.). Clearly, wicked kings and kingdoms are no match for the justice and holiness of God.

Chapter 13	Chapter 14	Chapter 15	Chapter 16
The Downfall of Babylon		The Desolation of Moab	
Predicted	Praised	Prophesied	Publicized
Gloom		Doom	

YOUR DAILY WALK There's something deliciously satisfying about seeing "the other guy" get his just deserts . . . or watching the speeding car ahead of you get pulled over . . . or learning that your obnoxious next-door neighbor is being audited . . . or reading about a corrupt politician landing in jail.

Knowledge humbles great people, astonishes common people, and puffs up little people.

But wait! Smugness in the face of another's calamity diminishes when you remember your own shortcomings and imperfections. God in his Word has included the bad with the good, the *condemnation* of nations as well as their *commendation*, that you might profit from their example. The fact that nations such as Babylon and Moab no longer exist should warn you that when God promises punishment for persistent sin, it is no idle threat.

Think of a recent calamity that has befallen someone you know because of his or her inattention to God's Word. How can you save yourself some grief by learning from that example?

INSIGHT Tomorrow's Headlines Prophesied Today
The gist of Isaiah's prophecy regarding Babylon is this: Media would supersede Babylon (13:17); and Babylon would disappear forever (13:19-22). Historically, Babylon conquered Assyria in 607 B.C. and fell to Medo-Persian armies in 538 B.C.

CHAPTER 13

Isaiah son of Amoz received this message concerning the destruction of Babylon:

2"See the flags waving as the enemy attacks. Cheer them on, O Israel! Wave to them as they march against Babylon to destroy the palaces of the high and mighty. 3I, the LORD, have assigned this task to these armies, and they will rejoice when I am exalted. I have called them to satisfy my anger."

4Hear the noise on the mountains! Listen, as the armies march! It is the noise and the shout of many nations. The LORD

Almighty has brought them here to form an army. 5They came from countries far away. They are the LORD's weapons; they carry his anger with them and will destroy the whole land. 6Scream in terror, for the LORD's time has arrived—the time for the Almighty to destroy. 7Every arm is paralyzed with fear. Even the strongest hearts melt 8and are afraid. Fear grips them with terrible pangs, like those of a woman about to give birth. They look helplessly at one another as the flames of the burning city reflect on their faces. 9For see, the day of the LORD is coming—the terrible day of his fury and fierce anger. The land will be destroyed and all the sinners with it. [10]The heavens will be black above them. No light will shine from stars or sun or moon.

[11]"I, the LORD, will punish the world for its evil and the wicked for their sin. I will crush the arrogance of the proud and the haughtiness of the mighty. [12]Few will be left alive when I have finished my work. People will be as scarce as gold—more rare than the gold of Ophir. [13]For I will shake the heavens, and the earth will move from its place. I, the LORD Almighty, will show my fury and fierce anger."

[14]Everyone will run until exhausted, rushing back to their own lands like hunted deer, wandering like sheep without a shepherd. [15]Anyone who is captured will be run through with a sword. [16]Their little children will be dashed to death right before their eyes. Their homes will be sacked and their wives raped by the attacking hordes. [17]For I will stir up the Medes against Babylon, and no amount of silver or gold will buy them off. [18]The attacking armies will shoot down the young people with arrows. They will have no mercy on helpless babies and will show no compassion for the children.

[19]Babylon, the most glorious of kingdoms, the flower of Chaldean culture, will be devastated like Sodom and Gomorrah when God destroyed them. [20]Babylon will never rise again. Generation after generation will come and go, but the land will never again be lived in. Nomads will refuse to camp there, and shepherds will not allow their sheep to stay overnight. [21]Wild animals of the desert will move into the ruined city. The houses will be haunted by howling creatures. Ostriches will live among the ruins, and wild goats will come there to dance. [22]Hyenas will howl in its fortresses, and jackals will make their dens in its palaces. Babylon's days are numbered; its time of destruction will soon arrive.

CHAPTER 14

But the LORD will have mercy on the descendants of Jacob. Israel will be his special people once again. He will bring them back to settle once again in their own land. And people from many different nations will come and join them there and become a part of the people of Israel.* [2]The nations of the world will help the LORD's people to return, and those who come to live in their land will serve them. Those who captured Israel will be captured, and Israel will rule over its enemies.

[3]In that wonderful day when the LORD gives his people rest from sorrow and fear, from slavery and chains, [4]you will taunt the king of Babylon. You will say, "The mighty man has been destroyed. Yes, your insolence is ended. [5]For the LORD has crushed your wicked power and broken your evil rule. [6]You persecuted the people with unceasing blows of rage and held the nations in your angry grip. Your tyranny was unrestrained. [7]But at last the land is at rest and is quiet. Finally it can sing again! [8]Even the trees of the forest—the cypress trees and the cedars of Lebanon—sing out this joyous song: 'Your power is broken! No one will come to cut us down now!'

[9]"In the place of the dead* there is excitement over your arrival. World leaders and mighty kings long dead are there to see you. [10]With one voice they all cry out, 'Now you are as weak as we are! [11]Your might and power are gone; they were buried with you. All the pleasant music in your palace has ceased. Now maggots are your sheet and worms your blanket.'

[12]"How you are fallen from heaven, O shining star, son of the morning! You have been thrown down to the earth, you who destroyed the nations of the world. [13]For you said to yourself, 'I will ascend to heaven and set my throne above God's stars. I will preside on the mountain of the gods far away in the north. [14]I will climb to the highest heavens and be like the Most High.' [15]But instead, you will be brought down to the place of the dead, down to its lowest depths. [16]Everyone there will stare at you and ask, 'Can this be the one who shook the earth and the kingdoms of the world? [17]Is this the one who destroyed the world and made it into a wilderness? Is this the king who demolished the world's greatest cities and had no mercy on his prisoners?'

[18]"The kings of the nations lie in stately glory in their tombs, [19]but you will be thrown out of your grave like a worthless branch. Like a corpse trampled underfoot, you will be dumped into a mass grave with those killed in battle. You will descend to

14:1 Hebrew *the house of Jacob.*　14:9 Hebrew *Sheol;* also in 14:15.

the pit. [20]You will not be given a proper burial, for you have destroyed your nation and slaughtered your people. Your son will not succeed you as king. [21]Kill the children of this sinner! Do not let them rise and conquer the land or rebuild the cities of the world."

[22]This is what the LORD Almighty says: "I, myself, have risen against him! I will destroy his children and his children's children, so they will never sit on his throne. [23]I will make Babylon into a desolate land, a place of porcupines, filled with swamps and marshes. I will sweep the land with the broom of destruction. I, the LORD Almighty, have spoken!"

[24]The LORD Almighty has sworn this oath: "It will all happen as I have planned. It will come about according to my purposes. [25]I will break the Assyrians when they are in Israel; I will trample them on my mountains. My people will no longer be their slaves. [26]I have a plan for the whole earth, for my mighty power reaches throughout the world. [27]The LORD Almighty has spoken—who can change his plans? When his hand moves, who can stop him?"

[28]This message came to me the year King Ahaz died:

[29]Do not rejoice, you Philistines, that the king who attacked you is dead. For even though that whip is broken, his son will be worse than his father ever was. From that snake a poisonous snake will be born, a fiery serpent to destroy you! [30]I will feed the poor in my pasture; the needy will lie down in peace. But as for you, I will wipe you out with famine. I will destroy the few who remain.

[31]Weep, you Philistine cities, for you are doomed! Melt in fear, for everyone will be destroyed. A powerful army is coming out of the north. Each soldier rushes forward ready to fight. [32]What should we tell the enemy messengers? Tell them that the LORD has built Jerusalem,* and that the poor of his people will find refuge in its walls.

CHAPTER 15
This message came to me concerning Moab:

In one night your cities of Ar and Kir will be destroyed. [2]Your people in Dibon will

mourn at their temples and shrines, weeping for the fate of Nebo and Medeba. They will shave their heads in sorrow and cut off their beards. [3]They will wear sackcloth as they wander the streets. From every home will come the sound of weeping. [4]The cries from the cities of Heshbon and Elealeh will be heard far away, even in Jahaz! The bravest warriors of Moab will cry out in utter terror.

[5]My heart weeps for Moab. Its people flee to Zoar and Eglath-shelishiyah. Weeping, they climb the road to Luhith. Their crying can be heard all along the road to Horonaim. [6]Even the waters of Nimrim are dried up! The grassy banks are scorched, and the tender plants are gone. [7]The desperate refugees take only the possessions they can carry and flee across the Ravine of Willows. [8]The whole land of Moab is a land of weeping from one end to the other—from Eglaim to Beer-elim. [9]The stream near Dibon* runs red with blood, but I am still not finished with Dibon! Lions will hunt down the survivors, both those who try to run and those who remain behind.

CHAPTER 16
Moab's refugees at Sela send lambs to Jerusalem* as a token of alliance with the king of Judah. [2]The women of Moab are left like homeless birds at the shallow crossings of the Arnon River. [3]"Help us," they cry. "Defend us against our enemies. Protect us from their relentless attack. Do not betray us. [4]Let our outcasts stay among you. Hide them from our enemies until the terror is past."

When oppression and destruction have ceased and enemy raiders have disappeared, [5]then David's throne will be established by love. From that throne a faithful king will reign, one who always does what is just and right.

[6]Is this Moab, the proud land we have heard so much about? Its pride and insolence are all gone now! [7]The entire land of Moab weeps. Yes, you people of Moab, mourn for the delicacies of Kir-hareseth. [8]Weep for the abandoned farms of Heshbon and the vineyards at Sibmah. The wine from those vineyards used to make the rulers of the nations drunk. Moab was once like a spreading grapevine. Her tendrils spread out as far as Jazer and trailed out

14:32 Hebrew *Zion.*   **15:9** As in Dead Sea Scrolls, some Greek manuscripts, and Latin Vulgate; Masoretic Text reads *Dimon;* also in 15:9b.   **16:1** Hebrew *to the daughter of Zion.*

into the desert. Her shoots once reached as far as the Dead Sea.* ⁹But now the enemy has completely destroyed that vine. So I wail and lament for Jazer and the vineyards of Sibmah. My tears will flow for Heshbon and Elealeh, for their summer fruits and harvests have all been destroyed.

¹⁰Gone now is the gladness; gone is the joy of harvest. The happy singing in the vineyards will be heard no more. The treading out of grapes in the winepresses has ceased forever. I have ended all their harvest joys. ¹¹I will weep for Moab. My sorrow for Kir-hareseth* will be very great. ¹²On the hilltops the people of Moab will pray in anguish to their idols, but it will do them no good. They will cry to the gods in their temples, but no one will come to save them.

¹³The LORD has already said this about Moab in the past. ¹⁴But now the LORD says, "Within three years, without fail, the glory of Moab will be ended, and few of its people will be left alive."

16:8 Hebrew *the sea.*   16:11 Hebrew *Kir-heres,* a variant name for Kir-hareseth.

JULY 18 ☐ DAY 200
ISAIAH 17–20
Collapse from Corruption

 OVERVIEW Damascus, Ethiopia, and Egypt are next to feel the hot blast of Isaiah's burdens of judgment. The glory of Damascus would be removed, leaving behind leanness of body and soul. But a handful would repent and—like the gleanings from an olive tree—provide hope for a future harvest. Ethiopia, though tall in stature and smooth of skin, would be pruned away like branches and one day return to Zion to pay homage to God and acknowledge him as her Sovereign. Egypt would experience civil war, economic ruin, and spiritual poverty, showing the bankruptcy of Egypt's false gods. But one day the Lord Almighty would declare, "Blessed be Egypt, my people" (19:25).

Chapter 17	Chapter 18	Chapter 19	Chapter 20
Doom for Damascus	Pruning for Ethiopia	Infamy for Egypt	Enemies for Egypt
Removal		Reproof	

 YOUR DAILY WALK The courtroom scene unfolds as it has countless times before.

The case is presented; the jury recesses; a verdict is reached: Guilty! But then the trial takes an unexpected twist. The presiding judge also happens to be the father of the convicted criminal. And just before his son reaches the bar, where the fine is to be assessed, the judge steps down from his seat, takes off his robe, and approaches the bar to pay the fine for his guilty son. Justice . . . and mercy!

Mercy without justice becomes unmerciful; justice without mercy, unjust.

That story illustrates a divine truth. The judge would not have been just if he had allowed his son to go free. But his love caused him to take his son's place in paying the fine. The same is true about God. He would not be just if he ignored the sins committed against him. At the same time, his great love shines forth in the gift of his Son to pay the price for humanity's sins.

Isaiah 14:1-8 is a message of mercy inserted between many dark chapters of judgment. God is just, but he is also loving toward all who trust him. In his love he has provided the answer to humanity's sin problem (11:10)—a Savior. What is your answer to him today?

INSIGHT Old Testament POWs
As part of his judgment on Egypt, God instructed Isaiah to dress like a prisoner of war—unclothed and barefoot—for three years as a sign of the calamity God was going to bring on Egypt (20:1-4).

CHAPTER 17
This message came to me concerning Damascus:

"Look, Damascus will disappear! It will become a heap of ruins. ²The cities of Aroer will be deserted. Sheep will graze in the streets and lie down unafraid. There will be no one to chase them away. ³The fortified cities of Israel* will also be destroyed, and the power of Damascus will end. The few left in Aram will share the fate of Israel's departed glory," says the LORD Almighty.

⁴"In that day the glory of Israel* will be very dim, for poverty will stalk the land. ⁵Israel will be abandoned like the grainfields in the valley of Rephaim after the harvest. ⁶Only a few of its people will be left, like the stray olives left on the tree after the harvest. Only two or three remain in the highest branches, four or five out on the tips of the limbs. Yes, Israel will be stripped bare of people," says the LORD, the God of Israel.

⁷Then at last the people will think of their Creator and have respect for the Holy One of Israel. ⁸They will no longer ask their idols for help or worship what their own hands have made. They will never again bow down to their Asherah poles or burn incense on the altars they built.

⁹Their largest cities will be as deserted as overgrown thickets. They will become like the cities the Amorites abandoned when the Israelites came here so long ago. ¹⁰Why? Because you have turned from the God who can save you—the Rock who can hide you. You may plant the finest imported grapevines, ¹¹and they may grow so well that they blossom on the very morning you plant them, but you will never pick any grapes from them. Your only harvest will be a load of grief and incurable pain.

¹²Look! The armies rush forward like waves thundering toward the shore. ¹³But though they roar like breakers on a beach, God will silence them. They will flee like chaff scattered by the wind or like dust whirling before a storm. ¹⁴In the evening Israel waits in terror, but by dawn its ene-

mies are dead. This is the just reward of those who plunder and destroy the people of God.

CHAPTER 18
Destruction is certain for the land of Ethiopia,* which lies at the headwaters of the Nile. Its winged sailboats glide along the river, ²and ambassadors are sent in fast boats down the Nile. Go home, swift messengers! Take a message to your land divided by rivers, to your tall, smooth-skinned people, who are feared far and wide for their conquests and destruction.

³When I raise my battle flag on the mountain, let all the world take notice. When I blow the trumpet, listen! ⁴For the LORD has told me this: "I will watch quietly from my dwelling place—as quietly as the heat rises on a summer day, or as the dew forms on an autumn morning during the harvest."

⁵Even before you begin your attack, while your plans are ripening like grapes, the LORD will cut you off as though with pruning shears. He will snip your spreading branches. ⁶Your mighty army will be left dead in the fields for the mountain birds and wild animals to eat. The vultures will tear at corpses all summer. The wild animals will gnaw at bones all winter.

⁷But the time will come when the LORD Almighty will receive gifts from this land divided by rivers, from this tall, smooth-skinned people, who are feared far and wide for their conquests and destruction. They will bring the gifts to the LORD Almighty in Jerusalem,* the place where his name dwells.

CHAPTER 19
This message came to me concerning Egypt:

Look! The LORD is advancing against Egypt, riding on a swift cloud. The idols of Egypt tremble. The hearts of the Egyptians melt with fear.

17:3 Hebrew *of Ephraim*, referring to the northern kingdom of Israel.   17:4 Hebrew *of Jacob*.   18:1 Hebrew *Cush*.   18:7 Hebrew *on Mount Zion.*

2"I will make the Egyptians fight against each other—brother against brother, neighbor against neighbor, city against city, province against province. ³The Egyptians will lose heart, and I will confuse their plans. They will plead with their idols for wisdom. They will call on spirits, mediums, and psychics to show them which way to turn. ⁴I will hand Egypt over to a hard, cruel master, to a fierce king," says the Lord, the LORD Almighty.

⁵The waters of the Nile will fail to rise and flood the fields. The riverbed will be parched and dry. ⁶The canals of the Nile will dry up, and the streams of Egypt will become foul with rotting reeds and rushes. ⁷All the greenery along the riverbank will wither and blow away. All the crops will dry up, and everything will die. ⁸The fishermen will weep for lack of work. Those who fish with hooks and those who use nets will all be unemployed. ⁹The weavers will have no flax or cotton, for the crops will fail. ¹⁰The weavers and all the workers will be sick at heart.

¹¹What fools are the counselors of Zoan! Their best counsel to the king of Egypt is stupid and wrong. Will they still boast of their wisdom? Will they dare tell Pharaoh about their long line of wise ancestors? ¹²What has happened to your wise counselors, Pharaoh? If they are so wise, let them tell you what the LORD Almighty is going to do to Egypt. ¹³The wise men from Zoan are fools, and those from Memphis* are deluded. The leaders of Egypt have ruined the land with their foolish counsel. ¹⁴The LORD has sent a spirit of foolishness on them, so all their suggestions are wrong. They cause the land of Egypt to stagger like a sick drunkard. ¹⁵Nobody in Egypt, whether rich or poor, important or unknown, can offer any help.

¹⁶In that day the Egyptians will be as weak as women. They will cower in fear beneath the upraised fist of the LORD Almighty. ¹⁷Just to speak the name of Israel will strike deep terror in their hearts, for the LORD Almighty has laid out his plans against them.

¹⁸In that day five of Egypt's cities will follow the LORD Almighty. They will even begin to speak the Hebrew language.* One of these will be Heliopolis, the City of the Sun. ¹⁹In that day there will be an altar to the LORD in the heart of Egypt, and there will be a monument to the LORD at its border. ²⁰It will be a sign and a witness to the LORD Almighty in the land of Egypt. When the people cry to the LORD for help against those who oppress them, he will send them a savior who will rescue them.

²¹In that day the LORD will make himself known to the Egyptians. Yes, they will know the LORD and will give their sacrifices and offerings to him. They will make promises to the LORD and keep them. ²²The LORD will strike Egypt in a way that will bring healing. For the Egyptians will turn to the LORD, and he will listen to their pleas and heal them.

²³In that day Egypt and Assyria will be connected by a highway. The Egyptians and Assyrians will move freely between their lands, and they will worship the same God. ²⁴And Israel will be their ally. The three will be together, and Israel will be a blessing to them. ²⁵For the LORD Almighty will say, "Blessed be Egypt, my people. Blessed be Assyria, the land I have made. Blessed be Israel, my special possession!"

CHAPTER 20

In the year when King Sargon of Assyria captured the Philistine city of Ashdod, ²the LORD told Isaiah son of Amoz, "Take off all your clothes, including your sandals." Isaiah did as he was told and walked around naked and barefoot.

³Then the LORD said, "My servant Isaiah has been walking around naked and barefoot for the last three years. This is a sign— a symbol of the terrible troubles I will bring upon Egypt and Ethiopia.* ⁴For the king of Assyria will take away the Egyptians and Ethiopians* as prisoners. He will make them walk naked and barefoot, both young and old, their buttocks uncovered, to the shame of Egypt. ⁵How dismayed will be the Philistines, who counted on the power of Ethiopia and boasted of their allies in Egypt! ⁶They will say, 'If this can happen to Egypt, what chance do we have? For we counted on Egypt to protect us from the king of Assyria.'"

19:13 Hebrew *Noph.*   **19:18** Hebrew *the language of Canaan.*   **20:3** Hebrew *Cush;* also in 20:5.   **20:4** Hebrew *Cushites.*

JULY 19 ☐ DAY 201
ISAIAH 21–23
Judgment Near and Far

OVERVIEW Isaiah is not finished yet with his woes for Judah's foes. In today's reading he mentions two more neighboring powers that are in line for God's chastening hand: Arabia and Tyre. But in the midst of his list of "endangered nations," Isaiah shocks his countrymen by including Jerusalem with the rest. Because of the careless indulgence of its inhabitants, the city would suffer siege and calamity.

Chapter 21	Chapter 22	Chapter 23
Down with Idolatry	Down with Insensitivity	Down with Pride
Arabia	Jerusalem	Tyre

Sin is the womb of our sorrows and the grave of our comforts.

YOUR DAILY WALK Have you ever wondered why you can feel so convicted *after* you sin but remain so indifferent *before* you sin? If there were only a way for you to reverse these conditions—to feel as remorseful before as you do after you disobey God—temptation would surely be easier to resist.

Well, God's verbal warnings are designed to do precisely that! He sent his prophets to paint in grim, unmistakable tones the calamity awaiting his people if they continued in their wicked ways. Pestilence, plague, defeat in battle, destruction of home and family—all these and more would be the wages they would richly deserve for their sin. Harsh prophecies of national catastrophe were designed by God to deter his people's mad dash for power and prestige at the expense of righteousness and justice. The pain of hearing about these promised calamities was God's way of breaking down indifference and bringing his people to the point of repentance.

If the specific wages of specific sins were revealed to you ahead of time, would you be as eager to earn them? Find a canceled payroll statement and on it write these words: "Is sin worth the pain it brings?" Leave those words in your billfold or purse as a reminder of the high price of unholy living—wages you can't afford to earn!

INSIGHT A Nickname That Makes Sense

Jerusalem was once called the "Valley of Vision." This was an apt description because the hill on which Jerusalem is situated is surrounded by valleys, with higher hills beyond. In addition, the Temple in Jerusalem was the place where God was "visible" to his people.

CHAPTER 21

This message came to me concerning the land of Babylonia*:

Disaster is roaring down on you from the desert, like a whirlwind sweeping in from the Negev. ²I see an awesome vision: I see you plundered and destroyed. Go ahead, you Elamites and Medes, take part in the siege. Babylon will fall, and the groaning of all the nations she enslaved will end. ³My stomach aches and burns with pain. Sharp

pangs of horror are upon me, like the pangs of a woman giving birth. I grow faint when I hear what God is planning; I am blinded with dismay. ⁴My mind reels; my heart races. The sleep I once enjoyed at night is now a faint memory. I lie awake, trembling.

⁵Look! They are preparing a great feast. They are spreading rugs for people to sit on. Everyone is eating and drinking. Quick! Grab your shields and prepare for battle! You are being attacked!

21:1 Hebrew *the desert of the sea.*

⁶Meanwhile, the Lord said to me, "Put a watchman on the city wall to shout out what he sees. ⁷Tell him to sound the alert when he sees chariots drawn by horses and warriors mounted on donkeys and camels."

⁸Then the watchman* called out, "Day after day I have stood on the watchtower, my lord. Night after night I have remained at my post. ⁹Now at last—look! Here come the chariots and warriors!" Then the watchman said, "Babylon is fallen! All the idols of Babylon lie broken on the ground!"

¹⁰O my people, threshed and winnowed, I have told you everything the LORD Almighty, the God of Israel, has said.

¹¹This message came to me concerning Edom*:

Someone from Edom* keeps calling to me, "Watchman, how much longer until morning? When will the night be over?"

¹²The watchman replies, "Morning is coming, but night will soon follow. If you wish to ask again, then come back and ask."

¹³This message came to me concerning Arabia:

O caravans from Dedan, hide in the deserts of Arabia. ¹⁴O people of Tema, bring food and water to these weary refugees. ¹⁵They have fled from drawn swords and sharp arrows and the terrors of war. ¹⁶"But within a year,"* says the Lord, "all the glory of Kedar will come to an end. ¹⁷Only a few of its courageous archers will survive. I, the LORD, the God of Israel, have spoken!"

CHAPTER 22

This message came to me concerning Jerusalem*:

What is happening? Why is everyone running to the rooftops? ²The whole city is in a terrible uproar. What do I see in this reveling city? Bodies are lying everywhere, killed by famine and disease.* ³All your leaders flee. They surrender without resistance. The people try to slip away, but they are captured, too. ⁴Leave me alone to weep; do not try to comfort me. Let me cry for my people as I watch them being destroyed.

⁵Oh, what a day of crushing trouble! What a day of confusion and terror the Lord, the LORD Almighty, has brought upon the Valley of Vision! The walls of Jerusalem have been broken, and cries of death echo from the mountainsides. ⁶Elamites are the archers; Arameans drive the chariots. The men of Kir hold up the shields. ⁷They fill your beautiful valleys and crowd against your gates. ⁸Judah's defenses have been stripped away. You run to the armory for your weapons. ⁹You inspect the walls of Jerusalem* to see what needs to be repaired. You store up water in the lower pool. ¹⁰You check the houses and tear some down to get stone to fix the walls. ¹¹Between the city walls, you build a reservoir for water from the old pool. But all your feverish plans are to no avail because you never ask God for help. He is the one who planned this long ago.

¹²The Lord, the LORD Almighty, called you to weep and mourn. He told you to shave your heads in sorrow for your sins and to wear clothes of sackcloth to show your remorse. ¹³But instead, you dance and play; you slaughter sacrificial animals, feast on meat, and drink wine. "Let's eat, drink, and be merry," you say. "What's the difference, for tomorrow we die." ¹⁴The LORD Almighty has revealed to me that this sin will never be forgiven you until the day you die. That is the judgment of the Lord, the LORD Almighty.

¹⁵Furthermore, the Lord, the LORD Almighty, told me to confront Shebna, the palace administrator, and to give him this message: ¹⁶"Who do you think you are, building a beautiful tomb for yourself in the rock? ¹⁷For the LORD is about to seize you and hurl you away. He is going to send you into captivity, you strong man! ¹⁸He will crumple you up into a ball and toss you away into a distant, barren land. There you will die, and there your glorious chariots will remain, broken and useless. You are a disgrace to your master.

¹⁹"Yes, I will drive you out of office," says the LORD. "I will pull you down from your high position. ²⁰And then I will call my servant Eliakim son of Hilkiah to replace you. ²¹He will have your royal robes, your title, and your authority. And he will be a father to the people of Jerusalem and Judah. ²²I will give him the key to the house

21:8 As in Dead Sea Scrolls and Syriac version; Masoretic Text reads *a lion.*   21:11a Hebrew *Dumah,* which means "silence" or "stillness." It is a wordplay on the word *Edom.*   21:11b Hebrew *Seir,* another name for Edom.   21:16 Hebrew *Within a year, like the years of a hired hand.* Some ancient manuscripts read *Within three years,* as in 16:14.   22:1 Hebrew *concerning the Valley of Vision.* 22:2 Hebrew *killed, but not by sword and not in battle.*   22:9 Hebrew *the city of David.*

of David—the highest position in the royal court. He will open doors, and no one will be able to shut them; he will close doors, and no one will be able to open them. ²³He will bring honor to his family name, for I will drive him firmly in place like a tent stake. ²⁴He will be loaded down with responsibility, and he will bring honor to even the lowliest members of his family."

²⁵The LORD Almighty says: "When that time comes, I will pull out the stake that seemed so firm. It will come out and fall to the ground. Everything it supports will fall with it. I, the LORD, have spoken!"

CHAPTER 23

This message came to me concerning Tyre:

Weep, O ships of Tarshish, returning home from distant lands! Weep for your harbor at Tyre because it is gone! The rumors you heard in Cyprus* are all true. ²Mourn in silence, you people of the coast and you merchants of Sidon. Your traders crossed the sea, ³sailing over deep waters. They brought you grain from Egypt* and harvests from along the Nile. You were the merchandise mart of the world.

⁴But now you are put to shame, city of Sidon, fortress on the sea. For the sea says, "Now I am childless; I have no sons or daughters." ⁵When Egypt hears the news about Tyre, there will be great sorrow. ⁶Flee now to Tarshish! Wail, you people who live by the sea! ⁷How can this silent ruin be all that is left of your once joyous city? What a history was yours! Think of all the colonists you sent to distant lands.

⁸Who has brought this disaster on Tyre,

empire builder and chief trader of the world? ⁹The LORD Almighty has done it to destroy your pride and show his contempt for all human greatness. ¹⁰Come, Tarshish, sweep over your mother Tyre like the flooding Nile, for the city is defenseless. ¹¹The LORD holds out his hand over the seas. He shakes the kingdoms of the earth. He has spoken out against Phoenicia* and depleted its strength. ¹²He says, "Never again will you rejoice, O daughter of Sidon. Once you were a lovely city, but you will never again be strong. Even if you flee to Cyprus, you will find no rest."

¹³Look at the land of Babylonia*—the people of that land are gone! The Assyrians have handed Babylon over to the wild beasts. They have built siege ramps against its walls, torn down its palaces, and turned it into a heap of rubble.

¹⁴Wail, O ships of Tarshish, for your home port is destroyed! ¹⁵For seventy years, the length of a king's life, Tyre will be forgotten. But then the city will come back to life and sing sweet songs like a prostitute. ¹⁶Long absent from her lovers, she will take a harp, walk the streets, and sing her songs, so that she will again be remembered. ¹⁷Yes, after seventy years the LORD will revive Tyre. But she will be no different than she was before. She will return again to all her evil ways around the world. ¹⁸But in the end her businesses will give their profits to the LORD. Her wealth will not be hoarded but will be used to provide good food and fine clothing for the LORD's priests.

23:1 Hebrew *Kittim;* also in 23:12.   23:3 Hebrew *from Shihor,* a branch of the Nile River.   23:11 Hebrew *Canaan.* 23:13 Or *Chaldea.*

JULY 20 □ DAY 202
ISAIAH 24–27
Judgment and Jubilation

OVERVIEW After eleven chapters of pronouncements upon specific nations, Isaiah's focus changes. There is coming a day when the entire earth will reel in judgment, its inhabitants quaking in terror and dismay. But the redeemed of the Lord will welcome that day and sing hymns of praise to the God of their salvation. "This is our God. We trusted in him, and he saved us. This is the LORD, in whom we trusted. Let us rejoice in the salvation he brings" (25:9). While the nations of the world writhe in judgment, Israel enjoys the benefits of peace and prosperity.

Chapter 24	Chapter 25	Chapter 26	Chapter 27
Day of the Lord	Devotion to the Lord	Delight in the Lord	Deliverance from the Lord
Reeling	Rejoicing	Singing	Saving

YOUR DAILY WALK During a violent thunderstorm, a mother tiptoed upstairs to her young son's bedroom, assuming he would need comfort from his fears. She found him kneeling by his bed talking to God—not in fear but in excitement. With each new flash of lightning, the mother heard her son exclaim, "Do it again, God! Do it again!"

You cannot have a holy country until you first have holy citizens.

In the midst of God's prophecy of a "thunderstorm" of judgment upon Israel and the surrounding nations, Isaiah pauses to praise God for his promise to overthrow the wicked ("Do it again, God!"). Isaiah knew it was meaningless to speak of judgment for sin on a national scale and ignore the fact that nations are made up of individuals, for to have a holy country, you must first have holy citizens.

Spend a few extra minutes today pondering chapter 26, Isaiah's hymn of praise for God's power "to punish the people of the earth for their sins" (26:21). And if you feel an uncomfortable pinching sensation as you read, maybe God is trying to speak to you!

INSIGHT There's Coming a Day
Isaiah 24–27 has been called "Isaiah's Apocalypse" because of the similarity of these chapters to the New Testament book of Revelation. One way Isaiah indicates he is prophesying is by using the phrase *in that day*. It occurs thirty times in the book as a whole; how many times can you find it in today's section? (Hint: Begin with the first verses of Isaiah 26 and 27.)

CHAPTER 24

Look! The LORD is about to destroy the earth and make it a vast wasteland. See how he is scattering the people over the face of the earth. ²Priests and laypeople, servants and masters, maids and mistresses, buyers and sellers, lenders and borrowers, bankers and debtors—none will be spared. ³The earth will be completely emptied and looted. The LORD has spoken!

⁴The earth dries up, the crops wither, the skies refuse to rain. ⁵The earth suffers for the sins of its people, for they have twisted the instructions of God, violated his laws, and broken his everlasting covenant. ⁶Therefore, a curse consumes the earth and its people. They are left desolate, destroyed by fire. Few will be left alive.

⁷All the joys of life will be gone. The grape harvest will fail, and there will be no wine. The merrymakers will sigh and mourn. ⁸The clash of tambourines will be stilled; the happy cries of celebration will be heard no more. The melodious chords of the harp will be silent. ⁹Gone are the joys of wine and song; strong drink now turns bitter in the mouth.

¹⁰The city writhes in chaos; every home is locked to keep out looters. ¹¹Mobs gather in the streets, crying out for wine. Joy has reached its lowest ebb. Gladness has been banished from the land. ¹²The city is left in ruins, with its gates battered down. ¹³Throughout the earth the story is the same—like the stray olives left on the tree or the few grapes left on the vine after harvest, only a remnant is left.

¹⁴But all who are left will shout and sing for joy. Those in the west will praise the LORD's majesty. ¹⁵In eastern lands, give glory to the LORD. In the coastlands of the sea, praise the name of the LORD, the God of Israel. ¹⁶Listen to them as they sing to the LORD from the ends of the earth. Hear them singing praises to the Righteous One!

But my heart is heavy with grief. I am discouraged, for evil still prevails, and treachery is everywhere. ¹⁷Terror and traps and snares will be your lot, you people of the earth. ¹⁸Those who flee in terror will fall into a trap, and those who escape the trap will step into a snare.

Destruction falls on you from the heavens. The world is shaken beneath you. ¹⁹The earth has broken down and has utterly collapsed. Everything is lost, abandoned, and confused. ²⁰The earth staggers like a drunkard. It trembles like a tent in a storm. It falls and will not rise again, for its sins are very great.

²¹In that day the LORD will punish the fallen angels in the heavens and the proud rulers of the nations on earth. ²²They will be rounded up and put in prison until they are tried and condemned. ²³Then the LORD Almighty will mount his throne on Mount Zion. He will rule gloriously in Jerusalem, in the sight of all the leaders of his people. There will be such glory that the brightness of the sun and moon will seem to fade away.

CHAPTER 25
O LORD, I will honor and praise your name, for you are my God. You do such wonderful things! You planned them long ago, and now you have accomplished them. ²You turn mighty cities into heaps of ruins. Cities with strong walls are turned to rubble. Beautiful palaces in distant lands disappear and will never be rebuilt. ³Therefore, strong nations will declare your glory; ruthless nations will revere you.

⁴But to the poor, O LORD, you are a refuge from the storm. To the needy in distress, you are a shelter from the rain and the heat. For the oppressive acts of ruthless people are like a storm beating against a wall, ⁵or like the relentless heat of the desert. But you silence the roar of foreign nations. You cool the land with the shade of a cloud. So the boastful songs of ruthless people are stilled.

⁶In Jerusalem,* the LORD Almighty will spread a wonderful feast for everyone around the world. It will be a delicious feast of good food, with clear, well-aged wine and choice beef. ⁷In that day he will remove the cloud of gloom, the shadow of death that hangs over the earth. ⁸He will swallow up death forever! The Sovereign LORD will wipe away all tears. He will remove forever all insults and mockery against his land and people. The LORD has spoken!

⁹In that day the people will proclaim, "This is our God. We trusted in him, and he saved us. This is the LORD, in whom we trusted. Let us rejoice in the salvation he brings!" ¹⁰For the LORD's good hand will rest on Jerusalem.

Moab will be crushed like trampled straw and left to rot. ¹¹God will push down Moab's people as a swimmer pushes down water with his hands. He will end their pride and all their evil works. ¹²The high walls of Moab will be demolished and ground to dust.

CHAPTER 26
In that day, everyone in the land of Judah will sing this song:

Our city is now strong!
   We are surrounded by the walls of God's salvation.
² Open the gates to all who are righteous;
   allow the faithful to enter.
³ You will keep in perfect peace all who trust in you,
   whose thoughts are fixed on you!
⁴ Trust in the LORD always,
   for the LORD GOD is the eternal Rock.
⁵ He humbles the proud
   and brings the arrogant city to the dust.
   Its walls come crashing down!
⁶   The poor and oppressed trample it underfoot.

⁷ But for those who are righteous,
   the path is not steep and rough.
   You are a God of justice,
   and you smooth out the road ahead of them.
⁸ LORD, we love to obey your laws;
   our heart's desire is to glorify your name.
⁹ All night long I search for you;
   earnestly I seek for God.
   For only when you come to judge the earth
   will people turn from wickedness and do what is right.
¹⁰ Your kindness to the wicked does not make them do good.
   They keep doing wrong and take no notice of the LORD's majesty.
¹¹ O LORD, they do not listen when you threaten.
   They do not see your upraised fist.

25:6 Hebrew *On this mountain;* also in 25:10.

Show them your eagerness to defend
your people.
Perhaps then they will be ashamed.
Let your fire consume your enemies.

¹² LORD, you will grant us peace,
for all we have accomplished is
really from you.
¹³ O LORD our God, others have ruled us,
but we worship you alone.
¹⁴ Those we served before are dead and
gone.
Never again will they return!
You attacked them and destroyed them,
and they are long forgotten.
¹⁵ We praise you, LORD!
You have made our nation great;
you have extended our borders!

¹⁶ LORD, in distress we searched for you.
We were bowed beneath the burden
of your discipline.
¹⁷ We were like a woman about to give
birth,
writhing and crying out in pain.
When we are in your presence, LORD,
¹⁸ we, too, writhe in agony,
but nothing comes of our suffering.
We have done nothing to rescue the
world;
no one has been born to populate the
earth.
¹⁹ Yet we have this assurance:
Those who belong to God will live;
their bodies will rise again!
Those who sleep in the earth
will rise up and sing for joy!
For God's light of life will fall like dew
on his people in the place of the dead!

²⁰Go home, my people, and lock your
doors! Hide until the LORD's anger against
your enemies has passed. ²¹Look! The
LORD is coming from heaven to punish the
people of the earth for their sins. The earth
will no longer hide those who have been
murdered. They will be brought out for all
to see.

27:9 Hebrew *Jacob's.*   27:12 Hebrew *the river.*

CHAPTER 27

In that day the LORD will take his terrible,
swift sword and punish Leviathan, the
swiftly moving serpent, the coiling, writhing serpent, the dragon of the sea.

²"In that day we will sing of the pleasant
vineyard. ³I, the LORD, will watch over it
and tend its fruitful vines. Each day I will
water them; day and night I will watch to
keep enemies away. ⁴My anger against Israel will be gone. If I find briers and thorns
bothering her, I will burn them up. ⁵These
enemies will be spared only if they surrender and beg for peace and protection."

⁶The time is coming when my people
will take root. Israel will bud and blossom
and fill the whole earth with her fruit! ⁷Has
the LORD punished Israel in the same way
he has punished her enemies? No, for he
devastated her enemies, ⁸but he has punished Israel only a little. He has exiled her
from her land as though blown away in a
storm from the east. ⁹The LORD did this to
purge away Israel's* sin. When he has finished, all the pagan altars will be crushed
to dust. There won't be an Asherah pole or
incense altar left standing. ¹⁰Israel's fortified cities will be silent and empty, the
houses abandoned, the streets covered
with grass. Cattle will graze there, chewing
on twigs and branches.

¹¹The people are like the dead branches
of a tree, broken off and used for kindling
beneath the cooking pots. Israel is a foolish
and stupid nation, for its people have
turned away from God. Therefore, the one
who made them will show them no pity or
mercy. ¹²Yet the time will come when the
LORD will gather them together one by one
like handpicked grain. He will bring them
to his great threshing floor—from the Euphrates River* in the east to the brook of
Egypt in the west. ¹³In that day the great
trumpet will sound. Many who were dying
in exile in Assyria and Egypt will return to
Jerusalem to worship the LORD on his holy
mountain.

JULY 21 ☐ DAY 203
As Good As Done

LOOK BACK It's hard to read Isaiah 5–27 without the aid of a good Bible atlas. Some of the nations and cities mentioned should be familiar because they still exist today (Damascus, Ethiopia, Egypt, Tyre, Arabia). Others have long since disappeared from the pages of history (Assyria, Babylon, Moab). Like a mighty threshing machine, the judgment of God falls upon small and great alike "in that day," punishing the arrogant, rewarding the faithful, and leading all humanity to worship the one who opens what no one can shut and shuts what no one can open (22:22).

Every loss leaves a space that can be filled by God's presence.

LOOK UP Do you remember where you were and what you were doing when you heard the news that the space shuttle *Challenger* had exploded?

For those of you over forty, do you remember where you were and what you were doing when you heard the news that President Kennedy had been assassinated?

Of course you do. Both events touched the heart and soul of the nation. In a moment frozen in time, the nation held its breath, hoping, praying that the headlines were a mistake.

Now read Isaiah 6:1: "In the year King Uzziah died . . ." One of the most beloved monarchs in Judah's history, a man who had ruled for more than half a century, was dead. The only ruler many in Judah had ever known had died a tragic death, leaving an enormous leadership vacuum in the nation. No doubt many questions filled the air: How will we get along without good king Uzziah? What will happen to us and our nation? What will the future hold? Everything seemed so uncertain, so frightening, so fragile.

But then Isaiah saw something more. He saw the Lord, "sitting on a lofty throne" (6:1). Suddenly his fears melted away and his questions seemed unimportant. Who was in control? *God was in control.* Even though the king of Judah had passed off the scene, the King of the universe would continue to rule forever.

LOOK AHEAD One wag has commented, "If you can keep your wits about you when everyone else around you is losing theirs, you obviously don't understand the situation." Perhaps. But it's equally possible you have a source of comfort and confidence that others around you haven't experienced. And that comforting Presence can give you a peace that defies human explanation, even in the face of tragedy (Philippians 4:6-7).

At a time when the nation of Judah was traumatized by front-page news, Isaiah was focusing on his holy, awesome, almighty God. The result was a quiet confidence that would fortify Isaiah for a lifetime of ministry to a hostile audience. How about you? Instead of reading a paper today, allow Isaiah's pen to be your eyes and ears as you look upon and listen to your mighty God. And don't be surprised if "peace like a river" is the result.

JULY 22 ☐ DAY 204
ISAIAH 28–30
A Painful Example

OVERVIEW Isaiah now declares a series of specific woes upon Israel and Judah. Targeting his messages for the capital cities of Samaria and Jerusalem (much like a modern reporter would speak of Washington, D.C., or Moscow), Isaiah declares that destruction is imminent. For "the drunkards of Israel" (28:1), it is too late to repent; judgment is inescapable. But Jerusalem can still learn from the fate of her sister nation. Lulled into a false sense of security by empty ritualism, Jerusalem must awake from spiritual stupor. Otherwise, it will follow Israel's fatal error of substituting foolish alliances for faith in God.

Chapter 28	Chapter 29	Chapter 30
No Time for Israel	Destruction for Jerusalem	Warning to Judah
"Too Late!"	"Shape Up!"	"Trust God!"

YOUR DAILY WALK When was the last time you tried to help God solve one of your problems? *After all,* you probably reasoned, *God must not know how desperate my situation really is! If he did, he would come to my rescue. But since I don't see him working, I'd better get in there and give him a helping hand. Right?*

Walking by faith means being prepared to trust where we are not permitted to see.

Wrong! That was precisely the mistake Judah made. To prevent the onslaught of Assyria, Judah looked to her pagan neighbors for alliances to offset Assyria's mighty armies. Look at 29:15-16 and you'll see that Judah thought she was doing this without God's knowledge. But God compares Judah's self-help program to a lump of clay trying to aid the potter who is shaping it!

Carry a shoestring with you today as a constant reminder of the danger of pulling yourself up by your own bootstraps. Rather, "in quietness and confidence is your strength" (30:15).

INSIGHT A Fitting Title for Judah's Capital
Ariel (29:1), literally "hearth of God," refers to Jerusalem. It can also be translated "altar," an apt description of the city where the Ark of God's presence resided and where all too soon the fire of God's judgment would fall with devastating fury.

CHAPTER 28
Destruction is certain for the city of Samaria—the pride and joy of the drunkards of Israel*! It sits in a rich valley, but its glorious beauty will suddenly disappear. Destruction is certain for that city—the pride of a people brought low by wine. ²For the Lord will send the mighty Assyrian army against it. Like a mighty hailstorm and a torrential rain, they will burst upon it and dash it to the ground. ³The proud city of Samaria—the pride and joy of the drunkards of Israel—will be trampled beneath its enemies' feet. ⁴It sits in a fertile

valley, but its glorious beauty will suddenly disappear. It will be greedily snatched up, as an early fig is hungrily picked and eaten.

⁵Then at last the LORD Almighty will himself be Israel's crowning glory. He will be the pride and joy of the remnant of his people. ⁶He will give a longing for justice to their judges. He will give great courage to their warriors who stand at the gates.

⁷Now, however, Israel is being led by drunks! The priests and prophets reel and stagger from beer and wine. They make stupid mistakes as they carry out their re-

28:1 Hebrew *of Ephraim,* referring to the northern kingdom of Israel; also in 28:3.

sponsibilities. ⁸Their tables are covered with vomit; filth is everywhere. ⁹They say, "Who does the LORD think we are? Why does he speak to us like this? Are we little children, barely old enough to talk? ¹⁰He tells us everything over and over again, a line at a time, in very simple words!*"

¹¹Since they refuse to listen, God will speak to them through foreign oppressors who speak an unknown language! ¹²God's people could have rest in their own land if they would only obey him, but they will not listen. ¹³So the LORD will spell out his message for them again, repeating it over and over, a line at a time, in very simple words. Yet they will stumble over this simple, straightforward message. They will be injured, trapped, and captured.

¹⁴Therefore, listen to this message from the LORD, you scoffing rulers in Jerusalem. ¹⁵You boast that you have struck a bargain to avoid death and have made a deal to dodge the grave.* You say, "The Assyrians can never touch us, for we have built a strong refuge made of lies and deception." ¹⁶Therefore, this is what the Sovereign LORD says: "Look! I am placing a foundation stone in Jerusalem.* It is firm, a tested and precious cornerstone that is safe to build on. Whoever believes need never run away again.*

¹⁷"I will take the measuring line of justice and the plumb line of righteousness to check the foundation wall you have built. Your refuge looks strong, but since it is made of lies, a hailstorm will knock it down. Since it is made of deception, the enemy will come like a flood to sweep it away. ¹⁸I will cancel the bargain you made to avoid death, and I will overturn your deal to dodge the grave. When the terrible enemy floods in, you will be trampled into the ground. ¹⁹Again and again that flood will come, morning after morning, day and night, until you are carried away."

This message will bring terror to your people. ²⁰For you have no place of refuge—the bed you have made is too short to lie on. The blankets are too narrow to cover you. ²¹The LORD will come suddenly and in anger, as he did against the Philistines at Mount Perazim and against the Amorites at Gibeon. He will come to do a strange,

unusual thing: He will destroy his own people! ²²So scoff no more, or your punishment will be even greater. For the Lord, the LORD Almighty, has plainly told me that he is determined to crush you.

²³Listen to me; listen as I plead! ²⁴Does a farmer always plow and never sow? Is he forever cultivating the soil and never planting it? ²⁵Does he not finally plant his seeds for dill, cummin, wheat, barley, and spelt, each in its own section of his land? ²⁶The farmer knows just what to do, for God has given him understanding. ²⁷He doesn't thresh all his crops the same way. A heavy sledge is never used on dill; rather, it is beaten with a light stick. A threshing wheel is never rolled on cummin; instead, it is beaten softly with a flail. ²⁸Bread grain is easily crushed, so he doesn't keep on pounding it. He threshes it under the wheels of a cart, but he doesn't pulverize it. ²⁹The LORD Almighty is a wonderful teacher, and he gives the farmer great wisdom.

CHAPTER 29
"Destruction is certain for Ariel,* the City of David. Year after year you offer your many sacrifices. ²Yet I will bring disaster upon you, and there will be much weeping and sorrow. For Jerusalem will become as her name Ariel means—an altar covered with blood. ³I will be your enemy, surrounding Jerusalem and attacking its walls. I will build siege towers around it and will destroy it. ⁴Your voice will whisper like a ghost from the earth where you will lie buried.

⁵"But suddenly, your ruthless enemies will be driven away like chaff before the wind. ⁶In an instant, I, the LORD Almighty, will come against them with thunder and earthquake and great noise, with whirlwind and storm and consuming fire. ⁷All the nations fighting against Jerusalem* will vanish like a dream! Those who are attacking her walls will vanish like a vision in the night. ⁸A hungry person dreams of eating but is still hungry. A thirsty person dreams of drinking but is still faint from thirst when morning comes. In the same way, your enemies will dream of a victorious conquest over Jerusalem,* but all to no avail."

28:10 The Hebrew text for this verse may simply be childish sounds that have no meaning, or perhaps a childish mimicking of the prophet's words. Also in 28:13.   28:15 Hebrew *Sheol;* also in 28:18.   28:16a Hebrew *in Zion.*   28:16b Greek version reads *Anyone who believes in him will not be disappointed.*   29:1 *Ariel* sounds like a Hebrew term that means "hearth" or "altar."   29:7 Hebrew *Ariel.*   29:8 Hebrew *Mount Zion.*

⁹Are you amazed and incredulous? Do you not believe it? Then go ahead and be blind if you must. You are stupid, but not from wine! You stagger, but not from beer! ¹⁰For the LORD has poured out on you a spirit of deep sleep. He has closed the eyes of your prophets and visionaries. ¹¹All these future events are a sealed book to them. When you give it to those who can read, they will say, "We can't read it because it is sealed." ¹²When you give it to those who cannot read, they will say, "Sorry, we don't know how to read."

¹³And so the Lord says, "These people say they are mine. They honor me with their lips, but their hearts are far away. And their worship of me amounts to nothing more than human laws learned by rote.* ¹⁴Because of this, I will do wonders among these hypocrites. I will show that human wisdom is foolish and even the most brilliant people lack understanding."

¹⁵Destruction is certain for those who try to hide their plans from the LORD, who try to keep him in the dark concerning what they do! "The LORD can't see us," you say to yourselves. "He doesn't know what is going on!" ¹⁶How stupid can you be? He is the Potter, and he is certainly greater than you. You are only the jars he makes! Should the thing that was created say to the one who made it, "He didn't make us"? Does a jar ever say, "The potter who made me is stupid"?

¹⁷Soon—and it will not be very long—the wilderness of Lebanon will be a fertile field once again. And the fertile fields will become a lush and fertile forest. ¹⁸In that day deaf people will hear words read from a book, and blind people will see through the gloom and darkness. ¹⁹The humble will be filled with fresh joy from the LORD. Those who are poor will rejoice in the Holy One of Israel. ²⁰Those who intimidate and harass will be gone, and all those who plot evil will be killed. ²¹Those who make the innocent guilty by their false testimony will disappear. And those who use trickery to pervert justice and tell lies to tear down the innocent will be no more.

²²That is why the LORD, who redeemed Abraham, says to the people of Israel,* "My people will no longer pale with fear or be ashamed. ²³For when they see their

many children and material blessings, they will recognize the holiness of the Holy One of Israel. They will stand in awe of the God of Israel. ²⁴Those in error will then believe the truth, and those who constantly complain will accept instruction.

CHAPTER 30

"Destruction is certain for my rebellious children," says the LORD. "You make plans that are contrary to my will. You weave a web of plans that are not from my Spirit, thus piling up your sins. ²For without consulting me, you have gone down to Egypt to find help. You have put your trust in Pharaoh for his protection. ³But in trusting Pharaoh, you will be humiliated and disgraced. ⁴For though his power extends to Zoan and Hanes, ⁵it will all turn out to your shame. He will not help you even one little bit."

⁶Look at the animals moving slowly across the terrible desert to Egypt—donkeys and camels loaded with treasure to pay for Egypt's aid. On through the wilderness they go, where lions and poisonous snakes live. All this, and Egypt will give you nothing in return. ⁷Egypt's promises are worthless! I call her the Harmless Dragon.*

⁸Now go and write down these words concerning Egypt. They will then stand until the end of time as a witness to Israel's unbelief. ⁹For these people are stubborn rebels who refuse to pay any attention to the LORD's instructions.

¹⁰They tell the prophets, "Shut up! We don't want any more of your reports." They say, "Don't tell us the truth. Tell us nice things. Tell us lies. ¹¹Forget all this gloom. We have heard more than enough about your 'Holy One of Israel.' We are tired of listening to what he has to say."

¹²This is the reply of the Holy One of Israel: "Because you despise what I tell you and trust instead in oppression and lies, ¹³calamity will come upon you suddenly. It will be like a bulging wall that bursts and falls. In an instant it will collapse and come crashing down. ¹⁴You will be smashed like a piece of pottery—shattered so completely that there won't be a piece left that is big enough to carry coals from a fireplace or a little water from the well."

29:13 Greek version reads *Their worship is a farce, for they merely teach human commands and teachings.* 29:22 Hebrew *of Jacob;* also in 29:23. 30:7 Hebrew *Rahab who sits still.* Rahab is the name of a mythical sea monster that represents chaos in ancient literature. The name is used here as a poetic name for Egypt.

¹⁵The Sovereign LORD, the Holy One of Israel, says, "Only in returning to me and waiting for me will you be saved. In quietness and confidence is your strength. But you would have none of it. ¹⁶You said, 'No, we will get our help from Egypt. They will give us swift horses for riding into battle.' But the only swiftness you are going to see is the swiftness of your enemies chasing you! ¹⁷One of them will chase a thousand of you. Five of them will make all of you flee. You will be left like a lonely flagpole on a distant mountaintop."

¹⁸But the LORD still waits for you to come to him so he can show you his love and compassion. For the LORD is a faithful God. Blessed are those who wait for him to help them.

¹⁹O people of Zion, who live in Jerusalem, you will weep no more. He will be gracious if you ask for help. He will respond instantly to the sound of your cries. ²⁰Though the Lord gave you adversity for food and affliction for drink, he will still be with you to teach you. You will see your teacher with your own eyes, ²¹and you will hear a voice say, "This is the way; turn around and walk here." ²²Then you will destroy all your silver idols and gold images. You will throw them out like filthy rags. "Ugh!" you will say to them. "Begone!"

²³Then the LORD will bless you with rain at planting time. There will be wonderful harvests and plenty of pastureland for your cattle. ²⁴The oxen and donkeys that till the ground will eat good grain, its chaff having been blown away by the wind. ²⁵In that day, when your enemies are slaughtered, there will be streams of water flowing down every mountain and hill. ²⁶The moon will be as bright as the sun, and the sun will be seven times brighter—like the light of seven days! So it will be when the LORD begins to heal his people and cure the wounds he gave them.

²⁷Look! The LORD is coming from far away, burning with anger, surrounded by a thick, rising smoke. His lips are filled with fury; his words consume like fire. ²⁸His anger pours out like a flood on his enemies, sweeping them all away. He will sift out the proud nations. He will bridle them and lead them off to their destruction.

²⁹But the people of God will sing a song of joy, like the songs at the holy festivals. You will be filled with joy, as when a flutist leads a group of pilgrims to Jerusalem—the mountain of the LORD—to the Rock of Israel. ³⁰And the LORD will make his majestic voice heard. With angry indignation he will bring down his mighty arm on his enemies. It will descend with devouring flames, with cloudbursts, thunderstorms, and huge hailstones, bringing their destruction. ³¹At the LORD's command, the Assyrians will be shattered. He will strike them down with his rod. ³²And as the LORD strikes them, his people will keep time with the music of tambourines and harps. ³³Topheth—the place of burning—has long been ready for the Assyrian king; it has been piled high with wood. The breath of the LORD, like fire from a volcano, will set it ablaze.

JULY 23 ☐ DAY 205
ISAIAH 31–35
Coming Destruction, Coming King

 OVERVIEW As Isaiah ponders the joyous prophecy of Israel's deliverance from Assyria, his thoughts naturally turn to the arrival of the much-prophesied future King whose rule and righteousness would be worldwide. In the light of this glorious future, Isaiah urges the people of Judah to remain strong in their trust of God, even though the gathering storm clouds of Assyrian invasion can be seen on the horizon. With faith in God they can wait expectantly for the promised era of restored prosperity when "sorrow and mourning will disappear" (35:10).

Chapter 31	Chapter 32	Chapters 33–34	Chapter 35
Coming Destruction	Coming King	Sword of the Lord	The Nation Restored
Egypt	Messiah	Assyria	Redeemed

YOUR DAILY WALK When your heart is disturbed by fear or worry, where do you turn to find peace and provision?

Faith is dead to doubt, dumb to discouragement, blind to impossibilities.

The story is told of an all-church meeting called to discuss an urgent matter. There were insufficient funds on hand to pay an important bill. Worried expressions furrowed many a brow. Where could the church turn? Suddenly, a wealthy businessman stood to his feet and offered to underwrite the full amount. Sighs of relief were heard throughout the room—until one older Christian reminded the members that God had promised to underwrite his work all along.

By nature it is easier for people to trust limited human resources than God's inexhaustible supply. Judah looked to the military might of Egypt for security, forgetting that the God of Israel had shown once before how fragile that "might" might prove (Exodus 14)!

What need is uppermost in your life right now? Are the resources of God enough to put your mind at ease, or are you seeking relief from another source? You wouldn't ask a child to do what only an adult is capable of doing. But are you trusting others to do what only God can—and will—do on your behalf? Talk to him about it.

INSIGHT No Smooth Path to Peace

The pampered women of 32:9 provide only one example of the self-indulgent society of Israel's day (see also 22:13; 28:15). But God cannot bring peace to a self-indulgent people. The ground must be cleared and resown with righteousness, of which peace is the fruit (32:16-17).

CHAPTER 31

Destruction is certain for those who look to Egypt for help, trusting their cavalry and chariots instead of looking to the LORD, the Holy One of Israel. ²In his wisdom, the LORD will send great disaster; he will not change his mind. He will rise against those who are wicked, and he will crush their allies, too. ³For these Egyptians are mere humans, not God! Their horses are puny flesh, not mighty spirits! When the LORD clenches his fist against them, they will stumble and fall among those they are trying to help. They will all fall down and die together.

⁴But the LORD has told me this: "When a lion, even a young one, kills a sheep, it pays no attention to the shepherd's shouts and noise. It just goes right on eating. In the same way, the LORD Almighty will come and fight on Mount Zion. He will not be frightened away! ⁵The LORD Almighty will hover over Jerusalem as a bird hovers around its nest. He will defend and save the city; he will pass over it and rescue it."

⁶Therefore, my people, though you are such wicked rebels, come and return to the LORD. ⁷I know the glorious day will come when every one of you will throw away the gold idols and silver images that your sinful hands have made.

⁸"The Assyrians will be destroyed, but not by the swords of men. The sword of God will strike them, and they will panic and flee. The strong young Assyrians will be taken away as captives. ⁹Even their generals will quake with terror and flee when they see the battle flags," says the LORD, whose flame burns brightly in Jerusalem.

CHAPTER 32

Look, a righteous king is coming! And honest princes will rule under him. ²He will shelter Israel from the storm and the wind. He will refresh her as a river in the desert and as the cool shadow of a large rock in a hot and weary land. ³Then everyone who can see will be looking for God, and those who can hear will listen to his voice. ⁴Even the hotheads among them will be full of sense and understanding. Those who stammer in uncertainty will speak out plainly.

⁵In that day ungodly fools will not be heroes. Wealthy cheaters will not be respected as outstanding citizens. ⁶Everyone will recognize ungodly fools for what they are. They spread lies about the LORD; they deprive the hungry of food and give no water to the thirsty. ⁷The smooth tricks of evil people will be exposed, including all the lies they use to oppress the poor in the courts. ⁸But good people will be generous to others and will be blessed for all they do.

⁹Listen, you women who lie around in lazy ease. Listen to me, and I will tell you of your reward. ¹⁰In a short time—in just a little more than a year—you careless ones will suddenly begin to care. For your fruit crop will fail, and the harvest will never take place. ¹¹Tremble, you women of ease; throw off your unconcern. Strip off your pretty clothes, and wear sackcloth in your grief. ¹²Beat your breasts in sorrow for your bountiful farms that will soon be gone, and for those fruitful vines of other years. ¹³For your land will be overgrown with thorns and briers. Your joyful homes and happy cities will be gone. ¹⁴The palace and the city will be deserted, and busy towns will be empty. Herds of donkeys and goats will graze on the hills where the watchtowers are, ¹⁵until at last the Spirit is poured down upon us from heaven. Then the wilderness will become a fertile field, and the fertile field will become a lush and fertile forest. ¹⁶Justice will rule in the wilderness and righteousness in the fertile field. ¹⁷And this righteousness will bring peace. Quietness and confidence will fill the land forever.

¹⁸My people will live in safety, quietly at home. They will be at rest. ¹⁹Even though the forest will be destroyed and the city torn down, ²⁰God will greatly bless his people. Wherever they plant seed, bountiful crops will spring up. Their flocks and herds will graze in green pastures.

CHAPTER 33
Destruction is certain for you Assyrians,* who have destroyed everything around you but have never felt destruction yourselves. You expect others to respect their promises to you, while you betray your promises to them. Now you, too, will be betrayed and destroyed!

²But LORD, be merciful to us, for we have waited for you. Be our strength each day and our salvation in times of trouble. ³The enemy runs at the sound of your voice. When you stand up, the nations flee! ⁴Just as locusts strip the fields and vines, so Jerusalem will strip the fallen army of Assyria!

⁵Though the LORD is very great and lives in heaven, he will make Jerusalem* his home of justice and righteousness. ⁶In that day he will be your sure foundation, providing a rich store of salvation, wisdom, and knowledge. The fear of the LORD is the key to this treasure.

⁷But now your ambassadors weep in bitter disappointment, for Assyria has refused their petition for peace. ⁸Your roads are deserted; no one travels them anymore. The Assyrians have broken their peace pact and care nothing for the promises they made before witnesses.* They have no respect for anyone. ⁹All the land of Israel is in trouble. Lebanon has been destroyed. The plain of Sharon is now a wilderness. Bashan and Carmel have been plundered.

¹⁰But the LORD says: "I will stand up and show my power and might. ¹¹You Assyrians will gain nothing by all your efforts. Your own breath will turn to fire and kill you. ¹²Your people will be burned up completely, like thorns cut down and tossed in a fire. ¹³Listen to what I have done, you nations far away! And you that are near, acknowledge my might!"

¹⁴The sinners in Jerusalem* shake with fear. "Which one of us," they cry, "can live here in the presence of this all-consuming fire?" ¹⁵The ones who can live here are those who are honest and fair, who reject making a profit by fraud, who stay far away from bribes, who refuse to listen to those who plot murder, who shut their eyes to all enticement to do wrong. ¹⁶These are the ones who will dwell on high. The rocks of the mountains will be their fortress of safety. Food will be supplied to them, and they will have water in abundance.

¹⁷Your eyes will see the king in all his splendor, and you will see a land that stretches into the distance. ¹⁸You will think back to this time of terror when the Assyrian officers outside your walls counted your towers and estimated how much

33:1 Hebrew *for you, O destroyer . . . O betrayer.* The Hebrew text does not specifically name Assyria as the object of this prophecy. **33:5** Hebrew *Zion.*   **33:8** As in Dead Sea Scrolls; Masoretic Text reads *care nothing for the cities.*   **33:14** Hebrew *in Zion.*

plunder they would get from your fallen city. [19]But soon they will all be gone. These fierce, violent people with a strange, unknown language will disappear.

[20]Instead, you will see Zion as a place of worship and celebration. You will see Jerusalem, a city quiet and secure. [21]The LORD will be our Mighty One. He will be like a wide river of protection that no enemy can cross. [22]For the LORD is our judge, our lawgiver, and our king. He will care for us and save us. [23]The enemies' sails hang loose on broken masts with useless tackle. Their treasure will be divided by the people of God. Even the lame will win their share! [24]The people of Israel will no longer say, "We are sick and helpless," for the LORD will forgive their sins.

CHAPTER 34

Come here and listen, O nations of the earth. Let the world and everything in it hear my words. [2]For the LORD is enraged against the nations. His fury is against all their armies. He will completely destroy* them, bringing about their slaughter. [3]Their dead will be left unburied, and the stench of rotting bodies will fill the land. The mountains will flow with their blood. [4]The heavens above will melt away and disappear like a rolled-up scroll. The stars will fall from the sky, just as withered leaves and fruit fall from a tree.

[5]And when my sword has finished its work in the heavens, then watch. It will fall upon Edom, the nation I have completely destroyed. [6]The sword of the LORD is drenched with blood. It is covered with fat as though it had been used for killing lambs and goats and rams for a sacrifice. Yes, the LORD will offer a great sacrifice in the rich city of Bozrah. He will make a mighty slaughter in Edom. [7]The strongest will die—veterans and young men, too. The land will be soaked with blood and the soil enriched with fat. [8]For it is the day of the LORD's vengeance, the year when Edom will be paid back for all it did to Israel.* [9]The streams of Edom will be filled with burning pitch, and the ground will be covered with fire.

[10]This judgment on Edom will never end; the smoke of its burning will rise forever. The land will lie deserted from generation to generation. No one will live there anymore. [11]It will be haunted by the horned owl, the hawk, the screech owl, and the raven.* For God will bring chaos and destruction to that land. [12]It will be called the Land of Nothing, and its princes soon will all be gone. [13]Thorns will overrun its palaces; nettles will grow in its forts. The ruins will become a haunt for jackals and a home for ostriches. [14]Wild animals of the desert will mingle there with hyenas, their howls filling the night. Wild goats will bleat at one another among the ruins, and night creatures will come there to rest. [15]There the owl will make her nest and lay her eggs. She will hatch her young and cover them with her wings. And the vultures will come, each one with its mate.

[16]Search the book of the LORD, and see what he will do. He will not miss a single detail. Not one of these birds and animals will be missing, and none will lack a mate, for the LORD has promised this. His Spirit will make it all come true. [17]He has surveyed and divided the land and deeded it over to those creatures. They will possess it forever, from generation to generation.

CHAPTER 35

Even the wilderness will rejoice in those days. The desert will blossom with flowers. [2]Yes, there will be an abundance of flowers and singing and joy! The deserts will become as green as the mountains of Lebanon, as lovely as Mount Carmel's pastures and the plain of Sharon. There the LORD will display his glory, the splendor of our God.

[3]With this news, strengthen those who have tired hands, and encourage those who have weak knees. [4]Say to those who are afraid, "Be strong, and do not fear, for your God is coming to destroy your enemies. He is coming to save you." [5]And when he comes, he will open the eyes of the blind and unstop the ears of the deaf. [6]The lame will leap like a deer, and those who cannot speak will shout and sing! Springs will gush forth in the wilderness, and streams will water the desert. [7]The parched ground will become a pool, and springs of water will satisfy the thirsty land. Marsh grass and reeds and rushes will flourish where desert jackals once lived.

34:2 The Hebrew term used here refers to the complete consecration of things or people to the LORD, either by destroying them or by giving them as an offering; also in 34:5.   **34:8** Hebrew *to Zion.*   **34:11** The identification of some of these birds is uncertain.

⁸And a main road will go through that once deserted land. It will be named the Highway of Holiness. Evil-hearted people will never travel on it. It will be only for those who walk in God's ways; fools will never walk there. ⁹Lions will not lurk along its course, and there will be no other dangers. Only the redeemed will follow it. ¹⁰Those who have been ransomed by the LORD will return to Jerusalem,* singing songs of everlasting joy. Sorrow and mourning will disappear, and they will be overcome with joy and gladness.

35:10 Hebrew *Zion*.

JULY 24 ☐ DAY 206
ISAIAH 36–39
Judah's Day of Judgment

OVERVIEW Today's reading represents a four-chapter interlude in Isaiah's prophecy—a historical parenthesis that shows the fulfillment of some of Isaiah's early prophecies and sets the stage for many of his later ones. The focus throughout is on godly king Hezekiah, perhaps the premier reformer of Judah. A man of prayer and principle, Hezekiah sees God destroy 185,000 Assyrian invaders and extend his own life by fifteen years. But by responding in foolish pride to Babylonian emissaries, Hezekiah seals the fate of his nation.

Chapter 36	Chapter 37	Chapter 38	Chapter 39
Arrogant Assyria	Divine Deliverance	A Mortal Illness	A Fatal Error
Hezekiah's Faithfulness		Hezekiah's Failure	

No one ever repented of being a Christian on his or her deathbed.

YOUR DAILY WALK Something happened (on the average) every twenty seconds last year. It affected the lives of 1.5 million Americans. Can you guess what it was? (Hint: It had nothing to do with Ronald McDonald!)

Answer: Every twenty seconds, someone in the United States suffered a heart attack . . . and suddenly came to realize that death was only a heartbeat away. And for six hundred thousand Americans that realization became a reality.

Death. It's a universally distasteful subject. But the fact remains that one out of one dies! For King Hezekiah—as with many people—the approach of death brought tears (38:1-3)—tears of regret . . . tears of remorse. So many good intentions . . . so many half-finished projects. God gave Hezekiah a gift of fifteen additional years—but that doesn't always happen. When it's time for you to die, will you be ready—or regretful—to see the Lord face-to-face? Find the obituary column in your newspaper, and pretend for a moment that your name is there (you may even want to write it in, just to emphasize the point). Now talk to God about how you want to spend the rest of your days!

INSIGHT A Historic Spot Revisited
King Sennacherib's field commander "stopped beside the aqueduct that feeds water into the upper pool, near the road leading to the field where cloth is bleached" when he shouted his arrogant threats (36:2). Twenty-three years earlier, God had told a man to stand in the same spot and declare his message. Do you remember who? (If you're stumped, check 7:3-9.)

CHAPTER 36

In the fourteenth year of King Hezekiah's reign, King Sennacherib of Assyria came to attack the fortified cities of Judah and conquered them. ²Then the king of Assyria sent his personal representative with a huge army from Lachish to confront King Hezekiah in Jerusalem. The Assyrians stopped beside the aqueduct that feeds water into the upper pool, near the road leading to the field where cloth is bleached.

³These are the officials who went out to meet with them: Eliakim son of Hilkiah, the palace administrator, Shebna the court secretary, and Joah son of Asaph, the royal historian. ⁴Then the Assyrian king's personal representative sent this message to King Hezekiah:

"This is what the great king of Assyria says: What are you trusting in that makes you so confident? ⁵Do you think that mere words can substitute for military skill and strength? Which of your allies will give you any military backing against Assyria? ⁶Will Egypt? If you lean on Egypt, you will find it to be a stick that breaks beneath your weight and pierces your hand. The Pharaoh of Egypt is completely unreliable!

⁷"But perhaps you will say, 'We are trusting in the LORD our God!' But isn't he the one who was insulted by King Hezekiah? Didn't Hezekiah tear down his shrines and altars and make everyone in Judah worship only at the altar here in Jerusalem?

⁸"I'll tell you what! My master, the king of Assyria, will strike a bargain with you. If you can find two thousand horsemen in your entire army, he will give you two thousand horses for them to ride on! ⁹With your tiny army, how can you think of challenging even the weakest contingent of my master's troops, even with the help of Egypt's chariots and horsemen*? ¹⁰What's more, do you think we have invaded your land without the LORD's direction? The LORD himself told us, 'Go and destroy it!'"

¹¹Then Eliakim, Shebna, and Joah said to the king's representative, "Please speak to us in Aramaic, for we understand it well. Don't speak in Hebrew, for the people on the wall will hear."

¹²But Sennacherib's representative replied, "My master wants everyone in Jerusalem to hear this, not just you. He wants them to know that if you do not surrender, this city will be put under siege. The people will become so hungry and thirsty that they will eat their own dung and drink their own urine."

¹³Then he stood and shouted in Hebrew to the people on the wall, "Listen to this message from the great king of Assyria! ¹⁴This is what the king says: Don't let King Hezekiah deceive you. He will never be able to rescue you. ¹⁵Don't let him fool you into trusting in the LORD by saying, 'The LORD will rescue us! This city will never be handed over to the Assyrian king.'

¹⁶"Don't listen to Hezekiah! These are the terms the king of Assyria is offering: Make peace with me—open the gates and come out. Then I will allow each of you to continue eating from your own garden and drinking from your own well. ¹⁷Then I will arrange to take you to another land like this one—a country with bountiful harvests of grain and wine, bread and vineyards—a land of plenty.

¹⁸"Don't let Hezekiah mislead you by saying, 'The LORD will rescue us!' Have the gods of any other nations ever saved their people from the king of Assyria? ¹⁹What happened to the gods of Hamath and Arpad? And what about the gods of Sepharvaim? Did they rescue Samaria from my power? ²⁰What god of any nation has ever been able to save its people from my power? Name just one! So what makes you think that the LORD can rescue Jerusalem?"

²¹But the people were silent and did not answer because Hezekiah had told them not to speak. ²²Then Eliakim son of Hilkiah, the palace administrator, Shebna the court secretary, and Joah son of Asaph, the royal historian, went back to Hezekiah. They tore their clothes in despair, and they went in to see the king and told him what the Assyrian representative had said.

CHAPTER 37

When King Hezekiah heard their report, he tore his clothes and put on sackcloth and went into the Temple of the LORD to pray. ²And he sent Eliakim the palace administrator, Shebna the court secretary, and the leading priests, all dressed in sackcloth, to

36:9 Or *and charioteers.*

the prophet Isaiah son of Amoz. [3]They told him, "This is what King Hezekiah says: This is a day of trouble, insult, and disgrace. It is like when a child is ready to be born, but the mother has no strength to deliver it. [4]But perhaps the LORD your God has heard the Assyrian representative defying the living God and will punish him for his words. Oh, pray for those of us who are left!"

[5]After King Hezekiah's officials delivered the king's message to Isaiah, [6]the prophet replied, "Say to your master, 'This is what the LORD says: Do not be disturbed by this blasphemous speech against me from the Assyrian king's messengers. [7]Listen! I myself will make sure that the king will receive a report from Assyria telling him that he is needed at home. Then I will make him want to return to his land, where I will have him killed with a sword.'"

[8]Meanwhile, the Assyrian representative left Jerusalem and went to consult his king, who had left Lachish and was attacking Libnah. [9]Soon afterward King Sennacherib received word that King Tirhakah of Ethiopia* was leading an army to fight against him. Before leaving to meet the attack, he sent this message back to Hezekiah in Jerusalem:

[10]"This message is for King Hezekiah of Judah. Don't let this God you trust deceive you with promises that Jerusalem will not be captured by the king of Assyria. [11]You know perfectly well what the kings of Assyria have done wherever they have gone. They have crushed everyone who stood in their way! Why should you be any different? [12]Have the gods of other nations rescued them—such nations as Gozan, Haran, Rezeph, and the people of Eden who were in Tel-assar? The former kings of Assyria destroyed them all! [13]What happened to the king of Hamath and the king of Arpad? What happened to the kings of Sepharvaim, Hena, and Ivvah?"

[14]After Hezekiah received the letter and read it, he went up to the LORD's Temple and spread it out before the LORD. [15]And Hezekiah prayed this prayer before the LORD: [16]"O LORD Almighty, God of Israel, you are enthroned between the mighty cherubim! You alone are God of all the kingdoms of the earth. You alone created the heavens and the earth. [17]Listen to me, O LORD, and hear! Open your eyes, O LORD, and see! Listen to Sennacherib's words of defiance against the living God.

[18]"It is true, LORD, that the kings of Assyria have destroyed all these nations, just as the message says. [19]And they have thrown the gods of these nations into the fire and burned them. But of course the Assyrians could destroy them! They were not gods at all—only idols of wood and stone shaped by human hands. [20]Now, O LORD our God, rescue us from his power; then all the kingdoms of the earth will know that you alone, O LORD, are God."

[21]Then Isaiah son of Amoz sent this message to Hezekiah: "This is what the LORD, the God of Israel, says: This is my answer to your prayer concerning King Sennacherib of Assyria. [22]This is the message that the LORD has spoken against him:

'The virgin daughter of Zion
    despises you and laughs at you.
The daughter of Jerusalem
    scoffs and shakes her head as you
        flee.
[23] 'Whom do you think you have been
        insulting and ridiculing?
    Against whom did you raise your
        voice?
    At whom did you look in such proud
        condescension?
    It was the Holy One of Israel!
[24] By your messengers you have mocked
        the Lord.
    You have said, "With my many
        chariots
    I have conquered the highest
        mountains—
    yes, the remotest peaks of Lebanon.
    I have cut down its tallest cedars
        and its choicest cypress trees.
    I have reached its farthest corners
        and explored its deepest forests.
[25] I have dug wells in many a foreign
        land
        and refreshed myself with their
            water.
    I even stopped up the rivers of Egypt
        so that my armies could go across!"

37:9 Hebrew *of Cush.*

26 'But have you not heard?
  It was I, the LORD, who decided this
    long ago.
  Long ago I planned what I am now
    causing to happen,
  that you should crush fortified cities
    into heaps of rubble.
27 That is why their people have so little
    power
  and are such easy prey for you.
  They are as helpless as the grass,
    as easily trampled as tender green
      shoots.
  They are like grass sprouting on a
    housetop,
    easily scorched by the sun.

28 'But I know you well—
    your comings and goings and all
      you do.
  I know the way you have raged
    against me.
29 And because of your arrogance
    against me,
    which I have heard for myself,
  I will put my hook in your nose
    and my bridle in your mouth.
  I will make you return
    by the road on which you came.'"

30 Then Isaiah said to Hezekiah, "Here
is the proof that the LORD will protect this
city from Assyria's king. This year you
will eat only what grows up by itself, and
next year you will eat what springs up
from that. But in the third year you will
plant crops and harvest them; you will
tend vineyards and eat their fruit. 31 And
you who are left in Judah, who have escaped the ravages of the siege, will take
root again in your own soil, and you will
flourish and multiply. 32 For a remnant of
my people will spread out from Jerusalem, a group of survivors from Mount
Zion. The passion of the LORD Almighty
will make this happen!
33 "And this is what the LORD says
about the king of Assyria: His armies
will not enter Jerusalem to shoot their
arrows. They will not march outside its
gates with their shields and build banks
of earth against its walls. 34 The king will
return to his own country by the road on
which he came. He will not enter this
city, says the LORD. 35 For my own honor

and for the sake of my servant David, I
will defend it."
36 That night the angel of the LORD
went out to the Assyrian camp and
killed 185,000 Assyrian troops. When
the surviving Assyrians* woke up the
next morning, they found corpses everywhere. 37 Then King Sennacherib of
Assyria broke camp and returned to his
own land. He went home to his capital
of Nineveh and stayed there. 38 One day
while he was worshiping in the temple
of his god Nisroch, his sons Adrammelech and Sharezer killed him with their
swords. They then escaped to the land
of Ararat, and another son, Esarhaddon,
became the next king of Assyria.

CHAPTER 38
About that time Hezekiah became
deathly ill, and the prophet Isaiah son of
Amoz went to visit him. He gave the king
this message: "This is what the LORD
says: Set your affairs in order, for you are
going to die. You will not recover from
this illness."
2 When Hezekiah heard this, he turned
his face to the wall and prayed to the LORD,
3 "Remember, O LORD, how I have always
tried to be faithful to you and do what is
pleasing in your sight." Then he broke
down and wept bitterly.
4 Then this message came to Isaiah from
the LORD: 5 "Go back to Hezekiah and tell
him, 'This is what the LORD, the God of
your ancestor David, says: I have heard
your prayer and seen your tears. I will add
fifteen years to your life, 6 and I will rescue
you and this city from the king of Assyria.
Yes, I will defend this city.
7 " 'And this is the sign that the LORD will
give you to prove he will do as he promised: 8 I will cause the sun's shadow to
move ten steps backward on the sundial of
Ahaz!'" So the shadow on the sundial
moved backward ten steps.
9 When King Hezekiah was well again,
he wrote this poem about his experience:

10 I said, "In the prime of my life,
    must I now enter the place of the
      dead?
  Am I to be robbed of my normal years?"
11 I said, "Never again will I see the LORD
    GOD
  while still in the land of the living.

37:36 Hebrew *When they.*

Never again will I see my friends
  or laugh with those who live in this
  world.
¹² My life has been blown away
  like a shepherd's tent in a storm.
It has been cut short,
  as when a weaver cuts cloth from
  a loom.
Suddenly, my life was over.
¹³ I waited patiently all night,
  but I was torn apart as though by
  lions.
Suddenly, my life was over.
¹⁴ Delirious, I chattered like a swallow
  or a crane,
  and then I moaned like a mourning
  dove.
My eyes grew tired of looking to
  heaven for help.
  I am in trouble, Lord. Help me!"

¹⁵ But what could I say?
  For he himself had sent this sickness.
Now I will walk humbly throughout
  my years
  because of this anguish I have felt.
¹⁶ Lord, your discipline is good,
  for it leads to life and health.
You have restored my health
  and have allowed me to live!
¹⁷ Yes, it was good for me to suffer this
  anguish,
  for you have rescued me from death
  and have forgiven all my sins.
¹⁸ For the dead cannot praise you;
  they cannot raise their voices in
  praise.
Those who go down to destruction
  can no longer hope in your
  faithfulness.
¹⁹ Only the living can praise you as I do
  today.
  Each generation can make known
  your faithfulness to the next.
²⁰ Think of it—the LORD has healed me!
  I will sing his praises with instruments

every day of my life
  in the Temple of the LORD.

²¹Isaiah had said to Hezekiah's servants, "Make an ointment from figs and spread it over the boil, and Hezekiah will recover." ²²And Hezekiah had asked, "What sign will prove that I will go to the Temple of the LORD three days from now?"

CHAPTER 39

Soon after this, Merodach-baladan son of Baladan, king of Babylon, sent Hezekiah his best wishes and a gift. He had heard that Hezekiah had been very sick and that he had recovered. ²Hezekiah welcomed the Babylonian envoys and showed them everything in his treasure-houses—the silver, the gold, the spices, and the aromatic oils. He also took them to see his armory and showed them all his other treasures—everything! There was nothing in his palace or kingdom that Hezekiah did not show them.

³Then Isaiah the prophet went to King Hezekiah and asked him, "What did those men want? Where were they from?"

Hezekiah replied, "They came from the distant land of Babylon."

⁴"What did they see in your palace?" asked Isaiah.

"They saw everything," Hezekiah replied. "I showed them everything I own—all my treasures."

⁵Then Isaiah said to Hezekiah, "Listen to this message from the LORD Almighty: ⁶The time is coming when everything you have—all the treasures stored up by your ancestors—will be carried off to Babylon. Nothing will be left, says the LORD. ⁷Some of your own descendants will be taken away into exile. They will become eunuchs who will serve in the palace of Babylon's king."

⁸Then Hezekiah said to Isaiah, "This message you have given me from the LORD is good." But the king was thinking, "At least there will be peace and security during my lifetime."

JULY 25 ☐ DAY 207
ISAIAH 40–43
Mighty Lord vs. Idle Idols

OVERVIEW Beginning with chapter 40, Isaiah changes the focus of his message. For thirty-nine chapters (much like the thirty-nine books of the Old Testament), his major message has been the condemnation resulting from the waywardness and wickedness of God's people. But now comes a heartwarming message of hope and comfort. Like the twenty-seven books of the New Testament, the next twenty-seven chapters declare the coming salvation of the Lord. He is sovereign over creation; he is sovereign in the selection and protection of his nation Israel. And thus there can be certainty that he will comfort and deliver his people.

Chapter 40	Chapter 41	Chapter 42	Chapter 43
God's Comfort for Israel	God's Case against Idols	God's Perfect Servant: Messiah	God's Wayward Servant: Israel
Consolation	Confrontation	Revelation	Restoration

YOUR DAILY WALK Today, rather than looking for a practical project in which to put God's truth to work, spend some quiet moments contemplating the greatness of the God who made you and whose you are. Here are some thoughts to prepare your mind for worship and reflection:

God is not made greater when you worship him, but you are made greater when you serve him.

The oceans of the world contain more than 340 quintillion gallons of water; yet God holds them in his hand (40:12).

The earth weighs 6 sextillion metric tons; yet to God it represents but dust on the scale (40:12, 15).

The known universe stretches more than 30 billion light years (200 sextillion miles); yet God has measured off that great expanse with his fingers (40:12).

That same universe contains at least 100 billion galaxies, each made up of approximately 100 billion stars—yet God knows them all by name (40:26).

Now do you see why it is absurd to offer the God of heaven your *advice* rather than your *worship?* Even so, he says to you: "Do not be afraid, for I have ransomed you. . . . You are mine" (43:1)!

INSIGHT A Key Verse for Isaiah 40–66
One verse (40:2) previews all of chapters 40–66: (1) "her sad days are gone" describes the *deliverance* of 40–48; (2) "her sins are pardoned" describes the *deliverer* of 49–57; (3) "the LORD has punished her in full" describes the end of Judah's punishment and the *delivered captives* of 58–66.

CHAPTER 40

"Comfort, comfort my people," says your God. ²"Speak tenderly to Jerusalem. Tell her that her sad days are gone and that her sins are pardoned. Yes, the LORD has punished her in full for all her sins."

³Listen! I hear the voice of someone shouting, "Make a highway for the LORD through the wilderness. Make a straight, smooth road through the desert for our God. ⁴Fill the valleys and level the hills. Straighten out the curves and smooth off the rough spots. ⁵Then the glory of the LORD will be revealed, and all people will see it together. The LORD has spoken!"

⁶A voice said, "Shout!"

I asked, "What should I shout?"

"Shout that people are like the grass that dies away. Their beauty fades as quickly as the beauty of flowers in a field. ⁷The grass withers, and the flowers fade beneath the breath of the LORD. And so it is with people. [8]The grass withers, and the flowers fade, but the word of our God stands forever."

[9]Messenger of good news, shout to Zion from the mountaintops! Shout louder to Jerusalem—do not be afraid. Tell the towns of Judah, "Your God is coming!" [10]Yes, the Sovereign LORD is coming in all his glorious power. He will rule with awesome strength. See, he brings his reward with him as he comes. [11]He will feed his flock like a shepherd. He will carry the lambs in his arms, holding them close to his heart. He will gently lead the mother sheep with their young.

[12]Who else has held the oceans in his hand? Who has measured off the heavens with his fingers? Who else knows the weight of the earth or has weighed out the mountains and the hills? [13]Who is able to advise the Spirit of the LORD? Who knows enough to be his teacher or counselor? [14]Has the LORD ever needed anyone's advice? Does he need instruction about what is good or what is best? [15]No, for all the nations of the world are nothing in comparison with him. They are but a drop in the bucket, dust on the scales. He picks up the islands as though they had no weight at all. [16]All Lebanon's forests do not contain sufficient fuel to consume a sacrifice large enough to honor him. All Lebanon's sacrificial animals would not make an offering worthy of our God. [17]The nations of the world are as nothing to him. In his eyes they are less than nothing—mere emptiness and froth.

[18]To whom, then, can we compare God? What image might we find to resemble him? [19]Can he be compared to an idol formed in a mold, overlaid with gold, and decorated with silver chains? [20]Or is a poor person's wooden idol better? Can God be compared to an idol that must be placed on a stand so it won't fall down?

[21]Have you never heard or understood? Are you deaf to the words of God—the words he gave before the world began? Are you so ignorant? [22]It is God who sits above the circle of the earth. The people below must seem to him like grasshoppers! He is the one who spreads out the heavens like a curtain and makes his tent from them. [23]He judges the great people of the world and brings them all to nothing. [24]They hardly get started, barely taking root, when he

blows on them and their work withers. The wind carries them off like straw.

[25]"To whom will you compare me? Who is my equal?" asks the Holy One.

[26]Look up into the heavens. Who created all the stars? He brings them out one after another, calling each by its name. And he counts them to see that none are lost or have strayed away.

[27]O Israel, how can you say the LORD does not see your troubles? How can you say God refuses to hear your case? [28]Have you never heard or understood? Don't you know that the LORD is the everlasting God, the Creator of all the earth? He never grows faint or weary. No one can measure the depths of his understanding. [29]He gives power to those who are tired and worn out; he offers strength to the weak. [30]Even youths will become exhausted, and young men will give up. [31]But those who wait on the LORD will find new strength. They will fly high on wings like eagles. They will run and not grow weary. They will walk and not faint.

CHAPTER 41

"Listen in silence before me, you lands beyond the sea. Bring your strongest arguments. Come now and speak. The court is ready for your case.

[2]"Who has stirred up this king from the east, who meets victory at every step? Who, indeed, but the LORD? He gives him victory over many nations and permits him to trample their kings underfoot. He puts entire armies to the sword. He scatters them in the wind with his bow. [3]He chases them away and goes on safely, though he is walking over unfamiliar ground. [4]Who has done such mighty deeds, directing the affairs of the human race as each new generation marches by? It is I, the LORD, the First and the Last. I alone am he."

[5]The lands beyond the sea watch in fear. Remote lands tremble and mobilize for war. [6]They encourage one another with the words, "Be strong!" [7]The craftsmen rush to make new idols. The carver hurries the goldsmith, and the molder helps at the anvil. "Good," they say. "It's coming along fine." Carefully they join the parts together, then fasten the thing in place so it won't fall over.

[8]"But as for you, Israel my servant, Jacob my chosen one, descended from my friend

Abraham, [9]I have called you back from the ends of the earth so you can serve me. For I have chosen you and will not throw you away. [10]Don't be afraid, for I am with you. Do not be dismayed, for I am your God. I will strengthen you. I will help you. I will uphold you with my victorious right hand.

[11]"See, all your angry enemies lie there, confused and ashamed. Anyone who opposes you will die. [12]You will look for them in vain. They will all be gone! [13]I am holding you by your right hand—I, the LORD your God. And I say to you, 'Do not be afraid. I am here to help you. [14]Despised though you are, O Israel, don't be afraid, for I will help you. I am the LORD, your Redeemer. I am the Holy One of Israel.' [15]You will be a new threshing instrument with many sharp teeth. You will tear all your enemies apart, making chaff of mountains. [16]You will toss them in the air, and the wind will blow them all away; a whirlwind will scatter them. And the joy of the LORD will fill you to overflowing. You will glory in the Holy One of Israel.

[17]"When the poor and needy search for water and there is none, and their tongues are parched from thirst, then I, the LORD, will answer them. I, the God of Israel, will never forsake them. [18]I will open up rivers for them on high plateaus. I will give them fountains of water in the valleys. In the deserts they will find pools of water. Rivers fed by springs will flow across the dry, parched ground. [19]I will plant trees—cedar, acacia, myrtle, olive, cypress, fir, and pine—on barren land. [20]Everyone will see this miracle and understand that it is the LORD, the Holy One of Israel, who did it.

[21]"Can your idols make such claims as these? Let them come and show what they can do!" says the LORD, the King of Israel.* [22]"Let them try to tell us what happened long ago or what the future holds. [23]Yes, that's it! If you are gods, tell what will occur in the days ahead. Or perform a mighty miracle that will fill us with amazement and fear. Do something, whether good or bad! [24]But no! You are less than nothing and can do nothing at all. Anyone who chooses you becomes filthy, just like you!

[25]"But I have stirred up a leader from the north and east. He will come against the nations and call on my name, and I will give him victory over kings and princes.

He will trample them as a potter treads on clay.

[26]"Who but I have told you this would happen? Who else predicted this, making you admit that he was right? No one else said a word! [27]I was the first to tell Jerusalem, 'Look! Help is on the way!' [28]Not one of your idols told you this. Not one gave any answer when I asked. [29]See, they are all foolish, worthless things. Your idols are all as empty as the wind.

CHAPTER 42

"Look at my servant, whom I strengthen. He is my chosen one, and I am pleased with him. I have put my Spirit upon him. He will reveal justice to the nations. [2]He will be gentle—he will not shout or raise his voice in public. [3]He will not crush those who are weak or quench the smallest hope. He will bring full justice to all who have been wronged. [4]He will not stop until truth and righteousness prevail throughout the earth. Even distant lands beyond the sea will wait for his instruction."

[5]God, the LORD, created the heavens and stretched them out. He created the earth and everything in it. He gives breath and life to everyone in all the world. And it is he who says, [6]"I, the LORD, have called you to demonstrate my righteousness. I will guard and support you, for I have given you to my people as the personal confirmation of my covenant with them. And you will be a light to guide all nations to me. [7]You will open the eyes of the blind and free the captives from prison. You will release those who sit in dark dungeons.

[8]"I am the LORD; that is my name! I will not give my glory to anyone else. I will not share my praise with carved idols. [9]Everything I prophesied has come true, and now I will prophesy again. I will tell you the future before it happens."

[10] Sing a new song to the LORD!
  Sing his praises from the ends of the earth!
Sing, all you who sail the seas,
  all you who live in distant coastlands.
[11] Join in the chorus, you desert towns;
  let the villages of Kedar rejoice!
Let the people of Sela sing for joy;
  shout praises from the mountaintops!
[12] Let the coastlands glorify the LORD;
  let them sing his praise.

41:21 Hebrew *the King of Jacob.*

¹³ The LORD will march forth like a
      mighty man;
   he will come out like a warrior, full
      of fury.
He will shout his thundering battle cry,
   and he will crush all his enemies.
¹⁴ He will say, "I have long been silent;
   yes, I have restrained myself.
But now I will give full vent to my fury;
   I will gasp and pant like a woman
      giving birth.
¹⁵ I will level the mountains and hills
   and bring a blight on all their
      greenery.
I will turn the rivers into dry land
   and will dry up all the pools.
¹⁶ I will lead blind Israel down a new
      path,
   guiding them along an unfamiliar
      way.
I will make the darkness bright before
      them
   and smooth out the road ahead of
      them.
Yes, I will indeed do these things;
   I will not forsake them.
¹⁷ But those who trust in idols,
   calling them their gods—
      they will be turned away in shame.

¹⁸"Oh, how deaf and blind you are to-ward me! Why won't you listen? Why do you refuse to see? ¹⁹Who in all the world is as blind as my own people, my servant? Who is as deaf as my messengers? Who is as blind as my chosen people, the servant of the LORD? ²⁰You see and understand what is right but refuse to act on it. You hear, but you don't really listen."

²¹The LORD has magnified his law and made it truly glorious. Through it he had planned to show the world that he is righteous. ²²But what a sight his people are, for they have been robbed, enslaved, imprisoned, and trapped. They are fair game for all and have no one to protect them. ²³Will not even one of you apply these lessons from the past and see the ruin that awaits you? ²⁴Who allowed Israel to be robbed and hurt? Was it not the LORD? It was the LORD whom we sinned against, for the people would not go where he sent them, nor would they obey his law. ²⁵That is why he poured out such fury on them and destroyed them in battle. They were set on fire and burned, but they still refused to understand.

CHAPTER 43

But now, O Israel, the LORD who created you says: "Do not be afraid, for I have ransomed you. I have called you by name; you are mine. ²When you go through deep waters and great trouble, I will be with you. When you go through rivers of difficulty, you will not drown! When you walk through the fire of oppression, you will not be burned up; the flames will not consume you. ³For I am the LORD, your God, the Holy One of Israel, your Savior. I gave Egypt, Ethiopia,* and Seba as a ransom for your freedom. ⁴Others died that you might live. I traded their lives for yours because you are precious to me. You are honored, and I love you.

⁵"Do not be afraid, for I am with you. I will gather you and your children from east and west ⁶and from north and south. I will bring my sons and daughters back to Israel from the distant corners of the earth. ⁷All who claim me as their God will come, for I have made them for my glory. It was I who created them."

⁸Bring out the people who have eyes but are blind, who have ears but are deaf. ⁹Gather the nations together! Which of their idols has ever foretold such things? Can any of them predict something even a single day in advance? Where are the witnesses of such predictions? Who can verify that they spoke the truth?

¹⁰"But you are my witnesses, O Israel!" says the LORD. "And you are my servant. You have been chosen to know me, believe in me, and understand that I alone am God. There is no other God; there never has been and never will be. ¹¹I am the LORD, and there is no other Savior. ¹²First I predicted your deliverance; I declared what I would do, and then I did it—I saved you. No foreign god has ever done this before. You are witnesses that I am the only God," says the LORD. ¹³"From eternity to eternity I am God. No one can oppose what I do. No one can reverse my actions."

¹⁴The LORD your Redeemer, the Holy One of Israel, says: "For your sakes I will send an invading army against Babylon. And the Babylonians* will be forced to flee in those ships they are so proud of. ¹⁵I am the LORD, your Holy One, Israel's Creator and King. ¹⁶I am the LORD, who opened a way through the waters, making a dry path

43:3 Hebrew *Cush.*   43:14 Or *Chaldeans.*

through the sea. [17]I called forth the mighty army of Egypt with all its chariots and horses. I drew them beneath the waves, and they drowned, their lives snuffed out like a smoldering candlewick.

[18]"But forget all that—it is nothing compared to what I am going to do. [19]For I am about to do a brand-new thing. See, I have already begun! Do you not see it? I will make a pathway through the wilderness for my people to come home. I will create rivers for them in the desert! [20]The wild animals in the fields will thank me, the jackals and ostriches, too, for giving them water in the wilderness. Yes, I will make springs in the desert, so that my chosen people can be refreshed. [21]I have made Israel for myself, and they will someday honor me before the whole world.

[22]"But, my dear people, you refuse to ask for my help. You have grown tired of me! [23]You have not brought me lambs for burnt offerings. You have not honored me with sacrifices, though I have not burdened and wearied you with my requests for grain offerings and incense. [24]You have not brought me fragrant incense or pleased me with the fat from sacrifices. Instead, you have burdened me with your sins and wearied me with your faults.

[25]"I—yes, I alone—am the one who blots out your sins for my own sake and will never think of them again. [26]Let us review the situation together, and you can present your case if you have one. [27]From the very beginning, your ancestors sinned against me—all your leaders broke my laws. [28]That is why I have disgraced your priests and assigned Israel a future of complete destruction* and shame.

43:28 The Hebrew term used here refers to the complete consecration of things or people to the Lord, either by destroying them or by giving them as an offering.

JULY 26 □ DAY 208
ISAIAH 44–48
God's Choice and Babylon's Fall

 OVERVIEW Isaiah next contrasts the impotence of idols with the omnipotence of Israel's God. From the same piece of wood a workman fashions gods to be worshiped and logs to be burned. By contrast, the God of creation predicts centuries in advance the agent of his comfort (Cyrus, king of Persia) and the means he will employ to deliver his oppressed people. Is it any wonder God calls forth judgment upon idolatrous Babylon, which would dare to substitute trees and rocks for the Lord Almighty, the Holy One of Israel?

Chapter 44	Chapter 45	Chapters 46–47	Chapter 48
The People's Choice	The Lord's Choice	Babylon's Calamity	Judah's Caution
Impotent Idols		Omnipotent God	

 YOUR DAILY WALK Have you ever wondered about the unusual way God uses people and events to accomplish his purposes on earth?

God used a wet piece of "wool" to call Gideon into his service (Judges 6:36-38). He used a talking donkey to rebuke Balaam (Numbers 22:28). He used a hungry fish to turn Jonah around (Jonah 1:17). He swept his spiritually dirty nation clean by using an even dirtier "broom"—the brutal Babylonians. And he raised up a heathen king to free his people from exile and rebuild his holy house of worship (Isaiah 45:1, 4)!

God can do more in a moment than people in a millennium.

Can you see God's purpose linked with personal events in your life or with international developments in the life of your nation? Go back through chapter 45, and circle the phrases *I have, I am,* and *I will* every time you find them. Then make three columns on a sheet of paper describing God's activities in the past ("I have . . ."), the present ("I am . . ."), and the future ("I will . . ."). When you're finished, you'll have a wonderful prayer and praise prompter: *Father, as I see your trustworthiness in the past, build my confidence in you to accomplish your purposes in the present and future as well!*

 INSIGHT Predicting the Rebuilding of a House Not Yet Toppled Cyrus, who ruled Medo-Persia from 546 to 530 B.C.—more than 150 years after Isaiah's specific prophecies concerning him—is announced as the one to command the rebuilding of the Jerusalem Temple, *which in Isaiah's day had not yet been destroyed* (44:28)!

CHAPTER 44

"But now, listen to me, Jacob my servant, Israel my chosen one. ²The LORD who made you and helps you says: O Jacob, my servant, do not be afraid. O Israel,* my chosen one, do not fear. ³For I will give you abundant water to quench your thirst and to moisten your parched fields. And I will pour out my Spirit and my blessings on your children. ⁴They will thrive like watered grass, like willows on a riverbank. ⁵Some will proudly claim, 'I belong to the LORD.' Others will say, 'I am a descendant of Jacob.' Some will write the LORD's name on their hands and will take the honored name of Israel as their own.

⁶"This is what the LORD, Israel's King and Redeemer, the LORD Almighty, says: I am the First and the Last; there is no other God. ⁷Who else can tell you what is going to happen in the days ahead? Let them tell you if they can and thus prove their power. Let them do as I have done since ancient times. ⁸Do not tremble; do not be afraid. Have I not proclaimed from ages past what my purposes are for you? You are my witnesses—is there any other God? No! There is no other Rock—not one!"

⁹How foolish are those who manufacture idols to be their gods. These highly valued objects are really worthless. They themselves are witnesses that this is so, for their idols neither see nor know. No wonder those who worship them are put to shame. ¹⁰Who but a fool would make his own god—an idol that cannot help him one bit! ¹¹All who worship idols will stand before the LORD in shame, along with all these craftsmen—mere humans—who claim they can make a god. Together they will stand in terror and shame.

¹²The blacksmith stands at his forge to make a sharp tool, pounding and shaping it with all his might. His work makes him hungry and thirsty, weak and faint. ¹³Then the wood-carver measures and marks out a block of wood, takes the tool, and carves the figure of a man. Now he has a wonderful idol that cannot even move from where it is placed! ¹⁴He cuts down cedars; he selects the cypress and the oak; he plants the cedar in the forest to be nourished by the rain. ¹⁵And after his care, he uses part of the wood to make a fire to warm himself and bake his bread. Then—yes, it's true—he takes the rest of it and makes himself a god for people to worship! He makes an idol and bows down and praises it! ¹⁶He burns part of the tree to roast his meat and to keep himself warm. ¹⁷Then he takes what's left and makes his god: a carved idol! He falls down in front of it, worshiping and praying to it. "Rescue me!" he says. "You are my god!"

¹⁸Such stupidity and ignorance! Their eyes are closed, and they cannot see. Their minds are shut, and they cannot think. ¹⁹The person who made the idol never stops to reflect, "Why, it's just a block of wood! I burned half of it for heat and used it to bake my bread and roast my meat. How can the rest of it be a god? Should I bow down to worship a chunk of wood?" ²⁰The poor, deluded fool feeds on ashes. He is trusting something that can give him no help at all. Yet he cannot bring himself to ask, "Is this thing, this idol that I'm holding in my hand, a lie?"

²¹"Pay attention, O Israel, for you are my servant. I, the LORD, made you, and I will not forget to help you. ²²I have swept away your sins like the morning mists. I have scattered your offenses like the clouds. Oh, return to me, for I have paid the price to set you free."

²³Sing, O heavens, for the LORD has done this wondrous thing. Shout, O earth! Break forth into song, O mountains and forests

44:2 Hebrew *Jeshurun,* a term of endearment for Israel.

and every tree! For the LORD has redeemed Jacob and is glorified in Israel.

²⁴The LORD, your Redeemer and Creator, says: "I am the LORD, who made all things. I alone stretched out the heavens. By myself I made the earth and everything in it. ²⁵I am the one who exposes the false prophets as liars by causing events to happen that are contrary to their predictions. I cause wise people to give bad advice, thus proving them to be fools. ²⁶But I carry out the predictions of my prophets! When they say Jerusalem will be saved and the towns of Judah will be lived in once again, it will be done! ²⁷When I speak to the rivers and say, 'Be dry!' they will be dry. ²⁸When I say of Cyrus, 'He is my shepherd,' he will certainly do as I say. He will command that Jerusalem be rebuilt and that the Temple be restored."

CHAPTER 45

This is what the LORD says to Cyrus, his anointed one, whose right hand he will empower. Before him, mighty kings will be paralyzed with fear. Their fortress gates will be opened, never again to shut against him. ²This is what the LORD says: "I will go before you, Cyrus, and level the mountains.* I will smash down gates of bronze and cut through bars of iron. ³And I will give you treasures hidden in the darkness—secret riches. I will do this so you may know that I am the LORD, the God of Israel, the one who calls you by name.

⁴"And why have I called you for this work? It is for the sake of Jacob my servant, Israel my chosen one. I called you by name when you did not know me. ⁵I am the LORD; there is no other God. I have prepared you, even though you do not know me, ⁶so all the world from east to west will know there is no other God. I am the LORD, and there is no other. ⁷I am the one who creates the light and makes the darkness. I am the one who sends good times and bad times. I, the LORD, am the one who does these things. ⁸Open up, O heavens, and pour out your righteousness. Let the earth open wide so salvation and righteousness can sprout up together. I, the LORD, created them.

⁹"Destruction is certain for those who argue with their Creator. Does a clay pot ever argue with its maker? Does the clay dispute with the one who shapes it, saying, 'Stop, you are doing it wrong!' Does the pot exclaim, 'How clumsy can you be!' ¹⁰How terrible it would be if a newborn baby said to its father and mother, 'Why was I born? Why did you make me this way?'"

¹¹This is what the LORD, the Creator and Holy One of Israel, says: "Do you question what I do? Do you give me orders about the work of my hands? ¹²I am the one who made the earth and created people to live on it. With my hands I stretched out the heavens. All the millions of stars are at my command. ¹³I will raise up Cyrus to fulfill my righteous purpose, and I will guide all his actions. He will restore my city and free my captive people—and not for a reward! I, the LORD Almighty, have spoken!"

¹⁴This is what the LORD says: "The Egyptians, Ethiopians,* and Sabeans will be subject to you. They will come to you with all their merchandise, and it will all be yours. They will follow you as prisoners in chains. They will fall to their knees in front of you and say, 'God is with you, and he is the only God.'"

¹⁵Truly, O God of Israel, our Savior, you work in strange and mysterious ways. ¹⁶All who make idols will be humiliated and disgraced. ¹⁷But the LORD will save the people of Israel with eternal salvation. They will never again be humiliated and disgraced throughout everlasting ages. ¹⁸For the LORD is God, and he created the heavens and earth and put everything in place. He made the world to be lived in, not to be a place of empty chaos.

"I am the LORD," he says, "and there is no other. ¹⁹I publicly proclaim bold promises. I do not whisper obscurities in some dark corner so no one can understand what I mean. And I did not tell the people of Israel* to ask me for something I did not plan to give. I, the LORD, speak only what is true and right.

²⁰"Gather together and come, you fugitives from surrounding nations. What fools they are who carry around their wooden idols and pray to gods that cannot save! ²¹Consult together, argue your case, and state your proofs that idol worship pays. Who made these things known long ago? What idol ever told you they would happen? Was it not I, the LORD? For there is no other God but me—a just God and a Sav-

45:2 As in Dead Sea Scrolls and Greek version; Masoretic Text reads *the swellings.*   45:14 Hebrew *Cushites.*   45:19 Hebrew *of Jacob.*

ior—no, not one! ²²Let all the world look to me for salvation! For I am God; there is no other. ²³I have sworn by my own name, and I will never go back on my word: Every knee will bow to me, and every tongue will confess allegiance to my name."

²⁴The people will declare, "The LORD is the source of all my righteousness and strength." And all who were angry with him will come to him and be ashamed. ²⁵In the LORD all the generations of Israel will be justified, and in him they will boast.

CHAPTER 46

The idols of Babylon, Bel and Nebo, are being hauled away on ox carts. But look! The beasts are staggering under the weight! ²Both the idols and the ones carrying them are bowed down. The gods cannot protect the people, and the people cannot protect the gods. They go off into captivity together.

³"Listen to me, all you who are left in Israel. I created you and have cared for you since before you were born. ⁴I will be your God throughout your lifetime—until your hair is white with age. I made you, and I will care for you. I will carry you along and save you.

⁵"To whom will you compare me? Who is my equal? ⁶Some people pour out their silver and gold and hire a craftsman to make a god from it. Then they bow down and worship it! ⁷They carry it around on their shoulders, and when they set it down, it stays there. It cannot even move! And when someone prays to it, there is no answer. It has no power to get anyone out of trouble.

⁸"Do not forget this, you guilty ones. ⁹And do not forget the things I have done throughout history. For I am God—I alone! I am God, and there is no one else like me. ¹⁰Only I can tell you what is going to happen even before it happens. Everything I plan will come to pass, for I do whatever I wish. ¹¹I will call a swift bird of prey from the east—a leader from a distant land who will come and do my bidding. I have said I would do it, and I will. ¹²Listen to me, you stubborn, evil people! ¹³For I am ready to set things right, not in the distant future, but right now! I am ready to save Jerusalem* and give my glory to Israel.

46:13 Hebrew *Zion*.   **47:1** Or *Chaldea*; also in 47:5.

CHAPTER 47

"Come, Babylon, unconquered one, sit in the dust. For your days of glory, pomp, and honor have ended. O daughter of Babylonia,* never again will you be the lovely princess, tender and delicate. ²Take heavy millstones and grind the corn. Remove your veil and strip off your robe. Expose yourself to public view. ³You will be naked and burdened with shame. I will take vengeance against you and will not negotiate."

⁴Our Redeemer, whose name is the LORD Almighty, is the Holy One of Israel.

⁵"O daughter of Babylonia, sit now in darkness and silence. Never again will you be known as the queen of kingdoms. ⁶For I was angry with my chosen people and began their punishment by letting them fall into your hands. But you, Babylon, showed them no mercy. You have forced even the elderly to carry heavy burdens. ⁷You thought, 'I will reign forever as queen of the world!' You did not care at all about my people or think about the consequences of your actions.

⁸"You are a pleasure-crazy kingdom, living at ease and feeling secure, bragging as if you were the greatest in the world! You say, 'I'm self-sufficient and not accountable to anyone! I will never be a widow or lose my children.' ⁹Well, those two things will come upon you in a moment: widowhood and the loss of your children. Yes, these calamities will come upon you, despite all your witchcraft and magic.

¹⁰"You felt secure in all your wickedness. 'No one sees me,' you said. Your 'wisdom' and 'knowledge' have caused you to turn away from me and claim, 'I am self-sufficient and not accountable to anyone!' ¹¹So disaster will overtake you suddenly, and you won't be able to charm it away. Calamity will fall upon you, and you won't be able to buy your way out. A catastrophe will arise so fast that you won't know what hit you.

¹²"Call out the demon hordes you have worshiped all these years. Ask them to help you strike terror into the hearts of people once again. ¹³You have more than enough advisers, astrologers, and stargazers. Let them stand up and save you from what the future holds. ¹⁴But they are as useless as dried grass burning in a fire. They cannot

even save themselves! You will get no help from them at all. Their hearth is not a place to sit for warmth. [15]And all your friends, those with whom you have done business since childhood, will slip away and disappear, unable to help.

CHAPTER 48

"Listen to me, O family of Jacob, who are called by the name of Israel and born into the family of Judah. Listen, you who take oaths in the name of the LORD and call on the God of Israel. You don't follow through on any of your promises, [2]even though you call yourself the holy city and talk about depending on the God of Israel, whose name is the LORD Almighty. [3]Time and again I warned you about what was going to happen in the future. Then suddenly I took action, and all my predictions came true.

[4]"I know how stubborn and obstinate you are. Your necks are as unbending as iron. You are as hardheaded as bronze. [5]That is why I told you ahead of time what I was going to do. That way, you could never say, 'My idols did it. My wooden image and metal god commanded it to happen!' [6]You have heard my predictions and seen them fulfilled, but you refuse to admit it. Now I will tell you new things I have not mentioned before, secrets you have not yet heard. [7]They are brand new, not things from the past. So you cannot say, 'We knew that all the time!'

[8]"Yes, I will tell you of things that are entirely new, for I know so well what traitors you are. You have been rebels from your earliest childhood, rotten through and through. [9]Yet for my own sake and for the honor of my name, I will hold back my anger and not wipe you out. [10]I have refined you but not in the way silver is refined. Rather, I have refined you in the furnace of suffering. [11]I will rescue you for my sake—yes, for my own sake! That way, the pagan nations will not be able to claim that their gods have conquered me. I will not let them have my glory!

[12]"Listen to me, O family of Jacob, Israel my chosen one! I alone am God, the First and the Last. [13]It was my hand that laid the foundations of the earth. The palm of my right hand spread out the heavens above. I spoke, and they came into being.

[14]"Have any of your idols ever told you this? Come, all of you, and listen: 'The LORD has chosen Cyrus as his ally. He will use him to put an end to the empire of Babylon, destroying the Babylonian* armies.' [15]I have said it: I am calling Cyrus! I will send him on this errand and will help him succeed. [16]Come closer and listen. I have always told you plainly what would happen so you would have no trouble understanding."

And now the Sovereign LORD and his Spirit have sent me with this message: [17]"The LORD, your Redeemer, the Holy One of Israel, says: I am the LORD your God, who teaches you what is good and leads you along the paths you should follow. [18]Oh, that you had listened to my commands! Then you would have had peace flowing like a gentle river and righteousness rolling like waves. [19]Then you would have become as numerous as the sands along the seashore—too many to count! There would have been no need for your destruction."

[20]Yet even now, be free from your captivity! Leave Babylon and the Babylonians,* singing as you go! Shout to the ends of the earth that the LORD has redeemed his servants, the people of Israel.* [21]They were not thirsty when he led them through the desert. He divided the rock, and water gushed out for them to drink.

[22]"But there is no peace for the wicked," says the LORD.

48:14 Or Chaldean.   48:20a Or the Chaldeans.   48:20b Hebrew his servant, Jacob.

JULY 27 □ DAY 209
ISAIAH 49–51
The Prince of Peace

OVERVIEW The first nine chapters of Isaiah's message of comfort have centered on God's deliverance of his people through Cyrus. Now Isaiah focuses on the one who will bring deliverance through his suffering and death (Isaiah 49–55). He would come as a Servant to his people and a Light to the surrounding nations, providing strength for the weary and compassion for the downcast. And as the crowning act of servanthood, he would offer himself as a sacrifice for sin.

Chapter 49	Chapter 50	Chapter 51
Call of the Servant	Commitment of the Servant	Consolation from the Servant
Salvation	Suffering	Solace

YOUR DAILY WALK Definition: A free country is a place where people can say whatever they think—provided they aren't overheard by a spouse, neighbor, minister, or boss.

Independence—the freedom to speak, write, assemble, and worship without fear of a tyrant's intervention—is a prized possession. But never forget as you enjoy your *independence* that you were also created to enjoy *dependence* under the lordship of Jesus Christ.

Freedom is a two-sided coin: On one side is privilege; on the other, responsibility.

A violin string, when totally "independent" of the violin for which it was created, is "free" to twist and turn—but not to do what a violin string is designed to do: produce music. By the same token, you are "free" when your life is uncommitted—but not free to be what God intended you to be.

Real freedom is not freedom *from* God, but freedom *with* God through the salvation that is in Jesus Christ (51:5-6, 8). In your travels today, look for a quiet place marked Free Parking, where you can pause and thank God for your independence as a citizen of earth—and your dependence as a citizen of heaven.

INSIGHT Isaiah, the Evangelical Prophet
Perhaps the most remarkable feature of Isaiah's lengthy book is the detailed way in which he describes Jesus Christ—more than seven centuries before his birth! Here are just a few of the dozens of "Snapshots of the Savior" you will find in the book: 7:14; 9:2, 6-7; 11:1-2; 35:4-6; 40:10-11; 42:1-4, 6-7; 50:6; 52:13–53:12; 61:1-2. Spend a few minutes looking these verses up and marking them. They may be just the key you need to open a door of witness to a Jewish friend or relative for whom you have been praying.

CHAPTER 49
Listen to me, all of you in far-off lands! The LORD called me before my birth; from within the womb he called me by name. [2]He made my words of judgment as sharp as a sword. He has hidden me in the shadow of his hand. I am like a sharp arrow in his quiver.

[3]He said to me, "You are my servant, Israel, and you will bring me glory."

[4]I replied, "But my work all seems so useless! I have spent my strength for nothing and to no purpose at all. Yet I leave it all in the LORD's hand; I will trust God for my reward."

[5]And now the LORD speaks—he who formed me in my mother's womb to be his servant, who commissioned me to bring his people of Israel back to him. The LORD has honored me, and my God has given me

strength. [6]He says, "You will do more than restore the people of Israel to me. I will make you a light to the Gentiles, and you will bring my salvation to the ends of the earth."

[7]The LORD, the Redeemer and Holy One of Israel, says to the one who is despised and rejected by a nation, to the one who is the servant of rulers: "Kings will stand at attention when you pass by. Princes will bow low because the LORD has chosen you. He, the faithful LORD, the Holy One of Israel, chooses you."

[8]This is what the LORD says: "At just the right time, I will respond to you. On the day of salvation, I will help you. I will give you as a token and pledge to Israel. This will prove that I will reestablish the land of Israel and reassign it to its own people again. [9]Through you I am saying to the prisoners of darkness, 'Come out! I am giving you your freedom!' They will be my sheep, grazing in green pastures and on hills that were previously bare. [10]They will neither hunger nor thirst. The searing sun and scorching desert winds will not reach them anymore. For the LORD in his mercy will lead them beside cool waters. [11]And I will make my mountains into level paths for them. The highways will be raised above the valleys. [12]See, my people will return from far away, from lands to the north and west, and from as far south as Egypt.*"

[13]Sing for joy, O heavens! Rejoice, O earth! Burst into song, O mountains! For the LORD has comforted his people and will have compassion on them in their sorrow.

[14]Yet Jerusalem* says, "The LORD has deserted us; the Lord has forgotten us."

[15]"Never! Can a mother forget her nursing child? Can she feel no love for a child she has borne? But even if that were possible, I would not forget you! [16]See, I have written your name on my hand. Ever before me is a picture of Jerusalem's walls in ruins. [17]Soon your descendants will come back, and all who are trying to destroy you will go away. [18]Look and see, for all your children will come back to you. As surely as I live," says the LORD, "they will be like jewels or bridal ornaments for you to display.

[19]"Even the most desolate parts of your abandoned land will soon be crowded with your people. Your enemies who enslaved you will be far away. [20]The generations born in exile will return and say, 'We need more room! It's crowded here!' [21]Then you will think to yourself, 'Who has given me all these descendants? For most of my children were killed, and the rest were carried away into exile. I was left here all alone. Who bore these children? Who raised them for me?'"

[22]This is what the Sovereign LORD says: "See, I will give a signal to the godless nations. They will carry your little sons back to you in their arms; they will bring your daughters on their shoulders. [23]Kings and queens will serve you. They will care for all your needs. They will bow to the earth before you and lick the dust from your feet. Then you will know that I am the LORD. Those who wait for me will never be put to shame."

[24]Who can snatch the plunder of war from the hands of a warrior? Who can demand that a tyrant* let his captives go? [25]But the LORD says, "The captives of warriors will be released, and the plunder of tyrants will be retrieved. For I will fight those who fight you, and I will save your children. [26]I will feed your enemies with their own flesh. They will be drunk with rivers of their own blood. All the world will know that I, the LORD, am your Savior and Redeemer, the Mighty One of Israel.*"

CHAPTER 50

The LORD asks, "Did I sell you as slaves to my creditors? Is that why you are not here? Is your mother gone because I divorced her and sent her away? No, you went away as captives because of your sins. And your mother, too, was taken because of your sins. [2]Was I too weak to save you? Is that why the house is silent and empty when I come home? Is it because I have no power to rescue? No, that is not the reason! For I can speak to the sea and make it dry! I can turn rivers into deserts covered with dying fish. [3]I am the one who sends darkness out across the skies, bringing it to a state of mourning."

[4]The Sovereign LORD has given me his words of wisdom, so that I know what to

---

49:12 As in Dead Sea Scrolls, which read *from the region of Aswan,* which is in southern Egypt. Masoretic Text reads *from the region of Sinim.*   **49:14** Hebrew *Zion.*   **49:24** As in Dead Sea Scrolls, Syriac version, and Latin Vulgate (also see 49:25); Masoretic Text reads *a righteous person.*   **49:26** Hebrew *of Jacob.*

say to all these weary ones. Morning by morning he wakens me and opens my understanding to his will. ⁵The Sovereign LORD has spoken to me, and I have listened. I do not rebel or turn away. ⁶I give my back to those who beat me and my cheeks to those who pull out my beard. I do not hide from shame, for they mock me and spit in my face.

⁷Because the Sovereign LORD helps me, I will not be dismayed. Therefore, I have set my face like a stone, determined to do his will. And I know that I will triumph. ⁸He who gives me justice is near. Who will dare to oppose me now? Where are my enemies? Let them appear! ⁹See, the Sovereign LORD is on my side! Who will declare me guilty? All my enemies will be destroyed like old clothes that have been eaten by moths!

¹⁰Who among you fears the LORD and obeys his servant? If you are walking in darkness, without a ray of light, trust in the LORD and rely on your God. ¹¹But watch out, you who live in your own light and warm yourselves by your own fires. This is the reward you will receive from me: You will soon lie down in great torment.

CHAPTER 51

"Listen to me, all who hope for deliverance—all who seek the LORD! Consider the quarry from which you were mined, the rock from which you were cut! ²Yes, think about your ancestors Abraham and Sarah, from whom you came. Abraham was alone when I called him. But when I blessed him, he became a great nation."

³The LORD will comfort Israel* again and make her deserts blossom. Her barren wilderness will become as beautiful as Eden—the garden of the LORD. Joy and gladness will be found there. Lovely songs of thanksgiving will fill the air.

⁴"Listen to me, my people. Hear me, Israel, for my law will be proclaimed, and my justice will become a light to the nations. ⁵My mercy and justice are coming soon. Your salvation is on the way. I will rule the nations. They will wait for me and long for my power. ⁶Look up to the skies above, and gaze down on the earth beneath. For the skies will disappear like smoke, and the earth will wear out like a

piece of clothing. The people of the earth will die like flies, but my salvation lasts forever. My righteous rule will never end!

⁷"Listen to me, you who know right from wrong and cherish my law in your hearts. Do not be afraid of people's scorn or their slanderous talk. ⁸For the moth will destroy them as it destroys clothing. The worm will eat away at them as it eats wool. But my righteousness will last forever. My salvation will continue from generation to generation."

⁹Wake up, LORD! Robe yourself with strength! Rouse yourself as in the days of old when you slew Egypt, the dragon of the Nile.* ¹⁰Are you not the same today, the one who dried up the sea, making a path of escape when you saved your people? ¹¹Those who have been ransomed by the LORD will return to Jerusalem,* singing songs of everlasting joy. Sorrow and mourning will disappear, and they will be overcome with joy and gladness.

¹²"I, even I, am the one who comforts you. So why are you afraid of mere humans, who wither like the grass and disappear? ¹³Yet you have forgotten the LORD, your Creator, the one who put the stars in the sky and established the earth. Will you remain in constant dread of human oppression? Will you continue to fear the anger of your enemies from morning till night? ¹⁴Soon all you captives will be released! Imprisonment, starvation, and death will not be your fate! ¹⁵For I am the LORD your God, who stirs up the sea, causing its waves to roar. My name is the LORD Almighty. ¹⁶And I have put my words in your mouth and hidden you safely within my hand. I set all the stars in space and established the earth. I am the one who says to Israel, 'You are mine!'"

¹⁷Wake up, wake up, O Jerusalem! You have drunk enough from the cup of the LORD's fury. You have drunk the cup of terror, tipping out its last drops. ¹⁸Not one of your children is left alive to help you or tell you what to do. ¹⁹These two things have been your lot: desolation and destruction, famine and war. And who is left to sympathize? Who is left to comfort you? ²⁰For your children have fainted and lie in the streets, helpless as antelopes caught in

---

51:3 Hebrew *Zion;* also in 51:16.   **51:9** Hebrew *slew Rahab the dragon.* Rahab is the name of a mythical sea monster that represents chaos in ancient literature. The name is used here as a poetic name for Egypt.   **51:11** Hebrew *Zion.*

a net. The LORD has poured out his fury; God has rebuked them.

²¹But now listen to this, you afflicted ones, who sit in a drunken stupor, though not from drinking wine. ²²This is what the Sovereign LORD, your God and Defender, says:

"See, I am taking the terrible cup from your hands. You will drink no more of my fury. It is gone at last! ²³But I will put that cup into the hands of those who tormented you. I will give it to those who trampled you into the dust and walked on your backs."

JULY 28 ☐ DAY 210
Walking in the Light

 LOOK BACK Disciplining an obstinate child is painful, both for the child and for the parent. God's loyal love for his people is tempered because of their heartache over the pain they are inflicting upon themselves because of their disobedience. They say the right words, but their lives betray their true allegiance. They substitute man-made rules for wholehearted worship. They know full well whom to trust and where to turn, but have willfully chosen not to do either. They look to foreign alliances for deliverance, rather than to the Lord Almighty.

Shining like a bright light in a dark room is righteous King Hezekiah. Faced with a tidal wave of Assyrian soldiers, Hezekiah turns to the one true Lifeguard—the living God. Faced with a life-threatening illness, Hezekiah turns to the Great Physician. In each case, the answer that comes can only have one explanation (God did it) and one outcome ("then all the kingdoms of the earth will know that you alone, O LORD, are God" 37:20). Indeed, comfort, instruction, and guidance are near at hand for all who look to the Holy One of Israel.

 LOOK UP How do you walk with a holy God? If he is truly a consuming fire (Hebrews 12:29), how do you stay in step with him, enjoying his company without being consumed by his glory? How do you talk with him? fellowship with him? please him? serve him?

A person should give a lot of thought to a sudden decision.

The answer is as close as Isaiah 33:15-16. Those who aspire to walk with God cannot be casual or indifferent about their conduct and conversation. The ones who long to please God in everything are the ones

• who are honest and fair;
• who reject making a profit by fraud;
• who stay far away from bribes; and
• who refuse to listen to those who plot murder, who shut their eyes to all enticement to do wrong.

And what reward awaits those willing to pay the high price for holy living?

• "[They] will dwell on high" (heaven will be their home).
• "Food will be supplied to them" (God will supply their physical needs, Philippians 4:19).
• "The rocks of the mountains will be their fortress of safety" (God will protect and defend them from their enemies).

 LOOK AHEAD It's not easy taking a stand for what's *right* when everyone around you is running after what's *wrong*. It's not fun swimming against the current of public opinion or walking against the wind of selfish pursuits. If the truth were known, it's hard work. But don't be quick to go with the flow. After all, it was Jesus who warned us that "the gateway to life is small, and the road is narrow, and only a few ever find it" (Matthew 7:14).

Even if you are the only one in your office or school who refuses to cheat and cut corners, *tell the truth.* Even if you are the only one in your dorm or class who has committed yourself to sexual abstinence until marriage, *be willing to wait.* Standing alone may not be popular, but it is always profitable for the man or woman who chooses to walk with God.

JULY 29 ☐ DAY 211
ISAIAH 52–57
The Suffering Servant

 OVERVIEW Isaiah the prophet—Isaac Watts the hymnist. More than twenty-four centuries separate their lives. And yet the words you will read today about the selfless sacrifice of the Suffering Servant bear a striking similarity to these familiar, yet ever-moving stanzas:

> When I survey the wondrous cross,
> On which the Prince of glory died,
> My richest gain I count but loss,
> And pour contempt on all my pride.
>
> See, from His head, His hands, His feet,
> Sorrow and love flow mingled down;
> Did e'er such love and sorrow meet,
> Or thorns compose so rich a crown?

Chapters 52–53	Chapters 54–56	Chapter 57
Redemption Accomplished	Redemption Applied	Redemption Rejected
Results	Response	

 YOUR DAILY WALK Consider Christopher Columbus writing a book about space traveler George Washington predicting the outcome of the 1996 presidential election.

Christ's blood is heaven's key.

Absurd? Of course! No one can predict events like those centuries in advance. No one, that is, except a prophet of God.

As you read chapters 52 and 53 of Isaiah's prophecy, the details appear so vivid as to make you think Isaiah is standing at the foot of the cross. In his mind the events are so clear that he narrates them in the past tense, as if Christ's death had already taken place. Yet Isaiah penned his prophecies fully seven centuries before!

Spend some thoughtful minutes meditating on today's reading.

Put yourself into the passage in Isaiah 53: "He was wounded and crushed for *my* sins. He was beaten that *I* might have peace. He was whipped, and *I* was healed." Then close your daily walk by giving God a heartfelt thank-you for sending his Son to die on the cross—for *you.*

 INSIGHT The Bull's-Eye of Comfort
In Isaiah's prophecies of comfort (40–66), locate the middle chapter and the middle verse. Wouldn't you agree that that's a good "central passage" on comfort? (In case you can't find it, it's 53:6!)

CHAPTER 52

Wake up, wake up, O Zion! Clothe yourselves with strength. Put on your beautiful clothes, O holy city of Jerusalem, for unclean and godless people will no longer enter your gates. ²Rise from the dust, O Jerusalem. Remove the slave bands from your neck, O captive daughter of Zion. ³For this is what the LORD says: "When I sold you into exile, I received no payment. Now I can redeem you without paying for you."

⁴This is what the Sovereign LORD says: "Long ago my people went to live as resident foreigners in Egypt. Now they have been oppressed without cause by Assyria. ⁵And now, what is this?" asks the LORD. "Why are my people enslaved again? Those who rule them shout in exultation. My name is being blasphemed all day long. ⁶But I will reveal my name to my people, and they will come to know its power. Then at last they will recognize that it is I who speaks to them."

⁷How beautiful on the mountains are the feet of those who bring good news of peace and salvation, the news that the God of Israel* reigns! ⁸The watchmen shout and sing with joy, for before their very eyes they see the LORD bringing his people home to Jerusalem.* ⁹Let the ruins of Jerusalem break into joyful song, for the LORD has comforted his people. He has redeemed Jerusalem. ¹⁰The LORD will demonstrate his holy power before the eyes of all the nations. The ends of the earth will see the salvation of our God.

¹¹Go now, leave your bonds and slavery. Put Babylon behind you, with everything it represents, for it is unclean to you. You are the LORD's holy people. Purify yourselves, you who carry home the vessels of the LORD. ¹²You will not leave in a hurry, running for your lives. For the LORD will go ahead of you, and the God of Israel will protect you from behind.

¹³See, my servant will prosper; he will be highly exalted. ¹⁴Many were amazed when they saw him*—beaten and bloodied, so disfigured one would scarcely know he was a person. ¹⁵And he will again startle* many nations. Kings will stand speechless in his presence. For they will see what they had not previously been told about; they will understand what they had not heard about.

CHAPTER 53

Who has believed our message? To whom will the LORD reveal his saving power? ²My servant grew up in the LORD's presence like a tender green shoot, sprouting from a root in dry and sterile ground. There was nothing beautiful or majestic about his appearance, nothing to attract us to him. ³He was despised and rejected—a man of sorrows, acquainted with bitterest grief. We turned our backs on him and looked the other way when he went by. He was despised, and we did not care.

⁴Yet it was our weaknesses he carried; it was our sorrows* that weighed him down. And we thought his troubles were a punishment from God for his own sins! ⁵But he was wounded and crushed for our sins. He was beaten that we might have peace. He was whipped, and we were healed! ⁶All of us have strayed away like sheep. We have left God's paths to follow our own. Yet the LORD laid on him the guilt and sins of us all.

⁷He was oppressed and treated harshly, yet he never said a word. He was led as a lamb to the slaughter. And as a sheep is silent before the shearers, he did not open his mouth. ⁸From prison and trial they led him away to his death. But who among the people realized that he was dying for their sins—that he was suffering their punishment? ⁹He had done no wrong, and he never deceived anyone. But he was buried like a criminal; he was put in a rich man's grave.

¹⁰But it was the LORD's good plan to crush him and fill him with grief. Yet when his life is made an offering for sin, he will have a multitude of children, many heirs. He will enjoy a long life, and the LORD's plan will prosper in his hands. ¹¹When he sees all that is accomplished by his anguish, he will be satisfied. And because of what he has experienced, my righteous servant will make it possible for many to be counted righteous, for he will bear all their sins. ¹²I will give him the honors of one who is mighty and great, because he exposed himself to death. He was counted among those who were sinners. He bore the sins of many and interceded for sinners.

CHAPTER 54

"Sing, O childless woman! Break forth into loud and joyful song, O Jerusalem, even though you never gave birth to a child. For

---

52:7 Hebrew *of Zion.*   **52:8** Hebrew *to Zion.*   **52:14** As in Syriac version; Hebrew reads *you.*   **52:15** Or *cleanse.*   **53:4** Or *Yet it was our sicknesses he carried; it was our diseases.*

the woman who could bear no children now has more than all the other women," says the LORD. ²"Enlarge your house; build an addition; spread out your home! ³For you will soon be bursting at the seams. Your descendants will take over other nations and live in their cities.

⁴"Fear not; you will no longer live in shame. The shame of your youth and the sorrows of widowhood will be remembered no more, ⁵for your Creator will be your husband. The LORD Almighty is his name! He is your Redeemer, the Holy One of Israel, the God of all the earth. ⁶For the LORD has called you back from your grief— as though you were a young wife abandoned by her husband," says your God. ⁷"For a brief moment I abandoned you, but with great compassion I will take you back. ⁸In a moment of anger I turned my face away for a little while. But with everlasting love I will have compassion on you," says the LORD, your Redeemer.

⁹"Just as I swore in the time of Noah that I would never again let a flood cover the earth and destroy its life, so now I swear that I will never again pour out my anger on you. ¹⁰For the mountains may depart and the hills disappear, but even then I will remain loyal to you. My covenant of blessing will never be broken," says the LORD, who has mercy on you.

¹¹"O storm-battered city, troubled and desolate! I will rebuild you on a foundation of sapphires and make the walls of your houses from precious jewels. ¹²I will make your towers of sparkling rubies and your gates and walls of shining gems. ¹³I will teach all your citizens, and their prosperity will be great. ¹⁴You will live under a government that is just and fair. Your enemies will stay far away; you will live in peace. Terror will not come near. ¹⁵If any nation comes to fight you, it will not be because I sent them to punish you. Your enemies will always be defeated because I am on your side. ¹⁶I have created the blacksmith who fans the coals beneath the forge and makes the weapons of destruction. And I have created the armies that destroy. ¹⁷But in that coming day, no weapon turned against you will succeed. And everyone who tells lies in court will be brought to justice. These benefits are enjoyed by the servants of the LORD; their vindication will come from me. I, the LORD, have spoken!

CHAPTER 55

"Is anyone thirsty? Come and drink—even if you have no money! Come, take your choice of wine or milk—it's all free! ²Why spend your money on food that does not give you strength? Why pay for food that does you no good? Listen, and I will tell you where to get food that is good for the soul!

³"Come to me with your ears wide open. Listen, for the life of your soul is at stake. I am ready to make an everlasting covenant with you. I will give you all the mercies and unfailing love that I promised to David. ⁴He displayed my power by being my witness and a leader among the nations. ⁵You also will command the nations, and they will come running to obey, because I, the LORD your God, the Holy One of Israel, have made you glorious."

⁶Seek the LORD while you can find him. Call on him now while he is near. ⁷Let the people turn from their wicked deeds. Let them banish from their minds the very thought of doing wrong! Let them turn to the LORD that he may have mercy on them. Yes, turn to our God, for he will abundantly pardon.

⁸"My thoughts are completely different from yours," says the LORD. "And my ways are far beyond anything you could imagine. ⁹For just as the heavens are higher than the earth, so are my ways higher than your ways and my thoughts higher than your thoughts.

¹⁰"The rain and snow come down from the heavens and stay on the ground to water the earth. They cause the grain to grow, producing seed for the farmer and bread for the hungry. ¹¹It is the same with my word. I send it out, and it always produces fruit. It will accomplish all I want it to, and it will prosper everywhere I send it. ¹²You will live in joy and peace. The mountains and hills will burst into song, and the trees of the field will clap their hands! ¹³Where once there were thorns, cypress trees will grow. Where briers grew, myrtles will sprout up. This miracle will bring great honor to the LORD's name; it will be an everlasting sign of his power and love.

CHAPTER 56

"Be just and fair to all," says the LORD. "Do what is right and good, for I am coming soon to rescue you. ²Blessed are those who are careful to do this. Blessed are those who honor my Sabbath days of rest by refusing to work. And blessed are those who keep themselves from doing wrong.

3"And my blessings are for Gentiles, too, when they commit themselves to the LORD. Do not let them think that I consider them second-class citizens. And my blessings are also for the eunuchs. They are as much mine as anyone else. 4For I say this to the eunuchs who keep my Sabbath days holy, who choose to do what pleases me and commit their lives to me: 5I will give them—in my house, within my walls—a memorial and a name far greater than the honor they would have received by having sons and daughters. For the name I give them is an everlasting one. It will never disappear!

6"I will also bless the Gentiles who commit themselves to the LORD and serve him and love his name, who worship him and do not desecrate the Sabbath day of rest, and who have accepted his covenant. 7I will bring them also to my holy mountain of Jerusalem and will fill them with joy in my house of prayer. I will accept their burnt offerings and sacrifices, because my Temple will be called a house of prayer for all nations. 8For the Sovereign LORD, who brings back the outcasts of Israel, says: I will bring others, too, besides my people Israel."

9Come, wild animals of the field! Come, wild animals of the forest! Come and devour my people! 10For the leaders of my people—the LORD's watchmen, his shepherds—are blind to every danger. They are like silent watchdogs that give no warning when danger comes. They love to lie around, sleeping and dreaming. 11And they are as greedy as dogs, never satisfied. They are stupid shepherds, all following their own path, all of them intent on personal gain.

12"Come," they say. "We will get some wine and have a party. Let's all get drunk. Let this go on and on, and tomorrow will be even better."

CHAPTER 57

The righteous pass away; the godly often die before their time. And no one seems to care or wonder why. No one seems to understand that God is protecting them from the evil to come. 2For the godly who die will rest in peace.

3"But you—come here, you witches' children, you offspring of adulterers and prostitutes! 4Whom do you mock, making faces and sticking out your tongues? You children of sinners and liars! 5You worship your idols with great passion beneath every green tree. You slaughter your children as human sacrifices down in the valleys, under overhanging rocks. 6Your gods are the smooth stones in the valleys. You worship them with drink offerings and grain offerings. They, not I, are your inheritance. Does all this make me happy? 7You have committed adultery on the mountaintops by worshiping idols there, and so you have been unfaithful to me. 8Behind closed doors, you have set up your idols and worship them instead of me. This is adultery, for you are loving these idols instead of loving me. You have climbed right into bed with these detestable gods. 9You have given olive oil and perfume to Molech* as your gift. You have traveled far, even into the world of the dead,* to find new gods to love. 10You grew weary in your search, but you never gave up. You strengthened yourself and went on. 11Why were you more afraid of them than of me? How is it that you don't even remember me or think about me? Is it because I have not corrected you that you have no fear of me?

12"Now I will expose your so-called good deeds that you consider so righteous. None of them will benefit or save you. 13Let's see if your idols can do anything for you when you cry to them for help. They are so helpless that a breath of wind can knock them down! But whoever trusts in me will possess the land and inherit my holy mountain. 14I will say, 'Rebuild the road! Clear away the rocks and stones so my people can return from captivity.'"

15The high and lofty one who inhabits eternity, the Holy One, says this: "I live in that high and holy place with those whose spirits are contrite and humble. I refresh the humble and give new courage to those with repentant hearts. 16For I will not fight against you forever; I will not always show my anger. If I did, all people would pass away—all the souls I have made. 17I was angry and punished these greedy people. I withdrew myself from them, but they went

57:9a Or to the king.   57:9b Hebrew into Sheol.

right on sinning. [18]I have seen what they do, but I will heal them anyway! I will lead them and comfort those who mourn. [19]Then words of praise will be on their lips. May they have peace, both near and far, for I will heal them all," says the LORD. [20]"But those who still reject me are like the restless sea. It is never still but continually churns up mire and dirt. [21]There is no peace for the wicked," says my God.

JULY 30 □ DAY 212
ISAIAH 58–62
Consummation of Judgment

 OVERVIEW Comfort is coming in the form of a deliverer (Cyrus, 40–48); comfort is coming in the form of a Suffering Servant (Messiah, 49–57); and finally, comfort is coming in the form of a delivered people (Judah, 58–66). Obedience to God's commands has always been the path to individual and corporate blessing. And the future of God's people is bright indeed! When the Messiah, the light of Jerusalem, comes, then righteousness and salvation will shine forth to the nations of the world (60:1; 62:1), and Jerusalem will be "the object of praise throughout the earth" (62:7).

Chapter 58	Chapter 59	Chapter 60	Chapters 61–62
Ungodly Worship	Ungodly Ways	A New Wealth	A New Name
Judah's Groan		Judah's Glory	

 YOUR DAILY WALK Some people are so indecisive, their favorite color is plaid. For instance, when a lady was asked, "Do you always have trouble making up your mind?" she replied, "Well, yes and no."

Repentance may be old-fashioned, but as long as there is sin, it will never be outdated.

But there comes a time when changing your mind is not only desirable, it is imperative—and that is when God tells you to!

Chapter 58 describes a nation of people who needed to change their minds about God, themselves, and the wickedness that characterized their lives. In a word, they needed to repent. Their worship was full of shallow formalism; their outward piety was not matched by inward purity; they fasted for public recognition while ignoring the needs of others all around them.

Whenever an improper attitude or action has crept into your life, it's time for a change. Do these three words describe your lifestyle before God today? *Pure . . . undefiled . . . unspotted.* If not, let James 1:27 point the way to an *outward* religion that is consistent with your *inward* relationship to Jesus Christ.

 INSIGHT A New Name Promised and Provided
In 62:2 the Lord promises the ransomed community of Zion "a new name." Keep reading and you'll discover not one new name but two, all contained in the same verse (62:12). What are they?

CHAPTER 58
"Shout with the voice of a trumpet blast. Tell my people Israel* of their sins! [2]Yet they act so pious! They come to the Temple every day and seem delighted to hear my laws. You would almost think this was a righteous nation that would never abandon its God. They love to make a show of

58:1 Hebrew *Jacob.*

coming to me and asking me to take action on their behalf. [3]'We have fasted before you!' they say. 'Why aren't you impressed? We have done much penance, and you don't even notice it!'

"I will tell you why! It's because you are living for yourselves even while you are fasting. You keep right on oppressing your workers. [4]What good is fasting when you keep on fighting and quarreling? This kind of fasting will never get you anywhere with me. [5]You humble yourselves by going through the motions of penance, bowing your heads like a blade of grass in the wind. You dress in sackcloth and cover yourselves with ashes. Is this what you call fasting? Do you really think this will please the LORD?

[6]"No, the kind of fasting I want calls you to free those who are wrongly imprisoned and to stop oppressing those who work for you. Treat them fairly and give them what they earn. [7]I want you to share your food with the hungry and to welcome poor wanderers into your homes. Give clothes to those who need them, and do not hide from relatives who need your help.

[8]"If you do these things, your salvation will come like the dawn. Yes, your healing will come quickly. Your godliness will lead you forward, and the glory of the LORD will protect you from behind. [9]Then when you call, the LORD will answer. 'Yes, I am here,' he will quickly reply.

"Stop oppressing the helpless and stop making false accusations and spreading vicious rumors! [10]Feed the hungry and help those in trouble. Then your light will shine out from the darkness, and the darkness around you will be as bright as day. [11]The LORD will guide you continually, watering your life when you are dry and keeping you healthy, too. You will be like a well-watered garden, like an ever-flowing spring. [12]Your children will rebuild the deserted ruins of your cities. Then you will be known as the people who rebuild their walls and cities.

[13]"Keep the Sabbath day holy. Don't pursue your own interests on that day, but enjoy the Sabbath and speak of it with delight as the LORD's holy day. Honor the LORD in everything you do, and don't follow your own desires or talk idly. If you do this, [14]the LORD will be your delight. I will give you great honor and give you your full share of the inheritance I promised to Jacob, your ancestor. I, the LORD, have spoken!"

CHAPTER 59

Listen! The LORD is not too weak to save you, and he is not becoming deaf. He can hear you when you call. [2]But there is a problem—your sins have cut you off from God. Because of your sin, he has turned away and will not listen anymore. [3]Your hands are the hands of murderers, and your fingers are filthy with sin. Your mouth is full of lies, and your lips are tainted with corruption.

[4]No one cares about being fair and honest. Their lawsuits are based on lies. They spend their time plotting evil deeds and then doing them. [5]They spend their time and energy spinning evil plans that end up in deadly actions. [6]They cheat and shortchange everyone. Nothing they do is productive; all their activity is filled with sin. Violence is their trademark. [7]Their feet run to do evil, and they rush to commit murder. They think only about sinning. Wherever they go, misery and destruction follow them. [8]They do not know what true peace is or what it means to be just and good. They continually do wrong, and those who follow them cannot experience a moment's peace.

[9]It is because of all this evil that deliverance is far from us. That is why God doesn't punish those who injure us. No wonder we are in darkness when we expected light. No wonder we are walking in the gloom. [10]No wonder we grope like blind people and stumble along. Even at brightest noontime, we fall down as though it were dark. No wonder we are like corpses when compared to vigorous young men! [11]We growl like hungry bears; we moan like mournful doves. We look for justice, but it is nowhere to be found. We look to be rescued, but it is far away from us. [12]For our sins are piled up before God and testify against us. Yes, we know what sinners we are. [13]We know that we have rebelled against the LORD. We have turned our backs on God. We know how unfair and oppressive we have been, carefully planning our deceitful lies. [14]Our courts oppose people who are righteous, and justice is nowhere to be found. Truth falls dead in the streets, and fairness has been outlawed. [15]Yes, truth is gone, and anyone who tries to live a godly life is soon attacked.

The LORD looked and was displeased to find that there was no justice. [16]He was amazed to see that no one intervened to help the oppressed. So he himself stepped in to save them with his mighty power and justice. [17]He put on righteousness as his body armor and placed the helmet of salvation on his head. He clothed himself with the robes of vengeance and godly fury. [18]He will repay his enemies for their evil deeds. His fury will fall on his foes in distant lands. [19]Then at last they will respect and glorify the name of the LORD throughout the world. For he will come like a flood tide driven by the breath of the LORD.

[20]"The Redeemer will come to Jerusalem,*" says the LORD, "to buy back those in Israel* who have turned from their sins. [21]And this is my covenant with them," says the LORD. "My Spirit will not leave them, and neither will these words I have given you. They will be on your lips and on the lips of your children and your children's children forever. I, the LORD, have spoken!

CHAPTER 60

"Arise, Jerusalem! Let your light shine for all the nations to see! For the glory of the LORD is shining upon you. [2]Darkness as black as night will cover all the nations of the earth, but the glory of the LORD will shine over you. [3]All nations will come to your light. Mighty kings will come to see your radiance.

[4]"Look and see, for everyone is coming home! Your sons are coming from distant lands; your little daughters will be carried home. [5]Your eyes will shine, and your hearts will thrill with joy, for merchants from around the world will come to you. They will bring you the wealth of many lands. [6]Vast caravans of camels will converge on you, the camels of Midian and Ephah. From Sheba they will bring gold and incense for the worship of the LORD. [7]The flocks of Kedar will be given to you, and the rams of Nebaioth will be brought for my altars. In that day I will make my Temple glorious.

[8]"And what do I see flying like clouds to Israel, like doves to their nests? [9]They are the ships of Tarshish, reserved to bring the people of Israel home. They will bring their wealth with them, and it will bring great honor to the LORD your God, the Holy One of Israel, for he will fill you with splendor.

[10]"Foreigners will come to rebuild your cities. Kings and rulers will send you aid. For though I have destroyed you in my anger, I will have mercy on you through my grace. [11]Your gates will stay open around the clock to receive the wealth of many lands. The kings of the world will be led as captives in a victory procession. [12]For the nations that refuse to be your allies will be destroyed. [13]The glory of Lebanon will be yours—the forests of cypress, fir, and pine—to beautify my sanctuary. My Temple will be glorious!

[14]"The children of your tormentors will come and bow before you. Those who despised you will kiss your feet. They will call you the City of the LORD, and Zion of the Holy One of Israel.

[15]"Though you were once despised and hated and rebuffed by all, you will be beautiful forever. You will be a joy to all generations, for I will make you so. [16]Powerful kings and mighty nations will bring the best of their goods to satisfy your every need. You will know at last that I, the LORD, am your Savior and Redeemer, the Mighty One of Israel.* [17]I will exchange your bronze for gold, your iron for silver, your wood for bronze, and your stones for iron. Peace and righteousness will be your leaders! [18]Violence will disappear from your land; the desolation and destruction of war will end. Salvation will surround you like city walls, and praise will be on the lips of all who enter there.

[19]"No longer will you need the sun or moon to give you light, for the LORD your God will be your everlasting light, and he will be your glory. [20]The sun will never set; the moon will not go down. For the LORD will be your everlasting light. Your days of mourning will come to an end. [21]All your people will be righteous. They will possess their land forever, for I will plant them there with my own hands in order to bring myself glory. [22]The smallest family will multiply into a large clan. The tiniest group will become a mighty nation. I, the LORD, will bring it all to pass at the right time."

CHAPTER 61

The Spirit of the Sovereign LORD is upon me, because the LORD has appointed me to bring good news to the poor. He has sent me to comfort the brokenhearted and to announce that captives will be released and

59:20a Hebrew *to Zion.*   59:20b Hebrew *in Jacob.*   60:16 Hebrew *of Jacob.*

prisoners will be freed.* [2]He has sent me to tell those who mourn that the time of the LORD's favor has come,* and with it, the day of God's anger against their enemies. [3]To all who mourn in Israel,* he will give beauty for ashes, joy instead of mourning, praise instead of despair. For the LORD has planted them like strong and graceful oaks for his own glory.

[4]They will rebuild the ancient ruins, repairing cities long ago destroyed. They will revive them, though they have been empty for many generations. [5]Foreigners will be your servants. They will feed your flocks and plow your fields and tend your vineyards. [6]You will be called priests of the LORD, ministers of our God. You will be fed with the treasures of the nations and will boast in their riches. [7]Instead of shame and dishonor, you will inherit a double portion of prosperity and everlasting joy.

[8]"For I, the LORD, love justice. I hate robbery and wrongdoing. I will faithfully reward my people for their suffering and make an everlasting covenant with them. [9]Their descendants will be known and honored among the nations. Everyone will realize that they are a people the LORD has blessed."

[10]I am overwhelmed with joy in the LORD my God! For he has dressed me with the clothing of salvation and draped me in a robe of righteousness. I am like a bridegroom in his wedding suit or a bride with her jewels. [11]The Sovereign LORD will show his justice to the nations of the world. Everyone will praise him! His righteousness will be like a garden in early spring, filled with young plants springing up everywhere.

CHAPTER 62

Because I love Zion, because my heart yearns for Jerusalem, I cannot remain silent. I will not stop praying for her until her righteousness shines like the dawn, and her salvation blazes like a burning torch.

[2]The nations will see your righteousness. Kings will be blinded by your glory. And the LORD will give you a new name. [3]The LORD will hold you in his hands for all to see—a splendid crown in the hands of God. [4]Never again will you be called the Godforsaken City* or the Desolate Land.* Your new name will be the City of God's Delight* and the Bride of God,* for the LORD delights in you and will claim you as his own. [5]Your children will care for you with joy, O Jerusalem, just as a young man cares for his bride. Then God will rejoice over you as a bridegroom rejoices over his bride.

[6]O Jerusalem, I have posted watchmen on your walls; they will pray to the LORD day and night for the fulfillment of his promises. Take no rest, all you who pray. [7]Give the LORD no rest until he makes Jerusalem the object of praise throughout the earth. [8]The LORD has sworn to Jerusalem by his own strength: "I will never again hand you over to your enemies. Never again will foreign warriors come and take away your grain and wine. [9]You raised it, and you will keep it, praising the LORD. Within the courtyards of the Temple, you yourselves will drink the wine that you have pressed."

[10]Go out! Prepare the highway for my people to return! Smooth out the road; pull out the boulders; raise a flag for all the nations to see. [11]The LORD has sent this message to every land: "Tell the people of Israel,* 'Look, your Savior is coming. See, he brings his reward with him as he comes.'" [12]They will be called the Holy People and the People Redeemed by the LORD. And Jerusalem will be known as the Desirable Place and the City No Longer Forsaken.

61:1 Greek version reads *and the blind will see.*   61:2 Or *to proclaim the acceptable year of the LORD.*   61:3 Hebrew *in Zion.*
62:4a Hebrew *Azubah,* which means "forsaken."   62:4b Hebrew *Shemamah,* which means "desolate."   62:4c Hebrew *Hephzibah,* which means "my delight is in her."   62:4d Hebrew *Beulah,* which means "married."   62:11 Hebrew *Tell the daughter of Zion.*

JULY 31 □ DAY 213
ISAIAH 63–66
Isaiah's Prayer and the Lord's Reply

OVERVIEW Isaiah closes his great prophetic work with a stirring prayer of intercession for the house of Israel. While acknowledging their waywardness and frequent rebellions, he nevertheless claims God's promises on their behalf to redeem them and to refashion them into a people for his glory. God's response is both stern and comforting. The rebels will be punished for ignoring God's frequent invitations. Idolatry, covetousness, rebellion, and disobedience will be rooted out of his people. In addition, a rich store of glory and blessing awaits God's faithful ones: a new heaven and earth, no more tears, no premature death, no want of food, and no violence in nature. Isaiah concludes by summarizing the major themes of his book: God exalts the humble and contrite; the Messiah is coming to avenge his enemies; all nations will see God's glory; and all flesh will one day worship the Lord.

Chapter 63	Chapter 64	Chapter 65	Chapter 66
"Redeem Your People"	"Remake Your People"	"I Will Restore My People"	"I Will Refashion My Creation"
Isaiah's Prayer for Redemption		The Lord's Powerful Reply	

YOUR DAILY WALK The book of Isaiah is a sobering reminder of the painful consequences of

Those who live in the Lord never see each other for the last time.

- taking God lightly;
- ignoring his promises (and thereby forfeiting his blessing);
- ignoring his warnings (and thereby incurring judgment); and
- ignoring his invitations (and thereby missing the joy of a personal family relationship with God).

Isaiah's prophecy is long. It contains more chapters than any other Old Testament prophetic book. But his message is simple and concise—judgment and comfort: judgment for those who fail to heed God's voice and comfort for those who do.

Give yourself a spiritual hearing test right now. Are you tuned in to hear God's voice? Do you answer when he calls (6:8), or is your line constantly busy? There will come a day when the phone quits ringing forever. Spend the next few minutes telling God what you have learned from the book of Isaiah.

INSIGHT An Old Testament "News" Paper
Notice how much "news" there is in chapters 65–66: new nations brought into the fold, a new name for God's people, a new heaven and earth for their inheritance, and a new order of worship!

CHAPTER 63

Who is this who comes from Edom, from the city of Bozrah, with his clothing stained red? Who is this in royal robes, marching in the greatness of his strength?

"It is I, the LORD, announcing your salvation! It is I, the LORD, who is mighty to save!"

²Why are your clothes so red, as if you have been treading out grapes?

³"I have trodden the winepress alone; no one was there to help me. In my anger I have trampled my enemies as if they were grapes. In my fury I have trampled my foes. It is their blood that has stained my clothes. ⁴For the time has come for me to avenge my people, to ransom them from their oppressors. ⁵I looked, but no one came to help my people. I was amazed and appalled at what I saw. So I executed

vengeance alone; unaided, I passed down judgment. [6]I crushed the nations in my anger and made them stagger and fall to the ground."

[7]I will tell of the LORD's unfailing love. I will praise the LORD for all he has done. I will rejoice in his great goodness to Israel, which he has granted according to his mercy and love. [8]He said, "They are my very own people. Surely they will not be false again." And he became their Savior. [9]In all their suffering he also suffered, and he personally rescued them. In his love and mercy he redeemed them. He lifted them up and carried them through all the years.

[10]But they rebelled against him and grieved his Holy Spirit. That is why he became their enemy and fought against them. [11]Then they remembered those days of old when Moses led his people out of Egypt. They cried out, "Where is the one who brought Israel through the sea, with Moses as their shepherd? Where is the one who sent his Holy Spirit to be among his people? [12]Where is the one whose power divided the sea before them, when Moses lifted up his hand, establishing his reputation forever? [13]Where is the one who led them through the bottom of the sea? They were like fine stallions racing through the desert, never stumbling. [14]As with cattle going down into a peaceful valley, the Spirit of the LORD gave them rest. You led your people, LORD, and gained a magnificent reputation."

[15]LORD, look down from heaven and see us from your holy, glorious home. Where is the passion and the might you used to show on our behalf? Where are your mercy and compassion now? [16]Surely you are still our Father! Even if Abraham and Jacob* would disown us, LORD, you would still be our Father. You are our Redeemer from ages past. [17]LORD, why have you allowed us to turn from your path? Why have you given us stubborn hearts so we no longer fear you? Return and help us, for we are your servants and your special possession. [18]How briefly your holy people possessed the holy place, and now our enemies have destroyed it. [19]LORD, why do you treat us as though we never belonged to you? Why do you act as though we had never been known as your people?

63:16 Hebrew *Israel.*

CHAPTER 64

Oh, that you would burst from the heavens and come down! How the mountains would quake in your presence! [2]As fire causes wood to burn and water to boil, your coming would make the nations tremble. Then your enemies would learn the reason for your fame! [3]When you came down long ago, you did awesome things beyond our highest expectations. And oh, how the mountains quaked! [4]For since the world began, no ear has heard, and no eye has seen a God like you, who works for those who wait for him! [5]You welcome those who cheerfully do good, who follow godly ways.

But we are not godly. We are constant sinners, so your anger is heavy on us. How can people like us be saved? [6]We are all infected and impure with sin. When we proudly display our righteous deeds, we find they are but filthy rags. Like autumn leaves, we wither and fall. And our sins, like the wind, sweep us away. [7]Yet no one calls on your name or pleads with you for mercy. Therefore, you have turned away from us and turned us over to our sins.

[8]And yet, LORD, you are our Father. We are the clay, and you are the potter. We are all formed by your hand. [9]Oh, don't be so angry with us, LORD. Please don't remember our sins forever. Look at us, we pray, and see that we are all your people.

[10]Your holy cities are destroyed; even Jerusalem is a desolate wilderness. [11]The holy, beautiful Temple where our ancestors praised you has been burned down, and all the things of beauty are destroyed. [12]After all this, LORD, must you still refuse to help us? Will you continue to be silent and punish us?

CHAPTER 65

The LORD says, "People who never before inquired about me are now asking about me. I am being found by people who were not looking for me. To them I have said, 'I am here!'

[2]"I opened my arms to my own people all day long, but they have rebelled. They follow their own evil paths and thoughts. [3]All day long they insult me to my face by worshiping idols in their sacred gardens. They burn incense on the rooftops of their homes. [4]At night they go out among the

graves and secret places to worship evil spirits. They also eat pork and other forbidden foods. [5]Yet they say to each other, 'Don't come too close or you will defile me! I am holier than you!' They are a stench in my nostrils, an acrid smell that never goes away.

[6]"Look, my decree is written out in front of me: I will not stand silent; I will repay them in full! Yes, I will repay them—[7]both for their own sins and for those of their ancestors," says the LORD. "For they also burned incense on the mountains and insulted me on the hills. I will pay them back in full!

[8]"But I will not destroy them all," says the LORD. "For just as good grapes are found among a cluster of bad ones (and someone will say, 'Don't throw them all away—there are some good grapes there!'), so I will not destroy all Israel. For I still have true servants there. [9]I will preserve a remnant of the people of Israel* and of Judah to possess my land. Those I choose will inherit it and serve me there. [10]For my people who have searched for me, the plain of Sharon will again be filled with flocks, and the valley of Achor will be a place to pasture herds.

[11]"But because the rest of you have forsaken the LORD and his Temple and worship the gods of Fate and Destiny, [12]I will 'destine' you to the sword. All of you will bow before the executioner, for when I called, you did not answer. When I spoke, you did not listen. You deliberately sinned—before my very eyes—and chose to do what you know I despise."

[13]Therefore, this is what the Sovereign LORD says: "You will starve, but my servants will eat. You will be thirsty, but they will drink. You will be sad and ashamed, but they will rejoice. [14]You will cry in sorrow and despair, while my servants sing for joy. [15]Your name will be a curse word among my people, for the Sovereign LORD will destroy you and call his true servants by another name. [16]All who invoke a blessing or take an oath will do so by the God of truth. For I will put aside my anger and forget the evil of earlier days.

[17]"Look! I am creating new heavens and a new earth—so wonderful that no one will even think about the old ones anymore. [18]Be glad; rejoice forever in my creation!

And look! I will create Jerusalem as a place of happiness. Her people will be a source of joy. [19]I will rejoice in Jerusalem and delight in my people. And the sound of weeping and crying will be heard no more.

[20]"No longer will babies die when only a few days old. No longer will adults die before they have lived a full life. No longer will people be considered old at one hundred! Only sinners will die that young! [21]In those days, people will live in the houses they build and eat the fruit of their own vineyards. [22]It will not be like the past, when invaders took the houses and confiscated the vineyards. For my people will live as long as trees and will have time to enjoy their hard-won gains. [23]They will not work in vain, and their children will not be doomed to misfortune. For they are people blessed by the LORD, and their children, too, will be blessed. [24]I will answer them before they even call to me. While they are still talking to me about their needs, I will go ahead and answer their prayers! [25]The wolf and lamb will feed together. The lion will eat straw like the ox. Poisonous snakes will strike no more. In those days, no one will be hurt or destroyed on my holy mountain. I, the LORD, have spoken!"

CHAPTER 66

This is what the LORD says: "Heaven is my throne, and the earth is my footstool. Could you ever build me a temple as good as that? Could you build a dwelling place for me? [2]My hands have made both heaven and earth, and they are mine. I, the LORD, have spoken!

"I will bless those who have humble and contrite hearts, who tremble at my word. [3]But those who choose their own ways, delighting in their sins, are cursed. Their offerings will not be accepted. When such people sacrifice an ox, it is no more acceptable than a human sacrifice. When they sacrifice a lamb or bring an offering of grain, it is as bad as putting a dog or the blood of a pig on the altar! When they burn incense, it is as if they had blessed an idol. [4]I will send great troubles against them—all the things they feared. For when I called, they did not answer. When I spoke, they did not listen. They deliberately sinned—

65:9 Hebrew *remnant of Jacob.*

before my very eyes—and chose to do what they know I despise."

[5]Hear this message from the LORD, and tremble at his words: "Your close relatives hate you and throw you out for being loyal to my name. 'Let the LORD be honored!' they scoff. 'Be joyful in him!' But they will be put to shame. [6]What is all the commotion in the city? What is that terrible noise from the Temple? It is the voice of the LORD taking vengeance against his enemies.

[7]"Before the birth pains even begin, Jerusalem gives birth to a son. [8]Who has ever seen or heard of anything as strange as this? Has a nation ever been born in a single day? Has a country ever come forth in a mere moment? But by the time Jerusalem's* birth pains begin, the baby will be born; the nation will come forth. [9]Would I ever bring this nation to the point of birth and then not deliver it?" asks the LORD. "No! I would never keep this nation from being born," says your God.

[10]"Rejoice with Jerusalem! Be glad with her, all you who love her and mourn for her. [11]Delight in Jerusalem! Drink deeply of her glory even as an infant drinks at its mother's generous breasts. [12]Peace and prosperity will overflow Jerusalem like a river," says the LORD. "The wealth of the nations will flow to her. Her children will be nursed at her breasts, carried in her arms, and treated with love. [13]I will comfort you there as a child is comforted by its mother."

[14]When you see these things, your heart will rejoice. Vigorous health will be yours! Everyone will see the good hand of the LORD on his people—and his anger against his enemies. [15]See, the LORD is coming with fire, and his swift chariots of destruction roar like a whirlwind. He will bring punishment with the fury of his anger and the flaming fire of his hot rebuke. [16]The LORD will punish the world by fire and by his sword, and many will be killed by the LORD.

[17]"Those who 'purify' themselves in a sacred garden, feasting on pork and rats and other forbidden meats, will come to a terrible end," says the LORD. [18]"I can see what they are doing, and I know what they are thinking. So I will gather all nations and peoples together, and they will see my glory. [19]I will perform a sign among them. And I will send those who survive to be messengers to the nations—to Tarshish, to the Libyans* and Lydians* (who are famous as archers), to Tubal and Greece,* and to all the lands beyond the sea that have not heard of my fame or seen my glory. There they will declare my glory to the nations. [20]They will bring the remnant of your people back from every nation. They will bring them to my holy mountain in Jerusalem as an offering to the LORD. They will ride on horses, in chariots and wagons, and on mules and camels," says the LORD. [21]"And I will appoint some of those who return to be my priests and Levites. I, the LORD, have spoken!

[22]"As surely as my new heavens and earth will remain, so will you always be my people, with a name that will never disappear," says the LORD. [23]"All humanity will come to worship me from week to week and from month to month. [24]And as they go out, they will see the dead bodies of those who have rebelled against me. For the worms that devour them will never die, and the fire that burns them will never go out. All who pass by will view them with utter horror."

66:8 Hebrew *Zion's*.　　66:19a As in some Greek manuscripts, which read *Put* [Libya]; Hebrew reads *Pul*.　　66:19b Hebrew *Lud*.
66:19c Hebrew *Javan*.

Jeremiah

THE BOOK of Jeremiah presents the life and ministry of one of Judah's greatest prophets as he preaches to his once-mighty nation now teetering on the brink of disaster. For more than forty years Jeremiah proclaims an unpopular message: Repent or perish. His sermons go unheeded by his headstrong countrymen, who do their best to silence Jeremiah once and for all. Opposed, hated, and imprisoned, the heartbroken prophet lives to see the cruel Babylonians carry away Judah's citizens.

Focus	Jeremiah's Sermons						Jeremiah's Experiences					
Divisions	Judah in Jeopardy	Judah in Idolatry	Judah in Rebellion	Judah in Potter's Hand	Judah in Leadership Crisis	Judah in Opposition	Hope amidst Judgment	Before the Fall	During the Fall	After the Fall	Gentiles in Judgment	Fall of Jerusalem
	1⎯6	7⎯10	11⎯15	16⎯20	21⎯25	26⎯29	30⎯33	34⎯36	37⎯39	40⎯45	46⎯51	52
Topics	Judgment						Hope	Judgment				
	Preaching							Portrayal			Prophecy	
Place	Judah											Babylonia
Time	About 42 Years (627–585 B.C.)											

AUGUST 1 ☐ DAY 214
JEREMIAH 1–6
Judah in Jeopardy of Judgment

OVERVIEW God has patiently sent warning after warning through his prophetic spokesmen in an attempt to turn Judah from her hard-hearted ways. Now for the last time, God sends an ultimatum through a tender man of steel: Jeremiah. The prophet from Anathoth tells the people exactly what they need to hear, but through tear-filled eyes: God can bear with the sins of the nation no longer. Even now, the gathering clouds of Babylonian conquest can be viewed on the horizon by those having eyes to see and hearts to repent.

Chapter 1	Chapters 2–3	Chapters 4–6
Messenger of Judgment	Message of Judgment	Means of Judgment
Jeremiah's Call	Jeremiah's Cry	Judah's Conqueror

YOUR DAILY WALK Working with people is not so difficult. All you need is inexhaustible patience, unfailing insight, unshakable stability, and a tremendous amount of experience!

There are no trivial assignments in the work of the Lord.

God could have chosen to do his work another way, but he didn't. He chose to use people. People like Moses . . . and Isaiah . . . and Jeremiah . . . and you! God asked Moses to walk boldly into the court of Pharaoh and announce, "Let my people go!" God asked Isaiah to volunteer for an important mission. God asked Jeremiah to prophesy to a rebellious nation. Moses said, "I won't." Isaiah said, "Woe is me!" Jeremiah said, "I can't." Yet God supplied a tailor-made program of training and encouragement to prepare each messenger to deliver his message.

What message is God asking you to deliver for him today? What is your response to his assignment? Have you answered, "I can't" . . . or "I won't" . . . or "I will"? As you begin your study of Jeremiah's life and ministry, take one of your "can'ts" or "won'ts" and turn it into a "will." In the last five minutes of your quiet time today, write a short note to God expressing your desire to be used by him. Then watch him work *in* you and *through* you.

INSIGHT Deaf Ears in the Palace
Jeremiah's ministry spanned the reigns of five kings in Judah: Josiah, Jehoahaz, Jehoiakim, Jehoiachin, and Zedekiah. All but Josiah were wicked kings who opposed or ignored the prophet's words.

CHAPTER 1

These are the words of Jeremiah son of Hilkiah, one of the priests from Anathoth, a town in the land of Benjamin. ²The LORD first gave messages to Jeremiah during the thirteenth year of King Josiah's reign in Judah.* ³He continued to give messages throughout the reign of Josiah's son, King Jehoiakim, until the eleventh year of King Zedekiah's reign in Judah. In August of that year,* the people of Jerusalem were taken away as captives.

1:2 The thirteenth year of Josiah's reign was 627 B.C. 1:3 Hebrew *In the fifth month,* of the Hebrew calendar. A number of events in Jeremiah can be cross-checked with dates in surviving Babylonian records and related accurately to our modern calendar. This month in the eleventh year of Zedekiah's reign occurred in August and September 586 B.C. Also see 52:12 and the note there.

⁴The LORD gave me a message. He said, ⁵"I knew you before I formed you in your mother's womb. Before you were born I set you apart and appointed you as my spokesman to the world."

⁶"O Sovereign LORD," I said, "I can't speak for you! I'm too young!"

⁷"Don't say that," the LORD replied, "for you must go wherever I send you and say whatever I tell you. ⁸And don't be afraid of the people, for I will be with you and take care of you. I, the LORD, have spoken!"

⁹Then the LORD touched my mouth and said, "See, I have put my words in your mouth! ¹⁰Today I appoint you to stand up against nations and kingdoms. You are to uproot some and tear them down, to destroy and overthrow them. You are to build others up and plant them."

¹¹Then the LORD said to me, "Look, Jeremiah! What do you see?"

And I replied, "I see a branch from an almond tree."

¹²And the LORD said, "That's right, and it means that I am watching,* and I will surely carry out my threats of punishment."

¹³Then the LORD spoke to me again and asked, "What do you see now?"

And I replied, "I see a pot of boiling water, tipping from the north."

¹⁴"Yes," the LORD said, "for terror from the north will boil out on the people of this land. ¹⁵Listen! I am calling the armies of the kingdoms of the north to come to Jerusalem. They will set their thrones at the gates of the city. They will attack its walls and all the other towns of Judah. ¹⁶I will pronounce judgment on my people for all their evil—for deserting me and worshiping other gods. Yes, they worship idols that they themselves have made!

¹⁷"Get up and get dressed. Go out, and tell them whatever I tell you to say. Do not be afraid of them, or I will make you look foolish in front of them. ¹⁸For see, today I have made you immune to their attacks. You are strong like a fortified city that cannot be captured, like an iron pillar or a bronze wall. None of the kings, officials, priests, or people of Judah will be able to stand against you. ¹⁹They will try, but they will fail. For I am with you, and I will take care of you. I, the LORD, have spoken!"

CHAPTER 2

The LORD gave me another message. He said, ²"Go and shout in Jerusalem's streets: 'This is what the LORD says: I remember how eager you were to please me as a young bride long ago, how you loved me and followed me even through the barren wilderness. ³In those days Israel was holy to the LORD, the first of my children.* All who harmed my people were considered guilty, and disaster fell upon them. I, the LORD, have spoken!'"

⁴Listen to the word of the LORD, people of Jacob—all you families of Israel! ⁵This is what the LORD says: "What sin did your ancestors find in me that led them to stray so far? They worshiped foolish idols, only to become foolish themselves. ⁶They did not ask, 'Where is the LORD who brought us safely out of Egypt and led us through the barren wilderness—a land of deserts and pits, of drought and death, where no one lives or even travels?'

⁷"And when I brought you into a fruitful land to enjoy its bounty and goodness, you defiled my land and corrupted the inheritance I had promised you. ⁸The priests did not ask, 'Where is the LORD?' The judges ignored me, the rulers turned against me, and the prophets spoke in the name of Baal, wasting their time on nonsense. ⁹Therefore, I will bring my case against you and will keep on accusing you, even against your children's children in the years to come. I, the LORD, have spoken!

¹⁰"Go west to the land of Cyprus*; go east to the land of Kedar. Think about what you see there. See if anyone has ever heard of anything as strange as this. ¹¹Has any nation ever exchanged its gods for another god, even though its gods are nothing? Yet my people have exchanged their glorious God* for worthless idols! ¹²The heavens are shocked at such a thing and shrink back in horror and dismay, says the LORD. ¹³For my people have done two evil things: They have forsaken me—the fountain of living water. And they have dug for themselves cracked cisterns that can hold no water at all!

¹⁴"Why has Israel become a nation of slaves? Why has she been carried away as plunder? ¹⁵Lions have roared against her. The land has been destroyed, and the cities are now in ruins. No one lives in them

1:12 The Hebrew word for "watching" sounds like the word for "almond tree."   2:3 Hebrew *the firstfruits of his harvest.*
2:10 Hebrew *Kittim.*   2:11 Hebrew *their Glory.*

anymore. [16]Egyptians, marching from their cities of Memphis* and Tahpanhes, have utterly destroyed Israel's glory and power. [17]And you have brought this on yourselves by rebelling against the LORD your God when he wanted to lead you and show you the way!

[18]"What have you gained by your alliances with Egypt and Assyria? What good to you are the waters of the Nile* and the Euphrates*? [19]Your own wickedness will punish you. You will see what an evil, bitter thing it is to forsake the LORD your God, having no fear of him. I, the Lord, the LORD Almighty, have spoken! [20]Long ago I broke your yoke and tore away the chains of your slavery, but still you would not obey me. On every hill and under every green tree, you have prostituted yourselves by bowing down to idols.

[21]"How could this happen? When I planted you, I chose a vine of the purest stock—the very best. How did you grow into this corrupt wild vine? [22]No amount of soap or lye can make you clean. You are stained with guilt that cannot be washed away. I, the Sovereign LORD, have spoken!

[23]"You say, 'That's not true! We haven't worshiped the images of Baal!' But how can you say that? Go and look in any valley in the land! Face the awful sins you have done. You are like a restless female camel, desperate for a male! [24]You are like a wild donkey, sniffing the wind at mating time. Who can restrain your lust? Those who desire you do not even need to search, for you come running to them! [25]Why do you refuse to turn from all this running after other gods? But you say, 'Don't waste your breath. I have fallen in love with these foreign gods, and I can't stop loving them now!'

[26]"Like a thief, Israel feels shame only when she gets caught. Kings, officials, priests, and prophets—all are alike in this. [27]To an image carved from a piece of wood they say, 'You are my father.' To an idol chiseled out of stone they say, 'You are my mother.' They turn their backs on me, but in times of trouble they cry out for me to save them! [28]Why don't you call on these gods you have made? When danger comes, let them save you if they can! For you have as many gods as there are cities and towns in Judah. [29]Why do you accuse me of doing

wrong? You are the ones who have rebelled, says the LORD. [30]I have punished your children, but it did them no good. They still refuse to obey. You yourselves have killed your prophets as a lion kills its prey.

[31]"O my people, listen to the words of the LORD! Have I been like a desert to Israel? Have I been to them a land of darkness? Why then do my people say, 'At last we are free from God! We won't have anything to do with him anymore!' [32]Does a young woman forget her jewelry? Does a bride hide her wedding dress? No! Yet for years on end my people have forgotten me.

[33]"How you plot and scheme to win your lovers. The most experienced prostitute could learn from you! [34]Your clothing is stained with the blood of the innocent and the poor. You killed them even though they didn't break into your houses! [35]And yet you say, 'I haven't done anything wrong. Surely he isn't angry with me!' Now I will punish you severely because you claim you have not sinned.

[36]"First here, then there—you flit from one ally to another asking for help. But your new friends in Egypt will let you down, just as Assyria did before. [37]In despair, you will be led into exile with your hands on your heads, for the LORD has rejected the nations you trust. You will not succeed despite their help.

CHAPTER 3

"If a man divorces a woman and she marries someone else, he is not to take her back again, for that would surely corrupt the land. But you have prostituted yourself with many lovers, says the LORD. Yet I am still calling you to come back to me.

[2]"Look all around you. Is there anywhere in the entire land where you have not been defiled by your adulteries? You sit like a prostitute beside the road waiting for a client. You sit alone like a nomad in the desert. You have polluted the land with your prostitution and wickedness. [3]That is why even the spring rains have failed. For you are a prostitute and are completely unashamed. [4]Yet you say to me, 'Father, you have been my guide since the days of my youth. [5]Surely you won't be angry about such a little thing! Surely you can

forget it!' So you talk, and keep right on doing all the evil you can."

⁶During the reign of King Josiah, the LORD said to me, "Have you seen what fickle Israel does? Like a wife who commits adultery, Israel has worshiped other gods on every hill and under every green tree. ⁷I thought that after she had done all this she would return to me. But she did not come back. And though her faithless sister Judah saw this, ⁸she paid no attention. She saw that I had divorced faithless Israel and sent her away. But now Judah, too, has left me and given herself to prostitution. ⁹Israel treated it all so lightly—she thought nothing of committing adultery by worshiping idols made of wood and stone. So now the land has been greatly defiled. ¹⁰But in spite of all this, her faithless sister Judah has never sincerely returned to me. She has only pretended to be sorry," says the LORD.

¹¹Then the LORD said to me, "Even faithless Israel is less guilty than treacherous Judah! ¹²Therefore, go and say these words to Israel,* 'This is what the LORD says: O Israel, my faithless people, come home to me again, for I am merciful. I will not be angry with you forever. ¹³Only acknowledge your guilt. Admit that you rebelled against the LORD your God and committed adultery against him by worshiping idols under every green tree. Confess that you refused to follow me. I, the LORD, have spoken!'"

¹⁴"Return home, you wayward children," says the LORD, "for I am your husband. I will bring you again to the land of Israel*—one from here and two from there, from wherever you are scattered. ¹⁵And I will give you leaders after my own heart, who will guide you with knowledge and understanding.

¹⁶"And when your land is once more filled with people," says the LORD, "you will no longer wish for 'the good old days' when you possessed the Ark of the LORD's covenant. Those days will not be missed or even thought about, and there will be no need to rebuild the Ark. ¹⁷In that day Jerusalem will be known as The Throne of the LORD. All nations will come there to honor the LORD. They will no longer stubbornly follow their own evil desires. ¹⁸In those days the people of Judah and Israel will return together from exile in the north.

They will return to the land I gave their ancestors as an inheritance forever.

¹⁹"I thought to myself, 'I would love to treat you as my own children!' I wanted nothing more than to give you this beautiful land—the finest inheritance in the world. I looked forward to your calling me 'Father,' and I thought you would never turn away from me again. ²⁰But you have betrayed me, you people of Israel! You have been like a faithless wife who leaves her husband," says the LORD.

²¹Voices are heard high on the windswept mountains, the weeping and pleading of Israel's people. For they have forgotten the LORD their God and wandered far from his ways.

²²"My wayward children," says the LORD, "come back to me, and I will heal your wayward hearts."

"Yes, we will come," the people reply, "for you are the LORD our God. ²³Our worship of idols and our religious orgies on the hills and mountains are completely false. Only in the LORD our God will Israel ever find salvation. ²⁴From childhood we have watched as everything our ancestors worked for—their flocks and herds, their sons and daughters—was squandered on a delusion. ²⁵Let us now lie down in shame and dishonor, for we and our ancestors have always sinned against the LORD our God. We have never obeyed him."

CHAPTER 4
"O Israel, come back to me," says the LORD. "If you will throw away your detestable idols and go astray no more, ²and if you will swear by my name alone, and begin to live good, honest lives and uphold justice, then you will be a blessing to the nations of the world, and all people will come and praise my name."

³This is what the LORD says to the people of Judah and Jerusalem: "Plow up the hard ground of your hearts! Do not waste your good seed among thorns. ⁴Cleanse your minds and hearts before the LORD, or my anger will burn like an unquenchable fire because of all your sins.

⁵"Shout to Jerusalem and to all Judah! Tell them to sound the alarm throughout the land: 'Run for your lives! Flee to the fortified cities!' ⁶Send a signal toward Jerusalem*: 'Flee now! Do not delay!' For I am

3:12 Hebrew *toward the north.*   **3:14** Hebrew *to Zion.*   **4:6** Hebrew *Zion.*

bringing terrible destruction upon you from the north."

[7]A lion stalks from its den, a destroyer of nations. And it is headed for your land! Your towns will lie in ruins, empty of people. [8]So put on clothes of mourning and weep with broken hearts, for the fierce anger of the LORD is still upon us.

[9]"In that day," says the LORD, "the king and the officials will tremble in fear. The priests and the prophets will be struck with horror."

[10]Then I said, "O Sovereign LORD, the people have been deceived by what you said, for you promised peace for Jerusalem. Yet the sword is even now poised to strike them dead!"

[11]The time is coming when the LORD will say to the people of Jerusalem, "A burning wind is blowing in from the desert. It is not a gentle breeze useful for winnowing grain. [12]It is a roaring blast sent by me! Now I will pronounce your destruction!"

[13]Our enemy rushes down on us like a storm wind! His chariots are like whirlwinds; his horses are swifter than eagles. How terrible it will be! Our destruction is sure! [14]O Jerusalem, cleanse your hearts that you may be saved. How long will you harbor your evil thoughts? [15]From Dan and the hill country of Ephraim, your destruction has been announced.

[16]"Warn the surrounding nations and announce to Jerusalem: 'The enemy is coming from a distant land, raising a battle cry against the towns of Judah. [17]They surround Jerusalem like watchmen surrounding a field, for my people have rebelled against me,'" says the LORD. [18]"Your own actions have brought this upon you. This punishment is a bitter dose of your own medicine. It has pierced you to the heart!"

[19]My heart, my heart—I writhe in pain! My heart pounds within me! I cannot be still. For I have heard the blast of enemy trumpets and the roar of their battle cries. [20]Waves of destruction roll over the land, until it lies in complete desolation. Suddenly, every tent is destroyed; in a moment, every shelter is crushed. [21]How long must this go on? How long must I be surrounded by war and death?

[22]"My people are foolish and do not know me," says the LORD. "They are senseless children who have no understanding.

They are clever enough at doing wrong, but they have no talent at all for doing right!"

[23]I looked at the earth, and it was empty and formless. I looked at the heavens, and there was no light. [24]I looked at the mountains and hills, and they trembled and shook. [25]I looked, and all the people were gone. All the birds of the sky had flown away. [26]I looked, and the fertile fields had become a wilderness. The cities lay in ruins, crushed by the LORD's fierce anger.

[27]This is what the LORD says: "The whole land will be ruined, but I will not destroy it completely. [28]The earth will mourn, the heavens will be draped in black, because of my decree against my people. I have made up my mind and will not change it."

[29]At the noise of marching armies, the people flee in terror from the cities. They hide in the bushes and run for the mountains. All the cities have been abandoned—not a person remains! [30]What are you doing, you who have been plundered? Why do you dress up in your most beautiful clothing and jewelry? Why do you brighten your eyes with mascara? It will do you no good! Your allies despise you and will kill you.

[31]I hear a great cry, like that of a woman giving birth to her first child. It is the cry of Jerusalem's people* gasping for breath, pleading for help, prostrate before their murderers.

CHAPTER 5

"Run up and down every street in Jerusalem," says the LORD. "Look high and low; search throughout the city! If you can find even one person who is just and honest, I will not destroy the city. [2]Even when they are under oath, saying, 'As surely as the LORD lives,' they all tell lies!"

[3]LORD, you are searching for honesty. You struck your people, but they paid no attention. You crushed them, but they refused to turn from sin. They are determined, with faces set like stone; they have refused to repent.

[4]Then I said, "But what can we expect from the poor and ignorant? They don't know the ways of the LORD. They don't understand what God expects of them. [5]I will go and speak to their leaders. Surely they will know the LORD's ways and what

4:31 Hebrew *the daughter of Zion.*

God requires of them." But the leaders, too, had utterly rejected their God. [6]So now a lion from the forest will attack them; a wolf from the desert will pounce on them. A leopard will lurk near their towns, tearing apart any who dare to venture out. For their rebellion is great, and their sins are many.

[7]"How can I pardon you? For even your children have turned from me. They have sworn by gods that are not gods at all! I fed my people until they were fully satisfied. But they thanked me by committing adultery and lining up at the city's brothels. [8]They are well-fed, lusty stallions, each neighing for his neighbor's wife. [9]Should I not punish them for this?" asks the LORD. "Should I not avenge myself against a nation such as this?

[10]"Go down the rows of the vineyards and destroy them, but leave a scattered few alive. Strip the branches from the vine, for they do not belong to the LORD. [11]The people of Israel and Judah are full of treachery against me," says the LORD. [12]"They have lied about the LORD and have said, 'He won't bother us! No disasters will come upon us! There will be no war or famine! [13]God's prophets are windbags full of words with no divine authority. Their predictions of disaster will fall on themselves!'"

[14]Therefore, this is what the LORD God Almighty says: "Because the people are talking like this, I will give you messages that will burn them up as if they were kindling wood. [15]O Israel, I will bring a distant nation against you," says the LORD. "It is a mighty nation, an ancient nation, a people whose language you do not know, whose speech you cannot understand. [16]Their weapons are deadly; their warriors are mighty. [17]They will eat your harvests and your children's bread, your flocks of sheep and your herds of cattle. Yes, they will eat your grapes and figs. And they will destroy your fortified cities, which you think are so safe.

[18]"Yet even in those days I will not blot you out completely," says the LORD. [19]"And when your people ask, 'Why is the LORD our God doing this to us?' you must reply, 'You rejected him and gave yourselves to foreign gods in your own land. Now you will serve foreigners in a land that is not your own.'

[20]"Make this announcement to Israel* and to Judah: [21]Listen, you foolish and senseless people—who have eyes but do not see, who have ears but do not hear. [22]Do you have no respect for me? Why do you not tremble in my presence? I, the LORD, am the one who defines the ocean's sandy shoreline, an everlasting boundary that the waters cannot cross. The waves may toss and roar, but they can never pass the bounds I set.

[23]"But my people have stubborn and rebellious hearts. They have turned against me and have chosen to practice idolatry. [24]They do not say from the heart, 'Let us live in awe of the LORD our God, for he gives us rain each spring and fall, assuring us of plentiful harvests.' [25]Your wickedness has deprived you of these wonderful blessings. Your sin has robbed you of all these good things.

[26]"Among my people are wicked men who lie in wait for victims like a hunter hiding in a blind. They are continually setting traps for other people. [27]Like a cage filled with birds, their homes are filled with evil plots. And the result? Now they are great and rich. [28]They are well fed and well groomed, and there is no limit to their wicked deeds. They refuse justice to orphans and deny the rights of the poor. [29]Should I not punish them for this?" asks the LORD. "Should I not avenge myself against a nation such as this?

[30]"A horrible and shocking thing has happened in this land—[31]the prophets give false prophecies, and the priests rule with an iron hand. And worse yet, my people like it that way! But what will you do when the end comes?

CHAPTER 6

"Run for your lives, you people of Benjamin! Flee from Jerusalem! Sound the alarm in Tekoa! Send up a signal at Bethhakkerem! Warn everyone that a powerful army is coming from the north to destroy this nation. [2]O Jerusalem,* you are my beautiful and delicate daughter—but I will destroy you! [3]Enemy shepherds will surround you. They will set up camp around the city and divide your pastures for their flocks. [4]They shout, 'Prepare for battle and

5:20 Hebrew *to the house of Jacob.*   6:2 Hebrew *Zion.*

attack at noon! But now the day is fading, and the evening shadows are falling. ⁵So let us attack by night and destroy her palaces!'"

⁶This is what the LORD Almighty says: "Cut down the trees for battering rams. Build ramps against the walls of Jerusalem. This is the city to be punished, for she is wicked through and through. ⁷She spouts evil like a fountain! Her streets echo with the sounds of violence and destruction. Her sickness and sores are ever before me. ⁸This is your last warning, Jerusalem! If you do not listen, I will empty the land."

⁹This is what the LORD Almighty says: "Disaster will fall upon you. Even the few who remain in Israel will be gleaned again, as when a harvester checks each vine a second time to pick the grapes that were missed."

¹⁰To whom can I give warning? Who will listen when I speak? Their ears are closed, and they cannot hear. They scorn the word of the LORD. They don't want to listen at all. ¹¹So now I am filled with the LORD's fury. Yes, I am weary of holding it in!

"I will pour out my fury over Jerusalem, even on children playing in the streets, on gatherings of young men, and on husbands and wives and grandparents. ¹²Their homes will be turned over to their enemies, and so will their fields and their wives. For I will punish the people of this land," says the LORD.

¹³"From the least to the greatest, they trick others to get what does not belong to them. Yes, even my prophets and priests are like that! ¹⁴They offer superficial treatments for my people's mortal wound. They give assurances of peace when all is war. ¹⁵Are they ashamed when they do these disgusting things? No, not at all—they don't even blush! Therefore, they will lie among the slaughtered. They will be humbled beneath my punishing anger," says the LORD.

¹⁶So now the LORD says, "Stop right where you are! Look for the old, godly way, and walk in it. Travel its path, and you will find rest for your souls. But you reply, 'No, that's not the road we want!' ¹⁷I set watchmen over you who said, 'Listen for the sound of the trumpet!' But you replied, 'No! We won't pay attention!'

¹⁸"Therefore, listen to this, all you nations. Take note of my people's condition. ¹⁹Listen, all the earth! I will bring disaster upon my people. It is the fruit of their own sin because they refuse to listen to me. They have rejected all my instructions. ²⁰There is no use now in offering me sweet incense from Sheba. Keep your expensive perfumes! I cannot accept your burnt offerings. Your sacrifices have no sweet fragrance for me."

²¹Therefore, this is what the LORD says: "I will put obstacles in my people's path. Fathers and sons will both fall over them. Neighbors and friends will collapse together."

²²This is what the LORD says: "See a great army marching from the north! A great nation is rising against you from far-off lands. ²³They are fully armed for slaughter. They are cruel and show no mercy. As they ride forward, the noise of their army is like a roaring sea. They are marching in battle formation to destroy you, Jerusalem.*"

²⁴We have heard reports about the enemy, and we are weak with fright. Fear and pain have gripped us, like that of a woman about to give birth. ²⁵Don't go out to the fields! Don't travel the roads! The enemy is everywhere, and they are ready to kill. We are terrorized at every turn! ²⁶Now my people, dress yourselves in sackcloth, and sit among the ashes. Mourn and weep bitterly, as for the loss of an only son. For suddenly, the destroying armies will be upon you!

²⁷"Jeremiah, I have made you a tester of metals, that you may determine the quality of my people. ²⁸Are they not the worst of rebels, full of slander? They are as insolent as bronze, as hard and cruel as iron. All of them lead others into corruption. ²⁹The bellows blow fiercely. The refining fire grows hotter. But it will never purify and cleanse them because there is no purity in them to refine. ³⁰I will label them 'Rejected Silver' because I, the LORD, am discarding them."

6:23 Hebrew *daughter of Zion.*

AUGUST 2 ☐ DAY 215
JEREMIAH 7–10
Judah in Idolatry

OVERVIEW The malignancy of idolatry and hypocrisy has permeated every segment of Judah's national life: families (7:18), teachers (8:9), shepherds (10:21), and even prophets and priests (8:10). Thinking that their privileged position as God's chosen people will ensure their immunity from God's wrath, they continue in a pattern of worthless worship. Because of their rebellion and indifference, their homeland will one day be reduced to a heap of ruins—a thought that reduces Jeremiah to a river of tears.

Chapter 7	Chapter 8	Chapter 9	Chapter 10
A Last Appeal	A Leaderless People	A Desolate Land	A Sovereign Lord
Judah's Shame			God's Glory

YOUR DAILY WALK Make a list of some of the things you have reason to take pride in (e.g., your financial success, physical strength, education, family, national heritage). Which item on your list gives you the greatest sense of satisfaction? Why?

As a neglected garden tends toward weeds, so the faithless life tends toward ungodly chaos.

Do you know there is something in which God wants you to glory? to "pop your buttons" over with pride? to derive an "ego boost" from every time you think about it? There is! But it isn't your bank account, your muscles, or your mind. It's your relationship with him.

"This is what the LORD says: 'Let not the wise man gloat in his wisdom, or the mighty man in his might, or the rich man in his riches. Let them boast in this alone: that they truly know me and understand that I am the LORD who is just and righteous, whose love is unfailing, and that I delight in these things. I, the LORD, have spoken'" (9:23-24).

Your personal relationship with the God of creation should be your source of greatest pride. But before you can enjoy that kind of relationship, you must first experience it through personal faith in his Son, Jesus. Turn to John 5:24 and read about the relationship that you can glory in today and every day.

INSIGHT Shiloh's Demise Recorded in the Digs
Shiloh (present-day Seilun), mentioned in 7:12, was the place where the Ark resided in the days of Joshua (Joshua 18:1; 1 Samuel 1:3). It was abandoned by God (Psalm 78:60) and destroyed by the Philistines in approximately 1050 B.C., probably after the battle of Ebenezer (1 Samuel 4:10-11).

CHAPTER 7

The LORD gave another message to Jeremiah. He said, ²"Go to the entrance of the LORD's Temple, and give this message to the people: 'O Judah, listen to this message from the LORD! Listen to it, all of you who worship here! ³The LORD Almighty, the God of Israel, says: Even now, if you quit your evil ways, I will let you stay in your own land. ⁴But do not be fooled by those who repeatedly promise your safety be-

cause the Temple of the LORD is here. ⁵I will be merciful only if you stop your wicked thoughts and deeds and are fair to others; ⁶and if you stop exploiting foreigners, orphans, and widows; and if you stop your murdering; and if you stop worshiping idols as you now do to your own harm. ⁷Then I will let you stay in this land that I gave to your ancestors to keep forever.

⁸"'Do you think that because the Temple is here you will never suffer?

Don't fool yourselves! [9]Do you really think you can steal, murder, commit adultery, lie, and worship Baal and all those other new gods of yours, [10]and then come here and stand before me in my Temple and chant, "We are safe!"—only to go right back to all those evils again? [11]Do you think this Temple, which honors my name, is a den of thieves? I see all the evil going on there, says the LORD.

[12]" 'Go to the place at Shiloh where I once put the Tabernacle to honor my name. See what I did there because of all the wickedness of my people, the Israelites. [13]While you were doing these wicked things, says the LORD, I spoke to you about it repeatedly, but you would not listen. I called out to you, but you refused to answer. [14]So just as I destroyed Shiloh, I will now destroy this Temple that was built to honor my name, this Temple that you trust for help, this place that I gave to you and your ancestors. [15]And I will send you into exile, just as I did your relatives, the people of Israel.*'

[16]"Pray no more for these people, Jeremiah. Do not weep or pray for them, and don't beg me to help them, for I will not listen to you. [17]Do you not see what they are doing throughout the towns of Judah and in the streets of Jerusalem? [18]No wonder I am so angry! Watch how the children gather wood and the fathers build sacrificial fires. See how the women knead dough and make cakes to offer to the Queen of Heaven. And they give drink offerings to their other idol gods! [19]Am I the one they are hurting?" asks the LORD. "Most of all, they hurt themselves, to their own shame."

[20]So the Sovereign LORD says: "I will pour out my terrible fury on this place. Its people, animals, trees, and crops will be consumed by the unquenchable fire of my anger."

[21]This is what the LORD Almighty, the God of Israel, says: "Away with your burnt offerings and sacrifices! Eat them yourselves! [22]When I led your ancestors out of Egypt, it was not burnt offerings and sacrifices I wanted from them. [23]This is what I told them: 'Obey me, and I will be your God, and you will be my people. Only do as I say, and all will be well!'

[24]"But my people would not listen to me. They kept on doing whatever they wanted, following the stubborn desires of their evil hearts. They went backward instead of forward. [25]From the day your ancestors left Egypt until now, I have continued to send my prophets—day in and day out. [26]But my people have not listened to me or even tried to hear. They have been stubborn and sinful—even worse than their ancestors.

[27]"Tell them all this, but do not expect them to listen. Shout out your warnings, but do not expect them to respond. [28]Say to them, 'This is the nation whose people will not obey the LORD their God and who refuse to be taught. Truth has vanished from among them; it is no longer heard on their lips. [29]O Jerusalem, shave your head in mourning, and weep alone on the mountains. For the LORD has rejected and forsaken this generation that has provoked his fury.'

[30]"The people of Judah have sinned before my very eyes," says the LORD. "They have set up their abominable idols right in my own Temple, defiling it. [31]They have built the pagan shrines of Topheth in the valley of the son of Hinnom, where they sacrifice their little sons and daughters in the fire. I have never commanded such a horrible deed; it never even crossed my mind to command such a thing! [32]So beware, for the time is coming," says the LORD, "when that place will no longer be called Topheth or the valley of the son of Hinnom, but the Valley of Slaughter. They will bury so many bodies in Topheth that there won't be room for all the graves. [33]The corpses of my people will be food for the vultures and wild animals, and no one will be left to scare them away. [34]I will put an end to the happy singing and laughter in the streets of Jerusalem. The joyful voices of bridegrooms and brides will no longer be heard in the towns of Judah. The land will lie in complete desolation.

CHAPTER 8

"In that day," says the LORD, "the enemy will break open the graves of the kings and officials of Judah, and the graves of the priests, prophets, and common people. [2]They will dig out their bones and spread them out on the ground before the sun, moon, and stars—the gods my people have loved, served, and worshiped. Their bones will not be gathered up again or buried but

7:15 Hebrew *of Ephraim,* referring to the northern kingdom of Israel.

will be scattered on the ground like dung. ³And the people of this evil nation who survive will wish to die rather than live where I will send them. I, the LORD Almighty, have spoken!

⁴"Jeremiah, say to the people, 'This is what the LORD says: When people fall down, don't they get up again? When they start down the wrong road and discover their mistake, don't they turn back? ⁵Then why do these people keep going along their self-destructive path, refusing to turn back, even though I have warned them? ⁶I listen to their conversations, and what do I hear? Is anyone sorry for sin? Does anyone say, "What a terrible thing I have done"? No! All are running down the path of sin as swiftly as a horse rushing into battle! ⁷The stork knows the time of her migration, as do the turtledove, the swallow, and the crane.* They all return at the proper time each year. But not my people! They do not know what the LORD requires of them.

⁸" 'How can you say, "We are wise because we have the law of the LORD," when your teachers have twisted it so badly? ⁹These wise teachers will be shamed by exile for their sin, for they have rejected the word of the LORD. Are they so wise after all? ¹⁰I will give their wives and their farms to others. From the least to the greatest, they trick others to get what does not belong to them. Yes, even my prophets and priests are like that. ¹¹They offer superficial treatments for my people's mortal wound. They give assurances of peace when all is war. ¹²Are they ashamed when they do these disgusting things? No, not at all—they don't even blush! Therefore, they will lie among the slaughtered. They will be humbled when they are punished, says the LORD. ¹³I will take away their rich harvests of figs and grapes. Their fruit trees will all die. All the good things I prepared for them will soon be gone. I, the LORD, have spoken!'

¹⁴"Then the people will say, 'Why should we wait here to die? Come, let's go to the fortified cities to die there. For the LORD our God has decreed our destruction and has given us a cup of poison to drink because we sinned against the LORD. ¹⁵We hoped for peace, but no peace came. We hoped for a time of healing, but found only terror. ¹⁶The snorting of the enemies' warhorses can be heard all the way from the land of Dan in the north! The whole land trembles at the approach of the terrible army, for it is coming to devour the land and everything in it—cities and people alike.'

¹⁷"I will send these enemy troops among you like poisonous snakes you cannot charm," says the LORD. "No matter what you do, they will bite you, and you will die."

¹⁸My grief is beyond healing; my heart is broken. ¹⁹Listen to the weeping of my people; it can be heard all across the land.

"Has the LORD abandoned Jerusalem*?" the people ask. "Is her King no longer there?"

"Oh, why have they angered me with their carved idols and worthless gods?" asks the LORD.

²⁰"The harvest is finished, and the summer is gone," the people cry, "yet we are not saved!"

²¹I weep for the hurt of my people. I am stunned and silent, mute with grief. ²²Is there no medicine in Gilead? Is there no physician there? Why is there no healing for the wounds of my people?

CHAPTER 9

Oh, that my eyes were a fountain of tears; I would weep forever! I would sob day and night for all my people who have been slaughtered. ²Oh, that I could go away and forget them and live in a shack in the desert, for they are all adulterous and treacherous.

³"My people bend their tongues like bows to shoot lies. They refuse to stand up for the truth. And they only go from bad to worse! They care nothing for me," says the LORD.

⁴"Beware of your neighbor! Beware of your brother! They all take advantage of one another and spread their slanderous lies. ⁵They all fool and defraud each other; no one tells the truth. With practiced tongues they tell lies; they wear themselves out with all their sinning. ⁶They pile lie upon lie and utterly refuse to come to me," says the LORD.

⁷Therefore, the LORD Almighty says, "See, I will melt them in a crucible and test them like metal. What else can I do with them? ⁸For their tongues aim lies like

8:7 The identification of some of these birds is uncertain.   8:19 Hebrew *Zion.*

poisoned arrows. They promise peace to their neighbors while planning to kill them. ⁹Should I not punish them for this?" asks the LORD. "Should I not avenge myself against a nation such as this?"

¹⁰I will weep for the mountains and wail for the desert pastures. For they are desolate and empty of life; the lowing of cattle is heard no more; the birds and wild animals all have fled.

¹¹"I will make Jerusalem into a heap of ruins," says the LORD. "It will be a place haunted by jackals. The towns of Judah will be ghost towns, with no one living in them."

¹²Who is wise enough to understand all this? Who has been instructed by the LORD and can explain it to others? Why has the land been ruined so completely that no one even dares to travel through it?

¹³The LORD replies, "This has happened because my people have abandoned the instructions I gave them; they have refused to obey my law. ¹⁴Instead, they have stubbornly followed their own desires and worshiped the images of Baal, as their ancestors taught them. ¹⁵So now, listen to what the LORD Almighty, the God of Israel, says: Look! I will feed them with bitterness and give them poison to drink. ¹⁶I will scatter them around the world, and they will be strangers in distant lands. Their enemies will chase them with the sword until I have destroyed them completely."

¹⁷This is what the LORD Almighty says: "Think about what is going on! Call for the mourners to come. ¹⁸Quick! Begin your weeping! Let the tears flow from your eyes. ¹⁹Hear the people of Jerusalem* crying in despair, 'We are ruined! Disaster has come upon us! We must leave our land, because our homes have been torn down.'"

²⁰Listen, you women, to the words of the LORD; open your ears to what he has to say. Teach your daughters to wail; teach one another how to lament. ²¹For death has crept in through our windows and has entered our mansions. It has killed off the flower of our youth: Children no longer play in the streets, and young men no longer gather in the squares. ²²And the LORD says, "Bodies will be scattered across the fields like dung, or like bundles of grain after the harvest. No one will be left to bury them."

²³This is what the LORD says: "Let not the wise man gloat in his wisdom, or the mighty man in his might, or the rich man in his riches. ²⁴Let them boast in this alone: that they truly know me and understand that I am the LORD who is just and righteous, whose love is unfailing, and that I delight in these things. I, the LORD, have spoken!

²⁵"A time is coming," says the LORD, "when I will punish all those who are circumcised in body but not in spirit—²⁶the Egyptians, Edomites, Ammonites, Moabites, the people who live in distant places,* and yes, even the people of Judah. Like all these pagan nations, the people of Israel also have uncircumcised hearts."

CHAPTER 10

Hear the word of the LORD, O Israel! ²This is what the LORD says: "Do not act like other nations who try to read their future in the stars. Do not be afraid of their predictions, even though other nations are terrified by them. ³Their ways are futile and foolish. They cut down a tree and carve an idol. ⁴They decorate it with gold and silver and then fasten it securely with hammer and nails so it won't fall over. ⁵There stands their god like a helpless scarecrow in a garden! It cannot speak, and it needs to be carried because it cannot walk. Do not be afraid of such gods, for they can neither harm you nor do you any good."

⁶LORD, there is no one like you! For you are great, and your name is full of power. ⁷Who would not fear you, O King of nations? That title belongs to you alone! Among all the wise people of the earth and in all the kingdoms of the world, there is no one like you.

⁸The wisest of people who worship idols are stupid and foolish. The things they worship are made of wood! ⁹They bring beaten sheets of silver from Tarshish and gold from Uphaz, and they give these materials to skillful craftsmen who make their idols. Then they dress these gods in royal purple robes made by expert tailors. ¹⁰But the LORD is the only true God, the living God. He is the everlasting King! The whole earth trembles at his anger. The nations hide before his wrath.

¹¹Say this to those who worship other gods: "Your so-called gods, who did not make the heavens and earth, will vanish from the earth."*

¹² But God made the earth by his power,
and he preserves it by his wisdom.

He has stretched out the heavens
  by his understanding.
¹³ When he speaks, there is thunder in the
  heavens.
  He causes the clouds to rise over the
    earth.
  He sends the lightning with the rain
    and releases the wind from his store-
    houses.
¹⁴ Compared to him, all people are foolish
    and have no knowledge at all!
  They make idols, but the idols will
    disgrace their makers,
    for they are frauds.
  They have no life or power in them.
¹⁵ Idols are worthless; they are lies!
  The time is coming when they will
    all be destroyed.
¹⁶ But the God of Israel* is no idol!
  He is the Creator of everything that
    exists,
    including Israel, his own special
    possession.
  The LORD Almighty is his name!

¹⁷"Pack your bag and prepare to leave;
the siege is about to begin," ¹⁸says the

10:16 Hebrew *the Portion of Jacob.*   10:25 Hebrew *Jacob.*

LORD. "For suddenly, I will fling you from
this land and pour great troubles upon
you. At last you will feel my anger."

¹⁹My wound is desperate, and my grief is
great. My sickness is incurable, but I must
bear it. ²⁰My home is gone, and no one is left
to help me rebuild it. My children have been
taken away, and I will never see them again.
²¹The shepherds of my people have lost their
senses. They no longer follow the LORD or
ask what he wants of them. Therefore, they
fail completely, and their flocks are scattered.
²²Listen! Hear the terrifying roar of great
armies as they roll down from the north. The
towns of Judah will be destroyed and will
become a haunt for jackals.

²³I know, LORD, that a person's life is not
his own. No one is able to plan his own
course. ²⁴So correct me, LORD, but please be
gentle. Do not correct me in anger, for I
would die. ²⁵Pour out your wrath on the
nations that refuse to recognize you—on
nations that do not call upon your name.
For they have utterly devoured your
people Israel,* making the land a desolate
wilderness.

AUGUST 3 ☐ DAY 216
JEREMIAH 11–15
Judah in Rebellion

OVERVIEW Through the prophet Jeremiah, God brings a stern accusation against his people: "They . . . have both broken the covenant"
(11:10). To shock the nation into realizing the seriousness of their sin,
God commands Jeremiah to provide them with two object lessons: a
rotten linen belt and full wineskins. God's judgment will be swift and
severe, involving drought, invasion, and exile. As Jeremiah laments over
the fate of his nation, God promises him personal strength and protection as he carries out his prophetic ministry of doom.

Chapters 11–12	Chapter 13	Chapters 14–15
Disregarding the Covenant	Demonstrating Judah's Sinfulness	Detailing God's Judgment
Accusation	Application	Anticipation

YOUR DAILY WALK Make a list of the five people who, in your opinion, are the most popular personalities in the world today. Then ask
yourself: How did they get where they are today? By being righteous?
. . . serving God? . . . working hard? . . . getting the breaks? . . . keeping the law? . . . breaking the law?

Unless the heart Now read Jeremiah's complaint to God in 12:1: "Why are the wicked
is full, even so prosperous? Why are evil people so happy?" In other words, why do
a rich person the ungodly prosper while the righteous are persecuted?
is poor. Long before Jeremiah's day, Job raised the same question. So did
Asaph (Psalm 73). So did Habakkuk. And God's answer to each of them
was basically the same: Consider the fate of the wicked. Granted, their
lifestyle today and their seeming prosperity are attractive. But in the
light of their eternal destiny, are you willing to trade places?

Never forget the sure outcome of those outside Christ. Make a list of
five blessings you are experiencing as a child of God that those who do
not belong to Christ know nothing about. Now thank God for the true
riches you enjoy.

 INSIGHT A Ruined Homecoming in Anathoth
Jeremiah's rude reception in his hometown is a grim reminder that
"a prophet is honored everywhere except in his own hometown"
(Matthew 13:57)—the same kind of treatment that Christ received
(John 1:11).

CHAPTER 11
The LORD gave another message to Jeremiah. He said, 2"Remind the people of
Judah and Jerusalem about the terms of
their covenant with me. 3Say to them, 'This
is what the LORD, the God of Israel, says:
Cursed is anyone who does not obey the
terms of my covenant! 4For I said to your
ancestors when I brought them out of slavery in Egypt, "If you obey me and do whatever I command you, then you will be my
people, and I will be your God." 5I said this
so I could keep my promise to your ancestors to give you a land flowing with milk
and honey—the land you live in today.'"

Then I replied, "So be it,* LORD!"

6Then the LORD said, "Broadcast this
message in the streets of Jerusalem. Go
from town to town throughout the land
and say, 'Remember the covenant your ancestors made, and do everything they
promised. 7For I solemnly warned your ancestors when I brought them out of Egypt,
repeating over and over again to this day:
"Obey me!" 8But your ancestors did not
pay any attention; they would not even
listen. Instead, they stubbornly followed
their own evil desires. And because they
refused to obey, I brought upon them all the
curses described in our covenant.'"

9Again the LORD spoke to me and said, "I
have discovered a conspiracy against me
among the people of Judah and Jerusalem.
10They have returned to the sins of their
forefathers. They have refused to listen to
me and are worshiping idols. Israel and
Judah have both broken the covenant I

made with their ancestors. 11Therefore,
says the LORD, I am going to bring calamity
upon them, and they will not escape.
Though they beg for mercy, I will not listen
to their cries. 12Then the people of Judah
and Jerusalem will pray to their idols and
offer incense before them. But the idols will
not save them when disaster strikes! 13Look
now, people of Judah, you have as many
gods as there are cities and towns. Your
altars of shame—altars for burning incense
to your god Baal—are along every street in
Jerusalem.

14"Pray no more for these people, Jeremiah. Do not weep or pray for them, for I
will not listen to them when they cry out to
me in distress. 15What right do my beloved
people have to come to my Temple, where
they have done so many immoral things?
Can their sacrifices avert their destruction?
They actually rejoice in doing evil!

16"I, the LORD, once called them a thriving olive tree, beautiful to see and full of
good fruit. But now I have sent the fury of
their enemies to burn them with fire, leaving them charred and broken. 17I, the LORD
Almighty, who planted this olive tree, have
ordered it destroyed. For the people of Israel and Judah have done evil, provoking
my anger by offering incense to Baal."

18Then the LORD told me about the plots
my enemies were making against me. 19I
had been as unaware as a lamb on the way
to its slaughter. I had no idea that they were
planning to kill me! "Let's destroy this man
and all his words," they said. "Let's kill
him, so his name will be forgotten forever."

11:5 Hebrew *Amen.*

²⁰O LORD Almighty, you are just, and you examine the deepest thoughts of hearts and minds. Let me see your vengeance against them, for I have committed my cause to you. ²¹The men of Anathoth wanted me dead. They said they would kill me if I did not stop speaking in the LORD's name. ²²So this is what the LORD Almighty says about them: "I will punish them! Their young men will die in battle, and their little boys and girls will starve. ²³Not one of these plotters from Anathoth will survive, for I will bring disaster upon them when their time of punishment comes."

CHAPTER 12

LORD, you always give me justice when I bring a case before you. Now let me bring you this complaint: Why are the wicked so prosperous? Why are evil people so happy? ²You have planted them, and they have taken root and prospered. Your name is on their lips, but in their hearts they give you no credit at all. ³But as for me, LORD, you know my heart. You see me and test my thoughts. Drag these people away like helpless sheep to be butchered! Set them aside to be slaughtered!

⁴How long must this land weep? Even the grass in the fields has withered. The wild animals and birds have disappeared because of the evil in the land. Yet the people say, "The LORD won't do anything!"

⁵Then the LORD replied to me, "If racing against mere men makes you tired, how will you race against horses? If you stumble and fall on open ground, what will you do in the thickets near the Jordan? ⁶Even your own brothers, members of your own family, have turned on you. They have plotted, raising a cry against you. Do not trust them, no matter how pleasantly they speak.

⁷"I have abandoned my people, my special possession. I have surrendered my dearest ones to their enemies. ⁸My chosen people have roared at me like a lion of the forest, so I have treated them as though I hated them. ⁹My chosen people have become as disgusting to me as a vulture. And indeed, they are surrounded by vultures. Bring on the wild beasts to pick their corpses clean!

¹⁰"Many rulers have ravaged my vine-yard, trampling down the vines and turning all its beauty into a barren wilderness. ¹¹They have made it an empty wasteland; I hear its mournful cry. The whole land is desolate, and no one even cares. ¹²Destroying armies plunder the land. The sword of the LORD kills people from one end of the nation to the other. No one will escape! ¹³My people have planted wheat but are harvesting thorns. They have worked hard, but it has done them no good. They will harvest a crop of shame, for the fierce anger of the LORD is upon them."

¹⁴Now this is what the LORD says: "As for all the evil nations reaching out for the inheritance I gave my people Israel, I will uproot them from their lands just as Judah will be uprooted from hers. ¹⁵But afterward I will return and have compassion on all of them. I will bring them home to their own lands again, each nation to its own inheritance. ¹⁶And if these nations quickly learn the ways of my people, and if they learn to swear by my name, saying, 'As surely as the LORD lives' (just as they taught my people to swear by the name of Baal), then they will be given a place among my people. ¹⁷But any nation who refuses to obey me will be uprooted and destroyed. I, the LORD, have spoken!"

CHAPTER 13

This is what the LORD said to me: "Go and buy a linen belt and put it around your waist, but do not wash it." ²So I bought the belt as the LORD directed me and put it around my waist. ³Then the LORD gave me another message: ⁴"Take the linen belt you are wearing, and go to the Euphrates River.* Hide it there in a hole in the rocks." ⁵So I went and hid it at the Euphrates as the LORD had instructed me.

⁶A long time afterward, the LORD said to me, "Go back to the Euphrates and get the linen belt that I told you to hide there." ⁷So I went to the Euphrates and dug it out of the hole where I had hidden it. But now it was mildewed and falling apart. The belt was useless.

⁸Then I received this message from the LORD: ⁹"The LORD says: This illustrates how I will rot away the pride of Judah and Jerusalem. ¹⁰These wicked people refuse to listen to me. They stubbornly follow their own desires and worship idols. Therefore,

13:4 Hebrew *Perath;* also in 13:5, 6, 7.

they will become like this linen belt—good for nothing! ¹¹As a belt clings to a person's waist, so I created Judah and Israel to cling to me," says the LORD. "They were to be my people, my pride, my glory—an honor to my name. But they would not listen to me.

¹²"So tell them, 'The LORD, the God of Israel, says: All your wineskins will be full of wine.' And they will reply, 'Of course, you don't need to tell us how prosperous we will be!' ¹³Then tell them, 'No, this is what the LORD means: I will make everyone in this land so confused that they will seem drunk—from the king sitting on David's throne and from the priests and the prophets, right on down to the common people. ¹⁴I will smash them one against the other, even parents against children, says the LORD. I will not let my pity or mercy or compassion keep me from destroying them.'"

¹⁵Listen! Do not be proud, for the LORD has spoken. ¹⁶Give glory to the LORD your God before it is too late. Acknowledge him before he brings darkness upon you, causing you to stumble and fall on the dark mountains. For then, when you look for light, you will find only terrible darkness. ¹⁷And if you still refuse to listen, I will weep alone because of your pride. My eyes will overflow with tears because the LORD's flock will be led away into exile.

¹⁸Say to the king and his mother, "Come down from your thrones and sit in the dust, for your glorious crowns will soon be snatched from your heads." ¹⁹The towns of the Negev will close their gates, and no one will be able to open them. The people of Judah will be taken away as captives. They will all be carried into exile.

²⁰See the armies marching down from the north! Where is your flock—your beautiful flock—that he gave you to care for? ²¹How will you feel when the LORD sets your foreign allies over you as rulers? You will writhe in pain like a woman giving birth! ²²You may ask yourself, "Why is all this happening to me?" It is because of your many sins! That is why you have been raped and destroyed by invading armies. ²³Can an Ethiopian* change the color of his skin? Can a leopard take away its spots? Neither can you start doing good, for you always do evil. ²⁴"I will scatter you, just as chaff is scattered by the winds blowing in from the desert. ²⁵This is your allotment, that which is due you," says the LORD. "I have mea-

sured it out especially for you, because you have forgotten me and put your trust in false gods. ²⁶I myself will expose you to shame. ²⁷I am keenly aware of your adultery and lust, and your abominable idol worship out in the fields and on the hills. Your destruction is sure, Jerusalem! How long will it be before you are pure?"

CHAPTER 14

This message came to Jeremiah from the LORD, explaining why he was holding back the rain: ²"Judah wilts; her businesses have ground to a halt. All the people sit on the ground in mourning, and a great cry rises from Jerusalem. ³The nobles send servants to get water, but all the wells are dry. The servants return with empty pitchers, confused and desperate, covering their heads in grief. ⁴The ground is parched and cracked for lack of rain. The farmers are afraid; they, too, cover their heads. ⁵The deer abandons her newborn fawn because there is no grass. ⁶The wild donkeys stand on the bare hills panting like thirsty jackals. They strain their eyes looking for grass to eat, but there is none to be found."

⁷The people say, "LORD, our wickedness has caught up with us. We have sinned against you. So please, help us for the sake of your own reputation. ⁸O Hope of Israel, our Savior in times of trouble! Why are you like a stranger to us? Why are you like someone passing through the land, stopping only for the night? ⁹Are you also confused? Are you helpless to save us? You are right here among us, LORD. We are known as your people. Please don't abandon us now!"

¹⁰So the LORD replies to his people, "You love to wander far from me and do not follow in my paths. Now I will no longer accept you as my people. I will remember all your wickedness and will punish you for your sins."

¹¹Then the LORD said to me, "Do not pray for these people anymore. ¹²When they fast in my presence, I will pay no attention. When they present their burnt offerings and grain offerings to me, I will not accept them. In return, I will give them only war, famine, and disease."

¹³Then I said, "O Sovereign LORD, their prophets are telling them, 'All is well—no war or famine will come. The LORD will surely send you peace.'"

13:23 Hebrew *a Cushite.*

¹⁴Then the LORD said, "These prophets are telling lies in my name. I did not send them or tell them to speak. I did not give them any messages. They prophesy of visions and revelations they have never seen or heard. They speak foolishness made up in their own lying hearts. ¹⁵Therefore, says the LORD, I will punish these lying prophets, for they have spoken in my name even though I never sent them. They say that no war or famine will come, but they themselves will die by war and famine! ¹⁶As for the people to whom they prophesy—their bodies will be thrown out into the streets of Jerusalem, victims of famine and war. There will be no one left to bury them. Husbands, wives, sons, and daughters—all will be gone. For I will pour out their own wickedness on them.

¹⁷"Now, Jeremiah, say this to them: 'Night and day my eyes overflow with tears. I cannot stop weeping, for my virgin daughter—my precious people—has been run through with a sword and lies mortally wounded on the ground. ¹⁸If I go out into the fields, I see the bodies of people slaughtered by the enemy. If I walk the city streets, there I see people who have died of starvation. The prophets and priests continue with their work, but they do not know what they are doing.'"

¹⁹LORD, have you completely rejected Judah? Do you really hate Jerusalem*? Why have you wounded us past all hope of healing? We hoped for peace, but no peace came. We hoped for a time of healing but found only terror.

²⁰LORD, we confess our wickedness and that of our ancestors, too. We all have sinned against you. ²¹For the sake of your own name, LORD, do not abandon us. Do not disgrace yourself and the throne of your glory. Do not break your covenant with us. Please don't forget us!

²²Can any of the foreign gods send us rain? Does it fall from the sky by itself? No, it comes from you, the LORD our God! Only you can do such things. So we will wait for you to help us.

CHAPTER 15

Then the LORD said to me, "Even if Moses and Samuel stood before me pleading for these people, I wouldn't help them. Away with them! Get them out of my sight! ²And if they say to you, 'But where can we go?' tell them, 'This is what the LORD says: Those who are destined for death, to death; those who are destined for war, to war; those who are destined for famine, to famine; those who are destined for captivity, to captivity.'

³"I will send four kinds of destroyers against them," says the LORD. "I will send the sword to kill, the dogs to drag away, the vultures to devour, and the wild animals to finish up what is left. ⁴Because of the wicked things Manasseh son of Hezekiah, king of Judah, did in Jerusalem, I will make my people an object of horror to all the kingdoms of the earth.

⁵"Who will feel sorry for you, Jerusalem? Who will weep for you? Who will even bother to ask how you are? ⁶You have forsaken me and turned your back on me," says the LORD. "Therefore, I will raise my clenched fists to destroy you. I am tired of always giving you another chance. ⁷I will winnow you like grain at the gates of your cities and take away everything you hold dear. I will destroy my own people, because they refuse to turn back to me from all their evil ways.

⁸"There will be more widows than the grains of sand along the seashore. At noontime I will bring a destroyer against the mothers of young men. I will cause anguish and terror to come upon them suddenly. ⁹The mother of seven grows faint and gasps for breath; her sun has gone down while it is yet day. She sits childless now, disgraced and humiliated. And those who are left, I will hand over to the enemy to be killed," says the LORD.

¹⁰Then I said, "What sadness is mine, my mother. Oh, that I had died at birth! I am hated everywhere I go. I am neither a lender who has threatened to foreclose nor a borrower who refuses to pay—yet they all curse me."

¹¹The LORD replied, "All will be well with you, Jeremiah. Your enemies will ask you to plead on their behalf in times of trouble and distress. ¹²Can a man break a bar of iron from the north, or a bar of bronze? ¹³Because of all my people's sins against me, I will hand over their wealth and treasures as plunder to the enemy. ¹⁴I will tell their enemies to take them as captives to a foreign land. For my anger blazes forth like fire, and it will consume them."

¹⁵Then I said, "LORD, you know I am

14:19 Hebrew *Zion*.

suffering for your sake. Punish my persecutors! Don't let them kill me! Be merciful to me and give them what they deserve! ¹⁶Your words are what sustain me. They bring me great joy and are my heart's delight, for I bear your name, O LORD God Almighty. ¹⁷I never joined the people in their merry feasts. I sat alone because your hand was on me. I burst with indignation at their sins. ¹⁸Why then does my suffering continue? Why is my wound so incurable? Your help seems as uncertain as a seasonal brook. It is like a spring that has gone dry."

¹⁹The LORD replied, "If you return to me, I will restore you so you can continue to serve me. If you speak words that are worthy, you will be my spokesman. You are to influence them; do not let them influence you! ²⁰They will fight against you like an attacking army, but I will make you as secure as a fortified wall. They will not conquer you, for I will protect and deliver you. I, the LORD, have spoken! ²¹Yes, I will certainly keep you safe from these wicked men. I will rescue you from their cruel hands."

AUGUST 4 ☐ DAY 217
JEREMIAH 16–20
Judah in the Potter's Hand

OVERVIEW Frequently God asked his prophets to do unusual things to illustrate the message they were bringing. It was all part of being God's mouthpiece to a wayward people. In today's section Jeremiah is not allowed to marry or to attend funerals or feasts. Visually, Jeremiah is showing the people that they will lose their personal freedoms when the day of judgment finally arrives. Attempting to emphasize the coming calamity, the prophet smashes a clay pot at the feet of the leaders. But the response Jeremiah receives is discouragingly predictable. In place of the repentance he seeks, there is only rejection on the part of the people— a sure sign that judgment is near.

Chapter 16	Chapters 17–18	Chapter 19	Chapter 20
Hope in the Lord	Heart of the Matter	Hand of the Potter	Hurt of the Prophet
Consolation	Controversy	Clay Pot	Complaint

YOUR DAILY WALK Though few homemakers would enjoy the prospects of a dirt floor in their kitchen, there is one thing to be said in favor of a dirt floor: You don't worry about it getting dirty. However, it is equally true that no matter how much you clean it, your floor will always be just as dirty as the day it was "installed." That is the nature of dirt floors.

The heart is a triangle that only the Trinity can fill.

What is true of dirt floors is equally true of the human heart. The more you "scrub" it, the worse it becomes. Jeremiah delivers the bad news: "The human heart is most deceitful and desperately wicked. Who really knows how bad it is?" (17:9).

But there is good news as well. The Lord is a heart specialist (17:10). He is in the business, not simply of repairing hearts, but of replacing them with new hearts that desire to know him, love him, and serve him. Have you experienced a spiritual heart transplant? If not, the Master Surgeon stands waiting to give you new life, hope, and a real purpose for living. Talk to him right now. Tell him you want to "believe in your heart . . . [and] be saved" (Romans 10:9). On the basis of his Word, that is exactly what will happen!

INSIGHT Now You Know . . . and Wish You Didn't
Today's reading mentions for the first time where Judah would spend its years of exile and who would lead the nation there. Can you find it? (Hint: Look in chapter 20.)

CHAPTER 16

The LORD gave me another message. He said, [2]"Do not marry or have children in this place. [3]For this is what the LORD says about the children born here in this city and about their mothers and fathers: [4]They will die from terrible diseases. No one will mourn for them or bury them, and they will lie scattered on the ground like dung. They will die from war and famine, and their bodies will be food for the vultures and wild animals.

[5]"Do not go to their funerals to mourn and show sympathy for them," says the LORD, "for I have removed my protection and peace from them. I have taken away my unfailing love and my mercy. [6]Both the great and the lowly will die in this land. No one will bury them or mourn for them. Their friends will not cut themselves or shave their heads in sadness. [7]No one will offer a meal to comfort those who mourn for the dead—not even for the death of a mother or a father. No one will send a cup of wine to console them.

[8]"And do not go to their feasts and parties. Do not eat and drink with them at all. [9]For the LORD Almighty, the God of Israel, says: In your own lifetime, before your very eyes, I will put an end to the happy singing and laughter in this land. The joyful voices of bridegrooms and brides will no longer be heard.

[10]"When you tell the people all these things, they will ask, 'Why has the LORD decreed such terrible things against us? What have we done to deserve such treatment? What is our sin against the LORD our God?' [11]Tell them that this is the LORD's reply: It is because your ancestors were unfaithful to me. They worshiped other gods and served them. They abandoned me. They did not keep my law. [12]And you are even worse than your ancestors! You stubbornly follow your own evil desires and refuse to listen to me. [13]So I will throw you out of this land and send you into a foreign land where you and your ancestors have never been. There you can worship idols all you like—and I will grant you no favors!

[14]"But the time is coming," says the LORD, "when people who are taking an oath will no longer say, 'As surely as the LORD lives, who rescued the people of Israel from the land of Egypt.' [15]Instead, they will say, 'As surely as the LORD lives, who brought the people of Israel back to their own land from the land of the north and from all the countries to which he had exiled them.' For I will bring them back to this land that I gave their ancestors.

[16]"But now I am sending for many fishermen who will catch them," says the LORD. "I am sending for hunters who will search for them in the forests and caves. [17]I am watching them closely, and I see every sin. They cannot hope to hide from me. [18]I will punish them doubly for all their sins, because they have defiled my land with lifeless images of their detestable gods and filled my inheritance with their evil deeds."

[19]LORD, you are my strength and fortress, my refuge in the day of trouble! Nations from around the world will come to you and say, "Our ancestors were foolish, for they worshiped worthless idols. [20]Can people make their own god? The gods they make are not real gods at all!"

[21]"So now I will show them my power and might," says the LORD. "At last they will know that I am the LORD."

CHAPTER 17

The LORD says, "My people act as though their evil ways are laws to be obeyed, inscribed with a diamond point on their stony hearts, or with an iron chisel on the corners of their altars. [2]Even their children go to worship at their sacred altars and Asherah poles, beneath every green tree and on every high hill. [3]So I will give all your wealth and treasures—together with your pagan shrines—as plunder to your enemies, for sin runs rampant in your land. [4]The wonderful inheritance I have reserved for you will slip out of your hands, and I will send you away as captives to a foreign land. For you have kindled my anger into a roaring fire that will burn forever."

5This is what the LORD says: "Cursed are those who put their trust in mere humans and turn their hearts away from the LORD. 6They are like stunted shrubs in the desert, with no hope for the future. They will live in the barren wilderness, on the salty flats where no one lives.

7"But blessed are those who trust in the LORD and have made the LORD their hope and confidence. 8They are like trees planted along a riverbank, with roots that reach deep into the water. Such trees are not bothered by the heat or worried by long months of drought. Their leaves stay green, and they go right on producing delicious fruit.

9"The human heart is most deceitful and desperately wicked. Who really knows how bad it is? 10But I know! I, the LORD, search all hearts and examine secret motives. I give all people their due rewards, according to what their actions deserve."

11Like a bird that hatches eggs she has not laid, so are those who get their wealth by unjust means. Sooner or later they will lose their riches and, at the end of their lives, will become poor old fools.

12But we worship at your throne—eternal, high, and glorious! 13O LORD, the hope of Israel, all who turn away from you will be disgraced and shamed. They will be buried in a dry and dusty grave, for they have forsaken the LORD, the fountain of living water.

14O LORD, you alone can heal me; you alone can save. My praises are for you alone! 15People scoff at me and say, "What is this 'message from the LORD' you keep talking about? Why don't your predictions come true?"

16LORD, I have not abandoned my job as a shepherd for your people. I have not urged you to send disaster. It is your message I have given them, not my own. 17LORD, do not desert me now! You alone are my hope in the day of disaster. 18Bring shame and terror on all who persecute me, but give me peace. Yes, bring double destruction upon them!

19Then the LORD said to me, "Go and stand in the gates of Jerusalem, first at the gate where the king goes out, and then at each of the other gates. 20Say to all the people, 'Listen to this message from the LORD, you kings of Judah and all you people of Judah and everyone living in Jerusalem. 21This is what the LORD says: Listen to my warning and live! Stop carrying on your trade at Jerusalem's gates on the Sabbath day. 22Do not do your work on the Sabbath, but make it a holy day. I gave this command to your ancestors, 23but they did not listen or obey. They stubbornly refused to pay attention and would not respond to discipline.

24"'But if you obey me, says the LORD, and do not carry on your trade or work on the Sabbath day, and if you keep it holy, 25then this nation will continue forever. There will always be a descendant of David sitting on the throne here in Jerusalem. Kings and their officials will always ride among the people of Judah in chariots and on horses, and this city will remain forever. 26And from all around Jerusalem, from the towns of Judah and Benjamin, from the western foothills* and the hill country and the Negev, the people will come with their burnt offerings and sacrifices. They will bring their grain offerings, incense, and thanksgiving offerings to the LORD's Temple.

27"'But if you do not listen to me and refuse to keep the Sabbath holy, and if on the Sabbath day you bring loads of merchandise through the gates of Jerusalem just as on other days, then I will set fire to these gates. The fire will spread to the palaces, and no one will be able to put out the roaring flames.'"

CHAPTER 18
The LORD gave another message to Jeremiah. He said, 2"Go down to the shop where clay pots and jars are made. I will speak to you while you are there." 3So I did as he told me and found the potter working at his wheel. 4But the jar he was making did not turn out as he had hoped, so the potter squashed the jar into a lump of clay and started again.

5Then the LORD gave me this message: 6"O Israel, can I not do to you as this potter has done to his clay? As the clay is in the potter's hand, so are you in my hand. 7If I announce that a certain nation or kingdom is to be uprooted, torn down, and destroyed, 8but then that nation renounces its evil ways, I will not destroy it as I had planned. 9And if I announce that I will

17:26 Hebrew the Shephelah.

build up and plant a certain nation or kingdom, making it strong and great, [10]but then that nation turns to evil and refuses to obey me, I will not bless that nation as I had said I would.

[11]"Therefore, Jeremiah, go and warn all Judah and Jerusalem. Say to them, 'This is what the LORD says: I am planning disaster against you instead of good. So turn from your evil ways, each of you, and do what is right.'"

[12]But they replied, "Don't waste your breath. We will continue to live as we want to, following our own evil desires."

[13]Then the LORD said, "Has anyone ever heard of such a thing, even among the pagan nations? My virgin Israel has done something too terrible to understand! [14]Does the snow ever melt high up in the mountains of Lebanon? Do the cold, flowing streams from the crags of Mount Hermon ever run dry? [15]These can be counted on, but not my people! For they have deserted me and turned to worthless idols. They have stumbled off the ancient highways of good, and they walk the muddy paths of sin. [16]Therefore, their land will become desolate, a monument to their stupidity. All who pass by will be astonished and shake their heads in amazement at its utter desolation. [17]I will scatter my people before their enemies as the east wind scatters dust. And in all their trouble I will turn my back on them and refuse to notice their distress."

[18]Then the people said, "Come on, let's find a way to stop Jeremiah. We have our own priests and wise men and prophets. We don't need him to teach the law and give us advice and prophecies. Let's spread rumors about him and ignore what he says."

[19]LORD, help me! Listen to what they are planning to do to me! [20]Should they repay evil for good? They have set a trap to kill me, though I pleaded for them and tried to protect them from your anger. [21]So let their children starve! Let the sword pour out their blood! Let their wives become widows without any children! Let their old men die in a plague, and let their young men be killed in battle! [22]Let screaming be heard from their homes as warriors come suddenly upon them. For they have dug a pit for me, and they have hidden traps along my path.

[23]LORD, you know all about their mur-

derous plots against me. Don't forgive their crimes and blot out their sins. Let them die before you. Deal with them in your anger.

CHAPTER 19

The LORD said to me, "Go and buy a clay jar. Then ask some of the leaders of the people and of the priests to follow you. [2]Go out into the valley of the son of Hinnom by the entrance to the Potsherd Gate, and repeat to them the words that I give you. [3]Say to them, 'Listen to this message from the LORD, you kings of Judah and citizens of Jerusalem! This is what the LORD Almighty, the God of Israel, says: I will bring such a terrible disaster on this place that the ears of those who hear about it will ring!

[4]" 'For Israel has forsaken me and turned this valley into a place of wickedness. The people burn incense to foreign gods—idols never before worshiped by this generation, by their ancestors, or by the kings of Judah. And they have filled this place with the blood of innocent children. [5]They have built pagan shrines to Baal, and there they burn their sons as sacrifices to Baal. I have never commanded such a horrible deed; it never even crossed my mind to command such a thing! [6]So beware, for the time is coming, says the LORD, when this place will no longer be called Topheth or the valley of the son of Hinnom, but the Valley of Slaughter. [7]For I will upset the battle plans of Judah and Jerusalem and let invading armies slaughter them. The enemy will leave the dead bodies as food for the vultures and wild animals. [8]I will wipe Jerusalem from the face of the earth, making it a monument to their stupidity. All who pass by will be appalled and will gasp at the destruction they see there. [9]I will see to it that your enemies lay siege to the city until all the food is gone. Then those trapped inside will have to eat their own sons and daughters and friends. They will be driven to utter despair.'

[10]"As these men watch, Jeremiah, smash the jar you brought with you. [11]Then say to them, 'This is what the LORD Almighty says: As this jar lies shattered, so I will shatter the people of Judah and Jerusalem beyond all hope of repair. They will bury the bodies in Topheth until there is no more room. [12]This is what I will do to this place and its people, says the LORD. I will cause this city to become defiled like Topheth.

13 Yes, all the houses in Jerusalem, including the palace of Judah's kings, will become like Topheth—all the houses where you burned incense on the rooftops to your star gods, and where drink offerings were poured out to your idols.'"

14 Then Jeremiah returned from Topheth where he had delivered this message, and he stopped in front of the Temple of the LORD. He said to the people there, 15 "This is what the LORD Almighty, the God of Israel, says: I will bring disaster upon this city and its surrounding towns just as I promised, because you have stubbornly refused to listen to me."

CHAPTER 20

Now Pashhur son of Immer, the priest in charge of the Temple of the LORD, heard what Jeremiah was saying. 2 So he arrested Jeremiah the prophet and had him whipped and put in stocks at the Benjamin Gate of the LORD's Temple.

3 The next day, when Pashhur finally released him, Jeremiah said, "Pashhur, the LORD has changed your name. From now on you are to be called 'The Man Who Lives in Terror.'* 4 For this is what the LORD says: I will send terror upon you and all your friends, and you will watch as they are slaughtered by the swords of the enemy. I will hand the people of Judah over to the king of Babylon. He will take them captive to Babylon or run them through with the sword. 5 And I will let your enemies plunder Jerusalem. All the famed treasures of the city—the precious jewels and gold and silver of your kings—will be carried off to Babylon. 6 As for you, Pashhur, you and all your household will go as captives to Babylon. There you will die and be buried, you and all your friends to whom you promised that everything would be all right."

7 O LORD, you persuaded me, and I allowed myself to be persuaded. You are stronger than I am, and you overpowered me. Now I am mocked by everyone in the city. 8 Whenever I speak, the words come out in a violent outburst. "Violence and destruction!" I shout. So these messages from the LORD have made me a household joke. 9 And I can't stop! If I say I'll never mention the LORD or speak in his name, his word burns in my heart like a fire. It's like a fire in my bones! I am weary of holding it in!

10 I have heard the many rumors about me. They call me "The Man Who Lives in Terror." And they say, "If you say anything, we will report it." Even my old friends are watching me, waiting for a fatal slip. "He will trap himself," they say, "and then we will get our revenge on him."

11 But the LORD stands beside me like a great warrior. Before him they will stumble. They cannot defeat me. They will be shamed and thoroughly humiliated. Their dishonor will never be forgotten. 12 O LORD Almighty! You know those who are righteous, and you examine the deepest thoughts of hearts and minds. Let me see your vengeance against them, for I have committed my cause to you. 13 Now I will sing out my thanks to the LORD! Praise the LORD! For though I was poor and needy, he delivered me from my oppressors.

14 Yet I curse the day I was born! May the day of my birth not be blessed. 15 I curse the messenger who told my father, "Good news—you have a son!" 16 Let him be destroyed like the cities of old that the LORD overthrew without mercy. Terrify him all day long with battle shouts, 17 for he did not kill me at birth. Oh, that I had died in my mother's womb, that her body had been my grave! 18 Why was I ever born? My entire life has been filled with trouble, sorrow, and shame.

20:3 Hebrew *Magor-missabib*, which means "surrounded by terror"; also in 20:10.

AUGUST 5 ☐ DAY 218
JEREMIAH 21–25
Judah in a Leadership Crisis

OVERVIEW Judah's downfall can ultimately be traced to the failure of its leadership—those wicked shepherds who plundered rather than protected the flock. In the midst of Jeremiah's dirge of doom upon the nation's false kings and prophets, he prophesies the coming of the Messiah, who will restore justice and righteousness. Exile is inevitable, but there is hope. In seventy years the deported will return to Judah, while their captors will feel God's wrath.

Chapters 21–22	Chapter 23	Chapter 24	Chapter 25
False Kings	False Prophets	Captive Nation	Condemned Nations
National Judgment		International Judgment	

The most dangerous of all false doctrines is that seasoned with a little truth.

YOUR DAILY WALK Turn on your radio or TV, and almost any day of the week (especially on Sunday) chances are good that you will find someone claiming, "God told me this" or "The Lord said to me that . . ." Perhaps you have been offered literature lately by someone claiming to have audibly heard from God and who therefore had an authoritative "word from God." With the ever-growing number of cults and "-isms," how can you be certain who is truly speaking for God?

In Jeremiah's day the people were plagued with false prophets, who claimed to know God's mind. Though these deceivers didn't have TV or radio to help propagate their statements, they still managed to lull the nation into complacency.

Jeremiah's warnings concerning false prophets are timely indeed! The next time you encounter someone who claims, "God told me . . . ," apply this twofold test: (1) Does his life match his words? (23:13); (2) does the Bible back up his statements? (23:21-22). If not, watch out! Read and remember 1 John 4:1-6. Don't just accept what someone says; learn to "test the spirits" and develop a discerning mind that won't be deceived.

INSIGHT No Secret about the Seventy
The duration of the Babylonian exile (25:11-12) was a matter of public record. In fact, Daniel, as the result of reading Jeremiah's prophecy of the seventy years, began to pray specifically that God would restore the people to the land (Daniel 9:1-3). God knows the end from the beginning!

CHAPTER 21

The LORD spoke through Jeremiah when King Zedekiah sent Pashhur son of Malkijah and Zephaniah son of Maaseiah, the priest, to speak with him. They begged Jeremiah, ²"Please ask the LORD to help us. King Nebuchadnezzar* of Babylon has begun his attack on Judah. Perhaps the LORD will be gracious and do a mighty miracle as he has done in the past. Perhaps he will force Nebuchadnezzar to withdraw his armies."

³Jeremiah replied, "Go back to King Zedekiah and tell him, ⁴'This is what the LORD, the God of Israel, says: I will make your weapons useless against the king of Babylon and the Babylonians* who are attacking you. Yes, I will bring your enemies right into the heart of this city. ⁵I myself will fight against you with great power, for I am very angry. You have made me furious! ⁶I will send a terrible plague upon this city, and both people and animals will die. ⁷And

21:2 Hebrew *Nebuchadrezzar*, a variant name for Nebuchadnezzar; also in 21:7.   21:4 Or *Chaldeans*; also in 21:9.

then, says the LORD, even after King Zedekiah, his officials, and everyone else in the city have survived war, famine, and disease, I will hand them over to King Nebuchadnezzar of Babylon. He will slaughter them all without mercy, pity, or compassion.'

8"Tell all the people, 'This is what the LORD says: Take your choice of life or death! 9Everyone who stays in Jerusalem will die from war, famine, or disease, but those who go out and surrender to the Babylonians will live. 10For I have decided to bring disaster and not good upon this city, says the LORD. It will be captured by the king of Babylon, and he will reduce it to ashes.'

11"Say to the royal family of Judah, 'Listen to this message from the LORD! 12This is what the LORD says to the dynasty of David: Give justice to the people you judge! Help those who have been robbed; rescue them from their oppressors. Do what is right, or my anger will burn like an unquenchable fire because of all your sins. 13I will fight against this city of Jerusalem that boasts, "We are safe on our mountain! No one can touch us here." 14And I myself will punish you for your sinfulness, says the LORD. I will light a fire in your forests that will burn up everything around you.'"

CHAPTER 22
Then the LORD said to me, "Go over and speak directly to the king of Judah. Say to him, 2'Listen to this message from the LORD, you king of Judah, sitting on David's throne. Let your officials and your people listen, too. 3This is what the LORD says: Be fair-minded and just. Do what is right! Help those who have been robbed; rescue them from their oppressors. Quit your evil deeds! Do not mistreat foreigners, orphans, and widows. Stop murdering the innocent! 4If you obey me, there will always be a descendant of David sitting on the throne here in Jerusalem. The king will ride through the palace gates in chariots and on horses, with his parade of officials and subjects. 5But if you refuse to pay attention to this warning, I swear by my own name, says the LORD, that this palace will become a pile of rubble.'"

6Now this is what the LORD says concerning the royal palace: "You are as beloved to me as fruitful Gilead and the green forests of Lebanon. But I will destroy you and leave you deserted, with no one living within your walls. 7I will call for wreckers, who will bring out their tools to dismantle you. They will tear out all your fine cedar beams and throw them on the fire. 8People from many nations will pass by the ruins of this city and say to one another, 'Why did the LORD destroy such a great city?' 9And the answer will be, 'Because they violated their covenant with the LORD their God by worshiping other gods.'"

10Do not weep for the dead king or mourn his loss. Instead, weep for the captive king being led away! For he will never return to see his native land again. 11For this is what the LORD says about Jehoahaz,* who succeeded his father, King Josiah, and was taken away as a captive: "He will never return. 12He will die in a distant land and never again see his own country."

13And the LORD says, "Destruction is certain for Jehoiakim,* who builds his palace with forced labor.* By not paying wages, he builds injustice into its walls and oppression into its doorframes and ceilings. 14He says, 'I will build a magnificent palace with huge rooms and many windows, paneled throughout with fragrant cedar and painted a lovely red.'

15"But a beautiful palace does not make a great king! Why did your father, Josiah, reign so long? Because he was just and right in all his dealings. That is why God blessed him. 16He made sure that justice and help were given to the poor and needy, and everything went well for him. Isn't that what it means to know me?" asks the LORD. 17"But you! You are full of selfish greed and dishonesty! You murder the innocent, oppress the poor, and reign ruthlessly."

18Therefore, this is the LORD's decree of punishment against King Jehoiakim, who succeeded his father, Josiah, on the throne: "His family will not weep for him when he dies. His subjects will not even care that he is dead. 19He will be buried like a dead donkey—dragged out of Jerusalem and dumped outside the gate! 20Weep, for your allies are all gone. Search for them in Lebanon. Shout for them at Bashan. Search for them in the regions east of the river.* See,

22:11 Hebrew *Shallum,* another name for Jehoahaz.   22:13a The brother and successor of the exiled Jehoahaz.   22:13b Hebrew *by unrighteousness.*   22:20 Hebrew *in Abarim.*

they are all destroyed. Not one is left to help you.

²¹"When you were prosperous, I warned you, but you replied, 'Don't bother me.' Since childhood you have been that way—you simply will not listen! ²²And now your allies have all disappeared with a puff of wind. All your friends have been taken away as captives. Surely at last you will see your wickedness and be ashamed. ²³It may be nice to live in a beautiful palace lined with lumber from the cedars of Lebanon, but soon you will cry and groan in anguish—anguish like that of a woman about to give birth.

²⁴"And as surely as I live," says the LORD, "I will abandon you, Jehoiachin* son of Jehoiakim, king of Judah. Even if you were the signet ring on my right hand, I would pull you off. ²⁵I will hand you over to those who seek to kill you, of whom you are so desperately afraid—to King Nebuchadnezzar* of Babylon and the mighty Babylonian* army. ²⁶I will expel you and your mother from this land, and you will die in a foreign country. ²⁷You will never again return to the land of your desire.

²⁸"Why is this man Jehoiachin like a discarded, broken dish? Why are he and his children to be exiled to distant lands? ²⁹O earth, earth, earth! Listen to this message from the LORD! ³⁰This is what the LORD says: Let the record show that this man Jehoiachin was childless, for none of his children will ever sit on the throne of David to rule in Judah. His life will amount to nothing."

CHAPTER 23

"I will send disaster upon the leaders of my people—the shepherds of my sheep—for they have destroyed and scattered the very ones they were expected to care for," says the LORD.

²This is what the LORD, the God of Israel, says to these shepherds: "Instead of leading my flock to safety, you have deserted them and driven them to destruction. Now I will pour out judgment on you for the evil you have done to them. ³But I will gather together the remnant of my flock from wherever I have driven them. I will bring them back into their own fold, and they will be fruitful and increase in number. ⁴Then I will appoint responsible shepherds to care for them, and they will never be afraid again. Not a single one of them will be lost or missing," says the LORD.

⁵"For the time is coming," says the LORD, "when I will place a righteous Branch on King David's throne. He will be a King who rules with wisdom. He will do what is just and right throughout the land. ⁶And this is his name: 'The LORD Is Our Righteousness.'* In that day Judah will be saved, and Israel will live in safety.

⁷"In that day," says the LORD, "when people are taking an oath, they will no longer say, 'As surely as the LORD lives, who rescued the people of Israel from the land of Egypt.' ⁸Instead, they will say, 'As surely as the LORD lives, who brought the people of Israel back to their own land from the land of the north and from all the countries to which he had exiled them.' Then they will live in their own land."

⁹My heart is broken because of the false prophets, and I tremble uncontrollably. I stagger like a drunkard, like someone overcome by wine, because of the holy words the LORD has spoken against them. ¹⁰For the land is full of adultery, and it lies under a curse. The land itself is in mourning—its pastures are dried up. For the prophets do evil and abuse their power.

¹¹"The priests are like the prophets, all ungodly, wicked men. I have seen their despicable acts right here in my own Temple," says the LORD. ¹²"Therefore, their paths will be dark and slippery. They will be chased down dark and treacherous trails, where they will fall. For I will bring disaster upon them when their time of punishment comes. I, the LORD, have spoken!

¹³"I saw that the prophets of Samaria were terribly evil, for they prophesied by Baal and led my people of Israel into sin. ¹⁴But now I see that the prophets of Jerusalem are even worse! They commit adultery, and they love dishonesty. They encourage those who are doing evil instead of turning them away from their sins. These prophets are as wicked as the people of Sodom and Gomorrah once were."

¹⁵Therefore, this is what the LORD Almighty says concerning the prophets: "I will feed them with bitterness and give them poison to drink. For it is because of Jerusalem's prophets that wickedness fills

22:24 Hebrew *Coniah*, a variant name for Jehoiachin; also in 22:28, 30.   22:25a Hebrew *Nebuchadrezzar*, a variant name for Nebuchadnezzar.   22:25b Or *Chaldean*.   23:6 Hebrew *Yahweh Tsidqenu*.

this land. [16]This is my warning to my people," says the LORD Almighty. "Do not listen to these prophets when they prophesy to you, filling you with futile hopes. They are making up everything they say. They do not speak for the LORD! [17]They keep saying to these rebels who despise my word, 'Don't worry! The LORD says you will have peace!' And to those who stubbornly follow their own evil desires, they say, 'No harm will come your way!'

[18]"But can you name even one of these prophets who knows the LORD well enough to hear what he is saying? Has even one of them cared enough to listen? [19]Look! The LORD's anger bursts out like a storm, a whirlwind that swirls down on the heads of the wicked. [20]The anger of the LORD will not diminish until it has finished all his plans. In the days to come, you will understand all this very clearly.

[21]"I have not sent these prophets, yet they claim to speak for me. I have given them no message, yet they prophesy. [22]If they had listened to me, they would have spoken my words and turned my people from their evil ways. [23]Am I a God who is only in one place?" asks the LORD. "Do they think I cannot see what they are doing? [24]Can anyone hide from me? Am I not everywhere in all the heavens and earth?" asks the LORD.

[25]"I have heard these prophets say, 'Listen to the dream I had from God last night.' And then they proceed to tell lies in my name. [26]How long will this go on? If they are prophets, they are prophets of deceit, inventing everything they say. [27]By telling these false dreams, they are trying to get my people to forget me, just as their ancestors did by worshiping the idols of Baal. [28]Let these false prophets tell their dreams, but let my true messengers faithfully proclaim my every word. There is a difference between chaff and wheat! [29]Does not my word burn like fire?" asks the LORD. "Is it not like a mighty hammer that smashes rock to pieces?

[30]"Therefore," says the LORD, "I stand against these prophets who get their messages from each other—[31]these smooth-tongued prophets who say, 'This prophecy is from the LORD!' [32]Their imaginary dreams are flagrant lies that lead my people into sin. I did not send or appoint them, and they

have no message at all for my people," says the LORD.

[33]"Suppose one of the people or one of the prophets or priests asks you, 'What prophecy has the LORD burdened you with now?' You must reply, 'You are the burden!* The LORD says he will abandon you!' [34]If any prophet, priest, or anyone else says, 'I have a prophecy from the LORD,' I will punish that person along with his entire family. [35]You should keep asking each other, 'What is the LORD's answer?' or 'What is the LORD saying?' [36]But stop using this phrase, 'prophecy from the LORD.' For people are using it to give authority to their own ideas, turning upside down the words of our God, the living God, the LORD Almighty.

[37]"This is what you should say to the prophets: 'What is the LORD's answer?' or 'What is the LORD saying?' [38]But suppose they respond, 'This is a prophecy from the LORD!' Then you should say, 'This is what the LORD says: Because you have used this phrase, "prophecy from the LORD," even though I warned you not to use it, [39]I will forget you completely. I will expel you from my presence, along with this city that I gave to you and your ancestors. [40]And I will make you an object of ridicule, and your name will be infamous throughout the ages.'"

CHAPTER 24

After King Nebuchadnezzar* of Babylon exiled Jehoiachin* son of Jehoiakim, king of Judah, to Babylon along with the princes of Judah and all the skilled craftsmen, the LORD gave me this vision. I saw two baskets of figs placed in front of the LORD's Temple in Jerusalem. [2]One basket was filled with fresh, ripe figs, while the other was filled with figs that were spoiled and could not be eaten.

[3]Then the LORD said to me, "What do you see, Jeremiah?"

I replied, "Figs, some very good and some very bad."

[4]Then the LORD gave me this message: [5]"This is what the LORD, the God of Israel, says: The good figs represent the exiles I sent from Judah to the land of the Babylonians.* [6]I have sent them into captivity for their own good. I will see that they are well

23:33 As in Greek version and Latin Vulgate; Hebrew reads *What burden?*   24:1a Hebrew *Nebuchadrezzar*, a variant name for Nebuchadnezzar.   24:1b Hebrew *Jeconiah*, a variant name for Jehoiachin.   24:5 Or *Chaldeans.*

treated, and I will bring them back here again. I will build them up and not tear them down. I will plant them and not uproot them. [7]I will give them hearts that will recognize me as the LORD. They will be my people, and I will be their God, for they will return to me wholeheartedly.

[8]"But the rotten figs," the LORD said, "represent King Zedekiah of Judah, his officials, all the people left in Jerusalem, and those who live in Egypt. I will treat them like spoiled figs, too rotten to eat. [9]I will make them an object of horror and evil to every nation on earth. They will be disgraced and mocked, taunted and cursed, wherever I send them. [10]I will send war, famine, and disease until they have vanished from the land of Israel, which I gave to them and their ancestors."

CHAPTER 25

This message for all the people of Judah came to Jeremiah from the LORD during the fourth year of Jehoiakim's reign* over Judah. This was the year when King Nebuchadnezzar* of Babylon began his reign.

[2]Jeremiah the prophet said to the people in Judah and Jerusalem, [3]"For the past twenty-three years—from the thirteenth year of Josiah son of Amon,* king of Judah, until now—the LORD has been giving me his messages. I have faithfully passed them on to you, but you have not listened.

[4]"Again and again, the LORD has sent you his prophets, but you have not listened or even tried to hear. [5]Each time the message was this: 'Turn from the evil road you are traveling and from the evil things you are doing. Only then will I let you live in this land that the LORD gave to you and your ancestors forever. [6]Do not make me angry by worshiping the idols you have made. Then I will not harm you.'

[7]"But you would not listen to me," says the LORD. "You made me furious by worshiping your idols, bringing on yourselves all the disasters you now suffer. [8]And now the LORD Almighty says: Because you have not listened to me, [9]I will gather together all the armies of the north under King Nebuchadnezzar of Babylon, whom I have appointed as my deputy. I will bring them all against this land and its people and against

the other nations near you. I will completely destroy* you and make you an object of horror and contempt and a ruin forever. [10]I will take away your happy singing and laughter. The joyful voices of bridegrooms and brides will no longer be heard. Your businesses will fail, and all your homes will stand silent and dark. [11]This entire land will become a desolate wasteland. Israel and her neighboring lands will serve the king of Babylon for seventy years.

[12]"Then, after the seventy years of captivity are over, I will punish the king of Babylon and his people for their sins, says the LORD. I will make the country of the Babylonians* an everlasting wasteland. [13]I will bring upon them all the terrors I have promised in this book—all the penalties announced by Jeremiah against the nations. [14]Many nations and great kings will enslave the Babylonians, just as they enslaved my people. I will punish them in proportion to the suffering they cause my people."

[15]Then the LORD, the God of Israel, said to me, "Take from my hand this cup filled to the brim with my anger, and make all the nations to whom I send you drink from it. [16]When they drink from it, they will stagger, crazed by the warfare I will send against them."

[17]So I took the cup of anger from the LORD and made all the nations drink from it—every nation the LORD sent me to. [18]I went to Jerusalem and the other towns of Judah, and their kings and officials drank from the cup. From that day until this, they have been a desolate ruin, an object of horror, contempt, and cursing. [19]I went to Egypt and spoke to Pharaoh, his officials, his princes, and his people. They, too, drank from that terrible cup, [20]along with all the foreigners living in that land. So did all the kings of the land of Uz and the kings of the Philistine cities of Ashkelon, Gaza, Ekron, and what remains of Ashdod. [21]Then I went to the nations of Edom, Moab, and Ammon, [22]and the kings of Tyre and Sidon, and the kings of the regions across the sea. [23]I went to Dedan, Tema, and Buz, and to the people who live in distant places.* [24]I went to the kings of Arabia, the kings of the nomadic tribes of the desert,

---

25:1a The fourth year of Jehoiakim's reign and the accession year of Nebuchadnezzar's reign was 605 B.C.   25:1b Hebrew *Nebuchadrezzar*, a variant name for Nebuchadnezzar; also in 25:9.   25:3 The thirteenth year of Josiah's reign was 627 B.C.   25:9 The Hebrew term used here refers to the complete consecration of things or people to the LORD, either by destroying them or by giving them as an offering.   25:12 Or *Chaldeans*.   25:23 Or *who clip the corners of their hair*.

²⁵and to the kings of Zimri, Elam, and Media. ²⁶And I went to the kings of the northern countries, far and near, one after the other—all the kingdoms of the world. And finally, the king of Babylon* himself drank from the cup of the LORD's anger.

²⁷Then the LORD said to me, "Now tell them, 'The LORD Almighty, the God of Israel, says: Drink from this cup of my anger. Get drunk and vomit, and you will fall to rise no more, for I am sending terrible wars against you.' ²⁸And if they refuse to accept the cup, tell them, 'The LORD Almighty says: You must drink from it. You cannot escape! ²⁹I have begun to punish Jerusalem, the city where my own name is honored. Now should I let you go unpunished? No, you will not escape disaster. I will call for war against all the nations of the earth. I, the LORD Almighty, have spoken!'

³⁰"Now prophesy all these things, and say to them, 'The LORD will roar loudly against his own land from his holy dwelling in heaven. He will shout against everyone on the earth, like the harvesters do as they crush juice from the grapes. ³¹His cry of judgment will reach the ends of the earth, for the LORD will bring his case

25:26 Hebrew *of Sheshach*, a code name for Babylon.

against all the nations. He will judge all the people of the earth, slaughtering the wicked with his sword. The LORD has spoken!'"

³²This is what the LORD Almighty says: "Look! Disaster will fall upon nation after nation! A great whirlwind of fury is rising from the most distant corners of the earth!"

³³In that day those the LORD has slaughtered will fill the earth from one end to the other. No one will mourn for them or gather up their bodies to bury them. They will be scattered like dung on the ground.

³⁴Weep and moan, you evil shepherds! Roll in the dust, you leaders of the flock! The time of your slaughter has arrived; you will fall and shatter like fragile pottery. ³⁵You will find no place to hide; there will be no way to escape.

³⁶Listen to the frantic cries of the shepherds, to the leaders of the flock shouting in despair, for the LORD is spoiling their pastures. ³⁷Peaceful meadows will be turned into a wasteland by the LORD's fierce anger. ³⁸He has left his den like a lion seeking its prey, and their land will be made desolate by the sword of the enemy and the LORD's fierce anger.

AUGUST 6 ☐ DAY 219
JEREMIAH 26–29
Judah in Opposition to Jeremiah

 OVERVIEW Preachers usually hope for some kind of response after delivering their message, and Jeremiah is no different. But in his case the audience's response is breathtaking—literally! After hearing his appeal for repentance, they rise up in unison and declare, "This man should die!" (26:11). Jeremiah is arrested and tried by a murderous crowd; his life hangs in the balance until he is vindicated. But the message must go forth. Wearing an ox yoke, Jeremiah stresses the importance of Judah and her neighbors' surrendering to (rather than revolting against) Babylon, for to do otherwise is to court certain death. Discredited by Hananiah, a prophet of false hope, Jeremiah pens a letter to the recent deportees urging them to settle down in Babylon.

Chapter 26	Chapter 27	Chapter 28	Chapter 29
A Plot against the Prophet	A Yoke upon the Prophet	A Prophecy against the Prophet	A Letter from the Prophet
Extermination	Exile	Hananiah	Hope

YOUR DAILY WALK "I have learned how to get along happily whether I have much or little" (Philippians 4:11). Do you recognize those words? They aren't the declaration of a plaster saint or the meaningless small talk of featherbed royalty. Rather, they are the carefully reasoned words of Paul—a man who had been beaten, stoned, shipwrecked, imperiled, and impoverished. He had learned the secret of being content, regardless of the circumstances swirling around him.

Those who truly aspire to be Christlike should not be surprised when the mob comes to crucify them.

Jeremiah was much like Paul. On trial for his life, slandered by a fellow prophet, faced with a howling mob demanding his blood, Jeremiah calmly went about delivering his God-given message of judgment and doom. He lived above his circumstances, not under them, in his walk with God.

Write the following words on a slip of paper, carry them with you today, and read them often: "Sometimes the Lord calms the storm; more often he lets the storm rage and calms the child." Now relax in the Lord.

INSIGHT The Babylonian Exile—Slavery or Something Else?
The Hebrew exiles in Babylon were not slaves but deportees who were free to live as they pleased (29:4-9). Some became wealthy merchants, and others attained high places in court.

CHAPTER 26

This message came to Jeremiah from the LORD early in the reign of Jehoiakim son of Josiah,* king of Judah. ²The LORD said, "Stand out in front of the Temple of the LORD, and make an announcement to the people who have come there to worship from all over Judah. Give them my entire message; include every word. ³Perhaps they will listen and turn from their evil ways. Then I will be able to withhold the disaster I am ready to pour out on them because of their sins.

⁴"Say to them, 'This is what the LORD says: If you will not listen to me and obey the law I have given you, ⁵and if you will not listen to my servants, the prophets—for I sent them again and again to warn you, but you would not listen to them—⁶then I will destroy this Temple as I destroyed Shiloh, the place where the Tabernacle was located. And I will make Jerusalem an object of cursing in every nation on earth.'"

⁷The priests, the prophets, and all the people listened to Jeremiah as he spoke in front of the LORD's Temple. ⁸But when Jeremiah had finished his message, saying everything the LORD had told him to say, the priests and prophets and all the people at the Temple mobbed him. "Kill him!" they shouted. ⁹"What right do you have to prophesy in the LORD's name that this Temple will be destroyed like Shiloh? What do you mean, saying that Jerusalem will be

destroyed?" And all the people threatened him as he stood in front of the Temple.

¹⁰When the officials of Judah heard what was happening, they rushed over from the palace and sat down at the New Gate of the Temple to hold court. ¹¹The priests and prophets presented their accusations to the officials and the people. "This man should die!" they said. "You have heard with your own ears what a traitor he is, for he has prophesied against this city."

¹²Then Jeremiah spoke in his own defense. "The LORD sent me to prophesy against this Temple and this city," he said. "The LORD gave me every word that I have spoken. ¹³But if you stop your sinning and begin to obey the LORD your God, he will cancel this disaster that he has announced against you. ¹⁴As for me, I am helpless and in your power—do with me as you think best. ¹⁵But if you kill me, rest assured that you will be killing an innocent man! The responsibility for such a deed will lie on you, on this city, and on every person living in it. For it is absolutely true that the LORD sent me to speak every word you have heard."

¹⁶Then the officials and the people said to the priests and prophets, "This man does not deserve the death sentence, for he has spoken to us in the name of the LORD our God."

¹⁷Then some of the wise old men stood and spoke to the people there. ¹⁸They said,

26:1 The first year of Jehoiakim's reign was 608 B.C.

"Think back to the days when Micah of Moresheth prophesied during the reign of King Hezekiah of Judah. He told the people of Judah, 'This is what the LORD Almighty says: Mount Zion will be plowed like an open field; Jerusalem will be reduced to rubble! A great forest will grow on the hilltop, where the Temple now stands.'* [19]But did King Hezekiah and the people kill him for saying this? No, they turned from their sins and worshiped the LORD. They begged him to have mercy on them. Then the LORD held back the terrible disaster he had pronounced against them. If we kill Jeremiah, who knows what will happen to us?"

[20](At this time, Uriah son of Shemaiah from Kiriath-jearim was also prophesying for the LORD. And he predicted the same terrible disaster against the city and nation as Jeremiah did. [21]When King Jehoiakim and the army officers and officials heard what he was saying, the king sent someone to kill him. But Uriah heard about the plot and escaped to Egypt. [22]Then King Jehoiakim sent Elnathan son of Acbor to Egypt along with several other men to capture Uriah. [23]They took him prisoner and brought him back to King Jehoiakim. The king then killed Uriah with a sword and had him buried in an unmarked grave.)

[24]Ahikam son of Shaphan also stood with Jeremiah and persuaded the court not to turn him over to the mob to be killed.

CHAPTER 27

This message came to Jeremiah from the LORD early in the reign of Zedekiah* son of Josiah, king of Judah.

[2]The LORD said to me, "Make a yoke, and fasten it on your neck with leather thongs. [3]Then send messages to the kings of Edom, Moab, Ammon, Tyre, and Sidon through their ambassadors to King Zedekiah in Jerusalem. [4]Give them this message for their masters: 'This is what the LORD Almighty, the God of Israel, says: [5]By my great power I have made the earth and all its people and every animal. I can give these things of mine to anyone I choose. [6]Now I will give your countries to King Nebuchadnezzar of Babylon, who is my servant. I have put everything, even the wild animals, under his control. [7]All

the nations will serve him and his son and his grandson until his time is up. But then many nations and great kings will conquer and rule over Babylon. [8]So you must submit to Babylon's king and serve him; put your neck under Babylon's yoke! I will punish any nation that refuses to be his slave, says the LORD. I will send war, famine, and disease upon that nation until Babylon has conquered it.

[9]"'Do not listen to your false prophets, fortune-tellers, interpreters of dreams, mediums, and sorcerers who say, "The king of Babylon will not conquer you." [10]They are all liars, and I will drive you from your land and send you far away to die. [11]But the people of any nation that submits to the king of Babylon will be allowed to stay in their own country to farm the land as usual. I, the LORD, have spoken!'"

[12]Then I repeated this same message to King Zedekiah of Judah. "If you want to live, submit to the king of Babylon and his people," I said. [13]"Why do you insist on dying—you and your people? Why should you choose war, famine, and disease, which the LORD will bring against every nation that refuses to submit to Babylon's king? [14]Do not listen to the false prophets who keep telling you, 'The king of Babylon will not conquer you.' They are liars. [15]This is what the LORD says: I have not sent these prophets! They are telling you lies in my name, so I will drive you from this land. You will all die—you and all these prophets, too."

[16]Then I spoke to the priests and the people and said, "This is what the LORD says: Do not listen to your prophets who claim that soon the gold utensils taken from my Temple will be returned from Babylon. It is all a lie! [17]Do not listen to them. Surrender to the king of Babylon, and you will live. Why should this whole city be destroyed? [18]If they really are the LORD's prophets, let them pray to the LORD Almighty about the gold utensils that are still left in the LORD's Temple and in the king's palace and in the palaces of Jerusalem. Let them pray that these remaining articles will not be carried away with you to Babylon!

[19]"For this is what the LORD Almighty says about the bronze pillars in front of the

26:18 Mic 3:12.   27:1 As in some Hebrew manuscripts and Syriac version (see also 27:3, 12); most Hebrew manuscripts read *Jehoiakim*.

Temple, the bronze Sea in the Temple court-yard, the bronze water carts, and all the other ceremonial articles. [20]King Nebuchadnezzar of Babylon left them here when he exiled Jehoiachin* son of Jehoiakim, king of Judah, to Babylon, along with all the other important people of Judah and Jerusalem. [21]Yes, this is what the LORD Almighty, the God of Israel, says about the precious things kept in the Temple and in the palace of Judah's king: [22]They will all be carried away to Babylon and will stay there until I send for them, says the LORD. But someday I will bring them back to Jerusalem again."

CHAPTER 28

One day in late summer* of that same year—the fourth year of the reign of Zedekiah, king of Judah—Hananiah son of Azzur, a prophet from Gibeon, addressed me publicly in the Temple while all the priests and people listened. He said, [2]"The LORD Almighty, the God of Israel, says: I will remove the yoke of the king of Babylon from your necks. [3]Within two years, I will bring back all the Temple treasures that King Nebuchadnezzar carried off to Babylon. [4]And I will bring back Jehoiachin* son of Jehoiakim, king of Judah, and all the other captives that were taken to Babylon. I will surely break the yoke that the king of Babylon has put on your necks. I, the LORD, have spoken!"

[5]Jeremiah responded to Hananiah as they stood in front of all the priests and people at the Temple. [6]He said, "Amen! May your prophecies come true! I hope the LORD does everything you say. I hope the LORD does bring back from Babylon the treasures of this Temple and all our loved ones. [7]But listen now to the solemn words I speak to you in the presence of all these people. [8]The ancient prophets who preceded you and me spoke against many nations, always warning of war, famine, and disease. [9]So a prophet who predicts peace must carry the burden of proof. Only when his predictions come true can it be known that he is really from the LORD."

[10]Then Hananiah the prophet took the yoke off Jeremiah's neck and broke it. [11]And Hananiah said again to the crowd that had gathered, "The LORD has promised that within two years he will break the yoke of oppression from all the nations now subject to King Nebuchadnezzar of Babylon." At that, Jeremiah left the Temple area.

[12]Soon afterward the LORD gave this message to Jeremiah: [13]"Go and tell Hananiah, 'This is what the LORD says: You have broken a wooden yoke, but you have replaced it with a yoke of iron. [14]The LORD Almighty, the God of Israel, says: I have put a yoke of iron on the necks of all these nations, forcing them into slavery under King Nebuchadnezzar of Babylon. I have put everything, even the wild animals, under his control.'"

[15]Then Jeremiah the prophet said to Hananiah, "Listen, Hananiah! The LORD has not sent you, but the people believe your lies. [16]Therefore, the LORD says you must die. Your life will end this very year because you have rebelled against the LORD."

[17]Two months later,* Hananiah died.

CHAPTER 29

Jeremiah wrote a letter from Jerusalem to the elders, priests, prophets, and all the people who had been exiled to Babylon by King Nebuchadnezzar. [2]This was after King Jehoiachin,* the queen mother, the court officials, the leaders of Judah, and all the craftsmen had been deported from Jerusalem. [3]He sent the letter with Elasah son of Shaphan and Gemariah son of Hilkiah, when they went to Babylon as King Zedekiah's ambassadors to Nebuchadnezzar. This is what Jeremiah's letter said:

[4]The LORD Almighty, the God of Israel, sends this message to all the captives he has exiled to Babylon from Jerusalem: [5]"Build homes, and plan to stay. Plant gardens, and eat the food you produce. [6]Marry, and have children. Then find spouses for them, and have many grandchildren. Multiply! Do not dwindle away! [7]And work for the peace and prosperity of Babylon. Pray to the LORD for that city where you are held captive, for if Babylon has peace, so will you."

[8]The LORD Almighty, the God of Israel, says, "Do not let the prophets and mediums who are there in Babylon

27:20 Hebrew *Jeconiah*, a variant name for Jehoiachin.   28:1 Hebrew *In the fifth month*, of the Hebrew calendar. This month in the fourth year of Zedekiah's reign occurred in August and September 593 B.C. Also see note on 1:3.   28:4 Hebrew *Jeconiah*, a variant name for Jehoiachin.   28:17 Hebrew *In the seventh month of that same year*. See 28:1 and the note there.   29:2 Hebrew *Jeconiah*, a variant name for Jehoiachin.

trick you. Do not listen to their dreams [9]because they prophesy lies in my name. I have not sent them," says the LORD. [10]"The truth is that you will be in Babylon for seventy years. But then I will come and do for you all the good things I have promised, and I will bring you home again. [11]For I know the plans I have for you," says the LORD. "They are plans for good and not for disaster, to give you a future and a hope. [12]In those days when you pray, I will listen. [13]If you look for me in earnest, you will find me when you seek me. [14]I will be found by you," says the LORD. "I will end your captivity and restore your fortunes. I will gather you out of the nations where I sent you and bring you home again to your own land."

[15]You may claim that the LORD has raised up prophets for you in Babylon. [16]But this is what the LORD says about the king who sits on David's throne and all those still living here in Jerusalem—your relatives who were not exiled to Babylon. [17]This is what the LORD Almighty says: "I will send war, famine, and disease upon them and make them like rotting figs—too bad to eat. [18]Yes, I will pursue them with war, famine, and disease, and I will scatter them around the world. In every nation where I send them, I will make them an object of damnation, horror, contempt, and mockery. [19]For they refuse to listen to me, though I have spoken to them repeatedly through my prophets. And you who are in exile have not listened either," says the LORD.

[20]Therefore, listen to this message from the LORD, all you captives there in Babylon. [21]This is what the LORD Almighty, the God of Israel, says about your prophets—Ahab son of Kolaiah and Zedekiah son of Maaseiah—who are telling you lies in my name: "I will turn them over to Nebuchadnezzar* for

a public execution. [22]Their terrible fate will become proverbial, so that whenever the Judean exiles want to curse someone they will say, 'May the LORD make you like Zedekiah and Ahab, whom the king of Babylon burned alive!' [23]For these men have done terrible things among my people. They have committed adultery with their neighbors' wives and have lied in my name. I am a witness to this," says the LORD.

[24]The LORD sent this message to Shemaiah the Nehelamite in Babylon: [25]"This is what the LORD Almighty, the God of Israel, says: You wrote a letter on your own authority to Zephaniah son of Maaseiah, the priest, and you sent copies to the other priests and people in Jerusalem. You said to Zephaniah, [26]'The LORD has appointed you to replace Jehoiada as the priest in charge of the house of the LORD. You are responsible to put anyone who claims to be a prophet in the stocks and neck irons. [27]So why have you done nothing to stop Jeremiah from Anathoth, who pretends to be a prophet among you? [28]Jeremiah sent a letter here to Babylon, predicting that our captivity will be a long one. He said we should build homes and plan to stay for many years. He said we should plant fruit trees, because we will be here to eat the fruit for many years to come.'"

[29]But when Zephaniah the priest received Shemaiah's letter, he took it to Jeremiah and read it to him. [30]Then the LORD gave this message to Jeremiah: [31]"Send an open letter to all the exiles in Babylon. Tell them, 'This is what the LORD says concerning Shemaiah the Nehelamite: Since he has prophesied to you when I did not send him and has tricked you into believing his lies, [32]I will punish him and his family. None of his descendants will see the good things I will do for my people, for he has taught you to rebel against me. I, the LORD, have spoken!'"

29:21 Hebrew *Nebuchadrezzar,* a variant name for Nebuchadnezzar.

AUGUST 7 ☐ DAY 220
The Death That Brings Life

LOOK BACK Ironically, the good news that brings peace begins with bad news that brings brutality. The word picture you read in Isaiah 53 includes a graphic depiction of the Suffering Servant and his violent death at the hands of wicked men. He was "despised . . . rejected . . . wounded . . . crushed . . . oppressed . . . led as a lamb to the slaughter" (53:3-8). But far from being a tragic accident of history, his death "was the LORD's good plan" (53:10) because he "bore the sins of many and interceded for sinners" (53:12). Like water to a thirsty pilgrim and healing to a broken heart, this glorious news needs to be made known to the nations, and that's where the people of God come in!

But often, God's people feel totally inadequate for the assignment—like Jeremiah, whose tender spirit and frequent tears make him an unlikely candidate for the demanding role of prophet and proclaimer. For every excuse Jeremiah can raise, God has a faith-building vision of what can happen through an obedient servant, even in the face of false accusations and death threats.

LOOK UP Have you discovered the liberating truth of God's patient promises?

As early as Genesis 3:15, God promised that one day the offspring of the woman would crush the head of the serpent—the Messiah would come to deal Satan a crushing blow and provide the bridge between sinful humanity and holy God. The promise was sure, but the wait would last thousands of years!

Patience is a tree whose root is bitter but whose fruit is very sweet.

Isaiah painted a prophetic portrait of the Suffering Servant hundreds of years before the birth of Christ. Crucifixion was unknown in Isaiah's day, yet he described the brutal procedure in minute detail. With unerring accuracy, Isaiah foretold details of Jesus' death as if he were at Calvary gazing upon the very scene.

Centuries later—right on schedule—it all came true just as Isaiah had predicted. With each passing year, the promise moved closer and closer to fulfillment, until at long last, "when the right time came, God sent his Son" (Galatians 4:4).

LOOK AHEAD Waiting for the fulfillment of a promise can be as exasperating as waiting for Christmas to come. Time can seem to "stand still" when something you long for is long awaited. But those with the patient endurance to keep their eyes on the prize will one day discover it was all well worth the wait.

When you read "this is what the LORD says" in the pages of his Word, mark it down—it will come to pass! And when the time is right, you won't have to wonder or wait. Pick a promise from the list below, and lay it alongside Isaiah 60:22: "I, the LORD, will bring it all to pass at the right time." Then wait with patient expectation, for in due season you will reap if you don't faint!

- "I am going to prepare a place for you. . . . I will come and get you" (John 14:2-3).
- "I will not abandon you as orphans—I will come to you" (John 14:18).
- "God will bring back with Jesus all the Christians who have died. . . . So comfort and encourage each other with these words" (1 Thessalonians 4:14, 18).

AUGUST 8 ☐ DAY 221
JEREMIAH 30–33
Hope amidst Judgment

OVERVIEW It's always darkest just before the dawn, and Jeremiah's prophecy is no exception. The opening lines of chapter 30 paint the blackest picture yet of Israel's coming calamity. The pinnacle of the nation's age-long sufferings will be a unique period of tribulation. But the bleakness of judgment will give way to the glory of restoration and blessing. The people will be replanted in their homeland (31:4-6, 8), their mourning will be turned to joy (31:13), and God will make a new covenant with them (31:31-34). As a sign of his confidence in the promises of God, Jeremiah buys a field—knowing full well it will soon fall into Babylonian hands.

Chapter 30	Chapter 31	Chapter 32	Chapter 33
Judah's Protection	Judah's Promotion	Jeremiah's Purchase	The Lord's Promise
Calamity	Covenant	Confidence	

YOUR DAILY WALK Are you building your life on God's promises or merely building a file full of them? One ambitious soul has counted all the promises contained in the Bible. How many do you suppose he found?

The possibilities of prayer run parallel with the promises of God.

There are, in fact, more than seven thousand promises buried in the Bible, most of which are targeted for you! But once you find a promise, don't just write it down, memorize it, or file it away. Claim it. Act upon it. Let it change your life.

Jeremiah received a promise from God. His nation, though faced with the prospect of being swept away by a Babylonian tidal wave, would not be annihilated. God would bring them back. So Jeremiah bought real estate at a rock-bottom price as if to declare to his nation, "I'm standing on the promises of God! He will restore us!"

Pick a promise from God that you may have read, filed away, and maybe even memorized—but never claimed. Now act upon it!

INSIGHT A Mother's Tears
Rachel, the mother of Joseph and Benjamin, is pictured weeping for her sons, signifying the attempt that was made to destroy the messianic line (31:15). Many years later other women of Ramah would weep as Herod slaughtered their children in an attempt to kill the promised Messiah (Matthew 2:16-18), a fulfillment of Jeremiah's prophecy.

CHAPTER 30
The LORD gave another message to Jeremiah. He said, ²"This is what the LORD, the God of Israel, says: Write down for the record everything I have said to you, Jeremiah. ³For the time is coming when I will restore the fortunes of my people of Israel and Judah. I will bring them home to this land that I gave to their ancestors, and they will possess it and live here again. I, the LORD, have spoken!"

⁴This is the message the LORD gave concerning Israel and Judah: ⁵"This is what the LORD says: I have heard the people crying; there is only fear and trembling. ⁶Now let me ask you a question: Do men give birth to babies? Then why do they stand there, ashen-faced, hands pressed against their sides like women about to give birth? ⁷In all history there has never been such a time of terror. It will be a time of trouble for my people Israel.* Yet in the end, they will be saved!

⁸"For in that day, says the LORD Al-

30:7 Hebrew *Jacob;* also in 30:10b.

mighty, I will break the yoke from their necks and snap their chains. Foreigners will no longer be their masters. [9]For my people will serve the LORD their God and David their king, whom I will raise up for them.

[10]"So do not be afraid, Jacob, my servant; do not be dismayed, Israel, says the LORD. For I will bring you home again from distant lands, and your children will return from their exile. Israel will return and will have peace and quiet in their own land, and no one will make them afraid. [11]For I am with you and will save you, says the LORD. I will completely destroy the nations where I have scattered you, but I will not destroy you. But I must discipline you; I cannot let you go unpunished.

[12]"This is what the LORD says: Yours is an incurable bruise, a terrible wound. [13]There is no one to help you or bind up your injury. You are beyond the help of any medicine. [14]All your allies have left you and do not care about you anymore. I have wounded you cruelly, as though I were your enemy. For your sins are many, and your guilt is great. [15]Why do you protest your punishment—this wound that has no cure? I have had to punish you because your sins are many and your guilt is great.

[16]"But in that coming day, all who destroy you will be destroyed, and all your enemies will be sent into exile. Those who plunder you will be plundered, and those who attack you will be attacked. [17]I will give you back your health and heal your wounds, says the LORD.

"Now you are called an outcast—'Jerusalem* for whom nobody cares.' [18]But the LORD says this: When I bring you home again from your captivity and restore your fortunes, Jerusalem will be rebuilt on her ruins. The palace will be reconstructed as it was before. [19]There will be joy and songs of thanksgiving, and I will multiply my people and make of them a great and honored nation. [20]Their children will prosper as they did long ago. I will establish them as a nation before me, and I will punish anyone who hurts them. [21]They will have their own ruler again, and he will not be a foreigner. I will invite him to approach me, says the LORD, for who would dare to come unless invited? [22]You will be my people, and I will be your God."

[23]Look! The LORD's anger bursts out like a storm, a driving wind that swirls down on the heads of the wicked. [24]The fierce anger of the LORD will not diminish until it has finished all his plans. In the days to come, you will understand all this.

CHAPTER 31

"In that day," says the LORD, "I will be the God of all the families of Israel, and they will be my people. [2]I will care for the survivors as they travel through the wilderness. I will again come to give rest to the people of Israel."

[3]Long ago the LORD said to Israel: "I have loved you, my people, with an everlasting love. With unfailing love I have drawn you to myself. [4]I will rebuild you, my virgin Israel. You will again be happy and dance merrily with tambourines. [5]Again you will plant your vineyards on the mountains of Samaria and eat from your own gardens there. [6]The day will come when watchmen will shout from the hill country of Ephraim, 'Come, let us go up to Jerusalem* to worship the LORD our God.'"

[7]Now this is what the LORD says: "Sing with joy for Israel*! Shout for the greatest of nations! Shout out with praise and joy: 'Save your people, O LORD, the remnant of Israel!' [8]For I will bring them from the north and from the distant corners of the earth. I will not forget the blind and lame, the expectant mothers and women about to give birth. A great company will return! [9]Tears of joy will stream down their faces, and I will lead them home with great care. They will walk beside quiet streams and not stumble. For I am Israel's father, and Ephraim is my oldest child.

[10]"Listen to this message from the LORD, you nations of the world; proclaim it in distant coastlands: The LORD, who scattered his people, will gather them together and watch over them as a shepherd does his flock. [11]For the LORD has redeemed Israel from those too strong for them. [12]They will come home and sing songs of joy on the heights of Jerusalem. They will be radiant because of the many gifts the LORD has given them—the good crops of wheat, wine, and oil, and the healthy flocks and herds. Their life will be like a watered garden, and all their sorrows will be gone. [13]The young women will dance for joy, and

30:17 Hebrew *Zion*.   31:6 Hebrew *Zion;* also in 31:12.   31:7 Hebrew *Jacob;* also in 31:11.

the men—old and young—will join in the celebration. I will turn their mourning into joy. I will comfort them and exchange their sorrow for rejoicing. [14]I will supply the priests with an abundance of offerings. I will satisfy my people with my bounty. I, the LORD, have spoken!"

[15]This is what the LORD says: "A cry of anguish is heard in Ramah—mourning and weeping unrestrained. Rachel weeps for her children, refusing to be comforted—for her children are dead."

[16]But now the LORD says, "Do not weep any longer, for I will reward you. Your children will come back to you from the distant land of the enemy. [17]There is hope for your future," says the LORD. "Your children will come again to their own land. [18]I have heard Israel* saying, 'You disciplined me severely, but I deserved it. I was like a calf that needed to be trained for the yoke and plow. Turn me again to you and restore me, for you alone are the LORD my God. [19]I turned away from God, but then I was sorry. I kicked myself for my stupidity! I was thoroughly ashamed of all I did in my younger days.'

[20]"Is not Israel still my son, my darling child?" asks the LORD. "I had to punish him, but I still love him. I long for him and surely will have mercy on him.

[21]"Set up road signs; put up guideposts. Mark well the path by which you came. Come back again, my virgin Israel; return to your cities here. [22]How long will you wander, my wayward daughter? For the LORD will cause something new and different to happen—Israel will embrace her God.*"

[23]This is what the LORD Almighty, the God of Israel, says: "When I bring them back again, the people of Judah and its cities will again say, 'The LORD bless you—O righteous home, O holy mountain!' [24]And city dwellers and farmers and shepherds alike will live together in peace and happiness. [25]For I have given rest to the weary and joy to the sorrowing."

[26]At this, I woke up and looked around. My sleep had been very sweet.

[27]"The time will come," says the LORD, "when I will greatly increase the population and multiply the number of cattle here in Israel and Judah. [28]In the past I uprooted and tore down this nation. I overthrew it,

destroyed it, and brought disaster upon it. But in the future I will plant it and build it up," says the LORD.

[29]"The people will no longer quote this proverb: 'The parents eat sour grapes, but their children's mouths pucker at the taste.' [30]All people will die for their own sins—those who eat the sour grapes will be the ones whose mouths will pucker.

[31]"The day will come," says the LORD, "when I will make a new covenant with the people of Israel and Judah. [32]This covenant will not be like the one I made with their ancestors when I took them by the hand and brought them out of the land of Egypt. They broke that covenant, though I loved them as a husband loves his wife," says the LORD.

[33]"But this is the new covenant I will make with the people of Israel on that day," says the LORD. "I will put my laws in their minds, and I will write them on their hearts. I will be their God, and they will be my people. [34]And they will not need to teach their neighbors, nor will they need to teach their family, saying, 'You should know the LORD.' For everyone, from the least to the greatest, will already know me," says the LORD. "And I will forgive their wickedness and will never again remember their sins."

[35]It is the LORD who provides the sun to light the day and the moon and stars to light the night. It is he who stirs the sea into roaring waves. His name is the LORD Almighty, and this is what he says: [36]"I am as likely to reject my people Israel as I am to do away with the laws of nature! [37]Just as the heavens cannot be measured and the foundation of the earth cannot be explored, so I will not consider casting them away forever for their sins. I, the LORD, have spoken!

[38]"The time is coming," says the LORD, "when all Jerusalem will be rebuilt for me, from the Tower of Hananel to the Corner Gate. [39]A measuring line will be stretched out over the hill of Gareb and across to Goah. [40]And the entire area—including the graveyard and ash dump in the valley, and all the fields out to the Kidron Valley on the east as far as the Horse Gate—will be holy to the LORD. The city will never again be captured or destroyed."

31:18 Hebrew *Ephraim*, referring to the northern kingdom of Israel; also in 31:20.   **31:22** Hebrew *a woman will court a suitor.*

CHAPTER 32

The following message came to Jeremiah from the LORD in the tenth year of the reign of Zedekiah,* king of Judah. This was also the eighteenth year of the reign of King Nebuchadnezzar.* ²Jerusalem was under siege from the Babylonian army, and Jeremiah was imprisoned in the courtyard of the guard in the royal palace. ³King Zedekiah had put him there because he continued to give this prophecy: "This is what the LORD says: I am about to hand this city over to the king of Babylon. ⁴King Zedekiah will be captured by the Babylonians* and taken to the king of Babylon to be judged and sentenced. ⁵I will take Zedekiah to Babylon and will deal with him there. If you fight against the Babylonians, you will never succeed."

⁶At that time the LORD sent me a message. He said, ⁷"Your cousin Hanamel son of Shallum will come and say to you, 'Buy my field at Anathoth. By law you have the right to buy it before it is offered to anyone else.'"

⁸Then, just as the LORD had said he would, Hanamel came and visited me in the prison. He said, "Buy my field at Anathoth in the land of Benjamin. By law you have the right to buy it before it is offered to anyone else, so buy it for yourself." Then I knew for sure that the message I had heard was from the LORD.

⁹So I bought the field at Anathoth, paying Hanamel seventeen pieces* of silver for it. ¹⁰I signed and sealed the deed of purchase before witnesses, weighed out the silver, and paid him. ¹¹Then I took the sealed deed and an unsealed copy of the deed, which contained the terms and conditions of the purchase, ¹²and I handed them to Baruch son of Neriah and grandson of Mahseiah. I did all this in the presence of my cousin Hanamel, the witnesses who had signed the deed, and all the men of Judah who were there.

¹³Then I said to Baruch as they all listened, ¹⁴"The LORD Almighty, the God of Israel, says: Take both this sealed deed and the unsealed copy, and put them into a pottery jar to preserve them for a long time. ¹⁵For the LORD Almighty, the God of Israel, says: Someday people will again own property here in this land and will buy and sell houses and vineyards and fields."

¹⁶Then after I had given the papers to Baruch, I prayed to the LORD: ¹⁷"O Sovereign LORD! You have made the heavens and earth by your great power. Nothing is too hard for you! ¹⁸You are loving and kind to thousands, though children suffer for their parents' sins. You are the great and powerful God, the LORD Almighty. ¹⁹You have all wisdom and do great and mighty miracles. You are very aware of the conduct of all people, and you reward them according to their deeds. ²⁰You performed miraculous signs and wonders in the land of Egypt—things still remembered to this day! And you have continued to do great miracles in Israel and all around the world. You have made your name very great, as it is today.

²¹"You brought Israel out of Egypt with mighty signs and wonders, with great power and overwhelming terror. ²²You gave the people of Israel this land that you had promised their ancestors long before—a land flowing with milk and honey. ²³Our ancestors came and conquered it and lived in it, but they refused to obey you or follow your law. They have hardly done one thing you told them to! That is why you have sent this terrible disaster upon them.

²⁴"See how the siege ramps have been built against the city walls! Because of war, famine, and disease, the city has been handed over to the Babylonians, who will conquer it. Everything has happened just as you said it would. ²⁵And yet, O Sovereign LORD, you have told me to buy the field—paying good money for it before these witnesses—even though the city will soon belong to the Babylonians."

²⁶Then this message came to Jeremiah from the LORD: ²⁷"I am the LORD, the God of all the peoples of the world. Is anything too hard for me? ²⁸I will hand this city over to the Babylonians and to Nebuchadnezzar, king of Babylon, and he will capture it. ²⁹The Babylonians outside the walls will come in and set fire to the city. They will burn down all these houses, where the people caused my fury to rise by offering incense to Baal on the rooftops and by pouring out drink offerings to other gods. ³⁰Israel and Judah have done nothing but wrong since their earliest days. They have infuriated me with all their evil deeds," says the LORD. ³¹"From the time this city was built until now, it has done

32:1a The tenth year of Zedekiah's reign and the eighteenth year of Nebuchadnezzar's reign was 587 B.C.   32:1b Hebrew *Nebuchadrezzar*, a variant name for Nebuchadnezzar; also in 32:28.   32:4 Or *Chaldeans*; also in 32:5, 24, 25, 28, 29, 43.
32:9 Hebrew 17 *shekels*, about 7 ounces or 194 grams in weight.

nothing but anger me, so I am determined to get rid of it.

[32] "The sins of Israel and Judah—the sins of the people of Jerusalem, the kings, the officials, the priests, and the prophets—stir up my anger. [33] My people have turned their backs on me and have refused to return. Day after day, year after year, I taught them right from wrong, but they would not listen or obey. [34] They have set up their abominable idols right in my own Temple, defiling it. [35] They have built pagan shrines to Baal in the valley of the son of Hinnom, and there they sacrifice their sons and daughters to Molech. I have never commanded such a horrible deed; it never even crossed my mind to command such a thing. What an incredible evil, causing Judah to sin so greatly!

[36] "Now I want to say something more about this city. You have been saying, 'It will fall to the king of Babylon through war, famine, and disease.' But this is what the LORD, the God of Israel, says: [37] I will surely bring my people back again from all the countries where I will scatter them in my fury. I will bring them back to this very city and let them live in peace and safety. [38] They will be my people, and I will be their God. [39] And I will give them one heart and mind to worship me forever, for their own good and for the good of all their descendants.

[40] "And I will make an everlasting covenant with them, promising not to stop doing good for them. I will put a desire in their hearts to worship me, and they will never leave me. [41] I will rejoice in doing good to them and will faithfully and wholeheartedly replant them in this land. [42] Just as I have sent all these calamities upon them, so I will do all the good I have promised them. I, the LORD, have spoken!

[43] "Fields will again be bought and sold in this land about which you now say, 'It has been ravaged by the Babylonians, a land where people and animals have all disappeared.' [44] Yes, fields will once again be bought and sold—deeds signed and sealed and witnessed—in the land of Benjamin and here in Jerusalem, in the towns of Judah and in the hill country, in the foothills of Judah* and in the Negev, too. For someday I will restore prosperity to them. I, the LORD, have spoken!"

CHAPTER 33

While Jeremiah was still confined in the courtyard of the guard, the LORD gave him this second message: [2] "The LORD, the Maker of the heavens and earth—the LORD is his name—says this: [3] Ask me and I will tell you some remarkable secrets about what is going to happen here. [4] For this is what the LORD, the God of Israel, says: Though you have torn down the houses of this city and even the king's palace to get materials to strengthen the walls against the siege weapons of the enemy, [5] the Babylonians* will still enter. The men of this city are already as good as dead, for I have determined to destroy them in my terrible anger. I have abandoned them because of all their wickedness.

[6] "Nevertheless, the time will come when I will heal Jerusalem's damage and give her prosperity and peace. [7] I will restore the fortunes of Judah and Israel and rebuild their cities. [8] I will cleanse away their sins against me, and I will forgive all their sins of rebellion. [9] Then this city will bring me joy, glory, and honor before all the nations of the earth! The people of the world will see the good I do for my people and will tremble with awe!

[10] "This is what the LORD says: You say, 'This land has been ravaged, and the people and animals have all disappeared.' Yet in the empty streets of Jerusalem and Judah's other towns, there will be heard once more [11] the sounds of joy and laughter. The joyful voices of bridegrooms and brides will be heard again, along with the joyous songs of people bringing thanksgiving offerings to the LORD. They will sing,

'Give thanks to the LORD Almighty,
    for the LORD is good.
    His faithful love endures forever!'

For I will restore the prosperity of this land to what it was in the past, says the LORD.

[12] "This is what the LORD Almighty says: This land—though it is now desolate and the people and animals have all disappeared—will once more see shepherds leading sheep and lambs. [13] Once again their flocks will prosper in the towns of the hill country, the foothills of Judah,* the Negev, the land of Benjamin, the vicinity of Jerusalem, and all the towns of Judah. I, the LORD, have spoken!

¹⁴"The day will come, says the LORD, when I will do for Israel and Judah all the good I have promised them. ¹⁵At that time I will bring to the throne of David a righteous descendant,* and he will do what is just and right throughout the land. ¹⁶In that day Judah will be saved, and Jerusalem will live in safety. And their motto will be 'The LORD is our righteousness!' ¹⁷For this is what the LORD says: David will forever have a descendant sitting on the throne of Israel. ¹⁸And there will always be Levitical priests to offer burnt offerings and grain offerings and sacrifices to me."

¹⁹Then this message came to Jeremiah from the LORD: ²⁰"If you can break my covenant with the day and the night so that they do not come on their usual schedule, ²¹only then will my covenant with David, my servant, be broken. Only then will he no longer have a descendant to reign on his throne. The same is true for my covenant with the Levitical priests who minister before me. ²²And as the stars cannot be counted and the sand on the seashores cannot be measured, so I will multiply the descendants of David, my servant, and the Levites who minister before me."

²³The LORD gave another message to Jeremiah. He said, ²⁴"Have you heard what people are saying?—'The LORD chose Judah and Israel and then abandoned them!' They are sneering and saying that Israel is not worthy to be counted as a nation. ²⁵But this is the LORD's reply: I would no more reject my people than I would change my laws of night and day, of earth and sky. ²⁶I will never abandon the descendants of Jacob or David, my servant, or change the plan that David's descendants will rule the descendants of Abraham, Isaac, and Jacob. Instead, I will restore them to their land and have mercy on them."

33:15 Hebrew *a righteous Branch.*

AUGUST 9 ☐ DAY 222
JEREMIAH 34–36
Before the Fall of Jerusalem

 OVERVIEW With the close of chapter 33, Jeremiah completes the written account of his preaching ministry to the rebellious nation. Throughout the rest of the book, the prophet emphasizes his personal experiences during the nation's last days. Three events point out the advanced state of Judah's decline: the broken covenant under Zedekiah, the contrasting faithfulness of the Recabite family, and the utter rebellion of Jehoiakim in burning the scroll of the Lord.

Chapter 34	Chapter 35	Chapter 36
A Nation's Treachery	A Family's Testimony	A King's Tyranny
Rebuke	Righteousness	Rebellion

 YOUR DAILY WALK The next time you read your Bible, try this exercise. Whenever you come to a passage that points out your sin or tells you what you ought to do, tear out that page and burn it!

Ridiculous? Of course. No one today would do to God's Word what Jehoiakim did to Jeremiah's scroll . . . or would they?

Have you ever read a command in God's Word you didn't like and just ignored it and kept on reading? That's a sure way to save on expensive Bibles—while accomplishing the same spiritual damage as the knife-wielding king Jehoiakim.

If your study of God's Word does not change the way you live, either you are already perfect or not studying correctly.

How should you read the Bible? The key is a responsive heart. God wants his Word to change your life as it convicts you of sin and instructs you in righteousness. Ignoring God's commands is dangerous business. In fact, it would be better not to know them at all than to know them and then not obey.

Is there a specific command from Scripture you have been avoiding? Jehoiakim learned the hard way that you cannot alter God's truth by ignoring it. Confess your sin of omission to God (James 4:17), and like the servants in John 2:5, make a fresh commitment to obedience. "Do whatever he tells you."

 INSIGHT God's Commendation of a Nonconformist Family
The Recabites made the nomadic way of life and abstinence from drink a religious obligation (Jeremiah 35). God commended them, not for their rules, but for their faithfulness to those rules—a striking contrast to Judah's infidelity.

CHAPTER 34

King Nebuchadnezzar of Babylon came with all the armies from the kingdoms he ruled, and he fought against Jerusalem and the towns of Judah. At that time this message came to Jeremiah from the LORD: ²"Go to King Zedekiah of Judah, and tell him, 'This is what the LORD, the God of Israel, says: I am about to hand this city over to the king of Babylon, and he will burn it. ³You will not escape his grasp but will be taken into captivity. You will stand before the king of Babylon to be judged and sentenced. Then you will be exiled to Babylon.'

⁴"But listen to this promise from the LORD, O Zedekiah, king of Judah. This is what the LORD says: 'You will not be killed in war ⁵but will die peacefully among your people. They will burn incense in your memory, just as they did for your ancestors. They will weep for you and say, "Alas, our king is dead!" This I have decreed, says the LORD.'"

⁶So Jeremiah the prophet delivered the message to King Zedekiah of Judah. ⁷At this time the Babylonian army was besieging Jerusalem, Lachish, and Azekah—the only cities of Judah with their walls still standing.

⁸This message came to Jeremiah from the LORD after King Zedekiah made a covenant with the people, proclaiming freedom for the slaves. ⁹He had ordered all the people to free their Hebrew slaves—both men and women. No one was to keep a fellow Judean in bondage. ¹⁰The officials and all the people had obeyed the king's command, ¹¹but later they changed their minds. They took back the people they had freed, making them slaves again.

¹²So the LORD gave them this message through Jeremiah: ¹³"This is what the LORD, the God of Israel, says: I made a covenant with your ancestors long ago when I rescued them from their slavery in Egypt. ¹⁴I told them that every Hebrew slave must be freed after serving six years. But this was never done. ¹⁵Recently you repented and did what was right, following my command. You freed your slaves and made a solemn covenant with me in my Temple. ¹⁶But now you have shrugged off your oath and defiled my name by taking back the men and women you had freed, making them slaves once again.

¹⁷"Therefore, this is what the LORD says: Since you have not obeyed me by setting your countrymen free, I will set you free to be destroyed by war, famine, and disease. You will be considered a disgrace by all the nations of the earth. ¹⁸Because you have refused the terms of our covenant, I will cut you apart just as you cut apart the calf when you walked between its halves to solemnize your vows. ¹⁹Yes, I will cut you apart, whether you are officials of Judah or Jerusalem, court officials, priests, or common people—for you have broken your oath. ²⁰I will give you to your enemies, and they will kill you. Your bodies will be food for the vultures and wild animals. ²¹I will hand over King Zedekiah of Judah and his officials to the army of the king of Babylon. And though Babylon's king has left this city for a while, ²²I will call the Babylonian armies back again. They will fight against this city and will capture and burn it. I will see to it that all the towns of Judah are destroyed and left completely empty."

CHAPTER 35

This is the message the LORD gave Jeremiah when Jehoiakim son of Josiah was king of Judah: ²"Go to the settlement where the families of the Recabites live, and invite them to the LORD's Temple. Take them into one of the inner rooms, and offer them some wine."

³So I went to see Jaazaniah son of Jeremiah and grandson of Habazziniah and all his brothers and sons—representing all the Recabite families. ⁴I took them to the Temple, and we went into the room assigned to the sons of Hanan son of Igdaliah, a man of God. This room was located next to the one used by the palace officials, directly above the room of Maaseiah son of Shallum, the Temple gatekeeper.

⁵I set cups and jugs of wine before them and invited them to have a drink, ⁶but they refused. "No," they said. "We don't drink wine, because Jehonadab* son of Recab, our ancestor, gave us this command: 'You and your descendants must never drink wine. ⁷And do not build houses or plant crops or vineyards, but always live in tents. If you follow these commands, you will live long, good lives in the land.' ⁸So we have obeyed him in all these things. We have never had a drink of wine since then, nor have our wives, our sons, or our daughters. ⁹We haven't built houses or owned vineyards or farms or planted crops. ¹⁰We have lived in tents and have fully obeyed all the commands of Jehonadab, our ancestor. ¹¹But when King Nebuchadnezzar* of Babylon arrived in this country, we were afraid of the Babylonian* and Aramean armies. So we decided to move to Jerusalem. That is why we are here."

¹²Then the LORD gave this message to Jeremiah: ¹³"The LORD Almighty, the God of Israel, says: Go and say to the people in Judah and Jerusalem, 'Come and learn a lesson about how to obey me. ¹⁴The Recabites do not drink wine because their ancestor Jehonadab told them not to. But I have spoken to you again and again, and you refuse to listen or obey. ¹⁵I have sent you prophet after prophet to tell you to turn from your wicked ways and to stop worshiping other gods, so that you might live in peace here in the land I gave to you and your ancestors. But you would not listen to me or obey. ¹⁶The families of Recab have obeyed their ancestor completely, but you have refused to listen to me.'

¹⁷"Therefore, the LORD God Almighty, the God of Israel, says: Because you refuse to listen or answer when I call, I will send upon Judah and Jerusalem all the disasters I have threatened."

¹⁸Then Jeremiah turned to the Recabites and said, "This is what the LORD Almighty, the God of Israel, says: You have obeyed your ancestor Jehonadab in every respect, following all his instructions. ¹⁹Because of this, Jehonadab son of Recab will always have descendants who serve me. I, the LORD Almighty, the God of Israel, have spoken!"

CHAPTER 36

During the fourth year that Jehoiakim son of Josiah was king in Judah,* the LORD gave this message to Jeremiah: ²"Get a scroll, and write down all my messages against Israel, Judah, and the other nations. Begin with the first message back in the days of Josiah, and write down every message you have given, right up to the present time. ³Perhaps the people of Judah will repent if they see in writing all the terrible things I have planned for them. Then I will be able to forgive their sins and wrongdoings."

⁴So Jeremiah sent for Baruch son of Neriah, and as Jeremiah dictated, Baruch wrote down all the prophecies that the LORD had given him. ⁵Then Jeremiah said to Baruch, "I am a prisoner here and unable to go to the Temple. ⁶So you go to the Temple on the next day of fasting, and read the messages from the LORD that are on this scroll. On that day people will be there from all over Judah. ⁷Perhaps even yet they will turn from their evil ways and ask the LORD's forgiveness before it is too late. For the LORD's terrible anger has been pronounced against them."

⁸Baruch did as Jeremiah told him and read these messages from the LORD to the people at the Temple. ⁹This happened on the day of sacred fasting held in late autumn,* during the fifth year of the reign of Jehoiakim son of Josiah. People from all over Judah came to attend the services at the Temple on that day. ¹⁰Baruch read Jeremiah's words to all the people from the Temple room of Gemariah son of Shaphan. This room was just off the

35:6 Hebrew *Jonadab*, a variant name for Jehonadab; also in 35:10, 14, 18, 19. See 2 Kgs 10:15.   **35:11a** Hebrew *Nebuchadrezzar*, a variant name for Nebuchadnezzar.   **35:11b** Or *Chaldean*.   **36:1** The fourth year of Jehoiakim's reign was 605 B.C.   **36:9** Hebrew *in the ninth month*, of the Hebrew calendar (also in 36:22). This month in the fifth year of Jehoiakim's reign occurred in November and December 604 B.C. Also see note on 1:3.

upper courtyard of the Temple, near the New Gate entrance.

[11] When Micaiah son of Gemariah and grandson of Shaphan heard the messages from the LORD, [12] he went down to the secretary's room in the palace where the administrative officials were meeting. Elishama the secretary was there, along with Delaiah son of Shemaiah, Elnathan son of Acbor, Gemariah son of Shaphan, Zedekiah son of Hananiah, and all the others with official responsibilities. [13] When Micaiah told them about the messages Baruch was reading to the people, [14] the officials sent Jehudi son of Nethaniah, grandson of Shelemiah, and great-grandson of Cushi, to ask Baruch to come and read the messages to them, too. So Baruch took the scroll and went to them. [15] "Sit down and read the scroll to us," the officials said, and Baruch did as they requested.

[16] By the time Baruch had finished reading, they were badly frightened. "We must tell the king what we have heard," they said. [17] "But first, tell us how you got these messages. Did they come directly from Jeremiah?"

[18] So Baruch explained, "Jeremiah dictated them to me word by word, and I wrote down his words with ink on this scroll."

[19] "You and Jeremiah should both hide," the officials told Baruch. "Don't tell anyone where you are!" [20] Then the officials left the scroll for safekeeping in the room of Elishama the secretary and went to tell the king.

[21] The king sent Jehudi to get the scroll. Jehudi brought it from Elishama's room and read it to the king as all his officials stood by. [22] It was late autumn, and the king was in a winterized part of the palace, sitting in front of a fire to keep warm. [23] Whenever Jehudi finished reading three or four columns, the king took his knife and cut off that section of the scroll. He then threw it into the fire, section by section, until the whole scroll was burned up. [24] Neither the king nor his officials showed any signs of fear or repentance at what they heard. [25] Even when Elnathan, Delaiah, and Gemariah begged the king not to burn the scroll, he wouldn't listen.

[26] Then the king commanded his son Jerahmeel, Seraiah son of Azriel, and Shelemiah son of Abdeel to arrest Baruch and Jeremiah. But the LORD had hidden them.

[27] After the king had burned Jeremiah's scroll, the LORD gave Jeremiah another message. He said, [28] "Get another scroll, and write everything again just as you did on the scroll King Jehoiakim burned. [29] Then say to the king, 'This is what the LORD says: You burned the scroll because it said the king of Babylon would destroy this land and everything in it. [30] Now this is what the LORD says about King Jehoiakim of Judah: He will have no heirs to sit on the throne of David. His dead body will be thrown out to lie unburied—exposed to hot days and frosty nights. [31] I will punish him and his family and his officials because of their sins. I will pour out on them and on all the people of Judah and Jerusalem all the disasters I have promised, for they would not listen to my warnings.'"

[32] Then Jeremiah took another scroll and dictated again to his secretary Baruch. He wrote everything that had been on the scroll King Jehoiakim had burned in the fire. Only this time, he added much more!

AUGUST 10 ☐ DAY 223
JEREMIAH 37–39
During the Fall of Jerusalem

OVERVIEW Jeremiah endures his worst persecution during the nation's last desperate days in the Babylonian siege. First, he is arrested on suspicion of treason. Next, his enemies conspire to throw him into a muddy cistern to die. Rescued at the last minute by order of King Zedekiah, Jeremiah offers yet again his familiar advice: "Surrender!" The king refuses, sealing the destruction of Jerusalem. All the horrors Jeremiah has so long predicted are now fully carried out by the merciless Babylonians, but Jeremiah himself is spared.

Chapter 37	Chapter 38	Chapter 39
Jeremiah's Arrest	Jeremiah's Abandonment	Judah's Annihilation
The King's Fearfulness		The King's Fate

Faith, like a muscle, grows by stretching.

YOUR DAILY WALK Have you ever received the pessimistic advice, "Cheer up, things could be worse"? So you cheered up, and sure enough, things got worse! Jeremiah could identify with your experience. No sooner had he left the prison court of King Zedekiah than he was thrown into the dungeon pit—from the frying pan into the mire, so to speak. He no doubt prayed things would get better, but instead they got "badder." Yet Jeremiah never wavered in his commitment to God or in his calling to preach an unpopular message. How was that possible?

Jeremiah's faith never wavered because his focus never wandered. Imprisonment and intimidation could not take his eyes off his Sovereign. With his gaze firmly fixed on God, Jeremiah could fearlessly proclaim God's message, trusting him to take care of the consequences.

In the midst of trials and discouragements, it's more important than ever to check your focus. Are you looking at your problem or your Problem Solver? Read Romans 8:37 right now, and underline the word *through*. Remember, it's not above or around all things, but *through* all things that we are more than conquerors through him who loved us.

INSIGHT The Obscure Man Who Made a Difference
It was not a Jew but an Ethiopian eunuch who persuaded the king to rescue Jeremiah from sure death in the cistern. For his faithfulness, Ebed-melech was promised personal safety during Jerusalem's fall and received an eternal memorial in God's Word (38:7-13).

CHAPTER 37

Zedekiah son of Josiah succeeded Jehoiachin* son of Jehoiakim as the king of Judah. He was appointed by King Nebuchadnezzar* of Babylon. ²But neither King Zedekiah nor his officials nor the people who were left in the land listened to what the LORD said through Jeremiah. ³Nevertheless, King Zedekiah sent Jehucal son of Shelemiah and Zephaniah the priest, son of Maaseiah, to ask Jeremiah, "Please pray to the LORD our God for us." ⁴Jeremiah had not yet been imprisoned, so he could come and go as he pleased.

⁵At this time the army of Pharaoh Hophra* of Egypt appeared at the southern border of Judah. When the Babylonian* army heard about it, they withdrew from their siege of Jerusalem. ⁶Then the LORD gave this message to Jeremiah: ⁷"This is what the LORD, the God of Israel, says: Tell the king of Judah, who sent you to ask me what is going to happen, that Pharaoh's army is about to return to Egypt, though he came here to help you. ⁸Then the Babyloni-

ans* will come back and capture this city and burn it to the ground. ⁹The LORD says: Do not fool yourselves that the Babylonians are gone for good. They aren't! ¹⁰Even if you were to destroy the entire Babylonian army, leaving only a handful of wounded survivors, they would still stagger from their tents and burn this city to the ground!"

¹¹When the Babylonian army left Jerusalem because of Pharaoh's approaching army, ¹²Jeremiah started to leave the city on his way to the land of Benjamin, to see the property he had bought. ¹³But as he was walking through the Benjamin Gate, a sentry arrested him and said, "You are defecting to the Babylonians!" The sentry making the arrest was Irijah son of Shelemiah and grandson of Hananiah.

¹⁴"That's not true!" Jeremiah protested. "I had no intention of doing any such thing." But Irijah wouldn't listen, and he took Jeremiah before the officials. ¹⁵They were furious with Jeremiah and had him flogged and imprisoned in the house of

37:1a Hebrew *Coniah*, a variant name for Jehoiachin.   **37:1b** Hebrew *Nebuchadrezzar*, a variant name for Nebuchadnezzar.
37:5a Hebrew *army of Pharaoh*; see 44:30.   **37:5b** Or *Chaldean*; also in 37:10, 11.   **37:8** Or *Chaldeans*; also in 37:9, 13.

Jonathan the secretary. Jonathan's house had been converted into a prison. [16]Jeremiah was put into a dungeon cell, where he remained for many days.

[17]Later King Zedekiah secretly requested that Jeremiah come to the palace, where the king asked him, "Do you have any messages from the LORD?"

"Yes, I do!" said Jeremiah. "You will be defeated by the king of Babylon."

[18]Then Jeremiah asked the king, "What crime have I committed? What have I done against you, your officials, or the people that I should be imprisoned like this? [19]Where are your prophets now who told you the king of Babylon would not attack you? [20]Listen, my lord the king, I beg you. Don't send me back to the dungeon in the house of Jonathan the secretary, for I will die there."

[21]So King Zedekiah commanded that Jeremiah not be returned to the dungeon. Instead, he was imprisoned in the courtyard of the guard in the royal palace. The king also commanded that Jeremiah be given a loaf of fresh bread every day as long as there was any left in the city. So Jeremiah was put in the palace prison.

CHAPTER 38

Now Shephatiah son of Mattan, Gedaliah son of Pashhur, Jehucal* son of Shelemiah, and Pashhur son of Malkijah heard what Jeremiah had been telling the people. He was saying, [2]"This is what the LORD says: Everyone who stays in Jerusalem will die from war, famine, or disease, but those who surrender to the Babylonians* will live. [3]The LORD also says: The city of Jerusalem will surely be handed over to the army of the king of Babylon, who will capture it."

[4]So these officials went to the king and said, "Sir, this man must die! That kind of talk will undermine the morale of the few fighting men we have left, as well as that of all the people, too. This man is a traitor!"

[5]So King Zedekiah agreed. "All right," he said. "Do as you like. I will do nothing to stop you."

[6]So the officials took Jeremiah from his cell and lowered him by ropes into an empty cistern in the prison yard. It belonged to Malkijah, a member of the royal family. There was no water in the cistern, but there was a thick layer of mud at the bottom, and Jeremiah sank down into it.

[7]But Ebed-melech the Ethiopian,* an important palace official, heard that Jeremiah was in the cistern. At that time the king was holding court at the Benjamin Gate, [8]so Ebed-melech rushed from the palace to speak with him. [9]"My lord the king," he said, "these men have done a very evil thing in putting Jeremiah the prophet into the cistern. He will soon die of hunger, for almost all the bread in the city is gone."

[10]So the king told Ebed-melech, "Take along thirty of my men, and pull Jeremiah out of the cistern before he dies."

[11]So Ebed-melech took the men with him and went to a room in the palace beneath the treasury, where he found some old rags and discarded clothing. He carried these to the cistern and lowered them to Jeremiah on a rope. [12]Ebed-melech called down to Jeremiah, "Put these rags under your armpits to protect you from the ropes." Then when Jeremiah was ready, [13]they pulled him out. So Jeremiah was returned to the courtyard of the guard—the palace prison—where he remained.

[14]One day King Zedekiah sent for Jeremiah to meet him at the third entrance of the LORD's Temple. "I want to ask you something," the king said. "And don't try to hide the truth."

[15]Jeremiah said, "If I tell you the truth, you will kill me. And if I give you advice, you won't listen to me anyway."

[16]So King Zedekiah secretly promised him, "As surely as the LORD our Creator lives, I will not kill you or hand you over to the men who want you dead."

[17]Then Jeremiah said to Zedekiah, "The LORD God Almighty, the God of Israel, says: If you surrender to Babylon, you and your family will live, and the city will not be burned. [18]But if you refuse to surrender, you will not escape! This city will be handed over to the Babylonians, and they will burn it to the ground."

[19]"But I am afraid to surrender," the king said, "for the Babylonians will hand me over to the Judeans who have defected to them. And who knows what they will do to me?"

[20]Jeremiah replied, "You won't be handed over to them if you choose to obey the LORD. Your life will be spared, and all

38:1 Hebrew *Jucal*, a variant name for Jehucal; see 37:3.   38:2 Or *Chaldeans*; also in 38:18, 19, 23.   38:7 Hebrew *the Cushite*.

will go well for you. [21]But if you refuse to surrender, this is what the LORD has revealed to me: [22]All the women left in your palace will be brought out and given to the officers of the Babylonian army. Then the women will taunt you, saying, 'What fine friends you have! They have betrayed and misled you. When your feet sank in the mud, they left you to your fate!' [23]All your wives and children will be led out to the Babylonians, and you will not escape. You will be seized by the king of Babylon, and this city will be burned."

[24]Then Zedekiah said to Jeremiah, "Don't tell anyone you told me this, or you will die! [25]My officials may hear that I spoke to you. Then they may say to you, 'Tell us what you and the king were talking about. If you don't tell us, we will kill you.' [26]If this happens, just tell them you begged me not to send you back to Jonathan's dungeon, for fear you would die there."

[27]Sure enough, it wasn't long before the king's officials came to Jeremiah and asked him why the king had called for him. But Jeremiah followed the king's instructions, and they left without finding out the truth. No one had overheard the conversation between Jeremiah and the king. [28]And Jeremiah remained a prisoner in the courtyard of the guard until the day Jerusalem was captured.

CHAPTER 39

It was in January* during the ninth year of King Zedekiah's reign that King Nebuchadnezzar* and his army returned to besiege Jerusalem. [2]Two and a half years later, on July 18,* the Babylonians broke through the wall, and the city fell. [3]All the officers of the Babylonian army came in and sat in triumph at the Middle Gate: Nergal-sharezer of Samgar, and Nebo-sarsekim,* a chief officer, and Nergal-sharezer, the king's adviser, and many others.

[4]King Zedekiah and his royal guard saw the Babylonians in the city gate, so they fled when the darkness of night arrived. They went out through a gate between the two walls behind the king's garden and headed toward the Jordan Valley.* [5]But the Babylonians* chased the king and caught him on the plains of Jericho. They took him to King Nebuchadnezzar of Babylon, who was at Riblah in the land of Hamath. There the king of Babylon pronounced judgment upon Zedekiah. [6]He made Zedekiah watch as they killed his sons and all the nobles of Judah. [7]Then he gouged out Zedekiah's eyes, bound him in chains, and sent him away to exile in Babylon.

[8]Meanwhile, the Babylonians burned Jerusalem, including the palace, and tore down the walls of the city. [9]Then Nebuzaradan, the captain of the guard, sent to Babylon the remnant of the population as well as those who had defected to him. [10]But Nebuzaradan left a few of the poorest people in Judah, and he assigned them fields and vineyards to care for.

[11]King Nebuchadnezzar had told Nebuzaradan to find Jeremiah. [12]"See that he isn't hurt," he had said. "Look after him well, and give him anything he wants." [13]So Nebuzaradan, the captain of the guard, and Nebushazban, a chief officer, and Nergal-sharezer, the king's adviser, and the other officers of Babylon's king [14]sent messengers to bring Jeremiah out of the prison. They put him under the care of Gedaliah son of Ahikam and grandson of Shaphan, who was to take him back to his home. So Jeremiah stayed in Judah among his own people.

[15]The LORD had given the following message to Jeremiah while he was still in prison: [16]"Say to Ebed-melech the Ethiopian,* 'The LORD Almighty, the God of Israel, says: I will do to this city everything I have threatened. I will send disaster, not prosperity. You will see its destruction, [17]but I will rescue you from those you fear so much. [18]Because you trusted me, I will preserve your life and keep you safe. I, the LORD, have spoken!'"

39:1a Hebrew *in the tenth month,* of the Hebrew calendar. A number of events in Jeremiah can be cross-checked with dates in surviving Babylonian records and related accurately to our modern calendar. This event occurred on January 15, 588 B.C.; see 52:4 and the note there.   **39:1b** Hebrew *Nebuchadrezzar,* a variant name for Nebuchadnezzar; also in 39:11.   **39:2** Hebrew *On the ninth day of the fourth month of the eleventh year of Zedekiah.* This event occurred on July 18, 586 B.C.; also see note on 39:1.   **39:3** Or *Nergal-sharezer, Samgar-nebo, Sarsekim.*   **39:4** Hebrew *the Arabah.*   **39:5** Or *Chaldeans;* also in 39:8.   **39:16** Hebrew *the Cushite.*

AUGUST 11 ☐ DAY 224
JEREMIAH 40–45
After the Fall of Jerusalem

OVERVIEW Jeremiah's ministry does not end with the fall of Jerusalem. Given carte blanche by the Babylonian king Nebuchadnezzar, he chooses to cast his lot with Gedaliah, the governor appointed to oversee Jerusalem. But after Gedaliah's brutal assassination by Ishmael, the Jewish remnant disregards God's specific command and flees into Egypt, taking Jeremiah along. This prompts Jeremiah to predict Egypt's destruction and the Jews' discipline at the hands of Jehovah.

Chapters 40–41	Chapter 42	Chapter 43	Chapters 44–45
Gathering around Gedaliah	The Plan	Escaping into Egypt	
		The Execution	The Aftermath
Safety in the City	Disaster through Disobedience		

There is no more difficult prayer to pray aright than "Thy will be done."

YOUR DAILY WALK Are you a "coin-collector Christian"? It is a common practice today for coin and stamp collectors (numismatists and philatelists, if you want to be proper!) to buy merchandise "on approval." That is, the company will send samples of coins or stamps through the mail. The buyer looks them over, keeps the ones he or she wants to buy, and returns the rest. If the buyer doesn't like what is sent, he or she just sends it all back.

Some Christians view God's will that way! They pray, "Lord, show me what you want me to do." And when he does, they decide whether they want to do *all* of it, *part* of it, or *none* of it!

After the fall of Jerusalem, the survivors came to Jeremiah and asked him to pray for them. They wanted to know God's will "on approval." They were looking for God to rubber-stamp what they had already decided to do: flee to Egypt! And when the answer came back *no!* they went anyway—with disastrous results.

Examine a decision you're wrestling with in prayer. Are you seeking God's will "on approval," or are you willing to go wherever he guides? Read Proverbs 3:5-6; then you decide.

INSIGHT The Word of the Lord Came . . . in Tahpanhes
Tahpanhes (43:8-13) has been linked with a site about ten miles west of the Suez Canal. In 1886 Sir Flinders Petrie uncovered the ruins of a large castle, in front of which was a great open platform of brickwork. According to Petrie, it is likely Jeremiah hid the stones there that he referred to in his prophecy of Egypt's downfall!

CHAPTER 40

The LORD gave a message to Jeremiah after Nebuzaradan, captain of the guard, had released him at Ramah. He had found Jeremiah bound in chains among the captives of Jerusalem and Judah who were being sent to exile in Babylon.

²The captain of the guard called for Jeremiah and said, "The LORD your God has brought this disaster on this land, ³just as he said he would. For these people have

sinned against the LORD and disobeyed him. That is why it happened. ⁴Now I am going to take off your chains and let you go. If you want to come with me to Babylon, you are welcome. I will see that you are well cared for. But if you don't want to come, you may stay here. The whole land is before you—go wherever you like. ⁵If you decide to stay, then return to Gedaliah son of Ahikam and grandson of Shaphan. He has been appointed governor of Judah by the king of Babylon. Stay there with the people he rules. But it's up to you; go wherever you like."

Then Nebuzaradan gave Jeremiah some food and money and let him go. [6]So Jeremiah returned to Gedaliah son of Ahikam at Mizpah and lived in Judah with the few who were still left in the land.

[7]The leaders of the Judean guerrilla bands in the countryside heard that the king of Babylon had appointed Gedaliah son of Ahikam as governor over the poor people who were left behind in Judah, and that he hadn't exiled everyone to Babylon. [8]So they came to see Gedaliah at Mizpah. These are the names of the leaders who came: Ishmael son of Nethaniah, Johanan and Jonathan, sons of Kareah, Seraiah son of Tanhumeth, the sons of Ephai the Netophathite, Jaazaniah* son of the Maacathite, and all their men.

[9]Gedaliah assured them that it would be safe for them to surrender to the Babylonians.* "Stay here, and serve the king of Babylon," he said, "and all will go well for you. [10]As for me, I will stay at Mizpah to represent you before the Babylonians who come to meet with us. Settle in any town you wish, and live off the land. Harvest the grapes and summer fruits and olives, and store them away."

[11]When the Judeans in Moab, Ammon, Edom, and the other nearby countries heard that the king of Babylon had left a few people in Judah and that Gedaliah was the governor, [12]they began to return to Judah from the places to which they had fled. They stopped at Mizpah to discuss their plans with Gedaliah and then went out into the Judean countryside to gather a great harvest of grapes and other crops.

[13]Soon after this, Johanan son of Kareah and the other guerrilla leaders came to Gedaliah at Mizpah. [14]They said to him, "Did you know that Baalis, king of Ammon, has sent Ishmael son of Nethaniah to assassinate you?" But Gedaliah refused to believe them.

[15]Later Johanan had a private conference with Gedaliah and volunteered to kill Ishmael secretly. "Why should we let him come and murder you?" Johanan asked. "What will happen then to the Judeans who have returned? Why should the few of us who are still left be scattered and lost?"

[16]But Gedaliah said to Johanan, "I forbid you to do any such thing, for you are lying about Ishmael."

CHAPTER 41

But in midautumn,* Ishmael son of Nethaniah and grandson of Elishama, who was a member of the royal family, arrived in Mizpah accompanied by ten men. Gedaliah invited them to dinner. While they were eating, [2]Ishmael and his ten men suddenly drew their swords and killed Gedaliah, whom the king of Babylon had appointed governor. [3]Then they went out and slaughtered all the Judean officials and Babylonian* soldiers who were with Gedaliah at Mizpah.

[4]The next day, before anyone had heard about Gedaliah's murder, [5]eighty men arrived from Shechem, Shiloh, and Samaria. They had come to worship at the Temple of the LORD. They had shaved off their beards, torn their clothes, and cut themselves, and had brought along grain offerings and incense. [6]Ishmael left Mizpah to meet them, weeping as he went. When he reached them, he said, "Oh, come and see what has happened to Gedaliah!"

[7]But as soon as they were all inside the town, Ishmael and his men killed all but ten of them and threw their bodies into a cistern. [8]The other ten had talked Ishmael into letting them go by promising to bring him their stores of wheat, barley, oil, and honey that they had hidden away. [9]The cistern where Ishmael dumped the bodies of the men he murdered was the large one made by King Asa when he fortified Mizpah to protect himself against King Baasha of Israel. Ishmael son of Nethaniah filled it with corpses.

[10]Ishmael made captives of the king's daughters and the other people who had been left under Gedaliah's care in Mizpah by Nebuzaradan, captain of the guard. Taking them with him, he started back toward the land of Ammon.

[11]But when Johanan son of Kareah and the rest of the guerrilla leaders heard what Ishmael had done, [12]they took all their men and set out to stop him. They caught up with him at the pool near Gibeon. [13]The

---

40:8 As in parallel text at 2 Kgs 25:23; Hebrew reads *Jezaniah,* a variant name for Jaazaniah.   40:9 Or *Chaldeans;* also in 40:10.
41:1 Hebrew *in the seventh month,* of the Hebrew calendar. This month occurred in October and November 586 B.C. Also see note on 39:1.   41:3 Or *Chaldean.*

people Ishmael had captured shouted for joy when they saw Johanan and his men. [14]And all the captives from Mizpah escaped and began to help Johanan. [15]Meanwhile, Ishmael and eight of his men escaped from Johanan into the land of Ammon.

[16]Then Johanan son of Kareah and his officers led away all the people they had rescued—warriors, women, children, and palace officials.* [17]They took them all to the village of Geruth-kimham near Bethlehem, where they prepared to leave for Egypt. [18]They were afraid of what the Babylonians* would do when they heard that Ishmael had killed Gedaliah, the governor appointed by the Babylonian king.

CHAPTER 42

Then all the army officers, including Johanan son of Kareah and Jezaniah* son of Hoshaiah, and all the people, from the least to the greatest, approached [2]Jeremiah the prophet. They said, "Please pray to the LORD your God for us. As you know, we are only a tiny remnant compared to what we were before. [3]Beg the LORD your God to show us what to do and where to go."

[4]"All right," Jeremiah replied. "I will pray to the LORD your God, and I will tell you everything he says. I will hide nothing from you."

[5]Then they said to Jeremiah, "May the LORD your God be a faithful witness against us if we refuse to obey whatever he tells us to do! [6]Whether we like it or not, we will obey the LORD our God to whom we send you with our plea. For if we obey him, everything will turn out well for us."

[7]Ten days later, the LORD gave his reply to Jeremiah. [8]So he called for Johanan son of Kareah and the army officers, and for all the people, from the least to the greatest. [9]He said to them, "You sent me to the LORD, the God of Israel, with your request, and this is his reply: [10]'Stay here in this land. If you do, I will build you up and not tear you down; I will plant you and not uproot you. For I am sorry for all the punishment I have had to bring upon you. [11]Do not fear the king of Babylon anymore, says the LORD. For I am with you and will save you and rescue you from his power. [12]I will be merciful to you by making him kind, so he will let you stay here in your land.'

[13]"But if you refuse to obey the LORD your God and say, 'We will not stay here,' [14]and if you insist on going to live in Egypt where you think you will be free from war, famine, and alarms, [15]then this is what the LORD says to the remnant of Judah. The LORD Almighty, the God of Israel, says: 'If you insist on going to Egypt, [16]the war and famine you fear will follow close behind you, and you will die there. [17]That is the fate awaiting every one of you who insists on going to live in Egypt. Yes, you will die from war, famine, and disease. None of you will escape from the disaster I will bring upon you there.'

[18]"For the LORD Almighty, the God of Israel, says: 'Just as my anger and fury were poured out on the people of Jerusalem, so they will be poured out on you when you enter Egypt. You will become an object of damnation, horror, cursing, and mockery. And you will never see your homeland again.'

[19]"Listen, you remnant of Judah. The LORD has told you: 'Do not go to Egypt!' Don't forget this warning I have given you today. [20]For you were deceitful when you sent me to pray to the LORD your God for you, saying, 'Just tell us what the LORD our God says, and we will do it!' [21]And today I have told you exactly what he said, but you will not obey the LORD your God any better now than you have in the past. [22]So you can be sure that you will die from war, famine, and disease in Egypt, where you insist on going."

CHAPTER 43

When Jeremiah had finished giving this message from the LORD their God to all the people, [2]Azariah son of Hoshaiah and Johanan son of Kareah and all the other proud men said to Jeremiah, "You lie! The LORD our God hasn't forbidden us to go to Egypt! [3]Baruch son of Neriah has convinced you to say this, so we will stay here and be killed by the Babylonians* or be carried off into exile."

[4]So Johanan and all the army officers and all the people refused to obey the LORD's command to stay in Judah. [5]Johanan and his officers took with them all the people who had returned from the nearby countries to which they had fled. [6]In the crowd were men, women, and children, the king's

daughters, and all those whom Nebuzar-adan, the captain of the guard, had left with Gedaliah. Also included were the prophet Jeremiah and Baruch. [7]The people refused to obey the LORD and went to Egypt, going as far as the city of Tahpanhes.

[8]Then at Tahpanhes, the LORD gave another message to Jeremiah. He said, [9]"While the people of Judah are watching, bury large rocks between the pavement stones at the entrance of Pharaoh's palace here in Tahpanhes. [10]Then say to the people of Judah, 'The LORD Almighty, the God of Israel, says: I will surely bring my servant Nebuchadnezzar,* king of Babylon, here to Egypt. I will set his throne on these stones that I have hidden. He will spread his royal canopy over them. [11]And when he comes, he will destroy the land of Egypt. He will bring death to those destined for death; he will bring captivity to those destined for captivity; he will bring the sword against those destined for the sword. [12]He will set fire to the temples of Egypt's gods, burning all their idols and carrying away the people as captives. He will pick clean the land of Egypt as a shepherd picks fleas from his cloak. And he himself will leave unharmed. [13]He will break down the sacred pillars standing in the temple of the sun* in Egypt, and he will burn down the temples of Egypt's gods.'"

CHAPTER 44

This is the message Jeremiah received concerning the Judeans living in northern Egypt in the cities of Migdol, Tahpanhes, and Memphis,* and throughout southern Egypt as well: [2]"This is what the LORD Almighty, the God of Israel, says: You saw what I did to Jerusalem and to all the towns of Judah. They now lie in ruins, and no one lives in them. [3]Because of all their wickedness, my anger rose high against them. They burned incense and worshiped other gods—gods that neither they nor you nor any of your ancestors have ever known.

[4]"Again and again I sent my servants, the prophets, to plead with them, 'Don't do these horrible things that I hate so much.' [5]But my people would not listen or turn back from their wicked ways. They kept right on burning incense to these gods. [6]And so my fury boiled over and fell like fire on the towns of Judah and into the streets of Jerusalem, and now they are a desolate ruin.

[7]"And now the LORD God Almighty, the God of Israel, asks you: Why are you destroying yourselves? For not one of you will survive—not a man, woman, or child among you who has come here from Judah, not even the babies in your arms. [8]Why arouse my anger by burning incense to the idols you have made here in Egypt? You will only destroy yourselves and make yourselves an object of cursing and mockery for all the nations of the earth. [9]Have you forgotten the sins of your ancestors, the sins of the kings and queens of Judah, and the sins you and your wives committed in Judah and Jerusalem? [10]To this very hour you have shown no remorse or reverence. No one has chosen to follow my law and the decrees I gave to you and your ancestors before you.

[11]"Therefore, the LORD Almighty, the God of Israel, says: I have made up my mind to destroy every one of you! [12]I will take this remnant of Judah that insisted on coming here to Egypt, and I will consume them. They will fall here in Egypt, killed by war and famine. All will die, from the least to the greatest. They will be an object of damnation, horror, cursing, and mockery. [13]I will punish them in Egypt just as I punished them in Jerusalem, by war, famine, and disease. [14]Of those who fled to Egypt with dreams of returning home to Judah, only a handful will escape."

[15]Then all the women present and all the men who knew that their wives had burned incense to idols—a great crowd of all the Judeans living in Pathros, the southern region of Egypt—answered Jeremiah, [16]"We will not listen to your messages from the LORD! [17]We will do whatever we want. We will burn incense to the Queen of Heaven and sacrifice to her just as much as we like—just as we and our ancestors did before us, and as our kings and princes have always done in the towns of Judah and in the streets of Jerusalem. For in those days we had plenty to eat, and we were well off and had no troubles! [18]But ever since we quit burning incense to the Queen of Heaven and stopped worshiping her, we have been in great trouble and have suffered the effects of war and famine."

[19]"And," the women added, "do you

43:10 Hebrew *Nebuchadrezzar*, a variant name for Nebuchadnezzar.   43:13 Or *in Heliopolis*.   44:1 Hebrew *Noph*.

suppose that we were worshiping the Queen of Heaven, pouring out drink offerings to her, and making cakes marked with her image, without our husbands knowing it and helping us? Of course not!"

20 Then Jeremiah said to all of them, men and women alike, who had given him that answer, 21 "Do you think the LORD did not know that you and your ancestors, your kings and officials, and all the people were burning incense to idols in the towns of Judah and in the streets of Jerusalem? 22 It was because the LORD could no longer bear all the evil things you were doing that he made your land an object of cursing—a desolate ruin without a single inhabitant—as it is today. 23 The very reason all these terrible things have happened to you is because you have burned incense to idols and sinned against the LORD, refusing to obey him and follow his instructions, laws, and stipulations."

24 Then Jeremiah said to them all, including the women, "Listen to this message from the LORD, all you citizens of Judah who live in Egypt. 25 The LORD Almighty, the God of Israel, says: You and your wives have said that you will never give up your devotion and sacrifices to the Queen of Heaven, and you have proved it by your actions. Then go ahead and carry out your promises and vows to her!

26 "But listen to this message from the LORD, all you Judeans now living in Egypt: I have sworn by my great name, says the LORD, that my name will no longer be spoken by any of the Judeans in the land of Egypt. None of you may invoke my name

or use this oath: 'As surely as the Sovereign LORD lives!' 27 For I will watch over you to bring you disaster and not good. You will suffer war and famine until all of you are dead.

28 "Only a small number will escape death and return to Judah from Egypt. Then all those who came to Egypt will find out whose words are true, mine or theirs! 29 And this is the proof I give you, says the LORD, that all I have threatened will happen to you and that I will punish you here: 30 I will turn Pharaoh Hophra, king of Egypt, over to his enemies who want to kill him, just as I turned King Zedekiah of Judah over to King Nebuchadnezzar* of Babylon. I, the LORD, have spoken!"

CHAPTER 45

The prophet Jeremiah gave a message to Baruch son of Neriah in the fourth year of the reign of Jehoiakim son of Josiah,* after Baruch had written down everything Jeremiah had dictated to him. He said, 2 "This is what the LORD, the God of Israel, says to you, Baruch: 3 You have said, 'I am overwhelmed with trouble! Haven't I had enough pain already? And now the LORD has added more! I am weary of my own sighing and can find no rest.'

4 "Baruch, this is what the LORD says: I will destroy this nation that I built. I will uproot what I planted. 5 Are you seeking great things for yourself? Don't do it! But don't be discouraged. I will bring great disaster upon all these people, but I will protect you wherever you go. I, the LORD, have spoken!"

44:30 Hebrew *Nebuchadrezzar*, a variant name for Nebuchadnezzar.   45:1 The fourth year of Jehoiakim's reign was 605 B.C.

AUGUST 12 □ DAY 225
JEREMIAH 46–52
The Fall of Jerusalem

OVERVIEW With a last, far-reaching sweep of his prophetic pen, Jeremiah outlines the judgments to come on many of the ungodly nations of the world: Egypt, Philistia, Moab, Ammon, and Babylon. All will feel the sting of God's chastening hand. Even Babylon, the mighty conqueror of God's people, will eventually fall. The final chapter of the book, like the final brush strokes of a dark and dreary painting, portrays the fall of Jerusalem in all its stark horror. But the book closes on a significant note of hope as the heir to Judah's throne enjoys kindly treatment at the hands of his Babylonian captors.

Chapter 46	Chapter 47	Chapter 48	Chapter 49	Chs. 50–51	Chapter 52
Discipline of God upon					
Egypt	Philistia	Moab	Ammon	Babylon	Jerusalem
Judah's Foes					Judah's Fall

YOUR DAILY WALK Immunity to disease is a wonderful thing. But there are some immunities you would be better off without.

One such immunity is typically—and tragically—found among those who regularly sit under the teaching of God's Word. Sunday by Sunday in church, conviction comes as God's truth "hits home" in your life. You promise to change—but don't. Conviction returns, and again you know what needs to happen—but somehow you never get around to doing it. After a time, you begin to see conviction as an end in itself. "Immunity" has set in.

The recognition of sin is only the beginning of salvation.

Think back over the way God has spoken to you through the life of Jeremiah this month. Then ask yourself this question: How many of the areas of my life about which I've been convicted have I actually attempted to change? Choose one neglected area to work on today. Don't allow spiritual immunity to rob you of spiritual vitality.

INSIGHT Nations Then and Now

With your Bible and a world map before you, notice these Old Testament designations for modern-day regions: Philistia (Gaza); Moab, Ammon, Edom, and Kedar (Jordan); Damascus (Syria); Elam and Babylon (Iraq/Iran). Of all the nations mentioned in chapters 46–49, Egypt is the only one to maintain its identity and name today!

CHAPTER 46

The following messages were given to Jeremiah the prophet from the LORD concerning foreign nations.

²This message concerning Egypt was given in the fourth year of the reign of Jehoiakim son of Josiah,* the king of Judah, on the occasion of the battle of Carchemish when Pharaoh Neco, king of Egypt, and his army were defeated beside the Euphrates River by King Nebuchadnezzar* of Babylon.

³"Buckle on your armor and advance into battle! ⁴Harness the horses, and prepare to mount them. Put on your helmets, sharpen your spears, and prepare your armor. ⁵But look! The Egyptian army flees in terror. The bravest of its fighting men run without a backward glance. They are terrorized at every turn, says the LORD. ⁶The swiftest cannot flee; the mightiest warriors cannot escape. By the Euphrates River to the north they stumble and fall.

⁷"Who is this, rising like the Nile River at floodtime, overflowing all the land? ⁸It is the Egyptian army, boasting that it will cover the earth like a flood, destroying every foe. ⁹Then come, you horses and chariots and mighty warriors of Egypt! Come, all you allies from Ethiopia, Libya, and Lydia* who are skilled with the shield and bow! ¹⁰For this is the day of the Lord, the LORD Almighty, a day of vengeance on his enemies. The sword will devour until it is satisfied, yes, drunk with your blood! The Lord, the LORD Almighty, will receive a sacrifice today in the north country beside the Euphrates River. ¹¹Go up to Gilead to get ointment, O virgin daughter of Egypt! But your many medicines will bring you no healing. ¹²The nations have heard of your shame. The earth is filled with your cries of despair. Your mightiest warriors will stumble across each other and fall together."

¹³Then the LORD gave the prophet Jeremiah this message about King Nebuchadnezzar's plans to attack Egypt.

¹⁴"Shout it out in Egypt! Publish it in the cities of Migdol, Memphis,* and Tahpanhes! Mobilize for battle, for the sword of destruction will devour everyone around you. ¹⁵Why have your warriors fled in terror?

46:2a The fourth year of Jehoiakim's reign was 605 B.C.   46:2b Hebrew *Nebuchadrezzar*, a variant name for Nebuchadnezzar; also in 46:13, 26.   46:9 Hebrew *Cush, Put, and Lud*.   46:14 Hebrew *Noph*; also in 46:19.

They cannot stand because the LORD has driven them away. [16]They stumble and fall over each other and say among themselves, 'Come, let's go back to our homeland where we were born. Let's get away from the sword of the enemy!' [17]There they will say, 'Pharaoh, the king of Egypt, is a loudmouth who missed his opportunity!'

[18]"As surely as I live," says the King, whose name is the LORD Almighty, "one is coming against Egypt who is as tall as Mount Tabor or Mount Carmel by the sea! [19]Pack up! Get ready to leave for exile, you citizens of Egypt! The city of Memphis will be destroyed, without a single person living there. [20]Egypt is as sleek as a young cow, but a gadfly from the north is on its way! [21]Egypt's famed mercenaries have become like fattened calves. They turn and run, for it is a day of great disaster for Egypt, a time of great punishment. [22]Silent as a serpent gliding away, Egypt flees. The invading army marches in; they come against her with axes like woodsmen. [23]They will cut down her people like trees," says the LORD, "for they are more numerous than grasshoppers. [24]Egypt will be humiliated; she will be handed over to men from the north."

[25]The LORD Almighty, the God of Israel, says: "I will punish Amon, the god of Thebes,* and all the other gods of Egypt. I will punish its rulers and Pharaoh, too, and all who trust in him. [26]I will hand them over to those who want them killed—to King Nebuchadnezzar of Babylon and his army. But afterward the land will recover from the ravages of war. I, the LORD, have spoken!

[27]"But do not be afraid, Jacob, my servant; do not be dismayed, Israel. For I will bring you home again from distant lands, and your children will return from their exile. Israel* will return and will have peace and quiet, and nothing will make them afraid. [28]Fear not, Jacob, my servant," says the LORD, "for I am with you. I will destroy the nations to which I have exiled you, but I will not destroy you. But I must discipline you; I cannot let you go unpunished."

CHAPTER 47

This is the LORD's message to the prophet Jeremiah concerning the Philistines of Gaza, before it was captured by the Egyptian army.

[2]This is what the LORD says: "A flood is coming from the north to overflow the land. It will destroy the land and everything in it—cities and people alike. People will scream in terror, and everyone in the land will weep. [3]Hear the clatter of hooves and the rumble of wheels as the chariots rush by. Terrified fathers run madly, without a backward glance at their helpless children.

[4]"The time has come for the Philistines to be destroyed, along with their allies from Tyre and Sidon. Yes, the LORD is destroying the Philistines, those colonists from Crete.* [5]The city of Gaza will be demolished; Ashkelon will lie in ruins. You remnant of the Mediterranean plain,* how long will you lament and mourn?

[6]"Now, O sword of the LORD, when will you be at rest again? Go back into your sheath; rest and be still! [7]But how can it be still when the LORD has sent it on an errand? For the city of Ashkelon and the people living along the sea must be destroyed."

CHAPTER 48

This message was given concerning Moab.

This is what the LORD Almighty, the God of Israel, says: "Destruction is certain for the city of Nebo; it will soon lie in ruins. The city of Kiriathaim will be humiliated and captured; the fortress will be humiliated and broken down. [2]No one will ever brag about Moab again, for there is a plot against her life. In Heshbon plans have been completed to destroy her. 'Come,' they say, 'we will cut her off from being a nation.' The city of Madmen,* too, will be silenced; the sword will follow you there. [3]And then the roar of battle will surge against Horonaim, [4]for all Moab is being destroyed. Her little ones will cry out.* [5]Her refugees will climb the hills of Luhith, weeping bitterly, while cries of terror rise from Horonaim below. [6]Flee for your lives! Hide in the wilderness!* [7]Because you have trusted in your wealth and skill, you will be taken captive. Your god Chemosh, with his priests and princes, will be exiled to distant lands!

[8]"All the towns will be destroyed, both on the plateaus and in the valleys, for the LORD has spoken. [9]Oh, that Moab had

46:25 Hebrew *No.*   46:27 Hebrew *Jacob.*   47:4 Hebrew *from Caphtor.*   47:5 Hebrew *the plain.*   48:2 *Madmen* sounds like the Hebrew word for "silence"; it should not be confused with the English word *madmen.*   48:4 Greek version reads *Her cries are heard as far away as Zoar.*   48:6 Or *Be like* [the town of] *Aroer in the wilderness.*

wings so she could fly away, for her cities will be left empty, with no one living in them. ¹⁰Cursed be those who refuse to do the work the LORD has given them, who hold back their swords from shedding blood!

¹¹"From her earliest history, Moab has lived in peace. She is like wine that has been allowed to settle. She has not been poured from flask to flask, and she is now fragrant and smooth. ¹²But the time is coming soon," says the LORD, "when I will send troublemakers to pour her from her jar. They will pour her out, then shatter the jar! ¹³At last Moab will be ashamed of her idol Chemosh, as Israel was ashamed of her gold calf at Bethel.*

¹⁴"You used to boast, 'We are heroes, mighty men of war.' ¹⁵But now Moab and her towns will be destroyed. Her most promising youth are doomed to slaughter," says the King, whose name is the LORD Almighty. ¹⁶"Calamity is coming fast to Moab; it threatens ominously.

¹⁷"You friends of Moab, weep for her and cry! See how the strong scepter is broken, how the beautiful staff is shattered! ¹⁸Come down from your glory and sit in the dust, you people of Dibon, for those who destroy Moab will shatter Dibon, too. They will tear down all your towers. ¹⁹The people of Aroer stand anxiously beside the road to watch. They shout to those who flee from Moab, 'What has happened there?'

²⁰"And the reply comes back, 'Moab lies in ruins; weep and wail! Tell it by the banks of the Arnon River: Moab has been destroyed!' ²¹All the cities of the plateau lie in ruins, too. Judgment has been poured out on them all—on Holon and Jahaz* and Mephaath, ²²and on Dibon and Nebo and Beth-diblathaim, ²³and on Kiriathaim and Beth-gamul and Beth-meon, ²⁴and on Kerioth and Bozrah—all the cities of Moab, far and near.

²⁵"The strength of Moab has ended. Her horns have been cut off, and her arms have been broken," says the LORD. ²⁶"Let her stagger and fall like a drunkard, for she has rebelled against the LORD. Moab will wallow in her own vomit, ridiculed by all. ²⁷Did you not make Israel the object of your ridicule? Was she caught in the company of thieves that you should despise her as you do?

²⁸"You people of Moab, flee from your cities and towns! Live in the caves like doves that nest in the clefts of the rocks. ²⁹We have heard of the pride of Moab, for it is very great. We know of her loftiness, her arrogance, and her haughty heart. ³⁰I know about her insolence," says the LORD, "but her boasts are false; they accomplish nothing. ³¹Yes, I wail for Moab; my heart is broken for the men of Kir-hareseth.*

³²"You people of Sibmah, rich in vineyards, I will weep for you even more than I did for Jazer. Your spreading vines once reached as far as the Dead Sea,* but the destroyer has stripped you bare! He has harvested your grapes and summer fruits. ³³Joy and gladness are gone from fruitful Moab. The presses yield no wine. No one treads the grapes with shouts of joy. There is shouting, yes, but not of joy. ³⁴Instead, their awful cries of terror can be heard from Heshbon clear across to Elealeh and Jahaz; from Zoar all the way to Horonaim and Eglath-shelishiyah. Even the waters of Nimrim are dried up now.

³⁵"I will put an end to Moab," says the LORD, "for they offer sacrifices at the pagan shrines and burn incense to their false gods. ³⁶My heart moans like a flute for Moab and Kir-hareseth, for all their wealth has disappeared. ³⁷They shave their heads and beards in mourning. They slash their hands and put on clothes made of sackcloth. ³⁸Crying and sorrow will be in every Moabite home and on every street. For I have smashed Moab like an old, unwanted bottle. ³⁹How it is broken! Hear the wailing! See the shame of Moab! She has become an object of ridicule, an example of ruin to all her neighbors.

⁴⁰"An eagle swoops down on the land of Moab," says the LORD. ⁴¹"Her cities will fall; her strongholds will be seized. Even the mightiest warriors will be as frightened as a woman about to give birth. ⁴²Moab will no longer be a nation, for she has boasted against the LORD.

⁴³"Terror and traps and snares will be your lot, O Moab," says the LORD. ⁴⁴"Those who flee in terror will fall into a trap, and those who escape the trap will step into a snare. I will see to it that you do not get away, for the time of your judgment has come," says the LORD. ⁴⁵"The people flee as far as Heshbon but are unable to go on. For

48:13 Hebrew *ashamed when they trusted in Bethel.*   **48:21** Hebrew *Jahzah,* a variant name for Jahaz.   **48:31** Hebrew *Kir-heres,* a variant name for Kir-hareseth; also in 48:36.   **48:32** Hebrew *the sea of Jazer.*

a fire comes from Heshbon, King Sihon's ancestral home, to devour the entire land with all its rebellious people.

⁴⁶"O Moab, your destruction is sure! The people of the god Chemosh are destroyed! Your sons and daughters have been taken away as captives. ⁴⁷But in the latter days I will restore the fortunes of Moab," says the LORD.

This is the end of Jeremiah's prophecy concerning Moab.

CHAPTER 49

This message was given concerning the Ammonites.

This is what the LORD says: "What are you doing? Are there no descendants of Israel to inherit the land of Gad? Why are you, who worship Molech,* living in its towns? ²I will punish you for this," says the LORD, "by destroying your city of Rabbah. It will become a desolate heap, and the neighboring towns will be burned. Then Israel will come and take back the land you took from her," says the LORD.

³"Cry out, O Heshbon, for the town of Ai is destroyed. Weep, O people of Rabbah! Put on your clothes of mourning. Weep and wail, hiding in the hedges, for your god Molech will be exiled along with his princes and priests. ⁴You are proud of your fertile valleys, but they will soon be ruined. You rebellious daughter, you trusted in your wealth and thought no one could ever harm you. ⁵But look! I will bring terror upon you," says the Lord, the LORD Almighty. "Your neighbors will chase you from your land, and no one will help your exiles as they flee. ⁶But afterward I will restore the fortunes of the Ammonites," says the LORD.

⁷This message was given concerning Edom.

This is what the LORD Almighty says: "Where are all the wise men of Teman? Is there no one left to give wise counsel? ⁸Turn and flee! Hide in deep caves, you people of Dedan! For when I bring disaster on Edom,* I will punish you, too! ⁹Those who harvest grapes always leave a few for the poor. If thieves came at night, even they would not take everything. ¹⁰But I will strip bare the land of Edom, and there will be no place left to hide. Its children, its brothers, and its neighbors—all will be destroyed—

and Edom itself will be no more. ¹¹But I will preserve the orphans who remain among you. Your widows, too, will be able to depend on me for help."

¹²And this is what the LORD says: "If the innocent must suffer, how much more must you! You will not go unpunished! You must drink this cup of judgment! ¹³For I have sworn by my own name," says the LORD, "that Bozrah will become an object of horror and a heap of rubble; it will be mocked and cursed. All its towns and villages will be desolate forever."

¹⁴I have heard a message from the LORD that an ambassador was sent to the nations to say, "Form a coalition against Edom, and prepare for battle!"

¹⁵This is what the LORD says: "I will cut you down to size among the nations, Edom. You will be despised by all. ¹⁶You are proud that you inspire fear in others. And you are proud because you live in a rock fortress and hide high in the mountains. But don't fool yourselves! Though you live among the peaks with the eagles, I will bring you crashing down," says the LORD.

¹⁷"Edom will be an object of horror. All who pass by will be appalled and will gasp at the destruction they see there. ¹⁸It will be like the destruction of Sodom and Gomorrah and their neighboring towns," says the LORD. "No one will live there anymore. ¹⁹I will come like a lion from the thickets of the Jordan, leaping on the sheep in the pasture. I will chase Edom from its land, and I will appoint the leader of my choice. For who is like me, and who can challenge me? What ruler can oppose my will?"

²⁰Listen to the LORD's plans for Edom and the people of Teman. Even the little children will be dragged off, and their homes will be empty. ²¹The earth will shake with the noise of Edom's fall, and its cry of despair will be heard all the way to the Red Sea.* ²²The enemy will come as swiftly as an eagle, and he will spread his wings against Bozrah. Even the mightiest warriors will be as frightened as a woman about to give birth.

²³This message was given concerning Damascus.

This is what the LORD says: "The towns of Hamath and Arpad are struck with fear, for they have heard the news of their de-

---

49:1 Hebrew *Milcom,* a variant name for Molech; also in 49:3.   **49:8** Hebrew *Esau;* also in 49:10.   **49:21** Hebrew *sea of reeds.*

struction. Their hearts are troubled like a wild sea in a raging storm. ²⁴Damascus has become feeble, and all her people turn to flee. Fear, anguish, and pain have gripped her as they do a woman giving birth. ²⁵That famous city, a city of joy, will be forsaken! ²⁶Her young men will fall in the streets and die. Her warriors will all be killed," says the LORD Almighty. ²⁷"And I will start a fire at the edge of Damascus that will burn up the palaces of Ben-hadad."

²⁸This message was given concerning Kedar and the kingdoms of Hazor, which were attacked by King Nebuchadnezzar* of Babylon.

This is what the LORD says: "Advance against Kedar! Blot out the warriors from the East! ²⁹Their flocks and tents will be captured, and their household goods and camels will be taken away. Everywhere shouts of panic will be heard: 'We are terrorized at every turn!' ³⁰Flee for your lives," says the LORD. "Hide yourselves in deep caves, you people of Hazor, for King Nebuchadnezzar of Babylon has plotted against you and is preparing to destroy you.

³¹"Go up and attack those self-sufficient nomadic tribes," says the LORD. "They live alone in the desert without walls or gates. ³²Their camels and cattle will all be yours. I will scatter to the winds these people who live in distant places.* I will bring calamity upon them from every direction," says the LORD. ³³"Hazor will be inhabited by jackals, and it will be desolate forever. No one will live there anymore."

³⁴This message concerning Elam came to the prophet Jeremiah from the LORD at the beginning of the reign of King Zedekiah of Judah.

³⁵This is what the LORD Almighty says: "I will destroy the archers of Elam—the best of their marksmen. ³⁶I will bring enemies from all directions, and I will scatter the people of Elam to the four winds. They will be exiled to countries around the world. ³⁷I myself will go with Elam's enemies to shatter it. My fierce anger will bring great disaster upon the people of Elam," says the LORD. "Their enemies will chase them with the sword until I have destroyed them completely. ³⁸I will set my throne in Elam," says the LORD,

"and I will destroy its king and princes. ³⁹But in the latter days I will restore the fortunes of Elam," says the LORD.

CHAPTER 50
The LORD gave Jeremiah the prophet this message concerning Babylon and the land of the Babylonians.*

²This is what the LORD says: "Tell the whole world, and keep nothing back! Raise a signal flag so everyone will know that Babylon will fall! Her images and idols will be shattered. Her gods Bel and Marduk will be utterly disgraced. ³For a nation will attack her from the north and bring such destruction that no one will live in her again. Everything will be gone; both people and animals will flee.

⁴"Then the people of Israel and Judah will join together," says the LORD, "weeping and seeking the LORD their God. ⁵They will ask the way to Jerusalem* and will start back home again. They will bind themselves to the LORD with an eternal covenant that will never again be broken.

⁶"My people have been lost sheep. Their shepherds have led them astray and turned them loose in the mountains. They have lost their way and cannot remember how to get back to the fold. ⁷All who found them devoured them. Their enemies said, 'We are allowed to attack them freely, for they have sinned against the LORD, their place of rest, the hope of their ancestors.'

⁸"But now, flee from Babylon! Leave the land of the Babylonians. Lead my people home again. ⁹For look, I am raising up an army of great nations from the north. I will bring them against Babylon to attack her, and she will be captured. The enemies' arrows will go straight to the mark; they will not miss! ¹⁰Babylonia* will be plundered until the attackers are glutted with plunder," says the LORD.

¹¹"You rejoice and are glad, you plunderers of my chosen people. You frisk about like a calf in a meadow and neigh like a stallion. ¹²But your homeland* will be overwhelmed with shame and disgrace. You will become the least of nations—a wilderness, a dry and desolate land. ¹³Because of the LORD's anger, Babylon will become a deserted wasteland. All who pass by will be horrified and will gasp at the destruction they see there.

¹⁴"Yes, prepare to attack Babylon, all you nations round about. Let your archers shoot at her. Spare no arrows, for she has sinned against the LORD. ¹⁵Shout against her from every side. Look! She surrenders! Her walls have fallen. The LORD has taken vengeance, so do not spare her. Do to her as she has done to others! ¹⁶Lead from Babylon all those who plant crops; send all the harvesters away. Let the captives escape the sword of the enemy and rush back to their own lands.

¹⁷"The Israelites are like sheep that have been scattered by lions. First the king of Assyria ate them up. Then King Nebuchadnezzar* of Babylon cracked their bones." ¹⁸Therefore, the LORD Almighty, the God of Israel, says: "Now I will punish the king of Babylon and his land, just as I punished the king of Assyria. ¹⁹And I will bring Israel home again to her own land, to feed in the fields of Carmel and Bashan, and to be satisfied once more on the hill country of Ephraim and Gilead. ²⁰In those days," says the LORD, "no sin will be found in Israel or in Judah, for I will forgive the remnant I preserve.

²¹"Go up, my warriors, against the land of Merathaim and against the people of Pekod. Yes, march against Babylon, the land of rebels, a land that I will judge! Pursue, kill, and completely destroy* them, as I have commanded you," says the LORD. ²²"Let the battle cry be heard in the land, a shout of great destruction. ²³Babylon, the mightiest hammer in all the earth, lies broken and shattered. Babylon is desolate among the nations! ²⁴Listen, Babylon, for I have set a trap for you. You are caught, for you have fought against the LORD.

²⁵"The LORD has opened his armory and brought out weapons to vent his fury against his enemies. The terror that falls upon the Babylonians will be the work of the Sovereign LORD Almighty. ²⁶Yes, come against her from distant lands. Break open her granaries. Crush her walls and houses into heaps of rubble. Destroy her completely, and leave nothing! ²⁷Even destroy her cattle—it will be terrible for them, too! Slaughter them all! For the time has come for Babylon to be devastated. ²⁸Listen to the people who have escaped from Babylon, as they declare in Jerusalem how the LORD

our God has taken vengeance against those who destroyed his Temple.

²⁹"Send out a call for archers to come to Babylon. Surround the city so none can escape. Do to her as she has done to others, for she has defied the LORD, the Holy One of Israel. ³⁰Her young men will fall in the streets and die. Her warriors will all be killed," says the LORD.

³¹"See, I am your enemy, O proud people," says the Lord, the LORD Almighty. "Your day of reckoning has arrived. ³²O land of pride, you will stumble and fall, and no one will raise you up. For I will light a fire in the cities of Babylon that will burn everything around them."

³³And now the LORD Almighty says this: "The people of Israel and Judah have been wronged. Their captors hold them and refuse to let them go. ³⁴But the one who redeems them is strong. His name is the LORD Almighty. He will defend them and give them rest again in Israel. But the people of Babylon—there will be no rest for them!

³⁵"The sword of destruction will strike the Babylonians," says the LORD. "It will strike the people of Babylon—her princes and wise men, too. ³⁶And when it strikes her wise counselors, they will become fools! When it strikes her mightiest warriors, panic will seize them! ³⁷When it strikes her horses and chariots, her allies from other lands will become as weak as women. When it strikes her treasures, they all will be plundered. ³⁸It will even strike her water supply, causing it to dry up. And why? Because the whole land is filled with idols, and the people are madly in love with them.

³⁹"Soon this city of Babylon will be inhabited by ostriches and jackals. It will be a home for the wild animals of the desert. Never again will people live there; it will lie desolate forever. ⁴⁰I will destroy it just as I* destroyed Sodom and Gomorrah and their neighboring towns," says the LORD. "No one will live there anymore.

⁴¹"Look! A great army is marching from the north! A great nation and many kings are rising against you from far-off lands. ⁴²They are fully armed for slaughter. They are cruel and show no mercy. As they ride forward, the noise of their army is like a roaring sea. They are marching in battle formation to destroy you, Babylon. ⁴³The

50:17 Hebrew *Nebuchadrezzar*, a variant name for Nebuchadnezzar.   50:21 The Hebrew term used here refers to the complete consecration of things or people to the LORD, either by destroying them or by giving them as an offering.   50:40 Hebrew *just as God*.

king of Babylon has received reports about the enemy, and he is weak with fright. Fear and pain have gripped him, like that of a woman about to give birth.

⁴⁴"I will come like a lion from the thickets of the Jordan, leaping on the sheep in the pasture. I will chase Babylon from its land, and I will appoint the leader of my choice. For who is like me, and who can challenge me? What ruler can oppose my will?"

⁴⁵Listen to the LORD's plans against Babylon and the land of the Babylonians. Even little children will be dragged off, and their homes will be empty. ⁴⁶The earth will shake with the noise of Babylon's fall, and her cry of despair will be heard around the world.

CHAPTER 51

This is what the LORD says: "I will stir up a destroyer against Babylon and the people of Babylonia.* ²Foreigners will come and winnow her, blowing her away as chaff. They will come from every side to rise against her in her day of trouble. ³Don't let the archers put on their armor or draw their bows. No one will be spared! Young and old alike will be completely destroyed.* ⁴They will fall dead in the land of the Babylonians,* slashed to death in her streets. ⁵For the LORD Almighty has not forsaken Israel and Judah. He is still their God, even though their land was filled with sin against the Holy One of Israel."

⁶Flee from Babylon! Save yourselves! Don't get trapped in her punishment! It is the LORD's time for vengeance; he will fully repay her. ⁷Babylon has been like a golden cup in the LORD's hands, a cup from which he made the whole earth drink and go mad. ⁸But now suddenly, Babylon, too, has fallen. Weep for her, and give her medicine. Perhaps she can yet be healed. ⁹We would have helped her if we could, but nothing can save her now. Let her go; abandon her. Return now to your own land, for her judgment will be so great it cannot be measured. ¹⁰The LORD has vindicated us. Come, let us announce in Jerusalem* everything the LORD our God has done.

¹¹Sharpen the arrows! Lift up the shields! For the LORD has stirred up the spirit of the kings of the Medes to march against Bab-

ylon and destroy her. This is his vengeance against those who desecrated his Temple. ¹²Raise the battle flag against Babylon! Reinforce the guard and station the watchmen. Prepare an ambush, for the LORD will fulfill all his plans against Babylon.

¹³You are a city rich with water, a great center of commerce, but your end has come. The thread of your life is cut. ¹⁴The LORD Almighty has taken this vow and has sworn to it by his own name: "Your cities will be filled with enemies, like fields filled with locusts, and they will lift their shouts of triumph over you."

¹⁵ He made the earth by his power,
    and he preserves it by his wisdom.
  He has stretched out the heavens
    by his understanding.
¹⁶ When he speaks, there is thunder in the
      heavens.
    He causes the clouds to rise over the
      earth.
  He sends the lightning with the rain
    and releases the wind from his store-
      houses.
¹⁷ Compared to him, all people are foolish
    and have no knowledge at all!
  They make idols, but the idols will
      disgrace their makers,
    for they are frauds.
  They have no life or power in them.
¹⁸ Idols are worthless; they are lies!
    The time is coming when they will
      all be destroyed.
¹⁹ But the God of Israel* is no idol!
    He is the Creator of everything that
      exists,
    including his people, his own special
      possession.
  The LORD Almighty is his name!

²⁰"You* are my battle-ax and sword," says the LORD. "With you I will shatter nations and destroy many kingdoms. ²¹With you I will shatter armies, destroying the horse and rider, the chariot and charioteer. ²²With you I will shatter men and women, old people and children, young men and maidens. ²³With you I will shatter shepherds and flocks, farmers and oxen, captains and rulers.

²⁴"As you watch, I will repay Babylon and the people of Babylonia* for all the

---

51:1 Hebrew *of Leb-kamai,* a code name for Babylonia.   **51:3** The Hebrew term used here refers to the complete consecration of things or people to the LORD, either by destroying them or by giving them as an offering.   **51:4** Or *Chaldeans;* also in 51:54.   **51:10** Hebrew *Zion;* also in 51:24, 35a.   **51:19** Hebrew *the Portion of Jacob.*   **51:20** Possibly Cyrus, who was used of God to conquer Babylon. Compare Isa 44:28; 45:1.   **51:24** Or *Chaldea;* also in 51:35.

wrong they have done to my people in Jerusalem," says the LORD.

25"Look, O mighty mountain, destroyer of the earth! I am your enemy," says the LORD. "I will raise my fist against you, to roll you down from the heights. When I am finished, you will be nothing but a heap of rubble. 26 You will be desolate forever. Even your stones will never again be used for building. You will be completely wiped out," says the LORD.

27Signal many nations to mobilize for war against Babylon. Sound the battle cry! Bring out the armies of Ararat, Minni, and Ashkenaz. Appoint a leader, and bring a multitude of horses! 28Bring against her the armies of the kings of the Medes and their generals, and the armies of all the countries they rule.

29Babylon trembles and writhes in pain, for everything the LORD has planned against her stands unchanged. Babylon will be left desolate without a single inhabitant. 30Her mightiest warriors no longer fight. They stay in their barracks. Their courage is gone. They have become as fearful as women. The invaders have burned the houses and broken down the city gates. 31Messengers from every side come running to the king to tell him all is lost! 32All the escape routes are blocked. The fortifications are burning, and the army is in panic.

33For the LORD Almighty, the God of Israel, says: "Babylon is like wheat on a threshing floor, about to be trampled. In just a little while her harvest will begin."

34"King Nebuchadnezzar* of Babylon has eaten and crushed us and emptied out our strength. He has swallowed us like a great monster and filled his belly with our riches. He has thrown us out of our own country. 35May Babylon be repaid for all the violence she did to us," say the people of Jerusalem. "May the people of Babylonia be paid in full for all the blood they spilled," says Jerusalem.

36The LORD says to Jerusalem, "I will be your lawyer to plead your case, and I will avenge you. I will dry up her river, her water supply, 37and Babylon will become a heap of rubble, haunted by jackals. It will be an object of horror and contempt, without a single person living there.

38"In their drunken feasts, the people of Babylon roar like lions. 39And while they lie inflamed with all their wine, I will prepare a different kind of feast for them. I will make them drink until they fall asleep, never again to waken," says the LORD. 40"I will bring them like lambs to the slaughter, like rams and goats to be sacrificed.

41"How Babylon* is fallen—great Babylon, praised throughout the earth! The world can scarcely believe its eyes at her fall! 42The sea has risen over Babylon; she is covered by its waves. 43Her cities now lie in ruins; she is a dry wilderness where no one lives or even passes by. 44And I will punish Bel, the god of Babylon, and pull from his mouth what he has taken. The nations will no longer come and worship him. The wall of Babylon has fallen.

45"Listen, my people, flee from Babylon. Save yourselves! Run from the LORD's fierce anger. 46But do not panic when you hear the first rumor of approaching forces. For rumors will keep coming year by year. Then there will be a time of violence as the leaders fight against each other. 47For the time is surely coming when I will punish this great city and all her idols. Her whole land will be disgraced, and her dead will lie in the streets. 48The heavens and earth will rejoice, for out of the north will come destroying armies against Babylon," says the LORD. 49"Just as Babylon killed the people of Israel and others throughout the world, so must her people be killed. 50Go, you who escaped the sword! Do not stand and watch—flee while you can! Remember the LORD, even though you are in a far-off land, and think about your home in Jerusalem."

51"We are ashamed," the people say. "We are insulted and disgraced because the LORD's Temple has been defiled by foreigners."

52"Yes," says the LORD, "but the time is coming when Babylon's idols will be destroyed. The groans of her wounded people will be heard throughout the land. 53Though Babylon reaches as high as the heavens, and though she increases her strength immeasurably, I will send enemies to plunder her," says the LORD.

54Listen! Hear the cry of Babylon, the sound of great destruction from the land of the Babylonians. 55For the LORD is destroying Babylon. He will silence her. Waves of enemies pound against her; the noise of battle rings through the city. 56Destroying

51:34 Hebrew *Nebuchadrezzar*, a variant name for Nebuchadnezzar.   51:41 Hebrew *Sheshach*, a code name for Babylon.

armies come against Babylon. Her mighty men are captured, and their weapons break in their hands. For the LORD is a God who gives just punishment, and he is giving Babylon all she deserves.

[57]"I will make drunk her officials, wise men, rulers, captains, and warriors," says the King, whose name is the LORD Almighty. "They will fall asleep and never wake up again!"

[58]This is what the LORD Almighty says: "The wide walls of Babylon will be leveled to the ground, and her high gates will be burned. The builders from many lands have worked in vain, for their work will be destroyed by fire!"

[59]The prophet Jeremiah gave this message to Zedekiah's staff officer, Seraiah son of Neriah and grandson of Mahseiah, when he went to Babylon with King Zedekiah of Judah. This was during the fourth year of Zedekiah's reign.* [60]Jeremiah had recorded on a scroll all the terrible disasters that would soon come upon Babylon. [61]He said to Seraiah, "When you get to Babylon, read aloud everything on this scroll. [62]Then say, 'LORD, you have said that you will destroy Babylon so that neither people nor animals will remain here. She will lie empty and abandoned forever.' [63]Then, when you have finished reading the scroll, tie it to a stone, and throw it into the Euphrates River. [64]Then say, 'In this same way Babylon and her people will sink, never again to rise, because of the disasters I will bring upon her.'"

This is the end of Jeremiah's messages.

CHAPTER 52

Zedekiah was twenty-one years old when he became king, and he reigned in Jerusalem eleven years. His mother's name was Hamutal, the daughter of Jeremiah from Libnah. [2]But Zedekiah did what was evil in the LORD's sight, just as Jehoiakim had done. [3]So the LORD, in his anger, finally banished the people of Jerusalem and Judah from his presence and sent them into exile.

Then Zedekiah rebelled against the king of Babylon. [4]So on January 15,* during the ninth year of Zedekiah's reign, King Nebuchadnezzar* of Babylon led his entire army against Jerusalem. They surrounded the city and built siege ramps against its walls. [5]Jerusalem was kept under siege until the eleventh year of King Zedekiah's reign.

[6]By July 18 of Zedekiah's eleventh year,* the famine in the city had become very severe, with the last of the food entirely gone. [7]Then a section of the city wall was broken down, and all the soldiers made plans to escape from the city. But since the city was surrounded by the Babylonians,* they waited for nightfall and fled through the gate between the two walls behind the king's gardens. They made a dash across the fields, in the direction of the Jordan Valley.*

[8]But the Babylonians chased after them and caught King Zedekiah on the plains of Jericho, for by then his men had all abandoned him. [9]They brought him to the king of Babylon at Riblah, in the land of Hamath, where sentence was passed against him. [10]There at Riblah, the king of Babylon made Zedekiah watch as all his sons were killed; they also killed all the other leaders of Judah. [11]Then they gouged out Zedekiah's eyes, bound him in bronze chains, and led him away to Babylon. Zedekiah remained there in prison for the rest of his life.

[12]On August 17 of that year,* which was the nineteenth year of Nebuchadnezzar's reign, Nebuzaradan, captain of the guard, an official of the Babylonian king, arrived in Jerusalem. [13]He burned down the Temple of the LORD, the royal palace, and all the houses of Jerusalem. He destroyed all the important buildings in the city. [14]Then the captain of the guard supervised the entire Babylonian* army as they tore down the walls of Jerusalem. [15]Nebuzaradan, captain of the guard, then took as exiles some of the poorest of the people and those who remained in the city, along with the rest of the craftsmen and the troops who had declared their allegiance to the king of Babylon. [16]But Nebuzaradan allowed some of the poorest people to stay

---

51:59 The fourth year of Zedekiah's reign was 593 B.C.   **52:4a** Hebrew *on the tenth day of the tenth month,* of the Hebrew calendar. A number of events in Jeremiah can be cross-checked with dates in surviving Babylonian records and related accurately to our modern calendar. This event occurred on January 15, 588 B.C.   **52:4b** Hebrew *Nebuchadrezzar,* a variant name for Nebuchadnezzar; also in 52:12, 28, 29, 30.   **52:6** Hebrew *By the ninth day of the fourth month* [of Zedekiah's eleventh year]. This event of the Hebrew lunar calendar occurred on July 18, 586 B.C.; also see note on 52:4a.   **52:7a** Or *Chaldeans;* also in 52:8, 17.   **52:7b** Hebrew *the Arabah.* **52:12** Hebrew *On the tenth day of the fifth month,* of the Hebrew calendar. This day was August 17, 586 B.C.; also see note on 52:4a. **52:14** Or *Chaldean.*

behind in Judah to care for the vineyards and fields.

¹⁷The Babylonians broke up the bronze pillars, the bronze water carts, and the bronze Sea that were at the LORD's Temple, and they carried all the bronze away to Babylon. ¹⁸They also took all the pots, shovels, lamp snuffers, basins, dishes, and all the other bronze utensils used for making sacrifices at the Temple. ¹⁹Nebuzaradan, captain of the guard, also took the small bowls, firepans, basins, pots, lampstands, dishes, bowls used for drink offerings, and all the other utensils made of pure gold or silver.

²⁰The bronze from the two pillars, the water carts, and the Sea with the twelve bulls beneath it was too great to be measured. These things had been made for the LORD's Temple in the days of King Solomon. ²¹Each of the pillars was 27 feet tall and 18 feet in circumference.* They were hollow, with walls 3 inches thick.* ²²The bronze capital on top of each pillar was 7½ feet* high and was decorated with a network of bronze pomegranates all the way around. ²³There were ninety-six pomegranates on the sides, and a total of one hundred on the network around the top.

²⁴The captain of the guard took with him as prisoners Seraiah the chief priest, his assistant Zephaniah, and the three chief gatekeepers. ²⁵And of the people still hiding in the city, he took an officer of the Judean army, seven of the king's personal advisers, the army commander's chief secretary, who was in charge of recruitment, and sixty other citizens. ²⁶Nebuzaradan the commander took them all to the king of Babylon at Riblah. ²⁷And there at Riblah in the land of Hamath, the king of Babylon had them all put to death. So the people of Judah were sent into exile from their land.

²⁸The number of captives taken to Babylon in the seventh year of Nebuchadnezzar's reign* was 3,023. ²⁹Then in Nebuchadnezzar's eighteenth year* he took 832 more. ³⁰In his twenty-third year* he sent Nebuzaradan, his captain of the guard, who took 745 more—a total of 4,600 captives in all.

³¹In the thirty-seventh year of King Jehoiachin's exile in Babylon, Evil-merodach ascended to the Babylonian throne. He was kind to Jehoiachin and released him from prison on March 31 of that year.* ³²He spoke pleasantly to Jehoiachin and gave him preferential treatment over all the other exiled kings in Babylon. ³³He supplied Jehoiachin with new clothes to replace his prison garb and allowed him to dine at the king's table for the rest of his life. ³⁴The Babylonian king also gave him a regular allowance to cover his living expenses until the day of his death.

52:21a Hebrew *18 cubits* [8.1 meters] *tall and 12 cubits* [5.4 meters] *in circumference.*   52:21b Hebrew *4 fingers thick* [8 centimeters]. 52:22 Hebrew *5 cubits* [2.3 meters].   52:28 This exile in the seventh year of Nebuchadnezzar's reign occurred in 597 B.C. 52:29 This exile in the eighteenth year of Nebuchadnezzar's reign occurred in 586 B.C.   52:30 This exile in the twenty-third year of Nebuchadnezzar's reign occurred in 581 B.C.   52:31 Hebrew *on the twenty-fifth day of the twelfth month,* of the Hebrew calendar. This day was March 31, 561 B.C.; also see note on 52:4a.

Lamentations

JEREMIAH the prophet had warned the people of Judah for years of their impending doom if they would not repent. When his prophecies were fulfilled and Jerusalem was destroyed by the Babylonians, Jeremiah wrote Lamentations, a funeral dirge for the city. Written in five poems, this is probably the saddest book of the Bible. However, Jeremiah saw ultimate reason and hope beyond the ruins of his city. God is sovereign—after all, he had described this judgment years before—and he is gracious. In his faithful mercy Jerusalem will be restored.

Focus	God's Chastening and Control				God's Character
Divisions	Destroyed City	Crushed Population	Lamenting Prophet	Lost Glory	Repentant Kingdom
	1:1 1:22	2:1 2:22	3:1 3:66	4:1 4:22	5:1 5:22
Topics	The Sorrow	The Reason	The Hope	The Contrast	The Plea
Place	Jerusalem				
Time	Approximately 586 B.C.				

AUGUST 13 □ DAY 226
LAMENTATIONS 1–5
Wailing without a Wall

OVERVIEW Lamentations describes the funeral of a city. It is a tear-stained portrait of once-proud Jerusalem, now reduced to a pile of rubble by the invading Babylonian hordes. In a five-poem dirge, Jeremiah lays bare his emotions. A death has occurred; Jerusalem lies barren. Jeremiah, traditionally acclaimed as the author of Lamentations, writes his lament in acrostic or alphabetical fashion. In the midst of this terrible holocaust, Jeremiah triumphantly cries out, "Great is [the Lord's] faithfulness" (3:23)! In the face of death and destruction, with life seeming to come apart at the seams, Jeremiah turns tragedy into a triumph of faith. God has never failed him in the past. God has promised to remain faithful in the future. In the light of the God he knows and loves, Jeremiah finds hope and comfort.

Chapter 1	Chapter 2	Chapter 3	Chapter 4	Chapter 5
Jerusalem Deserted	Jerusalem Destroyed	Triumphant Hope	Jerusalem Defeated	Jerusalem Distressed
Defeat		Victory	Defeat	

YOUR DAILY WALK It's a strange paradox that while the pages of Scripture are soaked with the tears of Jeremiah, David, Hezekiah, the Lord Jesus, and a host of others, crying today is often looked upon as a sign of weakness.

A Christian should show more concern for people than for creeds.

Psalm 56:8 tells us that God puts our tears in a bottle and keeps track of them in a book. Stoic insensitivity is nothing to be proud of. A man or woman with God's heart for people can't help but get emotionally involved. If you've never done so, ask God to break your heart for people—to give you the kind of compassion that caused Jeremiah and Jesus to cry over the city of Jerusalem.

INSIGHT Jeremiah's Two Glimpses of Jerusalem's Fall

Book of Jeremiah	*Book of Lamentations*
Looking ahead to the fall of Jerusalem (Warning)	Looking back at the fall of Jerusalem (Mourning)

CHAPTER 1

Jerusalem's streets, once bustling with people, are now silent. Like a widow broken with grief, she sits alone in her mourning. Once the queen of nations, she is now a slave.

²She sobs through the night; tears stream down her cheeks. Among all her lovers, there is no one left to help her. All her friends have betrayed her; they are now her enemies.

³Judah has been led away into captivity, afflicted and enslaved. She lives among foreign nations and has no place of rest.

1:1 Each of the first four chapters of this book is an acrostic, laid out in the order of the Hebrew alphabet. The first word of each verse begins with a successive Hebrew letter. Chapters 1, 2, and 4 have one verse for each of the 22 Hebrew letters. Chapter 3 contains 22 stanzas of three verses each. Though chapter 5 is not an acrostic, it also has 22 verses.

Her enemies have chased her down, and she has nowhere to turn.

⁴The roads to Jerusalem* are in mourning, no longer filled with crowds on their way to celebrate the Temple festivals. The city gates are silent, her priests groan, her young women are crying—how bitterly Jerusalem weeps!

⁵Her oppressors have become her masters, and her enemies prosper, for the LORD has punished Jerusalem for her many sins. Her children have been captured and taken away to distant lands.

⁶All the beauty and majesty of Jerusalem* are gone. Her princes are like starving deer searching for pasture, too weak to run from the pursuing enemy.

⁷And now in the midst of her sadness and wandering, Jerusalem remembers her ancient splendor. But then she fell to her enemy, and there was no one to help her. Her enemy struck her down and laughed as she fell.

⁸Jerusalem has sinned greatly, so she has been tossed away like a filthy rag. All who once honored her now despise her, for they have seen her stripped naked and humiliated. All she can do is groan and hide her face.

⁹She defiled herself with immorality with no thought of the punishment that would follow. Now she lies in the gutter with no one to lift her out. "LORD, see my deep misery," she cries. "The enemy has triumphed."

¹⁰The enemy has plundered her completely, taking everything precious that she owns. She has seen foreigners violate her sacred Temple, the place the LORD had forbidden them to enter.

¹¹Her people groan as they search for bread. They have sold their treasures for food to stay alive. "O LORD, look," she mourns, "and see how I am despised.

¹²"Is it nothing to you, all you who pass by? Look around and see if there is any suffering like mine, which the LORD brought on me in the day of his fierce anger.

¹³"He has sent fire from heaven that burns in my bones. He has placed a trap in my path and turned me back. He has made me desolate, racked with sickness all day long.

¹⁴"He wove my sins into ropes to hitch me to a yoke of captivity. The Lord sapped my strength and gave me to my enemies; I am helpless in their hands.

¹⁵"The Lord has treated my mighty men with contempt. At his command a great army has come to crush my young warriors. The Lord has trampled his beloved city* as grapes are trampled in a winepress.

¹⁶"For all these things I weep; tears flow down my cheeks. No one is here to comfort me; any who might encourage me are far away. My children have no future, for the enemy has conquered us."

¹⁷Jerusalem pleads for help, but no one comforts her. Regarding his people,* the LORD has said, "Let their neighbors be their enemies! Let them be thrown away like a filthy rag!"

¹⁸"And the LORD is right," she groans, "for I rebelled against him. Listen, people everywhere; look upon my anguish and despair, for my sons and daughters have been taken captive to distant lands.

¹⁹"I begged my allies for help, but they betrayed me. My priests and leaders starved to death in the city, even as they searched for food to save their lives.

²⁰"LORD, see my anguish! My heart is broken and my soul despairs, for I have rebelled against you. In the streets the sword kills, and at home there is only death.

²¹"Others heard my groans, but no one turned to comfort me. When my enemies heard of my troubles, they were happy to see what you had done. Oh, bring the day you promised, when you will destroy them as you have destroyed me.

²²"Look at all their evil deeds, LORD. Punish them, as you have punished me for all my sins. My groans are many, and my heart is faint."

CHAPTER 2

The Lord in his anger has cast a dark shadow over Jerusalem.* The fairest of Israel's cities lies in the dust, thrown down from the heights of heaven. In his day of awesome fury, the Lord has shown no mercy even to his Temple.*

²Without mercy the Lord has destroyed every home in Israel.* In his anger he has broken down the fortress walls of Jerusalem.* He has brought to dust the kingdom and all its rulers.

1:4 Hebrew *Zion;* also in 1:17.   1:6 Hebrew *the daughter of Zion.*   1:15 Hebrew *the virgin daughter of Judah.*   1:17 Hebrew *Jacob.*
2:1a Hebrew *the daughter of Zion;* also in 2:8, 10, 18.   2:1b Hebrew *footstool.*   2:2a Hebrew *Jacob;* also in 2:3.   2:2b Hebrew *the daughter of Judah;* also in 2:5.

³All the strength of Israel vanishes beneath his fury. The Lord has withdrawn his protection as the enemy attacks. He consumes the whole land of Israel like a raging fire.

⁴He bends his bow against his people as though he were their enemy. His strength is used against them to kill their finest youth. His fury is poured out like fire on beautiful Jerusalem.*

⁵Yes, the Lord has vanquished Israel like an enemy. He has destroyed her forts and palaces. He has brought unending sorrow and tears to Jerusalem.

⁶He has broken down his Temple as though it were merely a garden shelter. The LORD has blotted out all memory of the holy festivals and Sabbath days. Kings and priests fall together before his anger.

⁷The Lord has rejected his own altar; he despises his own sanctuary. He has given Jerusalem's palaces to her enemies. They shout in the LORD's Temple as though it were a day of celebration.

⁸The LORD was determined to destroy the walls of Jerusalem. He made careful plans for their destruction, then he went ahead and did it. Therefore, the ramparts and walls have fallen down before him.

⁹Jerusalem's gates have sunk into the ground. All their locks and bars are destroyed, for he has smashed them. Her kings and princes have been exiled to distant lands; the law is no more. Her prophets receive no more visions from the LORD.

¹⁰The leaders of Jerusalem sit on the ground in silence, clothed in sackcloth. They throw dust on their heads in sorrow and despair. The young women of Jerusalem hang their heads in shame.

¹¹I have cried until the tears no longer come. My heart is broken, my spirit poured out, as I see what has happened to my people. Little children and tiny babies are fainting and dying in the streets.

¹²"Mama, we want food," they cry, and then collapse in their mothers' arms. Their lives ebb away like the life of a warrior wounded in battle.

¹³In all the world has there ever been such sorrow? O daughter of Jerusalem, to what can I compare your anguish? O virgin daughter of Zion, how can I comfort you? For your wound is as deep as the sea. Who can heal you?

¹⁴Your "prophets" have said so many foolish things, false to the core. They did not try to hold you back from exile by pointing out your sins. Instead, they painted false pictures, filling you with false hope.

¹⁵All who pass by jeer at you. They scoff and insult Jerusalem,* saying, "Is this the city called 'Most Beautiful in All the World' and 'Joy of All the Earth'?"

¹⁶All your enemies deride you. They scoff and grind their teeth and say, "We have destroyed her at last! Long have we awaited this day, and it is finally here!"

¹⁷But it is the LORD who did it just as he warned. He has fulfilled the promises of disaster he made long ago. He has destroyed Jerusalem without mercy and caused her enemies to rejoice over her and boast of their power.

¹⁸Cry aloud* before the Lord, O walls of Jerusalem! Let your tears flow like a river. Give yourselves no rest from weeping day or night.

¹⁹Rise during the night and cry out. Pour out your hearts like water to the Lord. Lift up your hands to him in prayer. Plead for your children as they faint with hunger in the streets.

²⁰"O LORD, think about this!" Jerusalem cries. "You are doing this to your own people! Should mothers eat their little children, those they once bounced on their knees? Should priests and prophets die within the Lord's Temple?

²¹"See them lying in the streets—young and old, boys and girls, killed by the swords of the enemy. You have killed them in your anger, slaughtering them without mercy.

²²"You have invited terrors from all around as though you were calling them to a day of feasting. In the day of the LORD's anger, no one has escaped or survived. The enemy has killed all the children I bore and raised."

CHAPTER 3

I am the one who has seen the afflictions that come from the rod of the LORD's anger. ²He has brought me into deep darkness, shutting out all light. ³He has turned against me. Day and night his hand is heavy upon me.

⁴He has made my skin and flesh grow

2:4 Hebrew *on the tent of the daughter of Zion.*   2:15 Hebrew *the daughter of Jerusalem.*   2:18 Hebrew *Their heart cried.*

old. He has broken my bones. ⁵He has attacked me and surrounded me with anguish and distress. ⁶He has buried me in a dark place, like a person long dead.

⁷He has walled me in, and I cannot escape. He has bound me in heavy chains. ⁸And though I cry and shout, he shuts out my prayers. ⁹He has blocked my path with a high stone wall. He has twisted the road before me with many detours.

¹⁰He hid like a bear or a lion, waiting to attack me. ¹¹He dragged me off the path and tore me with his claws, leaving me helpless and desolate. ¹²He bent his bow and aimed it squarely at me.

¹³He shot his arrows deep into my heart. ¹⁴My own people laugh at me. All day long they sing their mocking songs. ¹⁵He has filled me with bitterness. He has given me a cup of deep sorrow to drink.

¹⁶He has made me grind my teeth on gravel. He has rolled me in the dust. ¹⁷Peace has been stripped away, and I have forgotten what prosperity is. ¹⁸I cry out, "My splendor is gone! Everything I had hoped for from the LORD is lost!"

¹⁹The thought of my suffering and homelessness is bitter beyond words.* ²⁰I will never forget this awful time, as I grieve over my loss. ²¹Yet I still dare to hope when I remember this:

²²The unfailing love of the LORD never ends! By his mercies we have been kept from complete destruction. ²³Great is his faithfulness; his mercies begin afresh each day. ²⁴I say to myself, "The LORD is my inheritance; therefore, I will hope in him!"

²⁵The LORD is wonderfully good to those who wait for him and seek him. ²⁶So it is good to wait quietly for salvation from the LORD. ²⁷And it is good for the young to submit to the yoke of his discipline.

²⁸Let them sit alone in silence beneath the LORD's demands. ²⁹Let them lie face down in the dust; then at last there is hope for them. ³⁰Let them turn the other cheek to those who strike them. Let them accept the insults of their enemies.

³¹For the Lord does not abandon anyone forever. ³²Though he brings grief, he also shows compassion according to the greatness of his unfailing love. ³³For he does not enjoy hurting people or causing them sorrow.

³⁴But the leaders of his people trampled prisoners underfoot. ³⁵They deprived people of their God-given rights in defiance of the Most High. ³⁶They perverted justice in the courts. Do they think the Lord didn't see it?

³⁷Can anything happen without the Lord's permission? ³⁸Is it not the Most High who helps one and harms another? ³⁹Then why should we, mere humans, complain when we are punished for our sins?

⁴⁰Instead, let us test and examine our ways. Let us turn again in repentance to the LORD. ⁴¹Let us lift our hearts and hands to God in heaven and say, ⁴²"We have sinned and rebelled, and you have not forgiven us.

⁴³"You have engulfed us with your anger, chased us down, and slaughtered us without mercy. ⁴⁴You have hidden yourself in a cloud so our prayers cannot reach you. ⁴⁵You have discarded us as refuse and garbage among the nations.

⁴⁶"All our enemies have spoken out against us. ⁴⁷We are filled with fear, for we are trapped, desolate, and ruined." ⁴⁸Streams of tears flow from my eyes because of the destruction of my people!

⁴⁹My tears flow down endlessly. They will not stop ⁵⁰until the LORD looks down from heaven and sees. ⁵¹My heart is breaking over the fate of all the women of Jerusalem.

⁵²My enemies, whom I have never harmed, chased me like a bird. ⁵³They threw me into a pit and dropped stones on me. ⁵⁴The water flowed above my head, and I cried out, "This is the end!"

⁵⁵But I called on your name, LORD, from deep within the well, ⁵⁶and you heard me! You listened to my pleading; you heard my weeping! ⁵⁷Yes, you came at my despairing cry and told me, "Do not fear."

⁵⁸Lord, you are my lawyer! Plead my case! For you have redeemed my life. ⁵⁹You have seen the wrong they have done to me, LORD. Be my judge, and prove me right. ⁶⁰You have seen the plots my enemies have laid against me.

⁶¹LORD, you have heard the vile names they call me. You know all about the plans they have made—⁶²the plots my enemies whisper and mutter against me all day long. ⁶³Look at them! In all their activities, they constantly mock me with their songs.

⁶⁴Pay them back, LORD, for all the evil

3:19 Hebrew is *wormwood and gall.*

they have done. 65Give them hard and stubborn hearts, and then let your curse fall upon them! 66Chase them down in your anger, destroying them from beneath the LORD's heavens.

CHAPTER 4

How the gold has lost its luster! Even the finest gold has become dull. The sacred gemstones lie scattered in the streets!

2See how the precious children of Jerusalem,* worth their weight in gold, are now treated like pots of clay.

3Even the jackals feed their young, but not my people Israel. They ignore their children's cries, like the ostriches of the desert.

4The parched tongues of their little ones stick with thirst to the roofs of their mouths. The children cry for bread, but no one has any to give them.

5The people who once ate only the richest foods now beg in the streets for anything they can get. Those who once lived in palaces now search the garbage pits for food.

6The guilt* of my people is greater than that of Sodom, where utter disaster struck in a moment with no one to help them.

7Our princes were once glowing with health; they were as clean as snow and as elegant as jewels.

8But now their faces are blacker than soot. No one even recognizes them. Their skin sticks to their bones; it is as dry and hard as wood.

9Those killed by the sword are far better off than those who die of hunger, wasting away for want of food.

10Tenderhearted women have cooked their own children and eaten them in order to survive the siege.

11But now the anger of the LORD is satisfied. His fiercest anger has now been poured out. He started a fire in Jerusalem* that burned the city to its foundations.

12Not a king in all the earth—no one in all the world—would have believed an enemy could march through the gates of Jerusalem.

13Yet it happened because of the sins of her prophets and priests, who defiled the city by shedding innocent blood.

14They wandered blindly through the streets, so defiled by blood that no one dared to touch them.

15"Get away!" the people shouted at them. "You are defiled! Don't touch us!" So they fled to distant lands and wandered there among foreign nations, but none would let them stay.

16The LORD himself has scattered them, and he no longer helps them. The priests and leaders are no longer honored and respected.

17We looked in vain for our allies to come and save us, but we were looking to nations that could offer no help at all.

18We couldn't go into the streets without danger to our lives. Our end was near; our days were numbered. We were doomed!

19Our enemies were swifter than the eagles. If we fled to the mountains, they found us. If we hid in the wilderness, they were waiting for us there.

20Our king, the LORD's anointed, the very life of our nation, was caught in their snares. We had foolishly boasted that under his protection we could hold our own against any nation on earth!

21Are you rejoicing in the land of Uz, O people of Edom? But you, too, must drink from the cup of the LORD's anger. You, too, will be stripped naked in your drunkenness.

22O Jerusalem,* your punishment will end; you will soon return from exile. But Edom, your punishment is just beginning; soon your many sins will be revealed.

CHAPTER 5

LORD, remember everything that has happened to us. See all the sorrows we bear! 2Our inheritance has been turned over to strangers, our homes to foreigners. 3We are orphaned and fatherless. Our mothers are widowed. 4We have to pay for water to drink, and even firewood is expensive. 5Those who pursue us are at our heels; we are exhausted but are given no rest. 6We submitted to Egypt and Assyria to get enough food to survive. 7It was our ancestors who sinned, but they died before the hand of judgment fell. We have suffered the punishment they deserved!

8Slaves have now become our masters; there is no one left to rescue us. 9We must hunt for food in the wilderness at the risk of our lives. 10Because of the famine, our skin has been blackened as though baked in an oven. 11Our enemies rape the

4:2 Hebrew *sons of Zion*.   4:6 Or *punishment*.   4:11 Hebrew *in Zion*.   4:22 Hebrew *daughter of Zion*.

women and young girls in Jerusalem* and throughout the towns of Judah. ¹²Our princes are being hanged by their thumbs, and the old men are treated with contempt. ¹³The young men are led away to work at millstones, and the children stagger under heavy loads of wood. ¹⁴The old men no longer sit in the city gates; young men no longer dance and sing.

¹⁵The joy of our hearts has ended; our dancing has turned to mourning. ¹⁶The garlands have* fallen from our heads. Disaster has fallen upon us because we have sinned. ¹⁷Our hearts are sick and weary, and our eyes grow dim with tears. ¹⁸For Jerusalem* is empty and desolate, a place haunted by jackals.

¹⁹But LORD, you remain the same forever! Your throne continues from generation to generation. ²⁰Why do you continue to forget us? Why have you forsaken us for so long? ²¹Restore us, O LORD, and bring us back to you again! Give us back the joys we once had! ²²Or have you utterly rejected us? Are you angry with us still?

5:11 Hebrew *Zion.*   **5:16** Or *The crown has.*   **5:18** Hebrew *Mount Zion.*

AUGUST 14 □ DAY 227
Light in the Darkest Hour

 LOOK BACK Sometimes through sermons, sometimes through silence and symbolic object lessons, Jeremiah confronts the people of Judah with the deadly consequences of their disobedience. His sermons are ignored by some and burned by others. His character is smeared and his motives questioned. Finally, Jeremiah is thrown into a muddy well, where he sinks to an all-time low (literally and figuratively). But through it all, God is at work in and through his choice messenger. When Jerusalem falls to the Babylonian onslaught, Jeremiah is freed and carried to Egypt. There he declares the future fortunes and misfortunes of Judah and her pagan neighbors. Though the present is grim, the future brims with hope if you know where to look (Jeremiah 52:31-34).

Lamentations is Jeremiah's "diary of disaster," penned as he watches calamity befall his beloved Jerusalem. You can almost wring out the pages, so soaked are they with Jeremiah's tears. But in the midst of Jeremiah's grief (Lamentations 3:22-23), he proclaims a truth so powerful, it has become the theme of one of the best-loved hymns of all time: "Great Is Thy Faithfulness." Governments rise and fall; economies crumble; even spiritual leaders disappoint us. But the Lord's mercies never fail!

 LOOK UP Have you ever experienced total darkness? You know, the kind you can *feel* as well as *see?*

Try it! Find an interior room, attic, or closet in your house where there is little or no natural light. Put a blindfold over your eyes and close your eyes tightly. What you have is absolute darkness—the absence of any glimmer of light.

Life is filled with shadows, but it is Sonshine that makes them all.

Metaphorically, the people of God were experiencing total darkness in Jeremiah 52 as they faced the Babylonian onslaught. After all, consider this:

- There was not a crust of bread left in the city (v. 6).
- The city's defenses were in shambles (v. 7).
- The army had all gone AWOL (v. 7).
- The king's family was slaughtered before his eyes. Then his eyes were gouged out, and he was deported in chains to a distant prison (vv. 10-11).

• The Temple, city walls, and chief buildings were burned down (vv. 13-14).
• The king's entire "cabinet" was taken prisoner and executed (vv. 24-27).
• Thousands of Jews were taken captive to a distant land (vv. 27-30).

Dark days for the people of God, to be sure. But don't miss the final four verses, for there you'll discover light in the darkness—hope in the midst of horror. Though Evil-merodach had no earthly reason to do so, the king of Babylon showed kindness and courtesy to the exiled king of Judah. Why? Because *God was not finished with his people.* He knew that they needed hope and a future.

 LOOK AHEAD When your health is frail, when your financial prospects are bleak, when your family and friends are far away, when your job is uncertain, when tomorrow looks no brighter than today, it's easy to be overwhelmed by the darkness. But the light of one match can illuminate an entire room!

Take a moment to bask in the light of Psalm 27:1. There you'll discover that darkness is no match for the Light of your life, the one in whom there is no darkness at all (1 John 1:5).

The LORD is my light and my salvation—
so why should I be afraid?
The LORD protects me from danger—
so why should I tremble?

Ezekiel

EZEKIEL'S ministry among the Jewish exiles in Babylonia during the last days of Judah's decline is similar to that of Jeremiah. But while Jeremiah delivers a chilling message of destruction, Ezekiel offers a warning message of reconstruction. Jeremiah is a man of tears; Ezekiel, a man of vision. And those visions stretch all the way from horrible condemnation of Judah's faithless leaders and godless foes to hopeful consolation regarding Judah's future restoration.

Focus	Judah's End					Judah's Enemies		Judah's Future			
Divisions	Ezekiel's Call	Sins and Sorrows	Signs and Sermons	Parables of Judgment	Swords and Signposts	Judgment East & West	Judgment on Egypt	Watchman on the Wall	Gog and Magog	New Temple for Israel	New Worship for Israel
	1 6	7 11	12 15	16 19	20 23	24 28	29 32	33 36	37 39	40 43	44 48
Topics	Before the Fall (592–587 B.C.)					During the Fall (586 B.C.)		After the Fall (585–570 B.C.)			
	Prophecies of Judgment							Promises of Restoration			
Place	Babylonia										
Time	About 22 Years										

AUGUST 15 ☐ DAY 228
EZEKIEL 1–6
Ezekiel's Vision and Call

OVERVIEW Six hundred miles from Jerusalem lives Ezekiel, another of God's handpicked mouthpieces. Ezekiel is called by God to preach both judgment and hope to the first Judean exiles in Babylonia. Because his prophetic assignment is so challenging, God first gives Ezekiel a most unusual vision of his greatness and glory. Fortified with a fresh glimpse of his great God, Ezekiel launches into his difficult task: explaining to the exiles why Jerusalem will fall and why the nation will spend the next seven decades in Babylonia.

Chapter 1	Chapters 2–3	Chapters 4–5	Chapter 6
Ezekiel's Vision	Ezekiel's Commission	Judgment Visualized	Judgment Explained
The Prophet		The Prophecy	

Life without purpose inevitably falls prey to the perverted ways of the uncommitted life.

YOUR DAILY WALK How many times a day do you put into practice a "this is what the Sovereign LORD says" principle? You know the kinds of situations: You're tempted to gossip . . . you feel yourself losing control of your temper . . . you're confronted by a close friend who is caught in the quicksand of a deep personal problem . . . you feel like telling a half-truth (which, in reality, is a whole untruth).

How do you tackle these and countless other sticky situations? Do you just ignore them and hope they'll go away? Do you share your own thoughts and wisdom on the subject? Or do you do what God told Ezekiel to do: "Go to your people in exile and say to them, 'This is what the Sovereign LORD says'" (3:11)?

This devotional guide can help you walk through the Bible, but how much of the *Bible* are you allowing to walk through *you* . . . in your thoughts, habits, speech, and conduct? Put these words on an index card for quick reference: "God said it, I believe it, I will do it, and that settles it." Then today, with God's help, translate a "this is what the Sovereign LORD says" into a "this is what my life says."

INSIGHT Repetition Is the Mother of Learning
Ezekiel's style of instruction might be summarized this way: "If a point is worth making, it is worth making at least four times!" It might be easy to miss the prophet's point if stated only once, but it is nearly impossible to miss when stated four times in one chapter (6:7, 10, 13-14)! Find it and state it in your own words.

CHAPTER 1
On July 31* of my thirtieth year,* while I was with the Judean exiles beside the Kebar River in Babylon, the heavens were opened to me, and I saw visions of God. ²This happened during the fifth year of King Jehoiachin's captivity. ³The LORD gave a message to me, Ezekiel son of Buzi,

1:1a Hebrew *On the fifth day of the fourth month*, of the Hebrew calendar. A number of dates in Ezekiel can be cross-checked with dates in surviving Babylonian records and related accurately to our modern calendar. This event occurred on July 31, 593 B.C. **1:1b** Or *in the thirtieth year*.

a priest, there beside the Kebar River in the land of the Babylonians,* and I felt the hand of the LORD take hold of me.

4As I looked, I saw a great storm coming toward me from the north, driving before it a huge cloud that flashed with lightning and shone with brilliant light. The fire inside the cloud glowed like gleaming amber. 5From the center of the cloud came four living beings that looked human, 6except that each had four faces and two pairs of wings. 7Their legs were straight like human legs, but their feet were split like calves' feet and shone like burnished bronze. 8Beneath each of their wings I could see human hands. 9The wings of each living being touched the wings of the two beings beside it. The living beings were able to fly in any direction without turning around. 10Each had a human face in the front, the face of a lion on the right side, the face of an ox on the left side, and the face of an eagle at the back. 11Each had two pairs of outstretched wings—one pair stretched out to touch the wings of the living beings on either side of it, and the other pair covered its body. 12They went in whatever direction the spirit chose, and they moved straight forward in all directions without having to turn around.

13The living beings looked like bright coals of fire or brilliant torches, and it looked as though lightning was flashing back and forth among them. 14And the living beings darted to and fro like flashes of lightning.

15As I looked at these beings, I saw four wheels on the ground beneath them, one wheel belonging to each. 16The wheels sparkled as if made of chrysolite. All four wheels looked the same; each wheel had a second wheel turning crosswise within it. 17The beings could move forward in any of the four directions they faced, without turning as they moved. 18The rims of the four wheels were awesomely tall, and they were covered with eyes all around the edges. 19When the four living beings moved, the wheels moved with them. When they flew upward, the wheels went up, too. 20The spirit of the four living beings was in the wheels. So wherever the spirit went, the wheels and the living beings went, too. 21When the living beings moved, the wheels moved. When the living

beings stopped, the wheels stopped. When the living beings flew into the air, the wheels rose up. For the spirit of the living beings was in the wheels.

22There was a surface spread out above them like the sky. It sparkled like crystal. 23Beneath this surface the wings of each living being stretched out to touch the others' wings, and each had two wings covering its body. 24As they flew their wings roared like waves crashing against the shore, or like the voice of the Almighty,* or like the shouting of a mighty army. When they stopped, they let down their wings. 25As they stood with their wings lowered, a voice spoke from beyond the crystal surface above them.

26Above the surface over their heads was what looked like a throne made of blue sapphire. And high above this throne was a figure whose appearance was like that of a man. 27From his waist up, he looked like gleaming amber, flickering like a fire. And from his waist down, he looked like a burning flame, shining with splendor. 28All around him was a glowing halo, like a rainbow shining through the clouds. This was the way the glory of the LORD appeared to me. When I saw it, I fell face down in the dust, and I heard someone's voice speaking to me.

CHAPTER 2

"Stand up, son of man," said the voice. "I want to speak with you." 2The Spirit came into me as he spoke and set me on my feet. I listened carefully to his words. 3"Son of man," he said, "I am sending you to the nation of Israel, a nation that is rebelling against me. Their ancestors have rebelled against me from the beginning, and they are still in revolt to this very day. 4They are a hard-hearted and stubborn people. But I am sending you to say to them, 'This is what the Sovereign LORD says!' 5And whether they listen or not—for remember, they are rebels—at least they will know they have had a prophet among them.

6"Son of man, do not fear them. Don't be afraid even though their threats are sharp as thorns and barbed like briers, and they sting like scorpions. Do not be dismayed by their dark scowls. For remember, they are rebels! 7You must give them my messages whether they listen or not. But they won't

1:3 Or *Chaldeans.*   1:24 Hebrew *Shaddai.*

listen, for they are completely rebellious! ⁸Son of man, listen to what I say to you. Do not join them in being a rebel. Open your mouth, and eat what I give you."

⁹Then I looked and saw a hand reaching out to me, and it held a scroll. ¹⁰He unrolled it, and I saw that both sides were covered with funeral songs, other words of sorrow, and pronouncements of doom.

CHAPTER 3

The voice said to me, "Son of man, eat what I am giving you—eat this scroll! Then go and give its message to the people of Israel." ²So I opened my mouth, and he fed me the scroll. ³"Eat it all," he said. And when I ate it, it tasted as sweet as honey.

⁴Then he said, "Son of man, go to the people of Israel with my messages. ⁵I am not sending you to some foreign people whose language you cannot understand. ⁶No, I am not sending you to people with strange and difficult speech. If I did, they would listen! ⁷I am sending you to the people of Israel, but they won't listen to you any more than they listen to me! For the whole lot of them are hard-hearted and stubborn. ⁸But look, I have made you as hard and stubborn as they are. ⁹I have made you as hard as rock! So don't be afraid of them or fear their angry looks, even though they are such rebels."

¹⁰Then he added, "Son of man, let all my words sink deep into your own heart first. Listen to them carefully for yourself. ¹¹Then go to your people in exile and say to them, 'This is what the Sovereign LORD says!' Do this whether they listen to you or not."

¹²Then the Spirit lifted me up, and I heard a loud rumbling sound behind me. (May the glory of the LORD be praised in his place!)* ¹³It was the sound of the wings of the living beings as they brushed against each other and the rumbling of their wheels beneath them.

¹⁴The Spirit lifted me up and took me away. I went in bitterness and turmoil, but the LORD's hold on me was strong. ¹⁵Then I came to the colony of Judean exiles in Tel-abib, beside the Kebar River. I sat there among them for seven days, overwhelmed.

¹⁶At the end of the seven days, the LORD gave me a message. He said, ¹⁷"Son of man, I have appointed you as a watchman for Israel. Whenever you receive a message from me, pass it on to the people immediately. ¹⁸If I warn the wicked, saying, 'You are under the penalty of death,' but you fail to deliver the warning, they will die in their sins. And I will hold you responsible, demanding your blood for theirs. ¹⁹If you warn them and they keep on sinning and refuse to repent, they will die in their sins. But you will have saved your life because you did what you were told to do. ²⁰If good people turn bad and don't listen to my warning, they will die. If you did not warn them of the consequences, then they will die in their sins. Their previous good deeds won't help them, and I will hold you responsible, demanding your blood for theirs. ²¹But if you warn them and they repent, they will live, and you will have saved your own life, too."

²²Then the LORD took hold of me, and he said to me, "Go out into the valley, and I will talk to you there." ²³So I got up and went, and there I saw the glory of the LORD, just as I had seen it in my first vision by the Kebar River. And I fell face down in the dust.

²⁴Then the Spirit came into me and set me on my feet. He talked to me and said, "Go, shut yourself up in your house. ²⁵There you will be bound with ropes so you cannot go out among the people. ²⁶And I will make your tongue stick to the roof of your mouth so you won't be able to pray for them, for they are rebellious. ²⁷But whenever I give you a message, I will loosen your tongue and let you speak. Then you will say to them, 'This is what the Sovereign LORD says!' Some of them will listen, but some will ignore you, for they are rebels.

CHAPTER 4

"And now, son of man, take a large brick and set it down in front of you. Then draw a map of the city of Jerusalem on it. ²Build siege ramps against the city walls. Surround it with enemy camps and battering rams. ³Then take an iron griddle and place it between you and the city. Turn toward it and demonstrate how the enemy will attack Jerusalem. This will be a warning to the people of Israel.

⁴"Now lie on your left side and place the sins of Israel on yourself. You are to bear

3:12 A likely reading for this verse is *Then the Spirit lifted me up, and as the glory of the LORD rose from its place, I heard behind me a loud rumbling sound.*

their sins for the number of days you lie there on your side. [5]You will bear Israel's sins for 390 days—one day for each year of their sin. [6]After that, turn over and lie on your right side for 40 days—one day for each year of Judah's sin.

[7]"Meanwhile, continue your demonstration of the siege of Jerusalem. Lie there with your arm bared and prophesy her destruction. [8]I will tie you up with ropes so you won't be able to turn from side to side until the days of your siege have been completed.

[9]"Now go and get some wheat, barley, beans, lentils, millet, and spelt, and mix them together in a storage jar. Use this food to make bread for yourself during the 390 days you will be lying on your side. [10]Ration this out to yourself, eight ounces* of food for each day, and eat it at set times. [11]Then measure out a jar* of water for each day, and drink it at set times. [12]Each day prepare your bread as you would barley cakes. While all the people are watching, bake it over a fire using dried human dung as fuel and then eat the bread. [13]For this is what the LORD says: Israel will eat defiled bread in the Gentile lands, where I will banish them!"

[14]Then I said, "O Sovereign LORD, must I be defiled by using human dung? For I have never been defiled before. From the time I was a child until now I have never eaten any animal that died of sickness or that I found dead. And I have never eaten any of the animals that our laws forbid."

[15]"All right," the LORD said. "You may bake your bread with cow dung instead of human dung." [16]Then he told me, "Son of man, I will cause food to be very scarce in Jerusalem. It will be weighed out with great care and eaten fearfully. The water will be portioned out drop by drop, and the people will drink it with dismay. [17]Food and water will be so scarce that the people will look at one another in terror, and they will waste away under their punishment.

CHAPTER 5

"Son of man, take a sharp sword and use it as a razor to shave your head and beard. Use a scale to weigh the hair into three equal parts. [2]Place a third of it at the center of your map of Jerusalem. After acting out the siege, burn it there. Scatter another third across your map and slash at it with a sword. Scatter the last third to the wind, for I will scatter my people with the sword. [3]Keep just a bit of the hair and tie it up in your robe. [4]Then take a few of these hairs out and throw them into the fire, burning them up. A fire will then spread from this remnant and destroy all of Israel.

[5]"This is what the Sovereign LORD says: This is an illustration of what will happen to Jerusalem. I placed her at the center of the nations, [6]but she has rebelled against my regulations and has been even more wicked than the surrounding nations. She has refused to obey the laws I gave her to follow. [7]So this is what the Sovereign LORD says: Since you have refused to obey my laws and regulations and have behaved even worse than your neighbors, [8]I myself, the Sovereign LORD, am now your enemy. I will punish you publicly while all the nations watch. [9]Because of your detestable idols, I will punish you more severely than I have punished anyone before or ever will again. [10]Parents will eat their own children, and children will eat their parents. And I will punish you by scattering the few who survive to the far reaches of the earth.

[11]"As surely as I live, says the Sovereign LORD, I will cut you off completely. I will show you no pity at all because you have defiled my Temple with idols and vile practices. [12]A third of your people will die in the city from famine and disease. A third of them will be slaughtered by the enemy outside the city walls. And I will scatter a third to the winds and chase them with my sword. [13]Then at last my anger will be spent, and I will be satisfied. And when my fury against them has subsided, all Israel will know that I, the LORD, have spoken to them in my jealous anger.

[14]"So I will turn you into a ruin, a mockery in the eyes of the surrounding nations and to everyone who travels by. [15]You will become an object of mockery and taunting and horror. You will be a warning to all the nations around you. They will see what happens when the LORD turns against a nation in furious rebuke. I, the LORD, have spoken!

[16]"I will shower you with the deadly arrows of famine to destroy you. The famine will become more and more severe until every crumb of food is gone. [17]And along

---

4:10 Hebrew *20 shekels* [228 grams].　　**4:11** Hebrew *⅙ of a hin*, about 1.3 pints or 0.6 liters.

with the famine, wild animals will attack you, robbing you of your children. Disease and war will stalk your land, and I will bring the sword of the enemy against you. I, the LORD, have spoken!"

CHAPTER 6

Again a message came to me from the LORD: ²"Son of man, look over toward the mountains of Israel and prophesy against them. ³Give the mountains of Israel this message from the Sovereign LORD. This is what the Sovereign LORD says to the mountains and hills and to the ravines and valleys: I am about to bring war upon you, and I will destroy your pagan shrines. ⁴All your altars will be demolished, and your incense altars will be smashed. I will kill your people in front of your idols. ⁵I will lay your corpses in front of your idols and scatter your bones around your altars. ⁶Wherever you live there will be desolation. I will destroy your pagan shrines, your altars, your idols, your incense altars, and all the other religious objects you have made. ⁷Then when the place is littered with corpses, you will know that I am the LORD.

⁸"But I will let a few of my people escape destruction, and they will be scattered among the nations of the world. ⁹Then when they are exiled among the nations, they will remember me. They will recognize how grieved I am by their unfaithful hearts and lustful eyes that long for other gods. Then at last they will hate themselves for all their wickedness. ¹⁰They will know that I alone am the LORD and that I was serious when I predicted that all this would happen to them.

¹¹"This is what the Sovereign LORD says: Clap your hands in horror, and stamp your feet. Cry out, 'Alas!' because of all the evil that the people of Israel have done. Now they are going to die from war and famine and disease. ¹²Disease will strike down those who are far away in exile. War will destroy those who are nearby. And anyone who survives will be killed by famine. So at last I will spend my fury on them. ¹³When their dead lie scattered among their idols and altars, on every hill and mountain and under every green tree and great oak where they offered incense to their gods, then they will know that I alone am the LORD. ¹⁴I will crush them and make their cities desolate from the wilderness in the south to Riblah* in the north. Then they will know that I am the LORD."

6:14 As in some Hebrew manuscripts; most Hebrew manuscripts read *Diblah.*

AUGUST 16 ☐ DAY 229
EZEKIEL 7–11
Sins and Sorrows

 OVERVIEW For wayward Judah, the end has come. Past sins now give way to crushing horrors as the city of Jerusalem falls in the midst of confusion and brutality. The Temple, God's abode among his people, no longer houses the glory of the Lord. Judah's leaders—blind leading the blind—watch helplessly as their beloved Jerusalem turns into a seething cauldron of death. Even the prophet Ezekiel wonders how any can survive such an onslaught. But the Word of the Lord returns in warming comfort: "I . . . will gather you back from the nations . . . and I will give you the land of Israel once again" (11:17).

Chapters 7–8	Chapter 9	Chapter 10	Chapter 11
Doom for Jerusalem	Death for the Guilty	Departure of God's Glory	Downfall of God's Leaders
Condemnation of Idolatry		Consequences of Idolatry	

YOUR DAILY WALK What is the longest distance you have ever walked or jogged without stopping? (If your answer is, "The distance from the couch to the refrigerator," read 1 Corinthians 9:27 . . . fast!)

To get through the hardest journey, take only one step at a time, but in God's strength keep on stepping.

There is a vast difference between training for a *sprint* (like the hundred-yard dash) and training for a *marathon* (which covers more than twenty-six miles). It means very little to a marathon runner if he covers the first hundred yards in ten seconds. A burst of speed is good, but in the long run it is the ability to stick with it mile after mile that counts. *Steadfastness,* not simply short-term *fastness,* determines the winner.

God told the prophet Ezekiel in advance that he was running a marathon (3:4, 7-9), not a sprint. His audience would be calloused, hard of hearing, and indifferent to his message. Ezekiel would need strength for the long run.

What about you today? Your race is described in Hebrews 12:1-2. Put on your sneakers for a few minutes' walk as you ponder the marathon God has set before you and the resources he has provided in his Son—strength for each step of the way!

INSIGHT A Strong Name for a Demanding Assignment

Ezekiel's name literally means "God strengthens" or "strengthened by God." And his name becomes the testimony of his life (3:8-9), for who but God could strengthen a man to deliver the crushing message of chapters 7–11 week after week . . . for more than twenty years!

CHAPTER 7

Then this message came to me from the LORD: [2]"Son of man, this is what the Sovereign LORD says to Israel: The end is here! Wherever you look—east, west, north, or south—your land is finished. [3]No hope remains, for I will unleash my anger against you. I will call you to account for all your disgusting behavior. [4]I will turn my eyes away and show no pity, repaying you in full for all your evil. Then you will know that I am the LORD!

[5]"This is what the Sovereign LORD says: With one blow after another I will bring total disaster! [6]The end has come! It has finally arrived! Your final doom is waiting! [7]O people of Israel, the day of your destruction is dawning. The time has come; the day of trouble is near. It will ring with shouts of anguish, not shouts of joy. [8]Soon I will pour out my fury to complete your punishment for all your disgusting behavior. [9]I will neither spare nor pity you. I will repay you for all your detestable practices. Then you will know that it is I, the LORD, who is striking the blow.

[10]"The day of judgment is here; your destruction awaits! The people's wickedness and pride have reached a climax. [11]Their violence will fall back on them as punishment for their wickedness. None of these proud and wicked people will survive. All their wealth will be swept away. [12]Yes, the time has come; the day is here! There is no reason for buyers to rejoice over the bargains they find or for sellers to grieve over their losses, for all of them will fall under my terrible anger. [13]And if any merchants should survive, they will never return to their business. For what God has said applies to everyone—it will not be changed! Not one person whose life is twisted by sin will recover.

[14]"The trumpets call Israel's army to mobilize, but no one listens, for my fury is against them all. [15]Any who leave the city walls will be killed by enemy swords. Those who stay inside will die of famine and disease. [16]The few who survive and escape to the mountains will moan like doves, weeping for their sins. [17]Everyone's hands will be feeble; their knees will be as weak as water. [18]They will dress themselves in sackcloth; horror and shame will cover them. They will shave their heads in sorrow and remorse.

[19]"They will throw away their money, tossing it out like worthless trash. It won't buy their deliverance in that day of the LORD's anger. It will neither satisfy nor feed them, for their love of money made them stumble into sin. [20]They were proud of their gold jewelry and used it to make vile and detestable idols. That is why I will make all their wealth disgusting to them. [21]I will give it as plunder to foreigners from the most wicked of nations, and they will defile it. [22]I will hide my eyes as

these robbers invade my treasured land and corrupt it.

²³"Prepare chains for my people, for the land is bloodied by terrible crimes. Jerusalem is filled with violence. ²⁴I will bring the most ruthless of nations to occupy their homes. I will break down their proud fortresses and defile their sanctuaries. ²⁵Terror and trembling will overcome my people. They will look for peace but will not find it. ²⁶Calamity will follow calamity; rumor will follow rumor. They will look in vain for a vision from the prophets. They will receive no teaching from the priests and no counsel from the leaders. ²⁷The king and the prince will stand helpless, weeping in despair, and the people's hands will tremble with fear. I will bring against them the evil they have done to others, and they will receive the punishment they so richly deserve. Then they will know that I am the LORD!"

CHAPTER 8
Then on September 17,* during the sixth year of King Jehoiachin's captivity, while the leaders of Judah were in my home, the Sovereign LORD took hold of me. ²I saw a figure that appeared to be a man. From the waist down he looked like a burning flame. From the waist up he looked like gleaming amber. ³He put out what seemed to be a hand and took me by the hair. Then the Spirit lifted me up into the sky and transported me in a vision of God to Jerusalem. I was taken to the north gate of the inner courtyard of the Temple, where there is a large idol that has made the LORD very angry. ⁴Suddenly, the glory of the God of Israel was there, just as I had seen it before in the valley.

⁵Then the LORD said to me, "Son of man, look toward the north." So I looked, and there to the north, beside the entrance to the gate of the altar, stood the idol that had made the LORD so angry.

⁶"Son of man," he said, "do you see what they are doing? Do you see the great sins the people of Israel are doing to drive me from my Temple? But come, and you will see even greater sins than these!" ⁷Then he brought me to the door of the Temple courtyard, where I could see an opening in the wall. ⁸He said to me, "Now, son of man, dig

into the wall." So I dug into the wall and uncovered a door to a hidden room.

⁹"Go in," he said, "and see the unspeakable wickedness going on in there!" ¹⁰So I went in and saw the walls engraved with all kinds of snakes, lizards, and hideous creatures. I also saw the various idols worshiped by the people of Israel. ¹¹Seventy leaders of Israel were standing there with Jaazaniah son of Shaphan in the middle. Each of them held an incense burner, so there was a thick cloud of incense above their heads.

¹²Then the LORD said to me, "Son of man, have you seen what the leaders of Israel are doing with their idols in dark rooms? They are saying, 'The LORD doesn't see us; he has deserted our land!'" ¹³Then he added, "Come, and I will show you greater sins than these!"

¹⁴He brought me to the north gate of the LORD's Temple, and some women were sitting there, weeping for the god Tammuz. ¹⁵"Have you seen this?" he asked. "But I will show you even greater sins than these!"

¹⁶Then he brought me into the inner courtyard of the LORD's Temple. At the entrance, between the foyer and the bronze altar, about twenty-five men were standing with their backs to the LORD's Temple. They were facing eastward, worshiping the sun!

¹⁷"Have you seen this, son of man?" he asked. "Is it nothing to the people of Judah that they commit these terrible sins, leading the whole nation into violence, thumbing their noses at me, and rousing my fury against them? ¹⁸Therefore, I will deal with them in fury. I will neither pity nor spare them. And though they scream for mercy, I will not listen."

CHAPTER 9
Then the LORD thundered, "Bring on the men appointed to punish the city! Tell them to bring their weapons with them!" ²Six men soon appeared from the upper gate that faces north, each carrying a battle club in his hand. One of them was dressed in linen and carried a writer's case strapped to his side. They all went into the Temple courtyard and stood beside the bronze altar.

³Then the glory of the God of Israel rose

8:1 Hebrew *on the fifth day of the sixth month*, of the Hebrew calendar. This event occurred on September 17, 592 B.C.; also see note on 1:1.

up from between the cherubim, where it had rested, and moved to the entrance of the Temple. And the LORD called to the man dressed in linen who was carrying the writer's case. [4]He said to him, "Walk through the streets of Jerusalem and put a mark on the foreheads of all those who weep and sigh because of the sins they see around them."

[5]Then I heard the LORD say to the other men, "Follow him through the city and kill everyone whose forehead is not marked. Show no mercy; have no pity! [6]Kill them all—old and young, girls and women and little children. But do not touch anyone with the mark. Begin your task right here at the Temple." So they began by killing the seventy leaders. [7]"Defile the Temple!" the LORD commanded. "Fill its courtyards with the bodies of those you kill! Go!" So they went throughout the city and did as they were told.

[8]While they were carrying out their orders, I was all alone. I fell face down in the dust and cried out, "O Sovereign LORD! Will your fury against Jerusalem wipe out everyone left in Israel?"

[9]Then he said to me, "The sins of the people of Israel and Judah are very great. The entire land is full of murder; the city is filled with injustice. They are saying, 'The LORD doesn't see it! The LORD has forsaken the land!' [10]So I will not spare them or have any pity on them. I will fully repay them for all they have done."

[11]Then the man in linen clothing, who carried the writer's case, reported back and said, "I have finished the work you gave me to do."

CHAPTER 10

As I looked, I saw what appeared to be a throne of blue sapphire above the crystal surface over the heads of the cherubim. [2]Then the LORD spoke to the man in linen clothing and said, "Go in between the whirling wheels beneath the cherubim, and take a handful of glowing coals and scatter them over the city." He did this as I watched. [3]The cherubim were standing at the south end of the Temple when the man went in, and the cloud of glory filled the inner courtyard. [4]Then the glory of the LORD rose up from above the cherubim and went over to the door of the Temple. The

Temple was filled with this cloud of glory, and the Temple courtyard glowed brightly with the glory of the LORD. [5]The moving wings of the cherubim sounded like the voice of God Almighty and could be heard clearly in the outer courtyard.

[6]The LORD said to the man in linen clothing, "Go between the cherubim and take some burning coals from between the wheels." So the man went in and stood beside one of the wheels. [7]Then one of the cherubim reached out his hand and took some live coals from the fire burning among them. He put the coals into the hands of the man in linen clothing, and the man took them and went out. [8](All the cherubim had what looked like human hands hidden beneath their wings.)

[9]Each of the four cherubim had a wheel beside him, and the wheels sparkled like chrysolite. [10]All four wheels looked the same; each wheel had a second wheel turning crosswise within it. [11]The cherubim could move forward in any of the four directions they faced, without turning as they moved. They went straight in the direction in which their heads were turned, never turning aside. [12]Both the cherubim and the wheels were covered with eyes. The cherubim had eyes all over their bodies, including their hands, their backs, and their wings. [13]I heard someone refer to the wheels as "the whirling wheels." [14]Each of the four cherubim had four faces—the first was the face of an ox,* the second was a human face, the third was the face of a lion, and the fourth was the face of an eagle.

[15]Then the cherubim rose upward. These were the same living beings I had seen beside the Kebar River. [16]When the cherubim moved, the wheels moved with them. When they rose into the air, the wheels stayed beside them, going with them as they flew. [17]When the cherubim stood still, the wheels also stopped, for the spirit of the living beings was in the wheels.

[18]Then the glory of the LORD moved from the door of the Temple and hovered above the cherubim. [19]And as I watched, the cherubim flew with their wheels to the east gate of the LORD's Temple. And the glory of the God of Israel hovered above them.

[20]These were the same living beings I had seen beneath the God of Israel when I

10:14 Hebrew *the face of a cherub;* compare 1:10.

was by the Kebar River. I knew they were cherubim, 21for each had four faces and four wings and what looked like human hands under their wings. 22Their faces, too, were just like the faces of the beings I had seen at the Kebar, and they traveled straight ahead, just as the others had.

CHAPTER 11

Then the Spirit lifted me and brought me over to the east gateway of the LORD's Temple, where I saw twenty-five prominent men of the city. Among them were Jaazaniah son of Azzur and Pelatiah son of Benaiah, who were leaders among the people.

2Then the Spirit said to me, "Son of man, these are the men who are responsible for the wicked counsel being given in this city. 3They say to the people, 'Is it not a good time to build houses? Our city is like an iron pot. Inside it we will be like meat— safe from all harm.*' 4Therefore, son of man, prophesy against them loudly and clearly."

5Then the Spirit of the LORD came upon me, and he told me to say, "This is what the LORD says to the people of Israel: Is that what you are saying? Yes, I know it is, for I know every thought that comes into your minds. 6You have murdered endlessly and filled your streets with the dead.

7"Therefore, this is what the Sovereign LORD says: This city is an iron pot, but the victims of your injustice are the pieces of meat. And you are not safe, for I will soon drag you from the city. 8I will expose you to the war you so greatly fear, says the Sovereign LORD. 9I will drive you out of Jerusalem and hand you over to foreigners who will carry out my judgments against you. 10You will be slaughtered all the way to the borders of Israel, and then you will know that I am the LORD. 11No, this city will not be an iron pot for you, and you will not be the meat, safe inside. I will judge you even

to the borders of Israel, 12and you will know that I am the LORD. For you have refused to obey me; instead, you have copied the sins of the nations around you."

13While I was still speaking, Pelatiah son of Benaiah suddenly died. Then I fell face down in the dust and cried out, "O Sovereign LORD, are you going to kill everyone in Israel?"

14Then this message came to me from the LORD: 15"Son of man, the people still left in Jerusalem are talking about their relatives in exile, saying, 'They are far away from the LORD, so now he has given their land to us!' 16Therefore, give the exiles this message from the Sovereign LORD: Although I have scattered you in the countries of the world, I will be a sanctuary to you during your time in exile. 17I, the Sovereign LORD, will gather you back from the nations where you are scattered, and I will give you the land of Israel once again.

18"When the people return to their homeland, they will remove every trace of their detestable idol worship. 19And I will give them singleness of heart and put a new spirit within them. I will take away their hearts of stone and give them tender hearts* instead, 20so they will obey my laws and regulations. Then they will truly be my people, and I will be their God. 21But as for those who long for idols, I will repay them fully for their sins, says the Sovereign LORD."

22Then the cherubim lifted their wings and rose into the air with their wheels beside them, and the glory of the God of Israel hovered above them. 23Then the glory of the LORD went up from the city and stopped above the mountain to the east.

24Afterward the Spirit of God carried me back again to Babylonia,* to the Judeans in exile there. And so ended the vision of my visit to Jerusalem. 25And I told the exiles everything the LORD had shown me.

11:3 Hebrew *This city is the pot, and we are the meat.*   **11:19** Hebrew *hearts of flesh.*   **11:24** Or *Chaldea.*

AUGUST 17 ☐ DAY 230
EZEKIEL 12–15
Signs and Sermons

OVERVIEW Jeremiah used object lessons extensively in his prophetic ministry. Ezekiel uses dramatic portrayals—divine charades designed to arouse the curiosity of the people and rivet their attention on the events soon to transpire in Jerusalem. Packing up his household belongings, Ezekiel heads for the city wall, where he digs a hole and climbs through—a picture of the soon-coming deportation of the people and the loss of all they called home.

Chapter 12	Chapter 13	Chapter 14	Chapter 15
Symbols of Exile	Sins Leading to Exile Involving		
	Prophets	Leaders	People
Destruction	Disobedience		

YOUR DAILY WALK Look around your house and see if you can find at least five things that are virtually useless: burned-out light bulbs, broken shoestrings, pens with no ink, husbands watching baseball games, etc.

People's character and their gardens both reflect the amount of weeding that was done during the growing season.

In chapter 15 Ezekiel likens Jerusalem to a useless vine. Vines are excellent for growing fruit, but when you stop and think about it, they are good for little else. You can't make furniture out of them, build a good fire with them, or turn them into anything particularly useful. In fact, a vine that is fruitless is practically worthless.

The inhabitants of Jerusalem were worthless to God because of their wickedness and idolatry. Planted in the land to be a testimony to his name, they failed to produce the fruit God expected from them. There was nothing left to do but remove them—a painful but necessary way for God to get across the message, "I am the LORD."

Check up on your UQ (Usefulness Quotient) today. Does God have free rein to produce the fruit of the Spirit in your life (Galatians 5:22-23)? Press a leaf between the pages of your Bible as a reminder that fruit-bearing is not just a good idea. It is one of the reasons God has placed you on this planet (John 15:1-6)!

INSIGHT Famous Names in Unfamiliar Places
In Jeremiah you learned that even if _____ and _____ had prayed on Judah's behalf, God would not have listened (Jeremiah 15:1). Now in Ezekiel you will learn that even if _____, _____, and _____ had lived in Jerusalem, their presence would not have saved the city (Ezekiel 14:14, 18, 20).

CHAPTER 12

Again a message came to me from the LORD: ²"Son of man, you live among rebels who could see the truth if they wanted to, but they don't want to. They could hear me if they would listen, but they won't listen because they are rebellious. ³So now put on a demonstration to show them what it will be like to go off into exile. Pack whatever you can carry on your back and leave your home to go on a journey. Make your preparations in broad daylight so the people can see you, for perhaps they will even yet consider what this means, even though they are such rebels. ⁴Bring your baggage outside during the day so they can watch you. Then as they are watching, leave your house in the evening, just as captives do when they begin a long march to distant lands. ⁵Dig a hole through the wall while they are watching and carry your possessions out through it. ⁶As they watch, lift your pack to your shoulders and walk away into the night. Cover your face and don't look around. All of these actions will be a sign for the people of Israel."

⁷So I did as I was told. In broad daylight I brought my pack outside, filled with the things I might carry into exile. Then in the evening while the people looked on, I dug through the wall with my hands and went out into the darkness with my pack on my shoulder.

⁸The next morning this message came to me from the LORD: ⁹"Son of man, these rebels, the people of Israel, have asked you what all this means. ¹⁰Say to them, 'This is what the Sovereign LORD says: These actions contain a message for Zedekiah in Jerusalem* and for all the people of Israel.' ¹¹Then explain that your actions are a demonstration of what will soon happen to them, for they will be driven from their homes and sent away into exile.

¹²"Even Zedekiah will leave Jerusalem at night through a hole in the wall, taking only what he can carry with him. He will cover his face, and his eyes will never see his homeland again. ¹³Then I will spread out my net and capture him in my snare. I will bring him to Babylon, the land of the Babylonians,* though he will never see it, and he will die there. ¹⁴I will scatter his servants and guards to the four winds and send the sword after them. ¹⁵And when I scatter them among the nations, they will know that I am the LORD. ¹⁶But I will spare a few of them from death by war, famine, or disease, so they can confess to their captors about how wicked they have been. Then they will know that I am the LORD!"

¹⁷Then this message came to me from the LORD: ¹⁸"Son of man, tremble as you eat your food. Drink your water with fear, as if it were your last. ¹⁹Give the people this message from the Sovereign LORD concerning those living in Israel and Jerusalem: They will eat their food with trembling and sip their tiny portions of water in utter despair, because their land will be stripped bare on account of their violence. ²⁰The cities will be destroyed and the farmland deserted. Then you will know that I am the LORD."

²¹Again a message came to me from the LORD: ²²"Son of man, what is that proverb they quote in Israel: 'Time passes, making a liar of every prophet'? ²³Give the people this message from the Sovereign LORD: I

will put an end to this proverb, and you will soon stop quoting it. Now give them this new proverb to replace the old one: 'The time has come for every prophecy to be fulfilled!'

²⁴"Then you will see what becomes of all the false visions and misleading predictions about peace in Israel. ²⁵For I am the LORD! What I threaten always happens. There will be no more delays, you rebels of Israel! I will fulfill my threat of destruction in your own lifetime, says the Sovereign LORD."

²⁶Then this message came to me from the LORD: ²⁷"Son of man, the people of Israel are saying, 'His visions won't come true for a long, long time.' ²⁸Therefore, give them this message from the Sovereign LORD: No more delay! I will now do everything I have threatened! I, the Sovereign LORD, have spoken!"

CHAPTER 13

Then this message came to me from the LORD: ²"Son of man, speak against the false prophets of Israel who are inventing their own prophecies. Tell them to listen to the word of the LORD. ³This is what the Sovereign LORD says: Destruction is certain for the false prophets who are following their own imaginations and have seen nothing at all!

⁴"O people of Israel, these prophets of yours are like jackals digging around in the ruins. ⁵They have done nothing to strengthen the breaks in the walls around the nation. They have not helped it to stand firm in battle on the day of the LORD. ⁶Instead, they have lied and said, 'My message is from the LORD,' even though the LORD never sent them. And yet they expect him to fulfill their prophecies! ⁷Can your visions be anything but false if you claim, 'This message is from the LORD,' when I have not even spoken to you?

⁸"Therefore, this is what the Sovereign LORD says: Because what you say is false and your visions are a lie, I will stand against you, says the Sovereign LORD. ⁹I will raise my fist against all the lying prophets, and they will be banished from the community of Israel. I will blot their names from Israel's record books, and they will never again see their own land. Then

12:10 Hebrew *the prince in Jerusalem;* also in 12:12.   **12:13** Or *Chaldeans.*

you will know that I am the Sovereign LORD!

¹⁰"These evil prophets deceive my people by saying, 'All is peaceful!' when there is no peace at all! It's as if the people have built a flimsy wall, and these prophets are trying to hold it together by covering it with whitewash! ¹¹Tell these whitewashers that their wall will soon fall down. A heavy rainstorm will undermine it; great hailstones and mighty winds will knock it down. ¹²And when the wall falls, the people will cry out, 'Where is the whitewash you applied?'

¹³"Therefore, this is what the Sovereign LORD says: I will sweep away your whitewashed wall with a storm of indignation, with a great flood of anger, and with hailstones of fury. ¹⁴I will break down your wall right to the foundation, and when it falls, it will crush you. Then you will know that I am the LORD! ¹⁵At last my anger against the wall and those who covered it with whitewash will be satisfied. Then I will say to you: 'The wall and those who whitewashed it are both gone. ¹⁶They were lying prophets who claimed peace would come to Jerusalem when there was no peace. I, the Sovereign LORD, have spoken!'

¹⁷"Now, son of man, also speak out against the women who prophesy from their own imaginations. ¹⁸This is what the Sovereign LORD says: Destruction is certain for you women who are ensnaring the souls of my people, both young and old alike. You tie magic charms on their wrists and furnish them with magic veils. Do you think you can trap others without bringing destruction on yourselves? ¹⁹You turn my people away from me for a few handfuls of barley or a piece of bread. By lying to my people who love to listen to lies, you kill those who should not die, and you promise life to those who should not live.

²⁰"And so the Sovereign LORD says: I am against all your magic charms, which you use to ensnare my people like birds. I will tear them from your arms, setting my people free like birds set free from a cage. ²¹I will tear off the magic veils and save my people from your grasp. They will no longer be your victims. Then you will know that I am the LORD. ²²You have discouraged the righteous with your lies, when I didn't want them to suffer grief. And you have encouraged the wicked by promising them life, even though they con-

tinue in their sins. ²³But you will no longer talk of seeing visions that you never saw, nor will you practice your magic. For I will rescue my people from your grasp. Then you will know that I am the LORD."

CHAPTER 14

Then some of the leaders of Israel visited me, and while they were there, ²this message came to me from the LORD: ³"Son of man, these leaders have set up idols in their hearts. They have embraced things that lead them into sin. Why should I let them ask me anything? ⁴Give them this message from the Sovereign LORD: I, the LORD, will punish the people of Israel who set up idols in their hearts so they fall into sin and then come to a prophet asking for help. ⁵I will do this to capture the minds and hearts of all my people who have turned from me to worship their detestable idols.

⁶"Therefore, give the people of Israel this message from the Sovereign LORD: Repent and turn away from your idols, and stop all your loathsome practices. ⁷I, the LORD, will punish all those, both Israelites and foreigners, who reject me and set up idols in their hearts so they fall into sin, and who then come to a prophet asking for my advice. ⁸I will turn against such people and make a terrible example of them, destroying them. Then you will know that I am the LORD. ⁹And if a prophet is deceived and gives a message anyway, it is because I, the LORD, have deceived that prophet. I will stand against such prophets and cut them off from the community of Israel. ¹⁰False prophets and hypocrites—evil people who claim to want my advice—will all be punished for their sins. ¹¹In this way, the people of Israel will learn not to stray from me, polluting themselves with sin. They will be my people, and I will be their God, says the Sovereign LORD."

¹²Then this message came to me from the LORD: ¹³"Son of man, suppose the people of a country were to sin against me, and I lifted my fist to crush them, cutting off their food supply and sending a famine to destroy both people and animals alike. ¹⁴Even if Noah, Daniel, and Job were there, their righteousness would save no one but themselves, declares the Sovereign LORD.

¹⁵"Or suppose I were to send an invasion of dangerous wild animals to devastate the land and kill the people. ¹⁶Even if these

three men were there, the Sovereign LORD swears that it would do no good—it wouldn't save the people from destruction. Those three alone would be saved, but the land would be devastated.

¹⁷"Or suppose I were to bring war against the land, and I told enemy armies to come and destroy everything. ¹⁸Even if these three men were in the land, the Sovereign LORD swears that they could not save the people. They alone would be saved.

¹⁹"Or suppose I were to pour out my fury by sending an epidemic of disease into the land, and the plague killed people and animals alike. ²⁰Even if Noah, Daniel, and Job were living there, the Sovereign LORD swears that they could not save the people. They alone would be saved by their righteousness.

²¹"Now this is what the Sovereign LORD says: How terrible it will be when all four of these fearsome punishments fall upon Jerusalem—war, famine, beasts, and plague—destroying all her people and animals. ²²Yet there will be survivors, and they will come here to join you as exiles in Babylon. You will see with your own eyes how wicked they are, and then you will feel

better about what I have done to Jerusalem. ²³When you meet them and see their behavior, you will agree that these things are not being done to Israel without cause, says the Sovereign LORD."

CHAPTER 15

Then this message came to me from the LORD: ²"Son of man, how does a grapevine compare to a tree? Is a vine's wood as useful as the wood of a tree? ³Can its wood be used for making things, like pegs to hang up pots and pans? ⁴No, it can only be used for fuel, and even as fuel, it burns too quickly. ⁵Vine branches are useless both before and after being put into the fire!

⁶"And this is what the Sovereign LORD says: The people of Jerusalem are like grapevines growing among the trees of the forest. Since they are useless, I have set them aside to be burned! ⁷And I will see to it that if they escape from one fire, they will fall into another. When this happens, you will know that I am the LORD. ⁸And I will make the land desolate because my people have been unfaithful to me, says the Sovereign LORD."

AUGUST 18 ☐ DAY 231
EZEKIEL 16–19
Parables of Judgment for Judah

 OVERVIEW Using a picturesque series of allegories and parables, Ezekiel continues his dual message of horror and hope. Like an unfaithful wife, God's people have gone after other gods. They have committed spiritual adultery and prostituted their privileged position. But God's love remains ever faithful for the objects of his delight. Using illustrations drawn from nature, the prophet portrays the reasons for God's coming discipline and gives the sobering reminder: "The one who sins is the one who dies" (18:20).

Chapter 16	Chapter 17	Chapter 18	Chapter 19
Parable of the Unfaithful Wife	Parable of the Eagles	Proverb of the Sour Grapes	Picture of the Lioness
Graphic Lessons			Grim Lament

YOUR DAILY WALK Perhaps God's providence is nowhere more evident than in the fact that he gives parents twelve years to develop a love for their children before he turns them into teenagers!

The best way to keep teens at home is to make home pleasant— and let the air out of the tires.

Chapter 18 contains some sobering words for teens . . . and for God's children of all ages. It's a reminder of personal accountability—of the fact that we cannot and dare not attempt to pin the blame for today's problems on yesterday's generation.

Are you the product of godly parents? Then thank God, but don't think he will condone your willful rebellion (18:5-13). Are you the child of rebellious or backslidden parents? Don't think you can use that as an excuse for avoiding the clear and insistent commands of God's Word (18:20).

Make an appointment to take a parent or child out for a special meal this week. (Or call a family member who is out of town.) If there is a root of bitterness between you, confess it. If there has been indifference or a lack of accountability in your relationship, forsake it.

INSIGHT The Madness of Israel's Unfaithfulness
You've heard the maxim: "Dog bites man, that's not news; man bites dog, that's news." A prostitute who is paid for her wickedness isn't newsworthy because she isn't unusual. On the other hand, a prostitute who pays those who come to her will definitely attract attention. In Ezekiel's day, Israel had become front-page material. She had committed such mad, willful idolatry that God likened her to a prostitute who paid her customers (16:33-34)!

CHAPTER 16

Then another message came to me from the LORD: ²"Son of man, confront Jerusalem with her loathsome sins. ³Give her this message from the Sovereign LORD: You are nothing but a Canaanite! Your father was an Amorite and your mother a Hittite! ⁴When you were born, no one cared about you. Your umbilical cord was left uncut, and you were never washed, rubbed with salt, and dressed in warm clothing. ⁵No one had the slightest interest in you; no one pitied you or cared for you. On the day you were born, you were dumped in a field and left to die, unwanted.

⁶"But I came by and saw you there, helplessly kicking about in your own blood. As you lay there, I said, 'Live!' ⁷And I helped you to thrive like a plant in the field. You grew up and became a beautiful jewel. Your breasts became full, and your hair grew, though you were still naked. ⁸And when I passed by and saw you again, you were old enough to be married. So I wrapped my cloak around you to cover your nakedness and declared my marriage vows. I made a covenant with you, says the Sovereign LORD, and you became mine.

⁹"Then I bathed you and washed off your blood, and I rubbed fragrant oils into your skin. ¹⁰I gave you expensive clothing of linen and silk, beautifully embroidered, and sandals made of fine leather. ¹¹I gave you lovely jewelry, bracelets, and beautiful necklaces, ¹²a ring for your nose and earrings for your ears, and a lovely crown for your head. ¹³And so you were made beautiful with gold and silver. Your clothes were made of fine linen and were beautifully embroidered. You ate the finest foods—fine flour, honey, and olive oil—and became more beautiful than ever. You looked like a queen, and so you were! ¹⁴Your fame soon spread throughout the world on account of your beauty, because the splendor I bestowed on you perfected your beauty, says the Sovereign LORD.

¹⁵"But you thought you could get along without me, so you trusted instead in your fame and beauty. You gave yourself as a prostitute to every man who came along. Your beauty was theirs for the asking! ¹⁶You used the lovely things I gave you to make shrines for idols, where you carried out your acts of prostitution. Unbelievable! How could such a thing ever happen? ¹⁷You took the very jewels and gold and silver ornaments I had given you and made statues of men and worshiped them, which is adultery against me. ¹⁸You used the beautifully embroidered clothes I gave you to cover your idols. Then you used my oil and incense to worship them. ¹⁹Imagine it! You set before them as a lovely sacrifice the

fine flour and oil and honey I had given you, says the Sovereign LORD.

²⁰"Then you took your sons and daughters—the children you had borne to me—and sacrificed them to your gods. Was it not enough that you should be a prostitute? ²¹Must you also slaughter my children by sacrificing them to idols? ²²In all your years of adultery and loathsome sin, you have not once thought of the days long ago when you lay naked in a field, kicking about in your own blood.

²³"Your destruction is certain, says the Sovereign LORD. In addition to all your other wickedness, ²⁴you built a pagan shrine and put altars to idols in every town square. ²⁵On every street corner you defiled your beauty, offering your body to every passerby in an endless stream of prostitution. ²⁶Then you added lustful Egypt to your lovers, fanning the flames of my anger with your increasing promiscuity. ²⁷That is why I struck you with my fist and reduced your boundaries. I handed you over to your enemies, the Philistines, and even they were shocked by your lewd conduct! ²⁸You have prostituted yourselves with the Assyrians, too. It seems you can never find enough new lovers! And after your prostitution there, you still were not satisfied. ²⁹You added to your lovers by embracing that great merchant land of Babylonia*—but you still weren't satisfied!

³⁰"What a sick heart you have, says the Sovereign LORD, to do such things as these, acting like a shameless prostitute. ³¹You build your pagan shrines on every street corner and your altars to idols in every square. You have been worse than a prostitute, so eager for sin that you have not even demanded payment for your love! ³²Yes, you are an adulterous wife who takes in strangers instead of her own husband. ³³Prostitutes charge for their services—but not you! You give gifts to your lovers, bribing them to come to you. ³⁴So you are the opposite of other prostitutes. No one pays you; instead, you pay them!

³⁵"Therefore, you prostitute, listen to this message from the LORD! ³⁶This is what the Sovereign LORD says: Because you have exposed yourself in prostitution to all your lovers, and because you have worshiped detestable idols, and because you have slaughtered your children as

sacrifices to your gods, ³⁷this is what I am going to do. I will gather together all your allies—these lovers of yours with whom you have sinned, both those you loved and those you hated—and I will strip you naked in front of them so they can stare at you. ³⁸I will punish you for your murder and adultery. I will cover you with blood in my jealous fury. ³⁹Then I will give you to your lovers—these many nations—and they will destroy you. They will knock down your pagan shrines and the altars to your idols. They will strip you and take your beautiful jewels, leaving you completely naked and ashamed. ⁴⁰They will band together in a mob to stone you and run you through with swords. ⁴¹They will burn your homes and punish you in front of many women. I will see to it that you stop your prostitution and end your payments to your many lovers.

⁴²"Then at last my fury against you will be spent, and my jealous anger will subside. I will be calm and will not be angry with you anymore. ⁴³But first, because you have not remembered your youth but have angered me by doing all these evil things, I will fully repay you for all of your sins, says the Sovereign LORD. For to all your disgusting sins, you have added these lewd acts. ⁴⁴Everyone who makes up proverbs will say of you, 'Like mother, like daughter.' ⁴⁵For your mother loathed her husband and her children, and so do you. And you are exactly like your sisters, for they despised their husbands and their children. Truly your mother must have been a Hittite and your father an Amorite.

⁴⁶"Your older sister was Samaria, who lived with her daughters in the north. Your younger sister was Sodom, who lived with her daughters in the south. ⁴⁷But you have not merely sinned as they did—no, that was nothing to you. In a very short time you far surpassed them! ⁴⁸As surely as I live, says the Sovereign LORD, Sodom and her daughters were never as wicked as you and your daughters. ⁴⁹Sodom's sins were pride, laziness, and gluttony, while the poor and needy suffered outside her door. ⁵⁰She was proud and did loathsome things, so I wiped her out, as you have seen.

⁵¹"Even Samaria did not commit half your sins. You have done far more loathsome things than your sisters ever did.

16:29 Or *Chaldea*.

They seem righteous compared to you! [52]You should be deeply ashamed because your sins are so terrible. In comparison, you make your sisters seem innocent!

[53]"But someday I will restore the fortunes of Sodom and Samaria, and I will restore you, too. [54]Then you will be truly ashamed of everything you have done, for your sins make them feel good in comparison. [55]Yes, your sisters, Sodom and Samaria, and all their people will be restored, and at that time you also will be restored. [56]In your proud days you held Sodom in contempt. [57]But now your greater wickedness has been exposed to all the world, and you are the one who is scorned—by Edom* and all her neighbors and by Philistia. [58]This is your punishment for all your disgusting sins, says the LORD.

[59]"Now this is what the Sovereign LORD says: I will give you what you deserve, for you have taken your solemn vows lightly by breaking your covenant. [60]Yet I will keep the covenant I made with you when you were young, and I will establish an everlasting covenant with you. [61]Then you will remember with shame all the evil you have done. I will make your sisters, Samaria and Sodom, to be your daughters, even though they are not part of our covenant. [62]And I will reaffirm my covenant with you, and you will know that I am the LORD. [63]You will remember your sins and cover your mouth in silence and shame when I forgive you of all that you have done, says the Sovereign LORD."

CHAPTER 17
Then this message came to me from the LORD: [2]"Son of man, tell this story to the people of Israel. [3]Give them this message from the Sovereign LORD: A great eagle with broad wings full of many-colored feathers came to Lebanon. He took hold of the highest branch of a cedar tree [4]and plucked off its topmost shoot. Then he carried it away to a city filled with merchants, where he planted it.

[5]"Then he planted one of its seedlings in fertile ground beside a broad river, where it would grow as quickly as a willow tree. [6]It took root there and grew into a low, spreading vine. Its branches turned up toward the eagle, and its roots grew

down beneath it. It soon produced strong branches and luxuriant leaves. [7]But then another great eagle with broad wings and full plumage came along. So the vine sent its roots and branches out toward him for water. [8]The vine did this even though it was already planted in good soil and had plenty of water so it could grow into a splendid vine and produce rich leaves and luscious fruit.

[9]"So now the Sovereign LORD asks: Should I let this vine grow and prosper? No! I will pull it out, roots and all! I will cut off its fruit and let its leaves wither and die. I will pull it out easily enough—it won't take a strong arm or a large army to do it. [10]Then when the vine is transplanted, will it thrive? No, it will wither away completely when the east wind blows against it. It will die in the same good soil where it had grown so well."

[11]Then this message came to me from the LORD: [12]"Say to these rebels of Israel: Don't you understand the meaning of this riddle of the eagles? I will tell you, says the Sovereign LORD. The king of Babylon came to Jerusalem, took away her king and princes, and brought them to Babylon. [13]He made a treaty with a member of the royal family and made him take an oath of loyalty. He also exiled Israel's most influential leaders, [14]so Israel would not become strong again and revolt. Only by keeping her treaty with Babylon could Israel maintain her national identity.

[15]"Nevertheless, this man of Israel's royal family rebelled against Babylon, sending ambassadors to Egypt to request a great army and many horses. Can Israel break her sworn treaties like that and get away with it? [16]No! For as surely as I live, says the Sovereign LORD, the king of Israel will die in Babylon, the land of the king who put him in power and whose treaty he despised and broke. [17]Pharaoh and all his mighty army will fail to help Israel when the king of Babylon lays siege to Jerusalem again and destroys the lives of many. [18]For the king of Israel broke his treaty after swearing to obey; therefore, he will not escape.

[19]"So this is what the Sovereign LORD says: As surely as I live, I will punish him for breaking my covenant and despising the solemn oath he made in my name. [20]I

16:57 Many ancient manuscripts read *Aram*.

will throw my net over him and capture him in my snare. I will bring him to Babylon and deal with him there for this treason against me. ²¹And all the best warriors of Israel will be killed in battle, and those remaining in the city will be scattered to the four winds. Then you will know that I, the LORD, have spoken these words.

²²"And the Sovereign LORD says: I will take a tender shoot from the top of a tall cedar, and I will plant it on the top of Israel's highest mountain. ²³It will become a noble cedar, sending forth its branches and producing seed. Birds of every sort will nest in it, finding shelter beneath its branches. ²⁴And all the trees will know that it is I, the LORD, who cuts down the tall tree and helps the short tree to grow tall. It is I who makes the green tree wither and gives new life to the dead tree. I, the LORD, have spoken! I will do what I have said."

CHAPTER 18
Then another message came to me from the LORD: ²"Why do you quote this proverb in the land of Israel: 'The parents have eaten sour grapes, but their children's mouths pucker at the taste'? ³As surely as I live, says the Sovereign LORD, you will not say this proverb anymore in Israel. ⁴For all people are mine to judge—both parents and children alike. And this is my rule: The person who sins will be the one who dies.

⁵"Suppose a certain man is just and does what is lawful and right, ⁶and he has not feasted in the mountains before Israel's idols or worshiped them. And suppose he does not commit adultery or have intercourse with a woman during her menstrual period. ⁷Suppose he is a merciful creditor, not keeping the items given in pledge by poor debtors, and does not rob the poor but instead gives food to the hungry and provides clothes for people in need. ⁸And suppose he grants loans without interest, stays away from injustice, is honest and fair when judging others, ⁹and faithfully obeys my laws and regulations. Anyone who does these things is just and will surely live, says the Sovereign LORD.

¹⁰"But suppose that man has a son who grows up to be a robber or murderer and refuses to do what is right. ¹¹And suppose that son does all the evil things his father

would never do—worships idols on the mountains, commits adultery, ¹²oppresses the poor and helpless, steals from debtors by refusing to let them redeem what they have given in pledge, worships idols and takes part in loathsome practices, ¹³and lends money at interest. Should such a sinful person live? No! He must die and must take full blame.

¹⁴"But suppose that sinful son, in turn, has a son who sees his father's wickedness but decides against that kind of life. ¹⁵Suppose this son refuses to worship idols on the mountains, does not commit adultery, ¹⁶and does not exploit the poor, but instead is fair to debtors and does not rob them. And suppose this son feeds the hungry, provides clothes for the needy, ¹⁷helps the poor, does not lend money at interest, and obeys all my regulations and laws. Such a person will not die because of his father's sins; he will surely live. ¹⁸But the father will die for the many sins he committed—for being cruel and robbing close relatives, doing what was clearly wrong among his people.

¹⁹"'What?' you ask. 'Doesn't the child pay for the parent's sins?' No! For if the child does what is right and keeps my laws, that child will surely live. ²⁰The one who sins is the one who dies. The child will not be punished for the parent's sins, and the parent will not be punished for the child's sins. Righteous people will be rewarded for their own goodness, and wicked people will be punished for their own wickedness. ²¹But if wicked people turn away from all their sins and begin to obey my laws and do what is just and right, they will surely live and not die. ²²All their past sins will be forgotten, and they will live because of the righteous things they have done.

²³"Do you think, asks the Sovereign LORD, that I like to see wicked people die? Of course not! I only want them to turn from their wicked ways and live. ²⁴However, if righteous people turn to sinful ways and start acting like other sinners, should they be allowed to live? No, of course not! All their previous goodness will be forgotten, and they will die for their sins.

²⁵"Yet you say, 'The Lord isn't being just!' Listen to me, O people of Israel. Am I the one who is unjust, or is it you? ²⁶When righteous people turn from being

good and start doing sinful things, they will die for it. Yes, they will die because of their sinful deeds. ²⁷ And if wicked people turn away from their wickedness, obey the law, and do what is just and right, they will save their lives. ²⁸ They will live, because after thinking it over, they decided to turn from their sins. Such people will not die. ²⁹ And yet the people of Israel keep saying, 'The Lord is unjust!' O people of Israel, it is you who are unjust, not I.

³⁰ "Therefore, I will judge each of you, O people of Israel, according to your actions, says the Sovereign LORD. Turn from your sins! Don't let them destroy you! ³¹ Put all your rebellion behind you, and get for yourselves a new heart and a new spirit. For why should you die, O people of Israel? ³² I don't want you to die, says the Sovereign LORD. Turn back and live!

CHAPTER 19

"Sing this funeral song for the princes of Israel:

² 'What is your mother?
     A lioness among lions!
   She lay down among the young lions
     and reared her cubs.
³ She raised one of her cubs
     to become a strong young lion.
   He learned to catch and devour prey,
     and he became a man-eater.
⁴ Then the nations heard about him,
     and he was trapped in their pit.
   They led him away in chains
     to the land of Egypt.

⁵ 'When the mother lion saw
     that all her hopes for him were gone,
   she took another of her cubs
     and taught him to be a strong lion.
⁶ He prowled among the other lions
     and became a leader among them.
   He learned to catch and devour prey,
     and he, too, became a man-eater.

19:7 As in Greek version; Hebrew reads *He consorted with widows.*

⁷ He demolished fortresses in nearby
        nations*
     and destroyed their towns and cities.
   Their farms were desolated,
     and their crops were destroyed.
   Everyone in the land trembled in fear
     when they heard him roar.
⁸ Then the armies of the nations attacked
        him,
     surrounding him from every
        direction.
   They spread out their nets for him
     and captured him in their pit.
⁹ With hooks, they dragged him into
        a cage
     and brought him before the king
        of Babylon.
   They held him in captivity,
     so his voice could never again be
        heard
     on the mountains of Israel.

¹⁰ 'Your mother was like a vine
        planted by the water's edge.
   It had lush, green foliage
     because of the abundant water.
¹¹ Its branches became very strong,
     strong enough to be a ruler's scepter.
   It soon became very tall,
     towering above all the others.
   It stood out because of its height
     and because of its many lush
        branches.
¹² But the vine was uprooted in fury
     and thrown down to the ground.
   The desert wind dried up its fruit
     and tore off its branches.
   Its stem was destroyed by fire.
¹³ Now the vine is growing in the
        wilderness,
     where the ground is hard and dry.
¹⁴ A fire has come from its branches
     and devoured its fruit.
   None of the remaining limbs
     is strong enough to be a ruler's
        scepter.'

This is a funeral song, and it is now time for the funeral."

AUGUST 19 ☐ DAY 232
EZEKIEL 20–23
Swords and Signposts

OVERVIEW Ezekiel the prophet often becomes Ezekiel the playwright as he uses a number of symbolic actions to dramatize the coming despair for Jerusalem. God's smelting furnace of wrath will refine the nation of Judah, burning away like dross her violence, immorality, and idolatry. Like an adulterous woman she has followed the lewd example of her sister, Israel. As a result, Babylon—God's sword of punishment—is posed to strike. God declares, "My sword is in my hand, and it will not return to its sheath until its work is finished" (21:5).

Chapter 20	Chapter 21	Chapter 22	Chapter 23
Reviewing Judah's Sins	Removing Judah's King	Parable of the Silver	Parable of the Sisters
Swords		Signposts	

YOUR DAILY WALK When do you know that punishment has accomplished its intention?
  a. When the person being punished begins to cry
  b. When the person being punished responds, "Ouch!"
  c. When the person being punished changes his or her mind about repeating a course of action

Repentance may be old-fashioned, but it is not outdated so long as there is sin.

Punishment is always *painful*. But whether or not it is *profitable* depends on the response of the offender. Repeatedly Ezekiel has tried—through pictures, parables, and illustrations—to visualize the agony of God's punishing hand. It is a sword, a smelting pot, a cauldron. But God's underlying purpose is not to inflict pain; he is looking for repentance—a change of mind, heart, and direction regarding a sinful action. Are you being prodded, refined, or simmered today?

INSIGHT Sign Language for Exiles
God told Ezekiel, "All [your] actions will be a sign for the people of Israel" (12:6). See if you can complete the chart below that lists Ezekiel's ten signs designed to teach the nation ten divine truths:

Reference	Sign
4:1-3	
4:4-8	
4:9-17	
5:1-17	
12:1-7	
21:1-17	
22:17-31	
24:1-14	
24:15-27	
37:15-17	

CHAPTER 20
On August 14,* during the seventh year of King Jehoiachin's captivity, some of the leaders of Israel came to request a message from the LORD. They sat down in front of me to wait for his reply. ²Then this message came to me from the LORD: ³"Son of man, give the leaders of Israel this message from the Sovereign LORD: How dare you come to ask for my help? As surely as I live, I will tell you nothing. This is the word of the Sovereign LORD!

20:1 Hebrew *In the fifth month, on the tenth day,* of the Hebrew calendar. This event occurred on August 14, 591 B.C.; also see note on 1:1.

⁴"Son of man, bring judgment against them and condemn them. Make them realize how loathsome the actions of their ancestors really were. ⁵Give them this message from the Sovereign LORD: When I chose Israel and revealed myself to her in Egypt, I swore that I, the LORD, would be her God. ⁶I promised that I would bring her and her descendants out of Egypt to a land I had discovered and explored for them—a good land, a land flowing with milk and honey, the best of all lands anywhere. ⁷Then I said to them, 'Each of you, get rid of your idols. Do not defile yourselves with the Egyptian gods, for I am the LORD your God.'

⁸"But they rebelled against me and would not listen. They did not get rid of their idols or forsake the gods of Egypt. Then I threatened to pour out my fury to satisfy my anger while they were still in Egypt. ⁹But I didn't do it, for I acted to protect the honor of my name. That way the surrounding nations wouldn't be able to laugh at Israel's God, who had promised to deliver his people. ¹⁰So I brought my people out of Egypt and led them into the wilderness. ¹¹There I gave them my laws so they could live by keeping them. Yes, all those who keep them will live! ¹²And I gave them my Sabbath days of rest as a sign between them and me. It was to remind them that I, the LORD, had set them apart to be holy, making them my special people.

¹³"But the people of Israel rebelled against me, and they refused to obey my laws there in the wilderness. They wouldn't obey my instructions even though obedience would have given them life. And they also violated my Sabbath days. So I threatened to pour out my fury on them, and I made plans to utterly consume them in the desert. ¹⁴But again I held back in order to protect the honor of my name. That way the nations who saw me lead my people out of Egypt wouldn't be able to claim I destroyed them because I couldn't take care of them. ¹⁵But I swore to them in the wilderness that I would not bring them into the land I had given them, a land flowing with milk and honey, the most beautiful place on earth. ¹⁶I told them this because they had rejected my laws, ignored my will for them, and violated my Sabbath days. Their hearts were given to their idols. ¹⁷Nevertheless, I pitied them and held back from destroying them in the wilderness.

¹⁸"Then I warned their children and told them not to follow in their parents' footsteps, defiling themselves with their idols. ¹⁹I am the LORD your God,' I told them. 'Follow my laws, pay attention to my instructions, ²⁰and keep my Sabbath days holy, for they are a sign to remind you that I am the LORD your God.'

²¹"But their children, too, rebelled against me. They refused to keep my laws and follow my instructions, even though obeying them would have given them life. And they also violated my Sabbath days. So again I threatened to pour out my fury on them in the wilderness. ²²Nevertheless, I withdrew my judgment against them to protect the honor of my name among the nations who had seen my power in bringing them out of Egypt. ²³But I took a solemn oath against them while they were in the wilderness. I vowed I would scatter them among all the nations ²⁴because they did not obey my laws. They scorned my instructions by violating my Sabbath days and longing for the idols of their ancestors. ²⁵I gave them over to worthless customs and laws that would not lead to life. ²⁶I let them pollute themselves with the very gifts I had given them, and I allowed them to give their firstborn children as offerings to their gods—so I might devastate them and show them that I alone am the LORD.

²⁷"Therefore, son of man, give the people of Israel this message from the Sovereign LORD: Your ancestors continued to blaspheme and betray me, ²⁸for when I brought them into the land I had promised them, they offered sacrifices and incense on every high hill and under every green tree they saw! They roused my fury as they offered up sacrifices to their gods. They brought their perfumes and incense and poured out their drink offerings to them! ²⁹I said to them, 'What is this high place where you are going?' (This idol shrine has been called Bamah—'high place'—ever since.)

³⁰"Therefore, give the people of Israel this message from the Sovereign LORD: Do you plan to pollute yourselves just as your ancestors did? Do you intend to keep prostituting yourselves by worshiping detestable idols? ³¹For when you offer gifts to them and give your little children to be burned as sacrifices,* you continue to pollute yourselves to this day. Should I listen to you or help you,

20:31 Or *and make your little children pass through the fire.*

O people of Israel? As surely as I live, says the Sovereign LORD, I will not give you a message even though you have come to me requesting one.

[32]"You say, 'We want to be like the nations all around us, who serve idols of wood and stone.' But what you have in mind will never happen. [33]As surely as I live, says the Sovereign LORD, I will rule you with an iron fist in great anger and with awesome power. [34]With might and fury I will bring you out from the lands where you are scattered. [35]I will bring you into the wilderness of the nations, and there I will judge you face to face. [36]I will judge you there just as I did your ancestors in the wilderness after bringing them out of Egypt, says the Sovereign LORD. [37]I will count you carefully and hold you to the terms of the covenant. [38]I will purge you of all those who rebel and sin against me. I will bring them out of the countries where they are in exile, but they will never enter the land of Israel. And when that happens, you will know that I am the LORD.

[39]"As for you, O people of Israel, this is what the Sovereign LORD says: If you insist, go right ahead and worship your idols, but then don't turn around and bring gifts to me. Such desecration of my holy name must stop! [40]For on my holy mountain, says the Sovereign LORD, the people of Israel will someday worship me, and I will accept them. There I will require that you bring me all your offerings and choice gifts and sacrifices. [41]When I bring you home from exile, you will be as pleasing to me as an offering of perfumed incense. And I will display my holiness in you as all the nations watch. [42]Then when I have brought you home to the land I promised your ancestors, you will know that I am the LORD. [43]You will look back at all your sins and hate yourselves because of the evil you have done. [44]You will know that I am the LORD, O people of Israel, when I have honored my name by treating you mercifully in spite of your wickedness, says the Sovereign LORD."

[45]Then this message came to me from the LORD: [46]"Son of man, look toward the south* and speak out against it; prophesy against the fields of the Negev. [47]Give the southern wilderness this message from the Sovereign LORD: Hear the word of the LORD! I will set you on fire, O forest, and every tree will be burned—green and dry trees alike. The ter-

rible flames will not be quenched; they will scorch everything from south to north. [48]And all the world will see that I, the LORD, have set this fire. It will not be put out."

[49]Then I said, "O Sovereign LORD, they are saying of me, 'He only talks in riddles!'"

CHAPTER 21

Then this message came to me from the LORD: [2]"Son of man, look toward Jerusalem and prophesy against Israel and her sanctuaries. [3]Give her this message from the LORD: I am your enemy, O Israel, and I am about to unsheath my sword to destroy your people—the righteous and the wicked alike. [4]Yes, I will not spare even the righteous! I will make a clean sweep throughout the land from south to north. [5]All the world will know that I am the LORD. My sword is in my hand, and it will not return to its sheath until its work is finished.

[6]"Son of man, groan before the people! Groan before them with bitter anguish and a broken heart. [7]When they ask you why, tell them, 'I groan because of the terrifying news I have heard. When it comes true, the boldest heart will melt with fear; all strength will disappear. Every spirit will faint; strong knees will tremble and become as weak as water. And the Sovereign LORD says: It is coming! It's on its way!'"

[8]Then the LORD said to me, [9]"Son of man, give the people this message from the LORD: A sword is being sharpened and polished. [10]It is being prepared for terrible slaughter; it will flash like lightning! Now will you laugh? Those far stronger than you have fallen beneath its power!* [11]Yes, the sword is now being sharpened and polished; it is being prepared for the executioner!

[12]"Son of man, cry out and wail; pound your thighs in anguish, for that sword will slaughter my people and their leaders— everyone will die! [13]It will put them all to the test! So now the Sovereign LORD asks: What chance do they have?*

[14]"Son of man, prophesy to them and clap your hands vigorously. Then take the sword and brandish it twice, even three times, to symbolize the great massacre they will face! [15]Let their hearts melt with terror, for the sword glitters at every gate. It flashes like lightning; it is polished for slaughter! [16]O sword, slash to the right, and slash to the left, wherever you will,

20:46 Hebrew *Teman.*   **21:10** The meaning of the Hebrew is uncertain.   **21:13** The meaning of the Hebrew is uncertain.

wherever you want. [17]I, too, will clap my hands, and I will satisfy my fury. I, the LORD, have spoken!"

[18]Then this message came to me from the LORD: [19]"Son of man, make a map and trace two routes on it for the sword of Babylon's king to follow. Put a signpost on the road that comes out of Babylon where the road forks into two—[20]one road going to Ammon and its capital, Rabbah, and the other to Judah and fortified Jerusalem. [21]The king of Babylon now stands at the fork, uncertain whether to attack Jerusalem or Rabbah. He will call his magicians to use divination. They will cast lots by shaking arrows from the quiver. They will inspect the livers of their animal sacrifices. [22]Then they will decide to turn toward Jerusalem! With battering rams they will go against the gates, shouting for the kill. They will put up siege towers and build ramps against the walls to reach the top. [23]The people of Jerusalem will think it is a mistake, because of their treaty with the Babylonians. But the king of Babylon will remind the people of their rebellion. Then he will attack and capture them.

[24]"Therefore, this is what the Sovereign LORD says: Again and again your guilt cries out against you, for you are not ashamed of your sin. You don't even try to hide it! Wherever you go, whatever you do, all your actions are filled with sin. So now the time of your punishment has come!

[25]"O you corrupt and wicked prince of Israel, your final day of reckoning is here! [26]Take off your jeweled crown, says the Sovereign LORD. The old order changes— now the lowly are exalted, and the mighty are brought low. [27]Destruction! Destruction! I will surely destroy the kingdom. And it will not be restored until the one appears who has the right to judge it. Then I will hand it over to him.

[28]"And now, son of man, prophesy concerning the Ammonites and their mockery. Give them this message from the Sovereign LORD: My sword is drawn for your slaughter; it is sharpened to destroy, flashing like lightning! [29]Your magicians and false prophets have given false visions and told lies about the sword. And now it will fall with even greater force on the wicked for whom the day of final reckoning has come. [30]Should I return my sword to its sheath before I deal with you? No, I will destroy you in your own country, the land of your birth. [31]I will pour out my fury on you and blow on

you with the fire of my anger. I will hand you over to cruel men who are skilled in destruction. [32]You are fuel for the fire, and your blood will be spilled in your own land. You will be utterly wiped out, your memory lost to history. I, the LORD, have spoken!"

CHAPTER 22

Now this message came to me from the LORD: [2]"Son of man, are you ready to judge Jerusalem? Are you ready to judge this city of murderers? Denounce her terrible deeds in public, [3]and give her this message from the Sovereign LORD: O city of murderers, doomed and damned—city of idols, filthy and foul—[4]you are guilty of both murder and idolatry. Your day of destruction has come! You have reached the end of your years. I will make you an object of mockery throughout the world. [5]O infamous city, filled with confusion, you will be mocked by people both far and near.

[6]"Every leader in Israel who lives within your walls is bent on murder. [7]Fathers and mothers are contemptuously ignored. Resident foreigners are forced to pay for protection. Orphans and widows are wronged and oppressed. [8]Inside your walls you despise my holy things and violate my Sabbath days of rest. [9]People accuse others falsely and send them to their death. You are filled with idol worshipers and people who take part in lewd activities. [10]Men sleep with their fathers' wives and have intercourse with women who are menstruating. [11]Within your walls live men who commit adultery with their neighbors' wives, who defile their daughters-in-law or who rape their own sisters. [12]There are hired murderers, loan racketeers, and extortioners everywhere! They never even think of me and my commands, says the Sovereign LORD.

[13]"But now I clap my hands in indignation over your dishonest gain and bloodshed. [14]How strong and courageous will you be in my day of reckoning? I, the LORD, have spoken! I will do what I have said. [15]I will scatter you among the nations and purge you of your wickedness. [16]And when you have been dishonored among the nations, you will know that I am the LORD."

[17]Then this message came to me from the LORD: [18]"Son of man, the people of Israel are the worthless slag that remains after silver is smelted. They are the dross that is left over—a useless mixture of copper, tin,

iron, and lead. ¹⁹So give them this message from the Sovereign LORD: Because you are all worthless slag, I will bring you to my crucible in Jerusalem. ²⁰I will melt you down in the heat of my fury, just as copper, tin, iron, and lead are melted down in a furnace. ²¹I will gather you together and blow the fire of my anger upon you, ²²and you will melt like silver in fierce heat. Then you will know that I, the LORD, have poured out my fury on you."

²³Again a message came to me from the LORD: ²⁴"Son of man, give the people of Israel this message: In the day of my indignation, you will become like an uncleared wilderness or a desert without rain. ²⁵Your princes* plot conspiracies just as lions stalk their prey. They devour innocent people, seizing treasures and extorting wealth. They increase the number of widows in the land. ²⁶Your priests have violated my laws and defiled my holy things. To them there is no difference between what is holy and what is not. And they do not teach my people the difference between what is ceremonially clean and unclean. They disregard my Sabbath days so that my holy name is greatly dishonored among them. ²⁷Your leaders are like wolves, who tear apart their victims. They actually destroy people's lives for profit! ²⁸And your prophets announce false visions and speak false messages. They say, 'My message is from the Sovereign LORD,' when the LORD hasn't spoken a single word to them. They repair cracked walls with whitewash! ²⁹Even common people oppress the poor, rob the needy, and deprive foreigners of justice.

³⁰"I looked for someone who might rebuild the wall of righteousness that guards the land. I searched for someone to stand in the gap in the wall so I wouldn't have to destroy the land, but I found no one. ³¹So now I will pour out my fury on them, consuming them in the fire of my anger. I will heap on them the full penalty for all their sins, says the Sovereign LORD."

CHAPTER 23

This message came to me from the LORD: ²"Son of man, once there were two sisters who were daughters of the same mother. ³They became prostitutes in Egypt. Even as young girls, they allowed themselves to be fondled and caressed. ⁴The older girl was named Oholah, and her sister was Oholibah. I married them, and they bore me sons and daughters. I am speaking of Samaria and Jerusalem, for Oholah is Samaria and Oholibah is Jerusalem.

⁵"Then Oholah lusted after other lovers instead of me, and she gave her love to the Assyrians, her neighbors. ⁶They were all attractive young men, captains and commanders dressed in handsome blue, dashing about on their horses. ⁷And so she prostituted herself with the most desirable men of Assyria, worshiping their idols and defiling herself. ⁸For when she left Egypt, she did not leave her spirit of prostitution behind. She was still as lewd as in her youth, when the Egyptians satisfied their lusts with her and robbed her of her virginity. ⁹And so I handed her over to her Assyrian lovers, whom she desired so much. ¹⁰They stripped her and killed her and took away her children as their slaves. Her name was known to every woman in the land as a sinner who had received what she deserved.

¹¹"Yet even though Oholibah saw what had happened to Oholah, her sister, she followed right in her footsteps. And she was even more depraved, abandoning herself to her lust and prostitution. ¹²She fawned over her Assyrian neighbors, those handsome young men on fine horses, those captains and commanders in handsome uniforms—all of them desirable. ¹³I saw the way she was going, defiling herself just like her older sister.

¹⁴"Then she carried her prostitution even further. She fell in love with pictures that were painted on a wall—pictures of Babylonian* military officers, outfitted in striking red uniforms. ¹⁵Handsome belts encircled their waists, and flowing turbans crowned their heads. They were dressed like chariot officers from the land of Babylonia.* ¹⁶When she saw these paintings, she longed to give herself to them, so she sent messengers to Babylonia to invite them to come to her. ¹⁷So they came and committed adultery with her, defiling her in the bed of love. But later, she became disgusted with them and broke off their relationship.

¹⁸"So I became disgusted with Oholibah, just as I was with her sister, because she flaunted herself before them and gave herself to satisfy their lusts. ¹⁹But that didn't bother her. She turned to even greater pros-

22:25 As in Greek version; Hebrew reads *prophets.*   23:14 Or *Chaldean.*   23:15 Or *Chaldea;* also in 23:16.

titution, remembering her youth when she was a prostitute in Egypt. ²⁰She lusted after lovers whose attentions were gross and bestial. ²¹And so, Oholibah, you celebrated your former days as a young girl in Egypt, when you first allowed yourself to be fondled and caressed.

²²"Therefore, Oholibah, this is what the Sovereign LORD says: I will send your lovers against you—those very nations from which you turned away in disgust. ²³For the Babylonians will come with all the Chaldeans from Pekod and Shoa and Koa. And all the Assyrians will come with them—handsome young captains, commanders, chariot officers, and other high-ranking officers, riding their horses. ²⁴They will all come against you from the north with chariots, wagons, and a great army fully prepared for attack. They will take up positions on every side, surrounding you with men armed for battle. And I will hand you over to them so they can do with you as they please. ²⁵I will turn my jealous anger against you, and they will deal furiously with you. They will cut off your nose and ears, and any survivors will then be slaughtered by the sword. Your children will be taken away as captives, and everything that is left will be burned. ²⁶They will strip you of your beautiful clothes and jewels. ²⁷In this way, I will put a stop to the lewdness and prostitution you brought from Egypt. You will never again cast longing eyes on those things or fondly remember your time in Egypt.

²⁸"For this is what the Sovereign LORD says: I will surely hand you over to your enemies, to those you loathe. ²⁹They will deal with you in hatred and rob you of all you own, leaving you naked and bare. The shame of your prostitution will be exposed to all the world. ³⁰You brought all this on yourself by prostituting yourself to other nations, defiling yourself with all their idols. ³¹Because you have followed in your sister's footsteps, I will punish you with the same terrors that destroyed her.

³²"Yes, this is what the Sovereign LORD says: You will drink from the same cup of terror as your sister—a cup that is large and deep. And all the world will mock and scorn you in your desolation. ³³You will reel like a drunkard beneath the awful blows of sorrow and distress, just as your sister Samaria did. ³⁴In deep anguish you will drain that cup of terror to the very

bottom. Then you will smash it to pieces and beat your breast in anguish. For I, the Sovereign LORD, have spoken! ³⁵And because you have forgotten me and turned your back on me, says the Sovereign LORD, you must bear the consequences of all your lewdness and prostitution."

³⁶The LORD said to me, "Son of man, you must accuse Oholah and Oholibah of all their awful deeds. ³⁷They have committed both adultery and murder—adultery by worshiping idols and murder by burning their children as sacrifices on their altars. ³⁸Then after doing these terrible things, they defiled my Temple and violated my Sabbath day! ³⁹On the very day that they murdered their children in front of their idols, they boldly came into my Temple to worship! They came in and defiled my house!

⁴⁰"You sisters sent messengers to distant lands to get men. Then when they arrived, you bathed yourselves, painted your eyelids, and put on your finest jewels for them. ⁴¹You sat with them on a beautifully embroidered couch and put my incense and my oil on a table that was spread before you. ⁴²From your room came the sound of many men carousing. They were lustful men and drunkards from the wilderness, who put bracelets on your wrists and beautiful crowns on your heads. ⁴³Then I said, 'If they really want to sleep with worn-out, old prostitutes like these, let them!' ⁴⁴And that is what they did. They slept with Oholah and Oholibah, these shameless prostitutes, with all the zest of lustful young men. ⁴⁵But righteous people will judge these sister cities for what they really are—adulteresses and murderers. They will sentence them to all the punishment they deserve.

⁴⁶"Now this is what the Sovereign LORD says: Bring an army against them and hand them over to be terrorized and plundered. ⁴⁷For their enemies will stone them and kill them with swords. They will butcher their sons and daughters and burn their homes. ⁴⁸In this way, I will put an end to lewdness and idolatry in the land, and my judgment will be a warning to others not to follow their wicked example. ⁴⁹You will be fully repaid for all your prostitution—your worship of idols. Yes, you will suffer the full penalty! Then you will know that I am the Sovereign LORD."

AUGUST 20 □ DAY 233
EZEKIEL 24 –28
Judgment East and West

OVERVIEW Gloating over the fate of another is one sure way to share that fate! Judah's neighbors, smug in their arrogance, stand next in line for Ezekiel's declaration of doom. Ammon, Moab, Edom, Philistia, Tyre—none will escape God's wrath according to Ezekiel's vision of doom. Age-old adversaries and great commercial empires alike will topple to show the world that God's justice cannot be thwarted.

Chapter 24	Chapter 25	Chapters 26–27	Chapter 28
Tears for Ezekiel	Terror for Ammon, Moab, Edom, Philistia	Toppling of Tyre's Pride	King
Dead Wife	Deadly Warfare	Deadly "Wisdom"	

YOUR DAILY WALK Do you have a problem with pride? If you answered no, are you proud of that fact?

Consider for a moment these insightful words on the subject of pride—a problem not limited to Ezekiel's day:

Humility is the embarrassment we feel when we tell others how wonderful we are.

Pride is a vice not limited to the emperors of far-flung realms. Almost anyone, by comparing himself or herself with those who have less talent, less success, less popularity, can emerge with a feeling of satisfaction that is the very opposite of humility.

What is the remedy for pride? You'll find the prescription in 1 Corinthians 4:7. It's the daily realization that all you are and have is a gift from God. The king of Tyre got into "pride problems" by forgetting that fact. Ezekiel 28:12-19 shows numerous ways in which pride tripped up the king of Tyre. Are you in danger of being tripped as well? Then spend a few minutes reviewing these potent proverbs about pride and its pitfalls: Proverbs 8:13; 11:2; 13:10; 14:3; 16:18; 29:23.

INSIGHT When Ezekiel Talks, People Listen!

Tyre, located sixty miles northwest of Nazareth, was actually a split city—half on an island and half on the mainland with a channel in between. At the zenith of its power, Tyre controlled virtually all commerce on the Mediterranean and boasted colonies in Africa, Spain, and Britain. After the Babylonian siege, however, it never regained its former glory. Today, the once-proud city is nothing more than a bare rock where fishermen spread their nets (26:4-5, 14)—a remarkable fulfillment of Ezekiel's prophecy (26:14, 21; 27:36).

CHAPTER 24

On January 15,* during the ninth year of King Jehoiachin's captivity, this message came to me from the LORD: ²"Son of man, write down today's date, because on this very day the king of Babylon is beginning his attack against Jerusalem. ³Then show these rebels an illustration; give them a message from the Sovereign LORD. Put a pot of water on the fire to boil. ⁴Fill it with choice meat—the rump and the shoulder

and all the most tender cuts. ⁵Use only the best sheep from the flock and heap fuel on the fire beneath the pot. Bring the pot to a boil, and cook the bones along with the meat.

⁶"Now this is what the Sovereign LORD says: Destruction is certain for Jerusalem, the city of murderers! She is a pot filled with corruption. So take the meat out chunk by chunk in whatever order it comes, ⁷for her wickedness is evident to all.

24:1 Hebrew *On the tenth day of the tenth month,* of the Hebrew calendar. This event occurred on January 15, 588 B.C.; also see note on 1:1.

She murders boldly, leaving blood on the rocks for all to see. She doesn't even try to cover it! 8So I will splash her blood on a rock as an open expression of my anger and vengeance against her.

9"This is what the Sovereign LORD says: Destruction is certain for Jerusalem, the city of murderers! I myself will pile up the fuel beneath her. 10Yes, heap on the wood! Let the fire roar to make the pot boil. Cook the meat well with many spices. Then empty the pot and burn the bones. 11Now set the empty pot on the coals to scorch away the filth and corruption. 12But it's hopeless; the corruption remains. So throw it into the fire! 13It is the filth and corruption of your lewdness and idolatry. And now, because I tried to cleanse you but you refused, you will remain filthy until my fury against you has been satisfied. 14I, the LORD, have spoken! The time has come and I won't hold back; I will not change my mind. You will be judged on the basis of all your wicked actions, says the Sovereign LORD."

15Then this message came to me from the LORD: 16"Son of man, I am going to take away your dearest treasure. Suddenly she will die. Yet you must not show any sorrow. Do not weep; let there be no tears. 17You may sigh but only quietly. Let there be no wailing at her grave. Do not uncover your head or take off your sandals. Do not perform the rituals of mourning or accept any food brought to you by consoling friends."

18So I proclaimed this to the people the next morning, and in the evening my wife died. The next morning I did everything I had been told to do. 19Then the people asked, "What does all this mean? What are you trying to tell us?"

20So I said to them, "A message came to me from the LORD, 21and I was told to give this message to the people of Israel. This is what the Sovereign LORD says: I will desecrate my Temple, the source of your security and pride. Your sons and daughters in Judea will be slaughtered by the sword. 22Then you will do as Ezekiel has done. You will not mourn in public or console yourselves by eating the food brought to you by sympathetic friends. 23Your heads must remain covered, and your sandals must not be taken off. You will not mourn or weep, but you will waste away because of your sins. You will mourn privately for all the evil you have done. 24Ezekiel is an example

for you to follow; you will do as he has done. And when that time comes, you will know that I am the LORD."

25Then the LORD said to me, "Son of man, on the day I take away their stronghold—their joy and glory, their heart's desire, their dearest treasure—I will also take away their sons and daughters. 26And on that day a refugee from Jerusalem will come to you in Babylon and tell you what has happened. 27And when he arrives, your voice will suddenly return so you can talk to him, and you will be a symbol for these people. Then they will know that I am the LORD."

CHAPTER 25

Then this message came to me from the LORD: 2"Son of man, look toward the land of Ammon and prophesy against its people. 3Give the Ammonites this message from the Sovereign LORD: Hear the word of the Sovereign LORD! Because you scoffed when my Temple was desecrated, mocked Israel in her desolation, and laughed at Judah as she went away into exile, 4I will allow nomads from the eastern deserts to overrun your country. They will set up their camps among you and pitch their tents on your land. They will harvest all your fruit and steal your livestock. 5And I will turn the city of Rabbah into a pasture for camels, and all the land of the Ammonites into an enclosure for sheep. Then you will know that I am the LORD.

6"And the Sovereign LORD says: Because you clapped and stamped and cheered with glee at the destruction of my people, 7I will lift up my fist against you. I will give you as plunder to many nations. I will cut you off from being a nation and destroy you completely. Then you will know that I am the LORD.

8"And the Sovereign LORD says: Because the people of Moab have said that Judah is just like all the other nations, 9I will open up their eastern flank and wipe out their glorious frontier cities—Beth-jeshimoth, Baal-meon, and Kiriathaim. 10And I will hand Moab over to nomads from the eastern deserts, just as I handed over Ammon. Yes, the Ammonites will no longer be counted among the nations. 11And in the same way, I will bring my judgment down on the Moabites. Then they will know that I am the LORD.

¹²"And the Sovereign LORD says: The people of Edom have sinned greatly by avenging themselves against the people of Judah. ¹³Therefore, says the Sovereign LORD, I will raise my fist of judgment against Edom. I will wipe out their people, cattle, and flocks with the sword. I will make a wasteland of everything from Teman to Dedan. ¹⁴By the hand of my people of Israel, I will accomplish this. They will carry out my furious vengeance, and Edom will know it is from me. I, the Sovereign LORD, have spoken!

¹⁵"And the Sovereign LORD says: The people of Philistia have acted against Judah out of revenge and long-standing contempt. ¹⁶Therefore, says the Sovereign LORD, I will raise my fist of judgment against the land of the Philistines. I will wipe out the Kerethites and utterly destroy the people who live by the sea. ¹⁷I will execute terrible vengeance against them to rebuke them for what they have done. And when I have inflicted my revenge, then they will know that I am the LORD."

CHAPTER 26

On February 3, during the twelfth year of King Jehoiachin's captivity,* this message came to me from the LORD: ²"Son of man, Tyre has rejoiced over the fall of Jerusalem, saying, 'Ha! She who controlled the rich trade routes to the east has been broken, and I am the heir! Because she has been destroyed, I will become wealthy!'

³"Therefore, this is what the Sovereign LORD says: I am your enemy, O Tyre, and I will bring many nations against you, like the waves of the sea crashing against your shoreline. ⁴They will destroy the walls of Tyre and tear down its towers. I will scrape away its soil and make it a bare rock! ⁵The island of Tyre will become uninhabited. It will be a place for fishermen to spread their nets, for I have spoken, says the Sovereign LORD. Tyre will become the prey of many nations, ⁶and its mainland villages will be destroyed by the sword. Then they will know that I am the LORD.

⁷"For the Sovereign LORD says: I will bring King Nebuchadnezzar* of Babylon— the king of kings from the north—against Tyre with his cavalry, chariots, and great army. ⁸First he will destroy your mainland villages. Then he will attack you by building a siege wall, constructing a ramp, and raising a roof of shields against you. ⁹He will pound your walls with battering rams and demolish your towers with sledgehammers. ¹⁰The hooves of his cavalry will choke the city with dust, and your walls will shake as the horses gallop through your broken gates, pulling chariots behind them. ¹¹His horsemen will trample every street in the city. They will butcher your people, and your famous pillars will topple.

¹²"They will plunder all your riches and merchandise and break down your walls. They will destroy your lovely homes and dump your stones and timbers and even your dust into the sea. ¹³I will stop the music of your songs. No more will the sound of harps be heard among your people. ¹⁴I will make your island a bare rock, a place for fishermen to spread their nets. You will never be rebuilt, for I, the LORD, have spoken! This is the word of the Sovereign LORD.

¹⁵"This is what the Sovereign LORD says to Tyre: The whole coastline will tremble at the sound of your fall, as the screams of the wounded echo in the continuing slaughter. ¹⁶All the seaport rulers will step down from their thrones and take off their royal robes and beautiful clothing. They will sit on the ground trembling with horror at what they have seen. ¹⁷Then they will wail for you, singing this funeral song:

'O famous island city,
    once ruler of the sea,
    how you have been destroyed!
Your people, with their naval power,
    once spread fear around the world.
¹⁸ Now the coastlands tremble at your fall.
    The islands are dismayed as you
        pass away.'

¹⁹"For the Sovereign LORD says: I will make Tyre an uninhabited ruin. You will sink beneath the terrible waves of enemy attack. Great seas will swallow you. ²⁰I will send you to the pit to lie there with those who descended there long ago. Your city will lie in ruins, buried beneath the earth, like those in the pit who have entered the

26:1 Hebrew *In the eleventh year, on the first day of the month,* of the Hebrew calendar year. Since an element is missing in the date formula here, scholars have reconstructed this probable reading: *In the eleventh [month of the twelfth] year, on the first day of the month.* This reading would put this message on February 3, 585 B.C.; also see note on 1:1.   **26:7** Hebrew *Nebuchadrezzar,* a variant name for Nebuchadnezzar.

world of the dead. Never again will you be given a position of respect here in the land of the living. ²¹I will bring you to a terrible end, and you will be no more. You will be looked for, but you will never be found. I, the Sovereign LORD, have spoken!"

CHAPTER 27

Then this message came to me from the LORD: ²"Son of man, sing a funeral song for Tyre, ³that mighty gateway to the sea, the trading center of the world. Give Tyre this message from the Sovereign LORD: You claimed, O Tyre, to be perfect in beauty. ⁴You extended your boundaries into the sea. Your builders made you glorious! ⁵You were like a great ship built of the finest cypress from Senir.* They took a cedar from Lebanon to make a mast for you. ⁶They carved oars for you from the oaks of Bashan. They made your deck of pine wood, brought from the southern coasts of Cyprus.* Then they inlaid it with ivory. ⁷Your sails were made of Egypt's finest linen, and they flew as a banner above you. You stood beneath blue and purple awnings made bright with dyes from the coasts of Elishah.

⁸"Your oarsmen came from Sidon and Arvad; your helmsmen were skilled men from Tyre itself. ⁹Wise old craftsmen from Gebal did all the caulking. Ships came with goods from every land to barter for your trade. ¹⁰Men from distant Persia, Lydia, and Libya* served in your great army. They hung their shields and helmets on your walls, giving you great honor. ¹¹Men from Arvad and from Helech stood on your walls as sentinels. Your towers were manned by men from Gammad. Their shields hung on your walls, perfecting your splendor.

¹²"Tarshish was your agent, trading your wares in exchange for silver, iron, tin, and lead. ¹³Merchants from Greece,* Tubal, and Meshech brought slaves and bronze dishes. ¹⁴From Togarmah came riding horses, chariot horses, and mules. All these things were exchanged for your manufactured goods. ¹⁵Merchants came to you from Dedan.* Numerous coastlands were your captive markets; they brought payment in ivory tusks and ebony wood.

¹⁶"Aram* sent merchants to buy your wares. They traded turquoise, purple dyes,

embroidery, fine linen, and jewelry of coral and rubies. ¹⁷Judah and Israel traded for your wares, offering wheat from Minnith, early figs,* honey, oil, and balm. ¹⁸Damascus traded for your rich variety of goods, bringing wine from Helbon and white wool from Zahar. ¹⁹Greeks from Uzal* came to trade for your merchandise. Wrought iron, cassia, and calamus were bartered for your wares. ²⁰Dedan traded their expensive saddle blankets with you.

²¹"The Arabians and the princes of Kedar brought lambs and rams and goats in trade for your goods. ²²The merchants of Sheba and Raamah came with all kinds of spices, jewels, and gold in exchange for your wares. ²³Haran, Canneh, Eden, Sheba, Asshur, and Kilmad came with their merchandise, too. ²⁴They brought choice fabrics to trade—blue cloth, embroidery, and many-colored carpets bound with cords and made secure. ²⁵The ships of Tarshish were your ocean caravans. Your island warehouse was filled to the brim!

²⁶"But look! Your oarsmen are rowing your ship of state into a hurricane! Your mighty vessel flounders in the heavy eastern gale. You are shipwrecked in the heart of the sea! ²⁷Everything is lost—your riches and wares, your sailors and helmsmen, your ship builders, merchants, and warriors. On that day of vast ruin, everyone on board sinks into the depths of the sea.

²⁸"Your cities by the sea tremble as your helmsmen cry out in terror. ²⁹All the oarsmen abandon their ships; the sailors and helmsmen come to stand on the shore. ³⁰They weep bitterly as they throw dust on their heads and roll in ashes. ³¹They shave their heads in grief because of you and dress themselves in sackcloth. They weep for you with bitter anguish and deep mourning. ³²As they wail and mourn, they sing this sad funeral song:

'Was there ever such a city as Tyre,
    now silent at the bottom of the sea?
³³ The merchandise you traded
    satisfied the needs of many nations.
Kings at the ends of the earth
    were enriched by your trade.
³⁴ Now you are a wrecked ship,
    broken at the bottom of the sea.
All your merchandise and your crew
    have passed away with you.

27:5 Or *Hermon.*   **27:6** Hebrew *Kittim.*   **27:10** Hebrew *Paras, Lud, and Put.*   **27:13** Hebrew *Javan.*   **27:15** Greek version reads *Rhodes.*   **27:16** Some manuscripts read *Edom.*   **27:17** The meaning of the Hebrew is uncertain.   **27:19** Hebrew *Vedan and Javan from Uzal.* The meaning of the Hebrew is uncertain.

³⁵ All who live along the coastlands
      are appalled at your terrible fate.
   Their kings are filled with horror
      and look on with twisted faces.
³⁶ The merchants of the nations
      shake their heads at the sight of you,*
   for you have come to a horrible end
      and will be no more.'"

CHAPTER 28

Then this message came to me from the
LORD: ²"Son of man, give the prince of Tyre
this message from the Sovereign LORD: In
your great pride you claim, 'I am a god! I sit
on a divine throne in the heart of the sea.'
But you are only a man and not a god,
though you boast that you are like a god.
³You regard yourself as wiser than Daniel
and think no secret is hidden from you.
⁴With your wisdom and understanding
you have amassed great wealth—gold and
silver for your treasuries. ⁵Yes, your wisdom has made you very rich, and your
riches have made you very proud.

⁶"Therefore, this is what the Sovereign
LORD says: Because you think you are as
wise as a god, ⁷I will bring against you an
enemy army, the terror of the nations. They
will suddenly draw their swords against
your marvelous wisdom and defile your
splendor! ⁸They will bring you down to the
pit, and you will die there on your island
home in the heart of the sea, pierced with
many wounds. ⁹Will you then boast, 'I am
a god!' to those who kill you? To them you
will be no god but merely a man! ¹⁰You will
die like an outcast at the hands of foreigners. I, the Sovereign LORD, have spoken!"

¹¹Then this further message came to me
from the LORD: ¹²"Son of man, weep for the
king of Tyre. Give him this message from
the Sovereign LORD: You were the perfection of wisdom and beauty. ¹³You were in
Eden, the garden of God. Your clothing was
adorned with every precious stone*—red
carnelian, chrysolite, white moonstone,
beryl, onyx, jasper, sapphire, turquoise,
and emerald—all beautifully crafted for
you and set in the finest gold. They were
given to you on the day you were created.
¹⁴I ordained and anointed you as the
mighty angelic guardian.* You had access

to the holy mountain of God and walked
among the stones of fire.

¹⁵"You were blameless in all you did
from the day you were created until the
day evil was found in you. ¹⁶Your great
wealth filled you with violence, and you
sinned. So I banished you from the mountain of God. I expelled you, O mighty
guardian, from your place among the
stones of fire. ¹⁷Your heart was filled with
pride because of all your beauty. You corrupted your wisdom for the sake of your
splendor. So I threw you to the earth and
exposed you to the curious gaze of kings.
¹⁸You defiled your sanctuaries with your
many sins and your dishonest trade. So I
brought fire from within you, and it consumed you. I let it burn you to ashes on the
ground in the sight of all who were watching. ¹⁹All who knew you are appalled at
your fate. You have come to a terrible end,
and you are no more."

²⁰Then another message came to me
from the LORD: ²¹"Son of man, look toward
the city of Sidon and prophesy against it.
²²Give the people of Sidon this message
from the Sovereign LORD: I am your enemy,
O Sidon, and I will reveal my glory by
what happens to you. When I bring judgment against you and reveal my holiness
among you, everyone watching will know
that I am the LORD. ²³I will send a plague
against you, and blood will be spilled in
your streets. The attack will come from
every direction, and your people will lie
slaughtered within your walls. Then everyone will know that I am the LORD. ²⁴No
longer will Israel's scornful neighbors
prick and tear at her like thorns and briers.
For then they will know that I am the Sovereign LORD.

²⁵"This is what the Sovereign LORD says:
The people of Israel will again live in their
own land, the land I gave my servant Jacob.
For I will gather them from the distant
lands where I have scattered them. I will
reveal to the nations of the world my holiness among my people. ²⁶They will live
safely in Israel and build their homes and
plant their vineyards. And when I punish
the neighboring nations that treated them
with contempt, they will know that I am
the LORD their God."

27:36 Hebrew *hiss at you.*   **28:13** The identification of some of these gemstones is uncertain.   **28:14** Hebrew *guardian cherub;*
also in 28:16.

AUGUST 21 ☐ DAY 234
Then You Will Know

LOOK BACK Isaiah, Jeremiah, Ezekiel—each shares a common experience. Early in their prophetic ministries, they experience a vision from God that shapes the entire course of their lives. Ezekiel discovers that the person God can use is awed by the glory of God . . . available to the Spirit of God . . . and acting on the Word of God. In signs and symbols, Ezekiel dramatizes the fate awaiting his countrymen: siege, enslavement, and a "very close shave"! Indeed, the end is near, and God is going out of his way to be sure the world knows who is behind it all—the sovereign Lord.

As the glory departs from the Temple, it is clear that judgment and exile for Judah's leaders cannot be far behind, for as go the leaders, so go the people. Jerusalem has been unfaithful and fruitless, but God has shown loyal love in the face of her spiritual prostitution. Lamenting loudly and repenting of its wicked ways are the only appropriate responses to God's undying love. They are responses that Judah and its pagan neighboring nations desperately need to learn.

LOOK UP *Specialization* has been defined as "the art of learning more and more about less and less." Wisdom comes more from living than from studying, and indeed, it is better to know some of the answers than all of the questions.

Draw a circle and get inside, then pray God will send revival within the circle.

There are many things God wants you to know, but perhaps the most important is the truth repeated dozens of times in the book of Ezekiel: "You will know that I am the LORD" (6:7). Whatever else you learn in life will be meaningless unless and until you discover that God exists and rewards those who diligently seek him (Hebrews 11:6).

Scan back through the chapters you have read this past week, and catalog a few of the things that should have led the people of God to the inescapable conclusion that there is a God and he is not silent. (All the references are in Ezekiel.)

5:13   _____
6:7   _____
7:4   _____
12:15 _____
13:14 _____
15:7   _____
16:62 _____
17:21 _____
20:20 _____
24:24 _____
28:24 _____

LOOK AHEAD God is sovereignly in control of what happens in your life, your family, and your nation. Did you know that? If so, what difference does it make?

God is holy, totally apart from sin, and totally committed to helping you find power over every sinful habit that still clings to your life. Did you know that? If so, what is his will for you today?

God knows all about you and still loves you unconditionally. Did you know that? If so, there's nothing he would rather hear than "I love you, Lord," flowing from your heart to his. Have you told him that today? If not, there's no time like the present.

AUGUST 22 □ DAY 235
EZEKIEL 29–32
Judgment on Egypt

OVERVIEW Ezekiel's concluding words to Judah's neighbors are addressed specifically to Egypt. The perennial enemy of God's people, Egypt would not be totally destroyed (as Ammon, Moab, Edom, Philistia, and Tyre would be). Instead, it would be reduced to insignificance after a time of dispersion and regathering. Never again would the glory of the pharaohs shine. Egypt's wealth would be given to the Babylonians as a "reward" for carrying out God's will.

Chapter 29	Chapter 30	Chapter 31	Chapter 32
Egypt's Downfall	Egypt's Lament	Pharaoh's Downfall	Pharaoh's Lament
Judgment on Egypt			

YOUR DAILY WALK God has always been in the business of working with the remnant, not the majority. Do you feel you're in the minority as a Christian? The next time you're tempted to say, "I'm a nobody . . . the church has so little influence . . . I'm insignificant," think about little Israel. Like Ezekiel, get your eyes off yourself and fix your focus on God. It will do wonders for your perspective!

INSIGHT Tiny Nation, Great God

If you don't climb the mountain, you can't see the view.

The prophet has devoted a large section, fully one-sixth of his prophecy, to a denunciation of Israel's neighbors. It may seem strange to you that so much attention should be given to pagan countries in a book written to bring encouragement to God's people in exile.

Consider the relationship of Israel to the world around it. Compared to its neighbors, Israel was a tiny nation only a few thousand square miles in size. But by being located on the primary Near Eastern trade routes, Israel became significant to the foreign affairs of Assyria, Babylonia, Egypt, and Persia.

Ezekiel's message to these great world powers is the same message God would proclaim to the nations today. The destiny of humankind does not rest in the control of kings and queens but in God alone. Secular historians may consider Israel of little consequence when compared with Babylonia and Egypt, the Soviet Union or the United States. But Ezekiel saw these world powers from God's perspective. Like specks of dust on the prophetic page, they would disappear from view, while God's program for his people lived on!

CHAPTER 29

On January 7,* during the tenth year of King Jehoiachin's captivity, this message came to me from the LORD: ²"Son of man, turn toward Egypt and prophesy against Pharaoh the king and all the people of Egypt. ³Give them this message from the Sovereign LORD: I am your enemy, O Pharaoh, king of Egypt—you great monster, lurking in the streams of the Nile. For you

have said, 'The Nile River is mine; I made it for myself!' ⁴I will put hooks in your jaws and drag you out on the land with fish sticking to your scales. ⁵I will leave you and all your fish stranded in the desert to die. You will lie unburied on the open ground, for I have given you as food to the wild animals and birds.

⁶"All the people of Egypt will discover that I am the LORD, for you collapsed like a

29:1 Hebrew *On the twelfth day of the tenth month,* of the Hebrew calendar. A number of dates in Ezekiel can be cross-checked with dates in surviving Babylonian records and related accurately to our modern calendar. This event occurred on January 7, 587 B.C.

reed when Israel looked to you for help. [7]Israel leaned on you, but like a cracked staff, you splintered and stabbed her in the armpit. When she put her weight on you, you gave way, and her back was thrown out of joint. [8]So now the Sovereign LORD says: I will bring an army against you, O Egypt, and destroy both people and animals. [9]The land of Egypt will become a desolate wasteland, and the Egyptians will know that I am the LORD.

"Because you said, 'The Nile River is mine; I made it,' [10]I am now the enemy of both you and your river. I will utterly destroy the land of Egypt, from Migdol to Aswan, as far south as the border of Ethiopia.* [11]For forty years not a soul will pass that way, neither people nor animals. It will be completely uninhabited. [12]I will make Egypt desolate, and it will be surrounded by other desolate nations. Its cities will be empty and desolate for forty years, surrounded by other desolate cities. I will scatter the Egyptians to distant lands.

[13]"But the Sovereign LORD also says: At the end of the forty years I will bring the Egyptians home again from the nations to which they have been scattered. [14]I will restore the prosperity of Egypt and bring its people back to the land of Pathros in southern Egypt from which they came. But Egypt will remain an unimportant, minor kingdom. [15]It will be the lowliest of all the nations, never again great enough to rise above its neighbors.

[16]"Then Israel will no longer be tempted to trust in Egypt for help. Egypt's shattered condition will remind Israel of how sinful she was to trust Egypt in earlier days. Then Israel will know that I alone am the Sovereign LORD."

[17]On April 26,* during the twenty-seventh year of King Jehoiachin's captivity, this message came to me from the LORD: [18]"Son of man, the army of King Nebuchadnezzar* of Babylon fought so hard against Tyre that the warriors' heads were rubbed bare and their shoulders were raw and blistered. Yet Nebuchadnezzar and his army won no plunder to compensate them for all their work. [19]Therefore, this is what the Sovereign LORD says: I will give the land of Egypt to Nebuchadnezzar, king of Babylon. He will carry off their wealth, plundering everything they have to pay his army. [20]Yes, I have given him the land of Egypt as a reward for his work, says the Sovereign LORD, because he was working for me when he destroyed Tyre.

[21]"And the day will come when I will cause the ancient glory of Israel to revive, and then at last your words will be respected. Then they will know that I am the LORD."

CHAPTER 30

This is another message that came to me from the LORD: [2]"Son of man, prophesy and give this message from the Sovereign LORD: Weep, [3]for the terrible day is almost here— the day of the LORD! It is a day of clouds and gloom, a day of despair for the nations! [4]A sword will come against Egypt, and those who are slaughtered will cover the ground. Their wealth will be carried away and their foundations destroyed. The land of Ethiopia* will be ravished. [5]Ethiopia, Libya,* Lydia,* and Arabia, with all their other allies, will be destroyed in that war.

[6]"For this is what the LORD says: All of Egypt's allies will fall, and the pride of their power will end. From Migdol to Aswan they will be slaughtered by the sword, says the Sovereign LORD. [7]Egypt will be desolate, surrounded by desolate nations, and its cities will be in ruins, surrounded by other ruined cities. [8]And the people of Egypt will know that I am the LORD when I have set Egypt on fire and destroyed all their allies. [9]At that time I will send swift messengers in ships to terrify the complacent Ethiopians. Great panic will come upon them on that day of Egypt's certain destruction.

[10]"For this is what the Sovereign LORD says: Through King Nebuchadnezzar* of Babylon, I will destroy the hordes of Egypt. [11]He and his armies—ruthless among the nations—have been sent to demolish the land. They will make war against Egypt until slaughtered Egyptians cover the ground. [12]I will dry up the Nile River and hand the land over to wicked men. I will destroy the land of Egypt and everything in it, using foreigners to do it. I, the LORD, have spoken!

29:10 Hebrew Cush.   29:17 Hebrew On the first day of the first month, of the Hebrew calendar. This event occurred on April 26, 571 B.C.; also see note on 29:1.   29:18 Hebrew Nebuchadrezzar, a variant name for Nebuchadnezzar; also in 29:19.   30:4 Hebrew Cush; also in 30:5, 9.   30:5a Hebrew Put . . . Kub. Both Put and Kub are associated with Libya.   30:5b Hebrew Lud.   30:10 Hebrew Nebuchadrezzar, a variant name for Nebuchadnezzar.

¹³"This is what the Sovereign LORD says: I will smash the idols of Egypt and the images at Memphis.* There will be no rulers left in Egypt; anarchy will prevail throughout the land! ¹⁴I will destroy Pathros, Zoan, and Thebes,* and they will lie in ruins, burned up by my anger. ¹⁵I will pour out my fury on Pelusium,* the strongest fortress of Egypt, and I will stamp out the people of Thebes. ¹⁶Yes, I will set fire to all Egypt! Pelusium will be racked with pain; Thebes will be torn apart; Memphis will live in constant terror. ¹⁷The young men of Heliopolis and Bubastis* will die in battle, and the women* will be taken away as slaves. ¹⁸When I come to break the proud strength of Egypt, it will be a dark day for Tahpanhes, too. A dark cloud will cover Tahpanhes, and its daughters will be led away as captives. ¹⁹And so I will greatly punish Egypt, and they will know that I am the LORD."

²⁰On April 29,* during the eleventh year of King Jehoiachin's captivity, this message came to me from the LORD: ²¹"Son of man, I have broken the arm of Pharaoh, the king of Egypt. His arm has not been put in a cast so that it may heal. Neither has it been bound up with a splint to make it strong enough to hold a sword. ²²Therefore, this is what the Sovereign LORD says: I am the enemy of Pharaoh, the king of Egypt! I will break both of his arms—the good arm along with the broken one—and I will make his sword clatter to the ground. ²³I will scatter the Egyptians to many lands throughout the world. ²⁴I will strengthen the arms of Babylon's king and put my sword in his hand. But I will break the arms of Pharaoh, king of Egypt, and he will lie there mortally wounded, groaning in pain. ²⁵I will strengthen the arms of the king of Babylon, while the arms of Pharaoh fall useless to his sides. And when I put my sword in the hand of Babylon's king and he brings it against the land of Egypt, Egypt will know that I am the LORD. ²⁶I will scatter the Egyptians among the nations. Then they will know that I am the LORD."

CHAPTER 31

On June 21,* during the eleventh year of King Jehoiachin's captivity, this message came to me from the LORD: ²"Son of man,

give this message to Pharaoh, king of Egypt, and all his people: To whom would you compare your greatness? ³You are as Assyria was—a great and mighty nation. Assyria, too, was once like a cedar of Lebanon, full of thick branches that cast deep forest shade with its top high among the clouds. ⁴Deep springs watered it and helped it to grow tall and luxuriant. The water was so abundant that there was enough for all the trees nearby. ⁵This great tree towered above all the other trees around it. It prospered and grew long thick branches because of all the water at its roots. ⁶The birds nested in its branches, and in its shade all the wild animals gave birth to their young. All the great nations of the world lived in its shadow. ⁷It was strong and beautiful, for its roots went deep into abundant water. ⁸This tree became taller than any of the other cedars in the garden of God. No cypress had branches equal to it; no plane tree had boughs to compare. No tree in the garden of God came close to it in beauty. ⁹Because of the magnificence I gave this tree, it was the envy of all the other trees of Eden, the garden of God.

¹⁰"Therefore, this is what the Sovereign LORD says: Because it became proud and arrogant, and because it set itself so high above the others, reaching to the clouds, ¹¹I handed it over to a mighty nation that destroyed it as its wickedness deserved. I myself discarded it. ¹²A foreign army—the terror of the nations—cut it down and left it fallen on the ground. Its branches were scattered across the mountains and valleys and ravines of the land. All those who lived beneath its shadow went away and left it lying there. ¹³The birds roosted on its fallen trunk, and the wild animals lay among its branches. ¹⁴Let no other nation proudly exult in its own prosperity, though it be higher than the clouds, for all are doomed. They will land in the pit along with all the proud people of the world.

¹⁵"This is what the Sovereign LORD says: When Assyria went down into the grave,* I made the deep places mourn, and I restrained the mighty waters. I clothed Lebanon in black and caused the trees of the field to wilt. ¹⁶I made the nations shake with fear at the sound of its fall, for I sent it

30:13 Hebrew *Noph;* also in 30:16.   30:14 Hebrew *No;* also in 30:15, 16.   30:15 Hebrew *Sin;* also in 30:16.   30:17a Hebrew *of Awen and Pi-beseth.*   30:17b Or *her cities.*   30:20 Hebrew *On the seventh day of the first month,* of the Hebrew calendar. This event occurred on April 29, 587 B.C.; also see note on 29:1.   31:1 Hebrew *On the first day of the third month,* of the Hebrew calendar. This event occurred on June 21, 587 B.C.; also see note on 29:1.   31:15 Hebrew *to Sheol;* also in 31:16, 17.

down to the grave with all the others like it. And all the other proud trees of Eden, the most beautiful and the best of Lebanon, the ones whose roots went deep into the water, were relieved to find it there with them in the pit. [17]Its allies, too, were all destroyed and had passed away. They had gone down to the grave—all those nations that had lived in its shade.

[18]"O Egypt, to which of the trees of Eden will you compare your strength and glory? You, too, will be brought down to the pit with all these other nations. You will lie there among the outcasts who have died by the sword. This will be the fate of Pharaoh and all his teeming hordes. I, the Sovereign LORD, have spoken!"

CHAPTER 32

On March 3,* during the twelfth year of King Jehoiachin's captivity, this message came to me from the LORD: [2]"Son of man, mourn for Pharaoh, king of Egypt, and give him this message: You think of yourself as a strong young lion among the nations, but you are really just a sea monster, heaving around in your own rivers, stirring up mud with your feet.

[3]"Therefore, this is what the Sovereign LORD says: I will send many people to catch you in my net and haul you out of the water. [4]I will leave you stranded on the land to die. All the birds of the heavens will land on you, and the wild animals of the whole earth will gorge themselves on you. [5]I will cover the hills with your flesh and fill the valleys with your bones. [6]I will drench the earth with your gushing blood all the way to the mountains, filling the ravines to the brim. [7]When I blot you out, I will veil the heavens and darken the stars. I will cover the sun with a cloud, and the moon will not give you its light. [8]Yes, I will bring darkness everywhere across your land. Even the brightest stars will become dark above you. I, the Sovereign LORD, have spoken!

[9]"And when I bring your shattered remains to distant nations that you have never seen, I will disturb many hearts. [10]Yes, I will bring terror to many lands, and their kings will be terrified because of all I

do to you. They will shudder in fear for their lives as I brandish my sword before them on the day of your fall.

[11]"For this is what the Sovereign LORD says: The sword of the king of Babylon will come against you. [12]I will destroy you with the swords of mighty warriors—the terror of the nations. They will shatter the pride of Egypt, and all its hordes will be destroyed. [13]I will destroy all your flocks and herds that graze beside the streams. Never again will people or animals disturb those waters with their feet. [14]Then I will let the waters of Egypt become calm again, and they will flow as smoothly as olive oil, says the Sovereign LORD. [15]And when I destroy Egypt and wipe out everything you have and strike down all your people, then you will know that I am the LORD. [16]Yes, this is the funeral song they will sing for Egypt. Let all the nations mourn for Egypt and its hordes. I, the Sovereign LORD, have spoken!"

[17]On March 17,* during the twelfth year, another message came to me from the LORD: [18]"Son of man, weep for the hordes of Egypt and for the other mighty nations. For I will send them down to the world below in company with those who descend to the pit. [19]Say to them, 'O Egypt, are you lovelier than the other nations? No! So go down to the pit and lie there among the outcasts.' [20]The Egyptians will fall with the many who have died by the sword, for the sword is drawn against them. Egypt will be dragged away to its judgment. [21]Down in the grave* mighty leaders will mockingly welcome Egypt and its allies, saying, 'They have come down; they lie among the outcasts, all victims of the sword.'

[22]"Assyria lies there surrounded by the graves of all its people, those who were slaughtered by the sword. [23]Their graves are in the depths of the pit, and they are surrounded by their allies. These mighty men who once struck terror in the hearts of people everywhere are now dead at the hands of their enemies.

[24]"Elam lies there buried with its hordes who descended as outcasts to the world below. They terrorized the nations while they lived, but now they lie in the pit and share

---

32:1 Hebrew *On the first day of the twelfth month,* of the Hebrew calendar. This event occurred on March 3, 585 B.C.; also see note on 29:1.   **32:17** Hebrew *On the fifteenth day of the month,* presumably in the twelfth month of the Hebrew calendar (see 32:1). This would put this message at the end of King Jehoiachin's twelfth year of captivity, on March 17, 585 B.C.; also see note on 29:1. Greek version reads *On the fifteenth day of the first month,* which would put this message on April 27, 586 B.C., at the beginning of Jehoiachin's twelfth year.   **32:21** Hebrew *in Sheol.*

the humiliation of those who have gone to the world of the dead. 25They have a resting place among the slaughtered, surrounded by the graves of all their people. Yes, they terrorized the nations while they lived, but now they lie in shame in the pit, all of them outcasts, slaughtered by the sword.

26"Meshech and Tubal are there, surrounded by the graves of all their hordes. They once struck terror into the hearts of all people. But now they are outcasts, all victims of the sword. 27They are not buried in honor like the fallen heroes of the outcasts, who went down to the grave* with their weapons—their shields covering their bodies,* and their swords beneath their heads. They brought terror to everyone while they were still alive.

28"You too, Egypt, will lie crushed and broken among the outcasts, all victims of the sword.

29"Edom is there with its kings and princes. Mighty as they were, they also lie among those killed by the sword, with the outcasts who have gone down to the pit. 30All the princes of the north and the Sidonians are there, all victims of the sword. Once a terror, they now lie there in shame. They lie there as outcasts with all the other dead who have descended to the pit.

31"When Pharaoh arrives, he will be relieved to find that he is not alone in having his entire army killed, says the Sovereign LORD. 32For I have caused my terror to fall upon all the living. And Pharaoh and his hordes will lie there among the outcasts who have died by the sword. I, the Sovereign LORD, have spoken!"

32:27a Hebrew *to Sheol.*   **32:27b** The meaning of the Hebrew phrase here is uncertain.

AUGUST 23 □ DAY 236
EZEKIEL 33–36
Watchman on the Wall

 OVERVIEW The fall of Jerusalem brings a significant shift in the focus of the prophet's message. Up to this point Ezekiel has declared coming calamity for Jerusalem's citizens (Ezekiel 1–32). But now he looks ahead to the day of coming comfort for Babylon's captives (Ezekiel 33–48). God is preparing a time of consolation—a time when he will regather, restore, and refresh his covenant people. Though the nation is presently experiencing groaning, there is coming a day of glory when even the mountains and hills, rivers and valleys will declare the greatness of the God of Israel.

Chapter 33	Chapter 34	Chapter 35	Chapter 36
Watchman on the Wall	Shepherds and Sheep	Edom's Doom	Israel's Delight
Duty	Denunciation	Calamity	Cleansing

 YOUR DAILY WALK Can you think of a promise you made to someone during the past month and then failed to keep?

Can you think of a promise someone made to you and then went back on?

One thing you can give and still keep is your word.

Can you think of a promise God made to you and then forgot about or failed to fulfill?

There is a wonderful *promise about promises* stated in Numbers 23:19 and illustrated in Ezekiel 33–36. "God is not a man, that he should lie." God is not fickle or vacillating in keeping his Word. When he states, "This is what the Sovereign LORD says," you can stake your life on it—every time!

Are you ready to become a prospector for the promises of God? Then here are some nuggets of gold to get you started. But be careful. Collecting and claiming God's promises can be contagious!

Matthew 6:14; 7:7-8   Philippians 1:6; 4:6-7, 13
Luke 6:38   James 1:12; 4:7-8; 5:16
John 14:2-3

 INSIGHT Where There's a "Will," There's a Promise!
At least twenty-one times in chapter 36 God declares, "I will [do something]" on behalf of his covenant people. Take two minutes and see how many of the twenty-one you can discover for yourself.

CHAPTER 33

Once again a message came to me from the LORD: ²"Son of man, give your people this message: When I bring an army against a country, the people of that land choose a watchman. ³When the watchman sees the enemy coming, he blows the alarm to warn the people. ⁴Then if those who hear the alarm refuse to take action—well, it is their own fault if they die. ⁵They heard the warning but wouldn't listen, so the responsibility is theirs. If they had listened to the warning, they could have saved their lives. ⁶But if the watchman sees the enemy coming and doesn't sound the alarm to warn the people, he is responsible for their deaths. They will die in their sins, but I will hold the watchman accountable.

⁷"Now, son of man, I am making you a watchman for the people of Israel. Therefore, listen to what I say and warn them for me. ⁸If I announce that some wicked people are sure to die and you fail to warn them about changing their ways, then they will die in their sins, but I will hold you responsible for their deaths. ⁹But if you warn them to repent and they don't repent, they will die in their sins, but you will not be held responsible.

¹⁰"Son of man, give the people of Israel this message: You are saying, 'Our sins are heavy upon us; we are wasting away! How can we survive?' ¹¹As surely as I live, says the Sovereign LORD, I take no pleasure in the death of wicked people. I only want them to turn from their wicked ways so they can live. Turn! Turn from your wickedness, O people of Israel! Why should you die?

¹²"Son of man, give your people this message: The good works of righteous people will not save them if they turn to sin, nor will the sins of evil people destroy them if they repent and turn from their

sins. ¹³When I tell righteous people that they will live, but then they sin, expecting their past righteousness to save them, then none of their good deeds will be remembered. I will destroy them for their sins. ¹⁴And suppose I tell some wicked people that they will surely die, but then they turn from their sins and do what is just and right. ¹⁵For instance, they might give back a borrower's pledge, return what they have stolen, and obey my life-giving laws, no longer doing what is evil. If they do this, then they will surely live and not die. ¹⁶None of their past sins will be brought up again, for they have done what is just and right, and they will surely live.

¹⁷"Your people are saying, 'The Lord is not just,' but it is they who are not just. ¹⁸For again I say, when righteous people turn to evil, they will die. ¹⁹But if wicked people turn from their wickedness and do what is just and right, they will live. ²⁰O people of Israel, you are saying, 'The Lord is not just.' But I will judge each of you according to your deeds."

²¹On January 8,* during the twelfth year of our captivity, a man who had escaped from Jerusalem came to me and said, "The city has fallen!" ²²The previous evening the LORD had taken hold of me and opened my mouth, so I would be able to speak when this man arrived the next morning.

²³Then this message came to me from the LORD: ²⁴"Son of man, the scattered remnants of Judah living among the ruined cities keep saying, 'Abraham was only one man, and yet he gained possession of the entire land! We are many; surely the land should be given to us as a possession.' ²⁵Now give these people this message from the Sovereign LORD: You eat meat with blood in it, you worship idols, and you murder the innocent. Do you really think the land should be yours? ²⁶Murderers!

33:21 Hebrew *On the fifth day of the tenth month,* of the Hebrew calendar. This event occurred on January 8, 585 B.C.; also see note on 29:1.

Idolaters! Adulterers! Should the land belong to you?

27"Give them this message from the Sovereign LORD: As surely as I live, those living in the ruins will die by the sword. Those living in the open fields will be eaten by wild animals. Those hiding in the forts and caves will die of disease. 28I will destroy the land and demolish her pride. Her arrogant power will come to an end. The mountains of Israel will be so ruined that no one will even travel through them. 29When I have ruined the land because of their disgusting sins, then they will know that I am the LORD.

30"Son of man, your people are whispering behind your back. They talk about you in their houses and whisper about you at the doors, saying, 'Come on, let's have some fun! Let's go hear the prophet tell us what the LORD is saying!' 31So they come pretending to be sincere and sit before you listening. But they have no intention of doing what I tell them. They express love with their mouths, but their hearts seek only after money. 32You are very entertaining to them, like someone who sings love songs with a beautiful voice or plays fine music on an instrument. They hear what you say, but they don't do it! 33But when all these terrible things happen to them—as they certainly will—then they will know a prophet has been among them."

CHAPTER 34

Then this message came to me from the LORD: 2"Son of man, prophesy against the shepherds, the leaders of Israel. Give them this message from the Sovereign LORD: Destruction is certain for you shepherds who feed yourselves instead of your flocks. Shouldn't shepherds feed their sheep? 3You drink the milk, wear the wool, and butcher the best animals, but you let your flocks starve. 4You have not taken care of the weak. You have not tended the sick or bound up the broken bones. You have not gone looking for those who have wandered away and are lost. Instead, you have ruled them with force and cruelty. 5So my sheep have been scattered without a shepherd. They are easy prey for any wild animal. 6They have wandered through the mountains and hills, across the face of the earth, yet no one has gone to search for them.

7"Therefore, you shepherds, hear the word of the LORD: 8As surely as I live, says the Sovereign LORD, you abandoned my flock and left them to be attacked by every wild animal. Though you were my shepherds, you didn't search for my sheep when they were lost. You took care of yourselves and left the sheep to starve. 9Therefore, you shepherds, hear the word of the LORD. 10This is what the Sovereign LORD says: I now consider these shepherds my enemies, and I will hold them responsible for what has happened to my flock. I will take away their right to feed the flock, along with their right to feed themselves. I will rescue my flock from their mouths; the sheep will no longer be their prey.

11"For this is what the Sovereign LORD says: I myself will search and find my sheep. 12I will be like a shepherd looking for his scattered flock. I will find my sheep and rescue them from all the places to which they were scattered on that dark and cloudy day. 13I will bring them back home to their own land of Israel from among the peoples and nations. I will feed them on the mountains of Israel and by the rivers in all the places where people live. 14Yes, I will give them good pastureland on the high hills of Israel. There they will lie down in pleasant places and feed in lush mountain pastures. 15I myself will tend my sheep and cause them to lie down in peace, says the Sovereign LORD. 16I will search for my lost ones who strayed away, and I will bring them safely home again. I will bind up the injured and strengthen the weak. But I will destroy those who are fat and powerful. I will feed them, yes—feed them justice!

17"And as for you, my flock, my people, this is what the Sovereign LORD says: I will judge between one sheep and another, separating the sheep from the goats. 18Is it not enough for you to keep the best of the pastures for yourselves? Must you also trample down the rest? Is it not enough for you to take the best water for yourselves? Must you also muddy the rest with your feet? 19All that is left for my flock to eat is what you have trampled down. All they have to drink is water that you have fouled.

20"Therefore, this is what the Sovereign LORD says: I will surely judge between the fat sheep and the scrawny sheep. 21For you fat sheep push and butt and crowd my sick and hungry flock until they are scattered to distant lands. 22So I will rescue my flock, and they will no longer be abused and destroyed. And I will judge between one sheep and another. ²³And I will set one shepherd over them, even my servant David. He will feed them and be a shepherd to them. ²⁴And I, the LORD, will be their God, and my servant David will be a prince among my people. I, the LORD, have spoken!

²⁵"I will make a covenant of peace with them and drive away the dangerous animals from the land. Then my people will be able to camp safely in the wildest places and sleep in the woods without fear. ²⁶I will cause my people and their homes around my holy hill to be a blessing. And I will send showers, showers of blessings, which will come just when they are needed. ²⁷The orchards and fields of my people will yield bumper crops, and everyone will live in safety. When I have broken their chains of slavery and rescued them from those who enslaved them, then they will know that I am the LORD. ²⁸They will no longer be prey for other nations, and wild animals will no longer attack them. They will live in safety, and no one will make them afraid.

²⁹"And I will give them a land famous for its crops, so my people will never again go hungry or be shamed by the scorn of foreign nations. ³⁰In this way, they will know that I, the LORD their God, am with them. And they will know that they, the people of Israel, are my people, says the Sovereign LORD. ³¹You are my flock, the sheep of my pasture. You are my people, and I am your God, says the Sovereign LORD."

CHAPTER 35

Again a message came to me from the LORD: ²"Son of man, turn toward Mount Seir, and prophesy against its people. ³Give them this message from the Sovereign LORD: I am your enemy, O Mount Seir, and I will raise my fist against you to destroy you completely. ⁴I will demolish your cities and make you desolate, and then you will know that I am the LORD. ⁵Your continual hatred for the people of Israel led you to butcher them when they were helpless, when I had already punished them for all their sins. ⁶As surely as I live, says the Sovereign LORD, since you show no distaste for blood, I will give you a bloodbath of your own. Your turn has

come! ⁷I will make Mount Seir utterly desolate, killing off all who try to escape and any who return. ⁸I will fill your mountains with the dead. Your hills, your valleys, and your streams will be filled with people slaughtered by the sword. ⁹I will make you desolate forever. Your cities will never be rebuilt. Then you will know that I am the LORD.

¹⁰"For you said, 'The lands of Israel and Judah will be ours. We will take possession of them. What do we care that the LORD is there!' ¹¹Therefore, as surely as I live, says the Sovereign LORD, I will pay back your angry deeds with mine. I will punish you for all your acts of anger, envy, and hatred. And I will bring honor to my name by what I do to you. ¹²Then you will know that I, the LORD, have heard every contemptuous word you spoke against the mountains of Israel. For you said, 'They have been destroyed; they have been given to us as food to eat!' ¹³In saying that, you boasted proudly against me, and I have heard it all!

¹⁴"This is what the Sovereign LORD says: The whole world will rejoice when I make you desolate. ¹⁵You rejoiced at the desolation of Israel's inheritance. Now I will rejoice at yours! You will be wiped out, you people of Mount Seir and all who live in Edom! Then you will know that I am the LORD!

CHAPTER 36

"Son of man, prophesy to Israel's mountains. Give them this message: O mountains of Israel, hear the word of the LORD! ²This is what the Sovereign LORD says: Your enemies have taunted you, saying, 'Aha! Now the ancient heights belong to us!' ³Therefore, son of man, give the mountains of Israel this message from the Sovereign LORD: Your enemies have attacked you from all directions, and now you are possessed by many nations. You are the object of much mocking and slander. ⁴Therefore, O mountains of Israel, hear the word of the Sovereign LORD. He speaks to the hills and mountains, ravines and valleys, and to ruined wastes and long-deserted cities that have been destroyed and mocked by foreign nations everywhere. ⁵This is what the Sovereign LORD says: My jealous anger is on fire against these nations, especially Edom, because they have shown utter contempt for me by gleefully taking my land for themselves as plunder.

6"Therefore, prophesy to the hills and mountains, the ravines and valleys of Israel. Give them this message from the Sovereign LORD: I am full of fury because you have suffered shame before the surrounding nations. 7Therefore, says the Sovereign LORD, I have raised my hand and sworn an oath that those nations will soon have their turn at suffering shame. 8But the mountains of Israel will produce heavy crops of fruit to prepare for my people's return—and they will be coming home again soon! 9See, I am concerned for you, and I will come to help you. Your ground will be tilled and your crops planted. 10I will greatly increase the population of Israel, and the ruined cities will be rebuilt and filled with people. 11Not only the people, but your flocks and herds will also greatly multiply. O mountains of Israel, I will bring people to live on you once again. I will make you even more prosperous than you were before. Then you will know that I am the LORD. 12I will cause my people to walk on you once again, and you will be their inheritance. You will never again devour their children.

13"This is what the Sovereign LORD says: Now the other nations taunt you, saying, 'Israel is a land that devours her own people!' 14But you will never again devour your people or bereave your nation, says the Sovereign LORD. 15I will not allow those foreign nations to sneer at you, and you will no longer be shamed by them or cause your nation to fall, says the Sovereign LORD."

16Then this further message came to me from the LORD: 17"Son of man, when the people of Israel were living in their own land, they defiled it by their evil deeds. To me their conduct was as filthy as a bloody rag. 18They polluted the land with murder and by worshiping idols, so I poured out my fury on them. 19I scattered them to many lands to punish them for the evil way they had lived. 20But when they were scattered among the nations, they brought dishonor to my holy name. For the nations said, 'These are the people of the LORD, and he couldn't keep them safe in his own land!' 21Then I was concerned for my holy name, which had been dis-

honored by my people throughout the world.

22"Therefore, give the people of Israel this message from the Sovereign LORD: I am bringing you back again but not because you deserve it. I am doing it to protect my holy name, which you dishonored while you were scattered among the nations. 23I will show how holy my great name is—the name you dishonored among the nations. And when I reveal my holiness through you before their very eyes, says the Sovereign LORD, then the nations will know that I am the LORD. 24For I will gather you up from all the nations and bring you home again to your land.

25"Then I will sprinkle clean water on you, and you will be clean. Your filth will be washed away, and you will no longer worship idols. 26And I will give you a new heart with new and right desires, and I will put a new spirit in you. I will take out your stony heart of sin and give you a new, obedient heart.* 27And I will put my Spirit in you so you will obey my laws and do whatever I command.

28"And you will live in Israel, the land I gave your ancestors long ago. You will be my people, and I will be your God. 29I will cleanse you of your filthy behavior. I will give you good crops, and I will abolish famine in the land. 30I will give you great harvests from your fruit trees and fields, and never again will the surrounding nations be able to scoff at your land for its famines. 31Then you will remember your past sins and hate yourselves for all the evil things you did. 32But remember, says the Sovereign LORD, I am not doing this because you deserve it. O my people of Israel, you should be utterly ashamed of all you have done!

33"This is what the Sovereign LORD says: When I cleanse you from your sins, I will bring people to live in your cities, and the ruins will be rebuilt. 34The fields that used to lie empty and desolate—a shock to all who passed by—will again be farmed. 35And when I bring you back, people will say, 'This godforsaken land is now like Eden's garden! The ruined cities now have strong walls, and they are filled with people!' 36Then the nations all around—all those still left—will know that I, the LORD, rebuilt the ruins and planted lush crops in

36:26 Hebrew *a heart of flesh.*

the wilderness. For I, the LORD, have promised this, and I will do it.

37"This is what the Sovereign LORD says: I am ready to hear Israel's prayers for these blessings, and I am ready to grant them their requests. 38I will multiply them like the sacred flocks that fill Jerusalem's streets at the time of her festivals. The ruined cities will be crowded with people once more, and everyone will know that I am the LORD."

AUGUST 24 ☐ DAY 237
EZEKIEL 37–39
Gog from Magog

 OVERVIEW Even if you have never read it, you have probably sung about it: "The foot bone's connected to the ankle bone; the ankle bone's connected to the leg bone . . ." Today you will read about Ezekiel's well-known vision of the valley of dry bones in chapter 37. This vision summarizes the entire message of the book. The dry bones symbolize the spiritual condition of the nation as the people languish in captivity. But even in the bleak valley of judgment, there is hope. As Ezekiel looks on, the bones begin to join themselves together, a picture of the future restoration of the nation. God will again breathe life into his people. Their present deadness because of sin and judgment will give way to future life as the nation is regathered.

Chapter 37	Chapter 38	Chapter 39
Valley of Dry Bones	Victory over Gog	
	The Attack	The Annihilation
Restoration	Rescue	

 YOUR DAILY WALK Have you ever composed a spiritual autobiography? There was a time when you, like those dead, dry bones in Ezekiel's vision, had no life, no hope, no purpose for living. But if you know Christ, there was a point at which he picked you up, put the pieces of your life together again, clothed you with his righteousness, and breathed into you the breath of spiritual life. From that day forward you have been a different person. You have been spiritually alive—a person with limitless hope for the future.

Many problems, like storms, never arrive in spite of threatening skies.

Take time today to write out a three-minute testimony of your spiritual pilgrimage: your life before you met Christ, the way in which you met Christ, and your life since you met Christ. Then share your "literary masterpiece" with your Sunday school class, your pastor, or a close Christian friend. You'll be surprised at how encouraged others will be upon reading your spiritual autobiography! (For an added challenge, share it with an unsaved friend or neighbor and watch what happens!)

If you can't yet write a spiritual autobiography, ask a Christian friend to share his or hers with you . . . and to help you take the first step in creating one of your own.

 INSIGHT Magog and a Cast of Thousands
Ezekiel describes an alliance between Magog (a great power from the north, 38:15) and Persia (Iran), Ethiopia, Libya, Gomer (Ukraine), and Beth-togarmah (southeast of the Black Sea). See Genesis 10 for the historical roots of these different nations.

CHAPTER 37

The LORD took hold of me, and I was carried away by the Spirit of the LORD to a valley filled with bones. [2]He led me around among the old, dry bones that covered the valley floor. They were scattered everywhere across the ground. [3]Then he asked me, "Son of man, can these bones become living people again?"

"O Sovereign LORD," I replied, "you alone know the answer to that."

[4]Then he said to me, "Speak to these bones and say, 'Dry bones, listen to the word of the LORD! [5]This is what the Sovereign LORD says: Look! I am going to breathe into you and make you live again! [6]I will put flesh and muscles on you and cover you with skin. I will put breath into you, and you will come to life. Then you will know that I am the LORD.'"

[7]So I spoke these words, just as he told me. Suddenly as I spoke, there was a rattling noise all across the valley. The bones of each body came together and attached themselves as they had been before. [8]Then as I watched, muscles and flesh formed over the bones. Then skin formed to cover their bodies, but they still had no breath in them.

[9]Then he said to me, "Speak to the winds and say: 'This is what the Sovereign LORD says: Come, O breath, from the four winds! Breathe into these dead bodies so that they may live again.'"

[10]So I spoke as he commanded me, and the wind entered the bodies, and they began to breathe. They all came to life and stood up on their feet—a great army of them.

[11]Then he said to me, "Son of man, these bones represent the people of Israel. They are saying, 'We have become old, dry bones—all hope is gone.' [12]Now give them this message from the Sovereign LORD: O my people, I will open your graves of exile and cause you to rise again. Then I will bring you back to the land of Israel. [13]When this happens, O my people, you will know that I am the LORD. [14]I will put my Spirit in you, and you will live and return home to your own land. Then you will know that I am the LORD. You will see that I have done everything just as I promised. I, the LORD, have spoken!"

[15]Again a message came to me from the LORD: [16]"Son of man, take a stick and carve on it these words: 'This stick represents Judah and its allied tribes.' Then take another stick and carve these words on it: 'This stick represents the northern tribes of Israel.'* [17]Now hold them together in your hand as one stick. [18]When your people ask you what your actions mean, [19]say to them, 'This is what the Sovereign LORD says: I will take the northern tribes and join them to Judah. I will make them one stick in my hand.' [20]Then hold out the sticks you have inscribed, so the people can see them. [21]And give them this message from the Sovereign LORD: I will gather the people of Israel from among the nations. I will bring them home to their own land from the places where they have been scattered. [22]I will unify them into one nation in the land. One king will rule them all; no longer will they be divided into two nations. [23]They will stop polluting themselves with their detestable idols and other sins, for I will save them from their sinful backsliding. I will cleanse them. Then they will truly be my people, and I will be their God.

[24]"My servant David will be their king, and they will have only one shepherd. They will obey my regulations and keep my laws. [25]They will live in the land of Israel where their ancestors lived, the land I gave my servant Jacob. They and their children and their grandchildren after them will live there forever, generation after generation. And my servant David will be their prince forever. [26]And I will make a covenant of peace with them, an everlasting covenant. I will give them their land and multiply them, and I will put my Temple among them forever. [27]I will make my home among them. I will be their God, and they will be my people. [28]And since my Temple will remain among them forever, the nations will know that I, the LORD, have set Israel apart for myself to be holy."

CHAPTER 38

This is another message that came to me from the LORD: [2]"Son of man, prophesy against Gog of the land of Magog, the prince who rules over the nations of Meshech and Tubal. [3]Give him this message from the Sovereign LORD: Gog, I am your enemy! [4]I will turn you around and put hooks into your jaws to lead you out to

37:16 Hebrew *Ephraim's stick, representing Joseph and all the house of Israel.*

your destruction. I will mobilize your troops and cavalry and make you a vast and mighty horde, all fully armed. [5]Persia, Ethiopia, and Libya* will join you, too, with all their weapons. [6]Gomer and all its hordes will also join you, along with the armies of Beth-togarmah from the distant north and many others.

[7]"Get ready; be prepared! Keep all the armies around you mobilized, and take command of them. [8]A long time from now you will be called into action. In the distant future you will swoop down on the land of Israel, which will be lying in peace after her recovery from war and after the return of her people from many lands. [9]You and all your allies—a vast and awesome horde—will roll down on them like a storm and cover the land like a cloud.

[10]"This is what the Sovereign LORD says: At that time evil thoughts will come to your mind, and you will devise a wicked scheme. [11]You will say, 'Israel is an unprotected land filled with unwalled villages! I will march against her and destroy these people who live in such confidence! [12]I will go to those once-desolate cities that are again filled with people who have returned from exile in many nations. I will capture vast amounts of plunder and take many slaves, for the people are rich with cattle now, and they think the whole world revolves around them!' [13]But Sheba and Dedan and the merchants of Tarshish will ask, 'Who are you to rob them of silver and gold? Who are you to drive away their cattle and seize their goods and make them poor?'

[14]"Therefore, son of man, prophesy against Gog. Give him this message from the Sovereign LORD: When my people are living in peace in their land, then you will rouse yourself.* [15]You will come from your homeland in the distant north with your vast cavalry and your mighty army, [16]and you will cover the land like a cloud. This will happen in the distant future. I will bring you against my land as everyone watches, and my holiness will be displayed by what happens to you. Then all the nations will know that I am the LORD.

[17]"This is what the Sovereign LORD says: You are the one I was talking about long ago, when I announced through Israel's prophets that in future days I would bring you against my people. [18]But when Gog invades the land of Israel, says the Sovereign LORD, my fury will rise! [19]For in my jealousy and blazing anger, I promise a mighty shaking in the land of Israel on that day. [20]All living things—all the fish, birds, animals, and people—will quake in terror at my presence. Mountains will be thrown down; cliffs will crumble; walls will fall to the earth. [21]I will summon the sword against you throughout Israel, says the Sovereign LORD. Your men will turn against each other in mortal combat. [22]I will punish you and your hordes with disease and bloodshed; I will send torrential rain, hailstones, fire, and burning sulfur! [23]Thus will I show my greatness and holiness, and I will make myself known to all the nations of the world. Then they will know that I am the LORD!

CHAPTER 39

"Son of man, prophesy against Gog. Give him this message from the Sovereign LORD: I am your enemy, O Gog, ruler of the nations of Meshech and Tubal. [2]I will turn you and drive you toward the mountains of Israel, bringing you from the distant north. [3]I will knock your weapons from your hands and leave you helpless. [4]You and all your vast hordes will die on the mountains. I will give you as food to the vultures and wild animals. [5]You will fall in the open fields, for I have spoken, says the Sovereign LORD. [6]And I will rain down fire on Magog and on all your allies who live safely on the coasts. Then they will know that I am the LORD.

[7]"Thus, I will make known my holy name among my people of Israel. I will not let it be desecrated anymore. And the nations, too, will know that I am the LORD, the Holy One of Israel. [8]That day of judgment will come, says the Sovereign LORD. Everything will happen just as I have declared it.

[9]"Then the people in the towns of Israel will go out and pick up your small and large shields, bows and arrows, javelins and spears, and they will use them for fuel. There will be enough to last them seven years! [10]They will need nothing else for their fires. They won't need to cut wood from the fields or forests, for these weapons will give them all they need. They will take

38:5 Hebrew *Paras, Cush,* and *Put.*   38:14 As in Greek version; Hebrew reads *then you will know.*

plunder from those who planned to plunder them, says the Sovereign LORD.

[11]"And I will make a vast graveyard for Gog and his hordes in the Valley of the Travelers, east of the Dead Sea.* The path of those who travel there will be blocked by this burial ground, and they will change the name of the place to the Valley of Gog's Hordes. [12]It will take seven months for the people of Israel to cleanse the land by burying the bodies. [13]Everyone in Israel will help, for it will be a glorious victory for Israel when I demonstrate my glory on that day, says the Sovereign LORD. [14]At the end of the seven months, special crews will be appointed to search the land for any skeletons and to bury them, so the land will be made clean again. [15]Whenever some bones are found, a marker will be set up beside them so the burial crews will see them and take them to be buried in the Valley of Gog's Hordes. [16](There will be a town there named Hamonah—which means 'horde.') And so the land will finally be cleansed.

[17]"And now, son of man, call all the birds and wild animals, says the Sovereign LORD. Say to them: Gather together for my great sacrificial feast. Come from far and near to the mountains of Israel, and there eat the flesh and drink the blood! [18]Eat the flesh of mighty men and drink the blood of princes as though they were rams, lambs, goats, and fat young bulls of Bashan! [19]Gorge yourselves with flesh until you are glutted; drink blood until you are drunk. This is the sacrificial feast I have prepared for you.

[20]Feast at my banquet table—feast on horses, riders, and valiant warriors, says the Sovereign LORD.

[21]"Thus, I will demonstrate my glory among the nations. Everyone will see the punishment I have inflicted on them and the power I have demonstrated. [22]And from that time on the people of Israel will know that I am the LORD their God. [23]The nations will then know why Israel was sent away to exile—it was punishment for sin, for they acted in treachery against their God. Therefore, I turned my back on them and let their enemies destroy them. [24]I turned my face away and punished them in proportion to the vileness of their sins.

[25]"So now the Sovereign LORD says: I will end the captivity of my people*; I will have mercy on Israel, for I am jealous for my holy reputation! [26]They will accept responsibility for their past shame and treachery against me after they come home to live in peace and safety in their own land. And then no one will bother them or make them afraid. [27]When I bring them home from the lands of their enemies, my holiness will be displayed to the nations. [28]Then my people will know that I am the LORD their God—responsible for sending them away to exile and responsible for bringing them home. I will leave none of my people behind. [29]And I will never again turn my back on them, for I will pour out my Spirit upon them, says the Sovereign LORD."

39:11 Hebrew *the sea.*   **39:25** Hebrew *of Jacob.*

AUGUST 25 □ DAY 238
EZEKIEL 40–43
New Temple for Israel

OVERVIEW Twenty years earlier, Ezekiel had been transported to Jerusalem in a vision to pronounce its doom (8:1-3). He now returns in a vision to the destroyed city to proclaim its reconstruction. Like a precise architect, Ezekiel carefully measures and records the dimensions and details. But his joy over the thought of a rebuilt Temple pales in comparison with the thrill of seeing the glory of God, long since departed (11:23), now return to take up residence in the Temple's Most Holy Place.

Chapters 40–41	Chapter 42	Chapter 43
Temple Court	Temple Rooms	Temple Consecration
Blueprint for Ezekiel's Temple		Glory in Ezekiel's Temple

YOUR DAILY WALK God has always desired to dwell in the midst of his people. Prove that to yourself!

It's when we rub shoulders with someone that we discover what that person has up his or her sleeve.

In the Garden of Eden, what was God doing in the cool of the day (Genesis 3:8)?

When the Tabernacle was completed, what happened to show that God was there (Exodus 40:34-35)?

When Solomon's Temple was finished, where was God to be found (2 Chronicles 7:1-3)?

And what does 1 Corinthians 6:19-20 say about the temple (tabernacle, abode) of God today?

God's presence is once again abiding in the midst of his people. In the Old Testament Tabernacle and Temple it was plain for all to see. Could that be said of your life as well? As you read the blueprint of Ezekiel's Temple, map out another blueprint. You could call this one "The blueprint for making a part of my life a showcase for God's glory today." Your tongue, temper, work habits, leisure time—each can show forth God's glory.

INSIGHT The Significance of Mountains

Ezekiel's vision was on a mountain. The giving of the Law to Moses, the Sermon on the Mount, the Transfiguration, and the Great Commission all occurred on mountains. These and other events point us toward the time when Jesus will reign and the mountain of the Lord's house will be supreme (Isaiah 2:2). Can you think of at least two other mountains mentioned in the Bible that are associated with significant events?

CHAPTER 40

On April 28,* during the twenty-fifth year of our captivity—fourteen years after the fall of Jerusalem—the LORD took hold of me. [2]In a vision of God he took me to the land of Israel and set me down on a very high mountain. From there I could see what appeared to be a city across from me toward the south. [3]As he brought me nearer, I saw a man whose face shone like bronze standing beside a gateway entrance. He was holding in his hand a measuring tape and a measuring rod.

[4]He said to me, "Son of man, watch and listen. Pay close attention to everything I show you. You have been brought here so I can show you many things. Then you will return to the people of Israel and tell them everything you have seen."

[5]I could see a wall completely surrounding the Temple area. The man took a measuring rod that was 10½ feet* long and measured the wall, and the wall was 10½ feet thick and 10½ feet high.

[6]Then he went over to the gateway that goes through the eastern wall. He climbed the steps and measured the threshold of the gateway; it was 10½ feet deep.* [7]There were guard alcoves on each side built into the gateway passage. Each of these alcoves was 10½ feet square, with a distance between them of 8¾ feet along the passage wall. The gateway's inner threshold, which led to the foyer at the inner end of the gateway passage, was 10½ feet deep. [8]He also measured the foyer of the gateway* [9]and found it to be 14 feet deep, with supporting columns 3½ feet thick. This foyer

40:1 Hebrew *At the beginning of the year, on the tenth day of the month,* of the Hebrew calendar. A number of dates in Ezekiel can be cross-checked with dates in surviving Babylonian records and related accurately to our modern calendar. This event occurred on April 28, 573 B.C.   **40:5** Hebrew *6 long cubits* [3.2 meters], *each being a cubit* [18 inches or 45 centimeters] *and a handbreadth* [3 inches or 8 centimeters] *in length.* In this chapter, the distance measures are calculated using the Hebrew long cubit, which equals 21 inches or 53 centimeters.   **40:6** Greek version; Hebrew reads *one rod* [10.5 feet or 3.2 meters] *deep, and one threshold, one rod deep.*   **40:8** Many Hebrew manuscripts add *which faced inward toward the Temple; it was one rod* [10.5 feet or 3.2 meters] *deep.* [9]*Then he measured the foyer of the gateway, . . .*

was at the inner end of the gateway structure, facing toward the Temple.

[10] There were three guard alcoves on each side of the gateway passage. Each had the same measurements, and the dividing walls separating them were also identical. [11] The man measured the gateway entrance, which was 17½ feet wide at the opening and 22¾ feet wide in the gateway passage. [12] In front of each of the guard alcoves was a 21-inch curb. The alcoves themselves were 10½ feet square.

[13] Then he measured the entire width of the gateway, measuring the distance between the back walls of facing guard alcoves; this distance was 43¾ feet. [14] He measured the dividing walls all along the inside of the gateway up to the gateway's foyer; this distance was 105 feet.* [15] The full length of the gateway passage was 87½ feet from one end to the other. [16] There were recessed windows that narrowed inward through the walls of the guard alcoves and their dividing walls. There were also windows in the foyer structure. The surfaces of the dividing walls were decorated with carved palm trees.

[17] Then the man brought me through the gateway into the outer courtyard of the Temple. A stone pavement ran along the walls of the courtyard, and thirty rooms were built against the walls, opening onto the pavement. [18] This pavement flanked the gates and extended out from the walls into the courtyard the same distance as the gateway entrance. This was the lower pavement. [19] Then the man measured across the Temple's outer courtyard between the outer and inner gateways; the distance was 175 feet.

[20] There was a gateway on the north just like the one on the east, and the man measured it. [21] Here, too, there were three guard alcoves on each side, with dividing walls and a foyer. All the measurements matched those of the east gateway. The gateway passage was 87½ feet long and 43¾ feet wide between the back walls of facing guard alcoves. [22] The windows, the foyer, and the palm tree decorations were identical to those in the east gateway. There were seven steps leading up to the gateway entrance, and the foyer was at the inner end of the gateway passage. [23] Here on the north side, just as on the east, there was another gateway leading to the Temple's inner courtyard directly opposite this outer gateway. The distance between the two gateways was 175 feet.

[24] Then the man took me around to the south gateway and measured its various parts, and he found they were exactly the same as in the others. [25] It had windows along the walls as the others did, and there was a foyer where the gateway passage opened into the outer courtyard. And like the others, the gateway passage was 87½ feet long and 43¾ feet wide between the back walls of facing guard alcoves. [26] This gateway also had a stairway of seven steps leading up to it, and there were palm tree decorations along the dividing walls. [27] And here again, directly opposite the outer gateway, was another gateway that led into the inner courtyard. The distance between the two gateways was 175 feet.

[28] Then the man took me to the south gateway leading into the inner courtyard. He measured it and found that it had the same measurements as the other gateways. [29] Its guard alcoves, dividing walls, and foyer were the same size as those in the others. It also had windows along its walls and in the foyer structure. And like the others, the gateway passage was 87½ feet long and 43¾ feet wide. [30] (The foyers of the gateways leading into the inner courtyard were 8¾ feet deep and 43¾ feet wide.) [31] The foyer of the south gateway faced into the outer courtyard. It had palm tree decorations on its columns, and there were eight steps leading to its entrance.

[32] Then he took me to the east gateway leading to the inner courtyard. He measured it and found that it had the same measurements as the other gateways. [33] Its guard alcoves, dividing walls, and foyer were the same size as those of the others, and there were windows along the walls and in the foyer structure. The gateway passage measured 87½ feet long and 43¾ feet wide. [34] Its foyer faced into the outer courtyard. It had palm tree decorations on its columns, and there were eight steps leading to its entrance.

[35] Then he took me around to the north gateway leading to the inner courtyard. He measured it and found that it had the same measurements as the other gateways. [36] The guard alcoves, dividing walls, and

40:14 The meaning of the Hebrew in this verse is uncertain.

foyer of this gateway had the same measurements as in the others and the same window arrangements. The gateway passage measured 87½ feet long and 43¾ feet wide. ³⁷Its foyer faced into the outer courtyard, and it had palm tree decorations on the columns. There were eight steps leading to its entrance.

³⁸A door led from the foyer of the inner gateway on the north side into a side room where the meat for sacrifices was washed before being taken to the altar. ³⁹On each side of this foyer were two tables, where the sacrificial animals were slaughtered for the burnt offerings, sin offerings, and guilt offerings. ⁴⁰Outside the foyer, on each side of the stairs going up to the north entrance, there were two more tables. ⁴¹So there were eight tables in all, four inside and four outside, where the sacrifices were cut up and prepared. ⁴²There were also four tables of hewn stone for preparation of the burnt offerings, each 31½ inches square and 21 inches high. On these tables were placed the butchering knives and other implements and the sacrificial animals. ⁴³There were hooks, each three inches* long, fastened to the foyer walls and set on the tables where the sacrificial meat was to be laid.

⁴⁴Inside the inner courtyard there were two one-room buildings for the singers, one beside the north gateway, facing south, and the other beside the south* gateway, facing north. ⁴⁵And the man said to me, "The building beside the north inner gate is for the priests who supervise the Temple maintenance. ⁴⁶The building beside the south inner gate is for the priests in charge of the altar—the descendants of Zadok—for they alone of all the Levites may approach the LORD to minister to him."

⁴⁷Then the man measured the inner courtyard and found it to be 175 feet square. The altar stood there in the courtyard in front of the Temple. ⁴⁸Then he brought me to the foyer of the Temple. He measured its supporting columns and found them to be 8¾ feet square. The entrance was 24½ feet wide with walls 5¼ feet thick. ⁴⁹The depth of the foyer was 35 feet and the width was 19¼ feet. There were ten steps leading up to it, with a column on each side.

CHAPTER 41

After that, the man brought me into the Holy Place, the large main room of the Temple, and he measured the columns that framed its doorway. They were 10½ feet* square. ²The entrance was 17½ feet wide, and the walls on each side were 8¾ feet wide. The Holy Place itself was 70 feet long and 35 feet wide.

³Then he went into the inner room at the end of the Holy Place. He measured the columns at the entrance and found them to be 3½ feet thick. The entrance was 10½ feet wide, and the walls on each side of the entrance extended 12¼ feet to the corners of the inner room. ⁴The inner room was 35 feet square. "This," he told me, "is the Most Holy Place."

⁵Then he measured the wall of the Temple and found that it was 10½ feet thick. There was a row of rooms along the outside wall; each room was 7 feet wide. ⁶These rooms were built in three levels, one above the other, with thirty rooms on each level. The supports for these rooms rested on ledges in the Temple wall, but the supports did not extend into the wall. ⁷Each level was wider than the one below it, corresponding to the narrowing of the Temple wall as it rose higher. A stairway led up from the bottom level through the middle level to the top level.

⁸I noticed that the Temple was built on a terrace, which provided a foundation for the side rooms. This terrace was 10½ feet high. ⁹The outer wall of the Temple's side rooms was 8¾ feet thick. This left an open area between these side rooms ¹⁰and the row of rooms along the outer wall of the inner courtyard. This open area measured 35 feet in width, and it went all the way around the Temple. ¹¹Two doors opened from the side rooms into the terrace yard, which was 8¾ feet wide. One door faced north and the other south.

¹²A large building stood on the west, facing the Temple courtyard. It was 122½ feet wide and 157½ feet long, and its walls were 8¾ feet thick. ¹³Then the man measured the Temple, and he found it to be 175 feet long. The courtyard around the building, including its walls, was an additional 175 feet in length. ¹⁴The inner courtyard to the east of the Temple was also 175 feet wide. ¹⁵The

40:43 Hebrew *a handbreadth* [8 centimeters].   40:44 As in Greek version; Hebrew reads *east*.   41:1 Hebrew *6 cubits* [3.2 meters].
In this chapter, the distance measures are calculated using the Hebrew long cubit, which equals 21 inches or 53 centimeters.

building to the west, including its two walls, was also 175 feet wide.

The Holy Place, the Most Holy Place, and the foyer of the Temple were all paneled with wood, [16]as were the frames of the recessed windows. The inner walls of the Temple were paneled with wood above and below the windows. [17]The space above the door leading into the Most Holy Place was also paneled. [18]All the walls were decorated with carvings of cherubim, each with two faces, and there was a palm tree carving between each of the cherubim. [19]One face— that of a man—looked toward the palm tree on one side. The other face—that of a young lion—looked toward the palm tree on the other side. The figures were carved all along the inside of the Temple, [20]from the floor to the top of the walls, including the outer wall of the Holy Place.

[21]There were square columns at the entrance to the Holy Place, and the ones at the entrance of the Most Holy Place were similar. [22]There was an altar made of wood, 3½ feet square and 5¼ feet high. Its corners, base, and sides were all made of wood. "This," the man told me, "is the table that stands in the LORD's presence."

[23]Both the Holy Place and the Most Holy Place had double doorways, [24]each with two swinging doors. [25]The doors leading into the Holy Place were decorated with carved cherubim and palm trees just as on the walls. And there was a wooden canopy over the front of the Temple's foyer. [26]On both sides of the foyer there were recessed windows decorated with carved palm trees.

CHAPTER 42

Then the man led me out of the Temple courtyard by way of the north gateway. We entered the outer courtyard and came to a group of rooms against the north wall of the inner courtyard. [2]This group of structures, whose entrance opened toward the north, was 175 feet long and 87½ feet wide.* [3]One block of rooms overlooked the 35-foot width of the inner courtyard. Another block of rooms looked out onto the pavement of the outer courtyard. The two blocks were built three levels high and stood across from each other. [4]Between the two blocks of rooms ran a walkway 17½ feet wide. It extended the entire 175 feet of the complex, and all the doors faced to-

ward the north. [5]Each of the two upper levels of rooms was narrower than the one beneath it because the upper levels had to allow space for walkways in front of them. [6]Since there were three levels and they did not have supporting columns as in the courtyards, each of the upper levels was set back from the level beneath it. [7]There was an outer wall that separated the rooms from the outer courtyard; it was 87½ feet long. [8]This wall added length to the outer block of rooms, which extended for only 87½ feet, while the inner block—the rooms toward the Temple—extended for 175 feet. [9]There was an entrance from the outer courtyard to these rooms from the east.

[10]On the south* side of the Temple there were two blocks of rooms just south of the inner courtyard between the Temple and the outer courtyard. These rooms were arranged just like the rooms on the north. [11]There was a walkway between the two blocks of rooms just like the complex on the north side of the Temple. This complex of rooms was the same length and width as the other one, and it had the same entrances and doors. The dimensions of each were identical. [12]So there was an entrance in the wall facing the doors of the inner block of rooms, and another on the east at the end of the interior walkway.

[13]Then the man told me, "These rooms that overlook the Temple from the north and south are holy. It is there that the priests who offer sacrifices to the LORD will eat the most holy offerings. And they will use these rooms to store the grain offerings, sin offerings, and guilt offerings because these rooms are holy. [14]When the priests leave the Holy Place, they must not go directly to the outer courtyard. They must first take off the clothes they wore while ministering because these clothes are holy. They must put on other clothes before entering the parts of the building complex open to the public."

[15]When the man had finished taking these measurements, he led me out through the east gateway to measure the entire Temple area. [16]He measured the east side; it was 875 feet long. [17]He also measured the north side and got the same measurement. [18]The south side was the same length, [19]and so was the west side. [20]So the area was 875 feet on each side with a wall all around it to separate the holy places from the common.

42:2 Hebrew *100 cubits* [53 meters] *long and 50 cubits* [26.5 meters] *wide*. In this chapter, the distance measures are calculated using the Hebrew long cubit, which equals 21 inches or 53 centimeters. **42:10** As in Greek version; Hebrew reads *east*.

CHAPTER 43

After this, the man brought me back around to the east gateway. [2]Suddenly, the glory of the God of Israel appeared from the east. The sound of his coming was like the roar of rushing waters, and the whole landscape shone with his glory. [3]This vision was just like the others I had seen, first by the Kebar River and then when he came to destroy Jerusalem. And I fell down before him with my face in the dust. [4]And the glory of the LORD came into the Temple through the east gateway.

[5]Then the Spirit took me up and brought me into the inner courtyard, and the glory of the LORD filled the Temple. [6]And I heard someone speaking to me from within the Temple. (The man who had been measuring was still standing beside me.) [7]And the LORD said to me, "Son of man, this is the place of my throne and the place where I will rest my feet. I will remain here forever, living among the people of Israel. They and their kings will not defile my holy name any longer by their adulterous worship of other gods or by raising monuments in honor of their dead kings.* [8]They put their idol altars right next to mine with only a wall between them and me. They defiled my holy name by such wickedness, so I consumed them in my anger. [9]Now let them put away their idols and the sacred pillars erected to honor their kings, and I will live among them forever.

[10]"Son of man, describe to the people of Israel the Temple I have shown you. Tell them its appearance and its plan so they will be ashamed of all their sins. [11]And if they are ashamed of what they have done, describe to them all the specifications of its construction—including its entrances and doors—and everything else about it. Write down all these specifications and directions as they watch so they will be sure to remember them. [12]And this is the basic law of the Temple: absolute holiness! The entire top of the hill where the Temple is built is holy. Yes, this is the primary law of the Temple.

[13]"These are the measurements of the altar*: There is a gutter all around the altar 21 inches wide and 21 inches deep, with a curb 9 inches* wide around its edge. And this is the height of the altar: [14]From the gutter the altar rises 3½ feet to a ledge that surrounds the altar; this lower ledge is 21 inches wide. From the lower ledge the altar rises 7 feet to the upper ledge; this upper ledge is also 21 inches wide. [15]The top of the altar, the hearth, rises still 7 feet higher, with a horn rising up from each of the four corners. [16]The top of the altar is square, measuring 21 feet by 21 feet. [17]The upper ledge also forms a square, measuring 24½ feet on each side, with a 21-inch gutter and a 10½-inch curb all around the edge. There are steps going up the east side of the altar."

[18]Then he said to me, "Son of man, this is what the Sovereign LORD says: These will be the regulations for the burning of offerings and the sprinkling of blood when the altar is built. [19]At that time, the Levitical priests of the family of Zadok, who minister before me, are to be given a young bull for a sin offering, says the Sovereign LORD. [20]You will take some of its blood and smear it on the four horns of the altar, the four corners of the upper ledge, and the curb that runs around that ledge. This will cleanse and make atonement for the altar. [21]Then take the young bull for the sin offering and burn it at the appointed place outside the Temple area.

[22]"On the second day, sacrifice as a sin offering a young male goat that has no physical defects. Then cleanse and make atonement for the altar again, just as you did with the young bull. [23]When you have finished the cleansing ceremony, offer another young bull that has no defects and a perfect ram from the flock. [24]You are to present them to the LORD, and the priests are to sprinkle salt on them and offer them as a burnt offering to the LORD.

[25]"Every day for seven days a male goat, a young bull, and a ram from the flock will be sacrificed as a sin offering. None of these animals may have physical defects of any kind. [26]Do this each day for seven days to cleanse and make atonement for the altar, thus setting it apart for holy use. [27]On the eighth day, and on each day afterward, the priests will sacrifice on the altar the burnt offerings and peace offerings of the people. Then I will accept you, says the Sovereign LORD."

43:7 Or *by raising pillars on their high places.*   43:13a Hebrew *measurements of the altar in long cubits, each being a cubit* [18 inches or 45 centimeters] *and a handbreadth* [3 inches or 8 centimeters] *in length.* In this chapter, the distance measures are calculated using the Hebrew long cubit, which equals 21 inches or 53 centimeters.   43:13b Hebrew *1 span* [23 centimeters].

AUGUST 26 ☐ DAY 239
EZEKIEL 44–48
New Worship for Israel

OVERVIEW The new Temple Ezekiel envisions is more than a religious shrine; it is the hub of activity in the rebuilt nation! The new order of worship, much like the worship in the days of Solomon, will involve priests, Levites, sacrifices, offerings, feasts, and designated portions and places for the priesthood. In that day the nation will occupy all the territory originally promised to Israel in the covenant God made with Abraham (Genesis 15:18-21; 17:8). And over the city will hang the name, "The LORD Is There"—a reminder of the burden Ezekiel has carried throughout his life and ministry, that men and women everywhere might see and acknowledge God as the Lord.

Chapter 44	Chapter 45	Chapter 46	Chapter 47	Chapter 48
Priestly Service	Priestly Supplies	Priestly Sacrifices	Boundaries of the Land	Boundaries of the Tribes
United in Service			Divided Inheritance	

God loves each of us as if there were only one of us.

YOUR DAILY WALK Using a measuring tape (or with the help of a floor plan), spend a few minutes reviewing the dimensions of your home: the length and width of your house; the size of your yard; the location of the doors, windows, sidewalks, and driveways. When you have finished, you will probably be the only human being who knows (or cares to know) those details.

But there is someone else who knows. He's the God who never loses track of the hairs on your head or the days of your life (Matthew 10:30; Job 14:5). He's waiting to share your hurts and carry your burdens. As Ezekiel learned, God cares about the smallest details of life. Share one of your "little hurts" with him now!

INSIGHT The Lord Is Here . . . There . . . Everywhere
The concluding statement of Ezekiel, "The LORD Is There" (48:35), becomes the recurring theme of John in the book of Revelation. God's abiding presence becomes the chief joy of those in the new heaven and new earth (Revelation 21:3-4, 7, 22-23; 22:3-5).

CHAPTER 44
Then the man brought me back to the east gateway in the outer wall, but it was closed. ²And the LORD said to me, "This gate must remain closed; it will never again be opened. No man will ever pass through it, for the LORD, the God of Israel, entered here. Thus, it must always remain shut. ³Only the prince himself may sit inside this gateway to feast in the LORD's presence. But he may come and go only through the gateway's foyer."

⁴Then the man brought me through the north gateway to the front of the Temple. I looked and saw that the glory of the LORD filled the Temple of the LORD, and I fell to the ground with my face in the dust.

⁵And the LORD said to me, "Son of man, take careful notice; use your eyes and ears. Listen to everything I tell you about the regulations concerning the LORD's Temple. Take careful note of who may be admitted to the Temple and who is to be excluded from it. ⁶And give these rebels, the people of Israel, this message from the Sovereign LORD: O people of Israel, enough of your disgusting sins! ⁷You have brought uncircumcised foreigners into my sanctuary—people who have no heart for God. In this way, you profaned my Temple even as you offered me my food, the fat and blood of sacrifices. Thus, in addition to all your other disgusting sins, you have broken my covenant. ⁸You have not kept the laws I

gave you concerning these sacred rituals, for you have hired foreigners to take charge of my sanctuary.

9"So this is what the Sovereign LORD says: No foreigners, including those who live among the people of Israel, will enter my sanctuary if they have not been circumcised and do not love the LORD. 10And the men of the tribe of Levi who abandoned me when Israel strayed away from me to worship idols must bear the consequences of their unfaithfulness. 11They may still be Temple guards and gatemen, and they may still slaughter the animals brought for burnt offerings and be present to help the people. 12But they encouraged my people to worship other gods, causing Israel to fall into deep sin. So I have raised my hand and taken an oath that they must bear the consequences for their sins, says the Sovereign LORD. 13They may not approach me to minister as priests. They may not touch any of my holy things or the holy offerings, for they must bear the shame of all the sins they have committed. 14They are to serve as the Temple caretakers and are relegated to doing maintenance work and helping the people in a general way.

15"However, the Levitical priests of the family of Zadok continued to minister faithfully in the Temple when Israel abandoned me for idols. These men will serve as my ministers. They will stand in my presence and offer the fat and blood of the sacrifices, says the Sovereign LORD. 16They are the ones who will enter my sanctuary and approach my table to serve me. They are the ones who will fulfill all my requirements. 17When they enter the gateway to the inner courtyard, they must wear only linen clothing. They must wear no wool while on duty in the inner courtyard or in the Temple itself. 18They must wear linen turbans and linen undergarments. They must not wear anything that would cause them to perspire. 19When they return to the outer courtyard where the people are, they must take off the clothes they wear while ministering to me. They must leave them in the sacred rooms and put on other clothes so they do not harm the people by transmitting holiness to them through this clothing.

20"They must neither let their hair grow too long nor shave it off completely. Instead, they must trim it regularly. 21The priests must never drink wine before entering the inner courtyard. 22They may choose their wives only from among the virgins of Israel or the widows of the priests. They may not marry other widows or divorced women. 23They will teach my people the difference between what is holy and what is common, what is ceremonially clean and unclean.

24"They will serve as judges to resolve any disagreements among my people. Their decisions must be based on my regulations. And the priests themselves must obey my instructions and laws at all the sacred festivals, and they will see to it that the Sabbath is set apart as a holy day. 25A priest must never defile himself by being in the presence of a dead person unless it is his father, mother, child, brother, or unmarried sister. In such cases it is permitted. 26But such a priest can only return to his Temple duties after being ritually cleansed and then waiting for seven days. 27The first day he returns to work and enters the inner courtyard and the sanctuary, he must offer a sin offering for himself, says the Sovereign LORD.

28"As to property, the priests will not have any, for I alone am their inheritance. 29Their food will come from the gifts and sacrifices brought to the Temple by the people—the grain offerings, the sin offerings, and the guilt offerings. Whatever anyone sets apart* for the LORD will belong to the priests. 30The first of the ripe fruits and all the gifts brought to the LORD will go to the priests. The first samples of each grain harvest and the first of your flour must also be given to the priests so the LORD will bless your homes. 31The priests may never eat meat from any bird or animal that dies a natural death or that dies after being attacked by another animal.

CHAPTER 45

"When you divide the land among the tribes of Israel, you must set aside a section of it for the LORD as his holy portion. This piece of land will be 8⅓ miles long and 6⅔ miles wide.* The entire area will be holy ground.

44:29 The Hebrew term used here refers to the complete consecration of things or people to the LORD, either by destroying them or by giving them as an offering.   **45:1** Reflecting the Greek reading *25,000 cubits* [13.3 kilometers] *long and 20,000 cubits* [10.6 kilometers] *wide;* Hebrew reads *25,000 cubits long and 10,000 cubits wide.* Compare 45:3, 5; 48:9. In this chapter, the distance measures are calculated using the Hebrew long cubit, which equals 21 inches or 53 centimeters.

2A section of this land, measuring 875 feet by 875 feet, will be set aside for the Temple. An additional strip of land 87½ feet wide is to be left empty all around it. 3Within the larger sacred area, measure out a portion of land 8⅓ miles long and 3⅓ miles wide. Within it the sanctuary of the Most Holy Place will be located. 4This area will be a holy land, set aside for the priests who minister to the LORD in the sanctuary. They will use it for their homes, and my Temple will be located within it. 5The strip of sacred land next to it, also 8⅓ miles long and 3⅓ miles wide, will be a living area for the Levites who work at the Temple. It will be their possession and a place for their towns.*

6"Adjacent to the larger sacred area will be a section of land 8⅓ miles long and 1⅔ miles wide. This will be set aside to be a city where anyone in Israel can come and live.

7"Two special sections of land will be set apart for the prince. One section will share a border with the east side of the sacred lands and city, and the second section will share a border on the west side. Then the far eastern and western borders of the prince's lands will line up with the eastern and western boundaries of the tribal areas. 8These sections of land will be the prince's allotment.

"My princes will no longer oppress and rob my people; they will assign the rest of the land to the people, giving an allotment to each tribe. 9For this is what the Sovereign LORD says: Enough, you princes of Israel! Stop all your violence and oppression and do what is just and right. Quit robbing and cheating my people out of their land! Stop expelling them from their homes! 10You must use only honest weights and scales, honest dry volume measures, and honest liquid volume measures.* 11The homer* will be your standard unit for measuring volume. The ephah and the bath* will each measure one-tenth of a homer. 12The standard unit for weight will be the silver shekel.* One shekel consists of twenty gerahs, and sixty shekels are equal to one mina.*

13"This is the tax you must give to the prince: one bushel of wheat or barley for every sixty* you harvest, 14one percent of your olive oil,* 15and one sheep for every two hundred in your flocks in Israel. These will be the grain offerings, burnt offerings, and peace offerings that will make atonement for the people who bring them, says the Sovereign LORD. 16All the people of Israel must join the prince in bringing their offerings. 17The prince will be required to provide offerings that are given at the religious festivals, the new moon celebrations, the Sabbath days, and all other similar occasions. He will provide the sin offerings, burnt offerings, grain offerings, drink offerings, and peace offerings to make reconciliation for the people of Israel.

18"This is what the Sovereign LORD says: In early spring, on the first day of each new year,* sacrifice a young bull with no physical defects to purify the Temple. 19The priest will take some of the blood of this sin offering and put it on the doorposts of the Temple, the four corners of the upper ledge on the altar, and the gateposts at the entrance to the inner courtyard. 20Do this also on the seventh day of the new year for anyone who has sinned through error or ignorance. In that way, you will make atonement for the Temple.

21"On the fourteenth day of the new year, you must celebrate the Passover. This festival will last for seven days. Only bread without yeast may be eaten during that time. 22On the day of Passover the prince will provide a young bull as a sin offering for himself and the people of Israel. 23On each of the seven days of the feast he will prepare a burnt offering to the LORD. This daily offering will consist of seven young bulls and seven rams without any defects. A male goat will also be given each day for a sin offering. 24The prince will provide a half bushel of flour as a grain offering and a gallon of olive oil* with each young bull and ram.

25"During the seven days of the Festival of Shelters, which occurs every year in early autumn,* the prince will provide these same sacrifices for the sin offering, the burnt offering, and the grain offering, along with the required olive oil.

CHAPTER 46

"This is what the Sovereign LORD says: The east gateway of the inner wall will be closed during the six workdays each week, but it will be open on Sabbath days and the days of new moon celebrations. ²The prince will enter the foyer of the gateway from the outside. Then he will stand by the gatepost while the priest offers his burnt offering and peace offering. He will worship inside the gateway passage and then go back out the way he came. The gateway will not be closed until evening. ³The common people will worship the LORD in front of this gateway on Sabbath days and the days of new moon celebrations.

⁴"Each Sabbath day the prince will present to the LORD a burnt offering of six lambs and one ram, all with no physical defects. ⁵He will present a grain offering of a half bushel of flour to go with the ram and whatever amount of flour he chooses to go with each lamb. He is to offer one gallon of olive oil* for each half bushel of flour. ⁶At the new moon celebrations, he will bring one young bull, six lambs, and one ram, all with no physical defects. ⁷With the young bull he must bring a half bushel of flour for a grain offering. With the ram he must bring another half bushel of flour. And with each lamb he is to bring whatever amount of flour that he decides to give. With each half bushel of flour he must offer one gallon of olive oil.

⁸"The prince must enter the gateway through the foyer, and he must leave the same way he came. ⁹But when the people come in through the north gateway to worship the LORD during the religious festivals, they must leave by the south gateway. And those who entered through the south gateway must leave by the north gateway. They must never leave by the same gateway they came in; they must always use the opposite gateway. ¹⁰The prince will enter and leave with the people on these occasions.

¹¹"So at the special feasts and sacred festivals, the grain offering will be a half bushel of flour with each young bull, another half bushel of flour with each ram, and as much flour as the prince chooses to give with each lamb. One gallon of oil is to be given with each half bushel of flour. ¹²Whenever the prince offers a voluntary burnt offering or peace offering to the LORD, the east gateway to the inner courtyard will be opened for him to enter, and he will offer his sacrifices just as he does on Sabbath days. Then he will turn and leave the way he entered, and the gateway will be shut behind him.

¹³"Each morning a year-old lamb with no physical defects must be sacrificed as a burnt offering to the LORD. ¹⁴With the lamb, a grain offering must also be given to the LORD—about two and a half quarts of flour with a third of a gallon of olive oil* to moisten the flour. This will be a permanent law for you. ¹⁵The lamb, the grain offering, and the olive oil must be given as a daily sacrifice every morning without fail.

¹⁶"This is what the Sovereign LORD says: If the prince gives a gift of land to one of his sons, it will belong to him and his descendants forever. ¹⁷But if he gives a gift of land to one of his servants, the servant may keep it only until the Year of Jubilee, which comes every fiftieth year.* At that time the servant will be set free, and the land will return to the prince. Only the gifts given to the prince's sons will be permanent. ¹⁸And the prince may never take anyone's property by force. If he gives property to his sons, it must be from his own land, for I do not want any of my people unjustly evicted from their property."

¹⁹Then the man brought me through the entrance beside the gateway and led me to the sacred rooms assigned to the priests, which faced toward the north. He showed me a place at the extreme west end of these rooms. ²⁰He explained, "This is where the priests will cook the meat from the guilt offerings and sin offerings and bake the flour from the grain offerings into bread. They will do it here to avoid carrying the sacrifices through the outer courtyard and harming the people by transmitting holiness to them."

²¹Then he brought me back to the outer courtyard and led me to each of its four corners. In each corner I saw an enclosure. ²²Each of these enclosures was 70 feet long and 52½ feet wide,* surrounded by walls.

46:5 Hebrew *an ephah* [18 liters] *of flour . . . a hin* [3.8 liters] *of olive oil;* also in 46:7, 11.   46:14 Hebrew *⅙ of an ephah* [2.9 liters] *of flour with ⅓ of a hin* [1.3 liters] *of olive oil.*   46:17 Hebrew *until the Year of Release;* see Lev 25:8-17.   46:22 Hebrew *40 cubits* [21.2 meters] *long and 30 cubits* [15.9 meters] *wide.* The distances are calculated using the Hebrew long cubit, which equals 21 inches or 53 centimeters.

²³Along the inside of these walls was a ledge of stone with fireplaces under the ledge all the way around. ²⁴The man said to me, "These are the kitchens to be used by the Temple assistants to boil the sacrifices offered by the people."

CHAPTER 47

Then the man brought me back to the entrance of the Temple. There I saw a stream flowing eastward from beneath the Temple threshold. This stream then passed to the right of the altar on its south side. ²The man brought me outside the wall through the north gateway and led me around to the eastern entrance. There I could see the stream flowing out through the south side of the east gateway. ³Measuring as he went, he led me along the stream for 1,750 feet* and told me to go across. At that point the water was up to my ankles. ⁴He measured off another 1,750 feet and told me to go across again. This time the water was up to my knees. After another 1,750 feet, it was up to my waist. ⁵Then he measured another 1,750 feet, and the river was too deep to cross without swimming.

⁶He told me to keep in mind what I had seen; then he led me back along the riverbank. ⁷Suddenly, to my surprise, many trees were now growing on both sides of the river! ⁸Then he said to me, "This river flows east through the desert into the Jordan Valley,* where it enters the Dead Sea.* The waters of this stream will heal the salty waters of the Dead Sea and make them fresh and pure. ⁹Everything that touches the water of this river will live. Fish will abound in the Dead Sea, for its waters will be healed. Wherever this water flows, everything will live. ¹⁰Fishermen will stand along the shores of the Dead Sea, fishing all the way from Engedi to En-eglaim. The shores will be covered with nets drying in the sun. Fish of every kind will fill the Dead Sea, just as they fill the Mediterranean*! ¹¹But the marshes and swamps will not be purified; they will be sources of salt. ¹²All kinds of fruit trees will grow along both sides of the river. The leaves of these trees will never turn brown and fall, and there will always be fruit on their branches. There will be a new crop every month, without fail! For they are watered by the river flowing from the Temple. The fruit will be for food and the leaves for healing."

¹³This is what the Sovereign LORD says: "Follow these instructions for dividing the land for the twelve tribes of Israel: The tribe of Joseph will be given two shares of land.* ¹⁴Otherwise each tribe will receive an equal share. I swore that I would give this land to your ancestors, and it will now come to you as your inheritance.

¹⁵"The northern border will run from the Mediterranean toward Hethlon, then on through Lebo-hamath to Zedad; ¹⁶then it will run to Berothah and Sibraim, which are on the border between Damascus and Hamath, and finally to Hazer-hatticon, on the border of Hauran. ¹⁷So the northern border will run from the Mediterranean to Hazar-enan, on the border between Hamath to the north and Damascus to the south.

¹⁸"The eastern border starts at a point between Hauran and Damascus and runs southward along the Jordan River between Israel and Gilead, past the Dead Sea* and as far south as Tamar.* This will be the eastern border.

¹⁹"The southern border will go west from Tamar to the waters of Meribah at Kadesh* and then follow the course of the brook of Egypt to the Mediterranean. This will be the southern border.

²⁰"On the west side the Mediterranean itself will be your border from the southern border to the point where the northern border begins, opposite Lebo-hamath.

²¹"Divide the land within these boundaries among the tribes of Israel. ²²Distribute the land as an inheritance for yourselves and for the foreigners who have joined you and are raising their families among you. They will be just like native-born Israelites to you, and they will receive an inheritance among the tribes. ²³All these immigrants are to be given land within the territory of the tribe with whom they now live. I, the Sovereign LORD, have spoken!

47:3 Hebrew *1,000 cubits* [530 meters]; also in 47:4, 5. The distances are calculated using the Hebrew long cubit, which equals 21 inches or 53 centimeters.　　**47:8a** Hebrew *the Arabah.*　　**47:8b** Hebrew *the sea*; also in 47:10.　　**47:10** Hebrew *the great sea*; also in 47:15, 17, 19, 20.　　**47:13** A share of land for each of Joseph's two oldest sons, Ephraim and Manasseh.　　**47:18a** Hebrew *the eastern sea.*　　**47:18b** As in Greek version; Hebrew reads *you will measure.*　　**47:19** Hebrew *waters of Meribath-kadesh.*

CHAPTER 48

"Here is the list of the tribes of Israel and the territory each is to receive. The territory of Dan is in the extreme north. Its boundary line follows the Hethlon road to Lebo-hamath and then runs on to Hazar-enan on the border of Damascus, with Hamath to the north. Dan's territory extends all the way across the land of Israel from east to west. ²Asher's territory lies south of Dan's and also extends from east to west. ³Naphtali's land lies south of Asher's, also extending from east to west. ⁴Then comes Manasseh south of Naphtali, and its territory also extends from east to west. ⁵South of Manasseh is Ephraim, ⁶and then Reuben, ⁷and then Judah, all of whose boundaries extend from east to west.

⁸"South of Judah is the land set aside for a special purpose. It will be 8⅓ miles wide and will extend as far east and west as the tribal territories, with the Temple at the center.

⁹"The area set aside for the LORD's Temple will be 8⅓ miles long and 6⅔ miles wide.* ¹⁰For the priests there will be a strip of land measuring 8⅓ miles long by 3⅓ miles wide, with the LORD's Temple at the center. ¹¹This area is set aside for the ordained priests, the descendants of Zadok who obeyed me and did not go astray when the people of Israel and the rest of the Levites did. ¹²It will be their special portion when the land is distributed, the most sacred land of all. Next to the priests' territory will lie the land where the other Levites will live. ¹³The land allotted to the Levites will be the same size and shape as that belonging to the priests—8⅓ miles long and 3⅓ miles wide. Together these portions of land will measure 8⅓ miles long by 6⅔ miles wide.* ¹⁴None of this special land will ever be sold or traded or used by others, for it belongs to the LORD; it is set apart as holy.

¹⁵"An additional strip of land 8⅓ miles long by 1⅔ miles wide, south of the sacred Temple area, will be allotted for public use—homes, pasturelands, and common lands, with a city at the center. ¹⁶The city will measure 1½ miles* on each side. ¹⁷Open lands will surround the city for 150 yards* in every direction. ¹⁸Outside the city there will be a farming area that stretches 3⅓ miles to the east and 3⅓ miles to the west along the bor-

der of the sacred area. This farmland will produce food for the people working in the city. ¹⁹Those who come from the various tribes to work in the city may farm it. ²⁰This entire area—including the sacred lands and the city—is a square that measures 8⅓ miles on each side.

²¹"The areas that remain, to the east and to the west of the sacred lands and the city, will belong to the prince. Each of these areas will be 8⅓ miles wide, extending in opposite directions to the eastern and western borders of Israel. ²²So the prince's land will include everything between the territories allotted to Judah and Benjamin, except for the areas set aside for the sacred lands and the city.

²³"These are the territories allotted to the rest of the tribes. Benjamin's territory lies just south of the prince's lands, and it extends across the entire land of Israel from east to west. ²⁴South of Benjamin's territory lies that of Simeon, also extending across the land from east to west. ²⁵Next is the territory of Issachar with the same eastern and western boundaries. ²⁶Then comes the territory of Zebulun, which also extends across the land from east to west. ²⁷The territory of Gad is just south of Zebulun with the same borders to the east and west. ²⁸The southern border of Gad runs from Tamar to the waters of Meribah at Kadesh* and then follows the brook of Egypt to the Mediterranean.* ²⁹These are the allotments that will be set aside for each tribe's inheritance, says the Sovereign LORD.

³⁰"These will be the exits to the city: On the north wall, which is 1½ miles long, ³¹there will be three gates, each one named after a tribe of Israel. The first will be named for Reuben, the second for Judah, and the third for Levi. ³²On the east wall, also 1½ miles long, the gates will be named for Joseph, Benjamin, and Dan. ³³The south wall, also 1½ miles long, will have gates named for Simeon, Issachar, and Zebulun. ³⁴And on the west wall, also 1½ miles long, the gates will be named for Gad, Asher, and Naphtali.

³⁵"The distance around the entire city will be six miles.* And from that day the name of the city will be 'The LORD Is There.'*"

48:9 Reflecting the Greek reading in 45:1: *25,000 cubits* [13.3 kilometers] *long and 20,000 cubits* [10.6 kilometers] *wide;* Hebrew reads *25,000 cubits long and 10,000 cubits wide.* Compare 45:1-5; 48:10-13. In this chapter, the distance measures are calculated using the Hebrew long cubit, which equals 21 inches or 53 centimeters.　　**48:13** See note on 48:9.　　**48:16** Hebrew *4,500 cubits* [2.4 kilometers]; also in 48:30, 32, 33, 34.　　**48:17** Hebrew *250 cubits* [133 meters].　　**48:28a** Hebrew *waters of Meribath-kadesh.* **48:28b** Hebrew *the great sea.*　　**48:35a** Hebrew *18,000 cubits* [9.6 kilometers].　　**48:35b** Hebrew *Yahweh Shammah.*

Daniel

TAKEN captive as a youth, Daniel is used by God as "the prophet in the palace" during the seventy-year period of Judah's exile in Babylon. Confronting pagan kings with God's worldwide rule, Daniel sets forth dreams and interpretations of dreams that unfold the world's history from Daniel's day far into the future—from here to eternity. But Daniel is more than a man of the future. He is also a man of faith, taking a courageous stand for God in the face of roaring lions.

Focus	Judgment upon the Gentiles		Hope for the Jews	
Divisions	Daniel's Friends in the Furnace	Daniel's Faith in the Lions' Den	Beasts, Kings, and Seventy Weeks	Previews of Israel's Future
	1 3	4 6	7 9	10 12
Topics	Convincing Gentiles of God's Power		Convincing Jews of God's Purpose	
	Daniel Interprets Others' Dreams		Angels Interpret Daniel's Dreams	
Place	Babylonia/Persia			
Time	At Least 70 Years			

AUGUST 27 □ DAY 240
DANIEL 1–3
Daniel's Friends in the Furnace

OVERVIEW Daniel lives and prophesies at the beginning of a unique period in world history—a time when Gentile nations rather than God's chosen people are dominant in the world. Cast away temporarily in judgment, the Jews must play spectator as God demonstrates his power before Gentile kings and kingdoms, showing that he is sovereign over all nations, not just his chosen nation. Daniel's ministry in Babylon spans at least seventy years. During that time he watches the reins of power pass from Babylon (Nebuchadnezzar and Belshazzar) to Media (Darius) to Persia (Cyrus), culminating in the invitation by Cyrus for the Jews to return to their homeland and rebuild their city and Temple. The section you will read today contains three familiar accounts from Daniel's life: his early days in the king's service, his interpretation of the king's dream, and his three friends in the blazing furnace.

Chapter 1	Chapter 2	Chapter 3
Daniel's Friends and Food	Daniel's Interpretation of Nebuchadnezzar's Dream	Daniel's Friends in the Blazing Furnace
Introduction	Historic Panorama	Historic Preservation

YOUR DAILY WALK Three times in the book, Daniel is described as "loved" by God (9:23; 10:11, 19). His life abounds with examples of godly behavior and outstanding character traits. As you begin your reading, start a notebook of "Godly Traits in Daniel's Life." List them day by day, and jot down ideas on how to build them into your own life. Better yet, find three friends (as Daniel did), and make it a team project!

INSIGHT Three Strikes and You're Out!
Both the books of Daniel and Ezekiel take place during the Babylonian exile, the seventy-year period of Jewish captivity and "transplanting" to Babylon after the destruction of Jerusalem. Actually, the downfall of Jerusalem came in three stages. In 605 B.C. Nebuchadnezzar overpowered the city and took back choice hostages, among them Daniel and his three friends (Daniel 1:1-6). In 597 B.C. Nebuchadnezzar returned to quell a rebellion; he then took ten thousand more captives, among them King Jehoiachin and the young prophet Ezekiel (Ezekiel 1:1-3; 2 Kings 24:8-16). Finally, in 586 B.C. Nebuchadnezzar besieged the city, destroyed the Temple, and reduced the Jewish community to rubble (Jeremiah 52:1-16).

True godliness is that which breeds the quarrel between God's children and the wicked.

CHAPTER 1

During the third year of King Jehoiakim's reign in Judah,* King Nebuchadnezzar of Babylon came to Jerusalem and besieged it with his armies. ²The Lord gave him victory over King Jehoiakim of Judah. When Nebuchadnezzar returned to Babylon, he took with him some of the sacred objects from the Temple of God and placed them in the treasure-house of his god in the land of Babylonia.*

³Then the king ordered Ashpenaz, who

1:1 The third year of Jehoiakim's reign, according to the Hebrew system of reckoning, was 605 B.C.   1:2 Hebrew *the land of Shinar.*

was in charge of the palace officials, to bring to the palace some of the young men of Judah's royal family and other noble families, who had been brought to Babylon as captives. [4]"Select only strong, healthy, and good-looking young men," he said. "Make sure they are well versed in every branch of learning, are gifted with knowledge and good sense, and have the poise needed to serve in the royal palace. Teach these young men the language and literature of the Babylonians.*" [5]The king assigned them a daily ration of the best food and wine from his own kitchens. They were to be trained for a three-year period, and then some of them would be made his advisers in the royal court.

[6]Daniel, Hananiah, Mishael, and Azariah were four of the young men chosen, all from the tribe of Judah. [7]The chief official renamed them with these Babylonian names:

Daniel was called Belteshazzar.
Hananiah was called Shadrach.
Mishael was called Meshach.
Azariah was called Abednego.

[8]But Daniel made up his mind not to defile himself by eating the food and wine given to them by the king. He asked the chief official for permission to eat other things instead. [9]Now God had given the chief official great respect for Daniel. [10]But he was alarmed by Daniel's suggestion. "My lord the king has ordered that you eat this food and wine," he said. "If you become pale and thin compared to the other youths your age, I am afraid the king will have me beheaded for neglecting my duties."

[11]Daniel talked it over with the attendant who had been appointed by the chief official to look after Daniel, Hananiah, Mishael, and Azariah. [12]"Test us for ten days on a diet of vegetables and water," Daniel said. [13]"At the end of the ten days, see how we look compared to the other young men who are eating the king's rich food. Then you can decide whether or not to let us continue eating our diet." [14]So the attendant agreed to Daniel's suggestion and tested them for ten days.

[15]At the end of the ten days, Daniel and his three friends looked healthier and better nourished than the young men who had been eating the food assigned by the king. [16]So after that, the attendant fed them only vegetables instead of the rich foods and wines. [17]God gave these four young men an unusual aptitude for learning the literature and science of the time. And God gave Daniel special ability in understanding the meanings of visions and dreams.

[18]When the three-year training period ordered by the king was completed, the chief official brought all the young men to King Nebuchadnezzar. [19]The king talked with each of them, and none of them impressed him as much as Daniel, Hananiah, Mishael, and Azariah. So they were appointed to his regular staff of advisers. [20]In all matters requiring wisdom and balanced judgment, the king found the advice of these young men to be ten times better than that of all the magicians and enchanters in his entire kingdom.

[21]Daniel remained there until the first year of King Cyrus's reign.*

CHAPTER 2
One night during the second year of his reign,* Nebuchadnezzar had a dream that disturbed him so much that he couldn't sleep. [2]He called in his magicians, enchanters, sorcerers, and astrologers,* and he demanded that they tell him what he had dreamed. As they stood before the king, [3]he said, "I have had a dream that troubles me. Tell me what I dreamed, for I must know what it means."

[4]Then the astrologers answered the king in Aramaic,* "Long live the king! Tell us the dream, and we will tell you what it means."

[5]But the king said to the astrologers, "I am serious about this. If you don't tell me what my dream was and what it means, you will be torn limb from limb, and your houses will be demolished into heaps of rubble! [6]But if you tell me what I dreamed and what the dream means, I will give you many wonderful gifts and honors. Just tell me the dream and what it means!"

[7]They said again, "Please, Your Majesty. Tell us the dream, and we will tell you what it means."

[8]The king replied, "I can see through your trick! You are trying to stall for time because you know I am serious about what I said. [9]If you don't tell me the dream, you

1:4 Or *of the Chaldeans*.   1:21 The first year of Cyrus's reign was 538 B.C.   2:1 The second year of Nebuchadnezzar's reign was 603 B.C.   2:2 Or *Chaldeans*; also in 2:4, 5, 10.   2:4 The original text from this point through chapter 7 is in Aramaic.

will be condemned. You have conspired to tell me lies in hopes that something will change. But tell me the dream, and then I will know that you can tell me what it means."

[10]The astrologers replied to the king, "There isn't a man alive who can tell Your Majesty his dream! And no king, however great and powerful, has ever asked such a thing of any magician, enchanter, or astrologer! [11]This is an impossible thing the king requires. No one except the gods can tell you your dream, and they do not live among people."

[12]The king was furious when he heard this, and he sent out orders to execute all the wise men of Babylon. [13]And because of the king's decree, men were sent to find and kill Daniel and his friends. [14]When Arioch, the commander of the king's guard, came to kill them, Daniel handled the situation with wisdom and discretion. [15]He asked Arioch, "Why has the king issued such a harsh decree?" So Arioch told him all that had happened. [16]Daniel went at once to see the king and requested more time so he could tell the king what the dream meant.

[17]Then Daniel went home and told his friends Hananiah, Mishael, and Azariah what had happened. [18]He urged them to ask the God of heaven to show them his mercy by telling them the secret, so they would not be executed along with the other wise men of Babylon. [19]That night the secret was revealed to Daniel in a vision. Then Daniel praised the God of heaven, [20]saying,

"Praise the name of God forever and ever,
    for he alone has all wisdom and power.
[21] He determines the course of world events;
    he removes kings and sets others on the throne.
He gives wisdom to the wise
    and knowledge to the scholars.
[22] He reveals deep and mysterious things
    and knows what lies hidden in darkness,
    though he himself is surrounded by light.
[23] I thank and praise you, God of my ancestors,

for you have given me wisdom and strength.
You have told me what we asked of you
    and revealed to us what the king demanded."

[24]Then Daniel went in to see Arioch, who had been ordered to execute the wise men of Babylon. Daniel said to him, "Don't kill the wise men. Take me to the king, and I will tell him the meaning of his dream."

[25]Then Arioch quickly took Daniel to the king and said, "I have found one of the captives from Judah who will tell Your Majesty the meaning of your dream!"

[26]The king said to Daniel (also known as Belteshazzar), "Is this true? Can you tell me what my dream was and what it means?"

[27]Daniel replied, "There are no wise men, enchanters, magicians, or fortune-tellers who can tell the king such things. [28]But there is a God in heaven who reveals secrets, and he has shown King Nebuchadnezzar what will happen in the future. Now I will tell you your dream and the visions you saw as you lay on your bed.

[29]"While Your Majesty was sleeping, you dreamed about coming events. The revealer of mysteries has shown you what is going to happen. [30]And it is not because I am wiser than any living person that I know the secret of your dream, but because God wanted you to understand what you were thinking about.

[31]"Your Majesty, in your vision you saw in front of you a huge and powerful statue of a man, shining brilliantly, frightening and awesome. [32]The head of the statue was made of fine gold, its chest and arms were of silver, its belly and thighs were of bronze, [33]its legs were of iron, and its feet were a combination of iron and clay. [34]But as you watched, a rock was cut from a mountain by supernatural means.* It struck the feet of iron and clay, smashing them to bits. [35]The whole statue collapsed into a heap of iron, clay, bronze, silver, and gold. The pieces were crushed as small as chaff on a threshing floor, and the wind blew them all away without a trace. But the rock that knocked the statue down became a great mountain that covered the whole earth.

[36]"That was the dream; now I will tell Your Majesty what it means. [37]Your Majesty,

2:34 Aramaic *not by human hands*; also in 2:45.

you are a king over many kings. The God of heaven has given you sovereignty, power, strength, and honor. ³⁸He has made you the ruler over all the inhabited world and has put even the animals and birds under your control. You are the head of gold.

³⁹"But after your kingdom comes to an end, another great kingdom, inferior to yours, will rise to take your place. After that kingdom has fallen, yet a third great kingdom, represented by the bronze belly and thighs, will rise to rule the world. ⁴⁰Following that kingdom, there will be a fourth great kingdom, as strong as iron. That kingdom will smash and crush all previous empires, just as iron smashes and crushes everything it strikes. ⁴¹The feet and toes you saw that were a combination of iron and clay show that this kingdom will be divided. ⁴²Some parts of it will be as strong as iron, and others as weak as clay. ⁴³This mixture of iron and clay also shows that these kingdoms will try to strengthen themselves by forming alliances with each other through intermarriage. But this will not succeed, just as iron and clay do not mix.

⁴⁴"During the reigns of those kings, the God of heaven will set up a kingdom that will never be destroyed; no one will ever conquer it. It will shatter all these kingdoms into nothingness, but it will stand forever. ⁴⁵That is the meaning of the rock cut from the mountain by supernatural means, crushing to dust the statue of iron, bronze, clay, silver, and gold.

"The great God has shown Your Majesty what will happen in the future. The dream is true, and its meaning is certain."

⁴⁶Then King Nebuchadnezzar bowed to the ground before Daniel and worshiped him, and he commanded his people to offer sacrifices and burn sweet incense before him. ⁴⁷The king said to Daniel, "Truly, your God is the God of gods, the Lord over kings, a revealer of mysteries, for you have been able to reveal this secret."

⁴⁸Then the king appointed Daniel to a high position and gave him many valuable gifts. He made Daniel ruler over the whole province of Babylon, as well as chief over all his wise men. ⁴⁹At Daniel's request, the king appointed Shadrach, Meshach, and Abednego to be in charge of all the affairs of the province of Babylon, while Daniel remained in the king's court.

CHAPTER 3

King Nebuchadnezzar made a gold statue ninety feet tall and nine feet wide* and set it up on the plain of Dura in the province of Babylon. ²Then he sent messages to the princes, prefects, governors, advisers, counselors, judges, magistrates, and all the provincial officials to come to the dedication of the statue he had set up. ³When all these officials* had arrived and were standing before the image King Nebuchadnezzar had set up, ⁴a herald shouted out, "People of all races and nations and languages, listen to the king's command! ⁵When you hear the sound of the horn, flute, zither, lyre, harp, pipes, and other instruments,* bow to the ground to worship King Nebuchadnezzar's gold statue. ⁶Anyone who refuses to obey will immediately be thrown into a blazing furnace."

⁷So at the sound of the musical instruments,* all the people, whatever their race or nation or language, bowed to the ground and worshiped the statue that King Nebuchadnezzar had set up.

⁸But some of the astrologers* went to the king and informed on the Jews. ⁹They said to King Nebuchadnezzar, "Long live the king! ¹⁰You issued a decree requiring all the people to bow down and worship the gold statue when they hear the sound of the musical instruments.* ¹¹That decree also states that those who refuse to obey must be thrown into a blazing furnace. ¹²But there are some Jews—Shadrach, Meshach, and Abednego—whom you have put in charge of the province of Babylon. They have defied Your Majesty by refusing to serve your gods or to worship the gold statue you have set up."

¹³Then Nebuchadnezzar flew into a rage and ordered Shadrach, Meshach, and Abednego to be brought before him. When they were brought in, ¹⁴Nebuchadnezzar said to them, "Is it true, Shadrach, Meshach, and Abednego, that you refuse to serve my gods or to worship the gold statue I have set up? ¹⁵I will give you one more chance. If you bow down and wor-

3:1 Aramaic *60 cubits* [27 meters] *tall and 6 cubits* [2.7 meters] *wide.* **3:3** Aramaic *the princes, prefects, governors, advisers, counselors,* *judges, magistrates, and all the provincial officials.* **3:5** The identification of some of these musical instruments is uncertain. **3:7** Aramaic *the horn, flute, zither, lyre, harp, and other instruments of the musical ensemble.* **3:8** Aramaic *Chaldeans.* **3:10** Aramaic *the horn, flute, zither, lyre, harp, pipes, and other instruments of the musical ensemble;* also in 3:15.

ship the statue I have made when you hear the sound of the musical instruments, all will be well. But if you refuse, you will be thrown immediately into the blazing furnace. What god will be able to rescue you from my power then?"

¹⁶Shadrach, Meshach, and Abednego replied, "O Nebuchadnezzar, we do not need to defend ourselves before you. ¹⁷If we are thrown into the blazing furnace, the God whom we serve is able to save us. He will rescue us from your power, Your Majesty. ¹⁸But even if he doesn't, Your Majesty can be sure that we will never serve your gods or worship the gold statue you have set up."

¹⁹Nebuchadnezzar was so furious with Shadrach, Meshach, and Abednego that his face became distorted with rage. He commanded that the furnace be heated seven times hotter than usual. ²⁰Then he ordered some of the strongest men of his army to bind Shadrach, Meshach, and Abednego and throw them into the blazing furnace. ²¹So they tied them up and threw them into the furnace, fully clothed. ²²And because the king, in his anger, had demanded such a hot fire in the furnace, the flames leaped out and killed the soldiers as they threw the three men in! ²³So Shadrach, Meshach, and Abednego, securely tied, fell down into the roaring flames.

²⁴But suddenly, as he was watching, Nebuchadnezzar jumped up in amazement and exclaimed to his advisers, "Didn't we tie up three men and throw them into the furnace?"

3:25 Aramaic *like a son of the gods.*

"Yes," they said, "we did indeed, Your Majesty."

²⁵"Look!" Nebuchadnezzar shouted. "I see four men, unbound, walking around in the fire. They aren't even hurt by the flames! And the fourth looks like a divine being*!"

²⁶Then Nebuchadnezzar came as close as he could to the door of the flaming furnace and shouted: "Shadrach, Meshach, and Abednego, servants of the Most High God, come out! Come here!" So Shadrach, Meshach, and Abednego stepped out of the fire. ²⁷Then the princes, prefects, governors, and advisers crowded around them and saw that the fire had not touched them. Not a hair on their heads was singed, and their clothing was not scorched. They didn't even smell of smoke!

²⁸Then Nebuchadnezzar said, "Praise to the God of Shadrach, Meshach, and Abednego! He sent his angel to rescue his servants who trusted in him. They defied the king's command and were willing to die rather than serve or worship any god except their own God. ²⁹Therefore, I make this decree: If any people, whatever their race or nation or language, speak a word against the God of Shadrach, Meshach, and Abednego, they will be torn limb from limb, and their houses will be crushed into heaps of rubble. There is no other god who can rescue like this!" ³⁰Then the king promoted Shadrach, Meshach, and Abednego to even higher positions in the province of Babylon.

AUGUST 28 ☐ DAY 241
Watching and Waiting

 LOOK BACK This past week you have seen Judah herself receive the full brunt of Ezekiel's assault. Like a diligent watchman, Ezekiel guards the house of Israel by warning of impending judgment. He calls and calls, but no one is listening. And finally the end has come, for "the city has fallen" (Ezekiel 33:21). They are curious to hear the word of the Lord but do not put it into practice.

Knowing what to do must be translated into doing what you know. Like sheep without a shepherd, like dry, lifeless, disconnected bones, the nation lies plundered and devoured by its pagan neighbors. But even in defeat, God's purposes shine through, for he wants the nations to know that God alone is the Lord. The book ends with a glorious display demonstrating that God is not finished with his people or their Temple.

By contrast, Daniel is torn from his beloved Jerusalem to begin a three-year "resident program" in Babylonian studies. In his diet and his dreams, Daniel demonstrates to his captors that "there is a God in heaven" (Daniel 2:28), who interprets the world's most difficult dreams and protects his exiled people far from home.

LOOK UP Life has been described as "a series of crises cleverly connected by the mundane of the everyday." In Daniel's young existence, the mundane of life in Jerusalem gave way almost overnight to the crisis of living out his faith in a foreign land.

A well-worn path is not necessarily the right one.

Captured as a prisoner of war, Daniel was soon confronted with numerous choices: Should I eat what they feed me? Should I accept the name they give me? Should I take the credit for being able to interpret dreams? Should I bow down to an idol of gold, at the risk of my life if I don't?

Daniel's parents could not possibly have anticipated the perils their son would encounter in Babylonia—but they would have been proud of his wise response in translating his faith into daily decisions. Little wonder that Daniel's reputation grew and grew. No longer merely a transplanted teenager, Daniel was growing into a man of God whose wisdom and tact were legendary.

LOOK AHEAD Though you never read of Daniel preaching a sermon, that's precisely what he did with his life—in the choices he made, the wisdom he demonstrated, the priority that he gave to prayer, and the diligence he demonstrated toward every task set before him.

"Dare to Be a Daniel" is more than a gospel song. It is a timeless challenge for each new generation intent on being God's "change agents" wherever he might send them. You may never see the inside of a kingly castle (or lions' den), but you can be sure your life will be full of excitement and challenge.

Daniel demonstrated by his dietary habits that his body was the temple of God. Your body is the only vehicle God will give you to do his will this side of heaven. Are you taking good care of it—eating a nourishing diet, getting adequate rest and exercise, and avoiding harmful substances? If not, study Daniel's example carefully, and then "dare to be a Daniel."

AUGUST 29 ☐ DAY 242
DANIEL 4–6
Daniel's Faith in the Lions' Den

OVERVIEW Today's section shows the sovereignty of the God of Israel in the affairs of people and nations. Because of Nebuchadnezzar's great pride, he is "put out to pasture" to live like the cattle of the field. When his reason returns to him, he voices a testimony of praise to the one who is God of heaven and earth. His grandson Belshazzar sees the hand of God (literally!) in a different way. In the midst of a drunken feast, God's finger appears to write Belshazzar's death sentence on the palace wall. That very night, Darius conquers Belshazzar, and the kingdom of Babylonia falls. During the reign of Darius, God displays his power of protection in Daniel's life by shutting the lions' mouths.

Chapter 4	Chapter 5	Chapter 6
Disciplined in the Pasture	Weighed in the Balance	Protected in the Lions' Den
Nebuchadnezzar	Belshazzar	Daniel

YOUR DAILY WALK The little girl was only weeks old when she contracted an eye disease. Her parents took her to a physician, and in the process of treatment the doctor accidentally prescribed the wrong medication. As a result, the girl became permanently blind. And yet, in spite of her blindness, she composed more than eight thousand hymns during her lifetime.

God grants with each burden the strength to bear it— seldom more, never less.

Toward the end of Fanny Crosby's life a friend asked her, "Do you ever feel any bitterness toward the doctor?" She replied, "No, you see, it may have been a mistake on the doctor's part, but not on God's part." Fanny Crosby's God was the God of Daniel—the God in perfect control of all things in heaven and earth.

Is Daniel's God your God? Do you have that same confidence in a sovereign Lord that sustained Fanny Crosby? Find a hymnal, turn to the author index, and select two or three hymns written by Fanny Crosby. Then prayerfully read some of the stanzas penned by a woman of God whose faith was unshakable. Does this testimony of praise express what is on your heart?

INSIGHT Not a Seal of Approval

Darius and his nobles sealed the lions' pit, which was to have been Daniel's tomb, to prevent outside interference. Hundreds of years later Pilate also sealed a tomb to prevent human interference with Jesus' body. But a mere king's seal cannot stop the power of God.

CHAPTER 4

King Nebuchadnezzar sent this message to the people of every race and nation and language throughout the world:

"Peace and prosperity to you!

2"I want you all to know about the miraculous signs and wonders the Most High God has performed for me.

3 How great are his signs,
       how powerful his wonders!
   His kingdom will last forever,
       his rule through all generations.

4"I, Nebuchadnezzar, was living in my palace in comfort and prosperity. 5But one night I had a dream that greatly frightened me; I saw visions that terrified me as I lay in my bed. 6So I issued an order calling in all the wise men of Babylon, so they could tell me what my dream meant. 7When all the magicians, enchanters, astrologers,* and fortune-tellers came in, I told them the dream, but they could not tell me

what it meant. 8At last Daniel came in before me, and I told him the dream. (He was named Belteshazzar after my god, and the spirit of the holy gods is in him.)

9"I said to him, 'O Belteshazzar, master magician, I know that the spirit of the holy gods is in you and that no mystery is too great for you to solve. Now tell me what my dream means.

10" 'While I was lying in my bed, this is what I dreamed. I saw a large tree in the middle of the earth. 11The tree grew very tall and strong, reaching high into the heavens for all the world to see. 12It had fresh green leaves, and it was loaded with fruit for all to eat. Wild animals lived in its shade, and birds nested in its branches. All the world was fed from this tree.

13" 'Then as I lay there dreaming, I saw a messenger,* a holy one, coming down from heaven. 14The messenger shouted, "Cut down the tree; lop off its branches! Shake off its leaves, and

4:7 Or *Chaldeans.*   **4:13** Aramaic *a watcher;* also in 4:23.

scatter its fruit! Chase the animals from its shade and the birds from its branches. [15]But leave the stump and the roots in the ground, bound with a band of iron and bronze and surrounded by tender grass. Now let him be drenched with the dew of heaven, and let him live like an animal among the plants of the fields. [16]For seven periods of time, let him have the mind of an animal instead of a human. [17]For this has been decreed by the messengers*; it is commanded by the holy ones. The purpose of this decree is that the whole world may understand that the Most High rules over the kingdoms of the world and gives them to anyone he chooses—even to the lowliest of humans.'

[18]" 'O Belteshazzar, that was the dream that I, King Nebuchadnezzar, had. Now tell me what it means, for no one else can help me. All the wisest men of my kingdom have failed me. But you can tell me because the spirit of the holy gods is in you.'

[19]"Upon hearing this, Daniel (also known as Belteshazzar) was overcome for a time, aghast at the meaning of the dream. Finally, the king said to him, 'Belteshazzar, don't be alarmed by the dream and what it means.'

"Belteshazzar replied, 'Oh, how I wish the events foreshadowed in this dream would happen to your enemies, my lord, and not to you! [20]You saw a tree growing very tall and strong, reaching high into the heavens for all the world to see. [21]It had fresh green leaves, and it was loaded with fruit for all to eat. Wild animals lived in its shade, and birds nested in its branches. [22]That tree, Your Majesty, is you. For you have grown strong and great; your greatness reaches up to heaven, and your rule to the ends of the earth.

[23]" 'Then you saw a messenger, a holy one, coming down from heaven and saying, "Cut down the tree and destroy it. But leave the stump and the roots in the ground, bound with a band of iron and bronze and surrounded by tender grass. Let him be drenched with the dew of heaven. Let him eat grass with the animals of the field for seven periods of time."

[24]" 'This is what the dream means, Your Majesty, and what the Most High has declared will happen to you. [25]You will be driven from human society, and you will live in the fields with the wild animals. You will eat grass like a cow, and you will be drenched with the dew of heaven. Seven periods of time will pass while you live this way, until you learn that the Most High rules over the kingdoms of the world and gives them to anyone he chooses. [26]But the stump and the roots were left in the ground. This means that you will receive your kingdom back again when you have learned that heaven rules.

[27]" 'O King Nebuchadnezzar, please listen to me. Stop sinning and do what is right. Break from your wicked past by being merciful to the poor. Perhaps then you will continue to prosper.'

[28]"But all these things did happen to King Nebuchadnezzar. [29]Twelve months later, he was taking a walk on the flat roof of the royal palace in Babylon. [30]As he looked out across the city, he said, 'Just look at this great city of Babylon! I, by my own mighty power, have built this beautiful city as my royal residence and as an expression of my royal splendor.'

[31]"While he was still speaking these words, a voice called down from heaven, 'O King Nebuchadnezzar, this message is for you! You are no longer ruler of this kingdom. [32]You will be driven from human society. You will live in the fields with the wild animals, and you will eat grass like a cow. Seven periods of time will pass while you live this way, until you learn that the Most High rules over the kingdoms of the world and gives them to anyone he chooses.'

[33]"That very same hour the prophecy was fulfilled, and Nebuchadnezzar was driven from human society. He ate grass like a cow, and he was drenched with the dew of heaven. He lived this way until his hair was as long as eagles' feathers and his nails were like birds' claws.

[34]"After this time had passed, I, Nebuchadnezzar, looked up to heaven. My sanity returned, and I praised and

4:17 Aramaic *the watchers.*

worshiped the Most High and honored the one who lives forever.

His rule is everlasting,
and his kingdom is eternal.
³⁵ All the people of the earth
are nothing compared to him.
He has the power to do as he pleases
among the angels of heaven
and with those who live on earth.
No one can stop him or challenge
him,
saying, 'What do you mean by
doing these things?'

³⁶"When my sanity returned to me, so did my honor and glory and kingdom. My advisers and officers sought me out, and I was reestablished as head of my kingdom, with even greater honor than before. ³⁷"Now I, Nebuchadnezzar, praise and glorify and honor the King of heaven. All his acts are just and true, and he is able to humble those who are proud."

CHAPTER 5
A number of years later, King Belshazzar gave a great feast for a thousand of his nobles and drank wine with them. ²While Belshazzar was drinking, he gave orders to bring in the gold and silver cups that his predecessor,* Nebuchadnezzar, had taken from the Temple in Jerusalem, so that he and his nobles, his wives, and his concubines might drink from them. ³So they brought these gold cups taken from the Temple of God in Jerusalem, and the king and his nobles, his wives, and his concubines drank from them. ⁴They drank toasts from them to honor their idols made of gold, silver, bronze, iron, wood, and stone.

⁵At that very moment they saw the fingers of a human hand writing on the plaster wall of the king's palace, near the lampstand. The king himself saw the hand as it wrote, ⁶and his face turned pale with fear. Such terror gripped him that his knees knocked together and his legs gave way beneath him.

⁷The king shouted for the enchanters, astrologers,* and fortune-tellers to be brought before him. He said to these wise men of Babylon, "Whoever can read this writing and tell me what it means will be

dressed in purple robes of royal honor and will wear a gold chain around his neck. He will become the third highest ruler in the kingdom!" ⁸But when all the king's wise men came in, none of them could read the writing or tell him what it meant. ⁹So the king grew even more alarmed, and his face turned ashen white. His nobles, too, were shaken.

¹⁰But when the queen mother heard what was happening, she hurried to the banquet hall. She said to Belshazzar, "Long live the king! Don't be so pale and afraid about this. ¹¹There is a man in your kingdom who has within him the spirit of the holy gods. During Nebuchadnezzar's reign, this man was found to have insight, understanding, and wisdom as though he himself were a god. Your predecessor, King Nebuchadnezzar, made him chief over all the magicians, enchanters, astrologers, and fortune-tellers of Babylon. ¹²This man Daniel, whom the king named Belteshazzar, has a sharp mind and is filled with divine knowledge and understanding. He can interpret dreams, explain riddles, and solve difficult problems. Call for Daniel, and he will tell you what the writing means."

¹³So Daniel was brought in before the king. The king asked him, "Are you Daniel, who was exiled from Judah by my predecessor, King Nebuchadnezzar? ¹⁴I have heard that you have the spirit of the gods within you and that you are filled with insight, understanding, and wisdom. ¹⁵My wise men and enchanters have tried to read this writing on the wall, but they cannot. ¹⁶I am told that you can give interpretations and solve difficult problems. If you can read these words and tell me their meaning, you will be clothed in purple robes of royal honor, and you will wear a gold chain around your neck. You will become the third highest ruler in the kingdom."

¹⁷Daniel answered the king, "Keep your gifts or give them to someone else, but I will tell you what the writing means. ¹⁸Your Majesty, the Most High God gave sovereignty, majesty, glory, and honor to your predecessor, Nebuchadnezzar. ¹⁹He made him so great that people of all races and nations and languages trembled before him in fear. He killed those he wanted to kill and spared those he wanted to spare. He honored those he wanted to honor and

5:2 Aramaic *father;* also in 5:11, 13, 18.   **5:7** Or *Chaldeans;* also in 5:11.

disgraced those he wanted to disgrace. [20]But when his heart and mind were hardened with pride, he was brought down from his royal throne and stripped of his glory. [21]He was driven from human society. He was given the mind of an animal, and he lived among the wild donkeys. He ate grass like a cow, and he was drenched with the dew of heaven, until he learned that the Most High God rules the kingdoms of the world and appoints anyone he desires to rule over them.

[22]"You are his successor,* O Belshazzar, and you knew all this, yet you have not humbled yourself. [23]For you have defied the Lord of heaven and have had these cups from his Temple brought before you. You and your nobles and your wives and concubines have been drinking wine from them while praising gods of silver, gold, bronze, iron, wood, and stone—gods that neither see nor hear nor know anything at all. But you have not honored the God who gives you the breath of life and controls your destiny! [24]So God has sent this hand to write a message.

[25]"This is the message that was written: MENE, MENE, TEKEL, PARSIN. [26]This is what these words mean:

> Mene means 'numbered'—God has numbered the days of your reign and has brought it to an end.
> [27] Tekel means 'weighed'—you have been weighed on the balances and have failed the test.
> [28] Parsin* means 'divided'—your kingdom has been divided and given to the Medes and Persians."

[29]Then at Belshazzar's command, Daniel was dressed in purple robes, a gold chain was hung around his neck, and he was proclaimed the third highest ruler in the kingdom.

[30]That very night Belshazzar, the Babylonian* king, was killed.* [31]And Darius the Mede took over the kingdom at the age of sixty-two.

CHAPTER 6

Darius the Mede decided to divide the kingdom into 120 provinces, and he appointed a prince to rule over each province. [2]The king also chose Daniel and two others as administrators to supervise the princes and to watch out for the king's interests. [3]Daniel soon proved himself more capable than all the other administrators and princes. Because of his great ability, the king made plans to place him over the entire empire. [4]Then the other administrators and princes began searching for some fault in the way Daniel was handling his affairs, but they couldn't find anything to criticize. He was faithful and honest and always responsible. [5]So they concluded, "Our only chance of finding grounds for accusing Daniel will be in connection with the requirements of his religion."

[6]So the administrators and princes went to the king and said, "Long live King Darius! [7]We administrators, prefects, princes, advisers, and other officials have unanimously agreed that Your Majesty should make a law that will be strictly enforced. Give orders that for the next thirty days anyone who prays to anyone, divine or human—except to Your Majesty—will be thrown to the lions. [8]And let Your Majesty issue and sign this law so it cannot be changed, a law of the Medes and Persians, which cannot be revoked." [9]So King Darius signed the law.

[10]But when Daniel learned that the law had been signed, he went home and knelt down as usual in his upstairs room, with its windows open toward Jerusalem. He prayed three times a day, just as he had always done, giving thanks to his God. [11]The officials went together to Daniel's house and found him praying and asking for God's help. [12]So they went back to the king and reminded him about his law. "Did you not sign a law that for the next thirty days anyone who prays to anyone, divine or human—except to Your Majesty—will be thrown to the lions?"

"Yes," the king replied, "that decision stands; it is a law of the Medes and Persians, which cannot be revoked."

[13]Then they told the king, "That man Daniel, one of the captives from Judah, is paying no attention to you or your law. He still prays to his God three times a day."

[14]Hearing this, the king was very angry with himself for signing the law, and he tried to find a way to save Daniel. He spent the rest of the day looking for a way to get Daniel out of this predicament. [15]In the evening the men went together to the king and

5:22 Aramaic son.   5:28 Aramaic Peres, the singular of Parsin.   5:30a Or Chaldean.   5:30b The Persians and Medes conquered Babylon in October 539 B.C.

said, "Your Majesty knows that according to the law of the Medes and the Persians, no law that the king signs can be changed."

[16]So at last the king gave orders for Daniel to be arrested and thrown into the den of lions. The king said to him, "May your God, whom you worship continually, rescue you." [17]A stone was brought and placed over the mouth of the den. The king sealed the stone with his own royal seal and the seals of his nobles, so that no one could rescue Daniel from the lions. [18]Then the king returned to his palace and spent the night fasting. He refused his usual entertainment and couldn't sleep at all that night.

[19]Very early the next morning, the king hurried out to the lions' den. [20]When he got there, he called out in anguish, "Daniel, servant of the living God! Was your God, whom you worship continually, able to rescue you from the lions?"

[21]Daniel answered, "Long live the king! [22]My God sent his angel to shut the lions' mouths so that they would not hurt me, for I have been found innocent in his sight. And I have not wronged you, Your Majesty."

[23]The king was overjoyed and ordered that Daniel be lifted from the den. Not a

6:28 Or of Darius, that is, the reign of Cyrus the Persian.

scratch was found on him because he had trusted in his God. [24]Then the king gave orders to arrest the men who had maliciously accused Daniel. He had them thrown into the lions' den, along with their wives and children. The lions leaped on them and tore them apart before they even hit the floor of the den.

[25]Then King Darius sent this message to the people of every race and nation and language throughout the world:

"Peace and prosperity to you!

[26]"I decree that everyone throughout my kingdom should tremble with fear before the God of Daniel.

> For he is the living God,
> and he will endure forever.
> His kingdom will never be destroyed,
> and his rule will never end.
> [27] He rescues and saves his people;
> he performs miraculous signs and
>   wonders
> in the heavens and on earth.
> He has rescued Daniel
> from the power of the lions."

[28]So Daniel prospered during the reign of Darius and the reign of Cyrus the Persian.*

AUGUST 30 ☐ DAY 243
DANIEL 7–9
Beasts, Kings, and Seventy Weeks

 OVERVIEW Today's section contains prophecies of breathtaking scope. Interestingly, much of what Daniel prophesied is explained right in the passage. Watch for keys to the interpretation of the various beasts and animals as you read through these chapters. Chapter 9 is a record of Daniel's prayer for himself and his countrymen based on the truth he encountered while reading the prophecy of Jeremiah. In response to Daniel's prayer, God sends the angel Gabriel to give Daniel added insight into coming events.

Chapter 7	Chapter 8	Chapter 9
The Lion, Bear, Leopard, and Beast	The Ram, Goat, and Little Horn	The Prayer, Angel, and Explanation
Daniel's Visions: History Foretold		

YOUR DAILY WALK One night a soldier was caught creeping back to his quarters from the nearby woods. Taken before his commanding officer, the soldier was charged with communicating with the enemy. The man pleaded that he had gone into the woods to pray alone. "Then you'd better start praying now!" roared the officer. "You never needed it so much!" Expecting certain death, the soldier knelt and poured out his soul in eloquent prayer. "You may go," said the officer when the soldier had finished. "I believe your story. If you hadn't drilled so often, you wouldn't be doing so well under fire."

Does your life affirm the reality of your God or refute it?

How well do you pray "on the spot"? Have you learned through practice and persistence to communicate often and long with your heavenly Father? Standing side by side with Daniel's confidence in God was his communication with God. The two are inseparable, for to trust God is to talk to him, and to talk to God is to trust him all the more.

How often have you talked to God in the last twenty-four hours? If the answer discourages you, then try this. Tape the words *Pray Now* to the face of your wristwatch. Then, as often as you are reminded, talk to your heavenly Father. You'll find your love for him and your trust in him growing with each passing hour.

INSIGHT Correlating the Creatures of Daniel
It may help you in your reading of chapters 7–8 to remember that both the leopard and the male goat represent Greece, while both the bear and the ram represent Medo-Persia.

CHAPTER 7

Earlier, during the first year of King Belshazzar's reign in Babylon, Daniel had a dream and saw visions as he lay in his bed. He wrote the dream down, and this is what he saw.

[2]In my vision that night, I, Daniel, saw a great storm churning the surface of a great sea, with strong winds blowing from every direction. [3]Then four huge beasts came up out of the water, each different from the others.

[4]The first beast was like a lion with eagles' wings. As I watched, its wings were pulled off, and it was left standing with its two hind feet on the ground, like a human being. And a human mind was given to it.

[5]Then I saw a second beast, and it looked like a bear. It was rearing up on one side, and it had three ribs in its mouth between its teeth. And I heard a voice saying to it, "Get up! Devour many people!"

[6]Then the third of these strange beasts appeared, and it looked like a leopard. It had four wings like birds' wings on its back, and it had four heads. Great authority was given to this beast.

[7]Then in my vision that night, I saw a fourth beast, terrifying, dreadful, and very strong. It devoured and crushed its victims with huge iron teeth and trampled what was left beneath its feet. It was different from any of the other beasts, and it had ten horns. [8]As I was looking at the horns, suddenly another small horn appeared among them. Three of the first horns were wrenched out, roots and all, to make room for it. This little horn had eyes like human eyes and a mouth that was boasting arrogantly.

[9]I watched as thrones were put in place and the Ancient One* sat down to judge. His clothing was as white as snow, his hair like whitest wool. He sat on a fiery throne with wheels of blazing fire, [10]and a river of fire flowed from his presence. Millions of angels ministered to him, and a hundred million stood to attend him. Then the court began its session, and the books were opened.

[11]I continued to watch because I could hear the little horn's boastful speech. I kept watching until the fourth beast was killed and its body was destroyed by fire. [12]As for the other three beasts, their authority was taken from them, but they were allowed to live for a while longer.*

[13]As my vision continued that night, I saw someone who looked like a man* coming with the clouds of heaven. He approached the Ancient One and was led into his presence. [14]He was given authority,

7:9 Aramaic *an Ancient of Days;* also in 7:13, 22.   7:12 Aramaic *for a season and a time.*   7:13 Or *a Son of Man;* Aramaic reads *a son of man.*

honor, and royal power over all the nations of the world, so that people of every race and nation and language would obey him. His rule is eternal—it will never end. His kingdom will never be destroyed.

[15] I, Daniel, was troubled by all I had seen, and my visions terrified me. [16] So I approached one of those standing beside the throne and asked him what it all meant. He explained it to me like this: [17] "These four huge beasts represent four kingdoms that will arise from the earth. [18] But in the end, the holy people of the Most High will be given the kingdom, and they will rule forever and ever."

[19] Then I wanted to know the true meaning of the fourth beast, the one so different from the others and so terrifying. It devoured and crushed its victims with iron teeth and bronze claws, and it trampled what was left beneath its feet. [20] I also asked about the ten horns on the fourth beast's head and the little horn that came up afterward and destroyed three of the other horns. This was the horn that seemed greater than the others and had human eyes and a mouth that was boasting arrogantly. [21] As I watched, this horn was waging war against the holy people and was defeating them, [22] until the Ancient One came and judged in favor of the holy people of the Most High. Then the time arrived for the holy people to take over the kingdom.

[23] Then he said to me, "This fourth beast is the fourth world power that will rule the earth. It will be different from all the others. It will devour the whole world, trampling everything in its path. [24] Its ten horns are ten kings that will rule that empire. Then another king will arise, different from the other ten, who will subdue three of them. [25] He will defy the Most High and wear down the holy people of the Most High. He will try to change their sacred festivals and laws, and they will be placed under his control for a time, times, and half a time.

[26] "But then the court will pass judgment, and all his power will be taken away and completely destroyed. [27] Then the sovereignty, power, and greatness of all the kingdoms under heaven will be given to the holy people of the Most High. They will rule forever, and all rulers will serve and obey them."

[28] That was the end of the vision. I, Daniel, was terrified by my thoughts and my face was pale with fear, but I kept these things to myself.

CHAPTER 8

During the third year of King Belshazzar's reign, I, Daniel, saw another vision, following the one that had already appeared to me. [2] This time I was at the fortress of Susa, in the province of Elam, standing beside the Ulai River.*

[3] As I looked up, I saw in front of me a ram with two long horns standing beside the river.* One of the horns was longer than the other, even though it had begun to grow later than the shorter one. [4] The ram butted everything out of its way to the west, to the north, and to the south, and no one could stand against it or help its victims. It did as it pleased and became very great.

[5] While I was watching, suddenly a male goat appeared from the west, crossing the land so swiftly that it didn't even touch the ground. This goat, which had one very large horn between its eyes, [6] headed toward the two-horned ram that I had seen standing beside the river. [7] The goat charged furiously at the ram and struck it, breaking off both its horns. Now the ram was helpless, and the goat knocked it down and trampled it. There was no one who could rescue the ram from the goat's power.

[8] The goat became very powerful. But at the height of its power, its large horn was broken off. In the large horn's place grew four prominent horns pointing in the four directions of the earth. [9] From one of the prominent horns came a small horn whose power grew very great. It extended toward the south and the east and toward the glorious land of Israel. [10] His power reached to the heavens where it attacked the heavenly armies, throwing some of the heavenly beings and stars to the ground and trampling them. [11] He even challenged the Commander of heaven's armies by canceling the daily sacrifices offered to him and by destroying his Temple. [12] But the army of heaven was restrained from destroying him for this sin. As a result, sacrilege was committed against the Temple ceremonies, and truth was overthrown. The horn succeeded in everything it did.*

8:2 Or the Ulai Gate; also in 8:16.　　8:3 Or the gate; also in 8:6.　　8:11-12 The meaning of the Hebrew for these verses is uncertain.

¹³Then I heard two of the holy ones talking to each other. One of them said, "How long will the events of this vision last? How long will the rebellion that causes desecration stop the daily sacrifices? How long will the Temple and heaven's armies be trampled on?"

¹⁴The other replied, "It will take twenty-three hundred evenings and mornings; then the Temple will be restored."

¹⁵As I, Daniel, was trying to understand the meaning of this vision, someone who looked like a man suddenly stood in front of me. ¹⁶And I heard a human voice calling out from the Ulai River, "Gabriel, tell this man the meaning of his vision."

¹⁷As Gabriel approached the place where I was standing, I became so terrified that I fell to the ground. "Son of man," he said, "you must understand that the events you have seen in your vision relate to the time of the end."

¹⁸While he was speaking, I fainted and lay there with my face to the ground. But Gabriel roused me with a touch and helped me to my feet. ¹⁹Then he said, "I am here to tell you what will happen later in the time of wrath. What you have seen pertains to the very end of time. ²⁰The two-horned ram represents the kings of Media and Persia. ²¹The shaggy male goat represents the king of Greece,* and the large horn between its eyes represents the first king of the Greek Empire. ²²The four prominent horns that replaced the one large horn show that the Greek Empire will break into four sections with four kings, none of them as great as the first.

²³"At the end of their rule, when their sin is at its height, a fierce king, a master of intrigue, will rise to power. ²⁴He will become very strong, but not by his own power. He will cause a shocking amount of destruction and succeed in everything he does. He will destroy powerful leaders and devastate the holy people. ²⁵He will be a master of deception, defeating many by catching them off guard. Without warning he will destroy them. He will even take on the Prince of princes in battle, but he will be broken, though not by human power.

²⁶"This vision about the twenty-three hundred evenings and mornings* is true. But none of these things will happen for a long time, so do not tell anyone about them yet."

²⁷Then I, Daniel, was overcome and lay sick for several days. Afterward I got up and performed my duties for the king, but I was greatly troubled by the vision and could not understand it.

CHAPTER 9

It was the first year of the reign of Darius the Mede, the son of Ahasuerus, who became king of the Babylonians.* ²During the first year of his reign, I, Daniel, was studying the writings of the prophets. I learned from the word of the LORD, as recorded by Jeremiah the prophet, that Jerusalem must lie desolate for seventy years.* ³So I turned to the Lord God and pleaded with him in prayer and fasting. I wore rough sackcloth and sprinkled myself with ashes.

⁴I prayed to the LORD my God and confessed: "O Lord, you are a great and awesome God! You always fulfill your promises of unfailing love to those who love you and keep your commands. ⁵But we have sinned and done wrong. We have rebelled against you and scorned your commands and regulations. ⁶We have refused to listen to your servants the prophets, who spoke your messages to our kings and princes and ancestors and to all the people of the land.

⁷"Lord, you are in the right; but our faces are covered with shame, just as you see us now. This is true of us all, including the people of Judah and Jerusalem and all Israel, scattered near and far, wherever you have driven us because of our disloyalty to you. ⁸O LORD, we and our kings, princes, and ancestors are covered with shame because we have sinned against you. ⁹But the Lord our God is merciful and forgiving, even though we have rebelled against him. ¹⁰We have not obeyed the LORD our God, for we have not followed the laws he gave us through his servants the prophets. ¹¹All Israel has disobeyed your law and turned away, refusing to listen to your voice.

"So now the solemn curses and judgments written in the law of Moses, the servant of God, have been poured out against us because of our sin. ¹²You have done exactly what you warned you would do against us and our rulers. Never in all history has there been a disaster like the one that happened in Jerusalem. ¹³Every curse written against us in the law of Moses has come true. All the troubles he predicted have taken place. But we have refused to seek mercy from the LORD our God by turning from our sins and recognizing his truth. ¹⁴The LORD has brought against us the disaster he prepared, for we did not obey him, and the LORD our God is just in everything he does.

¹⁵"O Lord our God, you brought lasting honor to your name by rescuing your people from Egypt in a great display of power. But we have sinned and are full of wickedness. ¹⁶In view of all your faithful mercies, Lord, please turn your furious anger away from your city of Jerusalem, your holy mountain. All the neighboring nations mock Jerusalem and your people because of our sins and the sins of our ancestors.

¹⁷"O our God, hear your servant's prayer! Listen as I plead. For your own sake, Lord, smile again on your desolate sanctuary.

¹⁸"O my God, listen to me and hear my request. Open your eyes and see our wretchedness. See how your city lies in ruins—for everyone knows that it is yours. We do not ask because we deserve help, but because you are so merciful.

¹⁹"O Lord, hear. O Lord, forgive. O Lord, listen and act! For your own sake, O my God, do not delay, for your people and your city bear your name."

²⁰I went on praying and confessing my sin and the sins of my people, pleading with the LORD my God for Jerusalem, his holy mountain. ²¹As I was praying, Ga-

briel, whom I had seen in the earlier vision, came swiftly to me at the time of the evening sacrifice. ²²He explained to me, "Daniel, I have come here to give you insight and understanding. ²³The moment you began praying, a command was given. I am here to tell you what it was, for God loves you very much. Now listen, so you can understand the meaning of your vision.

²⁴"A period of seventy sets of seven* has been decreed for your people and your holy city to put down rebellion, to bring an end to sin, to atone for guilt, to bring in everlasting righteousness, to confirm the prophetic vision, and to anoint the Most Holy Place.* ²⁵Now listen and understand! Seven sets of seven plus sixty-two sets of seven* will pass from the time the command is given to rebuild Jerusalem until the Anointed One* comes. Jerusalem will be rebuilt with streets and strong defenses,* despite the perilous times.

²⁶"After this period of sixty-two sets of seven,* the Anointed One will be killed, appearing to have accomplished nothing, and a ruler will arise whose armies will destroy the city and the Temple. The end will come with a flood, and war and its miseries are decreed from that time to the very end. ²⁷He will make a treaty with the people for a period of one set of seven,* but after half this time, he will put an end to the sacrifices and offerings. Then as a climax to all his terrible deeds,* he will set up a sacrilegious object that causes desecration,* until the end that has been decreed is poured out on this defiler."

9:24a Hebrew *70 sevens.*   **9:24b** Or *the Most Holy One.*   **9:25a** Hebrew *Seven sevens plus 62 sevens.*   **9:25b** Or *an anointed one.*   **9:25c** Or *and a moat,* or *and trenches.*   **9:26** Hebrew *After 62 sevens.*   **9:27a** Hebrew *for one seven.*   **9:27b** Hebrew *on the wing of abominations;* the meaning of the Hebrew is uncertain.   **9:27c** Hebrew *an abomination of desolation.*

AUGUST 31 ☐ DAY 244
DANIEL 10–12
Previews of Israel's Future

 OVERVIEW You may find comfort in knowing that even Daniel didn't understand everything that was revealed to him in his visions (12:8). (While you're at it, glance at 2 Peter 3:15-16, and notice that Peter had the same trouble with some of Paul's writings!) Don't be overly concerned about the parts of today's reading you don't understand. Instead, like Daniel, worry about the parts you do! In Daniel's final visions he sees a titanic struggle between kings from the south and north vying for control of "the glorious land" (11:41) in a climactic "time of anguish" (12:1). Though the final chapter of world history is not revealed to Daniel (12:9), the outcome is sure: purifying judgment.

Chapter 10	Chapter 11	Chapter 12
Daniel's Prayer and an Angel's Visit	Persia and Greece in Israel's Future	Punishment and Reward in Israel's Future
Preparation	Prophecy	Preview

YOUR DAILY WALK It does seem strange, but Daniel—God's great prophetic mouthpiece during the exile—probably knew less about his prophetic visions than you do.

No Bible subject matter holds more practical implications than prophecy.
Looking back over the course of history as it has transpired, with the great world powers all carefully documented by secular historians and archaeologists, you can match leaders and nations with parts of Daniel's visions in a way that Daniel never dreamed possible. Babylonia . . . Medo-Persia . . . Greece . . . Rome—much of their history was foretold centuries before from the mouth of a godly government servant in Babylon! Add to that the additional insight of the New Testament, and you have a sharper picture of the future course of this world than did any Old Testament prophet! What a privilege—what a responsibility.

Set aside some extra time to study a particularly difficult passage from the book of Daniel. Your pastor or local Christian bookstore can suggest a good commentary or two to make your time even more profitable.

INSIGHT Final Score: Daniel—100, Critics—0
Chapter 11 alone contains more than one hundred specific prophecies of historical events that literally came true! It is little wonder that some critics attempt to place Daniel two hundred years later in order to undermine the miraculous character of his prophecies.

CHAPTER 10
In the third year of the reign of King Cyrus of Persia, Daniel (also known as Belteshazzar) had another vision. It concerned events certain to happen in the future— times of war and great hardship—and Daniel understood what the vision meant.

²When this vision came to me, I, Daniel, had been in mourning for three weeks. ³All that time I had eaten no rich food or meat, had drunk no wine, and had used no fragrant oils. ⁴On April 23,* as I was standing beside the great Tigris River, ⁵I looked up and saw a man dressed in linen clothing, with a belt of pure gold around his waist. ⁶His body looked like a dazzling gem. From his face came flashes like lightning, and his eyes were like flaming torches. His arms and feet shone like polished bronze, and his voice was like the roaring of a vast multitude of people.

⁷I, Daniel, am the only one who saw this

vision. The men with me saw nothing, but they were suddenly terrified and ran away to hide. ⁸So I was left there all alone to watch this amazing vision. My strength left me, my face grew deathly pale, and I felt very weak. ⁹When I heard him speak, I fainted and lay there with my face to the ground.

¹⁰Just then a hand touched me and lifted me, still trembling, to my hands and knees. ¹¹And the man said to me, "O Daniel, greatly loved of God, listen carefully to what I have to say to you. Stand up, for I have been sent to you." When he said this to me, I stood up, still trembling with fear.

¹²Then he said, "Don't be afraid, Daniel. Since the first day you began to pray for understanding and to humble yourself before your God, your request has been heard in heaven. I have come in answer to your prayer. ¹³But for twenty-one days the spirit prince* of the kingdom of Persia blocked

10:4 Hebrew *On the twenty-fourth day of the first month.* This date in the book of Daniel can be cross-checked with dates in surviving Persian records and can be related accurately to our modern calendar. This day of the Hebrew lunar calendar occurred on April 23, 536 B.C.   10:13a Hebrew *the prince;* also in 10:13c, 20.

my way. Then Michael, one of the archangels,* came to help me, and I left him there with the spirit prince of the kingdom of Persia.* [14]Now I am here to explain what will happen to your people in the future, for this vision concerns a time yet to come."

[15]While he was speaking to me, I looked down at the ground, unable to say a word. [16]Then the one who looked like a man* touched my lips, and I opened my mouth and began to speak. I said to the one standing in front of me, "I am terrified by the vision I have seen, my lord, and I am very weak. [17]How can someone like me, your servant, talk to you, my lord? My strength is gone, and I can hardly breathe."

[18]Then the one who looked like a man touched me again, and I felt my strength returning. [19]"Don't be afraid," he said, "for you are deeply loved by God. Be at peace; take heart and be strong!"

As he spoke these words, I suddenly felt stronger and said to him, "Now you may speak, my lord, for you have strengthened me."

[20]He replied, "Do you know why I have come? Soon I must return to fight against the spirit prince of the kingdom of Persia, and then against the spirit prince of the kingdom of Greece.* [21]But before I do that, I will tell you what is written in the Book of Truth. (There is no one to help me against these spirit princes except Michael, your spirit prince.* [1]I have been standing beside Michael* as his support and defense since the first year of the reign of Darius the Mede.)

CHAPTER 11
[2]"Now then, I will reveal the truth to you. Three more Persian kings will reign, to be succeeded by a fourth, far richer than the others. Using his wealth for political advantage, he will stir up everyone to war against the kingdom of Greece.*

[3]"Then a mighty king will rise to power who will rule a vast kingdom and accomplish everything he sets out to do. [4]But at the height of his power, his kingdom will be broken apart and divided into four parts. It will not be ruled by the king's descendants, nor will the kingdom hold

the authority it once had. For his empire will be uprooted and given to others.

[5]"The king of the south will increase in power, but one of this king's own officials will become more powerful than he and will rule his kingdom with great strength.

[6]"Some years later, an alliance will be formed between the king of the north and the king of the south. The daughter of the king of the south will be given in marriage to the king of the north to secure the alliance, but she will lose her influence over him, and so will her father. She will be given up along with her supporters. [7]But when one of her relatives* becomes king of the south, he will raise an army and enter the fortress of the king of the north and defeat him. [8]When he returns again to Egypt, he will carry back their idols with him, along with priceless gold and silver dishes. For some years afterward he will leave the king of the north alone.

[9]"Later the king of the north will invade the realm of the king of the south but will soon return to his own land. [10]However, the sons of the king of the north will assemble a mighty army that will advance like a flood and carry the battle as far as the enemy's fortress. [11]Then the king of the south, in great anger, will rally against the vast forces assembled by the king of the north and will defeat them. [12]After the enemy army is swept away, the king of the south will be filled with pride and will have many thousands of his enemies killed. But his success will be short lived.

[13]"A few years later, the king of the north will return with a fully equipped army far greater than the one he lost. [14]At that time there will be a general uprising against the king of the south. Lawless ones among your own people will join them in order to fulfill the vision, but they will not succeed. [15]Then the king of the north will come and lay siege to a fortified city and capture it. The best troops of the south will not be able to stand in the face of the onslaught.

[16]"The king of the north will march onward unopposed; none will be able to stop him. He will pause in the glorious land of Israel, intent on destroying it. [17]He will make plans to come with the might of his entire kingdom and will form an alliance

---

10:13b Hebrew *the chief princes.*   10:13c As in one Greek version; Hebrew reads *and I was left there with the kings of Persia.* The meaning of the Hebrew is uncertain.   10:16 As in most manuscripts of the Masoretic Text; one manuscript of the Masoretic Text and one Greek version read *Then something that looked like a human hand.*   10:20 Hebrew *of Javan.*   10:21 Hebrew *against these except Michael, your prince.*   11:1 Hebrew *him.*   11:2 Hebrew *of Javan.*   11:7 Hebrew *a branch from her roots.*

with the king of the south. He will give him a daughter in marriage in order to overthrow the kingdom from within, but his plan will fail.

¹⁸"After this, he will turn his attention to the coastal cities and conquer many. But a commander from another land will put an end to his insolence and will cause him to retreat in shame. ¹⁹He will take refuge in his own fortresses but will stumble and fall, and he will be seen no more.

²⁰"His successor will be remembered as the king who sent a tax collector to maintain the royal splendor, but after a very brief reign, he will die, though neither in battle nor open conflict.

²¹"The next to come to power will be a despicable man who is not directly in line for royal succession. But he will slip in when least expected and take over the kingdom by flattery and intrigue. ²²Before him great armies will be swept away, including a covenant prince. ²³By making deceitful promises, he will make various alliances. With a mere handful of followers, he will become strong. ²⁴Without warning he will enter the richest areas of the land and do something that none of his predecessors ever did—distribute among his followers the plunder and wealth of the rich. He will plot the overthrow of strongholds, but this will last for only a short while.

²⁵"Then he will stir up his courage and raise a great army against the king of the south. The king of the south will go to battle with a mighty army, but to no avail, for plots against him will succeed. ²⁶Those of his own household will bring his downfall. His army will be swept away, and many will be killed. ²⁷Seeking nothing but each other's harm, these kings will plot against each other at the conference table, attempting to deceive each other. But it will make no difference, for an end will still come at the appointed time.

²⁸"The king of the north will then return home with great riches. On the way he will set himself against the people of the holy covenant, doing much damage before continuing his journey.

²⁹"Then at the appointed time he will once again invade the south, but this time the result will be different. ³⁰For warships from western coastlands* will scare him off, and he will withdraw and return home.

But he will vent his anger against the people of the holy covenant and reward those who forsake the covenant. ³¹His army will take over the Temple fortress, polluting the sanctuary, putting a stop to the daily sacrifices, and setting up the sacrilegious object that causes desecration.* ³²He will flatter those who have violated the covenant and win them over to his side. But the people who know their God will be strong and will resist him.

³³"Those who are wise will give instruction to many. But for a time many of these teachers will die by fire and sword, or they will be jailed and robbed. ³⁴While all these persecutions are going on, a little help will arrive, though many who join them will not be sincere. ³⁵And some who are wise will fall victim to persecution. In this way, they will be refined and cleansed and made pure until the time of the end, for the appointed time is still to come.

³⁶"The king will do as he pleases, exalting himself and claiming to be greater than every god there is, even blaspheming the God of gods. He will succeed—until the time of wrath is completed. For what has been determined will surely take place. ³⁷He will have no regard for the gods of his ancestors, or for the god beloved of women, or for any other god, for he will boast that he is greater than them all. ³⁸Instead of these, he will worship the god of fortresses—a god his ancestors never knew—and lavish on him gold, silver, precious stones, and costly gifts. ³⁹Claiming this foreign god's help, he will attack the strongest fortresses. He will honor those who submit to him, appointing them to positions of authority and dividing the land among them as their reward.*

⁴⁰"Then at the time of the end, the king of the south will attack him, and the king of the north will storm out against him with chariots, cavalry, and a vast navy. He will invade various lands and sweep through them like a flood. ⁴¹He will enter the glorious land of Israel, and many nations will fall, but Moab, Edom, and the best part of Ammon will escape. ⁴²He will conquer many countries, and Egypt will not escape. ⁴³He will gain control over the gold, silver, and treasures of Egypt, and the Libyans and Ethiopians* will be his servants.

⁴⁴"But then news from the east and the

11:30 Hebrew *from Kittim.*   **11:31** Hebrew *the abomination of desolation.*   **11:39** Or *at a price.*   **11:43** Hebrew *Cushites.*

north will alarm him, and he will set out in great anger to destroy many as he goes. [45]He will halt between the glorious holy mountain and the sea and will pitch his royal tents there, but while he is there, his time will suddenly run out, and there will be no one to help him.

CHAPTER 12

"At that time Michael, the archangel* who stands guard over your nation, will arise. Then there will be a time of anguish greater than any since nations first came into existence. But at that time every one of your people whose name is written in the book will be rescued. [2]Many of those whose bodies lie dead and buried will rise up, some to everlasting life and some to shame and everlasting contempt. [3]Those who are wise will shine as bright as the sky, and those who turn many to righteousness will shine like stars forever. [4]But you, Daniel, keep this prophecy a secret; seal up the book until the time of the end. Many will rush here and there, and knowledge will increase."

[5]Then I, Daniel, looked and saw two others standing on opposite banks of the river. [6]One of them asked the man dressed in linen, who was now standing above the river, "How long will it be until these shocking events happen?"

[7]The man dressed in linen, who was standing above the river, raised both his hands toward heaven and took this solemn oath by the one who lives forever: "It will go on for a time, times, and half a time. When the shattering of the holy people has finally come to an end, all these things will have happened."

[8]I heard what he said, but I did not understand what he meant. So I asked, "How will all this finally end, my lord?"

[9]But he said, "Go now, Daniel, for what I have said is for the time of the end. [10]Many will be purified, cleansed, and refined by these trials. But the wicked will continue in their wickedness, and none of them will understand. Only those who are wise will know what it means.

[11]"From the time the daily sacrifice is taken away and the sacrilegious object that causes desecration* is set up to be worshiped, there will be 1,290 days. [12]And blessed are those who wait and remain until the end of the 1,335 days!

[13]"As for you, go your way until the end. You will rest, and then at the end of the days, you will rise again to receive the inheritance set aside for you."

12:1 Hebrew *the great prince.*   **12:11** Hebrew *the abomination of desolation.*

Hosea

HOSEA'S book is a bittersweet story of unfaithfulness and undying love. It involves two similar relationships: the prophet Hosea to his adulterous wife, Gomer, and God to his faithless covenant people. Gomer abandons Hosea for other lovers; Israel abandons God by going after pagan idols. But perfect love keeps on loving even after being spurned. In Hosea's case, that means buying back his wayward wife from her lovers; for Israel, purifying punishment will be followed by restoration.

Focus	Harlotry and Hope in Hosea's Day				
Divisions	Moral Sins of Gomer	National Sins of Israel	International Sins of Israel	Promise of Israel's Ruin	Promise of Israel's Renewal
	1 3	4 6	7 8	9 11	12 14
Topics	Physical Adultery	Spiritual Adultery			
	Personal Tragedy	National Transgression			
Place	Northern Kingdom of Israel				
Time	About 45 Years (755–710 B.C.)				

SEPTEMBER 1 □ DAY 245
HOSEA 1–3
Moral Sins of Gomer

OVERVIEW Hosea's family life becomes a painful but accurate picture of the problems within his nation. He marries a woman named Gomer, who bears him three children appropriately named by God as signs to Israel: Jezreel, "God plants"; Lo-ruhamah, "not loved"; and Lo-ammi, "not my people." All too soon, Hosea's home is shattered by Gomer's unfaithfulness. She leaves her prophet-husband in search of other lovers and sinks to such depths that Hosea must redeem her from her lovers. Hosea's steadfast love in the face of such unfaithfulness parallels God's love for his people in the midst of their idolatry.

Chapter 1	Chapter 2	Chapter 3
Marriage of Hosea and Gomer	Unfaithfulness of Gomer	Undying Love of Hosea
Faithless Wife		Forgiving Husband

YOUR DAILY WALK What do the following have in common: a conversation with a brick wall . . . a telephone call answered by a recorded voice . . . and a debate with a corpse?

Like a delicate seismograph, Hosea's sensitive soul recorded the hidden and secret rumblings of divine judgment.

Answer: They all represent one-sided conversations. Try as you might, you will never get the brick wall, answering machine, or corpse to respond to you. Why? Because there is no life in them.

There is something pathetic about a one-sided relationship, the kind in which one partner remains faithful and committed, while the other fails to respond to that love. Does that describe God's relationship with you? Romans 5:8 states: "But God showed his great love for us by sending Christ to die for us while we were still sinners." God has demonstrated his love for you; have you responded to that love in kind? If *one-sided* describes God's relationship with you (as it did Hosea's relationship with Gomer and God's relationship with Israel), then why not respond today? By putting your faith in the fact of Christ's love and sacrificial death, you can become a child of God right now. A love like that is just too good to ignore (1 John 4:10)!

INSIGHT The Prophet Who Outlived His Audience
According to 1:1, Hosea ministered during the reigns of four kings in Judah (southern kingdom). Hosea's long career, therefore, spanned the reigns of the last six kings of Israel (northern kingdom), making him one of the few "ten-king prophets" in the Bible.

CHAPTER 1
The LORD gave these messages to Hosea son of Beeri during the years when Uzziah, Jotham, Ahaz, and Hezekiah were kings of Judah, and Jeroboam son of Jehoash* was king of Israel.

[2] When the LORD first began speaking to Israel through Hosea, he said to him, "Go and marry a prostitute,* so some of her children will be born to you from other men. This will illustrate the way my people have been untrue to me, openly

1:1 Hebrew *Joash,* a variant name for Jehoash.   1:2 Or *a promiscuous woman.*

committing adultery against the LORD by worshiping other gods."

³So Hosea married Gomer, the daughter of Diblaim, and she became pregnant and gave Hosea a son. ⁴And the LORD said, "Name the child Jezreel, for I am about to punish King Jehu's dynasty to avenge the murders he committed at Jezreel. ⁵In fact, I will put an end to Israel's independence by breaking its military power in the Jezreel Valley."

⁶Soon Gomer became pregnant again and gave birth to a daughter. And the LORD said to Hosea, "Name your daughter Lo-ruhamah—'Not loved'—for I will no longer show love to the people of Israel or forgive them. ⁷But I, the LORD their God, will show love to the people of Judah. I will personally free them from their enemies without any help from weapons or armies."

⁸After Gomer had weaned Lo-ruhamah, she again became pregnant and gave birth to a second son. ⁹And the LORD said, "Name him Lo-ammi—'Not my people'—for Israel is not my people, and I am not their God. ¹⁰Yet the time will come when Israel will prosper and become a great nation. In that day its people will be like the sands of the seashore—too many to count! Then, at the place where they were told, 'You are not my people,' it will be said, 'You are children of the living God.' ¹¹Then the people of Judah and Israel will unite under one leader, and they will return from exile together. What a day that will be—the day of Jezreel*— when God will again plant his people in his land. ¹In that day you will call your brothers Ammi—'My people.' And you will call your sisters Ruhamah—'The ones I love.'

CHAPTER 2
²"But now, call Israel* to account, for she is no longer my wife, and I am no longer her husband. Tell her to take off her garish makeup and suggestive clothing and to stop playing the prostitute. ³If she doesn't, I will strip her as naked as she was on the day she was born. I will leave her to die of thirst, as in a desert or a dry and barren wilderness. ⁴And I will not love her children as I would my own because they are not my children! They were conceived in

adultery. ⁵For their mother is a shameless prostitute and became pregnant in a shameful way. She said, 'I'll run after other lovers and sell myself to them for food and drink, for clothing of wool and linen, and for olive oil.'

⁶"But I will fence her in with thornbushes. I will block the road to make her lose her way. ⁷When she runs after her lovers, she won't be able to catch up with them. She will search for them but not find them. Then she will think, 'I might as well return to my husband because I was better off with him than I am now.' ⁸She doesn't realize that it was I who gave her everything she has—the grain, the wine, the olive oil. Even the gold and silver she used in worshiping the god Baal were gifts from me!

⁹"But now I will take back the wine and ripened grain I generously provided each harvest season. I will take away the linen and wool clothing I gave her to cover her nakedness. ¹⁰I will strip her naked in public, while all her lovers look on. No one will be able to rescue her from my hands. ¹¹I will put an end to her annual festivals, her new moon celebrations, and her Sabbath days—all her appointed festivals. ¹²I will destroy her vineyards and orchards, things she claims her lovers gave her. I will let them grow into tangled thickets, where only wild animals will eat the fruit. ¹³I will punish her for all the times she deserted me, when she burned incense to her images of Baal, put on her earrings and jewels, and went out looking for her lovers," says the LORD.

¹⁴"But then I will win her back once again. I will lead her out into the desert and speak tenderly to her there. ¹⁵I will return her vineyards to her and transform the Valley of Trouble* into a gateway of hope. She will give herself to me there, as she did long ago when she was young, when I freed her from her captivity in Egypt.

¹⁶"In that coming day," says the LORD, "you will call me 'my husband' instead of 'my master.'* ¹⁷O Israel, I will cause you to forget your images of Baal; even their names will no longer be spoken. ¹⁸At that time I will make a covenant with all the wild animals and the birds and the animals that scurry along the ground so that they

1:11 *Jezreel* means "God plants."   2:2 Hebrew *call your mother.*   2:15 Hebrew *valley of Achor.*   2:16 Hebrew *'my baal.'*

will not harm you. I will remove all weapons of war from the land, all swords and bows, so you can live unafraid in peace and safety. ¹⁹I will make you my wife forever, showing you righteousness and justice, unfailing love and compassion. ²⁰I will be faithful to you and make you mine, and you will finally know me as LORD.

²¹"In that day," says the LORD, "I will answer the pleading of the sky for clouds, which will pour down water on the earth in answer to its cries for rain. ²²Then the earth will answer the thirsty cries of the grain, the grapes, and the olive trees for moisture. And the whole grand chorus will sing together, 'Jezreel'—'God plants!'

²³"At that time I will plant a crop of Israelites and raise them for myself! I will show love to those I called 'Not loved.'* And to those I called 'Not my people,'* I will say, 'Now you are my people.' Then they will reply, 'You are our God!'"

CHAPTER 3

Then the LORD said to me, "Go and get your wife again. Bring her back to you and love her, even though she loves adultery. For the LORD still loves Israel even though the people have turned to other gods, offering them choice gifts.*"

²So I bought her back for fifteen pieces of silver* and about five bushels of barley and a measure of wine.* ³Then I said to her, "You must live in my house for many days and stop your prostitution. During this time, you will not have sexual intercourse with anyone, not even with me.*"

⁴This illustrates that Israel will be a long time without a king or prince, and without sacrifices, temple, priests, or even idols! ⁵But afterward the people will return to the LORD their God and to David's descendant, their king.* They will come trembling in awe to the LORD, and they will receive his good gifts in the last days.

2:23a Hebrew *Lo-ruhamah*; see 1:6.   **2:23b** Hebrew *Lo-ammi*; see 1:9.   **3:1** Hebrew *raisin cakes*.   **3:2a** Hebrew *15 shekels of silver*, about 6 ounces or 171 grams in weight.   **3:2b** As in Greek version, which reads *a homer* [182 liters] *of barley and a measure of wine*; Hebrew reads *a homer of barley and a lethech* [2.5 bushels or 91 liters] *of barley*.   **3:3** Or *and I will live with you*.   **3:5** Hebrew *to David their king*.

SEPTEMBER 2 ☐ DAY 246
HOSEA 4–6
National Sins of Israel

 OVERVIEW Because of his own painful experiences, Hosea is able to identify with the sorrow of God over the sinfulness of Israel. Hosea's loyal love for Gomer pictures God's undying love for his people. But Israel's sin-hardened populace refuses to respond to God's last gracious appeal. The people stand guilty and defenseless before God's accusations. Even now God is willing to heal and redeem them, but in their arrogance and idolatry they refuse to return.

Chapter 4	Chapter 5	Chapter 6
Guilty People and Priests	Rebellious Priests and Princes	Merciful God of Goodness
God's Indictment	God's Displeasure	God's Demands

 YOUR DAILY WALK Complete this sentence at least five different ways: "I know for certain that . . ."

The knowledge of God is far from the love of him.

Now examine the responses you gave. Is the level of your "knowledge" the same in all cases, or does it vary? Perhaps you said, "I know for certain that my name is Norman (or Norma) Christian." That is knowledge from firsthand experience. But is that the same kind of knowledge as represented in the statements "I know the world is round" and "I know my car will start tomorrow morning"?

Death and destruction were coming upon the people of Israel. Why? In God's own words: "My people are being destroyed because they don't know me" (4:6). In a nation founded by God, built upon godly principles, and centered around the Temple of God, it seems incredible to think there was no knowledge of God. But the issue was not facts *about* God; the issue was firsthand experience *with* God.

Might the shocking statement of Hosea 4:6 be true of your nation as well? Godly foundations and an abundance of churches are no guarantee of the knowledge of God. Remember, if the knowledge of God is to permeate your country, it first must be the experience of your life.

INSIGHT The Tattered Ten Commandments
Chapters 4–6 show how the nation has broken each of the Ten Commandments (Exodus 20:1-17). Can you find at least one statement corresponding to each broken command?

CHAPTER 4

Hear the word of the LORD, O people of Israel! The LORD has filed a lawsuit against you, saying: "There is no faithfulness, no kindness, no knowledge of God in your land. ²You curse and lie and kill and steal and commit adultery. There is violence everywhere, with one murder after another. ³That is why your land is not producing. It is filled with sadness, and all living things are becoming sick and dying. Even the animals, birds, and fish have begun to disappear.

⁴"Don't point your finger at someone else and try to pass the blame! Look, you priests, my complaint is with you!* ⁵As a sentence for your crimes, you will stumble in broad daylight, just as you might at night, and so will your false prophets. And I will destroy your mother, Israel. ⁶My people are being destroyed because they don't know me. It is all your fault, you priests, for you yourselves refuse to know me. Now I refuse to recognize you as my priests. Since you have forgotten the laws of your God, I will forget to bless your children. ⁷The more priests there are, the more they sin against me. They have exchanged* the glory of God for the disgrace of idols.

⁸"The priests get fed when the people sin and bring their sin offerings to them. So the priests are glad when the people sin! ⁹'Like priests, like people'—since the priests are wicked, the people are wicked, too. So now I will punish both priests and people for all their wicked deeds. ¹⁰They will eat and still be hungry. Though they do a big business as prostitutes, they will have no children, for they have deserted the LORD to worship other gods.

¹¹"Alcohol and prostitution have robbed my people of their brains. ¹²They are asking a piece of wood to tell them what to do! They think a stick can tell them the future! Longing after idols has made them foolish. They have played the prostitute, serving other gods and deserting their God. ¹³They offer sacrifices to idols on the tops of mountains. They go up into the hills to burn incense in the pleasant shade of oaks, poplars, and other trees.

"That is why your daughters turn to prostitution, and your daughters-in-law commit adultery. ¹⁴Why should I punish them? For you men are doing the same thing, sinning with whores and shrine prostitutes. O foolish people! You will be destroyed, for you refuse to understand.

¹⁵"Though Israel is a prostitute, may Judah avoid such guilt. O Judah, do not join with those who worship me insincerely at Gilgal and at Beth-aven.* Their worship is mere pretense as they take oaths in the LORD's name. ¹⁶Israel is as stubborn as a heifer, so the LORD will put her out to pasture. She will stand alone and unprotected, like a helpless lamb in an open field. ¹⁷Leave her alone because she is married to idolatry. ¹⁸The men of Israel finish up their drinking bouts and off they go to find some prostitutes. Their love for shame is greater than their love for honor.* ¹⁹So a mighty wind will sweep them away. They will die in shame because they offer sacrifices to idols.

CHAPTER 5

"Hear this, you priests and all of Israel's leaders! Listen, all you men of the royal family! These words of judgment are for

---

4:4 Hebrew *Your people are like those with a complaint against the priests.*   4:7 As in Syriac version and an ancient Hebrew tradition; Masoretic Text reads *I will exchange.*   4:15 *Beth-aven* means "house of wickedness"; it is being used as another name for Bethel, which means "house of God."   4:18 As in Greek version; the meaning of the Hebrew is uncertain.

you: You are doomed! For you have led the people into a snare by worshiping the idols at Mizpah and Tabor. [2]You have dug a deep pit to trap them at Acacia.* But never forget—I will settle with all of you for what you have done. [3]I know what you are like, O Israel! You have left me as a prostitute leaves her husband; you are utterly defiled. [4]Your deeds won't let you return to your God. You are a prostitute through and through, and you cannot know the LORD.

[5]"The arrogance of Israel* testifies against her; she will stumble under her load of guilt. Judah, too, will fall with her. [6]Then at last, they will come with their flocks and herds to offer sacrifices to the LORD. But it will be too late! They will not find him, because he has withdrawn from them, and they are now alone. [7]For they have betrayed the honor of the LORD, bearing children that aren't his. Now their false religion will devour them, along with their wealth.

[8]"Blow the ram's horn in Gibeah! Sound the alarm in Ramah! Raise the battle cry in Beth-aven*! Lead on into battle, O warriors of Benjamin! [9]One thing is certain, Israel*: When your day of punishment comes, you will become a heap of rubble.

[10]"The leaders of Judah have become as bad as thieves.* So I will pour my anger down on them like a waterfall. [11]The people of Israel will be crushed and broken by my judgment because they are determined to worship idols. [12]I will destroy Israel as a moth consumes wool. I will sap Judah's strength as dry rot weakens wood.

[13]"When Israel and Judah saw how sick they were, Israel turned to Assyria, to the great king there, but he could neither help nor cure them. [14]I will tear at Israel and Judah as a lion rips apart its prey. I will

carry them off, and there will be no one left to rescue them. [15]Then I will return to my place until they admit their guilt and look to me for help. For as soon as trouble comes, they will search for me."

CHAPTER 6

"Come, let us return to the LORD! He has torn us in pieces; now he will heal us. He has injured us; now he will bandage our wounds. [2]In just a short time, he will restore us so we can live in his presence. [3]Oh, that we might know the LORD! Let us press on to know him! Then he will respond to us as surely as the arrival of dawn or the coming of rains in early spring."

[4]"O Israel* and Judah, what should I do with you?" asks the LORD. "For your love vanishes like the morning mist and disappears like dew in the sunlight. [5]I sent my prophets to cut you to pieces. I have slaughtered you with my words, threatening you with death. My judgment will strike you as surely as day follows night. [6]I want you to be merciful; I don't want your sacrifices. I want you to know God; that's more important than burnt offerings.

[7]"But like Adam, you broke my covenant and rebelled against me. [8]Gilead is a city of sinners, tracked with footprints of blood. [9]Its citizens are bands of robbers, lying in ambush for their victims. Gangs of priests murder travelers along the road to Shechem and practice every kind of sin. [10]Yes, I have seen a horrible thing in Israel: My people have defiled themselves by chasing after other gods!

[11]"O Judah, a harvest of punishment is also waiting for you, though I wanted so much to restore the fortunes of my people!

5:2 Hebrew *at Shittim.* The meaning of the Hebrew for this sentence is uncertain.   **5:5** Hebrew *Israel and Ephraim.*   **5:8** *Beth-aven* means "house of wickedness"; it is being used as another name for Bethel, which means "house of God."   **5:9** Hebrew *Ephraim,* referring to the northern kingdom of Israel; also in 5:11, 12, 13, 14.   **5:10** Hebrew *have become as those who move a boundary marker.*   **6:4** Hebrew *Ephraim,* referring to the northern kingdom of Israel.

SEPTEMBER 3 ☐ DAY 247
HOSEA 7–8
International Sins of Israel

OVERVIEW Israel's sin remains the focus of Hosea's prophecy. The nation's iniquity is like a raging fire. Her rebellion has weakened her to the point of spiritual stupor. She is beyond realizing who God is or what he has done for her. For this idolatrous, sin-riddled nation there can be only one verdict: exile.

Chapter 7		Chapter 8	
Burning Sin	Betrayal of God	Blight of Idolatry	Banishment from the Land
1 10	11 16	1 7	8 14
Sowing the Wind		Reaping the Whirlwind	

By chastening, the Lord separates the sin that he hates from the sinner whom he loves.

YOUR DAILY WALK A bird lies fluttering on the ground, obviously injured. You respond to this pitiful sight by reaching out your hand to try and help. Instead of recognizing your intent, the bird jerks free in a frantic effort to escape. You are the only one who can help, and yet the bird refuses your assistance—perhaps at the cost of its life.

"How foolish! How wasteful!" you say. And yet that is precisely how God's people responded to God's overtures. "I wanted to heal Israel," cried the Lord, but Israel refused (7:1). Blinded by sin and devoured by wickedness, the people rejected God's gracious offers. And the heart of God grieved. Instead of compassion, he was forced to extend a hand of chastening—punishment in place of pardon, exile rather than encouragement.

Are you grieving the Lord today by your stubborn refusal to respond to his grace? Pinpoint a bad habit, an unchecked passion, a persistent sin that is saddening your Lord. Then remember the illustration of the injured bird. The choice is up to you. Yield to God's love before you feel his hand of discipline.

INSIGHT Will They Never Learn?

The gold calf, which nearly cost Aaron his life and resulted in the deaths of three thousand Israelites, was later destroyed (Exodus 32). But the idea lived on during the reign of Jeroboam, first king of the northern kingdom. He ordered similar gold calves to be erected at Dan (in the north) and Bethel (in the south). For years these calves were the focus of Israel's idolatrous worship (1 Kings 12:26-33). And perhaps it was in the very shadow of these same calves that Hosea stood as he prophesied destruction for idol and idolater alike (8:5-7).

CHAPTER 7

"I wanted to heal Israel, but its sins were far too great. Samaria is filled with liars, thieves, and bandits! ²Its people don't realize I am watching them. Their sinful deeds are all around them; I see them all! ³The people make the king glad with their wickedness. The princes laugh about the people's many lies. ⁴They are all adulterers, always aflame with lust. They are like an oven that is kept hot even while the baker is still kneading the dough.

⁵"On royal holidays, the princes get drunk. The king makes a fool of himself and drinks with those who are making fun of him. ⁶Their hearts blaze like a furnace with intrigue. Their plot smolders through the night, and in the morning it flames forth like a raging fire. ⁷They kill their kings one after another, and no one cries out to me for help.

⁸"My people of Israel* mingle with god-

7:8 Hebrew *Ephraim*, referring to the northern kingdom of Israel; also in 7:11.

less foreigners, picking up their evil ways. Now they have become as worthless as a half-baked cake! [9]Worshiping foreign gods has sapped their strength, but they don't even know it. Israel is like an old man with graying hair, unaware of how weak and old he has become. [10]His arrogance testifies against him, yet he doesn't return to the LORD his God or even try to find him.

[11]"The people of Israel have become like silly, witless doves, first calling to Egypt, then flying to Assyria. [12]But as they fly about, I will throw my net over them and bring them down like a bird from the sky. I will punish them for all their evil ways.*

[13]"How terrible it will be for my people who have deserted me! Let them die, for they have rebelled against me. I wanted to redeem them, but they have only spoken lies about me. [14]They do not cry out to me with sincere hearts. Instead, they sit on their couches and wail. They cut themselves, begging foreign gods for crops and prosperity.

[15]"I trained them and made them strong, yet now they plot evil against me. [16]They look everywhere except to heaven, to the Most High. They are like a crooked bow that always misses its target. Their leaders will be killed by their enemies because of their insolence toward me. Then the people of Egypt will laugh at them.

CHAPTER 8

"Sound the alarm! The enemy descends like an eagle on the people of the LORD, for they have broken my covenant and revolted against my law. [2]Now Israel pleads with me, 'Help us, for you are our God!' [3]But it is too late! The people of Israel have rejected what is good, and now their enemies will chase after them. [4]The people have appointed kings and princes, but not with my consent. By making idols for themselves from their silver and gold, they have brought about their own destruction.

[5]"O Samaria, I reject this calf—this idol you have made. My fury burns against you. How long will you be incapable of innocence? [6]This calf you worship was crafted by your own hands! It is not God! Therefore, it must be smashed to bits.

[7]"They have planted the wind and will harvest the whirlwind. The stalks of wheat wither, producing no grain. And if there is any grain, foreigners will eat it. [8]The people of Israel have been swallowed up; they lie among the nations like an old pot that no one wants. [9]Like a wild donkey looking for a mate, they have gone up to Assyria. The people of Israel* have sold themselves to many lovers. [10]But though they have sold themselves to many lands, I will now gather them together. Then they will writhe under the burden of the great king!

[11]"Israel has built many altars to take away sin, but these very altars became places for sinning! [12]Even though I gave them all my laws, they act as if those laws don't apply to them. [13]The people of Israel love their rituals of sacrifice, but to me their sacrifices are all meaningless! I will call my people to account for their sins, and I will punish them. They will go back down to Egypt.

[14]"Israel has built great palaces, and Judah has fortified its cities. But they have both forgotten their Maker. Therefore, I will send down fire on their palaces and burn their fortresses."

7:12 Hebrew *I will punish them because of what was reported against them in the assembly.*   **8:9** Hebrew *Ephraim,* referring to the northern kingdom of Israel; also in 8:11.

SEPTEMBER 4 □ DAY 248
HOSEA 9–11
Promise of Israel's Ruin

OVERVIEW Like the pounding of a hammer, Hosea's indictment of Israel continues. Worship has no meaning for God when offered by people with idolatrous hearts. The nation has been wasted by unchecked sin. Once a fruitful vine, Israel now lies spiritually barren and fruitless. Yet God remains loyal to his people. His love will not permit him to leave sin unpunished—just as a loving father must discipline his erring children. But in the midst of that painful process, God's promise shines brightly. Restoration and blessing await his people when the painful punishment is over.

Chapter 9	Chapter 10	Chapter 11
God's Hatred for Israel's Barrenness	God's Promise of Israel's Bondage	God's Heart for Israel's Blessing
Punishment Coming		Restoration Coming

YOUR DAILY WALK Contrast these two statements from today's reading: "There I began to hate them [Israel]" (9:15). "My heart is torn within me, and my compassion overflows [for Israel]" (11:8). How can you reconcile these verses? Is God contradicting himself?

A prophet deserves honor, not because he foresees the coming event, but because he sees the meaning within the current event.

The answer can be found in the ageless maxim "God hates the sin but loves the sinner." A holy God can never excuse or condone sin. Yet God never blurs the distinction between the sinner and his or her sin. His love for the sinner never ends, nor does his hatred for the sin.

How do you view those around you who have fallen into gross sin? Have you been so offended by their actions that you now shun them? Remember, "God showed his great love for us by sending Christ to die for us while we were still sinners" (Romans 5:8). Pick someone whose lifestyle would normally cause you to avoid him or her, and plan an activity to demonstrate God's love toward that person. Ask the Holy Spirit to cause the individual to see in your love the extended hand of a loving God, whose compassions never end!

INSIGHT Determined Declaration of Love
The concluding five verses of chapter 11 have been called "the finest presentation in the Old Testament of the tension between the love and justice of God." The final resolution of this tension is seen at the cross, for it is there that God becomes both "just and the justifier" (Romans 3:26, NKJV).

CHAPTER 9

O people of Israel, do not rejoice as others do. For you have been unfaithful to your God, hiring yourselves out like prostitutes, offering sacrifices to other gods on every threshing floor. ²So now your harvests will be too small to feed you. The grapes you gather will not quench your thirst. ³You may no longer stay here in this land of the LORD. You will be carried off to Egypt and Assyria, where you will live on food that is ceremonially unclean.

⁴There, far from home, you will not be allowed to pour out wine as a sacrifice to the LORD. None of the sacrifices you offer there will please him. Such sacrifices will be unclean, just as food touched by a person in mourning is unclean. All who present such sacrifices will be defiled. They may eat this food to feed themselves, but they may not offer it to the LORD.

⁵What then will you do on festival days? What will you do on days of feasting in the LORD's presence? ⁶Even if you escape destruction from Assyria, you will be conquered by Egypt. Memphis* will bury you. Briers will take over your treasures of silver; brambles will fill your homes.

⁷The time of Israel's punishment has come; the day of payment is almost here. Soon Israel will know this all too well. "The prophets are crazy!" the people shout. "The inspired men are mad!" So they taunt, for the nation is burdened with sin and shows only hatred for those who love God.

⁸The prophet is a watchman for my God over Israel,* yet traps are laid in front of him wherever he goes. He faces hostility even in the house of God. ⁹The things my people do are as depraved as what they did in Gibeah long ago. God will not forget. He will surely punish them for their sins.

9:6 Memphis was the capital of northern Egypt.   **9:8** Hebrew *Ephraim,* referring to the northern kingdom of Israel; also in 9:11, 13, 16.

¹⁰The LORD says, "O Israel, when I first found you, it was like finding fresh grapes in the desert! When I saw your ancestors, it was like seeing the first ripe figs of the season! But then they deserted me for Baal-peor, giving themselves to that shameful idol. Soon they became as vile as the god they worshiped. ¹¹The glory of Israel will fly away like a bird, for your children will die at birth or perish in the womb or never even be conceived. ¹²Even if your children do survive to grow up, I will take them from you. It will be a terrible day when I turn away and leave you alone. ¹³I have watched Israel become as beautiful and pleasant as Tyre. But now Israel will bring out her children to be slaughtered."

¹⁴O LORD, what should I request for your people? I will ask for wombs that don't give birth and breasts that give no milk.

¹⁵The LORD says, "All their wickedness began at Gilgal; there I began to hate them. I will drive them from my land because of their evil actions. I will love them no more because all their leaders are rebels. ¹⁶The people of Israel are stricken. Their roots are dried up; they will bear no more fruit. And if they give birth, I will slaughter their beloved children."

¹⁷My God will reject the people of Israel because they will not listen or obey. They will be wanderers, homeless among the nations.

CHAPTER 10

How prosperous Israel is—a luxuriant vine loaded with fruit! But the more wealth the people got, the more they poured it on the altars of their foreign gods. The richer the harvests they brought in, the more beautiful the statues and idols they built. ²The hearts of the people are fickle; they are guilty and must be punished. The LORD will break down their foreign altars and smash their many idols.

³Then they will say, "We have no king because we didn't fear the LORD. But what's the difference? What could a king do for us anyway?" ⁴They spout empty words and make promises they don't intend to keep. So perverted justice springs up among them like poisonous weeds in a farmer's field.

⁵The people of Samaria tremble for their calf idol at Beth-aven.* The people mourn over it, and the priests wail for it, because its glory will be stripped away. ⁶This idol they love so much will be carted away with them when they go as captives to Assyria, a gift to the great king there. Israel will be laughed at and shamed because its people have trusted in this idol. ⁷Samaria will be cut off, and its king will disappear like a chip of wood on an ocean wave. ⁸And the pagan shrines of Aven,* the place of Israel's sin, will crumble. Thorns and thistles will grow up around them. They will beg the mountains to bury them and the hills to fall on them.

⁹The LORD says, "O Israel, ever since that awful night in Gibeah, there has been only sin and more sin! You have made no progress whatsoever. Was it not right that the wicked men of Gibeah were attacked? ¹⁰Now I will attack you, too, for your rebellion and disobedience. I will call out the armies of the nations to punish you for your multiplied sins.

¹¹"Israel* is like a trained heifer accustomed to treading out the grain—an easy job that she loves. Now I will put a heavy yoke on her tender neck. I will drive her in front of the plow. Israel* and Judah must now break up the hard ground; their days of ease are gone. ¹²I said, 'Plant the good seeds of righteousness, and you will harvest a crop of my love. Plow up the hard ground of your hearts, for now is the time to seek the LORD, that he may come and shower righteousness upon you.'

¹³"But you have cultivated wickedness and raised a thriving crop of sins. You have eaten the fruit of lies—trusting in your military might, believing that great armies could make your nation safe! ¹⁴Now the terrors of war will rise among your people. All your fortifications will fall, just as they did when Shalman destroyed Beth-arbel. Even mothers and children were dashed to death there. ¹⁵You will share that fate, Bethel, because of your great wickedness. When the day of judgment dawns, the king of Israel will be completely destroyed.

CHAPTER 11

"When Israel was a child, I loved him as a son, and I called my son out of Egypt. ²But the more I* called to him, the more he rebelled, offering sacrifices to the images of Baal and burning incense to idols. ³It was I who taught Israel* how to walk, leading him along by the hand. But he doesn't know or even care that it was I who took care of him. ⁴I led Israel along with my ropes of kindness and love. I lifted the yoke from his neck, and I myself stooped to feed him.

⁵"But since my people refuse to return to me, they will go back to Egypt and will be forced to serve Assyria. ⁶War will swirl through their cities; their enemies will crash through their gates and destroy them, trapping them in their own evil plans. ⁷For my people are determined to desert me. They call me the Most High, but they don't truly honor me.

⁸"Oh, how can I give you up, Israel?

How can I let you go? How can I destroy you like Admah and Zeboiim? My heart is torn within me, and my compassion overflows. ⁹No, I will not punish you as much as my burning anger tells me to. I will not completely destroy Israel, for I am God and not a mere mortal. I am the Holy One living among you, and I will not come to destroy.

¹⁰"For someday the people will follow the LORD. I will roar like a lion, and my people will return trembling from the west. ¹¹Like a flock of birds, they will come from Egypt. Flying like doves, they will return from Assyria. And I will bring them home again," says the LORD.

¹²Israel surrounds me with lies and deceit, but Judah still walks with God and is faithful to the Holy One.*

11:3 Hebrew *Ephraim*, referring to the northern kingdom of Israel; also in 11:8, 9, 12.   11:12 Or *and Judah is unruly against God, the faithful Holy One.*

SEPTEMBER 5 ☐ DAY 249
HOSEA 12–14
Promise of Israel's Renewal

OVERVIEW Hosea ends his book the same way he began it—by driving home his three-part theme: Israel's past is stained with disobedience and rebellion; Israel's future holds the ominous threat of calamity; and Israel's present demands an immediate and complete change of heart if that calamity is to be averted. Hosea's heart has already been broken by the adultery and shame of his wife, Gomer. Now he pleads one last time with his countrymen that they not duplicate Gomer's folly: "Return, O Israel, to the LORD your God" (14:1).

Chapter 12	Chapter 13	Chapter 14
Israel's Past Recounted	Israel's Future Previewed	Israel's Present Responsibility
Rebellion	Removal	Repentance

YOUR DAILY WALK Few sentences in the English language are more difficult to say than the little two-word phrase *I'm sorry.* You've sinned; you've failed miserably. How do you tell God about it? How do you make it right with him so you can enjoy fellowship once again?

Hosea 14 has been called by some the backslider's chapter. It describes the steps necessary for God's erring people to be restored to fellowship with him:

1. Return to the Lord (14:1). Remember, if God seems distant from you, it must mean *you* have moved!
2. Confess your sins to the Lord (14:2). Agree with him that what you have done is wrong and needs to be forsaken.

As long as we live we should more and more be turning from all that is evil and to all that is good.

3. Put your confidence in the Lord (14:3). Trusting your own strength or understanding can only bring disappointment. Instead, lean on the Rock that can never be moved.

Are you, like Israel in Hosea's day, estranged from your God? Restoration is only a prayer away. Read chapter 14 twice. Then do business with God. He's waiting for you, and his door is always open.

 INSIGHT Great Truths in Tiny Capsules
Think through these fragments of thought from Hosea's pen. What great truths about God do they teach you?
"I want you to be merciful; I don't want your sacrifices" (6:6).
"How can I give you up?" (11:8).
"I will heal you of your idolatry and faithlessness" (14:4).

CHAPTER 12

The people of Israel* feed on the wind; they chase after the east wind all day long. They multiply lies and violence; they make alliances with Assyria and cut deals with the Egyptians.

²Now the LORD is bringing a lawsuit against Judah. He is about to punish Jacob* for all his deceitful ways. ³Before Jacob was born, he struggled with his brother; when he became a man, he even fought with God. ⁴Yes, he wrestled with the angel and won. He wept and pleaded for a blessing from him. There at Bethel he met God face to face, and God spoke to him*—⁵the LORD God Almighty, the LORD is his name! ⁶So now, come back to your God! Act on the principles of love and justice, and always live in confident dependence on your God.

⁷But no, the people are like crafty merchants selling from dishonest scales—they love to cheat. ⁸Israel boasts, "I am rich, and I've gotten it all by myself! No one can say I got it by cheating! My record is spotless!"

⁹"I am the LORD your God, who rescued you from your slavery in Egypt. And I will make you live in tents again, as you do each year when you celebrate the Festival of Shelters.* ¹⁰I sent my prophets to warn you with many visions and parables."

¹¹But Gilead is filled with sinners who worship idols. And in Gilgal, too, they sacrifice bulls; their altars are lined up like the heaps of stone along the edges of a plowed field. ¹²Jacob fled to the land of Aram and earned a wife by tending sheep. ¹³Then the LORD led Jacob's descendants, the Israelites, out of Egypt by a prophet, who guided

and protected them. ¹⁴But the people of Israel have bitterly provoked the LORD, so their Lord will now sentence them to death in payment for their sins.

CHAPTER 13

In the past when the tribe of Ephraim spoke, the people shook with fear because the other Israelite tribes looked up to them. But the people of Ephraim sinned by worshiping Baal and thus sealed their destruction. ²Now they keep on sinning by making silver idols to worship—images shaped skillfully with human hands. "Sacrifice to these," they cry, "and kiss the calf idols!" ³Therefore, they will disappear like the morning mist, like dew in the morning sun, like chaff blown by the wind, like smoke from a chimney.

⁴"I am the LORD your God, who rescued you from your slavery in Egypt. You have no God but me, for there is no other savior. ⁵I took care of you in the wilderness, in that dry and thirsty land. ⁶But when you had eaten and were satisfied, then you became proud and forgot me. ⁷So now I will attack you like a lion, or like a leopard that lurks along the road. ⁸I will rip you to pieces like a bear whose cubs have been taken away. I will tear you apart and devour you like a hungry lion.

⁹"You are about to be destroyed, O Israel, though I am your helper. ¹⁰Where now is* your king? Why don't you call on him for help? Where are all the leaders of the land? You asked for them, now let them save you! ¹¹In my anger I gave you kings, and in my fury I took them away.

¹²"The sins of Ephraim have been collected and stored away for punishment.

12:1 Hebrew *Ephraim,* referring to the northern kingdom of Israel; also in 12:8, 14.   **12:2** *Jacob* means "he grasps at the heel"; this can also figuratively mean "he deceives."   **12:4** As in Greek and Syriac versions; Hebrew reads *to us.*   **12:9** Hebrew *as in the days of your appointed feast.*   **13:10** As in Greek and Syriac versions and Latin Vulgate; Hebrew reads *I will be.*

¹³The people have been offered new birth, but they are like a child who resists being born. How stubborn they are! How foolish! ¹⁴Should I ransom them from the grave? Should I redeem them from death? O death, bring forth your terrors! O grave, bring forth your plagues! For I will not relent! ¹⁵Ephraim was the most fruitful of all his brothers, but the east wind—a blast from the LORD—will arise in the desert. It will blow hard against the people of Ephraim, drying up their land. All their flowing springs and wells will disappear. Every precious thing they have will be plundered and carried away. ¹⁶The people of Samaria must bear the consequences of their guilt because they rebelled against their God. They will be killed by an invading army, their little ones dashed to death against the ground, their pregnant women ripped open by swords."

CHAPTER 14

Return, O Israel, to the LORD your God, for your sins have brought you down. ²Bring your petitions, and return to the LORD. Say to him, "Forgive all our sins and graciously receive us, so that we may offer you the sacrifice of praise. ³Assyria cannot save us,

14:8 Hebrew *Ephraim,* referring to the northern kingdom of Israel.

nor can our strength in battle. Never again will we call the idols we have made 'our gods.' No, in you alone do the orphans find mercy."

⁴The LORD says, "Then I will heal you of your idolatry and faithlessness, and my love will know no bounds, for my anger will be gone forever! ⁵I will be to Israel like a refreshing dew from heaven. It will blossom like the lily; it will send roots deep into the soil like the cedars in Lebanon. ⁶Its branches will spread out like those of beautiful olive trees, as fragrant as the cedar forests of Lebanon. ⁷My people will return again to the safety of their land. They will flourish like grain and blossom like grapevines. They will be as fragrant as the wines of Lebanon.

⁸"O Israel,* stay away from idols! I am the one who looks after you and cares for you. I am like a tree that is always green, giving my fruit to you all through the year."

⁹Let those who are wise understand these things. Let those who are discerning listen carefully. The paths of the LORD are true and right, and righteous people live by walking in them. But sinners stumble and fall along the way.

Joel

THE LOCUSTS have come. And suddenly every green thing is gone. God's spokesman Joel uses this national disaster to bring a dire warning of a far worse catastrophe. Not locusts, but an army from the north will attack Judah. The only hope of escape in this day of the Lord is to repent: "Don't tear your clothing in your grief; instead, tear your hearts" (2:13). If his people will repent, God will send unparalleled blessing instead of devastating judgment. He will judge the nations that hurt his people and bring peace to Zion.

Focus	Past Judgment of God's People	Future Judgment and Restoration of God's People	
Divisions	Devastation of the Locusts	Day of the Lord	Doom of the Nations
	1:1 1:20	2:1 2:32	3:1 3:21
Topics	Israel's Review	Israel's Future	Gentiles' Future
	Historical Invasion	Prophetic Invasions	
Place	Southern Kingdom of Judah		
Time	Approximately 835 B.C.		

SEPTEMBER 6 □ DAY 250
JOEL 1–3
Locusts and the Day of the Lord

OVERVIEW Disaster struck the southern kingdom of Judah without warning. An ominous black cloud descended upon the land—the dreaded locusts. In a matter of hours, every green living thing had been stripped bare. Joel, God's spokesman during the reign of Joash (835–796 B.C.), seizes the occasion to proclaim God's message. The locust plague has been a terrible judgment for sin. Yet God's future judgments during the day of the Lord will make that plague pale by comparison. In that day God will destroy his enemies but bring unparalleled blessing to those who faithfully obey him.

Chapter 1	Chapter 2	Chapter 3
Devastation of the Locusts	Day of the Lord	Doom of the Nations
Israel's Present	Israel's Future	Gentiles' Future

The judgment of God shall turn topsy-turvy the judgments of people.

YOUR DAILY WALK After reading Joel's little three-chapter book, see if you can summarize its description of God in a single word: _____.

The book of Joel reads like the screenplay from a disaster movie: locust swarms, drought, famine, raging brush fires, invading armies, astronomical catastrophes. But why all these "fireworks"? Why this display of calamitous events? One reason becomes apparent at the end of the book: "Then you will know that I, the LORD your God, live in Zion" (3:17). You can't read Joel without coming to grips with the almighty God who sovereignly controls the course of history.

Not only is God big enough to move mountains, he is concerned enough to be "a welcoming refuge and a strong fortress" (3:16). That means he is your refuge, your stronghold, your fortress (all good words to choose for your one-word summary). Pick up a small rock and carry it with you today. Let it remind you that your rock and fortress is big enough to rule this mighty universe (and your own personal locust plagues), yet small enough to live within your heart.

INSIGHT Joel in the Old, Peter in the New
Peter, preaching on the Day of Pentecost (Acts 2), referred to Joel 2:28–32 to explain to the multitudes the miracle they were witnessing. Although the complete fulfillment of this prophecy would not occur until later, Joel's message showed that Pentecost was the work of God's Holy Spirit, not of alcoholic spirits.

CHAPTER 1
The LORD gave this message to Joel son of Pethuel.

²Hear this, you leaders of the people! Everyone listen! In all your history, has anything like this ever happened before? ³Tell your children about it in the years to come. Pass the awful story down from generation to generation. ⁴After the cutting locusts finished eating the crops, the swarming locusts took what was left! After them came the hopping locusts, and then the stripping locusts,* too!

⁵Wake up, you drunkards, and weep! All

1:4 The precise identification of the four kinds of locusts mentioned here is uncertain.

the grapes are ruined, and all your new wine is gone! [6]A vast army of locusts* has invaded my land. It is a terrible army, too numerous to count! Its teeth are as sharp as the teeth of lions! [7]They have destroyed my grapevines and fig trees, stripping their bark and leaving the branches white and bare.

[8]Weep with sorrow, as a virgin weeps when her fiancé has died. [9]There is no grain or wine to offer at the Temple of the LORD. The priests are mourning because there are no offerings. Listen to the weeping of these ministers of the LORD! [10]The fields are ruined and empty of crops. The grain, the wine, and the olive oil are gone.

[11]Despair, all you farmers! Wail, all you vine growers! Weep, because the wheat and barley—yes, all the field crops—are ruined. [12]The grapevines and the fig trees have all withered. The pomegranate trees, palm trees, and apple trees—yes, all the fruit trees—have dried up. All joy has dried up with them.

[13]Dress yourselves in sackcloth, you priests! Wail, you who serve before the altar! Come, spend the night in sackcloth, you ministers of my God! There is no grain or wine to offer at the Temple of your God. [14]Announce a time of fasting; call the people together for a solemn meeting. Bring the leaders and all the people into the Temple of the LORD your God, and cry out to him there. [15]The day of the LORD is on the way, the day when destruction comes from the Almighty. How terrible that day will be!

[16]We watch as our food disappears before our very eyes. There are no joyful celebrations in the house of our God. [17]The seeds die in the parched ground, and the grain crops fail. The barns and granaries stand empty and abandoned. [18]How the animals moan with hunger! The cattle wander about confused because there is no pasture for them. The sheep bleat in misery.

[19]LORD, help us! The fire has consumed the pastures and burned up all the trees. [20]Even the wild animals cry out to you because they have no water to drink. The streams have dried up, and fire has consumed the pastures.

CHAPTER 2

Blow the trumpet in Jerusalem*! Sound the alarm on my holy mountain! Let everyone tremble in fear because the day of the LORD is upon us. [2]It is a day of darkness and gloom, a day of thick clouds and deep blackness. Suddenly, like dawn spreading across the mountains, a mighty army appears! How great and powerful they are! The likes of them have not been seen before and never will be seen again.

[3]Fire burns in front of them and follows them in every direction! Ahead of them the land lies as fair as the Garden of Eden in all its beauty. Behind them is nothing but desolation; not one thing escapes. [4]They look like tiny horses, and they run as fast. [5]Look at them as they leap along the mountaintops! Listen to the noise they make—like the rumbling of chariots, like the roar of a fire sweeping across a field, or like a mighty army moving into battle.

[6]Fear grips all the people; every face grows pale with fright. [7]The attackers march like warriors and scale city walls like trained soldiers. Straight forward they march, never breaking rank. [8]They never jostle each other; each moves in exactly the right place. They lunge through the gaps, and no weapon can stop them. [9]They swarm over the city and run along its walls. They enter all the houses, climbing like thieves through the windows.

[10]The earth quakes as they advance, and the heavens tremble. The sun and moon grow dark, and the stars no longer shine. [11]The LORD leads them with a shout! This is his mighty army, and they follow his orders. The day of the LORD is an awesome, terrible thing. Who can endure it?

[12]That is why the LORD says, "Turn to me now, while there is time! Give me your hearts. Come with fasting, weeping, and mourning. [13]Don't tear your clothing in your grief; instead, tear your hearts." Return to the LORD your God, for he is gracious and merciful. He is not easily angered. He is filled with kindness and is eager not to punish you. [14]Who knows? Perhaps even yet he will give you a reprieve, sending you a blessing instead of this terrible curse. Perhaps he will give you so much that you will be able to offer grain and wine to the LORD your God as before!

[15]Blow the trumpet in Jerusalem! Announce a time of fasting; call the people together for a solemn meeting. [16]Bring everyone—the elders, the children, and even the babies. Call the bridegroom from

1:6 Hebrew *A nation.*   2:1 Hebrew *Zion;* also in 2:15, 23.

his quarters and the bride from her private room. [17]The priests, who minister in the LORD's presence, will stand between the people and the altar, weeping. Let them pray, "Spare your people, LORD! They belong to you, so don't let them become an object of mockery. Don't let their name become a proverb of unbelieving foreigners who say, 'Where is the God of Israel? He must be helpless!'"

[18]Then the LORD will pity his people and be indignant for the honor of his land! [19]He will reply, "Look! I am sending you grain and wine and olive oil, enough to satisfy your needs. You will no longer be an object of mockery among the surrounding nations. [20]I will remove these armies from the north and send them far away. I will drive them back into the parched wastelands, where they will die. Those in the rear will go into the Dead Sea; those at the front will go into the Mediterranean.* The stench of their rotting bodies will rise over the land."

Surely the LORD has done great things! [21]Don't be afraid, my people! Be glad now and rejoice because the LORD has done great things. [22]Don't be afraid, you animals of the field! The pastures will soon be green. The trees will again be filled with luscious fruit; fig trees and grapevines will flourish once more. [23]Rejoice, you people of Jerusalem! Rejoice in the LORD your God! For the rains he sends are an expression of his grace. Once more the autumn rains will come, as well as the rains of spring. [24]The threshing floors will again be piled high with grain, and the presses will overflow with wine and olive oil.

[25]The LORD says, "I will give you back what you lost to the stripping locusts, the cutting locusts, the swarming locusts, and the hopping locusts.* It was I who sent this great destroying army against you. [26]Once again you will have all the food you want, and you will praise the LORD your God, who does these miracles for you. Never again will my people be disgraced like this. [27]Then you will know that I am here among my people of Israel and that I alone am the LORD your God. My people will never again be disgraced like this.

[28]"Then after I have poured out my rains again, I will pour out my Spirit upon all people. Your sons and daughters will prophesy. Your old men will dream dreams.

Your young men will see visions. [29]In those days, I will pour out my Spirit even on servants, men and women alike.

[30]"I will cause wonders in the heavens and on the earth—blood and fire and pillars of smoke. [31]The sun will be turned into darkness, and the moon will turn bloodred before that great and terrible day of the LORD arrives. [32]And anyone who calls on the name of the LORD will be saved. There will be people on Mount Zion in Jerusalem who escape, just as the LORD has said. These will be among the survivors whom the LORD has called.

CHAPTER 3
"At that time, when I restore the prosperity of Judah and Jerusalem," says the LORD, [2]"I will gather the armies of the world into the valley of Jehoshaphat.* There I will judge them for harming my people, for scattering my inheritance among the nations, and for dividing up my land. [3]They cast lots to decide which of my people would be their slaves. They traded young boys for prostitutes and little girls for enough wine to get drunk.

[4]"What do you have against me, Tyre and Sidon and you cities of Philistia? Are you trying to take revenge on me? If you are, then watch out! I will strike swiftly and pay you back for everything you have done. [5]You have taken my silver and gold and all my precious treasures, and you have carried them off to your pagan temples. [6]You have sold the people of Judah and Jerusalem to the Greeks,* who took them far from their homeland. [7]But I will bring them back again from all these places to which you sold them, and I will pay you back for all you have done. [8]I will sell your sons and daughters to the people of Judah, and they will sell them to the peoples of Arabia,* a nation far away. I, the LORD, have spoken!"

[9]Say to the nations far and wide: "Get ready for war! Call out your best warriors! Let all your fighting men advance for the attack! [10]Beat your plowshares into swords and your pruning hooks into spears. Train even your weaklings to be warriors. [11]Come quickly, all you nations everywhere! Gather together in the valley."

And now, O LORD, call out your warriors!

2:20 Hebrew *the eastern sea; . . . the western sea.*   **2:25** The precise identification of the four kinds of locusts mentioned here is uncertain.   **3:2** *Jehoshaphat* means "the LORD judges."   **3:6** Hebrew *to the peoples of Javan.*   **3:8** Hebrew *to the Sabeans.*

¹²"Let the nations be called to arms. Let them march to the valley of Jehoshaphat. There I, the LORD, will sit to pronounce judgment on them all. ¹³Now let the sickle do its work, for the harvest is ripe. Come, tread the winepress because it is full. The storage vats are overflowing with the wickedness of these people."

¹⁴Thousands upon thousands are waiting in the valley of decision. It is there that the day of the LORD will soon arrive. ¹⁵The sun and moon will grow dark, and the stars will no longer shine. ¹⁶The LORD's voice will roar from Zion and thunder from Jerusalem, and the earth and heavens will begin to shake. But to his people of Israel, the LORD will be a welcoming refuge and a strong fortress.

¹⁷"Then you will know that I, the LORD your God, live in Zion, my holy mountain. Jerusalem will be holy forever, and foreign armies will never conquer her again. ¹⁸In that day the mountains will drip with sweet wine, and the hills will flow with milk. Water will fill the dry streambeds of Judah, and a fountain will burst forth from the LORD's Temple, watering the arid valley of acacias.* ¹⁹Egypt will become a wasteland and Edom a wilderness, because they attacked Judah and killed her innocent people. ²⁰"But Judah will remain forever, and Jerusalem will endure through all future generations. ²¹I will pardon my people's crimes, which I have not yet pardoned; and I, the LORD, will make my home in Jerusalem* with my people."

3:18 Hebrew *valley of Shittim.*   **3:21** Hebrew *Zion.*

SEPTEMBER 7 □ DAY 251
Faithfulness through the Years

 LOOK BACK Daniel first appeared in the book that bears his name as a transplanted teenager. By chapter 4, he was probably about seventy-six years old. And by the end of the book, he was a spry ninety-three!

Again and again Daniel demonstrated the *power* of God in the life of the *child* of God, enabling him to read writing on the banquet room wall . . . untangle beastly visions . . . decipher dreams involving seventies and sevens.

Daniel's life of singleness and single-minded devotion contrasts with Hosea's life as father of three and husband of an unfaithful wife. Hosea's fractured home became the backdrop for preaching to a fractured and faithless nation. God would heal, God would restore—if only Judah were interested in being cured. But her unrelenting disobedience and indifference left room for only one conclusion: "God will reject the people of Israel because they will not listen or obey" (Hosea 9:17).

In the wake of a devastating locust plague, Joel wrote his message of comfort and caution to the southern kingdom of Judah. Joy and gladness had evaporated from the house of the Lord, and the day of his vengeance was near. But the solution has always been the same, in Joel's generation and in yours: "Anyone who calls on the name of the LORD will be saved" (Joel 2:32).

 LOOK UP What's in a name? If you're a character in the pages of Scripture, the likely answer is "Plenty!" Here is a cast of characters from the book of Hosea and a suggested meaning for each name. Can you retell the story of the book of Hosea and his family experience just by using the names of his family members? Try it!

Love is a fabric that doesn't fade when washed in the water of adversity and grief.

Hosea means "salvation."
Gomer (his wife) means "completion."
Jezreel (his son) means "God plants."
Lo-ruhamah (his daughter) means "not loved."
Lo-ammi (his other son) means "not my people."

LOOK AHEAD There are no perfect families in the Bible because there are no perfect people. Regardless of your family background, you'll find something to identify with in the pages of the Bible.

Did you come from a home filled with jealousy and backbiting? You're in good company. So did the shepherd boy David and the eleventh of twelve brothers, Joseph.

Were your parents perhaps unfaithful to one another? Join the ranks with Jephthah, whose mother was a prostitute (Judges 11:1).

Has one of your parents been married more than once? Welcome to the club. The Samaritan woman whom Jesus met one day by a well in Sychar had been married and divorced *five times* and at the time was living with a sixth man (John 4:16-18).

The Bible does not condone this behavior, but neither does it seek to conceal the real family situation. And the point is clear: Regardless of the family situation from which you have come, God has a wonderful family in mind for your future—the family of God. His unconditional, undying love for you is modeled in Hosea's love for his unfaithful wife. It's a love that doesn't know when to quit! Do the members of your earthly family know about God's love yet? They can, you know, even without your saying a word (1 Peter 3:1).

Amos

TIMES were good in Israel. The nation basked in peace, prosperity, strength, and security. Then came Amos, breaking through the facade of respectability and exposing the rotten core of immorality, injustice, false optimism, and shallow piety. To those who had grown soft and lax in luxurious living, Amos declares God's terrible warning and issues God's last call to repentance. But the people fail to respond, and Amos announces God's unwelcome but necessary discipline.

Focus	Judgment Is Sure		Judgment Is Soon	
Divisions	Funnel of Fire	Fallen Family	Woes and Warnings	Rejection and Restoration
	1　　　　　　2	3　　　　　　5	6　　　　　　7	8　　　　　　9
Topics	Vengeance	Vindication	Visions	Victory
	Pronouncements		Pictures	
Place	Neighboring Nations	Northern Kingdom of Israel		
Time	About 10 Years (760–750 B.C.)			

SEPTEMBER 8 □ DAY 252
AMOS 1–2
The Funnel of Fire

OVERVIEW Amos, a southern shepherd sent north with God's awful message for Israel, begins with a series of stinging judgments on Israel's neighbors. In characteristically prophetic fashion, he harshly condemns the transgressions of the seven nations that surround Israel, and then he gradually "zeros in" on Israel itself. Each of his eight oracles in today's two chapters begins with the words, "The people of . . . have sinned again and again," meaning that each nation is full of sin. Therefore each nation receives the same sentence of doom: "I will send down fire" (1:4, 7, 10, 12, 14; 2:2, 5).

Chapter 1						Chapter 2	
Fiery Judgment on the Nations of							
Damascus	Gaza	Tyre	Edom	Ammon	Moab	Judah	Israel
1 5	6 8	9 10	11 12	13 15	1 3	4 5	6 16
Gentiles						Jews	

YOUR DAILY WALK Imagine Amos standing on your street corner loudly condemning the sins of your neighbors. He names your friends house by house, moving steadily around the block: "the Hoovers . . . the Kirks . . . the Wallaces . . . the Holmeses . . ." And then, horrified, you hear him name . . . you!

There is no such thing as a little sin because there is no such person as a little God to sin against.

What would Amos say about you? Mentally list those shortcomings, failures, and excesses that would embarrass you the most if announced from your street corner. Announce them yourself right now to God! There's no need to wait for fire to fall—or a prophet to knock—before you tend to an area of your life overdue for change!

INSIGHT Amos's Funnel of Fire
God is concerned for all nations, and they all must answer to his justice and judgment. Amos begins his "Rogues Gallery" with Israel's neighbors on all sides, then spirals inward, leaving the judgment of Israel for last. Can you sense the expectation building as Amos moves ever closer to the principal target of his sermon?

CHAPTER 1

This message was given to Amos, a shepherd from the town of Tekoa in Judah. He received this message in visions two years before the earthquake, when Uzziah was king of Judah and Jeroboam II, the son of Jehoash,* was king of Israel.

²This is his report of what he saw and heard: "The LORD's voice roars from his Temple on Mount Zion; he thunders from Jerusalem! Suddenly, the lush pastures of the shepherds dry up. All the grass on Mount Carmel withers and dies."

³This is what the LORD says: "The people of Damascus have sinned again and again, and I will not forget it. I will not let them go unpunished any longer! They beat down my people in Gilead as grain is threshed with threshing sledges of iron. ⁴So I will send down fire on King Hazael's palace, and the fortresses of King Ben-hadad will be destroyed. ⁵I will break down the gates of Damascus and slaughter its people all the way to the valley of Aven.* I will destroy the ruler in Beth-eden, and the people of Aram will return to Kir as slaves. I, the LORD, have spoken!"

1:1 Hebrew *Joash,* a variant name for Jehoash.   **1:5** *Aven* means "wickedness."

⁶This is what the LORD says: "The people of Gaza have sinned again and again, and I will not forget it. I will not let them go unpunished any longer! They sent my people into exile, selling them as slaves in Edom. ⁷So I will send down fire on the walls of Gaza, and all its fortresses will be destroyed. ⁸I will slaughter the people of Ashdod and destroy the king of Ashkelon. Then I will turn to attack Ekron, and the few Philistines still left will be killed. I, the Sovereign LORD, have spoken!"

⁹This is what the LORD says: "The people of Tyre have sinned again and again, and I will not forget it. I will not let them go unpunished any longer! They broke their treaty of brotherhood with Israel, selling whole villages as slaves to Edom. ¹⁰So I will send down fire on the walls of Tyre, and all its fortresses will be destroyed."

¹¹This is what the LORD says: "The people of Edom have sinned again and again, and I will not forget it. I will not let them go unpunished any longer! They chased down their relatives, the Israelites, with swords. They showed them no mercy and were unrelenting in their anger. ¹²So I will send down fire on Teman, and the fortresses of Bozrah will be destroyed."

¹³This is what the LORD says: "The people of Ammon have sinned again and again, and I will not forget it. I will not let them go unpunished any longer! When they attacked Gilead to extend their borders, they committed cruel crimes, ripping open pregnant women with their swords. ¹⁴So I will send down fire on the walls of Rabbah, and all its fortresses will be destroyed. There will be wild shouts during the battle, swirling like a whirlwind in a mighty storm. ¹⁵And their king* and his princes will go into exile together. I, the LORD, have spoken!"

CHAPTER 2

This is what the LORD says: "The people of Moab have sinned again and again, and I will not forget it. I will not let them go unpunished any longer! They desecrated the tomb of Edom's king and burned his bones to ashes. ²So I will send down fire on the land of Moab, and all the fortresses in Kerioth will be destroyed. The people will fall in the noise of battle, as the warriors shout and the trumpets blare. ³And I will destroy their king and slaughter all their princes. I, the LORD, have spoken!"

⁴This is what the LORD says: "The people of Judah have sinned again and again, and I will not forget it. I will not let them go unpunished any longer! They have rejected the laws of the LORD, refusing to obey him. They have been led astray by the same lies that deceived their ancestors. ⁵So I will send down fire on Judah, and all the fortresses of Jerusalem will be destroyed."

⁶This is what the LORD says: "The people of Israel have sinned again and again, and I will not forget it. I will not let them go unpunished any longer! They have perverted justice by selling honest people for silver and poor people for a pair of sandals. ⁷They trample helpless people in the dust and deny justice to those who are oppressed. Both father and son sleep with the same woman, corrupting my holy name. ⁸At their religious festivals, they lounge around in clothing stolen from their debtors. In the house of their god, they present offerings of wine purchased with stolen money.

⁹"Yet think of all I did for my people! I destroyed the Amorites before my people arrived in the land. The Amorites were as tall as cedar trees and strong as oaks, but I destroyed their fruit and dug out their roots. ¹⁰It was I who rescued you from Egypt and led you through the desert for forty years so you could possess the land of the Amorites. ¹¹I chose some of your sons to be prophets and others to be Nazirites. Can you deny this, my people of Israel?" asks the LORD. ¹²"But you caused the Nazirites to sin by making them drink your wine, and you said to my prophets, 'Shut up!'

¹³"So I will make you groan as a wagon groans when it is loaded down with grain. ¹⁴Your fastest runners will not get away. The strongest among you will become weak. Even the mightiest warriors will be unable to save themselves. ¹⁵The archers will fail to stand their ground. The swiftest soldiers won't be fast enough to escape. Even warriors on horses won't be able to outrun the danger. ¹⁶On that day, the most courageous of your fighting men will drop their weapons and run for their lives. I, the LORD, have spoken!"

1:15 Hebrew *malcam*, possibly referring to their god Molech.

SEPTEMBER 9 □ DAY 253
AMOS 3–5
A Fallen Family

OVERVIEW Many times over God has tried to bring the self-satisfied family of Israel to repentance. Famine, pestilence, drought, blight, death, defeat—and still the people of God cling to their sin. Violence and injustice, drunkenness and greed remain the hallmarks of their decadent way of life. The prophet has only one message left: "Prepare to meet your God as he comes in judgment, you people of Israel!" (4:12).

Chapter 3	Chapter 4	Chapter 5
Israel's Rebellion	God's Rejection	Resulting Retribution
Guilty	Judged	Sentenced

YOUR DAILY WALK Your car stalls repeatedly, so you go to a mechanic. He takes it for a test drive, and sure enough, while ascending a hill, the engine dies. Stepping on the brakes, he turns and announces to you cheerily, "Well, it's not so bad. After all, you could be rolling backwards!"

Do all the good you can, in all the ways you can, to all the people you can, as long as you can.

How would you evaluate that "mechanic"?

After reading today's section dealing with the sins of the fallen family of Israel, you may be tempted to conclude, "Well, at least I'm not that bad!" And you may be right. But are you "stalled" on the upward road of righteousness, your brakes firmly set—not really running after wickedness, but not actively pursuing godliness either?

Amos proposed to the people that they "do what is good . . . that you may live" (5:14). It is not enough, Amos declared, to avoid evil; you must also actively "do what is good." And that never happens by accident!

Across the top of the next five daily readings, write the name of one person you'll see each day. Then think of an "active good" you can do in the life of that individual: Offer a helping hand, a sincere compliment, a free lunch, an expression of friendship. Now let off those brakes and start again, confident that the Lord will be with you as you "spend your time and energy in training yourself for spiritual fitness" (1 Timothy 4:7).

INSIGHT The Hand That Rocks the Cradle Steadies the Nation
A comment by J. E. McFayden is cogent, and Amos 4:1-3 provides a case in point: "All the Hebrew prophets knew that for the temper and quality of a civilization, the women are greatly responsible. A country is largely what its women make it; if they are careless or unwomanly, the country is on the road to ruin." Think about that!

CHAPTER 3

Listen to this message that the LORD has spoken against you, O people of Israel and Judah—the entire family I rescued from Egypt: ²"From among all the families on the earth, I chose you alone. That is why I must punish you for all your sins."

³Can two people walk together without agreeing on the direction? ⁴Does a lion ever roar in a thicket without first finding a victim? Does a young lion growl in its den without first catching its prey? ⁵Does a bird ever get caught in a trap that has no bait? Does a trap ever spring shut when there's nothing there to catch? ⁶When the war trumpet blares, shouldn't the people be alarmed? When disaster comes to a city, isn't it because the LORD planned it?

⁷"But always, first of all, I warn you through my servants the prophets. I, the Sovereign LORD, have now done this."

[8]The lion has roared—tremble in fear! The Sovereign LORD has spoken—I dare not refuse to proclaim his message!

[9]Announce this to the leaders of Philistia* and Egypt: "Take your seats now on the hills around Samaria, and witness the scandalous spectacle of all Israel's crimes."

[10]"My people have forgotten what it means to do right," says the LORD. "Their fortresses are filled with wealth taken by theft and violence. [11]Therefore," says the Sovereign LORD, "an enemy is coming! He will surround them and shatter their defenses. Then he will plunder all their fortresses."

[12]This is what the LORD says: "A shepherd who tries to rescue a sheep from a lion's mouth will recover only two legs and a piece of ear. So it will be when the Israelites in Samaria are rescued with only a broken chair and a tattered pillow. [13]Now listen to this, and announce it throughout all Israel,*" says the Lord, the LORD God Almighty. [14]"On the very day I punish Israel for its sins, I will destroy the pagan altars at Bethel. The horns of the altar will be cut off and fall to the ground. [15]And I will destroy the beautiful homes of the wealthy—their winter mansions and their summer houses, too—all their palaces filled with ivory. I, the LORD, have spoken!"

CHAPTER 4

Listen to me, you "fat cows" of Samaria, you women who oppress the poor and crush the needy and who are always asking your husbands for another drink! [2]The Sovereign LORD has sworn this by his holiness: "The time will come when you will be led away with hooks in your noses. Every last one of you will be dragged away like a fish on a hook! [3]You will leave by going straight through the breaks in the wall; you will be thrown from your fortresses.* I, the LORD, have spoken!

[4]"Go ahead and offer your sacrifices to the idols at Bethel and Gilgal. Keep on disobeying—your sins are mounting up! Offer sacrifices each morning and bring your tithes every three days! [5]Present your bread made with yeast as an offering of thanksgiving. Then give your extra voluntary offerings so you can brag about it

everywhere! This is the kind of thing you Israelites love to do," says the Sovereign LORD.

[6]"I brought hunger to every city and famine to every town. But still you wouldn't return to me," says the LORD.

[7]"I kept the rain from falling when you needed it the most, ruining all your crops. I sent rain on one town but withheld it from another. Rain fell on one field, while another field withered away. [8]People staggered from one town to another for a drink of water, but there was never enough. But still you wouldn't return to me," says the LORD.

[9]"I struck your farms and vineyards with blight and mildew. Locusts devoured all your fig and olive trees. But still you wouldn't return to me," says the LORD.

[10]"I sent plagues against you like the plagues I sent against Egypt long ago. I killed your young men in war and slaughtered all your horses. The stench of death filled the air! But still you wouldn't return to me," says the LORD.

[11]"I destroyed some of your cities, as I destroyed* Sodom and Gomorrah. Those of you who survived were like half-burned sticks snatched from a fire. But still you wouldn't return to me," says the LORD.

[12]"Therefore, I will bring upon you all these further disasters I have announced. Prepare to meet your God as he comes in judgment, you people of Israel!"

[13]For the LORD is the one who shaped the mountains, stirs up the winds, and reveals his every thought. He turns the light of dawn into darkness and treads the mountains under his feet. The LORD God Almighty is his name!

CHAPTER 5

Listen, you people of Israel! Listen to this funeral song I am singing:

[2] "The virgin Israel has fallen,
    never to rise again!
  She lies forsaken on the ground,
    with none to raise her up."

[3]The Sovereign LORD says: "When one of your cities sends a thousand men to battle, only a hundred will return. When a town sends a hundred, only ten will come back alive."

3:9 Hebrew *Ashdod.*   **3:13** Hebrew *the house of Jacob.*   **4:3** Hebrew *thrown out toward Harmon,* possibly a reference to Mount Hermon.   **4:11** Hebrew *as when God destroyed.*

[4]Now this is what the LORD says to the family of Israel: "Come back to me and live! [5]Don't go to worship the idols of Bethel, Gilgal, or Beersheba. For the people of Gilgal will be dragged off into exile, and the people of Bethel will come to nothing."

[6]Come back to the LORD and live! If you don't, he will roar through Israel* like a fire, devouring you completely. Your gods in Bethel certainly won't be able to quench the flames! [7]You wicked people! You twist justice, making it a bitter pill for the poor and oppressed. Righteousness and fair play are meaningless fictions to you.

[8]It is the LORD who created the stars, the Pleiades and Orion. It is he who turns darkness into morning and day into night. It is he who draws up water from the oceans and pours it down as rain on the land. The LORD is his name! [9]With blinding speed and power he destroys the strong, crushing all their defenses.

[10]How you hate honest judges! How you despise people who tell the truth! [11]You trample the poor and steal what little they have through taxes and unfair rent. Therefore, you will never live in the beautiful stone houses you are building. You will never drink wine from the lush vineyards you are planting. [12]For I know the vast number of your sins and rebellions. You oppress good people by taking bribes and deprive the poor of justice in the courts. [13]So those who are wise will keep quiet, for it is an evil time.

[14]Do what is good and run from evil—that you may live! Then the LORD God Almighty will truly be your helper, just as you have claimed he is. [15]Hate evil and love what is good; remodel your courts into true halls of justice. Perhaps even yet the LORD God Almighty will have mercy on his people who remain.*

[16]Therefore, this is what the Lord, the LORD God Almighty, says: "There will be crying in all the public squares and in every street. Call for the farmers to weep with you, and summon professional mourners to wail and lament. [17]There will be wailing in every vineyard, for I will pass through and destroy them all. I, the LORD, have spoken!"

[18]How terrible it will be for you who say, "If only the day of the LORD were here! For then the LORD would rescue us from all our enemies." But you have no idea what you are wishing for. That day will not bring light and prosperity, but darkness and disaster. [19]In that day you will be like a man who runs from a lion—only to meet a bear. After escaping the bear, he leans his hand against a wall in his house—and is bitten by a snake. [20]Yes, the day of the LORD will be a dark and hopeless day, without a ray of joy or hope.

[21]"I hate all your show and pretense—the hypocrisy of your religious festivals and solemn assemblies. [22]I will not accept your burnt offerings and grain offerings. I won't even notice all your choice peace offerings. [23]Away with your hymns of praise! They are only noise to my ears. I will not listen to your music, no matter how lovely it is. [24]Instead, I want to see a mighty flood of justice, a river of righteous living that will never run dry.

[25]"Was it to me you were bringing sacrifices and offerings during the forty years in the wilderness, Israel? [26]No, your real interest was in your pagan gods—Sakkuth your king god and Kaiwan your star god—the images you yourselves made.* [27]So I will send you into exile, to a land east of Damascus," says the LORD, whose name is God Almighty.

5:6 Hebrew *the house of Joseph.*   5:15 Hebrew *on the remnant of Joseph.*   5:26 Greek version reads *You took up the shrine of Molech,* *and the star of your god Rephan, and the images you made for yourselves.*

SEPTEMBER 10 ☐ DAY 254
AMOS 6–7
Woes and Warnings

OVERVIEW Israel has grown fat, apathetic, and proud, choking on its own luxury. God's verdict is fitting: "Therefore, you will be the first to be led away as captives. Suddenly, all your revelry will end" (6:7). The prophet relates a series of visions in which God stays his hand of punishment repeatedly—but no more. The plumb line of his righteousness shows how far out of line the people have drifted, prompting Amos to report God's new resolve: "I will no longer ignore all their sins" (7:8).

Chapter 6		Chapter 7
Woe to the Complacent	Woe to the Proud	Three Warnings of Doom
1 7	8 14	
Violations of God's Law		Visions of God's Wrath

YOUR DAILY WALK A wife and mother looks for employment in order to help pay for the family's second car—a car purchased so that she would have good transportation to and from her new job! A man works double shifts and weekends so that his overtime income will cover the payments on his new camper and boat. But when vacation time comes, he's too exhausted to drive to the lake.

Close your eyes and you will see everything you actually possess.

A wealthy executive relates how, as a young man, he recklessly spent his health to make millions—and now, later in life, he finds himself spending the millions he earned to regain the health he lost.

Each of these stories illustrates the subtle effects of materialism—a sickness characterized by an overwhelming desire to own things that all too often turn around and begin to "own" you!

Luxury-loving Israel was so "owned" by its possessions and materialistic lifestyle that God had become the "previous owner." Enjoying *things* from God had replaced enjoying *God himself*.

You may proudly think of your house, your car, your boat, your (whatever) as being "owned by me," but never forget it is also "loaned by God"! Wouldn't now be a good time to consider a "transfer of ownership"?

INSIGHT Wine by the Bowlful
For the gluttonous people of God, an ordinary cup was not large enough (6:6), so they used enormous vessels customarily reserved for sacrificial purposes (Exodus 38:3; Zechariah 14:20).

CHAPTER 6

How terrible it will be for you who lounge in luxury and think you are secure in Jerusalem* and Samaria! You are famous and popular in Israel, you to whom the people go for help. ²Go over to Calneh and see what happened there. Then go to the great city of Hamath and on down to the Philistine city of Gath. You are no better than they were, and look at how they were destroyed. ³You push away every thought of

coming disaster, but your actions only bring the day of judgment closer.

⁴How terrible it will be for you who sprawl on ivory beds surrounded with luxury, eating the meat of tender lambs and choice calves. ⁵You sing idle songs to the sound of the harp, and you fancy yourselves to be great musicians, as King David was. ⁶You drink wine by the bowlful, and you perfume yourselves with exotic fragrances, caring nothing at all that

6:1 Hebrew *Zion.*

your nation* is going to ruin. ⁷Therefore, you will be the first to be led away as captives. Suddenly, all your revelry will end.

⁸The Sovereign LORD has sworn by his own name, and this is what he, the LORD God Almighty, says: "I despise the pride and false glory of Israel,* and I hate their beautiful homes. I will give this city and everything in it to their enemies."

⁹If there are ten men left in one house, they will all die. ¹⁰And when a close relative—one who is responsible for burning the dead—goes into the house to carry away a dead body, he will ask the last survivor, "Is there anyone else with you?" And the person will answer, "No!" Then he will say, "Hush! Don't even whisper the name of the LORD. He might hear you!"

¹¹When the LORD gives the command, homes both great and small will be smashed to pieces. ¹²Can horses gallop over rocks? Can oxen be used to plow rocks? Stupid even to ask—but that's how stupid you are when you turn justice into poison and make bitter the sweet fruit of righteousness. ¹³And just as stupid is this bragging about your conquest of Lo-debar.* You boast, "Didn't we take Karnaim* by our own strength and power?"

¹⁴"O people of Israel, I am about to bring an enemy nation against you," says the LORD God Almighty. "It will oppress you bitterly throughout your land—from Lebo-hamath in the north to the Arabah Valley in the south."

CHAPTER 7

The Sovereign LORD showed me a vision. I saw him preparing to send a vast swarm of locusts over the land. This was after the king's share had been harvested from the fields and as the main crop was coming up. ²In my vision the locusts ate everything in sight that was green. Then I said, "O Sovereign LORD, please forgive your people! Unless you relent, Israel* will not survive, for we are only a small nation."

³So the LORD relented and did not fulfill the vision. "I won't do it," he said.

⁴Then the Sovereign LORD showed me another vision. I saw him preparing to punish his people with a great fire. The fire had burned up the depths of the sea and was devouring the entire land. ⁵Then I said, "O Sovereign LORD, please don't do it. Unless you relent, Israel will not survive, for we are only a small nation."

⁶Then the LORD turned from this plan, too. "I won't do that either," said the Sovereign LORD.

⁷Then he showed me another vision. I saw the Lord standing beside a wall that had been built using a plumb line. He was checking it with a plumb line to see if it was straight. ⁸And the LORD said to me, "Amos, what do you see?"

I answered, "A plumb line."

And the Lord replied, "I will test my people with this plumb line. I will no longer ignore all their sins. ⁹The pagan shrines of your ancestors* and the temples of Israel will be destroyed, and I will bring the dynasty of King Jeroboam to a sudden end."

¹⁰But when Amaziah, the priest of Bethel, heard what Amos was saying, he rushed a message to King Jeroboam: "Amos is hatching a plot against you right here on your very doorstep! What he is saying is intolerable. It will lead to rebellion all across the land. ¹¹He is saying, 'Jeroboam will soon be killed and the people of Israel will be sent away into exile.'"

¹²Then Amaziah sent orders to Amos: "Get out of here, you seer! Go on back to the land of Judah and do your preaching there! ¹³Don't bother us here in Bethel with your prophecies, especially not here where the royal sanctuary is!"

¹⁴But Amos replied, "I'm not one of your professional prophets. I certainly never trained to be one. I'm just a shepherd, and I take care of fig trees. ¹⁵But the LORD called me away from my flock and told me, 'Go and prophesy to my people in Israel.'

¹⁶"Now then, listen to this message from the LORD! You say, 'Don't prophesy against Israel. Stop preaching against my people.*' ¹⁷But this is what the LORD says: Because you have refused to listen, your wife will become a prostitute in this city, and your sons and daughters will be killed. Your land will be divided up, and you yourself will die in a foreign land. And the people of Israel will certainly become captives in exile, far from their homeland."

6:6 Hebrew *Joseph.*   6:8 Hebrew *Jacob.*   6:13a *Lo-debar* means "nothing."   6:13b *Karnaim* means "horns," a term that symbolizes strength.   7:2 Hebrew *Jacob;* also in 7:5.   7:9 Hebrew *of Isaac.*   7:16 Hebrew *against the house of Isaac.*

SEPTEMBER 11 □ DAY 255
AMOS 8–9
Visions of Horror and Hope

OVERVIEW Amos's series of visions concludes with a picture of the people's irreversible corruption (basket of ripe fruit) and a sign of God's inescapable judgment (the Lord on the altar). Disaster will come like a flood, leaving the people in helpless despair. And yet, through the present darkness comes a prophetic glimmer of hope: "'In that day I will restore the fallen kingdom of David. . . . I will bring my exiled people of Israel back from distant lands. . . . I will firmly plant them there in the land I have given them,' says the LORD your God" (9:11, 14-15).

Chapter 8		Chapter 9	
Judgment Is Ripe	1	The Lord Is Right	10 | 11 Israel Is Restored	15
No Escape		No Partiality	New Prosperity

YOUR DAILY WALK God pursues. His love causes him to pursue us in order to show his mercy. And when we reject his gracious overtures, his holiness causes him to pursue us in order to show his justice.

How do you run away from the God who is everywhere? "Even if they dig down to the place of the dead, I will reach down and pull them up. Even if they climb up into the heavens, I will bring them down" (9:2). Climb the highest mountain or plunge the deepest depth, and even there you will find the pursuing God.

Have you been seeking to elude God? Amos's message is clear: Run *to* him, not *from* him. He stands ready to restore, to forgive, to cleanse— if you will just let him. The nation of Israel refused to acknowledge God's pursuit, and the rest is sordid history. Talk to God now about what you want the outcome of his pursuit to be in your life.

This is the fundamental thing, the most serious thing of all, that we are always in the presence of God.

INSIGHT Law Enforcement God's Way
The first six verses of chapter 9 paint the darkest picture yet of Israel's coming captivity. There will be total destruction and death—no possible way of escape, no spiritual refuge or earthly security. God's people will learn—the hard way—that the God who is big enough to declare such threats in advance is also powerful enough to put his threats into effect!

CHAPTER 8
Then the Sovereign LORD showed me another vision. In it I saw a basket filled with ripe fruit. ²"What do you see, Amos?" he asked.

I replied, "A basket full of ripe fruit."

Then the LORD said, "This fruit represents my people of Israel—ripe for punishment! I will not delay their punishment again. ³In that day the riotous sounds of singing in the Temple will turn to wailing. Dead bodies will be scattered everywhere. They will be carried out of the city in silence. I, the Sovereign LORD, have spoken!"

⁴Listen to this, you who rob the poor and

trample the needy! ⁵You can't wait for the Sabbath day to be over and the religious festivals to end so you can get back to cheating the helpless. You measure out your grain in false measures and weigh it out on dishonest scales. ⁶And you mix the wheat you sell with chaff swept from the floor! Then you enslave poor people for a debt of one piece of silver or a pair of sandals.

⁷Now the LORD has sworn this oath by his own name, the Pride of Israel*: "I will never forget the wicked things you have done! ⁸The earth will tremble for your deeds, and everyone will mourn. The land

8:7 Hebrew *the pride of Jacob.*

will rise up like the Nile River at floodtime, toss about, and sink again. ⁹At that time," says the Sovereign LORD, "I will make the sun go down at noon and darken the earth while it is still day. ¹⁰I will turn your celebrations into times of mourning, and your songs of joy will be turned to weeping. You will wear funeral clothes and shave your heads as signs of sorrow, as if your only son had died. How very bitter that day will be!

¹¹"The time is surely coming," says the Sovereign LORD, "when I will send a famine on the land—not a famine of bread or water but of hearing the words of the LORD. ¹²People will stagger everywhere from sea to sea, searching for the word of the LORD, running here and going there, but they will not find it. ¹³Beautiful girls and fine young men will grow faint and weary, thirsting for the LORD's word. ¹⁴And those who worship and swear by the idols of Samaria, Dan, and Beersheba will fall down, never to rise again."

CHAPTER 9

Then I saw a vision of the Lord standing beside the altar. He said, "Strike the tops of the Temple columns so hard that the foundation will shake. Smash the columns so the roof will crash down on the people below. Then those who survive will be slaughtered in battle. No one will escape!

²"Even if they dig down to the place of the dead,* I will reach down and pull them up. Even if they climb up into the heavens, I will bring them down. ³Even if they hide at the very top of Mount Carmel, I will search them out and capture them. Even if they hide at the bottom of the ocean, I will send the great sea serpent after them to bite and destroy them. ⁴Even if they are driven into exile, I will command the sword to kill them there. I am determined to bring disaster upon them and not to help them."

⁵The Lord, the LORD Almighty, touches

the land and it melts, and all its people mourn. The ground rises like the Nile River at floodtime, and then it sinks again. ⁶The upper stories of the LORD's home are in the heavens, while its foundation is on the earth. He draws up water from the oceans and pours it down as rain on the land. The LORD is his name!

⁷"Do you Israelites think you are more important to me than the Ethiopians*?" asks the LORD. "I brought you out of Egypt, but have I not done as much for other nations, too? I brought the Philistines from Crete* and led the Arameans out of Kir.

⁸"I, the Sovereign LORD, am watching this sinful nation of Israel, and I will uproot it and scatter its people across the earth. Yet I have promised that I will never completely destroy the family of Israel,*" says the LORD. ⁹"For I have commanded that Israel be persecuted by the other nations as grain is sifted in a sieve, yet not one true kernel will be lost. ¹⁰But all the sinners will die by the sword—all those who say, 'Nothing bad will happen to us.'

¹¹"In that day I will restore the fallen kingdom of David. It is now like a house in ruins, but I will rebuild its walls and restore its former glory. ¹²And Israel will possess what is left of Edom and all the nations I have called to be mine. I, the LORD, have spoken, and I will do these things.

¹³"The time will come," says the LORD, "when the grain and grapes will grow faster than they can be harvested. Then the terraced vineyards on the hills of Israel will drip with sweet wine! ¹⁴I will bring my exiled people of Israel back from distant lands, and they will rebuild their ruined cities and live in them again. They will plant vineyards and gardens; they will eat their crops and drink their wine. ¹⁵I will firmly plant them there in the land I have given them," says the LORD your God. "Then they will never be uprooted again."

9:2 Hebrew *to Sheol.*   9:7a Hebrew *the Cushites.*   9:7b Hebrew *Caphtor.*   9:8 Hebrew *the house of Jacob.*

Obadiah

EDOM and Israel should have existed in brotherly harmony as neighbors. After all, they are in the same family: Edom is descended from Esau and Israel from Jacob. But in a moment of urgent need, with Israel's enemies knocking at the gates of Jerusalem, the Edomites rush in to help . . . the enemy! As a result, God sends his prophet Obadiah to predict extinction for the haughty Edomites. In contrast, God promises that his people will ultimately destroy their enemies and live in peace.

Focus	Destruction of Edom		Success of Israel	
Divisions	Destruction Predicted	Destruction Explained	Judgment on Nations	Restoration of Israel
	1 9	10 14	15 16	17 21
Topics	Edom's Arrogance	Edom's Antagonism	Edom's Annihilation	
	Defeat of Israel		Victory of Israel	
Place	Edom and Israel			
Time	Approximately 840 B.C.			

SEPTEMBER 12 ☐ DAY 256
OBADIAH
An Ancient Family Feud

OVERVIEW A struggle that began in the womb between twin brothers, Esau and Jacob, grows into a struggle between their respective descendants, the Edomites and the Israelites. Obadiah soundly condemns the Edomites for their stubborn refusal to aid Israel, first during the time of wilderness wandering (Numbers 20:14-21) and later during a time of invasion. This little-known prophet describes the Edomites' crimes, tries their case, and pronounces their judgment: total destruction. Did the prophet's prediction of doom come true? To find out, you need only look at a map of the world today.

Verses 1-9	Verses 10-14	Verses 15-21
Edom's Arrogance	Edom's Antagonism	Edom's Annihilation
Condemnation	Charge	Consummation

YOUR DAILY WALK *Family Feud* (definition #1): a TV game show that pits two families against each other. The goal: huge sums of prize money. Ratings: high. Future prospects: syndicated reruns.

Hating others is like burning down your house to get rid of a rat.

Family Feud (definition #2): an ancient struggle between two brother nations. The goal: preserving personal pride. Ratings: low (audience of one—God himself!). Future prospects: soon to be canceled (v. 10).

What a tragedy that the strife between Esau and Jacob, a contention settled in their own lifetimes (Genesis 32–33), should reappear in the form of bitter jealousy and hatred between their respective nations. Esau's offspring maintained their enmity toward Israel for more than a thousand years!

How are things in your immediate family? Is there someone—brother, sister, parent, child, in-law—with whom you are holding a family feud? Let Psalm 133:1 show you a time-tested way to resolve that conflict. Learn from the doom of Edom.

INSIGHT A Major Distinction for a Minor Prophet
Evidence indicates that Obadiah's message against Edom was probably delivered in response to the Edomites' opposition to Israel (and collaboration with the Philistines in a raid on Jerusalem) during Jehoram's reign about 845 B.C. (See 2 Chronicles 21:8-10, 16-17.) If so, this would make Obadiah the earliest of the minor prophets.

This is the vision that the Sovereign LORD revealed to Obadiah concerning the land of Edom.

We have heard a message from the LORD that an ambassador was sent to the nations to say, "Get ready, everyone! Let's assemble our armies and attack Edom!"

²The LORD says, "I will cut you down to size among the nations, Edom; you will be small and despised. ³You are proud because you live in a rock fortress and make your home high in the mountains. 'Who can ever reach us way up here?' you ask boastfully. Don't fool yourselves! ⁴Though you

soar as high as eagles and build your nest among the stars, I will bring you crashing down. I, the LORD, have spoken!

[5]"If thieves came at night and robbed you, they would not take everything. Those who harvest grapes always leave a few for the poor. But your enemies will wipe you out completely! [6]Every nook and cranny of Edom* will be searched and looted. Every treasure will be found and taken.

[7]"All your allies will turn against you. They will help to chase you from your land. They will promise you peace, while plotting your destruction. Your trusted friends will set traps for you, and you won't even know about it. [8]At that time not a single wise person will be left in the whole land of Edom!" says the LORD. "For on the mountains of Edom I will destroy everyone who has wisdom and understanding. [9]The mightiest warriors of Teman will be terrified, and everyone on the mountains of Edom will be cut down in the slaughter.

[10]"And why? Because of the violence you did to your close relatives in Israel.* Now you will be destroyed completely and filled with shame forever. [11]For you deserted your relatives in Israel during their time of greatest need. You stood aloof, refusing to lift a finger to help when foreign invaders carried off their wealth and cast lots to divide up Jerusalem. You acted as though you were one of Israel's enemies.

[12]"You shouldn't have done this! You shouldn't have gloated when they exiled your relatives to distant lands. You shouldn't have rejoiced because they were suffering such misfortune. You shouldn't have crowed over them as they suffered these disasters. [13]You shouldn't have plundered the land of Israel when they were suffering such calamity. You shouldn't have gloated over the destruction of your relatives, looting their homes and making yourselves rich at their expense. [14]You shouldn't have stood at the crossroads, killing those who tried to escape. You shouldn't have captured the survivors, handing them over to their enemies in that terrible time of trouble.

[15]"The day is near when I, the LORD, will judge the godless nations! As you have done to Israel, so it will be done to you. All your evil deeds will fall back on your own heads. [16]Just as you swallowed up my people on my holy mountain, so you and the surrounding nations will swallow the punishment I pour out on you. Yes, you nations will drink and stagger and disappear from history, as though you had never even existed.

[17]"But Jerusalem* will become a refuge for those who escape; it will be a holy place. And the people of Israel* will come back to reclaim their inheritance. [18]At that time Israel will be a raging fire, and Edom, a field of dry stubble. The fire will roar across the field, devouring everything and leaving no survivors in Edom. I, the LORD, have spoken!

[19]"Then my people living in the Negev will occupy the mountains of Edom. Those living in the foothills of Judah* will possess the Philistine plains and take over the fields of Ephraim and Samaria. And the people of Benjamin will occupy the land of Gilead. [20]The exiles of Israel will return to their land and occupy the Phoenician coast as far north as Zarephath. The captives from Jerusalem exiled in the north* will return to their homeland and resettle the villages of the Negev. [21]Deliverers will go up to* Mount Zion in Jerusalem to rule over the mountains of Edom. And the LORD himself will be king!"

6 Hebrew *Esau;* also in 8b, 9, 18, 19, 21.   **10** Hebrew *your brother Jacob.*   **17a** Hebrew *Mount Zion.*   **17b** Hebrew *house of Jacob;* also in 18.   **19** Hebrew *the Shephelah.*   **20** Hebrew *in Sepharad.*   **21** Or *from.*

Jonah

JONAH despised the brutal Assyrian city of Nineveh. So when God tells him to go warn them of their impending destruction, Jonah sets sail in the opposite direction. God sends a storm to fetch him back, and at his own request Jonah is tossed overboard. A great fish swallows God's prophet and deposits him on dry land. Result: Jonah goes straight to Nineveh. When the people repent, God mercifully withholds punishment. God then teaches the resentful Jonah firsthand of his compassion.

Focus	Revival for a Prophet				Revival for a Pagan City			
Divisions	Prophet's Disobedience	Prophet's Danger	Prophet's Prayer	Prophet's Deliverance	Prophet's Obedience	Pagans' Repentance	Prophet's Complaint	Prophet's Rebuke
	1:1 1:3	1:4 1:17	2:1 2:9	2:10	3:1 3:4	3:5 3:10	4:1 4:5	4:6 4:11
Topics	Mercy on Jonah				Mercy on Nineveh			
	Jonah in the Ship		Jonah in the Fish		Jonah in the City		Jonah in the Suburbs	
Place	The Sea				The City			
Time	Approximately 760 B.C.							

SEPTEMBER 13 ☐ DAY 257

JONAH 1–4
God's Reaching Mercy

OVERVIEW When God assigns Jonah to preach a revival in Nineveh, the reluctant prophet ships out instead for Tarshish—precisely in the opposite direction! But God pursues him. He uses a fierce wind and a hungry fish to deposit Jonah on shore once again, ready now to respond to God's directive. Using a divinely given one-sentence sermon, Jonah watches in amazement as one of the greatest revivals in history takes place—"from the greatest to the least" of the inhabitants of Nineveh (3:5). But rather than rejoice at Nineveh's spiritual awakening, Jonah is disappointed that Israel's archenemy now will not be destroyed. God must teach his pouting prophet a lesson on divine mercy.

Chapter 1	Chapter 2	Chapter 3	Chapter 4
Jonah's Disobedience	Jonah's Distress	Jonah's Declaration	Jonah's Displeasure
In the Ship	In the Fish	In the City	In the Sunlight

YOUR DAILY WALK God has a marvelous way of bringing his children great opportunities brilliantly disguised as impossible situations!

Consider Jonah. Summoned by God on short notice to preach to Israel's cruelest foe, Jonah hits the panic button and runs for cover. Finally turned around by God and sent by "special delivery" to Nineveh, Jonah reluctantly preaches his message of repentance. Once again, God does the unexpected by bringing sweeping revival to the city. But instead of rejoicing over the salvation of lost souls, Jonah withdraws to grumble at God.

Mercy imitates God and disappoints Satan.

Are you prepared to handle a "mission impossible" today? a shift in plans? an unexpected interruption? an opportunity cleverly disguised as an imposition? Today, the first time something unexpected happens (and it will!), resist the urge to hit the panic button. Instead, look for the door of opportunity God is opening to you, and take it. Let others experience God's mercy through you!

INSIGHT Jonah's Story—*Did* It Happen? *Could* It Happen?
There are at least two documented cases of men who were swallowed by sharks or whales and lived to tell about it. In answer to the question, Did it happen? check Matthew 12:38-41 for confirmation from an irrefutable source!

CHAPTER 1
The LORD gave this message to Jonah son of Amittai: ²"Get up and go to the great city of Nineveh! Announce my judgment against it because I have seen how wicked its people are."

³But Jonah got up and went in the opposite direction in order to get away from the LORD. He went down to the seacoast, to the port of Joppa, where he found a ship leaving for Tarshish. He bought a ticket and went on board, hoping that by going away to the west he could escape from the LORD.

⁴But as the ship was sailing along, suddenly the LORD flung a powerful wind over the sea, causing a violent storm that threatened to send them to the bottom.

⁵Fearing for their lives, the desperate sailors shouted to their gods for help and threw the cargo overboard to lighten the ship. And all this time Jonah was sound asleep down in the hold. ⁶So the captain went down after him. "How can you sleep at a time like this?" he shouted. "Get up and pray to your god! Maybe he will have mercy on us and spare our lives."

⁷Then the crew cast lots to see which of them had offended the gods and caused the terrible storm. When they did this, Jonah lost the toss. ⁸"What have you done to bring this awful storm down on us?" they demanded. "Who are you? What is your line of work? What country are you from? What is your nationality?"

⁹And Jonah answered, "I am a Hebrew, and I worship the LORD, the God of heaven, who made the sea and the land." ¹⁰Then he told them that he was running away from the LORD.

The sailors were terrified when they heard this. "Oh, why did you do it?" they groaned. ¹¹And since the storm was getting worse all the time, they asked him, "What should we do to you to stop this storm?"

¹²"Throw me into the sea," Jonah said, "and it will become calm again. For I know that this terrible storm is all my fault."

¹³Instead, the sailors tried even harder to row the boat ashore. But the stormy sea was too violent for them, and they couldn't make it. ¹⁴Then they cried out to the LORD, Jonah's God. "O LORD," they pleaded, "don't make us die for this man's sin. And don't hold us responsible for his death, because it isn't our fault. O LORD, you have sent this storm upon him for your own good reasons."

¹⁵Then the sailors picked Jonah up and threw him into the raging sea, and the storm stopped at once! ¹⁶The sailors were awestruck by the LORD's great power, and they offered him a sacrifice and vowed to serve him.

¹⁷Now the LORD had arranged for a great fish to swallow Jonah. And Jonah was inside the fish for three days and three nights.

CHAPTER 2

Then Jonah prayed to the LORD his God from inside the fish. ²He said, "I cried out to the LORD in my great trouble, and he answered me. I called to you from the

world of the dead,* and LORD, you heard me! ³You threw me into the ocean depths, and I sank down to the heart of the sea. I was buried beneath your wild and stormy waves. ⁴Then I said, 'O LORD, you have driven me from your presence. How will I ever again see your holy Temple?'

⁵"I sank beneath the waves, and death was very near. The waters closed in around me, and seaweed wrapped itself around my head. ⁶I sank down to the very roots of the mountains. I was locked out of life and imprisoned in the land of the dead. But you, O LORD my God, have snatched me from the yawning jaws of death!

⁷"When I had lost all hope, I turned my thoughts once more to the LORD. And my earnest prayer went out to you in your holy Temple. ⁸Those who worship false gods turn their backs on all God's mercies. ⁹But I will offer sacrifices to you with songs of praise, and I will fulfill all my vows. For my salvation comes from the LORD alone."

¹⁰Then the LORD ordered the fish to spit up Jonah on the beach, and it did.

CHAPTER 3

Then the LORD spoke to Jonah a second time: ²"Get up and go to the great city of Nineveh, and deliver the message of judgment I have given you."

³This time Jonah obeyed the LORD's command and went to Nineveh, a city so large that it took three days to see it all. ⁴On the day Jonah entered the city, he shouted to the crowds: "Forty days from now Nineveh will be destroyed!" ⁵The people of Nineveh believed God's message, and from the greatest to the least, they decided to go without food and wear sackcloth to show their sorrow.

⁶When the king of Nineveh heard what Jonah was saying, he stepped down from his throne and took off his royal robes. He dressed himself in sackcloth and sat on a heap of ashes. ⁷Then the king and his nobles sent this decree throughout the city: "No one, not even the animals, may eat or drink anything at all. ⁸Everyone is required to wear sackcloth and pray earnestly to God. Everyone must turn from their evil ways and stop all their violence. ⁹Who can tell? Perhaps even yet God will have pity

2:2 Hebrew *from Sheol.*

on us and hold back his fierce anger from destroying us."

¹⁰When God saw that they had put a stop to their evil ways, he had mercy on them and didn't carry out the destruction he had threatened.

CHAPTER 4

This change of plans upset Jonah, and he became very angry. ²So he complained to the LORD about it: "Didn't I say before I left home that you would do this, LORD? That is why I ran away to Tarshish! I knew that you were a gracious and compassionate God, slow to get angry and filled with unfailing love. I knew how easily you could cancel your plans for destroying these people. ³Just kill me now, LORD! I'd rather be dead than alive because nothing I predicted is going to happen."

⁴The LORD replied, "Is it right for you to be angry about this?"

⁵Then Jonah went out to the east side of the city and made a shelter to sit under as he waited to see if anything would happen to the city. ⁶And the LORD God arranged for

4:11 Hebrew *people who don't know their right hands from their left.*

a leafy plant to grow there, and soon it spread its broad leaves over Jonah's head, shading him from the sun. This eased some of his discomfort, and Jonah was very grateful for the plant.

⁷But God also prepared a worm! The next morning at dawn the worm ate through the stem of the plant, so that it soon died and withered away. ⁸And as the sun grew hot, God sent a scorching east wind to blow on Jonah. The sun beat down on his head until he grew faint and wished to die. "Death is certainly better than this!" he exclaimed.

⁹Then God said to Jonah, "Is it right for you to be angry because the plant died?"

"Yes," Jonah retorted, "even angry enough to die!"

¹⁰Then the LORD said, "You feel sorry about the plant, though you did nothing to put it there. And a plant is only, at best, short lived. ¹¹But Nineveh has more than 120,000 people living in spiritual darkness,* not to mention all the animals. Shouldn't I feel sorry for such a great city?"

SEPTEMBER 14 □ DAY 258
Loving Others as Only God Can

 LOOK BACK Amos, Obadiah, and Jonah were three minor prophets with a message of major importance. Amos (whose name means "burden bearer") leaves his country roots as a shepherd and fig picker to bring a fiery message of judgment upon the northern kingdom of Israel. Obadiah ("servant of the Lord") declares a scathing indictment upon the Edomites for their cruelty toward their brother nation Israel; and Jonah ("dove") takes a boat ride and a "whale" of a thrill ride before he arrives in Nineveh to announce a forty-day countdown to calamity for the mighty nation of Assyria.

Amos uses three sermons and five visions to portray in graphic detail Israel's unavoidable judgment. Obadiah, though the shortest book in the Old Testament, carries one of the strongest messages of judgment, offering Edom no plea to return and no promise of avoiding national calamity. Jonah, the only Old Testament prophetic book that revolves exclusively around a Gentile nation, shows it is possible for the audience (Nineveh) to repent, even though the preacher (Jonah) is hesitant to preach!

God invites us to burden him with what burdens us.

LOOK UP "The world would be a better place if only God would destroy _____ ."

Few of us are bold enough to *utter* those words, but most of us have *considered* that thought at one time or another. If only God would get rid of the world powers that threaten the safety of our nation . . . the criminals who kill without conscience . . . the doctors who terminate life rather than protect it . . . the political and social zealots who murder for their cause . . . the parents who abuse and even murder their children.

The book of Jonah addresses our desire for revenge and retribution upon evildoers. The Assyrians were the most brutal, bloodthirsty power on earth in Jonah's day. Given the chance, Jonah would have asked God to destroy them—and felt good about his request! But God had other ideas. He wanted Jonah to see the Ninevites as God saw them: lost, desperate, without hope, spiritually naïve, in need of mercy, and worthy of saving.

Jonah's prejudice toward the Assyrians ran deep. His hatred was intense, and he longed to see God's mercy withheld from his enemies. For four chapters, God patiently worked with his stubborn prophet. When the book closes, the issue is still in doubt. What do you think? Do you suppose Jonah ever got on God's "wavelength" regarding the Ninevites?

LOOK AHEAD Don't allow an individual or a group of people who are objects of God's love to become objects of your hatred or revenge. That doesn't mean condoning conduct that God condemns. But it does mean releasing any bitterness or unforgiveness you may be harboring toward those whom God loves. Regardless of the *reason* for your hatred, the *response* should be the same: seeing others as God sees them and loving others as God loves them.

The psalmist David prayed this way: "Search me, O God, and know my heart; test me and know my thoughts. Point out anything in me that offends you, and lead me along the path of everlasting life" (Psalm 139:23-24). Don't allow Jonah's "hardening of the attitudes" to poison your heart as well. Life is too short to spend it hating the very people God longs to love and save.

Micah

THE MESSAGE of Micah, like that of prophets before him, is neither pleasant nor popular: God knows the sins of his people, and terrible judgment is close at hand. For continued social injustice, oppression, exploitation, and the self-serving interests of leaders and false prophets, the nation will experience destruction and a generation of captivity. But in the midst of this, Micah offers a word of hope. A divine Deliverer is coming, and when he does, righteousness and justice will prevail.

Focus	Violence		Victory		Vindication	
Divisions	Judah's Day of Judgment		Judah's Day of Triumph		Judah's Day in Court	
	1	2	3	5	6	7
Topics	Condemnation		Consolation		Conflict	
	Punishment for Injustice		Promise of a Justice-Bringer		Preservation of Justice	
Place	Judah and Israel					
Time	About 25 Years (735–710 B.C.)					

SEPTEMBER 15 □ DAY 259
MICAH 1–2
Judah's Day of Judgment

OVERVIEW The southern kingdom has begun the final "countdown to captivity." In the face of anarchy from within and annihilation from without, Micah emerges with a message from the Lord. God's day of judgment upon his complacent people is fast approaching, and woe to the one upon whom the judgment falls. It is too late to turn over a new leaf, too late to repent. Judah's wound is incurable, and only divine surgery can remove the malignancy of sin.

Chapter 1		Chapter 2	
Incurable Wounds	Inescapable Wrath	Indicted Princes	Ingathered People
1 7	8 16	1 11	12 13
Rebellion	Rebuke		Reward

We lose the peace of years when we hunt after the rapture of moments.

YOUR DAILY WALK What do you think about when you're not think-ing about anything? Where does your mind wander during the moments before you fall asleep? What is the first thing that crosses your mind when you awaken in the morning? Answer those questions honestly, and you will discover the greatest passion in your life.

What was it that consumed David's thoughts morning and evening? (See Psalm 63:1; 139:17-18.)

Where did the thoughts of Judah's leaders turn throughout the day? (See Micah 2:1-2.)

And where does your mind focus when you wake up . . . when you pause from the frantic pace of your day . . . when you lie down to rest at night? Paul urged Timothy, his son in the faith, to "spend [his] time and energy in training [himself] for spiritual fitness" (1 Timothy 4:7). And to the Colossians he wrote, "Let heaven fill your thoughts" (Colos-sians 3:2). Filling your mind with the things of God takes a deliberate act of the will; it won't happen by accident! Take a brisk walk sometime today, and as you exercise your body, exercise your mind as well with Bible verses, hymns, and thoughts of God. It's habit-forming.

INSIGHT Don't Fool Around with the Farms
Israel was primarily an agrarian society in which each family owned a portion of land. Only under extreme conditions was a family to give up its land. Micah condemns those who exploited the poor by acquiring their land (2:1-2), thus creating an impoverished, landless class that would be a burden on society. See Leviticus 25:25-28.

CHAPTER 1

The LORD gave these messages to Micah of Moresheth during the years when Jotham, Ahaz, and Hezekiah were kings of Judah. The messages concerned both Samaria and Jerusalem, and they came to Micah in the form of visions.

²Attention! Let all the people of the world listen! The Sovereign LORD has made accusations against you; the Lord speaks from his holy Temple.

³Look! The LORD is coming! He leaves his throne in heaven and comes to earth, walking on the high places. ⁴They melt

beneath his feet and flow into the valleys like wax in a fire, like water pouring down a hill.

⁵And why is this happening? Because of the sins and rebellion of Israel and Judah.* Who is to blame for Israel's rebellion? Samaria, its capital city! Where is the center of idolatry in Judah? In Jerusalem, its capital!

⁶"So I, the LORD, will make the city of Samaria a heap of rubble. Her streets will be plowed up for planting vineyards. I will roll the stones of her walls down into the valley below, exposing all her foundations. ⁷All her carved images will be smashed to pieces. All her sacred treasures will be burned up. These things were bought with the money earned by her prostitution, and they will now be carried away to pay prostitutes elsewhere."

⁸Because of all this, I will mourn and lament. I will walk around naked and barefoot in sorrow and shame. I will howl like a jackal and wail like an ostrich. ⁹For my people's wound is far too deep to heal. It has reached into Judah, even to the gates of Jerusalem.

¹⁰Don't tell our enemies in the city of Gath*; don't weep at all.* You people in Beth-leaphrah,* roll in the dust to show your anguish and despair. ¹¹You people of Shaphir,* go as captives into exile—naked and ashamed. The people of Zaanan* dare not come outside their walls. The people of Beth-ezel* mourn because the very foundations of their city have been swept away. ¹²The people of Maroth* anxiously wait for relief, but only bitterness awaits them as the LORD's judgment reaches even to the gates of Jerusalem.

¹³Quick! Use your swiftest chariots and flee, you people of Lachish.* You were the first city in Judah to follow Israel in the sin of idol worship, and so you led Jerusalem* into sin. ¹⁴Send a farewell gift to Moresheth-gath; there is no hope of saving it. The town of Aczib* has deceived the kings of Israel, for it promised help it could not give. ¹⁵You people of Mareshah,* I will bring a conqueror to capture your town. And the leaders* of Israel will go to Adullam.

¹⁶Weep, you people of Judah! Shave your heads in sorrow, for the children you love will be snatched away, and you will never see them again. Make yourselves as bald as an eagle, for your little ones will be exiled to distant lands.

CHAPTER 2

How terrible it will be for you who lie awake at night, thinking up evil plans. You rise at dawn and hurry to carry out any of the wicked schemes you have power to accomplish. ²When you want a certain piece of land, you find a way to seize it. When you want someone's house, you take it by fraud and violence. No one's family or inheritance is safe with you around!

³But this is what the LORD says: "I will reward your evil with evil; you won't be able to escape! After I am through with you, none of you will ever again walk proudly in the streets."

⁴In that day your enemies will make fun of you by singing this song of despair about your experience:

"We are finished,
     completely ruined!
God has confiscated our land,
     taking it from us.
He has given our fields
     to those who betrayed us.*"

⁵Others will set your boundaries then, and the LORD's people will have no say in how the land is divided.

⁶"Don't say such things," the people say. "Don't prophesy like that. Such disasters will never come our way!"

⁷Should you talk that way, O family of Israel*? Will the LORD have patience with such behavior? If you would do what is right, you would find my words to be good. ⁸Yet to this very hour my people rise against me! You steal the shirts right off the backs of those who trusted you, making them as ragged as men who have just come home from battle. ⁹You have evicted women from their homes and stripped their children of all their God-given rights. ¹⁰Up! Begone! This is no longer your land and home, for you have filled it with sin and ruined it completely.

1:5 Hebrew *and Jacob.*   **1:10a** *Gath* sounds like the Hebrew term for "tell."   **1:10b** Greek version reads *weep not in Acco.* **1:10c** *Beth-leaphrah* means "house of dust."   **1:11a** *Shaphir* means "pleasant."   **1:11b** *Zaanan* sounds like the Hebrew term for "come out."   **1:11c** *Beth-ezel* means "adjoining house."   **1:12** *Maroth* sounds like the Hebrew term for "bitter." **1:13a** *Lachish* sounds like the Hebrew term for "team of horses."   **1:13b** Hebrew *the daughter of Zion.*   **1:14** *Aczib* means "deception."   **1:15a** *Mareshah* sounds like the Hebrew term for "conqueror."   **1:15b** Hebrew *the glory.*   **2:4** Or *to those who took us captive.*   **2:7** Hebrew *house of Jacob.*

¹¹Suppose a prophet full of lies were to say to you, "I'll preach to you the joys of wine and drink!" That's just the kind of prophet you would like!

¹²"Someday, O Israel, I will gather the few of you who are left. I will bring you together again like sheep in a fold, like a flock in its pasture. Yes, your land will again be filled with noisy crowds! ¹³Your leader will break out and lead you out of exile. He will bring you through the gates of your cities of captivity, back to your own land. Your king will lead you; the LORD himself will guide you."

SEPTEMBER 16 ☐ DAY 260
MICAH 3–5
Judah's Day of Triumph

 OVERVIEW Like princes, like people. Micah knows that the nation's morals can be no stronger than the nation's leaders. But prince and priest alike pervert justice, oppress the helpless, and minister for bribes. For their greed and injustice, Micah declares their judgment will be swift and severe. By contrast, in the last days righteousness will be a way of life, and the afflicted will be the objects of God's special attention. Messiah will emerge from the obscurity of Bethlehem to be "ruler of Israel" (5:2) and executor of vengeance upon the heathen (5:15).

Chapter 3	Chapter 4	Chapter 5
Rebuking False Prophets	Restoring True Religion	Ruling Jacob's Remnant
False Peace	Kingdom of Peace	Prince of Peace

 YOUR DAILY WALK A good leader is someone who
- balances sensitivity with responsibility;
- has earned the confidence of others through integrity;
- facilitates development in others through being a servant;
- takes more than his share of the blame and less than his share of the credit; and
- keeps hope alive in others.

Good leaders take more than their share of blame and less than their share of credit.

Using that list of definitions, spend a few extra minutes evaluating Judah's leaders. Where did they fail in their God-given assignment and why? Now add to the list of definitions one more: A leader is someone who is willing to learn from those who won't.

Take a hard look at one of your personal leadership roles: in the home, at the office, in the dorm, at the church. Can you spot one error, committed centuries ago by Judah's leaders, that you are in danger of duplicating today? If your ability to lead as God intended depends on your willingness to learn from the mistakes of others, then what will you do with that insight, beginning right now?

 INSIGHT Prophet of Birth, Prophet of Death
Micah and Isaiah ministered at the same time (and perhaps, on occasion, side by side) to the nation of Judah. While their books are similar in style and content, Micah is best known for his prophecies regarding the birth of Christ (5:2), Isaiah for his prophecies describing the death of Christ (Isaiah 52:13–53:12).

CHAPTER 3

Listen, you leaders of Israel! You are supposed to know right from wrong, ²but you are the very ones who hate good and love evil. You skin my people alive and tear the flesh off their bones. ³You eat my people's flesh, cut away their skin, and break their bones. You chop them up like meat for the cooking pot. ⁴Then you beg the LORD for help in times of trouble! Do you really expect him to listen? After all the evil you have done, he won't even look at you!

⁵This is what the LORD says to you false prophets: "You are leading my people astray! You promise peace for those who give you food, but you declare war on anyone who refuses to pay you. ⁶Now the night will close around you, cutting off all your visions. Darkness will cover you, making it impossible for you to predict the future. The sun will set for you prophets, and your day will come to an end. ⁷Then you seers will cover your faces in shame, and you diviners will be disgraced. And you will admit that your messages were not from God."

⁸But as for me, I am filled with power and the Spirit of the LORD. I am filled with justice and might, fearlessly pointing out Israel's sin and rebellion. ⁹Listen to me, you leaders of Israel! You hate justice and twist all that is right. ¹⁰You are building Jerusalem on a foundation of murder and corruption. ¹¹You rulers govern for the bribes you can get; you priests teach God's laws only for a price; you prophets won't prophesy unless you are paid. Yet all of you claim you are depending on the LORD. "No harm can come to us," you say, "for the LORD is here among us."

¹²So because of you, Mount Zion will be plowed like an open field; Jerusalem will be reduced to rubble! A great forest will grow on the hilltop, where the Temple now stands.

CHAPTER 4

In the last days, the Temple of the LORD in Jerusalem will become the most important place on earth. People from all over the world will go there to worship. ²Many nations will come and say, "Come, let us go up to the mountain of the LORD, to the Temple of the God of Israel.* There he will teach us his ways, so that we may obey him." For in those days the LORD's teaching and his word will go out from Jerusalem.

³The LORD will settle international disputes. All the nations will beat their swords into plowshares and their spears into pruning hooks. All wars will stop, and military training will come to an end. ⁴Everyone will live quietly in their own homes in peace and prosperity, for there will be nothing to fear. The LORD Almighty has promised this! ⁵Even though the nations around us worship idols, we will follow the LORD our God forever and ever.

⁶"In that coming day," says the LORD, "I will gather together my people who are lame, who have been exiles, filled with grief. ⁷They are weak and far from home, but I will make them strong again, a mighty nation. Then I, the LORD, will rule from Jerusalem* as their king forever."

⁸As for you, O Jerusalem, the citadel of God's people, your royal might and power will come back to you again. The kingship will be restored to my precious Jerusalem. ⁹But why are you now screaming in terror? Have you no king to lead you? He is dead! Have you no wise people to counsel you? All are gone! Pain has gripped you like it does a woman in labor. ¹⁰Writhe and groan in terrible pain, you people of Jerusalem,* for you must leave this city to live in the open fields. You will soon be sent into exile in distant Babylon. But the LORD will rescue you there; he will redeem you from the grip of your enemies.

¹¹True, many nations have gathered together against you, calling for your blood, eager to gloat over your destruction. ¹²But they do not know the LORD's thoughts or understand his plan. These nations don't know that he is gathering them together to be beaten and trampled like bundles of grain on a threshing floor.

¹³"Rise up and destroy the nations, O Jerusalem!"* says the LORD. "For I will give you iron horns and bronze hooves, so you can trample many nations to pieces. Then you will give all the wealth they acquired as offerings to me, the Lord of all the earth."

CHAPTER 5

Mobilize! Marshal your troops! The enemy is laying siege to Jerusalem. With a rod they will strike the leader of Israel in the face.

4:2 Hebrew *of Jacob.*   **4:7** Hebrew *Mount Zion.*   **4:10** Hebrew *O daughter of Zion.*   **4:13** Hebrew *"Rise up and thresh, O daughter of Zion."*

²But you, O Bethlehem Ephrathah, are only a small village in Judah. Yet a ruler of Israel will come from you, one whose origins are from the distant past. ³The people of Israel will be abandoned to their enemies until the time when the woman in labor gives birth to her son. Then at last his fellow countrymen will return from exile to their own land. ⁴And he will stand to lead his flock with the LORD's strength, in the majesty of the name of the LORD his God. Then his people will live there undisturbed, for he will be highly honored all around the world. ⁵And he will be the source of our peace.

When the Assyrians invade our land and break through our defenses, we will appoint seven rulers to watch over us, eight princes to lead us. ⁶They will rule Assyria with drawn swords and enter the gates of the land of Nimrod. They* will rescue us from the Assyrians when they pour over the borders to invade our land.

⁷Then the few left in Israel* will go out among the nations. They will be like dew sent by the LORD or like rain falling on the grass, which no one can hold back. ⁸The remnant of Israel will go out among the nations and be as strong as a lion. And the other nations will be like helpless sheep, with no one to rescue them. ⁹The people of Israel will stand up to their foes, and all their enemies will be wiped out.

¹⁰"At that same time," says the LORD, "I will destroy all your weapons—your horses and chariots. ¹¹I will tear down your walls and demolish the defenses of your cities. ¹²I will put an end to all witchcraft; there will be no more fortune-tellers to consult. ¹³I will destroy all your idols and sacred pillars, so you will never again worship the work of your own hands. ¹⁴I will abolish your pagan shrines with their Asherah poles and destroy the cities where your idol temples stand. ¹⁵I will pour out my vengeance on all the nations that refuse to obey me."

5:6 Hebrew *He.*   5:7 Hebrew *Jacob;* also in 5:8.

SEPTEMBER 17 □ DAY 261
MICAH 6–7
Judah's Day in Court

OVERVIEW Micah's prophecy closes with a courtroom scene. God has a controversy with his people, and he calls the mountains and hills together to sit in judgment on the case. The people have replaced wholehearted worship with halfhearted ritual. They have divorced God's righteous standards from their daily business transactions in order to justify their greed and corruption. In short, they have failed to understand what God requires of his covenant people.

Chapter 6		Chapter 7	
Judah's Ingratitude	Judah's Injustice	The Lord's Verdict	Judah's Victory
1 8	9 16	1 7	8 20
God's Justice		God's Mercy	

YOUR DAILY WALK Picture this scene. You are sharing with another person the deepest burden of your heart. Suddenly, for no apparent reason, the hearer turns away and puts his fingers in his ears. What do you conclude? And would that dampen your enthusiasm to share again?

Micah prophesied to Judah during the reigns of three kings over a period of at least twenty-five years (1:1). Like his contemporary Isaiah, he saw little fruit from his ministry. Most of his hearers turned away in

What a person believes, he or she will die for. What a person merely thinks, he or she will change his mind about.

unbelief (2:6) or indifference (3:11). But Micah firmly believed his task was a divine mandate, not simply a hobby or religious activity. Fortified with that conviction, Micah could stand for God even when no one was willing to listen and take his message to heart.

Micah's confidence is reflected in his prayer: "As for me, I look to the LORD for his help. I wait confidently for God to save me, and my God will certainly hear me" (7:7). Use his example as a motivation to start (or an encouragement to continue) sharing the claims of Christ with an unsaved friend, neighbor, or relative.

INSIGHT John 3:16 of the Old Testament
In the New Testament, John 3:16 answers the question, How can sinful man and holy God be restored to fellowship with one another? In the Old Testament, Micah 6:8 answers the same question for God's covenant people.

CHAPTER 6

Listen to what the LORD is saying: "Stand up and state your case against me. Let the mountains and hills be called to witness your complaints.

2"And now, O mountains, listen to the LORD's complaint! He has a case against his people Israel! He will prosecute them to the full extent of the law. 3O my people, what have I done to make you turn from me? Tell me why your patience is exhausted! Answer me! 4For I brought you out of Egypt and redeemed you from your slavery. I sent Moses, Aaron, and Miriam to help you.

5"Don't you remember, my people, how King Balak of Moab tried to have you cursed and how Balaam son of Beor blessed you instead? And remember your journey from Acacia* to Gilgal, when I, the LORD, did everything I could to teach you about my faithfulness."

6What can we bring to the LORD to make up for what we've done? Should we bow before God with offerings of yearling calves? 7Should we offer him thousands of rams and tens of thousands of rivers of olive oil? Would that please the LORD? Should we sacrifice our firstborn children to pay for the sins of our souls? Would that make him glad?

8No, O people, the LORD has already told you what is good, and this is what he requires: to do what is right, to love mercy, and to walk humbly with your God.

9Listen! Fear the LORD if you are wise! His voice is calling out to everyone in Jerusalem: "The armies of destruction are coming; the LORD is sending them.* 10Will there

be no end of your getting rich by cheating? The homes of the wicked are filled with treasures gained by dishonestly measuring out grain in short measures.* 11And how can I tolerate all your merchants who use dishonest scales and weights? 12The rich among you have become wealthy through extortion and violence. Your citizens are so used to lying that their tongues can no longer tell the truth.

13"Therefore, I will wound you! I will bring you to ruin for all your sins. 14You will eat but never have enough. Your hunger pangs and emptiness will still remain. And though you try to save your money, it will come to nothing in the end. You will save a little, but I will give it to those who conquer you. 15You will plant crops but not harvest them. You will press your olives but not get enough oil to anoint yourselves. You will trample the grapes but get no juice to make your wine.

16"The only laws you keep are those of evil King Omri; the only example you follow is that of wicked King Ahab! Therefore, I will make an example of you, bringing you to complete ruin. You will be treated with contempt, mocked by all who see you."

CHAPTER 7

What misery is mine! I feel like the fruit picker after the harvest who can find nothing to eat. Not a cluster of grapes or a single fig can be found to satisfy my hunger. 2The godly people have all disappeared; not one fair-minded person is left on the earth. They are all murderers, even setting traps for their own brothers. 3They go about

6:5 Hebrew *Shittim.*   6:9 Hebrew *"Listen to the rod. Who appointed it?"*   6:10 Hebrew *by using the short ephah;* the ephah was a unit for measuring grain.

their evil deeds with both hands. How skilled they are at using them! Officials and judges alike demand bribes. The people with money and influence pay them off, and together they scheme to twist justice. [4]Even the best of them is like a brier; the straightest is more crooked than a hedge of thorns. But your judgment day is coming swiftly now. Your time of punishment is here.

[5]Don't trust anyone—not your best friend or even your wife! [6]For the son despises his father. The daughter defies her mother. The daughter-in-law defies her mother-in-law. Your enemies will be right in your own household.

[7]As for me, I look to the LORD for his help. I wait confidently for God to save me, and my God will certainly hear me. [8]Do not gloat over me, my enemies! For though I fall, I will rise again. Though I sit in darkness, the LORD himself will be my light. [9]I will be patient as the LORD punishes me, for I have sinned against him. But after that, he will take up my case and punish my enemies for all the evil they have done to me. The LORD will bring me out of my darkness into the light, and I will see his righteousness. [10]Then my enemies will see that the LORD is on my side. They will be ashamed that they taunted me, saying, "Where is the LORD—that God of yours?" With my own eyes I will see them trampled down like mud in the streets.

[11]In that day, Israel, your cities will be rebuilt, and your borders will be extended. [12]People from many lands will come and honor you—from Assyria all the way to the towns of Egypt, and from Egypt all the way to the Euphrates River,* and from many distant seas and mountains. [13]But the land* will become empty and desolate because of the wickedness of those who live there.

[14]O LORD, come and rule your people; lead your flock in green pastures. Help them to live in peace and prosperity. Let them enjoy the fertile pastures of Bashan and Gilead as they did long ago.

[15]"Yes," says the LORD, "I will do mighty miracles for you, like those I did when I rescued you from slavery in Egypt."

[16]All the nations of the world will stand amazed at what the LORD will do for you. They will be embarrassed that their power is so insignificant. They will stand in silent awe, deaf to everything around them. [17]They will come to realize what lowly creatures they really are. Like snakes crawling from their holes, they will come out to meet the LORD our God. They will fear him greatly, trembling in terror at his presence.

[18]Where is another God like you, who pardons the sins of the survivors among his people? You cannot stay angry with your people forever, because you delight in showing mercy. [19]Once again you will have compassion on us. You will trample our sins under your feet and throw them into the depths of the ocean! [20]You will show us your faithfulness and unfailing love as you promised with an oath to our ancestors Abraham and Jacob long ago.

7:12 Hebrew *the river.*   7:13 Or *earth.*

Nahum

IT HAS been about a century since Nineveh had repented under the preaching of Jonah, and Nineveh is as wicked a city as it has ever been. The inhabitants fear no judgment; after all, the walls are wide and high, and they are surrounded by a deep moat. But God speaks of Nineveh's destruction through Nahum—and his message is not a warning of doom that could be averted like Jonah's, but a description of certain coming death. God's prophecy comes true to the letter, and Nineveh's grave is so effectively dug that it will lie undiscovered for twenty-five hundred years.

Focus	God's Displeasure Proclaimed		Nineveh's Doom Predicted		Nineveh's Downfall Portrayed	
Divisions	Praise for God's Justice	Joy for Nineveh's Destruction	Destruction of Nineveh	Contrast with Former Glory	Sins of Nineveh	Inevitability of Destruction
	1:1 1:7	1:8 1:15	2:1 2:10	2:11 2:13	3:1 3:4	3:5 3:19
Topics	Sentence of Judgment		Sight of Judgment		Sense of Judgment	
	Psalm of Justice		Description of Justice		Reason for Justice	
Place	In Judah against Nineveh, capital of Assyria					
Time	Approximately 660 B.C.					

SEPTEMBER 18 □ DAY 262
NAHUM 1–3
A Flood of Judgment on Nineveh

OVERVIEW More than a century has passed since Jonah preached his way through the streets of Nineveh. Though revival came in Jonah's day, the repentance was short-lived. At last God's patience runs out, and he sends another prophet—Nahum (whose name means "burden")—to deliver an ominous decree. Nineveh's end will come "in an overwhelming flood" (1:8).

Chapter 1	Chapter 2	Chapter 3
Wrath against Nineveh	Warning to Nineveh	Woe to Nineveh
Destruction	Dirge	Doom

YOUR DAILY WALK The book of Nahum provides God's evaluation of the widely held view that "might makes right." If ever there was a nation that deserved the title "Most Likely to Survive," Assyria was it! Its vast armies and fortified defenses made it virtually impregnable—from a human point of view. But because the Assyrians boasted in their might and would not acknowledge their pride and brutality, from God's point of view the nation's fall was inevitable. One good rainstorm, and the mightiest military power on earth was conquered and demolished.

Trusting God is not faith without evidence; it is commitment without reservation.

   If the great Assyrian Empire couldn't shake its fist in the face of God and get away with it, what does that suggest about your chances of doing the same today? Rebellion in God's eyes is as abominable as witchcraft, and stubbornness as intolerable as idolatry (1 Samuel 15:23). But those who put their trust in him find him a faithful and forgiving refuge (Nahum 1:7). What are you relying on: your *might*, or your *Mighty One?* It's easy to tell, for the former will fail you often, while the latter remains forever faithful!

INSIGHT A Literal and Figurative Flood
The prophecy of Nahum 1:8—that Nineveh's end would come "in an overwhelming flood"—literally came true. In 612 B.C. heavy rains caused the Tigris to overflow its banks and destroy a portion of the city wall, allowing both the river and the invading Babylonians to sweep in like floods. Truly "the LORD is slow to get angry, but his power is great" (1:3).

CHAPTER 1

This message concerning Nineveh came as a vision to Nahum, who lived in Elkosh.

²The LORD is a jealous God, filled with vengeance and wrath. He takes revenge on all who oppose him and furiously destroys his enemies! ³The LORD is slow to get angry, but his power is great, and he never lets the guilty go unpunished. He displays his power in the whirlwind and the storm. The billowing clouds are the dust beneath his feet. ⁴At his command the oceans and rivers dry up, the lush pastures of Bashan and Carmel fade, and the green forests of Lebanon wilt. ⁵In his presence the mountains quake, and the hills melt away; the earth trembles, and its people are destroyed. ⁶Who can stand before his fierce anger? Who can survive his burning fury? His rage blazes forth like

fire, and the mountains crumble to dust in his presence.

⁷The LORD is good. When trouble comes, he is a strong refuge. And he knows everyone who trusts in him. ⁸But he sweeps away his enemies in an overwhelming flood. He pursues his foes into the darkness of night.

⁹Why are you scheming against the LORD? He will destroy you with one blow; he won't need to strike twice! ¹⁰His enemies, tangled up like thorns, staggering like drunks, will be burned like dry straw in a field. ¹¹Who is this king of yours who dares to plot evil against the LORD?

¹²This is what the LORD says: "Even though the Assyrians have many allies, they will be destroyed and disappear. O my people, I have already punished you once, and I will not do it again. ¹³Now I will break your chains and release you from Assyrian oppression."

¹⁴And this is what the LORD says concerning the Assyrians in Nineveh: "You will have no more children to carry on your name. I will destroy all the idols in the temples of your gods. I am preparing a grave for you because you are despicable and don't deserve to live!"

¹⁵Look! A messenger is coming over the mountains with good news! He is bringing a message of peace. Celebrate your festivals, O people of Judah, and fulfill all your vows, for your enemies from Nineveh will never invade your land again. They have been completely destroyed!

CHAPTER 2

Nineveh, you are already surrounded by enemy armies! Sound the alarm! Man the ramparts! Muster your defenses, and keep a sharp watch for the enemy attack to begin! ²For the land of Israel lies empty and broken after your attacks, but the LORD will restore its honor and power again.

³Shields flash red in the sunlight! The attack begins! See their scarlet uniforms! Watch as their glittering chariots move into position, with a forest of spears waving above them. ⁴The chariots race recklessly along the streets and through the squares, swift as lightning, flickering like torches. ⁵The king shouts to his officers; they stumble in their haste, rushing to the walls to set up their defenses. ⁶But too late! The river

gates are open! The enemy has entered! The palace is about to collapse!

⁷Nineveh's exile has been decreed, and all the servant girls mourn its capture. Listen to them moan like doves; watch them beat their breasts in sorrow. ⁸Nineveh is like a leaking water reservoir! The people are slipping away. "Stop, stop!" someone shouts, but the people just keep on running.

⁹Loot the silver! Plunder the gold! There seems no end to Nineveh's many treasures—its vast, uncounted wealth. ¹⁰Soon the city is an empty shambles, stripped of its wealth. Hearts melt in horror, and knees shake. The people stand aghast, their faces pale and trembling.

¹¹Where now is that great Nineveh, lion of the nations, full of fight and boldness, where the old and feeble and the young and tender lived with nothing to fear? ¹²O Nineveh, you were once a mighty lion! You crushed your enemies to feed your cubs and your mate. You filled your city and your homes with captives and plunder.

¹³"I am your enemy!" says the LORD Almighty. "Your chariots will soon go up in smoke. The finest of your youth will be killed in battle. Never again will you bring back plunder from conquered nations. Never again will the voices of your proud messengers be heard."

CHAPTER 3

How terrible it will be for Nineveh, the city of murder and lies! She is crammed with wealth to be plundered. ²Listen! Hear the crack of the whips as the chariots rush forward against her. Wheels rumble, horses' hooves pound, and chariots clatter as they bump wildly through the streets. ³See the flashing swords and glittering spears in the upraised arms of the cavalry! The dead are lying in the streets—dead bodies, heaps of bodies, everywhere. People stumble over them, scramble to their feet, and fall again. ⁴All this because Nineveh, the beautiful and faithless city, mistress of deadly charms, enticed the nations with her beauty. She taught them all to worship her false gods, enchanting people everywhere.

⁵"No wonder I am your enemy!" declares the LORD Almighty. "And now I will lift your skirts so all the earth will see your nakedness and shame. ⁶I will cover you

with filth and show the world how vile you really are. 7All who see you will shrink back in horror and say, 'Nineveh lies in utter ruin.' Yet no one anywhere will regret your destruction."

8Are you any better than Thebes,* surrounded by rivers, protected by water on all sides? 9Ethiopia* and the land of Egypt were the source of her strength, which seemed without limit. The nations of Put and Libya also helped and supported her. 10Yet Thebes fell, and her people were led away as captives. Her babies were dashed to death against the stones of the streets. Soldiers cast lots to see who would get the Egyptian officers as servants. All their leaders were bound in chains.

11And you, Nineveh, will also stagger like a drunkard. You will hide for fear of the attacking enemy. 12All your fortresses will fall. They will be devoured like the ripe figs that fall into the mouths of those who shake the trees. 13Your troops will be as weak and helpless as women. The gates of your land will be opened wide to the enemy and set on fire and burned.

14Get ready for the siege! Store up wa-

3:8 Hebrew *No-amon;* also in 3:10.   3:9 Hebrew *Cush.*

ter! Strengthen the defenses! Make bricks to repair the walls! Go into the pits to trample clay, and pack it into molds! 15But in the middle of your preparations, the fire will devour you; the sword will cut you down. The enemy will consume you like locusts, devouring everything they see. There will be no escape, even if you multiply like grasshoppers. 16Merchants, as numerous as the stars, have filled your city with vast wealth. But like a swarm of locusts, they strip the land and then fly away. 17Your princes and officials are also like locusts, crowding together in the hedges to survive the cold. But like locusts that fly away when the sun comes up to warm the earth, all of them will fly away and disappear.

18O Assyrian king, your princes lie dead in the dust. Your people are scattered across the mountains. There is no longer a shepherd to gather them together. 19There is no healing for your wound; your injury is fatal. All who hear of your destruction will clap their hands for joy. Where can anyone be found who has not suffered from your cruelty?

Habakkuk

HABAKKUK ministers during Judah's death throes. Though repeatedly called to repentance, the nation stubbornly refuses to change its sinful ways. Habakkuk, knowing the hard-heartedness of his countrymen, asks God how long this intolerable condition can be tolerated. God replies that the Babylonians will be his chastening rod upon the nation—an announcement that sends the prophet to his knees, where he acknowledges that the just in any generation will live by faith, not by sight.

Focus	Habakkuk's Perplexity				Habakkuk's Prayer
Divisions	First Question: Israel's Sin	First Response: Babylonian Invasion	Second Question: Babylon's Sin	Second Response: Babylon's Destruction	Prayer and Praise
	1:1 1:4	1:5 1:11	1:12 2:1	2:2 2:20	3:1 3:19
Topics	Sweeping a Dirty Nation Clean . . .		Using an Even Dirtier Broom . . .		As Only God Can Do!
	Questions and Answers				Wonder and Worship
Place	Judah				
Time	Approximately 607 B.C.				

SEPTEMBER 19 ☐ DAY 263
HABAKKUK 1–3
Living by Faith in Hard Times

OVERVIEW Habakkuk prophesies in Judah just before its final destruction at the hands of the Babylonians. Like Job, he honestly raises the perplexing issue of why a just God is silent, and why the cries of the faithful seem to go unheard (1:2) "while the wicked destroy people who are more righteous than they" (1:13). In reply, God declares to his prophet a timeless principle of trust in his sovereignty. The wicked will be dealt with—in God's own way, in God's own time. But in the meantime, "the righteous will live by their faith" (2:4).

Chapter 1	Chapter 2	Chapter 3
Questions and Answers	Woes and Warnings	Wonder and Worship
Dialogue	Monologue	Devotion

Faith is reason at rest with God.

YOUR DAILY WALK A swimmer far from shore flails helplessly in the water. A lifeguard rushes to his aid—and is greeted with this surprising retort: "Why don't you mind your own business?" Of course, the correct response from the lifeguard would be: "I *am* minding my own business—and you're part of it! You may not fully understand what I am doing, but just trust me to bring you to shore."

Life is filled with occasions when you are called upon to put your trust in a *person* even though you may not fully understand the *process*. A surgeon's scalpel, a pilot's skill, a doctor's prescription—these are all things you have learned to trust. Doesn't it make sense, therefore, to trust God when it comes to the "business" he specializes in?

Habakkuk was distraught at seeing the wicked get away with murder. But the prophet's focus sharpened when he saw that he was trying to mind God's business instead of the business God had entrusted to him—the business of walking by faith!

"Mind your own business." It may sound harsh, but perhaps it's just the reminder you need today to stay on target in your walk with God!

INSIGHT May I Quote You, Mr. Habakkuk?
The last half of 2:4 is so significant that it's quoted three times in the New Testament: twice by Paul (Romans 1:17; Galatians 3:11) and once by the writer to the Hebrews (Hebrews 10:38).

CHAPTER 1

This is the message that the prophet Habakkuk received from the LORD in a vision.

²How long, O LORD, must I call for help? But you do not listen! "Violence!" I cry, but you do not come to save. ³Must I forever see this sin and misery all around me? Wherever I look, I see destruction and violence. I am surrounded by people who love to argue and fight. ⁴The law has become paralyzed and useless, and there is no justice given in the courts. The wicked far outnumber the righteous, and justice is perverted with bribes and trickery.

⁵The LORD replied, "Look at the nations and be amazed! Watch and be astounded at what I will do! For I am doing some-

thing in your own day, something you wouldn't believe even if someone told you about it. [6]I am raising up the Babylonians* to be a new power on the world scene. They are a cruel and violent nation who will march across the world and conquer it. [7]They are notorious for their cruelty. They do as they like, and no one can stop them. [8]Their horses are swifter than leopards. They are a fierce people, more fierce than wolves at dusk. Their horsemen race forward from distant places. Like eagles they swoop down to pounce on their prey.

[9]"On they come, all of them bent on violence. Their hordes advance like a wind from the desert, sweeping captives ahead of them like sand. [10]They scoff at kings and princes and scorn all their defenses. They simply pile ramps of earth against their walls and capture them! [11]They sweep past like the wind and are gone. But they are deeply guilty, for their own strength is their god."

[12]O LORD my God, my Holy One, you who are eternal—is your plan in all of this to wipe us out? Surely not! O LORD our Rock, you have decreed the rise of these Babylonians to punish and correct us for our terrible sins. [13]You are perfectly just in this. But will you, who cannot allow sin in any form, stand idly by while they swallow us up? Should you be silent while the wicked destroy people who are more righteous than they?

[14]Are we but fish to be caught and killed? Are we but creeping things that have no leader to defend them from their enemies? [15]Must we be strung up on their hooks and dragged out in their nets while they rejoice? [16]Then they will worship their nets and burn incense in front of them. "These nets are the gods who have made us rich!" they will claim.

[17]Will you let them get away with this forever? Will they succeed forever in their heartless conquests?

CHAPTER 2

I will climb up into my watchtower now and wait to see what the LORD will say to me and how he will answer my complaint.

[2]Then the LORD said to me, "Write my answer in large, clear letters on a tablet, so that a runner can read it and tell everyone else. [3]But these things I plan won't happen right away. Slowly, steadily, surely, the time approaches when the vision will be fulfilled. If it seems slow, wait patiently, for it will surely take place. It will not be delayed.

[4]"Look at the proud! They trust in themselves, and their lives are crooked;* but the righteous will live by their faith.* [5]Wealth* is treacherous, and the arrogant are never at rest. They range far and wide, with their mouths opened as wide as death,* but they are never satisfied. In their greed they have gathered up many nations and peoples. [6]But the time is coming when all their captives will taunt them, saying, 'You thieves! At last justice has caught up with you! Now you will get what you deserve for your oppression and extortion!' [7]Suddenly, your debtors will rise up in anger. They will turn on you and take all you have, while you stand trembling and helpless. [8]You have plundered many nations; now they will plunder you. You murderers! You have filled the countryside with violence and all the cities, too.

[9]"How terrible it will be for you who get rich by unjust means! You believe your wealth will buy security, putting your families beyond the reach of danger. [10]But by the murders you committed, you have shamed your name and forfeited your lives. [11]The very stones in the walls of your houses cry out against you, and the beams in the ceilings echo the complaint.

[12]"How terrible it will be for you who build cities with money gained by murder and corruption! [13]Has not the LORD Almighty promised that the wealth of nations will turn to ashes? They work so hard, but all in vain! [14]For the time will come when all the earth will be filled, as the waters fill the sea, with an awareness of the glory of the LORD.

[15]"How terrible it will be for you who make your neighbors drunk! You force your cup on them so that you can gloat over their nakedness and shame. [16]But soon it will be your turn! Come, drink and be exposed! Drink from the cup of the LORD's judgment, and all your glory will be turned to shame. [17]You cut down the forests of Lebanon. Now you will be cut

1:6 Or Chaldeans. **2:4a** Greek version reads I will have no pleasure in anyone who turns away. **2:4b** Or the just will live by their faithfulness. **2:5a** As in Dead Sea Scroll 1QpHab; other Hebrew manuscripts read Wine. **2:5b** Hebrew as Sheol.

down! You terrified the wild animals you caught in your traps. Now terror will strike you because of your murder and violence in cities everywhere!

[18] "What have you gained by worshiping all your man-made idols? How foolish to trust in something made by your own hands! What fools you are to believe such lies! [19] How terrible it will be for you who beg lifeless wooden idols to save you. You ask speechless stone images to tell you what to do. Can an idol speak for God? They may be overlaid with gold and silver, but they are lifeless inside. [20] But the LORD is in his holy Temple. Let all the earth be silent before him."

CHAPTER 3

This prayer was sung by the prophet Habakkuk:*

[2] I have heard all about you, LORD, and I am filled with awe by the amazing things you have done. In this time of our deep need, begin again to help us, as you did in years gone by. Show us your power to save us. And in your anger, remember your mercy.

[3] I see God, the Holy One, moving across the deserts from Edom* and Mount Paran.* His brilliant splendor fills the heavens, and the earth is filled with his praise! What a wonderful God he is! [4] Rays of brilliant light flash from his hands. He rejoices in his awesome power.* [5] Pestilence marches before him; plague follows close behind. [6] When he stops, the earth shakes. When he looks, the nations tremble. He shatters the everlasting mountains and levels the eternal hills. But his power is not diminished in the least! [7] I see the peoples of Cushan and Midian trembling in terror.

[8] Was it in anger, LORD, that you struck the rivers and parted the sea? Were you displeased with them? No, you were sending your chariots of salvation! [9] You were commanding your weapons of power! You split open the earth with flowing rivers! [10] The mountains watched and trembled. Onward swept the raging waters. The mighty deep cried out, lifting its hands to the LORD. [11] The lofty sun and moon began to fade, obscured by brilliance from your arrows and the flashing of your glittering spear.

[12] You marched across the land in awesome anger and trampled the nations in your fury. [13] You went out to rescue your chosen people, to save your anointed ones. You crushed the heads of the wicked and laid bare their bones from head to toe. [14] With their own weapons, you destroyed those who rushed out like a whirlwind, thinking Israel would be easy prey. [15] You trampled the sea with your horses, and the mighty waters piled high.

[16] I trembled inside when I heard all this; my lips quivered with fear. My legs gave way beneath me,* and I shook in terror. I will wait quietly for the coming day when disaster will strike the people who invade us. [17] Even though the fig trees have no blossoms, and there are no grapes on the vine; even though the olive crop fails, and the fields lie empty and barren; even though the flocks die in the fields, and the cattle barns are empty, [18] yet I will rejoice in the LORD! I will be joyful in the God of my salvation! [19] The Sovereign LORD is my strength! He will make me as surefooted as a deer* and bring me safely over the mountains.

(For the choir director: This prayer is to be accompanied by stringed instruments.)

3:1 Hebrew adds *according to shigionoth*, probably indicating the musical setting for the prayer.   3:3a Hebrew *Teman*.
3:3b Hebrew adds *selah*; also in 3:9, 13. The meaning of this Hebrew term is uncertain; it is probably a musical or literary term.   3:4 Or *He veils his awesome power*.   3:16 Hebrew *Decay entered my bones*.   3:19 Or *will give me the speed of a deer*.

Zephaniah

ZEPHANIAH is possessed by one passion, motivated by one concern: the impending day of the Lord. That day signifies God's final judgment of the earth and the ensuing time of blessing and peace. He shudders at Judah's flouting God, moving from him instead of toward him. Judah will be punished. But beyond that cloud brightness blazes: God will purify his people; he will restore their fortunes; he will rejoice over them with shouts of joy; he will make them great; he will be in their midst. Beyond judgment there is joy.

Focus	The Judgment of the Day of the Lord			The Salvation of the Day of the Lord		
Divisions	Judgment of Whole Earth	Judgment of Judah	Judgment of Nations	Need of Salvation	Promise of Salvation	Promise of Restoration
	1:1　1:3	1:4　　2:3	2:4　　2:15	3:1　3:8	3:9　3:13	3:14　3:20
Topics	God's Wrath on Judah		God's Woes on the Nations	God's Will for the Remnant		
	Retribution and Judgment			Restoration and Joy		
Place	Judah and the Nations					
Time	Approximately 630 B.C.					

SEPTEMBER 20 □ DAY 264
ZEPHANIAH 1–3
Judgment Day Is Coming

OVERVIEW During Judah's hectic political and religious history, reform would come from time to time. Zephaniah's forceful prophecy may have been a factor in the reform that occurred during Josiah's reign—a "revival" that produced outward change but could not remove the inward heart of corruption that characterized the leadership of the nation. Zephaniah hammers home his message repeatedly that the day of the Lord—Judgment Day—is coming when the malignancy of sin will be dealt with. Israel and her Gentile neighbors will soon experience the crushing hand of God's wrath. But after the chastening process is complete, blessing will come in the person of the Messiah, who will be the cause for praise and singing.

Chapter 1	Chapter 2	Chapter 3
God's Wrath on Judah	God's Woes on the Nations	God's Will for the Remnant
Judgment		Joy

The calm that puts us to sleep may be more deadly than a storm that keeps us wide awake.

YOUR DAILY WALK When it comes to responding to spiritual truth, there are three "temperatures" of individuals: hot (responsive), cold (rebellious), and lukewarm (indifferent). God rewards the hot, reaches out to the cold, but rejects the lukewarm (Revelation 3:14-16)!

The people of Jerusalem during Zephaniah's day had become lukewarm—indifferent toward the Lord (1:12). Their problem was not a lack of *knowledge* about God's will, but rather a lack of *willingness* to do what they knew to be right.

What would Zephaniah have to say about your "spiritual temperature"? Have you reached a plateau, a leveling off, a point of complacency in your spiritual life? Are you stimulated by God's Word or stagnant toward it? Complete this sentence: "If I knew I had to face my God and Judge tomorrow and account for my life, I would spend my time today [doing what?]." There's no time like the present to leave lukewarmness behind!

INSIGHT Hidden Meaning in a Hidden Name
Zephaniah's name, which means "the Lord hides," had great significance for his message. In the midst of a graphic description of divine judgment "on that day," Zephaniah inserts a note of hope for the righteous remnant. Read about it in 2:3!

CHAPTER 1

The LORD gave these messages to Zephaniah when Josiah son of Amon was king of Judah. Zephaniah was the son of Cushi, son of Gedaliah, son of Amariah, son of Hezekiah.

²"I will sweep away everything in all

your land," says the LORD. ³"I will sweep away both people and animals alike. Even the birds of the air and the fish in the sea will die. I will reduce the wicked to heaps of rubble,* along with the rest of humanity," says the LORD. ⁴"I will crush Judah and Jerusalem with my fist and destroy

1:3 The meaning of the Hebrew is uncertain.

every last trace of their Baal worship. I will put an end to all the idolatrous priests, so that even the memory of them will disappear. [5]For they go up to their roofs and bow to the sun, moon, and stars. They claim to follow the LORD, but then they worship Molech,* too. So now I will destroy them! [6]And I will destroy those who used to worship me but now no longer do. They no longer ask for the LORD's guidance or seek my blessings."

[7]Stand in silence in the presence of the Sovereign LORD, for the awesome day of the LORD's judgment has come. The LORD has prepared his people for a great slaughter and has chosen their executioners.* [8]"On that day of judgment," says the LORD, "I will punish the leaders and princes of Judah and all those following pagan customs. [9]Yes, I will punish those who participate in pagan worship ceremonies, and those who steal and kill to fill their masters' homes with loot.

[10]"On that day," says the LORD, "a cry of alarm will come from the Fish Gate and echo throughout the newer Mishneh section* of the city. And a great crashing sound will come from the surrounding hills. [11]Wail in sorrow, all you who live in the market area, for all who buy and sell there will die.

[12]"I will search with lanterns in Jerusalem's darkest corners to find and punish those who sit contented in their sins, indifferent to the LORD, thinking he will do nothing at all to them. [13]They are the very ones whose property will be plundered by the enemy, whose homes will be ransacked. They will never have a chance to live in the new homes they have built. They will never drink wine from the vineyards they have planted.

[14]"That terrible day of the LORD is near. Swiftly it comes—a day when strong men will cry bitterly. [15]It is a day when the LORD's anger will be poured out. It is a day of terrible distress and anguish, a day of ruin and desolation, a day of darkness and gloom, of clouds, blackness, [16]trumpet calls, and battle cries. Down go the walled cities and strongest battlements!

[17]"Because you have sinned against the LORD, I will make you as helpless as a blind man searching for a path. Your blood will be poured out into the dust, and your bodies will lie there rotting on the ground."

[18]Your silver and gold will be of no use to you on that day of the LORD's anger. For the whole land will be devoured by the fire of his jealousy. He will make a terrifying end of all the people on earth.*

CHAPTER 2

Gather together and pray, you shameless nation. [2]Gather while there is still time, before judgment begins and your opportunity is blown away like chaff. Act now, before the fierce fury of the LORD falls and the terrible day of the LORD's anger begins. [3]Beg the LORD to save you—all you who are humble, all you who uphold justice. Walk humbly and do what is right. Perhaps even yet the LORD will protect you from his anger on that day of destruction.

[4]Gaza, Ashkelon, Ashdod, Ekron—these Philistine cities, too, will be rooted out and left in desolation. [5]And how terrible it will be for you Philistines* who live along the coast and in the land of Canaan, for this judgment is against you, too! The LORD will destroy you until not one of you is left. [6]The coastal area will become a pasture, a place of shepherd camps and enclosures for sheep.

[7]The few survivors of the tribe of Judah will pasture there. They will lie down to rest in the abandoned houses in Ashkelon. For the LORD their God will visit his people in kindness and restore their prosperity again.

[8]"I have heard the taunts of the people of Moab and Ammon, mocking my people and invading their borders. [9]Now, as surely as I live," says the LORD Almighty, the God of Israel, "Moab and Ammon will be destroyed as completely as Sodom and Gomorrah. Their land will become a place of stinging nettles, salt pits, and eternal desolation. Those of my people who are left will plunder them and take their land."

[10]They will receive the wages of their pride, for they have scoffed at the people of the LORD Almighty. [11]The LORD will terrify them as he destroys all the gods in the land. Then people from nations around the world will worship the LORD, each in their own land.

1:5 Hebrew *Malcam,* another name for Molech; or it could possibly mean *their king, and sanctified his guests.* **1:10** Or *the Second Quarter,* a newer section of Jerusalem. **2:5** Hebrew *Kerethites.*   **1:7** Hebrew *has prepared a sacrifice* **1:18** Or *the people living in the land.*

¹²"You Ethiopians* will also be slaughtered by my sword," says the LORD.

¹³And the LORD will strike the lands of the north with his fist. He will destroy Assyria and make its great capital, Nineveh, a desolate wasteland, parched like a desert. ¹⁴The city that once was so proud will become a pasture for sheep and cattle. All sorts of wild animals will settle there. Owls of many kinds will live among the ruins of its palaces, hooting from the gaping windows. Rubble will block all the doorways, and the cedar paneling will lie open to the wind and weather.

¹⁵This is the fate of that boisterous city, once so secure. "In all the world there is no city as great as I," it boasted. But now, look how it has become an utter ruin, a place where animals live! Everyone passing that way will laugh in derision or shake a defiant fist.

CHAPTER 3

How terrible it will be for rebellious, polluted Jerusalem, the city of violence and crime. ²It proudly refuses to listen even to the voice of the LORD. No one can tell it anything; it refuses all correction. It does not trust in the LORD or draw near to its God.

³Its leaders are like roaring lions hunting for their victims—out for everything they can get. Its judges are like ravenous wolves at evening time, who by dawn have left no trace of their prey. ⁴Its prophets are arrogant liars seeking their own gain. Its priests defile the Temple by disobeying God's laws. ⁵But the LORD is still there in the city, and he does no wrong. Day by day his justice is more evident, but no one takes notice—the wicked know no shame.

⁶"I have wiped out many nations, devastating their fortress walls and towers. Their cities are now deserted; their streets are in silent ruin. There are no survivors to even tell what happened. ⁷I thought, 'Surely they will have reverence for me now! Surely they will listen to my warnings, so I won't need to strike again.' But no; however much I punish them, they continue their evil practices from dawn till dusk and dusk till dawn." ⁸So now the LORD says: "Be patient; the time is coming soon when I will stand up and accuse these evil nations. For it is my decision to gather together the kingdoms of the earth and pour out my fiercest anger and fury on them. All the earth will be devoured by the fire of my jealousy.

⁹"On that day I will purify the lips of all people, so that everyone will be able to worship the LORD together. ¹⁰My scattered people who live beyond the rivers of Ethiopia* will come to present their offerings. ¹¹And then you will no longer need to be ashamed of yourselves, for you will no longer be rebels against me. I will remove all the proud and arrogant people from among you. There will be no pride on my holy mountain. ¹²Those who are left will be the lowly and the humble, for it is they who trust in the name of the LORD. ¹³The people of Israel who survive will do no wrong to each other, never telling lies or deceiving one another. They will live peaceful lives, lying down to sleep in safety; there will be no one to make them afraid."

¹⁴Sing, O daughter of Zion; shout aloud, O Israel! Be glad and rejoice with all your heart, O daughter of Jerusalem! ¹⁵For the LORD will remove his hand of judgment and will disperse the armies of your enemy. And the LORD himself, the King of Israel, will live among you! At last your troubles will be over, and you will fear disaster no more.

¹⁶On that day the announcement to Jerusalem will be, "Cheer up, Zion! Don't be afraid! ¹⁷For the LORD your God has arrived to live among you. He is a mighty savior. He will rejoice over you with great gladness. With his love, he will calm all your fears. He will exult over you by singing a happy song."

¹⁸"I will gather you who mourn for the appointed festivals; you will be disgraced no more.* ¹⁹And I will deal severely with all who have oppressed you. I will save the weak and helpless ones; I will bring together those who were chased away. I will give glory and renown to my former exiles, who have been mocked and shamed. ²⁰On that day I will gather you together and bring you home again. I will give you a good name, a name of distinction among all the nations of the earth. They will praise you as I restore your fortunes before their very eyes. I, the LORD, have spoken!"

2:12 Hebrew *Cushites.*   **3:10** Hebrew *Cush.*   **3:18** The meaning of the Hebrew for this verse is uncertain.

SEPTEMBER 21 ☐ DAY 265
Mercy and Justice for All

LOOK BACK   Micah (whose name means "who is like the Lord?") has been called the prophet for the exploited and downtrodden. Corrupt kings, false prophets, bribed judges, and pilfering priests all become targets of Micah's prophetic barbs. Every level of Judah's society has been taken captive by greed and opportunism.

Nahum ("burden") concludes the saga begun more than a century earlier in the book of Jonah. The Ninevites, who have experienced a short-lived repentance, now face a tidal wave of judgment. Total destruction is sure, and escape is impossible.

Habakkuk ("embrace") is not afraid to wrestle with tough issues that test his faith. His questions of "Why?" and "How long?" are met by comforting descriptions of the person and program of God. The more Habakkuk knows about the plan of God, the more he can relax in the loving arms of the Planner, for indeed, "the righteous will live by their faith" (Habakkuk 2:4).

Zephaniah ("the Lord hides") paints a grim picture of death, destruction, and darkness for wayward Judah. He looks in all four directions before focusing on Jerusalem, the focus of God's chastening and the object of God's love.

LOOK UP   Last week you read the book of Jonah and discovered that God delights to show his love to even the most wicked.

Perhaps it surprised you to read this week that the city of Nineveh, which was the object of God's love in the book of Jonah, became the object of his wrath and judgment in the book of Nahum. How can this be? Is God fickle in his feelings? How could God be angry with Jonah for failing to show mercy to the Ninevites, then turn around and act precisely the same way himself?

Those who see God's hand in everything can best leave everything in God's hand.

The key is found back in Exodus 34:6-7. There you will learn how the mercy of God and the justice of God blend together perfectly: "I am the LORD, I am the LORD, the merciful and gracious God. I am slow to anger and rich in unfailing love and faithfulness. I show this unfailing love to many thousands by forgiving every kind of sin and rebellion. Even so I do not leave sin unpunished, but I punish the children for the sins of their parents to the third and fourth generations [just like the book of Nahum presents him]."

LOOK AHEAD   How can so many people get away with murder today? Because it is "today." The time is coming when God will settle all accounts equitably, when it will be too late for mercy, and in its place justice will prevail. For the Ninevites, that "day of reckoning" came approximately 150 years after Jonah's memorable visit. The Assyrians' change of heart in the days of Jonah became "business as usual" within a handful of years. God's patience is great, but it is not endless. And while he may be *long-suffering* today, you can be sure there is coming a day when others will be doing the *suffering* if they have not gotten right with him!

On a three-by-five-inch card, make a list of any grievances you are carrying against others that, from your perspective, are as yet unsettled. Now take your list of "unrighted wrongs," commit each to the Lord in prayer, and then tear up the list. Practice showing mercy; leave justice to God.

Haggai

HAVING just returned from exile in Babylonia, the people are confronted by a heartbreaking sight. Nebuchadnezzar had made a shambles of their city, including the glorious structure that was once Solomon's Temple. Work progresses on a new Temple until opposition arises. For sixteen years the Jews ignore the unfinished Temple to pursue personal prosperity. Onto the scene steps Haggai, an aged, straight-talking prophet of God, who minces no words in his call to "finish what you have begun," for future blessing is promised to the obedient.

Focus	Finishing God's House		Finding God's Blessing	
Divisions	A Call to Build	A Promise of Glory	A Problem with Defilement	A Promise to a Servant
	1:1 1:15	2:1 2:9	2:10 2:19	2:20 2:23
Topics	Wrong Priorities	Wrong Perspectives	Incomplete Purity	Encouraging Promises
	". . . rebuild my house. Then I will take pleasure in it and be honored" (1:8).			
Place	Jerusalem			
Time	September 1, 520 B.C.	October 21, 520 B.C.	December 24, 520 B.C.	

SEPTEMBER 22 ☐ DAY 266
HAGGAI 1–2
Don't Throw in the Trowel!

 OVERVIEW The final three Old Testament books are known as the post-exilic prophets because their messages are addressed to the returnees in Jerusalem following the Babylonian exile. The people waste no time beginning to restore their beloved Temple. But delays and distractions soon undermine the work, setting the stage for Haggai to appear with a new word from the Lord. In four brief but powerful messages, Haggai exhorts the people to put first things first. With renewed courage and commitment, the citizens respond by completing the Temple—and clearing a place for God in their hearts.

Chapter 1		Chapter 2	
Wrong Priorities	Wrong Perspectives	Incomplete Purity	Encouraging Promises
1	9 | 10	19 | 20	23

"Rebuild my house. Then I will . . . be honored" (1:8).

 YOUR DAILY WALK It has been well said, "If you aim at nothing, you will hit it every time." You will often accomplish what you set out to do, but you will rarely (if ever) accomplish that which you never even intended to do.

Some people dream of worthy accomplishments, while others stay awake and do them.

Every person has exactly the same number of hours in a week: 168. Why is it that some people accomplish so much more with those same hours than others do?

Answer: *Priorities!* Achievers determine in advance what they want to do, then tackle their tasks in the order of importance.

Haggai's contemporaries built a Temple in the midst of stiff opposition because that was their number one priority. Now transfer that concept to your spiritual life. What do you want to be able to look back on when you reach the age of forty? . . . fifty-five? . . . seventy? A deep familiarity with the Bible? A consistent prayer life? A family that is walking with God? If someone were to determine your priorities by looking at the way you spent the last 168 hours, what would they decide? And what will be your priorities as you spend the next 168?

 INSIGHT Words That Carry Clout

Four times Haggai introduces his words with the phrase "the LORD sent"; five times he uses "this is what the LORD Almighty says" and twelve times "says the LORD." Mark these twenty-one phrases in your Bible, for they give the key to the prophet's power. He was speaking for none other than the Lord Almighty.

CHAPTER 1
On August 29* of the second year of King Darius's reign, the LORD gave a message through the prophet Haggai to Zerubbabel son of Shealtiel, governor of Judah, and to Jeshua* son of Jehozadak, the high priest. ²"This is what the LORD Almighty says: The people are saying, 'The time has not

1:1a Hebrew *On the first day of the sixth month,* of the Hebrew calendar. A number of dates in Haggai can be cross-checked with dates in surviving Persian records and related accurately to our modern calendar. This event occurred on August 29, 520 B.C.
1:1b Hebrew *Joshua,* a variant name for Jeshua; also in 1:12, 14.

yet come to rebuild the LORD's house—the Temple.'"

³So the LORD sent this message through the prophet Haggai: ⁴"Why are you living in luxurious houses while my house lies in ruins? ⁵This is what the LORD Almighty says: Consider how things are going for you! ⁶You have planted much but harvested little. You have food to eat, but not enough to fill you up. You have wine to drink, but not enough to satisfy your thirst. You have clothing to wear, but not enough to keep you warm. Your wages disappear as though you were putting them in pockets filled with holes!

⁷"This is what the LORD Almighty says: Consider how things are going for you! ⁸Now go up into the hills, bring down timber, and rebuild my house. Then I will take pleasure in it and be honored, says the LORD. ⁹You hoped for rich harvests, but they were poor. And when you brought your harvest home, I blew it away. Why? Because my house lies in ruins, says the LORD Almighty, while you are all busy building your own fine houses. ¹⁰That is why the heavens have withheld the dew and the earth has withheld its crops. ¹¹I have called for a drought on your fields and hills—a drought to wither the grain and grapes and olives and all your other crops, a drought to starve both you and your cattle and to ruin everything you have worked so hard to get."

¹²Then Zerubbabel son of Shealtiel, Jeshua son of Jehozadak, the high priest, and the whole remnant of God's people obeyed the message from the LORD their God. It had been delivered by the prophet Haggai, whom the LORD their God had sent, and the people worshiped the LORD in earnest. ¹³Then Haggai, the LORD's messenger, gave the people this message from the LORD: "I am with you, says the LORD!" ¹⁴So the LORD sparked the enthusiasm of Zerubbabel son of Shealtiel, governor of Judah, Jeshua son of Jehozadak, the high priest, and the whole remnant of God's people. They came and began their work on the house of the LORD Almighty, their God. ¹⁵This was on September 21* of the second year of King Darius's reign.

CHAPTER 2

Then on October 17* of that same year, the LORD sent another message through the prophet Haggai. ²"Say this to Zerubbabel son of Shealtiel, governor of Judah, and to Jeshua* son of Jehozadak, the high priest, and to the remnant of God's people there in the land: ³Is there anyone who can remember this house—the Temple—as it was before? In comparison, how does it look to you now? It must seem like nothing at all! ⁴But now take courage, Zerubbabel, says the LORD. Take courage, Jeshua son of Jehozadak, the high priest. Take courage, all you people still left in the land, says the LORD. Take courage and work, for I am with you, says the LORD Almighty. ⁵My Spirit remains among you, just as I promised when you came out of Egypt. So do not be afraid.

⁶"For this is what the LORD Almighty says: In just a little while I will again shake the heavens and the earth. I will shake the oceans and the dry land, too. ⁷I will shake all the nations, and the treasures of all the nations will come to this Temple. I will fill this place with glory, says the LORD Almighty. ⁸The silver is mine, and the gold is mine, says the LORD Almighty. ⁹The future glory of this Temple will be greater than its past glory, says the LORD Almighty. And in this place I will bring peace. I, the LORD Almighty, have spoken!"

¹⁰On December 18* of the second year of King Darius's reign, the LORD sent this message to the prophet Haggai: ¹¹"This is what the LORD Almighty says! Ask the priests this question about the law: ¹²If one of you is carrying a holy sacrifice in his robes and happens to brush against some bread or stew, wine or oil, or any other kind of food, will it also become holy?"

The priests replied, "No."

¹³Then Haggai asked, "But if someone becomes ceremonially unclean by touching a dead person and then brushes against any of the things mentioned, will it be defiled?"

And the priests answered, "Yes."

¹⁴Then Haggai said, "That is how it is with this people and this nation, says the LORD. Everything they do and everything they offer is defiled. ¹⁵So think about this

1:15 Hebrew *on the twenty-fourth day of the sixth month*, of the Hebrew calendar. This event occurred on September 21, 520 B.C.; also see note on 1:1a.   **2:1** Hebrew *on the twenty-first day of the seventh month*, of the Hebrew calendar. This event occurred on October 17, 520 B.C.; also see note on 1:1a.   **2:2** Hebrew *Joshua*, a variant name for Jeshua; also in 2:4.   **2:10** Hebrew *On the twenty-fourth day of the ninth month*, of the Hebrew calendar (also in 2:18). This event occurred on December 18, 520 B.C.; also see note on 1:1a.

from now on—consider how things were going for you before you began to lay the foundation of the LORD's Temple. ¹⁶When you hoped for a twenty-bushel crop, you harvested only ten. When you expected to draw fifty gallons from the winepress, you found only twenty. ¹⁷I sent blight and mildew and hail to destroy all the produce of your labor. Yet, even so, you refused to return to me, says the LORD.

¹⁸"On this eighteenth day of December—the day when the foundation of the LORD's Temple was laid—carefully consider this: ¹⁹I am giving you a promise now while the seed is still in the barn, before you have harvested your grain and before the grapevine, the fig tree, the pomegranate,

2:20 Hebrew *on the twenty-fourth day of the month;* see note on 2:10.

and the olive tree have produced their crops. From this day onward I will bless you."

²⁰The LORD sent this second message to Haggai on December 18*: ²¹"Tell Zerubbabel, the governor of Judah, that I am about to shake the heavens and the earth. ²²I will overthrow royal thrones, destroying the power of foreign kingdoms. I will overturn their chariots and charioteers. The horses will fall, and their riders will kill each other. ²³But when this happens, says the LORD Almighty, I will honor you, Zerubbabel son of Shealtiel, my servant. I will treat you like a signet ring on my finger, says the LORD, for I have specially chosen you. I, the LORD Almighty, have spoken!"

Zechariah

THE TEMPLE rebuilding had begun amid great excitement in 536 B.C. But the early enthusiasm had waned, and sixteen years later the only movement in the unfinished building was the stirring of the wind. Enter Zechariah, commissioned by God to join Haggai in motivating the workers to finish what they had begun. His message is one of consolation: The Temple will be no ordinary building, but will house Messiah himself. All hands to the task, for "look, your king is coming to you" (9:9).

Focus	Corrections			Directions	
Divisions	Visions of Horses and Horns	Visions of Scrolls and Chariots	To Fast or Not to Fast	Israel's Coming King and Shepherd	Israel's Coming Consolation
	1　　2	3　　6	7　　8	9　　11	12　　14
Topics	Eight Visions		Four Sermons	Two Burdens	
	Present Problems			Future Promises	
Place	Jerusalem				
Time	While Rebuilding the Temple (520–518 B.C.)			After Rebuilding the Temple (480–410 B.C.)	

SEPTEMBER 23 ☐ DAY 267
ZECHARIAH 1–2
Visions of Horses and Horns

OVERVIEW Zechariah, the longest of the minor prophets, contains a message of encouragement to the temple builders after the exile. A younger contemporary of Haggai, Zechariah delivers a similar message in a strikingly different manner. Haggai uses sermons; Zechariah uses visions. Haggai is an exhorter; Zechariah is an encourager. Haggai proclaims a strong message of rebuke; Zechariah brings a soothing message of restoration. Haggai is concerned with the present: "Take part and finish the Temple!" Zechariah is concerned with the future: "Take heart. Messiah is coming." The first six chapters of Zechariah's prophecy contain night visions describing Israel's fortunes and future both in Zechariah's day and the days to come.

Chapter 1		Chapter 2	
Vision of the Horses	Vision of the Horns	Vision of the Surveyor	Survey of the Visions
1 17	18 21	1 5	6 13
Israel's Fortunes and Future			

YOUR DAILY WALK On a scale of 1 to 10 (1 = hopeless; 10 = excellent), how would you rate your managerial skills in the following areas?

Buoyant and zealous, Zechariah had the soul of an artist and the eyes of a seer.

_____ Getting your family to help around the house
_____ Supervising your subordinates at work
_____ Motivating committee members to do their jobs
_____ Encouraging members of your Sunday school class

Not all of these situations may apply to you, but here is one that does: challenging others to follow the Lord. Zechariah's task, in a nutshell, was to encourage his countrymen not to "throw in the trowel" in their walk with God. You can do the same!

Look for a small but significant (and sincere) compliment you can pay to each person you encounter today. Watch how attitudes change as others see you seeking to build them up, rather than trying to tear them down. After all, we are put on this earth, not to *see through* one another, but to *see* one another *through*—and encouragement helps!

INSIGHT Zechariah, Alias Smith and Jones
With the aid of a Bible concordance or Bible dictionary, do some "Scripture sleuthing" to see how many different people you can find in the Bible named Zechariah. The answer will surprise you. (Hint: When you get to twenty, you've only just begun.)

CHAPTER 1
In midautumn* of the second year of King Darius's reign, the LORD gave this message to the prophet Zechariah son of Berekiah and grandson of Iddo.

²"I, the LORD, was very angry with your ancestors. ³Therefore, say to the people, 'This is what the LORD Almighty says: Return to me, and I will return to you, says the LORD Almighty.' ⁴Do not be like

1:1 Hebrew *In the eighth month.* A number of dates in Zechariah can be cross-checked with dates in surviving Persian records and related accurately to our modern calendar. This month of the Hebrew lunar calendar occurred in October and November 520 B.C.

your ancestors who would not listen when the earlier prophets said to them, 'This is what the LORD Almighty says: Turn from your evil ways and stop all your evil practices.'

⁵"Your ancestors and their prophets are now long dead. ⁶But all the things I said through my servants the prophets happened to your ancestors, just as I said they would. As a result, they repented and said, 'We have received what we deserved from the LORD Almighty. He has done what he said he would do.' "

⁷Then on February 15* of the second year of King Darius's reign, the LORD sent another message to the prophet Zechariah son of Berekiah and grandson of Iddo. Zechariah said:

⁸In a vision during the night, I saw a man sitting on a red horse that was standing among some myrtle trees in a small valley. Behind him were red, brown, and white horses, each with its own rider. ⁹I asked the angel who was talking with me, "My lord, what are all those horses for?"

"I will show you," the angel replied.

¹⁰So the man standing among the myrtle trees explained, "They are the ones the LORD has sent out to patrol the earth."

¹¹Then the other riders reported to the angel of the LORD, who was standing among the myrtle trees, "We have patrolled the earth, and the whole earth is at peace."

¹²Upon hearing this, the angel of the LORD prayed this prayer: "O LORD Almighty, for seventy years now you have been angry with Jerusalem and the towns of Judah. How long will it be until you again show mercy to them?" ¹³And the LORD spoke kind and comforting words to the angel who talked with me.

¹⁴Then the angel said to me, "Shout this message for all to hear: 'This is what the LORD Almighty says: My love for Jerusalem and Mount Zion is passionate and strong. ¹⁵But I am very angry with the other nations that enjoy peace and security. I was only a little angry with my people, but the nations punished them far beyond my intentions.

¹⁶" 'Therefore, this is what the LORD says: I have returned to show mercy to Jerusalem. My Temple will be rebuilt, says

the LORD Almighty, and plans will be made for the reconstruction of Jerusalem.*' ¹⁷Say this also: 'This is what the LORD Almighty says: The towns of Israel will again overflow with prosperity, and the LORD will again comfort Zion and choose Jerusalem as his own.'"

¹⁸Then I looked up and saw four animal horns. ¹⁹"What are these?" I asked the angel who was talking with me.

He replied, "These horns represent the world powers that scattered Judah, Israel, and Jerusalem."

²⁰Then the LORD showed me four blacksmiths. ²¹"What are these men coming to do?" I asked.

The angel replied, "The blacksmiths have come to terrify the four horns that scattered and humbled Judah. They will throw them down and destroy them."

CHAPTER 2

When I looked around me again, I saw a man with a measuring line in his hand. ²"Where are you going?" I asked.

He replied, "I am going to measure Jerusalem, to see how wide and how long it is."

³Then the angel who was with me went to meet a second angel who was coming toward him. ⁴The other angel said, "Hurry, and say to that young man, 'Jerusalem will someday be so full of people that it won't have room enough for everyone! Many will live outside the city walls, with all their livestock—and yet they will be safe. ⁵For I, myself, will be a wall of fire around Jerusalem, says the LORD. And I will be the glory inside the city!'"

⁶The LORD says, "Come away! Flee from the north, for I have scattered you to the four winds. ⁷Come away! Escape to Jerusalem,* you who are exiled in Babylon!"

⁸"After a period of glory, the LORD Almighty sent me against the nations who oppressed you. For he said, 'Anyone who harms you harms my most precious possession.* ⁹I will raise my fist to crush them, and their own slaves will plunder them.' Then you will know that the LORD Almighty has sent me."

¹⁰The LORD says, "Shout and rejoice, O Jerusalem,* for I am coming to live among you. ¹¹Many nations will join themselves to the LORD on that day, and they,

---

1:7 Hebrew *on the twenty-fourth day of the eleventh month, the month of Shebat,* of the Hebrew calendar. This event occurred on February 15, 519 B.C.; also see note on 1:1.   **1:16** Hebrew *and the measuring line will be stretched out over Jerusalem.*   **2:7** Hebrew *to Zion.*   **2:8** Hebrew *harms the apple of my eye.*   **2:10** Hebrew *O daughter of Zion.*

too, will be my people. I will live among you, and you will know that the LORD Almighty sent me to you. [12]The land of Judah will be the LORD's inheritance in the holy land, and he will once again choose Jerusalem to be his own city. [13]Be silent before the LORD, all humanity, for he is springing into action from his holy dwelling."

SEPTEMBER 24 ☐ DAY 268
ZECHARIAH 3–4
Visions of Priests and Olive Trees

 OVERVIEW In his eight-part series that might be titled "Visions to Revitalize a Nation," Zechariah uses an assortment of symbols and signs to portray the future of his people. Certain themes emerge repeatedly: the need for cleansing, the certainty of judgment, the sovereignty of God over sinful men and women. Like a candlestick in a darkened room, Israel will bear light to a darkened world, "not by force nor by strength, but by my Spirit, says the LORD Almighty" (4:6).

Chapter 3	Chapter 4
Vision of the High Priest	Vision of the Lampstand and Olive Trees
Zechariah's Night Visions	

 YOUR DAILY WALK Becoming a Christian has been likened to taking a step into the unknown . . . and landing on a Rock. There are many things about the Bible you may not fully understand. You may have many questions about points of theology. But the all-important issue you must face is simply this: Is Jesus Christ who he claimed to be? Either you will accept his claim as Messiah (as amply supported by the many specific prophecies in Zechariah), or you will reject it. But you cannot straddle the fence. What will you do with Jesus today?

 INSIGHT The Messiah in Zechariah
With the exception of Isaiah, no other Old Testament book contains more specific prophecies regarding the coming Messiah than Zechariah does. You may want to mark the following passages for quick reference:

The person who insists upon seeing with perfect clearness before he or she decides never decides.

Reference in Zechariah	Picture of Messiah
3:8	Servant (Mark 10:45)
6:13	Priest (Hebrews 6:20–7:1)
6:13; 9:9-10	King (Matthew 21:4-5)
11:12-13	Betrayed (Matthew 27:5-10)
12:10	Pierced (John 19:34, 37)
13:1	Fountain (Revelation 21:6)
13:7	Shepherd (John 10:11)
13:7-9	God (John 1:1)
14:9	King over All (Revelation 11:15)

CHAPTER 3
Then the angel showed me Jeshua* the high priest standing before the angel of the LORD. Satan* was there at the angel's right hand, accusing Jeshua of many things. [2]And the LORD said to Satan, "I, the LORD, reject your accusations, Satan. Yes, the LORD, who has chosen Jerusalem, rebukes

3:1a Hebrew *Joshua*, a variant name for Jeshua; also in 3:3, 4, 6, 8, 9.   **3:1b** Or *The Accuser*; Hebrew reads *The Adversary*; also in 3:2.

you. This man is like a burning stick that has been snatched from a fire."

³Jeshua's clothing was filthy as he stood there before the angel. ⁴So the angel said to the others standing there, "Take off his filthy clothes." And turning to Jeshua he said, "See, I have taken away your sins, and now I am giving you these fine new clothes."

⁵Then I said, "Please, could he also have a clean turban on his head?" So they put a clean priestly turban on his head and dressed him in new clothes while the angel of the LORD stood by.

⁶Then the angel of the LORD spoke very solemnly to Jeshua and said, ⁷"This is what the LORD Almighty says: If you follow my ways and obey my requirements, then you will be given authority over my Temple and its courtyards. I will let you walk in and out of my presence along with these others standing here. ⁸Listen to me, O Jeshua the high priest, and all you other priests. You are symbols of the good things to come. Soon I am going to bring my servant, the Branch. ⁹Now look at the jewel I have set before Jeshua, a single stone with seven facets.* I will engrave an inscription on it, says the LORD Almighty, and I will remove the sins of this land in a single day. ¹⁰And on that day, says the LORD Almighty, each of you will invite your neighbor into your home to share your peace and prosperity."

CHAPTER 4

Then the angel who had been talking with me returned and woke me, as though I had been asleep. ²"What do you see now?" he asked.

3:9 Hebrew 7 *eyes.*

I answered, "I see a solid gold lampstand with a bowl of oil on top of it. Around the bowl are seven lamps, each one having seven spouts with wicks. ³And I see two olive trees, one on each side of the bowl."

⁴Then I asked the angel, "What are these, my lord? What do they mean?"

⁵"Don't you know?" the angel asked.

"No, my lord," I replied.

⁶Then he said to me, "This is what the LORD says to Zerubbabel: It is not by force nor by strength, but by my Spirit, says the LORD Almighty. ⁷Nothing, not even a mighty mountain, will stand in Zerubbabel's way; it will flatten out before him! Then Zerubbabel will set the final stone of the Temple in place, and the people will shout: 'May God bless it! May God bless it!'"

⁸Then another message came to me from the LORD: ⁹"Zerubbabel is the one who laid the foundation of this Temple, and he will complete it. Then you will know that the LORD Almighty has sent me. ¹⁰Do not despise these small beginnings, for the LORD rejoices to see the work begin, to see the plumb line in Zerubbabel's hand. For these seven lamps represent the eyes of the LORD that search all around the world."

¹¹Then I asked the angel, "What are these two olive trees on each side of the lampstand, ¹²and what are the two olive branches that pour out golden oil through two gold tubes?"

¹³"Don't you know?" he asked.

"No, my lord," I replied.

¹⁴Then he said to me, "They represent the two anointed ones who assist the Lord of all the earth."

SEPTEMBER 25 ☐ DAY 269
ZECHARIAH 5–6
Visions of Scrolls and Chariots

OVERVIEW You'll notice a distinct change in emphasis in today's section. All of Zechariah's visions so far have revolved around the nation of Israel: its Temple, its future, its Messiah. But now the focus shifts to include all the earth. God's program is not limited merely to his chosen people. He is the Sovereign of *all* nations. The balance of Zechariah's book represents a concentrated package of messianic prophecies designed to encourage and motivate God's people to complete the task of erecting the Temple.

Chapter 5		Chapter 6	
Vision of the Flying Scroll	Vision of the Woman	Vision of the Chariots	Parable of the Crowns
1 4	5 11	1 8	9 15
Zechariah's Night Visions (cont.)			

Today's preparation determines tomorrow's achievement.

YOUR DAILY WALK Often in the pages of Scripture you will find God preparing a worker for a particular task by displaying a dramatic picture of himself. Think back over the experiences of Isaiah (Isaiah 6:1-7), Ezekiel (Ezekiel 1:1–2:1), and Moses (Exodus 3:1-8). Throughout history God has prepared the workers before he turned them loose to do the work. Armed with a fresh, clear understanding of the great God they served, his men and women then confidently marched forth to perform the task for which God had selected and equipped them.

If your fervor and commitment for God's work have been waning, chances are you need to stop and refocus on the wonderful character of God. Before you tackle your Sunday school lesson, Bible study, sermon notes, or other ministry preparation this week, set aside some quiet moments alone with your Lord. Read from his Word, talk to him openly and honestly about your fears and frustrations, and fall in love with him all over again.

INSIGHT Behold the Man . . .
The crowning of Joshua (6:9-14) prefigures the dual role of the coming man "called the Branch." He will be both priest and king, and peace will result from the union of the kingly and priestly functions in the one person.

CHAPTER 5

I looked up again and saw a scroll flying through the air.

²"What do you see?" the angel asked.

"I see a flying scroll," I replied. "It appears to be about thirty feet long and fifteen feet wide.*"

³Then he said to me, "This scroll contains the curse that is going out over the entire land. One side says that those who steal will be banished from the land; the other side says that those who swear falsely will be banished from the land. ⁴And this is what the LORD Almighty says: I am sending this curse into the house of every thief and into the house of everyone who swears falsely by my name. And my curse will remain in that house until it is completely destroyed—even its timbers and stones."

⁵Then the angel who was talking with me came forward and said, "Look up! Something is appearing in the sky."

⁶"What is it?" I asked.

He replied, "It is a basket for measuring grain,* and it is filled with the sins* of everyone throughout the land."

⁷When the heavy lead cover was lifted off the basket, there was a woman sitting inside it. ⁸The angel said, "The woman's name is Wickedness," and he pushed her back into the basket and closed the heavy lid again.

⁹Then I looked up and saw two women flying toward us, with wings gliding on the wind. Their wings were like those of a stork, and they picked up the basket and flew with it into the sky.

¹⁰"Where are they taking the basket?" I asked the angel.

¹¹He replied, "To the land of Babylonia,* where they will build a temple for the basket. And when the temple is ready, they will set the basket there on its pedestal."

CHAPTER 6

Then I looked up again and saw four chariots coming from between two bronze mountains. ²The first chariot was pulled by red horses, the second by black horses, ³the third by white horses, and the fourth by dappled-gray horses. ⁴"And what are these, my lord?" I asked the angel who was talking with me.

5:2 Hebrew *20 cubits* [9 meters] *long and 10 cubits* [4.5 meters] *wide.*   5:6a Hebrew *an ephah,* about half a bushel or 18 liters; also in 5:7, 8, 9, 10, 11.   5:6b As in Greek version; Hebrew reads *the appearance.*   5:11 Hebrew *the land of Shinar.*

⁵He replied, "These are the four spirits* of heaven who stand before the Lord of all the earth. They are going out to do his work. ⁶The chariot with black horses is going north, the chariot with white horses is going west,* and the chariot with dappled-gray horses is going south."

⁷The powerful horses were eager to be off, to patrol back and forth across the earth. And the LORD said, "Go and patrol the earth!" So they left at once on their patrol.

⁸Then the LORD summoned me and said, "Those who went north have vented the anger of my Spirit* there."

⁹Then I received another message from the LORD: ¹⁰"Heldai, Tobijah, and Jedaiah will bring gifts of silver and gold from the Jews exiled in Babylon. As soon as they arrive, meet them at the home of Josiah son of Zephaniah. ¹¹Accept their gifts and

make a crown* from the silver and gold. Then put the crown on the head of Jeshua* son of Jehozadak, the high priest. ¹²Tell him that the LORD Almighty says: Here is the man called the Branch. He will branch out where he is and build the Temple of the LORD. ¹³He will build the LORD's Temple, and he will receive royal honor and will rule as king from his throne. He will also serve as priest from his throne,* and there will be perfect harmony between the two.

¹⁴"The crown will be a memorial in the Temple of the LORD to honor those who gave it—Heldai,* Tobijah, Jedaiah, and Josiah* son of Zephaniah."

¹⁵Many will come from distant lands to rebuild the Temple of the LORD. And when this happens, you will know my messages have been from the LORD Almighty. All this will happen if you carefully obey the commands of the LORD your God.

6:5 Or *the four winds.*   **6:6** Hebrew *is going after them.*   **6:8** Hebrew *have given my Spirit rest.*   **6:11a** As in Greek and Syriac versions; Hebrew reads *crowns.*   **6:11b** Hebrew *Joshua,* a variant name for Jeshua.   **6:13** Or *There will be a priest by his throne.*   **6:14a** As in Syriac version (compare 6:10); Hebrew reads *Helem.*   **6:14b** As in Syriac version (compare 6:10); Hebrew reads *Hen.*

SEPTEMBER 26 ☐ DAY 270
ZECHARIAH 7–8
To Fast or Not to Fast

OVERVIEW Two years after his night visions, Zechariah is commanded by God to deliver four messages to his people on the subject of fasting. The people are fasting in the fourth, fifth, seventh, and tenth months to commemorate events surrounding the siege and destruction of Jerusalem. Now that they have returned to the land and rebuilt the city, the question naturally arises, "Should we continue to observe the fasts as before?" God's reply through Zechariah is both sobering and comforting. The object of fasting is the key (7:5-7). The way you *live* is more important than the way you *fast* (7:8-14). God's blessing falls on those who exercise truth and love—not empty rituals (8:1-17). True fasting can take place even during feasting (8:18-23)!

Chapter 7		Chapter 8	
Insincere Fasts	Incomplete Obedience	Complete Restoration	Complete Righteousness
1 7	8 14	1 17	18 23
Present Problems		Future Problems	

YOUR DAILY WALK Have you ever been so captivated by the Lord's presence, so absorbed by his Word or engrossed in talking with him, that you skipped a meal? Then whether you knew it or not, you were fasting!

Today's section gives God's commentary on fasting. At its heart, fast-

The prophets of God were fearless men who believed that one plus God was always a majority.

ing is more an *attitude* than an *action.* You can go days without food and never be fasting if your motive is wrong (remember the hypocrites in Matthew 6:16-18?). Conversely, you can be in an attitude of true fasting even as you enjoy a banquet!

Using a good concordance, take an expedition through the Bible to discover what else it has to say about fasting. (You'll discover that David, Hezekiah, Ezra, Nehemiah, Esther, Jesus, and many others fasted.) Notice especially *why* these individuals fasted. Then ask God what the role of fasting should be in your life.

INSIGHT Giving Credit (or Placing Blame) Where It's Due
Here is a tricky question with a significant answer: Who was responsible for scattering the nation of Israel in judgment? According to Zechariah 7:8-14, there is a three-part answer: God initiated the judgment (7:14); God's enemies executed the judgment (7:14); and God's people are charged with the ultimate responsibility for the judgment because their sins were the underlying cause (7:11-13).

CHAPTER 7

On December 7* of the fourth year of King Darius's reign, another message came to Zechariah from the LORD. ²The people of Bethel had sent Sharezer and Regemmelech,* along with their men, to seek the LORD's favor. ³They were to ask this question of the prophets and of the priests at the Temple of the LORD Almighty: "Should we continue to mourn and fast each summer on the anniversary of the Temple's destruction,* as we have done for so many years?"

⁴The LORD Almighty sent me this message: ⁵"Say to all your people and your priests, 'During those seventy years of exile, when you fasted and mourned in the summer and at the festival in early autumn,* was it really for me that you were fasting? ⁶And even now in your holy festivals, you don't think about me but only of pleasing yourselves. ⁷Isn't this the same message the LORD proclaimed through the prophets years ago when Jerusalem and the towns of Judah were bustling with people, and the Negev and the foothills of Judah* were populated areas?'"

⁸Then this message came to Zechariah from the LORD: ⁹"This is what the LORD Almighty says: Judge fairly and honestly, and show mercy and kindness to one another. ¹⁰Do not oppress widows, orphans, foreigners, and poor people. And do not make evil plans to harm each other.

¹¹"Your ancestors would not listen to this

message. They turned stubbornly away and put their fingers in their ears to keep from hearing. ¹²They made their hearts as hard as stone, so they could not hear the law or the messages that the LORD Almighty had sent them by his Spirit through the earlier prophets. That is why the LORD Almighty was so angry with them.

¹³"Since they refused to listen when I called to them, I would not listen when they called to me, says the LORD Almighty. ¹⁴I scattered them as with a whirlwind among the distant nations, where they lived as strangers. Their land became so desolate that no one even traveled through it. The land that had been so pleasant became a desert."

CHAPTER 8

Then another message came to me from the LORD Almighty: ²"This is what the LORD Almighty says: My love for Mount Zion is passionate and strong; I am consumed with passion for Jerusalem! ³And now the LORD says: I am returning to Mount Zion, and I will live in Jerusalem. Then Jerusalem will be called the Faithful City; the mountain of the LORD Almighty will be called the Holy Mountain. ⁴This is what the LORD Almighty says: Once again old men and women will walk Jerusalem's streets with a cane and sit together in the city squares. ⁵And the streets of the city will be filled with boys and girls at play.

7:1 Hebrew *On the fourth day of the ninth month, the month of Kislev,* of the Hebrew calendar. This event occurred on December 7, 518 B.C.; also see note on 1:1.   **7:2** Or *Bethel-sharezer had sent Regemmelech.*   **7:3** Hebrew *mourn and fast in the fifth month.* This month of the Hebrew lunar calendar usually occurs in July and August.   **7:5** Hebrew *fasted and mourned in the fifth and seventh months.* The fifth month of the Hebrew lunar calendar usually occurs in July and August. The seventh month usually occurs in September and October; both the Day of Atonement and the Festival of Shelters were celebrated in the seventh month.   **7:7** Hebrew *the Shephelah.*

6"This is what the LORD Almighty says: All this may seem impossible to you now, a small and discouraged remnant of God's people. But do you think this is impossible for me, the LORD Almighty? 7This is what the LORD Almighty says: You can be sure that I will rescue my people from the east and from the west. 8I will bring them home again to live safely in Jerusalem. They will be my people, and I will be faithful and just toward them as their God.

9"This is what the LORD Almighty says: Take heart and finish the task! You have heard what the prophets have been saying about building the Temple of the LORD Almighty ever since the foundation was laid. 10Before the work on the Temple began, there were no jobs and no wages for either people or animals. No traveler was safe from the enemy, for there were enemies on all sides. I had turned everyone against each other. 11But now I will not treat the remnant of my people as I treated them before, says the LORD Almighty. 12For I am planting seeds of peace and prosperity among you. The grapevines will be heavy with fruit. The earth will produce its crops, and the sky will release the dew. Once more I will make the remnant in Judah and Israel the heirs of these blessings. 13Among the nations, Judah and Israel had become symbols of what it means to be cursed. But no longer! Now I will rescue you and make you both a symbol and a source of blessing! So don't be afraid or discouraged, but instead get on with rebuilding the Temple!

14"For this is what the LORD Almighty says: I did not change my mind when your ancestors angered me and I promised to punish them, says the LORD Almighty. 15Neither will I change my decision to bless Jerusalem and the people of Judah. So don't be afraid. 16But this is what you must do: Tell the truth to each other. Render verdicts in your courts that are just and that lead to peace. 17Do not make evil plots to harm each other. And stop this habit of swearing to things that are false. I hate all these things, says the LORD."

18Here is another message that came to me from the LORD Almighty. 19"This is what the LORD Almighty says: The traditional fasts and times of mourning you have kept in early summer, midsummer, autumn, and winter* are now ended. They will become festivals of joy and celebration for the people of Judah. So love truth and peace.

20"This is what the LORD Almighty says: People from nations and cities around the world will travel to Jerusalem. 21The people of one city will say to the people in another, 'Let us go to Jerusalem to ask the LORD to bless us and to seek the LORD Almighty. We are planning to go ourselves.' 22People from many nations, even powerful nations, will come to Jerusalem to seek the LORD Almighty and to ask the LORD to bless them.

23"This is what the LORD Almighty says: In those days ten people from nations and languages around the world will clutch at the hem of one Jew's robe. And they will say, 'Please let us walk with you, for we have heard that God is with you.'"

8:19 Hebrew *in the fourth, fifth, seventh, and tenth months.* The fourth month of the Hebrew lunar calendar usually occurs in June and July. The fifth month usually occurs in July and August. The seventh month usually occurs in September and October. The tenth month usually occurs in December and January.

SEPTEMBER 27 ☐ DAY 271
ZECHARIAH 9–11
Israel's Coming King and Shepherd

OVERVIEW In an amazingly specific series of prophecies, Zechariah foretells Israel's immediate future. Israel's neighbors would be defeated by an invading force, while Israel would be preserved to the day of the coming Messiah. He would arrive on the colt of a donkey, coming to defend his people and defeat his enemies, as he had promised. Tragically, he would be rejected by the people and betrayed for thirty pieces of silver. In his place false shepherds would emerge to scatter the flock and lead his people astray.

Chapter 9		Chapter 10	Chapter 11
Coming Calamity	Coming King	Messiah's Redemption	Messiah's Rejection
1 8	9 17		
Judgment and Justice		Salvation and Suffering	

 YOUR DAILY WALK Does God have limitations? Is there anything God cannot do? A seminary student, wrestling with those difficult questions, posed the problem to his professor in the form of a riddle: "Professor, can God make a rock so big that he cannot pick it up?" To which the teacher wisely responded, "Yes . . . and then he would pick it up anyway!"

The prophets laid bare the moral and spiritual condition of the nation.

God is infinite, all-powerful, all-knowing, almighty. But he does have limitations: He cannot act contrary to his promises; he will never contradict his written Word; and he will not release individuals from the consequences of (and responsibility for) their personal choices in life.

This explains why Jesus, the fulfillment of prophecy, God's only Son, the Messiah, could be rejected by Israel. God would not force the nation to accept him if it chose instead to reject him. But though the people were free to make the choice, they were powerless to escape the consequences of that choice.

Where in your life has God made his will clear to you through his Word, parental or pastoral counsel, or prayer—and yet you are resisting it? Zechariah would be the first to tell you that it is dangerous to say no to God.

 INSIGHT Greece, a Sticky Problem for the Critics
Like Daniel (Daniel 8:21; 10:20; 11:2), Zechariah mentions a nation's rise to power (Greece, in 9:13) long before it occurred. And like Daniel, he receives the critics' doubts for this supernatural insight!

CHAPTER 9

This is the message* from the LORD against the land of Aram* and the city of Damascus, for the eyes of all humanity, including the people of Israel, are on the LORD. ²Doom is certain for Hamath, near Damascus, and for the cities of Tyre and Sidon, too, though they are so clever. ³Tyre has built a strong fortress and has piled up so much silver and gold that it is as common as dust in the streets! ⁴But now the Lord will strip away Tyre's possessions and hurl its fortifications into the Mediterranean Sea.* Tyre will be set on fire and burned to the ground.

⁵The city of Ashkelon will see Tyre fall and will be filled with fear. Gaza will shake with terror, and so will Ekron, for their hopes will be dashed. Gaza will be con-quered and its king killed, and Ashkelon will be completely deserted. ⁶Foreigners will occupy the city of Ashdod. Thus, I will destroy the pride of the Philistines. ⁷They will no longer eat meat with blood in it or feed on other forbidden foods. All the surviving Philistines will worship our God and be adopted as a new clan in Judah.* And the Philistines of Ekron will join my people, just as the Jebusites once did. ⁸I will guard my Temple and protect it from invading armies. I am closely watching their movements. No foreign oppressor will ever again overrun my people's land.

⁹Rejoice greatly, O people* of Zion! Shout in triumph, O people of Jerusalem! Look, your king is coming to you. He is righteous and victorious, yet he is humble, riding on a donkey—even on a donkey's

9:1a Hebrew *An Oracle: The message.* **9:1b** Hebrew *land of Hadrach.* **9:4** Hebrew *the sea.* **9:7** Hebrew *and will become a leader in Judah.* **9:9** Hebrew *daughter.*

colt. ¹⁰I will remove the battle chariots from Israel* and the warhorses from Jerusalem, and I will destroy all the weapons used in battle. Your king will bring peace to the nations. His realm will stretch from sea to sea and from the Euphrates River* to the ends of the earth.*

¹¹Because of the covenant I made with you, sealed with blood, I will free your prisoners from death in a waterless dungeon. ¹²Come back to the place of safety, all you prisoners, for there is yet hope! I promise this very day that I will repay you two mercies for each of your woes! ¹³Judah is my bow, and Israel is my arrow! Jerusalem* is my sword, and like a warrior, I will brandish it against the Greeks.*

¹⁴The LORD will appear above his people; his arrows will fly like lightning! The Sovereign LORD will sound the trumpet; he will go out against his enemies like a whirlwind from the southern desert. ¹⁵The LORD Almighty will protect his people, and they will subdue their enemies with sling stones. They will shout in battle as though drunk with wine, shedding the blood of their enemies. They will be filled with blood like a bowl, drenched with blood like the corners of the altar.

¹⁶When that day arrives, the LORD their God will rescue his people, just as a shepherd rescues his sheep. They will sparkle in his land like jewels in a crown. ¹⁷How wonderful and beautiful they will be! The young men and women will thrive on the abundance of grain and new wine.

CHAPTER 10

Ask the LORD for rain in the spring, and he will give it. It is the LORD who makes storm clouds that drop showers of rain so that every field becomes a lush pasture.

²Household gods give false advice, fortune-tellers predict only lies, and interpreters of dreams pronounce comfortless falsehoods. So my people are wandering like lost sheep, without a shepherd to protect and guide them.

³"My anger burns against your shepherds, and I will punish these leaders.* For the LORD Almighty has arrived to look after his flock of Judah; he will make them strong and glorious, like a proud warhorse in battle. ⁴From Judah will come the corner-

stone, the tent peg, the battle bow, and all the rulers. ⁵They will be like mighty warriors in battle, trampling their enemies in the mud under their feet. Since the LORD is with them as they fight, they will overthrow even the horsemen of the enemy.

⁶"I will strengthen Judah and save Israel*; I will reestablish them because I love them. It will be as though I had never rejected them, for I am the LORD their God, who will hear their cries. ⁷The people of Israel* will become like mighty warriors, and their hearts will be happy as if by wine. Their children, too, will see it all and be glad; their hearts will rejoice in the LORD. ⁸When I whistle to them, they will come running, for I have redeemed them. From the few that are left, their population will grow again to its former size. ⁹Though I have scattered them like seeds among the nations, still they will remember me in distant lands. With their children, they will survive and come home again to Israel. ¹⁰I will bring them back from Egypt and Assyria and resettle them in Gilead and Lebanon. There won't be enough room for them all! ¹¹They will pass safely through the sea of distress,* for the waves of the sea will be held back. And the waters of the Nile will become dry. The pride of Assyria will be crushed, and the rule of Egypt will end. ¹²I will make my people strong in my power, and they will go wherever they wish by my authority. I, the LORD, have spoken!"

CHAPTER 11

Open your doors, Lebanon, so that fire may sweep through your cedar forests. ²Weep, you cypress trees, for all the ruined cedars; the tallest and most beautiful of them are fallen. Weep, you oaks of Bashan, as you watch the thickest forests being felled. ³Listen to the wailing of the shepherds, for their wealth is gone. Hear the young lions roaring, for their thickets in the Jordan Valley have been destroyed.

⁴This is what the LORD my God says: "Go and care for a flock that is intended for slaughter. ⁵The buyers will slaughter their sheep without remorse. The sellers will say, 'Praise the LORD, I am now rich!' Even the shepherds have no compassion for them. ⁶And likewise, I will no longer have pity on the inhabitants of the land," says the LORD.

9:10a Hebrew *from Ephraim;* also in 9:13.   9:10b Hebrew *the river.*   9:10c Or *the end of the land.*   9:13a Hebrew *Zion.*
9:13b Hebrew *the sons of Javan.*   10:3 Or *these male goats.*   10:6 Hebrew *save the house of Joseph.*   10:7 Hebrew *of Ephraim.*
10:11 Or *the sea of Egypt,* referring to the Red Sea.

"I will let them fall into each other's clutches, as well as into the clutches of their king. They will turn the land into a wilderness, and I will not protect them."

⁷So I cared for the flock intended for slaughter—the flock that was oppressed. Then I took two shepherd's staffs and named one Favor and the other Union. ⁸I got rid of their three evil shepherds in a single month. But I became impatient with these sheep—this nation—and they hated me, too. ⁹So I told them, "I won't be your shepherd any longer. If you die, you die. If you are killed, you are killed. And those who remain will devour each other!"

¹⁰Then I took my staff called Favor and snapped it in two, showing that I had revoked the covenant I had made with all the nations. ¹¹That was the end of my covenant with them. Those who bought and sold sheep were watching me, and they knew that the LORD was speaking to them through my actions. ¹²And I said to them, "If you like, give me my wages, whatever I am worth; but only if you want to." So they counted out for my wages thirty pieces* of silver.

¹³And the LORD said to me, "Throw it to the potters*"—this magnificent sum at which they valued me! So I took the thirty coins and threw them to the potters in the Temple of the LORD. ¹⁴Then I broke my other staff, Union, to show that the bond of unity between Judah and Israel was broken.

¹⁵Then the LORD said to me, "Go again and play the part of a worthless shepherd. ¹⁶This will illustrate how I will give this nation a shepherd who will not care for the sheep that are threatened by death, nor look after the young, nor heal the injured, nor feed the healthy. Instead, this shepherd will eat the meat of the fattest sheep and tear off their hooves. ¹⁷Doom is certain for this worthless shepherd who abandons the flock! The sword will cut his arm and pierce his right eye! His arm will become useless, and his right eye completely blind!"

11:12 Hebrew *30 shekels*, about 12 ounces or 342 grams in weight.   **11:13** Syriac version reads *into the treasury;* also in 11:13b.

SEPTEMBER 28 ☐ DAY 272
Finishing Touches

 LOOK BACK Haggai (whose name means "festive") and Zechariah ("the Lord remembers") are prophetic contemporaries with contrasting styles and messages. Haggai delivers a powerful call to arms, urging the people of Judah to *take part* and complete the rebuilding of the Temple. Zechariah, by contrast, uses a series of visions, messages, and burdens to gently urge the people of Judah to *take heart,* regain courage, and see the future as bright with the promises of God. Haggai exhorts the people to action with strong words of rebuke; Zechariah urges the people to action with gentle reminders of the future importance of the Temple.

Haggai, the second shortest book in the Old Testament, jars the nation out of its complacency and preoccupation. Because of Judah's misplaced priorities, the Temple that should have been finished years earlier still stands half-completed and useless. By contrast, Zechariah reminds the nation of God's covenant faithfulness. When times are tough and the future is uncertain, it's always safe to trust the Lord. Together, these prophets urge God's people to rise up and complete the rebuilding of the Temple. And, indeed, that is precisely what they did!

 LOOK UP Here is a simple three-question quiz with a profound point to it:
- How long does it take to cook a one-minute steak? _____
- How long does it take to complete a four-year bachelor's degree? _____

- How long does it take to read the Bible all the way through with the help of a through-the-Bible-in-a-year devotional program? _____

To do nothing is tiresome because you cannot stop and take a rest.

The answer to each question is the same: No one knows for sure! It all depends on your attentiveness and persistence.

A one-minute steak *should* take about a minute . . . unless the cook gets distracted or interrupted, in which case the steak might cook indefinitely (with predictable results).

A four-year degree program *ought* to be completed in about four years, but many who start with the best of intentions find themselves mired in a half-completed program after more than a decade.

A through-the-Bible-in-a-year reading plan *can* be completed in a year, if it remains a daily priority with the reader! But allow the goal to grow fuzzy or other priorities to compete for the necessary twenty minutes a day, and the goal may prove elusive indeed.

LOOK AHEAD Even a goal as worthy as rebuilding the Temple has a way of becoming slippery and elusive when other priorities are allowed to compete. As the project dragged on year after year, the homes and comforts of God's people became more important than the Temple and glory of God. And the result? Sixteen years after Cyrus had issued the proclamation launching the project, there were *weeds* instead of *walls* growing from the foundation.

Haggai and Zechariah held their countrymen accountable to finish what they had begun. Haggai (with exhortation) and Zechariah (with encouragement) both urged the builders not to "throw in the trowel." If you're having trouble completing a long-term project you began more than a year ago, why not enlist the help of a friend or family member? A weekly time of accountability and progress reporting might be just the thing you need to stay on target and bring to completion a worthy endeavor.

SEPTEMBER 29 ☐ DAY 273
ZECHARIAH 12–14
Israel's Coming Consolation

OVERVIEW Consolation is coming for the people of God, and Zechariah closes his prophecy with a stirring portrayal of what will happen "on that day." God will destroy Jerusalem's enemies; the nation will be cleansed of idols and false prophets; mountains will move; hard hearts will melt; and the Lord will be king over all the earth (14:9). What began as a vision of horror in chapters 1 and 2 ends as a vision of hope.

Chapter 12	Chapter 13	Chapter 14
"Jerusalem [Has] Found Strength"	"The LORD Is Our God"	"The LORD Will Be King"
Deliverance	Delight	Dominion

YOUR DAILY WALK If you had to select the three strongest men in the Bible, whom would you pick?

Chances are the names you listed are examples of physical strength. Perhaps you chose men like Samson . . . or David . . . or Joshua—men of might, men of warfare, men of the outdoors. But did you ever stop to think that some of the strongest men in the Bible were, from a physical point of view, some of the weakest? Daniel (whose greatest claim to

Let us pray not for lighter burdens but for stronger backs. fame was sitting quietly in the corner of a lions' den); Jeremiah (who turned into a fountain of tears at the thought of his exiled people, yet preached with fire and faithfulness for forty years); Timothy (who stood toe-to-toe with heretics in spite of his young age, poor health, and timid temperament).

As Zechariah looks ahead on the prophetic calendar, he predicts, "The weakest among them wil be as mighty as King David" (12:8). Their strength will come, not from physical, material, or military superiority, but from their relationship to God. Is that true of you today? Regardless of your physical stamina or financial condition, you can be strong in the Lord. Place these words next to your medicine cabinet: *My strength is in the Lord Almighty.* Then every time you reach for a pill or prescription, you'll be reminded of the strength that's available in limitless supply!

 INSIGHT Jerusalem in the Forefront
In chapter 14 you will find at least eight specific references to the city of Jerusalem—an important clue to the original intent of Zechariah's visions and to God's program "on that day."

CHAPTER 12
This* message concerning the fate of Israel came from the LORD: "This message is from the LORD, who stretched out the heavens, laid the foundations of the earth, and formed the spirit within humans. ²I will make Jerusalem and Judah like an intoxicating drink to all the nearby nations that send their armies to besiege Jerusalem. ³On that day I will make Jerusalem a heavy stone, a burden for the world. None of the nations who try to lift it will escape unscathed.

⁴"On that day, says the LORD, I will cause every horse to panic and every rider to lose his nerve. I will watch over the people of Judah, but I will blind the horses of her enemies. ⁵And the clans of Judah will say to themselves, 'The people of Jerusalem have found strength in the LORD Almighty, their God.'

⁶"On that day I will make the clans of Judah like a brazier that sets a woodpile ablaze or like a burning torch among sheaves of grain. They will burn up all the neighboring nations right and left, while the people living in Jerusalem remain secure. ⁷The LORD will give victory to the rest of Judah first, before Jerusalem, so that the people of Jerusalem and the royal line of David will not have greater honor than the rest of Judah. ⁸On that day the LORD will defend the people of Jerusalem; the weakest among them will be as mighty as King David! And the royal descendants will be like God, like the angel of the LORD who goes before them! ⁹For my plan is to destroy all the nations that come against Jerusalem.

¹⁰"Then I will pour out a spirit of grace and prayer on the family of David and on all the people of Jerusalem. They will look on me whom they have pierced and mourn for him as for an only son. They will grieve bitterly for him as for a firstborn son who has died. ¹¹The sorrow and mourning in Jerusalem on that day will be like the grievous mourning of Hadad-rimmon in the valley of Megiddo.

¹²"All Israel will weep in profound sorrow, each family by itself, with the husbands and wives in separate groups. The family of David will mourn, along with the family of Nathan, ¹³the family of Levi, and the family of Shimei. ¹⁴Each of the surviving families from Judah will mourn separately, husbands and wives apart.

CHAPTER 13
"On that day a fountain will be opened for the dynasty of David and for the people of Jerusalem, a fountain to cleanse them from all their sins and defilement.

²"And on that day, says the LORD Almighty, I will get rid of every trace of idol worship throughout the land, so that even the names of the idols will be forgotten. I will remove from the land all false prophets and the unclean spirits that inspire them. ³If anyone begins prophesying again, his own father and mother will tell him, 'You must die, for you have prophesied lies in the name of the LORD.' Then his own father and mother will stab him.

⁴"No one will be boasting then of a prophetic gift! No one will wear prophet's

12:1 Hebrew *An Oracle: This.*

clothes to try to fool the people. [5]'No,' he will say. 'I'm not a prophet; I'm a farmer. The soil has been my means of livelihood from my earliest youth.' [6]And if someone asks, 'Then what are those scars on your chest*?' he will say, 'I was wounded at the home of friends!'

[7]"Awake, O sword, against my shepherd, the man who is my partner, says the LORD Almighty. Strike down the shepherd, and the sheep will be scattered, and I will turn against the lambs. [8]Two-thirds of the people in the land will be cut off and die, says the LORD. But a third will be left in the land. [9]I will bring that group through the fire and make them pure, just as gold and silver are refined and purified by fire. They will call on my name, and I will answer them. I will say, 'These are my people,' and they will say, 'The LORD is our God.'"

CHAPTER 14
Watch, for the day of the LORD is coming when your possessions will be plundered right in front of you! [2]On that day I will gather all the nations to fight against Jerusalem. The city will be taken, the houses plundered, and the women raped. Half the population will be taken away into captivity, and half will be left among the ruins of the city.

[3]Then the LORD will go out to fight against those nations, as he has fought in times past. [4]On that day his feet will stand on the Mount of Olives, which faces Jerusalem on the east. And the Mount of Olives will split apart, making a wide valley running from east to west, for half the mountain will move toward the north and half toward the south. [5]You will flee through this valley, for it will reach across to Azal.* Yes, you will flee as you did from the earthquake in the days of King Uzziah of Judah. Then the LORD my God will come, and all his holy ones with him.*

[6]On that day the sources of light will no longer shine,* [7]yet there will be continuous day! Only the LORD knows how this could happen! There will be no normal day and night, for at evening time it will still be light. [8]On that day life-giving waters will flow out from Jerusalem, half toward the Dead Sea and half toward the Mediterranean,* flowing continuously both in summer and in winter.

[9]And the LORD will be king over all the earth. On that day there will be one LORD— his name alone will be worshiped. [10]All the land from Geba, north of Judah, to Rimmon, south of Jerusalem, will become one vast plain. But Jerusalem will be raised up in its original place and will be inhabited all the way from the Benjamin Gate over to the site of the old gate, then to the Corner Gate, and from the Tower of Hananel to the king's winepresses. [11]And Jerusalem will be filled, safe at last, never again to be cursed and destroyed.

[12]And the LORD will send a plague on all the nations that fought against Jerusalem. Their people will become like walking corpses, their flesh rotting away. Their eyes will shrivel in their sockets, and their tongues will decay in their mouths. [13]On that day they will be terrified, stricken by the LORD with great panic. They will fight against each other in hand-to-hand combat; [14]Judah, too, will be fighting at Jerusalem. The wealth of all the neighboring nations will be captured—great quantities of gold and silver and fine clothing. [15]This same plague will strike the horses, mules, camels, donkeys, and all the other animals in the enemy camps.

[16]In the end, the enemies of Jerusalem who survive the plague will go up to Jerusalem each year to worship the King, the LORD Almighty, and to celebrate the Festival of Shelters. [17]And any nation anywhere in the world that refuses to come to Jerusalem to worship the King, the LORD Almighty, will have no rain. [18]And if the people of Egypt refuse to attend the festival, the LORD will punish them with the same plague that he sends on the other nations who refuse to go. [19]Egypt and the other nations will all be punished if they don't go to celebrate the festival.

[20]On that day even the harness bells of the horses will be inscribed with these words: SET APART AS HOLY TO THE LORD. And the cooking pots in the Temple of the LORD will be as sacred as the basins used beside the altar. [21]In fact, every cooking pot in Jerusalem and Judah will be set apart as holy to the LORD Almighty. All who come to worship will be free to use any of these pots to boil their sacrifices. And on that day there will no longer be traders* in the Temple of the LORD Almighty.

13:6 Or *scars between your hands.*   **14:5a** The meaning of the Hebrew is uncertain.   **14:5b** As in Greek version; Hebrew reads *with you.*   **14:6** Hebrew *there will be no light, no cold or frost.* The meaning of the Hebrew is uncertain.   **14:8** Hebrew *half toward the eastern sea and half toward the western sea.*   **14:21** Hebrew *Canaanites.*

Malachi

IT HAS been years since God restored his people to their land. But they have lapsed into the very sins that brought about their captivity. God sends Malachi to remind his people that he loves them, but they have not returned his love. The priests have dishonored him and led his people astray. The men have married heathen women. And all have hardened their hearts to persist in their sins. Malachi gives them a final warning of the purifying day of the Lord, after which God's people would hear no more from him for four hundred years.

Focus	God's Love	God's Rebuke		God's Promise		
Divisions	God's Love for the People	Rebuke of the Priests	Rebuke of the People	Righteous Remembered	Wicked Destroyed	Elijah Coming
	1:1 1:5	1:6 2:9	2:10 3:15	3:16 3:18	4:1 4:3	4:4 4:6
Topics	Past	Present		Future		
	Questions and Answers			Invitation and Warning		
Place	Jerusalem					
Time	Approximately 432–425 B.C.					

SEPTEMBER 30 ☐ DAY 274
MALACHI 1–4
Hard Words for Hearts of Stone

OVERVIEW Malachi marks the sunset of Old Testament prophecy. Malachi the prophet and Nehemiah the builder were contemporaries, and the situations Nehemiah faced—corrupt priests, mixed marriages, neglected tithes—formed the basis for Malachi's sermons. The book is constructed around a three-part pattern involving accusation, interrogation, and refutation. For example:

Accusation: "In Judah, in Israel, and in Jerusalem there is treachery" (2:11).

Interrogation: "You cry out, 'Why has the LORD abandoned us?'" (2:14).

Refutation: "Because the LORD witnessed the vows you and your wife made to each other on your wedding day. . . . But you have been disloyal to her" (2:14). Can you find more examples in the book?

Arrogant insensitivity shows that the nation has hit rock bottom spiritually. The people have become so sin-hardened that God's proddings no longer prick their conscience. With his intense, convicting words, Malachi ushers in four hundred years of silence, which will be broken at last when John the Baptist emerges to proclaim, "Look! There is the Lamb of God who takes away the sin of the world!" (John 1:29).

Chapter 1	Chapter 2	Chapter 3	Chapter 4
Sins of the Priests	Sins of the People	Payday for the People	Coming Day of the Lord
Questions and Answers			Invitation and Warning

Malachi's prophecy, like a morning dawn, brings with it the promise of a new and more glorious day.

YOUR DAILY WALK It is fitting that the last word of the Old Testament should be *curse*. A curse is something to be avoided—the result of a neglected command or disobedient action. Malachi brings down the curtain on the Old Testament with a final reminder that sin must be dealt with. When the New Testament opens, the scene will be set for the one who alone can cure humanity's sin sickness: Jesus the Messiah.

Close your study of Malachi with a time of prayer. If you know Christ as Savior, tell him how much he means to you. If you don't, wouldn't now be a perfect time to put your trust in him?

INSIGHT Will the Real Elijah Please Stand Up?
John the Baptist was the fulfillment of Malachi's prophecy that Elijah would come as Messiah's forerunner (4:5; Matthew 17:12). And according to Malachi, another Elijah-like forerunner will precede Christ's second coming as well (4:6; Matthew 17:11)!

CHAPTER 1

This is the message* that the LORD gave to Israel through the prophet Malachi.*

²"I have loved you deeply," says the LORD.

But you retort, "Really? How have you loved us?"

And the LORD replies, "I showed my love for you by loving your ancestor Jacob. Yet Esau was Jacob's brother, ³and I

1:1a Hebrew *An Oracle: The message.*   **1:1b** *Malachi* means "my messenger."

rejected Esau and devastated his hill country. I turned Esau's inheritance into a desert for jackals."

[4] And Esau's descendants in Edom may say, "We have been shattered, but we will rebuild the ruins."

But this is what the LORD Almighty says: "They may try to rebuild, but I will demolish them again! Their country will be known as 'The Land of Wickedness,' and their people will be called 'The People with Whom the LORD Is Forever Angry.' [5] When you see the destruction for yourselves, you will say, 'Truly, the LORD's great power reaches far beyond our borders!'"

[6] The LORD Almighty says to the priests: "A son honors his father, and a servant respects his master. I am your father and master, but where are the honor and respect I deserve? You have despised my name!

"But you ask, 'How have we ever despised your name?'

[7] "You have despised my name by offering defiled sacrifices on my altar.

"Then you ask, 'How have we defiled the sacrifices*?'

"You defile them by saying the altar of the LORD deserves no respect. [8] When you give blind animals as sacrifices, isn't that wrong? And isn't it wrong to offer animals that are crippled and diseased? Try giving gifts like that to your governor, and see how pleased he is!" says the LORD Almighty.

[9] "Go ahead, beg God to be merciful to you! But when you bring that kind of offering, why should he show you any favor at all?" asks the LORD Almighty.

[10] "I wish that someone among you would just shut the Temple doors so that these worthless sacrifices could not be offered! I am not at all pleased with you," says the LORD Almighty, "and I will not accept your offerings. [11] But my name is honored by people of other nations from morning till night. All around the world they offer sweet incense and pure offerings in honor of my name. For my name is great among the nations," says the LORD Almighty. [12] "But you dishonor my name with your actions. By bringing contemptible food, you are saying it's all right to defile the Lord's table. [13] You say, 'It's too hard to serve the LORD,' and you turn up your

noses at his commands," says the LORD Almighty. "Think of it! Animals that are stolen and mutilated, crippled and sick— presented as offerings! Should I accept from you such offerings as these?" asks the LORD. [14] "Cursed is the cheat who promises to give a fine ram from his flock but then sacrifices a defective one to the Lord. For I am a great king," says the LORD Almighty, "and my name is feared among the nations!

CHAPTER 2

"Listen, you priests; this command is for you! [2] Listen to me and take it to heart. Honor my name," says the LORD Almighty, "or I will bring a terrible curse against you. I will curse even the blessings you receive. Indeed, I have already cursed them, because you have not taken my warning seriously. [3] I will rebuke your descendants and splatter your faces with the dung of your festival sacrifices, and I will add you to the dung heap. [4] Then at last you will know it was I who sent you this warning so that my covenant with the Levites may continue," says the LORD Almighty.

[5] "The purpose of my covenant with the Levites was to bring life and peace, and this is what I gave them. This called for reverence from them, and they greatly revered me and stood in awe of my name. [6] They passed on to the people all the truth they received from me. They did not lie or cheat; they walked with me, living good and righteous lives, and they turned many from lives of sin. [7] The priests' lips should guard knowledge, and people should go to them for instruction, for the priests are the messengers of the LORD Almighty. [8] But not you! You have left God's paths. Your 'guidance' has caused many to stumble into sin. You have corrupted the covenant I made with the Levites," says the LORD Almighty. [9] "So I have made you despised and humiliated in the eyes of all the people. For you have not obeyed me but have shown partiality in your interpretation of the law."

[10] Are we not all children of the same Father? Are we not all created by the same God? Then why are we faithless to each other, violating the covenant of our ancestors? [11] In Judah, in Israel, and in Jerusalem there is treachery, for the men of Judah have defiled the LORD's beloved sanctuary

---

1:7 As in Greek version; Hebrew reads *defiled you.*

by marrying women who worship idols. [12]May the LORD cut off from the nation of Israel* every last man who has done this and yet brings an offering to the LORD Almighty.

[13]Here is another thing you do. You cover the LORD's altar with tears, weeping and groaning because he pays no attention to your offerings, and he doesn't accept them with pleasure. [14]You cry out, "Why has the LORD abandoned us?" I'll tell you why! Because the LORD witnessed the vows you and your wife made to each other on your wedding day when you were young. But you have been disloyal to her, though she remained your faithful companion, the wife of your marriage vows. [15]Didn't the LORD make you one with your wife? In body and spirit you are his.* And what does he want? Godly children from your union. So guard yourself; remain loyal to the wife of your youth. [16]"For I hate divorce!" says the LORD, the God of Israel. "It is as cruel as putting on a victim's bloodstained coat," says the LORD Almighty. "So guard yourself; always remain loyal to your wife."

[17]You have wearied the LORD with your words.

"Wearied him?" you ask. "How have we wearied him?"

You have wearied him by suggesting that the LORD favors evildoers since he does not punish them. You have wearied him by asking, "Where is the God of justice?"

CHAPTER 3

"Look! I am sending my messenger, and he will prepare the way before me. Then the Lord you are seeking will suddenly come to his Temple. The messenger of the covenant, whom you look for so eagerly, is surely coming," says the LORD Almighty. [2]"But who will be able to endure it when he comes? Who will be able to stand and face him when he appears? For he will be like a blazing fire that refines metal or like a strong soap that whitens clothes. [3]He will sit and judge like a refiner of silver, watching closely as the dross is burned away. He will purify the Levites, refining them like gold or silver, so that they may once again offer acceptable sacrifices to the LORD. [4]Then once more the LORD will accept the offerings brought to him by the people of Judah and Jerusalem, as he did in former times. [5]At that time I will put you on trial. I will be a ready witness against all sorcerers and adulterers and liars. I will speak against those who cheat employees of their wages, who oppress widows and orphans, or who deprive the foreigners living among you of justice, for these people do not fear me," says the LORD Almighty.

[6]"I am the LORD, and I do not change. That is why you descendants of Jacob are not already completely destroyed. [7]Ever since the days of your ancestors, you have scorned my laws and failed to obey them. Now return to me, and I will return to you," says the LORD Almighty.

"But you ask, 'How can we return when we have never gone away?'

[8]"Should people cheat God? Yet you have cheated me!

"But you ask, 'What do you mean? When did we ever cheat you?'

"You have cheated me of the tithes and offerings due to me. [9]You are under a curse, for your whole nation has been cheating me. [10]Bring all the tithes into the storehouse so there will be enough food in my Temple. If you do," says the LORD Almighty, "I will open the windows of heaven for you. I will pour out a blessing so great you won't have enough room to take it in! Try it! Let me prove it to you! [11]Your crops will be abundant, for I will guard them from insects and disease.* Your grapes will not shrivel before they are ripe," says the LORD Almighty. [12]"Then all nations will call you blessed, for your land will be such a delight," says the LORD Almighty.

[13]"You have said terrible things about me," says the LORD.

"But you say, 'What do you mean? How have we spoken against you?'

[14]"You have said, 'What's the use of serving God? What have we gained by obeying his commands or by trying to show the LORD Almighty that we are sorry for our sins? [15]From now on we will say, "Blessed are the arrogant." For those who do evil get rich, and those who dare God to punish them go free of harm.'"

[16]Then those who feared the LORD spoke with each other, and the LORD listened to what they said. In his presence, a scroll of remembrance was written to record the

2:12 Hebrew *from the tents of Jacob.*   **2:15** Or *Did not one God make us and preserve our life and breath?* or *Did not one God make her, both flesh and spirit?* The meaning of the Hebrew is uncertain.   **3:11** Hebrew *from the devourer.*

names of those who feared him and loved to think about him. [17]"They will be my people," says the LORD Almighty. "On the day when I act, they will be my own special treasure. I will spare them as a father spares an obedient and dutiful child. [18]Then you will again see the difference between the righteous and the wicked, between those who serve God and those who do not."

CHAPTER 4

The LORD Almighty says, "The day of judgment is coming, burning like a furnace. The arrogant and the wicked will be burned up like straw on that day. They will be consumed like a tree—roots and all. [2]"But for you who fear my name, the Sun of Righteousness will rise with healing in his wings.* And you will go free, leaping with joy like calves let out to pasture. [3]On the day when I act, you will tread upon the wicked as if they were dust under your feet," says the LORD Almighty.

[4]"Remember to obey the instructions of my servant Moses, all the laws and regulations that I gave him on Mount Sinai* for all Israel.

[5]"Look, I am sending you the prophet Elijah before the great and dreadful day of the LORD arrives. [6]His preaching will turn the hearts of parents* to their children, and the hearts of children to their parents. Otherwise I will come and strike the land with a curse."

4:2 Or *the sun of righteousness will rise with healing in its wings.*   **4:4** Hebrew *Horeb,* another name for Sinai.   **4:6** Hebrew *fathers;* also in 4:6b.

Matthew

THE FIRST verse of the Gospel of Matthew announces the event predicted by Old Testament prophets and long awaited by Israel: the coming of the Anointed One, "Jesus the Messiah, a descendant of King David and of Abraham." Under the Spirit's guidance, Matthew carefully documents Christ's claim to be the Messiah: He possesses the credentials of the Messiah and ministers in the predicted pattern of the Messiah. He preaches messages only the Messiah could deliver and finally dies the death only the Messiah could die.

Focus	Preparation	Pattern			Proclamation		Passion
Divisions	Pedigree of the King	Preaching of the King	Power of the King	Parables of the King	Principles of the King	Predictions of the King	Passion of the King
	1　　　　　4	5　　7	8　　11	12　　15	16　　　19	20　　　25	26　　　28
Topics	Teaching the Throngs	Teaching the Twelve					
	Growing Reception	Growing Rejection					
Place	Bethlehem and Nazareth	Galilee				Jerusalem	
Time	4 B.C.–A.D. 33						

OCTOBER 1 □ DAY 275
MATTHEW 1–4
Pedigree of the King

OVERVIEW What was *anticipated* in the last book of the Old Testament (Malachi) now *arrives* in the first book of the New Testament (Matthew): the Messiah of God. He must come from the kingly line—and Jesus does. He must bear the name of royalty—and Jesus' name means "the LORD saves." He must be worthy of worship—and wise men from the east travel great distances to pay homage to him. He must be a light to the Gentiles, be announced by a forerunner, and demonstrate power over Satan, demons, disease, and death—and Jesus does all this and more. The Messiah has come!

Chapter 1	Chapter 2	Chapter 3	Chapter 4
Pedigree of the King	Presentation of the King	Proclamation of the King	Power of the King
Joseph	Wise Men	John	Satan

You can never starve the person who feeds on God's promises.

YOUR DAILY WALK How well do you know your Old Testament? That may seem like an unusual question to ask as you begin reading the New Testament. But you'll quickly discover that the key to unlocking the *New* is a foundational knowledge of the *Old!* In order to persuade his fellow Jews to believe in Jesus as their long-awaited King and Messiah, Matthew used the Old Testament as proof. When Jesus faced the triple temptation by Satan in the wilderness, he used Scripture from the fifth book of the Old Testament (Deuteronomy) as his basis of defense.

Underline each Old Testament quotation you find in today's reading. (Hint: Watch for such phrases as "this happened to fulfill the Lord's message through his prophet.") Then spend a few extra minutes looking up those Old Testament prophecies that became New Testament realities. Wouldn't it be fitting to close your time in God's Word today by thanking God that his centuries-old promises are trustworthy? Do that right now!

INSIGHT Great Expectations . . . Unfulfilled!
The Jewish world of Jesus' day longed for a deliverer from the iron heel of Roman oppression. But many thought the Messiah would not arrive until they were good enough to "deserve" him. One commonly held notion was that the Messiah would only come when the nation had kept the Sabbath for *four consecutive weeks*. There was just one problem. No one could keep all the Mosaic Laws for even *one day!* God sent the Savior as a gift for the godless—not as a reward for the righteous.

CHAPTER 1
This is a record of the ancestors of Jesus the Messiah, a descendant of King David and of Abraham:

² Abraham was the father of Isaac.
  Isaac was the father of Jacob.
  Jacob was the father of Judah and his brothers.

3 Judah was the father of Perez and
   Zerah (their mother was Tamar).
   Perez was the father of Hezron.
   Hezron was the father of Ram.*
4 Ram was the father of Amminadab.
   Amminadab was the father of Nahshon.
   Nahshon was the father of Salmon.
5 Salmon was the father of Boaz (his
   mother was Rahab).
   Boaz was the father of Obed (his
   mother was Ruth).
   Obed was the father of Jesse.
6 Jesse was the father of King David.
   David was the father of Solomon (his
   mother was Bathsheba, the widow of
   Uriah).
7 Solomon was the father of Rehoboam.
   Rehoboam was the father of Abijah.
   Abijah was the father of Asaph.*
8 Asaph was the father of Jehoshaphat.
   Jehoshaphat was the father of Jehoram.*
   Jehoram was the father* of Uzziah.
9 Uzziah was the father of Jotham.
   Jotham was the father of Ahaz.
   Ahaz was the father of Hezekiah.
10 Hezekiah was the father of Manasseh.
   Manasseh was the father of Amos.*
   Amos was the father of Josiah.
11 Josiah was the father of Jehoiachin* and
   his brothers (born at the time of the
   exile to Babylon).
12 After the Babylonian exile:
   Jehoiachin was the father of Shealtiel.
   Shealtiel was the father of Zerubbabel.
13 Zerubbabel was the father of Abiud.
   Abiud was the father of Eliakim.
   Eliakim was the father of Azor.
14 Azor was the father of Zadok.
   Zadok was the father of Akim.
   Akim was the father of Eliud.
15 Eliud was the father of Eleazar.
   Eleazar was the father of Matthan.
   Matthan was the father of Jacob.
16 Jacob was the father of Joseph, the
   husband of Mary.
   Mary was the mother of Jesus, who is
   called the Messiah.

17All those listed above include fourteen
generations from Abraham to King David,
and fourteen from David's time to the Babylonian exile, and fourteen from the Babylonian exile to the Messiah.

18Now this is how Jesus the Messiah was
born. His mother, Mary, was engaged to be
married to Joseph. But while she was still a
virgin, she became pregnant by the Holy
Spirit. 19Joseph, her fiancé, being a just
man, decided to break the engagement quietly, so as not to disgrace her publicly.

20As he considered this, he fell asleep,
and an angel of the Lord appeared to him
in a dream. "Joseph, son of David," the
angel said, "do not be afraid to go ahead
with your marriage to Mary. For the child
within her has been conceived by the Holy
Spirit. 21And she will have a son, and you
are to name him Jesus,* for he will save his
people from their sins." 22All of this happened to fulfill the Lord's message through
his prophet:

23 "Look! The virgin will conceive a child!
     She will give birth to a son,
   and he will be called Immanuel*
     (meaning, God is with us)."

24When Joseph woke up, he did what the
angel of the Lord commanded. He brought
Mary home to be his wife, 25but she remained a virgin until her son was born.
And Joseph named him Jesus.

CHAPTER 2

Jesus was born in the town of Bethlehem in
Judea, during the reign of King Herod.
About that time some wise men* from eastern lands arrived in Jerusalem, asking,
2"Where is the newborn king of the Jews?
We have seen his star as it arose,* and we
have come to worship him."

3Herod was deeply disturbed by their
question, as was all of Jerusalem. 4He
called a meeting of the leading priests and
teachers of religious law. "Where did the
prophets say the Messiah would be born?"
he asked them.

5"In Bethlehem," they said, "for this is
what the prophet wrote:

6 'O Bethlehem of Judah,
     you are not just a lowly village in
       Judah,
   for a ruler will come from you
     who will be the shepherd for my
       people Israel.'*"

7Then Herod sent a private message to
the wise men, asking them to come see him.

1:3 Greek *Aram;* also in 1:4. See 1 Chr 2:9-10.   1:7 *Asaph* is the same person as Asa; also in 1:8. See 1 Chr 3:10.   1:8a Greek *Joram.*
See 1 Kgs 22:50 and note at 1 Chr 3:11.   1:8b Or *ancestor;* also in 1:11.   1:10 *Amos* is the same person as Amon. See 1 Chr 3:14.
1:11 Greek *Jeconiah;* also in 1:12. See 2 Kgs 24:6 and note at 1 Chr 3:16.   1:21 *Jesus* means "The LORD saves."   1:23 Isa 7:14; 8:8, 10.
2:1 Or *royal astrologers;* Greek reads *magi;* also in 2:7, 16.   2:2 Or *in the east.*   2:6 Mic 5:2; 2 Sam 5:2.

At this meeting he learned the exact time when they first saw the star. [8]Then he told them, "Go to Bethlehem and search carefully for the child. And when you find him, come back and tell me so that I can go and worship him, too!"

[9]After this interview the wise men went their way. Once again the star appeared to them, guiding them to Bethlehem. It went ahead of them and stopped over the place where the child was. [10]When they saw the star, they were filled with joy! [11]They entered the house where the child and his mother, Mary, were, and they fell down before him and worshiped him. Then they opened their treasure chests and gave him gifts of gold, frankincense, and myrrh. [12]But when it was time to leave, they went home another way, because God had warned them in a dream not to return to Herod.

[13]After the wise men were gone, an angel of the Lord appeared to Joseph in a dream. "Get up and flee to Egypt with the child and his mother," the angel said. "Stay there until I tell you to return, because Herod is going to try to kill the child." [14]That night Joseph left for Egypt with the child and Mary, his mother, [15]and they stayed there until Herod's death. This fulfilled what the Lord had spoken through the prophet: "I called my Son out of Egypt."*

[16]Herod was furious when he learned that the wise men had outwitted him. He sent soldiers to kill all the boys in and around Bethlehem who were two years old and under, because the wise men had told him the star first appeared to them about two years earlier.* [17]Herod's brutal action fulfilled the prophecy of Jeremiah:

[18] "A cry of anguish is heard in Ramah—
　　weeping and mourning unrestrained.
　　Rachel weeps for her children,
　　　refusing to be comforted—for they
　　　are dead."*

[19]When Herod died, an angel of the Lord appeared in a dream to Joseph in Egypt and told him, [20]"Get up and take the child and his mother back to the land of Israel, because those who were trying to kill the child are dead." [21]So Joseph returned immediately to Israel with Jesus and his mother. [22]But when he learned that the new ruler was Herod's son Archelaus, he was afraid. Then, in another dream, he was warned to go to Galilee. [23]So they went and lived in a town called Nazareth. This fulfilled what was spoken by the prophets concerning the Messiah: "He will be called a Nazarene."

CHAPTER 3

In those days John the Baptist began preaching in the Judean wilderness. His message was, [2]"Turn from your sins and turn to God, because the Kingdom of Heaven is near.*" [3]Isaiah had spoken of John when he said,

"He is a voice shouting in the
　　wilderness:
'Prepare a pathway for the Lord's
　　coming!
　　Make a straight road for him!'"*

[4]John's clothes were woven from camel hair, and he wore a leather belt; his food was locusts and wild honey. [5]People from Jerusalem and from every section of Judea and from all over the Jordan Valley went out to the wilderness to hear him preach. [6]And when they confessed their sins, he baptized them in the Jordan River.

[7]But when he saw many Pharisees and Sadducees coming to be baptized, he denounced them. "You brood of snakes!" he exclaimed. "Who warned you to flee God's coming judgment? [8]Prove by the way you live that you have really turned from your sins and turned to God. [9]Don't just say, 'We're safe—we're the descendants of Abraham.' That proves nothing. God can change these stones here into children of Abraham. [10]Even now the ax of God's judgment is poised, ready to sever your roots. Yes, every tree that does not produce good fruit will be chopped down and thrown into the fire.

[11]"I baptize with* water those who turn from their sins and turn to God. But someone is coming soon who is far greater than I am—so much greater that I am not even worthy to be his slave.* He will baptize you with the Holy Spirit and with fire.* [12]He is ready to separate the chaff from the grain with his winnowing fork. Then he will clean up the threshing area, storing the grain in his barn but burning the chaff with never-ending fire."

[13]Then Jesus went from Galilee to the

2:15 Hos 11:1.　**2:16** Or *according to the time he calculated from the wise men.*　**2:18** Jer 31:15.　**3:2** Or *has come* or *is coming soon.*
3:3 Isa 40:3.　**3:11a** Or *in.*　**3:11b** Greek *to carry his sandals.*　**3:11c** Or *in the Holy Spirit and in fire.*

Jordan River to be baptized by John. [14]But John didn't want to baptize him. "I am the one who needs to be baptized by you," he said, "so why are you coming to me?"

[15]But Jesus said, "It must be done, because we must do everything that is right.*" So then John baptized him.

[16]After his baptism, as Jesus came up out of the water, the heavens were opened and he saw the Spirit of God descending like a dove and settling on him. [17]And a voice from heaven said, "This is my beloved Son, and I am fully pleased with him."

CHAPTER 4

Then Jesus was led out into the wilderness by the Holy Spirit to be tempted there by the Devil. [2]For forty days and forty nights he ate nothing and became very hungry. [3]Then the Devil* came and said to him, "If you are the Son of God, change these stones into loaves of bread."

[4]But Jesus told him, "No! The Scriptures say,

'People need more than bread for their life;
    they must feed on every word of God.'*"

[5]Then the Devil took him to Jerusalem, to the highest point of the Temple, [6]and said, "If you are the Son of God, jump off! For the Scriptures say,

'He orders his angels to protect you.
And they will hold you with their hands
    to keep you from striking your foot
        on a stone.'*"

[7]Jesus responded, "The Scriptures also say, 'Do not test the Lord your God.'*"

[8]Next the Devil took him to the peak of a very high mountain and showed him the nations of the world and all their glory. [9]"I will give it all to you," he said, "if you will only kneel down and worship me."

[10]"Get out of here, Satan," Jesus told him. "For the Scriptures say,

'You must worship the Lord your God;
    serve only him.'*"

[11]Then the Devil went away, and angels came and cared for Jesus.

[12]When Jesus heard that John had been arrested, he left Judea and returned to Galilee. [13]But instead of going to Nazareth, he went to Capernaum, beside the Sea of Galilee, in the region of Zebulun and Naphtali. [14]This fulfilled Isaiah's prophecy:

[15] "In the land of Zebulun and of
        Naphtali,
    beside the sea, beyond the Jordan
        River—
    in Galilee where so many Gentiles
        live—
[16] the people who sat in darkness
    have seen a great light.
And for those who lived in the land
    where death casts its shadow,
    a light has shined."*

[17]From then on, Jesus began to preach, "Turn from your sins and turn to God, because the Kingdom of Heaven is near.*"

[18]One day as Jesus was walking along the shore beside the Sea of Galilee, he saw two brothers—Simon, also called Peter, and Andrew—fishing with a net, for they were commercial fishermen. [19]Jesus called out to them, "Come, be my disciples, and I will show you how to fish for people!" [20]And they left their nets at once and went with him.

[21]A little farther up the shore he saw two other brothers, James and John, sitting in a boat with their father, Zebedee, mending their nets. And he called them to come, too. [22]They immediately followed him, leaving the boat and their father behind.

[23]Jesus traveled throughout Galilee teaching in the synagogues, preaching everywhere the Good News about the Kingdom. And he healed people who had every kind of sickness and disease. [24]News about him spread far beyond the borders of Galilee so that the sick were soon coming to be healed from as far away as Syria. And whatever their illness and pain, or if they were possessed by demons, or were epileptics, or were paralyzed—he healed them all. [25]Large crowds followed him wherever he went—people from Galilee, the Ten Towns,* Jerusalem, from all over Judea, and from east of the Jordan River.

3:15 Or *we must fulfill all righteousness.*   **4:3** Greek *the tempter.*   **4:4** Deut 8:3.   **4:6** Ps 91:11-12.   **4:7** Deut 6:16.   **4:10** Deut 6:13.
4:15-16 Isa 9:1-2.   **4:17** Or *has come* or *is coming soon.*   **4:25** Greek *Decapolis.*

OCTOBER 2 ☐ DAY 276
MATTHEW 5–7
Preaching of the King

 OVERVIEW Matthew's Gospel is not primarily chronological in its arrangement but topical, alternating between Jesus' deeds and his discourses, between his miracles and his messages. Today's reading, traditionally called the Sermon on the Mount, is really ten "sermonettes" in one and was preached on a mountainside overlooking the Sea of Galilee (5:1).

Chapter 5	Chapter 6	Chapter 7
How We Stand before the Law	How We Stand before the World	How We Stand before God
Holy Actions	Holy Attitudes	Holy Judgment

 YOUR DAILY WALK Try this quiz on attitudes and actions:
1. True or False: It is possible to do the right thing for the wrong reason.
2. True or False: It is possible to do the wrong thing for the right reason.

Although disciples are to be seen doing good works, they must not do good works in order to be seen.

If spirituality were measured in units of activity, surely the Pharisees of Jesus' day were candidates for spiritual greatness! They gave a tithe of all they possessed, right down to the herbs on their shelves (Luke 11:42), and they fasted twice weekly (Luke 18:12). Judging from the externals, they were models of holy zeal. But inwardly, where only God can see, they were like "whitewashed tombs . . . filled on the inside with dead people's bones" (Matthew 23:27).

That's why Jesus said, "Unless you obey God better than the teachers of religious law and the Pharisees do, you can't enter the Kingdom of Heaven at all" (Matthew 5:20).

It's not that we need to do more than the Pharisees or discard what they did in favor of something better (Luke 11:42), but we must couple their outer zeal with an inner heart for God's love and justice—the kind of heart portrayed in the Beatitudes of Matthew 5:3-12. Think of these as "Be Attitudes"—attitudes God wants you to demonstrate in your life and service for him. Pick one (there are eight to choose from), write it in your own words, and with God's help make it your holy "exercise project" for today.

 INSIGHT Open Mouth, Open Heart
Matthew introduces Jesus' sermon by saying, "This is what he taught them" (5:2)—a phrase in Greek that refers to an utterance from deep within the heart and soul of a person.

CHAPTER 5
One day as the crowds were gathering, Jesus went up the mountainside with his disciples and sat down to teach them. ²This is what he taught them:

³ "God blesses those who realize their need for him,*
for the Kingdom of Heaven is given to them.

⁴ God blesses those who mourn,
for they will be comforted.
⁵ God blesses those who are gentle and lowly,
for the whole earth will belong to them.
⁶ God blesses those who are hungry and thirsty for justice,
for they will receive it in full.

5:3 Greek *the poor in spirit.*

7 God blesses those who are merciful,
    for they will be shown mercy.
8 God blesses those whose hearts are pure,
    for they will see God.
9 God blesses those who work for peace,
    for they will be called the children of
    God.
10 God blesses those who are persecuted
    because they live for God,
    for the Kingdom of Heaven is theirs.

11"God blesses you when you are
mocked and persecuted and lied about because you are my followers. 12Be happy
about it! Be very glad! For a great reward
awaits you in heaven. And remember, the
ancient prophets were persecuted, too.

13"You are the salt of the earth. But what
good is salt if it has lost its flavor? Can you
make it useful again? It will be thrown out
and trampled underfoot as worthless.
14You are the light of the world—like a city
on a mountain, glowing in the night for all
to see. 15Don't hide your light under a basket! Instead, put it on a stand and let it
shine for all. 16In the same way, let your
good deeds shine out for all to see, so that
everyone will praise your heavenly Father.

17"Don't misunderstand why I have
come. I did not come to abolish the law of
Moses or the writings of the prophets. No,
I came to fulfill them. 18I assure you, until
heaven and earth disappear, even the
smallest detail of God's law will remain
until its purpose is achieved. 19So if you
break the smallest commandment and
teach others to do the same, you will be the
least in the Kingdom of Heaven. But anyone who obeys God's laws and teaches
them will be great in the Kingdom of
Heaven.

20"But I warn you—unless you obey God
better than the teachers of religious law
and the Pharisees do, you can't enter the
Kingdom of Heaven at all!

21"You have heard that the law of Moses
says, 'Do not murder. If you commit murder, you are subject to judgment.'* 22But I
say, if you are angry with someone,* you
are subject to judgment! If you call someone an idiot,* you are in danger of being
brought before the high council. And if you
curse someone,* you are in danger of the
fires of hell.

23"So if you are standing before the altar
in the Temple, offering a sacrifice to God,
and you suddenly remember that someone
has something against you, 24leave your
sacrifice there beside the altar. Go and be
reconciled to that person. Then come and
offer your sacrifice to God. 25Come to terms
quickly with your enemy before it is too
late and you are dragged into court,
handed over to an officer, and thrown in
jail. 26I assure you that you won't be free
again until you have paid the last penny.

27"You have heard that the law of Moses
says, 'Do not commit adultery.'* 28But I say,
anyone who even looks at a woman with
lust in his eye has already committed adultery with her in his heart. 29So if your eye—
even if it is your good eye*—causes you to
lust, gouge it out and throw it away. It is
better for you to lose one part of your body
than for your whole body to be thrown into
hell. 30And if your hand—even if it is your
stronger hand*—causes you to sin, cut it off
and throw it away. It is better for you to lose
one part of your body than for your whole
body to be thrown into hell.

31"You have heard that the law of Moses
says, 'A man can divorce his wife by merely
giving her a letter of divorce.'* 32But I say
that a man who divorces his wife, unless
she has been unfaithful, causes her to commit adultery. And anyone who marries a
divorced woman commits adultery.

33"Again, you have heard that the law of
Moses says, 'Do not break your vows; you
must carry out the vows you have made to
the Lord.'* 34But I say, don't make any
vows! If you say, 'By heaven!' it is a sacred
vow because heaven is God's throne.
35And if you say, 'By the earth!' it is a sacred
vow because the earth is his footstool. And
don't swear, 'By Jerusalem!' for Jerusalem
is the city of the great King. 36Don't even
swear, 'By my head!' for you can't turn one
hair white or black. 37Just say a simple,
'Yes, I will,' or 'No, I won't.' Your word is
enough. To strengthen your promise with a
vow shows that something is wrong.*

38"You have heard that the law of Moses
says, 'If an eye is injured, injure the eye of
the person who did it. If a tooth gets
knocked out, knock out the tooth of the
person who did it.'* 39But I say, don't resist

an evil person! If you are slapped on the right cheek, turn the other, too. ⁴⁰If you are ordered to court and your shirt is taken from you, give your coat, too. ⁴¹If a soldier demands that you carry his gear for a mile,* carry it two miles. ⁴²Give to those who ask, and don't turn away from those who want to borrow.

⁴³"You have heard that the law of Moses says, 'Love your neighbor'* and hate your enemy. ⁴⁴But I say, love your enemies!* Pray for those who persecute you! ⁴⁵In that way, you will be acting as true children of your Father in heaven. For he gives his sunlight to both the evil and the good, and he sends rain on the just and on the unjust, too. ⁴⁶If you love only those who love you, what good is that? Even corrupt tax collectors do that much. ⁴⁷If you are kind only to your friends,* how are you different from anyone else? Even pagans do that. ⁴⁸But you are to be perfect, even as your Father in heaven is perfect.

CHAPTER 6

"Take care! Don't do your good deeds publicly, to be admired, because then you will lose the reward from your Father in heaven. ²When you give a gift to someone in need, don't shout about it as the hypocrites do—blowing trumpets in the synagogues and streets to call attention to their acts of charity! I assure you, they have received all the reward they will ever get. ³But when you give to someone, don't tell your left hand what your right hand is doing. ⁴Give your gifts in secret, and your Father, who knows all secrets, will reward you.

⁵"And now about prayer. When you pray, don't be like the hypocrites who love to pray publicly on street corners and in the synagogues where everyone can see them. I assure you, that is all the reward they will ever get. ⁶But when you pray, go away by yourself, shut the door behind you, and pray to your Father secretly. Then your Father, who knows all secrets, will reward you.

⁷"When you pray, don't babble on and on as people of other religions do. They think their prayers are answered only by repeating their words again and again. ⁸Don't be like them, because your Father

knows exactly what you need even before you ask him! ⁹Pray like this:

Our Father in heaven,
　　may your name be honored.
¹⁰ May your Kingdom come soon.
May your will be done here on earth,
　　just as it is in heaven.
¹¹ Give us our food for today,*
¹² and forgive us our sins,
　　just as we have forgiven those who
　　　have sinned against us.
¹³ And don't let us yield to temptation,
　　but deliver us from the evil one.*

¹⁴"If you forgive those who sin against you, your heavenly Father will forgive you. ¹⁵But if you refuse to forgive others, your Father will not forgive your sins.

¹⁶"And when you fast, don't make it obvious, as the hypocrites do, who try to look pale and disheveled so people will admire them for their fasting. I assure you, that is the only reward they will ever get. ¹⁷But when you fast, comb your hair and wash your face. ¹⁸Then no one will suspect you are fasting, except your Father, who knows what you do in secret. And your Father, who knows all secrets, will reward you.

¹⁹"Don't store up treasures here on earth, where they can be eaten by moths and get rusty, and where thieves break in and steal. ²⁰Store your treasures in heaven, where they will never become moth-eaten or rusty and where they will be safe from thieves. ²¹Wherever your treasure is, there your heart and thoughts will also be.

²²"Your eye is a lamp for your body. A pure eye lets sunshine into your soul. ²³But an evil eye shuts out the light and plunges you into darkness. If the light you think you have is really darkness, how deep that darkness will be!

²⁴"No one can serve two masters. For you will hate one and love the other, or be devoted to one and despise the other. You cannot serve both God and money.

²⁵"So I tell you, don't worry about everyday life—whether you have enough food, drink, and clothes. Doesn't life consist of more than food and clothing? ²⁶Look at the birds. They don't need to plant or harvest or put food in barns because your heavenly Father feeds them. And you are far more valuable to him than they are. ²⁷Can all

---

5:41 Greek *milion* [4,854 feet or 1,478 meters].　　5:47 Greek *your brothers*.　　5:43 Lev 19:18.　　5:44 Some manuscripts add *Bless those who curse you, do good to those who hate you*.　　6:11 Or *for tomorrow*.　　6:13 Or *from evil*. Some manuscripts add *For yours is the kingdom and the power and the glory forever. Amen*.

your worries add a single moment to your life? Of course not.

²⁸"And why worry about your clothes? Look at the lilies and how they grow. They don't work or make their clothing, ²⁹yet Solomon in all his glory was not dressed as beautifully as they are. ³⁰And if God cares so wonderfully for flowers that are here today and gone tomorrow, won't he more surely care for you? You have so little faith!

³¹"So don't worry about having enough food or drink or clothing. ³²Why be like the pagans who are so deeply concerned about these things? Your heavenly Father already knows all your needs, ³³and he will give you all you need from day to day if you live for him and make the Kingdom of God your primary concern.

³⁴"So don't worry about tomorrow, for tomorrow will bring its own worries. Today's trouble is enough for today.

CHAPTER 7

"Stop judging others, and you will not be judged. ²For others will treat you as you treat them.* Whatever measure you use in judging others, it will be used to measure how you are judged. ³And why worry about a speck in your friend's eye* when you have a log in your own? ⁴How can you think of saying, 'Let me help you get rid of that speck in your eye,' when you can't see past the log in your own eye? ⁵Hypocrite! First get rid of the log from your own eye; then perhaps you will see well enough to deal with the speck in your friend's eye.

⁶"Don't give what is holy to unholy people.* Don't give pearls to swine! They will trample the pearls, then turn and attack you.

⁷"Keep on asking, and you will be given what you ask for. Keep on looking, and you will find. Keep on knocking, and the door will be opened. ⁸For everyone who asks, receives. Everyone who seeks, finds. And the door is opened to everyone who knocks. ⁹You parents—if your children ask for a loaf of bread, do you give them a stone instead? ¹⁰Or if they ask for a fish, do you give them a snake? Of course not! ¹¹If you sinful people know how to give good gifts to your chil-

dren, how much more will your heavenly Father give good gifts to those who ask him.

¹²"Do for others what you would like them to do for you. This is a summary of all that is taught in the law and the prophets.

¹³"You can enter God's Kingdom only through the narrow gate. The highway to hell* is broad, and its gate is wide for the many who choose the easy way. ¹⁴But the gateway to life is small, and the road is narrow, and only a few ever find it.

¹⁵"Beware of false prophets who come disguised as harmless sheep, but are really wolves that will tear you apart. ¹⁶You can detect them by the way they act, just as you can identify a tree by its fruit. You don't pick grapes from thornbushes, or figs from thistles. ¹⁷A healthy tree produces good fruit, and an unhealthy tree produces bad fruit. ¹⁸A good tree can't produce bad fruit, and a bad tree can't produce good fruit. ¹⁹So every tree that does not produce good fruit is chopped down and thrown into the fire. ²⁰Yes, the way to identify a tree or a person is by the kind of fruit that is produced.

²¹"Not all people who sound religious are really godly. They may refer to me as 'Lord,' but they still won't enter the Kingdom of Heaven. The decisive issue is whether they obey my Father in heaven. ²²On judgment day many will tell me, 'Lord, Lord, we prophesied in your name and cast out demons in your name and performed many miracles in your name.' ²³But I will reply, 'I never knew you. Go away; the things you did were unauthorized.*'

²⁴"Anyone who listens to my teaching and obeys me is wise, like a person who builds a house on solid rock. ²⁵Though the rain comes in torrents and the floodwaters rise and the winds beat against that house, it won't collapse, because it is built on rock. ²⁶But anyone who hears my teaching and ignores it is foolish, like a person who builds a house on sand. ²⁷When the rains and floods come and the winds beat against that house, it will fall with a mighty crash."

²⁸After Jesus finished speaking, the crowds were amazed at his teaching, ²⁹for he taught as one who had real authority— quite unlike the teachers of religious law.

7:2 Or *For God will treat you as you treat others;* Greek reads *For with the judgment you judge you will be judged.*   **7:3** Greek *your brother's eye;* also in 7:5.   **7:6** Greek *Don't give the sacred to dogs.*   **7:13** Greek *The way that leads to destruction.*   **7:23** Or *unlawful.*

OCTOBER 3 ☐ DAY 277
MATTHEW 8–11
Power of the King

OVERVIEW It is one thing for a preacher to proclaim the words contained in the Sermon on the Mount; it is something else to be able to back up those words with power—power that could only come from God. Jesus' miracles serve at least two vital functions: (1) They demonstrate his authority over sin, sickness, demons, and nature; and (2) they show his heart of compassion toward the objects of his love. An incurable leper . . . a disillusioned woman who had a hemorrhage for twelve years . . . a timid band of disciples on the raging Sea of Galilee—each receives comfort and consolation from the powerful words of the Savior.

Chapter 8	Chapter 9	Chapter 10	Chapter 11
Christ Supreme over Nature	Christ Supreme over Death	Christ Multiplied in His Men	Christ Justified in His Deeds
Jesus Shows His Love		Jesus Sends His Disciples	

YOUR DAILY WALK Put yourself in the sandals of one of Jesus' disciples for a moment. You have just been informed by the Master, "I have been given complete authority in heaven and on earth" (as he will tell them in 28:18).

A religion without wonders is false. A theology without wonders is heretical.

Taken in isolation, that statement might seem like the proud boast of an egotist. But in this case, it has been preceded by no fewer than nine miracles! You have watched hopeless medical cases healed, violent storms silenced, even dead people raised to life. *Now* how do you react to Christ's words?

Seeing is believing. One of the strongest encouragements for trusting God today is seeing God's power in the past. Below are spaces for you to record the nine miracles found in today's reading plus a tenth from the hand of God in your own life over the past week. If you can't think of one, then ask him to make your life a miracle today!

1. _____ 4. _____ 7. _____
2. _____ 5. _____ 8. _____
3. _____ 6. _____ 9. _____
And in my life . . . 10. _____

INSIGHT "If You Refuse to Take Up Your Cross"
The cross casts its terrible shadow across all four Gospels. In Matthew it's mentioned numerous times, as in 10:38, for example. Jesus knew he would die by crucifixion when he spoke these words, but only much later would his disciples see the deep significance of his statement.

CHAPTER 8
Large crowds followed Jesus as he came down the mountainside. ²Suddenly, a man with leprosy approached Jesus. He knelt before him, worshiping. "Lord," the man said, "if you want to, you can make me well again."

³Jesus touched him. "I want to," he said. "Be healed!" And instantly the leprosy dis-

appeared. ⁴Then Jesus said to him, "Go right over to the priest and let him examine you. Don't talk to anyone along the way. Take along the offering required in the law of Moses for those who have been healed of leprosy, so everyone will have proof of your healing."

⁵When Jesus arrived in Capernaum, a Roman officer came and pleaded with him,

[6]"Lord, my young servant lies in bed, paralyzed and racked with pain."

[7]Jesus said, "I will come and heal him."

[8]Then the officer said, "Lord, I am not worthy to have you come into my home. Just say the word from where you are, and my servant will be healed! [9]I know, because I am under the authority of my superior officers and I have authority over my soldiers. I only need to say, 'Go,' and they go, or 'Come,' and they come. And if I say to my slaves, 'Do this or that,' they do it."

[10]When Jesus heard this, he was amazed. Turning to the crowd, he said, "I tell you the truth, I haven't seen faith like this in all the land of Israel! [11]And I tell you this, that many Gentiles will come from all over the world and sit down with Abraham, Isaac, and Jacob at the feast in the Kingdom of Heaven. [12]But many Israelites—those for whom the Kingdom was prepared—will be cast into outer darkness, where there will be weeping and gnashing of teeth."

[13]Then Jesus said to the Roman officer, "Go on home. What you have believed has happened." And the young servant was healed that same hour.

[14]When Jesus arrived at Peter's house, Peter's mother-in-law was in bed with a high fever. [15]But when Jesus touched her hand, the fever left her. Then she got up and prepared a meal for him.

[16]That evening many demon-possessed people were brought to Jesus. All the spirits fled when he commanded them to leave; and he healed all the sick. [17]This fulfilled the word of the Lord through Isaiah, who said, "He took our sicknesses and removed our diseases."*

[18]When Jesus noticed how large the crowd was growing, he instructed his disciples to cross to the other side of the lake.

[19]Then one of the teachers of religious law said to him, "Teacher, I will follow you no matter where you go!"

[20]But Jesus said, "Foxes have dens to live in, and birds have nests, but I, the Son of Man, have no home of my own, not even a place to lay my head."

[21]Another of his disciples said, "Lord, first let me return home and bury my father."

[22]But Jesus told him, "Follow me now! Let those who are spiritually dead care for their own dead."*

[23]Then Jesus got into the boat and started across the lake with his disciples. [24]Suddenly, a terrible storm came up, with waves breaking into the boat. But Jesus was sleeping. [25]The disciples went to him and woke him up, shouting, "Lord, save us! We're going to drown!"

[26]And Jesus answered, "Why are you afraid? You have so little faith!" Then he stood up and rebuked the wind and waves, and suddenly all was calm. [27]The disciples just sat there in awe. "Who is this?" they asked themselves. "Even the wind and waves obey him!"

[28]When Jesus arrived on the other side of the lake in the land of the Gadarenes,* two men who were possessed by demons met him. They lived in a cemetery and were so dangerous that no one could go through that area. [29]They began screaming at him, "Why are you bothering us, Son of God? You have no right to torture us before God's appointed time!" [30]A large herd of pigs was feeding in the distance, [31]so the demons begged, "If you cast us out, send us into that herd of pigs."

[32]"All right, go!" Jesus commanded them. So the demons came out of the men and entered the pigs, and the whole herd plunged down the steep hillside into the lake and drowned in the water. [33]The herdsmen fled to the nearby city, telling everyone what happened to the demon-possessed men. [34]The entire town came out to meet Jesus, but they begged him to go away and leave them alone.

CHAPTER 9

Jesus climbed into a boat and went back across the lake to his own town. [2]Some people brought to him a paralyzed man on a mat. Seeing their faith, Jesus said to the paralyzed man, "Take heart, son! Your sins are forgiven."

[3]"Blasphemy! This man talks like he is God!" some of the teachers of religious law said among themselves.

[4]Jesus knew what they were thinking, so he asked them, "Why are you thinking such evil thoughts? [5]Is it easier to say, 'Your sins are forgiven' or 'Get up and walk'? [6]I will prove that I, the Son of Man, have the authority on earth to forgive sins." Then Jesus turned to the paralyzed man and

---

8:17 Isa 53:4.   **8:22** Greek *Let the dead bury their own dead.*   **8:28** Some manuscripts read *Gerasenes;* other manuscripts read *Gergesenes.* See Mark 5:1; Luke 8:26.

said, "Stand up, take your mat, and go on home, because you are healed!"

⁷And the man jumped up and went home! ⁸Fear swept through the crowd as they saw this happen right before their eyes. They praised God for sending a man with such great authority.

⁹As Jesus was going down the road, he saw Matthew sitting at his tax-collection booth. "Come, be my disciple," Jesus said to him. So Matthew got up and followed him.

¹⁰That night Matthew invited Jesus and his disciples to be his dinner guests, along with his fellow tax collectors and many other notorious sinners. ¹¹The Pharisees were indignant. "Why does your teacher eat with such scum*?" they asked his disciples.

¹²When he heard this, Jesus replied, "Healthy people don't need a doctor—sick people do." ¹³Then he added, "Now go and learn the meaning of this Scripture: 'I want you to be merciful; I don't want your sacrifices.'* For I have come to call sinners, not those who think they are already good enough."

¹⁴One day the disciples of John the Baptist came to Jesus and asked him, "Why do we and the Pharisees fast, but your disciples don't fast?"

¹⁵Jesus responded, "Should the wedding guests mourn while celebrating with the groom? Someday he will be taken from them, and then they will fast. ¹⁶And who would patch an old garment with unshrunk cloth? For the patch shrinks and pulls away from the old cloth, leaving an even bigger hole than before. ¹⁷And no one puts new wine into old wineskins. The old skins would burst from the pressure, spilling the wine and ruining the skins. New wine must be stored in new wineskins. That way both the wine and the wineskins are preserved."

¹⁸As Jesus was saying this, the leader of a synagogue came and knelt down before him. "My daughter has just died," he said, "but you can bring her back to life again if you just come and lay your hand upon her."

¹⁹As Jesus and the disciples were going to the official's home, ²⁰a woman who had had a hemorrhage for twelve years came up behind him. She touched the fringe of his robe, ²¹for she thought, "If I can just touch his robe, I will be healed."

²²Jesus turned around and said to her, "Daughter, be encouraged! Your faith has made you well." And the woman was healed at that moment.

²³When Jesus arrived at the official's home, he noticed the noisy crowds and heard the funeral music. ²⁴He said, "Go away, for the girl isn't dead; she's only asleep." But the crowd laughed at him. ²⁵When the crowd was finally outside, Jesus went in and took the girl by the hand, and she stood up! ²⁶The report of this miracle swept through the entire countryside.

²⁷After Jesus left the girl's home, two blind men followed along behind him, shouting, "Son of David, have mercy on us!"

²⁸They went right into the house where he was staying, and Jesus asked them, "Do you believe I can make you see?"

"Yes, Lord," they told him, "we do."

²⁹Then he touched their eyes and said, "Because of your faith, it will happen." ³⁰And suddenly they could see! Jesus sternly warned them, "Don't tell anyone about this." ³¹But instead, they spread his fame all over the region.

³²When they left, some people brought to him a man who couldn't speak because he was possessed by a demon. ³³So Jesus cast out the demon, and instantly the man could talk. The crowds marveled. "Nothing like this has ever happened in Israel!" they exclaimed.

³⁴But the Pharisees said, "He can cast out demons because he is empowered by the prince of demons."

³⁵Jesus traveled through all the cities and villages of that area, teaching in the synagogues and announcing the Good News about the Kingdom. And wherever he went, he healed people of every sort of disease and illness. ³⁶He felt great pity for the crowds that came, because their problems were so great and they didn't know where to go for help. They were like sheep without a shepherd. ³⁷He said to his disciples, "The harvest is so great, but the workers are so few. ³⁸So pray to the Lord who is in charge of the harvest; ask him to send out more workers for his fields."

CHAPTER 10

Jesus called his twelve disciples to him and gave them authority to cast out evil spirits and to heal every kind of disease and illness. ²Here are the names of the twelve apostles:

9:11 Greek *with tax collectors and sinners.* **9:13** Hos 6:6.

first Simon (also called Peter),
then Andrew (Peter's brother),
James (son of Zebedee),
John (James's brother),
3 Philip,
Bartholomew,
Thomas,
Matthew (the tax collector),
James (son of Alphaeus),
Thaddaeus,
4 Simon (the Zealot*),
Judas Iscariot (who later betrayed him).

5Jesus sent the twelve disciples out with these instructions: "Don't go to the Gentiles or the Samaritans, 6but only to the people of Israel—God's lost sheep. 7Go and announce to them that the Kingdom of Heaven is near.* 8Heal the sick, raise the dead, cure those with leprosy, and cast out demons. Give as freely as you have received!

9"Don't take any money with you. 10Don't carry a traveler's bag with an extra coat and sandals or even a walking stick. Don't hesitate to accept hospitality, because those who work deserve to be fed.* 11Whenever you enter a city or village, search for a worthy man and stay in his home until you leave for the next town. 12When you are invited into someone's home, give it your blessing. 13If it turns out to be a worthy home, let your blessing stand; if it is not, take back the blessing. 14If a village doesn't welcome you or listen to you, shake off the dust of that place from your feet as you leave. 15I assure you, the wicked cities of Sodom and Gomorrah will be better off on the judgment day than that place will be.

16"Look, I am sending you out as sheep among wolves. Be as wary as snakes and harmless as doves. 17But beware! For you will be handed over to the courts and beaten in the synagogues. 18And you must stand trial before governors and kings because you are my followers. This will be your opportunity to tell them about me—yes, to witness to the world. 19When you are arrested, don't worry about what to say in your defense, because you will be given the right words at the right time. 20For it won't be you doing the talking—it will be the Spirit of your Father speaking through you.

21"Brother will betray brother to death, fathers will betray their own children, and children will rise against their parents and cause them to be killed. 22And everyone will hate you because of your allegiance to me. But those who endure to the end will be saved. 23When you are persecuted in one town, flee to the next. I assure you that I, the Son of Man, will return before you have reached all the towns of Israel.

24"A student is not greater than the teacher. A servant is not greater than the master. 25The student shares the teacher's fate. The servant shares the master's fate. And since I, the master of the household, have been called the prince of demons,* how much more will it happen to you, the members of the household! 26But don't be afraid of those who threaten you. For the time is coming when everything will be revealed; all that is secret will be made public. 27What I tell you now in the darkness, shout abroad when daybreak comes. What I whisper in your ears, shout from the housetops for all to hear!

28"Don't be afraid of those who want to kill you. They can only kill your body; they cannot touch your soul. Fear only God, who can destroy both soul and body in hell. 29Not even a sparrow, worth only half a penny, can fall to the ground without your Father knowing it. 30And the very hairs on your head are all numbered. 31So don't be afraid; you are more valuable to him than a whole flock of sparrows.

32"If anyone acknowledges me publicly here on earth, I will openly acknowledge that person before my Father in heaven. 33But if anyone denies me here on earth, I will deny that person before my Father in heaven.

34"Don't imagine that I came to bring peace to the earth! No, I came to bring a sword. 35I have come to set a man against his father, and a daughter against her mother, and a daughter-in-law against her mother-in-law. 36Your enemies will be right in your own household! 37If you love your father or mother more than you love me, you are not worthy of being mine; or if you love your son or daughter more than me, you are not worthy of being mine. 38If you refuse to take up your cross and follow me, you are not worthy of being mine. 39If you cling to your life, you will lose it; but if you give it up for me, you will find it.

40"Anyone who welcomes you is wel-

10:4 Greek the Cananean.   10:7 Or has come or is coming soon.   10:10 Or the worker is worthy of support.   10:25 Greek Beelzeboul.

coming me, and anyone who welcomes me is welcoming the Father who sent me. [41]If you welcome a prophet as one who speaks for God,* you will receive the same reward a prophet gets. And if you welcome good and godly people because of their godliness, you will be given a reward like theirs. [42]And if you give even a cup of cold water to one of the least of my followers, you will surely be rewarded."

CHAPTER 11

When Jesus had finished giving these instructions to his twelve disciples, he went off teaching and preaching in towns throughout the country.

[2]John the Baptist, who was now in prison, heard about all the things the Messiah was doing. So he sent his disciples to ask Jesus, [3]"Are you really the Messiah we've been waiting for, or should we keep looking for someone else?"

[4]Jesus told them, "Go back to John and tell him about what you have heard and seen— [5]the blind see, the lame walk, the lepers are cured, the deaf hear, the dead are raised to life, and the Good News is being preached to the poor. [6]And tell him: 'God blesses those who are not offended by me.*'"

[7]When John's disciples had gone, Jesus began talking about him to the crowds. "Who is this man in the wilderness that you went out to see? Did you find him weak as a reed, moved by every breath of wind? [8]Or were you expecting to see a man dressed in expensive clothes? Those who dress like that live in palaces, not out in the wilderness. [9]Were you looking for a prophet? Yes, and he is more than a prophet. [10]John is the man to whom the Scriptures refer when they say,

'Look, I am sending my messenger
    before you,
  and he will prepare your way before
    you.'*

[11]"I assure you, of all who have ever lived, none is greater than John the Baptist. Yet even the most insignificant person in the Kingdom of Heaven is greater than he is! [12]And from the time John the Baptist began preaching and baptizing until now, the Kingdom of Heaven has been forcefully advancing, and violent people attack it.* [13]For before John came, all the teachings of the Scriptures looked forward to this present time. [14]And if you are willing to accept what I say, he is Elijah, the one the prophets said would come.* [15]Anyone who is willing to hear should listen and understand!

[16]"How shall I describe this generation? These people are like a group of children playing a game in the public square. They complain to their friends, [17]'We played wedding songs, and you weren't happy, so we played funeral songs, but you weren't sad.' [18]For John the Baptist didn't drink wine and he often fasted, and you say, 'He's demon possessed.' [19]And I, the Son of Man, feast and drink, and you say, 'He's a glutton and a drunkard, and a friend of the worst sort of sinners!' But wisdom is shown to be right by what results from it."

[20]Then Jesus began to denounce the cities where he had done most of his miracles, because they hadn't turned from their sins and turned to God. [21]"What horrors await you, Korazin and Bethsaida! For if the miracles I did in you had been done in wicked Tyre and Sidon, their people would have sat in deep repentance long ago, clothed in sackcloth and throwing ashes on their heads to show their remorse. [22]I assure you, Tyre and Sidon will be better off on the judgment day than you! [23]And you people of Capernaum, will you be exalted to heaven? No, you will be brought down to the place of the dead.* For if the miracles I did for you had been done in Sodom, it would still be here today. [24]I assure you, Sodom will be better off on the judgment day than you."

[25]Then Jesus prayed this prayer: "O Father, Lord of heaven and earth, thank you for hiding the truth from those who think themselves so wise and clever, and for revealing it to the childlike. [26]Yes, Father, it pleased you to do it this way!

[27]"My Father has given me authority over everything. No one really knows the Son except the Father, and no one really knows the Father except the Son and those to whom the Son chooses to reveal him."

[28]Then Jesus said, "Come to me, all of you who are weary and carry heavy burdens, and I will give you rest. [29]Take my yoke upon you. Let me teach you, because I am humble and gentle, and you will find rest for your souls. [30]For my yoke fits perfectly, and the burden I give you is light."

10:41 Greek *welcome a prophet in the name of a prophet.*   **11:6** Or *who don't fall away because of me.*   **11:10** Mal 3:1.   **11:12** Or *until now, eager multitudes have been pressing into the Kingdom of Heaven.*   **11:14** See Mal 4:5.   **11:23** Greek *to Hades.*

OCTOBER 4 ☐ DAY 278
MATTHEW 12–15
Parables of the King

OVERVIEW Even as the multitudes press around Jesus to experience his healing touch, the religious leaders are plotting his downfall and ultimate destruction. Those who refuse to acknowledge the clear evidence of his miracles have no choice but to attribute his power to Satan. To them, Jesus responds with warnings of judgment and condemnation. But to all who will accept his claims, he offers rest and forgiveness. In the midst of this drama involving both growing reception and growing rejection, Jesus portrays his kingdom program in seven parables—earthly stories portraying heavenly realities.

Chapter 12	Chapter 13	Chapter 14	Chapter 15
Suppressors of the Truth	Expressions of the Truth	Feeding the 5,000	Feeling Compassion
Pharisees	Parables	Miracles	

YOUR DAILY WALK "There are none so blind as those who will not see."

Faith is to believe what we do not see, and the reward of this faith is to see what we believe.

It's one thing to have a legitimate question for which you are seeking an answer. Jesus welcomed seekers and questioners (7:7), promising to teach them, take their burdens, and grant them rest. But it's quite another thing to demand a sign and refuse to be convinced when the evidence is ample (12:38-42).

Think about your own relationship with God. In what ways are you honestly and sincerely seeking answers from God with a humble disposition to obey? In what areas are you demanding that God conform to your will, with an attitude that says, "My mind is made up, God, so don't confuse me with your plan for my life"?

A number of groups are portrayed in the passage you are reading today—and each responded with a different heart attitude.

The teachers of religious law said, "We want you to show us a miraculous sign" (12:38).

The people of Nazareth said, "He's just a carpenter's son" (13:55).

The apostle Peter exclaimed, "Tell me to come to you" (14:28). Which "seekers" found what they sought? Which seeker will you seek to emulate today as you walk humbly with God?

INSIGHT Teaching Techniques from the Master Teacher
Notice in Jesus' parables how his teaching was characterized by simplicity, informality, and specificity. His goal was to communicate truth, not to impress his audience. Is that your goal in teaching?

CHAPTER 12

At about that time Jesus was walking through some grainfields on the Sabbath. His disciples were hungry, so they began breaking off heads of wheat and eating the grain. ²Some Pharisees saw them do it and protested, "Your disciples shouldn't be doing that! It's against the law to work by harvesting grain on the Sabbath."

³But Jesus said to them, "Haven't you ever read in the Scriptures what King David did when he and his companions were hungry? ⁴He went into the house of God, and they ate the special bread reserved for the priests alone. That was breaking the law, too. ⁵And haven't you ever read in the law of Moses that the priests on duty in the Temple may work on the Sabbath? ⁶I tell you, there is one here who is even greater than the Temple! ⁷But

you would not have condemned those who aren't guilty if you knew the meaning of this Scripture: 'I want you to be merciful; I don't want your sacrifices.'* ⁸For I, the Son of Man, am master even of the Sabbath."

⁹Then he went over to the synagogue, ¹⁰where he noticed a man with a deformed hand. The Pharisees asked Jesus, "Is it legal to work by healing on the Sabbath day?" (They were, of course, hoping he would say yes, so they could bring charges against him.)

¹¹And he answered, "If you had one sheep, and it fell into a well on the Sabbath, wouldn't you get to work and pull it out? Of course you would. ¹²And how much more valuable is a person than a sheep! Yes, it is right to do good on the Sabbath." ¹³Then he said to the man, "Reach out your hand." The man reached out his hand, and it became normal, just like the other one. ¹⁴Then the Pharisees called a meeting and discussed plans for killing Jesus.

¹⁵But Jesus knew what they were planning. He left that area, and many people followed him. He healed all the sick among them, ¹⁶but he warned them not to say who he was. ¹⁷This fulfilled the prophecy of Isaiah concerning him:

¹⁸ "Look at my Servant,
  whom I have chosen.
He is my Beloved,
  and I am very pleased with him.
I will put my Spirit upon him,
  and he will proclaim justice to the
    nations.
¹⁹ He will not fight or shout;
  he will not raise his voice in public.
²⁰ He will not crush those who are weak,
  or quench the smallest hope,
until he brings full justice with his
    final victory.
²¹ And his name will be the hope
  of all the world."*

²²Then a demon-possessed man, who was both blind and unable to talk, was brought to Jesus. He healed the man so that he could both speak and see. ²³The crowd was amazed. "Could it be that Jesus is the Son of David, the Messiah?" they wondered out loud.

²⁴But when the Pharisees heard about the miracle, they said, "No wonder he can cast out demons. He gets his power from Satan,* the prince of demons."

²⁵Jesus knew their thoughts and replied, "Any kingdom at war with itself is doomed. A city or home divided against itself is doomed. ²⁶And if Satan is casting out Satan, he is fighting against himself. His own kingdom will not survive. ²⁷And if I am empowered by the prince of demons,* what about your own followers? They cast out demons, too, so they will judge you for what you have said. ²⁸But if I am casting out demons by the Spirit of God, then the Kingdom of God has arrived among you. ²⁹Let me illustrate this. You can't enter a strong man's house and rob him without first tying him up. Only then can his house be robbed!* ³⁰Anyone who isn't helping me opposes me, and anyone who isn't working with me is actually working against me.

³¹"Every sin or blasphemy can be forgiven—except blasphemy against the Holy Spirit, which can never be forgiven. ³²Anyone who blasphemes against me, the Son of Man, can be forgiven, but blasphemy against the Holy Spirit will never be forgiven, either in this world or in the world to come.

³³"A tree is identified by its fruit. Make a tree good, and its fruit will be good. Make a tree bad, and its fruit will be bad. ³⁴You brood of snakes! How could evil men like you speak what is good and right? For whatever is in your heart determines what you say. ³⁵A good person produces good words from a good heart, and an evil person produces evil words from an evil heart. ³⁶And I tell you this, that you must give an account on judgment day of every idle word you speak. ³⁷The words you say now reflect your fate then; either you will be justified by them or you will be condemned."

³⁸One day some teachers of religious law and Pharisees came to Jesus and said, "Teacher, we want you to show us a miraculous sign to prove that you are from God."

³⁹But Jesus replied, "Only an evil, faithless generation would ask for a miraculous sign; but the only sign I will give them is the sign of the prophet Jonah. ⁴⁰For as Jonah was in the belly of the great fish for three days and three nights, so I, the Son of Man, will be in the heart of the earth for

---

12:7 Hos 6:6.   **12:18-21** Isa 42:1-4.   **12:24** Greek *Beelzeboul*.   **12:27** Greek *by Beelzeboul*.   **12:29** Or *One cannot rob Satan's kingdom without first tying him up. Only then can his demons be cast out.*

three days and three nights. ⁴¹The people of Nineveh will rise up against this generation on judgment day and condemn it, because they repented at the preaching of Jonah. And now someone greater than Jonah is here—and you refuse to repent. ⁴²The queen of Sheba* will also rise up against this generation on judgment day and condemn it, because she came from a distant land to hear the wisdom of Solomon. And now someone greater than Solomon is here—and you refuse to listen to him.

⁴³"When an evil spirit leaves a person, it goes into the desert, seeking rest but finding none. ⁴⁴Then it says, 'I will return to the person I came from.' So it returns and finds its former home empty, swept, and clean. ⁴⁵Then the spirit finds seven other spirits more evil than itself, and they all enter the person and live there. And so that person is worse off than before. That will be the experience of this evil generation."

⁴⁶As Jesus was speaking to the crowd, his mother and brothers were outside, wanting to talk with him. ⁴⁷Someone told Jesus, "Your mother and your brothers are outside, and they want to speak to you."

⁴⁸Jesus asked, "Who is my mother? Who are my brothers?" ⁴⁹Then he pointed to his disciples and said, "These are my mother and brothers. ⁵⁰Anyone who does the will of my Father in heaven is my brother and sister and mother!"

CHAPTER 13

Later that same day, Jesus left the house and went down to the shore, ²where an immense crowd soon gathered. He got into a boat, where he sat and taught as the people listened on the shore. ³He told many stories such as this one:

"A farmer went out to plant some seed. ⁴As he scattered it across his field, some seeds fell on a footpath, and the birds came and ate them. ⁵Other seeds fell on shallow soil with underlying rock. The plants sprang up quickly, ⁶but they soon wilted beneath the hot sun and died because the roots had no nourishment in the shallow soil. ⁷Other seeds fell among thorns that shot up and choked out the tender blades. ⁸But some seeds fell on fertile soil and produced a crop that was thirty, sixty, and even a hundred times as much as had been planted. ⁹Anyone who is willing to hear should listen and understand!"

¹⁰His disciples came and asked him, "Why do you always tell stories when you talk to the people?"

¹¹Then he explained to them, "You have been permitted to understand the secrets of the Kingdom of Heaven, but others have not. ¹²To those who are open to my teaching, more understanding will be given, and they will have an abundance of knowledge. But to those who are not listening, even what they have will be taken away from them. ¹³That is why I tell these stories, because people see what I do, but they don't really see. They hear what I say, but they don't really hear, and they don't understand. ¹⁴This fulfills the prophecy of Isaiah, which says:

'You will hear my words,
  but you will not understand;
you will see what I do,
  but you will not perceive its meaning.
¹⁵ For the hearts of these people are
    hardened,
  and their ears cannot hear,
  and they have closed their eyes—
so their eyes cannot see,
  and their ears cannot hear,
  and their hearts cannot understand,
and they cannot turn to me
  and let me heal them.'*

¹⁶"But blessed are your eyes, because they see; and your ears, because they hear. ¹⁷I assure you, many prophets and godly people have longed to see and hear what you have seen and heard, but they could not.

¹⁸"Now here is the explanation of the story I told about the farmer sowing grain: ¹⁹The seed that fell on the hard path represents those who hear the Good News about the Kingdom and don't understand it. Then the evil one comes and snatches the seed away from their hearts. ²⁰The rocky soil represents those who hear the message and receive it with joy. ²¹But like young plants in such soil, their roots don't go very deep. At first they get along fine, but they wilt as soon as they have problems or are persecuted because they believe the word. ²²The thorny ground represents those who hear and accept the Good News, but all too quickly the message is crowded out by the

12:42 Greek *The queen of the south.*   **13:14-15** Isa 6:9-10.

cares of this life and the lure of wealth, so no crop is produced. 23The good soil represents the hearts of those who truly accept God's message and produce a huge harvest—thirty, sixty, or even a hundred times as much as had been planted."

24Here is another story Jesus told: "The Kingdom of Heaven is like a farmer who planted good seed in his field. 25But that night as everyone slept, his enemy came and planted weeds among the wheat. 26When the crop began to grow and produce grain, the weeds also grew. 27The farmer's servants came and told him, 'Sir, the field where you planted that good seed is full of weeds!'

28" 'An enemy has done it!' the farmer exclaimed.

" 'Shall we pull out the weeds?' they asked.

29"He replied, 'No, you'll hurt the wheat if you do. 30Let both grow together until the harvest. Then I will tell the harvesters to sort out the weeds and burn them and to put the wheat in the barn.'"

31Here is another illustration Jesus used: "The Kingdom of Heaven is like a mustard seed planted in a field. 32It is the smallest of all seeds, but it becomes the largest of garden plants and grows into a tree where birds can come and find shelter in its branches."

33Jesus also used this illustration: "The Kingdom of Heaven is like yeast used by a woman making bread. Even though she used a large amount* of flour, the yeast permeated every part of the dough."

34Jesus always used stories and illustrations like these when speaking to the crowds. In fact, he never spoke to them without using such parables. 35This fulfilled the prophecy that said,

"I will speak to you in parables.
    I will explain mysteries hidden since
        the creation of the world."*

36Then, leaving the crowds outside, Jesus went into the house. His disciples said, "Please explain the story of the weeds in the field."

37"All right," he said. "I, the Son of Man, am the farmer who plants the good seed. 38The field is the world, and the good seed represents the people of the Kingdom. The weeds are the people who belong to the evil

one. 39The enemy who planted the weeds among the wheat is the Devil. The harvest is the end of the world, and the harvesters are the angels.

40"Just as the weeds are separated out and burned, so it will be at the end of the world. 41I, the Son of Man, will send my angels, and they will remove from my Kingdom everything that causes sin and all who do evil, 42and they will throw them into the furnace and burn them. There will be weeping and gnashing of teeth. 43Then the godly will shine like the sun in their Father's Kingdom. Anyone who is willing to hear should listen and understand!

44"The Kingdom of Heaven is like a treasure that a man discovered hidden in a field. In his excitement, he hid it again and sold everything he owned to get enough money to buy the field—and to get the treasure, too!

45"Again, the Kingdom of Heaven is like a pearl merchant on the lookout for choice pearls. 46When he discovered a pearl of great value, he sold everything he owned and bought it!

47"Again, the Kingdom of Heaven is like a fishing net that is thrown into the water and gathers fish of every kind. 48When the net is full, they drag it up onto the shore, sit down, sort the good fish into crates, and throw the bad ones away. 49That is the way it will be at the end of the world. The angels will come and separate the wicked people from the godly, 50throwing the wicked into the fire. There will be weeping and gnashing of teeth. 51Do you understand?"

"Yes," they said, "we do."

52Then he added, "Every teacher of religious law who has become a disciple in the Kingdom of Heaven is like a person who brings out of the storehouse the new teachings as well as the old."

53When Jesus had finished telling these stories, he left that part of the country. 54He returned to Nazareth, his hometown. When he taught there in the synagogue, everyone was astonished and said, "Where does he get his wisdom and his miracles? 55He's just a carpenter's son, and we know Mary, his mother, and his brothers—James, Joseph, Simon, and Judas. 56All his sisters live right here among us. What makes him so great?" 57And they were deeply offended and refused to believe in him.

13:33 Greek *3 measures.*   **13:35** Ps 78:2.

Then Jesus told them, "A prophet is honored everywhere except in his own hometown and among his own family." [58]And so he did only a few miracles there because of their unbelief.

CHAPTER 14

When Herod Antipas* heard about Jesus, [2]he said to his advisers, "This must be John the Baptist come back to life again! That is why he can do such miracles." [3]For Herod had arrested and imprisoned John as a favor to his wife Herodias (the former wife of Herod's brother Philip). [4]John kept telling Herod, "It is illegal for you to marry her." [5]Herod would have executed John, but he was afraid of a riot, because all the people believed John was a prophet.

[6]But at a birthday party for Herod, Herodias's daughter performed a dance that greatly pleased him, [7]so he promised with an oath to give her anything she wanted. [8]At her mother's urging, the girl asked, "I want the head of John the Baptist on a tray!" [9]The king was sorry, but because of his oath and because he didn't want to back down in front of his guests, he issued the necessary orders. [10]So John was beheaded in the prison, [11]and his head was brought on a tray and given to the girl, who took it to her mother. [12]John's disciples came for his body and buried it. Then they told Jesus what had happened.

[13]As soon as Jesus heard the news, he went off by himself in a boat to a remote area to be alone. But the crowds heard where he was headed and followed by land from many villages. [14]A vast crowd was there as he stepped from the boat, and he had compassion on them and healed their sick.

[15]That evening the disciples came to him and said, "This is a desolate place, and it is getting late. Send the crowds away so they can go to the villages and buy food for themselves."

[16]But Jesus replied, "That isn't necessary—you feed them."

[17]"Impossible!" they exclaimed. "We have only five loaves of bread and two fish!"

[18]"Bring them here," he said. [19]Then he told the people to sit down on the grass. And he took the five loaves and two fish, looked up toward heaven, and asked God's blessing on the food. Breaking the loaves into pieces, he gave some of the bread and fish to each disciple, and the disciples gave them to the people. [20]They all ate as much as they wanted, and they picked up twelve baskets of leftovers. [21]About five thousand men had eaten from those five loaves, in addition to all the women and children!

[22]Immediately after this, Jesus made his disciples get back into the boat and cross to the other side of the lake while he sent the people home. [23]Afterward he went up into the hills by himself to pray. Night fell while he was there alone. [24]Meanwhile, the disciples were in trouble far away from land, for a strong wind had risen, and they were fighting heavy waves.

[25]About three o'clock in the morning* Jesus came to them, walking on the water. [26]When the disciples saw him, they screamed in terror, thinking he was a ghost. [27]But Jesus spoke to them at once. "It's all right," he said. "I am here! Don't be afraid."

[28]Then Peter called to him, "Lord, if it's really you, tell me to come to you by walking on water."

[29]"All right, come," Jesus said.

So Peter went over the side of the boat and walked on the water toward Jesus. [30]But when he looked around at the high waves, he was terrified and began to sink. "Save me, Lord!" he shouted.

[31]Instantly Jesus reached out his hand and grabbed him. "You don't have much faith," Jesus said. "Why did you doubt me?" [32]And when they climbed back into the boat, the wind stopped.

[33]Then the disciples worshiped him. "You really are the Son of God!" they exclaimed.

[34]After they had crossed the lake, they landed at Gennesaret. [35]The news of their arrival spread quickly throughout the whole surrounding area, and soon people were bringing all their sick to be healed. [36]The sick begged him to let them touch even the fringe of his robe, and all who touched it were healed.

CHAPTER 15

Some Pharisees and teachers of religious law now arrived from Jerusalem to interview Jesus. [2]"Why do your disciples dis-

14:1 Greek *Herod the tetrarch*. He was a son of King Herod and was ruler over one of the four districts in Palestine.   14:25 Greek *In the fourth watch of the night*.

obey our age-old traditions?" they demanded. "They ignore our tradition of ceremonial hand washing before they eat."

3Jesus replied, "And why do you, by your traditions, violate the direct commandments of God? 4For instance, God says, 'Honor your father and mother,' and 'Anyone who speaks evil of father or mother must be put to death.'* 5But you say, 'You don't need to honor your parents by caring for their needs if you give the money to God instead.' 6And so, by your own tradition, you nullify the direct commandment of God. 7You hypocrites! Isaiah was prophesying about you when he said,

8 'These people honor me with their lips,
    but their hearts are far away.
9 Their worship is a farce,
    for they replace God's commands
    with their own man-made
    teachings.'*"

10Then Jesus called to the crowds and said, "Listen to what I say and try to understand. 11You are not defiled by what you eat; you are defiled by what you say and do.*"

12Then the disciples came to him and asked, "Do you realize you offended the Pharisees by what you just said?"

13Jesus replied, "Every plant not planted by my heavenly Father will be rooted up, 14so ignore them. They are blind guides leading the blind, and if one blind person guides another, they will both fall into a ditch."

15Then Peter asked Jesus, "Explain what you meant when you said people aren't defiled by what they eat."

16"Don't you understand?" Jesus asked him. 17"Anything you eat passes through the stomach and then goes out of the body. 18But evil words come from an evil heart and defile the person who says them. 19For from the heart come evil thoughts, murder, adultery, all other sexual immorality, theft, lying, and slander. 20These are what defile you. Eating with unwashed hands could never defile you and make you unacceptable to God!"

21Jesus then left Galilee and went north to the region of Tyre and Sidon. 22A Gentile* woman who lived there came to him, pleading, "Have mercy on me, O Lord, Son of David! For my daughter has a demon in her, and it is severely tormenting her."

23But Jesus gave her no reply—not even a word. Then his disciples urged him to send her away. "Tell her to leave," they said. "She is bothering us with all her begging."

24Then he said to the woman, "I was sent only to help the people of Israel—God's lost sheep—not the Gentiles."

25But she came and worshiped him and pleaded again, "Lord, help me!"

26"It isn't right to take food from the children and throw it to the dogs," he said.

27"Yes, Lord," she replied, "but even dogs are permitted to eat crumbs that fall beneath their master's table."

28"Woman," Jesus said to her, "your faith is great. Your request is granted." And her daughter was instantly healed.

29Jesus returned to the Sea of Galilee and climbed a hill and sat down. 30A vast crowd brought him the lame, blind, crippled, mute, and many others with physical difficulties, and they laid them before Jesus. And he healed them all. 31The crowd was amazed! Those who hadn't been able to speak were talking, the crippled were made well, the lame were walking around, and those who had been blind could see again! And they praised the God of Israel.

32Then Jesus called his disciples to him and said, "I feel sorry for these people. They have been here with me for three days, and they have nothing left to eat. I don't want to send them away hungry, or they will faint along the road."

33The disciples replied, "And where would we get enough food out here in the wilderness for all of them to eat?"

34Jesus asked, "How many loaves of bread do you have?"

They replied, "Seven, and a few small fish." 35So Jesus told all the people to sit down on the ground. 36Then he took the seven loaves and the fish, thanked God for them, broke them into pieces, and gave them to the disciples, who distributed the food to the crowd.

37They all ate until they were full, and when the scraps were picked up, there were seven large baskets of food left over! 38There were four thousand men who were fed that day, in addition to all the women and children. 39Then Jesus sent the people home, and he got into a boat and crossed over to the region of Magadan.

15:4 Exod 20:12; 21:17; Lev 20:9; Deut 5:16.   **15:8-9** Isa 29:13.   **15:11** Or *what comes out of the mouth defiles a person.*   **15:22** Greek *Canaanite.*

OCTOBER 5 ☐ DAY 279
MATTHEW 16–19
Principles of the King

OVERVIEW Though Jesus takes time to minister to hungry crowds, confront the increasingly hostile Pharisees, and comfort the believing Canaanite woman, it is clear that his primary concern is for the disciples—those he will soon leave behind to continue the work he has begun. His miracles and parables, healings and discourses all focus on his faithful followers to prepare them for difficult days just ahead.

Chapter 16	Chapter 17	Chapter 18	Chapter 19
Accusation of the King	Affirmation of the King	Instruction on the Kingdom	Correction for Kingdom Dwellers
Test	Transfiguration	Devotion	Divorce

Christ is the meeting point between the Trinity and the sinner's soul.

YOUR DAILY WALK Think of the book of Matthew as a mountain with the action rising to a peak and then subsiding. Some commentators have suggested you'll find the "peak," the pivotal climax of the book, in the dramatic confession of Peter in chapter 16.

Up to this point Jesus has been seeking to prove his claim of messiahship through words and deeds. Now it is time to see if the lesson has been learned.

Jesus gives his disciples a "public opinion" survey: "Who do people say that the Son of Man is?" (16:13). The disciples report that public opinion is divided. Some say he's John, others Elijah or one of the prophets. Then Jesus cuts to the heart of the matter: "Who do you say I am?" And suddenly the disciples have no public opinion to hide behind. They must make an intelligent personal choice based on Christ's miracles and messages.

On the basis of what you have read in the first half of Matthew's Gospel, what would be your response to Jesus' penetrating question: "Who do you say I am?"

Now check 16:16 to find the correct answer to the question. Take a few moments to memorize it—and make it your own answer!

INSIGHT An Inspired Commentary on the Transfiguration
What does the transfiguration of Jesus mean (17:1-9)? Peter, one of the observers, gives the inspired explanation in 2 Peter 1:17-18. It was the unveiling of the glory of Jesus, a "sneak preview" of what heaven will be like!

CHAPTER 16
One day the Pharisees and Sadducees came to test Jesus' claims by asking him to show them a miraculous sign from heaven.

²He replied, "You know the saying, 'Red sky at night means fair weather tomorrow, ³red sky in the morning means foul weather all day.' You are good at reading the weather signs in the sky, but you can't read the obvious signs of the times!* ⁴Only an evil, faithless generation would ask for a miraculous sign, but the only sign I will

give them is the sign of the prophet Jonah." Then Jesus left them and went away.

⁵Later, after they crossed to the other side of the lake, the disciples discovered they had forgotten to bring any food. ⁶"Watch out!" Jesus warned them. "Beware of the yeast of the Pharisees and Sadducees."

⁷They decided he was saying this because they hadn't brought any bread. ⁸Jesus knew what they were thinking, so he said, "You have so little faith! Why are you worried about having no food? ⁹Won't you

16:2-3 Several manuscripts do not include any of the words in 16:2-3 after *He replied*.

ever understand? Don't you remember the five thousand I fed with five loaves, and the baskets of food that were left over? [10]Don't you remember the four thousand I fed with seven loaves, with baskets of food left over? [11]How could you even think I was talking about food? So again I say, 'Beware of the yeast of the Pharisees and Sadducees.'"

[12]Then at last they understood that he wasn't speaking about yeast or bread but about the false teaching of the Pharisees and Sadducees.

[13]When Jesus came to the region of Caesarea Philippi, he asked his disciples, "Who do people say that the Son of Man is?"

[14]"Well," they replied, "some say John the Baptist, some say Elijah, and others say Jeremiah or one of the other prophets."

[15]Then he asked them, "Who do you say I am?"

[16]Simon Peter answered, "You are the Messiah, the Son of the living God."

[17]Jesus replied, "You are blessed, Simon son of John,* because my Father in heaven has revealed this to you. You did not learn this from any human being. [18]Now I say to you that you are Peter,* and upon this rock I will build my church, and all the powers of hell* will not conquer it. [19]And I will give you the keys of the Kingdom of Heaven. Whatever you lock on earth will be locked in heaven, and whatever you open on earth will be opened in heaven." [20]Then he sternly warned them not to tell anyone that he was the Messiah.

[21]From then on Jesus began to tell his disciples plainly that he had to go to Jerusalem, and he told them what would happen to him there. He would suffer at the hands of the leaders and the leading priests and the teachers of religious law. He would be killed, and he would be raised on the third day.

[22]But Peter took him aside and corrected him. "Heaven forbid, Lord," he said. "This will never happen to you!"

[23]Jesus turned to Peter and said, "Get away from me, Satan! You are a dangerous trap to me. You are seeing things merely from a human point of view, and not from God's."

[24]Then Jesus said to the disciples, "If any of you wants to be my follower, you must put aside your selfish ambition, shoulder your cross, and follow me. [25]If you try to keep your life for yourself, you will lose it. But if you give up your life for me, you will find true life. [26]And how do you benefit if you gain the whole world but lose your own soul* in the process? Is anything worth more than your soul? [27]For I, the Son of Man, will come in the glory of my Father with his angels and will judge all people according to their deeds. [28]And I assure you that some of you standing here right now will not die before you see me, the Son of Man, coming in my Kingdom."

CHAPTER 17

Six days later Jesus took Peter and the two brothers, James and John, and led them up a high mountain. [2]As the men watched, Jesus' appearance changed so that his face shone like the sun, and his clothing became dazzling white. [3]Suddenly, Moses and Elijah appeared and began talking with Jesus. [4]Peter blurted out, "Lord, this is wonderful! If you want me to, I'll make three shrines,* one for you, one for Moses, and one for Elijah."

[5]But even as he said it, a bright cloud came over them, and a voice from the cloud said, "This is my beloved Son, and I am fully pleased with him. Listen to him." [6]The disciples were terrified and fell face down on the ground.

[7]Jesus came over and touched them. "Get up," he said, "don't be afraid." [8]And when they looked, they saw only Jesus with them. [9]As they descended the mountain, Jesus commanded them, "Don't tell anyone what you have seen until I, the Son of Man, have been raised from the dead."

[10]His disciples asked, "Why do the teachers of religious law insist that Elijah must return before the Messiah comes*?"

[11]Jesus replied, "Elijah is indeed coming first to set everything in order. [12]But I tell you, he has already come, but he wasn't recognized, and he was badly mistreated. And soon the Son of Man will also suffer at their hands." [13]Then the disciples realized he had been speaking of John the Baptist.

[14]When they arrived at the foot of the mountain, a huge crowd was waiting for them. A man came and knelt before Jesus and said, [15]"Lord, have mercy on my son, because he has seizures and suffers terribly.

16:17 Greek *Simon son of Jonah;* see John 1:42; 21:15-17.   **16:18a** *Peter* means "stone" or "rock."   **16:18b** Greek *and the gates of Hades.*   **16:26** Or *your life;* also in 16:26b.   **17:4** Or *shelters;* Greek reads *tabernacles.*   **17:10** Greek *that Elijah must come first.*

He often falls into the fire or into the water. ¹⁶So I brought him to your disciples, but they couldn't heal him."

¹⁷Jesus replied, "You stubborn, faithless people! How long must I be with you until you believe? How long must I put up with you? Bring the boy to me." ¹⁸Then Jesus rebuked the demon in the boy, and it left him. From that moment the boy was well.

¹⁹Afterward the disciples asked Jesus privately, "Why couldn't we cast out that demon?"

²⁰"You didn't have enough faith," Jesus told them. "I assure you, even if you had faith as small as a mustard seed you could say to this mountain, 'Move from here to there,' and it would move. Nothing would be impossible."*

²²One day after they had returned to Galilee, Jesus told them, "The Son of Man is going to be betrayed. ²³He will be killed, but three days later he will be raised from the dead." And the disciples' hearts were filled with grief.

²⁴On their arrival in Capernaum, the tax collectors for the Temple tax came to Peter and asked him, "Doesn't your teacher pay the Temple tax?"

²⁵"Of course he does," Peter replied. Then he went into the house to talk to Jesus about it.

But before he had a chance to speak, Jesus asked him, "What do you think, Peter*? Do kings tax their own people or the foreigners they have conquered?"

²⁶"They tax the foreigners," Peter replied.

"Well, then," Jesus said, "the citizens are free! ²⁷However, we don't want to offend them, so go down to the lake and throw in a line. Open the mouth of the first fish you catch, and you will find a coin. Take the coin and pay the tax for both of us."

CHAPTER 18

About that time the disciples came to Jesus and asked, "Which of us is greatest in the Kingdom of Heaven?"

²Jesus called a small child over to him and put the child among them. ³Then he said, "I assure you, unless you turn from your sins and become as little children, you will never get into the Kingdom of Heaven. ⁴Therefore, anyone who becomes as humble as this little child is the greatest in the

Kingdom of Heaven. ⁵And anyone who welcomes a little child like this on my behalf is welcoming me. ⁶But if anyone causes one of these little ones who trusts in me to lose faith, it would be better for that person to be thrown into the sea with a large millstone tied around the neck.

⁷"How terrible it will be for anyone who causes others to sin. Temptation to do wrong is inevitable, but how terrible it will be for the person who does the tempting. ⁸So if your hand or foot causes you to sin, cut it off and throw it away. It is better to enter heaven* crippled or lame than to be thrown into the unquenchable fire with both of your hands and feet. ⁹And if your eye causes you to sin, gouge it out and throw it away. It is better to enter heaven half blind than to have two eyes and be thrown into hell.

¹⁰"Beware that you don't despise a single one of these little ones. For I tell you that in heaven their angels are always in the presence of my heavenly Father.*

¹²"If a shepherd has one hundred sheep, and one wanders away and is lost, what will he do? Won't he leave the ninety-nine others and go out into the hills to search for the lost one? ¹³And if he finds it, he will surely rejoice over it more than over the ninety-nine that didn't wander away! ¹⁴In the same way, it is not my heavenly Father's will that even one of these little ones should perish.

¹⁵"If another believer* sins against you, go privately and point out the fault. If the other person listens and confesses it, you have won that person back. ¹⁶But if you are unsuccessful, take one or two others with you and go back again, so that everything you say may be confirmed by two or three witnesses. ¹⁷If that person still refuses to listen, take your case to the church. If the church decides you are right, but the other person won't accept it, treat that person as a pagan or a corrupt tax collector. ¹⁸I tell you this: Whatever you prohibit on earth is prohibited in heaven, and whatever you allow on earth is allowed in heaven.

¹⁹"I also tell you this: If two of you agree down here on earth concerning anything you ask, my Father in heaven will do it for you. ²⁰For where two or three gather together because they are mine,* I am there among them."

17:20 Some manuscripts add verse 21, *But this kind of demon won't leave unless you have prayed and fasted.*   17:25 Greek *Simon.*
18:8 Greek *enter life; also in 18:9.*   18:10 Some manuscripts add verse 11, *And I, the Son of Man, have come to save the lost.*
18:15 Greek *your brother.*   18:20 Greek *gather together in my name.*

²¹Then Peter came to him and asked, "Lord, how often should I forgive someone* who sins against me? Seven times?"

²²"No!" Jesus replied, "seventy times seven!*

²³"For this reason, the Kingdom of Heaven can be compared to a king who decided to bring his accounts up to date with servants who had borrowed money from him. ²⁴In the process, one of his debtors was brought in who owed him millions of dollars.* ²⁵He couldn't pay, so the king ordered that he, his wife, his children, and everything he had be sold to pay the debt. ²⁶But the man fell down before the king and begged him, 'Oh, sir, be patient with me, and I will pay it all.' ²⁷Then the king was filled with pity for him, and he released him and forgave his debt.

²⁸"But when the man left the king, he went to a fellow servant who owed him a few thousand dollars.* He grabbed him by the throat and demanded instant payment. ²⁹His fellow servant fell down before him and begged for a little more time. 'Be patient and I will pay it,' he pleaded. ³⁰But his creditor wouldn't wait. He had the man arrested and jailed until the debt could be paid in full.

³¹"When some of the other servants saw this, they were very upset. They went to the king and told him what had happened. ³²Then the king called in the man he had forgiven and said, 'You evil servant! I forgave you that tremendous debt because you pleaded with me. ³³Shouldn't you have mercy on your fellow servant, just as I had mercy on you?' ³⁴Then the angry king sent the man to prison until he had paid every penny.

³⁵"That's what my heavenly Father will do to you if you refuse to forgive your brothers and sisters in your heart."

C H A P T E R   19
After Jesus had finished saying these things, he left Galilee and went southward to the region of Judea and into the area east of the Jordan River. ²Vast crowds followed him there, and he healed their sick.

³Some Pharisees came and tried to trap him with this question: "Should a man be allowed to divorce his wife for any reason?"

⁴"Haven't you read the Scriptures?"

Jesus replied. "They record that from the beginning 'God made them male and female.'* ⁵And he said, 'This explains why a man leaves his father and mother and is joined to his wife, and the two are united into one.'* ⁶Since they are no longer two but one, let no one separate them, for God has joined them together."

⁷"Then why did Moses say a man could merely write an official letter of divorce and send her away?"* they asked.

⁸Jesus replied, "Moses permitted divorce as a concession to your hard-hearted wickedness, but it was not what God had originally intended. ⁹And I tell you this, a man who divorces his wife and marries another commits adultery—unless his wife has been unfaithful.*"

¹⁰Jesus' disciples then said to him, "Then it is better not to marry!"

¹¹"Not everyone can accept this statement," Jesus said. "Only those whom God helps. ¹²Some are born as eunuchs, some have been made that way by others, and some choose not to marry for the sake of the Kingdom of Heaven. Let anyone who can, accept this statement."

¹³Some children were brought to Jesus so he could lay his hands on them and pray for them. The disciples told them not to bother him. ¹⁴But Jesus said, "Let the children come to me. Don't stop them! For the Kingdom of Heaven belongs to such as these." ¹⁵And he put his hands on their heads and blessed them before he left.

¹⁶Someone came to Jesus with this question: "Teacher,* what good things must I do to have eternal life?"

¹⁷"Why ask me about what is good?" Jesus replied. "Only God is good. But to answer your question, you can receive eternal life if you keep the commandments."

¹⁸"Which ones?" the man asked.

And Jesus replied: " 'Do not murder. Do not commit adultery. Do not steal. Do not testify falsely. ¹⁹Honor your father and mother. Love your neighbor as yourself.'*"

²⁰"I've obeyed all these commandments," the young man replied. "What else must I do?"

²¹Jesus told him, "If you want to be perfect, go and sell all you have and give the money to the poor, and you will have treasure in heaven. Then come, follow me."

18:21 Greek *your brother.*   **18:22** Or *77 times.*   **18:24** Greek *10,000 talents.*   **18:28** Greek *100 denarii.* A denarius was the equivalent of a full day's wage.   **19:4** Gen 1:27; 5:2.   **19:5** Gen 2:24.   **19:7** Deut 24:1.   **19:9** Some manuscripts add *And the man who marries a divorced woman commits adultery.*   **19:16** Some manuscripts read *Good Teacher.*   **19:18-19** Exod 20:12-16; Lev 19:18; Deut 5:16-20.

²²But when the young man heard this, he went sadly away because he had many possessions.

²³Then Jesus said to his disciples, "I tell you the truth, it is very hard for a rich person to get into the Kingdom of Heaven. ²⁴I say it again—it is easier for a camel to go through the eye of a needle than for a rich person to enter the Kingdom of God!"

²⁵The disciples were astounded. "Then who in the world can be saved?" they asked.

²⁶Jesus looked at them intently and said, "Humanly speaking, it is impossible. But with God everything is possible."

²⁷Then Peter said to him, "We've given up everything to follow you. What will we get out of it?"

²⁸And Jesus replied, "I assure you that when I, the Son of Man, sit upon my glorious throne in the Kingdom,* you who have been my followers will also sit on twelve thrones, judging the twelve tribes of Israel. ²⁹And everyone who has given up houses or brothers or sisters or father or mother or children or property, for my sake, will receive a hundred times as much in return and will have eternal life. ³⁰But many who seem to be important now will be the least important then, and those who are considered least here will be the greatest then.*

19:28 Greek *in the regeneration.*   19:30 Greek *But many who are first will be last; and the last, first.*

OCTOBER 6 □ DAY 280
MATTHEW 20–23
More Parables of the King

OVERVIEW Though public opinion regarding Jesus is divided, there can be no mistaking the murderous intent of the religious teachers and Pharisees. Jesus repeatedly warns his men of the soon coming dark days of his suffering and death (16:21; 20:18-19). Arriving in Jerusalem to a hero's welcome, Jesus is hailed as King while making his entrance into the city. But even in the midst of this joyful reception, he mourns over the fickleness and fate of his countrymen.

Chapter 20	Chapter 21	Chapter 22	Chapter 23
Privilege before the King	Presentation of the King	Tricky Questions from Opponents	Harsh Words for Hypocrites
Pride	Humility	Interrogation	Condemnation

The more your heart is washed, the more you'll sense its remaining defilement.

YOUR DAILY WALK A voice of authority (a teacher, parent, boss, church leader) speaks . . . and one of three things happens: (1) Because of *inattention* you fail to hear and heed the leader's words; (2) because of *irritation* you refuse to obey; or (3) because of *conviction* you respond obediently. Which response(s) do you see modeled in the parable of the vineyard (20:1-16)? the parable of the two sons (21:28-32)? the parable of the tenants (21:33-46)?

God's Word has a way of being irritatingly convicting. You wish you could ignore its truth, but there it is—persistent, penetrating, uncompromising. And until you respond in obedience, you will feel uncomfortable and without peace. Like the Pharisees whom Christ called "blind guides," "hypocrites," and "whitewashed tombs," you will either find a way to silence the Preacher . . . or submit your life to the truth of his sermon!

Is there a burr under your spiritual saddle today? Don't ignore it; God has placed it there for a purpose—to make it too painful *not* to change! So how will you respond?

INSIGHT Condemned by Jews, Crucified by Gentiles
Jesus' declaration of his coming death (20:18-19) was accurate in every detail. The crime of which Jesus was accused by the Jews—blasphemy—was punishable by death. But since only the Roman civil authorities could execute such a sentence, Jesus was taken before Pilate and Herod—Roman rulers of his day—to gain the necessary permission for his crucifixion.

CHAPTER 20

"For the Kingdom of Heaven is like the owner of an estate who went out early one morning to hire workers for his vineyard. ²He agreed to pay the normal daily wage* and sent them out to work.

³"At nine o'clock in the morning he was passing through the marketplace and saw some people standing around doing nothing. ⁴So he hired them, telling them he would pay them whatever was right at the end of the day. ⁵At noon and again around three o'clock he did the same thing. ⁶At five o'clock that evening he was in town again and saw some more people standing around. He asked them, 'Why haven't you been working today?'

⁷"They replied, 'Because no one hired us.'

"The owner of the estate told them, 'Then go on out and join the others in my vineyard.'

⁸"That evening he told the foreman to call the workers in and pay them, beginning with the last workers first. ⁹When those hired at five o'clock were paid, each received a full day's wage. ¹⁰When those hired earlier came to get their pay, they assumed they would receive more. But they, too, were paid a day's wage. ¹¹When they received their pay, they protested, ¹²'Those people worked only one hour, and yet you've paid them just as much as you paid us who worked all day in the scorching heat.'

¹³"He answered one of them, 'Friend, I haven't been unfair! Didn't you agree to work all day for the usual wage? ¹⁴Take it and go. I wanted to pay this last worker the same as you. ¹⁵Is it against the law for me to do what I want with my money? Should you be angry because I am kind?'

¹⁶"And so it is, that many who are first now will be last then; and those who are last now will be first then."

¹⁷As Jesus was on the way to Jerusalem, he took the twelve disciples aside privately and told them what was going to happen to him. ¹⁸"When we get to Jerusalem," he said, "the Son of Man will be betrayed to the leading priests and the teachers of religious law. They will sentence him to die. ¹⁹Then they will hand him over to the Romans to be mocked, whipped, and crucified. But on the third day he will be raised from the dead."

²⁰Then the mother of James and John, the sons of Zebedee, came to Jesus with her sons. She knelt respectfully to ask a favor. ²¹"What is your request?" he asked.

She replied, "In your Kingdom, will you let my two sons sit in places of honor next to you, one at your right and the other at your left?"

²²But Jesus told them, "You don't know what you are asking! Are you able to drink from the bitter cup of sorrow I am about to drink?"

"Oh yes," they replied, "we are able!"

²³"You will indeed drink from it," he told them. "But I have no right to say who will sit on the thrones next to mine. My Father has prepared those places for the ones he has chosen."

²⁴When the ten other disciples heard what James and John had asked, they were indignant. ²⁵But Jesus called them together and said, "You know that in this world kings are tyrants, and officials lord it over the people beneath them. ²⁶But among you it should be quite different. Whoever wants to be a leader among you must be your servant, ²⁷and whoever wants to be first must become your slave. ²⁸For even I, the Son of Man, came here not to be served but to serve others, and to give my life as a ransom for many."

²⁹As Jesus and the disciples left the city of Jericho, a huge crowd followed behind. ³⁰Two blind men were sitting beside the road. When they heard that Jesus was coming that way, they began shouting, "Lord, Son of David, have mercy on us!" ³¹The crowd told them to be quiet, but they only shouted louder, "Lord, Son of David, have mercy on us!"

20:2 Greek *a denarius*, the payment for a full day's labor; also in 20:9, 10, 13.

[32]Jesus stopped in the road and called, "What do you want me to do for you?"

[33]"Lord," they said, "we want to see!" [34]Jesus felt sorry for them and touched their eyes. Instantly they could see! Then they followed him.

CHAPTER 21

As Jesus and the disciples approached Jerusalem, they came to the town of Bethphage on the Mount of Olives. Jesus sent two of them on ahead. [2]"Go into the village over there," he said, "and you will see a donkey tied there, with its colt beside it. Untie them and bring them here. [3]If anyone asks what you are doing, just say, 'The Lord needs them,' and he will immediately send them." [4]This was done to fulfill the prophecy,

[5] "Tell the people of Israel,*

'Look, your King is coming to you.
He is humble, riding on a donkey—
even on a donkey's colt.'"*

[6]The two disciples did as Jesus said. [7]They brought the animals to him and threw their garments over the colt, and he sat on it.*

[8]Most of the crowd spread their coats on the road ahead of Jesus, and others cut branches from the trees and spread them on the road. [9]He was in the center of the procession, and the crowds all around him were shouting,

"Praise God* for the Son of David!
Bless the one who comes in the name of
the Lord!
Praise God in highest heaven!"*

[10]The entire city of Jerusalem was stirred as he entered. "Who is this?" they asked.

[11]And the crowds replied, "It's Jesus, the prophet from Nazareth in Galilee."

[12]Jesus entered the Temple and began to drive out the merchants and their customers. He knocked over the tables of the money changers and the stalls of those selling doves. [13]He said, "The Scriptures declare, 'My Temple will be called a place of prayer,' but you have turned it into a den of thieves!"*

[14]The blind and the lame came to him, and he healed them there in the Temple. [15]The leading priests and the teachers of religious law saw these wonderful miracles and heard even the little children in the Temple shouting, "Praise God for the Son of David." But they were indignant [16]and asked Jesus, "Do you hear what these children are saying?"

"Yes," Jesus replied. "Haven't you ever read the Scriptures? For they say, 'You have taught children and infants to give you praise.'*" [17]Then he returned to Bethany, where he stayed overnight.

[18]In the morning, as Jesus was returning to Jerusalem, he was hungry, [19]and he noticed a fig tree beside the road. He went over to see if there were any figs on it, but there were only leaves. Then he said to it, "May you never bear fruit again!" And immediately the fig tree withered up.

[20]The disciples were amazed when they saw this and asked, "How did the fig tree wither so quickly?"

[21]Then Jesus told them, "I assure you, if you have faith and don't doubt, you can do things like this and much more. You can even say to this mountain, 'May God lift you up and throw you into the sea,' and it will happen. [22]If you believe, you will receive whatever you ask for in prayer."

[23]When Jesus returned to the Temple and began teaching, the leading priests and other leaders came up to him. They demanded, "By whose authority did you drive out the merchants from the Temple?* Who gave you such authority?"

[24]"I'll tell you who gave me the authority to do these things if you answer one question," Jesus replied. [25]"Did John's baptism come from heaven or was it merely human?"

They talked it over among themselves. "If we say it was from heaven, he will ask why we didn't believe him. [26]But if we say it was merely human, we'll be mobbed, because the people think he was a prophet." [27]So they finally replied, "We don't know."

And Jesus responded, "Then I won't answer your question either.

[28]"But what do you think about this? A man with two sons told the older boy, 'Son, go out and work in the vineyard today.' [29]The son answered, 'No, I won't go,' but later he changed his mind and went anyway. [30]Then the father told the other son,

21:5a Greek *Tell the daughter of Zion.* Isa 62:11.   **21:5b** Zech 9:9.   **21:7** Greek *over them, and he sat on them.*   **21:9a** Greek *Hosanna,* an exclamation of praise that literally means "save now"; also in 21:9b, 15.   **21:9b** Pss 118:25-26; 148:1.   **21:13** Isa 56:7; Jer 7:11. **21:16** Ps 8:2.   **21:23** Or *By whose authority do you do these things?*

'You go,' and he said, 'Yes, sir, I will.' But he didn't go. ³¹Which of the two was obeying his father?"

They replied, "The first, of course."

Then Jesus explained his meaning: "I assure you, corrupt tax collectors and prostitutes will get into the Kingdom of God before you do. ³²For John the Baptist came and showed you the way to life, and you didn't believe him, while tax collectors and prostitutes did. And even when you saw this happening, you refused to turn from your sins and believe him.

³³"Now listen to this story. A certain landowner planted a vineyard, built a wall around it, dug a pit for pressing out the grape juice, and built a lookout tower. Then he leased the vineyard to tenant farmers and moved to another country. ³⁴At the time of the grape harvest he sent his servants to collect his share of the crop. ³⁵But the farmers grabbed his servants, beat one, killed one, and stoned another. ³⁶So the landowner sent a larger group of his servants to collect for him, but the results were the same.

³⁷"Finally, the owner sent his son, thinking, 'Surely they will respect my son.'

³⁸"But when the farmers saw his son coming, they said to one another, 'Here comes the heir to this estate. Come on, let's kill him and get the estate for ourselves!' ³⁹So they grabbed him, took him out of the vineyard, and murdered him.

⁴⁰"When the owner of the vineyard returns," Jesus asked, "what do you think he will do to those farmers?"

⁴¹The religious leaders replied, "He will put the wicked men to a horrible death and lease the vineyard to others who will give him his share of the crop after each harvest."

⁴²Then Jesus asked them, "Didn't you ever read this in the Scriptures?

'The stone rejected by the builders
   has now become the cornerstone.
This is the Lord's doing,
   and it is marvelous to see.'*

⁴³What I mean is that the Kingdom of God will be taken away from you and given to a nation that will produce the proper fruit. ⁴⁴Anyone who stumbles over that stone will be broken to pieces, and it will crush anyone on whom it falls.*"

⁴⁵When the leading priests and Pharisees heard Jesus, they realized he was pointing at them—that they were the farmers in his story. ⁴⁶They wanted to arrest him, but they were afraid to try because the crowds considered Jesus to be a prophet.

CHAPTER 22
Jesus told them several other stories to illustrate the Kingdom. He said, ²"The Kingdom of Heaven can be illustrated by the story of a king who prepared a great wedding feast for his son. ³Many guests were invited, and when the banquet was ready, he sent his servants to notify everyone that it was time to come. But they all refused! ⁴So he sent other servants to tell them, 'The feast has been prepared, and choice meats have been cooked. Everything is ready. Hurry!' ⁵But the guests he had invited ignored them and went about their business, one to his farm, another to his store. ⁶Others seized his messengers and treated them shamefully, even killing some of them.

⁷"Then the king became furious. He sent out his army to destroy the murderers and burn their city. ⁸And he said to his servants, 'The wedding feast is ready, and the guests I invited aren't worthy of the honor. ⁹Now go out to the street corners and invite everyone you see.'

¹⁰"So the servants brought in everyone they could find, good and bad alike, and the banquet hall was filled with guests. ¹¹But when the king came in to meet the guests, he noticed a man who wasn't wearing the proper clothes for a wedding. ¹²'Friend,' he asked, 'how is it that you are here without wedding clothes?' And the man had no reply. ¹³Then the king said to his aides, 'Bind him hand and foot and throw him out into the outer darkness, where there is weeping and gnashing of teeth.' ¹⁴For many are called, but few are chosen."

¹⁵Then the Pharisees met together to think of a way to trap Jesus into saying something for which they could accuse him. ¹⁶They decided to send some of their disciples, along with the supporters of Herod, to ask him this question: "Teacher, we know how honest you are. You teach about the way of God regardless of the consequences. You are impartial and don't

21:42 Ps 118:22-23.   **21:44** This verse is omitted in some early manuscripts.

play favorites. ¹⁷Now tell us what you think about this: Is it right to pay taxes to the Roman government or not?"

¹⁸But Jesus knew their evil motives. "You hypocrites!" he said. "Whom are you trying to fool with your trick questions? ¹⁹Here, show me the Roman coin used for the tax." When they handed him the coin,* ²⁰he asked, "Whose picture and title are stamped on it?"

²¹"Caesar's," they replied.

"Well, then," he said, "give to Caesar what belongs to him. But everything that belongs to God must be given to God." ²²His reply amazed them, and they went away.

²³That same day some Sadducees stepped forward—a group of Jews who say there is no resurrection after death. They posed this question: ²⁴"Teacher, Moses said, 'If a man dies without children, his brother should marry the widow and have a child who will be the brother's heir.'* ²⁵Well, there were seven brothers. The oldest married and then died without children, so the second brother married the widow. ²⁶This brother also died without children, and the wife was married to the next brother, and so on until she had been the wife of each of them. ²⁷And then she also died. ²⁸So tell us, whose wife will she be in the resurrection? For she was the wife of all seven of them!"

²⁹Jesus replied, "Your problem is that you don't know the Scriptures, and you don't know the power of God. ³⁰For when the dead rise, they won't be married. They will be like the angels in heaven. ³¹But now, as to whether there will be a resurrection of the dead—haven't you ever read about this in the Scriptures? Long after Abraham, Isaac, and Jacob had died, God said,* ³²'I am the God of Abraham, the God of Isaac, and the God of Jacob.'* So he is the God of the living, not the dead."

³³When the crowds heard him, they were impressed with his teaching.

³⁴But when the Pharisees heard that he had silenced the Sadducees with his reply, they thought up a fresh question of their own to ask him. ³⁵One of them, an expert in religious law, tried to trap him with this question: ³⁶"Teacher, which is the most im-

portant commandment in the law of Moses?"

³⁷Jesus replied, " 'You must love the Lord your God with all your heart, all your soul, and all your mind.'* ³⁸This is the first and greatest commandment. ³⁹A second is equally important: 'Love your neighbor as yourself.'* ⁴⁰All the other commandments and all the demands of the prophets are based on these two commandments."

⁴¹Then, surrounded by the Pharisees, Jesus asked them a question: ⁴²"What do you think about the Messiah? Whose son is he?"

They replied, "He is the son of David."

⁴³Jesus responded, "Then why does David, speaking under the inspiration of the Holy Spirit, call him Lord? For David said,

⁴⁴ 'The LORD said to my Lord,
    Sit in honor at my right hand
        until I humble your enemies beneath
            your feet.'*

⁴⁵Since David called him Lord, how can he be his son at the same time?"

⁴⁶No one could answer him. And after that, no one dared to ask him any more questions.

CHAPTER 23
Then Jesus said to the crowds and to his disciples, ²"The teachers of religious law and the Pharisees are the official interpreters of the Scriptures. ³So practice and obey whatever they say to you, but don't follow their example. For they don't practice what they teach. ⁴They crush you with impossible religious demands and never lift a finger to help ease the burden.

⁵"Everything they do is for show. On their arms they wear extra wide prayer boxes with Scripture verses inside,* and they wear extra long tassels on their robes. ⁶And how they love to sit at the head table at banquets and in the most prominent seats in the synagogue! ⁷They enjoy the attention they get on the streets, and they enjoy being called 'Rabbi.'* ⁸Don't ever let anyone call you 'Rabbi,' for you have only one teacher, and all of you are on the same level as brothers and sisters. ⁹And don't address anyone here on earth as 'Father,' for only God in heaven is your spiritual

Father. [10]And don't let anyone call you 'Master,' for there is only one master, the Messiah. [11]The greatest among you must be a servant. [12]But those who exalt themselves will be humbled, and those who humble themselves will be exalted.

[13]"How terrible it will be for you teachers of religious law and you Pharisees. Hypocrites! For you won't let others enter the Kingdom of Heaven, and you won't go in yourselves.* [15]Yes, how terrible it will be for you teachers of religious law and you Pharisees. For you cross land and sea to make one convert, and then you turn him into twice the son of hell as you yourselves are.

[16]"Blind guides! How terrible it will be for you! For you say that it means nothing to swear 'by God's Temple'—you can break that oath. But then you say that it is binding to swear 'by the gold in the Temple.' [17]Blind fools! Which is greater, the gold, or the Temple that makes the gold sacred? [18]And you say that to take an oath 'by the altar' can be broken, but to swear 'by the gifts on the altar' is binding! [19]How blind! For which is greater, the gift on the altar, or the altar that makes the gift sacred? [20]When you swear 'by the altar,' you are swearing by it and by everything on it. [21]And when you swear 'by the Temple,' you are swearing by it and by God, who lives in it. [22]And when you swear 'by heaven,' you are swearing by the throne of God and by God, who sits on the throne.

[23]"How terrible it will be for you teachers of religious law and you Pharisees. Hypocrites! For you are careful to tithe even the tiniest part of your income,* but you ignore the important things of the law—justice, mercy, and faith. You should tithe, yes, but you should not leave undone the more important things. [24]Blind guides! You strain your water so you won't accidentally swallow a gnat; then you swallow a camel!

[25]"How terrible it will be for you teachers of religious law and you Pharisees. Hypocrites! You are so careful to clean the outside of the cup and the dish, but inside you are filthy—full of greed and self-indulgence! [26]Blind Pharisees! First wash the inside of the cup, and then the outside will become clean, too.

[27]"How terrible it will be for you teachers of religious law and you Pharisees. Hypocrites! You are like whitewashed tombs—beautiful on the outside but filled on the inside with dead people's bones and all sorts of impurity. [28]You try to look like upright people outwardly, but inside your hearts are filled with hypocrisy and lawlessness.

[29]"How terrible it will be for you teachers of religious law and you Pharisees. Hypocrites! For you build tombs for the prophets your ancestors killed and decorate the graves of the godly people your ancestors destroyed. [30]Then you say, 'We never would have joined them in killing the prophets.'

[31]"In saying that, you are accusing yourselves of being the descendants of those who murdered the prophets. [32]Go ahead. Finish what they started. [33]Snakes! Sons of vipers! How will you escape the judgment of hell? [34]I will send you prophets and wise men and teachers of religious law. You will kill some by crucifixion and whip others in your synagogues, chasing them from city to city. [35]As a result, you will become guilty of murdering all the godly people from righteous Abel to Zechariah son of Barachiah, whom you murdered in the Temple between the altar and the sanctuary. [36]I assure you, all the accumulated judgment of the centuries will break upon the heads of this very generation.

[37]"O Jerusalem, Jerusalem, the city that kills the prophets and stones God's messengers! How often I have wanted to gather your children together as a hen protects her chicks beneath her wings, but you wouldn't let me. [38]And now look, your house is left to you, empty and desolate. [39]For I tell you this, you will never see me again until you say, 'Bless the one who comes in the name of the Lord!'*"

23:13 Some manuscripts add verse 14, *How terrible it will be for you teachers of religious law and you Pharisees. Hypocrites! You shamelessly cheat widows out of their property, and then, to cover up the kind of people you really are, you make long prayers in public. Because of this, your punishment will be the greater.*   **23:23** Greek *to tithe the mint, the dill, and the cumin.*   **23:39** Ps 118:26.

OCTOBER 7 ☐ DAY 281
Something Old, Something New

 LOOK BACK "The Old is in the New revealed; the New is in the Old concealed." With those words, one poet has attempted to explain the relationship between the two halves of the Bible. The Old Testament prophets provided hundreds of details about the coming Messiah: where he would be born, how he would be born, how he would live, how he would die, and what would be accomplished by his death. Now as you read the book of Matthew, you will see predictions that were *concealed* in the Old Testament and *revealed* in the New Testament.

Matthew, a Jewish tax collector, writes to a Jewish audience presenting Jesus as the promised King of the Jews. As with any king, his genealogy, upbringing, and demeanor come under intense scrutiny to determine whether he has the qualifications to be king. By word and deed, by public miracle and private message, Jesus validates his credentials, setting the stage for the dramatic conclusion of his earthly life and mission.

 LOOK UP Find the last verse in the Old Testament. Write the reference to it here: _____

Now find the first verse in the New Testament. Write the reference to it here: _____

We are never alone when we are alone with Jesus.

How far apart are those two verses in your Bible? In terms of inches, the answer may be as short as the thickness of one or two sheets of paper. But in terms of time, between Malachi 4:6 and Matthew 1:1 there is an "intermission" of no less than four hundred years! Four long centuries come and go before the silence that begins with the last verse of Malachi is broken by the first verse of Matthew.

Galatians 4:4 tells us why the long intermission was necessary between the close of the Old Testament and the opening of the New Testament. "But when the right time came, God sent his Son . . ." Like a pregnant woman awaiting the precise moment when her child is due to enter the world, so God was awaiting the precise moment when the world was uniquely prepared for the coming of his Son.

If the good news of his coming was to spread quickly around the world, there had to be a language common to all. And there was! It was called Koine Greek.

If the good news of his coming was to be carried to the farthest corners of the known world, there had to be an extensive network of roads. And there was! The Roman legions had seen to that.

 LOOK AHEAD If Jesus were walking the earth in bodily form today instead of in the first century A.D., just think what a stir his presence would create! Imagine how many television cameras would follow his every move . . . how many talk shows would clamor for interviews . . . the crowds that would shadow his every step.

But God knew that the perfect moment for his Son to enter human history was not the twentieth (or twenty-first!) century but the first. As you continue to read about Jesus' encounters with men and women, boys and girls, don't overlook the fact that today he longs to welcome all who will come to him in childlike faith (Matthew 19:14). His arms are open . . . to you!

OCTOBER 8 ☐ DAY 282
MATTHEW 24 –25
Predictions of the King

OVERVIEW Prominent in Jesus' day was the magnificent Temple of Herod. The disciples, duly impressed with its immense splendor, are stunned by Jesus' words that it will one day lie in rubble. This naturally raises questions in their minds regarding how and when such destruction will occur—an occasion Jesus seizes upon to teach them about events even more significant than the conquest of Jerusalem. He goes on to instruct them about his future second coming to earth and the unmistakable signs preceding it.

Chapter 24		Chapter 25
Predictions of Coming Calamity	Preparation for Coming Calamity	Parables of the Kingdom of Heaven
"Beware!"	"Be Watchful!"	"Be Working!"

YOUR DAILY WALK It has been well said, "A person can live forty days without food, seven days without water, and a few minutes without air; but he cannot live one second without hope."

"Hope" is biblical shorthand for "unconditional certainty."

There is no medicine like hope—the expectation that tomorrow will be better than today. And for the Christian, that hope is no idle dream. Your future can brim with expectation because of Jesus' promise, "I will come and get you" (John 14:3). But in the meantime, you need the daily reminder and encouragement that your waiting is not in vain. In Jesus' response to his disciples' questions, he offers several principles to help them—and you—pass the time until his return:

1. Don't get sidetracked (24:4). False christs will abound, but there will be no doubt when Jesus returns (24:24-31).

2. Don't become a date-setter (24:36). Only God himself knows when that great event will happen.

3. Do be a wise steward of your time and opportunities (24:14, 45-46). God wants you to sow seed, not scan the horizon!

On your appointment calendar, pick a date later in October and add this memo line: "It's later than it's ever been before. Am I more prepared than I've ever been before?"

INSIGHT Something Old, Something New
Chapters 20–23 employ at least eleven quotations from the Old Testament. All together, Matthew contains about seventy-four such quotations and allusions—more than any other New Testament book.

CHAPTER 24
As Jesus was leaving the Temple grounds, his disciples pointed out to him the various Temple buildings. ²But he told them, "Do you see all these buildings? I assure you, they will be so completely demolished that not one stone will be left on top of another!"

³Later, Jesus sat on the slopes of the Mount of Olives. His disciples came to him privately and asked, "When will all this

take place? And will there be any sign ahead of time to signal your return and the end of the world*?"

⁴Jesus told them, "Don't let anyone mislead you. ⁵For many will come in my name, saying, 'I am the Messiah.' They will lead many astray. ⁶And wars will break out near and far, but don't panic. Yes, these things must come, but the end won't follow immediately. ⁷The nations and kingdoms will proclaim war against each other, and there

24:3 Or *the age.*

will be famines and earthquakes in many parts of the world. [8]But all this will be only the beginning of the horrors to come.

[9]"Then you will be arrested, persecuted, and killed. You will be hated all over the world because of your allegiance to me. [10]And many will turn away from me and betray and hate each other. [11]And many false prophets will appear and will lead many people astray. [12]Sin will be rampant everywhere, and the love of many will grow cold. [13]But those who endure to the end will be saved. [14]And the Good News about the Kingdom will be preached throughout the whole world, so that all nations will hear it; and then, finally, the end will come.

[15]"The time will come when you will see what Daniel the prophet spoke about: the sacrilegious object that causes desecration* standing in the Holy Place"—reader, pay attention! [16]Then those in Judea must flee to the hills. [17]A person outside the house* must not go inside to pack. [18]A person in the field must not return even to get a coat. [19]How terrible it will be for pregnant women and for mothers nursing their babies in those days. [20]And pray that your flight will not be in winter or on the Sabbath. [21]For that will be a time of greater horror than anything the world has ever seen or will ever see again. [22]In fact, unless that time of calamity is shortened, the entire human race will be destroyed. But it will be shortened for the sake of God's chosen ones.

[23]"Then if anyone tells you, 'Look, here is the Messiah,' or 'There he is,' don't pay any attention. [24]For false messiahs and false prophets will rise up and perform great miraculous signs and wonders so as to deceive, if possible, even God's chosen ones. [25]See, I have warned you.

[26]"So if someone tells you, 'Look, the Messiah is out in the desert,' don't bother to go and look. Or, 'Look, he is hiding here,' don't believe it! [27]For as the lightning lights up the entire sky, so it will be when the Son of Man comes. [28]Just as the gathering of vultures shows there is a carcass nearby, so these signs indicate that the end is near.*

[29]"Immediately after those horrible days end,

the sun will be darkened,
the moon will not give light,

the stars will fall from the sky,
and the powers of heaven will be shaken.*

[30]And then at last, the sign of the coming of the Son of Man will appear in the heavens, and there will be deep mourning among all the nations of the earth. And they will see the Son of Man arrive on the clouds of heaven with power and great glory.* [31]And he will send forth his angels with the sound of a mighty trumpet blast, and they will gather together his chosen ones from the farthest ends of the earth and heaven.

[32]"Now learn a lesson from the fig tree. When its buds become tender and its leaves begin to sprout, you know without being told that summer is near. [33]Just so, when you see the events I've described beginning to happen, you can know his return is very near, right at the door. [34]I assure you, this generation* will not pass from the scene before all these things take place. [35]Heaven and earth will disappear, but my words will remain forever.

[36]"However, no one knows the day or the hour when these things will happen, not even the angels in heaven or the Son himself.* Only the Father knows.

[37]"When the Son of Man returns, it will be like it was in Noah's day. [38]In those days before the Flood, the people were enjoying banquets and parties and weddings right up to the time Noah entered his boat. [39]People didn't realize what was going to happen until the Flood came and swept them all away. That is the way it will be when the Son of Man comes.

[40]"Two men will be working together in the field; one will be taken, the other left. [41]Two women will be grinding flour at the mill; one will be taken, the other left. [42]So be prepared, because you don't know what day your Lord is coming.

[43]"Know this: A homeowner who knew exactly when a burglar was coming would stay alert and not permit the house to be broken into. [44]You also must be ready all the time. For the Son of Man will come when least expected.

[45]"Who is a faithful, sensible servant, to whom the master can give the responsibility of managing his household and feeding his family? [46]If the master returns and finds that the servant has done a good job, there

---

24:15 Greek *the abomination of desolation.* See Dan 9:27; 11:31; 12:11.   **24:17** Greek *on the roof.*   **24:28** Greek *Wherever the carcass is, the vultures gather.*   **24:29** See Isa 13:10; 34:4; Joel 2:10.   **24:30** See Dan 7:13.   **24:34** Or *this age,* or *this nation.*   **24:36** Some manuscripts omit the phrase *or the Son himself.*

will be a reward. [47]I assure you, the master will put that servant in charge of all he owns. [48]But if the servant is evil and thinks, 'My master won't be back for a while,' [49]and begins oppressing the other servants, partying, and getting drunk—[50]well, the master will return unannounced and unexpected. [51]He will tear the servant apart and banish him with the hypocrites. In that place there will be weeping and gnashing of teeth.

CHAPTER 25

"The Kingdom of Heaven can be illustrated by the story of ten bridesmaids* who took their lamps and went to meet the bridegroom. [2]Five of them were foolish, and five were wise. [3]The five who were foolish took no oil for their lamps, [4]but the other five were wise enough to take along extra oil. [5]When the bridegroom was delayed, they all lay down and slept. [6]At midnight they were roused by the shout, 'Look, the bridegroom is coming! Come out and welcome him!'

[7]"All the bridesmaids got up and prepared their lamps. [8]Then the five foolish ones asked the others, 'Please give us some of your oil because our lamps are going out.' [9]But the others replied, 'We don't have enough for all of us. Go to a shop and buy some for yourselves.'

[10]"But while they were gone to buy oil, the bridegroom came, and those who were ready went in with him to the marriage feast, and the door was locked. [11]Later, when the other five bridesmaids returned, they stood outside, calling, 'Sir, open the door for us!' [12]But he called back, 'I don't know you!'

[13]"So stay awake and be prepared, because you do not know the day or hour of my return.

[14]"Again, the Kingdom of Heaven can be illustrated by the story of a man going on a trip. He called together his servants and gave them money to invest for him while he was gone. [15]He gave five bags of gold* to one, two bags of gold to another, and one bag of gold to the last—dividing it in proportion to their abilities—and then left on his trip. [16]The servant who received the five bags of gold began immediately to invest the money and soon doubled it. [17]The servant with two bags of gold also went

right to work and doubled the money. [18]But the servant who received the one bag of gold dug a hole in the ground and hid the master's money for safekeeping.

[19]"After a long time their master returned from his trip and called them to give an account of how they had used his money. [20]The servant to whom he had entrusted the five bags of gold said, 'Sir, you gave me five bags of gold to invest, and I have doubled the amount.' [21]The master was full of praise. 'Well done, my good and faithful servant. You have been faithful in handling this small amount, so now I will give you many more responsibilities. Let's celebrate together!'

[22]"Next came the servant who had received the two bags of gold, with the report, 'Sir, you gave me two bags of gold to invest, and I have doubled the amount.' [23]The master said, 'Well done, my good and faithful servant. You have been faithful in handling this small amount, so now I will give you many more responsibilities. Let's celebrate together!'

[24]"Then the servant with the one bag of gold came and said, 'Sir, I know you are a hard man, harvesting crops you didn't plant and gathering crops you didn't cultivate. [25]I was afraid I would lose your money, so I hid it in the earth and here it is.'

[26]"But the master replied, 'You wicked and lazy servant! You think I'm a hard man, do you, harvesting crops I didn't plant and gathering crops I didn't cultivate? [27]Well, you should at least have put my money into the bank so I could have some interest. [28]Take the money from this servant and give it to the one with the ten bags of gold. [29]To those who use well what they are given, even more will be given, and they will have an abundance. But from those who are unfaithful,* even what little they have will be taken away. [30]Now throw this useless servant into outer darkness, where there will be weeping and gnashing of teeth.'

[31]"But when the Son of Man comes in his glory, and all the angels with him, then he will sit upon his glorious throne. [32]All the nations will be gathered in his presence, and he will separate them as a shepherd separates the sheep from the goats. [33]He will place the sheep at his right hand and the goats at his left. [34]Then the King will

---

25:1 Or *virgins;* also in 25:7, 11.   **25:15** Greek *talents;* also throughout the story. A talent is equal to 75 pounds or 34 kilograms.
25:29 Or *who have nothing.*

say to those on the right, 'Come, you who are blessed by my Father, inherit the Kingdom prepared for you from the foundation of the world. ³⁵For I was hungry, and you fed me. I was thirsty, and you gave me a drink. I was a stranger, and you invited me into your home. ³⁶I was naked, and you gave me clothing. I was sick, and you cared for me. I was in prison, and you visited me.'

³⁷"Then these righteous ones will reply, 'Lord, when did we ever see you hungry and feed you? Or thirsty and give you something to drink? ³⁸Or a stranger and show you hospitality? Or naked and give you clothing? ³⁹When did we ever see you sick or in prison, and visit you?' ⁴⁰And the King will tell them, 'I assure you, when you did it to one of the least of these my brothers and sisters, you were doing it to me!'

⁴¹"Then the King will turn to those on the left and say, 'Away with you, you cursed ones, into the eternal fire prepared for the Devil and his demons! ⁴²For I was hungry, and you didn't feed me. I was thirsty, and you didn't give me anything to drink. ⁴³I was a stranger, and you didn't invite me into your home. I was naked, and you gave me no clothing. I was sick and in prison, and you didn't visit me.'

⁴⁴"Then they will reply, 'Lord, when did we ever see you hungry or thirsty or a stranger or naked or sick or in prison, and not help you?' ⁴⁵And he will answer, 'I assure you, when you refused to help the least of these my brothers and sisters, you were refusing to help me.' ⁴⁶And they will go away into eternal punishment, but the righteous will go into eternal life."

OCTOBER 9 ☐ DAY 283
MATTHEW 26–28
Passion of the King

OVERVIEW The one who only days before was hailed as King now experiences arrest, scourging, ridicule, and crucifixion as "criminal." His royal title hangs in mockery from the top of his rugged cross. And in his death, he fulfills more Old Testament prophecies than he did in his lifetime. Not one of his bones is broken, as befitting the Passover lamb. And at the moment of his death, the veil in the Temple is split from top to bottom, indicating free and unlimited access to God through him. Buried in haste in a borrowed tomb and mourned by his followers for three dark days, he rises in victory at dawn on that first Easter morning, later commissioning all who have put their saving trust in him to go and teach all nations (28:19-20).

Chapter 26	Chapter 27	Chapter 28
The King's Last Supper	The King's Crucifixion	The King's Resurrection
Passover	Passion	Proclamation

YOUR DAILY WALK Perhaps the worst time to celebrate Christmas is at Christmas!

Why? Because the truth of that great event all too often gets lost in the tinsel and trappings.

Death died when Christ arose.

Similarly, the worst time to celebrate Easter is when the bunnies, baskets, and bonnets are in abundance! Which means right now would be a wonderful time to celebrate the resurrection!

Don't hurry through today's reading. The story of Jesus' crucifixion is one of the most graphic depictions of love ever penned. Ask the Holy Spirit to take the familiar phrases of the Calvary story and infuse them with fresh meaning and life for you. If you can, read the three chapters in today's section straight through at a single sitting. Then, with your Bible open and your heart brimming with gratitude, offer God a sacrifice of praise for the Savior, whose suffering and death made it all possible. "He has been raised from the dead" (28:7), so rejoice!

 INSIGHT Taunting the King with the Truth
Over the head of every victim of Roman crucifixion was inscribed his crime. In Jesus' case the indictment was made in mockery: "This is Jesus, the King of the Jews" (27:37). How little did the unbelieving soldiers realize the truth of their taunt!

CHAPTER 26

When Jesus had finished saying these things, he said to his disciples, ²"As you know, the Passover celebration begins in two days, and I, the Son of Man, will be betrayed and crucified."

³At that same time the leading priests and other leaders were meeting at the residence of Caiaphas, the high priest, ⁴to discuss how to capture Jesus secretly and put him to death. ⁵"But not during the Passover," they agreed, "or there will be a riot."

⁶Meanwhile, Jesus was in Bethany at the home of Simon, a man who had leprosy. ⁷During supper, a woman came in with a beautiful jar* of expensive perfume and poured it over his head. ⁸The disciples were indignant when they saw this. "What a waste of money," they said. ⁹"She could have sold it for a fortune and given the money to the poor."

¹⁰But Jesus replied, "Why berate her for doing such a good thing to me? ¹¹You will always have the poor among you, but I will not be here with you much longer. ¹²She has poured this perfume on me to prepare my body for burial. ¹³I assure you, wherever the Good News is preached throughout the world, this woman's deed will be talked about in her memory."

¹⁴Then Judas Iscariot, one of the twelve disciples, went to the leading priests ¹⁵and asked, "How much will you pay me to betray Jesus to you?" And they gave him thirty pieces of silver. ¹⁶From that time on, Judas began looking for the right time and place to betray Jesus.

¹⁷On the first day of the Festival of Unleavened Bread, the disciples came to Jesus and asked, "Where do you want us to prepare the Passover supper?"

¹⁸"As you go into the city," he told them, "you will see a certain man. Tell him, 'The Teacher says, My time has come, and I will eat the Passover meal with my disciples at your house.'" ¹⁹So the disciples did as Jesus told them and prepared the Passover supper there.

²⁰When it was evening, Jesus sat down at the table with the twelve disciples. ²¹While they were eating, he said, "The truth is, one of you will betray me."

²²Greatly distressed, one by one they began to ask him, "I'm not the one, am I, Lord?"

²³He replied, "One of you who is eating with me now* will betray me. ²⁴For I, the Son of Man, must die, as the Scriptures declared long ago. But how terrible it will be for my betrayer. Far better for him if he had never been born!"

²⁵Judas, the one who would betray him, also asked, "Teacher, I'm not the one, am I?"

And Jesus told him, "You have said it yourself."

²⁶As they were eating, Jesus took a loaf of bread and asked God's blessing on it. Then he broke it in pieces and gave it to the disciples, saying, "Take it and eat it, for this is my body." ²⁷And he took a cup of wine and gave thanks to God for it. He gave it to them and said, "Each of you drink from it, ²⁸for this is my blood, which seals the covenant* between God and his people. It is poured out to forgive the sins of many. ²⁹Mark my words—I will not drink wine again until the day I drink it new with you in my Father's Kingdom." ³⁰Then they sang a hymn and went out to the Mount of Olives.

³¹"Tonight all of you will desert me," Jesus told them. "For the Scriptures say,

'God* will strike the Shepherd,
　and the sheep of the flock will be
　scattered.'*

26:7 Greek *an alabaster jar.*　　26:23 Or *The one who has dipped his hand in the bowl with me.*　　26:28 Some manuscripts read *the new covenant.*　　26:31a Greek *I.*　　26:31b Zech 13:7.

³²But after I have been raised from the dead, I will go ahead of you to Galilee and meet you there."

³³Peter declared, "Even if everyone else deserts you, I never will."

³⁴"Peter," Jesus replied, "the truth is, this very night, before the rooster crows, you will deny me three times."

³⁵"No!" Peter insisted. "Not even if I have to die with you! I will never deny you!" And all the other disciples vowed the same.

³⁶Then Jesus brought them to an olive grove called Gethsemane, and he said, "Sit here while I go on ahead to pray." ³⁷He took Peter and Zebedee's two sons, James and John, and he began to be filled with anguish and deep distress. ³⁸He told them, "My soul is crushed with grief to the point of death. Stay here and watch with me."

³⁹He went on a little farther and fell face down on the ground, praying, "My Father! If it is possible, let this cup of suffering be taken away from me. Yet I want your will, not mine." ⁴⁰Then he returned to the disciples and found them asleep. He said to Peter, "Couldn't you stay awake and watch with me even one hour? ⁴¹Keep alert and pray. Otherwise temptation will overpower you. For though the spirit is willing enough, the body is weak!"

⁴²Again he left them and prayed, "My Father! If this cup cannot be taken away until I drink it, your will be done." ⁴³He returned to them again and found them sleeping, for they just couldn't keep their eyes open.

⁴⁴So he went back to pray a third time, saying the same things again. ⁴⁵Then he came to the disciples and said, "Still sleeping? Still resting?* Look, the time has come. I, the Son of Man, am betrayed into the hands of sinners. ⁴⁶Up, let's be going. See, my betrayer is here!"

⁴⁷And even as he said this, Judas, one of the twelve disciples, arrived with a mob that was armed with swords and clubs. They had been sent out by the leading priests and other leaders of the people. ⁴⁸Judas had given them a prearranged signal: "You will know which one to arrest when I go over and give him the kiss of greeting." ⁴⁹So Judas came straight to Jesus. "Greetings, Teacher!" he exclaimed and gave him the kiss.

⁵⁰Jesus said, "My friend, go ahead and do what you have come for." Then the others grabbed Jesus and arrested him. ⁵¹One of the men with Jesus pulled out a sword and slashed off an ear of the high priest's servant.

⁵²"Put away your sword," Jesus told him. "Those who use the sword will be killed by the sword. ⁵³Don't you realize that I could ask my Father for thousands* of angels to protect us, and he would send them instantly? ⁵⁴But if I did, how would the Scriptures be fulfilled that describe what must happen now?"

⁵⁵Then Jesus said to the crowd, "Am I some dangerous criminal, that you have come armed with swords and clubs to arrest me? Why didn't you arrest me in the Temple? I was there teaching every day. ⁵⁶But this is all happening to fulfill the words of the prophets as recorded in the Scriptures." At that point, all the disciples deserted him and fled.

⁵⁷Then the people who had arrested Jesus led him to the home of Caiaphas, the high priest, where the teachers of religious law and other leaders had gathered. ⁵⁸Meanwhile, Peter was following far behind and eventually came to the courtyard of the high priest's house. He went in, sat with the guards, and waited to see what was going to happen to Jesus.

⁵⁹Inside, the leading priests and the entire high council* were trying to find witnesses who would lie about Jesus, so they could put him to death. ⁶⁰But even though they found many who agreed to give false witness, there was no testimony they could use. Finally, two men were found ⁶¹who declared, "This man said, 'I am able to destroy the Temple of God and rebuild it in three days.'"

⁶²Then the high priest stood up and said to Jesus, "Well, aren't you going to answer these charges? What do you have to say for yourself?" ⁶³But Jesus remained silent. Then the high priest said to him, "I demand in the name of the living God that you tell us whether you are the Messiah, the Son of God."

⁶⁴Jesus replied, "Yes, it is as you say. And in the future you will see me, the Son of Man, sitting at God's right hand in the place of power and coming back on the clouds of heaven."*

26:45 Or *Sleep on, take your rest.*   **26:53** Greek *12 legions.*   **26:59** Greek *the Sanhedrin.*   **26:64** See Ps 110:1; Dan 7:13.

⁶⁵Then the high priest tore his clothing to show his horror, shouting, "Blasphemy! Why do we need other witnesses? You have all heard his blasphemy. ⁶⁶What is your verdict?"

"Guilty!" they shouted. "He must die!"

⁶⁷Then they spit in Jesus' face and hit him with their fists. And some slapped him, ⁶⁸saying, "Prophesy to us, you Messiah! Who hit you that time?"

⁶⁹Meanwhile, as Peter was sitting outside in the courtyard, a servant girl came over and said to him, "You were one of those with Jesus the Galilean."

⁷⁰But Peter denied it in front of everyone. "I don't know what you are talking about," he said.

⁷¹Later, out by the gate, another servant girl noticed him and said to those standing around, "This man was with Jesus of Nazareth."

⁷²Again Peter denied it, this time with an oath. "I don't even know the man," he said.

⁷³A little later some other bystanders came over to him and said, "You must be one of them; we can tell by your Galilean accent."

⁷⁴Peter said, "I swear by God, I don't know the man." And immediately the rooster crowed. ⁷⁵Suddenly, Jesus' words flashed through Peter's mind: "Before the rooster crows, you will deny me three times." And he went away, crying bitterly.

CHAPTER 27

Very early in the morning, the leading priests and other leaders met again to discuss how to persuade the Roman government to sentence Jesus to death. ²Then they bound him and took him to Pilate, the Roman governor.

³When Judas, who had betrayed him, realized that Jesus had been condemned to die, he was filled with remorse. So he took the thirty pieces of silver back to the leading priests and other leaders. ⁴"I have sinned," he declared, "for I have betrayed an innocent man."

"What do we care?" they retorted. "That's your problem." ⁵Then Judas threw the money onto the floor of the Temple and went out and hanged himself. ⁶The leading priests picked up the money. "We can't put it in the Temple treasury," they said, "since it's against the law to accept money paid for

murder." ⁷After some discussion they finally decided to buy the potter's field, and they made it into a cemetery for foreigners. ⁸That is why the field is still called the Field of Blood. ⁹This fulfilled the prophecy of Jeremiah that says,

> "They took* the thirty pieces of silver—
>   the price at which he was valued by
>   the people of Israel—
> ¹⁰ and purchased the potter's field,
>   as the Lord directed.*"

¹¹Now Jesus was standing before Pilate, the Roman governor. "Are you the King of the Jews?" the governor asked him.

Jesus replied, "Yes, it is as you say."

¹²But when the leading priests and other leaders made their accusations against him, Jesus remained silent. ¹³"Don't you hear their many charges against you?" Pilate demanded. ¹⁴But Jesus said nothing, much to the governor's great surprise.

¹⁵Now it was the governor's custom to release one prisoner to the crowd each year during the Passover celebration—anyone they wanted. ¹⁶This year there was a notorious criminal in prison, a man named Barabbas.* ¹⁷As the crowds gathered before Pilate's house that morning, he asked them, "Which one do you want me to release to you—Barabbas, or Jesus who is called the Messiah?" ¹⁸(He knew very well that the Jewish leaders had arrested Jesus out of envy.)

¹⁹Just then, as Pilate was sitting on the judgment seat, his wife sent him this message: "Leave that innocent man alone, because I had a terrible nightmare about him last night."

²⁰Meanwhile, the leading priests and other leaders persuaded the crowds to ask for Barabbas to be released and for Jesus to be put to death. ²¹So when the governor asked again, "Which of these two do you want me to release to you?" the crowd shouted back their reply: "Barabbas!"

²²"But if I release Barabbas," Pilate asked them, "what should I do with Jesus who is called the Messiah?"

And they all shouted, "Crucify him!"

²³"Why?" Pilate demanded. "What crime has he committed?"

But the crowd only roared the louder, "Crucify him!"

²⁴Pilate saw that he wasn't getting

27:9 Or I took.   27:9-10 Greek *as the Lord directed me*. Zech 11:12-13; Jer 32:6-9.   27:16 Some manuscripts read *Jesus Barabbas*; also in 27:17.

anywhere and that a riot was developing. So he sent for a bowl of water and washed his hands before the crowd, saying, "I am innocent of the blood of this man. The responsibility is yours!"

25And all the people yelled back, "We will take responsibility for his death—we and our children!"*

26So Pilate released Barabbas to them. He ordered Jesus flogged with a lead-tipped whip, then turned him over to the Roman soldiers to crucify him.

27Some of the governor's soldiers took Jesus into their headquarters and called out the entire battalion. 28They stripped him and put a scarlet robe on him. 29They made a crown of long, sharp thorns and put it on his head, and they placed a stick in his right hand as a scepter. Then they knelt before him in mockery, yelling, "Hail! King of the Jews!" 30And they spit on him and grabbed the stick and beat him on the head with it. 31When they were finally tired of mocking him, they took off the robe and put his own clothes on him again. Then they led him away to be crucified.

32As they were on the way, they came across a man named Simon, who was from Cyrene,* and they forced him to carry Jesus' cross. 33Then they went out to a place called Golgotha (which means Skull Hill). 34The soldiers gave him wine mixed with bitter gall, but when he had tasted it, he refused to drink it.

35After they had nailed him to the cross, the soldiers gambled for his clothes by throwing dice.* 36Then they sat around and kept guard as he hung there. 37A signboard was fastened to the cross above Jesus' head, announcing the charge against him. It read: "This is Jesus, the King of the Jews."

38Two criminals were crucified with him, their crosses on either side of his. 39And the people passing by shouted abuse, shaking their heads in mockery. 40"So! You can destroy the Temple and build it again in three days, can you? Well then, if you are the Son of God, save yourself and come down from the cross!"

41The leading priests, the teachers of religious law, and the other leaders also mocked Jesus. 42"He saved others," they scoffed, "but he can't save himself! So he is the king of Israel, is he? Let him come down from the cross, and we will believe in him! 43He trusted God—let God show his approval by delivering him! For he said, 'I am the Son of God.'" 44And the criminals who were crucified with him also shouted the same insults at him.

45At noon, darkness fell across the whole land until three o'clock. 46At about three o'clock, Jesus called out with a loud voice, "Eli, Eli, lema sabachthani?" which means, "My God, my God, why have you forsaken me?"*

47Some of the bystanders misunderstood and thought he was calling for the prophet Elijah. 48One of them ran and filled a sponge with sour wine, holding it up to him on a stick so he could drink. 49But the rest said, "Leave him alone. Let's see whether Elijah will come and save him."*

50Then Jesus shouted out again, and he gave up his spirit. 51At that moment the curtain in the Temple was torn in two, from top to bottom. The earth shook, rocks split apart, 52and tombs opened. The bodies of many godly men and women who had died were raised from the dead 53after Jesus' resurrection. They left the cemetery, went into the holy city of Jerusalem, and appeared to many people.*

54The Roman officer and the other soldiers at the crucifixion were terrified by the earthquake and all that had happened. They said, "Truly, this was the Son of God!"

55And many women who had come from Galilee with Jesus to care for him were watching from a distance. 56Among them were Mary Magdalene, Mary (the mother of James and Joseph), and Zebedee's wife, the mother of James and John.

57As evening approached, Joseph, a rich man from Arimathea who was one of Jesus' followers, 58went to Pilate and asked for Jesus' body. And Pilate issued an order to release it to him. 59Joseph took the body and wrapped it in a long linen cloth. 60He placed it in his own new tomb, which had been carved out of the rock. Then he rolled a great stone across the entrance as he left. 61Both Mary Magdalene and the other Mary were sitting nearby watching.

27:25 Greek "His blood be on us and on our children."   27:32 Cyrene was a city in northern Africa.   27:35 Greek by casting lots.
A few late manuscripts add This fulfilled the word of the prophet: "They divided my clothes among themselves and cast lots for my robe."
See Ps 22:18.   27:46 Ps 22:1.   27:49 Some manuscripts add And another took a spear and pierced his side, and out came water and blood.   27:51-53 Or The earth shook, rocks split apart, tombs opened, and the bodies of many godly men and women who had died were raised from the dead. After Jesus' resurrection, they left the cemetery, went into the holy city of Jerusalem, and appeared to many people.

⁶²The next day—on the first day of the Passover ceremonies*—the leading priests and Pharisees went to see Pilate. ⁶³They told him, "Sir, we remember what that deceiver once said while he was still alive: 'After three days I will be raised from the dead.' ⁶⁴So we request that you seal the tomb until the third day. This will prevent his disciples from coming and stealing his body and then telling everyone he came back to life! If that happens, we'll be worse off than we were at first."

⁶⁵Pilate replied, "Take guards and secure it the best you can." ⁶⁶So they sealed the tomb and posted guards to protect it.

CHAPTER 28

Early on Sunday morning,* as the new day was dawning, Mary Magdalene and the other Mary went out to see the tomb. ²Suddenly there was a great earthquake, because an angel of the Lord came down from heaven and rolled aside the stone and sat on it. ³His face shone like lightning, and his clothing was as white as snow. ⁴The guards shook with fear when they saw him, and they fell into a dead faint.

⁵Then the angel spoke to the women. "Don't be afraid!" he said. "I know you are looking for Jesus, who was crucified. ⁶He isn't here! He has been raised from the dead, just as he said would happen. Come, see where his body was lying. ⁷And now, go quickly and tell his disciples he has been raised from the dead, and he is going ahead of you to Galilee. You will see him there. Remember, I have told you."

⁸The women ran quickly from the tomb.

They were very frightened but also filled with great joy, and they rushed to find the disciples to give them the angel's message. ⁹And as they went, Jesus met them. "Greetings!" he said. And they ran to him, held his feet, and worshiped him. ¹⁰Then Jesus said to them, "Don't be afraid! Go tell my brothers to leave for Galilee, and they will see me there."

¹¹As the women were on their way into the city, some of the men who had been guarding the tomb went to the leading priests and told them what had happened. ¹²A meeting of all the religious leaders was called, and they decided to bribe the soldiers. ¹³They told the soldiers, "You must say, 'Jesus' disciples came during the night while we were sleeping, and they stole his body.' ¹⁴If the governor hears about it, we'll stand up for you and everything will be all right." ¹⁵So the guards accepted the bribe and said what they were told to say. Their story spread widely among the Jews, and they still tell it today.

¹⁶Then the eleven disciples left for Galilee, going to the mountain where Jesus had told them to go. ¹⁷When they saw him, they worshiped him—but some of them still doubted!

¹⁸Jesus came and told his disciples, "I have been given complete authority in heaven and on earth. ¹⁹Therefore, go and make disciples of all the nations, baptizing them in the name of the Father and the Son and the Holy Spirit. ²⁰Teach these new disciples to obey all the commands I have given you. And be sure of this: I am with you always, even to the end of the age."

27:62 Or *On the next day, which is after the Preparation.*   **28:1** Greek *After the Sabbath, on the first day of the week.*

Mark

WRITING in the present tense, Mark involves his readers in the dramatic immediacy of Christ's life. He sets forth in convincing style the credentials of Jesus of Nazareth, the Servant of God. In pithy statements and brief paragraphs, Mark captures the ministry of Jesus but focuses more on what Jesus does than on what he says. The theme of Mark's Gospel is that Jesus' service and sacrifice provide the pattern of living for his followers (16:20).

Focus	Proclamation		Rejection		Exaltation
Divisions	Power of the Servant	Compassion of the Servant	Teaching of the Servant	Signs of the Servant	Suffering of the Servant
	1 — 3	4 — 7	8 — 10	11 — 13	14 — 16
Topics	Servant to the Multitudes		Servant to the Disciples	Sacrifice for the World	
	Ministry to Individuals				Ministry to Humankind
Place	Galilee and Perea			Jerusalem	
Time	A.D. 29–33				

OCTOBER 10 ☐ DAY 284
MARK 1–3
Power of the Servant

OVERVIEW Mark's unadorned opening to his account ("Here begins the Good News about Jesus the Messiah, the Son of God") introduces the character of his entire book: brisk, vivid, and to the point—just like the character and conduct of an active servant. For this is the biography of Jesus Christ, the Perfect Servant. Over and over, Mark uses the word *immediately* to accelerate the pace of events in the book. He omits details of Christ's genealogy and childhood (of what relevance is that for a servant?) and plunges immediately into Christ's public ministry in the region of Galilee.

Chapter 1	Chapter 2	Chapter 3
Preparation of the Servant	Power and Preaching of the Servant	Opposition to the Servant
"Beloved Son"	"Son of Man"	"Son of God"

YOUR DAILY WALK Do you have a balanced view of Jesus Christ? Down through the centuries, Christians have wrestled with the incarnation of Jesus Christ, trying to describe adequately that unique blend of perfect humanity and undiminished deity that he possessed as he walked the face of the earth. Some Christians emphasize his deity, focusing on the attributes and actions that could only belong to God and forgetting that Jesus ate, slept, and wept like other men. Others focus on his humanity, neglecting the many things Jesus did that only God could do.

I have a great need for Christ; I have a great Christ for my need.

Today's reading portrays both attributes of Jesus: his *deity* (e.g., healing the sick and casting out demons, 1:11, 29-34) and his *humanity* (e.g., rising early the next morning to pray, 1:35). Mark alerts his readers at the very beginning of the book to the power behind Jesus' ministry.

What about you? Are you engaged in a busy schedule of ministry for God? Are you taking the necessary time in prayer and preparation first? If Jesus needed to pray, how can we expect to minister effectively without prayer? Have your own fifteen-minute prayer retreat right now.

INSIGHT Mark, a Gospel of Actions, Not Words
Of the seventy parables the Gospel writers recorded, only eighteen are contained in Mark, and many are only one sentence in length. However, of Jesus' thirty-five recorded miracles, Mark gives an account of more than half.

CHAPTER 1
Here begins the Good News about Jesus the Messiah, the Son of God.*
²In the book of the prophet Isaiah, God said,

"Look, I am sending my messenger
    before you,
    and he will prepare your way.*
³ He is a voice shouting in the
    wilderness:

1:1 Some manuscripts do not include *the Son of God*.   **1:2** Mal 3:1.

'Prepare a pathway for the Lord's
  coming!
Make a straight road for him!'*"

[4] This messenger was John the Baptist. He lived in the wilderness and was preaching that people should be baptized to show that they had turned from their sins and turned to God to be forgiven.* [5] People from Jerusalem and from all over Judea traveled out into the wilderness to see and hear John. And when they confessed their sins, he baptized them in the Jordan River. [6] His clothes were woven from camel hair, and he wore a leather belt; his food was locusts and wild honey. [7] He announced: "Someone is coming soon who is far greater than I am—so much greater that I am not even worthy to be his slave.* [8] I baptize you with* water, but he will baptize you with the Holy Spirit!"

[9] One day Jesus came from Nazareth in Galilee, and he was baptized by John in the Jordan River. [10] And when Jesus came up out of the water, he saw the heavens split open and the Holy Spirit descending like a dove on him. [11] And a voice came from heaven saying, "You are my beloved Son, and I am fully pleased with you."

[12] Immediately the Holy Spirit compelled Jesus to go into the wilderness. [13] He was there for forty days, being tempted by Satan. He was out among the wild animals, and angels took care of him.

[14] Later on, after John was arrested by Herod Antipas, Jesus went to Galilee to preach God's Good News. [15] "At last the time has come!" he announced. "The Kingdom of God is near! Turn from your sins and believe this Good News!"

[16] One day as Jesus was walking along the shores of the Sea of Galilee, he saw Simon* and his brother, Andrew, fishing with a net, for they were commercial fishermen. [17] Jesus called out to them, "Come, be my disciples, and I will show you how to fish for people!" [18] And they left their nets at once and went with him.

[19] A little farther up the shore Jesus saw Zebedee's sons, James and John, in a boat mending their nets. [20] He called them, too, and immediately they left their father, Zebedee, in the boat with the hired men and went with him.

[21] Jesus and his companions went to the town of Capernaum, and every Sabbath day he went into the synagogue and taught the people. [22] They were amazed at his teaching, for he taught as one who had real authority—quite unlike the teachers of religious law.

[23] A man possessed by an evil spirit was in the synagogue, [24] and he began shouting, "Why are you bothering us, Jesus of Nazareth? Have you come to destroy us? I know who you are—the Holy One sent from God!"

[25] Jesus cut him short. "Be silent! Come out of the man." [26] At that, the evil spirit screamed and threw the man into a convulsion, but then he left him.

[27] Amazement gripped the audience, and they began to discuss what had happened. "What sort of new teaching is this?" they asked excitedly. "It has such authority! Even evil spirits obey his orders!" [28] The news of what he had done spread quickly through that entire area of Galilee.

[29] After Jesus and his disciples left the synagogue, they went over to Simon and Andrew's home, and James and John were with them. [30] Simon's mother-in-law was sick in bed with a high fever. They told Jesus about her right away. [31] He went to her bedside, and as he took her by the hand and helped her to sit up, the fever suddenly left, and she got up and prepared a meal for them.

[32] That evening at sunset, many sick and demon-possessed people were brought to Jesus. [33] And a huge crowd of people from all over Capernaum gathered outside the door to watch. [34] So Jesus healed great numbers of sick people who had many different kinds of diseases, and he ordered many demons to come out of their victims. But because they knew who he was, he refused to allow the demons to speak.

[35] The next morning Jesus awoke long before daybreak and went out alone into the wilderness to pray. [36] Later Simon and the others went out to find him. [37] They said, "Everyone is asking for you."

[38] But he replied, "We must go on to other towns as well, and I will preach to them, too, because that is why I came." [39] So he traveled throughout the region of Galilee, preaching in the synagogues and expelling demons from many people.

[40] A man with leprosy came and knelt in

1:3 Isa 40:3.   1:4 Greek *preaching a baptism of repentance for the forgiveness of sins.*   1:7 Greek *to stoop down and untie his sandals.*
1:8 Or *in*; also in 1:8b.   1:16 *Simon* is called *Peter* in 3:16 and thereafter.

front of Jesus, begging to be healed. "If you want to, you can make me well again," he said.

[41] Moved with pity,* Jesus touched him. "I want to," he said. "Be healed!" [42] Instantly the leprosy disappeared—the man was healed. [43] Then Jesus sent him on his way and told him sternly, [44] "Go right over to the priest and let him examine you. Don't talk to anyone along the way. Take along the offering required in the law of Moses for those who have been healed of leprosy, so everyone will have proof of your healing."

[45] But as the man went on his way, he spread the news, telling everyone what had happened to him. As a result, such crowds soon surrounded Jesus that he couldn't enter a town anywhere publicly. He had to stay out in the secluded places, and people from everywhere came to him there.

CHAPTER 2

Several days later Jesus returned to Capernaum, and the news of his arrival spread quickly through the town. [2] Soon the house where he was staying was so packed with visitors that there wasn't room for one more person, not even outside the door. And he preached the word to them. [3] Four men arrived carrying a paralyzed man on a mat. [4] They couldn't get to Jesus through the crowd, so they dug through the clay roof above his head. Then they lowered the sick man on his mat, right down in front of Jesus. [5] Seeing their faith, Jesus said to the paralyzed man, "My son, your sins are forgiven."

[6] But some of the teachers of religious law who were sitting there said to themselves, [7] "What? This is blasphemy! Who but God can forgive sins!"

[8] Jesus knew what they were discussing among themselves, so he said to them, "Why do you think this is blasphemy? [9] Is it easier to say to the paralyzed man, 'Your sins are forgiven' or 'Get up, pick up your mat, and walk'? [10] I will prove that I, the Son of Man, have the authority on earth to forgive sins." Then Jesus turned to the paralyzed man and said, [11] "Stand up, take your mat, and go on home, because you are healed!"

[12] The man jumped up, took the mat, and pushed his way through the stunned on-

lookers. Then they all praised God. "We've never seen anything like this before!" they exclaimed.

[13] Then Jesus went out to the lakeshore again and taught the crowds that gathered around him. [14] As he walked along, he saw Levi son of Alphaeus sitting at his tax-collection booth. "Come, be my disciple," Jesus said to him. So Levi got up and followed him.

[15] That night Levi invited Jesus and his disciples to be his dinner guests, along with his fellow tax collectors and many other notorious sinners. (There were many people of this kind among the crowds that followed Jesus.) [16] But when some of the teachers of religious law who were Pharisees* saw him eating with people like that, they said to his disciples, "Why does he eat with such scum*?"

[17] When Jesus heard this, he told them, "Healthy people don't need a doctor—sick people do. I have come to call sinners, not those who think they are already good enough."

[18] John's disciples and the Pharisees sometimes fasted. One day some people came to Jesus and asked, "Why do John's disciples and the Pharisees fast, but your disciples don't fast?"

[19] Jesus replied, "Do wedding guests fast while celebrating with the groom? Of course not. They can't fast while they are with the groom. [20] But someday he will be taken away from them, and then they will fast. [21] And who would patch an old garment with unshrunk cloth? For the new patch shrinks and pulls away from the old cloth, leaving an even bigger hole than before. [22] And no one puts new wine into old wineskins. The wine would burst the wineskins, spilling the wine and ruining the skins. New wine needs new wineskins."

[23] One Sabbath day as Jesus was walking through some grainfields, his disciples began breaking off heads of wheat. [24] But the Pharisees said to Jesus, "They shouldn't be doing that! It's against the law to work by harvesting grain on the Sabbath."

[25] But Jesus replied, "Haven't you ever read in the Scriptures what King David did when he and his companions were hungry? [26] He went into the house of God (during the days when Abiathar was high priest), ate the special bread reserved for

1:41 Some manuscripts read *Moved with anger.*   2:16a Greek *the scribes of the Pharisees.*   2:16b Greek *with tax collectors and sinners.*

the priests alone, and then gave some to his companions. That was breaking the law, too." ²⁷Then he said to them, "The Sabbath was made to benefit people, and not people to benefit the Sabbath. ²⁸And I, the Son of Man, am master even of the Sabbath!"

CHAPTER 3

Jesus went into the synagogue again and noticed a man with a deformed hand. ²Since it was the Sabbath, Jesus' enemies watched him closely. Would he heal the man's hand on the Sabbath? If he did, they planned to condemn him. ³Jesus said to the man, "Come and stand in front of everyone." ⁴Then he turned to his critics and asked, "Is it legal to do good deeds on the Sabbath, or is it a day for doing harm? Is this a day to save life or to destroy it?" But they wouldn't answer him. ⁵He looked around at them angrily, because he was deeply disturbed by their hard hearts. Then he said to the man, "Reach out your hand." The man reached out his hand, and it became normal again! ⁶At once the Pharisees went away and met with the supporters of Herod to discuss plans for killing Jesus.

⁷Jesus and his disciples went out to the lake, followed by a huge crowd from all over Galilee, Judea, ⁸Jerusalem, Idumea, from east of the Jordan River, and even from as far away as Tyre and Sidon. The news about his miracles had spread far and wide, and vast numbers of people came to see him for themselves.

⁹Jesus instructed his disciples to bring around a boat and to have it ready in case he was crowded off the beach. ¹⁰There had been many healings that day. As a result, many sick people were crowding around him, trying to touch him. ¹¹And whenever those possessed by evil spirits caught sight of him, they would fall down in front of him shrieking, "You are the Son of God!" ¹²But Jesus strictly warned them not to say who he was.

¹³Afterward Jesus went up on a mountain and called the ones he wanted to go with him. And they came to him. ¹⁴Then he selected twelve of them to be his regular companions, calling them apostles.* He sent them out to preach, ¹⁵and he gave them authority to cast out demons. ¹⁶These are the names of the twelve he chose:

Simon (he renamed him Peter),
¹⁷ James and John (the sons of Zebedee, but Jesus nicknamed them "Sons of Thunder"*),
¹⁸ Andrew,
Philip,
Bartholomew,
Matthew,
Thomas,
James (son of Alphaeus),
Thaddaeus,
Simon (the Zealot*),
¹⁹ Judas Iscariot (who later betrayed him).

²⁰When Jesus returned to the house where he was staying, the crowds began to gather again, and soon he and his disciples couldn't even find time to eat. ²¹When his family heard what was happening, they tried to take him home with them. "He's out of his mind," they said.

²²But the teachers of religious law who had arrived from Jerusalem said, "He's possessed by Satan,* the prince of demons. That's where he gets the power to cast out demons."

²³Jesus called them over and said to them by way of illustration, "How can Satan cast out Satan? ²⁴A kingdom at war with itself will collapse. ²⁵A home divided against itself is doomed. ²⁶And if Satan is fighting against himself, how can he stand? He would never survive. ²⁷Let me illustrate this. You can't enter a strong man's house and rob him without first tying him up. Only then can his house be robbed!*

²⁸"I assure you that any sin can be forgiven, including blasphemy; ²⁹but anyone who blasphemes against the Holy Spirit will never be forgiven. It is an eternal sin." ³⁰He told them this because they were saying he had an evil spirit.

³¹Jesus' mother and brothers arrived at the house where he was teaching. They stood outside and sent word for him to come out and talk with them. ³²There was a crowd around Jesus, and someone said, "Your mother and your brothers and sisters* are outside, asking for you."

³³Jesus replied, "Who is my mother? Who are my brothers?" ³⁴Then he looked at those around him and said, "These are my mother and brothers. ³⁵Anyone who does God's will is my brother and sister and mother."

3:14 Some manuscripts do not include *calling them apostles.*   3:17 Greek *whom he named Boanerges, which means Sons of Thunder.*
3:18 Greek *the Cananean.*   3:22 Greek *Beelzeboul.*   3:27 Or *One cannot rob Satan's kingdom without first tying him up. Only then can his demons be cast out.*   3:32 Some manuscripts do not include *and sisters.*

OCTOBER 11 ☐ DAY 285
MARK 4–7
Compassion of the Servant

OVERVIEW Beginning with chapter 4, Mark pauses in his rapid portrayal of Jesus' life and ministry to focus briefly on his teaching concerning the Kingdom of God. Returning to his action-packed narrative, Mark then relates four miracles that reveal Jesus' power over nature, demons, disease, and death. After a brief (and discouraging) visit to his hometown of Nazareth, Jesus multiplies his ministry by sending out the twelve disciples to teach and to heal. Upon their return, Jesus performs a different kind of ministry of multiplication as he takes a boy's lunch and increases it to feed a multitude of hungry seekers.

Chapter 4	Chapter 5	Chapter 6	Chapter 7
Ministry of Teaching	Ministry of Healing	Ministry of Multiplying	Ministry of Diagnosing
Parables	Miracles		Debates

YOUR DAILY WALK The Sea of Galilee is fifteen miles long by seven miles wide, cradled between hills that tower more than two thousand feet above the shore. Usually calm and tranquil, it can become treacherous when violent storms spring up without warning. The Sea of Galilee is like life itself: beautiful and tranquil at times, stormy and threatening at others.

No trial troubles the child of God who knows God has a reason for allowing it.

At the end of a long day of instruction on the shores of Galilee, Jesus and his disciples got into a boat (4:35-36). After pushing away from the shore, Jesus fell asleep . . . just as a storm exploded in full fury. Twelve frightened men rushed to the Savior and exclaimed in unison, "Teacher, don't you even care that we are going to drown?" (4:38). Now go back and reread verse 35. What was it Christ had said to his disciples just before entering the boat? "Let us go to the middle of the lake and drown"? Of course not! "Let's cross to the other side of the lake."

What stormy, unexpected event in your life has you feeling panicked and fretful? Remember, Christ intends to take you to the other side safe and secure and not let you drown. Invite him into your "boat" right now, and let him calm your anxieties and still your storms of doubt.

INSIGHT The Tower of Peace
The command Jesus gives to the storm in today's reading is the same command (in Greek) that he uses to heal the tortured soul in Mark 1:25. Is it any wonder Paul identifies this powerful peace as that "which is far more wonderful than the human mind can understand" (Philippians 4:7)?

CHAPTER 4
Once again Jesus began teaching by the lakeshore. There was such a large crowd along the shore that he got into a boat and sat down and spoke from there. ²He began to teach the people by telling many stories such as this one:

³"Listen! A farmer went out to plant some seed. ⁴As he scattered it across his field, some seed fell on a footpath, and the birds came and ate it. ⁵Other seed fell on shallow soil with underlying rock. The plant sprang up quickly, ⁶but it soon wilted beneath the hot sun and died because the roots had no nourishment in the shallow soil. ⁷Other seed fell among thorns that shot up and choked out the tender blades so that it produced no grain. ⁸Still other

seed fell on fertile soil and produced a crop that was thirty, sixty, and even a hundred times as much as had been planted." Then he said, [9]"Anyone who is willing to hear should listen and understand!"

[10]Later, when Jesus was alone with the twelve disciples and with the others who were gathered around, they asked him, "What do your stories mean?"

[11]He replied, "You are permitted to understand the secret about the Kingdom of God. But I am using these stories to conceal everything about it from outsiders, [12]so that the Scriptures might be fulfilled:

'They see what I do,
    but they don't perceive its meaning.
They hear my words,
    but they don't understand.
So they will not turn from their sins
    and be forgiven.'*

[13]"But if you can't understand this story, how will you understand all the others I am going to tell? [14]The farmer I talked about is the one who brings God's message to others. [15]The seed that fell on the hard path represents those who hear the message, but then Satan comes at once and takes it away from them. [16]The rocky soil represents those who hear the message and receive it with joy. [17]But like young plants in such soil, their roots don't go very deep. At first they get along fine, but they wilt as soon as they have problems or are persecuted because they believe the word. [18]The thorny ground represents those who hear and accept the Good News, [19]but all too quickly the message is crowded out by the cares of this life, the lure of wealth, and the desire for nice things, so no crop is produced. [20]But the good soil represents those who hear and accept God's message and produce a huge harvest—thirty, sixty, or even a hundred times as much as had been planted."

[21]Then Jesus asked them, "Would anyone light a lamp and then put it under a basket or under a bed to shut out the light? Of course not! A lamp is placed on a stand, where its light will shine.

[22]"Everything that is now hidden or secret will eventually be brought to light. [23]Anyone who is willing to hear should listen and understand! [24]And be sure to pay attention to what you hear. The more

you do this, the more you will understand—and even more, besides. [25]To those who are open to my teaching, more understanding will be given. But to those who are not listening, even what they have will be taken away from them."

[26]Jesus also said, "Here is another illustration of what the Kingdom of God is like: A farmer planted seeds in a field, [27]and then he went on with his other activities. As the days went by, the seeds sprouted and grew without the farmer's help, [28]because the earth produces crops on its own. First a leaf blade pushes through, then the heads of wheat are formed, and finally the grain ripens. [29]And as soon as the grain is ready, the farmer comes and harvests it with a sickle."

[30]Jesus asked, "How can I describe the Kingdom of God? What story should I use to illustrate it? [31]It is like a tiny mustard seed. Though this is one of the smallest of seeds, [32]it grows to become one of the largest of plants, with long branches where birds can come and find shelter."

[33]He used many such stories and illustrations to teach the people as much as they were able to understand. [34]In fact, in his public teaching he taught only with parables, but afterward when he was alone with his disciples, he explained the meaning to them.

[35]As evening came, Jesus said to his disciples, "Let's cross to the other side of the lake." [36]He was already in the boat, so they started out, leaving the crowds behind (although other boats followed). [37]But soon a fierce storm arose. High waves began to break into the boat until it was nearly full of water.

[38]Jesus was sleeping at the back of the boat with his head on a cushion. Frantically they woke him up, shouting, "Teacher, don't you even care that we are going to drown?"

[39]When he woke up, he rebuked the wind and said to the water, "Quiet down!" Suddenly the wind stopped, and there was a great calm. [40]And he asked them, "Why are you so afraid? Do you still not have faith in me?"

[41]And they were filled with awe and said among themselves, "Who is this man, that even the wind and waves obey him?"

4:12 Isa 6:9-10.

CHAPTER 5

So they arrived at the other side of the lake, in the land of the Gerasenes.* ²Just as Jesus was climbing from the boat, a man possessed by an evil spirit ran out from a cemetery to meet him. ³This man lived among the tombs and could not be restrained, even with a chain. ⁴Whenever he was put into chains and shackles—as he often was—he snapped the chains from his wrists and smashed the shackles. No one was strong enough to control him. ⁵All day long and throughout the night, he would wander among the tombs and in the hills, screaming and hitting himself with stones.

⁶When Jesus was still some distance away, the man saw him. He ran to meet Jesus and fell down before him. ⁷He gave a terrible scream, shrieking, "Why are you bothering me, Jesus, Son of the Most High God? For God's sake, don't torture me!" ⁸For Jesus had already said to the spirit, "Come out of the man, you evil spirit."

⁹Then Jesus asked, "What is your name?"

And the spirit replied, "Legion, because there are many of us here inside this man." ¹⁰Then the spirits begged him again and again not to send them to some distant place. ¹¹There happened to be a large herd of pigs feeding on the hillside nearby. ¹²"Send us into those pigs," the evil spirits begged. ¹³Jesus gave them permission. So the evil spirits came out of the man and entered the pigs, and the entire herd of two thousand pigs plunged down the steep hillside into the lake, where they drowned.

¹⁴The herdsmen fled to the nearby city and the surrounding countryside, spreading the news as they ran. Everyone rushed out to see for themselves. ¹⁵A crowd soon gathered around Jesus, but they were frightened when they saw the man who had been demon possessed, for he was sitting there fully clothed and perfectly sane. ¹⁶Those who had seen what happened to the man and to the pigs told everyone about it, ¹⁷and the crowd began pleading with Jesus to go away and leave them alone.

¹⁸When Jesus got back into the boat, the man who had been demon possessed begged to go, too. ¹⁹But Jesus said, "No, go home to your friends, and tell them what wonderful things the Lord has done for you and how merciful he has been." ²⁰So the man started off to visit the Ten Towns* of that region and began to tell everyone about the great things Jesus had done for him; and everyone was amazed at what he told them.

²¹When Jesus went back across to the other side of the lake, a large crowd gathered around him on the shore. ²²A leader of the local synagogue, whose name was Jairus, came and fell down before him, ²³pleading with him to heal his little daughter. "She is about to die," he said in desperation. "Please come and place your hands on her; heal her so she can live."

²⁴Jesus went with him, and the crowd thronged behind. ²⁵And there was a woman in the crowd who had had a hemorrhage for twelve years. ²⁶She had suffered a great deal from many doctors through the years and had spent everything she had to pay them, but she had gotten no better. In fact, she was worse. ²⁷She had heard about Jesus, so she came up behind him through the crowd and touched the fringe of his robe. ²⁸For she thought to herself, "If I can just touch his clothing, I will be healed." ²⁹Immediately the bleeding stopped, and she could feel that she had been healed!

³⁰Jesus realized at once that healing power had gone out from him, so he turned around in the crowd and asked, "Who touched my clothes?"

³¹His disciples said to him, "All this crowd is pressing around you. How can you ask, 'Who touched me?'"

³²But he kept on looking around to see who had done it. ³³Then the frightened woman, trembling at the realization of what had happened to her, came and fell at his feet and told him what she had done. ³⁴And he said to her, "Daughter, your faith has made you well. Go in peace. You have been healed."

³⁵While he was still speaking to her, messengers arrived from Jairus's home with the message, "Your daughter is dead. There's no use troubling the Teacher now."

³⁶But Jesus ignored their comments and said to Jairus, "Don't be afraid. Just trust me." ³⁷Then Jesus stopped the crowd and wouldn't let anyone go with him except Peter and James and John. ³⁸When they came to the home of the synagogue leader, Jesus saw the commotion and the weeping

---

5:1 Some manuscripts read *Gadarenes;* others read *Gergesenes.* See Matt 8:28; Luke 8:26.   5:20 Greek *Decapolis.*

and wailing. [39]He went inside and spoke to the people. "Why all this weeping and commotion?" he asked. "The child isn't dead; she is only asleep."

[40]The crowd laughed at him, but he told them all to go outside. Then he took the girl's father and mother and his three disciples into the room where the girl was lying. [41]Holding her hand, he said to her, "Get up, little girl!"* [42]And the girl, who was twelve years old, immediately stood up and walked around! Her parents were absolutely overwhelmed. [43]Jesus commanded them not to tell anyone what had happened, and he told them to give her something to eat.

CHAPTER 6

Jesus left that part of the country and returned with his disciples to Nazareth, his hometown. [2]The next Sabbath he began teaching in the synagogue, and many who heard him were astonished. They asked, "Where did he get all his wisdom and the power to perform such miracles? [3]He's just the carpenter, the son of Mary and brother of James, Joseph,* Judas, and Simon. And his sisters live right here among us." They were deeply offended and refused to believe in him.

[4]Then Jesus told them, "A prophet is honored everywhere except in his own hometown and among his relatives and his own family." [5]And because of their unbelief, he couldn't do any mighty miracles among them except to place his hands on a few sick people and heal them. [6]And he was amazed at their unbelief.

Then Jesus went out from village to village, teaching. [7]And he called his twelve disciples together and sent them out two by two, with authority to cast out evil spirits. [8]He told them to take nothing with them except a walking stick—no food, no traveler's bag, no money. [9]He told them to wear sandals but not to take even an extra coat. [10]"When you enter each village, be a guest in only one home," he said. [11]"And if a village won't welcome you or listen to you, shake off its dust from your feet as you leave. It is a sign that you have abandoned that village to its fate."

[12]So the disciples went out, telling all they met to turn from their sins. [13]And they cast out many demons and healed many sick people, anointing them with olive oil.

[14]Herod Antipas, the king, soon heard about Jesus, because people everywhere were talking about him. Some were saying,* "This must be John the Baptist come back to life again. That is why he can do such miracles." [15]Others thought Jesus was the ancient prophet Elijah. Still others thought he was a prophet like the other great prophets of the past. [16]When Herod heard about Jesus, he said, "John, the man I beheaded, has come back from the dead." [17]For Herod had sent soldiers to arrest and imprison John as a favor to Herodias. She had been his brother Philip's wife, but Herod had married her. [18]John kept telling Herod, "It is illegal for you to marry your brother's wife." [19]Herodias was enraged and wanted John killed in revenge, but without Herod's approval she was powerless. [20]And Herod respected John, knowing that he was a good and holy man, so he kept him under his protection. Herod was disturbed whenever he talked with John, but even so, he liked to listen to him.

[21]Herodias's chance finally came. It was Herod's birthday, and he gave a party for his palace aides, army officers, and the leading citizens of Galilee. [22]Then his daughter, also named Herodias,* came in and performed a dance that greatly pleased them all. "Ask me for anything you like," the king said to the girl, "and I will give it to you." [23]Then he promised, "I will give you whatever you ask, up to half of my kingdom!"

[24]She went out and asked her mother, "What should I ask for?"

Her mother told her, "Ask for John the Baptist's head!"

[25]So the girl hurried back to the king and told him, "I want the head of John the Baptist, right now, on a tray!"

[26]Then the king was very sorry, but he was embarrassed to break his oath in front of his guests. [27]So he sent an executioner to the prison to cut off John's head and bring it to him. The soldier beheaded John in the prison, [28]brought his head on a tray, and gave it to the girl, who took it to her mother. [29]When John's disciples heard what had happened, they came for his body and buried it in a tomb.

[30]The apostles returned to Jesus from their ministry tour and told him all they had done and what they had taught. [31]Then Jesus said, "Let's get away from the

---

5:41 Greek text uses Aramaic *Talitha cumi* and then translates it as "Get up, little girl."   6:3 Greek *Joses;* see Matt 13:55.
6:14 Some manuscripts read *He was saying.*   6:22 Some manuscripts read *the daughter of Herodias herself.*

crowds for a while and rest." There were so many people coming and going that Jesus and his apostles didn't even have time to eat. [32]They left by boat for a quieter spot. [33]But many people saw them leaving, and people from many towns ran ahead along the shore and met them as they landed. [34]A vast crowd was there as he stepped from the boat, and he had compassion on them because they were like sheep without a shepherd. So he taught them many things.

[35]Late in the afternoon his disciples came to him and said, "This is a desolate place, and it is getting late. [36]Send the crowds away so they can go to the nearby farms and villages and buy themselves some food."

[37]But Jesus said, "You feed them."

"With what?" they asked. "It would take a small fortune* to buy food for all this crowd!"

[38]"How much food do you have?" he asked. "Go and find out."

They came back and reported, "We have five loaves of bread and two fish." [39]Then Jesus told the crowd to sit down in groups on the green grass. [40]So they sat in groups of fifty or a hundred.

[41]Jesus took the five loaves and two fish, looked up toward heaven, and asked God's blessing on the food. Breaking the loaves into pieces, he kept giving the bread and fish to the disciples to give to the people. [42]They all ate as much as they wanted, [43]and they picked up twelve baskets of leftover bread and fish. [44]Five thousand men had eaten from those five loaves!

[45]Immediately after this, Jesus made his disciples get back into the boat and head out across the lake to Bethsaida, while he sent the people home. [46]Afterward he went up into the hills by himself to pray.

[47]During the night, the disciples were in their boat out in the middle of the lake, and Jesus was alone on land. [48]He saw that they were in serious trouble, rowing hard and struggling against the wind and waves. About three o'clock in the morning* he came to them, walking on the water. He started to go past them, [49]but when they saw him walking on the water, they screamed in terror, thinking he was a ghost. [50]They were all terrified when they saw him. But Jesus spoke to them at once. "It's all right," he said. "I am here! Don't be afraid." [51]Then he

climbed into the boat, and the wind stopped. They were astonished at what they saw. [52]They still didn't understand the significance of the miracle of the multiplied loaves, for their hearts were hard and they did not believe.

[53]When they arrived at Gennesaret on the other side of the lake, they anchored the boat [54]and climbed out. The people standing there recognized him at once, [55]and they ran throughout the whole area and began carrying sick people to him on mats. [56]Wherever he went—in villages and cities and out on the farms—they laid the sick in the market plazas and streets. The sick begged him to let them at least touch the fringe of his robe, and all who touched it were healed.

CHAPTER 7

One day some Pharisees and teachers of religious law arrived from Jerusalem to confront Jesus. [2]They noticed that some of Jesus' disciples failed to follow the usual Jewish ritual of hand washing before eating. [3](The Jews, especially the Pharisees, do not eat until they have poured water over their cupped hands,* as required by their ancient traditions. [4]Similarly, they eat nothing bought from the market unless they have immersed their hands in water. This is but one of many traditions they have clung to—such as their ceremony of washing cups, pitchers, and kettles.*) [5]So the Pharisees and teachers of religious law asked him, "Why don't your disciples follow our age-old customs? For they eat without first performing the hand-washing ceremony."

[6]Jesus replied, "You hypocrites! Isaiah was prophesying about you when he said,

[7] 'These people honor me with their lips,
     but their hearts are far away.
Their worship is a farce,
     for they replace God's commands
       with their own man-made
       teachings.'*

[8]For you ignore God's specific laws and substitute your own traditions."

[9]Then he said, "You reject God's laws in order to hold on to your own traditions. [10]For instance, Moses gave you this law from God: 'Honor your father and mother,' and 'Anyone who speaks evil of father or mother must be put to death.'* [11]But you

---

6:37 Greek *200 denarii*. A denarius was the equivalent of a full day's wage.   6:48 Greek *About the fourth watch of the night.*
7:3 Greek *washed with the fist.*   7:4 Some Greek manuscripts add *and dining couches.*   7:7 Isa 29:13.   7:10 Exod 20:12; 21:17;
Lev 20:9; Deut 5:16.

say it is all right for people to say to their parents, 'Sorry, I can't help you. For I have vowed to give to God what I could have given to you.'* [12]You let them disregard their needy parents. [13]As such, you break the law of God in order to protect your own tradition. And this is only one example. There are many, many others."

[14]Then Jesus called to the crowd to come and hear. "All of you listen," he said, "and try to understand. [15]You are not defiled by what you eat; you are defiled by what you say and do!*"

[17]Then Jesus went into a house to get away from the crowds, and his disciples asked him what he meant by the statement he had made. [18]"Don't you understand either?" he asked. "Can't you see that what you eat won't defile you? [19]Food doesn't come in contact with your heart, but only passes through the stomach and then comes out again." (By saying this, he showed that every kind of food is acceptable.)

[20]And then he added, "It is the thought-life that defiles you. [21]For from within, out of a person's heart, come evil thoughts, sexual immorality, theft, murder, [22]adultery, greed, wickedness, deceit, eagerness for lustful pleasure, envy, slander, pride, and foolishness. [23]All these vile things come from within; they are what defile you and make you unacceptable to God."

[24]Then Jesus left Galilee and went north to the region of Tyre.* He tried to keep it secret that he was there, but he couldn't. As usual, the news of his arrival spread fast. [25]Right away a woman came to him whose little girl was possessed by an evil spirit. She had heard about Jesus, and now she came and fell at his feet. [26]She begged him to release her child from the demon's control.

Since she was a Gentile, born in Syrian Phoenicia, [27]Jesus told her, "First I should help my own family, the Jews.* It isn't right to take food from the children and throw it to the dogs."

[28]She replied, "That's true, Lord, but even the dogs under the table are given some crumbs from the children's plates."

[29]"Good answer!" he said. "And because you have answered so well, I have healed your daughter." [30]And when she arrived home, her little girl was lying quietly in bed, and the demon was gone.

[31]Jesus left Tyre and went to Sidon, then back to the Sea of Galilee and the region of the Ten Towns.* [32]A deaf man with a speech impediment was brought to him, and the people begged Jesus to lay his hands on the man to heal him. [33]Jesus led him to a private place away from the crowd. He put his fingers into the man's ears. Then, spitting onto his own fingers, he touched the man's tongue with the spittle. [34]And looking up to heaven, he sighed and commanded, "Be opened!"* [35]Instantly the man could hear perfectly and speak plainly!

[36]Jesus told the crowd not to tell anyone, but the more he told them not to, the more they spread the news, [37]for they were completely amazed. Again and again they said, "Everything he does is wonderful. He even heals those who are deaf and mute."

7:11 Greek *'What I could have given to you is Corban' (that is, a gift).* 7:15 Some manuscripts add verse 16, *Anyone who is willing to hear should listen and understand.* 7:24 Some Greek manuscripts add *and Sidon.* 7:27 Greek *Let the children eat first.* 7:31 Greek *Decapolis.* 7:34 Greek text uses Aramaic *"Ephphatha"* and then translates it as *"Be opened."*

OCTOBER 12 ☐ DAY 286
MARK 8–10
Teaching of the Servant

 OVERVIEW Many of Christ's sayings and sermons are uttered in response to the questions and attacks of the Pharisees. The same is true of his discussions with the disciples—conversations that lead to important teachings on such subjects as discipleship, humility, stumbling blocks, and proper priorities. But even as he teaches, Jesus is constantly on the move, traveling across the Sea of Galilee to Caesarea Philippi and finally through Perea to Jerusalem.

Chapter 8	Chapter 9	Chapter 10
Lessons from the Loaves	Lessons on Prayer and Pride	Lessons on Servanthood
"Be Careful!"	"Be Prayerful!"	"Be Available!"

If someone's sense of security depends on having all people speak well of him or her, he or she can never be secure following Christ.

YOUR DAILY WALK Ask a truck driver, a senior citizen, and a teenager how to get from point A to point B, and you will probably get three different answers. The truck driver may suggest, "Take the freeway"; the senior citizen, "Take the bus"; and the teenager, "You can't get there from here!" Same goal, but different paths to achieve it.

In today's section you will read two accounts of Jesus healing blind men (8:22-26; 10:46-52). In the case of the blind man of Bethsaida, Jesus led the man out of town, spit on his eyes, and placed his hands on the man's face twice before his sight was fully restored. With Bartimaeus of Jericho, full healing came with but the speaking of a word.

So it is with spiritual lessons God wants to teach us. God may teach your friend to depend on him through financial problems; you learn the same lesson through illness. Another Christian learns to walk by faith in affluence; you learn it in poverty. One person learns patience through being single; another learns it through having a spouse . . . and little spouslings! In each case, it is dangerous to compare—rather than commit to—God's perfect curriculum. Every time you see an Under Construction sign next to a building or highway this month, let it remind you that God is not finished with you yet!

INSIGHT The Toughest of the Ten
The rich young man (10:17-22) gloried in his observance of the Ten Commandments, but he had never really gotten past the first one (Exodus 20:3). His possessions had become his god . . . his idol . . . the focus of his affections. Read 1 John 5:21 and restate it in your own words.

CHAPTER 8

About this time another great crowd had gathered, and the people ran out of food again. Jesus called his disciples and told them, ²"I feel sorry for these people. They have been here with me for three days, and they have nothing left to eat. ³And if I send them home without feeding them, they will faint along the road. For some of them have come a long distance."

⁴"How are we supposed to find enough food for them here in the wilderness?" his disciples asked.

⁵"How many loaves of bread do you have?" he asked.

"Seven," they replied. ⁶So Jesus told all the people to sit down on the ground. Then he took the seven loaves, thanked God for them, broke them into pieces, and gave them to his disciples, who distributed the bread to the crowd. ⁷A few small fish were found, too, so Jesus also blessed these and told the disciples to pass them out.

⁸They ate until they were full, and when the scraps were picked up, there were seven large baskets of food left over! ⁹There were about four thousand people in the crowd that day, and he sent them home after they had eaten. ¹⁰Immediately after this, he got into a boat with his disciples and crossed over to the region of Dalmanutha.

¹¹When the Pharisees heard that Jesus had arrived, they came to argue with him. Testing him to see if he was from God, they demanded, "Give us a miraculous sign from heaven to prove yourself."

¹²When he heard this, he sighed deeply and said, "Why do you people keep demanding a miraculous sign? I assure you, I will not give this generation any such sign." ¹³So he got back into the boat and left them, and he crossed to the other side of the lake.

¹⁴But the disciples discovered they had forgotten to bring any food, so there was

only one loaf of bread with them in the boat. ¹⁵As they were crossing the lake, Jesus warned them, "Beware of the yeast of the Pharisees and of Herod."

¹⁶They decided he was saying this because they hadn't brought any bread. ¹⁷Jesus knew what they were thinking, so he said, "Why are you so worried about having no food? Won't you ever learn or understand? Are your hearts too hard to take it in? ¹⁸'You have eyes—can't you see? You have ears—can't you hear?'* Don't you remember anything at all? ¹⁹What about the five thousand men I fed with five loaves of bread? How many baskets of leftovers did you pick up afterward?"

"Twelve," they said.

²⁰"And when I fed the four thousand with seven loaves, how many large baskets of leftovers did you pick up?"

"Seven," they said.

²¹"Don't you understand even yet?" he asked them.

²²When they arrived at Bethsaida, some people brought a blind man to Jesus, and they begged him to touch and heal the man. ²³Jesus took the blind man by the hand and led him out of the village. Then, spitting on the man's eyes, he laid his hands on him and asked, "Can you see anything now?"

²⁴The man looked around. "Yes," he said, "I see people, but I can't see them very clearly. They look like trees walking around."

²⁵Then Jesus placed his hands over the man's eyes again. As the man stared intently, his sight was completely restored, and he could see everything clearly. ²⁶Jesus sent him home, saying, "Don't go back into the village on your way home."

²⁷Jesus and his disciples left Galilee and went up to the villages of Caesarea Philippi. As they were walking along, he asked them, "Who do people say I am?"

²⁸"Well," they replied, "some say John the Baptist, some say Elijah, and others say you are one of the other prophets."

²⁹Then Jesus asked, "Who do you say I am?"

Peter replied, "You are the Messiah."
³⁰But Jesus warned them not to tell anyone about him.

³¹Then Jesus began to tell them that he, the Son of Man, would suffer many terrible things and be rejected by the leaders, the leading priests, and the teachers of religious law. He would be killed, and three days later he would rise again. ³²As he talked about this openly with his disciples, Peter took him aside and told him he shouldn't say things like that.*

³³Jesus turned and looked at his disciples and then said to Peter very sternly, "Get away from me, Satan! You are seeing things merely from a human point of view, not from God's."

³⁴Then he called his disciples and the crowds to come over and listen. "If any of you wants to be my follower," he told them, "you must put aside your selfish ambition, shoulder your cross, and follow me. ³⁵If you try to keep your life for yourself, you will lose it. But if you give up your life for my sake and for the sake of the Good News, you will find true life. ³⁶And how do you benefit if you gain the whole world but lose your own soul* in the process? ³⁷Is anything worth more than your soul? ³⁸If a person is ashamed of me and my message in these adulterous and sinful days, I, the Son of Man, will be ashamed of that person when I return in the glory of my Father with the holy angels."

CHAPTER 9

Jesus went on to say, "I assure you that some of you standing here right now will not die before you see the Kingdom of God arrive in great power!"

²Six days later Jesus took Peter, James, and John to the top of a mountain. No one else was there. As the men watched, Jesus' appearance changed, ³and his clothing became dazzling white, far whiter than any earthly process could ever make it. ⁴Then Elijah and Moses appeared and began talking with Jesus.

⁵"Teacher, this is wonderful!" Peter exclaimed. "We will make three shrines*— one for you, one for Moses, and one for Elijah." ⁶He didn't really know what to say, for they were all terribly afraid.

⁷Then a cloud came over them, and a voice from the cloud said, "This is my beloved Son. Listen to him." ⁸Suddenly they looked around, and Moses and Elijah were gone, and only Jesus was with them. ⁹As they descended the mountainside, he told them not to tell anyone what they had seen

8:18 Jer 5:21.   **8:32** Or *and began to correct him.*   **8:36** Or *your life;* also in 8:37.   **9:5** Or *shelters;* Greek reads *tabernacles.*

until he, the Son of Man, had risen from the dead. [10]So they kept it to themselves, but they often asked each other what he meant by "rising from the dead."

[11]Now they began asking him, "Why do the teachers of religious law insist that Elijah must return before the Messiah comes?"

[12]Jesus responded, "Elijah is indeed coming first to set everything in order. Why then is it written in the Scriptures that the Son of Man must suffer and be treated with utter contempt? [13]But I tell you, Elijah has already come, and he was badly mistreated, just as the Scriptures predicted."

[14]At the foot of the mountain they found a great crowd surrounding the other disciples, as some teachers of religious law were arguing with them. [15]The crowd watched Jesus in awe as he came toward them, and then they ran to greet him. [16]"What is all this arguing about?" he asked.

[17]One of the men in the crowd spoke up and said, "Teacher, I brought my son for you to heal him. He can't speak because he is possessed by an evil spirit that won't let him talk. [18]And whenever this evil spirit seizes him, it throws him violently to the ground and makes him foam at the mouth and grind his teeth and become rigid.* So I asked your disciples to cast out the evil spirit, but they couldn't do it."

[19]Jesus said to them, "You faithless people! How long must I be with you until you believe? How long must I put up with you? Bring the boy to me." [20]So they brought the boy. But when the evil spirit saw Jesus, it threw the child into a violent convulsion, and he fell to the ground, writhing and foaming at the mouth. [21]"How long has this been happening?" Jesus asked the boy's father.

He replied, "Since he was very small. [22]The evil spirit often makes him fall into the fire or into water, trying to kill him. Have mercy on us and help us. Do something if you can."

[23]"What do you mean, 'If I can'?" Jesus asked. "Anything is possible if a person believes."

[24]The father instantly replied, "I do believe, but help me not to doubt!"

[25]When Jesus saw that the crowd of onlookers was growing, he rebuked the evil spirit. "Spirit of deafness and muteness,"

he said, "I command you to come out of this child and never enter him again!" [26]Then the spirit screamed and threw the boy into another violent convulsion and left him. The boy lay there motionless, and he appeared to be dead. A murmur ran through the crowd, "He's dead." [27]But Jesus took him by the hand and helped him to his feet, and he stood up.

[28]Afterward, when Jesus was alone in the house with his disciples, they asked him, "Why couldn't we cast out that evil spirit?"

[29]Jesus replied, "This kind can be cast out only by prayer.*"

[30]Leaving that region, they traveled through Galilee. Jesus tried to avoid all publicity [31]in order to spend more time with his disciples and teach them. He said to them, "The Son of Man is going to be betrayed. He will be killed, but three days later he will rise from the dead." [32]But they didn't understand what he was saying, and they were afraid to ask him what he meant.

[33]After they arrived at Capernaum, Jesus and his disciples settled in the house where they would be staying. Jesus asked them, "What were you discussing out on the road?" [34]But they didn't answer, because they had been arguing about which of them was the greatest. [35]He sat down and called the twelve disciples over to him. Then he said, "Anyone who wants to be the first must take last place and be the servant of everyone else."

[36]Then he put a little child among them. Taking the child in his arms, he said to them, [37]"Anyone who welcomes a little child like this on my behalf welcomes me, and anyone who welcomes me welcomes my Father who sent me."

[38]John said to Jesus, "Teacher, we saw a man using your name to cast out demons, but we told him to stop because he isn't one of our group."

[39]"Don't stop him!" Jesus said. "No one who performs miracles in my name will soon be able to speak evil of me. [40]Anyone who is not against us is for us. [41]If anyone gives you even a cup of water because you belong to the Messiah, I assure you, that person will be rewarded.

[42]"But if anyone causes one of these little ones who trusts in me to lose faith, it would be better for that person to be

9:18 Or *become weak.*   **9:29** Some manuscripts add *and fasting.*

thrown into the sea with a large millstone tied around the neck. [43]If your hand causes you to sin, cut it off. It is better to enter heaven* with only one hand than to go into the unquenchable fires of hell with two hands.* [45]If your foot causes you to sin, cut it off. It is better to enter heaven with only one foot than to be thrown into hell with two feet.* [47]And if your eye causes you to sin, gouge it out. It is better to enter the Kingdom of God half blind than to have two eyes and be thrown into hell, [48]'where the worm never dies and the fire never goes out.'*

[49]"For everyone will be purified with fire.* [50]Salt is good for seasoning. But if it loses its flavor, how do you make it salty again? You must have the qualities of salt among yourselves and live in peace with each other."

CHAPTER 10
Then Jesus left Capernaum and went southward to the region of Judea and into the area east of the Jordan River. As always there were the crowds, and as usual he taught them.

[2]Some Pharisees came and tried to trap him with this question: "Should a man be allowed to divorce his wife?"

[3]"What did Moses say about divorce?" Jesus asked them.

[4]"Well, he permitted it," they replied. "He said a man merely has to write his wife an official letter of divorce and send her away."*

[5]But Jesus responded, "He wrote those instructions only as a concession to your hard-hearted wickedness. [6]But God's plan was seen from the beginning of creation, for 'He made them male and female.'* [7]This explains why a man leaves his father and mother and is joined to his wife,* [8]and the two are united into one.'* Since they are no longer two but one, [9]let no one separate them, for God has joined them together."

[10]Later, when he was alone with his disciples in the house, they brought up the subject again. [11]He told them, "Whoever divorces his wife and marries someone else commits adultery against her. [12]And

if a woman divorces her husband and remarries, she commits adultery."

[13]One day some parents brought their children to Jesus so he could touch them and bless them, but the disciples told them not to bother him. [14]But when Jesus saw what was happening, he was very displeased with his disciples. He said to them, "Let the children come to me. Don't stop them! For the Kingdom of God belongs to such as these. [15]I assure you, anyone who doesn't have their kind of faith will never get into the Kingdom of God." [16]Then he took the children into his arms and placed his hands on their heads and blessed them.

[17]As he was starting out on a trip, a man came running up to Jesus, knelt down, and asked, "Good Teacher, what should I do to get eternal life?"

[18]"Why do you call me good?" Jesus asked. "Only God is truly good. [19]But as for your question, you know the commandments: 'Do not murder. Do not commit adultery. Do not steal. Do not testify falsely. Do not cheat. Honor your father and mother.'*"

[20]"Teacher," the man replied, "I've obeyed all these commandments since I was a child."

[21]Jesus felt genuine love for this man as he looked at him. "You lack only one thing," he told him. "Go and sell all you have and give the money to the poor, and you will have treasure in heaven. Then come, follow me." [22]At this, the man's face fell, and he went sadly away because he had many possessions.

[23]Jesus looked around and said to his disciples, "How hard it is for rich people to get into the Kingdom of God!" [24]This amazed them. But Jesus said again, "Dear children, it is very hard* to get into the Kingdom of God. [25]It is easier for a camel to go through the eye of a needle than for a rich person to enter the Kingdom of God!"

[26]The disciples were astounded. "Then who in the world can be saved?" they asked.

[27]Jesus looked at them intently and said, "Humanly speaking, it is impossible. But

9:43a Greek *enter life;* also in 9:45.   **9:43b** Some manuscripts add verse 44 (which is identical with 9:48).   **9:45** Some manuscripts add verse 46 (which is identical with 9:48).   **9:48** Isa 66:24.   **9:49** Greek *salted with fire.* Some manuscripts add *and every sacrifice will be salted with salt.*   **10:4** Deut 24:1.   **10:6** Gen 1:27; 5:2.   **10:7** Some manuscripts do not include *and is joined to his wife.* **10:7-8** Gen 2:24.   **10:19** Exod 20:12-16; Deut 5:16-20.   **10:24** Some manuscripts add *for those who trust in riches.*

not with God. Everything is possible with God."

28 Then Peter began to mention all that he and the other disciples had left behind. "We've given up everything to follow you," he said.

29 And Jesus replied, "I assure you that everyone who has given up house or brothers or sisters or mother or father or children or property, for my sake and for the Good News, 30 will receive now in return, a hundred times over, houses, brothers, sisters, mothers, children, and property—with persecutions. And in the world to come they will have eternal life. 31 But many who seem to be important now will be the least important then, and those who are considered least here will be the greatest then.*"

32 They were now on the way to Jerusalem, and Jesus was walking ahead of them. The disciples were filled with dread and the people following behind were overwhelmed with fear. Taking the twelve disciples aside, Jesus once more began to describe everything that was about to happen to him in Jerusalem. 33 "When we get to Jerusalem," he told them, "the Son of Man will be betrayed to the leading priests and the teachers of religious law. They will sentence him to die and hand him over to the Romans. 34 They will mock him, spit on him, beat him with their whips, and kill him, but after three days he will rise again."

35 Then James and John, the sons of Zebedee, came over and spoke to him. "Teacher," they said, "we want you to do us a favor."

36 "What is it?" he asked.

37 "In your glorious Kingdom, we want to sit in places of honor next to you," they said, "one at your right and the other at your left."

38 But Jesus answered, "You don't know what you are asking! Are you able to drink from the bitter cup of sorrow I am about to drink? Are you able to be bap-

tized with the baptism of suffering I must be baptized with?"

39 "Oh yes," they said, "we are able!"

And Jesus said, "You will indeed drink from my cup and be baptized with my baptism, 40 but I have no right to say who will sit on the thrones next to mine. God has prepared those places for the ones he has chosen."

41 When the ten other disciples discovered what James and John had asked, they were indignant. 42 So Jesus called them together and said, "You know that in this world kings are tyrants, and officials lord it over the people beneath them. 43 But among you it should be quite different. Whoever wants to be a leader among you must be your servant, 44 and whoever wants to be first must be the slave of all. 45 For even I, the Son of Man, came here not to be served but to serve others, and to give my life as a ransom for many."

46 And so they reached Jericho. Later, as Jesus and his disciples left town, a great crowd was following. A blind beggar named Bartimaeus (son of Timaeus) was sitting beside the road as Jesus was going by. 47 When Bartimaeus heard that Jesus from Nazareth was nearby, he began to shout out, "Jesus, Son of David, have mercy on me!"

48 "Be quiet!" some of the people yelled at him.

But he only shouted louder, "Son of David, have mercy on me!"

49 When Jesus heard him, he stopped and said, "Tell him to come here."

So they called the blind man. "Cheer up," they said. "Come on, he's calling you!" 50 Bartimaeus threw aside his coat, jumped up, and came to Jesus.

51 "What do you want me to do for you?" Jesus asked.

"Teacher," the blind man said, "I want to see!"

52 And Jesus said to him, "Go your way. Your faith has healed you." And instantly the blind man could see! Then he followed Jesus down the road.*

10:31 Greek *But many who are first will be last; and the last, first.*   10:52 Or *on the way.*

OCTOBER 13 ☐ DAY 287
MARK 11–13
Signs of the Servant

OVERVIEW Mark, who has written seven chapters covering the first three years of Jesus' active ministry and three chapters describing the next six months, now devotes six chapters—fully 40 percent of his book—to the final eight days! Throughout this last week Jesus' activities revolve around the Temple as he confronts "the leading priests, teachers of religious law, and the other leaders" with his irrefutable claims. Though the adoring cries of "Praise God" announce his arrival in Jerusalem, only a few days later he will hear the frenzied cry "Crucify him!" Jesus is now taking his final steps to the cross.

Chapter 11	Chapter 12	Chapter 13
Arrival in Jerusalem	Antagonism from the Jews	Anticipation of the Future
Triumph	Turmoil	Tribulation

Jesus Christ is God's everything for everyone's total need.

YOUR DAILY WALK Sometimes it's difficult to remember that the people living in Jesus' day did not have the New Testament to read. They knew no John 3:16 to declare the good news of the gospel . . . no Romans 3:23-24 to explain the significance of the cross . . . no Ephesians 2:1-7 to describe the miracle of new life in Jesus Christ. All they had to help them anticipate and understand the events of their day was the Old Testament: the law of Moses . . . the predictions of the prophets . . . the word pictures contained in the Psalms.

Mark draws heavily on that vital material to show the significance of events during Christ's final days on earth. Put yourself in the sandals of a first-century Jew. See if you can walk your way through today's section by reading these Old Testament passages in sequence: Psalm 118:25-26; Isaiah 56:7; Jeremiah 7:11; Isaiah 5:1-7; Psalm 118:22-23; Deuteronomy 6:4-5; Leviticus 19:18; Psalm 110:1; Daniel 9:27; 11:31; 12:11; Isaiah 13:10.

INSIGHT The Unridden Donkey
In Old Testament times an object to be consecrated to God—that is, set apart for special service—could never have been used previously for common purposes (Numbers 19:2; 1 Samuel 6:7). This may explain why Christ selected a young colt that had never been ridden (Mark 11:2) and why he would later be buried in a new tomb that had never been occupied (Luke 23:53).

CHAPTER 11

As Jesus and his disciples approached Jerusalem, they came to the towns of Bethphage and Bethany, on the Mount of Olives. Jesus sent two of them on ahead. ²"Go into that village over there," he told them, "and as soon as you enter it, you will see a colt tied there that has never been ridden. Untie it and bring it here. ³If anyone asks what you are doing, just say, 'The Lord needs it and will return it soon.'"

⁴The two disciples left and found the colt standing in the street, tied outside a house. ⁵As they were untying it, some bystanders demanded, "What are you doing, untying that colt?" ⁶They said what Jesus had told them to say, and they were permitted to take it. ⁷Then they brought the colt to Jesus and threw their garments over it, and he sat on it.

⁸Many in the crowd spread their coats on the road ahead of Jesus, and others cut leafy branches in the fields and spread them along the way. ⁹He was in the center

of the procession, and the crowds all around him were shouting,

"Praise God!*
  Bless the one who comes in the name
    of the Lord!
[10] Bless the coming kingdom of our
    ancestor David!
  Praise God in highest heaven!"*

[11]So Jesus came to Jerusalem and went into the Temple. He looked around carefully at everything, and then he left because it was late in the afternoon. Then he went out to Bethany with the twelve disciples.

[12]The next morning as they were leaving Bethany, Jesus felt hungry. [13]He noticed a fig tree a little way off that was in full leaf, so he went over to see if he could find any figs on it. But there were only leaves because it was too early in the season for fruit. [14]Then Jesus said to the tree, "May no one ever eat your fruit again!" And the disciples heard him say it.

[15]When they arrived back in Jerusalem, Jesus entered the Temple and began to drive out the merchants and their customers. He knocked over the tables of the money changers and the stalls of those selling doves, [16]and he stopped everyone from bringing in merchandise. [17]He taught them, "The Scriptures declare, 'My Temple will be called a place of prayer for all nations,' but you have turned it into a den of thieves."*

[18]When the leading priests and teachers of religious law heard what Jesus had done, they began planning how to kill him. But they were afraid of him because the people were so enthusiastic about Jesus' teaching. [19]That evening Jesus and the disciples* left the city.

[20]The next morning as they passed by the fig tree he had cursed, the disciples noticed it was withered from the roots. [21]Peter remembered what Jesus had said to the tree on the previous day and exclaimed, "Look, Teacher! The fig tree you cursed has withered!"

[22]Then Jesus said to the disciples, "Have faith in God. [23]I assure you that you can say to this mountain, 'May God lift you up and throw you into the sea,' and your command will be obeyed. All that's required is

that you really believe and do not doubt in your heart. [24]Listen to me! You can pray for anything, and if you believe, you will have it. [25]But when you are praying, first forgive anyone you are holding a grudge against, so that your Father in heaven will forgive your sins, too.*"

[27]By this time they had arrived in Jerusalem again. As Jesus was walking through the Temple area, the leading priests, the teachers of religious law, and the other leaders came up to him. They demanded, [28]"By whose authority did you drive out the merchants from the Temple?* Who gave you such authority?"

[29]"I'll tell who gave me authority to do these things if you answer one question," Jesus replied. [30]"Did John's baptism come from heaven or was it merely human? Answer me!"

[31]They talked it over among themselves. "If we say it was from heaven, he will ask why we didn't believe him. [32]But do we dare say it was merely human?" For they were afraid that the people would start a riot, since everyone thought that John was a prophet. [33]So they finally replied, "We don't know."

And Jesus responded, "Then I won't answer your question either."

CHAPTER 12

Then Jesus began telling them stories: "A man planted a vineyard, built a wall around it, dug a pit for pressing out the grape juice, and built a lookout tower. Then he leased the vineyard to tenant farmers and moved to another country. [2]At grape-picking time he sent one of his servants to collect his share of the crop. [3]But the farmers grabbed the servant, beat him up, and sent him back empty-handed.

[4]"The owner then sent another servant, but they beat him over the head and treated him shamefully. [5]The next servant he sent was killed. Others who were sent were either beaten or killed, [6]until there was only one left—his son whom he loved dearly. The owner finally sent him, thinking, 'Surely they will respect my son.'

[7]"But the farmers said to one another, 'Here comes the heir to this estate. Let's kill him and get the estate for ourselves!' [8]So

11:9 Greek *Hosanna*, an exclamation of praise that literally means "save now"; also in 11:10.   **11:9-10** Pss 118:25-26; 148:1.
11:17 Isa 56:7; Jer 7:11.   **11:19** Greek *they;* some manuscripts read *he.*   **11:25** Some manuscripts add verse 26, *But if you do not forgive, neither will your Father who is in heaven forgive your sins.*   **11:28** Or *By whose authority do you do these things?*

they grabbed him and murdered him and threw his body out of the vineyard.

⁹"What do you suppose the owner of the vineyard will do?" Jesus asked. "I'll tell you—he will come and kill them all and lease the vineyard to others. ¹⁰Didn't you ever read this in the Scriptures?

'The stone rejected by the builders
   has now become the cornerstone.
¹¹ This is the Lord's doing,
   and it is marvelous to see.'*"

¹²The Jewish leaders wanted to arrest him for using this illustration because they realized he was pointing at them—they were the wicked farmers in his story. But they were afraid to touch him because of the crowds. So they left him and went away.

¹³The leaders sent some Pharisees and supporters of Herod to try to trap Jesus into saying something for which he could be arrested. ¹⁴"Teacher," these men said, "we know how honest you are. You are impartial and don't play favorites. You sincerely teach the ways of God. Now tell us—is it right to pay taxes to the Roman government or not? ¹⁵Should we pay them, or should we not?"

Jesus saw through their hypocrisy and said, "Whom are you trying to fool with your trick questions? Show me a Roman coin,* and I'll tell you." ¹⁶When they handed it to him, he asked, "Whose picture and title are stamped on it?"

"Caesar's," they replied.

¹⁷"Well, then," Jesus said, "give to Caesar what belongs to him. But everything that belongs to God must be given to God." This reply completely amazed them.

¹⁸Then the Sadducees stepped forward— a group of Jews who say there is no resurrection after death. They posed this question: ¹⁹"Teacher, Moses gave us a law that if a man dies, leaving a wife without children, his brother should marry the widow and have a child who will be the brother's heir.* ²⁰Well, there were seven brothers. The oldest of them married and then died without children. ²¹So the second brother married the widow, but soon he too died and left no children. Then the next brother married her and died without children. ²²This continued until all the brothers had married her and died, and still there were no children. Last of

all, the woman died, too. ²³So tell us, whose wife will she be in the resurrection? For all seven were married to her."

²⁴Jesus replied, "Your problem is that you don't know the Scriptures, and you don't know the power of God. ²⁵For when the dead rise, they won't be married. They will be like the angels in heaven. ²⁶But now, as to whether the dead will be raised— haven't you ever read about this in the writings of Moses, in the story of the burning bush? Long after Abraham, Isaac, and Jacob had died, God said to Moses,* 'I am the God of Abraham, the God of Isaac, and the God of Jacob.'* ²⁷So he is the God of the living, not the dead. You have made a serious error."

²⁸One of the teachers of religious law was standing there listening to the discussion. He realized that Jesus had answered well, so he asked, "Of all the commandments, which is the most important?"

²⁹Jesus replied, "The most important commandment is this: 'Hear, O Israel! The Lord our God is the one and only Lord. ³⁰And you must love the Lord your God with all your heart, all your soul, all your mind, and all your strength.'* ³¹The second is equally important: 'Love your neighbor as yourself.'* No other commandment is greater than these."

³²The teacher of religious law replied, "Well said, Teacher. You have spoken the truth by saying that there is only one God and no other. ³³And I know it is important to love him with all my heart and all my understanding and all my strength, and to love my neighbors as myself. This is more important than to offer all of the burnt offerings and sacrifices required in the law."

³⁴Realizing this man's understanding, Jesus said to him, "You are not far from the Kingdom of God." And after that, no one dared to ask him any more questions.

³⁵Later, as Jesus was teaching the people in the Temple, he asked, "Why do the teachers of religious law claim that the Messiah will be the son of David? ³⁶For David himself, speaking under the inspiration of the Holy Spirit, said,

'The LORD said to my Lord,
Sit in honor at my right hand
   until I humble your enemies beneath
     your feet.'*

12:10-11 Ps 118:22-23.   **12:15** Greek *a denarius.*   **12:19** Deut 25:5-6.   **12:26a** Greek *in the story of the bush? God said to him.*
12:26b Exod 3:6.   **12:29-30** Deut 6:4-5.   **12:31** Lev 19:18.   **12:36** Ps 110:1.

³⁷Since David himself called him Lord, how can he be his son at the same time?" And the crowd listened to him with great interest.

³⁸Here are some of the other things he taught them at this time: "Beware of these teachers of religious law! For they love to parade in flowing robes and to have everyone bow to them as they walk in the marketplaces. ³⁹And how they love the seats of honor in the synagogues and at banquets. ⁴⁰But they shamelessly cheat widows out of their property, and then, to cover up the kind of people they really are, they make long prayers in public. Because of this, their punishment will be the greater."

⁴¹Jesus went over to the collection box in the Temple and sat and watched as the crowds dropped in their money. Many rich people put in large amounts. ⁴²Then a poor widow came and dropped in two pennies.* ⁴³He called his disciples to him and said, "I assure you, this poor widow has given more than all the others have given. ⁴⁴For they gave a tiny part of their surplus, but she, poor as she is, has given everything she has."

CHAPTER 13

As Jesus was leaving the Temple that day, one of his disciples said, "Teacher, look at these tremendous buildings! Look at the massive stones in the walls!"

²Jesus replied, "These magnificent buildings will be so completely demolished that not one stone will be left on top of another."

³Later, Jesus sat on the slopes of the Mount of Olives across the valley from the Temple. Peter, James, John, and Andrew came to him privately and asked him, ⁴"When will all this take place? And will there be any sign ahead of time to show us when all this will be fulfilled?"

⁵Jesus replied, "Don't let anyone mislead you, ⁶because many will come in my name, claiming to be the Messiah.* They will lead many astray. ⁷And wars will break out near and far, but don't panic. Yes, these things must come, but the end won't follow immediately. ⁸Nations and kingdoms will proclaim war against each other, and there will be earthquakes in many parts of the world, and famines. But all this will be only the beginning of the horrors to come. ⁹But

when these things begin to happen, watch out! You will be handed over to the courts and beaten in the synagogues. You will be accused before governors and kings of being my followers. This will be your opportunity to tell them about me.* ¹⁰And the Good News must first be preached to every nation. ¹¹But when you are arrested and stand trial, don't worry about what to say in your defense. Just say what God tells you to. Then it is not you who will be speaking, but the Holy Spirit.

¹²"Brother will betray brother to death, fathers will betray their own children, and children will rise against their parents and cause them to be killed. ¹³And everyone will hate you because of your allegiance to me. But those who endure to the end will be saved.

¹⁴"The time will come when you will see the sacrilegious object that causes desecration* standing where it should not be"—reader, pay attention! "Then those in Judea must flee to the hills. ¹⁵A person outside the house* must not go back into the house to pack. ¹⁶A person in the field must not return even to get a coat. ¹⁷How terrible it will be for pregnant women and for mothers nursing their babies in those days. ¹⁸And pray that your flight will not be in winter. ¹⁹For those will be days of greater horror than at any time since God created the world. And it will never happen again. ²⁰In fact, unless the Lord shortens that time of calamity, the entire human race will be destroyed. But for the sake of his chosen ones he has shortened those days.

²¹"And then if anyone tells you, 'Look, here is the Messiah,' or, 'There he is,' don't pay any attention. ²²For false messiahs and false prophets will rise up and perform miraculous signs and wonders so as to deceive, if possible, even God's chosen ones. ²³Watch out! I have warned you!

²⁴"At that time, after those horrible days end,

the sun will be darkened,
　the moon will not give light,
²⁵ the stars will fall from the sky,
　and the powers of heaven will be
　　shaken.*

²⁶Then everyone will see the Son of Man arrive on the clouds with great power and

12:42 Greek *2 lepta, which is a kodrantes.* **13:6** Greek *name, saying, 'I am.'* **13:9** Or *This will be your testimony against them.* **13:14** Greek *the abomination of desolation.* See Dan 9:27; 11:31; 12:11. **13:15** Greek *on the roof.* **13:24-25** See Isa 13:10; 34:4; Joel 2:10.

glory.* [27]And he will send forth his angels to gather together his chosen ones from all over the world—from the farthest ends of the earth and heaven.

[28]"Now, learn a lesson from the fig tree. When its buds become tender and its leaves begin to sprout, you know without being told that summer is near. [29]Just so, when you see the events I've described beginning to happen, you can be sure that his return is very near, right at the door. [30]I assure you, this generation* will not pass from the scene until all these events have taken place. [31]Heaven and earth will disappear, but my words will remain forever.

[32]"However, no one knows the day or hour when these things will happen, not even the angels in heaven or the Son himself. Only the Father knows. [33]And since you don't know when they will happen, stay alert and keep watch.*

[34]"The coming of the Son of Man can be compared with that of a man who left home to go on a trip. He gave each of his employees instructions about the work they were to do, and he told the gatekeeper to watch for his return. [35]So keep a sharp lookout! For you do not know when the homeowner will return—at evening, midnight, early dawn, or late daybreak. [36]Don't let him find you sleeping when he arrives without warning. [37]What I say to you I say to everyone: Watch for his return!"

13:26 See Dan 7:13.   13:30 Or *this age*, or *this nation*.   13:33 Some manuscripts add *and pray*.

OCTOBER 14 ☐ DAY 288
Committed to the Task

 LOOK BACK The final week of Jesus' life is so important, fully 40 percent of the verses in the four Gospel accounts focus on the "week that changed the world." This past week you have read Matthew's account, and tomorrow you will read Mark's (and in the next three weeks you'll come to Luke's and John's). Notice which elements are repeated, which are omitted, and which are elaborated upon by the different Gospel writers. In each case, the author's intent is not to confuse you but to convince you that Jesus is indeed
  • the King of the Jews (Matthew)
  • the Selfless Servant (Mark)
  • the Son of Man (Luke)
  • the Son of God (John)
As you see the final days of Jesus' life through the eyes of a tax collector (Matthew), a missionary (Mark), a physician (Luke), and a fisherman (John), don't be surprised if your vision is sharpened to see his purpose in coming and his purpose for leaving you here on earth until his return.

 LOOK UP *Last* words have a tendency to be *lasting* words. And the final utterances of Jesus are no different.

Those on the road to heaven will not be content to go there alone.

The *Great Commission* is the name given to the final marching orders Jesus delivered to his disciples just before his death. You'll find the Great Commission in each of the four Gospel accounts and (for good measure) in the book of Acts. Take a few moments to look up each of the following verses, and write down in your own words what Jesus told his disciples to do while he was away preparing an eternal home for them:

  • Matthew 28:19-20 _____
_____

  • Mark 16:15 _____
_____

• Luke 24:47 ———————————————————
—————————————————————————
• John 20:21 ——————————————————
—————————————————————————
• Acts 1:8 ——————————————————
—————————————————————————

 LOOK AHEAD Coca-Cola . . . General Motors . . . IBM . . . Why is it that a cola or car or computer can become a household word in places most people can hardly find on a map, while the good news of Jesus Christ remains a mystery to millions nearly twenty centuries after the news first broke?

Is it because their "product" has a better name than ours? Not likely. After all, we're introducing people to the one whose name is so majestic that it fills the earth (Psalm 8:1).

Is it because their "product" is better for you than ours? Hardly. We have the privilege of introducing people to the bread of life and the living water.

Is it because their budget is bigger than ours? Maybe. And yet, more than $2 billion is invested in world missions every year.

Or is it perhaps because they are simply more committed to *their* commission than we as Christians are committed to *ours?* It's well worth pondering and praying over.

OCTOBER 15 □ DAY 289
MARK 14–16
Suffering of the Servant

 OVERVIEW While the devout Jews prepare for a feast, the chief priests prepare for an execution. The target of their conspiracy: Jesus of Nazareth, the Passover lamb of God. Judas's treachery and Jesus' last supper with his disciples set the stage for his arrest, trial, denial, flogging, crucifixion, burial, and resurrection. But the story is not finished, for now his disciples are commissioned to bear the glad tidings worldwide—"the Lord worked with them" (16:20)—servants in partnership with the Master Servant.

Chapter 14		Chapter 15	Chapter 16	
Servant's Anointing	Servant's Arrest	Servant's Abuse	Servant's Arising	Servant's Appearing
1 9	10 72	1	8	9 20
Preparation		Crucifixion	Resurrection	

 YOUR DAILY WALK What if . . . ? Pretend for a moment that the book of Mark ended at 15:37, rather than 16:20. Would that change the way you face life today?

Jesus Christ changed sunset into sunrise.

The apostle Paul wrote an entire chapter probing the question "What if Jesus had died . . . and that was all?" See if you agree with his conclusions (1 Corinthians 15:12-19):

• Faith in Christ would be useless (v. 14).
• Christians would be liars (v. 15).

• Christians would still be condemned for their sins (v. 17).
• Deceased Christians would be hopelessly lost (v. 18).
• Christians would be the most miserable people alive (v. 19).
Now read Paul's triumphant declaration in verse 20 (the same message Mark declares in 15:38–16:20). The heart of Christianity is Christ's resurrection. In the margin jot down three life-changing implications of that truth from 1 Corinthians 15:20-28. The message of Easter is not "what if . . . ?" but "because he lives!"

INSIGHT A Passover Population Bulge
Why did the chief priests want to wait till after the Passover to apprehend Jesus? Perhaps because Jerusalem's population skyrocketed from about fifty thousand to several hundred thousand each year during the Passover and the Festival of Unleavened Bread. With pilgrims from different districts and tribes mixing with Jews who had traveled in from other regions, any disturbances could have caused a large-scale riot.

CHAPTER 14
It was now two days before the Passover celebration and the Festival of Unleavened Bread. The leading priests and the teachers of religious law were still looking for an opportunity to capture Jesus secretly and put him to death. 2"But not during the Passover," they agreed, "or there will be a riot."

3Meanwhile, Jesus was in Bethany at the home of Simon, a man who had leprosy. During supper, a woman came in with a beautiful jar of expensive perfume.* She broke the seal and poured the perfume over his head. 4Some of those at the table were indignant. "Why was this expensive perfume wasted?" they asked. 5"She could have sold it for a small fortune* and given the money to the poor!" And they scolded her harshly.

6But Jesus replied, "Leave her alone. Why berate her for doing such a good thing to me? 7You will always have the poor among you, and you can help them whenever you want to. But I will not be here with you much longer. 8She has done what she could and has anointed my body for burial ahead of time. 9I assure you, wherever the Good News is preached throughout the world, this woman's deed will be talked about in her memory."

10Then Judas Iscariot, one of the twelve disciples, went to the leading priests to arrange to betray Jesus to them. 11The leading priests were delighted when they heard why he had come, and they promised him a reward. So he began looking for the right time and place to betray Jesus.

12On the first day of the Festival of Unleavened Bread (the day the Passover lambs were sacrificed), Jesus' disciples asked him, "Where do you want us to go to prepare the Passover supper?"

13So Jesus sent two of them into Jerusalem to make the arrangements. "As you go into the city," he told them, "a man carrying a pitcher of water will meet you. Follow him. 14At the house he enters, say to the owner, 'The Teacher asks, Where is the guest room where I can eat the Passover meal with my disciples?' 15He will take you upstairs to a large room that is already set up. That is the place; go ahead and prepare our supper there." 16So the two disciples went on ahead into the city and found everything just as Jesus had said, and they prepared the Passover supper there.

17In the evening Jesus arrived with the twelve disciples. 18As they were sitting around the table eating, Jesus said, "The truth is, one of you will betray me, one of you who is here eating with me."

19Greatly distressed, one by one they began to ask him, "I'm not the one, am I?"

20He replied, "It is one of you twelve, one who is eating with me now.* 21For I, the Son of Man, must die, as the Scriptures declared long ago. But how terrible it will be for my betrayer. Far better for him if he had never been born!"

22As they were eating, Jesus took a loaf of bread and asked God's blessing on it. Then he broke it in pieces and gave it to the disciples, saying, "Take it, for this is my body."

23And he took a cup of wine and gave

14:3 Greek *an alabaster jar of expensive ointment, pure nard.*   14:5 Greek *300 denarii.* A denarius was the equivalent of a full day's wage.   14:20 Or *one who is dipping bread into the bowl with me.*

thanks to God for it. He gave it to them, and they all drank from it. ²⁴And he said to them, "This is my blood, poured out for many, sealing the covenant* between God and his people. ²⁵I solemnly declare that I will not drink wine again until that day when I drink it new in the Kingdom of God." ²⁶Then they sang a hymn and went out to the Mount of Olives.

²⁷"All of you will desert me," Jesus told them. "For the Scriptures say,

'God* will strike the Shepherd,
   and the sheep will be scattered.'*

²⁸But after I am raised from the dead, I will go ahead of you to Galilee and meet you there."

²⁹Peter said to him, "Even if everyone else deserts you, I never will."

³⁰"Peter," Jesus replied, "the truth is, this very night, before the rooster crows twice, you will deny me three times."

³¹"No!" Peter insisted. "Not even if I have to die with you! I will never deny you!" And all the others vowed the same.

³²And they came to an olive grove called Gethsemane, and Jesus said, "Sit here while I go and pray." ³³He took Peter, James, and John with him, and he began to be filled with horror and deep distress. ³⁴He told them, "My soul is crushed with grief to the point of death. Stay here and watch with me."

³⁵He went on a little farther and fell face down on the ground. He prayed that, if it were possible, the awful hour awaiting him might pass him by. ³⁶"Abba,* Father," he said, "everything is possible for you. Please take this cup of suffering away from me. Yet I want your will, not mine."

³⁷Then he returned and found the disciples asleep. "Simon!" he said to Peter. "Are you asleep? Couldn't you stay awake and watch with me even one hour? ³⁸Keep alert and pray. Otherwise temptation will overpower you. For though the spirit is willing enough, the body is weak."

³⁹Then Jesus left them again and prayed, repeating his pleadings. ⁴⁰Again he returned to them and found them sleeping, for they just couldn't keep their eyes open. And they didn't know what to say.

⁴¹When he returned to them the third time, he said, "Still sleeping? Still resting?* Enough! The time has come. I, the Son of Man, am betrayed into the hands of sinners. ⁴²Up, let's be going. See, my betrayer is here!"

⁴³And immediately, as he said this, Judas, one of the twelve disciples, arrived with a mob that was armed with swords and clubs. They had been sent out by the leading priests, the teachers of religious law, and the other leaders. ⁴⁴Judas had given them a prearranged signal: "You will know which one to arrest when I go over and give him the kiss of greeting. Then you can take him away under guard."

⁴⁵As soon as they arrived, Judas walked up to Jesus. "Teacher!" he exclaimed, and gave him the kiss. ⁴⁶Then the others grabbed Jesus and arrested him. ⁴⁷But someone pulled out a sword and slashed off an ear of the high priest's servant.

⁴⁸Jesus asked them, "Am I some dangerous criminal, that you come armed with swords and clubs to arrest me? ⁴⁹Why didn't you arrest me in the Temple? I was there teaching every day. But these things are happening to fulfill what the Scriptures say about me."

⁵⁰Meanwhile, all his disciples deserted him and ran away. ⁵¹There was a young man following along behind, clothed only in a linen nightshirt. When the mob tried to grab him, ⁵²they tore off his clothes, but he escaped and ran away naked.

⁵³Jesus was led to the high priest's home where the leading priests, other leaders, and teachers of religious law had gathered. ⁵⁴Meanwhile, Peter followed far behind and then slipped inside the gates of the high priest's courtyard. For a while he sat with the guards, warming himself by the fire.

⁵⁵Inside, the leading priests and the entire high council* were trying to find witnesses who would testify against Jesus, so they could put him to death. But their efforts were in vain. ⁵⁶Many false witnesses spoke against him, but they contradicted each other. ⁵⁷Finally, some men stood up to testify against him with this lie: ⁵⁸"We heard him say, 'I will destroy this Temple made with human hands, and in three days I will build another, made without human hands.'" ⁵⁹But even then they didn't get their stories straight!

⁶⁰Then the high priest stood up before the others and asked Jesus, "Well, aren't

---

14:24 Some manuscripts read *the new covenant.*   **14:27a** Greek *I.*   **14:27b** Zech 13:7.   **14:36** *Abba* is an Aramaic term for "father."
14:41 Or *Sleep on, take your rest.*   **14:55** Greek *the Sanhedrin.*

you going to answer these charges? What do you have to say for yourself?" [61]Jesus made no reply. Then the high priest asked him, "Are you the Messiah, the Son of the blessed God?"

[62]Jesus said, "I am, and you will see me, the Son of Man, sitting at God's right hand in the place of power and coming back on the clouds of heaven."*

[63]Then the high priest tore his clothing to show his horror and said, "Why do we need other witnesses? [64]You have all heard his blasphemy. What is your verdict?" And they all condemned him to death.

[65]Then some of them began to spit at him, and they blindfolded him and hit his face with their fists. "Who hit you that time, you prophet?" they jeered. And even the guards were hitting him as they led him away.

[66]Meanwhile, Peter was below in the courtyard. One of the servant girls who worked for the high priest [67]noticed Peter warming himself at the fire. She looked at him closely and then said, "You were one of those with Jesus, the Nazarene."

[68]Peter denied it. "I don't know what you're talking about," he said, and he went out into the entryway. Just then, a rooster crowed.*

[69]The servant girl saw him standing there and began telling the others, "That man is definitely one of them!" [70]Peter denied it again.

A little later some other bystanders began saying to Peter, "You must be one of them because you are from Galilee."

[71]Peter said, "I swear by God, I don't know this man you're talking about."
[72]And immediately the rooster crowed the second time. Suddenly, Jesus' words flashed through Peter's mind: "Before the rooster crows twice, you will deny me three times." And he broke down and cried.

CHAPTER 15
Very early in the morning the leading priests, other leaders, and teachers of religious law—the entire high council*—met to discuss their next step. They bound Jesus and took him to Pilate, the Roman governor.

[2]Pilate asked Jesus, "Are you the King of the Jews?"

Jesus replied, "Yes, it is as you say."

[3]Then the leading priests accused him of many crimes, [4]and Pilate asked him, "Aren't you going to say something? What about all these charges against you?" [5]But Jesus said nothing, much to Pilate's surprise.

[6]Now it was the governor's custom to release one prisoner each year at Passover time—anyone the people requested. [7]One of the prisoners at that time was Barabbas, convicted along with others for murder during an insurrection. [8]The mob began to crowd in toward Pilate, asking him to release a prisoner as usual. [9]"Should I give you the King of the Jews?" Pilate asked. [10](For he realized by now that the leading priests had arrested Jesus out of envy.) [11]But at this point the leading priests stirred up the mob to demand the release of Barabbas instead of Jesus.

[12]"But if I release Barabbas," Pilate asked them, "what should I do with this man you call the King of the Jews?"

[13]They shouted back, "Crucify him!"

[14]"Why?" Pilate demanded. "What crime has he committed?"

But the crowd only roared the louder, "Crucify him!"

[15]So Pilate, anxious to please the crowd, released Barabbas to them. He ordered Jesus flogged with a lead-tipped whip, then turned him over to the Roman soldiers to crucify him.

[16]The soldiers took him into their headquarters* and called out the entire battalion. [17]They dressed him in a purple robe and made a crown of long, sharp thorns and put it on his head. [18]Then they saluted, yelling, "Hail! King of the Jews!" [19]And they beat him on the head with a stick, spit on him, and dropped to their knees in mock worship. [20]When they were finally tired of mocking him, they took off the purple robe and put his own clothes on him again. Then they led him away to be crucified.

[21]A man named Simon, who was from Cyrene,* was coming in from the country just then, and they forced him to carry Jesus' cross. (Simon is the father of Alexander and Rufus.) [22]And they brought Jesus to a place called Golgotha (which means Skull Hill). [23]They offered him wine drugged with myrrh, but he refused

14:62 See Ps 110:1; Dan 7:13.   **14:68** Some manuscripts do not include *Just then, a rooster crowed.*   **15:1** Greek *the Sanhedrin;* also in 15:43.   **15:16** Greek *the courtyard, which is the praetorium.*   **15:21** *Cyrene* was a city in northern Africa.

it. ²⁴Then they nailed him to the cross. They gambled for his clothes, throwing dice* to decide who would get them.

²⁵It was nine o'clock in the morning when the crucifixion took place. ²⁶A signboard was fastened to the cross above Jesus' head, announcing the charge against him. It read: "The King of the Jews." ²⁷Two criminals were crucified with him, their crosses on either side of his.* ²⁹And the people passing by shouted abuse, shaking their heads in mockery. "Ha! Look at you now!" they yelled at him. "You can destroy the Temple and rebuild it in three days, can you? ³⁰Well then, save yourself and come down from the cross!"

³¹The leading priests and teachers of religious law also mocked Jesus. "He saved others," they scoffed, "but he can't save himself! ³²Let this Messiah, this king of Israel, come down from the cross so we can see it and believe him!" Even the two criminals who were being crucified with Jesus ridiculed him.

³³At noon, darkness fell across the whole land until three o'clock. ³⁴Then, at that time Jesus called out with a loud voice, "*Eloi, Eloi, lema sabachthani?*" which means, "My God, my God, why have you forsaken me?"*

³⁵Some of the bystanders misunderstood and thought he was calling for the prophet Elijah. ³⁶One of them ran and filled a sponge with sour wine, holding it up to him on a stick so he could drink. "Leave him alone. Let's see whether Elijah will come and take him down!" he said.

³⁷Then Jesus uttered another loud cry and breathed his last. ³⁸And the curtain in the Temple was torn in two, from top to bottom. ³⁹When the Roman officer who stood facing him saw how he had died, he exclaimed, "Truly, this was the Son of God!"

⁴⁰Some women were there, watching from a distance, including Mary Magdalene, Mary (the mother of James the younger and of Joseph*), and Salome. ⁴¹They had been followers of Jesus and had cared for him while he was in Galilee. Then they and many other women had come with him to Jerusalem.

⁴²This all happened on Friday, the day

of preparation,* the day before the Sabbath. As evening approached, ⁴³an honored member of the high council, Joseph from Arimathea (who was waiting for the Kingdom of God to come), gathered his courage and went to Pilate to ask for Jesus' body. ⁴⁴Pilate couldn't believe that Jesus was already dead, so he called for the Roman military officer in charge and asked him. ⁴⁵The officer confirmed the fact, and Pilate told Joseph he could have the body. ⁴⁶Joseph bought a long sheet of linen cloth, and taking Jesus' body down from the cross, he wrapped it in the cloth and laid it in a tomb that had been carved out of the rock. Then he rolled a stone in front of the entrance. ⁴⁷Mary Magdalene and Mary the mother of Joseph saw where Jesus' body was laid.

CHAPTER 16

The next evening, when the Sabbath ended, Mary Magdalene and Salome and Mary the mother of James went out and purchased burial spices to put on Jesus' body. ²Very early on Sunday morning,* just at sunrise, they came to the tomb. ³On the way they were discussing who would roll the stone away from the entrance to the tomb. ⁴But when they arrived, they looked up and saw that the stone—a very large one—had already been rolled aside. ⁵So they entered the tomb, and there on the right sat a young man clothed in a white robe. The women were startled, ⁶but the angel said, "Do not be so surprised. You are looking for Jesus, the Nazarene, who was crucified. He isn't here! He has been raised from the dead! Look, this is where they laid his body. ⁷Now go and give this message to his disciples, including Peter: Jesus is going ahead of you to Galilee. You will see him there, just as he told you before he died!" ⁸The women fled from the tomb, trembling and bewildered, saying nothing to anyone because they were too frightened to talk.*

[Shorter Ending of Mark]

Then they reported all these instructions briefly to Peter and his companions. Afterward Jesus himself sent them out

15:24 Greek *casting lots*. See Ps 22:18.   15:27 Some manuscripts add verse 28, *And the Scripture was fulfilled that said, "He was counted among those who were rebels."* See Isa 53:12.   15:34 Ps 22:1.   15:40 Greek *Joses*; also in 15:47. See Matt 27:56.   15:42 Greek *on the day of preparation*.   16:2 Greek *on the first day of the week*; also in 16:9.   16:8 The most reliable early manuscripts conclude the Gospel of Mark at verse 8. Other manuscripts include various endings to the Gospel. Two of the more noteworthy endings are printed here.

from east to west with the sacred and unfailing message of salvation that gives eternal life. Amen.

[*Longer Ending of Mark*]

[9]It was early on Sunday morning when Jesus rose from the dead, and the first person who saw him was Mary Magdalene, the woman from whom he had cast out seven demons. [10]She went and found the disciples, who were grieving and weeping. [11]But when she told them that Jesus was alive and she had seen him, they didn't believe her.

[12]Afterward he appeared to two who were walking from Jerusalem into the country, but they didn't recognize him at first because he had changed his appearance. [13]When they realized who he was, they rushed back to tell the others, but no one believed them.

[14]Still later he appeared to the eleven disciples as they were eating together. He rebuked them for their unbelief—their stubborn refusal to believe those who had seen him after he had risen.

[15]And then he told them, "Go into all the world and preach the Good News to everyone, everywhere. [16]Anyone who believes and is baptized will be saved. But anyone who refuses to believe will be condemned. [17]These signs will accompany those who believe: They will cast out demons in my name, and they will speak new languages.* [18]They will be able to handle snakes with safety, and if they drink anything poisonous, it won't hurt them. They will be able to place their hands on the sick and heal them."

[19]When the Lord Jesus had finished talking with them, he was taken up into heaven and sat down in the place of honor at God's right hand. [20]And the disciples went everywhere and preached, and the Lord worked with them, confirming what they said by many miraculous signs.

16:17 Or *new tongues.* Some manuscripts omit *new.*

Luke

LUKE, a Greek physician and missionary companion of the apostle Paul, intends his Gospel—along with the book of Acts—to be a primer for a new Christian named Theophilus. Luke stresses the humanity of Jesus as the one who understands people's weaknesses and cares for their needs. Luke's interest in historical accuracy leads him under divine inspiration to research and record the details of Jesus' life, including his family tree, social contacts, and inner life of prayer and compassion.

Focus	Presentation		Exhortation						Resur-rection
Divisions	Advent of the Son of Man	Authority of the Son of Man	Activities of the Son of Man	Antagonism toward the Son of Man	Parables of the Son of Man (Part 1)	Parables of the Son of Man (Part 2)	Praise for the Son of Man	Passion of the Son of Man	
	1 2	3 6	7 9	10 12	13 15	16 18	19 21	22 24	
Topics	Miracles Prominent			Parables Prominent					
	Early Years		Earthly Ministry						Last Days
Place	Judea		Samaria and Perea						Jerusalem
Time	5 B.C–A.D. 33								

OCTOBER 16 ☐ DAY 290
LUKE 1–2
Advent of the Son of Man

OVERVIEW A careful historian, Luke seeks to relate the story of Christ's life in chronological order. He begins with the angelic announcements of two miraculous births: John the forerunner, who would prepare the way for Messiah, and Jesus the Christ, who would be born of a virgin. The arrival of the Christ child is described in meticulous detail, as you would expect from a physician. Angelic hosts and humble shepherds proclaim his arrival. The law is fulfilled in the infant Jesus' circumcision. Simeon and Anna, representatives of Israel's godly remnant, proclaim his identity. The silent years of growth in Nazareth are broken only by the incident in the Temple at age twelve, an event that foreshadows the ministry of the Perfect Man.

	Chapter 1			Chapter 2
A Son for a Priest		A Son for a Virgin		A Prophet Named John		A Savior Named Jesus
1 25	26 56	57 80	
Angelic Announcements		Miraculous Births	

YOUR DAILY WALK How abandoned are you to the will of God? How much of your life is available for God to direct—or redirect? Have you given him your finances? . . . your dating life? . . . your career plans? . . . your family?

When you pray, make sure your will is in neutral so God can shift it.

Consider the case of a young Jewish maiden named Mary. God-fearing, virtuous, engaged, and no doubt full of cherished dreams for the future, Mary was confronted by the angel Gabriel who announced she was God's choice to conceive and bear the Messiah. What must have gone through her mind at that point? *Who will believe I have conceived as a virgin? How will Joseph react to the news? What will happen to our wedding plans? What will my parents and friends think?* In spite of her questions, Mary's response was faith inspired. "I am the Lord's servant . . . May everything you have said come true" (1:38).

God will never ask of you what he did of Mary, but he desires the same attitude from you: abandonment . . . availability . . . allegiance. Now go back and reread the questions in the first paragraph.

INSIGHT Know Your Angels by Name
Three angels are named in the Bible: Gabriel, the revealing angel (Daniel 8:16; 9:21; Luke 1:19, 26); Lucifer, the fallen angel (Isaiah 14:12); and Michael, the archangel (Daniel 10:13, 21; 12:1; Jude 9; Revelation 12:7).

CHAPTER 1
Most honorable Theophilus:
Many people have written accounts about the events that took place* among us. ²They used as their source material the re-

ports circulating among us from the early disciples and other eyewitnesses of what God has done in fulfillment of his promises. ³Having carefully investigated all of these accounts from the beginning, I have

1:1 Or *have been fulfilled.*

decided to write a careful summary for you, [4]to reassure you of the truth of all you were taught.

[5]It all begins with a Jewish priest, Zechariah, who lived when Herod was king of Judea. Zechariah was a member of the priestly order of Abijah. His wife, Elizabeth, was also from the priestly line of Aaron. [6]Zechariah and Elizabeth were righteous in God's eyes, careful to obey all of the Lord's commandments and regulations. [7]They had no children because Elizabeth was barren, and now they were both very old.

[8]One day Zechariah was serving God in the Temple, for his order was on duty that week. [9]As was the custom of the priests, he was chosen by lot to enter the sanctuary and burn incense in the Lord's presence. [10]While the incense was being burned, a great crowd stood outside, praying.

[11]Zechariah was in the sanctuary when an angel of the Lord appeared, standing to the right of the incense altar. [12]Zechariah was overwhelmed with fear. [13]But the angel said, "Don't be afraid, Zechariah! For God has heard your prayer, and your wife, Elizabeth, will bear you a son! And you are to name him John. [14]You will have great joy and gladness, and many will rejoice with you at his birth, [15]for he will be great in the eyes of the Lord. He must never touch wine or hard liquor, and he will be filled with the Holy Spirit, even before his birth.* [16]And he will persuade many Israelites to turn to the Lord their God. [17]He will be a man with the spirit and power of Elijah, the prophet of old. He will precede the coming of the Lord, preparing the people for his arrival. He will turn the hearts of the fathers to their children, and he will change disobedient minds to accept godly wisdom."*

[18]Zechariah said to the angel, "How can I know this will happen? I'm an old man now, and my wife is also well along in years."

[19]Then the angel said, "I am Gabriel! I stand in the very presence of God. It was he who sent me to bring you this good news! [20]And now, since you didn't believe what I said, you won't be able to speak until the child is born. For my words will certainly come true at the proper time."

[21]Meanwhile, the people were waiting for Zechariah to come out, wondering why he was taking so long. [22]When he finally did come out, he couldn't speak to them. Then they realized from his gestures that he must have seen a vision in the Temple sanctuary.

[23]He stayed at the Temple until his term of service was over, and then he returned home. [24]Soon afterward his wife, Elizabeth, became pregnant and went into seclusion for five months. [25]"How kind the Lord is!" she exclaimed. "He has taken away my disgrace of having no children!"

[26]In the sixth month of Elizabeth's pregnancy, God sent the angel Gabriel to Nazareth, a village in Galilee, [27]to a virgin named Mary. She was engaged to be married to a man named Joseph, a descendant of King David. [28]Gabriel appeared to her and said, "Greetings, favored woman! The Lord is with you!*"

[29]Confused and disturbed, Mary tried to think what the angel could mean. [30]"Don't be frightened, Mary," the angel told her, "for God has decided to bless you! [31]You will become pregnant and have a son, and you are to name him Jesus. [32]He will be very great and will be called the Son of the Most High. And the Lord God will give him the throne of his ancestor David. [33]And he will reign over Israel* forever; his Kingdom will never end!"

[34]Mary asked the angel, "But how can I have a baby? I am a virgin."

[35]The angel replied, "The Holy Spirit will come upon you, and the power of the Most High will overshadow you. So the baby born to you will be holy, and he will be called the Son of God. [36]What's more, your relative Elizabeth has become pregnant in her old age! People used to say she was barren, but she's already in her sixth month. [37]For nothing is impossible with God."

[38]Mary responded, "I am the Lord's servant, and I am willing to accept whatever he wants. May everything you have said come true." And then the angel left.

[39]A few days later Mary hurried to the hill country of Judea, to the town [40]where Zechariah lived. She entered the house and greeted Elizabeth. [41]At the sound of Mary's greeting, Elizabeth's child leaped within her, and Elizabeth was filled with the Holy Spirit.

1:15 Or *even from birth.*   **1:17** See Mal 4:5-6.   **1:28** Some manuscripts add *Blessed are you among women.*   **1:33** Greek *over the house of Jacob.*

[42] Elizabeth gave a glad cry and exclaimed to Mary, "You are blessed by God above all other women, and your child is blessed. [43] What an honor this is, that the mother of my Lord should visit me! [44] When you came in and greeted me, my baby jumped for joy the instant I heard your voice! [45] You are blessed, because you believed that the Lord would do what he said."

[46] Mary responded,

"Oh, how I praise the Lord.
[47]   How I rejoice in God my Savior!
[48] For he took notice of his lowly servant
        girl,
        and now generation after generation
            will call me blessed.
[49] For he, the Mighty One, is holy,
        and he has done great things for me.
[50] His mercy goes on from generation to
        generation,
        to all who fear him.
[51] His mighty arm does tremendous
        things!
    How he scatters the proud and
        haughty ones!
[52] He has taken princes from their thrones
        and exalted the lowly.
[53] He has satisfied the hungry with good
        things
        and sent the rich away with empty
            hands.
[54] And how he has helped his servant
        Israel!
    He has not forgotten his promise
        to be merciful.
[55] For he promised our
        ancestors—Abraham and his
        children—
        to be merciful to them forever."

[56] Mary stayed with Elizabeth about three months and then went back to her own home.

[57] Now it was time for Elizabeth's baby to be born, and it was a boy. [58] The word spread quickly to her neighbors and relatives that the Lord had been very kind to her, and everyone rejoiced with her.

[59] When the baby was eight days old, all the relatives and friends came for the circumcision ceremony. They wanted to name him Zechariah, after his father. [60] But Elizabeth said, "No! His name is John!"

[61] "What?" they exclaimed. "There is no one in all your family by that name." [62] So they asked the baby's father, communicat-

ing to him by making gestures. [63] He motioned for a writing tablet, and to everyone's surprise he wrote, "His name is John!" [64] Instantly Zechariah could speak again, and he began praising God.

[65] Wonder fell upon the whole neighborhood, and the news of what had happened spread throughout the Judean hills. [66] Everyone who heard about it reflected on these events and asked, "I wonder what this child will turn out to be? For the hand of the Lord is surely upon him in a special way."

[67] Then his father, Zechariah, was filled with the Holy Spirit and gave this prophecy:

[68] "Praise the Lord, the God of Israel,
        because he has visited his people
            and redeemed them.
[69] He has sent us a mighty Savior
        from the royal line of his servant
            David,
[70] just as he promised
        through his holy prophets long ago.
[71] Now we will be saved from our
        enemies
        and from all who hate us.
[72] He has been merciful to our ancestors
        by remembering his sacred covenant
            with them,
[73]   the covenant he gave to our ancestor
            Abraham.
[74] We have been rescued from our
        enemies,
        so we can serve God without fear,
[75]   in holiness and righteousness forever.
[76] "And you, my little son,
        will be called the prophet of the
            Most High,
        because you will prepare the way
            for the Lord.
[77] You will tell his people how to find
        salvation
        through forgiveness of their sins.
[78] Because of God's tender mercy,
        the light from heaven is about to
            break upon us,
[79] to give light to those who sit in
        darkness and in the shadow of
            death,
        and to guide us to the path of peace."

[80] John grew up and became strong in spirit. Then he lived out in the wilderness until he began his public ministry to Israel.

CHAPTER 2

At that time the Roman emperor, Augustus, decreed that a census should be taken throughout the Roman Empire. ²(This was the first census taken when Quirinius was governor of Syria.) ³All returned to their own towns to register for this census. ⁴And because Joseph was a descendant of King David, he had to go to Bethlehem in Judea, David's ancient home. He traveled there from the village of Nazareth in Galilee. ⁵He took with him Mary, his fiancée, who was obviously pregnant by this time.

⁶And while they were there, the time came for her baby to be born. ⁷She gave birth to her first child, a son. She wrapped him snugly in strips of cloth and laid him in a manger, because there was no room for them in the village inn.

⁸That night some shepherds were in the fields outside the village, guarding their flocks of sheep. ⁹Suddenly, an angel of the Lord appeared among them, and the radiance of the Lord's glory surrounded them. They were terribly frightened, ¹⁰but the angel reassured them. "Don't be afraid!" he said. "I bring you good news of great joy for everyone! ¹¹The Savior—yes, the Messiah, the Lord—has been born tonight in Bethlehem, the city of David! ¹²And this is how you will recognize him: You will find a baby lying in a manger, wrapped snugly in strips of cloth!"

¹³Suddenly, the angel was joined by a vast host of others—the armies of heaven—praising God:

¹⁴ "Glory to God in the highest heaven,
    and peace on earth to all whom God
        favors.*"

¹⁵When the angels had returned to heaven, the shepherds said to each other, "Come on, let's go to Bethlehem! Let's see this wonderful thing that has happened, which the Lord has told us about."

¹⁶They ran to the village and found Mary and Joseph. And there was the baby, lying in the manger. ¹⁷Then the shepherds told everyone what had happened and what the angel had said to them about this child. ¹⁸All who heard the shepherds' story were astonished, ¹⁹but Mary quietly treasured these things in her heart and thought about them often. ²⁰The shepherds went back to their fields and flocks, glorifying and praising God for what the angels had told them, and because they had seen the child, just as the angel had said.

²¹Eight days later, when the baby was circumcised, he was named Jesus, the name given him by the angel even before he was conceived.

²²Then it was time for the purification offering, as required by the law of Moses after the birth of a child; so his parents took him to Jerusalem to present him to the Lord. ²³The law of the Lord says, "If a woman's first child is a boy, he must be dedicated to the Lord."* ²⁴So they offered a sacrifice according to what was required in the law of the Lord—"either a pair of turtledoves or two young pigeons."*

²⁵Now there was a man named Simeon who lived in Jerusalem. He was a righteous man and very devout. He was filled with the Holy Spirit, and he eagerly expected the Messiah to come and rescue Israel. ²⁶The Holy Spirit had revealed to him that he would not die until he had seen the Lord's Messiah. ²⁷That day the Spirit led him to the Temple. So when Mary and Joseph came to present the baby Jesus to the Lord as the law required, ²⁸Simeon was there. He took the child in his arms and praised God, saying,

²⁹ "Lord, now I can die in peace!
        As you promised me,
³⁰ I have seen the Savior
³¹   you have given to all people.
³² He is a light to reveal God to the nations,
        and he is the glory of your people
            Israel!"

³³Joseph and Mary were amazed at what was being said about Jesus. ³⁴Then Simeon blessed them, and he said to Mary, "This child will be rejected by many in Israel, and it will be their undoing. But he will be the greatest joy to many others. ³⁵Thus, the deepest thoughts of many hearts will be revealed. And a sword will pierce your very soul."

³⁶Anna, a prophet, was also there in the Temple. She was the daughter of Phanuel, of the tribe of Asher, and was very old. She was a widow, for her husband had died when they had been married only seven years. ³⁷She was now eighty-four years old. She never left the Temple but stayed there day and night, worshiping

2:14 Or *and peace on earth for all those pleasing God.* Some manuscripts read *and peace on earth, goodwill among people.*   2:23 Exod 13:2.
2:24 Lev 12:8.

God with fasting and prayer. ³⁸She came along just as Simeon was talking with Mary and Joseph, and she began praising God. She talked about Jesus to everyone who had been waiting for the promised King to come and deliver Jerusalem.

³⁹When Jesus' parents had fulfilled all the requirements of the law of the Lord, they returned home to Nazareth in Galilee. ⁴⁰There the child grew up healthy and strong. He was filled with wisdom beyond his years, and God placed his special favor upon him.

⁴¹Every year Jesus' parents went to Jerusalem for the Passover festival. ⁴²When Jesus was twelve years old, they attended the festival as usual. ⁴³After the celebration was over, they started home to Nazareth, but Jesus stayed behind in Jerusalem. His parents didn't miss him at first, ⁴⁴because they assumed he was with friends among the other travelers. But when he didn't show up that evening, they started to look for him among their relatives and friends.

⁴⁵When they couldn't find him, they went back to Jerusalem to search for him there. ⁴⁶Three days later they finally discovered him. He was in the Temple, sitting among the religious teachers, discussing deep questions with them. ⁴⁷And all who heard him were amazed at his understanding and his answers.

⁴⁸His parents didn't know what to think. "Son!" his mother said to him. "Why have you done this to us? Your father and I have been frantic, searching for you everywhere."

⁴⁹"But why did you need to search?" he asked. "You should have known that I would be in my Father's house."* ⁵⁰But they didn't understand what he meant.

⁵¹Then he returned to Nazareth with them and was obedient to them; and his mother stored all these things in her heart. ⁵²So Jesus grew both in height and in wisdom, and he was loved by God and by all who knew him.

2:49 Or *"Didn't you realize that I should be involved with my Father's affairs?"*

OCTOBER 17 □ DAY 291
LUKE 3–6
Authority of the Son of Man

OVERVIEW Before Jesus can begin his public ministry, he undertakes a period of preparation to show that he is worthy to minister. John, the promised forerunner, baptizes Jesus in the Jordan—an occasion marked by an audible voice from heaven declaring God's approval of his beloved Son. The character and obedience of Christ are tested through a series of temptations by Satan in the wilderness. Again Jesus emerges victorious. Returning "to Galilee, filled with the Holy Spirit's power" (4:14), Jesus is ready to begin his earthly ministry as the obedient, approved Savior sent from God.

Chapter 3		Chapter 4	Chapter 5	Chapter 6
Preaching of John	Baptism of Jesus	Temptation of Jesus	Healing of Jesus	Teaching of Jesus
1 20	21 38			
Preparation			Practice	

YOUR DAILY WALK How important is Scripture memory in your personal schedule? Is it something you do hit-or-miss? (Usually that will result in missing more than you hit!)

Study carefully Christ's defense against the attacks of Satan (4:1-13). He did not preach; he did not argue; he merely quoted Scripture

Apply yourself wholly to the Scriptures and the Scriptures wholly to yourself.

passages from the Old Testament. Three times Christ responded, "The Scriptures say" (4:4, 8, 12). Even more surprising, he quoted from a book of the Old Testament that most Christians have trouble spelling, much less explaining. (What is it?)

How well stocked are you with scriptural ammunition to counter the attacks of Satan? One good source of ammunition is a supply of memorized verses. Stop by your local Christian bookstore, or ask your pastor to recommend a plan. Also consider asking a friend or family member to listen as you recite your verses from time to time. Begin with a single verse and learn it well. You might want to start with one of the three verses that Christ found to be valuable in his own personal struggles with Satan: Deuteronomy 6:13, 16; 8:3. Memorizing Scripture takes time, but it's a habit worth developing.

 INSIGHT Significant Preparation for a Significant Decision
What steps of preparation do you take before making a major decision in your life? Notice what Jesus did the night before he selected the twelve disciples: "One day soon afterward Jesus went to a mountain to pray, and he prayed to God all night" (6:12).

CHAPTER 3

It was now the fifteenth year of the reign of Tiberius, the Roman emperor. Pilate was governor over Judea; Herod Antipas was ruler* over Galilee; his brother Philip was ruler* over Iturea and Traconitis; Lysanias was ruler over Abilene. ²Annas and Caiaphas were the high priests. At this time a message from God came to John son of Zechariah, who was living out in the wilderness. ³Then John went from place to place on both sides of the Jordan River, preaching that people should be baptized to show that they had turned from their sins and turned to God to be forgiven.* ⁴Isaiah had spoken of John when he said,

"He is a voice shouting in the
        wilderness:
'Prepare a pathway for the Lord's
        coming!
    Make a straight road for him!
⁵ Fill in the valleys,
    and level the mountains and hills!
Straighten the curves,
    and smooth out the rough places!
⁶ And then all people will see
    the salvation sent from God.'"*

⁷Here is a sample of John's preaching to the crowds that came for baptism: "You brood of snakes! Who warned you to flee God's coming judgment? ⁸Prove by the way you live that you have really turned from your sins and turned to God. Don't just say, 'We're safe—we're the descen-

dants of Abraham.' That proves nothing. God can change these stones here into children of Abraham. ⁹Even now the ax of God's judgment is poised, ready to sever your roots. Yes, every tree that does not produce good fruit will be chopped down and thrown into the fire."

¹⁰The crowd asked, "What should we do?"

¹¹John replied, "If you have two coats, give one to the poor. If you have food, share it with those who are hungry."

¹²Even corrupt tax collectors came to be baptized and asked, "Teacher, what should we do?"

¹³"Show your honesty," he replied. "Make sure you collect no more taxes than the Roman government requires you to."

¹⁴"What should we do?" asked some soldiers.

John replied, "Don't extort money, and don't accuse people of things you know they didn't do. And be content with your pay."

¹⁵Everyone was expecting the Messiah to come soon, and they were eager to know whether John might be the Messiah. ¹⁶John answered their questions by saying, "I baptize with* water; but someone is coming soon who is greater than I am—so much greater that I am not even worthy to be his slave.* He will baptize you with the Holy Spirit and with fire.* ¹⁷He is ready to separate the chaff from the grain with his winnowing fork. Then he will clean up the

---

3:1a Greek *Herod was tetrarch.* Herod Antipas was a son of King Herod.   **3:1b** Greek *tetrarch;* also in 3:1c, 19.   **3:3** Greek *preaching a baptism of repentance for the forgiveness of sins.*   **3:4-6** Isa 40:3-5.   **3:16a** Or *in.*   **3:16b** Greek *to untie his sandals.*   **3:16c** Or *in the Holy Spirit and in fire.*

threshing area, storing the grain in his barn but burning the chaff with never-ending fire." [18]John used many such warnings as he announced the Good News to the people.

[19]John also publicly criticized Herod Antipas, ruler of Galilee, for marrying Herodias, his brother's wife, and for many other wrongs he had done. [20]So Herod put John in prison, adding this sin to his many others.

[21]One day when the crowds were being baptized, Jesus himself was baptized. As he was praying, the heavens opened, [22]and the Holy Spirit descended on him in the form of a dove. And a voice from heaven said, "You are my beloved Son, and I am fully pleased with you.*"

[23]Jesus was about thirty years old when he began his public ministry.

Jesus was known as the son of Joseph.
Joseph was the son of Heli.
[24] Heli was the son of Matthat.
Matthat was the son of Levi.
Levi was the son of Melki.
Melki was the son of Jannai.
Jannai was the son of Joseph.
[25] Joseph was the son of Mattathias.
Mattathias was the son of Amos.
Amos was the son of Nahum.
Nahum was the son of Esli.
Esli was the son of Naggai.
[26] Naggai was the son of Maath.
Maath was the son of Mattathias.
Mattathias was the son of Semein.
Semein was the son of Josech.
Josech was the son of Joda.
[27] Joda was the son of Joanan.
Joanan was the son of Rhesa.
Rhesa was the son of Zerubbabel.
Zerubbabel was the son of Shealtiel.
Shealtiel was the son of Neri.
[28] Neri was the son of Melki.
Melki was the son of Addi.
Addi was the son of Cosam.
Cosam was the son of Elmadam.
Elmadam was the son of Er.
[29] Er was the son of Joshua.
Joshua was the son of Eliezer.
Eliezer was the son of Jorim.
Jorim was the son of Matthat.
Matthat was the son of Levi.
[30] Levi was the son of Simeon.
Simeon was the son of Judah.

Judah was the son of Joseph.
Joseph was the son of Jonam.
Jonam was the son of Eliakim.
[31] Eliakim was the son of Melea.
Melea was the son of Menna.
Menna was the son of Mattatha.
Mattatha was the son of Nathan.
Nathan was the son of David.
[32] David was the son of Jesse.
Jesse was the son of Obed.
Obed was the son of Boaz.
Boaz was the son of Salmon.*
Salmon was the son of Nahshon.
[33] Nahshon was the son of Amminadab.
Amminadab was the son of Admin.
Admin was the son of Arni.*
Arni was the son of Hezron.
Hezron was the son of Perez.
Perez was the son of Judah.
[34] Judah was the son of Jacob.
Jacob was the son of Isaac.
Isaac was the son of Abraham.
Abraham was the son of Terah.
Terah was the son of Nahor.
[35] Nahor was the son of Serug.
Serug was the son of Reu.
Reu was the son of Peleg.
Peleg was the son of Eber.
Eber was the son of Shelah.
[36] Shelah was the son of Cainan.
Cainan was the son of Arphaxad.
Arphaxad was the son of Shem.
Shem was the son of Noah.
Noah was the son of Lamech.
[37] Lamech was the son of Methuselah.
Methuselah was the son of Enoch.
Enoch was the son of Jared.
Jared was the son of Mahalalel.
Mahalalel was the son of Kenan.
[38] Kenan was the son of Enosh.*
Enosh was the son of Seth.
Seth was the son of Adam.
Adam was the son of God.

CHAPTER 4

Then Jesus, full of the Holy Spirit, left the Jordan River. He was led by the Spirit to go out into the wilderness, [2]where the Devil tempted him for forty days. He ate nothing all that time and was very hungry.

[3]Then the Devil said to him, "If you are the Son of God, change this stone into a loaf of bread."

[4]But Jesus told him, "No! The Scriptures

3:22 Some manuscripts read *and today I have become your Father.*   **3:32** Greek *Sala;* see Ruth 4:22.   **3:33** *Arni* is the same person as Ram; see 1 Chr 2:9-10.   **3:38** Greek *Enos;* see Gen 5:6.

say, 'People need more than bread for their life.'*"

5 Then the Devil took him up and revealed to him all the kingdoms of the world in a moment of time. 6 The Devil told him, "I will give you the glory of these kingdoms and authority over them—because they are mine to give to anyone I please. 7 I will give it all to you if you will bow down and worship me."

8 Jesus replied, "The Scriptures say,

'You must worship the Lord your God; serve only him.'*"

9 Then the Devil took him to Jerusalem, to the highest point of the Temple, and said, "If you are the Son of God, jump off! 10 For the Scriptures say,

'He orders his angels to protect and guard you.
11 And they will hold you with their hands
    to keep you from striking your foot on a stone.'*"

12 Jesus responded, "The Scriptures also say, 'Do not test the Lord your God.'*"

13 When the Devil had finished tempting Jesus, he left him until the next opportunity came.

14 Then Jesus returned to Galilee, filled with the Holy Spirit's power. Soon he became well known throughout the surrounding country. 15 He taught in their synagogues and was praised by everyone.

16 When he came to the village of Nazareth, his boyhood home, he went as usual to the synagogue on the Sabbath and stood up to read the Scriptures. 17 The scroll containing the messages of Isaiah the prophet was handed to him, and he unrolled the scroll to the place where it says:

18 "The Spirit of the Lord is upon me,
    for he has appointed me to preach Good News to the poor.
  He has sent me to proclaim
    that captives will be released,
    that the blind will see,
    that the downtrodden will be freed from their oppressors,
19   and that the time of the Lord's favor has come.*"

20 He rolled up the scroll, handed it back to the attendant, and sat down. Everyone in the synagogue stared at him intently. 21 Then he said, "This Scripture has come true today before your very eyes!"

22 All who were there spoke well of him and were amazed by the gracious words that fell from his lips. "How can this be?" they asked. "Isn't this Joseph's son?"

23 Then he said, "Probably you will quote me that proverb, 'Physician, heal yourself'—meaning, 'Why don't you do miracles here in your hometown like those you did in Capernaum?' 24 But the truth is, no prophet is accepted in his own hometown.

25 "Certainly there were many widows in Israel who needed help in Elijah's time, when there was no rain for three and a half years and hunger stalked the land. 26 Yet Elijah was not sent to any of them. He was sent instead to a widow of Zarephath—a foreigner in the land of Sidon. 27 Or think of the prophet Elisha, who healed Naaman, a Syrian, rather than the many lepers in Israel who needed help."

28 When they heard this, the people in the synagogue were furious. 29 Jumping up, they mobbed him and took him to the edge of the hill on which the city was built. They intended to push him over the cliff, 30 but he slipped away through the crowd and left them.

31 Then Jesus went to Capernaum, a town in Galilee, and taught there in the synagogue every Sabbath day. 32 There, too, the people were amazed at the things he said, because he spoke with authority.

33 Once when he was in the synagogue, a man possessed by a demon began shouting at Jesus, 34 "Go away! Why are you bothering us, Jesus of Nazareth? Have you come to destroy us? I know who you are—the Holy One sent from God."

35 Jesus cut him short. "Be silent!" he told the demon. "Come out of the man!" The demon threw the man to the floor as the crowd watched; then it left him without hurting him further.

36 Amazed, the people exclaimed, "What authority and power this man's words possess! Even evil spirits obey him and flee at his command!" 37 The story of what he had done spread like wildfire throughout the whole region.

38 After leaving the synagogue that day, Jesus went to Simon's home, where he found Simon's mother-in-law very sick with a high

4:4 Deut 8:3.   4:8 Deut 6:13.   4:10-11 Ps 91:11-12.   4:12 Deut 6:16.   4:18-19 Or *and to proclaim the acceptable year of the Lord.* Isa 61:1-2.

fever. "Please heal her," everyone begged. [39]Standing at her bedside, he spoke to the fever, rebuking it, and immediately her temperature returned to normal. She got up at once and prepared a meal for them.

[40]As the sun went down that evening, people throughout the village brought sick family members to Jesus. No matter what their diseases were, the touch of his hand healed every one. [41]Some were possessed by demons; and the demons came out at his command, shouting, "You are the Son of God." But because they knew he was the Messiah, he stopped them and told them to be silent.

[42]Early the next morning Jesus went out into the wilderness. The crowds searched everywhere for him, and when they finally found him, they begged him not to leave them. [43]But he replied, "I must preach the Good News of the Kingdom of God in other places, too, because that is why I was sent." [44]So he continued to travel around, preaching in synagogues throughout Judea.*

CHAPTER 5

One day as Jesus was preaching on the shore of the Sea of Galilee,* great crowds pressed in on him to listen to the word of God. [2]He noticed two empty boats at the water's edge, for the fishermen had left them and were washing their nets. [3]Stepping into one of the boats, Jesus asked Simon,* its owner, to push it out into the water. So he sat in the boat and taught the crowds from there.

[4]When he had finished speaking, he said to Simon, "Now go out where it is deeper and let down your nets, and you will catch many fish."

[5]"Master," Simon replied, "we worked hard all last night and didn't catch a thing. But if you say so, we'll try again." [6]And this time their nets were so full they began to tear! [7]A shout for help brought their partners in the other boat, and soon both boats were filled with fish and on the verge of sinking.

[8]When Simon Peter realized what had happened, he fell to his knees before Jesus and said, "Oh, Lord, please leave me—I'm too much of a sinner to be around you." [9]For he was awestruck by the size of their catch, as were the others with him. [10]His partners, James and John, the sons of Zebedee, were also amazed.

Jesus replied to Simon, "Don't be afraid! From now on you'll be fishing for people!" [11]And as soon as they landed, they left everything and followed Jesus.

[12]In one of the villages, Jesus met a man with an advanced case of leprosy. When the man saw Jesus, he fell to the ground, face down in the dust, begging to be healed. "Lord," he said, "if you want to, you can make me well again."

[13]Jesus reached out and touched the man. "I want to," he said. "Be healed!" And instantly the leprosy disappeared. [14]Then Jesus instructed him not to tell anyone what had happened. He said, "Go right to the priest and let him examine you. Take along the offering required in the law of Moses for those who have been healed of leprosy, so everyone will have proof of your healing." [15]Yet despite Jesus' instructions, the report of his power spread even faster, and vast crowds came to hear him preach and to be healed of their diseases. [16]But Jesus often withdrew to the wilderness for prayer.

[17]One day while Jesus was teaching, some Pharisees and teachers of religious law were sitting nearby. (It seemed that these men showed up from every village in all Galilee and Judea, as well as from Jerusalem.) And the Lord's healing power was strongly with Jesus. [18]Some men came carrying a paralyzed man on a sleeping mat. They tried to push through the crowd to Jesus, [19]but they couldn't reach him. So they went up to the roof, took off some tiles, and lowered the sick man down into the crowd, still on his mat, right in front of Jesus. [20]Seeing their faith, Jesus said to the man, "Son, your sins are forgiven."

[21]"Who does this man think he is?" the Pharisees and teachers of religious law said to each other. "This is blasphemy! Who but God can forgive sins?"

[22]Jesus knew what they were thinking, so he asked them, "Why do you think this is blasphemy? [23]Is it easier to say, 'Your sins are forgiven' or 'Get up and walk'? [24]I will prove that I, the Son of Man, have the authority on earth to forgive sins." Then Jesus turned to the paralyzed man and said, "Stand up, take your mat, and go on home, because you are healed!"

[25]And immediately, as everyone watched, the man jumped to his feet, picked up his mat, and went home praising God. [26]Every-

4:44 Some manuscripts read *Galilee.*   5:1 Greek *Lake Gennesaret,* another name for the Sea of Galilee.   5:3 *Simon* is called *Peter* in 6:14 and thereafter.

one was gripped with great wonder and awe. And they praised God, saying over and over again, "We have seen amazing things today."

²⁷Later, as Jesus left the town, he saw a tax collector named Levi sitting at his tax-collection booth. "Come, be my disciple!" Jesus said to him. ²⁸So Levi got up, left everything, and followed him.

²⁹Soon Levi held a banquet in his home with Jesus as the guest of honor. Many of Levi's fellow tax collectors and other guests were there. ³⁰But the Pharisees and their teachers of religious law complained bitterly to Jesus' disciples, "Why do you eat and drink with such scum*?"

³¹Jesus answered them, "Healthy people don't need a doctor—sick people do. ³²I have come to call sinners to turn from their sins, not to spend my time with those who think they are already good enough."

³³The religious leaders complained that Jesus' disciples were feasting instead of fasting. "John the Baptist's disciples always fast and pray," they declared, "and so do the disciples of the Pharisees. Why are yours always feasting?"

³⁴Jesus asked, "Do wedding guests fast while celebrating with the groom? ³⁵Someday he will be taken away from them, and then they will fast."

³⁶Then Jesus gave them this illustration: "No one tears a piece of cloth from a new garment and uses it to patch an old garment. For then the new garment would be torn, and the patch wouldn't even match the old garment. ³⁷And no one puts new wine into old wineskins. The new wine would burst the old skins, spilling the wine and ruining the skins. ³⁸New wine must be put into new wineskins. ³⁹But no one who drinks the old wine seems to want the fresh and the new. 'The old is better,' they say."

CHAPTER 6

One Sabbath day as Jesus was walking through some grainfields, his disciples broke off heads of wheat, rubbed off the husks in their hands, and ate the grains. ²But some Pharisees said, "You shouldn't be doing that! It's against the law to work by harvesting grain on the Sabbath."

³Jesus replied, "Haven't you ever read in the Scriptures what King David did when he and his companions were hungry? ⁴He went

5:30 Greek *with tax collectors and sinners.*

into the house of God, ate the special bread reserved for the priests alone, and then gave some to his friends. That was breaking the law, too." ⁵And Jesus added, "I, the Son of Man, am master even of the Sabbath."

⁶On another Sabbath day, a man with a deformed right hand was in the synagogue while Jesus was teaching. ⁷The teachers of religious law and the Pharisees watched closely to see whether Jesus would heal the man on the Sabbath, because they were eager to find some legal charge to bring against him. ⁸But Jesus knew their thoughts. He said to the man with the deformed hand, "Come and stand here where everyone can see." So the man came forward. ⁹Then Jesus said to his critics, "I have a question for you. Is it legal to do good deeds on the Sabbath, or is it a day for doing harm? Is this a day to save life or to destroy it?" ¹⁰He looked around at them one by one and then said to the man, "Reach out your hand." The man reached out his hand, and it became normal again! ¹¹At this, the enemies of Jesus were wild with rage and began to discuss what to do with him.

¹²One day soon afterward Jesus went to a mountain to pray, and he prayed to God all night. ¹³At daybreak he called together all of his disciples and chose twelve of them to be apostles. Here are their names:

¹⁴ Simon (he also called him Peter),
   Andrew (Peter's brother),
   James,
   John,
   Philip,
   Bartholomew,
¹⁵ Matthew,
   Thomas,
   James (son of Alphaeus),
   Simon (the Zealot),
¹⁶ Judas (son of James),
   Judas Iscariot (who later betrayed him).

¹⁷When they came down the slopes of the mountain, the disciples stood with Jesus on a large, level area, surrounded by many of his followers and by the crowds. There were people from all over Judea and from Jerusalem and from as far north as the seacoasts of Tyre and Sidon. ¹⁸They had come to hear him and to be healed, and Jesus cast out many evil spirits. ¹⁹Everyone was trying to touch him, because healing power went out from him, and they were all cured.

²⁰Then Jesus turned to his disciples and said,

"God blesses you who are poor,
  for the Kingdom of God is given to you.
²¹ God blesses you who are hungry now,
  for you will be satisfied.
God blesses you who weep now,
  for the time will come when you will laugh with joy.
²² God blesses you who are hated and
  excluded and mocked and cursed
  because you are identified with me,
  the Son of Man.

²³"When that happens, rejoice! Yes, leap for joy! For a great reward awaits you in heaven. And remember, the ancient prophets were also treated that way by your ancestors.

²⁴ "What sorrows await you who are rich,
  for you have your only happiness now.
²⁵ What sorrows await you who are
  satisfied and prosperous now,
  for a time of awful hunger is before you.
What sorrows await you who laugh carelessly,
  for your laughing will turn to mourning and sorrow.
²⁶ What sorrows await you who are
  praised by the crowds,
  for their ancestors also praised false prophets.

²⁷"But if you are willing to listen, I say, love your enemies. Do good to those who hate you. ²⁸Pray for the happiness of those who curse you. Pray for those who hurt you. ²⁹If someone slaps you on one cheek, turn the other cheek. If someone demands your coat, offer your shirt also. ³⁰Give what you have to anyone who asks you for it; and when things are taken away from you, don't try to get them back. ³¹Do for others as you would like them to do for you.

³²"Do you think you deserve credit merely for loving those who love you? Even the sinners do that! ³³And if you do good only to those who do good to you, is that so wonderful? Even sinners do that much! ³⁴And if you lend money only to those who can repay you, what good is that? Even sinners will lend to their own kind for a full return.

³⁵"Love your enemies! Do good to them!

Lend to them! And don't be concerned that they might not repay. Then your reward from heaven will be very great, and you will truly be acting as children of the Most High, for he is kind to the unthankful and to those who are wicked. ³⁶You must be compassionate, just as your Father is compassionate.

³⁷"Stop judging others, and you will not be judged. Stop criticizing others, or it will all come back on you. If you forgive others, you will be forgiven. ³⁸If you give, you will receive. Your gift will return to you in full measure, pressed down, shaken together to make room for more, and running over. Whatever measure you use in giving—large or small—it will be used to measure what is given back to you."

³⁹Then Jesus gave the following illustration: "What good is it for one blind person to lead another? The first one will fall into a ditch and pull the other down also. ⁴⁰A student is not greater than the teacher. But the student who works hard will become like the teacher.

⁴¹"And why worry about a speck in your friend's eye* when you have a log in your own? ⁴²How can you think of saying, 'Friend,* let me help you get rid of that speck in your eye,' when you can't see past the log in your own eye? Hypocrite! First get rid of the log from your own eye; then perhaps you will see well enough to deal with the speck in your friend's eye.

⁴³"A good tree can't produce bad fruit, and a bad tree can't produce good fruit. ⁴⁴A tree is identified by the kind of fruit it produces. Figs never grow on thornbushes or grapes on bramble bushes. ⁴⁵A good person produces good deeds from a good heart, and an evil person produces evil deeds from an evil heart. Whatever is in your heart determines what you say.

⁴⁶"So why do you call me 'Lord,' when you won't obey me? ⁴⁷I will show you what it's like when someone comes to me, listens to my teaching, and then obeys me. ⁴⁸It is like a person who builds a house on a strong foundation laid upon the underlying rock. When the floodwaters rise and break against the house, it stands firm because it is well built. ⁴⁹But anyone who listens and doesn't obey is like a person who builds a house without a foundation. When the floods sweep down against that house, it will crumble into a heap of ruins."

6:41 Greek *your brother's eye;* also in 6:42. **6:42** Greek *Brother.*

OCTOBER 18 ☐ DAY 292
LUKE 7–9
Activities of the Son of Man

OVERVIEW Today's reading may leave you just a little breathless. In the space of these three chapters Jesus travels from the region of Galilee to the surrounding provinces east of the Sea of Galilee, north to Caesarea Philippi, and finally south through Samaria. As he travels, the demands on him increase. He is busily engaged in healing the sick, raising the dead, teaching through parables, calming storms, and casting out demons. But Jesus knows his days on earth will be short. So he chooses twelve men—disciples—to whom he delegates his power and authority to minister. This is no halfhearted call to discipleship, for the terms of commitment are drastic indeed (9:23-26, 57-62).

Chapter 7	Chapter 8	Chapter 9
The Testimony of Working	The Testimony of Teaching	The Testimony of Training
The Son of Man Has Not Come to Destroy Men's Lives, but to Save Them (9:56).		

YOUR DAILY WALK What would be different about your life if you were a "drastic disciple" of Jesus Christ?

God deserves the same place in your heart that he holds in the universe.

The lessons for disciples and tests of discipleship that are contained in chapter 9 do not make for easy reading. They are painfully pointed, calling for commitment in matters of allegiance, lifestyle, and goals. Christ made the terms of discipleship unmistakably clear. Read the following verses prayerfully, asking yourself, How do I need to change if my Christian life is to reflect that kind of commitment?

"If any of you wants to be my follower, you must put aside your selfish ambition, shoulder your cross daily, and follow me" (9:23).

"If a person is ashamed of me and my message, I, the Son of Man, will be ashamed of that person" (9:26).

"Anyone who puts a hand to the plow and then looks back is not fit for the Kingdom of God" (9:62).

INSIGHT The Messiah of Many Names

Look for the variety of names and titles ascribed to Jesus in these chapters. Can you find the two times he is identified as the Son of God? How about the six occurrences of Jesus' favorite name for himself, *Son of Man?* How many times does *Lord* occur? There is only one use of the word *Christ* ("the Anointed One") in these chapters. Can you find it? What other names and titles can you find?

CHAPTER 7

When Jesus had finished saying all this, he went back to Capernaum. ²Now the highly valued slave of a Roman officer was sick and near death. ³When the officer heard about Jesus, he sent some respected Jewish leaders to ask him to come and heal his slave. ⁴So they earnestly begged Jesus to come with them and help the man. "If anyone deserves your help, it is he," they said, ⁵"for he loves the Jews and even built a synagogue for us."

⁶So Jesus went with them. But just before they arrived at the house, the officer sent some friends to say, "Lord, don't trouble yourself by coming to my home, for I am not worthy of such an honor. ⁷I am not even worthy to come and meet you. Just say the word from where you are, and my servant will be healed. ⁸I know because I am under the authority of my superior officers, and I have authority over my soldiers. I only need to say, 'Go,' and they go, or 'Come,'

and they come. And if I say to my slaves, 'Do this or that,' they do it."

⁹When Jesus heard this, he was amazed. Turning to the crowd, he said, "I tell you, I haven't seen faith like this in all the land of Israel!" ¹⁰And when the officer's friends returned to his house, they found the slave completely healed.

¹¹Soon afterward Jesus went with his disciples to the village of Nain, with a great crowd following him. ¹²A funeral procession was coming out as he approached the village gate. The boy who had died was the only son of a widow, and many mourners from the village were with her. ¹³When the Lord saw her, his heart overflowed with compassion. "Don't cry!" he said. ¹⁴Then he walked over to the coffin and touched it, and the bearers stopped. "Young man," he said, "get up." ¹⁵Then the dead boy sat up and began to talk to those around him! And Jesus gave him back to his mother.

¹⁶Great fear swept the crowd, and they praised God, saying, "A mighty prophet has risen among us," and "We have seen the hand of God at work today." ¹⁷The report of what Jesus had done that day spread all over Judea and even out across its borders.

¹⁸The disciples of John the Baptist told John about everything Jesus was doing. So John called for two of his disciples, ¹⁹and he sent them to the Lord to ask him, "Are you the Messiah we've been expecting, or should we keep looking for someone else?"

²⁰John's two disciples found Jesus and said to him, "John the Baptist sent us to ask, 'Are you the Messiah we've been expecting, or should we keep looking for someone else?'"

²¹At that very time, he cured many people of their various diseases, and he cast out evil spirits and restored sight to the blind. ²²Then he told John's disciples, "Go back to John and tell him what you have seen and heard—the blind see, the lame walk, the lepers are cured, the deaf hear, the dead are raised to life, and the Good News is being preached to the poor. ²³And tell him, 'God blesses those who are not offended by me.*'"

²⁴After they left, Jesus talked to the crowd about John. "Who is this man in the wilderness that you went out to see? Did you find him weak as a reed, moved by every breath of wind? ²⁵Or were you expecting to see a man dressed in expensive clothes? No, people who wear beautiful clothes and live in luxury are found in palaces, not in the wilderness. ²⁶Were you looking for a prophet? Yes, and he is more than a prophet. ²⁷John is the man to whom the Scriptures refer when they say,

'Look, I am sending my messenger
    before you,
and he will prepare your way before
    you.'*

²⁸I tell you, of all who have ever lived, none is greater than John. Yet even the most insignificant person in the Kingdom of God is greater than he is!"

²⁹When they heard this, all the people, including the unjust tax collectors, agreed that God's plan was right,* for they had been baptized by John. ³⁰But the Pharisees and experts in religious law had rejected God's plan for them, for they had refused John's baptism.

³¹"How shall I describe this generation?" Jesus asked. "With what will I compare them? ³²They are like a group of children playing a game in the public square. They complain to their friends, 'We played wedding songs, and you weren't happy, so we played funeral songs, but you weren't sad.' ³³For John the Baptist didn't drink wine and he often fasted, and you say, 'He's demon possessed.' ³⁴And I, the Son of Man, feast and drink, and you say, 'He's a glutton and a drunkard, and a friend of the worst sort of sinners!' ³⁵But wisdom is shown to be right by the lives of those who follow it.*"

³⁶One of the Pharisees asked Jesus to come to his home for a meal, so Jesus accepted the invitation and sat down to eat. ³⁷A certain immoral woman heard he was there and brought a beautiful jar* filled with expensive perfume. ³⁸Then she knelt behind him at his feet, weeping. Her tears fell on his feet, and she wiped them off with her hair. Then she kept kissing his feet and putting perfume on them.

³⁹When the Pharisee who was the host saw what was happening and who the woman was, he said to himself, "This proves that Jesus is no prophet. If God had really sent him, he would know what kind of woman is touching him. She's a sinner!"

7:23 Or *who don't fall away because of me.*   **7:27** Mal 3:1.   **7:29** Or *praised God.*   **7:35** Or *But wisdom is justified by all her children.*
7:37 Greek *an alabaster jar.*

[40] Then Jesus spoke up and answered his thoughts. "Simon," he said to the Pharisee, "I have something to say to you."

"All right, Teacher," Simon replied, "go ahead."

[41] Then Jesus told him this story: "A man loaned money to two people—five hundred pieces of silver* to one and fifty pieces to the other. [42] But neither of them could repay him, so he kindly forgave them both, canceling their debts. Who do you suppose loved him more after that?"

[43] Simon answered, "I suppose the one for whom he canceled the larger debt."

"That's right," Jesus said. [44] Then he turned to the woman and said to Simon, "Look at this woman kneeling here. When I entered your home, you didn't offer me water to wash the dust from my feet, but she has washed them with her tears and wiped them with her hair. [45] You didn't give me a kiss of greeting, but she has kissed my feet again and again from the time I first came in. [46] You neglected the courtesy of olive oil to anoint my head, but she has anointed my feet with rare perfume. [47] I tell you, her sins—and they are many—have been forgiven, so she has shown me much love. But a person who is forgiven little shows only little love." [48] Then Jesus said to the woman, "Your sins are forgiven."

[49] The men at the table said among themselves, "Who does this man think he is, going around forgiving sins?"

[50] And Jesus said to the woman, "Your faith has saved you; go in peace."

CHAPTER 8

Not long afterward Jesus began a tour of the nearby cities and villages to announce the Good News concerning the Kingdom of God. He took his twelve disciples with him, [2] along with some women he had healed and from whom he had cast out evil spirits. Among them were Mary Magdalene, from whom he had cast out seven demons; [3] Joanna, the wife of Chuza, Herod's business manager; Susanna; and many others who were contributing from their own resources to support Jesus and his disciples.

[4] One day Jesus told this story to a large crowd that had gathered from many towns to hear him: [5] "A farmer went out to plant some seed. As he scattered it across his field, some seed fell on a footpath, where it was stepped on, and the birds came and ate it. [6] Other seed fell on shallow soil with underlying rock. This seed began to grow, but soon it withered and died for lack of moisture. [7] Other seed fell among thorns that shot up and choked out the tender blades. [8] Still other seed fell on fertile soil. This seed grew and produced a crop one hundred times as much as had been planted." When he had said this, he called out, "Anyone who is willing to hear should listen and understand!"

[9] His disciples asked him what the story meant. [10] He replied, "You have been permitted to understand the secrets of the Kingdom of God. But I am using these stories to conceal everything about it from outsiders, so that the Scriptures might be fulfilled:

'They see what I do,
    but they don't really see;
they hear what I say,
    but they don't understand.'*

[11] "This is the meaning of the story: The seed is God's message. [12] The seed that fell on the hard path represents those who hear the message, but then the Devil comes and steals it away and prevents them from believing and being saved. [13] The rocky soil represents those who hear the message with joy. But like young plants in such soil, their roots don't go very deep. They believe for a while, but they wilt when the hot winds of testing blow. [14] The thorny ground represents those who hear and accept the message, but all too quickly the message is crowded out by the cares and riches and pleasures of this life. And so they never grow into maturity. [15] But the good soil represents honest, good-hearted people who hear God's message, cling to it, and steadily produce a huge harvest.

[16] "No one would light a lamp and then cover it up or put it under a bed. No, lamps are mounted in the open, where they can be seen by those entering the house. [17] For everything that is hidden or secret will eventually be brought to light and made plain to all. [18] So be sure to pay attention to what you hear. To those who are open to my teaching, more understanding will be given. But to those who are not listening,

7:41 Greek *500 denarii*. A denarius was the equivalent of a full day's wage.   8:10 Isa 6:9.

even what they think they have will be taken away from them."

[19] Once when Jesus' mother and brothers came to see him, they couldn't get to him because of the crowds. [20] Someone told Jesus, "Your mother and your brothers are outside, and they want to see you."

[21] Jesus replied, "My mother and my brothers are all those who hear the message of God and obey it."

[22] One day Jesus said to his disciples, "Let's cross over to the other side of the lake." So they got into a boat and started out. [23] On the way across, Jesus lay down for a nap, and while he was sleeping the wind began to rise. A fierce storm developed that threatened to swamp them, and they were in real danger.

[24] The disciples woke him up, shouting, "Master, Master, we're going to drown!"

So Jesus rebuked the wind and the raging waves. The storm stopped and all was calm! [25] Then he asked them, "Where is your faith?"

And they were filled with awe and amazement. They said to one another, "Who is this man, that even the winds and waves obey him?"

[26] So they arrived in the land of the Gerasenes,* across the lake from Galilee. [27] As Jesus was climbing out of the boat, a man who was possessed by demons came out to meet him. Homeless and naked, he had lived in a cemetery for a long time. [28] As soon as he saw Jesus, he shrieked and fell to the ground before him, screaming, "Why are you bothering me, Jesus, Son of the Most High God? Please, I beg you, don't torture me!" [29] For Jesus had already commanded the evil spirit to come out of him. This spirit had often taken control of the man. Even when he was shackled with chains, he simply broke them and rushed out into the wilderness, completely under the demon's power.

[30] "What is your name?" Jesus asked.

"Legion," he replied—for the man was filled with many demons. [31] The demons kept begging Jesus not to send them into the Bottomless Pit. [32] A large herd of pigs was feeding on the hillside nearby, and the demons pleaded with him to let them enter into the pigs. Jesus gave them permission. [33] So the demons came out of the man and entered the pigs, and the whole herd plunged down the steep hillside into the lake, where they drowned.

[34] When the herdsmen saw it, they fled to the nearby city and the surrounding countryside, spreading the news as they ran. [35] A crowd soon gathered around Jesus, for they wanted to see for themselves what had happened. And they saw the man who had been possessed by demons sitting quietly at Jesus' feet, clothed and sane. And the whole crowd was afraid. [36] Then those who had seen what happened told the others how the demon-possessed man had been healed. [37] And all the people in that region begged Jesus to go away and leave them alone, for a great wave of fear swept over them.

So Jesus returned to the boat and left, crossing back to the other side of the lake. [38] The man who had been demon possessed begged to go, too, but Jesus said, [39] "No, go back to your family and tell them all the wonderful things God has done for you." So he went all through the city telling about the great thing Jesus had done for him.

[40] On the other side of the lake the crowds received Jesus with open arms because they had been waiting for him. [41] And now a man named Jairus, a leader of the local synagogue, came and fell down at Jesus' feet, begging him to come home with him. [42] His only child was dying, a little girl twelve years old.

As Jesus went with him, he was surrounded by the crowds. [43] And there was a woman in the crowd who had had a hemorrhage for twelve years. She had spent everything she had on doctors* and still could find no cure. [44] She came up behind Jesus and touched the fringe of his robe. Immediately, the bleeding stopped.

[45] "Who touched me?" Jesus asked.

Everyone denied it, and Peter said, "Master, this whole crowd is pressing up against you."

[46] But Jesus told him, "No, someone deliberately touched me, for I felt healing power go out from me." [47] When the woman realized that Jesus knew, she began to tremble and fell to her knees before him. The whole crowd heard her explain why she had touched him and that she had been immediately healed. [48] "Daughter," he said to her, "your faith has made you well. Go in peace."

[49] While he was still speaking to her, a

8:26 Some manuscripts read *Gadarenes*; other manuscripts read *Gergesenes*. See Matt 8:28; Mark 5:1.   8:43 Some manuscripts omit *She had spent everything she had on doctors.*

messenger arrived from Jairus's home with the message, "Your little girl is dead. There's no use troubling the Teacher now."

⁵⁰But when Jesus heard what had happened, he said to Jairus, "Don't be afraid. Just trust me, and she will be all right."

⁵¹When they arrived at the house, Jesus wouldn't let anyone go in with him except Peter, James, John, and the little girl's father and mother. ⁵²The house was filled with people weeping and wailing, but he said, "Stop the weeping! She isn't dead; she is only asleep."

⁵³But the crowd laughed at him because they all knew she had died. ⁵⁴Then Jesus took her by the hand and said in a loud voice, "Get up, my child!" ⁵⁵And at that moment her life returned, and she immediately stood up! Then Jesus told them to give her something to eat. ⁵⁶Her parents were overwhelmed, but Jesus insisted that they not tell anyone what had happened.

CHAPTER 9

One day Jesus called together his twelve apostles and gave them power and authority to cast out demons and to heal all diseases. ²Then he sent them out to tell everyone about the coming of the Kingdom of God and to heal the sick. ³"Don't even take along a walking stick," he instructed them, "nor a traveler's bag, nor food, nor money. Not even an extra coat. ⁴When you enter each village, be a guest in only one home. ⁵If the people of the village won't receive your message when you enter it, shake off its dust from your feet as you leave. It is a sign that you have abandoned that village to its fate."

⁶So they began their circuit of the villages, preaching the Good News and healing the sick.

⁷When reports of Jesus' miracles reached Herod Antipas,* he was worried and puzzled because some were saying, "This is John the Baptist come back to life again." ⁸Others were saying, "It is Elijah or some other ancient prophet risen from the dead." ⁹"I beheaded John," Herod said, "so who is this man about whom I hear such strange stories?" And he tried to see him.

¹⁰When the apostles returned, they told Jesus everything they had done. Then he slipped quietly away with them toward the town of Bethsaida. ¹¹But the crowds found out where he was going, and they followed him. And he welcomed them, teaching them about the Kingdom of God and curing those who were ill. ¹²Late in the afternoon the twelve disciples came to him and said, "Send the crowds away to the nearby villages and farms, so they can find food and lodging for the night. There is nothing to eat here in this deserted place."

¹³But Jesus said, "You feed them."

"Impossible!" they protested. "We have only five loaves of bread and two fish. Or are you expecting us to go and buy enough food for this whole crowd?" ¹⁴For there were about five thousand men there.

"Just tell them to sit down on the ground in groups of about fifty each," Jesus replied. ¹⁵So the people all sat down. ¹⁶Jesus took the five loaves and two fish, looked up toward heaven, and asked God's blessing on the food. Breaking the loaves into pieces, he kept giving the bread and fish to the disciples to give to the people. ¹⁷They all ate as much as they wanted, and they picked up twelve baskets of leftovers!

¹⁸One day as Jesus was alone, praying, he came over to his disciples and asked them, "Who do people say I am?"

¹⁹"Well," they replied, "some say John the Baptist, some say Elijah, and others say you are one of the other ancient prophets risen from the dead."

²⁰Then he asked them, "Who do you say I am?"

Peter replied, "You are the Messiah sent from God!"

²¹Jesus warned them not to tell anyone about this. ²²"For I, the Son of Man, must suffer many terrible things," he said. "I will be rejected by the leaders, the leading priests, and the teachers of religious law. I will be killed, but three days later I will be raised from the dead."

²³Then he said to the crowd, "If any of you wants to be my follower, you must put aside your selfish ambition, shoulder your cross daily, and follow me. ²⁴If you try to keep your life for yourself, you will lose it. But if you give up your life for me, you will find true life. ²⁵And how do you benefit if you gain the whole world but lose or forfeit your own soul in the process? ²⁶If a person is ashamed of me and my message, I, the Son of Man, will be ashamed of that person when I return in my glory and in the glory

9:7 Greek *Herod the tetrarch*. He was a son of King Herod and was ruler over one of the four districts in Palestine.

of the Father and the holy angels. ²⁷And I assure you that some of you standing here right now will not die before you see the Kingdom of God."

²⁸About eight days later Jesus took Peter, James, and John to a mountain to pray. ²⁹And as he was praying, the appearance of his face changed, and his clothing became dazzling white. ³⁰Then two men, Moses and Elijah, appeared and began talking with Jesus. ³¹They were glorious to see. And they were speaking of how he was about to fulfill God's plan by dying in Jerusalem.

³²Peter and the others were very drowsy and had fallen asleep. Now they woke up and saw Jesus' glory and the two men standing with him. ³³As Moses and Elijah were starting to leave, Peter, not even knowing what he was saying, blurted out, "Master, this is wonderful! We will make three shrines*—one for you, one for Moses, and one for Elijah." ³⁴But even as he was saying this, a cloud came over them; and terror gripped them as it covered them.

³⁵Then a voice from the cloud said, "This is my Son, my Chosen One.* Listen to him." ³⁶When the voice died away, Jesus was there alone. They didn't tell anyone what they had seen until long after this happened.

³⁷The next day, after they had come down the mountain, a huge crowd met Jesus. ³⁸A man in the crowd called out to him, "Teacher, look at my boy, who is my only son. ³⁹An evil spirit keeps seizing him, making him scream. It throws him into convulsions so that he foams at the mouth. It is always hitting and injuring him. It hardly ever leaves him alone. ⁴⁰I begged your disciples to cast the spirit out, but they couldn't do it."

⁴¹"You stubborn, faithless people," Jesus said, "how long must I be with you and put up with you? Bring him here." ⁴²As the boy came forward, the demon knocked him to the ground and threw him into a violent convulsion. But Jesus rebuked the evil spirit and healed the boy. Then he gave him back to his father. ⁴³Awe gripped the people as they saw this display of God's power.

While everyone was marveling over all the wonderful things he was doing, Jesus said to his disciples, ⁴⁴"Listen to me and remember what I say. The Son of Man is going to be betrayed." ⁴⁵But they didn't know what he meant. Its significance was hidden from them, so they could not understand it, and they were afraid to ask him about it.

⁴⁶Then there was an argument among them as to which of them would be the greatest. ⁴⁷But Jesus knew their thoughts, so he brought a little child to his side. ⁴⁸Then he said to them, "Anyone who welcomes a little child like this on my behalf welcomes me, and anyone who welcomes me welcomes my Father who sent me. Whoever is the least among you is the greatest."

⁴⁹John said to Jesus, "Master, we saw someone using your name to cast out demons. We tried to stop him because he isn't in our group."

⁵⁰But Jesus said, "Don't stop him! Anyone who is not against you is for you."

⁵¹As the time drew near for his return to heaven, Jesus resolutely set out for Jerusalem. ⁵²He sent messengers ahead to a Samaritan village to prepare for his arrival. ⁵³But they were turned away. The people of the village refused to have anything to do with Jesus because he had resolved to go to Jerusalem. ⁵⁴When James and John heard about it, they said to Jesus, "Lord, should we order down fire from heaven to burn them up*?" ⁵⁵But Jesus turned and rebuked them.* ⁵⁶So they went on to another village.

⁵⁷As they were walking along someone said to Jesus, "I will follow you no matter where you go."

⁵⁸But Jesus replied, "Foxes have dens to live in, and birds have nests, but I, the Son of Man, have no home of my own, not even a place to lay my head."

⁵⁹He said to another person, "Come, be my disciple."

The man agreed, but he said, "Lord, first let me return home and bury my father."

⁶⁰Jesus replied, "Let those who are spiritually dead care for their own dead.* Your duty is to go and preach the coming of the Kingdom of God."

⁶¹Another said, "Yes, Lord, I will follow you, but first let me say good-bye to my family."

⁶²But Jesus told him, "Anyone who puts a hand to the plow and then looks back is not fit for the Kingdom of God."

9:33 Or *shelters;* Greek reads *tabernacles.*   **9:35** Some manuscripts read *This is my beloved Son.*   **9:54** Some manuscripts add *as Elijah did.*   **9:55** Some manuscripts add *And he said, "You don't realize what your hearts are like.* ⁵⁶*For the Son of Man has not come to destroy men's lives, but to save them."*   **9:60** Greek *Let the dead bury their own dead.*

OCTOBER 19 ☐ DAY 293
LUKE 10–12
Antagonism toward the Son of Man

OVERVIEW The corps of disciples expands as Jesus sends out thirty-five pairs of ministers to prepare the way before him. As the opportunities for ministry increase, so too does the opposition. Open rejection by the Pharisees leads Christ to pronounce woes on the hypocritical religious leaders and to warn his disciples of the Pharisees' damaging influence. This leads to a series of parables and warnings concerning the future judgment of God on those who are indifferent or unfaithful in their service for God.

Chapter 10	Chapter 11	Chapter 12
Denouncing the Unresponsive	Denouncing the Insincere	Denouncing the Unfaithful
Capernaum	Pharisees	Parables

YOUR DAILY WALK What do sparrows, hairs, ravens, lilies, and you have in common?

Answer: They are all objects of God's special care.

Go to the nearest window and watch for a bird. Then ponder this: God has the welfare of that tiny creature on his mind (12:6).

Faith never knows where it is being led, but it loves and knows the one who is leading.

Pull out your comb or hair brush, run it through your hair several times and notice the hairs that were pulled out. Then ponder this: God knows exactly how many hairs you have left (12:7).

Take a walk on your lunch hour today to enjoy the beauties of nature around you. Then ponder this: God is making sure that the flowers have rain and the birds have food (12:24, 27-28).

Now stand in front of a mirror to see one of God's creations about which he cares infinitely more than the flowers and birds: *you!* If God expends such energy and tender attention on the less important parts of his creation, how much more must he be interested in your welfare and happiness?

Spend a few extra minutes meditating on 12:22-31 until your "little faith" is rekindled in the constant loving care of your heavenly Father.

INSIGHT Something's Fishy about This Sign

Luke records Jesus' words comparing himself with the prophet Jonah and speaking of the "sign of Jonah" (11:29-30). But what is the sign of Jonah? Luke doesn't say. Check Matthew 12:38-40. Could you explain it to a non-Christian friend? Try it.

CHAPTER 10

The Lord now chose seventy-two* other disciples and sent them on ahead in pairs to all the towns and villages he planned to visit. ²These were his instructions to them: "The harvest is so great, but the workers are so few. Pray to the Lord who is in charge of the harvest, and ask him to send out more workers for his fields. ³Go now, and remember that I am sending you out as lambs among wolves. ⁴Don't take

along any money, or a traveler's bag, or even an extra pair of sandals. And don't stop to greet anyone on the road.

⁵"Whenever you enter a home, give it your blessing. ⁶If those who live there are worthy, the blessing will stand; if they are not, the blessing will return to you. ⁷When you enter a town, don't move around from home to home. Stay in one place, eating and drinking what they provide you. Don't hesitate to accept

10:1 Some manuscripts read *70;* also in 10:17.

hospitality, because those who work deserve their pay.

8"If a town welcomes you, eat whatever is set before you 9and heal the sick. As you heal them, say, 'The Kingdom of God is near you now.' 10But if a town refuses to welcome you, go out into its streets and say, 11'We wipe the dust of your town from our feet as a public announcement of your doom. And don't forget the Kingdom of God is near!' 12The truth is, even wicked Sodom will be better off than such a town on the judgment day.

13"What horrors await you, Korazin and Bethsaida! For if the miracles I did in you had been done in wicked Tyre and Sidon, their people would have sat in deep repentance long ago, clothed in sackcloth and throwing ashes on their heads to show their remorse. 14Yes, Tyre and Sidon will be better off on the judgment day than you. 15And you people of Capernaum, will you be exalted to heaven? No, you will be brought down to the place of the dead.*"

16Then he said to the disciples, "Anyone who accepts your message is also accepting me. And anyone who rejects you is rejecting me. And anyone who rejects me is rejecting God who sent me."

17When the seventy-two disciples returned, they joyfully reported to him, "Lord, even the demons obey us when we use your name!"

18"Yes," he told them, "I saw Satan falling from heaven as a flash of lightning! 19And I have given you authority over all the power of the enemy, and you can walk among snakes and scorpions and crush them. Nothing will injure you. 20But don't rejoice just because evil spirits obey you; rejoice because your names are registered as citizens of heaven."

21Then Jesus was filled with the joy of the Holy Spirit and said, "O Father, Lord of heaven and earth, thank you for hiding the truth from those who think themselves so wise and clever, and for revealing it to the childlike. Yes, Father, it pleased you to do it this way.

22"My Father has given me authority over everything. No one really knows the Son except the Father, and no one really knows the Father except the Son and those to whom the Son chooses to reveal him."

23Then when they were alone, he turned to the disciples and said, "How privileged you are to see what you have seen. 24I tell you, many prophets and kings have longed to see and hear what you have seen and heard, but they could not."

25One day an expert in religious law stood up to test Jesus by asking him this question: "Teacher, what must I do to receive eternal life?"

26Jesus replied, "What does the law of Moses say? How do you read it?"

27The man answered, " 'You must love the Lord your God with all your heart, all your soul, all your strength, and all your mind.' And, 'Love your neighbor as yourself.'"*

28"Right!" Jesus told him. "Do this and you will live!"

29The man wanted to justify his actions, so he asked Jesus, "And who is my neighbor?"

30Jesus replied with an illustration: "A Jewish man was traveling on a trip from Jerusalem to Jericho, and he was attacked by bandits. They stripped him of his clothes and money, beat him up, and left him half dead beside the road.

31"By chance a Jewish priest came along; but when he saw the man lying there, he crossed to the other side of the road and passed him by. 32A Temple assistant* walked over and looked at him lying there, but he also passed by on the other side.

33"Then a despised Samaritan came along, and when he saw the man, he felt deep pity. 34Kneeling beside him, the Samaritan soothed his wounds with medicine and bandaged them. Then he put the man on his own donkey and took him to an inn, where he took care of him. 35The next day he handed the innkeeper two pieces of silver* and told him to take care of the man. 'If his bill runs higher than that,' he said, 'I'll pay the difference the next time I am here.'

36"Now which of these three would you say was a neighbor to the man who was attacked by bandits?" Jesus asked.

37The man replied, "The one who showed him mercy."

Then Jesus said, "Yes, now go and do the same."

38As Jesus and the disciples continued on their way to Jerusalem, they came to a village where a woman named Martha wel-

---

10:15 Greek *to Hades.*   10:27 Deut 6:5; Lev 19:18.   10:32 Greek *A Levite.*   10:35 Greek *2 denarii.* A denarius was the equivalent of a full day's wage.

comed them into her home. [39]Her sister, Mary, sat at the Lord's feet, listening to what he taught. [40]But Martha was worrying over the big dinner she was preparing. She came to Jesus and said, "Lord, doesn't it seem unfair to you that my sister just sits here while I do all the work? Tell her to come and help me."

[41]But the Lord said to her, "My dear Martha, you are so upset over all these details! [42]There is really only one thing worth being concerned about. Mary has discovered it— and I won't take it away from her."

CHAPTER 11

Once when Jesus had been out praying, one of his disciples came to him as he finished and said, "Lord, teach us to pray, just as John taught his disciples."

[2]He said, "This is how you should pray:

"Father, may your name be honored.
    May your Kingdom come soon.
[3] Give us our food day by day.
[4] And forgive us our sins—
    just as we forgive those who have
        sinned against us.
And don't let us yield to temptation.*"

[5]Then, teaching them more about prayer, he used this illustration: "Suppose you went to a friend's house at midnight, wanting to borrow three loaves of bread. You would say to him, [6]'A friend of mine has just arrived for a visit, and I have nothing for him to eat.' [7]He would call out from his bedroom, 'Don't bother me. The door is locked for the night, and we are all in bed. I can't help you this time.' [8]But I tell you this—though he won't do it as a friend, if you keep knocking long enough, he will get up and give you what you want so his reputation won't be damaged.*

[9]"And so I tell you, keep on asking, and you will be given what you ask for. Keep on looking, and you will find. Keep on knocking, and the door will be opened. [10]For everyone who asks, receives. Everyone who seeks, finds. And the door is opened to everyone who knocks.

[11]"You fathers—if your children ask* for a fish, do you give them a snake instead? [12]Or if they ask for an egg, do you give them a scorpion? Of course not! [13]If you sinful people know how to give good gifts to your children, how much more will your heavenly Father give the Holy Spirit to those who ask him."

[14]One day Jesus cast a demon out of a man who couldn't speak, and the man's voice returned to him. The crowd was amazed, [15]but some said, "No wonder he can cast out demons. He gets his power from Satan,* the prince of demons!" [16]Trying to test Jesus, others asked for a miraculous sign from heaven to see if he was from God.

[17]He knew their thoughts, so he said, "Any kingdom at war with itself is doomed. A divided home is also doomed. [18]You say I am empowered by the prince of demons.* But if Satan is fighting against himself by empowering me to cast out his demons, how can his kingdom survive? [19]And if I am empowered by the prince of demons, what about your own followers? They cast out demons, too, so they will judge you for what you have said. [20]But if I am casting out demons by the power of God, then the Kingdom of God has arrived among you. [21]For when Satan,* who is completely armed, guards his palace, it is safe—[22]until someone who is stronger attacks and overpowers him, strips him of his weapons, and carries off his belongings.

[23]"Anyone who isn't helping me opposes me, and anyone who isn't working with me is actually working against me.

[24]"When an evil spirit leaves a person, it goes into the desert, searching for rest. But when it finds none, it says, 'I will return to the person I came from.' [25]So it returns and finds that its former home is all swept and clean. [26]Then the spirit finds seven other spirits more evil than itself, and they all enter the person and live there. And so that person is worse off than before."

[27]As he was speaking, a woman in the crowd called out, "God bless your mother— the womb from which you came, and the breasts that nursed you!"

[28]He replied, "But even more blessed are all who hear the word of God and put it into practice."

[29]As the crowd pressed in on Jesus, he said, "These are evil times, and this evil generation keeps asking me to show them a miraculous sign. But the only sign I will give them is the sign of the prophet Jonah.

11:2-4 Some manuscripts add additional portions of the Lord's Prayer as it reads in Matt 6:9-13.   11:8 Greek *in order to avoid shame,* or *because of [your] persistence.*   11:11 Some manuscripts add *for bread, do you give them a stone? Or if they ask.*   11:15 Greek *Beelzeboul.*   11:18 Greek *by Beelzeboul;* also in 11:19.   11:21 Greek *the strong one.*

30 What happened to him was a sign to the people of Nineveh that God had sent him. What happens to me will be a sign that God has sent me, the Son of Man, to these people.

31 "The queen of Sheba* will rise up against this generation on judgment day and condemn it, because she came from a distant land to hear the wisdom of Solomon. And now someone greater than Solomon is here—and you refuse to listen to him. 32 The people of Nineveh, too, will rise up against this generation on judgment day and condemn it, because they repented at the preaching of Jonah. And now someone greater than Jonah is here—and you refuse to repent.

33 "No one lights a lamp and then hides it or puts it under a basket. Instead, it is put on a lampstand to give light to all who enter the room. 34 Your eye is a lamp for your body. A pure eye lets sunshine into your soul. But an evil eye shuts out the light and plunges you into darkness. 35 Make sure that the light you think you have is not really darkness. 36 If you are filled with light, with no dark corners, then your whole life will be radiant, as though a floodlight is shining on you."

37 As Jesus was speaking, one of the Pharisees invited him home for a meal. So he went in and took his place at the table. 38 His host was amazed to see that he sat down to eat without first performing the ceremonial washing required by Jewish custom. 39 Then the Lord said to him, "You Pharisees are so careful to clean the outside of the cup and the dish, but inside you are still filthy—full of greed and wickedness! 40 Fools! Didn't God make the inside as well as the outside? 41 So give to the needy what you greedily possess, and you will be clean all over.

42 "But how terrible it will be for you Pharisees! For you are careful to tithe even the tiniest part of your income,* but you completely forget about justice and the love of God. You should tithe, yes, but you should not leave undone the more important things.

43 "How terrible it will be for you Pharisees! For how you love the seats of honor in the synagogues and the respectful greetings from everyone as you walk through the markets! 44 Yes, how terrible it will be for you. For you are like hidden graves in a field. People walk over them without knowing the corruption they are stepping on."

45 "Teacher," said an expert in religious law, "you have insulted us, too, in what you just said."

46 "Yes," said Jesus, "how terrible it will be for you experts in religious law! For you crush people beneath impossible religious demands, and you never lift a finger to help ease the burden. 47 How terrible it will be for you! For you build tombs for the very prophets your ancestors killed long ago. 48 Murderers! You agree with your ancestors that what they did was right. You would have done the same yourselves. 49 This is what God in his wisdom said about you:* 'I will send prophets and apostles to them, and they will kill some and persecute the others.'

50 "And you of this generation will be held responsible for the murder of all God's prophets from the creation of the world—51 from the murder of Abel to the murder of Zechariah, who was killed between the altar and the sanctuary. Yes, it will surely be charged against you.

52 "How terrible it will be for you experts in religious law! For you hide the key to knowledge from the people. You don't enter the Kingdom yourselves, and you prevent others from entering."

53 As Jesus finished speaking, the Pharisees and teachers of religious law were furious. From that time on they grilled him with many hostile questions, 54 trying to trap him into saying something they could use against him.

CHAPTER 12

Meanwhile, the crowds grew until thousands were milling about and crushing each other. Jesus turned first to his disciples and warned them, "Beware of the yeast of the Pharisees—beware of their hypocrisy. 2 The time is coming when everything will be revealed; all that is secret will be made public. 3 Whatever you have said in the dark will be heard in the light, and what you have whispered behind closed doors will be shouted from the housetops for all to hear!

4 "Dear friends, don't be afraid of those who want to kill you. They can only kill the body; they cannot do any more to you. 5 But

11:31 Greek *the queen of the south.*   11:42 Greek *to tithe the mint and the rue and every herb.*   11:49 Greek *Therefore, the wisdom of God said.*

I'll tell you whom to fear. Fear God, who has the power to kill people and then throw them into hell.

⁶"What is the price of five sparrows? A couple of pennies? Yet God does not forget a single one of them. ⁷And the very hairs on your head are all numbered. So don't be afraid; you are more valuable to him than a whole flock of sparrows.

⁸"And I assure you of this: If anyone acknowledges me publicly here on earth, I, the Son of Man, will openly acknowledge that person in the presence of God's angels. ⁹But if anyone denies me here on earth, I will deny that person before God's angels. ¹⁰Yet those who speak against the Son of Man may be forgiven, but anyone who speaks blasphemies against the Holy Spirit will never be forgiven.

¹¹"And when you are brought to trial in the synagogues and before rulers and authorities, don't worry about what to say in your defense, ¹²for the Holy Spirit will teach you what needs to be said even as you are standing there."

¹³Then someone called from the crowd, "Teacher, please tell my brother to divide our father's estate with me."

¹⁴Jesus replied, "Friend, who made me a judge over you to decide such things as that?" ¹⁵Then he said, "Beware! Don't be greedy for what you don't have. Real life is not measured by how much we own."

¹⁶And he gave an illustration: "A rich man had a fertile farm that produced fine crops. ¹⁷In fact, his barns were full to overflowing. ¹⁸So he said, 'I know! I'll tear down my barns and build bigger ones. Then I'll have room enough to store everything. ¹⁹And I'll sit back and say to myself, My friend, you have enough stored away for years to come. Now take it easy! Eat, drink, and be merry!'

²⁰"But God said to him, 'You fool! You will die this very night. Then who will get it all?'

²¹"Yes, a person is a fool to store up earthly wealth but not have a rich relationship with God."

²²Then turning to his disciples, Jesus said, "So I tell you, don't worry about everyday life—whether you have enough food to eat or clothes to wear. ²³For life consists of far more than food and clothing. ²⁴Look at the ravens. They don't need to plant or harvest or put food in barns because God feeds them. And you are far more valuable to him than any birds! ²⁵Can all your worries add a single moment to your life? Of course not! ²⁶And if worry can't do little things like that, what's the use of worrying over bigger things?

²⁷"Look at the lilies and how they grow. They don't work or make their clothing, yet Solomon in all his glory was not dressed as beautifully as they are. ²⁸And if God cares so wonderfully for flowers that are here today and gone tomorrow, won't he more surely care for you? You have so little faith! ²⁹And don't worry about food—what to eat and drink. Don't worry whether God will provide it for you. ³⁰These things dominate the thoughts of most people, but your Father already knows your needs. ³¹He will give you all you need from day to day if you make the Kingdom of God your primary concern.

³²"So don't be afraid, little flock. For it gives your Father great happiness to give you the Kingdom.

³³"Sell what you have and give to those in need. This will store up treasure for you in heaven! And the purses of heaven have no holes in them. Your treasure will be safe—no thief can steal it and no moth can destroy it. ³⁴Wherever your treasure is, there your heart and thoughts will also be.

³⁵"Be dressed for service and well prepared, ³⁶as though you were waiting for your master to return from the wedding feast. Then you will be ready to open the door and let him in the moment he arrives and knocks. ³⁷There will be special favor for those who are ready and waiting for his return. I tell you, he himself will seat them, put on an apron, and serve them as they sit and eat! ³⁸He may come in the middle of the night or just before dawn.* But whenever he comes, there will be special favor for his servants who are ready!

³⁹"Know this: A homeowner who knew exactly when a burglar was coming would not permit the house to be broken into. ⁴⁰You must be ready all the time, for the Son of Man will come when least expected."

⁴¹Peter asked, "Lord, is this illustration just for us or for everyone?"

⁴²And the Lord replied, "I'm talking to any faithful, sensible servant to whom the master gives the responsibility of managing his household and feeding his family.

12:38 Greek *in the second or third watch.*

⁴³If the master returns and finds that the servant has done a good job, there will be a reward. ⁴⁴I assure you, the master will put that servant in charge of all he owns. ⁴⁵But if the servant thinks, 'My master won't be back for a while,' and begins oppressing the other servants, partying, and getting drunk—⁴⁶well, the master will return unannounced and unexpected. He will tear the servant apart and banish him with the unfaithful. ⁴⁷The servant will be severely punished, for though he knew his duty, he refused to do it.

⁴⁸"But people who are not aware that they are doing wrong will be punished only lightly. Much is required from those to whom much is given, and much more is required from those to whom much more is given.

⁴⁹"I have come to bring fire to the earth, and I wish that my task were already completed! ⁵⁰There is a terrible baptism ahead of me, and I am under a heavy burden until it is accomplished. ⁵¹Do you think I have

come to bring peace to the earth? No, I have come to bring strife and division! ⁵²From now on families will be split apart, three in favor of me, and two against—or the other way around. ⁵³There will be a division between father and son, mother and daughter, mother-in-law and daughter-in-law."

⁵⁴Then Jesus turned to the crowd and said, "When you see clouds beginning to form in the west, you say, 'Here comes a shower.' And you are right. ⁵⁵When the south wind blows, you say, 'Today will be a scorcher.' And it is. ⁵⁶You hypocrites! You know how to interpret the appearance of the earth and the sky, but you can't interpret these present times.

⁵⁷"Why can't you decide for yourselves what is right? ⁵⁸If you are on the way to court and you meet your accuser, try to settle the matter before it reaches the judge, or you may be sentenced and handed over to an officer and thrown in jail. ⁵⁹And if that happens, you won't be free again until you have paid the last penny."

OCTOBER 20 □ DAY 294
LUKE 13–15
Parables of the Son of Man (Part 1)

 OVERVIEW Jesus uses a recent report of Pilate's slaughter of some Galileans to emphasize the need for repentance. God is patient, but his sense of justice is perfect. Though it may sometimes seem overdue, justice will indeed come—a truth that brings tears to the Savior's eyes as he gazes at the hard-hearted city of Jerusalem. Jesus knows that, just as the people have spurned his message, so, too, they will treat his disciples with contempt. Discipleship will be costly for those who take up their cross to follow him. But in God's sight, every lost sinner is a cause for seeking, and every converted sinner a cause for heavenly rejoicing.

Chapter 13	Chapter 14	Chapter 15
The Need for Repentance	The Price of Discipleship	The Value of the Individual
Counting the Cost		Seeking the Lost

 YOUR DAILY WALK In military operations the machinery, equipment, supplies, and even personnel are commonly considered "expendable" for the sake of the battle in order to insure the ultimate victory.

Contrast that with spiritual warfare in which each human being is infinitely valuable. In spiritual conflict only one person was deemed "expendable"—the Lord Jesus Christ—and even his seeming defeat on the cross was turned to victory three days later.

You can give
without loving,
but you cannot
love without
giving.

How great is God's love for lost men? "But God showed his great love for us by sending Christ to die for us while we were still sinners" (Romans 5:8).

How can you help to send this good news of sins forgiven to an unsaved friend across the street . . . or halfway around the world? Why not send a special gift to the mission agency of your choice today and take a baked treat (and a word of witness) to a neighbor, so that sinners far and near might learn of God's love firsthand? After all, what if you had been considered "expendable" by the one who shared the gospel with you?

INSIGHT More than Mere Gifts
The lost son's father had more in mind than simply providing for his son's needs when he gave him a robe, a ring, and sandals. The gifts symbolized how he again accepted him as a son: A robe signified honor; a ring, power; and sandals set him apart from the barefooted servants.

CHAPTER 13

About this time Jesus was informed that Pilate had murdered some people from Galilee as they were sacrificing at the Temple in Jerusalem. [2]"Do you think those Galileans were worse sinners than other people from Galilee?" he asked. "Is that why they suffered? [3]Not at all! And you will also perish unless you turn from your evil ways and turn to God. [4]And what about the eighteen men who died when the Tower of Siloam fell on them? Were they the worst sinners in Jerusalem? [5]No, and I tell you again that unless you repent, you will also perish."

[6]Then Jesus used this illustration: "A man planted a fig tree in his garden and came again and again to see if there was any fruit on it, but he was always disappointed. [7]Finally, he said to his gardener, 'I've waited three years, and there hasn't been a single fig! Cut it down. It's taking up space we can use for something else.'

[8]"The gardener answered, 'Give it one more chance. Leave it another year, and I'll give it special attention and plenty of fertilizer. [9]If we get figs next year, fine. If not, you can cut it down.'"

[10]One Sabbath day as Jesus was teaching in a synagogue, [11]he saw a woman who had been crippled by an evil spirit. She had been bent double for eighteen years and was unable to stand up straight. [12]When Jesus saw her, he called her over and said, "Woman, you are healed of your sickness!" [13]Then he touched her, and instantly she could stand straight. How she praised and thanked God!

[14]But the leader in charge of the synagogue was indignant that Jesus had healed her on the Sabbath day. "There are six days of the week for working," he said to the crowd. "Come on those days to be healed, not on the Sabbath."

[15]But the Lord replied, "You hypocrite! You work on the Sabbath day! Don't you untie your ox or your donkey from their stalls on the Sabbath and lead them out for water? [16]Wasn't it necessary for me, even on the Sabbath day, to free this dear woman* from the bondage in which Satan has held her for eighteen years?" [17]This shamed his enemies. And all the people rejoiced at the wonderful things he did.

[18]Then Jesus said, "What is the Kingdom of God like? How can I illustrate it? [19]It is like a tiny mustard seed planted in a garden; it grows and becomes a tree, and the birds come and find shelter among its branches."

[20]He also asked, "What else is the Kingdom of God like? [21]It is like yeast used by a woman making bread. Even though she used a large amount* of flour, the yeast permeated every part of the dough."

[22]Jesus went through the towns and villages, teaching as he went, always pressing on toward Jerusalem. [23]Someone asked him, "Lord, will only a few be saved?"

He replied, [24]"The door to heaven is narrow. Work hard to get in, because many will try to enter, [25]but when the head of the house has locked the door, it will be too late. Then you will stand outside knocking and pleading, 'Lord, open the door for us!' But he will reply, 'I do not know you.' [26]You

13:16 Greek *this woman, a daughter of Abraham.*   **13:21** Greek *3 measures.*

will say, 'But we ate and drank with you, and you taught in our streets.' ²⁷And he will reply, 'I tell you, I don't know you. Go away, all you who do evil.'

²⁸"And there will be great weeping and gnashing of teeth, for you will see Abraham, Isaac, Jacob, and all the prophets within the Kingdom of God, but you will be thrown out. ²⁹Then people will come from all over the world to take their places in the Kingdom of God. ³⁰And note this: Some who are despised now will be greatly honored then; and some who are greatly honored now will be despised then.*"

³¹A few minutes later some Pharisees said to him, "Get out of here if you want to live, because Herod Antipas wants to kill you!"

³²Jesus replied, "Go tell that fox that I will keep on casting out demons and doing miracles of healing today and tomorrow; and the third day I will accomplish my purpose. ³³Yes, today, tomorrow, and the next day I must proceed on my way. For it wouldn't do for a prophet of God to be killed except in Jerusalem!

³⁴"O Jerusalem, Jerusalem, the city that kills the prophets and stones God's messengers! How often I have wanted to gather your children together as a hen protects her chicks beneath her wings, but you wouldn't let me. ³⁵And now look, your house is left to you empty. And you will never see me again until you say, 'Bless the one who comes in the name of the Lord!'*"

CHAPTER 14
One Sabbath day Jesus was in the home of a leader of the Pharisees. The people were watching him closely, ²because there was a man there whose arms and legs were swollen.* ³Jesus asked the Pharisees and experts in religious law, "Well, is it permitted in the law to heal people on the Sabbath day, or not?" ⁴When they refused to answer, Jesus touched the sick man and healed him and sent him away. ⁵Then he turned to them and asked, "Which of you doesn't work on the Sabbath? If your son* or your cow falls into a pit, don't you proceed at once to get him out?" ⁶Again they had no answer.

⁷When Jesus noticed that all who had come to the dinner were trying to sit near the head of the table, he gave them this advice: ⁸"If you are invited to a wedding feast, don't always head for the best seat. What if someone more respected than you has also been invited? ⁹The host will say, 'Let this person sit here instead.' Then you will be embarrassed and will have to take whatever seat is left at the foot of the table!

¹⁰"Do this instead—sit at the foot of the table. Then when your host sees you, he will come and say, 'Friend, we have a better place than this for you!' Then you will be honored in front of all the other guests. ¹¹For the proud will be humbled, but the humble will be honored."

¹²Then he turned to his host. "When you put on a luncheon or a dinner," he said, "don't invite your friends, brothers, relatives, and rich neighbors. For they will repay you by inviting you back. ¹³Instead, invite the poor, the crippled, the lame, and the blind. ¹⁴Then at the resurrection of the godly, God will reward you for inviting those who could not repay you."

¹⁵Hearing this, a man sitting at the table with Jesus exclaimed, "What a privilege it would be to have a share in the Kingdom of God!"

¹⁶Jesus replied with this illustration: "A man prepared a great feast and sent out many invitations. ¹⁷When all was ready, he sent his servant around to notify the guests that it was time for them to come. ¹⁸But they all began making excuses. One said he had just bought a field and wanted to inspect it, so he asked to be excused. ¹⁹Another said he had just bought five pair of oxen and wanted to try them out. ²⁰Another had just been married, so he said he couldn't come.

²¹"The servant returned and told his master what they had said. His master was angry and said, 'Go quickly into the streets and alleys of the city and invite the poor, the crippled, the lame, and the blind.' ²²After the servant had done this, he reported, 'There is still room for more.' ²³So his master said, 'Go out into the country lanes and behind the hedges and urge anyone you find to come, so that the house will be full. ²⁴For none of those I invited first will get even the smallest taste of what I had prepared for them.'"

²⁵Great crowds were following Jesus. He turned around and said to them, ²⁶"If you want to be my follower you must love me more than* your own father and mother,

---

13:30 Greek *Some are last who will be first, and some are first who will be last.*   **13:35** Ps 118:26.   **14:2** Traditionally translated *who had dropsy.*   **14:5** Some manuscripts read *donkey.*   **14:26** Greek *you must hate.*

wife and children, brothers and sisters—yes, more than your own life. Otherwise, you cannot be my disciple. ²⁷And you cannot be my disciple if you do not carry your own cross and follow me.

²⁸"But don't begin until you count the cost. For who would begin construction of a building without first getting estimates and then checking to see if there is enough money to pay the bills? ²⁹Otherwise, you might complete only the foundation before running out of funds. And then how everyone would laugh at you! ³⁰They would say, 'There's the person who started that building and ran out of money before it was finished!'

³¹"Or what king would ever dream of going to war without first sitting down with his counselors and discussing whether his army of ten thousand is strong enough to defeat the twenty thousand soldiers who are marching against him? ³²If he is not able, then while the enemy is still far away, he will send a delegation to discuss terms of peace. ³³So no one can become my disciple without giving up everything for me.

³⁴"Salt is good for seasoning. But if it loses its flavor, how do you make it salty again? ³⁵Flavorless salt is good neither for the soil nor for fertilizer. It is thrown away. Anyone who is willing to hear should listen and understand!"

CHAPTER 15

Tax collectors and other notorious sinners often came to listen to Jesus teach. ²This made the Pharisees and teachers of religious law complain that he was associating with such despicable people—even eating with them!

³So Jesus used this illustration: ⁴"If you had one hundred sheep, and one of them strayed away and was lost in the wilderness, wouldn't you leave the ninety-nine others to go and search for the lost one until you found it? ⁵And then you would joyfully carry it home on your shoulders. ⁶When you arrived, you would call together your friends and neighbors to rejoice with you because your lost sheep was found. ⁷In the same way, heaven will be happier over one lost sinner who returns to God than over ninety-nine others who are righteous and haven't strayed away!

⁸"Or suppose a woman has ten valuable silver coins* and loses one. Won't she light a lamp and look in every corner of the house and sweep every nook and cranny until she finds it? ⁹And when she finds it, she will call in her friends and neighbors to rejoice with her because she has found her lost coin. ¹⁰In the same way, there is joy in the presence of God's angels when even one sinner repents."

¹¹To illustrate the point further, Jesus told them this story: "A man had two sons. ¹²The younger son told his father, 'I want my share of your estate now, instead of waiting until you die.' So his father agreed to divide his wealth between his sons.

¹³"A few days later this younger son packed all his belongings and took a trip to a distant land, and there he wasted all his money on wild living. ¹⁴About the time his money ran out, a great famine swept over the land, and he began to starve. ¹⁵He persuaded a local farmer to hire him to feed his pigs. ¹⁶The boy became so hungry that even the pods he was feeding the pigs looked good to him. But no one gave him anything.

¹⁷"When he finally came to his senses, he said to himself, 'At home even the hired men have food enough to spare, and here I am, dying of hunger! ¹⁸I will go home to my father and say, "Father, I have sinned against both heaven and you, ¹⁹and I am no longer worthy of being called your son. Please take me on as a hired man."'

²⁰"So he returned home to his father. And while he was still a long distance away, his father saw him coming. Filled with love and compassion, he ran to his son, embraced him, and kissed him. ²¹His son said to him, 'Father, I have sinned against both heaven and you, and I am no longer worthy of being called your son.*'

²²"But his father said to the servants, 'Quick! Bring the finest robe in the house and put it on him. Get a ring for his finger, and sandals for his feet. ²³And kill the calf we have been fattening in the pen. We must celebrate with a feast, ²⁴for this son of mine was dead and has now returned to life. He was lost, but now he is found.' So the party began.

²⁵"Meanwhile, the older son was in the fields working. When he returned home, he heard music and dancing in the house, ²⁶and he asked one of the servants what was going on. ²⁷'Your brother is back,' he was told, 'and

15:8 Greek *10 drachmas.* A drachma was the equivalent of a full day's wage.   **15:21** Some manuscripts add *Please take me on as a hired man.*

your father has killed the calf we were fattening and has prepared a great feast. We are celebrating because of his safe return.'

²⁸"The older brother was angry and wouldn't go in. His father came out and begged him, ²⁹but he replied, 'All these years I've worked hard for you and never once refused to do a single thing you told me to. And in all that time you never gave me even one young goat for a feast

with my friends. ³⁰Yet when this son of yours comes back after squandering your money on prostitutes, you celebrate by killing the finest calf we have.'

³¹"His father said to him, 'Look, dear son, you and I are very close, and everything I have is yours. ³²We had to celebrate this happy day. For your brother was dead and has come back to life! He was lost, but now he is found!'"

OCTOBER 21 □ DAY 295
Going with the Gospel

LOOK BACK Mark presents Jesus as the Selfless Servant, instantly obedient to the will of his Father. (The word *immediately* appears nearly a dozen times in the book.) "For even I, the Son of Man, came here not to be served but to serve others, and to give my life as a ransom for many" (Mark 10:45).

Luke presents Jesus as the Perfect Man, keenly interested in the human condition. (The phrase *Son of Man* occurs twenty-seven times in the book.) "And I, the Son of Man, have come to seek and save those like him who are lost" (Luke 19:10).

Mark and Luke are two of the "synoptic Gospels" (Matthew being the third), so called because they recount many of the same events from the life and ministry of Jesus and as such can be profitably studied side by side (*synoptic* comes from the root idea "to see side by side").

LOOK UP Be careful where you get your information, for your facts will be no more reliable than your source.

It is good to be a Christian and know it; it is better to be a Christian and show it.

After reading the Christmas accounts in the Gospels, try this Christmas Story Trivia Quiz. It may surprise you to learn how many of the "facts" you thought you knew are merely the stuff of Christmas cards and carols!

_____ 1. How did Joseph and Mary travel to Bethlehem? *(a)* by donkey, *(b)* by camel, *(c)* on foot, *(d)* the Bible doesn't say.

_____ 2. Which animals were present at Jesus' birth? *(a)* cows, sheep, goats, *(b)* cows, donkeys, sheep, *(c)* sheep and goats, *(d)* the Bible doesn't say.

_____ 3. What did the angels sing? *(a)* "Joy to the World," *(b)* "Alleluia," *(c)* "For unto Us a Child Is Born," *(d)* "Glory to God in the Highest," *(e)* none of the above.

_____ 4. How many wise men came to see Jesus? *(a)* three, *(b)* more than three, *(c)* less than three, *(d)* the Bible doesn't say.

_____ 5. Where did the wise men find Jesus? *(a)* in the manger, *(b)* in a stable, *(c)* in a house, *(d)* in an inn.

_____ 6. What is frankincense? *(a)* a precious metal, *(b)* a precious fabric, *(c)* a precious perfume, *(d)* an Eastern monster.

_____ 7. Where do we find the Christmas story in order to check up on all these facts? *(a)* Matthew; *(b)* Mark; *(c)* Luke; *(d)* John; *(e)* all of these; *(f)* only *a* and *b*; *(g)* only *a* and *c*; *(h)* only *a, b,* and *c;* *(i)* none of the above.

Answers: 1. *d,* 2. *d,* 3. *e* (the Bible doesn't say they sang), 4. *d,* 5. *c,* 6. *c,* 7. *g*

LOOK AHEAD Good news deserves to be shared. As you continue to read through the Gospels, notice how Jesus engages in conversations with those who need to know God's love firsthand. Some individuals come to him with questions and needs (Luke 8:4; 10:25); other times, Jesus initiates the conversation (Luke 9:1-5).

Today, you will likely experience both kinds of encounters: those you initiate (such as shopping at a store or filling your tank at a gas station) and those initiated by others (such as delivering your mail or keeping an appointment at your office). In both cases, follow the advice of 1 Peter 3:15. "And if you are asked about your Christian hope, always be ready to explain it." After all, the first two letters in the word *gospel* spell GO!

OCTOBER 22 ☐ DAY 296
LUKE 16–18
Parables of the Son of Man (Part 2)

OVERVIEW Christ continues his "School of Discipleship" with an assortment of parables designed to teach his men stewardship of money, time, and talents; the importance of forgiveness and faith; and the primacy of prayer in a disciple's life. The curriculum is concentrated because time is short. Just beyond Jericho lies the city of Jerusalem, where the final dramatic events in the life of the Son of Man will soon be played out.

Chapter 16	Chapter 17	Chapter 18
Serving Two Masters	Waiting for the Son of Man	Praying with Persistence
"You Can't!"	"Be Ready!"	"Don't Forget!"

YOUR DAILY WALK Select the proper response to complete this verse (1 Corinthians 4:2): "Now, a person who is put in charge as a manager must be . . ." *(a)* gifted, *(b)* dynamic, *(c)* faithful, *(d)* famous, *(e)* educated, *(f)* wealthy.

Give according to your income lest God make your income according to your giving.

The correct answer, of course, is *(c)* faithful; in other words, trustworthy, dependable.

But how do you know if you are faithful, the kind of steward God is looking for? Luke 16 will help you. There you'll find the threefold test of a faithful man or woman, boy or girl. Take this "trustworthiness checkup" for yourself; then enlist the aid of your spouse, child, or friend in helping you work on an area that is weak. They'll be delighted to help.

- Are you faithful in little things (v. 10)? little promises? small amounts of time, talent, and responsibility?
- Are you faithful with money (v. 11)? God's Word has much to say on money matters.
- Are you faithful in the affairs of others (v. 12)? Are you as careful with their possessions and reputations as you are with your own?

INSIGHT The Big "Little Horn" of the Scriptures
The *tittle* (Greek *keraian,* "little horn," 16:17) is a small projection or "hook" that distinguishes one Hebrew letter from another. Jesus was saying that, even down to the smallest detail, God's Word will maintain its reliability "until heaven and earth disappear" (Matthew 5:18).

CHAPTER 16

Jesus told this story to his disciples: "A rich man hired a manager to handle his affairs, but soon a rumor went around that the manager was thoroughly dishonest. ²So his employer called him in and said, 'What's this I hear about your stealing from me? Get your report in order, because you are going to be dismissed.'

³"The manager thought to himself, 'Now what? I'm through here, and I don't have the strength to go out and dig ditches, and I'm too proud to beg. ⁴I know just the thing! And then I'll have plenty of friends to take care of me when I leave!'

⁵"So he invited each person who owed money to his employer to come and discuss the situation. He asked the first one, 'How much do you owe him?' ⁶The man replied, 'I owe him eight hundred gallons of olive oil.' So the manager told him, 'Tear up that bill and write another one for four hundred gallons.*'

⁷" 'And how much do you owe my employer?' he asked the next man. 'A thousand bushels of wheat,' was the reply. 'Here,' the manager said, 'take your bill and replace it with one for only eight hundred bushels.*'

⁸"The rich man had to admire the dishonest rascal for being so shrewd. And it is true that the citizens of this world are more shrewd than the godly are. ⁹I tell you, use your worldly resources to benefit others and make friends. In this way, your generosity stores up a reward for you in heaven.*

¹⁰"Unless you are faithful in small matters, you won't be faithful in large ones. If you cheat even a little, you won't be honest with greater responsibilities. ¹¹And if you are untrustworthy about worldly wealth, who will trust you with the true riches of heaven? ¹²And if you are not faithful with other people's money, why should you be trusted with money of your own?

¹³"No one can serve two masters. For you will hate one and love the other, or be devoted to one and despise the other. You cannot serve both God and money."

¹⁴The Pharisees, who dearly loved their money, naturally scoffed at all this. ¹⁵Then he said to them, "You like to look good in public, but God knows your evil hearts. What this world honors is an abomination in the sight of God.

¹⁶"Until John the Baptist began to preach, the laws of Moses and the messages of the prophets were your guides. But now the Good News of the Kingdom of God is preached, and eager multitudes are forcing their way in. ¹⁷But that doesn't mean that the law has lost its force in even the smallest point. It is stronger and more permanent than heaven and earth.

¹⁸"Anyone who divorces his wife and marries someone else commits adultery, and anyone who marries a divorced woman commits adultery."

¹⁹Jesus said, "There was a certain rich man who was splendidly clothed and who lived each day in luxury. ²⁰At his door lay a diseased beggar named Lazarus. ²¹As Lazarus lay there longing for scraps from the rich man's table, the dogs would come and lick his open sores. ²²Finally, the beggar died and was carried by the angels to be with Abraham.* The rich man also died and was buried, ²³and his soul went to the place of the dead.* There, in torment, he saw Lazarus in the far distance with Abraham.

²⁴"The rich man shouted, 'Father Abraham, have some pity! Send Lazarus over here to dip the tip of his finger in water and cool my tongue, because I am in anguish in these flames.'

²⁵"But Abraham said to him, 'Son, remember that during your lifetime you had everything you wanted, and Lazarus had nothing. So now he is here being comforted, and you are in anguish. ²⁶And besides, there is a great chasm separating us. Anyone who wanted to cross over to you from here is stopped at its edge, and no one there can cross over to us.'

²⁷"Then the rich man said, 'Please, Father Abraham, send him to my father's home. ²⁸For I have five brothers, and I want

16:6 Greek *100 baths . . . 50 [baths].*   **16:7** Greek *100 korous . . . 80 [korous].*   **16:9** Or *Then when you run out at the end of this life, your friends will welcome you into eternal homes.*   **16:22** Greek *into Abraham's bosom.*   **16:23** Greek *to Hades.*

him to warn them about this place of torment so they won't have to come here when they die.'

²⁹"But Abraham said, 'Moses and the prophets have warned them. Your brothers can read their writings anytime they want to.'

³⁰"The rich man replied, 'No, Father Abraham! But if someone is sent to them from the dead, then they will turn from their sins.'

³¹"But Abraham said, 'If they won't listen to Moses and the prophets, they won't listen even if someone rises from the dead.'"

CHAPTER 17

One day Jesus said to his disciples, "There will always be temptations to sin, but how terrible it will be for the person who does the tempting. ²It would be better to be thrown into the sea with a large millstone tied around the neck than to face the punishment in store for harming one of these little ones. ³I am warning you! If another believer* sins, rebuke him; then if he repents, forgive him. ⁴Even if he wrongs you seven times a day and each time turns again and asks forgiveness, forgive him."

⁵One day the apostles said to the Lord, "We need more faith; tell us how to get it."

⁶"Even if you had faith as small as a mustard seed," the Lord answered, "you could say to this mulberry tree, 'May God uproot you and throw you into the sea,' and it would obey you!

⁷"When a servant comes in from plowing or taking care of sheep, he doesn't just sit down and eat. ⁸He must first prepare his master's meal and serve him his supper before eating his own. ⁹And the servant is not even thanked, because he is merely doing what he is supposed to do. ¹⁰In the same way, when you obey me you should say, 'We are not worthy of praise. We are servants who have simply done our duty.'"

¹¹As Jesus continued on toward Jerusalem, he reached the border between Galilee and Samaria. ¹²As he entered a village there, ten lepers stood at a distance, ¹³crying out, "Jesus, Master, have mercy on us!"

¹⁴He looked at them and said, "Go show yourselves to the priests." And as they went, their leprosy disappeared.

¹⁵One of them, when he saw that he was healed, came back to Jesus, shouting, "Praise God, I'm healed!" ¹⁶He fell face down on the ground at Jesus' feet, thanking him for what he had done. This man was a Samaritan.

¹⁷Jesus asked, "Didn't I heal ten men? Where are the other nine? ¹⁸Does only this foreigner return to give glory to God?" ¹⁹And Jesus said to the man, "Stand up and go. Your faith has made you well."

²⁰One day the Pharisees asked Jesus, "When will the Kingdom of God come?"

Jesus replied, "The Kingdom of God isn't ushered in with visible signs.* ²¹You won't be able to say, 'Here it is!' or 'It's over there!' For the Kingdom of God is among you.*"

²²Later he talked again about this with his disciples. "The time is coming when you will long to share in the days of the Son of Man, but you won't be able to," he said. ²³"Reports will reach you that the Son of Man has returned and that he is in this place or that. Don't believe such reports or go out to look for him. ²⁴For when the Son of Man returns, you will know it beyond all doubt. It will be as evident as the lightning that flashes across the sky. ²⁵But first the Son of Man must suffer terribly* and be rejected by this generation.

²⁶"When the Son of Man returns, the world will be like the people were in Noah's day. ²⁷In those days before the flood, the people enjoyed banquets and parties and weddings right up to the time Noah entered his boat and the flood came to destroy them all.

²⁸"And the world will be as it was in the days of Lot. People went about their daily business—eating and drinking, buying and selling, farming and building—²⁹until the morning Lot left Sodom. Then fire and burning sulfur rained down from heaven and destroyed them all. ³⁰Yes, it will be 'business as usual' right up to the hour when the Son of Man returns.* ³¹On that day a person outside the house* must not go into the house to pack. A person in the field must not return to town. ³²Remember what happened to Lot's wife! ³³Whoever clings to this life will lose it, and whoever loses this life will save it. ³⁴That night two people will be asleep in one bed; one will be taken away, and the other will be left. ³⁵Two women will be

grinding flour together at the mill; one will be taken, the other left.*"

37"Lord, where will this happen?" the disciples asked.

Jesus replied, "Just as the gathering of vultures shows there is a carcass nearby, so these signs indicate that the end is near."*

CHAPTER 18

One day Jesus told his disciples a story to illustrate their need for constant prayer and to show them that they must never give up. 2"There was a judge in a certain city," he said, "who was a godless man with great contempt for everyone. 3A widow of that city came to him repeatedly, appealing for justice against someone who had harmed her. 4The judge ignored her for a while, but eventually she wore him out. 'I fear neither God nor man,' he said to himself, 5'but this woman is driving me crazy. I'm going to see that she gets justice, because she is wearing me out with her constant requests!'"

6Then the Lord said, "Learn a lesson from this evil judge. 7Even he rendered a just decision in the end, so don't you think God will surely give justice to his chosen people who plead with him day and night? Will he keep putting them off? 8I tell you, he will grant justice to them quickly! But when I, the Son of Man, return, how many will I find who have faith?"

9Then Jesus told this story to some who had great self-confidence and scorned everyone else: 10"Two men went to the Temple to pray. One was a Pharisee, and the other was a dishonest tax collector. 11The proud Pharisee stood by himself and prayed this prayer: 'I thank you, God, that I am not a sinner like everyone else, especially like that tax collector over there! For I never cheat, I don't sin, I don't commit adultery, 12I fast twice a week, and I give you a tenth of my income.'

13"But the tax collector stood at a distance and dared not even lift his eyes to heaven as he prayed. Instead, he beat his chest in sorrow, saying, 'O God, be merciful to me, for I am a sinner.' 14I tell you, this sinner, not the Pharisee, returned home justified before God. For the proud will be humbled, but the humble will be honored."

15One day some parents brought their little children to Jesus so he could touch them and bless them, but the disciples told

them not to bother him. 16Then Jesus called for the children and said to the disciples, "Let the children come to me. Don't stop them! For the Kingdom of God belongs to such as these. 17I assure you, anyone who doesn't have their kind of faith will never get into the Kingdom of God."

18Once a religious leader asked Jesus this question: "Good teacher, what should I do to get eternal life?"

19"Why do you call me good?" Jesus asked him. "Only God is truly good. 20But as for your question, you know the commandments: 'Do not commit adultery. Do not murder. Do not steal. Do not testify falsely. Honor your father and mother.'*"

21The man replied, "I've obeyed all these commandments since I was a child."

22"There is still one thing you lack," Jesus said. "Sell all you have and give the money to the poor, and you will have treasure in heaven. Then come, follow me." 23But when the man heard this, he became sad because he was very rich.

24Jesus watched him go and then said to his disciples, "How hard it is for rich people to get into the Kingdom of God! 25It is easier for a camel to go through the eye of a needle than for a rich person to enter the Kingdom of God!"

26Those who heard this said, "Then who in the world can be saved?"

27He replied, "What is impossible from a human perspective is possible with God."

28Peter said, "We have left our homes and followed you."

29"Yes," Jesus replied, "and I assure you, everyone who has given up house or wife or brothers or parents or children, for the sake of the Kingdom of God, 30will be repaid many times over in this life, as well as receiving eternal life in the world to come."

31Gathering the twelve disciples around him, Jesus told them, "As you know, we are going to Jerusalem. And when we get there, all the predictions of the ancient prophets concerning the Son of Man will come true. 32He will be handed over to the Romans to be mocked, treated shamefully, and spit upon. 33They will whip him and kill him, but on the third day he will rise again."

34But they didn't understand a thing he said. Its significance was hidden from them, and they failed to grasp what he was talking about.

17:37 Greek Wherever the carcass is, the vultures gather.   18:20 Exod 20:12-16; Deut 5:16-20.

³⁵As they approached Jericho, a blind beggar was sitting beside the road. ³⁶When he heard the noise of a crowd going past, he asked what was happening. ³⁷They told him that Jesus of Nazareth was going by. ³⁸So he began shouting, "Jesus, Son of David, have mercy on me!" ³⁹The crowds ahead of Jesus tried to hush the man, but he only shouted louder, "Son of David, have mercy on me!"

⁴⁰When Jesus heard him, he stopped and ordered that the man be brought to him. ⁴¹Then Jesus asked the man, "What do you want me to do for you?"

"Lord," he pleaded, "I want to see!"

⁴²And Jesus said, "All right, you can see! Your faith has healed you." ⁴³Instantly the man could see, and he followed Jesus, praising God. And all who saw it praised God, too.

OCTOBER 23 ☐ DAY 297
LUKE 19–21
Praise for the Son of Man

OVERVIEW People don't just "peacefully coexist" with the Son of Man. They either embrace his claims and call him Messiah or reject his claims and become his enemy. A Jewish tax collector named Zacchaeus finds new life in Jesus . . . while the Jewish religious leaders plot to destroy him. The disciples of Christ flock to the streets to welcome their Teacher . . . while his enemies question his authority at every turn. In less than a week, the Triumphal Entry will turn into a tragic exit as the Son of Man becomes the sacrifice for sin.

Chapter 19	Chapter 20	Chapter 21
Acclamation for the Son of Man	Authority of the Son of Man	Appearing of the Son of Man
Triumphal Entry	Testing Questions	Timely Signs

YOUR DAILY WALK Today's section might well be titled "Money—Its Use and Abuse." Notice how prominent earthly wealth becomes in the final days of Jesus' ministry: Zacchaeus's use of money becomes a testimony of his new faith in Christ (19:8-10); the parable of the ten servants teaches the disciples to use it (for God's glory) or lose it (19:11-27); Jesus cleanses the Temple of those who have turned his Father's house into a supermarket of animals and moneychangers (19:45-48); paying taxes to Caesar becomes a test of Christ's authority (20:20-26); and the widow's offering of two pennies becomes an object lesson of sacrificial giving—the kind God is pleased with (21:1-4).

Money alone has never yet made anyone rich.

Why is your use of money such a good barometer of your walk with God? Because "wherever your treasure is, there your heart and thoughts will also be" (Matthew 6:21). Type a verse dealing with money from today's section on an index card (you might want to use 20:25 or 21:3-4), but instead of striking the s key, strike the dollar sign ($). Let that card remind you throughout the day of God'$ principle$ regarding the u$e . . . and abu$e . . . of hi$ material ble$$ing$.

INSIGHT The Clearest Cloudy Day on Record
Jesus predicted that he would come back to earth "on the clouds with power and great glory" (21:27). The cloud would not obscure the event but rather make it unmistakably clear (Acts 1:9-11; Revelation 1:7). Do you remember another occasion in Luke's Gospel when a cloud highlighted, rather than hid, Jesus' identity? (See Luke 9:28-36.)

CHAPTER 19

Jesus entered Jericho and made his way through the town. ²There was a man there named Zacchaeus. He was one of the most influential Jews in the Roman tax-collecting business, and he had become very rich. ³He tried to get a look at Jesus, but he was too short to see over the crowds. ⁴So he ran ahead and climbed a sycamore tree beside the road, so he could watch from there.

⁵When Jesus came by, he looked up at Zacchaeus and called him by name. "Zacchaeus!" he said. "Quick, come down! For I must be a guest in your home today."

⁶Zacchaeus quickly climbed down and took Jesus to his house in great excitement and joy. ⁷But the crowds were displeased. "He has gone to be the guest of a notorious sinner," they grumbled.

⁸Meanwhile, Zacchaeus stood there and said to the Lord, "I will give half my wealth to the poor, Lord, and if I have overcharged people on their taxes, I will give them back four times as much!"

⁹Jesus responded, "Salvation has come to this home today, for this man has shown himself to be a son of Abraham. ¹⁰And I, the Son of Man, have come to seek and save those like him who are lost."

¹¹The crowd was listening to everything Jesus said. And because he was nearing Jerusalem, he told a story to correct the impression that the Kingdom of God would begin right away. ¹²He said, "A nobleman was called away to a distant empire to be crowned king and then return. ¹³Before he left, he called together ten servants and gave them ten pounds of silver* to invest for him while he was gone. ¹⁴But his people hated him and sent a delegation after him to say they did not want him to be their king.

¹⁵"When he returned, the king called in the servants to whom he had given the money. He wanted to find out what they had done with the money and what their profits were. ¹⁶The first servant reported a tremendous gain—ten times as much as the original amount! ¹⁷'Well done!' the king exclaimed. 'You are a trustworthy servant. You have been faithful with the little I entrusted to you, so you will be governor of ten cities as your reward.'

¹⁸"The next servant also reported a good gain—five times the original amount.

¹⁹'Well done!' the king said. 'You can be governor over five cities.'

²⁰"But the third servant brought back only the original amount of money and said, 'I hid it and kept it safe. ²¹I was afraid because you are a hard man to deal with, taking what isn't yours and harvesting crops you didn't plant.'

²²"'You wicked servant!' the king roared. 'Hard, am I? If you knew so much about me and how tough I am, ²³why didn't you deposit the money in the bank so I could at least get some interest on it?' ²⁴Then turning to the others standing nearby, the king ordered, 'Take the money from this servant, and give it to the one who earned the most.'

²⁵"'But, master,' they said, 'that servant has enough already!'

²⁶"'Yes,' the king replied, 'but to those who use well what they are given, even more will be given. But from those who are unfaithful,* even what little they have will be taken away. ²⁷And now about these enemies of mine who didn't want me to be their king—bring them in and execute them right here in my presence.'"

²⁸After telling this story, Jesus went on toward Jerusalem, walking ahead of his disciples. ²⁹As they came to the towns of Bethphage and Bethany, on the Mount of Olives, he sent two disciples ahead. ³⁰"Go into that village over there," he told them, "and as you enter it, you will see a colt tied there that has never been ridden. Untie it and bring it here. ³¹If anyone asks what you are doing, just say, 'The Lord needs it.'"

³²So they went and found the colt, just as Jesus had said. ³³And sure enough, as they were untying it, the owners asked them, "Why are you untying our colt?"

³⁴And the disciples simply replied, "The Lord needs it." ³⁵So they brought the colt to Jesus and threw their garments over it for him to ride on.

³⁶Then the crowds spread out their coats on the road ahead of Jesus. ³⁷As they reached the place where the road started down from the Mount of Olives, all of his followers began to shout and sing as they walked along, praising God for all the wonderful miracles they had seen.

³⁸ "Bless the King who comes in the name
    of the Lord!
Peace in heaven
    and glory in highest heaven!"*

19:13 Greek *10 minas;* 1 mina was was worth about 3 months' wages.   **19:26** Or *who have nothing.*   **19:38** Pss 118:26; 148:1.

³⁹But some of the Pharisees among the crowd said, "Teacher, rebuke your followers for saying things like that!"

⁴⁰He replied, "If they kept quiet, the stones along the road would burst into cheers!"

⁴¹But as they came closer to Jerusalem and Jesus saw the city ahead, he began to cry. ⁴²"I wish that even today you would find the way of peace. But now it is too late, and peace is hidden from you. ⁴³Before long your enemies will build ramparts against your walls and encircle you and close in on you. ⁴⁴They will crush you to the ground, and your children with you. Your enemies will not leave a single stone in place, because you have rejected the opportunity God offered you."

⁴⁵Then Jesus entered the Temple and began to drive out the merchants from their stalls. ⁴⁶He told them, "The Scriptures declare, 'My Temple will be a place of prayer,' but you have turned it into a den of thieves."*

⁴⁷After that, he taught daily in the Temple, but the leading priests, the teachers of religious law, and the other leaders of the people began planning how to kill him. ⁴⁸But they could think of nothing, because all the people hung on every word he said.

CHAPTER 20

One day as Jesus was teaching and preaching the Good News in the Temple, the leading priests and teachers of religious law and other leaders came up to him. ²They demanded, "By whose authority did you drive out the merchants from the Temple?* Who gave you such authority?"

³"Let me ask you a question first," he replied. ⁴"Did John's baptism come from heaven, or was it merely human?"

⁵They talked it over among themselves. "If we say it was from heaven, he will ask why we didn't believe him. ⁶But if we say it was merely human, the people will stone us, because they are convinced he was a prophet." ⁷Finally they replied, "We don't know."

⁸And Jesus responded, "Then I won't answer your question either."

⁹Now Jesus turned to the people again and told them this story: "A man planted a vineyard, leased it out to tenant farmers, and moved to another country to live for several years. ¹⁰At grape-picking time, he sent one of his servants to collect his share of the crop. But the farmers attacked the servant, beat him up, and sent him back empty-handed. ¹¹So the owner sent another servant, but the same thing happened; he was beaten up and treated shamefully, and he went away empty-handed. ¹²A third man was sent and the same thing happened. He, too, was wounded and chased away.

¹³" 'What will I do?' the owner asked himself. 'I know! I'll send my cherished son. Surely they will respect him.'

¹⁴"But when the farmers saw his son, they said to each other, 'Here comes the heir to this estate. Let's kill him and get the estate for ourselves!' ¹⁵So they dragged him out of the vineyard and murdered him.

"What do you suppose the owner of the vineyard will do to those farmers?" Jesus asked. ¹⁶"I'll tell you—he will come and kill them all and lease the vineyard to others."

"But God forbid that such a thing should ever happen," his listeners protested.

¹⁷Jesus looked at them and said, "Then what do the Scriptures mean?

'The stone rejected by the builders
   has now become the cornerstone.'*

¹⁸All who stumble over that stone will be broken to pieces, and it will crush anyone on whom it falls."

¹⁹When the teachers of religious law and the leading priests heard this story, they wanted to arrest Jesus immediately because they realized he was pointing at them—that they were the farmers in the story. But they were afraid there would be a riot if they arrested him.

²⁰Watching for their opportunity, the leaders sent secret agents pretending to be honest men. They tried to get Jesus to say something that could be reported to the Roman governor so he would arrest Jesus. ²¹They said, "Teacher, we know that you speak and teach what is right and are not influenced by what others think. You sincerely teach the ways of God. ²²Now tell us—is it right to pay taxes to the Roman government or not?"

²³He saw through their trickery and said, ²⁴"Show me a Roman coin.* Whose picture and title are stamped on it?"

19:46 Isa 56:7; Jer 7:11.   **20:2** Or *By whose authority do you do these things?*   **20:17** Ps 118:22.   **20:24** Greek *a denarius.*

"Caesar's," they replied.

25"Well then," he said, "give to Caesar what belongs to him. But everything that belongs to God must be given to God." 26So they failed to trap him in the presence of the people. Instead, they were amazed by his answer, and they were silenced.

27Then some Sadducees stepped forward—a group of Jews who say there is no resurrection after death. 28They posed this question: "Teacher, Moses gave us a law that if a man dies, leaving a wife but no children, his brother should marry the widow and have a child who will be the brother's heir.* 29Well, there were seven brothers. The oldest married and then died without children. 30His brother married the widow, but he also died. Still no children. 31And so it went, one after the other, until each of the seven had married her and died, leaving no children. 32Finally, the woman died, too. 33So tell us, whose wife will she be in the resurrection? For all seven were married to her!"

34Jesus replied, "Marriage is for people here on earth. 35But that is not the way it will be in the age to come. For those worthy of being raised from the dead won't be married then. 36And they will never die again. In these respects they are like angels. They are children of God raised up to new life. 37But now, as to whether the dead will be raised—even Moses proved this when he wrote about the burning bush. Long after Abraham, Isaac, and Jacob had died, he referred to the Lord* as 'the God of Abraham, the God of Isaac, and the God of Jacob.'* 38So he is the God of the living, not the dead. They are all alive to him."

39"Well said, Teacher!" remarked some of the teachers of religious law who were standing there. 40And that ended their questions; no one dared to ask any more.

41Then Jesus presented them with a question. "Why is it," he asked, "that the Messiah is said to be the son of David? 42For David himself wrote in the book of Psalms:

'The LORD said to my Lord,
Sit in honor at my right hand
43   until I humble your enemies,
    making them a footstool under your
        feet.'*

44Since David called him Lord, how can he be his son at the same time?"

45Then, with the crowds listening, he turned to his disciples and said, 46"Beware of these teachers of religious law! For they love to parade in flowing robes and to have everyone bow to them as they walk in the marketplaces. And how they love the seats of honor in the synagogues and at banquets. 47But they shamelessly cheat widows out of their property, and then, to cover up the kind of people they really are, they make long prayers in public. Because of this, their punishment will be the greater."

CHAPTER 21

While Jesus was in the Temple, he watched the rich people putting their gifts into the collection box. 2Then a poor widow came by and dropped in two pennies.* 3"I assure you," he said, "this poor widow has given more than all the rest of them. 4For they have given a tiny part of their surplus, but she, poor as she is, has given everything she has."

5Some of his disciples began talking about the beautiful stonework of the Temple and the memorial decorations on the walls. But Jesus said, 6"The time is coming when all these things will be so completely demolished that not one stone will be left on top of another."

7"Teacher," they asked, "when will all this take place? And will there be any sign ahead of time?"

8He replied, "Don't let anyone mislead you. For many will come in my name, claiming to be the Messiah* and saying, 'The time has come!' But don't believe them. 9And when you hear of wars and insurrections, don't panic. Yes, these things must come, but the end won't follow immediately." 10Then he added, "Nations and kingdoms will proclaim war against each other. 11There will be great earthquakes, and there will be famines and epidemics in many lands, and there will be terrifying things and great miraculous signs in the heavens.

12"But before all this occurs, there will be a time of great persecution. You will be dragged into synagogues and prisons, and you will be accused before kings and governors of being my followers. 13This

20:28 Deut 25:5-6.   20:37a Greek *when he wrote about the bush. He referred to the Lord.*   20:37b Exod 3:6.   20:42-43 Ps 110:1.
21:2 Greek *2 lepta.*   21:8 Greek *name, saying, 'I am.'*

will be your opportunity to tell them about me. ¹⁴So don't worry about how to answer the charges against you, ¹⁵for I will give you the right words and such wisdom that none of your opponents will be able to reply! ¹⁶Even those closest to you—your parents, brothers, relatives, and friends—will betray you. And some of you will be killed. ¹⁷And everyone will hate you because of your allegiance to me. ¹⁸But not a hair of your head will perish! ¹⁹By standing firm, you will win your souls.

²⁰"And when you see Jerusalem surrounded by armies, then you will know that the time of its destruction has arrived. ²¹Then those in Judea must flee to the hills. Let those in Jerusalem escape, and those outside the city should not enter it for shelter. ²²For those will be days of God's vengeance, and the prophetic words of the Scriptures will be fulfilled. ²³How terrible it will be for pregnant women and for mothers nursing their babies. For there will be great distress in the land and wrath upon this people. ²⁴They will be brutally killed by the sword or sent away as captives to all the nations of the world. And Jerusalem will be conquered and trampled down by the Gentiles until the age of the Gentiles comes to an end.

²⁵"And there will be strange events in the skies—signs in the sun, moon, and stars. And down here on earth the nations will be in turmoil, perplexed by the roar-

ing seas and strange tides. ²⁶The courage of many people will falter because of the fearful fate they see coming upon the earth, because the stability of the very heavens will be broken up. ²⁷Then everyone will see the Son of Man arrive on the clouds with power and great glory.* ²⁸So when all these things begin to happen, stand straight and look up, for your salvation is near!"

²⁹Then he gave them this illustration: "Notice the fig tree, or any other tree. ³⁰When the leaves come out, you know without being told that summer is near. ³¹Just so, when you see the events I've described taking place, you can be sure that the Kingdom of God is near. ³²I assure you, this generation* will not pass from the scene until all these events have taken place. ³³Heaven and earth will disappear, but my words will remain forever.

³⁴"Watch out! Don't let me find you living in careless ease and drunkenness, and filled with the worries of this life. Don't let that day catch you unaware, ³⁵as in a trap. For that day will come upon everyone living on the earth. ³⁶Keep a constant watch. And pray that, if possible, you may escape these horrors and stand before the Son of Man."

³⁷Every day Jesus went to the Temple to teach, and each evening he returned to spend the night on the Mount of Olives. ³⁸The crowds gathered early each morning to hear him.

21:27 See Dan 7:13.   21:32 Or *this age*, or *this nation*.

OCTOBER 24 ☐ DAY 298
LUKE 22–24
Passion of the Son of Man

 In his account of the closing days of Jesus' earthly ministry, Luke includes a number of details not given by the other Gospel writers. Only Luke records the verbal strife among the disciples as they jostle for positions of honor in the Kingdom of God. Only Luke records Jesus' warning to Peter of Satan's desire to use him. Only Luke records the healing of the high priest's servant. Only Luke provides the details of Jesus' trial before Herod Antipas. Only Luke reveals the repentance of one of the two thieves crucified with Jesus. And only Luke presents the resurrection day appearance to the two disciples on the road to Emmaus.

Chapter 22	Chapter 23	Chapter 24
Condemnation by the Jews	Execution by the Romans	Exaltation by the God of Heaven
Passover Lamb	King of the Jews	Risen Redeemer

When you don't feel like reading your Bible, that's the time to read it.

YOUR DAILY WALK Do you have difficulty from time to time understanding the Word of God as you read it in this devotional Bible? You're not alone! The two on the road to Emmaus were called "foolish people" (24:25) by none other than Jesus Christ, who had to explain to them the things concerning himself (24:27). The Ethiopian eunuch confessed to Philip that he did not understand what he read from the book of Isaiah (Acts 8:30-31). Even the apostle Peter admitted that some of the letters written by Paul were weighty and difficult to understand (2 Peter 3:15-16)!

Two elements are necessary if you are to understand the Word of God. On your part there must be a diligent reading and study of the Scriptures. (This may include the use of tools like Bible concordances, reference works, and commentaries penned by godly Bible scholars.) On God's part there will be the illuminating work of the Holy Spirit, providing spiritual insight and understanding (John 16:13-15). God has promised to do his part; are you doing yours? Today would be a good day to drop by your church library or local Christian bookstore to find a tool that will help you in your daily study and application of God's Word.

INSIGHT End of Volume I, Beginning of Volume II

Luke closes his Gospel of the incarnate Son of God with a report of Jesus' ascension to heaven (24:51), exactly the same event he will use to open his continuing account of the Acts of the Apostles (Acts 1:1-2).

CHAPTER 22

The Festival of Unleavened Bread, which begins with the Passover celebration, was drawing near. ²The leading priests and teachers of religious law were actively plotting Jesus' murder. But they wanted to kill him without starting a riot, a possibility they greatly feared.

³Then Satan entered into Judas Iscariot, who was one of the twelve disciples, ⁴and he went over to the leading priests and captains of the Temple guard to discuss the best way to betray Jesus to them. ⁵They were delighted that he was ready to help them, and they promised him a reward. ⁶So he began looking for an opportunity to betray Jesus so they could arrest him quietly when the crowds weren't around.

⁷Now the Festival of Unleavened Bread arrived, when the Passover lambs were sacrificed. ⁸Jesus sent Peter and John ahead and said, "Go and prepare the Passover meal, so we can eat it together."

⁹"Where do you want us to go?" they asked him.

¹⁰He replied, "As soon as you enter Jerusalem, a man carrying a pitcher of water will meet you. Follow him. At the house he enters, ¹¹say to the owner, 'The Teacher asks, Where is the guest room where I can eat the Passover meal with my disciples?' ¹²He will take you upstairs to a large room that is already set up. That is the place. Go ahead and prepare our supper there." ¹³They went off to the city and found everything just as Jesus had said, and they prepared the Passover supper there.

¹⁴Then at the proper time Jesus and the twelve apostles sat down together at the table. ¹⁵Jesus said, "I have looked forward to this hour with deep longing, anxious to eat this Passover meal with you before my suffering begins. ¹⁶For I tell you now that I won't eat it again until it comes to fulfillment in the Kingdom of God."

¹⁷Then he took a cup of wine, and when he had given thanks for it, he said, "Take this and share it among yourselves. ¹⁸For I will not drink wine again until the Kingdom of God has come."

[19]Then he took a loaf of bread; and when he had thanked God for it, he broke it in pieces and gave it to the disciples, saying, "This is my body, given for you. Do this in remembrance of me." [20]After supper he took another cup of wine and said, "This wine is the token of God's new covenant to save you—an agreement sealed with the blood I will pour out for you.*

[21]"But here at this table, sitting among us as a friend, is the man who will betray me. [22]For I, the Son of Man, must die since it is part of God's plan. But how terrible it will be for my betrayer!" [23]Then the disciples began to ask each other which of them would ever do such a thing.

[24]And they began to argue among themselves as to who would be the greatest in the coming Kingdom. [25]Jesus told them, "In this world the kings and great men order their people around, and yet they are called 'friends of the people.' [26]But among you, those who are the greatest should take the lowest rank, and the leader should be like a servant. [27]Normally the master sits at the table and is served by his servants. But not here! For I am your servant. [28]You have remained true to me in my time of trial. [29]And just as my Father has granted me a Kingdom, I now grant you the right [30]to eat and drink at my table in that Kingdom. And you will sit on thrones, judging the twelve tribes of Israel.

[31]"Simon, Simon, Satan has asked to have all of you, to sift you like wheat. [32]But I have pleaded in prayer for you, Simon, that your faith should not fail. So when you have repented and turned to me again, strengthen and build up your brothers."

[33]Peter said, "Lord, I am ready to go to prison with you, and even to die with you."

[34]But Jesus said, "Peter, let me tell you something. The rooster will not crow tomorrow morning until you have denied three times that you even know me."

[35]Then Jesus asked them, "When I sent you out to preach the Good News and you did not have money, a traveler's bag, or extra clothing, did you lack anything?"

"No," they replied.

[36]"But now," he said, "take your money and a traveler's bag. And if you don't have a sword, sell your clothes and buy one! [37]For the time has come for this prophecy about me to be fulfilled: 'He was counted among those who were rebels.'* Yes, everything written about me by the prophets will come true."

[38]"Lord," they replied, "we have two swords among us."

"That's enough," he said.

[39]Then, accompanied by the disciples, Jesus left the upstairs room and went as usual to the Mount of Olives. [40]There he told them, "Pray that you will not be overcome by temptation."

[41]He walked away, about a stone's throw, and knelt down and prayed, [42]"Father, if you are willing, please take this cup of suffering away from me. Yet I want your will, not mine." [43]Then an angel from heaven appeared and strengthened him. [44]He prayed more fervently, and he was in such agony of spirit that his sweat fell to the ground like great drops of blood.* [45]At last he stood up again and returned to the disciples, only to find them asleep, exhausted from grief. [46]"Why are you sleeping?" he asked. "Get up and pray. Otherwise temptation will overpower you."

[47]But even as he said this, a mob approached, led by Judas, one of his twelve disciples. Judas walked over to Jesus and greeted him with a kiss. [48]But Jesus said, "Judas, how can you betray me, the Son of Man, with a kiss?"

[49]When the other disciples saw what was about to happen, they exclaimed, "Lord, should we fight? We brought the swords!" [50]And one of them slashed at the high priest's servant and cut off his right ear.

[51]But Jesus said, "Don't resist anymore." And he touched the place where the man's ear had been and healed him. [52]Then Jesus spoke to the leading priests and captains of the Temple guard and the other leaders who headed the mob. "Am I some dangerous criminal," he asked, "that you have come armed with swords and clubs to arrest me? [53]Why didn't you arrest me in the Temple? I was there every day. But this is your moment, the time when the power of darkness reigns."

[54]So they arrested him and led him to the high priest's residence, and Peter was following far behind. [55]The guards lit a fire in the courtyard and sat around it, and Peter joined them there. [56]A servant girl noticed him in the firelight and began staring at

---

22:19-20 Some manuscripts omit 22:19b-20, *given for you . . . I will pour out for you.*   **22:37** Isa 53:12.   **22:43-44** These verses are not included in many ancient manuscripts.

him. Finally she said, "This man was one of Jesus' followers!"

[57] Peter denied it. "Woman," he said, "I don't even know the man!"

[58] After a while someone else looked at him and said, "You must be one of them!"

"No, man, I'm not!" Peter replied.

[59] About an hour later someone else insisted, "This must be one of Jesus' disciples because he is a Galilean, too."

[60] But Peter said, "Man, I don't know what you are talking about." And as soon as he said these words, the rooster crowed. [61] At that moment the Lord turned and looked at Peter. Then Peter remembered that the Lord had said, "Before the rooster crows tomorrow morning, you will deny me three times." [62] And Peter left the courtyard, crying bitterly.

[63] Now the guards in charge of Jesus began mocking and beating him. [64] They blindfolded him; then they hit him and asked, "Who hit you that time, you prophet?" [65] And they threw all sorts of terrible insults at him.

[66] At daybreak all the leaders of the people assembled, including the leading priests and the teachers of religious law. Jesus was led before this high council,* [67] and they said, "Tell us if you are the Messiah."

But he replied, "If I tell you, you won't believe me. [68] And if I ask you a question, you won't answer. [69] But the time is soon coming when I, the Son of Man, will be sitting at God's right hand in the place of power."*

[70] They all shouted, "Then you claim you are the Son of God?"

And he replied, "You are right in saying that I am."

[71] "What need do we have for other witnesses?" they shouted. "We ourselves heard him say it."

CHAPTER 23

Then the entire council took Jesus over to Pilate, the Roman governor. [2] They began at once to state their case: "This man has been leading our people to ruin by telling them not to pay their taxes to the Roman government and by claiming he is the Messiah, a king."

[3] So Pilate asked him, "Are you the King of the Jews?"

Jesus replied, "Yes, it is as you say."

[4] Pilate turned to the leading priests and to the crowd and said, "I find nothing wrong with this man!"

[5] Then they became desperate. "But he is causing riots everywhere he goes, all over Judea, from Galilee to Jerusalem!"

[6] "Oh, is he a Galilean?" Pilate asked. [7] When they answered that he was, Pilate sent him to Herod Antipas, because Galilee was under Herod's jurisdiction, and Herod happened to be in Jerusalem at the time.

[8] Herod was delighted at the opportunity to see Jesus, because he had heard about him and had been hoping for a long time to see him perform a miracle. [9] He asked Jesus question after question, but Jesus refused to answer. [10] Meanwhile, the leading priests and the teachers of religious law stood there shouting their accusations. [11] Now Herod and his soldiers began mocking and ridiculing Jesus. Then they put a royal robe on him and sent him back to Pilate. [12] Herod and Pilate, who had been enemies before, became friends that day.

[13] Then Pilate called together the leading priests and other religious leaders, along with the people, [14] and he announced his verdict. "You brought this man to me, accusing him of leading a revolt. I have examined him thoroughly on this point in your presence and find him innocent. [15] Herod came to the same conclusion and sent him back to us. Nothing this man has done calls for the death penalty. [16] So I will have him flogged, but then I will release him."*

[18] Then a mighty roar rose from the crowd, and with one voice they shouted, "Kill him, and release Barabbas to us!" [19] (Barabbas was in prison for murder and for taking part in an insurrection in Jerusalem against the government.) [20] Pilate argued with them, because he wanted to release Jesus. [21] But they shouted, "Crucify him! Crucify him!"

[22] For the third time he demanded, "Why? What crime has he committed? I have found no reason to sentence him to death. I will therefore flog him and let him go."

22:66 Greek *before their Sanhedrin.*   22:69 See Ps 110:1.   23:16 Some manuscripts add verse 17, *For it was necessary for him to release one [prisoner] for them during the feast.*

23But the crowd shouted louder and louder for Jesus' death, and their voices prevailed. 24So Pilate sentenced Jesus to die as they demanded. 25As they had requested, he released Barabbas, the man in prison for insurrection and murder. But he delivered Jesus over to them to do as they wished.

26As they led Jesus away, Simon of Cyrene,* who was coming in from the country just then, was forced to follow Jesus and carry his cross. 27Great crowds trailed along behind, including many grief-stricken women. 28But Jesus turned and said to them, "Daughters of Jerusalem, don't weep for me, but weep for yourselves and for your children. 29For the days are coming when they will say, 'Fortunate indeed are the women who are childless, the wombs that have not borne a child and the breasts that have never nursed.' 30People will beg the mountains to fall on them and the hills to bury them. 31For if these things are done when the tree is green, what will happen when it is dry?*"

32Two others, both criminals, were led out to be executed with him. 33Finally, they came to a place called The Skull.* All three were crucified there—Jesus on the center cross, and the two criminals on either side.

34Jesus said, "Father, forgive these people, because they don't know what they are doing."* And the soldiers gambled for his clothes by throwing dice.*

35The crowd watched, and the leaders laughed and scoffed. "He saved others," they said, "let him save himself if he is really God's Chosen One, the Messiah." 36The soldiers mocked him, too, by offering him a drink of sour wine. 37They called out to him, "If you are the King of the Jews, save yourself!" 38A signboard was nailed to the cross above him with these words: "This is the King of the Jews."

39One of the criminals hanging beside him scoffed, "So you're the Messiah, are you? Prove it by saving yourself—and us, too, while you're at it!"

40But the other criminal protested, "Don't you fear God even when you are dying? 41We deserve to die for our evil deeds, but this man hasn't done anything wrong." 42Then he said, "Jesus, remember me when you come into your Kingdom."

43And Jesus replied, "I assure you, today you will be with me in paradise."

44By this time it was noon, and darkness fell across the whole land until three o'clock. 45The light from the sun was gone. And suddenly, the thick veil hanging in the Temple was torn apart. 46Then Jesus shouted, "Father, I entrust my spirit into your hands!"* And with those words he breathed his last.

47When the captain of the Roman soldiers handling the executions saw what had happened, he praised God and said, "Surely this man was innocent.*" 48And when the crowd that came to see the crucifixion saw all that had happened, they went home in deep sorrow.* 49But Jesus' friends, including the women who had followed him from Galilee, stood at a distance watching.

50Now there was a good and righteous man named Joseph. He was a member of the Jewish high council, 51but he had not agreed with the decision and actions of the other religious leaders. He was from the town of Arimathea in Judea, and he had been waiting for the Kingdom of God to come. 52He went to Pilate and asked for Jesus' body. 53Then he took the body down from the cross and wrapped it in a long linen cloth and laid it in a new tomb that had been carved out of rock. 54This was done late on Friday afternoon, the day of preparation* for the Sabbath.

55As his body was taken away, the women from Galilee followed and saw the tomb where they placed his body. 56Then they went home and prepared spices and ointments to embalm him. But by the time they were finished it was the Sabbath, so they rested all that day as required by the law.

CHAPTER 24

But very early on Sunday morning* the women came to the tomb, taking the spices they had prepared. 2They found that the stone covering the entrance had been rolled aside. ³So they went in, but they couldn't find the body of the Lord Jesus. ⁴They were puzzled, trying to think what could have happened to it. Suddenly, two men appeared to them, clothed in dazzling robes. ⁵The women were terrified and bowed low before them. Then the men asked, "Why are you looking in a tomb for someone who is alive? ⁶He isn't here! He has risen from the dead! Don't you remember what he told you back in Galilee, ⁷that the Son of Man must be betrayed into the hands of sinful men and be crucified, and that he would rise again the third day?"

⁸Then they remembered that he had said this. ⁹So they rushed back to tell his eleven disciples—and everyone else— what had happened. ¹⁰The women who went to the tomb were Mary Magdalene, Joanna, Mary the mother of James, and several others. They told the apostles what had happened, ¹¹but the story sounded like nonsense, so they didn't believe it. ¹²However, Peter ran to the tomb to look. Stooping, he peered in and saw the empty linen wrappings; then he went home again, wondering what had happened.*

¹³That same day two of Jesus' followers were walking to the village of Emmaus, seven miles* out of Jerusalem. ¹⁴As they walked along they were talking about everything that had happened. ¹⁵Suddenly, Jesus himself came along and joined them and began walking beside them. ¹⁶But they didn't know who he was, because God kept them from recognizing him.

¹⁷"You seem to be in a deep discussion about something," he said. "What are you so concerned about?"

They stopped short, sadness written across their faces. ¹⁸Then one of them, Cleopas, replied, "You must be the only person in Jerusalem who hasn't heard about all the things that have happened there the last few days."

¹⁹"What things?" Jesus asked.

"The things that happened to Jesus, the man from Nazareth," they said. "He was a prophet who did wonderful miracles. He was a mighty teacher, highly regarded by both God and all the people. ²⁰But our leading priests and other religious leaders

arrested him and handed him over to be condemned to death, and they crucified him. ²¹We had thought he was the Messiah who had come to rescue Israel. That all happened three days ago. ²²Then some women from our group of his followers were at his tomb early this morning, and they came back with an amazing report. ²³They said his body was missing, and they had seen angels who told them Jesus is alive! ²⁴Some of our men ran out to see, and sure enough, Jesus' body was gone, just as the women had said."

²⁵Then Jesus said to them, "You are such foolish people! You find it so hard to believe all that the prophets wrote in the Scriptures. ²⁶Wasn't it clearly predicted by the prophets that the Messiah would have to suffer all these things before entering his time of glory?" ²⁷Then Jesus quoted passages from the writings of Moses and all the prophets, explaining what all the Scriptures said about himself.

²⁸By this time they were nearing Emmaus and the end of their journey. Jesus would have gone on, ²⁹but they begged him to stay the night with them, since it was getting late. So he went home with them. ³⁰As they sat down to eat, he took a small loaf of bread, asked God's blessing on it, broke it, then gave it to them. ³¹Suddenly, their eyes were opened, and they recognized him. And at that moment he disappeared!

³²They said to each other, "Didn't our hearts feel strangely warm as he talked with us on the road and explained the Scriptures to us?" ³³And within the hour they were on their way back to Jerusalem, where the eleven disciples and the other followers of Jesus were gathered. When they arrived, they were greeted with the report, ³⁴"The Lord has really risen! He appeared to Peter*!"

³⁵Then the two from Emmaus told their story of how Jesus had appeared to them as they were walking along the road and how they had recognized him as he was breaking the bread. ³⁶And just as they were telling about it, Jesus himself was suddenly standing there among them. He said, "Peace be with you."* ³⁷But the whole group was terribly frightened, thinking they were seeing a ghost! ³⁸"Why are you frightened?" he asked. "Why do you doubt

---

24:12 Some manuscripts do not include this verse.   24:13 Greek 60 stadia [11.1 kilometers].   24:34 Greek Simon.   24:36 Some manuscripts do not include He said, "Peace be with you."

who I am? [39]Look at my hands. Look at my feet. You can see that it's really me. Touch me and make sure that I am not a ghost, because ghosts don't have bodies, as you see that I do!" [40]As he spoke, he held out his hands for them to see, and he showed them his feet.*

[41]Still they stood there doubting, filled with joy and wonder. Then he asked them, "Do you have anything here to eat?" [42]They gave him a piece of broiled fish, [43]and he ate it as they watched.

[44]Then he said, "When I was with you before, I told you that everything written about me by Moses and the prophets and in the Psalms must all come true." [45]Then he opened their minds to understand these many Scriptures. [46]And he said, "Yes, it was written long ago that the Mes-

siah must suffer and die and rise again from the dead on the third day. [47]With my authority, take this message of repentance to all the nations, beginning in Jerusalem: 'There is forgiveness of sins for all who turn to me.' [48]You are witnesses of all these things.

[49]"And now I will send the Holy Spirit, just as my Father promised. But stay here in the city until the Holy Spirit comes and fills you with power from heaven."

[50]Then Jesus led them to Bethany, and lifting his hands to heaven, he blessed them. [51]While he was blessing them, he left them and was taken up to heaven.* [52]They worshiped him and* then returned to Jerusalem filled with great joy. [53]And they spent all of their time in the Temple, praising God.

24:40 Some manuscripts do not include this verse.   **24:51** Some manuscripts do not include *and was taken up to heaven.*
24:52 Some manuscripts do not include *worshiped him and.*

John

EVEN though the book of John covers the same basic outline of Jesus' life as the other three Gospels, it displays marked differences in content and viewpoint. John highlights many encounters with the Son of God that are found nowhere else: the miracle at Cana, the visit by Nicodemus, the Samaritan woman at the well, a lame man at the pool of Bethesda, the man born blind, the beloved Lazarus. Why this selectivity? "But these are written so that you may believe that Jesus is the Messiah, the Son of God" (20:31).

Focus	Ministry to Many				Ministry to Few	
Divisions	Manifestation of the Son of God	Ministry to Individuals by God's Son	Ministry to the Multitudes by God's Son	Mounting Anger toward God's Son	Ministry to the Disciples by God's Son	The Resurrected Son of God
	1　　　　2	3　　　　5	6　　　　8	9　　　　12	13　　　17	18　　　21
Topics	Signs				Sermons	Sacrifice
	Public Ministry				Private Ministry	Paschal Ministry
Place	Galilee and Judea				Jerusalem	
Time	About 3½ Years				Only a Few Days	

OCTOBER 25 ☐ DAY 299
JOHN 1–2
Manifestation of the Son of God

 OVERVIEW The opening of John's Gospel makes it clear he is giving a different perspective on the life and ministry of Jesus Christ than did the other three Gospel writers. John begins with the preexistence and deity of the Word, the one who became human to show God to people and to fulfill God's promises of a Messiah to Israel. Proclaiming the identity of Jesus as the Word is the ministry of John the Baptist, who directs his disciples to become Jesus' first followers. At a wedding in Cana, Jesus demonstrates his miraculous power for the first time. Later in Jerusalem, his zeal for his Father's house causes him to challenge the status quo, an act which forces an early confrontation over his claims.

Chapter 1			Chapter 2
The Identity of the Son of God			The Authority of the Son of God
Affirmed 1 18	Proclaimed 19 34	Acknowledged 35 51	
By God	By John	By Disciples	Over Nature

 YOUR DAILY WALK Turn to Acts 1:13. There you will find the names of eleven of the twelve disciples of Jesus. Glance down the list, and see if you can recall one significant fact about each man. (For example, Peter—walked on the water, etc.) Which disciples come up "anonymous" in your mind?

The object in witnessing is not to win arguments but to win disciples.

Chances are, Andrew fits that category. Although he was one of the twelve apostles, he lived his life in the shadow of his brother, Peter. Outside of John's Gospel he is mentioned only in the lists of the apostles. He was an ordinary and little-known person. And yet Andrew was distinctive in at least one way: He was constantly bringing people to Jesus. First his brother (John 1:40-42) and later a little boy (6:8-9) came to the Savior because of Andrew's invitation.

Witnessing for Christ may sound like a scary assignment. But could you "invite" another person to meet a Friend who has changed your life? This week invite a neighbor to go to church with you. You'll both be glad you did!

 INSIGHT A Handy Outline in a Handy Place

Prologue	Description	Expanded in . . .
1:1-4	Revelation of the Son of God	1:19–6:71
1:5-11	Rejection of the Son of God	7:1–12:50
1:12-18	Acceptance of the Son of God	13:1–21:25

CHAPTER 1

In the beginning the Word already existed. He was with God, and he was God. ²He was in the beginning with God. ³He created everything there is. Nothing exists that he didn't make. ⁴Life itself was in him, and this life gives light to everyone. ⁵The

light shines through the darkness, and the darkness can never extinguish it.

⁶God sent John the Baptist ⁷to tell everyone about the light so that everyone might believe because of his testimony. ⁸John himself was not the light; he was only a witness to the light. ⁹The one who is the

true light, who gives light to everyone, was going to come into the world.

¹⁰But although the world was made through him, the world didn't recognize him when he came. ¹¹Even in his own land and among his own people, he was not accepted. ¹²But to all who believed him and accepted him, he gave the right to become children of God. ¹³They are reborn! This is not a physical birth resulting from human passion or plan—this rebirth comes from God.

¹⁴So the Word became human and lived here on earth among us. He was full of unfailing love and faithfulness.* And we have seen his glory, the glory of the only Son of the Father.

¹⁵John pointed him out to the people. He shouted to the crowds, "This is the one I was talking about when I said, 'Someone is coming who is far greater than I am, for he existed long before I did.'"

¹⁶We have all benefited from the rich blessings he brought to us—one gracious blessing after another.* ¹⁷For the law was given through Moses; God's unfailing love and faithfulness came through Jesus Christ. ¹⁸No one has ever seen God. But his only Son, who is himself God,* is near to the Father's heart; he has told us about him.

¹⁹This was the testimony of John when the Jewish leaders sent priests and Temple assistants* from Jerusalem to ask John whether he claimed to be the Messiah. ²⁰He flatly denied it. "I am not the Messiah," he said.

²¹"Well then, who are you?" they asked. "Are you Elijah?"

"No," he replied.

"Are you the Prophet?"*

"No."

²²"Then who are you? Tell us, so we can give an answer to those who sent us. What do you have to say about yourself?"

²³John replied in the words of Isaiah:

"I am a voice shouting in the
   wilderness,
   'Prepare a straight pathway for the
   Lord's coming!'"*

²⁴Then those who were sent by the Pharisees ²⁵asked him, "If you aren't the Mes-

siah or Elijah or the Prophet, what right do you have to baptize?"

²⁶John told them, "I baptize with* water, but right here in the crowd is someone you do not know, ²⁷who will soon begin his ministry. I am not even worthy to be his slave.*" ²⁸This incident took place at Bethany, a village east of the Jordan River, where John was baptizing.

²⁹The next day John saw Jesus coming toward him and said, "Look! There is the Lamb of God who takes away the sin of the world! ³⁰He is the one I was talking about when I said, 'Soon a man is coming who is far greater than I am, for he existed long before I did.' ³¹I didn't know he was the one, but I have been baptizing with water in order to point him out to Israel."

³²Then John said, "I saw the Holy Spirit descending like a dove from heaven and resting upon him. ³³I didn't know he was the one, but when God sent me to baptize with water, he told me, 'When you see the Holy Spirit descending and resting upon someone, he is the one you are looking for. He is the one who baptizes with the Holy Spirit.' ³⁴I saw this happen to Jesus, so I testify that he is the Son of God.*"

³⁵The following day, John was again standing with two of his disciples. ³⁶As Jesus walked by, John looked at him and then declared, "Look! There is the Lamb of God!" ³⁷Then John's two disciples turned and followed Jesus.

³⁸Jesus looked around and saw them following. "What do you want?" he asked them.

They replied, "Rabbi" (which means Teacher), "where are you staying?"

³⁹"Come and see," he said. It was about four o'clock in the afternoon when they went with him to the place, and they stayed there the rest of the day.

⁴⁰Andrew, Simon Peter's brother, was one of these men who had heard what John said and then followed Jesus. ⁴¹The first thing Andrew did was to find his brother, Simon, and tell him, "We have found the Messiah" (which means the Christ).

⁴²Then Andrew brought Simon to meet Jesus. Looking intently at Simon, Jesus said, "You are Simon, the son of John—but you will be called Cephas" (which means Peter*).

[43]The next day Jesus decided to go to Galilee. He found Philip and said to him, "Come, be my disciple." [44]Philip was from Bethsaida, Andrew and Peter's hometown.

[45]Philip went off to look for Nathanael and told him, "We have found the very person Moses and the prophets wrote about! His name is Jesus, the son of Joseph from Nazareth."

[46]"Nazareth!" exclaimed Nathanael. "Can anything good come from there?"

"Just come and see for yourself," Philip said.

[47]As they approached, Jesus said, "Here comes an honest man—a true son of Israel."

[48]"How do you know about me?" Nathanael asked.

And Jesus replied, "I could see you under the fig tree before Philip found you."

[49]Nathanael replied, "Teacher, you are the Son of God—the King of Israel!"

[50]Jesus asked him, "Do you believe all this just because I told you I had seen you under the fig tree? You will see greater things than this." [51]Then he said, "The truth is, you will all see heaven open and the angels of God going up and down upon the Son of Man."*

CHAPTER 2

The next day* Jesus' mother was a guest at a wedding celebration in the village of Cana in Galilee. [2]Jesus and his disciples were also invited to the celebration. [3]The wine supply ran out during the festivities, so Jesus' mother spoke to him about the problem. "They have no more wine," she told him.

[4]"How does that concern you and me?" Jesus asked. "My time has not yet come."

[5]But his mother told the servants, "Do whatever he tells you."

[6]Six stone waterpots were standing there; they were used for Jewish ceremonial purposes and held twenty to thirty gallons* each. [7]Jesus told the servants, "Fill the jars with water." When the jars had been filled to the brim, [8]he said, "Dip some out and take it to the master of ceremonies." So they followed his instructions.

[9]When the master of ceremonies tasted the water that was now wine, not knowing where it had come from (though, of course, the servants knew), he called the bridegroom over. [10]"Usually a host serves the best wine first," he said. "Then, when everyone is full and doesn't care, he brings out the less expensive wines. But you have kept the best until now!"

[11]This miraculous sign at Cana in Galilee was Jesus' first display of his glory. And his disciples believed in him.

[12]After the wedding he went to Capernaum for a few days with his mother, his brothers, and his disciples.

[13]It was time for the annual Passover celebration, and Jesus went to Jerusalem. [14]In the Temple area he saw merchants selling cattle, sheep, and doves for sacrifices; and he saw money changers behind their counters. [15]Jesus made a whip from some ropes and chased them all out of the Temple. He drove out the sheep and oxen, scattered the money changers' coins over the floor, and turned over their tables. [16]Then, going over to the people who sold doves, he told them, "Get these things out of here. Don't turn my Father's house into a marketplace!"

[17]Then his disciples remembered this prophecy from the Scriptures: "Passion for God's house burns within me."*

[18]"What right do you have to do these things?" the Jewish leaders demanded. "If you have this authority from God, show us a miraculous sign to prove it."

[19]"All right," Jesus replied. "Destroy this temple, and in three days I will raise it up."

[20]"What!" they exclaimed. "It took forty-six years to build this Temple, and you can do it in three days?" [21]But by "this temple," Jesus meant his body. [22]After he was raised from the dead, the disciples remembered that he had said this. And they believed both Jesus and the Scriptures.

[23]Because of the miraculous signs he did in Jerusalem at the Passover celebration, many people were convinced that he was indeed the Messiah. [24]But Jesus didn't trust them, because he knew what people were really like. [25]No one needed to tell him about human nature.

1:51 See Gen 28:10-17, the account of Jacob's ladder.   **2:1** Greek *On the third day;* see 1:35, 43.   **2:6** Greek *2 or 3 measures* [75 to 113 liters].   **2:17** Or *"Concern for God's house will be my undoing."* Ps 69:9.

OCTOBER 26 □ DAY 300
JOHN 3–5
Ministry to Individuals by God's Son

OVERVIEW Today's section centers around Jesus' encounters with three individuals: Nicodemus, the Samaritan woman at the well, and the lame man at the pool of Bethesda. In each instance, Christ's dealings with the individual have a far-reaching impact on others as well. His contact with the Samaritan woman (John 4) leads to the evangelization of the town of Sychar. The healing of the lame man (John 5) produces an angry confrontation with Jews intent on killing Jesus. Christ's night visit from Nicodemus (John 3) provides the context for one of the most beloved verses in all of Scripture: John 3:16—"For God so loved the world that he gave his only Son. . . ."

Chapter 3	Chapter 4	Chapter 5
Life for the Seeker	Cleansing for the Sinner	Healing for the Sick
Nicodemus	Samaritan Woman	Lame Man

"God has sent you to teach us," said Nicodemus of Jesus. Jesus was more— he was God come to teach.

YOUR DAILY WALK Have you ever used a freeway on-ramp? (If you've tried to enter a freeway at rush hour, you perhaps have felt like you *lived* on an on-ramp!) Though the on-ramp is not technically part of the freeway itself, without it the freeway would be virtually useless. On-ramps get you onto the freeway. They provide access to the highway itself.

Now think of the gospel of Jesus Christ as a freeway. How are you at finding "on-ramps" to share that Good News with others? In each of the three chapters you will read today, Jesus uses an on-ramp to open a door of opportunity for his listener to hear and receive the gospel. Can you discover the on-ramps Jesus used? And can you suggest one you might use with a friend or fellow worker today?

INSIGHT Tracing the Roots of the Samaritans

The Samaritans were a mixed race of people, resulting from the inter-marriage of Jews with the pagan colonists the Assyrians used to repop-ulate the northern kingdom after its dispersal in 722 B.C. Racial hatred ensued, causing the Samaritans to form their own national and religious identity, complete with their own holy mountain and sacred writings. Though Samaria was considered off-limits to devout Jews, Jesus and his disciples passed through it in order to keep a divine appointment (4:4).

CHAPTER 3

After dark one evening, a Jewish religious leader named Nicodemus, a Pharisee, ²came to speak with Jesus. "Teacher," he said, "we all know that God has sent you to teach us. Your miraculous signs are proof enough that God is with you."

³Jesus replied, "I assure you, unless you are born again,* you can never see the Kingdom of God."

⁴"What do you mean?" exclaimed Nic-odemus. "How can an old man go back into his mother's womb and be born again?"

⁵Jesus replied, "The truth is, no one can enter the Kingdom of God without being born of water and the Spirit.* ⁶Humans can reproduce only human life, but the Holy Spirit gives new life from heaven. ⁷So don't be surprised at my statement that you* must be born again. ⁸Just as you can hear the wind but can't tell where it comes from or where it is going, so you can't explain how people are born of the Spirit."

3:3 Or *born from above*; also in 3:7.   **3:5** Or *spirit*. The Greek word for *Spirit* can also be translated *wind*; see 3:8.   **3:7** The Greek word for *you* is plural; also in 3:12.

⁹"What do you mean?" Nicodemus asked.

¹⁰Jesus replied, "You are a respected Jewish teacher, and yet you don't understand these things? ¹¹I assure you, I am telling you what we know and have seen, and yet you won't believe us. ¹²But if you don't even believe me when I tell you about things that happen here on earth, how can you possibly believe if I tell you what is going on in heaven? ¹³For only I, the Son of Man,* have come to earth and will return to heaven again. ¹⁴And as Moses lifted up the bronze snake on a pole in the wilderness, so I, the Son of Man, must be lifted up on a pole,* ¹⁵so that everyone who believes in me will have eternal life.

¹⁶"For God so loved the world that he gave his only Son, so that everyone who believes in him will not perish but have eternal life. ¹⁷God did not send his Son into the world to condemn it, but to save it.

¹⁸"There is no judgment awaiting those who trust him. But those who do not trust him have already been judged for not believing in the only Son of God. ¹⁹Their judgment is based on this fact: The light from heaven came into the world, but they loved the darkness more than the light, for their actions were evil. ²⁰They hate the light because they want to sin in the darkness. They stay away from the light for fear their sins will be exposed and they will be punished. ²¹But those who do what is right come to the light gladly, so everyone can see that they are doing what God wants."

²²Afterward Jesus and his disciples left Jerusalem, but they stayed in Judea for a while and baptized there.

²³At this time John the Baptist was baptizing at Aenon, near Salim, because there was plenty of water there and people kept coming to him for baptism. ²⁴This was before John was put into prison. ²⁵At that time a certain Jew began an argument with John's disciples over ceremonial cleansing. ²⁶John's disciples came to him and said, "Teacher, the man you met on the other side of the Jordan River, the one you said was the Messiah, is also baptizing people. And everybody is going over there instead of coming here to us."

²⁷John replied, "God in heaven appoints each person's work. ²⁸You yourselves know how plainly I told you that I am not the

Messiah. I am here to prepare the way for him—that is all. ²⁹The bride will go where the bridegroom is. A bridegroom's friend rejoices with him. I am the bridegroom's friend, and I am filled with joy at his success. ³⁰He must become greater and greater, and I must become less and less.

³¹"He has come from above and is greater than anyone else. I am of the earth, and my understanding is limited to the things of earth, but he has come from heaven.* ³²He tells what he has seen and heard, but how few believe what he tells them! ³³Those who believe him discover that God is true. ³⁴For he is sent by God. He speaks God's words, for God's Spirit is upon him without measure or limit. ³⁵The Father loves his Son, and he has given him authority over everything. ³⁶And all who believe in God's Son have eternal life. Those who don't obey the Son will never experience eternal life, but the wrath of God remains upon them."

CHAPTER 4
Jesus* learned that the Pharisees had heard, "Jesus is baptizing and making more disciples than John" ²(though Jesus himself didn't baptize them—his disciples did). ³So he left Judea to return to Galilee.

⁴He had to go through Samaria on the way. ⁵Eventually he came to the Samaritan village of Sychar, near the parcel of ground that Jacob gave to his son Joseph. ⁶Jacob's well was there; and Jesus, tired from the long walk, sat wearily beside the well about noontime. ⁷Soon a Samaritan woman came to draw water, and Jesus said to her, "Please give me a drink." ⁸He was alone at the time because his disciples had gone into the village to buy some food.

⁹The woman was surprised, for Jews refuse to have anything to do with Samaritans. She said to Jesus, "You are a Jew, and I am a Samaritan woman. Why are you asking me for a drink?"

¹⁰Jesus replied, "If you only knew the gift God has for you and who I am, you would ask me, and I would give you living water."

¹¹"But sir, you don't have a rope or a bucket," she said, "and this is a very deep well. Where would you get this living water? ¹²And besides, are you greater than our

3:13 Some manuscripts add *who lives in heaven.*   3:14 Greek *must be lifted up.*   3:31 Some manuscripts omit *but he has come from heaven.*   4:1 Some manuscripts read *The Lord.*

ancestor Jacob who gave us this well? How can you offer better water than he and his sons and his cattle enjoyed?"

¹³Jesus replied, "People soon become thirsty again after drinking this water. ¹⁴But the water I give them takes away thirst altogether. It becomes a perpetual spring within them, giving them eternal life."

¹⁵"Please, sir," the woman said, "give me some of that water! Then I'll never be thirsty again, and I won't have to come here to haul water."

¹⁶"Go and get your husband," Jesus told her.

¹⁷"I don't have a husband," the woman replied.

Jesus said, "You're right! You don't have a husband—¹⁸for you have had five husbands, and you aren't even married to the man you're living with now."

¹⁹"Sir," the woman said, "you must be a prophet. ²⁰So tell me, why is it that you Jews insist that Jerusalem is the only place of worship, while we Samaritans claim it is here at Mount Gerizim,* where our ancestors worshiped?"

²¹Jesus replied, "Believe me, the time is coming when it will no longer matter whether you worship the Father here or in Jerusalem. ²²You Samaritans know so little about the one you worship, while we Jews know all about him, for salvation comes through the Jews. ²³But the time is coming and is already here when true worshipers will worship the Father in spirit and in truth. The Father is looking for anyone who will worship him that way. ²⁴For God is Spirit, so those who worship him must worship in spirit and in truth."

²⁵The woman said, "I know the Messiah will come—the one who is called Christ. When he comes, he will explain everything to us."

²⁶Then Jesus told her, "I am the Messiah!"*

²⁷Just then his disciples arrived. They were astonished to find him talking to a woman, but none of them asked him why he was doing it or what they had been discussing. ²⁸The woman left her water jar beside the well and went back to the village and told everyone, ²⁹"Come and meet a man who told me everything I ever did!

Can this be the Messiah?" ³⁰So the people came streaming from the village to see him.

³¹Meanwhile, the disciples were urging Jesus to eat. ³²"No," he said, "I have food you don't know about."

³³"Who brought it to him?" the disciples asked each other.

³⁴Then Jesus explained: "My nourishment comes from doing the will of God, who sent me, and from finishing his work. ³⁵Do you think the work of harvesting will not begin until the summer ends four months from now? Look around you! Vast fields are ripening all around us and are ready now for the harvest. ³⁶The harvesters are paid good wages, and the fruit they harvest is people brought to eternal life. What joy awaits both the planter and the harvester alike! ³⁷You know the saying, 'One person plants and someone else harvests.' And it's true. ³⁸I sent you to harvest where you didn't plant; others had already done the work, and you will gather the harvest."

³⁹Many Samaritans from the village believed in Jesus because the woman had said, "He told me everything I ever did!" ⁴⁰When they came out to see him, they begged him to stay at their village. So he stayed for two days, ⁴¹long enough for many of them to hear his message and believe. ⁴²Then they said to the woman, "Now we believe because we have heard him ourselves, not just because of what you told us. He is indeed the Savior of the world."

⁴³At the end of the two days' stay, Jesus went on into Galilee. ⁴⁴He had previously said, "A prophet is honored everywhere except in his own country." ⁴⁵The Galileans welcomed him, for they had been in Jerusalem at the Passover celebration and had seen all his miraculous signs.

⁴⁶In the course of his journey through Galilee, he arrived at the town of Cana, where he had turned the water into wine. There was a government official in the city of Capernaum whose son was very sick. ⁴⁷When he heard that Jesus had come from Judea and was traveling in Galilee, he went over to Cana. He found Jesus and begged him to come to Capernaum with him to heal his son, who was about to die.

⁴⁸Jesus asked, "Must I do miraculous

4:20 Greek *on this mountain.*   **4:26** Greek *"I am, the one speaking to you."*

signs and wonders before you people will believe in me?"

⁴⁹The official pleaded, "Lord, please come now before my little boy dies."

⁵⁰Then Jesus told him, "Go back home. Your son will live!" And the man believed Jesus' word and started home.

⁵¹While he was on his way, some of his servants met him with the news that his son was alive and well. ⁵²He asked them when the boy had begun to feel better, and they replied, "Yesterday afternoon at one o'clock his fever suddenly disappeared!" ⁵³Then the father realized it was the same time that Jesus had told him, "Your son will live." And the officer and his entire household believed in Jesus. ⁵⁴This was Jesus' second miraculous sign in Galilee after coming from Judea.

CHAPTER 5

Afterward Jesus returned to Jerusalem for one of the Jewish holy days. ²Inside the city, near the Sheep Gate, was the pool of Bethesda,* with five covered porches. ³Crowds of sick people—blind, lame, or paralyzed—lay on the porches.* ⁵One of the men lying there had been sick for thirty-eight years. ⁶When Jesus saw him and knew how long he had been ill, he asked him, "Would you like to get well?"

⁷"I can't, sir," the sick man said, "for I have no one to help me into the pool when the water is stirred up. While I am trying to get there, someone else always gets in ahead of me."

⁸Jesus told him, "Stand up, pick up your sleeping mat, and walk!"

⁹Instantly, the man was healed! He rolled up the mat and began walking! But this miracle happened on the Sabbath day. ¹⁰So the Jewish leaders objected. They said to the man who was cured, "You can't work on the Sabbath! It's illegal to carry that sleeping mat!"

¹¹He replied, "The man who healed me said to me, 'Pick up your sleeping mat and walk.'"

¹²"Who said such a thing as that?" they demanded.

¹³The man didn't know, for Jesus had disappeared into the crowd. ¹⁴But afterward Jesus found him in the Temple and told him, "Now you are well; so stop sinning, or something even worse may hap-

pen to you." ¹⁵Then the man went to find the Jewish leaders and told them it was Jesus who had healed him.

¹⁶So the Jewish leaders began harassing Jesus for breaking the Sabbath rules. ¹⁷But Jesus replied, "My Father never stops working, so why should I?" ¹⁸So the Jewish leaders tried all the more to kill him. In addition to disobeying the Sabbath rules, he had spoken of God as his Father, thereby making himself equal with God.

¹⁹Jesus replied, "I assure you, the Son can do nothing by himself. He does only what he sees the Father doing. Whatever the Father does, the Son also does. ²⁰For the Father loves the Son and tells him everything he is doing, and the Son will do far greater things than healing this man. You will be astonished at what he does. ²¹He will even raise from the dead anyone he wants to, just as the Father does. ²²And the Father leaves all judgment to his Son, ²³so that everyone will honor the Son, just as they honor the Father. But if you refuse to honor the Son, then you are certainly not honoring the Father who sent him.

²⁴"I assure you, those who listen to my message and believe in God who sent me have eternal life. They will never be condemned for their sins, but they have already passed from death into life.

²⁵"And I assure you that the time is coming, in fact it is here, when the dead will hear my voice—the voice of the Son of God. And those who listen will live. ²⁶The Father has life in himself, and he has granted his Son to have life in himself. ²⁷And he has given him authority to judge all mankind because he is the Son of Man. ²⁸Don't be so surprised! Indeed, the time is coming when all the dead in their graves will hear the voice of God's Son, ²⁹and they will rise again. Those who have done good will rise to eternal life, and those who have continued in evil will rise to judgment. ³⁰But I do nothing without consulting the Father. I judge as I am told. And my judgment is absolutely just, because it is according to the will of God who sent me; it is not merely my own.

³¹"If I were to testify on my own behalf, my testimony would not be valid. ³²But someone else is also testifying about me, and I can assure you that everything he

---

5:2 Some manuscripts read *Beth-zatha*; other manuscripts read *Bethsaida*.   5:3 Some manuscripts add *waiting for a certain movement of the water, ⁴for an angel of the Lord came from time to time and stirred up the water. And the first person to step down into it afterward was healed.*

says about me is true. ³³In fact, you sent messengers to listen to John the Baptist, and he preached the truth. ³⁴But the best testimony about me is not from a man, though I have reminded you about John's testimony so you might be saved. ³⁵John shone brightly for a while, and you benefited and rejoiced. ³⁶But I have a greater witness than John—my teachings and my miracles. They have been assigned to me by the Father, and they testify that the Father has sent me. ³⁷And the Father himself has also testified about me. You have never heard his voice or seen him face to face, ³⁸and you do not have his message in your hearts, because you do not believe me—the one he sent to you.

³⁹"You search the Scriptures because you believe they give you eternal life. But the Scriptures point to me! ⁴⁰Yet you refuse to come to me so that I can give you this eternal life.

⁴¹"Your approval or disapproval means nothing to me, ⁴²because I know you don't have God's love within you. ⁴³For I have come to you representing my Father, and you refuse to welcome me, even though you readily accept others who represent only themselves. ⁴⁴No wonder you can't believe! For you gladly honor each other, but you don't care about the honor that comes from God alone.

⁴⁵"Yet it is not I who will accuse you of this before the Father. Moses will accuse you! Yes, Moses, on whom you set your hopes. ⁴⁶But if you had believed Moses, you would have believed me because he wrote about me. ⁴⁷And since you don't believe what he wrote, how will you believe what I say?"

OCTOBER 27 ☐ DAY 301
JOHN 6–8
Ministry to the Multitudes by God's Son

OVERVIEW John relates his record of Jesus' life and ministry to the major festivals of the Jews. The feeding of the five thousand and Jesus' discourse on the true bread of life take place during the Passover (6:4). The discourses of chapters 7 and 8 are given during Jesus' visit to Jerusalem for the Festival of Shelters (7:2, 10). Though in both cases it is a time for feasting, clearly the temperament of the Jewish leaders is more akin to murder than to merriment as they take up rocks to stone Christ (8:59).

Chapter 6	Chapter 7	Chapter 8
The Bread of Life	The Living Water	The Light of the World
Festival of Passover	Festival of Shelters	

YOUR DAILY WALK Do you stand alone in your family circle as a Christian? And do you find your home environment hard on your spiritual life and growth? Then take heart. The Lord Jesus faced the same discouraging problem in his earthly family (7:5). His mother, Mary, of course, knew her Son's true identity. But none of his brothers believed he was the Messiah until after his resurrection. Not only were they unbelieving, but they made fun of his claims and ministry.

The way Jesus dealt with unbelief and sarcasm in his family will work for you, too. First, he ignored their taunts. Do not respond to scoffing, either in anger or in rebuttal. Response is what the scoffers want. It only feeds the fires of antagonism. Second, Jesus quietly and consistently continued his ministry for God. Do not be intimidated by unbelieving

Wherever you see persecution, there is more than a probability that truth is on the persecuted side.

family members. Ask God to enable you to be faithful to him and to live a consistent, vibrant Christian life before them as a witness. Remember, you may be the only "Bible" your unsaved family will ever read. Third, Jesus drew strength and encouragement from his believers (Matthew 12:46-50). Can you hope to grow spiritually without doing the same? Schedule a time of prayer with one of your brothers or sisters in Christ. You need it—and so do they!

 INSIGHT "I AM" in the Old, "I AM" in the New
In Exodus 3:14 God reveals his name to Moses as "I AM," the self-existent, all-sufficient God. The claims of Jesus in today's section (6:35, 48; 8:12) make it clear he is identifying himself as the same person—a claim the Jewish leaders understand all too clearly.

CHAPTER 6

After this, Jesus crossed over the Sea of Galilee, also known as the Sea of Tiberias. ²And a huge crowd kept following him wherever he went, because they saw his miracles as he healed the sick. ³Then Jesus went up into the hills and sat down with his disciples around him. ⁴(It was nearly time for the annual Passover celebration.) ⁵Jesus soon saw a great crowd of people climbing the hill, looking for him. Turning to Philip, he asked, "Philip, where can we buy bread to feed all these people?" ⁶He was testing Philip, for he already knew what he was going to do.

⁷Philip replied, "It would take a small fortune* to feed them!"

⁸Then Andrew, Simon Peter's brother, spoke up. ⁹"There's a young boy here with five barley loaves and two fish. But what good is that with this huge crowd?"

¹⁰"Tell everyone to sit down," Jesus ordered. So all of them—the men alone numbered five thousand—sat down on the grassy slopes. ¹¹Then Jesus took the loaves, gave thanks to God, and passed them out to the people. Afterward he did the same with the fish. And they all ate until they were full. ¹²"Now gather the leftovers," Jesus told his disciples, "so that nothing is wasted." ¹³There were only five barley loaves to start with, but twelve baskets were filled with the pieces of bread the people did not eat!

¹⁴When the people saw this miraculous sign, they exclaimed, "Surely, he is the Prophet* we have been expecting!" ¹⁵Jesus saw that they were ready to take him by force and make him king, so he went higher into the hills alone.

¹⁶That evening his disciples went down to the shore to wait for him. ¹⁷But as darkness fell and Jesus still hadn't come back, they got into the boat and headed out across the lake toward Capernaum. ¹⁸Soon a gale swept down upon them as they rowed, and the sea grew very rough. ¹⁹They were three or four miles* out when suddenly they saw Jesus walking on the water toward the boat. They were terrified, ²⁰but he called out to them, "I am here! Don't be afraid." ²¹Then they were eager to let him in, and immediately the boat arrived at their destination!

²²The next morning, back across the lake, crowds began gathering on the shore, waiting to see Jesus. For they knew that he and his disciples had come over together and that the disciples had gone off in their boat, leaving him behind. ²³Several boats from Tiberias landed near the place where the Lord had blessed the bread and the people had eaten. ²⁴When the crowd saw that Jesus wasn't there, nor his disciples, they got into the boats and went across to Capernaum to look for him. ²⁵When they arrived and found him, they asked, "Teacher, how did you get here?"

²⁶Jesus replied, "The truth is, you want to be with me because I fed you, not because you saw the miraculous sign. ²⁷But you shouldn't be so concerned about perishable things like food. Spend your energy seeking the eternal life that I, the Son of Man, can give you. For God the Father has sent me for that very purpose."

²⁸They replied, "What does God want us to do?"

²⁹Jesus told them, "This is what God wants you to do: Believe in the one he has sent."

³⁰They replied, "You must show us a

6:7 Greek *200 denarii.* A denarius was the equivalent of a full day's wage.   **6:14** See Deut 18:15, 18.   **6:19** Greek *25 or 30 stadia* [4.6 or 5.5 kilometers].

miraculous sign if you want us to believe in you. What will you do for us? [31]After all, our ancestors ate manna while they journeyed through the wilderness! As the Scriptures say, 'Moses gave them bread from heaven to eat.'*"

[32]Jesus said, "I assure you, Moses didn't give them bread from heaven. My Father did. And now he offers you the true bread from heaven. [33]The true bread of God is the one who comes down from heaven and gives life to the world."

[34]"Sir," they said, "give us that bread every day of our lives."

[35]Jesus replied, "I am the bread of life. No one who comes to me will ever be hungry again. Those who believe in me will never thirst. [36]But you haven't believed in me even though you have seen me. [37]However, those the Father has given me will come to me, and I will never reject them. [38]For I have come down from heaven to do the will of God who sent me, not to do what I want. [39]And this is the will of God, that I should not lose even one of all those he has given me, but that I should raise them to eternal life at the last day. [40]For it is my Father's will that all who see his Son and believe in him should have eternal life— that I should raise them at the last day."

[41]Then the people* began to murmur in disagreement because he had said, "I am the bread from heaven." [42]They said, "This is Jesus, the son of Joseph. We know his father and mother. How can he say, 'I came down from heaven'?"

[43]But Jesus replied, "Don't complain about what I said. [44]For people can't come to me unless the Father who sent me draws them to me, and at the last day I will raise them from the dead. [45]As it is written in the Scriptures, 'They will all be taught by God.'* Everyone who hears and learns from the Father comes to me. [46](Not that anyone has ever seen the Father; only I, who was sent from God, have seen him.)

[47]"I assure you, anyone who believes in me already has eternal life. [48]Yes, I am the bread of life! [49]Your ancestors ate manna in the wilderness, but they all died. [50]However, the bread from heaven gives eternal life to everyone who eats it. [51]I am the living bread that came down out of heaven. Anyone who eats this bread will live for-

ever; this bread is my flesh, offered so the world may live."

[52]Then the people began arguing with each other about what he meant. "How can this man give us his flesh to eat?" they asked.

[53]So Jesus said again, "I assure you, unless you eat the flesh of the Son of Man and drink his blood, you cannot have eternal life within you. [54]But those who eat my flesh and drink my blood have eternal life, and I will raise them at the last day. [55]For my flesh is the true food, and my blood is the true drink. [56]All who eat my flesh and drink my blood remain in me, and I in them. [57]I live by the power of the living Father who sent me; in the same way, those who partake of me will live because of me. [58]I am the true bread from heaven. Anyone who eats this bread will live forever and not die as your ancestors did, even though they ate the manna."

[59]He said these things while he was teaching in the synagogue in Capernaum.

[60]Even his disciples said, "This is very hard to understand. How can anyone accept it?"

[61]Jesus knew within himself that his disciples were complaining, so he said to them, "Does this offend you? [62]Then what will you think if you see me, the Son of Man, return to heaven again? [63]It is the Spirit who gives eternal life. Human effort accomplishes nothing. And the very words I have spoken to you are spirit and life. [64]But some of you don't believe me." (For Jesus knew from the beginning who didn't believe, and he knew who would betray him.) [65]Then he said, "That is what I meant when I said that people can't come to me unless the Father brings them to me."

[66]At this point many of his disciples turned away and deserted him. [67]Then Jesus turned to the Twelve and asked, "Are you going to leave, too?"

[68]Simon Peter replied, "Lord, to whom would we go? You alone have the words that give eternal life. [69]We believe them, and we know you are the Holy One of God."

[70]Then Jesus said, "I chose the twelve of you, but one is a devil." [71]He was speaking of Judas, son of Simon Iscariot, one of the Twelve, who would betray him.

6:31 Exod 16:4; Ps 78:24.   **6:41** Greek *Jewish people;* also in 6:52.   **6:45** Isa 54:13.

CHAPTER 7

After this, Jesus stayed in Galilee, going from village to village. He wanted to stay out of Judea where the Jewish leaders were plotting his death. [2]But soon it was time for the Festival of Shelters, [3]and Jesus' brothers urged him to go to Judea for the celebration. "Go where your followers can see your miracles!" they scoffed. [4]"You can't become a public figure if you hide like this! If you can do such wonderful things, prove it to the world!" [5]For even his brothers didn't believe in him.

[6]Jesus replied, "Now is not the right time for me to go. But you can go anytime, and it will make no difference. [7]The world can't hate you, but it does hate me because I accuse it of sin and evil. [8]You go on. I am not yet* ready to go to this festival, because my time has not yet come." [9]So Jesus remained in Galilee.

[10]But after his brothers had left for the festival, Jesus also went, though secretly, staying out of public view. [11]The Jewish leaders tried to find him at the festival and kept asking if anyone had seen him. [12]There was a lot of discussion about him among the crowds. Some said, "He's a wonderful man," while others said, "He's nothing but a fraud, deceiving the people." [13]But no one had the courage to speak favorably about him in public, for they were afraid of getting in trouble with the Jewish leaders.

[14]Then, midway through the festival, Jesus went up to the Temple and began to teach. [15]The Jewish leaders were surprised when they heard him. "How does he know so much when he hasn't studied everything we've studied?" they asked.

[16]So Jesus told them, "I'm not teaching my own ideas, but those of God who sent me. [17]Anyone who wants to do the will of God will know whether my teaching is from God or is merely my own. [18]Those who present their own ideas are looking for praise for themselves, but those who seek to honor the one who sent them are good and genuine. [19]None of you obeys the law of Moses! In fact, you are trying to kill me."

[20]The crowd replied, "You're demon possessed! Who's trying to kill you?"

[21]Jesus replied, "I worked on the Sabbath by healing a man, and you were offended. [22]But you work on the Sabbath, too, when you obey Moses' law of circumcision. (Actually, this tradition of circumcision is older than the law of Moses; it goes back to Abraham.) [23]For if the correct time for circumcising your son falls on the Sabbath, you go ahead and do it, so as not to break the law of Moses. So why should I be condemned for making a man completely well on the Sabbath? [24]Think this through and you will see that I am right."

[25]Some of the people who lived there in Jerusalem said among themselves, "Isn't this the man they are trying to kill? [26]But here he is, speaking in public, and they say nothing to him. Can it be that our leaders know that he really is the Messiah? [27]But how could he be? For we know where this man comes from. When the Messiah comes, he will simply appear; no one will know where he comes from."

[28]While Jesus was teaching in the Temple, he called out, "Yes, you know me, and you know where I come from. But I represent one you don't know, and he is true. [29]I know him because I have come from him, and he sent me to you." [30]Then the leaders tried to arrest him; but no one laid a hand on him, because his time had not yet come.

[31]Many among the crowds at the Temple believed in him. "After all," they said, "would you expect the Messiah to do more miraculous signs than this man has done?"

[32]When the Pharisees heard that the crowds were murmuring such things, they and the leading priests sent Temple guards to arrest Jesus. [33]But Jesus told them, "I will be here a little longer. Then I will return to the one who sent me. [34]You will search for me but not find me. And you won't be able to come where I am."

[35]The Jewish leaders were puzzled by this statement. "Where is he planning to go?" they asked. "Maybe he is thinking of leaving the country and going to the Jews in other lands, or maybe even to the Gentiles! [36]What does he mean when he says, 'You will search for me but not find me,' and 'You won't be able to come where I am'?"

[37]On the last day, the climax of the festival, Jesus stood and shouted to the crowds, "If you are thirsty, come to me! [38]If you believe in me, come and drink! For the Scriptures declare that rivers of living water will flow out from within."* [39](When he

7:8 Some manuscripts omit *yet.*   7:37-38 Or *"Let anyone who is thirsty come to me and drink.* [38]*For the Scriptures declare that rivers of living water will flow from the heart of those who believe in me."*

said "living water," he was speaking of the Spirit, who would be given to everyone believing in him. But the Spirit had not yet been given, because Jesus had not yet entered into his glory.)

[40] When the crowds heard him say this, some of them declared, "This man surely is the Prophet."* [41] Others said, "He is the Messiah." Still others said, "But he can't be! Will the Messiah come from Galilee? [42] For the Scriptures clearly state that the Messiah will be born of the royal line of David, in Bethlehem, the village where King David was born."* [43] So the crowd was divided in their opinion about him. [44] And some wanted him arrested, but no one touched him.

[45] The Temple guards who had been sent to arrest him returned to the leading priests and Pharisees. "Why didn't you bring him in?" they demanded.

[46] "We have never heard anyone talk like this!" the guards responded.

[47] "Have you been led astray, too?" the Pharisees mocked. [48] "Is there a single one of us rulers or Pharisees who believes in him? [49] These ignorant crowds do, but what do they know about it? A curse on them anyway!"

[50] Nicodemus, the leader who had met with Jesus earlier, then spoke up. [51] "Is it legal to convict a man before he is given a hearing?" he asked.

[52] They replied, "Are you from Galilee, too? Search the Scriptures and see for yourself—no prophet ever comes from Galilee!"

[The most ancient Greek manuscripts do not include John 7:53–8:11.]

[53] Then the meeting broke up and everybody went home.

CHAPTER 8

Jesus returned to the Mount of Olives, [2] but early the next morning he was back again at the Temple. A crowd soon gathered, and he sat down and taught them. [3] As he was speaking, the teachers of religious law and Pharisees brought a woman they had caught in the act of adultery. They put her in front of the crowd.

[4] "Teacher," they said to Jesus, "this woman was caught in the very act of adultery. [5] The law of Moses says to stone her. What do you say?"

[6] They were trying to trap him into saying something they could use against him, but Jesus stooped down and wrote in the dust with his finger. [7] They kept demanding an answer, so he stood up again and said, "All right, stone her. But let those who have never sinned throw the first stones!" [8] Then he stooped down again and wrote in the dust.

[9] When the accusers heard this, they slipped away one by one, beginning with the oldest, until only Jesus was left in the middle of the crowd with the woman. [10] Then Jesus stood up again and said to her, "Where are your accusers? Didn't even one of them condemn you?"

[11] "No, Lord," she said.

And Jesus said, "Neither do I. Go and sin no more."

[12] Jesus said to the people, "I am the light of the world. If you follow me, you won't be stumbling through the darkness, because you will have the light that leads to life."

[13] The Pharisees replied, "You are making false claims about yourself!"

[14] Jesus told them, "These claims are valid even though I make them about myself. For I know where I came from and where I am going, but you don't know this about me. [15] You judge me with all your human limitations,* but I am not judging anyone. [16] And if I did, my judgment would be correct in every respect because I am not alone—I have with me the Father who sent me. [17] Your own law says that if two people agree about something, their witness is accepted as fact.* [18] I am one witness, and my Father who sent me is the other."

[19] "Where is your father?" they asked.

Jesus answered, "Since you don't know who I am, you don't know who my Father is. If you knew me, then you would know my Father, too." [20] Jesus made these statements while he was teaching in the section of the Temple known as the Treasury. But he was not arrested, because his time had not yet come.

[21] Later Jesus said to them again, "I am going away. You will search for me and die in your sin. You cannot come where I am going."

[22] The Jewish leaders asked, "Is he planning to commit suicide? What does he mean, 'You cannot come where I am going'?"

7:40 See Deut 18:15, 18.   7:42 See Mic 5:2.   8:15 Or judge me by human standards.   8:17 See Deut 19:15.

²³Then he said to them, "You are from below; I am from above. You are of this world; I am not. ²⁴That is why I said that you will die in your sins; for unless you believe that I am who I say I am, you will die in your sins."

²⁵"Tell us who you are," they demanded.

Jesus replied, "I am the one I have always claimed to be.* ²⁶I have much to say about you and much to condemn, but I won't. For I say only what I have heard from the one who sent me, and he is true." ²⁷But they still didn't understand that he was talking to them about his Father.

²⁸So Jesus said, "When you have lifted up the Son of Man on the cross, then you will realize that I am he and that I do nothing on my own, but I speak what the Father taught me. ²⁹And the one who sent me is with me—he has not deserted me. For I always do those things that are pleasing to him." ³⁰Then many who heard him say these things believed in him.

³¹Jesus said to the people* who believed in him, "You are truly my disciples if you keep obeying my teachings. ³²And you will know the truth, and the truth will set you free."

³³"But we are descendants of Abraham," they said. "We have never been slaves to anyone on earth. What do you mean, 'set free'?"

³⁴Jesus replied, "I assure you that everyone who sins is a slave of sin. ³⁵A slave is not a permanent member of the family, but a son is part of the family forever. ³⁶So if the Son sets you free, you will indeed be free. ³⁷Yes, I realize that you are descendants of Abraham. And yet some of you are trying to kill me because my message does not find a place in your hearts. ³⁸I am telling you what I saw when I was with my Father. But you are following the advice of your father."

³⁹"Our father is Abraham," they declared.

"No," Jesus replied, "for if you were children of Abraham, you would follow his good example.* ⁴⁰I told you the truth I heard from God, but you are trying to kill me. Abraham wouldn't do a thing like that. ⁴¹No, you are obeying your real father when you act that way."

They replied, "We were not born out of wedlock! Our true Father is God himself."

⁴²Jesus told them, "If God were your Father, you would love me, because I have come to you from God. I am not here on my own, but he sent me. ⁴³Why can't you understand what I am saying? It is because you are unable to do so! ⁴⁴For you are the children of your father the Devil, and you love to do the evil things he does. He was a murderer from the beginning and has always hated the truth. There is no truth in him. When he lies, it is consistent with his character; for he is a liar and the father of lies. ⁴⁵So when I tell the truth, you just naturally don't believe me! ⁴⁶Which of you can truthfully accuse me of sin? And since I am telling you the truth, why don't you believe me? ⁴⁷Anyone whose Father is God listens gladly to the words of God. Since you don't, it proves you aren't God's children."

⁴⁸The people retorted, "You Samaritan devil! Didn't we say all along that you were possessed by a demon?"

⁴⁹"No," Jesus said, "I have no demon in me. For I honor my Father—and you dishonor me. ⁵⁰And though I have no wish to glorify myself, God wants to glorify me. Let him be the judge. ⁵¹I assure you, anyone who obeys my teaching will never die!"

⁵²The people said, "Now we know you are possessed by a demon. Even Abraham and the prophets died, but you say that those who obey your teaching will never die! ⁵³Are you greater than our father Abraham, who died? Are you greater than the prophets, who died? Who do you think you are?"

⁵⁴Jesus answered, "If I am merely boasting about myself, it doesn't count. But it is my Father who says these glorious things about me. You say, 'He is our God,' ⁵⁵but you do not even know him. I know him. If I said otherwise, I would be as great a liar as you! But it is true—I know him and obey him. ⁵⁶Your ancestor Abraham rejoiced as he looked forward to my coming. He saw it and was glad."

⁵⁷The people said, "You aren't even fifty years old. How can you say you have seen Abraham?*"

⁵⁸Jesus answered, "The truth is, I existed before Abraham was even born!"* ⁵⁹At that point they picked up stones to kill him. But Jesus hid himself from them and left the Temple.

8:25 Or "Why do I speak to you at all?"   8:31 Greek *Jewish people*; also in 8:48, 52, 57.   8:39 Some manuscripts read *if you are children of Abraham, follow his example.*   8:57 Some manuscripts read *How can you say Abraham has seen you?*   8:58 Or "Truly, truly, before Abraham was, I am."

OCTOBER 28 □ DAY 302
Ready with an Answer

LOOK BACK In contrast to the synoptic Gospels (Matthew, Mark, and Luke), John's Gospel might well be called the *supplemental* Gospel, for about 93 percent of John's account is found nowhere else in the Gospel records. Such favorite characters as the woman at the well, Nicodemus, Jesus' dear friend Lazarus, and the nameless Good Samaritan are found in John's Gospel alone.

Luke writes with the precision of a careful historian as he documents the life and times of Jesus, for that is his purpose: "to write a careful summary for you, to reassure you of the truth of all you were taught" (Luke 1:3-4). By contrast, John focuses on the miraculous signs Jesus performed (seven in the first twelve chapters alone) "that you may believe that Jesus is the Messiah, the Son of God, and that by believing in him you will have life" (John 20:31).

Many verses you have read this past week would make excellent memory work projects. Why not hide a bit of God's Word in your heart this next week, beginning with one of the following verses: Luke 16:13; 18:16; 19:10; 20:25; John 1:12, 14; 3:16, 36; 5:24; 8:32.

Your mission field is the next unsaved person you meet.

LOOK UP There is a knock at your door. It is late, and visitors at night are rare. But this visitor turns out to be your minister or religious leader. After a few minutes of polite conversation, the discussion takes a serious turn. He asks you, "How can I know I am a Christian?"

Would you be surprised? Of course you would! After all, ministers and religious leaders are supposed to know the answers to spiritual questions. But here is a man asking the very questions he should have been prepared to answer.

In John 3 you've read a true account that in many ways parallels the fictitious story about your minister. Nicodemus was a Pharisee, a religious man. Trained in the Mosaic Law, he was an expert in the Old Testament Scriptures. Quite likely he taught children in the synagogue school. But here he was asking Jesus the very question he should have been prepared to answer himself: "How can an old man go back into his mother's womb and be born again?" (John 3:4). In other words, how can a person experience the second birth and be born again?

Jesus' answer has become the most familiar verse in the entire Bible—John 3:16. There you will find the best piece of good news ever broadcast to the world. Do you know what it is?

LOOK AHEAD Here is a handy way to remember what Jesus told Nicodemus during that evening encounter. By writing down the letters in the word *gospel,* you are not only ready to discover the Good News for yourself, but to share it with anyone who will listen to you for two minutes!

G_____ so loved the world that he gave his

O_____

S_____, so that everyone who believes in him will not

P_____ but have

E_____

L_____

If you have put your confident trust in Jesus as your Sin Bearer, it means that you have experienced the second birth. Eternal life is God's gift to all who acknowledge their need of a Savior and turn to Jesus in believing faith. Have you heard the Good News? Good! Now pass it on to someone else who has yet to hear.

OCTOBER 29 ☐ DAY 303
JOHN 9–12
Mounting Anger toward God's Son

OVERVIEW Continuing his ministry in Jerusalem following the Festival of Shelters, Jesus first gives physical sight to a blind man, then opens spiritual eyes as well. This leads to a discussion with the Jews about "the blind leading the blind" and the importance of a Shepherd who both guides and guards his sheep. Jesus' seventh and climactic miracle takes place in Bethany, where he raises Lazarus from the dead. Though Bethany is astir with wonderment and belief, from this point on Jesus is a marked man (11:53), his every step leading closer to the cross.

Chapter 9	Chapter 10	Chapter 11	Chapter 12
"I Am the Light"	"I Am the Gate"	"I Am the Resurrection"	"Here Comes the King"
Blind Man	Lost Sheep	Lazarus	Last Week

YOUR DAILY WALK Mary of Bethany is a woman every Christian should emulate. She is mentioned three separate times in the Gospels, and each time she is described as being at the feet of Jesus (Luke 10:39; John 11:32; 12:3). In this position she worshiped him, received instruction from him, and experienced his comfort in the midst of sorrow. You cannot literally take the position of Mary, but in attitude you can. It is the position of submission and dependence.

We must not only give what we have; we must also give what we are.

Mary also was willing to sacrifice her most precious and costly possession in an act of devotion to Jesus. The twelve-ounce jar of expensive perfume was worth hundreds of dollars by today's standards. It may well have been her dowry in anticipation of a wedding proposal. Yet she poured it over the feet of Jesus in an offering of love.

Perhaps you are wondering, *What do I have that I can give to Jesus as an act of worship?* The most precious thing you possess is yourself. If you have never done so before, assume the posture of Mary as you prayerfully read Romans 12:1, and give yourself as an offering today. It's an act of worship God never grows tired of receiving.

INSIGHT The Door-less Door of the Sheep
In ancient times the sheepfold was a circular stone corral with a single narrow opening. After the sheep were inside, the shepherd would lie down across the opening, using his own body to form the gate or "door" of the sheepfold. Nothing could enter or leave the fold without the shepherd knowing about it. Keep that image in mind as you read Jesus' words in 10:7.

CHAPTER 9

As Jesus was walking along, he saw a man who had been blind from birth. 2"Teacher," his disciples asked him, "why was this man born blind? Was it a result of his own sins or those of his parents?"

3"It was not because of his sins or his parents' sins," Jesus answered. "He was born blind so the power of God could be seen in him. 4All of us must quickly carry out the tasks assigned us by the one who sent me, because there is little time left before the night falls and all work comes to an end. 5But while I am still here in the world, I am the light of the world."

6Then he spit on the ground, made mud with the saliva, and smoothed the mud over the blind man's eyes. 7He told him, "Go and wash in the pool of Siloam" (Siloam means Sent). So the man went and washed, and came back seeing!

8His neighbors and others who knew

him as a blind beggar asked each other, "Is this the same man—that beggar?" [9]Some said he was, and others said, "No, but he surely looks like him!"

And the beggar kept saying, "I am the same man!"

[10]They asked, "Who healed you? What happened?"

[11]He told them, "The man they call Jesus made mud and smoothed it over my eyes and told me, 'Go to the pool of Siloam and wash off the mud.' I went and washed, and now I can see!"

[12]"Where is he now?" they asked.

"I don't know," he replied.

[13]Then they took the man to the Pharisees. [14]Now as it happened, Jesus had healed the man on a Sabbath. [15]The Pharisees asked the man all about it. So he told them, "He smoothed the mud over my eyes, and when it was washed away, I could see!"

[16]Some of the Pharisees said, "This man Jesus is not from God, for he is working on the Sabbath." Others said, "But how could an ordinary sinner do such miraculous signs?" So there was a deep division of opinion among them.

[17]Then the Pharisees once again questioned the man who had been blind and demanded, "This man who opened your eyes—who do you say he is?"

The man replied, "I think he must be a prophet."

[18]The Jewish leaders wouldn't believe he had been blind, so they called in his parents. [19]They asked them, "Is this your son? Was he born blind? If so, how can he see?"

[20]His parents replied, "We know this is our son and that he was born blind, [21]but we don't know how he can see or who healed him. He is old enough to speak for himself. Ask him." [22]They said this because they were afraid of the Jewish leaders, who had announced that anyone saying Jesus was the Messiah would be expelled from the synagogue. [23]That's why they said, "He is old enough to speak for himself. Ask him."

[24]So for the second time they called in the man who had been blind and told him, "Give glory to God by telling the truth,* because we know Jesus is a sinner."

[25]"I don't know whether he is a sinner,"

the man replied. "But I know this: I was blind, and now I can see!"

[26]"But what did he do?" they asked. "How did he heal you?"

[27]"Look!" the man exclaimed. "I told you once. Didn't you listen? Why do you want to hear it again? Do you want to become his disciples, too?"

[28]Then they cursed him and said, "You are his disciple, but we are disciples of Moses. [29]We know God spoke to Moses, but as for this man, we don't know anything about him."

[30]"Why, that's very strange!" the man replied. "He healed my eyes, and yet you don't know anything about him! [31]Well, God doesn't listen to sinners, but he is ready to hear those who worship him and do his will. [32]Never since the world began has anyone been able to open the eyes of someone born blind. [33]If this man were not from God, he couldn't do it."

[34]"You were born in sin!" they answered. "Are you trying to teach us?" And they threw him out of the synagogue.

[35]When Jesus heard what had happened, he found the man and said, "Do you believe in the Son of Man*?"

[36]The man answered, "Who is he, sir, because I would like to."

[37]"You have seen him," Jesus said, "and he is speaking to you!"

[38]"Yes, Lord," the man said, "I believe!" And he worshiped Jesus.

[39]Then Jesus told him, "I have come to judge the world. I have come to give sight to the blind and to show those who think they see that they are blind."

[40]The Pharisees who were standing there heard him and asked, "Are you saying we are blind?"

[41]"If you were blind, you wouldn't be guilty," Jesus replied. "But you remain guilty because you claim you can see.

CHAPTER 10

"I assure you, anyone who sneaks over the wall of a sheepfold, rather than going through the gate, must surely be a thief and a robber! [2]For a shepherd enters through the gate. [3]The gatekeeper opens the gate for him, and the sheep hear his voice and come to him. He calls his own sheep by name and leads them out. [4]After he has gathered his own flock, he walks ahead of

9:24 Or *Give glory to God, not to Jesus;* Greek reads *Give glory to God.*   **9:35** Some manuscripts read *the Son of God.*

them, and they follow him because they recognize his voice. [5]They won't follow a stranger; they will run from him because they don't recognize his voice."

[6]Those who heard Jesus use this illustration didn't understand what he meant, [7]so he explained it to them. "I assure you, I am the gate for the sheep," he said. [8]"All others who came before me were thieves and robbers. But the true sheep did not listen to them. [9]Yes, I am the gate. Those who come in through me will be saved. Wherever they go, they will find green pastures. [10]The thief's purpose is to steal and kill and destroy. My purpose is to give life in all its fullness.

[11]"I am the good shepherd. The good shepherd lays down his life for the sheep. [12]A hired hand will run when he sees a wolf coming. He will leave the sheep because they aren't his and he isn't their shepherd. And so the wolf attacks them and scatters the flock. [13]The hired hand runs away because he is merely hired and has no real concern for the sheep.

[14]"I am the good shepherd; I know my own sheep, and they know me, [15]just as my Father knows me and I know the Father. And I lay down my life for the sheep. [16]I have other sheep, too, that are not in this sheepfold. I must bring them also, and they will listen to my voice; and there will be one flock with one shepherd.

[17]"The Father loves me because I lay down my life that I may have it back again. [18]No one can take my life from me. I lay down my life voluntarily. For I have the right to lay it down when I want to and also the power to take it again. For my Father has given me this command."

[19]When he said these things, the people* were again divided in their opinions about him. [20]Some of them said, "He has a demon, or he's crazy. Why listen to a man like that?" [21]Others said, "This doesn't sound like a man possessed by a demon! Can a demon open the eyes of the blind?"

[22]It was now winter, and Jesus was in Jerusalem at the time of Hanukkah.* [23]He was at the Temple, walking through the section known as Solomon's Colonnade. [24]The Jewish leaders surrounded him and asked, "How long are you going to keep us in suspense? If you are the Messiah, tell us plainly."

[25]Jesus replied, "I have already told you, and you don't believe me. The proof is what I do in the name of my Father. [26]But you don't believe me because you are not part of my flock. [27]My sheep recognize my voice; I know them, and they follow me. [28]I give them eternal life, and they will never perish. No one will snatch them away from me, [29]for my Father has given them to me, and he is more powerful than anyone else. So no one can take them from me. [30]The Father and I are one."

[31]Once again the Jewish leaders picked up stones to kill him. [32]Jesus said, "At my Father's direction I have done many things to help the people. For which one of these good deeds are you killing me?"

[33]They replied, "Not for any good work, but for blasphemy, because you, a mere man, have made yourself God."

[34]Jesus replied, "It is written in your own law that God said to certain leaders of the people, 'I say, you are gods!'* [35]And you know that the Scriptures cannot be altered. So if those people, who received God's message, were called 'gods,' [36]why do you call it blasphemy when the Holy One who was sent into the world by the Father says, 'I am the Son of God'? [37]Don't believe me unless I carry out my Father's work. [38]But if I do his work, believe in what I have done, even if you don't believe me. Then you will realize that the Father is in me, and I am in the Father."

[39]Once again they tried to arrest him, but he got away and left them. [40]He went beyond the Jordan River to stay near the place where John was first baptizing. [41]And many followed him. "John didn't do miracles," they remarked to one another, "but all his predictions about this man have come true." [42]And many believed in him there.

CHAPTER 11

A man named Lazarus was sick. He lived in Bethany with his sisters, Mary and Martha. [2]This is the Mary who poured the expensive perfume on the Lord's feet and wiped them with her hair.* Her brother, Lazarus, was sick. [3]So the two sisters sent a message to Jesus telling him, "Lord, the one you love is very sick."

[4]But when Jesus heard about it he said, "Lazarus's sickness will not end in death.

10:19 Greek *Jewish people.*   **10:22** Or *the Festival of Dedication.*   **10:34** Ps 82:6.   **11:2** This incident is recorded in chapter 12.

No, it is for the glory of God. I, the Son of God, will receive glory from this." [5]Although Jesus loved Martha, Mary, and Lazarus, [6]he stayed where he was for the next two days and did not go to them. [7]Finally after two days, he said to his disciples, "Let's go to Judea again."

[8]But his disciples objected. "Teacher," they said, "only a few days ago the Jewish leaders in Judea were trying to kill you. Are you going there again?"

[9]Jesus replied, "There are twelve hours of daylight every day. As long as it is light, people can walk safely. They can see because they have the light of this world. [10]Only at night is there danger of stumbling because there is no light." [11]Then he said, "Our friend Lazarus has fallen asleep, but now I will go and wake him up."

[12]The disciples said, "Lord, if he is sleeping, that means he is getting better!" [13]They thought Jesus meant Lazarus was having a good night's rest, but Jesus meant Lazarus had died.

[14]Then he told them plainly, "Lazarus is dead. [15]And for your sake, I am glad I wasn't there, because this will give you another opportunity to believe in me. Come, let's go see him."

[16]Thomas, nicknamed the Twin,* said to his fellow disciples, "Let's go, too—and die with Jesus."

[17]When Jesus arrived at Bethany, he was told that Lazarus had already been in his grave for four days. [18]Bethany was only a few miles* down the road from Jerusalem, [19]and many of the people* had come to pay their respects and console Martha and Mary on their loss. [20]When Martha got word that Jesus was coming, she went to meet him. But Mary stayed at home. [21]Martha said to Jesus, "Lord, if you had been here, my brother would not have died. [22]But even now I know that God will give you whatever you ask."

[23]Jesus told her, "Your brother will rise again."

[24]"Yes," Martha said, "when everyone else rises, on resurrection day."

[25]Jesus told her, "I am the resurrection and the life.* Those who believe in me, even though they die like everyone else, will live again. [26]They are given eternal life for believing in me and will never perish. Do you believe this, Martha?"

[27]"Yes, Lord," she told him. "I have always believed you are the Messiah, the Son of God, the one who has come into the world from God." [28]Then she left him and returned to Mary. She called Mary aside from the mourners and told her, "The Teacher is here and wants to see you." [29]So Mary immediately went to him.

[30]Now Jesus had stayed outside the village, at the place where Martha met him. [31]When the people who were at the house trying to console Mary saw her leave so hastily, they assumed she was going to Lazarus's grave to weep. So they followed her there. [32]When Mary arrived and saw Jesus, she fell down at his feet and said, "Lord, if you had been here, my brother would not have died."

[33]When Jesus saw her weeping and saw the other people wailing with her, he was moved with indignation and was deeply troubled. [34]"Where have you put him?" he asked them.

They told him, "Lord, come and see." [35]Then Jesus wept. [36]The people who were standing nearby said, "See how much he loved him." [37]But some said, "This man healed a blind man. Why couldn't he keep Lazarus from dying?"

[38]And again Jesus was deeply troubled. Then they came to the grave. It was a cave with a stone rolled across its entrance. [39]"Roll the stone aside," Jesus told them.

But Martha, the dead man's sister, said, "Lord, by now the smell will be terrible because he has been dead for four days."

[40]Jesus responded, "Didn't I tell you that you will see God's glory if you believe?" [41]So they rolled the stone aside. Then Jesus looked up to heaven and said, "Father, thank you for hearing me. [42]You always hear me, but I said it out loud for the sake of all these people standing here, so they will believe you sent me." [43]Then Jesus shouted, "Lazarus, come out!" [44]And Lazarus came out, bound in graveclothes, his face wrapped in a headcloth. Jesus told them, "Unwrap him and let him go!"

[45]Many of the people who were with Mary believed in Jesus when they saw this happen. [46]But some went to the Pharisees and told them what Jesus had done. [47]Then the leading priests and Pharisees called the high council* together to dis-

11:16 Greek *the one who was called Didymus.*   **11:18** Greek *was about 15 stadia* [about 2.8 kilometers].   **11:19** Greek *Jewish people;* also 11:31, 33, 36, 45, 54.   **11:25** Some manuscripts do not include *and the life.*   **11:47** Greek *the Sanhedrin.*

cuss the situation. "What are we going to do?" they asked each other. "This man certainly performs many miraculous signs. [48]If we leave him alone, the whole nation will follow him, and then the Roman army will come and destroy both our Temple and our nation."

[49]And one of them, Caiaphas, who was high priest that year, said, "How can you be so stupid? [50]Why should the whole nation be destroyed? Let this one man die for the people."

[51]This prophecy that Jesus should die for the entire nation came from Caiaphas in his position as high priest. He didn't think of it himself; he was inspired to say it. [52]It was a prediction that Jesus' death would be not for Israel only, but for the gathering together of all the children of God scattered around the world.

[53]So from that time on the Jewish leaders began to plot Jesus' death. [54]As a result, Jesus stopped his public ministry among the people and left Jerusalem. He went to a place near the wilderness, to the village of Ephraim, and stayed there with his disciples.

[55]It was now almost time for the celebration of Passover, and many people from the country arrived in Jerusalem several days early so they could go through the cleansing ceremony before the Passover began. [56]They wanted to see Jesus, and as they talked in the Temple, they asked each other, "What do you think? Will he come for the Passover?" [57]Meanwhile, the leading priests and Pharisees had publicly announced that anyone seeing Jesus must report him immediately so they could arrest him.

CHAPTER 12
Six days before the Passover ceremonies began, Jesus arrived in Bethany, the home of Lazarus—the man he had raised from the dead. [2]A dinner was prepared in Jesus' honor. Martha served, and Lazarus sat at the table with him. [3]Then Mary took a twelve-ounce jar* of expensive perfume made from essence of nard, and she anointed Jesus' feet with it and wiped his feet with her hair. And the house was filled with fragrance.

[4]But Judas Iscariot, one of his disci-

ples—the one who would betray him— said, [5]"That perfume was worth a small fortune.* It should have been sold and the money given to the poor." [6]Not that he cared for the poor—he was a thief who was in charge of the disciples' funds, and he often took some for his own use.

[7]Jesus replied, "Leave her alone. She did it in preparation for my burial. [8]You will always have the poor among you, but I will not be here with you much longer."

[9]When all the people* heard of Jesus' arrival, they flocked to see him and also to see Lazarus, the man Jesus had raised from the dead. [10]Then the leading priests decided to kill Lazarus, too, [11]for it was because of him that many of the people had deserted them and believed in Jesus.

[12]The next day, the news that Jesus was on the way to Jerusalem swept through the city. A huge crowd of Passover visitors [13]took palm branches and went down the road to meet him. They shouted,

"Praise God!*
Bless the one who comes in the name of
    the Lord!
Hail to the King of Israel!"*

[14]Jesus found a young donkey and sat on it, fulfilling the prophecy that said:

[15] "Don't be afraid, people of Israel.*
Look, your King is coming,
    sitting on a donkey's colt."*

[16]His disciples didn't realize at the time that this was a fulfillment of prophecy. But after Jesus entered into his glory, they remembered that these Scriptures had come true before their eyes.

[17]Those in the crowd who had seen Jesus call Lazarus back to life were telling others all about it. [18]That was the main reason so many went out to meet him—because they had heard about this mighty miracle. [19]Then the Pharisees said to each other, "We've lost. Look, the whole world has gone after him!"

[20]Some Greeks who had come to Jerusalem to attend the Passover [21]paid a visit to Philip, who was from Bethsaida in Galilee. They said, "Sir, we want to meet Jesus." [22]Philip told Andrew about it, and they went together to ask Jesus.

12:3 Greek *took 1 litra* [327 grams].   **12:5** Greek *300 denarii.* A denarius was equivalent to a full day's wage.   **12:9** Greek *Jewish people;* also in 12:11.   **12:13a** Greek *Hosanna,* an exclamation of praise that literally means "save now."   **12:13b** Ps 118:25-26; Zeph 3:15.   **12:15a** Greek *daughter of Zion.*   **12:15b** Zech 9:9.

[23]Jesus replied, "The time has come for the Son of Man to enter into his glory. [24]The truth is, a kernel of wheat must be planted in the soil. Unless it dies it will be alone—a single seed. But its death will produce many new kernels—a plentiful harvest of new lives. [25]Those who love their life in this world will lose it. Those who despise their life in this world will keep it for eternal life. [26]All those who want to be my disciples must come and follow me, because my servants must be where I am. And if they follow me, the Father will honor them. [27]Now my soul is deeply troubled. Should I pray, 'Father, save me from what lies ahead'? But that is the very reason why I came! [28]Father, bring glory to your name."

Then a voice spoke from heaven, saying, "I have already brought it glory, and I will do it again." [29]When the crowd heard the voice, some thought it was thunder, while others declared an angel had spoken to him.

[30]Then Jesus told them, "The voice was for your benefit, not mine. [31]The time of judgment for the world has come, when the prince of this world* will be cast out. [32]And when I am lifted up on the cross,* I will draw everyone to myself." [33]He said this to indicate how he was going to die.

[34]"Die?" asked the crowd. "We understood from Scripture that the Messiah would live forever. Why are you saying the Son of Man will die? Who is this Son of Man you are talking about?"

[35]Jesus replied, "My light will shine out for you just a little while longer. Walk in it while you can, so you will not stumble when the darkness falls. If you walk in the darkness, you cannot see where you are going. [36]Believe in the light while there is still time; then you will become children of the light." After saying these things, Jesus went away and was hidden from them.

[37]But despite all the miraculous signs he had done, most of the people did not believe in him. [38]This is exactly what Isaiah the prophet had predicted:

"Lord, who has believed our message?
    To whom will the Lord reveal his
        saving power?"*

[39]But the people couldn't believe, for as Isaiah also said,

[40] "The Lord has blinded their eyes
        and hardened their hearts—
    so their eyes cannot see,
        and their hearts cannot understand,
    and they cannot turn to me
        and let me heal them."*

[41]Isaiah was referring to Jesus when he made this prediction, because he was given a vision of the Messiah's glory. [42]Many people, including some of the Jewish leaders, believed in him. But they wouldn't admit it to anyone because of their fear that the Pharisees would expel them from the synagogue. [43]For they loved human praise more than the praise of God.

[44]Jesus shouted to the crowds, "If you trust me, you are really trusting God who sent me. [45]For when you see me, you are seeing the one who sent me. [46]I have come as a light to shine in this dark world, so that all who put their trust in me will no longer remain in the darkness. [47]If anyone hears me and doesn't obey me, I am not his judge—for I have come to save the world and not to judge it. [48]But all who reject me and my message will be judged at the day of judgment by the truth I have spoken. [49]I don't speak on my own authority. The Father who sent me gave me his own instructions as to what I should say. [50]And I know his instructions lead to eternal life; so I say whatever the Father tells me to say!"

12:31 *The prince of this world* is a name for Satan.   **12:32** Greek *lifted up from the earth.*   **12:38** Isa 53:1.   **12:40** Isa 6:10.

OCTOBER 30 ☐ DAY 304
JOHN 13–17
Ministry to the Disciples by God's Son

 OVERVIEW Today's section, traditionally called the Upper Room Discourse, actually takes place partly in an upper room (John 13–14) and partly in an unspecified location (John 15–17; see 14:31). These verses constitute Jesus' final instructions to his disciples before his death. In them you will read of the importance of a servant's heart, the necessity of Christ's return to heaven, and the provision of the Holy Spirit in Christ's absence. There are many spiritual insights yet to be grasped by the disciples—a realization that drives Christ to his knees as he prays for his followers both present and future.

Chapter 13	Chapters 14–15	Chapter 16	Chapter 17
Instructions to the Disciples Regarding			Intercession for the Disciples
Foot Washing	Fruit Bearing	Future Events	
Talking to the Disciples			Talking to God

 YOUR DAILY WALK Reflect upon this thought-provoking statement by Robert Murray McCheyne: "If I could hear Christ praying for me in the next room, I would not fear a million enemies. Yet distance makes no difference. He is praying for me."

If Christ be not divine, every impulse of the Christian world falls to a lower octave.

In John 17, Jesus Christ prayed fervently and specifically for his disciples—those he would leave behind to continue the work in his absence. And that means he was praying for you. Read the chapter that way, inserting your name in the appropriate places beginning with verse 6:
I have told _____ about you. _____ was always yours, and you gave _____ to me. . . . My prayer is not for the world, but for _____, whom you have given me. . . . Now I am departing the world; I am leaving _____ behind. . . . I'm not asking you to take _____ out of the world, but to keep _____ safe from the evil one.

 INSIGHT Mission Accomplished . . . Cross Yet to Come
In his prayer to God the Father, Jesus reported, "I brought glory to you here on earth by doing everything you told me to do" (17:4). Though Jesus' death was still a day away, victory was certain as the Savior bathed each step to the cross in prayer. You can face today with confidence, too!

CHAPTER 13
Before the Passover celebration, Jesus knew that his hour had come to leave this world and return to his Father. He now showed the disciples the full extent of his love.* ²It was time for supper, and the Devil had already enticed Judas, son of Simon Iscariot, to carry out his plan to betray Jesus. ³Jesus knew that the Father had given him authority over everything and that he had come from God and would return to God. ⁴So he got up from the table, took off his robe, wrapped a towel around his waist, ⁵and poured water into a basin. Then he began to wash the disciples' feet and to wipe them with the towel he had around him.

⁶When he came to Simon Peter, Peter said to him, "Lord, why are you going to wash my feet?"

⁷Jesus replied, "You don't understand now why I am doing it; someday you will."

⁸"No," Peter protested, "you will never wash my feet!"

Jesus replied, "But if I don't wash you, you won't belong to me."

13:1 Or *He loved his disciples to the very end.*

⁹Simon Peter exclaimed, "Then wash my hands and head as well, Lord, not just my feet!"

¹⁰Jesus replied, "A person who has bathed all over does not need to wash, except for the feet,* to be entirely clean. And you are clean, but that isn't true of everyone here." ¹¹For Jesus knew who would betray him. That is what he meant when he said, "Not all of you are clean."

¹²After washing their feet, he put on his robe again and sat down and asked, "Do you understand what I was doing? ¹³You call me 'Teacher' and 'Lord,' and you are right, because it is true. ¹⁴And since I, the Lord and Teacher, have washed your feet, you ought to wash each other's feet. ¹⁵I have given you an example to follow. Do as I have done to you. ¹⁶How true it is that a servant is not greater than the master. Nor are messengers more important than the one who sends them. ¹⁷You know these things—now do them! That is the path of blessing.

¹⁸"I am not saying these things to all of you; I know so well each one of you I chose. The Scriptures declare, 'The one who shares my food has turned against me,'* and this will soon come true. ¹⁹I tell you this now, so that when it happens you will believe I am the Messiah. ²⁰Truly, anyone who welcomes my messenger is welcoming me, and anyone who welcomes me is welcoming the Father who sent me."

²¹Now Jesus was in great anguish of spirit, and he exclaimed, "The truth is, one of you will betray me!"

²²The disciples looked at each other, wondering whom he could mean. ²³One of Jesus' disciples, the one Jesus loved, was sitting next to Jesus at the table.* ²⁴Simon Peter motioned to him to ask who would do this terrible thing. ²⁵Leaning toward Jesus, he asked, "Lord, who is it?"

²⁶Jesus said, "It is the one to whom I give the bread dipped in the sauce." And when he had dipped it, he gave it to Judas, son of Simon Iscariot. ²⁷As soon as Judas had eaten the bread, Satan entered into him. Then Jesus told him, "Hurry. Do it now." ²⁸None of the others at the table knew what Jesus meant. ²⁹Since Judas was their treasurer, some thought Jesus was telling him to go and pay for the food or to give some

money to the poor. ³⁰So Judas left at once, going out into the night.

³¹As soon as Judas left the room, Jesus said, "The time has come for me, the Son of Man, to enter into my glory, and God will receive glory because of all that happens to me. ³²And God will bring* me into my glory very soon. ³³Dear children, how brief are these moments before I must go away and leave you! Then, though you search for me, you cannot come to me—just as I told the Jewish leaders. ³⁴So now I am giving you a new commandment: Love each other. Just as I have loved you, you should love each other. ³⁵Your love for one another will prove to the world that you are my disciples."

³⁶Simon Peter said, "Lord, where are you going?"

And Jesus replied, "You can't go with me now, but you will follow me later."

³⁷"But why can't I come now, Lord?" he asked. "I am ready to die for you."

³⁸Jesus answered, "Die for me? No, before the rooster crows tomorrow morning, you will deny three times that you even know me.

CHAPTER 14
"Don't be troubled. You trust God, now trust in me. ²There are many rooms in my Father's home, and I am going to prepare a place for you. If this were not so, I would tell you plainly. ³When everything is ready, I will come and get you, so that you will always be with me where I am. ⁴And you know where I am going and how to get there."

⁵"No, we don't know, Lord," Thomas said. "We haven't any idea where you are going, so how can we know the way?"

⁶Jesus told him, "I am the way, the truth, and the life. No one can come to the Father except through me. ⁷If you had known who I am, then you would have known who my Father is.* From now on you know him and have seen him!"

⁸Philip said, "Lord, show us the Father and we will be satisfied."

⁹Jesus replied, "Philip, don't you even yet know who I am, even after all the time I have been with you? Anyone who has seen me has seen the Father! So why are you asking to see him? ¹⁰Don't you be-

---

13:10 Some manuscripts do not include *except for the feet.*   13:18 Ps 41:9.   13:23 Greek *was reclining on Jesus' bosom.* The "disciple whom Jesus loved" was probably John.   13:32 Some manuscripts read *And if God is glorified in him [the Son of Man], God will bring.*
14:7 Some manuscripts read *If you really have known me, you will know who my Father is.*

lieve that I am in the Father and the Father is in me? The words I say are not my own, but my Father who lives in me does his work through me. [11]Just believe that I am in the Father and the Father is in me. Or at least believe because of what you have seen me do.

[12]"The truth is, anyone who believes in me will do the same works I have done, and even greater works, because I am going to be with the Father. [13]You can ask for anything in my name, and I will do it, because the work of the Son brings glory to the Father. [14]Yes, ask anything in my name, and I will do it!

[15]"If you love me, obey my commandments. [16]And I will ask the Father, and he will give you another Counselor,* who will never leave you. [17]He is the Holy Spirit, who leads into all truth. The world at large cannot receive him, because it isn't looking for him and doesn't recognize him. But you do, because he lives with you now and later will be in you. [18]No, I will not abandon you as orphans—I will come to you. [19]In just a little while the world will not see me again, but you will. For I will live again, and you will, too. [20]When I am raised to life again, you will know that I am in my Father, and you are in me, and I am in you. [21]Those who obey my commandments are the ones who love me. And because they love me, my Father will love them, and I will love them. And I will reveal myself to each one of them."

[22]Judas (not Judas Iscariot, but the other disciple with that name) said to him, "Lord, why are you going to reveal yourself only to us and not to the world at large?"

[23]Jesus replied, "All those who love me will do what I say. My Father will love them, and we will come to them and live with them. [24]Anyone who doesn't love me will not do what I say. And remember, my words are not my own. This message is from the Father who sent me. [25]I am telling you these things now while I am still with you. [26]But when the Father sends the Counselor as my representative—and by the Counselor I mean the Holy Spirit—he will teach you everything and will remind you of everything I myself have told you.

[27]"I am leaving you with a gift—peace of mind and heart. And the peace I give isn't like the peace the world gives. So don't be troubled or afraid. [28]Remember what I told you: I am going away, but I will come back to you again. If you really love me, you will be very happy for me, because now I can go to the Father, who is greater than I am. [29]I have told you these things before they happen so that you will believe when they do happen.

[30]"I don't have much more time to talk to you, because the prince of this world approaches. He has no power over me, [31]but I will do what the Father requires of me, so that the world will know that I love the Father. Come, let's be going.

CHAPTER 15

"I am the true vine, and my Father is the gardener. [2]He cuts off every branch that doesn't produce fruit, and he prunes the branches that do bear fruit so they will produce even more. [3]You have already been pruned for greater fruitfulness by the message I have given you. [4]Remain in me, and I will remain in you. For a branch cannot produce fruit if it is severed from the vine, and you cannot be fruitful apart from me.

[5]"Yes, I am the vine; you are the branches. Those who remain in me, and I in them, will produce much fruit. For apart from me you can do nothing. [6]Anyone who parts from me is thrown away like a useless branch and withers. Such branches are gathered into a pile to be burned. [7]But if you stay joined to me and my words remain in you, you may ask any request you like, and it will be granted! [8]My true disciples produce much fruit. This brings great glory to my Father.

[9]"I have loved you even as the Father has loved me. Remain in my love. [10]When you obey me, you remain in my love, just as I obey my Father and remain in his love. [11]I have told you this so that you will be filled with my joy. Yes, your joy will overflow! [12]I command you to love each other in the same way that I love you. [13]And here is how to measure it—the greatest love is shown when people lay down their lives for their friends. [14]You are my friends if you obey me. [15]I no longer call you servants, because a master doesn't confide in his servants. Now you are my friends, since I have told you everything the Father told

14:16 Or Comforter, or Encourager, or Advocate. Greek Paraclete; also in 14:26.

me. [16] You didn't choose me. I chose you. I appointed you to go and produce fruit that will last, so that the Father will give you whatever you ask for, using my name. [17] I command you to love each other.

[18] "When the world hates you, remember it hated me before it hated you. [19] The world would love you if you belonged to it, but you don't. I chose you to come out of the world, and so it hates you. [20] Do you remember what I told you? 'A servant is not greater than the master.' Since they persecuted me, naturally they will persecute you. And if they had listened to me, they would listen to you! [21] The people of the world will hate you because you belong to me, for they don't know God who sent me. [22] They would not be guilty if I had not come and spoken to them. But now they have no excuse for their sin. [23] Anyone who hates me hates my Father, too. [24] If I hadn't done such miraculous signs among them that no one else could do, they would not be counted guilty. But as it is, they saw all that I did and yet hated both of us—me and my Father. [25] This has fulfilled what the Scriptures said: 'They hated me without cause.'*

[26] "But I will send you the Counselor*— the Spirit of truth. He will come to you from the Father and will tell you all about me. [27] And you must also tell others about me because you have been with me from the beginning.

CHAPTER 16

"I have told you these things so that you won't fall away. [2] For you will be expelled from the synagogues, and the time is coming when those who kill you will think they are doing God a service. [3] This is because they have never known the Father or me. [4] Yes, I'm telling you these things now, so that when they happen, you will remember I warned you. I didn't tell you earlier because I was going to be with you for a while longer.

[5] "But now I am going away to the one who sent me, and none of you has asked me where I am going. [6] Instead, you are very sad. [7] But it is actually best for you that I go away, because if I don't, the Counselor* won't come. If I do go away, he will come because I will send him to you. [8] And when he comes, he will convince the world of its

sin, and of God's righteousness, and of the coming judgment. [9] The world's sin is unbelief in me. [10] Righteousness is available because I go to the Father, and you will see me no more. [11] Judgment will come because the prince of this world has already been judged.

[12] "Oh, there is so much more I want to tell you, but you can't bear it now. [13] When the Spirit of truth comes, he will guide you into all truth. He will not be presenting his own ideas; he will be telling you what he has heard. He will tell you about the future. [14] He will bring me glory by revealing to you whatever he receives from me. [15] All that the Father has is mine; this is what I mean when I say that the Spirit will reveal to you whatever he receives from me.

[16] "In just a little while I will be gone, and you won't see me anymore. Then, just a little while after that, you will see me again."

[17] The disciples asked each other, "What does he mean when he says, 'You won't see me, and then you will see me'? And what does he mean when he says, 'I am going to the Father'? [18] And what does he mean by 'a little while'? We don't understand."

[19] Jesus realized they wanted to ask him, so he said, "Are you asking yourselves what I meant? I said in just a little while I will be gone, and you won't see me anymore. Then, just a little while after that, you will see me again. [20] Truly, you will weep and mourn over what is going to happen to me, but the world will rejoice. You will grieve, but your grief will suddenly turn to wonderful joy when you see me again. [21] It will be like a woman experiencing the pains of labor. When her child is born, her anguish gives place to joy because she has brought a new person into the world. [22] You have sorrow now, but I will see you again; then you will rejoice, and no one can rob you of that joy. [23] At that time you won't need to ask me for anything. The truth is, you can go directly to the Father and ask him, and he will grant your request because you use my name. [24] You haven't done this before. Ask, using my name, and you will receive, and you will have abundant joy.

[25] "I have spoken of these matters in parables, but the time will come when this will not be necessary, and I will tell you

15:25 Pss 35:19; 69:4.   **15:26** Or *Comforter,* or *Encourager,* or *Advocate.* Greek *Paraclete.*   **16:7** Or *Comforter,* or *Encourager,* or *Advocate.* Greek *Paraclete.*

plainly all about the Father. ²⁶Then you will ask in my name. I'm not saying I will ask the Father on your behalf, ²⁷for the Father himself loves you dearly because you love me and believe that I came from God. ²⁸Yes, I came from the Father into the world, and I will leave the world and return to the Father."

²⁹Then his disciples said, "At last you are speaking plainly and not in parables. ³⁰Now we understand that you know everything and don't need anyone to tell you anything.* From this we believe that you came from God."

³¹Jesus asked, "Do you finally believe? ³²But the time is coming—in fact, it is already here—when you will be scattered, each one going his own way, leaving me alone. Yet I am not alone because the Father is with me. ³³I have told you all this so that you may have peace in me. Here on earth you will have many trials and sorrows. But take heart, because I have overcome the world."

CHAPTER 17

When Jesus had finished saying all these things, he looked up to heaven and said, "Father, the time has come. Glorify your Son so he can give glory back to you. ²For you have given him authority over everyone in all the earth. He gives eternal life to each one you have given him. ³And this is the way to have eternal life—to know you, the only true God, and Jesus Christ, the one you sent to earth. ⁴I brought glory to you here on earth by doing everything you told me to do. ⁵And now, Father, bring me into the glory we shared before the world began.

⁶"I have told these men about you. They were in the world, but then you gave them to me. Actually, they were always yours, and you gave them to me; and they have kept your word. ⁷Now they know that everything I have is a gift from you, ⁸for I have passed on to them the words you gave me; and they accepted them and know that I came from you, and they believe you sent me.

⁹"My prayer is not for the world, but for those you have given me, because they be-

long to you. ¹⁰And all of them, since they are mine, belong to you; and you have given them back to me, so they are my glory! ¹¹Now I am departing the world; I am leaving them behind and coming to you. Holy Father, keep them and care for them—all those you have given me—so that they will be united just as we are. ¹²During my time here, I have kept them safe.* I guarded them so that not one was lost, except the one headed for destruction, as the Scriptures foretold.

¹³"And now I am coming to you. I have told them many things while I was with them so they would be filled with my joy. ¹⁴I have given them your word. And the world hates them because they do not belong to the world, just as I do not. ¹⁵I'm not asking you to take them out of the world, but to keep them safe from the evil one. ¹⁶They are not part of this world any more than I am. ¹⁷Make them pure and holy by teaching them your words of truth. ¹⁸As you sent me into the world, I am sending them into the world. ¹⁹And I give myself entirely to you so they also might be entirely yours.

²⁰"I am praying not only for these disciples but also for all who will ever believe in me because of their testimony. ²¹My prayer for all of them is that they will be one, just as you and I are one, Father—that just as you are in me and I am in you, so they will be in us, and the world will believe you sent me.

²²"I have given them the glory you gave me, so that they may be one, as we are—²³I in them and you in me, all being perfected into one. Then the world will know that you sent me and will understand that you love them as much as you love me. ²⁴Father, I want these whom you've given me to be with me, so they can see my glory. You gave me the glory because you loved me even before the world began!

²⁵"O righteous Father, the world doesn't know you, but I do; and these disciples know you sent me. ²⁶And I have revealed you to them and will keep on revealing you. I will do this so that your love for me may be in them and I in them."

16:30 Or *don't need that anyone should ask you anything.*   **17:12** Greek *I have kept in your name those whom you have given me.*

OCTOBER 31 □ DAY 305
JOHN 18–21
The Resurrected Son of God

OVERVIEW After reading the closing events of Christ's life in each of the other three Gospels, you may be tempted to skim John's account. But don't! Put yourself in the sandals of the key individuals in the narrative, and feel the emotions as the crucifixion unfolds: Judas's disillusionment . . . Peter's denial . . . Pilate's concession . . . the crowd's frenzied screams . . . the rugged cross . . . the nail-pierced hands . . . the bleeding side . . . the hurried burial. Experience with the women the shock of finding the tomb empty. Follow Thomas's transformation from a doubting disciple to a devoted believer. Listen as Peter receives his marching orders—to feed God's flock until the Shepherd returns.

Chapter 18	Chapter 19	Chapters 20–21	
Arrest and Trials	Crucifixion and Burial	Disappearance of the Corpse	Appearance of the Christ
		20:1 20:10	20:11 21:25
The Crucified King		The Risen Savior	

If ever a man was God, or God man, Jesus was both.

YOUR DAILY WALK Read John 20:30-31 carefully to refresh your memory regarding John's purpose in writing. He is not merely trying to satisfy your curiosity about the historical person of Christ or fill your head with little-known facts about him or teach you all the events from Bethlehem to Calvary in chronological order. Rather, John is seeking to move you to a point of commitment. Unless Jesus Christ has invaded your life, you are lost in your sins: without God, without life, without hope of heaven.

Becoming a Christian is not simply joining a church, signing a card, or walking an aisle—though these can certainly be valid expressions of your desire to become a Christian. But true faith comes as the result of believing on Jesus Christ, God's Son, to solve your sin problem. It is trusting him to do something for you that you cannot do yourself. Have you done that? If not, what better way to close your reading of the Gospels than by opening your heart to the Savior of whom those Gospels speak: Jesus Christ.

INSIGHT Evidence Enough for John
John records that he saw the graveclothes and head cloth lying undisturbed in Jesus' tomb with a space between them. For him this was clear and convincing evidence that Jesus' body had passed through them and that Jesus was alive. John saw and believed!

CHAPTER 18

After saying these things, Jesus crossed the Kidron Valley with his disciples and entered a grove of olive trees. ²Judas, the betrayer, knew this place, because Jesus had gone there many times with his disciples. ³The leading priests and Pharisees had given Judas a battalion of Roman soldiers and Temple guards to accompany him. Now with blazing torches, lanterns, and weapons, they arrived at the olive grove.

⁴Jesus fully realized all that was going to happen to him. Stepping forward to meet them, he asked, "Whom are you looking for?"

⁵"Jesus of Nazareth," they replied.

"I am he,"* Jesus said. Judas was standing there with them when Jesus identified himself. ⁶And as he said, "I am he," they all fell backward to the ground! ⁷Once more he asked them, "Whom are you searching for?"

18:5 Greek *I am;* also in 18:6, 8.

And again they replied, "Jesus of Nazareth."

[8]"I told you that I am he," Jesus said. "And since I am the one you want, let these others go." [9]He did this to fulfill his own statement: "I have not lost a single one of those you gave me."*

[10]Then Simon Peter drew a sword and slashed off the right ear of Malchus, the high priest's servant. [11]But Jesus said to Peter, "Put your sword back into its sheath. Shall I not drink from the cup the Father has given me?"

[12]So the soldiers, their commanding officer, and the Temple guards arrested Jesus and tied him up. [13]First they took him to Annas, the father-in-law of Caiaphas, the high priest that year. [14]Caiaphas was the one who had told the other Jewish leaders, "Better that one should die for all."

[15]Simon Peter followed along behind, as did another of the disciples. That other disciple was acquainted with the high priest, so he was allowed to enter the courtyard with Jesus. [16]Peter stood outside the gate. Then the other disciple spoke to the woman watching at the gate, and she let Peter in. [17]The woman asked Peter, "Aren't you one of Jesus' disciples?"

"No," he said, "I am not."

[18]The guards and the household servants were standing around a charcoal fire they had made because it was cold. And Peter stood there with them, warming himself.

[19]Inside, the high priest began asking Jesus about his followers and what he had been teaching them. [20]Jesus replied, "What I teach is widely known, because I have preached regularly in the synagogues and the Temple. I have been heard by people* everywhere, and I teach nothing in private that I have not said in public. [21]Why are you asking me this question? Ask those who heard me. They know what I said."

[22]One of the Temple guards standing there struck Jesus on the face. "Is that the way to answer the high priest?" he demanded.

[23]Jesus replied, "If I said anything wrong, you must give evidence for it. Should you hit a man for telling the truth?"

[24]Then Annas bound Jesus and sent him to Caiaphas, the high priest.

[25]Meanwhile, as Simon Peter was standing by the fire, they asked him again, "Aren't you one of his disciples?"

"I am not," he said.

[26]But one of the household servants of the high priest, a relative of the man whose ear Peter had cut off, asked, "Didn't I see you out there in the olive grove with Jesus?" [27]Again Peter denied it. And immediately a rooster crowed.

[28]Jesus' trial before Caiaphas ended in the early hours of the morning. Then he was taken to the headquarters of the Roman governor. His accusers didn't go in themselves because it would defile them, and they wouldn't be allowed to celebrate the Passover feast. [29]So Pilate, the governor, went out to them and asked, "What is your charge against this man?"

[30]"We wouldn't have handed him over to you if he weren't a criminal!" they retorted.

[31]"Then take him away and judge him by your own laws," Pilate told them.

"Only the Romans are permitted to execute someone," the Jewish leaders replied. [32]This fulfilled Jesus' prediction about the way he would die.*

[33]Then Pilate went back inside and called for Jesus to be brought to him. "Are you the King of the Jews?" he asked him.

[34]Jesus replied, "Is this your own question, or did others tell you about me?"

[35]"Am I a Jew?" Pilate asked. "Your own people and their leading priests brought you here. Why? What have you done?"

[36]Then Jesus answered, "I am not an earthly king. If I were, my followers would have fought when I was arrested by the Jewish leaders. But my Kingdom is not of this world."

[37]Pilate replied, "You are a king then?"

"You say that I am a king, and you are right," Jesus said. "I was born for that purpose. And I came to bring truth to the world. All who love the truth recognize that what I say is true."

[38]"What is truth?" Pilate asked. Then he went out again to the people and told them, "He is not guilty of any crime. [39]But you have a custom of asking me to release someone from prison each year at Passover. So if you want me to, I'll release the King of the Jews."

[40]But they shouted back, "No! Not this man, but Barabbas!" (Barabbas was a criminal.)

18:9 See John 6:39 and 17:12.   **18:20** Greek *Jewish people;* also in 18:38.   **18:32** See John 12:32-33.

CHAPTER 19

Then Pilate had Jesus flogged with a lead-tipped whip. [2]The soldiers made a crown of long, sharp thorns and put it on his head, and they put a royal purple robe on him. [3]"Hail! King of the Jews!" they mocked, and they hit him with their fists.

[4]Pilate went outside again and said to the people, "I am going to bring him out to you now, but understand clearly that I find him not guilty." [5]Then Jesus came out wearing the crown of thorns and the purple robe. And Pilate said, "Here is the man!"

[6]When they saw him, the leading priests and Temple guards began shouting, "Crucify! Crucify!"

"You crucify him," Pilate said. "I find him not guilty."

[7]The Jewish leaders replied, "By our laws he ought to die because he called himself the Son of God."

[8]When Pilate heard this, he was more frightened than ever. [9]He took Jesus back into the headquarters again and asked him, "Where are you from?" But Jesus gave no answer. [10]"You won't talk to me?" Pilate demanded. "Don't you realize that I have the power to release you or to crucify you?"

[11]Then Jesus said, "You would have no power over me at all unless it were given to you from above. So the one who brought me to you has the greater sin."

[12]Then Pilate tried to release him, but the Jewish leaders told him, "If you release this man, you are not a friend of Caesar. Anyone who declares himself a king is a rebel against Caesar."

[13]When they said this, Pilate brought Jesus out to them again. Then Pilate sat down on the judgment seat on the platform that is called the Stone Pavement (in Hebrew, *Gabbatha*). [14]It was now about noon of the day of preparation for the Passover. And Pilate said to the people,* "Here is your king!"

[15]"Away with him," they yelled. "Away with him—crucify him!"

"What? Crucify your king?" Pilate asked.

"We have no king but Caesar," the leading priests shouted back.

[16]Then Pilate gave Jesus to them to be crucified.

So they took Jesus and led him away. [17]Carrying the cross by himself, Jesus went to the place called Skull Hill (in Hebrew, *Golgotha*). [18]There they crucified him. There were two others crucified with him, one on either side, with Jesus between them. [19]And Pilate posted a sign over him that read, "Jesus of Nazareth, the King of the Jews." [20]The place where Jesus was crucified was near the city; and the sign was written in Hebrew, Latin, and Greek, so that many people could read it.

[21]Then the leading priests said to Pilate, "Change it from 'The King of the Jews' to 'He said, I am King of the Jews.'"

[22]Pilate replied, "What I have written, I have written. It stays exactly as it is."

[23]When the soldiers had crucified Jesus, they divided his clothes among the four of them. They also took his robe, but it was seamless, woven in one piece from the top. [24]So they said, "Let's not tear it but throw dice* to see who gets it." This fulfilled the Scripture that says, "They divided my clothes among themselves and threw dice for my robe."* So that is what they did.

[25]Standing near the cross were Jesus' mother, and his mother's sister, Mary (the wife of Clopas), and Mary Magdalene. [26]When Jesus saw his mother standing there beside the disciple he loved, he said to her, "Woman, he is your son." [27]And he said to this disciple, "She is your mother." And from then on this disciple took her into his home.

[28]Jesus knew that everything was now finished, and to fulfill the Scriptures he said, "I am thirsty."* [29]A jar of sour wine was sitting there, so they soaked a sponge in it, put it on a hyssop branch, and held it up to his lips. [30]When Jesus had tasted it, he said, "It is finished!" Then he bowed his head and gave up his spirit.

[31]The Jewish leaders didn't want the victims hanging there the next day, which was the Sabbath (and a very special Sabbath at that, because it was the Passover), so they asked Pilate to hasten their deaths by ordering that their legs be broken. Then their bodies could be taken down. [32]So the soldiers came and broke the legs of the two men crucified with Jesus. [33]But when they came to Jesus, they saw that he was dead already, so they didn't break his legs. [34]One of the soldiers, however, pierced his side with a spear, and blood and water flowed out. [35]This report is from an eyewitness

19:14 Greek *Jewish people;* also in 19:20.   **19:24a** Greek *cast lots.*   **19:24b** Ps 22:18.   **19:28** See Pss 22:15; 69:21.

giving an accurate account; it is presented so that you also can believe. [36] These things happened in fulfillment of the Scriptures that say, "Not one of his bones will be broken,"* [37] and "They will look on him whom they pierced."*

[38] Afterward Joseph of Arimathea, who had been a secret disciple of Jesus (because he feared the Jewish leaders), asked Pilate for permission to take Jesus' body down. When Pilate gave him permission, he came and took the body away. [39] Nicodemus, the man who had come to Jesus at night, also came, bringing about seventy-five pounds* of embalming ointment made from myrrh and aloes. [40] Together they wrapped Jesus' body in a long linen cloth with the spices, as is the Jewish custom of burial. [41] The place of crucifixion was near a garden, where there was a new tomb, never used before. [42] And so, because it was the day of preparation before the Passover and since the tomb was close at hand, they laid Jesus there.

CHAPTER 20

Early Sunday morning,* while it was still dark, Mary Magdalene came to the tomb and found that the stone had been rolled away from the entrance. [2] She ran and found Simon Peter and the other disciple, the one whom Jesus loved. She said, "They have taken the Lord's body out of the tomb, and I don't know where they have put him!"

[3] Peter and the other disciple ran to the tomb to see. [4] The other disciple outran Peter and got there first. [5] He stooped and looked in and saw the linen cloth lying there, but he didn't go in. [6] Then Simon Peter arrived and went inside. He also noticed the linen wrappings lying there, [7] while the cloth that had covered Jesus' head was folded up and lying to the side. [8] Then the other disciple also went in, and he saw and believed— [9] for until then they hadn't realized that the Scriptures said he would rise from the dead. [10] Then they went home.

[11] Mary was standing outside the tomb crying, and as she wept, she stooped and looked in. [12] She saw two white-robed angels sitting at the head and foot of the place where the body of Jesus had been lying. [13] "Why are you crying?" the angels asked her.

"Because they have taken away my Lord," she replied, "and I don't know where they have put him."

[14] She glanced over her shoulder and saw someone standing behind her. It was Jesus, but she didn't recognize him. [15] "Why are you crying?" Jesus asked her. "Who are you looking for?"

She thought he was the gardener. "Sir," she said, "if you have taken him away, tell me where you have put him, and I will go and get him."

[16] "Mary!" Jesus said.

She turned toward him and exclaimed, "Teacher!"*

[17] "Don't cling to me," Jesus said, "for I haven't yet ascended to the Father. But go find my brothers and tell them that I am ascending to my Father and your Father, my God and your God."

[18] Mary Magdalene found the disciples and told them, "I have seen the Lord!" Then she gave them his message.

[19] That evening, on the first day of the week, the disciples were meeting behind locked doors because they were afraid of the Jewish leaders. Suddenly, Jesus was standing there among them! "Peace be with you," he said. [20] As he spoke, he held out his hands for them to see, and he showed them his side. They were filled with joy when they saw their Lord! [21] He spoke to them again and said, "Peace be with you. As the Father has sent me, so I send you." [22] Then he breathed on them and said to them, "Receive the Holy Spirit. [23] If you forgive anyone's sins, they are forgiven. If you refuse to forgive them, they are unforgiven."

[24] One of the disciples, Thomas (nicknamed the Twin*), was not with the others when Jesus came. [25] They told him, "We have seen the Lord!" But he replied, "I won't believe it unless I see the nail wounds in his hands, put my fingers into them, and place my hand into the wound in his side."

[26] Eight days later the disciples were together again, and this time Thomas was with them. The doors were locked; but suddenly, as before, Jesus was standing among them. He said, "Peace be with you." [27] Then he said to Thomas, "Put your finger here and see my hands. Put your hand into the

19:36 Exod 12:46; Num 9:12; Ps 34:20.   **19:37** Zech 12:10.   **19:39** Greek *100 litras* [32.7 kilograms].   **20:1** Greek *On the first day of the week.*   **20:16** Greek *and said in Hebrew, "Rabboni," which means "Teacher."*   **20:24** Greek *the one who was called Didymus.*

wound in my side. Don't be faithless any longer. Believe!"

[28]"My Lord and my God!" Thomas exclaimed.

[29]Then Jesus told him, "You believe because you have seen me. Blessed are those who haven't seen me and believe anyway."

[30]Jesus' disciples saw him do many other miraculous signs besides the ones recorded in this book. [31]But these are written so that you may believe* that Jesus is the Messiah, the Son of God, and that by believing in him you will have life.

CHAPTER 21

Later Jesus appeared again to the disciples beside the Sea of Galilee.* This is how it happened. [2]Several of the disciples were there—Simon Peter, Thomas (nicknamed the Twin*), Nathanael from Cana in Galilee, the sons of Zebedee, and two other disciples.

[3]Simon Peter said, "I'm going fishing."

"We'll come, too," they all said. So they went out in the boat, but they caught nothing all night.

[4]At dawn the disciples saw Jesus standing on the beach, but they couldn't see who he was. [5]He called out, "Friends, have you caught any fish?"

"No," they replied.

[6]Then he said, "Throw out your net on the right-hand side of the boat, and you'll get plenty of fish!" So they did, and they couldn't draw in the net because there were so many fish in it.

[7]Then the disciple whom Jesus loved said to Peter, "It is the Lord!" When Simon Peter heard that it was the Lord, he put on his tunic (for he had stripped for work), jumped into the water, and swam ashore. [8]The others stayed with the boat and pulled the loaded net to the shore, for they were only out about three hundred feet.* [9]When they got there, they saw that a charcoal fire was burning and fish were frying over it, and there was bread.

[10]"Bring some of the fish you've just caught," Jesus said. [11]So Simon Peter went aboard and dragged the net to the shore. There were 153 large fish, and yet the net hadn't torn.

[12]"Now come and have some breakfast!" Jesus said. And no one dared ask him if he really was the Lord because they were sure of it. [13]Then Jesus served them the bread and the fish. [14]This was the third time Jesus had appeared to his disciples since he had been raised from the dead.

[15]After breakfast Jesus said to Simon Peter, "Simon son of John, do you love me more than these?"

"Yes, Lord," Peter replied, "you know I love you."

"Then feed my lambs," Jesus told him.

[16]Jesus repeated the question: "Simon son of John, do you love me?"

"Yes, Lord," Peter said, "you know I love you."

"Then take care of my sheep," Jesus said.

[17]Once more he asked him, "Simon son of John, do you love me?"

Peter was grieved that Jesus asked the question a third time. He said, "Lord, you know everything. You know I love you."

Jesus said, "Then feed my sheep. [18]The truth is, when you were young, you were able to do as you liked and go wherever you wanted to. But when you are old, you will stretch out your hands, and others will direct you and take you where you don't want to go." [19]Jesus said this to let him know what kind of death he would die to glorify God. Then Jesus told him, "Follow me."

[20]Peter turned around and saw the disciple Jesus loved following them—the one who had leaned over to Jesus during supper and asked, "Lord, who among us will betray you?" [21]Peter asked Jesus, "What about him, Lord?"

[22]Jesus replied, "If I want him to remain alive until I return, what is that to you? You follow me." [23]So the rumor spread among the community of believers* that that disciple wouldn't die. But that isn't what Jesus said at all. He only said, "If I want him to remain alive until I return, what is that to you?"

[24]This is that disciple who saw these events and recorded them here. And we all know that his account of these things is accurate.

[25]And I suppose that if all the other things Jesus did were written down, the whole world could not contain the books.

20:31 Some manuscripts read *may continue to believe.*   21:1 Greek *Sea of Tiberias,* another name for the Sea of Galilee.   21:2 Greek *the one who was called Didymus.*   21:8 Greek *200 cubits* [90 meters].   21:23 Greek *the brothers.*

Acts

WITH the coming of the Holy Spirit at Pentecost, Jesus' small band of disciples is empowered and emboldened to take the Good News of the risen Savior to Jerusalem, Judea, Samaria, and "to the ends of the earth" (1:8). Paul, apostle to the Gentiles, spearheads the gospel's advance on three far-reaching missionary journeys. The book of Acts ends in Rome with Paul's imprisonment. Paul's ministry is drawing to a close, but an unstoppable message is just beginning.

Focus	Peter		Philip		Paul					
Divisions	Power of the Church	Progress of the Church	Persecution of the Church	Propagation of the Church	Paul's First Journey	Paul's Second Journey	Paul's Third Journey	Paul's Arrest	Paul's Three Trials	Paul's Trip to Rome
	1　　4	5　　7	8　　9	10　　12	13　15	16　18	19　20	21　23	24　26	27　28
Topics	History of the Church				History of a Church Planter					
	Establish-ment	Extension			Expansion		Explanation			
Place	Jerusalem	Judea and Samaria			Uttermost Part					
Time	2 Years (A.D. 33–35)	13 Years (A.D. 35–48)			14 Years (A.D. 48–62)					

NOVEMBER 1 □ DAY 306
ACTS 1–4
Power of the Church

OVERVIEW Luke's two books, the Gospel of Luke and the book of Acts, might well be called a two-volume "History of the New Testament Church"—Volume 1: *The History of the Founder of the Church;* Volume 2: *The History of the Followers of the Church.* With the ascension of Jesus Christ into heaven, the disciples are left in Jerusalem with Good News to share and a command to obey: "Do not leave Jerusalem until the Father sends you what he promised" (1:4). True to Christ's word, on the day of Pentecost the Holy Spirit arrives, accompanied by dramatic signs. With the Spirit's empowerment, the disciples move out to proclaim the glad tidings.

Chapter 1	Chapter 2	Chapter 3	Chapter 4
Waiting for Power	Witnessing Power	Powerful Healing	Powerful Appeal
Holy Spirit		Holy Boldness	

Without God, we are inadequate; with him, we are invincible.

YOUR DAILY WALK Is your life a wonder to those around you? Is there anything about your lifestyle—the way you use your time . . . spend your money . . . treat your family . . . love your neighbors—that causes others to sit up and take notice?

There was no ignoring the powerful witness of those first-century Christians. "A deep sense of awe came over them all" when they saw the "many miraculous signs and wonders" the apostles did in their midst (2:43). One such sign in chapter 3 involved a lame man—a man who begged for alms but who received legs instead! As others looked at his changed life, "they were absolutely astounded" (3:10). Peter's preaching turned that casual encounter by the Beautiful Gate into a wonderful revival with hundreds responding to the Good News of a risen Savior. But it all began with one changed life.

It's never too late for revival to break in your family or neighborhood. All God needs is one life to use as a showcase for his transforming power. Are you willing to let that revival begin with you? Then write God a note in the margin and tell him so.

INSIGHT A Bit of Arithmetic in Acts
In 1:15 the band of disciples consisted of 120. In 2:41, their number had swelled to more than three thousand. By 4:4 that total had increased by several thousand more. At first, disciples were *added* daily (2:47). But soon the believers were *increasing* rapidly (6:7)!

CHAPTER 1
Dear Theophilus:
In my first book* I told you about everything Jesus began to do and teach ²until the day he ascended to heaven after giving his

chosen apostles further instructions from the Holy Spirit. ³During the forty days after his crucifixion, he appeared to the apostles from time to time and proved to them in many ways that he was actually alive. On

1:1 The reference is to the book of Luke.

these occasions he talked to them about the Kingdom of God.

[4] In one of these meetings as he was eating a meal with them, he told them, "Do not leave Jerusalem until the Father sends you what he promised. Remember, I have told you about this before. [5] John baptized with* water, but in just a few days you will be baptized with the Holy Spirit."

[6] When the apostles were with Jesus, they kept asking him, "Lord, are you going to free Israel now and restore our kingdom?"

[7] "The Father sets those dates," he replied, "and they are not for you to know. [8] But when the Holy Spirit has come upon you, you will receive power and will tell people about me everywhere—in Jerusalem, throughout Judea, in Samaria, and to the ends of the earth."

[9] It was not long after he said this that he was taken up into the sky while they were watching, and he disappeared into a cloud. [10] As they were straining their eyes to see him, two white-robed men suddenly stood there among them. [11] They said, "Men of Galilee, why are you standing here staring at the sky? Jesus has been taken away from you into heaven. And someday, just as you saw him go, he will return!"

[12] The apostles were at the Mount of Olives when this happened, so they walked the half mile* back to Jerusalem. [13] Then they went to the upstairs room of the house where they were staying. Here is the list of those who were present:

Peter,
John,
James,
Andrew,
Philip,
Thomas,
Bartholomew,
Matthew,
James (son of Alphaeus),
Simon (the Zealot),
and Judas (son of James).

[14] They all met together continually for prayer, along with Mary the mother of Jesus, several other women, and the brothers of Jesus.

[15] During this time, on a day when about 120 believers* were present, Peter stood up and addressed them as follows:

[16] "Brothers, it was necessary for the Scriptures to be fulfilled concerning Judas, who guided the Temple police to arrest Jesus. This was predicted long ago by the Holy Spirit, speaking through King David. [17] Judas was one of us, chosen to share in the ministry with us."

[18] (Judas bought a field with the money he received for his treachery, and falling there, he burst open, spilling out his intestines. [19] The news of his death spread rapidly among all the people of Jerusalem, and they gave the place the Aramaic name *Akeldama*, which means "Field of Blood.")

[20] Peter continued, "This was predicted in the book of Psalms, where it says, 'Let his home become desolate, with no one living in it.' And again, 'Let his position be given to someone else.'*

[21] "So now we must choose someone else to take Judas's place. It must be someone who has been with us all the time that we were with the Lord Jesus—[22] from the time he was baptized by John until the day he was taken from us into heaven. Whoever is chosen will join us as a witness of Jesus' resurrection."

[23] So they nominated two men: Joseph called Barsabbas (also known as Justus) and Matthias. [24] Then they all prayed for the right man to be chosen. "O Lord," they said, "you know every heart. Show us which of these men you have chosen [25] as an apostle to replace Judas the traitor in this ministry, for he has deserted us and gone where he belongs." [26] Then they cast lots, and in this way Matthias was chosen and became an apostle with the other eleven.

CHAPTER 2

On the day of Pentecost, seven weeks after Jesus' resurrection,* the believers were meeting together in one place. [2] Suddenly, there was a sound from heaven like the roaring of a mighty windstorm in the skies above them, and it filled the house where they were meeting. [3] Then, what looked like flames or tongues of fire appeared and settled on each of them. [4] And everyone present was filled with the Holy Spirit and began speaking in other languages,* as the Holy Spirit gave them this ability.

[5] Godly Jews from many nations were

1:5 Or *in;* also in 1:5b.   **1:12** Greek *a Sabbath day's journey.*   **1:15** Greek *brothers.*   **1:20** Pss 69:25; 109:8.   **2:1** Greek *When the day of Pentecost arrived.* This annual celebration came 50 days after the Passover ceremonies. See Lev 23:16.   **2:4** Or *in other tongues.*

living in Jerusalem at that time. ⁶When they heard this sound, they came running to see what it was all about, and they were bewildered to hear their own languages being spoken by the believers.

⁷They were beside themselves with wonder. "How can this be?" they exclaimed. "These people are all from Galilee, ⁸and yet we hear them speaking the languages of the lands where we were born! ⁹Here we are—Parthians, Medes, Elamites, people from Mesopotamia, Judea, Cappadocia, Pontus, the province of Asia, ¹⁰Phrygia, Pamphylia, Egypt, and the areas of Libya toward Cyrene, visitors from Rome (both Jews and converts to Judaism), ¹¹Cretans, and Arabians. And we all hear these people speaking in our own languages about the wonderful things God has done!" ¹²They stood there amazed and perplexed. "What can this mean?" they asked each other. ¹³But others in the crowd were mocking. "They're drunk, that's all!" they said.

¹⁴Then Peter stepped forward with the eleven other apostles and shouted to the crowd, "Listen carefully, all of you, fellow Jews and residents of Jerusalem! Make no mistake about this. ¹⁵Some of you are saying these people are drunk. It isn't true! It's much too early for that. People don't get drunk by nine o'clock in the morning. ¹⁶No, what you see this morning was predicted centuries ago by the prophet Joel:

¹⁷ 'In the last days, God said,
   I will pour out my Spirit upon all
      people.
   Your sons and daughters will prophesy,
      your young men will see visions,
      and your old men will dream dreams.
¹⁸ In those days I will pour out my Spirit
      upon all my servants, men and
         women alike,
      and they will prophesy.
¹⁹ And I will cause wonders in the
      heavens above
      and signs on the earth below—
      blood and fire and clouds of smoke.
²⁰ The sun will be turned into darkness,
      and the moon will turn bloodred,
      before that great and glorious day
         of the Lord arrives.
²¹ And anyone who calls on the name
      of the Lord
      will be saved.'*

²²"People of Israel, listen! God publicly endorsed Jesus of Nazareth by doing wonderful miracles, wonders, and signs through him, as you well know. ²³But you followed God's prearranged plan. With the help of lawless Gentiles, you nailed him to the cross and murdered him. ²⁴However, God released him from the horrors of death and raised him back to life again, for death could not keep him in its grip. ²⁵King David said this about him:

   'I know the Lord is always with me.
      I will not be shaken, for he is right
         beside me.
²⁶ No wonder my heart is filled with joy,
      and my mouth shouts his praises!
      My body rests in hope.
²⁷ For you will not leave my soul among
         the dead*
      or allow your Holy One to rot in the
         grave.
²⁸ You have shown me the way of life,
      and you will give me wonderful joy
         in your presence.'*

²⁹"Dear brothers, think about this! David wasn't referring to himself when he spoke these words I have quoted, for he died and was buried, and his tomb is still here among us. ³⁰But he was a prophet, and he knew God had promised with an oath that one of David's own descendants would sit on David's throne as the Messiah. ³¹David was looking into the future and predicting the Messiah's resurrection. He was saying that the Messiah would not be left among the dead and that his body would not rot in the grave.

³²"This prophecy was speaking of Jesus, whom God raised from the dead, and we all are witnesses of this. ³³Now he sits on the throne of highest honor in heaven, at God's right hand. And the Father, as he had promised, gave him the Holy Spirit to pour out upon us, just as you see and hear today. ³⁴For David himself never ascended into heaven, yet he said,

   'The LORD said to my Lord,
   Sit in honor at my right hand
³⁵   until I humble your enemies,
      making them a footstool under your
         feet.'*

³⁶So let it be clearly known by everyone in Israel that God has made this Jesus whom

2:17-21 Joel 2:28-32.   **2:27** Greek *in Hades;* also in 2:31.   **2:25-28** Ps 16:8-11.   **2:34-35** Ps 110:1.

you crucified to be both Lord and Messiah!"

37Peter's words convicted them deeply, and they said to him and to the other apostles, "Brothers, what should we do?"

38Peter replied, "Each of you must turn from your sins and turn to God, and be baptized in the name of Jesus Christ for the forgiveness of your sins. Then you will receive the gift of the Holy Spirit. 39This promise is to you and to your children, and even to the Gentiles*—all who have been called by the Lord our God." 40Then Peter continued preaching for a long time, strongly urging all his listeners, "Save yourselves from this generation that has gone astray!"

41Those who believed what Peter said were baptized and added to the church— about three thousand in all. 42They joined with the other believers and devoted themselves to the apostles' teaching and fellowship, sharing in the Lord's Supper and in prayer.

43A deep sense of awe came over them all, and the apostles performed many miraculous signs and wonders. 44And all the believers met together constantly and shared everything they had. 45They sold their possessions and shared the proceeds with those in need. 46They worshiped together at the Temple each day, met in homes for the Lord's Supper, and shared their meals with great joy and generosity— 47all the while praising God and enjoying the goodwill of all the people. And each day the Lord added to their group those who were being saved.

CHAPTER 3

Peter and John went to the Temple one afternoon to take part in the three o'clock prayer service. 2As they approached the Temple, a man lame from birth was being carried in. Each day he was put beside the Temple gate, the one called the Beautiful Gate, so he could beg from the people going into the Temple. 3When he saw Peter and John about to enter, he asked them for some money.

4Peter and John looked at him intently, and Peter said, "Look at us!" 5The lame man looked at them eagerly, expecting a gift. 6But Peter said, "I don't have any money for you. But I'll give you what I

have. In the name of Jesus Christ of Nazareth, get up and walk!"

7Then Peter took the lame man by the right hand and helped him up. And as he did, the man's feet and anklebones were healed and strengthened. 8He jumped up, stood on his feet, and began to walk! Then, walking, leaping, and praising God, he went into the Temple with them.

9All the people saw him walking and heard him praising God. 10When they realized he was the lame beggar they had seen so often at the Beautiful Gate, they were absolutely astounded! 11They all rushed out to Solomon's Colonnade, where he was holding tightly to Peter and John. Everyone stood there in awe of the wonderful thing that had happened.

12Peter saw his opportunity and addressed the crowd. "People of Israel," he said, "what is so astounding about this? And why look at us as though we had made this man walk by our own power and godliness? 13For it is the God of Abraham, the God of Isaac, the God of Jacob, the God of all our ancestors who has brought glory to his servant Jesus by doing this. This is the same Jesus whom you handed over and rejected before Pilate, despite Pilate's decision to release him. 14You rejected this holy, righteous one and instead demanded the release of a murderer. 15You killed the author of life, but God raised him to life. And we are witnesses of this fact!

16"The name of Jesus has healed this man—and you know how lame he was before. Faith in Jesus' name has caused this healing before your very eyes.

17"Friends,* I realize that what you did to Jesus was done in ignorance; and the same can be said of your leaders. 18But God was fulfilling what all the prophets had declared about the Messiah beforehand—that he must suffer all these things. 19Now turn from your sins and turn to God, so you can be cleansed of your sins. 20Then wonderful times of refreshment will come from the presence of the Lord, and he will send Jesus your Messiah to you again. 21For he must remain in heaven until the time for the final restoration of all things, as God promised long ago through his prophets. 22Moses said, 'The Lord your God will raise up a Prophet like me from among your own people. Listen carefully to everything he

2:39 Greek *to those far away.*   3:17 Greek *Brothers.*

tells you.'* ²³Then Moses said, 'Anyone who will not listen to that Prophet will be cut off from God's people and utterly destroyed.'*

²⁴"Starting with Samuel, every prophet spoke about what is happening today. ²⁵You are the children of those prophets, and you are included in the covenant God promised to your ancestors. For God said to Abraham, 'Through your descendants all the families on earth will be blessed.'* ²⁶When God raised up his servant, he sent him first to you people of Israel, to bless you by turning each of you back from your sinful ways."

CHAPTER 4

While Peter and John were speaking to the people, the leading priests, the captain of the Temple guard, and some of the Sadducees came over to them. ²They were very disturbed that Peter and John were claiming, on the authority of Jesus, that there is a resurrection of the dead. ³They arrested them and, since it was already evening, jailed them until morning. ⁴But many of the people who heard their message believed it, so that the number of believers totaled about five thousand men, not counting women and children.*

⁵The next day the council of all the rulers and elders and teachers of religious law met in Jerusalem. ⁶Annas the high priest was there, along with Caiaphas, John, Alexander, and other relatives of the high priest. ⁷They brought in the two disciples and demanded, "By what power, or in whose name, have you done this?"

⁸Then Peter, filled with the Holy Spirit, said to them, "Leaders and elders of our nation, ⁹are we being questioned because we've done a good deed for a crippled man? Do you want to know how he was healed? ¹⁰Let me clearly state to you and to all the people of Israel that he was healed in the name and power of Jesus Christ from Nazareth, the man you crucified, but whom God raised from the dead. ¹¹For Jesus is the one referred to in the Scriptures, where it says,

'The stone that you builders rejected
    has now become the cornerstone.'*

¹²There is salvation in no one else! There is no other name in all of heaven for people to call on to save them."

¹³The members of the council were amazed when they saw the boldness of Peter and John, for they could see that they were ordinary men who had had no special training. They also recognized them as men who had been with Jesus. ¹⁴But since the man who had been healed was standing right there among them, the council had nothing to say. ¹⁵So they sent Peter and John out of the council chamber* and conferred among themselves.

¹⁶"What should we do with these men?" they asked each other. "We can't deny they have done a miraculous sign, and everybody in Jerusalem knows about it. ¹⁷But perhaps we can stop them from spreading their propaganda. We'll warn them not to speak to anyone in Jesus' name again." ¹⁸So they called the apostles back in and told them never again to speak or teach about Jesus.

¹⁹But Peter and John replied, "Do you think God wants us to obey you rather than him? ²⁰We cannot stop telling about the wonderful things we have seen and heard."

²¹The council then threatened them further, but they finally let them go because they didn't know how to punish them without starting a riot. For everyone was praising God ²²for this miraculous sign— the healing of a man who had been lame for more than forty years.

²³As soon as they were freed, Peter and John found the other believers and told them what the leading priests and elders had said. ²⁴Then all the believers were united as they lifted their voices in prayer: "O Sovereign Lord, Creator of heaven and earth, the sea, and everything in them— ²⁵you spoke long ago by the Holy Spirit through our ancestor King David, your servant, saying,

'Why did the nations rage?
  Why did the people waste their time
    with futile plans?
²⁶ The kings of the earth prepared for
    battle;
  the rulers gathered together
against the Lord
  and against his Messiah.'*

²⁷"That is what has happened here in this city! For Herod Antipas, Pontius Pilate the governor, the Gentiles, and the people of Israel were all united against Jesus, your holy servant, whom you anointed. ²⁸In fact,

3:22 Deut 18:15.   **3:23** Deut 18:19; Lev 23:29.   **3:25** Gen 22:18.   **4:4** Greek *5,000 adult males.*   **4:11** Ps 118:22.   **4:15** Greek *the Sanhedrin.*   **4:25-26** Ps 2:1-2.

everything they did occurred according to your eternal will and plan. [29]And now, O Lord, hear their threats, and give your servants great boldness in their preaching. [30]Send your healing power; may miraculous signs and wonders be done through the name of your holy servant Jesus."

[31]After this prayer, the building where they were meeting shook, and they were all filled with the Holy Spirit. And they preached God's message with boldness.

[32]All the believers were of one heart and mind, and they felt that what they owned was not their own; they shared everything

they had. [33]And the apostles gave powerful witness to the resurrection of the Lord Jesus, and God's great favor was upon them all. [34]There was no poverty among them, because people who owned land or houses sold them [35]and brought the money to the apostles to give to others in need.

[36]For instance, there was Joseph, the one the apostles nicknamed Barnabas (which means "Son of Encouragement"). He was from the tribe of Levi and came from the island of Cyprus. [37]He sold a field he owned and brought the money to the apostles for those in need.

NOVEMBER 2 ☐ DAY 307
ACTS 5–7
Progress of the Church

 OVERVIEW Every church has its problems, and the newly organized church in Jerusalem is no exception. On the heels of Peter's miraculous healing of a lame man, several waves of trouble arrive: scandal in the church involving Ananias and Sapphira, sharp dissension between Jews and Greeks over the provision for widows in the church, and the brutal martyrdom of Stephen after his eloquent and convicting address before the Sanhedrin. But even in the face of such strong adversity, God is at work. One of the witnesses of Stephen's death is Saul, the Jewish persecutor who would soon become one of the chief figures in the expanding church!

Chapter 5	Chapter 6	Chapter 7
Embezzlement in the Church	Overlooked Needs in the Church	Opposition outside the Church
Discipline	Deacons	Death

 YOUR DAILY WALK Two pastors were exchanging the latest news. Said one, "Did you hear about the revival we had at our church?" "No," replied the other, "how many new members did you add?" "None," responded the first, "but we had some very helpful subtractions!"

Revival is nothing more than a new beginning of obedience to God.

The early chapters of Acts are marked by both kinds of "revival." There was dramatic growth by *addition:* at first three thousand, then five thousand more were added. But don't overlook the growth by *subtraction.* Ananias and Sapphira felt God's disciplining hand, and "more people believed and were brought to the Lord" (5:14). Stephen, the church's spokesman, died a terrible death by stoning, and consequently "the believers who had fled Jerusalem went everywhere preaching the Good News about Jesus" (8:4).

Start a revival in your own life today by either *adding* something that is sorely missing (like making time to read good Christian books) or *subtracting* something that is hindering your walk with God (like too much television or too many late-night activities).

INSIGHT Stephen's Sermon—The Old Testament in a Nugget
With the help of this Bible, "walk" your way through the Old Testament
with Stephen, marking in Acts 7 where each Old Testament book begins
and ends. For example, Genesis begins with verse 1 and ends with
verse 16. See how many more you can find. Have fun!

CHAPTER 5

There was also a man named Ananias who, with his wife, Sapphira, sold some property. [2]He brought part of the money to the apostles, but he claimed it was the full amount. His wife had agreed to this deception.

[3]Then Peter said, "Ananias, why has Satan filled your heart? You lied to the Holy Spirit, and you kept some of the money for yourself. [4]The property was yours to sell or not sell, as you wished. And after selling it, the money was yours to give away. How could you do a thing like this? You weren't lying to us but to God."

[5]As soon as Ananias heard these words, he fell to the floor and died. Everyone who heard about it was terrified. [6]Then some young men wrapped him in a sheet and took him out and buried him.

[7]About three hours later his wife came in, not knowing what had happened. [8]Peter asked her, "Was this the price you and your husband received for your land?"

"Yes," she replied, "that was the price."

[9]And Peter said, "How could the two of you even think of doing a thing like this—conspiring together to test the Spirit of the Lord? Just outside that door are the young men who buried your husband, and they will carry you out, too."

[10]Instantly, she fell to the floor and died. When the young men came in and saw that she was dead, they carried her out and buried her beside her husband. [11]Great fear gripped the entire church and all others who heard what had happened.

[12]Meanwhile, the apostles were performing many miraculous signs and wonders among the people. And the believers were meeting regularly at the Temple in the area known as Solomon's Colonnade. [13]No one else dared to join them, though everyone had high regard for them. [14]And more and more people believed and were brought to the Lord—crowds of both men and women. [15]As a result of the apostles' work, sick people were brought out into the streets on beds and mats so that Peter's

shadow might fall across some of them as he went by. [16]Crowds came in from the villages around Jerusalem, bringing their sick and those possessed by evil spirits, and they were all healed.

[17]The high priest and his friends, who were Sadducees, reacted with violent jealousy. [18]They arrested the apostles and put them in the jail. [19]But an angel of the Lord came at night, opened the gates of the jail, and brought them out. Then he told them, [20]"Go to the Temple and give the people this message of life!" [21]So the apostles entered the Temple about daybreak and immediately began teaching.

When the high priest and his officials arrived, they convened the high council,* along with all the elders of Israel. Then they sent for the apostles to be brought for trial. [22]But when the Temple guards went to the jail, the men were gone. So they returned to the council and reported, [23]"The jail was locked, with the guards standing outside, but when we opened the gates, no one was there!"

[24]When the captain of the Temple guard and the leading priests heard this, they were perplexed, wondering where it would all end. [25]Then someone arrived with the news that the men they had jailed were out in the Temple, teaching the people.

[26]The captain went with his Temple guards and arrested them, but without violence, for they were afraid the people would kill them if they treated the apostles roughly. [27]Then they brought the apostles in before the council. [28]"Didn't we tell you never again to teach in this man's name?" the high priest demanded. "Instead, you have filled all Jerusalem with your teaching about Jesus, and you intend to blame us for his death!"

[29]But Peter and the apostles replied, "We must obey God rather than human authority. [30]The God of our ancestors raised Jesus from the dead after you killed him by crucifying him. [31]Then God put him in the place of honor at his right hand as Prince

5:21 Greek *Sanhedrin*; also in 5:27, 41.

and Savior. He did this to give the people of Israel an opportunity to turn from their sins and turn to God so their sins would be forgiven. [32]We are witnesses of these things and so is the Holy Spirit, who is given by God to those who obey him."

[33]At this, the high council was furious and decided to kill them. [34]But one member had a different perspective. He was a Pharisee named Gamaliel, who was an expert on religious law and was very popular with the people. He stood up and ordered that the apostles be sent outside the council chamber for a while. [35]Then he addressed his colleagues as follows: "Men of Israel, take care what you are planning to do to these men! [36]Some time ago there was that fellow Theudas, who pretended to be someone great. About four hundred others joined him, but he was killed, and his followers went their various ways. The whole movement came to nothing. [37]After him, at the time of the census, there was Judas of Galilee. He got some people to follow him, but he was killed, too, and all his followers were scattered.

[38]"So my advice is, leave these men alone. If they are teaching and doing these things merely on their own, it will soon be overthrown. [39]But if it is of God, you will not be able to stop them. You may even find yourselves fighting against God."

[40]The council accepted his advice. They called in the apostles and had them flogged. Then they ordered them never again to speak in the name of Jesus, and they let them go. [41]The apostles left the high council rejoicing that God had counted them worthy to suffer dishonor for the name of Jesus. [42]And every day, in the Temple and in their homes,* they continued to teach and preach this message: "The Messiah you are looking for is Jesus."

CHAPTER 6

But as the believers* rapidly multiplied, there were rumblings of discontent. Those who spoke Greek complained against those who spoke Hebrew, saying that their widows were being discriminated against in the daily distribution of food. [2]So the Twelve called a meeting of all the believers.

"We apostles should spend our time preaching and teaching the word of God, not administering a food program," they said. [3]"Now look around among yourselves, brothers, and select seven men who are well respected and are full of the Holy Spirit and wisdom. We will put them in charge of this business. [4]Then we can spend our time in prayer and preaching and teaching the word."

[5]This idea pleased the whole group, and they chose the following: Stephen (a man full of faith and the Holy Spirit), Philip, Procorus, Nicanor, Timon, Parmenas, and Nicolas of Antioch (a Gentile convert to the Jewish faith, who had now become a Christian). [6]These seven were presented to the apostles, who prayed for them as they laid their hands on them.

[7]God's message was preached in ever-widening circles. The number of believers greatly increased in Jerusalem, and many of the Jewish priests were converted, too.

[8]Stephen, a man full of God's grace and power, performed amazing miracles and signs among the people. [9]But one day some men from the Synagogue of Freed Slaves, as it was called, started to debate with him. They were Jews from Cyrene, Alexandria, Cilicia, and the province of Asia. [10]None of them was able to stand against the wisdom and Spirit by which Stephen spoke.

[11]So they persuaded some men to lie about Stephen, saying, "We heard him blaspheme Moses, and even God." [12]Naturally, this roused the crowds, the elders, and the teachers of religious law. So they arrested Stephen and brought him before the high council.* [13]The lying witnesses said, "This man is always speaking against the Temple and against the law of Moses. [14]We have heard him say that this Jesus of Nazareth will destroy the Temple and change the customs Moses handed down to us." [15]At this point everyone in the council stared at Stephen because his face became as bright as an angel's.

CHAPTER 7

Then the high priest asked Stephen, "Are these accusations true?"

[2]This was Stephen's reply: "Brothers and honorable fathers, listen to me. Our glorious God appeared to our ancestor Abraham in Mesopotamia before he moved to Haran.* [3]God told him, 'Leave your native land and your relatives, and come to the land that I will show you.'* [4]So Abraham

5:42 Greek *from house to house.*   **6:1** Greek *disciples;* also in 6:2, 7.   **6:12** Greek *Sanhedrin;* also in 6:15.   **7:2** *Mesopotamia* was the region now called Iraq. *Haran* was a city in what is now called Syria.   **7:3** Gen 12:1.

left the land of the Chaldeans and lived in Haran until his father died. Then God brought him here to the land where you now live. [5]But God gave him no inheritance here, not even one square foot of land. God did promise, however, that eventually the whole country would belong to Abraham and his descendants—though he had no children yet. [6]But God also told him that his descendants would live in a foreign country where they would be mistreated as slaves for four hundred years. [7]'But I will punish the nation that enslaves them,' God told him, 'and in the end they will come out and worship me in this place.'* [8]God also gave Abraham the covenant of circumcision at that time. And so Isaac, Abraham's son, was circumcised when he was eight days old. Isaac became the father of Jacob, and Jacob was the father of the twelve patriarchs of the Jewish nation.

[9]"These sons of Jacob were very jealous of their brother Joseph, and they sold him to be a slave in Egypt. But God was with him [10]and delivered him from his anguish. And God gave him favor before Pharaoh, king of Egypt. God also gave Joseph unusual wisdom, so that Pharaoh appointed him governor over all of Egypt and put him in charge of all the affairs of the palace.

[11]"But a famine came upon Egypt and Canaan. There was great misery for our ancestors, as they ran out of food. [12]Jacob heard that there was still grain in Egypt, so he sent his sons* to buy some. [13]The second time they went, Joseph revealed his identity to his brothers, and they were introduced to Pharaoh. [14]Then Joseph sent for his father, Jacob, and all his relatives to come to Egypt, seventy-five persons in all. [15]So Jacob went to Egypt. He died there, as did all his sons. [16]All of them were taken to Shechem and buried in the tomb Abraham had bought from the sons of Hamor in Shechem.

[17]"As the time drew near when God would fulfill his promise to Abraham, the number of our people in Egypt greatly increased. [18]But then a new king came to the throne of Egypt who knew nothing about Joseph. [19]This king plotted against our people and forced parents to abandon their newborn babies so they would die.

[20]"At that time Moses was born—a beautiful child in God's eyes. His parents cared for him at home for three months. [21]When at last they had to abandon him, Pharaoh's daughter found him and raised him as her own son. [22]Moses was taught all the wisdom of the Egyptians, and he became mighty in both speech and action.

[23]"One day when he was forty years old, he decided to visit his relatives, the people of Israel. [24]During this visit, he saw an Egyptian mistreating a man of Israel. So Moses came to his defense and avenged him, killing the Egyptian. [25]Moses assumed his brothers would realize that God had sent him to rescue them, but they didn't.

[26]"The next day he visited them again and saw two men of Israel fighting. He tried to be a peacemaker. 'Men,' he said, 'you are brothers. Why are you hurting each other?'

[27]"But the man in the wrong pushed Moses aside and told him to mind his own business. 'Who made you a ruler and judge over us?' he asked. [28]'Are you going to kill me as you killed that Egyptian yesterday?' [29]When Moses heard that, he fled the country and lived as a foreigner in the land of Midian, where his two sons were born.

[30]"Forty years later, in the desert near Mount Sinai, an angel appeared to Moses in the flame of a burning bush. [31]Moses saw it and wondered what it was. As he went to see, the voice of the Lord called out to him, [32]'I am the God of your ancestors—the God of Abraham, Isaac, and Jacob.' Moses shook with terror and dared not look.

[33]"And the Lord said to him, 'Take off your sandals, for you are standing on holy ground. [34]You can be sure that I have seen the misery of my people in Egypt. I have heard their cries. So I have come to rescue them. Now go, for I will send you to Egypt.'* [35]And so God sent back the same man his people had previously rejected by demanding, 'Who made you a ruler and judge over us?' Through the angel who appeared to him in the burning bush, Moses was sent to be their ruler and savior. [36]And by means of many miraculous signs and wonders, he led them out of Egypt, through the Red Sea, and back and forth through the wilderness for forty years.

[37]"Moses himself told the people of Israel, 'God will raise up a Prophet like me from among your own people.'* [38]Moses was with the assembly of God's people in

the wilderness. He was the mediator between the people of Israel and the angel who gave him life-giving words on Mount Sinai to pass on to us.

³⁹"But our ancestors rejected Moses and wanted to return to Egypt. ⁴⁰They told Aaron, 'Make us some gods who can lead us, for we don't know what has become of this Moses, who brought us out of Egypt.' ⁴¹So they made an idol shaped like a calf, and they sacrificed to it and rejoiced in this thing they had made. ⁴²Then God turned away from them and gave them up to serve the sun, moon, and stars as their gods! In the book of the prophets it is written,

'Was it to me you were bringing
　　sacrifices
　　during those forty years in the
　　　wilderness, Israel?
⁴³ No, your real interest was in your
　　　pagan gods—
　　the shrine of Molech,
　　the star god Rephan,
　　and the images you made to worship
　　　them.
So I will send you into captivity
　　far away in Babylon.'*

⁴⁴"Our ancestors carried the Tabernacle* with them through the wilderness. It was constructed in exact accordance with the plan shown to Moses by God. ⁴⁵Years later, when Joshua led the battles against the Gentile nations that God drove out of this land, the Tabernacle was taken with them into their new territory. And it was used there until the time of King David.

⁴⁶"David found favor with God and asked for the privilege of building a permanent Temple for the God of Jacob.* ⁴⁷But it was Solomon who actually built it. ⁴⁸However, the Most High doesn't live in temples made by human hands. As the prophet says,

⁴⁹ 'Heaven is my throne,
　　and the earth is my footstool.
Could you ever build me a temple as
　　good as that?'
　asks the Lord.
'Could you build a dwelling place for
　　me?
⁵⁰　Didn't I make everything in heaven
　　and earth?'*

⁵¹"You stubborn people! You are heathen at heart and deaf to the truth. Must you forever resist the Holy Spirit? But your ancestors did, and so do you! ⁵²Name one prophet your ancestors didn't persecute! They even killed the ones who predicted the coming of the Righteous One—the Messiah whom you betrayed and murdered. ⁵³You deliberately disobeyed God's law, though you received it from the hands of angels.*"

⁵⁴The Jewish leaders were infuriated by Stephen's accusation, and they shook their fists in rage.* ⁵⁵But Stephen, full of the Holy Spirit, gazed steadily upward into heaven and saw the glory of God, and he saw Jesus standing in the place of honor at God's right hand. ⁵⁶And he told them, "Look, I see the heavens opened and the Son of Man standing in the place of honor at God's right hand!"

⁵⁷Then they put their hands over their ears, and drowning out his voice with their shouts, they rushed at him. ⁵⁸They dragged him out of the city and began to stone him. The official witnesses took off their coats and laid them at the feet of a young man named Saul.*

⁵⁹And as they stoned him, Stephen prayed, "Lord Jesus, receive my spirit." ⁶⁰And he fell to his knees, shouting, "Lord, don't charge them with this sin!" And with that, he died.

7:42-43 Amos 5:25-27.　　**7:44** Greek *the tent of witness.*　　**7:46** Some manuscripts read *the house of Jacob.*　　**7:49-50** Isa 66:1-2.
7:53 Greek *received the Law as it was ordained by angels.*　　**7:54** Greek *they were grinding their teeth against him.*　　**7:58** *Saul* is later
called Paul; see 13:9.

NOVEMBER 3 ☐ DAY 308
ACTS 8–9
Persecution of the Church

OVERVIEW Saul's intense persecution against the Christians in Jerusalem forces them to scatter to the regions of Judea and Samaria—exactly as Christ had predicted in 1:8. Philip the evangelist becomes God's instrument to lead many to faith in the city of Samaria, and later he shares the Good News with an Ethiopian eunuch on the road to Gaza. But the most strategic conversion takes place more than a hundred miles to the north, where Saul comes face-to-face with the very Lord whose cause he has persecuted.

Chapter 8		Chapter 9	
Evangelism in Samaria	Evangelism in the Desert	Encounter near Damascus	Escape in a Basket
1 25	26 40	1 18	19 43
Philip's Preaching		Saul's Conversion	

To know God is to know that he should be obeyed.

YOUR DAILY WALK What does the Second Law of Thermodynamics ("the greater the heat, the greater the expansion") have to do with the book of Acts?

Answer: It is an accurate description of the process by which the gospel message expanded beyond the city of Jerusalem.

Two years after Jesus spoke the words recorded in Acts 1:8, the disciples resided only in Jerusalem . . . and so the Good News they were commissioned to share stayed within the city walls. But that meant that only phase one of the Great Commission was being accomplished. So God allowed a little "heat" in the form of persecution to encourage the expansion of the gospel into the regions of Judea and Samaria.

Postponed obedience to the command of God is disobedience. And God has many loving (but often painful) ways to encourage you to obey. The choice is yours: You can "beat the heat" by doing his bidding or "feel the heat" of his chastening hand. Five times in today's passage an individual is commanded to "go" and do something. Locate and circle the response in each case, and let that guide your response the next time you receive a similar command!

INSIGHT Why Down Is Up in Palestine
We read in 8:5 that Philip "went to the city of Samaria." Even though Samaria is *north* of Jerusalem, Israelites traveling to that city would say that they were going down to Samaria. This makes sense when we realize that Israel's capital city is located atop a hill, and Samaria lies in a low plain. Moreover, we draw our maps with the top facing north, but the Palestinians drew them with the top facing east, looking inland from the Mediterranean.

CHAPTER 8
Saul was one of the official witnesses at the killing of Stephen.

A great wave of persecution began that day, sweeping over the church in Jerusalem, and all the believers except the apostles fled into Judea and Samaria. ²(Some godly people came and buried Stephen with loud weeping.) ³Saul was going everywhere to devastate the church. He went from house to house, dragging out both men and women to throw them into jail.

⁴But the believers who had fled Jerusalem went everywhere preaching the Good News about Jesus. ⁵Philip, for example,

went to the city of Samaria and told the people there about the Messiah. 6Crowds listened intently to what he had to say because of the miracles he did. 7Many evil spirits were cast out, screaming as they left their victims. And many who had been paralyzed or lame were healed. 8So there was great joy in that city.

9A man named Simon had been a sorcerer there for many years, claiming to be someone great. 10The Samaritan people, from the least to the greatest, often spoke of him as "the Great One—the Power of God." 11He was very influential because of the magic he performed. 12But now the people believed Philip's message of Good News concerning the Kingdom of God and the name of Jesus Christ. As a result, many men and women were baptized. 13Then Simon himself believed and was baptized. He began following Philip wherever he went, and he was amazed by the great miracles and signs Philip performed.

14When the apostles back in Jerusalem heard that the people of Samaria had accepted God's message, they sent Peter and John there. 15As soon as they arrived, they prayed for these new Christians to receive the Holy Spirit. 16The Holy Spirit had not yet come upon any of them, for they had only been baptized in the name of the Lord Jesus. 17Then Peter and John laid their hands upon these believers, and they received the Holy Spirit.

18When Simon saw that the Holy Spirit was given when the apostles placed their hands upon people's heads, he offered money to buy this power. 19"Let me have this power, too," he exclaimed, "so that when I lay my hands on people, they will receive the Holy Spirit!"

20But Peter replied, "May your money perish with you for thinking God's gift can be bought! 21You can have no part in this, for your heart is not right before God. 22Turn from your wickedness and pray to the Lord. Perhaps he will forgive your evil thoughts, 23for I can see that you are full of bitterness and held captive by sin."

24"Pray to the Lord for me," Simon exclaimed, "that these terrible things won't happen to me!"

25After testifying and preaching the word of the Lord in Samaria, Peter and John returned to Jerusalem. And they stopped in many Samaritan villages along the way to preach the Good News to them, too.

26As for Philip, an angel of the Lord said to him, "Go south* down the desert road that runs from Jerusalem to Gaza." 27So he did, and he met the treasurer of Ethiopia, a eunuch of great authority under the queen of Ethiopia.* The eunuch had gone to Jerusalem to worship, 28and he was now returning. Seated in his carriage, he was reading aloud from the book of the prophet Isaiah.

29The Holy Spirit said to Philip, "Go over and walk along beside the carriage."

30Philip ran over and heard the man reading from the prophet Isaiah; so he asked, "Do you understand what you are reading?"

31The man replied, "How can I, when there is no one to instruct me?" And he begged Philip to come up into the carriage and sit with him. 32The passage of Scripture he had been reading was this:

"He was led as a sheep to the slaughter.
    And as a lamb is silent before the
       shearers,
    he did not open his mouth.
33 He was humiliated and received no
      justice.
    Who can speak of his descendants?
    For his life was taken from the
      earth."*

34The eunuch asked Philip, "Was Isaiah talking about himself or someone else?" 35So Philip began with this same Scripture and then used many others to tell him the Good News about Jesus.

36As they rode along, they came to some water, and the eunuch said, "Look! There's some water! Why can't I be baptized?"* 38He ordered the carriage to stop, and they went down into the water, and Philip baptized him. 39When they came up out of the water, the Spirit of the Lord caught Philip away. The eunuch never saw him again but went on his way rejoicing. 40Meanwhile, Philip found himself farther north at the city of Azotus! He preached the Good News there and in every city along the way until he came to Caesarea.

8:26 Or *Go at noon.*   8:27 Greek *under the Candace, the queen of Ethiopia.*   8:32-33 Isa 53:7-8.   8:36 Some manuscripts add verse 37, *"You can," Philip answered, "if you believe with all your heart." And the eunuch replied, "I believe that Jesus Christ is the Son of God."*

CHAPTER 9

Meanwhile, Saul was uttering threats with every breath. He was eager to destroy the Lord's followers,* so he went to the high priest. ²He requested letters addressed to the synagogues in Damascus, asking their cooperation in the arrest of any followers of the Way he found there. He wanted to bring them—both men and women—back to Jerusalem in chains.

³As he was nearing Damascus on this mission, a brilliant light from heaven suddenly beamed down upon him! ⁴He fell to the ground and heard a voice saying to him, "Saul! Saul! Why are you persecuting me?"

⁵"Who are you, sir?" Saul asked.

And the voice replied, "I am Jesus, the one you are persecuting! ⁶Now get up and go into the city, and you will be told what you are to do."

⁷The men with Saul stood speechless with surprise, for they heard the sound of someone's voice, but they saw no one! ⁸As Saul picked himself up off the ground, he found that he was blind. ⁹So his companions led him by the hand to Damascus. He remained there blind for three days. And all that time he went without food and water.

¹⁰Now there was a believer* in Damascus named Ananias. The Lord spoke to him in a vision, calling, "Ananias!"

"Yes, Lord!" he replied.

¹¹The Lord said, "Go over to Straight Street, to the house of Judas. When you arrive, ask for Saul of Tarsus. He is praying to me right now. ¹²I have shown him a vision of a man named Ananias coming in and laying his hands on him so that he can see again."

¹³"But Lord," exclaimed Ananias, "I've heard about the terrible things this man has done to the believers in Jerusalem! ¹⁴And we hear that he is authorized by the leading priests to arrest every believer in Damascus."

¹⁵But the Lord said, "Go and do what I say. For Saul is my chosen instrument to take my message to the Gentiles and to kings, as well as to the people of Israel. ¹⁶And I will show him how much he must suffer for me."

¹⁷So Ananias went and found Saul. He laid his hands on him and said, "Brother Saul, the Lord Jesus, who appeared to you on the road, has sent me so that you may get your sight back and be filled with the Holy Spirit." ¹⁸Instantly something like scales fell from Saul's eyes, and he regained his sight. Then he got up and was baptized. ¹⁹Afterward he ate some food and was strengthened.

Saul stayed with the believers* in Damascus for a few days. ²⁰And immediately he began preaching about Jesus in the synagogues, saying, "He is indeed the Son of God!"

²¹All who heard him were amazed. "Isn't this the same man who persecuted Jesus' followers with such devastation in Jerusalem?" they asked. "And we understand that he came here to arrest them and take them in chains to the leading priests."

²²Saul's preaching became more and more powerful, and the Jews in Damascus couldn't refute his proofs that Jesus was indeed the Messiah. ²³After a while the Jewish leaders decided to kill him. ²⁴But Saul was told about their plot, and that they were watching for him day and night at the city gate so they could murder him. ²⁵So during the night, some of the other believers* let him down in a large basket through an opening in the city wall.

²⁶When Saul arrived in Jerusalem, he tried to meet with the believers, but they were all afraid of him. They thought he was only pretending to be a believer! ²⁷Then Barnabas brought him to the apostles and told them how Saul had seen the Lord on the way to Damascus. Barnabas also told them what the Lord had said to Saul and how he boldly preached in the name of Jesus in Damascus. ²⁸Then the apostles accepted Saul, and after that he was constantly with them in Jerusalem, preaching boldly in the name of the Lord. ²⁹He debated with some Greek-speaking Jews, but they plotted to murder him. ³⁰When the believers* heard about it, however, they took him to Caesarea and sent him on to his hometown of Tarsus.

³¹The church then had peace throughout Judea, Galilee, and Samaria, and it grew in strength and numbers. The believers were walking in the fear of the Lord and in the comfort of the Holy Spirit.

³²Peter traveled from place to place to visit the believers, and in his travels he came to the Lord's people in the town of

---

9:1 Greek *disciples.*   **9:10** Greek *disciple;* also in 9:36.   **9:19** Greek *disciples;* also in 9:26.   **9:25** Greek *his disciples.*
9:30 Greek *brothers.*

Lydda. [33]There he met a man named Aeneas, who had been paralyzed and bedridden for eight years. [34]Peter said to him, "Aeneas, Jesus Christ heals you! Get up and make your bed!" And he was healed instantly. [35]Then the whole population of Lydda and Sharon turned to the Lord when they saw Aeneas walking around.

[36]There was a believer in Joppa named Tabitha (which in Greek is Dorcas*). She was always doing kind things for others and helping the poor. [37]About this time she became ill and died. Her friends prepared her for burial and laid her in an upstairs room. [38]But they had heard that Peter was nearby at Lydda, so they sent two men to beg him, "Please come as soon as possible!"

[39]So Peter returned with them; and as soon as he arrived, they took him to the upstairs room. The room was filled with widows who were weeping and showing him the coats and other garments Dorcas had made for them. [40]But Peter asked them all to leave the room; then he knelt and prayed. Turning to the body he said, "Get up, Tabitha." And she opened her eyes! When she saw Peter, she sat up! [41]He gave her his hand and helped her up. Then he called in the widows and all the believers, and he showed them that she was alive.

[42]The news raced through the whole town, and many believed in the Lord. [43]And Peter stayed a long time in Joppa, living with Simon, a leatherworker.

9:36 The names *Tabitha* in Aramaic and *Dorcas* in Greek both mean "gazelle."

NOVEMBER 4 □ DAY 309
ACTS 10–12
Propagation of the Church

OVERVIEW After his encounter with the Ethiopian, Philip the evangelist leaves for Caesarea and is not mentioned again until chapter 21. Another resident of Caesarea—a Gentile centurion named Cornelius—becomes the first non-Jewish convert to Christianity. God sends a thrice-repeated vision to Peter to break down centuries of deep-seated prejudice between Jew and Gentile, setting the stage for the third and most expansive phase of the gospel advance—this time to the remotest corners of the known world.

Chapter 10	Chapter 11	Chapter 12
Peter's Revelation	Peter's Explanation	Peter's Incarceration
Vision	Vindication	Vast Expansion

YOUR DAILY WALK Using a dictionary (or better yet, a medical dictionary), look up the following words: *spleen, pancreas, kidney, pituitary gland, hypothalamus.*

We find it easier to go to church than to be the church.

What do they all have in common? Here are two suggestions:
1. They are hidden from view.
2. They are essential to the proper functioning of the body.

It's easy to be aware of the visible parts of an organism—whether it's a human body or the body of Christ. But just as vital—and perhaps more so—are those parts you never see and seldom think about.

A diabetic may look perfectly healthy at a casual glance. But deep within his or her body a single organ has ceased to make its essential contribution, and, as a result, the entire body suffers. In the church at Antioch, Barnabas and Saul taught (11:26), but countless others exercised the gifts of giving, helps, mercy, and prayer to undergird their ministry (11:29; 12:5). One without the other would have left the church anemic and ineffective. Have you discovered the role God wants you to play in your local church? If not, your minister or church leader would be delighted to help you find it . . . and fill it!

INSIGHT The Third Time's a Charm
For Peter, almost every major lesson had to be repeated three times before he got the message. Three times he denied the Lord (Matthew 26:69-75); three times he was commanded by Christ to feed God's flock (John 21:15-17); and three times the sheet rose and fell before Peter saw the significance of it (Acts 10:9-16).

CHAPTER 10

In Caesarea there lived a Roman army officer named Cornelius, who was a captain of the Italian Regiment. ²He was a devout man who feared the God of Israel, as did his entire household. He gave generously to charity and was a man who regularly prayed to God. ³One afternoon about three o'clock, he had a vision in which he saw an angel of God coming toward him. "Cornelius!" the angel said.

⁴Cornelius stared at him in terror. "What is it, sir?" he asked the angel.

And the angel replied, "Your prayers and gifts to the poor have not gone unnoticed by God! ⁵Now send some men down to Joppa to find a man named Simon Peter. ⁶He is staying with Simon, a leatherworker who lives near the shore. Ask him to come and visit you."

⁷As soon as the angel was gone, Cornelius called two of his household servants and a devout soldier, one of his personal attendants. ⁸He told them what had happened and sent them off to Joppa.

⁹The next day as Cornelius's messengers were nearing the city, Peter went up to the flat roof to pray. It was about noon, ¹⁰and he was hungry. But while lunch was being prepared, he fell into a trance. ¹¹He saw the sky open, and something like a large sheet was let down by its four corners. ¹²In the sheet were all sorts of animals, reptiles, and birds. ¹³Then a voice said to him, "Get up, Peter; kill and eat them."

¹⁴"Never, Lord," Peter declared. "I have never in all my life eaten anything forbidden by our Jewish laws.*"

¹⁵The voice spoke again, "If God says something is acceptable, don't say it isn't."*
¹⁶The same vision was repeated three times. Then the sheet was pulled up again to heaven.

¹⁷Peter was very perplexed. What could the vision mean? Just then the men sent by Cornelius found the house and stood outside at the gate. ¹⁸They asked if this was the place where Simon Peter was staying. ¹⁹Meanwhile, as Peter was puzzling over the vision, the Holy Spirit said to him, "Three men have come looking for you. ²⁰Go down and go with them without hesitation. All is well, for I have sent them."

²¹So Peter went down and said, "I'm the man you are looking for. Why have you come?"

²²They said, "We were sent by Cornelius, a Roman officer. He is a devout man who fears the God of Israel and is well respected by all the Jews. A holy angel instructed him to send for you so you can go to his house and give him a message." ²³So Peter invited the men to be his guests for the night. The next day he went with them, accompanied by some other believers* from Joppa.

²⁴They arrived in Caesarea the following day. Cornelius was waiting for him and had called together his relatives and close friends to meet Peter. ²⁵As Peter entered his home, Cornelius fell to the floor before him in worship. ²⁶But Peter pulled him up and said, "Stand up! I'm a human being like you!" ²⁷So Cornelius got up, and they talked together and went inside where the others were assembled.

²⁸Peter told them, "You know it is against the Jewish laws for me to come into a Gentile home like this. But God has shown me that I should never think of anyone as impure. ²⁹So I came as soon as I was sent for. Now tell me why you sent for me."

³⁰Cornelius replied, "Four days ago I was praying in my house at three o'clock in the afternoon. Suddenly, a man in dazzling clothes was standing in front of me. ³¹He told me, 'Cornelius, your prayers have been heard, and your gifts to the poor have been noticed by God! ³²Now send some

10:14 Greek *anything common and unclean.*   10:15 Greek *"What God calls clean you must not call unclean."*   10:23 Greek *brothers.*

men to Joppa and summon Simon Peter. He is staying in the home of Simon, a leatherworker who lives near the shore.' ³³So I sent for you at once, and it was good of you to come. Now here we are, waiting before God to hear the message the Lord has given you."

³⁴Then Peter replied, "I see very clearly that God doesn't show partiality. ³⁵In every nation he accepts those who fear him and do what is right. ³⁶I'm sure you have heard about the Good News for the people of Israel—that there is peace with God through Jesus Christ, who is Lord of all. ³⁷You know what happened all through Judea, beginning in Galilee after John the Baptist began preaching. ³⁸And no doubt you know that God anointed Jesus of Nazareth with the Holy Spirit and with power. Then Jesus went around doing good and healing all who were oppressed by the Devil, for God was with him.

³⁹"And we apostles are witnesses of all he did throughout Israel and in Jerusalem. They put him to death by crucifying him, ⁴⁰but God raised him to life three days later. Then God allowed him to appear, ⁴¹not to the general public,* but to us whom God had chosen beforehand to be his witnesses. We were those who ate and drank with him after he rose from the dead. ⁴²And he ordered us to preach everywhere and to testify that Jesus is ordained of God to be the judge of all—the living and the dead. ⁴³He is the one all the prophets testified about, saying that everyone who believes in him will have their sins forgiven through his name."

⁴⁴Even as Peter was saying these things, the Holy Spirit fell upon all who had heard the message. ⁴⁵The Jewish believers who came with Peter were amazed that the gift of the Holy Spirit had been poured out upon the Gentiles, too. ⁴⁶And there could be no doubt about it, for they heard them speaking in tongues and praising God.

Then Peter asked, ⁴⁷"Can anyone object to their being baptized, now that they have received the Holy Spirit just as we did?" ⁴⁸So he gave orders for them to be baptized in the name of Jesus Christ. Afterward Cornelius asked him to stay with them for several days.

CHAPTER 11

Soon the news reached the apostles and other believers* in Judea that the Gentiles had received the word of God. ²But when Peter arrived back in Jerusalem, some of the Jewish believers* criticized him. ³"You entered the home of Gentiles* and even ate with them!" they said.

⁴Then Peter told them exactly what had happened. ⁵"One day in Joppa," he said, "while I was praying, I went into a trance and saw a vision. Something like a large sheet was let down by its four corners from the sky. And it came right down to me. ⁶When I looked inside the sheet, I saw all sorts of small animals, wild animals, reptiles, and birds that are not allowed to eat. ⁷And I heard a voice say, 'Get up, Peter; kill and eat them.'

⁸"'Never, Lord,' I replied. 'I have never eaten anything forbidden by our Jewish laws.*'

⁹"But the voice from heaven came again, 'If God says something is acceptable, don't say it isn't.'*

¹⁰"This happened three times before the sheet and all it contained was pulled back up to heaven. ¹¹Just then three men who had been sent from Caesarea arrived at the house where I was staying. ¹²The Holy Spirit told me to go with them and not to worry about their being Gentiles. These six brothers here accompanied me, and we soon arrived at the home of the man who had sent for us. ¹³He told us how an angel had appeared to him in his home and had told him, 'Send messengers to Joppa to find Simon Peter. ¹⁴He will tell you how you and all your household will be saved!'

¹⁵"Well, I began telling them the Good News, but just as I was getting started, the Holy Spirit fell on them, just as he fell on us at the beginning. ¹⁶Then I thought of the Lord's words when he said, 'John baptized with* water, but you will be baptized with the Holy Spirit.' ¹⁷And since God gave these Gentiles the same gift he gave us when we believed in the Lord Jesus Christ, who was I to argue?"

¹⁸When the others heard this, all their objections were answered and they began praising God. They said, "God has also given the Gentiles the privilege of turning from sin and receiving eternal life."

¹⁹Meanwhile, the believers who had fled

10:41 Greek *the people.*   **11:1** Greek *brothers.*   **11:2** Greek *those of the circumcision.*   **11:3** Greek *of uncircumcised men.*   **11:8** Greek *anything common or unclean.*   **11:9** Greek *'What God calls clean you must not call unclean.'*   **11:16** Or *in;* also in 11:16b.

from Jerusalem during the persecution after Stephen's death traveled as far as Phoenicia, Cyprus, and Antioch of Syria. They preached the Good News, but only to Jews. [20]However, some of the believers who went to Antioch from Cyprus and Cyrene began preaching to Gentiles* about the Lord Jesus. [21]The power of the Lord was upon them, and large numbers of these Gentiles believed and turned to the Lord.

[22]When the church at Jerusalem heard what had happened, they sent Barnabas to Antioch. [23]When he arrived and saw this proof of God's favor, he was filled with joy, and he encouraged the believers to stay true to the Lord. [24]Barnabas was a good man, full of the Holy Spirit and strong in faith. And large numbers of people were brought to the Lord.

[25]Then Barnabas went on to Tarsus to find Saul. [26]When he found him, he brought him back to Antioch. Both of them stayed there with the church for a full year, teaching great numbers of people. (It was there at Antioch that the believers* were first called Christians.)

[27]During this time, some prophets traveled from Jerusalem to Antioch. [28]One of them named Agabus stood up in one of the meetings to predict by the Spirit that a great famine was coming upon the entire Roman world. (This was fulfilled during the reign of Claudius.) [29]So the believers in Antioch decided to send relief to the brothers and sisters in Judea, everyone giving as much as they could. [30]This they did, entrusting their gifts to Barnabas and Saul to take to the elders of the church in Jerusalem.

CHAPTER 12

About that time King Herod Agrippa* began to persecute some believers in the church. [2]He had the apostle James (John's brother) killed with a sword. [3]When Herod saw how much this pleased the Jewish leaders, he arrested Peter during the Passover celebration* [4]and imprisoned him, placing him under the guard of four squads of four soldiers each. Herod's intention was to bring Peter out for public trial after the Passover. [5]But while Peter was in prison, the church prayed very earnestly for him.

[6]The night before Peter was to be placed on trial, he was asleep, chained between two soldiers, with others standing guard at the prison gate. [7]Suddenly, there was a bright light in the cell, and an angel of the Lord stood before Peter. The angel tapped him on the side to awaken him and said, "Quick! Get up!" And the chains fell off his wrists. [8]Then the angel told him, "Get dressed and put on your sandals." And he did. "Now put on your coat and follow me," the angel ordered.

[9]So Peter left the cell, following the angel. But all the time he thought it was a vision. He didn't realize it was really happening. [10]They passed the first and second guard posts and came to the iron gate to the street, and this opened to them all by itself. So they passed through and started walking down the street, and then the angel suddenly left him.

[11]Peter finally realized what had happened. "It's really true!" he said to himself. "The Lord has sent his angel and saved me from Herod and from what the Jews were hoping to do to me!"

[12]After a little thought, he went to the home of Mary, the mother of John Mark, where many were gathered for prayer. [13]He knocked at the door in the gate, and a servant girl named Rhoda came to open it. [14]When she recognized Peter's voice, she was so overjoyed that, instead of opening the door, she ran back inside and told everyone, "Peter is standing at the door!"

[15]"You're out of your mind," they said. When she insisted, they decided, "It must be his angel."

[16]Meanwhile, Peter continued knocking. When they finally went out and opened the door, they were amazed. [17]He motioned for them to quiet down and told them what had happened and how the Lord had led him out of jail. "Tell James and the other brothers what happened," he said. And then he went to another place.

[18]At dawn, there was a great commotion among the soldiers about what had happened to Peter. [19]Herod Agrippa ordered a thorough search for him. When he couldn't be found, Herod interrogated the guards and sentenced them to death. Afterward Herod left Judea to stay in Caesarea for a while.

[20]Now Herod was very angry with the people of Tyre and Sidon. So they sent a

---

11:20 Greek *the Greeks;* other manuscripts read *the Hellenists.*   **11:26** Greek *disciples;* also in 11:29a.   **12:1** Greek *Herod the king.* He was the nephew of Herod Antipas and a grandson of Herod the Great.   **12:3** Greek *the days of unleavened bread.*

delegation to make peace with him because their cities were dependent upon Herod's country for their food. They made friends with Blastus, Herod's personal assistant, [21]and an appointment with Herod was granted. When the day arrived, Herod put on his royal robes, sat on his throne, and made a speech to them. [22]The people gave him a great ovation, shouting, "It is the voice of a god, not of a man!"

[23]Instantly, an angel of the Lord struck Herod with a sickness, because he accepted the people's worship instead of giving the glory to God. So he was consumed with worms and died.

[24]But God's Good News was spreading rapidly, and there were many new believers.

[25]When Barnabas and Saul had finished their mission in Jerusalem, they returned to Antioch, taking John Mark with them.

NOVEMBER 5 □ DAY 310
ACTS 13–15
Paul's First Journey

 OVERVIEW Beginning with chapter 13, Syrian Antioch replaces Jerusalem as the missionary headquarters of the church. While five men are ministering in the church at Antioch, the Holy Spirit selects two to spearhead phase three of the gospel advance, this time "to the ends of the earth" (1:8). Paul and Barnabas leave for Cyprus, making stops in Antioch, Iconium, Lystra, and Derbe before returning home to Jerusalem. There they find that their success in making Gentile converts has caused a major dispute among Jewish believers, prompting an all-church council to settle the matter.

Chapter 13	Chapter 14	Chapter 15
Commission of Paul and Barnabas	Mission to Lystra and Derbe	Circumcision in Question
First Missionary Journey		First Church Council

 YOUR DAILY WALK Ask ten Christians, "Who is the greatest missionary in the New Testament apart from Jesus Christ?" and chances are at least nine will answer without hesitation, "The apostle Paul!"

The more we know the mind of Christ, the more missionary-minded we become.

But did you ever stop to consider that missionaries today face even greater challenges than Paul did in his day? For example:

Paul did not need to learn a foreign language. Every part of the known world spoke the same universal language—Greek.

Paul did not need to adjust to a foreign culture. Rome ruled the known world, providing the same rights and privileges for Roman citizens worldwide. A little bit of Rome awaited Paul everywhere he went. Not so for today's overseas missionaries!

Repeatedly in his letters, Paul asked for prayer as he traveled and ministered (see Colossians 4:3 and 1 Thessalonians 5:25, for example). Don't your missionaries today deserve the same? Locate a picture of a missionary family you or your church supports, and place it in a prominent place at your home or office. Then make Philippians 1:3-4 your daily discipline in prayer on their behalf!

INSIGHT A Preview of Paul's Travels

Journey	Length	Locale	Personnel
#1	2 years	Galatia	Paul and Barnabas
#2	3 years	Macedonia/Achaia	Paul and Silas
#3	4 years	Asia Minor	Paul and others

CHAPTER 13

Among the prophets and teachers of the church at Antioch of Syria were Barnabas, Simeon (called "the black man"*), Lucius (from Cyrene), Manaen (the childhood companion of King Herod Antipas*), and Saul. ²One day as these men were worshiping the Lord and fasting, the Holy Spirit said, "Dedicate Barnabas and Saul for the special work I have for them." ³So after more fasting and prayer, the men laid their hands on them and sent them on their way.

⁴Sent out by the Holy Spirit, Saul and Barnabas went down to the seaport of Seleucia and then sailed for the island of Cyprus. ⁵There, in the town of Salamis, they went to the Jewish synagogues and preached the word of God. (John Mark went with them as their assistant.)

⁶Afterward they preached from town to town across the entire island until finally they reached Paphos, where they met a Jewish sorcerer, a false prophet named Bar-Jesus. ⁷He had attached himself to the governor, Sergius Paulus, a man of considerable insight and understanding. The governor invited Barnabas and Saul to visit him, for he wanted to hear the word of God. ⁸But Elymas, the sorcerer (as his name means in Greek), interfered and urged the governor to pay no attention to what Saul and Barnabas said. He was trying to turn the governor away from the Christian faith.

⁹Then Saul, also known as Paul, filled with the Holy Spirit, looked the sorcerer in the eye and said, ¹⁰"You son of the Devil, full of every sort of trickery and villainy, enemy of all that is good, will you never stop perverting the true ways of the Lord? ¹¹And now the Lord has laid his hand of punishment upon you, and you will be stricken awhile with blindness." Instantly mist and darkness fell upon him, and he began wandering around begging for someone to take his hand and lead him. ¹²When the governor saw what had hap-

pened, he believed and was astonished at what he learned about the Lord.

¹³Now Paul and those with him left Paphos by ship for Pamphylia,* landing at the port town of Perga. There John Mark left them and returned to Jerusalem. ¹⁴But Barnabas and Paul traveled inland to Antioch of Pisidia.*

On the Sabbath they went to the synagogue for the services. ¹⁵After the usual readings from the books of Moses and from the Prophets, those in charge of the service sent them this message: "Brothers, if you have any word of encouragement for us, come and give it!"

¹⁶So Paul stood, lifted his hand to quiet them, and started speaking. "People of Israel," he said, "and you devout Gentiles who fear the God of Israel, listen to me.

¹⁷"The God of this nation of Israel chose our ancestors and made them prosper in Egypt. Then he powerfully led them out of their slavery. ¹⁸He put up with them* through forty years of wandering around in the wilderness. ¹⁹Then he destroyed seven nations in Canaan and gave their land to Israel as an inheritance. ²⁰All this took about 450 years. After that, judges ruled until the time of Samuel the prophet. ²¹Then the people begged for a king, and God gave them Saul son of Kish, a man of the tribe of Benjamin, who reigned for forty years. ²²But God removed him from the kingship and replaced him with David, a man about whom God said, 'David son of Jesse is a man after my own heart, for he will do everything I want him to.'*

²³"And it is one of King David's descendants, Jesus, who is God's promised Savior of Israel! ²⁴But before he came, John the Baptist preached the need for everyone in Israel to turn from sin and turn to God and be baptized. ²⁵As John was finishing his ministry he asked, 'Do you think I am the Messiah? No! But he is coming soon—and I am not even worthy to be his slave.'*

²⁶"Brothers—you sons of Abraham, and also all of you devout Gentiles who fear the

---

13:1a Greek *who was called Niger.*   **13:1b** Greek *Herod the tetrarch.*   **13:13-14** *Pamphylia* and *Pisidia* were districts in the land now called Turkey.   **13:18** Other manuscripts read *He cared for them;* compare Deut 1:31.   **13:22** 1 Sam 13:14.   **13:25** Greek *to untie his sandals.*

God of Israel—this salvation is for us! [27] The people in Jerusalem and their leaders fulfilled prophecy by condemning Jesus to death. They didn't recognize him or realize that he is the one the prophets had written about, though they hear the prophets' words read every Sabbath. [28] They found no just cause to execute him, but they asked Pilate to have him killed anyway.

[29] "When they had fulfilled all the prophecies concerning his death, they took him down from the cross and placed him in a tomb. [30] But God raised him from the dead! [31] And he appeared over a period of many days to those who had gone with him from Galilee to Jerusalem—these are his witnesses to the people of Israel.

[32] "And now Barnabas and I are here to bring you this Good News. God's promise to our ancestors has come true in our own time, [33] in that God raised Jesus. This is what the second psalm is talking about when it says concerning Jesus,

'You are my Son.
    Today I have become your Father.*'

[34] For God had promised to raise him from the dead, never again to die. This is stated in the Scripture that says, 'I will give you the sacred blessings I promised to David.'* [35] Another psalm explains more fully, saying, 'You will not allow your Holy One to rot in the grave.'* [36] Now this is not a reference to David, for after David had served his generation according to the will of God, he died and was buried, and his body decayed. [37] No, it was a reference to someone else—someone whom God raised and whose body did not decay.

[38] "Brothers, listen! In this man Jesus there is forgiveness for your sins. [39] Everyone who believes in him is freed from all guilt and declared right with God—something the Jewish law could never do. [40] Be careful! Don't let the prophets' words apply to you. For they said,

[41] 'Look you mockers,
    be amazed and die!
For I am doing something in your own day,
    something you wouldn't believe
    even if someone told you about it.*'

[42] As Paul and Barnabas left the synagogue that day, the people asked them to return again and speak about these things the next week. [43] Many Jews and godly converts to Judaism who worshiped at the synagogue followed Paul and Barnabas, and the two men urged them, "By God's grace, remain faithful."

[44] The following week almost the entire city turned out to hear them preach the word of the Lord. [45] But when the Jewish leaders saw the crowds, they were jealous; so they slandered Paul and argued against whatever he said.

[46] Then Paul and Barnabas spoke out boldly and declared, "It was necessary that this Good News from God be given first to you Jews. But since you have rejected it and judged yourselves unworthy of eternal life—well, we will offer it to Gentiles. [47] For this is as the Lord commanded us when he said,

'I have made you a light to the Gentiles,
    to bring salvation to the farthest
        corners of the earth.'*"

[48] When the Gentiles heard this, they were very glad and thanked the Lord for his message; and all who were appointed to eternal life became believers. [49] So the Lord's message spread throughout that region.

[50] Then the Jewish leaders stirred up both the influential religious women and the leaders of the city, and they incited a mob against Paul and Barnabas and ran them out of town. [51] But they shook off the dust of their feet against them and went to the city of Iconium. [52] And the believers* were filled with joy and with the Holy Spirit.

CHAPTER 14

In Iconium,* Paul and Barnabas went together to the synagogue and preached with such power that a great number of both Jews and Gentiles believed. [2] But the Jews who spurned God's message stirred up distrust among the Gentiles against Paul and Barnabas, saying all sorts of evil things about them. [3] The apostles stayed there a long time, preaching boldly about the grace of the Lord. The Lord proved their message was true by giving them power to do miraculous signs and wonders. [4] But the people of the city were divided in their opinion about them. Some sided with the Jews, and some with the apostles.

13:33 Or *Today I reveal you as my Son.* Ps 2:7.   **13:34** Isa 55:3.   **13:35** Ps 16:10.   **13:41** Hab 1:5.   **13:47** Isa 49:6.   **13:52** Greek *the disciples.*   **14:1** *Iconium,* as well as *Lystra* and *Derbe* (14:6), were cities in the land now called Turkey.

⁵A mob of Gentiles and Jews, along with their leaders, decided to attack and stone them. ⁶When the apostles learned of it, they fled for their lives. They went to the region of Lycaonia, to the cities of Lystra and Derbe and the surrounding area, ⁷and they preached the Good News there.

⁸While they were at Lystra, Paul and Barnabas came upon a man with crippled feet. He had been that way from birth, so he had never walked. ⁹He was listening as Paul preached, and Paul noticed him and realized he had faith to be healed. ¹⁰So Paul called to him in a loud voice, "Stand up!" And the man jumped to his feet and started walking.

¹¹When the listening crowd saw what Paul had done, they shouted in their local dialect, "These men are gods in human bodies!" ¹²They decided that Barnabas was the Greek god Zeus and that Paul, because he was the chief speaker, was Hermes. ¹³The temple of Zeus was located on the outskirts of the city. The priest of the temple and the crowd brought oxen and wreaths of flowers, and they prepared to sacrifice to the apostles at the city gates.

¹⁴But when Barnabas and Paul heard what was happening, they tore their clothing in dismay and ran out among the people, shouting, ¹⁵"Friends,* why are you doing this? We are merely human beings like yourselves! We have come to bring you the Good News that you should turn from these worthless things to the living God, who made heaven and earth, the sea, and everything in them. ¹⁶In earlier days he permitted all the nations to go their own ways, ¹⁷but he never left himself without a witness. There were always his reminders, such as sending you rain and good crops and giving you food and joyful hearts." ¹⁸But even so, Paul and Barnabas could scarcely restrain the people from sacrificing to them.

¹⁹Now some Jews arrived from Antioch and Iconium and turned the crowds into a murderous mob. They stoned Paul and dragged him out of the city, apparently dead. ²⁰But as the believers* stood around him, he got up and went back into the city. The next day he left with Barnabas for Derbe.

²¹After preaching the Good News in Derbe and making many disciples, Paul and Barnabas returned again to Lystra, Iconium, and Antioch of Pisidia, ²²where they strengthened the believers. They encouraged them to continue in the faith, reminding them that they must enter into the Kingdom of God through many tribulations. ²³Paul and Barnabas also appointed elders in every church and prayed for them with fasting, turning them over to the care of the Lord, in whom they had come to trust. ²⁴Then they traveled back through Pisidia to Pamphylia. ²⁵They preached again in Perga, then went on to Attalia.

²⁶Finally, they returned by ship to Antioch of Syria, where their journey had begun and where they had been committed to the grace of God for the work they had now completed. ²⁷Upon arriving in Antioch, they called the church together and reported about their trip, telling all that God had done and how he had opened the door of faith to the Gentiles, too. ²⁸And they stayed there with the believers in Antioch for a long time.

CHAPTER 15

While Paul and Barnabas were at Antioch of Syria, some men from Judea arrived and began to teach the Christians*: "Unless you keep the ancient Jewish custom of circumcision taught by Moses, you cannot be saved." ²Paul and Barnabas, disagreeing with them, argued forcefully and at length. Finally, Paul and Barnabas were sent to Jerusalem, accompanied by some local believers, to talk to the apostles and elders about this question. ³The church sent the delegates to Jerusalem, and they stopped along the way in Phoenicia and Samaria to visit the believers.* They told them—much to everyone's joy—that the Gentiles, too, were being converted.

⁴When they arrived in Jerusalem, Paul and Barnabas were welcomed by the whole church, including the apostles and elders. They reported on what God had been doing through their ministry. ⁵But then some of the men who had been Pharisees before their conversion stood up and declared that all Gentile converts must be circumcised and be required to follow the law of Moses.

14:15 Greek *Men.* **14:20** Greek *disciples;* also in 14:22, 28. **15:1** Greek *brothers;* also in 15:32, 33. **15:3** Greek *brothers;* also in 15:23, 36, 40.

[6]So the apostles and church elders got together to decide this question. [7]At the meeting, after a long discussion, Peter stood and addressed them as follows: "Brothers, you all know that God chose me from among you some time ago to preach to the Gentiles so that they could hear the Good News and believe. [8]God, who knows people's hearts, confirmed that he accepts Gentiles by giving them the Holy Spirit, just as he gave him to us. [9]He made no distinction between us and them, for he also cleansed their hearts through faith. [10]Why are you now questioning God's way by burdening the Gentile believers* with a yoke that neither we nor our ancestors were able to bear? [11]We believe that we are all saved the same way, by the special favor of the Lord Jesus."

[12]There was no further discussion, and everyone listened as Barnabas and Paul told about the miraculous signs and wonders God had done through them among the Gentiles.

[13]When they had finished, James stood and said, "Brothers, listen to me. [14]Peter* has told you about the time God first visited the Gentiles to take from them a people for himself. [15]And this conversion of Gentiles agrees with what the prophets predicted. For instance, it is written:

[16] 'Afterward I will return,
       and I will restore the fallen kingdom
         of David.
    From the ruins I will rebuild it,
       and I will restore it,
[17] so that the rest of humanity might find
       the Lord,
    including the Gentiles—
       all those I have called to be mine.
    This is what the Lord says,
[18]   he who made these things known
       long ago.'*

[19]And so my judgment is that we should stop troubling the Gentiles who turn to God, [20]except that we should write to them and tell them to abstain from eating meat sacrificed to idols, from sexual immorality, and from consuming blood or eating the meat of strangled animals. [21]For these laws of Moses have been preached in Jewish synagogues in every city on every Sabbath for many generations."

[22]Then the apostles and elders and the whole church in Jerusalem chose delegates, and they sent them to Antioch of Syria with Paul and Barnabas to report on this decision. The men chosen were two of the church leaders*—Judas (also called Barsabbas) and Silas. [23]This is the letter they took along with them:

"This letter is from the apostles and elders, your brothers in Jerusalem. It is written to the Gentile believers in Antioch, Syria, and Cilicia. Greetings!

[24]"We understand that some men from here have troubled you and upset you with their teaching, but they had no such instructions from us. [25]So it seemed good to us, having unanimously agreed on our decision, to send you these official representatives, along with our beloved Barnabas and Paul, [26]who have risked their lives for the sake of our Lord Jesus Christ. [27]So we are sending Judas and Silas to tell you what we have decided concerning your question.

[28]"For it seemed good to the Holy Spirit and to us to lay no greater burden on you than these requirements: [29]You must abstain from eating food offered to idols, from consuming blood or eating the meat of strangled animals, and from sexual immorality. If you do this, you will do well. Farewell."

[30]The four messengers went at once to Antioch, where they called a general meeting of the Christians and delivered the letter. [31]And there was great joy throughout the church that day as they read this encouraging message.

[32]Then Judas and Silas, both being prophets, spoke extensively to the Christians, encouraging and strengthening their faith. [33]They stayed for a while, and then Judas and Silas were sent back to Jerusalem, with the blessings of the Christians, to those who had sent them.* [35]Paul and Barnabas stayed in Antioch to assist many others who were teaching and preaching the word of the Lord there.

[36]After some time Paul said to Barnabas, "Let's return to each city where we previously preached the word of the Lord, to see how the new believers are getting along." [37]Barnabas agreed and wanted to take along John Mark. [38]But

15:10 Greek *disciples*.   15:14 Greek *Simon*.   15:16-18 Amos 9:11-12; Isa 45:21.   15:22 Greek *were leaders among the brothers*.
15:33 Some manuscripts add verse 34, *But Silas decided to stay there*.

Paul disagreed strongly, since John Mark had deserted them in Pamphylia and had not shared in their work. [39] Their disagreement over this was so sharp that they separated. Barnabas took John Mark with him and sailed for Cyprus. [40]Paul chose Silas, and the believers sent them off, entrusting them to the Lord's grace. [41]So they traveled throughout Syria and Cilicia to strengthen the churches there.

NOVEMBER 6 ☐ DAY 311
ACTS 16–18
Paul's Second Journey

OVERVIEW John Mark, Barnabas's cousin and a traveling companion for part of the first journey, becomes the focus of a sharp dispute between Paul and Barnabas. As a result, the two veteran missionaries part company. Barnabas stays with Mark and sails for Cyprus. Paul, accompanied by Silas and Timothy, travels more than three thousand miles, planting and building up churches in Macedonia, Achaia, and Greece.

Chapter 16	Chapter 17	Chapter 18
Entrance to Europe	Trouble in Thessalonica	Co-laborers in Corinth
Paul's Second Missionary Journey		

YOUR DAILY WALK Disagreements in the church are nothing new. Even Paul and Barnabas had a falling-out! But we can learn much from the way they wisely resolved their conflict.

Force may subdue, but love gains; and the person that forgives first wins the laurel.

The reason for their sharp disagreement was John Mark, who had left the team midway through the first journey. Barnabas (whose name means "son of encouragement") was concerned primarily for the *worker* and wanted to give his cousin a second chance. Paul, on the other hand, was more concerned about the *work*, not wanting to lose the momentum of the first journey through another desertion. In the end they parted company to form two gospel teams instead of one. The impact of Paul's second journey is well documented in today's section. And in Colossians 4:10 and 2 Timothy 4:11, Paul himself warmly notes John Mark's contribution to his ministry.

Being reconciled does not always mean holding the same view. Sometimes it can mean agreeing to disagree in a spirit of love and humility. Are you having a disagreement today? Take the first step toward reconciling it by assuring the other person, "I accept you as you are; let's support one another as we labor for God's glory."

INSIGHT Called by a Man, Confronted by a Woman
In his vision Paul saw a "man from Macedonia" (16:9) pleading with him to come to Europe with the message of Good News. But when Paul arrived in Philippi, there were no God-fearing men to be found. Undaunted, Paul began working instead with women. Result: The first Macedonian convert to Christianity was not a man at all! (Can you find her name in today's section?)

CHAPTER 16

Paul and Silas went first to Derbe and then on to Lystra. There they met Timothy, a young disciple whose mother was a Jewish believer, but whose father was a Greek. [2]Timothy was well thought of by the believers* in Lystra and Iconium, [3]so Paul wanted him to join them on their journey. In deference to the Jews of the area, he arranged for Timothy to be circumcised before they left, for everyone knew that his father was a Greek. [4]Then they went from town to town, explaining the decision regarding the commandments that were to be obeyed, as decided by the apostles and elders in Jerusalem. [5]So the churches were strengthened in their faith and grew daily in numbers.

[6]Next Paul and Silas traveled through the area of Phrygia and Galatia, because the Holy Spirit had told them not to go into the province of Asia at that time. [7]Then coming to the borders of Mysia, they headed for the province of Bithynia,* but again the Spirit of Jesus did not let them go. [8]So instead, they went on through Mysia to the city of Troas.

[9]That night Paul had a vision. He saw a man from Macedonia in northern Greece, pleading with him, "Come over here and help us." [10]So we* decided to leave for Macedonia at once, for we could only conclude that God was calling us to preach the Good News there.

[11]We boarded a boat at Troas and sailed straight across to the island of Samothrace, and the next day we landed at Neapolis. [12]From there we reached Philippi, a major city of the district of Macedonia and a Roman colony; we stayed there several days.

[13]On the Sabbath we went a little way outside the city to a riverbank, where we supposed that some people met for prayer, and we sat down to speak with some women who had come together. [14]One of them was Lydia from Thyatira, a merchant of expensive purple cloth. She was a worshiper of God. As she listened to us, the Lord opened her heart, and she accepted what Paul was saying. [15]She was baptized along with other members of her household, and she asked us to be her guests. "If you agree that I am faithful to the Lord," she said, "come and stay at my home." And she urged us until we did.

[16]One day as we were going down to the place of prayer, we met a demon-possessed slave girl. She was a fortune-teller who earned a lot of money for her masters. [17]She followed along behind us shouting, "These men are servants of the Most High God, and they have come to tell you how to be saved."

[18]This went on day after day until Paul got so exasperated that he turned and spoke to the demon within her. "I command you in the name of Jesus Christ to come out of her," he said. And instantly it left her.

[19]Her masters' hopes of wealth were now shattered, so they grabbed Paul and Silas and dragged them before the authorities at the marketplace. [20]"The whole city is in an uproar because of these Jews!" they shouted. [21]"They are teaching the people to do things that are against Roman customs."

[22]A mob quickly formed against Paul and Silas, and the city officials ordered them stripped and beaten with wooden rods. [23]They were severely beaten, and then they were thrown into prison. The jailer was ordered to make sure they didn't escape. [24]So he took no chances but put them into the inner dungeon and clamped their feet in the stocks.

[25]Around midnight, Paul and Silas were praying and singing hymns to God, and the other prisoners were listening. [26]Suddenly, there was a great earthquake, and the prison was shaken to its foundations. All the doors flew open, and the chains of every prisoner fell off! [27]The jailer woke up to see the prison doors wide open. He assumed the prisoners had escaped, so he drew his sword to kill himself. [28]But Paul shouted to him, "Don't do it! We are all here!"

[29]Trembling with fear, the jailer called for lights and ran to the dungeon and fell down before Paul and Silas. [30]He brought them out and asked, "Sirs, what must I do to be saved?"

[31]They replied, "Believe on the Lord Jesus and you will be saved, along with your entire household." [32]Then they shared the word of the Lord with him and all who lived in his household. [33]That same hour the jailer washed their wounds, and he and everyone in his household were

16:2 Greek brothers; also in 16:40.   16:6-7 Phrygia, Galatia, Asia, Mysia, and Bithynia were all districts in the land now called Turkey. 16:10 Luke, the writer of this book, here joined Paul and accompanied him on his journey.

immediately baptized. [34]Then he brought them into his house and set a meal before them. He and his entire household rejoiced because they all believed in God.

[35]The next morning the city officials sent the police to tell the jailer, "Let those men go!" [36]So the jailer told Paul, "You and Silas are free to leave. Go in peace."

[37]But Paul replied, "They have publicly beaten us without trial and jailed us—and we are Roman citizens. So now they want us to leave secretly? Certainly not! Let them come themselves to release us!"

[38]When the police made their report, the city officials were alarmed to learn that Paul and Silas were Roman citizens. [39]They came to the jail and apologized to them. Then they brought them out and begged them to leave the city. [40]Paul and Silas then returned to the home of Lydia, where they met with the believers and encouraged them once more before leaving town.

CHAPTER 17
Now Paul and Silas traveled through the towns of Amphipolis and Apollonia and came to Thessalonica, where there was a Jewish synagogue. [2]As was Paul's custom, he went to the synagogue service, and for three Sabbaths in a row he interpreted the Scriptures to the people. [3]He was explaining and proving the prophecies about the sufferings of the Messiah and his rising from the dead. He said, "This Jesus I'm telling you about is the Messiah." [4]Some who listened were persuaded and became converts, including a large number of godly Greek men and also many important women of the city.*

[5]But the Jewish leaders were jealous, so they gathered some worthless fellows from the streets to form a mob and start a riot. They attacked the home of Jason, searching for Paul and Silas so they could drag them out to the crowd.* [6]Not finding them there, they dragged out Jason and some of the other believers* instead and took them before the city council. "Paul and Silas have turned the rest of the world upside down, and now they are here disturbing our city," they shouted. [7]"And Jason has let them into his home. They are all guilty of treason against Caesar, for they profess allegiance to another king, Jesus."

[8]The people of the city, as well as the city officials, were thrown into turmoil by these reports. [9]But the officials released Jason and the other believers after they had posted bail.

[10]That very night the believers sent Paul and Silas to Berea. When they arrived there, they went to the synagogue. [11]And the people of Berea were more open-minded than those in Thessalonica, and they listened eagerly to Paul's message. They searched the Scriptures day after day to check up on Paul and Silas, to see if they were really teaching the truth. [12]As a result, many Jews believed, as did some of the prominent Greek women and many men.

[13]But when some Jews in Thessalonica learned that Paul was preaching the word of God in Berea, they went there and stirred up trouble. [14]The believers acted at once, sending Paul on to the coast, while Silas and Timothy remained behind. [15]Those escorting Paul went with him to Athens; then they returned to Berea with a message for Silas and Timothy to hurry and join him.

[16]While Paul was waiting for them in Athens, he was deeply troubled by all the idols he saw everywhere in the city. [17]He went to the synagogue to debate with the Jews and the God-fearing Gentiles, and he spoke daily in the public square to all who happened to be there.

[18]He also had a debate with some of the Epicurean and Stoic philosophers. When he told them about Jesus and his resurrection, they said, "This babbler has picked up some strange ideas." Others said, "He's pushing some foreign religion."

[19]Then they took him to the Council of Philosophers.* "Come and tell us more about this new religion," they said. [20]"You are saying some rather startling things, and we want to know what it's all about." [21](It should be explained that all the Athenians as well as the foreigners in Athens seemed to spend all their time discussing the latest ideas.)

[22]So Paul, standing before the Council,* addressed them as follows: "Men of Athens, I notice that you are very religious, [23]for as I was walking along I saw your many altars. And one of them had this inscription on it—'To an Unknown God.' You have been worshiping him without knowing who he is, and now I wish to tell you about him.

17:4 Some manuscripts read *many of the wives of the leading men.*   17:5 Or *the city council.*   17:6 Greek *brothers;* also in 17:10, 14. 17:19 Greek *the Areopagus.*   17:22 Or *in the middle of Mars Hill;* Greek reads *in the middle of the Areopagus.*

²⁴"He is the God who made the world and everything in it. Since he is Lord of heaven and earth, he doesn't live in man-made temples, ²⁵and human hands can't serve his needs—for he has no needs. He himself gives life and breath to everything, and he satisfies every need there is. ²⁶From one man he created all the nations throughout the whole earth. He decided beforehand which should rise and fall, and he determined their boundaries.

²⁷"His purpose in all of this was that the nations should seek after God and perhaps feel their way toward him and find him—though he is not far from any one of us. ²⁸For in him we live and move and exist. As one of your own poets says, 'We are his offspring.' ²⁹And since this is true, we shouldn't think of God as an idol designed by craftsmen from gold or silver or stone. ³⁰God overlooked people's former ignorance about these things, but now he commands everyone everywhere to turn away from idols and turn to him.* ³¹For he has set a day for judging the world with justice by the man he has appointed, and he proved to everyone who this is by raising him from the dead."

³²When they heard Paul speak of the resurrection of a person who had been dead, some laughed, but others said, "We want to hear more about this later." ³³That ended Paul's discussion with them, ³⁴but some joined him and became believers. Among them were Dionysius, a member of the Council,* a woman named Damaris, and others.

CHAPTER 18

Then Paul left Athens and went to Corinth.* ²There he became acquainted with a Jew named Aquila, born in Pontus, who had recently arrived from Italy with his wife, Priscilla. They had been expelled from Italy as a result of Claudius Caesar's order to deport all Jews from Rome. ³Paul lived and worked with them, for they were tentmakers* just as he was.

⁴Each Sabbath found Paul at the synagogue, trying to convince the Jews and Greeks alike. ⁵And after Silas and Timothy came down from Macedonia, Paul spent his full time preaching and testifying to the Jews, telling them, "The Messiah you are

looking for is Jesus." ⁶But when the Jews opposed him and insulted him, Paul shook the dust from his robe and said, "Your blood be upon your own heads—I am innocent. From now on I will go to the Gentiles."

⁷After that he stayed with Titius Justus, a Gentile who worshiped God and lived next door to the synagogue. ⁸Crispus, the leader of the synagogue, and all his household believed in the Lord. Many others in Corinth also became believers and were baptized.

⁹One night the Lord spoke to Paul in a vision and told him, "Don't be afraid! Speak out! Don't be silent! ¹⁰For I am with you, and no one will harm you because many people here in this city belong to me." ¹¹So Paul stayed there for the next year and a half, teaching the word of God.

¹²But when Gallio became governor of Achaia, some Jews rose in concerted action against Paul and brought him before the governor for judgment. ¹³They accused Paul of "persuading people to worship God in ways that are contrary to the law." ¹⁴But just as Paul started to make his defense, Gallio turned to Paul's accusers and said, "Listen, you Jews, if this were a case involving some wrongdoing or a serious crime, I would be obliged to listen to you. ¹⁵But since it is merely a question of words and names and your Jewish laws, you take care of it. I refuse to judge such matters." ¹⁶And he drove them out of the courtroom. ¹⁷The mob had grabbed Sosthenes, the leader of the synagogue, and had beaten him right there in the courtroom. But Gallio paid no attention.

¹⁸Paul stayed in Corinth for some time after that and then said good-bye to the brothers and sisters and sailed for the coast of Syria, taking Priscilla and Aquila with him. (Earlier, at Cenchrea, Paul had shaved his head according to Jewish custom, for he had taken a vow.) ¹⁹When they arrived at the port of Ephesus, Paul left the others behind. But while he was there, he went to the synagogue to debate with the Jews. ²⁰They asked him to stay longer, but he declined. ²¹So he left, saying, "I will come back later,* God willing." Then he set sail from Ephesus. ²²The next stop was at the port of Caesarea. From there he went up

17:30 Greek *everywhere to repent.*   17:34 Greek *an Areopagite.*   18:1 *Athens* and *Corinth* were major cities in Achaia, the region on the southern end of the Greek peninsula.   18:3 Or *leatherworkers.*   18:21 Some manuscripts read *"I must by all means be at Jerusalem for the upcoming festival, but I will come back later."*

and visited the church at Jerusalem* and then went back to Antioch.

²³After spending some time in Antioch, Paul went back to Galatia and Phrygia, visiting all the believers,* encouraging them and helping them to grow in the Lord.

²⁴Meanwhile, a Jew named Apollos, an eloquent speaker who knew the Scriptures well, had just arrived in Ephesus from Alexandria in Egypt. ²⁵He had been taught the way of the Lord and talked to others with great enthusiasm and accuracy about Jesus. However, he knew only about John's baptism. ²⁶When Priscilla and Aquila heard him preaching boldly in the synagogue, they took him aside and explained the way of God more accurately.

²⁷Apollos had been thinking about going to Achaia, and the brothers and sisters in Ephesus encouraged him in this. They wrote to the believers in Achaia, asking them to welcome him. When he arrived there, he proved to be of great benefit to those who, by God's grace, had believed. ²⁸He refuted all the Jews with powerful arguments in public debate. Using the Scriptures, he explained to them, "The Messiah you are looking for is Jesus."

18:22 Greek *the church.*   **18:23** Greek *disciples*; also in 18:27.

NOVEMBER 7 □ DAY 312
Seeing and Hearing Is Believing

 LOOK BACK Jesus' *miracles* were designed to validate his *message.* When he said, "I am the resurrection and the life" (John 11:25), he meant it! And to validate his claim that he was the source of life, he raised Lazarus from the grave.

John's account of the death, burial, and resurrection of Jesus is poignant and personal, as befitting the one who was nicknamed the disciple whom "Jesus loved" (John 13:23). The final chapter of John's Gospel tells of a breakfast meeting between Jesus and seven of his disciples. They came to that encounter discouraged and ready to quit; they left fortified with courage to follow their Lord even unto death.

The book of Acts continues the story of Jesus' followers as they go forth in the power of the Spirit to broadcast the news about their risen Leader and Lord. First in Jerusalem, then in Judea and Samaria, and finally to the farthest corners of the known world, the New Testament church carries out its marching orders in spite of persecution from without and problems from within.

 LOOK UP Two cars collide in the intersection in front of you. From the safety of your own car, you see the entire drama unfold. Now answer the following questions:

Do not expect God to use you as a lighthouse somewhere else if God cannot use you as a candle right where you are.

1. Are you a witness to the accident?
2. If yes, why are you a witness?
3. What did you have to do to become a witness?
4. How sure are you that you are a witness?
5. Would you know what to say if called to the witness stand?
6. And what would that be?

Being a witness for your Lord is no different. Only those who have seen and heard something firsthand about Jesus Christ are eligible to be his witnesses. "We saw him with our own eyes and touched him with our own hands. He is Jesus Christ, the Word of life. . . . We are telling you about what we ourselves have actually seen and heard, so that you may have fellowship with us" (1 John 1:1, 3). If you have seen the miracle of new birth in your own life, then you are a candidate to be a witness for your Lord.

LOOK AHEAD The book of Acts is the exciting account of men and women who bore testimony of the truth they had experienced first-hand. Most of them were not trained preachers or educated philosophers. They were simple people whose lives had been simply touched and transformed for eternity!

After they met Jesus in a life-changing way, he told them to "go and tell." And so, they went and told. And everywhere they went, the power of God was evident. They testified as much by the quality of their lives as by the testimony of their lips.

It's the same today. People all around you may never visit a church or tune in to a Christian radio or television program. But they will listen to the gospel according to you—in your office . . . your home . . . your neighborhood . . . your school. Why? Because they know you, and they can see with their own eyes and hear with their own ears the difference Jesus has made in your life. They've seen the difference; now they need to know what (or rather, who) has made the difference.

Well, what do you say, witness?

NOVEMBER 8 □ DAY 313
ACTS 19–20
Paul's Third Journey

 OVERVIEW Turn back to Acts 18:23 to pick up the beginning of Paul's third journey—an expedition that takes him throughout the province of Asia, where he visits churches founded on previous trips. The church at Ephesus hosts Paul for nearly three years, while he conducts a ministry so successful that "people throughtout the province of Asia—both Jews and Greeks—heard the Lord's message" (19:10). Leaving Ephesus, Paul visits churches in Macedonia and Achaia before setting sail for Jerusalem and an uncertain future.

Chapter 19		Chapter 20	
Persuasion at Ephesus	Persecution at Ephesus	Travels to Greece	Testimonial to Ephesians
1 22	23 41	1 16	17 38
Paul's Third Missionary Journey			

 YOUR DAILY WALK Put yourself in the following situation. You have just received word that an adult bookstore is opening next door to your house or apartment. What is your response? Are you indifferent or indignant? What action would you take?

Our sense of sin is in proportion to our nearness to God.

Paul was surrounded by sinful influences and corrupting pressures during his public ministry. Corinth was notorious for its immorality, Ephesus for its idolatry, Athens for its polytheism. And yet, through the power of the Holy Spirit, Paul was able to move among sinful people, making an impact on their lives for Jesus Christ. In Corinth and Ephesus he left behind growing young churches.

What impact is your life making on sinful people and sinful situations around you? Is your influence for God being felt? Make a list of three or four corrupting influences in your neighborhood that you would like to see changed. Select one item from your list, and make it the focus of your prayer time. Then write your mayor, city council member, or congressional representative, and tell him or her about your concern.

INSIGHT Standing Room Only in Ephesus
The Grand Theatre in Ephesus, site of the famous "pro-Artemis, anti-Paul rally," was a large outdoor amphitheater that seated more than twenty-five thousand people—all of whom screamed for two hours, "Great is Artemis of the Ephesians!" (19:34). The site still stands today near Selcuk, Turkey.

CHAPTER 19

While Apollos was in Corinth, Paul traveled through the interior provinces. Finally, he came to Ephesus, where he found several believers.* ²"Did you receive the Holy Spirit when you believed?" he asked them.

"No," they replied, "we don't know what you mean. We haven't even heard that there is a Holy Spirit."

³"Then what baptism did you experience?" he asked.

And they replied, "The baptism of John."

⁴Paul said, "John's baptism was to demonstrate a desire to turn from sin and turn to God. John himself told the people to believe in Jesus, the one John said would come later."

⁵As soon as they heard this, they were baptized in the name of the Lord Jesus. ⁶Then when Paul laid his hands on them, the Holy Spirit came on them, and they spoke in other tongues and prophesied. ⁷There were about twelve men in all.

⁸Then Paul went to the synagogue and preached boldly for the next three months, arguing persuasively about the Kingdom of God. ⁹But some rejected his message and publicly spoke against the Way, so Paul left the synagogue and took the believers with him. Then he began preaching daily at the lecture hall of Tyrannus. ¹⁰This went on for the next two years, so that people throughout the province of Asia—both Jews and Greeks—heard the Lord's message.

¹¹God gave Paul the power to do unusual miracles, ¹²so that even when handkerchiefs or cloths that had touched his skin were placed on sick people, they were healed of their diseases, and any evil spirits within them came out.

¹³A team of Jews who were traveling from town to town casting out evil spirits tried to use the name of the Lord Jesus. The incantation they used was this: "I command you by Jesus, whom Paul preaches, to come out!" ¹⁴Seven sons of Sceva, a leading priest, were doing this. ¹⁵But when they tried it on a man possessed by an evil spirit,

the spirit replied, "I know Jesus, and I know Paul. But who are you?" ¹⁶And he leaped on them and attacked them with such violence that they fled from the house, naked and badly injured.

¹⁷The story of what happened spread quickly all through Ephesus, to Jews and Greeks alike. A solemn fear descended on the city, and the name of the Lord Jesus was greatly honored. ¹⁸Many who became believers confessed their sinful practices. ¹⁹A number of them who had been practicing magic brought their incantation books and burned them at a public bonfire. The value of the books was several million dollars.* ²⁰So the message about the Lord spread widely and had a powerful effect.

²¹Afterward Paul felt impelled by the Holy Spirit* to go over to Macedonia and Achaia before returning to Jerusalem. "And after that," he said, "I must go on to Rome!" ²²He sent his two assistants, Timothy and Erastus, on ahead to Macedonia while he stayed awhile longer in the province of Asia.

²³But about that time, serious trouble developed in Ephesus concerning the Way. ²⁴It began with Demetrius, a silversmith who had a large business manufacturing silver shrines of the Greek goddess Artemis.* He kept many craftsmen busy. ²⁵He called the craftsmen together, along with others employed in related trades, and addressed them as follows:

"Gentlemen, you know that our wealth comes from this business. ²⁶As you have seen and heard, this man Paul has persuaded many people that handmade gods aren't gods at all. And this is happening not only here in Ephesus but throughout the entire province! ²⁷Of course, I'm not just talking about the loss of public respect for our business. I'm also concerned that the temple of the great goddess Artemis will lose its influence and that Artemis—this magnificent goddess worshiped throughout the province of Asia and all around the world—will be robbed of her prestige!"

19:1 Greek *disciples;* also in 19:9, 30. 19:19 Greek *50,000 pieces of silver,* each of which was the equivalent of a day's wage.
19:21 Or *purposed in his spirit.* 19:24 *Artemis* is otherwise known as Diana.

²⁸At this their anger boiled, and they began shouting, "Great is Artemis of the Ephesians!" ²⁹A crowd began to gather, and soon the city was filled with confusion. Everyone rushed to the amphitheater, dragging along Gaius and Aristarchus, who were Paul's traveling companions from Macedonia. ³⁰Paul wanted to go in, but the believers wouldn't let him. ³¹Some of the officials of the province, friends of Paul, also sent a message to him, begging him not to risk his life by entering the amphitheater.

³²Inside, the people were all shouting, some one thing and some another. Everything was in confusion. In fact, most of them didn't even know why they were there. ³³Alexander was thrust forward by some of the Jews, who encouraged him to explain the situation. He motioned for silence and tried to speak in defense. ³⁴But when the crowd realized he was a Jew, they started shouting again and kept it up for two hours: "Great is Artemis of the Ephesians! Great is Artemis of the Ephesians!"

³⁵At last the mayor was able to quiet them down enough to speak. "Citizens of Ephesus," he said. "Everyone knows that Ephesus is the official guardian of the temple of the great Artemis, whose image fell down to us from heaven. ³⁶Since this is an indisputable fact, you shouldn't be disturbed, no matter what is said. Don't do anything rash. ³⁷You have brought these men here, but they have stolen nothing from the temple and have not spoken against our goddess. ³⁸If Demetrius and the craftsmen have a case against them, the courts are in session and the judges can take the case at once. Let them go through legal channels. ³⁹And if there are complaints about other matters, they can be settled in a legal assembly. ⁴⁰I am afraid we are in danger of being charged with rioting by the Roman government, since there is no cause for all this commotion. And if Rome demands an explanation, we won't know what to say." ⁴¹Then he dismissed them, and they dispersed.

CHAPTER 20
When it was all over, Paul sent for the believers* and encouraged them. Then he said good-bye and left for Macedonia. ²Along the way, he encouraged the believ-

ers in all the towns he passed through. Then he traveled down to Greece, ³where he stayed for three months. He was preparing to sail back to Syria when he discovered a plot by some Jews against his life, so he decided to return through Macedonia.

⁴Several men were traveling with him. They were Sopater of Berea, the son of Pyrrhus; Aristarchus and Secundus, from Thessalonica; Gaius, from Derbe; Timothy; and Tychicus and Trophimus, who were from the province of Asia. ⁵They went ahead and waited for us at Troas. ⁶As soon as the Passover season* ended, we boarded a ship at Philippi in Macedonia and five days later arrived in Troas, where we stayed a week.

⁷On the first day of the week, we gathered to observe the Lord's Supper.* Paul was preaching; and since he was leaving the next day, he talked until midnight. ⁸The upstairs room where we met was lighted with many flickering lamps. ⁹As Paul spoke on and on, a young man named Eutychus, sitting on the windowsill, became very drowsy. Finally, he sank into a deep sleep and fell three stories to his death below. ¹⁰Paul went down, bent over him, and took him into his arms. "Don't worry," he said, "he's alive!" ¹¹Then they all went back upstairs and ate the Lord's Supper together.* And Paul continued talking to them until dawn; then he left. ¹²Meanwhile, the young man was taken home unhurt, and everyone was greatly relieved.

¹³Paul went by land to Assos, where he had arranged for us to join him, and we went on ahead by ship. ¹⁴He joined us there and we sailed together to Mitylene. ¹⁵The next day we passed the island of Kios. The following day, we crossed to the island of Samos. And a day later we arrived at Miletus.

¹⁶Paul had decided against stopping at Ephesus this time because he didn't want to spend further time in the province of Asia. He was hurrying to get to Jerusalem, if possible, for the Festival of Pentecost. ¹⁷But when we landed at Miletus, he sent a message to the elders of the church at Ephesus, asking them to come down to meet him.

¹⁸When they arrived he declared, "You know that from the day I set foot in the province of Asia until now ¹⁹I have done

20:1 Greek disciples.   20:6 Greek the days of unleavened bread.   20:7 Greek to break bread.   20:11 Greek broke the bread.

the Lord's work humbly—yes, and with tears. I have endured the trials that came to me from the plots of the Jews. ²⁰Yet I never shrank from telling you the truth, either publicly or in your homes. ²¹I have had one message for Jews and Gentiles alike—the necessity of turning from sin and turning to God, and of faith in our Lord Jesus.

²²"And now I am going to Jerusalem, drawn there irresistibly by the Holy Spirit,* not knowing what awaits me, ²³except that the Holy Spirit has told me in city after city that jail and suffering lie ahead. ²⁴But my life is worth nothing unless I use it for doing the work assigned me by the Lord Jesus—the work of telling others the Good News about God's wonderful kindness and love.

²⁵"And now I know that none of you to whom I have preached the Kingdom will ever see me again. ²⁶Let me say plainly that I have been faithful. No one's damnation can be blamed on me,* ²⁷for I didn't shrink from declaring all that God wants for you.

²⁸"And now beware! Be sure that you feed and shepherd God's flock—his church, purchased with his blood—over whom the Holy Spirit has appointed you as elders.* ²⁹I know full well that false

teachers, like vicious wolves, will come in among you after I leave, not sparing the flock. ³⁰Even some of you will distort the truth in order to draw a following. ³¹Watch out! Remember the three years I was with you—my constant watch and care over you night and day, and my many tears for you.

³²"And now I entrust you to God and the word of his grace—his message that is able to build you up and give you an inheritance with all those he has set apart for himself.

³³"I have never coveted anyone's money or fine clothing. ³⁴You know that these hands of mine have worked to pay my own way, and I have even supplied the needs of those who were with me. ³⁵And I have been a constant example of how you can help the poor by working hard. You should remember the words of the Lord Jesus: 'It is more blessed to give than to receive.'"

³⁶When he had finished speaking, he knelt and prayed with them. ³⁷They wept aloud as they embraced him in farewell, ³⁸sad most of all because he had said that they would never see him again. Then they accompanied him down to the ship.

20:22 Or *by my spirit, or by an inner compulsion.* Greek reads *by the spirit.*   **20:26** Greek *I am innocent of the blood of all.*   **20:28** Greek *overseers.*

NOVEMBER 9 □ DAY 314
ACTS 21–23
Paul's Arrest

 OVERVIEW Ominous signs accompany Paul's third missionary journey. A prophet named Agabus binds himself with Paul's belt, demonstrating the fate awaiting Paul in Jerusalem. True to the prophet's word, Paul's arrival sparks angry opposition and false accusations. Once before the crowd and again before the Sanhedrin, Paul attempts to defend himself. But after narrowly averting an assassination plot, he finds himself in prison, awaiting the opportunity to declare the gospel before governors, kings, and Caesar himself.

Chapter 21	Chapter 22	Chapter 23
Paul's Arrest	Paul's Accusers	Paul's Attempted Assassination
Jerusalem	Jews	Jeopardy

YOUR DAILY WALK "Timely advice is as lovely as golden apples in a silver basket" (Proverbs 25:11). That verse would provide a fitting title for Acts 21–28—chapters in which Paul speaks before many different audiences: mobs and councils, governors and kings, prisoners and sailors. In each case his speech is appropriate to the occasion: gracious praise for those in authority, terse commands to those on the ship, and courteous apology to the high priest.

People like not only to be loved but also to be told they are loved; the realm of silence is large enough beyond the grave.

Paul knew that words are easy to cast but difficult to reel in! Munch on an apple, and think about how you have been communicating with those around you lately. Have your words been golden apples or crab apples? List below "timely advice" that you can share this week with your

- boss or co-worker: _____
- parent or teacher: _____
- pastor or minister: _____
- spouse or friend: _____
- unsaved neighbor: _____

INSIGHT Tale of Two Journeys
A striking series of parallels can be drawn between the last journeys to Jerusalem of Paul and Jesus. The outcomes of both journeys were predicted in advance (21:10-11; Mark 10:33). Both men were bound by the Jews and delivered to the Gentiles. And both desired above all else that the will of God be done (21:14; Luke 22:42).

CHAPTER 21

After saying farewell to the Ephesian elders, we sailed straight to the island of Cos. The next day we reached Rhodes and then went to Patara. ²There we boarded a ship sailing for the Syrian province of Phoenicia. ³We sighted the island of Cyprus, passed it on our left, and landed at the harbor of Tyre, in Syria, where the ship was to unload. ⁴We went ashore, found the local believers,* and stayed with them a week. These disciples prophesied through the Holy Spirit that Paul should not go on to Jerusalem. ⁵When we returned to the ship at the end of the week, the entire congregation, including wives and children, came down to the shore with us. There we knelt, prayed, ⁶and said our farewells. Then we went aboard, and they returned home.

⁷The next stop after leaving Tyre was Ptolemais, where we greeted the brothers and sisters but stayed only one day. ⁸Then we went on to Caesarea and stayed at the home of Philip the Evangelist, one of the seven men who had been chosen to distribute food. ⁹He had four unmarried daughters who had the gift of prophecy.

¹⁰During our stay of several days, a man named Agabus, who also had the gift of

prophecy, arrived from Judea. ¹¹When he visited us, he took Paul's belt and bound his own feet and hands with it. Then he said, "The Holy Spirit declares, 'So shall the owner of this belt be bound by the Jewish leaders in Jerusalem and turned over to the Romans.'" ¹²When we heard this, we who were traveling with him, as well as the local believers, begged Paul not to go on to Jerusalem.

¹³But he said, "Why all this weeping? You are breaking my heart! For I am ready not only to be jailed at Jerusalem but also to die for the sake of the Lord Jesus." ¹⁴When it was clear that we couldn't persuade him, we gave up and said, "The will of the Lord be done."

¹⁵Shortly afterward we packed our things and left for Jerusalem. ¹⁶Some believers from Caesarea accompanied us, and they took us to the home of Mnason, a man originally from Cyprus and one of the early disciples. ¹⁷All the brothers and sisters in Jerusalem welcomed us cordially.

¹⁸The next day Paul went in with us to meet with James, and all the elders of the Jerusalem church were present. ¹⁹After greetings were exchanged, Paul gave a detailed account of the things God had

21:4 Greek *disciples*; also in 21:16.

accomplished among the Gentiles through his ministry.

20After hearing this, they praised God. But then they said, "You know, dear brother, how many thousands of Jews have also believed, and they all take the law of Moses very seriously. 21Our Jewish Christians here at Jerusalem have been told that you are teaching all the Jews living in the Gentile world to turn their backs on the laws of Moses. They say that you teach people not to circumcise their children or follow other Jewish customs. 22Now what can be done? For they will certainly hear that you have come.

23"Here's our suggestion. We have four men here who have taken a vow and are preparing to shave their heads. 24Go with them to the Temple and join them in the purification ceremony, and pay for them to have their heads shaved. Then everyone will know that the rumors are all false and that you yourself observe the Jewish laws.

25"As for the Gentile Christians, all we ask of them is what we already told them in a letter: They should not eat food offered to idols, nor consume blood, nor eat meat from strangled animals, and they should stay away from all sexual immorality."

26So Paul agreed to their request, and the next day he went through the purification ritual with the men and went to the Temple. Then he publicly announced the date when their vows would end and sacrifices would be offered for each of them.

27The seven days were almost ended when some Jews from the province of Asia saw Paul in the Temple and roused a mob against him. They grabbed him, 28yelling, "Men of Israel! Help! This is the man who teaches against our people and tells everybody to disobey the Jewish laws. He speaks against the Temple—and he even defiles it by bringing Gentiles in!" 29(For earlier that day they had seen him in the city with Trophimus, a Gentile from Ephesus,* and they assumed Paul had taken him into the Temple.)

30The whole population of the city was rocked by these accusations, and a great riot followed. Paul was dragged out of the Temple, and immediately the gates were closed behind him. 31As they were trying to kill him, word reached the commander of the Roman regiment that all Jerusalem was

in an uproar. 32He immediately called out his soldiers and officers and ran down among the crowd. When the mob saw the commander and the troops coming, they stopped beating Paul. 33The commander arrested him and ordered him bound with two chains. Then he asked the crowd who he was and what he had done. 34Some shouted one thing and some another. He couldn't find out the truth in all the uproar and confusion, so he ordered Paul to be taken to the fortress. 35As they reached the stairs, the mob grew so violent the soldiers had to lift Paul to their shoulders to protect him. 36And the crowd followed behind shouting, "Kill him, kill him!"

37As Paul was about to be taken inside, he said to the commander, "May I have a word with you?"

"Do you know Greek?" the commander asked, surprised. 38"Aren't you the Egyptian who led a rebellion some time ago and took four thousand members of the Assassins out into the desert?"

39"No," Paul replied, "I am a Jew from Tarsus in Cilicia, which is an important city. Please, let me talk to these people." 40The commander agreed, so Paul stood on the stairs and motioned to the people to be quiet. Soon a deep silence enveloped the crowd, and he addressed them in their own language, Aramaic.*

CHAPTER 22

"Brothers and esteemed fathers," Paul said, "listen to me as I offer my defense." 2When they heard him speaking in their own language,* the silence was even greater. 3"I am a Jew, born in Tarsus, a city in Cilicia, and I was brought up and educated here in Jerusalem under Gamaliel. At his feet I learned to follow our Jewish laws and customs very carefully. I became very zealous to honor God in everything I did, just as all of you are today. 4And I persecuted the followers of the Way, hounding some to death, binding and delivering both men and women to prison. 5The high priest and the whole council of leaders can testify that this is so. For I received letters from them to our Jewish brothers in Damascus, authorizing me to bring the Christians from there to Jerusalem, in chains, to be punished.

6"As I was on the road, nearing Damas-

21:29 Greek *Trophimus, the Ephesian.*   21:40 Or *Hebrew.*   22:2 Greek *in Aramaic.*

cus, about noon a very bright light from heaven suddenly shone around me. [7]I fell to the ground and heard a voice saying to me, 'Saul, Saul, why are you persecuting me?'

[8]"'Who are you, sir?' I asked. And he replied, 'I am Jesus of Nazareth, the one you are persecuting.' [9]The people with me saw the light but didn't hear the voice.

[10]"I said, 'What shall I do, Lord?' And the Lord told me, 'Get up and go into Damascus, and there you will be told all that you are to do.'

[11]"I was blinded by the intense light and had to be led into Damascus by my companions. [12]A man named Ananias lived there. He was a godly man in his devotion to the law, and he was well thought of by all the Jews of Damascus. [13]He came to me and stood beside me and said, 'Brother Saul, receive your sight.' And that very hour I could see him!

[14]"Then he told me, 'The God of our ancestors has chosen you to know his will and to see the Righteous One and hear him speak. [15]You are to take his message everywhere, telling the whole world what you have seen and heard. [16]And now, why delay? Get up and be baptized, and have your sins washed away, calling on the name of the Lord.'

[17]"One day after I returned to Jerusalem, I was praying in the Temple, and I fell into a trance. [18]I saw a vision of Jesus saying to me, 'Hurry! Leave Jerusalem, for the people here won't believe you when you give them your testimony about me.'

[19]"'But Lord,' I argued, 'they certainly know that I imprisoned and beat those in every synagogue who believed on you. [20]And when your witness Stephen was killed, I was standing there agreeing. I kept the coats they laid aside as they stoned him.'

[21]"But the Lord said to me, 'Leave Jerusalem, for I will send you far away to the Gentiles!'"

[22]The crowd listened until Paul came to that word; then with one voice they shouted, "Away with such a fellow! Kill him! He isn't fit to live!" [23]They yelled, threw off their coats, and tossed handfuls of dust into the air.

[24]The commander brought Paul inside and ordered him lashed with whips to make him confess his crime. He wanted to find out why the crowd had become so furious. [25]As they tied Paul down to lash him, Paul said to the officer standing there, "Is it legal for you to whip a Roman citizen who hasn't even been tried?"

[26]The officer went to the commander and asked, "What are you doing? This man is a Roman citizen!"

[27]So the commander went over and asked Paul, "Tell me, are you a Roman citizen?"

"Yes, I certainly am," Paul replied.

[28]"I am, too," the commander muttered, "and it cost me plenty!"

"But I am a citizen by birth!"

[29]The soldiers who were about to interrogate Paul quickly withdrew when they heard he was a Roman citizen, and the commander was frightened because he had ordered him bound and whipped.

[30]The next day the commander freed Paul from his chains and ordered the leading priests into session with the Jewish high council.* He had Paul brought in before them to try to find out what the trouble was all about.

CHAPTER 23
Gazing intently at the high council,* Paul began: "Brothers, I have always lived before God in all good conscience!"

[2]Instantly Ananias the high priest commanded those close to Paul to slap him on the mouth. [3]But Paul said to him, "God will slap you, you whitewashed wall! What kind of judge are you to break the law yourself by ordering me struck like that?"

[4]Those standing near Paul said to him, "Is that the way to talk to God's high priest?"

[5]"I'm sorry, brothers. I didn't realize he was the high priest," Paul replied, "for the Scriptures say, 'Do not speak evil of anyone who rules over you.'*"

[6]Paul realized that some members of the high council were Sadducees and some were Pharisees, so he shouted, "Brothers, I am a Pharisee, as were all my ancestors! And I am on trial because my hope is in the resurrection of the dead!"

[7]This divided the council—the Pharisees against the Sadducees—[8]for the Sadducees say there is no resurrection or angels or spirits, but the Pharisees believe in all of

---

22:30 Greek *Sanhedrin.*   **23:1** Greek *Sanhedrin;* also in 23:6, 15, 20, 28.   **23:5** Exod 22:28.

these. ⁹So a great clamor arose. Some of the teachers of religious law who were Pharisees jumped up to argue that Paul was all right. "We see nothing wrong with him," they shouted. "Perhaps a spirit or an angel spoke to him." ¹⁰The shouting grew louder and louder, and the men were tugging at Paul from both sides, pulling him this way and that. Finally, the commander, fearing they would tear him apart, ordered his soldiers to take him away from them and bring him back to the fortress.

¹¹That night the Lord appeared to Paul and said, "Be encouraged, Paul. Just as you have told the people about me here in Jerusalem, you must preach the Good News in Rome."

¹²The next morning a group of Jews got together and bound themselves with an oath to neither eat nor drink until they had killed Paul. ¹³There were more than forty of them. ¹⁴They went to the leading priests and other leaders and told them what they had done. "We have bound ourselves under oath to neither eat nor drink until we have killed Paul. ¹⁵You and the high council should tell the commander to bring Paul back to the council again," they requested. "Pretend you want to examine his case more fully. We will kill him on the way."

¹⁶But Paul's nephew heard of their plan and went to the fortress and told Paul. ¹⁷Paul called one of the officers and said, "Take this young man to the commander. He has something important to tell him."

¹⁸So the officer did, explaining, "Paul, the prisoner, called me over and asked me to bring this young man to you because he has something to tell you."

¹⁹The commander took him by the arm, led him aside, and asked, "What is it you want to tell me?"

²⁰Paul's nephew told him, "Some Jews are going to ask you to bring Paul before the Jewish high council tomorrow, pretending they want to get some more information. ²¹But don't do it! There are more than

forty men hiding along the way ready to jump him and kill him. They have vowed not to eat or drink until they kill him. They are ready, expecting you to agree to their request."

²²"Don't let a soul know you told me this," the commander warned the young man as he sent him away.

²³Then the commander called two of his officers and ordered, "Get two hundred soldiers ready to leave for Caesarea at nine o'clock tonight. Also take two hundred spearmen and seventy horsemen. ²⁴Provide horses for Paul to ride, and get him safely to Governor Felix." ²⁵Then he wrote this letter to the governor:

²⁶"From Claudius Lysias, to his Excellency, Governor Felix. Greetings! ²⁷This man was seized by some Jews, and they were about to kill him when I arrived with the troops. When I learned that he was a Roman citizen, I removed him to safety. ²⁸Then I took him to their high council to try to find out what he had done. ²⁹I soon discovered it was something regarding their religious law—certainly nothing worthy of imprisonment or death. ³⁰But when I was informed of a plot to kill him, I immediately sent him on to you. I have told his accusers to bring their charges before you."

³¹So that night, as ordered, the soldiers took Paul as far as Antipatris. ³²They returned to the fortress the next morning, while the horsemen took him on to Caesarea. ³³When they arrived in Caesarea, they presented Paul and the letter to Governor Felix. ³⁴He read it and then asked Paul what province he was from. "Cilicia," Paul answered.

³⁵"I will hear your case myself when your accusers arrive," the governor told him. Then the governor ordered him kept in the prison at Herod's headquarters.

NOVEMBER 10 ☐ DAY 315
ACTS 24–26
Paul's Three Trials

 OVERVIEW Two years pass before Paul's case reaches the courtroom. But political pressure keeps two governors, Felix and Festus, from resolving the issue. When Festus suggests the case be sent back to Jerusalem— an almost certain death sentence—there can be only one response from Paul: "I appeal to Caesar" (25:11). While preparations are being made for the two-thousand-mile journey to Rome, King Agrippa arrives, giving Paul yet another opportunity to defend the gospel.

Chapter 24	Chapter 25	Chapter 26
Trial before Governor Felix	Trial before Governor Festus	Trial before King Agrippa
Almost Released	Almost Murdered	Almost Persuaded

 YOUR DAILY WALK Doctor to parent: "And how is your little boy doing at controlling his behavior this week?"

Parent: "He's trying, doctor."

Doctor: "Good, I'm glad to hear it."

Only the willingness to suffer can conquer suffering.

Parent: "Yes, Doc, he's very, *very* trying!"

Trials. They come in all shapes and sizes. But the bottom line is the same: God wants you to rise above them, persevere through them, and emerge stronger from them. Peter puts it this way: "Your faith is far more precious to God than mere gold. So if your faith remains strong after being tried by fiery trials, it will bring you much praise and glory and honor on the day when Jesus Christ is revealed to the whole world" (1 Peter 1:7).

Paul could have viewed his three trials as a bother. Instead, he welcomed them as a blessing—not because they were pleasant, but because he knew they were purposeful. Developing a faith like gold requires the fiery heat of refining situations. If you have a fireplace, build a fire this evening as you consider this question: "Is God finding that I am trying to cooperate with him . . . or that I'm just plain *trying?*"

 INSIGHT: "The Power of a King with the Mind of a Slave"

The historian Tacitus made the above statement about Felix, and Felix's treatment of Paul in 24:24-27 seems to bear out this character analysis. He often met with Paul, not to wrestle with the issues that Paul raised, but to give Paul an opportunity to bribe him. Paul, of course, did not oblige and thus had to sit in prison for two years.

CHAPTER 24

Five days later Ananias, the high priest, arrived with some of the Jewish leaders and the lawyer* Tertullus, to press charges against Paul. [2]When Paul was called in, Tertullus laid charges against Paul in the following address to the governor:

"Your Excellency, you have given peace to us Jews and have enacted reforms for us. [3]And for all of this we are very grateful to you. [4]But lest I bore you, kindly give me your attention for only a moment as I briefly outline our case against this man. [5]For we have found him to be a troublemaker, a man who is constantly inciting the Jews throughout the world to riots and rebellions against the Roman government. He is a ringleader of the sect known as the Nazarenes. [6]Moreover he was trying to defile the Temple when we arrested him.*

24:1 Greek *some elders and an orator.*   24:6 Some manuscripts add *We would have judged him by our law,* [7]*but Lysias, the commander of the garrison, came and took him violently away from us,* [8]*commanding his accusers to come before you.*

⁸You can find out the truth of our accusations by examining him yourself." ⁹Then the other Jews chimed in, declaring that everything Tertullus said was true.

¹⁰Now it was Paul's turn. The governor motioned for him to rise and speak. Paul said, "I know, sir, that you have been a judge of Jewish affairs for many years, and this gives me confidence as I make my defense. ¹¹You can quickly discover that it was no more than twelve days ago that I arrived in Jerusalem to worship at the Temple. ¹²I didn't argue with anyone in the Temple, nor did I incite a riot in any synagogue or on the streets of the city. ¹³These men certainly cannot prove the things they accuse me of doing.

¹⁴"But I admit that I follow the Way, which they call a sect. I worship the God of our ancestors, and I firmly believe the Jewish law and everything written in the books of prophecy. ¹⁵I have hope in God, just as these men do, that he will raise both the righteous and the ungodly. ¹⁶Because of this, I always try to maintain a clear conscience before God and everyone else.

¹⁷"After several years away, I returned to Jerusalem with money to aid my people and to offer sacrifices to God. ¹⁸My accusers saw me in the Temple as I was completing a purification ritual. There was no crowd around me and no rioting. ¹⁹But some Jews from the province of Asia were there—and they ought to be here to bring charges if they have anything against me! ²⁰Ask these men here what wrongdoing the Jewish high council* found in me, ²¹except for one thing I said when I shouted out, 'I am on trial before you today because I believe in the resurrection of the dead!'"

²²Felix, who was quite familiar with the Way, adjourned the hearing and said, "Wait until Lysias, the garrison commander, arrives. Then I will decide the case." ²³He ordered an officer to keep Paul in custody but to give him some freedom and allow his friends to visit him and take care of his needs.

²⁴A few days later Felix came with his wife, Drusilla, who was Jewish. Sending for Paul, they listened as he told them about faith in Christ Jesus. ²⁵As he reasoned with them about righteousness and self-control and the judgment to come, Felix was terrified. "Go away for now," he

replied. "When it is more convenient, I'll call for you again." ²⁶He also hoped that Paul would bribe him, so he sent for him quite often and talked with him.

²⁷Two years went by in this way; then Felix was succeeded by Porcius Festus. And because Felix wanted to gain favor with the Jewish leaders, he left Paul in prison.

CHAPTER 25

Three days after Festus arrived in Caesarea to take over his new responsibilities, he left for Jerusalem, ²where the leading priests and other Jewish leaders met with him and made their accusations against Paul. ³They asked Festus as a favor to transfer Paul to Jerusalem. (Their plan was to waylay and kill him.) ⁴But Festus replied that Paul was at Caesarea and he himself would be returning there soon. ⁵So he said, "Those of you in authority can return with me. If Paul has done anything wrong, you can make your accusations."

⁶Eight or ten days later he returned to Caesarea, and on the following day Paul's trial began. ⁷On Paul's arrival in court, the Jewish leaders from Jerusalem gathered around and made many serious accusations they couldn't prove. ⁸Paul denied the charges. "I am not guilty," he said. "I have committed no crime against the Jewish laws or the Temple or the Roman government."

⁹Then Festus, wanting to please the Jews, asked him, "Are you willing to go to Jerusalem and stand trial before me there?"

¹⁰But Paul replied, "No! This is the official Roman court, so I ought to be tried right here. You know very well I am not guilty. ¹¹If I have done something worthy of death, I don't refuse to die. But if I am innocent, neither you nor anyone else has a right to turn me over to these men to kill me. I appeal to Caesar!"

¹²Festus conferred with his advisers and then replied, "Very well! You have appealed to Caesar, and to Caesar you shall go!"

¹³A few days later King Agrippa arrived with his sister, Bernice,* to pay their respects to Festus. ¹⁴During their stay of several days, Festus discussed Paul's case with the king. "There is a prisoner here," he told him, "whose case was left for me by Felix.

24:20 Greek *Sanhedrin.*   25:13 Greek *Agrippa the king and Bernice arrived.*

[15]When I was in Jerusalem, the leading priests and other Jewish leaders pressed charges against him and asked me to sentence him. [16]Of course, I quickly pointed out to them that Roman law does not convict people without a trial. They are given an opportunity to defend themselves face to face with their accusers.

[17]"When they came here for the trial, I called the case the very next day and ordered Paul brought in. [18]But the accusations made against him weren't at all what I expected. [19]It was something about their religion and about someone called Jesus who died, but whom Paul insists is alive. [20]I was perplexed as to how to conduct an investigation of this kind, and I asked him whether he would be willing to stand trial on these charges in Jerusalem. [21]But Paul appealed to the emperor. So I ordered him back to jail until I could arrange to send him to Caesar."

[22]"I'd like to hear the man myself," Agrippa said.

And Festus replied, "You shall—tomorrow!"

[23]So the next day Agrippa and Bernice arrived at the auditorium with great pomp, accompanied by military officers and prominent men of the city. Festus ordered that Paul be brought in. [24]Then Festus said, "King Agrippa and all present, this is the man whose death is demanded both by the local Jews and by those in Jerusalem. [25]But in my opinion he has done nothing worthy of death. However, he appealed his case to the emperor, and I decided to send him. [26]But what shall I write the emperor? For there is no real charge against him. So I have brought him before all of you, and especially you, King Agrippa, so that after we examine him, I might have something to write. [27]For it doesn't seem reasonable to send a prisoner to the emperor without specifying the charges against him!"

CHAPTER 26
Then Agrippa said to Paul, "You may speak in your defense."

So Paul, with a gesture of his hand, started his defense: [2]"I am fortunate, King Agrippa, that you are the one hearing my defense against all these accusations made by the Jewish leaders, [3]for I know you are an expert on Jewish customs and controversies. Now please listen to me patiently!

[4]"As the Jewish leaders are well aware, I was given a thorough Jewish training from my earliest childhood among my own people and in Jerusalem. [5]If they would admit it, they know that I have been a member of the Pharisees, the strictest sect of our religion. [6]Now I am on trial because I am looking forward to the fulfillment of God's promise made to our ancestors. [7]In fact, that is why the twelve tribes of Israel worship God night and day, and they share the same hope I have. Yet, O king, they say it is wrong for me to have this hope! [8]Why does it seem incredible to any of you that God can raise the dead?

[9]"I used to believe that I ought to do everything I could to oppose the followers of Jesus of Nazareth.* [10]Authorized by the leading priests, I caused many of the believers in Jerusalem to be sent to prison. And I cast my vote against them when they were condemned to death. [11]Many times I had them whipped in the synagogues to try to get them to curse Christ. I was so violently opposed to them that I even hounded them in distant cities of foreign lands.

[12]"One day I was on such a mission to Damascus, armed with the authority and commission of the leading priests. [13]About noon, Your Majesty, a light from heaven brighter than the sun shone down on me and my companions. [14]We all fell down, and I heard a voice saying to me in Aramaic,* 'Saul, Saul, why are you persecuting me? It is hard for you to fight against my will.*'

[15]"'Who are you, sir?' I asked.

"And the Lord replied, 'I am Jesus, the one you are persecuting. [16]Now stand up! For I have appeared to you to appoint you as my servant and my witness. You are to tell the world about this experience and about other times I will appear to you. [17]And I will protect you from both your own people and the Gentiles. Yes, I am going to send you to the Gentiles, [18]to open their eyes so they may turn from darkness to light, and from the power of Satan to God. Then they will receive forgiveness for their sins and be given a place among God's people, who are set apart by faith in me.'

[19]"And so, O King Agrippa, I was not disobedient to that vision from heaven. [20]I

26:9 Greek *oppose the name of Jesus the Nazarene.*   26:14a Or *Hebrew.*   26:14b Greek *It is hard for you to kick against the oxgoads.*

preached first to those in Damascus, then in Jerusalem and throughout all Judea, and also to the Gentiles, that all must turn from their sins and turn to God—and prove they have changed by the good things they do. [21]Some Jews arrested me in the Temple for preaching this, and they tried to kill me. [22]But God protected me so that I am still alive today to tell these facts to everyone, from the least to the greatest. I teach nothing except what the prophets and Moses said would happen—[23]that the Messiah would suffer and be the first to rise from the dead as a light to Jews and Gentiles alike."

[24]Suddenly, Festus shouted, "Paul, you are insane. Too much study has made you crazy!"

[25]But Paul replied, "I am not insane, Most Excellent Festus. I am speaking the sober truth. [26]And King Agrippa knows about these things. I speak frankly, for I am sure these events are all familiar to him, for they were not done in a corner! [27]King Agrippa, do you believe the prophets? I know you do—"

[28]Agrippa interrupted him. "Do you think you can make me a Christian so quickly?"*

[29]Paul replied, "Whether quickly or not, I pray to God that both you and everyone here in this audience might become the same as I am, except for these chains."

[30]Then the king, the governor, Bernice, and all the others stood and left. [31]As they talked it over they agreed, "This man hasn't done anything worthy of death or imprisonment." [32]And Agrippa said to Festus, "He could be set free if he hadn't appealed to Caesar!"

26:28 Or *"A little more, and your arguments would make me a Christian."*

NOVEMBER 11 ☐ DAY 316
ACTS 27–28
Paul's Trip to Rome

OVERVIEW During the perilous voyage by sea to Rome, God assures Paul in a dream that he will stand before Caesar to bear witness to the gospel. What God does not tell Paul is that before he arrives in Rome, he will experience shipwreck and snakebite! The account closes with Paul under house arrest for two years, "proclaiming the Kingdom of God with all boldness and teaching about the Lord Jesus Christ. And no one tried to stop him" (28:31).

Chapter 27		Chapter 28	
Sailing for Rome	Shipwrecked on Malta	Reception in Rome	House Arrest in Rome
1 26	27 44	1 16	17 31
Peril in the Water		Peril on the Land	

YOUR DAILY WALK Even the best seeds germinate only in the proper soil.

We conquer not in any brilliant fashion—we conquer by continuing.

Acts 28:24 is a summary of the response to Paul's "seed sowing" in the city of Rome: "Some believed and some didn't." It's a reminder that even the apostle Paul couldn't persuade a person into heaven if that individual was not willing to "see . . . hear . . . understand . . . and . . . turn" (28:27).

You can expect the same response as you venture forth with the words of life! Some will believe, for God has promised that his Word will prosper everywhere (Isaiah 55:11). And some will not believe—not because the message is deficient, but because they are unwilling to repent. Don't be discouraged at the latter; and don't be surprised at the former! Like Paul, keep praying, sharing, and looking up.

INSIGHT Acts beyond the Book of Acts
Chapter 28 concludes Luke's account, but significant events continued to transpire in the life of Paul and the New Testament church. The following is a suggested chronology:

Paul's First Roman Imprisonment (Acts 28:30) . . . . A.D. 60–62
(Ephesians, Philippians, Colossians, and Philemon written)
Paul's Freedom from Imprisonment 62–67
(1 Timothy and Titus written)
Burning of Rome 64
Second Roman Imprisonment 67–68
(2 Timothy written)
Paul's Death 68
Destruction of Jerusalem 70

CHAPTER 27

When the time came, we set sail for Italy. Paul and several other prisoners were placed in the custody of an army officer named Julius, a captain of the Imperial Regiment. ²And Aristarchus, a Macedonian from Thessalonica, was also with us. We left on a boat whose home port was Adramyttium; it was scheduled to make several stops at ports along the coast of the province of Asia.

³The next day when we docked at Sidon, Julius was very kind to Paul and let him go ashore to visit with friends so they could provide for his needs. ⁴Putting out to sea from there, we encountered headwinds that made it difficult to keep the ship on course, so we sailed north of Cyprus between the island and the mainland. ⁵We passed along the coast of the provinces of Cilicia and Pamphylia, landing at Myra, in the province of Lycia. ⁶There the officer found an Egyptian ship from Alexandria that was bound for Italy, and he put us on board.

⁷We had several days of rough sailing, and after great difficulty we finally neared Cnidus. But the wind was against us, so we sailed down to the leeward side of Crete, past the cape of Salmone. ⁸We struggled along the coast with great difficulty and finally arrived at Fair Havens, near the city of Lasea. ⁹We had lost a lot of time. The weather was becoming dangerous for long voyages by then because it was so late in the fall,* and Paul spoke to the ship's officers about it.

¹⁰"Sirs," he said, "I believe there is trouble ahead if we go on—shipwreck, loss of cargo, injuries, and danger to our lives."

¹¹But the officer in charge of the prisoners listened more to the ship's captain and the owner than to Paul. ¹²And since Fair Havens was an exposed harbor—a poor place to spend the winter—most of the crew wanted to go to Phoenix, farther up the coast of Crete, and spend the winter there. Phoenix was a good harbor with only a southwest and northwest exposure.

¹³When a light wind began blowing from the south, the sailors thought they could make it. So they pulled up anchor and sailed along close to shore. ¹⁴But the weather changed abruptly, and a wind of typhoon strength (a "northeaster," they called it) caught the ship and blew it out to sea. ¹⁵They couldn't turn the ship into the wind, so they gave up and let it run before the gale.

¹⁶We sailed behind a small island named Cauda,* where with great difficulty we hoisted aboard the lifeboat that was being towed behind us. ¹⁷Then we banded the ship with ropes to strengthen the hull. The sailors were afraid of being driven across to the sandbars of Syrtis off the African coast, so they lowered the sea anchor and were thus driven before the wind.

¹⁸The next day, as gale-force winds continued to batter the ship, the crew began throwing the cargo overboard. ¹⁹The following day they even threw out the ship's equipment and anything else they could lay their hands on. ²⁰The terrible storm raged unabated for many days, blotting out the sun and the stars, until at last all hope was gone.

²¹No one had eaten for a long time. Finally, Paul called the crew together and said, "Men, you should have listened to me

27:9 Greek *because the fast was now already gone by.* This fast happened on the Day of Atonement (*Yom Kippur*), which occurred in late September or early October.   **27:16** Some manuscripts read *Clauda.*

in the first place and not left Fair Havens. You would have avoided all this injury and loss. [22]But take courage! None of you will lose your lives, even though the ship will go down. [23]For last night an angel of the God to whom I belong and whom I serve stood beside me, [24]and he said, 'Don't be afraid, Paul, for you will surely stand trial before Caesar! What's more, God in his goodness has granted safety to everyone sailing with you.' [25]So take courage! For I believe God. It will be just as he said. [26]But we will be shipwrecked on an island."

[27]About midnight on the fourteenth night of the storm, as we were being driven across the Sea of Adria,* the sailors sensed land was near. [28]They took soundings and found the water was only 120 feet deep. A little later they sounded again and found only 90 feet.* [29]At this rate they were afraid we would soon be driven against the rocks along the shore, so they threw out four anchors from the stern and prayed for daylight. [30]Then the sailors tried to abandon the ship; they lowered the lifeboat as though they were going to put out anchors from the prow. [31]But Paul said to the commanding officer and the soldiers, "You will all die unless the sailors stay aboard." [32]So the soldiers cut the ropes and let the boat fall off.

[33]As the darkness gave way to the early morning light, Paul begged everyone to eat. "You haven't touched food for two weeks," he said. [34]"Please eat something now for your own good. For not a hair of your heads will perish." [35]Then he took some bread, gave thanks to God before them all, and broke off a piece and ate it. [36]Then everyone was encouraged, [37]and all 276 of us began eating—for that is the number we had aboard. [38]After eating, the crew lightened the ship further by throwing the cargo of wheat overboard.

[39]When morning dawned, they didn't recognize the coastline, but they saw a bay with a beach and wondered if they could get between the rocks and get the ship safely to shore. [40]So they cut off the anchors and left them in the sea. Then they lowered the rudders, raised the foresail, and headed toward shore. [41]But the ship hit a shoal and ran aground. The bow of the ship stuck fast, while the stern was repeatedly smashed by the force of the waves and began to break apart.

[42]The soldiers wanted to kill the prisoners to make sure they didn't swim ashore and escape. [43]But the commanding officer wanted to spare Paul, so he didn't let them carry out their plan. Then he ordered all who could swim to jump overboard first and make for land, [44]and he told the others to try for it on planks and debris from the broken ship. So everyone escaped safely ashore!

CHAPTER 28

Once we were safe on shore, we learned that we were on the island of Malta. [2]The people of the island were very kind to us. It was cold and rainy, so they built a fire on the shore to welcome us and warm us.

[3]As Paul gathered an armful of sticks and was laying them on the fire, a poisonous snake, driven out by the heat, fastened itself onto his hand. [4]The people of the island saw it hanging there and said to each other, "A murderer, no doubt! Though he escaped the sea, justice will not permit him to live." [5]But Paul shook off the snake into the fire and was unharmed. [6]The people waited for him to swell up or suddenly drop dead. But when they had waited a long time and saw no harm come to him, they changed their minds and decided he was a god.

[7]Near the shore where we landed was an estate belonging to Publius, the chief official of the island. He welcomed us courteously and fed us for three days. [8]As it happened, Publius's father was ill with fever and dysentery. Paul went in and prayed for him, and laying his hands on him, he healed him. [9]Then all the other sick people on the island came and were cured. [10]As a result we were showered with honors, and when the time came to sail, people put on board all sorts of things we would need for the trip.

[11]It was three months after the shipwreck that we set sail on another ship that had wintered at the island—an Alexandrian ship with the twin gods* as its figurehead. [12]Our first stop was Syracuse,* where we stayed three days. [13]From there we sailed across to Rhegium.* A day later a south wind began blowing, so the following day we sailed up the coast to Puteoli. [14]There

27:27 The *Sea of Adria* is in the central Mediterranean; it is not to be confused with the Adriatic Sea.   27:28 Greek *20 fathoms . . .*
15 fathoms [37 meters . . . 27 meters].   28:11 The *twin gods* were the Roman gods Castor and Pollux.   28:12 *Syracuse* was on the
island of Sicily.   28:13 *Rhegium* was on the southern tip of Italy.

we found some believers,* who invited us to stay with them seven days. And so we came to Rome.

¹⁵ The brothers and sisters in Rome had heard we were coming, and they came to meet us at the Forum* on the Appian Way. Others joined us at The Three Taverns.* When Paul saw them, he thanked God and took courage.

¹⁶ When we arrived in Rome, Paul was permitted to have his own private lodging, though he was guarded by a soldier.

¹⁷ Three days after Paul's arrival, he called together the local Jewish leaders. He said to them, "Brothers, I was arrested in Jerusalem and handed over to the Roman government, even though I had done nothing against our people or the customs of our ancestors. ¹⁸ The Romans tried me and wanted to release me, for they found no cause for the death sentence. ¹⁹ But when the Jewish leaders protested the decision, I felt it necessary to appeal to Caesar, even though I had no desire to press charges against my own people. ²⁰ I asked you to come here today so we could get acquainted and so I could tell you that I am bound with this chain because I believe that the hope of Israel—the Messiah—has already come."

²¹ They replied, "We have heard nothing against you. We have had no letters from Judea or reports from anyone who has arrived here. ²² But we want to hear what you believe, for the only thing we know about these Christians* is that they are denounced everywhere."

²³ So a time was set, and on that day a large number of people came to Paul's house. He told them about the Kingdom of God and taught them about Jesus from the Scriptures—from the five books of Moses and the books of the prophets. He began lecturing in the morning and went on into the evening. ²⁴ Some believed and some didn't. ²⁵ But after they had argued back and forth among themselves, they left with this final word from Paul: "The Holy Spirit was right when he said to our ancestors through Isaiah the prophet,

²⁶ 'Go and say to my people,
You will hear my words,
    but you will not understand;
you will see what I do,
    but you will not perceive its meaning.
²⁷ For the hearts of these people are
        hardened,
    and their ears cannot hear,
    and they have closed their eyes—
so their eyes cannot see,
    and their ears cannot hear,
    and their hearts cannot understand,
and they cannot turn to me
    and let me heal them.'*

²⁸ So I want you to realize that this salvation from God is also available to the Gentiles, and they will accept it."*

³⁰ For the next two years, Paul lived in his own rented house.* He welcomed all who visited him, ³¹ proclaiming the Kingdom of God with all boldness and teaching about the Lord Jesus Christ. And no one tried to stop him.

28:14 Greek *brothers.*   28:15a *The Forum* was about 43 miles (70 kilometers) from Rome.   28:15b *The Three Taverns* was about 35 miles (57 kilometers) from Rome.   28:22 Greek *this sect.*   28:26-27 Isa 6:9-10.   —28:28 Some manuscripts add verse 29, *And when he had said these words, the Jews departed, greatly disagreeing with each other.*   28:30 Or *at his own expense.*

Romans

WHILE the four Gospels recount the life of Jesus Christ, the book of Romans explores the significance of his sacrificial death. As such, it has been called "the gospel according to Paul." In a question and answer format, Romans is the most systematic presentation of doctrine in the Bible. But the Good News is more than a theology to be pondered; it is a life to be lived—a life of righteousness befitting one whom God declares "not guilty" (3:24).

Focus	Sin	Salvation	Struggle	Sovereignty	Service
Divisions	Humankind's Need of Righteousness	God's Provision of Righteousness	God's Power for Righteous Living	God's Plan of Righteousness	Practical Outworking of Righteousness
	1 3	4 5	6 8	9 11	12 16
Topics	Basis of the Gospel			Behavior of the Gospel	
	Condemnation	Justification	Sanctification	Vindication	Application
Place	Probably Corinth				
Time	A.D. 57				

NOVEMBER 12 ☐ DAY 317
ROMANS 1–3
Man's Need of Righteousness

 OVERVIEW Unlike most of Paul's letters, Romans is addressed to believers Paul has never met. Resembling a doctrinal treatise more than a personal letter, it explores in carefully worded phrases the need, provision, and outworking of God's grace. Paul begins with God's wrath upon sinful humanity. Without exception, all have sinned and face the condemnation of God. But there is hope in the person of Jesus Christ, by whom God provides righteousness to all who believe (3:22).

Chapter 1		Chapter 2	Chapter 3
Nature of the Gospel	Need for the Gospel	Objects of the Gospel	Outcome of the Gospel
1 17	18 32		
Judgment			Grace

 YOUR DAILY WALK Webster defines the verb *to earn* this way: "To receive as return for work done or services rendered." With that in mind, go on an expedition through the Scriptures to discover what God says about an unsaved people's good works.

All the sorrows of faith put together do not equal in bitterness one drop of the sorrows of sin.

Their righteous deeds are like _____ (Isaiah 64:6).
Their sins are red as _____ (Isaiah 1:18).
Their hearts are _____ and desperately _____ (Jeremiah 17:9).
In short, the verdict of Paul the apostle, echoing the words of David the psalmist, is this: "No one is good—not even one" (Romans 3:10; see also Psalms 14:3; 53:3). And what are the wages that that sinful, unrighteous condition earns? (See Romans 6:23.)

Now do you understand why it is so important to view your sinfulness the way God views it? Not as a character weakness . . . or an unfortunate setback . . . but as a terminal condition.

The prognosis is grim—unless Jesus is your Savior. Is he? If not, new life is only a prayer away. Take him at his word right now. All you have to lose is a hopeless eternity (John 3:16-18).

 INSIGHT Glad Tidings Oft Told
Romans has been called "the gospel according to Paul" with good reason. Sixteen times in the book you'll find the phrase *Good News,* referring specifically to salvation in Jesus. This is a significant number of occurrences, considering that the four Gospels combined use the phrase only twenty-six times!

CHAPTER 1
This letter is from Paul, Jesus Christ's slave, chosen by God to be an apostle and sent out to preach his Good News. ²This Good News was promised long ago by God through his prophets in the holy Scriptures. ³It is the Good News about his Son, Jesus,

who came as a man, born into King David's royal family line. ⁴And Jesus Christ our Lord was shown to be the Son of God when God powerfully raised him from the dead by means of the Holy Spirit.* ⁵Through Christ, God has given us the privilege and authority to tell Gentiles everywhere what

1:4 Or *the Spirit of holiness.*

God has done for them, so that they will believe and obey him, bringing glory to his name.

[6] You are among those who have been called to belong to Jesus Christ, [7] dear friends in Rome. God loves you dearly, and he has called you to be his very own people.

May grace and peace be yours from God our Father and the Lord Jesus Christ.

[8] Let me say first of all that your faith in God is becoming known throughout the world. How I thank God through Jesus Christ for each one of you. [9] God knows how often I pray for you. Day and night I bring you and your needs in prayer to God, whom I serve with all my heart* by telling others the Good News about his Son.

[10] One of the things I always pray for is the opportunity, God willing, to come at last to see you. [11] For I long to visit you so I can share a spiritual blessing with you that will help you grow strong in the Lord. [12] I'm eager to encourage you in your faith, but I also want to be encouraged by yours. In this way, each of us will be a blessing to the other.

[13] I want you to know, dear brothers and sisters, that I planned many times to visit you, but I was prevented until now. I want to work among you and see good results, just as I have done among other Gentiles. [14] For I have a great sense of obligation to people in our culture and to people in other cultures,* to the educated and uneducated alike. [15] So I am eager to come to you in Rome, too, to preach God's Good News.

[16] For I am not ashamed of this Good News about Christ. It is the power of God at work, saving everyone who believes— Jews first and also Gentiles. [17] This Good News tells us how God makes us right in his sight. This is accomplished from start to finish by faith. As the Scriptures say, "It is through faith that a righteous person has life."*

[18] But God shows his anger from heaven against all sinful, wicked people who push the truth away from themselves.* [19] For the truth about God is known to them instinctively.* God has put this knowledge in their hearts. [20] From the time the world was created, people have seen the earth and sky and all that God made. They can clearly see

his invisible qualities—his eternal power and divine nature. So they have no excuse whatsoever for not knowing God.

[21] Yes, they knew God, but they wouldn't worship him as God or even give him thanks. And they began to think up foolish ideas of what God was like. The result was that their minds became dark and confused. [22] Claiming to be wise, they became utter fools instead. [23] And instead of worshiping the glorious, ever-living God, they worshiped idols made to look like mere people, or birds and animals and snakes.

[24] So God let them go ahead and do whatever shameful things their hearts desired. As a result, they did vile and degrading things with each other's bodies. [25] Instead of believing what they knew was the truth about God, they deliberately chose to believe lies. So they worshiped the things God made but not the Creator himself, who is to be praised forever. Amen.

[26] That is why God abandoned them to their shameful desires. Even the women turned against the natural way to have sex and instead indulged in sex with each other. [27] And the men, instead of having normal sexual relationships with women, burned with lust for each other. Men did shameful things with other men and, as a result, suffered within themselves the penalty they so richly deserved.

[28] When they refused to acknowledge God, he abandoned them to their evil minds and let them do things that should never be done. [29] Their lives became full of every kind of wickedness, sin, greed, hate, envy, murder, fighting, deception, malicious behavior, and gossip. [30] They are backstabbers, haters of God, insolent, proud, and boastful. They are forever inventing new ways of sinning and are disobedient to their parents. [31] They refuse to understand, break their promises, and are heartless and unforgiving. [32] They are fully aware of God's death penalty for those who do these things, yet they go right ahead and do them anyway. And, worse yet, they encourage others to do them, too.

CHAPTER 2
You may be saying, "What terrible people you have been talking about!" But you are just as bad, and you have no excuse! When you say they are wicked and should be

1:9 Or *in my spirit.*   **1:14** Greek *to Greeks and to barbarians.*   **1:17** Hab 2:4.   **1:18** Or *who prevent the truth from being known.*
1:19 Greek *is manifest in them.*

punished, you are condemning yourself, for you do these very same things. [2]And we know that God, in his justice, will punish anyone who does such things. [3]Do you think that God will judge and condemn others for doing them and not judge you when you do them, too? [4]Don't you realize how kind, tolerant, and patient God is with you? Or don't you care? Can't you see how kind he has been in giving you time to turn from your sin?

[5]But no, you won't listen. So you are storing up terrible punishment for yourself because of your stubbornness in refusing to turn from your sin. For there is going to come a day of judgment when God, the just judge of all the world, [6]will judge all people according to what they have done. [7]He will give eternal life to those who persist in doing what is good, seeking after the glory and honor and immortality that God offers. [8]But he will pour out his anger and wrath on those who live for themselves, who refuse to obey the truth and practice evil deeds. [9]There will be trouble and calamity for everyone who keeps on sinning—for the Jew first and also for the Gentile. [10]But there will be glory and honor and peace from God for all who do good—for the Jew first and also for the Gentile. [11]For God does not show favoritism.

[12]God will punish the Gentiles when they sin, even though they never had God's written law. And he will punish the Jews when they sin, for they do have the law. [13]For it is not merely knowing the law that brings God's approval. Those who obey the law will be declared right in God's sight. [14]Even when Gentiles, who do not have God's written law, instinctively follow what the law says, they show that in their hearts they know right from wrong. [15]They demonstrate that God's law is written within them, for their own consciences either accuse them or tell them they are doing what is right. [16]The day will surely come when God, by Jesus Christ, will judge everyone's secret life. This is my message.

[17]If you are a Jew, you are relying on God's law for your special relationship with him. You boast that all is well between yourself and God. [18]Yes, you know what he wants; you know right from wrong because you have been taught his law. [19]You are convinced that you are a guide for the blind and a beacon light for people who are lost in darkness without God. [20]You think you can instruct the ignorant and teach children the ways of God. For you are certain that in God's law you have complete knowledge and truth.

[21]Well then, if you teach others, why don't you teach yourself? You tell others not to steal, but do you steal? [22]You say it is wrong to commit adultery, but do you do it? You condemn idolatry, but do you steal from pagan temples? [23]You are so proud of knowing the law, but you dishonor God by breaking it. [24]No wonder the Scriptures say, "The world blasphemes the name of God because of you."*

[25]The Jewish ceremony of circumcision is worth something only if you obey God's law. But if you don't obey God's law, you are no better off than an uncircumcised Gentile. [26]And if the Gentiles obey God's law, won't God give them all the rights and honors of being his own people? [27]In fact, uncircumcised Gentiles who keep God's law will be much better off than you Jews who are circumcised and know so much about God's law but don't obey it.

[28]For you are not a true Jew just because you were born of Jewish parents or because you have gone through the Jewish ceremony of circumcision. [29]No, a true Jew is one whose heart is right with God. And true circumcision is not a cutting of the body but a change of heart produced by God's Spirit. Whoever has that kind of change seeks praise from God, not from people.

CHAPTER 3
Then what's the advantage of being a Jew? Is there any value in the Jewish ceremony of circumcision? [2]Yes, being a Jew has many advantages. First of all, the Jews were entrusted with the whole revelation of God.*

[3]True, some of them were unfaithful; but just because they broke their promises, does that mean God will break his promises? [4]Of course not! Though everyone else in the world is a liar, God is true. As the Scriptures say, "He will be proved right in what he says, and he will win his case in court."*

[5]"But," some say, "our sins serve a good purpose, for people will see God's goodness

2:24 Isa 52:5.　　3:2 Greek *the oracles of God.*　　3:4 Ps 51:4.

when he declares us sinners to be innocent. Isn't it unfair, then, for God to punish us?" (That is actually the way some people talk.) [6]Of course not! If God is not just, how is he qualified to judge the world? [7]"But," some might still argue, "how can God judge and condemn me as a sinner if my dishonesty highlights his truthfulness and brings him more glory?" [8]If you follow that kind of thinking, however, you might as well say that the more we sin the better it is! Those who say such things deserve to be condemned, yet some slander me by saying this is what I preach!

[9]Well then, are we Jews better than others?* No, not at all, for we have already shown that all people, whether Jews or Gentiles, are under the power of sin. [10]As the Scriptures say,

"No one is good—
    not even one.
[11] No one has real understanding;
    no one is seeking God.
[12] All have turned away from God;
    all have gone wrong.
  No one does good,
    not even one."*
[13] "Their talk is foul, like the stench from
    an open grave.
  Their speech is filled with lies."*
  "The poison of a deadly snake drips
    from their lips."*
[14]   "Their mouths are full of cursing
    and bitterness."*
[15] "They are quick to commit murder.
[16]   Wherever they go, destruction and
    misery follow them.
[17] They do not know what true peace is."*
[18]   "They have no fear of God to
    restrain them."*

[19]Obviously, the law applies to those to whom it was given, for its purpose is to keep people from having excuses and to bring the entire world into judgment before God. [20]For no one can ever be made

right in God's sight by doing what his law commands. For the more we know God's law, the clearer it becomes that we aren't obeying it.

[21]But now God has shown us a different way of being right in his sight—not by obeying the law but by the way promised in the Scriptures long ago. [22]We are made right in God's sight when we trust in Jesus Christ to take away our sins. And we all can be saved in this same way, no matter who we are or what we have done.

[23]For all have sinned; all fall short of God's glorious standard. [24]Yet now God in his gracious kindness declares us not guilty. He has done this through Christ Jesus, who has freed us by taking away our sins. [25]For God sent Jesus to take the punishment for our sins and to satisfy God's anger against us. We are made right with God when we believe that Jesus shed his blood, sacrificing his life for us. God was being entirely fair and just when he did not punish those who sinned in former times. [26]And he is entirely fair and just in this present time when he declares sinners to be right in his sight because they believe in Jesus.

[27]Can we boast, then, that we have done anything to be accepted by God? No, because our acquittal is not based on our good deeds. It is based on our faith. [28]So we are made right with God through faith and not by obeying the law.

[29]After all, God is not the God of the Jews only, is he? Isn't he also the God of the Gentiles? Of course he is. [30]There is only one God, and there is only one way of being accepted by him. He makes people right with himself only by faith, whether they are Jews or Gentiles. [31]Well then, if we emphasize faith, does this mean that we can forget about the law? Of course not! In fact, only when we have faith do we truly fulfill the law.

3:9 Greek *Are we better?*   **3:10-12** Pss 14:1-3; 53:1-3.   **3:13** Pss 5:9; 140:3.   **3:14** Ps 10:7.   **3:15-17** Isa 59:7-8.   **3:18** Ps 36:1.

NOVEMBER 13 □ DAY 318
ROMANS 4–5
God's Provision of Righteousness

OVERVIEW In today's reading, Paul illustrates the doctrine of justification by citing Abraham as one who "believed God, so God declared him to be righteous" (4:3). Abraham's faith points to two changeless truths: (1) Since the beginning of time, God's method of salvation has been justification by faith. (2) Justification results in peace between God and humans. Paul discusses that peace in chapter 5, then contrasts the disobedience of Adam with the obedience of Christ. Adam's sin caused humanity's alienation from God; Christ's death provides reconciliation to God.

Chapter 4	Chapter 5	
Justifying Faith Illustrated	Justifying Faith Demonstrated	Justifying Faith Contrasted
1	11 12	21
Abraham	All Believers	Adam

YOUR DAILY WALK "Only forty shopping days till Christmas!" Though Christmas is still more than a month away, perhaps you have already begun your Christmas shopping. Who is on your Christmas list this year: your immediate family members . . . close relatives . . .

We make a living by what we get; we make a life by what we give.

intimate friends? Those are the obvious choices. But what about the person at work who rubs you the wrong way? . . . the neighbor next door who has a questionable lifestyle? . . . the relative who holds a grudge against you? Are they high on your gift list? Probably not, for gift giving is usually directed to those you love.

But God's gift to mankind—salvation—was provided "while we were still sinners" (5:8) . . . when there was nothing lovely about us at all! Paul describes those for whom Christ died as sinners and enemies of God (5:8, 10).

With God's love as a model, make a "Christmas list" of five people you know who need to receive God's free gift of salvation. By the end of the day, try to share God's plan of salvation with one of the five. Make it your goal to share the Good News of Christ with everyone on your list by Christmas Day!

INSIGHT All Roads Lead to Rome
Romans is one of the few epistles written by Paul to a church he had not previously visited, and yet in chapter 16 he includes a long list of personal greetings—twenty-six in all!

CHAPTER 4
Abraham was, humanly speaking, the founder of our Jewish nation. What were his experiences concerning this question of being saved by faith? ²Was it because of his good deeds that God accepted him? If so, he would have had something to boast about. But from God's point of view Abraham had no basis at all for pride. ³For the Scriptures tell us, "Abraham believed God, so God declared him to be righteous."*

⁴When people work, their wages are not a gift. Workers earn what they receive. ⁵But people are declared righteous because of their faith, not because of their work.

⁶King David spoke of this, describing the happiness of an undeserving sinner who is declared to be righteous:

4:3 Gen 15:6.

7 "Oh, what joy for those whose
        disobedience is forgiven,
    whose sins are put out of sight.
8 Yes, what joy for those
    whose sin is no longer counted
        against them by the Lord."*

⁹Now then, is this blessing only for the
Jews, or is it for Gentiles, too? Well, what
about Abraham? We have been saying he
was declared righteous by God because of
his faith. ¹⁰But how did his faith help him?
Was he declared righteous only after he
had been circumcised, or was it before he
was circumcised? The answer is that God
accepted him first, and then he was circumcised later!

¹¹The circumcision ceremony was a sign
that Abraham already had faith and that
God had already accepted him and declared him to be righteous—even before he
was circumcised. So Abraham is the spiritual father of those who have faith but have
not been circumcised. They are made right
with God by faith. ¹²And Abraham is also
the spiritual father of those who have been
circumcised, but only if they have the same
kind of faith Abraham had before he was
circumcised.

¹³It is clear, then, that God's promise to
give the whole earth to Abraham and his
descendants was not based on obedience to
God's law, but on the new relationship
with God that comes by faith. ¹⁴So if you
claim that God's promise is for those who
obey God's law and think they are "good
enough" in God's sight, then you are saying that faith is useless. And in that case,
the promise is also meaningless. ¹⁵But the
law brings punishment on those who try to
obey it. (The only way to avoid breaking
the law is to have no law to break!)

¹⁶So that's why faith is the key! God's
promise is given to us as a free gift. And we
are certain to receive it, whether or not we
follow Jewish customs, if we have faith like
Abraham's. For Abraham is the father of all
who believe. ¹⁷That is what the Scriptures
mean when God told him, "I have made
you the father of many nations."* This happened because Abraham believed in the
God who brings the dead back to life and
who brings into existence what didn't exist
before.

¹⁸When God promised Abraham that he
would become the father of many nations,

Abraham believed him. God had also said,
"Your descendants will be as numerous as
the stars,"* even though such a promise
seemed utterly impossible! ¹⁹And Abraham's faith did not weaken, even though
he knew that he was too old to be a father
at the age of one hundred and that Sarah,
his wife, had never been able to have children.

²⁰Abraham never wavered in believing
God's promise. In fact, his faith grew
stronger, and in this he brought glory to
God. ²¹He was absolutely convinced that
God was able to do anything he promised.
²²And because of Abraham's faith, God declared him to be righteous.

²³Now this wonderful truth—that God
declared him to be righteous—wasn't just
for Abraham's benefit. ²⁴It was for us, too,
assuring us that God will also declare us to
be righteous if we believe in God, who
brought Jesus our Lord back from the dead.
²⁵He was handed over to die because of our
sins, and he was raised from the dead to
make us right with God.

CHAPTER 5
Therefore, since we have been made right
in God's sight by faith, we have peace with
God because of what Jesus Christ our Lord
has done for us. ²Because of our faith,
Christ has brought us into this place of
highest privilege where we now stand, and
we confidently and joyfully look forward
to sharing God's glory.

³We can rejoice, too, when we run into
problems and trials, for we know that they
are good for us—they help us learn to endure. ⁴And endurance develops strength of
character in us, and character strengthens
our confident expectation of salvation.
⁵And this expectation will not disappoint
us. For we know how dearly God loves us,
because he has given us the Holy Spirit to
fill our hearts with his love.

⁶When we were utterly helpless, Christ
came at just the right time and died for us
sinners. ⁷Now, no one is likely to die for a
good person, though someone might be
willing to die for a person who is especially
good. ⁸But God showed his great love for us
by sending Christ to die for us while we
were still sinners. ⁹And since we have been
made right in God's sight by the blood of
Christ, he will certainly save us from God's

4:7-8 Ps 32:1-2.   **4:17** Gen 17:5.   **4:18** Gen 15:5.

judgment. ¹⁰For since we were restored to friendship with God by the death of his Son while we were still his enemies, we will certainly be delivered from eternal punishment by his life. ¹¹So now we can rejoice in our wonderful new relationship with God—all because of what our Lord Jesus Christ has done for us in making us friends of God.

¹²When Adam sinned, sin entered the entire human race. Adam's sin brought death, so death spread to everyone, for everyone sinned. ¹³Yes, people sinned even before the law was given. And though there was no law to break, since it had not yet been given, ¹⁴they all died anyway—even though they did not disobey an explicit commandment of God, as Adam did. What a contrast between Adam and Christ, who was yet to come! ¹⁵And what a difference between our sin and God's generous gift of forgiveness. For this one man, Adam, brought death to many through his sin. But this other man, Jesus Christ, brought forgiveness to many through God's bountiful gift. ¹⁶And the result of God's gracious gift is very different from the result of that one man's sin. For Adam's sin led to condemnation, but we have the free gift of being accepted by God, even though we are guilty of many sins. ¹⁷The sin of this one man, Adam, caused death to rule over us, but all who receive God's wonderful, gracious gift of righteousness will live in triumph over sin and death through this one man, Jesus Christ.

¹⁸Yes, Adam's one sin brought condemnation upon everyone, but Christ's one act of righteousness makes all people right in God's sight and gives them life. ¹⁹Because one person disobeyed God, many people became sinners. But because one other person obeyed God, many people will be made right in God's sight.

²⁰God's law was given so that all people could see how sinful they were. But as people sinned more and more, God's wonderful kindness became more abundant. ²¹So just as sin ruled over all people and brought them to death, now God's wonderful kindness rules instead, giving us right standing with God and resulting in eternal life through Jesus Christ our Lord.

NOVEMBER 14 ☐ DAY 319
Unreservedly Available

 LOOK BACK Saul the persecutor becomes Paul the apostle to the Gentiles. His "travel diary" reads like a modern-day adventure novel as he faces mobs and magistrates, stonings and shipwreck for the privilege of spreading the Good News from Antioch to Rome.

Paul's missionary journeys cover thousands of miles and more than a decade of his life. Following his trips to such areas as Galatia, Macedonia, and Asia, Paul is arrested in Jerusalem and faces a series of trials at the hands of Felix, Festus, and Agrippa. Failing to find justice in the courts, Paul declares, "I appeal to Caesar" (Acts 25:11), and to Rome he goes! The journey by land and sea is fraught with peril, but at last Paul arrives to await trial. During his imprisonment in Rome, he is not free to travel but is able to meet with his spiritual children and prepare them for the ministry that will soon be passed to them.

The *epistles* (letters) of Paul correspond to the *expeditions* of Paul. On his first journey, he writes the book of Galatians. On his second journey, he writes the books of 1 and 2 Thessalonians. On his third journey, he writes the books of Romans and 1 and 2 Corinthians. As you read these epistles in the coming weeks, turn back to the corresponding chapter in Acts to establish the settings for the letters.

 LOOK UP Imagine that you are part of a military unit stationed on the edge of enemy territory. To make matters worse, the enemy is headed your way—fast.

You await orders to retreat, but instead you hear your commanding

True greatness is to serve unnoticed and to work unseen.

officer give these orders: "Men, you are to stay right where you are and fight as hard as you can, as long as you can, until you are killed or captured." (Incidentally, a situation very similar to this actually happened during World War II. You'll find it documented in the book and movie entitled *They Were Expendable*.)

How would you feel about such an assignment? It's definitely not a role for the fainthearted. But those willing to look death in the face and become "walking dead men" can wreak havoc on the enemy. Why? Because death holds no sway over them. They are fearless and focused. They have nothing to lose and everything to gain. They have already counted the cost of service. In short, they are a dangerous foe because they are expendable.

 LOOK AHEAD The apostles and disciples in the book of Acts saw themselves as expendable in the service of their Lord. Self-preservation was the last thought on their minds. They were totally, unreservedly available to their Lord. You can see that attitude in a number of verses from Paul's letters:

"I myself no longer live, but Christ lives in me. So I live my life in this earthly body by trusting in the Son of God, who loved me and gave himself for me" (Galatians 2:20).

"For to me, living is for Christ, and dying is even better" (Philippians 1:21).

If self-promotion or self-preservation is your goal in life, you have yet to discover the liberating power of expendability. But once you see your time, talents, and treasure as 100 percent available in the service of your Lord, then you'll be able to say with Paul: "But my life is worth nothing unless I use it for doing the work assigned me by the Lord Jesus—the work of telling others the Good News about God's wonderful kindness and love" (Acts 20:24).

NOVEMBER 15 □ DAY 320
ROMANS 6–8
God's Power for Righteous Living

 OVERVIEW Paul, the gifted debater, anticipates the logical questions that will follow his explanation of justification by faith: Since grace abounds, may I continue to sin? Can I sin because I am no longer under the law, but under grace? Is the law sinful? After answering these and other questions, Paul moves on to discuss the constant struggle between the two natures: the flesh and the spirit. He concludes his arguments by revealing two liberating facts: "There is no condemnation for those who belong to Christ Jesus" (8:1); and nothing on earth or in heaven can separate us from the love of God (8:39).

Chapter 6	Chapter 7	Chapter 8
The Potential for Holy Living	The Problem with Holy Living	The Power for Holy Living
Perfect Christ	Wretched People	Ministering Spirit

YOUR DAILY WALK In the margin, write down the name of a former employer, someone you *used* to work for. Now suppose you were to walk into your former employer's office and he or she told you, "All right, don't just stand there. Get to work!" What would you do?

If sin rules us, it will inevitably ruin us.

Probably you'd do absolutely nothing . . . except walk out of the building. Why? Because you no longer work for your former employer. When you were under your former employer's authority, you did whatever he or she told you to do. But now that you work for someone else, the old boss has lost that position of authority. You answer to another boss now!

Now read 6:16-18. Do you see the parallel? Formerly you were a servant to sin. Sin was your master, your employer. But now in Christ you have been set free from that slavery in order to become a "slave" to righteousness. Christ is your new Employer, and your responsibility is to answer to him!

Are you still taking orders from your old employer, sin, as if it had ultimate control over you? Write out the words of 6:13, put them in a prominent place, and make them your "marching orders" for today. You might even share them with your boss at work!

INSIGHT The Winning Team for Nearly 2,000 Years
The apostle Paul encouraged the Roman believers with these words: "Overwhelming victory is ours through Christ" (8:37). His words are still true today. No matter how bad your situation is, you can have victory over your circumstances through Christ. Let this truth encourage you daily.

C H A P T E R 6
Well then, should we keep on sinning so that God can show us more and more kindness and forgiveness? [2]Of course not! Since we have died to sin, how can we continue to live in it? [3]Or have you forgotten that when we became Christians and were baptized to become one with Christ Jesus, we died with him? [4]For we died and were buried with Christ by baptism. And just as Christ was raised from the dead by the glorious power of the Father, now we also may live new lives.

[5]Since we have been united with him in his death, we will also be raised as he was. [6]Our old sinful selves were crucified with Christ so that sin might lose its power in our lives. We are no longer slaves to sin. [7]For when we died with Christ we were set free from the power of sin. [8]And since we died with Christ, we know we will also share his new life. [9]We are sure of this because Christ rose from the dead, and he will never die again. Death no longer has any power over him. [10]He died once to defeat sin, and now he lives for the glory of God. [11]So you should consider yourselves dead to sin and able to live for the glory of God through Christ Jesus.

[12]Do not let sin control the way you live;*

do not give in to its lustful desires. [13]Do not let any part of your body become a tool of wickedness, to be used for sinning. Instead, give yourselves completely to God since you have been given new life. And use your whole body as a tool to do what is right for the glory of God. [14]Sin is no longer your master, for you are no longer subject to the law, which enslaves you to sin. Instead, you are free by God's grace.

[15]So since God's grace has set us free from the law, does this mean we can go on sinning? Of course not! [16]Don't you realize that whatever you choose to obey becomes your master? You can choose sin, which leads to death, or you can choose to obey God and receive his approval. [17]Thank God! Once you were slaves of sin, but now you have obeyed with all your heart the new teaching God has given you. [18]Now you are free from sin, your old master, and you have become slaves to your new master, righteousness.

[19]I speak this way, using the illustration of slaves and masters, because it is easy to understand. Before, you let yourselves be slaves of impurity and lawlessness. Now you must choose to be slaves of righteousness so that you will become holy.

[20]In those days, when you were slaves of

6:12 Or *Do not let sin reign in your body, which is subject to death.*

sin, you weren't concerned with doing what was right. ²¹And what was the result? It was not good, since now you are ashamed of the things you used to do, things that end in eternal doom. ²²But now you are free from the power of sin and have become slaves of God. Now you do those things that lead to holiness and result in eternal life. ²³For the wages of sin is death, but the free gift of God is eternal life through Christ Jesus our Lord.

CHAPTER 7

Now, dear brothers and sisters—you who are familiar with the law—don't you know that the law applies only to a person who is still living? ²Let me illustrate. When a woman marries, the law binds her to her husband as long as he is alive. But if he dies, the laws of marriage no longer apply to her. ³So while her husband is alive, she would be committing adultery if she married another man. But if her husband dies, she is free from that law and does not commit adultery when she remarries.

⁴So this is the point: The law no longer holds you in its power, because you died to its power when you died with Christ on the cross. And now you are united with the one who was raised from the dead. As a result, you can produce good fruit, that is, good deeds for God. ⁵When we were controlled by our old nature, sinful desires were at work within us, and the law aroused these evil desires that produced sinful deeds, resulting in death. ⁶But now we have been released from the law, for we died with Christ, and we are no longer captive to its power. Now we can really serve God, not in the old way by obeying the letter of the law, but in the new way, by the Spirit.

⁷Well then, am I suggesting that the law of God is evil? Of course not! The law is not sinful, but it was the law that showed me my sin. I would never have known that coveting is wrong if the law had not said, "Do not covet."* ⁸But sin took advantage of this law and aroused all kinds of forbidden desires within me! If there were no law, sin would not have that power.

⁹I felt fine when I did not understand what the law demanded. But when I learned the truth, I realized I had broken the law and was a sinner, doomed to die.

¹⁰So the good law, which was supposed to show me the way of life, instead gave me the death penalty. ¹¹Sin took advantage of the law and fooled me; it took the good law and used it to make me guilty of death. ¹²But still, the law itself is holy and right and good.

¹³But how can that be? Did the law, which is good, cause my doom? Of course not! Sin used what was good to bring about my condemnation. So we can see how terrible sin really is. It uses God's good commandment for its own evil purposes.

¹⁴The law is good, then. The trouble is not with the law but with me, because I am sold into slavery, with sin as my master. ¹⁵I don't understand myself at all, for I really want to do what is right, but I don't do it. Instead, I do the very thing I hate. ¹⁶I know perfectly well that what I am doing is wrong, and my bad conscience shows that I agree that the law is good. ¹⁷But I can't help myself, because it is sin inside me that makes me do these evil things.

¹⁸I know I am rotten through and through so far as my old sinful nature is concerned. No matter which way I turn, I can't make myself do right. I want to, but I can't. ¹⁹When I want to do good, I don't. And when I try not to do wrong, I do it anyway. ²⁰But if I am doing what I don't want to do, I am not really the one doing it; the sin within me is doing it.

²¹It seems to be a fact of life that when I want to do what is right, I inevitably do what is wrong. ²²I love God's law with all my heart. ²³But there is another law at work within me that is at war with my mind. This law wins the fight and makes me a slave to the sin that is still within me. ²⁴Oh, what a miserable person I am! Who will free me from this life that is dominated by sin?* ²⁵Thank God! The answer is in Jesus Christ our Lord. So you see how it is: In my mind I really want to obey God's law, but because of my sinful nature I am a slave to sin.

CHAPTER 8

So now there is no condemnation for those who belong to Christ Jesus. ²For the power* of the life-giving Spirit has freed you* through Christ Jesus from the power of sin that leads to death. ³The law of Moses could not save us, because of our

7:7 Exod 20:17; Deut 5:21.   7:24 Greek *from this body of death?*   8:2a Greek *the law;* also in 8:2b.   8:2b Some manuscripts read *me.*

sinful nature. But God put into effect a different plan to save us. He sent his own Son in a human body like ours, except that ours are sinful. God destroyed sin's control over us by giving his Son as a sacrifice for our sins. [4]He did this so that the requirement of the law would be fully accomplished for us* who no longer follow our sinful nature but instead follow the Spirit.

[5]Those who are dominated by the sinful nature think about sinful things, but those who are controlled by the Holy Spirit think about things that please the Spirit. [6]If your sinful nature controls your mind, there is death. But if the Holy Spirit controls your mind, there is life and peace. [7]For the sinful nature is always hostile to God. It never did obey God's laws, and it never will. [8]That's why those who are still under the control of their sinful nature can never please God.

[9]But you are not controlled by your sinful nature. You are controlled by the Spirit if you have the Spirit of God living in you. (And remember that those who do not have the Spirit of Christ living in them are not Christians at all.) [10]Since Christ lives within you, even though your body will die because of sin, your spirit is alive* because you have been made right with God. [11]The Spirit of God, who raised Jesus from the dead, lives in you. And just as he raised Christ from the dead, he will give life to your mortal body by this same Spirit living within you.

[12]So, dear brothers and sisters, you have no obligation whatsoever to do what your sinful nature urges you to do. [13]For if you keep on following it, you will perish. But if through the power of the Holy Spirit you turn from it* and its evil deeds, you will live. [14]For all who are led by the Spirit of God are children of God.

[15]So you should not be like cowering, fearful slaves. You should behave instead like God's very own children, adopted into his family—calling him "Father, dear Father."* [16]For his Holy Spirit speaks to us deep in our hearts and tells us that we are God's children. [17]And since we are his children, we will share his treasures—for everything God gives to his Son, Christ, is ours, too. But if we are to share his glory, we must also share his suffering.

[18]Yet what we suffer now is nothing compared to the glory he will give us later. [19]For all creation is waiting eagerly for that future day when God will reveal who his children really are. [20]Against its will, everything on earth was subjected to God's curse. [21]All creation anticipates the day when it will join God's children in glorious freedom from death and decay. [22]For we know that all creation has been groaning as in the pains of childbirth right up to the present time. [23]And even we Christians, although we have the Holy Spirit within us as a foretaste of future glory, also groan to be released from pain and suffering. We, too, wait anxiously for that day when God will give us our full rights as his children, including the new bodies he has promised us. [24]Now that we are saved, we eagerly look forward to this freedom. For if you already have something, you don't need to hope for it. [25]But if we look forward to something we don't have yet, we must wait patiently and confidently.

[26]And the Holy Spirit helps us in our distress. For we don't even know what we should pray for, nor how we should pray. But the Holy Spirit prays for us with groanings that cannot be expressed in words. [27]And the Father who knows all hearts knows what the Spirit is saying, for the Spirit pleads for us believers in harmony with God's own will. [28]And we know that God causes everything to work together* for the good of those who love God and are called according to his purpose for them. [29]For God knew his people in advance, and he chose them to become like his Son, so that his Son would be the firstborn, with many brothers and sisters. [30]And having chosen them, he called them to come to him. And he gave them right standing with himself, and he promised them his glory.

[31]What can we say about such wonderful things as these? If God is for us, who can ever be against us? [32]Since God did not spare even his own Son but gave him up for us all, won't God, who gave us Christ, also give us everything else?

[33]Who dares accuse us whom God has chosen for his own? Will God? No! He is the one who has given us right standing with himself. [34]Who then will condemn us?

8:4 Or *accomplished by us.*   **8:10** Or *the Spirit will bring you eternal life.*   **8:13** Greek *put it to death.*   **8:15** Greek *"Abba, Father."* Abba *is an Aramaic term for "father."*   **8:28** Some manuscripts read *And we know that everything works together.*

Will Christ Jesus? No, for he is the one who died for us and was raised to life for us and is sitting at the place of highest honor next to God, pleading for us.

³⁵Can anything ever separate us from Christ's love? Does it mean he no longer loves us if we have trouble or calamity, or are persecuted, or are hungry or cold or in danger or threatened with death? ³⁶(Even the Scriptures say, "For your sake we are killed every day; we are being slaughtered like sheep."*) ³⁷No, despite all these things,

8:36 Ps 44:22.

overwhelming victory is ours through Christ, who loved us.

³⁸And I am convinced that nothing can ever separate us from his love. Death can't, and life can't. The angels can't, and the demons can't. Our fears for today, our worries about tomorrow, and even the powers of hell can't keep God's love away. ³⁹Whether we are high above the sky or in the deepest ocean, nothing in all creation will ever be able to separate us from the love of God that is revealed in Christ Jesus our Lord.

NOVEMBER 16 □ DAY 321
ROMANS 9–11
God's Plan of Righteousness

OVERVIEW In one sense Romans 9–11 resembles a parenthesis because of the way chapters 8 and 12 flow together. (Read 8:39 and 12:1). Even so, these chapters are essential to Paul's argument and are strategically placed in the epistle. Paul has said that salvation is by grace—God's undeserved favor from start to finish! This raises the question: If God's people (the Jews) have rejected his grace, then hasn't God also discarded his people? Paul answers with three observations:

1. God chose the Jews by sovereign selection.
2. The Jews turned away from God by willful rejection.
3. God's rejection of his people is both incomplete (there is a remnant) and temporary (they will be restored).

Paul then concludes the section with praise to God for his incomprehensible ways—an appropriate response!

Chapter 9	Chapter 10	Chapter 11
Israel's Past	Israel's Present	Israel's Future
Selection	Rejection	Restoration

The authority for faith is the revelation of God.

YOUR DAILY WALK It hurts to see someone reject the gospel. It hurts even more when that "someone" is part of your family. But it hurts most when that "someone" who rejects the gospel prides him or herself on being religious!

Paul lamented that his own people, the Jews, had rejected the gospel. Though their religious zeal was exemplary, it was based on something other than Christ. It was a zeal without knowledge—activity without reality—which only led to self-deception and false pride. No one could doubt the sincerity of their beliefs and actions. But they were sincerely wrong . . . and so they died in their sins.

The best way to combat such misplaced confidence is by a clear proclamation of the gospel. Using 10:13-15 as your model, look for one sincere—but sincerely wrong—individual to whom you can bring "Good News" today!

INSIGHT Paul, the Old Testament Whiz
In the space of these three chapters, Paul demonstrates his thorough
knowledge of the Old Testament Scriptures by quoting from ten different books. How many can you identify? Have fun!

CHAPTER 9

In the presence of Christ, I speak with utter truthfulness—I do not lie—and my conscience and the Holy Spirit confirm that what I am saying is true. [2]My heart is filled with bitter sorrow and unending grief [3]for my people, my Jewish brothers and sisters. I would be willing to be forever cursed—cut off from Christ!—if that would save them. [4]They are the people of Israel, chosen to be God's special children. God revealed his glory to them. He made covenants with them and gave his law to them. They have the privilege of worshiping him and receiving his wonderful promises. [5]Their ancestors were great people of God, and Christ himself was a Jew as far as his human nature is concerned. And he is God, who rules over everything and is worthy of eternal praise! Amen.*

[6]Well then, has God failed to fulfill his promise to the Jews? No, for not everyone born into a Jewish family is truly a Jew! [7]Just the fact that they are descendants of Abraham doesn't make them truly Abraham's children. For the Scriptures say, "Isaac is the son through whom your descendants will be counted,"* though Abraham had other children, too. [8]This means that Abraham's physical descendants are not necessarily children of God. It is the children of the promise who are considered to be Abraham's children. [9]For God had promised, "Next year I will return, and Sarah will have a son."*

[10]This son was our ancestor Isaac. When he grew up, he married Rebekah, who gave birth to twins. [11]But before they were born, before they had done anything good or bad, she received a message from God. (This message proves that God chooses according to his own plan, [12]not according to our good or bad works.) She was told, "The descendants of your older son will serve the descendants of your younger son."* [13]In the words of the Scriptures, "I loved Jacob, but I rejected Esau."*

[14]What can we say? Was God being unfair? Of course not! [15]For God said to Moses,

"I will show mercy to anyone I choose,
  and I will show compassion to
      anyone I choose."*

[16]So receiving God's promise is not up to us. We can't get it by choosing it or working hard for it. God will show mercy to anyone he chooses.

[17]For the Scriptures say that God told Pharaoh, "I have appointed you for the very purpose of displaying my power in you, and so that my fame might spread throughout the earth."* [18]So you see, God shows mercy to some just because he wants to, and he chooses to make some people refuse to listen.

[19]Well then, you might say, "Why does God blame people for not listening? Haven't they simply done what he made them do?"

[20]No, don't say that. Who are you, a mere human being, to criticize God? Should the thing that was created say to the one who made it, "Why have you made me like this?" [21]When a potter makes jars out of clay, doesn't he have a right to use the same lump of clay to make one jar for decoration and another to throw garbage into? [22]God has every right to exercise his judgment and his power, but he also has the right to be very patient with those who are the objects of his judgment and are fit only for destruction. [23]He also has the right to pour out the riches of his glory upon those he prepared to be the objects of his mercy—[24]even upon us, whom he selected, both from the Jews and from the Gentiles.

[25]Concerning the Gentiles, God says in the prophecy of Hosea,

"Those who were not my people,
  I will now call my people.
And I will love those
  whom I did not love before."*

[26]And,

"Once they were told,
  'You are not my people.'
But now he will say,
  'You are children of the living
      God.'"*

9:5 Or *May God, who rules over everything, be praised forever. Amen.*   **9:7** Gen 21:12.   **9:9** Gen 18:10, 14.   **9:12** Gen 25:23.
9:13 Mal 1:2-3.   **9:15** Exod 33:19.   **9:17** Exod 9:16.   **9:25** Hos 2:23.   **9:26** Hos 1:10.

²⁷Concerning Israel, Isaiah the prophet cried out,

> "Though the people of Israel are as
>   numerous as the sand on the
>   seashore,
>   only a small number will be saved.
> ²⁸ For the Lord will carry out his sentence
>   upon the earth
>   quickly and with finality."*

²⁹And Isaiah said in another place,

> "If the Lord Almighty
>   had not spared a few of us,
> we would have been wiped out
>   as completely as Sodom and
>   Gomorrah."*

³⁰Well then, what shall we say about these things? Just this: The Gentiles have been made right with God by faith, even though they were not seeking him. ³¹But the Jews, who tried so hard to get right with God by keeping the law, never succeeded. ³²Why not? Because they were trying to get right with God by keeping the law and being good instead of by depending on faith. They stumbled over the great rock in their path. ³³God warned them of this in the Scriptures when he said,

> "I am placing a stone in Jerusalem* that
>   causes people to stumble,
>   and a rock that makes them fall.*
> But anyone who believes in him
>   will not be disappointed.*"

CHAPTER 10

Dear brothers and sisters, the longing of my heart and my prayer to God is that the Jewish people might be saved. ²I know what enthusiasm they have for God, but it is misdirected zeal. ³For they don't understand God's way of making people right with himself. Instead, they are clinging to their own way of getting right with God by trying to keep the law. They won't go along with God's way. ⁴For Christ has accomplished the whole purpose* of the law. All who believe in him are made right with God.

⁵For Moses wrote that the law's way of making a person right with God requires obedience to all of its commands.* ⁶But the way of getting right with God through

faith says, "You don't need to go to heaven" (to find Christ and bring him down to help you). ⁷And it says, "You don't need to go to the place of the dead" (to bring Christ back to life again). ⁸Salvation that comes from trusting Christ—which is the message we preach—is already within easy reach. In fact, the Scriptures say, "The message is close at hand; it is on your lips and in your heart."*

⁹For if you confess with your mouth that Jesus is Lord and believe in your heart that God raised him from the dead, you will be saved. ¹⁰For it is by believing in your heart that you are made right with God, and it is by confessing with your mouth that you are saved. ¹¹As the Scriptures tell us, "Anyone who believes in him will not be disappointed.*" ¹²Jew and Gentile are the same in this respect. They all have the same Lord, who generously gives his riches to all who ask for them. ¹³For "Anyone who calls on the name of the Lord will be saved."*

¹⁴But how can they call on him to save them unless they believe in him? And how can they believe in him if they have never heard about him? And how can they hear about him unless someone tells them? ¹⁵And how will anyone go and tell them without being sent? That is what the Scriptures mean when they say, "How beautiful are the feet of those who bring good news!"*

¹⁶But not everyone welcomes the Good News, for Isaiah the prophet said, "Lord, who has believed our message?"* ¹⁷Yet faith comes from listening to this message of good news—the Good News about Christ.

¹⁸But what about the Jews? Have they actually heard the message? Yes, they have:

> "The message of God's creation has
>   gone out to everyone,
>   and its words to all the world."*

¹⁹But did the people of Israel really understand? Yes, they did, for even in the time of Moses, God had said,

> "I will rouse your jealousy by blessing
>   other nations.
> I will make you angry by blessing
>   the foolish Gentiles."*

9:27-28 Isa 10:22-23.　9:29 Isa 1:9.　9:33a Greek *in Zion.*　9:33b Isa 8:14.　9:33c Or *will not be put to shame.* Isa 28:16.
10:4 Or *the end.*　10:5 Lev 18:5.　10:6-8 Deut 30:12-14.　10:11 Or *will not be put to shame.* Isa 28:16.　10:13 Joel 2:32.
10:15 Isa 52:7.　10:16 Isa 53:1.　10:18 Ps 19:4.　10:19 Deut 32:21.

²⁰And later Isaiah spoke boldly for God:

> "I was found by people
>> who were not looking for me.
> I showed myself to those
>> who were not asking for me."*

²¹But regarding Israel, God said,

> "All day long I opened my arms to
>> them,
> but they kept disobeying me and
>> arguing with me."*

CHAPTER 11

I ask, then, has God rejected his people, the Jews? Of course not! Remember that I myself am a Jew, a descendant of Abraham and a member of the tribe of Benjamin.

²No, God has not rejected his own people, whom he chose from the very beginning. Do you remember what the Scriptures say about this? Elijah the prophet complained to God about the people of Israel and said, ³"Lord, they have killed your prophets and torn down your altars. I alone am left, and now they are trying to kill me, too."*

⁴And do you remember God's reply? He said, "You are not the only one left. I have seven thousand others who have never bowed down to Baal!"*

⁵It is the same today, for not all the Jews have turned away from God. A few* are being saved as a result of God's kindness in choosing them. ⁶And if they are saved by God's kindness, then it is not by their good works. For in that case, God's wonderful kindness would not be what it really is— free and undeserved.

⁷So this is the situation: Most of the Jews have not found the favor of God they are looking for so earnestly. A few have—the ones God has chosen—but the rest were made unresponsive. ⁸As the Scriptures say,

> "God has put them into a deep sleep.
> To this very day he has shut their eyes
>> so they do not see,
>> and closed their ears so they do not
>>> hear."*

⁹David spoke of this same thing when he said,

> "Let their bountiful table become a
>> snare,

a trap that makes them think all is
>> well.
> Let their blessings cause them to
>> stumble.
¹⁰ Let their eyes go blind so they cannot
>> see,
> and let their backs grow weaker and
>> weaker."*

¹¹Did God's people stumble and fall beyond recovery? Of course not! His purpose was to make his salvation available to the Gentiles, and then the Jews would be jealous and want it for themselves. ¹²Now if the Gentiles were enriched because the Jews turned down God's offer of salvation, think how much greater a blessing the world will share when the Jews finally accept it.

¹³I am saying all of this especially for you Gentiles. God has appointed me as the apostle to the Gentiles. I lay great stress on this, ¹⁴for I want to find a way to make the Jews want what you Gentiles have, and in that way I might save some of them. ¹⁵For since the Jews' rejection meant that God offered salvation to the rest of the world, how much more wonderful their acceptance will be. It will be life for those who were dead! ¹⁶And since Abraham and the other patriarchs were holy, their children will also be holy.* For if the roots of the tree are holy, the branches will be, too.

¹⁷But some of these branches from Abraham's tree, some of the Jews, have been broken off. And you Gentiles, who were branches from a wild olive tree, were grafted in. So now you also receive the blessing God has promised Abraham and his children, sharing in God's rich nourishment of his special olive tree. ¹⁸But you must be careful not to brag about being grafted in to replace the branches that were broken off. Remember, you are just a branch, not the root.

¹⁹"Well," you may say, "those branches were broken off to make room for me." ²⁰Yes, but remember—those branches, the Jews, were broken off because they didn't believe God, and you are there because you do believe. Don't think highly of yourself, but fear what could happen. ²¹For if God did not spare the branches he put there in the first place, he won't spare you either. ²²Notice how God is both kind and

---

10:20 Isa 65:1.   10:21 Isa 65:2.   11:3 1 Kgs 19:10, 14.   11:4 1 Kgs 19:18.   11:5 Greek *A remnant*.   11:8 Deut 29:4; Isa 29:10.
11:9-10 Ps 69:22-23.   11:16 Greek *If the dough offered as firstfruits is holy, so is the whole lump.*

severe. He is severe to those who disobeyed, but kind to you as you continue
to trust in his kindness. But if you stop
trusting, you also will be cut off. ²³And if
the Jews turn from their unbelief, God
will graft them back into the tree again.
He has the power to do it.

²⁴For if God was willing to take you who
were, by nature, branches from a wild olive
tree and graft you into his own good tree—
a very unusual thing to do—he will be far
more eager to graft the Jews back into the
tree where they belong.

²⁵I want you to understand this mystery,
dear brothers and sisters, so that you will
not feel proud and start bragging. Some of
the Jews have hard hearts, but this will last
only until the complete number of Gentiles
comes to Christ. ²⁶And so all Israel will be
saved. Do you remember what the prophets said about this?

"A Deliverer will come from
    Jerusalem,*
  and he will turn Israel* from all
    ungodliness.
²⁷ And then I will keep my covenant with
    them
  and take away their sins."*

²⁸Many of the Jews are now enemies of
the Good News. But this has been to your
benefit, for God has given his gifts to you
Gentiles. Yet the Jews are still his chosen
people because of his promises to Abraham, Isaac, and Jacob. ²⁹For God's gifts and
his call can never be withdrawn. ³⁰Once,
you Gentiles were rebels against God, but
when the Jews refused his mercy, God was
merciful to you instead. ³¹And now, in the
same way, the Jews are the rebels, and
God's mercy has come to you. But someday they,* too, will share in God's mercy.
³²For God has imprisoned all people in
their own disobedience so he could have
mercy on everyone.

³³Oh, what a wonderful God we have!
How great are his riches and wisdom and
knowledge! How impossible it is for us to
understand his decisions and his methods!
³⁴For who can know what the Lord is thinking? Who knows enough to be his counselor?* ³⁵And who could ever give him so
much that he would have to pay it back?
³⁶For everything comes from him; everything exists by his power and is intended
for his glory. To him be glory evermore.
Amen.

11:26a Greek *from Zion.*   **11:26b** Greek *Jacob.*   **11:26-27** Isa 59:20-21.   **11:31** Some manuscripts read *But now they;* other
manuscripts read *But they.*   **11:34** See Isa 40:13.

NOVEMBER 17 ☐ DAY 322
ROMANS 12–16
Practical Outworking of Righteousness

 OVERVIEW In the first eleven chapters, Paul has discussed the key
doctrines of the Christian faith. But Christian living requires more than
theory; it demands attention to duty as well, the daily outworking of
applied doctrine. To Paul, what you believe and how you behave are
inseparable. Doctrine dictates that love must control a believer's conduct both inside and outside the church (Romans 12), that a Christian
must be a good citizen (Romans 13), and that a Christian must make
proper ethical choices in consideration of weaker believers (Romans
14). Paul concludes his letter with a summary of his travel plans, a list
of personal greetings, and a warning against false teachers.

Chapter 12	Chapter 13	Chapters 14–15	Chapter 16
Serve One Another	Submit to Authority	Support the Weak	Salute the Saints
Practical Appeals			Personal Postscripts

YOUR DAILY WALK "WANTED: DEAD AND ALIVE!" Do you detect anything peculiar about a "wanted" poster like this?

Sacrifice is the ecstasy of giving the best we have to the one we love the most.

God wants you dead (to sin and self), but he also wants you alive (for service). In the Old Testament, animals were offered for sacrifices, and they had no say-so in the matter! But now, based on God's abundant mercies on your behalf, he is calling you to become a voluntary living sacrifice as a reasonable expression of your gratitude for all he has done for you and through you.

The trouble with being a living sacrifice is that, when the heat's on, the tendency is to crawl off the altar! If you have trouble volunteering for such an assignment, chances are you need to review God's mercies in your life. Thumb back through the pages of Romans, and see if you can discover at least six of those mercies . . . but don't stop there!

1. _____ (3:24)   4. _____ (   )
2. _____ (5:1)   5. _____ (   )
3. _____ (8:1)   6. _____ (   )

INSIGHT A Doxology of Doxologies
The word *doxology* comes from a Greek word meaning "brightness, radiance, splendor, glory." Notice how frequently Paul breaks forth in a spontaneous doxology (11:33-36; 15:9-13; 16:25-27) and whose glory is in view!

CHAPTER 12

And so, dear brothers and sisters, I plead with you to give your bodies to God. Let them be a living and holy sacrifice—the kind he will accept. When you think of what he has done for you, is this too much to ask? ²Don't copy the behavior and customs of this world, but let God transform you into a new person by changing the way you think. Then you will know what God wants you to do, and you will know how good and pleasing and perfect his will really is.

³As God's messenger, I give each of you this warning: Be honest in your estimate of yourselves, measuring your value by how much faith God has given you. ⁴Just as our bodies have many parts and each part has a special function, ⁵so it is with Christ's body. We are all parts of his one body, and each of us has different work to do. And since we are all one body in Christ, we belong to each other, and each of us needs all the others.

⁶God has given each of us the ability to do certain things well. So if God has given you the ability to prophesy, speak out when you have faith that God is speaking through you. ⁷If your gift is that of serving others, serve them well. If you are a teacher, do a good job of teaching. ⁸If your gift is to encourage others, do it! If you have money, share it generously. If God

has given you leadership ability, take the responsibility seriously. And if you have a gift for showing kindness to others, do it gladly.

⁹Don't just pretend that you love others. Really love them. Hate what is wrong. Stand on the side of the good. ¹⁰Love each other with genuine affection,* and take delight in honoring each other. ¹¹Never be lazy in your work, but serve the Lord enthusiastically.

¹²Be glad for all God is planning for you. Be patient in trouble, and always be prayerful. ¹³When God's children are in need, be the one to help them out. And get into the habit of inviting guests home for dinner or, if they need lodging, for the night.

¹⁴If people persecute you because you are a Christian, don't curse them; pray that God will bless them. ¹⁵When others are happy, be happy with them. If they are sad, share their sorrow. ¹⁶Live in harmony with each other. Don't try to act important, but enjoy the company of ordinary people. And don't think you know it all!

¹⁷Never pay back evil for evil to anyone. Do things in such a way that everyone can see you are honorable. ¹⁸Do your part to live in peace with everyone, as much as possible.

¹⁹Dear friends, never avenge yourselves. Leave that to God. For it is written,

12:10 Greek *with brotherly love.*

"I will take vengeance;
 I will repay those who deserve it,"*
 says the Lord.

20Instead, do what the Scriptures say:

"If your enemies are hungry, feed them.
 If they are thirsty, give them something
    to drink,
 and they will be ashamed of what
    they have done to you."*

21Don't let evil get the best of you, but conquer evil by doing good.

CHAPTER 13

Obey the government, for God is the one who put it there. All governments have been placed in power by God. 2So those who refuse to obey the laws of the land are refusing to obey God, and punishment will follow. 3For the authorities do not frighten people who are doing right, but they frighten those who do wrong. So do what they say, and you will get along well. 4The authorities are sent by God to help you. But if you are doing something wrong, of course you should be afraid, for you will be punished. The authorities are established by God for that very purpose, to punish those who do wrong. 5So you must obey the government for two reasons: to keep from being punished and to keep a clear conscience.

6Pay your taxes, too, for these same reasons. For government workers need to be paid so they can keep on doing the work God intended them to do. 7Give to everyone what you owe them: Pay your taxes and import duties, and give respect and honor to all to whom it is due.

8Pay all your debts, except the debt of love for others. You can never finish paying that! If you love your neighbor, you will fulfill all the requirements of God's law. 9For the commandments against adultery and murder and stealing and coveting—and any other commandment—are all summed up in this one commandment: "Love your neighbor as yourself."* 10Love does no wrong to anyone, so love satisfies all of God's requirements.

11Another reason for right living is that you know how late it is; time is running out. Wake up, for the coming of our salvation is nearer now than when we first be-

lieved. 12The night is almost gone; the day of salvation will soon be here. So don't live in darkness. Get rid of your evil deeds. Shed them like dirty clothes. Clothe yourselves with the armor of right living, as those who live in the light. 13We should be decent and true in everything we do, so that everyone can approve of our behavior. Don't participate in wild parties and getting drunk, or in adultery and immoral living, or in fighting and jealousy. 14But let the Lord Jesus Christ take control of you, and don't think of ways to indulge your evil desires.

CHAPTER 14

Accept Christians who are weak in faith, and don't argue with them about what they think is right or wrong. 2For instance, one person believes it is all right to eat anything. But another believer who has a sensitive conscience will eat only vegetables. 3Those who think it is all right to eat anything must not look down on those who won't. And those who won't eat certain foods must not condemn those who do, for God has accepted them. 4Who are you to condemn God's servants? They are responsible to the Lord, so let him tell them whether they are right or wrong. The Lord's power will help them do as they should.

5In the same way, some think one day is more holy than another day, while others think every day is alike. Each person should have a personal conviction about this matter. 6Those who have a special day for worshiping the Lord are trying to honor him. Those who eat all kinds of food do so to honor the Lord, since they give thanks to God before eating. And those who won't eat everything also want to please the Lord and give thanks to God. 7For we are not our own masters when we live or when we die. 8While we live, we live to please the Lord. And when we die, we go to be with the Lord. So in life and in death, we belong to the Lord. 9Christ died and rose again for this very purpose, so that he might be Lord of those who are alive and of those who have died.

10So why do you condemn another Christian*? Why do you look down on another Christian? Remember, each of us will

12:19 Deut 32:35.   12:20 Greek *and you will heap burning coals on their heads.* Prov 25:21-22.   13:9 Lev 19:18.   14:10 Greek *your brother; also in 14:10b, 13, 15, 21.*

stand personally before the judgment seat of God. [11]For the Scriptures say,

> "'As surely as I live,' says the Lord,
> 'every knee will bow to me
> 　and every tongue will confess
> 　　allegiance to God.'"*

[12]Yes, each of us will have to give a personal account to God. [13]So don't condemn each other anymore. Decide instead to live in such a way that you will not put an obstacle in another Christian's path.

[14]I know and am perfectly sure on the authority of the Lord Jesus that no food, in and of itself, is wrong to eat. But if someone believes it is wrong, then for that person it is wrong. [15]And if another Christian is distressed by what you eat, you are not acting in love if you eat it. Don't let your eating ruin someone for whom Christ died. [16]Then you will not be condemned for doing something you know is all right.

[17]For the Kingdom of God is not a matter of what we eat or drink, but of living a life of goodness and peace and joy in the Holy Spirit. [18]If you serve Christ with this attitude, you will please God. And other people will approve of you, too. [19]So then, let us aim for harmony in the church and try to build each other up.

[20]Don't tear apart the work of God over what you eat. Remember, there is nothing wrong with these things in themselves. But it is wrong to eat anything if it makes another person stumble. [21]Don't eat meat or drink wine or do anything else if it might cause another Christian to stumble. [22]You may have the faith to believe that there is nothing wrong with what you are doing, but keep it between yourself and God. Blessed are those who do not condemn themselves by doing something they know is all right. [23]But if people have doubts about whether they should eat something, they shouldn't eat it. They would be condemned for not acting in faith before God. If you do anything you believe is not right, you are sinning.

CHAPTER 15

We may know that these things make no difference, but we cannot just go ahead and do them to please ourselves. We must be considerate of the doubts and fears of those who think these things are wrong. [2]We

should please others. If we do what helps them, we will build them up in the Lord. [3]For even Christ didn't please himself. As the Scriptures say, "Those who insult you are also insulting me."* [4]Such things were written in the Scriptures long ago to teach us. They give us hope and encouragement as we wait patiently for God's promises.

[5]May God, who gives this patience and encouragement, help you live in complete harmony with each other—each with the attitude of Christ Jesus toward the other. [6]Then all of you can join together with one voice, giving praise and glory to God, the Father of our Lord Jesus Christ.

[7]So accept each other just as Christ has accepted you; then God will be glorified. [8]Remember that Christ came as a servant to the Jews to show that God is true to the promises he made to their ancestors. [9]And he came so the Gentiles might also give glory to God for his mercies to them. That is what the psalmist meant when he wrote:

> "I will praise you among the Gentiles;
> 　I will sing praises to your name."*

[10]And in another place it is written,

> "Rejoice, O you Gentiles,
> 　along with his people, the Jews."*

[11]And yet again,

> "Praise the Lord, all you Gentiles;
> 　praise him, all you people of the
> 　　earth."*

[12]And the prophet Isaiah said,

> "The heir to David's throne* will come,
> 　and he will rule over the Gentiles.
> 　They will place their hopes on him."*

[13]So I pray that God, who gives you hope, will keep you happy and full of peace as you believe in him. May you overflow with hope through the power of the Holy Spirit.

[14]I am fully convinced, dear brothers and sisters, that you are full of goodness. You know these things so well that you are able to teach others all about them. [15]Even so, I have been bold enough to emphasize some of these points, knowing that all you need is this reminder from me. For I am, by God's grace, [16]a special messenger from Christ Jesus to you Gentiles. I bring you the Good News and offer you up as a fragrant

---

14:11 Isa 45:23.　　15:3 Ps 69:9.　　15:9 Ps 18:49.　　15:10 Deut 32:43.　　15:11 Ps 117:1.　　15:12a Greek *The root of Jesse.*
15:12b Isa 11:10.

sacrifice to God so that you might be pure and pleasing to him by the Holy Spirit. ¹⁷So it is right for me to be enthusiastic about all Christ Jesus has done through me in my service to God. ¹⁸I dare not boast of anything else. I have brought the Gentiles to God by my message and by the way I lived before them. ¹⁹I have won them over by the miracles done through me as signs from God—all by the power of God's Spirit. In this way, I have fully presented the Good News of Christ all the way from Jerusalem clear over into Illyricum.*

²⁰My ambition has always been to preach the Good News where the name of Christ has never been heard, rather than where a church has already been started by someone else. ²¹I have been following the plan spoken of in the Scriptures, where it says,

"Those who have never been told
    about him will see,
and those who have never heard of
    him will understand."*

²²In fact, my visit to you has been delayed so long because I have been preaching in these places. ²³But now I have finished my work in these regions, and after all these long years of waiting, I am eager to visit you. ²⁴I am planning to go to Spain, and when I do, I will stop off in Rome. And after I have enjoyed your fellowship for a little while, you can send me on my way again. ²⁵But before I come, I must go down to Jerusalem to take a gift to the Christians there. ²⁶For you see, the believers in Greece* have eagerly taken up an offering for the Christians in Jerusalem, who are going through such hard times. ²⁷They were very glad to do this because they feel they owe a real debt to them. Since the Gentiles received the wonderful spiritual blessings of the Good News from the Jewish Christians, they feel the least they can do in return is help them financially. ²⁸As soon as I have delivered this money and completed this good deed of theirs, I will come to see you on my way to Spain. ²⁹And I am sure that when I come, Christ will give me a great blessing for you.

³⁰Dear brothers and sisters, I urge you in the name of our Lord Jesus Christ to join me in my struggle by praying to God for me. Do this because of your love for me,

given to you by the Holy Spirit. ³¹Pray that I will be rescued from those in Judea who refuse to obey God. Pray also that the Christians there will be willing to accept the donation I am bringing them. ³²Then, by the will of God, I will be able to come to you with a happy heart, and we will be an encouragement to each other.

³³And now may God, who gives us his peace, be with you all. Amen.

CHAPTER 16

Our sister Phoebe, a deacon in the church in Cenchrea, will be coming to see you soon. ²Receive her in the Lord, as one who is worthy of high honor. Help her in every way you can, for she has helped many in their needs, including me.

³Greet Priscilla and Aquila. They have been co-workers in my ministry for Christ Jesus. ⁴In fact, they risked their lives for me. I am not the only one who is thankful to them; so are all the Gentile churches. ⁵Please give my greetings to the church that meets in their home.

Greet my dear friend Epenetus. He was the very first person to become a Christian in the province of Asia. ⁶Give my greetings to Mary, who has worked so hard for your benefit. ⁷Then there are Andronicus and Junia,* my relatives,* who were in prison with me. They are respected among the apostles and became Christians before I did. Please give them my greetings. ⁸Say hello to Ampliatus, whom I love as one of the Lord's own children, ⁹and Urbanus, our co-worker in Christ, and beloved Stachys.

¹⁰Give my greetings to Apelles, a good man whom Christ approves. And give my best regards to the members of the household of Aristobulus. ¹¹Greet Herodion, my relative.* Greet the Christians in the household of Narcissus. ¹²Say hello to Tryphena and Tryphosa, the Lord's workers, and to dear Persis, who has worked so hard for the Lord. ¹³Greet Rufus, whom the Lord picked out to be his very own; and also his dear mother, who has been a mother to me.

¹⁴And please give my greetings to Asyncritus, Phlegon, Hermes, Patrobas, Hermas, and the brothers and sisters who are with them. ¹⁵Give my greetings to Philologus, Julia, Nereus and his sister, and to Olympas and all the other believers who

15:19 Illyricum was a region northeast of Italy.   15:21 Isa 52:15.   15:26 Greek Macedonia and Achaia, the northern and southern regions of Greece.   16:7a Or Junias; some manuscripts read Julia.   16:7b Or compatriots; also in 16:21.   16:11 Or compatriot.

are with them. [16]Greet each other in Christian love.* All the churches of Christ send you their greetings.

[17]And now I make one more appeal, my dear brothers and sisters. Watch out for people who cause divisions and upset people's faith by teaching things that are contrary to what you have been taught. Stay away from them. [18]Such people are not serving Christ our Lord; they are serving their own personal interests. By smooth talk and glowing words they deceive innocent people. [19]But everyone knows that you are obedient to the Lord. This makes me very happy. I want you to see clearly what is right and to stay innocent of any wrong. [20]The God of peace will soon crush Satan under your feet. May the grace of our Lord Jesus Christ be with you.

[21]Timothy, my fellow worker, and Lu-cius, Jason, and Sosipater, my relatives, send you their good wishes.

[22]I, Tertius, the one who is writing this letter for Paul, send my greetings, too, as a Christian brother.

[23]Gaius says hello to you. I am his guest, and the church meets here in his home. Erastus, the city treasurer, sends you his greetings, and so does Quartus, a Christian brother.*

[25]God is able to make you strong, just as the Good News says. It is the message about Jesus Christ and his plan for you Gentiles, a plan kept secret from the beginning of time. [26]But now as the prophets* foretold and as the eternal God has commanded, this message is made known to all Gentiles everywhere, so that they might believe and obey Christ. [27]To God, who alone is wise, be the glory forever through Jesus Christ. Amen.

16:16 Greek *with a sacred kiss.*   **16:23** Some manuscripts add verse 24, *May the grace of our Lord Jesus Christ be with you all. Amen.* **16:26** Greek *the prophetic writings.*

1 Corinthians

FAMOUS as a commercial center, Corinth was also infamous for immorality and paganism. But despite great obstacles, Paul planted a Christian church there in his second missionary journey (Acts 18:1-17). Though gifted and growing, the church was plagued with problems—moral and ethical, doctrinal and practical, corporate and private. Paul writes this letter to deal with some of the disorders and to answer questions the Christians at Corinth had raised.

Focus	Disruptions		Debates		Doubts	
Divisions	Problems with Divisions	Problems with Immorality	Problems with Marriage	Problems with Food and Idols	Problems with Worship and Gifts	Problems with Doctrinal Error
	1 4	5 6	7	8 10	11 14	15 16
Topics	In the Body	In the Home			In the Church	
	Responding to Reports			Answering Questions		
Place	Written in Ephesus					
Time	About A.D. 56					

NOVEMBER 18 ☐ DAY 323
1 CORINTHIANS 1–6
Problems with Divisions

OVERVIEW Despite all the problems in the church at Corinth, the believers there had received God's generous gift of grace (1:4) and were "holy" (1:2). The existence of factions in the church was caused by exalting human leaders and embracing human wisdom. This practice, Paul points out, opposes the wisdom of God. Human leaders are only instruments to accomplish God's work. They are his stewards, and their faithfulness will one day be judged by him. But factions are not the only problem in the Corinthian fellowship. Gross immorality and lawsuits between believers are also causing disunity in the church—a condition Paul finds intolerable.

Chapters 1–2	Chapters 3–4	Chapter 5	Chapter 6
Worldly Wisdom	Carnal Co-laborers	Moral Misconduct	Unjust Judges
Divisions in the Church		Disorders in the Church	

No person is living at his or her best who is not living at his or her best spiritually.

YOUR DAILY WALK There are three kinds of people in the business world: those who make things happen, those who watch things happen, and those who ask, "What happened?" Which kind are you?

There are three kinds of people in the spiritual world: those who are spiritually dead (natural man, 2:14); those who are spiritually immature (carnal man, 3:1); and those who are spiritually discerning (spiritual man, 2:15-16). Which kind are you?

The *natural* person does not have the Spirit of God and cannot understand or apply spiritual truth. The *carnal* person is a Christian who is acting like a natural person (3:3). This person's growth in Christ is stunted. The carnal person is still feeding on spiritual "milk" when he or she should be eating "meat." The *spiritual* person has "the mind of Christ" (2:16) and is able to take the truths of God's Word and translate them into obedient action. In the margin of your Bible place your name next to the verse that most accurately describes your life today. Then talk to God about what needs to change before you could be described as "he [or she] who is spiritual."

INSIGHT Apollos Would Have Been Appalled!
The "Apollos party" (3:4-5) claimed allegiance to Apollos, an Alexandrian Jew who was a gifted orator. Apollos had known the message of John the Baptist and had been instructed more fully in the truth of Jesus Christ by Aquila and Priscilla (Acts 18:24–19:1).

CHAPTER 1
This letter is from Paul, chosen by the will of God to be an apostle of Christ Jesus, and from our brother Sosthenes.

²We are writing to the church of God in Corinth, you who have been called by God to be his own holy people. He made you holy by means of Christ Jesus, just as he did all Christians everywhere—whoever calls upon the name of Jesus Christ, our Lord and theirs.

³May God our Father and the Lord Jesus Christ give you his grace and peace.

⁴I can never stop thanking God for all the generous gifts he has given you, now that you belong to Christ Jesus. ⁵He has enriched your church with the gifts of eloquence and every kind of knowledge. ⁶This shows that what I told you about Christ is true. ⁷Now you have every spiritual gift you need as you eagerly wait for the return of our Lord Jesus Christ. ⁸He will keep you strong right up to the end, and he will keep you free from all blame on the great day when our Lord Jesus Christ returns. ⁹God will surely do this for you, for he always does just what he says, and he is the one who invited you into this wonderful friendship with his Son, Jesus Christ our Lord.

¹⁰Now, dear brothers and sisters, I appeal to you by the authority of the Lord Jesus Christ to stop arguing among yourselves. Let there be real harmony so there won't be divisions in the church. I plead with you to be of one mind, united in thought and purpose. ¹¹For some members of Chloe's household have told me about your arguments, dear brothers and sisters. ¹²Some of you are saying, "I am a follower of Paul." Others are saying, "I follow Apollos," or "I follow Peter,*" or "I follow only Christ." ¹³Can Christ be divided into pieces?

Was I, Paul, crucified for you? Were any of you baptized in the name of Paul? ¹⁴I thank God that I did not baptize any of you except Crispus and Gaius, ¹⁵for now no one can say they were baptized in my name. ¹⁶(Oh yes, I also baptized the household of Stephanas. I don't remember baptizing anyone else.) ¹⁷For Christ didn't send me to baptize, but to preach the Good News—and not with clever speeches and high-sounding ideas, for fear that the cross of Christ would lose its power.

¹⁸I know very well how foolish the message of the cross sounds to those who are on the road to destruction. But we who are being saved recognize this message as the very power of God. ¹⁹As the Scriptures say,

"I will destroy human wisdom
    and discard their most brilliant
        ideas."*

²⁰So where does this leave the philosophers, the scholars, and the world's bril-

liant debaters? God has made them all look foolish and has shown their wisdom to be useless nonsense. ²¹Since God in his wisdom saw to it that the world would never find him through human wisdom, he has used our foolish preaching to save all who believe. ²²God's way seems foolish to the Jews because they want a sign from heaven to prove it is true. And it is foolish to the Greeks because they believe only what agrees with their own wisdom. ²³So when we preach that Christ was crucified, the Jews are offended, and the Gentiles say it's all nonsense. ²⁴But to those called by God to salvation, both Jews and Gentiles,* Christ is the mighty power of God and the wonderful wisdom of God. ²⁵This "foolish" plan of God is far wiser than the wisest of human plans, and God's weakness is far stronger than the greatest of human strength.

²⁶Remember, dear brothers and sisters, that few of you were wise in the world's eyes, or powerful, or wealthy when God called you. ²⁷Instead, God deliberately chose things the world considers foolish in order to shame those who think they are wise. And he chose those who are powerless to shame those who are powerful. ²⁸God chose things despised by the world, things counted as nothing at all, and used them to bring to nothing what the world considers important, ²⁹so that no one can ever boast in the presence of God.

³⁰God alone made it possible for you to be in Christ Jesus. For our benefit God made Christ to be wisdom itself. He is the one who made us acceptable to God. He made us pure and holy, and he gave himself to purchase our freedom. ³¹As the Scriptures say,

"The person who wishes to boast
    should boast only of what the Lord
        has done."*

CHAPTER 2
Dear brothers and sisters, when I first came to you I didn't use lofty words and brilliant ideas to tell you God's message.* ²For I decided to concentrate only on Jesus Christ and his death on the cross. ³I came to you in weakness—timid and trembling. ⁴And my message and my preaching were very plain. I did not use wise and persuasive

speeches, but the Holy Spirit was powerful among you. [5]I did this so that you might trust the power of God rather than human wisdom.

[6]Yet when I am among mature Christians, I do speak with words of wisdom, but not the kind of wisdom that belongs to this world, and not the kind that appeals to the rulers of this world, who are being brought to nothing. [7]No, the wisdom we speak of is the secret wisdom of God,* which was hidden in former times, though he made it for our benefit before the world began. [8]But the rulers of this world have not understood it; if they had, they would never have crucified our glorious Lord. [9]That is what the Scriptures mean when they say,

"No eye has seen, no ear has heard,
　and no mind has imagined
what God has prepared
　for those who love him."*

[10]But we know these things because God has revealed them to us by his Spirit, and his Spirit searches out everything and shows us even God's deep secrets. [11]No one can know what anyone else is really thinking except that person alone, and no one can know God's thoughts except God's own Spirit. [12]And God has actually given us his Spirit (not the world's spirit) so we can know the wonderful things God has freely given us. [13]When we tell you this, we do not use words of human wisdom. We speak words given to us by the Spirit, using the Spirit's words to explain spiritual truths.* [14]But people who aren't Christians can't understand these truths from God's Spirit. It all sounds foolish to them because only those who have the Spirit can understand what the Spirit means. [15]We who have the Spirit understand these things, but others can't understand us at all. [16]How could they? For,

"Who can know what the Lord is
　thinking?
　Who can give him counsel?"*

But we can understand these things, for we have the mind of Christ.

CHAPTER 3

Dear brothers and sisters, when I was with you I couldn't talk to you as I would to mature Christians. I had to talk as though you belonged to this world or as though you were infants in the Christian life.* [2]I had to feed you with milk and not with solid food, because you couldn't handle anything stronger. And you still aren't ready, [3]for you are still controlled by your own sinful desires. You are jealous of one another and quarrel with each other. Doesn't that prove you are controlled by your own desires? You are acting like people who don't belong to the Lord. [4]When one of you says, "I am a follower of Paul," and another says, "I prefer Apollos," aren't you acting like those who are not Christians?*

[5]Who is Apollos, and who is Paul, that we should be the cause of such quarrels? Why, we're only servants. Through us God caused you to believe. Each of us did the work the Lord gave us. [6]My job was to plant the seed in your hearts, and Apollos watered it, but it was God, not we, who made it grow. [7]The ones who do the planting or watering aren't important, but God is important because he is the one who makes the seed grow. [8]The one who plants and the one who waters work as a team with the same purpose. Yet they will be rewarded individually, according to their own hard work. [9]We work together as partners who belong to God. You are God's field, God's building—not ours.

[10]Because of God's special favor to me, I have laid the foundation like an expert builder. Now others are building on it. But whoever is building on this foundation must be very careful. [11]For no one can lay any other foundation than the one we already have—Jesus Christ. [12]Now anyone who builds on that foundation may use gold, silver, jewels, wood, hay, or straw. [13]But there is going to come a time of testing at the judgment day to see what kind of work each builder has done. Everyone's work will be put through the fire to see whether or not it keeps its value. [14]If the work survives the fire, that builder will receive a reward. [15]But if the work is burned up, the builder will suffer great loss. The builders themselves will be saved, but like someone escaping through a wall of flames.

[16]Don't you realize that all of you together are the temple of God and that the Spirit of God lives in* you? [17]God will bring

2:7 Greek *we speak God's wisdom in a mystery.*　　**2:9** Isa 64:4.　　**2:13** Or *explaining spiritual truths in spiritual language,* or *explaining spiritual truths to spiritual people.*　　**2:16** Isa 40:13.　　**3:1** Greek *in Christ.*　　**3:4** Greek *aren't you merely human?*　　**3:16** Or *among.*

ruin upon anyone who ruins this temple. For God's temple is holy, and you Christians are that temple.

[18]Stop fooling yourselves. If you think you are wise by this world's standards, you will have to become a fool so you can become wise by God's standards. [19]For the wisdom of this world is foolishness to God. As the Scriptures say,

> "God catches those who think they are wise
>   in their own cleverness."*

[20]And again,

> "The Lord knows the thoughts of the wise,
>   that they are worthless."*

[21]So don't take pride in following a particular leader. Everything belongs to you: [22]Paul and Apollos and Peter*; the whole world and life and death; the present and the future. Everything belongs to you, [23]and you belong to Christ, and Christ belongs to God.

CHAPTER 4

So look at Apollos and me as mere servants of Christ who have been put in charge of explaining God's secrets. [2]Now, a person who is put in charge as a manager must be faithful. [3]What about me? Have I been faithful? Well, it matters very little what you or anyone else thinks. I don't even trust my own judgment on this point. [4]My conscience is clear, but that isn't what matters. It is the Lord himself who will examine me and decide.

[5]So be careful not to jump to conclusions before the Lord returns as to whether or not someone is faithful. When the Lord comes, he will bring our deepest secrets to light and will reveal our private motives. And then God will give to everyone whatever praise is due.

[6]Dear brothers and sisters, I have used Apollos and myself to illustrate what I've been saying. If you pay attention to the Scriptures,* you won't brag about one of your leaders at the expense of another. [7]What makes you better than anyone else? What do you have that God hasn't given you? And if all you have is from God, why boast as though you have accomplished something on your own?

[8]You think you already have everything you need! You are already rich! Without us you have become kings! I wish you really were on your thrones already, for then we would be reigning with you! [9]But sometimes I think God has put us apostles on display, like prisoners of war at the end of a victor's parade, condemned to die. We have become a spectacle to the entire world—to people and angels alike.

[10]Our dedication to Christ makes us look like fools, but you are so wise! We are weak, but you are so powerful! You are well thought of, but we are laughed at. [11]To this very hour we go hungry and thirsty, without enough clothes to keep us warm. We have endured many beatings, and we have no homes of our own. [12]We have worked wearily with our own hands to earn our living. We bless those who curse us. We are patient with those who abuse us. [13]We respond gently when evil things are said about us. Yet we are treated like the world's garbage, like everybody's trash—right up to the present moment.

[14]I am not writing these things to shame you, but to warn you as my beloved children. [15]For even if you had ten thousand others to teach you about Christ, you have only one spiritual father. For I became your father in Christ Jesus when I preached the Good News to you. [16]So I ask you to follow my example and do as I do.

[17]That is the very reason I am sending Timothy—to help you do this. For he is my beloved and trustworthy child in the Lord. He will remind you of what I teach about Christ Jesus in all the churches wherever I go.

[18]I know that some of you have become arrogant, thinking I will never visit you again. [19]But I will come—and soon—if the Lord will let me, and then I'll find out whether these arrogant people are just big talkers or whether they really have God's power. [20]For the Kingdom of God is not just fancy talk; it is living by God's power. [21]Which do you choose? Should I come with punishment and scolding, or should I come with quiet love and gentleness?

CHAPTER 5

I can hardly believe the report about the sexual immorality going on among you, something so evil that even the pagans

3:19 Job 5:13.   **3:20** Ps 94:11.   **3:22** Greek *Cephas.*   **4:6** Or *You must learn not to go beyond "what is written,"* so that.

don't do it. I am told that you have a man in your church who is living in sin with his father's wife. ²And you are so proud of yourselves! Why aren't you mourning in sorrow and shame? And why haven't you removed this man from your fellowship?

³Even though I am not there with you in person, I am with you in the Spirit.* Concerning the one who has done this, I have already passed judgment ⁴in the name of the Lord Jesus. You are to call a meeting of the church,* and I will be there in spirit, and the power of the Lord Jesus will be with you as you meet. ⁵Then you must cast this man out of the church and into Satan's hands, so that his sinful nature will be destroyed* and he himself* will be saved when the Lord returns.

⁶How terrible that you should boast about your spirituality, and yet you let this sort of thing go on. Don't you realize that if even one person is allowed to go on sinning, soon all will be affected? ⁷Remove this wicked person from among you so that you can stay pure.* Christ, our Passover Lamb, has been sacrificed for us. ⁸So let us celebrate the festival, not by eating the old bread* of wickedness and evil, but by eating the new bread* of purity and truth.

⁹When I wrote to you before, I told you not to associate with people who indulge in sexual sin. ¹⁰But I wasn't talking about unbelievers who indulge in sexual sin, or who are greedy or are swindlers or idol worshipers. You would have to leave this world to avoid people like that. ¹¹What I meant was that you are not to associate with anyone who claims to be a Christian* yet indulges in sexual sin, or is greedy, or worships idols, or is abusive, or a drunkard, or a swindler. Don't even eat with such people.

¹²It isn't my responsibility to judge outsiders, but it certainly is your job to judge those inside the church who are sinning in these ways. ¹³God will judge those on the outside; but as the Scriptures say, "You must remove the evil person from among you."*

CHAPTER 6

When you have something against another Christian, why do you file a lawsuit and ask a secular court to decide the matter, instead of taking it to other Christians to decide who is right? ²Don't you know that someday we Christians are going to judge the world? And since you are going to judge the world, can't you decide these little things among yourselves? ³Don't you realize that we Christians will judge angels? So you should surely be able to resolve ordinary disagreements here on earth. ⁴If you have legal disputes about such matters, why do you go to outside judges who are not respected by the church? ⁵I am saying this to shame you. Isn't there anyone in all the church who is wise enough to decide these arguments? ⁶But instead, one Christian* sues another—right in front of unbelievers!

⁷To have such lawsuits at all is a real defeat for you. Why not just accept the injustice and leave it at that? Why not let yourselves be cheated? ⁸But instead, you yourselves are the ones who do wrong and cheat even your own Christian brothers and sisters.

⁹Don't you know that those who do wrong will have no share in the Kingdom of God? Don't fool yourselves. Those who indulge in sexual sin, who are idol worshipers, adulterers, male prostitutes, homosexuals, ¹⁰thieves, greedy people, drunkards, abusers, and swindlers—none of these will have a share in the Kingdom of God. ¹¹There was a time when some of you were just like that, but now your sins have been washed away,* and you have been set apart for God. You have been made right with God because of what the Lord Jesus Christ and the Spirit of our God have done for you.

¹²You may say, "I am allowed to do anything." But I reply, "Not everything is good for you." And even though "I am allowed to do anything," I must not become a slave to anything. ¹³You say, "Food is for the stomach, and the stomach is for food." This is true, though someday God will do away with both of them. But our bodies were not made for sexual immorality. They were made for the Lord, and the Lord cares about our bodies. ¹⁴And God will raise our bodies from the dead by his marvelous power, just

---

5:3 Or *in spirit.*   **5:4** Or *In the name of the Lord Jesus, you are to call a meeting of the church.*   **5:5a** Or *so that he will die;* Greek reads for the destruction of the flesh.   **5:5b** Greek *and the spirit.*   **5:6-7** Greek *Don't you realize that even a little leaven spreads quickly through the whole batch of dough? ⁷Purge out the old leaven so that you can be a new batch of dough, just as you are already unleavened.*   **5:8a** Greek *not with old leaven.*   **5:8b** Greek *but with unleavened [bread].*   **5:11** Greek *a brother.*   **5:13** Deut 17:7.   **6:6** Greek *one brother.*   **6:11** Or *you have been cleansed.*

as he raised our Lord from the dead. ¹⁵Don't you realize that your bodies are actually parts of Christ? Should a man take his body, which belongs to Christ, and join it to a prostitute? Never! ¹⁶And don't you know that if a man joins himself to a prostitute, he becomes one body with her? For the Scriptures say, "The two are united into one."* ¹⁷But the person who is joined to the Lord becomes one spirit with him.

6:16 Gen 2:24.

¹⁸Run away from sexual sin! No other sin so clearly affects the body as this one does. For sexual immorality is a sin against your own body. ¹⁹Or don't you know that your body is the temple of the Holy Spirit, who lives in you and was given to you by God? You do not belong to yourself, ²⁰for God bought you with a high price. So you must honor God with your body.

NOVEMBER 19 ☐ DAY 324
1 CORINTHIANS 7–10
Problems with Daily Life

 OVERVIEW Beginning with chapter 7, Paul answers a series of questions raised by the believers at Corinth that neither the Old Testament nor the words of Christ resolve: Is celibacy better than marriage? Is it permissible for Christians to eat meat offered to idols? Is it proper for a minister of the gospel to derive his living from the gospel? If an action is lawful, is it therefore permissible? Paul draws upon Old Testament passages, the teaching of Christ, and his own apostolic authority to set forth principles for the proper use of Christian liberty.

Chapter 7	Chapter 8	Chapter 9	Chapter 10
Counsel and Commands Regarding			
Marriage	Meat	Ministers	Murmuring
It Is a Gift	Take Heed	Share with Them	Learn from the Past

 YOUR DAILY WALK There are several God-ordained institutions in the pages of Scripture, but perhaps the two most important are the *church* and the *home*. So it is no coincidence that they are interrelated. Leadership ability in the home is a prerequisite for leadership in the church (1 Timothy 3:4-5); love and submission in the home are to be patterned after the relationship between Christ and the church.

If the young could be old for a day, they would neither fear so much growing old, nor foolishly squander the days of their youth.

Chapter 7 is an important passage on marriage. Regardless of your marital status (single, married, divorced, widowed, remarried), you'll find helpful counsel for dealing with the stresses and decisions of marriage. Set aside a few extra minutes today to concentrate on these forty verses. You might want to divide a sheet of paper into five columns and label them: Marriage, Celibacy, Mixed Marriage, Divorce, Remarriage. Now catalog what Paul has to say about each topic, paying careful attention to the column you are in . . . or plan to join! Then prayerfully apply your study to a decision you may be facing.

 INSIGHT Where Did Paul Get His Advice on Marriage?
Notice in 7:6, 10, 12, 25, 40 the origin of Paul's counsel. On certain matters he had no written or oral command from Christ (such as in Matthew 19:6, used in 7:10). In such cases, however, he made it clear that his "judgment" (opinion) was Spirit-guided (7:25, 40) and therefore authoritative. This is not merely a first-century "Dear Abby" column but rather inspired Scripture and fully authoritative for your life!

CHAPTER 7

Now about the questions you asked in your letter. Yes, it is good to live a celibate life. ²But because there is so much sexual immorality, each man should have his own wife, and each woman should have her own husband.

³The husband should not deprive his wife of sexual intimacy, which is her right as a married woman, nor should the wife deprive her husband. ⁴The wife gives authority over her body to her husband, and the husband also gives authority over his body to his wife. ⁵So do not deprive each other of sexual relations. The only exception to this rule would be the agreement of both husband and wife to refrain from sexual intimacy for a limited time, so they can give themselves more completely to prayer. Afterward they should come together again so that Satan won't be able to tempt them because of their lack of self-control. ⁶This is only my suggestion. It's not meant to be an absolute rule. ⁷I wish everyone could get along without marrying, just as I do. But we are not all the same. God gives some the gift of marriage, and to others he gives the gift of singleness.

⁸Now I say to those who aren't married and to widows—it's better to stay unmarried, just as I am. ⁹But if they can't control themselves, they should go ahead and marry. It's better to marry than to burn with lust.

¹⁰Now, for those who are married I have a command that comes not from me, but from the Lord.* A wife must not leave her husband. ¹¹But if she does leave him, let her remain single or else go back to him. And the husband must not leave his wife.

¹²Now, I will speak to the rest of you, though I do not have a direct command from the Lord. If a Christian man* has a wife who is an unbeliever and she is willing to continue living with him, he must not leave her. ¹³And if a Christian woman has a husband who is an unbeliever, and he is willing to continue living with her, she must not leave him. ¹⁴For the Christian wife brings holiness to her marriage, and the Christian husband brings holiness to his marriage. Otherwise, your children would not have a godly influence, but now they are set apart for him. ¹⁵(But if the husband or wife who isn't a Christian insists

on leaving, let them go. In such cases the Christian husband or wife is not required to stay with them, for God wants his children to live in peace.) ¹⁶You wives must remember that your husbands might be converted because of you. And you husbands must remember that your wives might be converted because of you.

¹⁷You must accept whatever situation the Lord has put you in, and continue on as you were when God first called you. This is my rule for all the churches. ¹⁸For instance, a man who was circumcised before he became a believer should not try to reverse it. And the man who was uncircumcised when he became a believer should not be circumcised now. ¹⁹For it makes no difference whether or not a man has been circumcised. The important thing is to keep God's commandments.

²⁰You should continue on as you were when God called you. ²¹Are you a slave? Don't let that worry you—but if you get a chance to be free, take it. ²²And remember, if you were a slave when the Lord called you, the Lord has now set you free from the awful power of sin. And if you were free when the Lord called you, you are now a slave of Christ. ²³God purchased you at a high price. Don't be enslaved by the world.* ²⁴So, dear brothers and sisters, whatever situation you were in when you became a believer, stay there in your new relationship with God.

²⁵Now, about the young women who are not yet married. I do not have a command from the Lord for them. But the Lord in his kindness has given me wisdom that can be trusted, and I will share it with you. ²⁶Because of the present crisis,* I think it is best to remain just as you are. ²⁷If you have a wife, do not end the marriage. If you do not have a wife, do not get married. ²⁸But if you do get married, it is not a sin.. And if a young woman gets married, it is not a sin. However, I am trying to spare you the extra problems that come with marriage.

²⁹Now let me say this, dear brothers and sisters: The time that remains is very short, so husbands should not let marriage be their major concern. ³⁰Happiness or sadness or wealth should not keep anyone from doing God's work. ³¹Those in frequent contact with the things of the world should make good use of them without

7:10 See Matt 5:32; 19:9; Mark 10:11-12; Luke 16:18.   7:12 Greek *a brother.*   7:23 Greek *don't become slaves of people.*   7:26 Or *pressures of life.*

becoming attached to them, for this world and all it contains will pass away. ³²In everything you do, I want you to be free from the concerns of this life. An unmarried man can spend his time doing the Lord's work and thinking how to please him. ³³But a married man can't do that so well. He has to think about his earthly responsibilities and how to please his wife. ³⁴His interests are divided. In the same way, a woman who is no longer married or has never been married can be more devoted to the Lord in body and in spirit, while the married woman must be concerned about her earthly responsibilities and how to please her husband.

³⁵I am saying this for your benefit, not to place restrictions on you. I want you to do whatever will help you serve the Lord best, with as few distractions as possible. ³⁶But if a man thinks he ought to marry his fiancée because he has trouble controlling his passions and time is passing, it is all right; it is not a sin. Let them marry. ³⁷But if he has decided firmly not to marry and there is no urgency and he can control his passion, he does well not to marry. ³⁸So the person who marries does well, and the person who doesn't marry does even better.

³⁹A wife is married to her husband as long as he lives. If her husband dies, she is free to marry whomever she wishes, but this must be a marriage acceptable to the Lord.* ⁴⁰But in my opinion it will be better for her if she doesn't marry again, and I think I am giving you counsel from God's Spirit when I say this.

CHAPTER 8

Now let's talk about food that has been sacrificed to idols. You think that everyone should agree with your perfect knowledge. While knowledge may make us feel important, it is love that really builds up the church. ²Anyone who claims to know all the answers doesn't really know very much. ³But the person who loves God is the one God knows and cares for.

⁴So now, what about it? Should we eat meat that has been sacrificed to idols? Well, we all know that an idol is not really a god and that there is only one God and no other. ⁵According to some people, there are many so-called gods and many lords, both in heaven and on earth. ⁶But we know that there is only one God, the Father, who created everything, and we exist for him. And there is only one Lord, Jesus Christ, through whom God made everything and through whom we have been given life.

⁷However, not all Christians realize this. Some are accustomed to thinking of idols as being real, so when they eat food that has been offered to idols, they think of it as the worship of real gods, and their weak consciences are violated. ⁸It's true that we can't win God's approval by what we eat. We don't miss out on anything if we don't eat it, and we don't gain anything if we do. ⁹But you must be careful with this freedom of yours. Do not cause a brother or sister with a weaker conscience to stumble.

¹⁰You see, this is what can happen: Weak Christians who think it is wrong to eat this food will see you eating in the temple of an idol. You know there's nothing wrong with it, but they will be encouraged to violate their conscience by eating food that has been dedicated to the idol. ¹¹So because of your superior knowledge, a weak Christian,* for whom Christ died, will be destroyed. ¹²And you are sinning against Christ when you sin against other Christians* by encouraging them to do something they believe is wrong. ¹³If what I eat is going to make another Christian sin, I will never eat meat again as long as I live—for I don't want to make another Christian stumble.

CHAPTER 9

Do I not have as much freedom as anyone else?* Am I not an apostle? Haven't I seen Jesus our Lord with my own eyes? Isn't it because of my hard work that you are in the Lord? ²Even if others think I am not an apostle, I certainly am to you, for you are living proof that I am the Lord's apostle.

³This is my answer to those who question my authority as an apostle.* ⁴Don't we have the right to live in your homes and share your meals? ⁵Don't we have the right to bring a Christian wife* along with us as the other disciples and the Lord's brothers and Peter* do? ⁶Or is it only Barnabas and I who have to work to support ourselves? ⁷What soldier has to pay his own expenses? And have you ever heard of a farmer who harvests his crop and doesn't have the right to eat some of it? What shep-

---

7:39 Or *but only to a Christian;* Greek reads *but only in the Lord.*   **8:11** Greek *brother;* also in 8:13.   **8:12** Greek *brothers.*   **9:1** Greek *Am I not free?*   **9:3** Greek *those who examine me.*   **9:5a** Greek *a sister, a wife.*   **9:5b** Greek *Cephas.*

herd takes care of a flock of sheep and isn't allowed to drink some of the milk? ⁸And this isn't merely human opinion. Doesn't God's law say the same thing? ⁹For the law of Moses says, "Do not keep an ox from eating as it treads out the grain."* Do you suppose God was thinking only about oxen when he said this? ¹⁰Wasn't he also speaking to us? Of course he was. Just as farm workers who plow fields and thresh the grain expect a share of the harvest, Christian workers should be paid by those they serve.

¹¹We have planted good spiritual seed among you. Is it too much to ask, in return, for mere food and clothing? ¹²If you support others who preach to you, shouldn't we have an even greater right to be supported? Yet we have never used this right. We would rather put up with anything than put an obstacle in the way of the Good News about Christ.

¹³Don't you know that those who work in the Temple get their meals from the food brought to the Temple as offerings? And those who serve at the altar get a share of the sacrificial offerings. ¹⁴In the same way, the Lord gave orders that those who preach the Good News should be supported by those who benefit from it. ¹⁵Yet I have never used any of these rights. And I am not writing this to suggest that I would like to start now. In fact, I would rather die than lose my distinction of preaching without charge. ¹⁶For preaching the Good News is not something I can boast about. I am compelled by God to do it. How terrible for me if I didn't do it!

¹⁷If I were doing this of my own free will, then I would deserve payment. But God has chosen me and given me this sacred trust, and I have no choice. ¹⁸What then is my pay? It is the satisfaction I get from preaching the Good News without expense to anyone, never demanding my rights as a preacher.

¹⁹This means I am not bound to obey people just because they pay me, yet I have become a servant of everyone so that I can bring them to Christ. ²⁰When I am with the Jews, I become one of them so that I can bring them to Christ. When I am with those who follow the Jewish laws, I do the same, even though I am not subject to the law, so that I can bring them to Christ. ²¹When I am

with the Gentiles who do not have the Jewish law,* I fit in with them as much as I can. In this way, I gain their confidence and bring them to Christ. But I do not discard the law of God; I obey the law of Christ.

²²When I am with those who are oppressed, I share their oppression so that I might bring them to Christ. Yes, I try to find common ground with everyone so that I might bring them to Christ. ²³I do all this to spread the Good News, and in doing so I enjoy its blessings.

²⁴Remember that in a race everyone runs, but only one person gets the prize. You also must run in such a way that you will win. ²⁵All athletes practice strict self-control. They do it to win a prize that will fade away, but we do it for an eternal prize. ²⁶So I run straight to the goal with purpose in every step. I am not like a boxer who misses his punches.* ²⁷I discipline my body like an athlete, training it to do what it should. Otherwise, I fear that after preaching to others I myself might be disqualified.

CHAPTER 10

I don't want you to forget, dear brothers and sisters, what happened to our ancestors in the wilderness long ago. God guided all of them by sending a cloud that moved along ahead of them, and he brought them all safely through the waters of the sea on dry ground. ²As followers of Moses, they were all baptized in the cloud and the sea. ³And all of them ate the same miraculous* food, ⁴and all of them drank the same miraculous water. For they all drank from the miraculous rock that traveled with them, and that rock was Christ. ⁵Yet after all this, God was not pleased with most of them, and he destroyed them in the wilderness.

⁶These events happened as a warning to us, so that we would not crave evil things as they did ⁷or worship idols as some of them did. For the Scriptures say, "The people celebrated with feasting and drinking, and they indulged themselves in pagan revelry."* ⁸And we must not engage in sexual immorality as some of them did, causing 23,000 of them to die in one day. ⁹Nor should we put Christ* to the test, as some of them did and then died from snakebites. ¹⁰And don't grumble as some of them did, for that is why God sent his

---

9:9 Deut 25:4.　　**9:21** Greek *those without the law.*　　**9:26** Or *I am not just shadowboxing.*　　**10:3** Greek *spiritual;* also in 10:4.
10:7 Exod 32:6.　　**10:9** Some manuscripts read *the Lord.*

angel of death to destroy them. ¹¹All these events happened to them as examples for us. They were written down to warn us, who live at the time when this age is drawing to a close.

¹²If you think you are standing strong, be careful, for you, too, may fall into the same sin. ¹³But remember that the temptations that come into your life are no different from what others experience. And God is faithful. He will keep the temptation from becoming so strong that you can't stand up against it. When you are tempted, he will show you a way out so that you will not give in to it.

¹⁴So, my dear friends, flee from the worship of idols. ¹⁵You are reasonable people. Decide for yourselves if what I am about to say is true. ¹⁶When we bless the cup at the Lord's Table, aren't we sharing in the benefits of the blood of Christ? And when we break the loaf of bread, aren't we sharing in the benefits of the body of Christ? ¹⁷And we all eat from one loaf, showing that we are one body. ¹⁸And think about the nation of Israel; all who eat the sacrifices are united by that act.

¹⁹What am I trying to say? Am I saying that the idols to whom the pagans bring sacrifices are real gods and that these sacrifices are of some value? ²⁰No, not at all. What I am saying is that these sacrifices are offered to demons, not to God. And I don't want any of you to be partners with demons. ²¹You cannot drink from the cup of the Lord and from the cup of demons, too. You cannot eat at the Lord's Table and at the table of demons, too. ²²What? Do you

10:26 Ps 24:1.

dare to rouse the Lord's jealousy as Israel did? Do you think we are stronger than he is?

²³You say, "I am allowed to do anything"—but not everything is helpful. You say, "I am allowed to do anything"—but not everything is beneficial. ²⁴Don't think only of your own good. Think of other Christians and what is best for them.

²⁵Here's what you should do. You may eat any meat that is sold in the marketplace. Don't ask whether or not it was offered to idols, and then your conscience won't be bothered. ²⁶For "the earth is the Lord's, and everything in it."*

²⁷If someone who isn't a Christian asks you home for dinner, go ahead; accept the invitation if you want to. Eat whatever is offered to you and don't ask any questions about it. Your conscience should not be bothered by this. ²⁸But suppose someone warns you that this meat has been offered to an idol. Don't eat it, out of consideration for the conscience of the one who told you. ²⁹It might not be a matter of conscience for you, but it is for the other person.

Now, why should my freedom be limited by what someone else thinks? ³⁰If I can thank God for the food and enjoy it, why should I be condemned for eating it? ³¹Whatever you eat or drink or whatever you do, you must do all for the glory of God. ³²Don't give offense to Jews or Gentiles or the church of God. ³³That is the plan I follow, too. I try to please everyone in everything I do. I don't just do what I like or what is best for me, but what is best for them so they may be saved.

NOVEMBER 20 ☐ DAY 325
1 CORINTHIANS 11–14
Problems with Worship and Gifts

OVERVIEW In previous chapters Paul has dealt with the Corinthians' personal problems. Now he turns his attention to problems of a public nature, specifically, disorder in the church's worship. In chapter 11 he answers questions regarding the role of women in the church, then gives a sharp rebuke for the Corinthians' misconduct during the Lord's Supper. In chapters 12–14 Paul addresses the issue of spiritual gifts in the church, emphasizing the diversity of gifts and the fundamental test of love in the exercise of spiritual gifts. Orderliness should characterize all Christian worship (14:40).

Chapter 11		Chapter 12	Chapter 13	Chapter 14
The Role of Women	The Sanctity of Communion	The Use of Spiritual Gifts		
1　　　　16	17　　　　34	in Question	in Love	in Church
Submission	Examination	Participation		

YOUR DAILY WALK Imagine that you have given your best friend a gift for his or her birthday. The big day arrives, and you call to find out how your gift was received. To your surprise, the reply comes, "Oh, I don't know, I haven't opened it yet. I decided to keep it wrapped up." Encouraging your friend to open it, you wait another day or two and call again, this time to ask if your gift (a clock radio) was being put to good use. Instead, you hear these discouraging words: "Oh, I opened it all right, but I decided to leave it in the closet."

God's gift to you is often God's gift to others through you.

God doesn't give spiritual gifts (1 Corinthians 12–14) merely to have them left undiscovered or unused. Just as he has given you eyes, ears, and feet to be used in your physical body, so, too, he has given you gifts to be employed in the spiritual body, his church. In which areas of ministry has God gifted you? Is your local church profiting from the use of those gifts, or are your gifts still unwrapped and unused? Talk to your pastor, Sunday school teacher, or a close friend about the way you can begin to put your gifts to work this week.

INSIGHT Does Your Gift Lack the Key Ingredient?
Paul lists four classes of spiritual gifts: ecstatic (tongues), instructive (prophecy), wonder-working (faith), and helps (giving). But without love, the results of such gifts are futile: I convey nothing (13:1); I am nothing (13:2); I gain nothing (13:3).

CHAPTER 11
And you should follow my example, just as I follow Christ's.

²I am so glad, dear friends, that you always keep me in your thoughts and you are following the Christian teaching I passed on to you. ³But there is one thing I want you to know: A man is responsible to Christ, a woman is responsible to her husband, and Christ is responsible to God. ⁴A man dishonors Christ* if he covers his head while praying or prophesying. ⁵But a woman dishonors her husband* if she prays or prophesies without a covering on her head, for this is the same as shaving her head. ⁶Yes, if she refuses to wear a head covering, she should cut off all her hair. And since it is shameful for a woman to have her hair cut or her head shaved, then she should wear a covering.* ⁷A man should not wear anything on his head when worshiping, for man is God's glory, made in God's own image, but woman is the glory of man. ⁸For the first man didn't come from woman, but the first woman came from man. ⁹And man was not made

for woman's benefit, but woman was made for man. ¹⁰So a woman should wear a covering on her head as a sign of authority because the angels are watching.

¹¹But in relationships among the Lord's people, women are not independent of men, and men are not independent of women. ¹²For although the first woman came from man, all men have been born from women ever since, and everything comes from God.

¹³What do you think about this? Is it right for a woman to pray to God in public without covering her head? ¹⁴Isn't it obvious that it's disgraceful for a man to have long hair? ¹⁵And isn't it obvious that long hair is a woman's pride and joy? For it has been given to her as a covering. ¹⁶But if anyone wants to argue about this, all I can say is that we have no other custom than this, and all the churches of God feel the same way about it.

¹⁷But now when I mention this next issue, I cannot praise you. For it sounds as if more harm than good is done when you meet together. ¹⁸First of all, I hear that there

11:4 Greek *his head.*　　**11:5** Greek *her head.*　　**11:6** Or *then she should have long hair.*

are divisions among you when you meet as a church, and to some extent I believe it. [19]But, of course, there must be divisions among you so that those of you who are right will be recognized!

[20]It's not the Lord's Supper you are concerned about when you come together. [21]For I am told that some of you hurry to eat your own meal without sharing with others. As a result, some go hungry while others get drunk. [22]What? Is this really true? Don't you have your own homes for eating and drinking? Or do you really want to disgrace the church of God and shame the poor? What am I supposed to say about these things? Do you want me to praise you? Well, I certainly do not!

[23]For this is what the Lord himself said, and I pass it on to you just as I received it. On the night when he was betrayed, the Lord Jesus took a loaf of bread, [24]and when he had given thanks, he broke it and said, "This is my body, which is given* for you. Do this in remembrance of me." [25]In the same way, he took the cup of wine after supper, saying, "This cup is the new covenant between God and you, sealed by the shedding of my blood. Do this in remembrance of me as often as you drink it." [26]For every time you eat this bread and drink this cup, you are announcing the Lord's death until he comes again.

[27]So if anyone eats this bread or drinks this cup of the Lord unworthily, that person is guilty of sinning against the body and the blood of the Lord. [28]That is why you should examine yourself before eating the bread and drinking from the cup. [29]For if you eat the bread or drink the cup unworthily, not honoring the body of Christ,* you are eating and drinking God's judgment upon yourself. [30]That is why many of you are weak and sick and some have even died.

[31]But if we examine ourselves, we will not be examined by God and judged in this way. [32]But when we are judged and disciplined by the Lord, we will not be condemned with the world. [33]So, dear brothers and sisters, when you gather for the Lord's Supper, wait for each other. [34]If you are really hungry, eat at home so you won't bring judgment upon yourselves when you meet together.

I'll give you instructions about the other matters after I arrive.

CHAPTER 12

And now, dear brothers and sisters, I will write about the special abilities the Holy Spirit gives to each of us, for I must correct your misunderstandings about them. [2]You know that when you were still pagans you were led astray and swept along in worshiping speechless idols. [3]So I want you to know how to discern what is truly from God: No one speaking by the Spirit of God can curse Jesus, and no one is able to say, "Jesus is Lord," except by the Holy Spirit.

[4]Now there are different kinds of spiritual gifts, but it is the same Holy Spirit who is the source of them all. [5]There are different kinds of service in the church, but it is the same Lord we are serving. [6]There are different ways God works in our lives, but it is the same God who does the work through all of us. [7]A spiritual gift is given to each of us as a means of helping the entire church.

[8]To one person the Spirit gives the ability to give wise advice; to another he gives the gift of special knowledge. [9]The Spirit gives special faith to another, and to someone else he gives the power to heal the sick. [10]He gives one person the power to perform miracles, and to another the ability to prophesy. He gives someone else the ability to know whether it is really the Spirit of God or another spirit that is speaking. Still another person is given the ability to speak in unknown languages,* and another is given the ability to interpret what is being said. [11]It is the one and only Holy Spirit who distributes these gifts. He alone decides which gift each person should have.

[12]The human body has many parts, but the many parts make up only one body. So it is with the body of Christ. [13]Some of us are Jews, some are Gentiles, some are slaves, and some are free. But we have all been baptized into Christ's body by one Spirit, and we have all received the same Spirit.*

[14]Yes, the body has many different parts, not just one part. [15]If the foot says, "I am not a part of the body because I am not a hand," that does not make it any less a part of the body. [16]And if the ear says, "I am not part of the body because I am only an ear and not an eye," would that make it any less a part of the body? [17]Suppose the whole body were an eye—then how

---

11:24 Some manuscripts read *broken.*   **11:29** Greek *the body;* some manuscripts read *the Lord's body.*   **12:10** Or *in tongues;* also in 12:28, 30.   **12:13** Greek *we were all given one Spirit to drink.*

would you hear? Or if your whole body were just one big ear, how could you smell anything? [18]But God made our bodies with many parts, and he has put each part just where he wants it. [19]What a strange thing a body would be if it had only one part! [20]Yes, there are many parts, but only one body. [21]The eye can never say to the hand, "I don't need you." The head can't say to the feet, "I don't need you."

[22]In fact, some of the parts that seem weakest and least important are really the most necessary. [23]And the parts we regard as less honorable are those we clothe with the greatest care. So we carefully protect from the eyes of others those parts that should not be seen, [24]while other parts do not require this special care. So God has put the body together in such a way that extra honor and care are given to those parts that have less dignity. [25]This makes for harmony among the members, so that all the members care for each other equally. [26]If one part suffers, all the parts suffer with it, and if one part is honored, all the parts are glad.

[27]Now all of you together are Christ's body, and each one of you is a separate and necessary part of it. [28]Here is a list of some of the members that God has placed in the body of Christ:

> first are apostles,
> second are prophets,
> third are teachers,
> then those who do miracles,
> those who have the gift of healing,
> those who can help others,
> those who can get others to work
>   together,
> those who speak in unknown
>   languages.

[29]Is everyone an apostle? Of course not. Is everyone a prophet? No. Are all teachers? Does everyone have the power to do miracles? [30]Does everyone have the gift of healing? Of course not. Does God give all of us the ability to speak in unknown languages? Can everyone interpret unknown languages? No! [31]And in any event, you should desire the most helpful gifts.

First, however, let me tell you about something else that is better than any of them!

CHAPTER 13

If I could speak in any language in heaven or on earth* but didn't love others, I would only be making meaningless noise like a loud gong or a clanging cymbal. [2]If I had the gift of prophecy, and if I knew all the mysteries of the future and knew everything about everything, but didn't love others, what good would I be? And if I had the gift of faith so that I could speak to a mountain and make it move, without love I would be no good to anybody. [3]If I gave everything I have to the poor and even sacrificed my body, I could boast about it;* but if I didn't love others, I would be of no value whatsoever.

[4]Love is patient and kind. Love is not jealous or boastful or proud [5]or rude. Love does not demand its own way. Love is not irritable, and it keeps no record of when it has been wronged. [6]It is never glad about injustice but rejoices whenever the truth wins out. [7]Love never gives up, never loses faith, is always hopeful, and endures through every circumstance.

[8]Love will last forever, but prophecy and speaking in unknown languages* and special knowledge will all disappear. [9]Now we know only a little, and even the gift of prophecy reveals little! [10]But when the end comes, these special gifts will all disappear.

[11]It's like this: When I was a child, I spoke and thought and reasoned as a child does. But when I grew up, I put away childish things. [12]Now we see things imperfectly as in a poor mirror, but then we will see everything with perfect clarity.* All that I know now is partial and incomplete, but then I will know everything completely, just as God knows me now.

[13]There are three things that will endure—faith, hope, and love—and the greatest of these is love.

CHAPTER 14

Let love be your highest goal, but also desire the special abilities the Spirit gives, especially the gift of prophecy. [2]For if your gift is the ability to speak in tongues,* you will be talking to God but not to people, since they won't be able to understand you. You will be speaking by the power of the Spirit, but it will all be mysterious. [3]But one who prophesies is helping others grow in the Lord, encouraging and comforting

---

13:1 Greek *in tongues of people and angels.*   **13:3** Some manuscripts read *and even gave my body to be burned.*   **13:8** Or *in tongues.*
13:12 Greek *see face to face.*   **14:2** Or *in unknown languages;* also in 14:4, 5, 13, 14, 18, 22, 28, 39.

them. ⁴A person who speaks in tongues is strengthened personally in the Lord, but one who speaks a word of prophecy strengthens the entire church.

⁵I wish you all had the gift of speaking in tongues, but even more I wish you were all able to prophesy. For prophecy is a greater and more useful gift than speaking in tongues, unless someone interprets what you are saying so that the whole church can get some good out of it.

⁶Dear brothers and sisters, if I should come to you talking in an unknown language,* how would that help you? But if I bring you some revelation or some special knowledge or some prophecy or some teaching—that is what will help you. ⁷Even musical instruments like the flute or the harp, though they are lifeless, are examples of the need for speaking in plain language. For no one will recognize the melody unless the notes are played clearly. ⁸And if the bugler doesn't sound a clear call, how will the soldiers know they are being called to battle? ⁹And it's the same for you. If you talk to people in a language they don't understand, how will they know what you mean? You might as well be talking to an empty room.

¹⁰There are so many different languages in the world, and all are excellent for those who understand them, ¹¹but to me they mean nothing. I will not understand people who speak those languages, and they will not understand me. ¹²Since you are so eager to have spiritual gifts, ask God for those that will be of real help to the whole church.

¹³So anyone who has the gift of speaking in tongues should pray also for the gift of interpretation in order to tell people plainly what has been said. ¹⁴For if I pray in tongues, my spirit is praying, but I don't understand what I am saying.

¹⁵Well then, what shall I do? I will do both. I will pray in the spirit,* and I will pray in words I understand. I will sing in the spirit, and I will sing in words I understand. ¹⁶For if you praise God only in the spirit, how can those who don't understand you praise God along with you? How can they join you in giving thanks when they don't understand what you are saying? ¹⁷You will be giving thanks very

nicely, no doubt, but it doesn't help the other people present.

¹⁸I thank God that I speak in tongues more than all of you. ¹⁹But in a church meeting I would much rather speak five understandable words that will help others than ten thousand words in an unknown language.

²⁰Dear brothers and sisters, don't be childish in your understanding of these things. Be innocent as babies when it comes to evil, but be mature and wise in understanding matters of this kind. ²¹It is written in the Scriptures,*

"I will speak to my own people
    through unknown languages
    and through the lips of foreigners.
But even then, they will not listen to
    me,"*
    says the Lord.

²²So you see that speaking in tongues is a sign, not for believers, but for unbelievers; prophecy, however, is for the benefit of believers, not unbelievers. ²³Even so, if unbelievers or people who don't understand these things come into your meeting and hear everyone talking in an unknown language, they will think you are crazy. ²⁴But if all of you are prophesying, and unbelievers or people who don't understand these things come into your meeting, they will be convicted of sin, and they will be condemned by what you say. ²⁵As they listen, their secret thoughts will be laid bare, and they will fall down on their knees and worship God, declaring, "God is really here among you."

²⁶Well, my brothers and sisters, let's summarize what I am saying. When you meet, one will sing, another will teach, another will tell some special revelation God has given, one will speak in an unknown language, while another will interpret what is said. But everything that is done must be useful to all and build them up in the Lord. ²⁷No more than two or three should speak in an unknown language. They must speak one at a time, and someone must be ready to interpret what they are saying. ²⁸But if no one is present who can interpret, they must be silent in your church meeting and speak in tongues to God privately.

²⁹Let two or three prophesy, and let the

14:6 Or *in tongues*; also in 14:19, 23, 26, 27.   14:15 Or *in the Spirit*; also in 14:15b, 16.   14:21a Greek *in the law*.   14:21b Isa 28:11-12.

others evaluate what is said. ³⁰But if someone is prophesying and another person receives a revelation from the Lord, the one
who is speaking must stop. ³¹In this way, all
who prophesy will have a turn to speak,
one after the other, so that everyone will
learn and be encouraged. ³²Remember that
people who prophesy are in control of their
spirit and can wait their turn. ³³For God is
not a God of disorder but of peace, as in all
the other churches.*

³⁴Women should be silent during the
church meetings. It is not proper for them
to speak. They should be submissive, just
as the law says. ³⁵If they have any questions to ask, let them ask their husbands at
home, for it is improper for women to
speak in church meetings.*

³⁶Do you think that the knowledge of
God's word begins and ends with you Corinthians? Well, you are mistaken! ³⁷If you
claim to be a prophet or think you are very
spiritual, you should recognize that what I
am saying is a command from the Lord
himself. ³⁸But if you do not recognize this,
you will not be recognized.*

³⁹So, dear brothers and sisters, be eager
to prophesy, and don't forbid speaking in
tongues. ⁴⁰But be sure that everything is
done properly and in order.

14:33 The phrase *as in all the other churches* could be joined to the beginning of 14:34.   **14:35** Some manuscripts place verses 34-35
after 14:40.   **14:38** Some manuscripts read *If you are ignorant of this, stay in your ignorance.*

NOVEMBER 21 ☐ DAY 326
Questions and Answers

LOOK BACK Romans has been called "the gospel according to Paul."
Writing like a trained lawyer, Paul probes the significance of Jesus' death
and resurrection. All people stand condemned before a holy God. Jew
and Gentile alike are without excuse.

But what the human race was powerless to do for itself, God did in
the person of his Son, Jesus. Through his sinless life and sacrificial death
we are declared "not guilty" before God—not because of anything we
have done, but because of his love and grace. We had a debt we could
not pay; Jesus paid a debt he did not owe. And the result? Sin's power
has been broken, freeing us to live a new life in him.

But that new life is not a problem-free life, as you'll learn by reading
Paul's letter to the Corinthians. Here, a church that was "called by God
to be his own holy people" (1 Corinthians 1:2) was nonetheless beset
by a myriad of sins and excesses that needed Paul's discipline and direction. Clearly, the *wealth* of the believer must be translated into a *worthy
walk* for the believer.

LOOK UP What is one of the most effective teaching methods?
Answer: The use of question and answer.

Romans 8 is one of the richest "mother lodes" in the Bible. There
you'll discover nugget after nugget of truth for the Christian: the limitless boundaries of God's love, the proven way to be an overcomer in
any circumstance, the role of the Holy Spirit in the life of the Christian.

*Every day
holds the
possibility
of miracles.*

There you'll also find the answers to several important questions.
According to Romans 8:31-39,

• if God is for us, who can ever be against us?
• who dares accuse us whom God has chosen?
• can anything ever separate us from Christ's love?

In case you had trouble with the above exercise, the answer to all
three questions is the same: *no one!*

LOOK AHEAD The challenge is often to take what we know about God from the pages of his Word and apply it to real-life situations that have us baffled and anxious. For example:

- Who is seemingly against you and out to get you today? (Answer: my boss, my spouse, my rebellious teenager, the IRS, my business competitors—in short, *everyone!*)
- But in reality, if God is for you, who can be against you?
- Who is accusing you falsely today of things you never did or said?
- But in reality, who can bring any charge against God's chosen, and make it stick?
- Who or what is trying to drive a wedge between you and your Lord today?
- But in reality, who or what can separate you from the love of Christ?

NOVEMBER 22 □ DAY 327
1 CORINTHIANS 15–16
Problems with Doctrinal Error

OVERVIEW Two final matters attract Paul's attention as he closes his letter: the problem of disbelief in the resurrection and of distribution to the needs of the saints at Jerusalem. Paul relates a string of consequences that will result like a row of falling dominoes if, in fact, there is no resurrection of the dead: If Christ did not rise from the dead, preaching about him is meaningless, your faith is empty, you are still in your sins, those who have died believing in Christ are without hope, and you are to be pitied for your delusion. Then with one gentle nudge, Paul refutes the first fallen domino ("Christ has been raised from the dead") and watches the rest of his conclusions fall over as well! Our hope in Christ is as secure as the historical foundation of our faith.

Chapter 15			Chapter 16	
Prominence of Resurrection	Proofs of Resurrection	Power of Resurrection	Liberal Giving	Loving Greetings
1 4	5 19	20 58	1 4	5 24
Errors concerning the Gospel			Errors concerning Money	

Our friends take us to the grave and leave us there, but God will not.

YOUR DAILY WALK No doubt you are aware that God has a future program for your soul (salvation). But did you know he has a program for your body as well (resurrection)? Chapter 15 describes the future body God has in store for you—and it is exciting to consider!

- It will not decay (15:42) and won't wrinkle, age, wear out, or fall apart.
- It will be full of glory and power (15:43), eternally beautiful, and supernaturally strong.
- It will be a spiritual body (15:44), not limited by flesh and blood, time or space.
- It will be a body over which death and sin have no power (15:54-57).
- And best of all, you will be fitted with it "in a moment, in the blinking of an eye" (15:52), with no waiting in line!

Do you know a Christian who is physically limited by age, illness, or injury? Why not invite that person over for a meal—and encourage him or her with God's promise of a resurrected body!

INSIGHT Living Today in the Light of Tomorrow's Promises
In 1 Corinthians 15:58 you'll find a call to *action* and a call to *immobility*.
Why are both appropriate responses to Paul's appeal?

CHAPTER 15

Now let me remind you, dear brothers and sisters, of the Good News I preached to you before. You welcomed it then and still do now, for your faith is built on this wonderful message. ²And it is this Good News that saves you if you firmly believe it—unless, of course, you believed something that was never true in the first place.

³I passed on to you what was most important and what had also been passed on to me—that Christ died for our sins, just as the Scriptures said. ⁴He was buried, and he was raised from the dead on the third day, as the Scriptures said. ⁵He was seen by Peter* and then by the twelve apostles. ⁶After that, he was seen by more than five hundred of his followers* at one time, most of whom are still alive, though some have died by now. ⁷Then he was seen by James and later by all the apostles. ⁸Last of all, I saw him, too, long after the others, as though I had been born at the wrong time. ⁹For I am the least of all the apostles, and I am not worthy to be called an apostle after the way I persecuted the church of God.

¹⁰But whatever I am now, it is all because God poured out his special favor on me—and not without results. For I have worked harder than all the other apostles, yet it was not I but God who was working through me by his grace. ¹¹So it makes no difference whether I preach or they preach. The important thing is that you believed what we preached to you.

¹²But tell me this—since we preach that Christ rose from the dead, why are some of you saying there will be no resurrection of the dead? ¹³For if there is no resurrection of the dead, then Christ has not been raised either. ¹⁴And if Christ was not raised, then all our preaching is useless, and your trust in God is useless. ¹⁵And we apostles would all be lying about God, for we have said that God raised Christ from the grave, but that can't be true if there is no resurrection of the dead. ¹⁶If there is no resurrection of the dead, then Christ has not been raised. ¹⁷And if Christ has not been raised, then your faith is useless, and you are still under condemnation for your sins. ¹⁸In that case,

all who have died believing in Christ have perished! ¹⁹And if we have hope in Christ only for this life, we are the most miserable people in the world.

²⁰But the fact is that Christ has been raised from the dead. He has become the first of a great harvest of those who will be raised to life again.

²¹So you see, just as death came into the world through a man, Adam, now the resurrection from the dead has begun through another man, Christ. ²²Everyone dies because all of us are related to Adam, the first man. But all who are related to Christ, the other man, will be given new life. ²³But there is an order to this resurrection: Christ was raised first; then when Christ comes back, all his people will be raised.

²⁴After that the end will come, when he will turn the Kingdom over to God the Father, having put down all enemies of every kind.* ²⁵For Christ must reign until he humbles all his enemies beneath his feet. ²⁶And the last enemy to be destroyed is death. ²⁷For the Scriptures say, "God has given him authority over all things."* (Of course, when it says "authority over all things," it does not include God himself, who gave Christ his authority.) ²⁸Then, when he has conquered all things, the Son will present himself to God, so that God, who gave his Son authority over all things, will be utterly supreme over everything everywhere.

²⁹If the dead will not be raised, then what point is there in people being baptized for those who are dead? Why do it unless the dead will someday rise again?

³⁰And why should we ourselves be continually risking our lives, facing death hour by hour? ³¹For I swear, dear brothers and sisters, I face death daily. This is as certain as my pride in what the Lord Jesus Christ has done in you. ³²And what value was there in fighting wild beasts—those men of Ephesus*—if there will be no resurrection from the dead? If there is no resurrection,

"Let's feast and get drunk,
  for tomorrow we die!"*

15:5 Greek *Cephas.*   **15:6** Greek *the brothers.*   **15:24** Greek *every ruler and every authority and power.*   **15:27** Ps 8:6.   **15:32a** Greek *fighting wild beasts in Ephesus.*   **15:32b** Isa 22:13.

³³Don't be fooled by those who say such things, for "bad company corrupts good character." ³⁴Come to your senses and stop sinning. For to your shame I say that some of you don't even know God.

³⁵But someone may ask, "How will the dead be raised? What kind of bodies will they have?" ³⁶What a foolish question! When you put a seed into the ground, it doesn't grow into a plant unless it dies first. ³⁷And what you put in the ground is not the plant that will grow, but only a dry little seed of wheat or whatever it is you are planting. ³⁸Then God gives it a new body— just the kind he wants it to have. A different kind of plant grows from each kind of seed. ³⁹And just as there are different kinds of seeds and plants, so also there are different kinds of flesh—whether of humans, animals, birds, or fish.

⁴⁰There are bodies in the heavens, and there are bodies on earth. The glory of the heavenly bodies is different from the beauty of the earthly bodies. ⁴¹The sun has one kind of glory, while the moon and stars each have another kind. And even the stars differ from each other in their beauty and brightness.

⁴²It is the same way for the resurrection of the dead. Our earthly bodies, which die and decay, will be different when they are resurrected, for they will never die. ⁴³Our bodies now disappoint us, but when they are raised, they will be full of glory. They are weak now, but when they are raised, they will be full of power. ⁴⁴They are natural human bodies now, but when they are raised, they will be spiritual bodies. For just as there are natural bodies, so also there are spiritual bodies.

⁴⁵The Scriptures tell us, "The first man, Adam, became a living person."* But the last Adam—that is, Christ—is a life-giving Spirit. ⁴⁶What came first was the natural body, then the spiritual body comes later. ⁴⁷Adam, the first man, was made from the dust of the earth, while Christ, the second man, came from heaven. ⁴⁸Every human being has an earthly body just like Adam's, but our heavenly bodies will be just like Christ's. ⁴⁹Just as we are now like Adam, the man of the earth, so we will someday be like Christ, the man from heaven.

⁵⁰What I am saying, dear brothers and sisters, is that flesh and blood cannot inherit the Kingdom of God. These perishable bodies of ours are not able to live forever.

⁵¹But let me tell you a wonderful secret God has revealed to us. Not all of us will die, but we will all be transformed. ⁵²It will happen in a moment, in the blinking of an eye, when the last trumpet is blown. For when the trumpet sounds, the Christians who have died* will be raised with transformed bodies. And then we who are living will be transformed so that we will never die. ⁵³For our perishable earthly bodies must be transformed into heavenly bodies that will never die.

⁵⁴When this happens—when our perishable earthly bodies have been transformed into heavenly bodies that will never die— then at last the Scriptures will come true:

"Death is swallowed up in victory.*
⁵⁵ O death, where is your victory?
    O death, where is your sting?"*

⁵⁶For sin is the sting that results in death, and the law gives sin its power. ⁵⁷How we thank God, who gives us victory over sin and death through Jesus Christ our Lord!

⁵⁸So, my dear brothers and sisters, be strong and steady, always enthusiastic about the Lord's work, for you know that nothing you do for the Lord is ever useless.

CHAPTER 16

Now about the money being collected for the Christians in Jerusalem: You should follow the same procedures I gave to the churches in Galatia. ²On every Lord's Day,* each of you should put aside some amount of money in relation to what you have earned and save it for this offering. Don't wait until I get there and then try to collect it all at once. ³When I come I will write letters of recommendation for the messengers you choose to deliver your gift to Jerusalem. ⁴And if it seems appropriate for me also to go along, then we can travel together.

⁵I am coming to visit you after I have been to Macedonia, for I am planning to travel through Macedonia. ⁶It could be that I will stay awhile with you, perhaps all winter, and then you can send me on my way to the next destination. ⁷This time I don't want to make just a short visit and then go right on. I want to come and stay

15:45 Gen 2:7.   **15:52** Greek *the dead*.   **15:54** Isa 25:8.   **15:55** Hos 13:14.   **16:2** Greek *every first day of the week*.

awhile, if the Lord will let me. [8]In the meantime, I will be staying here at Ephesus until the Festival of Pentecost, [9]for there is a wide-open door for a great work here, and many people are responding. But there are many who oppose me.

[10]When Timothy comes, treat him with respect. He is doing the Lord's work, just as I am. [11]Don't let anyone despise him. Send him on his way with your blessings when he returns to me. I am looking forward to seeing him soon, along with the other brothers.

[12]Now about our brother Apollos—I urged him to join the other brothers when they visit you, but he was not willing to come right now. He will be seeing you later, when the time is right.

[13]Be on guard. Stand true to what you believe. Be courageous. Be strong. [14]And everything you do must be done with love.

[15]You know that Stephanas and his household were the first to become Christians in Greece,* and they are spending their lives in service to other Christians. I urge you, dear brothers and sisters, [16]to respect them fully and others like them who serve with such real devotion. [17]I am so glad that Stephanas, Fortunatus, and Achaicus have come here. They have been making up for the help you weren't here to give me. [18]They have been a wonderful encouragement to me, as they have been to you, too. You must give proper honor to all who serve so well.

[19]The churches here in the province of Asia* greet you heartily in the Lord, along with Aquila and Priscilla and all the others who gather in their home for church meetings. [20]All the brothers and sisters here have asked me to greet you for them. Greet each other in Christian love.*

[21]Here is my greeting, which I write with my own hand—PAUL.

[22]If anyone does not love the Lord, that person is cursed. Our Lord, come!*

[23]May the grace of the Lord Jesus be with you.

[24]My love to all of you in Christ Jesus.*

16:15 Greek *were the firstfruits in Achaia,* the southern region of the Greek peninsula.   **16:19** *Asia* was a Roman province in what is now western Turkey.   **16:20** Greek *with a sacred kiss.*   **16:22** From Aramaic, *Marana tha.*   **16:24** Some manuscripts add *Amen.*

2 Corinthians

FALSE teachers in Corinth—angered by Paul's first letter—swayed the people against him. They claimed Paul was fickle, proud, unimpressive in appearance and speech, dishonest, and unqualified as an apostle. After Paul sent Titus to deal with the situation, he rejoiced to hear of the Corinthians' change of heart. Paul wrote this letter to thank the repentant majority for their support and to appeal to the rebellious minority to accept his authority, as he defends his conduct, character, and calling.

Focus	Ministry of the Gospel		Minister of the Gospel
Divisions	Paul's Attitudes in Ministry	Paul's Motivation and Model in Ministry	Paul's Authority in Ministry
	1 5	6 9	10 13
Topics	Character	Commitment	Credentials
	Explanation	Exhortation	Vindication
Place	Written in Macedonia		
Time	About A.D. 56		

NOVEMBER 23 □ DAY 328
2 CORINTHIANS 1–5
Vindication: Paul's Attitude in Ministry

OVERVIEW The numerous problems in the church at Corinth, coupled with Paul's personal conflicts with certain individuals, were weighing heavily upon him. Nevertheless, God had comforted him so that he in turn could comfort others. Despite the most trying circumstances, the faithful minister for God can enjoy daily strength and victory—not that he or she might be comfortable, but that he or she might be a comforter. The gospel ministry is a ministry of glory that seeks to exalt Jesus Christ in all things. Motivated by Christ's example of love and living daily in the fear of the Lord, the faithful minister can rejoice in his role as an ambassador for Christ—proclaiming reconciliation and restoration for estranged sinners.

Chapters 1–2	Chapters 3–4	Chapter 5
A Ministry of Comfort	A Ministry of Glory	A Ministry of Reconciliation
Triumph in Christ	Temple of Christ	

YOUR DAILY WALK Your best friend's marriage is in trouble. Your friend's spouse moves out; the couple seeks professional help. Then you hear the welcome news: They have been *reconciled*. What does that mean?

It takes two sides to make a lasting peace, but it only takes one to make the first step.

A union goes on strike for higher wages and shorter hours. The management refuses to meet the union's demands. The two sides sit down to negotiate. At last an announcement is made: They *reconciled* their differences. What does that mean?

An estranged sinner has gone his or her own way (Isaiah 53:6), wandering far from the God who made him or her. You as an ambassador of Jesus Christ come to share with him or her the Good News that a bridge has been provided to restore fellowship between sinful humanity and holy God (5:19). You extend the invitation, "Will you be *reconciled* to God?" What are you asking the person to do?

Yours is the precious privilege of inviting others to be *reconciled* to God. Have you reported for work yet today?

INSIGHT They Didn't Even Like His Looks!
Paul's need to write 2 Corinthians becomes clear when you note the severity of the charges against him: fickleness (1:17-23), pride (3:1), weakness (10:10), rude speech (11:6), meanness (7:8-10), dishonesty (12:16-19), and mental instability (5:13).

CHAPTER 1
This letter is from Paul, appointed by God to be an apostle of Christ Jesus, and from our dear brother Timothy.

We are writing to God's church in Corinth and to all the Christians throughout Greece.*

²May God our Father and the Lord Jesus Christ give you his grace and peace.

³All praise to the God and Father of our Lord Jesus Christ. He is the source* of every mercy and the God who comforts us. ⁴He

1:1 Greek *Achaia,* the southern region of the Greek peninsula.   **1:3** Greek *the Father.*

comforts us in all our troubles so that we can comfort others. When others are troubled, we will be able to give them the same comfort God has given us. [5]You can be sure that the more we suffer for Christ, the more God will shower us with his comfort through Christ. [6]So when we are weighed down with troubles, it is for your benefit and salvation! For when God comforts us, it is so that we, in turn, can be an encouragement to you. Then you can patiently endure the same things we suffer. [7]We are confident that as you share in suffering, you will also share God's comfort.

[8]I think you ought to know, dear brothers and sisters, about the trouble we went through in the province of Asia. We were crushed and completely overwhelmed, and we thought we would never live through it. [9]In fact, we expected to die. But as a result, we learned not to rely on ourselves, but on God who can raise the dead. [10]And he did deliver us from mortal danger. And we are confident that he will continue to deliver us. [11]He will rescue us because you are helping by praying for us. As a result, many will give thanks to God because so many people's prayers for our safety have been answered.

[12]We can say with confidence and a clear conscience that we have been honest* and sincere in all our dealings. We have depended on God's grace, not on our own earthly wisdom. That is how we have acted toward everyone, and especially toward you. [13]My letters have been straightforward, and there is nothing written between the lines and nothing you can't understand. I hope someday you will fully understand us, [14]even if you don't fully understand us now. Then on the day when our Lord Jesus comes back again, you will be proud of us in the same way we are proud of you.

[15]Since I was so sure of your understanding and trust, I wanted to give you a double blessing. [16]I wanted to stop and see you on my way to Macedonia and again on my return trip. Then you could send me on my way to Judea.

[17]You may be asking why I changed my plan. Hadn't I made up my mind yet? Or am I like people of the world who say yes when they really mean no? [18]As surely as God is true, I am not that sort of person. My yes means yes [19]because Jesus Christ, the Son of God, never wavers between yes and no. He is the one whom Timothy, Silas,* and I preached to you, and he is the divine Yes—God's affirmation. [20]For all of God's promises have been fulfilled in him. That is why we say "Amen" when we give glory to God through Christ. [21]It is God who gives us, along with you, the ability to stand firm for Christ.* He has commissioned us, [22]and he has identified us as his own by placing the Holy Spirit in our hearts as the first installment of everything he will give us.

[23]Now I call upon God as my witness that I am telling the truth. The reason I didn't return to Corinth was to spare you from a severe rebuke. [24]But that does not mean we want to tell you exactly how to put your faith into practice.* We want to work together with you so you will be full of joy as you stand firm in your faith.

CHAPTER 2

So I said to myself, "No, I won't do it. I won't make them unhappy with another painful visit." [2]For if I cause you pain and make you sad, who is going to make me glad? [3]That is why I wrote as I did in my last letter, so that when I do come, I will not be made sad by the very ones who ought to give me the greatest joy. Surely you know that my happiness depends on your happiness. [4]How painful it was to write that letter! Heartbroken, I cried over it. I didn't want to hurt you, but I wanted you to know how very much I love you.

[5]I am not overstating it when I say that the man who caused all the trouble hurt your entire church more than he hurt me. [6]He was punished enough when most of you were united in your judgment against him. [7]Now it is time to forgive him and comfort him. Otherwise he may become so discouraged that he won't be able to recover. [8]Now show him that you still love him.

[9]I wrote to you as I did to find out how far you would go in obeying me. [10]When you forgive this man, I forgive him, too. And when I forgive him (for whatever is to be forgiven), I do so with Christ's authority for your benefit, [11]so that Satan will not

---

1:12 Some manuscripts read *holy.*   **1:19** Greek *Silvanus.*   **1:21** Or *who has identified us and you as genuine Christians.*   **1:24** Greek *want to lord it over your faith.*

outsmart us. For we are very familiar with his evil schemes.

¹²Well, when I came to the city of Troas to preach the Good News of Christ, the Lord gave me tremendous opportunities. ¹³But I couldn't rest because my dear brother Titus hadn't yet arrived with a report from you. So I said good-bye and went on to Macedonia to find him.

¹⁴But thanks be to God, who made us his captives and leads us along in Christ's triumphal procession. Now wherever we go he uses us to tell others about the Lord and to spread the Good News like a sweet perfume. ¹⁵Our lives are a fragrance presented by Christ to God. But this fragrance is perceived differently by those being saved and by those perishing. ¹⁶To those who are perishing we are a fearful smell of death and doom. But to those who are being saved we are a life-giving perfume. And who is adequate for such a task as this? ¹⁷You see, we are not like those hucksters—and there are many of them—who preach just to make money. We preach God's message with sincerity and with Christ's authority. And we know that the God who sent us is watching us.

CHAPTER 3

Are we beginning again to tell you how good we are? Some people need to bring letters of recommendation with them or ask you to write letters of recommendation for them. ²But the only letter of recommendation we need is you yourselves! Your lives are a letter written in our* hearts, and everyone can read it and recognize our good work among you. ³Clearly, you are a letter from Christ prepared by us. It is written not with pen and ink, but with the Spirit of the living God. It is carved not on stone, but on human hearts.

⁴We are confident of all this because of our great trust in God through Christ. ⁵It is not that we think we can do anything of lasting value by ourselves. Our only power and success come from God. ⁶He is the one who has enabled us to represent his new covenant. This is a covenant, not of written laws, but of the Spirit. The old way ends in death; in the new way, the Holy Spirit gives life.

⁷That old system of law etched in stone led to death, yet it began with such glory that the people of Israel could not bear to look at Moses' face. For his face shone with the glory of God, even though the brightness was already fading away. ⁸Shouldn't we expect far greater glory when the Holy Spirit is giving life? ⁹If the old covenant, which brings condemnation, was glorious, how much more glorious is the new covenant, which makes us right with God! ¹⁰In fact, that first glory was not glorious at all compared with the overwhelming glory of the new covenant. ¹¹So if the old covenant, which has been set aside, was full of glory, then the new covenant, which remains forever, has far greater glory.

¹²Since this new covenant gives us such confidence, we can be very bold. ¹³We are not like Moses, who put a veil over his face so the people of Israel would not see the glory fading away. ¹⁴But the people's minds were hardened, and even to this day whenever the old covenant is being read, a veil covers their minds so they cannot understand the truth. And this veil can be removed only by believing in Christ. ¹⁵Yes, even today when they read Moses' writings, their hearts are covered with that veil, and they do not understand.

¹⁶But whenever anyone turns to the Lord, then the veil is taken away. ¹⁷Now, the Lord is the Spirit, and wherever the Spirit of the Lord is, he gives freedom. ¹⁸And all of us have had that veil removed so that we can be mirrors that brightly reflect* the glory of the Lord. And as the Spirit of the Lord works within us, we become more and more like him and reflect his glory even more.

CHAPTER 4

And so, since God in his mercy has given us this wonderful ministry, we never give up. ²We reject all shameful and underhanded methods. We do not try to trick anyone, and we do not distort the word of God. We tell the truth before God, and all who are honest know that.

³If the Good News we preach is veiled from anyone, it is a sign that they are perishing. ⁴Satan, the god of this evil world, has blinded the minds of those who don't believe, so they are unable to see the glorious light of the Good News that is shining upon them. They don't understand the

3:2 Some manuscripts read *your.*   3:18 Or *so that we can see in a mirror.*

message we preach about the glory of Christ, who is the exact likeness of God.

[5]We don't go around preaching about ourselves; we preach Christ Jesus, the Lord. All we say about ourselves is that we are your servants because of what Jesus has done for us. [6]For God, who said, "Let there be light in the darkness," has made us understand that this light is the brightness of the glory of God that is seen in the face of Jesus Christ.

[7]But this precious treasure—this light and power that now shine within us—is held in perishable containers, that is, in our weak bodies.* So everyone can see that our glorious power is from God and is not our own.

[8]We are pressed on every side by troubles, but we are not crushed and broken. We are perplexed, but we don't give up and quit. [9]We are hunted down, but God never abandons us. We get knocked down, but we get up again and keep going. [10]Through suffering, these bodies of ours constantly share in the death of Jesus so that the life of Jesus may also be seen in our bodies.

[11]Yes, we live under constant danger of death because we serve Jesus, so that the life of Jesus will be obvious in our dying bodies. [12]So we live in the face of death, but it has resulted in eternal life for you.

[13]But we continue to preach because we have the same kind of faith the psalmist had when he said, "I believed in God, and so I speak."* [14]We know that the same God who raised our Lord Jesus will also raise us with Jesus and present us to himself along with you. [15]All of these things are for your benefit. And as God's grace brings more and more people to Christ, there will be great thanksgiving, and God will receive more and more glory.

[16]That is why we never give up. Though our bodies are dying, our spirits are* being renewed every day. [17]For our present troubles are quite small and won't last very long. Yet they produce for us an immeasurably great glory that will last forever! [18]So we don't look at the troubles we can see right now; rather, we look forward to what we have not yet seen. For the troubles we see will soon be over, but the joys to come will last forever.

CHAPTER 5

For we know that when this earthly tent we live in is taken down—when we die and leave these bodies—we will have a home in heaven, an eternal body made for us by God himself and not by human hands. [2]We grow weary in our present bodies, and we long for the day when we will put on our heavenly bodies like new clothing. [3]For we will not be spirits without bodies, but we will put on new heavenly bodies. [4]Our dying bodies make us groan and sigh, but it's not that we want to die and have no bodies at all. We want to slip into our new bodies so that these dying bodies will be swallowed up by everlasting life. [5]God himself has prepared us for this, and as a guarantee he has given us his Holy Spirit.

[6]So we are always confident, even though we know that as long as we live in these bodies we are not at home with the Lord. [7]That is why we live by believing and not by seeing. [8]Yes, we are fully confident, and we would rather be away from these bodies, for then we will be at home with the Lord. [9]So our aim is to please him always, whether we are here in this body or away from this body. [10]For we must all stand before Christ to be judged. We will each receive whatever we deserve for the good or evil we have done in our bodies.

[11]It is because we know this solemn fear of the Lord that we work so hard to persuade others. God knows we are sincere, and I hope you know this, too. [12]Are we trying to pat ourselves on the back again? No, we are giving you a reason to be proud of us, so you can answer those who brag about having a spectacular ministry rather than having a sincere heart before God. [13]If it seems that we are crazy, it is to bring glory to God. And if we are in our right minds, it is for your benefit. [14]Whatever we do, it is because Christ's love controls us.* Since we believe that Christ died for everyone, we also believe that we have all died to the old life we used to live.* [15]He died for everyone so that those who receive his new life will no longer live to please themselves. Instead, they will live to please Christ, who died and was raised for them.

[16]So we have stopped evaluating others by what the world thinks about them. Once I mistakenly thought of Christ that way, as though he were merely a human being.

4:7 Greek *But we have this treasure in earthen vessels.*   4:13 Ps 116:10.   4:16 Greek *our inner being is.*   5:14a Or *urges us on.*
5:14b Greek *Since one died on behalf of all, then all died.*

How differently I think about him now! [17]What this means is that those who become Christians become new persons. They are not the same anymore, for the old life is gone. A new life has begun! [18]All this newness of life is from God, who brought us back to himself through what Christ did. And God has given us the task of reconciling people to him. [19]For God was in Christ, reconciling the world to himself, no longer counting people's sins against them. This is the wonderful message he has given us to tell others. [20]We are Christ's ambassadors, and God is using us to speak to you. We urge you, as though Christ himself were here pleading with you, "Be reconciled to God!" [21]For God made Christ, who never sinned, to be the offering for our sin, so that we could be made right with God through Christ.

NOVEMBER 24 ☐ DAY 329
2 CORINTHIANS 6–9
Paul's Motivation and Model

OVERVIEW Being a partner in the gospel means, first and foremost, allowing the gospel to have its life-changing effect on you. As a fellow worker in the gospel ministry, Paul exhorts the Corinthians not to receive the grace of God in an empty, purposeless way. Fellowship with darkness, filthiness of the flesh, and insensitivity to financial needs around you are all inconsistent with the grace of God. Those truly motivated by the gospel will seek to exercise generosity toward those in need.

Chapter 6	Chapter 7	Chapter 8	Chapter 9
A Ministry of Purity	A Message of Praise	A Ministry of Giving	A Method of Giving
Separation		Stewardship	

YOUR DAILY WALK A man complained to his pastor, "It's getting to be just one continuous 'give, give, give.'"

To which the pastor replied, "Say, that's one of the best descriptions of Christianity I've ever heard!"

Here are some sermons-in-a-sentence on the subject of giving:

All we can hold in our cold, dead hands is what we have given away.

- Only by giving of oneself is enough taken away to make room for receiving more.
- Discontentment makes rich men poor; contentment makes poor men rich.
- Two telltale marks of a Christian are giving and forgiving, for the world knows little about either.

The average American churchgoer gives 3 percent of his or her income to church and charity. If 2 Corinthians 8:1-2 were being written about you and your church—rather than the churches of Macedonia—what would Paul say? And would you be pleased or pained to know others were reading about your model of giving? Write the words of 2 Corinthians 9:7 inside your checkbook. Let them remind you that cheerful giving comes from the heart, not just the checkbook!

INSIGHT Grace: The Gift That Keeps On Giving

The Christians in Macedonia were so moved by the grace God had shown them that they actually *begged* Paul for the privilege of showing God's grace to the believers in Jerusalem (8:1-5).

CHAPTER 6

As God's partners,* we beg you not to reject this marvelous message of God's great kindness. ²For God says,

"At just the right time, I heard you.
    On the day of salvation, I helped
    you."*

Indeed, God is ready to help you right now. Today is the day of salvation.

³We try to live in such a way that no one will be hindered from finding the Lord by the way we act, and so no one can find fault with our ministry. ⁴In everything we do we try to show that we are true ministers of God. We patiently endure troubles and hardships and calamities of every kind. ⁵We have been beaten, been put in jail, faced angry mobs, worked to exhaustion, endured sleepless nights, and gone without food. ⁶We have proved ourselves by our purity, our understanding, our patience, our kindness, our sincere love, and the power of the Holy Spirit.* ⁷We have faithfully preached the truth. God's power has been working in us. We have righteousness as our weapon, both to attack and to defend ourselves. ⁸We serve God whether people honor us or despise us, whether they slander us or praise us. We are honest, but they call us impostors. ⁹We are well known, but we are treated as unknown. We live close to death, but here we are, still alive. We have been beaten within an inch of our lives. ¹⁰Our hearts ache, but we always have joy. We are poor, but we give spiritual riches to others. We own nothing, and yet we have everything.

¹¹Oh, dear Corinthian friends! We have spoken honestly with you. Our hearts are open to you. ¹²If there is a problem between us, it is not because of a lack of love on our part, but because you have withheld your love from us. ¹³I am talking now as I would to my own children. Open your hearts to us!

¹⁴Don't team up with those who are unbelievers. How can goodness be a partner with wickedness? How can light live with darkness? ¹⁵What harmony can there be between Christ and the Devil*? How can a believer be a partner with an unbeliever? ¹⁶And what union can there be between God's temple and idols? For we are the temple of the living God. As God said:

"I will live in them
    and walk among them.
I will be their God,
    and they will be my people.*
¹⁷ Therefore, come out from them
    and separate yourselves from them,
    says the Lord.
Don't touch their filthy things,
    and I will welcome you.*
¹⁸ And I will be your Father,
    and you will be my sons and
    daughters,
    says the Lord Almighty.*"

CHAPTER 7

Because we have these promises, dear friends, let us cleanse ourselves from everything that can defile our body or spirit. And let us work toward complete purity because we fear God.

²Please open your hearts to us. We have not done wrong to anyone. We have not led anyone astray. We have not taken advantage of anyone. ³I'm not saying this to condemn you, for I said before that you are in our hearts forever. We live or die together with you. ⁴I have the highest confidence in you, and my pride in you is great. You have greatly encouraged me; you have made me happy despite all our troubles.

⁵When we arrived in Macedonia there was no rest for us. Outside there was conflict from every direction, and inside there was fear. ⁶But God, who encourages those who are discouraged, encouraged us by the arrival of Titus. ⁷His presence was a joy, but so was the news he brought of the encouragement he received from you. When he told me how much you were looking forward to my visit, and how sorry you were about what had happened, and how loyal your love is for me, I was filled with joy!

⁸I am no longer sorry that I sent that letter to you, though I was sorry for a time, for I know that it was painful to you for a little while. ⁹Now I am glad I sent it, not because it hurt you, but because the pain caused you to have remorse and change your ways. It was the kind of sorrow God wants his people to have, so you were not harmed by us in any way. ¹⁰For God can use sorrow in our lives to help us turn away from sin and seek salvation. We will never regret that kind of sorrow. But sor-

6:1 Or *As we work together.*   **6:2** Isa 49:8.   **6:6** Or *the holiness of spirit.*   **6:15** Greek *and Beliar.*   **6:16** Lev 26:12; Ezek 37:27.
6:17 Isa 52:11; Ezek 20:34.   **6:18** 2 Sam 7:14.

row without repentance is the kind that results in death.

[11]Just see what this godly sorrow produced in you! Such earnestness, such concern to clear yourselves, such indignation, such alarm, such longing to see me, such zeal, and such a readiness to punish the wrongdoer. You showed that you have done everything you could to make things right. [12]My purpose was not to write about who did the wrong or who was wronged. I wrote to you so that in the sight of God you could show how much you really do care for us. [13]We have been encouraged by this.

In addition to our own encouragement, we were especially delighted to see how happy Titus was at the way you welcomed him and set his mind at ease. [14]I had told him how proud I was of you—and you didn't disappoint me. I have always told you the truth, and now my boasting to Titus has also proved true! [15]Now he cares for you more than ever when he remembers the way you listened to him and welcomed him with such respect and deep concern. [16]I am very happy now because I have complete confidence in you.

CHAPTER 8
Now I want to tell you, dear brothers and sisters, what God in his kindness has done for the churches in Macedonia. [2]Though they have been going through much trouble and hard times, their wonderful joy and deep poverty have overflowed in rich generosity. [3]For I can testify that they gave not only what they could afford but far more. And they did it of their own free will. [4]They begged us again and again for the gracious privilege of sharing in the gift for the Christians in Jerusalem. [5]Best of all, they went beyond our highest hopes, for their first action was to dedicate themselves to the Lord and to us for whatever directions God might give them.

[6]So we have urged Titus, who encouraged your giving in the first place, to return to you and encourage you to complete your share in this ministry of giving. [7]Since you excel in so many ways—you have so much faith, such gifted speakers, such knowledge, such enthusiasm, and such love for us*—now I want you to excel also in this gracious ministry of giving. [8]I am not saying you must do it, even though the other

churches are eager to do it. This is one way to prove your love is real.

[9]You know how full of love and kindness our Lord Jesus Christ was. Though he was very rich, yet for your sakes he became poor, so that by his poverty he could make you rich.

[10]I suggest that you finish what you started a year ago, for you were the first to propose this idea, and you were the first to begin doing something about it. [11]Now you should carry this project through to completion just as enthusiastically as you began it. Give whatever you can according to what you have. [12]If you are really eager to give, it isn't important how much you are able to give. God wants you to give what you have, not what you don't have. [13]Of course, I don't mean you should give so much that you suffer from having too little. I only mean that there should be some equality. [14]Right now you have plenty and can help them. Then at some other time they can share with you when you need it. In this way, everyone's needs will be met. [15]Do you remember what the Scriptures say about this? "Those who gathered a lot had nothing left over, and those who gathered only a little had enough."*

[16]I am thankful to God that he has given Titus the same enthusiasm for you that I have. [17]He welcomed our request that he visit you again. In fact, he himself was eager to go and see you. [18]We are also sending another brother with Titus. He is highly praised in all the churches as a preacher of the Good News. [19]He was appointed by the churches to accompany us as we take the offering to Jerusalem*—a service that glorifies the Lord and shows our eagerness to help. [20]By traveling together we will guard against any suspicion, for we are anxious that no one should find fault with the way we are handling this generous gift. [21]We are careful to be honorable before the Lord, but we also want everyone else to know we are honorable.

[22]And we are also sending with them another brother who has been thoroughly tested and has shown how earnest he is on many occasions. He is now even more enthusiastic because of his increased confidence in you. [23]If anyone asks about Titus, say that he is my partner who works with me to help you. And these brothers are

8:7 Some manuscripts read *love from us to you.*   **8:15** Exod 16:18.   **8:19** See 1 Cor 16:3-4.

representatives* of the churches. They are splendid examples of those who bring glory to Christ. ²⁴So show them your love, and prove to all the churches that our boasting about you is justified.

CHAPTER 9

I really don't need to write to you about this gift for the Christians in Jerusalem.* ²For I know how eager you are to help, and I have been boasting to our friends in Macedonia that you Christians in Greece* were ready to send an offering a year ago. In fact, it was your enthusiasm that stirred up many of them to begin helping. ³But I am sending these brothers just to be sure that you really are ready, as I told them you would be, with your money all collected. I don't want it to turn out that I was wrong in my boasting about you. ⁴I would be humiliated—and so would you—if some Macedonian Christians came with me, only to find that you still weren't ready after all I had told them! ⁵So I thought I should send these brothers ahead of me to make sure the gift you promised is ready. But I want it to be a willing gift, not one given under pressure.

⁶Remember this—a farmer who plants only a few seeds will get a small crop. But the one who plants generously will get a generous crop. ⁷You must each make up your own mind as to how much you should give. Don't give reluctantly or in response to pressure. For God loves the person who gives cheerfully. ⁸And God will generously provide all you need. Then you will always have everything you need and plenty left over to share with others. ⁹As the Scriptures say,

"Godly people give generously to the poor.
    Their good deeds will never be forgotten."*

¹⁰For God is the one who gives seed to the farmer and then bread to eat. In the same way, he will give you many opportunities to do good, and he will produce a great harvest of generosity* in you.

¹¹Yes, you will be enriched so that you can give even more generously. And when we take your gifts to those who need them, they will break out in thanksgiving to God. ¹²So two good things will happen—the needs of the Christians in Jerusalem will be met, and they will joyfully express their thanksgiving to God. ¹³You will be glorifying God through your generous gifts. For your generosity to them will prove that you are obedient to the Good News of Christ. ¹⁴And they will pray for you with deep affection because of the wonderful grace of God shown through you.

¹⁵Thank God for his Son—a gift too wonderful for words!*

8:23 Greek *apostles.*   9:1 Greek *about the offering for the saints.*   9:2 Greek *Achaia,* the southern region of the Greek peninsula.
9:9 Ps 112:9.   9:10 Greek *righteousness.*   9:15 Greek *Thank God for his indescribable gift.*

NOVEMBER 25 □ DAY 330
2 CORINTHIANS 10–13
Paul's Authority in Ministry

OVERVIEW Discipline is never pleasant, but the task becomes doubly difficult when the authority of the disciplinarian is under attack. In order to defend his authority as an apostle of Jesus Christ, Paul relates certain events from his background, including his heavenly visions and thorn in the flesh. His letter closes with a warning that he will soon make his third visit to Corinth, and so he urges the believers there to take his exhortations to heart.

Chapter 10	Chapter 11	Chapter 12	Chapter 13
Authority Declared	Authority Defended	Authority Dramatized	A Visit Described
Paul, the Minister		Paul, the Messenger	

YOUR DAILY WALK How are splinters, thorns, and chewing gum alike? *Answer:* It's easier to get attached to them than to get rid of them! Paul's thorn in the flesh has been the subject of much speculation. Though the biblical account is brief, this much is clear:

The person who would have nothing to do with thorns must never attempt to gather flowers.

- God allowed it for a purpose—to promote humility in Paul's life and keep him from exalting himself above measure (12:7).
- It was of satanic origin—similar to Job's loss of wealth, health, family, and status (12:7; Job 1–2).
- No amount of prayer would remove it (12:8)—regardless of how fervent or frequent the petition.
- It was used to show the sufficiency of God in the face of human weakness (12:9-10).

The exact nature of Paul's thorn is unclear—perhaps so you can learn a lesson from your own "thorny" situation. A lingering illness, a physical handicap, a speech impediment—God is adequate for them all. Carry a stick of gum today to remind you that God's strength is a promise that will "stick" with you. Now that's a thought worth chewing on!

INSIGHT What's in a Thorn?
The list of suggestions regarding Paul's thorn in the flesh reads like a medical dictionary. Ideas include epilepsy, eye disease, malaria, leprosy, migraine headaches, depression, and stammering.

CHAPTER 10

Now I, Paul, plead with you. I plead with the gentleness and kindness that Christ himself would use, even though some of you say I am bold in my letters but timid in person. [2]I hope it won't be necessary, but when I come I may have to be very bold with those who think we act from purely human motives. [3]We are human, but we don't wage war with human plans and methods. [4]We use God's mighty weapons, not mere worldly weapons, to knock down the Devil's strongholds. [5]With these weapons we break down every proud argument that keeps people from knowing God. With these weapons we conquer their rebellious ideas, and we teach them to obey Christ. [6]And we will punish those who remained disobedient after the rest of you became loyal and obedient.

[7]The trouble with you is that you make your decisions on the basis of appearance.* You must recognize that we belong to Christ just as much as those who proudly declare that they belong to Christ. [8]I may seem to be boasting too much about the authority given to us by the Lord. But this authority is to build you up, not to tear you down. And I will not be put to shame by having my work among you destroyed.

[9]Now this is not just an attempt to frighten you by my letters. [10]For some say,

"Don't worry about Paul. His letters are demanding and forceful, but in person he is weak, and his speeches are really bad!" [11]The ones who say this must realize that we will be just as demanding and forceful in person as we are in our letters.

[12]Oh, don't worry; I wouldn't dare say that I am as wonderful as these other men who tell you how important they are! But they are only comparing themselves with each other, and measuring themselves by themselves. What foolishness!

[13]But we will not boast of authority we do not have. Our goal is to stay within the boundaries of God's plan for us, and this plan includes our working there with you. [14]We are not going too far when we claim authority over you, for we were the first to travel all the way to you with the Good News of Christ. [15]Nor do we claim credit for the work someone else has done. Instead, we hope that your faith will grow and that our work among you will be greatly enlarged. [16]Then we will be able to go and preach the Good News in other places that are far beyond you, where no one else is working. Then there will be no question about being in someone else's territory. [17]As the Scriptures say,

"The person who wishes to boast
should boast only of what the Lord
has done."*

10:7 Or *Look at the obvious facts.*　　**10:17** Jer 9:24.

¹⁸When people boast about themselves, it doesn't count for much. But when the Lord commends someone, that's different!

CHAPTER 11

I hope you will be patient with me as I keep on talking like a fool. Please bear with me. ²I am jealous for you with the jealousy of God himself. For I promised you as a pure bride* to one husband, Christ. ³But I fear that somehow you will be led away from your pure and simple devotion to Christ, just as Eve was deceived by the serpent. ⁴You seem to believe whatever anyone tells you, even if they preach about a different Jesus than the one we preach, or a different Spirit than the one you received, or a different kind of gospel than the one you believed. ⁵But I don't think I am inferior to these "super apostles." ⁶I may not be a trained speaker, but I know what I am talking about. I think you realize this by now, for we have proved it again and again.

⁷Did I do wrong when I humbled myself and honored you by preaching God's Good News to you without expecting anything in return? ⁸I "robbed" other churches by accepting their contributions so I could serve you at no cost. ⁹And when I was with you and didn't have enough to live on, I did not ask you to help me. For the brothers who came from Macedonia brought me another gift. I have never yet asked you for any support, and I never will. ¹⁰As surely as the truth of Christ is in me, I will never stop boasting about this all over Greece.* ¹¹Why? Because I don't love you? God knows I do.

¹²But I will continue doing this to cut the ground out from under the feet of those who boast that their work is just like ours. ¹³These people are false apostles. They have fooled you by disguising themselves as apostles of Christ. ¹⁴But I am not surprised! Even Satan can disguise himself as an angel of light. ¹⁵So it is no wonder his servants can also do it by pretending to be godly ministers. In the end they will get every bit of punishment their wicked deeds deserve.

¹⁶Once again, don't think that I have lost my wits to talk like this. But even if you do, listen to me, as you would to a foolish person, while I also boast a little.

¹⁷Such bragging is not something the Lord wants, but I am acting like a fool. ¹⁸And since others boast about their human achievements, I will, too. ¹⁹After all, you, who think you are so wise, enjoy listening to fools! ²⁰You put up with it when they make you their slaves, take everything you have, take advantage of you, put on airs, and slap you in the face. ²¹I'm ashamed to say that we were not strong enough to do that!

But whatever they dare to boast about—I'm talking like a fool again—I can boast about it, too. ²²They say they are Hebrews, do they? So am I. And they say they are Israelites? So am I. And they are descendants of Abraham? So am I. ²³They say they serve Christ? I know I sound like a madman, but I have served him far more! I have worked harder, been put in jail more often, been whipped times without number, and faced death again and again. ²⁴Five different times the Jews gave me thirty-nine lashes. ²⁵Three times I was beaten with rods. Once I was stoned. Three times I was shipwrecked. Once I spent a whole night and a day adrift at sea. ²⁶I have traveled many weary miles. I have faced danger from flooded rivers and from robbers. I have faced danger from my own people, the Jews, as well as from the Gentiles. I have faced danger in the cities, in the deserts, and on the stormy seas. And I have faced danger from men who claim to be Christians but are not.* ²⁷I have lived with weariness and pain and sleepless nights. Often I have been hungry and thirsty and have gone without food. Often I have shivered with cold, without enough clothing to keep me warm.

²⁸Then, besides all this, I have the daily burden of how the churches are getting along. ²⁹Who is weak without my feeling that weakness? Who is led astray, and I do not burn with anger?

³⁰If I must boast, I would rather boast about the things that show how weak I am. ³¹God, the Father of our Lord Jesus, who is to be praised forever, knows I tell the truth. ³²When I was in Damascus, the governor under King Aretas kept guards at the city gates to catch me. ³³But I was lowered in a basket through a window in the city wall, and that's how I got away!

11:2 Greek *a virgin.*   **11:10** Greek *Achaia.*   **11:26** Greek *from false brothers.*

CHAPTER 12

This boasting is all so foolish, but let me go on. Let me tell about the visions and revelations I received from the Lord. ²I* was caught up into the third heaven fourteen years ago. ³Whether my body was there or just my spirit, I don't know; only God knows. ⁴But I do know that I* was caught up into paradise and heard things so astounding that they cannot be told. ⁵That experience is something worth boasting about, but I am not going to do it. I am going to boast only about my weaknesses. ⁶I have plenty to boast about and would be no fool in doing it, because I would be telling the truth. But I won't do it. I don't want anyone to think more highly of me than what they can actually see in my life and my message, ⁷even though I have received wonderful revelations from God. But to keep me from getting puffed up, I was given a thorn in my flesh, a messenger from Satan to torment me and keep me from getting proud.

⁸Three different times I begged the Lord to take it away. ⁹Each time he said, "My gracious favor is all you need. My power works best in your weakness." So now I am glad to boast about my weaknesses, so that the power of Christ may work through me. ¹⁰Since I know it is all for Christ's good, I am quite content with my weaknesses and with insults, hardships, persecutions, and calamities. For when I am weak, then I am strong.

¹¹You have made me act like a fool—boasting like this. You ought to be writing commendations for me, for I am not at all inferior to these "super apostles," even though I am nothing at all. ¹²When I was with you, I certainly gave you every proof that I am truly an apostle, sent to you by God himself. For I patiently did many signs and wonders and miracles among you. ¹³The only thing I didn't do, which I do in the other churches, was to become a burden to you. Please forgive me for this wrong!

¹⁴Now I am coming to you for the third time, and I will not be a burden to you. I don't want what you have; I want you. And anyway, little children don't pay for their parents' food. It's the other way around; parents supply food for their children. ¹⁵I will gladly spend myself and all I have for your spiritual good, even though it seems that the more I love you, the less you love me.

¹⁶Some of you admit I was not a burden to you. But they still think I was sneaky and took advantage of you by trickery. ¹⁷But how? Did any of the men I sent to you take advantage of you? ¹⁸When I urged Titus to visit you and sent our other brother with him, did Titus take advantage of you? No, of course not! For we both have the same Spirit and walk in each other's steps, doing things the same way.

¹⁹Perhaps you think we are saying all this just to defend ourselves. That isn't it at all. We tell you this as Christ's servants, and we know that God is listening. Everything we do, dear friends, is for your benefit. ²⁰For I am afraid that when I come to visit you I won't like what I find, and then you won't like my response. I am afraid that I will find quarreling, jealousy, outbursts of anger, selfishness, backstabbing, gossip, conceit, and disorderly behavior. ²¹Yes, I am afraid that when I come, God will humble me again because of you. And I will have to grieve because many of you who sinned earlier have not repented of your impurity, sexual immorality, and eagerness for lustful pleasure.

CHAPTER 13

This is the third time I am coming to visit you. As the Scriptures say, "The facts of every case must be established by the testimony of two or three witnesses."* ²I have already warned those who had been sinning when I was there on my second visit. Now I again warn them and all others, just as I did before, that this next time I will not spare them.

³I will give you all the proof you want that Christ speaks through me. Christ is not weak in his dealings with you; he is a mighty power among you. ⁴Although he died on the cross in weakness, he now lives by the mighty power of God. We, too, are weak, but we live in him and have God's power—the power we use in dealing with you.

⁵Examine yourselves to see if your faith is really genuine. Test yourselves. If you cannot tell that Jesus Christ is among you,* it means you have failed the test. ⁶I hope you recognize that we have passed the test and are approved by God.

⁷We pray to God that you will not do anything wrong. We pray this, not to show that our ministry to you has been successful, but because we want you to do right even if

12:2 Greek *I know a man in Christ who.*   12:4 Greek *he.*   13:1 Deut 19:15.   13:5 Or *in you.*

we ourselves seem to have failed. [8]Our responsibility is never to oppose the truth, but to stand for the truth at all times. [9]We are glad to be weak, if you are really strong. What we pray for is your restoration to maturity.

[10]I am writing this to you before I come, hoping that I won't need to deal harshly with you when I do come. For I want to use the authority the Lord has given me to build you up, not to tear you down.

[11]Dear brothers and sisters, I close my letter with these last words: Rejoice. Change your ways. Encourage each other. Live in harmony and peace. Then the God of love and peace will be with you.

[12]Greet each other in Christian love.* All the Christians here send you their greetings.

[13]May the grace of our Lord Jesus Christ, the love of God, and the fellowship of the Holy Spirit be with you all.*

13:12 Greek with a sacred kiss. **13:12-13** Some English versions divide verse 12 into verses 12 and 13, and then verse 13 becomes verse 14.

Galatians

PAUL'S epistle to the Galatians is an attempt to avert disaster. Having launched their Christian experience by faith, the Galatians now seem willing to leave their faith voyage and chart a new and misguided course based on works. Paul blends boldness with benevolence as he repudiates the bondage the Galatians have imposed on themselves. After reminding them that it is through grace, not law, that heaven is obtained, Paul goes on to show that it is in the Spirit, not the flesh, that the Christian life is successfully lived. Freedom in Christ means freedom to produce the fruits of righteousness through a Spirit-led lifestyle.

Focus	Defending the Gospel Minister		Defending the Gospel's Message		Demonstrating the Gospel's Might	
Divisions	Perverters' Renunciation	Paul's Apostleship	Law Cannot Set Free	Grace Sets Free	Peril to Freedom	Practice in Freedom
	1:1 1:10	1:11 2:21	3:1 4:20	4:21 4:31	5:1 5:12	5:13 6:18
Topics	Autobiography		Argument		Application	
	Authority, Not Opinion		Freedom, Not Slavery		Spirit, Not Flesh	
Place	South Galatian Theory: Syrian Antioch North Galatian Theory: Ephesus or Macedonia					
Time	South Galatian Theory: A.D. 49 North Galatian Theory: A.D. 53–56					

NOVEMBER 26 ☐ DAY 331
GALATIANS 1–6
Unshackled in Christ

OVERVIEW After Paul's first missionary journey, the Jerusalem council (Acts 15) reached a landmark decision in which it acknowledged that a person does not first have to become a Jew in order to become a Christian. However, the apostle Paul continued to struggle with those who would add the requirement of Jewish law to the simple message of salvation. It is not through keeping the Mosaic law that the Christian faith is either begun or continued. The law enslaves; faith in Jesus Christ liberates. But liberty is not license to sin.

Chapters 1–2	Chapters 3–4	Chapters 5–6
Defending the Gospel's Minister	Defending the Gospel's Message	Demonstrating the Gospel's Might
Autobiography	Authority	Application

Legalism is bound to produce pride of heart.

YOUR DAILY WALK Imagine for a moment that you have been invited to witness a most unusual wedding ceremony. The bride and groom are there in all their finery. But before the ceremony begins, each hands the other a contract detailing the rules of their new relationship and life together. The husband-to-be reads, "You must help with the dishes each evening; you must cut the lawn each Saturday; you must not soil the carpets with your muddy fishing boots." And conversely, the wife-to-be reads, with shock and dismay, "You must cook the meals; you must keep a clean house; you must make the beds. . . ." What's the problem here? They are trying to legislate what love would cause them to do willingly in the first place!

Now carry that illustration over into the spiritual realm. A Spirit-controlled person needs no law to make him or her live a righteous life. Why? Because the motivation to do so comes from within.

Take a hard look at your walk with God. Is it characterized by a growing list of *rules* or a growing love *relationship*? Remember, without the fruit of the Spirit you are just a religious noise (1 Corinthians 13:1)! Pick one characteristic listed in 5:22-23 to cultivate today.

INSIGHT Galatians: The Large-Print Edition
Verses such as 6:11 seem to indicate that Paul suffered from poor eyesight. As a result he usually dictated his letters (Romans 16:22), adding a handwritten greeting (1 Corinthians 16:21). This evidence leads some commentators to believe that Paul's "thorn in the flesh" may have been an eye disease.

C H A P T E R 1
This letter is from Paul, an apostle. I was not appointed by any group or by human authority. My call is from Jesus Christ himself and from God the Father, who raised Jesus from the dead.

²All the brothers and sisters here join me in sending greetings to the churches of Galatia.

³May grace and peace be yours from God our Father and from the Lord Jesus Christ. ⁴He died for our sins, just as God

our Father planned, in order to rescue us from this evil world in which we live. [5]That is why all glory belongs to God through all the ages of eternity. Amen.

[6]I am shocked that you are turning away so soon from God, who in his love and mercy called you to share the eternal life he gives through Christ. You are already following a different way [7]that pretends to be the Good News but is not the Good News at all. You are being fooled by those who twist and change the truth concerning Christ.

[8]Let God's curse fall on anyone, including myself, who preaches any other message than the one we told you about. Even if an angel comes from heaven and preaches any other message, let him be forever cursed. [9]I will say it again: If anyone preaches any other gospel than the one you welcomed, let God's curse fall upon that person.

[10]Obviously, I'm not trying to be a people pleaser! No, I am trying to please God. If I were still trying to please people, I would not be Christ's servant.

[11]Dear brothers and sisters, I solemnly assure you that the Good News of salvation which I preach is not based on mere human reasoning or logic. [12]For my message came by a direct revelation from Jesus Christ himself. No one else taught me.

[13]You know what I was like when I followed the Jewish religion—how I violently persecuted the Christians.* I did my best to get rid of them. [14]I was one of the most religious Jews of my own age, and I tried as hard as possible to follow all the old traditions of my religion.

[15]But then something happened! For it pleased God in his kindness to choose me and call me, even before I was born! What undeserved mercy! [16]Then he revealed his Son to me* so that I could proclaim the Good News about Jesus to the Gentiles. When all this happened to me, I did not rush out to consult with anyone else; [17]nor did I go up to Jerusalem to consult with those who were apostles before I was. No, I went away into Arabia and later returned to the city of Damascus. [18]It was not until three years later that I finally went to Jerusalem for a visit with Peter* and stayed there with him for fifteen days. [19]And the only other apostle I met at that time was James, our Lord's brother. [20]You must believe what I am saying, for I declare before God that I am not lying. [21]Then after this visit, I went north into the provinces of Syria and Cilicia. [22]And still the Christians in the churches in Judea didn't know me personally. [23]All they knew was that people were saying, "The one who used to persecute us now preaches the very faith he tried to destroy!" [24]And they gave glory to God because of me.

CHAPTER 2

Then fourteen years later I went back to Jerusalem again, this time with Barnabas; and Titus came along, too. [2]I went there because God revealed to me that I should go. While I was there I talked privately with the leaders of the church. I wanted them to understand what I had been preaching to the Gentiles. I wanted to make sure they did not disagree, or my ministry would have been useless. [3]And they did agree. They did not even demand that my companion Titus be circumcised, though he was a Gentile.*

[4]Even that question wouldn't have come up except for some so-called Christians there—false ones, really*—who came to spy on us and see our freedom in Christ Jesus. They wanted to force us, like slaves, to follow their Jewish regulations. [5]But we refused to listen to them for a single moment. We wanted to preserve the truth of the Good News for you.

[6]And the leaders of the church who were there had nothing to add to what I was preaching. (By the way, their reputation as great leaders made no difference to me, for God has no favorites.) [7]They saw that God had given me the responsibility of preaching the Good News to the Gentiles, just as he had given Peter the responsibility of preaching to the Jews. [8]For the same God who worked through Peter for the benefit of the Jews worked through me for the benefit of the Gentiles. [9]In fact, James, Peter,* and John, who were known as pillars of the church, recognized the gift God had given me, and they accepted Barnabas and me as their co-workers. They encouraged us to keep preaching to the Gentiles, while they continued their work with the Jews.

1:13 Greek *the church of God.*   **1:16** Or *in me.*   **1:18** Greek *Cephas.*   **2:3** Greek *a Greek.*   **2:4** Greek *some false brothers.*   **2:9** Greek *Cephas; also in 2:11, 14.*

¹⁰The only thing they suggested was that we remember to help the poor, and I have certainly been eager to do that.

¹¹But when Peter came to Antioch, I had to oppose him publicly, speaking strongly against what he was doing, for it was very wrong. ¹²When he first arrived, he ate with the Gentile Christians, who don't bother with circumcision. But afterward, when some Jewish friends of James came, Peter wouldn't eat with the Gentiles anymore because he was afraid of what these legalists would say. ¹³Then the other Jewish Christians followed Peter's hypocrisy, and even Barnabas was influenced to join them in their hypocrisy.

¹⁴When I saw that they were not following the truth of the Good News, I said to Peter in front of all the others, "Since you, a Jew by birth, have discarded the Jewish laws and are living like a Gentile, why are you trying to make these Gentiles obey the Jewish laws you abandoned? ¹⁵You and I are Jews by birth, not 'sinners' like the Gentiles. ¹⁶And yet we Jewish Christians know that we become right with God, not by doing what the law commands, but by faith in Jesus Christ. So we have believed in Christ Jesus, that we might be accepted by God because of our faith in Christ—and not because we have obeyed the law. For no one will ever be saved by obeying the law."*

¹⁷But what if we seek to be made right with God through faith in Christ and then find out that we are still sinners? Has Christ led us into sin? Of course not! ¹⁸Rather, I make myself guilty if I rebuild the old system I already tore down. ¹⁹For when I tried to keep the law, I realized I could never earn God's approval. So I died to the law so that I might live for God. I have been crucified with Christ. ²⁰I myself no longer live, but Christ lives in me. So I live my life in this earthly body by trusting in the Son of God, who loved me and gave himself for me. ²¹I am not one of those who treats the grace of God as meaningless. For if we could be saved by keeping the law, then there was no need for Christ to die.

CHAPTER 3

Oh, foolish Galatians! What magician has cast an evil spell on you? For you used to see the meaning of Jesus Christ's death as clearly as though I had shown you a sign-board with a picture of Christ dying on the cross. ²Let me ask you this one question: Did you receive the Holy Spirit by keeping the law? Of course not, for the Holy Spirit came upon you only after you believed the message you heard about Christ. ³Have you lost your senses? After starting your Christian lives in the Spirit, why are you now trying to become perfect by your own human effort? ⁴You have suffered so much for the Good News. Surely it was not in vain, was it? Are you now going to just throw it all away?

⁵I ask you again, does God give you the Holy Spirit and work miracles among you because you obey the law of Moses? Of course not! It is because you believe the message you heard about Christ.

⁶In the same way, "Abraham believed God, so God declared him righteous because of his faith."* ⁷The real children of Abraham, then, are all those who put their faith in God.

⁸What's more, the Scriptures looked forward to this time when God would accept the Gentiles, too, on the basis of their faith. God promised this good news to Abraham long ago when he said, "All nations will be blessed through you."* ⁹And so it is: All who put their faith in Christ share the same blessing Abraham received because of his faith.

¹⁰But those who depend on the law to make them right with God are under his curse, for the Scriptures say, "Cursed is everyone who does not observe and obey all these commands that are written in God's Book of the Law."* ¹¹Consequently, it is clear that no one can ever be right with God by trying to keep the law. For the Scriptures say, "It is through faith that a righteous person has life."* ¹²How different from this way of faith is the way of law, which says, "If you wish to find life by obeying the law, you must obey all of its commands."* ¹³But Christ has rescued us from the curse pronounced by the law. When he was hung on the cross, he took upon himself the curse for our wrongdoing. For it is written in the Scriptures, "Cursed is everyone who is hung on a tree."* ¹⁴Through the work of Christ Jesus, God has blessed the Gentiles with the same blessing he promised to Abraham, and we

2:16 Some translators hold that the quotation extends through verse 14; others through verse 16; and still others through verse 21. **3:6** Gen 15:6.   **3:8** Gen 12:3; 18:18; 22:18.   **3:10** Deut 27:26.   **3:11** Hab 2:4.   **3:12** Lev 18:5.   **3:13** Deut 21:23.

Christians receive the promised Holy Spirit through faith.

¹⁵Dear brothers and sisters, here's an example from everyday life. Just as no one can set aside or amend an irrevocable agreement, so it is in this case. ¹⁶God gave the promise to Abraham and his child.* And notice that it doesn't say the promise was to his children,* as if it meant many descendants. But the promise was to his child—and that, of course, means Christ. ¹⁷This is what I am trying to say: The agreement God made with Abraham could not be canceled 430 years later when God gave the law to Moses. God would be breaking his promise. ¹⁸For if the inheritance could be received only by keeping the law, then it would not be the result of accepting God's promise. But God gave it to Abraham as a promise.

¹⁹Well then, why was the law given? It was given to show people how guilty they are. But this system of law was to last only until the coming of the child to whom God's promise was made. And there is this further difference. God gave his laws to angels to give to Moses, who was the mediator between God and the people. ²⁰Now a mediator is needed if two people enter into an agreement, but God acted on his own when he made his promise to Abraham.

²¹Well then, is there a conflict between God's law and God's promises? Absolutely not! If the law could have given us new life, we could have been made right with God by obeying it. ²²But the Scriptures have declared that we are all prisoners of sin, so the only way to receive God's promise is to believe in Jesus Christ.

²³Until faith in Christ was shown to us as the way of becoming right with God, we were guarded by the law. We were kept in protective custody, so to speak, until we could put our faith in the coming Savior.

²⁴Let me put it another way. The law was our guardian and teacher to lead us until Christ came. So now, through faith in Christ, we are made right with God. ²⁵But now that faith in Christ has come, we no longer need the law as our guardian. ²⁶So you are all children of God through faith in Christ Jesus. ²⁷And all who have been united with Christ in baptism have been made like him. ²⁸There is no longer Jew or Gentile,* slave or free, male or female. For

you are all Christians—you are one in Christ Jesus. ²⁹And now that you belong to Christ, you are the true children of Abraham. You are his heirs, and now all the promises God gave to him belong to you.

CHAPTER 4
Think of it this way. If a father dies and leaves great wealth for his young children, those children are not much better off than slaves until they grow up, even though they actually own everything their father had. ²They have to obey their guardians until they reach whatever age their father set.

³And that's the way it was with us before Christ came. We were slaves to the spiritual powers of this world. ⁴But when the right time came, God sent his Son, born of a woman, subject to the law. ⁵God sent him to buy freedom for us who were slaves to the law, so that he could adopt us as his very own children. ⁶And because you Gentiles have become his children, God has sent the Spirit of his Son into your hearts, and now you can call God your dear Father.* ⁷Now you are no longer a slave but God's own child. And since you are his child, everything he has belongs to you.

⁸Before you Gentiles knew God, you were slaves to so-called gods that do not even exist. ⁹And now that you have found God (or should I say, now that God has found you), why do you want to go back again and become slaves once more to the weak and useless spiritual powers of this world? ¹⁰You are trying to find favor with God by what you do or don't do on certain days or months or seasons or years. ¹¹I fear for you. I am afraid that all my hard work for you was worth nothing. ¹²Dear brothers and sisters, I plead with you to live as I do in freedom from these things, for I have become like you Gentiles were—free from the law.

You did not mistreat me when I first preached to you. ¹³Surely you remember that I was sick when I first brought you the Good News of Christ. ¹⁴But even though my sickness was revolting to you, you did not reject me and turn me away. No, you took me in and cared for me as though I were an angel from God or even Christ Jesus himself. ¹⁵Where is that joyful spirit we felt together then? In those days, I know you would gladly have taken out your own eyes and given them to me if it had been possible. [16]Have I now become your enemy because I am telling you the truth?

[17]Those false teachers who are so anxious to win your favor are not doing it for your good. They are trying to shut you off from me so that you will pay more attention to them. [18]Now it's wonderful if you are eager to do good, and especially when I am not with you. [19]But oh, my dear children! I feel as if I am going through labor pains for you again, and they will continue until Christ is fully developed in your lives. [20]How I wish I were there with you right now, so that I could be more gentle with you. But at this distance I frankly don't know what else to do.

[21]Listen to me, you who want to live under the law. Do you know what the law really says? [22]The Scriptures say that Abraham had two sons, one from his slave-wife and one from his freeborn wife.* [23]The son of the slave-wife was born in a human attempt to bring about the fulfillment of God's promise. But the son of the freeborn wife was born as God's own fulfillment of his promise.

[24]Now these two women serve as an illustration of God's two covenants. Hagar, the slave-wife, represents Mount Sinai where people first became enslaved to the law. [25]And now Jerusalem is just like Mount Sinai in Arabia, because she and her children live in slavery. [26]But Sarah, the free woman, represents the heavenly Jerusalem. And she is our mother. [27]That is what Isaiah meant when he prophesied,

"Rejoice, O childless woman!
Break forth into loud and joyful song,
   even though you never gave birth to
   a child.
For the woman who could bear no
   children
   now has more than all the other
   women!"*

[28]And you, dear brothers and sisters, are children of the promise, just like Isaac. [29]And we who are born of the Holy Spirit are persecuted by those who want us to keep the law, just as Isaac, the child of promise, was persecuted by Ishmael, the son of the slave-wife. [30]But what do the Scriptures say about

that? "Get rid of the slave and her son, for the son of the slave woman will not share the family inheritance with the free woman's son."* [31]So, dear brothers and sisters, we are not children of the slave woman, obligated to the law. We are children of the free woman, acceptable to God because of our faith.

CHAPTER 5

So Christ has really set us free. Now make sure that you stay free, and don't get tied up again in slavery to the law.

[2]Listen! I, Paul, tell you this: If you are counting on circumcision to make you right with God, then Christ cannot help you. [3]I'll say it again. If you are trying to find favor with God by being circumcised, you must obey all of the regulations in the whole law of Moses. [4]For if you are trying to make yourselves right with God by keeping the law, you have been cut off from Christ! You have fallen away from God's grace.

[5]But we who live by the Spirit eagerly wait to receive everything promised to us who are right with God through faith. [6]For when we place our faith in Christ Jesus, it makes no difference to God whether we are circumcised or not circumcised. What is important is faith expressing itself in love.

[7]You were getting along so well. Who has interfered with you to hold you back from following the truth? [8]It certainly isn't God, for he is the one who called you to freedom. [9]But it takes only one wrong person among you to infect all the others—a little yeast spreads quickly through the whole batch of dough! [10]I am trusting the Lord to bring you back to believing as I do about these things. God will judge that person, whoever it is, who has been troubling and confusing you.

[11]Dear brothers and sisters, if I were still preaching that you must be circumcised— as some say I do—why would the Jews persecute me? The fact that I am still being persecuted proves that I am still preaching salvation through the cross of Christ alone. [12]I only wish that those troublemakers who want to mutilate you by circumcision would mutilate themselves.*

[13]For you have been called to live in freedom—not freedom to satisfy your sinful nature, but freedom to serve one another in

---

4:22 See Gen 16:15; 21:2-3.   **4:27** Isa 54:1.   **4:30** Gen 21:10.   **5:12** Or *castrate themselves*; Greek reads *cut themselves off.*

love. [14]For the whole law can be summed up in this one command: "Love your neighbor as yourself."* [15]But if instead of showing love among yourselves you are always biting and devouring one another, watch out! Beware of destroying one another.

[16]So I advise you to live according to your new life in the Holy Spirit. Then you won't be doing what your sinful nature craves. [17]The old sinful nature loves to do evil, which is just opposite from what the Holy Spirit wants. And the Spirit gives us desires that are opposite from what the sinful nature desires. These two forces are constantly fighting each other, and your choices are never free from this conflict. [18]But when you are directed by the Holy Spirit, you are no longer subject to the law.

[19]When you follow the desires of your sinful nature, your lives will produce these evil results: sexual immorality, impure thoughts, eagerness for lustful pleasure, [20]idolatry, participation in demonic activities, hostility, quarreling, jealousy, outbursts of anger, selfish ambition, divisions, the feeling that everyone is wrong except those in your own little group, [21]envy, drunkenness, wild parties, and other kinds of sin. Let me tell you again, as I have before, that anyone living that sort of life will not inherit the Kingdom of God.

[22]But when the Holy Spirit controls our lives, he will produce this kind of fruit in us: love, joy, peace, patience, kindness, goodness, faithfulness, [23]gentleness, and self-control. Here there is no conflict with the law.

[24]Those who belong to Christ Jesus have nailed the passions and desires of their sinful nature to his cross and crucified them there. [25]If we are living now by the Holy Spirit, let us follow the Holy Spirit's leading in every part of our lives. [26]Let us not become conceited, or irritate one another, or be jealous of one another.

CHAPTER 6

Dear brothers and sisters, if another Christian* is overcome by some sin, you who are godly should gently and humbly help that person back onto the right path. And be careful not to fall into the same temptation yourself. [2]Share each other's troubles and problems, and in this way obey the law of Christ. [3]If you think you are too important to help someone in need, you are only fooling yourself. You are really a nobody.

[4]Be sure to do what you should, for then you will enjoy the personal satisfaction of having done your work well, and you won't need to compare yourself to anyone else. [5]For we are each responsible for our own conduct.

[6]Those who are taught the word of God should help their teachers by paying them.

[7]Don't be misled. Remember that you can't ignore God and get away with it. You will always reap what you sow! [8]Those who live only to satisfy their own sinful desires will harvest the consequences of decay and death. But those who live to please the Spirit will harvest everlasting life from the Spirit. [9]So don't get tired of doing what is good. Don't get discouraged and give up, for we will reap a harvest of blessing at the appropriate time. [10]Whenever we have the opportunity, we should do good to everyone, especially to our Christian brothers and sisters.

[11]Notice what large letters I use as I write these closing words in my own handwriting. [12]Those who are trying to force you to be circumcised are doing it for just one reason. They don't want to be persecuted for teaching that the cross of Christ alone can save. [13]And even those who advocate circumcision don't really keep the whole law. They only want you to be circumcised so they can brag about it and claim you as their disciples.

[14]As for me, God forbid that I should boast about anything except the cross of our Lord Jesus Christ. Because of that cross,* my interest in this world died long ago, and the world's interest in me is also long dead. [15]It doesn't make any difference now whether we have been circumcised or not. What counts is whether we really have been changed into new and different people. [16]May God's mercy and peace be upon all those who live by this principle. They are the new people of God.*

[17]From now on, don't let anyone trouble me with these things. For I bear on my body the scars that show I belong to Jesus.

[18]My dear brothers and sisters, may the grace of our Lord Jesus Christ be with you all. Amen.

5:14 Lev 19:18.   **6:1** Greek *if a man.*   **6:14** Or *Because of him.*   **6:16** Greek *the Israel of God.*

Ephesians

ALL who have trusted in Christ possess the priceless bounty of "every spiritual blessing in the heavenly realms" (1:3). Yet many continue to live like spiritual paupers. Paul writes this epistle to make Christians more aware of their heavenly wealth in Christ and to motivate them to draw upon those resources in their earthly walk. Chapters 1–3 outline the believer's heavenly possessions: adoption, redemption, inheritance, power, life, citizenship. Chapters 4–6 urge the children of God to conduct themselves according to their calling.

Focus	The Christian's Wealth			The Christian's Walk			
Divisions	Thanksgiving for Wealth	Wealth of Salvation	Wealth of the Church	Walk at Church	Walk in Holiness	Walk at Home and Work	Walk in Warfare
	1:1 1:23	2:1 2:22	3:1 3:21	4:1 4:16	4:17 5:21	5:22 6:9	6:10 6:24
Topics	Calling			Conduct			
	Privileges			Practicalities			
Place	Rome						
Time	A.D. 60–61						

NOVEMBER 27 ☐ DAY 332
EPHESIANS 1–6
Unity in Christ

 OVERVIEW There once was an old farmer who became a millionaire overnight when oil was discovered beneath his land. The wealth had always been there, but the farmer never knew it. So, too, the Ephesians possessed a wealth of spiritual blessings but had never recognized their own abundance. Their spiritual condition prompts Paul to write a letter in which he describes the believer's incredible wealth in Christ. The doctrinal truths of chapters 1–3 are followed by practical applications of those truths in chapters 4–6.

Chapter 1	Chapter 2	Chapter 3	Chapter 4	Chapter 5	Chapter 6
Blessings in Christ	Oneness in Christ	Mission for Christ	Unity in Diversity	Holiness in Life	Preparation for War
Belief			Behavior		

 YOUR DAILY WALK Have you ever tried to hammer a nail with your shoe? or tighten a screw with your fingernail file? or shield yourself from a rainstorm with just a newspaper? When you need a hammer or screwdriver or umbrella, nothing else will quite do. Are you living your spiritual life that way, using shoes for hammers and newspapers for umbrellas? God has provided the implements necessary for successful Christian living, but perhaps you have tried to make do by substituting your own tools and plans.

Why is it we spend so much time focusing on the concerns of the world we'll soon leave and so little time on the eternity we're headed for?

Even though Ephesians 6:10-20 may be familiar to you, read it with a new sense of urgency today. As Paul comes to each implement for successful Christian living, write it on a sheet of paper. Then think of a "shoe" or "hammer" you may have been substituting for God's spiritual weapons. A shoelace or nail carried with you today will remind you of the importance of using your spiritual wealth the way God intended it to be used.

 INSIGHT The Watermark of Paul's Style
As you read Ephesians, watch for the phrase *in Christ Jesus* and its equivalents. The phrase implies not only personal identification of Paul with Christ, but in some contexts it indicates the body of Christ (see 1 Corinthians 12:12).

CHAPTER 1
This letter is from Paul, chosen by God to be an apostle of Christ Jesus.

It is written to God's holy people in Ephesus,* who are faithful followers of Christ Jesus.

²May grace and peace be yours, sent to you from God our Father and Jesus Christ our Lord.

³How we praise God, the Father of our Lord Jesus Christ, who has blessed us with every spiritual blessing in the heavenly realms because we belong to Christ. ⁴Long ago, even before he made the world, God loved us and chose us in Christ to be holy and without fault in his eyes. ⁵His unchanging plan has always been to adopt us into his own family by bringing us to

1:1 Some manuscripts do not include *in Ephesus*.

himself through Jesus Christ. And this gave him great pleasure.

[6]So we praise God for the wonderful kindness he has poured out on us because we belong to his dearly loved Son. [7]He is so rich in kindness that he purchased our freedom through the blood of his Son, and our sins are forgiven. [8]He has showered his kindness on us, along with all wisdom and understanding.

[9]God's secret plan has now been revealed to us; it is a plan centered on Christ, designed long ago according to his good pleasure. [10]And this is his plan: At the right time he will bring everything together under the authority of Christ—everything in heaven and on earth. [11]Furthermore, because of Christ, we have received an inheritance from God,* for he chose us from the beginning, and all things happen just as he decided long ago. [12]God's purpose was that we who were the first to trust in Christ should praise our glorious God. [13]And now you also have heard the truth, the Good News that God saves you. And when you believed in Christ, he identified you as his own by giving you the Holy Spirit, whom he promised long ago. [14]The Spirit is God's guarantee that he will give us everything he promised and that he has purchased us to be his own people. This is just one more reason for us to praise our glorious God.

[15]Ever since I first heard of your strong faith in the Lord Jesus and your love for Christians everywhere, [16]I have never stopped thanking God for you. I pray for you constantly, [17]asking God, the glorious Father of our Lord Jesus Christ, to give you spiritual wisdom and understanding, so that you might grow in your knowledge of God. [18]I pray that your hearts will be flooded with light so that you can understand the wonderful future he has promised to those he called. I want you to realize what a rich and glorious inheritance he has given to his people.*

[19]I pray that you will begin to understand the incredible greatness of his power for us who believe him. This is the same mighty power [20]that raised Christ from the dead and seated him in the place of honor at God's right hand in the heavenly realms. [21]Now he is far above any ruler or authority or power or leader or anything else in this world or in the world to come. [22]And God has put all things under the authority of Christ, and he gave him this authority for the benefit of the church. [23]And the church is his body; it is filled by Christ, who fills everything everywhere with his presence.

CHAPTER 2

Once you were dead, doomed forever because of your many sins. [2]You used to live just like the rest of the world, full of sin, obeying Satan, the mighty prince of the power of the air. He is the spirit at work in the hearts of those who refuse to obey God. [3]All of us used to live that way, following the passions and desires of our evil nature. We were born with an evil nature, and we were under God's anger just like everyone else.

[4]But God is so rich in mercy, and he loved us so very much, [5]that even while we were dead because of our sins, he gave us life when he raised Christ from the dead. (It is only by God's special favor that you have been saved!) [6]For he raised us from the dead along with Christ, and we are seated with him in the heavenly realms—all because we are one with Christ Jesus. [7]And so God can always point to us as examples of the incredible wealth of his favor and kindness toward us, as shown in all he has done for us through Christ Jesus.

[8]God saved you by his special favor when you believed. And you can't take credit for this; it is a gift from God. [9]Salvation is not a reward for the good things we have done, so none of us can boast about it. [10]For we are God's masterpiece. He has created us anew in Christ Jesus, so that we can do the good things he planned for us long ago.

[11]Don't forget that you Gentiles used to be outsiders by birth. You were called "the uncircumcised ones" by the Jews, who were proud of their circumcision, even though it affected only their bodies and not their hearts. [12]In those days you were living apart from Christ. You were excluded from God's people, Israel, and you did not know the promises God had made to them. You lived in this world without God and without hope. [13]But now you belong to Christ Jesus. Though you once were far away from God, now you have been brought near to him because of the blood of Christ.

1:11 Or *we have become God's inheritance.*   **1:18** Or *realize how much God has been honored by acquiring his people.*

[14]For Christ himself has made peace between us Jews and you Gentiles by making us all one people. He has broken down the wall of hostility that used to separate us. [15]By his death he ended the whole system of Jewish law that excluded the Gentiles. His purpose was to make peace between Jews and Gentiles by creating in himself one new person from the two groups. [16]Together as one body, Christ reconciled both groups to God by means of his death, and our hostility toward each other was put to death. [17]He has brought this Good News of peace to you Gentiles who were far away from him, and to us Jews who were near. [18]Now all of us, both Jews and Gentiles, may come to the Father through the same Holy Spirit because of what Christ has done for us.

[19]So now you Gentiles are no longer strangers and foreigners. You are citizens along with all of God's holy people. You are members of God's family. [20]We are his house, built on the foundation of the apostles and the prophets. And the cornerstone is Christ Jesus himself. [21]We who believe are carefully joined together, becoming a holy temple for the Lord. [22]Through him you Gentiles are also joined together as part of this dwelling where God lives by his Spirit.

CHAPTER 3

I, Paul, am a prisoner of Christ Jesus because of my preaching to you Gentiles. [2]As you already know, God has given me this special ministry of announcing his favor to you Gentiles. [3]As I briefly mentioned earlier in this letter, God himself revealed his secret plan to me. [4]As you read what I have written, you will understand what I know about this plan regarding Christ. [5]God did not reveal it to previous generations, but now he has revealed it by the Holy Spirit to his holy apostles and prophets.

[6]And this is the secret plan: The Gentiles have an equal share with the Jews in all the riches inherited by God's children. Both groups have believed the Good News, and both are part of the same body and enjoy together the promise of blessings through Christ Jesus. [7]By God's special favor and mighty power, I have been given the wonderful privilege of serving him by spreading this Good News.

[8]Just think! Though I did nothing to deserve it, and though I am the least deserving Christian there is, I was chosen for this special joy of telling the Gentiles about the endless treasures available to them in Christ. [9]I was chosen to explain to everyone this plan that God, the Creator of all things, had kept secret from the beginning.

[10]God's purpose was to show his wisdom in all its rich variety to all the rulers and authorities in the heavenly realms. They will see this when Jews and Gentiles are joined together in his church. [11]This was his plan from all eternity, and it has now been carried out through Christ Jesus our Lord.

[12]Because of Christ and our faith in him, we can now come fearlessly into God's presence, assured of his glad welcome. [13]So please don't despair because of what they are doing to me here. It is for you that I am suffering, so you should feel honored and encouraged.

[14]When I think of the wisdom and scope of God's plan, I fall to my knees and pray to the Father,* [15]the Creator of everything in heaven and on earth. [16]I pray that from his glorious, unlimited resources he will give you mighty inner strength through his Holy Spirit. [17]And I pray that Christ will be more and more at home in your hearts as you trust in him. May your roots go down deep into the soil of God's marvelous love. [18]And may you have the power to understand, as all God's people should, how wide, how long, how high, and how deep his love really is. [19]May you experience the love of Christ, though it is so great you will never fully understand it. Then you will be filled with the fullness of life and power that comes from God.

[20]Now glory be to God! By his mighty power at work within us, he is able to accomplish infinitely more than we would ever dare to ask or hope. [21]May he be given glory in the church and in Christ Jesus forever and ever through endless ages. Amen.

CHAPTER 4

Therefore I, a prisoner for serving the Lord, beg you to lead a life worthy of your calling, for you have been called by God. [2]Be humble and gentle. Be patient with each other, making allowance for each other's faults because of your love. [3]Always keep

3:14 Some manuscripts read *the Father of our Lord Jesus Christ.*

yourselves united in the Holy Spirit, and bind yourselves together with peace.

⁴We are all one body, we have the same Spirit, and we have all been called to the same glorious future. ⁵There is only one Lord, one faith, one baptism, ⁶and there is only one God and Father, who is over us all and in us all and living through us all. ⁷However, he has given each one of us a special gift according to the generosity of Christ. ⁸That is why the Scriptures say,

"When he ascended to the heights,
  he led a crowd of captives
  and gave gifts to his people."*

⁹Notice that it says "he ascended." This means that Christ first came down to the lowly world in which we live.* ¹⁰The same one who came down is the one who ascended higher than all the heavens, so that his rule might fill the entire universe.

¹¹He is the one who gave these gifts to the church: the apostles, the prophets, the evangelists, and the pastors and teachers. ¹²Their responsibility is to equip God's people to do his work and build up the church, the body of Christ, ¹³until we come to such unity in our faith and knowledge of God's Son that we will be mature and full grown in the Lord, measuring up to the full stature of Christ.

¹⁴Then we will no longer be like children, forever changing our minds about what we believe because someone has told us something different or because someone has cleverly lied to us and made the lie sound like the truth. ¹⁵Instead, we will hold to the truth in love, becoming more and more in every way like Christ, who is the head of his body, the church. ¹⁶Under his direction, the whole body is fitted together perfectly. As each part does its own special work, it helps the other parts grow, so that the whole body is healthy and growing and full of love.

¹⁷With the Lord's authority let me say this: Live no longer as the ungodly* do, for they are hopelessly confused. ¹⁸Their closed minds are full of darkness; they are far away from the life of God because they have shut their minds and hardened their hearts against him. ¹⁹They don't care anymore about right and wrong, and they have given themselves over to immoral ways.

Their lives are filled with all kinds of impurity and greed.

²⁰But that isn't what you were taught when you learned about Christ. ²¹Since you have heard all about him and have learned the truth that is in Jesus, ²²throw off your old evil nature and your former way of life, which is rotten through and through, full of lust and deception. ²³Instead, there must be a spiritual renewal of your thoughts and attitudes. ²⁴You must display a new nature because you are a new person, created in God's likeness—righteous, holy, and true.

²⁵So put away all falsehood and "tell your neighbor the truth"* because we belong to each other. ²⁶And "don't sin by letting anger gain control over you."* Don't let the sun go down while you are still angry, ²⁷for anger gives a mighty foothold to the Devil.

²⁸If you are a thief, stop stealing. Begin using your hands for honest work, and then give generously to others in need. ²⁹Don't use foul or abusive language. Let everything you say be good and helpful, so that your words will be an encouragement to those who hear them.

³⁰And do not bring sorrow to God's Holy Spirit by the way you live. Remember, he is the one who has identified you as his own, guaranteeing that you will be saved on the day of redemption.

³¹Get rid of all bitterness, rage, anger, harsh words, and slander, as well as all types of malicious behavior. ³²Instead, be kind to each other, tenderhearted, forgiving one another, just as God through Christ has forgiven you.

CHAPTER 5

Follow God's example in everything you do, because you are his dear children. ²Live a life filled with love for others, following the example of Christ, who loved you and gave himself as a sacrifice to take away your sins. And God was pleased, because that sacrifice was like sweet perfume to him.

³Let there be no sexual immorality, impurity, or greed among you. Such sins have no place among God's people. ⁴Obscene stories, foolish talk, and coarse jokes— these are not for you. Instead, let there be thankfulness to God. ⁵You can be sure that no immoral, impure, or greedy person will

4:8 Ps 68:18.   **4:9** Or *to the lowest parts of the earth.*   **4:17** Greek *Gentiles.*   **4:25** Zech 8:16.   **4:26** Ps 4:4.

inherit the Kingdom of Christ and of God. For a greedy person is really an idolater who worships the things of this world. [6]Don't be fooled by those who try to excuse these sins, for the terrible anger of God comes upon all those who disobey him. [7]Don't participate in the things these people do. [8]For though your hearts were once full of darkness, now you are full of light from the Lord, and your behavior should show it! [9]For this light within you produces only what is good and right and true.

[10]Try to find out what is pleasing to the Lord. [11]Take no part in the worthless deeds of evil and darkness; instead, rebuke and expose them. [12]It is shameful even to talk about the things that ungodly people do in secret. [13]But when the light shines on them, it becomes clear how evil these things are. [14]And where your light shines, it will expose their evil deeds. This is why it is said,

> "Awake, O sleeper,
> rise up from the dead,
> and Christ will give you light."

[15]So be careful how you live, not as fools but as those who are wise. [16]Make the most of every opportunity for doing good in these evil days. [17]Don't act thoughtlessly, but try to understand what the Lord wants you to do. [18]Don't be drunk with wine, because that will ruin your life. Instead, let the Holy Spirit fill and control you. [19]Then you will sing psalms and hymns and spiritual songs among yourselves, making music to the Lord in your hearts. [20]And you will always give thanks for everything to God the Father in the name of our Lord Jesus Christ.

[21]And further, you will submit to one another out of reverence for Christ. [22]You wives will submit to your husbands as you do to the Lord. [23]For a husband is the head of his wife as Christ is the head of his body, the church; he gave his life to be her Savior. [24]As the church submits to Christ, so you wives must submit to your husbands in everything.

[25]And you husbands must love your wives with the same love Christ showed the church. He gave up his life for her [26]to make her holy and clean, washed by baptism and God's word.* [27]He did this to present her to himself as a glorious church

without a spot or wrinkle or any other blemish. Instead, she will be holy and without fault. [28]In the same way, husbands ought to love their wives as they love their own bodies. For a man is actually loving himself when he loves his wife. [29]No one hates his own body but lovingly cares for it, just as Christ cares for his body, which is the church. [30]And we are his body.

[31]As the Scriptures say, "A man leaves his father and mother and is joined to his wife, and the two are united into one."* [32]This is a great mystery, but it is an illustration of the way Christ and the church are one. [33]So again I say, each man must love his wife as he loves himself, and the wife must respect her husband.

CHAPTER 6

Children, obey your parents because you belong to the Lord, for this is the right thing to do. [2]"Honor your father and mother." This is the first of the Ten Commandments that ends with a promise. [3]And this is the promise: If you honor your father and mother, "you will live a long life, full of blessing."*

[4]And now a word to you fathers. Don't make your children angry by the way you treat them. Rather, bring them up with the discipline and instruction approved by the Lord.

[5]Slaves, obey your earthly masters with deep respect and fear. Serve them sincerely as you would serve Christ. [6]Work hard, but not just to please your masters when they are watching. As slaves of Christ, do the will of God with all your heart. [7]Work with enthusiasm, as though you were working for the Lord rather than for people. [8]Remember that the Lord will reward each one of us for the good we do, whether we are slaves or free.

[9]And in the same way, you masters must treat your slaves right. Don't threaten them; remember, you both have the same Master in heaven, and he has no favorites.

[10]A final word: Be strong with the Lord's mighty power. [11]Put on all of God's armor so that you will be able to stand firm against all strategies and tricks of the Devil. [12]For we are not fighting against people made of flesh and blood, but against the evil rulers and authorities of the unseen world, against those mighty powers of

---

5:26 Greek *having cleansed her by the washing of water with the word.*   **5:31** Gen 2:24.   **6:2-3** Exod 20:12; Deut 5:16.

darkness who rule this world, and against wicked spirits in the heavenly realms.

¹³Use every piece of God's armor to resist the enemy in the time of evil, so that after the battle you will still be standing firm. ¹⁴Stand your ground, putting on the sturdy belt of truth and the body armor of God's righteousness. ¹⁵For shoes, put on the peace that comes from the Good News, so that you will be fully prepared.* ¹⁶In every battle you will need faith as your shield to stop the fiery arrows aimed at you by Satan.* ¹⁷Put on salvation as your helmet, and take the sword of the Spirit, which is the word of God. ¹⁸Pray at all times and on every occasion in the power of the Holy Spirit. Stay alert and be persistent in your prayers for all Christians everywhere.

¹⁹And pray for me, too. Ask God to give me the right words as I boldly explain God's secret plan that the Good News is for the Gentiles, too.* ²⁰I am in chains now for preaching this message as God's ambassador. But pray that I will keep on speaking boldly for him, as I should.

²¹Tychicus, a much loved brother and faithful helper in the Lord's work, will tell you all about how I am getting along. ²²I am sending him to you for just this purpose. He will let you know how we are, and he will encourage you.

²³May God give you peace, dear brothers and sisters, and love with faith, from God the Father and the Lord Jesus Christ. ²⁴May God's grace be upon all who love our Lord Jesus Christ with an undying love.

6:15 Or *For shoes, put on the readiness to preach the Good News of peace with God.*   6:16 Greek *by the evil one.*   6:19 Greek *explain the mystery of the gospel.*

NOVEMBER 28   □   DAY 333
Eternal Riches

LOOK BACK Everything you have read this past week was from the potent pen of the apostle Paul, the most prolific of the New Testament writers. At least thirteen letters (epistles) were written by Paul during the course of his three missionary journeys and numerous imprisonments.

In 1 Corinthians, Paul is confronting the saints at Corinth about their lifestyle of disobedience. Divisions, disorders, and difficulties abound in the Corinthian church. The reaction to Paul's first letter prompts him to write yet another (2 Corinthians) in which he sets forth the "anatomy of an apostle," explaining the authority by which he wrote his earlier letter.

Galatians has been called the Christian's "emancipation proclamation." There Paul explains the liberty that comes through the redemption that is in Christ Jesus. We are neither saved nor sanctified by embracing the false gospel of works—a message directed to anyone willing to give up his or her freedom in Christ for slavery to the law.

In Christ Jesus we are "unshackled" from the law (Galatians) and indescribably rich in the family of God (Ephesians). Our heavenly inheritance includes adoption and redemption, power and position, citizenship in heaven and spiritual resources on earth to live out the love of Christ in our daily lives.

LOOK UP How rich are you *in dollars and cents?* (That's what is often called your "net worth"—how much you *own* less how much you *owe.*)

How rich are you *in family and friends?* (That's the circle of lives you have touched that would otherwise be impoverished for not having known you. It's the theme developed in the timeless movie *It's a Wonderful Life.*)

How rich are you *in Christ?* (That's your spiritual inheritance as part of God's family of faith. Through faith in Christ you are a child of God and a fellow heir with Christ. Think of it—all the fullness of Christ is yours because you are in him.)

A Christian is one who does not have to consult a bank book to see how wealthy he or she really is.

All the wealth in the world will not buy you a cup of coffee unless you *know* you are rich and you know how to *appropriate* that wealth. Take it from a man in east Texas who died in abject poverty . . . and lived till his dying day in a house that sat just a few feet above the largest undiscovered oil reserve in the world! Wealthy, yet living like a pauper. It's the sad condition of many a Christian as well.

 LOOK AHEAD Take a few minutes to review the book of Ephesians and inventory all that you are and have because you are "in Christ." It's as simple as reviewing all the occurrences of the little phrase *in Christ* or *in him,* which you located yesterday. Use what you have discovered to complete this sentence: "Because I am in Christ, I have _____

_____, and to show it, today with God's help I will

_____. (Example from Ephesians 1:7—

"Because I am in Christ, I have forgiveness of sins, and to show it, today with God's help I will forgive someone else who doesn't deserve my forgiveness but needs it nonetheless.")

If you can find five "nuggets" in Ephesians, you are doing well; six to ten nuggets, you are a first-class prospector; eleven to fifteen nuggets, you are a super sleuth; more than fifteen, you deserve a gold medal!

Philippians

PHILIPPIANS is a letter of joy written by Paul from a Roman prison to a church he founded on his second missionary journey (Acts 16). In spite of his circumstances, he encourages the Philippians in the midst of persecution to "always be full of joy in the Lord" (4:4). After all, Paul has much to be thankful for: their financial assistance, the hope of visiting them soon, their steadfast testimony for the gospel. Though that testimony is threatened by divisions, Paul is confident their unity will be restored as they imitate the humble servanthood of Christ.

Focus	Rejoice in God's Will				Relax in God's Peace		
Divisions	Paul and Philippians	Paul and Prison	Christ and Living	Timothy and Epaphroditus	Philippians and Errors	Philippians and Holiness	Paul and a Gift
	1:1 1:11	1:12 1:26	1:27 2:18	2:19 2:30	3:1 4:1	4:2 4:9	4:10 4:23
Topics	Information	Appeal	Plans	Warning	Exhortation	Thanks	
	Rejoicing in Affliction	Rejoicing in Ministry		Rejoicing in Jesus	Rejoicing in Blessings		
Place	Rome						
Time	Approximately A.D. 62						

NOVEMBER 29 ☐ DAY 334
PHILIPPIANS 1–4
Joy in Christ

OVERVIEW Philippians is unique among Paul's epistles for at least two reasons: (1) It is virtually "problem-free," lacking the usual disciplinary tone of Paul's letters; (2) it is filled with joyful statements, even though Paul is chained in prison! Paul has learned that joy comes, not as the result of external conditions, but from internal confidence that God is in control. Being a good teacher, Paul not only exhorts the Philippians to rejoice always, but he also exemplifies the very principle he is preaching.

Chapter 1		Chapter 2		Chapter 3	Chapter 4
Paul's Prayer	Paul's Plea	Christ's Pattern	Paul's Plan	Paul's Example	Paul's Exhortation
1 11	12 30	1 18	19 30		
Rejoice in God's Will			Relax in God's Peace		

Worry and worship are mutually exclusive.

YOUR DAILY WALK A lady walks into a downtown department store, seeks out the customer service counter, and announces, "I don't want this item."

"Fine," responds the clerk. "If you'll just give it to me, I'll be happy to help you find something else you do like."

"No," answers the lady, "I don't want to give this up."

Perhaps you're as confused as the salesclerk by now! But did you know that is how many Christians pray? "Lord, I have a problem that I'm worried about."

"Fine," responds the Lord. "Exchange those worries for my matchless peace."

"Oh no, I'd rather keep worrying!"

Philippians 4:6-7 makes it clear that you and God can't "worry" about the same problem at the same time. Either *you* will (and forfeit his peace in the process), or *he* will (leaving you free to relax in his strong arms). That's a good reason for you to make a "worry list" of the anxieties you're nursing right now and turn it into a prayer list! Then you, too, can enjoy "God's peace" (4:7), which is only possible by knowing the "God of peace" (4:9).

INSIGHT It's All in Your Head!

Two key words in Philippians 4 are *rejoice* and *mind.* Do you see the connection? Joy is not simply a smile on the lips; it is peace in the heart as a result of our mind being continually kept on Christ. And that's peace no circumstance can shatter!

CHAPTER 1

This letter is from Paul and Timothy, slaves of Christ Jesus.

It is written to all of God's people in Philippi, who believe in Christ Jesus, and to the elders* and deacons.

1:1 Greek *overseers.*

²May God our Father and the Lord Jesus Christ give you grace and peace.

³Every time I think of you, I give thanks to my God. ⁴I always pray for you, and I make my requests with a heart full of joy

⁵because you have been my partners in spreading the Good News about Christ from the time you first heard it until now. ⁶And I am sure that God, who began the good work within you, will continue his work until it is finally finished on that day when Christ Jesus comes back again.

⁷It is right that I should feel as I do about all of you, for you have a very special place in my heart. We have shared together the blessings of God, both when I was in prison and when I was out, defending the truth and telling others the Good News. ⁸God knows how much I love you and long for you with the tender compassion of Christ Jesus. ⁹I pray that your love for each other will overflow more and more, and that you will keep on growing in your knowledge and understanding. ¹⁰For I want you to understand what really matters, so that you may live pure and blameless lives until Christ returns. ¹¹May you always be filled with the fruit of your salvation*—those good things that are produced in your life by Jesus Christ—for this will bring much glory and praise to God.

¹²And I want you to know, dear brothers and sisters, that everything that has happened to me here has helped to spread the Good News. ¹³For everyone here, including all the soldiers in the palace guard, knows that I am in chains because of Christ. ¹⁴And because of my imprisonment, many of the Christians* here have gained confidence and become more bold in telling others about Christ.

¹⁵Some are preaching out of jealousy and rivalry. But others preach about Christ with pure motives. ¹⁶They preach because they love me, for they know the Lord brought me here to defend the Good News. ¹⁷Those others do not have pure motives as they preach about Christ. They preach with selfish ambition, not sincerely, intending to make my chains more painful to me. ¹⁸But whether or not their motives are pure, the fact remains that the message about Christ is being preached, so I rejoice. And I will continue to rejoice. ¹⁹For I know that as you pray for me and as the Spirit of Jesus Christ helps me, this will all turn out for my deliverance.

²⁰For I live in eager expectation and hope that I will never do anything that causes me shame, but that I will always be bold for Christ, as I have been in the past, and that my life will always honor Christ, whether I live or I die. ²¹For to me, living is for Christ, and dying is even better. ²²Yet if I live, that means fruitful service for Christ. I really don't know which is better. ²³I'm torn between two desires: Sometimes I want to live, and sometimes I long to go and be with Christ. That would be far better for me, ²⁴but it is better for you that I live.

²⁵I am convinced of this, so I will continue with you so that you will grow and experience the joy of your faith. ²⁶Then when I return to you, you will have even more reason to boast about what Christ Jesus has done for me.

²⁷But whatever happens to me, you must live in a manner worthy of the Good News about Christ, as citizens of heaven. Then, whether I come and see you again or only hear about you, I will know that you are standing side by side, fighting together for the Good News. ²⁸Don't be intimidated by your enemies. This will be a sign to them that they are going to be destroyed, but that you are going to be saved, even by God himself. ²⁹For you have been given not only the privilege of trusting in Christ but also the privilege of suffering for him. ³⁰We are in this fight together. You have seen me suffer for him in the past, and you know that I am still in the midst of this great struggle.

CHAPTER 2

Is there any encouragement from belonging to Christ? Any comfort from his love? Any fellowship together in the Spirit? Are your hearts tender and sympathetic? ²Then make me truly happy by agreeing wholeheartedly with each other, loving one another, and working together with one heart and purpose.

³Don't be selfish; don't live to make a good impression on others. Be humble, thinking of others as better than yourself. ⁴Don't think only about your own affairs, but be interested in others, too, and what they are doing.

⁵Your attitude should be the same that Christ Jesus had. ⁶Though he was God, he did not demand and cling to his rights as God. ⁷He made himself nothing;* he took the humble position of a slave and ap-

1:11 Greek *the fruit of righteousness.*   **1:14** Greek *brothers in the Lord.*   **2:7a** Or *He laid aside his mighty power and glory.*

peared in human form.* [8]And in human form he obediently humbled himself even further by dying a criminal's death on a cross. [9]Because of this, God raised him up to the heights of heaven and gave him a name that is above every other name, [10]so that at the name of Jesus every knee will bow, in heaven and on earth and under the earth, [11]and every tongue will confess that Jesus Christ is Lord, to the glory of God the Father.

[12]Dearest friends, you were always so careful to follow my instructions when I was with you. And now that I am away you must be even more careful to put into action God's saving work in your lives, obeying God with deep reverence and fear. [13]For God is working in you, giving you the desire to obey him and the power to do what pleases him.

[14]In everything you do, stay away from complaining and arguing, [15]so that no one can speak a word of blame against you. You are to live clean, innocent lives as children of God in a dark world full of crooked and perverse people. Let your lives shine brightly before them. [16]Hold tightly to the word of life, so that when Christ returns, I will be proud that I did not lose the race and that my work was not useless. [17]But even if my life is to be poured out like a drink offering to complete the sacrifice of your faithful service (that is, if I am to die for you), I will rejoice, and I want to share my joy with all of you. [18]And you should be happy about this and rejoice with me.

[19]If the Lord Jesus is willing, I hope to send Timothy to you soon. Then when he comes back, he can cheer me up by telling me how you are getting along. [20]I have no one else like Timothy, who genuinely cares about your welfare. [21]All the others care only for themselves and not for what matters to Jesus Christ. [22]But you know how Timothy has proved himself. Like a son with his father, he has helped me in preaching the Good News. [23]I hope to send him to you just as soon as I find out what is going to happen to me here. [24]And I have confidence from the Lord that I myself will come to see you soon.

[25]Meanwhile, I thought I should send Epaphroditus back to you. He is a true brother, a faithful worker, and a courageous soldier. And he was your messen-

ger to help me in my need. [26]Now I am sending him home again, for he has been longing to see you, and he was very distressed that you heard he was ill. [27]And he surely was ill; in fact, he almost died. But God had mercy on him—and also on me, so that I would not have such unbearable sorrow.

[28]So I am all the more anxious to send him back to you, for I know you will be glad to see him, and that will lighten all my cares. [29]Welcome him with Christian love* and with great joy, and be sure to honor people like him. [30]For he risked his life for the work of Christ, and he was at the point of death while trying to do for me the things you couldn't do because you were far away.

CHAPTER 3

Whatever happens, dear brothers and sisters, may the Lord give you joy. I never get tired of telling you this. I am doing this for your own good.

[2]Watch out for those dogs, those wicked men and their evil deeds, those mutilators who say you must be circumcised to be saved. [3]For we who worship God in the Spirit* are the only ones who are truly circumcised. We put no confidence in human effort. Instead, we boast about what Christ Jesus has done for us.

[4]Yet I could have confidence in myself if anyone could. If others have reason for confidence in their own efforts, I have even more! [5]For I was circumcised when I was eight days old, having been born into a pure-blooded Jewish family that is a branch of the tribe of Benjamin. So I am a real Jew if there ever was one! What's more, I was a member of the Pharisees, who demand the strictest obedience to the Jewish law. [6]And zealous? Yes, in fact, I harshly persecuted the church. And I obeyed the Jewish law so carefully that I was never accused of any fault.

[7]I once thought all these things were so very important, but now I consider them worthless because of what Christ has done. [8]Yes, everything else is worthless when compared with the priceless gain of knowing Christ Jesus my Lord. I have discarded everything else, counting it all as garbage, so that I may have Christ [9]and become one with him. I no longer count on my own

2:7b Greek *and was born in the likeness of men and was found in appearance as a man.*   **2:29** Greek *in the Lord.*   **3:3** Or *in spirit;* some manuscripts read *worship by the Spirit of God.*

goodness or my ability to obey God's law, but I trust Christ to save me. For God's way of making us right with himself depends on faith. [10]As a result, I can really know Christ and experience the mighty power that raised him from the dead. I can learn what it means to suffer with him, sharing in his death, [11]so that, somehow, I can experience the resurrection from the dead!

[12]I don't mean to say that I have already achieved these things or that I have already reached perfection! But I keep working toward that day when I will finally be all that Christ Jesus saved me for and wants me to be. [13]No, dear brothers and sisters, I am still not all I should be,* but I am focusing all my energies on this one thing: Forgetting the past and looking forward to what lies ahead, [14]I strain to reach the end of the race and receive the prize for which God, through Christ Jesus, is calling us up to heaven.*

[15]I hope all of you who are mature Christians will agree on these things. If you disagree on some point, I believe God will make it plain to you. [16]But we must be sure to obey the truth we have learned already.

[17]Dear brothers and sisters, pattern your lives after mine, and learn from those who follow our example. [18]For I have told you often before, and I say it again with tears in my eyes, that there are many whose conduct shows they are really enemies of the cross of Christ. [19]Their future is eternal destruction. Their god is their appetite, they brag about shameful things, and all they think about is this life here on earth. [20]But we are citizens of heaven, where the Lord Jesus Christ lives. And we are eagerly waiting for him to return as our Savior. [21]He will take these weak mortal bodies of ours and change them into glorious bodies like his own, using the same mighty power that he will use to conquer everything, everywhere.

CHAPTER 4

Dear brothers and sisters, I love you and long to see you, for you are my joy and the reward for my work. So please stay true to the Lord, my dear friends.

[2]And now I want to plead with those two women, Euodia and Syntyche. Please, because you belong to the Lord, settle your disagreement. [3]And I ask you, my true teammate,* to help these women, for they worked hard with me in telling others the Good News. And they worked with Clement and the rest of my co-workers, whose names are written in the Book of Life.

[4]Always be full of joy in the Lord. I say it again—rejoice! [5]Let everyone see that you are considerate in all you do. Remember, the Lord is coming soon.

[6]Don't worry about anything; instead, pray about everything. Tell God what you need, and thank him for all he has done. [7]If you do this, you will experience God's peace, which is far more wonderful than the human mind can understand. His peace will guard your hearts and minds as you live in Christ Jesus.

[8]And now, dear brothers and sisters, let me say one more thing as I close this letter. Fix your thoughts on what is true and honorable and right. Think about things that are pure and lovely and admirable. Think about things that are excellent and worthy of praise. [9]Keep putting into practice all you learned from me and heard from me and saw me doing, and the God of peace will be with you.

[10]How grateful I am, and how I praise the Lord that you are concerned about me again. I know you have always been concerned for me, but for a while you didn't have the chance to help me. [11]Not that I was ever in need, for I have learned how to get along happily whether I have much or little. [12]I know how to live on almost nothing or with everything. I have learned the secret of living in every situation, whether it is with a full stomach or empty, with plenty or little. [13]For I can do everything with the help of Christ who gives me the strength I need. [14]But even so, you have done well to share with me in my present difficulty.

[15]As you know, you Philippians were the only ones who gave me financial help when I brought you the Good News and then traveled on from Macedonia. No other church did this. [16]Even when I was in Thessalonica you sent help more than once. [17]I don't say this because I want a gift from you. What I want is for you to receive a well-earned reward because of your kindness.

[18]At the moment I have all I need—more than I need! I am generously supplied with the gifts you sent me with Epaphroditus. They are a sweet-smelling sacrifice that is

3:13 Some manuscripts read *I am not all I should be.*   3:14 Or *from heaven.*   4:3 Greek *true yokefellow,* or *loyal Syzygus.*

acceptable to God and pleases him. [19]And this same God who takes care of me will supply all your needs from his glorious riches, which have been given to us in Christ Jesus. [20]Now glory be to God our Father forever and ever. Amen.

[21]Give my greetings to all the Christians there. The brothers who are with me here send you their greetings. [22]And all the other Christians send their greetings, too, especially those who work in Caesar's palace.

[23]May the grace of the Lord Jesus Christ be with your spirit.

Colossians

ALL is not well in Colosse. A heresy is growing that promotes empty ritual, useless asceticism, and false mysticism. In order to encourage the Colossians to hold on to the truth, Paul refutes the heresy in a positive way—he shows them who Christ is. Christ as Lord of all gives complete salvation, and he is sufficient for every need. And if Christ is all that matters, then he ought to be in all we say, do, and think. So Paul encourages the Colossians to pursue a godly lifestyle befitting those who "have been raised to new life with Christ" (3:1).

Focus	Christ, the Lord of the Universe			Christ, the Lord of Life			
Divisions	Prayer to Father of Christ	Supremacy of Christ	Sufficiency of Christ	New Life	Home Life	Christian Life	Conclusion
	1:1 — 1:12	1:13 — 2:3	2:4 — 2:23	3:1 — 3:17	3:18 — 4:1	4:2 — 4:6	4:7 — 4:18
Topics	Transforming Relationship			Transformed Relationships			
	Consistent Doctrine			Consistent Life			
Place	Rome						
Time	A.D. 60–61						

NOVEMBER 30 □ DAY 335
COLOSSIANS 1–4
Christ, the Head of the Body

 OVERVIEW If Ephesians can be described as portraying the "church of Christ," then Colossians must surely portray the "Christ of the church." Ephesians focuses on the body; Colossians, on the head. Like Ephesians, the little book of Colossians divides neatly in half, with the first portion being doctrinal (Colossians 1–2) and the second, practical (Colossians 3–4). Paul's purpose is to show that Christ is preeminent—first and foremost in everything—and the Christian's life should reflect that priority. Because believers are rooted in him, built up in him, dead in him, risen with him, alive with him, hidden in him, and complete in him, it is utterly inconsistent for them to live without him. Clothed in his love, with his peace ruling in their hearts, they are equipped to make Christ preeminent in every walk of life.

Chapter 1	Chapter 2	Chapters 3–4
Christ, the Head of the Body	Christ, the Lord of the Universe	Christ, the Head of the Home
Christ . . . Preeminent in All Things		

 YOUR DAILY WALK Here are twelve words to think about today: "Christ is all that matters, and he lives in all of us" (3:11).

In Christ we see God's purpose in making the world and in making us.

Notice how Paul expands that thought throughout his letter. In the space of a single paragraph (1:15-18), he lists at least eight evidences of Christ's preeminence: He created you, set you free, and forgave you; he is the image of God and the firstborn of all creation; he preceded all things, designed all things, and holds all things together. In short, he is all that matters!

And that means he wants to be in all you say, do, or think. Concentrate on your thought life today. Each time you finish a phone call, recite quietly to yourself a favorite Bible verse or stanza of a hymn about Christ.

 INSIGHT Being a Friend Means Being Informed
"I have sent him [Tychicus] on this special trip to let you know how we are doing and to encourage you. I am also sending Onesimus. . . . He [Onesimus] and Tychicus will give you all the latest news" (4:8-9). These two verses show us that communication is a vital element of a healthy friendship. Is a letter or phone call to a friend overdue? Invest a few minutes now!

CHAPTER 1
This letter is from Paul, chosen by God to be an apostle of Christ Jesus, and from our brother Timothy.

²It is written to God's holy people in the city of Colosse, who are faithful brothers and sisters in Christ.

May God our Father give you grace and peace.

³We always pray for you, and we give thanks to God the Father of our Lord Jesus Christ, ⁴for we have heard that you trust in Christ Jesus and that you love all of God's

people. [5]You do this because you are looking forward to the joys of heaven—as you have been ever since you first heard the truth of the Good News. [6]This same Good News that came to you is going out all over the world. It is changing lives everywhere, just as it changed yours that very first day you heard and understood the truth about God's great kindness to sinners.

[7]Epaphras, our much loved co-worker, was the one who brought you the Good News. He is Christ's faithful servant, and he is helping us in your place.* [8]He is the one who told us about the great love for others that the Holy Spirit has given you.

[9]So we have continued praying for you ever since we first heard about you. We ask God to give you a complete understanding of what he wants to do in your lives, and we ask him to make you wise with spiritual wisdom. [10]Then the way you live will always honor and please the Lord, and you will continually do good, kind things for others. All the while, you will learn to know God better and better.

[11]We also pray that you will be strengthened with his glorious power so that you will have all the patience and endurance you need. May you be filled with joy, [12]always thanking the Father, who has enabled you to share the inheritance that belongs to God's holy people, who live in the light. [13]For he has rescued us from the one who rules in the kingdom of darkness, and he has brought us into the Kingdom of his dear Son. [14]God has purchased our freedom with his blood* and has forgiven all our sins.

[15]Christ is the visible image of the invisible God. He existed before God made anything at all and is supreme over all creation.* [16]Christ is the one through whom God created everything in heaven and earth. He made the things we can see and the things we can't see—kings, kingdoms, rulers, and authorities. Everything has been created through him and for him. [17]He existed before everything else began, and he holds all creation together.

[18]Christ is the head of the church, which is his body. He is the first of all who will rise from the dead,* so he is first in everything. [19]For God in all his fullness was pleased to live in Christ, [20]and by him God reconciled everything to himself. He made peace with everything in heaven and on earth by means of his blood on the cross. [21]This includes you who were once so far away from God. You were his enemies, separated from him by your evil thoughts and actions, [22]yet now he has brought you back as his friends. He has done this through his death on the cross in his own human body. As a result, he has brought you into the very presence of God, and you are holy and blameless as you stand before him without a single fault. [23]But you must continue to believe this truth and stand in it firmly. Don't drift away from the assurance you received when you heard the Good News. The Good News has been preached all over the world, and I, Paul, have been appointed by God to proclaim it.

[24]I am glad when I suffer for you in my body, for I am completing what remains of Christ's sufferings for his body, the church. [25]God has given me the responsibility of serving his church by proclaiming his message in all its fullness to you Gentiles. [26]This message was kept secret for centuries and generations past, but now it has been revealed to his own holy people. [27]For it has pleased God to tell his people that the riches and glory of Christ are for you Gentiles, too. For this is the secret: Christ lives in you, and this is your assurance that you will share in his glory.

[28]So everywhere we go, we tell everyone about Christ. We warn them and teach them with all the wisdom God has given us, for we want to present them to God, perfect* in their relationship to Christ. [29]I work very hard at this, as I depend on Christ's mighty power that works within me.

CHAPTER 2

I want you to know how much I have agonized for you and for the church at Laodicea, and for many other friends who have never known me personally. [2]My goal is that they will be encouraged and knit together by strong ties of love. I want them to have full confidence because they have complete understanding of God's secret plan, which is Christ himself. [3]In him lie hidden all the treasures of wisdom and knowledge.

1:7 Greek *he is ministering on your behalf*; other manuscripts read *he is ministering on our behalf*.   1:14 Some manuscripts do not include *with his blood*.   1:15 Greek *He is the firstborn of all creation*.   1:18 Greek *He is the beginning, the firstborn from the dead*.   1:28 Or *mature*.

[4]I am telling you this so that no one will be able to deceive you with persuasive arguments. [5]For though I am far away from you, my heart is with you. And I am very happy because you are living as you should and because of your strong faith in Christ.

[6]And now, just as you accepted Christ Jesus as your Lord, you must continue to live in obedience to him. [7]Let your roots grow down into him and draw up nourishment from him, so you will grow in faith, strong and vigorous in the truth you were taught. Let your lives overflow with thanksgiving for all he has done.

[8]Don't let anyone lead you astray with empty philosophy and high-sounding nonsense that come from human thinking and from the evil powers of this world,* and not from Christ. [9]For in Christ the fullness of God lives in a human body,* [10]and you are complete through your union with Christ. He is the Lord over every ruler and authority in the universe.

[11]When you came to Christ, you were "circumcised," but not by a physical procedure. It was a spiritual procedure—the cutting away of your sinful nature. [12]For you were buried with Christ when you were baptized. And with him you were raised to a new life because you trusted the mighty power of God, who raised Christ from the dead.

[13]You were dead because of your sins and because your sinful nature was not yet cut away. Then God made you alive with Christ. He forgave all our sins. [14]He canceled the record that contained the charges against us. He took it and destroyed it by nailing it to Christ's cross. [15]In this way, God disarmed the evil rulers and authorities. He shamed them publicly by his victory over them on the cross of Christ.

[16]So don't let anyone condemn you for what you eat or drink, or for not celebrating certain holy days or new-moon ceremonies or Sabbaths. [17]For these rules were only shadows of the real thing, Christ himself. [18]Don't let anyone condemn you by insisting on self-denial. And don't let anyone say you must worship angels, even though they say they have had visions about this. These people claim to be so humble, but their sinful minds have made them proud. [19]But they are not connected to Christ, the head of the body. For we are joined together in his body by his strong sinews, and we grow only as we get our nourishment and strength from God.

[20]You have died with Christ, and he has set you free from the evil powers of this world. So why do you keep on following rules of the world, such as, [21]"Don't handle, don't eat, don't touch." [22]Such rules are mere human teaching about things that are gone as soon as we use them. [23]These rules may seem wise because they require strong devotion, humility, and severe bodily discipline. But they have no effect when it comes to conquering a person's evil thoughts and desires.

CHAPTER 3

Since you have been raised to new life with Christ, set your sights on the realities of heaven, where Christ sits at God's right hand in the place of honor and power. [2]Let heaven fill your thoughts. Do not think only about things down here on earth. [3]For you died when Christ died, and your real life is hidden with Christ in God. [4]And when Christ, who is your* real life, is revealed to the whole world, you will share in all his glory.

[5]So put to death the sinful, earthly things lurking within you. Have nothing to do with sexual sin, impurity, lust, and shameful desires. Don't be greedy for the good things of this life, for that is idolatry. [6]God's terrible anger will come upon those who do such things. [7]You used to do them when your life was still part of this world. [8]But now is the time to get rid of anger, rage, malicious behavior, slander, and dirty language. [9]Don't lie to each other, for you have stripped off your old evil nature and all its wicked deeds. [10]In its place you have clothed yourselves with a brand-new nature that is continually being renewed as you learn more and more about Christ, who created this new nature within you. [11]In this new life, it doesn't matter if you are a Jew or a Gentile,* circumcised or uncircumcised, barbaric, uncivilized,* slave, or free. Christ is all that matters, and he lives in all of us.

[12]Since God chose you to be the holy people whom he loves, you must clothe yourselves with tenderhearted mercy, kindness, humility, gentleness, and patience.

2:8 Or *from the basic principles of this world;* also in 2:20.   **2:9** Greek *in him dwells all the fullness of the Godhead bodily.*   **3:4** Some manuscripts read *our.*   **3:11a** Greek *Greek.*   **3:11b** Greek *Barbarian, Scythian.*

[13]You must make allowance for each other's faults and forgive the person who offends you. Remember, the Lord forgave you, so you must forgive others. [14]And the most important piece of clothing you must wear is love. Love is what binds us all together in perfect harmony. [15]And let the peace that comes from Christ rule in your hearts. For as members of one body you are all called to live in peace. And always be thankful.

[16]Let the words of Christ, in all their richness, live in your hearts and make you wise. Use his words to teach and counsel each other. Sing psalms and hymns and spiritual songs to God with thankful hearts. [17]And whatever you do or say, let it be as a representative of the Lord Jesus, all the while giving thanks through him to God the Father.

[18]You wives must submit to your husbands, as is fitting for those who belong to the Lord. [19]And you husbands must love your wives and never treat them harshly.

[20]You children must always obey your parents, for this is what pleases the Lord. [21]Fathers, don't aggravate your children. If you do, they will become discouraged and quit trying.

[22]You slaves must obey your earthly masters in everything you do. Try to please them all the time, not just when they are watching you. Obey them willingly because of your reverent fear of the Lord. [23]Work hard and cheerfully at whatever you do, as though you were working for the Lord rather than for people. [24]Remember that the Lord will give you an inheritance as your reward, and the Master you are serving is Christ. [25]But if you do what is wrong, you will be paid back for the wrong you have done. For God has no favorites who can get away with evil.

CHAPTER 4

You slave owners must be just and fair to your slaves. Remember that you also have a Master—in heaven.

[2]Devote yourselves to prayer with an alert mind and a thankful heart. [3]Don't forget to pray for us, too, that God will give us many opportunities to preach about his secret plan—that Christ is also for you Gentiles. That is why I am here in chains. [4]Pray that I will proclaim this message as clearly as I should.

[5]Live wisely among those who are not Christians, and make the most of every opportunity. [6]Let your conversation be gracious and effective so that you will have the right answer for everyone.

[7]Tychicus, a much loved brother, will tell you how I am getting along. He is a faithful helper who serves the Lord with me. [8]I have sent him on this special trip to let you know how we are doing and to encourage you. [9]I am also sending Onesimus, a faithful and much loved brother, one of your own people. He and Tychicus will give you all the latest news.

[10]Aristarchus, who is in prison with me, sends you his greetings, and so does Mark, Barnabas's cousin. And as you were instructed before, make Mark welcome if he comes your way. [11]Jesus (the one we call Justus) also sends his greetings. These are the only Jewish Christians among my coworkers; they are working with me here for the Kingdom of God. And what a comfort they have been!

[12]Epaphras, from your city, a servant of Christ Jesus, sends you his greetings. He always prays earnestly for you, asking God to make you strong and perfect, fully confident of the whole will of God. [13]I can assure you that he has agonized for you and also for the Christians in Laodicea and Hierapolis.

[14]Dear Doctor Luke sends his greetings, and so does Demas. [15]Please give my greetings to our Christian brothers and sisters at Laodicea, and to Nympha and those who meet in her house.

[16]After you have read this letter, pass it on to the church at Laodicea so they can read it, too. And you should read the letter I wrote to them. [17]And say to Archippus, "Be sure to carry out the work the Lord gave you."

[18]Here is my greeting in my own handwriting—PAUL.

Remember my chains.

May the grace of God be with you.

1 Thessalonians

PROSPEROUS, prominent, and thoroughly pagan, the seaport city of Thessalonica first heard the gospel on Paul's second missionary journey. A dynamic fellowship developed there, becoming a continual joy to Paul. He writes 1 Thessalonians to encourage them. They are being persecuted; he urges them to persevere. They have heard slander about Paul; he refutes it. Their city is full of sensual temptation; he exhorts them to hold to Christian standards. Finally, he corrects some misunderstandings about the return of Christ.

Focus	Personal Relations to the Thessalonians		Practical Instructions to the Thessalonians		
Divisions	Paul's Memories	Paul's Methods	Paul's Directions	Christ's Return	Paul's Reminders
	1:1 1:10	2:1 3:13	4:1 4:12	4:13 5:11	5:12 5:28
Topics	Personal	Parental		Prophetic	Practical
	A Saving Hope	A Purifying Hope		A Comforting Hope	
Place	Corinth				
Time	Approximately A.D. 51				

DECEMBER 1 ☐ DAY 336
1 THESSALONIANS 1–5
Stay on Target

OVERVIEW The church at Thessalonica was in many ways a model church. Paul had many things to commend the believers for: their exemplary faith, diligent service, patient steadfastness, and overflowing joy. But in the midst of his commendation, Paul voices a word of caution. Abounding in the work of the Lord is only one step removed from abandoning the work of the Lord through complacency. Thus, Paul exhorts the Thessalonians to excel in their faith, to increase in their love for one another, and to give thanks for all things. At the same time, to know Christ must always be their primary goal. In short, Paul encourages them to "stay on target" as they labor for the Lord.

Chapter 1	Chapters 2–3	Chapter 4	Chapter 5
Paul's Memories	Paul's Methods	Christ's Return	Paul's Reminders
Personal	Parental	Prophetic	Practical

YOUR DAILY WALK Do you *believe* Jesus Christ is coming again? Do you *behave* as if Jesus Christ is coming again?

If your behavior does not reflect your beliefs, then your beliefs are of no value.

The first question is straightforward and simple to answer. Either you do or you don't. But the second is more difficult because it involves looking for practical, everyday ways to translate your belief into behavior and then making those activities and attitudes a priority in your daily Christian life.

Each of the five chapters of 1 Thessalonians ends with an exhortation based on the fact that Jesus Christ is coming again. Read the indicated verses prayerfully; then write out a step of *behavior* you can begin today to put your *beliefs* to work!

- 1:9-10   I will look for someone to serve as I wait for God's Son.
- 2:19-20   _____ .
- 3:11-13   _____ .
- 4:13-18   I will comfort someone today with the thought of Christ's coming.
- 5:23-24   _____ .

INSIGHT Graduate Course for Kindergarten Christians
Prophecy is often considered a weighty subject that is reserved for mature, well-taught Christians and seminary graduates. But Paul spent considerable time teaching prophecy to new converts (5:1-2). How knowledgeable are you of God's blueprint for future events?

CHAPTER 1
This letter is from Paul, Silas,* and Timothy.

It is written to the church in Thessalo-nica, you who belong to God the Father and the Lord Jesus Christ.

May his grace and peace be yours.

1:1 Greek *Silvanus.*

[2] We always thank God for all of you and pray for you constantly. [3] As we talk to our God and Father about you, we think of your faithful work, your loving deeds, and your continual anticipation of the return of our Lord Jesus Christ.

[4] We know that God loves you, dear brothers and sisters, and that he chose you to be his own people. [5] For when we brought you the Good News, it was not only with words but also with power, for the Holy Spirit gave you full assurance that what we said was true. And you know that the way we lived among you was further proof of the truth of our message. [6] So you received the message with joy from the Holy Spirit in spite of the severe suffering it brought you. In this way, you imitated both us and the Lord. [7] As a result, you yourselves became an example to all the Christians in Greece.* [8] And now the word of the Lord is ringing out from you to people everywhere, even beyond Greece, for wherever we go we find people telling us about your faith in God. We don't need to tell them about it, [9] for they themselves keep talking about the wonderful welcome you gave us and how you turned away from idols to serve the true and living God. [10] And they speak of how you are looking forward to the coming of God's Son from heaven—Jesus, whom God raised from the dead. He is the one who has rescued us from the terrors of the coming judgment.

CHAPTER 2
You yourselves know, dear brothers and sisters, that our visit to you was not a failure. [2] You know how badly we had been treated at Philippi just before we came to you and how much we suffered there. Yet our God gave us the courage to declare his Good News to you boldly, even though we were surrounded by many who opposed us. [3] So you can see that we were not preaching with any deceit or impure purposes or trickery.

[4] For we speak as messengers who have been approved by God to be entrusted with the Good News. Our purpose is to please God, not people. He is the one who examines the motives of our hearts. [5] Never once did we try to win you with flattery, as you very well know. And God is our witness that we were not just pretending to be your

friends so you would give us money! [6] As for praise, we have never asked for it from you or anyone else. [7] As apostles of Christ we certainly had a right to make some demands of you, but we were as gentle among you as a mother* feeding and caring for her own children. [8] We loved you so much that we gave you not only God's Good News but our own lives, too.

[9] Don't you remember, dear brothers and sisters, how hard we worked among you? Night and day we toiled to earn a living so that our expenses would not be a burden to anyone there as we preached God's Good News among you. [10] You yourselves are our witnesses—and so is God—that we were pure and honest and faultless toward all of you believers. [11] And you know that we treated each of you as a father treats his own children. [12] We pleaded with you, encouraged you, and urged you to live your lives in a way that God would consider worthy. For he called you into his Kingdom to share his glory.

[13] And we will never stop thanking God that when we preached his message to you, you didn't think of the words we spoke as being just our own. You accepted what we said as the very word of God—which, of course, it was. And this word continues to work in you who believe.

[14] And then, dear brothers and sisters, you suffered persecution from your own countrymen. In this way, you imitated the believers in God's churches in Judea who, because of their belief in Christ Jesus, suffered from their own people, the Jews. [15] For some of the Jews had killed their own prophets, and some even killed the Lord Jesus. Now they have persecuted us and driven us out. They displease God and oppose everyone [16] by trying to keep us from preaching the Good News to the Gentiles, for fear some might be saved. By doing this, they continue to pile up their sins. But the anger of God has caught up with them at last.

[17] Dear brothers and sisters, after we were separated from you for a little while (though our hearts never left you), we tried very hard to come back because of our intense longing to see you again. [18] We wanted very much to come, and I, Paul, tried again and again, but Satan prevented us. [19] After all, what gives us hope and joy,

---

1:7 Greek *Macedonia and Achaia*, the northern and southern regions of Greece; also in 1:8.   **2:7** Some manuscripts read *we were as infants among you; we were as a mother*.

and what is our proud reward and crown? It is you! Yes, you will bring us much joy as we stand together before our Lord Jesus when he comes back again. [20]For you are our pride and joy.

CHAPTER 3

Finally, when we could stand it no longer, we decided that I should stay alone in Athens, [2]and we sent Timothy to visit you. He is our co-worker for God and our brother in proclaiming the Good News of Christ. We sent him to strengthen you, to encourage you in your faith, [3]and to keep you from becoming disturbed by the troubles you were going through. But, of course, you know that such troubles are going to happen to us Christians. [4]Even while we were with you, we warned you that troubles would soon come—and they did, as you well know.

[5]That is why, when I could bear it no longer, I sent Timothy to find out whether your faith was still strong. I was afraid that the Tempter had gotten the best of you and that all our work had been useless. [6]Now Timothy has just returned, bringing the good news that your faith and love are as strong as ever. He reports that you remember our visit with joy and that you want to see us just as much as we want to see you. [7]So we have been greatly comforted, dear brothers and sisters, in all of our own crushing troubles and suffering, because you have remained strong in your faith. [8]It gives us new life, knowing you remain strong in the Lord.

[9]How we thank God for you! Because of you we have great joy in the presence of God. [10]Night and day we pray earnestly for you, asking God to let us see you again to fill up anything that may still be missing in your faith.

[11]May God himself, our Father, and our Lord Jesus make it possible for us to come to you very soon. [12]And may the Lord make your love grow and overflow to each other and to everyone else, just as our love overflows toward you. [13]As a result, Christ will make your hearts strong, blameless, and holy when you stand before God our Father on that day when our Lord Jesus comes with all those who belong to him.

CHAPTER 4

Finally, dear brothers and sisters, we urge you in the name of the Lord Jesus to live in a way that pleases God, as we have taught you. You are doing this already, and we encourage you to do so more and more. [2]For you remember what we taught you in the name of the Lord Jesus. [3]God wants you to be holy, so you should keep clear of all sexual sin. [4]Then each of you will control your body* and live in holiness and honor—[5]not in lustful passion as the pagans do, in their ignorance of God and his ways.

[6]Never cheat a Christian brother in this matter by taking his wife, for the Lord avenges all such sins, as we have solemnly warned you before. [7]God has called us to be holy, not to live impure lives. [8]Anyone who refuses to live by these rules is not disobeying human rules but is rejecting God, who gives his Holy Spirit to you.

[9]But I don't need to write to you about the Christian love* that should be shown among God's people. For God himself has taught you to love one another. [10]Indeed, your love is already strong toward all the Christians* in all of Macedonia. Even so, dear brothers and sisters, we beg you to love them more and more. [11]This should be your ambition: to live a quiet life, minding your own business and working with your hands, just as we commanded you before. [12]As a result, people who are not Christians will respect the way you live, and you will not need to depend on others to meet your financial needs.

[13]And now, brothers and sisters, I want you to know what will happen to the Christians who have died so you will not be full of sorrow like people who have no hope. [14]For since we believe that Jesus died and was raised to life again, we also believe that when Jesus comes, God will bring back with Jesus all the Christians who have died.

[15]I can tell you this directly from the Lord: We who are still living when the Lord returns will not rise to meet him ahead of those who are in their graves. [16]For the Lord himself will come down from heaven with a commanding shout, with the call of the archangel, and with the trumpet call of God. First, all the Christians who have died will rise from

4:4 Or *will know how to take a wife for himself;* Greek reads *will know how to possess his own vessel.*   **4:9** Greek *brotherly love.*
4:10 Greek *the brothers.*

their graves. [17]Then, together with them, we who are still alive and remain on the earth will be caught up in the clouds to meet the Lord in the air and remain with him forever. [18]So comfort and encourage each other with these words.

CHAPTER 5

I really don't need to write to you about how and when all this will happen, dear brothers and sisters. [2]For you know quite well that the day of the Lord will come unexpectedly, like a thief in the night. [3]When people are saying, "All is well; everything is peaceful and secure," then disaster will fall upon them as suddenly as a woman's birth pains begin when her child is about to be born. And there will be no escape.

[4]But you aren't in the dark about these things, dear brothers and sisters, and you won't be surprised when the day of the Lord comes like a thief. [5]For you are all children of the light and of the day; we don't belong to darkness and night. [6]So be on your guard, not asleep like the others. Stay alert and be sober. [7]Night is the time for sleep and the time when people get drunk. [8]But let us who live in the light think clearly, protected by the body armor of faith and love, and wearing as our helmet the confidence of our salvation. [9]For God decided to save us through our Lord Jesus Christ, not to pour out his anger on us. [10]He died for us so that we can live with him forever, whether we are dead or alive at the time of his return. [11]So encour-

age each other and build each other up, just as you are already doing.

[12]Dear brothers and sisters, honor those who are your leaders in the Lord's work. They work hard among you and warn you against all that is wrong. [13]Think highly of them and give them your wholehearted love because of their work. And remember to live peaceably with each other.

[14]Brothers and sisters, we urge you to warn those who are lazy. Encourage those who are timid. Take tender care of those who are weak. Be patient with everyone. [15]See that no one pays back evil for evil, but always try to do good to each other and to everyone else.

[16]Always be joyful. [17]Keep on praying. [18]No matter what happens, always be thankful, for this is God's will for you who belong to Christ Jesus.

[19]Do not stifle the Holy Spirit. [20]Do not scoff at prophecies, [21]but test everything that is said. Hold on to what is good. [22]Keep away from every kind of evil.

[23]Now may the God of peace make you holy in every way, and may your whole spirit and soul and body be kept blameless until that day when our Lord Jesus Christ comes again. [24]God, who calls you, is faithful; he will do this.

[25]Dear brothers and sisters, pray for us.

[26]Greet all the brothers and sisters in Christian love.*

[27]I command you in the name of the Lord to read this letter to all the brothers and sisters.

[28]And may the grace of our Lord Jesus Christ be with all of you.

5:26 Greek *with a holy kiss.*

2 Thessalonians

PAUL opens this letter by encouraging the Thessalonians in the midst of their persecution that God's judgment would more than even the score. However, because some had been teaching that the day of the Lord had already arrived, many were quitting their jobs and interfering with those who continued to work. Paul instructs them about the future and exhorts them not to sit back and wait for Christ's coming but to take advantage of the limited time available now.

Focus	Commendation		Instruction		Correction	
Divisions	Return of Christ		Revelation of Antichrist		Return to Work	
	1:1	1:12	2:1	2:17	3:1	3:18
Topics	Strengthening the Stressed		Comforting the Confused		Disciplining the Disorderly	
	Encouragement		Explanation		Exhortation	
Place	Corinth					
Time	Approximately A.D. 51					

DECEMBER 2 ☐ DAY 337
2 THESSALONIANS 1–3
Work While You Wait

OVERVIEW The Thessalonians were waiting expectantly for Christ's return, and that was good. But in addition, some were waiting unproductively, and that was bad. False teachers had come claiming that the "day of the Lord" had already come. Paul refutes their teaching by reminding the Thessalonians of the events that must precede the coming of the Lord. But how should they respond in the light of that joyful expectation? Not with lazy resignation, but with renewed labor for the Lord. Therefore, Paul urges, "Never get tired of doing good" (3:13).

Chapter 1	Chapter 2	Chapter 3
Strengthening the Stressed	Comforting the Confused	Disciplining the Disorderly
Commendation	Instruction	Correction

Live every moment as if expecting him at any moment.

YOUR DAILY WALK Is there at least one other person you pray for every day? Is there at least one time every day (apart from mealtimes) when you regularly pray? Is there at least one person you regularly pray with about mutually shared problems and praise items?

Paul entreated the Thessalonian Christians, "Pray for us" (3:1). He also asked for prayer in 1 Thessalonians (5:25), in Colossians (4:3-4), and in Ephesians (6:18-20). The apostle Paul was acutely aware of his need for prayer support to undergird his ministry for Jesus Christ. And he labored daily for the Lord, knowing that dozens of people in congregations scattered throughout the Roman Empire were praying for him by name.

Do you pray regularly for your spouse? for your children? for your roommate? for your pastor and church staff? for the leaders of strategic Christian schools and organizations? They need your prayers just as badly as Paul needed the prayers of the Thessalonians. Take your calendar for December, and write the name of one person you will pray for on each day of the month.

INSIGHT The Mark of Authenticity
Although Paul sometimes dictated his letters to a secretary (or *amanuensis* such as Tertius, Romans 16:22), he always added a handwritten salutation and signature in order to identify his letters as genuine (3:17; compare 1 Corinthians 16:21 and Colossians 4:18).

CHAPTER 1
This letter is from Paul, Silas,* and Timothy.

It is written to the church in Thessalonica, you who belong to God our Father and the Lord Jesus Christ.

²May God our Father and the Lord Jesus Christ give you grace and peace.

1:1 Greek *Silvanus*.

³Dear brothers and sisters, we always thank God for you, as is right, for we are thankful that your faith is flourishing and you are all growing in love for each other. ⁴We proudly tell God's other churches about your endurance and faithfulness in all the persecutions and hardships you are

suffering. [5]But God will use this persecution to show his justice. For he will make you worthy of his Kingdom, for which you are suffering, [6]and in his justice he will punish those who persecute you. [7]And God will provide rest for you who are being persecuted and also for us when the Lord Jesus appears from heaven. He will come with his mighty angels, [8]in flaming fire, bringing judgment on those who don't know God and on those who refuse to obey the Good News of our Lord Jesus. [9]They will be punished with everlasting destruction, forever separated from the Lord and from his glorious power [10]when he comes to receive glory and praise from his holy people. And you will be among those praising him on that day, for you believed what we testified about him.

[11]And so we keep on praying for you, that our God will make you worthy of the life to which he called you. And we pray that God, by his power, will fulfill all your good intentions and faithful deeds. [12]Then everyone will give honor to the name of our Lord Jesus because of you, and you will be honored along with him. This is all made possible because of the undeserved favor of our God and Lord, Jesus Christ.*

C H A P T E R 2
And now, brothers and sisters, let us tell you about the coming again of our Lord Jesus Christ and how we will be gathered together to meet him. [2]Please don't be so easily shaken and troubled by those who say that the day of the Lord has already begun. Even if they claim to have had a vision, a revelation, or a letter supposedly from us, don't believe them. [3]Don't be fooled by what they say.

For that day will not come until there is a great rebellion against God and the man of lawlessness is revealed—the one who brings destruction.* [4]He will exalt himself and defy every god there is and tear down every object of adoration and worship. He will position himself in the temple of God, claiming that he himself is God. [5]Don't you remember that I told you this when I was with you? [6]And you know what is holding him back, for he can be revealed only when his time comes.

[7]For this lawlessness is already at work secretly, and it will remain secret until the one who is holding it back steps out of the way. [8]Then the man of lawlessness will be revealed, whom the Lord Jesus will consume with the breath of his mouth and destroy by the splendor of his coming. [9]This evil man will come to do the work of Satan with counterfeit power and signs and miracles. [10]He will use every kind of wicked deception to fool those who are on their way to destruction because they refuse to believe the truth that would save them. [11]So God will send great deception upon them, and they will believe all these lies. [12]Then they will be condemned for not believing the truth and for enjoying the evil they do.

[13]As for us, we always thank God for you, dear brothers and sisters loved by the Lord. We are thankful that God chose you to be among the first* to experience salvation, a salvation that came through the Spirit who makes you holy and by your belief in the truth. [14]He called you to salvation when we told you the Good News; now you can share in the glory of our Lord Jesus Christ.

[15]With all these things in mind, dear brothers and sisters, stand firm and keep a strong grip on everything we taught you both in person and by letter.

[16]May our Lord Jesus Christ and God our Father, who loved us and in his special favor gave us everlasting comfort and good hope, [17]comfort your hearts and give you strength in every good thing you do and say.

C H A P T E R 3
Finally, dear brothers and sisters, I ask you to pray for us. Pray first that the Lord's message will spread rapidly and be honored wherever it goes, just as when it came to you. [2]Pray, too, that we will be saved from wicked and evil people, for not everyone believes in the Lord. [3]But the Lord is faithful; he will make you strong and guard you from the evil one.* [4]And we are confident in the Lord that you are practicing the things we commanded you, and that you always will. [5]May the Lord bring you into an ever deeper understanding of the love of God and the endurance that comes from Christ.

[6]And now, dear brothers and sisters, we give you this command with the authority of our Lord Jesus Christ: Stay away from any Christian* who lives in idleness and doesn't follow the tradition of hard work

---

1:12 Or of our God and the Lord Jesus Christ.   **2:3** Greek the son of destruction.   **2:13** Some manuscripts read God chose you from the very beginning.   **3:3** Or from evil.   **3:6** Greek brother; also in 3:15.

we gave you. [7]For you know that you ought to follow our example. We were never lazy when we were with you. [8]We never accepted food from anyone without paying for it. We worked hard day and night so that we would not be a burden to any of you. [9]It wasn't that we didn't have the right to ask you to feed us, but we wanted to give you an example to follow. [10]Even while we were with you, we gave you this rule: "Whoever does not work should not eat."

[11]Yet we hear that some of you are living idle lives, refusing to work and wasting time meddling in other people's business. [12]In the name of the Lord Jesus Christ, we appeal to such people—no, we command them: Settle down and get to work. Earn your own living. [13]And I say to the rest of you, dear brothers and sisters, never get tired of doing good.

[14]Take note of those who refuse to obey what we say in this letter. Stay away from them so they will be ashamed. [15]Don't think of them as enemies, but speak to them as you would to a Christian who needs to be warned.

[16]May the Lord of peace himself always give you his peace no matter what happens. The Lord be with you all.

[17]Now here is my greeting, which I write with my own hand—PAUL. I do this at the end of all my letters to prove that they really are from me.

[18]May the grace of our Lord Jesus Christ be with you all.

1 Timothy

TIMOTHY, a young disciple discovered by Paul on his second missionary journey (Acts 16:1), enjoyed a unique relationship with the apostle. Referred to by Paul as "my true child in the faith," Timothy ministered side by side with Paul as a missionary and later received the challenging assignment of pastoring the church at Ephesus. Paul's first letter to him resembles a manual for building church leadership. But more generally, it is a rich mine of principles for anyone who wishes to have a spiritual impact in the lives of others.

Focus	Organization in the Church			Operation of the Church		
Divisions	Law and Grace	Worship and Women	Elders and Deacons	False Teaching in the Church	Age Groups in the Church	Areas of Conflict in the Church
	1:1 1:20	2:1 2:15	3:1 3:16	4:1 4:16	5:1 5:25	6:1 6:21
Topics	Life of the Church		Leaders of the Church	Apostasy of the Church	Groups in the Church	Example to the Church
	Plans			Problems		
Place	Macedonia					
Time	Approximately A.D. 62–63					

DECEMBER 3 ☐ DAY 338
1 TIMOTHY 1–3
The Pastor and Church Government

OVERVIEW Timothy, Paul's child in the faith, was facing a heavy burden of responsibility in the church at Ephesus. False doctrine and numerous disorders required his prayerful attention. But Timothy was facing an even greater challenge in selecting and developing leadership in the church. Paul's first letter to Timothy is, in many ways, a "leadership manual" describing the qualifications of leaders in the household of God. Family life and finances, attitudes and habits, reputation both inside and outside the church—all provide evidence of a person's readiness to serve as a leader in the church of Jesus Christ.

Chapter 1	Chapter 2	Chapter 3
Law and Grace	Worship and Women	Elders and Deacons
"How people must conduct themselves in the household of God" (3:15).		

Our God has a big eraser.

YOUR DAILY WALK If you had to select a candidate for the title "The Worst Sinner Who Ever Lived," who would you choose and why?

Now consider this. The man who penned more books of the Bible than any other person . . . the man considered by many to be the greatest church leader who ever lived . . . the man who, during his lifetime, carried the gospel to the farthest reaches of the known world, by his own estimation deserved the title "World's Worst Sinner." Listen to these remarkable words from Paul: "Christ Jesus came into the world to save sinners—and I was the worst of them all" (1:15).

The tendency is to focus on what Paul *became in Christ* while overlooking the horrible background from which Paul *came to Christ:* "I used to scoff at the name of Christ. I hunted down his people, harming them in every way I could" (1:13). Regardless of your background or past sins, Jesus stands ready to save you, a sinner like Paul, if you will only accept his invitation. Will you come to Christ today—just as you are? You'll find a Savior eager to forgive you, even if you are the "World's Worst Sinner."

INSIGHT Who's Who among Elders and Deacons
Though later separated into two levels of responsibility in the history of the church, the terms *deacon* and *elder* originally referred to the same position in the early church. (Compare 1 Timothy 3:1; Acts 20:17, 28; Titus 1:5, 7.) The same role was alternately referred to as *overseer.*

CHAPTER 1
This letter is from Paul, an apostle of Christ Jesus, appointed by the command of God our Savior and by Christ Jesus our hope. ²It is written to Timothy, my true child in the faith.

May God our Father and Christ Jesus our Lord give you grace, mercy, and peace.

³When I left for Macedonia, I urged you to stay there in Ephesus and stop those who are teaching wrong doctrine. ⁴Don't

let people waste time in endless speculation over myths and spiritual pedigrees.* For these things only cause arguments; they don't help people live a life of faith in God.* ⁵The purpose of my instruction is that all the Christians there would be filled with love that comes from a pure heart, a clear conscience, and sincere faith.

⁶But some teachers have missed this whole point. They have turned away from these things and spend their time arguing and talking foolishness. ⁷They want to be known as teachers of the law of Moses, but they don't know what they are talking about, even though they seem so confident. ⁸We know these laws are good when they are used as God intended. ⁹But they were not made for people who do what is right. They are for people who are disobedient and rebellious, who are ungodly and sinful, who consider nothing sacred and defile what is holy, who murder their father or mother or other people. ¹⁰These laws are for people who are sexually immoral, for homosexuals and slave traders, for liars and oath breakers, and for those who do anything else that contradicts the right teaching ¹¹that comes from the glorious Good News entrusted to me by our blessed God.

¹²How thankful I am to Christ Jesus our Lord for considering me trustworthy and appointing me to serve him, ¹³even though I used to scoff at the name of Christ. I hunted down his people, harming them in every way I could. But God had mercy on me because I did it in ignorance and unbelief. ¹⁴Oh, how kind and gracious the Lord was! He filled me completely with faith and the love of Christ Jesus.

¹⁵This is a true saying, and everyone should believe it: Christ Jesus came into the world to save sinners—and I was the worst of them all. ¹⁶But that is why God had mercy on me, so that Christ Jesus could use me as a prime example of his great patience with even the worst sinners. Then others will realize that they, too, can believe in him and receive eternal life. ¹⁷Glory and honor to God forever and ever. He is the eternal King, the unseen one who never dies; he alone is God. Amen.

¹⁸Timothy, my son, here are my instructions for you, based on the prophetic words spoken about you earlier. May they give you the confidence to fight well in the Lord's battles. ¹⁹Cling tightly to your faith in Christ, and always keep your conscience clear. For some people have deliberately violated their consciences; as a result, their faith has been shipwrecked. ²⁰Hymenaeus and Alexander are two examples of this. I turned them over to Satan so they would learn not to blaspheme God.

CHAPTER 2

I urge you, first of all, to pray for all people. As you make your requests, plead for God's mercy upon them, and give thanks. ²Pray this way for kings and all others who are in authority, so that we can live in peace and quietness, in godliness and dignity. ³This is good and pleases God our Savior, ⁴for he wants everyone to be saved and to understand the truth. ⁵For there is only one God and one Mediator who can reconcile God and people. He is the man Christ Jesus. ⁶He gave his life to purchase freedom for everyone. This is the message that God gave to the world at the proper time. ⁷And I have been chosen—this is the absolute truth—as a preacher and apostle to teach the Gentiles about faith and truth.

⁸So wherever you assemble, I want men to pray with holy hands lifted up to God, free from anger and controversy. ⁹And I want women to be modest in their appearance. They should wear decent and appropriate clothing and not draw attention to themselves by the way they fix their hair or by wearing gold or pearls or expensive clothes. ¹⁰For women who claim to be devoted to God should make themselves attractive by the good things they do.

¹¹Women should listen and learn quietly and submissively. ¹²I do not let women teach men or have authority over them. Let them listen quietly. ¹³For God made Adam first, and afterward he made Eve. ¹⁴And it was the woman, not Adam, who was deceived by Satan, and sin was the result. ¹⁵But women will be saved through childbearing* and by continuing to live in faith, love, holiness, and modesty.

CHAPTER 3

It is a true saying that if someone wants to be an elder,* he desires an honorable responsibility. ²For an elder must be a man

---

1:4a Greek *in myths and endless genealogies, which cause speculation.* **1:4b** Greek *a stewardship of God in faith.* **2:15** Or *will be saved by* *accepting their role as mothers,* or *will be saved by the birth of the Child.* **3:1** Greek *overseer; also in 3:2.*

whose life cannot be spoken against. He must be faithful to his wife.* He must exhibit self-control, live wisely, and have a good reputation. He must enjoy having guests in his home and must be able to teach. ³He must not be a heavy drinker or be violent. He must be gentle, peace loving, and not one who loves money. ⁴He must manage his own family well, with children who respect and obey him. ⁵For if a man cannot manage his own household, how can he take care of God's church?

⁶An elder must not be a new Christian, because he might be proud of being chosen so soon, and the Devil will use that pride to make him fall.* ⁷Also, people outside the church must speak well of him so that he will not fall into the Devil's trap and be disgraced.

⁸In the same way, deacons must be people who are respected and have integrity. They must not be heavy drinkers and must not be greedy for money. ⁹They must be committed to the revealed truths of the Christian faith and must live with a clear conscience. ¹⁰Before they are appointed as deacons, they should be given other responsibilities in the church as a test of their character and ability. If they do well, then they may serve as deacons.

¹¹In the same way, their wives* must be respected and must not speak evil of others. They must exercise self-control and be faithful in everything they do.

¹²A deacon must be faithful to his wife, and he must manage his children and household well. ¹³Those who do well as deacons will be rewarded with respect from others and will have increased confidence in their faith in Christ Jesus.

¹⁴I am writing these things to you now, even though I hope to be with you soon, ¹⁵so that if I can't come for a while, you will know how people must conduct themselves in the household of God. This is the church of the living God, which is the pillar and support of the truth.

¹⁶Without question, this is the great mystery of our faith:

> Christ* appeared in the flesh
>   and was shown to be righteous by
>   the Spirit.*
> He was seen by angels
>   and was announced to the nations.
> He was believed on in the world
>   and was taken up into heaven.*

3:2 Greek *be the husband of one wife*; also in 3:12.   **3:6** Or *he might fall into the same judgment as the Devil.*   **3:11** Or *the women deacons.* The Greek word can be translated *women* or *wives*.   **3:16a** Greek *Who*; some manuscripts read *God.*   **3:16b** Or *in his spirit.* **3:16c** Greek *in glory.*

DECEMBER 4 □ DAY 339
1 TIMOTHY 4 – 6
The Pastor and Personal Progress

 OVERVIEW No single letter (even one from the apostle Paul) could hope to cover all the potential problem areas in a church congregation. But Paul does the next best thing. He warns Timothy of some of the major dangers he is sure to face in the "last times" (4:1)—a period filled with obstacles and opportunities. False teaching, frivolous speculation, improper conduct, inconsistent example, and greedy motives must be dealt with decisively. There are certain things from which Timothy and his congregation must flee, and there are others they must pursue if they are to "fight the good fight for what [they] believe" (6:12).

Chapter 4	Chapter 5	Chapter 6
Apostasy in the Church	Age Groups in the Church	Areas of Conflict in the Church
"Be an example to all believers" (4:12).		

YOUR DAILY WALK Do you have a written (or unwritten) code of conduct at your house, a set of rules each family member is expected to know and abide by? Here is one family's "Five Commandments for Household Survival":

The best form of spiritual exercise is to touch the floor regularly with your knees.

1. Eat a little of whatever is cooked.
2. No dessert until Rule 1 is observed.
3. Sleeping with the dog is forbidden.
4. Telephone calls limited to 5 minutes' duration.
5. If you got it dirty, you get it clean!

In the same way, the church—the household of God—needs guidelines if its conduct is to bring glory to God (3:15). Read today's section with pencil in hand, and circle each command that Paul delivers to Timothy. Pick one that speaks to a specific need in your local congregation, and ask God what he would have you do to promote harmony and growth in the family of God. And don't forget to check up on your own conduct first. You can't be part of the solution if you are part of the problem.

INSIGHT A Majestic Doxology to Your Majestic Lord
The mere mention of the second coming of Jesus (6:14) immediately catapults Paul into one of the most majestic doxologies to be found anywhere in the Scriptures. Its theme is the incomparable glory of God. Worship this King over all kings and Lord over all lords by reading verses 15 and 16 aloud—"to him be honor and power forever. Amen."

CHAPTER 4

Now the Holy Spirit tells us clearly that in the last times some will turn away from what we believe; they will follow lying spirits and teachings that come from demons. [2]These teachers are hypocrites and liars. They pretend to be religious, but their consciences are dead.*

[3]They will say it is wrong to be married and wrong to eat certain foods. But God created those foods to be eaten with thanksgiving by people who know and believe the truth. [4]Since everything God created is good, we should not reject any of it. We may receive it gladly, with thankful hearts. [5]For we know it is made holy by the word of God and prayer.

[6]If you explain this to the brothers and sisters, you will be doing your duty as a worthy servant of Christ Jesus, one who is fed by the message of faith and the true teaching you have followed. [7]Do not waste time arguing over godless ideas and old wives' tales. Spend your time and energy in training yourself for spiritual fitness. [8]Physical exercise has some value, but spiritual exercise is much more important, for it promises a reward in both this life and the next. [9]This is true, and everyone should accept it. [10]We work hard and suffer much* in order that people will believe the truth,

for our hope is in the living God, who is the Savior of all people, and particularly of those who believe.

[11]Teach these things and insist that everyone learn them. [12]Don't let anyone think less of you because you are young. Be an example to all believers in what you teach, in the way you live, in your love, your faith, and your purity. [13]Until I get there, focus on reading the Scriptures to the church, encouraging the believers, and teaching them.

[14]Do not neglect the spiritual gift you received through the prophecies spoken to you when the elders of the church laid their hands on you. [15]Give your complete attention to these matters. Throw yourself into your tasks so that everyone will see your progress. [16]Keep a close watch on yourself and on your teaching. Stay true to what is right, and God will save you and those who hear you.

CHAPTER 5

Never speak harshly to an older man,* but appeal to him respectfully as though he were your own father. Talk to the younger men as you would to your own brothers. [2]Treat the older women as you would your mother, and treat the younger women with all purity as your own sisters.

[3]The church should care for any widow

4:2 Greek *are seared.*   4:10 Some manuscripts read *and strive.*   5:1 Or *an elder.*

who has no one else to care for her. ⁴But if she has children or grandchildren, their first responsibility is to show godliness at home and repay their parents by taking care of them. This is something that pleases God very much.

⁵But a woman who is a true widow, one who is truly alone in this world, has placed her hope in God. Night and day she asks God for help and spends much time in prayer. ⁶But the widow who lives only for pleasure is spiritually dead. ⁷Give these instructions to the church so that the widows you support* will not be criticized.

⁸But those who won't care for their own relatives, especially those living in the same household, have denied what we believe. Such people are worse than unbelievers.

⁹A widow who is put on the list for support must be a woman who is at least sixty years old and was faithful to her husband.* ¹⁰She must be well respected by everyone because of the good she has done. Has she brought up her children well? Has she been kind to strangers? Has she served other Christians humbly?* Has she helped those who are in trouble? Has she always been ready to do good?

¹¹The younger widows should not be on the list, because their physical desires will overpower their devotion to Christ and they will want to remarry. ¹²Then they would be guilty of breaking their previous pledge. ¹³Besides, they are likely to become lazy and spend their time gossiping from house to house, getting into other people's business and saying things they shouldn't. ¹⁴So I advise these younger widows to marry again, have children, and take care of their own homes. Then the enemy will not be able to say anything against them. ¹⁵For I am afraid that some of them have already gone astray and now follow Satan.

¹⁶If a Christian woman has relatives who are widows, she must take care of them and not put the responsibility on the church. Then the church can care for widows who are truly alone.

¹⁷Elders who do their work well should be paid well,* especially those who work hard at both preaching and teaching. ¹⁸For the Scripture says, "Do not keep an ox from eating as it treads out the grain." And in another place, "Those who work deserve their pay!"*

¹⁹Do not listen to complaints against an elder unless there are two or three witnesses to accuse him. ²⁰Anyone who sins should be rebuked in front of the whole church so that others will have a proper fear of God.

²¹I solemnly command you in the presence of God and Christ Jesus and the holy angels to obey these instructions without taking sides or showing special favor to anyone. ²²Never be in a hurry about appointing an elder. Do not participate in the sins of others. Keep yourself pure.

²³Don't drink only water. You ought to drink a little wine for the sake of your stomach because you are sick so often.

²⁴Remember that some people lead sinful lives, and everyone knows they will be judged. But there are others whose sin will not be revealed until later. ²⁵In the same way, everyone knows how much good some people do, but there are others whose good deeds won't be known until later.

CHAPTER 6

Christians who are slaves should give their masters full respect so that the name of God and his teaching will not be shamed. ²If your master is a Christian, that is no excuse for being disrespectful. You should work all the harder because you are helping another believer* by your efforts.

Teach these truths, Timothy, and encourage everyone to obey them. ³Some false teachers may deny these things, but these are the sound, wholesome teachings of the Lord Jesus Christ, and they are the foundation for a godly life. ⁴Anyone who teaches anything different is both conceited and ignorant. Such a person has an unhealthy desire to quibble over the meaning of words. This stirs up arguments ending in jealousy, fighting, slander, and evil suspicions. ⁵These people always cause trouble. Their minds are corrupt, and they don't tell the truth. To them religion is just a way to get rich.

⁶Yet true religion with contentment is great wealth. ⁷After all, we didn't bring anything with us when we came into the world, and we certainly cannot carry anything with us when we die. ⁸So if we have enough food and clothing, let us be

---

5:7 Or *so the church*; Greek reads *so they.*   5:9 Greek *was the wife of one man.*   5:10 Greek *Has she washed the feet of saints?*
5:17 Greek *should be worthy of double honor.*   5:18 Deut 25:4; Luke 10:7.   6:2 Greek *a brother.*

content. [9]But people who long to be rich fall into temptation and are trapped by many foolish and harmful desires that plunge them into ruin and destruction. [10]For the love of money is at the root of all kinds of evil. And some people, craving money, have wandered from the faith and pierced themselves with many sorrows.

[11]But you, Timothy, belong to God; so run from all these evil things, and follow what is right and good. Pursue a godly life, along with faith, love, perseverance, and gentleness. [12]Fight the good fight for what we believe. Hold tightly to the eternal life that God has given you, which you have confessed so well before many witnesses. [13]And I command you before God, who gives life to all, and before Christ Jesus, who gave a good testimony before Pontius Pilate, [14]that you obey his commands with all purity. Then no one can find fault with you from now until our Lord Jesus Christ returns. [15]For at the right time Christ will be revealed from heaven by the blessed and only almighty God, the King of kings and Lord of lords. [16]He alone can never die, and he lives in light so brilliant that no human can approach him. No one has ever seen him, nor ever will. To him be honor and power forever. Amen.

[17]Tell those who are rich in this world not to be proud and not to trust in their money, which will soon be gone. But their trust should be in the living God, who richly gives us all we need for our enjoyment. [18]Tell them to use their money to do good. They should be rich in good works and should give generously to those in need, always being ready to share with others whatever God has given them. [19]By doing this they will be storing up their treasure as a good foundation for the future so that they may take hold of real life.

[20]Timothy, guard what God has entrusted to you. Avoid godless, foolish discussions with those who oppose you with their so-called knowledge. [21]Some people have wandered from the faith by following such foolishness.

May God's grace be with you all.

2 Timothy

SECOND Timothy is the dying appeal of Paul to his young co-worker. Underlying each theme is the importance of God's Word. Paul encourages Timothy, naturally timid and facing persecution, to find in Scripture all he needs to persevere. In the same pages he would find what he needs to preach and to practice. Lonely in his death-row cell, Paul asks Timothy to visit as soon as possible—and to bring him a copy of the Word. He offers a stirring testimony of how God has used his life to spread that Word—and of the reward awaiting him.

Focus	Be Steadfast in Your Ministry			Be Steadfast in Your Doctrine		
Divisions	Thanksgiving for Timothy	Exhortation to Timothy	Duties of Timothy	False Teachers and Timothy	Charge to Timothy	Death of Timothy's Friend
	1:1 1:5	1:6 1:18	2:1 2:13	2:14 3:17	4:1 4:5	4:6 4:22
Topics	Hold Fast the Gospel		Pass on the Gospel	Protect the Gospel	Preach the Gospel	
	Foundation		Faithfulness	Foes	Fearlessness	
Place	Roman Prison					
Time	Approximately A.D. 67					

DECEMBER 5 □ DAY 340
2 TIMOTHY 1–4
Paul's Combat Manual

OVERVIEW Chronologically, 2 Timothy is Paul's final epistle. Written from a Roman prison cell, it contains words of wisdom and encouragement for Timothy, who is laboring in the midst of hardship and opposition in Ephesus. Paul stresses the importance of godly living, consistent biblical preaching, and adequate preparation for difficult days yet to come. Underlying all that Paul says is the importance of God's Word—the only foundation strong enough to stand upon in perilous times.

Chapter 1	Chapter 2	Chapter 3	Chapter 4
Power of the Truth	Practice of the Truth	Persecution of the Truth	Preaching of the Truth
Foundation	Faithfulness	Foes	Fearlessness

YOUR DAILY WALK "'Tis the season to be jolly," exclaims the Christmas chorus.

You do not choose to be in the business of bringing others to Christ; you choose Christ and you are at once in the business.

Football season . . . holiday season . . . planting season . . . harvesting season . . . there's a time and season for everything (Ecclesiastes 3:1). Everything, that is, except sharing the Good News of Jesus Christ; that important task is *always* "in season."

Paul exhorts young Timothy, "Preach the word of God. Be persistent, whether the time is favorable or not" (4:2). There will be occasions when you have virtually all the time you need to prepare what you want to say about Jesus Christ. A Sunday school lesson, sermon manuscript, magazine article, study group devotional—each represents an opportunity to "preach the word" . . . *in season.* But what about those times when you are suddenly called upon to speak for your Lord—and there isn't a Bible in sight? Paul's counsel to you is the same: "Preach the word of God. Be persistent, *whether the time is favorable or not."* In short, be prepared to share the Good News whenever and wherever the occasion might arise!

Get a head start on that assignment by writing out your personal testimony today as you would want to share it with another person. You may find the opportunity to do precisely that!

INSIGHT A Warm Coat for a Cold Apostle
Writing in the fall, Paul was naturally concerned about staying warm during the coming winter. His unheated underground cell, believed to be in the Mamertine Prison, probably measured only ten by nineteen feet and was six feet high. It was accessible through only a hole in the ceiling. Now reread 4:9-13 . . . with feeling!

CHAPTER 1

This letter is from Paul, an apostle of Christ Jesus by God's will, sent out to tell others about the life he has promised through faith in Christ Jesus. ²It is written to Timothy, my dear son.

May God our Father and Christ Jesus our Lord give you grace, mercy, and peace.

³Timothy, I thank God for you. He is the God I serve with a clear conscience, just as my ancestors did. Night and day I con-

stantly remember you in my prayers. ⁴I long to see you again, for I remember your tears as we parted. And I will be filled with joy when we are together again.

⁵I know that you sincerely trust the Lord, for you have the faith of your mother, Eunice, and your grandmother, Lois. ⁶This is why I remind you to fan into flames the spiritual gift God gave you when I laid my hands on you. ⁷For God has not given us a spirit of fear and timidity, but of power, love, and self-discipline. ⁸So you must never be ashamed to tell others about our Lord. And don't be ashamed of me, either, even though I'm in prison for Christ. With the strength God gives you, be ready to suffer with me for the proclamation of the Good News.

⁹It is God who saved us and chose us to live a holy life. He did this not because we deserved it, but because that was his plan long before the world began—to show his love and kindness to us through Christ Jesus. ¹⁰And now he has made all of this plain to us by the coming of Christ Jesus, our Savior, who broke the power of death and showed us the way to everlasting life through the Good News. ¹¹And God chose me to be a preacher, an apostle, and a teacher of this Good News.

¹²And that is why I am suffering here in prison. But I am not ashamed of it, for I know the one in whom I trust, and I am sure that he is able to guard what I have entrusted to him* until the day of his return.

¹³Hold on to the pattern of right teaching you learned from me. And remember to live in the faith and love that you have in Christ Jesus. ¹⁴With the help of the Holy Spirit who lives within us, carefully guard what has been entrusted to you.

¹⁵As you know, all the Christians who came here from the province of Asia have deserted me; even Phygelus and Hermogenes are gone. ¹⁶May the Lord show special kindness to Onesiphorus and all his family because he often visited and encouraged me. He was never ashamed of me because I was in prison. ¹⁷When he came to Rome, he searched everywhere until he found me. ¹⁸May the Lord show him special kindness on the day of Christ's return. And you know how much he helped me at Ephesus.

CHAPTER 2
Timothy, my dear son, be strong with the special favor God gives you in Christ Jesus. ²You have heard me teach many things that have been confirmed by many reliable witnesses. Teach these great truths to trustworthy people who are able to pass them on to others.

³Endure suffering along with me, as a good soldier of Christ Jesus. ⁴And as Christ's soldier, do not let yourself become tied up in the affairs of this life, for then you cannot satisfy the one who has enlisted you in his army. ⁵Follow the Lord's rules for doing his work, just as an athlete either follows the rules or is disqualified and wins no prize. ⁶Hardworking farmers are the first to enjoy the fruit of their labor. ⁷Think about what I am saying. The Lord will give you understanding in all these things.

⁸Never forget that Jesus Christ was a man born into King David's family and that he was raised from the dead. This is the Good News I preach. ⁹And because I preach this Good News, I am suffering and have been chained like a criminal. But the word of God cannot be chained. ¹⁰I am willing to endure anything if it will bring salvation and eternal glory in Christ Jesus to those God has chosen.

¹¹This is a true saying:

If we die with him,
    we will also live with him.
¹² If we endure hardship,
    we will reign with him.
If we deny him,
    he will deny us.
¹³ If we are unfaithful,
    he remains faithful,
    for he cannot deny himself.

¹⁴Remind everyone of these things, and command them in God's name to stop fighting over words. Such arguments are useless, and they can ruin those who hear them. ¹⁵Work hard so God can approve you. Be a good worker, one who does not need to be ashamed and who correctly explains the word of truth. ¹⁶Avoid godless, foolish discussions that lead to more and more ungodliness. ¹⁷This kind of talk spreads like cancer. Hymenaeus and Philetus are examples of this. ¹⁸They have left the path of truth, preaching the lie that the

1:12 Or *what has been entrusted to me.*

resurrection of the dead has already occurred; and they have undermined the faith of some.

[19]But God's truth stands firm like a foundation stone with this inscription: "The Lord knows those who are his,"* and "Those who claim they belong to the Lord must turn away from all wickedness."*

[20]In a wealthy home some utensils are made of gold and silver, and some are made of wood and clay. The expensive utensils are used for special occasions, and the cheap ones are for everyday use. [21]If you keep yourself pure, you will be a utensil God can use for his purpose. Your life will be clean, and you will be ready for the Master to use you for every good work.

[22]Run from anything that stimulates youthful lust. Follow anything that makes you want to do right. Pursue faith and love and peace, and enjoy the companionship of those who call on the Lord with pure hearts.

[23]Again I say, don't get involved in foolish, ignorant arguments that only start fights. [24]The Lord's servants must not quarrel but must be kind to everyone. They must be able to teach effectively and be patient with difficult people. [25]They should gently teach those who oppose the truth. Perhaps God will change those people's hearts, and they will believe the truth. [26]Then they will come to their senses and escape from the Devil's trap. For they have been held captive by him to do whatever he wants.

CHAPTER 3

You should also know this, Timothy, that in the last days there will be very difficult times. [2]For people will love only themselves and their money. They will be boastful and proud, scoffing at God, disobedient to their parents, and ungrateful. They will consider nothing sacred. [3]They will be unloving and unforgiving; they will slander others and have no self-control; they will be cruel and have no interest in what is good. [4]They will betray their friends, be reckless, be puffed up with pride, and love pleasure rather than God. [5]They will act as if they are religious, but they will reject the power that could make them godly. You must stay away from people like that.

[6]They are the kind who work their way into people's homes and win the confidence of* vulnerable women who are burdened with the guilt of sin and controlled by many desires. [7]Such women are forever following new teachings, but they never understand the truth. [8]And these teachers fight the truth just as Jannes and Jambres fought against Moses. Their minds are depraved, and their faith is counterfeit. [9]But they won't get away with this for long. Someday everyone will recognize what fools they are, just as happened with Jannes and Jambres.

[10]But you know what I teach, Timothy, and how I live, and what my purpose in life is. You know my faith and how long I have suffered. You know my love and my patient endurance. [11]You know how much persecution and suffering I have endured. You know all about how I was persecuted in Antioch, Iconium, and Lystra—but the Lord delivered me from all of it. [12]Yes, and everyone who wants to live a godly life in Christ Jesus will suffer persecution. [13]But evil people and impostors will flourish. They will go on deceiving others, and they themselves will be deceived.

[14]But you must remain faithful to the things you have been taught. You know they are true, for you know you can trust those who taught you. [15]You have been taught the holy Scriptures from childhood, and they have given you the wisdom to receive the salvation that comes by trusting in Christ Jesus. [16]All Scripture is inspired by God and is useful to teach us what is true and to make us realize what is wrong in our lives. It straightens us out and teaches us to do what is right. [17]It is God's way of preparing us in every way, fully equipped for every good thing God wants us to do.

CHAPTER 4

And so I solemnly urge you before God and before Christ Jesus—who will someday judge the living and the dead when he appears to set up his Kingdom: [2]Preach the word of God. Be persistent, whether the time is favorable or not. Patiently correct, rebuke, and encourage your people with good teaching.

[3]For a time is coming when people will no longer listen to right teaching. They will follow their own desires and will look for

2:19a Num 16:5.   2:19b See Isa 52:11.   3:6 Greek *and take captive.*

teachers who will tell them whatever they want to hear. [4]They will reject the truth and follow strange myths.

[5]But you should keep a clear mind in every situation. Don't be afraid of suffering for the Lord. Work at bringing others to Christ. Complete the ministry God has given you.

[6]As for me, my life has already been poured out as an offering to God. The time of my death is near. [7]I have fought a good fight, I have finished the race, and I have remained faithful. [8]And now the prize awaits me—the crown of righteousness that the Lord, the righteous Judge, will give me on that great day of his return. And the prize is not just for me but for all who eagerly look forward to his glorious return.

[9]Please come as soon as you can. [10]Demas has deserted me because he loves the things of this life and has gone to Thessalonica. Crescens has gone to Galatia, and Titus has gone to Dalmatia. [11]Only Luke is with me. Bring Mark with you when you come, for he will be helpful to me. [12]I sent Tychicus to Ephesus. [13]When you come, be sure to bring the coat I left with Carpus at Troas. Also bring my books, and especially my papers.*

[14]Alexander the coppersmith has done me much harm, but the Lord will judge him for what he has done. [15]Be careful of him, for he fought against everything we said.

[16]The first time I was brought before the judge, no one was with me. Everyone had abandoned me. I hope it will not be counted against them. [17]But the Lord stood with me and gave me strength, that I might preach the Good News in all its fullness for all the Gentiles to hear. And he saved me from certain death.* [18]Yes, and the Lord will deliver me from every evil attack and will bring me safely to his heavenly Kingdom. To God be the glory forever and ever. Amen.

[19]Give my greetings to Priscilla and Aquila and those living at the household of Onesiphorus. [20]Erastus stayed at Corinth, and I left Trophimus sick at Miletus.

[21]Hurry so you can get here before winter. Eubulus sends you greetings, and so do Pudens, Linus, Claudia, and all the brothers and sisters.

[22]May the Lord be with your spirit. Grace be with you all.

4:13 Greek *especially the parchments.*   **4:17** Greek *from the mouth of a lion.*

Titus

TITUS lived among a people who had one of the worst reputations in the world. He was organizing and shepherding the new believers on Crete, the largest island in the Mediterranean. Paul writes to authorize him for this work and instruct him in it. Titus was to appoint spiritual leaders as elders and to promote sound teaching. False teachers should be quickly detected and removed, and all must be encouraged to live worthy of the gospel. The epistle to Titus is known for its summary of Christian doctrine and its emphasis on holy living.

Focus	Duties of Church Leaders		Duties of Church Members	
Divisions	Elders Designated	Heresy Described	Good Works Demanded	Heretics Denounced
	1:1 .... 1:9	1:10 .... 1:16	2:1 .... 2:15	3:1 .... 3:15
Topics	Servants		Service	Salvation
	Preservation of Truth		Use of Truth	
Place	Probably Written in Corinth			
Time	Approximately A.D. 63			

DECEMBER 6 □ DAY 341
TITUS 1–3
Practicing the Faith

OVERVIEW Titus, a young minister, is left on the Mediterranean island of Crete by Paul to begin the challenging task of organizing new converts into local churches. In this letter, Paul shares with Titus some practical wisdom regarding church organization and administration. For example: Leaders must be chosen on the basis of proven character and conduct; false teachers must be quickly detected and removed; church members of all ages must be encouraged to live in a way that is worthy of the gospel they claim to believe. Young and old, leader and laity, all must demonstrate the reality of their faith by being "careful to do good deeds all the time" (3:8).

Chapter 1		Chapter 2	Chapter 3
Elders Designated	Heresy Described	Good Works Demanded	Heretics Denounced
1 9	10 16		
The Church Organized		The Church in Operation	

YOUR DAILY WALK True or False: Good works cannot save you.
True or False: Good works for the Christian are unimportant.
True or False: Good works come naturally for a child of God.

To keep the faith we must teach the faith.

Perhaps you found the first questions easy (the first is true, 3:5, and the second, false, 3:8). But the third one may have been more difficult! In 2 Corinthians 5:17 Paul makes it clear that a new Christian is a new creation, with new desires, ambitions, and enablement to live for God. But just as children need guidance and training by their parents if they are to develop normally, so spiritual children must be taught "right teaching" (2:1). New believers of all ages in the church at Crete needed instruction in proper Christian conduct.

Paul has some timely words for you as well, regardless of your age, gender, or level of maturity as a Christian. As you read, watch for his exhortations aimed straight at you and your peers. Write them in a notebook or on a sheet of paper. If possible, find another daily walker and discuss together what you have learned.

INSIGHT Parallel Epistles with Parallel Emphases

	1 Timothy	*Titus*
False Teachers	1:6-11, 19-20; 6:3-5	1:10-16; 3:9-11
Faithful Leaders	3:1-13	1:6-9
Faithful Believers	5:1–6:2	2:1-15

CHAPTER 1

This letter is from Paul, a slave of God and an apostle of Jesus Christ. I have been sent to bring faith to those God has chosen and to teach them to know the truth that shows them how to live godly lives. ²This truth gives them the confidence of eternal life, which God promised them before the world began—and he cannot lie. ³And now at the right time he has revealed this Good News, and we announce it to everyone. It is by the command of God our Savior that I have been trusted to do this work for him.

⁴This letter is written to Titus, my true child in the faith that we share.

May God the Father and Christ Jesus our Savior give you grace and peace.

⁵I left you on the island of Crete so you could complete our work there and appoint elders in each town as I instructed you. ⁶An elder must be well thought of for his good life. He must be faithful to his wife,* and his children must be believers who are not wild or rebellious. ⁷An elder* must live a blameless life because he is God's minister. He must not be arrogant or quick-tempered; he must not be a heavy drinker, violent, or greedy for money. ⁸He must enjoy having guests in his home and must love all that is good. He must live wisely and be fair. He must live a devout and disciplined life. ⁹He must have a strong and steadfast belief in the trustworthy message he was taught; then he will be able to encourage others with right teaching and show those who oppose it where they are wrong.

¹⁰For there are many who rebel against right teaching; they engage in useless talk and deceive people. This is especially true of those who insist on circumcision for salvation. ¹¹They must be silenced. By their wrong teaching, they have already turned whole families away from the truth. Such teachers only want your money. ¹²One of their own men, a prophet from Crete, has said about them, "The people of Crete are all liars; they are cruel animals and lazy gluttons." ¹³This is true. So rebuke them as sternly as necessary to make them strong in the faith. ¹⁴They must stop listening to Jewish myths and the commands of people who have turned their backs on the truth.

¹⁵Everything is pure to those whose hearts are pure. But nothing is pure to those who are corrupt and unbelieving, because their minds and consciences are defiled. ¹⁶Such people claim they know God, but they deny him by the way they live. They are despicable and disobedient, worthless for doing anything good.

CHAPTER 2

But as for you, promote the kind of living that reflects right teaching. ²Teach the older men to exercise self-control, to be worthy of respect, and to live wisely. They must have strong faith and be filled with love and patience.

³Similarly, teach the older women to live in a way that is appropriate for someone serving the Lord. They must not go around speaking evil of others and must not be heavy drinkers. Instead, they should teach others what is good. ⁴These older women must train the younger women to love their husbands and their children, ⁵to live wisely and be pure, to take care of their homes, to do good, and to be submissive to their husbands. Then they will not bring shame on the word of God.

⁶In the same way, encourage the young men to live wisely in all they do. ⁷And you yourself must be an example to them by doing good deeds of every kind. Let everything you do reflect the integrity and seriousness of your teaching. ⁸Let your teaching be so correct that it can't be criticized. Then those who want to argue will be ashamed because they won't have anything bad to say about us.

⁹Slaves must obey their masters and do their best to please them. They must not talk back ¹⁰or steal, but they must show themselves to be entirely trustworthy and good. Then they will make the teaching about God our Savior attractive in every way.

¹¹For the grace of God has been revealed, bringing salvation to all people. ¹²And we are instructed to turn from godless living and sinful pleasures. We should live in this evil world with self-control, right conduct, and devotion to God, ¹³while we look forward to that wonderful event when the glory of our great God and Savior, Jesus Christ, will be revealed. ¹⁴He gave his life to free us from every kind of sin, to cleanse us, and to make us his very own people, totally committed to doing what is right. ¹⁵You must teach these things and encourage your people to do them, correcting them when necessary. You have the authority to do this, so don't let anyone ignore you or disregard what you say.

CHAPTER 3

Remind your people to submit to the government and its officers. They should be obedient, always ready to do what is good. ²They must not speak evil of anyone, and they must avoid quarreling. Instead, they

---

1:6 Or *have only one wife,* or *be married only once;* Greek reads *be the husband of one wife.*   **1:7** Greek *overseer.*

should be gentle and show true humility to everyone.

³Once we, too, were foolish and disobedient. We were misled by others and became slaves to many wicked desires and evil pleasures. Our lives were full of evil and envy. We hated others, and they hated us.

⁴But then God our Savior showed us his kindness and love. ⁵He saved us, not because of the good things we did, but because of his mercy. He washed away our sins and gave us a new life through the Holy Spirit.* ⁶He generously poured out the Spirit upon us because of what Jesus Christ our Savior did. ⁷He declared us not guilty because of his great kindness. And now we know that we will inherit eternal life. ⁸These things I have told you are all true. I want you to insist on them so that everyone who trusts in God will be careful to do good deeds all the time. These things are good and beneficial for everyone.

⁹Do not get involved in foolish discussions about spiritual pedigrees* or in quarrels and fights about obedience to Jewish laws. These kinds of things are useless and a waste of time. ¹⁰If anyone is causing divisions among you, give a first and second warning. After that, have nothing more to do with that person. ¹¹For people like that have turned away from the truth. They are sinning, and they condemn themselves.

¹²I am planning to send either Artemas or Tychicus to you. As soon as one of them arrives, do your best to meet me at Nicopolis as quickly as you can, for I have decided to stay there for the winter. ¹³Do everything you can to help Zenas the lawyer and Apollos with their trip. See that they are given everything they need. ¹⁴For our people should not have unproductive lives. They must learn to do good by helping others who have urgent needs.

¹⁵Everybody here sends greetings. Please give my greetings to all of the believers who love us.

May God's grace be with you all.

3:5 Greek *He saved us through the washing of regeneration and renewing of the Holy Spirit.*　　**3:9** Greek *discussions and genealogies.*

DECEMBER 7 ☐ DAY 342
Happily Humble

 LOOK BACK The Pauline Epistles have been the focus of your reading over the past couple of weeks. Here's a "key" to help you unlock and remember each book:

Philippians: "Happily Humble" (The path of true happiness for the Christian is the path of genuine humility modeled by Jesus Christ.)

Colossians: "Commander in Chief" (Jesus is preeminent in everything and deserves first place in your life.)

1 Thessalonians: "Stay on Target" (Don't become distracted or discouraged as you seek to make faith, hope, and love the hallmarks of your faith.)

2 Thessalonians: "Work While You Wait" (There is work to be done in the harvest fields of the Lord as you await his return.)

1 Timothy: "Leadership Manual" (How to know when you are ready to assume leadership responsibility in the household of faith)

2 Timothy: "Combat Manual" (How to do battle with the enemy as you live for Jesus)

Titus: "Conduct Manual" (How to behave in the household of faith)

 LOOK UP Find two glasses of differing shapes, and fill one with water. Now pour the full glass into the empty glass. What you now have is all of the water from the first glass contained in a new "form."

In a crude way, that illustrates what happened when Jesus Christ, the Second Person of the Godhead, took upon himself human form and

To grow tall spiritually, a Christian must first learn to kneel.

became a man. Without in any way ceasing to be *divine* (his original nature), he took upon himself a new form (*flesh,* human nature). And the result? When Jesus walked the earth, in reality he was all of God in a human body—"the Incarnation." He was God come in the flesh, total divinity combined with perfect humanity. Jesus "emptied" himself of the use of many of his divine attributes (such as omnipotence and omnipresence) in order to dwell among the objects of his love: men and women, boys and girls (John 1:14).

And the result? A series of glorious ironies! The Christ of creation (John 1:3) was laid in a manger made from one of the trees he created. The Carpenter from Nazareth is busy today preparing our eternal "condominium" (John 14:1-4).

 LOOK AHEAD Philippians 2:5-11 describes Christ's example of humility as he emptied himself of his divine rights and privileges (remember our illustration with the glasses?) and made himself of no reputation. By rights, Jesus could have demanded that every knee bow to his authority. Instead, he suffered and died at the hands of wicked men in order that our response to him would be out of love, not coercion. He was willing to renounce his heavenly citizenship for an earthly one. Now he asks his followers to do just the opposite!

What price are you willing to pay today to follow in his footsteps? Are you willing to be inconvenienced by someone who calls or drops by unannounced with a need for your time and attention? Are you willing to rearrange your priorities in order to serve the needs of someone else? Are you willing to use money you were saving for a personal purchase to meet someone else's need?

Taking the form of a servant may not earn you any applause or fanfare, but it will demonstrate that you are serious about having the mind of Christ (Philippians 2:5). And after you read verse 9, perhaps you will agree that that's definitely the mind to have!

Philemon

ONESIMUS is a desperate slave who has wronged his master, Philemon. Slaves were crucified for lesser offenses than his! He had run away to Rome, where he found—through Paul—a glorious new slavery: to Jesus Christ. In gratefulness, Onesimus serves Paul. He repents, but he has not made restitution. Paul sends him back to his master with this letter, asking Philemon to forgive and accept him as a fellow brother in the Lord. This "postcard" provides a glimpse of Paul's affectionate heart and reminds us of our forgiveness in Christ.

Focus	Praise for Philemon		Plea for Onesimus		Preparation for Paul
Divisions	Paul's Preface	Paul's Commendation	Paul's Intercession	Paul's Promise	Paul's Messages
	1　　　3	4　　　7	8　　　16	17　　　21	22　　　25
Topics	Greetings	Gratitude	Grace		Good Words
	Courtesy	Compliment	Counsel		Conclusion
Place	Rome				
Time	Approximately A.D. 60–61				

DECEMBER 8 □ DAY 343
PHILEMON
Forgiveness in the Church

OVERVIEW Philemon is the shortest and one of the most personal of Paul's letters. Paul has befriended Onesimus, a runaway slave and new convert to Christianity. Now Onesimus must deal with his obligations to his former master, Philemon, who is also a Christian. Paul sends Onesimus back with a brief note in which Paul appeals for leniency based on love: Philemon's love for Paul and God's love for Philemon. Knowing the reality of Philemon's faith, Paul is confident that brotherly love will carry the day.

Verses 1-3	Verses 4-7	Verses 8-21	Verses 22-25
Paul's Courtesy	Paul's Compliment	Paul's Counsel	Paul's Conclusion
Salutation	Commendation	Intercession	Anticipation

YOUR DAILY WALK Place a check next to each item for which you have received an "overdue notice" in the past year:
- Library book
- Loan repayment
- Charge account
- Debt of restitution

Those who profess repentance must practice it.

Were you puzzled by the last item? Allow the life of Onesimus to demonstrate what restitution is and why it is so important.

When the runaway slave was confronted with the claims of Christ and responded in believing faith, many things changed. His sins were forgiven by God; he became a part of the family of God (with many new brothers and sisters in Christ, including Paul and Philemon); he received a whole new motivation for living! But some things did not change. He was still Philemon's servant—and a runaway servant at that. He was still a thief, with a debt to repay to his master. There were "overdue" accounts to settle involving restitution, repentance, and a return to Philemon's authority.

Is there an overdue account from your "B.C." (before Christ) days? Take a moment to honor the Christ who settled your heavenly debt by settling an earthly one today!

INSIGHT The Man Who Lived Up to His Name
Onesimus literally means "useful," which explains Paul's play on words in verse 11. A person who was formerly not "of much use" to Philemon is now "useful" to both Philemon and Paul!

This letter is from Paul, in prison for preaching the Good News about Christ Jesus, and from our brother Timothy.

It is written to Philemon, our much loved co-worker, ²and to our sister Apphia and to Archippus, a fellow soldier of the cross. I am also writing to the church that meets in your house.

³May God our Father and the Lord Jesus Christ give you grace and peace.

[4]I always thank God when I pray for you, Philemon, [5]because I keep hearing of your trust in the Lord Jesus and your love for all of God's people. [6]You are generous because of your faith. And I am praying that you will really put your generosity to work, for in so doing you will come to an understanding of all the good things we can do for Christ. [7]I myself have gained much joy and comfort from your love, my brother, because your kindness has so often refreshed the hearts of God's people.

[8]That is why I am boldly asking a favor of you. I could demand it in the name of Christ because it is the right thing for you to do, [9]but because of our love, I prefer just to ask you. So take this as a request from your friend Paul, an old man, now in prison for the sake of Christ Jesus.

[10]My plea is that you show kindness to Onesimus. I think of him as my own son because he became a believer as a result of my ministry here in prison. [11]Onesimus* hasn't been of much use to you in the past, but now he is very useful to both of us. [12]I am sending him back to you, and with him comes my own heart.

[13]I really wanted to keep him here with me while I am in these chains for preaching the Good News, and he would have helped me on your behalf. [14]But I didn't want to do

11 *Onesimus* means "useful."

anything without your consent. And I didn't want you to help because you were forced to do it but because you wanted to. [15]Perhaps you could think of it this way: Onesimus ran away for a little while so you could have him back forever. [16]He is no longer just a slave; he is a beloved brother, especially to me. Now he will mean much more to you, both as a slave and as a brother in the Lord.

[17]So if you consider me your partner, give him the same welcome you would give me if I were coming. [18]If he has harmed you in any way or stolen anything from you, charge me for it. [19]I, Paul, write this in my own handwriting: "I will repay it." And I won't mention that you owe me your very soul!

[20]Yes, dear brother, please do me this favor for the Lord's sake. Give me this encouragement in Christ. [21]I am confident as I write this letter that you will do what I ask and even more!

[22]Please keep a guest room ready for me, for I am hoping that God will answer your prayers and let me return to you soon.

[23]Epaphras, my fellow prisoner in Christ Jesus, sends you his greetings. [24]So do Mark, Aristarchus, Demas, and Luke, my co-workers.

[25]The grace of the Lord Jesus Christ be with your spirit.

Hebrews

THE ANONYMOUS first-century writer of Hebrews sent this letter of exhortation to professing Jewish Christians suffering persecution for their faith in Christ. Many, in fact, were considering renouncing their profession in order to return to the safety of Judaism (10:38-39). The writer exhorts them to hold fast to their faith and press on to spiritual maturity. The Christian faith is the true worship and service of the living God. Jesus Christ, as both the sacrifice and High Priest of the new covenant, is superior in every way to the Mosaic system.

Focus	"Jesus, on whom our faith depends from start to finish" (12:2).				
Divisions	Christ, Superior to the Angels	Christ, Superior to Moses and Joshua	Christ, Superior to Aaron's Priesthood	Christ, Superior to the Mosaic Law	Christ, the Secret of a Superior Lifestyle
	1 2	3 4	5 7	8 10	11 13
Topics	Revelation	Leader	Priest	Sacrifice	Example
	A Better Way				A Living Way
Place	Written to Scattered Jewish Christians				
Time	About A.D. 64–68				

DECEMBER 9 □ DAY 344
HEBREWS 1–2
Christ, Superior to Angels

 OVERVIEW God has revealed himself and his plans in many ways through long centuries of Old Testament history, but now he has provided the climactic chapter in the person of his Son. Angels have frequently been involved in God's program, but none of them could claim to be a royal Son of the King or suffer and die as the Savior of humankind. Only Jesus Christ could do that! Though made a little lower than the angels for a time, he provided the way to lift both Jews and Gentiles into the family of God through his sacrificial death.

Chapter 1				Chapter 2			
Christ, the Superior							
Message		Messenger		Savior		Sufferer	
1	3	4	14	1	8	9	18
Better than the Angels				A Little Lower than the Angels			

 YOUR DAILY WALK Can you complete this comparison chart from the first two verses of the book of Hebrews?

God has spoken . . .
in time past   in these last days
to the fathers   _____
by the prophets   _____

In the creation, the Lord made humans like himself; but in the redemption he made himself like humans.

What God has said in the past is important, but what he is saying *today* through his Son is even more important! As you read today's passage, look for statements describing who Christ is and what he has accomplished. You might want to share the results of your study with a friend who is seriously considering the claims of Christ. It might be just the evidence that person needs to find new life in the one before whom even angels bow!

 INSIGHT "Let Me Express It This Way. . . ." Hebrews 1:3 says that "The Son reflects God's own glory, and everything about him represents God exactly." Do you want to know what the character of the invisible God is like? Just study the character of his Son, who came in the flesh.

CHAPTER 1
Long ago God spoke many times and in many ways to our ancestors through the prophets. ²But now in these final days, he has spoken to us through his Son. God promised everything to the Son as an inheritance, and through the Son he made the universe and everything in it. ³The Son reflects God's own glory, and everything about him represents God exactly. He sustains the universe by the mighty power of his command. After he died to cleanse us from the stain of sin, he sat down in the place of honor at the right hand of the majestic God of heaven.

⁴This shows that God's Son is far greater than the angels, just as the name God gave him is far greater than their names. ⁵For God never said to any angel what he said to Jesus:

"You are my Son.
     Today I have become your Father.*"

1:5a Or *Today I reveal you as my Son.* Ps 2:7.

And again God said,

"I will be his Father,
   and he will be my Son."*

[6] And then, when he presented his honored* Son to the world, God said, "Let all the angels of God worship him."* [7] God calls his angels

"messengers swift as the wind,
   and servants made of flaming fire."*

[8] But to his Son he says,

"Your throne, O God, endures forever
   and ever.
Your royal power is expressed in
   righteousness.
[9] You love what is right and hate what is
   wrong.
Therefore God, your God, has anointed
   you,
pouring out the oil of joy on you
   more than on anyone else."*

[10] And,

"Lord, in the beginning you laid the
   foundation of the earth,
and the heavens are the work of your
   hands.
[11] Even they will perish, but you remain
   forever.
They will wear out like old clothing.
[12] You will roll them up like an old coat.
They will fade away like old clothing.
But you are always the same;
   you will never grow old."*

[13] And God never said to an angel, as he did to his Son,

"Sit in honor at my right hand
   until I humble your enemies,
   making them a footstool under your
   feet."*

[14] But angels are only servants. They are spirits sent from God to care for those who will receive salvation.

CHAPTER 2

So we must listen very carefully to the truth we have heard, or we may drift away from it. [2] The message God delivered through angels has always proved true, and the people were punished for every violation of the law and every act of disobedience. [3] What makes us think that we can escape if we are indifferent to this great salvation that was announced by the Lord Jesus himself? It was passed on* to us by those who heard him speak, [4] and God verified the message by signs and wonders and various miracles and by giving gifts of the Holy Spirit whenever he chose to do so.

[5] And furthermore, the future world we are talking about will not be controlled by angels. [6] For somewhere in the Scriptures it says,

"What is man that you should think of
   him,
and the son of man* that you should
   care for him?
[7] For a little while you made him lower
   than the angels,
and you crowned him with glory
   and honor.*
[8] You gave him authority over all
   things."*

Now when it says "all things," it means nothing is left out. But we have not yet seen all of this happen. [9] What we do see is Jesus, who "for a little while was made lower than the angels" and now is "crowned with glory and honor" because he suffered death for us. Yes, by God's grace, Jesus tasted death for everyone in all the world. [10] And it was only right that God—who made everything and for whom everything was made—should bring his many children into glory. Through the suffering of Jesus, God made him a perfect leader, one fit to bring them into their salvation.

[11] So now Jesus and the ones he makes holy have the same Father. That is why Jesus is not ashamed to call them his brothers and sisters.* [12] For he said to God,

"I will declare the wonder of your
   name to my brothers and sisters.*
I will praise you among all your
   people."

[13] He also said, "I will put my trust in him." And in the same context he said, "Here I am—together with the children God has given me."*

[14] Because God's children are human beings—made of flesh and blood—Jesus

1:5b 2 Sam 7:14.   1:6a Greek *firstborn*.   1:6b Deut 32:43.   1:7 Ps 104:4.   1:8-9 Ps 45:6-7.   1:10-12 Ps 102:25-27.   1:13 Ps 110:1.
2:3 Or *and confirmed*.   2:6 Or *Son of Man*.   2:7 Some manuscripts add *You put him in charge of everything you made*.   2:6-8 Ps 8:4-6.
2:11 Greek *his brothers*; also in 2:17.   2:12 Greek *my brothers*. Ps 22:22.   2:13 Isa 8:17-18.

also became flesh and blood by being born in human form. For only as a human being could he die, and only by dying could he break the power of the Devil, who had the power of death. [15]Only in this way could he deliver those who have lived all their lives as slaves to the fear of dying.

[16]We all know that Jesus came to help the descendants of Abraham, not to help the angels. [17]Therefore, it was necessary for Jesus to be in every respect like us, his brothers and sisters, so that he could be our merciful and faithful High Priest before God. He then could offer a sacrifice that would take away the sins of the people. [18]Since he himself has gone through suffering and temptation, he is able to help us when we are being tempted.

DECEMBER 10 □ DAY 345
HEBREWS 3–4
Christ, Superior to Moses and Joshua

OVERVIEW Humanly speaking, Israel's two greatest leaders during its establishment as a nation were Moses and Joshua. Moses was the great deliverer from Egyptian slavery—Israel's savior from captivity. Joshua was Israel's commander in chief during the conquest of Canaan—Israel's provider of peace. But both were merely servants and ministers of God in caring for his people. By contrast, Jesus is the Son of God who formed the people in the first place! Because of the nation's unbelief, Moses and Joshua were unable to provide the ultimate peace and rest that the people sought. Today "there is a special rest still waiting for the people of God" (4:9)—a rest found only in Jesus Christ.

Chapter 3	Chapter 4
Christ, Superior Because	
He Is the Son, Not the Servant	He Passes the "Rest Test"
Better than Moses	Better than Joshua

A field that has rested gives a bountiful crop.

YOUR DAILY WALK Sit down in a comfortable chair, grab a pencil or pen, and in the margin of this page note all the ways you can think of in which you are resting today. (For example, "Resting my tired feet, resting in my faith in Christ, resting in the confidence that God never rests . . .")

The writer to the Hebrews declares, "There is a special rest still waiting for the people of God" (4:9). This relates first to the individual's ceasing from all his or her efforts to *earn* salvation (an impossible task) and appropriating with restful faith the finished work of Jesus Christ. Is that a rest you are enjoying today?

But for the people of God, there is a second rest—a rest the wandering Israelites never experienced because they never learned to be content. It is the rest of walking day by day in God's strength rather than your own. Philippians 4:13 says it all: "For I can do everything with the help of [and rest confidently in] Christ who gives me the strength I need." Is that a rest you know firsthand?

INSIGHT The Results of Christ's Priestly Work
In Old Testament times only the priests were able to approach God in
worshipful service. But because Jesus suffered and knows what we are
going through, we now can "come boldly to the throne of our gracious
God" (4:15-16). The right of priestly approach is extended to all Christians.
Are you taking full advantage of this marvelous privilege?

C H A P T E R 3

And so, dear brothers and sisters who belong to God* and are bound for heaven, think about this Jesus whom we declare to be God's Messenger and High Priest. ²For he was faithful to God, who appointed him, just as Moses served faithfully and was entrusted with God's entire house. ³But Jesus deserves far more glory than Moses, just as a person who builds a fine house deserves more praise than the house itself. ⁴For every house has a builder, but God is the one who made everything.

⁵Moses was certainly faithful in God's house, but only as a servant. His work was an illustration of the truths God would reveal later. ⁶But Christ, the faithful Son, was in charge of the entire household. And we are God's household, if we keep up our courage and remain confident in our hope in Christ. ⁷That is why the Holy Spirit says,

"Today you must listen to his voice.
⁸ Don't harden your hearts against him
   as Israel did when they rebelled,
   when they tested God's patience
   in the wilderness.
⁹ There your ancestors tried my patience,
   even though they saw my miracles
   for forty years.
¹⁰ So I was angry with them, and I said,
   'Their hearts always turn away from
   me.
   They refuse to do what I tell them.'
¹¹ So in my anger I made a vow:
   'They will never enter my place of
   rest.'"*

¹²Be careful then, dear brothers and sisters. Make sure that your own hearts are not evil and unbelieving, turning you away from the living God. ¹³You must warn each other every day, as long as it is called "today," so that none of you will be deceived by sin and hardened against God. ¹⁴For if we are faithful to the end, trusting God just as firmly as when we first believed, we will

share in all that belongs to Christ. ¹⁵But never forget the warning:

"Today you must listen to his voice.
   Don't harden your hearts against him
   as Israel did when they rebelled."*

¹⁶And who were those people who rebelled against God, even though they heard his voice? Weren't they the ones Moses led out of Egypt? ¹⁷And who made God angry for forty years? Wasn't it the people who sinned, whose bodies fell in the wilderness? ¹⁸And to whom was God speaking when he vowed that they would never enter his place of rest? He was speaking to those who disobeyed him. ¹⁹So we see that they were not allowed to enter his rest because of their unbelief.

C H A P T E R 4

God's promise of entering his place of rest still stands, so we ought to tremble with fear that some of you might fail to get there. ²For this Good News—that God has prepared a place of rest—has been announced to us just as it was to them. But it did them no good because they didn't believe what God told them.* ³For only we who believe can enter his place of rest. As for those who didn't believe, God said,

"In my anger I made a vow:
   'They will never enter my place of
   rest,'"*

even though his place of rest has been ready since he made the world. ⁴We know it is ready because the Scriptures mention the seventh day, saying, "On the seventh day God rested from all his work."* ⁵But in the other passage God said, "They will never enter my place of rest."* ⁶So God's rest is there for people to enter. But those who formerly heard the Good News failed to enter because they disobeyed God. ⁷So God set another time for entering his place of rest, and that time is today. God announced this through David a long time later in the words already quoted:

3:1 Greek *And so, holy brothers.*   3:7-11 Ps 95:7-11.   3:15 Ps 95:7-8.   4:2 Some manuscripts read *they didn't share the faith of those who listened [to God].*   4:3 Ps 95:11.   4:4 Gen 2:2.   4:5 Ps 95:11.

"Today you must listen to his voice. Don't harden your hearts against him."*

⁸This new place of rest was not the land of Canaan, where Joshua led them. If it had been, God would not have spoken later about another day of rest. ⁹So there is a special rest* still waiting for the people of God. ¹⁰For all who enter into God's rest will find rest from their labors, just as God rested after creating the world. ¹¹Let us do our best to enter that place of rest. For anyone who disobeys God, as the people of Israel did, will fall.

¹²For the word of God is full of living power. It is sharper than the sharpest knife,

4:7 Ps 95:7-8.   4:9 Or *Sabbath rest.*

cutting deep into our innermost thoughts and desires. It exposes us for what we really are. ¹³Nothing in all creation can hide from him. Everything is naked and exposed before his eyes. This is the God to whom we must explain all that we have done.

¹⁴That is why we have a great High Priest who has gone to heaven, Jesus the Son of God. Let us cling to him and never stop trusting him. ¹⁵This High Priest of ours understands our weaknesses, for he faced all of the same temptations we do, yet he did not sin. ¹⁶So let us come boldly to the throne of our gracious God. There we will receive his mercy, and we will find grace to help us when we need it.

DECEMBER 11 □ DAY 346
HEBREWS 5–7
Christ, Superior to Aaron

 OVERVIEW At the center of Israel's life was its worship in the Tabernacle and later in the Temple. Crucial to that worship was the priesthood, beginning with the high priest, Aaron, and his sons. But the Lord Jesus Christ is a superior Priest because he belongs to a superior order: the order of Melchizedek, the king-priest (Genesis 14:18-20). Why? Because Melchizedek came before Aaron, and his priesthood was a timeless one without beginning or end. In the same way, Christ is an eternal Priest, who died once for all time as the eternal sacrifice for sin. These difficult truths, the writer of Hebrews admits, require maturity to grasp but are life-changing in their impact.

Chapter 5	Chapter 6	Chapter 7
Christ, the High Priest	"Grow Up in Christ!"	Christ, the Eternal Priest
A Better Priest	A Better Response	A Better Priesthood

 YOUR DAILY WALK Complete the following sentences:
- The priest's job was to . . .
- The priest's job was never finished because . . .
- The priest acted as a bridge builder between holy God and sinful humanity by . . .

The true meaning of the gospel is not what a person says about it, but what he or she does with it.

One of the doctrines recaptured and reemphasized in the Reformation was the priesthood of the believer. Each Christian, as a member of the body of Christ, is given the role of a priest (1 Peter 2:9), serving under Jesus Christ, the great High Priest, by praying for others (1 Timothy 2:1) and showing others what true worship is all about (1 Peter 2:9).

Now put your name in place of "the priest" in the three statements above, and complete them again:
- My job is to . . .
- My job is never finished because . . .
- I am to act as a bridge builder between holy God and sinful humanity by . . .

 INSIGHT High Marks for a High Priest
The writer to the Hebrews lists these identifying marks for the high priest: (1) He was a man chosen by God. (2) He represented mankind to God. (3) He offered gifts and sacrifices to God on behalf of humankind. (4) He exercised compassion in his ministry for God.

CHAPTER 5

Now a high priest is a man chosen to represent other human beings in their dealings with God. He presents their gifts to God and offers their sacrifices for sins. ²And because he is human, he is able to deal gently with the people, though they are ignorant and wayward. For he is subject to the same weaknesses they have. ³That is why he has to offer sacrifices, both for their sins and for his own sins. ⁴And no one can become a high priest simply because he wants such an honor. He has to be called by God for this work, just as Aaron was.

⁵That is why Christ did not exalt himself to become High Priest. No, he was chosen by God, who said to him,

"You are my Son.
    Today I have become your Father.*"

⁶And in another passage God said to him,

"You are a priest forever
    in the line of Melchizedek."*

⁷While Jesus was here on earth, he offered prayers and pleadings, with a loud cry and tears, to the one who could deliver him out of death. And God heard his prayers because of his reverence for God. ⁸So even though Jesus was God's Son, he learned obedience from the things he suffered. ⁹In this way, God qualified him as a perfect High Priest, and he became the source of eternal salvation for all those who obey him. ¹⁰And God designated him to be a High Priest in the line of Melchizedek.

¹¹There is so much more we would like to say about this. But you don't seem to listen, so it's hard to make you understand. ¹²You have been Christians a long time now, and you ought to be teaching others. Instead, you need someone to teach you again the basic things a beginner must

learn about the Scriptures.* You are like babies who drink only milk and cannot eat solid food. ¹³And a person who is living on milk isn't very far along in the Christian life and doesn't know much about doing what is right. ¹⁴Solid food is for those who are mature, who have trained themselves to recognize the difference between right and wrong and then do what is right.

CHAPTER 6

So let us stop going over the basics of Christianity* again and again. Let us go on instead and become mature in our understanding. Surely we don't need to start all over again with the importance of turning away from evil deeds and placing our faith in God. ²You don't need further instruction about baptisms, the laying on of hands, the resurrection of the dead, and eternal judgment. ³And so, God willing, we will move forward to further understanding.

⁴For it is impossible to restore to repentance those who were once enlightened—those who have experienced the good things of heaven and shared in the Holy Spirit, ⁵who have tasted the goodness of the word of God and the power of the age to come—⁶and who then turn away from God. It is impossible to bring such people to repentance again because they are nailing the Son of God to the cross again by rejecting him, holding him up to public shame.

⁷When the ground soaks up the rain that falls on it and bears a good crop for the farmer, it has the blessing of God. ⁸But if a field bears thistles and thorns, it is useless. The farmer will condemn that field and burn it.

⁹Dear friends, even though we are talking like this, we really don't believe that it

5:5 Or Today I reveal you as my Son. Ps 2:7.   **5:6** Ps 110:4.   **5:12** Or about the oracles of God.   **6:1** Or the basics about Christ.

applies to you. We are confident that you are meant for better things, things that come with salvation. [10]For God is not unfair. He will not forget how hard you have worked for him and how you have shown your love to him by caring for other Christians, as you still do. [11]Our great desire is that you will keep right on loving others as long as life lasts, in order to make certain that what you hope for will come true. [12]Then you will not become spiritually dull and indifferent. Instead, you will follow the example of those who are going to inherit God's promises because of their faith and patience.

[13]For example, there was God's promise to Abraham. Since there was no one greater to swear by, God took an oath in his own name, saying:

[14] "I will certainly bless you richly,
and I will multiply your descendants into countless millions."*

[15]Then Abraham waited patiently, and he received what God had promised.

[16]When people take an oath, they call on someone greater than themselves to hold them to it. And without any question that oath is binding. [17]God also bound himself with an oath, so that those who received the promise could be perfectly sure that he would never change his mind. [18]So God has given us both his promise and his oath. These two things are unchangeable because it is impossible for God to lie. Therefore, we who have fled to him for refuge can take new courage, for we can hold on to his promise with confidence.

[19]This confidence is like a strong and trustworthy anchor for our souls. It leads us through the curtain of heaven into God's inner sanctuary. [20]Jesus has already gone in there for us. He has become our eternal High Priest in the line of Melchizedek.

CHAPTER 7

This Melchizedek was king of the city of Salem and also a priest of God Most High. When Abraham was returning home after winning a great battle against many kings, Melchizedek met him and blessed him. [2]Then Abraham took a tenth of all he had won in the battle and gave it to Melchizedek. His name means "king of justice." He is also "king of peace" because *Salem*

means "peace." [3]There is no record of his father or mother or any of his ancestors—no beginning or end to his life. He remains a priest forever, resembling the Son of God.

[4]Consider then how great this Melchizedek was. Even Abraham, the great patriarch of Israel, recognized how great Melchizedek was by giving him a tenth of what he had taken in battle. [5]Now the priests, who are descendants of Levi, are commanded in the law of Moses to collect a tithe from all the people, even though they are their own relatives.* [6]But Melchizedek, who was not even related to Levi, collected a tenth from Abraham. And Melchizedek placed a blessing upon Abraham, the one who had already received the promises of God. [7]And without question, the person who has the power to bless is always greater than the person who is blessed.

[8]In the case of Jewish priests, tithes are paid to men who will die. But Melchizedek is greater than they are, because we are told that he lives on. [9]In addition, we might even say that Levi's descendants, the ones who collect the tithe, paid a tithe to Melchizedek through their ancestor Abraham. [10]For although Levi wasn't born yet, the seed from which he came was in Abraham's loins when Melchizedek collected the tithe from him.

[11]And finally, if the priesthood of Levi could have achieved God's purposes—and it was that priesthood on which the law was based—why did God need to send a different priest from the line of Melchizedek, instead of from the line of Levi and Aaron?*

[12]And when the priesthood is changed, the law must also be changed to permit it. [13]For the one we are talking about belongs to a different tribe, whose members do not serve at the altar. [14]What I mean is, our Lord came from the tribe of Judah, and Moses never mentioned Judah in connection with the priesthood.

[15]The change in God's law is even more evident from the fact that a different priest, who is like Melchizedek, has now come. [16]He became a priest, not by meeting the old requirement of belonging to the tribe of Levi, but by the power of a life that cannot be destroyed. [17]And the psalmist pointed this out when he said of Christ,

"You are a priest forever
in the line of Melchizedek."*

[18] Yes, the old requirement about the priesthood was set aside because it was weak and useless. [19] For the law made nothing perfect, and now a better hope has taken its place. And that is how we draw near to God.

[20] God took an oath that Christ would always be a priest, but he never did this for any other priest. [21] Only to Jesus did he say,

"The Lord has taken an oath
and will not break his vow:
'You are a priest forever.'"*

[22] Because of God's oath, it is Jesus who guarantees the effectiveness of this better covenant.

[23] Another difference is that there were many priests under the old system. When one priest died, another had to take his place. [24] But Jesus remains a priest forever; his priesthood will never end. [25] Therefore he is able, once and forever, to save* everyone who comes to God through him. He lives forever to plead with God on their behalf.

[26] He is the kind of high priest we need because he is holy and blameless, unstained by sin. He has now been set apart from sinners, and he has been given the highest place of honor in heaven. [27] He does not need to offer sacrifices every day like the other high priests. They did this for their own sins first and then for the sins of the people. But Jesus did this once for all when he sacrificed himself on the cross. [28] Those who were high priests under the law of Moses were limited by human weakness. But after the law was given, God appointed his Son with an oath, and his Son has been made perfect forever.

7:17 Ps 110:4.   **7:21** Ps 110:4.   **7:25** Or *able to save completely.*

DECEMBER 12 ☐ DAY 347
HEBREWS 8–10
Christ, Superior to the Mosaic Law

 OVERVIEW Aaron and his sons ministered in a Tabernacle built according to the specifications God gave to Moses. They offered animal and meal sacrifices in accordance with divine regulations. All of this was part of the Mosaic law that God established as a covenant with his people on Mount Sinai. Consequently, if Jesus Christ is superior to both Moses and Aaron, it follows that God has established with him a superior covenant based upon a superior sacrifice. Even the Old Testament bore witness that the Mosaic system was temporary and would be replaced by a new covenant—a covenant made with the Messiah and based upon the once-for-all-time sacrifice of his life.

Chapter 8	Chapter 9	Chapter 10
A Better Covenant	A Better Tabernacle	A Better Sacrifice
Christ	Better than the Old Covenant	

 YOUR DAILY WALK Hebrews 10 has been described as the "lettuce" chapter. Three times in the space of four verses (22-25) you'll find the phrase "Let us . . ." And whenever you do, you can be sure the author has provided ample reason to do precisely that! "And so, dear friends, we can boldly enter . . . because of the blood of Jesus. . . . And since we

The faintest whisper of encouragement uttered to a Christian brother or sister is heard in heaven.

have a great High Priest who rules over God's people, let us go right into the presence of God . . . let us hold tightly to the hope we say we have. . . . Think of ways to encourage one another to outbursts of love and good deeds. And let us not neglect our meeting together" (10:19-25). The two elements—exhortation and explanation—are inseparable, for without the second, there is no motivation to do the first. Duty in the Christian life flows naturally from doctrine.

Notice in each case the author uses the word *us.* There is a mutual responsibility for Christians to consider one another . . . be accountable to one another . . . encourage one another. Ask someone to help you with your memory work or a personal-growth project this week by checking up on your progress each day. You'll both be glad you did!

 INSIGHT The Timely, Superior New Covenant
God's covenant with Jesus Christ is obviously *new* in point of time; but the Greek word translated "new" also emphasizes its newness "in respect to form or quality" and, therefore, its superiority to the old covenant, which it supersedes.

CHAPTER 8

Here is the main point: Our High Priest sat down in the place of highest honor in heaven, at God's right hand. ²There he ministers in the sacred tent, the true place of worship that was built by the Lord and not by human hands.

³And since every high priest is required to offer gifts and sacrifices, our High Priest must make an offering, too. ⁴If he were here on earth, he would not even be a priest, since there already are priests who offer the gifts required by the law of Moses. ⁵They serve in a place of worship that is only a copy, a shadow of the real one in heaven. For when Moses was getting ready to build the Tabernacle, God gave him this warning: "Be sure that you make everything according to the design I have shown you here on the mountain."* ⁶But our High Priest has been given a ministry that is far superior to the ministry of those who serve under the old laws, for he is the one who guarantees for us a better covenant with God, based on better promises.

⁷If the first covenant had been faultless, there would have been no need for a second covenant to replace it. ⁸But God himself found fault with the old one when he said:

"The day will come, says the Lord,
    when I will make a new covenant
    with the people of Israel and Judah.
⁹ This covenant will not be like the one
    I made with their ancestors
    when I took them by the hand

and led them out of the land of
    Egypt.
They did not remain faithful to my
    covenant,
    so I turned my back on them, says
    the Lord.
¹⁰ But this is the new covenant I will make
    with the people of Israel on that day,
    says the Lord:
I will put my laws in their minds
    so they will understand them,
and I will write them on their hearts
    so they will obey them.
I will be their God,
    and they will be my people.
¹¹ And they will not need to teach their
    neighbors,
    nor will they need to teach their
    family,
    saying, 'You should know the Lord.'
For everyone, from the least to the
    greatest,
    will already know me.
¹² And I will forgive their wrongdoings,
    and I will never again remember
    their sins."*

¹³When God speaks of a new covenant, it means he has made the first one obsolete. It is now out of date and ready to be put aside.

CHAPTER 9

Now in that first covenant between God and Israel, there were regulations for worship and a sacred tent here on earth. ²There were two rooms in this tent. In the first room were a lampstand, a table, and loaves

8:5 Exod 25:40; 26:30.   8:8-12 Jer 31:31-34.

of holy bread on the table. This was called the Holy Place. [3]Then there was a curtain, and behind the curtain was the second room called the Most Holy Place. [4]In that room were a gold incense altar and a wooden chest called the Ark of the Covenant, which was covered with gold on all sides. Inside the Ark were a gold jar containing some manna, Aaron's staff that sprouted leaves, and the stone tablets of the covenant with the Ten Commandments written on them. [5]The glorious cherubim were above the Ark. Their wings were stretched out over the Ark's cover, the place of atonement. But we cannot explain all of these things now.

[6]When these things were all in place, the priests went in and out of the first room* regularly as they performed their religious duties. [7]But only the high priest goes into the Most Holy Place, and only once a year, and always with blood, which he offers to God to cover his own sins and the sins the people have committed in ignorance. [8]By these regulations the Holy Spirit revealed that the Most Holy Place was not open to the people as long as the first room and the entire system it represents were still in use.

[9]This is an illustration pointing to the present time. For the gifts and sacrifices that the priests offer are not able to cleanse the consciences of the people who bring them. [10]For that old system deals only with food and drink and ritual washing—external regulations that are in effect only until their limitations can be corrected.

[11]So Christ has now become the High Priest over all the good things that have come. He has entered that great, perfect sanctuary in heaven, not made by human hands and not part of this created world. [12]Once for all time he took blood into that Most Holy Place, but not the blood of goats and calves. He took his own blood, and with it he secured our salvation forever.

[13]Under the old system, the blood of goats and bulls and the ashes of a young cow could cleanse people's bodies from ritual defilement. [14]Just think how much more the blood of Christ will purify our hearts from deeds that lead to death so that we can worship the living God. For by the power of the eternal Spirit, Christ offered himself to God as a perfect sacrifice for our sins. [15]That is why he is the one who medi-

ates the new covenant between God and people, so that all who are invited can receive the eternal inheritance God has promised them. For Christ died to set them free from the penalty of the sins they had committed under that first covenant.

[16]Now when someone dies and leaves a will, no one gets anything until it is proved that the person who wrote the will* is dead.* [17]The will goes into effect only after the death of the person who wrote it. While the person is still alive, no one can use the will to get any of the things promised to them.

[18]That is why blood was required under the first covenant as a proof of death. [19]For after Moses had given the people all of God's laws, he took the blood of calves and goats, along with water, and sprinkled both the book of God's laws and all the people, using branches of hyssop bushes and scarlet wool. [20]Then he said, "This blood confirms the covenant God has made with you."* [21]And in the same way, he sprinkled blood on the sacred tent and on everything used for worship. [22]In fact, we can say that according to the law of Moses, nearly everything was purified by sprinkling with blood. Without the shedding of blood, there is no forgiveness of sins.

[23]That is why the earthly tent and everything in it—which were copies of things in heaven—had to be purified by the blood of animals. But the real things in heaven had to be purified with far better sacrifices than the blood of animals.

[24]For Christ has entered into heaven itself to appear now before God as our Advocate.* He did not go into the earthly place of worship, for that was merely a copy of the real Temple in heaven. [25]Nor did he enter heaven to offer himself again and again, like the earthly high priest who enters the Most Holy Place year after year to offer the blood of an animal. [26]If that had been necessary, he would have had to die again and again, ever since the world began. But no! He came once for all time, at the end of the age, to remove the power of sin forever by his sacrificial death for us.

[27]And just as it is destined that each person dies only once and after that comes judgment, [28]so also Christ died only once as a sacrifice to take away the sins of many people. He will come again but not to deal

9:6 Greek *first tent;* also in 9:8.   **9:16a** Or *covenant.*   **9:16b** Or *Now when someone makes a covenant, it is necessary to ratify it with the death of a sacrifice.*   **9:20** Exod 24:8.   **9:24** Greek *on our behalf.*

with our sins again. This time he will bring salvation to all those who are eagerly waiting for him.

CHAPTER 10

The old system in the law of Moses was only a shadow of the things to come, not the reality of the good things Christ has done for us. The sacrifices under the old system were repeated again and again, year after year, but they were never able to provide perfect cleansing for those who came to worship. ²If they could have provided perfect cleansing, the sacrifices would have stopped, for the worshipers would have been purified once for all time, and their feelings of guilt would have disappeared.

³But just the opposite happened. Those yearly sacrifices reminded them of their sins year after year. ⁴For it is not possible for the blood of bulls and goats to take away sins. ⁵That is why Christ, when he came into the world, said,

"You did not want animal sacrifices
    and grain offerings.
But you have given me a body so
    that I may obey you.
⁶ No, you were not pleased with animals
    burned on the altar
    or with other offerings for sin.
⁷ Then I said, 'Look, I have come to do
    your will, O God—
    just as it is written about me in the
    Scriptures.'"*

⁸Christ said, "You did not want animal sacrifices or grain offerings or animals burned on the altar or other offerings for sin, nor were you pleased with them" (though they are required by the law of Moses). ⁹Then he added, "Look, I have come to do your will." He cancels the first covenant in order to establish the second. ¹⁰And what God wants is for us to be made holy by the sacrifice of the body of Jesus Christ once for all time.

¹¹Under the old covenant, the priest stands before the altar day after day, offering sacrifices that can never take away sins. ¹²But our High Priest offered himself to God as one sacrifice for sins, good for all time. Then he sat down at the place of highest honor at God's right hand. ¹³There he waits until his enemies are humbled as a footstool under his feet. ¹⁴For by that one offering he perfected forever all those whom he is making holy.

¹⁵And the Holy Spirit also testifies that this is so. First he says,

¹⁶ "This is the new covenant I will make
    with my people on that day, says the
        Lord:
I will put my laws in their hearts
    so they will understand them,
and I will write them on their minds
    so they will obey them."

¹⁷Then he adds,

"I will never again remember
    their sins and lawless deeds."*

¹⁸Now when sins have been forgiven, there is no need to offer any more sacrifices.

¹⁹And so, dear brothers and sisters, we can boldly enter heaven's Most Holy Place because of the blood of Jesus. ²⁰This is the new, life-giving way that Christ has opened up for us through the sacred curtain, by means of his death for us.*

²¹And since we have a great High Priest who rules over God's people, ²²let us go right into the presence of God, with true hearts fully trusting him. For our evil consciences have been sprinkled with Christ's blood to make us clean, and our bodies have been washed with pure water.

²³Without wavering, let us hold tightly to the hope we say we have, for God can be trusted to keep his promise. ²⁴Think of ways to encourage one another to outbursts of love and good deeds. ²⁵And let us not neglect our meeting together, as some people do, but encourage and warn each other, especially now that the day of his coming back again is drawing near.

²⁶Dear friends, if we deliberately continue sinning after we have received a full knowledge of the truth, there is no other sacrifice that will cover these sins. ²⁷There will be nothing to look forward to but the terrible expectation of God's judgment and the raging fire that will consume his enemies. ²⁸Anyone who refused to obey the law of Moses was put to death without mercy on the testimony of two or three witnesses. ²⁹Think how much more terrible the punishment will be for those who have trampled on the Son of God and have treated the blood of the covenant as if it were common and unholy. Such people

10:5-7 Ps 40:6-8.   **10:16-17** Jer 31:33-34.   **10:20** Greek *his flesh.*

have insulted and enraged the Holy Spirit who brings God's mercy to his people.

³⁰For we know the one who said,

"I will take vengeance.
I will repay those who deserve it."

He also said,

"The Lord will judge his own people."*

³¹It is a terrible thing to fall into the hands of the living God.

³²Don't ever forget those early days when you first learned about Christ. Remember how you remained faithful even though it meant terrible suffering. ³³Sometimes you were exposed to public ridicule and were beaten, and sometimes you helped others who were suffering the same things. ³⁴You suffered along with those who were thrown into jail. When all you

10:30 Deut 32:35-36.   10:37-38 Hab 2:3-4.

owned was taken from you, you accepted it with joy. You knew you had better things waiting for you in eternity.

³⁵Do not throw away this confident trust in the Lord, no matter what happens. Remember the great reward it brings you! ³⁶Patient endurance is what you need now, so you will continue to do God's will. Then you will receive all that he has promised.

³⁷ "For in just a little while,
     the Coming One will come and not
        delay.
³⁸ And a righteous person will live by
        faith.
     But I will have no pleasure in anyone
        who turns away."*

³⁹But we are not like those who turn their backs on God and seal their fate. We have faith that assures our salvation.

DECEMBER 13 □ DAY 348
HEBREWS 11–13
Christ, Supreme Example of Faith

OVERVIEW The letter to the Hebrews closes with an appeal to leave behind the obsolete order of the old covenant and to approach God by the new and living way Jesus made possible through his death. Through steadfast hope and faith it is possible to have a firm assurance of those eternal truths that are invisible to the outward eye. Such forward-looking faith characterized the Old Testament saints who gained God's approval. They lived their lives on the basis of God's promises—promises whose fulfillment came centuries later—and it is their example and Christ's that you are called to follow.

Chapter 11	Chapter 12	Chapter 13
Requirement for Fellowship	Pattern for Fellowship	Proof of Fellowship
Confession	Christ	Conduct

Live your life in such a way that it would not make sense if God did not exist.

YOUR DAILY WALK In Cooperstown, New York, stands a monument to the great men who have excelled at the game of baseball. They are all there—Ruth . . . DiMaggio . . . Cobb—men who helped make baseball a household word, filling the Baseball Hall of Fame and providing encouragement for those who would seek to follow in their steps. If you have any doubts that it is humanly possible to hit sixty home runs in a year or bat safely in fifty-six consecutive games, you have only to visit Cooperstown to remove your doubts. It can be done. They did it!

Are you discouraged in your walk with God? Have you almost

concluded that the Christian life is a hopeless assignment, that walking by faith in a godless society is impossible? Then spend some long moments in the Believers' Hall of Fame—Hebrews 11. There you'll find those who excelled at the life of faith: Enoch . . . Abraham . . . Joseph . . . and many others. If you have any doubts that it is spiritually possible to walk by faith, just study their lives!

Then join their ranks by writing a short paragraph about yourself as you'd want it to appear in Hebrews 11: "By faith [who?] walked with God by obediently [doing what?]."

 INSIGHT Faith at Work in a Workaday World
Hebrews 11 describes the faith-inspired steps of a shepherd, prophet, shipbuilder, itinerant rancher, and prince-turned-deliverer. Try to match up each profession with the right person.

CHAPTER 11

What is faith? It is the confident assurance that what we hope for is going to happen. It is the evidence of things we cannot yet see. ²God gave his approval to people in days of old because of their faith.

³By faith we understand that the entire universe was formed at God's command, that what we now see did not come from anything that can be seen.

⁴It was by faith that Abel brought a more acceptable offering to God than Cain did. God accepted Abel's offering to show that he was a righteous man. And although Abel is long dead, he still speaks to us because of his faith.

⁵It was by faith that Enoch was taken up to heaven without dying—"suddenly he disappeared because God took him."* But before he was taken up, he was approved as pleasing to God. ⁶So, you see, it is impossible to please God without faith. Anyone who wants to come to him must believe that there is a God and that he rewards those who sincerely seek him.

⁷It was by faith that Noah built an ark to save his family from the flood. He obeyed God, who warned him about something that had never happened before. By his faith he condemned the rest of the world and was made right in God's sight.

⁸It was by faith that Abraham obeyed when God called him to leave home and go to another land that God would give him as his inheritance. He went without knowing where he was going. ⁹And even when he reached the land God promised him, he lived there by faith—for he was like a foreigner, living in a tent. And so did Isaac and Jacob, to whom God gave the same prom-

ise. ¹⁰Abraham did this because he was confidently looking forward to a city with eternal foundations, a city designed and built by God.

¹¹It was by faith that Sarah together with Abraham was able to have a child, even though they were too old and Sarah was barren. Abraham believed that God would keep his promise.* ¹²And so a whole nation came from this one man, Abraham, who was too old to have any children—a nation with so many people that, like the stars of the sky and the sand on the seashore, there is no way to count them.

¹³All these faithful ones died without receiving what God had promised them, but they saw it all from a distance and welcomed the promises of God. They agreed that they were no more than foreigners and nomads here on earth. ¹⁴And obviously people who talk like that are looking forward to a country they can call their own. ¹⁵If they had meant the country they came from, they would have found a way to go back. ¹⁶But they were looking for a better place, a heavenly homeland. That is why God is not ashamed to be called their God, for he has prepared a heavenly city for them.

¹⁷It was by faith that Abraham offered Isaac as a sacrifice when God was testing him. Abraham, who had received God's promises, was ready to sacrifice his only son, Isaac, ¹⁸though God had promised him, "Isaac is the son through whom your descendants will be counted."* ¹⁹Abraham assumed that if Isaac died, God was able to bring him back to life again. And in a sense, Abraham did receive his son back from the dead.

11:5 Gen 5:24.   **11:11** Some manuscripts read *It was by faith that Sarah was able to have a child, even though she was too old and barren. Sarah believed that God would keep his promise.*   **11:18** Gen 21:12.

²⁰It was by faith that Isaac blessed his two sons, Jacob and Esau. He had confidence in what God was going to do in the future. ²¹It was by faith that Jacob, when he was old and dying, blessed each of Joseph's sons and bowed in worship as he leaned on his staff. ²²And it was by faith that Joseph, when he was about to die, confidently spoke of God's bringing the people of Israel out of Egypt. He was so sure of it that he commanded them to carry his bones with them when they left! ²³It was by faith that Moses' parents hid him for three months. They saw that God had given them an unusual child, and they were not afraid of what the king might do. ²⁴It was by faith that Moses, when he grew up, refused to be treated as the son of Pharaoh's daughter. ²⁵He chose to share the oppression of God's people instead of enjoying the fleeting pleasures of sin. ²⁶He thought it was better to suffer for the sake of the Messiah than to own the treasures of Egypt, for he was looking ahead to the great reward that God would give him. ²⁷It was by faith that Moses left the land of Egypt. He was not afraid of the king. Moses kept right on going because he kept his eyes on the one who is invisible. ²⁸It was by faith that Moses commanded the people of Israel to keep the Passover and to sprinkle blood on the doorposts so that the angel of death would not kill their firstborn sons. ²⁹It was by faith that the people of Israel went right through the Red Sea as though they were on dry ground. But when the Egyptians followed, they were all drowned. ³⁰It was by faith that the people of Israel marched around Jericho seven days, and the walls came crashing down. ³¹It was by faith that Rahab the prostitute did not die with all the others in her city who refused to obey God. For she had given a friendly welcome to the spies.

³²Well, how much more do I need to say? It would take too long to recount the stories of the faith of Gideon, Barak, Samson, Jephthah, David, Samuel, and all the prophets. ³³By faith these people overthrew kingdoms, ruled with justice, and received what God had promised them. They shut the mouths of lions, ³⁴quenched the flames of fire, and escaped death by the edge of the sword. Their weakness was turned to strength. They became strong in battle and put whole armies to flight. ³⁵Women received their loved ones back again from death.

But others trusted God and were tortured, preferring to die rather than turn from God and be free. They placed their hope in the resurrection to a better life. ³⁶Some were mocked, and their backs were cut open with whips. Others were chained in dungeons. ³⁷Some died by stoning, and some were sawed in half; others were killed with the sword. Some went about in skins of sheep and goats, hungry and oppressed and mistreated. ³⁸They were too good for this world. They wandered over deserts and mountains, hiding in caves and holes in the ground.

³⁹All of these people we have mentioned received God's approval because of their faith, yet none of them received all that God had promised. ⁴⁰For God had far better things in mind for us that would also benefit them, for they can't receive the prize at the end of the race until we finish the race.*

CHAPTER 12

Therefore, since we are surrounded by such a huge crowd of witnesses to the life of faith, let us strip off every weight that slows us down, especially the sin that so easily hinders our progress. And let us run with endurance the race that God has set before us. ²We do this by keeping our eyes on Jesus, on whom our faith depends from start to finish.* He was willing to die a shameful death on the cross because of the joy he knew would be his afterward. Now he is seated in the place of highest honor beside God's throne in heaven. ³Think about all he endured when sinful people did such terrible things to him, so that you don't become weary and give up. ⁴After all, you have not yet given your lives in your struggle against sin.

⁵And have you entirely forgotten the encouraging words God spoke to you, his children? He said,

"My child, don't ignore it when the
    Lord disciplines you,
and don't be discouraged when he
    corrects you.

11:40 Greek *for us, for they apart from us can't finish.*   12:2 Or *Jesus, the Originator and Perfecter of our faith.*

6 For the Lord disciplines those he loves,
    and he punishes those he accepts as
    his children."*

7As you endure this divine discipline, remember that God is treating you as his own children. Whoever heard of a child who was never disciplined? 8If God doesn't discipline you as he does all of his children, it means that you are illegitimate and are not really his children after all. 9Since we respect our earthly fathers who disciplined us, should we not all the more cheerfully submit to the discipline of our heavenly Father and live forever*?

10For our earthly fathers disciplined us for a few years, doing the best they knew how. But God's discipline is always right and good for us because it means we will share in his holiness. 11No discipline is enjoyable while it is happening—it is painful! But afterward there will be a quiet harvest of right living for those who are trained in this way.

12So take a new grip with your tired hands and stand firm on your shaky legs. 13Mark out a straight path for your feet. Then those who follow you, though they are weak and lame, will not stumble and fall but will become strong.

14Try to live in peace with everyone, and seek to live a clean and holy life, for those who are not holy will not see the Lord. 15Look after each other so that none of you will miss out on the special favor of God. Watch out that no bitter root of unbelief rises up among you, for whenever it springs up, many are corrupted by its poison. 16Make sure that no one is immoral or godless like Esau. He traded his birthright as the oldest son for a single meal. 17And afterward, when he wanted his father's blessing, he was rejected. It was too late for repentance, even though he wept bitter tears.

18You have not come to a physical mountain, to a place of flaming fire, darkness, gloom, and whirlwind, as the Israelites did at Mount Sinai when God gave them his laws. 19For they heard an awesome trumpet blast and a voice with a message so terrible that they begged God to stop speaking. 20They staggered back under God's command: "If even an animal touches the mountain, it must be stoned to death."* 21Moses himself was so frightened at the sight that he said, "I am terrified and trembling."*

22No, you have come to Mount Zion, to the city of the living God, the heavenly Jerusalem, and to thousands of angels in joyful assembly. 23You have come to the assembly of God's firstborn children, whose names are written in heaven. You have come to God himself, who is the judge of all people. And you have come to the spirits of the redeemed in heaven who have now been made perfect. 24You have come to Jesus, the one who mediates the new covenant between God and people, and to the sprinkled blood, which graciously forgives instead of crying out for vengeance as the blood of Abel did.

25See to it that you obey God, the one who is speaking to you. For if the people of Israel did not escape when they refused to listen to Moses, the earthly messenger, how terrible our danger if we reject the One who speaks to us from heaven! 26When God spoke from Mount Sinai his voice shook the earth, but now he makes another promise: "Once again I will shake not only the earth but the heavens also."* 27This means that the things on earth will be shaken, so that only eternal things will be left.

28Since we are receiving a kingdom that cannot be destroyed, let us be thankful and please God by worshiping him with holy fear and awe. 29For our God is a consuming fire.

CHAPTER 13

Continue to love each other with true Christian love.* 2Don't forget to show hospitality to strangers, for some who have done this have entertained angels without realizing it! 3Don't forget about those in prison. Suffer with them as though you were there yourself. Share the sorrow of those being mistreated, as though you feel their pain in your own bodies.

4Give honor to marriage, and remain faithful to one another in marriage. God will surely judge people who are immoral and those who commit adultery.

5Stay away from the love of money; be satisfied with what you have. For God has said,

"I will never fail you.
    I will never forsake you."*

12:5-6 Prov 3:11-12.   **12:9** Or *really live.*   **12:20** Exod 19:13.   **12:21** Deut 9:19.   **12:26** Hag 2:6.   **13:1** Greek *with brotherly love.*
13:5 Deut 31:6, 8.

⁶That is why we can say with confidence,

"The Lord is my helper,
so I will not be afraid.
What can mere mortals do to me?"*

⁷Remember your leaders who first taught you the word of God. Think of all the good that has come from their lives, and trust the Lord as they do.

⁸Jesus Christ is the same yesterday, today, and forever. ⁹So do not be attracted by strange, new ideas. Your spiritual strength comes from God's special favor, not from ceremonial rules about food, which don't help those who follow them.

¹⁰We have an altar from which the priests in the Temple on earth have no right to eat. ¹¹Under the system of Jewish laws, the high priest brought the blood of animals into the Holy Place as a sacrifice for sin, but the bodies of the animals were burned outside the camp. ¹²So also Jesus suffered and died outside the city gates in order to make his people holy by shedding his own blood. ¹³So let us go out to him outside the camp and bear the disgrace he bore. ¹⁴For this world is not our home; we are looking forward to our city in heaven, which is yet to come.

¹⁵With Jesus' help, let us continually offer our sacrifice of praise to God by proclaiming the glory of his name. ¹⁶Don't forget to do good and to share what you

13:6 Ps 118:6.

have with those in need, for such sacrifices are very pleasing to God.

¹⁷Obey your spiritual leaders and do what they say. Their work is to watch over your souls, and they know they are accountable to God. Give them reason to do this joyfully and not with sorrow. That would certainly not be for your benefit.

¹⁸Pray for us, for our conscience is clear and we want to live honorably in everything we do. ¹⁹I especially need your prayers right now so that I can come back to you soon.

²⁰⁻²¹And now, may the God of peace, who brought again from the dead our Lord Jesus, equip you with all you need for doing his will. May he produce in you, through the power of Jesus Christ, all that is pleasing to him. Jesus is the great Shepherd of the sheep by an everlasting covenant, signed with his blood. To him be glory forever and ever. Amen.

²²I urge you, dear brothers and sisters, please listen carefully to what I have said in this brief letter.

²³I want you to know that our brother Timothy is now out of jail. If he comes here soon, I will bring him with me to see you.

²⁴Give my greetings to all your leaders and to the other believers there. The Christians from Italy send you their greetings.

²⁵May God's grace be with you all.

DECEMBER 14 ☐ DAY 349
Enduring Faith

 LOOK BACK Though the authorship of Hebrews remains a mystery, the thrust of its message could not be clearer. Spiritual birth is only the beginning. It is imperative that Christians go on to maturity and develop a grown-up and growing relationship with Jesus Christ. Don't be tempted to return to your pre-Christian past, for the path of Jesus is better in every way. Jesus is better than the angels . . . better than Moses . . . better than Joshua . . . better than the prophets. He offers a better way . . . a better sacrifice . . . a better work . . . a better rest. And because of that, the author is "confident that [Christians] are meant for better things" (6:9) as they press on to maturity in Christ.

The path is well trod by Old Testament martyrs and models, whose faith and perseverance can become a constant source of encouragement. In them we discover the liberating truth that "anyone who wants to come to him must believe that there is a God and that he rewards those who sincerely seek him" (11:6).

LOOK UP   What is the longest distance you have ever run without stopping? And how did you feel when the run was finally over?

Chances are, your answer was something less than a marathon (26.2 miles). And even if you have run a marathon sometime in your life, when it was over you probably had no desire to repeat the experience anytime soon!

Faith is the daring of the soul to go farther than it can see.

The Christian life would be a breeze if it were only a sprint—a hundred-yard dash of endurance, a quarter mile of patience, half a lap of steadfastness. Unfortunately, that's just not the case. The Christian life is more like a marathon. For Moses, it turned out to be a 120-year "hike" from Egypt to Midian, back to Egypt, and on to Moab. For Noah, it involved a century-long shipbuilding project under God's watchful eye. For Abraham, it meant a wait of twenty-five years for a promised son. No sprint, to be sure, but an exercise in endurance. And it was their enduring faith over the long haul that provided these heroes of the Old Testament with an enduring testimony that continues right up to the present.

LOOK AHEAD   When you think of models of enduring faith from your own generation, who comes to mind? Here are some suggestions of worthy candidates:

- a minister who has faithfully preached the gospel for forty years
- a couple who has stayed married and worked through their problems, rather than allowing those problems to drive them apart
- a missionary who has labored in a harvest field of the world for thirty years
- the Sunday school teacher who has faithfully taught class after class of fifth graders (including the fifth-grade children of those who once upon a time were his or her fifth graders!)

Why not honor their faithfulness today with a special phone call or note of appreciation? Their lives are living examples of Hebrews 12:1-2 in action. And it would no doubt make their day to know that you are following in their footsteps.

James

FAITH without works isn't really faith. It is dead, and a dead faith is worse than no faith at all. Faith must work; it must produce; it must be visible. Verbal faith is not enough; mental faith is insufficient. Faith must move into action. Throughout his epistle to Jewish believers, James integrates true faith and everyday practical experience by stressing that true faith "works" because it produces doers of the Word.

Focus	Tests of Faith						
Divisions	Trials and Temptations	Test of Attitude toward Bible	Test of Social Distinctions	Test of Works	Test of Self-Control	Test of Reactions to World	Test of Prayer
	1:1 1:18	1:19 1:27	2:1 2:13	2:14 2:26	3:1 3:18	4:1 5:12	5:13 5:20
Topics	Wisdom		Works		Words	Walk	Wait
	Faith Tested		Faith Displayed		Faith Proved	Faith Con-trasted	Faith Re-warded
Place	Probably Jerusalem						
Time	A.D. 46–49						

DECEMBER 15 □ DAY 350
JAMES 1–5
Doers of the Word

OVERVIEW James recognizes there can be a dangerous false conclusion from the simple equation "salvation = faith + nothing." One may conclude, "As long as I have faith, it doesn't matter how I act." But James responds with ringing clarity that a faith that produces no change in attitude is really no faith at all. Partiality, neglect of the poor, quarreling, a bitter tongue, a proud attitude—all are inconsistent with the royal law of love that Christ proclaimed.

Chapter 1	Chapter 2	Chapter 3	Chapter 4	Chapter 5
Trials of Faith	Works of Faith	Words of Faith	Walk of Faith	Waiting Faith
"It is a message to obey, not just to listen to" (1:22).				

More can be learned from life's trials than from its triumphs.

YOUR DAILY WALK In the Chinese picture-letter alphabet, the symbol for *crisis* is a combination of two characters—one meaning "danger" and the other "opportunity." You can look at it either way.

The same can be said of trials in the Christian life. A crisis that appears to one Christian as a calamity may be viewed by another as an opportunity. You can see your problems as purposeful and joyful if you see them from God's perspective. Tested faith produces patience (1:3), maturity (1:4), and God's rich reward (1:12).

As you read through the book of James, how would you catalog the various tests of faith you discover? Do you find some of the same crises you are presently facing?

Next to the ones on your list that look painfully familiar, put a check mark. Then ponder this question: If God intends these problems as *opportunities* for me to grow rather than *dangers* for me to fear, how can I cooperate with him to make the most of these faith-stretching trials? Then close your time with God by telling him what you intend to do about your new perspective on your problems.

INSIGHT Was James Eavesdropping on the Mount?
Four verses in the book of James correspond to passages from Jesus' famous Sermon on the Mount. Read Matthew 5:10-12, 34-37; 7:16-20, 24, 26. Can you find the four corresponding allusions in today's reading?

CHAPTER 1
This letter is from James, a slave of God and of the Lord Jesus Christ.

It is written to Jewish Christians scattered among the nations.*

Greetings!

²Dear brothers and sisters, whenever trouble comes your way, let it be an opportunity for joy. ³For when your faith is tested, your endurance has a chance to grow. ⁴So let it grow, for when your endurance is fully developed, you will be strong in character and ready for anything.

⁵If you need wisdom—if you want to know what God wants you to do—ask him, and he will gladly tell you. He will not resent your asking. ⁶But when you ask him,

1:1 Greek *To the twelve tribes in the dispersion.*

be sure that you really expect him to answer, for a doubtful mind is as unsettled as a wave of the sea that is driven and tossed by the wind. [7]People like that should not expect to receive anything from the Lord. [8]They can't make up their minds. They waver back and forth in everything they do.

[9]Christians who are* poor should be glad, for God has honored them. [10]And those who are rich should be glad, for God has humbled them. They will fade away like a flower in the field. [11]The hot sun rises and dries up the grass; the flower withers, and its beauty fades away. So also, wealthy people will fade away with all of their achievements.

[12]God blesses the people who patiently endure testing. Afterward they will receive the crown of life that God has promised to those who love him. [13]And remember, no one who wants to do wrong should ever say, "God is tempting me." God is never tempted to do wrong, and he never tempts anyone else either. [14]Temptation comes from the lure of our own evil desires. [15]These evil desires lead to evil actions, and evil actions lead to death. [16]So don't be misled, my dear brothers and sisters.

[17]Whatever is good and perfect comes to us from God above, who created all heaven's lights.* Unlike them, he never changes or casts shifting shadows. [18]In his goodness he chose to make us his own children by giving us his true word. And we, out of all creation, became his choice possession.

[19]My dear brothers and sisters, be quick to listen, slow to speak, and slow to get angry. [20]Your anger can never make things right in God's sight.

[21]So get rid of all the filth and evil in your lives, and humbly accept the message God has planted in your hearts, for it is strong enough to save your souls.

[22]And remember, it is a message to obey, not just to listen to. If you don't obey, you are only fooling yourself. [23]For if you just listen and don't obey, it is like looking at your face in a mirror but doing nothing to improve your appearance. [24]You see yourself, walk away, and forget what you look like. [25]But if you keep looking steadily into God's perfect law—the law that sets you free—and if you do what it says and don't forget what you heard, then God will bless you for doing it.

[26]If you claim to be religious but don't control your tongue, you are just fooling yourself, and your religion is worthless. [27]Pure and lasting religion in the sight of God our Father means that we must care for orphans and widows in their troubles, and refuse to let the world corrupt us.

CHAPTER 2

My dear brothers and sisters, how can you claim that you have faith in our glorious Lord Jesus Christ if you favor some people more than others?

[2]For instance, suppose someone comes into your meeting* dressed in fancy clothes and expensive jewelry, and another comes in who is poor and dressed in shabby clothes. [3]If you give special attention and a good seat to the rich person, but you say to the poor one, "You can stand over there, or else sit on the floor"—well, [4]doesn't this discrimination show that you are guided by wrong motives?

[5]Listen to me, dear brothers and sisters. Hasn't God chosen the poor in this world to be rich in faith? Aren't they the ones who will inherit the kingdom God promised to those who love him? [6]And yet, you insult the poor man! Isn't it the rich who oppress you and drag you into court? [7]Aren't they the ones who slander Jesus Christ, whose noble name you bear?

[8]Yes indeed, it is good when you truly obey our Lord's royal command found in the Scriptures: "Love your neighbor as yourself."* [9]But if you pay special attention to the rich, you are committing a sin, for you are guilty of breaking that law.

[10]And the person who keeps all of the laws except one is as guilty as the person who has broken all of God's laws. [11]For the same God who said, "Do not commit adultery," also said, "Do not murder."* So if you murder someone, you have broken the entire law, even if you do not commit adultery.

[12]So whenever you speak, or whatever you do, remember that you will be judged by the law of love, the law that set you free. [13]For there will be no mercy for you if you have not been merciful to others. But if you have been merciful, then God's mercy toward you will win out over his judgment against you.

[14]Dear brothers and sisters, what's the use of saying you have faith if you don't

---

1:9 Greek *The brother who is.*   **1:17** Greek *from above, from the Father of lights.*   **2:2** Greek *synagogue.*   **2:8** Lev 19:18.   **2:11** Exod 20:13-14; Deut 5:17-18.

prove it by your actions? That kind of faith can't save anyone. ¹⁵Suppose you see a brother or sister who needs food or clothing, ¹⁶and you say, "Well, good-bye and God bless you; stay warm and eat well"— but then you don't give that person any food or clothing. What good does that do?

¹⁷So you see, it isn't enough just to have faith. Faith that doesn't show itself by good deeds is no faith at all—it is dead and useless.

¹⁸Now someone may argue, "Some people have faith; others have good deeds." I say, "I can't see your faith if you don't have good deeds, but I will show you my faith through my good deeds."

¹⁹Do you still think it's enough just to believe that there is one God? Well, even the demons believe this, and they tremble in terror! ²⁰Fool! When will you ever learn that faith that does not result in good deeds is useless?

²¹Don't you remember that our ancestor Abraham was declared right with God because of what he did when he offered his son Isaac on the altar? ²²You see, he was trusting God so much that he was willing to do whatever God told him to do. His faith was made complete by what he did— by his actions. ²³And so it happened just as the Scriptures say: "Abraham believed God, so God declared him to be righteous."* He was even called "the friend of God."* ²⁴So you see, we are made right with God by what we do, not by faith alone.

²⁵Rahab the prostitute is another example of this. She was made right with God by her actions—when she hid those messengers and sent them safely away by a different road. ²⁶Just as the body is dead without a spirit, so also faith is dead without good deeds.

CHAPTER 3

Dear brothers and sisters, not many of you should become teachers in the church, for we who teach will be judged by God with greater strictness.

²We all make many mistakes, but those who control their tongues can also control themselves in every other way. ³We can make a large horse turn around and go wherever we want by means of a small bit in its mouth. ⁴And a tiny rudder makes a huge ship turn wherever the pilot wants it to go, even though the winds are strong. ⁵So also, the tongue is a small thing, but what enormous damage it can do. A tiny spark can set a great forest on fire. ⁶And the tongue is a flame of fire. It is full of wickedness that can ruin your whole life. It can turn the entire course of your life into a blazing flame of destruction, for it is set on fire by hell itself.

⁷People can tame all kinds of animals and birds and reptiles and fish, ⁸but no one can tame the tongue. It is an uncontrollable evil, full of deadly poison. ⁹Sometimes it praises our Lord and Father, and sometimes it breaks out into curses against those who have been made in the image of God. ¹⁰And so blessing and cursing come pouring out of the same mouth. Surely, my brothers and sisters, this is not right! ¹¹Does a spring of water bubble out with both fresh water and bitter water? ¹²Can you pick olives from a fig tree or figs from a grapevine? No, and you can't draw fresh water from a salty pool.

¹³If you are wise and understand God's ways, live a life of steady goodness so that only good deeds will pour forth. And if you don't brag about the good you do, then you will be truly wise! ¹⁴But if you are bitterly jealous and there is selfish ambition in your hearts, don't brag about being wise. That is the worst kind of lie. ¹⁵For jealousy and selfishness are not God's kind of wisdom. Such things are earthly, unspiritual, and motivated by the Devil. ¹⁶For wherever there is jealousy and selfish ambition, there you will find disorder and every kind of evil.

¹⁷But the wisdom that comes from heaven is first of all pure. It is also peace loving, gentle at all times, and willing to yield to others. It is full of mercy and good deeds. It shows no partiality and is always sincere. ¹⁸And those who are peacemakers will plant seeds of peace and reap a harvest of goodness.

CHAPTER 4

What is causing the quarrels and fights among you? Isn't it the whole army of evil desires at war within you? ²You want what you don't have, so you scheme and kill to get it. You are jealous for what others have, and you can't possess it, so you fight and

2:23a Gen 15:6.   2:23b See Isa 41:8.

quarrel to take it away from them. And yet the reason you don't have what you want is that you don't ask God for it. ³And even when you do ask, you don't get it because your whole motive is wrong—you want only what will give you pleasure.

⁴You adulterers! Don't you realize that friendship with this world makes you an enemy of God? I say it again, that if your aim is to enjoy this world, you can't be a friend of God. ⁵What do you think the Scriptures mean when they say that the Holy Spirit, whom God has placed within us, jealously longs for us to be faithful*? ⁶He gives us more and more strength to stand against such evil desires. As the Scriptures say,

"God sets himself against the proud,
   but he shows favor to the humble."*

⁷So humble yourselves before God. Resist the Devil, and he will flee from you. ⁸Draw close to God, and God will draw close to you. Wash your hands, you sinners; purify your hearts, you hypocrites. ⁹Let there be tears for the wrong things you have done. Let there be sorrow and deep grief. Let there be sadness instead of laughter, and gloom instead of joy. ¹⁰When you bow down before the Lord and admit your dependence on him, he will lift you up and give you honor.

¹¹Don't speak evil against each other, my dear brothers and sisters. If you criticize each other and condemn each other, then you are criticizing and condemning God's law. But you are not a judge who can decide whether the law is right or wrong. Your job is to obey it. ¹²God alone, who made the law, can rightly judge among us. He alone has the power to save or to destroy. So what right do you have to condemn your neighbor?

¹³Look here, you people who say, "Today or tomorrow we are going to a certain town and will stay there a year. We will do business there and make a profit." ¹⁴How do you know what will happen tomorrow? For your life is like the morning fog—it's here a little while, then it's gone. ¹⁵What you ought to say is, "If the Lord wants us to, we will live and do this or that." ¹⁶Otherwise you will be boasting about your own plans, and all such boasting is evil.

¹⁷Remember, it is sin to know what you ought to do and then not do it.

CHAPTER 5

Look here, you rich people, weep and groan with anguish because of all the terrible troubles ahead of you. ²Your wealth is rotting away, and your fine clothes are moth-eaten rags. ³Your gold and silver have become worthless. The very wealth you were counting on will eat away your flesh in hell.* This treasure you have accumulated will stand as evidence against you on the day of judgment. ⁴For listen! Hear the cries of the field workers whom you have cheated of their pay. The wages you held back cry out against you. The cries of the reapers have reached the ears of the Lord Almighty.

⁵You have spent your years on earth in luxury, satisfying your every whim. Now your hearts are nice and fat, ready for the slaughter. ⁶You have condemned and killed good people who had no power to defend themselves against you.

⁷Dear brothers and sisters, you must be patient as you wait for the Lord's return. Consider the farmers who eagerly look for the rains in the fall and in the spring. They patiently wait for the precious harvest to ripen. ⁸You, too, must be patient. And take courage, for the coming of the Lord is near.

⁹Don't grumble about each other, my brothers and sisters, or God will judge you. For look! The great Judge is coming. He is standing at the door!

¹⁰For examples of patience in suffering, dear brothers and sisters, look at the prophets who spoke in the name of the Lord. ¹¹We give great honor to those who endure under suffering. Job is an example of a man who endured patiently. From his experience we see how the Lord's plan finally ended in good, for he is full of tenderness and mercy.

¹²But most of all, my brothers and sisters, never take an oath, by heaven or earth or anything else. Just say a simple yes or no, so that you will not sin and be condemned for it.

¹³Are any among you suffering? They should keep on praying about it. And those who have reason to be thankful should continually sing praises to the Lord.

¹⁴Are any among you sick? They should call for the elders of the church and have them pray over them, anointing them with oil in the name of the Lord. ¹⁵And their prayer offered in faith will heal the sick,

4:5 Or *the spirit that God placed within us tends to envy,* or *the Holy Spirit, whom God has placed within us, opposes our envy.*
4:6 Prov 3:34.   5:3 Or *will eat your flesh like fire.*

and the Lord will make them well. And anyone who has committed sins will be forgiven.

[16]Confess your sins to each other and pray for each other so that you may be healed. The earnest prayer of a righteous person has great power and wonderful results. [17]Elijah was as human as we are, and yet when he prayed earnestly that no rain would fall, none fell for the next three and a half years! [18]Then he prayed for rain, and down it poured. The grass turned green, and the crops began to grow again.

[19]My dear brothers and sisters, if anyone among you wanders away from the truth and is brought back again, [20]you can be sure that the one who brings that person back will save that sinner from death and bring about the forgiveness of many sins.

1 Peter

THE APOSTLE PETER writes to scattered Jewish Christians, who are undergoing intense persecution for their faith. He reminds his readers that God has given them the privilege of being born again. Therefore, they shouldn't be surprised when suffering comes their way; they should expect it, prepare for it, and respond to it correctly. He also encourages them to imitate Christ through a submissive spirit toward one another. If they do, God will richly reward them when the trials of life are over.

Focus	Christian Salvation		Christian Relationships				Christian Suffering			Christian Discipline	
Divisions	Salvation	Sanctification	World	State	Home	Church	Blessings	Example	Encouragement	Church	Individual
	1:1 — 1:12	1:13 — 2:10	2:11 2:12	2:13 2:17	2:18 3:7	3:8 3:12	3:13 3:17	3:18 3:22	4:1 4:19	5:1 5:6	5:7 5:14
Topics	New Birth		New Building				Necessary Bulwark				
	Salvation		Submission				Suffering				
Place	Rome or Babylon										
Time	Approximately A.D. 63–64										

DECEMBER 16 ☐ DAY 351
1 PETER 1–5
Courage in Suffering

OVERVIEW Persecution can cause you either to grow or to grumble in the Christian life. It all depends on your response! In writing to Jewish believers struggling in the midst of persecution, Peter reminds them of their "roots." They have been born again to a living hope, and therefore both their character and conduct should be above reproach as they imitate the Holy One who called them. Since they are God's special people, their lives should be marked by submission to others, producing law-abiding citizens, obedient employees, submissive wives, and understanding husbands.

Chapter 1	Chapters 2–3	Chapters 4–5
Called to Salvation	Called to Submission	Called to Suffering
Belief	Behavior	Buffeting

Getting into hot water occasionally has a way of keeping a person clean.

YOUR DAILY WALK The book of 1 Peter might well be titled "A Survival Manual for Suffering Saints." It presents God's time-tested strategy for holding up, rather than folding up, in the midst of difficulties.

If you want to get in shape physically, there are some helpful steps you can take: Eat properly, get adequate sleep, take a multi-vitamin capsule every day. But in the final analysis, there is no substitute for exercise—working against a resistance. The same is true in the Christian life. Proper nourishment from the Word is essential, but so is "exercise"—in God's strength, facing and conquering trials and difficulties. God—the perfect Coach—knows exactly what kind of "workout" you need in order to turn an area of weakness into an area of Christlikeness.

Before you go to bed this evening, write out the words of 1 Peter 1:7, and place them in one of the shoes you'll wear tomorrow. When you awake, let that note remind you that God wants to "tone up" your faith today—and trials may well be part of the workout!

INSIGHT The All-Important Cornerstone
Peter makes an obvious allusion to Christ when he quotes Isaiah 28:16: "I am placing a stone in Jerusalem, a chosen cornerstone" (2:6). In biblical times a stone was put where two walls met. More than just a foundation, the cornerstone helped align the building horizontally and vertically and held it together. Thus, Christ is the all-important one on whom we, as "living stones," are built into a spiritual house.

CHAPTER 1
This letter is from Peter, an apostle of Jesus Christ.

I am writing to God's chosen people who are living as foreigners in the lands of Pontus, Galatia, Cappadocia, the province of Asia, and Bithynia. [2]God the Father chose you long ago, and the Spirit has made you holy. As a result, you have obeyed Jesus Christ and are cleansed by his blood.

May you have more and more of God's special favor and wonderful peace.

³All honor to the God and Father of our Lord Jesus Christ, for it is by his boundless mercy that God has given us the privilege of being born again. Now we live with a wonderful expectation because Jesus Christ rose again from the dead. ⁴For God has reserved a priceless inheritance for his children. It is kept in heaven for you, pure and undefiled, beyond the reach of change and decay. ⁵And God, in his mighty power, will protect you until you receive this salvation, because you are trusting him. It will be revealed on the last day for all to see. ⁶So be truly glad!* There is wonderful joy ahead, even though it is necessary for you to endure many trials for a while.

⁷These trials are only to test your faith, to show that it is strong and pure. It is being tested as fire tests and purifies gold—and your faith is far more precious to God than mere gold. So if your faith remains strong after being tried by fiery trials, it will bring you much praise and glory and honor on the day when Jesus Christ is revealed to the whole world.

⁸You love him even though you have never seen him. Though you do not see him, you trust him; and even now you are happy with a glorious, inexpressible joy. ⁹Your reward for trusting him will be the salvation of your souls.

¹⁰This salvation was something the prophets wanted to know more about. They prophesied about this gracious salvation prepared for you, even though they had many questions as to what it all could mean. ¹¹They wondered what the Spirit of Christ within them was talking about when he told them in advance about Christ's suffering and his great glory afterward. They wondered when and to whom all this would happen.

¹²They were told that these things would not happen during their lifetime, but many years later, during yours. And now this Good News has been announced by those who preached to you in the power of the Holy Spirit sent from heaven. It is all so wonderful that even the angels are eagerly watching these things happen.

¹³So think clearly and exercise self-control. Look forward to the special blessings that will come to you at the return of Jesus Christ. ¹⁴Obey God because you are his children. Don't slip back into your old ways of doing evil; you didn't know any better then. ¹⁵But now you must be holy in everything you do, just as God—who chose you to be his children—is holy. ¹⁶For he himself has said, "You must be holy because I am holy."*

¹⁷And remember that the heavenly Father to whom you pray has no favorites when he judges. He will judge or reward you according to what you do. So you must live in reverent fear of him during your time as foreigners here on earth. ¹⁸For you know that God paid a ransom to save you from the empty life you inherited from your ancestors. And the ransom he paid was not mere gold or silver. ¹⁹He paid for you with the precious lifeblood of Christ, the sinless, spotless Lamb of God. ²⁰God chose him for this purpose long before the world began, but now in these final days, he was sent to the earth for all to see. And he did this for you.

²¹Through Christ you have come to trust in God. And because God raised Christ from the dead and gave him great glory, your faith and hope can be placed confidently in God. ²²Now you can have sincere love for each other as brothers and sisters because you were cleansed from your sins when you accepted the truth of the Good News. So see to it that you really do love each other intensely with all your hearts.*

²³For you have been born again. Your new life did not come from your earthly parents because the life they gave you will end in death. But this new life will last forever because it comes from the eternal, living word of God. ²⁴As the prophet says,

"People are like grass that dies away;
 their beauty fades as quickly as the
 beauty of wildflowers.
The grass withers,
 and the flowers fall away.
²⁵ But the word of the Lord will last
 forever."*

And that word is the Good News that was preached to you.

CHAPTER 2
So get rid of all malicious behavior and deceit. Don't just pretend to be good! Be done with hypocrisy and jealousy and backstabbing. ²You must crave pure spiritual milk so that you can grow into the

1:6 Or *So you are truly glad.*   **1:16** Lev 11:44-45; 19:2; 20:7.   **1:22** Some manuscripts read *with a pure heart.*   **1:24-25** Isa 40:6-8.

fullness of your salvation. Cry out for this nourishment as a baby cries for milk, ³now that you have had a taste of the Lord's kindness.

⁴Come to Christ, who is the living cornerstone of God's temple. He was rejected by the people, but he is precious to God who chose him.

⁵And now God is building you, as living stones, into his spiritual temple. What's more, you are God's holy priests, who offer the spiritual sacrifices that please him because of Jesus Christ. ⁶As the Scriptures express it,

"I am placing a stone in Jerusalem,*
    a chosen cornerstone,
and anyone who believes in him
    will never be disappointed.*"

⁷Yes, he is very precious to you who believe. But for those who reject him,

"The stone that was rejected by the
    builders
    has now become the cornerstone."*

⁸And the Scriptures also say,

"He is the stone that makes people
    stumble,
    the rock that will make them fall."*

They stumble because they do not listen to God's word or obey it, and so they meet the fate that has been planned for them.

⁹But you are not like that, for you are a chosen people. You are a kingdom of priests, God's holy nation, his very own possession. This is so you can show others the goodness of God, for he called you out of the darkness into his wonderful light.

¹⁰ "Once you were not a people;
    now you are the people of God.
Once you received none of God's
        mercy;
    now you have received his mercy."*

¹¹Dear brothers and sisters, you are foreigners and aliens here. So I warn you to keep away from evil desires because they fight against your very souls. ¹²Be careful how you live among your unbelieving neighbors. Even if they accuse you of doing wrong, they will see your honorable behavior, and they will believe and give honor to God when he comes to judge the world.*

¹³For the Lord's sake, accept all authority—the king as head of state, ¹⁴and the officials he has appointed. For the king has sent them to punish all who do wrong and to honor those who do right.

¹⁵It is God's will that your good lives should silence those who make foolish accusations against you. ¹⁶You are not slaves; you are free. But your freedom is not an excuse to do evil. You are free to live as God's slaves. ¹⁷Show respect for everyone. Love your Christian brothers and sisters. Fear God. Show respect for the king.

¹⁸You who are slaves must accept the authority of your masters. Do whatever they tell you—not only if they are kind and reasonable, but even if they are harsh. ¹⁹For God is pleased with you when, for the sake of your conscience, you patiently endure unfair treatment. ²⁰Of course, you get no credit for being patient if you are beaten for doing wrong. But if you suffer for doing right and are patient beneath the blows, God is pleased with you.

²¹This suffering is all part of what God has called you to. Christ, who suffered for you, is your example. Follow in his steps. ²²He never sinned, and he never deceived anyone. ²³He did not retaliate when he was insulted. When he suffered, he did not threaten to get even. He left his case in the hands of God, who always judges fairly. ²⁴He personally carried away our sins in his own body on the cross so we can be dead to sin and live for what is right. You have been healed by his wounds! ²⁵Once you were wandering like lost sheep. But now you have turned to your Shepherd, the Guardian of your souls.

CHAPTER 3
In the same way, you wives must accept the authority of your husbands, even those who refuse to accept the Good News. Your godly lives will speak to them better than any words. They will be won over ²by watching your pure, godly behavior.

³Don't be concerned about the outward beauty that depends on fancy hairstyles, expensive jewelry, or beautiful clothes. ⁴You should be known for the beauty that comes from within, the unfading beauty of a gentle and quiet spirit, which is so precious to God. ⁵That is the way the holy women of old made themselves beautiful.

2:6a Greek *in Zion.*   **2:6b** Or *will never be put to shame.* Isa 28:16.   **2:7** Ps 118:22.   **2:8** Isa 8:14.   **2:10** Hos 1:6, 9; 2:23.
2:12 Or *on the day of visitation.*

They trusted God and accepted the authority of their husbands. 6For instance, Sarah obeyed her husband, Abraham, when she called him her master. You are her daughters when you do what is right without fear of what your husbands might do.

7In the same way, you husbands must give honor to your wives. Treat her with understanding as you live together. She may be weaker than you are, but she is your equal partner in God's gift of new life. If you don't treat her as you should, your prayers will not be heard.

8Finally, all of you should be of one mind, full of sympathy toward each other, loving one another with tender hearts and humble minds. 9Don't repay evil for evil. Don't retaliate when people say unkind things about you. Instead, pay them back with a blessing. That is what God wants you to do, and he will bless you for it. 10For the Scriptures say,

"If you want a happy life and good
        days,
    keep your tongue from speaking evil,
    and keep your lips from telling lies.
11 Turn away from evil and do good.
    Work hard at living in peace with
        others.
12 The eyes of the Lord watch over those
        who do right,
    and his ears are open to their prayers.
    But the Lord turns his face
        against those who do evil."*

13Now, who will want to harm you if you are eager to do good? 14But even if you suffer for doing what is right, God will reward you for it. So don't be afraid and don't worry. 15Instead, you must worship Christ as Lord of your life. And if you are asked about your Christian hope, always be ready to explain it. 16But you must do this in a gentle and respectful way. Keep your conscience clear. Then if people speak evil against you, they will be ashamed when they see what a good life you live because you belong to Christ. 17Remember, it is better to suffer for doing good, if that is what God wants, than to suffer for doing wrong!

18Christ also suffered when he died for our sins once for all time. He never sinned, but he died for sinners that he might bring us safely home to God. He suffered physi-

cal death, but he was raised to life in the Spirit.*

19So he went and preached to the spirits in prison—20those who disobeyed God long ago when God waited patiently while Noah was building his boat. Only eight people were saved from drowning in that terrible flood.* 21And this is a picture of baptism, which now saves you by the power of Jesus Christ's resurrection. Baptism is not a removal of dirt from your body; it is an appeal to God from* a clean conscience.

22Now Christ has gone to heaven. He is seated in the place of honor next to God, and all the angels and authorities and powers are bowing before him.

CHAPTER 4
So then, since Christ suffered physical pain, you must arm yourselves with the same attitude he had, and be ready to suffer, too. For if you are willing to suffer for Christ, you have decided to stop sinning. 2And you won't spend the rest of your life chasing after evil desires, but you will be anxious to do the will of God. 3You have had enough in the past of the evil things that godless people enjoy—their immorality and lust, their feasting and drunkenness and wild parties, and their terrible worship of idols.

4Of course, your former friends are very surprised when you no longer join them in the wicked things they do, and they say evil things about you. 5But just remember that they will have to face God, who will judge everyone, both the living and the dead. 6That is why the Good News was preached even to those who have died—so that although their bodies were punished with death, they could still live in the spirit as God does.

7The end of the world is coming soon. Therefore, be earnest and disciplined in your prayers. 8Most important of all, continue to show deep love for each other, for love covers a multitude of sins. 9Cheerfully share your home with those who need a meal or a place to stay.

10God has given gifts to each of you from his great variety of spiritual gifts. Manage them well so that God's generosity can flow through you. 11Are you called to be a speaker? Then speak as though God him-

---

3:10-12 Ps 34:12-16.   **3:18** Or *spirit.*   **3:20** Greek *saved through water.*   **3:21** Or *for.*

self were speaking through you. Are you called to help others? Do it with all the strength and energy that God supplies. Then God will be given glory in everything through Jesus Christ. All glory and power belong to him forever and ever. Amen.

[12]Dear friends, don't be surprised at the fiery trials you are going through, as if something strange were happening to you. [13]Instead, be very glad—because these trials will make you partners with Christ in his suffering, and afterward you will have the wonderful joy of sharing his glory when it is displayed to all the world.

[14]Be happy if you are insulted for being a Christian, for then the glorious Spirit of God will come upon you. [15]If you suffer, however, it must not be for murder, stealing, making trouble, or prying into other people's affairs. [16]But it is no shame to suffer for being a Christian. Praise God for the privilege of being called by his wonderful name! [17]For the time has come for judgment, and it must begin first among God's own children. And if even we Christians must be judged, what terrible fate awaits those who have never believed God's Good News? [18]And

"If the righteous are barely saved,
    what chance will the godless and
        sinners have?"*

[19]So if you are suffering according to God's will, keep on doing what is right, and trust yourself to the God who made you, for he will never fail you.

CHAPTER 5

And now, a word to you who are elders in the churches. I, too, am an elder and a witness to the sufferings of Christ. And I, too, will share his glory and his honor when he returns. As a fellow elder, this is my appeal to you: [2]Care for the flock of God entrusted to you. Watch over it willingly, not grudgingly—not for what you will get out of it, but because you are eager to serve God. [3]Don't lord it over the people assigned to your care, but lead them by your good example. [4]And when the head Shepherd comes, your reward will be a never-ending share in his glory and honor.

[5]You younger men, accept the authority of the elders. And all of you, serve each other in humility, for

"God sets himself against the proud,
    but he shows favor to the humble."*

[6]So humble yourselves under the mighty power of God, and in his good time he will honor you. [7]Give all your worries and cares to God, for he cares about what happens to you.

[8]Be careful! Watch out for attacks from the Devil, your great enemy. He prowls around like a roaring lion, looking for some victim to devour. [9]Take a firm stand against him, and be strong in your faith. Remember that your Christian brothers and sisters all over the world are going through the same kind of suffering you are.

[10]In his kindness God called you to his eternal glory by means of Jesus Christ. After you have suffered a little while, he will restore, support, and strengthen you, and he will place you on a firm foundation. [11]All power is his forever and ever. Amen.

[12]I have written this short letter to you with the help of Silas,* whom I consider a faithful brother. My purpose in writing is to encourage you and assure you that the grace of God is with you no matter what happens.

[13]Your sister church here in Rome* sends you greetings, and so does my son Mark. [14]Greet each other in Christian love.*

Peace be to all of you who are in Christ.

4:18 Prov 11:31.   **5:5** Prov 3:34.   **5:12** Greek *Silvanus.*   **5:13** Greek *The elect one in Babylon.* Babylon was probably a code name for Rome.   **5:14** Greek *with a kiss of love.*

2 Peter

IN HIS first letter Peter taught his readers to endure external enemies with hope; 2 Peter teaches the same audience to oppose internal enemies with knowledge of the truth. Apostasy within the church can be much more devastating than persecution against the church. Peter warns against the moral perversions and denial of Christ's return that false teachers propagate, then exhorts his readers to resist errors by growing in grace and knowledge. Knowledge is the prominent theme of this letter and the best antidote for heresies.

Focus	True Knowledge			False Knowledge			Challenge		
Divisions	Salutation	Growth in Knowledge	Source of Knowledge	Fear of False Teachers	Fate of False Teachers	Facts about False Teachers	Denial of Return	Truth of Return	Application of Return
	1:1	1:2 1:3	1:11 1:12	1:21 2:1 2:3	2:4 2:9	2:10 2:22	3:1 3:7	3:8 3:10	3:11 3:18
Topics	Growing in Grace			Growing in Knowledge			Growing in Expectation		
	"Grow Up!"			"Watch Out!"			"Look Up!"		
Place	Probably Rome								
Time	Approximately A.D. 64–66								

DECEMBER 17 □ DAY 352
2 PETER 1–3
Poison in the Pew

OVERVIEW Peter's second letter warns against the heretical teachers who are making inroads in the church by preaching false doctrine and practicing immorality. To refute these "peddlers of poison," Peter affirms the true knowledge of the Christian faith. Those who are growing in their knowledge and love of God will not fall prey to doctrinal error. But woe to those who attempt to introduce such destructive ways! Their punishment will be swift and severe, like that of Sodom and Gomorrah. What is the Christian's responsibility in the face of such danger? "Watch out" (3:17).

Chapter 1	Chapter 2	Chapter 3
Faith Considered	Faith Contradicted	Faith Consummated
"Add to It!"	"Guard It!"	"Watch for It!"

YOUR DAILY WALK How are your mathematical skills? If the third of your three R's—reading, (w)riting, and (a)rithmetic—has grown a little dusty from lack of use, 2 Peter 1 will give you a chance to dust it off. In the space of a single chapter, you will learn about addition and subtraction . . . from a spiritual point of view.

There is a world of difference between activity and progress.

In chapter one, Peter reminds you that the Christian life is largely a matter of addition. Verses 5-7 list seven characteristics that God wants you to add to your life, building upon the foundation of your faith in Jesus Christ. Why? Because growth in grace is the surest way to avoid error and prepare for the Lord's return.

The Christian life is not just one of addition though. Peter also reminds you that the Christian life involves subtraction, in particular the subtraction of sin: "God has cleansed them from their old life of sin" (1:9).

It's not enough to ask for godly character (like the person who prayed, "God, give me patience, and give it to me NOW!"). Rather, it demands daily attention in your Christian life. Pick a virtue from Peter's list, and add one activity to your "Must Do" list for today that will help you cultivate that Christlike quality.

INSIGHT Last Letters from Peter and Paul
Second Peter is the "swan song" of Peter, just as 2 Timothy is that of Paul. Both warn of apostasy, both speak in a joyful manner of approaching death, and both anchor the church to the immovable rock of Scripture as the only sure defense against false doctrine.

CHAPTER 1
This letter is from Simon* Peter, a slave and apostle of Jesus Christ.

I am writing to all of you who share the same precious faith we have, faith given to us by Jesus Christ, our God and Savior, who makes us right with God.

²May God bless you with his special favor and wonderful peace as you come to know Jesus, our God and Lord,* better and better.

1:1 Greek *Simeon*.   **1:2** Or *come to know God and Jesus our Lord.*

[3]As we know Jesus better, his divine power gives us everything we need for living a godly life. He has called us to receive his own glory and goodness! [4]And by that same mighty power, he has given us all of his rich and wonderful promises. He has promised that you will escape the decadence all around you caused by evil desires and that you will share in his divine nature.

[5]So make every effort to apply the benefits of these promises to your life. Then your faith will produce a life of moral excellence. A life of moral excellence leads to knowing God better. [6]Knowing God leads to self-control. Self-control leads to patient endurance, and patient endurance leads to godliness. [7]Godliness leads to love for other Christians,* and finally you will grow to have genuine love for everyone. [8]The more you grow like this, the more you will become productive and useful in your knowledge of our Lord Jesus Christ. [9]But those who fail to develop these virtues are blind or, at least, very shortsighted. They have already forgotten that God has cleansed them from their old life of sin.

[10]So, dear brothers and sisters, work hard to prove that you really are among those God has called and chosen. Doing this, you will never stumble or fall away. [11]And God will open wide the gates of heaven for you to enter into the eternal Kingdom of our Lord and Savior Jesus Christ.

[12]I plan to keep on reminding you of these things—even though you already know them and are standing firm in the truth. [13]Yes, I believe I should keep on reminding you of these things as long as I live. [14]But the Lord Jesus Christ has shown me that my days here on earth are numbered and I am soon to die.* [15]So I will work hard to make these things clear to you. I want you to remember them long after I am gone.

[16]For we were not making up clever stories when we told you about the power of our Lord Jesus Christ and his coming again. We have seen his majestic splendor with our own eyes. [17]And he received honor and glory from God the Father when God's glorious, majestic voice called down from heaven, "This is my beloved Son; I am fully pleased with him." [18]We ourselves heard the voice when we were there with him on the holy mountain.

[19]Because of that, we have even greater confidence in the message proclaimed by the prophets. Pay close attention to what they wrote, for their words are like a light shining in a dark place—until the day Christ appears and his brilliant light shines in your hearts.* [20]Above all, you must understand that no prophecy in Scripture ever came from the prophets themselves* [21]or because they wanted to prophesy. It was the Holy Spirit who moved the prophets to speak from God.

CHAPTER 2

But there were also false prophets in Israel, just as there will be false teachers among you. They will cleverly teach their destructive heresies about God and even turn against their Master who bought them. Theirs will be a swift and terrible end. [2]Many will follow their evil teaching and shameful immorality. And because of them, Christ and his true way will be slandered. [3]In their greed they will make up clever lies to get hold of your money. But God condemned them long ago, and their destruction is on the way.

[4]For God did not spare even the angels when they sinned; he threw them into hell,* in gloomy caves* and darkness until the judgment day. [5]And God did not spare the ancient world—except for Noah and his family of seven. Noah warned the world of God's righteous judgment. Then God destroyed the whole world of ungodly people with a vast flood. [6]Later, he turned the cities of Sodom and Gomorrah into heaps of ashes and swept them off the face of the earth. He made them an example of what will happen to ungodly people. [7]But at the same time, God rescued Lot out of Sodom because he was a good man who was sick of all the immorality and wickedness around him. [8]Yes, he was a righteous man who was distressed by the wickedness he saw and heard day after day.

[9]So you see, the Lord knows how to rescue godly people from their trials, even while punishing the wicked right up until the day of judgment. [10]He is especially hard on those who follow their own evil, lustful desires and who despise authority. These people are proud and arro-

1:7 Greek *brotherly love.*   **1:14** Greek *I must soon put off this earthly tent.*   **1:19** Or *until the day dawns and the morning star rises in your hearts.*   **1:20** Or *is a matter of one's own interpretation.*   **2:4a** Greek *Tartaros.*   **2:4b** Some manuscripts read *chains of gloom.*

gant, daring even to scoff at the glorious ones* without so much as trembling. [11]But the angels, even though they are far greater in power and strength than these false teachers, never speak out disrespectfully against* the glorious ones.

[12]These false teachers are like unthinking animals, creatures of instinct, who are born to be caught and killed. They laugh at the terrifying powers they know so little about, and they will be destroyed along with them. [13]Their destruction is their reward for the harm they have done. They love to indulge in evil pleasures in broad daylight. They are a disgrace and a stain among you. They revel in deceitfulness while they feast with you. [14]They commit adultery with their eyes, and their lust is never satisfied. They make a game of luring unstable people into sin. They train themselves to be greedy; they are doomed and cursed. [15]They have wandered off the right road and followed the way of Balaam son of Beor,* who loved to earn money by doing wrong. [16]But Balaam was stopped from his mad course when his donkey rebuked him with a human voice.

[17]These people are as useless as dried-up springs of water or as clouds blown away by the wind—promising much and delivering nothing. They are doomed to blackest darkness. [18]They brag about themselves with empty, foolish boasting. With lustful desire as their bait, they lure back into sin those who have just escaped from such wicked living. [19]They promise freedom, but they themselves are slaves to sin and corruption. For you are a slave to whatever controls you. [20]And when people escape from the wicked ways of the world by learning about our Lord and Savior Jesus Christ and then get tangled up with sin and become its slave again, they are worse off than before. [21]It would be better if they had never known the right way to live than to know it and then reject the holy commandments that were given to them. [22]They make these proverbs come true: "A dog returns to its vomit,"* and "A washed pig returns to the mud."

CHAPTER 3

This is my second letter to you, dear friends, and in both of them I have tried to stimulate your wholesome thinking and refresh your memory. [2]I want you to remember and understand what the holy prophets said long ago and what our Lord and Savior commanded through your apostles.

[3]First, I want to remind you that in the last days there will be scoffers who will laugh at the truth and do every evil thing they desire. [4]This will be their argument: "Jesus promised to come back, did he? Then where is he? Why, as far back as anyone can remember, everything has remained exactly the same since the world was first created."

[5]They deliberately forget that God made the heavens by the word of his command, and he brought the earth up from the water and surrounded it with water. [6]Then he used the water to destroy the world with a mighty flood. [7]And God has also commanded that the heavens and the earth will be consumed by fire on the day of judgment, when ungodly people will perish.

[8]But you must not forget, dear friends, that a day is like a thousand years to the Lord, and a thousand years is like a day. [9]The Lord isn't really being slow about his promise to return, as some people think. No, he is being patient for your sake. He does not want anyone to perish, so he is giving more time for everyone to repent. [10]But the day of the Lord will come as unexpectedly as a thief. Then the heavens will pass away with a terrible noise, and everything in them will disappear in fire, and the earth and everything on it will be exposed to judgment.*

[11]Since everything around us is going to melt away, what holy, godly lives you should be living! [12]You should look forward to that day and hurry it along—the day when God will set the heavens on fire and the elements will melt away in the flames. [13]But we are looking forward to the new heavens and new earth he has promised, a world where everyone is right with God.

[14]And so, dear friends, while you are waiting for these things to happen, make every effort to live a pure and blameless life. And be at peace with God.

[15]And remember, the Lord is waiting so that people have time to be saved. This is just as our beloved brother Paul wrote to you with the wisdom God gave him—[16]speaking of these things in all of his

letters. Some of his comments are hard to understand, and those who are ignorant and unstable have twisted his letters around to mean something quite different from what he meant, just as they do the other parts of Scripture—and the result is disaster for them.

[17]I am warning you ahead of time, dear friends, so that you can watch out and not be carried away by the errors of these wicked people. I don't want you to lose your own secure footing. [18]But grow in the special favor and knowledge of our Lord and Savior Jesus Christ.

To him be all glory and honor, both now and forevermore. Amen.

1 John

JOHN, "the disciple Jesus loved," had long known and enjoyed fellowship with the Lord. He writes 1 John to help his spiritual brothers and sisters in their walk with the God who is light, love, and life. He wants them to be grounded in the assurance of their salvation, experiencing victory over sin and the full joys of the Christian life. He reminds them that all these gems can be dimmed by false teaching and that belief should be based on the facts about Christ's incarnation and accompanied by the responsibility to walk like Christ.

Focus	Assurance through Fellowship		Assurance through Conflict			Assurance through Love		Assurance through Spirit	
Divisions	Basis of Fellowship	Obedience of Fellowship	Truth vs. Error	Purity vs. Impurity	Fact vs. Falsehood	God's Love	Our Love	Exernal Witness	Internal Witness
	1:1　　2:2	2:3　　2:17	2:18 2:28	2:29 3:24	4:1 4:6	4:7 4:16	4:17 5:5	5:6　5:9	5:10 5:21
Topics	Walking		Warring			Wooing		Witnessing	
	Abiding in Christ		Abiding in Truth			Abiding in Love		Abiding Assurance	
Place	Ephesus								
Time	Approximately A.D. 90								

DECEMBER 18 ☐ DAY 353
1 JOHN 1–5
Fellowship Barometer

OVERVIEW John, the beloved apostle with a pastor's heart, writes to his "dear children" (2:1, 18, 28; 3:7, 18; 5:21) and "dear friends" in the faith (3:2, 21; 4:1, 7, 11). His letter has at least five stated purposes: to promote fellowship (1:3), to produce joy (1:4), to protect holiness (2:1), to prevent heresy (2:26), and to provide hope (5:13). Fellowship with God is not a vague, nebulous experience. It can be an objective, daily reality. John sets forth three tests that can act as a "fellowship barometer" for his spiritual children in their walk with God: (1) Have I confessed all known sins to God (1:9)? (2) Am I walking in obedience to the light of God's Word (2:4-5)? (3) Am I demonstrating a love for other Christians (2:9-10)?

Chapter 1	Chapters 2–3	Chapters 4–5
Requirement for Fellowship	Pattern for Fellowship	Proof of Fellowship
Confession	Christ	Conduct

The Son of God became the Son of Man so that sons of men might become sons of God.

YOUR DAILY WALK Here is a reminder you could probably do without: Christmas is less than a week away! No doubt you have pondered and puzzled over *who* should get *what* as you celebrate the birth of the Savior. Here is a gift-giving suggestion you may have overlooked: Why not offer an unsaved friend or family member the gift of eternal life?

At perhaps no other time during the year will your loved ones' thoughts turn more readily to spiritual things than at Christmas. Perhaps all that is keeping them from coming to faith in Jesus Christ is a clear, convincing presentation of who he is and why he came to earth—a presentation you could share via a letter . . . over the phone . . . or just sitting around the Christmas tree. Begin to pray right now that Christmas Day will mark more than the birth of the Savior; pray that it will mark the spiritual birth of someone you love.

INSIGHT Contrasting John's Gospel with His First Epistle

The Gospel of John
- Written to spark belief (20:31)
- Emphasizes miracles
- Historical
- Addressed to "whoever" (3:16)

The Epistle of 1 John
- Written to promote joy (1:4)
- Emphasizes love
- Experiential
- Addressed to "my dear children" (2:1, 18, 28)

CHAPTER 1

The one who existed from the beginning* is the one we have heard and seen. We saw him with our own eyes and touched him with our own hands. He is Jesus Christ, the Word of life. ²This one who is life from God was shown to us, and we have seen him. And now we testify and announce to you that he is the one who is eternal life. He was with the Father, and then he was shown to us. ³We are telling you about what we ourselves have actually seen and heard, so that you may have fellowship with us. And our fellowship is

1:1 Greek *What was from the beginning.*

with the Father and with his Son, Jesus Christ.

⁴We are writing these things so that our* joy will be complete.

⁵This is the message he has given us to announce to you: God is light and there is no darkness in him at all. ⁶So we are lying if we say we have fellowship with God but go on living in spiritual darkness. We are not living in the truth. ⁷But if we are living in the light of God's presence, just as Christ is, then we have fellowship with each other, and the blood of Jesus, his Son, cleanses us from every sin.

⁸If we say we have no sin, we are only fooling ourselves and refusing to accept the truth. ⁹But if we confess our sins to him, he is faithful and just to forgive us and to cleanse us from every wrong. ¹⁰If we claim we have not sinned, we are calling God a liar and showing that his word has no place in our hearts.

CHAPTER 2

My dear children, I am writing this to you so that you will not sin. But if you do sin, there is someone to plead for you before the Father. He is Jesus Christ, the one who pleases God completely.* ²He is the sacrifice for our sins. He takes away not only our sins but the sins of all the world.

³And how can we be sure that we belong to him? By obeying his commandments. ⁴If someone says, "I belong to God," but doesn't obey God's commandments, that person is a liar and does not live in the truth. ⁵But those who obey God's word really do love him. That is the way to know whether or not we live in him. ⁶Those who say they live in God should live their lives as Christ did.

⁷Dear friends, I am not writing a new commandment, for it is an old one you have always had, right from the beginning. This commandment—to love one another—is the same message you heard before. ⁸Yet it is also new. This commandment is true in Christ and is true among you, because the darkness is disappearing and the true light is already shining.

⁹If anyone says, "I am living in the light," but hates a Christian brother or sister, that person is still living in darkness. ¹⁰Anyone who loves other Christians* is living in

the light and does not cause anyone to stumble. ¹¹Anyone who hates a Christian brother or sister is living and walking in darkness. Such a person is lost, having been blinded by the darkness.

¹²I am writing to you, my dear children, because your sins have been forgiven because of Jesus.

¹³I am writing to you who are mature because you know Christ, the one who is from the beginning.

I am writing to you who are young because you have won your battle with Satan.

¹⁴I have written to you, children, because you have known the Father.

I have written to you who are mature because you know Christ, the one who is from the beginning.

I have written to you who are young because you are strong with God's word living in your hearts, and you have won your battle with Satan.

¹⁵Stop loving this evil world and all that it offers you, for when you love the world, you show that you do not have the love of the Father in you. ¹⁶For the world offers only the lust for physical pleasure, the lust for everything we see, and pride in our possessions. These are not from the Father. They are from this evil world. ¹⁷And this world is fading away, along with everything it craves. But if you do the will of God, you will live forever.

¹⁸Dear children, the last hour is here. You have heard that the Antichrist is coming, and already many such antichrists have appeared. From this we know that the end of the world has come. ¹⁹These people left our churches because they never really belonged with us; otherwise they would have stayed with us. When they left us, it proved that they do not belong with us. ²⁰But you are not like that, for the Holy Spirit has come upon you,* and all of you know the truth. ²¹So I am writing to you not because you don't know the truth but because you know the difference between truth and falsehood. ²²And who is the great liar? The one who says that Jesus is not the Christ. Such people are antichrists, for they have

1:4 Some manuscripts read *your.*   **2:1** Greek *Jesus Christ, the righteous.*   **2:10** Greek *his brother.*   **2:20** Greek *But you have an anointing from the Holy One.*

denied the Father and the Son. ²³Anyone who denies the Son doesn't have the Father either. But anyone who confesses the Son has the Father also.

²⁴So you must remain faithful to what you have been taught from the beginning. If you do, you will continue to live in fellowship with the Son and with the Father. ²⁵And in this fellowship we enjoy the eternal life he promised us.

²⁶I have written these things to you because you need to be aware of those who want to lead you astray. ²⁷But you have received the Holy Spirit,* and he lives within you, so you don't need anyone to teach you what is true. For the Spirit teaches you all things, and what he teaches is true—it is not a lie. So continue in what he has taught you, and continue to live in Christ.

²⁸And now, dear children, continue to live in fellowship with Christ so that when he returns, you will be full of courage and not shrink back from him in shame. ²⁹Since we know that God is always right, we also know that all who do what is right are his children.

CHAPTER 3
See how very much our heavenly Father loves us, for he allows us to be called his children, and we really are! But the people who belong to this world don't know God, so they don't understand that we are his children. ²Yes, dear friends, we are already God's children, and we can't even imagine what we will be like when Christ returns. But we do know that when he comes we will be like him, for we will see him as he really is. ³And all who believe this will keep themselves pure, just as Christ is pure.

⁴Those who sin are opposed to the law of God, for all sin opposes the law of God. ⁵And you know that Jesus came to take away our sins, for there is no sin in him. ⁶So if we continue to live in him, we won't sin either. But those who keep on sinning have never known him or understood who he is.

⁷Dear children, don't let anyone deceive you about this: When people do what is right, it is because they are righteous, even as Christ is righteous. ⁸But when people keep on sinning, it shows they belong to the Devil, who has been sinning since the beginning. But the Son of God came to destroy these works of the Devil. ⁹Those who

have been born into God's family do not sin, because God's life is in them. So they can't keep on sinning, because they have been born of God. ¹⁰So now we can tell who are children of God and who are children of the Devil. Anyone who does not obey God's commands and does not love other Christians* does not belong to God.

¹¹This is the message we have heard from the beginning: We should love one another. ¹²We must not be like Cain, who belonged to the evil one and killed his brother. And why did he kill him? Because Cain had been doing what was evil, and his brother had been doing what was right. ¹³So don't be surprised, dear brothers and sisters, if the world hates you.

¹⁴If we love our Christian brothers and sisters, it proves that we have passed from death to eternal life. But a person who has no love is still dead. ¹⁵Anyone who hates another Christian* is really a murderer at heart. And you know that murderers don't have eternal life within them. ¹⁶We know what real love is because Christ gave up his life for us. And so we also ought to give up our lives for our Christian brothers and sisters. ¹⁷But if anyone has enough money to live well and sees a brother or sister in need and refuses to help—how can God's love be in that person?

¹⁸Dear children, let us stop just saying we love each other; let us really show it by our actions. ¹⁹It is by our actions that we know we are living in the truth, so we will be confident when we stand before the Lord, ²⁰even if our hearts condemn us. For God is greater than our hearts, and he knows everything.

²¹Dear friends, if our conscience is clear, we can come to God with bold confidence. ²²And we will receive whatever we request because we obey him and do the things that please him. ²³And this is his commandment: We must believe in the name of his Son, Jesus Christ, and love one another, just as he commanded us. ²⁴Those who obey God's commandments live in fellowship with him, and he with them. And we know he lives in us because the Holy Spirit lives in us.

CHAPTER 4
Dear friends, do not believe everyone who claims to speak by the Spirit. You must test them to see if the spirit they have comes

2:27 Greek *the anointing.*   **3:10** Greek *his brother.*   **3:15** Greek *his brother.*

from God. For there are many false prophets in the world. ²This is the way to find out if they have the Spirit of God: If a prophet acknowledges that Jesus Christ became a human being, that person has the Spirit of God. ³If a prophet does not acknowledge Jesus, that person is not from God. Such a person has the spirit of the Antichrist. You have heard that he is going to come into the world, and he is already here.

⁴But you belong to God, my dear children. You have already won your fight with these false prophets, because the Spirit who lives in you is greater than the spirit who lives in the world. ⁵These people belong to this world, so they speak from the world's viewpoint, and the world listens to them. ⁶But we belong to God; that is why those who know God listen to us. If they do not belong to God, they do not listen to us. That is how we know if someone has the Spirit of truth or the spirit of deception.

⁷Dear friends, let us continue to love one another, for love comes from God. Anyone who loves is born of God and knows God. ⁸But anyone who does not love does not know God—for God is love.

⁹God showed how much he loved us by sending his only Son into the world so that we might have eternal life through him. ¹⁰This is real love. It is not that we loved God, but that he loved us and sent his Son as a sacrifice to take away our sins.

¹¹Dear friends, since God loved us that much, we surely ought to love each other. ¹²No one has ever seen God. But if we love each other, God lives in us, and his love has been brought to full expression through us.

¹³And God has given us his Spirit as proof that we live in him and he in us. ¹⁴Furthermore, we have seen with our own eyes and now testify that the Father sent his Son to be the Savior of the world. ¹⁵All who proclaim that Jesus is the Son of God have God living in them, and they live in God. ¹⁶We know how much God loves us, and we have put our trust in him.

God is love, and all who live in love live in God, and God lives in them. ¹⁷And as we live in God, our love grows more perfect. So we will not be afraid on the day of judgment, but we can face him with confidence because we are like Christ here in this world.

¹⁸Such love has no fear because perfect love expels all fear. If we are afraid, it is for fear of judgment, and this shows that his love has not been perfected in us. ¹⁹We love each other* as a result of his loving us first.

²⁰If someone says, "I love God," but hates a Christian brother or sister, that person is a liar; for if we don't love people we can see, how can we love God, whom we have not seen? ²¹And God himself has commanded that we must love not only him but our Christian brothers and sisters, too.

CHAPTER 5

Everyone who believes that Jesus is the Christ is a child of God. And everyone who loves the Father loves his children, too. ²We know we love God's children if we love God and obey his commandments. ³Loving God means keeping his commandments, and really, that isn't difficult. ⁴For every child of God defeats this evil world by trusting Christ to give the victory. ⁵And the ones who win this battle against the world are the ones who believe that Jesus is the Son of God.

⁶And Jesus Christ was revealed as God's Son by his baptism in water and by shedding his blood on the cross*—not by water only, but by water and blood. And the Spirit also gives us the testimony that this is true. ⁷So we have these three witnesses*—⁸the Spirit, the water, and the blood—and all three agree. ⁹Since we believe human testimony, surely we can believe the testimony that comes from God. And God has testified about his Son. ¹⁰All who believe in the Son of God know that this is true. Those who don't believe this are actually calling God a liar because they don't believe what God has testified about his Son.

¹¹And this is what God has testified: He has given us eternal life, and this life is in his Son. ¹²So whoever has God's Son has life; whoever does not have his Son does not have life.

¹³I write this to you who believe in the Son of God, so that you may know you have eternal life. ¹⁴And we can be confident that he will listen to us whenever we ask him for anything in line with his will. ¹⁵And if we know he is listening when we

---

4:19 Or *We love him;* Greek reads *We love.*   **5:6** Greek *This is he who came by water and blood.*   **5:7** Some very late manuscripts add *in heaven—the Father, the Word, and the Holy Spirit, and these three are one. And we have three witnesses on earth.*

make our requests, we can be sure that he will give us what we ask for.

[16]If you see a Christian brother or sister sinning in a way that does not lead to death, you should pray, and God will give that person life. But there is a sin that leads to death, and I am not saying you should pray for those who commit it. [17]Every wrong is sin, but not all sin leads to death.

[18]We know that those who have become part of God's family do not make a practice of sinning, for God's Son holds them se-

5:21 Greek *keep yourselves from idols.*

curely, and the evil one cannot get his hands on them. [19]We know that we are children of God and that the world around us is under the power and control of the evil one. [20]And we know that the Son of God has come, and he has given us understanding so that we can know the true God. And now we are in God because we are in his Son, Jesus Christ. He is the only true God, and he is eternal life.

[21]Dear children, keep away from anything that might take God's place in your hearts.*

2 John

"IF YOU think you are standing strong, be careful, for you, too, may fall into the same sin." These words of Paul (1 Corinthians 10:12) could be a subtitle for 2 John, a brief letter from the apostle John that stresses the importance of balance. The readers, a "chosen lady" and "her children," are walking in the truth, and John commends them for it. But he warns them not to aid false teachers who deny the true humanity of Christ. John exhorts the readers to love God and one another and to obey God's commandments but warns them not to encourage false teachers in any way, whereby they would open the door to false teaching and share in their evil work.

Focus	Practicing the Truth	Protecting the Truth			
Divisions	Greeting	Exhortation	Wrong Doctrine	Right Response	Conclusion
	1 3	4 6	7 9	10 11	12 13
Topics	Living in Truth and Love		Learning to Detect False Teaching		Looking for John's Coming
	Important Command		Timely Caution		Tender Conclusion
Place	Ephesus				
Time	Approximately A.D. 90				

DECEMBER 19 ☐ DAY 354
2 JOHN
Fellowship with Enemies

OVERVIEW John's first epistle was written to a group of believers in danger of following false teachers. His second letter is addressed to a "chosen lady and to her children" who are undergoing similar temptations. John wastes no words in making his point: "If someone comes to your meeting and does not teach the truth about Christ, don't invite him into your house or encourage him in any way" (v. 10). Though John commends love as a necessary ingredient of the Christian life, it must not sentimentally embrace those who willfully seek to destroy the truth. To do so is to diminish the proper love that Christians must have for one another. John's warning is stern, but he knows a letter is not the best place to elaborate. He promises to deal more fully with the problem when he makes a personal visit.

Verses 1-6	Verses 7-11	Verses 12-13
Living in Truth and Love	Learning to Detect False Teaching	Looking for John's Coming
"Love means doing what God has commanded us" (v. 6).		

The fruit of our righteousness is obedience to God and love toward others.

YOUR DAILY WALK The point of John's second epistle is that love must be discerning. Love cannot be divorced from truth. God's love is not blind sentiment; it is just, truthful, demanding. God's love motivated him to send his Son to Calvary; but those who do not believe are condemned. Calvary and condemnation are both aspects of love. The one represents love extended; the other signifies love rejected.

How wise and discerning has your love been lately? Are you being too easy on yourself or other Christians in the name of love and acceptance? Are you silently condoning error because you have been unwilling to "speak the truth in love"?

Check up on your love relationships today, and make sure they're truly biblical, not merely sentimental.

INSIGHT "Dear You-Know-Who . . ."
One possible reason why the recipient's name is not given in 2 John has to do with the persecution suffered by the church at the time. If the letter had fallen into the wrong hands, those who were to receive it might have been ill-treated. By not identifying the recipient, John reduced that possibility.

This letter is from John the Elder.*
   It is written to the chosen lady and to her children,* whom I love in the truth, as does everyone else who knows God's truth—²the truth that lives in us and will be in our hearts forever.

1a Greek *From the elder.*   **1b** Or *the church God has chosen and her members,* or *the chosen Kyria and her children.*

[3]May grace, mercy, and peace, which come from God our Father and from Jesus Christ his Son, be with us who live in truth and love.

[4]How happy I was to meet some of your children and find them living in the truth, just as we have been commanded by the Father.

[5]And now I want to urge you, dear lady, that we should love one another. This is not a new commandment, but one we had from the beginning. [6]Love means doing what God has commanded us, and he has commanded us to love one another, just as you heard from the beginning.

[7]Many deceivers have gone out into the world. They do not believe that Jesus Christ came to earth in a real body. Such a person is a deceiver and an antichrist. [8]Watch out, so that you do not lose the prize for which we* have been working so hard. Be diligent so that you will receive your full reward. [9]For if you wander beyond the teaching of Christ, you will not have fellowship with God. But if you continue in the teaching of Christ, you will have fellowship with both the Father and the Son.

[10]If someone comes to your meeting and does not teach the truth about Christ, don't invite him into your house or encourage him in any way. [11]Anyone who encourages him becomes a partner in his evil work.

[12]Well, I have much more to say to you, but I don't want to say it in a letter. For I hope to visit you soon and to talk with you face to face. Then our joy will be complete.

[13]Greetings from the children of your sister,* chosen by God.

8 Some manuscripts read *you.*   **13** Or *from the members of your sister church.*

3 John

THE SHORTEST of John's epistles begins with the expressed desire for Gaius's prosperity (v. 2) and ends with a longing for Gaius's presence (v. 14). In between, John commends him and Demetrius for their faithful witness and good testimony and makes note of one disruptive individual. John concludes his letter by promising that when he makes a personal visit, he will speak face-to-face with them about the things he could not cover in writing.

Focus	Hospitality		Haughtiness	Holiness	
Divisions	Greeting	Commendation	Censuring	Compliment	Close
	1　　　　　　2	8	9　　　　　　10	11　　　　12	13　　　　　15
Topics	Commendation of Gaius		Censuring of Diotrephes	Compliment of Demetrius	
	Helping through Hospitality		Harming through Haughtiness	Honoring Holiness	
Place	Ephesus				
Time	Approximately A.D. 90				

DECEMBER 20 □ DAY 355
3 JOHN
Open the Door in the Name of the Lord

OVERVIEW Far from being problem-free, the church of John's day had its share of shortcomings, contentious saints, and false teachers. In his third epistle, John makes a special note of one such disruptive individual named Diotrephes, a gossiper "who loves to be the leader" (v. 9). But there are two shining examples of commendable saints in 3 John. Gaius is a constant source of joy to John because he walks in the truth (v. 3), and Demetrius is a faithful servant in the church, one who has a good testimony from all (v. 12). John concludes his letter by promising that the things he could not cover in writing, he will deal with face-to-face.

Verses 1- 8	Verses 9-10	Verses 11-15
Helping through Hospitality	Harming through Haughtiness	Honoring Holiness
Gaius	Diotrephes	Demetrius

YOUR DAILY WALK Hospitality speaks volumes about a person's Christianity. A Christian who practices hospitality is saying in effect, "My house or apartment may not be a candidate for *Better Homes and Gardens,* but I care enough about you to share it with you." Hospitality is other-oriented, for it seeks to benefit others who are in need. To help you practice hospitality, sit down with your calendar, and select one date in the next few weeks when you will share your home with others. Reserve that date, telephone someone you've been meaning to invite, and plan your own "Operation Gaius."

Hospitals should not have a monopoly on hospitality.

INSIGHT "If I've Said It Once, I've Said It a Dozen Times!"
Notice the repetition of three themes in John's writings:

John	1 John	2 John	3 John
Love 13:34-35	2:7-11; 3:10-14; 4:7–5:3	5-6	1
Truth 1:17; 3:21; 14:6, 17	1:6-7; 2:4, 21, 27; 4:6	1-4	3, 8, 12
Joy 16:24; 17:13	1:4		12

This letter is from John the Elder.*

It is written to Gaius, my dear friend, whom I love in the truth.

²Dear friend, I am praying that all is well with you and that your body is as healthy as I know your soul is. ³Some of the brothers recently returned and made me very happy by telling me about your faithfulness and that you are living in the truth. ⁴I could have no greater joy than to hear that my children live in the truth.

⁵Dear friend, you are doing a good work for God when you take care of the traveling teachers* who are passing through, even though they are strangers to you. ⁶They have told the church here of your friendship and your loving deeds. You do well to send them on their way in a manner that pleases God. ⁷For they are traveling for the Lord* and accept nothing from those who are not Christians.* ⁸So we ourselves should support them so that we may become partners with them for the truth.

⁹I sent a brief letter to the church about this, but Diotrephes, who loves to be the leader, does not acknowledge our authority.

1 Greek *From the elder.*   **5** Greek *the brothers;* also in verse 10.   **7a** Greek *the Name.*   **7b** Greek *from Gentiles.*

[10]When I come, I will report some of the things he is doing and the wicked things he is saying about us. He not only refuses to welcome the traveling teachers, he also tells others not to help them. And when they do help, he puts them out of the church.

[11]Dear friend, don't let this bad example influence you. Follow only what is good. Remember that those who do good prove that they are God's children, and those who do evil prove that they do not know God.

[12]But everyone speaks highly of Demetrius, even truth itself. We ourselves can say the same for him, and you know we speak the truth.

[13]I have much to tell you, but I don't want to do it in a letter. [14]For I hope to see you soon, and then we will talk face to face.

[15]May God's peace be with you.

Your friends here send you their greetings. Please give my personal greetings to each of our friends there.

DECEMBER 21 □ DAY 356
Unscrambling the Truth

LOOK BACK This week's selection of readings is from the "General Epistles," so called because the letters are typically addressed to scattered Christians generally, rather than to a specific individual or church. In contrast to Paul's letters, where the name of the book tells you the *recipient* of the letter, these books have names that indicate the *writer* of the letter: James, Peter, John. Here are six keys to help you unlock each book and remember its theme:

James: "Faith Gauge" (how to know if you have a living, breathing faith in God)

1 Peter: "Pain with a Purpose" (how to face painful circumstances that invade your life)

2 Peter: "Poison in the Pew" (how to deal with false teaching and false teachers that arise from within your church)

1 John: "Fellowship Barometer" (how to know if you are walking in fellowship with God, and what to do if you aren't)

2 John: "Bolt the Door" (how to be discerning and wise about false teachers)

3 John: "Open the Door" (how to be hospitable and supportive toward genuine teachers)

LOOK UP Try your hand at a little word quiz. Rearrange the letters in each word or phrase to form the name of a book of the Bible. You have one minute. Go!

We should have regular checkups to avoid truth-decay.

- CATS = the book of _ _ _ _.
- MT. WHEAT is no mountain at all but the book of _ _ _ _ _ _ _.
- LAMPSS is a bright idea for the book of _ _ _ _ _ _.
- NEUTER MOODY is a funny way to mix up the book of _ _ _ _ _ _ _ _ _ _ _.
- SEE SING is not the name of a new prison but the book of _ _ _ _ _ _ _.
- AH HAZE PIN is a sharp idea for scrambling the book of _ _ _ _ _ _ _ _ _.

Now that you've got the idea, why not try your hand at a few others? It's a fun way to help a friend or family member learn the books of the Bible. (Be sure there is a copy of the Table of Contents to the Bible handy for ready reference!)

(*Answers:* Acts, Matthew, Psalms, Deuteronomy, Genesis, Zephaniah)

LOOK AHEAD The epistles you have read this past week at first may seem to have confusing and even contradictory messages.

"After all," you might ask, "am I supposed to 'Bolt the Door' (2 John) or 'Open the Door' (3 John)? Am I supposed to give thanks for painful circumstances (1 Peter) or avoid the source of that pain (2 Peter)? If good works can't save me (James), then what are good works really good for anyway?" The key is in the context.

You should bolt the door if someone is selling you poison (and certainly, false teaching is every bit as lethal as poison), but you should open the door to faithful teachers and preachers of the truth.

You should give thanks for circumstances you *cannot* change, but you should work hard to change things you *can* change—such as the presence of false teachers in your church.

You should remember that good works cannot save you, but you are saved for the purpose of good works.

Take a letter you have read this past week, and make it your marching orders for the coming week. Don't just traffic in the truth—be a doer of it!

Jude

JUDE writes a fiery letter about the war the church must fight against destroyers in its own ranks. These corrupt teachers have a perverted view of God's grace and liberty, using salvation as an opportunity to sin with safety. Because they prefer their own ideas to God's truths, their beliefs result in shocking immorality. Jude reminds his readers of God's severe judgment on such hypocrites. He tells true believers to do two things: keep themselves from such sin and rescue others stumbling toward it.

Focus	Emergency	Examples	Exhortations
Divisions	Announcement of Falling Away	Anatomy of Falling Away	Antidote for Falling Away
	1　　　　　　4	5　　　　　　16	17　　　　　　25
Topics	Why Contend for the Faith		How to Contend for the Faith
	Contention	Condemnation	Caution
Place	Unknown		
Time	Approximately A.D. 66–80		

DECEMBER 22 ☐ DAY 357
JUDE
Contending for the Faith

OVERVIEW When the truth of God is under attack, it is time to enter the spiritual battle and fight for the faith. But beware! Only believers who are spiritually "in shape" will be ready to answer the summons. Jude begins a letter about the mutual mercy, peace, and love shared by all believers. But instead he feels compelled to challenge them to contend for the faith. The danger is real: False teachers have crept into the church, turning God's grace into license to do as they please. Jude reminds such people of God's past dealings with faithless Israel, disobedient angels, and wicked Sodom. In the face of such warnings, Christians have no excuse to be caught off guard.

Verses 1-4	Verses 5-16	Verses 17-25
Announcement of Falling Away	Anatomy of Falling Away	Antidote for Falling Away
Emergency	Examples	Exhortations

YOUR DAILY WALK Arrange a postage stamp, a sheet of paper, an envelope, and a pen before you. Then prayerfully read the following:

Lay hold of the Bible until the Bible lays hold of you.

"If Christ comes to rule the hearts of men, it will be because we take him with us on the tractor, behind the desk, when we're making a sale to a customer, or when we're driving on the road."—Alexander Nunn

"The deathless Book has survived three great dangers: the negligence of its friends; the false systems built upon it; and the warfare of those who have hated it."—Isaac Taylor

"I have a very simple thing to ask of you. I ask every man and woman that from this day on they will realize that part of the destiny of America lies in their daily perusal of this great Book."—Woodrow Wilson

Is the "faith of our fathers" worth proclaiming? Take ten minutes right now . . . and write someone a letter about it!

INSIGHT Triads of Trouble
Jude illustrates his message in threes: three examples of judgment (Egypt, angels, Sodom); three declarations of woe (Cain, Balaam, Korah); and three exhortations to caution (what are they?).

This letter is from Jude, a slave of Jesus Christ and a brother of James.

I am writing to all who are called to live in the love of God the Father and the care of Jesus Christ.

²May you receive more and more of God's mercy, peace, and love.

³Dearly loved friends, I had been eagerly planning to write to you about the salvation we all share. But now I find that I must write about something else, urging you to defend the truth of the Good News.* God gave this unchanging truth once for all time to his holy people. ⁴I say this because some godless people have wormed their way in among you, saying that God's forgiveness allows us to live immoral lives. The fate of such people was determined long ago, for they have

3 Greek *to contend for the faith.*

turned against our only Master and Lord, Jesus Christ.

[5]I must remind you—and you know it well—that even though the Lord* rescued the whole nation of Israel from Egypt, he later destroyed every one of those who did not remain faithful. [6]And I remind you of the angels who did not stay within the limits of authority God gave them but left the place where they belonged. God has kept them chained in prisons of darkness, waiting for the day of judgment. [7]And don't forget the cities of Sodom and Gomorrah and their neighboring towns, which were filled with sexual immorality and every kind of sexual perversion. Those cities were destroyed by fire and are a warning of the eternal fire that will punish all who are evil.

[8]Yet these false teachers, who claim authority from their dreams, live immoral lives, defy authority, and scoff at the power of the glorious ones.* [9]But even Michael, one of the mightiest of the angels, did not dare accuse Satan of blasphemy, but simply said, "The Lord rebuke you." (This took place when Michael was arguing with Satan about Moses' body.) [10]But these people mock and curse the things they do not understand. Like animals, they do whatever their instincts tell them, and they bring about their own destruction. [11]How terrible it will be for them! For they follow the evil example of Cain, who killed his brother. Like Balaam, they will do anything for money. And like Korah, they will perish because of their rebellion.

[12]When these people join you in fellowship meals celebrating the love of the Lord, they are like dangerous reefs that can shipwreck you.* They are shameless in the way they care only about themselves. They are like clouds blowing over dry land without giving rain, promising much but producing nothing. They are like trees without fruit at harvesttime. They are not only dead but doubly dead, for they have been pulled out by the roots. [13]They are like wild waves of the sea, churning up the dirty foam of their shameful deeds. They are wandering stars, heading for everlasting gloom and darkness.

[14]Now Enoch, who lived seven generations after Adam, prophesied about these people. He said,

"Look, the Lord is coming
      with thousands of his holy ones.
[15] He will bring the people of the world
      to judgment.
He will convict the ungodly of all the
      evil things
      they have done in rebellion
and of all the insults that godless
      sinners
      have spoken against him."*

[16]These people are grumblers and complainers, doing whatever evil they feel like. They are loudmouthed braggarts, and they flatter others to get favors in return.

[17]But you, my dear friends, must remember what the apostles of our Lord Jesus Christ told you, [18]that in the last times there would be scoffers whose purpose in life is to enjoy themselves in every evil way imaginable. [19]Now they are here, and they are the ones who are creating divisions among you. They live by natural instinct because they do not have God's Spirit living in them.

[20]But you, dear friends, must continue to build your lives on the foundation of your holy faith. And continue to pray as you are directed by the Holy Spirit.* [21]Live in such a way that God's love can bless you as you wait for the eternal life that our Lord Jesus Christ in his mercy is going to give you. [22]Show mercy to those whose faith is wavering. [23]Rescue others by snatching them from the flames of judgment. There are still others to whom you need to show mercy, but be careful that you aren't contaminated by their sins.*

[24]And now, all glory to God, who is able to keep you from stumbling, and who will bring you into his glorious presence innocent of sin and with great joy. [25]All glory to him, who alone is God our Savior, through Jesus Christ our Lord. Yes, glory, majesty, power, and authority belong to him, in the beginning, now, and forevermore. Amen.

---

5 Some manuscripts read *Jesus*.   8 *The glorious ones* are probably evil angels.   12 Or *they are contaminants among you*, or *they are stains*.   14-15 The quotation comes from the Apocrypha: Enoch 1:9.   20 Greek *Pray in the Holy Spirit*.   23 Greek *mercy, hating even the clothing stained by the flesh*.

Revelation

JOHN, while exiled on the island of Patmos, receives the visions contained in the book of Revelation. As the first verse states, through a dramatic series of pictures, signs, and symbols, Jesus Christ reveals to John—and to all subsequent readers—what will happen at the end of time. John depicts cataclysmic judgment upon the earth, the final destruction of satanic forces, and the beginning of a new heaven and new earth.

Focus	Heaven	Earth					New Heaven and Earth
Divisions	Letters to Seven Churches	Opening the Seven Seals	Blowing the Seven Trumpets	Describing the Seven Signs	Pouring Out the Seven Bowls	Destroying God's Enemies	Making All Things New
	1 3	4 6	7 9	10 13	14 16	17 19	20 22
Topics	Coming King	Coming Calamity					Coming Kingdom
	Judge	Judgment					Joy
Place		Aegean Island of Patmos					
Time		About A.D. 95–96					

DECEMBER 23 □ DAY 358
REVELATION 1–3
Letters to Seven Churches

OVERVIEW John's opening words provide the theme for the book. "This is a Revelation from Jesus Christ" in all his power and holiness, majesty and justice. John is commanded to write seven letters, each containing a message of reproof, rebuke, or reassurance, to seven first-century churches in Asia Minor. The Lord of the church knows the condition of the church. Like a skilled physician, he diagnoses the sin that must be dealt with if each congregation is to overcome, rather than be overcome, in the evil day.

Chapter 1	Chapters 2–3
Standing among the Churches	Speaking to the Churches: Ephesus, Smyrna, Pergamum, Thyatira, Sardis, Philadelphia, Laodicea
Seven Lampstands	Seven Letters

YOUR DAILY WALK If someone were to evaluate your Christian life today, which of the seven churches addressed in Revelation 2–3 would they say it most closely resembles?

When your work speaks for itself, don't interrupt.

- Ephesus (where love for Christ had grown cold)?
- Sardis (where the church was like a morgue)?
- Laodicea (where Christians were yawning and self-satisfied)?

Once you've thought about the *diagnosis* of your spiritual life, don't stop there! Read on to discover the specific *cure* Christ recommends for that spiritual ill. Then, with God's help, put that cure to work today so that your light can burn brightly for the Savior.

INSIGHT The Five Books of John
The apostle John wrote about the message of life in three different kinds of Scripture: the *Gospel* of John (biography), which speaks of eternal life; the *Epistles* of John (letters), which speak of the Christian life; and the *prophecies* of Revelation (visions), which speak of victorious life now and for eternity.

CHAPTER 1

This is a revelation from* Jesus Christ, which God gave him concerning the events that will happen soon. An angel was sent to God's servant John so that John could share the revelation with God's other servants. ²John faithfully reported the word of God and the testimony of Jesus Christ—everything he saw.

³God blesses the one who reads this prophecy to the church, and he blesses all who listen to it and obey what it says. For the time is near when these things will happen.

⁴This letter is from John to the seven churches in the province of Asia. Grace and peace from the one who is, who always was, and who is still to come; from the sevenfold Spirit* before his throne; ⁵and from Jesus Christ, who is the faithful witness to these things, the first to rise from the dead, and the commander of all the rulers of the world.

All praise to him who loves us and has freed us from our sins by shedding his blood for us. ⁶He has made us his kingdom and his priests who serve before God his

1:1 Or *of.*   **1:4** Greek *the seven spirits.*

Father. Give to him everlasting glory! He rules forever and ever! Amen!

⁷Look! He comes with the clouds of heaven. And everyone will see him—even those who pierced him. And all the nations of the earth will weep because of him. Yes! Amen!

⁸"I am the Alpha and the Omega—the beginning and the end," says the Lord God. "I am the one who is, who always was, and who is still to come, the Almighty One."

⁹I am John, your brother. In Jesus we are partners in suffering and in the Kingdom and in patient endurance. I was exiled to the island of Patmos for preaching the word of God and speaking about Jesus. ¹⁰It was the Lord's Day, and I was worshiping in the Spirit.* Suddenly, I heard a loud voice behind me, a voice that sounded like a trumpet blast. ¹¹It said, "Write down what you see, and send it to the seven churches: Ephesus, Smyrna, Pergamum, Thyatira, Sardis, Philadelphia, and Laodicea."

¹²When I turned to see who was speaking to me, I saw seven gold lampstands. ¹³And standing in the middle of the lampstands was the Son of Man.* He was wearing a long robe with a gold sash across his chest. ¹⁴His head and his hair were white like wool, as white as snow. And his eyes were bright like flames of fire. ¹⁵His feet were as bright as bronze refined in a furnace, and his voice thundered like mighty ocean waves. ¹⁶He held seven stars in his right hand, and a sharp two-edged sword came from his mouth. And his face was as bright as the sun in all its brilliance.

¹⁷When I saw him, I fell at his feet as dead. But he laid his right hand on me and said, "Don't be afraid! I am the First and the Last. ¹⁸I am the living one who died. Look, I am alive forever and ever! And I hold the keys of death and the grave.* ¹⁹Write down what you have seen—both the things that are now happening and the things that will happen later. ²⁰This is the meaning of the seven stars you saw in my right hand and the seven gold lampstands: The seven stars are the angels of* the seven churches, and the seven lampstands are the seven churches.

CHAPTER 2

"Write this letter to the angel of* the church in Ephesus. This is the message from the one who holds the seven stars in his right hand, the one who walks among the seven gold lampstands:

²"I know all the things you do. I have seen your hard work and your patient endurance. I know you don't tolerate evil people. You have examined the claims of those who say they are apostles but are not. You have discovered they are liars. ³You have patiently suffered for me without quitting. ⁴But I have this complaint against you. You don't love me or each other as you did at first! ⁵Look how far you have fallen from your first love! Turn back to me again and work as you did at first. If you don't, I will come and remove your lampstand from its place among the churches. ⁶But there is this about you that is good: You hate the deeds of the immoral Nicolaitans, just as I do.

⁷"Anyone who is willing to hear should listen to the Spirit and understand what the Spirit is saying to the churches. Everyone who is victorious will eat from the tree of life in the paradise of God.

⁸"Write this letter to the angel of the church in Smyrna. This is the message from the one who is the First and the Last, who died and is alive:

⁹"I know about your suffering and your poverty—but you are rich! I know the slander of those opposing you. They say they are Jews, but they really aren't because theirs is a synagogue of Satan. ¹⁰Don't be afraid of what you are about to suffer. The Devil will throw some of you into prison and put you to the test. You will be persecuted for 'ten days.' Remain faithful even when facing death, and I will give you the crown of life.

¹¹"Anyone who is willing to hear should listen to the Spirit and understand what the Spirit is saying to the churches. Whoever is victorious will not be hurt by the second death.

¹²"Write this letter to the angel of the church in Pergamum. This is the message

---

1:10 Or *in spirit.*   **1:13** Or *one who looked like a man;* Greek reads *one like a son of man.*   **1:18** Greek *and Hades.*   **1:20** Or *the messengers for.*   **2:1** Or *the messenger for;* also in 2:8, 12, 18.

from the one who has a sharp two-edged sword:

¹³"I know that you live in the city where that great throne of Satan is located, and yet you have remained loyal to me. And you refused to deny me even when Antipas, my faithful witness, was martyred among you by Satan's followers. ¹⁴And yet I have a few complaints against you. You tolerate some among you who are like Balaam, who showed Balak how to trip up the people of Israel. He taught them to worship idols by eating food offered to idols and by committing sexual sin. ¹⁵In the same way, you have some Nicolaitans among you—people who follow the same teaching and commit the same sins. ¹⁶Repent, or I will come to you suddenly and fight against them with the sword of my mouth.

¹⁷"Anyone who is willing to hear should listen to the Spirit and understand what the Spirit is saying to the churches. Everyone who is victorious will eat of the manna that has been hidden away in heaven. And I will give to each one a white stone, and on the stone will be engraved a new name that no one knows except the one who receives it.

¹⁸"Write this letter to the angel of the church in Thyatira. This is the message from the Son of God, whose eyes are bright like flames of fire, whose feet are like polished bronze:

¹⁹"I know all the things you do—your love, your faith, your service, and your patient endurance. And I can see your constant improvement in all these things. ²⁰But I have this complaint against you. You are permitting that woman—that Jezebel who calls herself a prophet—to lead my servants astray. She is encouraging them to worship idols, eat food offered to idols, and commit sexual sin. ²¹I gave her time to repent, but she would not turn away from her immorality. ²²Therefore, I will throw her upon a sickbed, and she will suffer greatly with all who commit adultery with her, unless they turn away from all their evil deeds. ²³I will strike her children dead. And all the churches will know that I am the one who searches out the thoughts and intentions of every person. And I will give to each of you whatever you deserve. ²⁴But I also have a message for the rest of you in Thyatira who have not followed this false teaching ('deeper truths,' as they call them—depths of Satan, really). I will ask nothing more of you ²⁵except that you hold tightly to what you have until I come.

²⁶"To all who are victorious, who obey me to the very end, I will give authority over all the nations. ²⁷They will rule the nations with an iron rod and smash them like clay pots. ²⁸They will have the same authority I received from my Father, and I will also give them the morning star! ²⁹Anyone who is willing to hear should listen to the Spirit and understand what the Spirit is saying to the churches.

CHAPTER 3

"Write this letter to the angel of* the church in Sardis. This is the message from the one who has the sevenfold Spirit* of God and the seven stars:

"I know all the things you do, and that you have a reputation for being alive—but you are dead. ²Now wake up! Strengthen what little remains, for even what is left is at the point of death. Your deeds are far from right in the sight of God. ³Go back to what you heard and believed at first; hold to it firmly and turn to me again. Unless you do, I will come upon you suddenly, as unexpected as a thief.

⁴"Yet even in Sardis there are some who have not soiled their garments with evil deeds. They will walk with me in white, for they are worthy. ⁵All who are victorious will be clothed in white. I will never erase their names from the Book of Life, but I will announce before my Father and his angels that they are mine. ⁶Anyone who is willing to hear should listen to the Spirit and understand what the Spirit is saying to the churches.

⁷"Write this letter to the angel of the church in Philadelphia. This is the message from the one who is holy and true. He is the one who has the key of David. He opens doors, and no one can shut them; he shuts doors, and no one can open them.

3:1a Or *the messenger for;* also in 3:7, 14.   **3:1b** Greek *the seven spirits.*

[8]"I know all the things you do, and I have opened a door for you that no one can shut. You have little strength, yet you obeyed my word and did not deny me. [9]Look! I will force those who belong to Satan—those liars who say they are Jews but are not—to come and bow down at your feet. They will acknowledge that you are the ones I love.

[10]"Because you have obeyed my command to persevere, I will protect you from the great time of testing that will come upon the whole world to test those who belong to this world. [11]Look, I am coming quickly. Hold on to what you have, so that no one will take away your crown. [12]All who are victorious will become pillars in the Temple of my God, and they will never have to leave it. And I will write my God's name on them, and they will be citizens in the city of my God—the new Jerusalem that comes down from heaven from my God. And they will have my new name inscribed upon them. [13]Anyone who is willing to hear should listen to the Spirit and understand what the Spirit is saying to the churches.

[14]"Write this letter to the angel of the church in Laodicea. This is the message from

3:14 Or *the source.*

the one who is the Amen—the faithful and true witness, the ruler* of God's creation:

[15]"I know all the things you do, that you are neither hot nor cold. I wish you were one or the other! [16]But since you are like lukewarm water, I will spit you out of my mouth! [17]You say, 'I am rich. I have everything I want. I don't need a thing!' And you don't realize that you are wretched and miserable and poor and blind and naked. [18]I advise you to buy gold from me—gold that has been purified by fire. Then you will be rich. And also buy white garments so you will not be shamed by your nakedness. And buy ointment for your eyes so you will be able to see. [19]I am the one who corrects and disciplines everyone I love. Be diligent and turn from your indifference.

[20]"Look! Here I stand at the door and knock. If you hear me calling and open the door, I will come in, and we will share a meal as friends. [21]I will invite everyone who is victorious to sit with me on my throne, just as I was victorious and sat with my Father on his throne. [22]Anyone who is willing to hear should listen to the Spirit and understand what the Spirit is saying to the churches."

DECEMBER 24 ☐ DAY 359
REVELATION 4–6
Opening the Seven Seals

 OVERVIEW Beginning with chapter 4, John is invited to "come up here" in order to see "what must happen after these things" (4:1). Transported in the spirit, John first sees a "technicolor" vision of the sovereign God upon his heavenly throne, holding a scroll in which are written his judgments for the earth. No one is qualified to open the seals of the scroll and execute God's judgments except the Lamb, "the Lion of the tribe of Judah" (5:5). One by one he breaks the seals, and horrible judgments fall upon the earth and its inhabitants.

Chapter 4	Chapter 5	Chapter 6
The One Who Sits on the Throne	The Lamb Who Opens the Scroll	The Plagues of the Seven Seals
Majestic	Worthy	Devastating

YOUR DAILY WALK Here is a thought worthy of your consideration: The elders who surround the throne of God proclaim, "You are worthy, O Lord our God" (4:11). Later they say to the Lamb, "You are worthy" (5:9), and still later all the hosts of heaven exclaim, "The Lamb is worthy" (5:12). What makes the God of heaven and the Lamb of God so worthy of receiving worship and adoration?

We are not Christ's lawyers; we are his witnesses.

First, God is worthy because of who he is—the God of infinite perfection and holiness. Second, God is worthy because of what he has done—the Father in creation, and his Son, the Lamb, in redemption and salvation.

The question to ponder is this: How can I show in my daily walk that I serve a worthy God? Is my speech worthy of him? Is my conduct worthy of my privileged position in the family of God? Do I talk about him often? worship him wholeheartedly? seek to please him daily?

Tape the words of Revelation 4:11 to your dashboard or mirror to remind you frequently that God is deserving of your greatest devotion and act of service. Indeed, he is worthy.

INSIGHT The Invisible God Made Visible
The Bible describes God as "invisible" (Colossians 1:15), reminding us that "no one has ever seen God" (John 1:18). Thus, John's awesome and majestic description of God the Father upon the throne (Revelation 4:2-3) is perhaps as much of God as humans will ever see this side of heaven.

CHAPTER 4

Then as I looked, I saw a door standing open in heaven, and the same voice I had heard before spoke to me with the sound of a mighty trumpet blast. The voice said, "Come up here, and I will show you what must happen after these things." ²And instantly I was in the Spirit,* and I saw a throne in heaven and someone sitting on it! ³The one sitting on the throne was as brilliant as gemstones—jasper and carnelian. And the glow of an emerald circled his throne like a rainbow. ⁴Twenty-four thrones surrounded him, and twenty-four elders sat on them. They were all clothed in white and had gold crowns on their heads. ⁵And from the throne came flashes of lightning and the rumble of thunder. And in front of the throne were seven lampstands with burning flames. They are the seven spirits* of God. ⁶In front of the throne was a shiny sea of glass, sparkling like crystal.

In the center and around the throne were four living beings, each covered with eyes, front and back. ⁷The first of these living beings had the form of a lion; the second looked like an ox; the third had a human face; and the fourth had the form of an eagle with wings spread out as though in flight. ⁸Each of these living beings had six wings, and their wings were covered with

eyes, inside and out. Day after day and night after night they keep on saying,

> "Holy, holy, holy is the Lord God
> Almighty—
> the one who always was, who is, and
> who is still to come."

⁹Whenever the living beings give glory and honor and thanks to the one sitting on the throne, the one who lives forever and ever, ¹⁰the twenty-four elders fall down and worship the one who lives forever and ever. And they lay their crowns before the throne and say,

> ¹¹ "You are worthy, O Lord our God,
> to receive glory and honor and
> power.
> For you created everything,
> and it is for your pleasure that they
> exist and were created."

CHAPTER 5

And I saw a scroll in the right hand of the one who was sitting on the throne. There was writing on the inside and the outside of the scroll, and it was sealed with seven seals. ²And I saw a strong angel, who shouted with a loud voice: "Who is worthy to break the seals on this scroll and unroll it?" ³But no one in heaven or on earth or

4:2 Or *in spirit.*   4:5 See 1:4 and 3:1, where the same expression is translated *the sevenfold Spirit.*

under the earth was able to open the scroll and read it.

[4]Then I wept because no one could be found who was worthy to open the scroll and read it. [5]But one of the twenty-four elders said to me, "Stop weeping! Look, the Lion of the tribe of Judah, the heir to David's throne,* has conquered. He is worthy to open the scroll and break its seven seals."

[6]I looked and I saw a Lamb that had been killed but was now standing between the throne and the four living beings and among the twenty-four elders. He had seven horns and seven eyes, which are the seven spirits* of God that are sent out into every part of the earth. [7]He stepped forward and took the scroll from the right hand of the one sitting on the throne. [8]And as he took the scroll, the four living beings and the twenty-four elders fell down before the Lamb. Each one had a harp, and they held gold bowls filled with incense— the prayers of God's people!

[9]And they sang a new song with these words:

"You are worthy to take the scroll
    and break its seals and open it.
For you were killed, and your blood
    has ransomed people for God
    from every tribe and language and
        people and nation.
[10] And you have caused them to become
        God's kingdom and his priests.
    And they will reign* on the earth."

[11]Then I looked again, and I heard the singing of thousands and millions of angels around the throne and the living beings and the elders. [12]And they sang in a mighty chorus:

"The Lamb is worthy—the Lamb who
        was killed.
    He is worthy to receive power and
        riches
    and wisdom and strength
    and honor and glory and blessing."

[13]And then I heard every creature in heaven and on earth and under the earth and in the sea. They also sang:

"Blessing and honor and glory and
        power
    belong to the one sitting on the throne
    and to the Lamb forever and ever."

[14]And the four living beings said, "Amen!" And the twenty-four elders fell down and worshiped God and the Lamb.

CHAPTER 6

As I watched, the Lamb broke the first of the seven seals on the scroll. Then one of the four living beings called out with a voice that sounded like thunder, "Come!" [2]I looked up and saw a white horse. Its rider carried a bow, and a crown was placed on his head. He rode out to win many battles and gain the victory.

[3]When the Lamb broke the second seal, I heard the second living being say, "Come!" [4]And another horse appeared, a red one. Its rider was given a mighty sword and the authority to remove peace from the earth. And there was war and slaughter everywhere.

[5]When the Lamb broke the third seal, I heard the third living being say, "Come!" And I looked up and saw a black horse, and its rider was holding a pair of scales in his hand. [6]And a voice from among the four living beings said, "A loaf of wheat bread or three loaves of barley for a day's pay.* And don't waste* the olive oil and wine."

[7]And when the Lamb broke the fourth seal, I heard the fourth living being say, "Come!" [8]And I looked up and saw a horse whose color was pale green like a corpse. And Death was the name of its rider, who was followed around by the Grave.* They were given authority over one-fourth of the earth, to kill with the sword and famine and disease* and wild animals.

[9]And when the Lamb broke the fifth seal, I saw under the altar the souls of all who had been martyred for the word of God and for being faithful in their witness. [10]They called loudly to the Lord and said, "O Sovereign Lord, holy and true, how long will it be before you judge the people who belong to this world for what they have done to us? When will you avenge our blood against these people?" [11]Then a white robe was given to each of them. And they were told to rest a little longer until the full number of their brothers and sisters—their fellow servants of Jesus—had been martyred.

[12]I watched as the Lamb broke the sixth seal, and there was a great earthquake. The sun became as dark as black cloth, and the moon became as red as blood.

5:5 Greek *the root of David.*   5:6 See note on 4:5.   5:10 Some manuscripts read *they are reigning.*   6:6a Greek *A choinix of wheat for a denarius, and 3 choinix of barley for a denarius.*   6:6b Or *hurt.*   6:8a Greek *by Hades.*   6:8b Greek *death.*

¹³Then the stars of the sky fell to the earth like green figs falling from trees shaken by mighty winds. ¹⁴And the sky was rolled up like a scroll and taken away. And all of the mountains and all of the islands disappeared. ¹⁵Then the kings of the earth, the rulers, the generals, the wealthy people, the people with great power, and every slave and every free person—all hid themselves in the caves and among the rocks of the mountains. ¹⁶And they cried to the mountains and the rocks, "Fall on us and hide us from the face of the one who sits on the throne and from the wrath of the Lamb. ¹⁷For the great day of their wrath has come, and who will be able to survive?"

DECEMBER 25 ☐ DAY 360
MATTHEW 1:18–2:12; LUKE 2:1-10
The Original Christmas Present

OVERVIEW On this most important of birthdays, we interrupt our normal Bible reading schedule to reflect on the two Gospel accounts of our Lord's birth.

In Matthew we see him as a King to be worshiped. Tracing his genealogy back to Abraham shows that Jesus is indeed in line to be King of the Jews. His miraculous conception fulfills the prophecy made by Isaiah that he would be born of a virgin. His name, *Immanuel* ("God with us"), reminds us of his divine mission. The place of his birth (Bethlehem) fulfills Micah's prediction. His flight to Egypt to escape the death threat of crazed King Herod fulfills Hosea's word and Jeremiah's heartrending lament.

In Luke we see Jesus as a baby lying in a manger. Caesar's census causes Jesus' earthly parents to return to the city of David to register. There, with no "emergency room" but a stable and no "attendants" but barn animals, God becomes a man . . . a Savior . . . Christ the Lord.

The angels greet his birth by saying, "Glory to God in the highest heaven"; the shepherds announce his arrival by "glorifying and praising God for what the angels had told them, and because they had seen the child." How will you respond to the joyous news that a Savior has come into the world?

Jesus is God spelling himself out in language the world can understand.

YOUR DAILY WALK Who, in your opinion, is Jesus of Nazareth? How would you describe him to a person who had never met him? And if he came knocking at the door of your heart this Christmas season, would he find room in the inn . . . or a No Vacancy sign prominently displayed?

Singing and reciting the songs of the season are marvelous ways to tune your heart for Christmas. Before you close your quiet time today, find a hymnbook and a quiet place where you can be alone. Read out loud (or sing softly) a verse or two of the following Christmas favorites. Let the words remind you of the "reason for the season"—the matchless Savior who is Jesus.

- "Thou Didst Leave Thy Throne"
- "Silent Night, Holy Night"
- "O Little Town of Bethlehem"
- "While Shepherds Watched Their Flocks"
- "Away in a Manger"
- "The First Noel the Angel Did Say"

INSIGHT Who Do You Say That He Is?
Down through the centuries, the miraculous account of Jesus' birth and life has prompted men and women to respond in praise and worship. Listen to what the sons of men have said about the Son of God:

"If Shakespeare should come into this room, we would all rise; but if Jesus Christ should come in, we would all kneel."—Charles Lamb

"I know men; and I tell you that Jesus Christ is no mere man. Between him and every other person in the world there is no possible term of comparison."—Napoléon

"Man's ultimate destiny depends not on whether he can learn new lessons or make new discoveries and conquests, but on his acceptance of the lesson taught him close upon two thousand years ago."—Inscription at the eastern entrance of Rockefeller Center, New York City

MATTHEW 1:18–2:12

¹⁸Now this is how Jesus the Messiah was born. His mother, Mary, was engaged to be married to Joseph. But while she was still a virgin, she became pregnant by the Holy Spirit. ¹⁹Joseph, her fiancé, being a just man, decided to break the engagement quietly, so as not to disgrace her publicly.

²⁰As he considered this, he fell asleep, and an angel of the Lord appeared to him in a dream. "Joseph, son of David," the angel said, "do not be afraid to go ahead with your marriage to Mary. For the child within her has been conceived by the Holy Spirit. ²¹And she will have a son, and you are to name him Jesus,* for he will save his people from their sins." ²²All of this happened to fulfill the Lord's message through his prophet:

²³ "Look! The virgin will conceive a child!
    She will give birth to a son,
 and he will be called Immanuel*
    (meaning, God is with us)."

²⁴When Joseph woke up, he did what the angel of the Lord commanded. He brought Mary home to be his wife, ²⁵but she remained a virgin until her son was born. And Joseph named him Jesus.

CHAPTER 2

Jesus was born in the town of Bethlehem in Judea, during the reign of King Herod. About that time some wise men* from eastern lands arrived in Jerusalem, asking, ²"Where is the newborn king of the Jews? We have seen his star as it arose,* and we have come to worship him."

³Herod was deeply disturbed by their question, as was all of Jerusalem. ⁴He called a meeting of the leading priests and teachers of religious law. "Where did the prophets say the Messiah would be born?" he asked them.

⁵"In Bethlehem," they said, "for this is what the prophet wrote:

⁶ 'O Bethlehem of Judah,
    you are not just a lowly village in
        Judah,
 for a ruler will come from you
    who will be the shepherd for my
        people Israel.'*"

⁷Then Herod sent a private message to the wise men, asking them to come see him. At this meeting he learned the exact time when they first saw the star. ⁸Then he told them, "Go to Bethlehem and search carefully for the child. And when you find him, come back and tell me so that I can go and worship him, too!"

⁹After this interview the wise men went their way. Once again the star appeared to them, guiding them to Bethlehem. It went ahead of them and stopped over the place where the child was. ¹⁰When they saw the star, they were filled with joy! ¹¹They entered the house where the child and his mother, Mary, were, and they fell down before him and worshiped him. Then they opened their treasure chests and gave him gifts of gold, frankincense, and myrrh. ¹²But when it was time to leave, they went home another way, because God had warned them in a dream not to return to Herod.

LUKE 2:1-10

At that time the Roman emperor, Augustus, decreed that a census should be taken throughout the Roman Empire. ²(This was the first census taken when Quirinius

---

1:21 *Jesus* means "The LORD saves." **1:23** Isa 7:14; 8:8, 10. **2:1** Or *royal astrologers;* Greek reads *magi;* also in 2:7, 16. **2:2** Or *in the east.* **2:6** Mic 5:2; 2 Sam 5:2.

was governor of Syria.) ³All returned to their own towns to register for this census. ⁴And because Joseph was a descendant of King David, he had to go to Bethlehem in Judea, David's ancient home. He traveled there from the village of Nazareth in Galilee. ⁵He took with him Mary, his fiancée, who was obviously pregnant by this time.

⁶And while they were there, the time came for her baby to be born. ⁷She gave birth to her first child, a son. She wrapped him snugly in strips of cloth and laid him in a manger, because there was no room for them in the village inn.

⁸That night some shepherds were in the fields outside the village, guarding their flocks of sheep. ⁹Suddenly, an angel of the Lord appeared among them, and the radiance of the Lord's glory surrounded them. They were terribly frightened, ¹⁰but the angel reassured them. "Don't be afraid!" he said. "I bring you good news of great joy for everyone!

DECEMBER 26 ☐ DAY 361
REVELATION 7–9
Blowing the Seven Trumpets

OVERVIEW The book of Revelation is organized around a series of cycles interrupted by parenthetical sections. Three cycles of judgments (seals, trumpets, and bowls) emerge like three sections of a telescope, each more severe and far-reaching than the previous cycle. Before the seventh seal is opened, John sees four angels place a seal upon 144,000 servants of God, 12,000 from each of the twelve tribes of Israel (7:3-4). In contrast to this, John next sees a vast, innumerable host of martyrs "coming out of the great tribulation" (7:14) for the cause of Christ. At last, the breaking of the seventh seal releases seven trumpets of judgment, which bring death and darkness, tears and torment upon humanity.

Chapter 7		Chapters 8–9	
Numbering a Multitude	A Numberless Multitude	The Seventh Seal	The Seven Trumpets
1 8	9 17	8:1 8:5	8:6 9:21
Sealed	Saved	Silence	Woes

Prayer is listening to what God might want to say to you.

YOUR DAILY WALK How many "purposes for prayer" can you think of? In the margin, see if you can list at least ten before reading on.

There are prayers of praise, thanksgiving, worship, and rejoicing. There are prayers of confession and repentance. There are prayers for personal needs, such as food, health, strength, wisdom, and forgiveness. There are prayers of intercession for the needs of others, for the salvation of unsaved loved ones, and for the ministry of local churches, missionaries, and schools.

Your prayers are a sweet fragrance to God (8:4) as you admit your own inadequacy and lean upon God's promises of provision and power. If you have not already done so, make prayer an indispensable part of your daily time with God. Five minutes on a daily basis represents more than thirty hours in a year . . . and, by any standard, that's a lot of praise, thanksgiving, worship, and rejoicing! Begin today, and every day, with prayer.

INSIGHT Seventh Seal—Seven Angels and Seven Trumpets
Seven was a sacred number to the ancient Hebrew people. It often
symbolized perfection, fullness, abundance, rest, and completion. The
number seven also had a ritual importance to the Hebrews. Since the
number seven is so symbolic in nature, it is no coincidence that it
appears frequently in Revelation, a book noted for its rich symbolism
and imagery.

CHAPTER 7

Then I saw four angels standing at the four corners of the earth, holding back the four winds from blowing upon the earth. Not a leaf rustled in the trees, and the sea became as smooth as glass. ²And I saw another angel coming from the east, carrying the seal of the living God. And he shouted out to those four angels who had been given power to injure land and sea, ³"Wait! Don't hurt the land or the sea or the trees until we have placed the seal of God on the fore-heads of his servants."

⁴And I heard how many were marked with the seal of God. There were 144,000 who were sealed from all the tribes of Israel:

⁵	from Judah	12,000
	from Reuben	12,000
	from Gad	12,000
⁶	from Asher	12,000
	from Naphtali	12,000
	from Manasseh	12,000
⁷	from Simeon	12,000
	from Levi	12,000
	from Issachar	12,000
⁸	from Zebulun	12,000
	from Joseph	12,000
	from Benjamin	12,000

⁹After this I saw a vast crowd, too great to count, from every nation and tribe and people and language, standing in front of the throne and before the Lamb. They were clothed in white and held palm branches in their hands. ¹⁰And they were shouting with a mighty shout, "Salvation comes from our God on the throne and from the Lamb!"

¹¹And all the angels were standing around the throne and around the elders and the four living beings. And they fell face down before the throne and worshiped God. ¹²They said,

"Amen! Blessing and glory and wisdom
    and thanksgiving and honor and
        power and strength
    belong to our God forever and
        forever. Amen!"

¹³Then one of the twenty-four elders asked me, "Who are these who are clothed in white? Where do they come from?"

¹⁴And I said to him, "Sir, you are the one who knows."

Then he said to me, "These are the ones coming out of the great tribulation. They washed their robes in the blood of the Lamb and made them white. ¹⁵That is why they are standing in front of the throne of God, serving him day and night in his Temple. And he who sits on the throne will live among them and shelter them. ¹⁶They will never again be hungry or thirsty, and they will be fully protected from the scorching noontime heat. ¹⁷For the Lamb who stands in front of the throne will be their Shepherd. He will lead them to the springs of life-giving water. And God will wipe away all their tears."

CHAPTER 8

When the Lamb broke the seventh seal, there was silence throughout heaven for about half an hour. ²And I saw the seven angels who stand before God, and they were given seven trumpets.

³Then another angel with a gold incense burner came and stood at the altar. And a great quantity of incense was given to him to mix with the prayers of God's people, to be offered on the gold altar before the throne. ⁴The smoke of the incense, mixed with the prayers of the saints, ascended up to God from the altar where the angel had poured them out. ⁵Then the angel filled the incense burner with fire from the altar and threw it down upon the earth; and thunder crashed, lightning flashed, and there was a terrible earthquake.

⁶Then the seven angels with the seven trumpets prepared to blow their mighty blasts.

⁷The first angel blew his trumpet, and hail and fire mixed with blood were thrown down upon the earth, and one-third of the earth was set on fire. One-third

of the trees were burned, and all the grass was burned.

[8] Then the second angel blew his trumpet, and a great mountain of fire was thrown into the sea. And one-third of the water in the sea became blood. [9] And one-third of all things living in the sea died. And one-third of all the ships on the sea were destroyed.

[10] Then the third angel blew his trumpet, and a great flaming star fell out of the sky, burning like a torch. It fell upon one-third of the rivers and on the springs of water. [11] The name of the star was Bitterness.* It made one-third of the water bitter, and many people died because the water was so bitter.

[12] Then the fourth angel blew his trumpet, and one-third of the sun was struck, and one-third of the moon, and one-third of the stars, and they became dark. And one-third of the day was dark and one-third of the night also.

[13] Then I looked up. And I heard a single eagle crying loudly as it flew through the air, "Terror, terror, terror to all who belong to this world because of what will happen when the last three angels blow their trumpets."

CHAPTER 9

Then the fifth angel blew his trumpet, and I saw a star that had fallen to earth from the sky, and he was given the key to the shaft of the bottomless pit. [2] When he opened it, smoke poured out as though from a huge furnace, and the sunlight and air were darkened by the smoke.

[3] Then locusts came from the smoke and descended on the earth, and they were given power to sting like scorpions. [4] They were told not to hurt the grass or plants or trees but to attack all the people who did not have the seal of God on their foreheads. [5] They were told not to kill them but to torture them for five months with agony like the pain of scorpion stings. [6] In those days people will seek death but will not find it. They will long to die, but death will flee away!

[7] The locusts looked like horses armed

8:11 Greek *Wormwood.*

for battle. They had gold crowns on their heads, and they had human faces. [8] Their hair was long like the hair of a woman, and their teeth were like the teeth of a lion. [9] They wore armor made of iron, and their wings roared like an army of chariots rushing into battle. [10] They had tails that stung like scorpions, with power to torture people. This power was given to them for five months. [11] Their king is the angel from the bottomless pit; his name in Hebrew is *Abaddon,* and in Greek, *Apollyon*—the Destroyer.

[12] The first terror is past, but look, two more terrors are coming!

[13] Then the sixth angel blew his trumpet, and I heard a voice speaking from the four horns of the gold altar that stands in the presence of God. [14] And the voice spoke to the sixth angel who held the trumpet: "Release the four angels who are bound at the great Euphrates River." [15] And the four angels who had been prepared for this hour and day and month and year were turned loose to kill one-third of all the people on earth. [16] They led an army of 200 million mounted troops—I heard an announcement of how many there were.

[17] And in my vision, I saw the horses and the riders sitting on them. The riders wore armor that was fiery red and sky blue and yellow. The horses' heads were like the heads of lions, and fire and smoke and burning sulfur billowed from their mouths. [18] One-third of all the people on earth were killed by these three plagues—by the fire and the smoke and burning sulfur that came from the mouths of the horses. [19] Their power was in their mouths, but also in their tails. For their tails had heads like snakes, with the power to injure people.

[20] But the people who did not die in these plagues still refused to turn from their evil deeds. They continued to worship demons and idols made of gold, silver, bronze, stone, and wood—idols that neither see nor hear nor walk! [21] And they did not repent of their murders or their witchcraft or their immorality or their thefts.

DECEMBER 27 □ DAY 362
REVELATION 10–13
Describing the Seven Signs

OVERVIEW Before the seventh trumpet sounds, John sees a vision of a mighty angel and a small scroll. John is instructed to eat the scroll, which proves sweet to the taste but sour to the stomach. Next, John sees two witnesses who have an astonishing ministry on earth for 1,260 days but then are martyred for their testimony. The sounding of the seventh trumpet is followed by a description of seven persons in chapters 12 and 13. The first four (a sun-clothed woman, a dragon, a male child, and the angel Michael) are all engaged in a struggle that begins in heaven and ends on earth, where the dragon displays his wrath against the fifth, the "rest of [the woman's] children" (12:17). John then sees the final two figures in the drama: the beast from the sea (13:1-10) and the second beast from the earth (13:11-18).

Chapter 10	Chapter 11	Chapter 12	Chapter 13
The Small Scroll	The Two Witnesses	The Terrible Conflict	The Two Beasts
Bitterness	Boldness	Birth	Blasphemies

Seek neither more nor less than God's will for you.

YOUR DAILY WALK Here is a thought worth clipping and pondering: You are indestructible until God's purpose for your life is completed.

Nowhere is that statement more eloquently illustrated than in the lives of the two witnesses John describes in 11:3-12. Though they face a seeming "suicide mission," they are divinely protected until they "complete their testimony" (11:7). Only then are the forces of evil permitted to "conquer them and kill them." But no power on earth can hold them in the grave! At the appointed time, they ascend to heaven to receive God's commendation: Mission accomplished!

You are under this same umbrella of God's protection today. He has a purpose for your life on this earth; and no matter what the obstacles, *he will preserve you until your mission is accomplished.* Let that assurance of God's hand on your life give you added boldness as you testify for him today. But remember, time is short. There is no guarantee that you, like the two witnesses, have 1,260 days to finish your God-given mission!

INSIGHT Revelation, a Beastly Book
Of the forty-two occurrences of the word *beast* in the New Testament, forty-one of them are found in the book of Revelation!

C H A P T E R 10
Then I saw another mighty angel coming down from heaven, surrounded by a cloud, with a rainbow over his head. His face shone like the sun, and his feet were like pillars of fire. ²And in his hand was a small scroll, which he had unrolled. He stood with his right foot on the sea and his left foot on the land. ³And he gave a great shout, like the roar of a lion. And when he shouted, the seven thunders answered.

⁴When the seven thunders spoke, I was about to write. But a voice from heaven called to me: "Keep secret what the seven thunders said. Do not write it down."

⁵Then the mighty angel standing on the sea and on the land lifted his right hand to heaven. ⁶And he swore an oath in the name of the one who lives forever and ever, who created heaven and everything in it, the earth and everything in it, and the sea and everything in it. He said, "God will wait no longer. ⁷But when the seventh angel blows his trumpet, God's mysterious plan will be fulfilled. It will happen just as he announced it to his servants the prophets."

[8] Then the voice from heaven called to me again: "Go and take the unrolled scroll from the angel who is standing on the sea and on the land."

[9] So I approached him and asked him to give me the little scroll. "Yes, take it and eat it," he said. "At first it will taste like honey, but when you swallow it, it will make your stomach sour!" [10] So I took the little scroll from the hands of the angel, and I ate it! It was sweet in my mouth, but it made my stomach sour. [11] Then he said to me, "You must prophesy again about many peoples, nations, languages, and kings."

CHAPTER 11

Then I was given a measuring stick, and I was told, "Go and measure the Temple of God and the altar, and count the number of worshipers. [2] But do not measure the outer courtyard, for it has been turned over to the nations. They will trample the holy city for 42 months. [3] And I will give power to my two witnesses, and they will be clothed in sackcloth and will prophesy during those 1,260 days."

[4] These two prophets are the two olive trees and the two lampstands that stand before the Lord of all the earth. [5] If anyone tries to harm them, fire flashes from the mouths of the prophets and consumes their enemies. This is how anyone who tries to harm them must die. [6] They have power to shut the skies so that no rain will fall for as long as they prophesy. And they have the power to turn the rivers and oceans into blood, and to send every kind of plague upon the earth as often as they wish.

[7] When they complete their testimony, the beast that comes up out of the bottomless pit will declare war against them. He will conquer them and kill them. [8] And their bodies will lie in the main street of Jerusalem,* the city which is called "Sodom" and "Egypt," the city where their Lord was crucified. [9] And for three and a half days, all peoples, tribes, languages, and nations will come to stare at their bodies. No one will be allowed to bury them. [10] All the people who belong to this world will give presents to each other to celebrate the death of the two prophets who had tormented them.

[11] But after three and a half days, the spirit of life from God entered them, and they stood up! And terror struck all who were staring at them. [12] Then a loud voice shouted from heaven, "Come up here!" And they rose to heaven in a cloud as their enemies watched.

[13] And in the same hour there was a terrible earthquake that destroyed a tenth of the city. Seven thousand people died in that earthquake. And everyone who did not die was terrified and gave glory to the God of heaven.

[14] The second terror is past, but look, now the third terror is coming quickly.

[15] Then the seventh angel blew his trumpet, and there were loud voices shouting in heaven: "The whole world has now become the kingdom of our Lord and of his Christ, and he will reign forever and ever."

[16] And the twenty-four elders sitting on their thrones before God fell on their faces and worshiped him. [17] And they said,

"We give thanks to you, Lord God Almighty,
   the one who is and who always was,
for now you have assumed your great power
   and have begun to reign.
[18] The nations were angry with you,
   but now the time of your wrath has come.
It is time to judge the dead and reward your servants.
You will reward your prophets and your holy people,
   all who fear your name, from the least to the greatest.
And you will destroy all who have caused destruction on the earth."

[19] Then, in heaven, the Temple of God was opened and the Ark of his covenant could be seen inside the Temple. Lightning flashed, thunder crashed and roared; there was a great hailstorm, and the world was shaken by a mighty earthquake.

CHAPTER 12

Then I witnessed in heaven an event of great significance. I saw a woman clothed with the sun, with the moon beneath her feet, and a crown of twelve stars on her head. [2] She was pregnant, and she cried out in the pain of labor as she awaited her delivery.

[3] Suddenly, I witnessed in heaven an-

11:8 Greek *the great city.*

other significant event. I saw a large red dragon with seven heads and ten horns, with seven crowns on his heads. ⁴His tail dragged down one-third of the stars, which he threw to the earth. He stood before the woman as she was about to give birth to her child, ready to devour the baby as soon as it was born.

⁵She gave birth to a boy who was to rule all nations with an iron rod. And the child was snatched away from the dragon and was caught up to God and to his throne. ⁶And the woman fled into the wilderness, where God had prepared a place to give her care for 1,260 days.

⁷Then there was war in heaven. Michael and the angels under his command fought the dragon and his angels. ⁸And the dragon lost the battle and was forced out of heaven. ⁹This great dragon—the ancient serpent called the Devil, or Satan, the one deceiving the whole world—was thrown down to the earth with all his angels.

¹⁰Then I heard a loud voice shouting across the heavens,

"It has happened at last—the salvation and power and kingdom of our God, and the authority of his Christ! For the Accuser has been thrown down to earth—the one who accused our brothers and sisters before our God day and night. ¹¹And they have defeated him because of the blood of the Lamb and because of their testimony. And they were not afraid to die. ¹²Rejoice, O heavens! And you who live in the heavens, rejoice! But terror will come on the earth and the sea. For the Devil has come down to you in great anger, and he knows that he has little time."

¹³And when the dragon realized that he had been thrown down to the earth, he pursued the woman who had given birth to the child. ¹⁴But she was given two wings like those of a great eagle. This allowed her to fly to a place prepared for her in the wilderness, where she would be cared for and protected from the dragon* for a time, times, and half a time. ¹⁵Then the dragon tried to drown the woman with a flood of water that flowed from its mouth. ¹⁶But the earth helped her by opening its mouth and swallowing the river that gushed out from the mouth of the

dragon. ¹⁷Then the dragon became angry at the woman, and he declared war against the rest of her children—all who keep God's commandments and confess that they belong to Jesus.

¹⁸Then he stood* waiting on the shore of the sea.

CHAPTER 13

And now in my vision I saw a beast rising up out of the sea. It had seven heads and ten horns, with ten crowns on its horns. And written on each head were names that blasphemed God. ²This beast looked like a leopard, but it had bear's feet and a lion's mouth! And the dragon gave him his own power and throne and great authority.

³I saw that one of the heads of the beast seemed wounded beyond recovery—but the fatal wound was healed! All the world marveled at this miracle and followed the beast in awe. ⁴They worshiped the dragon for giving the beast such power, and they worshiped the beast. "Is there anyone as great as the beast?" they exclaimed. "Who is able to fight against him?"

⁵Then the beast was allowed to speak great blasphemies against God. And he was given authority to do what he wanted for forty-two months. ⁶And he spoke terrible words of blasphemy against God, slandering his name and all who live in heaven, who are his temple. ⁷And the beast was allowed to wage war against God's holy people and to overcome them. And he was given authority to rule over every tribe and people and language and nation. ⁸And all the people who belong to this world worshiped the beast. They are the ones whose names were not written in the Book of Life, which belongs to the Lamb who was killed before the world was made.

⁹Anyone who is willing to hear should listen and understand. ¹⁰The people who are destined for prison will be arrested and taken away. Those who are destined for death will be killed. But do not be dismayed, for here is your opportunity to have endurance and faith.

¹¹Then I saw another beast come up out of the earth. He had two horns like those of a lamb, and he spoke with the voice of a dragon. ¹²He exercised all the authority of the first beast. And he required all the earth and those who belong to this world

12:14 Greek *the serpent;* also in 12:15. See 12:9.   **12:18** Some manuscripts read *Then I stood,* and some translations put this entire sentence into 13:1.

to worship the first beast, whose death-wound had been healed. [13]He did astounding miracles, such as making fire flash down to earth from heaven while everyone was watching. [14]And with all the miracles he was allowed to perform on behalf of the first beast, he deceived all the people who belong to this world. He ordered the people of the world to make a great statue of the first beast, who was fatally wounded and then came back to life. [15]He was permitted to give life to this statue so that it could speak. Then the statue commanded that anyone refusing to worship it must die.

[16]He required everyone—great and small, rich and poor, slave and free—to be given a mark on the right hand or on the forehead. [17]And no one could buy or sell anything without that mark, which was either the name of the beast or the number representing his name. [18]Wisdom is needed to understand this. Let the one who has understanding solve the number of the beast, for it is the number of a man.* His number is 666.*

13:18a Or *of humanity.*　　**13:18b** Some manuscripts read *616.*

DECEMBER 28 ☐ DAY 363
Alpha and Omega

LOOK BACK　The final two books of the New Testament are the "long and the short of it"—the powerful little book of Jude and the awe-inspiring book of Revelation. Jude challenges his readers to "fight for the faith" because it is a faith worth fighting for. False teachers prowl like ravaging wolves, looking for the weak and unprepared. Christians dare not be naive about the danger, for the Old Testament shows clearly what happened to the fallen angels and the wicked cities of Sodom and Gomorrah.

One of God's titles is "the Alpha and the Omega—the beginning and the end" (Revelation 1:8). What began in the book of Genesis now comes to completion in the book of Revelation. John the "beloved apostle" (the same man who wrote the Gospel of John and the three Epistles of John) writes from his island exile, unveiling "the things which you have seen [Revelation 1], and the things which are [Revelation 2–3], and the things which will take place after this [Revelation 4–22]." Highlights of the book include seven letters to seven churches and three cycles of judgment upon the earth.

Revelation concludes with a final glimpse of God's grandeur, an invitation to the reader, and a warning to all who would attempt to add to, or delete from, the message of the book. Though the story of the Bible has stretched over sixty-six books, one day the curtain on human history will drop and "The End" will come. "Amen! Come, Lord Jesus!" (Revelation 22:20).

LOOK UP　Earlier in your journey through the New Testament, you read these words from the apostle Paul: "And I am sure that God, who began the good work within you, will continue his work until it is finally finished on that day when Christ Jesus comes back again" (Philippians 1:6).

In a word, God finishes what he starts. To see that more clearly, notice this startling series of contrasts between the first three chapters of the Bible (Genesis 1–3) and the final three chapters (Revelation 20–22):

Where there is no faith in the future, there is no power in the present.

In Genesis We Read . . .	In Revelation We Read . . .
"In the beginning God created the heavens and the earth" (1:1)	"I saw a new heaven and a new earth" (21:1)
"God called . . . the darkness 'night'" (1:5)	"No night" (22:5)
"God made two great lights [sun and moon]" (1:16)	"The city has no need of sun or moon" (21:23)
"You will surely die" (2:17)	"No more death" (21:4)
"You will [have] . . . intense pain" (3:16)	"No more . . . pain" (21:4)
"I have placed a curse on the ground" (3:17)	"No longer will anything be cursed" (22:3)
"God banished Adam and his wife from the Garden" (3:23)	"They will see his face" (22:4)

 LOOK AHEAD Over the past year, you've developed a new habit of holiness—the habit of consistently reading and obeying God's Word. Congratulations! As the New Year begins, why not retrace your steps through the sixty-six books of the Bible? This time have a question in mind as you read: What does the Bible say about managing my money? being a godly spouse and parent? making wise decisions? praying prayers God delights to answer?

Keep a journal of your discoveries, and expect God to meet you each day along your *daily walk*.

DECEMBER 29 □ DAY 364
REVELATION 14–16
Pouring Out the Seven Bowls

 OVERVIEW Accompanied by the singing of the 144,000, the final outpouring of God's wrath begins. The earth is ripe in its wickedness and richly deserving of the calamities that are about to befall it. Seven angels arrive with seven bowls full of plagues, pestilence, disease, and death. As the bowls of God's wrath are poured out—judgments that are "true and just" (16:7)—people refuse to acknowledge the Creator, but instead curse "the God of heaven for their pains and sores" (16:11). Following the seventh bowl, a loud voice from heaven declares, "It is finished!" (16:17).

Chapter 14	Chapter 15	Chapter 16
The Judge Is Coming	Judgment Is Coming	Judgment Is Here
Lamb of God	Wrath of God	Bowls of God's Wrath

 YOUR DAILY WALK When was the last time your spouse was angry with you? Do you recall the circumstances? How about the last time your boss was mad at you? What was the outcome?

Anger can be a fearful emotion, whether expressed by a spouse or child, friend or foe. Now imagine that it is not another human being

Sinners may who is angry with you, but the God of the universe . . . the God who
oppose God's created you from dust . . . the God who will one day destroy "the
ways, but not elements . . . in the flames" (2 Peter 3:10, 12). How would you face
his wrath. that kind of anger? Where would you go to escape it? The answer, of
course, is *nowhere!*

Today God offers his love and mercy, but there is coming a day when
his wrath and judgment will pour down upon all who have ignored his
invitation. That means *you* if you have spurned his offer of salvation in
Jesus Christ. That means your unsaved family members and friends. And
that means there is no better time than *now* to warn those you love of
the peril they face by continuing in their unbelief. Can you afford to wait?

 INSIGHT Armageddon—the Big Little Mountain
Apart from its significance in Bible times, during which it witnessed two
great victories (Judges 4:15; 7:1-25) and two stunning defeats (1 Samuel
31:4-10; 2 Kings 23:29-30), the hill of Meggido has been the site of
battles involving Pompey, Napoléon, Alexander the Great, and (more
recently) Lord Allenby in 1917.

CHAPTER 14

Then I saw the Lamb standing on Mount
Zion, and with him were 144,000 who had
his name and his Father's name written on
their foreheads. ²And I heard a sound from
heaven like the roaring of a great waterfall
or the rolling of mighty thunder. It was like
the sound of many harpists playing together.

³This great choir sang a wonderful new
song in front of the throne of God and
before the four living beings and the
twenty-four elders. And no one could
learn this song except those 144,000 who
had been redeemed from the earth. ⁴For
they are spiritually undefiled, pure as virgins,* following the Lamb wherever he
goes. They have been purchased from
among the people on the earth as a special
offering* to God and to the Lamb. ⁵No
falsehood can be charged against them;
they are blameless.

⁶And I saw another angel flying through
the heavens, carrying the everlasting Good
News to preach to the people who belong
to this world—to every nation, tribe, language, and people. ⁷"Fear God," he
shouted. "Give glory to him. For the time
has come when he will sit as judge. Worship him who made heaven and earth, the
sea, and all the springs of water."

⁸Then another angel followed him
through the skies, shouting, "Babylon is
fallen—that great city is fallen—because
she seduced the nations of the world and
made them drink the wine of her passionate immorality."

⁹Then a third angel followed them,
shouting, "Anyone who worships the beast
and his statue or who accepts his mark on
the forehead or the hand ¹⁰must drink the
wine of God's wrath. It is poured out undi-
luted into God's cup of wrath. And they
will be tormented with fire and burning
sulfur in the presence of the holy angels
and the Lamb. ¹¹The smoke of their torment rises forever and ever, and they will
have no relief day or night, for they have
worshiped the beast and his statue and
have accepted the mark of his name. ¹²Let
this encourage God's holy people to endure persecution patiently and remain firm
to the end, obeying his commands and
trusting in Jesus."

¹³And I heard a voice from heaven saying, "Write this down: Blessed are those
who die in the Lord from now on. Yes, says
the Spirit, they are blessed indeed, for they
will rest from all their toils and trials; for
their good deeds follow them!"

¹⁴Then I saw the Son of Man* sitting on a
white cloud. He had a gold crown on his
head and a sharp sickle in his hand.

¹⁵Then an angel came from the Temple
and called out in a loud voice to the one
sitting on the cloud, "Use the sickle, for
the time has come for you to harvest; the
crop is ripe on the earth." ¹⁶So the one
sitting on the cloud swung his sickle over
the earth, and the whole earth was harvested.

¹⁷After that, another angel came from the
Temple in heaven, and he also had a sharp
sickle. ¹⁸Then another angel, who has

14:4a Greek *they are virgins who have not defiled themselves with women.*   **14:4b** Greek *as firstfruits.*   **14:14** Or *one who looked like*
a man; Greek reads *one like a son of man.*

power to destroy the world with fire, shouted to the angel with the sickle, "Use your sickle now to gather the clusters of grapes from the vines of the earth, for they are fully ripe for judgment." ¹⁹So the angel swung his sickle on the earth and loaded the grapes into the great winepress of God's wrath. ²⁰And the grapes were trodden in the winepress outside the city, and blood flowed from the winepress in a stream about 180 miles* long and as high as a horse's bridle.

CHAPTER 15

Then I saw in heaven another significant event, and it was great and marvelous. Seven angels were holding the seven last plagues, which would bring God's wrath to completion. ²I saw before me what seemed to be a crystal sea mixed with fire. And on it stood all the people who had been victorious over the beast and his statue and the number representing his name. They were all holding harps that God had given them. ³And they were singing the song of Moses, the servant of God, and the song of the Lamb:

"Great and marvelous are your actions,
  Lord God Almighty.
Just and true are your ways,
  O King of the nations.*
⁴ Who will not fear, O Lord, and glorify
  your name?
  For you alone are holy.
All nations will come and worship
  before you,
  for your righteous deeds have been
  revealed."

⁵Then I looked and saw that the Temple in heaven, God's Tabernacle, was thrown wide open! ⁶The seven angels who were holding the bowls of the seven plagues came from the Temple, clothed in spotless white linen* with gold belts across their chests. ⁷And one of the four living beings handed each of the seven angels a gold bowl filled with the terrible wrath of God, who lives forever and forever. ⁸The Temple was filled with smoke from God's glory and power. No one could enter the Temple until the seven angels had completed pouring out the seven plagues.

CHAPTER 16

Then I heard a mighty voice shouting from the Temple to the seven angels, "Now go your ways and empty out the seven bowls of God's wrath on the earth."

²So the first angel left the Temple and poured out his bowl over the earth, and horrible, malignant sores broke out on everyone who had the mark of the beast and who worshiped his statue.

³Then the second angel poured out his bowl on the sea, and it became like the blood of a corpse. And everything in the sea died.

⁴Then the third angel poured out his bowl on the rivers and springs, and they became blood. ⁵And I heard the angel who had authority over all water saying, "You are just in sending this judgment, O Holy One, who is and who always was. ⁶For your holy people and your prophets have been killed, and their blood was poured out on the earth. So you have given their murderers blood to drink. It is their just reward." ⁷And I heard a voice from the altar saying, "Yes, Lord God Almighty, your punishments are true and just."

⁸Then the fourth angel poured out his bowl on the sun, causing it to scorch everyone with its fire. ⁹Everyone was burned by this blast of heat, and they cursed the name of God, who sent all of these plagues. They did not repent and give him glory.

¹⁰Then the fifth angel poured out his bowl on the throne of the beast, and his kingdom was plunged into darkness. And his subjects ground their teeth in anguish, ¹¹and they cursed the God of heaven for their pains and sores. But they refused to repent of all their evil deeds.

¹²Then the sixth angel poured out his bowl on the great Euphrates River, and it dried up so that the kings from the east could march their armies westward without hindrance. ¹³And I saw three evil spirits that looked like frogs leap from the mouth of the dragon, the beast, and the false prophet. ¹⁴These miracle-working demons caused all the rulers of the world to gather for battle against the Lord on that great judgment day of God Almighty.

¹⁵"Take note: I will come as unexpectedly as a thief! Blessed are all who are watching for me, who keep their robes

14:20 Greek *1,600 stadia* [296 kilometers].   15:3 Some manuscripts read *King of the ages;* other manuscripts read *King of the saints.* 15:6 Some manuscripts read *in bright and sparkling stone.*

ready so they will not need to walk naked and ashamed."

¹⁶And they gathered all the rulers and their armies to a place called *Armageddon* in Hebrew.

¹⁷Then the seventh angel poured out his bowl into the air. And a mighty shout came from the throne of the Temple in heaven, saying, "It is finished!" ¹⁸Then the thunder crashed and rolled, and lightning flashed. And there was an earthquake greater than ever before in human history. ¹⁹The great

16:21 Greek *1 talent* [34 kilograms].

city of Babylon split into three pieces, and cities around the world fell into heaps of rubble. And so God remembered all of Babylon's sins, and he made her drink the cup that was filled with the wine of his fierce wrath. ²⁰And every island disappeared, and all the mountains were leveled. ²¹There was a terrible hailstorm, and hailstones weighing seventy-five pounds* fell from the sky onto the people below. They cursed God because of the hailstorm, which was a very terrible plague.

DECEMBER 30 ☐ DAY 365
REVELATION 17–19
Destroying God's Enemies

OVERVIEW John sees God's judgment poured out on more than just the physical universe. Babylon, headquarters of religious and civil authority, is warned by an angelic messenger of its approaching doom. The city's destruction—complete and irrevocable—is mourned by kings and merchants alike who profited from her rich trade and false religion. By contrast, heaven rejoices in the demise of the wicked city. After the marriage supper of the Lamb in heaven, the scene shifts back to the earth, where the King of kings comes to judge and destroy his human enemies.

Chapter 17	Chapter 18	Chapter 19	
Babylon's Description	Babylon's Destruction	Salvation from the Lord	A Feast for the Lamb
		1 5	6 21
Climax of Punishment		Commencement of Praise	

YOUR DAILY WALK In the cast of characters in the unfolding drama of God's plan of the ages, the leading role is played by the Lord Jesus Christ: the promised Messiah in the Old Testament, the Lamb of God in the New Testament, and the returning King of kings and Lord of lords (19:16). This is the significance of the angel's statement to John: "For the essence of prophecy is to give a clear witness for Jesus" (19:10). The totality of Scripture as the prophetic message of God to humankind centers on the person and ministry of the Lord Jesus Christ. Therefore, Jesus should be "visible" in every page of your Bible.

Time has no power over the name and deeds and words of Jesus Christ.

Try it! Thumb back through the books of the Bible you have studied this year, and see if you can suggest the way Jesus is pictured in each. For example, Genesis: the one who will crush Satan's head (3:15); Exodus: the Redeemer from bondage to sin; Leviticus: the Holy One of God, etc. Have fun!

INSIGHT The Supremely Appropriate Title
The woman dressed in purple "who sits on many waters" (17:1) is given
the title "Babylon the Great, Mother of All Prostitutes and Obscenities
in the World" (17:5)—a most appropriate caption for this mysterious
person who has prompted commentators to suggest a wide variety
of different identities, including: (1) the actual rebuilt city on the site
of ancient Babylon; (2) an actual city, but different from Babylon;
(3) a false religious system; (4) an atheistic political system.

CHAPTER 17
One of the seven angels who had poured
out the seven bowls came over and spoke
to me. "Come with me," he said, "and I
will show you the judgment that is going
to come on the great prostitute, who sits
on many waters. ²The rulers of the world
have had immoral relations with her, and
the people who belong to this world have
been made drunk by the wine of her immorality."

³So the angel took me in spirit* into the
wilderness. There I saw a woman sitting on
a scarlet beast that had seven heads and ten
horns, written all over with blasphemies
against God. ⁴The woman wore purple and
scarlet clothing and beautiful jewelry made
of gold and precious gems and pearls. She
held in her hand a gold goblet full of obscenities and the impurities of her immorality. ⁵A mysterious name was written on
her forehead: "Babylon the Great, Mother
of All Prostitutes and Obscenities in the
World." ⁶I could see that she was drunk—
drunk with the blood of God's holy people
who were witnesses for Jesus. I stared at
her completely amazed.

⁷"Why are you so amazed?" the angel
asked. "I will tell you the mystery of this
woman and of the beast with seven heads
and ten horns. ⁸The beast you saw was
alive but isn't now. And yet he will soon
come up out of the bottomless pit and go to
eternal destruction. And the people who
belong to this world, whose names were
not written in the Book of Life from before
the world began, will be amazed at the
reappearance of this beast who had died.

⁹"And now understand this: The seven
heads of the beast represent the seven hills
of the city where this woman rules. They
also represent seven kings. ¹⁰Five kings
have already fallen, the sixth now reigns,
and the seventh is yet to come, but his reign
will be brief. ¹¹The scarlet beast that was
alive and then died is the eighth king. He is
like the other seven, and he, too, will go to

his doom. ¹²His ten horns are ten kings
who have not yet risen to power; they will
be appointed to their kingdoms for one
brief moment to reign with the beast.
¹³They will all agree to give their power
and authority to him. ¹⁴Together they will
wage war against the Lamb, but the Lamb
will defeat them because he is Lord over all
lords and King over all kings, and his
people are the called and chosen and faithful ones."

¹⁵And the angel said to me, "The waters
where the prostitute is sitting represent
masses of people of every nation and language. ¹⁶The scarlet beast and his ten
horns—which represent ten kings who will
reign with him—all hate the prostitute.
They will strip her naked, eat her flesh, and
burn her remains with fire. ¹⁷For God has
put a plan into their minds, a plan that will
carry out his purposes. They will mutually
agree to give their authority to the scarlet
beast, and so the words of God will be
fulfilled. ¹⁸And this woman you saw in
your vision represents the great city that
rules over the kings of the earth."

CHAPTER 18
After all this I saw another angel come
down from heaven with great authority,
and the earth grew bright with his splendor. ²He gave a mighty shout, "Babylon is
fallen—that great city is fallen! She has become the hideout of demons and evil spirits, a nest for filthy buzzards, and a den for
dreadful beasts. ³For all the nations have
drunk the wine of her passionate immorality. The rulers of the world have committed
adultery with her, and merchants throughout the world have grown rich as a result of
her luxurious living."

⁴Then I heard another voice calling from
heaven, "Come away from her, my people.
Do not take part in her sins, or you will be
punished with her. ⁵For her sins are piled
as high as heaven, and God is ready to

17:3 Or *in the Spirit.*

judge her for her evil deeds. ⁶Do to her as she has done to your people. Give her a double penalty for all her evil deeds. She brewed a cup of terror for others, so give her twice as much as she gave out. ⁷She has lived in luxury and pleasure, so match it now with torments and sorrows. She boasts, 'I am queen on my throne. I am no helpless widow. I will not experience sorrow.' ⁸Therefore, the sorrows of death and mourning and famine will overtake her in a single day. She will be utterly consumed by fire, for the Lord God who judges her is mighty."

⁹And the rulers of the world who took part in her immoral acts and enjoyed her great luxury will mourn for her as they see the smoke rising from her charred remains. ¹⁰They will stand at a distance, terrified by her great torment. They will cry out, "How terrible, how terrible for Babylon, that great city! In one single moment God's judgment came on her."

¹¹The merchants of the world will weep and mourn for her, for there is no one left to buy their goods. ¹²She bought great quantities of gold, silver, jewels, pearls, fine linen, purple dye, silk, scarlet cloth, every kind of perfumed wood, ivory goods, objects made of expensive wood, bronze, iron, and marble. ¹³She also bought cinnamon, spice, incense, myrrh, frankincense, wine, olive oil, fine flour, wheat, cattle, sheep, horses, chariots, and slaves—yes, she even traded in human lives.

¹⁴"All the fancy things you loved so much are gone," they cry. "The luxuries and splendor that you prized so much will never be yours again. They are gone forever."

¹⁵The merchants who became wealthy by selling her these things will stand at a distance, terrified by her great torment. They will weep and cry. ¹⁶"How terrible, how terrible for that great city! She was so beautiful—like a woman clothed in finest purple and scarlet linens, decked out with gold and precious stones and pearls! ¹⁷And in one single moment all the wealth of the city is gone!"

And all the shipowners and captains of the merchant ships and their crews will stand at a distance. ¹⁸They will weep as they watch the smoke ascend, and they will say, "Where in all the world is there another city like this?" ¹⁹And they will throw dust on their heads to show their great sorrow. And they will say, "How terrible, how terrible for the great city! She made us all rich from her great wealth. And now in a single hour it is all gone."

²⁰But you, O heaven, rejoice over her fate. And you also rejoice, O holy people of God and apostles and prophets! For at last God has judged her on your behalf.

²¹Then a mighty angel picked up a boulder as large as a great millstone. He threw it into the ocean and shouted, "Babylon, the great city, will be thrown down as violently as I have thrown away this stone, and she will disappear forever. ²²Never again will the sound of music be heard there—no more harps, songs, flutes, or trumpets. There will be no industry of any kind, and no more milling of grain. ²³Her nights will be dark, without a single lamp. There will be no happy voices of brides and grooms. This will happen because her merchants, who were the greatest in the world, deceived the nations with her sorceries. ²⁴In her streets the blood of the prophets was spilled. She was the one who slaughtered God's people all over the world."

CHAPTER 19
After this, I heard the sound of a vast crowd in heaven shouting, "Hallelujah! Salvation is from our God. Glory and power belong to him alone. ²His judgments are just and true. He has punished the great prostitute who corrupted the earth with her immorality, and he has avenged the murder of his servants." ³Again and again their voices rang, "Hallelujah! The smoke from that city ascends forever and forever!"

⁴Then the twenty-four elders and the four living beings fell down and worshiped God, who was sitting on the throne. They cried out, "Amen! Hallelujah!"

⁵And from the throne came a voice that said, "Praise our God, all his servants, from the least to the greatest, all who fear him."

⁶Then I heard again what sounded like the shout of a huge crowd, or the roar of mighty ocean waves, or the crash of loud thunder: "Hallelujah! For the Lord our God, the Almighty, reigns. ⁷Let us be glad and rejoice and honor him. For the time has come for the wedding feast of the Lamb, and his bride has prepared herself. ⁸She is permitted to wear the finest white linen." (Fine linen represents the good deeds done by the people of God.)

⁹And the angel said, "Write this: Blessed are those who are invited to the wedding feast of the Lamb." And he added, "These are true words that come from God."

¹⁰Then I fell down at his feet to worship him, but he said, "No, don't worship me. For I am a servant of God, just like you and other brothers and sisters who testify of their faith in Jesus. Worship God. For the essence of prophecy is to give a clear witness for Jesus.*"

¹¹Then I saw heaven opened, and a white horse was standing there. And the one sitting on the horse was named Faithful and True. For he judges fairly and then goes to war. ¹²His eyes were bright like flames of fire, and on his head were many crowns. A name was written on him, and only he knew what it meant. ¹³He was clothed with a robe dipped in blood, and his title was the Word of God. ¹⁴The armies of heaven, dressed in pure white linen, followed him on white horses. ¹⁵From his mouth came a sharp sword, and with it he struck down the nations. He ruled them with an iron rod, and he trod the winepress of the fierce wrath of almighty God. ¹⁶On his robe and

19:10 Or *is the message confirmed by Jesus.*

thigh was written this title: King of kings and Lord of lords.

¹⁷Then I saw an angel standing in the sun, shouting to the vultures flying high in the sky: "Come! Gather together for the great banquet God has prepared. ¹⁸Come and eat the flesh of kings, captains, and strong warriors; of horses and their riders; and of all humanity, both free and slave, small and great."

¹⁹Then I saw the beast gathering the kings of the earth and their armies in order to fight against the one sitting on the horse and his army. ²⁰And the beast was captured, and with him the false prophet who did mighty miracles on behalf of the beast—miracles that deceived all who had accepted the mark of the beast and who worshiped his statue. Both the beast and his false prophet were thrown alive into the lake of fire that burns with sulfur. ²¹Their entire army was killed by the sharp sword that came out of the mouth of the one riding the white horse. And all the vultures of the sky gorged themselves on the dead bodies.

DECEMBER 31 □ DAY 366
REVELATION 20–22
Making All Things New

OVERVIEW The consummation of God's judgment includes the doom of two other enemies of humankind: the devil and death. Their being cast into the lake of fire (20:10, 14) paves the way for the introduction of a new heaven and earth where there is no night . . . no tears . . . no pain . . . no sun . . . no moon; a place where "nothing evil will be allowed to enter" (21:27). Once again, God and his people live in perfect, unbroken fellowship. John's book ends with the people of God assembled in the presence of God, worshiping him in holiness and reigning together over all he has created, much like Adam and Eve in the garden many centuries before. John, whose heart yearns for that day, is moved to write—even as millions have been moved to pray—"Amen! Come, Lord Jesus!" (22:20).

Chapter 20	Chapter 21	Chapter 22
The End of the Devil and Death	The Beginning of a New Heaven and Earth	A Final Warning "I Am Coming Soon"
Punishment	Pictures	Promises

YOUR DAILY WALK   Congratulations! If you began reading through the Bible last January (and have stayed on schedule), today you will finish reading the 31,173 verses in the New Living Translation of the Bible.

We are not at our best perched at the summit; we are climbers, at our best when the way is steep.

Perhaps occasionally, as you found yourself swimming through Psalms or jumping through Jeremiah, you were tempted to breathe the prayer that was on John's lips as he concluded writing down the lengthy book of Revelation: "Amen! Come, Lord Jesus" (22:20). But if Jesus tarries, the coming year will bring the exciting challenge of new steps of growth.

INSIGHT   Sadness in the Old, Gladness in the New
Perhaps the saddest words in the entire Old Testament are these: "So the LORD God banished Adam and his wife from the Garden of Eden" (Genesis 3:23). By contrast, some of the gladdest words in all the New Testament are found in today's section: "They will see his face" (Revelation 22:4). As one commentator put it, "Sin drove man from one garden. Grace brings man to an eternal Paradise." Are you ready for that day of gladness and joy?

CHAPTER 20

Then I saw an angel come down from heaven with the key to the bottomless pit and a heavy chain in his hand. ²He seized the dragon—that old serpent, the Devil, Satan—and bound him in chains for a thousand years. ³The angel threw him into the bottomless pit, which he then shut and locked so Satan could not deceive the nations anymore until the thousand years were finished. Afterward he would be released again for a little while.

⁴Then I saw thrones, and the people sitting on them had been given the authority to judge. And I saw the souls of those who had been beheaded for their testimony about Jesus, for proclaiming the word of God. And I saw the souls of those who had not worshiped the beast or his statue, nor accepted his mark on their forehead or their hands. They came to life again, and they reigned with Christ for a thousand years. ⁵This is the first resurrection. (The rest of the dead did not come back to life until the thousand years had ended.) ⁶Blessed and holy are those who share in the first resurrection. For them the second death holds no power, but they will be priests of God and of Christ and will reign with him a thousand years.

⁷When the thousand years end, Satan will be let out of his prison. ⁸He will go out to deceive the nations from every corner of the earth, which are called Gog and Magog. He will gather them together for battle—a mighty host, as numberless as sand along

the shore. ⁹And I saw them as they went up on the broad plain of the earth and surrounded God's people and the beloved city. But fire from heaven came down on the attacking armies and consumed them.

¹⁰Then the Devil, who betrayed them, was thrown into the lake of fire that burns with sulfur, joining the beast and the false prophet. There they will be tormented day and night forever and ever.

¹¹And I saw a great white throne, and I saw the one who was sitting on it. The earth and sky fled from his presence, but they found no place to hide. ¹²I saw the dead, both great and small, standing before God's throne. And the books were opened, including the Book of Life. And the dead were judged according to the things written in the books, according to what they had done. ¹³The sea gave up the dead in it, and death and the grave* gave up the dead in them. They were all judged according to their deeds. ¹⁴And death and the grave were thrown into the lake of fire. This is the second death—the lake of fire. ¹⁵And anyone whose name was not found recorded in the Book of Life was thrown into the lake of fire.

CHAPTER 21

Then I saw a new heaven and a new earth, for the old heaven and the old earth had disappeared. And the sea was also gone. ²And I saw the holy city, the new Jerusalem, coming down from God out of

20:13 Greek *and Hades;* also in 20:14.

heaven like a beautiful bride prepared for her husband.

³I heard a loud shout from the throne, saying, "Look, the home of God is now among his people! He will live with them, and they will be his people. God himself will be with them.* ⁴He will remove all of their sorrows, and there will be no more death or sorrow or crying or pain. For the old world and its evils are gone forever."

⁵And the one sitting on the throne said, "Look, I am making all things new!" And then he said to me, "Write this down, for what I tell you is trustworthy and true." ⁶And he also said, "It is finished! I am the Alpha and the Omega—the Beginning and the End. To all who are thirsty I will give the springs of the water of life without charge! ⁷All who are victorious will inherit all these blessings, and I will be their God, and they will be my children. ⁸But cowards who turn away from me, and unbelievers, and the corrupt, and murderers, and the immoral, and those who practice witchcraft, and idol worshipers, and all liars—their doom is in the lake that burns with fire and sulfur. This is the second death."

⁹Then one of the seven angels who held the seven bowls containing the seven last plagues came and said to me, "Come with me! I will show you the bride, the wife of the Lamb."

¹⁰So he took me in spirit* to a great, high mountain, and he showed me the holy city, Jerusalem, descending out of heaven from God. ¹¹It was filled with the glory of God and sparkled like a precious gem, crystal clear like jasper. ¹²Its walls were broad and high, with twelve gates guarded by twelve angels. And the names of the twelve tribes of Israel were written on the gates. ¹³There were three gates on each side—east, north, south, and west. ¹⁴The wall of the city had twelve foundation stones, and on them were written the names of the twelve apostles of the Lamb.

¹⁵The angel who talked to me held in his hand a gold measuring stick to measure the city, its gates, and its wall. ¹⁶When he measured it, he found it was a square, as wide as it was long. In fact, it was in the form of a cube, for its length and width and height were each 1,400 miles.* ¹⁷Then he measured the walls and found them to be 216

feet thick* (the angel used a standard human measure).

¹⁸The wall was made of jasper, and the city was pure gold, as clear as glass. ¹⁹The wall of the city was built on foundation stones inlaid with twelve gems: the first was jasper, the second sapphire, the third agate, the fourth emerald, ²⁰the fifth onyx, the sixth carnelian, the seventh chrysolite, the eighth beryl, the ninth topaz, the tenth chrysoprase, the eleventh jacinth, the twelfth amethyst.

²¹The twelve gates were made of pearls—each gate from a single pearl! And the main street was pure gold, as clear as glass.

²²No temple could be seen in the city, for the Lord God Almighty and the Lamb are its temple. ²³And the city has no need of sun or moon, for the glory of God illuminates the city, and the Lamb is its light. ²⁴The nations of the earth will walk in its light, and the rulers of the world will come and bring their glory to it. ²⁵Its gates never close at the end of day because there is no night. ²⁶And all the nations will bring their glory and honor into the city. ²⁷Nothing evil will be allowed to enter—no one who practices shameful idolatry and dishonesty—but only those whose names are written in the Lamb's Book of Life.

CHAPTER 22

And the angel showed me a pure river with the water of life, clear as crystal, flowing from the throne of God and of the Lamb, ²coursing down the center of the main street. On each side of the river grew a tree of life, bearing twelve crops of fruit,* with a fresh crop each month. The leaves were used for medicine to heal the nations.

³No longer will anything be cursed. For the throne of God and of the Lamb will be there, and his servants will worship him. ⁴And they will see his face, and his name will be written on their foreheads. ⁵And there will be no night there—no need for lamps or sun—for the Lord God will shine on them. And they will reign forever and ever.

⁶Then the angel said to me, "These words are trustworthy and true: 'The Lord God, who tells his prophets what the future holds, has sent his angel to tell you what will happen soon.'"

21:3 Some manuscripts read God himself will be with them, their God.   21:10 Or in the Spirit.   21:16 Greek 12,000 stadia [2,220 kilometers].   21:17 Greek 144 cubits [65 meters].   22:2 Or 12 kinds of fruit.

⁷"Look, I am coming soon! Blessed are those who obey the prophecy written in this scroll."

⁸I, John, am the one who saw and heard all these things. And when I saw and heard these things, I fell down to worship the angel who showed them to me. ⁹But again he said, "No, don't worship me. I am a servant of God, just like you and your brothers the prophets, as well as all who obey what is written in this scroll. Worship God!"

¹⁰Then he instructed me, "Do not seal up the prophetic words you have written, for the time is near. ¹¹Let the one who is doing wrong continue to do wrong; the one who is vile, continue to be vile; the one who is good, continue to do good; and the one who is holy, continue in holiness."

¹²"See, I am coming soon, and my reward is with me, to repay all according to their deeds. ¹³I am the Alpha and the Omega, the First and the Last, the Beginning and the End."

¹⁴Blessed are those who wash their robes so they can enter through the gates of the city and eat the fruit from the tree of life.

22:16 Greek *I am the root and offspring of David.*

¹⁵Outside the city are the dogs—the sorcerers, the sexually immoral, the murderers, the idol worshipers, and all who love to live a lie.

¹⁶"I, Jesus, have sent my angel to give you this message for the churches. I am both the source of David and the heir to his throne.* I am the bright morning star."

¹⁷The Spirit and the bride say, "Come." Let each one who hears them say, "Come." Let the thirsty ones come—anyone who wants to. Let them come and drink the water of life without charge. ¹⁸And I solemnly declare to everyone who hears the prophetic words of this book: If anyone adds anything to what is written here, God will add to that person the plagues described in this book. ¹⁹And if anyone removes any of the words of this prophetic book, God will remove that person's share in the tree of life and in the holy city that are described in this book.

²⁰He who is the faithful witness to all these things says, "Yes, I am coming soon!" Amen! Come, Lord Jesus!

²¹The grace of the Lord Jesus be with you all.